Standard & Poor's MidCap 400 Guide

1994 Edition

Standard & Poor's Corporation

McGraw-Hill, Inc.

New York San Francisco Washington, D.C. Auckland Bogotá
Caracas Lisbon London Madrid Mexico City Milan
Montreal New Delhi San Juan Singapore
Sydney Tokyo Toronto

Library of Congress Catalog Card Number

FOR STANDARD & POOR'S CORPORATION
Vice President, Products & Services: Elliott Shurgin
Vice President and Publisher: Ron Oliver
Managing Editor: Richard Albanese

1 2 3 4 5 6 7 8 9 0 DOH/DOH 9 9 8 7 6 5 4 3

ISBN 0-07-052095-X

The sponsoring editor for this book was David Conti, and the production supervisor was Thomas G. Kowalczyk. The front matter and introduction were set by North Market Street Graphics.

Printed and bound by R. R. Donnelley & Sons Company.

ABOUT THE AUTHOR

Standard & Poor's Corporation, a McGraw-Hill company, is the nation's leading securities information company. It provides a broad range of services, including the respected bond and stock ratings, advisory services, data guides, and the most closely watched and widely reported gauge of stock market activity—the S & P 500 Stock Index. S & P products are marketed around the world and used extensively by financial professionals and individual investors.

Introduction

by Alan J. Miller, C.F.A.

Most serious investors have heard of the Standard & Poor's 500 Composite Stock Index. Together with the Dow Jones Industrial Average, it is one of the two oldest stock market indices around (the DJIA having started in 1884 and the predecessor to the S&P 500 in 1923). It is the index of choice for measuring the performance of most professionally managed investment portfolios. And it is the basis upon which upwards of $250 billion in passive index funds are managed.

Moreover, there are few investors who have not at least heard of the most prominent components of the S&P 500. Their names read like a veritable "Who's Who" of American industry: AT&T, Aetna Life, ALCOA, American Brands, American Express, AMOCO, Anheuser-Busch, Apple Computer, Avon Products—and that's just a handful of the "A's"! Little wonder when the "average" S&P 500 company had a market value of $6.0 billion at the end of 1992, revenues of $7.0 billion in 1992, and net income of $264 million that year.

The S&P MidCap 400 Index, however, is not yet as well known. It has been around for less than three years, having been introduced in June 1991, and the companies which comprise it are not nearly as famous as their S&P 500 counterparts. Some of the "A's" in this lesser-known group include A&W Brands, Acuson Corporation, ADC Telecommunications, Adobe Systems, Aflac Inc., Air & Water Technologies, and Aldus Corporation. How many have you heard of?

This lack of recognition is unfortunate for several reasons:

1. Today's S&P MidCap 400 may well be the precursor of the S&P 500 of our grandchildren's time. The average market capitalization of companies in the S&P MidCap 400 is only about $1.1 billion (less than one-fifth of the $6.0 billion average for companies in the S&P 500). But while companies in the S&P MidCap 400 are much smaller than their S&P 500 counterparts today, they well may grow to be the giants of tomorrow.

   That is because many mid-capitalization stocks are in relatively fast-growing industries, offering superior earnings growth potential and boasting strong balance sheets and high returns on equity. Indeed, in the five years through 1991, the median earnings growth rate for the stocks in the MidCap 400 Index was 12.6% compared to 10.8% for stocks in the S&P 500. So investors who are willing to assume the incremental risk of investing in somewhat smaller and newer companies than the bluest of the blue chips in the S&P 500, in an attempt at realizing better than S&P 500 market returns, well might be advised to take a look at the stocks in this index.

2. The S&P 500 is probably the best equity index benchmark for the entire U.S. equities market. At year-end 1992, it represented approximately 70% of the total market value of all domestic stocks. However, it is largely dominated by large capitalization stocks, with over 50% of its total market value accounted for by the 50 largest stocks in the index. And it is the skewness toward large capitalization stocks which created a need for other means of indexing to capture the equity performance of the remaining U.S. equity market segments.

   That's where the S&P MidCap 400 came in. From a universe of 1,700 securities with 1990 year-end values ranging from $5 billion down to $200 million, the Standard & Poor's Corporation selected the 400 stock sample that came to comprise the S&P MidCap 400 Index, in order to better reflect the performance of the mid-sized market capitalization segment.

3. Prior to the creation of the S&P MidCap 400 Index, investors in mid-sized capitalization companies didn't really have a good benchmark against which to measure their investment managers' performance. The S&P MidCap 400 Index filled that void.

4. Investors who wish to invest in the mid-sized capitalization market without incurring the company-specific risk inherent in choosing individual stocks now can invest in passively managed index funds pegged to the S&P MidCap 400 Index. To be sure, such passively managed funds now amount to only about $2.5 billion (compared to 100 times as much currently indexed to the S&P 500), but remember that three years ago the opportunity to index a portfolio of mid-sized capitalization stocks didn't exist at all.

   Alternatively, investors who wish to invest in the mid-sized capitalization market without incurring specific company risk can invest directly in S&P MidCap 400 futures contracts or options on S&P MidCap 400 futures contracts. Both the futures contracts and the options are traded on the Chicago Mercantile Exchange.

5. Finally, there are those who may not even be investors, but who have all sorts of other reasons for needing to know how individual mid-sized capitalization companies are doing. Perhaps they are job hunters, seeking employment in companies like these which offer

above-average career opportunities. Perhaps they are salespeople or marketers, searching for new clients in rapidly growing industries. Perhaps they are the owners or managers of private or public companies who need to know how their competitors are doing. All of these people will find the companies which comprise the S&P MidCap 400 of interest to them.

How to Use This Book

In the pages that follow, you will find a wealth of information on each of the 400 companies which comprise the S&P MidCap 400 Index, information which will allow you to make reasoned investment, business, and personal judgments regarding these companies. But to get the most value from this book, you should take a few moments to familiarize yourself with just what you'll find on these pages.

The place to start is at the top of the left-hand page. That's where you'll find the following information, which is reasonably self-explanatory:

- The name of the company
- Where the company's stock is traded:
  - NYSE (New York Stock Exchange)
  - ASE (American Stock Exchange)
  - Nasdaq (The Nasdaq Stock Market)
- The stock's symbol
- Where options are traded and the monthly expiration dates

Directly below this information, you will find an array of the following seven bits of additional information:

Price

This is the price of the stock as of the date shown.

Range

The range within which the stock sold between January 1, 1993 and the price date above.

P-E Ratio

The price of the stock (as indicated in the price column) divided by the trailing 12-month earnings per share.

Dividend

The annual dividend rate as evidenced by the company's declaration policy.

Yield

The annual dividend divided by the price of the stock.

S&P Ranking

The investment process involves assessment of various factors—such as products and industry position, company resources and financial policy—with results that make some common stocks more highly esteemed than others. In this assessment, Standard & Poor's believes that earnings and dividend performance is the end result of the interplay of these factors and that, over the long run, the record of this performance has a considerable bearing on relative quality. The rankings, however, do not reflect all of the factors that may bear on stock quality.

Growth and stability of earnings and dividends are the key elements in Standard & Poor's earnings and dividend rankings for common stocks, which are designed to capsulize the nature of this record in a single symbol. It should be noted, however, that the process also takes into consideration certain adjustments and modifications deemed desirable in establishing such rankings.

These rankings are derived by means of a computerized scoring system based on per share earnings and dividend records of the most recent ten years. Basic scores are computed for earnings and dividends and then adjusted by a set of predetermined modifiers for growth, stability, and cyclicality. Adjusted scores for earnings and dividends are then combined to yield a final score.

The ranking system also makes allowance for the fact that, in general, corporate size imparts certain recognized advantages from an investment standpoint. Minimum size limits (in terms of corporate sales) are set for the various rankings, but exceptions may be made where a score reflects an outstanding earnings-dividend record.

The final score is then translated into one of the following rankings:

A+ Highest

A High

A− Above Average

B+ Average

B Below Average

B− Lower

C Lowest

D In Reorganization

NR No Ranking

In some instances, rankings may be modified by special considerations, such as natural disasters, massive strikes, or nonrecurring accounting adjustments.

It is important to note that a ranking is not a forecast of future market price performance, but is basically an appraisal of past performance of earnings and dividends and relative current standing. Consequently, rankings should not be used as market recommendations: a high-score stock may at times be so overpriced as to justify its sale while a low-score stock may be attractively priced for purchase. Rankings based upon earnings and dividends records are no substitute for complete analysis. They cannot take into account the potential effects of management changes, internal company policies not yet fully reflected in the earnings and dividend record, public relations standings, recent competitive shifts, and a host of other factors that may be relevant in investment decision making.

Beta

The beta coefficient is a measure of the volatility of the stock's price relative to the S&P 500 Index (a proxy for the overall market). An issue with a beta of 1.5, for example, tends to move 50% more than the overall market, in the same direction. An issue with a beta of 0.5 tends to move 50% less. If a stock moved exactly as the market moved, it would have a beta of 1.0. A stock with a negative beta tends to move in a direction opposite to that of the overall market.

Directly under this array of data, you will find a brief "Summary" of what and how the company is doing. Beneath that is a block of text and additional statistics summarizing the company's business and important corporate developments; reporting on and interpreting its current outlook and operations; analyzing its net sales (or revenues), common share earnings, dividends, finances, and capitalization; and (where appropriate) presenting net asset value per share and net investment income per share figures. Much of this information is wrapped around a stock price chart which indicates monthly price ranges, volume, and stock splits for the past seven years.

Arrayed across the bottom of the page are share statistics for the stock for each of the past ten years. Extensive additional statistical information, derived from balance sheets and 10K annual reports as filed with the Securities and Exchange Commission, appear in the top half of the right-hand page. The information presented varies, depending upon whether the company is an industrial enterprise, a financial institution, an investment company, or a public utility.

In these statistical arrays, these are the terms you'll be confronting and what they mean:

Per Share Data ($) Tables

Tangible Book Value; Book Value (See also: "Common Equity" under Industrial)—Indicates the theoretical dollar amount per common share one might expect to receive from a company's tangible "book" assets should liquidation take place. Generally, book value is determined by adding the stated value of the common stock, paid-in capital and retained earnings and then subtracting intangible assets (excess cost over equity of acquired companies, goodwill, and patents), preferred stock at liquidating value and unamortized debt discount. Divide that amount by the outstanding shares to get book value per common share.

Cash Flow—Net income plus depreciation, depletion, and amortization, divided by shares used to calculate earnings per common share. (Also see: "Cash Flow" for Industrial Companies)

Earnings—The amount a company reports as having been earned for the year on its common stock based on generally accepted accounting standards. Earnings may be indicated in terms of *primary* (common stock and common stock equivalents such as stock options and warrants) and *fully diluted* (reflecting dilution in earnings resulting if all contingent issuances of common stock materialized at the outset of the year), and are generally reported from continuing operations, before extraordinary items. INSURANCE companies report *operating earnings* before gains/losses on security transactions and *earnings* after such transactions.

Dividends—Generally total cash payments per share based on the ex-dividend dates over a twelve-months period. May also be reported on a declared basis where this has been established to be a company's payout policy.

Payout Ratio—Indicates the percentage of earnings paid out in dividends. It is calculated by dividing the annual dividend by the earnings. For INSURANCE companies *earnings* after gains/losses on security transactions are used.

Prices High/Low—Shows the calendar year high and low of a stock's market price.

P/E Ratio High/Low—The ratio of market price to earnings—essentially indicates the valuation investors place on a company's earnings. Obtained by dividing the annual earnings into the high and low market price for the year. For INSURANCE companies *operating earnings* before gains/losses on security transactions are used.

Net Asset Value—Appears on investment company reports and reflects the market value of stocks, bonds, and net cash divided by outstanding shares. The % DIFFERENCE indicates the percentage premium or discount of the market price over the net asset value.

Portfolio Turnover—Appears on investment company reports and indicates percentage of total security purchases and sales for the year to overall investment assets. Primarily mirrors trading aggressiveness.

Income/Balance Sheet Data Tables

Banks

Net Interest Income—Interest and dividend income, minus interest expense.

Loan Loss Provision—Amount charged to operating expenses to provide an adequate reserve to cover anticipated losses in the loan portfolio.

Taxable Equivalent Adjustment—Increase to render income from tax-exempt loans and securities comparable to fully taxed income.

Noninterest Income—Service fees, trading and other income, excluding gains/losses on securities transactions.

% Expenses/Op. Revenues—Noninterest expense as a percentage of taxable equivalent net interest income plus noninterest income (before securities gains/losses). A measure of cost control.

Commercial Loans—Commercial, industrial, financial, agricultural loans and leases, gross.

Other Loans—Gross consumer, real estate and foreign loans.

% Loan Loss Reserve—Contra-account to loan assets, built through provisions for loan losses, which serves as a cushion for possible future loan charge-offs.

% Loans/Deposits—Proportion of loans funded by deposits. A measure of liquidity and an indication of bank's ability to write more loans.

Earning Assets—Assets on which interest is earned.

Money Market Assets—Interest-bearing interbank deposits, federal funds sold, trading account securities.

Investment Securities—Federal, state, and local government bonds and other securities.

Gains/Losses on Securities Transactions—Realized losses on sales of securities, usually bonds.

Net Before Taxes—Amount remaining after operating expenses are deducted from income, including gains or losses on security transactions.

Effective Tax Rate—Actual income tax expense divided by net before taxes.

Net Income—The final profit before dividends (common/preferred) from all sources after deduction of expenses, taxes, and fixed charges, but before any discontinued operations or extraordinary items.

Net Interest Margin—A percentage computed by dividing net interest income, on a taxable equivalent basis, by average earning assets. Used as an analytical tool to measure profit margins from providing credit services.

% Return on Revenues—Net income divided by gross revenues.

% Return on Assets—Net income divided by average total assets. An analytical measure of asset-use efficiency and industry comparison.

% Return on Equity—Net income (minus preferred dividend requirements) divided by average common equity. Generally used to measure performance.

Total Assets—Includes interest-earning financial instruments—principally commercial, real estate, consumer loans and leases; investment securities/trading accounts; cash/money market investments; other owned assets.

Cash—Mainly vault cash, interest-bearing deposits placed with banks, reserves required by the Federal Reserve and items in the process of collection—generally referred to as float.

Government Securities—Includes United States Treasury securities and securities of other U.S. government agencies at book or carrying value. A bank's major "liquid asset."

State and Municipal Securities—State and municipal securities owned at book value.

Loans—All domestic and foreign loans (excluding leases), less unearned discount and reserve for possible losses. Generally considered a bank's principal asset.

Deposits—Primarily classified as either *demand* (payable at any time upon demand of depositor) or *time* (not payable within thirty days).

Deposits/Capital Funds—Average deposits divided by average capital funds. Capital funds include capital notes/debentures, other long-term debt, capital stock, surplus, and undivided profits. May be used as a "leverage" measure.

Long-Term Debt—Total borrowings for terms beyond one year including notes payable, mortgages, debentures, term loans, and capitalized lease obligations.

Common Equity—Includes common/capital surplus, undivided profits, reserve for contingencies and other capital reserves.

% Equity to Assets—Average common equity divided by average total assets. Used as a measure of capital adequacy.

% Equity to Loans—Average common equity divided by average loans. Reflects the degree of equity coverage to loans outstanding.

Industrial Companies

Following data is based on Form 10K Annual Report data as filed with SEC.

Revenues—Net sales and other operating revenues. Includes franchise/leased department income for retailers, and royalties for publishers and oil and mining companies. Excludes excise taxes for tobacco, liquor, and oil companies.

Operating Income—Net sales and operating revenues less cost of goods sold and operating expenses (including research and development, profit sharing, exploration and bad debt, but excluding depreciation and amortization).

% Operating Income of Revenues—Net sales and operating revenues divided into operating income. Used as a measure of operating profitability.

Capital Expenditures—The sum of additions at cost to property, plant and equipment and leaseholds, generally excluding amounts arising from acquisitions.

Depreciation—Includes noncash charges for obsolescence, wear on property, current portion of capitalized expenses (intangibles), and depletion charges.

Interest Expense—Includes all interest expense on short/long-term debt, amortization of debt discount/premium and deferred expenses (e.g., financing costs).

Net Before Taxes—Includes operating and nonoperating revenues (including extraordinary items not net of taxes), less all operating and nonoperating expenses, except income taxes and minority interest, but including equity in nonconsolidated subsidiaries.

Effective Tax Rate—Actual income tax charges divided by net before taxes.

Net Income—Profits derived from all sources after deduction of expenses, taxes, and fixed charges, but before any discontinued operations, extraordinary items, and dividends (preferred/common).

% Net Income of Revenues—Net income divided by sales/operating revenues.

Cash Flow—Net income (before extraordinary items and discontinued operations, and after preferred dividends) plus depreciation, depletion, and amortization.

Cash—Includes all cash and government and other marketable securities.

Current Assets—Those assets expected to be realized in cash or used up in the production of revenue within one year.

Current Liabilities—Generally includes all debts/obligations falling due within one year.

Current Ratio—Current assets divided by current liabilities. A measure of liquidity.

Total Assets—Current assets plus net plant and other noncurrent assets (intangibles and deferred items).

% Return on Assets—Net income divided by average total assets on a per common share basis. Used in industry analysis and as a measure of asset-use efficiency.

Long-Term Debt—Debts/obligations due after one year. Includes bonds, notes payable, mortgages, lease obligations, and industrial revenue bonds. Other Long-Term Debt, when reported as a separate account, is excluded. This account generally includes pension and retirement benefits.

Common Equity (See also: "Book Value" under Per Share Data Table)—Common stock plus capital surplus and retained earnings, less any difference between the carrying value and liquidating value of preferred stock.

Total Invested Capital—The sum of stockholders' equity plus long-term debt, capital lease obligations, deferred income taxes, investment credits, and minority interest.

% Long-Term Debt of Invested Capital—Long-term debt divided by total invested capital. Indicates how highly "lever aged" a business might be.

% Return on Equity—Net income less preferred dividend requirements divided by average common shareholders' equity on a per common share basis. Generally used to measure performance and industry comparisons.

Utilities

Operating Revenues—Represents the amount billed to customers by the utility.

Depreciation—Amounts charged to income to compensate for the decline in useful value of plant and equipment.

Maintenance—Amounts spent to keep plants in good operating condition.

Operating Ratio—Ratio of operating costs to operating revenues or the proportion of revenues absorbed by expenses. Obtained by dividing operating expenses including depreciation, maintenance, and taxes by revenues.

Fixed Charges Coverage—The number of times income before interest charges (operating income plus other income) after taxes covers total interest charges and preferred dividend requirements.

Construction Credits—Credits for interest charged to the cost of constructing new plant. A combination of allowance for equity funds used during construction and allowance for borrowed funds used during construction—credit.

Effective Tax Rate—Actual income tax expense divided by the total of net income and actual income tax expense.

Net Income—Amount of earnings for the year which is available for preferred and common dividend payments.

% Return on Revenues—Obtained by dividing net income for the year by revenues.

% Return on Invested Capital—Percentage obtained by dividing income available for fixed charges by average total invested capital.

% Return on Common Equity—Percentage obtained by dividing income available for common stock (net income less preferred dividend requirements) by average common equity.

Gross Property—Includes utility plant at cost, plant work in progress, and nuclear fuel.

Capital Expenditures—Represents the amounts spent on capital improvements to plant and funds for construction programs.

Net Property—Includes items in gross property less provision for depreciation.

% Earned on Net Property—Percentage obtained by dividing operating income by average net property for the year. A measure of plant efficiency.

Total Invested Capital—Sum of total capitalization (common-preferred-debt), accumulated deferred income taxes, accumulated investment tax credits, minority interest, contingency reserves, and contributions in aid of construction.

Total Capitalization—Combined sum of total common equity, preferred stock, and long-term debt.

Long-Term Debt—Debt obligations due beyond one year from balance sheet date.

Capitalization Ratios—Reflect the percentage of each type of debt/equity issues outstanding to total capitalization. % DEBT is obtained by dividing total debt by the sum of debt, preferred, common, paid-in capital and retained earnings. % PREFERRED is obtained by dividing the preferred stocks outstanding by total capitalization. % COMMON, divide the sum of common stocks, paid-in capital and retained earnings by total capitalization.

Finally, at the very bottom of the right-hand page, you'll find general information about the company: its address and telephone number, the names of its senior executive officers and directors (usually including the name of the investor contact), the transfer agent and registrar for the stock, and the state in which the company is incorporated.

How to Use This Book to Select Investments

And so, at last, we come to the most important question: given this vast array of data, how might a businessperson seeking to find out about her competition, a marketing manager looking for clients, a job seeker, or an investor use it to best serve their respective purposes?

If you fall into one of the first three of these categories—a businessperson seeking to find out information about her competition, a marketing manager looking for clients, or a job seeker—your task will be arduous, to be sure, but this book will provide you with an excellent starting point and your payoff can make it all worthwhile. You will have to go through this book page by page, looking for those companies that are in the industries in which you are interested, that are of the size and financial strength that appeal to you, that are located geographically in your territory or where you're willing to relocate, that have been profitable and growing, and so forth. And then you will have to read about just what's going on at those companies by referring to the appropriate "Current Outlook," "Business Summary," and "Important Developments" comments in these reports. But the companies you end up with can be those high-growth entities with the greatest potential.

Of course, this book won't do it *all* for you. It is, after all, just a starting point, not a conclusive summary of everything you might need to know. It is designed to educate, not to render advice or provide recommendations. But it will get you pointed in the right direction.

Finally, what about the investor who wants to use this book to find good individual investments from among the stocks in the S&P MidCap 400 Index? If you fall into that category, what should you do?

Well, you can approach your quest the same way that the businesswoman looking for information about her competitors, the marketing manager, and the job seeker approached theirs—by thumbing through this book page by page, looking for companies with high historic growth rates, generous dividend payout policies, wide profit margins, A+ S&P Rankings, or whatever other characteristics you consider desirable in stocks in which you might invest. In this case, however, we have made your job just a little bit easier.

We have already prescreened the 400 companies in this book for several of the stock characteristics in which investors generally are most interested, including S&P Earnings and Dividends Rankings, growth records, and dividend payment histories, and we're pleased to present on the next five pages lists of those companies which score highest on the bases of these criteria. So if you, like most investors, find these characteristics important in potential investments, you might want to turn first to the companies on these lists in your search for attractive investments.

One final thought: since many of these companies are less closely followed by Wall Street analysts, they may not be as efficiently priced as the better-known blue chips. Hence, they could include some interesting "hidden values" for those investors willing to accept some degree of incremental risk.

Good luck and happy investment returns!

Stocks With A+ or A Rankings

Based on the issues in this handbook, this screen shows stocks of all companies with Standard & Poor's earnings and dividend rankings of A+ or A.

Company	Business
Issues Ranked A+	
Bancorp Hawaii	Commercial bkg,Hawaii
Central Fidelity Banks	Commercial bkg,Virginia
Cintas Corp	Sales & rental of uniforms
Crompton & Knowles	Spec chemicals,ind'l mchy
Federal Signal	Special trucks,tools,signals
Fifth Third Bancorp	Comm'l bkg,Cincinnati,Ohio
First Alabama Bancshrs	Commercial bkg,Alabama
Hannaford Bros	Food dstr: partner supermkts
RPM, Inc	Protective coatings: fabrics
Schulman (A.)	Plastic mfr/merchant resins
Sigma-Aldrich	Biochemical & organic prod
State Str Boston	Comml bkg,Boston,Mass
Teleflex Inc	Aerospace ctrls: medical prod
Wilmington Trust Corp	Commercial bkg,Delaware
Issues Ranked A	
AFLAC Inc	Insurance & broadcasting
Betz Laboratories	Water treatment chemicals
Black Hills Corp	Electric utility:coal mining
Bob Evans Farms	Sausage prod: restaurants
Carter-Wallace	Drug and toiletry products
Century Telep Enterp	Tel svc in parts of 14 states
Cracker Brl Old Ctry	Restaurant & gift stores
Dauphin Deposit	Comm'l bkg,Pennsylvania
Dean Foods	Milk & dairy: food items
Donaldson Co	Engine air cleaners, mufflers
Dreyfus Corp	Manager, dstr Dreyfus Fund
Edwards(AG)Inc	Security broker: inv banker
Ennis Business Forms	Business forms: paper items
Equifax Inc	Risk mgmt & fin'l ctrl svs
First of America Bk	Commercial bkg,Michigan
First Virginia Banks	Commercial bkg,Virginia
Flightsafety Int'l	Aircraft & marine training
Heilig-Meyers	Retail furniture stores
Kelly Services'A'	Temporary office help
KeyCorp	Comml bkg in 8 states in NE&NW
Lance, Inc	Snack foods: vending
Leggett & Platt	Mfr springs,etc for furn,bed
Liberty Nat'l Bancorp	Comm'l bkg,Louisville,KY
Lincoln Telecommun	Telephone serv, Nebraska
Loctite Corp	Chemical sealants, adhesives
Marshall & Ilsley	Commercial bkg,Wisconsin
Mercantile Bankshares	Comm'l bkg,Baltimore, MD
Molex Inc	Terminals,connectors,switch
Nordson Corp	Industrial application eqp
Phillips-Van Heusen	Apparel mfr & retailer
Precision Castparts	Castings for aircraft engines
Ruddick Corp	Food supermkts,thread/yarn
Smucker (J.M.) Cl'A'	Preserves: jellies & fillings
Southern N.E. Telecom	Supplies telecommunic svcs
SouthTrust Corp	Commercial bkg,Alabama
Standard Register	Business forms & handl'g eq
Stanhome Inc	Consumer prd/household items
TECO Energy	Hldg co:Tampa Electric
Tyson Foods Cl'A'	Integrated poultry business
WPL Holdings	Utility hldg:Wisconsin Pwr/Lt
Wallace Computer Svc	Business forms:comm'l print
Washington Gas Lt	Natural gas:D.C.,Md,Va
Wausau Paper Mills	Print,write,specialty papers
Wisconsin Energy Corp	Hdlg:El & gas utility

Chart based on October 2, 1993 prices and data.

Companies With Five Consecutive Years of Earnings Increases

This table, compiled from a computer screen of the stocks in this handbook, shows companies that have recorded rising per-share earnings for five consecutive years, have a minimum 10% five-year EPS growth rate based on trailing 12-month earnings, have estimated 1993 EPS at least 10% above those reported for 1992, and pay dividends. The list is sorted by the five-year EPS growth rate.

Company	Business	Fiscal Year End	5 Yr. EPS Growth Rate %	— EPS $— 1992 Act.	1993 Est.	S&P Stock Rank	Price	P/E on 1993 Est.	% Yield
U.S. HealthCare	Health maintenance programs	Dec	121.95	1.85	2.40	B+	45.00	18.7	1.4
Intl Game Technology	Coin oper video/reel games	Sep	64.65	0.54	0.95	B	39.75	41.8	0.3
Amer Barrick Res	Gold prod'n U.S./Canada	Dec	47.33	0.62	0.75	B	24.87	33.1	0.2
Linear Technology Corp	Mfrs integrated circuits	Jun*	38.10	0.69	0.99	B	34.75	35.1	0.5
Mylan Labs	Pharmaceutical products	Mar#	32.46	0.92	1.15	A–	32.25	28.0	0.4
Crompton & Knowles	Spec chemicals,ind'l mchy	Dec	23.12	0.87	1.00	A+	18.37	18.3	2.1
Questar Corp	Nat'l gas dstr:oil/gas:mfg	Dec	22.69	1.79	2.10	A–	42.25	20.1	2.6
Sbarro Inc	Italian fast food restaurants	Dec	19.37	1.78	2.10	B+	39.62	18.8	2.0
Phillips–Van Heusen	Apparel mfr & retailer	Jan#	17.55	1.42	1.65	A	32.37	19.6	0.4
Franklin Resources	Mut'l fd inv advisory & svcs	Sep	17.43	1.59	1.95	A–	50.37	25.8	0.5
Heilig–Meyers	Retail furniture stores	Feb#	15.22	0.84	1.07	A	34.12	31.8	0.5
Tyson Foods Cl'A'	Integrated poultry business	Sep	14.95	1.16	1.30	A	21.37	16.4	0.1
Stewart & Stevenson	Diesel/turbine eng pwr sys	Jan#	14.71	1.35	1.70	B	47.50	27.9	0.5
Cintas Corp	Sales & rental of uniforms	May*	14.17	0.79	0.97	A+	27.75	28.6	0.5
Federal Signal	Special trucks,tools,signals	Dec	14.03	1.00	1.15	A+	26.75	23.2	1.7
Genl Motors Cl'E'	Business info systems	Dec	12.90	1.33	1.50	NR	29.12	19.4	1.3
Fifth Third Bancorp	Comm'l bkg,Cincinnati,Ohio	Dec	12.14	2.75	3.17	A+	53.75	16.9	2.0
Omnicom Group	Major int'l advertising co	Dec	9.81	2.31	2.75	B+	45.62	16.5	2.7
Transatlantic Holdings	Reinsur: property/casualty	Dec	9.70	3.13	3.50	NR	55.00	15.7	0.5
Arnold Indus*	Trucking–gen'l commodities	Dec	8.86	1.95	2.15	A–	40.25	18.7	1.6
RPM, Inc	Protective coatings: fabrics	May*	8.29	0.73	0.83	A+	17.87	21.5	2.9
NIPSCO Industries	Util hldg co:Elec/nat'l gas	Dec	8.23	2.00	2.30	B	33.12	14.4	3.9

*Actual 1993 EPS & estimated 1994 EPS; P/E based on estimated 1994 EPS. #Actual 1993 EPS; P/E based on 1993 actual EPS.

Chart based on October 2, 1993 prices and data.

Rapid Growth Stocks

The stocks listed below have shown strong and consistent earnings growth. Issues of rapidly growing companies tend to carry high price-earnings ratios and offer potential for substantial appreciation. At the same time, though, the stocks are subject to strong selling pressures should growth in earnings slow. Five-year earnings growth rates have been calculated for fiscal years 1988 through 1992 and the most current 12-month earnings.

Company	Business	S&P Stock Rank	Fiscal Year End	— EPS $ — 1992 Act.	1993 Est.	5 Yr. EPS % Growth	Price	P/E on 1993 Est.	% Yield
AFLAC Inc	Insurance & broadcasting	A	Dec	1.75	2.08	17.31	31.25	15.8	1.2
Amer Pwr Conversion	Mfr constant pwr supply prod	NR	Dec	0.30	0.50	61.06	22.00	55.0	....
BMC Software	Dvlp IBM compatible softwr	B+	Mar#	2.50	3.10	40.98	59.37	22.1	....
Brinker Int'l	Limited menu restaurants	B+	Jun*	0.76	1.03	28.93	38.50	37.3	....
Buffets Inc	Operates buffet–style rest'ts	NR	Dec	0.51	0.63	33.93	22.50	39.4	....
Cintas Corp	Sales & rental of uniforms	A+	May*	0.79	0.97	14.17	27.75	28.0	0.5
Clayton Homes	Produces/finances mfrd hms	B+	Jun*	0.90	1.18	21.25	26.50	22.4	....
Cracker Brl Old Ctry	Restaurant & gift stores	A	Jul*	0.61	0.78	35.02	27.25	34.9	....
Crompton & Knowles	Spec chemicals,ind'l mchy	A+	Dec	0.87	1.00	23.12	18.37	19.3	2.1
Franklin Resources	Mut'l fd inv advisory & svcs	A–	Sep	1.59	1.95	17.43	50.37	26.5	0.5
Heilig–Meyers	Retail furniture stores	A	Feb#	0.84	1.07	15.22	34.12	35.9	0.5
Linear Technology Corp	Mfrs integrated circuits	B	Jun*	0.69	0.99	38.10	34.75	35.1	0.5
McCormick & Co	Spices, flavoring, tea, mixes	A–	Nov	1.16	1.25	24.38	22.25	19.0	1.9
Phillips–Van Heusen	Apparel mfr & retailer	A	Jan#	1.42	1.65	17.55	32.37	22.3	0.4
Thermo Electron	Eng'd ind'l pr: environ instr	B+	Dec	2.27	2.55	17.34	63.25	25.4	....

*Actual 1993 EPS & estimated 1994 EPS; P/E based on estimated 1994 EPS. #Actual 1993 EPS; P/E based on 1993 actual EPS.

Chart based on October 2, 1993 prices and data.

Fast-Rising Dividends

Using the companies in this handbook, the companies below were chosen on the basis of their five-year annual growth rate in dividends from 1988 to the current 12-month indicated rate. All have increased their dividend payments each calendar year from 1988 to their current 12-month indicated rate.

Company	-- $ Divd. -- Paid 1988	Paid 1992	†Ind. Divd. Rate	* Divd. Growth Rate %	Price	% Yield
Penn Central	0.03	0.80	0.84	77.08	31.25	2.7
U.S. HealthCare	0.07	0.41	0.64	57.08	45.00	1.4
Crompton & Knowles	0.11	0.30	0.40	29.45	18.37	2.2
Kaydon Corp	0.10	0.30	0.36	28.25	19.62	1.8
McCormick& Co	0.13	0.38	0.44	27.89	22.25	2.0
Morgan Stanley Gr	0.32	0.95	1.08	26.17	88.50	1.2
Cintas Corp	0.04	0.11	0.14	25.96	27.75	0.5
Watts Industries'A'	0.12	0.28	0.36	23.38	43.75	0.8
Cardinal Distribution	0.04	0.08	0.10	21.92	40.00	0.3
Flightsafety Int'l	0.15	0.30	0.40	21.78	36.25	1.1
Arnold Indus	0.22	0.63	0.68	21.77	40.25	1.7
Dibrell Bros	0.28	0.57	0.72	20.81	27.00	2.7
TCA Cable TV	0.16	0.34	0.40	19.82	25.87	1.5
Savannah Foods & Ind	0.24	0.53	0.54	18.83	16.00	3.4
Federal Signal	0.21	0.41	0.48	18.31	26.75	1.8
Loctite Corp	0.33	0.72	0.80	17.52	36.75	2.2
Genl Motors Cl'E'	0.17	0.36	0.40	17.45	29.12	1.4
Schulman (A.)	0.14	0.28	0.32	17.35	29.25	1.1
Smucker (J.M.) Cl'A'	0.21	0.41	0.46	17.18	24.12	1.9
Hannaford Bros	0.16	0.30	0.34	16.91	23.37	1.5
Northern Trust	0.33	0.64	0.74	16.68	41.25	1.8
Franklin Resources	0.14	0.26	0.28	16.44	50.37	0.6
Wausau Paper Mills	0.13	0.26	0.28	16.36	39.50	0.7
NIPSCO Industries	0.60	1.24	1.32	16.08	33.12	4.0
Wilmington Trust	0.46	0.88	1.00	15.96	30.50	3.3
Fifth Third Bancorp	0.51	0.86	1.08	15.83	53.75	2.0
Univl Foods	0.43	0.85	0.92	15.46	33.12	2.8
Hanna (M.A.)Co	0.33	0.66	0.70	15.35	31.62	2.2
State Str Boston	0.25	0.43	0.52	15.22	36.37	1.4
Central Fidelity Bks	0.50	0.79	1.00	14.85	29.50	3.4
Lukens Inc	0.46	0.99	1.00	14.70	34.62	2.9

Company	-- $ Divd. -- Paid 1988	Paid 1992	†Ind. Divd. Rate	* Divd. Growth Rate %	Price	% Yield
AFLAC Inc	0.20	0.34	0.40	14.57	31.25	1.3
HON Indus	0.21	0.37	0.40	14.19	28.00	1.4
Lawson Products	0.23	0.40	0.48	13.81	26.75	1.8
Church & Dwight	0.23	0.38	0.44	13.74	24.00	1.8
Family Dollar Stores	0.15	0.25	0.30	13.62	15.87	1.9
Liberty Nat'l Bancorp	0.36	0.60	0.68	13.53	26.75	2.5
Donaldson Co	0.24	0.39	0.44	13.42	40.25	1.1
Edwards(AG)Inc	0.33	0.50	0.60	13.19	30.62	2.0
Heilig-Meyers	0.10	0.16	0.20	12.95	34.12	0.6
Ennis Business Forms	0.29	0.53	0.56	12.90	12.75	4.4
Bear Stearns Cos	0.35	0.57	0.60	12.83	24.75	2.4
Modine Mfg	0.25	0.41	0.46	12.76	25.25	1.8
Betz Laboratories	0.80	1.30	1.40	12.34	45.00	3.1
Sigma-Aldrich	0.16	0.25	0.29	12.28	46.25	0.6
Hartford Stm Boiler Ins	1.15	2.03	2.12	12.27	46.25	4.6
Stanhome Inc	0.56	0.94	1.00	12.14	28.00	3.6
Marshall & Ilsley	0.31	0.48	0.56	12.11	24.00	2.3
Teleflex Inc	0.26	0.41	0.46	11.90	33.00	1.4
Comerica Inc	0.60	0.94	1.12	11.87	28.37	3.9
Rollins Inc	0.34	0.40	0.44	11.86	23.37	1.9
Dean Foods	0.37	0.57	0.64	11.62	27.00	2.4
First Security	0.50	0.69	0.92	11.37	29.25	3.1
Nordson Corp	0.28	0.44	0.48	11.33	53.75	0.9
Tambrands Inc	0.97	1.40	1.68	11.27	43.75	3.8
RPM, Inc	0.31	0.46	0.52	11.10	17.87	2.9
First Tenn Nat'l	0.83	1.20	1.44	10.76	40.25	3.6
Wallace Computer Svc	0.35	0.55	0.58	10.48	27.00	2.1
First of America Bk	0.93	1.31	1.60	10.47	41.87	3.8
Kelly Services'A'	0.38	0.58	0.64	10.02	22.37	2.9
Provident L&C 'B'	0.67	1.00	1.04	10.02	28.12	3.7

†12-month indicated rate. *Five-year annual compounded growth rate.

Chart based on October 2, 1993 prices and data.

Higher Dividends For Ten Years

These companies have all paid higher cash dividends in each of the past ten calendar years and currently yield at least 2%. To be able to increase dividends under the difficult economic conditions that were experienced at times over the past ten years, indicates healthy finances and capable management.

Company	Price	†Ind. Divd. Rate	% Yield
Allegheny Power Sys	54.12	3.28	6.1
Angelica Corp	25.75	0.94	3.7
Atlanta Gas Light	37.00	2.08	5.6
Atlantic Energy	23.12	1.54	6.7
Betz Laboratories	45.00	1.40	3.1
Black Hills Corp	24.62	1.28	5.2
Brooklyn Union Gas	26.62	1.32	5.0
Carlisle Cos	31.50	0.72	2.3
Central Fidelity Banks	29.50	1.00	3.4
Central La Elec	25.87	1.42	5.5
Comerica Inc	28.37	1.12	3.9
Crompton & Knowles	18.37	0.40	2.2
Dean Foods	27.00	0.64	2.4
Dibrell Bros	27.00	0.72	2.7
Diebold, Inc	57.25	1.20	2.1
Ennis Business Forms	12.75	0.56	4.4
Fifth Third Bancorp	53.75	1.08	2.0
First Alabama Bancshrs	34.37	1.04	3.0
First of America Bk	41.87	1.60	3.8
First Tenn Nat'l	40.25	1.44	3.6
First Virginia Banks	39.75	1.12	2.8
Florida Progress	34.87	1.94	5.6
Flowers Indus	18.75	0.76	4.1
Hartford Stm Boiler Ins	46.25	2.12	4.6
Hawaiian Elec Indus	38.12	2.28	6.0
Indiana Energy	23.12	1.02	4.4
Kelly Services'A'	22.37	0.64	2.9
KeyCorp	36.62	1.24	3.4
Keystone Int'l	26.62	0.72	2.7
LG&E Energy	41.50	2.08	5.0
Lance, Inc	20.50	0.96	4.7
Liberty Nat'l Bancorp	26.75	0.68	2.5
Loctite Corp	36.75	0.80	2.2
Marshall & Ilsley	24.00	0.56	2.3
Mercantile Bankshares	21.25	0.68	3.2
Minnesota Pwr & Lt	34.25	1.98	5.8
Natl Fuel Gas	36.00	1.54	4.3
Pentair, Inc	33.75	0.68	2.0
Potomac Electric Pwr	27.75	1.64	5.9
Questar Corp	42.25	1.10	2.6
RPM, Inc	17.87	0.52	2.9
Rochester Telephone	45.87	1.58	3.4
SCANA Corp	50.87	2.74	5.4
Sonoco Products	21.12	0.54	2.6
SouthTrust Corp	19.50	0.60	3.1
Stanhome Inc	28.00	1.00	3.6
TECO Energy	25.25	0.96	3.8
Tambrands Inc	43.75	1.68	3.8
Univl Corp	24.25	0.88	3.6
WPL Holdings	35.12	1.90	5.4
Wallace Computer Svc	27.00	0.58	2.1
Washington Gas Lt	43.50	2.18	5.0
Wilmington Trust Corp	30.50	1.00	3.3

†12-month indicated rate

Chart based on October 2, 1993 prices and data.

ADC Telecommunications

NASDAQ Symbol ADCT (Incl. in Nat'l Market) Options on Pacific In S&P MidCap 400

Price	Range	P-E Ratio	Dividend	Yield	S&P Ranking	Beta
Oct. 14'93	1993					
42¾	42¾–18⅝	39	None	None	B	1.33

Summary

ADC makes copper-based and fiber optic products used by public telephone companies and large private telecommunications networks. Acquisitions have bolstered its product offerings in fiber optic internetworking backbone and intelligent hub products. Earnings surged in the first nine months of fiscal 1993, reflecting increased sales, wider gross margins, and the absence of a $3.8 million charge for personnel reduction. A two-for-one stock split was effected in June 1993.

Current Outlook

Earnings for fiscal 1993 are projected at $1.08 a share, up from 1992's $0.78 (as adjusted).

Dividends are not anticipated.

Revenues are expected to grow some 15% in fiscal 1993, to about $360 million, from $317 million in fiscal 1992. Gains should reflect increased expenditures by public telephone companies for ADC's products. Interest expense should decline as a result of efforts to reduce debt. The company expects capital outlays to increase to about $22 million in fiscal 1993, from $15.8 million in fiscal 1992.

Net Sales (Million $)

Quarter:	1992–93	1991–92	1990–91	1989–90
Jan.	78.6	64.8	72.9	62.0
Apr.	89.0	78.8	72.3	60.2
Jul.	93.4	83.8	73.8	65.8
Oct.	---	89.1	74.9	71.8
	---	316.5	293.8	259.8

Net sales in the nine months ended July 31, 1993, climbed 15%, year to year, reflecting increased sales to public telecommunications network providers. Gross margins widened due the increased volume and a more favorable product mix. Operating expenses were well controlled, and in the absence of $3,800,000 of personnel reduction expenses, pretax income soared 65%. After taxes at 36.6%, versus 39.0%, net income surged 71%, to $21,505,000 ($0.78 a share), from $12,568,000 ($0.46).

Common Share Earnings ($)

Quarter:	1992–93	1991–92	1990–91	1989–90
Jan.	0.19	d0.05	0.25	0.22
Apr.	0.26	0.23	0.25	0.18
Jul.	0.33	0.28	0.16	0.22
Oct.	E0.30	0.31	0.17	0.25
	E1.08	0.78	0.83	0.87

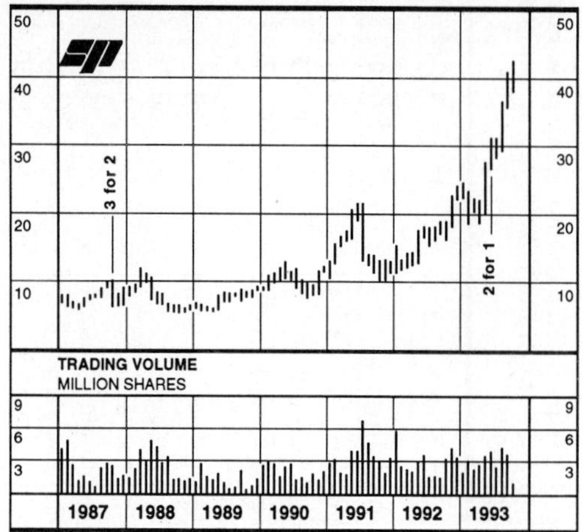

Important Developments

Jun. '93— ADC said it had signed a preliminary technology agreement with USA Video Corp. to pursue the development of an end-to-end video-dial-tone solution. The company intends to integrate its Homeworx access platform with USA Video's server and digital video receiver to create a commercially available, digital video-on-demand solution. The first customer for the product will be Rochester Telephone Corp., which announced a field test to begin in the fall of 1993, involving more than 100 homes in Rochester, N.Y. Separately, ADC's Kentrox unit purchased Radio Frequency technology and other assets from Waseca Technology, Inc.

Next earnings report expected in November.

Per Share Data ($)

Yr. End Oct. 31	1992	1991	[2]1990	[2]1989	1988	1987	1986	1985	1984	1983
Tangible Bk. Val.	**[1]6.70**	[1]5.90	[1]5.04	[1]4.18	3.58	2.93	2.34	1.87	1.57	1.42
Cash Flow	**1.36**	1.37	1.32	1.00	0.99	0.90	0.72	0.53	0.34	0.37
Earnings[3]	**0.78**	0.83	0.87	0.63	0.65	0.59	0.47	0.31	0.13	0.21
Dividends	**Nil**	Nil	Nil	Nil	Nil	Nil	Nil	Nil	Nil	Nil
Payout Ratio	**Nil**	Nil	Nil	Nil	Nil	Nil	Nil	Nil	Nil	Nil
Prices[4]—High	**24¼**	21⅝	13	9⅜	12	10¼	7¼	5	3 7/16	4⅜
Low	**11⅜**	10¼	7⅝	5⅝	5⅜	5 13/16	4⅜	2½	2 1/16	2 11/16
P/E Ratio—	**31–16**	26–12	15–9	15–9	18–8	17–10	16–9	16–8	27–16	21–13

Data as orig. reptd. Adj. for stk. divs. of 100% Jun. 1993, 50% Oct. 1987, 50% Apr. 1986, 50% May 1983. **1.** Incl. intangibles. **2.** Refl. merger or acq. **3.** Bef. results of disc. ops. of +0.02 in 1984, -0.24 in 1983. **4.** Cal. yr. d-Deficit. E-Estimated.

Income Data (Million $)

Year Ended Oct. 31	Revs.	Oper. Inc.	% Oper. Inc. of Revs.	Cap. Exp.	Depr.	Int. Exp.	Net Bef. Taxes	Eff. Tax Rate	Net Inc.	% Net Inc. of Revs.	Cash Flow
1992	**316**	**58.0**	**18.3**	**16.6**	**15.6**	**[4]0.94**	**34.7**	**39.5%**	**21.0**	**6.6**	**36.7**
1991	294	53.0	18.0	27.1	14.5	1.80	36.4	39.5%	22.0	7.5	36.5
[1]1990	260	49.7	19.1	15.3	12.0	0.62	38.2	40.0%	22.9	8.8	34.9
[1]1989	196	32.6	16.6	15.9	9.9	0.49	26.2	37.5%	16.4	8.4	26.3
1988	180	33.0	18.3	13.7	8.9	0.27	24.9	32.0%	[3]17.0	9.4	25.8
1987	167	32.4	19.4	11.5	7.9	0.46	25.4	40.0%	15.3	9.1	23.1
1986	144	28.4	19.8	11.1	6.6	1.40	21.0	42.9%	12.0	8.3	18.6
1985	125	20.4	16.4	8.5	5.8	1.50	12.9	39.0%	7.9	6.3	13.7
[2]1984	88	12.7	14.5	8.0	5.5	1.24	4.5	27.4%	3.2	3.7	8.8
[2]1983	76	13.3	17.5	6.7	4.0	0.62	9.0	39.2%	5.5	7.2	9.5

Balance Sheet Data (Million $)

Oct. 31	Cash	Curr. Assets	Curr. Liab.	Curr. Ratio	Total Assets	% Ret. on Assets	Long Term Debt	Common Equity	Total Cap.	% LT Debt of Cap.	% Ret. on Equity
1992	**20.5**	**115**	**40.1**	**2.9**	**241**	**8.6**	**14.1**	**182**	**201**	**7.0**	**12.3**
1991	30.1	120	40.5	2.9	247	10.2	43.6	158	207	21.1	15.0
1990	26.0	103	37.3	2.7	182	14.0	4.8	134	144	3.4	18.7
1989	17.6	76	23.9	3.2	144	12.4	4.7	110	120	3.9	16.0
1988	39.9	82	18.7	4.4	120	15.0	2.9	94	101	2.9	19.9
1987	26.2	72	22.1	3.2	105	16.0	3.2	76	83	3.8	22.4
1986	14.6	55	18.4	3.0	85	14.7	3.4	60	67	5.1	22.1
1985	10.0	50	16.2	3.1	77	11.0	10.6	48	61	17.4	17.8
1984	1.2	41	10.9	3.7	66	5.1	12.7	40	55	22.9	8.4
1983	2.2	36	14.6	2.4	61	9.4	6.3	37	46	13.7	15.1

Data as orig. reptd. **1.** Refl. merger or acq. **2.** Excl. disc. ops. **3.** Refl. acctg. change. **4.** Net.

Business Summary

ADC Telecommunications (formerly Magnetic Controls Co.) markets its products worldwide through its own direct sales force, as well as through distributors, dealer organizations and OEMs. The company's products are used in public telecommunciations networks by telephone operating companies and in private telecommunications networks by large businesses and government agencies. ADC has been selling more fiber optic products, shifting away from copper-based products. In fiscal 1992, fiber optic products accounted for 30% of total sales, up from from 21% in fiscal 1991. The company expects fiber optic sales to account for 50% of the total within a few years. Sales contributions by product line in recent fiscal years were:

	1992	1991	1990
Cable management products	54.3%	64.1%	69.9%
Networking products	26.6%	17.5%	17.3%
Transmission products	19.1%	18.4%	12.8%

Cable management products provide contact points for connecting different telecommunications system components and gaining access to telecommunications system circuits by electromechanical means for the purpose of testing, monitoring or reconfiguring such circuits. The majority of these products are designed for copper-based transmission systems.

The company's growth in networking products has been aided by acquisitions. In May 1991, ADC acquired Fibermux Corp., which makes private network "internetworking" backbone and intelligent hub products. Fibermux's Magnum 100 family of products transports multiple voice, data and video signals simultaneously over a 100-megabit fiber optic backbone, linking LANs, mainframes, minicomputers, PCs, telephone systems and video equipment using time-division multiplexing technology. In July 1989, Kentrox Industries, a manufacturer of network channel terminating equipment, was acquired. ADC also provides a patch/switch system used to gain access to, monitor, test and reconfigure digital circuits. Transmission products permit and enhance the generation of electronic signals and optical signals over a telecommunications circuit.

Exports represented 16%, 13% and 16% of total sales in fiscal 1992, 1991 and 1990, respectively.

Dividend Data

No cash has been paid.

Capitalization

Long Term Debt: $810,000 (7/93).

Common Stock: 27,648,991 shs. ($0.20 par).
State Farm Mutual Auto Ins. Co. holds 14%.
Institutions hold 73%.
Shareholders: 1,600 of record (12/92).

Office—4900 W. 78th St., Minneapolis, MN 55435. **Tel**—(612) 938-8080. **Chrmn**—C. M. Denny, Jr. **Pres, CEO**—W. J. Cadogan. **VP & CFO**—L. J. Morgan. **Treas & Investor Contact**—Aimee L. Gallogly (612-946-3338). **Secy**—Kathie J. Mikucki. **Dirs**—W. J. Cadogan, C. M. Denny, Jr., T. E. Holloran, B. K. Johnson, C. W. Oswald, D. M. Sullivan, W. F. Wheaton, J. D. Wunsch. **Transfer Agent & Registrar**—Norwest Bank Minnesota, South St. Paul. **Incorporated** in Minnesota in 1953. **Empl**—2,303.

 Kevin J. Gooley

AFLAC Inc.

NYSE Symbol AFL Options on ASE In S&P MidCap 400

Price	Range	P–E Ratio	Dividend	Yield	S&P Ranking	Beta
Aug. 9'93	1993					
31	32 3/16–26 3/8	15	0.40	1.3%	A	1.07

Summary

This holding company's principal asset is American Family Life Assurance Co., which offers supplemental cancer insurance in addition to other individual accident and health coverages. In 1992, AFL derived more than 80% of its revenues from Japan. Favorable policy persistency rates and contributions from an expanded U.S. product line will help offset a slowdown in new policy sales in Japan and lead to continued higher earnings in coming periods. The shares were split 5-for-4 in June 1993.

Current Outlook

Excluding realized investment gains or losses, operating earnings of $2.08 a share are expected for 1993, up from the $1.79 reported for 1992. Earnings could rise to $2.44 a share in 1994. All figures are adjusted for the June 1993 5-for-4 stock split.

The quarterly dividend was increased 14%, to $0.10 (adjusted), in June 1993.

The forecast for higher earnings in coming periods is predicated upon continued favorable persistency rates, which should offset a slowdown in new policy sales in Japan. AFL is the dominant underwriter of supplemental cancer insurance in Japan and has capitalized on that strength to exploit new market and product niches. In the U.S., a product expansion program away from solely cancer coverage, combined with stepped-up marketing efforts, aids the long-term premium growth outlook. Increased persistency rates and a maturing book of business will aid margin growth. While lower interest rates will limit investment income growth, writedowns in the portfolio are unlikely, since AFL is not exposed to either the junk bond or commercial real estate markets. Broadcast earnings, boosted in 1992 from political advertising, may improve further from cost controls and an uptick in advertising expenditures.

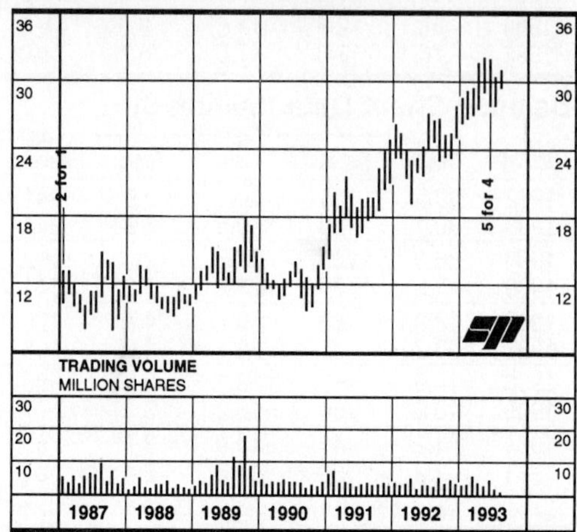

Common Share Earnings ($)

Quarter:	1993	1992	1991	1990
Mar.	0.51	0.42	0.33	0.26
Jun.	0.56	0.43	0.34	0.27
Sep.		0.46	0.38	0.30
Dec.		0.48	0.41	0.33
		1.79	1.46	1.15

Review of Operations

Revenues for the six months ended June 30, 1993, were up 25%, year to year, reflecting 25% growth in premiums, 28% higher investment income, a 5.8% rise in other income, and pretax realized investment gains of $770,000, versus losses of $1.8 million. Margins widened, and pretax earnings were up 32%. After taxes at 44.3%, versus 43.5%, net income advanced 30%. Share earnings were $1.07, compared with $0.85, before a special $0.11 gain in the 1993 interim from an accounting change. Per share net realized investment results were not material.

Important Developments

Jul. '93— AFL's annualized new premium sales for the first half of 1993 rose 3.1% in the U.S., but declined 0.6% in Japan (measured in dollars). The disappointing new sales in Japan primarily reflect a weakening Japanese economy. While this trend is likely to result in flat to only modestly higher sales growth in Japan for all of 1993, very high policy persistency rates and contributions from an expanded U.S. product line will allow AFL to meet its target of 15% revenue growth in 1993.

Next earnings report expected in early November.

Per Share Data ($)

Yr. End Dec. 31	1992	1991	1990	1989	1988	1987	1986	1985	1984	1983
Tangible Bk. Val.	**9.35**	7.86	6.54	5.63	5.25	4.89	3.86	2.82	2.37	1.97
Oper. Earnings	**1.79**	1.46	1.15	0.76	1.08	0.93	0.78	0.54	[1]0.54	0.31
Earnings[2]	**1.79**	1.46	1.15	0.80	1.08	1.02	1.01	0.54	0.56	0.32
Dividends	**0.344**	0.296	0.264	0.232	0.200	0.180	0.164	0.140	0.114	0.096
Payout Ratio	**19%**	20%	23%	29%	19%	18%	16%	26%	20%	30%
Prices—High	**27 7/8**	24 7/8	15 3/8	18	13 5/8	14 13/16	14 7/8	9 3/8	5 1/8	3 11/16
Low	**19 3/16**	14 5/16	9 11/16	10 11/16	9 3/16	7 7/8	8 5/16	4 11/16	2 13/16	2 5/16
P/E Ratio—[3]	**16–11**	17–10	13–8	23–13	13–9	16–9	19–11	17–9	9–5	12–7

Data as orig. reptd. Adj. for stk. divs. of 25% Jun. 1993, 100% Feb. 1987, 33 1/3% Mar. 1986, 50% Jun. 1985, 10% Oct. 1984, 20% Dec. 1983.
1. Incl. 0.11 (adj.) nonrecurring tax credit. **2.** Aft. gains/losses on securities trans. **3.** Based on oper. earns. prior to 1989.

Income Data (Million $)

Year Ended Dec. 31	Life Ins. In Force	Premium Income Life A & H	Other Income	Net Invest. Inc.	Total Revs.	Net Bef. Taxes	Net Oper. Inc.	Net Inc.	% Return On [1]Revs.	[1]Assets	[1]Equity
1992	**NA**	**3,369**	**87**	**533**	**3,986**	**325**	**183**	**183**	**4.6**	**1.7**	**18.3**
1991	9,659	2,765	87	431	3,283	265	148	149	4.5	1.6	17.3
1990	8,030	2,259	78	341	2,678	216	117	117	4.4	1.6	15.7
1989	6,914	2,033	103	296	2,438	178	77	81	3.3	1.3	12.0
1988	6,306	1,960	103	262	2,325	199	109	109	4.7	2.0	18.4
1987	5,206	1,606	77	193	1,876	163	93	102	5.0	2.2	18.7
1986	3,989	1,203	57	142	1,401	131	78	101	5.6	2.8	19.9
1985	3,524	815	47	92	955	95	54	55	5.7	2.8	17.7
1984	3,503	710	41	73	824	83	54	55	6.6	3.7	21.3
1983	3,137	615	34	55	704	60	31	32	4.5	2.6	14.1

Balance Sheet Data (Million $)

Dec. 31	Cash & Equiv.	Rec.	Investment Assets [2]Bonds	Stocks	[3]Loans	Total	Invest. Yield	Deferred Policy Costs	Total Assets	Debt	Common Equity
1992	**185**	**180**	**9,267**	**68**	**89.9**	**9,425**	**6.1**	**1,614**	**11,901**	**126**	**1,082**
1991	184	160	7,861	61	88.6	8,010	6.1	1,407	10,145	139	923
1990	136	144	6,105	55	83.1	6,243	6.1	1,164	8,035	158	791
1989	109	120	4,891	49	36.4	4,976	6.2	967	6,515	214	702
1988	94	115	4,484	113	29.9	4,627	6.2	913	6,074	174	642
1987	87	103	3,669	117	18.9	3,805	6.2	791	5,031	83	549
1986	50	83	2,274	99	13.5	2,387	7.2	581	3,302	65	446
1985	29	63	1,452	107	7.5	1,567	7.1	459	2,271	56	340
1984	32	43	975	52	6.1	1,033	7.8	381	1,592	25	274
1983	25	40	797	39	5.2	840	7.3	353	1,352	24	231

Data as orig. reptd. **1.** Based on oper. earns. prior to 1989. **2.** Incl. short-term invest. **3.** Incl. other long-term invest. NA-Not Available.

Business Summary

AFLAC Inc. (formerly American Family) is a holding company with insurance and broadcasting interests. Segment contributions before intercompany eliminations (pretax profits in millions) in 1992:

	Revs.	Profits
Insurance–Foreign	79%	$297
Insurance–U.S.	18%	67
Broadcasting & other	3%	–39

Foreign insurance operations consist primarily of the underwriting and sale of cancer insurance in Japan. AFL's policy pays cash directly to the policyholder to help defray certain out of pocket expenses (like private or at home nursing care or non-covered medicines) incurred in the treatment of cancer. During 1992, 88% of new cancer policy sales were made on a payroll-deduction basis through corporate-sponsored agencies. Under a plan to broaden its product base, the company in 1992 introduced a long term care/disability policy.

In the U.S., AFL has expanded its product line away from solely cancer insurance (which still remains a core offering), to an array of supplemental health insurance products, including hospital intensive care, home health care, accident and disability, Medicare supplemental, and long term care protection. During 1992, supplemental health products (other than cancer protection) accounted for about 67% of new premium sales.

Broadcast properties consist of seven network-affiliated television stations located primarily in the southeastern U.S.

Dividend Data

Cash dividends have been paid since 1973. A dividend reinvestment plan is available.

Amt of Divd. $	Date Decl.	Ex-divd. Date	Stock of Record	Payment Date
0.11	Oct. 28	Nov. 6	Nov. 13	Dec. 1'92
0.11	Jan. 29	Feb. 8	Feb. 12	Mar. 1'93
0.12½	Apr. 27	May 10	May 14	Jun. 1'93
5–for–4	Apr. 27	Jun. 15	Jun. 1	Jun. 14'93
0.10	Jul. 28	Aug. 9	Aug. 13	Sep. 1'93

Capitalization

Notes Payable: $142,913,000 (6/93).

Common Stock: 103,316,000 shs. ($0.10 par).
Institutions hold approximately 54%.
Shareholders of record: 24,474 (12/92).

Office—1932 Wynnton Rd., Columbus, GA 31999. **Tel**—(706) 323-3431; (800) 235-2667. **Chrmn**—P. Amos. **Pres & CEO**—D. P. Amos. **SVP-Secy**—J. M. Loudermilk. **EVP-CFO & Treas**—K. Cloninger III. **Investor Contacts**—K. S. Janke, Jr., J. K. Helmintoller. **Dirs**—D. P. Amos, J. S. Amos II, P. S. Amos, M. D. Edwards, G. W. Ford Jr., C. E. Garcia, J. F. Harris, E. J. Hudson, K. S. Janke Sr., C. B. Knapp, P. D. Morrow, Y. Otake, J. M. Pope, E. S. Purdom, J. S. Schiffman, H. C. Schwob, W. W. Shingleton, J. K. Spencer, K. Takahashi, G. Vaughn Jr. **Transfer Agent**—Company's office. **Registrar**—Columbus Bank & Trust Co. **Incorporated** in Georgia in 1955; reincorporated in 1973. **Empl**—3,618.

 Catherine A. Seifert

AST Research

NASDAQ Symbol ASTA (Incl. in Nat'l Market) Options on ASE In S&P MidCap 400

Price	Range	P-E Ratio	Dividend	Yield	S&P Ranking	Beta
Oct. 19'93	1993					
17	24¼–12¾	NM	None	None	B–	1.01

Summary

AST is a leading manufacturer of desktop, file server and notebook computers. The recently completed acquisition of Tandy Corp.'s computer manufacturing operations made the company the fourth largest U.S. PC manufacturer. Given continued strong demand for AST's PCs and the efficiencies resulting from the Tandy PC acquisition, earnings should improve strongly in fiscal 1994.

Current Outlook

Earnings for the fiscal year ending July 3, 1994, are estimated at $1.90 a share, versus fiscal 1993's $1.72 loss, which included a restructruing charge.

Initiation of cash dividends is not expected.

Revenue growth for fiscal 1994 is projected at about 50%, including results of the recently acquired Tandy PC operations. Gains will be fueled by strong demand for PCs, resulting from the PC price wars that began in the summer of 1992, as well as AST's expanded distribution channels and product offerings. In addition, AST is becoming a strong player in international markets, particularly in the Pacific Rim. Fiscal 1994 results should benefit from efficiencies of scale resulting from the acquisition of Tandy's computer manufacturing operations, but the first half of the fiscal year could be turbulent if AST has difficulties integrating the two disparate operations.

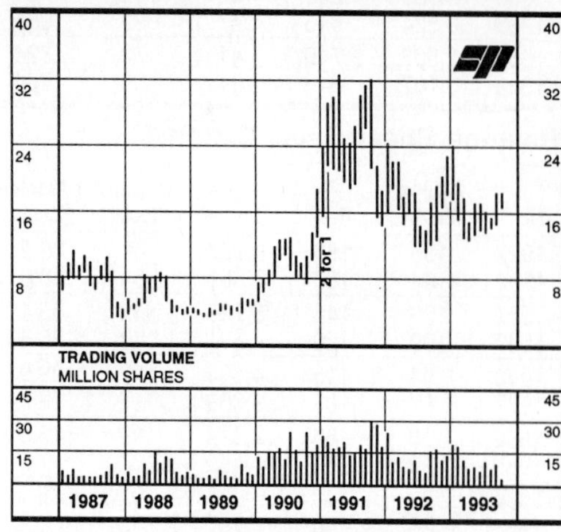

Net Sales (Million $)

13 Weeks:	1993–94	1992–93	1991–92	1990–91
Sep.	E458	[1]286	197	136
Dec.	E554	346	239	161
Mar.	E592	370	242	180
Jun.	E655	409	266	211
	E2,259	1,412	944	688

Net sales in the year ended July 3, 1993, soared 50% from those of the preceding year, as strong demand resulted from lower prices and wider distribution channels. Gross margins narrowed significantly, restricted by competitive pricing pressures, and operating expenses rose 15%. Following a $125 million restructuring charge related to the acquisition of Tandy's PC operations, and after tax credits of $11.5 million, versus taxes at 31.7%, a net loss of $53.7 million ($1.72 a share), replaced income of $68.5 million ($2.16).

Common Share Earnings ($)

13 Weeks:	1993–94	1992–93	1991–92	1990–91
Sep.	E0.27	[1]0.24	0.52	0.37
Dec.	E0.43	0.46	0.52	0.56
Mar.	E0.56	0.35	0.53	0.55
Jun.	E0.64	d2.76	0.59	0.64
	E1.90	d1.72	2.16	2.13

Important Developments

Oct. '93— AST expanded its PowerExec family of notebook computers by unveiling the PowerExec 4/33SL.

Sep. '93— AST announced the sale of its 5250 emulation board business to Micro-Integration Corp., a supplier of PC midrange connectivity solutions, for $525,000.

Next earnings report expected in late October.

Per Share Data ($)

Yr. End Jun. 30	1993	1992	1991	1990	1989	1988	1987	1986	1985	1984
Tangible Bk. Val.	**9.46**	11.80	9.33	6.30	4.60	4.94	4.21	3.61	2.47	0.44
Cash Flow	**d1.29**	2.53	2.50	1.89	0.17	0.92	0.78	1.31	1.07	0.38
Earnings	**d1.72**	2.16	2.13	[2]1.43	d0.32	0.64	0.57	1.17	0.99	0.35
Dividends	**Nil**	Nil	Nil	Nil	Nil	Nil	Nil	Nil	Nil	Nil
Payout Ratio	**Nil**	Nil	Nil	Nil	Nil	Nil	Nil	Nil	Nil	Nil
Prices[3]—High	**24¼**	24½	32¾	18⅞	5⅝	8⅝	11⅜	15¾	16⅜	4⅛
Low	**12¾**	11¼	14½	5¼	3⅜	3⅝	3⅛	5⅜	4	3½
P/E Ratio—	**NM**	11–5	15–7	13–4	NM	14–6	20–6	13–5	17–4	12–10

Data as orig. reptd. Adj. for stk. div. of 100% Feb. 1991. **1.** 14 wks. **2.** Ful. dil.: 1.21. **3.** Cal. yr. d-Deficit. NM-Not Meaningful. E-Estimated.

Income Data (Million $)

Year Ended Jun. 30	Revs.	Oper. Inc.	% Oper. Inc. of Revs.	Cap. Exp.	Depr.	Int. Exp.	Net Bef. Taxes	Eff. Tax Rate	Net Inc.	% Net Inc. of Revs.	Cash Flow
1993	**1,412**	**74**	**5.2**	**20.9**	**13.2**	**1.27**	**d65**	**NM**	**d53.7**	**NM**	**d40.5**
1992	944	109	11.6	[1]15.9	11.8	2.44	100	31.7%	68.5	7.3	80.3
1991	688	105	15.3	[1]8.9	11.3	3.67	98	34.2%	64.7	9.4	76.0
1990	534	66	12.3	11.1	11.3	5.97	52	32.0%	35.1	6.6	46.4
1989	457	10	2.2	11.8	11.3	7.57	d12	NM	d7.5	NM	3.9
1988	413	29	7.1	14.6	6.4	2.31	21	28.0%	15.1	3.7	21.5
1987	206	24	11.6	[1]6.3	4.8	0.16	22	40.0%	13.0	6.3	17.9
1986	172	50	28.8	[1]6.5	3.3	0.10	49	44.9%	27.2	15.8	30.5
1985	139	39	28.4	[1]2.7	1.5	0.30	38	50.0%	19.0	13.7	20.5
1984	64	12	18.1	2.2	0.5	0.28	11	47.6%	5.7	9.0	6.2

Balance Sheet Data (Million $)

Jun. 30	Cash	Curr. Assets	Curr. Liab.	Curr. Ratio	Total Assets	% Ret. on Assets	Long Term Debt	Common Equity	Total Cap.	% LT Debt of Cap.	% Ret. on Equity
1993	**122**	**761**	**460**	**1.7**	**886**	**NM**	**92.3**	**319**	**411**	**22.4**	**NM**
1992	141	515	182	2.8	581	12.7	2.4	363	366	0.7	21.1
1991	153	424	141	3.0	485	16.0	30.1	282	312	9.6	27.3
1990	92	262	77	3.4	324	10.5	30.1	193	223	13.5	20.9
1989	18	200	58	3.4	261	NM	81.0	109	190	42.7	NM
1988	20	235	87	2.7	272	7.2	61.3	115	185	33.1	14.0
1987	40	129	39	3.3	144	10.3	Nil	99	105	Nil	14.0
1986	48	96	19	4.9	109	29.2	NM	87	89	NM	37.6
1985	36	70	18	3.9	76	30.4	NM	57	58	0.1	55.7
1984	1	26	19	1.4	29	33.1	0.5	7	10	4.5	127.8

Data as orig. reptd. **1.** Net. d-Deficit. NM-Not Meaningful.

Business Summary

AST Research designs, manufactures and markets a broad line of IBM-compatible personal computers (PCs), including desktop, notebook and network server systems. Effective June 30, 1993, AST completed the purchase of Tandy Corp.'s (NYSE:TAN) PC manufacturing operations and the GRiD North American and GRiD/Victor European sales division for $15 million cash and a $90 million three-year promissory note. As part of the purchase agreement, AST will sell PCs to Tandy's Radio Shack, Computer City and Incredible Universe retail operations for three years. International business contributed 41% of the total in fiscal 1993, down from 44% in 1992.

The company has developed multiple brands which target a variety of price points and user requirements. These include the Advantage! product line, designed for the consumer retail market, the value oriented Bravo product line, the high-end Premium/Premmia product line and the Exec line of notebook computers. The recent Tandy/GRiD acquisition has expanded AST's product line to include handheld and pen-based systems as well as a full line of GRiD and Victor desktop and notebook products. Within the various brands, AST offers a range of portable and desktop products based on Intel microprocessors. In early fiscal 1993, the company announced its first fully symmetric multiprocessing system, the AST Manhattan SMP; based on open-system architecture, this system is aimed at LAN and multiuser UNIX environments.

In fiscal 1993, AST introduced ASTVision, a new line of low-radiation, multi-sync color monitors. The company's enhancement products provide various combinations of increased memory, additional input/output ports and other features.

Engineering and development expenses equaled 2.3% of net sales in fiscal 1993 (3.2% in 1992).

Dividend Data

No cash has been paid. A two-for-one stock split was effected in 1991.

Finances

During the fourth quarter of fiscal 1993, AST recorded a pretax restructuring charge of $125 million relating to the integration of the acquired Tandy PC manufacturing operations.

In October 1993, AST announced that its bank credit line had been increased to $225 million, from $175 million.

Capitalization

Long Term Debt: $92,258,000 (7/3/93).

Common Stock: 31,593,365 shs. ($0.01 par).
Insiders control 11.5%, inclduing 10.0% held by S.U. Qureshey.
Institutions hold 38%.
Shareholders: 1,222 of record (8/93).

Office—16215 Alton Parkway, Irvine, CA 92718. **Tels**—(714) 727-4141. **Chrmn**—C. J. Santoro. **Pres & CEO**—S. U. Qureshey. **SVP-Fin & CFO**—B. C. Edwards. **Secy & Treas**—D. R. Leibel. **Investor Contact**—Misty Omhart (714-727-7728). **Dirs**—R. J. Goeglein, J. W. Peltason, S. U. Qureshey, C. J. Santoro, D. W. Yocam. **Transfer Agent & Registrar**—American Stock Transfer & Trust Co., NYC. **Incorporated** in California in 1980; reincorporated in Delaware in 1987. **Empl**—4,509.

 Neeraj K. Vohra

Acuson Corp.

NYSE Symbol ACN Options on Pacific (Jan-Apr-Jul-Oct) In S&P MidCap 400

Price	Range	P-E Ratio	Dividend	Yield	S&P Ranking	Beta
Oct. 13'93	1993					
12⅛	16–10⅝	34	None	None	B	1.17

Summary

Acuson is a leading manufacturer and marketer of medical diagnostic ultrasound systems. A loss was incurred in the first half of 1993, reflecting weak demand from core markets and a $12 million restructuring charge. Despite new product introductions, soft demand for ultrasound products is expected to hurt results for the foreseeable future.

Current Outlook

Earnings are seen rising to $0.45 a share om 1994, following a plunge to $0.30 (after a restructuring charge of $0.27) expected in 1993.

Initiation of cash dividends is not likely.

Product sales for the balance of 1993 and into 1994 are not seen recovering to earlier levels. Demand from hospitals should remain weak, largely reflecting efforts to limit capital expenditures. Recently detailed U.S. healthcare policy encourages enrollment in HMO's and other managed care plans, and efforts by such plans to limit usage of procedures such as ultrasound by patients outside of the high risk category does not bode well for the fundamentals of ultrasound manufacturers. Patient demand for such procedures as fetal monitoring is expected to erode, on lower insurance reimbursement. However, ACN has a substantial installed base, strong management and significant level of service revenue. In addition, usage of ultrasound in high risk patients will drive future product sales.

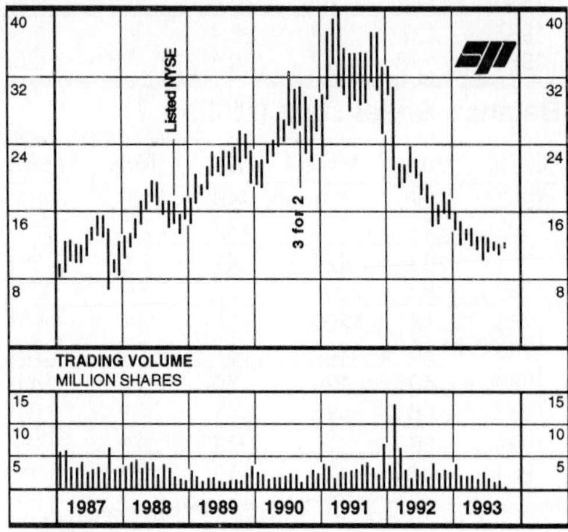

Net Sales (Million $)

Quarter:	1994	1993	1992	1991
Mar.	---	82.3	87.0	78.2
Jun.	---	72.1	87.7	82.7
Sep.	---	---	84.5	85.6
Dec.	---	---	83.6	89.9
	---	---	342.8	336.3

Net sales in the six months ended July 3, 1993, dropped 12%, year to year, reflecting protracted weakness in core markets. Gross margins narrowed, and product development spending climbed to $29.4 million, from $21.0 million. Net interest income was lower, and results were hurt by a $12 million pretax restructuring charge; a pretax loss contrasted with pretax income. After tax credits of $919,000, versus taxes at 37.0%, a net loss of $1,707,000 ($0.06 a share, on 18% fewer shares) replaced net income of $23,789,000 ($0.66).

Earnings Per Share ($)

Quarter:	1994	1993	1992	1991
Mar.	---	0.17	0.35	0.37
Jun.	---	d0.23	0.31	0.39
Sep.	---	E0.06	0.22	0.41
Dec.	---	E0.30	0.20	0.42
	E0.45	E0.30	1.08	1.59

Important Developments

Sep. '93— ACN introduced the 128XP/10sp, an ultrasound system designed to help surgeons avoid diseased areas of the heart by permitting direct observation of plaque in the aorta. The system is priced at $130,000 to $150,000.

Jul. '93— A net restructuring charge of $0.27 a share was recorded in the 1993 second quarter, for severance payments (the workforce was cut 15%) and other costs, reflecting worldwide weakness in medical ultrasound markets.

Next earnings report expected in late October.

Per Share Data ($)

Yr. End Dec. 31	1992	1991	1990	1989	1988	1987	1986	1985	1984	1983
Tangible Bk. Val.	**6.75**	[1]7.69	[1]5.75	[1]4.23	[1]3.01	2.11	1.59	NA	NA	NA
Cash Flow	**1.67**	1.98	1.67	1.35	0.99	0.61	0.33	0.17	NA	NA
Earnings[2]	**1.08**	1.59	1.33	1.07	0.78	0.49	0.27	0.07	d0.03	d0.25
Dividends	**Nil**	Nil	Nil	Nil	Nil	Nil	Nil	Nil	Nil	Nil
Payout Ratio	**Nil**	Nil	Nil	Nil	Nil	Nil	Nil	Nil	Nil	Nil
Prices—High	**33⅜**	40	32	25¹¹⁄₁₆	19¹¹⁄₁₆	15½	8¹³⁄₁₆	NA	NA	NA
Low	**14⅜**	22¾	18⅞	14¹¹⁄₁₆	10½	6¹³⁄₁₆	5	NA	NA	NA
P/E Ratio—	**31–13**	25–14	25–14	24–14	25–13	32–14	33–19	NA	NA	NA

Data as orig. reptd.; prior to 1986 data as reptd. in prosp. dated Sep. 16, 1986. Adj. for stk. div. of 50% Sep. 1990. **1.** Incl. intangibles. **2.** Bef. spec. items of +0.09 in 1986, +0.07 in 1985. d-Deficit. E-Estimated. NA-Not Available.

Income Data (Million $)

Year Ended Dec. 31	Revs.	Oper. Inc.	% Oper. Inc. of Revs.	Cap. Exp.	Depr.	Int. Exp.	Net Bef. Taxes	Eff. Tax Rate	2Net Inc.	% Net Inc. of Revs.	Cash Flow
1992	**343**	**71.3**	**20.8**	**35.2**	**20.4**	**0.12**	**58.3**	**36.8%**	**36.8**	**10.7**	**57.3**
1991	336	98.7	29.3	18.9	14.4	0.10	93.2	37.2%	58.5	17.4	72.9
1990	283	83.2	29.4	19.1	12.4	0.08	77.2	38.0%	47.8	16.9	60.2
1989	227	67.9	29.9	13.8	10.1	0.17	61.2	37.8%	38.1	16.7	48.2
1988	169	48.9	29.0	16.7	7.2	0.08	43.6	36.9%	27.5	16.3	34.7
1987	106	31.2	29.5	112.2	4.5	0.14	28.3	40.7%	16.8	15.9	21.3
1986	64	17.0	26.5	15.1	2.1	0.48	15.4	46.5%	8.2	12.8	10.3
1985	31	3.2	10.0	13.4	1.3	0.66	4.0	52.4%	1.9	6.1	3.2
1984	18	0.3	1.5	1.3	0.8	0.44	d0.6	Nil	d0.6	NM	NA
1983	3	d5.3	NM	2.0	0.3	0.15	d5.6	Nil	d5.6	NM	NA

Balance Sheet Data (Million $)

Dec. 31	Cash	Curr. Assets	Curr. Liab.	Curr. Ratio	Total Assets	% Ret. on Assets	Long Term Debt	Common Equity	Total Cap.	% LT Debt of Cap.	% Ret. on Equity
1992	**65**	**209**	**77.4**	**2.7**	**279**	**13.1**	**Nil**	**201**	**201**	**Nil**	**17.1**
1991	154	287	59.9	4.8	336	19.8	Nil	272	276	Nil	24.6
1990	98	212	49.3	4.3	249	22.0	Nil	200	200	Nil	27.6
1989	67	154	39.1	3.9	184	23.8	Nil	145	145	Nil	30.7
1988	28	108	31.3	3.5	134	24.4	Nil	102	102	Nil	31.7
1987	34	75	20.4	3.7	91	21.1	0.09	71	71	0.1	27.3
1986	35	59	14.8	4.0	68	17.0	0.52	53	53	1.0	NA
1985	9	24	6.8	3.5	29	8.8	8.65	d5	22	39.5	NA
1984	3	12	3.3	3.7	15	NM	2.02	d9	11	17.7	NM
1983	NA	NA	NA	NA	6	NM	1.87	NA	4	42.7	NM

Data as orig. reptd. **1.** Net of curr. yr. retirement and disposals. **2.** Bef. spec. items. d-Deficit. NM-Not Meaningful. NA-Not Available.

Business Summary

Acuson Corp. is a leader in the design, manufacture, and marketing of premium quality medical diagnostic ultrasound imaging systems. Such systems use low power, high-frequency sound waves to nonivasively generate real-time moving images of soft tissues, internal body organs and blood flows. Ultrasound is often the imaging technique of choice for many soft tissues and has common cardiac, abdominal (liver, kidney, spleen and gallbladder), gynecological, obstetrical, urological (prostate), and periferal vascular applications.

The company's systems use a hybrid analog/digital computer architechture designed to electronically form high resolution, real-time ultrasound images under software control. This basic architechture was utilized in the Acuson 128 system (introduced for radiology applications in 1983) and also forms the basis for its second generation 128XP system (launched in 1990 with expanded radiology capabilites). The 128XP systems can operate in all high resolution imaging formats, which include sector, Vector Array, linear array and High Performace Curved Array. ACN's systems can provide all of the major operating modalities, which include B-mode, spectral Doppler and color Doppler.

During 1992, ACN introduced its Transcranial Imaging technology for the examination of stroke and head trauma patients, which allows for direct visualization of blood vessels in the brain with color Doppler imaging. It also introduced the AEGIS system, which provides significant new capabilities for managing and storing ultrasound images and for preserving the quality of the images' diagnostic information. In the cardiology market, it began shipments of its new V510B probe, which provides high-resolution black and white images of the heart, as well as more sensitive Doppler and color Doppler blood flow data.

The company sells its products primarily to community and teaching hospitals and clinics. It employs a full-time sales, service and applications staff for the U.S., Australia, Canada, Finland, France, Germany, Italy, Norway, Sweden and the U.K., and sells through independent distributors in a number of countries. Foreign sales represented 17% of total sales and 4.2% of operating profits in 1992.

Dividend Data

The company has never paid a cash dividend.

Finances

During 1992, the repurchase of up to 8,000,000 common shares was authorized. As of July 3, 1993, 7,373,500 shares had been acquired.

Capitalization

Long Term Debt: None (7/93).

Common Stock: 28,678,125 shs. ($0.0001 par).
Officers and directors own 24%.
Institutions hold 39%.
Shareholders of record: 2,143 (2/93).

Office—1220 Charleston Rd. (PO Box 7393), Mountain View, CA 94039-7393. **Tel**—(415) 969-9112. **Pres & CEO**—S. H. Maslak. **EVP, CFO & Investor Contact**—Robert J. Gallagher (800-433-1447). **Secy**—C. H. Dearborn. **Dirs**—T. J. Perkins (Chrmn), W. H. Abbott, R. Diener, K. H. Johannsmeier, S. H. Maslak. **Transfer Agent & Registrar**—First National Bank of Boston, Boston, Mass. **Incorporated** in California in 1981; reincorporated in Delaware in 1986. **Empl**—1,472.

 Robert M. Gold

Adobe Systems

NASDAQ Symbol ADBE (Incl. in Nat'l Market) Options on Pacific In S&P MidCap 400

Price	Range	P-E Ratio	Dividend	Yield	S&P Ranking	Beta
Aug. 20'93	1993					
23¼	37–15⅝	24	0.20	0.9%	B	1.49

Summary

This company's systems and application software are used to print integrated text and graphics for high-quality electronic printing and publishing. Over 50% of revenues are derived from licensing its PostScript interpreter. Earnings dropped in fiscal 1992, reflecting slower sales growth, high R&D spending, charges related to acquisitions, and a real estate partnership writeoff. The release of new products should aid fiscal 1993 results.

Current Outlook

Earnings in the fiscal year ending November 30, 1994, are projected at $1.50 a share (adjusted), up from $1.30 estimated for fiscal 1993 and the $0.94 recorded in fiscal 1992 (which included charges and writeoffs totaling $0.17).

Dividends were raised 25%, to $0.05 a share (as adjusted), in March 1993.

Revenues are expected to rise through fiscal 1994, aided by new printers incorporating Adobe's PostScript page description language, the shipment of new applications (including Acrobat—formerly code-named "Carousel"— a document interchange product), and continued strong sales of Photoshop, Illustrator, Premiere, and other graphics and video products. Although margins are expected to be restricted in the near-term by higher sales and marketing expenses related to Acrobat and PostScript, long-term profitability should benefit from volume efficiencies and a more favorable product mix.

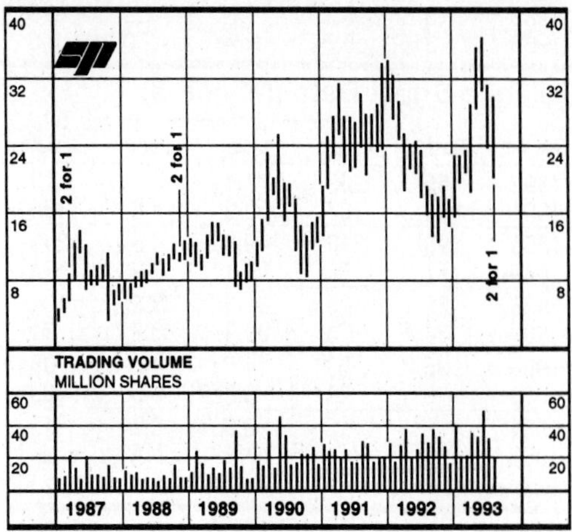

Revenues (Million $)

13 Weeks:	1992-93	1991-92	1990-91	1989-90
Feb.	68.5	62.6	52.6	37.2
May	79.6	69.6	57.1	35.3
Aug.		63.0	57.2	42.8
Nov.		70.7	62.7	53.4
		265.9	229.7	168.7

Revenues in the six months ended May 28, 1993, advanced 12%, year to year, reflecting 6.8% greater PostScript licensing revenues and a 19% increase in the sale of applications. Margins narrowed, as R&D spending climbed 36%, and sales, marketing and support costs rose 20%; despite sharply higher other income, including a $3,920,000 gain on the sale of an investment, the increase in pretax income was held to 7.1%. After taxes at 38.6%, versus 37.3%, net income was up 4.9%, to $29,912,000 ($0.65 a share, as adjusted), from $28,520,000 ($0.61).

Common Share Earnings ($)

13 Weeks:	1992-93	1991-92	1990-91	1989-90
Feb.	0.34	0.29	0.28	0.24
May	0.31	0.33	0.29	0.18
Aug.	E0.32	0.15	0.28	0.23
Nov.	E0.33	0.19	0.29	0.28
	E1.30	0.93	1.13	0.92

Important Developments

Jun. '93— The company said it had begun shipping its Acrobat family of document interchange products, which can communicate and describe documents across different types of computers, utilizing Adobe's Portable Document Format (PDF), a PostScript-based file format. Versions for Windows and Macintosh are currently available, with DOS and UNIX versions expected in late 1993.

Next earnings report expected in mid-September.

Per Share Data ($)

Yr. End Nov. 30	[2]1992	1991	1990	1989	[2]1988	1987	1986	1985
Tangible Bk. Val.	[1]5.06	[1]4.13	[1]2.57	1.47	1.07	0.58	0.34	d0.03
Cash Flow	1.13	1.27	1.03	0.86	0.54	0.24	0.11	0.03
Earnings	0.94	1.13	0.92	0.78	0.49	0.22	0.10	0.02
Dividends	0.160	0.150	0.115	0.095	0.040	Nil	Nil	Nil
Payout Ratio	17%	13%	13%	11%	8%	Nil	Nil	Nil
Prices[3]—High	34¼	33⅞	25⅜	15	12¾	14	3½	NA
Low	12⅝	13⅜	8½	7	5⅞	3³⁄₁₆	1⁷⁄₁₆	NA
P/E Ratio—	37-14	30-12	28-9	19-9	26-12	66-15	37-15	NA

Data as orig. reptd. Adj. for stk. divs. of 100% Aug. 1993, 100% Nov. 1988, 100% Mar. 1987, 100% Jun. 1986. **1.** Incl. intangibles. **2.** Refl. merger or acq. **3.** Cal. yr. E-Estimated d-Deficit. NA-Not Available.

Income Data (Million $)

Year Ended Nov. 30	Revs.	Oper. Inc.	% Oper. Inc. of Revs.	Cap. Exp.	Depr.	Int. Exp.	Net Bef. Taxes	Eff. Tax Rate	Net Inc.	% Net Inc. of Revs.	Cash Flow
[1]1992	**266**	**83.5**	**31.4**	**11.9**	**8.79**	**Nil**	**69.5**	**37.3%**	**43.6**	**16.4**	**52.4**
1991	230	84.6	36.8	12.2	6.68	NA	83.6	38.3%	51.6	22.5	58.3
1990	169	67.0	39.7	7.4	4.86	NA	66.3	39.6%	40.1	23.7	44.9
1989	121	55.3	45.6	5.2	3.73	NA	54.9	38.6%	33.7	27.8	37.4
[1]1988	83	36.2	43.4	5.0	2.09	NA	35.8	41.0%	21.1	25.3	23.2
1987	39	17.2	43.7	3.0	1.05	Nil	16.9	46.8%	9.0	22.8	10.0
1986	16	7.4	46.1	1.2	0.54	Nil	7.2	50.3%	3.6	22.3	4.1
1985	5	1.0	21.2	0.5	0.34	Nil	0.8	40.8%	0.5	10.8	0.8

Balance Sheet Data (Million $)

Nov. 30	Cash	Curr. Assets	Curr. Liab.	Curr. Ratio	Total Assets	% Ret. on Assets	Long Term Debt	Common Equity	Total Cap.	% LT Debt of Cap.	% Ret. on Equity
1992	**160**	**224**	**56.8**	**4.0**	**281**	**17.3**	**Nil**	**225**	**225**	**Nil**	**21.4**
1991	116	162	36.9	4.4	221	27.5	Nil	183	184	Nil	34.8
1990	70	109	37.0	2.9	146	32.9	0.25	108	109	0.2	47.4
1989	50	77	34.1	2.3	94	42.7	0.50	59	60	0.8	66.2
1988	35	52	19.0	2.7	65	42.9	0.86	44	46	1.9	61.9
1987	17	25	7.9	3.2	32	34.3	Nil	24	24	Nil	48.2
1986	13	17	5.1	3.2	20	18.2	Nil	14	15	Nil	57.0
1985	3	4	1.1	3.8	6	NA	Nil	NM	5	Nil	NA

Data as orig. reptd. **1.** Refl. merger or acq. NA-Not Available. NM-Not Meaningful.

Business Summary

Adobe Systems develops and supports computer software used to create, display, print and communicate all forms of electronic documents.

The company's principal product, the PostScript interpreter, executes page descriptions generated from applications that support the PostScript language to produce documents containing multiple typefaces and graphics, including charts, diagrams, drawings and photographic images. Because the PostScript page description language is device-independent, applications that have been written to support the PostScript language can be used with any raster output device that contains a PostScript interpreter.

The PostScript interpreter is typically implemented on a dedicated processor (controller) that has direct control over a printer. Adobe licenses the PostScript interpreter, typeface software and associated controller designs to computer, printer, imagesetter and film recorder manufacturers for incorporation into their products. As of January 31, 1993, the company had contracts with about 40 OEM customers. Royalties derived from the licensing of the PostScript interpreter accounted for 57% of revenues in fiscal 1992.

The Display PostScript system is a high-performance interactive version of PostScript software technology for use on workstation displays. This software is an extension of the PostScript language that incorporates a PostScript interpreter with other system software.

Approximately 340 software companies have introduced or announced the development of application programs that support the PostScript interpreter. More than 5,000 application programs support the PostScript interpreter and run on a variety of computers, including mainframes, minicomputers and Apple, IBM and IBM-compatible personal computers.

Adobe also offers application software packages including Illustrator, a graphics illustration program, Photoshop, an image enhancement tool, and downloadable typeface software programs that are licensed through retail distribution channels and directly to end-users. Revenues from product sales accounted for 43% of the total in fiscal 1992.

Dividend Data

A "poison pill" shareholder rights plan was adopted in 1990.

Amt of Divd. $	Date Decl.	Ex-divd. Date	Stock of Record	Payment Date
0.08	Sep. 14	Sep. 24	Sep. 30	Oct. 14'92
0.08	Jan. 12	Jan. 19	Jan. 25	Feb. 9'93
0.10	Mar. 16	Mar. 26	Apr. 1	Apr. 15'93
0.10	Jun. 16	Jun. 23	Jun. 29	Jul. 13'93
2-for-1	Jul. 9	Aug. 11	Jul. 27	Aug. 10'93

Finances

In fiscal 1992, Adobe wrote-off $6,000,000 ($0.08 a share, net, adjusted) for an investment in a real estate partnership and $6,325,000 ($0.09 a share, net, adjusted) for research and development in process at the time of its acquisitions of OCR Systems and Nonlinear Technologies.

Capitalization

Long Term Debt: None (5/93).

Common Stock: 44,597,726 shs.; adj. (no par).
Institutions hold 82%.
Shareholders: About 1,047 of record (1/93).

Office—1585 Charleston Rd., Mountain View, CA 94043-1225. **Tel**—(415) 961-4400. **Chrmn & CEO**—J. E. Warnock. **Pres & COO**—C. M. Geschke. **SVP-Fin, CFO, Treas & Investor Contact**—M. Bruce Nakao. **Secy**—C. M. Pouliot. **Dirs**—C. M. Geschke, W. R. Hambrecht, R. Sedgewick, W. J. Spencer, J. E. Warnock, D. W. Yocam. **Transfer Agent & Registrar**—Chemical Bank, SF. **Incorporated** in California in 1983. **Empl**—904.

 Peter C. Wood, CFA

Advanced Technology Labs.

NASDAQ Symbol ATLI (Incl. in Nat'l Market) Options on Phila In S&P MidCap 400

Price	Range	P–E Ratio	Dividend	Yield	S&P Ranking	Beta
Aug. 6'93	1993					
16¾	19–15½	28	None	None	NR	1.64

Summary

This company (formerly Westmark International) develops, manufactures, markets and services medical ultrasound systems widely used in hospitals, clinics and physicians' offices to diagnose a variety of conditions, such as tumors, inflammations, obstructions, cardiovascular diseases and fetal abnormalities. Results in recent periods were hurt by soft demand in the U.S. market due to the uncertain impact of pending healthcare reform. A common share repurchase program, begun in 1993's first quarter, is continuing.

Business Summary

Advanced Technology Laboratories, Inc. (ATL) is one of the world's leading suppliers of diagnostic ultrasound medical equipment. The company believes that it has become a worldwide leader in ultrasound technology through its proprietary position in digital, broad bandwidth beamforming and scanhead technologies.

Ultrasound systems provide a safe, noninvasive and painless means of observing soft tissues and internal body organs and assessing blood flow through the heart and vessels. These systems focus high-frequency sound waves at the internal structures being examined; echoes created are gathered and electronically processed by the system. Repeated scannings of the body interior at very high speeds produce moving, two-dimensional, black-and-white video images in real time. Ultrasound systems can also analyze blood flow characteristics using the Doppler principle. ATL's Ultramark product line serves all major diagnostic ultrasound clinical markets, including radiology, cardiology, obstetrics/gynecology and vascular.

ATL has pioneered the development of digital beamformers, which digitize the signals returning from the body prior to processing, and broad-bandwidth scanhead technologies, which complement the capability of its digital beamforming technology and allow physicians to see more of the tissue signature with greater clarity.

ATL's highest-performing system, the Ultramark 9 with High Definition Imaging (HDI; priced from $150,000 to $250,000 per unit) contains an ASIC-based digital beamformer and offers a series of high-performance scanheads for clinical applications in the radiology, perinatology and vascular segments of the ultrasound market. HDI captures and displays a broad tissue signature, enabling physicians to visualize anatomical detail, subtle tissue characteristics and disease processes that could not previously be seen or confidently identified with ultrasound. The Ultramark 4 is a highly

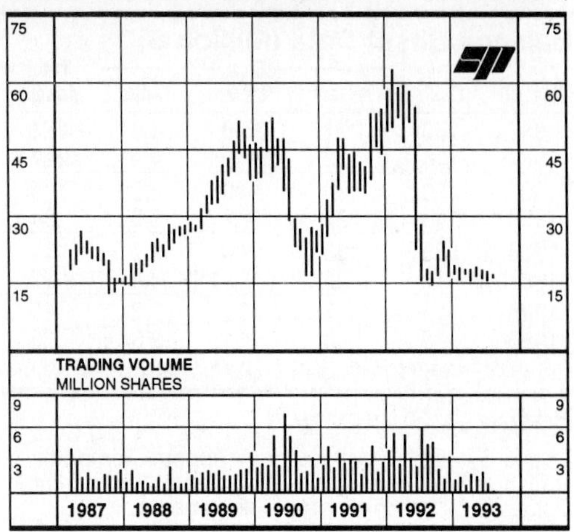

portable grayscale and Doppler system used principally in private ob/gyn offices and medical institutions ($30,000 to $60,000).

The company also offers products such as transducers, off-line analysis systems, used equipment and accessories and supplies.

Important Developments

May '93— ATL said it began customer deliveries of Extended Signal Processing (ESP), an upgrade of its digital Ultramark 9 HDI system. ESP uses real-time parallel processing and system software to optimize the image formation and extract further tissue information from the HDI broadband digital beamformer, eliminating "speckle noise" which restricts ultrasound image clarity. In addition, the company commenced shipments of its fifth broad bandwidth scanhead, the C7-4 Broadband Curved Array Scanhead for obstetrical, superficial abdominal and pediatric examinations.

Next earnings report expected in late October.

Per Share Data ($)

Yr. End Dec. 31	1992	1991	[1]1990	1989	1988	1987	1986
Tangible Bk. Val.	**18.04**	30.17	27.71	26.18	22.97	21.91	22.13
Cash Flow	**1.66**	3.61	3.00	2.99	2.01	0.24	NA
Earnings[2]	**0.67**	2.09	1.61	1.85	1.05	d0.67	d1.29
Dividends	**Nil**	Nil	Nil	Nil	Nil	Nil	Nil
Payout Ratio	**Nil**	Nil	Nil	Nil	Nil	Nil	Nil
Prices—High	**63**	54¼	52¼	51½	28¼	26¾	NA
Low	**14½**	21½	16¾	26½	14½	12¾	NA
P/E Ratio—	**94–22**	26–10	32–10	28–14	27–14	NM	NM

Data as orig. reptd. **1.** Refl. merger or acq. **2.** Bef. spec. items of +0.15 in 1991, +0.22 in 1990, +0.06 in 1989, +0.03 in 1988, +0.15 in 1986. d-Deficit. NM-Not Meaningful. NA-Not Available.

Income Data (Million $)

Year Ended Dec. 31	Revs.	Oper. Inc.	% Oper. Inc. of Revs.	Cap. Exp.	Depr.	Int. Exp.	[3]Net Bef. Taxes	Eff. Tax Rate	[4]Net Inc.	% Net Inc. of Revs.	Cash Flow
1992	**324**	**25.3**	**7.8**	**[2]10.2**	**11.0**	**0.79**	**9.5**	**22.1%**	**7.4**	**2.3**	**18.4**
1991	505	39.4	7.8	[2]24.0	15.5	1.61	34.0	37.0%	21.4	4.2	36.9
[1]1990	485	38.6	8.0	19.1	14.2	0.94	25.8	36.2%	16.4	3.4	30.7
1989	439	42.0	9.6	14.0	11.8	0.58	30.8	38.0%	19.1	4.3	30.9
1988	365	22.9	6.3	11.3	9.6	0.33	17.6	40.5%	10.4	2.9	20.1
1987	292	5.6	1.9	10.5	10.1	0.21	d3.8	NM	d7.2	NM	2.6
1986	244	8.6	3.5	16.8	6.9	2.75	d22.7	NM	d13.9	NM	d7.3

Balance Sheet Data (Million $)

Dec. 31	Cash	Curr. Assets	Curr. Liab.	Curr. Ratio	Total Assets	% Ret. on Assets	Long Term Debt	Common Equity	Total Cap.	% LT Debt of Cap.	% Ret. on Equity
1992	**77.4**	**249**	**89**	**2.8**	**296**	**1.8**	**Nil**	**204**	**207**	**Nil**	**2.6**
1991	74.8	350	119	2.9	452	4.9	13.3	314	333	4	7.1
1990	36.8	311	114	2.7	396	4.4	Nil	277	282	Nil	6.2
1989	48.7	292	92	3.2	365	5.5	Nil	268	274	Nil	7.5
1988	65.4	253	87	2.9	322	3.4	Nil	234	235	Nil	4.6
1987	62.6	237	71	3.4	303	NM	Nil	229	230	Nil	NM
1986	9.3	240	49	4.9	305	NM	Nil	254	254	Nil	NM

Data as orig. reptd. **1.** Refl. merger or acq. **2.** Net. **3.** Incl. equity in earns. of nonconsol. subs. **4.** Bef. spec. items. d-Deficit. NM-Not Meaningful.

Operating Revenues (Million $)

13 Weeks:	1993	[1]1992	1991	1990
Mar.	81	76	120	118
Jun.	75	77	114	126
Sep.		78	126	119
Dec.		93	145	122
		324	505	485

Revenues in the 26 weeks ended July 2, 1993, rose 2.6%, year to year, as lower product sales in the second quarter of 1993 reflected sluggish demand from U.S. hospitals and clinics; international sales improved. Gross margins narrowed, and after 19% greater R&D outlays, higher marketing and administrative expenses and lower net interest income, partially offset by the absence of stock distribution expenses of $1,195,000 and reorganization charges of $3,764,000, net income fell to $123,000 ($0.01 a share, on 5% more shares) from $989,000 ($0.09).

In April 1993, ATL was notified that a vendor would not be able to meet some commitments during 1993's second half for delivery of certain semiconductor devices used in the Ultramark 9 product. The company is attempting to minimize disruption of its shipment schedule.

Common Share Earnings ($)

13 Weeks:	1993	[1]1992	1991	1990
Mar.	0.17	0.25	0.60	0.48
Jun.	d0.16	d0.13	0.21	0.42
Sep.		0.11	0.42	0.32
Dec.		0.45	0.86	0.39
		0.67	2.09	1.61

Dividend Data

No cash has been paid. In June 1992, shareholders received one SpaceLabs Medical Inc. common share for each Westmark common share.

Finances

In February 1993, the company was authorized to repurchase up to 1,000,000 ATL common shares in the open market. As of July 2, 1993, 469,000 shares had been acquired.

Research and development expenditures amounted to $38.3 million (11.8% of revenues from ATL operations) in 1992, versus $35.2 (12.6%) in 1991.

ATL markets its products internationally through its direct sales force and service operations in Australia, Austria, Belgium, Canada, France, Germany, the Netherlands, Sweden and the United Kingdom, while other markets are covered through a dealer network. International revenues (including export sales) accounted for about 42% of total revenues in 1992, up from 41% in 1991.

Diagnostic ultrasound systems represented an estimated $1.9 billion worldwide market in 1992. Ultrasound is considered to be the fastest-growing major segment of the total medical imaging industry, with worldwide revenues estimated at more than $8 billion.

Capitalization

Long Term Debt: None (6/93).

Common Stock: 10,800,000 shs. ($0.01 par). Institutions hold 72%. Shareholders: 13,856 of record (2/93).

1. Excl. SpaceLabs Medical. d-Deficit.

Office—22100 Bothell-Everett Highway, P. O. Box 3003, Bothell, WA 98041-3003. **Tel**—(206) 487-7000. **Chrmn & CEO**—D. C. Fill. **Pres & COO**—D. M. Perozek. **SVP-Fin & CFO**—H. N. Gillis. **VP & Investor Contact**—Anne Marie Bugge (206) 487-7081. **Dirs**—R. M. Barford, K. L. Cramer, H. Feigenbaum, D. C. Fill, E. A. Larson, J. Miller, D. M. Perozek, H. Woolf. **Transfer Agent & Registrar**—First Chicago Trust Co. of New York. **Incorporated** in Delaware in 1983. **Empl**—2,136.

 Robert M. Gold

Affiliated Publications

NYSE Symbol AFP In S&P MidCap 400

Price	Range	P-E Ratio	Dividend	Yield	S&P Ranking	Beta
Jun. 28'93	1993					
13⅞	14½–11½	32	0.26	1.9%	NR	0.99

Summary

Affiliated owns The Boston Globe, the largest newspaper in New England, and a one-third interest in BPI Communications, a publisher of specialty magazines, books and directories. On June 10, 1993, directors agreed to a proposal by The New York Times Co. to acquire AFP for roughly $15.00 per share in stock and cash.

Current Outlook

Earnings for the company as presently constituted are expected to rise to $0.55 a share for 1993, versus the $0.40 (before special items) of 1992.

The quarterly dividend was recently raised to $0.06½ from $0.06.

Revenues for 1993 are expected to rise by roughly 6%, largely reflecting a continuing recovery in newspaper advertising. Margins should widen significantly, boosted by the revenue gains and operating economies, in spite of a gradual increase in newsprint costs. A full year of profitability for 33%-owned BPI Communications will sharply boost equity earnings.

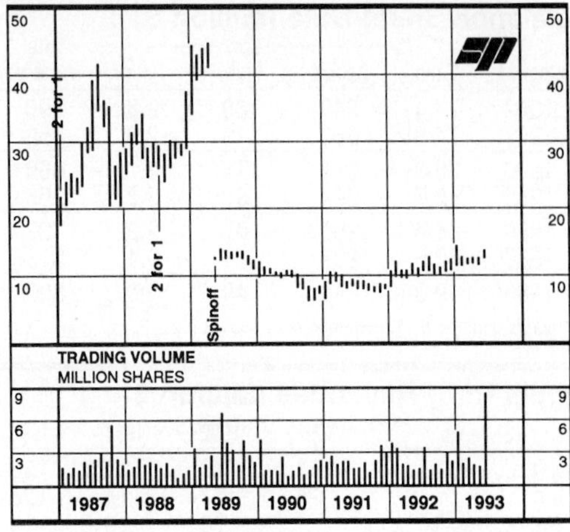

Operating Revenues (Million $)

13 Weeks:	1993	1992	1991	1990
Mar.	102.3	97.3	92.8	133.7
Jun.	---	106.8	100.7	132.1
Sep.	---	99.9	93.6	130.4
Dec.	---	109.9	105.8	139.8
	---	414.0	392.8	536.0

Revenues in the March 1993 quarter rose 5.2%, year to year. Operating costs rose less rapidly, and operating income advanced 27%. After other items, including 69% lower interest expense, and equity profits (instead of losses), pretax earnings climbed 67%. After taxes at 39.1%, against 36.4%, net income gained 60%. Results for 1992 exclude a $0.20 a share special charge from accounting changes.

Common Share Earnings ($)

13 Weeks:	1993	1992	1991	1990
Mar.	0.08	0.05	d0.01	0.09
Jun.	E0.14	0.10	0.04	0.11
Sep.	E0.11	0.08	d0.01	0.06
Dec.	E0.22	0.17	d0.97	0.09
	E0.55	0.40	d0.95	0.35

Acquisition Proposal

Jun. '93— AFP agreed to be acquired by The New York Times Co. in a transaction valued at roughly $1.1 billion, or $15 per share. Terms call for all of AFP's stockholders to receive $15 worth of Times Co. Class A Common Stock for each AFP share owned. Holders of AFP's Series A Common Stock will also have the option to elect cash, on a pro rata basis, in exchange for as much as 15% of the total number of shares of AFP's common stock. Stock transfers will be nontaxable, but cash payments will be taxable. The transaction, which is expected to be consummated by early fall 1993, is subject to shareholder approvals and other conditions. Under the agreement, the Globe newspaper will maintain full editorial autonomy and management responsibility for day-to-day operations.

Next earnings report expected in late July.

Per Share Data ($)

Yr. End Dec. 31	1992	1991	[1]1990	1989	1988	1987	1986	1985	1984	1983
Tangible Bk. Val.	**1.82**	1.84	0.04	0.43	0.80	3.16	2.69	1.97	1.74	1.47
Cash Flow	**0.67**	d0.66	0.65	0.90	1.03	2.30	0.78	0.62	0.53	0.41
Earnings[2]	**0.40**	d0.95	0.35	0.63	0.75	2.04	0.56	0.43	0.38	0.32
Dividends	**0.240**	0.240	0.240	0.220	0.200	0.160	0.110	0.100	0.089	0.073
Payout Ratio	**61%**	NM	70%	35%	27%	8%	20%	24%	24%	23%
Prices—High	**12⅞**	10⅝	12⅛	49½	37⅝	41⅞	18⅜	9½	5¾	5
Low	**8⅜**	6⅝	6¼	11	24	17⅝	8¾	5¼	4⅜	2⅞
P/E Ratio—	**32–21**	NM	35–18	79–17	50–32	20–9	33–16	22–12	15–11	16–9

Data as orig. reptd. Adj. for stk. divs. of 100% (Series B com.) Jul. 1988, 100% Jan. 1987, 50% Jan. 1986, of 50% Jan. 1985, 50% Feb. 1983. **1.** Refl. merger or acq. **2.** Bef. results of disc. ops. of -0.39 in 1989, -1.92 in 1988, +0.57 in 1987, +0.37 in 1986 & spec. items of -0.20 in 1992, +0.25 in 1987. d-Deficit. E-Estimated. NM-Not Meaningful.

Income Data (Million $)

Year Ended Dec. 31	Revs.	Oper. Inc.	% Oper. Inc. of Revs.	Cap. Exp.	Depr.	Int. Exp.	[3]Net Bef. Taxes	Eff. Tax Rate	[4]Net Inc.	% Net Inc. of Revs.	Cash Flow
1992	**414**	**71**	**17.0**	**17.2**	**19.6**	**8.7**	**45**	**38.6%**	**[5]28**	**6.7**	**47**
1991	393	51	12.9	19.7	20.6	13.7	d84	NM	d67	NM	d46
[1]1990	536	74	13.8	30.0	21.6	13.8	42	42.2%	24	4.5	46
[2]1989	542	101	18.7	33.5	19.5	11.9	74	40.7%	44	8.0	63
[2]1988	534	114	21.4	25.8	19.0	10.0	86	39.9%	52	9.7	71
[2]1987	490	124	25.4	30.1	17.9	6.1	191	24.7%	143	29.2	161
[2]1986	401	101	25.3	27.2	15.7	5.8	81	51.1%	[5]40	9.9	56
1985	367	80	21.8	22.4	14.8	4.7	66	53.2%	31	8.4	46
1984	344	72	20.9	43.1	11.6	2.1	57	51.8%	27	8.0	39
1983	294	57	19.5	32.8	6.9	1.9	46	52.2%	22	7.6	29

Balance Sheet Data (Million $)

Dec. 31	Cash	Curr. Assets	Curr. Liab.	Curr. Ratio	Total Assets	% Ret. on Assets	Long Term Debt	Common Equity	Total Cap.	% LT Debt of Cap.	% Ret. on Equity
1992	**47**	**111**	**55**	**2.0**	**308**	**8.1**	**50**	**132**	**186**	**26.8**	**21.2**
1991	109	189	156	1.2	381	NM	50	131	195	25.6	NM
[1]1990	5	97	80	1.2	498	5.0	154	213	384	40.0	11.7
1989	36	119	88	1.4	468	9.7	136	201	351	38.6	21.9
1988	11	99	60	1.7	425	10.8	116	194	329	35.2	20.0
1987	9	90	69	1.3	532	34.0	95	324	435	21.9	56.2
1986	40	113	59	1.9	318	13.4	30	190	239	12.5	23.0
1985	2	66	30	2.2	285	12.3	59	161	238	25.0	20.4
1984	6	61	30	2.0	219	10.9	22	143	173	12.4	16.7
1983	18	59	27	2.2	188	12.9	19	123	147	12.9	20.1

Data as orig. reptd. **1.** Refl. merger or acq. **2.** Excl. disc. ops. **3.** Incl. equity in earns. of nonconsol. subs. **4.** Bef. spec. items. **5.** Refl. acctg. change. d-Deficit. NM-Not Meaningful.

Business Summary

Affiliated Publications publishes The Boston Globe newspaper and owns a one-third equity interest in BPI Communications, a specialty publisher of magazines and books. In 1989, the company spun off to shareholders its 47.2% interest in McCaw Cellular Communications.

The Boston Globe has the largest combined daily and Sunday circulation of all newspapers in the Boston primary market, and it garners more than 80% of all advertising dollars placed in Boston newspapers. Average circulation in the 26 weeks ended September 30, 1992, was 508,867 daily and 812,021 Sunday.

In December 1991, AFP sold a two-thirds interest in BPI Communications, which was restructured as a limited partnership. Since AFP's purchase of Billboard Publications in 1987, BPI has expanded rapidly through acquisitions to become one of the leading U.S. information providers for the entertainment, arts and design fields. BPI owns 18 publications, including The Hollywood Reporter, Billboard, Amusement Business, Back Stage, Architecture, Music & Media, Musician, American Artist, AdWeek, Back Stage/Shoot, Marketing Computers, MediaWeek, Photo District News, Photo Business, Interiors, Brand Week, and Plants, Sites & Parks. It also publishes books, directories and special issues whose subjects relate to those of the magazines (through its subsidiary, Watson-Guptil Publications) and distributes information electronically worldwide.

Dividend Data

The company and its predecessor have paid dividends every year since 1882. Dividends are identical on the Series A and Series B common shares.

Amt. of Divd. $	Date Decl.	Ex–divd. Date	Stock of Record	Payment Date
0.06	Oct. 29	Nov. 6	Nov. 13	Dec. 1'92
0.06	Dec. 3	Feb. 8	Feb. 12	Mar. 1'93
0.06½	Mar. 25	May 10	May 15	Jun. 1'93
0.06½	Jun. 11	Aug. 9	Aug. 13	Sep. 1'93

Capitalization

Long Term Debt: $50,000,000 (3/93).

Series A Com. Stk.: 51,216,842 shs. ($0.01 par).

Series B Com. Stk.: 19,830,140 shs. ($0.01 par); 10 votes per sh.; limited transferability; conv. sh.-for-sh. into Series A.

About 81% of Series B is closely held (68% of total voting power), incl. some institutional holdings.

Institutions hold about 48% of both classes of stock.

Shareholders of record: 5,043 Series A; 3,053 Series B.

Office—135 Morrissey Blvd., P.O. Box 2378, Boston, MA 02107-2378. **Tel**—(617) 929-3300. **Chrmn & CEO**—W. O. Taylor. **Pres**—J. P. Giuggio. **EVP-CFO & Investor Contact**—William B. Huff. **Dirs**—H. E. Cox Jr., J. P. Giuggio, R. D. Grimm, A. F. Kingsbury, R. A. Lawrence, S. L. Lightfoot, E. E. Phillips, A. Simmons, R. Z. Sorenson, C. H. Taylor Jr., W. O. Taylor. **Transfer Agent & Registrar**—State Street Bank & Trust Co., Boston. **Incorporated** in Massachusetts in 1973. **Empl**—2,431.

Air & Water Technologies

ASE Symbol AWT In S&P MidCap 400

Price	Range	P-E Ratio	Dividend	Yield	S&P Ranking	Beta
Oct. 14'93	1993					
14⅛	15¼–9⅝	NM	None	None	NR	NA

Summary

This company provides a broad range of environmental services and technologies in the areas of air pollution control, water resources management, and the reuse of waste by-products. Services are provided mainly through Research-Cottrell Inc. and Metcalf & Eddy Cos. Inc. Following losses in the last two fiscal years, profitability was restored in the first nine months of fiscal 1993, reflecting an improved revenue mix at Metcalf & Eddy and cost control measures. In September 1993, Compagnie Generale des Eaux, which holds a 23% stake in AWT, said it intends to review the company's financial position and would consider influencing or controlling its management and policies.

Business Summary

Air & Water Technologies Corporation (AWT) is a leading environmental treatment and services company, providing a comprehensive range of services and technologies for controlling air pollution, protecting water resources, and disposing of or reusing certain waste by-products through the development of inert and environmentally sound products. Contributions to sales by division in recent fiscal years were:

	1992	1991
Research–Cottrell	37%	34%
Metcalf & Eddy	48%	57%
Residuals Management	15%	13%

Research-Cottrell provides air-related services and technologies, principally for the reduction of air pollution and the treatment of thermal discharges, the dispersion of airborne contaminants, the monitoring of emissions, and the provision of regulatory and engineering services. Services include identifying and analyzing air pollution problems and control options; designing treatment facilities and equipment; supervising equipment fabrication and installation; and providing overall project management and quality control.

Through Metcalf & Eddy Cos., AWT provides a comprehensive range of water-related services to governmental, commercial and industrial clients, including treatment process design, operation and ownership of facilities, and on-site and off-site remediation of environmental contamination. Activities include the collection, treatment and distribution of drinking water; the collection, treatment and disposal of wastewater and wastewater by-products, such as sludge; the treatment and disposal of hazardous and toxic wastes; and the management of non-hazardous solid wastes.

Residuals Management develops, acquires or utilizes new technologies for the reuse and ultimate disposal of by-products generated as a result of treatment processes or other industrial activities. Activities consist of asbestos abatement and removal services for utilities and industrial and commercial businesses, and the design, fabrication and service of natural gas compressor and other systems for industrial and governmental customers and for extracting commercially usable methane from landfills.

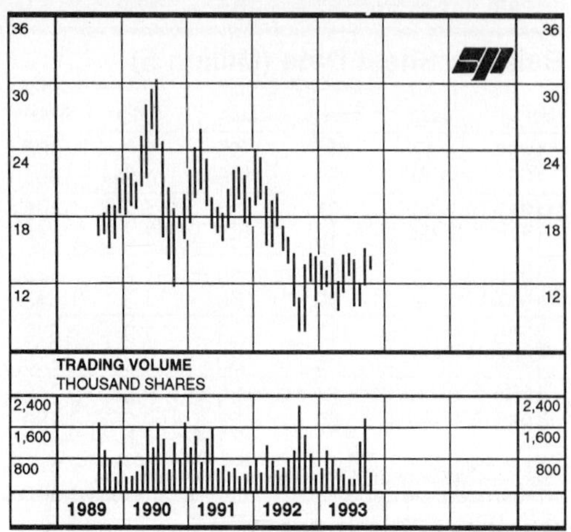

Important Developments

Sep. '93— Compagnie Generale des Eaux (CGE), which holds a 23% stake in AWT, said in a 13D filing with the SEC that it intends to review the company's financial position, and would consider influencing or controlling its management and policies, acquiring additional shares, or selling all or part of its shares.

Next earnings report expected in late December.

Per Share Data ($)

Yr. End Oct. 31	1992	[1]1991	1990	[1]1989	1988
Tangible Bk. Val.[4]	**8.72**	9.12	8.96	3.45	d0.59
Cash Flow	**0.27**	d0.48	1.01	d0.11	NA
Earnings[2]	**d0.40**	d1.15	0.35	d0.87	NA
Dividends	**Nil**	Nil	Nil	Nil	Nil
Payout Ratio	**Nil**	Nil	Nil	Nil	Nil
Prices[3]—High	**24⅛**	25⅞	30⅜	21½	NA
Low	**7¾**	15⅞	11¾	15¼	NA
P/E Ratio—	**NM**	NM	87–34	NM	NA

Data as orig. reptd. **1.** Refl. merger or acq. **2.** Bef. spec. items of -1.41 in 1990, +0.17 in 1989. **3.** Cal. yr. **4.** Incl. intangibles. d-Deficit. NM-Not Meaningful. NA-Not Available.

Income Data (Million $)

Year Ended Oct. 31	Revs.	Oper. Inc.	% Oper. Inc. of Revs.	Cap. Exp.	Depr.	Int. Exp.	Net Bef. Taxes	Eff. Tax Rate	[3]Net Inc.	% Net Inc. of Revs.	Cash Flow
1992	**719**	**39.3**	**5.5**	**9.2**	**16.9**	**23.1**	**[2]8.7**	**NM**	**d10.0**	**NM**	**6.8**
1991	657	27.7	4.2	12.0	15.1	22.0	[2]d23.9	NM	d25.9	NM	d10.8
1990	610	56.4	9.2	14.1	12.5	34.1	[2]17.3	47.9%	6.5	1.1	19.0
[1]1989	606	43.6	7.2	7.9	9.5	37.4	[2]4.3	126.0%	d3.2	NM	d1.4
1988	441	31.6	7.2	4.9	8.3	35.4	d4.6	NM	d7.1	NM	d3.7
1987	374	22.2	5.9	1.9	5.7	9.7	2.9	93.6%	0.2	Nil	4.8

Balance Sheet Data (Million $)

Oct. 31	Cash	Curr. Assets	Curr. Liab.	Curr. Ratio	Total Assets	% Ret. on Assets	Long Term Debt	Common Equity	Total Cap.	% LT Debt of Cap.	% Ret. on Equity
1992	**10.1**	**293**	**180**	**1.6**	**619**	**NM**	**222**	**216**	**439**	**50.6**	**NM**
1991	20.0	278	150	1.9	601	NM	225	226	451	49.9	NM
1990	66.3	319	143	2.2	600	1.0	226	201	458	49.4	4.7
1989	27.2	213	143	1.5	478	NM	254	55	335	76.0	NM
1988	37.1	181	133	1.4	434	NM	257	d6	302	85.2	NM
1987	24.1	188	373	0.5	415	0.1	7	4	42	17.3	NM

Data as orig. reptd. **1.** Refl. merger or acq. **2.** Incl. equity in earns. of nonconsol. subs. **3.** Bef. spec. items. d-Deficit. NM-Not Meaningful.

Net Sales (Million $)

Quarter:	1993	1992	1991	1990
Jan.	171	154	159	121
Apr.	188	173	162	148
Jul.	157	184	157	163
Oct.		208	179	178
		719	657	610

Sales in the nine months ended July 31, 1993, advanced 1.0%, year to year, as increases at Research-Cottrell and Residuals Management were largely offset by a decrease for Metcalf & Eddy. Growth at Research-Cottrell mainly reflected greater original equipment business, while gains at Residuals Management stemmed from increased volume in the asbestos abatement business; the decline for Metcalf & Eddy was due to a shift to more profitable segments of the remediation business. Margins widened, reflecting a more favorable revenue mix for Metcalf & Eddy, as well as cost control efforts. Income of $2,990,000 ($0.12 a share) replaced a loss of $2,510,000 ($0.10). Results exclude an extraordinary credit of $0.10 a share in the current interim.

Common Share Earnings ($)

Quarter:	1993	1992	1991	1990
Jan.	0.02	0.01	d0.09	d0.10
Apr.	0.05	d0.01	d1.06	0.09
Jul.	0.05	d0.09	d0.03	0.20
Oct.		d0.30	0.03	0.12
		d0.40	d1.15	0.35

Dividend Data

No cash dividends have been paid.

Finances

The company has a $70 million credit facility, including $40 million for working capital loans, under which $26,300,000 was available at July 31, 1993.

In August 1991, AWT acquired Laser Precision's analytical division for about $5 million.

In December 1990, Metcalf & Eddy notified the Puerto Rico Aqueduct & Sewer Authority (PRASA) that no further work would be done on a rehabilitation program unless PRASA makes substantial payments. Earlier, in September 1990, Metcalf filed suit against PRASA seeking $52 million in damages. In July 1991, Metcalf amended its action to seek $37.4 million, which represented the total amount of delinquent payments under the PRASA contract. A trial date was set for July 7, 1994.

In November 1990, the company acquired Regenerative Environmental Equipment Co. (REECO) for about $10 million. REECO provides volatile organic compound and air toxics control systems.

In its August 1989 initial public offering, the company sold 4,600,000 Class A common shares at $17 each, through underwriters led by Kidder, Peabody & Co. and Alex. Brown & Sons.

Capitalization

Long Term Debt: $223,851,000 (7/93), incl. $115,000,000 of 8% sub. debs. due 2015, conv. into com. at $30.00 a sh.

Minority Interest: $605,000 (7/93).

Cl. A Com. Stk.: 24,818,449 shs. ($0.001 par).
Officers and directors own 10%.
Compagnie Generale des Eaux holds 23%.
Institutions own 62%.
Shareholders: 795 of record (12/92).

d-Deficit.

Office—U.S. Highway 22 West and Station Rd., Branchburg, NJ 08876; P. O. Box 1500, Somerville, NJ 08876. **Tel**—(908) 685-4600. **Chrmn & CEO**—E. C. Beck. **Pres & COO**—A. L. Glenn. **VP, CFO & Contr**—A. D. DiMichele. **SVP & Secy**—J. Feldstein. **Treas**—J. M. Morena. **Dirs**—E. C. Beck, J. L. Boren, D. M. Costle, R. T. Dewling, R. M. Dowd, A. L. Glenn, H. Goldman, J. W. Morris, E. F. Senior, B. D. Young. **Transfer Agent**—First National Bank of Chicago. **Incorporated** in Delaware in 1987. **Empl**—3,500.

 Michael V. Pizzi

Airborne Freight

NYSE Symbol ABF Options on CBOE (Feb-May-Aug-Nov) In S&P MidCap 400

Price	Range	P-E Ratio	Dividend	Yield	S&P Ranking	Beta
Sep. 9'93	1993					
22⅝	27–18	30	0.30	1.4%	B	1.58

Summary

This company is a leader in the domestic express delivery industry, specializing in door-to-door, overnight and second-day deliveries of small packages and documents. It also operates an expanding international system. Rapid growth in recent years was spurred by offering large accounts rate reductions for volume shipments. A pickup in shipment growth, together with substantially improved margins, should lead to earnings growth in 1993 and 1994.

Current Outlook

Earnings for 1993 are estimated at $1.15 a share, up from $0.12 in 1992. For 1994, $1.60 is estimated.

Dividends should continue at $0.07½ quarterly.

Revenue gains of 11% to 12% should be seen in 1993. Domestic shipments should continue to increase at a fairly good pace in the second half, reflecting the gradually improving economy. International traffic is growing slowly as the result of continuing economic softness. Pressure on average revenue per shipment should lessen, as growth shifts more into overnight types of traffic. A rate increase implemented March 1, 1993, will also aid in stabilizing yields. Margins should benefit from continued efforts to reduce costs; the cost per shipment, down 12% in the 1993 first half, should continue to decline.

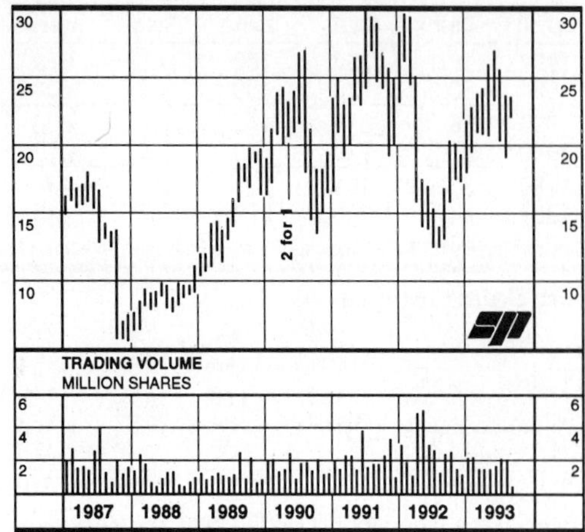

Revenues (Million $)

Quarter:	1993	1992	1991	1990
Mar.	399	360	318	272
Jun.	420	360	339	291
Sep.	---	372	350	302
Dec.	---	393	359	317
	---	1,484	1,367	1,182

Revenues in the six months ended June 30, 1993, advanced 14%, year to year. Margins widened, as the cost per shipment dropped 12%, and despite a 42% jump in net interest expense, net income of $9.9 million ($0.44 a share, after preferred dividends) contrasted with a loss of $2.4 million ($0.20). Results for 1993 exclude a special credit of $0.19.

Common Share Earnings ($)

Quarter:	1993	1992	1991	1990
Mar.	0.15	0.02	0.20	0.36
Jun.	0.29	d0.22	0.49	0.61
Sep.	E0.40	0.07	0.40	0.54
Dec.	E0.31	0.25	0.31	0.27
	E1.15	0.12	1.40	1.76

Important Developments

Aug. '93— IBM awarded Airborne a contract for U.S. export distribution in European, Middle Eastern, African and Asia Pacific areas. Services will include international air freight, ocean distribiution and other distribution services.

Jul. '93— ABF said domestic shipments in the 1993 second quarter climbed 28%, year to year, but average revenue per pound declined 4.8% as a result of fast growth in lower-priced select delivery service. International revenues were down 1.6% in the quarter because of a larger share of low revenue shipments, but margins improved 5% through competitive rate cuts from international carriers.

Mar. '93— The company implemented a general 5% rate increase, its first in two years.

Next earnings report expected in late October.

Per Share Data ($)

Yr. End Dec. 31	1992	1991	[1]1990	1989	[2]1988	1987	1986	1985	1984	1983
Tangible Bk. Val.	**14.88**	15.11	13.99	10.65	9.22	9.02	7.83	6.98	6.60	5.97
Cash Flow	**6.33**	6.49	5.61	5.14	4.23	3.54	3.31	2.29	2.25	2.05
Earnings	**0.12**	1.40	1.76	1.34	0.51	0.45	1.12	0.70	0.93	0.80
Dividends	**0.30**	0.30	0.30	0.30	0.30	0.30	0.30	0.30	0.30	0.30
Payout Ratio	**NM**	21%	18%	25%	59%	70%	27%	43%	32%	39%
Prices—High	**29¾**	30	27	19$^{13}/_{16}$	11⅛	18	16	12⅛	15¼	15⅜
Low	**12½**	16⅝	13½	10$^{7}/_{16}$	6⅜	5½	8	8¾	6½	6¾
P/E Ratio—	**NM**	21–12	15–8	15–8	22–13	40–12	14–7	18–13	16–7	19–9

Data as orig. reptd. Adj. for stk. div. of 100% May 1990. **1.** Refl. acctg. change. **2.** Refl. merger or acq. d-Deficit. E-Estimated. NM-Not Meaningful.

Airborne Freight Corporation

Income Data (Million $)

Year Ended Dec. 31	Revs.	Oper. Inc.	% Oper. Inc. of Revs.	Cap. Exp.	Depr.	[3]Int. Exp.	Net Bef. Taxes	Eff. Tax Rate	Net Inc.	% Net Inc. of Revs.	Cash Flow
1992	**1,484**	**148**	**10.0**	**255**	**121.0**	**21.2**	**[4]9.1**	**43.2%**	**5.2**	**0.3**	**123**
1991	1,367	158	11.6	253	99.0	15.3	[4]48.4	38.0%	30.0	2.2	126
[1]1990	1,182	140	11.8	225	75.3	13.0	[4]55.4	39.4%	33.6	2.8	106
1989	950	100	10.6	164	54.5	17.9	32.0	40.4%	19.1	2.0	74
[2]1988	768	74	9.6	92	52.0	13.9	11.5	39.0%	7.0	0.9	59
1987	632	59	9.4	100	40.6	9.5	10.1	41.6%	5.9	0.9	46
1986	542	52	9.6	87	26.0	6.0	23.7	44.2%	[1]13.2	2.4	39
1985	466	36	7.6	57	18.9	3.5	15.1	45.9%	8.2	1.8	27
1984	418	37	8.8	33	15.6	1.6	19.7	45.1%	10.8	2.6	26
1983	335	31	9.4	22	13.9	1.8	15.5	42.5%	8.9	2.7	23

Balance Sheet Data (Million $)

Dec. 31	Cash	Curr. Assets	Curr. Liab.	Curr. Ratio	Total Assets	% Ret. on Assets	Long Term Debt	Common Equity	Total Cap.	% LT Debt of Cap.	% Ret. on Equity
1992	**10.2**	**219**	**168**	**1.3**	**965**	**0.6**	**429**	**286**	**773**	**55.5**	**0.8**
1991	8.0	195	177	1.1	824	4.2	283	287	610	46.3	9.8
1990	8.8	176	152	1.2	614	5.7	124	263	428	29.0	13.4
1989	8.6	150	125	1.2	471	4.0	144	168	312	46.2	12.2
1988	6.4	126	93	1.4	422	1.8	171	127	298	57.2	5.6
1987	7.2	102	66	1.5	356	1.7	136	124	290	47.1	5.1
1986	3.1	78	62	1.2	272	5.4	91	92	209	43.6	15.2
1985	3.3	73	55	1.3	215	4.3	56	82	160	35.1	10.3
1984	1.2	55	41	1.3	166	7.4	29	76	125	23.2	14.9
1983	2.2	48	35	1.4	127	6.8	10	69	93	11.0	14.8

Data as orig. reptd. **1.** Refl. acctg. change. **2.** Refl. merger or acq. **3.** Net of int. inc. **4.** Incl. equity in earns. of nonconsol. subs.

Business Summary

Airborne Freight is an integrated air express transportation company, operating under the name Airborne Express. Revenues and operating profit contributions in 1992 were:

	Revs.	Profits
Domestic	85%	76%
International	15%	24%

Domestic operations consist primarily of express door-to-door, next-morning delivery of packages under 100 lbs. Next-afternoon or second-day delivery is offered at lower rates. The company also handles domestic shipments weighing over 100 lbs. The majority of shipments flow through ABF's airport and central sorting facility in Wilmington, Ohio. Ten regional hubs, handling about 17% of shipment weight, are operated at high-traffic areas.

Most shipments are carried on the company's own aircraft fleet, which as of December 31, 1992, consisted of 46 DC-9s, 23 DC-8s and 11 YS-11 turboprop aircraft. Pickup and delivery is handled by a fleet of more than 8,600 radio-dispatched vans.

ABF provides international express door-to-door delivery and door-to-airport freight services. It uses commercial airlines for international services. A joint venture with Mitsui & Co. and Tonami Transportation conducts operations in Japan.

Dividend Data

Dividends were initiated in 1974. A "poison pill" stock purchase right was adopted in 1986.

Amt of Divd. $	Date Decl.	Ex-divd. Date	Stock of Record	Payment Date
0.07½	Oct. 27	Nov. 4	Nov. 10	Nov. 24'92
0.07½	Feb. 9	Feb. 17	Feb. 23	Mar. 9'93
0.07½	Apr. 26	May 4	May 10	May 24'93
0.07½	Aug. 10	Aug. 18	Aug. 24	Sep. 7'93

Capitalization

Long Term Debt: $435,496,000 (6/93); incl. $115 million of debs. conv. into com. at $35.50 a sh.

$3.45 Conv. Pfd. Stock: 800,000 shs. ($50 par); ea. conv. into 2.14 com. shs.; owned by Mitsui & Co. & Tonami Transportation.

Common Stock: 19,254,541 shs. ($1 par).
Institutions hold 76%.
Shareholders of record: 1,891.

Office—3101 Western Ave., P.O. Box 662, Seattle, WA 98111-0662. **Tel**—(206) 285-4600. **Chrmn & CEO**—R. S. Cline. **Pres & COO**—R. G. Brazier. **Secy**—J. Wilbourne. **EVP, CFO & Investor Contact**—Roy C. Liljebeck. **Dirs**—R. G. Brazier, J. H. Carey, R. S. Cline, J. F. Gary, M. Kogetsu, C. M. Martenson, H. M. Messmer, Jr., A. H. Payne, R. M. Rosenberg, A. V. Smith. **Transfer Agent & Registrar**—First Interstate Bank of Washington, Seattle. **Incorporated** in Delaware in 1968. **Empl**—8,100.

 T. M. Canning, CFA

Alaska Air Group

NYSE Symbol ALK Options on ASE In S&P MidCap 400

Price	Range	P–E Ratio	Dividend	Yield	S&P Ranking	Beta
Sep. 16'93	1993					
13	18⅛–12¼	NM	[1]---	[1]---	B–	1.10

Summary

Alaska Air Group is the holding company for Alaska Airlines, the leading passenger carrier between Alaska and the lower 48 states, and Horizon Air, which serves smaller cities in the Northwest. ALK benefited in recent years from well managed route expansion, largely in West Coast and Mexican markets. However, the airline industry's extensive fare cutting resulted in a large loss for 1992. Moderate traffic growth and cuts in operating costs should reduce losses in 1993 and restore profitability in 1994.

Current Outlook

A loss of $1.30 a share is estimated for 1993, versus a loss of $6.53 in 1992. A profit of $1.00 a share is projected for 1994.

Dividends, omitted in December 1992, are not expected to be resumed in the near term.

Revenues for 1993 are expected to be slightly above 1992 levels. Traffic in the second half should up modestly, reflecting the contribution of some new routes. After improvement in the first half, yields have been affected by competitive pricing by new carriers and second-half yield gains will be small. The company has embarked on a program to reduce annual operating costs by more than $50 million through employee cuts and other steps, which should be effective in substantially improving margins.

Total Oper. Revenues (Million $)

Quarter:	1993	1992	1991	1990
Mar.	250	258	247	231
Jun.	277	277	278	263
Sep.	---	321	314	296
Dec.	---	259	265	257
	---	1,115	1,104	1,047

Revenues for the first six months of 1993 fell 1.4%, year to year. Passenger traffic decreased 12.2%, but yield gained 11.4%. Operating costs decreased 5.6%, and there was a net loss of $18.6 million ($1.59 a share), versus a net loss of $33.5 million ($2.77, before a $0.34 accounting charge).

Common Share Earnings ($)

Quarter:	1993	1992	1991	1990
Mar.	d1.25	d1.31	d0.88	d0.21
Jun.	d0.33	d1.46	0.21	0.59
Sep.	E0.55	d0.29	1.12	1.35
Dec.	Ed0.27	d3.47	d0.19	d0.90
	Ed1.30	d6.53	0.27	0.82

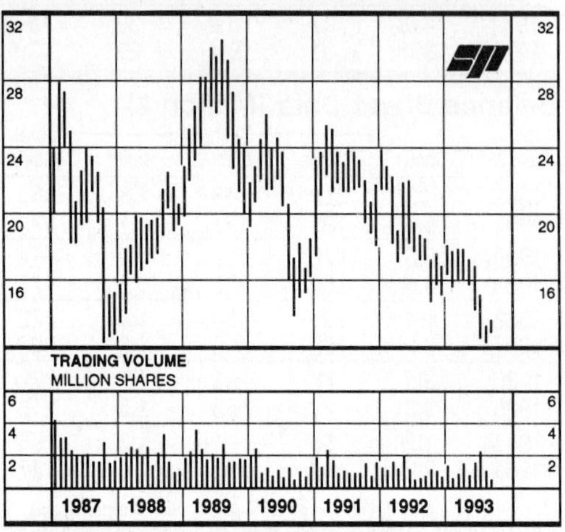

Important Developments

Sep. '93— Talks with the flight attendants' union concerning a new contract continued in recess following discontinuance in August. Work rule changes were imposed by the company in June.

Jun. '93— The company said it expected reductions in costs of about $55 million in 1993 from service cuts, reductions in staff, refinancing, schedule revisions and other measures.

Jun. '93— Alaska Airlines began new service to Reno, Las Vegas and Sacramento from Seattle.

May '93— The company redeemed its 1.2-million-share preferred stock issue. ILFC, holder of the shares, provided a $27 million loan to assist in the redemption.

Next earnings report expected in late October.

Per Share Data ($)

Yr. End Dec. 31	1992	1991	1990	1989	1988	1987	[2]1986	1985	1984	1983
Tangible Bk. Val.	**7.62**	13.78	13.02	16.51	14.50	12.00	7.81	13.05	10.12	8.05
Cash Flow	**d1.14**	5.05	5.09	5.89	5.22	3.56	3.99	3.83	3.66	2.69
Earnings[3]	**d6.53**	0.27	0.82	2.71	2.37	0.85	1.41	2.10	2.19	1.45
Dividends	**0.200**	0.200	0.200	0.200	0.160	0.160	0.160	0.120	0.140	0.125
Payout Ratio	**NM**	74%	24%	7%	7%	19%	11%	7%	6%	9%
Prices—High	**23⅞**	25⅜	26	30½	22½	27⅞	22¾	26⅜	17¼	18⅝
Low	**14¾**	17½	13⅞	19⅞	13½	12¼	14¼	14¼	9¼	10⅜
P/E Ratio—	**NM**	94–65	32–17	11–7	9–6	33–14	16–10	13–7	8–4	13–7

Data as orig. reptd. **1.** Omitted 12-1-92. **2.** Refl. merger or acq. **3.** Bef. spec. item(s) of -0.34 in 1992, +0.73 in 1987. d-Deficit. E-Estimated NM-Not Meaningful.

Alaska Air Group, Inc.

Income Data (Million $)

Year Ended Dec. 31	Revs.	Oper. Inc.	% Oper. Inc. of Revs.	Cap. Exp.	Depr.	Int. Exp.	Net Bef. Taxes	Eff. Tax Rate	[2]Net Inc.	% Net Inc. of Revs.	Cash Flow
1992	**1,115**	**3**	**0.3**	**278**	**71.8**	**43.2**	**d126.0**	**NM**	**[3]d80.3**	**NM**	**d15.1**
1991	1,104	99	8.9	213	64.0	40.2	16.2	36.2%	10.3	0.9	67.7
1990	1,047	87	8.3	249	58.5	20.3	27.9	38.5%	17.2	1.6	69.6
1989	917	120	13.1	144	50.5	19.4	69.4	38.1%	42.9	4.7	93.4
1988	814	115	14.2	128	44.9	19.2	62.5	40.0%	37.5	4.6	82.4
1987	710	77	10.8	76	42.3	23.9	22.2	39.9%	13.3	1.9	55.6
[1]1986	468	70	15.0	156	32.5	22.5	27.9	36.6%	17.7	3.8	50.2
1985	433	53	12.1	162	21.5	17.1	33.8	23.2%	25.9	6.0	47.4
1984	362	50	13.8	105	16.0	9.3	34.0	29.7%	23.9	6.6	39.9
1983	281	44	15.8	38	13.3	6.9	28.3	44.4%	15.7	5.6	29.1

Balance Sheet Data (Million $)

Dec. 31	Cash	Curr. Assets	Curr. Liab.	Curr. Ratio	Total Assets	% Ret. on Assets	Long Term Debt	Common Equity	Total Cap.	% LT Debt of Cap.	% Ret. on Equity
1992	**83**	**250**	**336**	**0.7**	**1,208**	**NM**	**488**	**195**	**775**	**63.0**	**NM**
1991	103	226	250	0.9	1,212	0.9	500	283	889	56.2	1.3
1990	52	168	296	0.6	1,021	1.9	282	278	665	42.4	3.9
1989	111	220	211	1.0	874	5.4	227	342	611	37.1	13.3
1988	48	144	174	0.8	730	5.2	171	307	523	32.7	13.0
1987	105	188	158	1.2	706	1.7	204	272	516	39.5	5.4
1986	66	130	138	0.9	672	2.9	292	177	516	56.6	10.5
1985	148	198	95	2.1	537	5.7	234	161	432	54.1	18.1
1984	61	100	77	1.3	326	8.3	102	109	245	41.5	24.4
1983	55	87	60	1.5	247	7.1	74	87	184	40.0	19.9

Data as orig. reptd. **1.** Refl. merger or acq. **2.** Bef. spec. item(s). **3.** Reflects acctg. change. d-Deficit. NM-Not Meaningful.

Business Summary

Alaska Air Group, Inc. is the holding company for Alaska Airlines and Horizon Air Industries (acquired in 1986). Alaska Airlines is the leading airline between Alaska and the lower 48 states. As of early 1993, it served 21 cities in Alaska, 13 cities in Washington, Oregon, California and Arizona (using Seattle, Portland and Anchorage as hubs), four cities in Mexico, and two in Russia (seasonally). It also serves Dallas/Ft. Worth, Houston, Chicago and Washington through an interchange agreement with American Airlines, using Seattle as the interchange point connecting with Anchorage and Fairbanks.

As of early 1993, Horizon Air served 35 airports in six western states and British Columbia, primarily connecting smaller cities to hubs in Seattle, Portland, Spokane and Boise.

Consolidated operating data in recent years (passenger and seat miles in billions):

	1992	1991	1990
Rev. pass. miles	6.02	5.35	4.85
Avail. seat miles	10.52	9.58	9.10
Load factor %	57.2	55.9	53.3
Rev. per RPM(¢)	16.6	18.7	19.6
Cost per ASM(¢).........	11.5	11.2	11.2

As of December 1992, the Alaska Airlines fleet included 72 aircraft—17 727s, 38 MD-80s and 17 737s; on order were six MD-80s, 12 737-400s and 10 MD-90s. Horizon's fleet included 31 Metroliner IIIs, 22 deHavilland Dash 8s and three F-28s; on order were 35 Dornier 328s.

Dividend Data

Dividends, resumed in 1982 after a three-year hiatus, were omitted in December 1992. A "poison pill" stock purchase right was issued in 1986. Payment in the past 12 months:

Amt of Divd. $	Date Decl.	Ex-divd. Date	Stock of Record	Payment Date
0.05	Sep. 14	Oct. 8	Oct. 15	Nov. 5'92

Capitalization

Long Term Debt: $498,448,000 (6/93).

Common Stock: 13,341,621 shs. ($1 par).
Institutions hold about 58%.
Shareholders of record: 6,855.

Office—19300 Pacific Highway South, Seattle, WA 98188. **Tel**—(206) 431-7040. **Chrmn, Pres & CEO**—R. J. Vecci. **VP-Secy**—M. E. Laws. **VP-CFO & Treas**—J. R. Vingo. **Dirs**—W. H. Clapp, R. F. Cosgrave, M. J. Fate, J. F. Kelly, B. R. Kennedy, R. M. Langland, B. I. Mallott, R. L. Parker Jr., R. J. Vecci, J. R. Vingo, R. A. Wien. **Transfer Agent & Registrar**—First National Bank of Boston. **Incorporated** in Alaska in 1937; reincorporated in Delaware in 1985. **Empl**—8,666.

 T.M. Canning, CFA

Albany International

NYSE Symbol AIN In S&P MidCap 400

Price	Range	P-E Ratio	Dividend	Yield	S&P Ranking	Beta
Oct. 15'93	1993					
17⅝	19–14¼	57	0.35	2.0%	NR	1.06

Summary

AIN is the world's largest producer of paper machine "clothing," or custom-designed, engineered fabrics essential to the paper-making process. Earnings for 1993's first six months improved significantly, reflecting AIN's work force reduction program and an acquisition. In September 1993, the company offered 4 million Class A shares at 17⅝ each.

Business Summary

Albany International designs, manufactures and markets paper machine "clothing," of which it is the world's largest producer. AIN believes it has a market share of 26% in the U.S. and Canada and 16% in the rest of the world. Revenues and operating income in 1992 were derived (in $ mil.):

	Revs.	Income
United States	39%	$15.3
Canada	12%	8.0
Rest of world	49%	–5.1

Paper machine clothing consists of large continuous belts of custom-designed, engineered fabrics that are installed on paper machines and carry the paper stock through the three primary stages of the paper production process: the forming of paperstock into a continuous sheet as it is being carried on the forming fabric; the pressing of the paper sheet between rollers as it is being transported on the press fabrics to partially reduce its water content; and the evaporation of most of the remaining water content as the paper sheet is held against a series of heated cylinders by the dryer fabrics.

Because interruptions of production impose significant costs on paper producers, key performance characteristics of paper machine clothing are its reliability, its average life-in-use, and the ease with which it can be replaced on a paper machine. Besides paper machine clothing, AIN makes other engineered fabrics and auxiliary equipment.

Sales and technical support are a major cost of operations, as Albany's sales and technical staff work directly with paper mill operating management in 21 countries. The company's U.S. technical service engineers also perform troubleshooting and application engineering in the field. Marketing and research efforts are concentrated on the forming and pressing sections of the papermaking process. Innovations in these areas have been more frequent than those in the drying section.

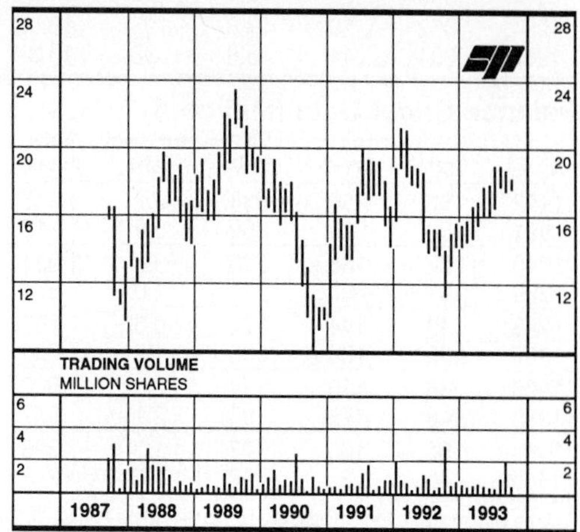

Over the past few years, paper manufactures have reduced the number of suppliers of paper machine clothing per machine position. AIN believes this trend has increased opportunities for market leaders, of which only six compete on a global basis. Manufacturing is conducted in 11 countries. AIN expects continued growth for the long term in world paper production.

Important Developments

Sep. '93— The company commenced a public offering of 4 million Class A shares at an initial price of $17⅝. Proceeds from the offering will be used for general corporate purposes and to reduce long-term indebtedness.

Next earnings report expected in late October.

Per Share Data ($)

Yr. End Dec. 31	1992	1991	1990	1989	1988	1987	1986	1985	1984	1983
Tangible Bk. Val.	**6.35**	8.73	8.66	8.27	6.06	4.85	1.81	1.35	NA	NA
Cash Flow	**1.89**	2.06	1.66	2.84	2.46	2.12	1.37	NA	NA	NA
Earnings[2]	**0.11**	0.41	0.30	1.75	1.46	1.15	0.59	0.45	0.33	[1]0.09
Dividends	**0.350**	0.350	0.350	0.313	0.263	0.063	Nil	Nil	Nil	Nil
Payout Ratio	**334%**	87%	116%	18%	18%	5%	Nil	Nil	Nil	Nil
Prices—High	**21¼**	20	19⅜	23½	19¾	16½	NA	NA	NA	NA
Low	**11¼**	10	8	15¾	12	9¾	NA	NA	NA	NA
P/E Ratio—	**NM**	49–24	65–27	13–9	14–8	14–8	NA	NA	NA	NA

Data as orig. reptd. **1.** From Aug. 5. **2.** Bef. spec. item(s) of -0.25 in 1992. NM-Not Meaningful. NA-Not Available.

Income Data (Million $)

Year Ended Dec. 31	Revs.	Oper. Inc.	% Oper. Inc. of Revs.	Cap. Exp.	Depr.	Int. Exp.	[3]Net Bef. Taxes	Eff. Tax Rate	[2]Net Inc.	% Net Inc. of Revs.	Cash Flow
1992	**570**	**86**	**15.1**	**20**	**45.5**	**20.6**	**2.7**	**35.7%**	**2.7**	**0.5**	**48.2**
1991	560	95	16.9	42	42.0	22.2	19.4	52.7%	10.3	1.8	52.3
1990	560	83	14.8	111	34.5	25.8	13.8	49.8%	7.6	1.4	42.1
1989	509	102	20.1	90	27.6	24.1	77.7	42.7%	44.5	8.7	72.1
1988	465	105	22.6	59	24.7	18.5	55.1	34.2%	36.3	7.8	61.0
1987	402	92	22.8	40	21.4	22.2	47.1	46.4%	25.2	6.3	46.6
1986	336	78	23.0	24	19.4	28.0	34.9	57.8%	14.7	4.4	34.1
1985	302	71	23.6	24	16.1	32.5	25.8	63.5%	11.4	3.8	NA
1984	267	55	20.4	19	12.7	29.5	19.7	67.8%	8.3	3.1	NA
[1]1983	105	NA	NA	NA	NA	10.3	7.5	75.0%	2.2	2.1	NA

Balance Sheet Data (Million $)

Dec. 31	Cash	Curr. Assets	Curr. Liab.	Curr. Ratio	Total Assets	% Ret. on Assets	Long Term Debt	Common Equity	Total Cap.	% LT Debt of Cap.	% Ret. on Equity
1992	**4.0**	**250**	**109**	**2.3**	**646**	**0.4**	**240**	**191**	**431**	**55.7**	**1.2**
1991	5.1	254	103	2.5	675	1.5	250	244	495	50.6	4.2
1990	4.2	273	104	2.6	703	1.2	262	243	506	47.4	3.2
1989	11.7	243	99	2.5	566	8.4	145	239	421	34.6	21.1
1988	8.5	207	85	2.4	477	8.0	158	178	360	43.8	22.0
1987	3.4	177	87	2.0	418	6.0	131	146	298	43.9	22.3
1986	3.5	150	70	2.2	360	4.6	173	67	253	68.4	23.7
1985	3.0	131	54	2.4	326	3.7	160	66	225	70.9	19.6
1984	NA	NA	NA	NA	296	2.8	NA	50	NA	NA	16.9
1983	NA	NA	NA	NA	304	NA	NA	48	NA	NA	NA

Data as orig. reptd. **1.** From Aug. 5. **2.** Bef. spec. items in 1992. **3.** Incl. equity in earns. of nonconsol. subs. NA-Not Available.

Net Sales (Million $)

Quarter:	1993	1992	1991	1990
Mar.	137	138	134	131
Jun.	150	140	143	134
Sep.		143	136	136
Dec.		141	145	155
		561	557	556

Sales in the six months ended June 30, 1993, rose 3.3%, year to year, reflecting the acquisition of the Mount Vernon Group, market share gains and product upgrades. Margins widened, due to work force reductions, and following lower interest expenses, pretax income replaced losses. After taxes at 39.4%, versus a benefit of $790,000, and minority and equity interests, net income was $4,705,000 ($0.18 a share) in contrast to a loss of $549,000 ($0.02, before a charge of $0.29 for accounting changes).

Common Share Earnings ($)

Quarter:	1993	1992	1991	1990
Mar.	0.01	NM	Nil	0.10
Jun.	0.17	d0.02	0.18	0.15
Sep.		0.09	0.10	0.05
Dec.		0.04	0.13	Nil
		0.11	0.41	0.30

Finances

In June 1993, AIN sold substantially all the assets of its Engineered Systems Division to Thermo Fibertek for $26.3 million. Subsequent to the sale, AIN and Thermo Fibertek entered into an alliance to coordinate product development and marketing.

In January 1993, AIN acquired Mount Vernon Group for $51 million and a lease valued at $4.5 million. In 1992, AIN reorganized its European operations, expecting to save at least $8 million per year when fully effective in 1994.

Dividend Data

Cash dividends, paid every year from 1926 until the company's leveraged buyout in 1983, were resumed in 1987 on the Class A common. Subsequent to September 1, 1991, Class A and B have equal rights to dividends. A dividend reinvestment plan is available.

Amt of Divd. $	Date Decl.	Ex-divd. Date	Stock of Record	Payment Date
0.08¾	Nov. 12	Dec. 7	Dec. 11	Jan. 4'93
0.08¾	Feb. 9	Mar. 9	Mar. 15	Apr. 1'93
0.08¾	May 13	May 26	Jun. 4	Jul. 1'93
0.08¾	Aug. 17	Aug. 30	Sep. 3	Oct. 1'93

Capitalization

Long Term Debt: $244,002,000 (6/93).

Class A Com. Stk.: 20,059,672 shs. ($0.001 par).
Institutions hold 62%.
Shareholders of record: 4,000.

Class B Com. Stk.: 5,658,515 shs. ($0.001 par).
10 votes per sh.; conv. sh.-for-sh. into Cl. A.
J.S. Standish controls 73% of the voting power.

NM-Not Meaningful.

Office—1373 Broadway, Albany, NY 12204. **Tel**—(518) 445-2200. **Chrmn**—J.S. Standish. **Pres**—F.L. McKone. **Sr VP-CFO**—M.C. Nahl. **VP-Secy & Investor Contact**—Charles B. Buchanan. **Dirs**—P. Bancroft III, T.R. Beecher Jr., C.B. Buchanan, S.I. Landgraf, F.L. McKone, J.S. Standish, A. Stenshamn, B.P. Wright. **Transfer Agent & Registrar**—Harris Trust and Savings Bank, Chicago. **Incorporated** in New York in 1895; reincorporated in Delaware in 1987. **Empl**—5,678.

 Joe Victor Shammas

Aldus Corp.

NASDAQ Symbol ALDC (Incl. in Nat'l Market) Options on Paciifc In S&P MidCap 400

Price	Range	P-E Ratio	Dividend	Yield	S&P Ranking	Beta
Aug. 20'93	1993					
17¼	20¾–13¼	66	None	None	NR	1.29

Summary

Aldus develops, markets and supports "PageMaker" desktop publishing software for Apple, IBM and IBM-compatible microcomputers. Other products include "FreeHand," a drawing program, and "Persuasion," a desktop presentations program. Earnings in recent periods were hurt by sluggish sales and narrower margins, but the shipment of new products, including new releases of PageMaker, should help operating results in the second half of 1993 and into 1994.

Current Outlook

Earnings for 1994 are projected at $0.90 a share, versus the $0.50 (including charges of $0.23) estimated for 1993 and compared with the $0.47 recorded in 1992.

Cash dividends are not anticipated.

Sales are expected to rise through 1994, spurred by the availability of PageMaker 5.0, a major upgrade of the company's flagship PageMaker desktop publishing program for both the Windows and Macintosh environments. Upgrades to Freehand, Photostyler and other products, as well as new offerings of less expensive "consumer software," will also aid results. Margins are expected to widen, benefiting from the greater volume and expense controls.

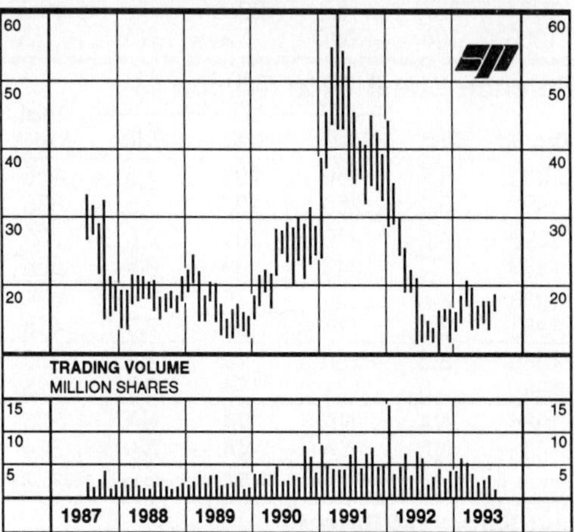

Net Sales (Million $)

13 Weeks:	1993	1992	1991	[1]1990
Mar.	41.6	44.1	40.3	25.5
Jun.	45.6	38.9	44.3	33.3
Sep.		45.9	40.3	36.7
Dec.		45.9	42.7	39.6
		174.1	167.5	135.0

Net sales in the six months ended July 2, 1993, rose 5.1%, year to year, as a strong second quarter, reflecting shipments of a new version of PageMaker for Windows, outweighed a weak first quarter, depressed in anticipation of this new version. Margins narrowed on the sluggish volume, a less favorable product mix and aggressive marketing programs, and with a $1,975,000 ($0.10 a share) charge for the acquisition of After Hours Software, a vendor of personal information management products, pretax income plunged 84%. After taxes at 33.0%, versus 31.0%, net income was down 85%, to $584,000 ($0.04 a share, on 12% fewer shares), from $3,805,000 ($0.25).

Common Share Earnings ($)

13 Weeks:	1993	1992	1991	[1]1990
Mar.	0.03	0.31	0.41	0.27
Jun.	0.02	d0.06	0.49	0.40
Sep.	E0.15	0.07	0.35	0.45
Dec.	E0.30	0.14	0.29	0.51
	E0.50	0.47	1.54	1.63

Important Developments

Jul. '93— Aldus said it expects to take a one-time charge of up to $2.3 million ($0.13 a share) in the third quarter of 1993 to reflect costs associated with its acquisition of CoSA, a developer of digital-video software tools. Separately, during the second quarter of 1993, Aldus repurchased 115,000 of its common shares, bringing to about 2.2 million shares the total number acquired under an authorization to buy up to 3 million shares.

Next earnings report expected in late October.

Per Share Data ($)

Yr. End Dec. 31	[2]1992	1991	[2]1990	1989	1988	[3]1987	1986	1985	1984
Tangible Bk. Val.	**9.18**	10.51	8.20	6.44	5.32	3.93	0.62	0.11	0.07
Cash Flow	**1.02**	1.95	1.91	1.43	1.31	0.73	0.22	NA	NA
Earnings[4]	**0.47**	1.54	1.63	1.21	1.15	0.66	0.21	0.04	[5]d0.02
Dividends	**Nil**	Nil	Nil	Nil	Nil	Nil	Nil	Nil	Nil
Payout Ratio	**Nil**	Nil	Nil	Nil	Nil	Nil	Nil	Nil	Nil
Prices—High	**44¼**	59⅞	31½	24½	21½	35¾	NA	NA	NA
Low	**10¼**	24	15	12¼	13½	15	NA	NA	NA
P/E Ratio—	**94–22**	39–16	19–9	20–10	19–12	54–23	NA	NA	NA

Data as orig. reptd. **1.** Refl. pooled acq. **2.** Refl. merger or acq. **3.** Refl. acctg. change. **4.** Bef. spec. item of +0.01 in 1985. **5.** From inception 2-27-84. d-Deficit. E-Estimated NA-Not Available.

Aldus Corporation

Income Data (Million $)

Year Ended Dec. 31	Revs.	Oper. Inc.	% Oper. Inc. of Revs.	Cap. Exp.	Depr.	Int. Exp.	Net Bef. Taxes	Eff. Tax Rate	[5]Net Inc.	% Net Inc. of Revs.	Cash Flow
[1]1992	**174**	**14.1**	**8.1**	**17.1**	**8.00**	**NA**	**9.9**	**31.6%**	**6.8**	**3.9**	**14.8**
1991	168	36.2	21.6	10.7	6.39	Nil	34.7	31.3%	23.8	14.2	30.2
[1]1990	135	34.7	25.7	9.2	3.99	NA	35.3	32.6%	23.8	17.6	27.7
1989	88	21.0	23.9	3.7	2.84	NA	[4]22.8	31.9%	15.5	17.6	18.3
1988	79	21.7	27.4	3.6	2.13	0.03	[4]21.3	31.5%	14.6	18.5	16.7
[2]1987	40	12.7	32.1	4.1	0.88	0.04	[4]12.6	37.9%	7.8	19.7	8.7
1986	11	4.1	36.7	0.8	0.13	Nil	4.1	42.6%	2.4	21.2	2.5
1985	2	0.7	31.0	0.2	0.04	Nil	0.7	36.6%	0.4	19.6	NA
[3]1984	NA	d0.2	NM	0.1	0.01	Nil	d0.2	Nil	d0.2	NM	NA

Balance Sheet Data (Million $)

Dec. 31	Cash	Curr. Assets	Curr. Liab.	Curr. Ratio	Total Assets	% Ret. on Assets	Long Term Debt	Common Equity	Total Cap.	% LT Debt of Cap.	% Ret. on Equity
1992	**71**	**108**	**28.1**	**3.9**	**156**	**4.3**	**Nil**	**127**	**128**	**Nil**	**5.1**
1991	106	146	19.3	7.6	179	14.6	Nil	155	159	Nil	17.2
1990	76	113	21.4	5.3	141	19.0	Nil	116	120	Nil	22.9
1989	59	80	12.8	6.3	95	18.0	Nil	80	82	Nil	21.2
1988	36	62	9.2	6.8	73	23.3	0.12	62	64	0.2	26.9
1987	32	42	4.3	9.9	49	24.1	0.22	43	45	0.5	31.2
1986	3	5	2.6	2.0	6	58.6	Nil	[6]4	4	Nil	97.0
1985	1	2	0.4	3.6	2	35.6	Nil	[6]1	1	Nil	43.9
1984	NA	NA	NA	NA	1	NM	Nil	[6]1	1	Nil	NM

Data as orig. reptd. **1.** Refl. merger or acq. **2.** Refl. acctg. change. **3.** From inception 2-27-84. **4.** Incl. equity in earns. of nonconsol. subs. **5.** Bef. spec. item. **6.** Refl. conv. of pfd. stk. d-Deficit. NA-Not Available. NM-Not Meaningful.

Business Summary

Aldus Corporation develops, markets and supports computer software products for the Apple Macintosh and for IBM and IBM-compatible microcomputers. Efforts are focused on graphic products for professional designers and production specialists; low-cost consumer products; and fee-based service products.

Professional graphics products include the company's best-known product, the "PageMaker" desktop publishing program for the Apple Machintosh and MS-Windows environment. Pagemaker allows the user to design, lay out and produce high-quality printed communications such as newsletters, brochures, manuals and other, more-complex technical documents. Other major products include "FreeHand," an illustration tool; "Persuasion," a business presentation graphics program; "Photostyler," a color image-processing program; "PrePaint," a program for generating four color separations; "PressWise," a page imposition program; and "TrapWise," a program that provides automatic trapping of color separations.

The consumer division develops and publishes entry-level graphics, multimedia and publishing software products. Products include "SuperPaint," a painting and drawing program; "SuperCard," a software toolkit for creating customized multimedia applications; "Digital Darkroom," an image-processing program; "Super 3D," a three-dimensional modeling and animation program; "Gallery Effects," a collection of image-processing filters; and "Personal Press," a desktop publishing program.

Aldus markets its products through distributors, resellers and OEMs. International sales accounted for 48% of net sales in 1992.

Dividend Data

No cash dividends have been paid. A shareholder rights plan was adopted in 1992.

Finances

In 1992, software development costs charged to operations totaled $27,812,000 (64% for R&D and 36% for software amortization), up from $23,413,000 (60% and 40%) in 1991. Capitalized software development costs, which are amortized on a product-by-product basis over 12 to 24 months, using the straight-line method, totaled $13,905,036 at December 31, 1992.

Capitalization

Long Term Debt: None (6/93).

Common Stock: 13,235,428 shs. ($0.01 par).
Officers and directors hold 26%, incl. 25% by P. Brainerd.
Institutions hold 33%.
Shareholders: About 1,067 of record (3/92).

Office—411 First Ave. South, Suite 200, Seattle, WA 98104. **Tel**—(206) 622-5500. **Pres & CEO**—P. Brainerd. **COO**—S. Smith. **VP-Fin, CFO & Secy**—W. H. McAleer. **Dirs**—G. P. Arnold, P. Brainerd, G. P. Carter, D. G. DeVivo, A. W. Smith. **Transfer Agent**—First Interstate Bank of Washington, Seattle. **Incorporated** in Washington in 1984. **Empl**—1,007.

 Peter C. Wood, CFA

Alexander & Baldwin

NASDAQ Symbol ALEX (Incl. in Nat'l Market) In S&P MidCap 400

Price	Range	P–E Ratio	Dividend	Yield	S&P Ranking	Beta
Sep. 8'93	1993					
23¼	28–22½	18	0.88	3.8%	A–	0.83

Summary

This company provides ocean shipping services between Hawaii and the U.S. Pacific Coast, is the largest Hawaiian sugar producer, and has interests in real estate and a growing container leasing business. In June 1993 ALEX purchased the 72% it did not already own of California and Hawaiian Sugar Co., a leading sugar refiner, for $63 million. Profits could remain under pressure in 1993 as weak tourism and sluggish construction activity curb shipping volumes and the expansion of Matson's fleet is accompanied by heavier fixed charges.

Current Outlook

Profits for 1993 are projected at $1.70 a share, versus $1.31 (after a $0.34 charge) reported for 1992. Profits could rebound to $2.15 in 1994.

Dividends, currently at $0.22 a share quarterly, are not expected to be raised before mid-1994.

Shipping profits could be flat in 1993, as recession in Japan and weak consumer confidence at home dampen tourism. Construction activity will remain sluggish apart from restoration work on Kauai in the wake of Hurricane Iniki. Supporting margins will be improved terminal productivity. Container profits will be flat as reduced equipment utilization and lower rates are offset by an expanded fleet. Real estate profits should post solid gains, reflecting high occupancy rates and lease income from Kmart and increased property sales. Sugar profits should advance as 1993's crop recovers from insect infestations and C&H makes positive contributions. Aiding comparisons will be the absence of 1992's hurricane-related losses.

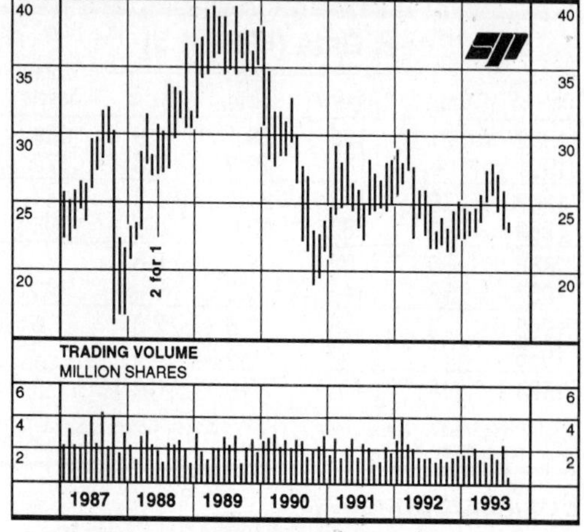

Revenues (Million $)

Quarter:	1993	1992	1991	1990
Mar.	186.4	170.0	163.8	203.4
Jun.	212.7	183.0	189.7	170.7
Sep.		195.4	194.9	192.2
Dec.		205.9	200.1	191.6
		754.4	748.5	758.0

Revenues for 1993's first half rose 13%, year to year. Net income fell 1.1% to $0.76 a share, from $0.78 (before a $0.90 special charge).

Common Share Earnings ($)

Quarter:	1993	1992	1991	1990
Mar.	0.39	0.33	0.29	1.02
Jun.	0.37	0.45	0.54	0.49
Sep.	E0.40	0.08	0.56	0.48
Dec.	E0.54	0.45	0.61	0.51
	E1.70	1.31	2.00	2.50

Important Developments

Aug. '93— ALEX purchased the S.S. Matsonia, a 760-foot containership operated under charter since 1973, for $22.8 million.

Jun. '93— ALEX acquired the 72% of California and Hawaiian Sugar Co. (C&H) that it did not already own from other members of the marketing cooperative for $63 million. C&H generated revenues of $446 million in 1992 on the sale of 735,000 tons of sugar products. Separately, ALEX bought 1,300 acres of property in California and and 20 acres in Hawaii from C&H for $21.5 million.

Oct. '92— ALEX took a $15.9 million ($0.34 a share) charge against third quarter net income to reflect losses associated with Hurricane Iniki.

Next earnings report expected in mid-October.

Per Share Data ($)

Yr. End Dec. 31	[3]1992	1991	1990	1989	1988	1987	1986	1985	1984	1983
Tangible Bk. Val.	**12.07**	15.90	[1]14.75	[1]13.12	11.96	9.79	9.98	8.98	7.96	7.17
Cash Flow	**3.15**	3.66	3.88	5.54	3.65	3.08	2.40	2.15	1.77	1.52
Earnings[2]	**1.31**	2.00	2.50	4.38	2.70	2.29	1.65	1.50	1.20	0.96
Dividends	**0.880**	0.880	0.860	0.800	0.770	0.680	0.660	0.468	0.400	0.325
Payout Ratio	**67%**	44%	34%	18%	29%	30%	40%	31%	33%	34%
Prices—High	**30½**	29½	38	39½	36¾	32	24½	14⅞	13¼	8⅝
Low	**21½**	21	19	31¼	20⅞	16	14⅛	10⅞	8¼	4⅞
P/E Ratio—	**23–16**	15–11	15–8	9–7	14–8	14–7	15–9	10–7	11–7	9–5

Data as orig. reptd. Adj. for stk. divs. of 100% Jun. 1988, 50% Jun. 1986, 100% Mar. 1984. 1. Incl. intangibles. 2. Bef. spec. items of -0.90 in 1992, +0.36 in 1988. 3. Refl. acctg. change. E-Estimated.

Income Data (Million $)

Year Ended Dec. 31	Revs.	Oper. Inc.	% Oper. Inc. of Revs.	Cap. Exp.	Depr.	Int. Exp.	[1]Net Bef. Taxes	Eff. Tax Rate	[2]Net Inc.	% Net Inc. of Revs.	Cash Flow
[3]1992	**731**	**195**	**26.6**	**234**	**85.4**	**31.6**	**84**	**28.1%**	**61**	**8.3**	**146**
1991	721	207	28.7	273	76.7	32.8	133	30.5%	92	12.8	169
1990	674	179	26.5	266	64.0	33.4	166	30.8%	115	17.1	179
1989	620	160	25.9	250	54.0	27.3	306	33.7%	203	32.7	257
1988	665	217	32.6	90	47.5	27.8	179	24.6%	135	20.3	183
1987	631	201	31.9	85	41.1	24.0	163	26.3%	120	19.1	161
1986	504	137	27.1	64	42.0	18.5	111	16.8%	92	18.3	134
1985	477	114	23.9	54	36.1	19.2	88	5.5%	84	17.5	120
1984	463	106	22.9	48	32.0	22.4	76	11.9%	67	14.4	99
1983	430	90	21.0	24	30.7	23.8	60	10.9%	53	12.3	84

Balance Sheet Data (Million $)

Dec. 31	Cash	Curr. Assets	Curr. Liab.	Curr. Ratio	Total Assets	% Ret. on Assets	Long Term Debt	Common Equity	Total Cap.	% LT Debt of Cap.	% Ret. on Equity
1992	**21.1**	**162**	**116**	**1.4**	**1,686**	**3.7**	**615**	**559**	**1,456**	**42.3**	**9.3**
1991	18.9	144	118	1.2	1,555	6.3	527	735	1,395	37.8	13.0
1990	47.5	170	119	1.4	1,371	9.2	407	683	1,211	33.6	17.9
1989	23.6	127	93	1.4	1,139	19.1	296	605	1,004	29.5	35.1
1988	22.8	131	95	1.4	1,070	13.2	278	599	939	29.6	24.8
1987	26.7	131	89	1.5	982	13.2	282	493	851	33.1	24.2
1986	34.5	144	76	1.9	934	10.2	188	560	822	22.8	17.4
1985	56.1	156	68	2.3	864	10.1	196	501	760	25.8	17.7
1984	65.4	169	82	2.1	787	8.7	183	443	690	26.5	15.8
1983	69.9	173	79	2.2	745	7.3	204	397	656	31.2	14.0

Data as orig. reptd. **1.** Incl. equity in earns. of nonconsol. subs. **2.** Bef. spec. items. **3.** Reflects acctg. change.

Business Summary

Contributions to operating profits (in millions) by business segment in recent years were:

	1992	1991	1990
Shipping	$97.2	$109.8	$124.4
Property	38.2	40.8	67.4
Food products	–26.2	16.1	18.5
Container leasing	12.5	6.7	0.7
Other	4.3	2.0	2.9

Matson Navigation Co. is the principal ocean carrier operating between Hawaii and the U.S. Pacific Coast. Service is also provided to Johnston Island and the Marshall Islands. Matson's fleet at 1992 year-end consisted of nine container or container/trailerships and four container barges. In 1992, Matson transported 236,000 containers (24-foot equivalent units), versus 229,000 units in 1991, and 111,000 automobiles, against 149,000.

Real estate operations include 93,000 acres of land (substantially all in Hawaii and used in sugar production or for other agricultural purposes). Some 2,100 acres of property are zoned for urban use, while 9,700 acres now zoned for conservation or agriculture have development potential in the foreseeable future. ALEX derived 52% of its real estate revenues in 1992 from the rental of 2.8 million square feet of commercial and industrial properties (75% located on U.S. mainland).

Through its Hawaiian Commercial & Sugar Co. and McBryde Sugar Co. units, which operate plantations on Maui and Kauai, ALEX produces 33% of Hawaii's raw sugar. California and Hawaiian Sugar Co. (100% owned) refines and markets sugar. In 1992, ALEX produced 216,329 tons of raw sugar and 57,422 of molasses. ALEX is test-marketing coffee grown from 4,850 acres.

ALEX is the world's ninth largest lessor of marine containers, managing a fleet of 133,000 20-foot equivalent units through a network of 62 depots.

Dividend Data

Cash has been paid each year since 1903. A "poison pill" stock purchase rights plan was adopted in 1989.

Amt of Divd. $	Date Decl.	Ex–divd. Date	Stock of Record	Payment Date
0.22	Oct. 23	Oct. 30	Nov. 5	Dec. 3'92
0.22	Jan. 28	Feb. 8	Feb. 12	Mar. 4'93
0.22	Apr. 23	Apr. 30	May 6	Jun. 3'93
0.22	Jun. 24	Jul. 30	Aug. 5	Sep. 2'93

Capitalization

Long Term Debt: $655,582,000 (6/93).

Common Stock: 46,338,445 shs. (no par).
Officers & directors own about 11%.
Institutions hold some 51%.
Shareholders: 7,507 of record (12/92).

Office—822 Bishop St., P.O. Box 3440, Honolulu, HI 96801. **Tel**—(808) 525-6611. **Chrmn**—R. J. Pfeiffer. **Pres & CEO**—J. C. Couch. **VP & Secy**—M. J. Marks. **VP-Treas & CFO**—G. R. Rogers. **VP & Investor Contact**—John B. Kelley (808-525-8422). **Dirs**—M. J. Chun, J. C. Couch, L. E. Denlea Jr., W. A. Dods Jr., C. G. King, C. R. McKissick, C. B. Mulholland, R. J. Pfeiffer, R. G. Reed III, M. G. Shaw, C. M. Stockholm. **Transfer Agents**—Bishop Trust Co. Ltd., Honolulu; Chemical Bank, NYC. **Registrars**—First Hawaiian Bank, Honolulu; Chemical Bank, NYC. **Incorporated** in Hawaii in 1900. **Empl**—2,859.

 Stephen R. Klein

Allegheny Ludlum

NYSE Symbol ALS Options on ASE, CBOE In S&P MidCap 400

Price	Range	P-E Ratio	Dividend	Yield	S&P Ranking	Beta
Aug. 20'93	1993					
21 1/8	23 3/8–17	23	0.48	2.3%	NR	1.38

Summary

Earnings of this leading U.S. producer of stainless steel have been recovering in recent periods, and the shares were split two for one in July 1993. An agreement to acquire Athlone Industries, primarily a manufacturer of specialty steels in plate form, was recently announced.

Current Outlook

Earnings for 1994 are projected at $1.30 a share, versus 1993's estimated earnings of $1.08.

Dividends should remain at $0.12 quarterly.

Sales for 1994 are expected to advance, reflecting the impact of a stronger economy on shipments and prices and the likely acquisition of Athlone Industries. Stable raw material costs, an improved product mix, more efficient use of plants, and other cost savings resulting from the merger should offset higher interest costs and share dilution. Accordingly, earnings should rise in 1994.

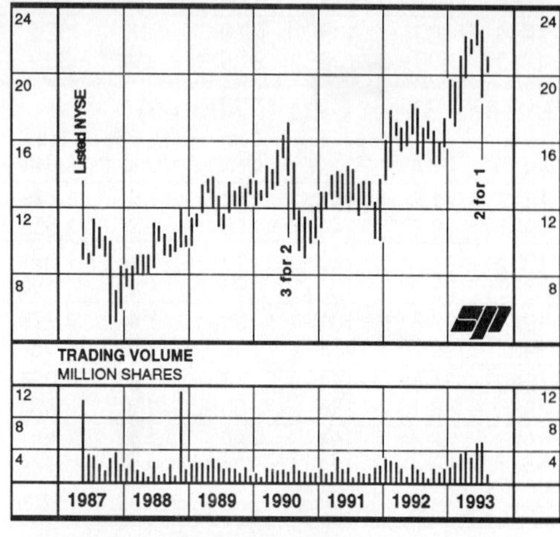

Net Sales (Million $)

Quarter:	1993	1992	1991	1990
Mar.	290	264	267	279
Jun.	280	261	265	296
Sep.		254	290	271
Dec.		[1]257	232	239
		1,036	1,005	1,084

Sales in the 26 weeks ended July 4, 1993, rose 8.5%, year to year, reflecting a 12% increase in tons shipped. Benefiting from lower raw material costs, and nonoperating income versus nonoperating expense, net income advanced 61%. Share earnings were $0.56 versus $0.35 (before a charge of $1.90 for accounting changes), as adjusted.

Common Share Earnings ($)

Quarter:	1993	1992	1991	1990
Mar.	0.28	0.17	0.19	0.35
Jun.	0.28	0.18	0.17	0.34
Sep.	E0.23	0.20	0.07	0.26
Dec.	E0.29	[1]0.17	0.20	0.10
	E1.08	0.71	0.63	1.04

Important Developments

Jun. '93— ALS signed a definitive agreement to acquire Athlone Industries (NYSE; ATH) through an exchange of stock valued at some $105 million, or about $17.50 of ALS common stock for each of the approximately 6,000,000 ATH shares outstanding. Athlone, a Washington, Pa., based producer of stainless steel plate, had net income of $5.7 million in 1992 on $207 million of sales. In the proposed merger, the final exchange ratio would be determined by dividing $17.50 by the average of the closing prices of ALS stock for the 15-day trading period ending two days prior to the closing. ALS would issue no more than 1.14604 nor less than 0.84726 of a share for each ATH share. The transaction, which is subject to various conditions, is expected to be completed in late 1993, with Athlone shareholders voting in October.

Next earnings report expected in late October.

Per Share Data ($)

Yr. End Dec. 31	1992	1991	1990	1989	1988	1987	1986
Tangible Bk. Val.	**3.91**	5.55	5.36	4.90	3.33	3.09	NA
Cash Flow	**1.13**	1.03	1.38	2.29	1.90	1.07	NA
Earnings[2]	**0.71**	0.63	1.04	1.98	1.61	0.76	0.26
Dividends	**0.440**	0.440	0.430	0.350	1.364	0.067	Nil
Payout Ratio	**62%**	70%	41%	18%	85%	10%	Nil
Prices—High	**18 5/16**	14 9/16	17 1/8	13 7/8	12 1/32	11 11/32	NA
Low	**13 3/4**	10 1/8	9 1/16	9 3/4	7 1/8	5 1/32	NA
P/E Ratio—	**26–19**	23–16	17–9	7–5	8–4	15–7	NA

Data as orig. reptd. Adj. for stk. divs. of 100% Jul. 1993, 50% Jul. 1990. **1.** 14 weeks. **2.** Bef. spec. item of -1.90 in 1992. E-Estimated. NA-Not Available.

Income Data (Million $)

Year Ended Dec. 31	Revs.	Oper. Inc.	% Oper. Inc. of Revs.	Cap. Exp.	Depr.	Int. Exp.	[1]Net Bef. Taxes	Eff. Tax Rate	[2]Net Inc.	% Net Inc. of Revs.	Cash Flow
1992	**1.036**	**104**	**10.0**	**26.0**	**27.6**	**8.0**	**79**	**40.5%**	**[3]47**	**4.5**	**74**
1991	1,005	100	9.9	36.5	26.2	5.4	72	43.2%	41	4.1	67
1990	1,085	134	12.3	57.0	22.7	6.2	110	37.2%	69	6.4	92
1989	1,180	230	19.5	35.4	21.0	6.8	218	38.6%	134	11.3	155
1988	1,208	195	16.1	24.4	19.9	6.4	175	37.8%	109	9.0	128
1987	867	110	12.7	9.8	19.0	14.6	77	40.1%	46	5.3	65
1986	732	63	8.6	NA	11.3	13.0	40	44.3%	22	3.1	NA

Balance Sheet Data (Million $)

Dec. 31	Cash	Curr. Assets	Curr. Liab.	Curr. Ratio	Total Assets	% Ret. on Assets	Long Term Debt	Common Equity	Total Cap.	% LT Debt of Cap.	% Ret. on Equity
1992	**124**	**460**	**160**	**2.9**	**871**	**5.7**	**138**	**257**	**395**	**35.0**	**15.1**
1991	3	385	192	2.0	764	5.3	49	364	476	10.2	11.5
1990	6	427	229	1.9	793	8.8	53	352	463	11.4	20.4
1989	79	458	220	2.1	785	18.0	68	329	449	15.2	48.4
1988	9	393	230	1.7	704	16.1	76	226	355	21.4	50.0
1987	28	343	184	1.9	649	NA	83	209	343	24.3	NA

Data as orig. reptd. **1.** Incl. equity in earns. of nonconsol. subs. **2.** Bef. spec. items. **3.** Refl. acctg. change. NA-Not Available.

Business Summary

Allegheny Ludlum is one of the largest U.S. producers of stainless steel, and a major producer of silicon electrical steels and other high technology alloys. Contributions from the three principal product lines in recent years:

	1992	1991	1990	1989
Stainless	80%	77%	74%	75%
Silicon electrical.....	16%	17%	19%	18%
Other specialty steel alloys........	4%	6%	7%	7%

Stainless steel products are sold in the form of sheet, strip and plate, as well as stampings and welded tubing. Stainless steel sheet is used in commercial kitchens, fast food restaurants, food processing equipment, chemical processing equipment, and storage tanks. Stainless steel strip is used in flatware, cookware, dishwashers, ranges, vacuum bottles, and a range of automotive components. Stainless steel plate is used primarily in industrial equipment that requires cleanliness or corrosion-resistant capabilities, including food processing equipment, pulp and paper equipment, chemical equipment, and power generation equipment.

Silicon electrical steel products are used primarily in applications in which electrical conductivity and magnetic properties are important. Users of ALS's silicon electrical steel products include manufacturers of transformers, motors, generators and communications equipment.

ALS produces tool steel, high temperature alloys, electronic and thermostatic alloys, and other special alloys in flat-rolled form. These specialty steel alloys are used primarily in applications that require high strength, hardness, heat resistance and special magnetic, electronic or expansion characteristics.

Principal markets in 1992 included steel service centers (40%), energy (16%), transportation (11%), converters (10%), commercial and domestic products (8%), exports (7%), industrial machinery and equipment (3%), construction and contractor products (3%), communications and electronic equipment (1%), and other (1%).

Dividend Data

Dividends were initiated in 1987.

Amt. of Divd. $	Date Decl.	Ex-divd. Date	Stock of Record	Payment Date
0.22	Nov. 12	Nov. 23	Nov. 30	Dec. 28'92
0.22	Feb. 11	Feb. 22	Feb. 26	Apr. 1'93
0.24	May 21	Jun. 2	Jun. 8	Jul. 1'93
2–for–1 Split	May 21	Jul. 2	Jun. 8	Jul. 1'93
0.12	Aug. 12	Aug. 25	Aug. 31	Oct. 1'93

Finances

Capital expenditures are expected to approximate $58 million in 1993.

In 1980, ALS's senior management and Tippins Machinery Co. purchased ALS from Allegheny International, Inc. and took the company private. At the end of 1986, the company purchased all of its common stock held by Tippins (about 86% of the shares then outstanding) and all of its preference stock. Subsequently, ALS went public on May 8, 1987.

Capitalization

Long Term Debt: $135,801,000 (7/4/93), incl. $90 million of 5.875% debs. due 2002, conv. into com. at $20.25 a sh.

Common Stock: 65,874,644 shs. ($0.10 par). Officers and directors own some 40.9%. Institutions hold about 45%. Shareholders of record: 991 (2/93).

Office—1000 Six PPG Place, Pittsburgh, PA 15222-5479. **Tel**—(412) 394-2800. **Chrmn**—R. P. Simmons. **Pres & CEO**—R. P. Bozzone. **SVP-CFO**—J. L. Murdy. **Secy**— J. D. Walton. **Investor Contact**—Herbert W. Delano. **Dirs**—A. H. Aronson, R. P. Bozzone, P. S. Brentlinger, C. F. Fetterolf, T. Marshall, W. C. McClelland, J. L. Murdy, R. K. Pitler, C. J. Queenan, J. E. Rohr, R. P. Simmons, G. W. Tippins, S. C. Wheelwright. **Transfer Agent & Registrar**—Mellon Bank, Pittsburgh. **Incorporated** in Pennsylvania in 1979. **Empl**—5,400.

 Leo Larkin

Allegheny Power System

NYSE Symbol AYP In S&P MidCap 400

Price	Range	P-E Ratio	Dividend	Yield	S&P Ranking	Beta
Aug. 5'93	1993					
54¾	54⅞–46⅞	15	3.24	5.9%	A–	0.37

Summary

This integrated coal-based electric utility system serves contiguous areas primarily in Pennsylvania, West Virginia and Maryland. With completion of the 40%-owned Bath County pumped-storage hydroelectric project in 1985, no additional generating capacity is expected to be needed until the late 1990s or beyond. Earnings should grow modestly in 1993, benefiting from rate increases and equitable rate orders.

Current Outlook

Share earnings for 1993 are estimated at $3.80, up from the $3.66 of 1992. Earnings for 1994 are projected at $3.85 a share.

The minimum expectation is for dividends to continue at $0.81 quarterly.

Higher earnings for 1993 should reflect rate increases totaling $85.7 million in additional annual revenues that became effective from mid-1992 to mid-1993, and a request for $9.97 million in extra annualized revenues, with interim rates effective in September 1993. Favorable conclusions by each of the subsidiaries' state regulatory commissions toward AYP's strategy to comply with Phase I of the Clean Air Act Amendments of 1990 removed major uncertainty concerning extensive cost recovery. Although regulatory lags may cause short delays in recovering compliance costs and permitting the company to book AFUDC income, they should not materially hinder 1993 earnings.

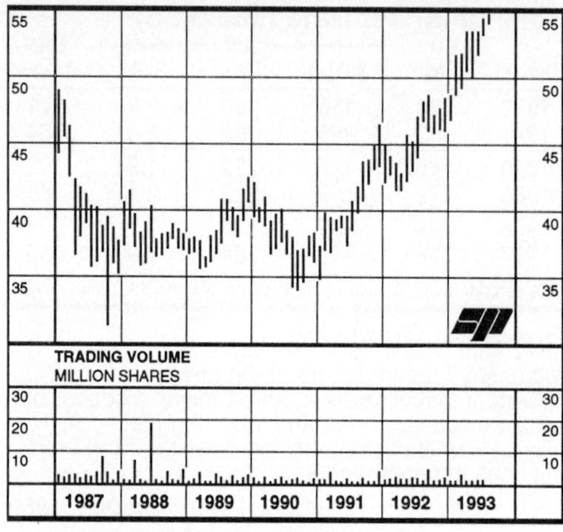

Operating Revenues (Million $)

Quarter:	1993	1992	1991	1990
Mar.	615	623	596	629
Jun.	552	556	548	550
Sep.		552	565	559
Dec.		576	572	560
		2,307	2,282	2,298

Total revenues for the six months ended June 30, 1993, fell marginally, year to year, as lower off-system sales offset higher retail revenues. Net income was up 2.0%. Share earnings were $1.96 (on 4.6% more average shares), versus $2.01.

Common Share Earnings ($)

Quarter:	1994	1993	1992	1991
Mar.	E1.25	1.19	1.24	1.12
Jun.	E0.80	0.78	0.77	0.77
Sep.	E0.90	Ed0.93	0.78	0.88
Dec.	E0.90	E0.90	0.87	0.84
	E3.85	E3.80	3.66	3.61

Important Developments

May '93— AYP reported that the Pennsylvania Public Utility Commission entered a final rate order granting its subsidiary, West Penn Power Co., rate increases that will result in an increase of $61.6 million in base revenues on an annual basis, which includes $7.5 million previously collected by a surcharge. The commission authorized a return on common equity of 11.5%. Included in the $61.6 million is more than $26 million in carrying charges for West Penn's share of facilities being built to comply with the Clean Air Act Amendments of 1990. The plan includes installing flue-gas desulfurization units (scrubbers) at the Harrison Power Station in West Virginia and low nitrogen-oxide burners and continuous emissions monitoring equipment at various other plants. Construction expenditures for 1993 are estimated at $596 million, $309.5 million of which is budgeted for environmental protection and $279 million is to be used on CAAA compliance costs.

Next earnings report expected in late October.

Per Share Data ($)

Yr. End Dec. 31	1992	1991	1990	1989	1988	1987	1986	1985	1984	1983
Tangible Bk. Val.	**31.17**	30.65	30.14	29.61	28.91	27.85	26.62	25.43	24.43	23.40
Earnings	**3.66**	3.61	3.61	3.72	3.96	4.05	4.03	3.59	3.61	3.54
Dividends	**3.210**	3.170	3.160	3.100	3.020	2.940	2.860	2.700	2.625	2.500
Payout Ratio	**88%**	88%	88%	83%	76%	73%	71%	75%	73%	71%
Prices—High	**48¾**	46½	42⅛	42½	41½	49	53½	34⅜	30	29
Low	**41½**	34⅞	34	35⅝	35⅞	31⅜	31⅝	28⅛	24⅝	22⅜
P/E Ratio—	**13–11**	13–10	12–9	11–10	10–9	12–8	13–8	10–8	8–7	8–6

Data as orig. reptd. d-Deficit. E-Estimated

Income Data (Million $)

Year Ended Dec. 31	Revs.	Depr.	Maint.	Oper. Ratio	[1]Fxd. Chgs. Cover.	Constr. Credits	Eff. Tax Rate	Net Inc.	% Return On Revs.	[2]Invest. Capital	Com. Equity
1992	**2,307**	**198**	**211**	**84.6%**	**2.94**	**17.6**	**34.2%**	**204**	**8.8**	**8.2**	**11.6**
1991	2,282	190	204	84.7%	2.95	7.9	35.9%	194	8.5	8.5	11.7
1990	2,298	181	182	85.1%	2.90	7.2	33.6%	191	8.3	8.6	11.9
1989	2,258	172	186	85.1%	2.86	7.7	29.4%	195	8.6	8.7	12.5
1988	2,170	166	167	83.8%	3.01	4.3	31.7%	205	9.4	9.1	13.8
1987	1,981	159	181	82.1%	3.27	5.1	37.4%	207	10.4	9.3	14.7
1986	1,704	151	165	79.4%	3.45	5.2	42.8%	204	12.0	9.5	15.3
1985	1,831	125	149	84.4%	3.08	46.5	36.7%	178	9.7	9.1	14.2
1984	1,721	119	131	83.3%	3.24	34.9	39.8%	176	10.2	9.5	14.9
1983	1,724	113	123	83.5%	3.17	26.0	39.5%	170	9.8	9.7	15.2

Balance Sheet Data (Million $)

Dec. 31	Gross Prop.	Capital Expend.	Net Prop.	% Earn. on Net Prop.	Total Cap.	Capitalization LT Debt	% LT Debt	Pfd.	% Pfd.	Com.	% Com.
1992	**6,680**	**488**	**4,440**	**8.3**	**4,645**	**1,952**	**48.1**	**278**	**6.9**	**1,828**	**45.0**
1991	6,256	338	4,162	8.5	4,271	1,748	47.3	264	7.1	1,686	45.6
1990	5,986	322	4,040	8.6	4,103	1,642	46.4	266	7.5	1,632	46.1
1989	5,721	303	3,914	8.7	3,998	1,578	46.1	266	7.7	1,582	46.2
1988	5,493	199	3,813	9.2	3,961	1,586	47.0	266	7.9	1,525	45.1
1987	5,320	219	3,781	9.5	3,911	1,604	48.3	266	8.0	1,452	43.7
1986	5,092	198	3,688	9.6	3,782	1,584	49.2	266	8.3	1,370	42.5
1985	4,917	520	3,641	8.3	3,688	1,601	49.8	319	9.9	1,293	40.3
1984	4,424	298	3,248	9.1	3,407	1,465	48.7	321	10.7	1,221	40.6
1983	4,135	207	3,048	9.5	3,249	1,418	49.1	321	11.1	1,149	39.8

Data as orig. reptd. **1.** Time int. exp. & pfd. divs. covered (pretax basis). **2.** Based on income bef. interest charges.

Business Summary

Allegheny Power System is an integrated electric utility holding company operating in Pennsylvania (44.7% of 1992 revenues), West Virginia (28.9%), Maryland (20.3%), and small adjacent sections of Virginia (4.5%) and Ohio (1.6%). Its subsidiaries, West Penn Power, Potomac Edison and Monongahela Power, serve 1.3 million customers in their highly industrialized service areas. Electric revenues in recent years were derived:

	1992	1991	1990	1989
Residential	32%	31%	28%	28%
Commercial	17%	17%	15%	15%
Industrial	28%	26%	25%	24%
Other	23%	26%	32%	33%

The system capacity mix in 1992 was 89% coal, 10% pumped storage, and 1% hydroelectric. Peak load in 1992 was 6,530 mw, and system capability was 7,991 mw, for a capacity margin of 18.3%.

AYP has a 40% interest in the 2,100 mw pumped-storage, hydroelectric generating facility in Bath County, Va., completed in December 1985. The entire project's cost was about $1.9 billion ($772 million for AYP). No additional generating capacity should be needed until the late 1990s or beyond.

Finances

During the first four months of 1993, AYP's subsidiaries issued $320 million of securities to refinance $307 of debt. AYP plans to fund the purchase of the subsidiaries' stock through the issuance of a substantial number of additional shares of common stock.

Dividend Data

Dividends have been paid since 1935. A dividend reinvestment plan is available.

Amt of Divd. $	Date Decl.	Ex-divd. Date	Stock of Record	Payment Date
0.80	Sep. 10	Sep. 14	Sep. 18	Sep. 30'92
0.81	Dec. 3	Dec. 8	Dec. 14	Dec. 30'92
0.81	Mar. 4	Mar. 9	Mar. 15	Mar. 31'93
0.81	Jun. 4	Jun. 8	Jun. 14	Jun. 30'93

Capitalization

Long Term Debt: $1,968,032,000 (3/93).

Subsidiary Pfd. Stk.: $278,091,000.

Common Stock: 57,126,229 shs. ($2.50 par).
Institutions hold about 37%.
Shareholders of record: 63,918 (12/92).

Office—12 East 49th St., New York, NY 10017. **Tel**—(212) 752-2121. **Pres & CEO**—K.Bergman. **Secy**—E. M. Beck. **VP-Fin**—S. I. Garnett. **Treas & Investor Contact**—Nancy Campbell (212-836-4305). **Dirs**—E. Baum, W. L. Bennett, K. Bergman, P. E. Lint, E.H. Malone, F. A. Metz Jr., C. F. Michalis, S. H. Rice, G. E. Sarsten. **Transfer Agents & Registrars**—Chemical Bank, NYC.;Chemical Trust Co. of California. **Incorporated** in Maryland in 1925. **Empl**—6,043.

 Ned Bancroft

Altera Corp.

NASDAQ Symbol ALTR (Incl. in Nat'l Market) Options on NYSE In S&P MidCap 400

Price	Range	P-E Ratio	Dividend	Yield	S&P Ranking	Beta
Sep. 10'93	1993					
28½	29¼–11⅞	54	None	None	NR	1.70

Summary

Altera is a leading designer and marketer of high-density programmable logic semiconductor chips. Using the company's proprietary software, customers can configure and program these logic chips in-house. Following five consecutive years of strong growth, earnings declined in 1992, reflecting weakness in the Japanese market and increased competition that put pressure on prices. Stronger industry conditions and a shift to a new generation of products should allow earnings to increase significantly in 1993. More moderate growth is likely in 1994 as competition increases.

Current Outlook

Earnings for 1994 should approximate $1.00 a share, up from the $0.85 projected for 1993.

Initiation of dividends is unlikely.

Sales for 1994 are expected to increase more than 20%, reflecting rapid growth in the programmable logic market and continued strong industry conditions in the U.S. and Europe. International sales should receive a further boost from a rebound in the Japanese semiconductor market, which is expected to grow only modestly in 1993. Sales should also benefit from greater shipments of the MAX 7000 family, which has higher prices than the MAX 5000 family. However, the programmable logic market is likely to become more competitive due to the entry of Motorola and start-ups into the product category. Margins are likely to narrow as pricing pressures increase due to the greater competition.

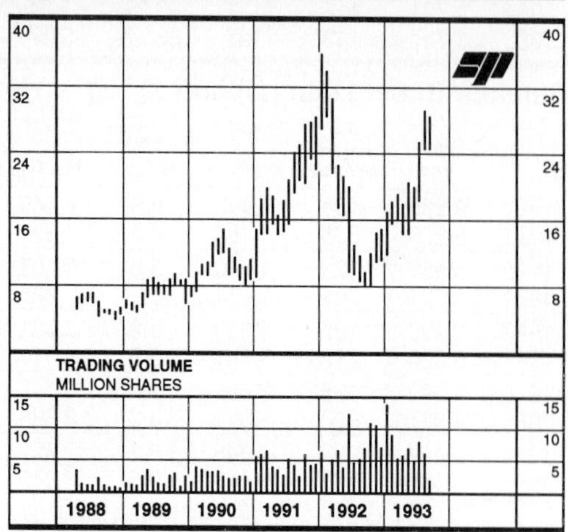

Net Sales (Million $)

Quarter:	1993	1992	1991	1990
Mar.	29.1	29.8	23.2	17.3
Jun.	33.1	23.0	26.0	19.3
Sep.	---	22.6	28.1	20.5
Dec.	---	26.0	29.6	21.2
	---	101.5	106.9	78.3

Sales for the six months ended June 30, 1993 increased 18%, year to year, led by the United States, although all geographic areas showed improvement. Margins narrowed due to continuing pressures on pricing in the first quarter and increases in expenses. Income from operations decreased 7.5%. Following a 21% decline in interest income (net), pretax income was 8.3% lower. After taxes at 36.0%, versus 37.0%, net income decreased 6.9%, to $0.37 a share from $0.40.

Common Share Earnings ($)

Quarter:	1993	1992	1991	1990
Mar.	0.15	0.25	0.18	0.15
Jun.	0.22	0.15	0.21	0.17
Sep.	E0.23	0.06	0.23	0.17
Dec.	E0.25	0.10	0.25	0.18
	E0.85	0.56	0.87	0.67

Important Developments

Jul. '93— Altera said that the 14% sequential increase in sales in 1993's second quarter reflected a 5% increase in units, combined with an 8% improvement in average selling prices. It added that its customers were continuing to move into products which offer higher capacity. It noted that sales of MAX 7000 products almost doubled from the prior quarter.

Next earnings report expected in mid-October.

Per Share Data ($)

Yr. End Dec. 31	1992	1991	1990	1989	1988	1987	1986	1985	1984	1983
Tangible Bk. Val.	**4.76**	4.11	3.14	2.46	1.88	[1]1.30	NA	NA	NA	NA
Cash Flow	**0.92**	1.15	0.90	0.72	0.51	0.16	d0.28	NA	NA	NA
Earnings[2]	**0.56**	0.87	0.67	0.55	0.38	0.07	d0.35	d0.35	d0.40	[3]d0.12
Dividends	**Nil**	Nil	Nil	Nil	Nil	Nil	Nil	Nil	Nil	Nil
Payout Ratio	**Nil**	Nil	Nil	Nil	Nil	Nil	Nil	Nil	Nil	Nil
Prices—High	**36**	28½	14⅞	9½	7⅛	NA	NA	NA	NA	NA
Low	**8⅛**	9⅛	6¾	4¾	3⅞	NA	NA	NA	NA	NA
P/E Ratio—	**64–15**	33–10	22–10	17–9	19–10	NA	NA	NA	NA	NA

Data as orig. reptd. **1.** Pro forma, aft. offering & conv. of pfd. stk. **2.** Bef. spec. item of +0.05 in 1987. **3.** From inception 6-3-83. E-Estimated d-Deficit. NA-Not Available.

Income Data (Million $)

Year Ended Dec. 31	Revs.	Oper. Inc.	% Oper. Inc. of Revs.	Cap. Exp.	Depr.	Int. Exp.	Net Bef. Taxes	Eff. Tax Rate	[2]Net Inc.	% Net Inc. of Revs.	Cash Flow
1992	**101**	**23.9**	**23.5**	**6.03**	**7.35**	**Nil**	**18.0**	**36.0%**	**11.5**	**11.4**	**18.9**
1991	107	32.0	30.0	7.80	5.81	Nil	27.8	36.0%	17.8	16.7	23.6
1990	78	23.6	30.1	8.08	4.62	Nil	20.7	35.4%	13.4	17.1	18.0
1989	59	16.9	28.7	5.61	3.43	0.04	15.4	29.9%	10.8	18.3	14.2
1988	38	9.3	24.5	5.17	2.48	0.23	8.2	13.6%	7.1	18.7	9.5
1987	21	3.3	16.0	1.70	1.41	0.48	2.2	44.3%	1.2	5.8	2.6
1986	10	d1.7	NM	1.79	0.92	0.44	d5.4	Nil	d5.4	NM	d4.5
1985	3	d4.3	NM	2.66	0.50	0.30	d4.5	Nil	d4.5	NM	NA
1984	NM	NA	NA	NA	NA	NA	d3.1	Nil	d3.1	NM	NA
[1]1983	Nil	NA	NA	NA	NA	NA	d0.6	Nil	d0.6	NM	NA

Balance Sheet Data (Million $)

Dec. 31	Cash	Curr. Assets	Curr. Liab.	Curr. Ratio	Total Assets	% Ret. on Assets	Long Term Debt	Common Equity	Total Cap.	% LT Debt of Cap.	% Ret. on Equity
1992	**50.6**	**85.6**	**19.1**	**4.5**	**115**	**10.6**	**Nil**	**95.6**	**95.6**	**Nil**	**12.9**
1991	40.1	72.2	20.8	3.5	102	19.9	Nil	81.5	81.5	Nil	24.8
1990	23.3	51.9	13.9	3.7	75	20.3	Nil	61.0	61.0	Nil	24.6
1989	26.0	45.8	8.8	5.2	56	21.2	Nil	46.6	46.6	Nil	27.2
1988	21.9	35.5	7.8	4.6	43	21.8	Nil	35.3	35.3	Nil	29.0
1987	8.7	14.6	6.1	2.4	22	6.1	2.36	[3]13.5	15.8	14.9	9.6
1986	8.4	11.0	3.0	3.7	18	NM	3.12	[3]11.4	14.5	21.5	NM
1985	NA	NA	NA	NA	14	NM	2.71	[3]9.1	11.8	23.1	NM
1984	NA	NA	NA	NA	6	NM	1.28	[3]3.6	4.8	26.4	NM
1983	NA	NA	NA	NA	10	NM	0.01	d0.7	d0.6	NM	NM

Data as orig. reptd. **1.** From inception 6-3-83. **2.** Bef. spec. item in 1987. **3.** Assumes conv. of pfd. stk. d-Deficit. NM-Not Meaningful. NA-Not Available.

Business Summary

Altera Corporation designs, develops and markets programmable logic integrated circuits and associated computer engineering development software and hardware.

The company's semiconductor products, which are known as Erasable Programmable Logic Devices (EPLDs) and FLEX (Flexible Logic Element matriX) devices, are standard logic chips that customers configure for specific end-use applications using the company's proprietary software. The company's customers enjoy the benefits of low development costs, short lead times and standard product inventories when compared to application-specific integrated circuits (ASICs) and high density and low power consumption when compared to transistor transistor logic (TTL).

Altera currently markets five families of CMOS programmable logic containing about 30 different standard integrated circuits, offered in various speed, package, and temperature variations, resulting in over 250 products.

A cornerstone of the company's strategy is the market penetration of its low-cost proprietary software design tools. As of the end of 1992, Altera had licensed over 13,000 of its development system software packages.

The company does not manufacture semiconductor wafers, but has them made by leading producers pursuant to technology exchange and foundry agreements. This eliminates the expense and inflexibility of in-house wafer fabrication.

Customers are in a broad range of market segments, including telecommunications (32% of sales), industrial (27%), office automation (21%), military (11%) and other (9%).

In 1992, exports accounted for approximately 48% of sales, with Europe representing 27% and Japan 13%.

Research and development spending totaled $15.8 million (15.6% of sales) in 1992, compared with $14.4 million (13.5%) in 1991.

Dividend Data

No cash dividends have been paid on the common shares.

Finances

At June 30, 1993, the company had cash and short-term investments of $62.9 million. It had no short-term debt at that date.

Capitalization

Long Term Debt: None (6/93).

Common Stock: 20,176,380 shs. (no par).
Officers, directors & employees own some 10%.
Institutions hold about 59%.
Shareholders: About 690 of record (12/92).

Office—2610 Orchard Pkwy., San Jose, CA 95134-2020. **Tel**—(408) 894-7000. **Chrmn, Pres & CEO**—R. Smith. **CFO & Investor Contact**—Thomas Nicoletti. **Dirs**—M. A. Ellison, J. B. Goodrich, P. Newhagen, R. Smith. **Transfer Agent & Registrar**—Chemical Trust Company of California, San Francisco. **Incorporated** in California in 1984. **Empl**—490.

 Paul H. Valentine, CFA

American Barrick

NYSE Symbol ABX Options on ASE (Jan-Apr-Jul-Oct), Toronto (Mar-Jun-Sep-Dec) In S&P MidCap 400

Price	Range	P-E Ratio	Dividend	Yield	S&P Ranking	Beta
Sep. 21'93	1993					
23¼	28½–13⅝	30	[1]0.08	[1]0.3%	B	0.11

Summary

This Canadian company is a leading North American gold producer with interests in four producing mines in the Southwestern U.S. and in Canada and a fifth under development in Nevada. With implementation of a new mining plan at the Goldstrike mine (Nev.), ABX is expected to produce 1.7 million ounces in 1994, and 1.5 million ounces in 1993, versus 1992's record 1.3 million ounces. Earnings growth should continue in 1993 and 1994 on the higher output.

Current Outlook

Even if average annual gold market prices are little changed, earnings for 1993 are estimated at $0.75 a share, up from 1992's $0.62 (adjusted for the 2-for-1 split in March 1993). Earnings for 1994 are projected at $0.85 a share.

Dividends should continue at $0.04 semiannually (in U.S. funds; before 15% Canadian tax).

Gold revenues for 1993 may rise moderately on an expected increase in gold production (1.5 million ounces, versus 1992's 1.3 million). The average gold price to be realized in 1993 under ABX's hedging program will probably be modestly below the relatively high average realization of 1992. The average price realized in 1992 was $422 an ounce, off from $438 in 1991. While a weakening U.S. dollar could have a temporary positive effect on the gold market, world deflationary forces would result in a continued downtrend for gold. With ABX's well-controlled unit costs, earnings should advance significantly on the greater output, despite lower realized prices.

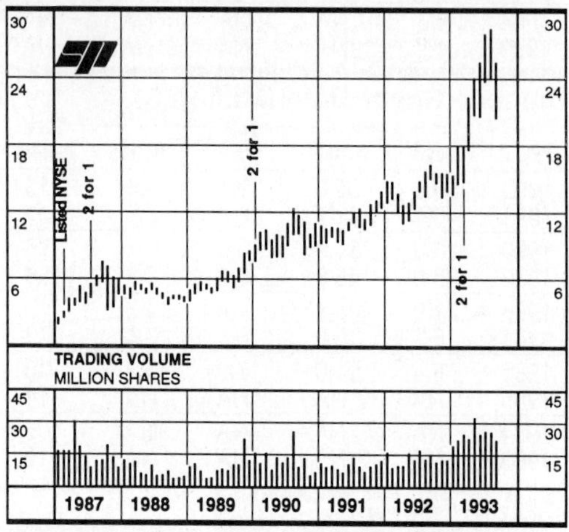

[2]Revenues (Million U.S. $)

Quarter:	1993	1992	1991	1990
Mar.	144.1	81.5	73.0	52.9
Jun.	175.2	115.5	90.2	61.4
Sep.	---	143.5	92.4	65.4
Dec.	---	199.9	89.1	71.9
	---	540.4	344.7	251.6

First-half 1993 gold revenues advanced 62%, year to year, as greater gold sales (778,942 ounces versus 465,161) more than offset lower average prices realized ($410 an ounce versus $424). With reduced unit operating costs ($172 an ounce versus $184) and lower unit depreciation, depletion and amortization expenses, net income rose 72%, to $0.36 a share from $0.21 (adjusted for the 2-for-1 split).

Common Share Earnings (U.S. $)

Quarter:	1993	1992	1991	1990
Mar.	0.16	0.08	0.06	0.05
Jun.	0.20	0.13	0.09	0.06
Sep.	E0.19	0.18	0.10	0.06
Dec.	E0.20	0.23	0.09	0.06
	E0.75	0.62	0.34	0.23

Important Developments

Aug. '93— Barrick Goldstrike Mines filed a Writ of Mandamus in Nevada Federal Court seeking a court order to require the Interior Secretary and the Bureau of Land Management to complete its Goldstrike patent applications promptly. In July 1993, ABX said that final preparations were made for shaft sinking of its Meikle mine, one mile north of Goldstrike, which would produce gold at a 400,000-ounce a year rate starting in 1996.

Next earnings report expected in mid-October.

Per Share Data (U.S. $)

Yr. End Dec. 31	1992	1991	1990	1989	1988	[3]1987	[3]1986	[3]1985	[3]1984
Tangible Bk. Val.	**3.50**	2.99	2.41	2.05	1.66	1.47	0.58	0.39	0.51
Cash Flow	**0.86**	0.52	0.39	0.32	0.24	0.18	0.14	0.08	0.02
Earnings[4]	**0.62**	0.34	0.23	0.15	0.13	0.10	0.07	0.02	d0.03
Dividends	**0.065**	0.055	0.043	0.032	0.022	0.010	Nil	Nil	Nil
Payout Ratio	**11%**	17%	20%	23%	16%	10%	Ni l	Nil	Nil
Prices—High	**16⅜**	14	12⅜	8⅝	5¾	7⅝	2⅛	1⅛	NA
Low	**11⅛**	9¼	7⅝	4⅛	3¾	1⅞	⅞	½	NA
P/E Ratio—	**26–18**	41–27	55–34	57–27	44–28	78–19	31–12	54–27	NA

Data as orig. reptd. Based on Canadian GAAP. Adj. for stk. div(s). of 100% Mar. 1993, 100% Jan. 1990, 100% Jul. 1987 & 1-for-5 reverse split Dec. 1985. **1.** In U.S. funds, bef. 15% Canadian tax on nonresidents. **2.** Excl. int. & other inc. **3.** Reflects merger or acquisition. **4.** Bef. results of disc. opers. of -0.13 in 1985, -0.09 in 1984; bef. spec. item(s) of -0.01 in 1987. E-Estimated. d-Deficit. NA-Not Available.

American Barrick Resources Corporation

Income Data (Million U.S. $)

Year Ended Dec. 31	Revs.	Oper. Inc.	% Oper. Inc. of Revs.	Cap. Exp.	Depr.	Int. Exp.	Net Bef. Taxes	Eff. Tax Rate	[4]Net Inc.	% Net Inc. of Revs.	Cash Flow
1992	**540**	**288**	**53.2**	**255**	**69.0**	**9.3**	**223**	**21.5%**	**175**	**32.4**	**244**
1991	345	156	45.2	264	51.3	9.4	115	19.6%	92	26.8	144
1990	252	107	42.7	170	48.6	12.8	78	24.9%	58	23.1	107
1989	206	86	41.8	224	40.6	12.8	45	20.8%	36	17.4	76
1988	148	60	40.9	196	25.7	10.7	39	22.5%	30	20.7	56
[1]1987	92	37	39.9	104	17.4	10.0	26	21.9%	21	22.3	38
[1]1986	65	24	36.0	56	11.2	3.6	[3]13	15.7%	11	16.8	22
[2]1985	35	10	30.0	55	8.3	2.7	[3]4	27.2%	3	8.3	11
[2]1984	15	4	24.5	110	4.4	4.8	[3]d4	NM	d3	NM	2

Balance Sheet Data (Million U.S. $)

Dec. 31	Cash	Curr. Assets	Curr. Liab.	Curr. Ratio	Total Assets	% Ret. on Assets	Long Term Debt	Common Equity	Total Cap.	% LT Debt of Cap.	% Ret. on Equity
1992	**288**	**353**	**139**	**2.5**	**1,504**	**12.4**	**317**	**993**	**1,360**	**23.3**	**19.0**
1991	252	328	112	2.9	1,306	7.4	306	841	1,189	25.7	12.2
1990	312	391	112	3.5	1,147	5.2	363	645	1,035	35.0	9.8
1989	305	368	89	4.1	1,050	3.9	419	526	961	43.6	7.5
1988	51	87	43	2.0	701	4.4	256	390	658	38.9	8.3
1987	167	239	53	4.6	676	3.9	279	338	623	44.8	8.7
1986	96	111	90	1.2	301	4.7	103	102	211	48.9	12.8
1985	2	13	15	0.8	148	1.8	68	60	130	52.2	4.1
1984	2	10	33	0.3	166	NA	46	77	133	34.7	NA

Data as orig. reptd. Based on Canadian GAAP. **1.** Reflects merger or acquisition. **2.** Excl. disc. opers. and reflects merger or acquisition. **3.** Incl. equity in earns. of nonconsol. subs. **4.** Bef. results of disc. opers. in 1985, 1984, and spec. item(s) in 1987. d-Deficit. NM-Not Meaningful. NA-Not Available.

Business Summary

American Barrick (ABX) has interests in four producing North American gold mines. Its share of 1992 output was 1,325,432 ounces, versus 789,846 oz. in 1991, and was expected to rise to 1.5 million oz. in 1993, 1.7 million in 1994 and 2.0 million in 1995. At year-end 1992, ABX's interest in total gold reserves was 27.2 million oz., including proven and probable of 25.7 million.

Gold output of ABX's Goldstrike (Nev.) mine was 1,108,219 oz. in 1992 at an operating cost of $143/oz., versus 1991's 546,146 oz. at $175. With commissioning of the final three of six autoclaves in the 1993 first quarter, the four-year Betze development plan was completed and the entire processing capacity converted to high grade sulphide ore, which will be the mainstay of Goldstrike operations. In December 1992, ABX signed an agreement with Newmont Gold (NGC) to jointly develop the northern Carlin Trend, where Goldstrike is located. As part of the NGC/ABX agreement, Goldstrike's mine plan has been revised and the Betze pit expanded to become the Betze-Post pit encompassing the Deep Post orebody, which straddles ABX and NGC land. As a result of this plan and higher grade identified in Betze-Post, Goldstrike is targeted to produce 1.3 million oz. in 1993, 1.5 million in 1994 and 1.8 million in 1995. At year-end 1992, Goldstrike's total reserves were 21.0 million oz.

The Mercur mine (Utah) is an open-pit operation. Output was 121,239 oz. in 1992 at an operating cost of $262/oz., versus 1991's 127,280 oz. at $240 and was estimated at 115,000 for 1993. In April 1993, Barrick Resources (USA) agreed to acquire Gold Standard, Inc.'s (GSI's) 15% net profits interest in Mercur and receive a full and complete release of all present and future claims by GSI relating to Mercur and Barrick for $4.7 million cash.

ABX's Holt-McDermott gold mine (Ontario) produced 46,325 oz. of gold in 1992 at an operating cost of $356/oz., versus 1991's 60,728 oz. at $331. Output is targeted at 60,000 oz. for 1993.

The 26.25%-owned Pinson mine (Nev.) consists of open pit operations. ABX's 1992 share of gold production was 13,376 ozs. at an average operating cost of $260/oz. ABX's Camflo mine (Quebec) depleted its reserves in December 1992 and the mill completed final processing in January 1993.

Dividend Data

Dividends were initiated in 1987. Semiannual payments in the past 12 months (in U.S. funds) before 15% Canadian nonresident tax:

Amt of Divd. $	Date Decl.	Ex-divd. Date	Stock of Record	Payment Date
0.06½	Sep. 16	Nov. 23	Nov. 30	Dec. 15'92
2-for-1	Feb. 8	Mar. 2	Feb. 19	Mar. 1'93
0.04	Feb. 8	May 24	May 31	Jun. 15'93

Capitalization

Long Term Liabilities: $273,050,000 (6/93).

Common Stock: 285,100,000 shs. (no par).
Horsham Corp. owns some 20%.
Institutions hold approximately 36%.

Office—24 Hazelton Ave., Toronto, ON, Canada M5R 2E2. **Tel**—(416) 923-9400. **Chrmn & CEO**—P. Munk. **Pres**—R. M. Smith. **VP-Secy**—W. R. Robertson. **EVP-CFO**—G. C. Wilkins. **SVP-Investor Contact**—Belle Mulligan. **Dirs**—H. L. Beck, C. W. D. Birchall, M. A. Cohen, D. J. Davies, J. T. Eyton, J. Garbutt, D. H. Gilmour, D. R. Hinde, A. A. MacNaughton, P. Munk, E. N. Ney, P. A. Novelly, J. L. Rotman, R. M. Smith, G. C. Wilkins. **Transfer Agent & Registrar**—Mellon Securities Trust Co., Ridgefield Park, NJ. **Incorporated** in Ontario in 1984. **Empl**—1,845.

 A.M. Sorrentino, CFA

American Power Conversion

NASDAQ Symbol APCC (Incl. in Nat'l Market) Options on ASE & CBOE In S&P MidCap 400

Price	Range	P-E Ratio	Dividend	Yield	S&P Ranking	Beta
Sep. 17'93	1993					
38½	48–21	48	None	None	NR	1.98

Summary

This company manufactures uninterruptible power supply (UPS) products that protect data in personal computers and other sensitive electronic devices from disruptions or surges in electric power. Sales and earnings have grown sharply in recent years, and further gains are expected in 1993, reflecting increased demand for UPS products, and penetration into international markets. In August 1993, APCC announced a two-for-one stock split, effective September 24, 1993.

Current Outlook

Earnings for 1993 are projected at $1.00 a share up from 1992's $0.61. For 1994, earnings are estimated at $1.35. (Unadjusted for the September 1993 two for one stock split).

Initiation of cash dividends is not expected.

Strong revenue growth is expected to continue for the remainder of 1993, reflecting increased demand for UPS products and expanding international business. Although APCC announced price reductions that went into effect in late July 1993, operating results are likely to benefit from this measure in the form of increased sales volumes and further market share gains. The company is pushing to improve market share overseas, where its share lags behind that held in the U.S. Specifically, overall revenue growth will be fueled by the continued proliferation of LANs and related power-sensitive networking equipment (routers, bridges and hubs) that rely on UPS products for protection against power anomalies and outages.

Net Sales (Million $)

Quarter:	1993	1992	1991	1990
Mar.	48.1	30.8	17.4	11.3
Jun.	57.0	33.3	21.3	14.5
Sep.	---	44.5	26.9	16.8
Dec.	---	48.9	28.1	16.7
	---	157.5	93.6	59.2

Net sales in the six months ended June 30, 1993, jumped 64%, year to year, reflecting increasing market share of UPS products in the computer networking, internetworking equipment and point of sale markets and strong international sales performance. Total operating expenses increased less rapidly than sales (59%), aided by realization of manufacturing efficiencies and stable gross margins. After taxes at 35.5% in both periods, net income surged 82%, to $18,716,683 ($0.41 a share), from $10,275,351 ($0.22).

Common Share Earnings ($)

Quarter:	1993	1992	1991	1990
Mar.	0.18	0.10	0.05	0.04
Jun.	0.23	0.13	0.07	0.05
Sep.	E0.27	0.17	0.10	0.07
Dec.	E0.32	0.22	0.12	0.08
	E1.00	0.61	0.34	0.22

Important Developments

Jul. '93— APCC lowered the prices on a selected number of its popular Smart-UPS products, by a range of 4-to-16%. The company said the realization of manufacturing cost savings allowed for the price reduction, and added that such measures may lead to increased sales volumes and market share.

Next earnings report expected in late October.

Per Share Data ($)

Yr. End Dec. 31	1992	1991	1990	1989	1988	1987
Tangible Bk. Val.	**1.73**	1.02	0.61	0.37	0.22	0.06
Cash Flow	**0.65**	0.37	0.23	0.16	0.09	0.04
Earnings[1]	**0.61**	0.34	0.22	0.15	0.08	0.04
Dividends	**Nil**	Nil	Nil	Nil	Nil	Nil
Payout Ratio	**Nil**	Nil	Nil	Nil	Nil	Nil
Prices—High	**28¾**	14⅛	4⅞	2⅛	⅝	NA
Low	**10⅜**	3⁹⁄₁₆	1¼	⅝	½	NA
P/E Ratio—	**47–17**	41–10	23–6	15–4	8–6	NA

Data as orig. reptd. Adj. for stk. divs. of 100% Dec. 1992, 100% Dec. 1991, 200% Oct. 1990, 25% Jun. 1989, 400% Jun. 1988. **1.** Bef. spec. item(s) of +0.01 in 1987. E-Estimated. NA-Not Available.

Income Data (Million $)

Year Ended Dec. 31	Revs.	Oper. Inc.	% Oper. Inc. of Revs.	Cap. Exp.	Depr.	Int. Exp.	Net Bef. Taxes	Eff. Tax Rate	[1]Net Inc.	% Net Inc. of Revs.	Cash Flow
1992	**157.0**	**44.7**	**28.4**	**6.43**	**1.82**	**0.07**	**43.1**	**35.5%**	**27.8**	**17.6**	**29.6**
1991	93.6	25.1	26.8	5.86	0.90	0.39	24.2	35.6%	15.6	16.6	16.5
1990	59.2	15.4	26.0	3.23	0.69	0.31	14.7	36.6%	9.3	15.8	10.0
1989	35.4	9.9	27.9	2.90	0.51	0.14	9.5	36.8%	6.0	17.0	6.5
1988	17.4	4.6	26.4	1.06	0.28	0.06	4.4	36.3%	2.8	16.0	3.1
1987	8.1	1.8	22.2	0.53	0.10	0.03	1.7	41.0%	1.0	12.2	1.1

Balance Sheet Data (Million $)

Dec. 31	Cash	Curr. Assets	Curr. Liab.	Curr. Ratio	Total Assets	% Ret. on Assets	Long Term Debt	Common Equity	Total Cap.	% LT Debt of Cap.	% Ret. on Equity
1992	**21.0**	**82.7**	**21.5**	**3.9**	**98.5**	**35.2**	**Nil**	**76.0**	**77.0**	**Nil**	**46.1**
1991	12.2	46.9	14.0	3.3	58.2	32.9	Nil	43.7	44.2	Nil	44.7
1990	3.0	29.5	7.1	4.1	35.9	30.7	3.04	25.6	28.7	10.6	45.7
1989	6.1	20.7	6.0	3.4	24.7	31.3	3.52	15.1	18.6	18.9	50.2
1988	5.2	11.9	4.6	2.6	13.4	28.9	0.14	8.7	8.8	1.6	50.6
1987	0.4	3.7	2.3	1.6	4.2	NA	0.21	1.7	1.9	11.0	NA

Data as orig. reptd. 1. Bef. spec. items. NA-Not Available.

Business Summary

American Power Conversion Corporation designs, develops, manufactures and markets a line of uninterruptible power supply (UPS) products and associated software and interface cables that are used with personal computers, engineering workstations, file servers, communications equipment and other sensitive electronic devices that rely on electric utility power.

As microcomputers have become increasingly important, it has become necessary to ensure that data stored in, and operating instructions for, microcomputers are protected from fluctuations in utility power. A UPS protects against these disturbances by providing continuous power automatically and virtually instantaneously after the electric power supply is interrupted or sags, as well as line filtering and protection against surges while the electric utility is operating.

The company's strategy has been to design and manufacture products that incorporate high performance and quality at competitive prices. In addition, its products are designed to be aesthetically pleasing and appropriate for use in an office environment. Products are engineered and extensively tested for compatibility with nearly all common microcomputers and small minicomputers. About 31 different UPS models are offered, ranging in capacity from 110 to 2,000 volt-amps and in end-user list price from $139 to $1,799.

APCC markets its products through a domestic and international network of computer distributors, computer dealers and catalog merchandisers. It also sells directly to some large value-added resellers, which integrate the company's products into specialized microcomputer systems and then market turnkey systems to selected vertical markets, and to manufacturers. In 1992, APCC sold products to more than 1000 customers, up from 650 in 1991; Ingram Micro D Corp., accounted for about 14% of sales in each of 1992, 1991 and 1990. Sales outside of North America accounted for 32% of the company's net sales in 1992, up from 25% in 1991.

Dividend Data

No cash dividends have been paid on the public shares. A two-for-one stock split is to be effected on September 24, 1993, for shareholders of record August 20. The shares had been split two for one in December 1992 and in December 1991, three for one in October 1990, five for four in 1989, and five for one in 1988.

Finances

The company had $15.0 million available for future borrowing under unsecured line-of-credit agreements at a floating interest rate equal to the bank's prime rate. No advances had been drawn on the credit facilities as of March 31, 1993.

R&D spending totaled $4,919,906 in 1992, up from $2,745,485 in 1991.

Capitalization

Long Term Debt: None (6/93).

Common Stock: 44,605,196 shs. ($0.01 par).
Officers and directors own 25%.
Institutions hold 52%.
Shareholders of record: About 1,970 (12/92).

Office—132 Fairgrounds Rd., West Kingston, RI 02892. **Tel**—(401) 789-5735. **Chrmn, Pres & CEO**—R. B. Dowdell, Jr. **VP, Treas & CFO**—E. W. Machala. **VP & Secy**—E. E. Landsman. **Dirs**—R. B. Dowdell, Jr., J. D. Gerson, E. E. Landsman, E. F. Lyon, N. E. Rasmussen. **Transfer Agent & Registrar**—Bank of Boston. **Incorporated** in Massachusetts in 1981. **Empl**—731.

 Samuel A. Dedio

American President

NYSE Symbol APS Options on Pacific In S&P MidCap 400

Price	Range	P-E Ratio	Dividend	Yield	S&P Ranking	Beta
Aug. 19'93	1993					
47⅞	57⅛–37⅛	11	0.60	1.3%	B–	1.89

Summary

This U.S.-flag containership operator serves trans-Pacific and intra-Asian routes and provides double-stack service. Plans to enter the Europe-Asia market were terminated in March 1993, because of poor market conditions. In July 1993, APS filed an application with the Maritime Administration to operate part of its existing fleet, and six vessels on order, under foreign registry. Profit comparisons in 1993 are being penalized by the absence of 1992's substantial nonrecurring income.

Current Outlook

Earnings for 1993 are estimated at $4.35 a share (including about $0.48 of nonrecurring income), versus the $4.86 (including $2.15 nonrecurring) of 1992. Profits could reach $5.00 in 1994.

The $0.15 quarterly dividend could be lifted moderately before 1993 year-end.

Container volumes should advance in 1993, primarily reflecting increased trade between China and its Asian neighbors and higher U.S. military cargo. Weak economic activity will limit trans-Pacific movements. Rates should firm on import containers, but remain under competitive pressure in the intra-Asian segment. Margins will benefit from the reduced costs for feeder service and lower spending on computer systems. Doublestack volumes will benefit from a stronger economy, increased volumes of automotive goods and traffic garnered under APS' new agreement with Burlington Motor Carriers. Hurting comparisons will be the absence of 1992 's nonrecurring income.

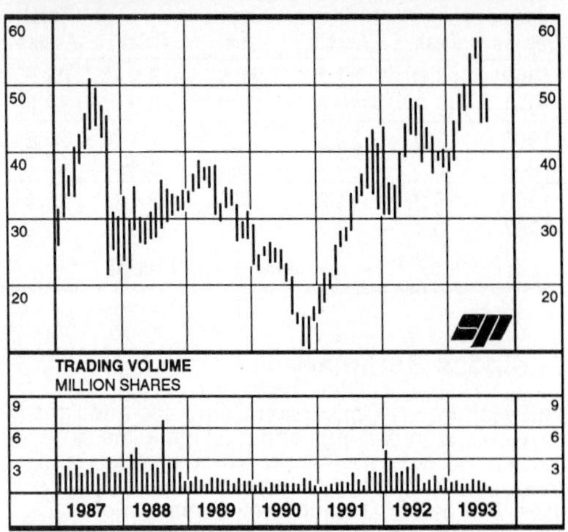

Revenues (Million $)

Quarter:	1993	1992	1991	1990
Mar.	629	660	624	587
Jun.	582	584	551	511
Sep.	---	591	605	539
Dec.	---	669	668	633
	---	2,505	2,449	2,270

Revenues for 1993's first half fell 2.7%, year to year. Net income was off 24%, to $2.19 a share, from $2.68 (before a $1.42 special charge).

Common Share Earnings ($)

Quarter:	1993	1992	1991	1990
Mar.	0.77	1.06	0.33	d0.21
Jun.	1.41	1.62	0.62	d0.01
Sep.	E1.45	1.50	2.16	d3.28
Dec.	E0.72	0.64	0.65	0.02
	E4.35	4.86	3.65	d3.46

Important Developments

Aug. '93— The House of Representatives passed a Maritime Administration (MarAd) funding bill containing an amendment barring the agency for 12 months from considering any applications by carriers to reflag their vessels. In July, APS notified MarAd that it wanted to transfer seven of its 15 U.S.-flag ships to foreign registry; six new vessels under construction also would bear foreign flags. APS said it is taking this action because the Clinton Administration has indicated that it would not renew carriers' operating subsidies. APS received $69.7 million in federal subsidies in 1992 under a contract expiring at 1997 year-end.

Mar. '93— Citing poor market conditions, APS terminated its proposed $100 million joint venture with East Asiatic Co. to provide containership service between Asia and Europe.

Next earnings report expected in mid-October.

Per Share Data ($)

Yr. End Dec. 31	1992	1991	1990	1989	1988	1987	1986	[1]1985	1984	1983
Tangible Bk. Val.	**29.93**	30.33	26.07	29.35	30.08	28.63	25.72	25.87	24.54	19.21
Cash Flow	**12.09**	10.39	2.17	5.91	7.55	6.85	3.81	4.51	8.12	3.60
Earnings[2]	**4.86**	3.65	d3.46	d0.04	3.46	3.42	0.71	1.86	5.78	1.51
Dividends	**0.60**	0.60	0.60	0.575	0.50	0.50	0.50	0.375	Nil	Nil
Payout Ratio	**12%**	15%	NM	NM	13%	15%	71%	20%	Nil	Nil
Prices—High	**48**	43⅜	29⅛	38¾	35⅞	51	29	29	24½	20½
Low	**30¼**	15¾	10⅜	26¾	22⅝	21⅝	16⅞	13⅞	14⅞	11⅞
P/E Ratio—	**10–6**	12–4	NM	NM	10–7	15–6	41–24	16–7	4–3	14–8

Data as orig. reptd. Adj. for stk. divs. of 50% May 1985, 3% Apr. 1984. **1.** Refl. merger or acq. **2.** Bef. spec. items of -1.47 in 1992, -0.65 in 1991. d-Deficit. E-Estimated. NM-Not Meaningful.

Income Data (Million $)

Year Ended Dec. 31	[1]Revs.	Oper. Inc.	% Oper. Inc. of Revs.	Cap. Exp.	Depr.	Int. Exp.	Net Bef. Taxes	Eff. Tax Rate	[4]Net Inc.	% Net Inc. of Revs.	Cash Flow
1992	**2,574**	**246**	**9.6**	**66**	**106**	**38.7**	**122**	**35.9%**	**78**	**3.0**	**177**
1991	2,518	256	10.2	20	106	44.0	107	40.0%	[5]64	2.5	163
1990	2,337	161	6.9	39	108	48.1	d93	NM	d60	NM	42
1989	2,300	164	7.1	111	104	52.6	22	47.9%	11	0.5	103
1988	2,194	247	11.2	247	85	48.1	136	40.1%	81	3.7	157
1987	1,891	236	12.5	281	72	43.5	[3]149	47.0%	79	4.2	144
1986	1,506	126	8.3	115	64	47.1	[3]41	56.7%	[5]18	1.2	79
[2]1985	1,235	128	10.3	134	55	34.4	[3]51	25.2%	38	3.1	94
1984	977	169	17.3	139	42	32.7	[3]115	10.4%	103	10.6	145
1983	806	84	10.4	59	36	29.9	[3]33	19.0%	26	3.3	63

Balance Sheet Data (Million $)

Dec. 31	Cash	Curr. Assets	Curr. Liab.	Curr. Ratio	Total Assets	% Ret. on Assets	Long Term Debt	Common Equity	Total Cap.	% LT Debt of Cap.	% Ret. on Equity
1992	**132**	**459**	**475**	**1.0**	**1,436**	**5.6**	**242**	**390**	**850**	**28.5**	**18.2**
1991	179	473	338	1.4	1,514	4.6	444	446	1,065	41.7	13.8
1990	118	467	373	1.3	1,590	NM	481	481	1,134	42.4	NM
1989	127	421	315	1.3	1,661	0.6	511	587	1,298	39.4	NM
1988	186	503	325	1.5	1,711	5.4	541	509	1,342	40.3	14.4
1987	287	536	275	2.0	1,599	5.4	372	600	1,158	32.1	12.7
1986	276	477	240	2.0	1,343	1.5	395	536	1,036	38.2	2.7
1985	67	218	192	1.1	1,060	3.7	290	538	828	35.0	7.3
1984	195	269	185	1.5	987	10.8	263	506	769	34.2	22.9
1983	107	199	124	1.6	790	3.5	305	335	641	47.7	8.2

Data as orig. reptd. **1.** Incl. Operating-Differential Subsidy. **2.** Refl. merger or acq. **3.** Incl. equity in earns. of nonconsol. subs. **4.** Bef. spec. items. **5.** Refl. acctg. change. d-Deficit. NM-Not Meaningful.

Business Summary

American President Companies is a leading U.S.-flag carrier, providing service to 37 nations over trans-Pacific and intra-Asian routes. The company also has certain real estate operations. Contributions to operating profits (in millions):

	1992	1991	1990
Transportation	$137	$131	–$64
Real estate	3	12	8

American President Lines is one of the largest containship operators serving the trans-Pacific market. APS handled 355,000 forty-foot equivalent containers (FEU) in trans-Pacific service in 1992, versus 375,000 units in 1991. In 1992, APS moved 146,000 FEUs in its intra-Asia service (138,000). APS' fleet consists of 102,500 containers, 51,700 chassis and 19 containerships having an aggregate capacity to transport 28,100 FEUs per voyage. APS also operates 11 foreign-flag feeder vessels on its intra-Asia service. In 1992, APS derived 51% of its shipping revenue from cargo imported to the U.S., 31% from U.S. export shipments and 18% from freight moving over intra-Asia routes.

APS provides doublestack service (the movement of containers via railroad) to 26 major commercial centers in the U.S. and three cities in Mexico. Operating a fleet of 1,172 railcars (transportation is performed by various railroads under contract), APS handled 508,000 (FEUs) in 1992, versus 509,000 in 1991. APS also provides domestic freight brokerage services, arranges transportation for time-sensitive freight for the automobile industry and consolidates small international shipments into full containerloads in 17 nations. APS also owns 185 acres of property in northern California.

Dividend Data

Dividends, which are subject to restrictions by the Maritime Administration and various loan agreements, were initiated in 1985. A new "poison pill" stock purchase right was adopted in 1988.

Amt. of Divd. $	Date Decl.	Ex-divd. Date	Stock of Record	Payment Date
0.15	Oct. 21	Nov. 6	Nov. 15	Nov. 30'92
0.15	Jan. 27	Feb. 8	Feb. 15	Feb. 28'93
0.15	Apr. 30	May 10	May 15	May 31'93
0.15	Jul. 28	Aug. 9	Aug. 15	Aug. 31'93

Capitalization

Long Term Debt: $228,819,000 (6/93), incl. $18.8 million of lease obligs.

9.0% Cum. Conv. Pfd. Stock: $75,000,000; conv. into 1,980,721 com.; privately held.

Common Stock: 13,339,701 shs. ($0.01 par).
Officers & directors own 15%.
Institutions hold about 68%.
Shareholders of record: 4,325 (3/93).

Office—1111 Broadway, Oakland, CA 94607. **Tel**—(510) 272-8000. **Chrmn & Pres**—J. M. Lillie. **VP-CFO**—W. M. Storey. **VP-Secy**—M. B. Cattani. **Investor Contact**—Randall K. Gausman. **Dirs**—C. S. Arledge, J. H. Barr, J. J. Hagenbuch, C. S. Hatch, J. Hayashi, F. W. Hellman, J. M. Lillie, T. J. Rhein, W. B. Seaton, F. N. Shumway, W. M. Storey, B. L. Williams. **Transfer Agent & Registrar**—Bank of Boston. **Incorporated** in Delaware in 1983. **Empl**—5,209.

American Waste Services

NYSE Symbol AW In S&P MidCap 400

Price	Range	P-E Ratio	Dividend	Yield	S&P Ranking	Beta
Aug. 5'93	1993					
2¼	3⅜–2	14	None	None	NR	NA

Summary

This company provides a full range of waste management services, including the operation of solid waste landfills, the transportation of special waste, and various analytical and remediation services. It is also a common carrier of general and bulk commodities. Net income declined in 1992, reflecting the effects of the weak economy, and continued to fall in the first half of 1993. Earnings for the balance of 1993 should continue to be penalized by competitive pricing pressures and weak disposal rates.

Current Outlook

Earnings for 1993 are projected at $0.15 a share, versus the $0.21 reported for 1992. Earnings for 1994 are expected at $0.20 a share.

Dividends are unlikely to be paid in the foreseeable future.

Revenue growth for the balance of 1993 is expected to be limited by continued softness in disposal rates and competitive pricing pressures. Profitability should continue to be negatively impacted by weak disposal and transportation brokerage volume, pricing pressures, a slow economic rebound, and a slightly higher tax rate, which will offset improved operating efficiencies.

Net Revenues (Million $)

Quarter:	1993	1992	1991	1990
Mar.	19.3	22.9	19.6	20.4
Jun.	21.3	24.6	22.0	23.0
Sep.	---	23.1	24.3	24.9
Dec.	---	21.9	24.7	26.5
	---	92.6	90.7	94.8

In the six months ended June 30, 1993, revenues declined 15%, year to year, primarily reflecting weak disposal and transportation brokerage volume. Profitability was penalized by soft disposal rates and stronger competitive pricing pressures, and pretax earnings were off 45%. After taxes at 41.5%, versus 38.0%, net income fell 48%, to $0.05 a share from $0.10.

Common Share Earnings ($)

Quarter:	1993	1992	1991	1990
Mar.	0.02	0.04	0.05	0.08
Jun.	0.03	0.07	0.07	0.09
Sep.	E0.03	0.06	0.08	0.11
Dec.	E0.07	0.05	0.07	0.09
	E0.15	0.21	0.27	0.37

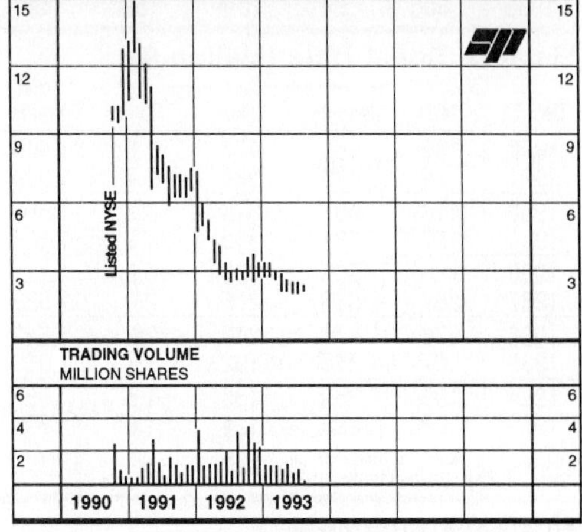

Important Developments

Aug. '93— American Waste said it expects competitive pressures for disposal services to continue during the next several months. The company said it will continue to focus on securing additional business for its landfills. In the second quarter of 1993, a 9% rise in disposal volumes was offset by an 11% decline in average disposal rates. The transportation group, which incurred a small loss in the quarter, implemented certain cost reduction measures at the end of the period to improve its profitability.

May '93— The company noted that its tire monofill facility at American Landfill became operational during the first quarter. The facility will have the capacity to dispose of 100 million shredded tires.

Next earnings report expected in early November.

Per Share Data ($)

Yr. End Dec. 31	[1]1992	1991	[1]1990	[1]1989
Tangible Bk. Val.	**2.40**	2.16	1.86	0.34
Cash Flow	**0.47**	0.45	0.51	0.24
Earnings	**0.21**	0.27	0.37	0.23
Dividends	**Nil**	Nil	Nil	Nil
Payout Ratio	**Nil**	Nil	Nil	Nil
Prices—High	**7⅜**	14⅞	12¾	NA
Low	**2½**	5⅞	9½	NA
P/E Ratio—	**35–12**	55–22	34–26	NA

Data as orig. reptd. **1.** Reflects merger or acquisition. E-Estimated NA-Not Available.

Income Data (Million $)

Year Ended Dec. 31	Revs.	Oper. Inc.	% Oper. Inc. of Revs.	Cap. Exp.	Depr.	Int. Exp.	Net Bef. Taxes	Eff. Tax Rate	Net Inc.	% Net Inc. of Revs.	Cash Flow
[1]1992	**92.6**	**19.5**	**21.0**	**17.7**	**7.87**	**3.08**	**9.9**	**37.9%**	**6.16**	**6.7**	**14.0**
1991	90.7	20.1	22.2	16.9	5.56	3.38	13.0	39.4%	7.90	8.7	13.5
[1]1990	94.8	22.7	23.9	21.2	3.58	4.68	15.4	40.3%	9.21	9.7	12.8
[1]1989	37.4	9.4	25.0	35.3	0.35	0.37	9.1	41.9%	5.29	14.1	5.6

Balance Sheet Data (Million $)

Dec. 31	Cash	Curr. Assets	Curr. Liab.	Curr. Ratio	Total Assets	% Ret. on Assets	Long Term Debt	Common Equity	Total Cap.	% LT Debt of Cap.	% Ret. on Equity
1992	**6.3**	**25.2**	**13.4**	**1.9**	**124**	**5.0**	**18.1**	**89.8**	**111**	**16.4**	**7.1**
1991	9.4	32.4	16.4	2.0	123	6.6	21.4	83.2	106	20.1	10.0
1990	20.6	39.4	15.9	2.5	116	10.3	24.3	75.0	100	24.3	21.7
1989	1.8	8.4	9.5	0.9	46	NA	29.2	7.3	37	80.0	NA

Data as orig. reptd. **1.** Reflects merger or acquisition. NA-Not Available.

Business Summary

American Waste Services provides waste management services to industrial, commercial, municipal and governmental customers primarily in selected eastern and midwestern markets. Principal activities include operation of nonhazardous solid waste landfills for the disposal of special waste, garbage and refuse; transportation and brokerage of hazardous and nonhazardous waste; and environmental engineering, site assessment, analytical laboratory and remediation services.

The company believes it is one of the largest transporters and disposers of special waste, which consists of all waste except hazardous waste, refuse and garbage. Examples of special waste include nonhazardous industrial waste products (such as those generated by air and water pollution control processes), combustion ashes, soils contaminated with petroleum and certain other chemicals, municipal and industrial sludges, demolition debris, asbestos and tires.

AW's waste disposal services currently utilize three nonhazardous solid waste disposal facilities in Ohio. The largest of such landfills, American Landfill, is owned by the company, as are Mahoning Landfill, which was acquired in January 1992 for $4.5 million, and East Liverpool Landfill, acquired in March 1993. Landfill customers are charged a tipping fee based on the amount of waste to be disposed of at the site. During 1992, 51% of the waste received by the company's landfills was generated in Ohio, down from 55% in 1991.

The company's transportation segment provides carrier services for waste removal on behalf of customers throughout the U.S. and parts of Canada. AW utilizes a variety of trucks, dump trailers, tankers and other equipment designed and constructed to transport hazardous waste. AW is also a nationwide carrier of general and bulk commodities, such as coal, salt, sand and ash, as well as steel products and heavy machinery, and engages in the brokerage of commodities transported by third parties.

The Earth Sciences Companies, acquired in 1990, provide various environmental services, including consulting, problem definition and assessment, analysis and cleanup, and also offer construction and remedial services.

Dividend Data

The company said in its initial offering prospectus in October 1990 that it did not intend to pay cash dividends in the foreseeable future, but would retain its earnings for reinvestment in its business.

Finances

In March 1993, AW completed the acquisition of the East Liverpool landfill for $1 million plus annual disposal fee payments of $600,000 over 20 years. The company said it would spend $5 million in 1993 on the landfill. Capacity at the plant was to be increased to 4,550 tons a day.

In its initial public offering on October 4, 1990, American Waste Services, Inc. sold 6,000,000 Class A common shares at $10 a share, including 4,800,000 shares in the U.S. and 1,200,000 outside the U.S. through underwriters led by Goldman, Sachs & Co., PaineWebber Inc., and First Analysis Securities Corp. Net proceeds of $55.0 million were used to purchase the Earth Sciences Companies ($20.1 million), to reduce debt ($22.5 million), and for working capital purposes ($4.1 million).

Capitalization

Long Term Debt: $23,510,000 (3/93).

Class A Common Stock: 22,029,013 shs. (no par).
Officers and directors own about 32%.
Institutions hold approximately 13%.
Shareholders of record: 791 (3/93).

Class B Common Stock: 7,656,715 shs. (no par); 10 votes per sh.; elects 75% of dirs.; transfer restricted; conv. sh.-for-sh. into Class A com.
Officers and directors own some 69%.

Office—One American Way, Warren, OH 44484. **Tel**—(216) 856-8800. **Chrmn & CEO**—R. E. Klingle. **Pres & COO**—D. D. Wilson. **EVP-Fin, Treas, CFO & Investor Contact**—Charles Boryenace. **EVP & Secy**—J. M. Grinstein. **Dirs**—D. J. Best, S. C. Blauvelt, C. Boryenace, S. B. Ferguson, J. A. Johnson, R. E. Klingle, J. R. Miller, F. O. Nicklin Jr., M. F. Schmidt, W. M. Thomas Jr., D. D. Wilson. **Transfer Agent & Registrar**—Society National Bank, Cleveland. **Incorporated** in Ohio in 1988. **Empl**—498.

 Stewart Scharf

AMETEK, Inc.

NYSE Symbol AME Options on Phila (Jan-Apr-Jul-Oct) In S&P MidCap 400

Price	Range	P–E Ratio	Dividend	Yield	S&P Ranking	Beta
Aug. 30'93	1993					
13¾	17½–12⅝	18	0.68	5.1%	B+	0.95

Summary

This diversified industrial company manufactures precision instruments, electro-mechanical products, and industrial materials. Very minimal share earnings progress was made during the nine-year period from 1984 to 1992, and book value declined. Profits are likely to be down sharply in 1993, reflecting weakness in key markets and expenses related to downsizing aerospace operations.

Current Outlook

Earnings for 1993 are estimated at about $0.65 a share, down significantly from 1992's $1.01. Partial recovery to $0.90 a share is projected for 1994.

Despite the recent lack of coverage, the dividend is expected to continue at $0.17 quarterly.

Sales for 1993 are likely to decrease, reflecting anticipated lower demand for both electro-mechanical and precision instruments products, which should more than offset a sales improvement for industrial materials. The electro-mechanical business is expected to be hurt by poor market conditions in the floorcare industry, customers rescheduling their orders, and the continuing recession in Europe. Precision instruments sales will probably continue to be affected by the worsening recession in commercial and military aerospace markets and unfavorable market conditions for process and analytical instruments (particularly in refining and petrochemical plants). Earnings will be penalized by the lower sales, nonrecurring charges related to downsizing the aerospace division, and start-up costs for a new electric motor plant.

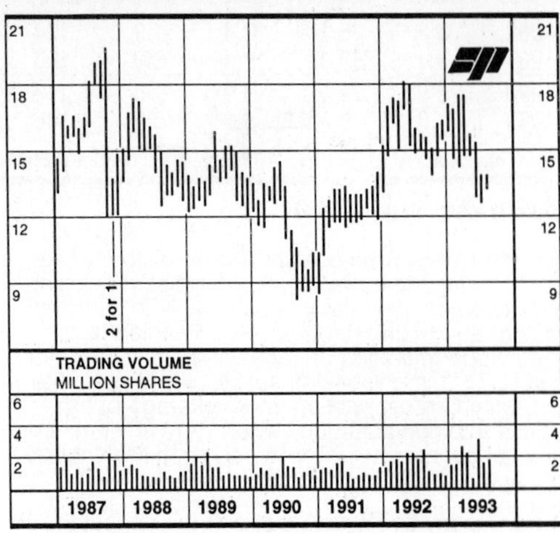

Net Sales (Million $)

Quarter:	1993	1992	1991	1990
Mar.	187.1	196.8	179.2	168.9
Jun.	186.8	195.3	182.1	157.6
Sep.	---	186.0	170.5	165.2
Dec.	---	191.5	183.4	169.1
	---	769.6	715.1	660.7

Sales for the six months ended June 30, 1993 declined 4.6%, year to year, primarily reflecting lower demand for electric motor products. Profits were down 21% for electromechanical and 73% for precision instruments, but industrial materials earnings edged up 2.6%. Overall operating profit dropped 40%. After 21% lower other expenses (net), pretax income fell 44%. With taxes at 37.3%, versus 34.2%, net income decreased 47%, to $0.28 a share from $0.52.

Common Share Earnings ($)

Quarter:	1993	1992	1991	1990
Mar.	0.14	0.26	0.20	0.22
Jun.	0.14	0.26	0.21	0.24
Sep.	E0.18	0.25	0.22	0.20
Dec.	E0.19	0.24	0.24	0.19
	E0.65	1.01	0.87	0.85

Important Developments

Apr. '93— AMETEK acquired certain assets of Revere Aerospace Inc. from Dobson Park Industries PLC, United Kingdom, for about $7 million in cash. Revere produces products for the aircraft industry, including electric, thermocouple, and fiber optic cable assemblies, as well as sensors for temperature, proximity, liquid level and flow monitoring.

Next earnings report expected in late October.

Per Share Data ($)

Yr. End Dec. 31	1992	1991	[1]1990	[1]1989	[2]1988	1987	1986	1985	1984	1983
Tangible Bk. Val.	**3.69**	3.54	3.30	3.03	3.34	4.87	4.38	4.01	4.33	4.05
Cash Flow	**1.67**	1.51	1.39	1.26	1.15	1.35	1.29	1.13	1.31	1.05
Earnings[3]	**1.01**	0.87	0.85	0.87	0.80	0.94	0.83	0.80	0.98	0.74
Dividends	**0.680**	0.660	0.640	0.620	0.600	0.525	0.500	0.425	0.400	0.350
Payout Ratio	**67%**	76%	75%	72%	75%	56%	60%	54%	41%	47%
Prices—High	**18⅛**	14	14½	15⅞	17⅜	19⅝	15½	14¾	15⅛	14⅛
Low	**13⅛**	8½	8¼	12	12½	12	11⅝	9⅞	10¾	8¼
P/E Ratio—	**18–13**	16–10	17–10	18–14	22–16	21–13	19–14	19–13	15–11	19–11

Data as orig. reptd. Adj. for stk. divs. of 100% Nov. 1987, 100% Jul. 1983. **1.** Reflects merger or acquisition. **2.** Reflects acctg. change. **3.** Bef. results of disc. ops. of -0.19 in 1988, and spec. items of +0.08 in 1988, +0.13 in 1983. E-Estimated

Income Data (Million $)

Year Ended Dec. 31	Revs.	Oper. Inc.	% Oper. Inc. of Revs.	Cap. Exp.	Depr.	Int. Exp.	Net Bef. Taxes	Eff. Tax Rate	[5]Net Inc.	% Net Inc. of Revs.	Cash Flow
1992	**770**	**109.0**	**14.1**	**24.0**	**29.4**	**19.7**	**66.7**	**33.5%**	**44.4**	**5.8**	**73.7**
1991	715	94.6	13.2	18.8	28.3	22.1	52.4	27.5%	38.0	5.3	66.3
[1]1990	661	92.4	14.0	35.7	24.1	20.8	56.7	34.1%	37.3	5.7	61.4
[1]1989	588	77.8	13.2	53.1	17.6	15.2	60.7	36.9%	38.3	6.5	55.9
[2,3]1988	520	68.9	13.2	41.9	15.3	13.0	55.8	37.1%	35.1	6.7	50.4
1987	620	84.3	13.6	35.4	18.4	13.9	[4]65.3	36.9%	41.2	6.6	59.5
1986	568	63.3	11.1	25.7	20.3	7.8	[4]54.5	32.8%	[3]36.6	6.4	56.9
1985	503	71.3	14.2	34.3	14.6	4.3	[4]61.8	43.4%	34.9	6.9	49.5
1984	504	76.3	15.1	18.5	14.5	4.4	[4]69.7	38.7%	42.7	8.5	57.2
1983	448	67.4	15.0	15.3	13.6	4.6	[4]58.2	44.9%	32.1	7.2	45.7

Balance Sheet Data (Million $)

Dec. 31	Cash	Curr. Assets	Curr. Liab.	Curr. Ratio	Total Assets	% Ret. on Assets	Long Term Debt	Common Equity	Total Cap.	% LT Debt of Cap.	% Ret. on Equity
1992	**116**	**319**	**138**	**2.3**	**595**	**7.3**	**187**	**210**	**432**	**43.3**	**21.0**
1991	107	319	138	2.3	612	6.2	205	211	452	45.3	18.4
1990	111	318	133	2.4	615	6.4	224	199	459	48.7	19.1
1989	116	316	101	3.1	563	7.6	220	195	447	49.2	20.3
1988	116	251	75	3.4	448	7.1	149	181	362	41.1	16.2
1987	175	338	84	4.0	538	7.8	156	253	450	34.6	17.0
1986	174	315	88	3.6	512	8.0	152	231	424	35.8	16.3
1985	60	203	101	2.0	401	9.4	39	220	299	12.9	16.6
1984	77	194	73	2.7	337	13.2	41	201	264	15.6	22.6
1983	73	190	66	2.9	309	10.7	47	176	243	19.2	19.3

Data as orig. reptd. **1.** Reflects merger or acquisition. **2.** Excl.disc. opers. **3.** Reflects acctg. change. **4.** Incl. equity in earns. of nonconsol. subs. prior. **5.** Bef. results of disc. opers. and spec. items.

Business Summary

AMETEK is a diversified multi-product manufacturer. Business segment contributions in 1992:

	Sales	Profits
Electro–mechanical	40%	50%
Precision instruments	39%	28%
Industrial materials.............	21%	22%

International business accounted for 15% of total sales in 1992.

Electro-mechanical products include motor-blower systems and injection-molded components (for manufacturers of floor care appliances) and electric and brushless D.C. fractional horsepower motors and motor blowers (used in computers, business machines, medical equipment, and high efficiency gas furnaces).

Precision Instruments products consist primarily of aircraft cockpit instruments and displays; pressure, temperature, flow, and liquid level sensors (for aircraft jet engine manufacturers and for airlines); and airborne electronics systems (to monitor and record flight and engine data). Other products include instruments and complete instrument panels (for heavy truck builders); process monitoring and display systems; combustion, gas analysis, moisture, and emissions monitoring systems; force and speed measuring instruments; air and noise monitors; pressure and temperature calibrators; pressure-indicating and digital manometers; and a mechanical pressure gauge.

Industrial Materials products include high temperature resistant materials and textiles; corrosion-resistant heat exchangers, tanks, and piping for process systems; lightweight foam sheet packaging material; filters for drinking water and other liquids; filter housings; high-purity metals and alloys in powder, strip and wire form for high performance aircraft, autos and electronics; and thermoplastic compounds.

Dividend Data

Dividends have been paid since 1942.

Amt of Divd. $	Date Decl.	Ex–divd. Date	Stock of Record	Payment Date
0.17	Nov. 18	Dec. 3	Dec. 9	Dec. 23'92
0.17	Feb. 24	Mar. 11	Mar. 17	Mar. 31'93
0.17	May 21	Jun. 10	Jun. 16	Jun. 30'93
0.17	Aug. 25	Sep. 10	Sep. 16	Sep. 30'93

Capitalization

Long Term Debt: $186,701,000 (6/93).

Common Stock: 43,636,229 shs. ($1 par).
Institutions hold about 50%.
Shareholders of record: 7,227.

Office—Station Square, Paoli, PA 19301. **Tel**—(215) 647-2121. **Chrmn**—J. H. Lux. **Pres & CEO**—W. E. Blankely. **EVP-CFO**—A. Kornfeld. **Secy**—W. E. Cowan. **Treas**—Deirdre D. Saunders. **Investor Contact**—William F. Cleary. **Dirs**—W. E. Blankely, L. G. Cole, H. N. Friedlaender, S. S. Gordon, C. D. Klein, D. P. Steinmann, E. R. Varet. **Transfer Agent & Registrar**—American Stock Transfer & Trust Co., NYC. **Incorporated** in Delaware in 1930. **Empl**—6,200.

 M. Graham Hackett

Anadarko Petroleum

NYSE Symbol APC Options on CBOE (Feb-May-Aug-Nov) In S&P MidCap 400

Price	Range	P–E Ratio	Dividend	Yield	S&P Ranking	Beta
Aug. 2'93	1993					
39½	44–25⅝	38	0.30	0.8%	B–	0.28

Summary

Anadarko Petroleum is a U.S.-based natural gas and crude oil production company. A significant portion of its reserves are in the Hugoton gas basin, the largest U.S. natural gas basin, with fields stretching across portions of Kansas, Texas and Oklahoma. The company's production profile is being expanded by development of oil fields overseas. Near-term earnings power has been enhanced by property acquisition in the U.S. Domestic natural gas fundamentals are seen in a secular upturn, and APC is well positioned to exploit strengthening U.S. natural gas markets.

Current Outlook

Share earnings for 1994 are projected at $1.25, up from 1993's estimated $1.00.

Dividends should continue at $0.07½ quarterly.

Revenues will climb in 1993 and 1994, reflecting greater natural gas and crude oil volumes. Profits should advance, benefiting from greater volumes. APC's strategy of integrating U.S. natural gas production with gas marketing should aid prospects. The U.S. natural gas business is seen being spurred by the Clinton administration because of plentiful North American supplies and the fuel's environmentally benign qualities.

Revenues (Million $)

Quarter:	1993	1992	1991	1990
Mar.	129.3	83.4	98.1	104.1
Jun.	112.5	69.6	67.0	72.0
Sep.		85.1	60.8	85.4
Dec.		137.2	110.6	126.9
		375.2	336.6	388.5

Revenues in the six months ended June 30, 1993, soared 58%, year to year, reflecting higher natural gas prices and increased volumes. Results benefited from improved natural gas fundamentals and greater oil volumes, and income of $27.6 million replaced a loss of $3.5 million. Share earnings were $0.50, before a credit of $1.39, versus a loss of $0.06.

Common Share Earnings ($)

Quarter:	1993	1992	1991	1990
Mar.	0.28	0.08	0.24	0.38
Jun.	0.22	d0.14	Nil	0.01
Sep.	E0.25	0.14	0.01	0.13
Dec.	E0.25	0.41	0.35	0.51
	E1.00	0.49	0.59	1.04

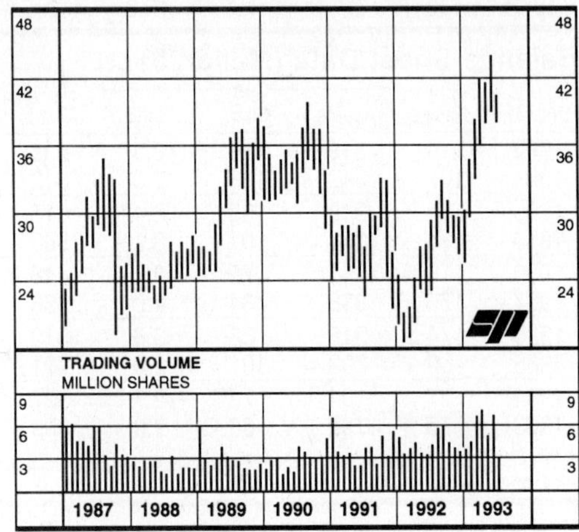

Important Developments

Jul. '93— APC's 1993 second quarter results benefited from higher natural gas prices and greater gas volumes. Natural gas prices averaged $2.05 per Mcf, versus $1.46 per Mcf a year earlier, while gas volumes rose to 34.8 Bcf, from 28.0 Bcf. Oil volumes also contributed to improved results; output climbed to 1,903,000 bbl., from 1,140,000 bbl. Increased oil and natural gas volumes were primarily due to 1992 property acquisitions from Atlantic Richfield Co. Oil prices dropped to $17.74 a bbl., from $18.86. Natural gas liquids output was about unchanged at 442,000 bbl., and the gas liquds price per gallon was unchanged at $0.31. Capital expenditures jumped to $70.3 million, from $53.3 million, while interest expense increased to $7.9 million, from $6.7 million.

Next earnings report expected in late October.

Per Share Data ($)

Yr. End Dec. 31	1992	1991	1990	1989	1988	1987	1986	1985	1984	1983
Tangible Bk. Val.	[1]**11.88**	[1]11.62	[1]11.25	9.47	8.74	8.21	8.37	8.63	8.08	7.19
Cash Flow	**2.90**	2.79	3.52	3.35	2.89	1.77	1.70	2.44	2.48	1.95
Earnings	**0.49**	0.59	1.04	0.92	0.76	0.18	0.21	0.91	1.08	0.80
Dividends	**0.300**	0.300	0.300	0.300	0.300	0.300	0.075	NA	NA	NA
Payout Ratio	**61%**	51%	30%	33%	39%	172%	38%	NA	NA	NA
Prices—High	**32⅞**	33⅛	39⅞	38½	28	34⅞	23	NA	NA	NA
Low	**18½**	21½	28⅝	24½	22	19¼	18⅜	NA	NA	NA
P/E Ratio—	**67–38**	56–36	38–28	42–27	37–29	NM	NM	NA	NA	NA

Data as orig. reptd.; prior to 1986 data. as reptd. in information statement dated Aug. 29, 1986, pro forma assuming 51.5 million com. shs. outstanding. **1.** Incl. intangibles. d-Deficit. E-Estimated. NM-Not Meaningful. NA-Not Available.

Anadarko Petroleum Corporation

Income Data (Million $)

Year Ended Dec. 31	Revs.	Oper. Inc.	% Oper. Inc. of Revs.	Cap. Exp.	Depr. Depl. & Amort.	Int. Exp.	Net Bef. Taxes	Eff. Tax Rate	Net Inc.	% Net Inc. of Revs.	Cash Flow
1992	**375**	**201**	**53.4**	**362**	**133**	**36.6**	**40**	**31.8%**	**27.3**	**7.3**	**160**
1991	337	194	57.7	170	121	36.8	48	32.9%	32.4	9.6	154
1990	388	252	64.8	213	132	42.9	84	34.4%	55.2	14.2	187
1989	330	217	65.7	203	127	50.9	72	33.2%	48.0	14.5	175
1988	304	202	66.6	161	124	58.1	61	34.8%	39.8	13.1	151
1987	230	141	61.2	120	82	52.0	[1]15	38.5%	9.1	4.0	92
1986	206	125	60.6	124	73	50.2	[1]17	39.0%	[2]10.1	4.9	83
1985	297	221	74.5	158	79	50.3	82	42.9%	46.9	15.8	126
1984	307	241	78.5	180	72	54.0	100	44.1%	55.7	18.1	128
1983	261	204	78.2	210	60	48.1	73	43.0%	41.4	15.8	101

Balance Sheet Data (Million $)

Dec. 31	Cash	Curr. Assets	Curr. Liab.	Curr. Ratio	Total Assets	% Ret. on Assets	Long Term Debt	Common Equity	Total Cap.	% LT Debt of Cap.	% Ret. on Equity
1992	**14.8**	**139**	**107**	**1.3**	**1,905**	**1.5**	**647**	**657**	**1,783**	**36.3**	**4.2**
1991	15.0	107	104	1.0	1,676	1.9	440	641	1,556	28.2	5.1
1990	13.0	120	118	1.0	1,647	3.4	427	618	1,512	28.2	9.7
1989	9.5	103	97	1.1	1,553	3.1	493	495	1,441	34.2	10.1
1988	6.3	109	100	1.1	1,490	2.7	493	455	1,378	35.8	9.0
1987	7.2	86	64	1.3	1,430	0.6	520	427	1,354	38.4	2.1
1986	10.3	69	48	1.4	1,376	Nil	485	432	1,318	36.8	Nil
1985	3.0	75	70	1.1	1,337	3.6	417	444	1,252	33.3	10.9
1984	4.3	76	91	0.8	1,263	4.6	388	416	1,158	33.5	14.2

Data as orig. reptd.; prior to 1986 data as reptd. in information statement dated Aug. 29, 1986. **1.** Incl. equity in earns. of nonconsol. subs. **2.** Reflects accounting change.

Business Summary

Anadarko Petroleum is engaged in crude oil and natural gas exploration, development and production. It has interest in 17 gas gathering systems, owns and operates six gas processing plants (with interests in others) and explores for geothermal energy. APC became an independent public company on October 1, 1986, when Panhandle Eastern Corp. spun off to Panhandle common shareholders all of outstanding APC shares on a share-for-share basis.

Production in 1992 amounted to 4,659,000 bbl. of oil, (4,968,000 bbl. in 1991), 146.4 Bcf of natural gas (137.9 Bcf), and 2,447,000 bbl. of natural gas liquids (1,957,000). At December 31, 1992, estimated proved reserves amounted to 80,300,000 bbl. of oil and condensate (45,800,000 in 1991) and 1,726 Bcf of natural gas (1,744).

The company's drilling program focuses on known petroleum and natural gas areas onshore in North America, primarily in the Anadarko Basin of Oklahoma, the Midcontinent region (Arkoma and Golden Trend Basins) of Arkansas and Oklahoma, the Permian Basin of West Texas and New Mexico, the Rocky Mountain regions of Nevada and Wyoming, and southern Alberta. APC also drills offshore in the Gulf of Mexico. It has also entered into overseas exploration joint ventures. A significant portion of APC's reserves is located in the Hugoton natural gas field, the largest natural gas field in the U.S.

During 1992, APC replaced 200% of total production with reserves of oil and natural gas, on an energy equivalent barrel (EEB) basis. The company's worldwide finding cost in 1992 was $5.43 per EEB. The U.S. oil and gas industry finding cost averaged $4.61 per EEB, compared with APC's five-year average U.S. finding cost of $4.46.

The capital budget for 1993 totals $290 million. Spending in 1992 came to $360 million, with $206 million used for producing property acquisitions, the largest of which was from Atlantic Richfield.

Dividend Data

Dividends were initiated in 1986. A new "poison pill" stock purchase right was adopted in 1988.

Amt. of Divd. $	Date Decl.	Ex-divd. Date	Stock of Record	Payment Date
0.07½	Oct. 30	Dec. 3	Dec. 9	Dec. 23'92
0.07½	Jan. 29	Mar. 4	Mar. 10	Mar. 24'93
0.07½	Apr. 29	Jun. 3	Jun. 9	Jun. 23'93
0.07½	Jul. 27	Sep. 1	Sep. 8	Sep. 22'93

Capitalization

Long Term Debt: $509,723,000 (3/93), excl. $100 million of 6¼% debs. that were converted into com. in July 1993.

Common Stock: 58,500,000 shs. ($0.10 par). Institutions hold 63%, incl. 11% by International Petroleum Investment Partnership. Shareholders of record: 9,200.

Office—Anadarko Tower, 17001 Northchase Dr. (P.O. Box 1330), Houston, TX 77251-1330. **Tel**—(713) 875-1101. **Chrmn, Pres & CEO**—R. J. Allison, Jr. **SVP-Fin & CFO**—M. E. Rose. **Secy**—Suzanne Suter. **VP & Investor Contact**—A. P. Taylor, Jr. **Dirs**—C. P. Albert, R. J. Allison, Jr., L. Barcus, R. Brown, J. L. Bryan, J. R. Gordon, C. M. Simmons. **Transfer Agent & Registrar**—Chemical Bank Shareholder Services Dept., NYC. **Incorporated** in Delaware in 1985. **Empl**—970.

 Edward G. Graves

Analog Devices

NYSE Symbol ADI Options on Phila (Mar-Jun-Sep-Dec) In S&P MidCap 400

Price	Range	P–E Ratio	Dividend	Yield	S&P Ranking	Beta
Aug. 24'93	1993					
24¼	26–15⅛	32	None	None	B–	1.61

Summary

This company is a leading manufacturer of high-performance linear and mixed-signal integrated circuits (ICs). The company also produces digital ICs, signal processing components, and a limited number of board-level subsystem products. Following higher earnings in 1992 that largely reflected the absence of restructuring charges, sharply higher results are likely in fiscal 1993 due to stronger industry conditions and well received new products. Those factors should again produce higher earnings in fiscal 1994.

Current Outlook

Earnings for the fiscal year ending October 31, 1994, should approximate $1.20 a share, up from the $0.85 projected for fiscal 1993.

Cash dividends have never been paid.

Sales for fiscal 1994 should increase approximately 20%, reflecting strong industry growth and an aggressive new product introduction program. The fastest growing products should be system level ICs, including digital signal processing and special purpose ICs. The gross margin should widen due to yield improvement and lower costs due to die shrinks. In addition, pricing pressures should lessen due to the stronger industry conditions and a focus on digital signal processing and special purpose ICs. Well controlled expenses should also allow for operating leverage on the higher volume. Longer-term growth should benefit from the growing need to interface real world phenomena with computers and the company's more focused new product introduction program.

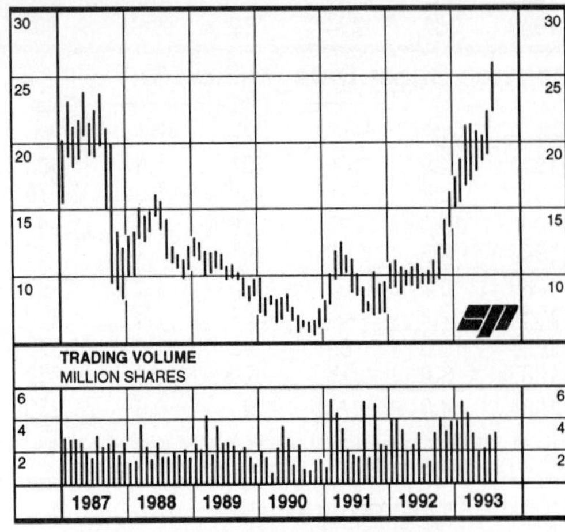

Net Sales (Million $)

Quarter:	1992–93	1991–92	1990–91	1989–90
Jan.	151.3	131.3	133.1	109.6
Apr.	162.9	142.9	142.1	116.4
Jul.	173.1	144.3	130.3	120.7
Oct.	---	148.8	132.2	138.5
	---	567.3	537.7	485.2

Sales for the nine months ended July 31, 1993, increased 16%, year to year, aided by new product introductions and stronger industry conditions. Gross margins widened on an improved product mix and expenses were well-controlled; pretax income increased 265%. After taxes at 20.8%, versus 25.0%, net income rose 286%, to $0.60 a share from $0.16.

Common Share Earnings ($)

Quarter:	1992–93	1991–92	1990–91	1989–90
Jan.	0.16	d0.02	0.08	0.02
Apr.	0.20	0.08	0.14	0.10
Jul.	0.24	0.10	0.01	0.11
Oct.	E0.24	0.15	d0.06	d0.51
	E0.85	0.31	0.17	d0.28

Important Development

Aug. '93— ADI said that during the third quarter bookings for system-level ICs rose 52% from the year earlier level, led by ICs used in signal computing applications and high-performance hard disk drives. Bookings for standard-function ICs rose 14%, as market penetration increased in the industrial distribution channel.

Next earnings report expected in early December.

Per Share Data ($)

Yr. End Oct. 31	1992	1991	[1]1990	1989	1988	1987	1986	1985	1984	1983
Tangible Bk. Val.	**7.31**	6.92	6.76	7.56	7.08	6.16	5.58	4.83	3.94	3.11
Cash Flow	**1.42**	1.24	0.70	1.43	1.55	1.12	1.12	1.15	1.17	0.75
Earnings	**0.31**	0.17	d0.28	0.58	0.80	0.40	0.51	0.65	0.83	0.44
Dividends	**Nil**	Nil	Nil	Nil	Nil	Nil	Nil	Nil	Nil	Nil
Payout Ratio	**Nil**	Nil	Nil	Nil	Nil	Nil	Nil	Nil	Nil	Nil
Prices[2]—High	**16¼**	12½	9⅞	12⅞	16⅛	23⅞	24¾	20⅝	18	18⅞
Low	**8⅝**	6½	5½	8⅛	9⅞	8⅜	14¼	13½	11⅝	7⅞
P/E Ratio—	**52-28**	74–38	NM	22–14	20–12	60–21	49–28	32–21	22–14	43–18

Data as orig. reptd. Adj. for stk. div(s) of 33⅓% Apr. 1986, 25% Apr. 1985, 33⅓% Apr. 1984, 50% Apr. 1983. **1.** Reflects merger or acquisition. **2.** Cal. yr. d-Deficit. E-Estimated. NM-Not Meaningful.

Income Data (Million $)

Year Ended Oct. 31	Revs.	Oper. Inc.	% Oper. Inc. of Revs.	Cap. Exp.	Depr.	Int. Exp.	Net Bef. Taxes	Eff. Tax Rate	Net Inc.	% Net Inc. of Revs.	Cash Flow
1992	**567**	**79.0**	**13.9**	**67.1**	**52.9**	**5.98**	**19.0**	**21.2%**	**14.9**	**2.6**	**67.8**
1991	538	74.4	13.8	57.9	50.0	4.78	[2]9.4	12.6%	8.2	1.5	58.2
[1]1990	485	73.4	15.1	59.4	45.7	3.19	[2]d13.6	NM	d12.9	NM	32.8
1989	453	84.7	18.7	51.7	40.9	2.02	[2]36.4	23.3%	27.9	6.1	68.8
1988	439	91.4	20.8	52.6	36.0	2.98	[2]51.6	26.4%	38.0	8.6	74.0
1987	370	68.0	18.4	44.3	33.6	3.99	[2]25.6	27.0%	18.7	5.0	52.3
1986	334	68.6	20.5	39.1	28.3	4.43	[2]32.1	27.0%	23.4	7.0	51.7
1985	322	69.5	21.5	73.5	22.8	4.87	[2]39.1	24.0%	[3]29.7	9.2	52.6
1984	313	72.4	23.1	58.5	15.4	3.99	54.9	32.0%	37.4	11.9	52.8
1983	214	45.8	21.4	22.1	13.2	5.84	27.1	32.0%	18.4	8.6	31.6

Balance Sheet Data (Million $)

Oct. 31	Cash	Curr. Assets	Curr. Liab.	Curr. Ratio	Total Assets	% Ret. on Assets	Long Term Debt	Common Equity	Total Cap.	% LT Debt of Cap.	% Ret. on Equity
1992	**17.7**	**297**	**100**	**3.0**	**562**	**2.8**	**70.6**	**375**	**458**	**15.4**	**4.1**
1991	16.5	249	97	2.6	503	1.6	36.8	354	403	9.1	2.3
1990	8.3	232	106	2.2	487	NM	24.1	343	378	6.4	NM
1989	30.1	223	63	3.5	453	6.1	12.2	361	388	3.1	8.0
1988	22.7	221	73	3.0	449	8.8	23.0	330	375	6.1	12.3
1987	5.8	176	58	3.1	397	4.8	30.1	278	339	8.9	7.0
1986	6.3	162	60	2.7	369	6.4	29.1	248	308	9.4	10.1
1985	11.3	152	59	2.6	348	9.2	42.9	210	288	14.9	15.6
1984	13.8	152	65	2.3	296	14.4	30.0	170	230	13.0	24.5
1983	24.2	128	38	3.3	223	9.2	27.7	135	184	15.0	17.0

Data as orig. reptd. **1.** Reflects merger or acquisition. **2.** Incl. equity in earns. of nonconsol. subs. **3.** Reflects acctg. change. d-Deficit. NM-Not Meaningful.

Business Summary

Analog Devices designs, manufactures and markets a broad line of high-performance linear, mixed signal and digital integrated circuits that address a wide range of real-world signal processing applications. The company also manufactures and markets devices using assembled product technology.

Real-world signal processing begins with analog, or continuously varying, electrical signals from sensors that detect real-world phenomena, such as temperature, pressure, sound, images, speed, acceleration, position and rotation. The signals are initially processed using analog methods that include amplification, filtering and shaping. They are typically then converted to digital form for input to a microprocessor, which is used to manipulate, store or display the information. In addition, digital signals are frequently converted to analog form to provide signals for visual display, sound or control functions.

The company's principal products include general-purpose, standard-function linear and mixed signal integrated circuits (SLICs) such as amplifiers and data converters; special-purpose ICs (SPLICs) and digital signal processing ICs (DSP ICs). Other products include hybrid devices, which combine unpackaged chips and other chip-level components in a single package.

Nearly all of the company's products are components, which are typically incorporated by original equipment manufacturers (OEMs) in a wide range of equipment and systems for use in industrial, instrumentation, military/aerospace, computer, telecommunication and high-performance consumer electronics applications.

Foreign operations accounted for 46% of sales and 78% of operating income in fiscal 1992.

Reseach and development spending totaled $88.2 million (15.5% of sales) in fiscal 1992, down from $89.0 million (16.6%) in fiscal 1991.

In October 1992, the company sold its MicroMac product line of measurement, data acquisition and control system products.

Dividend Data

No cash dividends have ever been paid. A "poison pill" stock purchase right was adopted in 1988.

Capitalization

Long Term Debt: $100,000,000 (7/93).

Common Stock: 48,472,171 shs. ($0.16⅔ par).
Officers and directors own about 5.6%.
Institutions hold approximately 68%.
Shareholders of record: 5,500.

Office—One Technology Way, Norwood, MA 02062-9106. **Tel**—(617) 329-4700. **Chrmn & CEO**—R. Stata. **Pres**—J. G. Fishman. **VP-Fin**—J. E. McDonough. **Clerk**—P. P. Brountas. **Investor Contact**—James Fishbeck (617) 461-3282. **Dirs**—M. Chang, J. D. Doyle, J. G. Fishman, P. L. Lowe, G. C. McKeague, J. Moses, R. Stata, L. C. Thurow. **Transfer Agent**—Bank of Boston, Boston, Mass. **Registrar**—Company's office. **Incorporated** in Massachusetts in 1965. **Empl**—5,300.

 Paul H. Valentine, CFA

Angelica Corp.

NYSE Symbol AGL In S&P MidCap 400

Price	Range	P-E Ratio	Dividend	Yield	S&P Ranking	Beta
Sep. 30'93	1993					
25⅛	27⅛–22½	23	0.94	3.7%	A–	0.87

Summary

This company is a leading manufacturer and marketer of uniforms and career apparel for a wide variety of institutions and businesses. It also provides textile rental and laundry services to healthcare institutions and is the largest operator of specialty retail stores offering uniforms and duty shoes primarily for nurses. AGL has suffered substantial earnings declines since the beginning of fiscal 1992-93, although gains are projected for 1993-94's second half.

Current Outlook

Earnings for the fiscal year ending January 31, 1994, are estimated at $1.34 a share, down from the $1.50 recorded in 1992-93 (excluding an accounting change credit of $0.21). Growth to $1.60 is projected for 1994-95.

The quarterly dividend was raised 2.2%, to $0.23½, with the October 1993 payment.

Sales and earnings should be off slightly in the the rental services area in 1993-94, as AGL's aggressive marketing effort and an easier second half comparison will not be able to completely offset the impact that two new West Coast competitors have had in recent periods (responsible for AGL's loss of two major customers in 1992-93's second half and pricing pressures). Earnings for the manufacturing and marketing segment will also be somewhat lower (despite a modest second half gain), as uncertainties in the health care market and continued poor business conditions in Canada and the U.K. will outweigh strengthening business from hospitality markets. Earnings should be higher in the retail sales segment, benefiting from the division's concentration on cost controls.

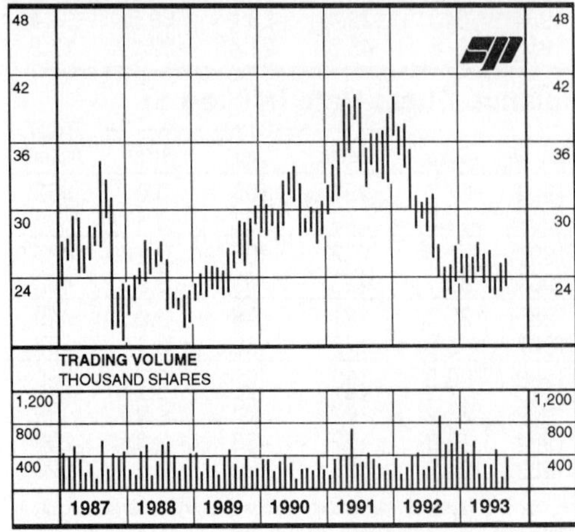

Sales & Revenues (Million $)

Quarter:	1993-94	1992-93	1991-92	1990-91
Apr.	104.1	110.3	107.2	101.6
Jul.	104.0	108.6	108.6	98.5
Oct.	---	109.3	107.1	109.6
Jan.	---	102.6	[1]111.5	103.9
	---	430.8	434.5	413.6

Revenues for the six months ended July 31, 1993, fell 5.0%, year to year, on the loss of two major rental services customers and continued sluggishness in the manufacturing and marketing segment. Margins narrowed considerably in both of those divisions, and net income plunged 45%, to $0.54 a share, from $0.95. Results for the 1992-93 period exclude a special credit of $0.21 from an accounting change.

Common Share Earnings ($)

Quarter:	1993-94	1992-93	1991-92	1990-91
Apr.	0.28	0.54	0.65	0.62
Jul.	0.26	0.41	0.57	0.56
Oct.	E0.45	0.42	0.67	0.67
Jan.	E0.35	0.13	[1]0.54	0.52
	E1.34	1.50	2.43	2.37

Important Developments

Aug. '93— Angelica reported that due to a competitive bidding situation, the manufacturing and marketing division recently lost its supply contract with Canada Post, its largest Canadian customer. AGL also noted that the retail division experienced a 2.1% decline in same store sales in 1993-94's second quarter, on a difficult year-earlier comparison and problems in generating new business.

Next earnings report expected in mid-November.

Per Share Data ($)

Yr. End Jan. 31	1993	[2]1992	[2]1991	[2]1990	1989	1988	1987	1986	1985	1984
Tangible Bk. Val.	**[3]20.87**	[3]20.43	[3]18.92	17.01	15.73	14.63	13.66	12.43	11.21	10.00
Cash Flow	**2.86**	3.68	3.47	3.08	2.70	2.66	2.59	2.51	2.37	2.13
Earnings[4]	**1.50**	2.43	2.37	2.06	1.79	1.85	1.79	1.84	1.76	1.63
Dividends	**0.92**	0.89	0.84	0.77	0.73	0.70	0.61	0.59	0.52	0.48
Payout Ratio	**60%**	37%	35%	37%	41%	38%	34%	32%	30%	29%
Calendar Years	**1992**	1991	1990	1989	1988	1987	1986	1985	1984	1983
Prices—High	**40**	40¼	33⅞	30⅜	27⅜	34⅜	29¾	27⅞	23¾	35
Low	**22 3/16**	29⅝	27	22	19⅝	18½	22	17	16¼	20¾
P/E Ratio—	**27–15**	17–12	14–11	15–11	15–11	19–10	17–12	15–9	13–9	21–13

Data as orig. reptd. **1.** 14 Wks. **2.** Refl. merger or acq. **3.** Incl. intangibles. **4.** Bef. special item(s) of +0.21 in 1993. E-Estimated.

Income Data (Million $)

Year Ended Jan. 31	Revs.	Oper. Inc.	% Oper. Inc. of Revs.	Cap. Exp.	Depr.	Int. Exp.	[2]Net Bef. Taxes	Eff. Tax Rate	[5]Net Inc.	% Net Inc. of Revs.	Cash Flow
1993	**431**	**45.0**	**10.5**	**[4]9.9**	**12.6**	**7.52**	**22.3**	**38.0%**	**13.8**	**3.2**	**26.4**
[1]1992	434	57.2	13.2	13.3	11.7	6.99	36.5	37.9%	22.7	5.2	34.4
[1]1991	414	53.4	12.9	14.1	10.3	6.27	35.9	38.5%	22.1	5.3	32.4
[1]1990	369	45.6	12.4	13.6	9.4	5.08	31.2	38.5%	19.2	5.2	28.6
1989	328	37.9	11.5	7.5	8.5	2.78	27.1	38.5%	16.6	5.1	25.2
1988	307	39.4	12.9	18.0	7.7	2.16	30.2	43.0%	[3]17.2	5.6	24.9
1987	292	39.6	13.6	13.3	7.5	2.36	32.1	47.9%	16.7	5.7	24.2
1986	269	39.0	14.5	15.0	6.3	2.46	32.4	47.0%	17.2	6.4	23.4
1985	246	35.4	14.4	8.6	5.7	2.63	30.8	47.0%	16.3	6.6	22.0
1984	220	32.4	14.7	16.0	4.6	2.80	28.6	47.1%	15.2	6.9	19.7

Balance Sheet Data (Million $)

Jan. 31	Cash	Curr. Assets	Curr. Liab.	Curr. Ratio	Total Assets	% Ret. on Assets	Long Term Debt	Common Equity	Total Cap.	% LT Debt of Cap.	% Ret. on Equity
1993	**2.7**	**205**	**43.7**	**4.7**	**327**	**4.2**	**78.2**	**189**	**273**	**28.7**	**7.4**
1992	6.1	211	50.4	4.2	335	6.9	80.5	190	275	29.3	12.4
1991	2.0	205	70.4	2.9	316	7.4	57.8	176	238	24.3	13.1
1990	6.9	184	53.7	3.4	279	7.5	50.6	161	218	23.2	12.4
1989	2.5	156	51.8	3.0	233	7.4	19.0	150	175	10.9	11.5
1988	3.2	141	45.3	3.1	216	8.4	21.6	139	166	13.0	12.9
1987	5.3	132	30.8	4.3	195	8.8	25.2	128	160	15.7	13.6
1986	14.0	125	30.7	4.1	183	9.9	26.8	117	149	17.9	15.5
1985	12.0	113	24.5	4.6	162	10.4	25.0	105	136	18.4	16.4
1984	17.5	107	23.5	4.6	152	10.3	27.8	94	127	21.9	17.1

Data as orig. reptd. **1.** Refl. merger or acq. **2.** Incl. equity in earns. of nonconsol. subs. **3.** Refl. acctg. change. **4.** Net of curr. year retirement and disposals. **5.** Bef. special item(s).

Business Summary

Angelica Corp. is a leading manufacturer and marketer of uniforms and business career apparel for a wide variety of institutions and businesses; provides textile rental and laundry services to health care institutions; and is the largest operator of specialty retail stores offering uniforms and duty shoes primarily for nurses and other health care professionals. Contributions in fiscal 1992-93 were:

	Sales	Profits
Manufacturing and marketing	39%	30%
Rental services	49%	58%
Retail sales	12%	12%

Important markets served are health services, including health services institutions and personnel; hospitality, including lodging, gaming and foodservice establishments and amusement parks; and other service industries such as retail, financial and transportation.

The company's manufacturing and marketing operations consist of the Angelica Uniform Group in the U.S., and companies in Canada and the U.K., all of which are involved in the production of uniforms and business career apparel for a wide variety of institutions and businesses.

The Rental Services division, with 32 plants in or near major U.S. metropolitan areas, provides textile rental and laundry services for health care institutions. It also provides general linen services in selected areas, principally to hotels, motels and restaurants.

The Life Retail Stores division is a specialty retailer offering uniforms and duty shoes primarily for nurses and other health care professionals. As of mid-May 1993, it was operating a total of 247 stores, located in malls, strip shopping centers and large hospitals.

Dividend Data

Dividends have been paid since 1954. A "poison pill" stock purchase rights plan was adopted in 1988.

Amt of Divd. $	Date Decl.	Ex-divd. Date	Stock of Record	Payment Date
0.23	Nov. 25	Dec. 9	Dec. 15	Jan. 1'93
0.23	Feb. 24	Mar. 9	Mar. 15	Apr. 1'93
0.23	May 26	Jun. 9	Jun. 15	Jul. 1'93
0.23½	Sep. 1	Sep. 9	Sep. 15	Oct. 1'93

Capitalization

Long Term Debt: $76,978,000 (7/93).

Common Stock: 9,082,411 shs. ($1 par).
Institutions hold about 77%.
Shareholders of record: 2,008 (1/93).

Office—424 So. Woods Mill Rd., Chesterfield, MO 63017. **Tel**—(314) 854-3800. **Chrmn & Pres**—L. J. Young. **SVP-Fin, CFO & Investor Contact**—Theodore M. Armstrong. **Treas**—T. M. Degnan. **VP-Secy**—J. Witter. **Dirs**—E. H. Harbison Jr, L. M. Liberman, L. F. Loewe, J. E. Stefoff, E. H. Stein, W. P. Stiritz, H. E. Trusheim, R. L. Virgil, R. C. West, L. J. Young. **Transfer Agent & Registrar**—Boatmen's Trust Co., St. Louis. **Incorporated** in Missouri in 1904; reincorporated in Missouri in 1968. **Empl**—9,000.

 Michael W. Jaffe

Anthem Electronics

NYSE Symbol ATM Options on NYSE & Phila In S&P MidCap 400

Price	Range	P-E Ratio	Dividend	Yield	S&P Ranking	Beta
Jul. 23'93	1993					
32¾	49¼–30½	15	None	None	B	1.87

Summary

Anthem is the fifth largest U.S. distributor of electronic components, including semiconductors, disk and tape drives, controller cards and video monitors. Aided by strong sales of semiconductors and subsystem products, sales and earnings reached record levels for the fifth consecutive year in 1992. Sales continued to rise in 1993's first half, but earnings were set back by narrower profit margins.

Business Summary

Anthem Electronics, Inc. manufactures, markets and distributes a broad range of semiconductor and subsystem products to original equipment manufacturers (OEMs), resellers and end-users worldwide. During 1992, the company reorganized its operations into two business units: Anthem Electronics Distribution and Eagle Technology. In both 1992 and 1991, Anthem Electronics Distribution provided 82% of the company's total net sales.

The company's activities include the distribution of electronic components pursuant to nonexclusive franchise agreements with several semiconductor and subsystem manufacturers; the sale of subsystem products that Anthem generally configures and assembles pursuant to customer-specific requirements; the sale of board-level products made by subcontractors for a limited number of customers pursuant to turnkey manufacturing agreements; and the sale of other value-added services related to the distribution of electronic components, such as kitting (selling in quantities that match the customer's required materials for a particular manufacturing job), testing and programming of semiconductors.

Subsystem products include disk and tape drives, disk drive controllers, video monitors and board-level products. The semiconductors and subsystems are used in electronic data processing equipment, other industrial products (including electronic instrumentation, telecommunications and process control equipment), consumer products and defense and aerospace equipment. Board-level products are produced for a limited number of customers on a turnkey basis. ATM procures the raw materials and subcontracts for the assembly of the products.

Eagle Technology manufactures and markets computer connectivity hardware products generally made pursuant to license agreements that grant the company manufacturing rights to such products. Eagle's current production is focused on network interface cards and HUBs.

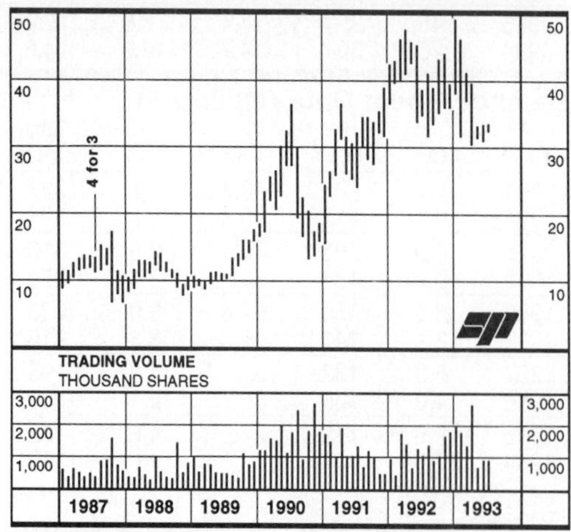

Anthem distributes its products to more than 7,000 customers. International sales, primarily to Europe, accounted for 10% of net sales in 1992, up from 8% in 1991.

In January 1993, the company announced the signing of an agreement with Intel Corp. to distribute Intel's full line of semiconductor and OEM system products. The distribution agreement became effective February 1, 1993. Also in early 1993, Anthem signed an agreement to become an authorized distributor for Quantum Corp., a maker of computer hard disk drives.

Next earnings report expected in mid-October.

Per Share Data ($)

Yr. End Dec. 31[1]	1992	1991	1990	1989	1988	[3]1987	[3]1986	1985	1984	1983
Tangible Bk. Val.	**[2]15.24**	[2]12.70	[2]10.53	[2]8.23	[2]7.16	5.36	3.57	4.35	4.05	3.43
Cash Flow	**2.71**	2.10	2.13	1.52	1.12	0.62	0.38	0.37	0.67	0.63
Earnings[4]	**2.48**	1.92	1.97	1.39	1.00	0.50	0.29	0.33	0.64	0.62
Dividends	**Nil**	Nil	Nil	Nil	Nil	Nil	Nil	0.03	0.03	0.026
Payout Ratio	**Nil**	Nil	Nil	Nil	Nil	Nil	Nil	9%	5%	5%
Prices[5]—High	**47¾**	39	36½	17¾	14⅜	17 ⅜	14⅜	13	12⅞	11⅝
Low	**31¾**	15¾	13⅜	8⅞	7⅞	6¾	6¼	7¾	6⅝	3½
P/E Ratio—	**19–13**	20–8	19–7	13–6	14–8	35–14	50–22	40–23	20–10	19–5

Data as orig. reptd. Adj. for stk. divs. of 33⅓% Jul. 1987, 100% Dec. 1983, 50% Apr. 1983. **1.** Yr. ended Mar. 31 of fol. cal. yr. prior to 1987. **2.** Incl. intangibles. **3.** Refl. merger or acq. **4.** Bef. spec. item of +0.05 in 1988. **5.** Cal. yr.

Income Data (Million $)

Year Ended Dec. 31[1]	Oper. Revs.	Oper. Inc.	% Oper. Inc. of Revs.	Cap. Exp.	Depr.	Int. Exp.	Net Bef. Taxes	Eff. Tax Rate	[3]Net Inc.	% Net Inc. of Revs.	Cash Flow
1992	**538**	**54.1**	**10.0**	**3.09**	**2.86**	**0.12**	**51.5**	**40.9%**	**30.4**	**5.7**	**33.3**
1991	420	41.4	9.9	5.91	2.15	0.27	39.4	40.9%	23.3	5.6	25.5
1990	408	41.2	10.1	6.82	1.91	0.42	39.3	40.9%	23.2	5.7	25.1
1989	319	28.2	8.9	8.47	1.52	0.55	26.6	40.7%	15.8	4.9	17.3
1988	265	21.4	8.1	0.72	1.30	1.05	19.1	40.8%	11.3	4.3	12.6
[2]1987	197	11.5	5.8	0.94	1.25	1.08	9.1	45.2%	5.0	2.5	6.3
[2]1986	149	7.4	5.0	0.41	0.93	1.03	5.6	52.0%	2.7	1.8	3.6
1985	104	6.4	6.2	0.72	0.43	0.08	6.3	49.9%	3.1	3.0	3.6
1984	120	13.1	10.9	0.63	0.35	0.45	12.3	50.5%	6.1	5.1	6.4
1983	95	11.3	11.9	1.03	0.20	0.32	10.9	50.0%	5.5	5.7	5.7

Balance Sheet Data (Million $)

Dec. 31[1]	Cash	Curr. Assets	Curr. Liab.	Curr. Ratio	Total Assets	% Ret. on Assets	Long Term Debt	Common Equity	Total Cap.	% LT Debt of Cap.	% Ret. on Equity
1992	**7.2**	**189**	**31.1**	**6.1**	**216**	**15.1**	**Nil**	**185**	**185**	**Nil**	**18.0**
1991	13.6	156	32.2	4.8	182	14.1	Nil	149	150	Nil	17.1
1990	1.5	124	25.1	4.9	146	17.5	Nil	121	121	Nil	21.6
1989	Nil	100	25.2	4.0	119	13.8	Nil	93	94	Nil	18.1
1988	Nil	96	19.5	4.9	110	11.2	8.9	81	90	9.9	15.1
1987	Nil	81	19.0	4.3	92	5.7	4.1	69	73	5.6	8.3
1986	Nil	59	14.1	4.2	72	4.6	13.4	45	58	23.0	6.3
1985	4.7	45	4.7	9.5	46	6.7	Nil	42	42	Nil	7.8
1984	Nil	46	7.2	6.4	48	13.5	1.5	39	40	3.7	17.0
1983	Nil	42	10.0	4.2	43	16.6	Nil	33	33	Nil	22.6

Data as orig. reptd. **1.** Yr. ended Mar. 31 of fol. cal. yr. prior to 1987. **2.** Refl. merger or acq. **3.** Bef. spec. item in 1988.

Net Sales (Million $)

Quarter:	1993	1992	1991	1990
Mar.	142	126	101	100
Jun.	161	122	102	110
Sep.		140	105	100
Dec.		150	112	98
		538	420	408

Net sales for the six months ended June 30, 1993, rose 22%, year to year, as a 37% increase in Anthem's distribution business more than offset a 34% decline at Eagle Technology. Gross margins narrowed, reflecting a negative shift in the product mix and product price decreases. After taxes at 41.2%, versus 40.9%, net income was down 19%, to $11,845,000 ($0.96 a share), from $14,648,000 ($1.20).

Common Share Earnings ($)

Quarter:	1993	1992	1991	1990
Mar.	0.45	0.62	0.47	0.48
Jun.	0.51	0.58	0.46	0.56
Sep.		0.64	0.48	0.46
Dec.		0.64	0.51	0.47
		2.48	1.92	1.97

Dividend Data

Dividends, initiated in 1982, were discontinued in 1986.

Finances

Results for 1992 marked the fifth consecutive year of record sales and earnings for Anthem. Improvement in productivity allowed sales per employee to climb to $850,000, from $708,000 during the year.

In 1987, Anthem sold 1,600,000 common shares at $13 each, with proceeds used to repay all bank debt.

Capitalization

Long Term Debt: None (6/93).

Common Stock: 12,173,311 shs. ($0.125 par). Institutions hold about 86%. Shareholders of record: 5,000 (12/92).

Office—1160 Ridder Park Drive, San Jose, CA 95131. **Tel**—(408) 453-1200. **Chrmn & CEO**—R. S. Throop. **Pres & COO**—P. L. Gannaway, **VP-CFO & Secy**—W. B. Snyder. **Investor Contacts**—Wayne B. Snyder & Robert S. Throop. **Dirs**—P. L. Gannaway, N. J. Hynes, A. R. McMillen, R. G. Teal. R. S. Throop. **Transfer Agent & Registrar**—First Interstate Bank of California, Los Angeles. **Incorporated** in California in 1968; reincorporated in Delaware in 1983. **Empl**—678.

 Samuel Dedio

Aon Corp.

NYSE Symbol AOC Options on Pacific In S&P MidCap 400

Price	Range	P–E Ratio	Dividend	Yield	S&P Ranking	Beta
Aug. 9'93	1993					
54⅜	56¾–50	18	1.80	3.3%	A–	0.88

Summary

Through its subsidiaries, Aon writes life, accident and health and specialty property-casualty insurance. Insurance brokerage operations are also important. As a result of the acquisition of a Netherlands-based insurance broker in late 1991 and Frank B. Hall & Co. in late 1992, AOC's Rollins Hudig Hall is now one of the world's largest insurance brokerage firms. Contributions from acquisitions paced the gain in earnings for 1993's first half. Continued revenue advances are expected for most segments in coming periods, and earnings should continue to trend upward.

Current Outlook

Earnings for 1993 (before realized capital gains and losses) are estimated at $4.25 a share, up from the $2.85 of 1992. Earnings could rise to $4.65 a share in 1994.

The quarterly dividend was increased 7.1%, to $0.45 a share, with the May 1993 payment.

Revenue growth is most segments is likely in 1993, and earnings will trend upward. Comparisons are also aided by the absence of an $86.5 million charge taken in 1992 to cover brokerage consolidations, staff cutbacks and insurance guaranty fund assessments. Demand for investment-oriented products, favorable interest rate spreads and expense controls will benefit life profits. Accident and health results are expected to be mixed, although demand for AOC's supplemental health products will not be adversely affected by health-care reform efforts. A pickup in consumer spending augurs well for auto and appliance warranty insurance. Long term, brokerage operations should benefit from expansion efforts. Near term, profit margins may be squeezed by the mildly dilutive effects of the Hall acquisition, weak p-c insurance pricing and tepid investment income growth.

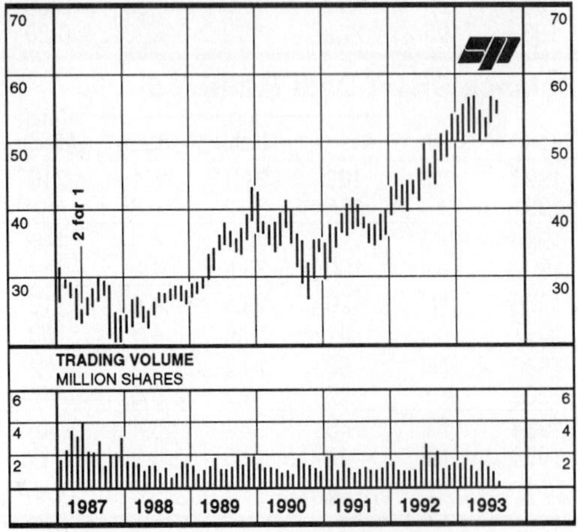

Common Share Earnings ($)

Quarter:	1993	1992	1991	1990
Mar.	1.18	1.08	0.91	0.89
Jun.	1.03	0.95	0.95	0.98
Sep.		0.91	0.97	0.93
Dec.		d0.04	0.89	0.81
		2.89	3.71	3.61

Review of Operations

Revenues for the six months ended June 30, 1993, rose 18%, year to year, reflecting an 84% surge in brokerage commissions and fees, 9.7% higher pretax realized investment gains, 3.8% growth in investment income, a 6.4% increase in other income and fractionally higher premiums. Margins widened, and pretax profits were up 21%. After taxes at 30.0%, versus 29.0%, income rose 19%. After preferred dividends, common share earnings were $2.20 ($2.17 of operating income), based on 1.7% more shares, compared with $2.03 ($2.00), excluding a $1.15 charge from accounting changes in the 1992 period.

Important Developments

Aug. '93— AOC's revenue growth in the first six months of 1993 was paced by contributions from acquisitions, most notably the November 1992 purchase of the operating assets of Frank B. Hall & Co. for $125 million in cash and $350 million of preferred stock. The purchase expanded AOC's presence in the U.S. and European brokerage markets and provided access to Mexican and South American commercial markets.

Next earnings report expected in early November.

Per Share Data ($)

Yr. End Dec. 31	1992	1991	1990	1989	1988	1987	1986	1985	1984	1983
Tangible Bk. Val.	**20.43**	20.06	18.24	18.50	16.67	15.13	15.23	12.75	10.52	8.87
Oper. Earnings[1]	**2.85**	3.66	3.56	3.49	3.18	2.80	2.76	2.42	2.49	1.93
Earnings[1,2]	**2.89**	3.71	3.61	3.54	2.79	2.36	3.70	2.74	2.46	1.67
Dividends	**1.66**	1.58	1.49	1.37	1.26	1.18	1.11	1.07	1.03	1.00
Payout Ratio	**57%**	43%	41%	39%	45%	50%	30%	39%	42%	60%
Prices—High	**54**	41¾	42⅝	43¼	28¾	31½	32⅞	26⅜	21⅞	21⅜
Low	**39⅛**	29¾	26¾	27	21⅞	20½	25½	18⅞	13⅝	13½
P/E Ratio[3]—	**19–14**	11–8	12–7	12–8	9–7	11–7	12–9	11–8	9–5	11–7

Data as orig. reptd. Adj. for stk. div. of 100% May 1987. **1.** Bef. spec. item of -1.15 in 1992. **2.** Aft. gains/losses on sec. trans. **3.** Based on oper. earns. prior to 1989.

Income Data (Million $)

Year Ended Dec. 31	Life Ins. In Force	Premium Income	Net Invest. Inc.	Other Oper. Revs.	Total Revs.	Net Bef. Taxes	[5]Net Oper. Inc.	[5]Net Inc.	% Return On [1]Revs.	% Return On [1]Assets	% Return On [1,2]Equity
1992	**NA**	**1,826**	**737**	**773**	**3,337**	**291**	**203**	**206**	**6.2**	**1.6**	**9.9**
1991	71,900	1,734	713	484	2,931	332	239	242	8.3	2.2	15.0
1990	74,791	1,559	661	407	2,626	325	235	239	9.1	2.4	16.6
1989	67,177	1,397	590	338	2,325	314	229	232	10.0	2.7	17.2
1988	65,812	1,939	503	290	2,732	278	204	180	7.5	2.7	16.9
1987	71,393	1,813	405	251	2,469	260	185	156	7.5	2.8	16.3
1986	60,621	1,303	311	192	1,806	263	184	247	10.2	4.0	17.4
1985	16,337	1,027	173	159	1,360	230	161	182	11.8	5.4	17.9
1984	14,173	1,009	152	127	1,288	190	164	162	12.7	6.3	22.5
1983	13,873	985	143	108	1,235	156	127	110	10.3	5.2	21.1

Balance Sheet Data (Million $)

Dec. 31	Cash & Equiv.	[3]Premiums Due	Investment Assets [4]Bonds	Investment Assets Stocks	Investment Assets Loans	Investment Assets Total	% Invest. Yield	Deferred Policy Costs	Total Assets	Debt	Common Equity
1992	**141**	**1,720**	**7,366**	**830**	**797**	**9,088**	**8.4**	**948**	**14,290**	**478**	**2,089**
1991	183	822	6,774	610	852	8,360	8.9	911	11,633	418	1,771
1990	224	594	6,038	628	894	7,704	9.2	868	10,432	430	1,457
1989	162	529	4,903	811	884	6,665	9.3	761	9,156	438	1,421
1988	141	473	4,449	731	824	6,065	9.0	699	8,266	380	1,253
1987	135	296	3,674	638	749	5,152	8.8	629	7,084	435	1,130
1986	125	327	2,557	729	700	4,078	10.2	518	5,905	264	1,142
1985	82	202	1,410	469	125	2,029	9.3	429	3,196	92	973
1984	53	142	1,195	328	143	1,685	9.5	375	2,721	31	822
1983	35	144	1,045	291	146	1,501	9.9	334	2,514	32	633

Data as orig. reptd. **1.** Based on oper. earns. prior to 1989. **2.** Common. **3.** Incl. other receivables. **4.** Incl. short-term invest. **5.** Bef. spec. item in 1992. NA-Not Available.

Business Summary

Aon Corp. (formerly Combined International) is a holding company that, through subsidiaries, writes accident and health, life and specialty property-casualty insurance. Other operations include insurance brokerage and related services. Pretax income (in millions) by segment in recent years were:

	1992	1991	1990
Accident & health	$159.5	$151.1	$142.1
Life insurance	93.1	75.8	67.0
Spec. prop.–cas.	37.3	34.0	33.2
Brokerage services	66.7	38.4	36.6
Corp. & other	16.4	59.5	46.3

Accident and health products (underwritten by Combined Insurance, Union Fidelity, Credit Life and Ryan Insurance Group) include Medicare supplemental insurance, disability, credit, cancer and accident and health supplemental insurance.

Life insurance, which is offered by Life of Virginina, Combined Insurance, Union Fidelity and Ryan Insurance Group, consists of capital accumulation products (such as universal life and annuities), ordinary life products and credit insurance.

Specialty property-casualty lines include automobile and appliance extended-warranty coverage and reinsurance.

Insurance brokerage and related services, conducted by Rollins Hudig Hall (formerly Rollins Burdick Hunter Co.) and affiliates (Aon Risk Services, Aon Specialty group, Godwins, Nicholson Chamberlain Colls Ltd. and Leslie Godwin Ltd.), provide commercial clients and specialty groups with risk management, reinsurance services and employee benefit consulting.

Dividend Data

Cash dividends have been paid since 1950. A dividend reinvestment plan is available.

Amt. of Divd. $	Date Decl.	Ex–divd. Date	Stock of Record	Payment Date
0.42	Sep. 18	Oct. 28	Nov. 3	Nov. 16'92
0.42	Jan. 15	Jan. 28	Feb. 3	Feb. 16'93
0.45	Mar. 19	Apr. 28	May 4	May 17'93
0.45	Jul. 16	Jul. 28	Aug. 3	Aug. 16'93

Capitalization

Long Term Debt: $596,700,000 (3/93, as adj.)

Preferred Stock: $15,100,000 (par value).

Common Stock: 65,757,588 shs. ($1 par).
P. G. Ryan owns about 14%.
Institutions hold approximately 49%.
Shareholders of record: 14,746 (12/92).

Office—123 North Wacker Drive, Chicago, IL 60606. **Tel**—(312) 701-3000. **Chrmn & Pres**—P. G. Ryan. **Sr VP-CFO & Treas**—H. N. Medvin. **Sr VP-Secy**—A. F. Quern. **VP-Investor Contact**—Joan E. Steel. **Dirs**—D. T. Carroll, F. A. Cole, P. J. Lewis, J. D. Manley, A. J. McKenna, N. N. Minow, P. Pedersen, D. S. Perkins, P. G. Ryan, G. A. Schaefer, R. I. Skilling, J. E. Swearingen, F. L. Turner, A. R. Weber. **Transfer Agent & Registrar**—First Chicago Trust Co. of New York, NYC. **Incorporated** in Illinois in 1949. **Empl**—11,000.

 Catherine A. Seifert

Apache Corp.

NYSE Symbol APA Options on NYSE, Phila (Jan-Apr-Jul-Oct) In S&P MidCap 400

Price	Range	P–E Ratio	Dividend	Yield	S&P Ranking	Beta
Sep. 14'93	1993					
28⅝	33½–17⅝	32	0.28	1.0%	B–	1.02

Summary

Apache is an independent energy company engaged in the exploration for and production and marketing of oil and natural gas, mostly on- and offshore the continental U.S.; it also holds international exploration interests. The company continues to seek acquisitions that fit with its strategic direction. In August 1993, APA acquired certain properties in the Gulf of Mexico and agreed to merge 68%-owned Hadson Energy Resources Corp. Long-term prospects are enhanced by expected increases in gas production and prices.

Current Outlook

Share earnings for 1993 are estimated at $0.95, down from 1992's $1.02 (including a $0.39 capital gain). An increase in share earnings to $1.25 is projected for 1994.

Dividends should continue at $0.07 quarterly.

Lower earnings are likely in 1993, in the absence of a prior-year gain of $0.39 a share from the sale of APA's interest in Natural Gas Clearinghouse. Operating profits should rise strongly, benefiting from a more profitable production mix, cost control efforts and a reduction in production taxes per barrel of oil equivalent. An increase of about 20% in average natural gas prices received, together with greater natural gas production, should aid margins. The effective tax rate is expected to be lower in 1993. The March 1993 sale of nearly 5.8 million shares is expected to be slightly dilutive, despite the application of proceeds to reduce debt and interest expense. Earnings for 1994 should benefit from continued growth in gas and oil production, partly reflecting acquisitions and higher gas prices; margins should widen, as operating costs per unit of energy produced remain level.

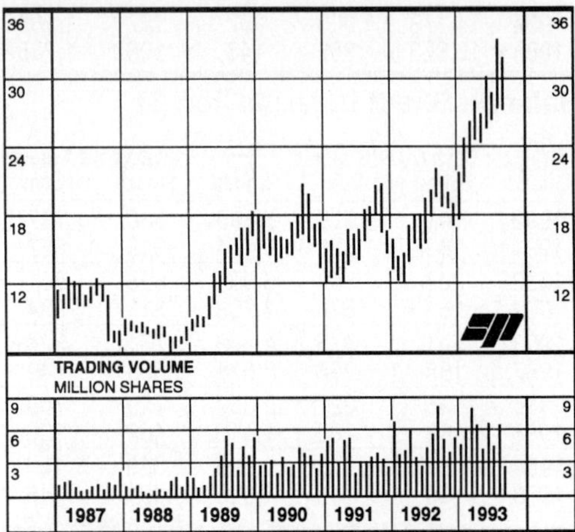

Total Revenues (Million $)

Quarter:	1993	1992	1991	1990
Mar.	108.6	92.2	68.0	69.0
Jun.	111.3	131.2	60.5	58.5
Sep.		111.3	111.9	65.0
Dec.		119.6	116.5	80.9
		454.3	356.9	273.4

Revenues for the six months ended June 30, 1993, declined 1.6%, year to year. The absence of a $0.39 a share gain on the sale of APA's interest in Natural Gas Clearinghouse more than offset benefits from improved oil and natural gas prices and natural gas production. Net income fell 18%, to $0.46 a share from $0.60.

Common Share Earnings ($)

Quarter:	1993	1992	1991	1990
Mar.	0.24	0.09	0.27	0.26
Jun.	0.22	0.51	0.15	0.17
Sep.	E0.21	0.18	0.02	0.21
Dec.	E0.28	0.24	0.32	0.26
	E0.95	1.02	0.76	0.90

Important Developments

Sep. '93— APA called for redemption on October 8, 1993, $150 million of convertible debt. In August, APA acquired Gulf of Mexico properties from Hall-Houston Oil Co. for $96.8 million, subject to adjustments. Hadson Energy Resources Corp. (ASE: HDX) agreed to the acquisition by APA of the remaining 32% of the HDX common shares it did not already own. Under the agreement, HDX shareholders would receive $15 in cash or APA common stock for each HDX share held.

Next earnings report expected in late October.

Per Share Data ($)

Yr. End Dec. 31	1992	[1]1991	1990	1989	[2]1988	1987	[2]1986	1985	1984	1983
Tangible Bk. Val.	**10.12**	9.39	8.65	7.97	6.28	4.92	10.21	11.02	10.91	10.26
Cash Flow	**4.63**	3.72	3.52	3.41	2.74	d1.36	2.72	2.59	2.80	2.42
Earnings[3]	**1.02**	0.76	0.90	0.64	0.23	d4.01	d0.49	0.45	1.00	0.93
Dividends	**0.28**	0.28	0.28	0.28	0.28	0.28	0.28	0.28	0.28	0.28
Payout Ratio	**27%**	38%	31%	56%	122%	NM	NM	61%	27%	30%
Prices—High	**22⅛**	20¾	20¾	18⅜	8⅞	12⅝	12	13⅜	14⅝	16⅜
Low	**12**	12	13⅜	7⅞	6	6⅝	7⅝	9⅞	9¼	8¼
P/E Ratio—	**22–12**	27–16	23–15	29–12	39–26	NM	NM	30–22	15–9	18–9

Data as orig. reptd. **1.** Refl. merger or acq. **2.** Refl. acctg. change. **3.** Bef. results of disc. ops. of +0.11 in 1988, +0.46 in 1987, -0.04 in 1986, -0.07 in 1985, +0.07 in 1983 & spec. items of +0.04 in 1988, +0.05 in 1987. E-Estimated. d-Deficit. NM-Not Meaningful.

Income Data (Million $)

Year Ended Dec. 31	Revs.	Oper. Inc.	% Oper. Inc. of Revs.	Cap. Exp.	Depr. Depl. & Amort.	Int. Exp.	[4]Net Bef. Taxes	Eff. Tax Rate	[5]Net Inc.	% Net Inc. of Revs.	Cash Flow
1992	**423**	**244**	**57.6**	**207**	**169**	**39.2**	**70**	**32.2%**	**47.8**	**11.3**	**217**
[1]1991	342	201	58.8	686	136	32.7	44	21.6%	34.6	10.1	170
1990	261	173	66.4	191	117	15.5	57	29.9%	40.3	15.4	157
1989	241	144	59.8	134	96	24.8	32	30.7%	22.1	9.2	118
[2,3]1988	142	84	57.3	288	60	20.1	7	22.9%	5.4	3.8	65
[3]1987	101	d75	NM	63	54	20.3	d144	NM	d81.5	NM	d28
[2,3]1986	172	64	37.4	323	66	24.4	d21	NM	d10.1	NM	55
[3]1985	128	59	46.2	107	44	10.8	13	30.2%	9.4	7.3	54
1984	116	77	67.0	9	38	11.8	35	39.2%	21.4	18.5	60
[3]1983	112	74	65.8	54	33	21.3	35	42.5%	20.3	18.1	53

Balance Sheet Data (Million $)

Dec. 31	Cash	Curr. Assets	Curr. Liab.	Curr. Ratio	Total Assets	% Ret. on Assets	Long Term Debt	Common Equity	Total Cap.	% LT Debt of Cap.	% Ret. on Equity
1992	**26.1**	**114**	**158**	**0.7**	**1,219**	**3.9**	**454**	**475**	**1,013**	**44.9**	**10.4**
1991	6.4	91	146	0.6	1,209	3.3	491	440	996	49.3	8.2
1990	85.2	138	123	1.1	830	5.0	195	387	648	30.1	10.8
1989	75.2	133	108	1.2	764	2.6	196	350	599	32.7	7.1
1988	34.9	109	98	1.1	702	0.7	309	207	555	55.7	2.9
1987	53.3	121	96	1.3	504	NM	236	99	399	59.2	NM
1986	17.7	177	143	1.2	729	NM	276	207	576	47.9	NM
1985	29.1	98	92	1.1	536	1.8	111	226	438	25.3	4.2
1984	20.6	86	73	1.2	489	4.3	80	228	408	19.6	9.7
1983	23.5	96	62	1.5	534	3.7	152	223	465	32.6	9.4

Data as orig. reptd. **1.** Refl. merger or acq. **2.** Refl. acctg. change. **3.** Excl. disc. ops. **4.** Incl. equity in earns. of nonconsol. subs. **5.** Bef. spec. items. d-Deficit. NM-Not Meaningful.

Business Summary

Apache Corp. is an independent energy company engaged in the exploration for and development, production, processing and marketing of natural gas and oil, mostly on- and offshore in the continental U.S. Through a subsidiary, the company holds international exploration interests.

At December 31, 1992, proved reserves aggregated 80,659,000 bbl. of crude oil (91% developed) and 643.3 Bcf of natural gas (91%), compared with 79,814,000 bbl. of oil (87%) and 602.0 Bcf of gas (91%) at year-end 1991. In 1991, the company acquired MW Petroleum Corp. in a transaction valued at about $545 million. APA continues to seek acquisitions that fit its strategic direction.

Acreage held under lease and rights at year-end 1992 totaled 1,224,051 gross (509,539 net) developed acres, mostly in the Midcontinent, Gulf Coast and Rocky Mountain regions in the U.S., and 12,887,946 gross (4,703,373 net) undeveloped acres (including international production-sharing contracts—Indonesia accounted for 5,124,190 gross and 1,835,298 net acres). At December 31, 1992, APA had 2,582 gross productive gas wells (901 net wells) and 4,194 gross productive oil wells (2,079 net). During 1992, it drilled 48 exploratory wells, of which 10 were productive, and drilled 161 developmental wells, with 145 productive.

Production in 1992 totaled 12,056,000 bbl. of oil and 96.0 Bcf of gas, versus 7,764,000 bbl. and 104.6 Bcf in 1991. The average price of oil was $18.16 per bbl. ($18.40 in 1990) and of gas $1.76 per Mcf ($1.58).

Apache International holds exploration interests in Angola, Australia, the Congo, France, Indonesia and Myanmar. International expenditures are targeted at 10% or less of the capital budget.

Dividend Data

Dividends have been paid since 1965. A dividend reinvestment plan is available. A "poison pill" stock purchase rights plan was adopted in 1986.

Amt of Divd. $	Date Decl.	Ex–divd. Date	Stock of Record	Payment Date
0.07	Sep. 10	Sep. 24	Sep. 30	Oct. 30'92
0.07	Dec. 9	Dec. 24	Dec. 31	Jan. 29'93
0.07	Feb. 3	Mar. 25	Mar. 31	Apr. 30'93
0.07	May 6	Jun. 24	Jun. 30	Jul. 30'93

Capitalization

Long Term Debt: $366,348,000 (6/93), incl. $150 million of 7.5% debs. conv. into com. at $19.18 a sh.

Common Stock: 52,790,992 shs. ($1.25 par). Institutions hold about 75%. Shareholders of record: 12,120.

Office—2000 Post Oak Blvd., Houston, TX 77056-4400. **Tel**—(713) 296-6000. **Chrmn & CEO**—R. Plank. **Pres & COO**—W. J. Johnson. **SVP & Secy**—G. J. Morgenthaler. **VP & Treas**—C. E. McKenzie. **Investor Contact**—Roger B. Plank. **Dirs**—F. M. Bohen, V. B. Day, R. M. Ferlic, E. C. Fiedorek, W. B. Fields, R. V. Gisselbeck, S. K. Hathaway, W. J. Johnson, J. A. Kocur, R. Plank, J. A. Precourt, J. A. Rice. **Transfer Agent & Registar**—Norwest Bank Minnesota, South St. Paul. **Incorporated** in Delaware in 1954. **Empl**—844.

 Mark Mattke

Applied Bioscience Int'l

NASDAQ Symbol APBI (Incl. in Nat'l Market) Options on Phila In S&P MidCap 400

Price	Range	P–E Ratio	Dividend	Yield	S&P Ranking	Beta
Aug. 31'93	1993					
6	10–4½	55	None	None	NR	1.48

Summary

This company provides a broad range of services to clients in the pharmaceutical, chemical, agrochemical, nutritional and other industries worldwide. Growth has been achieved through internal expansion and acquisitions, the most recent of which were the February 1992 purchase of Pharmaco Dynamics Research and the June 1992 acquisition of National Express Laboratories. Based on current business conditions, the company recently said its near term outlook is weaker than originally expected.

Business Summary

Applied Bioscience International Inc. provides a broad range of services, including biological safety testing; clinical research and development; management of agrochemical research and development; chemical risk assessment and risk management; and analytical laboratory services. Clients are engaged in pharmaceutical, general chemical, agrochemical, biotechnology and other industries worldwide. Operating revenues (net of subcontractor costs) in recent years were:

	1992	1991	1990
Life sciences..............	63%	66%	71%
Environmental sciences	37%	34%	29%

Following the acquisition of Pharmaco in February 1992, the company reorganized its operations. The Life Sciences Group, formerly comprised of Bio/dynamics, Inc., Life Science Research and Pharmaco, now operates as Pharmaco-LSR and provides contract biological safety (toxicological) testing services on a worldwide basis through two laboratories, one located in the U.K. and the other in the U.S. These studies are designed to produce the data needed to identify, quantify and evaluate the risks to humans and the environment resulting from the manufacture or use of pharmaceutical, chemical, biotechnology and other products. Other studies are designed to identify specific areas of adverse change, and include carcinogenicity, reproductive, metabolic and inhalation studies.

Pharmaco-LSR's clinical services division provides clinical research and development services to the pharmaceutical, biotechnology and consumer products industries. It is engaged in most aspects of the clinical development process, including analytical chemistry, evaluation of clinical data, data processing, biostatistical analysis and the preparation of supporting documentation for compliance with regulatory requirements. The operations of Clinical Science Research International Ltd., a wholly owned subsidiary of Pharmaco LSR Ltd., were combined with the operations of Pharmaco-LSR's U.K. clinical services subsidiary in March 1992.

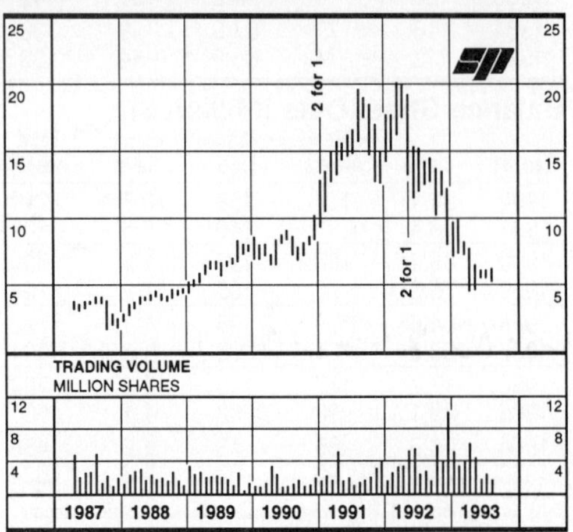

APBI's Environmental Sciences Group is comprised of Environ, an environmental and health sciences consulting firm; Landis International Inc., a provider of consulting services to agrochemical manufacuturers; and Environmental Testing and Certification Corp. (ETC), which operates five commercial testing laboratories to perform chemical analysis of contamination in soil, water and other environmental media.

Important Developments

Apr. '93— The company said the near term outlook for both of its business segments was weaker than expected, and it estimated that 1993 revenue growth would be between 5% and 8%. It also announced plans to implement aggressive expense reduction measures.

Next earnings report expected in early November.

Per Share Data ($)

Yr. End Dec. 31	1992	[1]1991	[1]1990	1989	1988	1987	1986
Tangible Bk. Val.	**3.28**	3.50	2.23	2.13	2.08	1.72	d2.12
Cash Flow	**0.55**	0.81	0.54	0.58	0.47	0.36	NA
Earnings[2]	**0.22**	0.54	0.31	[3]0.37	0.30	0.23	0.18
Dividends	**Nil**	Nil	Nil	Nil	Nil	Nil	Nil
Payout Ratio	**Nil**	Nil	Nil	Nil	Nil	Nil	Nil
Prices—High	**20⅛**	19⅝	10¼	8⅜	4¾	4⅛	NA
Low	**8**	9⅜	6½	4 7/16	2 5/16	1 11/16	NA
P/E Ratio—	**91–36**	36–17	33–21	23–12	16–8	18–7	NA

Data as orig. reptd. Adj. for stk. divs. of 100% Apr. 1992, 100% Jan. 1991. **1.** Refl. merger or acq. **2.** Bef. spec. item of +0.08 in 1990. **3.** Ful. dil.: 0.37. d-Deficit. NA-Not Available.

Income Data (Million $)

Year Ended Dec. 31	Revs.	Oper. Inc.	% Oper. Inc. of Revs.	Cap. Exp.	Depr.	Int. Exp.	Net Bef. Taxes	Eff. Tax Rate	[4]Net Inc.	% Net Inc. of Revs.	Cash Flow
1992	**181**	**33.9**	**18.7**	**17.8**	**9.86**	**1.04**	**12.4**	**47.6%**	**6.5**	**3.6**	**16.4**
[1]1991	114	24.9	21.9	8.8	6.15	0.65	19.7	36.5%	12.5	11.0	18.6
[1]1990	100	20.4	20.5	10.6	4.82	0.97	12.3	46.9%	6.6	6.6	11.4
1989	57	10.3	18.1	6.6	2.86	0.41	7.7	36.3%	4.9	8.6	7.8
1988	47	7.7	16.4	13.7	2.19	0.22	5.9	35.5%	3.8	8.1	6.0
1987	34	5.9	17.7	7.9	1.59	0.13	4.6	37.9%	2.9	8.6	4.5
[2]1986	26	4.6	17.7	[3]3.6	1.22	0.80	2.5	34.3%	1.7	6.4	2.9
1985	22	3.9	17.6	[3]1.5	1.12	1.72	1.2	38.3%	0.8	3.4	NA
1984	19	3.0	15.6	[3]2.1	1.04	1.65	0.5	81.5%	0.1	0.5	NA
1983	17	NA	NA	NA	NA	NA	NA	NA	d0.9	NM	NA

Balance Sheet Data (Million $)

Dec. 31	Cash	Curr. Assets	Curr. Liab.	Curr. Ratio	Total Assets	% Ret. on Assets	Long Term Debt	Common Equity	Total Cap.	% LT Debt of Cap.	% Ret. on Equity
1992	**12.90**	**94.0**	**57.4**	**1.6**	**196**	**3.3**	**14.00**	**112.0**	**137.0**	**10.2**	**6.3**
1991	15.30	63.6	36.7	1.7	139	9.6	4.15	84.2	101.0	4.1	17.9
1990	8.50	46.7	42.1	1.1	110	6.0	3.03	50.4	65.0	4.7	13.0
1989	6.30	24.7	24.9	1.0	70	7.5	2.35	32.9	45.0	5.2	16.2
1988	3.30	21.0	21.6	1.0	60	7.1	1.67	27.2	38.0	4.4	15.1
1987	6.20	19.2	15.6	1.2	47	7.2	1.20	22.7	32.0	3.8	NM
[1]1986	1.80	11.7	10.8	1.1	30	NA	1.43	d0.3	6.0	23.8	NA
1985	1.45	9.8	8.6	1.1	25	3.1	1.64	d1.5	0.1	NM	NM
1984	NA	NA	NA	NA	22	0.4	1.84	d1.6	0.2	NM	NM
1983	NA	NA	NA	NA	22	NM	2.05	d0.7	1.3	NM	NM

Data as orig. reptd. **1.** Refl. merger or acq. **2.** Pro forma, refl. acq. of predecessor co. & related transactions. **3.** Net. **4.** Bef. spec. item(s). d-Deficit. NA-Not Available. NM-Not Meaningful.

Operating Revenues (Million $)

Quarter:	1993	1992	1991	[1]1990
Mar.	45.5	42.2	26.5	22.7
Jun.	49.0	43.7	26.9	23.9
Sep.		46.2	27.6	25.3
Dec.		48.9	32.8	27.8
		181.0	113.8	99.7

For the six months ended June 30, 1993, operating revenues rose 8.2%, year to year. Results were penalized by a reserve for accounts receivable of $3.7 million, and despite the absence of $2.0 million of restructuring costs and $4.3 million of merger expenses, net income declined to $395,000 ($0.01 a share), from $3,435,000 ($0.12).

Common Share Earnings ($)

Quarter:	1993	1992	1991	[1]1990
Mar.	0.02	d0.03	0.12	0.11
Jun.	d0.01	0.15	0.13	0.12
Sep.		0.15	0.14	d0.02
Dec.		d0.05	0.15	0.12
		0.22	0.54	0.31

Dividend Data

No cash dividends have been paid. Two-for-one stock splits were effected in April 1992 and January 1991.

Finances

As of May 1993, the company had repurchased 1,440,000 shares of its common stock pursuant to a 2,000,000 share repurchase program initiated in January 1993.

In June 1992, APBI acquired National Express Laboratories Inc. (NATEX), for $5,671,000 in cash, subject to adjustments. In February, Pharmaco Dynamics Research Inc. was acquired for about 5.8 million (adjusted) common shares. APBI recorded a charge of $4,296,000 in the first quarter of 1992 for merger costs related to the Pharmaco transaction.

In a June 1992 public offering, 4,000,000 APBI common shares (including 2,900,000 for selling stockholders) were sold at $13.50 each. Proceeds were earmarked to reduce debt and for general corporate purposes and possible future acquisitions.

Capitalization

Long Term Debt: $7,318,000 (3/93).

Common Stock: 27,981,995 shs. ($0.01 par). Institutions hold about 63%. Shareholders: about 4,200 (3/93).

1. Interims restated. d-Deficit.

Office—4350 N. Fairfax Drive, Arlington, VA 22203-1627. **Tel**—(703) 516-2490. **Chrmn**—K. H. Harper. **Pres & CEO**—G. C. Wrenn. **CFO**—R. F. Amundsen Jr. **Secy**—C. E. Chason **SVP & Investor Contact**—John H. Timoney (609) 951-9090. **Dirs**—R. F. Amundsen Jr., S. T. Davis, S. A. Fleckman, F. Frank, K. H. Harper, J. H. Highland, G. K. Hogan, F. E. Loy, T. J. Russell Jr., J. H. Timoney, G. C. Wrenn. **Transfer Agent & Registrar**—Midlantic National Bank, Edison, N.J. **Incorporated** in Delaware in 1986. **Empl**—2,200.

 L. Feuer Nelson

Applied Materials

NASDAQ Symbol AMAT (Incl. in Nat'l Market) Options on Pacific In S&P MidCap 400

Price	Range	P–E Ratio	Dividend	Yield	S&P Ranking	Beta
Aug. 24'93	1993					
71⅜	74½–32¼	37	None	None	B–	2.03

Summary

A leading manufacturer of wafer fabrication equipment for the semiconductor industry, this company produces deposition, etching and ion implantation systems. Nearly two-thirds of revenues are derived from international sales. Following substantially higher earnings in fiscal 1992 due to well-received new products, earnings should more than double in fiscal 1994 as the company gains market share and industry growth resumes. Another substantial gain is forecast for fiscal 1994.

Current Outlook

Earnings for the fiscal year ending October 31, 1993, are expected to rise to $3.20 a share, from the $2.40 projected for fiscal 1993.

Initiation of cash dividends is not likely.

Fiscal 1994 sales are expected to advance at least 25%, as semiconductor capital spending rises and Applied's market share continues to increase. Sales will benefit not only from demand for capacity additions due to rapid growth in the semiconductor industry, but from a shift in the industry to a new generation of semiconductors that require more advanced equipment to manufacture. In addition, the company is likely to continue to increase its market share due to wide acceptance of its technologically advanced products. Margins should widen on the higher volume as cost increases remain under tight control. Long-term prospects should benefit from the company's global distribution capabilities, new product introductions and concentration in high-growth markets.

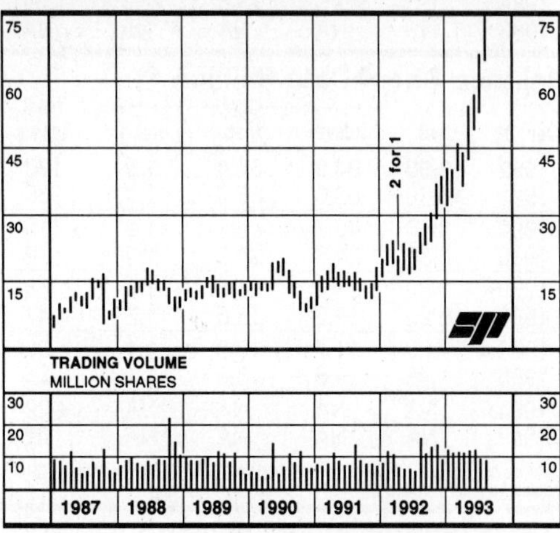

Net Sales (Million $)

13 Weeks:	1992–93	1992	1991	1990
Jan.	[1]216	167	145	139
Apr.	256	180	166	143
Jul.	281	194	167	144
Oct.	---	210	161	141
	---	751	639	567

For the nine months ended August 1, 1993, net sales increased 39%, year to year, led by gains for single-wafer, multi-chamber etch and deposition process equipment based on the Precision 5000 and Endura Masterfab platforms. Margins widened, and pretax income increased 146%. After taxes at 33.0% in both interims, net income also rose 146%. On 15% more share outstanding, share earnings were $1.59, versus $0.74.

Common Share Earnings ($)

13 Weeks:	1992–93	1992	1991	1990
Jan.	[1]0.36	0.18	0.13	0.33
Apr.	0.54	0.26	0.21	0.31
Jul.	0.68	0.30	0.24	0.28
Oct.	E0.82	0.34	0.18	0.09
	E2.40	1.09	0.76	1.00

Important Developments

Aug. '93— The company said that during its third quarter all product areas saw increased demand. Physical vapor deposition (PVD) system shipments more than doubled. Higher shipments were seen in dielectric and metal chemical vapor deposition (CVD), ion implantation, and etch systems when compared with the year earlier level.

Next earnings report expected in mid-November.

Per Share Data ($)

Yr. End Oct. 31	1992	1991	1990	1989	1988	1987	1986	1985	1984	1983
Tangible Bk. Val.	**12.13**	[2]9.65	[2]9.03	[2]7.85	[2]6.34	[2]4.97	[2]3.53	3.29	2.85	2.35
Cash Flow	**1.85**	1.47	1.48	1.90	1.58	0.33	0.33	0.54	0.70	0.30
Earnings	**1.09**	0.76	1.00	1.54	1.21	0.01	0.05	0.35	0.52	0.13
Dividends	**Nil**	Nil	Nil	Nil	Nil	Nil	Nil	Nil	Nil	Nil
Payout Ratio	**Nil**	Nil	Nil	Nil	Nil	Nil	Nil	Nil	Nil	Nil
Prices[3]—High	**38¾**	19	20¼	16⅜	18	16¾	8¼	9	9⅞	12¼
Low	**16⅛**	9¾	8¼	10¾	8⅜	4¾	4	4⅜	5¼	5½
P/E Ratio—	**36–15**	25–13	20–8	11–7	15–7	NM	NM	26–12	19–10	98–45

Data as orig. reptd. Adj. for stk. divs. of 100% Apr. 1992, 100% May 1986. **1.** 14 wks. **2.** Incl. intangibles. **3.** Cal. yr. E-Estimated NM-Not Meaningful.

Income Data (Million $)

Year Ended Oct. 31	Revs.	Oper. Inc.	% Oper. Inc. of Revs.	Cap. Exp.	Depr.	Int. Exp.	Net Bef. Taxes	Eff. Tax Rate	Net Inc.	% Net Inc. of Revs.	Cash Flow
1992	**751**	**96.1**	**12.8**	**67**	**27.7**	**15.2**	**58.9**	**33.0%**	**39.5**	**5.3**	**67.2**
1991	639	76.5	12.0	67	24.5	14.0	40.4	35.0%	26.2	4.1	50.7
1990	567	74.7	13.2	111	16.4	6.7	54.1	37.0%	34.1	6.0	50.5
1989	502	93.6	18.6	43	11.7	2.8	84.4	39.0%	51.5	10.3	63.6
1988	363	79.4	21.9	20	11.4	3.2	66.7	40.0%	40.0	11.0	52.0
1987	174	10.5	6.0	12	9.3	3.3	0.6	41.9%	0.3	0.2	9.1
1986	149	10.8	7.3	12	7.4	3.4	2.1	42.0%	1.2	0.8	8.6
1985	175	21.0	12.0	13	4.9	3.6	16.0	42.0%	9.3	5.3	14.1
1984	168	29.0	17.2	15	4.7	3.3	24.6	45.0%	13.5	8.0	18.2
1983	106	11.0	10.4	8	4.4	3.8	5.1	39.2%	3.1	2.9	7.5

Balance Sheet Data (Million $)

		Curr.									
Oct. 31	Cash	Assets	Liab.	Ratio	Total Assets	% Ret. on Assets	Long Term Debt	Common Equity	Total Cap.	% LT Debt of Cap.	% Ret. on Equity
1992	**223**	**582**	**248**	**2.3**	**854**	**4.9**	**118**	**474**	**599**	**19.8**	**9.3**
1991	140	434	200	2.2	661	4.3	124	325	456	27.2	8.3
1990	72	367	195	1.9	558	6.8	54	300	362	14.8	12.1
1989	107	343	143	2.4	434	13.2	29	254	290	10.2	22.4
1988	101	276	117	2.4	339	13.9	11	201	219	5.2	22.3
1987	71	179	48	3.7	233	0.2	21	154	183	11.5	0.3
1986	22	104	32	3.2	154	0.8	20	93	121	16.3	1.4
1985	36	109	41	2.7	150	6.4	17	86	108	15.6	11.5
1984	26	107	42	2.6	139	10.7	19	74	97	19.1	19.9
1983	39	94	35	2.7	113	3.1	16	62	78	20.9	6.0

Data as orig. reptd.

Business Summary

Applied Materials is a leading producer of wafer fabrication systems for the worldwide semiconductor industry. The company also sells related spare parts and services.

Contributions by geographic area in fiscal 1992 were:

	Sales	Profits
U.S.	40%	41%
Europe	18%	21%
Japan	30%	12%
Asia/Pacific	12%	26%

One of the fundamental steps in fabricating a semiconductor is deposition, a process in which a layer of either electrically insulating (dielectric) or electrically conductive material is deposited on a wafer. Deposition can be divided into several different categories, of which the company currently participates in three: chemical vapor deposition (CVD), physical vapor deposition (PVD) and epitaxial deposition.

Applied is a leader in dry etch systems. Etchers are used in conjunction with photo-resist and lithography equipment to create circuit paths in the semiconductor device by selectively removing materials from the wafer.

The company also manufactures ion implantation equipment, which adds impurities (dopants) to the silicon wafer to define the areas, or junctions, within the silicon that control the flow of electrical impulses through the circuit being built.

In January 1992, the company announced the formation of wholly owned Applied Display Technology Inc., which will develop thin-film manufacturing systems for the active matrix liquid crystal display segment of the flat-panel display market.

Dividend Data

No cash has been paid. Two-for-one stock splits were effected in 1992 and 1986. A "poison pill" stock purchase right was adopted in 1989.

Finances

At August 1, 1993, Applied Materials had cash, cash equivalents and short-term investments of $216.9 million and notes payable of $26.4 million.

In August 1992, the company sold publicly 3,925,000 common shares at $24 each. Proceeds were earmarked for general corporate purposes.

Capitalization

Long Term Debt: $122,854,000 (8/93).

Common Stock: 39,664,000 shs. (no par).
Institutions hold about 88%.
Shareholders of record: 981.

Office—3050 Bowers Ave., Santa Clara, CA 95054-3299. **Tel**—(408) 727-5555. **Chrmn & CEO**—J. C. Morgan. **Pres**—J. W. Bagley. **Sr VP, CFO & Investor Contact**—Gerald F. Taylor. **Secy**—D. A. Slichter. **Treas**—Nancy H. Handel. **Dirs**—J. W. Bagley, H. M. Dwight Jr., G. B. Farnsworth, P. V. Gerdine, P. R. Low, D. Maydan, J. C. Morgan, A. J. Stein, H. Toyoda. **Transfer Agent**—Harris Trust Co. of California, Los Angeles. **Incorporated** in California in 1967; reincorporated in Delaware in 1987. **Empl**—3,909.

 Paul H. Valentine, CFA

Arnold Industries

NASDAQ Symbol AIND (Incl. in Nat'l Market) In S&P MidCap 400

Price	Range	P-E Ratio	Dividend	Yield	S&P Ranking	Beta
Sep. 10'93	1993					
39½	40½–27	20	0.68	1.7%	A–	0.70

Summary

Arnold is a trucking company that provides less-than-truckload, truckload and warehouse services primarily in the northeastern U.S. Its important New Penn Motor Express subsidiary has been very profitable compared with other less-than-truckload carriers. Following record profits in 1992, another earnings gain is expected for 1993.

Current Outlook

Earnings for 1994 are estimated to reach $2.35, up from $2.15 a share expected for 1993.

Dividends should continue at the $0.17 quarterly rate in the near term.

Revenues for 1994 should increase at least 10%, reflecting the bankruptcy and exit of major competitor St. Johnsbury Trucking Co., Inc., the largest LTL carrier in the northeast, as well as gains from continued internal growth. Revenue comparisons for 1993 should benefit from a full year of contributions from the April 1992 acquisition of DW Freight. (Since the March 1992 acquisition of SilverEagle Transport was accounted for as a pooling of interests, that acquisition will not affect revenue comparisons.) Profitability should improve on the higher volumes and efficiencies resulting from implementation of better management systems—including management information and costing systems—at newly acquired DW Freight and SilverEagle. Arnold's long-term strategy includes expanding its services into contiguous geographic areas and increasing efficiencies.

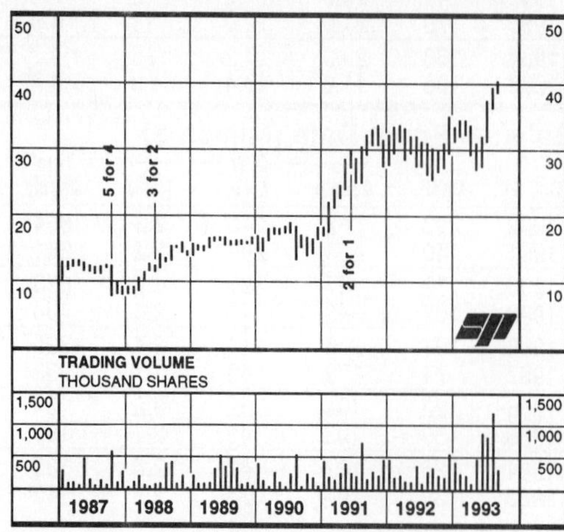

Operating Revenues (Million $)

Quarter:	1993	1992	1991	1990
Mar.	59.9	51.4	39.5	38.5
Jun.	66.9	59.9	42.2	39.1
Sep.	---	61.4	42.0	39.9
Dec.	---	60.9	41.1	41.3
	---	233.6	164.8	158.8

Revenues for the six months ended June 30, 1993, rose 14%, year to year. Operating income climbed 6.5%, aided by contributions from newly-acquired SilverEagle and DW subsidiaries. Lower interest expense was more than offset by a decline in other income, and pretax income advanced 4.7%. After taxes at 36.5% versus 36.7%, net income increased 5.0% to $13,258,887 ($1.00 a share) from $12,628,049 ($0.95).

Common Share Earnings ($)

Quarter:	1993	1992	1991	1990
Mar.	0.43	0.46	0.42	0.37
Jun.	0.57	0.49	0.47	0.41
Sep.	E0.55	0.46	0.43	0.39
Dec.	E0.60	0.54	0.45	0.45
	E2.15	1.95	1.77	1.62

Important Developments

Aug. '93— Arnold said that during 1993's second quarter, one half of the revenue gains were attributable to New Penn Motor Express, Inc., while the other half came from Arnold Logistics group, principally from SilverEagle Transport, Inc. and DW Freight Inc. The company was also able to capitalize on the exit from the industry of competitor St. Johnsbury, the largest less-than-truckload carrier in the Northeast, resulting in an increase in daily traffic volume in the area of about 15%-20%.

Next earnings report expected in early October.

Per Share Data ($)

Yr. End Dec. 31	[1]1992	1991	1990	1989	1988	1987	1986	1985	1984	[1]1983
Tangible Bk. Val.	**9.46**	8.83	7.64	6.51	5.43	4.24	3.55	2.91	2.36	2.08
Cash Flow	**2.99**	2.44	2.27	2.01	1.93	1.32	1.24	1.05	0.75	0.61
Earnings[2]	**1.95**	1.77	1.62	1.40	1.38	0.82	0.80	0.64	0.46	0.39
Dividends	**0.320**	0.575	0.500	0.435	0.220	0.120	0.100	0.080	0.080	0.064
Payout Ratio	**32%**	33%	31%	31%	16%	15%	13%	13%	14%	17%
Prices—High	**35**	33¾	19	16⅞	16	13⅜	12	6⅜	3⅞	3⅞
Low	**25½**	17	13⅜	14	8⅛	7⅞	5¾	3¾	3⅛	2¾
P/E Ratio—	**18–13**	19–10	12–8	12–10	12–6	16–10	15–7	10–6	9–7	10–7

Data as orig. reptd. Adj. for stk. divs. of 100% Jun. 1991, 50% Jun. 1988, 25% Oct. 1987, 100% May 1986. **1.** Refl. merger or acq. **2.** Bef. spec. item of +0.10 in 1989. E-Estimated.

Income Data (Million $)

Year Ended Dec. 31	Revs.	Oper. Inc.	% Oper. Inc. of Revs.	Cap. Exp.	Depr.	Int. Exp.	[2]Net Bef. Taxes	Eff. Tax Rate	[3]Net Inc.	% Net Inc. of Revs.	Cash Flow
[1]1992	**234**	**54.2**	**23.2**	**39.0**	**13.80**	**1.67**	**40.5**	**36.2%**	**25.8**	**11.1**	**39.7**
1991	165	43.0	26.1	6.7	8.74	0.15	36.4	36.5%	23.1	14.0	31.9
1990	159	41.8	26.3	17.2	8.47	0.18	33.8	37.3%	21.2	13.4	29.7
1989	144	35.5	24.7	20.1	8.04	0.18	29.2	37.5%	18.2	12.7	26.3
1988	128	30.5	23.8	16.9	7.13	0.20	28.2	37.3%	[4]17.7	13.8	24.8
1987	109	24.9	22.9	14.6	6.30	0.25	18.6	44.0%	10.4	9.6	16.7
1986	95	22.1	23.2	13.8	5.59	0.37	19.3	48.4%	[4]10.0	10.5	15.6
1985	84	19.4	23.0	8.0	5.16	0.66	14.6	45.4%	8.0	9.4	13.2
1984	77	16.2	21.1	9.1	4.49	0.57	12.6	44.3%	7.0	9.2	11.5
[1]1983	64	14.1	22.0	9.7	3.57	0.32	11.5	45.1%	6.3	9.8	9.9

Balance Sheet Data (Million $)

Dec. 31	Cash	Curr. Assets	Curr. Liab.	Curr. Ratio	Total Assets	% Ret. on Assets	Long Term Debt	Common Equity	Total Cap.	% LT Debt of Cap.	% Ret. on Equity
1992	**45.2**	**73.7**	**43.8**	**1.7**	**197**	**15.0**	**0.48**	**136**	**143**	**0.3**	**20.3**
1991	56.4	71.3	16.4	4.3	146	16.3	2.05	116	121	1.7	21.3
1990	43.6	59.9	30.2	2.0	137	17.0	2.27	100	107	2.1	22.8
1989	27.7	43.4	20.5	2.1	113	17.1	2.37	86	93	2.6	23.1
1988	24.7	40.9	17.3	2.4	99	19.8	2.57	71	82	3.1	27.8
1987	14.4	27.2	14.1	1.9	78	14.6	2.71	55	64	4.3	20.7
1986	10.9	22.2	9.8	2.3	65	16.9	4.08	46	55	7.4	24.0
1985	9.4	17.8	9.2	1.9	53	14.9	3.56	37	44	8.2	23.6
1984	14.1	22.0	17.7	1.2	54	15.2	4.29	30	37	11.7	24.8
1983	15.1	21.1	8.5	2.5	49	14.0	4.58	35	41	11.2	19.7

Data as orig. reptd. **1.** Refl. merger or acq. **2.** Incl. equity in earns. of nonconsol. subs. **3.** Bef. spec. item in 1989. **4.** Refl. acctg. change.

Business Summary

Arnold Industries is engaged in the trucking and warehousing business. Operations are conducted through four subsidiaries—one less-than-truckload carrier (LTL), New Penn Motor Express, and three truckload carriers (TL), Lebarnold, DW Freight (acquired April 1992 for cash) and SilverEagle Transport (acquired in March 1992 for common stock). Revenue contributions in recent years were:

	1992	1991	1990
LTL	59%	66%	66%
Truckload	33%	26%	25%
Warehousing/Related trucking	8%	8%	9%

New Penn is a less-than-truckload carrier transporting commodities primarily in interstate commerce in New England and the Middle Atlantic states, with extensive intrastate carriage in Pennsylvania and New York. The southeastern Atlantic states, Florida, Puerto Rico and certain areas of Canada are serviced by a specific carrier in each area that is on-line with New Penn's computer system. Commodities transported include food products, textiles, building products, metal products, paper products, pharmaceuticals, office equipment and supplies and wearing apparel.

Lebarnold, Inc. has two primary divisions, Lebarnold and ADW. Lebarnold is a Northeast TL carrier. Lebarnold closed down its pier container operation in 1992's, but has expanded its local Northeast operations. The division also expanded its Charlotte, North Carolina operation in 1992, an area which the company expects will provide growth in 1993 and beyond. ADW serves the assembly, distribution and warehousing needs of its customers from five separate warehouses in two operating locations in Pennsylvania.

SilverEagle is a regional dry freight TL carrier based in Jacksonville, Florida. Its customer base is in the food industry and it has terminals located in Florida, Georgia and North Carolina.

DW Freight's primary operating unit is Dalworth Trucking Co., a TL carrier, based in Fort Worth, Texas. The carrier's primary customer base is in the container business, and its main area of operation is in Texas and Oklahoma.

Dividend Data

Cash has been paid each year since 1972.

Amt of Divd. $	Date Decl.	Ex-divd. Date	Stock of Record	Payment Date
0.16	Feb. 5	Feb. 11	Feb. 18	Mar. 3'93
0.17	May 6	May 11	May 17	Jun. 2'93
0.17	Jul. 29	Aug. 16	Aug. 20	Sep. 3'93

Capitalization

Long Term Debt: $1,082,148 (6/93).

Common Stock: 13,281,137 shs. ($1 par).
Officers & directors own about 30%.
Institutions hold about 47%.
Shareholders of record: 700.

Office—625 South Fifth Ave., Lebanon, PA 17042. **Tel**—(717) 274-2521. **Chrmn & Pres**—E. H. Arnold. **Treas & Investor Contact**—Ronald E. Walborn (717) 236-7912. **Secy**—H. L. Allen. **Dirs**—H. L. Allen, E. H. Arnold, C. E. Hughes, K. F. Leedy, A. L. Peterson, R. E. Walborn. **Transfer Agent & Registrar**—Registrar & Transfer Co., Cranford, N.J. **Incorporated** in Pennsylvania in 1982. **Empl**—2,300.

 M. Graham Hackett

Arrow Electronics

NYSE Symbol ARW Options on ASE (Mar-Jun-Sep-Dec) In S&P MidCap 400

Price	Range	P-E Ratio	Dividend	Yield	S&P Ranking	Beta
Aug. 17'93	1993					
39	40–26½	18	None	None	B–	0.39

Summary

This company is one of the world's largest distributors of electronic components, systems and related products. Operations have been expanded substantially in the past several years by an aggressive program of acquisitions. Following sharply higher earnings in 1992, a further substantial gain is likely in 1993 due to rapid industry growth and contributions from acquisitions. The continuation of strong industry conditions and additional acquisitions should result in higher earnings again in 1994.

Current Outlook

Earnings for 1994 should approximate $2.90 a share, up from the $2.50 projected for 1993.

Early reinstatement of common dividends, omitted in 1986, is possible.

Sales are expected to rise 15% in 1994, led by semiconductors. The semiconductor industry is currently in the midst of a strong cyclical upturn that should continue through next year. Sales of computer products are also likely to be strong, although price declines will be somewhat offsetting. Passives sales should grow less rapidly reflecting the mature nature of that business. Sales growth should also be assisted by the consolidation of several acquisitions. Margins should be well maintained as the company continues to focus on cost containment. Longer-term prospects should benefit from consolidation in the distribution industry.

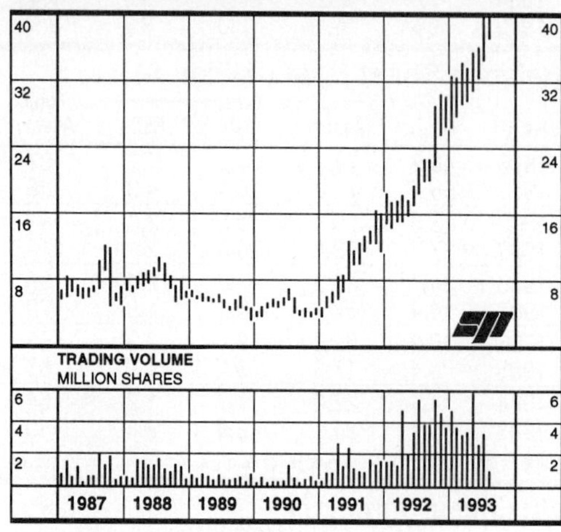

Net Sales (Million $)

Quarter:	1993	1992	1991	1990
Mar.	551	379	237	247
Jun.	584	382	233	242
Sep.	---	407	227	246
Dec.	---	453	347	236
	---	1,622	1,044	971

Sales for the six months ended June 30, 1993, increased 49%, year to year, reflecting strong internal growth and the consolidation of acquisitions. Margins widened, and pretax income more than doubled. After taxes at 39.6%, versus 36.7%, and minority interest in the 1993 interim, net income rose 78%. On 32% more average shares outstanding, share earnings were $1.21, versus $0.79. Results exclude a special charge of $0.11 in the 1992 interim.

Common Share Earnings ($)

Quarter:	1993	1992	1991	1990
Mar.	0.59	0.38	0.15	0.12
Jun.	0.62	0.41	0.16	0.13
Sep.	E0.60	0.47	d0.52	0.13
Dec.	E0.69	0.53	0.32	0.06
	E2.50	1.81	[1]0.28	0.44

Important Developments

Jun. '93— The company annouced that it had signed agreements in principle to acquire interests in three European electronic distribution concerns, which were expected to increase ARW's annual revenues by more than $75 million. The acquisitions would bring ARW's European sales to over $750 million.

Next earnings report expected in mid-October.

Per Share Data ($)

Yr. End Dec. 31	[2]1992	[2]1991	1990	[2]1989	[2]1988	1987	1986	1985	[2]1984	1983
Tangible Bk. Val.	**8.09**	4.23	3.41	2.18	2.49	3.59	4.40	10.24	11.75	9.92
Cash Flow	**2.29**	0.93	1.21	0.71	1.31	d2.57	d3.95	d1.13	2.56	1.51
Earnings[3]	**1.81**	0.28	0.44	d0.19	0.38	d3.17	d4.82	d1.69	2.00	0.85
Dividends	**Nil**	Nil	Nil	Nil	Nil	Nil	0.15	0.20	0.20	0.17
Payout Ratio	**Nil**	Nil	Nil	Nil	Nil	Nil	NM	NM	10%	20%
Prices—High	**30½**	16½	7	6¾	10¾	12⅛	17⅞	18¼	29⅜	34
Low	**14⅜**	3⅝	3⅝	3⅛	5⅜	4⅞	3	11¼	13¼	15½
P/E Ratio—	**17–8**	59–13	16–8	NM	28–14	NM	NM	NM	15–7	40–18

Data as orig. reptd. **1.** Quarters do not reconcile due to changes in no. of shs. outstanding. **2.** Reflects merger or acquisition. **3.** Bef. results of disc. opers. of +1.17 in 1988, +1.93 in 1987, bef. spec. item(s) of -0.21 in 1992, -0.56 in 1986. d-Deficit. E-Estimated. NM-Not Meaningful.

Income Data (Million $)

Year Ended Dec. 31	Revs.	Oper. Inc.	% Oper. Inc. of Revs.	[3]Cap. Exp.	Depr.	Int. Exp.	[4]Net Bef. Taxes	Eff. Tax Rate	[5]Net Inc.	% Net Inc. of Revs.	Cash Flow
[1]1992	**1,622**	**116.0**	**7.2**	**3.5**	**12.3**	**30.1**	**80.3**	**37.4%**	**50.2**	**3.1**	**58.6**
[1]1991	1,044	53.7	5.1	3.8	9.5	29.1	10.9	20.4%	8.7	0.8	13.5
1990	971	41.8	4.3	6.0	9.2	29.0	10.1	Nil	10.1	1.0	14.4
[1]1989	925	38.1	4.1	3.9	10.5	29.8	3.2	Nil	3.2	0.3	8.3
[1]1988	1,006	46.1	4.6	4.9	10.8	30.2	9.7	Nil	9.7	1.0	15.1
[2]1987	562	d9.9	NM	2.2	4.0	18.8	d15.8	NM	d15.8	NM	d17.2
1986	530	d5.7	NM	2.3	5.7	19.9	d28.3	NM	d28.3	NM	d25.8
1985	534	4.1	0.8	10.1	3.6	21.9	d20.0	NM	d10.9	NM	d7.2
[1]1984	740	46.1	6.2	10.9	3.6	20.1	22.4	42.9%	12.8	1.7	16.4
1983	567	27.1	4.8	3.5	4.9	13.8	8.3	38.6%	5.1	0.9	9.1

Balance Sheet Data (Million $)

Dec. 31	Cash	Curr. Assets	Curr. Liab.	Curr. Ratio	Total Assets	% Ret. on Assets	Long Term Debt	Common Equity	Total Cap.	% LT Debt of Cap.	% Ret. on Equity
1992	**3.4**	**549**	**180**	**3.1**	**781**	**5.4**	**225**	**335**	**577**	**39.1**	**16.0**
1991	1.5	512	186	2.8	745	1.1	304	167	530	57.4	2.6
1990	0.9	327	96	3.4	478	2.1	207	92	358	57.8	6.1
1989	4.6	357	110	3.2	498	0.6	216	78	363	59.3	NM
1988	9.7	382	117	3.3	530	1.7	240	78	388	61.9	7.0
1987	13.4	260	72	3.6	346	NM	167	26	269	62.1	NM
1986	32.0	246	63	3.9	337	NM	162	33	270	60.1	NM
1985	46.8	266	73	3.7	352	NM	201	69	275	73.1	NM
1984	24.0	297	83	3.6	345	4.1	173	80	257	67.3	17.4
1983	2.5	239	83	2.9	276	1.9	122	66	190	64.1	9.3

Data as orig. reptd. **1.** Reflects merger or acquisition. **2.** Excludes discontinued operations. **3.** Net of curr. yr. retirement and disposals after 1983. **4.** Incl. equity in nonconsol. subs. after 1984. **5.** Bef. results of disc. opers. in 1988, 1987, and spec. item(s) in 1992, 1986. d-Deficit. NM-Not Meaningful.

Business Summary

Arrow Electronics is one of the world's largest distributors of electronic components, systems and related products. Growth has benefited in recent years from acquisitions.

The company's electronics distribution networks, spanning both North America and Europe, incorporate 110 selling locations, nine primary U.S. distribution centers, and 3,500 remote on-line terminals that serve approximately 125,000 original equipment manufacturers (OEMs) and commercial customers worldwide.

About 57% of Arrow's consolidated sales are semiconductor products; industrial and commercial computer products account for approximately 30%; the remaining 13% of sales are passives, electromechanical, and connector products. In North America the company maintains an inventory of 300,000 different electronic components.

The company is also the largest participant in pan-European electronics distribution. These operations have been expanded in recent years through acquisitions.

Dividend Data

Common dividends were omitted in December 1986 after being initiated in 1977. A "poison pill" stock purchase right was adopted in 1988.

Finances

In May, 1993 the company sold 562,000 newly issued common shares for $32.50 each as part of a secondary offering in which Lex Service PLC of sold 4.7 million shares of ARW common stock.

In May, 1993 ARW acquired the high-reliability electronic component distributor and value-added service business of Zeus Components, Inc. This followed the January, 1993 acquisition of an additional 15% interest in Spoerle Electronic, Germany's largest electronics distributor, which brought ARW's interest in that company to 55%. In February 1992, the company acquired the European electronics distribution business of Lex Service PLC, which had sales of some $150 million. This followed the September 1991 purchase of Lex Service PLC's North American electronics distribution business, which had sales of $506 million in 1990.

Capitalization

Long Term Debt: $262,695,000 (6/93).

Minority Interest: $59,420,000.

Common Stock: 29,991,412 shs. ($1 par).
Officers and directors control some 6.8%.
Institutions hold approximately 56%.
Shareholders of record: 4,000.

Office—25 Hub Drive, Melville, NY 11747. **Tel**—(516) 391-1300. **Chrmn**—J. C. Waddell. **Pres & CEO**—S. P. Kaufman. **SVP-CFO, Secy & Investor Contact**—Robert E. Klatell. **Dirs**—T. M. Davidson, D. W. Duval, C. Giersch, J. S. Gould, S. P. Kaufman, L. R. Kem, R. E. Klatell, S. W. Menefee, R. S. Rosenbloom, J. C. Waddell. **Transfer Agent & Registrar**—Chemical Bank, NYC. **Incorporated** in New York in 1946. **Empl**—4,100.

 Paul H. Valentine, CFA

Arvin Industries

NYSE Symbol ARV Options on CBOE (Feb-May-Aug-Nov) In S&P MidCap 400

Price	Range	P–E Ratio	Dividend	Yield	S&P Ranking	Beta
Sep. 16'93	1993					
28¾	37¾–28¼	15	0.76	2.6%	B	1.02

Summary

This manufacturer of a broad line of automotive exhaust and ride control products, coated metals and other industrial products and services has expanded its European operations in recent years, and is well positioned to benefit from the implementation of U.S.-style emission controls in Europe as of January 1, 1993. Consolidation of certain European operations with those of competitors should increase the profits derived from those market segments in 1994.

Current Outlook

Earnings for 1993 are estimated at $1.80 a share, up from 1992's $1.70. A further rise to $2.15 is possible for 1994.

The dividend should continue at $0.19 quarterly.

Sales in 1994 should benefit from higher sales of original equipment catalytic converters as the European market recovers from the severe downturn experienced in 1993. Increased North American car and truck production should spur original equipment sales, but replacement parts sales may remain weak. Aided by contributions from recently formed joint ventures, earnings should advance strongly.

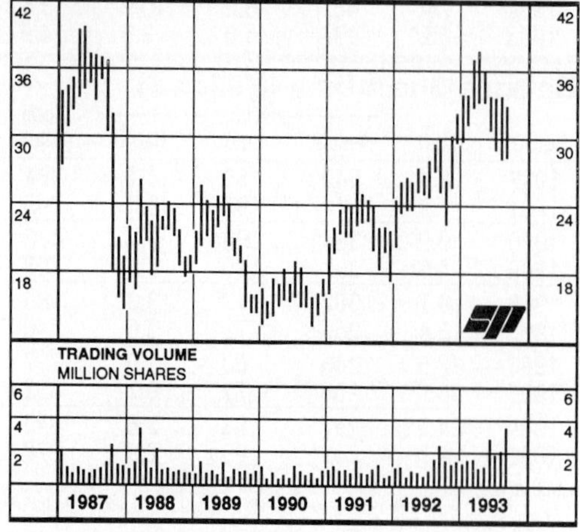

Net Sales (Million $)

Quarter:	1993	1992	1991	1990
Mar.	476	459	384	395
Jun.	521	500	450	445
Sep.	---	476	419	429
Dec.	---	455	424	418
	---	1,890	1,676	1,687

Net sales for the six months ended June 30, 1993, advanced 3.9%, year to year, as 19% higher automotive original equipment sales outweighed a 13% drop in replacement shipments. Total income from operations increased 8.9%. Net income increased 22%, to $1.02 a share, from $0.76 (as restated, before special charges of $1.74).

Common Share Earnings ($)

Quarter:	1993	1992	1991	1990
Mar.	0.28	0.09	d0.16	0.01
Jun.	0.74	0.67	0.30	0.48
Sep.	E0.25	0.51	0.32	0.43
Dec.	E0.53	0.43	0.29	0.43
	E1.80	1.70	0.75	1.35

Important Developments

Sep. '93— ARV said that third quarter earnings would be below 1992's third quarter because European original equipment catalytic converter sales were running below plan and due to costs related to recent consolidations and joint ventures. ARV still expects full year 1993 earnings to exceed those of 1992.

Jul. '93— ARV formed a 50%-owned joint venture with Sogefi, S.p.A. of Italy, combining their European replacement exhaust businesses: ARV's Timax Exhaust Systems division (the U.K. market leader) and Sogefi's Etablissements Rosi S.A. in France and Ansa Marmitte S.p.A. in Italy. Separately, ARV agreed to purchase 49.9% of Way Assauto, a division of IAO Industrie Riunite S.p.A. of Italy, which produces shock absorbers, MacPherson struts, rubber/metal parts and stampings.

Next earnings report expected in late October.

Per Share Data ($)

Yr. End Dec. 31	1992	1991	1990	[1]1989	[1]1988	1987	[1]1986	1985	1984	1983
Tangible Bk. Val.	**9.95**	10.44	10.22	8.34	9.75	18.36	[2]16.04	[2]14.85	[2]13.38	[2]12.05
Cash Flow	**5.14**	4.02	4.58	3.55	3.12	4.70	4.10	3.42	3.06	2.22
Earnings[3]	**1.70**	0.75	1.35	0.70	0.70	2.41	2.46	2.21	1.94	1.19
Dividends	**0.70**	0.68	0.68	0.68	0.68	0.68	0.65	0.61	0.57	0.56
Payout Ratio	**44%**	90%	50%	97%	97%	28%	26%	29%	29%	48%
Prices—High	**32¼**	26⅜	19	26¾	26¼	39¾	35	22¾	14⅞	15⅛
Low	**20⅜**	16¼	13⅜	14½	16½	14¾	19	13⅞	10⅝	8⅞
P/E Ratio—	**18–11**	35–22	14–10	38–21	38–24	16–6	14–8	10–6	8–5	13–7

Data as orig. reptd. Adj. for stk. divs. of 33⅓% Dec. 1985, 50% Dec. 1984. **1.** Reflects merger or acquisition. **2.** Includes intangibles. **3.** Bef. results of disc. opers. of +0.06 in 1991, +0.05 in 1990, -0.07 in 1989, -0.69 in 1988, bef. spec. item(s) of -1.67 in 1992. d-Deficit. E-Estimated.

Income Data (Million $)

Year Ended Dec. 31	Revs.	Oper. Inc.	% Oper. Inc. of Revs.	Cap. Exp.	Depr.	Int. Exp.	[3]Net Bef. Taxes	Eff. Tax Rate	[4]Net Inc.	% Net Inc. of Revs.	Cash Flow
1992	**1,890**	**181**	**9.6**	**101.0**	**68.9**	**40.8**	**66.5**	**40.0%**	**[5]39.9**	**2.1**	**103.0**
[1]1991	1,676	145	8.7	74.6	62.6	44.3	40.0	45.0%	22.0	1.3	76.8
1990	1,687	163	9.6	86.7	60.8	45.2	58.1	42.8%	33.2	2.0	86.3
[1,2]1989	1,541	132	8.6	85.6	53.7	42.3	36.2	45.6%	19.7	1.3	66.9
[1,2]1988	1,313	116	8.8	76.5	45.5	22.4	28.8	42.9%	16.5	1.3	58.5
1987	1,373	141	10.2	40.1	42.6	24.5	81.0	41.3%	47.6	3.5	87.3
[2]1986	996	113	11.4	30.9	27.3	11.4	76.0	45.8%	[5]41.2	4.1	68.3
1985	821	88	10.7	35.5	19.5	6.3	63.7	43.7%	35.9	4.4	55.0
1984	782	73	9.4	26.3	17.1	7.8	53.7	43.7%	30.2	3.9	46.8
1983	601	48	8.1	18.1	15.5	8.0	30.7	40.2%	18.3	3.1	33.1

Balance Sheet Data (Million $)

Dec. 31	Cash	Curr. Assets	Curr. Liab.	Curr. Ratio	Total Assets	% Ret. on Assets	Long Term Debt	Common Equity	Total Cap.	% LT Debt of Cap.	% Ret. on Equity
1992	**14.6**	**469**	**284**	**1.6**	**1,152**	**3.3**	**390**	**398**	**794**	**49.1**	**8.1**
1991	7.6	474	252	1.9	1,125	1.9	335	387	835	40.1	3.7
1990	17.2	541	338	1.6	1,193	2.9	321	386	851	37.7	6.9
1989	12.9	524	302	1.7	1,130	1.8	334	355	828	40.3	3.7
1988	22.2	497	278	1.8	1,058	1.8	345	359	780	44.2	3.6
1987	21.9	415	150	2.8	808	5.5	203	424	659	30.9	12.4
1986	30.4	419	199	2.1	803	7.2	317	259	605	52.5	16.9
1985	32.6	210	58	3.6	379	9.4	57	247	321	17.7	15.3
1984	21.0	200	71	2.8	354	8.9	64	203	284	22.5	15.5
1983	30.1	177	59	3.0	328	5.5	73	182	269	27.2	9.8

Data as orig. reptd. **1.** Excl. disc. opers. **2.** Reflects merger or acquisition. **3.** Incl. equity in earns. of nonconsol. subs. **4.** Bef. results of disc. opers. & spec. item(s). **5.** Reflects accounting change.

Business Summary

Arvin Industries is primarily a manufacturer of automotive products. Sales and profit contributions in 1992 were as follows:

	Sales	Profits
Automoti ve		
Original equipment	47%	33%
Replacement	36%	52%
Technology	11%	7%
Industrial	6%	8%

ARV supplies parts to the worldwide original equipment automotive market, including mufflers, exhaust pipes, catalytic converters, tubular manifolds, fuel filler tubes, tubeless tire valves, shock absorbers, MacPherson struts, gas springs, decorative trim parts, and coated coil steel for fabricating into body parts. Shipments to the automotive replacement market include mufflers, exhaust pipes, catalytic converters, shock absorbers, MacPherson struts, gas springs, brake and front end parts, tire valves and accessories.

The industrial segment provides tank valves, valve cores, bicycle valves, shock absorbers, pneumatic cylinders, vinyl metal laminate stampings, and precoated coils of steel and aluminum.

The company's Calspan unit, which provides research, development and testing services to the government and industrial customers in such areas as aerodynamics, automobile crash testing and accident research, aircraft systems, electronic systems analysis, and surface and laser chemistry, recently merged with Space Industries International, in which ARV now holds a 70% stake.

In 1992, 17.2% of sales were to Ford Motor Co., and 9.9% to the U.S. government. ARV also supplies General Motors, Chrysler and foreign-owned automakers. Foreign operations accounted for 38% of sales and 39% of profits in 1992.

Dividend Data

Dividends have been paid since 1925.

Amt of Divd. $	Date Decl.	Ex-divd. Date	Stock of Record	Payment Date
0.19	Nov. 12	Dec. 14	Dec. 18	Dec. 31'92
0.19	Feb. 11	Mar. 8	Mar. 12	Mar. 31'93
0.19	Apr. 8	Jun. 7	Jun. 11	Jun. 30'93
0.19	Sep. 9	Sep. 14	Sep. 20	Sep. 30'93

Capitalization

Long Term Debt: $388,588,000 (6/93), incl. $97.5 million of debs. conv. into com. stock.

Minority Interest: $4,066,000

Common Stock: 21,771,619 shs. ($2.50 par).
Institutions hold 59%.
Shareholders of record: 6,141.

Office—One Noblitt Plaza, Columbus, IN 47202-3000. **Tel**—(812) 379-3000. **Chrmn**—J. K. Baker. **Pres**—B. O. Pond. **VP & Secy**—R. R. Snyder. **VP-Fin & CFO**—R. A. Smith **Investor Contact**—John W. Brown. **Dirs**—J. P. Allen, J. K. Baker, S. C. Beering, J. P. Flannery, R. E. Fowler, Jr., R. W. Hanselman, T. A. Holmes, V. W. Hunt, D. J. Kacek, F. R. Meyer, B. O. Pond, R. M. Ringoen, R. A. Smith. **Transfer Agent & Registrar**—Harris Trust & Savings Bank, Chicago. **Incorporated** in Indiana in 1921. **Empl**—16,002.

 Joshua M. Harari, CFA

Atlanta Gas Light

NYSE Symbol ATG In S&P MidCap 400

Price	Range	P-E Ratio	Dividend	Yield	S&P Ranking	Beta
Sep. 29'93	1993					
38¼	42½–36½	17	2.08	5.4%	A–	0.35

Summary

This natural gas utility serves the principal industrial and metropolitan areas of Georgia, including Atlanta and Savannah, distributing about three-fourths of the natural gas consumed in the state. Long-term prospects are enhanced by an expected continuation of an above-average customer growth rate and the development of nontraditional gas markets. As a result of a recent disappointing rate increase award the company's string of consecutive annual dividend increases is expected to end in 1993.

Current Outlook

Share earnings for the fiscal year ending September 30, 1994, are projected at $2.25, up from an estimated $2.15 for fiscal 1993.

The disappointing rate decision in September 1993 is expected to result in the $0.52 quarterly dividend being maintained at the November meeting.

Utility profits are expected to increase slightly in fiscal 1994, reflecting some improvement in margins and higher gas deliveries. Margins are expected to benefit from the $11,166,000 (1.1%) rate hike; the disappointment in the size of the rate increase is likely to lead to significant cost-control measures. The customer growth rate should continue at an above-average 2.5%, as preparations for the 1996 Summer Olympics (to be held in Atlanta) should aid Atlanta's economy. The development of nontraditional gas markets, such as natural gas vehicles and gas air conditioning, is expected to enhance gas sales volume in the long-term, but growth in these markets is likely to affect gas sales in fiscal 1994 only slightly.

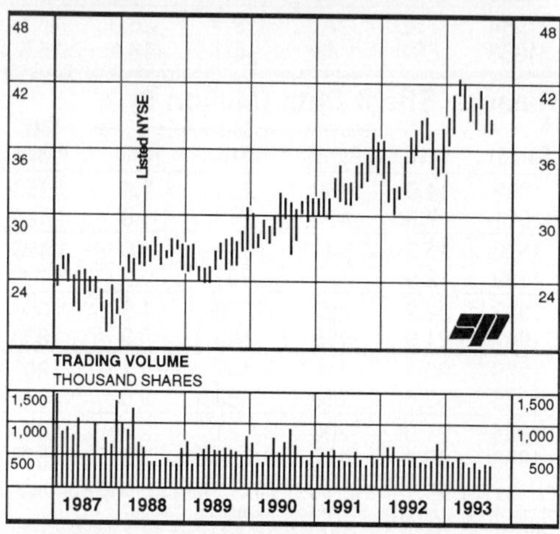

Operating Revenues (Million $)

Quarter:	1992–93	1991–92	1990–91	1989–90
Dec.	334	300	295	335
Mar.	448	395	379	375
Jun.	198	176	159	158
Sep.	---	123	130	133
	---	995	964	1,001

Revenues in the nine months ended June 30, 1993, rose 12%, year to year, on a 16% increase in gas costs (increases in gas costs are largely passed on to customers in the form of higher rates), and higher gas deliveries. Penalized by higher operating expenses, income from operations was up 1.0%. Following lower interest expenses, net income was up 3.5%. After higher preferred dividends, share earnings declined to $2.52, from $2.58.

Common Share Earnings ($)

Quarter:	1992–93	1991–92	1990–91	1989–90
Dec.	0.87	0.88	1.05	0.98
Mar.	1.79	1.79	1.47	1.63
Jun.	d0.14	d0.08	d0.11	d0.11
Sep.	Ed0.37	d0.31	d0.30	d0.46
	E2.15	2.26	2.07	2.02

Important Developments

Sep. '93— The Georgia Public Service Commission granted ATG a $11.2 million (1.1%) rate increase, effective October 1. The company orginally had filed for a $62.5 million rate hike, but reduced its request to about $47.0 million to include adjustments proposed by the commission's adversary staff, including a phase-in for postretirement benefit costs. The allowed rate of return was cut from 11.6% to 11.0%. The company planned to request the commission to reconsider its decision and appeal the decision to the courts.

Next earnings report expected in early November.

Per Share Data ($)

Yr. End Sep. 30	1992	1991	1990	1989	1988	1987	1986	1985	1984	1983
Tangible Bk. Val.	**20.91**	20.27	19.26	18.75	18.30	16.47	16.74	15.89	15.62	14.65
Earnings[1]	**2.26**	2.07	2.02	1.90	2.25	2.04	1.66	1.82	2.25	1.56
Dividends	**2.060**	2.040	1.960	1.880	1.760	1.600	1.400	1.260	1.075	0.960
Payout Ratio	**91%**	99%	97%	99%	78%	78%	84%	69%	48%	62%
Prices[2]—High	**39**	37⅝	32⅛	30¾	28	26⅜	24¼	19	14½	10⅜
Low	**30¼**	29¾	26½	23⅞	21½	19⅜	18½	14	9⅝	7⅞
P/E Ratio—	**17–13**	18–14	16–13	16–13	12–10	13–9	15–11	10–8	6–4	7–5

Data as orig. reptd. Adj. for stk. div. of 100% Dec. 1986. **1.** Bef. spec. item(s) of +0.15 in 1988, +0.36 in 1984. **2.** Cal. yr. d-Deficit. E-Estimated.

Income Data (Million $)

Year Ended Sep. 30	Revs.	Depr.	Maint.	Oper. Ratio	[1]Fxd. Chgs. Cover.	Constr. Credits	Eff. Tax Rate	[2]Net Inc.	% Return On Revs.	% Return On [3]Invest. Capital	% Return On [4]Com. Equity
1992	**995**	**54.9**	**29.5**	**89.9%**	**2.66**	**2.90**	**26.4%**	**55.4**	**5.6**	**9.6**	**11.8**
1991	964	50.2	28.6	90.2%	2.55	2.98	34.8%	49.4	5.1	9.1	11.4
1990	1,001	46.3	28.1	90.7%	2.47	1.25	31.7%	45.6	4.6	9.2	11.4
1989	939	43.2	25.3	91.7%	1.94	0.87	27.7%	42.1	4.5	8.9	10.8
1988	976	36.1	24.0	92.5%	2.30	4.98	31.8%	46.0	4.7	9.3	14.2
1987	983	31.2	22.4	93.3%	2.18	4.45	47.6%	39.4	4.0	9.3	13.2
1986	1,008	28.1	21.3	94.0%	1.76	1.11	46.0%	29.2	2.9	9.4	11.0
1985	1,165	24.9	18.0	95.2%	1.86	1.26	46.7%	29.7	2.5	10.6	13.7
1984	1,226	22.2	16.4	95.7%	1.89	0.87	47.7%	29.6	2.4	11.7	16.7
1983	1,114	21.0	15.0	96.5%	1.54	0.55	41.0%	18.0	1.6	9.9	11.9

Balance Sheet Data (Million $)

Sep. 30	[5]Gross Prop.	Capital Expend.	Net Prop.	% Earn. on Net Prop.	Total Cap.	LT Debt	% LT Debt	Capitalization Pfd.	% Pfd.	Com.	% Com.
1992	**1,679**	**132**	**1,202**	**8.6**	**1,019**	**326**	**40.2**	**14.2**	**1.7**	**472**	**58.1**
1991	1,559	141	1,123	8.8	1,113	456	49.6	14.5	1.6	448	48.8
1990	1,433	122	1,033	9.3	1,013	418	50.2	16.8	2.0	397	47.8
1989	1,331	162	962	8.7	950	369	47.9	18.0	2.3	383	49.8
1988	1,156	126	845	9.1	945	379	49.3	19.3	2.5	370	48.2
1987	1,036	139	758	9.4	756	271	46.2	20.5	3.5	296	50.3
1986	905	121	652	10.0	736	292	49.4	21.8	3.7	277	47.9
1985	790	95	561	10.7	616	243	49.8	23.1	4.7	222	45.5
1984	700	79	492	11.8	518	198	48.6	24.9	6.1	184	45.3
1983	628	57	437	9.2	488	218	55.6	26.9	6.9	147	37.5

Data as orig. reptd. **1.** Times int. exp. & pfd. divs. covered (aft. taxes). **2.** Bef. spec. item in 1988, 1984. **3.** Based on income before interest charges. **4.** As reptd. by Co. **5.** Utility plant.

Business Summary

Atlanta Gas Light is the largest gas distribution utility in the Southeast, serving more than 1.2 million customers in 227 cities and communities in Georgia, and through its Chattanooga Gas Co. subsidiary serving over 40,000 customers in Chattanooga and Cleveland, Tenn. Operating revenues by customer group in recent fiscal years were:

	1992	1991	1990
Residential	58%	57%	56%
Commercial	23%	23%	24%
Industrial	14%	15%	16%
Trans. & other	5%	5%	4%

Gas transported and sold in fiscal 1992 totaled 2,696 million therms, up from 2,540 million therms in fiscal 1991. An average of 1,248,400 customers were served during fiscal 1992, up from 1,218,500 in fiscal 1991.

The company's major gas suppliers, Southern Natural Gas Co., Transcontinental Gas Pipe Line, South Georgia Natural Gas and East Tennessee Natural Gas, provide for daily supply of 760,206 Mcf of pipeline gas. Supplemental gas supplies include underground storage, and liquefied natural gas. Throughput on ATG's system during fiscal 1992 consisted of 30% spot market gas, 37% traditional supplies and 33% transportation of customer-owned gas.

Other activities include the sale and installation of gas appliances, appliance service work; gas production; the sale of propane; and real estate development. Nonutility income totaled $1.8 million in fiscal 1992.

Variations in revenues due to abnormal weather during the heating season are largely offset by a weather normalization adjustment in rates.

Dividend Data

Dividends have been paid in each year since 1939. A dividend reinvestment plan is available.

Amt of Divd. $	Date Decl.	Ex-divd. Date	Stock of Record	Payment Date
0.52	Nov. 6	Nov. 16	Nov. 20	Dec. 1'92
0.52	Feb. 5	Feb. 12	Feb. 19	Mar. 1'93
0.52	May 7	May 17	May 21	Jun. 1'93
0.52	Aug. 6	Aug. 16	Aug. 20	Sep. 1'93

Capitalization

Long Term Debt: $516,000,000 (6/93).

Preferred Stock: $58,700,000.

Common Stock: 24,719,811 shs. ($5 par).
Institutions hold 20%.
Shareholders: 17,916.

Office—235 Peachtree St, N.E., Atlanta, GA 30303. **Tel**—(404) 584-4000. **Pres & CEO**—D. R. Jones. **Secy & Treas**—K. R. McKinley. **SVP-Fin, CFO & Investor Contact**—Robert L. Goocher. **Dirs**—F. Barron, Jr., W. W. Bradley, O. A. Brumby, Jr., L. L. Gellerstedt, Jr., D. R. Jones, K. D. Lewis, A. G. Norman, Jr., D. R. Riddle, B. L. Siegel, B. J. Tarbutton, Jr., C. M. Taylor, F. W. Ward, Jr. **Transfer Agent & Registrar**—Wachovia Bank of North Carolina, Winston-Salem. **Incorporated** in Georgia in 1856. **Empl**—3,748.

 Mark Mattke

Atlantic Southeast Airlines

NASDAQ Symbol ASAI (Incl. in Nat'l Market) Options on CBOE In S&P MidCap 400

Price	Range	P-E Ratio	Dividend	Yield	S&P Ranking	Beta
Sep. 3'93	1993					
28¼	39–20⅞	25	0.28	1.0%	B+	1.66

Summary

This regional air carrier provides regularly scheduled, high-frequency commuter service from hubs in Atlanta and Dallas/Ft. Worth. It is a member of the "Delta Connection" marketing program; Delta Air Lines has a 24% interest in the company. Atlantic Southeast has been consistently profitable, with operating margins among the highest in the industry. Operations at Dallas/Ft. Worth are being expanded substantially, which should boost earnings in 1993 and 1994.

Earnings for 1993 are estimated at $1.50 a share, up from 1992's $1.09 (as adjusted). A gain to $2.00 is projected for 1994.

The quarterly dividend should continue at least at the current $0.07 rate.

Revenues are expected to climb more than 15% in 1993. Traffic should continue to benefit from relatively good regional conditions. Expansion of operations at the DFW hub through new routes using the 66-seat ATR72 should boost traffic during the second half of 1993. Yields will benefit from less extreme fare discounting than in mid-1992. Margins will continue to reflect highly successful cost-containment efforts, which cut operating expense per seat-mile 2.4% during 1992.

Total Oper. Revenues (Million $)

Quarter:	1993	1992	1991	1990
Mar.	64.5	57.6	51.5	44.4
Jun.	69.9	57.5	58.2	48.7
Sep.	---	58.1	56.9	47.9
Dec.	---	62.3	55.3	46.2
	---	235.6	221.9	187.2

For the first six months of 1993, total operating revenues advanced 17% year to year. Operating expenses rose more rapidly, holding the gain in pretax income to 11%. After taxes at 37.5%, versus 38.0%, income was up 12%. Share earnings increased to $0.59 (before a credit of $0.12 from an accounting change), from $0.53 (as adjusted).

Common Share Earnings ($)

Quarter:	1993	1992	1991	1990
Mar.	0.21	0.24	0.20	0.17
Jun.	0.38	0.29	0.29	0.24
Sep.	E0.50	0.27	0.26	0.20
Dec.	E0.41	0.29	0.20	0.13
	E1.50	1.09	0.95	0.73

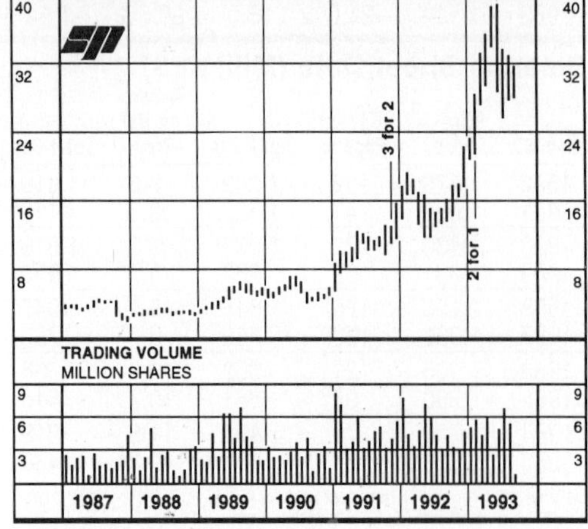

Important Developments

Jul. '93— The company inaugarated service from Dallas/Fort Worth to Lubbock, Amarillo, Oklahoma City and Wichita. Earlier, in June, service began to Corpus Christi and Tulsa. Service to Houston and San Antonio will start in October. New operations also include service from Atlanta to Jackson and Louisville, which began in April.

Apr. '93— ASA said 1993 first quarter share earnings were reduced by $0.18 for an accrual for the company's stock appreciation rights plan, reflecting a jump of about 50% in the common stock price during the first quarter of 1993.

Jul. '92— Directors authorized the repurchase of up to $15 million of the company's common stock through December 31, 1993.

Next earnings report expected in late October.

Per Share Data ($)

Yr. End Dec. 31	1992	1991	1990	1989	1988	1987	1986	1985	1984	1 1983
Tangible Bk. Val.	**5.14**	4.25	3.47	2.97	2.38	2.11	1.83	0.77	0.45	0.28
Cash Flow	**1.86**	1.70	1.38	1.29	0.74	0.57	0.47	0.44	0.23	0.13
Earnings	**1.09**	0.95	0.73	0.76	0.31	0.28	0.29	0.32	0.17	0.06
Dividends	**0.240**	0.200	0.159	0.080	Nil	Nil	Nil	Nil	Nil	Nil
Payout Ratio	**22%**	21%	21%	11%	Nil	Nil	Nil	Nil	Nil	Nil
Prices—High	**22⅜**	15¾	7⁹⁄₁₆	6⁹⁄₁₆	3⁹⁄₁₆	4⅝	5⅛	5½	1⁷⁄₁₆	1⅞
Low	**11¾**	5½	4	2⅞	2½	1¹⁵⁄₁₆	3¼	1¼	⅝	¹³⁄₁₆
P/E Ratio—	**21–11**	16–6	10–6	9–4	12–8	16–7	18–11	17–4	9–4	32–13

Data as orig. reptd. Adj. for stk. divs. of 100% Feb. 1993, 50% Nov. 1991, 33⅓% Aug. 1985, 100% Apr. 1985, 50% Nov. 1984. **1.** Refl. merger or acq. E-Estimated.

Income Data (Million $)

Year Ended Dec. 31	Revs.	Oper. Inc.	% Oper. Inc. of Revs.	Cap. Exp.	Depr.	Int. Exp.	Net Bef. Taxes	Eff. Tax Rate	Net Inc.	% Net Inc. of Revs.	Cash Flow
1992	**236**	**87.2**	**37.0**	**57.9**	**26.4**	**6.33**	**59.3**	**37.5%**	**37.1**	**15.7**	**63.4**
1991	222	78.0	35.1	52.1	25.4	7.01	51.6	37.0%	32.5	14.6	57.9
1990	187	62.6	33.4	52.6	22.7	6.51	41.0	38.1%	25.4	13.6	48.1
1989	180	63.2	35.1	53.2	19.3	5.91	44.5	38.0%	27.6	15.3	46.9
1988	137	35.5	25.9	35.4	16.2	5.29	18.6	38.0%	11.5	8.4	27.7
1987	119	30.0	25.7	84.6	11.3	3.96	18.0	37.5%	11.3	9.5	22.6
1986	92	24.9	27.0	39.7	6.4	2.56	18.3	42.5%	10.5	11.4	16.9
1985	75	19.0	25.2	35.3	3.8	1.09	15.1	31.6%	10.3	13.7	14.1
1984	44	12.8	29.2	2.9	2.1	1.16	10.3	48.4%	5.3	12.1	7.4
[1]1983	24	5.3	22.2	2.0	2.0	1.52	2.2	17.2%	1.8	7.6	3.8

Balance Sheet Data (Million $)

Dec. 31	Cash	Curr. Assets	Curr. Liab.	Curr. Ratio	Total Assets	% Ret. on Assets	Long Term Debt	Common Equity	Total Cap.	% LT Debt of Cap.	% Ret. on Equity
1992	**133**	**146**	**52.5**	**2.8**	**431**	**9.2**	**146**	**179**	**378**	**38.6**	**22.7**
1991	111	124	45.3	2.7	378	9.2	139	148	332	42.0	24.1
1990	88	99	39.1	2.5	325	8.5	128	120	286	44.6	22.7
1989	80	91	35.9	2.5	288	10.9	112	108	252	44.3	28.2
1988	58	68	25.7	2.6	231	5.4	90	92	205	44.0	13.3
1987	47	65	23.2	2.8	208	6.5	82	85	185	44.3	14.1
1986	53	65	14.6	4.4	144	8.7	40	77	129	31.0	18.7
1985	14	26	14.3	1.8	78	17.9	28	29	63	45.0	44.2
1984	11	17	9.4	1.9	38	16.2	7	18	29	25.7	34.1
1983	4	8	5.5	1.5	28	6.4	9	13	22	39.7	17.1

Data as orig. reptd. **1.** Refl. merger or acq.

Business Summary

Atlantic Southeast Airlines (ASA) is a regional air carrier that provides regularly scheduled, high-frequency commuter service from hubs in Atlanta and Dallas/Ft. Worth. As of March 1993, service was provided between Hartsfield Atlanta International Airport in Atlanta, Ga., and 36 other airports, in Georgia, Alabama, Florida, Indiana, Kentucky, North Carolina, South Carolina, Mississippi, Tennessee, Virginia and West Virginia. A similar hub-and-spoke operation from the Dallas/Ft. Worth International Airport served 15 other airports in Texas, Louisiana, Oklahoma and Arkansas.

Operating data for recent years were:

	1992	1991
Rev. passenger-miles (000s)	547,000	501,000
Available seat-miles (000s) .	1,077,000	1,020,000
Passenger load factor.........	50.8%	49.2%

As part of the "Delta Connection" program, ASA offers passengers connections and through-fares to major cities served by Delta from Atlanta and Dallas/Ft. Worth. During 1992, 80% of the company's passengers made connecting flights to other destinations; the remaining 20% originated or terminated their air travel in Atlanta or Dallas/Ft. Worth.

As of March 1993, the fleet consisted of 71 turboprop aircraft: 58 Embraer Brasilias (30-passenger capacity), two deHavilland Dash 7s (48-passenger) and 11 Embraer Bandeirantes (15-passenger).

Dividend Data

Cash payments were initiated in 1989.

Amt. of Divd. $	Date Decl.	Ex-divd. Date	Stock of Record	Payment Date
0.12	Oct. 28	Nov. 24	Dec. 1	Dec. 15'92
2-for-1 Split	Jan. 22	Feb. 19	Feb. 4	Feb. 18'93
0.07	Jan. 22	Feb. 23	Mar. 1	Mar. 15'93
0.07	May 20	May 25	Jun. 1	Jun. 15'93
0.07	Jul. 28	Aug. 26	Sep. 1	Sep. 15'93

Finances

In February 1993, the company agreed to acquire eight 66-passenger ATR72 turboprop aircraft during 1993, and took options on 20 additional ATR72s. It received operating lease financing from the manufacturer for the first eight planes.

Capitalization

Long Term Debt: $145,478,000 (3/93).

Common Stock: 34,333,812 shs. ($0.10 par).
Delta Air Lines owns 24%.
Institutions hold 59%.
Shareholders: 1,082 of record (3/93).

Office—100 Hartsfield Centre Parkway, Suite 800, Atlanta, GA 30354. **Tel**—(404) 766-1400. **Chrmn**—A. M. Voorhees. **Pres & CEO**—G. F. Pickett, Jr. **VP, Treas & CFO**—R. V. Sapp. **SVP, Secy & Investor Contact**—John W. Beiser. **Dirs**—J. W. Beiser, R. W. Coggin, J. P. Gwin, P. H. Petit, G. F. Pickett, Jr., A. M. Voorhees, R. W. Voorhees. **Transfer Agent & Registrar**—Trust Co. Bank, Atlanta. **Incorporated** in Georgia in 1979. **Empl**—1,755.

 T. M. Canning, CFA

Atlantic Energy

NYSE Symbol ATE In S&P MidCap 400

Price	Range	P-E Ratio	Dividend	Yield	S&P Ranking	Beta
Sep. 9'93	1993					
25	25⅛–21⅝	17	1.54	6.2%	A–	0.44

Summary

This utility holding company owns Atlantic City Electric, which supplies electricity to more than 455,000 customers in a 2,700 square mile area encompassing the southern third of New Jersey. Power generation is primarily coal and nuclear. A modest increase in earnings is expected in 1993 owing to a rate increase that became effective in late 1992. The continued loss of industrial customers to cogeneration plants could hinder earnings growth.

Current Outlook

Share earnings for 1993 are estimated at $1.75, up slightly from 1992's $1.67. Earnings for 1994 are projected at $1.75 a share.

Directors raised the quarterly cash dividend 1.3%, to $0.38½, from $0.38, with the July payment.

Earnings are projected to rise modestly in 1993, reflecting a $4.46 million rate increase which became effective in October 1992, pending rate requests and slightly lower interest expense resulting from refinancing $150 million of long term debt. Profitability will be limited by the loss of two large industrial customers and the prospective loss of others due to the development of independent power projects. As a result of soft economic conditions in the company's service area, kilowatt-hour sales growth will be limited. A sluggish regional economy has allowed the company to reduce its planned construction expenditures by 25%, and prudent cost controls will help earnings.

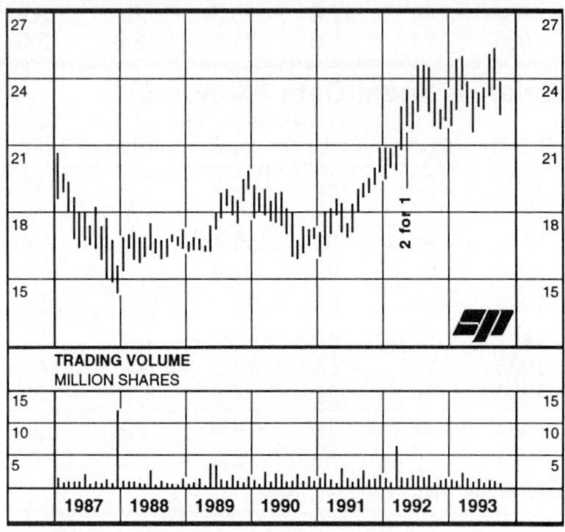

Operating Revenues (Million $)

Quarter:	1994	1993	1992	1991
Mar.	---	203.7	197.8	170.9
Jun.	---	192.5	187.4	175.7
Sep.	---	---	236.9	250.4
Dec.	---	---	194.7	181.0
	---	---	816.8	778.0

Operating revenues in the six months ended June 30, 1993, rose 2.8%, year to year, reflecting an increase in power sales. In the absence of a $0.15 contribution from the settlement of litigation, net income was off 20%. Share earnings fell to $0.59, on 2.5% more shares, from $0.76 (adjusted).

Common Share Earnings ($)

Quarter:	1994	1993	1992	1991
Mar.	E0.40	0.38	0.55	0.18
Jun.	E0.20	0.21	0.21	0.22
Sep.	E0.90	E0.91	0.76	1.08
Dec.	E0.25	E0.25	0.15	0.23
	1.75	E1.75	1.67	1.75

Important Developments

Mar. '93— ATE filed a petition with the New Jersey Board of Regulatory Commissioners requesting a $14.2 million increase in Levelized Energy Clause revenues for the period June 1, 1993 through May 31, 1994. ATE's request is based on a projected increase in fuel and energy costs and a reduction of the prior periods unrecovered energy costs currently being returned to ratepayers. Also included in ATE's request are: (1) an estimated payment of $569,000 expected to be made in October 1993 for ATE's assessment for the Department of Energy decommissioning and decontamination fund as required by the Energy Policy Act of 1992; and (2) a $48,000 penalty for 1992 nuclear operations as required by the Nuclear Performance Standard. A decision on this appeal is expected by January 1994. ATE cannot predict the outcome of this matter at this time.

Next earnings report expected in late October.

Per Share Data ($)

Yr. End Dec. 31	1992	1991	1990	1989	1988	1987	1986	1985	1984	1983
Tangible Bk. Val.	**14.50**	14.15	13.57	13.43	12.65	11.75	11.63	11.70	11.54	10.68
Earnings	**1.67**	1.75	1.51	1.87	1.84	2.02	1.75	1.50	1.60	1.74
Dividends	**1.515**	1.495	1.470	1.425	1.370	1.358	1.305	1.278	1.225	1.160
Payout Ratio	**91%**	86%	97%	76%	74%	67%	75%	85%	77%	67%
Prices—High	**24⅝**	20¹⁵⁄₁₆	19¼	19⅞	17½	20¹¹⁄₁₆	23⁵⁄₁₆	14⅞	12½	12¹⁵⁄₁₆
Low	**19½**	16	15¹⁵⁄₁₆	16¼	15⅜	14⅜	14⅛	11⅞	9¹⁵⁄₁₆	10³⁄₁₆
P/E Ratio—	**15–12**	12–9	13–11	11–9	10–8	10–7	13–8	10–8	8–6	7–6

Data as orig. reptd. Adj. for stk. div. of 100% May 1992. E-Estimated

Income Data (Million $)

Year Ended Dec. 31	Revs.	Depr.	Maint.	Oper. Ratio	[1]Fxd. Chgs. Cover.	Constr. Credits	Eff. Tax Rate	Net Inc.	% Return On Revs.	[2]Invest. Capital	Com. Equity
1992	**817**	**69.4**	**49.8**	**83.2%**	**2.70**	**3.8**	**30.4%**	**86.2**	**10.6**	**8.0**	**11.1**
1991	778	66.0	52.0	81.4%	2.79	4.9	26.5%	85.6	11.0	8.4	12.1
1990	717	62.1	52.4	82.6%	2.47	4.0	26.1%	68.9	9.6	7.8	10.6
1989	705	58.5	55.2	80.9%	2.75	2.8	20.6%	81.0	11.5	9.0	13.6
1988	676	54.8	59.6	81.8%	2.79	3.2	24.6%	72.2	10.7	9.3	14.2
1987	648	51.1	51.9	82.3%	3.43	3.2	38.4%	73.8	11.4	9.8	16.1
1986	583	42.5	44.8	83.6%	3.35	17.0	35.3%	69.6	11.9	8.9	13.9
1985	580	42.0	43.4	84.6%	3.16	11.2	37.5%	60.5	10.4	8.5	12.3
1984	550	38.3	39.2	83.4%	3.36	10.8	39.8%	63.3	11.5	9.2	13.4
1983	517	38.4	35.1	82.0%	3.74	9.2	42.6%	66.2	12.8	10.0	15.1

Balance Sheet Data (Million $)

Dec. 31	[3]Gross Prop.	[4]Capital Expend.	Net Prop.	% Earn. on Net Prop.	Total Cap.	Capitalization [5]LT Debt	[5]% LT Debt	Pfd.	% Pfd.	Com.	% Com.
1992	**2,281**	**131**	**1,682**	**8.3**	**2,036**	**680**	**40.0**	**230**	**13.5**	**792**	**46.5**
1991	2,176	172	1,630	9.2	1,919	618	38.5	231	14.4	755	47.1
1990	2,027	167	1,523	8.6	1,753	633	43.5	162	11.2	660	45.3
1989	1,846	145	1,387	10.1	1,668	639	45.8	113	8.1	643	46.1
1988	1,713	127	1,293	9.8	1,455	545	45.3	114	9.5	544	45.2
1987	1,603	102	1,214	9.7	1,291	526	49.8	59	5.5	472	44.7
1986	1,490	92	1,139	8.6	1,256	495	48.1	66	6.4	469	45.5
1985	1,407	94	1,076	8.6	1,151	437	45.3	76	7.8	452	46.9
1984	1,310	85	1,010	9.3	1,098	412	44.1	91	9.7	433	46.2
1983	1,226	74	951	10.0	1,018	380	43.1	94	10.7	407	46.2

Data as orig. reptd. **1.** Times int. exp. & pfd. divs. covered (pretax basis). **2.** Based on income bef. interest charges. **3.** Electric utility plant. **4.** Cash. **5.** Incl. capital lease oblig.

Business Summary

Atlantic Energy is the holding company formed in 1987 by Atlantic City Electric to facilitate diversification into nonutility businesses. Atlantic City Electric (ACE) supplies electricity in a 2,700 square mile area in southern New Jersey with a population of about 1,000,000. The territory includes a resort area along the Atlantic Seaboard and an industrial section in the Delaware River Valley, separated by an agricultural belt. Contributions by class of customers in recent years:

	1992	1991	1990	1989
Residential	47%	47%	47%	48%
Commercial	39%	38%	38%	37%
Industrial	13%	14%	14%	14%
Other	1%	1%	1%	1%

In 1992, ACE sold 7,655,137 mwh of electricity, down 3.5% from 1991. Coal and nuclear energy together provided about 59% of the utility's energy requirements in 1992. ACE is a co-owner of the Hope Creek (5.0% interest), Salem (7.41%), and Peach Bottom (7.51%) nuclear stations.

Atlantic Generation, Inc. is engaged in the development of cogeneration power projects. ATE Investment, Inc. manages capital investments for the company. Atlantic Southern Properties owns, develops and manages commercial real estate.

Finances

Construction expenditures for the 1993-1995 period have been estimated at $408.4 million, including $142.5 million for 1993. These estimates reflect funds needed to comply with the Clean Air Act Amendments of 1990, and $44.8 million of current commitments for the construction of major production and transmission facilities in 1993.

Dividend Data

Dividends have been paid since 1919. A dividend reinvestment plan is available.

Amt of Divd. $	Date Decl.	Ex-divd. Date	Stock of Record	Payment Date
0.38	Dec. 10	Dec. 15	Dec. 21	Jan. 15'93
0.38	Mar. 11	Mar. 16	Mar. 22	Apr. 15'93
0.38½	Jun. 10	Jun. 15	Jun. 21	Jul. 15'93
0.38½	Sep. 9	Sep. 14	Sep. 20	Oct. 15'93

Capitalization

Long Term Debt: $662,356,000 (3/93).

Subsid. Red. Cum. Preferred Stock: $190,250,000.

Subsid. Cum. Preferred Stock: $40,000,000.

Common Stock: 52,706,087 shs. ($3 par).
Institutions hold about 20%.
Shareholders of record: 46,524.

Office—6801 Black Horse Pike, Pleasantville, NJ 08232. **Tel**—(609) 645-4500. **Chrmn, Pres & CEO**—J. L. Jacobs. **VP-Treas & CFO**—J. G. Salomone. **Secy & Investor Contact**—S. M. McMillian. **Dirs**—J. M. Galvin Jr., G. A. Hale, M. Holden Jr., C. H. Holley, E. D. Huggard, J. L. Jacobs, K. MacDonnell, R. B. McGlynn, B. J. Morgan, H. J. Ravaché. **Transfer Agent & Registrar**—Company's office. **Incorporated** in New Jersey in 1907. **Empl**—2,023.

 Ned Bancroft

Avnet, Inc.

NYSE Symbol AVT Options on ASE (Feb-May-Aug-Nov) In S&P MidCap 400

Price	Range	P-E Ratio	Dividend	Yield	S&P Ranking	Beta
Sep. 2'93	1993					
40¼	41¾–29	21	0.60	1.5%	B+	0.85

Summary

Avnet is one of the world's largest distributors of electronic components and computer products. It also produces or distributes other electronic, electrical and video communications products. An aggressive program of acquisitions both in the U.S. and in Europe is being pursued. Following lower earnings in fiscal 1992, higher earnings were reported for fiscal 1993 due to strong growth in the semiconductor industry, less pressure on prices and contributions from recent acquisitions. Further growth is likely in fiscal 1994 as industry conditions continue to strengthen.

Current Outlook

Earnings for the fiscal year ending June 30, 1994, are expected to increase to $2.30 a share from the $1.91 reported for fiscal 1993.

Continuation of the $0.15 quarterly dividend is the minimum expectation.

Sales for fiscal 1994 are likely to increase significantly, due to strong growth in the semiconductor industry and acquisitions, including the purchase of Hall-Mark Electronics Corp. In addition, electronic marketing is benefiting from suppliers putting more of their sales through distributors, which particularly benefits Avnet because it has the technical abilities to provide field service. Recent acquisitions in the distribution industry have also allowed Avnet to obtain new suppliers because suppliers want to avoid using the same distributor as certain competitors. Margins should benefit from the higher volume, well-controlled costs and less price competition. The acquisition of Hall-Mark Electronics would also produce economies of scale that would further benefit margins.

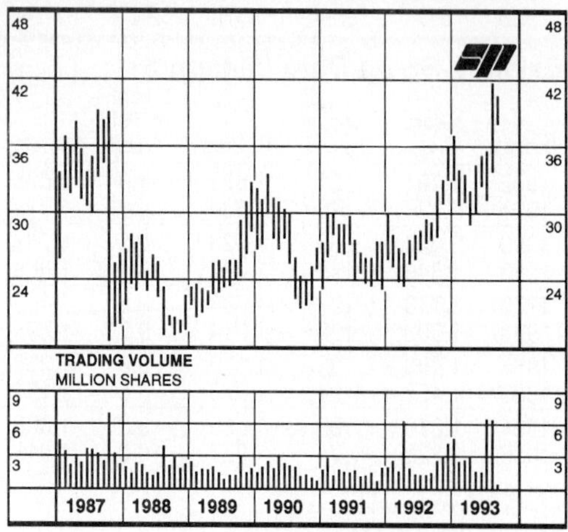

Net Sales (Million $)

Quarter:	1993–94	1992–93	1991–92	1990–91
Sep.	---	533	413	439
Dec.	---	527	415	436
Mar.	---	583	426	436
Jun.	---	596	505	431
	---	2,238	1,759	1,741

Sales for the fiscal year ended June 30, 1993 (preliminary), increased 27% from those of fiscal 1992, reflecting a 19% gain from continuing operations and $150 million in revenues from recently acquired French, Scandinavian and German operations. Despite a $1.15 million ($0.03 a share) charge to shutdown the video group's Far Eastern operations, margins widened on the higher volume, and pretax income increased 37. After taxes at 39.5%, versus 39.4%, net income was up 37%, to $1.91 a share from $1.42.

Common Share Earnings ($)

Quarter:	1993–94	1992–93	1991–92	1990–91
Sep.	E0.52	0.47	0.31	0.49
Dec.	E0.55	0.43	0.33	0.43
Mar.	E0.60	0.50	0.35	0.41
Jun.	E0.63	0.51	0.43	0.39
	E2.30	1.91	1.42	1.72

Important Developments

Jul. '93— AVT acquired Hall-Mark Electronics Corp., another electronics distributor with sales of $695 million and income before extraordinary items of $21.5 million in 1992. Each of Hall-Mark's approximately 10.1 million common shares was automatically converted into the right to receive $20 in cash plus 0.45 of a share of AVT common stock.

Next earnings report expected in early November.

Per Share Data ($)

Yr. End Jun. 30	1993	1992	[1]1991	1990	1989	1988	1987	1986	1985	1984
Tangible Bk. Val.	**NA**	22.60	21.83	20.93	20.05	18.89	17.78	17.53	17.25	16.35
Cash Flow	**NA**	2.09	2.25	2.20	2.34	2.28	1.40	1.34	1.90	2.76
Earnings	**1.91**	1.42	1.72	1.57	1.51	1.46	0.64	0.67	1.39	2.44
Dividends	**0.45**	0.60	0.60	0.60	0.50	0.50	0.50	0.50	0.50	0.50
Payout Ratio	**24%**	42%	35%	38%	33%	34%	78%	75%	36%	20%
Prices[2]—High	**41¾**	36	30	33½	32¾	28⅛	39¼	40⅜	38¼	49⅛
Low	**29**	23½	23¼	21½	20⅝	19	18½	25	27	27
P/E Ratio—	**22–15**	25–17	17–14	21–14	22–14	19–13	61–29	60–37	28–19	20–11

Data as orig. reptd. Adj. for stk. div. of 100% Feb. 1983. **1.** Refl. merger or acq. **2.** Cal. yr. NA-Not Available.

Income Data (Million $)

Year Ended Jun. 30	Revs.	Oper. Inc.	% Oper. Inc. of Revs.	Cap. Exp.	Depr.	Int. Exp.	Net Bef. Taxes	Eff. Tax Rate	Net Inc.	% Net Inc. of Revs.	Cash Flow
1992	**1,759**	**94**	**5.3**	**25.1**	**24.0**	**13.4**	**83**	**39.4%**	**50.5**	**2.9**	**75**
[1]1991	1,741	111	6.4	20.4	24.8	13.3	100	38.4%	61.6	3.5	86
1990	1,751	127	7.2	17.4	28.5	15.3	99	42.8%	56.5	3.2	85
1989	1,919	119	6.2	22.6	29.8	16.4	87	38.2%	54.0	2.8	84
1988	1,817	119	6.6	24.7	29.2	16.0	86	39.5%	52.2	2.9	81
1987	1,539	77	5.0	47.3	27.3	11.2	47	51.1%	22.8	1.5	50
1986	1,416	65	4.6	22.6	23.8	10.2	42	43.6%	[2]23.9	1.7	48
1985	1,534	114	7.4	40.7	18.3	11.1	93	46.9%	49.4	3.2	68
1984	1,636	174	10.6	33.0	14.7	9.0	166	47.6%	86.8	5.3	101
1983	1,165	92	7.9	13.3	10.3	4.7	92	45.4%	50.4	4.3	61

Balance Sheet Data (Million $)

Jun. 30	Cash	Curr. Assets	Curr. Liab.	Curr. Ratio	Total Assets	% Ret. on Assets	Long Term Debt	Common Equity	Total Cap.	% LT Debt of Cap.	% Ret. on Equity
1992	**305**	**1,079**	**230**	**4.7**	**1,243**	**4.2**	**175**	**837**	**1,013**	**17.3**	**6.2**
1991	341	1,038	179	5.8	1,181	5.3	201	801	1,002	20.1	7.9
1990	344	1,030	186	5.5	1,158	4.9	202	770	972	20.8	7.5
1989	237	983	179	5.5	1,126	4.7	211	735	947	22.3	7.5
1988	152	1,001	235	4.3	1,153	4.7	221	696	917	24.1	7.7
1987	213	906	181	5.0	1,062	2.3	224	658	882	25.4	3.5
1986	111	772	149	5.2	908	2.6	112	647	759	14.7	3.7
1985	128	782	166	4.7	917	5.4	112	638	751	15.0	7.9
1984	92	798	193	4.1	911	10.6	114	603	717	15.9	15.2
1983	106	620	164	3.8	710	7.5	17	528	546	3.1	9.9

Data as orig. reptd. **1.** Refl. merger or acq. **2.** Refl. acctg. change.

Business Summary

Avnet distributes electronic components and computer products. It also makes other electronic products. Contributions to sales and operating profit by segment in fiscal 1993 were:

	Sales	Profits
Electronic marketing	86%	96%
Electrical & industrial	8%	3%
Video communications	6%	1%

International operations accounted for 9.9% of sales and 4.9% of operating profits in fiscal 1992 (latest available).

The electronic marketing group distributes electronic components, connectors and passive and electromechanical devices. Components are shipped either as received or with assembly or other value added. It is also an international distributor of computer products.

The electrical and industrial group distributes electrical insulation, magnet wire, electric motors and supply parts. Industrial maintenance and factory supplies are also distributed.

The video communications group principally designs, develops and manufactures TV signal processing and audio equipment. Other products include private-label CD players and turntables.

Dividend Data

Dividends have been paid since 1961. A dividend reinvestment plan is available.

Amt of Divd. $	Date Decl.	Ex-divd. Date	Stock of Record	Payment Date
0.15	Nov. 18	Dec. 7	Dec. 11	Jan. 4'93
0.15	Jan. 27	Mar. 8	Mar. 12	Apr. 1'93
0.15	May 26	Jun. 7	Jun. 11	Jul. 1'93
0.15	Jul. 28	Sep. 3	Sep. 10	Oct. 1'93

Finances

In January 1993, the company acquired the components business of Electronic 2000 AG, which are located in Germany, Austria and Switzerland. Its combined sales were approximately $75 million in 1992. In September 1992, AVT began operating an electronics distribution business in the United Kingdom. This followed the July 1992 purchase of Nortec Group, the leading Scandinavian electronic components distributor, with annual sales of approximately $68 million. In April 1992, the company acquired F.H. Tec Composants, a French electronics distributor with annual sales of some $75 million.

Capitalization

Long Term Debt: $106,623,000 (6/93).

Common Stock: 40,176,000 shs. ($1 par).
Institutions hold about 73%.
Shareholders of record: 9,010 (8/92).

Office—80 Cutter Mill Rd., Great Neck, NY 11021. **Tel**—(516) 466-7000. **Chrmn & CEO**—L. Machiz. **Pres**—R. Vallee. **VP-Secy**—S. D. Herlihy. **VP-Treas & CFO**—J. Regazzi. **Investor Contact**—Irwin Lubalin. **Dirs**—S. Benerofe, G. J. Berkman, J. S. Berman, A. E. Friedman, S. D. Herlihy, J. W. Kenney, L. Machiz, S. J. Nuzzo, D. Shaw, H. Stein, R. Vallee, J. S. Webb, G. Weissman. **Transfer Agent & Registrar**—Bank of New York, NYC. **Incorporated** in New York in 1955. **Empl**—6,650.

 Paul H. Valentine, CFA

BJ Services

NYSE Symbol BJS In S&P MidCap 400

Price	Range	P-E Ratio	Dividend	Yield	S&P Ranking	Beta
Jul. 26'93	1993					
25¼	31⅝–13⅝	29	None	None	NR	NA

Summary

This company is a leading participant in the pressure pumping business, serving the petroleum industry worldwide. Its principal activities consist of well cementing and stimulation services, coiled tubing and casing and tubing services for the drilling and completion of oil and natural gas wells. After a loss in fiscal 1992, BJS returned to profitability in fiscal 1993's first nine months on increased activity in the U.S. and North Sea and the absence of a $15.7 million restructuring charge.

Business Summary

BJ Services provides pressure pumping services to the petroleum industry on a worldwide basis. Its principal activities consist of well cementing and stimulation services, coiled tubing and casing and tubing services for the drilling and completion of oil and natural gas wells, both onshore and offshore. BJS also provides commissioning and leak detection services on offshore platforms, pipelines and refineries. During fiscal 1992, the company restructured its U.S. operations with a sharp reduction in the workforce and the consolidation of several operating locations, and closed its Canadian operations. BJS was a subsidiary of Baker Hughes Inc. prior to its initial public offering in July 1990.

BJS's cementing services, which accounted for 49% of revenues in fiscal 1992, are utilized in a number of specific applications in oilfield operations, the most important of which is the cementing between the casing pipe and the wellbore during the drilling and completion phase of the well ("primary cementing"). Primary cementing provides structural support for the protective casing, prevents migration of fluids between productive formations, allows selective production among formations, and seals the casing from corrosive formation fluids. Cementing services are also utilized when a well is to be plugged and abandoned or when existing wells require remedial work.

Stimulation services, which accounted for 41% of revenues in fiscal 1992, consist of hydraulic fracturing, acidizing and nitrogen services to improve the flow of oil or natural gas from producing formations. Hydraulic fracturing is applied in formations and reservoirs with relatively low or impaired productive capabilities. Acidizing services are used to repair and unblock formations whose productivity has been lessened by damage or buildup over time of various materials in the formation. Nitrogen services are used principally in applications which support cement and fracturing services.

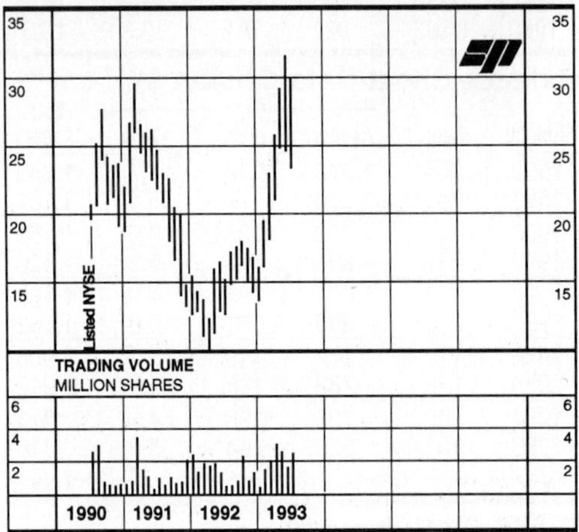

BJS's services are provided to customers in the major oil and gas producing regions of the U.S. (49% of fiscal 1992 revenues), Latin America and Canada (19%), Europe (15%), and other areas (17%). BJS believes that it is the third largest provider of pressure pumping services worldwide, with particularly strong market positions in a number of key, high margin regions such as the Alaskan North Slope, the North Sea and the Gulf of Mexico. BJS downsized its North American operations during fiscal 1992 and fiscal 1993 and focused its expansion efforts on international markets.

Important Developments

Jul. '93— BJS and Baroid Corp., a Houston-based oilfield services company, formed an alliance to provide a more complete line of drilling, completion, cementing and stimulation services.

Next earnings report expected in late October.

Per Share Data ($)

Yr. End Sep. 30	[4]1992	1991	1990	[1]1989
Tangible Bk. Val.	**8.99**	10.41	8.57	[2]7.33
Cash Flow	**0.89**	2.99	2.39	NA
Earnings	**d0.08**	1.88	1.42	0.45
Dividends	**Nil**	Nil	Nil	Nil
Payout Ratio	**Nil**	Nil	Nil	Nil
Prices[3]—High	**18**	29⅝	27¾	NA
Low	**10**	13¼	19⅛	NA
P/E Ratio—	**NM**	16–7	20–13	NA

Data as orig. reptd.; prior to 1990 data as reptd in prospectus dated Jul. 20, 1990. **1.** Pro forma. **2.** As of Mar. 31, 1990. **3.** Cal. yr. **4.** Reflects merger or acquisition. d-Deficit. NM-Not Meaningful. NA-Not Available.

Income Data (Million $)

Year Ended Sep. 30	Revs.	Oper. Inc.	% Oper. Inc. of Revs.	Cap. Exp.	Depr.	Int. Exp.	Net Bef. Taxes	Eff. Tax Rate	Net Inc.	% Net Inc. of Revs.	Cash Flow
[3]**1992**	**330**	**26.2**	**7.9**	**26.2**	**12.7**	**3.78**	[2]**d4.2**	**NM**	**d1.1**	**NM**	**11.6**
1991	390	44.8	11.5	34.6	14.5	3.89	[2]31.1	16.6%	24.4	6.3	38.9
1990	350	41.8	11.9	20.1	12.6	1.37	[2]28.8	31.9%	18.5	5.3	31.1
[1]1989	317	35.6	11.2	NA	13.7	3.87	15.7	56.4%	5.9	1.9	NA

Balance Sheet Data (Million $)

Sep. 30	Cash	Curr. Assets	Curr. Liab.	Curr. Ratio	Total Assets	% Ret. on Assets	Long Term Debt	Common Equity	Total Cap.	% LT Debt of Cap.	% Ret. on Equity
1992	**1.48**	**130**	**129**	**1.0**	**329**	**NM**	**55.5**	**135**	**200**	**27.8**	**NM**
1991	5.41	121	86	1.4	266	9.7	31.0	135	179	17.3	19.8
1990	3.09	112	90	1.2	239	NA	24.0	111	148	16.3	NA
[4]1989	0.05	91	74	1.2	211	NA	27.4	95	136	20.2	NA

Data as orig. reptd.; prior to 1990 data as reptd. in prospectus dated Jul. 20, 1990. **1.** Pro forma. **2.** Incl. equity in earns. of nonconsol. subs. **3.** Refl. merger or acquisition. **4.** As of Mar. 31, 1990, pro forma. d-Deficit. NM-Not Meaningful. NA-Not Available.

Revenues (Million $)

Quarter:	1992–93	1991–92	1990–91	1989–90
Dec.	94.4	88.7	102.1	86.4
Mar.	100.1	78.1	95.2	83.6
Jun.	96.7	79.4	94.9	83.3
Sep.		83.9	98.1	97.0
		330.0	390.3	350.2

Revenues for the nine months ended June 30, 1993, rose 18%, year to year, reflecting increased U.S. drilling activity, healthy North Sea stimulation work and acquisitions. Operating expenses advanced less rapidly while interest expense was up sharply. Other expense was down 94% and, in the absence of a $15.7 million restructuring charge, pretax income replaced a loss. After taxes at 18.9%, versus tax credits of $4.0 million, net income of $8,619,000 ($0.56 a share, based on 18% more shares) contrasted with a net loss of $4,978,000 ($0.38).

Common Share Earnings ($)

Quarter:	1992–93	1991–92	1990–91	1989–90
Dec.	0.21	0.17	0.49	0.31
Mar.	0.15	d0.75	0.26	0.23
Jun.	0.21	0.20	0.34	0.36
Sep.		0.30	0.79	0.53
		d0.08	1.88	1.42

Dividend Data

The company does not currently intend to pay dividends on its common shares. Any earnings, for the foreseeable future, will be retained for use in BJS's business. Also, the company's credit facilities restrict dividends.

Finances

In April 1993, the company acquired the assets, including existing service contracts, of Norsk Bronnservice A/S for $5.4 million. Norsk provides cementing, gravel packing and completion fluids services to the Norwegian oil and gas industry.

Fiscal 1993 capital spending is expected to be $42 million, with about 80% of the expenditures concentrated on international operations.

The company has a committed, unsecured credit facility totaling $85 million, of which $56 million was outstanding at March 31, 1993. BJS also has discretionary lines totaling $13 million, of which $7.9 million was outstanding at the end of fiscal 1993's second quarter.

In October 1992, BJS publicly offered 2.5 million common shares at $17.375 per share. Net proceeds of $40.8 million were used to repay debt, including $24.8 million of notes related to the Salvesen acquisition.

In September 1992, the company acquired Salvesen Ltd. (since renamed BJS Oilfield Technology Limited) for about $52 million. Salvesen provides services including casing and tubing, coiled tubing, and commissioning and leak detection to the oil and gas industry primarily in the U.K. North Sea. Beginning in fiscal 1993, Salvesen is expected to provide additional revenues of 8%-10%.

At September 30, 1992, BJS had about $77 million of U.S. tax net operating loss carryforwards expiring between 2004 and 2007. Foreign tax credits expiring between 1993 and 1997 totaled $3.1 million.

In July 1990, BJ Services Co., a wholly owned subsidiary of Baker Hughes Inc., offered 9,000,000 common shares at $20 each in its initial public offering.

Capitalization

Long Term Debt: $67,000,000 (3/93).

Minority Interest: $3,217,000.

Common Shares: 15,581,888 shs. ($0.10 par). Institutions hold about 94%, incl. 13% held by the Equitable Companies.
Shareholders of record: 387.

d-Deficit.

Office—5500 Northwest Central Drive, Houston, TX 77092; PO Box 4442, Houston, TX 77210-4442. **Tel**—(713) 462-4239. **Chrmn, Pres & CEO**—J. W. Stewart. **VP-Fin, CFO & Investor Contact**—Michael McShane. **VP-Secy**—D. H. Heard. **Treas**—T. M. Whichard III. **Dirs**—L. W. Heiligbrodt, J. R. Huff, D. D. Jordan, R. D. Kinder, J. E. McCormick, M. McShane, J. W. Stewart. **Transfer Agent & Registrar**—First Chicago Trust Co. of New York, NYC. **Incorporated** in Delaware in 1990. **Empl**—2,579.

 J.R. Jordan

BMC Software

NASDAQ Symbol BMCS (Incl. in Nat'l Market) Options on CBOE & Pacific In S&P MidCap 400

Price	Range	P-E Ratio	Dividend	Yield	S&P Ranking	Beta
Aug. 20'93	1993					
58¼	84⅛–38¾	22	None	None	B+	NA

Summary

This Texas-based company markets and supports systems software products to enhance IBM's database management and data communications systems, principally IMS, DB2 and CISC. Results for fiscal 1992-93 benefited from an expanded worldwide sales force and new product introductions. Higher revenues and steady margins should aid earnings in 1993-94.

Current Outlook

Earnings for the fiscal year ending March 31, 1994, are estimated at $3.10 a share, versus the $2.50 recorded for 1992-93.

Cash dividends are not currently anticipated.

Revenues for fiscal 1993-94 are expected to advance 25%-30%, aided by continued demand for IMS and DB2 mainframe database enhancement software programs, as well as new products that integrate and increase the performance of computer networks. License revenues are expected to grow in the 30%-35% range; maintenance revenues should advance at about 20%. The backlog of prospective new business remains healthy, and a focus on international operations bodes well. Margins should be maintained on volume efficiencies, despite continued investments in R&D.

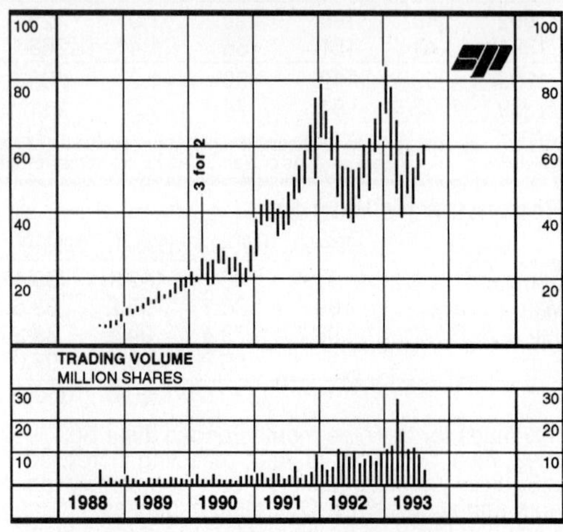

Revenues (Million $)

Quarter:	1993–94	1992–93	1991–92	[1]1990–91
Jun.	65.0	50.5	39.1	26.1
Sep.		57.5	43.8	29.3
Dec.		65.0	49.7	33.1
Mar.		65.5	56.0	41.6
		238.5	188.7	130.1

Revenues for the three months ended June 30 1993, advanced 29%, year to year, reflecting a 37% gain in licenses and a 20% increase in maintenance revenues. Margins widened on the higher volume, despite substantially increased R&D spending, and following greater interest and other income (net), pretax profits advanced 38%. After taxes at 30.0% in both periods, net income also rose 38%, to $18,201,000 ($0.69 a share), from $13,167,000 ($0.51).

Common Share Earnings ($)

Quarter:	1993–94	1992–93	1991–92	[1]1990–91
Jun.	0.69	0.51	0.36	0.22
Sep.		0.58	0.42	0.22
Dec.		0.66	0.51	0.24
Mar.		0.75	0.59	0.34
		2.50	1.88	1.02

Important Developments

Jul. '93— The company reported that combined revenues from its IMS and DB2 database management product lines accounted for about 70% of total revenues in the first quarter of 1993-94.

Apr. '93— During 1992-93, the company released seven new products and 23 new versions of existing products.

Next earnings report expected in late October.

Per Share Data ($)

Yr. End Mar. 31	1993	1992	[1]1991	1990	1989	1988
Tangible Bk. Val.	**8.52**	5.83	3.53	2.52	1.39	2.97
Cash Flow	**2.66**	2.06	1.15	0.91	0.60	0.37
Earnings	**2.50**	1.88	1.02	0.83	0.53	0.32
Dividends	**Nil**	Nil	Nil	Nil	Nil	Nil
Payout Ratio	**Nil**	Nil	Nil	Nil	Nil	Nil
Calendar Years	**1992**	1991	1990	1989	1988	1987
Prices—High	**79**	74¾	30¼	20½	9⅜	NA
Low	**37¼**	27	17¾	9⅛	5¼	NA
P/E Ratio—	**32–15**	40–14	30–17	25–11	18–10	NA

Data as orig. reptd. Adj. for stk. divs. of 50% Mar. 1990, 200% Aug. 1988. **1.** Refl. acctg. change. NA-Not Available.

Income Data (Million $)

Year Ended Mar. 31	Revs.	Oper. Inc.	% Oper. Inc. of Revs.	Cap. Exp.	Depr.	Int. Exp.	Net Bef. Taxes	Eff. Tax Rate	Net Inc.	% Net Inc. of Revs.	Cash Flow
1993	**239**	**90.4**	**37.9**	**39.6**	**4.28**	**Nil**	**93.4**	**30.0%**	**65.4**	**27.4**	**69.7**
1992	189	70.8	37.5	19.0	4.70	Nil	70.5	31.0%	48.6	25.8	53.3
[1]1991	130	37.7	28.9	9.0	3.46	Nil	38.2	33.2%	25.5	19.6	29.0
1990	93	30.0	32.2	4.1	1.85	NM	30.4	33.2%	20.3	21.8	22.1
1989	60	18.4	30.6	1.8	1.66	0.04	17.7	29.7%	12.4	20.6	14.1
1988	42	12.2	29.3	1.9	1.29	0.05	11.5	35.6%	7.4	17.8	8.7

Balance Sheet Data (Million $)

Mar. 31	Cash	Curr. Assets	Curr. Liab.	Curr. Ratio	Total Assets	% Ret. on Assets	Long Term Debt	Common Equity	Total Cap.	% LT Debt of Cap.	% Ret. on Equity
1993	**131**	**198**	**123.0**	**1.6**	**379**	**20.7**	**Nil**	**223**	**223**	**Nil**	**35.6**
1992	138	191	74.5	2.6	242	24.5	Nil	150	150	NM	40.5
1991	92	120	50.9	2.3	148	21.2	Nil	86	86	NM	34.6
1990	53	68	20.8	3.3	87	30.1	0.01	58	58	NM	45.5
1989	20	31	9.2	3.4	47	11.4	0.09	31	31	0.3	25.4
1988	5	15	8.8	1.7	23	NA	0.19	9	9	2.0	NA

Data as orig. reptd. 1. Refl. acctg. change. NM-Not Meaningful. NA-Not Available.

Business Summary

BMC Software, Inc. develops, markets and supports standard systems software products to enhance and increase the performance of large scale (mainframe) computer database management and data communications software systems.

Revenues by major product group in recent years were derived as follows:

	1992–93	1991–92	1990–91
IMS products	39%	43%	43%
DB2 products	33%	25%	21%
Network Performance Series	9%	11%	14%
Other	19%	21%	22%

BMC offers over 55 systems software products for use on IBM's primary mainframe operating system, MVS, and the principal MVS-based database management systems (DBMS), IMS/DB and DB2, and data communications systems, IMS/DC, VTAM, and CICS. The company's products facilitate database management and maintenance, increase the speed and efficiency of data network communications and compress data stored in direct access storage devices.

The company's core products are tools and utilities that address the IMS/DB and DB2 database management systems. These 23 products generated 72% of total revenues and 78% of license revenues in fiscal 1992-93.

IMS/DB is the most widely used production DBMS for IBM mainframe and compatible computers. However, the key deficiency of IMS/DB is its inflexibility; it is difficult to program to respond to new applications and queries. In fiscal 1992-93, the 10 IMS database utilities products contributed 39% of total revenues and 36% of license revenues.

DB2, IBM's second generation DBMS is easier to utilize than IMS/DB, and customers are accelerating their implementation of DB2 in production environments. The 13 tools and utilities in the "MasterPlan" for DB2 product group contributed 42% of license revenues and 33% of total revenues in fiscal 1992-93.

Other offerings include: network performance products which facilitate the transmission of data through telecommunications networks connecting mainframe computers with terminals and personal computers; data communications enhancements; and data compression products which reduce the space required to store data.

The company's products are designed to be marketed and supported by telephone rather than by direct sales.

International marketing efforts are conducted through nine wholly owned subsidiaries in Europe, Japan and Australia. In addition, the company is represented by independent agents in over 12 countries. Customers outside North America accounted for 43% of revenues in 1992-93, versus 44% in 1991-92.

Dividend Data

No cash dividends have been paid.

Finances

Research and development outlays totaled $38,131,000 (16% of revenues) in 1992-93, versus $24,144,000 (13%) the year before.

During 1992-93, $5,043,000 of software development costs were capitalized, up from $5,231,000 in 1991-92.

Capitalization

Long Term Debt: None (6/93).

Common Stock: 26,220,839 shs. ($0.01 par).
Institutions hold about 89%.
Shareholders: About 270 of record (5/93).

Office—One Sugar Creek Center Blvd., Sugar Land, TX 77478. **Tel**—(713) 240-8800. **Chrmn, Pres & CEO**—M. P. Watson Jr. **VP-CFO**—D. A. Farley. **VP-Secy**—M. B. Morse. **Investor Contact**—John Cox. **Dirs**—J. W. Barter, B. G. Cupp, D. A. Farley, M. K. Gafner, L. W. Gray, G. F. Raymond, M. P. Watson Jr. **Transfer Agent**—The First National Bank of Boston, Mass. **Incorporated** in Texas in 1980; reincorporated in Delaware in 1988. **Empl**—909.

 Peter C. Wood, CFA

Bancorp Hawaii

NYSE Symbol BOH In S&P MidCap 400

Price	Range	P-E Ratio	Dividend	Yield	S&P Ranking	Beta
Nov. 1'93	1993					
44¼	53⅞–40	11	1.38	3.1%	A+	1.18

Summary

Bancorp Hawaii is the holding company for Bank of Hawaii, the largest commercial bank in the state, and FirstFed America Inc. BOH provides varied financial services to customers in Hawaii and the South Pacific, and selected markets with economies similar to those of the Pacific-Basin. Earnings in 1994 are projected to rise to $4.90 a share, primarily due to lower loan loss provisions.

Current Outlook

Earnings for 1994 are projected at $4.90 a share, up from 1993's expected $4.55.

The minimum expectation for dividends is a continuation of the current quarterly rate of $0.34½.

Earnings for 1994 are expected to rise 7% to 10% from those of 1993, mostly as a result of lower loan loss provisions and reduced operating expenses. After charging-off a larger than anticipated amount of commerial real estate loans associated with one group of borrowers, BOH made additional loan loss provisions during 1993's third quarter to restore loan loss reserves to acceptable levels. With tourism still soft, and Southern California and Japan still mired in recessions, regional economic growth and the general lending environment is expected to be weak. BOH intends to continue to seek acquisition opportunities within Hawaii and the Asian and Pacific markets in which it operates.

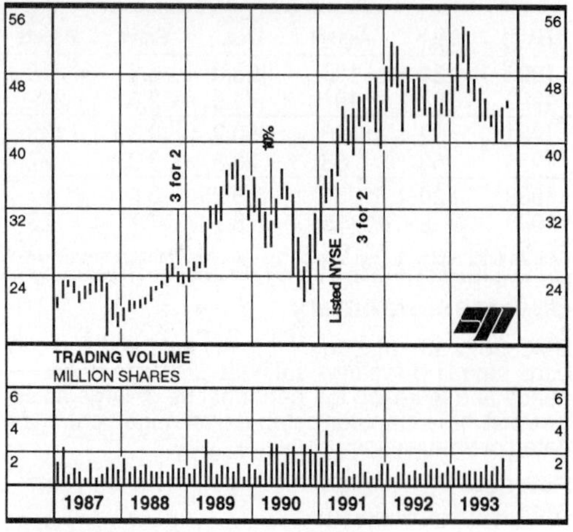

Review of Operations

In the nine months ended September 30, 1993, net interest income advanced 8.2%, year to year, reflecting a 2.4% decline in interest income and a 14% drop in interest expense. The loan loss provision increased to $45.1 million, from $26.1 million. Noninterest income rose 17%, due to higher fee income, and noninterest expense advanced 8.1%; pretax income was up 2.1%. After taxes at 37.8%, versus 38.2%, net income advanced 2.7%, to $96.9 million ($3.37 a share), from $94.3 million ($3.33). Results in the 1992 interim exclude a credit of $0.38 a share for an accounting change.

Common Share Earnings ($)

Quarter:	1994	1993	1992	1991
Mar.	E1.20	1.15	1.08	0.95
Jun.	E1.22	1.18	1.13	1.00
Sep.	E1.23	1.05	1.12	1.02
Dec.	E1.25	E1.17	0.79	1.07
	E4.90	E4.55	4.12	4.04

Important Developments

Oct. '93— Bancorp Hawaii issued $100 million of medium term bank notes, with an initial rate of 3.38%, due 1995.

Sep. '93— Directors eliminated the 5% discount on stock purchases available to participants in its dividend reinvestment plan, effective September 30. Additionally, the bank holding company announced plans to repurchase an unspecified number of common shares on the open market. The company estimates it will buy back several hundred thousand shares annually, depending on participation in company stock plans and share pricing.

Jun. '93— BOH discontinued discussions with International Holding Capital Corp. concerning the proposed acquisition of International by BOH. BOH had entered into a nonbinding letter of intent to acquire International in April.

Next earnings report expected in late January.

Per Share Data ($)

Yr. End Dec. 31	1992	1991	1990	1989	[1]1988	[2]1987	[2]1986	1985	1984	1983
Tangible Bk. Val.	**27.65**	24.56	20.78	19.24	16.57	14.95	13.30	11.75	10.51	9.61
Earnings[3]	**4.12**	4.04	3.67	3.28	3.18	2.31	2.05	1.74	1.52	1.50
Dividends	**1.268**	1.173	1.057	0.885	1.167	0.679	0.597	0.525	0.501	0.489
Payout Ratio	**31%**	29%	29%	27%	37%	29%	29%	30%	33%	33%
Prices—High	**52**	47¾	36⅞	37 15/16	25½	24	22½	15 7/16	10 13/16	11
Low	**40¼**	28⅜	21	23 5/16	18¾	17	14 5/16	10 5/16	7¼	8 9/16
P/E Ratio—	**13–10**	12–7	10–6	12–7	8–6	10–7	11–7	9–6	7–5	7–6

Data as orig. reptd. Adj. for stk. divs. of 50% Sep. 1991, 10% Apr. 1990, 50% Nov. 1988. **1.** Reflects acctg. change. **2.** Reflects merger or acquisition. **3.** Bef. spec. item(s) of +0.38 in 1992. NA-Not Available.

Income Data (Million $)

Year Ended Dec. 31	Net Int. Inc.	Tax Equiv. Adj.	Non Int. Inc.	Loan Loss Prov.	% Exp./ Op. Revs.	Net Bef. Taxes	Eff. Tax Rate	[3]Net Inc.	Net Int. Margin	—% Return On— Assets	Equity
1992	**441**	**3.3**	**109**	**50.1**	**56.8**	**189**	**38.2%**	**116.7**	**4.06**	**1.00**	**15.6**
1991	408	4.6	91	29.6	57.2	184	38.8%	112.7	4.05	1.04	16.5
1990	350	6.1	83	28.0	56.5	157	39.2%	95.7	4.14	1.04	17.0
1989	286	6.9	76	20.9	58.0	128	37.4%	79	4.49	1.14	17.6
[1]1988	242	7.7	110	31.0	54.8	124	39.6%	74.9	4.47	1.25	19.9
[2]1987	201	12.6	59	17.2	61.8	75	28.4%	53.9	4.39	1.03	16.2
[2]1986	175	19.6	83	28.2	59.5	65	28.5%	46.2	4.64	1.01	16.2
1985	157	17.9	51	20.2	60.9	50	23.0%	38.6	4.60	0.93	15.5
1984	141	11.6	32	14.4	62.8	42	22.0%	33.1	4.71	0.93	15.0
1983	130	10.7	28	9.4	63.6	41	25.2%	31.0	5.06	1.01	16.1

Balance Sheet Data (Million $)

Dec. 31	Total Assets	—Earning Assets— Mon. Mkt. Assets	Inv. Secs.	Com'l Loans	Other Loans	% Loan Loss Resv.	—Deposits— Demand	Time	% Loans/ Deposits	Long Term Debt	Common Equity	% Equity To Assets
1992	**12,713**	**2,037**	**3,036**	**2,257**	**4,707**	**1.85**	**1,257**	**6,633**	**86.6**	**84.1**	**828**	**6.74**
1991	11,409	1,472	2,545	2,104	4,655	1.74	1,251	7,416	76.5	75.5	724	6.31
1990	10,699	1,511	2,036	1,981	4,532	1.60	1,236	7,549	72.7	117.1	630	6.09
1989	8,317	1,471	1,364	1,826	3,150	1.73	1,127	5,897	69.6	47.6	483	6.35
1988	6,635	1,087	933	1,494	2,670	1.80	1,019	4,642	72.2	36.7	400	6.31
1987	5,826	1,075	936	1,266	2,170	1.61	922	3,996	68.8	56.5	347	6.36
1986	5,060	950	775	1,047	1,833	1.62	900	3,443	65.2	45.0	304	6.21
1985	4,439	787	755	839	1,630	1.18	712	3,145	63.5	38.6	262	5.99
1984	3,852	631	667	751	1,438	0.92	618	2,735	64.8	41.4	231	6.18
1983	3,377	586	524	582	1,305	0.96	606	2,385	62.5	46.2	206	6.12

Data as orig. reptd. **1.** Reflects acctg. change. **2.** Reflects merger or acquisition. **3.** Bef. spec. item(s).

Business Summary

Bancorp Hawaii owns all of the capital stock of Bank of Hawaii, the largest commercial bank in that state, and FirstFed America, Inc. Bank of Hawaii provides all customary services of a commercial bank. The bank has offices in Hawaii and branch or representative offices in 10 South Pacific island areas, plus locations in Tokyo, Seoul, Hong Kong, Singapore and Nassau, as well as affiliates in four other South Pacific locations. Gross loans totaled $6.96 billion at year-end 1992, compared with $6.76 billion the year before, and were divided:

	1992	1991
Real estate–mortgage.........	45.7%	45.6%
Commercial/industrial	26.8%	24.9%
Installment	9.4%	9.9%
Foreign............................	8.7%	10.2%
Lease financing................	5.6%	5.2%
Real estate–construction	3.7%	4.2%

The reserve for possible loan losses was $128.6 million at 1992 year-end (1.89% of gross loans outstanding), compared with $115.6 million (1.74%) a year earlier. Net loans charged off during 1992 came to $37.0 million (0.56% of average loans) versus $15.3 million (0.24%) during 1991. Nonperforming assets at December 31, 1992, totaled $93.0 million (0.73% of total assets), down from $42.0 million (0.37%) a year earlier.

Average deposits of $8.41 billion in 1992 were apportioned: interest-bearing demand 24.2%, public time CDs of $100,000 or more 18.7%, noninterest-bearing demand 14.6%, foreign 9.7%, private time CDs of $100,000 or more 6.5%, regular savings accounts 12.3%, and all other time and savings certificates 14.0%. On a tax-equivalent basis, the average yield on interest-earning assets was 7.59% in 1992 (9.18% in 1991), while the average rate paid on interest-bearing liabilities was 4.13% (5.97%), for a net spread of 3.46% (3.21%).

Dividend Data

Cash has been paid each year since 1899. A dividend reinvestment plan is available.

Amt. of Divd. $	Date Decl.	Ex–divd. Date	Stock of Record	Payment Date
0.32¼	Jan. 27	Feb. 11	Feb. 18	Mar. 12'93
0.34½	Apr. 28	May 13	May 19	Jun. 14'93
0.34½	Jul. 19	Aug. 18	Aug. 24	Sep. 15'93
0.34½	Nov. 1	Nov. 12	Nov. 18	Dec. 14'93

Capitalization

Long Term Debt: $253,500,000 (9/93).

Common Stock: 28,396,983 shs. ($2 par).
Institutions hold approximately 62%.
Shareholders of record: 5,814 (12/92).

Office—130 Merchant St, Honolulu, HI 96813. **Tel**—(808) 537-8111. **Chrmn & CEO**—H.H. Stephenson. **Pres**—L.M. Johnson. **EVP-CFO & Investor Contact**—Richard J. Dahl. **VP-Secy**—R.E. Miyashiro. **Dirs**—P.D. Baldwin, C.C. Cameron, S.I. Hashimoto, S.T.K. Ho, L.M. Johnson, F.J. Manaut, H.H. Stephenson, F.E. Trotter, M. Ulyshen, C.R. Wichman, K.T. Yee. **Transfer Agents & Registrars**—Bank of New York, NYC; Hawaiian Trust Co., Ltd., Honolulu. **Incorporated** in Hawaii in 1972; bank organized in 1897. **Empl**—4,275.

 Barry R. Haas

Bank of New York

NYSE Symbol BK Options on CBOE (Jan-Apr-Jul-Oct) In S&P MidCap 400

Price	Range	P-E Ratio	Dividend	Yield	S&P Ranking	Beta
Sep. 2'93	1993					
53¼	62½–50⅝	10	1.80	3.4%	B	1.78

Summary

At year-end 1992 Bank of New York was the 17th largest banking organization in the U.S. Lower 1991 earnings reflected a first-quarter loss due to higher nonperforming assets. Profits recovered in 1992 and are expected to rise in 1993 and 1994. In August 1993, the company completed the acquisition of National Community Banks, Inc., a $4 billion New Jersey based banking company, for about 10.2 million common shares.

Current Outlook

Earnings for 1993 are estimated at $5.55 a share, versus the $4.45 posted in 1992. For 1994, earnings could reach $6.10 a share.

In July 1993, the quarterly dividend was raised 18%, to $0.45 a share.

While commercial loan demand will probably remain depressed, gains in fee-based businesses (particularly securities processing) and a growing credit card business should lead to higher earnings in 1993 and 1994. The acquisition of Barclays 62 metro New York branches should also boost profits. Spreads should benefit from a better mix of earning assets. Further aiding the bottom line is improving asset quality. With reserves at 171% of NPLs, if credit quality continues to improve, (NP assets fell by $143 million in the second quarter to $717 million), the loan loss provision should continue to decline. Commercial real estate accounts for about 8% of loans (much less than its peers). Cost-conscious BK will continue to focus on operating costs in a slow growth revenue climate. While BK paid up for National Community Banks (about 2.3X book), it established a base in affluent Northern New Jersey from which to grow.

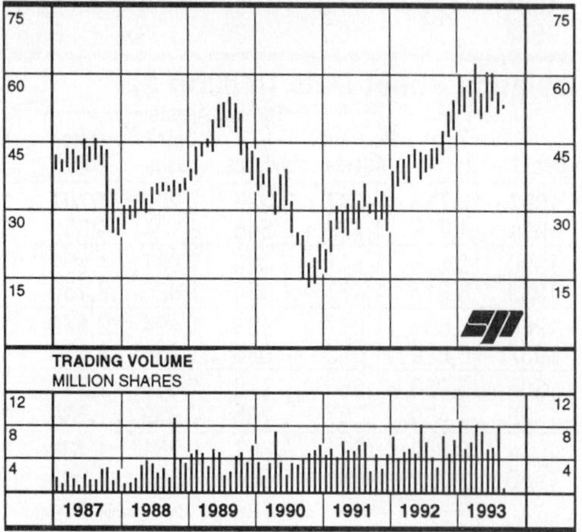

Review of Operations

Net interest income for the six months ended June 30, 1993, rose 12%, year to year, reflecting a wider net interest margin (3.73% versus 3.44%). Average earning assets were up 2.3% (average domestic loans increased 9.1%). The provision for loan losses declined 31%, to $165 million. (Net chargeoffs were $202 million.) Aided by an 13% rise in securities processing fees, higher securities gains and a $24 million gain from the sale of 20%,of the company's interest in a Hong Kong Bank, noninterest income advanced 15%. Paced by a 16% rise in salaries and employee benefits, noninterest expense was up 11%. Pretax earnings expanded 62%. After taxes at 37.7%, versus 34.0%, net income advanced 53%. Following preferred dividends, share earnings were $2.94 ($2.79 fully diluted), versus $2.13 ($2.02).

Common Share Earnings ($)

Quarter:	1993	1992	1991	1990
Mar.	1.45	1.02	d1.02	1.38
Jun.	1.49	1.11	0.75	0.90
Sep.	E1.30	1.12	0.72	0.90
Dec.	E1.31	1.20	0.82	0.82
	E5.55	4.45	1.28	3.98

Important Developments

Aug. '93— BK completed the acquisition of National Community Banks (NCBR), a 105-branch bank holding company based in New Jersey. BK exchanged 0.96 common share for each of NCBR's 10.66 million common shares outstanding. Separately, included in second quarter earnings was a pretax gain of $24 million related to the sale of 20% of BK's interest in a Hong Kong Bank.

Next earnings report expected in mid-October.

Per Share Data ($)

Yr. End Dec. 31	1992	1991	1990	1989	[1]1988	[2]1987	[2]1986	1985	1984	[1]1983
Tangible Bk. Val.	**39.70**	36.52	36.59	36.66	39.76	33.65	31.76	28.38	27.88	25.39
Earnings[3]	**4.45**	1.28	3.98	0.24	5.61	2.97	4.97	4.26	4.27	3.80
Dividends	**1.520**	1.670	2.120	1.970	1.830	1.710	1.560	1.400	1.260	1.158
Payout Ratio	**34%**	130%	53%	821%	33%	58%	31%	33%	30%	30%
Prices—High	**54⅝**	36⅛	41¾	55	37¼	45⅞	46¾	34⅞	24½	22⅛
Low	**30**	16½	13¼	36¾	25⅞	24½	32⅞	23¼	17½	15¾
P/E Ratio—	**12–7**	28–13	10–3	NM	7–5	15–8	9–7	8–5	6–4	6–4

Data as orig. reptd. Adj. for stk. div(s). of 50% Nov. 1986, 100% Oct. 1983. **1.** Reflects acctg. change. **2.** Reflects merger or acquisition and acctg. change. **3.** Ful. dil.: 4.23 in 1992, 1.36 in 1991, 5.21 in 1988, 2.81 in 1987, 4.54 in 1986, 4.02 in 1985, 3.57 in 1984, 3.15 in 1983. d-Deficit. E-Estimated. NM-Not Meaningful.

Income Data (Million $)

Year Ended Dec. 31	Net Int. Inc.	Tax Equiv. Adj.	Non Int. Inc.	Loan Loss Prov.	% Exp./ Op. Revs.	Net Bef. Taxes	Eff. Tax Rate	Net Inc.	% Net Int. Margin	—% Return On— Assets	Equity
1992	**1,224**	**62**	**1,091**	**427**	**57.7**	**559**	**34.0%**	**369**	**3.55**	**0.88**	**13.5**
1991	1,198	75	956	746	58.8	177	31.1%	122	3.43	0.29	4.2
1990	1,319	79	894	423	61.1	432	28.7%	308	3.29	0.63	13.0
1989	1,253	75	902	783	59.4	65	21.7%	51	3.09	0.10	0.7
[1]1988	729	64	508	168	62.0	298	28.6%	213	3.68	0.83	18.2
[2]1987	642	80	455	301	60.5	104	0.6%	103	3.77	0.46	9.7
[2]1986	536	116	346	142	56.8	183	15.1%	155	4.19	0.85	18.2
1985	463	87	258	117	52.8	174	25.1%	130	4.15	0.84	17.7
1984	404	72	243	94	56.6	147	26.7%	108	4.14	0.80	18.7
[1]1983	394	53	204	66	58.2	148	38.6%	91	4.21	0.71	17.0

Balance Sheet Data (Million $)

Dec. 31	Total Assets	—Earning Assets— Mon. Mkt. Assets	Inv. Secs.	Com'l Loans	Other Loans	% Loan Loss Resv.	—Deposits— Demand	Time	% Loans/ Deposits	Long Term Debt	Common Equity	% Equity To Assets
1992	**40,909**	**999**	**4,648**	**12,303**	**15,928**	**3.66**	**7,534**	**21,915**	**93.0**	**1,592**	**3,210**	**5.92**
1991	39,426	2,402	3,773	14,484	14,336	3.60	6,342	22,632	96.6	1,200	2,554	5.03
1990	45,390	2,661	3,287	15,219	18,613	3.14	7,355	26,666	97.0	840	2,537	4.33
1989	48,857	2,982	3,829	16,502	20,135	3.14	8,031	26,896	102.4	866	2,489	4.51
1988	47,388	3,023	4,274	14,405	19,322	2.84	8,229	24,478	101.0	1,121	2,517	4.26
1987	23,065	627	2,532	7,518	9,003	2.34	4,566	12,560	95.0	726	1,114	4.41
1986	20,709	1,098	2,069	7,016	7,060	1.57	4,834	10,279	91.2	502	953	4.48
1985	18,486	1,301	2,070	6,847	5,854	1.40	3,924	8,445	100.2	430	821	4.48
1984	15,157	1,502	1,481	5,527	4,973	1.27	2,870	7,658	97.9	169	660	3.94
1983	12,797	1,287	1,282	4,003	4,268	1.01	2,850	6,710	85.2	97	564	3.87

Data as orig. reptd. **1.** Reflects acctg. change. **2.** Reflects merger or acquisition and acctg. change.

Business Summary

The Bank of New York is the 17th largest bank holding company in the U.S., with assets at year-end 1992 of approximately $41 billion. Wholesale banking services are provided to corporate clients. Retail banking services are provided through 291 branches, largely in the suburbs of New York City. The company is also among the largest credit card issuers in the U.S., with 3.9 million credit card accounts. Securities lending and clearing and processing is an important part of business, as is corporate trust, mutual fund custody and stock transfer businesses. In 1990 BK discontinued its activities as a primary dealer in government securities. Nonbank subsidiaries include mortgage banking, factoring, and investment management services. International operations account for 14% of assets in 1992.

During 1992, average earning assets of $36.2 billion (down 2.3% from 1991) were divided: domestic loans 46%, foreign loans 32%, investment securities 14%, money market investments 8%. Sources of funds were interest-bearing deposits 54%, interest-free deposits 16%, short-term borrowings 14%, long-term debt 3%, equity 8% and other 5%.

At December 31, 1992, nonperforming assets were $931 million (3.4% of loans and related assets), versus $1.35 billion (4.8%) at year-end 1991. The allowance for loan losses was 3.66% compared with 3.60%. Net chargeoffs were $488 million (1.73% of average loans in 1992), versus $747 million (2.48%) in 1991.

Dividend Data

Dividends have been paid since 1785. A dividend reinvestment plan is available.

Amt of Divd. $	Date Decl.	Ex-divd. Date	Stock of Record	Payment Date
0.38	Oct. 13	Oct. 19	Oct. 23	Nov. 6'92
0.38	Jan. 12	Jan. 15	Jan. 22	Feb. 5'93
0.38	Apr. 13	Apr. 19	Apr. 23	May 5'93
0.45	Jul. 13	Jul. 19	Jul. 23	Aug. 6'93

Capitalization

Long Term Debt: $1,981,000,000 (6/93).

Preferred Stock: $267,000,000.

Common Stock: 83,051,304 shs. ($7.50 par).
Institutions hold about 81%.
Shareholders of record: 21,934.

Warrants: To purchase 14,099,037 com. shs. at $62 ea. to 1998.

Office—48 Wall St, New York, NY 10286. **Tel**—(212) 495-1784. **Chrmn & CEO**—J. C. Bacot. **Pres**—T. A. Renyi. **Secy**—C. E. Rappold. **VP-CFO**—D. D. Papageorge. **Investor Contacts**—M. M. Pascale, P. S. Brull. **Dirs**—J. C. Bacot, R. Barth, W. R. Chaney, S. F. Chevalier, A. S. D'Amato, A. P. Gammie, R. E. Gomory, A. R. Griffith, E. L. Hennessy Jr., J. C. Malone, D. L. Miller, H. B. Morley, M. T. Muse, C. A. Rein, T. A. Renyi, H. E. Sells, D. C. Staley, W. S. White Jr., S. H. Woolley. **Transfer Agent & Registrar**—Bank of New York, NYC. **Incorporated** in N.Y. in 1968; Bank of New York founded in 1784. **Empl**—14,310.

 Richard M. Levine, CFA

Banta Corp.

NASDAQ Symbol BNTA (Incl. in Nat'l Market) In S&P MidCap 400

Price	Range	P–E Ratio	Dividend	Yield	S&P Ranking	Beta
Sep. 20'93	1993					
32¾	33–26²¹⁄₃₂	17	0.48	1.5%	B+	0.92

Summary

Banta is a leading provider of printing and graphic arts services. Sales and earnings are expected to advance in 1993 and 1994, aided by increased market penetration, capacity gains, some economic improvement, and lower interest expense. In April 1993, the cash dividend was boosted 12.5% in conjunction with a 3-for-2 stock split.

Current Outlook

Earnings for 1993 are projected at $2.00 a share, up 11% from the $1.79 (adjusted) for 1992. About $2.25 is anticipated for 1994.

The cash dividend was raised 12.5% in conjunction with the April 1993 3-for-2 stock split. Another rise is possible in 1994.

Net sales for 1993 should rise roughly 7% from those of 1992 in spite of lingering softness in catalog production, point-of-purchase sales, and single-use products. Profitability will benefit from the higher volume overall, plus operating efficiencies. Interest expenses should drop by some 30%. A better economy, increased market penetration, and expanded capacity will aid 1994 operations.

Net Sales (Million $)

13 Weeks:	1993	1992	[1]1991	[1]1990
Mar.	162.0	152.5	138.4	139.3
Jun.	165.9	151.8	135.6	139.5
Sep.	---	166.2	144.0	155.3
Dec.	---	166.9	147.5	143.5
	---	637.4	565.5	577.6

Net sales for the 1993 first half rose 7.8%, year to year. Margins widened, and operating earnings advanced 14%. After other items, including a 16% drop in interest costs, pretax earnings rose 18%. Following taxes at 39.2%, against 39.1%, net income gained 18%. Share earnings were $0.93, versus $0.80.

Common Share Earnings ($)

13 Weeks:	1993	1992	[1]1991	[1]1990
Mar.	0.41	0.37	0.27	0.31
Jun.	0.52	0.43	0.36	0.41
Sep.	E0.58	0.53	0.43	0.46
Dec.	E0.49	0.45	0.38	0.35
	E2.00	1.79	1.44	1.53

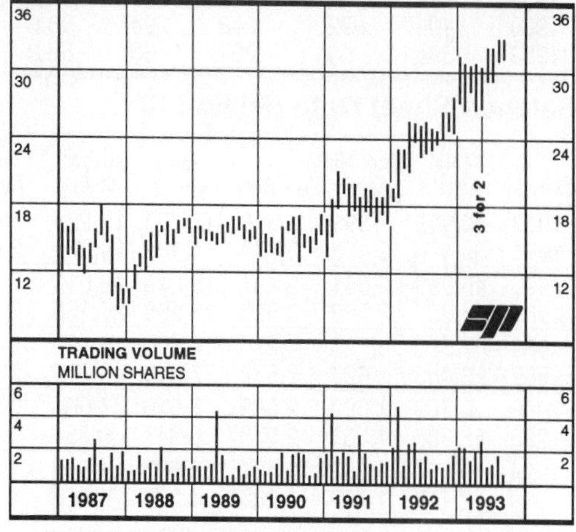

Important Developments

Aug. '93— Banta said that the outlook for 1993 remains upbeat, due in large part to the company's past investments in plants, equipment, and employee training. The company's confidence is tempered, however, by the uncertain economy. Banta said that the Direct Marketing Group was the top sales performer again in the second quarter, with double-digit gains, year to year. Softcover books were a close second, benefiting from stronger seasonal activity in educational products, and manuals for the computer software and hardware markets. Computer documentation and special-interest magazines also recorded gains. Capital expenditures of over $60 million are budgeted for 1993. Banta adopted FAS 106 accounting standards in the 1993 first quarter. The additional annual expense will approximate $1 million.

Next earnings report due in late October.

Per Share Data ($)

Yr. End Dec. 31	1992	1991	1990	1989	[2]1988	1987	1986	1985	[2]1984	1983
Tangible Bk. Val.	**12.10**	10.64	9.83	8.74	7.25	7.03	6.55	5.91	5.25	4.21
Cash Flow	**3.33**	2.89	2.91	2.90	2.51	1.93	1.75	1.68	1.67	1.12
Earnings[3]	**1.79**	1.44	1.53	1.24	1.14	0.97	0.91	0.97	1.17	0.67
Dividends	**0.407**	0.413	0.373	0.347	0.300	0.293	0.267	0.233	0.193	0.157
Payout Ratio	**23%**	29%	24%	28%	27%	30%	29%	24%	16%	24%
Prices—High	**27²⁷⁄₃₂**	21⁵⁄₃₂	17¹¹⁄₃₂	17	16²⁷⁄₃₂	18	16½	14½	9¹³⁄₃₂	8²¹⁄₃₂
Low	**18½**	13½	13	14½	9⁵⁄₃₂	8²¹⁄₃₂	11⁵⁄₃₂	8¾	5¹⁹⁄₃₂	4¾
P/E Ratio—	**16–10**	15–9	11–9	14–12	15–8	18–9	18–12	15–9	8–5	13–7

Data as orig. reptd. Adj. for stk. divs. of 50% May 1993, 100% May 1985. **1.** From continuing operations as of year-end. **2.** Refl. merger or acq. **3.** Bef. results of disc. ops. of -0.39 in 1991, -0.58 in 1990, +0.52 in 1989, +0.10 in 1988. E-Estimated.

Income Data (Million $)

Year Ended Dec. 31	Revs.	Oper. Inc.	% Oper. Inc. of Revs.	Cap. Exp.	Depr.	Int. Exp.	Net Bef. Taxes	Eff. Tax Rate	Net Inc.	% Net Inc. of Revs.	Cash Flow
1992	**637**	**94.0**	**14.8**	**33**	**30.8**	**6.5**	**58.5**	**39.0%**	**35.7**	**5.6**	**66.5**
[1]1991	565	80.1	14.2	32	28.6	5.7	46.2	38.9%	28.2	5.0	56.8
[1]1990	578	80.1	13.9	51	26.5	6.0	48.5	39.4%	29.4	5.1	55.8
[1]1989	568	76.5	13.5	56	31.8	11.0	39.2	39.4%	23.7	4.2	55.5
[1,2]1988	475	68.0	14.3	41	25.5	9.4	36.2	41.2%	21.3	4.5	46.7
1987	302	47.4	15.7	27	16.8	3.1	30.3	43.6%	17.1	5.6	33.9
1986	287	44.6	15.5	22	14.5	2.7	28.7	44.6%	[3]15.9	5.5	30.4
1985	276	44.6	16.2	19	11.9	3.5	31.1	45.7%	16.4	6.0	28.4
[2]1984	310	46.5	15.0	16	8.4	2.9	37.1	47.5%	19.5	6.3	27.8
1983	202	28.4	14.1	13	7.3	2.9	19.7	46.0%	10.6	5.3	17.9

Balance Sheet Data (Million $)

Dec. 31	Cash	Curr. Assets	Curr. Liab.	Curr. Ratio	Total Assets	% Ret. on Assets	Long Term Debt	Common Equity	Total Cap.	% LT Debt of Cap.	% Ret. on Equity
1992	**13.3**	**175**	**73**	**2.4**	**410**	**8.8**	**52.5**	**258**	**329**	**16.0**	**14.6**
1991	4.8	176	81	2.2	397	7.0	64.1	227	312	20.5	12.8
1990	1.5	181	91	2.0	398	7.5	75.4	207	302	25.0	14.6
1989	5.0	153	93	1.7	383	6.3	70.0	195	286	24.5	13.1
1988	0.3	158	100	1.6	370	7.2	82.0	166	266	30.8	13.8
1987	24.6	98	25	3.9	207	8.4	35.5	131	180	19.7	13.7
1986	29.5	97	26	3.7	197	8.7	38.1	118	169	22.6	14.4
1985	17.0	76	25	3.1	164	9.8	27.7	100	137	20.2	17.6
1984	12.4	89	49	1.8	169	13.3	24.9	86	119	21.0	24.8
1983	13.8	61	22	2.8	121	9.1	22.2	70	98	22.7	16.3

Data as orig. reptd. **1.** Excl. disc. ops. **2.** Refl. merger or acq. **3.** Refl. acctg. change.

Business Summary

Banta Corporation is one of the leading printing firms in the U.S. It provides a broad range of printing and graphic arts services to a variety of customers.

Products for the commercial market (46% of net sales in 1992) include catalogs and direct marketing materials. Bindery services provide ink-jet labeling and demographic binding. Healthcare products include plastic garment covers, gloves, stretcher sheets and examination table paper.

Book publishing (30%) is largely comprised of consumable grade-school workbooks. Other products for the educational market include textbooks (primarily soft-cover), testing materials and paperbound books. Banta Information Services Group serves the computer and software industries, printing manuals and offering complete turnkey servces. Multimedia products are also produced for educational publishers and industry, professional and trade associations. Other customers include publishers of religious books, trade books, cookbooks, manuals and fiction and nonfiction books.

Banta's magazine publishing segment (13%) prints more than 18.6 million magazines per month for publishers of specialty magazines. These magazines are primarily short- to medium-run publications (usually less than 350,000 copies), generally distributed to subscribers by mail.

Other operations (11%) include prepress services provided to publishers, printers, studios and advertising agencies; and KCS Industries, which produces point-of-purchase products.

Dividend Data

Cash has been paid each year since 1927. A dividend reinvestment plan is available.

Amt of Divd. $	Date Decl.	Ex–divd. Date	Stock of Record	Payment Date
0.16	Dec. 8	Jan. 11	Jan. 15	Jan. 29'93
0.18	Feb. 2	Apr. 19	Apr. 23	Apr. 30'93
3–for–2	Feb. 2	May 3	Apr. 23	Apr. 30'93
0.12	Apr. 27	Jul. 12	Jul. 16	Jul. 30'93
0.12	Jul. 27	Oct. 8	Oct. 15	Oct. 29'93

Finances

Banta said that capital spending for 1993 would be approximately $63 million.

Capitalization

Long Term Debt: $48,718,000 (7/93).

Common Stock: 19,931,990 shs. ($0.10 par).
Institutions hold some 72%.
Shareholders: 1,743 of record (2/93).

Office—River Place, Box 8003, Menasha, WI 54952-8003. **Tel**—(414) 722-7777. **Chrmn, Pres & CEO**—C. W. Aurand Jr. **VP & Secy**—R. D. Kneezel. **EVP & CFO**—G. A. Henseler. **Investor Contact**—Mark Fleming. **Dirs**—C. W. Aurand Jr., J. A. Baxter, G. T. Brophy, G. A. Henseler, B. S. Kubale, C. W. Tarr, D. Taylor, A. J. Williamson. **Transfer Agent**—Firstar Trust Co., Milwaukee. **Registrar**—Company's office. **Incorporated** in Wisconsin in 1901. **Empl**—4,172.

 William H. Donald

Baroid Corp.

NYSE Symbol BRC In S&P MidCap 400

Price	Range	P-E Ratio	Dividend	Yield	S&P Ranking	Beta
Oct. 1'93	1993					
8⅝	8¾–5⅛	32	0.20	2.3%	NR	NA

Summary

On September 7, 1993, Baroid Corp. and Dresser Industries, Inc. announced that they had signed a definitive merger agreement valued at approximately $900 million. Terms call for each BRC common share to be exchanged for 0.40 Dresser common share. The merger is subject to, among other things, completion of due diligence and approval by shareholders of both companies. Dresser Industries is a major supplier of products and services for the oil and natural gas industries.

Business Summary

Baroid Corp. supplies specialized products and services to the exploration and production segments of the oil and gas industry, through its drilling fluids, drilling services and products and offshore services businesses. During 1992, the company sold its oilfield equipment subsidiaries, Atlas Bradford Corp. and Shaffer, Inc. Business segment contributions in 1992:

	Sales	Profits
Drilling fluids	54%	69%
Drilling services	46%	31%

International activities accounted for 75% of revenues in 1992.

Drilling fluids operations are conducted through BRC's Baroid Drilling Fluids subsidiary. The primary products are drilling fluids, or "muds", that are used to lubricate and cool the drill bit, control downhole pressures, seal porous well formations and remove rock cuttings when drilling and completing oil and natural gas wells. BRC also provides a variety of related products and services for drilling in environmentally sensitive areas.

Sperry-Sun Drilling Services rents specialized steering and measurement-while-drilling tools and provides other directional drilling services worldwide for oil and gas wells.

Diamant Boart Stratabit was acquired in April 1991. Subsequently renamed DB Stratabit, Inc. (DBS), this subsidiary provides diamond drill bits and coring products and services worldwide to the oil and gas industry. The sale and rental of diamond drill bits accounted for 56% of 1992 sales.

At the end of 1992, the company formed Baroid Engineered Drilling Services, which combines the capabilities of its three operating divisions into a full-service package of drilling services.

In early 1993, BRC acquired Sub Sea International, Inc., a provider of diving and underwater engineering services to the offshore oil and gas industry, for 17.7 million common shares. Including Sub Sea, BRC's pro forma 1992 earnings from continuing operations were $0.24 a share.

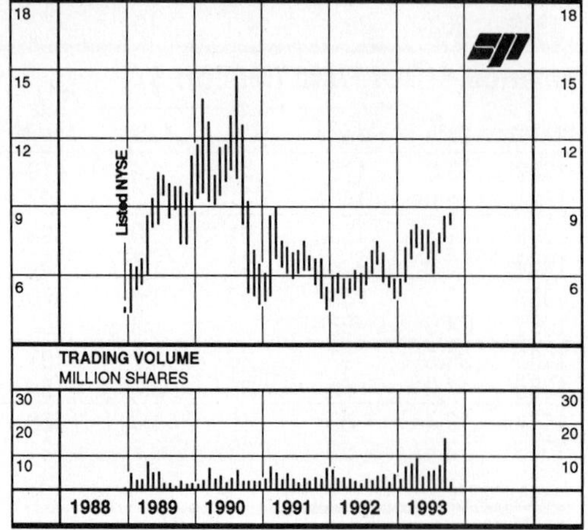

Important Developments

Sep. '93— Baroid and Dresser Industries, Inc. announced a definitive agreement for Dresser to acquire BRC in a transaction valued at about $900 million. Under the agreement, each BRC common share will be exchanged for 0.40 of a Dresser common share, subject to adjustment. The transaction is expected to close by mid-January 1994. Dresser Industries is a major global supplier of products and services for the oil and natural gas industry. Its earnings for the fiscal year ending October 31, 1993, are estimated at $0.75 a share, after a $0.30 nonrecurring charge. It currently pays a dividend of $0.15 quarterly.

Next earnings report expected in late October.

Per Share Data ($)

Yr. End Dec. 31	1992	[1]1991	[1]1990	1989	1988	1987
Tangible Bk. Val.[2]	**3.30**	3.45	3.53	5.44	5.36	NA
Cash Flow	**0.78**	0.80	0.76	0.80	NA	NA
Earnings[3]	**0.24**	0.24	0.28	0.25	[4]0.17	[4]d1.48
Dividends	**0.20**	0.20	0.20	0.20	Nil	NA
Payout Ratio	**84%**	84%	76%	81%	Nil	NA
Prices—High	**7½**	9	14¾	11¼	4⅝	NA
Low	**4⅞**	4½	4¾	4⅜	4⅜	NA
P/E Ratio—	**31–20**	38–19	53–17	45–18	27–26	NA

Data as orig. reptd.; for Baroid Corp. (Old) prior to 1990. **1.** Refl. merger or acq. **2.** Incl. intangibles. **3.** Bef. results of disc. ops. of -0.23 in 1991, +0.27 in 1990, -0.50 in 1987 & spec. items of +0.01 in 1991, +0.08 in 1990, +0.03 in 1989, +0.02 in 1988. **4.** Pro forma. d-Deficit. NA-Not Available.

Income Data (Million $)

Year Ended Dec. 31	Revs.	Oper. Inc.	% Oper. Inc. of Revs.	Cap. Exp.	Depr.	[3]Int. Exp.	Net Bef. Taxes	Eff. Tax Rate	[5]Net Inc.	% Net Inc. of Revs.	Cash Flow
1992	**614**	**70.4**	**11.5**	**34.5**	**40.5**	**15.3**	**[4]28.1**	**33.2%**	**17.7**	**2.9**	**58.2**
[1,2]1991	615	78.0	12.7	56.0	41.7	18.3	[4]26.5	32.4%	17.8	2.9	59.5
[1,2]1990	599	63.2	10.5	38.7	34.2	12.0	[4]34.8	37.8%	19.6	3.3	53.8
1989	489	39.6	8.1	22.4	33.7	8.7	[4]22.7	30.1%	[6]15.2	3.1	48.9
1988	492	39.3	8.0	16.6	35.8	7.4	18.1	39.0%	10.2	2.1	46.0
[2]1987	512	d42.9	NM	13.3	53.6	44.9	d61.4	NM	d89.5	NM	d35.8
[2]1986	549	d94.4	NM	24.5	79.0	23.5	d283.0	NM	d298.0	NM	NA
[2]1985	859	60.2	7.0	67.9	90.7	27.8	d42.0	NM	d47.0	NM	NA
[2]1984	887	NA	NA	NA	NA	NA	NA	NA	d152.0	NM	NA
[2]1983	884	NA	NA	NA	NA	NA	NA	NA	d66.0	NM	NA

Balance Sheet Data (Million $)

Dec. 31	Cash	Curr. Assets	Curr. Liab.	Curr. Ratio	Total Assets	% Ret. on Assets	Long Term Debt	Common Equity	Total Cap.	% LT Debt of Cap.	% Ret. on Equity
1992	**26.5**	**297**	**197**	**1.5**	**560**	**3.0**	**113**	**246**	**361**	**31.2**	**7.0**
1991	37.4	352	206	1.7	627	2.9	160	257	419	38.2	6.9
1990	55.5	331	176	1.9	591	2.9	145	262	413	35.1	5.9
1989	25.2	344	195	1.8	633	2.5	44	333	415	10.7	4.6
1988	19.3	248	159	1.6	562	Nil	49	325	377	12.9	Nil
1987	37.1	227	191	1.2	568	NM	31	308	343	9.1	NM
1986	100.0	293	375	0.8	831	NM	56	297	357	15.7	NM
1985	NA	NA	NA	NA	1,168	NM	92	729	NA	NA	NM
1984	NA	NA	NA	NA	1,301	NM	167	705	NA	NA	NM
1983	NA	NA	NA	NA	1,555	NM	222	922	NA	NA	NM

Data as orig. reptd.; for Baroid Corp. (Old) prior to 1990. **1.** Refl. merger or acq. **2.** Excl. disc. ops. **3.** Net of int. inc. **4.** Incl. equity in earns. of nonconsol. subs. **5.** Bef. spec. items. **6.** Refl. acctg. change. d-Deficit. NM-Not Meaningful. NA-Not Available.

Net Sales (Million $)

Quarter:	1993	1992	1991	1990
Mar.	176	170	134	124
Jun.	207	189	163	143
Sep.		193	151	155
Dec.		202	167	177
		755	615	599

Sales for the six months ended June 30, 1993, rose 6.5%, year to year, reflecting increased drilling activity in the Gulf of Mexico and improved pricing for certain product lines. SG&A expenses and interest expense were reduced, and pretax income advanced 15%. After taxes at 28.9% versus 27.5%, and sharply lower minority interest, net income climbed 22%, to $11.7 million ($0.13 a share) from $9.6 million ($0.10).

Common Share Earnings ($)

Quarter:	1993	1992	1991	1990
Mar.	0.05	0.04	0.04	0.02
Jun.	0.08	0.06	0.09	0.08
Sep.		0.07	0.08	0.08
Dec.		0.07	0.03	0.10
		0.24	0.24	0.28

Finances

The company acquired the bentonite mining operations of Tremont Corp. for $20 million in July 1993. In 1993's first quarter, BRC purchased the assets of a provider of offshore surveying services and of an industrial barite business for $7.2 million.

In November 1992, Valhi sold $379 million of zero coupon notes, secured by BRC shares, due 2007. Each $1,000 of the notes is convertible into 36.077 BRC common shares held by Valhi.

In October 1990, Baroid Corp. (Old) transferred its petroleum services business to Baroid Corp., a newly formed company, and distributed to its shareholders about 74.1 million shares of New Baroid. Old Baroid retained its titanium metals and bentonite mining businesses and changed its name to Tremont Corp.

Dividend Data

Dividends were initiated in 1988.

Amt of Divd. $	Date Decl.	Ex-divd. Date	Stock of Record	Payment Date
0.05	Oct. 29	Dec. 11	Dec. 17	Dec. 31'92
0.05	Feb. 4	Mar. 10	Mar. 16	Mar. 31'93
0.05	May 5	Jun. 10	Jun. 16	Jun. 30'93
0.05	Aug. 2	Sep. 10	Sep. 16	Sep. 30'93

Capitalization

Long Term Debt: $160,202,000 (6/93).

Minority Interest: $2,874,000.

Common Stock: 92,544,000 shs. ($0.10 par). Institutions hold 51%, including about 15% owned by Valhi, Inc. (controlled by H. C. Simmons). Shareholders of record: 15,000 (3/93).

Office—3000 North Sam Houston Parkway East, Houston, TX 77032. **Tel**—(713) 987-4000. **Chrmn & CEO**—J. L. Martin. **Pres & COO**—E. C. Hutcheson Jr. **VP-CFO**—J. S. Compofelice. **VP-Secy**—P. A. Lannie. **Investor Contact**—Robert P. Wallace. **Dirs**—F. A. Benevento II, E. C. Hutcheson Jr., J. A. Kellogg, H. J. Kelly, A. Manix, J. L. Martin, J. A. Precourt, P. M. Sacerdote, M. A. Snetzer. **Transfer Agent & Registrar**—First Chicago Trust Co. of New York, NYC. **Incorporated** in Delaware in 1990. **Empl**—4,600.

 J. R. Jordan

Battle Mountain Gold

NYSE Symbol BMG Options on CBOE (Jan-Apr-Jul-Oct) In S&P MidCap 400

Price	Range	P-E Ratio	Dividend	Yield	S&P Ranking	Beta
May 24'93	1993					
10	10⅛–4⅞	NM	0.05	0.5%	NR	0.07

Summary

In early 1993, this company brought into production the Kori Kollo sulfide gold mine (Bolivia) to replace its original Fortitude gold-silver property (Battle Mountain, Nev.), which was depleted in March 1993. Additional reserves at Kori Kollo, at the Battle Mountain complex and at the Red Dome gold mine (Australia), and successful development of promising large gold properties in Washington state and Papua New Guinea, provide potential for substantial growth of gold production by the mid-1990s.

Current Outlook

Assuming average annual gold market prices are little changed, a loss of $0.05 a share is estimated for 1993, versus 1992's loss of $0.44 (after a nonrecurring charge of $0.29).

Dividends should continue at $0.02½ semiannually.

Sales are likely to be flat in 1993, with little change expected in gold prices realized (despite greater hedging in futures markets) and in consolidated production (548,000 gold equivalent oz., versus 1992's 543,000). In 1993's first quarter, gold realizations averaged $347/oz., down from $356 a year earlier. Although inflation fears are aiding gold prices, higher real interest rates could lead to renewed downward pressure on prices. With anticipated lower exploration costs, and in the absence of a non-recurring charge, the loss should narrow, despite expected higher unit operating costs, flat gold sales and initial preferred dividends.

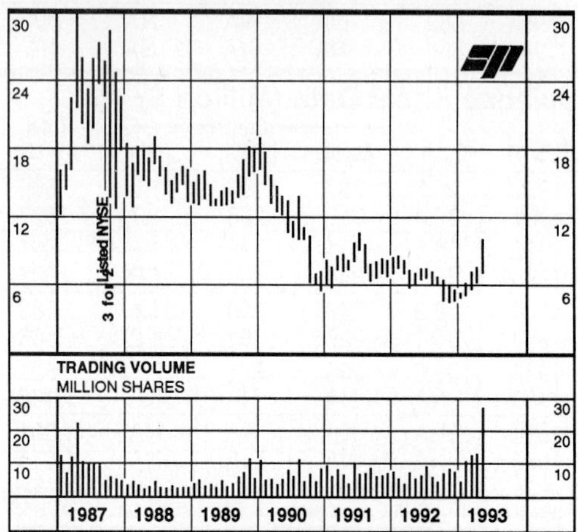

Net Sales (Million $)

Quarter:	1993	1992	1991	1990
Mar.	53.9	44.2	31.6	30.7
Jun.	---	43.3	45.2	36.1
Sep.	---	43.0	39.9	37.0
Dec.	---	51.3	53.5	39.0
	---	181.8	170.2	142.8

Net sales in the 1993 first quarter climbed 22%, year to year, as increased consolidated gold shipments (141,000 oz., versus 117,000) outweighed lower prices. Despite reduced exploration costs, With greater unit operating costs ($315/oz., versus $283), and interest expense, versus interest income, the pretax loss widened. After tax credits of $3.3 million, versus $595,000, and minority interest, the loss increased to $3.2 million ($0.04 a share), from $935,000 ($0.01, before a charge of $0.02 for accounting changes).

Common Share Earnings ($)

Quarter:	1993	1992	1991	1990
Mar.	d0.04	d0.01	0.06	0.09
Jun.	E0.01	d0.02	0.03	0.06
Sep.	Ed0.01	d0.40	d0.09	0.05
Dec.	Ed0.01	Nil	Nil	0.02
	Ed0.05	d0.44	d0.02	0.21

Important Developments

Apr. '93— BMG announced plans to develop the Reona heap leach project at its Battle Mountain complex, at a cost of $10 million. Average annual gold output of 40,000 oz. is expected over its six-year life, with startup slated for early 1994. Earlier, in March 1993, 56.5%-owned Niugini Mining Ltd. announced plans to extend the life of its Red Dome mine by pushing back a portion of the existing pit walls to access ore containing 190,000 oz. of gold, at a cost of $17 million.

Next earnings report expected in late July.

Per Share Data ($)

Yr. End Dec. 31	1992	1991	[1]1990	[2]1989	1988	1987	1986	1985
Tangible Bk. Val.	**3.37**	3.94	3.58	3.08	2.72	1.74	1.03	0.69
Cash Flow	**0.07**	0.36	0.45	0.79	1.16	0.86	0.56	0.34
Earnings[3]	**d0.44**	d0.02	0.21	0.40	0.91	0.74	0.42	0.25
Dividends	**0.100**	0.100	0.100	0.100	0.100	0.075	0.068	0.034
Payout Ratio	**NM**	NM	44%	25%	11%	10%	16%	14%
Prices—High	**8⅝**	10⅝	19	18¼	19⅛	29⅞	14⅞	9⅞
Low	**4½**	5¾	5½	13	12⅞	12¼	7¼	6¾
P/E Ratio—	**NM**	NM	90–26	46–33	21–14	40–17	35–17	40–27

Data as orig. reptd. Adj. for stk. div. of 50% Oct. 1987. **1.** Refl. acctg. change. **2.** Refl. merger or acq. **3.** Bef. spec. items of -0.02 in 1992,-0.45 in 1990. d-Deficit. E-Estimated. NM-Not Meaningful.

Income Data (Million $)

Year Ended Dec. 31	Revs.	Oper. Inc.	% Oper. Inc. of Revs.	Cap. Exp.	Depr.	Int. Exp.	Net Bef. Taxes	Eff. Tax Rate	Net Inc.	% Net Inc. of Revs.	Cash Flow
1992	**182**	**d5.1**	**NM**	**114**	**40.2**	**10.30**	**[4]d46.0**	**NM**	**[1]d34.9**	**NM**	**5.2**
1991	170	22.3	13.1	110	28.7	8.29	d5.5	NM	[5]d1.2	NM	27.5
[1]1990	143	22.9	16.0	130	17.5	6.79	[4]14.1	18.0%	[5]16.0	11.2	33.5
[2]1989	131	57.3	43.9	173	25.3	2.12	[4]39.0	31.7%	[5]26.4	20.2	51.7
1988	141	78.7	55.9	47	15.9	Nil	[4]70.8	16.1%	[5]59.4	42.2	75.3
1987	123	68.5	55.8	27	8.2	Nil	62.1	23.3%	[1,5]47.6	38.8	55.9
1986	91	44.1	48.5	10	8.9	NA	36.4	25.9%	[1,5]27.0	29.6	35.9
1985	78	27.8	35.9	5	5.7	NA	22.3	28.0%	[5]16.1	20.7	21.8
[3]1984	28	1.7	6.1	20	1.6	2.45	0.1	Nil	[5]0.1	0.3	NA

Balance Sheet Data (Million $)

Dec. 31	Cash	Curr. Assets	Curr. Liab.	Curr. Ratio	Total Assets	% Ret. on Assets	Long Term Debt	Common Equity	Total Cap.	% LT Debt of Cap.	% Ret. on Equity
1992	**45.4**	**86**	**50.1**	**1.7**	**577**	**NM**	**199**	**270**	**505**	**39.4**	**NM**
1991	28.7	58	31.9	1.8	525	NM	125	315	479	26.2	NM
1990	99.7	120	28.5	4.2	449	3.9	111	255	414	26.9	6.7
1989	39.6	56	9.7	5.8	351	9.5	50	204	338	14.8	13.8
1988	81.3	97	9.1	10.6	206	34.7	Nil	179	196	Nil	40.7
1987	52.2	61	8.3	7.4	135	43.1	Nil	113	126	Nil	53.2
1986	27.3	36	6.2	5.8	86	35.7	Nil	66	80	Nil	48.7
1985	5.4	14	5.4	2.5	65	26.6	Nil	45	59	Nil	38.9
1984	Nil	6	3.2	1.9	56	0.2	Nil	38	53	NM	NA

Data as orig. reptd. **1.** Refl. acctg. change. **2.** Refl. merger or acq. **3.** Battle Mountain Property. **4.** Incl. equity in earns. of nonconsol. subs. **5.** Bef. spec. items. d-Deficit. NM-Not Meaningful. NA-Not Available.

Business Summary

BMG and subsidiaries operate precious metals mines in the U.S., Australia and South America, and have precious metals prospects there and in the Pacific. The company's share of 1992 gold sales was 415,000 oz. (404,000 in 1991), at a total operating cost of $284/oz. ($242/oz.).

At the Battle Mountain gold mining complex (Nev.), the flagship Fortitude mine was depleted in March 1993. A small existing heap leach operation will continue for 1993. Gold output from the complex, 178,000 oz. in 1992, is estimated at 92,000 oz. for 1993. Mining at the open-pit Pajingo mine (Australia), which produced 47,000 oz. of gold in 1992, is expected to be concluded in mid-1993. Milling will continue from stockpiles through early 1994; output is put at 32,000 oz. for 1993. Operating problems at the San Luis (Colo.) gold mine hurt 1992 production (55,000 oz.); with their resolution, 1993 output is projected at 70,000 oz.

Empresa Minera Inti Raymi, S.A. of Bolivia (85%-owned) owns the Kori Kollo gold property. BMG's share of 1992 production mine was 46,000 oz., and its share of 1993 output is estimated at 153,000 oz. A new 245,000 oz./yr. mine and milling facility became operational in February 1993, at a total cost of $143 million.

BMG owns 56.5% of Niugini Mining (NM), which holds 20% of the Lihir gold discovery in Papua New Guinea (estimated reserves of 13.7 million oz.); talks on a mine development contract are progressing. Gold production at NM's Red Dome mine (Aus.), 104,000 oz. in 1992, is expected to fall to 37,000 oz. in 1993, as the original ore body nears depletion. Output at its San Cristobal heap leach gold mine (Chile) was 58,000 oz. in 1992, with 67,000 oz. targeted for 1993.

In March 1992, BMG proceeded with financing and $35 million development of its Crown Jewel gold project (Wash.) to earn a 51% interest. Output is expected to average 175,000 oz. a year, beginning by early 1995. At year-end 1992, the company's reserves were estimated at 7.21 million oz. of contained gold, distributed as follows: San Luis (5%), Battle Mountain complex (2%), Pajingo (1%), Kori Kollo (55%), Lihir (21%), Crown Jewel (11%), San Cristobal (4%) and Red Dome (1%).

Dividend Data

Dividends were initiated in 1985. A "poison pill" stock purchase right was adopted in 1988.

Amt. of Divd. $	Date Decl.	Ex-divd. Date	Stock of Record	Payment Date
0.02½	Apr. 21	Jul. 30	Aug. 5	Aug. 18'92
0.02½	Sep. 15	Oct. 30	Nov. 5	Nov. 18'92
0.02½	Nov. 19	Feb. 1	Feb. 5	Feb. 19'93

Capitalization

Long Term Debt: $215,048,000 (3/93), incl. $100 million of 6% debs. conv. into com. at $20⅝ a sh.

Minority Interest: $38,528,000.

$3.25 Cum. Preferred Stock: 2,300,000 shs.; conv. into 4.762 com. shs. ea.

Common Stock: 80,016,114 shs. ($0.10 par). Institutions hold 32%.

Office—333 Clay St., 42nd Floor, Houston, TX 77002. **Tel**—(713) 650-6400. **Chrmn & CEO**—K. E. Elers. **Pres & COO**—K. R. Werneburg. **VP-Fin & CFO**—R. D. O'Connell. **VP & Secy**—R. J. Quinn. **VP & Investor Contact**—Les Van Dyke. **Dirs**—D. J. Bourne, D. H. Caspary, C. E. Childers, J. R. Crosby, J. H. Elder, Jr., K. E. Elers, R. L. Gray, B. P. Kerr, J. H. Liedtke, T. H. Pate, Jr., K. R. Werneburg. **Transfer Agent & Registrar**—Bank of New York, NYC. **Incorporated** in Nevada in 1985. **Empl**—1,482.

 A.M. Sorrentino, CFA

Bear Stearns

NYSE Symbol BSC Options on CBOE (Jan-Apr-Jul-Oct) In S&P MidCap 400

Price	Range	P-E Ratio	Dividend	Yield	S&P Ranking	Beta
Oct. 20'93	1993					
22 3/8	26–15	7	0.60	2.7%	NR	1.45

Summary

Bear Stearns Companies is the holding company for Bear Stearns & Co., a leading investment banking and brokerage firm that ranked as the seventh largest NYSE member firm at December 31, 1992, as measured by total capital. The company's Bear Stearns Securities Corp. is one of the largest U.S. securities clearing organizations. Profits in the first quarter of fiscal 1994 benefited from strength in commissions, principal transactions and investment banking.

Business Summary

The Bear Stearns Companies is the holding company for Bear Stearns & Co., a leading investment banking and brokerage firm serving U.S. and foreign corporations, governments, and institutional and individual investors. Revenue contributions in recent fiscal years:

	1993	1992	1991
Commissions	15%	14%	14%
Principal transactions...	41%	36%	23%
Investment banking	12%	12%	8%
Interest & dividends.....	31%	37%	54%
Other.......................	1%	1%	1%

BSC provides brokerage services primarily to institutional and high net worth clients. Its registered representatives generate average gross commissions of over $450,000 a year. The company is a member of the NYSE and all other principal U.S. securities and commodities exchanges.

The company manages and participates in public offerings of debt and equity securities for a broad range of corporate clients, governments and agencies. BSC also provides advice and execution to clients on a wide range of financial matters.

Bear Stearns is one of the largest dealers making markets in corporate debt and equity securities, as well as mortgage-related and municipal securities. The company is also a "primary" dealer in U.S. government securities. BSC also conducts trading activities in Eurodollar securities in London and trading activities in foreign securities in the U.S. Other activities include fiduciary services, real estate brokerage and finance, securities research and insurance.

Bear Stearns Securities Corp., one of the largest clearing firms in the securities industry, clears and settles all of BSC's securities and commodities transactions, as well as its customers' and correspondent customers' transactions.

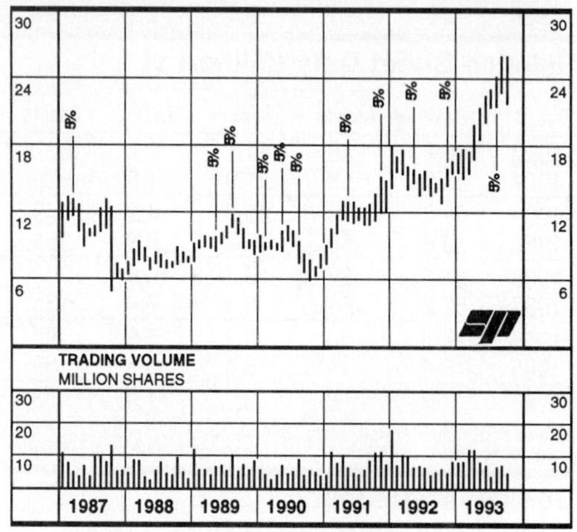

Important Developments

Oct. '93— Commenting on results of the September 1993 quarter, the company said that contributions from most of BSC's major business areas coupled with an unswerving focus on controlling operating costs aided the strong performance. Investment banking was helped by a high level of debt and equity underwriting activity during the quarter; The Correspondent Clearing, Institutional Sales and Private Client Services Departments all contributed to increased commissions; and higher principal transaction revenues were due to strong performances in the mortgage-backed securities, over-the-counter and foreign exchange areas.

Next earnings report expected in mid-July.

Per Share Data ($)

Yr. End Jun. 30[1]	1993	1992	1991	1990	1989	1988	1987	1986	1985
Tangible Bk. Val.	**14.13**	11.54	8.50	7.79	7.34	6.41	5.66	4.57	[2]4.67
Cash Flow	**NA**	NA	NA	NA	NA	NA	NA	NA	NA
Earnings[3]	**3.00**	2.45	1.12	0.86	1.21	0.95	1.26	0.95	0.64
Dividends	**0.558**	0.550	0.442	0.379	0.300	0.298	0.266	0.114	Nil
Payout Ratio	**19%**	22%	39%	44%	25%	31%	21%	12%	Nil
Prices[4]—High	**17 15/16**	17 31/32	15 1/4	10 25/32	11 27/32	9 11/32	13 9/32	15 17/32	9 11/32
Low	**12 13/16**	12 27/32	7 3/8	5 29/32	7 9/16	6 1/2	4 7/8	8 11/32	7 3/32
P/E Ratio—	**5–4**	7–5	12–6	13–7	10–6	10–7	11–4	16–9	14–11

Data as orig. reptd., prior to 1987, pro forma data as reptd. in 1986 Annual Report. Adj. for stk. divs. of 5% Aug. 1993, 5% Nov. 1992, 5% May 1992, 5% Nov. 1991, 5% May 1991, 5% Aug. 1990, May 1990, 5% Feb. 1990, 5% Aug. 1989, 5% Mar. 1987, 50% Jul. 1986, 5% Mar. 1986. **1.** Yrs. ended Apr. 30 prior to 1989. **2.** As reptd. by Co. as of Oct. 29, 1985 (adjusted for the stock offering). **3.** Bef. spec. items of -0.04 in 1987. **4.** Cal. yr. NA-Not Available.

Income Data (Million $)

Year Ended Jun. 30[1]	Commis-sions	Int. Inc.	Total Revs.	Int. Exp.	% Exp./ Op. Revs.	Net Bef. Taxes	Eff. Tax Rate	[2]Net Inc.	% Return On Revs.	% Return On Assets	% Return On [3]Equity
1993	**421**	**902**	**2,857**	**710**	**78.5**	**614**	**41.0%**	**362**	**12.7**	**0.7**	**27.7**
1992	375	997	2,677	835	81.0	508	42.0%	295	11.0	0.7	28.1
1991	339	1,279	2,380	1,141	90.4	230	37.7%	143	6.0	0.4	13.9
1990	338	1,384	2,386	1,217	91.9	193	38.0%	119	5.0	0.4	11.8
1989	347	1,254	2,365	1,090	87.8	287	40.0%	172	7.3	0.5	18.0
1988	404	846	1,888	668	89.3	201	29.0%	143	7.6	0.5	13.1
1987	350	684	1,774	550	81.4	329	46.4%	176	9.9	0.7	21.6
1986	267	1,438	2,164	1,218	89.5	227	41.9%	132	6.1	0.5	30.6
1985	202	1,309	1,804	1,173	92.1	143	38.4%	88	4.9	NA	NA

Balance Sheet Data (Million $)

Jun. 30[1]	Total Assets	Cash Items	Rec.	Secs. Owned	Sec. Borrowed	Due Brokers & Cust.	Other Liabs.	Capitalization [5]Debt	Capitalization [3]Equity	Capitalization Total
1993	**57,440**	**2,610**	**38,840**	**15,215**	**28,743**	**14,634**	**10,404**	**1,883**	**1,439**	**3,660**
1992	45,768	2,280	30,292	12,162	24,630	11,338	7,483	1,040	1,127	2,167
1991	39,285	2,331	27,317	8,792	24,077	9,011	4,443	682	1,001	1,754
1990	31,574	2,640	19,504	8,746	13,439	11,864	4,812	384	1,001	1,460
1989	36,410	1,614	24,325	9,733	17,254	8,875	8,831	385	964	1,451
1988	32,171	1,463	21,387	8,787	15,392	8,529	6,840	386	851	1,410
1987	25,247	446	15,517	8,921	11,929	6,637	5,357	387	736	1,325
1986	26,939	547	17,662	8,545	13,372	6,663	5,955	298	581	949
[4]1985	25,867	235	16,872	8,609	12,478	4,217	8,658	164	280	514

Data as orig. reptd. prior to 1987 pro forma data as reptd. in 1986 Annual Report. **1.** Years ended Apr. 30 of fol. cal. yr. prior to 1989. **2.** Bef. spec. item(s) in 1987. **3.** Common. **4.** As of Oct. 29, 1985. **5.** Incl. current portion. NA-Not Available.

Revenues (Million $)

Quarter:	1993–94	1992–93	1991–92	1990–91
Sep.	772	605	597	562
Dec.		632	698	587
Mar.		735	712	627
Jun.		885	670	605
		2,857	2,677	2,380

Total revenues in the three months ended September 24, 1993, rose 28%, year to year, reflecting a 27% increase in commissions, 15% higher revenues from principal transactions, 91% greater investment banking revenues, and a 19% increase in interest and dividend income. Net revenues (after deducting interest costs) were up 34%. Operating costs increased 24%, and pretax income was up 64%. After taxes at 41.4%, versus 42.0%, net income rose 66%. Share earnings were $0.81, on 1.4% more shares, versus $0.55.

Common Share Earnings ($)

Quarter:	1993–94	1992–93	1991–92	1990–91
Sep.	0.81	0.55	0.38	0.12
Dec.		0.52	0.64	0.12
Mar.		0.92	0.76	0.47
Jun.		1.02	0.68	0.42
		3.00	2.45	1.12

Dividend Data

Dividends were initiated in 1986.

Amt. of Divd. $	Date Decl.	Ex–divd. Date	Stock of Record	Payment Date
0.15	Oct. 27	Nov. 9	Nov. 16	Nov. 30'92
5% Stk.	Oct. 27	Nov. 9	Nov. 16	Nov. 30'92
0.15	Jan. 25	Feb. 8	Feb. 12	Feb. 26'93
0.15	Apr. 15	May 10	May 14	May 28'93
0.15	Aug. 3	Aug. 11	Aug. 17	Aug. 31'93
5% Stk.	Aug. 3	Aug. 11	Aug. 17	Aug. 31'93

Finances

At June 30, 1993, BSC's regulatory net capital of $885.5 million exceeded the minimum requirement by $873.1 million.

Profits and revenues are subject to wide fluctuations, reflecting securities markets conditions, the level and volatility of interest rates and other factors over which BSC has little control.

Capitalization

Long Term Debt: $1,883,123,000 (6/93).

Adj. Rate Cum. Preferred Stock: 881,450 shs. ($50 liquid. pref.).

7.88% Cum. Preferred, Series B: 937,500 shs. ($200 liquidation pref.).

Common Stock: 123,211,523 shs. ($1 par). Directors and officers own about 15%. Institutions hold approximately 57%. Shareholders of record: 3,854.

Office—245 Park Ave., New York, NY 10167. **Tel**—(212) 272-2000. **Chrmn**—A. C. Greenberg. **Pres & CEO**—J. E. Cayne. **Secy**—K. L. Edlow. **Treas**—M. Minikes. **Investor Contact**—Hannah Burns (212) 272-2395. **Dirs**—E. G. Bewkes III, D. A. Bovin, J. E. Cayne, M. R. Dabney, Jr., A. H. Einbender, G. J. Fippinger, C. D. Glickman, T. R. Green, A. C. Greenberg, R. Harriton, N. E. Havens-Hasty, J. Ilany, D. L. Keating, J. W. Kluge, D. A. Liebowitz, B. M. Lisman, M.J. Mancuso, V. J. Mattone, M. Minikes, W. J. Montgoris, R. B. Roberts, E. J. Rosenwald Jr., F. V. Salerno, A. D. Schwartz, J. C. Sites Jr., W. J. Spector, R. M. Steinberg, J. Steinhardt, M. L. Tarnopol, M. E. Tennenbaum, E. K. Wolk, U. Zucker. **Transfer Agent & Registrar**—Security Trust Co., Baltimore, Md. **Incorporated** in Delaware in 1985. **Empl**—6,306.

 Paul L. Huberman, CFA

Beckman Instruments

NYSE Symbol BEC Options on CBOE (Jan-Apr-Jul-Oct) In S&P MidCap 400

Price	Range	P-E Ratio	Dividend	Yield	S&P Ranking	Beta
Aug. 26'93	1993					
22⅛	25½–19⅝	14	0.36	1.7%	NR	NA

Summary

This company produces services laboratory systems for biological analysis and investigation into life processes. A new generation of diagnostic products and plant consolidations allowed earnings to increase significantly in 1992, despite continued weakness in public funding for research instrumentation. Another earnings gain is projected for 1993, on higher diagnostic sales, an improved product mix and lower costs. Further progress is likely in 1994.

Current Outlook

Earnings for 1994 should approximate $2.00, up from $1.75 projected for 1993.

An increase in the $0.09 quarterly dividend is likely in January 1994.

Sales are expected to increase about 5% in 1994, assuming that the dollar stabilizes. Sales to the life sciences market should benefit from the company's focus on pharmaceutical and biotechnology markets, which should outweigh continued weak demand from publicly funded universities and medical schools. Diagnostic sales are likely to increase only modestly. Although new product introductions are likely to allow BEC to boost its market share, the market itself is likely to decrease. Continued economic weakness in Europe will also have a negative impact. Margins are likely to widen, benefiting from newer products that have wider margins, and from aggressive efforts to reduce costs.

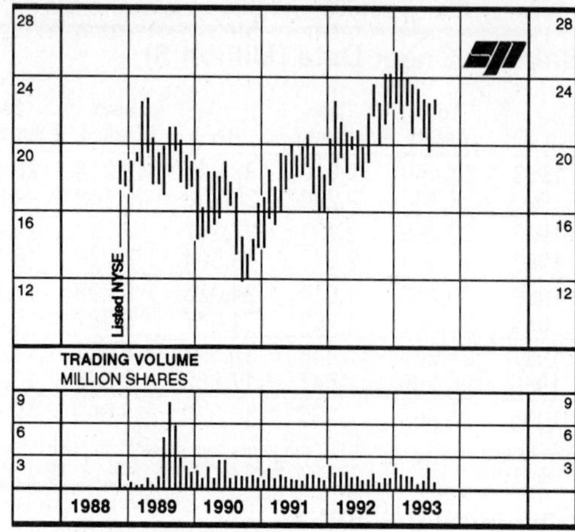

Revenues (Million $)

Quarter:	1993	1992	1991	1990
Mar.	201.7	213.0	195.9	185.5
Jun.	221.8	225.1	220.2	202.9
Sep.	---	220.5	208.1	201.0
Dec.	---	250.2	233.7	225.8
	---	908.8	857.9	815.2

Sales in the six months ended June 30, 1993, declined 3.3%, year to year, principally due to a strengthening of the U.S. dollar. With a more favorable product mix and lower marketing, administrative and general expenses, operating income increased 2.4%. Following an 11% decline in non-operating expense, pretax income rose 4.6%. After taxes at 36.0%, versus 38.8%, income advanced 9.5%, to $0.78 a share, from $0.69. Results in the 1993 interim exclude a net charge of $0.14 for accounting changes.

Earnings Per Share ($)

Quarter:	1993	1992	1991	1990
Mar.	0.36	0.32	0.28	0.28
Jun.	0.42	0.37	0.32	0.30
Sep.	E0.48	0.40	0.35	0.33
Dec.	E0.49	0.44	0.37	0.35
	E1.75	1.53	1.32	1.26

Important Developments

Jul. '93— BEC said life sciences sales in the U.S. in the 1993 second quarter rose more than 5%, year to year; sales outside the U.S. declined somewhat. Diagnostic sales outside the U.S. decreased, primarily because of a strengthening dollar and healthcare cost containment programs in key European markets. U.S. diagnostic sales were also down slightly.

Next earnings report expected in mid-October.

Per Share Data ($)

Yr. End Dec. 31	1992	1991	1990	1989	1988	1987
Tangible Bk. Val.	**12.51**	11.87	11.24	9.38	8.14	[1]6.27
Cash Flow	**3.76**	3.23	2.92	2.85	2.76	NA
Earnings[2]	**1.53**	1.32	1.26	1.47	1.49	1.06
Dividends	**0.30**	0.28	0.28	0.28	Nil	NA
Payout Ratio	**20%**	21%	22%	19%	Nil	NA
Prices—High	**24¼**	20⅝	19	22¾	19	NA
Low	**17⅝**	13⅞	11⅞	17⅛	17½	NA
P/E Ratio—	**16–12**	16–11	15–9	15–12	13–12	NA

Data as orig. reptd.; prior to 1988 pro forma data as reptd. in prospectus dated Nov. 4, 1988. **1.** As of Jun. 30, 1988. **2.** Bef. spec. items in 1987. E-Estimated. NA-Not Available.

Income Data (Million $)

Year Ended Dec. 31	Revs.	Oper. Inc.	% Oper. Inc. of Revs.	Cap. Exp.	Depr.	Int. Exp.	Net Bef. Taxes	Eff. Tax Rate	[2]Net Inc.	% Net Inc. of Revs.	Cash Flow
1992	**909**	**151**	**16.6**	**91.4**	**63.9**	**13.0**	**70.7**	**38.0%**	**43.8**	**4.8**	**108**
1991	858	130	15.2	69.7	55.5	15.3	63.8	40.3%	38.1	4.4	94
1990	815	119	14.6	67.3	47.6	17.1	61.4	41.0%	36.2	4.4	84
1989	786	123	15.7	56.6	39.2	17.1	72.3	42.0%	41.9	5.3	81
1988	770	119	15.5	47.5	36.2	13.9	74.2	42.7%	42.5	5.5	79
[1]1987	691	111	16.1	44.0	48.2	17.7	55.5	45.6%	30.2	4.4	83
1986	593	76	12.9	30.7	38.6	8.8	39.1	46.0%	21.1	3.6	NA
1985	551	70	12.7	34.3	34.1	8.9	45.3	51.2%	22.1	4.0	NA
1984	529	NA	NA	33.2	NA	NA	62.5	39.5%	37.8	7.1	NA
1983	547	NA	NA	NA	NA	NA	27.7	48.7%	14.2	2.6	NA

Balance Sheet Data (Million $)

Dec. 31	Cash	Curr. Assets	Curr. Liab.	Curr. Ratio	Total Assets	% Ret. on Assets	Long Term Debt	Common Equity	Total Cap.	% LT Debt of Cap.	% Ret. on Equity
1992	**46.0**	**509**	**281**	**1.8**	**738**	**6.1**	**59.5**	**357**	**430**	**13.8**	**12.6**
1991	33.9	492	264	1.9	712	5.5	59.0	343	409	14.4	11.4
1990	27.7	465	247	1.9	681	5.6	64.6	326	395	16.4	12.1
1989	17.8	412	225	1.8	607	7.1	75.9	269	350	21.7	16.7
1988	21.7	393	230	1.7	578	6.0	77.3	232	313	24.7	12.4
[1,3]1987	16.7	418	241	1.7	600	NA	24.0	179	333	44.0	NA
1986	39.2	383	179	2.1	637	3.2	28.8	386	445	6.5	5.2
1985	NA	NA	NA	NA	690	3.2	32.1	418	NA	NA	5.4
1984	NA	NA	NA	NA	704	5.3	36.1	394	NA	NA	10.1
1983	NA	NA	NA	NA	735	NA	43.8	357	NA	NA	NA

Data as orig. reptd.; prior to 1988 pro forma data as reptd. in prospectus dated Nov. 4, 1988. **1.** Pro forma, giving effect to the initial public offering and related transactions. **2.** Bef. spec. items. **3.** As of Jun. 30, 1988. NA-Not Available.

Business Summary

Beckman Instruments is one of the world's leading manufacturers of laboratory instruments.

The Bioanalytical Systems Group serves the life sciences laboratory market. Its products facilitate the whole range of laboratory processes in laboratories concerned with cells, subcellular particles and biochemical compounds fundamental to the dynamics of biology and the mechanisms of disease. BEC believes that it is one of the largest suppliers to the $3 billion worldwide market for life sciences laboratory products used by publicly funded researchers and private companies. Over 75 models of instruments are sold, in addition to a broad range of related accessories, consumable products and software.

Diagnostic Systems Group products detect and quantify various chemical substances of clinical interest (analytes) in human blood, urine and other body fluids. Products include a broad and flexible range of instrument systems and related products. Analytes are measured in vitro (which means that they are measured outside the body). The group concentrates in the area of clinical chemistry and immune disease testing, which is estimated to make up nearly 50% of the $15 billion worldwide market for vitro diagnostic products. In 1992, sales in the diagnostic laboratory market accounted for more than 55% of total company sales.

In 1992, foreign operations accounted for 45% of sales and 59% of operating income. However, all expenses for R&D and engineering ($85.9 million in 1992) are charged to U.S. operations.

Dividend Data

Dividends were initiated in February 1989. A "poison pill" stock purchase right was adopted in March 1989.

Amt. of Divd. $	Date Decl.	Ex-divd. Date	Stock of Record	Payment Date
0.08	Sep. 29	Nov. 6	Nov. 13	Dec. 3'92
0.09	Jan. 28	Feb. 8	Feb. 12	Mar. 4'93
0.09	Apr. 12	May 10	May 14	Jun. 3'93
0.09	Jul. 30	Aug. 9	Aug. 13	Sep. 2'93

Finances

In July 1989, SmithKline Beckman Corp. distributed its 84% interest in the Beckman Instruments to its shareholders at the rate of 0.18 of a BEC share for each SmithKline Beckman share held, in connection with a merger with Beecham Group plc.

Capitalization

Long Term Debt: $116,000,000 (6/93).

Common Stock: 28,301,117 shs. ($0.10 par).
Institutions hold 51%.
Shareholders of record: 11,852.

Office—2500 Harbor Blvd., Fullerton, CA 92634. **Tel**—(714) 871-4848. **Chrmn & Pres**—L. T. Rosso. **VP-Fin & CFO**—G. F. Kilmain. **VP & Secy**—W. H. May **Investor Contact**—Jay Steffenhagen (714-773-7764). **Dirs**—E. H. Clark, Jr., C. K. Davis. G. S. Herbert, G. F. Kilmain, F. P. Lucier, L. T. Rosso, D. S. Tappan Jr., H. Wendt. **Transfer Agent & Registrar**—First Chicago Trust Co. of New York, NYC. **Incorporated** in California in 1934; reincorporated in Delaware in 1988. **Empl**—6,879.

 Paul H. Valentine, CFA

Belo (A.H.) Corp.

NYSE Symbol BLC In S&P MidCap 400

Price	Range	P-E Ratio	Dividend	Yield	S&P Ranking	Beta
Aug. 25'93	1993					
47½	49⅝–38¾	22	0.56	1.2%	B	1.06

Summary

This newspaper and broadcasting concern publishes The Dallas Morning News, as well as several community newspapers. Broadcasting properties include five network-affiliated TV stations. Revenues and earnings through 1993 should continue to benefit from the late 1991 acquisition of substantially all of the assets of the publisher of the Dallas Times Herald, a former rival newspaper in that city. Prospects are also enhanced by above average economies in the company's major markets.

Current Outlook

Earnings for 1993 are projected at $2.30 a share, up 21% from 1992's $1.90. A gain to $2.75 is anticipated for 1994.

A modest increase in the $0.14 quarterly dividend is likely in the second half of 1993.

In the absence of a rival publisher in Dallas, and with a moderately growing economy, newspaper revenues are expected to gain at least 6% in 1993. TV advertising revenues will be boosted by strength in local markets and unusual political advertising. Belo continues to benefit from economies of scale realized upon the demise of its newspaper rival, but higher newsprint prices, particularly in the second half, will restrict margins. Interest expense will be substantially lower.

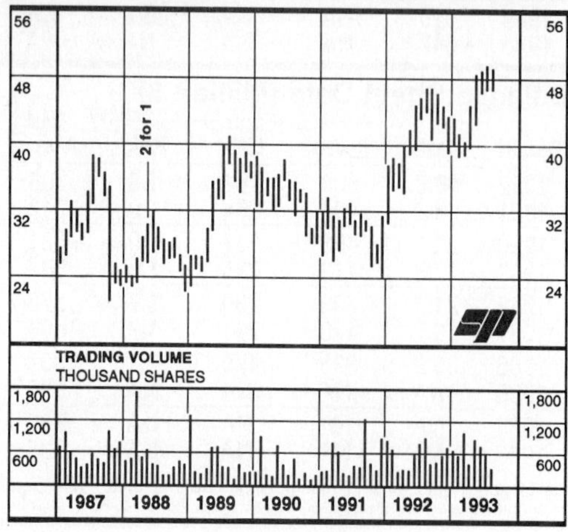

Operating Revenues (Million $)

Quarter:	1993	1992	1991	1989
Mar.	122.8	114.7	94.2	91.1
Jun.	143.8	134.2	111.9	109.3
Sep.		127.8	104.1	101.5
Dec.		139.3	121.4	115.2
		515.9	431.6	417.1

Revenues in the six months ended June 30, 1993, increased 7.1%, year to year. Profitability benefited from operating efficiencies, and operating earnings advanced 16%. Despite the absence of net income of $3.2 million from a claim settelement, results benefited from a a 41% drop in interest costs; pretax income climbed 22%. After taxes at 39.3%, versus 40.1%, net income soared 24%. Share earnings rose to $1.17 a share, from $0.95.

Common Share Earnings ($)

Quarter:	1993	1992	1991	1990
Mar.	0.37	0.33	d0.10	0.14
Jun.	0.80	0.63	0.34	0.45
Sep.	E0.44	0.36	0.10	0.29
Dec.	E0.69	0.56	0.31	0.67
	E2.30	1.90	0.65	1.55

Important Developments

Aug. '93— Belo said its president and COO, James P. Sheehan, would retire at the end of 1993. Robert W. Decherd, the company's chairman and CEO, will then assume the additional title of president, and the position of COO will be eliminated.

Jul. '93— The company said publishing revenues rose 5% in the 1993 second quarter, aided by gains in retail and classified advertising linage and higher advertising rates. Daily and Sunday circulation were up 3% and 1%, respectively. Higher newsprint prices hurt operating earnings, which declined 6.4%. Broadcast division revenues gained 11%, and second quarter earnings soared 29%, year to year. The gains stemmed from unusual political advertising in Texas and continued strength in the Houston market.

Next earnings report expected in late October.

Per Share Data ($)

Yr. End Dec. 31	1992	1991	1990	1989	1988	1987	1986	1985	1984	[1]1983
Tangible Bk. Val.	**d4.45**	d6.78	d7.72	d7.55	d7.89	d8.24	d7.64	d6.10	d7.22	8.47
Cash Flow	**3.74**	2.43	3.34	2.81	2.13	2.10	2.73	1.63	2.82	2.08
Earnings[2]	**1.90**	0.65	1.55	1.16	0.51	1.22	1.47	1.03	2.34	1.63
Dividends	**0.54**	0.52	0.48	0.44	0.43	0.40	0.40	0.40	0.36	0.36
Payout Ratio	**28%**	79%	30%	37%	84%	31%	26%	39%	15%	27%
Prices—High	**46⅞**	33¾	38⅝	41	32	38⅝	31⅛	28½	25⅛	25⅞
Low	**30⅝**	24¼	28¼	23	22⅜	21⅛	24¼	21⅛	17⅞	16⅞
P/E Ratio—	**25–16**	52–37	25–18	35–20	63–44	32–17	21–17	28–21	11–8	16–10

Data as orig. reptd. Adj. for stk. divs. of 100% May 1988 (Class B com. stk.) **1.** Refl. merger or acq. **2.** Bef. spec. items of -0.18 in 1987, -0.57 in 1986, +1.10 in 1984. d-Deficit. E-Estimated.

Income Data (Million $)

Year Ended Dec. 31	Revs.	Oper. Inc.	% Oper. Inc. of Revs.	Cap. Exp.	Depr.	Int. Exp.	Net Bef. Taxes	Eff. Tax Rate	[2]Net Inc.	% Net Inc. of Revs.	Cash Flow
1992	**516**	**118**	**22.8**	**55.9**	**36.0**	**24.6**	**61.6**	**39.6%**	**37.2**	**7.2**	**73.2**
1991	432	89	20.6	19.7	34.1	24.3	18.6	33.4%	12.4	2.9	46.5
1990	439	115	26.2	26.3	34.4	31.2	45.7	35.2%	29.6	6.7	63.9
1989	417	112	26.9	21.8	33.5	28.6	47.9	51.2%	23.4	5.6	56.9
1988	385	88	22.8	25.0	32.4	30.1	21.0	52.0%	10.1	2.6	42.5
1987	382	91	23.8	39.3	18.9	32.4	46.0	43.2%	26.1	6.8	45.0
1986	397	106	26.8	51.0	28.6	38.1	62.4	47.1%	[3]33.0	8.3	61.7
1985	385	99	25.6	33.1	14.2	41.0	44.4	46.3%	23.8	6.2	38.0
1984	354	102	28.8	61.0	11.1	40.9	96.2	43.7%	54.1	15.3	65.2
[1]1983	243	62	25.4	9.1	8.7	Nil	55.8	44.0%	31.2	12.9	40.0

Balance Sheet Data (Million $)

Dec. 31	Cash	Curr. Assets	Curr. Liab.	Curr. Ratio	Total Assets	% Ret. on Assets	Long Term Debt	Common Equity	Total Cap.	% LT Debt of Cap.	% Ret. on Equity
1992	**3**	**102**	**69.7**	**1.5**	**759**	**4.8**	**302**	**281**	**685**	**44.1**	**14.3**
1991	1	101	75.7	1.3	746	1.7	337	230	668	50.5	5.4
1990	3	91	61.7	1.5	694	4.3	280	224	622	45.1	13.2
1989	3	91	66.4	1.4	701	3.3	291	233	632	46.0	10.1
1988	8	94	61.4	1.5	720	1.4	327	235	653	50.0	4.3
1987	7	97	65.7	1.5	732	3.6	346	238	659	52.5	10.8
1986	6	112	67.1	1.7	757	4.6	357	266	683	52.2	12.1
1985	16	102	55.8	1.8	722	3.4	340	301	664	51.3	8.1
1984	3	83	49.3	1.7	692	11.2	349	286	643	54.2	20.6
1983	106	160	34.7	4.6	278	12.9	Nil	240	244	0.2	15.1

Data as orig. reptd. **1.** Refl. merger or acq. **2.** Bef. spec. items. **3.** Refl. acctg. change.

Business Summary

A.H. Belo's principal businesses are newspaper publishing and television broadcasting. Segment contributions in 1992 were:

	Revs.	Profits
Newspaper publishing.........	61%	43%
TV broadcasting	39%	57%

Belo's major newspaper property is The Dallas Morning News, the only major newspaper in Dallas since the closing of its rival in December 1991. Average paid circulation in the six-month period ended March 31, 1993, was 537,152 daily, and 834,035 Sunday, up 11% and 12%, respectively, from the year-earlier period. The company also publishes seven community newspapers, published three times per week, serving suburban communities in the Dallas-Fort Worth metropolitan area.

The companyh owns five network-affiliated television stations: WFAA-TV (an ABC affiliate), Dallas-Fort Worth; KHOU-TV (CBS), Houston; KXTV (CBS), Sacramento, Calif.; KOTV (CBS), Tulsa, Okla.; and WVEC-TV (ABC), Hampton-Norfolk, Va.

Finances

Belo said it may redeem its nearly $100 million in 8⅝% notes in December 1993 through borrowings under a revolving credit agreement.

In May 1992, the company began a $41 million expansion of its newspaper facility located in Plano, Tex. Completion is scheduled for the 1993 fourth quarter.

In May 1992, Belo entered into a partnership to acquire and operate cable systems. Its investment will total $23 million. The venture marks a strategic turnabout for the company, which in June 1984 sold a Clarksville, Tenn., cable system.

Dividend Data

Dividends have been paid since 1939. Payments are identical on the Class A and Class B shares. A "poison pill" stock purchase right was adopted in 1986.

Amt. of Divd. $	Date Decl.	Ex–divd. Date	Stock of Record	Payment Date
0.14	Sep. 23	Nov. 2	Nov. 6	Dec. 10'92
0.14	Feb. 24	Mar. 1	Mar. 5	Mar. 10'93
0.14	May 5	May 10	May 14	Jun. 10'93
0.14	Jul. 28	Aug. 2	Aug. 6	Sep. 10'93

Capitalization

Long Term Debt: $282,243,000 (3/31/93).

Class A Common Stk.: 13,602,340 shs. ($1.67 par).

Class B Common Stk.: 6,071,596 shs. ($1.67 par); 10 votes per sh.; limited transferability; conv. sh.-for-sh. into Cl. A.

About 26% of Cl. A and Cl. B stock closely held. Institutions hold 50% of both classes. Shareholders of record: 769.

Office—400 South Record St., Dallas, TX 75202. **Tel**—(214) 977-6600. **Chrmn & CEO**—R. W. Decherd. **Vice Chrmn**—W. L. Huey, Jr. **Pres & COO**—J. P. Sheehan. **SVP & CFO**—M. D. Perry. **SVP & Secy**—M. J. McCarthy. **Investor Contact**—Kelly Bitzer. **Dirs**—J. W. Bassett, Jr., J. L. Craven, J. M. Dealey, R. W. Decherd, D. D. Herndon, W. L. Huey, Jr., L. A. Levy, J. M. Moroney, Jr., B. Osborne, R. A. Overcash, Jr., H. G. Robinson, W. H. Seay, J. P. Sheehan, W. T. Solomon, T. B. Walker, Jr., J. M. Williams. **Transfer Agent & Registrar**—Chemical Bank, NYC. **Incorporated** in Texas in 1926; reincorporated in Delaware in 1987. **Empl**—2,788.

 William H. Donald

Bergen Brunswig

ASE Symbol BBC (Class A) Options on CBOE (Mar-Jun-Sep-Dec) In S&P MidCap 400

Price	Range	P–E Ratio	Dividend	Yield	S&P Ranking	Beta
Oct. 7'93	1993					
14¾	24⅜–14⅛	19	0.40	2.7%	B+	1.22

Summary

This company is the second largest pharmaceutical distributor in the U.S. The late 1992 acquisition of Durr-Fillauer Medical Inc., a distributor of pharmaceuticals and medical-surgical supplies, boosted annual revenues by about 20%. Earnings in fiscal 1993 were penalized by a significant one-time charge related to a planned restructuring of the drug distribution business.

Business Summary

Bergen Brunswig Corp. is the second largest U.S. distributor of health care products sold by institutional (hospital) and retail pharmacies. The company's home entertainment product distribution business was sold in June 1992.

Through Bergen Brunswig Drug Co. and Durr Drug Co. (a subsidiary of Durr-Fillauer Medical Inc., which was acquired in September 1992), the company distributes a full line of pharmaceuticals, proprietary medicines, cosmetics, toiletries, personal health products, sundries, and home healthcare supplies and equipment. These products are sold to a large number of hospital pharmacies, health maintenance organizations (HMOs), independent retail pharmacies, pharmacy chains, supermarkets, food-drug combination stores and other retailers located in 49 states, Washington, D.C. and Guam. Based on sales, Bergen is the second largest U.S. pharmaceutical distributor.

The company has been an innovator in the development and utilization of computer-based retailer order entry systems and electronic data interchange systems including computer-to-computer ordering systems with suppliers. Substantially all of the drug company's orders received from customers are received via electronic order entry systems. Bergen is expanding its electronic interface with its suppliers and now electronically processes a substantial portion of its purchase orders, invoices and payments.

In June 1992, Bergen sold its 81% interest in Commtron Corp., the largest U.S. distributor of prerecorded video cassettes and a national distributor of a wide range of consumer electronics items, to Ingram Industries. The company received total proceeds of about $63.9 million.

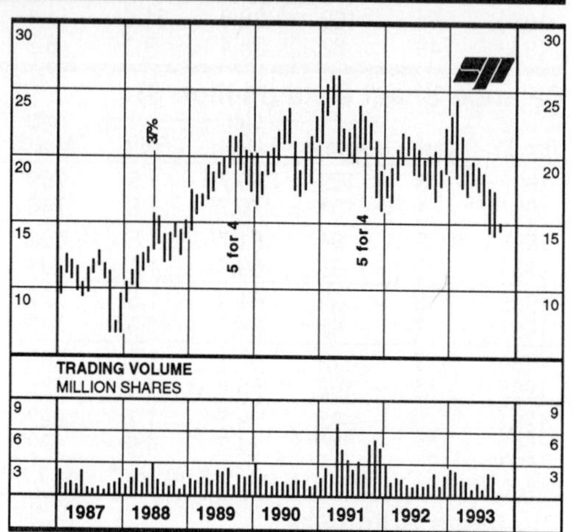

Important Developments

Sep. '93— The company announced plans to restructure its drug distribution business in response to current adverse trends affecting gross profit margins in the wholesale drug industry, including lower manufacturers' price increases and increased competition. The restructuring will include consolidation of distribution facilities, merging of duplicate operating systems, reduction of administrative support in areas not affecting valued services to customers, and the discontinuance of services and programs not meeting strategic and economic return objectives. Bergen recorded a one-time after-tax charge of $20.8 million related to the restructuring in the fourth quarter of fiscal 1993.

Next earnings report expected in mid-December.

Per Share Data ($)

Yr. End Aug. 31	1993	[1]1992	1991	1990	1989	1988	1987	1986	1985	1984
Tangible Bk. Val.	**NA**	9.22	9.35	8.70	7.55	4.82	3.60	3.10	3.82	4.74
Cash Flow	**NA**	1.81	1.85	1.76	1.86	1.56	0.98	1.10	1.06	0.97
Earnings[2,3]	**0.79**	1.41	1.50	1.46	1.48	1.14	0.56	0.72	[2,3]0.82	[2,3]0.82
Dividends	**0.400**	0.400	0.340	0.288	0.218	0.177	0.150	0.148	0.142	0.142
Payout Ratio	**51%**	28%	22%	20%	19%	15%	27%	20%	17%	17%
Prices[4]—High	**24⅜**	22¼	26¼	23¾	21¾	15¾	12⅞	7⅜	14½	12⁵⁄₁₆
Low	**14⅛**	16⅝	6	1⅜	14⅜	9	6¾	¹¹⁄₁₆	9¹³⁄₁₆	8½
P/E Ratio—	**31–18**	16–12	18–11	16–11	15–10	14–8	23–12	24–11	18–12	15–10

Data as orig. reptd. Adj. for stk. divs. of 25% Sep. 1991, 25% Sep. 1989, 37% Jun. 1988, 5% Jan. 1986, 25% Mar. 1983. **1.** Refl. merger or acquisition. **2.** Bef. results of disc. ops. of +0.21 in 1992, +0.06 in 1988, -0.18 in 1984, -0.05 in 1983, and spec. item(s) of +0.08 in 1990. **3.** Ful. dil.: 1.36 in 1992, 1.44 in 1991, 1.40 in 1990, 1.33 in 1989, 1.04 in 1988, 0.70 in 1986, 0.81 in 1985. **4.** Cal yr. NA-Not Available.

Income Data (Million $)

Year Ended Aug. 31	Revs.	Oper. Inc.	% Oper. Inc. of Revs.	Cap. Exp.	Depr.	Int. Exp.	Net Bef. Taxes	Eff. Tax Rate	[3]Net Inc.	% Net Inc. of Revs.	Cash Flow
[1,2]**1992**	**5,048**	**105**	**2.1**	**18.9**	**15.0**	**[5]6.9**	**83**	**36.5%**	**53.0**	**1.1**	**68.1**
1991	4,838	132	2.7	22.4	14.8	[5]14.5	102	35.8%	64.1	1.3	79.0
1990	4,442	127	2.9	30.1	12.9	[5]12.2	102	36.8%	62.6	1.4	75.5
1989	3,923	105	2.7	17.8	12.4	[5]13.8	79	37.5%	47.6	1.2	60.0
[1]1988	3,486	82	2.4	10.4	12.0	14.4	56	40.0%	[4]32.9	0.9	44.8
1987	3,376	61	1.8	10.1	12.1	16.5	33	50.0%	15.9	0.5	28.0
[2]1986	3,066	52	1.7	12.7	11.0	18.8	36	42.2%	20.7	0.7	31.6
[2]1985	2,435	60	2.5	13.3	6.8	7.6	46	49.0%	[4]23.3	1.0	30.0
[1,2]1984	1,703	51	3.0	7.8	4.0	2.3	45	48.0%	23.4	1.4	27.4
[1]1983	1,452	44	3.1	6.2	3.1	2.3	39	48.6%	20.0	1.4	23.1

Balance Sheet Data (Million $)

		Curr.									
Aug. 31	Cash	Assets	Liab.	Ratio	Total Assets	% Ret. on Assets	Long Term Debt	Common Equity	Total Cap.	% LT Debt of Cap.	% Ret. on Equity
1992	**308**	**1,192**	**771**	**1.5**	**1,412**	**4.1**	**224**	**395**	**631**	**35.5**	**13.4**
1991	304	1,119	610	1.8	1,322	5.1	211	455	698	30.2	14.5
1990	295	1,048	550	1.9	1,238	5.6	199	446	673	29.5	14.9
1989	130	818	509	1.6	986	4.2	48	391	465	10.3	13.3
1988	101	725	452	1.6	889	3.9	193	219	437	44.3	16.1
1987	59	614	378	1.6	785	2.0	198	189	407	48.6	8.7
1986	18	613	358	1.7	785	2.9	213	177	404	52.8	12.3
1985	38	514	309	1.7	629	4.6	147	160	307	47.9	15.5
1984	20	341	220	1.6	379	6.5	14	139	153	8.9	17.7
1983	18	313	200	1.6	345	6.0	15	124	141	10.8	18.1

Data as orig. reptd. **1.** Excl. disc. ops. **2.** Refl. merger or acq. **3.** Bef. spec. items. **4.** Refl. acctg. change. **5.** Net of interest income.

Revenues (Billion $)

Quarter:	1992–93	[1]1991–92	1990–91	1989–90
Nov.	1.60	1.15	1.18	1.09
Feb.	1.70	1.22	1.16	1.09
May	1.76	1.34	1.24	1.14
Aug.	1.76	1.34	1.25	1.13
	6.82	5.05	4.84	4.44

Based on a preliminary report, revenues for the fiscal year ended August 31, 1993, climbed 35% from those of the prior year, largely reflecting the Durr-Fillauer acquisition. Profitability was penalized by lower gross margins in the pharmaceutical distribution business and by a $20.8 million nonrecurring after-tax charge related to the planned restructuring of that business. Net income declined 46%, to $28,607,000 ($0.79 a share), from $53,012,000 ($1.41). Results exclude an extraordinary loss from the early extingusihment of debt of $0.07 a share and income from discontinued operations of $0.21 a share in the respective periods.

Common Share Earnings ($)

Quarter:	[1]1992–93	[1]1991–92	1990–91	1989–90
Nov.	0.33	0.16	0.39	0.34
Feb.	0.42	0.41	0.40	0.36
May	0.40	0.43	0.40	0.42
Aug.	d0.36	0.41	0.31	0.34
	0.79	1.41	1.50	1.46

1. From cont. ops. d-Deficit.

Dividend Data

Recent dividends on the Class A shares were:

Amt of Divd. $	Date Decl.	Ex–divd. Date	Stock of Record	Payment Date
0.10	Dec. 17	Jan. 26	Feb. 1	Mar. 1'93
0.10	Mar. 18	Apr. 27	May 3	Jun. 1'93
0.10	Jun. 17	Jul. 27	Aug. 2	Sep. 1'93

Finances

In September 1992, the company acquired Durr-Fillauer Medical Inc. for about $395 million in cash, plus expenses of $17 million and the assumption of long-term debt totaling $72 million. The acquisition was financed with $175 million borrowed under a $300 million credit line and with internally generated funds.

Capitalization

Long Term Debt: $312,834,000 (5/93).

Class A Common Stock: 35,492,406 shs. ($1.50 par).
Institutions hold 59%.
Shareholders: 3,500 (8/92).

Class B Common Stock: 100,492 shs. ($1.50 par); ea. conv. into 9.5285 Cl. A shs.

Office—4000 Metropolitan Dr., Orange, CA 92668-3510. **Tel**—(714) 385-4000. **Chrmn & CEO**—R. E. Martini. **Pres & COO**—D. A. Steffensen. **EVP, CFO & Investor Contact**—N. F. Dimick. **EVP & Secy**—M. A. Sawdei. **Dirs**—J. E. Blanco, R. H. Brady, J. Calasibetta, C. C. Edwards, C. J. Lee, G. R. Liddle, R. E. Martini, J. R. Mellor, G. E. Reinhardt, Jr., F. G. Rodgers, D. A. Steffensen. **Transfer Agent & Registrar**—Chemical Trust Co., LA. **Incorporated** in New Jersey in 1956. **Empl**—4,300.

 Adam J. Penn

Betz Laboratories

NYSE Symbol BTL Options on Pacific In S&P MidCap 400

Price	Range	P-E Ratio	Dividend	Yield	S&P Ranking	Beta
Sep. 17'93	1993					
46⅞	62⅞–44	18	1.40	3.0%	A	0.85

Summary

Betz is a leading supplier of specialty chemicals and engineered programs for the treatment of water, wastewater and process systems for use in a variety of industrial and commercial applications. Earnings were in a long uptrend in recent years, reflecting strength in industrial end-markets and growing environmental and conservation applications. However, 1993 first-half sales and earnings declined slightly on weakness in key U.S. industrial markets.

Business Summary

Betz Laboratories, Inc. primarily produces specialty chemicals and related products for the treatment of industrial and commercial water systems, industrial processes using water and the associated wastewater. Betz also provides chemical treatment for use in a variety of process systems and offers technical and laboratory services necessary to use its products effectively. Revenues from sales and services were divided as follows in recent years:

	1992	1991
Betz Industrial & Betz MetChem sales to basic industries	44%	47%
Betz PaperChem	15%	14%
Betz Entec commer. & light industrial markets	9%	9%
Betz Process Chemicals & Betz Energy Chemicals	9%	9%
International operations	18%	16%
Canadian operations	5%	5%

Foreign operations accounted for 21% of operating profits in 1992.

Specialty chemicals include products to control corrosion, scale and deposit formation and micro-organism growth in boiler systems, cooling systems, production processes and air-conditioning systems and feedstocks and chemicals used in production process systems. The company also formulates laboratory reagents and chemical test kits for analyzing industrial water, and it markets feeding, monitoring and control treatment systems for applying its chemicals. Customers are primarily in such industries as chemicals, paper, petrochemicals, petroleum and steel, as well as in the aircraft, automobile, building products, electronics, food, rubber, textile and utility industries.

A technical sales force of about 1,420 provides continuing guidance for effective use of Betz products. Engineering assistance, including water analysis, deposit identification and analysis, corrosion studies and microbiological studies, is available. The company also assists in training customer operating personnel. Betz has 13 plants in the U.S. and seven in other countries.

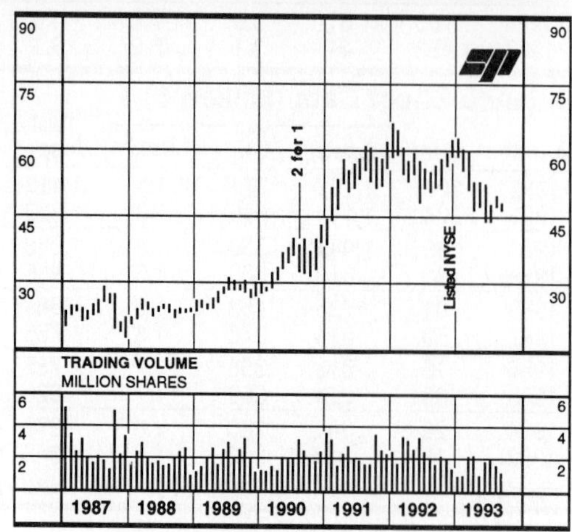

Important Developments

Jul. '93— Betz said that second-quarter results reflected continuing weakness in the industrial sector of the economy. Betz Industrial was down modestly, as new business gained during the quarter was more than offset by reduced consumption levels at existing accounts. PaperChem reported a modest decline in sales due to customer shutdowns and reduced treatment levels at existing accounts. The other U.S. units posted modest sales gains. Foreign operations posted sales gains in local currencies that were offset by unfavorable foreign exchange rates. The Canadian business continued to report strong increases in sales of process chemicals to the pulp and paper industry.

Next earnings report expected in late October.

Per Share Data ($)

Yr. End Dec. 31	1992	1991	1990	1989	1988	1987	1986	1985	1984	1983
Tangible Bk. Val.	**10.13**	8.80	7.46	6.07	7.12	6.34	6.48	6.14	5.43	5.06
Cash Flow	**3.95**	3.55	3.17	5.20	4.60	3.83	3.30	3.23	3.09	2.65
Earnings	**[1]2.71**	[1]2.47	[1]2.12	[1]1.77	1.58	1.30	1.12	1.17	1.17	1.04
Dividends	**1.30**	1.16	1.01	0.89	0.80	0.73	0.68	0.63	0.55	0.47
Payout Ratio	**50%**	49%	48%	50%	51%	56%	60%	54%	47%	45%
Prices—High	**66¼**	62	43¼	31¼	26¼	29⅛	22⅜	19⅛	19½	22⅜
Low	**48¼**	38¾	27¾	23⅝	20⅝	17½	17½	15⅛	13⅝	16⅛
P/E Ratio—	**24–18**	25–16	20–13	18–13	17–13	22–14	20–16	16–13	17–12	22–16

Data as orig. reptd. Adj. for stk. div. of 100% Aug. 1990. **1.** Ful. dil.: 2.58 in 1992, 2.36 in 1991, 2.02 in 1990, 1.73 in 1989.

Income Data (Million $)

Year Ended Dec. 31	Oper. Revs.	Oper. Inc.	% Oper. Inc. of Revs.	Cap. Exp.	Depr.	Int. Exp.	Net Bef. Taxes	Eff. Tax Rate	Net Inc.	% Net Inc. of Revs.	Cash Flow
1992	**707**	**170**	**24.0**	**[2]74.3**	**38.5**	**1.38**	**134**	**38.8%**	**82.0**	**11.6**	**113**
1991	666	153	23.0	58.4	33.8	1.53	124	39.0%	75.5	11.3	101
1990	597	134	22.5	57.5	29.9	2.86	107	39.0%	65.5	11.0	87
1989	517	113	21.9	53.0	25.9	2.22	91	38.6%	55.9	10.8	77
1988	448	99	22.1	43.5	23.0	1.16	79	38.6%	48.4	10.8	71
1987	386	88	22.7	25.4	20.1	0.12	71	42.4%	[1]40.6	10.5	60
1986	344	80	23.4	22.8	17.1	0.06	67	46.8%	35.5	10.3	53
1985	319	75	23.4	27.0	14.1	0.11	65	43.3%	36.8	11.5	51
1984	304	72	23.8	25.5	12.0	0.17	65	43.1%	36.7	12.1	49
1983	267	60	22.5	33.4	9.0	0.30	58	43.3%	33.1	12.4	42

Balance Sheet Data (Million $)

Dec. 31	Cash	Curr. Assets	Curr. Liab.	Curr. Ratio	Total Assets	% Ret. on Assets	Long Term Debt	Common Equity	Total Cap.	% LT Debt of Cap.	% Ret. on Equity
1992	**46.4**	**202**	**84.1**	**2.4**	**511**	**16.6**	**98.0**	**294**	**423**	**23.2**	**26.9**
1991	59.0	201	88.0	2.3	476	16.7	98.5	256	385	25.6	28.4
1990	39.8	176	77.4	2.3	427	16.4	99.0	219	348	28.5	28.4
1989	29.3	145	56.8	2.6	369	16.2	99.5	183	310	32.1	26.2
1988	8.5	120	59.6	2.0	319	15.9	Nil	231	256	Nil	22.1
1987	13.2	103	56.4	1.8	287	14.8	Nil	205	205	Nil	20.1
1986	34.1	104	42.1	2.5	270	13.6	Nil	204	204	Nil	17.9
1985	22.0	88	38.6	2.3	254	15.4	Nil	195	195	Nil	20.0
1984	16.4	76	33.5	2.3	221	17.4	0.3	171	171	0.2	22.3
1983	10.3	66	29.0	2.3	204	16.9	0.5	162	162	0.3	21.6

Data as orig. reptd. **1.** Refl. acctg. change. **2.** Net.

Net Sales (Million $)

Quarter:	1993	1992	1991	1990
Mar.	169	176	163	143
Jun.	171	176	166	148
Sep.		183	170	153
Dec.		173	166	152
		707	666	597

Sales for the first half of 1993 were off 3.3%, year to year, reflecting a 2% decline in volume and unfavorable foreign exchange rates. Foreign businesses posted sales gains in local currencies, led by Canadian operations. Domestic sales of industrial water treatment chemicals declined. With modest manufacturing costs increases and a less favorable product mix, operating profits decreased 7.5%. Pretax earnings fell 6.6%. After taxes at 38.5%, versus 38.8%, net income was off 6.2%, to $1.23 a share (before a net credit of $0.03 from accounting changes), from $1.33.

Common Share Earnings ($)

Quarter:	1993	1992	1991	1990
Mar.	0.62	0.66	0.60	0.50
Jun.	0.61	0.67	0.61	0.53
Sep.		0.71	0.65	0.57
Dec.		0.67	0.61	0.52
		2.71	2.47	2.12

Finances

In May 1993, Betz expected capital spending for 1993 of $80 million. Major projects include the completion of a plant expansion in Texas and a new plant in France and construction of a new plant in Korea, expected to be completed in 1994.

In June 1989, the company established a $100 million ESOP and sold 500,000 shares of convertible preferred stock to the plan.

Dividend Data

Dividends have been paid since 1958. A shareholder rights plan was adopted in 1988.

Amt. of Divd. $	Date Decl.	Ex-divd. Date	Stock of Record	Payment Date
0.34	Dec. 10	Jan. 22	Jan. 28	Feb. 11'93
0.34	Apr. 8	Apr. 23	Apr. 29	May 13'93
0.35	Jun. 10	Jul. 23	Jul. 29	Aug. 12'93
0.35	Aug. 12	Oct. 22	Oct. 28	Nov. 11'93

Capitalization

Long Term Debt: $97,500,000 (6/93).

ESOP Preferred Stock: 496,958 shs.; conv. into 2,747,000 com. shs.

Common Stock: 28,581,605 shs. ($0.10 par). Institutions hold about 67%. Stockholders of record: 4,044 (2/93).

Office—4636 Somerton Rd., Trevose, PA 19053. **Tel**—(215) 355-3300. **Chrmn & CEO**—J. F. McCaughan. **Pres**—W. R. Cook. **Secy**—W. C. Brafford. **VP-Fin, Treas & Investor Contact**—R. Dale Voncanon. **Dirs**—J. W. Boyer Jr., P. F. Brennan, C. S. Burger, G. A. Butler, W. R. Cook, J. F. McCaughan, J. A. Miller, T. B. Palmer III, J. Quarles, J. A. H. Shober, G. Stengel Jr., R. L. Yohe. **Transfer Agent & Registrar**—American Stock Transfer & Trust Co., NYC. **Incorporated** in Pennsylvania in 1957. **Empl**—4,170.

 Richard O'Reilly, CFA

Biogen, Inc.

NASDAQ Symbol BGEN (Incl. in Nat'l Market) Options on ASE, CBOE, Pacific In S&P MidCap 400

Price	Range	P-E Ratio	Dividend	Yield	S&P Ranking	Beta
Sep. 8'93	1993					
32¼	47¾–24¼	21	None	None	B–	2.09

Summary

This biotechnology company focuses on the development and commercialization of drugs produced through genetic engineering. Revenues are currently derived from royalties paid by licensees who sell five products based on technology developed by Biogen; the most important products are alpha interferon, sold by Schering-Plough, and hepatitis B vaccines, sold by Merck and SmithKline Beecham.

Current Outlook

Share earnings for 1994 are projected at $1.15 a share, up from $0.95 indicated for 1993.

Cash dividends are not anticipated.

Total revenues are expected to show further growth in 1994. Royalties from licensed products such as alpha interferon and hepatitis B vaccines should rise, on increased sales of these products by licensees. Despite large ongoing R&D outlays, improved profitability should be seen, reflecting the greater volume and the absence of nonrecurring charges. Earnings from licensed products should help fund R&D for promising new proprietary products such as hirulog cardiovascular and beta interferon.

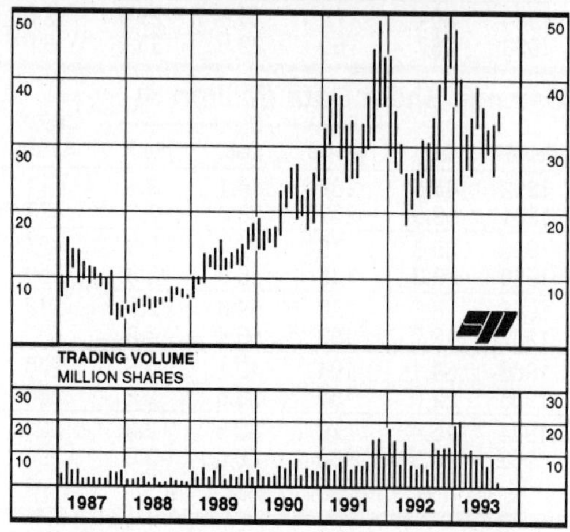

Total Revenues (Million $)

Quarter:	1993	1992	1991	1990
Mar.	35.4	19.1	18.1	14.1
Jun.	37.9	20.9	17.3	14.3
Sep.	---	40.6	16.6	14.8
Dec.	---	54.5	17.6	16.1
	---	135.1	69.6	59.4

Total revenues in the six months ended June 30, 1993, soared 83%, year to year, reflecting sharply higher royalties from licensee sales of hepatitis B vaccines and alpha interferon. Net income surged to $16,904,000 ($0.49 a share), from $1,479,000 ($0.04).

Common Share Earnings ($)

Quarter:	1993	1992	1991	1990
Mar.	0.32	0.02	0.05	0.01
Jun.	0.17	0.02	0.04	0.01
Sep.	E0.25	0.33	0.03	0.01
Dec.	E0.21	0.75	0.03	0.04
	E0.95	1.12	0.15	0.07

Important Developments

Sep. '93— Biogen said Phase III human clinical trials studying the company's Hirulog drug for the prevention of clot formation in unstable angina and angioplasty patients are expected continue into 1994, with an FDA filing for the drug possible during 1994. Biogen also has Phase III trials under way studying beta interferon for the treatment of multiple sclerosis, and Phase II trials evaluating beta interferon for the treatment of hepatitis. Separately, the company said 1993 second quarter earnings were reduced by a charge of $4.3 million ($0.12 a share) for certain obligations resulting from a recent patent settlement between Schering-Plough and Genentech involving alpha interferon. Future related obligations could involve payments of up to $11 million through 1996.

Next earnings report expected in mid-October.

Per Share Data ($)

Yr. End Dec. 31	1992	1991	1990	1989	1988	1987	1986	1985	1984	1983
Tangible Bk. Val.	**8.77**	7.53	3.06	2.91	2.88	2.90	3.90	3.91	4.78	5.44
Cash Flow	**1.33**	0.32	0.22	0.15	0.09	d0.85	d1.22	d0.78	d0.48	d0.52
Earnings[1]	**1.12**	0.15	0.07	0.01	d0.05	d1.02	d1.43	d1.03	d0.71	d0.67
Dividends	**Nil**	Nil	Nil	Nil	Nil	Nil	Nil	Nil	Nil	Nil
Payout Ratio	**Nil**	Nil	Nil	Nil	Nil	Nil	Nil	Nil	Nil	Nil
Prices—High	**49¾**	49	29⅜	18¼	8¾	16	20⅝	18⅝	14	23¼
Low	**18¼**	24¼	14⅜	7⅛	4¾	3¾	5⅞	5½	4¼	9¾
P/E Ratio—	**44–16**	NM	NM	NM	NM	NM	NM	NM	NM	NM

Data as orig. reptd. Adj. for stk. div. of 100% Jan. 1983. **1.** Bef. spec. item(s) of +0.02 in 1983. E-Estimated. d-Deficit. NM-Not Meaningful.

Income Data (Million $)

Year Ended Dec. 31	Revs.	Oper. Inc.	% Oper. Inc. of Revs.	Cap. Exp.	Depr.	Int. Exp.	[1]Net Bef. Taxes	Eff. Tax Rate	[2]Net Inc.	% Net Inc. of Revs.	Cash Flow
1992	**124**	**44.1**	**35.7**	**9.4**	**7.14**	**Nil**	**39.9**	**4.1%**	**38.3**	**31.0**	**45.5**
1991	61	3.9	6.3	8.4	5.06	Nil	7.4	3.5%	7.2	11.7	9.6
1990	50	4.6	9.1	11.1	3.79	Nil	8.0	3.6%	7.7	15.4	5.6
1989	28	d5.5	NM	3.1	3.33	Nil	3.4	5.8%	3.2	11.3	3.6
1988	21	d8.7	NM	2.7	3.12	Nil	d0.9	NM	d1.2	NM	1.9
1987	9	d20.4	NM	1.3	3.76	Nil	d22.4	NM	d22.6	NM	d18.8
1986	6	d24.9	NM	0.2	4.14	Nil	d27.8	NM	d28.2	NM	d24.0
1985	15	d19.4	NM	0.8	4.48	NA	d18.6	NM	d19.1	NM	d14.6
1984	23	d16.1	NM	4.8	4.22	NA	d12.4	NM	d13.1	NM	d8.9

Balance Sheet Data (Million $)

Dec. 31	Cash	Curr. Assets	Curr. Liab.	Curr. Ratio	Total Assets	% Ret. on Assets	Long Term Debt	Common Equity	Total Cap.	% LT Debt of Cap.	% Ret. on Equity
1992	**228**	**268**	**46.2**	**10.2**	**311**	**13.4**	**Nil**	**285**	**285**	**Nil**	**14.4**
1991	186	209	14.1	14.9	253	3.1	Nil	239	239	Nil	2.6
1990	104	121	12.7	9.5	158	5.0	Nil	76	146	Nil	2.5
1989	110	120	6.0	19.9	145	2.8	Nil	[3]70	139	Nil	0.3
1988	53	58	8.0	7.2	81	NM	4.82	68	73	6.6	NM
1987	54	58	7.6	7.6	81	NM	5.23	68	73	7.1	NM
1986	70	74	7.2	10.2	101	NM	4.43	89	94	4.7	NM
1985	53	57	7.4	7.7	86	NM	3.56	75	78	4.5	NM
1984	72	79	14.9	5.3	110	NM	2.97	92	95	3.1	NM

Data as orig. reptd. **1.** Incl. equity in earns. of nonconsol. subs. after 1983. **2.** Bef. spec. items. **3.** Aft. deduct. pfd. liquid. preference of 69.2. d-Deficit. NM-Not Meaningful. NA-Not Available.

Business Summary

Biogen Inc. is a leading biotechnology company, whose revenues are currently derived from products that are being sold by licensees or affiliates in various countries. During 1992, licensees generated total sales of about $1.3 billion from these products, up from about $700 million in 1991. In the future, the company expects to derive additional revenues from sales of proprietary products. The U.S. accounted for 37% of 1992 revenues, Europe for 34%, and other foreign for 29%. Revenues in 1992 were derived as follows:

	1992	1991	1990
Royalties & product sales	90%	81%	75%
R&D fees	2%	7%	9%
Interest	8%	12%	16%

Principal products are Intron-A alpha interferon and hepatitis B vaccines and diagnostics. The company holds patents covering the production of alpha interferon (a naturally occurring protein produced by normal white blood cells) through recombinant DNA techniques. Schering-Plough, Biogen's worldwide licensee for Intron-A, currently sells the product in 59 countries for 16 indications, including hairy cell leukemia, hepatitis B & C, genital warts and Kaposi's sarcoma. Schering-Plough's 1992 sales of Intron A totaled $478 million ($251 million in 1991), mostly generated outside the U.S.

Biogen holds several important patents related to hepatitis B antigens produced by genetic engineering techniques. These antigens are used in recombinant hepatitis B vaccines sold primarily by licensees SmithKline Beecham and Merck. The company has also licensed Abbott Laboratories and others to market hepatitis B diagnostic kits. Total licensee sales of hepatitis B vaccines and diagnostics exceeded $800 million in 1992.

Clinical trials are continuing on several products that the company plans to market itself. These include Hirulog, an antithrombotic for the treatment of various arterial and venous cardiovascular conditions; and recombinant beta inferferon, a protein being tested for use as a therapy for certain viruses and cancers. The R&D pipeline also includes LFA3TIP and VLA4 anti-inflammatory compounds; and 5A8, an AIDS therapeutic.

Dividend Data

No cash dividends have been paid on the common shares.

Capitalization

Long Term Debt: None (6/93).

Common Stock: 31,935,179 shs. ($0.01 par).
Institutions hold 68%.
Shareholders: 3,997 of record.

Warrants: To buy 2,405,300 com. shs.

Office—14 Cambridge Center, Cambridge, MA 02142. **Tel**—(617) 252-9200. **Chrmn & CEO**—J. L. Vincent. **VP-Fin, CFO & Treas**—T. M. Kish. **VP & Secy**—M. J. Astrue. **Investor Contact**—Amy S. Hedison. **Dirs**—A. G. Bearn, A. Belzer, H. W. Buirkle, W. Gilbert, R. H. Morley, K. Murray, P. A. Sharp, J. W. Stevens, J. L. Vincent. **Transfer Agent & Registrar**—State Street Bank & Trust Co., Boston. **Incorporated** in Massachusetts in 1988; predecessor company incorporated in the Netherlands Antilles in 1979. **Empl**—331.

 H. B. Saftlas

Black Hills Corp.

NYSE Symbol BKH In S&P MidCap 400

Price	Range	P-E Ratio	Dividend	Yield	S&P Ranking	Beta
Aug. 27'93	1993					
26⅝	28¼–24⅝	16	1.28	4.8%	A	0.55

Summary

This small utility serves rural communities in South Dakota, Wyoming and Montana. Profitability in recent years benefited from increased kwh sales and improved performance at the company's principal generating plant. BKH has restructured its nonutility businesses, which should enhance longer-term prospects. Cash flow is excellent, and electric sales are expected to benefit from demand growth in both the residential and commercial sectors.

Current Outlook

Share earnings for 1993 are projected at $1.65, down from the $1.73 reported for 1992. Share earnings could decline to $1.60 in 1994.

The quarterly dividend may be raised some 3.1%, to $0.33 from $0.32, effective with the January 1994 declaration.

Earnings for 1993 should reflect higher costs associated with the construction of the Neil Simpson Unit 2 coal-fired plant and lower interest income as funds are drawn down to finance that project, partially offset by higher kwh sales. A return to normal weather conditions would further aid results. Share earnings for 1994 should reflect higher kwh sales and increased AFUDC credits, more than offset by higher interest expense, more common shares outstanding and a maintenance outage at the Wyodak coal plant (scheduled for May, and expected to last about six weeks).

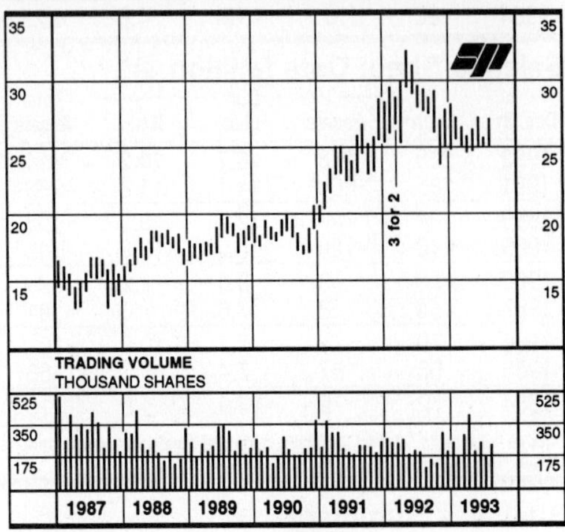

Revenues (Million $)

Quarter:	1993	1992	1991	1990
Mar.	34.4	32.5	33.8	32.3
Jun.	32.9	32.2	31.1	30.1
Sep.		35.4	35.2	33.2
Dec.		35.4	33.3	32.0
		135.3	133.4	127.5

Revenues for the six months to June 30, 1993, rose 4.1%, year to year, on increases in kwh sales and coal sales. However, in the absence of a pretax gain of $1.4 million related to a settlement with Pacificorp Coal, net income fell 4.4%. Share earnings were $0.78, versus $0.82.

Common Share Earnings ($)

Quarter:	1993	1992	1991	1990
Mar.	0.45	0.41	0.49	0.48
Jun.	0.33	0.41	0.31	0.34
Sep.	E0.45	0.46	0.51	0.46
Dec.	E0.42	0.45	0.35	0.40
	E1.65	1.73	1.66	1.68

Important Developments

Apr. '93— The company said the South Dakota PUC approved its request to withdraw a rate stability plan filed in October 1992, allowing the company to proceed with plans to build the 80 mw Neil Simpson Unit 2 coal-fired power plant. The new plant is to be located adjacent to its Wyodak Resources Development Corp. unit near Gillette, Wyoming. The South Dakota PUC also dismissed a proposal by Rosebud Enterprises of Boise, Idaho, to build an alternate facility near Edgemont, S.D., to provide power to Black Hills Power. BKH said the commission determined that Rosebud's proposal was not timely. In November 1992, the company said additional financing is expected to be needed from 1993 to 1996 for major capital expenditures, including more generating capacity.

Next earnings report expected in late October.

Per Share Data ($)

Yr. End Dec. 31	1992	1991	1990	1989	1988	1987	1986	1985	1984	1983
Tangible Bk. Val.	**10.89**	10.38	9.69	9.31	8.78	8.09	7.47	6.99	6.28	5.61
Earnings[1]	**1.73**	1.66	1.68	1.60	1.53	1.45	1.11	1.28	1.19	1.00
Dividends	**1.395**	1.173	1.093	1.013	0.933	0.827	0.760	0.640	0.560	0.440
Payout Ratio	**81%**	71%	65%	63%	61%	57%	69%	51%	48%	45%
Prices—High	**32¼**	28⅝	20¹¹⁄₁₆	19¹⁵⁄₁₆	18¹³⁄₁₆	16¹³⁄₁₆	19⁵⁄₁₆	13⁹⁄₁₆	9¼	8
Low	**23¾**	19⅜	17	16⁹⁄₁₆	15	13	12⁵⁄₁₆	8¾	6¹¹⁄₁₆	5¼
P/E Ratio—	**19–14**	17–12	12–10	12–10	12–10	12–9	17–11	11–7	8–6	8–5

Data as orig. reptd. adj. for stk. div(s). of 50% Mar. 1992, 100% Mar. 1986, 100% Jun. 1983. 1. Bef. results of disc. opers. of -0.06 in 1989, +0.09 in 1988, bef. spec. item(s) of +0.09 in 1986, +0.07 in 1983. E-Estimated

Income Data (Million $)

Year Ended Dec. 31	Revs.	Depr.	Maint.	Oper. Ratio	[3]Fxd. Chgs. Cover.	Constr. Credits	Eff. Tax Rate	[2]Net Inc.	% Return On Revs.	% Return On [4]Invest. Capital	% Return On [5]Com. Equity
1992	**135**	**13.9**	**6.51**	**79.4%**	**4.74**	**0.38**	**26.5%**	**23.6**	**17.5**	**11.6**	**15.8**
1991	133	12.0	6.73	79.8%	4.99	0.18	27.4%	22.7	17.0	11.5	16.0
1990	127	9.9	6.09	83.7%	7.66	0.26	27.6%	22.9	18.0	11.0	16.9
1989	[1]120	[1]9.5	6.78	83.9%	8.10	0.11	[1]27.5%	[1]22.0	18.3	10.7	16.6
1988	[1]284	[1]10.1	7.07	93.6%	7.99	0.15	[1]28.4%	[1]21.2	7.5	10.6	18.5
1987	122	10.4	6.05	NA	NA	NA	36.3%	20.4	16.6	NA	NA
1986	112	8.9	6.38	NA	NA	NA	39.7%	15.8	14.1	NA	NA
1985	114	8.4	7.09	NA	NA	NA	37.9%	18.0	15.8	NA	NA
1984	104	7.9	7.06	NA	NA	NA	38.8%	16.5	15.8	NA	NA
1983	85	6.9	NA	NA	NA	NA	40.3%	13.7	16.1	NA	NA

Balance Sheet Data (Million $)

Dec. 31	Gross Prop.	Capital Expend.	Net Prop.	% Earn. on Net Prop.	Total Cap.	Capitalization LT Debt	% LT Debt	Pfd.	% Pfd.	Com.	% Com.
1992	**413**	**25.6**	**280**	**10.2**	**282**	**88.8**	**37.3**	**Nil**	**Nil**	**149**	**62.7**
1991	391	25.6	268	10.5	276	88.8	39.6	Nil	Nil	142	60.4
1990	355	22.2	244	8.7	256	79.0	36.9	Nil	Nil	135	63.1
1989	331	10.1	230	8.8	247	78.9	38.3	Nil	Nil	127	61.7
1988	313	NA	220	8.6	245	85.1	41.5	Nil	Nil	120	58.5
1987	NA	NA	NA	NA	234	78.2	NA	NA	NA	110	NA
1986	NA	NA	NA	NA	226	78.7	NA	NA	NA	102	NA
1985	NA	NA	NA	NA	215	76.9	NA	NA	NA	95	NA
1984	NA	NA	NA	NA	197	74.2	NA	NA	NA	83	NA
1983	NA	NA	NA	NA	187	76.5	NA	NA	NA	73	NA

Data as orig. reptd. **1.** Excl. disc. ops. **2.** Bef. results of disc. opers. and spec. items. **3.** Times int. exp. & pfd. divs. covered (pretax basis). **4.** Based on income bef. interest charges. **5.** As reptd. by Co. NA-Not Available.

Business Summary

Black Hills Corp. provides electricity (72% of 1992 revenues; 47% of net income) to some 165,000 people in western South Dakota, northeastern Wyoming and southeastern Montana. The largest community served is Rapid City, S.D. Other operations include a coal mining business (21% of revenues; 49% of net income), and oil and gas production (7%; 4%). Electric revenue contributions:

	1992	1991	1990	1989
Residential	28%	29%	28%	28%
General/commercial	33%	33%	31%	31%
Industrial	30%	29%	28%	28%
Other	9%	9%	13%	13%

Peak demand in 1992 was 284 mw, and capability at peak totaled 313 mw, for a capacity margin of 9%. Internal generation was made up of 99% coal and 1% oil. BKH has a 40-year purchase agreement for 75 mw with PacifiCorp's Pacific Power & Light subsidiary.

In the 1991 second quarter, BKH purchased the 20% interest in the Wyodak generating plant which it had previously leased. At the company's request, the South Dakota Public Utilities Commission issued an order on December 17, 1990, allowing the full cost (approximately $42 million) of the Wyodak acquisition to be included in the rate base in future rate cases. The order prevented the company from filing in South Dakota for any general rate increases prior to January 1, 1992.

BKH's Wyodak Resources Development Corp. is a coal mining business with estimated reserves of 193.3 million tons, of which 34.4 million tons are committed to be sold to the Wyodak plant. It is also involved in energy production and distribution. Western Production Co. engages in oil and gas production.

Dividend Data

Dividends have been paid since 1942. A dividend reinvestment plan is available.

Amt of Divd. $	Date Decl.	Ex-divd. Date	Stock of Record	Payment Date
0.31	Oct. 22	Nov. 6	Nov. 13	Dec. 1'92
0.32	Jan. 26	Feb. 8	Feb. 12	Mar. 1'93
0.32	Apr. 27	May 10	May 14	Jun. 1'93
0.32	Aug. 2	Aug. 9	Aug. 13	Sep. 1'93

Capitalization

Long Term Debt: $86,783,000 (3/93).

Common Stock: 13,706,732 shs. ($1 par).
Institutions hold about 25%.
Shareholders of record: 7,034.

Office—625 Ninth St., Rapid City, SD 57709. **Tel**—(605) 348-1700. **Chrmn & Pres**—D. P. Landguth. **SVP-Fin, CFO & Investor Contact**—Dale E. Clement. **Secy-Treas**—R. R. Basham. **Dirs**—G. C. Barber, B. B. Brundage, D. E. Clement, M. B. Enzi, J. R. Howard, E. E. Hoyt, K. Jorgenson, D. P. Landguth, C. T. Undlin. **Transfer Agent & Registrar**—Chemical Bank, NYC. **Incorporated** in South Dakota in 1941. **Empl**—449.

 Christopher J. Grant

Bob Evans Farms

NASDAQ Symbol BOBE (Incl. in Nat'l Market) In S&P MidCap 400

Price	Range	P-E Ratio	Dividend	Yield	S&P Ranking	Beta
Sep. 20'93	1993					
18¼	21¾–16¾	17	0.27	1.5%	A	0.99

Summary

This company operates a chain of 293 family-style restaurants in 19 states and produces and distributes a variety of pork sausage products. Earnings continued a long uptrend in 1992-3, as higher sales reflected new restaurants in operation and contributions from acquisitions in the food products segment. The dividend was boosted 8% with the September 1993 payment.

Business Summary

Bob Evans Farms, Inc. operates family restaurants and produces a wide variety of pork sausage products. As a result of a general decline in the consumption of pork sausage, the company plans to continue to develop new food products to meet changes in consumer demand. In 1992-3, contributions to sales and pretax income by business segment were:

	Sales	Income
Restaurants	70%	75%
Food products	30%	25%

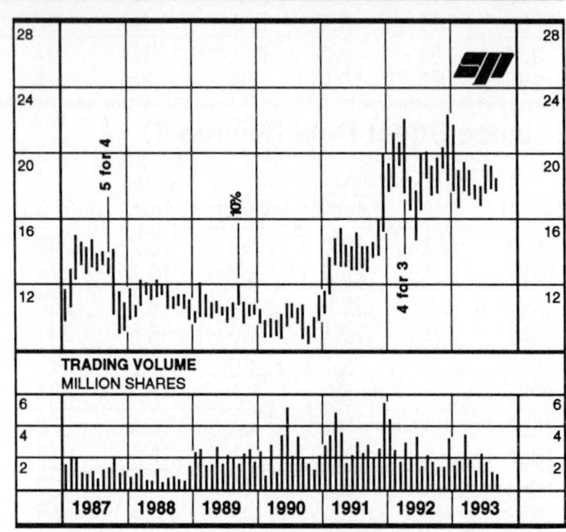

At July 30, 1993, BOBE was operating 293 family-style restaurants in 19 states, with the largest number of restaurants located in Ohio; other areas of concentration include Indiana, Michigan, Florida and Pennsylvania. The restaurants are typically open from 6 a.m. to 10 p.m. Sunday through Thursday, with extended hours on Friday and Saturday. Restaurants feature sausage products, with emphasis on breakfast entrees served all day. About half of total revenues are generated from 6 a.m. to 2 p.m.

New restaurant concepts continue to be developed. During 1990-1, the company opened its first Bob Evans General Store and Restaurant, combining a gift shop, bakery and 200 seat restaurant under one roof; eight General Stores were in operation at the end of 1992-3. The opening of the first Cantina del Rio in April 1992 was part of a planned chain of Mexican style restaurants located in Columbus, Ohio. A "small town" Bob Evans restaurant, designed to reduce building and operating costs, was developed in 1992-3. For 1993-4, the company planned to open 30 new restaurants, including 14 traditional Bob Evans Restaurants, 10 of the small-town units, and six Cantina del Rios.

The food products segment produces and distributes about 30 varieties of fresh, smoked and fully cooked pork sausage and ham products under the brand names Bob Evans Farms and Owens Country Sausage. In recent years, the company has begun to emphasize both new product development and sales of pork sausage and ham products to institutional and foodservice customers. In addition, the company has begun to explore the expansion of the products offered in its food products segment through the acquisition of companies producing food and food related products that complement the company's traditional sausage products.

Mrs. Giles Country Kitchens produces several lines of refrigerated delicatessen salads under the Mrs. Giles and Bob Evans Farms brand names. Hickory Specialties produces premium quality charcoal, wood smoking chips, natural smoke flavorings, gas grill ceramic briquets and grilling systems.

Through its own direct store delivery network, BOBE sells its products to more than 9,000 supermarkets and retail groceries.

Next earnings report expected in late November.

Per Share Data ($)

Yr. End Apr. 30	1993	[1]1992	1991	1990	1989	1988	[1]1987	1986	1985	1984
Tangible Bk. Val.	**7.04**	6.23	5.72	5.11	4.71	4.17	3.64	3.11	2.74	2.46
Cash Flow	**1.52**	1.37	1.22	1.05	1.11	1.03	0.78	0.72	0.62	0.55
Earnings[2]	**1.03**	0.94	0.80	0.65	0.72	0.68	0.52	0.50	0.44	0.39
Dividends	**0.240**	0.206	0.195	0.195	0.167	0.158	0.143	0.126	0.116	0.100
Payout Ratio	**23%**	22%	24%	30%	23%	23%	28%	25%	26%	25%
Calendar Years	**1992**	1991	1990	1989	1988	1987	1986	1985	1984	1983
Prices—High	**22⅜**	20	11⅜	12⅛	12⁵⁄₁₆	15	12¹¹⁄₁₆	10⅛	9½	10¹³⁄₁₆
Low	**14¾**	10¼	8⁷⁄₁₆	9¹¹⁄₁₆	9⅞	9	8¹⁵⁄₁₆	6¹⁵⁄₁₆	5¹³⁄₁₆	7¹¹⁄₁₆
P/E Ratio—	**22–14**	21–11	14–11	19–15	17–14	22–13	24–17	20–14	21–13	28–20

Data as orig. reptd. Adj. for stk. divs. of 33% Apr. 1992, 10% Sep. 1989, 25% Sep. 1987, 25% Sep. 1986, 10% Aug. 1985. **1.** Refl. merger or acq. **2.** Bef. spec. item of +0.05 in 1991.

Income Data (Million $)

Year Ended Apr. 30	Revs.	Oper. Inc.	% Oper. Inc. of Revs.	Cap. Exp.	Depr.	Int. Exp.	Net Bef. Taxes	Eff. Tax Rate	[2]Net Inc.	% Net Inc. of Revs.	Cash Flow
1993	**653**	**90.7**	**13.9**	**53.6**	**20.8**	**0.09**	**68.5**	**37.2%**	**43.1**	**6.6**	**63.8**
[1]1992	556	77.7	14.0	45.0	17.7	0.22	62.4	37.0%	39.3	7.1	57.0
1991	501	70.1	14.0	28.6	17.4	0.23	53.9	37.6%	33.6	6.7	51.0
1990	454	58.9	13.0	32.8	17.0	0.29	44.0	37.0%	27.7	6.1	44.8
1989	420	63.8	15.2	37.8	16.8	0.48	48.8	37.1%	30.7	7.3	47.4
1988	395	62.3	15.8	48.5	14.7	0.35	48.3	39.3%	29.3	7.4	44.0
[1]1987	327	50.5	15.4	57.7	11.1	NM	41.2	47.9%	21.5	6.6	32.6
1986	263	43.8	16.7	32.7	8.9	Nil	36.6	43.8%	20.6	7.8	29.5
1985	228	38.2	16.8	29.1	7.5	Nil	33.4	45.9%	18.1	7.9	25.6
1984	202	35.2	17.4	17.8	6.7	Nil	31.3	48.4%	16.1	8.0	22.9

Balance Sheet Data (Million $)

Apr. 30	Cash	Curr. Assets	Curr. Liab.	Curr. Ratio	Total Assets	% Ret. on Assets	Long Term Debt	Common Equity	Total Cap.	% LT Debt of Cap.	% Ret. on Equity
1993	**10.2**	**42.9**	**44.8**	**1.0**	**361**	**12.5**	**Nil**	**309**	**316**	**Nil**	**14.7**
1992	10.6	41.4	45.0	0.9	326	12.8	1.2	274	281	0.4	15.2
1991	25.2	46.2	38.5	1.2	287	12.4	1.6	242	249	0.6	14.7
1990	15.4	31.1	33.5	0.9	261	11.1	2.0	219	227	0.9	13.1
1989	13.8	28.1	30.8	0.9	244	13.2	2.4	205	213	1.1	15.8
1988	4.0	18.5	29.0	0.6	219	14.2	2.8	182	190	1.5	17.2
1987	11.1	24.8	26.6	0.9	193	12.3	3.2	159	166	1.9	14.7
1986	17.9	26.6	17.8	1.5	149	14.8	Nil	128	132	Nil	17.1
1985	21.1	29.2	14.8	2.0	129	14.7	Nil	112	114	Nil	17.0
1984	32.7	40.4	16.7	2.4	119	14.6	Nil	102	102	Nil	16.7

Data as orig. reptd. **1.** Refl. merger or acq. **2.** Bef. spec. items. NM-Not Meaningful.

Net Sales (Million $)

13 Weeks:	1993–94	1992–93	1991–92	1990–91
Jul.	178	159	131	123
Oct.		164	142	127
Jan.		170	141	126
Apr.		161	141	125
		653	556	501

Net sales in the 13 weeks ended July 30, 1993, rose 12%, year to year, reflecting additional restaurants in operation, higher same store restaurant sales and growth in sausage, fresh salad and charcoal sales. Wider margins in the restaurant segment were offset by deteriorating profitability at the food products unit due to higher live hog costs and lower margins on both fresh salad and foodservice products. Consolidated net income advanced 13%, to $11,815,000 ($0.28 a share), from $10,411,000 ($0.25).

Common Share Earnings ($)

13 Weeks:	1993–94	1992–93	1991–92	1990–91
Jul.	0.28	0.25	0.21	0.18
Oct.		0.26	0.25	0.21
Jan.		0.27	0.25	0.21
Apr.		0.25	0.23	0.20
		1.03	0.94	0.80

Dividend Data

Cash has been paid in each year since 1964. A dividend reinvestment plan is available.

Amt. of Divd. $	Date Decl.	Ex–divd. Date	Stock of Record	Payment Date
0.06¼	Nov. 16	Nov. 17	Nov. 23	Dec. 1'92
0.06¼	Jan. 15	Feb. 8	Feb. 12	Mar. 1'93
0.06¼	Apr. 30	May 10	May 14	Jun. 1'93
0.06¾	Aug. 9	Aug. 16	Aug. 20	Sep. 1'93

Finances

In July 1993, directors authorized the repurchase of up to 500,000 (1.2%) of the company's common shares outstanding.

At April 30, 1993, BOBE had bank lines of credit totaling $18 million, all of which was available.

In March 1992, the company purchased Tennessee- based Hickory Specialties, Inc., a producer of charcoal, wood smoking chips, natural smoke flavorings and grilling systems. In September 1991, BOBE acquired Mrs. Giles Country Kitchens. Mrs. Giles produces and distributes refrigerated delicatessen salads in the Southeast.

Capitalization

Long Term Debt: None (4/93).

Common Stock: 41,936,212 shs. ($0.01 par).
Officers and directors own 8%.
Institutions hold 38%.
Shareholders: 25,880 of record (5/93).

Office—3776 S. High St., Box 07863, Station G, Columbus, OH 43207-0863. **Tel**—(614) 491-2225. **Chrmn, CEO & Secy**—D. E. Evans. **CFO & Treas**—D. J. Radkoski. **Dirs**—L. E. Carroll, L. C. Corbin, D. E. Evans, J. T. Evans, D. A. Fronk, C. L. Krueger, G. R. Lucas II, S. K. Owens, R. S. Wood. **Transfer Agent & Registrar**—Co. itself. **Incorporated** in Ohio in 1957; reincorporated in Delaware in 1985. **Empl**—19,000.

 Gregg W. Bonardi

Borland International

NASDAQ Symbol BORL (Incl. in Nat'l Market) Options on CBOE In S&P MidCap 400

Price	Range	P-E Ratio	Dividend	Yield	S&P Ranking	Beta
Aug. 12'93	1993					
16¾	27¼–16½	NM	None	None	NR	NA

Summary

Borland designs personal computer software products that are marketed worldwide for use by businesses and by software developers. Operations were expanded significantly by the late 1991 acquisition of Ashton-Tate, the leading vendor of PC database software. Acquisition-related charges totaling $146 million penalized results in fiscal 1991-92. Losses continued in 1992-93, reflecting restructuring charges, but operations have been profitable in recent periods, and should remain so through fiscal 1993-94, on increased sales and a lower cost structure.

Current Outlook

Earnings for the fiscal year ending March 31, 1994, are projected at $0.90 a share, versus 1992-93's loss of $1.87 (including a $0.71 restructuring charge).

Cash dividends are not anticipated.

Revenues are expected to advance in fiscal 1993-94, aided by new software offerings for the important Windows operating environment. Windows versions of the Quattro Pro spreadsheet and Paradox database product are already available, and a Windows release of dBASE is expected near year-end. Profitability should benefit from the greater volume and from strict cost-containment programs; operating expense levels are targeted at approximately $85 million per quarter.

Net Revenues (Million $)

Quarter:	1993–94	1992–93	1991–92	1990–91
Jun.	123	115	[1]137	41
Sep.		128	114	53
Dec.		104	115	62
Mar.		117	117	71
		464	483	227

Net revenues for the three months ended June 30, 1993, rose 7.5%, year to year, aided by continued demand for Windows versions of Quattro Pro and Paradox, a new version of dBASE for the DOS market and contributions from Borland Office. Operating margins improved substantially, despite thinner gross margins resulting from lower average selling prices, as results benefited from a drop in SG&A as well as R&D expenses. Despite reduced interest income (net), the pretax profits soared to $8,252,000 from $2,301,000. After taxes at 25.0% in both periods, net income advanced to $6,189,000 ($0.22 a share, on 19% more average shares), from $1,726,000 ($0.06).

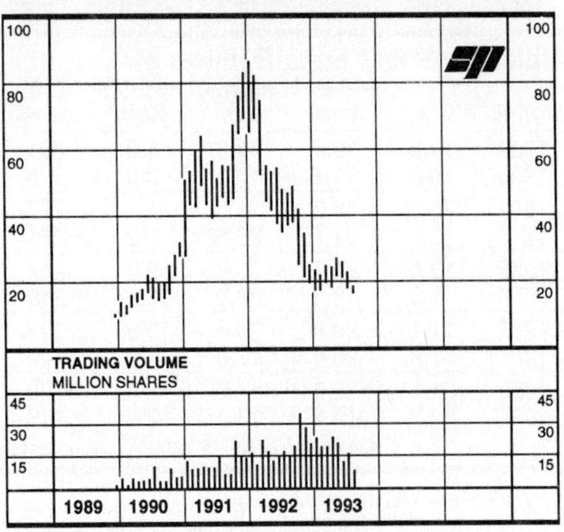

Common Share Earnings ($)

Quarter:	1993–94	1992–93	1991–92	1990–91
Jun.	0.22	0.06	[1]0.47	0.32
Sep.	E0.22	0.20	d4.21	0.41
Dec.	E0.23	d2.34	0.28	0.52
Mar.	E0.23	0.19	d1.05	0.55
	E0.90	d1.87	[2]d4.29	1.81

Important Developments

Jul. '93— Borland said that it expected to ship a version of its dBASE database software program for the Windows operating environment around the end of the year.

Next earnings report expected in mid-October.

Per Share Data ($)

Yr. End Mar. 31	1993	[3]1992	1991	1990	1989	[4]1988	1987	1986	1985
Tangible Bk. Val.	**7.01**	8.68	5.88	[5]4.03	[5]2.47	[5]2.75	[5]2.21	0.94	0.40
Cash Flow	**d1.01**	d3.09	2.16	1.19	0.07	0.37	0.45	NA	NA
Earnings	**d1.87**	d4.29	1.81	0.90	d0.25	0.15	0.35	0.10	0.13
Dividends	**Nil**	Nil	Nil	Nil	Nil	Nil	Nil	Nil	Nil
Payout Ratio	**Nil**	Nil	Nil	Nil	Nil	Nil	Nil	Nil	Nil
Calendar Years	**1992**	1991	1990	1989	1988	1987	1986	1985	1984
Prices—High	**86¾**	83½	32	10½	NA	NA	NA	NA	NA
Low	**19¾**	27⅞	9⅞	9⅝	NA	NA	NA	NA	NA
P/E Ratio—	**NM**	NM	18–5	12–10	NM	NM	NA	NA	NA

Data as orig. reptd. **1.** Restated. **2.** Sum of quarters does not equal full-year amount, due to change in shs. **3.** Major merger resulted in formation of new co. **4.** Refl. merger or acq. **5.** Incl. intangibles. d-Deficit. E-Estimated NM-Not Meaningful. NA-Not Available.

Income Data (Million $)

Year Ended Mar. 31	Revs.	Oper. Inc.	% Oper. Inc. of Revs.	Cap. Exp.	Depr.	Int. Exp.	Net Bef. Taxes	Eff. Tax Rate	Net Inc.	% Net Inc. of Revs.	Cash Flow
1993	**464**	**3.3**	**0.7**	**73.7**	**22.8**	**1.08**	**d41**	**NM**	**d49**	**NM**	**d26.5**
[1]1992	483	46.5	9.6	59.4	31.0	1.33	d125	NM	d110	NM	d79.5
1991	227	44.3	19.5	29.0	5.2	1.17	42	36.0%	27	11.8	32.0
1990	113	18.2	16.1	2.9	3.9	1.15	15	19.8%	12	10.4	15.7
1989	91	1.1	1.2	9.5	3.6	1.29	d4	NM	d3	NM	0.8
[2]1988	82	5.8	7.1	11.9	2.8	0.11	4	54.3%	2	2.1	4.6
1987	29	3.2	11.1	2.0	1.1	0.06	5	33.9%	3	10.7	4.2

Balance Sheet Data (Million $)

Mar. 31	Cash	Curr. Assets	Curr. Liab.	Curr. Ratio	Total Assets	% Ret. on Assets	Long Term Debt	Common Equity	Total Cap.	% LT Debt of Cap.	% Ret. on Equity
1993	**75**	**175**	**130**	**1.3**	**342**	**NM**	**9.8**	**188**	**198**	**4.9**	**NM**
1992	110	240	107	2.3	365	NM	9.8	228	238	4.1	NM
1991	42	83	40	2.1	136	23.7	10.0	85	95	10.5	38.0
1990	43	66	22	2.9	87	16.0	10.2	54	64	15.8	27.1
1989	10	29	12	2.3	53	NM	11.5	29	41	28.3	NM
1988	9	36	17	2.1	54	4.1	3.9	32	36	10.7	6.1
1987	15	20	5	3.8	28	NA	0.6	22	22	2.6	NA

Data as. orig. reptd. **1.** Major merger resulted in formation of new co. **2.** Refl. merger or acq. d-Deficit. NM-Not Meaningful. NA-Not Available.

Business Summary

Borland International designs and markets computer software products both for businesses and for software developers. Its key products run on personal computers that operate under the MS-DOS and OS/2 operating systems and the MS-Windows operating environment, although certain versions of the products also run under various UNIX-based operating systems. The company uses object-oriented programming techniques, which increases the functionality of its applications and simplifies the software development process.

The company has three principal product families: database, spreadsheet and language products. Database products include "dBASE IV" (acquired with Ashton-Tate in October 1991), a relational database management system that features the dBASE programming language, and "Paradox," a relational database management system known for its ease of use.

"Quattro Pro", Borland's electronic spreadsheet, offers extensive publishing and consolidation capabilities and is compatible with other spreadsheet programs.

The company is also a leader in the design and marketing of computer language compilers and other software development tools. Such products assist users in developing new programs in certain computer languages and in translating them into "machine language" (instructions capable of being read and executed by a computer). Products include "Borland C++," "Turbo C++," and "Turbo Pascal."

Other offerings include "SideKick," a utility program that performs simple tasks, such as calendar, calculator and notebook functions, and "Objectvision," an application development product.

Products are sold worldwide, primarily through independent distributors, dealers and original equipment manufacturers (OEMs), and also directly to corporate, governmental and educational customers and to individual end-users. International operations, including export sales and net foreign royalty income, totaled 53% and 49% of revenues in 1992-93 and 1991-92, respectively.

Dividend Data

No cash dividends have been paid.

Finances

In October 1991, the company completed the acquisition of Ashton-Tate Corp., the leading vendor of PC database software, in exchange for 9.6 million Borland common shares. During 1991-92, restructuring and pooling charges related to the acquisition totaling $146 million were recorded.

In April 1991, underwriters sold 1,000,000 Borland common shares (900,000 for the company) at $57.25 each.

Capitalization

Long Term Debt: $21,755,000 (6/93).

Common Stock: 26,603,265 shs. ($0.01 par).
P. Kahn owns or controls 10%.
Institutions hold about 40%.
Shareholders: 3,852 of record (6/93).

Office—1800 Green Hills Rd., Scotts Valley, CA 95066. **Tel**—(408) 438-8400. **Chrmn, Pres & CEO**—P. Kahn. **SVP-Fin, CFO & Investor Contact**—Alan S. Henricks. **VP & Secy**—R. H. Kohn. **Dirs**—S. M. Dow, G. Hara, D. Heller, P. R. Kahn. **Transfer Agents & Registrars**—Manufacturers Hanover Trust Co. of California, SF; Ravensbourne Registration Services Ltd., Beckenham, Kent, England. **Incorporated** in Delaware in 1989. **Empl**—1,885.

 Peter C. Wood, CFA

Bowater Inc.

NYSE Symbol BOW Options on Pacific (Mar-Jun-Sep-Dec) In S&P MidCap 400

Price	Range	P-E Ratio	Dividend	Yield	S&P Ranking	Beta
Oct. 27'93	1993					
19¼	24⅝–18	NM	0.60	3.1%	B–	1.41

Summary

This company is one of the largest producers of newsprint in North America, and makes coated publication papers, market pulp, and continuous computer forms. Sales and earnings are very sensitive to cyclical economic fluctuations; weakness in the U.S. economy and in pricing for paper products resulted in a significant loss in 1992. Another large deficit is expected in 1993, but losses should narrow as 1994 progresses.

Current Outlook

A loss of $0.40 a share is estimated for 1994, compared with the $2.40 loss projected for 1993.

The quarterly dividend, which was slashed 50% to $0.15 with the April 1993 payment, should remain at that level for the foreseeable future.

Sales in 1994 should rise modestly, assuming marginal recovery in newsprint and pulp pricing. Losses are expected to narrow as the year progresses, although high interest costs will continue to be a burden. The company is well positioned for an eventual recovery in its markets, but current industry overcapacity and weak demand may penalize earnings for some time. Overseas expansion and a renewed focus on markets such as directory paper should help boost long-term growth.

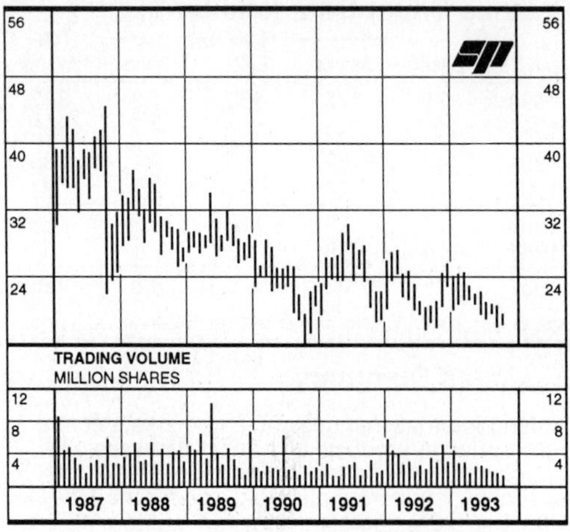

Net Sales (Million $)

Quarter:	1994	1993	1992	1991
Mar.	---	387	373	324
Jun.	---	363	356	326
Sep.	---	372	366	312
Dec.	---	---	399	326
	---	---	1,494	1,289

Sales for the nine months ended October 2, 1993, rose 2.4%, year to year, as strong demand for directory and uncoated specialty paper, improved pricing for coated paper and healthy lumber operations more than offset overcapacity, weak demand and low selling prices for newsprint and pulp. In the absence of a $0.21 a share charge for an equipment write-off and a $0.09 a share restructuring charge, the net loss narrowed to $69.4 million ($1.96 a share, after preferred dividend requirements) from a loss of $72.0 million ($2.05). Results for the 1992 period exclude a credit of $0.30 a share related to an accounting change.

Common Share Earnings ($)

Quarter:	1994	1993	1992	1991
Mar.	Ed0.25	d0.65	d0.84	0.43
Jun.	Ed0.15	d0.45	d0.70	0.54
Sep.	Ed0.05	d0.86	d0.51	0.17
Dec.	E0.05	Ed0.44	d0.59	0.02
	Ed0.40	Ed2.40	d2.64	1.15

Important Developments

Oct. '93— Management said that unless there is improvement in worldwide economic conditions, newsprint and pulp prices are likely to remain at "unacceptably low" levels.

Feb. '93— Directors cut the quarterly dividend 50%, citing prolonged pricing weakness for paper products and decreased cash flow.

Next earnings report expected in mid-February.

Per Share Data ($)

Yr. End Dec. 31	[2]1992	[1]1991	1990	1989	1988	[2]1987	1986	1985	1984	[1]1983
Tangible Bk. Val.	**20.90**	24.48	24.42	23.49	21.13	17.62	12.87	14.45	12.97	13.38
Cash Flow	**1.84**	4.84	5.61	6.83	7.07	4.50	3.60	3.94	3.83	3.15
Earnings[3]	**d2.64**	1.15	2.30	3.86	4.37	2.13	1.51	2.30	2.26	1.52
Dividends	**1.200**	1.200	1.200	1.140	0.970	0.830	0.720	0.720	0.359	NM
Payout Ratio	**NM**	104%	52%	29%	22%	39%	48%	31%	17%	NM
Prices—High	**27¼**	30⅜	28½	34⅛	36⅞	44½	33⅛	25⅞	25⅛	NA
Low	**17⅝**	18⅝	16⅛	25¾	25¼	22	23⅜	19⅞	14⅞	NA
P/E Ratio—	**NM**	26–16	12–7	9–7	8–6	21–10	22–15	11–9	11–7	NA

Data as orig. reptd.; prior to 1984 data as reptd. in preliminary prospectus dated 3-27-84, reflecting spin-off from Bowater Corp. plc. **1.** Reflects merger or acquisition. **2.** Reflects acctg. change. **3.** Bef. results of disc. opers. of +0.34 in 1984, and spec. item(s) of +0.30 in 1992, -0.25 in 1990. d-Deficit. E-Estimated. NM-Not Meaningful. NA-Not Available.

Income Data (Million $)

Year Ended Dec. 31	Revs.	Oper. Inc.	% Oper. Inc. of Revs.	Cap. Exp.	Depr.	Int. Exp.	[4]Net Bef. Taxes	Eff. Tax Rate	[5]Net Inc.	% Net Inc. of Revs.	Cash Flow
[2]1992	**1,494**	**93**	**6.2**	**139**	**162**	**79.7**	**d172**	**NM**	**d93**	**NM**	**67**
[1]1991	1,289	236	18.3	131	132	45.6	69	37.0%	46	3.5	174
1990	1,380	292	21.2	150	117	47.0	141	37.0%	87	6.3	200
1989	1,450	387	26.7	389	107	44.3	261	36.0%	145	10.0	245
1988	1,410	432	30.6	211	98	35.5	302	36.5%	164	11.7	257
[2]1987	1,231	304	24.7	62	85	46.8	177	43.0%	81	6.6	162
1986	920	186	20.2	223	62	50.5	91	30.2%	[2]49	5.4	106
1985	904	184	20.3	326	48	43.5	115	29.2%	68	7.5	115
[3]1984	888	181	20.4	153	43	29.1	118	38.8%	63	7.0	106
[1]1983	772	119	15.5	84	37	23.7	65	28.5%	38	4.9	79

Balance Sheet Data (Million $)

		Curr.									
Dec. 31	Cash	Assets	Liab.	Ratio	Total Assets	% Ret. on Assets	Long Term Debt	Common Equity	Total Cap.	% LT Debt of Cap.	% Ret. on Equity
1992	**166**	**459**	**266**	**1.7**	**2,882**	**NM**	**1,120**	**818**	**2,472**	**45.3**	**NM**
1991	28	386	282	1.4	2,780	1.8	840	943	2,428	34.6	4.4
1990	18	283	223	1.3	2,298	3.8	488	935	2,068	23.6	8.9
1989	92	357	246	1.5	2,284	7.0	504	907	2,030	24.8	16.0
1988	25	288	220	1.3	1,880	9.2	274	827	1,652	16.6	20.8
1987	33	267	161	1.7	1,700	4.4	350	713	1,532	22.9	12.0
1986	36	254	116	2.2	1,601	3.4	623	452	1,474	42.3	10.1
1985	59	237	197	1.2	1,315	5.8	322	423	1,101	29.2	16.8
1984	56	250	164	1.5	1,033	5.9	231	379	843	27.4	16.2
1983	37	254	207	1.2	935	4.2	194	334	723	26.8	11.0

Data as orig. reptd.; prior to 1984 data as reptd. in preliminary prospectus dated 3-27-84, reflecting spin-off from Bowater Corp. plc. **1.** Reflects merger or acquiition. **2.** Reflects acctg. change. **3.** Excl. disc. opers. **4.** Incl. equity in earns. of nonconsol. subs. prior to 1988. **5.** Bef. results of disc. opers. in 1984, and spec. item(s) in 1992, 1990. d-Deficit. NM-Not Meaningful.

Business Summary

Bowater Inc. is the largest producer of newsprint in the U.S., and the third largest in North America. Its annual newsprint capacity represents about 9% of the North American total. The company also produces coated paper, market pulp, continuous computer forms and lumber and other products. Segment contributions in 1992 (profits in million $):

	Sales	Profits
Pulp/paper & related products	86%	–$46.1
Communication papers	14%	–2.3

Export sales accounted for 18% of total revenues in 1992, versus 15% in 1991 and 13% in 1990.

The company manufactures pulp and paper products at facilities in Tennessee, South Carolina, Maine and Nova Scotia. All of its mills are fully integrated, and are supported by more than four million acres of owned and leased timberlands. A significant portion of BOW's newsprint tonnage is produced under joint venture arrangements with major publishers. These ventures include Calhoun Newsprint Co., which is 51%-owned by BOW and 49%-owned by the Newhouse Newspaper Group, and Mersey Paper Co., which is 49%-owned by The Washington Post.

Coated paper produced by BOW is used in special interest magazines, mail order catalogs, advertising pieces and coupons. Bowater Communication Papers makes continuous stock computer forms at eight plants in the U.S. Computer and other business communication papers are marketed through a network of 30 distribution centers. BOW also operates three sawmills that produce lumber.

In addition to its own pulp requirements, the company shipped 264,549 tons of bleached kraft market pulp in 1992 to manufacturers of fine papers, tissues and other paper products.

Dividend Data

Quarterly dividends were initiated in 1984. A dividend reinvestment plan is available. A "poison pill" stock purchase right was adopted in 1986.

Amt. of Divd. $	Date Decl.	Ex–divd. Date	Stock of Record	Payment Date
0.30	Nov. 18	Dec. 4	Dec. 10	Jan. 1'93
0.15	Feb. 26	Mar. 4	Mar. 10	Apr. 1'93
0.15	May 19	Jun. 4	Jun. 10	Jul. 1'93
0.15	Aug. 25	Sep. 3	Sep. 10	Oct. 1'93

Capitalization

Long Term Debt: $1,119,457,000 (7/93).

Minority Interests: $152,827,000.

LIBOR Preferred Stock: $74,314,000.

Common Stock: 36,394,999 shs. ($1 par).
Institutions hold approximately 64%.
Shareholders: 8,200.

Office—55 East Camperdown Way, P. O. Box 1028, Greenville, SC 29602. **Tel**—(803) 271-7733. **Chrmn & Pres**—A. P. Gammie. **Vice Chrmn**—R. D. McDonough. **SVP-CFO**—R. C. Lancaster. **Secy**—W. C. Shiba. **Investor Contact**—SuAnne B. Aune (803) 282-9560. **Dirs**—F. J. Aguilar, H. D. Aycock, R. Barth, K. M. Curtis, A. P. Gammie, R. Laster, H. G. MacNeill, R. D. McDonough, D. G. McMaster, D. R. Melville, J. A. Rolls, J. White. **Transfer Agent & Registrar**—Bank of New York, NYC. **Incorporated** in Delaware in 1964. **Empl**—6,900.

 Richard Spiegel

Brinker International

NYSE Symbol EAT Options on Pacific In S&P MidCap 400

Price	Range	P-E Ratio	Dividend	Yield	S&P Ranking	Beta
Aug. 26'93	1993					
35¾	37¼–27⅞	35	None	None	B+	1.69

Summary

This rapidly growing company operates and franchises the Chili's restaurant chain, which had 317 units open at June 30, 1993. EAT also operates more than 45 other restaurants under the Grady's American Grill, Romano's Macaroni Grill and Spageddies Italian Food names. Earnings have grown quickly in recent years, and further sizable advances are expected in the year ahead. The shares were split three for two in May 1993.

Current Outlook

Earnings for the fiscal year ending June 30, 1994, are estimated at $1.30 a share, up from fiscal 1993's $1.03.

Near-term initiation of a cash dividend is not expected.

Revenues in fiscal 1994 are expected to be fueled by additional EAT restaurants being open, plus improved sales at older units. In fiscal 1994, about 55 company-operated restaurants are expected to open, at least half of which are likely to be in the Chili's chain. In percentage terms, the number of units in EAT's three other restaurant chains is expected to grow faster, but off a lower base.

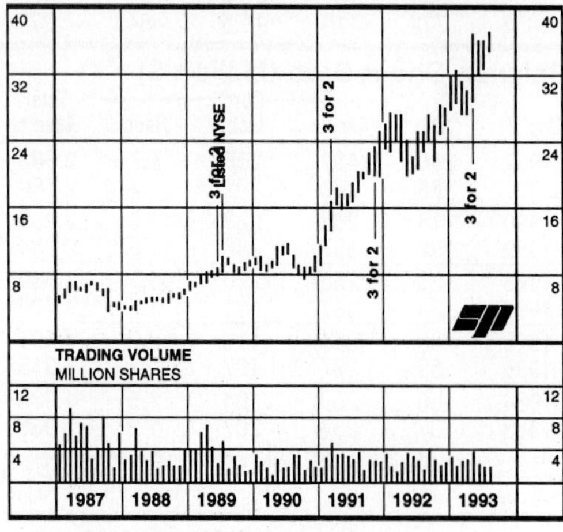

Revenues (Million $)

Quarter:	1992-3	1991-2	1990-1	1989-90
Sep.	151.2	124.1	101.6	83.4
Dec.	151.9	122.0	99.7	82.5
Mar.	164.7	131.9	107.2	85.5
Jun.	185.1	141.3	118.2	95.7
	652.9	519.3	426.8	347.1

Revenues for the fiscal year ended June 30, 1993 (preliminary), increased 26% from those of fiscal 1992. Net income advanced 37%, to $48.9 million ($1.03 a share, based on 2.1% more shares), from $35.7 million ($0.77, as adjusted).

Common Share Earnings ($)

Quarter:	1992-3	1991-2	1990-1	1989-90
Sep.	0.23	0.18	0.15	0.13
Dec.	0.23	0.16	0.13	0.11
Mar.	0.27	0.20	0.15	0.10
Jun.	0.30	0.22	0.19	0.15
	1.03	0.77	0.61	0.49

Important Developments

Aug. '93— In fiscal 1993's fourth quarter, comparable-unit sales at EAT's company-operated restaurants were up 5.4%, year to year. Also, EAT's 367 systemwide units (including franchises) at June 30, 1993, had fiscal 1993 sales totaling $812 million, up 25% from the $648 million generated by 305 restaurants the year before. In fiscal 1994, 45 to 48 Chili's units are expected to open, of which 30 would be company operated. Also, EAT expected to open six to eight Grady's restaurants, 12 to 15 Romano's and four to six Spageddies. EAT recently acquired full ownership of the Spageddies business through the issuance of 137,144 common shares. In May, Norman E. Brinker returned to the positions of chairman and CEO at Brinker International, following a polo match injury in January.

Next earnings report expected in late October.

Per Share Data ($)

Yr. End Jun. 30	1993	1992	1991	1990	[2]1989	1988	[2]1987	1986	1985	[2]1984
Tangible Bk. Val.	**NA**	5.87	4.87	[3]3.45	[3]2.36	[3]2.01	1.67	1.45	0.99	0.59
Cash Flow	**NA**	1.24	0.98	0.97	0.69	0.62	0.48	0.35	0.28	0.18
Earnings[4]	**1.03**	0.77	0.61	0.49	0.40	0.27	0.22	0.18	0.17	0.10
Dividends	**Nil**	Nil	Nil	Nil	Nil	Nil	Nil	Nil	Nil	Nil
Payout Ratio	**Nil**	Nil	Nil	Nil	Nil	Nil	Nil	Nil	Nil	Nil
Prices[1]—High	**37¼**	28½	25⅜	11⅞	10¼	6⅜	7⅛	5⅛	5¾	4⅞
Low	**27⅞**	19⅞	9⅛	7⅝	6⅛	3⅝	3⅝	3⅜	4	2½
P/E Ratio—	**36–27**	37–26	41–15	24–15	26–15	24–14	33–16	28–19	33–23	49–26

Data as orig. reptd. Adj. for stk. divs. of 50% May 1993. 50% Nov. 1991, 50% Mar. 1991, 50% Jun. 1989. **1.** Cal. yr. **2.** Refl. merger or acq. **3.** Incl. intangibles. **4.** Bef. spec. item of +0.02 in 1988. NA-Not Available.

Income Data (Million $)

Year Ended Jun. 30	Oper. Revs.	Oper. Inc.	% Oper. Inc. of Revs.	Cap. Exp.	Depr.	Int. Exp.	[3]Net Bef. Taxes	Eff. Tax Rate	[4]Net Inc.	% Net Inc. of Revs.	Cash Flow
1992	**519**	**73.5**	**14.1**	**91**	**22.2**	**1.30**	**54.5**	**34.5%**	**35.7**	**6.9**	**57.9**
1991	427	54.2	12.7	112	17.2	1.64	39.7	34.2%	26.1	6.1	43.3
1990	347	42.5	12.2	57	14.3	3.23	27.4	34.0%	18.1	5.2	32.4
[1]1989	285	32.4	11.4	32	10.1	3.37	20.9	32.8%	14.0	4.9	24.2
1988	218	26.0	11.9	27	10.8	3.76	12.4	34.4%	8.1	3.7	18.9
[1]1987	177	20.8	11.7	18	7.7	2.09	11.3	42.5%	6.5	3.7	14.2
1986	107	11.3	10.6	21	4.5	0.77	6.6	27.7%	4.8	4.5	9.3
1985	69	8.8	12.7	16	2.6	0.56	6.0	30.7%	4.1	6.0	6.7
[1]1984	43	5.4	12.6	8	1.6	0.88	2.9	32.4%	2.0	4.6	3.6
[2]1983	17	2.7	16.1	3	0.7	0.40	1.6	37.5%	1.0	5.9	NA

Balance Sheet Data (Million $)

Jun. 30	Cash	Curr. Assets	Curr. Liab.	Curr. Ratio	Total Assets	% Ret. on Assets	Long Term Debt	Common Equity	Total Cap.	% LT Debt of Cap.	% Ret. on Equity
1992	**10.1**	**30.9**	**62.2**	**0.5**	**337**	**11.7**	**4.2**	**254**	**270**	**1.5**	**15.4**
1991	23.9	42.3	40.1	1.1	266	10.7	4.8	207	221	2.2	14.7
1990	7.1	23.2	41.6	0.6	198	9.6	12.2	132	152	8.0	16.2
1989	6.5	23.0	28.8	0.8	154	9.5	40.3	79	125	32.3	19.3
1988	7.3	23.1	18.5	1.2	127	6.7	43.1	60	109	39.7	14.7
1987	27.1	39.3	13.6	2.9	111	7.2	43.3	49	98	44.4	14.2
1986	2.6	12.2	9.8	1.2	63	8.8	10.7	39	53	20.2	14.9
1985	0.3	8.1	6.6	1.2	41	12.5	8.5	23	34	24.8	22.2
1984	1.7	4.5	4.8	1.0	22	10.9	3.5	13	17	20.6	26.2
1983	1.1	4.0	3.1	1.3	14	NM	7.5	1	11	69.1	NM

Data as orig. reptd. **1.** Refl. merger or acq. **2.** Six mos. **3.** Incl. equity in earns. of nonconsol. subs. **4.** Bef. spec. item in 1988. NA-Not Available. NM-Not Meaningful.

Business Summary

Brinker International (formerly Chili's, Inc.) includes the Chili's Grill & Bar restaurant chain, which at June 30, 1993, had 317 units in operation. Of these, 235 were operated by EAT, and the remainder were joint-venture or franchise units. Also, EAT operated 49 other restaurants under the Grady's American Grill, Romano's Macaroni Grill and Spageddies Italian Food names. EAT is accelerating development of Spageddies, a moderately priced Italian-food concept, of which the first unit opened in July 1992.

The Chili's restaurant concept originated in 1975, when the first such unit opened in Dallas, Texas. The full-service, casual-atmosphere restaurants have a limited menu, including hamburgers, fajitas, chicken, seafood entrees, sandwiches, barbecued ribs, salads, appetizers and desserts. Entree prices range from about $3.85 to $9.95. Also, there is full bar service. Including alcoholic beverages, the average per-person revenue per meal has been about $8.10. In fiscal 1993, the Chili's chain grew by 42 units, including the opening of about 28 units owned and operated by EAT.

As of June 30, 1993, EAT also operated 24 Grady's American Grill restaurants, which are casual, upscale dinnerhouses. Average per-person revenue per meal has been about $10.60. EAT acquired Grady's Inc. in February 1989.

In November 1989, EAT acquired Romano's Macaroni Grill, an upscale Italian-theme restaurant in the San Antonio, Texas, area. As of June 30, 1993, there were 22 Romano's units in operation, including nine that opened in fiscal 1993. Average per-person revenue per meal has been about $13.90. Spageddies is a moderately priced Italian-food concept. The first such unit opened in July 1992, and as of June 30, 1993, there were three Spageddies open.

Dividend Data

No cash has been paid. Three-for-two stock splits were effected in May 1993, November and March 1991 and June 1989.

Finances

In March 1991, EAT completed a public offering of 2,923,650 new common shares (adjusted for subsequent stock splits) at $14.72 each. An additional 956,250 shares were sold by stockholders.

Capitalization

Long Term Debt: $3,855,000 (3/93).

Common Stock: About 45,668,000 shs. ($0.10 par).
Officers & directors own about 11%.
Institutions hold about 86%.
Shareholders of record: 1,245 (9/92).

Office—6820 LBJ Freeway, Dallas, TX 75240. **Tel**—(214) 980-9917. **Chrmn & CEO**—N. E. Brinker. **Pres & COO**—R. A. McDougall. **Exec VP-CFO & Investor Contact**—Debra Smithart. **VP-Secy**—R. L. Callaway. **Dirs**—N. E. Brinker, F. L. Cardwell Jr., J. W. Evans, R. F. Evans, C. L. Ford III, J. M. Haggar Jr., R. L. Hunt, R. A. McDougall, W. F. Regas, D. Smithart, R. Staubach. **Transfer Agent & Registrar**—Chemical Shareholder Services, Dallas. **Incorporated** in Delaware in 1983. **Empl**—28,000.

 Tom Graves, CFA

Brooklyn Union Gas

NYSE Symbol BU In S&P MidCap 400

Price	Range	P-E Ratio	Dividend	Yield	S&P Ranking	Beta
Sep. 1'93	1993					
27⅜	28½–21⁹⁄₁₆	16	1.32	4.8%	B+	0.39

Summary

This company distributes natural gas in the New York City boroughs of Brooklyn and Staten Island and a large part of Queens. Nonutility activities include exploration and production, participation in cogeneration projects, and gas marketing. Weather-normalized gas sales volumes are expected to grow at about 3.0% annually for the remainder of the decade. The shares were split 3-for-2 in July 1993.

Current Outlook

Share earnings for the fiscal year ending September 30, 1994, are projected at $1.76, up from an estimated $1.70 for fiscal 1993.

The $0.33 quarterly dividend is expected to be raised about 3.0% at the December 1993 meeting.

Utility profits for fiscal 1994 should be up slightly on growth in gas sales volumes stemming from the addition of some large customers, including multi-family dwelling complexes and schools; development of gas cooling and natural gas vehicles will yield minor benefits. BU's residential gas market is mature and likely to offer marginal growth in gas sales. Weather-normalized gas sales volumes should grow at a 3.0% annual pace for the remainder of the decade. Nonutility profits should benefit from higher wellhead gas prices, and increased gas marketing and storage activity.

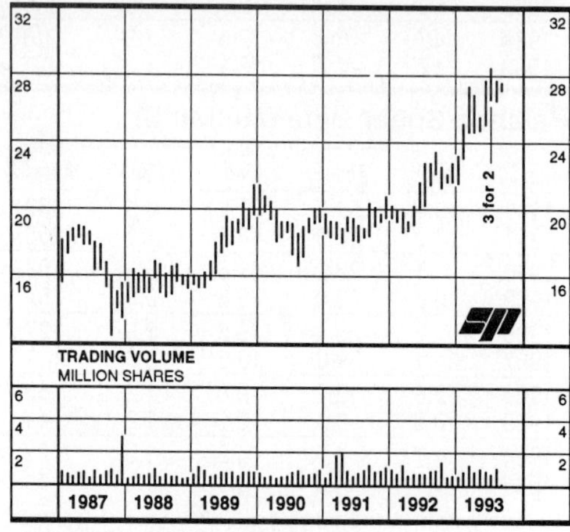

Operating Revenues (Million $)

Quarter:	1992–93	1991–92	1990–91	1989–90
Dec.	347	311	296	334
Mar.	489	433	403	366
Jun.	209	183	165	171
Sep.	---	148	127	122
	---	1,075	991	994

Operating revenues for the nine months ended June 30, 1993, rose 13%, year to year. Benefiting from the absence of a $13 million ($0.30 a share) writedown at energy production operations, net income advanced 17%, to $2.40 a share from $2.07 (adjusted).

Common Share Earnings ($)

Quarter:	1992–93	1991–92	1990–91	1989–90
Dec.	0.93	0.85	0.86	0.81
Mar.	1.63	1.35	1.61	1.64
Jun.	d0.15	d0.12	d0.20	d0.17
Sep.	Ed0.71	d0.71	d0.65	d0.83
	E1.70	1.35	[1]1.45	1.43

Important Developments

Aug. '93— BU's Solex Energy Corp. affiliate reached an agreement to sell gas properties in Alberta, Canada to Co-enerco Resources Ltd. for C$40 million; the properties have been producing about 10 million cubic feet of natural gas per day. Separately, BU planned to open a New York-based market hub for buyers and sellers of natural gas in the northeastern U.S.; operations were scheduled to begin October 1, 1993.

Jul. '93— BU said that Petroleum Heat and Power Co. (Petro) signed a letter of intent to acquire a substantial interest in and to assume the management of Star Gas Corp. Petro, along with certain other investors including the existing shareholders of Star Gas, will invest $30 million of additional equity in Star Gas. BU believed this development was an important step in the long-term restructuring of Star Gas and would position it for increased growth through internal marketing programs and acquisitions.

Next earnings report expected in late October.

Per Share Data ($)

Yr. End Sep. 30	1992	1991	1990	1989	1988	1987	1986	1985	1984	1983
Tangible Bk. Val.	**14.55**	14.37	13.69	13.36	12.77	12.19	11.53	11.27	10.62	10.11
Earnings	**1.35**	1.45	1.43	1.68	1.66	1.62	1.14	1.67	1.55	1.51
Dividends	**1.287**	1.257	1.217	1.177	1.147	1.107	1.070	1.030	0.993	0.967
Payout Ratio	**96%**	86%	85%	70%	69%	68%	94%	62%	64%	64%
Prices[2]—High	**23½**	20²⁷⁄₃₂	21½	21½	16²⁹⁄₃₂	19	19¼	14²⁹⁄₃₂	12	11¹¹⁄₃₂
Low	**18⅝**	18	16²¹⁄₃₂	15¹¹⁄₃₂	14¹³⁄₃₂	12¹³⁄₃₂	14	11¾	9¹¹⁄₃₂	9³⁄₃₂
P/E Ratio—	**17–14**	14–12	15–12	13–9	10–9	12–8	17–12	9–7	8–6	8–6

Data as orig. reptd. Adj. for stk. div(s). of 50% Jul. 1993, 100% Mar. 1986. **1.** Quarters do not add due to changes in number of shs. outstanding. **2.** Cal. yr. d-Deficit. E-Estimated.

Income Data (Million $)

Year Ended Sep. 30	Revs.	Depr.	Maint.	Oper. Ratio	[1]Fxd. Chgs. Cover.	Constr. Credits	Eff. Tax Rate	Net Inc.	% Return On Revs.	[2]Invest. Capital	[3]Com. Equity
1992	**1,075**	**54.2**	**53.0**	**90.8%**	**3.01**	**NA**	**32.8%**	**59.9**	**5.6**	**6.9**	**8.7**
1991	991	42.7	51.8	90.4%	2.91	NA	27.7%	61.8	6.2	7.6	9.6
1990	994	38.1	50.4	90.6%	2.46	NA	23.0%	56.4	5.7	8.3	9.8
1989	969	35.5	57.7	89.9%	2.85	NA	28.3%	64.3	6.6	9.3	12.1
1988	899	32.2	56.8	90.0%	2.97	NA	28.1%	61.7	6.9	9.9	12.6
1987	924	29.3	54.0	90.5%	3.28	NA	36.1%	59.1	6.4	10.3	12.9
1986	1,007	53.6	47.4	92.4%	2.43	NA	37.9%	44.7	4.4	9.5	9.4
1985	1,028	30.0	40.6	91.5%	3.32	NA	41.2%	60.1	5.8	11.4	14.3
1984	1,036	25.9	42.1	91.9%	2.94	NA	39.1%	54.3	5.2	12.1	14.0
1983	939	22.9	38.3	91.5%	2.74	NA	39.7%	49.1	5.2	12.7	14.1

Balance Sheet Data (Million $)

Sep. 30	Gross Prop.	Capital Expend.	Net Prop.	% Earn. on Net Prop.	Total Cap.	Capitalization LT Debt	% LT Debt	Pfd.	% Pfd.	Com.	% Com.
1992	**1,615**	**173**	**1,229**	**8.3**	**1,478**	**682**	**51.6**	**7.8**	**0.6**	**632**	**47.8**
1991	1,504	148	1,151	8.6	1,483	685	51.3	44.5	3.3	608	45.4
1990	1,381	134	1,063	9.1	1,223	534	49.0	45.4	4.2	510	46.8
1989	1,282	158	989	10.4	1,214	553	51.0	46.3	4.3	485	44.7
1988	1,211	125	897	10.6	1,067	445	47.2	48.0	5.1	450	47.7
1987	1,088	98	803	11.3	953	378	44.7	52.2	6.2	416	49.1
1986	1,023	78	759	10.2	878	344	44.2	53.9	6.9	381	48.9
1985	972	83	737	12.3	864	334	43.4	74.1	9.6	362	47.0
1984	897	76	686	12.6	753	272	40.3	76.5	11.3	327	48.4
1983	826	73	637	13.1	707	264	41.3	78.3	12.3	297	46.4

Data as orig. reptd. **1.** Times int. exp. & pfd. divs. covered (pretax basis). **2.** Based on income bef. interest charges. **3.** As reptd. by co. NA-Not Available.

Business Summary

Brooklyn Union distributes natural gas in a service area of about 187 square miles in New York City, including the boroughs of Brooklyn, Staten Island, and part of Queens, with an estimated population of 4 million. Firm volume sales in fiscal 1992 totaled 122.5 Bcf, up from 108.7 Bcf a year earlier, as the number of heating degree days increased to 4,659 (normal is 4,827) from 3,971. Interruptible and other sales were 8.6 Bcf, versus 6.4 Bcf.

Subsidiaries are: Gas Energy Inc., which participates in cogeneration projects and conducts fuel management services; Brooklyn Interstate Natural Gas Corp., which provides gas marketing services to pipelines and other customers; Star Energy Inc., which holds an interest in Star Gas Corp., a propane distributor; Fuel Resources Inc., which stores and markets gas and whose Brooklyn Union Exploration Co. unit is engaged in gas exploration and production; and North East Transmission Co., which holds an 11% interest in the Iroquois Gas Transmission System, a 370-mile pipeline which supplies about 600 MMcf of Canadian gas daily to 21 Northeastern utilities and power generators. U.S. nonutility operations accounted for a loss of $0.37 a share in fiscal 1992.

Pipeline gas and underground storage are provided under long-term contracts primarily with Transcontinental Gas Pipe Line Corp., Texas Eastern Transmission Corp., and Tennessee Gas Pipeline Co. Gas purchased on the spot market accounted for 22% of total supplies in fiscal 1992. Other sources of supply include Canadian gas, and BU's liquefied natural gas plant. In fiscal 1992, BU together with several other companies initiated plans for development of a pipeline across the lower New York Bay area.

Variations in revenues due to abnormal weather during the heating season are largely offset by a weather normalization adjustment in rates.

Dividend Data

Dividends have been paid since 1949. A dividend reinvestment plan is available.

Amt of Divd. $	Date Decl.	Ex–divd. Date	Stock of Record	Payment Date
0.48½	Sep. 23	Sep. 29	Oct. 5	Nov. 1'92
0.49½	Dec. 16	Dec. 28	Jan. 4	Feb. 1'93
0.49½	Mar. 24	Mar. 30	Apr. 5	May 1'93
3–for–2	Jun. 23	Jul. 21	Jul. 6	Jul. 20'93
0.33	Jun. 23	Jun. 29	Jul. 6	Aug. 1'93

Capitalization

Long Term Debt: $692,700,000 (6/93).

Red. Cum. Preferred Stock: $7,500,000.

Common Stock: 44,326,820 shs. ($0.33⅓ par).
Institutions hold about 27%.
Shareholders of record: 31,367.

Office—One MetroTech Center, Brooklyn, NY 11201-3851. **Tel**—(718) 403-2000. **Pres & CEO**—R. B. Catell. **EVP-CFO**—C. G. Matthews. **VP-Secy**—H. E. H. Knight Jr. **Investor Contact**—Jan C. Childress. **Dirs**— R. B. Catell, K. I. Chenault, A. S. Christensen, D. H. Elliott, A. H. Fishman, J. L. Larocca, W. A. Levin, E. H. Luntey, R. Pratt Jr., J. Q. Riordan. **Transfer Agent & Registrar**—First Chicago Trust Co. of New York, NYC. **Incorporated** in New York in 1895. **Empl**—3,626.

 Mark Mattke

Brush Wellman

NYSE Symbol BW In S&P MidCap 400

Price	Range	P-E Ratio	Dividend	Yield	S&P Ranking	Beta
Sep. 23'93	1993					
11⅝	17½–11	42	[1]0.20	[1]1.7%	B	0.97

Summary

This company is a leading worldwide supplier of beryllium alloys and beryllia for the electrical/electronics industry and metallic beryllium for aerospace and defense applications. BW remains focused on issues critical to its long-term success, including marketing, improved competitiveness, environmental management, and product/process development. Earnings may recover somewhat in 1994 from 1993's depressed level, which has reflected lower defense spending and temporary problems related to a new product line.

Current Outlook

Earnings for 1993 are estimated at $0.25 a share, down sharply from 1992's $0.65. Earnings for 1994 are projected at $0.50.

Dividends should continue at $0.05 quarterly; a $0.06 extra was paid in January 1993.

Sales for 1993 may rise modestly. Beryllium alloys receipts are likely to advance significantly, on growth of automotive electronics use and recovery in computer applications. Beryllium metal receipts will probably fall moderately, as diminished defense-related business outweighs introduction of aluminum beryllium material and unchanged sales to the U.S. stockpile. Margins should narrow in 1993 versus 1992, on a less profitable product mix.

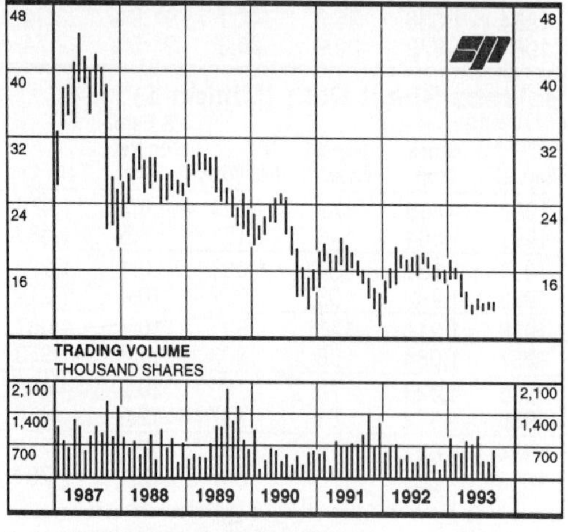

Net Sales (Million $)

Quarter:	1993	1992	1991	1990
Mar.	69.4	67.8	76.8	80.8
Jun.	70.9	67.3	69.2	78.4
Sep.	---	63.1	59.3	70.8
Dec.	---	66.8	62.2	67.4
	---	265.0	267.5	297.4

Sales for the six months ended July 4, 1993, rose 3.8%, year to year, on increased receipts from all product lines, except beryllium metal. With the lower sales and production volume of beryllium metal, coupled with problems in producing aluminum beryllium material disk drive components, pretax income fell 84%. After taxes at 20.4%, versus 28.0%, net income was down 82%, to $0.08 a share from $0.45.

Common Share Earnings ($)

Quarter:	1993	1992	1991	1990
Mar.	0.07	0.26	0.25	0.34
Jun.	0.01	0.19	0.13	0.41
Sep.	E0.02	0.07	d0.22	0.06
Dec.	E0.15	0.13	d1.88	0.27
	E0.25	0.65	d1.72	1.09

Important Developments

Jul. '93— BW said that for the rest of 1993, it should continue to achieve sales improvement compared with last year. Based on BW's order backlog, second half sales of beryllium metal should recover somewhat from their depressed first half level. These sales, combined with anticipated better performance on BW's new aluminum beryllium material, should help BW to increase profits in the second half over those of the first half of 1993. However, earnings for the year are expected to fall short of the 1992 level.

Oct. '92— The Defense Logistics Agency extended its contract with BW for an additional 26,000 pounds of vacuum hot-pressed beryllium billets to be delivered to the Strategic Materials Stockpile through June 1994. The additional amount brought the total to $46 million for 160,000 pounds. BW began providing material in December 1990.

Next earnings report expected in late October.

Per Share Data ($)

Yr. End Dec. 31	1992	[2]1991	1990	1989	1988	[2]1987	[3]1986	1985	1984	1983
Tangible Bk. Val.[5]	**10.49**	10.10	13.43	13.10	13.49	13.17	12.47	11.77	11.31	9.54
Cash Flow	**1.90**	d0.30	2.58	2.35	2.94	2.44	2.04	2.35	3.01	2.14
Earnings[4]	**0.65**	d1.72	1.09	1.10	1.79	1.38	1.20	1.48	2.20	1.39
Dividends	**0.26**	0.59	0.71	0.67	0.63	0.59	0.55	0.51	0.47	0.42
Payout Ratio	**40%**	NM	65%	58%	33%	42%	46%	34%	21%	30%
Prices—High	**19**	20	25¼	30¼	31	44½	39⅞	40⅜	39¾	29⅞
Low	**12¼**	9½	11½	20¼	22½	19	25⅛	29¼	25½	16½
P/E Ratio—	**29–19**	NM	23–11	28–18	17–13	32–14	33–21	27–20	18–12	21–12

Data as orig. reptd. Adj. for stk. div(s). of 100% Jun. 1984, 50% Jan. 1983. **1.** Excl. 0.06 extra paid Jan. 1993. **2.** Reflects accounting change. **3.** Reflects merger or acquisition. **4.** Bef. results of disc. opers. of -0.53 in 1985; bef. spec. item(s) of -1.02 in 1991. **5.** As reptd. by co. NM-Not Meaningful. d-Deficit. E-Estimated.

Income Data (Million $)

Year Ended Dec. 31	Revs.	Oper. Inc.	% Oper. Inc. of Revs.	Cap. Exp.	Depr.	Int. Exp.	4Net Bef. Taxes	Eff. Tax Rate	5Net Inc.	% Net Inc. of Revs.	Cash Flow
1992	**265**	**38.4**	**14.5**	**14.5**	**20.2**	**3.84**	**13.7**	**23.6%**	**10.5**	**4.0**	**30.7**
[1]1991	267	44.8	16.8	20.0	34.9	4.41	d36.2	NM	d27.5	NM	d4.8
1990	297	52.9	17.8	21.9	23.2	3.89	24.8	29.1%	17.6	5.9	41.6
1989	318	61.1	19.2	20.1	23.2	3.57	26.3	29.6%	18.5	5.8	39.7
1988	346	76.5	22.1	27.0	21.0	3.62	51.9	37.3%	32.5	9.4	53.6
[1]1987	308	68.6	22.3	19.1	20.1	3.57	45.8	42.9%	26.2	8.5	46.2
[2]1986	241	56.4	23.4	34.6	15.9	3.45	40.3	43.7%	[1]22.7	9.4	38.6
[3]1985	243	65.2	26.9	51.8	16.5	3.53	48.2	42.0%	27.9	11.5	44.4
1984	323	87.0	27.0	29.7	15.2	3.37	69.5	40.2%	41.5	12.9	56.7
1983	245	61.9	25.2	17.8	14.0	4.59	43.3	40.5%	25.8	10.5	39.8

Balance Sheet Data (Million $)

Dec. 31	Cash	Curr. Assets	Curr. Liab.	Curr. Ratio	Total Assets	% Ret. on Assets	Long Term Debt	Common Equity	Total Cap.	% LT Debt of Cap.	% Ret. on Equity
1992	**4.2**	**148**	**59.9**	**2.5**	**310**	**3.4**	**33.8**	**169**	**210**	**16.1**	**6.3**
1991	1.7	145	64.7	2.2	307	NM	34.9	162	205	17.1	NM
1990	1.9	152	62.8	2.4	339	5.2	26.7	216	267	10.0	8.2
1989	5.2	150	71.6	2.1	338	5.5	21.1	212	258	8.2	8.6
1988	5.4	156	63.9	2.4	358	9.3	29.9	233	284	10.5	14.1
1987	16.6	178	68.7	2.6	367	7.5	25.5	243	288	8.8	11.1
1986	22.2	157	56.8	2.8	336	7.1	26.6	235	279	9.5	9.9
1985	26.0	134	37.2	3.6	299	9.4	26.3	220	262	10.0	12.9
1984	16.2	152	44.6	3.4	294	15.2	27.6	211	250	11.1	21.4
1983	2.7	120	31.5	3.8	252	10.1	31.7	176	220	14.4	16.1

Data as orig. reptd. **1.** Reflects accounting change. **2.** Reflects merger or acquisition. **3.** Excl. disc. opers. **4.** Incl. equity in earns. of nonconsol. subs. **5.** Bef. results of disc. opers in 1985, and spec. item(s) in 1991. d-Deficit. NM-Not Meaningful.

Business Summary

Brush Wellman is the world's only fully integrated producer of products containing beryllium, and also supplies specialty metal systems and precious metal products. International sales comprised 27% of total sales in 1992 and 28% in 1991; the largest overseas customer concentrations are in Germany, the U.K., Japan and Switzerland.

Beryllium-containing products include beryllium alloys (principally beryllium copper), metallic beryllium and beryllia ceramic, which have high thermal and electrical conductivity, strength and hardness, excellent corrosion, wear and fatigue resistance, and good formability. Beryllium alloys are used in components such as connectors, switches, springs and relays in computers and in other electronic devices; and also by the motor vehicle electronics, telecommunications, energy development, and other consumer and industrial markets, including molds used by the plastics industry. Beryllium metal is the preferred material for many aerospace and defense components such as those used in guidance systems, satellite structures, optical platforms, mirrors and telescopes. BW's Electrofusion Corp. is a leading fabricator of beryllium structures for high performance applications. Beryllia ceramic is widely used with high density electronic circuits to dissipate heat; the January 1992 acquisition of Tegmen Corp. and its direct bonding technology should provide increased market opportunities.

Specialty clad metals produced by Technical Materials, Inc. are used for the high-speed production of complex electronic and electrical components. Williams Advanced Materials makes precious metal products used in BW's metals systems and by specialty stamping fabricators for the electronics industry as solder or braze material.

Proved beryllium-bearing bertrandite reserves were 6,787,000 tons at year-end 1992, after processing of 91,000 tons of ore in 1992.

Dividend Data

Dividends have been paid since 1972. A dividend reinvestment plan is available. A "poison pill" stock purchase right was amended in 1989.

Amt of Divd. $	Date Decl.	Ex-divd. Date	Stock of Record	Payment Date
0.05	Nov. 24	Dec. 15	Dec. 21	Jan. 4'93
0.06 Ext	Nov. 24	Dec. 15	Dec. 21	Jan. 4'93
0.05	Feb. 23	Mar. 8	Mar. 12	Mar. 26'93
0.05	Jun. 1	Jun. 7	Jun. 11	Jun. 25'93
0.05	Aug. 3	Sep. 3	Sep. 10	Sep. 24'93

Capitalization

Long Term Debt: $34,897,000 (7/4/93).

Common Stock: 16,087,015 shs. ($1 par). Institutions hold approximately 55%. Shareholders of record: 2,880.

Office—17876 St. Clair Ave., Cleveland, OH 44110. **Tel**—(216) 486-4200. **Chrmn & Pres**—G. D. Harnett. **SVP-CFO & Secy**—C. G. Waite. **Investor Contact**—Timothy J. Reid. **Dirs**—A. C. Bersticker, C. F. Brush III, F. B. Carr, G. D. Harnett, W. P. Madar, J. L. McCall, G. C. McDonough, R. M. McInnes, H. G. Piper, J. Sherwin Jr., C. G. Waite. **Transfer Agent & Registrar**—Society National Bank, Cleveland, Ohio. **Incorporated** in Ohio in 1931. **Empl**—1,831.

 A.M. Sorrentino, CFA

Buffets, Inc.

NASDAQ Symbol BOCB (Incl. in Nat'l Market) Options on CBOE In S&P MidCap 400

Price	Range	P–E Ratio	Dividend	Yield	S&P Ranking	Beta
Aug. 4'93	1993					
20¾	21–13¼	36	None	None	NR	2.02

Summary

This Minnesota-based company operates a rapidly expanding chain of more than 150 Old Country Buffet restaurants. Revenues and earnings have been in an uptrend since Buffets was established in 1983. BOCB is expected to open about 40 restaurants in 1993, and further large profit advances are expected in the year ahead. A 2-for-1 stock split was effected in June 1993, and in mid-1993, BOCB completed a public offering of 1.44 million common shares.

Current Outlook

Adjusted for a 2-for-1 stock split in June 1993, earnings for 1993 are estimated at $0.63 a share, up from 1992's $0.51. An increase to $0.85 is expected in 1994.

Initiation of cash dividends is not expected.

Sales are expected to increase close to 30% in 1993, largely reflecting the opening of more restaurants. Although there will be some disruption and cost from converting more older units to the "scatter format" for customer service, this effort should boost future sales and profits. Overall margins in 1993 are expected to narrow modestly from year-earlier levels, including first quarter weather-related weakness.

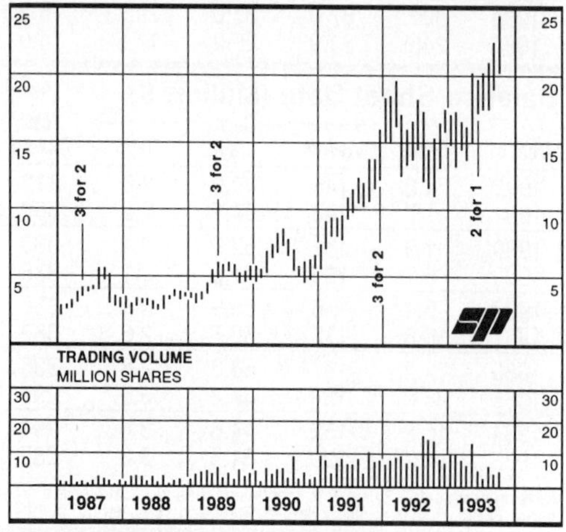

Net Sales (Million $)

Weeks:	1993	1992	1991	1990
16 Wks. Apr......	88.4	70.9	53.1	41.0
12 Wks. Jul.......	77.7	57.7	47.3	33.7
12 Wks. Oct......	---	60.3	48.1	34.5
12 Wks. Dec.....	---	58.6	47.7	36.0
	---	247.5	196.2	145.2

In the 28 weeks ended July 15, 1993, restaurant sales increased 29%, year to year. Pretax income was up 24%, and after taxes at 39.6% in both periods, net income also rose 24%, to $9.7 million ($0.32 a share), from $7.8 million ($0.26). Share earnings are adjusted for the recent stock split.

Common Share Earnings ($)

Weeks:	1993	1992	1991	1990
16 Wks. Apr......	0.15	0.13	0.09	0.08
12 Wks. Jul.......	0.17	0.13	0.11	0.08
12 Wks. Oct......	E0.17	0.14	0.10	0.07
12 Wks. Dec.....	E0.14	0.11	0.09	0.05
	E0.63	0.51	0.38	0.28

Important Developments

Jul. '93— In 1993's second quarter, BOCB opened 10 new restaurants. In all of 1993, 40 openings are expected, followed by 50 in 1995. Also in the quarter, BOCB converted 10 older units to the "scatter system" format, in which food is presented utilizing up to eight islands, thus reducing customer lines. By year-end 1993, all of BOCB's units are expected to be in the scatter format, including about 45 conversions of older restaurants during the year. BOCB's accelerated conversion schedule is expected to boost sales in 1994. In 1993's second quarter, average weekly sales of company-owned units was up 4.1%, largely due to higher prices. Meanwhile, in mid-1993, a public offering of 1.44 million BOCB common shares, at $18.25 each, was completed. Proceeds were to be used to repay debt, and to fund development and remodeling of restaurants.

Next earnings report expected in late October.

Per Share Data ($)

Yr. End Dec. 31	1992	1991	[1]1990	1989	1988	1987	1986	1985	1984
Tangible Bk. Val.	**2.22**	1.64	1.20	0.93	0.75	[2]0.61	[2]0.50	[2]0.29	[2]0.10
Cash Flow	**0.88**	0.67	0.50	0.36	0.24	0.17	0.10	0.07	0.02
Earnings	**0.51**	0.38	0.28	0.20	0.14	0.11	0.06	0.05	0.02
Dividends	**Nil**	Nil	Nil	Nil	Nil	Nil	Nil	Nil	Nil
Payout Ratio	**Nil**	Nil	Nil	Nil	Nil	Nil	Nil	Nil	Nil
Prices—High	**19⅝**	16	8 9/16	6 1/16	4 1/16	5 11/16	3⅛	1 9/16	NA
Low	**11**	5 9/16	4 9/16	3 1/16	2¼	2⅛	1½	1 3/16	NA
P/E Ratio—	**38–21**	42–15	31–17	31–16	29–16	53–20	57–28	35–26	NA

Data as orig. reptd. Adj. for stk. divs. of 50% Dec. 1991, 50% Jun. 1989, 50% May 1987, 50% Jun. 1986, 200% Aug. 1985. **1.** Refl. acctg. change. **2.** Incl. intangibles. E-Estimated NA-Not Available.

Income Data (Million $)

Year Ended Dec. 31	Revs.	Oper. Inc.	% Oper. Inc. of Revs.	Cap. Exp.	Depr.	Int. Exp.	Net Bef. Taxes	Eff. Tax Rate	Net Inc.	% Net Inc. of Revs.	Cash Flow
1992	**247**	**35.8**	**14.4**	**39.2**	**10.80**	**[2]0.04**	**25.2**	**39.6%**	**15.2**	**6.2**	**26.1**
1991	196	26.5	13.5	26.0	8.30	[2]0.09	18.4	39.6%	11.1	5.7	19.4
[1]1990	145	18.5	12.7	17.9	6.28	[2]0.04	[3]13.1	39.0%	8.0	5.5	14.3
1989	115	13.3	11.5	17.3	4.61	[2]0.04	[3]9.2	39.4%	5.6	4.8	10.2
1988	72	7.8	10.9	13.1	2.66	0.04	[3]6.1	36.6%	3.9	5.4	6.5
1987	48	6.0	12.6	6.7	1.72	0.00	[3]5.2	43.3%	2.9	6.1	4.6
1986	27	3.2	12.0	5.1	1.01	0.01	[3]2.9	50.8%	1.4	5.2	2.4
1985	13	1.7	12.7	3.9	0.50	0.04	[3]1.3	26.8%	1.0	7.2	1.5
1984	3	0.3	9.9	2.6	0.11	0.00	[3]0.3	14.6%	0.2	7.0	0.3

Balance Sheet Data (Million $)

Dec. 31	Cash	Curr. Assets	Curr. Liab.	Curr. Ratio	Total Assets	% Ret. on Assets	Long Term Debt	Common Equity	Total Cap.	% LT Debt of Cap.	% Ret. on Equity
1992	**4.91**	**13.10**	**24.5**	**0.5**	**113.0**	**15.9**	**12.00**	**69.1**	**88.2**	**13.6**	**25.3**
1991	2.05	7.73	17.8	0.4	78.3	15.9	5.00	50.9	60.5	8.3	25.0
1990	3.25	7.21	15.0	0.5	60.5	14.5	4.00	37.6	45.5	8.8	23.9
1989	4.75	7.39	12.3	0.6	48.7	13.9	4.00	28.6	36.4	11.0	22.5
1988	2.40	4.59	6.7	0.7	30.7	14.7	1.00	20.4	24.0	4.2	21.0
1987	4.30	6.01	3.8	1.6	21.8	15.0	Nil	16.5	18.0	Nil	19.6
1986	5.48	6.76	3.1	2.2	17.1	10.4	Nil	13.4	14.1	Nil	13.4
1985	2.77	3.26	2.0	1.7	9.2	15.3	0.01	7.0	7.2	0.1	20.1
1984	0.12	0.19	0.6	0.3	2.7	NA	0.01	2.0	2.1	0.6	NA

Data as orig. reptd. **1.** Refl. acctg. change. **2.** Net of int. inc. **3.** Incl. equity in earns. of nonconsol. subs. NA-Not Available.

Business Summary

Buffets, Inc., was established in October 1983 to develop and operate a chain of buffet-style restaurants. Its first restaurant opened in March 1984. The number of company-owned and franchised restaurants at the end of recent years was as follows:

	Owned	Franchised
1992	134	6
1991	108	6
1990	88	6
1989	69	8
1988	47	9
1987	30	6
1986	18	5
1985	12	2

The restaurants, generally operating under the name Old Country Buffet, offer a wide variety of food items, including soups, salads, entrees, vegetables, nonalcoholic beverages and desserts for one fixed all-inclusive price. Most restaurants are in strip or neighborhood shopping centers. Lunches typically cost about $4.89 to $5.29, while dinners are priced at about $6.39 to $6.99. Limited breakfast service is available. Customers pay prior to entering a buffet line and selecting the items and portions of their choice. In units opened after March 1990, a new concept called the "scatter" system has been used, in which food is presented utilizing up to eight food islands scattered throughout the restaurant, thus reducing long lines that occurred under an earlier format. Older units are being converted to the "scatter" concept. Historically, such older units presented food in a self-service, two-sided buffet line. Most restaurants range in size from 8,000 sq. ft. to 13,850 sq. ft., with seating for 260 to 390 people.

As of August 1993, the company was operating 155 restaurants in 24 states, and there were six franchises in Nebraska and Oklahoma. Buffets has not been actively seeking to grant additional franchises.

Dividend Data

Buffets has not paid any cash dividends on its common stock and, pursuant to its credit agreement, is restricted from doing so without the approval of its lender. Earnings are expected to be retained for the foreseeable future for use in expanding the company's business. A three-for-two stock split was effected in December 1991, and a 2-for-1 split was effected in June 1993.

Amt of Divd. $	Date Decl.	Ex-divd. Date	Stock of Record	Payment Date
2-for-1	Apr. 30	Jun. 1	May 17	May 28'93

Capitalization

Long Term Debt: None (7/14/93).

Minority Interest: $522,000.

Common Stock: 30,583,752 (8/23/93) ($0.01 par). Institutions hold about 85%, incl. a portion of the approximately 15%% owned by officers and directors.

Shareholders: About 10,442 (3/93).

Office—10260 Viking Drive, Suite 100, Eden Prairie, MN 55344. **Tel**—(612) 942-9760. **Chrmn & CEO**—R. H. Hatlen. **Pres & COO**—J. A. Conti, Sr. **VP-Fin, Treas & Investor Contact**—Clark C. Grant. **Dirs**—K. H. Erickson, R. H. Hatlen, R. A. Lipkin, A. S. McDowell, D. M. Winton. **Transfer Agent & Registrar**—American Stock Transfer & Trust Co., NYC. **Incorporated** in Minnesota in 1983. **Empl**—12,520.

 Tom Graves, CFA

Burlington Resources

NYSE Symbol BR Options on Phila (Feb-May-Aug-Nov) In S&P MidCap 400

Price	Range	P-E Ratio	Dividend	Yield	S&P Ranking	Beta
Oct. 19'93	1993					
43	53⅞–36½	18	0.55	1.3%	NR	0.24

Summary

Burlington Resources is primarily engaged in oil and gas exploration, development and marketing. A program of divesting noncore assets was essentially completed in 1992; proceeds from the sales totaled $1.4 billion. Earnings rose strongly in the first nine months of 1993, reflecting in part a large gain on the sale units of Burlington Resources Coal Seam Gas Royalty Trust. Operating profits are expected to increase in 1994. Long-term prospects are enhanced by a likely long-term gas price uptrend that began in 1992.

Current Outlook

Earnings from continuing operations in 1994 are projected at $1.95 a share, down from an estimated $2.00 (including nonrecurring gains of $0.59) for 1993.

The quarterly dividend is expected to be raised from $0.13¾ at the Janaury 1994 meeting.

Operating profits for 1994 are expected to be aided by the industry's tight balance between demand and supply, which should contribute to higher gas prices, and by BR's efforts to have more customers sign longer-term contracts, which command a price premium. Oil and natural gas production is expected to increase. Non-operating profits are expected to drop sharply, reflecting the absence of the $0.50 a share gain on the sale of units of the Coal Seam Gas Royalty Trust.

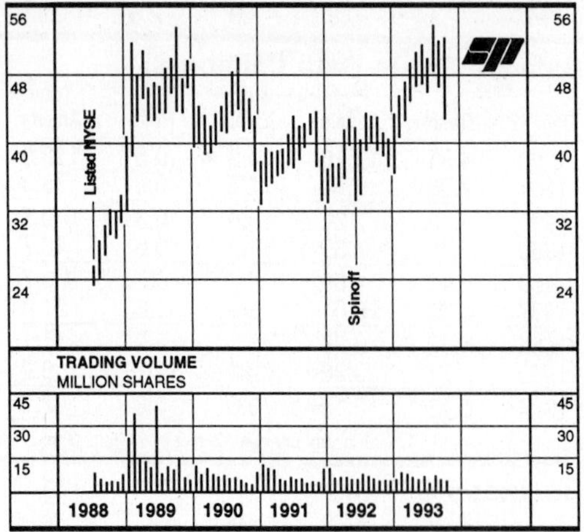

Revenues (Million $)

Quarter:	1993	1992	1991	1990
Mar.	316	270	467	514
Jun.	312	250	402	426
Sep.	309	284	409	420
Dec.	---	337	476	511
	---	1,141	1,754	1,871

Revenues in the nine months ended September 30, 1993, rose 17%, year to year, reflecting higher natural gas sales volumes and prices. Margins widened and, with sharply higher nonoperating income, net income from continuing operations was was up 118%, to $1.55 a share, from $0.71.

Common Share Earnings ($)

Quarter:	1993	1992	1991	1990
Mar.	0.35	0.23	0.49	0.47
Jun.	1.02	0.23	0.25	0.36
Sep.	0.18	0.25	0.37	0.27
Dec.	E0.45	0.73	0.37	0.36
	E2.00	1.44	1.48	1.46

Important Developments

Oct. '93— In the 1993 third quarter, net income from continuing operations was $24 million ($0.18 a share) versus $33 million ($0.25) in the year earlier period. The drop reflected a charge of $18 million ($0.14) from an increase in the tax rate due to the Budget Reconciliation Act of 1993. Natural gas sales averaged 890 MMcf/d, up 8.8% from the 1992 third quarter. Natural gas prices rose 14%, to $1.70 per mcf from $1.49. Oil sales increased to 41,100 b/d from 39,800 b/d, but oil prices declined 18%, to $15.76 per barrel from $19.13. Capital expenditures during the first nine months of 1993 totaled $427 million, versus $158 million in the year earlier period. The increase reflects higher development and reserve acquistion expenditures. As of October 7, 1993, cash flow from continuing operations during 1993 was $350 million, up from $281 million in the year earlier period.

Next earnings report expected in early Janaury.

Per Share Data ($)

Yr. End Dec. 31	1992	1991	1990	1989	1988
Tangible Bk. Val.	**18.67**	22.11	21.92	22.08	20.19
Cash Flow	**3.38**	3.64	3.43	2.74	2.09
Earnings[1]	**1.44**	1.48	1.46	0.99	0.46
Dividends	**0.60**	0.70	0.70	0.61	0.29
Payout Ratio	**41%**	47%	47%	61%	62%
Prices—High	**43½**	43¾	50⅛	53⅝	33⅞
Low	**33**	32⅞	36¾	32⅛	23⅜
P/E Ratio—	**30-23**	30-22	34-25	54-32	74-51

Data as orig. reptd.; prior to 1989, data from prospectus dated Jun. 2, 1988. **1.** Bef. results of disc. ops. of +0.52 in 1992, +0.06 in 1991, +0.15 in 1990, +2.07 in 1989. E-Estimated.

Income Data (Million $)

Year Ended Dec. 31	Revs.	Oper. Inc.	% Oper. Inc. of Revs.	Cap. Exp.	Depr.	Int. Exp.	Net Bef. Taxes	Eff. Tax Rate	[2]Net Inc.	% Net Inc. of Revs.	Cash Flow
[1]1992	**1,141**	**496**	**43.5**	**315**	**256**	**79**	**218**	**13.0%**	**190**	**16.6**	**446**
1991	1,754	662	37.7	806	289	122	256	23.0%	197	11.3	486
[1]1990	1,871	689	36.8	1,083	280	116	282	26.5%	208	11.1	487
[1]1989	1,715	553	32.2	656	261	77	201	25.8%	147	8.6	408
1988	2,167	627	28.9	588	244	89	101	28.5%	70	3.2	314
1987	2,371	701	29.6	217	238	115	371	37.7%	231	9.7	467
1986	3,046	63	2.1	240	269	141	d314	NM	d5	NM	263
1985	4,518	713	15.8	484	236	131	408	45.8%	221	4.9	458
1984	4,649	NA	NA	NA	NA	NA	NA	NA	134	2.9	NA
1983	396	NA	NA	NA	NA	NA	NA	NA	62	15.7	NA

Balance Sheet Data (Million $)

Dec. 31	Cash	Curr. Assets	Curr. Liab.	Curr. Ratio	Total Assets	% Ret. on Assets	[3]Long Term Debt	Common Equity	Total Cap.	% LT Debt of Cap.	% Ret. on Equity
1992	**32**	**370**	**346**	**1.1**	**4,470**	**3.6**	**1,003**	**2,406**	**3,977**	**25.2**	**7.2**
1991	17	760	916	0.8	6,290	3.2	1,548	2,907	5,135	30.1	6.8
1990	30	1,136	1,070	1.1	6,360	3.4	1,378	3,024	5,077	27.1	6.8
1989	160	893	1,155	0.8	6,098	2.5	718	3,223	4,694	15.3	4.8
1988	71	1,064	826	1.3	5,589	NA	668	3,020	4,339	15.4	NA
1987	502	1,383	1,135	1.2	5,250	4.6	615	2,548	3,836	16.0	10.0
1986	335	978	948	1.0	3,742	NM	864	2,037	3,537	24.4	NM
1985	NA	NA	NA	NA	5,474	4.4	925	3,162	NA	NA	5.1
1984	NA	NA	NA	NA	4,678	2.9	1,225	2,313	NA	NA	7.2
1983	NA	NA	NA	NA	4,562	NA	1,875	1,817	NA	NA	NA

Data as orig. reptd.; prior to 1989 data as reptd. in prospectus dated Jun. 2, 1988. **1.** Excl. disc. ops. **2.** Bef. results of disc. ops. and spec. items. **3.** Incl. red. pfd. stk. prior to 1988. d-Deficit. NM-Not Meaningful. NA-Not Available.

Business Summary

Burlington Resources is primarily engaged in the exploration, development and production of oil and natural gas. The company was formed by Burlington Northern Inc. (BNI) to consolidate its natural resources operations, and was spun off to BNI shareholders in 1988. In mid-1992, BR spun off its El Paso Natural Gas unit, and also sold virtually all of its coal operations.

Meridian Oil Holding is involved in oil and gas exploration and production, operation of intrastate natural gas and crude oil pipeline systems, and the extraction and marketing of natural gas liquids. Proved reserves (almost all in the U.S.) at 1992 year-end were estimated at 155.5 million bbl. of oil (141.1 million in 1991) and 5.1 Tcf of gas (4.9). The estimated present value of net cash flow from these reserves (discounted at 10%) was $3,138 million at December 31 1992. Production in 1992 amounted to 818 MMcf/d of gas (710 in 1991) and 40.6 Mbbl/d of oil (36.1). In 1992, BR's additions to reserves equaled 176% of its oil and gas production. Capital expenditures in 1993, projected at $420 million, are expected to consist of development of properties, reserve acquisitions, and processing plant and pipeline capacity expansions.

In 1992, the company essentially completed its program of selling nonstrategic real estate, minerals and forest products assets and reinvesting the net proceeds in oil and gas reserves and in the repurchase of its common stock; proceeds from the sales totaled about $1.4 billion.

Dividend Data

BR initiated dividends in 1988. A "poison pill" stock purchase right was adopted in 1988.

Amt of Divd. $	Date Decl.	Ex-divd. Date	Stock of Record	Payment Date
0.13¾	Jan. 13	Mar. 8	Mar. 12	Apr. 1'93
0.13¾	Apr. 7	Jun. 7	Jun. 11	Jul. 1'93
0.13¾	Jul. 7	Sep. 3	Sep. 10	Oct. 1'93
0.13¾	Oct. 7	Dec. 6	Dec. 10	Jan. 3'94

Finances

Between December 1988 and June 30, 1993, BR repurchased 23.4 million of its common shares under three 10 million-share repurchase programs; about 500,000 shares were bought in the first half of 1993.

Capitalization

Long Term Debt: $841,742,000 (9/93).

Common Stock: 130,301,663 shs. ($0.01 par).
Institutions hold 70%.
Shareholders of record: 28,915.

Office—999 Third Ave, Seattle, WA 98104. **Tel**—(206) 467-3838. **Chrmn & CEO**—T. H. O'Leary. **SVP & CFO**—G. E. Howison. **Secy**—L.S. Leland. **Investor Contact**—Donald L. Pope. **Dirs**—J. V. Byrne, J. C. Cushman III, S. P. Gilbert, J. F. McDonald, T. H. O'Leary, D. M. Roberts, W. Scott, Jr., W. E. Wall. **Transfer Agent & Registrar**—First National Bank of Boston. **Incorporated** in Delaware in 1988. **Empl**—1,705.

 Mark Mattke

CBI Industries

NYSE Symbol CBH Options on Phila (Mar-Jun-Sep-Dec) In S&P MidCap 400

Price	Range	P-E Ratio	Dividend	Yield	S&P Ranking	Beta
Aug. 30'93	1993					
28 7/8	30 3/4–21 3/4	23	0.48	1.7%	B	0.89

Summary

This company provides a wide variety of project management and other contracting services, and is the world's largest supplier of carbon dioxide through its Liquid Carbonic subsidiary. Earnings for 1993 are likley to be down sharply from 1992's strong level, reflecting lower revenues for contracting services due to weak economic conditions and customer confusion concerning environmental requirements.

Current Outlook

Earnings for 1993 are estimated at about $0.90 a share, down sharply from the $1.79 of 1992.

Dividends are expected to continue at $0.12 quarterly.

Revenues for 1993 should decline on decreased contracts services activity, due to weak economic conditions and customer confusion over environmental requirements and funding issues, causing projects delays. Contributions by the newly acquired businesses of MQS and Cooperheat, should somewhat offset the impact, as should improved profits by industrial gases and investments, as CBI continues to steadily reinvest in these segments.

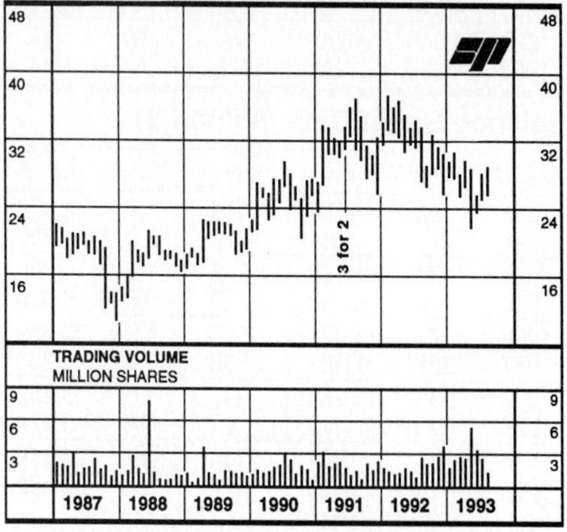

Revenues (Million $)

Quarter:	1993	1992	1991	1990
Mar.	398	398	375	375
Jun.	428	414	415	375
Sep.	---	429	405	416
Dec.	---	432	420	411
	---	1,673	1,615	1,576

Revenues for the first six months of 1993 were up 1.7%, year to year, as increased worldwide revenues from industrial gases, due to further market penetration, outweighed lower revenues from contracting services. Income from operations was down sharply, penalized by substantially reduced contributions from contracting services, and by higher SG&A expenses, due to the addition of newly acquired businesses. After greater interest expense, pretax income fell 49%. Following taxes at 49.0% versus 47.5%, and lower minority interest, net income was down 58%. After preferred dividends, share earnings were $0.30 ($0.28, fully diluted), down from $0.84 ($0.74). Results for 1992 exclude a $0.20 a share ($0.17) special charge from an accounting change.

Common Share Earnings ($)

Quarter:	1993	1992	1991	1990
Mar.	0.11	0.34	0.29	0.48
Jun.	0.19	0.50	0.40	0.37
Sep.	E0.25	0.51	0.40	0.38
Dec.	E0.35	0.44	0.45	0.35
	E0.90	1.79	1.54	1.58

Important Developments

May '93— CBI completed the purchase of Ershigs Inc., an engineering, manufacturing and construction company which specializes in fiberglass reinforced plastic (FRP) and dual laminate vessels, tanks and other structures for corrosion-resistant applications. Ershigs, which had sales of $22 million in 1992, is the leader in custom designed FRP products in the North American corrosion-resistant market.

Next earnings report expected in mid-October.

Per Share Data ($)

Yr. End Dec. 31	1992	1991	[1]1990	1989	1988	1987	[1]1986	1985	[2]1984	[2]1983
Tangible Bk. Val.	**18.55**	14.93	11.89	8.93	8.15	15.75	15.59	15.01	17.73	17.69
Cash Flow	**4.29**	3.92	4.14	3.48	2.85	2.14	2.18	0.65	3.30	3.10
Earnings[3]	**[4]1.79**	[4]1.54	[4]1.58	[4]0.94	0.58	0.25	0.49	d1.45	1.39	1.57
Dividends	**0.480**	0.440	0.400	0.400	0.400	0.400	0.400	0.800	1.033	1.033
Payout Ratio	**27%**	30%	27%	43%	66%	157%	82%	NM	86%	66%
Prices—High	**37 1/2**	37 1/8	29 9/16	22 9/16	21 1/4	22	21 1/4	19 5/16	22 9/16	28 9/16
Low	**25 3/4**	23 5/8	20 1/2	16 13/16	12 15/16	10 11/16	12 13/16	12 3/16	16 1/16	19 1/4
P/E Ratio—	**21–14**	24–15	19–13	24–18	37–22	87–42	44–26	NM	16–12	18–12

Data as orig. reptd. Adj. for stk. div. of 50% Jun. 1991. **1.** Reflects accounting change. **2.** Reflects merger or acquisition. **3.** Bef. spec. item(s) of -0.20 in 1992, +0.21 in 1986, +0.12 in 1983. **4.** Ful. dil.:1.59 in 1992, 1.38 in 1991, 1.41 in 1990, 0.86 in 1989. E-Estimated. d-Deficit. NM-Not Meaningful.

Income Data (Million $)

Year Ended Dec. 31	Revs.	Oper. Inc.	% Oper. Inc. of Revs.	Cap. Exp.	Depr.	Int. Exp.	[3]Net Bef. Taxes	Eff. Tax Rate	[4]Net Inc.	% Net Inc. of Revs.	Cash Flow
1992	**[5]1,666**	**251**	**15.1**	**271**	**91.6**	**20.8**	**146**	**43.1%**	**[1]71.1**	**4.3**	**157**
1991	1,608	243	15.1	165	82.6	30.6	137	44.0%	61.1	3.8	136
[1]1990	1,557	222	14.3	139	77.2	39.2	123	48.9%	55.1	3.5	125
1989	1,495	209	14.0	119	72.8	40.2	87	49.9%	34.3	2.3	100
1988	1,376	153	11.1	114	68.2	31.6	54	41.0%	27.5	2.0	86
1987	1,160	112	9.7	119	61.9	30.9	51	68.5%	[1]14.1	1.2	70
[1]1986	1,166	111	9.5	142	62.5	30.6	18	37.7%	8.9	0.8	71
1985	1,571	179	11.4	56	68.4	38.3	d72	NM	[1]d47.3	NM	21
[2]1984	960	143	14.9	451	53.1	25.1	64	27.3%	38.7	4.0	92
[2]1983	828	59	7.1	27	[1]40.0	3.5	63	28.5%	41.1	5.0	81

Balance Sheet Data (Million $)

Dec. 31	Cash	Curr. Assets	Curr. Liab.	Curr. Ratio	Total Assets	% Ret. on Assets	Long Term Debt	Common Equity	Total Cap.	% LT Debt of Cap.	% Ret. on Equity
1992	**38**	**434**	**325**	**1.3**	**1,685**	**4.5**	**411**	**681**	**1,255**	**32.8**	**9.8**
1991	41	457	338	1.4	1,479	4.0	260	542	1,085	23.9	11.0
1990	47	451	318	1.4	1,432	3.7	395	386	1,052	37.5	14.1
1989	62	429	291	1.5	1,359	2.5	466	256	1,015	45.9	11.0
1988	55	431	321	1.3	1,343	2.2	467	233	1,017	46.0	5.1
1987	85	406	267	1.5	1,266	1.2	261	507	995	26.3	1.6
1986	69	356	242	1.5	1,163	0.8	179	510	906	19.8	1.7
1985	45	333	240	1.4	1,104	NM	232	487	847	27.4	NM
1984	86	371	299	1.2	1,344	3.1	276	568	1,034	26.7	6.8
1983	197	380	309	1.2	917	4.3	3	465	608	0.4	9.0

Data as orig. reptd. **1.** Reflects accounting change. **2.** Reflects merger or acquisition. **3.** Incl. equity in earns. of nonconsol. subs. **4.** Bef. spec. items. **5.** Incl. other inc. d-Deficit. NM-Not Meaningful.

Business Summary

CBI Industries and its subsidiaries operate in three areas: contracting services, industrial gases, and investments. Segment contributions in 1992:

	Revs.	Profits
Contracting services	47%	41%
Industrial gases	45%	58%
Investments	8%	1%

Business outside of the U.S. accounted for about 50% of total revenues in 1992.

The Chicago Bridge & Iron subsidiary is a worldwide construction services group providing (through subsidiaries) contracting services, including design, engineering, fabrication, project management, general contracting and specialty construction services. This unit constructs a wide variety of fabricated metal plate structures (eg. elevated water tanks; penstocks and tunnel liners for hydroelectric dams; and low temperature and cryogenic vessels) used in the chemical, petroleum refining and petrochemical industries.

The Liquid Carbonic (LC) unit produces and sells carbon dioxide in various forms, and manufactures and/or markets a wide variety of other industrial and specialty gases, including oxygen, nitrogen, argon, hydrogen, acetylene, carbon monoxide and nitrous oxide; and assembles and sells related equipment. LC is the world's largest supplier of carbon dioxide.

Investments include interests in Statia Terminals (oil and gas storage and blending facilities and bunkering services, and special products terminal); and financial investments.

Finances

In June 1993, CBI sold $75 million of 7-year 6.321% senior notes.

Dividend Data

Dividends have been paid since 1953. A dividend reinvestment plan is available. A "poison pill" stock purchase right was issued in 1986.

Amt of Divd. $	Date Decl.	Ex–divd. Date	Stock of Record	Payment Date
0.12	Oct. 14	Nov. 12	Nov. 18	Dec. 11'92
0.12	Jan. 14	Feb. 10	Feb. 17	Mar. 12'93
0.12	Mar. 10	May 13	May 19	Jun. 11'93
0.12	May 13	Aug. 12	Aug. 18	Sep. 10'93

Capitalization

Long Term Debt: $506,385,000 (6/93).

Minority Interest: $63,586,000.

$2.27 Conv. Voting Preferred Stock: 3,750,695 shs. ($1 par). Held by ESOP.

Common Stock: 37,408,797 shs. ($2.50 par). Institutions hold approximately 69%. Shareholders of record: About 7,700.

Office—800 Jorie Blvd., Oak Brook, IL 60521-2268. **Tel**—(708) 572-7000. **Chrmn & Pres**—J. E. Jones. **EVP-CFO & Investor Contact**—George L. Schueppert. **Secy**—C. H. Toerber. **Dirs**—L. E. Akin, W. N. Caldwell, E. H. Clark Jr., R. J. Daniels, R. J. Day, J. T. Horton, J. E. Jones, G. E. MacDougal, E. J. Mooney Jr., J. F. Riordan, G. L. Schueppert, R. T. Stewart, R. G. Wallace. **Transfer Agent & Registrar**—First Chicago Trust Co. of New York, NYC. **Incorporated** in Illinois in 1889. **Empl**—14,100.

 M. Graham Hackett

CML Group

NYSE Symbol CML Options on Phila In S&P MidCap 400

Price	Range	P-E Ratio	Dividend	Yield	S&P Ranking	Beta
Oct. 20'93	1993					
29⅞	32⅜–17⅜	27	0.08	0.3%	B	1.92

Summary

CML is a specialty retailer conducting business through various store chains and by mail order. Earnings rose sharply in fiscal 1992, benefiting from strong sales for NordicTrack and The Nature Company and lower interest expense. The strong sales and earnings growth continued in fiscal 1993, fueled by new store openings and the absence of a $13.2 million restructuring charge. A three-for-two stock split was effected in August 1993.

Business Summary

CML Group, Inc. is a specialty retailing company that operates chains of stores under various trade names and also conducts mail-order operations. As of fiscal 1992 year-end, CML was operating 181 retail stores and 61 mall kiosks and had proprietary mail-order customer lists containing about 1.3 million names. In fiscal 1992, retail stores and mall kiosks accounted for 55.9% of total revenues and direct response and mail order for 44.1%.

Sales and operating income (in millions) for fiscal 1992 were derived as follows:

	Sales	Income
NordicTrack	54%	$82.8
Britches for Men	19%	2.1
Britches for Women	3%	–9.3
The Nature Company	23%	8.5
Mason & Sullivan	1%	–3.7

NordicTrack designs, manufactures and markets high-quality aerobic and anaerobic exercise equipment to customers through direct-response advertising in print and on TV and through its own specialty retail stores and kiosks. Products include eight models of cross-country ski exercisers, which range in price from $299 to $1,299 and three models of the NordicRow TBX.

Men's tailored professional clothing (natural-fiber suits, sport coats, trousers, shirts and neckties), men's sportswear and casual outdoor clothing and women's sportswear and casual weekend clothing are sold through about 70 stores in the mid-Atlantic and Southeastern states. During fiscal 1992, CML closed its Britches' Great Outdoor for Women division.

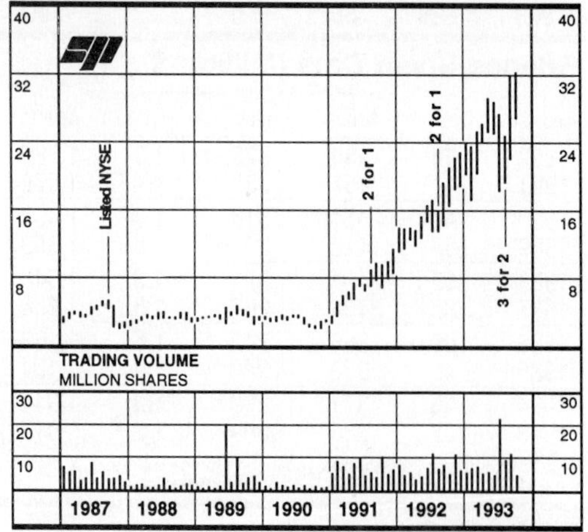

The Nature Company sells nature-related merchandise, including books, gifts, children's educational toys, music, clothing, accessories, backyard and garden items, minerals, sculpture, posters, optics, paper products, nature tapes and limited-edition prints. Mason & Sullivan sells do-it-yourself crafts kits and collectibles.

Important Developments

Sep. '93— In reporting results for fiscal 1993, CML cited numerous achievements, including nationwide retail expansion, infrastructure improvements to facilitate domestic and international growth and the broadening of its product base to include a larger assortment of proprietary and exclusive products.

Next earnings report expected in late November.

Per Share Data ($)

Yr. End Jul. 31	1993	1992	1991	1990	1989	1988	1987	[1]1986	1985	[1]1984
Tangible Bk. Val.	**NA**	2.11	0.50	d0.13	0.15	0.84	0.86	0.93	1.17	1.09
Cash Flow	**NA**	0.97	0.74	0.55	0.12	0.50	0.37	0.29	0.25	0.23
Earnings[2]	**1.11**	[4]0.73	[4]0.51	[4]0.35	d0.15	0.29	0.23	0.17	0.13	0.11
Dividends	**0.053**	0.02	Nil	Nil	Nil	Nil	Nil	Nil	Nil	Nil
Payout Ratio	**5%**	3%	Nil	Nil	Nil	Nil	Nil	Nil	Nil	Nil
Prices[3]—High	**32⅜**	22⅞	11½	3¾	4¾	4	5⅜	3¾	2⅛	2⅛
Low	**17⅜**	11⅛	2¾	2⅛	2½	2⅜	2	1⅞	1⅜	1⅛
P/E Ratio—	**29–16**	31–15	23–5	11–6	NM	14–8	24–9	21–11	17–11	20–10

Data as orig. reptd. Adj. for stk. divs. of 50% Aug. 1993, 100% Aug. 1992, 100% Aug. 1991, 33⅓% Sep. 1983. **1.** Refl. merger or acq. **2.** Bef. results of disc. ops. of -0.09 in 1992, -0.11 in 1991, -0.67 in 1990, -0.68 in 1989 & spec. items of +0.16 in 1992, +0.15 in 1991. **3.** Cal. yr. **4.** Ful. dil.: 0.71 in 1992, 0.45 in 1991, 0.33 in 1990. d-Deficit. NM-Not Meaningful. NA-Not Available.

Income Data (Million $)

Year Ended Jul. 31	Oper. Revs.	Oper. Inc.	% Oper. Inc. of Revs.	Cap. Exp.	Depr.	Int. Exp.	Net Bef. Taxes	Eff. Tax Rate	[3]Net Inc.	% Net Inc. of Revs.	Cash Flow
[1]**1992**	**494**	**90.4**	**18.3**	**43.3**	**12.1**	**1.35**	**63.7**	**42.3%**	**36.8**	**7.4**	**48.9**
[1]1991	339	52.4	15.5	19.7	9.3	7.72	35.4	41.9%	20.7	6.1	30.0
[1]1990	279	39.9	14.3	12.8	7.6	9.72	22.6	38.2%	14.0	5.0	21.5
[1]1989	235	34.3	14.6	10.5	10.2	7.04	d8.6	NM	d5.5	NM	4.6
1988	349	35.0	10.0	27.8	8.0	8.37	18.6	38.0%	11.6	3.3	19.5
1987	283	28.2	9.9	28.0	6.0	4.65	17.5	48.3%	9.0	3.2	15.1
[2]1986	232	21.0	9.1	13.7	4.6	3.89	12.5	45.5%	6.8	2.9	11.4
1985	191	14.5	7.6	11.0	3.8	3.60	7.1	44.8%	3.9	2.0	7.7
[2]1984	180	12.8	7.1	10.7	3.4	3.55	5.9	47.0%	3.1	1.7	6.4
[1]1983	125	14.0	9.1	4.0	2.4	3.24	5.7	47.7%	3.0	2.4	5.3

Balance Sheet Data (Million $)

Jul. 31	Cash	Curr. Assets	Curr. Liab.	Curr. Ratio	Total Assets	% Ret. on Assets	Long Term Debt	Common Equity	Total Cap.	% LT Debt of Cap.	% Ret. on Equity
1992	**3.52**	**89.8**	**63.4**	**1.4**	**219**	**17.7**	**5**	**130**	**135**	**4.0**	**38.7**
1991	2.01	58.5	41.6	1.4	164	12.2	59	50	108	54.1	54.8
1990	1.43	69.3	30.3	2.3	172	7.0	108	25	133	81.0	44.2
1989	1.03	65.0	72.3	0.9	221	NM	108	37	145	74.5	NM
1988	5.69	91.3	39.1	2.3	226	5.8	114	67	185	61.5	18.5
1987	5.57	78.4	44.7	1.8	181	5.8	72	60	135	53.2	16.3
1986	4.88	65.8	34.8	1.9	131	5.2	43	50	96	45.0	12.8
1985	1.91	59.1	26.6	2.2	104	3.9	30	45	77	39.6	9.1
1984	2.78	57.6	23.8	2.4	94	3.1	28	40	69	40.4	9.1
[2]1983	3.38	44.6	22.0	2.0	70	4.7	24	21	48	50.6	8.4

Data as orig. reptd. (pro forma in 1983 to incl. Britches of Georgetowne). **1.** Excl. disc. ops. **2.** Refl. merger or acq. **3.** Bef. spec. items. d-Deficit. NM-Not Meaningful.

Net Sales (Million $)

13 Weeks:	1992–3	1991–2	1990–1	1989–90
Oct.	107	85	72	54
Jan.	236	171	121	106
Apr.	169	139	77	58
Jul.	133	99	68	61
	645	494	339	279

Sales for the fiscal year ended July 31, 1993 (preliminary), advanced 31% from those of fiscal 1992. Margins widened, and pretax income was up 52%. After taxes at 40.0%, versus 42.3%, income rose 58%, to $1.11 a share, from $0.73 (as adjusted). Results for fiscal 1992 exclude a loss from discontinued operations of $0.09 a share and a credit from an accounting change of $0.16 a share.

Common Share Earnings ($)

13 Weeks:	1992–3	1991–2	1990–1	1989–90
Oct.	0.11	0.09	0.07	0.06
Jan.	0.63	0.43	0.35	0.27
Apr.	0.29	0.15	0.07	0.05
Jul.	0.09	0.06	0.01	d0.02
	1.11	0.73	0.51	0.35

Finances

In July 1993, directors authorized the repurchase of up to 1,500,000 (adjusted) CML common shares.

In January 1993, CML sold publicly $57.5 million of 5½% debentures, due 2003 and convertible into common stock at $25.92 a share (adjusted). In September 1991, CML called for redemption its 7½% debentures due 2012, all of which were converted into 7,236,672 (adjusted) common shares at $5.21 a share.

In fiscal 1992, CML began restructuring its Britches for Women and Mason & Sullivan divisions by eliminating product lines and consolidating facilities.

Dividend Data

Cash dividends were initiated in 1991. A "poison pill" stock purchase right was adopted in 1988. A dividend reinvestment plan is available.

Amt. of Divd. $	Date Decl.	Ex-divd. Date	Stock of Record	Payment Date
0.02	Dec. 3	Dec. 25	Mar. 3	Mar. 18'93
0.02	Mar. 16	May 25	Jun. 1	Jun. 18'93
0.02	Jun. 14	Aug. 31	Sep. 7	Sep. 22'93
3–for–2	Jul. 15	Aug. 17	Jul. 31	Aug. 16'93
0.02	Oct. 6	Nov. 23	Nov. 30	Dec. 16'93

Capitalization

Long Term Debt: $57,766,000 (5/1/93).

Common Stock: 50,614,158 shs. ($0.10 par).
Institutions hold about 78%.
Shareholders of record: 2,152.

d-Deficit.

Office—524 Main St., Acton, MA 01720. **Tel**—(508) 264-4155. **Chrmn & CEO**—C. M. Leighton. **Pres**—G. R. Tod. **Sr VP-Fin**—R. J. Samuelson. **Secy**—P. P. Brountas. **Investor Contact**—Nancy Wang. **Dirs**—H. H. Callaway, C. M. Leighton, R. W. Menninger, T. H. Lenagh, H. L. Luther Jr., G. R. Tod, R. F. Verni. **Transfer Agent & Registrar**—First National Bank of Boston. **Incorporated** in 1969. **Empl**—4,500.

 John D. Coyle, CFA

CMS Energy

NYSE Symbol CMS Options on NYSE (Mar-Jun-Sep-Dec) In S&P MidCap 400

Price	Range	P–E Ratio	Dividend	Yield	S&P Ranking	Beta
Aug. 6'93	1993					
25⅞	26⅝–18⅛	NM	0.72	2.8%	B	0.42

Summary

This electric and gas utility holding company has converted its Midland plant, originally designed as a nuclear station, to a gas-fired cogneration unit, and has a 49% stake in the project. In April 1993, CMS accepted the Michigan PSC's modified settlement in a dispute over power contract issues between its Consumers Power unit and the cogeneration venture. The settlement produced a net writeoff of $343 million ($4.30 a share) in the 1992 fourth quarter, but eliminated the future earnings impact of undercollection in Consumers Power's rates for power purchased from the cogeneration venture.

Current Outlook

Share earnings for 1993 are estimated at $1.85, versus 1992's loss of $3.72, which included a writeoff of $4.30 to resolve longstanding disputes related to the purchase of electricity from the Midland Cogeneration Venture. Earnings could rise to $1.95 in 1994.

The quarterly dividend was boosted 50%, to $0.18, in July 1993, as a result of the Midland settlement agreement. The dividend, omitted in 1984, was reinstated in late 1989.

Earnings in 1993 should reflect the absence of the Midland settlement writeoff, and the resultant elimination of the undercollection in Consumers Power's rates for power purchased from the MCV. However, higher negative accretion due to the agreement will partly offset these benefits. Share earnings should be aided by increased profits from CMS's non-utility units. Earnings for 1994 should reflect higher rates, kwh sales growth and greater profits from non-utility units.

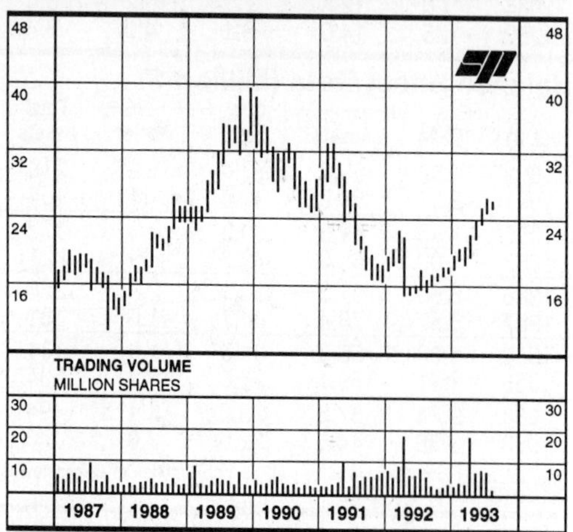

Operating Revenues (Million $)

Quarter:	1993	1992	1991	1990
Mar.	1,009	967	977	870
Jun.	742	664	635	642
Sep.	---	599	614	615
Dec.	---	843	715	850
	---	3,073	2,941	2,977

Revenues in the six months ended June 30, 1993, gained 8.1%, year to year. Results benefited from the Midland settlement order, and from higher profit contributions from non-utility units; net income soared 48%, to $1.20 a share, from $0.81.

Common Share Earnings ($)

Quarter:	1993	1992	1991	1990
Mar.	0.90	0.64	d2.56	1.23
Jun.	0.30	0.17	0.38	0.57
Sep.	E0.30	0.13	0.36	d0.45
Dec.	E0.35	d4.66	d1.43	d7.48
	E1.85	d3.72	d3.26	d6.07

Important Developments

Jul. '93— The company filed with the SEC for an offering of 4.6 million common shares.

May '93— The Michigan Public Service Commission (MPSC) reaffirmed its approval of an order settling electric rate issues between CMS's Consumer Power Co. unit and the Midland Cogeneration Venture (MCV). The settlement resolved longstanding disputes in several regulatory and court proceedings. The company recorded a related net writeoff of $343 million ($4.30 a share) in the 1992 fourth quarter. The settlement and writeoff eliminated the future earnings impact of undercollection in Consumers Power's rates for power purchased from MCV. Consumers Power effected a quasi-reorganization on December 31, 1992, allowing it to resume the payment of dividends to CMS as earnings are realized.

Next earnings report expected in late October.

Per Share Data ($)

Yr. End Dec. 31	1992	1991	1990	1989	1988	1987	1986	1985	1984	1983
Tangible Bk. Val.	**7.73**	13.23	17.28	23.86	20.10	24.41	21.88	21.38	25.79	25.92
Earnings[1]	**d3.72**	d3.26	d6.07	3.80	3.31	2.19	0.74	d4.42	1.14	3.12
Dividends	**0.48**	0.48	0.42	0.10	Nil	Nil	Nil	Nil	1.08	2.46
Payout Ratio	**NM**	NM	NM	3%	Nil	Nil	Nil	Nil	95%	79%
Prices—High	**22¾**	33	38½	39⅝	26½	20	17⅜	8⅞	16⅛	21⅞
Low	**14⅞**	16⅝	24⅞	22½	13½	10½	7½	4⅜	4⅛	13⅛
P/E Ratio—	**NM**	NM	NM	10–6	8–4	9–5	23–10	NM	14–4	7–4

Data as orig. reptd. 1. Bef. results of disc. ops. of -0.22 in 1990, and spec. items of -0.18 in 1991, -0.04 in 1987. d-Deficit. E-Estimated. NM-Not Meaningful.

Income Data (Million $)

Year Ended Dec. 31	Revs.	Depr.	Maint.	Oper. Ratio	[1]Fxd. Chgs. Cover.	Constr. Credits	Eff. Tax Rate	[2]Net Inc.	% Return On Revs.	% Return On [3]Invest. Capital	% Return On [4]Com. Equity
1992	**3,073**	**348**	**203**	**93.0%**	**NM**	**3**	**NM**	**d297**	**NM**	**NM**	**NM**
1991	2,941	283	172	91.8%	NM	5	NM	d262	NM	1.7	NM
1990	2,977	240	154	86.3%	NM	38	NM	d494	NM	NM	NM
1989	2,961	230	160	84.8%	3.56	177	34.0%	312	10.5	7.6	17.2
1988	2,943	219	163	84.5%	2.71	162	33.8%	272	9.2	8.2	17.8
1987	2,801	216	127	84.0%	1.99	NA	32.2%	187	6.7	6.9	9.3
1986	3,108	214	143	84.6%	1.42	1	45.9%	178	5.7	8.1	3.4
1985	3,298	201	146	85.2%	0.35	3	6.5%	d270	NM	2.5	NM
1984	3,236	206	134	84.8%	---	152	11.7%	221	6.8	7.7	4.3
1983	2,974	178	146	84.2%	---	242	8.2%	348	11.7	9.0	11.9

Balance Sheet Data (Million $)

Dec. 31	[5]Gross Prop.	Capital Expend.	Net Prop.	% Earn. on Net Prop.	Total Cap.	Capitalization LT Debt	% LT Debt	[6]Pfd.	[6]% Pfd.	Com.	% Com.
1992	**8,101**	**484**	**4,326**	**5.1**	**4,263**	**2,823**	**76.0**	**163**	**4.4**	**727**	**19.6**
1991	7,618	348	4,121	5.9	3,902	2,009	62.2	163	5.0	1,060	32.8
1990	7,310	387	4,033	10.4	5,928	3,389	68.5	156	3.2	1,402	28.3
1989	6,819	312	3,839	11.8	6,744	3,289	60.6	176	3.3	1,960	36.1
1988	6,574	275	3,780	12.1	6,404	3,113	61.1	322	6.3	1,663	32.6
1987	8,069	269	5,434	9.7	7,523	3,269	56.5	517	8.9	1,999	34.6
1986	6,200	191	3,764	12.6	6,970	3,285	53.6	911	14.9	1,936	31.5
1985	6,067	206	3,812	12.8	7,231	3,604	54.7	1,085	16.5	1,894	28.8
1984	5,820	622	3,817	9.0	7,772	3,717	52.4	1,099	15.5	2,282	32.1
1983	8,938	961	7,104	6.9	7,210	3,275	49.7	1,056	16.0	2,263	34.3

Data as orig. reptd. **1.** Times int. exp. & pfd. divs. covered (pretax basis). **2.** Bef. spec. items. **3.** Based on income before interest charges. **4.** As reptd. by Co. prior to 1989. **5.** Utility Plant; excl. Midland Nuclear Project. **6.** Incl. minority interest aft. 1986. d-Deficit. NM-Not Meaningful. NA-Not Available.

Business Summary

CMS Energy, the parent of Consumers Power Co., derived 61% of its 1992 revenues from electricity, 37% from gas, and 2% from other businesses. Electric revenues by customer class were:

	1992	1991	1990	1989
Residential	35%	36%	34%	34%
Commercial	30%	30%	30%	30%
Industrial	30%	29%	31%	32%
Other	5%	5%	5%	4%

Electric generation in 1992 was from coal (75%), nuclear (22%), hydro (2%) and oil/gas (1)%. Peak demand in 1992 was 5,939 mw, and capability was 7,365 mw, for a capacity margin of 19%. Gas sales and deliveries totaled 364,000 MMcf in 1992, up from 339,000 MMcf in 1991.

Part of CMS's Midland plant, originally designed as a nuclear facility and abandoned in 1984, was later converted into a 1,370 mw gas-fired cogeneration unit. The company has a 49% stake in the Midland plant, which began commercial operation in March 1990. CMS sought to recover $2.1 billion of abandoned Midland assets from its retail electric customers. In 1988, it charged $7.68 a share to 1986 earnings, reflecting the writeoff of return on the $2.1 billion investment. The charge will be amortized into earnings for 15 years beginning in 1986.

A Michigan PSC order in May 1991 allowed CMS to recover only $760 million of its $2.1 billion investment. In anticipation of the order, the company recorded net writedowns and reserves of $745 million in 1990. Another $294 million net writeoff was recorded in 1991. In 1992, CMS recorded a $343 million net writeoff, due to a modified settlement agreement for longstanding contract disputes between Consumers Power and Midland.

Dividend Data

Common dividends were resumed in November 1989, after having been omitted in 1984. A dividend reinvestment plan is available.

Amt. of Divd. $	Date Decl.	Ex-divd. Date	Stock of Record	Payment Date
0.12	Oct. 23	Oct. 27	Nov. 2	Nov. 23'92
0.12	Jan. 25	Feb. 1	Feb. 5	Feb. 22'93
0.12	Apr. 29	May 4	May 10	May 21'93
0.18	Jul. 30	Aug. 3	Aug. 9	Aug. 23'93

Capitalization

Long Term Debt: $2,730,000,000 (3/93).

Subsid. Preferred Stock: $163,000,000.

Common Stock: 80,070,974 shs. ($0.01 par). Institutions hold 61%. Shareholders of record: 70,801.

Office—Fairlane Plaza South, Suite 1100, 330 Town Center Drive, Dearborn, MI 48126. **Tel**—(313) 436-9261. **Chrmn & CEO**—W. T. McCormick, Jr. **Vice-Chrmn**—S. K. Smith, Jr. **Pres**—V. J. Fryling. **VP & CFO**—A. M. Wright. **Secy & Treas**—T. A. McNish. **Investor Contact**—Timothy Kohlitz (517-788-2590). **Dirs**—F. W. Buckman, J. M. Duderstadt, V. J. Fryling, E. D. Holton, L. A. Lund, W. T. McCormick, Jr., F. H. Merlotti, W. U. Parfet, P. A. Pierre, T. F. Russell, S. K. Smith, Jr., R. D. Tuttle, K. Whipple. **Transfer Agent & Registrar**—Co.'s office, Jackson, MI. **Incorporated** in Maine in 1910; reincorporated in Michigan in 1968. **Empl**—10,128.

 Christopher J. Grant

CPI Corp.

NYSE Symbol CPY In S&P MidCap 400

Price	Range	P-E Ratio	Dividend	Yield	S&P Ranking	Beta
Oct. 15'93	1993					
16½	20⅞–13¾	15	0.56	3.4%	B+	1.28

Summary

This company derives most of its income from the operation of portrait studios as a licensee of Sears, Roebuck and Co. It also operates one-hour photofinishing labs and high-tech copy stores and, through the May 1993 acquisition of Melville Corp.'s Prints Plus unit, operates a chain of prints, posters and framing stores. Results have been hurt in recent years by the lackluster economic recovery, competitive pressures, and certain unusual charges.

Business Summary

CPI Corp. derives the largest portion of its revenues from the operation of photographic studios in Sears, Roebuck and Co. department stores. It also operates one-hour photofinishing laboratories and conducts an electronic publishing business with retail stores. In May 1993, CPI acquired the Prints Plus chain of prints, posters and framing stores. Contributions to sales and operating profits (in millions) in 1992-3 were:

	Sales	Profits
Portrait studios	59%	$51.2
One-hour photofinishing	38%	12.6
Other products & services	3%	-3.9

In 1992-3, about 57% of CPI's sales and 85% of its operating profits were derived from the Sears Portrait Studios, which are engaged in professional portrait photography. CPI provides all studio furniture, equipment and fixtures and conducts advertising at its expense. The company is the only operator of Sears Portrait Studios in the U.S. and believes it is the largest participant in the $970 million preschool portrait market. The studios are operated under a license agreement with Sears, under which CPI pays a fee of 15% of net sales per fixed location studio and 7.5% of sales for freestanding studios in retail malls that operate under the Sears name. During 1992-3, CPI paid license fees of about $37.7 million. As of 1992-3 year-end, the company had 995 Sears Portrait Studios in the U.S., Puerto Rico and Canada. CPI expects to open about 15 new studios in 1993-4.

CPI is the largest U.S. owner/operator of one-hour photofinishing minilabs, operating 658 stores throughout the U.S. as of 1992-3 year-end. The stores are in major regional malls, strip shopping centers and freestanding buildings. The segment was substantially expanded through the August 1991 acquisition of Fox Photo Inc. for $61.3 million in cash. At the time of purchase, Fox was operating 306 one-hour photofinishing locations. CPI plans to open about 20 new minilabs in 1993-4.

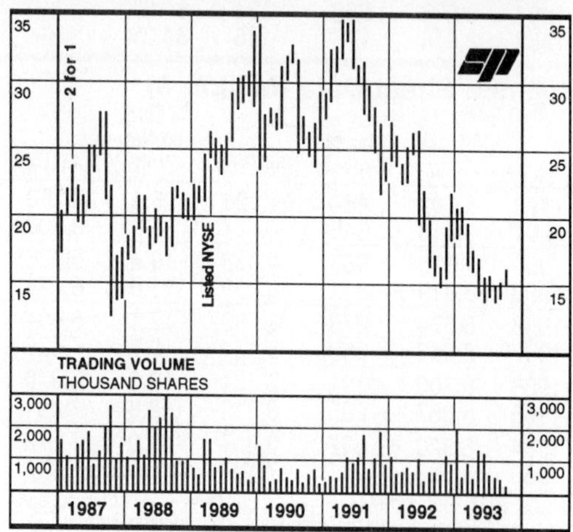

At 1992-3 year-end, the company was also operating a total of 45 high-tech copy stores in California, Dallas, Atlanta and the Midwest.

Important Developments

May '93— The company acquired Melville Corp.'s Prints Plus chain, which operates 102 prints, posters and framing stores in malls throughout the U.S. The unit was acquired for some $14.8 million, and CPI also entered into a noncompetition agreement with Melville for cash consideration of $1,050,000.

Next earnings report expected in mid-December.

Per Share Data ($)

Yr. End Jan. 31	1993	[1]1992	1991	1990	1989	1988	1987	1986	1985	1984
Tangible Bk. Val.	**7.33**	7.09	9.66	8.17	7.68	6.48	5.04	3.60	2.51	2.28
Cash Flow	**3.42**	3.46	3.66	3.32	2.95	2.53	2.02	1.59	1.17	0.95
Earnings[2]	**1.54**	1.80	2.19	1.97	1.81	1.46	1.11	0.90	0.65	0.73
Dividends	**0.560**	0.560	0.500	0.420	0.250	0.165	0.110	0.025	Nil	Nil
Payout Ratio	**36%**	30%	22%	21%	14%	11%	10%	3%	Nil	Nil
Calendar Years	**1992**	1991	1990	1989	1988	1987	1986	1985	1984	1983
Prices—High	**27⅛**	34¾	34⅜	33⅞	22¼	27¾	19	12⅞	13⅝	17⅛
Low	**14⅞**	21¾	23½	19¾	16¾	12½	11¾	7	7⅜	10⅜
P/E Ratio—	**18–10**	19–12	16–11	17–10	12–9	19–9	17–11	14–8	21–11	24–14

Data as orig. reptd. Adj. for stk. divs. of 100% Mar. 1987, 100% Feb. 1983. **1.** Refl. merger or acq. **2.** Bef. results of disc. opers. of -0.14 in 1990, +0.01 in 1987, +0.20 in 1986.

Income Data (Million $)

Year Ended Jan. 31	Revs.	Oper. Inc.	% Oper. Inc. of Revs.	Cap. Exp.	Depr.	Int. Exp.	Net Bef. Taxes	Eff. Tax Rate	Net Inc.	% Net Inc. of Revs.	Cash Flow
1993	**449**	**62.4**	**13.9**	[4]**13.3**	**27.5**	**0.17**	**36.5**	**38.1%**	**22.6**	**5.0**	**50.1**
[1]1992	415	64.4	15.5	40.6	26.5	0.15	43.3	37.3%	27.1	6.5	53.6
1991	374	69.6	18.6	20.3	22.6	0.09	53.5	37.1%	33.6	9.0	56.2
[2]1990	351	66.8	19.0	25.6	21.3	0.11	48.3	36.0%	30.9	8.8	52.2
1989	328	63.5	19.3	29.7	19.1	0.08	50.1	39.5%	30.3	9.2	49.4
1988	290	58.4	20.2	18.5	17.8	0.44	43.9	44.2%	24.5	8.5	42.3
[2]1987	258	50.9	19.8	27.0	15.0	0.24	36.9	50.7%	18.2	7.1	33.2
[2]1986	198	37.3	18.8	15.6	10.6	0.57	26.9	48.4%	13.9	7.0	24.5
1985	196	26.6	13.6	[3]32.3	8.0	1.32	17.9	44.1%	10.0	5.1	18.0
1984	153	22.4	14.7	17.2	3.7	0.10	20.1	44.8%	11.1	7.3	14.5

Balance Sheet Data (Million $)

Jan. 31	Cash	Curr. Assets	Curr. Liab.	Curr. Ratio	Total Assets	% Ret. on Assets	Long Term Debt	Common Equity	Total Cap.	% LT Debt of Cap.	% Ret. on Equity
1993	**21.0**	**73**	**56.8**	**1.3**	**238**	**9.5**	**0.34**	**172**	**175**	**0.2**	**13.6**
1992	31.2	84	67.1	1.2	239	12.0	0.56	160	165	0.3	17.6
1991	88.3	130	51.4	2.5	219	16.4	0.51	152	159	0.3	23.8
1990	70.0	106	47.8	2.2	196	16.2	0.29	133	141	0.2	23.6
1989	65.5	104	47.3	2.2	197	16.7	0.48	137	145	0.3	24.1
1988	59.6	90	39.9	2.3	169	15.8	0.17	117	125	0.1	23.2
1987	29.5	60	36.1	1.7	139	14.8	0.39	94	101	0.4	22.8
1986	14.7	36	30.5	1.2	99	15.4	0.45	61	67	0.7	26.2
1985	2.0	22	31.1	0.7	81	14.2	0.70	45	48	1.4	25.3
1984	13.2	30	22.5	1.3	59	21.8	0.13	34	36	0.4	38.8

Data as orig. reptd. **1.** Refl. merger or acq. **2.** Excl. disc. opers. **3.** Incl. 15.6 for PhotoFinish acquisition. **4.** Net of curr. year retirement and disposals.

Net Sales (Million $)

Weeks:	1993–4	1992–3	1991–2	1990–1
12 Apr.	88.8	92.6	80.6	75.5
12 Jul.	95.4	92.6	79.7	76.5
16 Nov.		126.5	129.9	113.8
12 Jan.		137.6	124.3	108.2
		449.4	414.5	374.0

In the 24 weeks ended July 24, 1993, net sales declined fractionally, year to year, as reduced portrait sittings and CPI's exit from certain businesses outweighed the inclusion of Prints Plus and Proex. Hampered by the lower portrait studio volume, acquisition-related costs and $1.4 million of one-time non-operating costs, a loss of $0.03 a share contrasted with earnings of $0.40. Results for the 1993 period exclude a credit of $0.14 a share from an accounting change.

Common Share Earnings ($)

Weeks:	1993–4	1992–3	1991–2	1990–1
12 Apr.	d0.17	0.15	0.30	0.29
12 Jul.	0.14	0.25	0.36	0.40
16 Nov.		0.42	0.45	0.67
12 Jan.		0.72	0.69	0.83
		1.54	1.80	2.19

Finances

In August 1993, CPI placed privately with two insurance companies $60 million of seven-year notes.

In December 1992, the company acquired the assets of Pemtom, Inc. for cash consideration of $19 million. The assets consisted of 25 one-hour photofinishing locations operating under the Proex name, 15 of which offer added services through adjacent Proex Portrait Studios. In a related transaction, CPI secured the services of the Pemtom management team for $4.8 million.

In April 1992, directors authorized the repurchase of two million CPI common shares, in addition to the 2.5 million shares authorized in September 1988. As of early February 1993, a total of 2,323,153 shares had been repurchased at a cost of $57.9 million.

Dividend Data

Dividends were initiated in 1985. A "poison pill" stock purchase rights plan was adopted in 1989.

Amt. of Divd. $	Date Decl.	Ex–divd. Date	Stock of Record	Payment Date
0.14	Nov. 2	Nov. 9	Nov. 16	Nov. 30'92
0.14	Feb. 4	Feb. 9	Feb. 16	Mar. 1'93
0.14	May 6	May 11	May 17	Jun. 1'93
0.14	Aug. 12	Aug. 17	Aug. 23	Sep. 7'93

Capitalization

Long Term Debt: $60,330,169 (8/93).

Common Stock: 14,655,572 shs. ($0.40 par). Institutions hold about 88%.

d-Deficit.

Office—1706 Washington Ave., St. Louis, MO 63103-1790. **Tel**—(314) 231-1575. **Chrmn & CEO**—A. V. Essman. **Pres**—R. Isaak. **EVP & CFO**—B. Arthur. **Secy**—J. E. Nelson. **Dirs**—M. Bohm, A. V. Essman, R. Isaak, L. M. Liberman, N. L. Redding, R. L. Virgil. **Transfer Agent & Registrar**—Continental Stock Transfer & Trust Co., NYC. **Incorporated** in Delaware in 1982. **Empl**—8,900.

 Michael W. Jaffe

CUC International

NYSE Symbol CU Options on Phila (Feb-May-Aug-Nov) In S&P MidCap 400

Price	Range	P–E Ratio	Dividend	Yield	S&P Ranking	Beta
Sep. 9'93	1993					
33⅛	35¾–16⅝	50	None	None	B	1.22

Summary

CUC International provides consumers with access to various services, including discount shopping, travel, automobile, dining, home improvement, credit card and checking account enhancement packages and discount coupon programs. Increased memberships and higher average membership fees contributed to strong earnings growth in recent periods. A 3-for-2 stock split was effected in April 1993.

Business Summary

CUC International is a membership-based consumer services company, providing more than 29 million individual customers with access to services such as discount shopping, travel, automobile discounts, dining, home improvement, vacation exchange, credit card and checking account enhancement packages, and discount coupon programs. The company also administers insurance package programs which are generally combined with discount shopping and travel memberships for credit union members and bank account holders. CU provides its services through individual, financial institution, credit union and group memberships.

The company's revenues are derived principally from membership fees, which vary depending upon the particular membership program. Annual fees generally range from $6 to $150 per year. CU arranges with client financial institutions, retailers, oil companies, credit unions, on-line networks, fundraisers and others to market certain membership services directly to such clients' individual account holders. Participating clients receive commissions on initial and renewal memberships, averaging twenty percent of the net membership fees.

Major membership services offered by the company include Shoppers Advantage, a discount shopping program that provides product price information and home shopping services; Travelers Advantage, a discount travel service program whereby members can obtain information on schedules and rates for major scheduled airlines, hotel chains and car rental agencies, tours, cruises, travel packages and short-notice travel arrangements; and AutoVantage, which offers comprehensive new car summaries and discounts on new domestic and foreign cars purchased through the company's independent dealer network, tire and parts discounts, and used car valuations.

Through its Comp-U-Card division, CU offers other membership services, including a dining service, a credit card registration service, Buyers Advantage, and a home service, all of which are consumer-oriented products similar to the company's shopping and travel membership services.

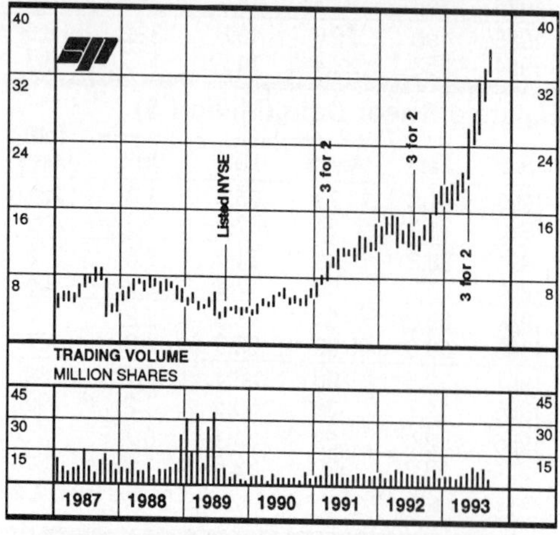

The company also sells enhancement package memberships through client financial institutions, which select a package of CU's products and services to be added to the clients' own services for use by checking account holders.

In January 1992, CU acquired Entertainment Publishing Corp., a provider of discount coupon programs, in exchange for 19,795,991 (adjusted) common shares. In December 1992, CU acquired Leaguestar plc, a provider of travel and exchange memberships and services, for $70 million in cash, and Sally Foster Gift Wrap LP, a producer of gift wrap products for school and club fundraising, for $31 million.

Next earnings report expected in early December.

Per Share Data ($)

Yr. End Jan. 31	[1]1993	[1]1992	1991	[1]1990	1989	[1]1988	[1]1987	[1]1986	1985	1984
Tangible Bk. Val.	**d0.27**	d0.70	d1.18	d1.37	0.69	0.79	0.39	0.69	0.42	0.33
Cash Flow	**0.73**	0.41	0.38	0.27	d0.04	0.36	0.23	0.10	0.06	0.01
Earnings[2]	**0.56**	0.26	0.24	0.12	d0.18	0.28	0.16	0.07	0.05	d0.01
Dividends	**Nil**	Nil	Nil	[3]1.48	Nil	Nil	Nil	Nil	Nil	Nil
Payout Ratio	**Nil**	Nil	Nil	NM	Nil	Nil	Nil	Nil	Nil	Nil
Calendar Years	**1992**	1991	1990	1989	1988	1987	1986	1985	1984	1983
Prices—High	**19 5/16**	14 11/16	6 13/16	6⅛	8 1/16	8 15/16	7 1/16	4¾	3 7/16	3 5/16
Low	**11½**	5 13/16	3 9/16	3⅛	4 15/16	3⅛	3 5/16	3⅛	1 13/16	2 7/16
P/E Ratio—	**34–21**	59–24	30–16	56–28	NM	34–12	49–23	89–58	80–42	NM

Data as orig. reptd. Adj. for stk. divs. of 50% May 1993, 50% Jul. 1992, 50% Mar. 1991, 50% Jul. 1986, 50% Mar. 1985. **1.** Reflects merger or acq. **2.** Bef. spec. items of +0.02 in 1987, +0.07 in 1986, +0.04 in 1985. **3.** Plus 2.07 face amt. of zero cpn. notes. d-Deficit. NM-Not Meaningful.

Income Data (Million $)

Year Ended Jan. 31	Revs.	Oper. Inc.	% Oper. Inc. of Revs.	Cap. Exp.	Depr.	Int. Exp.	Net Bef. Taxes	Eff. Tax Rate	[3]Net Inc.	% Net Inc. of Revs.	Cash Flow
[1]1993	**739**	**122.0**	**16.6**	**4.64**	**17.3**	**8.7**	**96.1**	**38.8%**	**58.8**	**8.0**	**76.1**
[1]1992	641	99.2	15.5	6.68	15.7	16.0	45.1	44.3%	25.1	3.9	40.8
1991	451	58.5	13.0	4.92	11.4	16.5	28.8	39.1%	17.5	3.9	28.9
[1]1990	365	38.6	10.6	4.13	10.9	12.1	13.7	41.2%	8.1	2.2	19.0
1989	269	44.1	16.4	7.38	9.1	1.4	d14.6	NM	d11.3	NM	d2.3
[1]1988	195	36.4	18.7	7.59	5.9	2.3	31.4	44.6%	17.4	8.9	23.4
[1]1987	138	20.0	14.4	5.08	4.8	2.7	16.0	45.9%	8.7	6.3	13.4
[1]1986	84	9.9	11.7	[2]5.29	2.0	1.5	7.3	61.0%	2.8	3.4	4.8
1985	28	3.0	10.6	[2]1.81	0.5	Nil	3.1	62.0%	1.5	5.4	2.0
1984	9	d0.3	NM	0.78	0.2	0.2	NM	NM	Nil	0.4	0.1

Balance Sheet Data (Million $)

Jan. 31	Cash	Curr. Assets	Curr. Liab.	Curr. Ratio	Total Assets	% Ret. on Assets	Long Term Debt	Common Equity	Total Cap.	% LT Debt of Cap.	% Ret. on Equity
1993	**28.6**	**243**	**127**	**1.9**	**479**	**14.1**	**37**	**150**	**187**	**19.9**	**NM**
1992	14.4	205	133	1.5	322	7.8	69	d1	68	101.4	NM
1991	13.3	143	103	1.4	239	8.0	101	d22	80	126.5	NM
1990	12.3	111	85	1.3	201	3.7	117	d41	78	NM	20.9
1989	38.1	125	68	1.9	216	NM	14	109	124	11.5	NM
1988	26.0	63	43	1.5	187	10.4	16	112	143	11.0	18.1
1987	14.8	42	26	1.6	132	7.7	27	72	105	25.7	15.4
1986	25.4	39	19	2.0	79	4.8	23	35	59	39.5	10.1
1985	6.5	16	12	1.3	27	6.8	Nil	15	15	1.2	11.4
1984	7.6	10	5	1.9	17	0.3	Nil	12	12	NM	NM

Data as orig. reptd. **1.** Reflects merger or acquisition. **2.** Net. **3.** Bef. spec. items. d-Deficit. NM-Not Meaningful.

Total Revenues (Million $)

Quarter:	1993–94	1992–93	1991–92	1990–91
Apr.	207.0	174.7	153.0	104.7
Jul.	215.8	181.2	158.1	110.6
Oct.		188.0	163.0	114.5
Jan.		198.4	170.0	123.7
		742.3	644.3	453.6

For the six months ended July 31, 1993, total revenues rose 19%, year to year, reflecting an increase in the membership base and aided by a 5% increase in the average annual fee. Total expenses rose less rapidly, and pretax income advanced 51%. After taxes at 38.8%, versus 39.1%, net income rose 52% to $39.4 million ($0.35 a share, based on 9.4% more shares) from $26.0 million ($0.25).

Common Share Earnings ($)

Quarter:	1993–94	1992–93	1991–92	1990–91
Apr.	0.17	0.12	0.09	0.04
Jul.	0.18	0.13	0.09	0.05
Oct.		0.15	0.10	0.06
Jan.		0.17	d0.03	0.07
		0.56	0.25	0.23

Dividend Data

In June 1989, CU paid special dividends of $1.48 a share cash and $2.07 face amount ($0.93 discount amount) of zero coupon notes due 1996 as part of its recapitalization plan (data adjusted). A 3-for-2 stock split was distributed on April 30, 1993, to shareholders of record April 16.

Finances

As of April 30, 1993, the company had repurchased 1,644,750 common shares under a 1991 authorization to acquire up to 6.75 million shares (adjusted).

In June 1989, CU completed a recapitalization plan which included the distribution to shareholders of $1.48 in cash and $2.07 face amount of zero coupon convertible subordinated notes due 1996 for each common share held. Each $100 principal amount of the zero coupon notes is convertible into 10.125 common shares (adjusted). The plan also included a restricted stock plan for employees.

Capitalization

Long Term Debt: $24,645,000 (net of $9,479,000 unamortized original issue discount) of zero coupon notes due 1996, conv. into 10.125 com. shs. per $100 face amount (7/93).

Common Stock: 109,226,778 shs. ($0.01 par).
Institutions hold about 83%.
Shareholders of record: 2,056 (3/93).

d-Deficit.

Office—707 Summer St., Stamford, CT 06901. **Tel**—(203) 324-9261. **Chrmn & CEO**—W. A. Forbes. **Pres & COO**—E. K. Shelton. **EVP & CFO**—S. L. Bell. **Secy**—R. T. Tucker. **VP & Investor Contact**—Sandra Morgan (203) 965-5114. **Dirs**—B. Burnap, T. B. Donnelley, W. A. Forbes, S. A. Greyser, W. B. King, H. C. McCall, B. C. Perfit, R. P. Rittereiser, S. M. Rumbough Jr. **Transfer Agent & Registrar**—First National Bank of Boston, Boston, Mass. **Incorporated** in Delaware in 1974. **Empl**—6,000.

 L. Feuer Nelson

Cabletron Systems

NYSE Symbol CS Options on ASE, NYSE & Pacific In S&P MidCap 400

Price	Range	P-E Ratio	Dividend	Yield	S&P Ranking	Beta
Sep. 21'93	1993					
108¾	119–74½	33	None	None	NR	NA

Summary

This leading intelligent hub maker develops and manufactures Ethernet, Token Ring, FDDI and ATM networking products based on its Integrated Network Architecture (INA). Sales and earnings have risen sharply each year since 1986 on growing acceptance of the company's products, and should continue to do so in the current year.

Current Outlook

Earnings for 1993-94 are estimated at $4.00 a share, up from 1992-93's $2.97.

Initiation of dividends is not expected.

Results should improve further as the computer networking industry continues to grow rapidly. According to one survey, at companies with more than 1,000 employees, some 63% of personal computers were connected to Local Area Networks (LANs) in 1992. It is likely CS's sales will increase some 40% in 1993-94, in line with expected industry growth rates, reflecting strong acceptance of the company's Multi Media Access Centers (MMAC) and the introduction of new products as the year progresses. Despite increasing competition, gross margins will probably decline just fractionally. Operating costs should remain well controlled—at about 20% of sales—leading to net margins of some 20%.

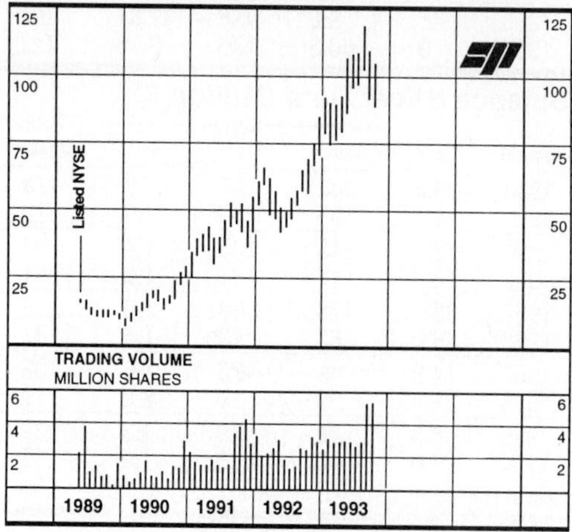

Net Sales (Million $)

Quarter:	1993-94	1992-93	1991-92	1990-91
May	131.5	88.0	60.6	35.5
Aug.	E139.3	96.7	69.6	42.4
Nov.	E151.8	110.4	78.0	48.2
Feb.	E159.9	123.0	82.3	54.4
	E582.5	418.2	290.5	180.5

Net sales in the quarter ended May 31, 1993, advanced 49%, year to year, reflecting strong market acceptance of Multi Media Access Centers (MMAC) and related items. Gross margins narrowed slightly, and, with a 50% increase in operating expenses, pretax income advanced 47%. After taxes at 35.4%, versus 36.5%, net income climbed 49%, to $26,229,000 ($0.93 a share), from $17,589,00 ($0.63).

Common Share Earnings ($)

Quarter:	1993-94	1992-93	1991-92	1990-91
May	0.93	0.63	0.44	0.27
Aug.	E0.96	0.69	0.50	0.32
Nov.	E1.02	0.79	0.55	0.36
Feb.	E1.09	0.87	0.59	0.40
	E4.00	2.97	2.08	1.35

Important Developments

Aug. '93— CS filed with the SEC for a public offering of 2,000,000 shares, all of which are to be offered by stockholders. Separately, the company announced plans to unveil SPECTRUM for Open Systems — the industry's first network management application to operate across multiple management platforms.

Next earnings report expected in mid-September.

Per Share Data ($)

Yr. End Feb. 28	1993	1992	1991	1990	1989	1988	1987	1986	1985
Tangible Bk. Val.	**10.22**	7.25	5.03	2.56	0.74	0.10	NA	NA	NA
Cash Flow	**3.38**	2.33	1.49	0.93	0.51	0.18	0.03	NA	NA
Earnings	**[1]2.97**	[1]2.08	[1]1.35	0.87	0.48	0.17	0.03	0.01	Nil
Dividends	**Nil**	Nil	Nil	Nil	Nil	Nil	Nil	Nil	Nil
Payout Ratio	**Nil**	Nil	Nil	Nil	Nil	Nil	Nil	Nil	Nil
Calendar Years	**1992**	1991	1990	1989	1988	1987	1986	1985	1984
Prices—High	**85¼**	55¼	29¼	16¾	NA	NA	NA	NA	NA
Low	**42⅛**	25½	6⅞	9¼	NA	NA	NA	NA	NA
P/E Ratio—	**29–14**	27–12	22-5	19–11	NA	NA	NA	NA	NA

Data as orig. reptd.; prior to 1990, pro forma data as reptd. in prospectus dated 5-30-89. **1.** Ful. dil.: 2.90 in 1993, 2.04 in 1992, 1.33 in 1991. NA-Not Available.

Income Data (Million $)

Year Ended Feb. 28	Revs.	Oper. Inc.	% Oper. Inc. of Revs.	Cap. Exp.	Depr.	Int. Exp.	Net Bef. Taxes	Eff. Tax Rate	Net Inc.	% Net Inc. of Revs.	Cash Flow
1993	**418**	**137.0**	**32.8**	**28.3**	**11.70**	**Nil**	**130.0**	**35.7%**	**83.5**	**20.0**	**95.2**
1992	291	95.0	32.7	25.5	7.05	Nil	91.8	36.9%	58.0	20.0	65.1
1991	181	59.3	32.9	14.5	3.58	0.01	57.3	37.3%	35.9	19.9	39.5
1990	105	36.0	34.4	10.8	1.46	0.39	33.0	31.9%	22.5	21.5	24.0
1989	55	19.8	36.2	4.9	0.58	0.13	19.1	38.5%	11.8	21.5	12.4
1988	25	7.4	29.8	0.7	0.32	0.21	6.9	41.6%	4.0	16.2	4.4
1987	10	1.5	15.9	0.3	0.08	0.15	1.3	42.9%	0.7	7.8	0.8
1986	4	NA	NA	NA	NA	NA	0.3	44.9%	0.2	4.9	NA

Balance Sheet Data (Million $)

Feb. 28	Cash	Curr. Assets	Curr. Liab.	Curr. Ratio	Total Assets	% Ret. on Assets	Long Term Debt	Common Equity	Total Cap.	% LT Debt of Cap.	% Ret. on Equity
1993	**154.0**	**285**	**51.3**	**5.5**	**343**	**28.7**	**Nil**	**289**	**292**	**Nil**	**33.8**
1992	90.9	193	30.7	6.3	236	29.7	Nil	204	206	Nil	33.6
1991	60.5	129	13.5	9.5	154	29.2	Nil	140	140	Nil	34.0
1990	15.8	73	19.7	3.7	87	34.5	Nil	67	68	Nil	51.8
1989	2.3	35	22.0	1.6	40	45.3	0.09	18	18	0.5	113.8
1988	0.1	11	7.4	1.5	12	45.7	1.86	3	4	42.6	235.2
1987	NA	NA	NA	NA	6	17.7	0.11	1	1	10.3	NM
1986	NA	NA	NA	NA	2	13.1	0.01	NM	NM	NM	195.9

Data as orig. reptd.; prior to 1990, pro forma data as reptd. in prospectus dated 5-30-89. NA-Not Available. NM-Not Meaningful.

Business Summary

Cabletron Systems, Inc. develops, manufactures, markets, installs and supports a wide range of standards-based local area network (LAN) connectivity products. Contributions to sales by product line in recent fiscal years were:

	1992–93	1991–92	1990–91
Interconnection	93.9%	93.2%	87.2%
Cables	2.8%	3.4%	4.8%
Test equipment & services	3.3%	3.4%	8.0%

Customers outside the U.S. accounted for 30% of sales in 1992-93, up from 28% in 1991-92.

The company's networking products are based on the concept of an Integrated Network Architecture (INA), which permits interconnection, integration, internetworking and expansion of LANs without regard to the transmission media or network protocols incorporated in the LANs. A key component of INA is Cabletron's Multi Media Access Center (MMAC), an intelligent hub that allows the integration of multiple network standards such as Ethernet, Token Ring and FDDI. The MMAC is complemented by Cabletron's network management software products.

Other interconnection products include multiport repeaters designed to increase the distance of a geograpically dispersed LAN; bridges, which perform high-speed filtering and data transmission; stand-alone transceivers, which attach to personal computers in a network enabling the user to communicate with other users in the LAN; and desktop network interface cards, which provide a high-speed data connection for personal computer platforms.

The company offers cable assemblies and various cables, such as coaxial, shielded-twisted pair (IBM-type) wire, unshielded twisted-pair wire (telephone-type) and optical fiber cut to specific lengths as well as connectors and accessories for the cable. Test equipment offered is designed to analyze and verify proper installation and operation of the company's products. Services include LAN installation and consulting.

Products are distributed primarily through a sales force to end-users. Research and development expenses were $41,318,000 (9.9% of net sales) in 1992-93, up from $27,298,000 (9.4%) in 1991-92.

Dividend Data

The company has never paid a cash dividend and intends to reinvest all of its earnings for use in its business to finance growth.

Finances

In November 1992, CS completed a secondary offering of two million common shares, priced at $73.25 each, through underwriters led by Merrill Lynch. All the shares were sold by three insiders: the president and CEO, the chairman and COO, and the director of national accounts. The overallotment option for 300,000 shares was not exercised.

Capitalization

Long Term Debt: None (5/93).

Common Stock: 28,332,714 shs. ($0.01 par). Officers & directors control 40%. Institutions hold approximately 51%. Shareholders: 1,205 of record (2/93).

Office—35 Industrial Way, Rochester, NH 03867. **Tel**—(603) 332-9400. **Chrmn, COO & Treas**—C. R. Benson. **Pres & CEO**—S. R. Levine. **CFO**—D. J. Kirkpatrick. **Secy**—M. D. Myerow. **Investor Contact**—Ed Cortes (603-335-6311). **Dirs**—C. R. Benson, P. R. Duncan, S. R. Levine, D. F. McGuinness, M. D. Myerow. **Transfer Agent & Registrar**—State Street Bank & Trust Co., Boston. **Incorporated** in Delaware in 1988. **Empl**—2,625.

 Neeraj K. Vohra

Cabot Corp.

NYSE Symbol CBT In S&P MidCap 400

Price	Range	P-E Ratio	Dividend	Yield	S&P Ranking	Beta
Aug. 12'93	1993					
51½	51½–37⅛	20	1.04	2.1%	B	0.84

Summary

Cabot has interests in specialty chemicals and materials (including carbon black and fumed silica), energy (liquefied natural gas importing operations and coal handling) and safety products. Fiscal 1993 earnings will be reduced as a result of the European recession, lower demand for LNG, and a likely fourth quarter restructuring charge, but fiscal 1994 prospects are more positive.

Current Outlook

Share earnings for the fiscal year ending September 30, 1994, are projected to exceed $3.00, up from the $2.65 (before likely fourth quarter charges) expected for fiscal 1993.

Dividends should continue at $0.26 quarterly.

Fiscal 1994 profits of the chemical segment are expected to rise on higher demand and wider margins for carbon blacks and other chemicals in most areas of the world, but the weak European economy may continue to impact demand for carbon black, plastics and silica in 1994. Restructuring actions in Europe would help to reduce costs. Cabot Safety is being adversely affected by lower U.S. industrial employment. LNG profits may rebound with more favorable industry conditions following the 1993 implementation of new federal energy regulations; new cogeneration contracts will help to even out seasonal LNG demand.

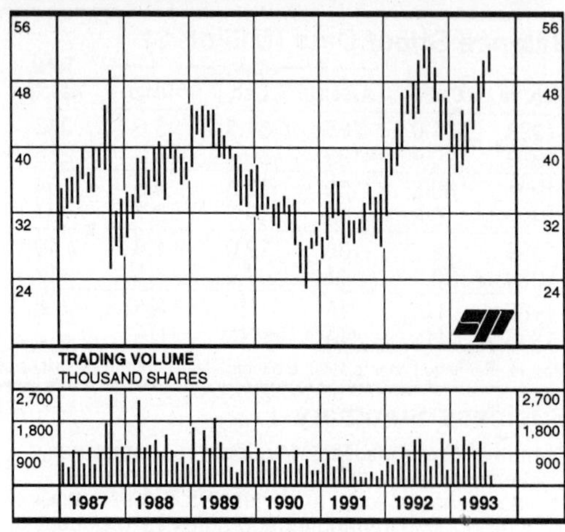

Sales & Oper. Revenues (Million $)

Quarter:	1992–93	1991–92	1990–91	1989–90
Dec.	396	385	400	407
Mar.	408	418	411	445
Jun.	419	371	347	421
Sep.	---	383	324	400
	---	1,557	1,482	1,673

Sales for the nine months ended June 30, 1993, rose 4.2%, year to year, on higher sales in the LNG and U.S. chemical businesses. With lower profits in both chemicals and energy, net income was off 20%, to $2.23 a share, from $2.85.

Common Share Earnings ($)

Quarter:	1992–93	1991–92	1990–91	1989–90
Dec.	0.59	0.86	0.52	0.71
Mar.	0.70	1.15	0.60	1.03
Jun.	0.94	0.84	0.30	0.62
Sep.	E0.42	0.34	0.17	0.37
	E2.65	3.18	1.69	2.73

Important Developments

Jul. '93— Cabot was pleased to report encouraging results in the fiscal third quarter despite no signs of improvement in the depressed business environments in Europe and Japan. Chemicals profits rose from the year-earlier level, reflecting stronger margins and volumes in North America and Latin America offset by weakness in Europe and Japan. The energy group reported an operating profit, versus a slight loss, due to higher LNG sales resulting from stronger spring pricing. CBT indicated that in light of the current business climate, it may close several production lines and/or an entire plant, and that should the latter action become necessary, the total restructuring accrual could be as much as $30 million after tax. CBT also expected to adopt FAS 106 in fiscal 1993, and estimated a one-time charge of about $45 million after tax for the entire cumulative effect.

Next earnings report expected in early November.

Per Share Data ($)

Yr. End Sep. 30	[2]1992	1991	[1]1990	1989	1988	1987	1986	1985	[1,2]1984	1983
Tangible Bk. Val.	**18.02**	13.95	16.00	16.10	22.06	20.88	20.48	18.88	21.88	20.47
Cash Flow	**7.75**	5.47	6.02	3.38	6.29	4.96	5.51	4.84	5.48	4.33
Earnings[3]	**[5]3.18**	[5]1.69	[5]2.73	d0.40	2.27	1.42	2.56	2.22	3.02	2.00
Dividends	**1.04**	1.04	1.04	1.01	0.92	0.92	0.92	0.92	0.92	0.92
Payout Ratio	**33%**	52%	38%	NM	41%	65%	35%	41%	30%	46%
Prices[4]—High	**52⅜**	35⅞	37⅞	45⅛	41¾	49¼	35⅜	33¾	28⅞	30⅞
Low	**31¾**	26⅝	23	32⅞	29⅛	25¼	23⅜	20½	22⅝	20½
P/E Ratio—	**16–10**	21–16	14–8	NM	18–13	35–18	14–9	15–9	10–7	15–10

Data as orig. reptd. 1. Refl. merger or acq. 2. Refl. acctg. change. 3. Bef. results of disc. ops. of +4.11 in 1991, +0.95 in 1989, -4.92 in 1985 & spec. items of -0.03 in 1988, -0.38 in 1987, -0.07 in 1986. 4. Cal. yr. 5. Ful. dil.: 2.97 in 1992, 1.63 in 1991, 2.61 in 1990. E-Estimated. d-Deficit. NM-Not Meaningful.

Income Data (Million $)

Year Ended Sep. 30	Revs.	Oper. Inc.	% Oper. Inc. of Revs.	Cap. Exp.	Depr.	Int. Exp.	[4]Net Bef. Taxes	Eff. Tax Rate	[5]Net Inc.	% Net Inc. of Revs.	Cash Flow
[3]1992	**1,557**	**242**	**15.6**	**78**	**84**	**45.7**	**117**	**46.7%**	**62.2**	**4.0**	**143**
[1]1991	1,482	188	12.7	198	80	47.4	71	43.8%	39.8	2.7	116
[2]1990	1,673	242	14.5	174	81	51.1	121	41.2%	71.0	4.2	148
[1]1989	1,937	225	11.6	214	98	42.2	4	248.2%	d6.5	NM	87
1988	1,677	205	12.3	170	109	39.8	113	45.6%	61.2	3.6	170
1987	1,424	225	15.8	81	98	35.4	71	44.8%	39.2	2.8	138
1986	1,310	247	18.8	73	84	41.6	129	43.3%	[3]73.1	5.6	157
[1]1985	1,408	240	17.1	155	84	34.0	125	43.1%	71.3	5.1	155
[2,3]1984	1,753	262	14.9	485	79	34.4	158	38.7%	97.1	5.5	176
1983	1,558	218	14.0	77	75	35.8	109	41.2%	64.2	4.1	139

Balance Sheet Data (Million $)

Sep. 30	Cash	Curr. Assets	Curr. Liab.	Curr. Ratio	Total Assets	% Ret. on Assets	Long Term Debt	Common Equity	Total Cap.	% LT Debt of Cap.	% Ret. on Equity
1992	**31**	**555**	**361**	**1.5**	**1,555**	**4.1**	**480**	**418**	**1,103**	**43.5**	**15.2**
1991	39	494	501	1.0	1,462	2.9	370	352	870	42.5	10.0
1990	48	579	444	1.3	1,732	4.5	481	495	1,184	40.6	14.8
1989	16	487	360	1.4	1,417	NM	386	414	975	39.6	NM
1988	66	548	394	1.4	1,543	4.1	320	607	1,066	30.0	10.3
1987	82	561	417	1.3	1,463	2.7	221	591	991	22.3	6.7
1986	123	586	287	2.0	1,510	5.0	426	591	1,151	37.1	12.8
1985	28	634	338	1.9	1,595	4.3	382	626	1,141	33.5	10.6
1984	4	637	357	1.8	1,752	6.4	337	720	1,235	27.3	14.0
1983	47	591	224	2.6	1,310	4.9	246	676	1,066	23.1	9.7

Data as orig. reptd. **1.** Excl. disc. ops. **2.** Rel. merger or acq. **3.** Refl. acctg. change. **4.** Incl. equity in earns. of nonconsol. subs. **5.** Bef. spec. items. d-Deficit. NM-Not Meaningful.

Business Summary

Cabot Corporation has operations in specialty chemicals and materials and energy. In April 1991, CBT completed the divestiture of 82%-owned Cabot Oil & Gas Corp. Segment contributions in fiscal 1992 were:

	Sales	Profits
Specialty chemicals & materials	76%	89%
Energy	24%	11%

International operations accounted for 44% of sales and 36% of profits in fiscal 1992.

Cabot is the world's largest producer of carbon black, an essential reinforcing agent used in tires and rubber products and as a pigment in inks, coatings, and plastics, with about one-fourth of the worldwide production capacity. CBT is also the world's second largest producer of fumed silica (used as a reinforcing and thickening agent in a variety of products), a major producer of electronic materials and refractory metals (primarily tantalum for electrolytic capacitors) and a leading European producer of plastic concentrates and compounds. Cabot Safety makes safety eyewear, hearing protection and industrial noise control products.

Cabot LNG is a liquefied natural gas importing and terminaling operation located in the northeastern U.S., and TUCO is a coal handling and distribution business. A 36% interest is held in American Oil & Gas Corp., a gas transmission company.

Dividend Data

Dividends have been paid since 1931. A dividend reinvestment plan is available. A "poison pill" stock purchase right was adopted in 1986.

Amt of Divd. $	Date Decl.	Ex-divd. Date	Stock of Record	Payment Date
0.26	Nov. 13	Nov. 20	Nov. 27	Dec. 11'92
0.26	Feb. 12	Feb. 22	Feb. 26	Mar. 12'93
0.26	May 14	May 24	May 28	Jun. 11'93
0.26	Jul. 9	Aug. 23	Aug. 27	Sep. 10'93

Capitalization

Long Term Debt: $480,841,000 (6/93).

ESOP 7.75% Preferred Stock: $72,592,000; conv. into approx. 1.6 million com. shs.

Common Stock: 18,535,787 shs. ($1 par).
Officers & directors control about 11%.
Institutions hold some 62%.
Shareholders of record: 2,300.

Office—75 State St., Boston, MA 02109-1806. **Tel**—(617) 345-0100. **Chrmn & CEO**—S. W. Bodman. **Secy**—C. D. Gerlinger. **Vice Chrmn & CFO**—J. G. L. Cabot. **Investor Contact**—Kathryn I. Davis. **Dirs**—D. Ames, S. W. Bodman, J. C. Bradley, K. F. Burnes, J. G. L. Cabot, R. A. Charpie, J. D. Curtin Jr., R. P Henderson, A. C. Hiatt, G. Jeelof, J. H. McArthur, J. F. O'Brien, D. V. Ragone, C. P. Siess Jr., M. Tanenbaum. **Transfer Agent & Registrar**—First National Bank of Boston. **Incorporated** in Delaware in 1960. **Empl**—5,400.

 Richard O'Reilly, CFA

Cadence Design Systems

NYSE Symbol CDN Options on ASE & CBOE (Feb-May-Aug-Nov) In S&P MidCap 400

Price	Range	P-E Ratio	Dividend	Yield	S&P Ranking	Beta
Sep. 24'93	1993					
10⅝	24⅜–8¼	NM	None	None	B	2.26

Summary

Cadence Design Systems is the leading producer of electronic design automation (EDA) software. Operations were significantly expanded through the acquisition of Valid Logic Systems in late 1991. Results in the first half of 1993 were hurt by sharply lower product revenues and a restructuring charge, but profitability should recover somewhat during the remainder of 1993 and in 1994, as steps taken by management to improve the cost structure yield results.

Current Outlook

A loss of $0.13 a share is projected for 1993. Earnings of $0.80 a share are estimated for 1994.

Initiation of cash dividends is not expected.

Following a decline of 17% in the first half of 1993, revenues for the full year are expected to be off 10%. European demand for EDA products will show little improvement, if any, reflecting the continued recessionary environment there. The firming of CDN's Japanese market in 1993's first half was better than anticipated, and order rates and inquiries suggest this will continue for the remainder of 1993. Steps taken by management to improve the cost structure should allow for sequential earnings gains in the third and fourth quarters of 1993, although comparisons with 1992 will still be unfavorable.

Total Revenues (Million $)

Quarter:	1993	1992	1991	1990
Mar.	79.3	101.4	94.1	50.2
Jun.	91.7	105.9	91.3	52.3
Sep.		106.5	96.5	59.6
Dec.		120.8	110.4	69.3
		434.5	392.3	231.4

Total revenues in the six months ended June 30, 1993, fell 17%, year to year, as a 29% decline in product revenue more than offset a 22% rise in maintenance fees. Gross margins fell to 71% of revenues, from 75%, principally because of the lower sales volume. SG&A expenses were higher, and following a $13.4 million restructuring charge absorbed in the first quarter, a pretax loss contrasted with earnings. After a tax credit of $5,440,000 versus taxes of $6,023,000, a net loss of $15,484,000 replaced net income of $22,657,000. After preferred dividend requirements in the 1992 period only, a per share loss of $0.36 was incurred, against earnings of $0.49 a share.

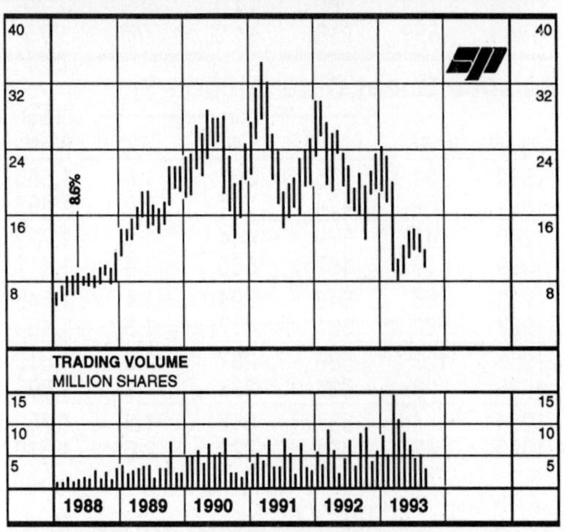

Common Share Earnings ($)

Quarter:	1993	1992	1991	1990
Mar.	d0.37	0.21	0.16	0.26
Jun.	0.02	0.28	0.09	0.24
Sep.	E0.08	0.28	0.15	0.33
Dec.	E0.14	0.44	d0.97	0.36
	Ed0.13	1.20	d0.56	1.19

Important Developments

Sep. '93— Cadence said that bookings were ahead of company plan during the first two months of 1993's third quarter. CDN added that it expects gross margin to be improved for the remainder of 1993.

Next earnings report expected in late October.

Per Share Data ($)

Yr. End Dec. 31	[1]1992	[1]1991	[1]1990	[1]1989	[1]1988	1987	1986
Tangible Bk. Val.	**[2]5.67**	[2]4.48	[2]5.30	[2]3.76	2.38	2.45	0.01
Cash Flow	**1.73**	0.06	1.64	1.24	0.81	0.50	0.33
Earnings	**1.20**	d0.56	1.19	0.93	0.58	0.30	0.16
Dividends	**Nil**	Nil	Nil	Nil	Nil	Nil	Nil
Payout Ratio	**Nil**	Nil	Nil	Nil	Nil	Nil	Nil
Prices—High	**29⅞**	34⅝	28⅞	22	11½	10⅝	NA
Low	**13⅛**	14½	13¼	11⅛	5⅛	3⅝	NA
P/E Ratio—	**25–11**	NM	24–11	24–12	20–9	35–12	NA

Data as orig. reptd. Adj. for stk. div. of 8.6% May 1988. **1.** Reflects merger or acquisition. **2.** Incl. intangibles. d-Deficit. E-Estimated. NM-Not Meaningful. NA-Not Available.

Income Data (Million $)

Year Ended Dec. 31	Revs.	Oper. Inc.	% Oper. Inc. of Revs.	Cap. Exp.	Depr.	Int. Exp.	Net Bef. Taxes	Eff. Tax Rate	Net Inc.	% Net Inc. of Revs.	Cash Flow
[1]1992	**435**	**89.9**	**20.7**	**31.4**	**24.2**	**0.93**	**[2]68.5**	**18.9%**	**55.4**	**12.7**	**79.0**
[1]1991	392	61.5	15.7	29.6	25.6	2.70	[2]d11.8	NM	d21.7	NM	2.6
[1]1990	231	67.1	29.0	22.2	14.5	0.94	[2]56.3	32.5%	38.0	16.4	52.5
[1]1989	143	50.3	35.2	6.2	9.6	0.77	[2]42.3	34.4%	27.8	19.4	37.3
[1]1988	67	24.9	37.1	9.6	5.0	0.53	19.1	31.2%	13.1	19.5	18.1
1987	24	6.6	27.6	2.4	2.1	0.22	4.7	33.0%	3.2	13.2	5.3
1986	17	3.9	23.5	3.9	1.6	0.18	2.3	36.2%	[3]1.5	9.0	3.1

Balance Sheet Data (Million $)

Dec. 31	Cash	Curr. Assets	Curr. Liab.	Curr. Ratio	Total Assets	% Ret. on Assets	Long Term Debt	Common Equity	Total Cap.	% LT Debt of Cap.	% Ret. on Equity
1992	**92**	**249**	**95**	**2.6**	**370**	**15.1**	**6.01**	**249**	**263**	**2.3**	**24.6**
1991	111	246	123	2.0	350	NM	4.13	189	212	1.9	NM
1990	91	166	58	2.9	234	18.7	7.92	158	174	4.6	28.1
1989	63	109	41	2.7	159	21.8	9.35	104	118	7.9	32.8
1988	37	55	20	2.8	75	17.9	2.25	51	55	4.1	25.2
1987	16	25	6	4.1	34	10.0	1.10	25	28	3.9	25.0
1986	5	10	4	2.9	17	NA	1.50	NM	13	11.2	NA

Data as orig. reptd. **1.** Reflects merger or acquisition. **2.** Incl. equity in earns. of nonconsol. subs. **3.** Reflects acctg. change. d-Deficit. NM-Not Meaningful. NA-Not Available.

Business Summary

Cadence Design Systems develops, markets and supports computer software products that automate and accelerate the design and verification of integrated circuits (ICs) and electronic systems. The company is the largest supplier of Electronic Design Automation (EDA) software and a market leader in the Integrated Circuit Design Automation (ICDA) segment of EDA.

EDA refers to the use of computers and engineering software to design electronic circuits and systems. Virtually all complex computer, telecommunication, aerospace and semiconductor projects depend on EDA solutions to handle the large amounts of data associated with such designs.

Cadence's Design Framework II software offers customers the ability to link and manage a variety of design tools under a graphical user interface.

CDN offers a full line of integrated EDA solutions for three basic design areas: IC design for digital, analog and mixed signal devices; system design for both analog and digital systems; and application specific integrated circuit (ASIC) design, particularly for high-performance sub-micron ASICs.

CDN's products operate on workstations made by Digital Equipment Corp., Hewlett Packard/Apollo, IBM, NEC and Sun Microsystems, Inc. Cadence believes it is well positioned to port its system quickly to other UNIX-based workstations that may gain customer acceptance in the future.

Customers include computer manufacturers, consumer electronics companies, defense electronics firms, merchant semiconductor manufacturers, application-specific IC foundries, and telecommunications companies.

Products are marketed by a direct sales force in North America and through a network of majority owned subsidiaries and licensed distributors in Europe and Asia.

Revenue from international sources represented about 50% of Cadence's total revenue in 1992, 1991 and 1990.

Dividend Data

Cadence has never paid cash dividends.

Finances

In April 1993, directors authorized the repurchase of up to 4 million common shares. As of June 30, 1993, 2,500,000 shares had been repurchased at a cost of about $22,000,000.

Effective December 31, 1991, Cadence acquired Valid Logic Systems Inc. (VLID) in a transaction that resulted in the issuance of some 11.8 million common shares. VLID supplies software used to develop electronic systems and printed circuit boards.

Capitalization

Long Term Debt: $18,373,000, incl. $12,097,000 of lease obligs. (6/93).

Common Stock: 42,894,443 shs. ($0.01 par).
Institutions hold approximately 76%.
Shareholders of record: 2,400 (12/92).

Options: To purchase 7,834,951 shs. at $0.41 to $28.75 ea.

Office—555 River Oaks Parkway, San Jose, CA 95134. **Tel**—(408) 943-1234. **Chrmn**—D. L. Lucas. **Pres & CEO**—J. B. Costello. **CFO & Investor Contact**—H. Raymond Bingham. **Dirs**—B. J. Cassin, J. B. Costello, W. D. Hajjar, L. Y. W. Liu, D. L. Lucas, A. Sangiovanni-Vincentelli, G. M. Scalise, J. R. Shoven, J. E. Solomon. **Transfer Agent**—Harris Trust & Savings Bank, Chicago. **Incorporated** in Delaware in 1987. **Empl**—2,460.

 Samuel A. Dedio

Caesars World

NYSE Symbol CAW Options on ASE (Feb-May-Aug-Nov) In S&P MidCap 400

Price	Range	P-E Ratio	Dividend	Yield	S&P Ranking	Beta
Oct. 11'93	1993					
48¼	51¼–37⅝	14	None	None	B	1.80

Summary

This major gaming company has two casino/hotels in Nevada, one in Atlantic City, and four resort hotels in the Pocono Mountains. Also, CAW is looking to operate or participate in casinos in various other areas. In light of new casino/hotels being opened by others in Las Vegas, CAW's earnings in fiscal 1994 are expected to approximate those of fiscal 1993.

Current Outlook

Share earnings for the fiscal year ending July 31, 1994, are expected to approximate fiscal 1993's $3.40.

Payment of a cash dividend is not expected.

In fiscal 1994, CAW's operating profit is expected to decline modestly, as the impact of three large new casino/hotels in Las Vegas dilutes the presence of Caesars Palace there. However, CAW should continue to have formidable presence with high-end customers, and its overall Las Vegas business should be bolstered by a shopping complex which opened in May 1992 adjacent to Caesars Palace. Earnings improvement of close to 10% is projected from Atlantic City, and CAW's interest expense is expected to decline again. Future growth prospects for CAW include a potential management contract for a casino in the Bahamas and various new casino markets.

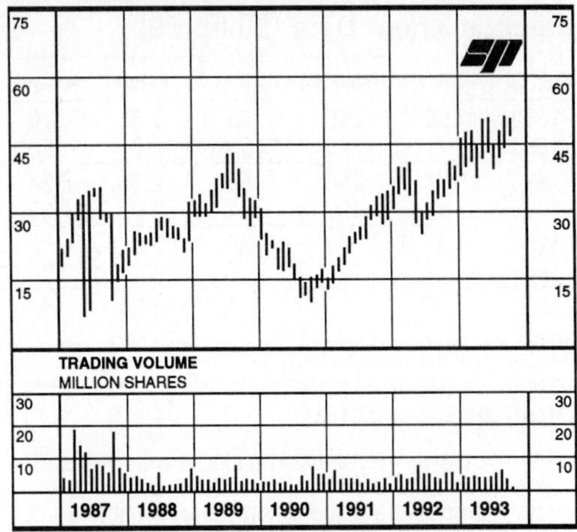

Net Revenues (Million $)

Quarter:	1992–93	1991–92	1990–91	1989–90
Oct.	232.6	233.1	235.6	225.7
Jan.	264.5	253.5	207.9	202.9
Apr.	224.4	197.9	220.2	217.9
Jul.	262.0	244.0	244.6	223.7
	983.5	928.5	908.3	870.2

Revenues for the fiscal year ended July 31, 1993 (preliminary) increased 5.4%, year to year. Net income was up 14%, to $3.40 a share from $3.01, excluding a $0.28 special charge in fiscal 1992.

Common Share Earnings ($)

Quarter:	1992–93	1991–92	1990–91	1989–90
Oct.	0.62	0.95	0.60	0.71
Jan.	1.05	0.96	0.17	0.06
Apr.	0.69	0.40	0.56	0.44
Jul.	1.04	0.71	0.77	0.31
	3.40	3.01	2.09	1.52

Important Developments

Oct. '93— CAW and Casino Magic Corp. intend to form a joint venture to develop a dockside riverboat casino and entertainment complex in St. Louis. Also, CAW and Hilton Hotels have jointly applied to operate a casino in Michigan City, Ind. Various approvals would be needed for such projects. Meanwhile, it appears that CAW will not be a participant in a large land-based casino project to be developed in New Orleans. A New Orleans casino riverboat that would be operated by CAW may open by the summer of 1994. Developer Christopher Hemmeter is prospectively involved in both that project and the land-based casino. Also, CAW has signed a letter of intent to manage a casino/hotel in The Bahamas; has agreed to fund and manage a proposed gambling facility on Indian land in Palm Springs, Cal.; and is part of a joint bid to develop a casino in Windsor, Ontario.

Next earnings report expected in mid-November.

Per Share Data ($)

Yr. End Jul. 31	1993	1992	1991	1990	1989	1988	1987	1986	1985	1984
Tangible Bk. Val.	**NA**	13.64	10.84	9.04	8.01	5.19	10.59	7.49	6.12	5.03
Cash Flow	**NA**	5.29	4.35	3.46	4.33	4.47	2.66	2.62	2.21	1.62
Earnings[1]	**3.40**	3.01	2.09	1.52	2.72	2.90	1.30	1.36	1.07	0.66
Dividends	**Nil**	Nil	Nil	Nil	Nil	Nil	Nil	Nil	Nil	Nil
Payout Ratio	**Nil**	Nil	Nil	Nil	Nil	Nil	Nil	Nil	Nil	Nil
Prices[2]—High	**51¼**	41¼	34¾	30⅞	43¼	32⅜	35¾	24	17⅜	13⅝
Low	**37⅝**	25	12⅞	10⅛	27	18⅜	10½	14¾	9⅛	8¼
P/E Ratio—	**15–11**	14–8	17–6	20–7	16–10	11–6	28–8	18–11	16–9	21–13

Data as orig. reptd. **1.** Bef. results of disc. opers. of -0.08 in 1983, and spec. items of -0.28 in 1992, -0.22 in 1987, -0.49 in 1983. **2.** Cal. yr.
NA-Not Available.

Income Data (Million $)

Year Ended Jul. 31	Revs.	Oper. Inc.	% Oper. Inc. of Revs.	Cap. Exp.	Depr.	Int. Exp.	Net Bef. Taxes	Eff. Tax Rate	[1]Net Inc.	% Net Inc. of Revs.	Cash Flow
1992	**928**	**215**	**23.2**	**40**	**55.2**	**43.6**	**117**	**38.0%**	**72.7**	**7.8**	**128**
1991	908	185	20.3	32	53.8	50.5	82	38.0%	49.6	5.5	103
1990	870	157	18.0	142	47.1	52.4	66	38.0%	36.8	4.2	84
1989	902	193	21.4	130	39.8	56.0	115	37.5%	66.9	7.4	107
1988	833	207	24.9	46	41.8	48.3	128	36.7%	77.0	9.2	119
1987	780	179	22.9	47	42.1	35.8	83	49.4%	40.4	5.2	83
1986	688	149	21.7	53	37.9	37.7	80	46.5%	41.0	6.0	79
1985	655	139	21.2	88	34.1	42.4	70	52.5%	31.8	4.9	66
1984	617	111	17.9	91	27.8	40.8	47	55.3%	18.8	3.2	47
1983	565	62	11.0	51	26.9	46.4	d8	NM	d8.6	NM	18

Balance Sheet Data (Million $)

Jul. 31	Cash	Curr. Assets	Curr. Liab.	Curr. Ratio	Total Assets	% Ret. on Assets	Long Term Debt	Common Equity	Total Cap.	% LT Debt of Cap.	% Ret. on Equity
1992	**52**	**185**	**183**	**1.0**	**902**	**8.1**	**271**	**385**	**686**	**39.5**	**20.7**
1991	41	157	187	0.8	888	5.6	325	313	671	48.4	17.3
1990	25	146	166	0.9	877	4.2	365	259	685	53.3	15.0
1989	164	267	167	1.6	901	7.7	415	244	712	58.3	32.0
1988	192	283	169	1.7	831	11.6	431	172	649	66.4	33.2
1987	86	162	149	1.1	712	5.0	92	417	551	16.6	11.0
1986	169	225	123	1.8	767	5.9	332	270	639	51.9	16.4
1985	46	103	130	0.8	619	5.1	237	226	488	48.5	15.1
1984	100	155	147	1.1	619	3.2	255	193	470	54.2	10.7
1983	24	96	150	0.6	497	NM	186	138	333	56.0	NM

Data as orig. reptd. **1.** Bef. results of disc. opers. in 1983, and extra. items in 1992, 1987, 1983. d-Deficit. NM-Not Meaningful.

Business Summary

This major gaming company operates two casino/hotels in Nevada and a casino/hotel in Atlantic City, N.J. Also, CAW is pursuing growth opportunities in a number of other gaming jurisdictions. CAW's non-casino interests include four resorts in Pennsylvania's Pocono Mountains. Business segment contributions in fiscal 1993:

	Revs.	Profits
Nevada casino/hotels	58%	67%
Caesars New Jersey	35%	38%
Pocono resorts..................	4%	6%
Other (incl. corp. exp).	2%	–11%

Caesars Palace in Las Vegas has about 118,000 sq. ft. of casino space, including a 40,000-sq.-ft. expansion completed in 1989. In fiscal 1990, CAW completed a refurbishment or total remodeling of virtually all of its rooms and suites there, of which there are now about 1,518. Caesars Palace includes a showroom, a theater, restaurants, bars, shops, meeting rooms, and athletic facilities. A new shopping complex built by a third party near Caesars Palace opened in May 1992. In Las Vegas, other industry participants will be opening three new large casino/hotels in 1993-94.

Caesars Tahoe has about 440 rooms and suites. The facility also includes a 40,000-sq.-ft. casino, a showroom, convention space, and recreation facilities.

Caesars Atlantic City had about a 10.3% share of Atlantic City's casino revenues in calendar 1992. It is one of 12 casino/hotels operating there. The Caesars facility includes about 637 rooms and suites, a 60,000-sq.-ft. casino, an 1,100-seat showroom, shops, and other recreational facilities. A casino expansion is expected to open in the fall of 1993.

CAW's four resort hotels in the Pocono Mountains are Cove Haven, Paradise Stream, Pocono Palace and Caesars Brookdale.

Dividend Data

No dividends have been paid since 1962. A "poison pill" stock purchase right was adopted in 1989.

Finances

In December 1990, CAW acquired full ownership of Caesars New Jersey (CJN), through a cash tender offer for the 2.18 million shares of CJN that it did not already own.

Capitalization

Long Term Debt: $254,060,000, incl. $10.9 million of capitalized leases (4/93).

Common Stock: 24,616,791 shs. ($0.10 par).
Institutions hold about 85%.
Shareholders of record: About 7,600.

Office—1801 Century Park East, Suite 2600, Los Angeles, CA 90067. **Tel**—(310) 552-2711. **Chrmn & CEO**—H. Gluck. **Pres**—J. T. Lanni. **SVP-Secy**—P. L. Ball. **SVP-Fin & Investor Contact**—Roger Lee. **Dirs**—P. L. Ball, I. Buchalter, T. Burman, W. E. Chaikin, P. Echeverria, H. Gluck, J. T. Lanni, R. Lee, S. Sevilla. **Transfer Agent & Registrar**—First Chicago Trust Co. of New York, NYC. **Incorporated** in Florida in 1958. **Empl**—9,673.

 Tom Graves, CFA

Calgon Carbon

NYSE Symbol CCC Options on Phila (Feb-May-Aug-Nov) In S&P MidCap 400

Price	Range	P-E Ratio	Dividend	Yield	S&P Ranking	Beta
Sep. 27'93	1993					
11⅛	18⅞–10½	20	0.16	1.4%	NR	1.18

Summary

This company, the world's largest manufacturer of activated carbon products, also provides related equipment and services that employ activated carbon technology. Activated carbons are used to purify products in the manufacturing process and to control air and water pollutants, and are also incorporated into other products. Earnings are expected to continue to decline in 1993, reflecting weak economies worldwide.

Current Outlook

Earnings for 1993 are projected to decline further, to $0.55 a share, from 1992's depressed $0.70. A partial recovery to $0.70 is seen for 1994.

Dividends should continue at $0.04 quarterly.

Sales are expected to decline about 10% in 1993, reflecting continuing weakness in economies in the U.S. and Europe, which has hurt all major markets served, and excess capacity in the carbon industry. Resulting reduced demand, primarily from industrial processors, has led to competitive pricing pressures, which will likely continue for the remainder of the year. Greater demand for water purification applications, especially in Europe, and a full-year contribution from the new Pearl River plant should partly offset weaker overall demand. Margins will be restricted by the lower prices, and the tax rate will rise. Long-term prospects appear favorable, aided by international expansion efforts and more-stringent clean water and air legislation.

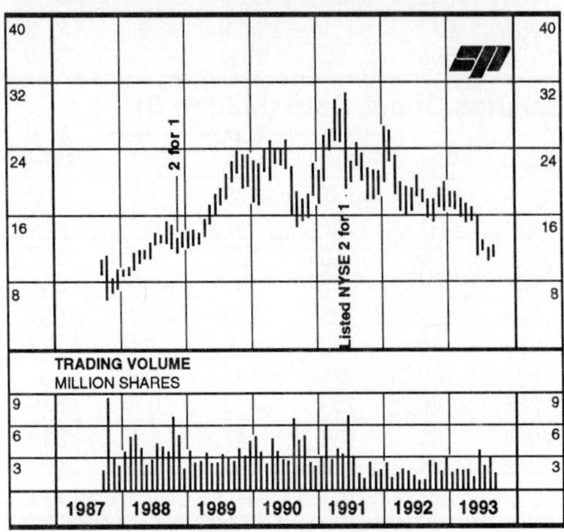

Net Sales (Million $)

Quarter:	1993	1992	1991	1990
Mar.	63.7	70.1	77.2	63.5
Jun.	72.7	79.4	77.5	74.7
Sep.	---	77.7	73.2	67.0
Dec.	---	71.1	80.5	79.7
	---	298.4	308.4	284.9

Net sales in the six months ended June 30, 1993, decreased 8.8%, year to year, as price and volume declines reflected the effects of the recession and excess capacity in the carbon industry. Margins narrowed, restricted by lower prices and a less favorable product mix; operating income dropped 21%. With higher depreciation charges, pretax income fell 32%. After taxes at 37.1%, versus 35.6%, income plunged 33%, to $0.27 a share, from $0.40 (before a charge of $0.26 from an accounting change).

Common Share Earnings ($)

Quarter:	1993	1992	1991	1990
Mar.	0.13	0.16	0.24	0.21
Jun.	0.14	0.24	0.23	0.27
Sep.	E0.14	0.19	0.23	0.22
Dec.	E0.14	0.11	0.24	0.28
	E0.55	0.70	0.94	0.97

Important Developments

Jul. '93— CCC said, in reporting lower sales and earnings, year to year, for the 1993 second quarter, that it did not foresee significant changes in the general economic climate that would markedly improve its operating results. The company added that it expects no changes in revenues in the near-term, other than greater shipments of activated carbon to potable water plants and declining seasonal demand for charcoal in Germany.

Next earnings report expected in late October.

Per Share Data ($)

Yr. End Dec. 31	1992	1991	1990	1989	1988	1987	1986
Tangible Bk. Val.[1]	**5.84**	5.67	4.92	3.99	3.01	2.27	1.31
Cash Flow	**1.10**	1.24	1.23	1.07	0.94	0.63	0.44
Earnings[2]	**0.70**	0.94	0.97	0.87	0.74	0.48	0.29
Dividends	**0.160**	0.160	0.150	0.110	0.053	0.025	Nil
Payout Ratio	**23%**	17%	15%	13%	7%	5%	Nil
Prices—High	**26¾**	30¾	25⅛	23¾	15⁵⁄₁₆	11⅛	NA
Low	**15¼**	17½	14⅝	12⅛	8¾	5½	NA
P/E Ratio—	**38–22**	33–19	26–15	27–14	21–12	23–11	NA

Data as orig. reptd. Adj. for stk. divs. of 100% Jun. 1991, 100% Nov. 1988. **1.** Incl. intangibles. **2.** Bef. spec. items of -0.26 in 1992, -0.03 in 1990, -0.02 in 1987. E-Estimated NA-Not Available.

Income Data (Million $)

Year Ended Dec. 31	Revs.	Oper. Inc.	% Oper. Inc. of Revs.	Cap. Exp.	Depr.	Int. Exp.	[1]Net Bef. Taxes	Eff. Tax Rate	[2]Net Inc.	% Net Inc. of Revs.	Cash Flow
1992	**298**	**68.0**	**22.8**	**24.0**	**16.1**	**1.35**	**44.0**	**34.9%**	**28.6**	**9.6**	**44.8**
1991	308	73.7	23.9	70.6	12.5	1.04	60.7	37.2%	38.1	12.4	50.6
1990	285	72.8	25.6	47.6	10.4	1.34	63.2	37.4%	39.6	13.9	49.9
1989	253	64.9	25.6	24.3	8.2	3.52	55.4	36.5%	35.2	13.9	43.4
1988	226	59.1	26.1	16.0	7.9	3.88	48.4	39.2%	29.5	13.0	37.4
1987	171	46.2	27.1	4.4	7.0	7.22	32.8	46.3%	17.6	10.3	24.2
1986	138	37.3	27.0	2.5	5.4	8.55	23.7	52.1%	[3]11.4	8.2	16.0

Balance Sheet Data (Million $)

Dec. 31	Cash	Curr. Assets	Curr. Liab.	Curr. Ratio	Total Assets	% Ret. on Assets	Long Term Debt	Common Equity	Total Cap.	% LT Debt of Cap.	% Ret. on Equity
1992	**8.2**	**120**	**45.1**	**2.7**	**335**	**8.5**	**6.8**	**239**	**280**	**2.4**	**12.2**
1991	8.2	124	46.5	2.7	336	12.3	27.7	231	279	9.9	17.7
1990	22.0	129	46.9	2.8	285	15.2	11.2	200	227	5.0	21.9
1989	44.2	129	38.6	3.3	234	16.3	17.7	162	188	9.4	24.8
1988	32.5	107	35.5	3.0	196	16.8	27.0	120	156	17.3	27.9
1987	20.1	75	30.5	2.5	153	8.8	22.5	90	123	18.3	24.2
1986	14.9	56	29.4	1.9	134	NA	58.7	28	101	57.9	NA

Data as orig. reptd. **1.** Incl. equity in earns. of nonconsol. subs **2.** Bef. spec. items. **3.** Refl. acctg. change. NA-Not Available.

Business Summary

Calgon Carbon is the world's largest manufacturer and supplier of granular activated carbon products. It also provides related adsorption equipment and services that utilize activated carbon technology. Manufacturing facilities are located in the U.S., Germany, Belgium and the U.K. Business segment contributions to sales in recent years were:

	1992	1991
Activated carbon	58%	55%
Services	24%	22%
Equipment	11%	16%
Charcoal/liquids	7%	7%

Sales to international customers, primarily in western Europe, accounted for 40% of sales in 1992 (38% in 1991) and 22% of operating income (26%).

CCC's activated carbons consist of a broad range of untreated, impregnated or acid-washed carbons, in either powder, granular or pellet form. The company also provides carbon reactivation services and designs, assembles and sells on-site purification, filtration and extraction systems and related services. Charcoal is sold to retail consumers in Germany for outdoor barbecue grilling. CCC's total annual activated carbon production capacity exceeds 200 million pounds, and approximately 90% of total production is granular, which can be reactivated and used over and over again by its customers.

Principal markets served include the environmental market (44% of sales in 1992); original equipment manufacturers (18%); food (12%); and chemical and pharmaceutical (9%). Products can be used to purify sweeteners, chemicals and pharmaceuticals; to decaffeinate coffee; to remove impurities from natural gas; and for gold recovery. Activated carbon can also be incorporated into products, such as water filters, cigarette filters, industrial and military respirators and evaporative emissions control canisters in automobiles. CCC's activated carbon, services and equipment are used by municipalities to purify drinking water and to control sewage odor and by other companies to control air pollution and wastewater discharges.

Dividend Data

Dividends have been paid since 1987.

Amt. of Divd. $	Date Decl.	Ex-divd. Date	Stock of Record	Payment Date
0.04	Oct. 14	Dec. 8	Dec. 14	Jan. 4'93
0.04	Feb. 12	Mar. 8	Mar. 12	Apr. 1'93
0.04	Apr. 20	Jun. 7	Jun. 11	Jun. 30'93
0.04	Jul. 13	Sep. 3	Sep. 10	Oct. 1'93

Finances

Capital expenditures in the first half of 1993 totaled $5.3 million, down from $16.9 million in the year-earlier period. CCC projected expenditures for all of 1993 at about $19 million.

Capitalization

Long Term Debt: $6,626,000 (6/93).

Class A Stock: 12,257,356 shs. ($0.01 par); 10 votes per sh.; conv. sh.-for-sh. into com. on 3/1/95; controlled by T.A. McConomy.

Common Stock: 28,781,204 shs. ($0.01 par).
Institutions hold 63%.
Shareholders of record: 1,503.

Office—400 Calgon Carbon Drive, Pittsburgh, PA 15205. **Tel**—(412) 787-6700. **Pres & CEO**—T. A. McConomy. **SVP-Fin & CFO**—C. P. Shannon. **VP & Secy**—J. A. Fischette. **Investor Contact**—Gail A. Gerono (412-787-6795). **Dirs**—C. Bailey, R. W. Cruickshank, W. J. Gilliam, A. L. Goeschel, T. A. McConomy, N. H. Prater, R. R. Tisch, H. H. Weil, R. H. Zanitsch. **Transfer Agent**—First Chicago Trust Co. of New York, NYC. **Incorporated** in Delaware in 1967. **Empl**—1,480.

 Michael V. Pizzi

CalMat Co.

NYSE Symbol CZM In S&P MidCap 400

Price	Range	P–E Ratio	Dividend	Yield	S&P Ranking	Beta
Aug. 6'93	1993					
18¼	22⅝–16½	NM	0.40	2.2%	B	1.16

Summary

CalMat is a major producer of aggregates, asphalt and ready-mixed concrete in California and neighboring states. The Dan Murphy Foundation holds about 18% of the outstanding shares. Earnings in recent years have been hurt by poor construction markets and economic weakness in California. However, operations improved in the second quarter of 1993, and long-term prospects are enhanced by an anticipated increase in infrastructure spending in the U.S.

Current Outlook

Earnings for 1993 are estimated at $0.45 a share, versus the $0.45 loss recorded for 1992. In 1994, earnings are projected at $0.90 a share.

Dividends, which were reduced 38% to $0.10 quarterly from $0.16 with the April 1993 payment, are expected to continue at the current level.

Revenues in the second half of 1993 should recover somewhat from recent depressed levels. Margins are expected to benefit from ongoing cost reduction efforts. Earnings in future years should receive a boost from the leaner cost structure, increased infrastructure spending, and a strengthening of demand in construction markets. However, the anticipated recovery in operations is likely to prove uneven and fitful, given uncertain economic conditions in CZM's California market.

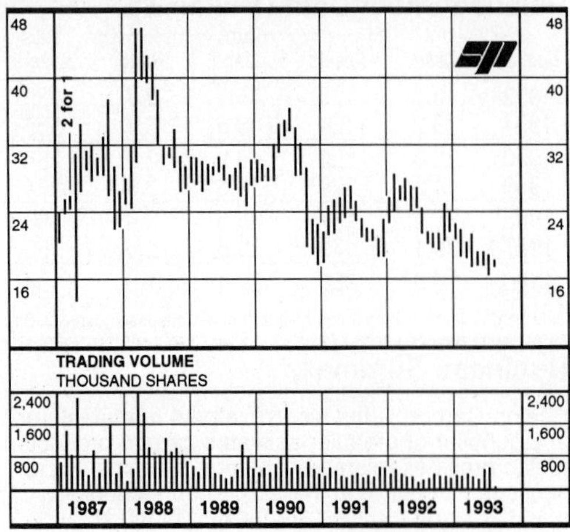

Total Revenues (Million $)

Quarter:	1994	1993	1992	1991
Mar.	---	62.0	65.6	76.8
Jun.	---	96.4	95.5	96.8
Sep.	---	---	101.6	109.9
Dec.	---	---	81.8	89.3
	---	---	344.5	372.8

Revenues for the six months ended June 30, 1993, declined 3.7%, year to year (as restated), reflecting sluggish construction activity in California and unfavorable weather. Lower unit production costs for aggregates and ready-mixed concrete, increased gains on property sales and higher profits from rental and landfill operations more than offset increased production costs in the asphalt division, and net income rose 5.2%. Share earnings were $0.09 in each interim. Results exclude a credit of $0.04 a share and a charge of $0.26 in the respective periods related to accounting changes.

Common Share Earnings ($)

Quarter:	1994	1993	1992	1991
Mar.	E0.10	d0.15	d0.10	0.08
Jun.	E0.25	0.24	0.19	0.24
Sep.	E0.35	E0.20	d0.20	0.39
Dec.	E0.20	E0.16	d0.35	0.10
	E0.90	E0.45	d0.45	0.81

Important Developments

Jul. '93— CZM said trends appear to be improving in Arizona and New Mexico in the residential and heavy construction sectors. The company added that second quarter earnings would have amounted to $0.20 a share, versus $0.13 in the same period a year earlier, if real estate gains and gains on assets held for sale were excluded in both periods.

Next earnings report expected in late October.

Per Share Data ($)

Yr. End Dec. 31	1992	1991	1990	1989	1988	1987	[1]1986	1985	1984	1983
Tangible Bk. Val.	**12.70**	14.50	14.41	15.81	14.10	13.20	11.24	11.15	10.14	9.78
Cash Flow	**0.75**	1.93	2.44	3.86	2.98	3.65	2.50	2.16	1.32	0.98
Earnings[2]	**d0.45**	0.81	1.08	2.52	1.82	2.53	1.44	1.34	0.45	0.25
Dividends	**0.64**	0.64	0.74	0.56	0.48	0.40	0.34	0.30	0.15	NA
Payout Ratio	**NM**	79%	57%	22%	26%	16%	24%	22%	33%	NA
Prices—High	**28⅝**	27⅛	36⅜	30⅝	46⅛	37½	21½	17¼	12½	NA
Low	**19½**	18	17¾	24¾	24½	20⅜	13⅜	9⅝	9⅛	NA
P/E Ratio—	**NM**	33–22	34–16	12–10	25–13	15–8	15–9	13–7	28–20	NA

Data as orig. reptd.; data prior to 1984 pro-forma (comb. opers. of California Portland Cement and Conrock) as reptd. in proxy dated 5-25-84. Adj. for stk. div(s). of 100% Apr. 1987. **1.** Reflects merger and acquisition and accounting change. **2.** Bef. results of disc. opers. of +1.79 in 1990 and spec. item(s) of -0.26 in 1992. d-Deficit. E-Estimated NM-Not Meaningful. NA-Not Available.

Income Data (Million $)

Year Ended Dec. 31	Revs.	Oper. Inc.	% Oper. Inc. of Revs.	Cap. Exp.	Depr.	Int. Exp.	Net Bef. Taxes	Eff. Tax Rate	[5]Net Inc.	% Net Inc. of Revs.	Cash Flow
1992	**342**	**38**	**11.2**	**32.1**	**27.9**	**3.49**	**d18**	**NM**	**[6]d10.5**	**NM**	**17**
1991	369	61	16.6	32.4	26.2	3.67	31	40.0%	18.9	5.1	45
[1]1990	422	77	18.4	76.6	38.3	6.25	51	39.8%	30.4	7.2	69
1989	682	134	19.6	46.8	43.3	8.61	126	37.9%	78.1	11.5	119
1988	655	129	19.7	75.5	36.1	7.26	[4]90	37.5%	56.4	8.6	93
1987	602	105	17.4	59.7	34.6	4.68	[4]121	35.5%	78.1	13.0	113
[2]1986	613	123	20.1	58.9	32.2	4.27	[4]91	33.7%	44.1	7.2	76
1985	415	67	16.3	53.7	24.9	6.05	[4]63	35.5%	40.5	9.8	65
1984	327	44	13.4	57.7	25.9	8.99	[4]17	22.9%	13.5	4.1	39
1983	266	[3]9	[3]3.2	NA	NA	9.30	11	37.3%	7.1	2.7	16

Balance Sheet Data (Million $)

		Curr.									
Dec. 31	Cash	Assets	Liab.	Ratio	Total Assets	% Ret. on Assets	Long Term Debt	Common Equity	Total Cap.	% LT Debt of Cap.	% Ret. on Equity
1992	**4.1**	**85**	**51.6**	**1.6**	**585**	**NM**	**116.0**	**351**	**522**	**22.2**	**NM**
1991	12.1	92	51.0	1.8	540	3.5	37.7	384	421	9.0	4.9
1990	3.3	95	59.7	1.6	548	5.2	40.0	387	427	9.4	7.7
1989	13.3	181	87.5	2.1	809	10.0	82.7	527	609	13.6	15.6
1988	4.7	156	80.0	2.0	765	7.9	95.4	482	682	14.0	12.2
1987	4.9	150	66.8	2.2	663	11.9	54.8	438	584	9.4	19.3
1986	10.5	169	90.3	1.9	647	7.5	61.7	371	526	11.7	12.4
1985	44.0	144	55.9	2.6	520	8.1	38.6	336	446	8.7	12.6
1984	13.3	103	49.2	2.1	481	3.9	76.7	304	432	17.8	5.7
1983	19.8	114	51.0	2.2	462	NA	68.7	292	411	16.7	NA

Data as orig. reptd.; data prior to 1984 pro-forma (comb. opers. of California Portland Cement and Conrock) as reptd. in proxy dated 5-25-84. **1.** Excludes discontinued operations. **2.** Reflects merger or acquisition and accounting change. **3.** Aft. depr. not separately reported. **4.** Incl. equity in earnings of nonconsol. subs. **5.** Bef. results of disc. opers. and spec. item(s). **6.** Reflects acctg. change. d-Deficit. NM-Not Meaningful. NA-Not Available.

Business Summary

CalMat is a major producer and supplier to the construction industry of aggregates, asphalt and ready-mixed concrete in California, Arizona and New Mexico. The company also has real estate operations. Segment contributions in 1992:

	Revs.	Profits
Asphalt	40%	58%
Concrete & aggregates	56%	7%
Properties	4%	35%

The asphalt division is the third largest supplier of hot mix asphalt to the construction industry nationwide, and the largest commercial supplier west of the Mississippi. CZM locates its plants near aggregates sites, as well as near major metropolitan regions. At December 31, 1992, it was operating 36 asphalt plants in metropolitan Los Angeles and San Diego, the San Francisco Bay and San Joaquin Valley areas of California, and in Phoenix and Tucson, Arizona, and Albuquerque, New Mexico. CZM also manufactures a specialty coating material called Guardtop, which is used for sealing asphalt paving to prevent water damage and erosion, and is the exclusive distributor in Los Angeles of a polypropylene reinforcing fabric used in resurfacing pavements.

The concrete and aggregates division operates aggregates processing plants at 33 locations in the major markets of California and in Phoenix, Tucson and Albuquerque. Ready-mixed concrete batch plants are operated at 35 locations in these markets except for the Los Angeles and San Francisco Bay areas. CZM produces and sells construction aggregates and supplies ready-mixed concrete for use in commercial and residential construction, public construction projects and projects to build and repair roads and highways.

The properties division is involved in the management of CZM's real estate portfolio, with activity in permitting, acquisitions, sales and leasing.

Dividend Data

A "poison pill" stock purchase right was adopted in 1987.

Amt of Divd. $	Date Decl.	Ex-divd. Date	Stock of Record	Payment Date
0.16	Aug. 26	Sep. 1	Sep. 8	Oct. 2'92
0.16	Nov. 24	Dec. 3	Dec. 9	Jan. 5'93
0.10	Feb. 17	Mar. 3	Mar. 9	Apr. 2'93
0.10	May 25	Jun. 2	Jun. 8	Jul. 2'93

Capitalization

Long Term Debt: $124,857,000 (3/93).

Common Stock: 23,109,294 shs. ($1 par).
The Dan Murphy Foundation owns 18%; institutions hold approximately 42%.
Shareholders of record: 1,463.

Office—3200 San Fernando Rd., Los Angeles, CA 90065. **Tel**—(213) 258-2777. **Chrmn & Pres**—A. F. Gerstell. **EVP-CFO & Investor Contact**—Ronald C. Hadfield. **VP-Secy**—P. Stanford. **Dirs**—J. C. Argue, H. M. Conger, R. S. Dezember, A. F. Gerstell, B. A. Getz, R. A. Grant Jr., G. R. Heyler, W. T. Huston, W. Jenkins, O. T. Lawler, T. L. Lee, T. M. Linden, S. T. Peeler. **Transfer Agent & Registrar**—First Chicago Trust Co. of N.Y., NYC. **Incorporated** in Delaware in 1984. **Empl**—1,668.

Cardinal Distribution

NASDAQ Symbol CDIC (Incl. in Nat'l Market) In S&P MidCap 400

Price	Range	P-E Ratio	Dividend	Yield	S&P Ranking	Beta
Aug. 27'93	1993					
33½	35–24½	18	0.10	0.3%	A–	1.29

Summary

Cardinal is a wholesale distributor of pharmaceuticals, medical/surgical supplies and related health products, serving customers primarily in the eastern U.S. Revenues and earnings have been in a long uptrend, reflecting both internal growth and acquisitions. In May 1993, the company acquired a Savannah, Ga.-based wholesale drug distributor, strengthening its presence in the Southeast.

Business Summary

Cardinal Distribution, Inc. is a full-service wholesaler distributing a broad line of pharmaceuticals, surgical and hospital supplies, health and beauty care products, and other items typically sold by retail drug stores, hospitals and other healthcare providers. Operations were expanded through the acquisitions of James W. Daly, Inc. in 1986, Marmac Distributors, Inc. in 1988, Ohio Valley-Clarksburg, Inc. in 1990, Chapman Drug Co. in 1991, and Solomons Co. in 1993. In 1988, the company sold its food distribution operations in order to concentrate on the pharmaceutical and medical/surgical supplies distribution business.

Cardinal distributes products from its 12 distribution centers and separate specialty facilities to drug stores, hospitals, alternate care centers, and the pharmacy departments of supermarkets and mass merchandisers located primarily in the eastern U.S. The company purchases products in quantities which enable it to obtain favorable prices and sells them at prices reflecting these savings. An important component of the company's distribution activites is the broad range of support services it offers to its customers, which are designed to assist the customers in maintaining and improving their market positions. Independent drug stores and chains accounted for about 66% of 1992-3 sales volume, with hospitals accounting for 34%.

Cardinal provides a wide range of custom-tailored support services designed to assist its customers, such as order entry and confirmation, customer inventory control, automatic monitoring and implementation of pricing strategies and financial reporting systems and controls. A comprehensive in-pharmacy computer system is designed to provide pharmacists with prescription pricing information, patient profiles, accounts receivable and third-party billing services, financial management, and other data.

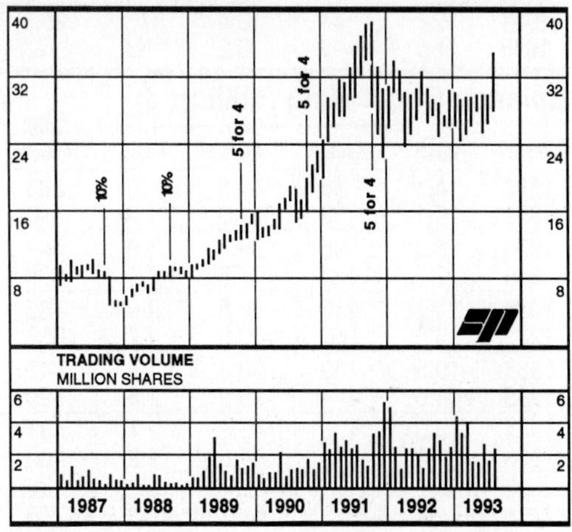

The company's five largest suppliers accounted for about 26% of sales in 1992-3. The loss of certain suppliers could adversely affect Cardinal's business, since many suppliers are its sole source of various pharmaceutical and medical/surgical products.

Important Developments

May '93— Cardinal acquired Solomons Co., a Savannah, Ga.-based wholesale drug distributor, in exchange for approximately 849,000 common shares. The company said the acquisition, which adds about $180 million of annual revenues, will complement its existing market presence in the Southeast, particularly in Georgia, South Carolina and Florida.

Next earnings report expected in late October.

Per Share Data ($)

Yr. End Mar. 31	1993	2 1992	2 1991	1990	1989	2 1988	2 1987	1986	2 1985	1984
Tangible Bk. Val.	1 **13.38**	10.40	9.20	6.79	5.04	3.81	3.75	3.73	3.24	2.27
Cash Flow	**2.15**	1.64	1.32	1.29	1.29	0.80	1.08	0.95	0.64	0.58
Earnings[3]	**1.77**	1.34	1.05	0.83	0.78	0.45	0.52	0.58	0.39	0.35
Dividends	**0.090**	0.076	0.061	0.049	0.040	0.037	0.034	0.032	0.022	0.067
Payout Ratio	**5%**	6%	7%	6%	5%	8%	7%	6%	6%	2%
Calendar Years	**1992**	1991	1990	1989	1988	1987	1986	1985	1984	1983
Prices—High	**34**	38¾	23¼	15¾	9⅜	10¼	10¾	7½	6½	6¾
Low	**23¾**	20	12⅝	8¼	4⅞	4⅝	6¼	4⅝	4¼	4⅜
P/E Ratio—	**20–14**	29–15	22–12	19–10	12–6	23–10	21–12	13–8	17–11	19–12

Data as orig. reptd. Adj. for stk. divs. of 25% Oct. 1991, 25% Oct. 1990, 25% Oct. 1989, 10% Sep. 1988, 10% Sep. 1987, 10% Feb. 1986, 10% Mar. 1985. **1.** Includes intangibles. **2.** Refl. merger or acq. **3.** Bef. results of disc. ops. of +0.43 in 1989, +0.17 in 1988.

Income Data (Million $)

Year Ended Mar. 31	Revs.	Oper. Inc.	% Oper. Inc. of Revs.	Cap. Exp.	Depr.	Int. Exp.	Net Bef. Taxes	Eff. Tax Rate	Net Inc.	% Net Inc. of Revs.	Cash Flow
1993	**1,967**	**66.3**	**3.4**	**5.3**	**7.20**	**13.4**	**54.1**	**37.8%**	**33.6**	**1.7**	**40.8**
[1]1992	1,648	53.0	3.2	8.9	5.65	11.8	41.0	38.5%	25.2	1.5	30.8
[1]1991	1,184	39.3	3.3	10.9	4.61	10.6	28.5	39.0%	17.4	1.5	22.0
1990	874	27.9	3.2	3.8	3.08	5.9	20.9	39.0%	12.8	1.5	15.9
[2]1989	700	21.1	3.0	8.1	2.76	6.6	13.6	37.5%	8.5	1.2	11.3
[1,2]1988	525	15.0	2.9	1.8	1.96	6.0	[4]8.2	41.6%	4.8	0.9	6.7
[1]1987	652	15.9	2.4	9.4	3.65	5.7	[4]9.8	57.3%	[3]5.4	0.8	9.1
1986	429	10.4	2.4	5.9	1.99	3.3	[4]9.9	39.6%	6.0	1.4	8.0
[1]1985	320	7.2	2.3	2.0	1.17	0.7	[4]6.2	40.7%	3.7	1.1	4.9
1984	243	4.8	2.0	2.1	0.84	0.5	[4]4.3	39.9%	2.6	1.1	3.4

Balance Sheet Data (Million $)

Mar. 31	Cash	Curr. Assets	Curr. Liab.	Curr. Ratio	Total Assets	% Ret. on Assets	Long Term Debt	Common Equity	Total Cap.	% LT Debt of Cap.	% Ret. on Equity
1993	**104.0**	**579**	**214**	**2.7**	**656**	**5.4**	**185**	**256**	**442**	**41.9**	**14.1**
1992	4.7	503	168	3.0	577	4.9	188	219	408	46.1	12.2
1991	78.3	385	163	2.4	446	4.8	90	193	283	31.6	10.4
1990	11.3	213	121	1.8	251	4.2	5	125	130	3.6	11.2
1989	9.3	199	115	1.7	233	4.0	50	68	118	42.3	13.9
1988	4.0	162	86	1.9	190	2.6	50	54	105	48.1	9.4
1987	10.5	140	72	1.9	177	3.5	55	47	105	52.9	12.3
1986	46.5	116	46	2.5	138	5.6	46	41	91	50.6	15.6
1985	5.9	64	39	1.7	79	5.7	4	36	40	9.3	12.3
1984	7.6	31	17	1.8	39	6.5	3	19	22	13.3	18.2

Data as orig. reptd. **1.** Refl. merger or acq. **2.** Excl. disc. ops. **3.** Refl. acctg. change. **4.** Incl. equity in earns. of nonconsol. subs.

Net Sales (Million $)

Quarter:	1993–94	1992–93	1991–92	1990–91
Jun.	550	474	345	242
Sep.		482	366	285
Dec.		512	453	316
Mar.		499	483	341
		1,967	1,648	1,184

Net sales for the three months ended June 30, 1993, rose 16%, year to year, reflecting internal growth and the May 1993 Solomons acquisition. Gross margins narrowed on moderating drug price inflation and competitive market conditions; but aided by cost containment measures and lower interest expense, pretax income advanced 22%. After taxes at 37.0%, versus 39.0%, net income was up 27%, to $7,771,000 ($0.41 a share; $0.38 fully diluted), from $6,145,000 ($0.33; $0.31). Results in the 1992-93 period exclude a charge of $10,000,000 ($0.53; $0.51) for the cumulative effect of an accounting change.

Common Share Earnings ($)

Quarter:	1993–94	1992–93	1991–92	1990–91
Jun.	0.41	0.33	0.26	0.20
Sep.		0.47	0.28	0.22
Dec.		0.42	0.35	0.27
Mar.		0.55	0.45	0.35
		1.77	1.34	1.05

Finances

In June 1993, the company called for redemption all of its $75 million outstanding of 7¼% convertible subordinated debentures, due 2015. In addition to a redemption for cash, holders of the debentures had the right to convert them into 45.68 Cardinal common shares for each $1,000 principal amount through July 2, 1993, the redemption date.

In May 1993, Cardinal registered with the SEC a shelf offering under which it may offer publicly, from time to time, an aggregate of up to $150 million of debt securities.

Dividend Data

Cash has been paid each year since 1983.

Amt. of Divd. $	Date Decl.	Ex-divd. Date	Stock of Record	Payment Date
0.02½	Nov. 11	Dec. 24	Jan. 1	Jan. 15'93
0.02½	Feb. 25	Mar. 26	Apr. 1	Apr. 15'93
0.02½	May 19	Jun. 25	Jul. 1	Jul. 15'93
0.02½	Aug. 11	Sep. 27	Oct. 1	Oct. 15'93

Capitalization

Long Term Debt: $184,441,000 (6/92).

Common Stock: 19,381,370 shs. (no par).
Officers & directors own about 15%.
Institutions hold some 65%.
Shareholders: About 1,160 of record (6/93).

Office—655 Metro Place S., Suite 925, Dublin, OH 43017. **Tel**—(614) 761-8700. **Chrmn & CEO**—R. D. Walter. **Pres & COO**—J. C. Kane. **Sr VP, CFO & Investor Contact**—David Bearman. **Secy**—M. E. Moritz. **Dirs**—R. L. Gerbig, J. F. Havens, J. L. Heskett, J. C. Kane, G. R. Manser, J. B. McCoy, M. E. Moritz, J. E. Robertson, L. J. Van Fossen, R. D. Walter. **Transfer Agent**—Bank One, Indianapolis. **Incorporated** in Ohio in 1971 (reincorporated in 1982). **Empl**—1,600.

 Adam J. Penn

Carlisle Companies

NYSE Symbol CSL In S&P MidCap 400

Price	Range	P–E Ratio	Dividend	Yield	S&P Ranking	Beta
Aug. 6'93	1993					
30½	31¾–23¹⁄₁₆	18	0.72	2.4%	B	0.92

Summary

Carlisle is a diversified manufacturer of rubber, plastics and friction materials for construction, transportation and general industry markets. Important product lines include automotive brake products, rubber roofing systems, and food service plastic products. CSL recently effected a 2-for-1 stock split and the dividend was increased 5.9% with the September 1, 1993 payment.

Current Outlook

Earnings for 1993 may increase to $1.75 a share from 1992's $1.58. A further rise to $2.00 a share is possible in 1994.

The quarterly dividend was raised 5.9% to $0.18 from $0.17 (adjusted). A 2-for-1 stock split was distributed June 1, 1993.

Sales should advance in 1993 as the recovery in the U.S. economy increases demand for friction materials and general industry products. Construction materials will remain dependent on repair and replacement demand, as the nonresidential construction market is expected to remain depressed. Margins should widen on improved manufacturing efficiencies following the integration of recent acquisitions.

Net Sales (Million $)

Quarter:	1993	1992	1991	1990
Mar.	138.4	132.6	115.2	150.7
Jun.	160.8	142.2	127.3	161.1
Sep.	---	134.0	133.2	157.7
Dec.	---	119.3	125.1	151.6
	---	528.1	500.8	621.1

Sales in the half ended June 30, 1993, were up 8.9%, year to year, on a 16% rise in general industry sales and a 14% increase in construction materials. Aided by sharply higher earnings in the general industry segment, pretax income rose 14%. After taxes at 39.5%, against 39.0%, share earnings were $0.87 a share, up from $0.77 (before a $0.03 special credit in 1992), as adjusted.

Common Share Earnings ($)

Quarter:	1993	1992	1991	1990
Mar.	0.39	0.35	0.20	0.26
Jun.	0.48	0.43	0.30	0.41
Sep.	E0.47	0.43	d0.39	0.40
Dec.	E0.41	0.38	0.32	0.37
	E1.75	1.58	0.43	1.43

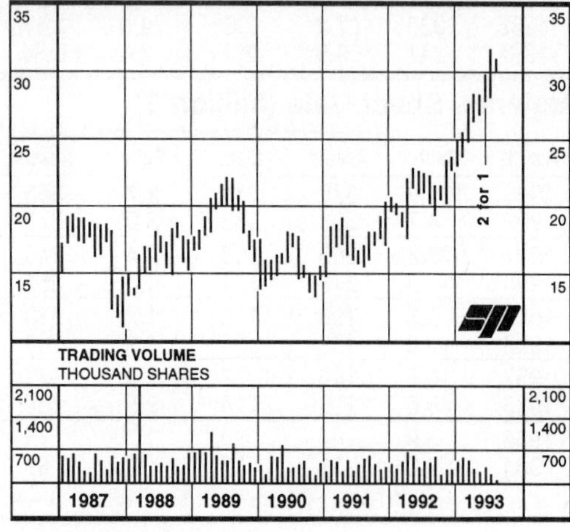

Important Developments

Jul. '93— As of June 30, the backlog of orders totaled $89.1 million, up 39% from $64 million a year earlier. The increase reflected market share gains and increased orders for specialty tire and wheels products and the impact of two recent acquisitions. CSL said that the outlook for the remainder of 1993 was favorable despite the persistent overall economic sluggishness. Some improvement in roofing sales was predicted due to indications of a recent pickup in demand. Stronger transportation sales were also likely in the absence of labor unrest in the auto industry, which was negotiating new union contracts during the summer months. CSL expected to benefit from internal cost control efforts and improvement in roofing, aided by integration of acquisitions.

Next earnings report expected in late October.

Per Share Data ($)

Yr. End Dec. 31	1992	1991	1990	1989	1988	1987	1986	1985	1984	1983
Tangible Bk. Val.	[1]**13.36**	[1]12.46	[1]13.65	[1]12.93	10.85	9.95	9.32	10.14	[1]9.93	[1]8.82
Cash Flow	**2.70**	1.58	2.62	2.77	2.28	2.39	2.09	2.33	2.64	1.98
Earnings[2]	**1.58**	0.43	1.43	1.67	1.08	1.13	1.08	1.31	1.76	1.23
Dividends	**0.660**	0.630	0.610	0.590	0.570	0.555	0.545	0.525	0.495	0.470
Payout Ratio	**42%**	147%	41%	35%	53%	48%	46%	40%	28%	38%
Prices—High	**23¾**	20⅜	18⅛	22³⁄₁₆	18¹³⁄₁₆	19⁷⁄₁₆	19¹¹⁄₁₆	20⅛	18¼	19¾
Low	**17⅝**	14¹³⁄₁₆	13⁵⁄₁₆	15¹⁵⁄₁₆	13⅜	11	14¼	13⅝	12¹⁄₁₆	11⁷⁄₁₆
P/E Ratio—	**15–11**	47–34	13–9	13–10	17–12	17–10	18–13	15–10	10–7	16–9

Data as orig. reptd. Adj. for stk. div(s). of 100% Jun. 1993. **1.** Incl. intangibles. **2.** Bef. results of disc. opers. of +0.03 in 1992, -0.98 in 1991. d-Deficit. E-Estimated

Income Data (Million $)

Year Ended Dec. 31	Revs.	Oper. Inc.	% Oper. Inc. of Revs.	Cap. Exp.	Depr.	Int. Exp.	Net Bef. Taxes	Eff. Tax Rate	[3]Net Inc.	% Net Inc. of Revs.	Cash Flow
[1]1992	**528**	**58.4**	**11.1**	**19.9**	**17.2**	**5.17**	**39.7**	**39.0%**	**24.2**	**4.6**	**41.4**
[1]1991	501	50.9	10.2	19.7	17.5	4.38	10.6	37.9%	6.6	1.3	24.1
1990	621	56.4	9.1	21.0	18.9	3.32	36.7	38.0%	22.7	3.7	41.6
1989	554	48.7	8.8	19.6	17.7	2.43	43.5	38.0%	27.0	4.9	44.7
1988	567	56.7	10.0	15.6	[2]19.3	3.69	28.6	39.2%	17.4	3.1	36.7
1987	543	55.1	10.1	21.3	21.0	4.27	31.9	41.0%	18.8	3.5	39.8
1986	466	53.7	11.5	17.5	18.4	4.25	34.6	43.2%	[2]19.7	4.2	38.1
1985	482	72.9	15.1	16.9	18.8	5.06	46.8	48.4%	24.1	5.0	42.9
1984	527	81.4	15.4	18.5	16.4	5.20	61.4	47.1%	32.5	6.2	49.0
1983	412	58.0	14.1	17.6	13.8	4.47	41.6	45.5%	22.7	5.5	36.5

Balance Sheet Data (Million $)

Dec. 31	Cash	Curr. Assets	Curr. Liab.	Curr. Ratio	Total Assets	% Ret. on Assets	Long Term Debt	Common Equity	Total Cap.	% LT Debt of Cap.	% Ret. on Equity
1992	**90.6**	**237**	**75.1**	**3.2**	**384**	**6.5**	**69.1**	**204**	**273**	**25.3**	**12.3**
1991	14.4	197	82.1	2.4	356	1.8	48.6	190	239	20.4	3.3
1990	17.6	213	92.0	2.3	374	6.6	44.5	207	252	17.7	11.2
1989	24.1	203	86.7	2.3	338	8.1	17.4	209	226	7.7	13.5
1988	32.3	200	83.4	2.4	325	5.5	21.7	191	213	10.2	9.3
1987	16.5	165	69.3	2.4	309	6.0	28.1	186	214	13.1	10.4
1986	21.3	173	79.1	2.2	322	6.5	36.6	181	218	16.8	10.9
1985	49.5	183	50.1	3.7	313	8.1	42.8	197	240	17.8	12.7
1984	16.4	162	52.2	3.1	287	11.9	45.3	183	232	19.5	18.8
1983	27.4	151	46.4	3.2	259	9.3	46.3	162	210	22.1	14.6

Data as orig. reptd. **1.** Excl. disc. opers. **2.** Reflects accounting change. **3.** Bef. results of disc. opers.

Business Summary

Carlisle Companies (formerly Carlisle Corp.) derived its sales and profits from continuing operations from the following markets in 1992:

	Sales	Profits
Construction materials	37.6%	49.4%
Transportation products	32.7%	24.2%
General industry	29.6%	26.4%

Construction materials includes Carlisle SynTec Systems, which makes elastomeric membranes (EPDM), adhesives and related items for roofing systems and water barrier applications. It is the largest U.S. producer in the single-ply roofing market. The business was expanded in early 1993 with the acquisition of Goodyear Tire & Rubbber's roofing business. Re-roofing demand represents about two-thirds of the market for nonresidential roofing materials. CSL has a joint venture to produce EPDM roofing in Russia. Other products include outdoor recreational tiles and insulated cable products.

Transportation products include brake linings for heavy-duty trucks, trailers and off-road vehicles; dry disc brakes and actuation systems for construction equipment; custom rubber and plastic components for use in passenger cars, appliances and other purposes; specialty industrial friction products, and insulated wire products.

General industry includes molded plastic foodservice products and melamine dinnerware; small pneumatic tires and stamped and roll-formed wheels used by most major lawn and garden equipment manufacturers; and insulated wire and cable products.

In 1991, CSL discontinued most of its data communications/electronics products operations. By June 30, 1992, CSL had sold all of the discontinued operations comprised of the digital controls operation, the Carlisle Memory Services division, and the half- and quarter-inch magnetic computer tape cartridge operations.

Dividend Data

Dividends have been paid since 1950.

Amt of Divd. $	Date Decl.	Ex-divd. Date	Stock of Record	Payment Date
0.34	Nov. 4	Nov. 10	Nov. 17	Dec. 1'92
0.34	Feb. 10	Feb. 16	Feb. 22	Mar. 1'93
0.34	Apr. 28	May 5	May 11	Jun. 1'93
2-for-1	Apr. 20	Jun. 2	May 11	Jun. 1'93
0.18	Aug. 4	Aug. 12	Aug. 18	Sep. 1'93

Capitalization

Long Term Debt: $57,048,000 (6/93).

Common Stock: 15,314,564 shs. ($1 par).
Officers and directors control about 15%.
Institutions hold about 61%.
Shareholders of record: 2,557.

Office—101 South Salina Street, Suite 800, Syracuse, NY 13202. **Tel**—(315) 474-2500. **Chrmn**—E. D. Kenna. **Pres & CEO**—S. P. Munn. **Secy**—S. C. Selbach. **EVP-CFO & Investor Contact**—Dennis J. Hall. **Dirs**— M. O. Bryant, D. G. Calder, P. J. Choquette Jr., E. D. Kenna, S. P. Munn, G. L. Ohrstrom, E. R. Scocimara, D. G. Thomas, E. N. White Jr. **Transfer Agent & Registrar**—Harris Trust Co., NYC. **Incorporated** in Delaware in 1917. **Empl**—4,607.

 Joshua M. Harari, CFA

Carpenter Technology

NYSE Symbol CRS In S&P MidCap 400

Price	Range	P–E Ratio	Dividend	Yield	S&P Ranking	Beta
Aug. 26'93	1993					
51	56⅜–47⅜	16	2.40	4.7%	B	0.67

Summary

Carpenter Technology produces stainless and tool steels, high temperature and electronic alloys, and other special purpose metals. Major markets include the electronics and electrical equipment, transportation, general industrial machinery, aerospace, fabricated metal products, and power generation industries. Earnings rose in fiscal 1993, reflecting higher sales, the absence of restructuring charges, and $1.67 a share in LIFO credits. Sales and earnings should rise again in fiscal 1994.

Current Outlook

Earnings for the fiscal year ending June 30, 1994, are projected at $3.50 a share, up from fiscal 1993's earnings of $3.11.

Dividends should remain at $0.60 quarterly.

Sales are expected to advance in fiscal 1994, reflecting growing demand from the automotive market, a recovery in demand from aerospace and energy markets, and a lower level of imports. Greater volume, firmer pricing, an improved product mix, stable raw materials costs, and increased utilization should aid margins. With level interest charges and a flat tax rate, fiscal 1994 earnings should grow.

Net Sales (Million $)

Quarter:	1992–93	1991–92	1990–91	1989–90
Sep.	139.4	126.5	125.4	133.6
Dec.	123.0	134.1	140.4	139.4
Mar.	155.4	162.8	146.8	157.0
Jun.	158.5	146.7	149.9	154.3
	576.3	570.2	562.5	584.4

Sales for the fiscal year ended June 30, 1993 (preliminary) rose 1.1% from those of fiscal 1992 as weak pricing offset a 6.0% increase in unit volume shipments. Aided by realization of LIFO credits, margins widened, and pretax income advanced 87%. After taxes at 38.1%, versus 34.8%, net income was up 78%. Share earnings were $3.11 (before a $9.32 charge for accounting changes), versus $1.63 (before an extraordinary charge of $0.15).

Common Share Earnings ($)

Quarter:	1992–93	1991–92	1990–91	1989–90
Sep.	---	0.24	0.76	0.86
Dec.	---	0.70	1.12	1.21
Mar.	[3]1.69	0.83	0.75	1.61
Jun.	1.42	d0.14	0.89	1.37
	3.11	1.63	3.52	5.05

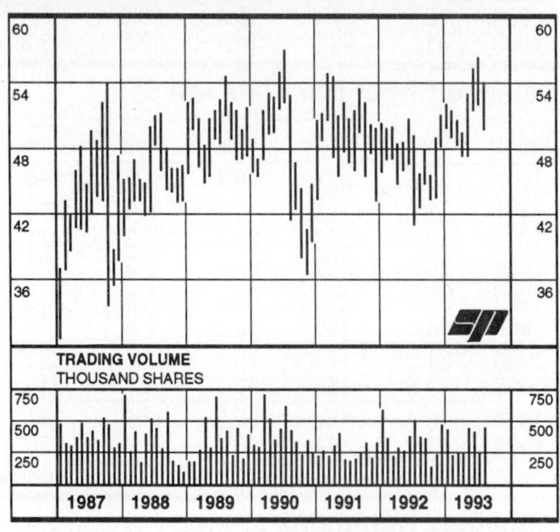

Important Developments

Jul. '93— CRS said that it had agreed to acquire the equity of Aceros Fortuna, S.A. de C.V., a Mexican steel distribution company and two related companies for $20.4 million in cash and the assumption of $2 million in debt. Aceros Fortuna, based in Mexico City, is Mexico's largest distributor of specialty steel bar, rod and wire. CRS stated that the acquisition would have a positive impact on fiscal 1994's earnings. Earlier, the company announced the formation of a manufacturing and distribution joint venture with Walsin Lihwa Corp. in Taiwan. CRS will provide technical and marketing assistance to the joint venture in exchange for royalty payments. The company would initially pay $47.5 million for a 19% interest, and would retain an option to increase its stake to 35%, prior to July 1, 1996.

Next earnings report expected in late October.

Per Share Data ($)

Yr. End Jun. 30	1993	1992	1991	1990	1989	1988	1987	1986	>1985	1984
Tangible Bk. Val.	**NA**	32.56	37.44	36.43	34.68	33.61	33.00	34.62	35.85	35.10
Cash Flow	**NA**	4.70	6.34	7.64	5.59	5.51	3.46	3.49	4.87	5.79
Earnings	**3.11**	[1]1.63	[1]3.52	[1]5.05	[1]3.16	[1]2.67	[1]0.50	[1]1.10	[1]2.77	[1]3.84
Dividends	**2.400**	2.400	2.400	2.325	2.100	2.100	2.100	2.100	2.100	2.100
Payout Ratio	**77%**	145%	68%	44%	66%	79%	425%	193%	76%	55%
Prices—High	**56⅜**	[2]51⅛	[2]54⅞	[2]57	[2]54⅝	[2]51¼	[2]53⅞	[2]37¾	[2]48	[2]58¼
Low	**47⅜**	[2]41	[2]43¼	[2]36½	[2]44⅞	[2]40	[2]30⅝	[2]28½	[2]29⅜	[2]36⅝
P/E Ratio—	**18–15**	31–25	16–12	11–7	17–14	19–15	NM	34–26	17–11	15–10

Data as orig. reptd. **1.** Bef. spec. item(s) of -9.32 in 1993, -0.15 in 1992, -0.24 in 1986. **2.** Cal. yr. **3.** Nine mos. d-Deficit. NM-Not Meaningful. NA-Not Available.

Income Data (Million $)

Year Ended Jun. 30	Revs.	Oper. Inc.	% Oper. Inc. of Revs.	Cap. Exp.	Depr.	Int. Exp.	Net Bef. Taxes	Eff. Tax Rate	[1]Net Inc.	% Net Inc. of Revs.	Cash Flow
1992	**570**	**75**	**13.2**	**35.0**	**25.7**	**20.6**	**22.8**	**34.8%**	**14.9**	**2.6**	**39.2**
1991	562	97	17.3	31.3	24.1	20.1	46.7	35.6%	30.1	5.3	54.2
1990	584	116	19.9	22.6	23.1	19.9	73.2	38.5%	45.0	7.7	68.1
1989	634	112	17.6	36.2	22.3	19.6	48.4	40.2%	29.0	4.6	51.3
1988	556	85	15.2	36.3	26.0	18.5	41.2	40.9%	24.3	4.4	50.3
1987	481	67	13.9	28.2	26.8	19.4	9.2	51.2%	[2]4.5	0.9	31.3
1986	517	45	8.7	64.4	21.5	20.6	10.7	8.3%	9.8	1.9	31.3
1985	557	81	14.5	70.1	18.6	18.0	42.3	42.1%	24.5	4.4	43.1
1984	529	80	15.0	49.0	17.0	12.6	59.7	44.0%	33.4	6.3	50.4
1983	397	38	9.6	71.9	14.6	8.0	21.6	25.7%	16.0	4.0	30.6

Balance Sheet Data (Million $)

Jun. 30	Cash	Curr. Assets	Curr. Liab.	Curr. Ratio	Total Assets	% Ret. on Assets	Long Term Debt	Common Equity	Total Cap.	% LT Debt of Cap.	% Ret. on Equity
1992	**9.3**	**234**	**80**	**2.9**	**715**	**2.1**	**197**	**267**	**626**	**31.4**	**4.7**
1991	4.7	263	137	1.9	717	4.3	123	320	573	21.4	9.5
1990	3.7	258	127	2.0	695	6.8	127	314	565	22.4	14.7
1989	3.7	249	110	2.3	674	4.4	130	319	558	23.3	9.2
1988	6.7	228	94	2.4	635	3.9	131	307	532	24.6	8.0
1987	5.9	206	80	2.6	602	0.7	130	300	514	25.3	1.5
1986	7.8	247	123	2.0	646	1.5	130	312	512	25.5	3.1
1985	6.7	265	107	2.5	622	4.1	126	319	505	24.9	7.8
1984	9.6	257	80	3.2	563	6.5	126	307	480	26.3	11.2
1983	8.0	182	71	2.6	456	3.6	61	289	383	15.9	5.5

Data as orig. reptd. **1.** Bef. spec. item(s) in 1992, 1986. **2.** Reflects acctg. change.

Business Summary

CRS is a leading manufacturer, fabricator, and international marketer of specialty steels and metals in a broad range of types, forms, and sizes for a variety of end-use markets. Revenues by product line in recent fiscal years were:

	1992	1991	1990	1989
Stainless steel	57%	58%	56%	58%
Special alloys	36%	36%	37%	35%
Tool steel	7%	6%	7%	7%

In fiscal 1992, aerospace accounted for 16% of sales, the transportation equipment market for 13% of sales, metal producing and distribution 11%, electrical/electronic equipment 12%, general industrial equipment 11%, chemical and petroleum processing 6%, power generation and distribution 7%, metalworking equipment 6%, consumer durables 5%, instruments and controls 5%, housing and construction 3%, and miscellaneous 5%.

Stainless steels include a broad range of corrosion resistant alloys, including conventional stainless steels and many proprietary grades for special applications.

Special alloys include those other than stainless steels that are used in critical components such as bearings and fasteners; heat resistant alloys such as those with a complex nickel or cobalt base; alloys for electronic/electrical applications; and zirconium base alloys for nuclear reactors.

Tool steels include extremely hard alloys used for tooling and other wear-resisting components in stamping, extrusion, and machining operations.

Dividend Data

Dividends have been paid since 1907. A dividend reinvestment plan is available. A "poison pill" stock purchase right was adopted in 1986.

Amt of Divd. $	Date Decl.	Ex-divd. Date	Stock of Record	Payment Date
0.60	Oct. 27	Nov. 2	Nov. 6	Dec. 3'92
0.60	Jan. 26	Feb. 1	Feb. 5	May 4'93
0.60	Apr. 27	May 3	May 7	Jun. 3'93
0.60	Aug. 12	Aug. 18	Aug. 24	Sep. 2'93

Capitalization

Long Term Debt: $192,812,000 (3/93), incl. $55.6 million of 12⅞% debs. due 2014.

8.25% Conv. Preferred Stock: $30,000,000; conv. into 461,500 com. shs. Held by ESOP.

Common Stock: 7,957,808 shs. ($5 par).
Institutions hold 67%.
Shareholders of record: 6,548 (6/92).

Office—101 West Bern St., Reading, PA 19612-4662. **Tel**—(215) 208-2000. **Chrmn, Pres & CEO**—R. W. Cardy. **SVP & CFO**—G. W. Cottrell. **Secy**—W. J. Pendleton. **Treas & Investor Contact**—John A. Schuler. **Dirs**— T. Beaver Jr., R. W. Cardy, D. M. Draeger, C. McCollister Evarts, C. R. Garr, W. J. Hudson, Jr., A. E. Humphrey, E. W. Kay, F. C. Langenberg, M. Miller, Jr., P. R. Roedel. **Transfer Agent & Registrar**—First Chicago Trust Co. of New York., NYC. **Incorporated** in New Jersey in 1904; reincorporated in Delaware in 1968. **Empl**—3,534.

 Leo Larkin

Carter-Wallace

NYSE Symbol CAR Options on CBOE In S&P MidCap 400

Price	Range	P-E Ratio	Dividend	Yield	S&P Ranking	Beta
Sep. 27'93	1993					
30¾	36⅝–22⅞	38	0.333	1.1%	A	1.30

Summary

This company generally derives well over half its earnings from a broad range of ethical drugs, and is well established in the highly competitive consumer products market with its Arrid antiperspirants and deodorants, Trojan condoms, and numerous other lines. Despite sales and margin pressure in fiscal 1992-93, earnings growth should resume in 1993-94, aided by royalty fees and the initial distribution of Felbatol (felbamate), a drug to treat epilepsy that was approved by the U.S. Food & Drug Administration in August 1993.

Current Outlook

Earnings for the fiscal year ending March 31, 1994, are estimated at $1.50 a share (excluding a special charge of $0.96), up from 1992-93's $1.03 (including a $0.13 nonrecurring gain). Earnings for 1994-95 could reach $1.80.

An increase in the $0.0833 quarterly dividend is likely.

Sales for 1993-94 should rise moderately, reflecting the initial distribution of Felbatol, a drug to treat epilepsy, in North America. Sales should also be boosted by royalty income from Schering-Plough, which has exclusive marketing rights to distribute Felbatol in all markets but North America. Sales of existing health products may continue to decline, mainly reflecting generic competition. Sales of consumer products may also be under pressure, due to an industrywide decline in sales of condoms, despite efforts to promote their use in combating the spread of AIDS. Despite ongoing competitive pricing pressures, margins should improve somewhat on a more profitable product mix. Interest charges could be lower. Earnings comparisons will be hurt by the absence of a $0.13 nonrecurring gain.

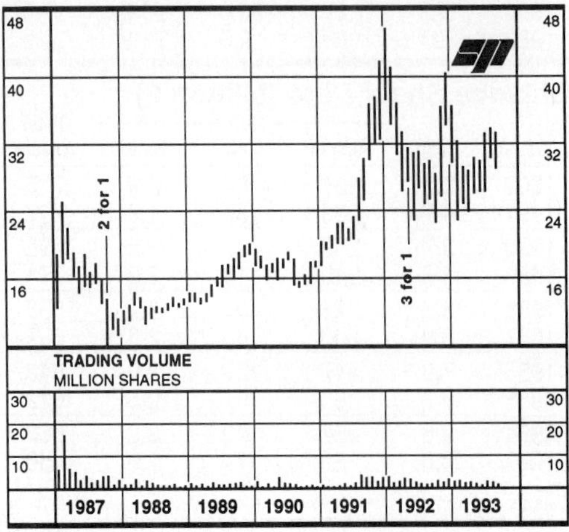

Net Sales (Million $)

Quarter:	1993–94	1992–93	1991–92	1990–91
Jun.	163	157	171	153
Sep.	---	167	172	158
Dec.	---	160	158	157
Mar.	---	169	173	166
	---	654	673	635

Sales for the first three months of fiscal 1993-94 advanced 3.5%, year to year. Margins narrowed substantially, and with the absence of a $10.0 million nonrecurring gain related to a licensing agreement with Schering-Plough, pretax income was off 64%. After taxes of 31.0% in both interims, net income was also down 64%, to $0.13 a share from $0.35. Results for the 1993 interim exclude a special charge of $0.96.

Common Share Earnings ($)

Quarter:	1993–94	1992–93	1991–92	1990–91
Jun.	0.13	0.35	0.34	0.31
Sep.	E0.35	0.22	0.17	0.34
Dec.	E0.47	0.29	0.30	0.29
Mar.	E0.55	0.17	0.19	0.18
	E1.50	1.03	1.00	1.12

Important Developments

Aug. '93— The U.S. Food & Drug Administration (FDA) approved CAR's new drug Felbatol (felbamate) to treat epilepsy, a disorder affecting about two million Americans. This is the first new epilepsy drug in 10 years.

Dec. '92— CAR filed a new drug application with the FDA to sell Asteln (azelastine) to treat allergic rhinitis.

Next earnings report expected in late October.

Per Share Data ($)

Yr. End Mar. 31	1993	1992	1991	1990	1989	1988	1987	[1]1986	1985	[1]1984
Tangible Bk. Val.	**6.84**	6.32	5.67	6.12	5.55	4.84	4.09	3.54	2.97	2.70
Cash Flow	**1.60**	1.53	1.57	1.42	1.25	1.08	0.94	0.77	0.61	0.53
Earnings	**1.03**	1.00	1.12	1.10	0.99	0.83	0.71	0.61	0.44	0.40
Dividends	**0.333**	0.327	0.298	0.262	0.215	0.168	0.125	0.097	0.082	0.077
Payout Ratio	**32%**	33%	26%	24%	22%	20%	18%	16%	18%	19%
Calendar Years	**1992**	1991	1990	1989	1988	1987	1986	1985	1984	1983
Prices—High	**45 13/16**	41⅞	19½	20⅛	14⅜	25⅛	14⅜	8½	4⅝	4⅞
Low	**22 19/32**	17½	15	13	10⅝	8	8	4⅛	3¼	3
P/E Ratio—	**44–21**	42–18	17–13	18–12	15–11	30–10	20–11	14–7	10–7	12–7

Data as orig. reptd. Adj. for stk. divs. of 200% May 1992, 100% Oct. 1987 (Cl. B com.). **1.** Refl. merger or acq. E-Estimated.

Income Data (Million $)

Year Ended Mar. 31	Revs.	Oper. Inc.	% Oper. Inc. of Revs.	Cap. Exp.	Depr.	Int. Exp.	Net Bef. Taxes	Eff. Tax Rate	Net Inc.	% Net Inc. of Revs.	Cash Flow
1993	**656**	**91**	**13.9**	**25.5**	**25.8**	**1.79**	**68.4**	**31.0%**	**47.2**	**7.2**	**73.0**
1992	673	108	16.0	22.3	24.5	3.37	67.3	32.0%	45.7	6.8	70.2
1991	635	99	15.6	18.7	20.5	4.14	76.1	32.0%	51.8	8.2	72.2
1990	555	86	15.6	34.9	14.6	4.26	75.6	33.5%	50.3	9.1	64.9
1989	515	79	15.3	22.9	12.0	3.12	69.3	35.0%	45.1	8.7	57.1
1988	483	73	15.2	19.8	11.2	3.23	61.0	38.0%	37.8	7.8	49.1
1987	451	68	15.3	11.9	10.4	3.95	[2]54.3	40.5%	32.3	7.2	42.7
[1]1986	400	50	14.9	9.1	7.4	3.37	[2]46.0	40.0%	27.6	6.9	35.0
1985	349	45	12.9	7.8	4.7	2.30	[2]36.3	42.9%	20.7	5.9	28.6
[1]1984	323	35	10.8	7.3	4.3	2.04	[2]31.2	40.9%	18.4	5.7	25.0

Balance Sheet Data (Million $)

Mar. 31	Cash	Curr. Assets	Curr. Liab.	Curr. Ratio	Total Assets	% Ret. on Assets	Long Term Debt	Common Equity	Total Cap.	% LT Debt of Cap.	% Ret. on Equity
1993	**36**	**316**	**132**	**2.4**	**601**	**8.0**	**13.4**	**431**	**444**	**3.0**	**11.2**
1992	39	305	134	2.3	582	8.0	15.2	409	424	3.6	11.6
1991	30	290	138	2.1	562	9.6	17.0	383	400	4.2	14.2
1990	108	316	131	2.4	516	10.2	21.3	345	367	5.8	15.5
1989	120	310	123	2.5	462	10.3	21.3	301	322	6.6	15.9
1988	90	276	108	2.6	409	9.7	23.2	265	288	8.1	15.3
1987	70	251	106	2.4	372	9.1	24.8	231	256	9.7	14.9
1986	44	206	91	2.3	335	9.1	31.7	202	234	13.6	14.5
1985	34	170	78	2.2	274	7.9	10.2	179	189	5.4	12.0
1984	18	149	62	2.4	254	7.7	13.7	170	184	7.4	11.3

Data as orig. reptd. **1.** Refl. merger or acq. **2.** Incl. equity in earns. of nonconsol. subs.

Business Summary

Business segment contributions (profits in millions) in fiscal 1992-93 were:

	Sales	Profits
Health care	43%	$46.5
Antiperspirants & deodorants	20%	−1.5
Other consumer	37%	58.3

Operations outside the U.S. accounted for about 26% of sales and 15% of operating profits in 1992-93. R&D equaled 7.6% of sales in 1992-93, slightly less than 1991-92's 7.7%.

Health care products include tranquilizers, muscle relaxants, laxatives, expectorants/mucolytics, topical antibacterial and antifungal agents, drugs for rheumatoid arthritis, antihypertensives, xanthine bronchodilators, cough/cold products, throat lozenges, sedatives, analgesics, anti-ulcer drugs, antacids, dietary supplements, antiflatulents, decongestants, anti-nauseant drugs and toothbrushes. Also produced are tests for pregnancy, herpes, streptococcal infections, rheumatoid factor, mononucleosis, meningitis, rubella and other ailments.

The consumer products segment is heavily dependent upon the Arrid line of antiperspirants and deodorants, which are available in sprays, roll-ons and creams. Other consumer products include Trojan condoms (which have over half of the U.S. retail market) and Pearl Drops tooth polish. Also produced are laxatives, depilatories, pregnancy tests and ovulation kits, lubricating jellies, skin care products, oral hygiene products, tapes and bandages, footcare products, shampoos, hair lotion, and footcare and pet care items.

Dividend Data

Dividends have been paid since 1883.

Amt of Divd. $	Date Decl.	Ex-divd. Date	Stock of Record	Payment Date
0.0833	Oct. 22	Oct. 27	Nov. 2	Nov. 25'92
0.0833	Jan. 19	Feb. 5	Feb. 11	Mar. 5'93
0.0833	Apr. 15	Apr. 28	May 4	Jun. 1'93
0.0833	Jul. 21	Jul. 30	Aug. 5	Aug. 31'93

Capitalization

Long Term Debt: $13,375,000 (6/93).

Common Stock: 33,108,000 shs. ($1 par).
Institutions hold about 55%.
Shareholders of record: 3,184.

Class B Common Stk.: 12,666,000 shs. ($1 par); 10 votes per sh.; transfer restricted; conv. sh.-for-sh. into com.

The Hoyt family owns 93% of the Class B and 36% of the common stock.

Office—1345 Ave. of the Americas, New York, NY 10105. **Tel**—(212) 339-5000. **Chrmn & CEO**—H. H. Hoyt Jr. **Pres**—D. J. Black. **VP-Secy & Investor Contact**—Ralph Levine. **VP-Treas**—J. L. Wagar. **Dirs**—D. M. Baldwin, D. J. Black, R. L. Cruess, C. O. Hoyt, H. H. Hoyt Jr., S. C. Hoyt, R. Levine, H. M. Rinaldi, P. A. Veteri. **Transfer Agent & Registrar**—Bank of New York, NYC. **Incorporated** in Maryland in 1937; reincorporated in Delaware in 1968. **Empl**—4,020.

 E.A. Vandeventer

Centocor

NASDAQ Symbol CNTO (Incl. in Nat'l Market) Options on CBOE In S&P MidCap 400

Price	Range	P–E Ratio	Dividend	Yield	S&P Ranking	Beta
Aug. 9'93	1993					
7⅝	60¼–5¼	NM	None	None	C	1.24

Summary

This biotechnology company is developing innovative therapeutics and diagnostic products both independently and in collaboration with others. Clinical trials of Centoxin, its lead product, for the treatment of septic shock and gram negative bacteremia were suspended in early 1993.

Business Summary

Centocor Inc. is a biopharmaceutical company that is developing and commercializing monoclonal antibody-based products to meet critical human healthcare needs. It also performs research activities in the field of small peptide molecule-based pharmaceutical products. The company focuses on four major disease areas—infectious, cardiovascular, autoimmune and cancer. During 1992, it implemented a new business strategy utilizing, among other things, alliances with established pharmaceutical companies.

In the area of infectious disease therapy, products under development include HA-1A, a product intended for the treatment of patients with severe sepsis who are dying from endotoxemia. In early 1993, Phase III trials of HA-1A were suspended, as results reflected an excess of mortality among patients who received HA-1A who did not have Gram-negative bacteremia, compared with placebo-treated patients. The company is evaluating clinical parameters, such as organ failure, and diagnostic tests that measure endotoxemia, to better identify patients who can benefit from HA-1A and to improve the timing of HA-1A administration, but resumption of clinical trials is not assured. Sales of the product in Europe have also been suspended.

During the 1993 first quarter, Centocor completed a Phase III trial involving CentoRx, a cardiovascular agent designed to reduce blood-clot related complications in high-risk coronary angioplasty. Product license applications (PLA's) for CentoRx are expected to be filed in the U.S. and Europe during 1993. A separate Phase III trial is in progress in patients with refractory unstable angina who are scheduled to undergo angioplasty. Eli Lilly & Co. has exercised an option to be the worldwide distributor of CentoRx, and will assist the company in regulatory filings and continued development of the product for various clinical indications.

The company is developing and clinically evaluating Panorex, a product designed to treat colorectal cancer. In the area of autoimmune disease therapy, two products are being developed as therapeutic agents for diseases such as rheumatoid arthritis and Crohn's disease: Centara and CenTNF.

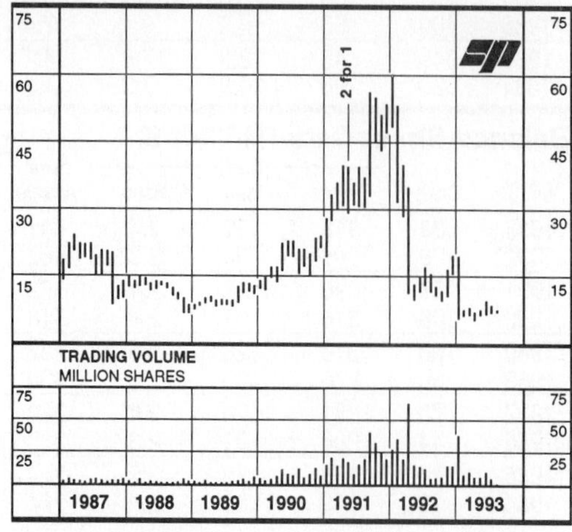

Using technology to modify monoclonal antibodies so that they may be coupled with radioactive isotopes and used with contrast agents in diagnostic imaging procedures, Centocor has received marketing approvals for Myoscint (a cardiac imaging agent) in several European countries; a PLA is under FDA review.

Cancer blood tests produced and sold include Ovarian Cancer Test CA 125, for clinical use in the U.S., certain European countries and Japan; Pancreatic Cancer Test CA 19-9, Breast Cancer Test CA 15-3 and Gastric Cancer Test CA 72-4, all sold for clinical use in certain European countries and Japan; and Multidrug Resistance Test P-glycoCHEK and Lung Cancer Test CYFRA 21-1, both available for investigational use in certain European countries and Japan.

Next earnings report expected in late October.

Per Share Data ($)

Yr. End Dec. 31	[1]1992	1991	1990	1989	1988	1987	[2]1986	1985	1984	1983
Tangible Bk. Val.	**0.31**	3.67	5.78	5.31	5.27	5.11	4.59	2.98	1.64	1.59
Cash Flow	**d4.48**	d5.36	d4.47	0.24	0.38	0.42	d1.99	0.19	0.05	d0.05
Earnings[3]	**d4.90**	d5.72	d5.10	0.01	0.18	0.31	d2.09	0.13	0.03	d0.06
Dividends	**Nil**	Nil	Nil	Nil	Nil	Nil	Nil	Nil	Nil	Nil
Payout Ratio	**Nil**	Nil	Nil	Nil	Nil	Nil	Nil	Nil	Nil	Nil
Prices—High	**60¼**	56¼	24⅛	13½	15	24¼	22¾	13⅝	8⅛	12¾
Low	**9½**	19⅜	11⅞	7½	6¹¹⁄₁₆	8½	10¾	4⅛	4	6⅛
P/E Ratio—	**NM**	NM	NM	NM	83–37	80–28	NM	NM	NM	NM

Data as orig. reptd. Adj. for stk. div. of 100% May 1991. **1.** Refl. merger or acq. **2.** Refl. acctg. change. **3.** Bef. spec. items of +0.05 in 1987, +0.10 in 1985, +0.02 in 1984. NM-Not Meaningful. d-Deficit.

Income Data (Million $)

Year Ended Dec. 31	Oper. Revs.	Oper. Inc.	% Oper. Inc. of Revs.	Cap. Exp.	Depr. & Amort.	Int. Exp.	Net Bef. Taxes	Eff. Tax Rate	[4]Net Inc.	% Net Inc. of Revs.	Cash Flow
[1]1992	**76.2**	**d123**	**NM**	**23.3**	**16.7**	**19.8**	**d194**	**NM**	**d194**	**NM**	**d177**
1991	53.2	d111	NM	32.5	12.4	11.4	d196	NM	d196	NM	d183
1990	64.6	d15	NM	47.8	16.3	[3]1.9	d134	NM	d132	NM	d116
1989	72.0	3	4.1	15.4	5.3	1.6	NM	43.1%	NM	0.2	5
1988	55.2	4	6.9	19.4	4.5	[3]1.1	7	40.3%	4	7.5	9
1987	51.6	11	20.7	8.2	3.4	[3]0.5	13	43.3%	7	13.4	10
[2]1986	27.1	d1	1.0	17.2	1.7	[3]0.1	d39	NM	d39	NM	d37
1985	20.0	2	9.6	2.9	0.8	Nil	4	41.8%	2	10.0	3
1984	10.9	d1	NM	0.9	0.3	Nil	1	43.2%	NM	3.7	1
1983	5.5	d3	NM	0.8	0.2	Nil	d1	NM	d1	NM	d1

Balance Sheet Data (Million $)

Dec. 31	Cash	Curr. Assets	Curr. Liab.	Curr. Ratio	Total Assets	% Ret. on Assets	Long Term Debt	Common Equity	Total Cap.	% LT Debt of Cap.	% Ret. on Equity
1992	**150**	**187**	**77.1**	**2.4**	**349**	**NM**	**238**	**31**	**269**	**88.4**	**NM**
1991	181	284	63.6	4.5	473	NM	259	144	405	64.0	NM
1990	96	158	43.6	3.6	273	NM	42	169	215	19.6	NM
1989	64	88	17.9	4.9	180	0.1	23	133	160	14.0	0.1
1988	45	72	12.4	5.8	153	2.7	13	122	137	9.5	3.4
1987	40	57	16.0	3.6	149	5.1	7	115	127	5.6	6.4
1986	81	92	6.6	13.9	121	NM	6	102	112	5.1	NM
1985	50	57	3.4	16.8	64	4.5	1	49	53	2.2	5.5
1984	10	13	1.7	7.9	25	1.6	Nil	24	24	Nil	1.7

Data as orig. reptd. **1.** Refl. merger or acq. **2.** Refl. acctg. change. **3.** Net of int. inc. **4.** Bef. spec. items. d-Deficit. NM-Not Meaningful.

Revenues (Million $)

Quarter:	1993	1992	1991	1990
Mar.	15.0	21.7	14.7	16.7
Jun.	13.8	20.5	9.8	12.9
Sep.		50.7	11.1	18.0
Dec.		33.4	17.6	17.0
		126.2	53.2	64.6

Total revenues in the six months ended June 30, 1993, fell 32%, year to year, reflecting the suspension of HA-1A product sales and a decrease in contract revenues. With lower marketing and general and administrative costs, and a reduced level of special charges, the loss narrowed to $51,550,000 ($1.25 a share, on 7.2% more shares), from $85,490,000 ($2.22).

Common Share Earnings ($)

Quarter:	1993	1992	1991	1990
Mar.	d0.62	d1.20	d0.60	Nil
Jun.	d0.63	d1.02	d2.96	0.01
Sep.		d0.47	d0.97	Nil
Dec.		d2.18	d1.19	d5.11
		d4.90	d5.72	d5.10

Dividend Data

No cash has been paid.

Finances

During the first half of 1992, the company recorded restructuring charges of $9.4 million related to facilities, equipment, and severance costs resulting from a work force reduction of about 300 employees.

Under a strategic alliance formed in July 1992, Eli Lilly & Co. paid Centocor $50 million for 2,000,000 common shares and $50 million to fund R&D of HA-1A. Lilly will market and distribute the product, if approved, while the company will manfacture and conduct clinical trials. An additional $25 million may be paid for similar arrangements for CentoRx.

In 1992, the company recorded charges of $64.9 million related to HA-1A inventory; $15.3 million for restructuring; and $11.2 million related to the proposed settlement of certain litigation.

Centocor has licensed certain technology related to small peptide molecule-based pharmaceutical products to Tocor II Inc., and performs research and development with respect to such technology on Tocor II's behalf. Tocor II holds the rights to licensed technology and the results of research and development realted thereto.

Capitalization

Long Term Debt: $238,150,000 (3/93).

Minority Interest: $503,000.

Common Stock: 41,289,447 shs. ($0.01 par).
Shareholders: 5,990 of record (3/93).

d-Deficit.

Office—200 Great Valley Parkway, Malvern, PA 19355. **Tel**—(215) 651-6000. **Chrmn**—H. J. P. Schoemaker. **Pres & CEO**—D. P. Holveck. **SVP & CFO**—M. R. Dougherty. **VP & Secy**—G. D. Hobbs. **Dirs**—A. B. Evnin, W. F. Hamilton, A. T. Knoppers, H. J. P. Schoemaker, L. Steinman, M. A. Wall. **Transfer Agent & Registrar**—First National Bank of Boston, Canton, MA. **Founded** in 1979. **Empl**—600.

 Robert M. Gold

Central Fidelity Banks

NASDAQ Symbol CFBS (Incl. in Nat'l Market) In S&P MidCap 400

Price	Range	P-E Ratio	Dividend	Yield	S&P Ranking	Beta
Oct. 7'93	1993					
30	35¼–26	12	1.00	3.3%	A+	0.86

Summary

This Richmond-based bank holding company is one of Virginia's largest banking organizations, with 230 branches throughout the state. Earnings rose in 1992 for the 18th consecutive year and advanced more than 40% in 1993's first half. In September 1993, the company finalized an application with the Office of the Comptroller of the Currency (OCC) for a national charter for its main subsidiary, Central Fidelity Bank. At the same time, to comply with strict OCC standards, CFBS substantially raised its nonperforming assets and wrote down a large amount of other real estate owned.

Business Summary

Central Fidelity Banks, Inc. is a bank holding company headquartered in Richmond, Va. At December 31, 1992, the company was operating 230 branch offices throughout the state.

Loans outstanding totaled $3.95 billion at 1992 year-end and were divided:

Commercial & commercial real estate	40%
Residential real estate	15%
Installment	15%
Bank card	11%
Consumer second mortgage	10%
Construction	9%

The provision for loan losses at December 31, 1992, totaled $101,800,000 (2.58% of net loans outstanding), compared with $61,000,000 (1.69%) a year earlier. Net chargeoffs in 1992 amounted to $58,957,000 ($49,616,000 in 1991), equal to 1.58% (1.38%) of average net loans. At December 31, 1992, nonperforming assets amounted to $112.3 million (1.29% of total assets), up from $62.2 million (1.01%) a year earlier.

Consolidated deposits of $6.67 billion at 1992 year-end were apportioned: 12% demand, 10% interest checking, 11% regular savings, 41% consumer certificates, 18% money-market accounts and 8% certificates of deposit $100,000 and over.

Total income for 1992 was derived 51% from interest and fees on loans, 23% from investment securities, 8% from securities available for sale, 1% from money-market and trading-account securities, 4% from deposit fees and charges, 2% from trust income, 8% from profits on securities available for sale and trading account securities and 3% from other income.

On a taxable-equivalent basis, the average yield on interest-earning assets in 1992 was 8.52% (10.12% in 1991), while the average rate paid on interest-bearing liabilities was 4.64% (6.32%), for a net spread of 3.88% (3.80%).

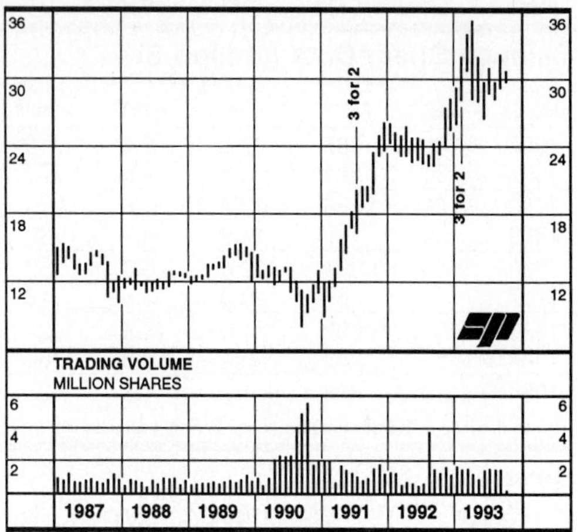

Important Developments

Sep. '93— The company finalized its application with the Office of the Comptroller of the Currency (OCC) for a national bank charter to be effective in 1993's fourth quarter for Central Fidelity Bank, its main subsidiary. Separately, to comply with the OCC's standards and in anticipation of continuing economic weakness in 1994, CFBS raised its nonperforming assets by a net of $23 million to about $135 million, or 1.5% of assets. Also, certain real estate-related loans and other real estate owned were written down about $40 million, reflecting a soft real estate market, especially in northern Virginia.

Next earnings report expected in mid-October.

Per Share Data ($)

Yr. End Dec. 31	1992	1991	1990	1989	1988	1987	1986	[1]1985	[1]1984	[1]1983
Tangible Bk. Val.	**15.71**	13.13	11.83	10.90	9.88	9.01	8.18	6.78	6.11	5.51
Earnings	**2.25**	1.87	1.65	1.57	1.42	1.34	1.23	1.09	1.01	0.89
Dividends	**0.807**	0.729	0.618	0.542	0.507	0.467	0.413	0.363	0.323	0.282
Payout Ratio	**36%**	39%	37%	35%	36%	35%	34%	33%	32%	32%
Prices—High	**28⅜**	26⅛	14½	15⅜	13⅛	15⅜	16¼	13⅞	8½	7⅛
Low	**22⅜**	8⅞	8	11⅞	11	10⅛	11	8½	5⅝	3⅞
P/E Ratio—	**13–10**	14–5	9–5	10–8	9–8	12–8	13–9	13–8	8–6	8–4

Data as orig. reptd. Adj. for stk. divs. of 50% Feb. 1993, 50% Jul. 1991, 50% Jun. 1985, 50% Sep. 1983. **1.** Refl. merger or acq.

Income Data (Million $)

Year Ended Dec. 31	Net Int. Inc.	Tax Equiv. Adj.	Non Int. Inc.	Loan Loss Prov.	% Exp./ Op. Revs.	Net Bef. Taxes	Eff. Tax Rate	Net Inc.	% Net Int. Margin	—% Return On— Assets	Equity
1992	**294**	**10.9**	**65.6**	**99.8**	**54.1**	**109**	**28.2%**	**78.5**	**4.40**	**1.06**	**15.5**
1991	241	13.2	61.2	49.9	60.9	79	23.8%	60.4	4.48	0.99	14.9
1990	208	15.8	64.7	45.0	58.1	69	19.6%	55.8	4.44	1.02	14.5
1989	196	17.9	53.3	17.3	61.0	70	22.5%	54.4	4.88	1.14	15.0
1988	170	18.6	44.7	17.1	60.1	59	16.5%	49.5	4.78	1.15	15.0
1987	162	28.4	42.3	23.4	57.7	53	10.6%	47.3	5.28	1.20	15.5
1986	137	45.5	42.7	20.9	56.5	36	NM	41.7	5.57	1.16	15.8
[1]1985	120	29.0	38.3	15.7	59.7	34	3.0%	33.3	5.13	1.04	16.8
[1]1984	111	16.5	30.8	9.8	61.5	34	14.3%	29.2	5.14	1.06	17.3
[1]1983	94	14.2	29.4	4.6	63.9	30	19.5%	24.5	4.55	0.93	17.0

Balance Sheet Data (Million $)

		—Earning Assets—				% Loan	—Deposits—			Long		
Dec. 31	Total Assets	Mon. Mkt. Assets	Inv. Secs.	Com'l Loans	Other Loans	Loss Resv.	Demand	Time	% Loans/ Deposits	Term Debt	Common Equity	% Equity To Assets
1992	**8,712**	**283**	**3,903**	**1,577**	**2,377**	**2.58**	**823**	**5,849**	**59.3**	**168**	**604**	**6.81**
1991	6,806	213	2,480	1,538	2,082	1.69	672	4,506	69.9	23	429	6.69
1990	6,173	382	1,592	1,583	1,994	1.70	602	3,931	78.9	27	382	7.06
1989	5,335	237	1,124	1,634	1,899	1.00	610	3,532	85.2	31	378	7.59
1988	4,731	381	748	1,556	1,668	1.00	608	3,136	85.8	36	343	7.64
1987	4,287	363	552	1,433	1,551	1.07	574	2,808	87.1	38	315	7.75
1986	4,137	569	649	1,140	1,461	1.25	602	2,634	78.4	42	289	7.32
1985	3,511	362	707	983	1,235	1.25	498	2,216	79.0	47	208	6.16
1984	2,951	294	475	776	1,147	1.02	451	1,879	79.3	57	181	6.09
1983	2,702	503	511	592	869	1.07	395	1,679	67.5	57	151	5.42

Data as orig. reptd. **1.** Refl. merger or acq. NM-Not Meaningful.

Review of Operations

For the six months ended June 30, 1993, net interest income rose 21%, year to year, as strong growth in assets, especially residential first mortgage loans, outweighed a decline in the net interest margin. The loan loss provision fell 36%, to $31.3 million, from $48.7 million. Noninterest income dropped 28% on much lower securities gains and, after 8.2% higher noninterest expense, pretax income climbed 48%. After taxes at 30.0%, versus 27.0%, net income advanced 42%, to $50.4 million ($1.31 a share, based on 17% more shares), from $35.6 million ($1.08, as adjusted).

Common Share Earnings ($)

Quarter:	1993	1992	1991	1990
Mar.	0.63	0.48	0.46	0.41
Jun.	0.68	0.60	0.47	0.41
Sep.		0.58	0.48	0.42
Dec.		0.58	0.46	0.41
		2.25	1.87	1.65

Finances

In September 1993, to reduce interest rate risk, CFBS sold $600 million of long term securities realizing a gross profit of about $50 million.

In August 1992, Central Fidelity sold publicly 5,175,000 (adjusted) common shares at $23 each through Robinson-Humphrey. Net proceeds were approximately $113 million.

In July 1992, CFBS acquired from Resolution Trust Corp. the branch network and $871 million in core deposits of Investors Federal Savings Bank.

Dividend Data

Central Fidelity or its predecessors have paid dividends every year since 1911. A dividend reinvestment plan is available.

Amt of Divd. $	Date Decl.	Ex-divd. Date	Stock of Record	Payment Date
0.31	Nov. 11	Dec. 14	Dec. 18	Jan. 2'93
3-for-2	Jan. 13	Feb. 23	Jan. 29	Feb. 22'93
0.25	Jan. 13	Mar. 15	Mar. 19	Apr. 1'93
0.25	May 12	Jun. 14	Jun. 18	Jul. 1'93
0.25	Jul. 27	Sep. 13	Sep. 17	Oct. 1'93

Capitalization

Long Term Debt: $167,774,000 (6/93), incl. $9,351,000 of lease obligs.

Common Stock: 38,820,992 shs. ($5 par).
Institutions hold about 35%.
Shareholders: 15,966 of record (12/92).

Offices—1021 E. Cary St., Richmond, VA 23219. **Tel**—(804) 782-4000. **Chrmn & CEO**—C. L. Saine. **Pres**—L. N. Miller Jr. **Treas, CFO & Investor Contact**—Charles W. Tysinger. **Secy**—W. N. Stoyko. **Dirs**—J. F. Betts, A. R. Clements, R. C. Dawson, P. A. Ellison, J. H. Ferguson, R. L. Freeman, T. R. Glass, M. B. Lane, G. R. Lewis, G. B. Miller, L. N. Miller Jr., T. J. Moore Jr., R. L. Morrill, L. U. Noland III, W. G. Reynolds Jr., C. L. Saine, W. F. Shumadine Jr., K. S. White. **Transfer Agent**—Central Fidelity Bank, Richmond. **Incorporated** in Virginia in 1978. **Empl**—3,400.

 C. Orgielewicz

Central Louisiana Electric

NYSE Symbol CNL In S&P MidCap 400

Price	Range	P-E Ratio	Dividend	Yield	S&P Ranking	Beta
Oct. 21'93	1993					
26⅞	27⅛–23½	14	1.42	5.3%	A–	0.45

Summary

This electric utility serves some 214,000 customers in west-central and southeastern Louisiana. About half of its electric power supply is derived from coal and lignite, with most of the balance from natural gas. CNL intends to remain a low-cost producer and position itself to benefit from open transmission lines and increased competition among electric utilities for wholesale customers.

Current Outlook

Share earnings for 1993 are estimated at $1.95, up slightly from the $1.93 of 1992. Earnings for 1994 are projected at $1.95 a share.

Directors raised the quarterly dividend 2.9%, to $0.35½ a share, with the April 1993 payment.

Customer growth could lead to a kilowatt-hour sales increase of 2.5% in 1993. Earnings should be aided by lower interest expense resulting from the refinancing of $97 million of debt during 1992. Being among the lowest-cost producers in its region will position the company for greater competition expected from passage of the Energy Policy Act of 1992. To protect against customer erosion from stiffer competition brought on by deregulation, CNL recently began implementing a restructuring plan to ensure a favorable cost structure.

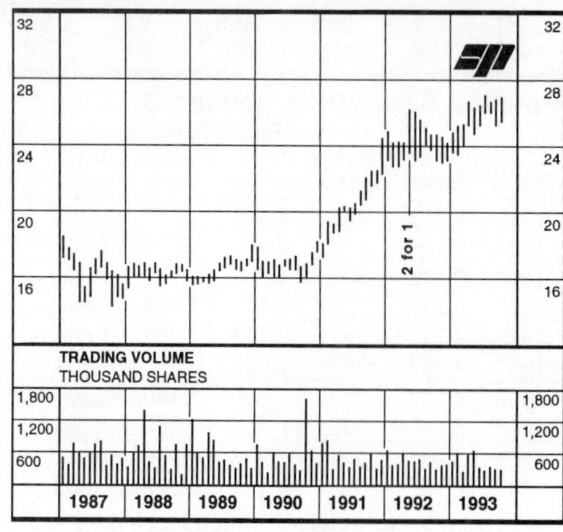

Operating Revenues (Million $)

Quarter:	1994	1993	1992	1991
Mar.	---	75.5	75.8	72.9
Jun.	---	92.1	85.7	85.7
Sep.	---	---	105.7	100.8
Dec.	---	---	84.4	78.0
	---	---	351.6	337.3

Operating revenues for the six months ended June 30, 1993, were up 3.7%, year to year, due to fuel adjustment clause increases. Profitability benefited from lower interest charges, as a result of refinancing debt; net income advanced fractionally (0.6%). Share earnings, after lower preferred dividends, were $0.83, versus $0.82 (as adjusted).

Common Share Earnings ($)

Quarter:	1994	1993	1992	1991
Mar.	E0.30	0.31	0.29	0.29
Jun.	E0.50	0.52	0.53	0.52
Sep.	E0.85	E0.82	0.83	0.81
Dec.	E0.30	E0.30	0.28	0.31
	E1.95	E1.95	1.93	1.92

Important Developments

Jun. '93— CNL announced the completion of a six-month organizational effectiveness study. Implementation of the study's recommendations will begin immediately. The study identified 100 to 150 positions to be eliminated over the next two years, which represents a reduction of about 10% of the company's workforce. Reductions will be achieved through attrition, early retirement, and voluntary severance. Program costs are expected to result in a one-time after-tax charge of $6 million in the third quarter of 1993. The restructuring and accompanying improvements in company work processes will substantially reduce operating costs, allowing for recovery of the one-time charge within the next 18 months. The company said its goal in the restructuring is not only to maintain good financial performance, but to protect its very competitive customer rates.

Next earnings report expected in late October.

Per Share Data ($)

Yr. End Dec. 31	1992	1991	1990	1989	1988	1987	1986	1985	1984	1983
Tangible Bk. Val.	**15.35**	14.81	14.31	13.74	13.12	12.46	11.97	11.27	10.45	9.64
Earnings[1]	**1.93**	1.92	1.85	1.78	1.80	1.76	1.61	1.83	1.81	1.43
Dividends	**1.370**	1.325	1.265	1.205	1.145	1.070	1.040	1.025	0.950	0.905
Payout Ratio	**71%**	69%	68%	68%	64%	61%	65%	56%	52%	64%
Prices—High	**26¼**	24½	18¼	18	16¹⁵⁄₁₆	18½	19	15⅛	11⅛	9¾
Low	**22¾**	17¼	15¾	15⁹⁄₁₆	15⅜	14¼	14¼	10⅝	8¹³⁄₁₆	7⁵⁄₁₆
P/E Ratio—	**14–12**	13–9	10–9	10–9	9	11–8	12–9	8–6	6–5	7–5

Data as orig. reptd. Adj. for stk. divd. of 100% May 1992. **1.** Bef. spec. item(s) of +0.14 in 1986. E-Estimated.

Income Data (Million $)

Year Ended Dec. 31	Revs.	Depr.	Maint.	Oper. Ratio	[1]Fxd. Chgs. Cover.	Constr. Credits	Eff. Tax Rate	[2]Net Inc.	% Return On Revs.	% Return On [3]Invest. Capital	% Return On Com. Equity
1992	**352**	**34.8**	**26.2**	**80.0%**	**3.05**	**2.0**	**29.1%**	**45.2**	**12.9**	**8.6**	**12.8**
1991	337	34.0	25.8	78.3%	2.90	1.0	29.6%	44.9	13.3	9.0	13.2
1990	334	32.9	22.0	78.0%	2.85	0.9	30.5%	42.5	12.7	9.8	13.2
1989	316	31.8	21.5	76.8%	2.70	1.8	30.8%	41.5	13.1	10.0	13.2
1988	301	30.4	20.0	76.3%	2.77	1.9	30.4%	43.1	14.3	9.6	14.0
1987	304	29.8	20.9	76.1%	2.78	1.6	35.8%	45.0	14.8	9.8	14.4
1986	297	25.5	16.5	78.7%	2.55	10.1	33.4%	42.5	14.3	9.9	13.9
1985	315	18.6	16.7	84.0%	3.04	22.1	27.3%	47.2	15.0	10.3	16.8
1984	331	17.9	15.1	84.8%	3.56	15.5	36.5%	43.7	13.2	11.0	18.0
1983	304	17.4	14.7	86.4%	3.57	7.6	40.3%	33.0	10.8	10.0	14.9

Balance Sheet Data (Million $)

Dec. 31	Gross Prop.	Capital Expend.	Net Prop.	% Earn. on Net Prop.	Total Cap.	Capitalization LT Debt	Capitalization % LT Debt	Capitalization Pfd.	Capitalization % Pfd.	Capitalization Com.	Capitalization % Com.
1992	**1,236**	**64**	**879**	**8.1**	**819**	**311**	**46.8**	**10.1**	**1.5**	**343**	**51.7**
1991	1,178	55	851	8.7	883	387	52.9	14.9	2.0	330	45.1
1990	1,129	49	828	9.0	798	315	48.3	14.8	2.3	322	49.4
1989	1,088	50	814	9.1	720	256	44.1	15.4	2.7	309	53.2
1988	1,044	49	798	9.0	765	298	47.3	37.1	5.9	295	46.8
1987	1,005	49	783	9.4	771	319	49.7	42.7	6.7	279	43.6
1986	961	71	765	8.5	778	322	49.2	66.2	10.1	267	40.7
1985	893	94	720	7.4	699	272	46.1	67.8	11.5	250	42.4
1984	803	131	648	8.5	629	242	45.2	69.4	13.0	224	41.8
1983	692	93	538	8.1	519	197	44.5	46.0	10.4	200	45.1

Data as orig. reptd. **1.** Times int. exp. & pfd. divs. covered (pretax basis). **2.** Bef. spec. item(s) in 1986. **3.** Based on income bef. interest charges.

Business Summary

Central Louisiana Electric provides electric service in Louisiana to some 214,000 customers in a service area that measures about 14,000 square miles and contains primarily small communities and adjacent rural areas. Contributions to electric revenues by class of customers in recent years were:

	1992	1991	1990	1989
Residential	44%	45%	45%	45%
Commercial	19%	19%	19%	19%
Industrial	23%	23%	24%	24%
Other	14%	13%	12%	11%

Sources of electric generation in 1992 were coal and lignite 52%, natural gas 41% and purchased power 7%. Peak demand in 1992 was 1,308 mw and generating capability totaled 1,706 mw, for a capacity margin of 23%. During 1992, CNL sold 6,098 million kwh of electricity, up from 6,010 million kwh in 1991. Over half of the company's industrial sales are made to the paper industry.

CNL estimated construction expenditures for 1993-1997 at $235 million, including $62 million for 1993. Internally generated funds should provide substantially all of the company's capital needs in 1993-1997. Outlays are primarily for transmission and distribution facilities. Generating capacity should be sufficient until the year 2000.

Finances

On May 5, 1993, the company priced for settlement on May 19, 1993, $25 million of medium-term notes to be issued in two tranches: $10 million 5.9% notes due 1999 and $15 million 6.55% notes due 2003. Proceeds were to be used to redeem higher coupon debt.

Dividend Data

Cash dividends have been paid since 1935. A dividend reinvestment plan is available.

Amt. of Divd. $	Date Decl.	Ex-divd. Date	Stock of Record	Payment Date
0.34½	Jan. 25	Jan. 26	Feb. 1	Feb. 15'93
0.35½	Apr. 23	Apr. 27	May 3	May 15'93
0.35½	Jul. 23	Jul. 27	Aug. 2	Aug. 15'93
0.35½	Oct. 22	Oct. 26	Nov. 1	Nov. 15'93

Capitalization

Long Term Debt: $310,322,000 (3/93).

Red. Preferred Stock: $7,400,000.

Cum. Preferred Stock: $30,982,000.

Common Stock: 22,334,795 shs. ($2 par).
Institutions hold about 34%.
Shareholders of record: 12,820.

Office—2030 Donahue Ferry Rd., Pineville, LA 71360-5226. **Tel**—(318) 484-7400. **Pres & CEO**—G. L. Nesbitt. **VP-Fin, Treas & Investor Contact**—David M. Eppler (800) 253-2652; in La. (800) 331-4132. **Secy**—V. J. Whittington. **Dirs**—J. P. Garrett, F. B. James Jr., H. J. Kelly, W. A. Lockwood, A. D. Martin Jr., G. L. Nesbitt, R. T. Ratcliff, E. M. Simmons, E. L. Williamson. **Transfer Agent & Registrar**—First Chicago Trust Co. of New York, NYC. **Incorporated** in Louisiana in 1934. **Empl**—1,322.

 Ned Bancroft

Central Maine Power

NYSE Symbol CTP In S&P MidCap 400

Price	Range	P-E Ratio	Dividend	Yield	S&P Ranking	Beta
Jul. 28'93	1993					
22⅞	24½–21	13	1.56	6.8%	B	0.63

Summary

This utility provides electric power to a service area that includes approximately 75% of Maine's population and the bulk of the state's industrial centers. About 26% of power in 1992 was generated by nuclear plants. Profitability in 1993 should benefit from a rate boost and lower costs stemming from refinancing debt, closing an inefficient nuclear facility, and terminating unneeded power purchase contracts.

Current Outlook

Earnings for 1993 are projected at $1.95 a share, up from $1.85 in 1992. Earnings for 1994 are projected at $1.95 a share.

Dividends should continue at $0.39 quarterly.

Higher earnings for 1993 should reflect a $41.5 million rate increase, effective July 1, 1993, and continued success in cutting and controlling costs. Through attrition, early retirement and layoffs, CTP has reduced its work force by 10% since 1991. The company initiated a base rate proceeding on March 1, 1993, to request a $95 million increase. Under Maine regulatory practices, new rates could be effective December 1, 1993. With the Maine economy still sluggish, weak kwh sales growth will limit earnings, and construction expenditures will be restricted to 1992 levels.

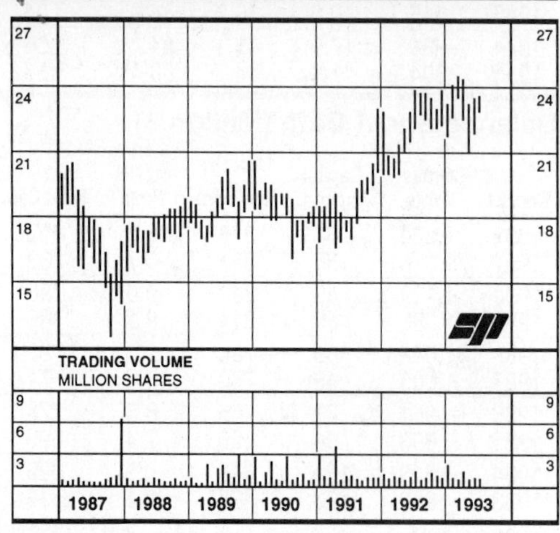

Operating Revenues (Million $)

Quarter:	1994	1993	1992	1991
Mar.	---	236.0	246.6	229.2
Jun.	---	199.0	203.8	203.0
Sep.	---	---	207.2	203.1
Dec.	---	---	220.1	231.2
	---	---	877.7	866.5

Revenues in the six months ended June 30, 1993, fell 3.4%, year to year, as lower residential and commercial sales offset higher industrial sales to the pulp and paper industry. Operation and maintenance expenses declined at a slower pace, and following higher preferred dividends, net income was down 3.7%. After significantly higher preferred dividends, earnings per share were $0.98, on 3.7% more common shares outstanding, compared with $1.11.

Common Share Earnings ($)

Quarter:	1994	1993	1992	1991
Mar.	E0.70	0.62	0.67	0.51
Jun.	E0.40	0.37	0.45	0.48
Sep.	E0.45	E0.56	0.44	0.41
Dec.	E0.40	E0.40	0.30	0.42
	E1.95	E1.95	1.85	1.82

Important Developments

Mar. '93— In a strategic move to reduce costs, CTP terminated a power purchase agreement with Caithness-King for an 80 mw generator Caithness had intended to install in Topsham, Me. Power deliveries were scheduled to begin on November 1, 1996, and present value savings to customers were about $85 million over the 30 year period beginning in 1996. During 1992, the company bought out five power purchase contracts with non-utility generators, saving CTP customers more than $44 million in fuel costs over the next four years, a reduction of 35% in the anticipated fuel increases for the period. Also in 1992, the company joined other owners in voting to close the small, high-cost Yankee Rowe atomic power station for present savings of $5 million. Refunding of certain of the company's outstanding mortgage bonds should save CTP $1 million a year in interest expense in each of the next five years.

Next earnings report expected in late October.

Per Share Data ($)

Yr. End Dec. 31	1992	1991	1990	1989	1988	1987	1986	1985	1984	1983
Tangible Bk. Val.	**16.68**	12.42	12.17	11.67	10.21	15.07	14.69	14.58	16.17	16.68
Earnings	**1.85**	1.82	1.68	1.92	1.83	1.79	1.54	0.08	1.99	2.51
Dividends	**1.56**	1.56	1.56	1.52	1.48	1.40	1.40	1.40	1.82	1.88
Payout Ratio	**84%**	86%	93%	79%	81%	78%	91%	NM	91%	75%
Prices—High	**23⅞**	23	20⅝	20⅜	18⅞	20½	20	14⅜	14¾	17
Low	**19⅞**	16⅝	16⅛	16⅞	15½	12½	13⅜	9¼	7⅞	14⅜
P/E Ratio—	**13–11**	13–9	12–10	11–9	10–8	11–7	13–9	NM	7–4	7–6

Data as orig. reptd. E-Estimated NM-Not Meaningful.

Income Data (Million $)

Year Ended Dec. 31	Revs.	Depr.	Maint.	Oper. Ratio	[1]Fxd. Chgs. Cover.	Constr. Credits	Eff. Tax Rate	Net Inc.	% Return On— Revs.	[2]Invest. Capital	Com. Equity
1992	**878**	**50.4**	**40.7**	**87.7%**	**2.24**	**2.8**	**19.7%**	**63.6**	**7.2**	**9.0**	**11.3**
1991	867	47.9	37.4	87.8%	2.22	1.6	23.2%	59.1	6.8	9.4	11.3
1990	766	44.4	34.1	88.5%	1.90	3.5	9.7%	48.8	6.4	9.1	10.3
1989	704	43.0	35.0	87.5%	2.16	3.4	22.5%	48.6	6.9	9.6	11.8
1988	654	43.6	36.2	87.1%	2.23	1.5	26.5%	45.8	7.0	9.4	12.0
1987	598	40.6	29.3	85.6%	2.38	0.4	34.6%	46.5	7.8	9.9	12.0
1986	509	38.1	26.9	82.2%	2.08	12.6	35.5%	45.3	8.9	9.8	10.5
1985	536	33.6	24.6	84.6%	0.93	26.9	NM	12.4	2.3	5.9	0.5
1984	515	25.8	21.2	85.9%	2.21	34.8	27.9%	51.0	9.9	9.2	12.3
1983	456	25.8	20.8	85.4%	2.55	29.3	25.1%	52.2	11.5	10.0	15.3

Balance Sheet Data (Million $)

Dec. 31	Gross Prop.	Capital Expend.	Net Prop.	% Earn. on Net Prop.	Total Cap.	Capitalization— LT Debt	% LT Debt	Pfd.	% Pfd.	Com.	% Com.
1992	**1,553**	**72**	**1,079**	**10.1**	**1,347**	**499**	**42.6**	**151**	**12.9**	**520**	**44.5**
1991	1,500	76	1,053	11.0	1,254	519	47.7	79	7.3	490	45.0
1990	1,445	105	1,017	9.7	1,200	496	47.7	80	7.7	464	44.6
1989	1,350	117	951	10.5	1,038	431	48.2	47	5.3	415	46.5
1988	1,226	96	845	11.1	1,022	476	53.7	58	6.6	353	39.7
1987	1,123	69	779	12.0	940	414	50.6	60	7.3	345	42.1
1986	1,051	85	734	11.6	909	390	48.2	82	10.2	336	41.6
1985	1,220	101	924	9.7	1,017	480	52.0	114	12.4	329	35.6
1984	1,192	121	917	8.7	1,046	485	51.2	117	12.4	344	36.4
1983	1,116	124	861	8.7	900	380	47.2	119	14.7	307	38.1

Data as orig. reptd. **1.** Times int. exp. & pfd. divs. covered (pretax basis). **2.** Based on income bef. interest chgs. NM-Not Meaningful.

Business Summary

Central Maine Power supplies electricity in central and southern Maine in an 11,000-square-mile area with a population of about 929,000 (roughly 75% of the state's population). Revenue contributions by class of customers in recent years:

	1992	1991	1990	1989
Residential	41%	40%	41%	42%
Industrial	30%	31%	30%	29%
Commercial	27%	27%	27%	26%
Other	2%	2%	2%	2%

The generation mix in 1992 was 26% nuclear, 38% cogeneration/small power producers, 19% oil, 15% hydro and 2% other purchased power. Peak demand in 1992 was 1,400 mw, and capability at time of peak was 1,855 mw, for a capacity margin of 32%. At 1992 year-end, the company had 496,669 customers, up from 490,506 in 1991.

The company's service area contains the bulk of Maine's industrial centers, including Portland, the state's largest city. CTP's industrial and commercial customers include major producers of pulp and paper products, manufacturers of chemicals, plastics, electronic components, processed food and footwear, and shipbuilders.

CTP's construction program for 1993-97 has been estimated to cost $350 million, with outlays for 1993 consistent with the $73 million spent in 1992. The company expects a substantial portion of the construction program requirements to be provided through internally generated funds.

Finances

In May 1993, CTP sold $50 million of 7⅞% general and refunding mortgage bonds through underwriters Lehman Brothers and Kidder, Peabody & Co. Proceeds from the sale will be used to refinance higher coupon debt.

Dividend Data

Dividends have been paid since 1943. A dividend reinvestment plan is available.

Amt of Divd. $	Date Decl.	Ex–divd. Date	Stock of Record	Payment Date
0.39	Sep. 23	Oct. 5	Oct. 9	Oct. 30'92
0.39	Dec. 16	Jan. 4	Jan. 8	Jan. 29'93
0.39	Mar. 17	Apr. 2	Apr. 9	Apr. 30'93
0.39	Jun. 16	Jul. 2	Jul. 9	Jul. 30'93

Capitalization

Long Term Debt: $521,727,000 (3/93).

Red. Cum. Preferred Stock: $35,000,000.

Cum. Preferred Stock: $110,571,000.

Common Stock: 31,678,523 shs. ($5 par). Institutions hold about 23%. Shareholders of record: 37,382.

Office—Edison Drive, Augusta, ME 04336. **Tel**—(207) 623-3521. **Chrmn**—C. D. Reed Jr. **Pres & CEO**—M. Hunter. **SVP-CFO**—D. E. Marsh. **Secy**—W. M. Finn. **Treas & Investor Contact**—Ann C. McCulloch. **Dirs**—C. H. Abbott, K. S. Axelson, C. M. Chase, E. J. Dufour, R. H. Gardiner, G. H. Gillespie, M. Hunter, D. M. Jagger, C.E. Monty, C. D. Reed Jr., R. H. Reny, K. M. Weare. **Transfer Agent**—Company itself. **Registrar**—Chemical Bank, NYC. **Incorporated** in Maine in 1905. **Empl**—2,376.

 Ned Bancroft

Century Telephone Enterprises

NYSE Symbol CTL Options on Pacific (Jan-Apr-Jul-Oct) In S&P MidCap 400

Price	Range	P-E Ratio	Dividend	Yield	S&P Ranking	Beta
Aug. 31'93	1993					
29⅝	33⅜–26	21	0.31	1.0%	A	1.44

Summary

This holding company provides local telephone services in designated areas of 15 states; other operations include cellular telephone and paging units. Century's strategy of acquisitions and clustering of operations to gain efficiencies should contribute to further earnings growth.

Current Outlook

Earnings for 1993 are estimated at $1.35 a share, versus 1992's $1.25. For 1994, earnings are forecast to reach $1.50.

The $0.07¾ quarterly dividend is expected to be maintained.

Telephone revenues are expected to continue to post strong growth in 1993, reflecting a full year's inclusion of the Ohio operations and the April 1993 San Marcos acquisition; however, regulatory changes could restrict revenue growth in the second half of the year. Margins may narrow, reflecting higher depreciation rates and increased costs associated with new operations. Mobile revenues are expected to grow rapidly, reflecting increased coverage areas. Mobile profit contributions should increase faster, on lower costs associated with the development of the RSA markets and efforts to reduce customer acquisition costs. Interest costs will rise. Share earnings will reflect additional shares outstanding.

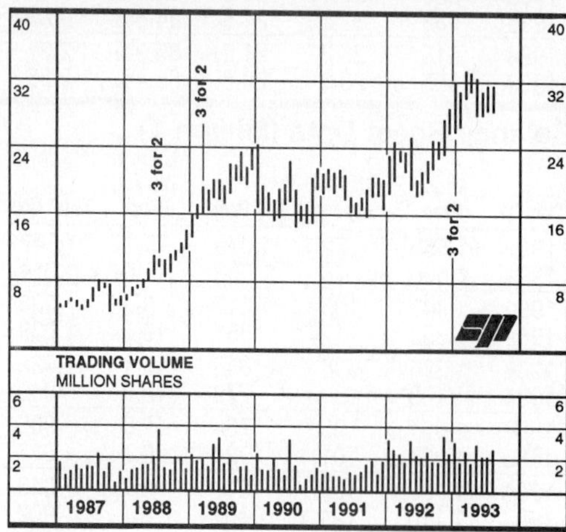

Revenues (Million $)

Quarter:	1993	1992	1991	1990
Mar.	96.8	75.4	64.8	60.4
Jun.	107.3	88.4	69.1	60.7
Sep.		92.8	72.4	62.8
Dec.		100.1	74.8	64.8
		356.8	281.0	248.8

Revenues for the six months to June 30, 1993, rose 24%, year to year, on a 22% gain in telephone revenues and a 36% increase in cellular revenues. Margins narrowed, primarily reflecting higher depreciation rates used in the telephone operations. A $1.7 million gain on the sale of assets and higher net other income outweighed a 9.0% increase in interest expense. Pretax income advanced 32%. After taxes, net income also was up 32%. Share earnings were $0.64 based on 4.6% more shares, versus $0.51 (before a $0.33 special charge for accounting changes).

Common Share Earnings ($)

Quarter:	1993	1992	1991	1990
Mar.	0.32	0.24	0.15	0.15
Jun.	0.32	0.26	0.18	0.19
Sep.	E0.34	0.31	0.21	0.16
Dec.	E0.37	0.44	0.26	0.18
	E1.35	1.25	0.80	0.67

Important Developments

Aug. '93— CTL signed an agreement to acquire Celutel, Inc. for about $105 million in cash and common shares. Celutel provides cellular service to about 20,000 customers in Texas and Mississippi. CTL anticipated that the acquisition would result in dilution of $0.09 to $0.11 per share in 1994. Separately, CTL expected to complete the acquisitions of majority interests in the Biloxi and Pascagoula, Miss., cellular operations shortly; the total purchase price of $36 million will be paid 40% in cash and 60% in common shares.

Next earnings report expected in early November.

Per Share Data ($)

Yr. End Dec. 31	1992	1991	1990	1989	1988	1987	1986	1985	1984	1983
Tangible Bk. Val.	**3.42**	4.36	3.69	3.21	2.96	2.82	2.71	2.51	2.21	2.01
Earnings[1]	**1.25**	0.80	0.67	0.49	0.57	0.58	0.44	0.43	0.40	0.31
Dividends	**0.293**	0.287	0.280	0.272	0.264	0.253	0.247	0.237	0.231	0.226
Payout Ratio	**23%**	36%	42%	55%	46%	44%	56%	54%	58%	71%
Prices—High	**28⅞**	21⅝	24⅜	24	14⅛	8⅛	5⅝	4¼	2⅞	3⅜
Low	**18⅜**	15⅞	14⅝	13⅜	5¾	4⅜	3⅞	2¾	2¼	2⅜
P/E Ratio—	**23–15**	27–20	36–22	49–27	25–10	14–8	13–9	10–6	7–6	11–8

Data as orig. reptd. Adj. for stk. divs. of 50% Jan. 1993, 50% Mar. 1989, 50% Aug. 1988. 1. Bef. spec. item of -0.33 in 1992.

Income Data (Million $)

Year Ended Dec. 31	[1]Access Lines	Util. & NonUtil— Util. Revs.	Non–Util.	Total Revs.	Constr. Credits	Eff. Tax Rate	[2]Net Inc.	—% Return On— Revs.	Assets	[3]Equity
1992	**397**	**298**	**59.3**	**357**	**NA**	**35.2%**	**60.0**	**16.8**	**6.6**	**17.0**
1991	315	236	45.2	281	NA	34.9%	37.4	13.3	5.1	12.5
1990	305	216	33.0	249	NA	35.9%	31.1	12.5	4.4	11.6
1989	296	191	22.7	213	NA	32.6%	22.2	10.4	3.7	10.8
1988	239	173	10.6	184	NA	32.1%	23.4	12.7	4.8	15.6
1987	232	157	61.9	219	1.20	34.7%	23.3	10.7	5.0	16.9
1986	227	146	60.5	207	1.60	38.1%	17.2	8.3	3.9	14.2
1985	224	135	59.1	194	1.38	38.1%	15.5	8.0	3.8	14.5
1984	201	111	49.4	160	1.44	37.5%	13.7	8.6	3.7	14.1
1983	198	100	47.5	147	0.52	39.1%	10.5	7.2	3.1	11.6

Balance Sheet Data (Million $)

Dec. 31	Gross Prop.	Depr. Reserve	Net Prop.	Capital Expend.	Total Invest. Capital	—Capitalization— LT Debt	% LT Debt	[4]Pfd.	[4]% Pfd.	Com.	% Com.
1992	**1,004**	**329**	**676**	**140**	**828**	**392**	**50.4**	**0.5**	**0.1**	**385**	**49.5**
1991	796	261	535	96	676	255	44.3	0.5	0.1	320	55.6
1990	735	244	491	65	612	231	45.1	0.5	0.1	280	54.8
1989	696	222	474	62	615	258	50.0	2.1	0.4	256	49.6
1988	580	179	401	57	426	180	53.6	3.7	1.1	152	45.3
1987	529	148	380	63	417	182	54.9	4.5	1.4	145	43.7
1986	503	139	364	46	412	195	58.5	9.6	2.9	129	38.6
1985	473	128	345	46	399	208	63.0	13.5	4.1	108	32.9
1984	400	106	294	44	345	184	62.1	19.5	6.6	93	31.3
1983	364	92	272	42	326	179	63.1	19.8	7.0	85	29.9

Data as orig. reptd. **1.** In thousands. **2.** Bef. spec. item in 1992. **3.** Common. **4.** Incl. minority interest. NA-Not Available.

Business Summary

Century Telephone Enterprises' telephone subsidiaries serve parts of 15 states. Through Century Cellunet, the company also provides cellular mobile telephone service and wide-area/nationwide radio paging services. Business segment contributions in 1992 were:

	Revs.	Profits
Telephone	83%	95%
Mobile	17%	5%

CTL provides local telephone service in 15 states, the most important being Wisconsin, Louisiana, Michigan, Ohio and Arkansas. At June 30, 1993, CTL's telephone subsidiaries served about 426,000 access lines. The territories served are largely rural and suburban.

As of June 30, 1993, cellular mobile telephone service was being provided to more than 88,000 subscribers. CTL's cellular operations are in franchised areas with a total of 5.5 million POPs (population of the service area, adjusted for percent ownership), with operations concentrated in Michigan and Louisiana.

CTL also provides wide-area and nationwide paging services in Michigan and Louisiana. Florida paging operations were sold during 1991. Paging service subscribers are able to receive messages in over 150 markets across the U.S.

Finances

CTL's budgeted capital expenditures for 1993 (exclusive of acquisitions) were $132 million for telephone operations, $50 million for mobile communications and $16 million for other operations.

Dividend Data

Dividends have been paid since 1974. A dividend reinvestment plan is available. A "poison pill" stock purchase right was adopted in 1986.

Amt of Divd. $	Date Decl.	Ex–divd. Date	Stock of Record	Payment Date
0.11	Nov. 24	Nov. 30	Dec. 4	Dec. 18'92
3–for–2	Nov. 24	Jan. 4	Dec. 10	Dec. 31'92
0.07¾	Feb. 23	Mar. 1	Mar. 5	Mar. 19'93
0.07¾	May 25	May 28	Jun. 4	Jun. 18'93
0.07¾	Aug. 24	Aug. 30	Sep. 3	Sep. 17'93

Capitalization

Long Term Debt: $438,569,000 (6/93).

Cum. Preferred Stock: $454,000.

Common Stock: 51,191,276 shs. ($1 par).
Institutions hold about 63%.
Shareholders of record: 5,370.

Office—100 Century Park Drive, P.O. Box 4065, Monroe, LA 71211-4065. **Tels**—(318) 388-9500; (800) 833-1188. **Chrmn**—C. M. Williams. **Pres & CEO**—G. F. Post III. **Sr VP-CFO**—R. S. Ewing Jr. **Secy**—H. P. Perry. **Investor Contact**—Robert E. Fudickar. **Dirs**—W. R. Boles Jr., E. Butler Jr., C. Czeschin, J. B. Gardner, W. B. Hanks, R. L. Hargrove Jr., J. Hebert, F. E. Hogan, T. S. Lovett, C. G. Melville Jr., H. P. Perry, G. F. Post III, J. D. Reppond, C. M. Williams. **Transfer Agent**—Society Shareholder Services, Dallas. **Incorporated** in Louisiana in 1968. **Empl**—2,378.

 Susan Stahl Gibney

Chesapeake Corp.

NYSE Symbol CSK In S&P MidCap 400

Price	Range	P-E Ratio	Dividend	Yield	S&P Ranking	Beta
Oct. 19'93	1993					
19¾	23⅛–17⅛	NM	0.72	3.7%	B–	0.95

Summary

Chesapeake produces paper, paperboard, pulp and corrugated containers, as well as wood products. In recent years, it has shifted its emphasis from commodity products to high margin, value-added products for niche markets. Operations were marginally profitable in the first half of 1993, with weak product pricing continuing to pressure results. Assuming some strengthening in paper industry conditions, earnings are expected to begin to rebound in 1994.

Current Outlook

Earnings for 1993 are projected at $0.32 a share, down from $0.63 (before special items) in 1992. In 1994, earnings should reach $1.00 a share.

Although not fully covered by recent earnings, dividends are expected to continue at $0.18 quarterly.

Sales are likely to continue to increase modestly in the second half of 1993, with higher volume expected to be largely offset by weak pricing. Margins will remain under pressure during the remainder of this year, but are expected to show some improvement in 1994 if the company's markets begin to turn around as expected. Efforts to lessen reliance on commodity-type products may improve profitability in the long term, but a return to peak earnings levels reached in the late 1980s is not expected soon.

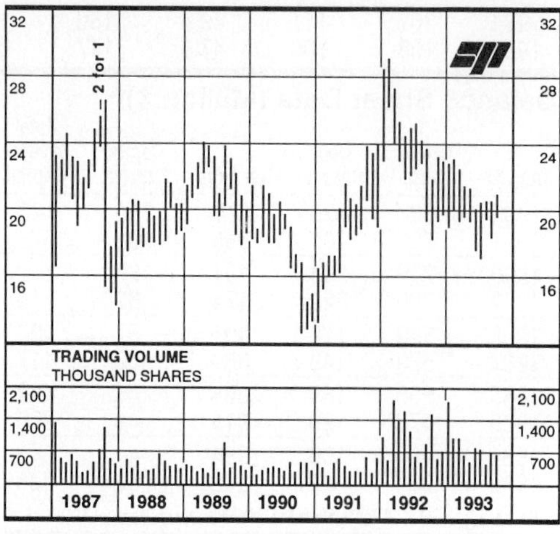

Net Sales (Million $)

Quarter:	1993	1992	1991	1990
Mar.	209	210	198	204
Jun.	236	229	219	223
Sep.	238	236	220	216
Dec.	---	213	204	199
	---	888	841	841

Sales for the six months ended June 30, 1993, rose 1.4%, year to year, reflecting higher shipments of tissue, kraft and packaging products. However, operating expenses increased more rapidly, and following higher interest charges, pretax income dropped 89%. After taxes at 54.9%, versus 36.0%, net income fell 92%, to $0.02 a share from $0.30. Results for the 1992 period exclude a special charge of $0.46 a share.

Common Share Earnings ($)

Quarter:	1994	1993	1992	1991
Mar.	E0.10	d0.03	0.11	0.12
Jun.	E0.30	0.05	0.19	0.12
Sep.	E0.40	0.11	0.28	0.23
Dec.	E0.20	E0.10	0.05	0.28
	E1.00	E0.32	0.63	0.75

Important Developments

Jul. '93— Management said that kraft products continued to be sold at "ridiculously low" prices, but tissue prices improved in the second quarter of 1993, with further improvement expected in the third quarter. Tissue product shipments rose 5% in 1993's first half over year-earlier levels, while kraft product shipments were up 9% and packaging product shipments increased 2%. CSK's tissue mill operated at over 100% of rated capacity in the second quarter. The company believes that improved pricing remains the key to improved earnings. According to CSK, earnings during the first half of 1993 were penalized by nearly $19 million of price erosion. However, cash flow was positive, enabling CSK to reduce long-term debt by $13 million from first quarter levels. Separately, CSK's capital expenditures in the first six months of 1993 totaled $38 million, versus $50 million in 1992's first half.

Next earnings report expected in mid-October.

Per Share Data ($)

Yr. End Dec. 31	1992	1991	1990	1989	1988	[1]1987	1986	[1]1985	1984	1983
Tangible Bk. Val.	**14.51**	13.80	13.63	13.45	12.12	10.06	8.87	8.44	9.78	9.09
Cash Flow	**3.66**	3.92	3.68	4.78	4.65	3.71	2.87	2.42	2.35	1.55
Earnings[2]	**0.63**	0.75	0.81	2.31	2.51	1.47	0.68	0.79	1.12	0.45
Dividends	**0.720**	0.720	0.720	0.680	0.500	0.450	0.420	0.415	0.388	0.368
Payout Ratio	**117%**	96%	88%	29%	20%	30%	62%	53%	35%	85%
Prices—High	**29⅛**	24	21½	24⅛	21⅞	26⅝	18½	13⅜	13¼	13½
Low	**18¼**	13¼	12⅝	17⅞	16⅜	14¼	12¾	10¾	10½	9¼
P/E Ratio—	**46–29**	32–18	27–16	10–8	9–7	18–10	27–19	17–14	12–9	30–21

Data as orig. reptd. Adj. for stk. divs. of 100% Sep. 1987, 50% Nov. 1986. **1.** Refl.merger or acq. **2.** Bef. spec. items of -0.43 in 1992, +0.21 in 1983. d-Deficit. E-Estimated.

Chesapeake Corporation

Income Data (Million $)

Year Ended Dec. 31	Revs.	Oper. Inc.	% Oper. Inc. of Revs.	Cap. Exp.	Depr.	Int. Exp.	Net Bef. Taxes	Eff. Tax Rate	[3]Net Inc.	% Net Inc. of Revs.	Cash Flow
1992	**888**	**121**	**13.6**	**85**	**68.6**	**35.1**	**22.5**	**36.0%**	**[4]14.4**	**1.6**	**83.0**
1991	841	124	14.7	92	65.2	37.9	26.1	41.0%	15.4	1.8	80.6
1990	841	118	14.0	125	59.0	34.9	29.1	42.6%	16.7	2.0	75.7
1989	813	153	18.9	148	50.8	27.7	78.5	39.4%	47.6	5.9	98.4
1988	711	148	20.7	72	44.0	22.1	84.1	38.8%	51.5	7.2	95.5
[1]1987	676	125	18.5	42	45.9	26.3	[2]56.2	46.3%	30.2	4.5	76.1
1986	600	89	14.8	43	44.2	30.2	[2]21.9	37.4%	13.7	2.3	57.9
[1]1985	454	64	14.1	244	32.5	17.7	[2]17.1	8.2%	15.7	3.5	48.2
1984	350	60	17.1	51	24.4	5.3	[2]33.6	34.2%	22.1	6.3	46.5
1983	274	37	13.5	28	21.2	6.0	[2]12.6	32.5%	8.5	3.1	29.7

Balance Sheet Data (Million $)

		Curr.									
Dec. 31	Cash	Assets	Liab.	Ratio	Total Assets	% Ret. on Assets	Long Term Debt	Common Equity	Total Cap.	% LT Debt of Cap.	% Ret. on Equity
1992	**0.7**	**212**	**89.7**	**2.4**	**959**	**1.4**	**383**	**370**	**850**	**45.1**	**3.9**
1991	1.0	196	94.7	2.1	916	1.7	416	318	821	50.7	4.8
1990	0.8	185	92.2	2.0	876	2.0	381	314	784	48.6	5.3
1989	0.5	184	85.3	2.2	790	6.5	301	314	704	42.7	16.0
1988	1.1	165	65.8	2.5	662	8.2	232	279	596	38.9	19.9
1987	0.4	126	57.1	2.2	591	4.9	226	239	534	42.3	13.3
1986	0.2	127	50.9	2.5	626	2.2	303	215	573	52.8	6.5
1985	2.8	115	51.8	2.2	618	3.3	309	207	561	55.1	7.7
1984	2.7	75	29.0	2.6	331	7.0	61	197	298	20.4	11.6
1983	9.1	70	28.0	2.5	296	2.9	52	182	268	19.4	4.8

Data as orig. reptd. **1.** Refl. merger or acq. **2.** Incl. equity in earns. of nonconsol. subs. **3.** Bef. spec. items. **4.** Refl. acctg. change.

Business Summary

Chesapeake Corp. is an integrated forest products company, with paper, paperboard, pulp, tissue products, corrugated container and lumber producing operations. In recent years, the company has shifted its emphasis from commod ity products to more profitable, value-added products for niche markets. Business segment contributions in 1992 were:

	Sales	Profits
Paper	56%	80%
Converted products	32%	15%
Wood products	12%	5%

Mill products produced at CSK's West Point, Va., complex consist of kraft and white top paperboard, kraft paper, corrugating medium and bleached hardwood pulp. Paperboard and corrugating medium are sold to independent and company-owned container and packaging plants. Kraft paper is sold to paper converters to make bags and wrappings. Bleached hardwood pulp is sold to mannufacturers of printing and writing paper. Wisconsin Tissue Mills produces napkins, tablecovers, towels and facial and bathroom tissue for commercial and industrial markets.

Converted products operations include three point-of-sale display and packaging manufacturing plants and four assembly plants which serve major consumer products companies. The company's Color-Box facility supplies consumer graphic packaging to customers requiring full litho-laminated point-of-sale packaging. Six corrugated container plants produce corrugated boxes and specialty packaging. CSK also sells napkins, plates and other products in consumer markets.

CSK operates four sawmills in Virginia and Maryland, manufacturing pine and hardwood lumber using materials provided from both company-owned timberlands and other landowners.

Dividend Data

Dividends have been paid since 1933. A dividend reinvestment plan is available. A "poison pill" stock purchase right was adopted in 1988.

Amt. of Divd. $	Date Decl.	Ex-divd. Date	Stock of Record	Payment Date
0.18	Dec. 8	Jan. 11	Jan. 18	Feb. 12'93
0.18	Feb. 9	Apr. 13	Apr. 19	May 14'93
0.18	Jun. 8	Jun. 13	Jul. 19	Aug. 13'93
0.18	Aug. 10	Oct. 12	Oct. 18	Nov. 15'93

Capitalization

Long Term Debt: $382,700,000 (6/93).

Common Stock: 23,329,558 shs. ($1 par).
S.G. Olsson controls some 11%.
Institutions hold 55%.
Shareholders of record: 7,706.

Office—1021 East Cary St., Box 2350, Richmond VA 23218-2350. **Tel**—(804) 697-1000. **Chrmn**—S. G. Olsson. **Pres & CEO**—J. C. Fox. **EVP & COO**—P. A. Dresser, Jr. **VP, CFO & Investor Contact**—Andrew J. Kohut. **Secy**—J. P. Causey, Jr. **Treas**—L. K. Matherne, Jr. **Dirs**—P. A. Dresser, Jr., J. C. Fox, R. L. Hintz, W. D. McCoy, S. G. Olsson, J. W. Rosenblum, F. S. Royal, W. Stettinius, J. H. Stookey, R. G. Tilghman, J.P. Viviano, H. H. Warner. **Transfer Agent & Registrar**—Harris Trust and Savings Bank, Chicago. **Incorporated** in Virginia in 1918. **Empl**—5,062.

 Richard Spiegel

Chiron Corp.

NASDAQ Symbol CHIR (Incl. in Nat'l Market) Options on ASE, CBOE, NY In S&P MidCap 400

Price	Range	P-E Ratio	Dividend	Yield	S&P Ranking	Beta
Sep. 8'93	1993					
66¾	70–40	NM	None	None	C	1.35

Summary

This leading biotechnology company applies genetic engineering and other technologies to develop products that diagnose, prevent and treat disease. Chiron operates in four principal markets: diagnostics, vaccines, therapeutics and ophthalmics. The sales base was substantially enlarged by the late 1991 acquisition of Cetus Corp., a leader in cancer research. Widening acceptance of existing products and contributions from new products enhance long-term prospects.

Current Outlook

Earnings are projected at $1.25 a share for 1994, up from $0.48 estimated for 1993.

Initiation of cash dividends is not anticipated.

Total revenues are expected to post another healthy gain in 1994, led by a sharp increase in sales of the company's new Betaseron drug for the treatment for multiple sclerosis. Sales of blood screening products should continue to grow, as should sales of Proleukin anticancer drug, vaccines and ophthalmic products. Despite heavy ongoing R&D outlays, profitability should benefit from the greater volume and an improved product mix.

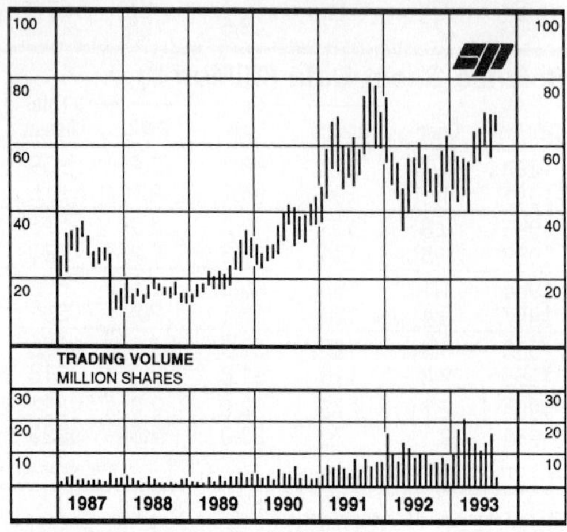

Total Revenues (Million $)

Quarter:	1993	1992	1991	1990
Mar.	69.1	56.7	23.7	14.2
Jun.	76.8	68.8	28.7	17.8
Sep.	---	61.3	29.9	19.1
Dec.	---	61.3	36.3	27.5
	---	248.2	118.5	78.5

Total revenues in the six months ended June 30, 1993, climbed 16%, year to year, primarily reflecting increased product sales and greater funding for Biocine Co. from Ciba-Geigy (Chiron's joint venture partner in Biocine). Net income of $7,900,000 ($0.24 a share) replaced a net loss of $44,857,000 ($1.52).

Common Share Earnings ($)

Quarter:	1993	1992	1991	1990
Mar.	0.08	d1.46	0.15	d0.29
Jun.	0.16	d0.13	0.16	0.20
Sep.	E0.11	d0.17	0.17	0.16
Dec.	E0.13	d1.42	d19.99	0.14
	E0.48	d3.18	[1]d22.12	[1]0.24

Important Developments

Sep. '93— Chiron formed a new R&D collaboration with Syntex Corp. to develop drugs for the treatment of arthritis, invasive malignant tumors and certain other diseases. Chiron's own R&D pipeline includes vaccines for herpes and HIV, and new DNA probe diagnostic tests to measure the amount of virus in blood samples.

Jul. '93— The FDA approved Betaseron, a new treatment for relapsing/remitting multiple sclerosis, developed by Cetus and Schering AG. Under terms of its agreement with Schering, Chiron will manufacture the drug and receive 30% of sales. Berlex Laboratories (a unit of Schering), will market the drug and receive 70% of sales.

Next earnings report expected in early November.

Per Share Data ($)

Yr. End Dec. 31[2]	[5]1992	1991	1990	1989	1988	1987	1986	1985	1984	1983
Tangible Bk. Val.	**[3]15.54**	[3]17.87	[3]7.39	[3]6.82	5.44	5.29	6.19	4.08	2.31	2.65
Cash Flow	**d2.36**	d21.68	0.57	d1.17	d0.95	d0.70	d0.53	d0.40	d0.18	d0.52
Earnings[4]	**d3.18**	d22.12	0.24	d1.51	d1.32	d0.97	d0.68	d0.53	d0.31	d0.61
Dividends	**Nil**	Nil	Nil	Nil	Nil	Nil	Nil	Nil	Nil	Nil
Payout Ratio	**Nil**	Nil	Nil	Nil	Nil	Nil	Nil	Nil	Nil	Nil
Prices—High	**74½**	79	44¾	34½	20⅛	37¼	31¾	15⅛	8¾	12
Low	**34¾**	37¼	23½	13	12¼	8¾	12⅛	4½	4⅜	6
P/E Ratio—	**NM**	NM	NM	NM	NM	NM	NM	NM	NM	NM

Data as orig. reptd. **1.** Does not reconcile bec. of changes in shares outstanding. **2.** Prior to 1989, yrs. ended Apr. 30 of fol. cal. yr. **3.** Incl. intangibles. **4.** Bef. spec. items of -0.22 in 1992, +0.01 in 1991, +0.16 in 1990. **5.** Refl. merger or acq. d-Deficit. E-Estimated. NM-Not Meaningful.

Income Data (Million $)

Year Ended Dec. 31[1]	Revs.	Oper. Inc.	% Oper. Inc. of Revs.	Cap. Exp.	Depr.	Int. Exp.	Net Bef. Taxes	Eff. Tax Rate	[4]Net Inc.	% Net Inc. of Revs.	Cash Flow
[2]1992	**174.0**	**d109.0**	**NM**	**24.7**	**24.70**	**17.30**	**[3]d92**	**NM**	**d96**	**NM**	**d71**
[2]1991	68.6	d54.1	NM	14.3	8.34	9.41	[3]d424	NM	d425	NM	d417
1990	52.4	d20.5	NM	9.4	5.23	4.49	[3]7	43%	4	7.7	10
1989	35.5	d21.9	NM	5.5	4.88	0.08	[3]d22	NM	d22	NM	d17
1988	35.7	d9.6	NM	4.3	4.41	0.03	[3]d16	NM	d16	NM	d12
1987	21.7	d10.5	NM	13.5	3.12	0.05	[3]d11	NM	d11	NM	d8
1986	10.5	d8.5	NM	6.7	1.65	0.09	[3]d7	Nil	d7	NM	d6
1985	7.1	d4.1	NM	2.0	1.03	0.13	d4	Nil	d4	NM	d3
1984	5.9	d2.7	NM	2.9	0.90	0.11	d2	Nil	d2	NM	d1
1983	2.5	d3.9	NM	1.8	0.46	0.09	d3	Nil	d3	NM	d3

Balance Sheet Data (Million $)

Dec. 31	Cash	Curr. Assets	Curr. Liab.	Curr. Ratio	Total Assets	% Ret. on Assets	Long Term Debt	Common Equity	Total Cap.	% LT Debt of Cap.	% Ret. on Equity
1992	**257**	**349**	**105**	**3.3**	**712**	**NM**	**107**	**493**	**600**	**17.9**	**NM**
1991	558	617	125	5.0	895	NM	239	524	763	31.3	NM
1990	154	174	21	8.3	265	2.1	122	120	242	50.3	3.5
1989	89	101	12	8.2	124	NM	Nil	109	109	NM	NM
1988	39	55	8	6.7	82	NM	Nil	71	71	NM	NM
1987	37	46	6	8.1	70	NM	Nil	62	62	0.3	NM
1986	64	66	6	10.8	80	NM	Nil	73	73	0.6	NM
1985	32	34	2	16.2	42	NM	Nil	39	40	2.0	NM
1984	13	14	3	5.1	21	NM	Nil	17	18	4.1	NM
1983	17	17	1	11.9	21	NM	Nil	19	20	3.3	NM

Data as orig. reptd. **1.** Prior to 1989, yrs. ended Apr. of fol. cal. yr. **2.** Reflects merger or acquisition. **3.** Incl. equity in earns. of nonconsol. subs. **4.** Bef. spec. items. d-Deficit. NM-Not Meaningful.

Business Summary

Chiron is a leading biotechnology company that focuses on the development of products in four key areas—diagnostics, vaccines, therapeutics and ophthalmics. Cetus Corp., a leader in cancer research, was acquired in late 1991. Total revenues in recent years were derived as follows:

	1992	1991	1990
Product sales	45%	24%	19%
Equity in unconsol. units	30%	42%	33%
Collaborative research	16%	26%	39%
Other	9%	8%	9%

Foreign operations accounted for 18% of total revenues in 1992. The company's principal customer, Johnson & Johnson, provided 38% of the 1992 total. R&D spending equaled 58% of 1992 revenues.

Product sales include ophthalmic surgical products used in cataract, corneal, refractive and vitreoretinal surgeries (26% of total revenues in 1992); drugs such as Cetus' Proleukin treatment for kidney cancer and other chemotherapeutics; and diagnostic kits and antigens.

Equity in unconsolidated joint businesses consists chiefly of Chiron's share in the earnings of Chiron—Ortho, a joint venture with the Ortho Diagnostics unit of Johnson & Johnson. Chiron—Ortho is the world's largest supplier of microplate blood screening tests for hepatitis and AIDS. The company's share of profits totaled $73.6 million in 1992, of which over 80% was derived from hepatitis C tests. Other joint ventures market generic anticancer drugs and sell pediatric vaccines.

Collaborative research revenues consist of funds provided Chiron by other firms to research specified projects in exchange for licenses to market resulting products. Collaborations include an agreement with Daiichi Pure Chemicals, Ltd. to develop DNA probe tests, a venture with CIBA-GEIGY which is working on new vaccines for herpes and AIDS, and a venture with Syntex to develop drugs for arthritis, cancer and other ailments. Other revenues include royalties under license agreements, sales fees and government R&D grants.

Dividend Data

No cash dividends have been paid.

Capitalization

Long Term Debt: $111,725,000 (6/93).

Common Stock: 32,016,092 shs. ($0.01 par). Institutions hold 58%. Shareholders of record: 10,218.

Office—4560 Horton St., Emeryville, CA 94608. **Tel**—(510) 655-8730. **Chrmn**—W. J. Rutter. **Pres & CEO**—E. E. Penhoet. **SVP-Fin & CFO**—D. L. Winger. **SVP & Secy**—W. G. Green. **Investor Contact**—Larry Kurtz. **Dirs**—G. F. Amelio, L. W. Coleman, D.A. Glaser, E. E. Penhoet, W. J. Rutter, H. Schramek, J. W. Schuler, P. J. Strijkert. **Transfer Agent & Registrar**—Chemical Trsut Co. of California, SF. **Reincorporated** in Delaware in 1987. **Empl**—1,867.

 Herman Saftlas

Chris-Craft Industries

NYSE Symbol CCN Options on CBOE (Jan-Apr-Jul-Oct) In S&P MidCap 400

Price	Range	P-E Ratio	Dividend	Yield	S&P Ranking	Beta
Oct. 28'93	1993					
42¼	43⅜–30⁷⁄₃₂	8	[1]---	[1]---	B–	0.90

Summary

This company is primarily engaged in television broadcasting, through its 69% ownership of ASE-listed BHC Communications Inc. BHC is the largest non-network TV group in the U.S. Over $1.14 billion in holdings of marketable securities and cash, derived from the disposition of Time Warner shares, places CCN in a strong position to expand operations, but creates a drag on profitability in the current low-interest-rate environment.

Current Outlook

Earnings for 1994 are projected at $2.30 a share, compared to the $5.15 estimated for 1993 (including about $3.00 of nonrecurring gains).

A stock dividend of 2% - 5% is likely to be distributed in the spring of 1994.

Television advertising revenues should continue to grow in 1994, in spite of continuing softness in the California market. A smaller rise in programming and other costs will contribute to an improvement in profitability. Interest and other income will be substantially lower.

Revenues (Million $)

Quarter:	1993	1992	1991	1990
Mar.	96.3	61.1	63.3	64.1
Jun.	120.3	75.8	76.1	80.1
Sep.	106.7	84.2	64.4	70.5
Dec.		110.5	80.1	82.8
		331.5	283.8	297.6

Revenues for the nine months ended September 20, 1993 advanced 46%, year to year, largely reflecting the inclusion of WWOR-TV. Operating earnings benefited from a 13% drop in programming costs, other than WWOR. After a nearly 3-fold increase in interest and other income, primarily gains from disposition of Time Warner convertible preferred shares, taxes at 39.5% against 25.6%, and higher minority interest, net income climbed to $124,987,000 ($4.55 a share) from 47,413,000 ($1.74).

Common Share Earnings ($)

Quarter:	1993	1992	1991	1990
Mar.	1.81	0.39	0.45	0.75
Jun.	2.29	0.63	0.53	0.74
Sep.	0.47	0.71	0.50	0.66
Dec.	E0.58	0.65	0.63	0.64
	E5.15	2.39	2.12	10.57

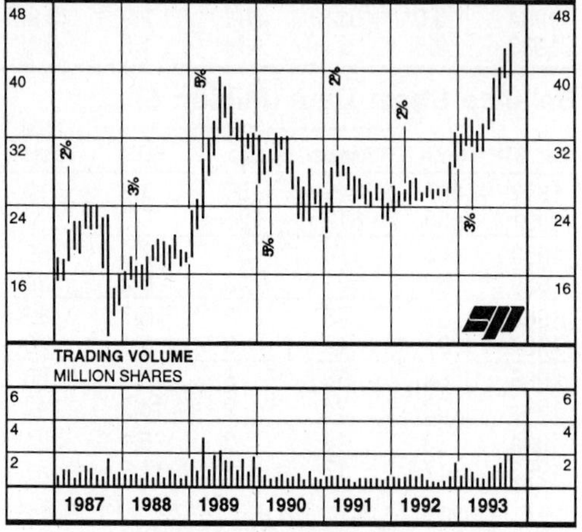

Important Developments

Oct. '93— CCN and Paramount Communications announced plans to launch a 5th TV network in January 1995, based on their 10 owned TV stations and Paramount's programming.

Jul. '93— BHC reported that its first-half earnings included pretax gains from the redemption of Time Warner convertible preferred stock of $93.7 million in the first quarter and $121.3 million in the second quarter. CCN said that it intends to expand its operations in the media, entertainment and communications industries, and to explore business opportunities in other industries. CCN has substantial holdings of cash and marketable securities, amounting to more than $1.14 billion at June 30, 1993, and has no debt. In the current low interest rate environment, however, CCN's large portfolio of government securities creates a drag on profitability.

Next earnings report expected in mid-January.

Per Share Data ($)

Yr. End Dec. 31[2]	1992	1991	1990	1989	1988	1987	1986	1985	1984	1983
Tangible Bk. Val.	**25.54**	37.63	34.12	24.86	1.67	0.64	d0.05	d0.71	d0.74	1.79
Cash Flow	**4.05**	2.41	10.87	17.43	1.12	0.75	0.90	0.97	0.42	0.24
Earnings[3]	**2.39**	2.11	10.57	17.13	0.78	0.38	0.54	0.68	0.16	0.20
Dividends	**Nil**	Nil	Nil	Nil	Nil	Nil	Nil	Nil	Nil	Nil
Payout Ratio	**Nil**	Nil	Nil	Nil	Nil	Nil	Nil	Nil	Nil	Nil
Prices—High	**32¹¹⁄₁₆**	30	32½	39⁹⁄₁₆	20½	24⁹⁄₁₆	20¹¹⁄₁₆	15¹³⁄₃₂	9⁹⁄₃₂	7½
Low	**23¹³⁄₃₂**	21	22⁵⁄₁₆	18⁹⁄₃₂	14⁹⁄₁₆	8¹⁹⁄₃₂	13¹⁹⁄₃₂	8¹¹⁄₁₆	6⁵⁄₁₆	4¹¹⁄₁₆
P/E Ratio—	**14–10**	14–10	3–2	2–1	26–18	64–23	39–25	23–13	60–42	38–23

Data as orig. reptd. Adj. for stk. divs. of 3% Mar. 1993, 2% Mar. 1992, 2% Mar. 1991, 5% Mar. 1990, 5% Mar. 1989, 3% Mar. 1988, 2% Mar. 1987, 200% Nov. 1986 (Cl. B com. shs.), 2% Apr. 1986, 2% Oct. 1984. **1.** Pays stock. **2.** Prior to 1985, fis. yr. ended Aug. **3.** Bef. results of disc. ops. of -0.68 in 1984, -0.08 in 1983, +0.01 in 1982. E-Estimated. d-Deficit.

Income Data (Million $)

Year Ended Dec. 31[1]	Revs.	Oper. Inc.	% Oper. Inc. of Revs.	Cap. Exp.	Depr.	Int. Exp.	Net Bef. Taxes	Eff. Tax Rate	Net Inc.	% Net Inc. of Revs.	Cash Flow
[6]1992	**332**	**30.2**	**9.1**	**[3]11.1**	**13.40**	**2.3**	**145**	**26.0%**	**65**	**19.7**	**78**
1991	284	4.3	1.5	[3]11.6	8.12	2.4	133	25.8%	58	20.5	66
1990	298	30.3	10.2	[3]8.4	8.44	2.6	777	35.6%	292	98.0	300
1989	267	16.6	6.2	4.8	9.31	20.9	[4]1,349	37.2%	473	176.9	481
1988	251	36.2	14.4	4.1	9.21	25.0	[4]50	20.6%	21	8.5	30
1987	241	35.3	14.6	[3]4.8	9.96	26.5	[4]33	17.6%	11	4.4	20
1986	224	38.1	17.0	[3]4.5	9.44	28.3	[4]41	24.0%	[5]15	6.6	24
1985	190	35.7	18.8	[3]15.1	7.55	31.7	[4]35	13.1%	18	9.6	25
[2]1984	166	40.1	24.1	6.0	6.65	25.8	[4]20	48.7%	5	2.8	11
[2]1983	84	13.7	16.2	2.9	1.33	10.1	[4]12	48.0%	6	7.2	7

Balance Sheet Data (Million $)

Dec. 31[1]	Cash	Curr. Assets	Curr. Liab.	Curr. Ratio	Total Assets	% Ret. on Assets	Long Term Debt	Common Equity	Total Cap.	% LT Debt of Cap.	% Ret. on Equity
1992	**984**	**1,229**	**330**	**3.7**	**2,161**	**3.1**	**Nil**	**1,103**	**1,677**	**Nil**	**6.0**
1991	962	1,168	229	5.1	2,050	2.9	16	1,044	1,698	0.9	5.8
1990	870	1,088	242	4.5	1,939	16.4	18	965	1,597	1.1	34.5
1989	1,057	1,260	245	5.2	1,613	37.4	19	721	1,265	1.5	115.5
1988	51	216	153	1.4	909	2.4	211	97	658	32.1	24.8
1987	49	188	141	1.3	862	1.2	225	70	624	36.0	15.9
1986	67	191	139	1.4	828	1.8	237	53	620	38.2	30.3
1985	64	168	133	1.3	805	2.4	259	39	611	42.3	47.2
1984	94	159	83	1.9	711	1.0	256	36	596	43.0	9.3
1983	72	103	51	2.0	204	3.1	66	50	128	51.6	10.4

Data as orig. reptd. **1.** Prior to 1985 fis. yr. ended Aug. **2.** Excl. disc. ops. **3.** Net of curr. yr. retirement and disposals. **4.** Incl. equity in earns. of nonconsol. subs. **5.** Refl. acctg. change. **6.** Reflects merger or acquisition.

Business Summary

Chris-Craft Industries is primarily engaged in television broadcasting, and also produces plastics. Its interest in Warner Communications, Inc. was sold to Time Warner Inc. in 1989 and 1990 for some $2.4 billion in cash and securities. Industry segment contributions in 1992 were:

	Sales	Profits
Television	93%	95%
Industrial	7%	5%

BHC Communications Inc. (69%-owned) operates VHF television stations in Los Angeles (KCOP), New York (WWOR-TV, acquired in August, 1992) and Portland, Ore. (KPTV). United Television (UTV), which is 53%-owned by BHC, owns and operates three VHF and two UHF television stations: KMSP Minneapolis, KTVX Salt Lake City, KMOL San Antonio, KBHK San Francisco and KUTP Phoenix. CCN is the fourth largest TV station group owner in the U.S., with coverage of roughly 20% of TV households. In alliances with others, the company is also involved in the development of new programming, such as The Montel Williams Show, launched in 1991.

The industrial division manufactures plastic flexible films, water-disposable hospital laundry bags, nonwoven sound control and insulation padding, and fiber carpet underlay.

Dividend Data

No cash dividends have been paid on the common since 1969. Stock dividends have been paid regularly, most recently a stock dividend of 3% on April 2, 1993, to stockholders of record March 19.

Amt. of Divd. $	Date Decl.	Ex-divd. Date	Stock of Record	Payment Date
3% Stk	Jan. 28	Jun. 9	Mar. 19	Apr. 2'93

Finances

At December 31, 1992, 1,034,302 common shares remained available for purchase under an earlier authorization.

Capitalization

Long Term Debt: None (6/93).

Minority Interest: $610,025,000.

$1 Cum. Prior Pfd. Stk.: 73,399 shs. (no par).

$1.40 Conv. Pfd. Stk.: 301,471 shs. (no par); red. at $40; ea. conv. into 29.21 com. shs.

Common Stock: 19,452,483 shs. ($0.50 par).

Class B Common Stock: 7,528,869 shs. ($0.50 par); 10 votes per sh.; limited transferability; conv. sh.-for-sh. into com.

Officers and directors hold 45%, and institutions hold 44% of com. and Cl. B.

Shareholders of record: 3,395 (2,465 Cl. B).

Office—600 Madison Ave., New York, NY 10022. **Tel**—(212) 421-0200. **Chrmn & Pres**—H. J. Siegel. **Secy**—B. C. Kelly. **VP & Treas**—Joelen K. Merkel. **Tel**—(305) 946-4000. **Dirs**—H. Arvey, L. R. Barnett, D. F. Linowes, N. Perlmutter, J. J. Rochlis, A. R. Rozelle, H. J. Siegel, E. C. Thompson. **Transfer Agents**—First Chicago Trust Co. of New York, NYC. **Incorporated** in Delaware in 1928. **Empl**—941.

 William H. Donald

Church & Dwight

NYSE Symbol CHD In S&P MidCap 400

Price	Range	P-E Ratio	Dividend	Yield	S&P Ranking	Beta
Oct. 19'93	1993					
23⅜	32⅞–22⅞	16	0.44	1.9%	A–	0.80

Summary

Church & Dwight sells baking soda and sodium bicarbonate-based products under the Arm & Hammer label to consumer and industrial markets. Earnings for 1993's first half were restricted by increased marketing expenses for most consumer products. The quarterly dividend was raised 10% in July 1993.

Current Outlook

Share earnings for 1994 are projected to rise to $1.75, up from the $1.53 expected for 1993.

The quarterly dividend was raised 10%, to $0.11 from $0.10, with the September 1993 payment.

Sales should continue to advance moderately in coming quarters, helped by contributions from Arm & Hammer Dental Care and the specialty products business. Sales of the company's best selling product, powder laundry detergent, may continue to slow, as the popularity of liquid detergents, particularly concentrates, increases. The recent introduction of a concentrated A&H Power Fresh liquid detergent should contribute to sales growth in 1994. Despite increased pricing pressures, margins could widen, reflecting a more favorable product mix associated with the volume growth of the dental care and baking soda products. Earnings gains, however, will likely be restricted, as continued intense competitive conditions in the laundry detergent and dentrifice segments will result in increased marketing expenditures. Long term earnings growth should be aided by line extensions, foreign expansion, and pro-environment specialty products.

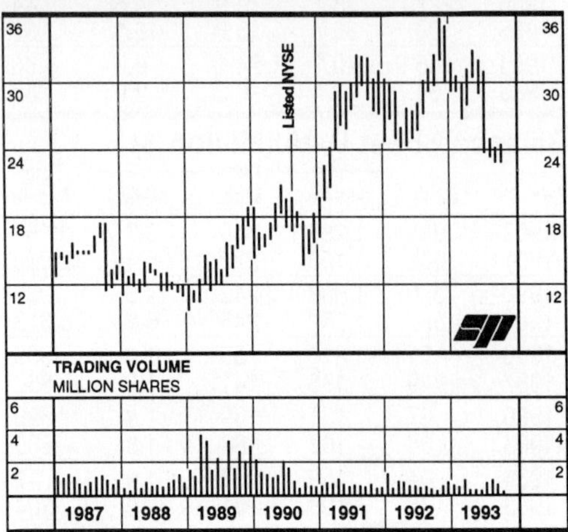

Net Sales (Million $)

Quarter:	1994	1993	1992	1991
Mar.	---	128	116	109
Jun.	---	136	128	118
Sep.	---	---	133	123
Dec.	---	---	139	135
	---	---	516	486

Sales for the six months ended July 2, 1993, rose 8.3%, year to year, led by A&H Dental Care, with contributions from baking soda, carpet deodorizers, and the specialty products business. Margins were restricted by higher marketing support for most major A&H consumer products. Net income was up 6.3%, to $0.62 a share from $0.58. Results for the 1993 period exclude a $0.13 a share net charge from the cumulative effect of accounting changes.

Common Share Earnings ($)

Quarter:	1994	1993	1992	1991
Mar.	E0.35	0.30	0.22	0.33
Jun.	E0.40	0.32	0.36	0.29
Sep.	E0.52	E0.45	0.46	0.38
Dec.	E0.48	E0.46	0.41	0.32
	E1.75	E1.53	1.45	1.34

Important Developments

Jun. '93— The company reported that it was responding to the growing demand for its water treatment method by trademarking its sodium bicarbonate for corrosion control under the new brand name Akalinity First. The treatment is currently being used by numerous municipalities in the U.S. to lower lead and copper levels in drinking water supplies.

Next earnings report expected in late October.

Per Share Data ($)

Yr. End Dec. 31	1992	1991	1990	1989	1988	1987	[1]1986	1985	1984	1983
Tangible Bk. Val.	[4]7.82	6.66	5.67	5.18	4.97	4.90	4.40	3.47	3.48	3.15
Cash Flow	1.92	1.79	1.54	0.83	1.12	0.97	0.86	0.48	0.75	0.70
Earnings[2]	[3]1.45	[3]1.34	[3]1.13	0.42	0.75	0.64	0.60	0.23	0.55	0.50
Dividends	0.380	0.340	0.300	0.260	0.230	0.215	0.205	0.195	0.183	0.168
Payout Ratio	26%	26%	26%	62%	29%	34%	35%	84%	32%	33%
Prices—High	35¾	32½	20⅞	18⅞	14	17½	15⅝	12¾	7½	6½
Low	24¼	16¼	13¾	9¾	11	11½	10¾	6⅜	5	3½
P/E Ratio—	25–17	24–12	18–12	45–23	19–15	27–18	26–18	55–28	14–9	13–7

Data as orig. reptd. Adj. for stk. divs. of 100% Mar. 1986, 50% Sep. 1984, 50% Jun. 1983. **1.** Reflects merger or acquisition. **2.** Bef. spec. item of -0.04 in 1990. **3.** Ful. dil.:1.42 in 1992, 1.29 in 1991, 1.08 in 1990. **4.** Incl. intangibles. E-Estimated.

Church & Dwight Co., Inc.

Income Data (Million $)

Year Ended Dec. 31	Revs.	Oper. Inc.	% Oper. Inc. of Revs.	Cap. Exp.	Depr.	Int. Exp.	Net Bef. Taxes	Eff. Tax Rate	[3]Net Inc.	% Net Inc. of Revs.	Cash Flow
1992	**517**	**55.0**	**10.6**	**17.5**	**9.62**	**0.40**	**[2]47.2**	**37.4%**	**29.5**	**5.7**	**39.1**
1991	487	50.5	10.4	20.5	9.06	1.67	[2]42.0	37.0%	26.5	5.4	35.5
1990	429	42.1	9.8	10.6	8.26	3.62	[2]39.0	40.5%	23.2	5.4	31.5
1989	388	38.7	10.0	11.6	8.48	4.34	[2]17.1	49.3%	8.6	2.2	17.1
1988	347	35.0	10.1	12.7	8.05	4.46	[2]24.9	33.9%	16.5	4.8	24.5
1987	319	30.6	9.6	14.2	7.38	4.76	[2]23.3	39.9%	14.0	4.4	21.4
[1]1986	275	23.9	8.7	38.2	5.59	4.07	[2]19.7	35.1%	12.8	4.6	18.4
1985	231	26.6	11.5	8.6	5.16	2.17	[2]7.1	34.4%	4.7	2.0	9.8
1984	185	21.7	11.8	3.5	4.17	2.08	18.7	40.1%	11.2	6.1	15.4
1983	152	20.1	13.2	5.6	4.17	2.10	16.3	38.0%	10.1	6.6	14.3

Balance Sheet Data (Million $)

Dec. 31	Cash	Curr. Assets	Curr. Liab.	Curr. Ratio	Total Assets	% Ret. on Assets	Long Term Debt	Common Equity	Total Cap.	% LT Debt of Cap.	% Ret. on Equity
1992	**25.6**	**124**	**76.6**	**1.6**	**262**	**11.6**	**7.5**	**159**	**184**	**4.1**	**19.8**
1991	8.7	117	78.7	1.5	245	10.6	7.8	139	164	4.8	20.5
1990	45.7	133	84.0	1.6	253	9.4	29.6	119	167	17.8	20.4
1989	43.3	130	59.8	2.2	245	3.6	52.2	112	184	28.3	7.8
1988	25.9	113	51.1	2.2	244	6.9	55.6	112	192	28.9	14.8
1987	45.7	118	46.0	2.6	246	5.9	56.8	116	200	28.5	12.7
1986	41.8	106	40.0	2.6	230	6.5	59.2	105	189	31.2	13.8
1985	26.0	73	31.4	2.3	149	3.2	20.8	74	117	17.7	6.3
1984	28.6	60	27.2	2.2	142	8.3	22.3	73	115	19.4	16.2
1983	32.6	59	20.0	3.0	128	8.5	26.2	66	108	24.3	16.2

Data as orig. reptd. **1.** Reflects merger or acquisition. **2.** Incl. equity in earns. of nonconsol. subs. **3.** Bef. spec. item(s).

Business Summary

Founded in 1846, Church & Dwight Co., Inc. is the world's leading producer of sodium bicarbonate, or baking soda. CHD specializes in sodium bicarbonate and sodium bicarbonate-based products, along with other products that use the same raw materials or technology or are sold into the same markets. Consumer and specialty products accounted for 79% and 21% of 1992 sales, respectively. The company does approximately 97% of its business in the U.S. and Canada.

Consumer products sold under the Arm & Hammer name include baking soda, dental care products, carpet and room deodorizer, deodorizer spray, laundry detergent powder and laundry detergent liquid. Arm & Hammer baking soda performs a wide variety of uses in the home, including refrigerator and freezer deodorizer, scratchless cleaner and deodorizer for kitchen surfaces and cooking appliances, bath additive, dentifrice, cat litter deodorizer and swimming pool pH stabilizer. The company's largest consumer business is in the laundry detergent market, where it makes products for use in various stages of the laundry cycle.

The specialty products business consists primarily of the manufacture and sale of sodium bicarbonate in a range of grades and granulations for use in industrial markets and animal feed. In industrial markets, sodium bicarbonate is used as a leavening agent for commercial baked goods, an antacid in pharmaceuticals, a carbon dioxide release agent in fire extinguishers and an alkaline agent in swimming pool chemicals, detergents and various textile and tanning applications. A special grade of sodium bicarbonate is sold to the animal feed market for use as a buffer, or antacid, for dairy cattle. MEGALAC Rumen Bypass Fat, introduced in 1986, is a nutritional supplement that allows cows to maintain energy levels during high milk prodution periods. CHD is the sole U.S. producer of ammonium bicarbonate, used principally as a leavening agent in the food industry, and produces other chemicals related to sodium bicarbonate.

Dividend Data

Cash has been paid each year by the company or its predecessor since 1901. A "poison pill" stock purchase right was adopted in 1989.

Amt. of Divd. $	Date Decl.	Ex-divd. Date	Stock of Record	Payment Date
0.10	Oct. 29	Nov. 6	Nov. 13	Dec. 1'92
0.10	Jan. 28	Feb. 5	Feb. 11	Mar. 1'93
0.10	Apr. 29	May 10	May 14	Jun. 1'93
0.11	Jul. 29	Aug. 12	Aug. 18	Sep. 1'93

Capitalization

Long Term Debt: $7,639,000 (7/2/93).

Common Stock: 20,229,174 shs. ($1 par).
Institutions hold some 42%.
Shareholders of record: 10,400 (12/92).

Office—469 North Harrison St., Princeton, NJ 08543-5297. **Tel**—(609) 683-5900. **Chrmn, Pres & CEO**—D. C. Minton. **VP-Fin, CFO & Investor Contact**—Anthony P. Deasey (609) 683-7069. **VP-Secy**—M. A. Bilawsky. **Dirs**—C. C. Baldwin Jr., W. R. Becklean, R. H. Beeby, R. B. Dixon, J. R. Leaman Jr., J. D. Leggett III, R. A. McCabe, D. C. Minton, D. P. Phypers, J. J. Slade, J. O. Whitney. **Transfer Agent & Registrar**—Chemical Bank, NYC. **Incorporated** in Delaware in 1925 as the successor to a business founded in 1846. **Empl**—1,092.

 L. Feuer Nelson

Cincinnati Gas & Electric

NYSE Symbol CIN In S&P MidCap 400

Price	Range	P–E Ratio	Dividend	Yield	S&P Ranking	Beta
Aug. 26'93	1993					
28⅛	28⅝–23⅞	14	1.66	5.9%	B+	0.39

Summary

On August 23, 1993, Indianapolis-based IPALCO Enteprises (IPL) terminated its hostile tender offer to purchase all of the common stock of PSI Resources,Indiana's largest electric utility holding company, after it became apparent that IPL's nominees would not be elected to PSI's board of directors. On August 17, this Ohio utility and PSI adjusted the terms of their proposed friendly merger in order to match a previous IPL bid.

Current Outlook

Share earnings for 1993 are projected at $2.05 (before a possible Zimmer-related writeoff of up to $2.60 a share), versus the $2.04 recorded for 1992. Share earnings could rise to $2.15 in 1994.

The $0.41½ quarterly dividend is the minimum expected.

Share earnings for 1993 may rise slightly, as rate increases, more normal weather conditions and cost savings via staff reductions more than offset sharply lower AFUDC credits. However, a Zimmer writeoff may be taken if an appeal of a May 1992 rate order is unsuccessful. Share earnings for 1994 should benefit from the full-year effect of the aforementioned rate increases.

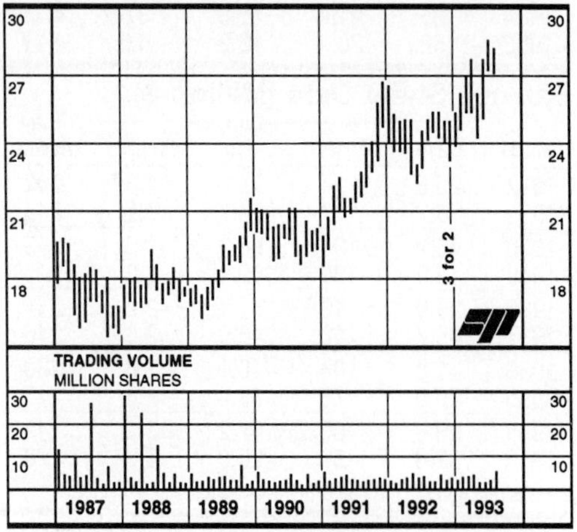

Operating Revenues (Million $)

Quarter:	1993	1992	1991	1990
Mar.	493	447	444	398
Jun.	367	334	328	316
Sep.	---	352	351	343
Dec.	---	420	395	382
	---	1,553	1,518	1,438

Revenues in the six months to June 30, 1993, rose 10%, year to year. With 7.5% higher operating costs, operating income rose 25%. After 52% lower other income and only slighlty lower interest charges, net income was down 2.5%. Share earnings were $1.10, versus $1.14, as adjusted to reflect a three-for-two stock split in December 1992.

Common Share Earnings ($)

Quarter:	1993	1992	1991	1990
Mar.	0.71	0.70	0.99	0.77
Jun.	0.38	0.43	0.38	0.48
Sep.	E0.50	0.45	0.53	0.73
Dec.	E0.46	0.45	0.33	0.76
	E2.05	2.04	2.21	2.75

Important Developments

Aug. '93— On August 23, IPALCO Enterprises, Inc. (IPL) terminated its hostile offer to acquire PSI Resources for $30.50 in cash and IPL common stock after it became apparent that its nominees would not be elected to PSI's board. On August 17, CIN and PSI adjusted the terms of their merger plan in order to match a previous sweetened IPL bid. Under the revised terms, CIN raised its friendly buyout offer to $28 a share from $25. But, the exchange ratio — 1.023 CIN shares for each PSI common share — would remain intact up to the point where CIN shares reached $33.76. In July, CIN and PSI entered into an amended merger agreement (to satisfy Indiana Utility Regulatory Commission requirements) that would create a registered holding company for their merger. Under such a structure, CIN may need to divest its gas operations, but the firms will seek approval from the SEC to keep the gas business.

Next earnings report expected in late October.

Per Share Data ($)

Yr. End Dec. 31	1992	1991	1990	1989	1988	1987	1986	1985	1984	1983
Tangible Bk. Val.	**19.01**	18.55	17.75	16.59	15.19	13.53	13.27	12.44	13.57	13.49
Earnings[1]	**2.04**	2.21	2.75	2.89	2.88	1.37	2.25	2.20	1.63	1.96
Dividends	**1.650**	1.653	1.600	1.533	1.487	1.453	1.440	1.440	1.440	1.440
Payout Ratio	**81%**	75%	58%	53%	52%	106%	64%	65%	88%	73%
Prices—High	**26 19/32**	26¾	21⅛	21⅝	19⅜	19⅞	20¾	14⅞	10⅛	12⅞
Low	**22¼**	18⅝	18⅝	16¼	16¼	15⅜	13⅝	9¼	5⅞	7⅞
P/E Ratio—	**13–11**	12–8	8–7	7–6	7–6	15–11	9–6	7–4	6–4	7–4

Data as orig. reptd. Adj. for stk. div. of 50% Dec. 1992. **1.** Bef. spec. items of +0.25 in 1987, -2.17 in 1985. E-Estimated.

Income Data (Million $)

Year Ended Dec. 31	Revs.	Depr.	Maint.	Oper. Ratio	[1]Fxd. Chgs. Cover.	Constr. Credits	Eff. Tax Rate	[2]Net Inc.	% Return On Revs.	[3]Invest. Capital	[4]Com. Equity
1992	**1,553**	**141**	**105**	**83.3%**	**2.31**	**18**	**25.0%**	**202**	**13.0**	**8.7**	**10.8**
1991	1,518	131	121	86.0%	2.91	68	19.2%	207	13.6	7.8	12.2
1990	1,438	94	120	84.2%	3.01	136	16.4%	235	16.3	9.8	15.9
1989	1,438	90	115	83.3%	3.34	113	20.6%	240	16.7	10.9	18.1
1988	1,386	89	107	82.8%	3.41	92	23.9%	227	16.4	11.3	19.8
1987	1,357	86	103	82.3%	1.96	69	16.8%	114	8.4	8.0	10.1
1986	1,403	83	86	83.7%	2.92	57	37.7%	173	12.3	10.7	17.4
1985	1,397	80	85	84.3%	2.88	52	36.7%	168	12.1	10.3	15.6
1984	1,419	78	87	86.2%	2.31	40	36.2%	129	9.1	9.2	12.0
1983	1,369	76	82	86.2%	2.49	64	30.6%	146	10.7	9.8	14.7

Balance Sheet Data (Million $)

Dec. 31	Gross Prop.	Capital Expend.	Net Prop.	% Earn. on Net Prop.	Total Cap.	Capitalization LT Debt	% LT Debt	Pfd.	% Pfd.	Com.	% Com.
1992	**5,308**	**230**	**3,945**	**6.7**	**4,250**	**1,810**	**47.7**	**330**	**8.7**	**1,655**	**43.6**
1991	5,110	410	3,861	5.7	4,047	1,734	47.5	330	9.1	1,584	43.4
1990	4,729	467	3,579	6.7	3,717	1,651	49.4	290	8.7	1,399	41.9
1989	4,286	441	3,203	7.9	3,236	1,348	47.0	241	8.4	1,279	44.6
1988	3,865	416	2,851	8.8	2,968	1,225	46.8	243	9.3	1,146	43.9
1987	3,513	297	2,557	9.7	2,733	1,199	50.3	244	10.2	941	39.5
1986	3,301	193	2,406	9.7	2,678	1,183	50.7	246	10.5	904	38.8
1985	3,161	155	2,333	9.7	2,596	1,173	51.5	277	12.2	826	36.3
1984	2,959	162	2,198	8.4	2,673	1,156	50.0	279	12.0	880	38.0
1983	3,199	234	2,504	7.8	2,559	1,171	50.8	280	12.1	855	37.1

Data as orig. reptd. **1.** Times int. exp. & pfd. divs. covered (pretax basis). **2.** Bef. spec. items. **3.** Based on income bef. interest charges. **4.** As reptd. by co. in 1985-1983.

Business Summary

Cincinnati Gas & Electric and its subsidiaries supply electricity and natural gas in the southwestern portion of Ohio and adjacent areas in Kentucky and Indiana. Of 1992 revenues, electricity accounted for some 75% and gas 25%. Electric revenues by customer in recent years were:

	1992	1991	1990	1989
Residential	38%	40%	36%	40%
Commercial	28%	28%	27%	28%
Industrial	23%	21%	22%	22%
Other	11%	11%	15%	10%

In 1992, nearly all of CIN's electric generation was fueled by coal. Peak load in 1992 was 4,002 mw, and system capability at time of peak totaled 5,040 mw, for a capacity margin of 21%. Gas sales in 1992 totaled 74,213 MMcf, up from 72,066 MMcf in 1991.

CIN's 46.5%-owned Zimmer generating station, begun as a nuclear facility, was canceled in 1984. Subsequently, CIN, together with construction partners American Electric Power and DPL Inc., received approval to convert the unit to a coal-fired plant at an additional cost of $1.7 billion. Including some $1.9 billion of sunk costs, CIN agreed to a cost cap of $3.6 billion for the unit. In 1985, CIN wrote off $142 million ($2.17 a share, as adjusted) of disallowed Zimmer costs. In November 1987, the lawsuit filed by CIN and the project's partners against General Electric Co. and Sargent & Lundy Engineers for defects with Zimmer's nuclear equipment was settled. At that time, CIN wrote off some $91 million ($1.34 a share, adjusted) for the balance of unrecoverable Zimmer costs.

Dividend Data

Dividends have been paid since 1853. A dividend reinvestment plan is available.

Amt. of Divd. $	Date Decl.	Ex–divd. Date	Stock of Record	Payment Date
0.62	Oct. 21	Oct. 27	Nov. 2	Nov. 15'92
3–for–2	Oct. 21	Dec. 3	Nov. 2	Dec. 2'92
0.41½	Jan. 20	Jan. 26	Feb. 1	Feb. 15'93
0.41½	Apr. 23	Apr. 27	May 3	May 15'93
0.41½	Jul. 21	Jul. 27	Aug. 2	Aug. 15'93

Capitalization

Long Term Debt: $1,810,293,000 (6/93).

Red. Cum. Preferred Stock: $210,000,000.

Cum. Preferred Stock: $120,000,000.

Common Stock: 87,339,574 shs. ($8.50 par).
Institutions hold about 39%.
Shareholders of record: 58,000.

Office—139 East Fourth St., Cincinnati, OH 45202. **Tel**—(513) 381-2000. **Pres & CEO**—J. H. Randolph. **Secy**—D. R. Blum. **VP-Fin & Investor Contact**—C. Robert Everman. **Dirs**—N. A. Armstrong, O. W. Birckhead, C. L. Buenger, C. R. Everman, G. C. Juilfs, T. E. Petry, J. H. Randolph, J. L. Rees, J. J. Schiff Jr., D. S. Taft, O. W. Waddell. **Transfer Agent**—Company's office. **Registrar**—Fifth Third Bank, Cincinnati. **Incorporated** in Ohio in 1837. **Empl**—4,900.

 Christopher J. Grant

Cirrus Logic

NASDAQ Symbol CRUS (Incl. in Nat'l Market) Options on CBOE, NY, Pac In S&P MidCap 400

Price	Range	P-E Ratio	Dividend	Yield	S&P Ranking	Beta
Aug. 6'93	1993					
26½	39¾–13¼	51	None	None	NR	NA

Summary

Cirrus Logic develops innovative architectures using VLSI circuits for applications such as mass storage, user interfaces, communications and data acquisition. Earnings are expected to decline in 1993-4 in the face of increasing competition and $10 million in inventory writedowns.

Current Outlook

Share earnings for 1993-4 are expected to decline to $0.60, excluding a $0.30 gain from an accounting change, from last year's $0.81.

Dividends are not anticipated.

Increased competition and a $10 million first quarter charge for addtional inventory reserves, due to a change in a customer's production schedule, are expected to limit earnings in 1993-4. However, the remainder of the fiscal year should see sequential growth in revenues and profitability on strong demand for newer, higher margin products, particularly in the graphics, audio and modem product lines. Long term prospects are bolstered by the company's strong market position and the continued introduction of new and innovative products.

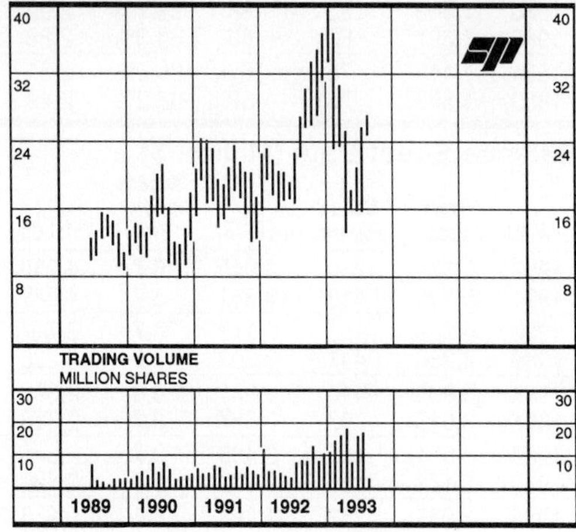

Net Sales (Million $)

Quarter:	1993-94	1992-93	1991-92	1990-91
Jun.	99.2	67.3	46.4	31.0
Sep.	---	83.2	44.5	34.6
Dec.	---	99.6	36.6	37.0
Mar.	---	104.6	44.0	39.2
	---	354.8	171.6	141.8

Net sales in the three months ended July 3, 1993, climbed 47%, year to year, reflecting strong demand for graphics and audio products. Gross margins narrowed due to a $10 million addition to inventory reserves, and operating expenses rose 78%. Results benefited from a $2,456,000 gain on the sale of an investment. After tax benefits of $1,849,000, versus taxes at 36.2%, a net loss of $3,709,000 ($0.15) replaced net income of $3,390,000 ($0.14). Results for 1993 exclude a credit of $7,550,000 ($0.30) for a change in the method of accounting for income taxes.

Common Share Earnings ($)

Quarter:	1993-94	1992-93	1991-92	1990-91
Jun.	d0.15	0.14	0.32	0.27
Sep.	E0.18	0.29	0.28	0.28
Dec.	E0.24	0.28	0.06	0.31
Mar.	E0.33	0.10	0.16	0.33
	E0.60	0.81	0.82	1.18

Important Developments

Jun. '93— CRUS introduced the CL-MD9624ECP, the industry's first intelligent data/fax/voice modem chip set dedicated to PCMCIA standard 2.0 applications. Separately, Intel said it will use the CL-GD5424 for its new Energy Efficient PC Platform, which is designed to meet the requirements of the EPA's Energy Star Computer Program.

May '93— IBM selected Cirrus graphics accelerators for its new PS/1 personal computer systems. Separately, two shareholder class action lawsuits were filed against the company, alleging violations of federal securities laws.

Feb. '93— Cirrus announced a new proprietary technology, using digital synchronous read/write channel electronics, that provides a 40% density increase for hard disk drives while reducing part count, power and board space.

Next earnings report expected in late October.

Per Share Data ($)

Yr. End Mar. 31	[2]1993	[2]1992	1991	1990	1989	1988	1987	1986	1985
Tangible Bk. Val.	**5.95**	5.24	4.85	3.51	[1]2.22	NA	NA	NM	NM
Cash Flow	**1.40**	1.26	1.50	1.28	NA	NA	NA	NA	NA
Earnings	**0.81**	0.82	1.18	1.03	0.32	d0.68	d0.68	d0.64	d0.34
Dividends	**Nil**	Nil	Nil	Nil	Nil	Nil	Nil	Nil	Nil
Payout Ratio	**Nil**	Nil	Nil	Nil	Nil	Nil	Nil	Nil	Nil
Ca lendar Years	**1992**	1991	1990	1989	1988	1987	1986	1985	1984
Prices—High	**36⅞**	24⅜	21⅜	15⅝	NA	NA	NA	NA	NA
Low	**15⅞**	12¼	7⅞	8⅞	NA	NA	NA	NA	NA
P/E Ratio—	**45–20**	30–15	18–7	15–9	NA	NA	NA	NA	NA

Data as orig. reptd. **1.** Pro forma. **2.** Reflects merger or acq. d-Deficit. E-Estimated. NA-Not Available. NM-Not Meaningful.

Income Data (Million $)

Year Ended Mar. 31	Revs.	Oper. Inc.	% Oper. Inc. of Revs.	Cap. Exp.	Depr.	Int. Exp.	Net Bef. Taxes	Eff. Tax Rate	Net Inc.	% Net Inc. of Revs.	Cash Flow
[1]**1993**	**355**	**49.8**	**14.0**	**26.7**	**15.2**	**1.61**	**32.9**	**37.3%**	**20.6**	**5.8**	**35.7**
[1]1992	172	32.0	18.6	5.5	8.4	0.83	23.0	32.1%	15.6	9.1	24.0
1991	142	31.7	22.3	10.9	5.1	1.00	29.1	35.4%	18.8	13.3	23.9
1990	85	19.9	23.4	7.3	3.8	0.66	18.0	14.5%	15.4	18.6	19.2
1989	37	6.7	18.2	0.9	2.3	0.60	4.3	6.0%	4.1	11.0	NA
1988	9	d6.7	NM	0.4	1.7	0.63	d8.4	Nil	d8.4	NM	NA
1987	5	d5.7	NM	0.2	0.8	0.16	d6.4	Nil	d6.4	NM	NA

Balance Sheet Data (Million $)

Mar. 31	Cash	Curr. Assets	Curr. Liab.	Curr. Ratio	Total Assets	% Ret. on Assets	Long Term Debt	[2]Common Equity	Total Cap.	% LT Debt of Cap.	% Ret. on Equity
1993	**72.7**	**194**	**95.8**	**2.0**	**256**	**9.4**	**18.1**	**143**	**161**	**11.3**	**16**
1992	48.3	99	32.9	3.0	141	11.5	11.9	96	107	11.1	17
1991	54.9	91	25.9	3.5	109	20.0	9.3	74	83	11.2	30
1990	40.8	67	21.7	3.1	78	31.2	3.1	52	55	5.6	48
1989	6.7	15	6.4	2.4	21	22.3	2.3	12	14	15.9	41
1988	4.9	10	4.8	2.1	15	NM	2.1	8	10	21.1	NM
1987	NA	NA	NA	NA	11	NM	2.0	6	8	26.0	NM

Data as orig. reptd. **1.** Reflects merger or acq. **2.** Refl. conv. of pfd. stk. upon public offering. d-Deficit. NA-Not Available. NM-Not Meaningful.

Business Summary

Cirrus Logic, Inc. develops innovative architectures for analog and digital systems functions and implements those architectures in very-large-scale integrated (VLSI) circuits for applications that include mass storage, user interface (graphics, audio and video), communications and data acquisition. Export sales accounted for 56% of total sales in 1992-3, compared to 59% in 1991-2 and 79% in 1990-1.

In the mass storage market, Cirrus supplies VLSI circuit products for embedded intelligent controllers used principally in high-performance, high-capacity hard disk drives in personal computers, workstations and other office automation products. Conner Peripherals and Seagate Technologies each accounted for more than 10% of 1992-3 and 1991-2 sales. CRUS has commenced volume production of next-generation low power circuits for 2.5-inch, 1.8-inch and 1.3-inch disk drives for notebook, laptop and palmtop computers.

In 1992-3, Cirrus introduced the industry's first true single-chip host adaptor interfaces for the new Personal Computer Memory Card International Association (PCMCIA) 2.0 standard, which provides a simple way to add extra functions to notebook computers via a small personal computer card.

The company's display graphics controllers provide compatibility both with new IBM-compatible video graphics array (VGA) software and monitor standards. During 1992, Cirrus began work in multimedia for desktop PCs. In April 1992, it acquired Acumos Inc., which had a complementary desktop graphics product portfolio.

Through the 1991 acquisition of Crystal Semiconductor, Cirrus became a market leader in audio analog-to-digital converters (ADC) and digital-to-analog converters (DAC) used in digital audio systems (such as compact disc players and digital audio tape players). Audio processing systems such as multimedia computers and consumer digital amplifiers require both DACs and ADCs. In addition, Crystal's ADCs are used in data acquisition to analyze DC signals and for image processing.

The company also offers high-performance controllers for multichannel and multiprotocol communications. During 1991-2, Cirrus introduced an intelligent data/fax/voice modem chip set designed for the notebook PC market. In addition, through Crystal, the company offers T1 transceivers and specialized quartz crystals used in telecommunications applications, as well as Ethernet LAN transceivers. Cirrus recently acquired Pacific Communication Sciences, Inc. (PCSI), a supplier of products and technologies for use in advanced wireless communications and telecommunications systems, including emerging worldwide personal communications.

Dividend Data

No cash dividends have been paid.

Finances

In February 1993, the company acquired Pacific Communication Sciences, Inc. (PCSI) of San Diego, for 1,746,481 shares of Cirrus common stock.

Capitalization

Long Term Obligs.: $17,558,000 (7/3/93).

Common Stock: 23,963,000 shs. (no par).
Officers and directors own 7.2%.
Institutions hold 64%.
Shareholders: 950 of record (3/93).

Options: To buy 3,707,000 shs. at an average price of $14.92 ea. (3/93).

Office—3100 West Warren Ave., Fremont, CA 94538. **Tel**—(510) 623-8300. **EVP & Chrmn**—S. S. Patil. **Pres & CEO**—M. L. Hackworth. **VP-Fin, CFO, Treas & Secy**—S. S. Srinivasan. **Investor Contact**—Paula Jones. **Dirs**—H. B. Cash, D. J. Guzy, M. L. Hackworth, M. S. Lee, D. L. Lyon, S. S. Patil, C. W. Rea, Jr., R. H. Smith. **Transfer Agent & Registrar**—First National Bank of Boston. **Incorporated** in California in 1984. **Empl**—1,353.

 Kevin J. Gooley

Cisco Systems

NASDAQ Symbol CSCO (Incl. in Nat'l Market) In S&P MidCap 400

Price	Range	P-E Ratio	Dividend	Yield	S&P Ranking	Beta
Sep. 8'93	1993					
43¼	59¼–38⅛	33	None	None	NR	NA

Summary

This company manufactures high-performance routers that connect and manage communications among local and wide area computer networks employing a variety of protocols, media interfaces, topologies and cabling systems. Share earnings, which have been growing since 1988, doubled in fiscal 1993, and might grow 50% in fiscal 1994 as demand for routers continues to be strong.

Current Outlook

Share earnings of $2.00 are estimated for the fiscal year ending July 31, 1994, up from $1.33 in fiscal 1993.

Initiation of dividends is not expected.

Cisco should be able to continue building on its reputation as the leading provider of routers for the Local Area Networking (LAN) marketplace. We estimate the company might grow sales some 65% in fiscal 1994 as organizations continue to tie their disparate computer networks together. Being one of the first entrants to this marketplace, Cisco should be able to fend off new competition that is being attracted by the high profitability of this industry segment. However, Cisco will probably see some erosion in its gross margins as the company protects its turf. With an increase expected in its research and development expenditures and a slightly higher anticipated tax rate, net margins could drop to some 24% from 26.5% in fiscal 1993. Given this scenario, earnings per share should climb some 50% in fiscal 1994.

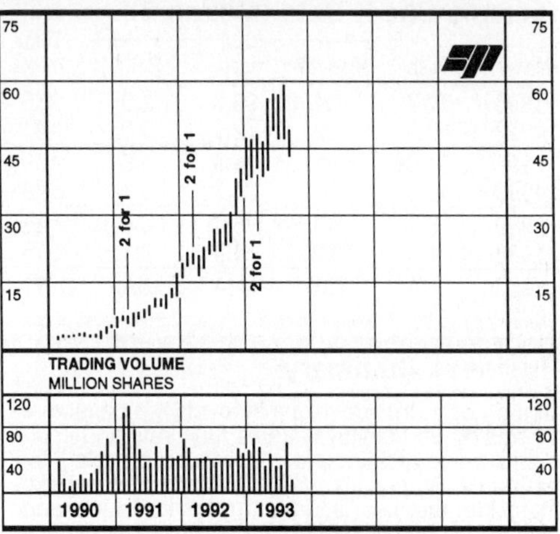

Net Sales (Million $)

13 Weeks:	1993-94	1992-93	1991-92	1990-91
Oct.	E221.2	126.4	63.6	32.8
Jan.	E246.6	145.1	74.0	43.9
Apr.	E284.4	172.4	91.4	49.7
Jul.	E328.4	205.2	110.6	56.8
	E1,081	649.0	339.6	183.2

Based on a preliminary report, net sales for the year ended July 31, 1993, rose 91% from those of the preceding year, reflecting continued growth of the internetworking market. Gross margins widened fractionally and operating expenses rose less rapidy than sales. Following higher net interest and other income, pretax income soared 102%. After taxes at 37.5%, versus 38.0%, net income surged 104%, to $171,955,000 ($1.33 a share), from $84,386,000 ($0.66).

Common Share Earnings ($)

13 Weeks:	1993-94	1992-93	1991-92	1990-91
Oct.	E0.43	0.26	0.13	0.07
Jan.	E0.47	0.30	0.15	0.08
Apr.	E0.52	0.36	0.18	0.10
Jul.	E0.58	0.41	0.22	0.11
	E2.00	1.33	0.67	0.35

Important Developments

Aug. '93— Cisco and Novell entered a strategic partnership aimed at ensuring interoperability between Cisco's routers and Novell's NetWare. Separately, Cisco and IBM signed an OEM agreement under which Cisco is licensing IBM's Advanced Peer-to-Peer Networking (APPN) technology for use in its routers.

Next earnings report expected in early November.

Per Share Data ($)

Yr. End Jul. 31	1993	1992	1991	1990	1989	1988	1987	1986	1985
Tangible Bk. Val.	**NA**	2.05	1.12	0.65	0.10	0.05	0.01	0.01	0.01
Cash Flow	**NA**	0.72	0.37	0.14	0.05	0.02	0.01	NA	NA
Earnings	**1.33**	0.67	0.35	0.13	0.05	0.01	0.01	d0.01	[1]0.01
Dividends	**Nil**	Nil	Nil	Nil	Nil	Nil	Nil	Nil	Nil
Payout Ratio	**Nil**	Nil	Nil	Nil	Nil	Nil	Nil	Nil	Nil
Prices[2]—High	**59¼**	40⅜	17⁷⁄₁₆	5⅝	NA	NA	NA	NA	NA
Low	**38⅛**	16⅛	4⅞	2¼	NA	NA	NA	NA	NA
P/E Ratio—	**45–29**	60–24	40–14	45–18	NA	NA	NA	NA	NA

Data as orig. reptd. Adj. for stk. divs. of 100% Mar. 1993, 100% Mar. 1992, 100% Mar. 1991. **1.** From inception 12-10-84. **2.** Cal. yr. NA-Not Available. d-Deficit. E-Estimated.

Income Data (Million $)

Year Ended Jul. 31	Revs.	Oper. Inc.	% Oper. Inc. of Revs.	Cap. Exp.	Depr.	Int. Exp.	Net Bef. Taxes	Eff. Tax Rate	Net Inc.	% Net Inc. of Revs.	Cash Flow
1992	**340**	**136**	**40.0**	**21.6**	**6.46**	**NA**	**136**	**38.0%**	**84.4**	**24.8**	**90.8**
1991	183	69	37.8	11.3	3.05	NA	71	39.0%	43.2	23.6	46.2
1990	70	22	31.8	4.1	0.80	0.02	23	40.8%	13.9	19.9	14.7
1989	28	7	24.9	0.3	0.13	NA	7	39.9%	4.2	15.1	4.3
1988	6	1	11.6	0.3	0.08	NA	1	40.1%	0.4	7.1	0.5
1987	2	Nil	10.0	0.1	0.02	NA	Nil	33.9%	0.1	5.6	0.1
1986	Nil	NA	NA	NA	NA	Nil	NM	NM	NM	NM	NA
[1]1985	Nil	NA	NA	NA	NA	Nil	Nil	11.6%	0.1	NM	NA

Balance Sheet Data (Million $)

Jul. 31	Cash	Curr. Assets	Curr. Liab.	Curr. Ratio	Total Assets	% Ret. on Assets	Long Term Debt	Common Equity	Total Cap.	% LT Debt of Cap.	% Ret. on Equity
1992	**156**	**247**	**78.3**	**3.2**	**324**	**34.7**	**Nil**	**246**	**246**	**Nil**	**44.4**
1991	91	141	26.3	5.4	154	36.5	Nil	128	128	Nil	43.9
1990	57	78	13.2	5.9	83	23.2	0.12	69	69	0.2	34.8
1989	4	16	8.8	1.8	17	39.2	0.21	8	8	2.7	78.9
1988	2	5	1.7	2.6	5	14.0	Nil	3	3	Nil	23.8
1987	NA	NA	NA	NA	1	19.1	Nil	Nil	Nil	Nil	86.5
1986	NA	NA	NA	NA	Nil	NM	Nil	Nil	Nil	Nil	NM
1985	NA	NA	NA	NA	Nil	NA	Nil	Nil	Nil	Nil	NA

Data as orig. reptd. 1. From inception 12-10-84. NA-Not Available. NM-Not Meaningful.

Business Summary

Cisco Systems develops, manufactures, markets and supports high-performance, multiprotocol internetworking systems that enable customers to build large-scale integrated networks of computer networks. Its products connect and manage communications among local and wide area networks that employ a variety of protocols, media interfaces, network topologies and cabling systems.

International sales accounted for 36% of net sales in each of fiscal 1992 and fiscal 1991.

Organized in 1984, Cisco began shipping products in commercial volumes during the second half of fiscal 1987. The product technology originated from efforts at Stanford University to integrate computers of various manufacturers into one of the first campuswide integrated systems.

The company's product family includes routers, routers with concurrent bridging, protocol translation and communication servers, all of which support multiprotocol multiple media connectivity in multivendor environments. An internetwork created by Cisco's product enables different devices using common protocols to communicate. The use of modular system design enables the company to configure media interfaces, protocol software and port capacity to meet customer needs for networks of varying size and different media.

High-performance, intelligent routers interconnect networks using different protocols and media. Cisco's routers can be configured to function simultaneously as a router and a bridge. Distributed processing architecture, protocol software and specialized high-performance network interfaces permit the construction of complex networks that can link thousands of network subsegments and connected devices. Routers range in unit list price from about $5,000 to $104,000.

The company currently markets its products in the U.S. mainly through a national direct sales force, supplemented by a small number of original equipment manufacturers (OEMs) and systems integrators, and internationally through distributors in about 45 countries. Cisco's internetworking systems have been installed by more than 3,000 customers in the industrial, financial, governmental and university sectors.

Dividend Data

No cash dividends have been paid. Two-for-one stock splits were effected in March 1993, March 1992 and March 1991.

Finances

In December 1992, Cisco and British Telecommunications PLC (BT) entered into a supply agreement whereby BT would become a worldwide OEM supplier for the company's internetworking products.

In its February 1990 initial public stock offering, Cisco sold 25,760,000 common shares (including 2,960,000 for selling stockholders) at $2.25 each (all as adjusted).

Capitalization

Long Term Debt: None (7/93).

Common Stock: 123,418,002 shs. (no par).
Institutions hold 86%.
Shareholders of record: 1,240 (7/92).

Options: To purchase 12,598,000 (adj.) shs. at $0.01 to $24.25 ea. (7/92).

Office—1525 O'Brien Drive, Menlo Park, CA 94025. **Tel**—(415) 326-1941. **Chrmn**—D. T. Valentine. **Pres & CEO**—J. P. Morgridge. **VP-Fin, Secy & Investor Contact**—J. M. Russell. **Dirs**—M. S. Frankel, J. Gibbons, J. P. Morgridge, W. O'Meara, R. L. Puette, R. G. Sweifach, D. T. Valentine. **Transfer Agent & Registrar**—Bank of Boston. **Incorporated** in California in 1984. **Empl**—882.

 Neeraj K. Vohra

Cintas Corporation

NASDAQ Symbol CTAS (Incl. in Nat'l Market) In S&P MidCap 400

Price	Range	P–E Ratio	Dividend	Yield	S&P Ranking	Beta
Oct. 11'93	1993					
27⅝	31–24¾	28	0.14	0.5%	A+	1.20

Summary

Besides engaging in uniform rentals, custom uniform sales and non-uniform rentals to customers with more than one million uniformed personnel, Cintas provides design, planning and implementation services for corporate-identity uniform programs. The company plans to add five uniform rental facilities and a manufacturing facility in 1993-4.

Business Summary

Cintas Corporation is a leader in the uniform rental and sales business, with particular expertise in designing, planning and implementing corporate-identity uniform programs. It concentrates on uniform rental services and custom uniform sales. Rental products and services are provided through a network of service centers located in many of the largest U.S. cities and the Province of Ontario. Uniforms are manufactured at three facilities located in Kentucky and are sold to customers nationwide through distribution centers located in Cincinnati and Los Angeles. At May 31, 1993, the company's customers provided uniforms for about 1.3 million personnel.

Total revenues in recent fiscal years were derived as follows:

	1992–3	1991–2	1990–1
Uniform rentals..........	68%	68%	70%
Non–uniform rentals....	20%	19%	19%
Uniform sales............	11%	12%	10%
Other......................	1%	1%	1%

Cintas helps customers determine the fabrics, color combinations, embroidered insignia and uniform designs that best meet their specific needs. Complete uniform service programs are offered, generally including the maintenance of appropriate inventories, periodic cleaning, replacement of worn items, adjustment of the program to match the customer's employment level and the redesign or modernization of uniform styles. Cintas provides such service either on a rental basis or by selling the uniforms to the customer. It also rents non-uniform items, such as wiping cloths, entrance mats, dust mops and linens. Generally, the company's rental contracts provide for 24- to 36-month terms.

Geographic expansion has been one of the company's highest priorities. It believes it is one of the few uniform rental companies with a national presence and infrastructure that is capable of providing service to large national corporations. As of May 31, 1993, Cintas occupied 102 facilities in 33

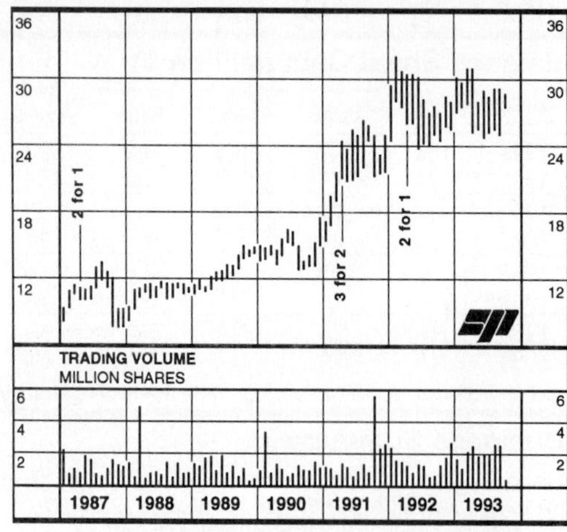

states. During 1992-3, 1991-2 and 1990-1, it acquired 17, eight and 10 uniform rental businesses, respectively. In October 1991, the company acquired Rental Uniform Service of Greenville, S.C. (annual revenues $30 million), for 2.6 million (adjusted) common shares. In March 1992, Cintas acquired Uniwear Inc., an Akron, Ohio, uniform rental firm. In late 1992, Seattle-based Maryatt Industries, whose operations are primarily in the Pacific Northwest, California and Arizona and which does about $28 million in annual volume, was acquired for about $30 million.

Important Developments

Sep. '93— The company said that it is in various stages of building uniform rental facilities in Baton Rouge, La., and Akron, Ohio, and a fourth manufacturing facility, in Hazard, Ky. During 1993-4, Cintas plans to construct three additional uniform rental facilities to accommodate growth.

Next earnings report expected in late December.

Per Share Data ($)

Yr. End May 31	1993	[1]1992	[1]1991	[1]1990	[1]1989	[1]1988	[1]1987	[1]1986	1985	[1]1984
Tangible Bk. Val.[3]	**5.69**	4.89	4.28	3.70	3.16	2.37	1.99	1.66	1.39	1.18
Cash Flow	**1.56**	1.21	1.12	0.92	0.77	0.64	0.53	0.43	0.34	0.27
Earnings[2]	**0.97**	0.79	0.74	0.63	0.53	0.44	0.36	0.29	0.24	0.20
Dividends	**0.14**	0.11	0.095	0.077	0.057	0.044	0.03	0.025	0.02	0.016
Payout Ratio	**15%**	14%	13%	12%	11%	10%	8%	9%	8%	9%
Calendar Years	**1992**	1991	1990	1989	1988	1987	1986	1985	1984	1983
Prices—High	**32⅛**	26⅜	17⅝	15	11¾	13½	10	7½	4½	3⅞
Low	**23¾**	15⅜	12⅞	10⅝	8⅛	7⅝	7⅛	4¼	3¼	2⅞
P/E Ratio—	**33–24**	33–20	24–17	24–17	22–16	31–18	28–20	26–15	19–14	20–15

Data as orig. reptd. Adj. for stk. divs. of 100% Apr. 1992, 50% Apr. 1991, 100% Apr. 1987. **1.** Refl. merger or acq. **2.** Bef. spec. item of +0.06 in 1992; ful. dil: 0.95 in 1993, 0.72 in 1991, 0.61 in 1990, 0.52 in 1989, 0.42 in 1988, 0.35 in 1987. **3.** Incl. intangibles after 1987.

Income Data (Million $)

Year Ended May 31	Oper. Revs.	Oper. Inc.	% Oper. Inc. of Revs.	Cap. Exp.	Depr.	Int. Exp.	[2]Net Bef. Taxes	Eff. Tax Rate	[3]Net Inc.	% Net Inc. of Revs.	Cash Flow
1993	**453**	**104**	**23.1**	**31.5**	**27.5**	**7.46**	**71.3**	**37.1%**	**44.9**	**9.9**	**72.3**
[1]1992	402	86	21.4	31.8	22.6	6.12	58.2	37.3%	36.5	9.1	59.1
[1]1991	322	69	21.5	57.9	19.2	5.65	48.8	35.6%	31.4	9.7	50.6
[1]1990	285	58	20.4	42.3	15.1	4.28	41.6	36.1%	26.6	9.4	41.7
[1]1989	244	51	20.8	29.0	13.9	3.53	34.8	36.6%	22.1	9.1	36.0
[1]1988	205	40	19.6	21.5	9.8	3.91	27.7	38.0%	17.2	8.4	27.0
[1]1987	163	34	20.6	22.0	6.6	3.57	25.1	44.4%	13.9	8.5	20.5
[1]1986	124	26	21.3	10.9	5.3	2.68	20.0	43.8%	11.3	9.1	16.5
1985	108	21	19.8	14.2	4.1	1.72	16.6	44.4%	9.2	8.6	13.3
[1]1984	83	17	20.3	9.3	2.9	1.23	13.9	46.9%	7.4	8.8	10.2

Balance Sheet Data (Million $)

May 31	Cash	Curr. Assets	Curr. Liab.	Ratio	Total Assets	% Ret. on Assets	Long Term Debt	Common Equity	Total Cap.	% LT Debt of Cap.	% Ret. on Equity
1993	**55.0**	**187**	**65.2**	**2.9**	**454**	**11.0**	**104**	**265**	**389**	**26.6**	**18.2**
1992	22.9	139	51.9	2.7	363	10.9	68	226	309	21.9	17.7
1991	18.4	118	53.4	2.2	306	11.1	59	186	252	23.3	18.1
1990	30.4	115	46.8	2.5	254	11.4	44	157	207	21.0	18.2
1989	30.1	105	37.9	2.8	214	10.9	37	134	176	21.0	18.8
1988	18.9	86	33.1	2.6	180	10.0	49	94	147	33.1	19.8
1987	26.9	77	30.1	2.6	162	9.5	51	78	132	38.8	19.5
1986	33.7	71	22.2	3.2	131	10.1	41	65	108	38.0	18.9
1985	11.4	46	20.2	2.3	92	10.9	15	55	72	21.2	18.3
1984	12.2	39	15.8	2.5	77	12.0	13	46	61	21.9	21.0

Data as orig. reptd. **1.** Refl. merger or acq. **2.** Incl. equity in earns. of nonconsol. subs. **3.** Bef. spec. item in 1992.

Revenues (Million $)

Quarter:	1993–4	1992–3	1991–2	1990–1
Aug.	122	105	94	76
Nov.		111	104	81
Feb.		113	99	80
May		124	104	85
		453	402	322

Revenues for the three months ended August 31, 1993, advanced 17%, year to year, reflecting an expanded customer base and acquisitions. Following a retroactive tax adjustment, net income rose 10%, to $10,543,000 ($0.23 a share), from $9,565,000 ($0.21).

Common Share Earnings ($)

Quarter:	1993–4	1992–3	1991–2	1990–1
Aug.	0.23	0.21	0.14	0.17
Nov.		0.25	0.21	0.18
Feb.		0.24	0.20	0.18
May		0.27	0.24	0.22
		0.97	0.79	0.74

Finances

Capital expenditures for 1992-3 totaled $29.7 million. Management expected capital outlays for 1993-4 would approximate $45 million.

During 1992-3, Cintas borrowed $38.4 million to make acquisitions (including $20 million associated with the acquisition of Maryatt) or refinance existing indebtedness to take advantage of lower interest rates.

In October 1991, directors authorized the company's ESOP to purchase up to 200,000 (adjusted) Cintas common shares.

Dividend Data

Annual cash dividends were initiated to the public in 1984. Three-for-two and two-for-one stock splits were effected in April 1991 and April 1992, respectively.

Amt. of Divd. $	Date Decl.	Ex–divd. Date	Stock of Record	Payment Date
0.14	Feb. 19	Mar. 3	Mar. 9	Apr. 2'93

Capitalization

Long Term Debt: $103,611,000 (5/93).

Common Stock: 46,666,606 shs. (no par).
Officers & directors own or control about 36%, incl. 29% held by R. T. Farmer.
Institutions hold about 37%.
Shareholders: 1,500 of record.

Office—6800 Cintas Blvd., P.O. Box 625737, Cincinnati, OH 45262-5737. **Tel**—(513) 459-1200. **Chrmn & CEO**—R. T. Farmer. **Pres & Secy**—R. J. Kohlhepp. **Sr VP-Fin & Investor Contact**—David T. Jeanmougin. **Dirs**—G. V. Dirvin, R. T. Farmer, J. J. Gardner, R. L. Howe, D. P. Klekamp, R. J. Kohlhepp, J. S. Lillard. **Transfer Agent**—Fifth Third Bank, Cincinnati. **Incorporated** in Ohio in 1968; reincorporated in Washington in 1986. **Empl**—7,797.

 L. Feuer Nelson

Circus Circus Enterprises

NYSE Symbol CIR Options on ASE In S&P MidCap 400

Price	Range	P–E Ratio	Dividend	Yield	S&P Ranking	Beta
Oct. 11'93	1993					
47⅜	49¾–27 19/32	33	None	None	B+	1.87

Summary

In October 1993, this major Nevada gaming company is expected to open a large, new pyramid-shaped casino/hotel in Las Vegas, following the August debut of a theme park attraction at another Las Vegas site. The company, which currently operates seven gaming facilities, is also planning a joint-venture casino/hotel in Reno and is looking to participate in casino developments outside of Nevada. A three-for-two stock split took effect in July 1993.

Current Outlook

Excluding any preopening charges for new facilities, earnings for the fiscal year ending January 31, 1994, are estimated at $1.60 a share, up from 1992-93's $1.41 (adjusted). An increase to $2.00 is expected for 1994-95.

Initiation of cash dividends is not expected soon.

Operating profit growth in the year ahead is expected to be fueled primarily by the opening of new facilities in Las Vegas. However, in addition to CIR's Luxor casino/hotel, two large, new casino/hotels operated by other industry participants will be opening in Las Vegas in the latter part of 1993.

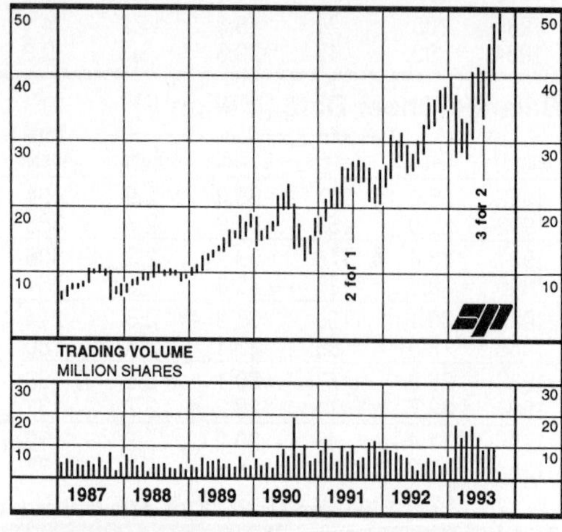

Revenues (Million $)

Quarter:	1993–94	1992–93	1991–92	1990–91
Apr.	210	206	197	133
Jul.	228	222	210	176
Oct.	---	224	211	206
Jan.	---	191	188	176
	---	843	806	692

Net revenues for the six months ended July 31, 1993, increased 2.4%, year to year. Operating profit was down 2.3%, but with a 76% decrease in interest expense, net income advanced 8.2%, to $0.80 a share (adjusted and based on 2.3% more shares), from $0.76. Results for the 1992-93 period exclude a $0.04 a share special charge from the early extinguishment of debt.

Common Share Earnings ($)

Quarter:	1993–94	1992–93	1991–92	1990–91
Apr.	0.37	0.35	0.32	0.23
Jul.	0.43	0.41	0.35	0.20
Oct.	E0.48	0.42	0.35	0.31
Jan.	E0.32	0.23	0.23	0.18
	E1.60	1.41	1.23	0.93

Important Developments

Oct. '93— CIR is about to open the pyramid-shaped Luxor casino/hotel on the Las Vegas Strip, adjacent to CIR's Excalibur facility. This is expected to be one of three large, new casino/hotels opening in Las Vegas during the final three months of 1993. Earlier in August, CIR's new Grand Slam Canyon water theme park opened near the Circus Circus casino/hotel in Las Vegas. Also, a joint venture of CIR and Eldorado Hotel/Casino is expected to develop a large, new casino/hotel in Reno, Nev.; completion is expected in the spring of 1995. In addition, CIR has expressed interest in several riverboat casino projects outside of Nevada and in the development of casino projects in Sydney, Australia, and Windsor, Ontario. The opening of a Mississippi casino is projected to modestly help CIR's 1994-95 earnings.

Next earnings report expected in late November.

Per Share Data ($)

Yr. End Jan. 31	1993	1992	1991	1990	1989	1988	1987	1986	1985	[1]1984
Tangible Bk. Val.	**5.49**	3.71	2.11	1.74	1.47	2.35	1.89	1.64	1.29	1.01
Cash Flow	**1.97**	1.81	1.44	1.24	1.11	0.81	0.54	0.50	0.41	0.34
Earnings[2]	**1.41**	1.23	0.93	0.87	0.77	0.55	0.32	0.33	0.28	0.23
Dividends	**Nil**	Nil	Nil	Nil	Nil	Nil	Nil	Nil	Nil	Nil
Payout Ratio	**Nil**	Nil	Nil	Nil	Nil	Nil	Nil	Nil	Nil	Nil
Calendar Years	**1992**	1991	1990	1989	1988	1987	1986	1985	1984	1983
Prices—High	**38½**	27 11/32	23⅝	19	11 19/32	11 5/32	7 3/32	5⅛	3 9/32	2 27/32
Low	**23 11/32**	16	11 29/32	9 19/32	6 31/32	5 27/32	4 15/32	2 29/32	2 9/32	2 13/32
P/E Ratio—	**27–17**	22–13	25–13	22–11	15–9	20–11	22–14	15–9	12–8	12–10

Data as orig. reptd. Adj. for stk. divs. of 50% Jul. 1993, 100% Jul. 1991, 100% Jul. 1986. **1.** Refl. merger or acq. **2.** Bef. spec. items of -0.04 in 1992, -0.10 in 1989, -0.05 in 1988, -0.07 in 1987. E-Estimated.

Income Data (Million $)

Year Ended Jan. 31	Revs.	Oper. Inc.	% Oper. Inc. of Revs.	Cap. Exp.	Depr.	Int. Exp.	Net Bef. Taxes	Eff. Tax Rate	[2]Net Inc.	% Net Inc. of Revs.	Cash Flow
1993	**843**	**254**	**30.1**	**209**	**48.2**	**31.0**	**183**	**34.0%**	**121.0**	**14.4**	**169**
1992	806	249	30.9	27	48.9	44.8	157	24.2%	103.0	12.8	152
1991	692	212	30.6	149	42.4	51.4	116	34.2%	76.3	11.0	119
1990	522	171	32.8	197	32.3	36.5	113	33.7%	75.1	14.4	107
1989	512	169	32.9	76	31.8	29.7	110	34.1%	72.5	14.2	105
1988	459	145	31.5	50	29.4	20.4	101	38.5%	61.9	13.5	92
1987	374	112	29.9	79	24.9	26.1	66	45.0%	36.1	9.7	61
1986	307	94	30.5	119	18.4	34.3	60	37.3%	37.4	12.2	56
1985	274	82	29.9	55	14.6	31.5	52	40.9%	31.0	11.3	46
[1]1984	230	65	28.1	110	11.2	16.6	40	43.0%	23.0	10.0	34

Balance Sheet Data (Million $)

Jan. 31	Cash	Curr. Assets	Curr. Liab.	Curr. Ratio	Total Assets	% Ret. on Assets	Long Term Debt	Common Equity	Total Cap.	% LT Debt of Cap.	% Ret. on Equity
1993	**43**	**78**	**87.5**	**0.9**	**950**	**13.8**	**308**	**490**	**862**	**35.7**	**29.3**
1992	34	68	59.5	1.1	783	12.9	338	326	723	46.7	40.0
1991	18	54	61.5	0.9	792	10.6	497	185	730	68.1	44.9
1990	19	41	62.1	0.7	675	12.8	408	161	612	66.8	50.4
1989	21	48	42.6	1.1	524	15.3	296	145	480	61.7	39.6
1988	74	97	41.5	2.3	529	12.4	169	278	486	34.7	24.7
1987	39	57	43.8	1.3	465	7.5	166	222	420	39.4	17.4
1986	106	123	43.9	2.8	490	8.0	229	192	445	51.5	21.6
1985	163	180	37.8	4.8	447	8.2	240	153	409	58.9	22.6
1984	67	77	26.4	2.9	308	9.2	151	122	281	53.9	23.6

Data as orig. reptd. **1.** Refl. merger or acq. **2.** Bef. spec. items.

Business Summary

Circus Circus Enterprises operates seven Nevada gaming facilities, which have about 11,138 hotel rooms and about 436,000 sq. ft. of casino space. In October 1993, CIR is expected to open another large casino/hotel (the Egyptian-themed Luxor) in Las Vegas. CIR typically attracts business by providing reasonably priced hotel rooms, food and alternative entertainment in combination with gaming activity. Free circus acts are offered at one Las Vegas casino/hotel and in Reno, and several other facilities also have themes. Gross revenue contributions (before deducting complimentary allowances) in recent fiscal years were:

	1992–93	1991–92	1990–91
Casino	57%	57%	58%
Rooms	17%	17%	15%
Food and beverage	16%	16%	16%
Other	10%	11%	11%

In Las Vegas, CIR's operations include the castle-themed Excalibur casino/hotel (4,032 hotel rooms and 110,000 sq. ft. of casino space), which opened in June 1990. Also, the older Circus Circus—Las Vegas facility has 2,793 hotel rooms, 110,000 sq. ft. of casino space and a recreational vehicle area. In August 1993, CIR opened a water theme park near this facility. In addition, CIR operates two smaller casinos in Las Vegas—the Silver City Casino and the Slots-A-Fun.

Circus Circus-Reno has 60,600 sq. ft. of casino space and 1,625 hotel rooms. In Laughlin, the company operates two casino/hotels—the riverboat-themed Colorado Belle, with 64,000 sq. ft. of casino space and 1,234 rooms, and the adjacent Edgewater Hotel and Casino, with more than 57,000 sq. ft. of casino space and about 1,450 rooms. Also, CIR has expressed interest in various new gaming markets.

Dividend Data

No cash dividends have ever been paid. A three-for-two stock split was effected in July 1993.

Finances

In October 1993, CIR said that it had arranged $750 million in unsecured bank credit facilities to back up commercial paper to be used to fund capital expenditures and investments in new ventures, and for general corporate purposes.

Since late 1987, the company has spent $335 million to repurchase about 32.7 million (adjusted) common shares, including about 21 million shares acquired from two principal stockholders.

Capitalization

Long Term Debt: $454,871,000 (7/93).

Common Stock: 87,365,045 shs. ($0.017 par).
W. G. Bennett owns about 6.9%.
Institutions hold about 86%.
Shareholders of record: 3,554.

Office—2880 Las Vegas Blvd. South, Las Vegas, NV 89109-1120. **Tel**—(702) 734-0410. **Chrmn & CEO**—W. G. Bennett. **Pres, CFO & Investor Contact**—Clyde T. Turner. **VP-Treas**—T. L. Caudill. **VP & Secy**—M. Sloan. **Dirs**—W. G. Bennett, J. Cashman III, T. Coelho, C. F. Dodge, W. N. Pennington, A. M. Smith Jr., F. W. Smith, C. T. Turner. **Transfer Agent & Registrar**—First Chicago Trust Co., NYC. **Incorporated** in Nevada in 1974. **Empl**—13,600.

 Tom Graves, CFA

City National Corp.

NYSE Symbol CYN In S&P MidCap 400

Price	Range	P–E Ratio	Dividend	Yield	S&P Ranking	Beta
Sep. 1'93	1993					
6⅞	11⅝–6⅜	NM	None	None	C	0.93

Summary

This holding company owns City National Bank, which operates 23 branches in Southern California serving Los Angeles, Orange and San Diego counties. A net loss occurred in 1992, reflecting the continued decline in real estate values in CYN's markets. Following a large first-quarter loss, profitability should continue for the remainder of 1993, benefiting from strengthened interest margins, higher noninterest income and the implementation of cost cutting measures. Goldsmith family interests continue to hold about 16% of the common stock.

Current Outlook

A loss of $0.21 a share is projected for 1993, versus a loss of $1.84 in 1992.

Quarterly dividends were omitted in August 1991. No payments are expected in the near future.

Earnings should rebound slowly in 1993, primarily as a result of declining loan loss provisions and reduced noninterest expenses. Despite the bank's conservative lending stance, loan loss provisions are likely to continue as Southern California is beset by further contraction in real estate values; management does not expect a meaningful regional economic recovery for the balance of the year. Although the rate of construction is falling, office vacancy rates still range between 15% to 25%. Higher-cost time deposits should continue to shift into transactional savings and money market deposits, effectively lowering the cost of funds. Noninterest income is anticipated to remain flat. Under a capital adequacy plan agreed to with federal regulators, CYN considerably strengthened the balance sheet of its subsidiary bank by raising $65 million in Tier 1 Capital in June 1993.

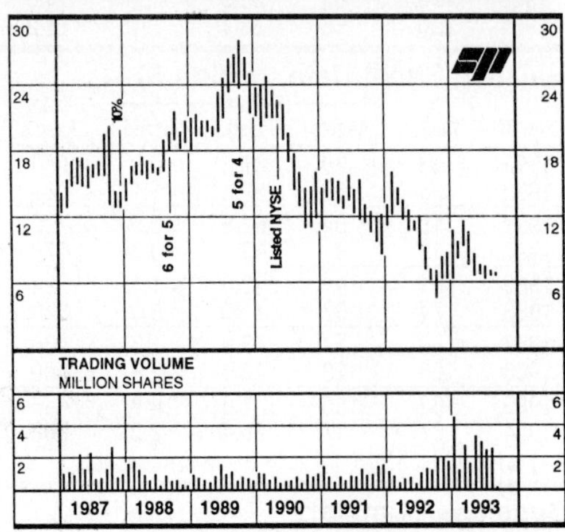

Common Share Earnings ($)

Quarter:	1993	1992	1991	1990
Mar.	d0.80	0.14	0.15	0.44
Jun.	0.30	d1.94	0.18	0.42
Sep.	E0.13	d0.07	d0.25	0.45
Dec.	E0.16	0.03	d0.74	0.04
	Ed0.21	d1.84	d0.66	1.35

Review of Operations

In the six months ended June 30, 1993, net interest income fell 19%, year to year, due to a decrease in the size of the loan portfolio and persistant weakness in the southern California economy and real estate markets. The provision for loan losses dropped to $19.0 million, from $99.5 million. Noninterest income rose 17%, and noninterest expense fell 20%; a $40.3 million writeoff of nonperforming real estate assets compared with one of $9.0 million a year earlier. There was a pretax loss of $34.8 million, versus $88.5 million. After a tax credit of $12.7 million, against $30.1 million, the loss from continuing operations narrowed to $22.1 million ($0.65 a share), from $58.3 million ($1.81).

Important Developments

Jun. 30'93— CYN reported a leverage ratio of 10.35% and a Tier 1 capital ratio of 14.61%. Under a written agreement with the Office of the Comptroller of the Currency (OCC), CYN generated $65 million in new Tier 1 capital, so as to comply with minimum regulatory requirements of 7.00% leverage ratios and a 10.00% Tier 1 capital ratios. The source of the new capital was a rights offering of CYN shares in June.

Next earnings report expected in mid-October.

Per Share Data ($)

Yr. End Dec. 31	1992	1991	1990	1989	1988	1987	1986	1985	1984	1983
Book Value	**7.07**	8.91	9.89	9.06	7.68	6.53	5.58	4.90	4.35	3.93
Earnings	**d1.84**	d0.66	1.35	1.86	1.62	1.34	0.98	0.80	0.66	0.58
Dividends	**Nil**	0.320	0.640	0.576	0.469	0.398	0.303	0.255	0.233	0.221
Payout Ratio	**NM**	NM	47%	31%	29%	30%	31%	32%	35%	38%
Prices—High	**16**	15¾	24¾	28	21⅝	20¼	4⅛	10¼	7⅜	8¾
Low	**4⅝**	8⅝	11	18	13½	12⅜	9⅜	6¼	5⅝	5½
P/E Ratio—	**NM**	NM	18–8	15–10	13–8	15–9	14–10	13–8	11–8	15–9

Data as orig. reptd. Adj. for stk. divs. of 25% Oct. 1989, 20% Sep. 1988, 10% Dec. 1987, 100% Jul. 1986, 10% Sep. 1985, 10% Sep. 1984. NM-Not Meaningful. E-Estimated. d-Deficit.

Income Data (Million $)

Year Ended Dec. 31	Net Int. Inc.	Tax Equiv. Adj.	Non Int. Inc.	Loan Loss Prov.	% Exp./ Op. Revs.	Net Bef. Taxes	Eff. Tax Rate	Net Inc.	Net Int. Margin	—% Return On— Assets	Equity
1992	**149**	**4.2**	**45.4**	**114.5**	**87.6**	**d92.6**	**NM**	**d60.1**	**4.41**	**NM**	**NM**
1991	181	6.2	75.7	118.0	68.9	d42.7	NM	d21.2	4.48	NM	NM
1990	197	6.5	75.9	43.0	58.5	66.4	33.8%	44.0	4.99	0.96	14.1
1989	184	7.2	73.7	15.0	56.3	93.4	36.7%	59.1	5.19	1.42	22.7
1988	156	6.8	70.4	12.0	59.3	76.1	35.2%	49.3	5.29	1.41	22.8
1987	123	14.2	77.5	10.3	59.6	62.1	34.2%	40.9	5.29	1.37	22.2
1986	104	13.8	66.6	11.1	63.9	41.5	28.4%	29.7	5.25	1.14	18.8
1985	90	11.2	56.0	5.6	67.2	36.3	33.4%	24.2	5.28	1.08	17.5
1984	73	14.7	47.5	5.5	67.9	24.1	17.7%	19.8	5.03	0.98	16.0
1983	65	18.4	40.2	7.9	66.5	15.5	NM	17.3	5.12	0.92	15.5

Balance Sheet Data (Million $)

Dec. 31	Total Assets	Earning Assets— Mon. Mkt. Assets	Inv. Secs.	Com'l Loans	Other Loans	% Loan Loss Resv.	—Deposits— Demand	Time	% Loans/ Deposits	Long Term Debt	Common Equity	% Equity To Assets
1992	**3,514**	**494**	**444**	**1,192**	**897**	**6.51**	**1,260**	**1,652**	**71.8**	**Nil**	**228**	**6.63**
1991	4,565	617	731	1,501	1,129	4.78	1,238	2,426	71.8	Nil	287	6.93
1990	4,956	874	622	1,766	1,312	1.95	1,196	2,906	75.0	0.43	318	6.80
1989	4,699	918	555	1,574	1,148	1.32	1,169	2,685	70.6	0.54	281	6.28
1988	4,296	843	518	1,508	930	1.15	1,112	2,353	70.4	0.66	236	6.16
1987	3,485	490	603	1,242	742	1.02	897	1,906	70.8	1.17	199	6.16
1986	3,142	363	640	1,028	511	0.97	937	1,732	57.6	1.66	169	6.04
1985	2,473	317	595	831	399	1.01	618	1,373	61.8	2.23	148	6.18
1984	2,225	382	552	734	312	0.96	543	1,261	58.0	5.87	131	6.11
1983	2,071	332	528	679	263	0.96	494	1,124	58.2	7.08	119	5.92

Data as orig. reptd. d-Deficit. NM-Not Meaningful.

Business Summary

City National Corp. is the holding company for City National Bank ($2.9 billion in assets at June 30, 1993), a commercial bank that conducts business in Southern California through 23 offices in Los Angeles County (20), Orange County (2), and San Diego County. Emphasis in recent years has been directed to the commercial sector rather than the retail segment. In 1993's second quarter, CYN sold its data processing business, recording an aftertax gain of $7.1 million. Total loans of $2.1 billion at 1992 year-end were divided:

	1992	1991
Commercial	57%	57%
Real estate – mortgage	28%	28%
Real estate – construction	5%	12%
Equity lines of credit, held for sale	8%	Nil
Installment	3%	3%

The reserve for loan losses at December 31, 1992, was $136.1 million (equal to 6.56% of gross loans outstanding), up from $125.8 million (4.81%) a year earlier. Net chargeoffs in 1992 totaled $104.2 million (4.50% of average loans), versus $52.3 million (1.83%) in 1991. Nonaccrual loans at December 31, 1992, were $160.3 million (7.72% of gross loans), compared with $152.6 million (5.83%) a year earlier.

Average deposits during 1992 were apportioned: time deposits 21%, money market deposits 33%, noninterest-bearing demand 33%, interest-bearing checking 10% and savings 3%. On a tax-equivalent basis, the average yield on interest-earning assets in 1992 was 6.85% (8.81% in 1991), while the average rate paid on interest-bearing liabilities was 3.24% (5.48%), for a net spread of 3.61% (3.33%).

Dividend Data

Cash dividends, paid each year since 1963, were omitted by directors on August 28, 1991. The most recent payment was $0.16 on July 15, 1991. A February 1993 Memorandum of Understanding with the Federal Reserve Bank of San Francisco requires CYN to give prior notice to the Bank of any cash dividends.

Capitalization

Long Term Debt: None (3/93).

Common Stock: 32,304,291 shs. ($1 par).
Officers & directors hold about 22%, incl. some 16% owned by Goldsmith family interests.
Institutions hold about 26%.
Shareholders of record: 2,619 (2/93).

Office—400 North Roxbury Drive, Beverly Hills, CA 90210. **Tel**—(310) 550-5400. **Chrmn & CEO**—B. Goldsmith. **Vice Chrmn**—A. L. Kyman. **Pres**—G. H. Benter Jr. **EVP-Secy**—C. D. Kenny. **EVP-CFO & Investor Contact**—F. P. Pekny. **Dirs**—G. H. Benter Jr., R. L. Bloch, S. D. Broidy, S. D. Buchalter, B. Goldsmith, R. D. Goldsmith, B. S. Horwitch, A. J. Perenchio, C. E. Rickershauser Jr., E. Sanders, S. A. Wainer, K. Ziffren. **Transfer Agent**—City National Bank. **Incorporated** in Delaware in 1968. **Empl**—1,650.

 Barry R. Haas

Claire's Stores

NYSE Symbol CLE Options on NYSE In S&P MidCap 400

Price	Range	P-E Ratio	Dividend	Yield	S&P Ranking	Beta
Oct. 21'93	1993					
17⅞	17⅞–12	20	0.10	0.6%	B+	2.50

Summary

This company operates the largest chain of specialty retail stores in the U.S. devoted solely to the sale of inexpensive fashion accessories. Its graphic arts stores were disposed of in early 1992. Following the sharp rebound in 1992-3, profits continued to advance in the first half of 1993-4, aided by higher same-store sales, strong inventory management and well-controlled operating expenses.

Business Summary

Claire's Stores, Inc. is a leading mall-based retailer of women's popular-priced fashion accessories. As of March 31, 1993, CLE was operating 1,036 stores in 48 states, consisting of 830 Claire's Boutiques stores, 157 Topkapi stores and 35 Dara Michelle stores (collectively the fashion accessory stores), as well as 14 Arcadia, Art Explosion or E. 57th stores (the trend gift stores, which are being converted or closed). Total stores in operation at the end of recent fiscal years were:

1993....	1,038	1990....	751	1987....	439
1992....	995	1989....	633	1986....	326
1991....	916	1988....	555	1985....	243

In 1992-3, costume jewelry (including hair ornaments, pierced earrings and fees for piercing ears) accounted for 65% of sales, other fashion accessories for 21%, trend gifts for 11% and totebags for 2%.

The fashion accessory stores average about 870 sq. ft. and carry merchandise designed to appeal to females aged 13 to 40. The average product is priced below $4. The Dara Michelle and Topkapi stores are similar in size and format to the Claire's Boutiques stores and give CLE the ability to add a second store in the malls that have a successful Claire's Boutiques store. The trend gift stores sell T-shirts, unframed posters, calendars, stationery products and seasonal items. Most sales are in the $5 to $10 range.

Merchandise, which is purchased from approximately 400 suppliers, is primarily either imported directly or purchased from importers. The majority of tote bags are purchased from importers. All merchandise is shipped to the company's distribution center in Wood Dale, Ill., a suburb of Chicago. After inspection, merchandise is shipped via common carrier to the individual stores. Stores typically receive three to five shipments a week.

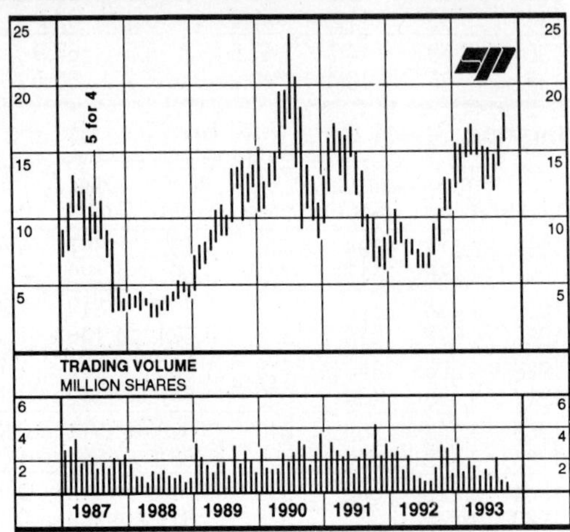

In February 1992, CLE sold its graphic arts stores (1991 sales of $20 million), which sold fine art posters, graphic reproductions and original lithographs.

Important Developments

Oct. '93— CLE reported total sales for the five weeks ended September 30, 1993, of $23.6 million, up 12%, year to year, on a same-store sales gain of 6%. For the eight months ended September 30, total sales rose 13%, year to year, on an 8% increase in same-store sales.

Aug. '93— CLE said it expects a continuation of strong sales and earnings comparisons in 1993-4's second half and also hinted of an accelerated pace of store openings in 1994-5. In 1993-4, the company expects to open 73 stores, close 17 and remodel 60. At July 31, 1993, CLE was operating 1,054 stores.

Next earnings report expected in mid-November.

Per Share Data ($)

Yr. End Jan. 31	1993	1992	1991	[1]1990	1989	1988	1987	1986	1985	1984
Tangible Bk. Val.	**3.75**	3.12	3.62	[2]2.69	1.67	1.40	1.17	1.00	0.81	0.47
Cash Flow	**1.34**	0.88	1.60	1.40	0.66	0.52	0.42	0.45	0.38	0.25
Earnings[3]	**0.71**	0.26	1.01	0.97	0.36	0.29	0.26	0.36	0.33	0.19
Dividends	**0.10**	0.10	0.10	0.10	0.10	0.095	0.08	0.067	0.025	Nil
Payout Ratio	**14%**	39%	10%	10%	28%	33%	30%	18%	7%	Nil
Calendar Years	**1992**	1991	1990	1989	1988	1987	1986	1985	1984	1983
Prices—High	**13**	17⅛	23⅞	14⅜	5⅜	13⅜	9⅜	15¾	7⅜	2¾
Low	**6¼**	6⅛	8½	4⅝	2⅝	3	5	6¾	2	¼
P/E Ratio—	**18–9**	66–24	24–8	15–5	15–7	46–10	35–19	44–19	23–6	15–1

Data as orig. reptd. Adj. for stk. divs. of 25% Jul. 1987 (Cl. A stk.), 50% Oct. 1985, 100% Feb. 1985, 50% Jul. 1984, 50% Apr. 1984. **1.** Refl. merger or acq. **2.** Incl. intangibles. **3.** Bef. results of disc. ops. of -0.68 in 1992 & spec. items of +0.03 in 1988, +0.04 in 1984.

Income Data (Million $)

Year Ended Jan. 31	Oper. Revs.	Oper. Inc.	% Oper. Inc. of Revs.	Cap. Exp.	Depr.	Int. Exp.	Net Bef. Taxes	Eff. Tax Rate	[4]Net Inc.	% Net Inc. of Revs.	Cash Flow
1993	**248**	**38.2**	**15.4**	**8.2**	**13.0**	**[3]1.72**	**23.5**	**38.0%**	**14.6**	**5.9**	**27.6**
[1]1992	234	24.0	10.2	14.2	12.8	[3]2.82	8.4	37.9%	5.2	2.2	18.0
1991	255	47.6	18.7	32.9	12.1	2.52	33.0	38.0%	20.5	8.0	32.6
[2]1990	190	41.4	21.7	28.3	8.5	1.23	31.6	38.5%	19.5	10.2	27.9
1989	127	19.1	15.0	12.1	6.0	[3]1.46	11.7	39.2%	7.1	5.6	13.1
1988	103	15.1	14.6	15.4	4.7	1.02	9.4	39.1%	5.7	5.5	10.4
1987	87	13.9	16.0	11.2	3.1	0.41	10.4	48.9%	5.3	6.1	8.4
1986	75	15.7	21.0	9.4	2.0	0.05	13.8	45.7%	7.5	10.0	9.4
1985	56	13.9	24.8	6.0	1.2	0.22	12.7	48.1%	6.6	11.8	7.8
1984	36	7.0	19.5	1.6	1.0	0.74	5.5	40.1%	3.3	9.2	4.3

Balance Sheet Data (Million $)

Jan. 31	Cash	Curr. Assets	Curr. Liab.	Curr. Ratio	Total Assets	% Ret. on Assets	Long Term Debt	Common Equity	Total Cap.	% LT Debt of Cap.	% Ret. on Equity
1993	**39.0**	**64.0**	**40.8**	**1.6**	**129**	**12.1**	**10.0**	**76.8**	**88**	**11.4**	**20.7**
1992	14.5	40.4	19.8	2.0	112	4.2	25.0	64.0	92	27.2	7.6
1991	1.9	46.3	26.0	1.8	134	17.2	28.9	73.6	108	26.7	31.8
1990	2.4	35.3	35.1	1.0	103	23.3	5.8	54.6	68	8.7	43.9
1989	2.5	20.6	14.8	1.4	63	12.4	7.0	33.6	49	14.4	22.9
1988	1.3	13.9	8.6	1.6	51	12.5	11.3	28.2	42	26.7	22.0
1987	1.4	13.4	14.2	0.9	40	14.6	Nil	23.6	26	Nil	24.3
1986	1.4	14.3	11.3	1.3	33	25.6	Nil	20.3	22	Nil	40.6
1985	6.3	14.4	8.4	1.7	26	29.8	Nil	16.6	17	Nil	49.8
1984	5.6	11.5	8.0	1.4	18	19.8	0.2	9.3	10	1.8	NM

Data as orig. reptd. **1.** Excl. disc. ops. **2.** Refl. merger or acq. **3.** Net of int. inc. **4.** Bef. spec. items. NM-Not Meaningful.

Net Sales (Million $)

13 Weeks:	1993–4	1992–3	1991–2	1990–1
Apr.	58.1	51.5	52.1	53.5
Jul.	61.8	53.6	55.9	55.2
Oct.		57.5	51.8	58.2
Jan.		85.3	74.3	88.3
		248.0	234.2	255.2

Sales for the 26 weeks ended July 31, 1993, advanced 14%, year to year, reflecting a 9% gain in same-store sales and more stores in operation. Margins benefited from fewer markdowns, well-controlled SG&A costs and a 74% decline in interest expense. Net income expanded to $4,670,000 ($0.23 a share), from $1,301,000 ($0.06).

Common Share Earnings ($)

13 Weeks:	1993–4	1992–3	1991–2	1990–1
Apr.	0.10	0.03	0.10	0.16
Jul.	0.13	0.04	0.04	0.17
Oct.		0.08	d0.10	0.18
Jan.		0.57	0.22	0.50
		0.71	0.26	1.01

Dividend Data

Dividends were initiated in 1984.

Amt. of Divd. $	Date Decl.	Ex-divd. Date	Stock of Record	Payment Date
0.025	Oct. 20	Oct. 29	Nov. 4	Nov. 18'92
0.025	Jan. 13	Jan. 28	Feb. 3	Feb. 17'93
0.025	Apr. 14	Apr. 29	May 5	May 19'93
0.025	Jul. 27	Jul. 30	Aug. 5	Aug. 19'93

Capitalization

Long Term Debt: $6,000,000 of 8½% sub. notes due 2001 & conv. into com. at $18 a sh. (7/93).

Class A Common Stock: 1,358,310 shs. ($0.05 par); 10 votes per sh.; conv. into com. sh. for sh.; max. divd. 50% of com. divd.; limited transferability.
About 77% is controlled by the Schaefer family.
Shareholders of record: 1,236.

Common Stock: 19,257,378 shs. ($0.05 par).
About 21% is controlled by the Schaefer family.
Institutions hold some 58%.
Shareholders of record: 2,401.

d-Deficit.

Office—3 S.W. 129th Ave., Pembroke Pines, FL 33027. **Tel**—(305) 433-3900. **Chrmn & Pres**—R. Schaefer. **Secy**—H. E. Berritt. **CFO & Treas**—I. Kaplan. **Investor Contact**—David A. Buchsbaum. **Dirs**—H. E. Berritt, F. D. Hirt, B. G. Miller, M. L. Schaefer, R. Schaefer, S. Schaefer, J. J. Silver. **Transfer Agent & Registrar**—First Union National Bank, Charlotte, N.C. **Incorporated** in Delaware in 1961. **Empl**—5,200.

 John D. Coyle, CFA

Clayton Homes

NYSE Symbol CMH Options on NYSE (Feb-May-Aug-Nov) In S&P MidCap 400

Price	Range	P-E Ratio	Dividend	Yield	S&P Ranking	Beta
Aug. 17'93	1993					
30	30¾–20⅝	25	None	None	B+	0.86

Summary

This producer and retailer of low- to medium-priced manufactured homes in the southern and eastern U.S. also provides related financing and insurance services, and develops, markets and manages communities of manufactured housing. Operations in recent periods have benefited from low mortgage interest rates and resultant strong home demand. In March 1993, CMH announced the acquisition of two plants that were expected to boost its annual production capacity by 3,000 homes. A long earnings uptrend is expected to continue in fiscal 1994. CMH chairman J.L. Clayton owns 29% of the shares.

Current Outlook

Earnings for the fiscal year ending June 30, 1994, are projected at $1.50 a share, up from the $1.18 of fiscal 1993.

No cash dividends are anticipated.

Sales are expected to increase at least 20% in fiscal 1994, aided by strong demand for the company's relatively low-cost homes, low mortgage interest rates, the addition of new independent dealers, a greater number of company-owned sales centers, increased financial services income and increased investment in manufactured housing communities. Margins are expected to continue to widen on the higher volume, aided by cost control efforts, and earnings will benefit from decreased interest expense. The company's long record of annual earnings gains is likely to continue over the next few years assuming the interest rate environment remains favorable and consumer confidence is sustained.

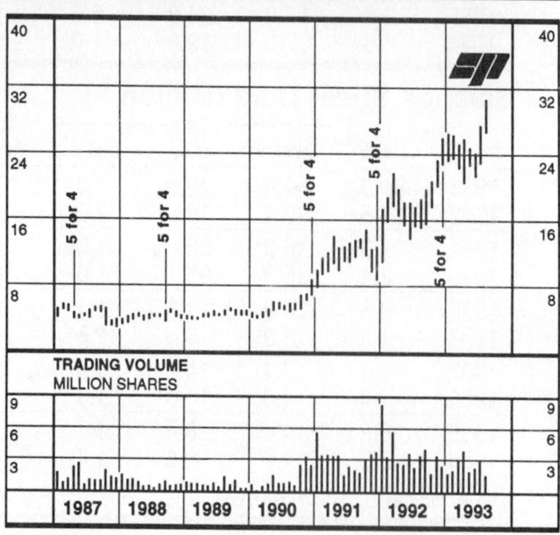

Total Revenues (Million $)

Quarter:	1993-94	1992-93	1991-92	1990-91
Sep.	---	109.8	89.8	76.6
Dec.	---	106.0	82.5	74.7
Mar.	---	112.2	84.9	70.7
Jun.	---	148.2	114.0	98.5
	---	476.3	371.2	320.6

Total revenues for the fiscal year ended June 30, 1993 (preliminary) rose 28% from those of the preceding year, reflecting a 30% increase in manufactured housing revenues and a 24% rise in financial services and other income. Costs and expenses increased less rapidly than revenues, and pretax income was up 39%. After taxes at 35.5%, against 34.6%, net income advanced 37%. Share earnings were $1.18 on 5.3% more shares, versus $0.90.

Common Share Earnings ($)

Quarter:	1993-94	1992-93	1991-92	1990-91
Sep.	E0.32	0.25	0.19	0.18
Dec.	E0.28	0.22	0.17	0.15
Mar.	E0.38	0.30	0.22	0.19
Jun.	E0.52	0.41	0.33	0.29
	E1.50	1.18	0.90	0.81

Important Developments

Aug. '93— Two CMH directors resigned following a disagreement with other members of the board over how an investigation of CMH's failure to pay certain state sales taxes should be handled. The investigation stemmed from an audit of Clayton's returns for 1988 through 1991 in which it was found that CMH did not file returns or gave incorrect information for six of its manufactured housing communities.

Next earnings report expected in mid-October.

Per Share Data ($)

Yr. End Jun. 30	1993	1992	[1]1991	1990	[1]1989	1988	1987	1986	1985	1984
Tangible Bk. Val.	**NA**	6.57	4.88	3.47	2.84	2.31	1.88	1.58	1.30	1.07
Cash Flow	**NA**	0.98	0.88	0.70	0.59	0.50	0.37	0.30	0.26	0.18
Earnings	**1.18**	0.90	0.81	0.62	0.52	0.45	0.32	0.27	0.23	0.18
Dividends	**Nil**	Nil	Nil	Nil	Nil	Nil	Nil	Nil	Nil	Nil
Payout Ratio	**Nil**	Nil	Nil	Nil	Nil	Nil	Nil	Nil	Nil	Nil
Prices[2]—High	**29¾**	26	14⅞	8⅞	5¼	5⅛	5¾	6⅞	4½	2⅞
Low	**20⅝**	11	7¾	4	3⅞	3¼	2⅞	3½	2¼	1⅜
P/E Ratio—	**25–17**	29–12	18–10	14–6	10–8	11–7	18–9	26–13	20–10	16–8

Data as orig. reptd. Adj. for stk. divs of 25% Dec. 1992, 25% Dec. 1991, 25% Dec. 1990, 25% Sep. 1988, Apr. 1987, 25% Jun. 1986, 25% Sep. 1985, 25% Oct. 1984. **1.** Reflects accounting change. **2.** Cal. yr. NA-Not Available. E-Estimated.

Income Data (Million $)

Year Ended Jun. 30	Revs.	Oper. Inc.	% Oper. Inc. of Revs.	Cap. Exp.	Depr.	Int. Exp.	[4]Net Bef. Taxes	Eff. Tax Rate	Net Inc.	% Net Inc. of Revs.	Cash Flow
1992	**371**	**80.5**	**21.7**	**[5]19.10**	**3.44**	**20.2**	**60.1**	**34.6%**	**39.3**	**10.6**	**42.8**
[1]1991	321	66.8	20.8	4.90	2.78	21.7	44.6	35.9%	28.6	8.9	31.4
1990	260	46.9	18.0	4.28	2.44	16.0	31.4	36.7%	19.9	7.6	22.3
[1]1989	243	39.5	16.3	2.96	2.26	14.1	26.0	37.4%	16.3	6.7	18.5
1988	[2]203	15.9	7.8	8.71	1.75	3.7	20.0	30.2%	14.0	6.9	15.7
1987	[2]172	16.1	9.3	5.83	1.43	2.7	18.2	41.8%	10.4	6.0	11.8
1986	[2]158	12.5	7.9	5.31	1.12	1.3	13.9	38.6%	8.4	5.3	9.5
1985	[2]115	10.6	9.2	1.74	0.83	0.3	12.3	41.5%	7.1	6.2	8.0
1984	[2]86	7.4	8.6	4.53	0.45	0.1	9.6	42.3%	5.5	6.4	5.9
1983	[2]72	6.2	8.6	0.41	0.40	[3]0.7	5.6	40.9%	3.2	4.4	3.6

Balance Sheet Data (Million $)

Jun. 30	Cash	Curr. Assets	Curr. Liab.	Curr. Ratio	Total Assets	% Ret. on Assets	Long Term Debt	Common Equity	Total Cap.	% LT Debt of Cap.	% Ret. on Equity
1992	**63.4**	**NA**	**NA**	**NA**	**555**	**7.3**	**163**	**293**	**462**	**35.4**	**15.4**
1991	57.5	NA	NA	NA	489	6.1	[6]227	201	435	52.3	16.6
1990	60.8	NA	NA	NA	339	6.2	[6]177	108	296	59.9	20.2
1989	37.7	NA	NA	NA	295	7.0	[6]163	87	265	61.7	20.5
1988	39.6	112	21.5	5.2	166	8.8	52	71	139	37.7	21.8
1987	44.0	109	15.2	7.1	152	8.0	54	59	132	41.0	19.3
1986	24.9	77	10.0	7.7	107	9.3	28	49	92	30.5	18.6
1985	20.3	53	10.7	4.9	72	11.3	5	41	56	8.6	19.2
1984	15.4	39	6.9	5.7	54	11.1	2	34	41	3.9	17.8
1983	19.4	34	6.4	5.2	44	9.0	Nil	28	31	0.7	18.4

Data as orig. reptd. **1.** Reflects acctg. change. **2.** Inc. other inc. **3.** Net of interest income. **4.** Inc. equity in earns. of nonconsol. subs. **5.** Net of curr. yr. retirement and disposals. **6.** Inc. curr. portion of long term debt. NA-Not Available.

Business Summary

Clayton Homes is a vertically integrated producer and retailer of low- to medium-priced manufactured homes in the southern and eastern U.S. It provides complete financing and insurance services to its retail customers, and develops communities for manufactured housing. Contributions to revenues in recent years were:

	1992	1991	1990
Retail sales	56%	55%	55%
Wholesale sales	24%	25%	29%
Financial services and other	20%	20%	16%

A manufactured home is a factory-built, completely furnished dwelling, constructed to be transported by trucks, and designed as a permanent, primary residence when sited and attached to utilities. CMH makes over 125 models of single- and multi-section homes. Retail prices range from $11,500 to $55,000, with sizes from 672 to 1,904 sq. ft. At the end of fiscal 1992, CMH was operating seven plants in Tennessee, two in North Carolina, and one each in Georgia and Texas, with a capacity to produce 26,000 floor sections per year.

At June 30, 1992, the company sold homes through 127 company-owned retail centers in 10 states, and through 312 independent dealers in 24 states. It sold 10,671 manufactured homes in fiscal 1992 (52% to independent dealers), up from 9,972 (54%) in fiscal 1991.

CMH offers retail customers a variety of home purchase finance programs through conventional lenders and directly through its finance subsidiary, Vanderbilt Mortgage and Finance, Inc. In fiscal 1992, 67% of retail home sales were financed through Vanderbilt. At June 30, 1992, Vanderbilt was servicing about 63,000 contracts with an aggregate dollar amount of $882 million.

In fiscal 1992, the company acquired about 3,300 sites in 10 manufactured housing communities, bringing total sites owned at June 30, 1992, to 5,353; CMH had also reserved marketing rights to an additional 480 sites. Occupancy at the sites at the end of fiscal 1992 was 58%.

Dividend Data

No cash dividends have been paid. The shares were split five-for-four in December of each of the past three years.

Capitalization

Long Term Liabilities: $147,662,000 (3/93), incl. $40,000,000 of 7.75% sub. debs. conv. into com. at $12.54 a sh.

Common Stock: 44,743,996 shs. ($0.10 par).
J.L. Clayton owns 29%.
Institutions hold about 67%.
Shareholders of record: 1,430.

Office—New Topside Drive at Alcoa Highway (P.O. Box 15169), Knoxville, TN 37901. **Tel**—(615) 970-7200. **Chrmn, Pres & CEO**—J. L. Clayton. **EVP-Fin, CFO & Investor Contact**—Richard B. Ray, Jr. **Secy-Treas**—W. O. Henry. **Dirs**—B. J. Clayton, J. L. Clayton, J. D. Cockman, D. W. Evins, E. T. Kelly, C. W. Neel, R. B. Ray, Jr., J. H. Stegmayer. **Transfer Agent & Registrar**—Trust Co. Bank, Atlanta. **Incorporated** in Tennessee in 1968. **Empl**—2,679.

 Richard Spiegel

Cleveland-Cliffs

NYSE Symbol CLF In S&P MidCap 400

Price	Range	P–E Ratio	Dividend	Yield	S&P Ranking	Beta
Sep. 16'93	1993					
30¼	36⅞–28¾	8	[4]1.20	[4]4.0%	B	0.96

Summary

Cleveland-Cliffs is the largest independent manager, processor and lessor of iron ore reserves in North America. CLF reported sharply higher earnings for 1993's first half as an after-tax gain of $1.91 a share from the recovery of the LTV bankruptcy claim more than offset the adverse impact of lower volume and prices. Although volume and pricing are expected to improve in 1994, the absence of the large gain on bankruptcy claims will cause reported earnings for 1994 to trail 1993.

Current Outlook

Earnings for 1994 are projected at $3.25 a share, versus 1993's estimated earnings of $4.25, which includes $1.91 non-operating income.

Dividends should remain at $0.30 quarterly. Special dividends of $1.00 in cash and 0.1249 common share of LTV Corp. were paid in July 1993.

Total revenues for 1994 are expected to decline, reflecting the absence of a bankruptcy claim recovery. Operating revenues should increase, however, on higher iron ore production from both managed and owned mines. Benefiting from higher operating rates and a probable increase in prices, operating profit should rise. But, the absence a gain on bankruptcy claims will cause reported earnings to trail those of1993.

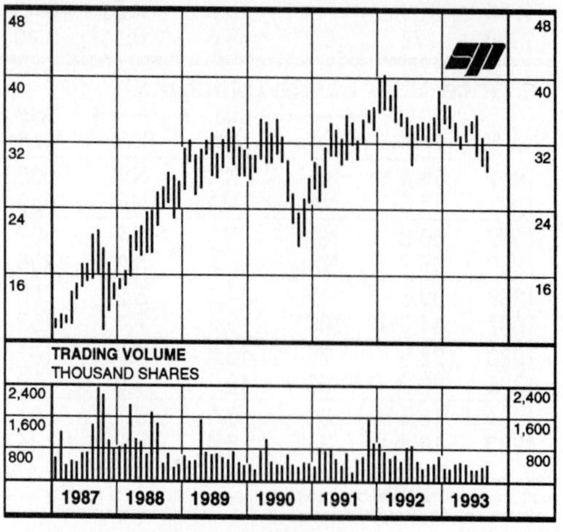

Total Revenues (Million $)

Quarter:	1993	1992	1991	1990
Mar.	43.3	53.4	85.9	59.5
Jun.	121.7	93.7	85.7	89.3
Sep.	---	107.7	102.2	96.3
Dec.	---	72.2	89.5	155.1
	---	327.0	363.3	400.2

Total revenues for the six months ended June 30, 1993, rose 12%, year to year, solely reflecting the recovery of a bankruptcy claim. Gross margins narrowed due to lower volume and prices. However, aided by a $1.91 a share after-tax gain on the LTV claim and absence of large bad debt expense, net income rose to $33.4 million ($2.78 a share) from $16.8 million ($1.41). Earnings for 1992 exclude a $3.23 a share charge for FAS 106.

Common Share Earnings ($)

Quarter:	1993	1992	1991	1990
Mar.	d0.01	0.43	1.56	0.47
Jun.	2.79	0.98	0.95	1.21
Sep.	E0.65	1.21	1.08	0.36
Dec.	E0.82	d0.05	0.96	4.27
	E4.25	2.57	4.55	6.31

Important Developments

Sep. '93— CLF announced that tentative contract agreements had been reached between the United Steelworkers of America and the company's iron ore mining partnerships. Union members had been on strike since the contract expired on July 31, 1993. Terms of the settlements, which apply to the Empire and Tilden Mines in Michigan and the Hibbing Taconite Mine in Minnesota, were not disclosed. The contracts, which are yet to be ratified by the members, will extend for six years and contain a provision for renegotiation or binding arbitration of certain economic terms after three years. CLF stated that the contract costs would be offset by improved efficiencies, capital equipment upgrades, and research applications.

Next earnings report expected in late October.

Per Share Data ($)

Yr. End Dec. 31	1992	1991	1990	1989	1988	1987	[1]1986	1985	1984	1983
Tangible Bk. Val.	**22.49**	24.40	24.88	19.36	14.53	21.02	22.16	25.74	25.78	24.70
Cash Flow	**2.80**	4.80	6.50	5.58	3.61	2.11	d2.38	2.93	3.97	d1.98
Earnings[2]	**2.57**	4.55	6.31	5.37	3.28	1.91	d3.76	1.46	2.30	d3.70
Dividends	**1.175**	[3]5.025	0.800	0.400	Nil	Nil	0.350	1.000	1.000	1.000
Payout Ratio	**46%**	111%	13%	7%	Nil	Nil	NM	69%	43%	NM
Prices—High	**40⅜**	36½	35	34	28⅜	21⅜	19⅜	22¼	26	25¼
Low	**29½**	25	19⅝	25¾	14¼	9¼	6	16⅝	17	18⅛
P/E Ratio—	**16–11**	8–5	6–3	6–5	9–4	11–5	NM	15–11	11–7	NM

Data as orig. reptd. **1.** Reflects merger or acquisition. **2.** Bef. results of disc. opers. of -0.17 in 1989, -0.42 in 1988, -1.34 in 1987; bef. spec. items of -3.23 in 1992, +0.32 in 1983. **3.** Incl. 4.00 spec. **4.** Excl. special divs. in Jul.1993. d-Deficit. E-Estimated NM-Not Meaningful.

Income Data (Million $)

Year Ended Dec. 31	Revs.	Oper. Inc.	% Oper. Inc. of Revs.	Cap. Exp.	Depr.	Int. Exp.	[3]Net Bef. Taxes	Eff. Tax Rate	[4]Net Inc.	% Net Inc. of Revs.	Cash Flow
1992	**311**	**38.3**	**12.3**	**2.9**	**2.8**	**5.0**	**41**	**25.6%**	**30.8**	**9.9**	**33.6**
1991	317	45.2	14.2	2.9	2.8	3.8	70	23.3%	53.8	17.0	56.6
1990	310	32.5	10.5	2.5	2.3	6.1	107	30.8%	73.8	23.8	76.1
[1]1989	351	94.9	27.1	2.9	2.2	11.0	87	28.1%	62.5	17.8	64.7
[1]1988	393	76.5	19.5	1.5	4.5	12.7	64	30.5%	44.7	11.4	47.7
[1]1987	363	15.1	4.2	Nil	2.7	12.2	49	37.4%	[5]30.6	8.4	28.3
[2]1986	267	d34.2	NM	7.0	17.2	7.3	d56	NM	[5]d41.7	NM	d29.5
1985	326	38.5	11.8	6.0	18.1	7.5	22	8.6%	20.1	6.2	36.3
1984	389	58.6	15.1	14.0	20.6	10.1	38	23.7%	28.6	7.4	49.2
1983	311	8.4	2.7	9.0	21.2	13.0	d75	NM	[5]d45.8	NM	d24.5

Balance Sheet Data (Million $)

Dec. 31	Cash	Curr. Assets	Curr. Liab.	Curr. Ratio	Total Assets	% Ret. on Assets	Long Term Debt	Common Equity	Total Cap.	% LT Debt of Cap.	% Ret. on Equity
1992	**129**	**249**	**60**	**4.1**	**537**	**6.1**	**75**	**270**	**345**	**21.8**	**11.0**
1991	96	206	66	3.1	473	10.9	29	291	358	8.2	18.3
1990	98	266	941	2.8	508	16.1	41	291	366	11.3	28.5
1989	96	178	79	2.3	411	15.6	53	226	313	16.9	31.6
1988	52	154	79	1.9	390	10.5	94	169	285	32.9	20.9
1987	109	320	84	3.8	657	4.3	122	345	539	22.7	7.2
1986	87	229	99	2.3	585	NM	80	276	447	17.9	NM
1985	48	184	68	2.7	560	3.6	37	320	464	7.9	5.7
1984	35	163	83	2.0	549	5.2	48	320	425	11.2	9.1
1983	10	159	76	2.1	542	NM	61	306	419	14.7	NM

Data as orig. reptd. **1.** Excludes discontinued operations. **2.** Reflects merger or acquisition. **3.** Incl. equity in earns. of nonconsol. subs. **4.** Bef. spec. items. **5.** Reflects accounting change. d-Deficit. NM-Not Meaningful.

Business Summary

Cleveland-Cliffs is the largest independent manager and lessor of iron ore reserves in North America. Its principal business is the production and sale of iron ore pellets.

Through subsidiaries, CLF manages the development, construction and operation of six iron ore mines, including five in North America and one in Australia, and the concentrating and pelletizing plants to produce iron ore pellets for steelmakers. The subsidiaries are reimbursed by the participants of the various mining ventures for substantially all expenses directly and indirectly incurred in operating the respective mines. Additionally, they are paid a management fee based on the number of tons of iron ore produced, which is subject to quarterly adjustment.

Following the pact with Weirton and other new contracts, multi-year contracts cover some 80% of CLF's equity interest in active production capacity in North America.

Iron ore pellet production from the six mines managed by CLF totaled 34.4 million tons in 1992, versus 33.4 million in 1991. Sales from CLF's own mines were 7.3 million in 1992 and 1991. Capacity utilization at North American mines was 93% in 1992, versus 90% in 1991. CLF's mines accounted for 45% of all the pellets produced in North America in 1992.

In February 1993 CLF sold its last remaining coal property.

Dividend Data

Dividends were resumed in 1989 after having been omitted in 1986. A dividend reinvestment plan is available. A revised "poison pill" stock purchase rights plan was adopted in 1991.

Amt of Divd. $	Date Decl.	Ex–divd. Date	Stock of Record	Payment Date
0.30	Nov. 10	Dec. 8	Dec. 14	Dec. 28'92
0.30	Jan. 12	Feb. 16	Feb. 22	Mar. 5'93
0.30	May 11	May 19	May 25	Jun. 9'93
*Stk	Jun. 18	Jul. 14	Jul. 1	Jul. 13'93
1.00 Spl	Jun. 18	Jul. 14	Jul. 1	Jul. 13'93
0.30	Jul. 13	Aug. 16	Aug. 20	Sep. 10'93

*0.1249 LTV com. sh. (new).

Finances

In 1992, CLF said that the agreement to supply iron ore pellets to Weirton Steel for 12 years would produce revenue of $400 to $500 million.

Capitalization

Long Term Debt: $75,000,000 (6/93).

Common Stock: 12,020,315 shs. ($1 par). Institutions hold about 90%. Shareholders of record: 3,973 (12/92).

Office—1100 Superior Ave., 18th Floor, Cleveland, OH 44114-2589. **Tel**—(216) 694-5700. **Chrmn & CEO**—M. T. Moore. **Secy**—J. E. Lenhard. **EVP-CFO**—J. S. Brinzo. **Investor Contact**—F. Rice. **Dirs**—R. S. Colman, E. M. deWindt, J. D. Ireland III, E. B. Jones, L. L. Kanuk, G. H. Lamphere, M. T. Moore, S. B. Oresman, A. Schwartz, S. K. Scovil, J. H. Wade, A. W. Whitehouse Jr. **Transfer Agent & Registrar**—Society National Bank, Cleveland. **Incorporated** in Ohio in 1947; reincorporated in Ohio in 1985. **Empl**—6,388.

 Leo Larkin

Coca-Cola Enterprises

NYSE Symbol CCE Options on CBOE In S&P MidCap 400

Price	Range	P–E Ratio	Dividend	Yield	S&P Ranking	Beta
Sep. 15'93	1993					
14⅝	15⅞–11¾	NM	0.05	0.3%	NR	1.40

Summary

This company is the world's largest bottler of Coca-Cola soft drinks, with a marketing territory covering over 50% of the population of the U.S. In June 1993, CCE acquired two bottling companies from the Coca-Cola Co. for a total of $366 million. Assuming favorable economic conditions, CCE profits are expected to trend upward through 1994. Coca-Cola Co. holds some 43% of CCE's outstanding common stock.

Current Outlook

Earnings for 1994 are projected to rise to $0.20 a share from the $0.07 estimated for 1993.

Dividends at $0.01¼ quarterly are the minimum expected.

Assuming favorable economic conditions, operating income is expected to trend higher through 1994, aided by higher case and fountain gallon volumes, as well as lower unit costs. However, a high level of acquisition-related depreciation, amortization and net interest expense will restrain share earnings gains.

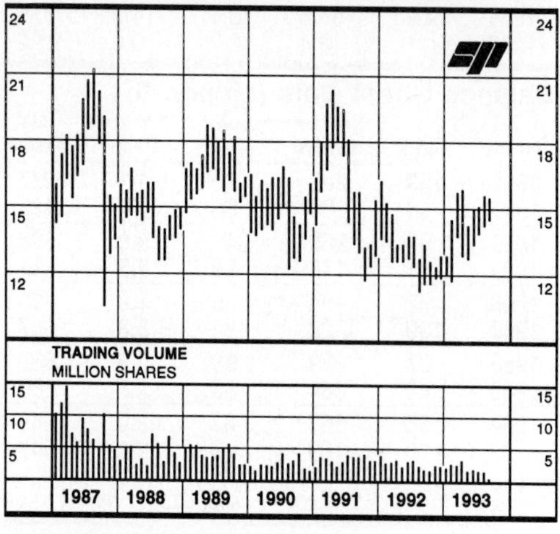

Net Oper. Revenues (Million $)

Quarter:	1993	1992	1991	1990
Mar.	1,208	1,112	905	906
Jun.	1,448	1,386	1,119	1,125
Sep.	---	1,351	1,079	1,067
Dec.	---	1,279	948	935
	---	5,127	4,051	4,034

Net operating revenues for the six months ended June 30, 1993, rose 6.4%, year to year, reflecting increased unit sales volume. Unit costs declined 2% on favorable packaging and ingredient trends, and pretax income was $37 million, versus a negligible amount. After taxes at 67.6%, against taxes of $1 million, income of $12 million ($0.09 a share) contrasted with a loss of $1 million (less than $0.01, excluding accounting charges totaling $1.33).

Common Share Earnings ($)

Quarter:	1993	1992	1991	1990
Mar.	d0.04	0.20	0.06	0.03
Jun.	0.13	d0.20	0.27	0.42
Sep.	E0.02	0.13	d0.04	0.13
Dec.	Ed0.04	d0.24	d1.07	0.06
	E0.07	d0.11	d0.79	0.65

Important Developments

Jul. '93— Management reported that cash operating profit (operating income plus depreciation and amortization charges) for 1993's first half rose 16%, year to year, benefiting from increases in both case bottle/can volume and fountain gallon volume. Management noted that 1993 second-quarter volumes were significantly positively affected by Fourth of July holiday sales, which were recorded in the third quarter in 1992. On a constant territory and fiscal period basis, 1993 first-half physical case bottle/can volume and fountain gallon volume would have exceeded comparable volume from 1992's first half by approximately 3% and 9%, respectively. In response to competitive pricing initiatives, net price per case did not change materially, year to year, in 1993's first half.

Next earnings report expected in late October.

Per Share Data ($)

Yr. End Dec. 31	[1]1992	[1]1991	1990	[1]1989	[1]1988	1987	[1]1986	1985	1984	1983
Tangible Bk. Val.	[3]**9.70**	d21.41	d14.55	d11.77	d10.36	d8.33	d7.24	NA	NA	NA
Cash Flow	**2.90**	1.38	2.62	2.18	2.65	2.01	1.56	NA	NA	NA
Earnings[2]	**d0.11**	d0.79	0.65	0.41	1.03	0.63	0.36	0.52	0.36	0.28
Dividends	**0.05**	0.05	0.05	0.05	0.05	0.05	Nil	NA	NA	NA
Payout Ratio	**NM**	NM	7%	11%	5%	8%	Nil	NA	NA	NA
Prices—High	**16¼**	20⅜	16⅞	18¾	16¾	21¼	16½	NA	NA	NA
Low	**11¼**	11¾	12¼	14¾	12⅝	10½	13⅞	NA	NA	NA
P/E Ratio—	**NM**	NM	26–19	46–36	16–12	34–17	46–39	NA	NA	NA

Data as orig. reptd. **1.** Refl. merger or acq. **2.** Bef. spec. item of -1.33 in 1992. **3.** Incl. intangibles. d-Deficit. E-Estimated. NM-Not Meaningful. NA-Not Available.

Income Data (Million $)

Year Ended Dec. 31	Oper. Revs.	Oper. Inc.	% Oper. Inc. of Revs.	Cap. Exp.	Depr.	Int. Exp.	Net Bef. Taxes	Eff. Tax Rate	[5]Net Inc.	% Net Inc. of Revs.	Cash Flow
[1]1992	**5,127**	**695**	**13.6**	**291**	**389**	**[4]312**	**d12**	**NM**	**d15**	**NM**	**374**
[1]1991	4,051	538	13.3	238	251	215	d91	NM	d82	NM	160
1990	4,034	582	14.4	259	236	207	[2]184	49.3%	93	2.3	313
[1]1989	3,882	539	13.9	273	229	200	[2]138	48.0%	72	1.8	283
[1]1988	3,874	606	15.7	273	225	211	[2]268	43.0%	153	3.9	368
1987	3,329	531	16.0	206	194	171	[2]173	48.9%	[3]88	2.7	282
[1]1986	1,951	260	13.3	136	92	83	85	67.2%	28	1.4	120
1985	1,272	140	11.0	79	55	32	64	43.6%	36	2.8	91
1984	872	92	10.5	47	36	11	47	46.6%	25	2.8	0
1983	684	73	10.6	40	28	5	39	50.4%	19	2.8	0

Balance Sheet Data (Million $)

Dec. 31	Cash	Curr. Assets	Curr. Liab.	Curr. Ratio	Total Assets	% Ret. on Assets	Long Term Debt	Common Equity	Total Cap.	% LT Debt of Cap.	% Ret. on Equity
1992	**6.0**	**701**	**1,304**	**0.5**	**8,805**	**NM**	**3,509**	**1,254**	**6,330**	**55.4**	**NM**
1991	64.1	706	1,385	0.5	6,677	NM	3,407	1,443	5,141	66.3	NM
1990	0.5	495	1,055	0.5	5,021	2.0	1,960	1,376	3,922	50.0	5.7
1989	9.7	493	996	0.5	4,732	1.6	1,756	1,430	3,702	47.4	3.7
1988	0.2	488	550	0.9	4,669	3.5	2,062	1,558	4,092	50.4	9.5
1987	11.3	452	474	1.0	4,250	2.2	2,091	1,526	3,770	55.5	5.9
1986	7.6	423	523	0.8	3,811	1.0	1,780	1,448	3,288	54.1	2.4
1985	20.7	205	137	1.5	780	NA	195	403	643	30.4	NA
1984	0.6	158	127	1.2	691	4.9	189	337	564	33.6	9.0

Data as orig. reptd. **1.** Refl. merger or acq. **2.** Incl. equity in earns. of nonconsol. subs. **3.** Refl. acctg. change. **4.** Net of int. inc. **5.** Bef. spec. item in 1992. d-Deficit. NM-Not Meaningful. NA-Not Available.

Business Summary

Coca Cola Enterprises is the world's largest bottler of Coca-Cola soft drinks. With the December 1991 acquisition of Johnston Coca-Cola Bottling Group, Inc., CCE distributes approximately 54% of all bottle/can volume of carbonated soft-drink products of Coca-Cola Co. (KO).

CCE's bottling territories include portions of 38 states, the District of Columbia and the U.S. Virgin Islands. These territories include about 131 million people, or about 52% of the U.S. population. In 1992, about 73% of CCE's equivalent case sales represented products bearing the "Coca-Cola" or "Coke" trademarks, approximately 16% were of other soft drinks of KO and about 11% represented products of other soft-drink firms.

The company conducts its business primarily under bottle contracts with KO, whereby CCE receives the exclusive right to produce and market Coca-Cola soft drinks in authorized containers in specified territories and provide KO with the ability, in its sole discretion, to set prices for concentrates and syrups, the terms of payment and other terms and conditions under which CCE purchases concentrates and syrups for KO soft-drink products. CCE operates 43 soft-drink production facilities, 16 of which are solely production facilities and 27 of which are combination production/distribution facilities, and also operates 213 facilities that are solely distribution facilities.

Dividend Data

Dividends were initiated in 1987. A dividend reinvestment plan is available.

Amt. of Divd. $	Date Decl.	Ex–divd. Date	Stock of Record	Payment Date
0.0125	Oct. 13	Dec. 10	Dec. 16	Dec. 29'92
0.0125	Feb. 23	Mar. 16	Mar. 22	Apr. 1'93
0.0125	Apr. 20	Jun. 15	Jun. 21	Jul. 1'93
0.0125	Jul. 21	Sep. 15	Sep. 21	Oct. 1'93

Finances

On June 30, 1993, CCE acquired from KO, the stock of Coca-Cola Beverages Nederland B.V. in the Netherlands (1992 net revenues of $327 million); Roddy Coca-Cola Bottling Company, Inc. in Knoxville, Tennessee; and the Coca-Cola Bottling Company of Johnson City, in Johnson City, Tennessee (Roddy/Johnson City Cos. combined 1992 net revenues were $84 million) for an aggregate purchase price of approximately $366 million in cash and assumed debt. The acquisition was accounted for under the purchase method.

Capitalization

Long Term Debt: $4,102,000,000 (7/2/93).

Common Stock: 129,366,619 shs. ($1 par).
The Coca-Cola Co. owns about 43%.
Institutions hold some 36%.
Shareholders of record: 9,946.

Office—Coca-Cola Plaza, N.W., Atlanta, GA 30313. **Tel**—(404) 676-2100. **Vice Chrmn & CEO**—S. K. Johnston Jr. **Pres**—H. A. Schimberg. **Sr VP-CFO**—J. R. Alm. **Secy**—J. G. Beatty Jr. **Investor Contact**—Margaret Carton. **Dirs**—J. L. Clendenin, J. B. Cole, T. M. Hahn Jr., C. M. Halle, L. P. Humann, E. N. Isdell, J. E. Jacob, S. K. Johnston Jr., R. A. Keller, W. D. Looney, S. L. Probasco Jr., H. A. Schimberg, F. A. Tarkenton. **Transfer Agent & Registrar**—First Chicago Trust Co. of New York, NYC. **Incorporated** in Delaware in 1944. **Empl**—26,000.

 Kenneth A. Shea

Comdisco, Inc.

NYSE Symbol CDO Options on Pacific (Jan-Apr-Jul-Oct) In S&P MidCap 400

Price	Range	P-E Ratio	Dividend	Yield	S&P Ranking	Beta
Jul. 28'93	1993					
14⅞	17⅜–13⅛	8	[1]0.32	[1]2.2%	B	1.34

Summary

Comdisco is primarily involved in buying, selling and leasing new and used computer and high-technology equipment. It also provides disaster recovery services for computer users. Share earnings for fiscal 1993 should be much improved from fiscal 1992's depressed level, and further growth is projected for fiscal 1994. In July 1993, the cash dividend was increased 14%.

Current Outlook

Earnings for the fiscal year ending September 30, 1993, are estimated at $1.99 a share, up from fiscal 1992's depressed $0.49 which was after $80 million of nonrecurring pretax charges. Earnings for fiscal 1994 are projected at $2.15 a share.

Dividends were raised 14%, to $0.08 from $0.07, with the July 1993 declaration.

Total revenues for fiscal 1993 are expected to fall about 3%, primarily due to lower volumes of initial leases of mainframe computers; revenues are expected to remain flat in fiscal 1994. While overall leasing volume improvement will be largely contingent upon whether or not worldwide economic conditions improve, margins should continue to widen as the company recognizes greater profits from equipment that is being re-leased. Contributions from the disaster recovery group should be more significant in fiscal 1994, as steps currently being taken by management to cut costs reduce operating burden going forward.

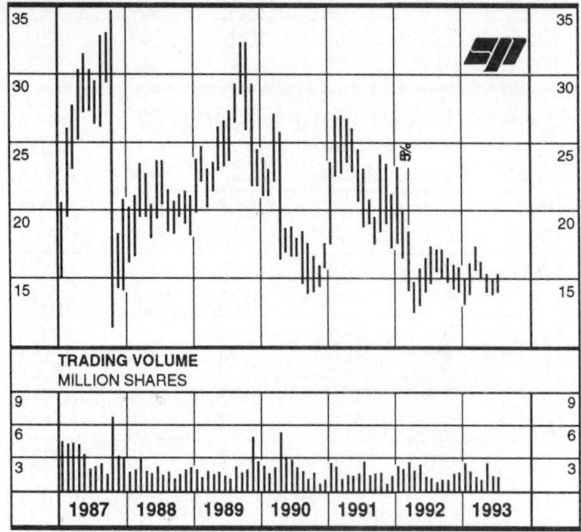

Total Revenues (Million $)

Quarter:	1992-93	1991-92	1990-91	1989-90
Dec.	571	553	527	458
Mar.	530	534	580	471
Jun.	513	561	517	489
Sep.		557	550	517
		2,205	2,174	1,935

Total revenues for the nine months ended June 30, 1993, were down 2.1%, year to year, as increased volume in the disaster recovery segment was more than offset by lower leasing volume, which resulted from a decline in the number of "big ticket" lease contracts. With declines in interest and SG&A costs and in the absence of $80 million of restructuring and other nonrecurring charges, net income totaled $64 million ($1.44 a share), up from $2 million ($0.05). Results for the 1992-93 period exclude a special credit of $0.49 a share from the cumulative effect of a change in accounting for income taxes; 1991-92 results exclude an $0.11 per share special charge.

Common Share Earnings ($)

Quarter:	1992-93	1991-92	1990-91	1989-90
Dec.	0.46	0.50	0.54	0.57
Mar.	0.48	d0.86	0.56	0.43
Jun.	0.50	0.41	0.45	0.48
Sep.	E0.55	0.44	0.48	0.51
	E1.99	0.49	2.03	1.99

Important Developments

Jun. '93— Comdisco sold 1,000,000 shares of 8¾% cumulative preferred stock at $25 a share. Proceeds were used to reduce short-term debt and for other corporate purposes. Separately, CDO said that it had repurchased 1.2 million common shares at a cost of about $16 million, under an April 1993, repurchase authorization.

Next earnings report expected in late October.

Per Share Data ($)

Yr. End Sep. 30	1992	1991	1990	[2]1989	[2]1988	1987	1986	1985	1984	1983
Tangible Bk. Val.	**15.38**	15.63	14.38	12.56	10.37	10.71	8.25	6.44	4.45	4.22
Cash Flow	**20.88**	20.99	17.40	13.58	10.65	10.00	9.12	7.09	5.72	4.88
Earnings[3]	**0.49**	2.03	1.99	2.45	2.10	1.76	1.82	1.34	0.67	1.13
Dividends	**0.273**	0.267	0.257	0.229	0.219	0.181	0.147	0.128	0.122	0.095
Payout Ratio	**56%**	13%	12%	9%	10%	10%	8%	9%	17%	8%
Prices[4]—High	**23¼**	27	27⅛	32⅜	23¾	34¾	23¾	18⅞	13⅝	26⅝
Low	**12½**	17¼	14	19⅞	16¼	11⅜	11⅜	7⅜	5⅛	10½
P/E Ratio—	**47–26**	13–9	14–7	13–8	11–8	20–6	13–6	14–5	20–8	24–9

Data as orig. reptd. Adj. for stk. divs. of 5% Mar. 1992, 50% Mar. 1986, 100% Mar. 1983. **1.** Plus 5% stk. in Mar. 1992. **2.** Reflects merger or acquisition. **3.** Bef. results of disc. opers. of -0.34 in 1991, -1.71 in 1988, +0.39 in 1987, extra. item(s) of -0.70 in 1992, +0.24 in 1990, +0.70 in 1985. **4.** Cal. yr. d-Deficit. E-Estimated

Income Data (Million $)

Year Ended Sep. 30	[1]Revs.	Oper. Inc.	% Oper. Inc. of Revs.	Cap. Exp.	Depr.	Int. Exp.	Net Bef. Taxes	Eff. Tax Rate	[6]Net Inc.	% Net Inc. of Revs.	Cash Flow
1992	**2,205**	**1,297**	**58.8**	**1,294**	**833**	**350**	**[5]34**	**41.2%**	**20**	**0.9**	**853**
1991	2,174	1,278	58.8	1,604	776	366	[5]136	39.0%	83	3.8	859
1990	1,935	1,132	58.5	1,268	657	338	[5]137	38.0%	85	4.4	742
[2]1989	1,678	950	56.6	1,108	490	290	170	36.5%	108	6.4	598
[2,3]1988	1,309	764	58.4	758	374	237	153	39.9%	92	7.0	466
[3]1987	1,175	708	60.3	542	359	[4]226	[5]123	37.4%	77	6.6	436
1986	902	519	57.5	655	316	104	[5]99	20.2%	79	8.8	395
1985	603	384	63.7	448	245	81	[5]58	1.0%	57	9.5	302
1984	558	332	59.5	373	225	71	[5]37	19.1%	30	5.3	254
1983	543	287	52.9	306	175	54	59	11.9%	52	9.5	227

Balance Sheet Data (Million $)

Sep. 30	Cash	Curr. Assets	Curr. Liab.	Curr. Ratio	Total Assets	% Ret. on Assets	[7]Long Term Debt	Common Equity	Total Cap.	% LT Debt of Cap.	% Ret. on Equity
1992	**142**	**NA**	**NA**	**NA**	**5,236**	**0.4**	**2,048**	**624**	**2,966**	**69.0**	**3.2**
1991	141	NA	NA	NA	5,006	1.7	2,199	634	3,057	71.9	13.6
1990	75	NA	NA	NA	4,785	2.0	2,070	589	2,832	73.1	15.4
1989	21	NA	NA	NA	4,045	2.9	1,629	548	2,335	69.8	21.6
1988	37	NA	NA	NA	3,488	2.8	1,527	450	2,084	73.3	20.1
1987	41	NA	NA	NA	3,023	3.2	2,100	466	2,614	80.3	18.7
1986	166	NA	NA	NA	1,700	5.7	1,028	351	1,422	72.3	25.3
1985	31	NA	NA	NA	1,077	5.6	610	272	914	66.7	25.0
1984	18	NA	NA	NA	974	3.2	672	188	864	77.8	16.2
1983	233	NA	NA	NA	975	6.4	633	191	843	75.1	34.2

Data as orig. reptd. **1.** Incl. other inc. **2.** Refl. merg. or acq. **3.** Excl. disc. opers. **4.** Refl. acctg. change. **5.** Incl. equity in earns. of nonconsol. subs. **6.** Bef. results of disc. opers. ands spec. items. **7.** Prior to 1988 incl. curr. portion. NA-Not Available.

Business Summary

Comdisco is primarily involved in buying, selling and leasing new and used computer and other high-technology equipment and in providing disaster recovery services. The company also provides systems consulting and strategic planning services. Revenue sources in recent fiscal years were:

	1992	1991
Leasing	75%	75%
Sales	14%	17%
Disaster recovery	9%	7%
Other	2%	1%

CDO buys or leases and, in turn, sells, leases or subleases IBM computer equipment, as well as computer equipment manufactured by others. Sales and lease transactions include mainframe central processing units and/or various peripherals, such as printers, tape and disk drives and other equipment used with a mainframe. CDO emphasizes the larger and more advanced mainframe models from IBM and Amdahl Corp., including the IBM ES/9000, the IBM 3090 series and related upgrades, the Amdahl 5995/4550 and a full range of peripheral equipment.

CDO leases other high-technology equipment, primarily telecommunications and other office and communications products, including PCs, workstations, point-of-sale devices and satellite earth stations. Through subsidiaries, the company leases and refurbishes medical equipment.

Comdisco also provides disaster recovery services to support a customer's data processing needs in the event of fire, flood, power outage or other disaster. Services include emergency data processing backup, voice recovery and consulting services.

Dividend Data

Amt of Divd. $	Date Decl.	Ex-divd. Date	Stock of Record	Payment Date
0.07	Jul. 27	Aug. 4	Aug. 10	Sep. 7'92
0.07	Nov. 12	Nov. 16	Nov. 20	Dec. 7'92
0.07	Jan. 22	Feb. 8	Feb. 15	Mar. 15'93
0.07	Apr. 26	May 24	May 28	Jun. 21'93
0.08	Jul. 20	Aug. 3	Aug. 9	Sep. 7'93

Capitalization

Total Debt: $1,911,000,000 (6/93).

Discounted Lease Rentals: $1,695,000,000.

8.75% Cum. Pfd. Stk, Ser. A.: 3,000,000 shs. ($25 liquidation preference).

8.75% Cum. Pfd. Stk, Ser. B.: 1,000,000 shs. ($25 liquidation preference).

Common Stock: 39,288,069 shs. ($0.10 par). About 29% controlled by officers & directors. Institutions hold approximately 50%. Shareholders of record: 2,802.

Office—6111 North River Rd., Rosemont, IL 60018. **Tel**—(708) 698-3000. **Chrmn & Pres**—K. N. Pontikes. **Secy**—P. A. Hewes **Sr VP & CFO**—J. J. Vosicky. **VP-Investor Contact**—James J. Hyland. **Dirs**—A. J. Andreini, R. A. Bardagy, E. H. Fiedler Jr., C. K. Hartley, P. A. Hewes, R. R. Hipp, R. Kash, T. H. Patrick, K. N. Pontikes, W. N. Pontikes, J. F. Slevin, B. R. Twist Jr., J. J. Vosicky. **Registrar & Principal Transfer Agent**—Chemical Bank, NYC. **Incorporated** in Delaware in 1971. **Empl**—2,087.

 Samuel A. Dedio

Comerica Inc.

NYSE Symbol CMA Options on Phila (Feb-May-Aug-Nov) In S&P MidCap 400

Price	Range	P-E Ratio	Dividend	Yield	S&P Ranking	Beta
Sep. 22'93	1993					
27⅜	35¼–26⅞	10	1.12	4.1%	A–	1.18

Summary

This holding company owns Comerica Bank (Michigan), one of the largest in the state, as well as Comerica Banks in Illinois, Texas, California and Florida, and other subsidiaries. In June 1992, the company nearly doubled in size with the acquisition of Manufacturers National Corp., a Detroit-based bank holding company with assets of $13.5 billion. Except for a restructuring charge related to the acquisition, earnings have continued to advance to new record levels. In July 1993, the dividend was raised 9.8%.

Business Summary

Comerica Inc. is the parent of Comerica Bank (Michigan), one of the largest in the state, as well as Comerica Banks in Illinois, Texas, California and Florida. Other subsidiaries provides brokerage, credit card, leasing, mortgage banking, investment banking, investment advisory and management services. In June 1992, CMA acquired Detroit-based Manufacturers National Corp., a $13.5 billion bank holding company. At year-end 1992, Comerica had assets of $26.6 billion, with 423 banking locations.

Total loans at December 31, 1992, amounted to $17.81 billion, versus $16.91 billion a year earlier and were divided:

	1992	1991
Commercial	46%	46%
Consumer	21%	21%
Comm'l. real estate	17%	16%
Res. mortgages	12%	14%
International	4%	3%

Total deposits of $20.39 billion at year-end 1992 consisted of noninterest-bearing demand 21%, domestic interest-bearing deposits 74%, and foreign deposits 5%.

On a tax-equivalent basis, the average yield on interest-earning assets in 1992 was 8.07% (9.51% a year earlier), while the average cost of funds (both interest and noninterest bearing liabilities) was 3.32% (4.99%). The net interest margin was 4.75% (4.52%).

Nonperforming assets at year-end 1992 totaled $264 million (1.48% of loans and related assets), up from $238 million a year earlier (1.41%). The allowance for loan losses at December 31, 1992, was $298.1 million (1.67% of loans), up from $266.5 million at year-end 1991 (1.58%). Net

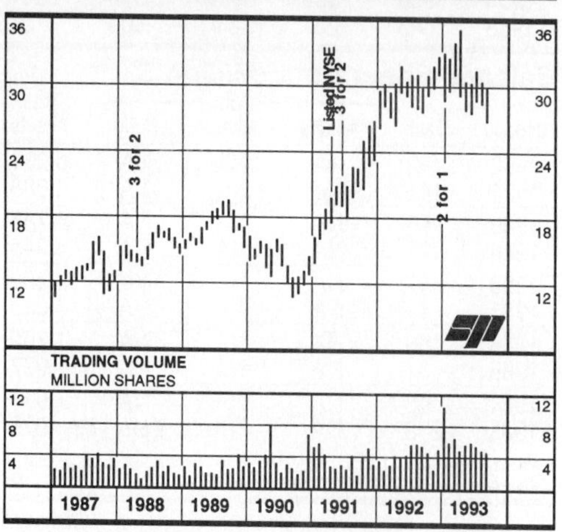

chargeoffs during 1992 totaled $98 million (0.58% of average loans), up from $93 million in 1991 (0.58%), and included $51 million of consumer loan net chargeoffs and $38 million of commercial loan net chargeoffs.

Important Developments

Sep. '93— The company agreed to acquire Pacific Western Bankshares (PWB) a $1 billion bank holding company based in San Jose, Calif. PWB shareholders will receive approximately 4,585,000 shares of CMA common stock. The transaction is expected to be completed in the spring of 1994. In May, CMA completed the acquisition of NorthPark National Corp., the parent of NorthPark National Bank, the largest independent bank in north Texas (assets of $719 million) for approximately $79 million in CMA common stock.

Next earnings report expected in mid-October.

Per Share Data ($)

Yr. End Dec. 31	[1]1992	[1]1991	[1]1990	[1]1989	[2]1988	1987	1986	1985	1984	[1,2]1983
Tangible Bk. Val.	**15.46**	13.51	12.78	11.32	11.15	10.05	9.84	9.83	9.25	8.63
Earnings[3]	**1.92**	2.52	2.52	1.55	2.26	1.38	1.21	1.00	1.07	0.98
Dividends	**1.665**	0.922	0.867	0.767	0.634	0.511	0.489	0.473	0.450	0.429
Payout Ratio	**50%**	37%	34%	49%	28%	37%	40%	47%	42%	44%
Prices—High	**32¾**	26⅞	16¹¹⁄₃₂	19¹⁹⁄₃₂	17⁵⁄₃₂	16⅛	13½	10⅛	7¾	6¾
Low	**26¼**	13¹⁵⁄₁₆	10¾	15³⁄₃₂	13¹⁄₃₂	10¹⁷⁄₃₂	8¹⁹⁄₃₂	7¹⁹⁄₃₂	5²⁵⁄₃₂	4³¹⁄₃₂
P/E Ratio—	**17–14**	11–6	6–4	13–10	8–6	12–8	11–7	10–8	7–5	7–5

Data as orig. reptd. Adj. for stk. divs. of 100% Jan. 1993, 50% Jun. 1991, 50% Apr. 1988, 5% Dec. 1983. **1.** Reflects merger or acquisition. **2.** Reflects accounting change. **3.** Bef. spec. item(s) of +0.09 in 1985.

Income Data (Million $)

Year Ended Dec. 31	Net Int. Inc.	Tax Equiv. Adj.	Non Int. Inc.	Loan Loss Prov.	% Exp./ Op. Revs.	Net Bef. Taxes	Eff. Tax Rate	[3]Net Inc.	% Net Int. Margin	—% Return On— Assets	Equity
[1]1992	**1,086**	**37.3**	**395**	**113**	**69.8**	**313**	**27.7%**	**226**	**4.75**	**0.88**	**12.0**
[1]1991	595	21.0	182	58	63.0	217	29.4%	153	4.87	1.12	16.6
[1]1990	492	24.3	158	57	62.6	171	25.1%	128	4.59	1.06	17.8
[1]1989	447	24.5	134	103	63.1	96	19.3%	78	4.54	0.69	12.0
[2]1988	396	26.8	126	39	60.8	148	24.1%	112	4.46	1.10	19.2
1987	369	35.4	130	79	60.8	87	18.3%	71	4.48	0.74	12.7
1986	323	48.7	117	64	65.1	72	13.7%	62	4.39	0.67	12.0
1985	326	43.2	110	52	68.2	57	7.7%	53	4.28	0.55	10.4
1984	287	40.7	98	29	67.0	71	19.5%	57	4.07	0.63	12.0
[1,2]1983	206	38.4	69	7	68.3	54	9.2%	49	3.56	0.65	11.8

Balance Sheet Data (Million $)

Dec. 31	Total Assets	———Earning Assets——— Mon. Mkt. Assets	Inv. Secs.	Com'l Loans	Other Loans	% Loan Loss Resv.	—Deposits— Demand	Time	% Loans/ Deposits	Long Term Debt	Common Equity	% Equity To Assets
1992	**26,587**	**1,481**	**4,749**	**8,184**	**9,859**	**1.65**	**4,366**	**16,029**	**88.5**	**737**	**1,988**	**7.27**
1991	14,451	722	3,115	4,049	5,464	1.31	1,920	9,521	81.9	239	1,010	6.61
1990	13,300	706	3,145	4,638	3,833	1.29	1,806	8,949	77.6	264	749	5.77
1989	12,150	666	2,519	4,349	3,721	2.48	1,742	8,141	80.4	274	663	5.46
1988	11,146	1,421	1,841	3,327	3,711	1.81	1,670	7,580	74.8	276	595	5.43
1987	10,116	1,725	1,614	2,874	3,209	1.91	1,505	6,898	71.0	194	520	5.34
1986	9,983	1,791	1,444	2,862	3,118	1.26	1,594	6,717	70.5	122	499	5.13
1985	9,770	1,549	1,580	2,625	3,204	1.06	1,449	6,624	70.7	130	461	4.70
1984	9,631	2,015	1,366	2,281	3,051	1.01	1,332	6,289	67.8	56	431	4.62
1983	8,557	2,399	1,348	1,533	2,334	1.06	1,211	5,756	54.4	72	403	5.15

Data as orig. reptd. **1.** Reflects merger or acquisition. **2.** Reflects acctg. change. **3.** Bef spec. items.

Review of Operations

Net interest income in the six months ended June 30, 1993, rose 1.4%, year to year, as a wider net interest margin (4.75% versus 4.65%), largely reflecting a 115 basis point decline in the funding costs for interest bearing deposits, offset a 1.1% decline in average earning assets. The provision for loan losses fell 34%, to $40.0 million. Aided by an 9.6% increase in service charges on deposits and a 17% increase in other noninterest income, total+ noninterest income advanced 8.7%. Noninterest expense was 17% lower, entirely due to the absence of 1992's $128 million restructuring charge, and pretax earnings increased 161%. After taxes at 30.2%, versus 27.9%, net income gained 153%. After preferred dividends, earnings per share were $1.39, versus $0.54 (restated and adjusted for the January 1993 2-for-1 stock split).

Common Share Earnings ($)

Quarter:	1993	[1]1992	1991	1990
Mar.	0.69	0.64	0.62	0.62
Jun.	0.70	d0.14	0.65	0.64
Sep.	---	0.71	0.60	0.66
Dec.	---	0.72	0.66	0.61
		1.92	2.52	2.52

1. Reflects MNTL acq. d-Deficit.

Dividend Data

Dividends have been paid since 1936. A dividend reinvestment plan is available. A "poison pill" stock purchase rights plan was adopted in 1988.

Amt of Divd. $	Date Decl.	Ex-divd. Date	Stock of Record	Payment Date
2-for-1	Nov. 20	Jan. 5	Dec. 15	Jan. 4'93
0.25½	Nov. 20	Dec. 9	Dec. 15	Jan. 4'93
0.25½	Jan. 15	Mar. 9	Mar. 15	Apr. 1'93
0.25½	May 21	Jun. 9	Jun. 15	Jul. 1'93
0.28	Jul. 16	Sep. 9	Sep. 15	Oct. 1'93

Finances

At June 30, 1993, the Tier 1 risk-based capital ratio stood at 8.92%, up from 8.83% at 1992 year end. The total risk-based capital ratio was 11.87% versus 11.82%. Non-performing assets totaled $248.1 million (1.34% of loans and related assets). The allowance for loan losses was $308.1 million.

Capitalization

Long Term Debt: $1,103,274,000 (6/93).

Common Stock: 118,821,678 shs. ($5 par). Institutions hold about 58%. Shareholders of record: 12,853.

Office—100 Renaissance Center, Suite 3800, Detroit, MI 48243. **Tel**—(313) 222-4000. **Chrmn & CEO**—G.V. MacDonald. **Pres**—E. A. Miller. **EVP & CFO**—P. H. Martzowka. **Treas & Investor Contact**—Leonard Carleton. **Dirs**—E. P. Casey, J. F. Cordes, J. P. DiNapoli, M. M. Fisher, P. Shontz Longe, W. B Lyon, G. V. MacDonald, D. R. Mandich, E. A. Miller, A. A. Piergallini, D. E. Richardson, T. F. Russell, A. E. Schwartz, F. Sims. **Transfer Agent & Registrar**—Comerica Bank-Detroit. **Incorporated** in Delaware in 1972. **Empl**—12,903.

 Richard M. Levine, CFA

COMSAT Corp.

NYSE Symbol CQ Options on Phila (Jan-Apr-Jul-Oct) In S&P MidCap 400

Price	Range	P-E Ratio	Dividend	Yield	S&P Ranking	Beta
Aug. 31'93	1993					
30½	31⅞–23¾	25	0.74	2.4%	B	0.86

Summary

COMSAT (formerly Communications Satellite) provides international, domestic, maritime and aeronautical communications and information services. Through minority ownership in two international satellite organizations, CQ links the U.S. by satellite with 180 nations and more than 25,000 mobile terminals. A 2-for-1 stock split was effected in June 1993.

Current Outlook

Earnings for 1993 are estimated at $1.85 a share, versus 1992's $1.09 (which included a $0.60 restructuring charge). For 1994, earnings are projected at $2.10.

A 2-for-1 stock split was effected in June 1993. The $0.18½ quarterly dividend should continue.

Revenues from international communications are expected to increase in the high single-digit range in 1993 on 3% to 5% growth from World Systems and continued double-digit growth from mobile communications services. Revenues from the newly combined systems and labs units are anticipated to show moderate growth; video entertainment revenues will benefit from increased ownership in On Command Video and higher penetration of the hospitality market. Margins should widen, reflecting cost savings from restructuring measures implemented in 1992 and anticipated profitability from the video unit, and the absence of a $39.0 million restructuring charge; depreciation charges will be up on additional satellites in orbit.

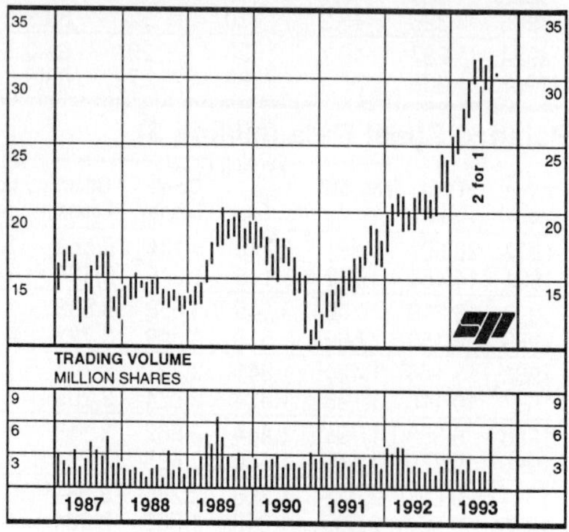

Operating Revenues (Million $)

Quarter:	1993	1992	1991	1990
Mar.	166.3	127.9	126.9	110.8
Jun.	154.1	133.2	127.6	116.8
Sep.	---	146.0	127.1	112.4
Dec.	---	156.5	141.3	116.8
	---	563.6	522.9	456.8

Revenues for the six months ended June 30, 1993, rose 23%, year to year, reflecting growth across all operating segments. Margins narrowed; higher depreciation charges impacted profitability at the mobile communications unit. Lower interest capitalized and higher interest charges offset the benefits from higher net other income and pretax earnings were up 22%. After taxes at 39.0%, versus 37.3%, net income advanced 19%. Share earnings, as adjusted for 2-for-1 stock split in June 1993, were $0.95 (before a $0.03 special credit from an accounting change), versus $0.83.

Common Share Earnings ($)

Quarter:	1993	1992	1991	1990
Mar.	0.46	0.40	0.48	0.51
Jun.	0.50	0.43	0.50	0.50
Sep.	E0.42	d0.17	0.50	0.33
Dec.	E0.47	0.43	0.41	d1.78
	E1.85	1.09	1.88	d0.44

Important Developments

Aug. '93— CQ reached an agreement with AT&T for a 10-year contract to provide international voice and data circuits on the INTELSAT system. The contract includes substantial rate reductions and increased operating flexibility in exchange for a longer commitment. The rate reductions would be offset, in part, by an expected increase in traffic over the system. AT&T also agreed to withdraw its comments in CQ's incentive rate proceeding before the FCC; this should increase the likeihood that the rate case will be approved.

Next earnings report expected in mid-October.

Per Share Data ($)

Yr. End Dec. 31	[1]1992	1991	1990	1989	1988	1987	1986	1985	1984	1983
Tangible Bk. Val.	**14.13**	15.36	16.29	16.80	15.81	14.64	16.66	15.57	17.09	14.44
Cash Flow	**4.27**	4.77	2.47	4.01	3.92	2.66	4.27	1.78	3.15	3.26
Earnings[2]	**1.09**	1.88	d0.44	1.68	1.68	0.49	1.48	d0.53	1.25	1.39
Dividends	**0.700**	0.670	0.660	0.660	0.630	0.600	0.600	0.600	0.600	0.588
Payout Ratio	**64%**	36%	NM	36%	34%	112%	41%	NM	48%	42%
Prices—High	**24 7/16**	19	19¼	20 5/16	15⅜	17 5/16	20¼	19 3/16	17¼	22 11/16
Low	**17⅛**	11 7/16	10 3/16	13	12 9/16	10⅞	14 1/16	12¾	10⅜	14 15/16
P/E Ratio—	**22–16**	10–6	NM	12–8	9–8	36–22	14–10	NM	14–8	16–11

Data as orig. reptd. Adj. for stk divs. of 100% Jun. 1993, 100% Jun. 1983. 1. Refl. acctg. change. 2. Bef. results of disc. ops. of -1.78 in 1987, +0.14 in 1986, -0.62 in 1985, +0.17 in 1984 & spec. item of -0.70 in 1991. d-Deficit. E-Estimated. NM-Not Meaningful.

Income Data (Million $)

Year Ended Dec. 31	Revs.	Oper. Inc.	% Oper. Inc. of Revs.	Cap. Exp.	Depr.	Int. Exp.	[3]Net Bef. Taxes	Eff. Tax Rate	[4]Net Inc.	% Net Inc. of Revs.	Cash Flow
[2]1992	**564**	**252**	**44.8**	**233**	**125**	**46.2**	**67**	**35.7%**	**42.9**	**7.6**	**168**
1991	523	238	45.5	282	110	46.9	103	30.7%	[2]71.4	13.7	182
1990	457	194	42.4	203	109	37.5	d16	NM	d16.3	NM	92
1989	412	173	42.1	227	87	41.4	91	31.5%	62.5	15.2	150
1988	359	163	45.5	218	83	40.5	85	27.0%	61.9	17.3	144
[1,2]1987	334	145	43.4	148	80	40.3	NM	NM	17.8	5.3	97
[1]1986	466	188	40.3	181	102	39.8	80	32.7%	[2]54.0	11.6	156
[1]1985	459	187	40.8	160	83	43.7	d12	NM	d19.0	NM	64
[1]1984	442	153	34.6	200	69	29.2	70	35.5%	45.2	10.2	114
1983	440	176	39.9	300	68	11.8	79	36.4%	50.1	11.4	118

Balance Sheet Data (Million $)

Dec. 31	Cash	Curr. Assets	Curr. Liab.	Curr. Ratio	Total Assets	% Ret. on Assets	Long Term Debt	Common Equity	Total Cap.	% LT Debt of Cap.	% Ret. on Equity
1992	**4**	**165**	**170**	**1.0**	**1,543**	**2.9**	**486**	**621**	**1,210**	**40.2**	**7.0**
1991	7	159	214	0.7	1,393	5.4	383	585	1,055	36.3	12.4
1990	2	161	142	1.1	1,229	NM	375	558	1,020	36.8	NM
1989	6	170	129	1.3	1,261	5.1	368	595	1,063	34.6	10.8
1988	60	176	95	1.9	1,163	5.4	369	553	997	37.0	11.6
1987	131	242	140	1.7	1,110	1.5	327	512	896	36.5	3.3
1986	113	257	106	2.4	1,214	4.5	335	579	1,023	32.7	9.6
1985	102	245	112	2.2	1,162	NM	354	536	1,006	35.2	NM
1984	63	211	136	1.6	1,166	4.1	258	599	981	26.3	7.7
1983	57	183	144	1.3	1,044	5.6	159	569	862	18.4	9.5

Data as orig. reptd. **1.** Excl. disc. ops. **2.** Refl. acctg. change. **3.** Incl. equity in earns. of nonconsol. subs. **4.** Bef. spec. item in 1991. d-Deficit. NM-Not Meaningful.

Business Summary

COMSAT (formerly Communications Satellite) provides regulated and unregulated satellite communications services and provides information services. Contributions (operating profits in million $) by business segment in 1992:

	Revs.	Profits
International	69%	$123.0
Technology Services	18%	−13.2
Video entertainment	13%	−8.2

The international segment provides telephone, data, video and audio communications services to U.S. communications carriers, U.S. and foreign broadcasters, and others using the INTELSAT (21.8%-owned as of March 1993) satellite system; and telecommunications services for maritime, aeronautical, and land mobile applications using the Inmarsat (23.1%) satellite system and COMSAT's land earth stations in Connecticut, California and Turkey. These businesses are subject to rate regulation by the FCC. The segment also includes COMSAT International Ventures, which forms non-U.S. ventures with public telecommunications authorities and private concerns to provide international and domestic digital communications services.

The technology services segment provides turnkey satellite communications systems to emerging markets and specialized technical consulting. Through COMSAT Laboratories, the unit also conducts research and development activities for the telecommunications industry.

Video entertainment operations consist of the distribution of interactive entertainment and information services to hotels throughout the U.S. CQ also holds a 100% interest in the Denver Nuggets—a team in the National Basketball Association.

Dividend Data

Dividends were initiated in 1970. A dividend reinvestment plan is available.

Amt of Divd. $	Date Decl.	Ex–divd. Date	Stock of Record	Payment Date
0.35	Oct. 16	Nov. 6	Nov. 13	Dec. 14'92
0.37	Jan. 15	Feb. 8	Feb. 12	Mar. 8'93
0.37	Apr. 16	May 10	May 14	Jun. 14'93
2–for–1	Jan. 15	Jun. 25	Jun. 1	Jun. 24'93
0.18½	Jul. 23	Aug. 9	Aug. 13	Sep. 13'93

Capitalization

Long Term Debt: $474,400,000 (6/93).

Common Stock: 39,864,204 shs. (no par). Institutions hold approximately 83%. Shareholders of record: 44,035.

Office—950 L'Enfant Plaza, SW Washington DC, 20024. **Tel**—(202) 863-6800. **Chrmn**—M. R. Laird. **Pres & CEO**—B. L. Crockett. **VP-CFO**—C. T. Faulders III. **VP-Secy**—J. W. Breslow. **Investor Contact**—Janine Anderson-Bays. **Dirs**—L. W. Benson, R. E. Boschwitz, E. I. Colodny, B. L. Crockett, F. B. Dent, J. B. Edwards, N. B. Freeman, B. M. Goldwater, A. Hauspurg, M. R. Laird, P. W. Likins, H. M. Love, R. Robinson Jr., R. G. Schwartz, C. J. Silas. **Transfer Agent & Registrar**—The Bank of New York, NYC. **Incorporated** in Washington, D.C. in 1963. **Empl**—1,644.

 Susan Stahl Gibney

Conner Peripherals

NYSE Symbol CNR Options on Pac (Jan-Apr-Jul-Oct) In S&P MidCap 400

Price	Range	P–E Ratio	Dividend	Yield	S&P Ranking	Beta
Jul. 30'93	1993					
11¼	25½–9	NM	None	None	NR	1.94

Summary

This company is a leading manufacturer of high-performance 2½- and 3½-inch Winchester disk drives, data storage devices for notebook, laptop, portable and desktop microcomputers, and high-performance workstations. Following the December 1992 acquisition of Archive Corp., Conner also became a leading vendor of tape drives and related subsystems, primarily for backup storage applications. Following strong 1992 earnings, a loss was recorded in the first half of 1993 on sharp declines in average selling prices. Greater than normal price pressures will restrain results through 1993 year-end.

Current Outlook

A loss of $2.00 is estimated for 1993, versus earnings of $2.19 (including a $0.73 acquisition charge) reported for 1992. Earnings of $1.00 a share are projected for 1994.

Initiation of dividends is not expected.

Sales should rise in 1993, reflecting higher unit shipments of disk drives and contributions from Archive's tape drive products. Operations should be unprofitable, however, reflecting fierce competitive pricing pressures, notably in drives under 200 MBs, caused in large part by industry-wide excess manufacturing capacity. Moderating price pressures, cost controls, and the absence of restructuring charges should return the company to profitability in 1994.

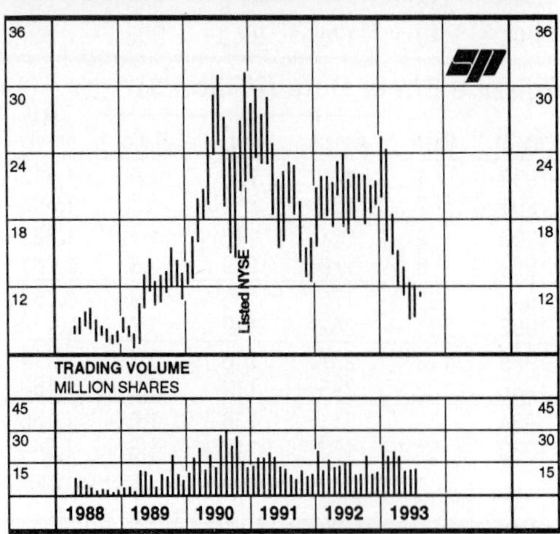

Net Sales (Million $)

Quarter:	1993	1992	1991	1990
Mar.	558	441	382	235
Jun.	491	551	405	304
Sep.	---	625	395	380
Dec.	---	620	417	418
	---	2,238	1,599	1,338

Sales for the six months ended June 30, 1993, advanced 5.7%, year to year, reflecting higher unit shipments of disk drives resulting from increased sales of personal computers, as well as contributions from the acquisition of Archive Corp. Profits, however, were penalized by a sharp decline in average selling prices, and following charges totaling $48.4 million for restructuring costs and inventory write-offs, and $12.9 million for the amortization of goodwill and other intangibles, there was a pretax loss of $91.0 million, against a pretax profit of $96.2 million. After a tax credit, versus a charge, the net loss was $81.4 million ($1.66 a share on 18% fewer shares), against net income of $70.7 million ($1.19; $1.05 fully diluted).

Common Share Earnings ($)

Quarter:	1993	1992	1991	1990
Mar.	d0.46	0.42	0.60	0.37
Jun.	d1.19	0.77	0.45	0.54
Sep.	Ed0.30	0.79	0.30	0.71
Dec.	Ed0.05	0.17	0.23	0.81
	Ed2.00	2.19	1.57	2.51

Important Developments

Jul.'93— In the second quarter of 1993, CNR recorded a $12 million charge to write-down inventories of older disk drives. In the first quarter, the company recorded charges of $36.4 million related to actions management took to restructure and downsize operations, including a 10% workforce cut, and to accelerate the transition of certain product lines, including the write-down of obsolete inventory.

Next earnings report expected in mid-October.

Per Share Data ($)

Yr. End Dec. 31	[4]1992	1991	1990	[2]1989	1988	1987	1986	1985
Tangible Bk. Val.	**7.48**	12.27	10.64	5.04	3.08	1.61	0.37	NA
Cash Flow	**3.46**	2.42	3.17	1.50	0.72	0.47	NA	NA
Earnings	**[3]2.19**	[3]1.57	[3]2.51	[3]1.09	0.58	0.43	d0.33	[1]d0.08
Dividends	**Nil**	Nil	Nil	Nil	Nil	Nil	Nil	Nil
Payout Ratio	**Nil**	Nil	Nil	Nil	Nil	Nil	Nil	Nil
Prices—High	**23⅞**	29¾	31¼	15½	10⅛	NA	NA	NA
Low	**15⅝**	12½	12¼	6½	6⅞	NA	NA	NA
P/E Ratio—	**11–7**	19–8	12–5	14–6	17–12	NA	NA	NA

Data as orig. reptd. **1.** From inception 6-18-85. **2.** Refl. acctg. change. **3.** Ful. dil.: 1.89 in 1992, 1.54 in 1991, 2.41 in 1990, 1.00 in 1989. **4.** Reflects merger or acquis. d-Deficit. E-Estimated NA-Not Available.

Income Data (Million $)

Year Ended Dec. 31	Revs.	Oper. Inc.	% Oper. Inc. of Revs.	Cap. Exp.	Depr.	Int. Exp.	Net Bef. Taxes	Eff. Tax Rate	Net Inc.	% Net Inc. of Revs.	Cash Flow
[4]1992	**2,238**	**281**	**12.6**	**116.0**	**70.3**	**46.9**	**[3]162**	**21.4%**	**121**	**5.4**	**191**
1991	1,599	177	11.1	87.7	50.1	23.3	128	26.0%	92	5.8	143
1990	1,338	207	15.5	95.9	34.0	7.0	[3]179	26.2%	130	9.7	164
[1]1989	705	79	11.2	80.7	15.6	9.2	[3]57	25.8%	41	5.9	57
1988	257	32	12.5	31.0	5.0	1.2	[3]27	27.6%	20	7.7	25
1987	113	18	15.8	17.7	1.2	0.3	[3]17	33.8%	11	10.0	13
1986	Nil	d4	NM	1.8	0.1	Nil	[3]d4	Nil	d4	NM	NA
[2]1985	Nil	NM	NM	NM	NM	Nil	[3]NM	Nil	NM	NM	NA

Balance Sheet Data (Million $)

Dec. 31	Cash	Curr. Assets	Curr. Liab.	Curr. Ratio	Total Assets	% Ret. on Assets	Long Term Debt	Common Equity	Total Cap.	% LT Debt of Cap.	% Ret. on Equity
1992	**615**	**1,388**	**436**	**3.2**	**1,905**	**8.0**	**705**	**626**	**1,463**	**48.2**	**19.9**
1991	570	1,124	169	6.7	1,335	8.3	368	713	1,162	31.7	13.9
1990	237	721	183	3.9	880	16.8	37	604	693	5.3	29.2
1989	104	366	124	3.0	468	11.9	123	201	341	36.0	25.6
1988	10	151	68	2.2	198	12.7	19	105	129	15.1	24.6
1987	30	75	43	1.7	94	21.5	4	46	50	7.8	42.5
1986	5	10	4	2.7	12	NM	NM	8	8	0.8	NM
1985	NA	NM	NM	5.4	NM	NM	Nil	NM	NM	Nil	NM

Data as orig. reptd. **1.** Refl. acctg. change. **2.** From inception 6-18-85. **3.** Incl. equity in earns. of nonconsol. subs. **4.** Reflects merger or acquis. d-Deficit. NM-Not Meaningful. NA-Not Available.

Business Summary

Conner Peripherals is engaged primarily in the design and manufacture of high-performance 2½- and 3½-inch Winchester disk drives, which are used to record, store and retrieve digital information that cannot be stored entirely in a computer system's central memory unit.

The company's disk drives address the requirements of high performance notebook, laptop, portable, desktop and workstation-class microcomputers for greater storage capacity, faster access time, lower power consumption and smaller size, utilizing proprietary microcode to implement various drive and controller functions traditionally handled by hardware.

The company's product line consists primarily of disk drives with formatted storage capacities ranging from 40 megabytes (MBs) to 545 MBs.

Conner's products are marketed mainly through direct sales to original equipment manufacturers (OEMs) and also through distributors. In 1992 Compaq Computer accounted for 15% of sales and Conner Peripherals Europe Gmbh, the company's European distributor, accounted for 12%.

Manufacturing facilities are in Singapore, Malaysia, Scotland, Italy and San Jose, Calif.

Conner holds a 51% interest in Conner Peripherals Europe, a joint venture with Ing. C. Olivetti & Co., S.P.A., formed in July 1988 to produce and sell Conner's drives in Europe. The manufacturing facility is located in Italy.

Following the late 1992 acquisition of Archive Corp., Conner assumed a leading position in the market for tape drives and related subsystems, used primarily for backup storage applications.

Foreign sales represented 61% and 64% of total sales in 1992 and 1991, respectively.

Dividend Data

No dividends have been paid, and Conner does not expect to pay dividends in the foreseeable future.

Finances

In November 1992, CNR acquired Archive Corp., a leading maker of tape drives and related subsystems with annual revenues of about $380 million, for approximately $176 million in cash. In the fourth quarter of 1992, CNR recorded an aftertax charge of $35.7 million (about $0.73 a share) for in-process R&D incurred in connection with the acquisition.

Capitalization

Long Term Debt: $672,289,000 (6/93), incl. $345 million of 6½% sub. debs. conv. into com. at $24 a sh. & $230 million of 6¾% sub. debs. conv. into com. at $29 a sh.

Minority Interest: $16,789,000.

Common Stock: 49,704,661 shs. ($0.001 par).
Institutions hold approximately 80%.
Shareholders of record: 2,375

Office—3081 Zanker Rd., San Jose, CA 95134. **Tel**—(408) 456-4500. **Chrmn & CEO**—F. F. Conner. **Pres**—D. T. Mitchell. **Sr VP-Investor Contact**—Regina Gindin. **Dirs**—W. S. Anderson, L. P. Bremer, F. F. Conner, L. W. Hart, D. T. Mitchell, R. S. Penske, M. S. Rossi, W. J. Schroeder, J. P. Squires. **Transfer Agent & Registrar**—First National Bank of Boston. **Incorporated** in California in 1985; reincorporated in Delaware 1992. **Empl**—10,300.

 Peter C. Wood, CFA

Consolidated Papers

NASDAQ Symbol CPER (Incl. in Nat'l Market) Options on Pacific In S&P MidCap 400

Price	Range	P-E Ratio	Dividend	Yield	S&P Ranking	Beta
Oct. 22'93	1993					
41	54¼–37½	30	1.28	3.1%	B+	0.65

Summary

This leading producer of enamel papers for the print communications industry and coated specialty papers for food and consumer product packaging also makes corrugated containers, paperboard and paperboard products, as well as pulp, primarily for its own production needs. Earnings declined in the third quarter of 1993 due to a higher federal tax rate and poor demand for lightweight coated paper. However, growth is expected to resume in 1994 and long-term prospects are bright.

Current Outlook

Earnings for 1994 are estimated at $2.50 a share, compared with the $1.45 projected for 1993.

Quarterly dividends should remain at $0.32 a share.

Sales for 1994 are expected to rise moderately, assuming some recovery in demand from magazine publishers. Margins should widen as the year progresses and excess industry capacity is absorbed. Profits are likely to recover significantly from the depressed levels of recent years. With its focus on the printed communications industry, recent capital investments and very strong financial position, the company's long-term growth prospects are bright.

Net Sales (Million $)

Quarter:	1994	1993	1992	1991
Mar.	---	242	217	230
Jun.	---	260	222	221
Sep.	---	229	233	217
Dec.	---	---	232	204
	---	---	904	872

Sales for the nine months ended September 30, 1993, rose 8.7%, year to year, reflecting higher shipments of coated printing paper in the first half of 1993. Benefiting from the absence of start-up costs of an expansion program completed in 1992, as well as cost control efforts, pretax income climbed 34%. After taxes at 42.4%, against 37.8%, net income was up 24%, to $1.15 a share from $0.93. Results for the 1992 period exclude a net charge of $0.87 a share related to accounting changes.

Common Share Earnings ($)

Quarter:	1994	1993	1992	1991
Mar.	E0.45	0.40	0.33	0.59
Jun.	E0.60	0.58	0.35	0.56
Sep.	E0.70	0.17	0.25	0.45
Dec.	E0.75	E0.30	0.22	0.50
	E2.50	E1.45	1.15	2.10

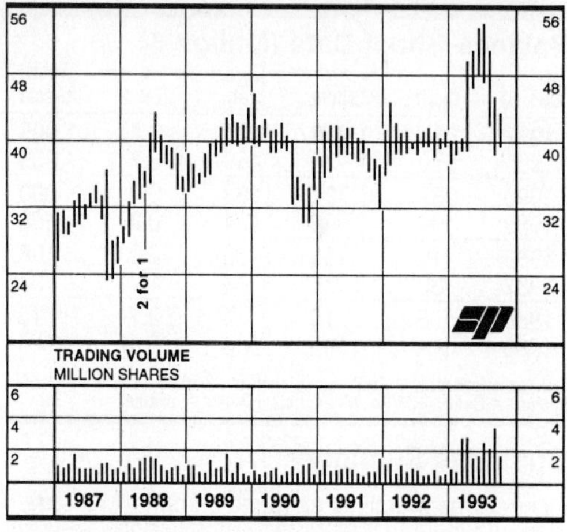

Important Developments

Oct. '93— Management attributed the decline in earnings for the third quarter of 1993 to a higher tax rate, weak markets for lightweight coated paper sold to magazine publishers and increased competition from imports. CPER said that due to sluggish economic conditions, some of its magazine customers have seen a significant drop in advertising pages. Also pressuring the market for coated paper in the third quarter was high inventory levels coming into the period. The company anticipated that the weak market for magazine paper would continue in the fourth quarter.

Apr. '93— Consolidated projected that earnings over the next few years would benefit from improvements in productivity, higher operating rates and a more favorable product mix. However, CPER cautioned that growth in the economy is necessary for continued operating gains.

Next earnings report expected in late January.

Per Share Data ($)

Yr. End Dec. 31	1992	1991	1990	1989	1988	1987	1986	1985	1984	1983
Tangible Bk. Val.	**21.03**	21.97	21.10	19.07	16.46	13.96	12.60	11.32	9.59	8.34
Cash Flow	**3.20**	3.58	4.56	5.02	4.47	3.18	2.75	3.11	2.43	1.69
Earnings[1]	**1.15**	2.10	3.27	3.85	3.44	2.20	2.01	2.46	1.90	1.13
Dividends	**1.280**	1.280	1.260	1.150	0.950	0.800	0.785	0.715	0.598	0.525
Payout Ratio	**111%**	61%	39%	30%	28%	36%	39%	29%	32%	47%
Prices—High	**44¾**	42	45¾	44	43½	36⅝	29¾	27¾	17⅞	13⁷⁄₁₆
Low	**36**	32	30¼	34	27¾	23⅜	24¼	16⅜	12⅝	8
P/E Ratio—	**39–31**	20–15	14–9	11–9	13–8	17–11	15–12	11–7	10–7	12–7

Data as orig. reptd. Adj. for stk. divs. of 100% May 1988, 100% Dec. 1984. **1.** Bef. spec. item of -0.87 (net) in 1992. E-Estimated.

Income Data (Million $)

Year Ended Dec. 31	Revs.	Oper. Inc.	% Oper. Inc. of Revs.	Cap. Exp.	Depr.	Int. Exp.	[1]Net Bef. Taxes	Eff. Tax Rate	[3]Net Inc.	% Net Inc. of Revs.	Cash Flow
[2]1992	**904**	**175**	**19.3**	**137**	**89.5**	**8.88**	**81**	**37.9%**	**50**	**5.6**	**140**
1991	872	202	23.2	280	64.9	7.00	146	37.2%	91	10.5	156
1990	949	269	28.3	331	56.5	0.16	228	37.4%	142	15.0	199
1989	953	294	30.8	150	51.1	1.05	263	36.2%	168	17.6	219
1988	897	264	29.5	112	45.1	0.18	237	36.7%	150	16.7	195
1987	743	194	26.2	69	42.8	1.07	164	41.6%	[2]96	12.9	139
1986	653	178	27.2	151	32.4	1.28	153	42.9%	88	13.4	120
1985	716	203	28.3	138	28.4	1.34	186	42.6%	107	14.9	135
1984	686	173	25.2	59	25.3	1.65	153	47.5%	81	11.7	106
1983	573	103	18.0	42	24.7	1.79	87	43.4%	49	8.5	74

Balance Sheet Data (Million $)

Dec. 31	Cash	Curr. Assets	Curr. Liab.	Curr. Ratio	Total Assets	% Ret. on Assets	Long Term Debt	Common Equity	Total Cap.	% LT Debt of Cap.	% Ret. on Equity
1992	**2**	**185**	**158**	**1.2**	**1,487**	**3.5**	**171**	**922**	**1,226**	**13.9**	**5.4**
1991	7	162	83	2.0	1,411	7.0	178	960	1,321	13.5	9.7
1990	12	163	91	1.8	1,192	12.5	Nil	920	1,095	Nil	16.3
1989	195	336	91	3.7	1,086	16.6	Nil	832	990	Nil	21.7
1988	147	287	71	4.1	935	17.2	Nil	717	861	Nil	22.6
1987	104	231	66	3.5	804	12.5	Nil	608	735	Nil	16.6
1986	64	185	68	2.7	723	12.8	4	547	652	0.6	16.8
1985	126	225	68	3.3	640	18.0	9	493	570	1.5	23.5
1984	124	230	61	3.8	548	15.6	12	417	486	2.4	20.7
1983	98	199	57	3.5	486	10.4	15	363	427	3.4	14.0

Data as orig. reptd. **1.** Incl. equity in earns. of nonconsol. subs. **2.** Refl. acctg. change. **3.** Bef. spec. items in 1992.

Business Summary

Consolidated Papers is a leading producer of enamel papers for the printed communications industry and of coated specialty papers used largely in the packaging and labeling of food and consumer products. It also manufactures corrugated displays and containers and paperboard products. Company shipments (in tons) in recent years were:

	1992	1991
Enamel papers	860,198	769,222
Specialty papers	81,531	67,102
Paperboard	5,749	4,870
Paperboard products	33,162	32,335
Corrugated products	34,028	32,634

The company's coated printing papers are used in magazines, books, brochures, advertising and corporate annual reports. Enamel printing paper sales represented 81% of CPER's total sales in 1992. These papers are sold directly to magazine publishers and through paper merchants to publishers and commercial printers. Direct sales to publisher accounts represented 61% of printing paper sales in 1992. Company shipments of enamel printing paper in 1992 represented about 12% of such paper sold in the U.S.

At 1992 year-end, the company was operating seven manufacturing plants in five Wisconsin municipalities. Equipment included 15 paper machines, two continuous kraft-pulp digesters, one paperboard machine, one corrugating machine and power production facilities with an aggregate rated capacity of 185,840 KW. Capacity utilization for enamel papers in 1992 was 89.4%.

Consolidated owns and manages 672,991 acres of timberland in Wisconsin, Michigan, Minnesota and Ontario. Company lands provided 16% of wood used in CPER's pulp mills in 1992.

Planned capital spending for 1993 is $95 million, down from expenditures of $137 million in 1992 and $280 million in 1991.

Dividend Data

Cash dividends have been paid in all years save two since 1906.

Amt. of Divd. $	Date Decl.	Ex–divd. Date	Stock of Record	Payment Date
0.32	Oct. 21	Nov. 2	Nov. 6	Nov. 20'92
0.32	Feb. 11	Feb. 16	Feb. 22	Mar. 5'93
0.32	Apr. 26	May 3	May 7	May 21'93
0.32	Jul. 20	Aug. 3	Aug. 6	Aug. 20'93
0.32	Oct. 19	Nov. 1	Nov. 5	Nov. 19'93

Capitalization

Long Term Debt: $108,000,000 (9/93).

Common Stock: 43,991,987 shs. ($1 par).
The Mead Voting Trust owns about 37%.
Institutions hold approximately 27%.
Shareholders of record: 7,546.

Office—P.O. Box 8050, Wisconsin Rapids, WI 54495-8050. **Tel**—(715) 422-3111. **Chrmn**—G. W. Mead. **Pres & CEO**—P. F. Brennan. **VP-Fin**—R. J. Kenney. **Secy**—C. H. Wartman. **Investor Contact**—Daniel P. Meyer (715) 422-3368. **Dirs**—R. B. Barker, P. F. Brennan, W. N. Caldwell, S. M. Hands, B. S. Kubale, D. R. Mead Jr., G. D. Mead, G. W. Mead, L. R. Nash. **Transfer Agent**—Harris Trust & Savings Bank, Chicago. **Incorporated** in Wisconsin in 1894. **Empl**—4,900.

 Richard Spiegel

Continental Bank

NYSE Symbol CBK Options on CBOE (Mar-Jun-Sep-Dec) In S&P MidCap 400

Price	Range	P-E Ratio	Dividend	Yield	S&P Ranking	Beta
Sep. 27'93	1993					
26¼	28⅜–19½	7	0.60	2.3%	B–	1.48

Summary

This bank holding company, among the 35 largest in the nation, owns Chicago's Continental Bank. Since the 1984 FDIC-aided restructuring, CBK has focused on three principal areas: corporate finance, market making and risk management, and specialized financial services. The loan loss provision rose 65% in 1993's first half, year to year, reflecting concern over the bank's California residential real estate portfolio, however, earnings improved 13%, as results were aided by an $8 million tax credit.

Business Summary

This bank holding company (formerly Continental Illinois Corp.), the 26th largest in the U.S., is the parent of Continental Bank. Since its FDIC-aided restructuring in 1984, CBK has focused on its traditional strengths in wholesale banking, targeted mainly at mid-sized corporations, complemented by investment banking-like businesses, including corporate finance, risk management and market-making.

Average earning assets of $18.6 billion in 1992 were divided: domestic loans 62%, foreign loans 9%, interest bearing deposits 10%, investment securities 6%, Federal funds sold and repurchase agreements 6%, and trading account assets 7%. Average sources of funds were: savings and time deposits 36%, Federal funds purchased and securities sold under repurchase agreements 9%, foreign accounts 19%, long term and other debt 10%, demand deposits 11%, equity and other 15%.

Nonperforming loans at year-end 1992 totaled $661 million (5.3% of loans; 16% were loans to less developed countries, 31% were HLT's), down from $733 million (5.3%) a year earlier. The reserve for loan losses was 3.0% of total loans, flat with a year ago. Net chargeoffs during 1992 were 1.19% of average loans, versus 1.53% in 1991. Total nonperforming assets at the end of 1992, including other real estate owned, were $834 million, up from $814 million a year before.

Under a restructuring plan adopted in 1984 after the company suffered a run on deposits due to a sharp increase in nonperforming loans, the Federal Deposit Insurance Corp. (FDIC) assumed $3.5 billion of problem loans and infused $1 billion of new capital into the bank. In exchange the FDIC received an 80% equity interest, which was subsequently reduced to 26%. In June 1991, the FDIC disposed of its remaining 26% interest in CBK by offering publicly the approximately 14.2 million CBK common shares it held

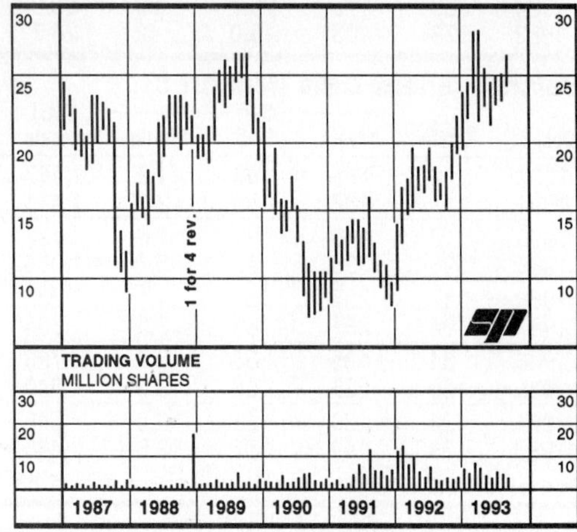

Important Developments

Aug. '93— CBK reported an increase in earnings for 1993's first half as a tax credit replaced tax expense. Pretax income decreased 3.4% as net interest income fell on declines in the value of interest-free funds and narrower Latin American net interest rate spreads. Results were penalized by the $36 million increase in the credit loss provision, due to continuing concerns over the bank's California residential real estate portfolio, bringing the reserve for loan losses to 3.1% of total loans as of June 30, 1993, from 3.0% at December 31, 1992, and 3.2% a year ago. Nonperforming assets fell to $768 million (6.55% of total loans) from $834 million (5.33%) at year-end 1992. The decrease was largely due to a drop in highly leveraged transaction loans and the transfer of Brazilian loans to trading account assets.

Next earnings report expected in mid-October.

Per Share Data ($)

Yr. End Dec. 31	1992	1991	1990	1989	[2]1988	1987	[3]1986	1985	1984	1983
Tangible Bk. Val.	[1]**24.07**	[1]20.89	[1]23.73	[1]24.01	[1]22.23	[1]17.76	[1]30.48	[1]28.36	[1]26.56	171.34
Earnings[4]	**3.44**	d2.03	0.95	4.64	5.19	d24.28	1.20	1.72	d107.96	9.84
Dividends	**0.60**	0.80	1.00	0.85	0.44	0.32	0.08	Nil	2.00	8.00
Payout Ratio	**17%**	NM	105%	18%	8%	NM	7%	Nil	Nil	81%
Prices—High	**22**	16	21½	26⅝	23½	24½	41	40½	91	103½
Low	**9⅛**	8	7⅛	18½	11	9	20	23	11	74
P/E Ratio—	**6–3**	NM	23–7	6–4	5–2	NM	34–17	24–13	NM	11–8

Data as orig. reptd. Adj. for 1-for-4 reverse split in 1988. **1.** As reptd. by co., assumes conv. of pref. stk. **2.** Reflects acctg. change. **3.** Reflects merger or acquisition. **4.** Bef. results of disc. opers. and/or spec. item(s) of -0.05 in 1991, -0.25 in 1990, -2.58 in 1989, +1.20 in 1986, +0.40 in 1985. d-Deficit. NM-Not Meaningful.

Income Data (Million $)

Year Ended Dec. 31	Net Int. Inc.	Tax Equiv. Adj.	Non Int. Inc.	Loan Loss Prov.	% Exp./ Op. Revs.	Net Bef. Taxes	Eff. Tax Rate	[3]Net Inc.	% Net Int. Margin	—% Return On— Assets	Equity
1992	**489**	**4**	**466**	**125**	**61.1**	**242**	**8.3%**	**222**	**2.66**	**1.01**	**15.61**
[1]1991	487	7	455	340	70.1	d56	NM	d73	2.33	NM	NM
1990	498	13	458	117	74.5	94	6.4%	88	1.98	0.30	4.24
1989	540	12	450	44	65.0	297	3.5%	286	2.20	1.01	21.41
1988	644	13	530	34	68.3	329	3.9%	316	2.37	1.03	38.20
[1]1987	598	19	440	824	77.3	d597	NM	d610	2.16	NM	NM
[2]1986	607	31	322	105	69.6	177	44.3%	99	2.55	0.35	6.80
1985	677	42	230	118	66.0	166	19.3%	134	2.83	0.47	13.10
1984	621	63	458	1,226	76.4	d1,047	NM	d1,087	2.10	NM	NM
1983	830	81	402	395	54.9	118	14.5%	101	2.52	0.25	5.90

Balance Sheet Data (Million $)

Dec. 31	Total Assets	—Earning Assets— Mon. Mkt. Assets	Inv. Secs.	Com'l Loans	Other Loans	% Loan Loss Resv.	—Deposits— Demand	Time	% Loans/ Deposits	Long Term Debt	Common Equity	% Equity To Assets
1992	**22,467**	**5,292**	**1,002**	**8,183**	**4,236**	**3.03**	**2,921**	**11,223**	**87.8**	**980**	**1,299**	**5.46**
1991	24,008	5,784	1,051	8,359	5,542	2.96	2,544	13,191	88.2	952	1,123	4.79
1990	27,143	6,593	1,458	8,895	6,461	1.88	2,995	13,103	95.2	917	1,203	4.05
1989	29,549	7,656	2,387	8,958	6,644	1.65	2,654	14,522	90.7	1,103	1,218	4.00
1988	30,578	7,249	1,952	9,029	7,579	5.98	2,933	14,034	97.7	942	960	2.30
1987	32,391	4,949	2,403	10,073	10,050	5.62	3,308	16,316	102.3	523	470	2.80
1986	32,809	3,909	3,057	10,281	10,462	2.15	3,319	14,713	114.5	1,145	1,154	3.40
1985	30,528	4,710	1,908	10,081	10,449	2.04	3,562	14,197	115.3	1,708	742	2.50
1984	30,413	1,398	1,534	12,352	12,077	1.50	3,612	11,444	161.6	2,456	648	1.50
1983	42,097	4,825	1,762	15,211	16,217	1.23	4,491	24,940	105.9	1,256	1,732	4.20

Data as orig. reptd. **1.** Reflects acctg. change. **2.** Reflects merger or acquisition. **3.** Bef. results of disc. opers. and/or spec. item(s) in 1990, 1989, 1986, 1985, 1983. d-Deficit. NM-Not Meaningful.

Review of Operations

Net interest income for the six months to June 30, 1993, fell 6.4%, year to year. The loan loss provision jumped 65%. Noninterest income climbed 33%, largely on higher trading revenues. Operating expenses rose 7.9% due to greater costs related to nonperforming assets. Pretax income declined 3.4%. After an $8 million tax credit, versus tax at 8.5%, net income was up 13.0%, to $122 million ($1.90 a share), from $108 million ($1.67). Results in 1993 exclude a $1.45 a share gain from the adoption of SFAS 109.

Common Share Earnings ($)

Quarter:	1993	1992	1991	1990
Mar.	0.96	0.90	0.41	0.99
Jun.	0.95	0.78	0.41	d1.03
Sep.		0.82	d3.61	0.58
Dec.		0.95	0.77	0.41
		3.44	d2.03	0.95

Finances

The rise in the loan loss provision in the first half of 1993 was due to higher charge-offs, mainly on loans to residential developers in California and on highly leveraged transaction loans. The loan loss reserve totaled $368 million at June 30, 1993, or about 48% of total nonperforming assets.

Dividend Data

Common dividends resumed in 1986. In 1991, a "poison pill" stock purchase right was adopted.

Amt of Divd. $	Date Decl.	Ex-divd. Date	Stock of Record	Payment Date
0.15	Oct. 26	Dec. 8	Dec. 14	Dec. 31'92
0.15	Feb. 22	Mar. 5	Mar. 11	Mar. 31'93
0.15	Apr. 27	Jun. 7	Jun. 11	Jun. 30'93
0.15	Aug. 17	Sep. 8	Sep. 14	Sep. 30'93

Capitalization

Long Term Debt: $1,130,000,000 (6/93).

Adj. Rate Pfd. Stock, Series 1: 1,788,000 shs. ($50 stated value).

Adj. Rate Cum. Pfd. Stock, Series 2: 3,000,000 shs. ($100 stated value).

Common Stock: 52,347,545 shs. ($4 par).
Executives and officers hold as a group 5.2%
Institutions hold approximately 63%.
Shareholders of record: 10,690 (12/92).

d-Deficit.

Office—231 South LaSalle St, Chicago, IL 60697. **Tel**—(312) 828-1614. **Chrmn & CEO**—T. C. Theobald. **Secy**—R. S. Brennan. **CFO**—H. W. Rademacher. **Investor Contact**—J. W. Alaimo (312) 828-4764. **Dirs**—J. W. Cozad, B. A. Getz, T. A. Gidlehaus, R. B. Goergen, W. M. Goodyear, R. L. Huber, M. L. Marsh, R. H. Morley, M. J. Murray, L. J. Rice, J. M. Richman, G. I. Segal, T. C. Theobald, J. L. Vincent. **Transfer Agent & Registrar**—Mellon Securities Trust Company, New Jersey. **Incorporated** in 1968; Bank chartered under National Bank Act in 1932. **Empl**—4,189.

 C. Orgielewicz

Continental Medical Systems

NYSE Symbol CNM In S&P MidCap 400

Price	Range	P-E Ratio	Dividend	Yield	S&P Ranking	Beta
Aug. 12'93	1993					
8	18¼–7⅛	14	None	None	NR	2.05

Summary

Continental is the leading independent provider of comprehensive medical rehabilitation programs and services in the U.S. A net loss in the fourth quarter of fiscal 1993 largely reflected a $14.5 million non-recurring charge related to the abandonment of development projects. Earnings were also penalized by weakness in the company's locum tenens business and at some inpatient hospitals.

Business Summary

Continental Medical Systems, Inc. is the largest provider of comprehensive medical rehabilitation programs and services in the U.S., with significant presence in each of the rehabilitation industry's three principal sectors—inpatient rehabilitation care, outpatient rehabilitation care and contract services.

The company has developed and provides inpatient and outpatient rehabilitation programs and services for patients suffering from stroke and other neurological disorders, orthopedic problems, head injuries, spinal cord injuries, work-related disabilities and multiple trauma. These programs and services are provided to patients through a plan of treatment developed by an interdisciplinary team that includes physician specialists, therapists and other medical personnel as determined by the individual patient's needs.

As of August 1993, Continental was operating 36 freestanding comprehensive inpatient medical rehabilitation hospitals and had three additional hospitals under construction. Many of the company's hospitals are operated through joint ventures with local general acute-care hospitals, physicians or other investors. The company also was providing outpatient rehabilitation services at more than 125 locations and managing 12 inpatient rehabilitation units for general acute care hospitals. The company was providing its rehabilitation services in 21 states.

Through its contract services business, the company provides physical, occupational, speech and respiratory therapy services on a contract basis to skilled nursing facilities, general acute-care hospitals, schools, home health agencies, inpatient rehabilitation hospitals and outpatient clinics. The contract services group also provides temporary physician and allied health professional staffing (locum tenens) services to hospitals and physician practice groups throughout the U.S.

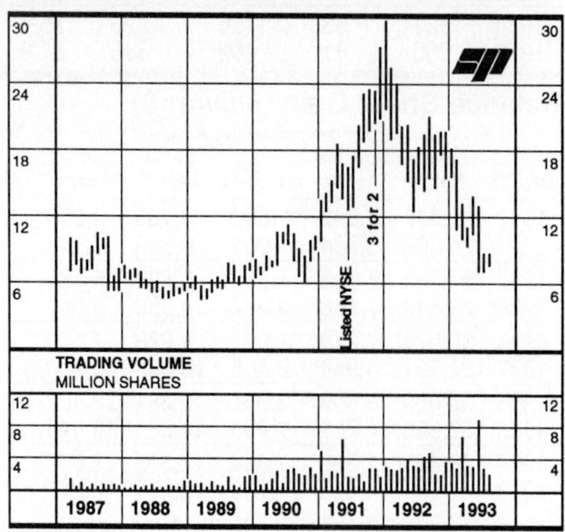

Important Developments

Aug. '93— The company noted that results for the fourth quarter of fiscal 1993 included non-recurring pretax charges of $14.5 million for the writedown or abandonment of about 30 development projects and $5 million related to the sale of facilities (reflected as an extraordinary item, net of the income tax effect). Earnings for the fourth quarter were also penalized by weaker than expected performances in the company's locum tenens business and at some inpatient hospitals. Continental said its decision to abandon the development projects was a result of changes in its strategy designed to significantly reduce the number of new hospital projects and pursue less capital intensive growth.

Next earnings report expected in late October.

Per Share Data ($)

Yr. End Jun. 30	1993	[1]1992	[1]1991	[1]1990	1989	[1]1988	[1]1987
Tangible Bk. Val.	**NA**	5.30	5.00	1.77	0.99	0.61	0.86
Cash Flow	**NA**	0.95	0.78	0.60	0.25	0.37	0.15
Earnings	**0.59**	[2]0.73	[2]0.57	[2]0.41	[2]0.03	[2]0.24	[2]0.07
Dividends	**Nil**	Nil	Nil	Nil	Nil	Nil	Nil
Payout Ratio	**Nil**	Nil	Nil	Nil	Nil	Nil	Nil
Prices—High	**NA**	[3]29¾	[3]27⅜	[3]11 5/16	[3]7 13/16	[3]7 9/16	[3]10½
Low	**NA**	[3]12½	[3]9⅞	[3]6 3/16	[3]4½	[3]4 11/16	[3]4 15/16
P/E Ratio—	**NA**	41–17	46–17	27–15	NM	32–19	NM

Data as orig. reptd. Adj. for stk. div. of 50% Nov. 1991. **1.** Refl. merger or acq. **2.** Bef. spec. items of -0.03 in 1989, +0.02 in 1987. **3.** Cal. yr.
NA-Not Available. NM-Not Meaningful.

Income Data (Million $)

Year Ended Jun. 30	Revs.	Oper. Inc.	% Oper. Inc. of Revs.	Cap. Exp.	Depr.	Int. Exp.	[2]Net Bef. Taxes	Eff. Tax Rate	[3]Net Inc.	% Net Inc. of Revs.	Cash Flow
[1]1992	**659**	**63.4**	**9.6**	**85.9**	**7.81**	**7.4**	**48.0**	**30.9%**	**26.4**	**4.0**	**34.2**
[1]1991	341	39.3	11.5	9.8	4.76	10.5	26.9	32.8%	14.8	4.3	19.5
[1]1990	227	28.9	12.7	8.2	4.18	9.8	16.9	39.7%	9.0	4.0	13.2
1989	151	21.5	14.2	9.8	4.36	9.0	2.4	77.4%	[4]0.6	0.4	5.0
[1]1988	112	18.3	16.3	30.6	2.78	7.6	8.8	45.7%	4.8	4.3	7.6
[1]1987	51	6.0	11.8	62.2	1.42	2.7	3.0	57.8%	1.3	2.5	2.7

Balance Sheet Data (Million $)

Jun. 30	Cash	Curr. Assets	Curr. Liab.	Curr. Ratio	Total Assets	% Ret. on Assets	Long Term Debt	Common Equity	Total Cap.	% LT Debt of Cap.	% Ret. on Equity
1992	**35.7**	**205**	**87.9**	**2.3**	**468**	**6.4**	**134**	**224**	**372**	**35.9**	**12.2**
1991	44.3	143	54.4	2.6	313	4.8	56	186	252	22.3	10.6
1990	13.3	69	39.0	1.8	209	4.4	90	64	162	56.2	15.1
1989	9.5	54	29.5	1.8	191	0.3	96	52	153	63.1	1.2
1988	15.9	44	32.7	1.3	177	2.9	89	51	140	63.4	9.9
1987	18.3	36	31.3	1.2	151	NA	73	46	120	61.2	NA

Data as orig. reptd. **1.** Refl. merger or acq. **2.** Incl. equity in earns. of nonconsol. subs. **3.** Bef. spec. items. **4.** Refl. acctg. change. NA-Not Available.

[1]Net Oper. Revenues (Million $)

Quarter:	1992–93	1991–92	1990–91	1989–90
Sep.	---	140	65	52
Dec.	[2]429	156	81	56
Mar.	232	176	89	60
Jun.	241	186	105	59
	901	659	341	227

Net operating revenues (preliminary) for the fiscal year ended June 30, 1993, rose 32% from those of the prior year (restated), reflecting continued expansion of the inpatient and outpatient rehabilitation and contract services businesses. Penalized by significantly higher interest expense and depreciation and amortization charges, and a $14.5 million non-recurring charge related to the writedown or abandonment of development projects, net income fell 16%, to $22,723,000 ($0.59 a share), from $27,091,000 ($0.72), excluding an extraordinary charge of $0.08 a share in fiscal 1993 for the cumulative effect of an accounting change.

Common Share Earnings ($)

Quarter:	1992–93	1991–92	1990–91	1989–90
Sep.	0.24	0.19	0.11	0.07
Dec.	0.26	0.18	0.15	0.09
Mar.	0.20	0.20	0.16	0.12
Jun.	d0.11	0.15	0.16	0.13
	0.59	0.73	0.57	0.41

Dividend Data

No cash dividends have ever been paid. A three-for-two stock split was effected in 1991. A "poison pill" stock purchase right was adopted in 1991.

Finances

In March 1993, Continental issued $150 million of 10⅜% notes, due 2003. In August 1992, it issued $200 million of 10⅞% notes, due 2002. The company used the aggregate proceeds from both issuances to repay all outstanding amounts under its revolving credit facility at the time of each sale (totaling about $277 million), with the ramainder to be used for general corporate purposes.

In February 1993, the company acquired Kron Medical Corp. in exchange for 1,268,331 common shares. Kron, which had 1992 revenues of $25 million, offers contract staffing services by physicians and other allied health professionals.

During fiscal 1992, Medicare accounted for 40% of the company's net patient revenues, private patients 54%, Medicaid 3% and other 3%.

In fiscal 1992, the company began development of its hospitals using a structure in which it constructs, owns and operates the hospitals. Historically, Continental has structured its operating companies with minority owners, and it intends to continue this policy where appropriate. The company believes its new on-balance-sheet financing structure will result in lower project costs and reduce its overall cost of capital.

Capitalization

Long Term Debt: $382,602,000 (6/93).

Minority Interest: $12,838,000.

Common Stock: 36,894,233 shs. ($0.01 par).
Institutions hold about 74%.
Stockholders of record: 611 (9/92).

1. Net of provisions for doubtful accounts & contractual adjustments. **2.** Six mos. d-Deficit.

Office—600 Wilson Lane, P.O. Box 715, Mechanicsburg, PA 17055. **Tel**—(717) 790-8300. **Chrmn & CEO**—Rocco A. Ortenzio. **Pres & COO**—Robert A. Ortenzio. **Sr VP-CFO**—D. L. Lehman. **Secy**—W. M. Goldstein. **Investor Contact**—Roger Breed (717) 790-8433. **Dirs**—K. F. Barber, R. L. Carson, B. C. Cressey, F. DeFazio, W. M. Goldstein, Robert A. Ortenzio, Rocco A. Ortenzio. **Transfer Agent & Registrar**—Security Trust, Baltimore. **Incorporated** in Delaware in 1985. **Empl**—10,000.

 Adam J. Penn

Convex Computer

NYSE Symbol CNX Options on Phila (Mar-Jun-Sep-Dec) In S&P MidCap 400

Price	Range	P-E Ratio	Dividend	Yield	S&P Ranking	Beta
Oct. 14'93	1993					
5⅝	8¾–3⅝	NM	None	None	B–	1.75

Summary

This company designs, manufactures, markets and services a line of supercomputers for use in various engineering, scientific and technical applications. Earnings in 1993 will be penalized by the difficult economic and competitive environment affecting the supercomputer industry and by the $32 million restructuring charge the company took in the second quarter. New products are scheduled for shipment in 1994.

Current Outlook

A loss of $1.90 a share, including a restructuring charge of $1.25, is projected for 1993, versus income of $0.11 in 1992. Share earnings of $0.25 are possible in 1994.

Initiation of cash dividends is not expected.

Results through at least the end of 1993 will continue to be restricted by a difficult economic and competitive environment affecting the supercomputer industry. These factors will lead to lower revenues and gross margins; operating costs should decline due to restructuring actions taken during the second quarter. The 16% workforce reduction should result in savings of some $22 million on an annualized basis by the fourth quarter of 1993. During the first half of 1994, the company is scheduled to start shipping the next generation C4 family of supercomputers, as well as the SPP System, CNX's implementation of massively parallel processing (MPP) technology. However, many other vendors, including IBM, have also announced plans for MPP machines for delivery in 1994.

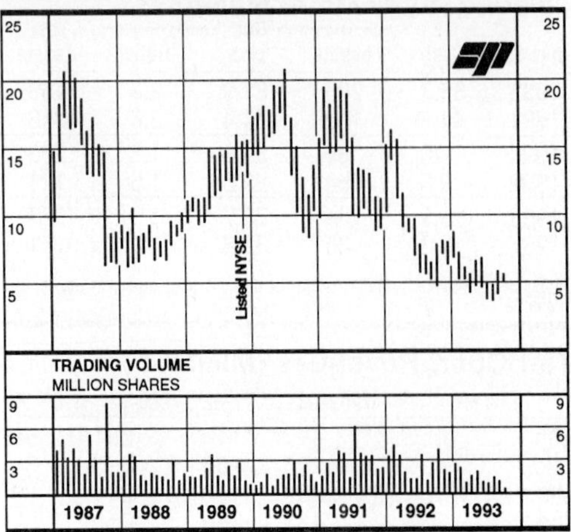

Revenues (Million $)

Quarter:	1993	1992	1991	1990
Mar.	59.1	54.5	55.6	48.6
Jun.	45.1	57.5	50.5	51.9
Sep.	---	57.9	40.2	53.3
Dec.	---	62.0	51.7	55.5
	---	231.8	198.1	209.3

Revenues in the six months ended March 31, 1993, fell 7.0%, year to year; product revenues declined 20%, while service revenues climbed 38%. Gross margins narrowed, and operating costs rose 5.7%. Following a $31.5 million restructuring charge, a pretax loss replaced pretax income. After a tax benefit of $1.6 million, versus taxes at 36.6%, a net loss of $41.8 million ($1.67 a share, on 4.0% more shares), contrasted with income of $1.2 million ($0.05).

Common Share Earnings ($)

Quarter:	1993	1992	1991	1990
Mar.	Nil	0.02	0.17	0.20
Jun.	d1.67	0.03	d0.06	0.22
Sep.	---	0.03	d0.38	0.23
Dec.	---	0.03	d0.04	0.23
	Ed1.90	0.11	d0.31	0.88

Important Developments

Sep. '93— CNX announced a broad range of data management solutions, the Dataseries, consisting of hardware, robotic tape systems, software and support systems based on Hewlett-Packard's Apollo 9000 Series 700 workstations at the low end and CNX's C Series systems for high-throughput, high-capacity applications.

Next earnings report expected in late October.

Per Share Data ($)

Yr. End Dec. 31	1992	1991	1990	1989	1988	1987	1986	1985
Tangible Bk. Val.	**7.03**	6.48	6.67	4.36	3.63	3.26	2.73	NA
Cash Flow	**0.67**	0.31	1.54	1.22	0.65	0.51	0.36	d0.30
Earnings[1]	**0.11**	d0.31	0.88	0.60	0.32	0.31	0.15	d0.44
Dividends	**Nil**	Nil	Nil	Nil	Nil	Nil	Nil	Nil
Payout Ratio	**Nil**	Nil	Nil	Nil	Nil	Nil	Nil	Nil
Prices—High	**16⅝**	19¾	20⅞	16	10⅝	22	10½	NA
Low	**4¾**	8⅞	8⅜	9⅜	6¼	6⅜	7½	NA
P/E Ratio—	**NM**	NM	24–10	27–16	33–20	71–21	70–50	NM

Data as orig. reptd. **1.** Bef. spec. items of +0.02 in 1989, +0.02 in 1988, +0.18 in 1987, +0.12 in 1986. d-Deficit. E-Estimated. NM-Not Meaningful. NA-Not Available.

Income Data (Million $)

Year Ended Dec. 31	Revs.	Oper. Inc.	% Oper. Inc. of Revs.	Cap. Exp.	Depr.	Int. Exp.	Net Bef. Taxes	Eff. Tax Rate	[2]Net Inc.	% Net Inc. of Revs.	Cash Flow
1992	**232**	**20.0**	**8.6**	**[1]17.7**	**13.8**	**7.93**	**4.1**	**32.0%**	**2.8**	**1.2**	**16.6**
1991	198	4.7	2.4	[1]16.2	13.7	6.83	d9.1	NM	d6.9	NM	6.8
1990	209	38.8	18.6	[1]25.1	13.8	5.59	27.3	32.5%	18.4	8.8	32.2
1989	159	29.1	18.3	[1]15.3	11.7	4.55	16.9	32.1%	11.5	7.2	23.2
1988	106	15.2	14.4	[1]16.1	5.9	4.67	9.0	35.9%	5.7	5.4	11.7
1987	70	10.4	15.0	[1]8.3	3.7	3.35	8.9	38.2%	5.5	7.9	9.2
1986	40	7.0	17.3	[1]6.6	3.1	0.30	4.3	47.6%	2.3	5.6	5.4
1985	14	d4.6	NM	4.0	1.7	0.23	d5.6	Nil	d5.6	NM	d3.8

Balance Sheet Data (Million $)

Dec. 31	Cash	Curr. Assets	Curr. Liab.	Curr. Ratio	Total Assets	% Ret. on Assets	Long Term Debt	Common Equity	Total Cap.	% LT Debt of Cap.	% Ret. on Equity
1992	**78**	**219**	**67.4**	**3.2**	**312**	**0.9**	**71.1**	**174**	**245**	**29.0**	**1.7**
1991	74	207	63.0	3.3	273	NM	63.8	146	210	30.4	NM
1990	108	211	59.8	3.5	267	7.8	64.0	143	207	31.0	15.6
1989	48	137	31.5	4.3	173	6.7	61.3	80	141	43.5	15.7
1988	63	132	24.8	5.3	161	3.7	71.3	64	135	52.8	9.5
1987	78	130	23.0	5.7	149	5.2	68.5	56	124	55.2	10.8
1986	28	52	10.7	4.9	63	2.5	3.9	46	50	7.7	NA
1985	11	21	4.2	5.0	25	NM	3.0	NA	NA	NA	NM

Data as orig. reptd. **1.** Net. **2.** Bef. spec. item(s) in 1989, 1988, 1987, 1986. d-Deficit. NM-Not Meaningful. NA-Not Available.

Business Summary

Convex Computer designs, manufactures, sells and services a family of affordable supercomputers for engineering, scientific and technical users. As of April 1993, the company had delivered nearly 1,200 systems to more than 600 customers. Domestic revenues accounted for about 53% of the total in 1992.

The Convex C3 Series supercomputers comprise three families of products: the high-end C3800 family, including the entry-level C3800/ES, which provides a growth path to high-end supercomputing; the departmental C3400 family; and the low-cost C3200 family. The C3 Series supercomputers, which are upward and downward binary compatible, range in price from $300,000 to over $8 million. The Convex Meta Series, introduced in 1992, combines the high-end server capabilities of a C Series supercomputer with the high-performance technology of Hewlett-Packard's PA-RISC cluster to provide the appropriate computing resource for solving a wide range of problems.

The company's systems provide a smooth growth path from a single-processor scalar/vector machine to a high-end, eight-processor, tightly-coupled, parallel supercomputer. These systems integrate the three forms of processing common in scientific and engineering applications: scalar, in which operations are performed on one element at a time; vector, in which simultaneous operations occur on arrays of data; and parallel, in which two or more processors simultaneously operate on different parts of a program. Other features include automatic self-allocating processors, to ensure maximum throughput, and a memory subsystem for improved performance in large-scale simulations.

The foundation of the CNX software environment is the ConvexOS operating system, an enhanced version of UNIX 4.2 and 4.3bsd. The company also provides compilers and networking products.

Dividend Data

No cash dividends have been paid.

Finances

In March 1992, the company and Hewlett-Packard Co. (HWP) entered into extensive business and technology agreements, and HWP purchased 1.2 million CNX common shares (5%).

Capitalization

Long Term Debt: $68,368,000 (6/93), incl. $53.5 million of 6% sub. debs. conv. into com. at $21.75 a sh.

Common Stock: 25,112,798 shs. ($0.01 par).
Officers and directors own 10%.
Institutions hold 45%.
Shareholders of record: 1,992 (12/92).

Options: To buy 3,749,898 shs. at $6.125 to $14.375 ea. (12/92).

Office—3000 Waterview Parkway, Richardson, TX 75080. **Tel**—(214) 497-4000. **Chrmn & CEO**—R. J. Paluck. **Pres**—T. L. Rock. **VP & Secy**—P. N. Cardman. **Dirs**—E. Bloch, H. B. Cash, R. P. McKenna, R. J. Paluck, S. K. Smith, S. J. Wallach, H. D. Wolfe. **Transfer Agent & Registrar & Registrar**—Bank of Boston. **Incorporated** in Delaware in 1982. **Empl**—1,164.

 Neeraj K. Vohra

Cordis Corp.

NASDAQ Symbol CORD (Incl. in Nat'l Market) Options on Phila In S&P MidCap 400

Price	Range	P-E Ratio	Dividend	Yield	S&P Ranking	Beta
Oct. 13'93	1993					
37¼	40¼–21¼	19	None	None	B–	1.09

Summary

This Miami-based company primarily manufactures and markets various medical devices and systems for the angiographic and neuroscience markets. Its line of catheters has expanded significantly with recent FDA approval of several new products, most recently a line of angioplasty catheters approved in August. Sales and earnings continued their impressive climb in fiscal 1993, aided by improved foreign sales and expanded operating margins.

Business Summary

Cordis Corporation designs, manufactures and sells medical products and devices, primarily angiographic catheters, neuroscience devices and other related medical instrumentation. Sales from continuing operations in recent fiscal years were derived as follows:

	1993	1992	1991	1990
Angiographic products	93%	92%	91%	90%
Neuroscience products	7%	8%	9%	10%

Cordis manufactures a wide range of angiographic devices for the diagnosis of various cardiovascular diseases and for use in interventional angiography. The diagnostic devices include catheters and related equipment that are inserted into a patient's circulatory system to allow introduction of contrast media that enable a physician to study the heart, blood vessels and other soft-tissue organs for the purpose of determining the proper treatment of patients exhibiting disorders of such tissues. The interventional devices include balloon dilatation catheters, guiding catheters, steerable guidewires and accessory products.

The company's neuroscience products include implantable cerebrospinal fluid (CSF) shunt systems for the treatment of hydrocephalus (an excess accumulation of CSF in the ventricles of the brain), and disposable intracranial pressure monitoring and drainage systems.

Products are sold worldwide to hospitals and other medical institutions and physicians. In fiscal 1993, foreign operations contributed 51% of net sales (49% in fiscal 1992) and 48% (45%) of operating profits.

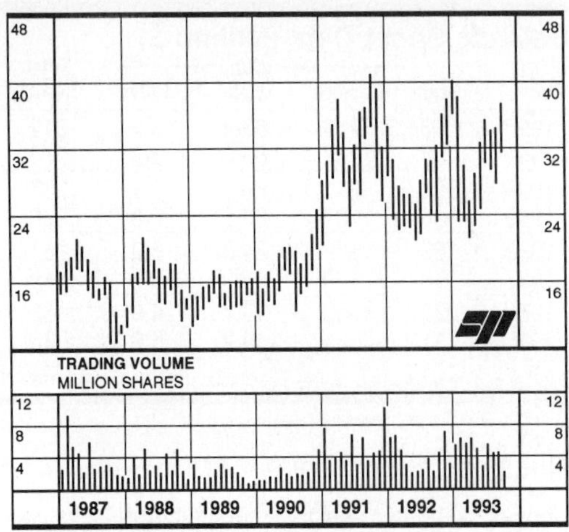

During fiscal 1993 and fiscal 1992, the company spent about $19.1 million (7.5% of revenues) and $19.3 million (8.7%), respectively, on research and development.

Important Developments

Aug. '93— Cordis announced the receipt of FDA approval to market its Predator PTCA Dilatation Catheters with 3 cm and 4 cm balloons (long balloons). The approval brings to 10 the number of angioplasty catheters to receive FDA approval for marketing. In July, the FDA approved the U.S. market release of Sleek PTCA Dilatation Catheters with 3 cm and 4 cm balloons, as well as standard Sleek catheters, which feature 2 cm balloons. Both devices are compatible with up to a 0.014 inch guidewire and thus compete in the largest segment of the U.S. angioplasty market.

Next earnings report due in mid-November.

Per Share Data ($)

Yr. End Jun. 30	1993	1992	1991	1990	1989	1988	1987	1986	1985	1984
Tangible Bk. Val.	**9.85**	8.29	5.74	5.15	3.88	4.40	4.25	8.11	8.06	7.57
Cash Flow	**2.65**	2.28	1.96	1.31	0.99	0.84	0.31	0.51	1.27	2.01
Earnings[1]	**2.00**	1.67	1.38	0.75	0.49	0.37	d0.13	d0.22	0.60	1.44
Dividends	**Nil**	Nil	Nil	Nil	Nil	Nil	Nil	Nil	Nil	Nil
Payout Ratio	**Nil**	Nil	Nil	Nil	Nil	Nil	Nil	Nil	Nil	Nil
Prices[2]—High	**40¼**	38	41	24¾	17½	21½	21¼	19¼	12¼	24¼
Low	**21¼**	21	20½	12	10¾	10⅝	8⅝	9⅜	7¾	6¾
P/E Ratio—	**20–11**	23–13	30–15	33–16	36–22	58–29	NM	NM	20–13	17–5

Data as orig. reptd. **1.** Bef. results of disc. ops of -0.70 in 1991, -0.87 in 1989, -0.25 in 1988, -4.09 in 1987, -0.19 in 1986, and spec. item of +0.06 in 1988. **2.** Cal. yr. d-Deficit. NM-Not Meaningful.

Income Data (Million $)

Year Ended Jun. 30	Revs.	Oper. Inc.	% Oper. Inc. of Revs.	Cap. Exp.	Depr.	Int. Exp.	[2]Net Bef. Taxes	Eff. Tax Rate	[3]Net Inc.	% Net Inc. of Revs.	Cash Flow
1993	**255**	**53.7**	**21.0**	**14.1**	**9.52**	**1.64**	**38.7**	**24.9%**	**29.1**	**11.4**	**38.6**
1992	223	41.5	18.6	10.8	8.67	3.20	32.3	25.6%	24.0	10.8	32.7
[1]1991	199	36.4	18.3	9.1	8.09	2.90	26.0	25.6%	19.3	9.7	27.4
1990	164	27.5	16.8	6.1	7.50	5.00	14.3	29.1%	10.2	6.2	17.7
[1]1989	141	20.7	14.6	10.7	6.75	6.50	6.9	5.7%	6.5	4.6	13.3
[1]1988	132	27.2	20.6	10.2	6.23	6.30	12.7	60.3%	5.0	3.8	11.3
[1]1987	107	15.5	14.5	19.8	5.88	6.30	1.8	NM	[4]d1.7	NM	4.2
[1]1986	188	5.9	3.2	17.2	9.71	7.40	d7.8	NM	d2.9	NM	6.8
1985	202	27.0	13.4	11.6	8.82	6.40	11.7	29.4%	7.9	3.9	16.7
1984	204	45.2	22.2	16.1	7.53	7.20	32.6	41.7%	19.0	9.3	26.5

Balance Sheet Data (Million $)

Jun. 30	Cash	Curr. Assets	Curr. Liab.	Curr. Ratio	Total Assets	% Ret. on Assets	Long Term Debt	Common Equity	Total Cap.	% LT Debt of Cap.	% Ret. on Equity
1993	**38.4**	**143**	**55.6**	**2.6**	**204**	**15.5**	**1.1**	**141**	**142**	**0.8**	**22.4**
1992	13.1	107	42.2	2.5	168	15.4	2.2	116	119	1.8	24.4
1991	11.6	84	32.4	2.6	142	13.3	15.6	80	97	16.2	25.6
1990	9.2	84	39.3	2.1	146	7.3	31.6	70	103	30.7	16.6
1989	1.0	71	37.2	1.9	130	4.9	36.9	52	91	40.8	11.8
1988	8.4	76	39.0	2.0	135	3.6	31.3	59	92	34.0	8.7
1987	7.0	85	45.0	1.9	143	NM	34.4	57	93	36.9	NM
1986	17.4	131	42.9	3.1	220	NM	58.4	107	168	34.8	NM
1985	32.7	134	34.1	3.9	213	3.9	62.0	107	171	36.1	7.7
1984	15.2	115	38.8	3.0	195	10.2	50.7	100	152	33.4	21.1

Data as orig. reptd. **1.** Excl. disc. ops. **2.** Incl. equity in earns. of nonconsol. subs. **3.** Bef. spec. items. **4.** Refl. acctg. change. d-Deficit. NM-Not Meaningful.

Net Sales (Million $)

Quarter:	1992–93	1991–92	1990–91	1989–90
Sep.	62.5	50.1	45.7	35.7
Dec.	62.0	55.3	49.2	37.9
Mar.	64.2	59.1	52.8	43.9
Jun.	66.8	58.5	51.3	46.1
	255.5	223.0	198.9	163.7

Net sales in the fiscal year ended June 30, 1993, rose 15%, boosted by the successful introduction of angioplasty products in foreign markets (U.S. marketing approval was received subsequent to year-end), which offset somewhat sluggish demand in domestic markets. Gross profit margins improved to 41% of sales, from 40%, and after lower R&D expenditures, increased SG&A expenses, and reduced interest charges, net income was ahead 21%, to $29,060,000 ($2.00 a s hare) from $24,014,000 ($1.67).

Common Share Earnings ($)

Quarter:	1992–93	1991–92	1990–91	1989–90
Sep.	0.42	0.33	0.25	0.16
Dec.	0.47	0.38	0.33	0.12
Mar.	0.53	0.46	0.38	0.18
Jun.	0.58	0.50	0.42	0.29
	2.00	1.67	1.38	0.75

Dividend Data

No cash has been paid.

Finances

Cash generated from operations amounted to $30.2 million in fiscal 1993. In addition, cash proceeds from net additions to debt and the exercise of stock options were $6.7 million and $6.4 million, respectively. Cash was used for additions to property, plant and equipment of $14.1 million and for the repurchase of common stock of $4.9 million (authorization to repurchase up to 500,000 shares was granted in April 1993).

At fiscal 1993 year-end, the company had unused and available credit lines aggregating $13.2 million in Europe and $25.0 million in the U.S.

In 1987, Cordis initiated a plan to dispose of all businesses outside of its angiographic and neuroscience product lines, including the disposal of the worldwide cardiac pacing operations, whose major asset was its Administrative and Technical Center (ATC) in Florida. In September 1991, Cordis agreed to sublease ATC to a third party, resulting in a $9.8 million charge for discontinued operations fiscal 1991's fourth quarter.

Capitalization

Long Term Debt: $1,112,000 (6/93).

Common Stock: 14,257,313 shs. ($1 par).
Institutions hold 73%.
Shareholders: 1,327 of record (8/93).

Options: To purchase 975,225 shs. at $14.50 to $36.75 ea. (6/93).

Office—14201 N. W. 60th Ave., Miami Lakes, FL 33014. **Tel**—(305) 824-2000. **Chrmn**—R. Q. Marston. **Pres & CEO**—R. C. Strauss. **VP-CFO & Treas**—A. J. Novak. **VP-Secy**—D. G. Hall. **VP-Asst Secy & Investor Contact**—Chick McDowell. **Dirs**—D. R. Challoner, R. W. Foxen, D. F. Malin, Jr., R. Q. Marston, P. G. Rogers, J. L. de Ruyter van Steveninck, R. C. Strauss, P. K. Woolf. **Transfer Agent & Registrar**—Chemical Bank, NYC. **Incorporated** in Florida in 1959. **Empl**—2,650.

 Robert M. Gold

Costco Wholesale

NASDAQ Symbol COST (Incl. in Nat'l Market) Options on ASE In S&P MidCap 400

Price	Range	P–E Ratio	Dividend	Yield	S&P Ranking	Beta
Sep. 3'93	1993					
17¾	25¼–15¾	19	None	None	NR	1.50

Summary

In June 1993, this fast-growing chain of wholesale cash-and-carry membership warehouses agreed to merge with The Price Company to form a 195 warehouse club entity with annual sales of $16 billion. Under terms of the plan, existing Costco shareholders will receive one share of the new entity for each share held. Earnings rose only slightly in fiscal 1993's first nine months, restricted by increased operating costs and substantially higher interest expense.

Business Summary

Costco Wholesale Corporation was operating 100 wholesale cash-and-carry membership warehouses as of December 31, 1992, in California (37), Washington (13), Florida (11), Oregon (7), Massachusetts (4), Nevada (3), Montana (2), New Hampshire (2), Alaska (2), Hawaii (2), Alberta (5), British Columbia (4), Manitoba (2) and one each in Connecticut, Utah, Idaho, New York, New Jersey and Saskatchewan. The company's strategy has been to offer a wide range of high-quality, nationally branded merchandise at prices consistently lower than those of traditional wholesalers.

Sales in fiscal 1992 were derived as follows:

	1992
Food	33%
Sundries, incl. alcoholic beverages, tobacco & snack foods	31%
Hardlines, incl. major appliances, electronics & auto supplies	22%
Softlines, incl. apparel, cameras, jewelry, housewares & books	12%
Other	2%

Marketing efforts are directed primarily at business customers ("wholesale members") and individuals belonging to selected employee groups. At August 30, 1992, Costco had some 1,404,000 wholesale members (excluding supplemental cardholders) and 2,370,000 group and gold card members, who have generally paid an annual membership fee of $25-$30 and $30-35, respectively.

Various strategies are used by Costco to operate effectively at low gross margins, including rapid inventory turnover, reduced working capital requirements (as of August 30, 1992, about 77% of inventories were financed with trade accounts payable), direct purchasing and low-cost warehouse operations (warehouses have a standardized floor plan occupying about 110,000 to 125,000 sq. ft. and are located in areas with relatively low property costs).

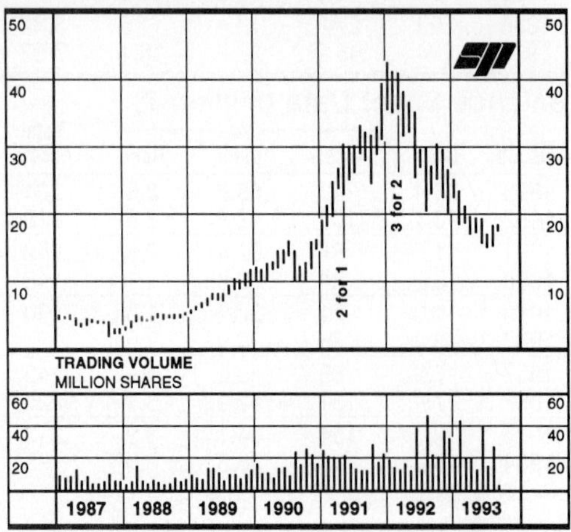

Costco opened its first warehouse on September 15, 1983, and had 89 units (77 owned and 22 leased) in operation at fiscal 1992 year-end. COST's strategy is to establish a strong market position by clustering warehouses in geographic areas.

Important Developments

Aug. '93— The company ended fiscal year 1993 with a total of 109 warehouses. Costco planned to record a reserve for the closing of a warehouse in Worcester, Massachusetts in the fourth quarter of fiscal 1993. In June, the company agreed to merge with The Price Company (PCLB, 35, NYSE) to form a new holding company called Price/Costco. Under terms of the merger, which is scheduled to be completed by 1993 year end, Costco shareholders will receive one share of the new company for each COST share held while Price Company holders will be issued 2.13 shares of the new company for each PCLB share held.

Next earnings report expected in late October.

Per Share Data ($)

Yr. End Aug. 31	1992	1991	1990	1989	1988	1987	1986	1985	1984	1983
Tangible Bk. Val.	**6.91**	5.93	3.77	2.61	1.44	1.22	1.14	NM	NM	NM
Cash Flow	**1.21**	0.95	0.64	0.48	0.26	0.13	0.09	d0.12	NA	NA
Earnings[1]	**0.93**	[2]0.74	0.47	[2]0.33	0.15	0.05	0.05	d0.17	d0.09	[3]d0.01
Dividends	**Nil**	Nil	Nil	Nil	Nil	Nil	Nil	Nil	Nil	Nil
Payout Ratio	**Nil**	Nil	Nil	Nil	Nil	Nil	Nil	Nil	Nil	Nil
Prices[4]—High	**42⅝**	39½	16⅜	11⅞	5⅜	5⅛	6½	4⅜	NA	NA
Low	**20¼**	15⅛	10	5¼	2¾	1⅞	2⅞	3⅜	NA	NA
P/E Ratio—	**46–22**	53–20	35–21	37–16	35–18	NM	NM	NM	NM	NM

Data as orig. reptd. Adj. for stk. divs. of 50% Mar. 1992, 100% May 1991. **1.** Bef. spec. items of +0.04 in 1988, +0.02 in 1987, +0.01 in 1986. **2.** Ful. dil.: 0.73 in 1991, 0.32 in 1989. **3.** From inception 2-28-83. **4.** Cal. yr. d-Deficit. NM-Not Meaningful. NA-Not Available.

Income Data (Million $)

Year Ended Aug. 31	[1]Revs.	Oper. Inc.	% Oper. Inc. of Revs.	Cap. Exp.	Depr.	Int. Exp.	Net Bef. Taxes	Eff. Tax Rate	[4]Net Inc.	% Net Inc. of Revs.	Cash Flow
1992	**6,621**	**219**	**3.3**	**274**	**34.0**	**9.7**	**186**	**39.0%**	**113**	**1.7**	**147**
1991	5,305	163	3.1	154	25.0	6.6	141	40.0%	85	1.6	110
1990	4,133	111	2.7	103	18.5	10.8	81	39.5%	49	1.2	68
1989	3,000	68	2.3	126	12.6	16.9	43	37.5%	27	0.9	40
1988	2,030	39	1.9	54	8.1	12.6	17	32.8%	12	0.6	20
1987	1,401	17	1.2	107	6.0	[3]9.3	5	31.9%	4	0.3	10
1986	762	8	1.1	55	2.5	[3]4.5	4	22.8%	4	0.5	6
1985	371	d1	NM	20	2.1	[3]2.1	d6	Nil	d6	NM	d4
1984	102	d3	NM	9	0.5	0.1	d3	Nil	d3	NM	NA
[2]1983	Nil	d1	NM	1	NM	Nil	NM	Nil	NM	NM	NA

Balance Sheet Data (Million $)

Aug. 31	Cash	Curr. Assets	Curr. Liab.	Curr. Ratio	Total Assets	% Ret. on Assets	Long Term Debt	Common Equity	Total Cap.	% LT Debt of Cap.	% Ret. on Equity
1992	**277**	**831**	**519**	**1.6**	**1,649**	**8.1**	**301**	**812**	**1,127**	**26.7**	**15.0**
1991	145	573	438	1.3	1,141	8.3	4	687	700	0.6	15.1
1990	14	371	344	1.1	820	6.5	76	392	474	16.0	14.8
1989	1	266	243	1.1	624	4.5	133	243	378	35.3	14.3
1988	1	203	216	0.9	452	2.8	128	106	234	54.6	11.8
1987	1	168	146	1.2	373	1.1	136	89	224	60.5	4.2
1986	85	171	71	2.4	277	1.4	122	83	204	59.6	11.3
1985	10	67	47	1.4	96	NM	24	[5]25	49	49.4	NM
1984	3	31	20	1.5	43	NM	Nil	[5]20	21	1.6	NM
1983	6	7	1	5.4	8	NM	Nil	NA	NA	NA	NM

Data as orig. reptd. **1.** Incl. membership fees & other revs. **2.** From inception 2-28-83. **3.** Net of int. inc. **4.** Bef. spec. items. **5.** Refl. conv. of pfd. stk. d-Deficit. NM-Not Meaningful. NA-Not Available.

Net Sales (Million $)

Weeks:	1992–93	1991–92	1990–91	1989–90
12 Wks. Nov. ...	1,670	1,402	1,101	818
12 Wks. Feb.	1,798	1,543	1,226	961
12 Wks. May.....	1,674	1,474	1,172	932
16 Wks. Aug.		2,082	1,717	1,350
		6,500	5,215	4,060

Revenues in the 36 weeks ended May 9, 1993, advanced 16%, year to year, reflecting a 3.0% increase in comparable-unit sales, and contributions from 16 new warehouses. Gross margins widened, but higher SG&A and pre-opening costs as a percentage of sales held the gain in operating income to 6.0%. Following a $10.7 million increase in interest expense, net income rose only 0.5%, to $74,495,000 ($0.61 a share), from $74,123,000 ($0.61, as adjusted).

Sales in the fourth quarter ended August 29, 1993 rose 14% rose, year to year; on a same-store basis, sales increased 2%.

Common Share Earnings ($)

Weeks:	1992–93	1991–92	1990–91	1989–90
12 Wks. Nov.	0.19	0.17	0.13	0.07
12 Wks. Feb.	0.28	0.27	0.20	0.15
12 Wks. May.....	0.15	0.17	0.14	0.05
16 Wks. Aug.		0.32	0.27	0.20
		0.93	0.74	0.47

Dividend Data

No cash dividends have been paid. A three-for-two stock split was effected in March 1992 and a two-for-one split in May 1991.

Finances

In May 1992, the company sold publicly $300 million of 5¾% subordinated debentures, due 2002 convertible into common stock at $41.25 per share.

In March 1991, COST sold publicly 10,350,000 (adjusted) common shares at $19.67 each. In December 1989, COST completed a public offering of 9,766,500 (adjusted) common shares (9,594,000 new financing). In December 1985, the company sold publicly 11,490,000 (adjusted) common shares. An additional 8,000,001 (adjusted) shares were issued upon conversion of a $20,000,000 subordinated note in March 1986. Virtually all of COST's 7½% subordinated debentures (issued in May 1986) were converted into common stock at $6 per share (adjusted) during 1989, resulting in 18,067,179 common shares being issued.

Capitalization

Long Term Debt: $300,092,000 (5/9/93).

Common Stock: 118,924,252 shs. ($0.0033 par). Carrefour S.A. owns about 18%. Institutions hold some 46%. Shareholders: 8,669 of record (11/92).

Office—10809 120th Ave. N.E., Kirkland, WA 98033. **Tel**—(206) 828-8100. **Chrmn**—J. H. Brotman. **Pres & CEO**—J. D. Sinegal. **SVP, CFO, Treas & Investor Contact**—Richard A. Galanti. **Secy**—J. R. Osterhaus. **Dirs**—J. H. Brotman, D. L. Defforey, R. D. DiCerchio, H. E. James, J. W. Meisenbach, F. O. Paulsell Jr., D. Pulver, R. R. Shaw, J. D. Sinegal. **Transfer Agent**—First Interstate Bank of Washington, Seattle. **Incorporated** in Washington in 1983; reincorporated in Delaware in 1986. **Empl**—18,100.

 John D. Coyle, CFA

Cracker Barrel Old Country

NASDAQ Symbol CBRL (Incl. in Nat'l Market) Options on Pacific In S&P MidCap 400

Price	Range	P-E Ratio	Dividend	Yield	S&P Ranking	Beta
Sep. 17'93	1993					
25¾	34¼–22½	33	0.02	0.1%	A	1.70

Summary

This company operates more than 150 full-service "country store" restaurants, primarily in the southeastern U.S. Cracker Barrel has achieved strong earnings growth in recent periods, aided by increased same-store sales and an ongoing expansion program. Another sizable earnings advance is expected in fiscal 1994. A three-for-two stock split was effected in March 1993, and a public offering of 2.59 million (adjusted) shares was completed in January 1993.

Current Outlook

Earnings for the fiscal year ending July 29, 1994, are estimated at $0.97 a share, up from fiscal 1993's $0.78.

A dividend of $0.005 quarterly is the minimum expected.

Sales increases in fiscal 1994 are expected to be largely fueled by more stores being open. The number of units open should increase by about 20%, following a 20% rise in fiscal 1993. Also, comparable sales of existing units are projected to increase further, but at lower rates of growth than in fiscal 1993. Economies of scale are expected to contribute to modest margin improvement.

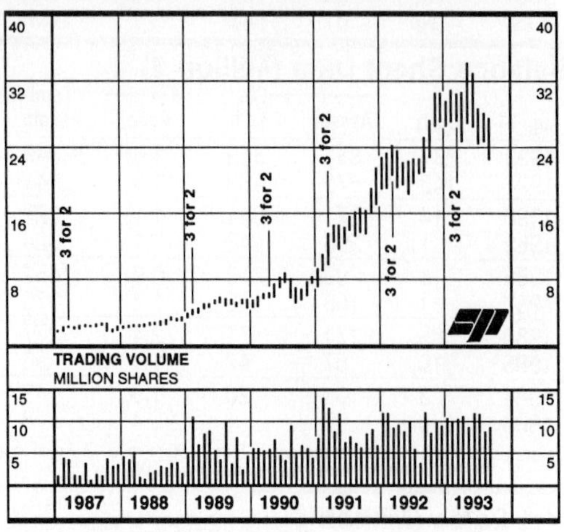

Net Sales (Million $)

13 Weeks:	1992-93	1991-92	1990-91	1989-90
Oct.	123	92	69	51
Jan.	120	89	66	48
Apr.	125	100	74	54
Jul.	150	120	92	[1]72
	518	401	300	226

Net sales (preliminary) for the fiscal year ended July 30, 1993, increased 29% from those of the prior year. Pretax income rose 35%, and after taxes at 37.4% in both periods, net income was up 34%, to $45.7 million, from $33.9 million. Per share earnings, on 4.6% more shares, rose 30%, to $0.78, from $0.60, as adjusted.

Common Share Earnings ($)

13 Weeks:	1992-93	1991-92	1990-91	1989-90
Oct.	0.18	0.13	0.11	0.08
Jan.	0.13	0.09	0.06	0.03
Apr.	0.17	0.14	0.10	0.06
Jul.	0.29	0.24	0.17	[1]0.14
	0.78	0.61	0.45	0.31

Important Developments

Sep. '93— In fiscal 1993's fourth quarter, CBRL's same-store restaurant sales were up 6.3% (3.0% after adjusting for price increases), following a 5.0% third quarter rise. Also, in the fourth quarter, same-store gift shop sales increased 4.9%. CBRL's fourth quarter operating margin (including general and administrative expense) widened to 18.7%, from a year-earlier 18.3. Five new CBRL restaurants opened during the quarter, bringing the year-end total to 152 units operating, which reflects 25 openings during the year. In fiscal 1994, about 30 units are expected to debut, which would again increase the number of units by close to 20%. Earlier, In January 1993, CBRL completed a public offering of 2.59 million common shares at $28 each (both adjusted).

Next earnings report expected in mid-November.

Per Share Data ($)

Yr. End Jul. 31	1993	1992	1991	1990	1989	1988	1987	1986	1985	1984
Tangible Bk. Val.	**NA**	4.05	3.35	2.10	1.79	1.25	1.09	0.99	0.91	0.71
Cash Flow	**NA**	0.83	0.63	0.45	0.38	0.29	0.21	0.17	0.13	0.14
Earnings	**0.78**	0.61	0.45	0.31	0.25	0.18	0.11	0.09	0.06	0.09
Dividends	**0.018**	0.016	0.015	0.014	0.014	0.013	0.013	0.013	0.013	0.013
Payout Ratio	**2%**	3%	3%	4%	6%	7%	11%	14%	21%	14%
Prices[2]—High	**34¼**	30⅝	21⅝	8⅞	5⅞	3⅝	2¾	2	1⅜	2⅛
Low	**22½**	18⅜	7⅛	4⅝	3⅜	2⅛	1⅝	1⅛	⅝	1
P/E Ratio—	**44-29**	51–30	49–16	28–15	24–13	20–12	24–14	22–13	23–14	24–12

Data as orig. reptd. Adj. for stk. divs. of 50% Mar. 1993, 50% Mar. 1992, 50% Mar. 1991, 50% Apr. 1990, 50% Feb. 1989, 50% Mar. 1987, 50% Jul. 1983. 1. 14 wks. 2. Cal. yr. NA-Not Available.

Income Data (Million $)

Year Ended Jul. 31	Revs.	Oper. Inc.	% Oper. Inc. of Revs.	Cap. Exp.	Depr.	Int. Exp.	Net Bef. Taxes	Eff. Tax Rate	Net Inc.	% Net Inc. of Revs.	Cash Flow
1992	**401**	**67.7**	**16.9**	**71.5**	**12.5**	**13.37**	**54.2**	**37.4%**	**33.9**	**8.5**	**46.4**
1991	300	47.0	15.7	64.0	9.3	12.84	36.6	37.4%	22.9	7.6	32.2
1990	226	31.1	13.8	38.4	6.7	11.34	24.1	36.6%	15.3	6.8	21.9
1989	170	24.0	14.1	25.9	5.7	12.24	16.9	35.5%	10.9	6.4	16.6
1988	126	17.3	13.7	24.8	4.5	11.35	11.5	37.0%	7.2	5.8	11.8
1987	99	13.5	13.6	17.9	3.6	1.10	9.2	49.1%	4.7	4.7	8.3
1986	81	9.9	12.3	9.3	3.2	1.30	6.3	42.5%	3.6	4.5	6.8
1985	68	6.4	9.5	11.4	2.5	1.28	3.9	37.1%	2.4	3.6	4.9
1984	57	6.4	11.3	11.1	1.9	1.14	4.4	37.6%	2.7	4.8	4.6
1983	46	4.9	10.7	6.1	1.4	0.95	3.3	37.4%	2.0	4.5	3.5

Balance Sheet Data (Million $)

Jul. 31	Cash	Curr. Assets	Curr. Liab.	Curr. Ratio	Total Assets	% Ret. on Assets	Long Term Debt	Common Equity	Total Cap.	% LT Debt of Cap.	% Ret. on Equity
1992	**50.6**	**76.1**	**43.5**	**1.7**	**313**	**11.7**	**43.3**	**222**	**270**	**16.1**	**16.7**
1991	67.4	85.3	35.0	2.4	265	10.7	44.5	180	230	19.4	15.6
1990	5.4	18.9	24.7	0.8	145	11.3	16.0	100	120	13.2	16.5
1989	19.9	30.4	18.6	1.6	125	9.8	17.3	85	107	15.2	15.2
1988	1.6	9.8	15.4	0.6	84	9.5	14.1	51	69	20.4	15.1
1987	5.1	12.3	11.1	1.1	68	7.4	8.6	44	56	15.3	11.1
1986	11.2	15.7	8.1	1.9	60	6.4	9.1	40	51	17.7	9.4
1985	9.6	14.2	4.7	3.0	53	4.8	9.9	37	48	20.6	7.3
1984	5.0	8.4	4.5	1.9	38	7.8	10.4	23	34	30.7	12.6
1983	10.8	14.1	3.4	4.1	32	6.9	7.4	21	28	26.2	12.4

Data as orig. reptd. **1.** Net of int. inc.

Business Summary

Cracker Barrel Old Country Store, Inc. owns and operates a chain of full-service "country store" restaurants with gift shops, located largely in the southeastern and midwestern sections of the U.S., near interstate highways. As of July 1993, the company was operating 157 restaurants.

The restaurant portion of the units generates close to 80% of total CBRL sales. CBRL typically serves breakfast, lunch and dinner, between 6:00 a.m. and 10:00 p.m. The restaurants feature home-style country cooking prepared on the premises from the company's own recipes. The moderately priced menu items include country ham, chicken, fish, barbecue pork ribs, roast beef, beans, turnip greens, vegetable plates and sandwiches. The restaurants do not serve alcoholic beverages.

CBRL's gift shops (about 20% of total sales) offer a wide variety of items, consisting primarily of reproductions of early American and rural-style glassware, wrought-iron products, toys, soaps, woodcrafts and candles, as well as various candies, preserves, cheeses and other foodstuffs.

Cracker Barrel units are typically freestanding. Store interiors are subdivided into a two-section dining area consisting of about 25% of the total interior space and a gift shop area consisting of about 22% of the space. The balance of the space consists of kitchen and storage areas. The recent average cost for a new store has been about $2.4 million, including land, building and equipment.

Comparable same-store restaurant sales increased 7.1% in fiscal 1993, including a real sales increase of 3.9%. Same-store gift shop sales increased 12.1%.

Dividend Data

Cash has been paid each year since 1972.

Amt of Divd. $	Date Decl.	Ex-divd. Date	Stock of Record	Payment Date
0.00⅝	Nov. 24	Dec. 8	Dec. 14	Jan. 4'93
3-for-2	Jan. 29	Mar. 22	Mar. 5	Mar. 19'93
0.00½	Feb. 26	Mar. 8	Mar. 12	Mar. 26'93
0.00½	May 28	Jun. 7	Jun. 11	Jun. 25'93
0.00½	Aug. 27	Sep. 7	Sep. 13	Sep. 24'93

Finances

At April 30, 1993, CBRL had cash and temporary investments totaling $120 million. Earlier, in January 1993, a public offering of 2.59 million CBRL shares was completed, at $28 a share. From this, CBRL received proceeds of about $69.5 million.

Capitalization

Long Term Debt: $38,396,967 (4/93), incl. $1,815,444 of lease obligs.

Common Stock: 59,319,201 shs. ($0.33 par).
Officers & directors own about 11%.
Institutions hold about 52%.
Shareholders: 8,175 of record (9/92).

Office—Hartmann Dr., P.O. Box 787, Lebanon, TN 37088-0787. **Tel**—(615) 444-5533. **Chrmn, Pres & CEO**—D. W. Evins. **Sr VP & COO**—D. M. Turner. **Sr VP-Fin, CFO & Investor Contact**—Jimmie D. White. **VP-Treas**—B. Van Winkle. **Secy**—Evalena C. Bennett. **Dirs**—J. C. Bradshaw, R. V. Dale, D. W. Evins, E. W. Evins, W. D. Heydel, R. C. Hilton, C. E. Jones Jr., C. T. Lowe Jr., B. F. Lowery, G. L. Miller, J. H. Stewart. **Transfer Agent**—Trust Company Bank, Atlanta. **Incorporated** in Tennessee in 1969. **Empl**—14,508.

 Tom Graves, CFA

Crestar Financial Corp.

NYSE Symbol CF In S&P MidCap 400

Price	Range	P-E Ratio	Dividend	Yield	S&P Ranking	Beta
Aug. 23'93	1993					
43⅝	46½–35⅛	14	1.12	2.6%	B+	1.22

Summary

Crestar is one of the largest bank holding companies in the Virginia/Maryland/Washington, D.C., area. As part of its strategy of growth within existing territories, CF recently acquired CFS Financial Corp. (assets of $843 million). An expanding asset base and improving credit quality should lead to continued earnings gains into 1994. Trading moved to the NYSE from The Nasdaq Stock Market on July 28, 1993.

Current Outlook

Earnings for 1993 are projected at $3.45 a share, up from $2.32 reported for 1992. For 1994, earnings are expected to reach $3.85.

The cash dividend, raised 25% in January 1993, was increased an additional 12% to $0.28 a share quarterly in April 1993.

Continued improvement in credit quality and a rapidly expanding asset base should provide for further earnings gains into 1994. Nonperforming assets were $162.8 million at June 30, 1993, down 48% from the year earlier level, reflecting aggressive efforts to work out problem loans. The May 1993 acquisition of CFS Financial Corp., which added about $843 million in assets and 19 branches to Crestar's network, expanded the company's presence in Northern Virginia and fits well with a strategy of growth within existing service terrritories. Benefits from the consolidation should be seen in the latter half of 1993. With an expanding asset base and improving credit quality, earnings should continue their advance into 1994.

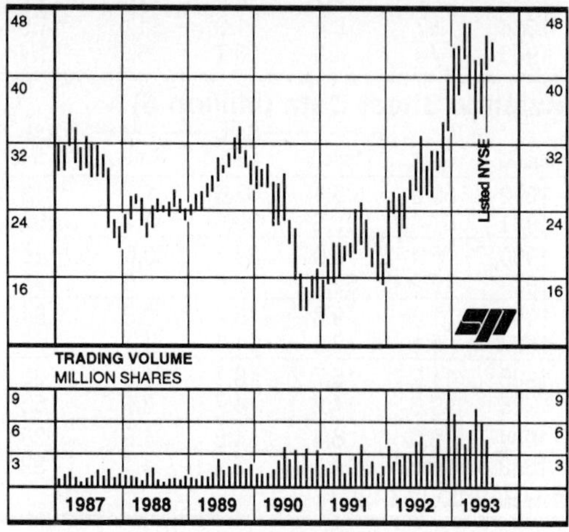

Review of Operations

Net interest income for the six months ended June 30, 1993, advanced 10%, year to year, aided by growth in earning assets and a wider net interest margin (4.71% vs. 4.41%). The provision for loan losses fell 67%, to $21.5 million. Noninterest income rose 14%, and with 12% lower noninterest expense, pretax income increased 142%. After taxes at 29.4%, against 19.4%, net income climbed 112%, to $64.6 million ($1.71 a share, based on 14% more shares; after preferred dividends), from $30.4 million ($0.90).

Common Share Earnings ($)

Quarter:	1993	1992	1991	1990
Mar.	0.83	0.40	0.36	0.85
Jun.	0.88	0.50	0.36	0.26
Sep.	E0.86	0.64	0.05	0.76
Dec.	E0.88	0.78	0.21	NM
	E3.45	2.32	0.98	1.87

Important Developments

Jun. '93— Crestar said it acquired all of the $22.2 million of deposits of the former City National Bank of Washington, D.C., from the FDIC.

May '93— The company said it acquired CFS Financial Corp. (assets of $843 million), the parent of Continental Federal Savings Bank, in a transaction whereby Crestar paid CFS shareholders $21.50 for each share held, with at least 85% of the payment in the form of Crestar common stock and the balance in cash. The transaction had an indicated value of about $66 million. The acquisition added 19 branches to the company's network in Northern Virginia.

Apr. '93— Directors authorized the repurchase of up to 500,000 CF common shares on the open market over the next 12 months to meet requirements of the company's dividend reinvestment and employee stock plans.

Next earnings report expected in mid-October.

Per Share Data ($)

Yr. End Dec. 31	1992	1991	[1]1990	[1]1989	[2]1988	[1]1987	[1,2]1986	[1]1985	1984	[1]1983
Tangible Bk. Val.	**23.00**	20.52	20.21	19.83	18.29	16.33	14.93	13.39	13.16	13.38
Earnings	**2.32**	0.98	1.87	[3]3.28	[3]2.96	[3]1.92	[3]2.92	[3]2.65	[3]2.33	[3]2.12
Divide nds	**0.800**	1.190	1.290	1.180	1.100	1.010	0.895	0.795	0.700	0.620
Payout Ratio	**34%**	121%	69%	36%	37%	53%	31%	30%	30%	29%
Prices—High	**39¾**	25	29⅝	34⅛	26½	35½	35⅞	24⅛	17½	15⅞
Low	**17¼**	11¼	12⅛	23½	20⅞	19⅝	22¾	17⅜	12½	11½
P/E Ratio—	**17–7**	26–11	16–6	10–7	9–7	18–10	12–8	9–7	7–5	8–5

Data as orig. reptd. Adj. for stk. divs. of 100% May 1986, 100% Jun. 1983. **1.** Refl. merger or acq. **2.** Refl. acctg. change. **3.** Ful. dil.: 3.25 in 1989, 2.92 in 1988, 1.90 in 1987, 2.87 in 1986, 2.60 in 1985, 2.26 in 1984, 2.05 in 1983.

Income Data (Million $)

Year Ended Dec. 31	Net Int. Inc.	Tax Equiv. Adj.	Non Int. Inc.	Loan Loss Prov.	% Exp./ Op. Revs.	Net Bef. Taxes	Eff. Tax Rate	Net Inc.	% Net Int. Margin	—% Return On— Assets	Equity
1992	**482**	**16.0**	**215**	**99.2**	**70.4**	**99.5**	**19.8%**	**79.8**	**4.67**	**0.67**	**10.3**
1991	421	22.1	186	210.0	64.5	40.0	15.2%	34.0	4.29	0.30	4.5
[1]1990	414	28.0	154	131.0	63.5	71.0	14.0%	61.0	4.22	0.52	8.5
[1]1989	380	33.3	146	45.0	64.7	121.0	14.1%	104.0	4.36	0.97	16.3
[2]1988	342	37.4	139	51.0	62.9	102.0	14.9%	87.0	4.29	0.87	16.0
[1]1987	328	51.1	136	73.0	64.6	63.0	9.5%	57.0	4.58	0.60	11.0
[1,2]1986	294	74.8	121	32.0	61.5	87.0	5.9%	82.0	5.04	0.97	18.3
[1]1985	253	52.0	73	27.0	60.8	72.0	6.7%	68.0	5.45	1.05	18.4
1984	224	41.8	61	17.0	62.7	63.0	9.3%	57.0	5.51	1.01	17.1
[1]1983	204	35.3	53	13.0	65.0	55.0	5.9%	52.0	5.64	1.03	17.3

Balance Sheet Data (Million $)

Dec. 31	Total Assets	—Earning Assets— Mon. Mkt. Assets	Inv. Secs.	Com'l Loans	Other Loans	% Loan Loss Resv.	—Deposits— Demand	Time	% Loans/ Deposits	Long Term Debt	Common Equity	% Equity To Assets
1992	**12,675**	**790**	**3,620**	**2,924**	**4,025**	**2.95**	**1,997**	**7,584**	**72.5**	**210**	**914**	**6.29**
1991	11,828	978	2,043	3,388	3,840	2.91	1,753	7,137	81.3	162	750	6.11
1990	11,881	271	2,184	3,842	3,963	1.91	1,675	6,831	91.8	168	726	5.88
1989	11,361	62	1,962	4,032	3,867	1.18	1,701	6,766	93.3	170	705	5.82
1988	10,408	141	1,330	3,776	3,769	1.15	1,704	6,278	94.5	168	603	5.18
1987	9,740	30	1,336	3,588	3,745	1.45	1,657	5,699	99.7	168	542	5.12
1986	9,413	51	1,486	3,303	3,346	1.16	1,954	4,943	94.2	172	510	5.07
1985	8,100	68	1,128	3,132	2,824	1.10	1,544	4,413	97.7	134	449	5.56
1984	5,941	20	720	2,442	2,054	1.05	1,088	3,286	99.7	55	363	5.78
1983	5,415	60	753	1,986	1,902	1.04	1,046	2,958	93.7	69	319	5.82

Data as orig. reptd. **1.** Refl. merger or acq. **2.** Refl. acctg. change.

Business Summary

Crestar Financial Corporation owns Crestar Bank of Virginia (one of the largest banks in that state), Crestar Bank, N.A. of Washington, D.C., and Crestar Bank of Maryland. As of mid-1993, the company had 308 banking branches, with the large majority in Virginia. Other subsidiaries provide insurance, discount brokerage, mortgage banking and investment advisory services.

Total loans (net of unearned income) amounted to $6.58 billion at year-end 1992 and were divided:

Commercial	40%
Tax–exempt	4%
Installment	21%
Bank card	9%
Real estate—mortgage	23%
Real estate—construction	3%

At the end of 1992, the allowance for loan losses totaled $205,017,000 (3.11% of loans outstanding), versus $210,004,000 (2.97%) a year earlier. Net chargeoffs were $113,929,000 in 1992 ($150,743,000 in 1991), equal to 1.69% (2.07%) of average loans. As of December 31, 1992, nonperforming assets amounted to $220,812,000 (3.32% of loans outstanding plus foreclosed properties), versus $349,959,000 (4.90%) a year earlier.

Deposits totaling $9.58 billion at December 31, 1992, were apportioned: demand 21%, interest-bearing demand 17%, money-market deposits 24%, regular savings 9%, other domestic time deposits 22%, CDs of $100,000 or more 1% and money-market certificates 6%.

On a tax-equivalent basis, the net interest margin was 4.67% in 1992, versus 4.29% in 1991.

Dividend Data

Dividends have been paid by the company and its predecessors since 1870. A dividend reinvestment plan is available.

Amt. of Divd. $	Date Decl.	Ex–divd. Date	Stock of Record	Payment Date
0.20	Oct. 23	Oct. 27	Nov. 2	Nov. 21'92
0.25	Jan. 22	Jan. 26	Feb. 1	Feb. 19'93
0.28	Apr. 23	Apr. 27	May 3	May 21'93
0.28	Jul. 23	Jul. 27	Aug. 2	Aug. 21'93

Capitalization

Long Term Debt: $260,758,000 (6/93).

Series B Adj. Rate Cum. Pfd. Stk.: 900,000 shs. ($50 stated value).

Common Stock: 37,720,229 shs. ($5 par). Institutions hold about 47%. Shareholders of record: 12,139 (12/92).

Office—919 E. Main St., Richmond, VA 23261-6665. **Tel**—(804) 782-5000. **Chrmn & CEO**—R. G. Tilghman. **Pres**—J. M. Wells III. **Vice Chrmn & CFO**—P. D. Giblin. **Exec VP-Contr & Treas**—J. D. Barr. **Sr VP & Secy**—J. C. Clark III. **Dirs**—R. M. Bagley, W. R. Battle, J. C. Fox, P. D. Giblin, G. T. Halpin, G. A. James, H. G. Leggett Jr., C. R. Longsworth, P. J. Maher, F. E. McCarthy, G. G. Minor III, G. F. Rainey Jr., F. S. Royal, R. G. Tilghman, E. P. Trani, W. F. Vosbeck, L. D. Walker, E. Walters, J. M. Wells III, K. H. Williams. **Transfer Agent**—Mellon Bank, Pittsburgh. **Incorporated** in Virginia in 1963. **Empl**—6,122.

 Stephen R. Biggar

Crompton & Knowles

NYSE Symbol CNK In S&P MidCap 400

Price	Range	P-E Ratio	Dividend	Yield	S&P Ranking	Beta
Sep. 29'93	1993					
18⅜	27¼–18	19	0.40	2.2%	A+	1.28

Summary

This company produces and markets specialty chemicals, primarily fabric dyes and ingredients for the food industry, and specialty equipment and controls. CNK is expected to continue earnings growth in the next two years, reflecting continued sales gains in established market niches, improving operating performance, and lower debt levels.

Current Outlook

Share earnings for 1994 are projected to advance to $1.12 from $1.00 expected for 1993.

The dividend has been raised 25%, to $0.10 quarterly from $0.08, with the May 1993 payment.

Revenues in 1994 are expected to continue their uptrend as U.S. dye sales remain strong, especially to the carpet and apparel industries, which will offset lower sales in European markets, primarily in the first half of the year. The specialty ingredient segment is expected to grow at a single-digit rate. Specialty process equipment and controls should continue to benefit from demand in U.S. markets. Operating margins will improve as much of the costs to increase the ingredient business were expensed in prior periods and as the French dye operation is integrated. Earnings should also be partly offset by a higher tax rate. Earnings for the remainder of 1993 will be aided by higher demand for specialty process equipment and controls, which will be partly offset by the soft European die market and higher taxes.

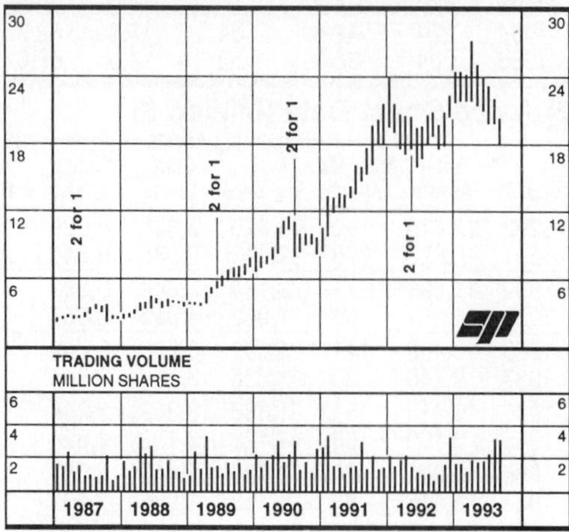

Net Sales (Million $)

Quarter:	1993	1992	1991	1990
Mar.	134	114	106	94
Jun.	148	135	119	98
Sep.	---	132	115	96
Dec.	---	138	110	101
	---	518	450	390

Sales for the six months ended June 26, 1993, advanced 13%, year to year, reflecting a strong rise in specialty process equipment sales, especially in export sales to the Far East. Operating profits in the specialty process equipment segment grew on the higher volume, and specialty chemicals' profits rise primarily reflected the May 1992 acquisition. Following 80% lower interest expense, pretax income was up 23%. After taxes at 36.9% in both periods, net income grew 23%, to $0.54 a share from $0.46. Results for the prior-year period were before a charge of $0.12 a share from the cumulative effect of an accounting change.

Common Share Earnings ($)

Quarter:	1993	1992	1991	1990
Mar.	0.24	0.20	0.17	0.14
Jun.	0.30	0.26	0.22	0.18
Sep.	E0.23	0.20	0.17	0.14
Dec.	E0.23	0.21	0.18	0.15
	E1.00	0.87	0.73	0.61

Important Developments

Sep. '93— CNK stated that the specialty process equipment and control backlog totaled $45 million at June 26, 1993, up from $34 million at 1992 year-end. While higher demand from the Far East boosted equipment sales in the first half of 1993, current backlog reflects higher domestic demand.

Next earnings report expected in mid-October.

Per Share Data ($)

Yr. End Dec. 31	[1]1992	[1]1991	[1]1990	1989	[1]1988	1987	1986	1985	1984	1983
Tangible Bk. Val.	**3.46**	2.26	1.83	1.50	1.15	1.44	1.26	1.15	1.08	1.05
Cash Flow	**1.10**	0.94	0.77	0.64	0.48	0.33	0.25	0.23	0.24	0.21
Earnings[2]	**0.87**	0.73	0.61	0.50	0.36	0.25	0.17	0.14	0.15	0.12
Dividends	**0.305**	0.248	0.197	0.145	0.108	0.084	0.079	0.075	0.072	0.067
Payout Ratio	**36%**	33%	31%	29%	30%	34%	45%	55%	49%	59%
Prices—High	**23⅞**	21⅝	11⁹⁄₁₆	7⅞	4½	3¹³⁄₁₆	2½	1¾	1½	1¹³⁄₁₆
Low	**16**	8½	6¹¹⁄₁₆	3¾	2⁹⁄₁₆	2¼	1⁹⁄₁₆	1³⁄₁₆	1¼	1³⁄₁₆
P/E Ratio—	**27–18**	30–12	19–11	16–7	13–7	16–9	15–9	12–8	10–8	16–10

Data as orig. reptd. Adj. for stk. divs. of 100% May 1992, 100% Aug. 1990, 100% Jun. 1989, 100% Jun. 1987. **1.** Reflects merger or acquisition. **2.** Bef. results of disc. opers. of -0.07 in 1988, -0.31 in 1986, and spec. item(s) of -0.18 in 1992. E-Estimated.

Income Data (Million $)

Year Ended Dec. 31	Revs.	Oper. Inc.	% Oper. Inc. of Revs.	Cap. Exp.	Depr.	Int. Exp.	[4]Net Bef. Taxes	Eff. Tax Rate	[6]Net Inc.	% Net Inc. of Revs.	Cash Flow
[1]1992	**518**	**84.4**	**16.3**	**12.8**	**11.6**	**6.98**	**68.3**	**36.7%**	**[5]43.3**	**8.4**	**54.9**
[1]1991	450	71.7	15.9	13.1	10.0	7.42	56.6	36.5%	35.9	8.0	46.0
[1]1990	390	59.4	15.2	16.4	8.0	5.84	47.3	36.5%	30.0	7.7	38.0
1989	356	48.9	13.7	13.4	6.5	6.01	38.6	36.5%	24.5	6.9	31.0
[2]1988	290	34.6	11.9	7.1	4.7	3.61	26.9	37.5%	16.8	5.8	22.5
1987	237	24.9	10.5	3.6	4.1	2.59	20.1	41.5%	11.8	4.9	15.9
[3]1986	213	21.0	9.8	3.5	3.7	1.28	16.1	44.7%	8.9	4.2	12.9
1985	231	20.0	8.6	3.4	3.8	2.12	14.5	47.7%	7.6	3.3	11.6
1984	230	20.3	8.8	3.9	3.8	2.75	14.4	45.2%	7.9	3.4	12.0
1983	231	19.4	8.4	3.0	3.8	3.05	12.1	47.8%	6.3	2.7	10.3

Balance Sheet Data (Million $)

Dec. 31	Cash	Curr. Assets	Curr. Liab.	Curr. Ratio	Total Assets	% Ret. on Assets	Long Term Debt	Common Equity	Total Cap.	% LT Debt of Cap.	% Ret. on Equity
1992	**2.4**	**207**	**103**	**2.0**	**351**	**12.7**	**24.0**	**211**	**239**	**10.0**	**23.9**
1991	8.5	185	86	2.2	309	12.1	76.1	141	223	34.2	27.7
1990	11.3	164	88	1.9	283	12.0	70.3	118	194	36.2	27.7
1989	4.9	127	71	1.8	218	11.5	41.2	99	147	28.1	26.9
1988	7.7	121	72	1.7	206	9.9	44.6	82	133	33.5	21.5
1987	3.3	94	41	2.3	135	8.8	12.9	76	94	13.7	16.4
1986	1.0	96	42	2.3	135	7.0	19.5	69	93	20.9	12.7
1985	3.4	87	32	2.7	130	6.0	19.1	69	98	19.6	10.5
1984	4.7	82	30	2.7	124	6.3	20.3	65	94	21.7	11.5
1983	4.4	82	30	2.8	126	4.9	24.5	64	97	25.3	8.9

Data as orig. reptd. **1.** Reflects merger or acquisition. **2.** Excl. disc. opers. and reflects merger or acquisition. **3.** Excl. disc. opers. **4.** Incl. equity in earns of nonconsol. subs. prior to 1988. **5.** Reflects acctg. change. **6.** Bef. results of disc. opers. and spec. item(s).

Business Summary

Crompton & Knowles produces dyes, specialty foods and pharmaceutical ingredients, and manufactures specialty extrusion equipment and control systems. Business segment contributions in 1992:

	Sales	Profits
Specialty chemicals............	76%	76%
Specialty process equipment & controls.....................	24%	24%

Foreign operations contributed 20% of sales and 18% of profits in 1992.

CNK's specialty chemicals segment manufactures and sells dyes used on synthetic and natural fibers for knit and woven garments, home furnishings (carpets, draperies and upholstery) and automotive furnishings. Industrial dyes and chemicals are marketed to the paper, leather and ink industries for use on stationery, tissue, towels and other products. A line of chemical auxiliaries (leveling agents, dye fixatives and scouring agents) is also marketed to the textile industry. The company also makes and sells reaction and compounded flavor ingredients for the food processing, bakery, beverage, pharmaceutical and tobacco industries, as well as food colorings and fragrance formulations. It is a leading supplier of specialty sweeteners, as well as seasonings and seasoning blends, for the bakery, confectionery and food processing industries.

Specialty process equipment and controls include extruders and processing systems used to insulate wire and cable and to process plastic resins into various shapes. Wire and cable insulating systems apply plastic or rubber insulation to high voltage power cable for electrical utilities and to wire for the communications, construction, automotive and appliance industries. Plastic processing systems produce plastic sheeting used in appliances, automobiles, home construction, sports equipment and furniture; blown film used for commercial packaging; plastic pipe; and other extruded shapes used as house siding and substitutes for wood molding.

Dividend Data

Dividends have been paid since 1933. A dividend reinvestment plan is available. A "poison pill" stock purchase right was issued in 1988.

Amt of Divd. $	Date Decl.	Ex–divd. Date	Stock of Record	Payment Date
0.08	Oct. 21	Nov. 2	Nov. 6	Nov. 27'92
0.08	Jan. 19	Feb. 8	Feb. 12	Feb. 26'93
0.10	Apr. 13	May 3	May 7	May 28'93
0.10	Jul. 21	Aug. 2	Aug. 6	Aug. 27'93

Capitalization

Long Term Debt: $24,000,000 (6/93).

Common Stock: 51,320,258 shs. ($0.10 par).
Institutions hold 58%.
Shareholders of record: 3,100.

Office—One Station Place, Metro Center, Stamford, CT 06902. **Tel**—(203) 353-5400. **Chrmn & Pres**—V. A. Calarco. **VP-Fin & CFO**—C. J. Marsden. **Secy**—J. T. Ferguson II. **Investor Contact**—Yanis Bibelnieks (212-949-2295). **Dirs**—J. A. Bitonti, H. W. Buchanan, V. A. Calarco, R. A. Fox, R. L. Headrick, M. W. Huber, W. A. Law, C. J. Marsden, C.A. Piccolo, H. B. Wentz, Jr. **Transfer Agent & Registrar**—Mellon Securities Transfew Services, Pittsburgh, PA. **Incorporated** in Massachusetts in 1900. **Empl**—2,309.

 Shayna J. Malnak

Cross (A.T.) Co.

ASE Symbol ATX.A In S&P MidCap 400

Price	Range	P-E Ratio	Dividend	Yield	S&P Ranking	Beta
Aug. 5'93	1993					
14	20¼–14	NM	0.64	4.6%	B+	0.87

Summary

This leading manufacturer of fine writing instruments also markets luggage and leather accessories. A loss is expected for 1993, reflecting weak markets for the company's products, particularly in Europe and Japan. The unprofitable Mark Cross unit was recently sold.

Current Outlook

A loss of $0.15 is projected for 1993, versus earnings of $0.64 in 1992. Earnings of $0.80 are seen for 1994.

The quarterly dividend was slashed 50%, to $0.16, with the August 1993 payment.

Net sales are expected to decline in 1993, reflecting weak markets for the company's products, particularly in Europe and Japan, despite potential added revenues from new product introductions. The downtrend in sales is not likely to reverse until foreign economies improve. Lower sales and reduced interest and other income will likely outweigh the absence of a $2.5 million pretax charge (related to a work force reduction). Proposed higher taxes could also hurt sales. Long-term strategy includes introducing a steady stream of new products, expanding channels of distribution in the U.S., and increasing sales in foreign markets.

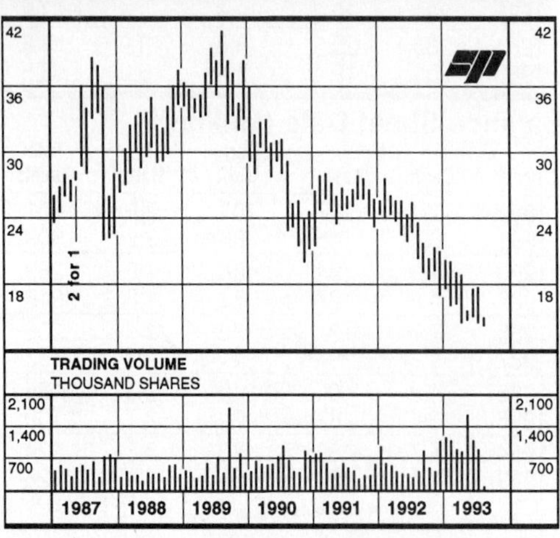

Net Sales (Million $)

Quarter:	1993	1992	1991	1990
Mar.	39.1	45.7	47.0	48.7
Jun.	37.3	46.6	51.4	53.2
Sep.	---	45.6	45.8	44.6
Dec.	---	62.5	72.9	76.1
	---	200.4	217.1	222.7

Net sales in the six months ended June 30, 1993, fell 15%, year to year, reflecting reduced worldwide demand for writing instruments. Results were penalized by a $9.6 million charge related to costs of productivity programs. A loss from continuing operations of $5,841,000 ($0.35 a share) replaced income of $6,024,000 ($0.36). Results exclude losses from discontinued operations of $4,000,000 ($0.23) and $934,000 ($0.06) in the respective periods.

Cl. A & B Share Earnings ($)

Quarter:	1993	1992	1991	1990
Mar.	---	0.13	0.15	0.22
Jun.	[1]d0.35	0.17	0.21	0.38
Sep.	E0.07	0.15	0.22	0.25
Dec.	E0.13	0.19	0.68	0.77
	Ed0.15	0.64	1.26	1.62

Important Developments

Jul. '93— Cross said it had sold its unprofitable Mark Cross unit to Sara Lee Corp., for about $8 million. The company incurred a related loss of $2.5 million. Cross said its departure from the retail store business would let it concentrate on manufacturing and selling writing instruments, and, through its Manetti-Farrow subsidiary, on the distribution of Fendi leather products.

Next earnings report expected in late October.

Per Share Data ($)

Yr. End Dec. 31	1992	1991	1990	1989	1988	1987	1986	1985	1984	1983
Tangible Bk. Val.	**8.64**	9.33	9.60	[2]9.20	7.65	7.09	6.24	5.72	5.00	[1]4.88
Cash Flow	**0.98**	1.58	1.93	2.64	2.48	2.00	1.50	1.34	1.23	1.11
Earnings	**0.64**	1.26	1.62	2.15	2.13	1.74	1.29	1.14	1.03	0.95
Dividends	**1.280**	1.280	1.250	1.180	1.060	0.860	0.760	0.690	0.630	0.575
Payout Ratio	**200%**	102%	77%	55%	50%	49%	59%	61%	61%	61%
Prices—High	**27⅞**	28⅛	36	41	37½	38⅝	24⅞	18½	16⅜	17¾
Low	**17**	21½	20	32	26⅜	22	17¼	12⅞	11⅞	12¼
P/E Ratio—	**43–27**	22–17	22–12	19–15	18–12	22–13	19–13	16–11	16–12	19–13

Data as orig. reptd. Adj. for stk. div. of 100% May 1987. **1.** Six mos. **2.** Incl. intangibles. d-Deficit. E-Estimated.

Income Data (Million $)

Year Ended Dec. 31	Revs.	Oper. Inc.	% Oper. Inc. of Revs.	Cap. Exp.	Depr.	Int. Exp.	Net Bef. Taxes	Eff. Tax Rate	Net Inc.	% Net Inc. of Revs.	Cash Flow
1992	**200**	**20.7**	**10.3**	**5.4**	**5.74**	**Nil**	**16.0**	**32.4%**	**10.8**	**5.4**	**16.6**
1991	217	29.9	13.8	8.4	5.49	Nil	29.6	28.5%	21.2	9.8	26.7
1990	223	38.5	17.3	5.9	5.17	Nil	38.4	29.0%	27.2	12.2	32.4
1989	247	53.7	21.7	9.8	5.19	Nil	[2]53.7	33.0%	36.0	14.6	41.2
1988	228	54.2	23.8	12.8	5.83	0.38	52.1	32.1%	35.4	15.6	41.2
1987	187	46.0	24.6	5.7	4.24	0.46	44.8	35.6%	28.9	15.4	33.1
1986	155	36.4	23.4	3.4	3.42	Nil	36.0	40.6%	[3]21.4	13.8	24.8
1985	139	32.4	23.3	3.0	3.35	Nil	32.0	41.2%	18.8	13.6	22.2
1984	133	31.5	23.7	2.1	3.51	Nil	30.7	44.8%	16.9	12.7	20.2
[1]1983	118	28.9	24.4	2.4	2.65	Nil	28.3	45.1%	15.6	13.1	18.1

Balance Sheet Data (Million $)

Dec. 31	Cash	Curr. Assets	Curr. Liab.	Curr. Ratio	Total Assets	% Ret. on Assets	Long Term Debt	Common Equity	Total Cap.	% LT Debt of Cap.	% Ret. on Equity
1992	**65.2**	**144**	**39.8**	**3.6**	**194**	**5.4**	**Nil**	**151**	**151**	**Nil**	**6.9**
1991	65.9	157	42.7	3.7	208	10.2	Nil	162	162	Nil	13.1
1990	70.4	158	41.5	3.8	207	13.5	Nil	162	162	Nil	17.2
1989	64.5	149	38.4	3.9	196	19.3	Nil	154	154	Nil	24.7
1988	64.9	134	36.2	3.7	176	21.3	Nil	136	136	Nil	27.8
1987	57.8	123	35.9	3.4	156	19.9	Nil	118	118	Nil	26.1
1986	56.0	109	23.8	4.6	133	16.9	3.39	103	107	3.2	21.6
1985	44.6	95	19.0	5.0	119	16.5	3.08	94	98	3.1	20.7
1984	35.1	85	16.5	5.1	109	16.1	2.79	87	90	3.1	20.3
1983	22.6	77	16.0	4.8	101	16.6	2.53	80	83	3.1	20.2

Data as orig. reptd. **1.** Refl. merger or acq. **2.** Incl. equity in earns. of nonconsol. subs. **3.** Refl. acctg. change.

Business Summary

A. T. Cross manufactures fine writing instruments and markets quality leather products and other gift items. Business segment contributions (profits in millions) in 1992 were:

	Sales	Profits
Writing instruments	84%	$18.2
Leather products and other gift items	16%	–2.4

Foreign business accounted for 25% of sales in 1992.

Writing instruments include ball-point pens, mechanical pencils, rolling/porous-point pens, and fountain pens. The signature series is crafted in 22 karat heavy gold electroplate and black lacquer, diamond cut 22 karat heavy gold electroplate finish, black lacquer, and burgundy lacquer. Writing instruments in the traditional Cross line are available in 18 and 14 karat gold; 18, 14 and 10 karat gold filled; Classic Black, gray, blue, burgundy, chrome and gold Medalist; and lustrous chrome. The company also produces desk sets with bases made of walnut, onyx, cherry and marble.

A leather business is conducted by the Manetti-Farrow subsidiary. Manetti-Farrow distributes the Fendi brand of leather products and fashion accessories in the U.S. and Canada. The Mark Cross unit, which markets quality luggage, leather goods and other distinctive gifts for personal and business use through stores in 26 retail locations in the U.S., was sold in June 1993.

Dividend Data

Cash dividends were increased each year from 1968 to 1990. The class A and class B common issues share equally in all disbursements.

Amt. of Divd. $	Date Decl.	Ex-divd. Date	Stock of Record	Payment Date
0.32	Oct. 22	Oct. 30	Nov. 5	Nov. 19'92
0.32	Dec. 8	Jan. 22	Jan. 28	Feb. 11'93
0.32	Apr. 22	Apr. 30	May 6	May 20'93
0.16	Jul. 22	Jul. 30	Aug. 5	Aug. 19'93

Capitalization

Long Term Debt: None (6/93).

Class B Common Stock: 1,804,800 shs. ($1 par); conv. into Cl. A sh.-for-sh.; elects two-thirds of directors; entirely owned by the Boss family.

Class A Common Stock: 15,114,328 shs. ($1 par).
The Boss family owns 16%.
Institutions own 69%.
Shareholders of record: 2,238.

Office—One Albion Rd., Lincoln, RI 02865. **Tel**—(401) 333-1200. **Chrmn**—B. R. Boss. **Pres & CEO**—R. A. Boss. **EVP & COO**—J. E. Buckley. **VP-Fin, Treas & CFO**—M. El-Hillow. **Secy**—Tina C. Benik. **Dirs**—B. R. Boss, R. A. Boss, J. E. Buckley, B. V. Buonanno, Jr., J. J. Burgdoerfer, H. F. Krimendahl II, T. C. McDermott, J. T. Murray, E. M. Watson. **Transfer Agents**—Fleet National Bank of Rhode Island, Providence; Mellon Financial Securities, NYC. **Registrar**—Citizens Trust Co., Providence. **Incorporated** in Rhode Island in 1916. **Empl**—1,800.

 M. Graham Hackett

Cypress Semiconductor

NYSE Symbol CY Options on CBOE In S&P MidCap 400

Price	Range	P-E Ratio	Dividend	Yield	S&P Ranking	Beta
Jun. 15'93	1993					
13⅞	14⅝–8⅝	NM	None	None	B	1.62

Summary

Cypress manufactures a broad line of high-performance integrated circuits. The loss sustained in 1992 reflected $39.7 million of restructuring and other nonrecurring charges, although poorly received new products, pricing pressures and a sluggish business environment also depressed results. Stronger industry conditions, an aggressive program of new product introductions and reduced pricing competition, as well as the absence of nonrecurring charges, should allow profitability to be restored in 1993. The company recently agreed to sell its microprocessor operations.

Current Outlook

Earnings for 1993 should approximate $0.60 a share, in contrast to the $0.56 loss sustained in 1992.

Initiation of cash dividends is unlikely.

Revenues should increase only slightly in 1993, as stronger industry conditions and new product introductions are largely offset by sharply lower sales of microprocessors due to weak demand and the planned sale of those operations. Profitability should be restored on lessened pricing pressures, the company's yield improvement program, cost savings from the relocation of U.S. assembly and test operations to Thailand and the absence of $39.7 million of restructuring and other nonrecurring charges. Failure to complete the sale of microprocessor operations would have a negative effect on results, since those operations are currently losing money.

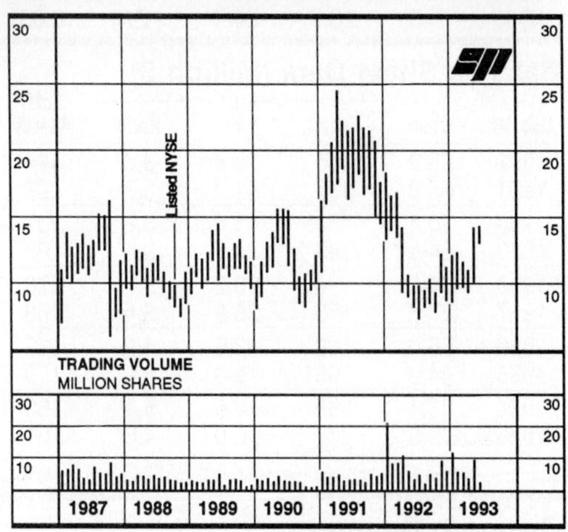

Revenues (Million $)

13 Weeks:	1993	1992	1991	1990
Mar.	69.7	73.8	69.1	52.8
Jun.	---	65.8	75.1	53.8
Sep.	---	65.3	71.6	55.6
Dec.	---	67.4	71.0	63.0
	---	272.2	286.8	225.2

Revenues for the 13 weeks ended March 29, 1993, declined 5.6%, year to year, as lower microprocessor shipments outweighed higher revenues for static random access memories (SRAMs), programmable logic devices (PLDs) and programmable read-only memories (PROMs). Margins narrowed on the lower volume and an unfavorable product mix, and pretax income was 34% lower. After taxes at 37.6%, versus 34.0%, net income decreased 37%, to $0.07 a share (based on 6.9% fewer shares), from $0.10.

Common Shares Earnings ($)

13 Weeks:	1993	1992	1991	1990
Mar.	0.07	0.10	0.23	0.22
Jun.	E0.10	d0.04	0.25	0.22
Sep.	E0.19	0.01	0.23	0.22
Dec.	E0.24	d0.66	0.15	0.22
	E0.60	d0.56	0.85	0.88

Important Developments

May '93— Cypress and Fujitsu Limited signed a letter of intent for Fujitsu to purchase CY's SPARC microprocessor subsidiary, Ross Technology, for approximately $23 million. The companies also agreed on the continuation of a joint development program focused on a complex logic-oriented product.

Next earnings report expected in mid-July.

Per Share Data ($)

Yr. End Dec. 31	1992	1991	1990	1989	1988	1987	1986	1985	1984	1983
Tangible Bk. Val.	**7.27**	7.89	6.77	5.95	5.09	4.49	3.35	NM	NM	NM
Cash Flow	**0.71**	1.78	1.67	1.44	0.99	0.61	0.42	d0.06	NA	NA
Earnings[1]	**d0.56**	0.85	0.87	0.80	0.56	0.32	0.25	d0.23	d0.49	d0.19
Dividends	**Nil**	Nil	Nil	Nil	Nil	Nil	Nil	Nil	Nil	Nil
Payout Ratio	**Nil**	Nil	Nil	Nil	Nil	Nil	Nil	Nil	Nil	Nil
Prices—High	**18⅜**	24½	15⅝	14½	12½	16¼	10½	NA	NA	NA
Low	**7⅜**	10⅞	8⅛	9¼	7½	6	6½	NA	NA	NA
P/E Ratio—	**NM**	29–13	18–9	18–12	22–13	51–19	42–26	NA	NA	NA

Data as orig. reptd. 1. Bef. spec. items of +0.05 in 1987, +0.20 in 1986. d-Deficit. E-Estimated. NM-Not Meaningful. NA-Not Available.

Income Data (Million $)

Year Ended Dec. 31	[1]Revs.	Oper. Inc.	% Oper. Inc. of Revs.	Cap. Exp.	Depr.	Int. Exp.	Net Bef. Taxes	Eff. Tax Rate	[2]Net Inc.	% Net Inc. of Revs.	Cash Flow
1992	**272**	**51.7**	**19.0**	**31.9**	**47.6**	**0.44**	**d32.9**	**NM**	**d21.0**	**NM**	**26.6**
1991	287	82.3	28.7	79.5	37.6	1.00	51.8	34.0%	34.2	11.9	71.7
1990	225	72.8	32.3	36.6	30.5	1.09	50.3	34.0%	33.2	14.8	63.8
1989	199	65.0	32.6	32.9	24.5	1.79	46.6	34.1%	30.7	15.4	55.2
1988	139	43.2	31.0	39.9	16.1	2.17	32.0	35.0%	20.8	14.9	36.9
1987	77	23.9	30.9	25.3	10.7	2.47	17.4	33.9%	11.5	14.9	22.3
1986	51	18.3	35.9	32.3	5.1	1.41	14.7	50.7%	7.3	14.3	12.4
1985	17	d0.1	NM	7.9	4.0	1.78	d5.3	Nil	d5.3	NM	d1.3
1984	3	d7.7	NM	17.6	1.7	0.84	d9.7	Nil	d9.7	NM	NA
1983	Nil	d2.8	NM	4.4	0.1	0.02	d2.5	Nil	d2.5	NM	NA

Balance Sheet Data (Million $)

Dec. 31	Cash	Curr. Assets	Curr. Liab.	Curr. Ratio	Total Assets	% Ret. on Assets	Long Term Debt	Common Equity	Total Inv. Capital	% LT Debt of Cap.	% Ret. on Equity
1992	**82**	**184**	**50.0**	**3.7**	**321**	**NM**	**1.6**	**262**	**271**	**0.6**	**NM**
1991	104	212	61.6	3.4	375	9.7	3.3	299	313	1.1	12.3
1990	92	192	52.8	3.6	309	11.3	5.4	242	257	2.1	14.6
1989	97	179	50.3	3.6	286	11.5	9.3	219	235	3.9	15.1
1988	89	150	39.4	3.8	245	9.0	14.3	185	205	6.9	11.9
1987	108	144	31.2	4.6	216	6.0	19.2	163	185	10.4	8.1
1986	76	98	21.5	4.5	151	3.0	19.8	110	129	15.3	11.4
1985	8	18	9.9	1.8	42	NM	14.3	[3]18	32	44.9	NM
1984	NM	11	5.8	1.9	31	NM	12.0	[3]13	25	47.1	NM
1983	NA	NA	NA	NA	9	NM	1.9	[3]5	7	27.4	NM

Data as orig. reptd. **1.** Incl. tech. licenses. **2.** Bef. spec. items. **3.** Refl. conv. of pfd. stk. at time of public offering. d-Deficit. NM-Not Meaningful. NA-Not Available.

Business Summary

Cypress Semiconductor designs, develops, manufactures and sells high-performance digital integrated circuits used in computers, telecommunications, instrumentation and military systems.

At the end of 1992, Cypress was shipping 263 products in seven distinct product areas: static random access memories (SRAMs), programmable read-only memories (PROMs), programmable logic devices (PLDs), data communications devices, SPARC RISC (reduced instruction set computing) microprocessors and peripherals, multichip modules and BiCMOS ECL (emitter coupled logic) and TTL (transistor transistor logic) devices. The company has agreed to sell its microprocessor operations.

High-speed SRAMs are used for storage and retrieval of data in computers and other electronic systems. PROMs are used in computers and telecommunications systems to store fixed data that is not altered during machine operations. PLDs perform non-memory functions, such as floating-point mathematics. The data communications and logic family consists of four different categories of fixed-function (non-programmable), high-speed standard logic products. RISC microprocessors use a smaller instruction set, enabling a computer to operate four times more efficiently than a standard machine. Multichip modules combine multiple chips into high-performance standard and custom memory subsystems. ECL logic and memory devices are typically used in the fastest available computers, where speed of computation and information retrieval is critical. TTL circuits are pervasive in most electronic applications.

International sales represented 27% of revenues in 1992, up from 25% in 1991.

Research and development spending declined to $65.0 million (23.9% of sales) in 1992, from $71.8 million (25.0%) in 1991.

Dividend Data

No cash dividends have ever been paid.

Finances

In April 1993, directors authorized the repurchase of 500,000 Cypress common shares, following the acquisition of 2.9 million shares in 1992.

Capitalization

Long Term Debt: $1,204,000 of lease obligs. (3/93).

Minority Interest: $4,749,000.

Common Stock: 35,562,000 shs. ($0.01 par).
Officers & directors own 4.7%.
Institutions hold about 42%.
Shareholders of record: 3,062.

Office—3901 North First St., San Jose, CA 95134. **Tel**—(408) 943-2600. **Pres & CEO**—T. J. Rodgers. **CFO**—P. Verderico. **Secy**—R. Foreman. **Dirs**— P. R. Lamond (Chrmn), F. B. Bialek, L. J. Doerr, T. J. Rodgers. **Transfer Agent & Registrar**—First National Bank of Boston. **Incorporated** in California in 1982; reincorporated in Delaware in 1987. **Empl**—1,529.

 Paul Valentine, CFA

Danaher Corp.

NYSE Symbol DHR Options on Phila In S&P MidCap 400

Price	Range	P-E Ratio	Dividend	Yield	S&P Ranking	Beta
Jul. 21'93	1993					
32⅜	33¼–24⅛	23	0.12	0.4%	B	1.02

Summary

Danaher is a leading manufacturer of hand tools, automotive and transportation products, and process and environmental controls. As of 1992, DHR's tool group was appointed the sole supplier of Sears Craftsman tools. DHR is also a major supplier to NAPA. Earnings should continue to benefit from gains in manufacturing efficiency as new production methods are adopted and from increased sales to Sears. The Rales Brothers own about 44% of the shares.

Current Outlook

Earnings for 1993 are estimated at $1.55 a share, up from 1992's $1.10. Earnings could rise to $1.75 a share in 1994.

Dividends were resumed in March 1993 at a $0.03 quarterly rate.

Demand for automotive and precision components should increase in 1993, and contributions by Danaher Tools should rise as sales to Sears, Roebuck & Co. continue to climb. Newer items, such as the Allen-brand hand tools, should aid comparisons, as should greater sales of Jacobs keyless chucks. Margins should widen as DHR benefits from higher capacity utilization and from investments in technologies that allow lower inventories and more frequent inventory turns. Amortization of goodwill will remain a constraint on earnings.

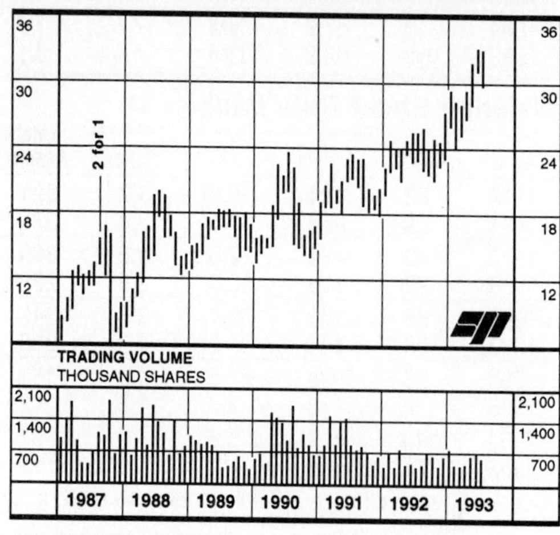

Net Sales (Million $)

Quarter:	1993	1992	1991	1990
Mar.	248	212	204	181
Jun.	259	237	202	203
Sep.	---	246	208	230
Dec.	---	261	224	227
	---	956	837	840

Revenues for the six months ended June 30, 1993, rose 13%, year to year, on improvement in all three segments. Aided by double digit operating profit improvement in all the groups, pretax income gained 73%. After taxes at 42.0% in both periods, net income also increased 73%, to $0.79 a share (before a $1.25 accounting charge) from $0.46.

Common Share Earnings ($)

Quarter:	1993	1992	1991	1990
Mar.	0.35	0.18	0.14	0.46
Jun.	0.44	0.28	0.15	0.46
Sep.	E0.40	0.34	0.15	0.40
Dec.	E0.36	0.30	0.03	0.06
	E1.55	1.10	0.47	1.34

Important Developments

Jul. '93— DHR said that despite economic uncertainty, each of its business groups had grown faster than the industries in which they participate, and each achieved double digit gains in operating profits in 1993's second quarter. DHR expected continued favorable earnings comparisons.

Jun. '93— DHR purchased four controls and instruments businesses from Mark IV Industries for approximately $35 million in cash. With about $50 million in annual sales, the businesses will be combined with DHR's Partlow/Anderson and Danaher Controls units. The acquisitions—Eagle Industrial, Rustrak, LFE and West Instruments—offer a broad range of process controllers, timers, data loggers and other instruments. About 20% of the sales of these units are manufactured in the United Kingdom.

Next earnings report expected in late October.

Per Share Data ($)

Yr. End Dec. 31	1992	1991	[1]1990	1989	1988	[1]1987	[1]1986	1985	[1]1984	1983
Tangible Bk. Val.	**0.98**	0.44	d0.02	d0.53	d2.10	d5.10	d6.47	1.35	1.43	1.04
Cash Flow	**2.08**	1.63	2.30	2.79	2.42	1.53	0.88	0.58	0.17	d0.26
Earnings[2]	**1.10**	0.47	1.34	1.98	1.68	0.92	0.43	0.27	0.09	d0.27
Dividends	**Nil**	Nil	Nil	Nil	Nil	Nil	Nil	Nil	Nil	Nil
Payout Ratio	**Nil**	Nil	Nil	Nil	Nil	Nil	Nil	Nil	Nil	Nil
Prices—High	**27⅞**	23½	23⅝	18⅜	20	16¾	6¾	4⅞	3⅞	2½
Low	**19¾**	15¾	13½	12⅞	7½	6	3½	3⅜	2¼	1⅜
P/E Ratio—	**25–18**	50–34	18–10	9–7	12–4	18–7	16–8	18–12	46–26	NM

Data as orig. reptd. Adj. for stk. div(s). of 100% Sep. 1987. **1.** Reflects merger or acquisition. **2.** Bef. results of disc. opers. of +0.59 in 1989, -0.04 in 1988, -0.02 in 1987, and spec. item(s) of +0.21 in 1988, -0.05 in 1987, +0.33 in 1986, +0.39 in 1985, +0.09 in 1984. E-Estimated d-Deficit. NM-Not Meaningful.

Income Data (Million $)

Year Ended Dec. 31	[1]Revs.	Oper. Inc.	% Oper. Inc. of Revs.	Cap. Exp.	Depr.	Int. Exp.	[6]Net Bef. Taxes	Eff. Tax Rate	[7]Net Inc.	% Net Inc. of Revs.	Cash Flow
1992	**954**	**98**	**10.2**	**33.9**	**28.1**	**[5]10.9**	**56.7**	**44.3%**	**31.6**	**3.3**	**59.7**
1991	836	73	8.7	41.8	33.2	[5]14.5	26.3	49.4%	13.3	1.6	46.5
[2]1990	845	107	12.6	33.0	25.6	25.6	62.1	42.5%	35.7	4.2	61.3
1989	756	120	15.9	22.9	19.1	27.9	79.1	40.4%	47.1	6.2	66.3
[3]1988	716	123	17.2	17.5	17.6	37.3	73.0	45.2%	40.0	5.6	57.6
[4]1987	617	100	16.2	17.8	13.5	48.1	43.4	52.9%	20.5	3.3	33.9
[2]1986	454	50	11.1	10.6	9.3	31.1	17.7	51.1%	8.7	1.9	17.9
1985	305	33	10.8	7.0	6.3	15.9	14.0	60.4%	5.6	1.8	11.8
[2]1984	91	10	10.9	2.6	1.5	5.5	3.0	52.7%	1.4	1.5	2.9
1983	24	3	13.0	Nil	Nil	6.9	d3.7	NM	d3.7	NM	d3.9

Balance Sheet Data (Million $)

Dec. 31	Cash	Curr. Assets	Curr. Liab.	Curr. Ratio	Total Assets	% Ret. on Assets	Long Term Debt	Common Equity	Total Cap.	% LT Debt of Cap.	% Ret. on Equity
1992	**1.7**	**230**	**212**	**1.1**	**770**	**4.2**	**137**	**348**	**486**	**28.3**	**9.4**
1991	Nil	216	174	1.2	735	1.8	182	319	501	36.3	4.3
1990	0.6	237	181	1.3	745	5.2	186	305	527	35.3	13.3
1989	4.8	169	144	1.2	507	9.0	143	192	335	42.7	27.8
1988	24.1	213	145	1.5	576	6.2	246	156	402	61.3	30.0
1987	13.0	286	141	2.0	655	2.8	393	103	496	79.2	23.2
1986	46.5	389	266	1.5	741	1.7	398	65	463	85.9	15.1
1985	94.6	176	50	3.5	269	2.4	167	50	217	77.0	12.9
1984	2.7	89	89	1.0	187	1.1	57	36	93	60.7	4.6
1983	0.7	NA	NA	NA	54	NM	[8]32	18	52	60.7	NM

Data as orig. reptd. **1.** Incl. other inc. prior to 1991. **2.** Reflects merger or acquisition. **3.** Excl. disc. opers. **4.** Excl. disc. opers. and reflects merger or acquisition. **5.** Net of interest inc. **6.** Incl. equity in earns. of nonconsol. subs. 1989-1984. **7.** Bef. results of disc. opers. in 1989, 1988, 1987, and spec. item(s) in 1988, 1987, 1986, 1985, 1984. **8.** Incl. current portion of lt. debt. d-Deficit. NM-Not Meaningful. NA-Not Available.

Business Summary

Segment contributions (profits in million $) in 1992:

	Sales	Profits
Tools	48%	$33.7
Transportation	30%	15.7
Process/environmental controls	22%	32.2

Danaher Tools manufactures a broad range of hand tools, tool holders, fasteners and components for consumer, industrial and professional markets. The group consists of Iseli, Jacobs Chuck, Matco Tools, Professional Tools and Special Markets. Products are sold under the Sears Craftsman, NAPA, Allen, Jacobs, Matco, K-D and Holo-Krome names. The company is the sole supplier of Sears, Roebuck's Craftsman mechanics' hand tools, which accounted for sales of $170 million in 1992, versus $120 million in 1991. Matco professional mechanics' tools are distributed by about 1,100 independent mobile distributors. Proprietary brands include Allen wrenches and Jacobs drill chucks.

Transportation includes Fayette Tubular (which makes original equipment automobile air conditioning components), Hennessy Industries (Coats and Ammco tire changers, wheel aligners and balancers, brake lathes and lifts) and Jacobs Brake (Jake Brake diesel engine retarders).

Process/Environmental Controls includes Danaher Controls, Veeder-Root, Partlow/Anderson, Qualitrol and A.L. Hyde. Storage tank leak detection systems, temperature, level and position sensing devices, liquid flow measuring devices and electronic and mechanical counters and controllers are produced.

Dividend Data

Dividends were resumed in March 1993 after omission since 1974.

Amt of Divd. $	Date Decl.	Ex-divd. Date	Stock of Record	Payment Date
0.03	Mar. 15	Mar. 22	Mar. 26	Apr. 16'93
0.03	Jun. 3	Jun. 21	Jun. 25	Jul. 16'93

Capitalization

Long Term Debt: $169,000,000 (4/2/93).

Common Stock: 28,421,305 shs. ($0.01 par). Mitchell & Steven Rales own about 44%. Institutions hold some 39%. Shareholders of record: 4,600.

Office—1250 24th St., N.W., Washington, DC 20037. **Tel**—(202) 828-0850. **Chrmn**—S. M. Rales. **Pres & CEO**—G. M. Sherman. **VP-CFO & Secy**—P. W. Allender. **VP-Contr & Investor Contact**—C. Scott Brannan. **Dirs**—M. M. Caplin, D. J. Ehrlich, W. G. Lohr Jr., M. P. Rales, S. M. Rales, G. M. Sherman, A. E. Stephenson Jr. **Transfer Agent**—Mellon Securities Trust Co., Pittsburgh, Pa. **Organized** in Massachusetts in 1969; reincorporated in Delaware in 1986. **Empl**—7,296.

 Joshua M. Harari, CFA

Datascope

NASDAQ Symbol DSCP (Incl. in Nat'l Market) Options on ASE, Pacific, Phila In S&P MidCap 400

Price	Range	P-E Ratio	Dividend	Yield	S&P Ranking	Beta
Aug. 4'93	1993					
13¾	26½–11¾	14	None	None	B	1.18

Summary

This company makes products for the clinical healthcare markets in anesthesiology, emergency medicine, invasive cardiology and cardiovascular surgery. The company's angioplasty division was recently sold for a net gain of $2.3 million.

Business Summary

Datascope Corp. is a manufacturer of proprietary products for the clinical health care markets in interventional cardiology, anesthesiology and cardiovascular and vascular surgery.

In the area of cardiac assist products (47% of fiscal 1992 sales), the company is a pioneer in intra-aortic balloon pumping (IABP) technology. Its primary product is an IABP system used in the treatment of cardiac shock, heart failure, cardiac arrhythmia, and in cardiac surgery and coronary angioplasty. As part of its IABP system, Datascope provides a line of disposable intra-aortic balloon (IAB) catheters. During the first quarter of fiscal 1993, the company began shipping the System 95 balloon pump, an advanced pump that replaces an earlier product, System 90. Datascope also makes and sells the System 90T, a lighter, transportable balloon pump.

Datascope makes and markets a broad line of multifunction patient safety monitor products (43%), which are capable of continuous and simultaneous measurement of multiple parameters in various hospital settings. In fiscal 1992, the company introduced the VISA, a central station monitor that can be connected to up to eight PASSPORT transportable monitors. The PASSPORT units, which measure EKG, blood pressure, temperature and respiration, and pulse oximetry, were also introduced in fiscal 1992. The top of the line operating room monitor is the 3000A, a product that measures invasive and non-invasive blood pressure, blood oxygen saturation, heart rate, EKG and temperature. Other monitors include FLEXISENSOR and SENSOR GUARD, which offer a low cost, disposable sensor system for pulse oximetry; MULTINEX, an advanced integrated respiratory gas monitor that combines the measurement of blood gas with pulse oximetry; and ACCUTORR, offering non-invasive measurement of blood pressure and heart rate measurement.

In October 1992, the FDA granted the company marketing approval for its PASSPORT/CO_2 monitor, which can monitor carbon dioxide. In July

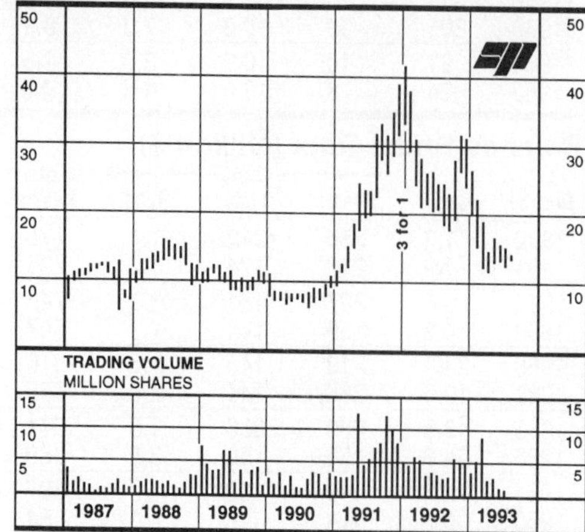

1993, Datascope introduced the PASSPORT D (fib), believed to be the lightest and most compact multi-parameter monitor/defibrilator combination available.

The InterVascular subsidiary makes a proprietary line of knitted, woven dacron vascular grafts and patches for reconstructive vascular and cardiovascular surgery. Another subsidiary, Bioplex, makes a collagen hemostat pad sold in the U.S. for use in surgical applications other than neurological, urological and opthalmological.

Important Developments

Jun. '93— Datascope said it had sold its angioplasty division to Boston Scientific Corp. It received an initial payment that resulted in a net gain of $2.3 million ($0.14 a share). Additional payments are contingent upon certain events, including FDA approval for Boston Scientific to market certain products. Operations of the angioplasty division were suspended in July 1992.

Next earnings report expected in late October.

Per Share Data ($)

Yr. End Jun. 30	1993	1992	1991	1990	1989	1988	1987	1986	1985	1984
Tangible Bk. Val.	**NA**	[1]7.01	[1]6.46	[1]5.99	[1]5.36	[1]4.01	3.31	2.24	1.96	1.81
Cash Flow	**NA**	0.76	0.82	0.98	0.95	0.97	0.65	0.48	0.31	0.25
Earnings[2,3]	**0.97**	0.47	0.55	0.60	0.69	0.73	0.45	0.26	0.14	0.12
Dividends	**Nil**	Nil	Nil	Nil	Nil	Nil	Nil	Nil	Nil	Nil
Payout Ratio	**NA**	Nil	Nil	Nil	Nil	Nil	Nil	Nil	Nil	Nil
Prices[4]—High	**26½**	41¾	39⅛	11³⁄₁₆	12⁷⁄₁₆	16¹⁄₁₆	12¹³⁄₁₆	8⁵⁄₁₆	6¹¹⁄₁₆	3¹⁵⁄₁₆
Low	**11¾**	17¾	9½	6¼	8½	9⁷⁄₁₆	5¹¹⁄₁₆	5¹¹⁄₁₆	2¹¹⁄₁₆	2⁷⁄₁₆
P/E Ratio—	**27–12**	89–38	71–17	19–10	18–12	22–13	29–13	32–22	48–20	34–21

Data as orig. reptd. Adj. for stk. divs. of 200% Jan. 1992, 50% Sept. 1986. **1.** Incl. intangibles. **2.** Bef. spec. items of +0.01 in 1985, +0.06 in 1984. **3.** Ful. dil.: 0.67 in 1989, 0.68 in 1988, 0.42 in 1987. **4.** Cal. yr. NA-Not Available.

Income Data (Million $)

Year Ended Jun. 30	Revs.	Oper. Inc.	% Oper. Inc. of Revs.	Cap. Exp.	Depr.	Int. Exp.	Net Bef. Taxes	Eff. Tax Rate	[3]Net Inc.	% Net Inc. of Revs.	Cash Flow
1992	**157**	**20.9**	**13.4**	**[1]5.34**	**4.77**	**0.18**	**10.6**	**27.6%**	**7.7**	**4.9**	**12.5**
1991	135	13.6	10.1	[1]4.22	4.28	0.18	12.5	31.0%	8.6	6.4	12.9
1990	120	12.4	10.3	[1]9.35	5.87	0.23	14.1	34.2%	9.3	7.7	15.2
1989	113	18.8	16.7	[1]8.49	3.83	0.06	16.0	34.5%	10.5	9.3	14.3
1988	105	18.7	17.8	[1]3.94	3.30	[2]0.06	15.6	38.0%	9.7	9.2	13.0
1987	88	12.9	14.8	[1]5.30	2.47	[2]0.71	10.1	46.0%	5.5	6.2	7.9
1986	67	8.3	12.4	[1]4.67	2.51	[2]0.95	5.0	39.5%	3.0	4.5	5.5
1985	51	4.5	9.0	4.19	1.86	[2]0.42	2.3	32.8%	1.5	3.0	3.4
1984	42	3.6	8.6	2.95	1.48	[2]0.19	2.0	35.9%	[4]1.3	3.0	2.7
1983	38	4.9	12.9	2.50	1.29	[2]0.24	3.4	37.7%	2.1	5.5	3.4

Balance Sheet Data (Million $)

Jun. 30	Cash	Curr. Assets	Curr. Liab.	Curr. Ratio	Total Assets	% Ret. on Assets	Long Term Debt	Common Equity	Total Cap.	% LT Debt of Cap.	% Ret. on Equity
1992	**32.1**	**110**	**25.5**	**4.3**	**141**	**5.7**	**Nil**	**110**	**110**	**Nil**	**7.3**
1991	28.7	98	23.9	4.1	128	6.8	Nil	100	100	Nil	8.9
1990	19.3	92	27.0	3.4	124	8.2	0.1	92	93	0.1	10.7
1989	13.1	79	17.7	4.5	104	9.7	0.4	82	83	0.5	14.6
1988	22.2	76	19.6	3.9	96	10.7	19.7	52	73	26.9	20.2
1987	20.7	66	18.2	3.6	83	7.3	19.6	42	63	31.1	15.5
1986	2.8	43	18.1	2.4	56	5.8	11.5	25	38	30.7	13.2
1985	5.3	37	13.0	2.8	48	3.4	12.0	21	34	34.8	7.5
1984	8.8	34	9.2	3.7	43	3.0	12.9	20	33	38.8	6.8
1983	13.7	36	8.4	4.2	42	6.5	16.0	18	34	47.3	12.7

Data as orig. reptd. **1.** Net. **2.** Net of int. inc. **3.** Bef. spec. items. **4.** Refl. acctg. change.

Sales (Million $)

Quarter:	1992–93	1991–92	1990–91	1989–90
Sep.	36.0	31.5	27.6	25.2
Dec.	42.7	38.8	33.1	27.3
Mar.	41.9	41.1	35.6	32.0
Jun.	45.4	45.1	39.2	35.7
	166.0	156.5	135.5	120.2

Based on a preliminary report, net sales in the fiscal year ended June 30, 1993 rose 6.1% from those of the preceding year. With a net gain of $2.3 million from the sale of the angioplasty division, and in the absence of charges of $4.1 million related to the suspension of operations of the angioplasty division and the termination of a distributor in Japan, net income surged 105%, to $15,740,000 ($0.83 a share), from $7,685,000 ($0.72, as adjusted).

Common Share Earnings ($)

Quarter:	1992–93	1991–92	1990–91	1989–90
Sep.	0.13	0.09	0.03	0.06
Dec.	0.21	0.16	0.12	0.10
Mar.	0.20	0.21	0.15	0.32
Jun.	0.43	0.01	0.23	0.12
	0.97	0.47	0.55	0.60

Dividend Data

No cash has been paid. A three-for-one stock split was effected in January 1992.

Finances

In the fourth quarter of fiscal 1992, the company recorded net charges of $4.1 million ($0.25 a share), including $2.4 million ($0.15) related to the suspension of the angioplasty division and $1.7 million ($0.10) related to the termination of a distributor in Japan.

During fiscal 1992 and 1991, Datascope's R&D spending totaled $14,176,000 (10.5% of sales) and $11,749,000 (9.7%), respectively.

Foreign sales represented 30% and 25% of total sales in fiscal 1992 and 1991, respectively.

Capitalization

Long Term Debt: None (3/93).

Common Stock: 16,031,529 shs. ($0.01 par);
L. Saper owns 16%.
Institutions hold 47%.
Shareholders: about 920 of record (8/92).

Office—14 Philips Pkwy., Montvale, NJ 07645. **Tel**—(201) 391-8100. **Chrmn & CEO**—L. Saper. **VP-Fin & Treas**—R. L. Smernoff. **SVP & Secy**—G. Heller. **Dirs**—D. Altschiller, W. L. Asmundson, J. Grayzel, G. Heller, A. J. Patricof, L. Saper, N. M. Schneider. **Transfer Agent**—Continental Stock Transfer & Trust Co., NYC. **Incorporated** in New York in 1964. **Empl**—1,100.

 Robert M. Gold

Dauphin Deposit Corp.

NASDAQ Symbol DAPN (Incl. in Nat'l Market) In S&P MidCap 400

Price	Range	P–E Ratio	Dividend	Yield	S&P Ranking	Beta
Sep. 17'93	1993					
24½	28–22½	12	0.80	3.3%	A	0.66

Summary

Headquartered in Harrisburg, this holding company owns Dauphin Deposit Bank & Trust Co., which includes the Bank of Pennsylvania Division, and Farmers Bank and Trust Company of Hanover. The banks operate 99 branch offices in Pennsylvania. Share earnings have risen steadily for 21 consecutive years. In late 1992, a two-for-one stock split was effected and the cash dividend was raised 5.3%.

Business Summary

Dauphin Deposit Corporation is a bank holding company headquartered in Harrisburg, Pa. Its principal subsidiary is Dauphin Deposit Bank & Trust Co. The bank, which includes the Bank of Pennsylvania Division, and Farmers Bank and Trust Company of Hanover operate 99 offices in the counties of Berks, Chester, Cumberland, Dauphin, Lancaster, Lebanon, Lehigh, Montgomery, Northampton and York. Nonbank subsidiaries include Dauphin Life Insurance Co., Dauphin Investment Co., Financial Realty, Inc. and Hopper Soliday & Co. (acquired in 1991), the largest underwriter of general obligation municipal bonds in Pennsylvania.

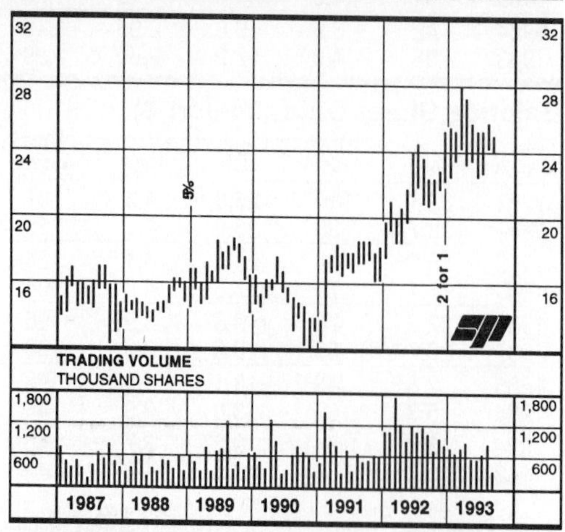

Loans outstanding (net of unearned income) amounted to $2.20 billion at 1992 year-end and were divided:

Commercial, financial & agricultural..	47%
Real estate–residential	31%
Real estate–construction...............	6%
Consumer..................................	15%
Lease financing...........................	1%

The allowance for loan losses totaled $33,624,000 at the end of 1992 (compared with $29,920,000 a year earlier) and was equal to 1.53% (1.36%) of loans at year-end. Net chargeoffs were $7,240,000 in 1992 ($7,840,000 in 1991), or 0.33% (0.37%) of average loans. As of December 31, 1992, nonperforming loans aggregated $24,154,000 (1.10% of outstanding loans), compared with $16,881,000 (0.77%) a year earlier.

Deposits amounted to $3.40 billion at the end of 1992 and were apportioned: 12% noninterest-bearing demand, 15% NOW accounts, 11% savings, 17% money-market accounts, 36% time and 9% time deposits of $100,000 or more.

Interest and fees on loans contributed 49% of total income for 1992, interest and dividends on investment securities 35%, other interest income 1%, income from fiduciary activities 4%, service charges on deposit accounts 3% and other noninterest income 8%.

On a tax-equivalent basis, the average yield on total interest-earning assets was 8.22% in 1992 (9.52% in 1991), while the average rate paid on interest-bearing liabilities was 4.72% (6.22%), for an interest rate spread of 3.50% (3.30%).

Important Developments

Jun. '93— The company signed a definitive agreement to acquire Valley Bancorp., Inc. (assets of $327 million), and its Valley Bank & Trust Co. subsidiary (Chambersburg, Pa.), in a stock transaction valued at $68.8 million.

Next earnings report expected in mid-October.

Per Share Data ($)

Yr. End Dec. 31	[1]1992	1991	1990	1989	[1,2]1988	[1]1987	1986	1985	1984	[1]1983
Tangible Bk. Val.	**14.47**	13.40	12.25	11.39	10.37	9.30	8.68	7.71	6.51	6.96
Earnings	**1.93**	1.84	1.78	1.71	1.57	1.49	1.38	1.22	1.06	0.98
Dividends	**0.770**	0.745	0.718	0.688	0.619	0.582	0.529	0.479	0.438	0.400
Payout Ratio	**40%**	41%	40%	40%	39%	39%	38%	39%	41%	41%
Prices—High	**25¼**	18⅝	17⅝	18¾	16⁵⁄₁₆	17	18¹¹⁄₁₆	13⁹⁄₁₆	7⅞	8⁹⁄₁₆
Low	**17⅝**	12½	12	14³⁄₁₆	13⁹⁄₁₆	12¼	13⁷⁄₁₆	7⅞	6	5¹¹⁄₁₆
P/E Ratio—	**13–9**	10–7	10–7	11–8	10–9	11–8	14–10	11–6	7–6	9–6

Data as orig. reptd. Adj. for stk. divs. of 100% Dec. 1992, 5% Jan. 1989, 100% Aug. 1985, 100% May 1983. **1.** Refl. merger or acq. **2.** Refl. acctg. change.

Income Data (Million $)

Year Ended Dec. 31	Net Int. Inc.	Tax Equiv. Adj.	Non Int. Inc.	Loan Loss Prov.	% Exp./ Op. Revs.	Net Bef. Taxes	Eff. Tax Rate	Net Inc.	% Net Int. Margin	—% Return On— Assets	Equity
[1]**1992**	**153**	**14.2**	**50.0**	**10.90**	**56.1**	**74.4**	**23.1%**	**57.2**	**4.11**	**1.31**	**14.1**
1991	118	12.9	37.8	7.90	55.5	57.0	19.8%	45.7	4.01	1.30	14.4
1990	110	11.4	34.5	6.45	52.9	57.8	21.5%	45.4	3.98	1.37	15.2
1989	109	8.6	31.7	6.18	51.3	60.1	26.1%	44.4	3.96	1.39	15.9
[1,2]1988	105	8.0	25.2	6.79	51.2	54.9	26.0%	40.7	3.92	1.31	16.0
[1]1987	96	10.1	20.0	4.29	51.5	49.3	29.4%	34.9	4.08	1.24	16.1
1986	84	14.5	16.4	4.75	50.0	40.1	26.7%	29.4	4.17	1.15	15.7
1985	75	12.5	14.3	3.70	53.0	32.8	25.7%	24.3	3.99	1.02	15.4
1984	61	14.7	12.9	2.40	55.5	23.7	13.0%	20.6	3.67	0.93	14.7
[1]1983	44	15.3	8.5	1.32	54.2	15.6	NM	16.7	3.77	0.99	14.9

Balance Sheet Data (Million $)

Dec. 31	Total Assets	—Earning Assets— Mon. Mkt. Assets	Inv. Secs.	Com'l Loans	Other Loans	% Loan Loss Resv.	—Deposits— Demand	Time	% Loans/ Deposits	Long Term Debt	Common Equity	% Equity To Assets
1992	**4,573**	**92**	**1,961**	**1,027**	**1,168**	**153.00**	**420**	**2,981**	**64.5**	**92.9**	**431**	**9.34**
1991	3,612	23	1,506	899	917	1.22	354	2,469	64.2	36.1	334	9.00
1990	3,489	80	1,363	865	893	1.21	329	2,401	64.3	40.3	304	9.00
1989	3,259	186	1,129	792	883	1.20	331	2,283	63.9	47.3	296	8.70
1988	3,336	207	1,270	772	826	1.11	356	2,189	62.5	47.9	269	8.20
1987	2,905	168	1,034	700	781	1.13	352	1,987	63.3	48.5	229	7.80
1986	2,654	149	939	626	705	1.15	322	1,840	61.6	48.8	197	7.30
1985	2,598	308	911	576	601	1.15	280	1,820	56.1	20.4	179	6.70
1984	2,285	232	845	353	707	1.18	257	1,686	52.2	20.9	147	6.30
1983	2,260	351	761	345	664	1.16	239	1,613	52.1	21.3	135	6.70

Data as orig. reptd. **1.** Refl. merger or acq. **2.** Refl. acctg. change. NM-Not Meaningful.

Review of Operations

Total interest income for the six months ended June 30, 1993, declined 8.1%, year to year. Total interest expense was down 20%, and net interest income rose 5.8%. The provision for loan losses increased 9.2%, and with 4.8% higher noninterest income and 1.2% lower noninterest expense, pretax income expanded 16%. After taxes at 24.2%, versus 23.7%, net income was also up 16%, to $33,174,000 ($1.11 a share, based on 2.0% more shares), from $28,706,000 ($0.98, as adjusted).

Common Share Earnings ($)

Quarter:	1993	1992	1991	1990
Mar.	0.56	0.49	0.45	0.42
Jun.	0.55	0.49	0.45	0.42
Sep.		0.47	0.45	0.48
Dec.		0.48	0.49	0.47
		1.93	1.84	1.78

Finances

In July 1992, the company acquired FB&T Corp. (Hanover, Pa.) for 3,953,182 shares of its common stock and $35,000 in cash. The purchase added $677 million in assets and 17 banking offices, extending Dauphin's presence in central Pennsylvania.

During 1992's first quarter, Dauphin issued 700,000 (adjusted) shares of its previously acquired treasury stock in a public offering. The net proceeds from the issuance amounted to $12.6 million and were earmarked for general corporate purposes.

Dividend Data

Cash has been paid each year by the company or its predecessor banks since 1910. A dividend reinvestment plan is available.

Amt. of Divd. $	Date Decl.	Ex-divd. Date	Stock of Record	Payment Date
2-for-1	Oct. 26	Dec. 7	Nov. 20	Dec. 4'92
0.20	Oct. 26	Dec. 18	Dec. 24	Jan. 15'93
0.20	Jan. 25	Mar. 22	Mar. 26	Apr. 16'93
0.20	Apr. 26	Jul. 2	Jul. 9	Jul. 16'93
0.20	Jul. 26	Sep. 20	Sep. 24	Oct. 15'93

Capitalization

Long Term Debt: $92,541,000 (6/93).

Common Stock: 29,891,793 shs. ($5 par). Institutions hold about 25%. Shareholders: 9,712 of record (12/92).

Office—213 Market St., Harrisburg, PA 17105. **Tel**—(717) 255-2121. **Chrmn & CEO**—W. J. King. **Pres & COO**—C. R. Jennings. **Exec VP & CFO**—D. L. Dinger. **Sr VP & Treas**—J. T. Lysczek Jr. **Sr VP & Secy**—Claire D. Flemming. **Dirs**—W. H. Alexander, J. A. Arnold, J. J. Burdge, J. O. Green, A. G. Hemmerich, L. H. Javitch, C. R. Jennings, W. J. King, W. T. Kirchoff, L. J. LaMaina Jr., J. E. Marley, F. E. Masland III, R. F. Nation, E. E. Naugle, W. F. Raab, P. C. Raub, H. W. Rhoads, R. C. Sheridan Jr. **Transfer Agent**—Dauphin Deposit Bank & Trust Co., Harrisburg. **Formed** in Pennsylvania in 1974. **Empl**—1,894.

 Stephen R. Biggar

Dean Foods

NYSE Symbol DF Options on Pacific (Feb-May-Aug-Nov) In S&P MidCap 400

Price	Range	P-E Ratio	Dividend	Yield	S&P Ranking	Beta
Sep. 27'93	1993					
26⅞	29¼–23⅛	17	0.64	2.4%	A	0.66

Summary

This company is a major producer of dairy goods, and also processes canned and frozen vegetables and other food items. Acquisitions have made a significant contribution to growth in recent years. Earnings are expected to make modest progress as 1993-94 progresses, primarily reflecting a projected improvement in vegetable product profits, helped by reduced industrywide supplies.

Current Outlook

Share earnings for the fiscal year ending May 31, 1994 are projected at $1.75, up from 1992-93's $1.73.

The quarterly dividend was raised 6.7%, to $0.16 with the September 1993 payment.

Sales should rise modestly in 1993-94, principally reflecting moderate volume growth and contributions from acquisitions. Adequate raw milk supplies should help dairy profits, and a projected reduction in industrywide supply of vegetable products should ease recent pressures on vegetable product selling prices. Continued acquisitions should enhance future earnings prospects.

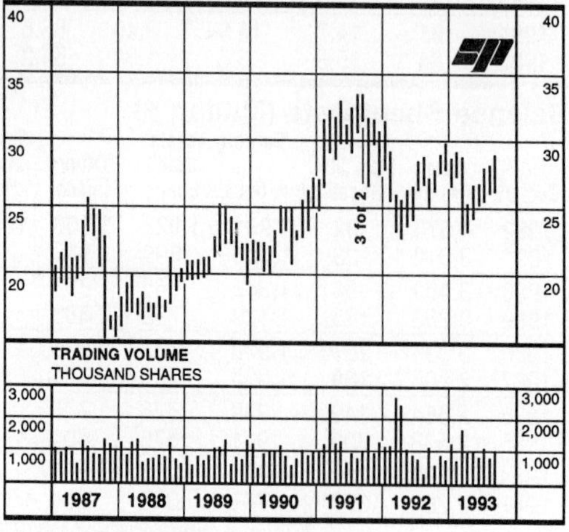

Net Sales (Million $)

Quarter:	1993–94	1992–93	1991–92	1990–91
Aug.	560	543	531	518
Nov.	---	572	551	555
Feb.	---	567	566	521
May	---	592	641	564
	---	2,274	2,289	2,158

Sales for the three months ended August 29, 1993 rose 3.0%, year to year. Margins narrowed, and despite a 6.1% reduction in interest expense, pretax profits fell 25%. After taxes at 45.9%, versus 40.7%, net income was down 31%, to $0.27 a share (before a $0.03 a share credit from accounting changes) from $0.39.

Common Share Earnings ($)

Quarter:	1993–94	1992–93	1991–92	1990–91
Aug.	0.27	0.39	0.42	0.39
Nov.	E0.43	0.43	0.39	0.41
Feb.	E0.48	0.41	0.33	0.41
May	E0.57	0.50	0.39	0.58
	E1.75	1.73	1.53	1.79

Important Developments

Sep. '93— DF attributed lower earnings in fiscal 1993-94's first quarter principally to higher costs in its vegetable and pickle businesses, which reflected weather related crop shortages and harvesting delays in the company's Midwest growing region. Dairy margins declined in the quarter, as volatility in raw milk costs reflected the weather related instability of milk supplies early in the quarter. Management added that there is fundamental improvement in the outlook for DF's vegetable business, as industry-wide inventory levels are better balanced as a result of the reduced crop processed in 1993. Separately, first quarter results include a $1.5 million charge ($0.04 per share) to reflect recently enacted budget legislation which taxes earnings at a higher rate, retroactive to January 1, 1993.

Next earnings report expected in mid-December.

Per Share Data ($)

Yr. End May 31[1]	1993	1992	[2]1991	[2]1990	1989	1988	1987	1986	1985	1984
Tangible Bk. Val.	**11.11**	10.00	9.36	8.15	7.26	6.41	5.60	4.90	4.65	3.90
Cash Flow	**3.03**	2.72	2.88	2.41	2.30	1.79	1.66	1.59	1.59	1.36
Earnings	**1.73**	1.53	1.79	1.53	1.52	1.07	1.03	1.02	1.03	0.86
Dividends	**0.600**	0.560	0.493	0.440	0.400	0.360	0.320	0.263	0.240	0.205
Payout Ratio	**35%**	36%	28%	29%	26%	34%	31%	26%	23%	24%
Calendar Years	**1992**	1991	1990	1989	1988	1987	1986	1985	1984	1983
Prices—High	**31½**	33½	27¼	25¼	21¼	25¹¹⁄₁₆	22⁷⁄₁₆	19¹⁵⁄₁₆	13	11¹³⁄₁₆
Low	**22¾**	24⅞	20⅛	19¼	16	15³⁄₁₆	16¾	11	8⁹⁄₁₆	7
P/E Ratio—	**18–13**	22–16	15–11	17–13	14–11	24–14	22–16	19–11	15–10	16–10

Data as orig. reptd. Adj. for stk. divs. of 50% Sep. 1991, 50% Jun. 1986, 50% Apr. 1984, 50% May 1983. **1.** Yrs. ended Dec. 31 prior to 1986. **2.** Reflects merger or acquisition. E-Estimated NA-Not Available.

Income Data (Million $)

Year Ended May 31[1]	Revs.	Oper. Inc.	% Oper. Inc. of Revs.	Cap. Exp.	Depr.	Int. Exp.	Net Bef. Taxes	Eff. Tax Rate	Net Inc.	% Net Inc. of Revs.	Cash Flow
1993	**2,274**	**178**	**7.8**	**75**	**51.8**	**14.9**	**115**	**40.4%**	**68.4**	**3.0**	**120**
1992	2,289	175	7.6	78	48.3	15.6	106	41.2%	62.0	2.7	110
[2]1991	2,158	180	8.4	94	44.5	16.8	124	41.7%	72.5	3.4	117
[2]1990	1,988	147	7.4	122	35.6	12.7	102	40.0%	61.2	3.1	97
1989	1,684	127	7.6	78	31.0	7.6	102	40.6%	60.4	3.6	91
1988	1,552	121	7.8	48	29.0	6.1	77	44.1%	42.8	2.8	72
1987	1,435	111	7.8	54	25.6	5.8	83	50.4%	41.1	2.9	67
1986	1,269	104	8.2	45	22.3	6.5	78	47.6%	40.7	3.2	49
1985	1,034	77	7.4	33	17.4	4.7	59	45.9%	31.8	3.1	49
1984	923	66	7.1	19	15.5	4.7	49	46.4%	26.5	2.9	42

Balance Sheet Data (Million $)

May 31[1]	Cash	Curr. Assets	Curr. Liab.	Curr. Ratio	Total Assets	% Ret. on Assets	Long Term Debt	Common Equity	Total Cap.	% LT Debt of Cap.	% Ret. on Equity
1993	**41.6**	**406**	**208**	**2.0**	**893**	**7.8**	**151**	**476**	**674**	**22.4**	**15.1**
1992	34.0	397	213	1.9	857	7.5	155	430	627	24.8	14.8
1991	44.1	399	201	2.0	817	9.3	150	417	599	25.0	18.6
1990	43.5	372	190	2.0	745	9.1	147	363	539	27.2	18.4
1989	70.0	320	164	2.0	587	11.2	84	293	404	20.8	21.8
1988	53.8	270	140	1.9	499	9.0	49	266	336	14.6	17.0
1987	51.1	239	124	1.9	450	9.5	47	236	299	15.7	18.8
1986	21.0	221	114	1.9	408	10.5	49	207	269	18.2	21.3
1985	37.5	177	99	1.8	322	10.6	37	155	200	18.7	22.4
1984	33.3	157	91	1.7	280	10.0	36	129	171	20.8	22.2

Data as orig. reptd. **1.** Yrs. ended Dec. 31 prior to 1986. **2.** Reflects merger or acquisition.

Business Summary

Dean Foods produces and distributes dairy and specialty food products. Contributions to sales and profits (in million $) by business segment in 1992-93 were:

	Sales	Profits
Dairy products	63%	$82.6
Specialty foods	35%	57.2
Other corporate	2%	–25.0

Fluid milk and specialty dairy products account for approximately 86% of total Dairy products group sales. Products include homogenized, lowfat and skimmed milk, regular and low fat cottage cheese, yogurt, half and half, buttermilk, chocolate milk, sour cream and egg nog. Ice cream products, which include ice milk, fruit sherberts, frozen dessert novelties, yogurt, and a non-fat frozen dairy dessert, account for the remainder of Dairy product sales. The Baskin Robbins franchise was sold in mid-1989, but the company continues to supply product to the franchise.

Specialty foods include canned and frozen vegetables (15% of sales), pickles, relishes and salad dressings (13%), which are sold in the Midwest, South and Southwest. Other categories include puddings, dips, and sauces (3%), and powdered products (4%), mainly non-dairy coffee creamers.

Corporate and other sales reflect DF's transportation subsidiary, and sales of canned meats processed under bid contracts with the federal government.

Dividend Data

Dividends have been paid since 1941. A dividend reinvestment plan is available. A "poison pill" stock purchase right was adopted in 1988 and amended in 1989.

Amt. of Divd. $	Date Decl.	Ex–divd. Date	Stock of Record	Payment Date
0.15	Dec. 4	Dec. 14	Dec. 18	Jan. 5'93
0.15	Jan. 25	Feb. 12	Feb. 19	Mar. 15'93
0.15	Mar. 29	May 17	May 21	Jun. 15'93
0.16	Jul. 23	Aug. 16	Aug. 20	Sep. 14'93

Capitalization

Long Term Obligations: $150,541,000 (8/93).

Common Stock: 39,688,829 shs. ($1 par).
Institutions hold 37%.
Shareholders of record: 8,654.

Office—3600 North River Rd., Franklin Park, IL 60131. **Tel**—(312) 625-6200. **Chrmn & CEO**—H. M. Dean. **Pres**—W. D. Fischer. **VP-Secy**—E. A. Blanchard. **VP-Fin & Investor Contact**—Timothy J. Bondy. **Dirs**—L. M. Collens, P. H. Crown, H. M. Dean, W. D. Fischer, J. P. Frazee, B. A. Getz, A. J. McKenna, T. A. Ravencroft, T. L. Rose, D. C. Staley, A. J. Vogl. **Transfer Agent & Registrar**—Harris Trust & Savings Bank, Chicago. **Incorporated** in Ill. in 1929; reincorporated in Del. in 1968. **Empl**—10,500.

 Kenneth A. Shea

Dell Computer

NASDAQ Symbol DELL (Incl. in Nat'l Market) Options on Phila In S&P MidCap 400

Price	Range	P–E Ratio	Dividend	Yield	S&P Ranking	Beta
Aug. 23'93	1993					
18¾	49⅞–13⅞	NM	None	None	NR	1.69

Summary

This company makes and direct markets high-performance personal computers compatible with industry standards established by IBM. Sales have been in an uptrend, and another record is anticipated for 1993-94. However, a loss is expected for the year, reflecting restructuring charges of $91 million taken in the first half, a shift in the business model, and continued competitive pressures.

Current Outlook

A loss of $1.45 a share, including unusual charges, is expected for the year ending January 31, 1994, versus earnings of $2.59 in 1992-93. Earnings of $1.85 are projected for 1994-95.

Initiation of cash dividends is not expected.

Earnings in the 1993-94 first half were significantly below expectations, reflecting charges related to restructuring provisions, inventory writedowns due to systems and process issues, and costs associated with delayed and canceled notebook projects. The company is no longer selling notebook computers and does not expect to do so until early 1994-95. Partly because it has had difficulty coping with recent rapid growth, Dell said it would now deemphasize growth in favor of liquidity and profitability by being less aggressive with pricing. However, the company is no longer a price leader — Gateway 2000, Compaq and Ambra are. We expect Dell will have a turbulent second half and be unprofitable until the fourth quarter.

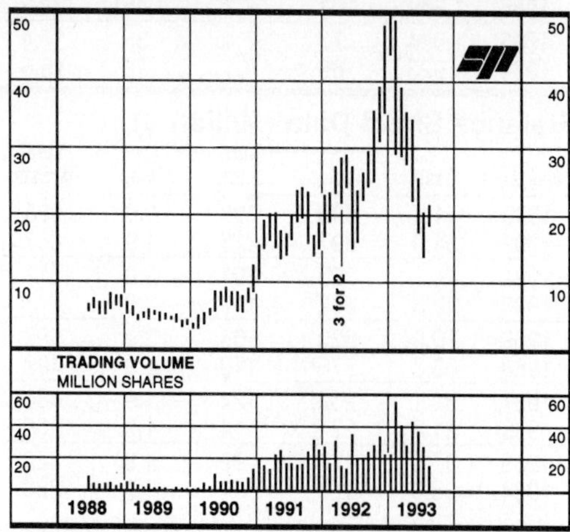

Net Sales (Million $)

13 Weeks:	1993–94	1992–93	1991–92	1990–91
Apr.	672	366	175	120
Jul.	701	458	200	122
Oct.	E741	570	229	137
Jan.	E837	620	286	167
	E2,951	2,014	890	546

Net sales in the 26 weeks ended August 1, 1993, surged 67%, year to year, spurred by strong domestic and international demand for desktop PCs. Results were penalized by price reductions and by $91 million of charges related to restructuring provisions, inventory writedowns, and costs associated with delayed and canceled notebook projects. With net financing and other expense replacing income, a pretax loss replaced income. After a tax credit of $20.5 million, versus taxes at 29.1%, a net loss of $65.5 million ($1.76 a share) contrasted with net income of $41.7 million ($1.09).

Common Share Earnings ($)

13 Weeks:	1993–94	1992–93	1991–92	1990–91
Apr.	0.25	0.52	0.31	0.19
Jul.	d2.03	0.57	0.33	0.21
Oct.	Ed0.05	0.72	0.35	0.23
Jan.	E0.38	0.77	0.41	0.28
	Ed1.45	2.59	1.41	0.91

Important Developments

Aug.'93— Dell announced a new marketing strategy that segments customers according to their technical needs, and introduced three new product lines: the Dell NetPlex, the Dell OptiPlex and the Dell Dimension XPS. Each line addresses specific needs within the segmentation strategy.

Next earnings report expected in mid-November.

Per Share Data ($)

Yr. End Jan. 31	1993	1992	1991	1990	1989	1988	1987	1986
Tangible Bk. Val.	**10.02**	7.66	3.86	2.83	2.69	0.57	0.17	0.05
Cash Flow	**3.09**	1.78	1.17	0.37	0.61	0.53	NA	NA
Earnings	**2.59**	1.40	0.91	0.18	0.53	0.48	0.13	0.05
Dividends	**Nil**	Nil	Nil	Nil	Nil	Nil	Nil	Nil
Payout Ratio	**Nil**	Nil	Nil	Nil	Nil	Nil	Nil	Nil
Calendar Years	**1992**	1991	1990	1989	1988	1987	1986	1985
Prices—High	**48**	24⅛	12⅝	7⅛	8⅜	NA	NA	NA
Low	**15**	10½	3⅛	3 ⅜	5⅛	NA	NA	NA
P/E Ratio—	**19–6**	17–8	14–3	39–19	16–10	NA	NA	NA

Data as orig. reptd. Adj. for stk. divs. of 50% Apr. 1992, 15% May 1987. d-Deficit. E-Estimated NA-Not Available. NM-Not Meaningful.

Income Data (Million $)

Year Ended Jan. 31	Revs.	Oper. Inc.	% Oper. Inc. of Revs.	Cap. Exp.	Depr.	Int. Exp.	Net Bef. Taxes	Eff. Tax Rate	Net Inc.	% Net Inc. of Revs.	Cash Flow
1993	**2,014**	**159**	**7.9**	**47.3**	**19.6**	**7.87**	**143**	**29.1%**	**102**	**5.0**	**121**
1992	890	83	9.3	32.6	13.8	1.78	73	30.7%	51	5.7	65
1991	546	53	9.8	9.5	7.9	1.53	44	37.5%	27	5.0	35
1990	389	18	4.7	13.6	5.4	3.36	8	38.2%	5	1.3	11
1989	258	25	9.7	6.6	2.1	1.29	21	31.8%	14	5.6	17
1988	159	18	11.4	2.2	1.0	0.87	15	38.0%	9	5.9	10
1987	69	5	6.4	0.6	0.3	0.27	4	44.1%	2	3.1	NA
1986	34	1	4.1	0.5	0.1	0.02	1	41.7%	1	2.3	NA

Balance Sheet Data (Million $)

Jan. 31	Cash	Curr. Assets	Curr. Liab.	Curr. Ratio	Total Assets	% Ret. on Assets	Long Term Debt	Common Equity	Total Cap.	% LT Debt of Cap.	% Ret. on Equity
1993	**95**	**853**	**494**	**1.7**	**927**	**13.5**	**48.4**	**369**	**418**	**11.6**	**31.2**
1992	155	512	230	2.2	560	11.5	41.5	274	316	13.1	24.7
1991	37	236	141	1.7	264	12.3	4.2	112	116	3.6	28.1
1990	Nil	143	85	1.7	172	3.0	6.0	80	86	7.0	6.6
1989	36	149	86	1.7	167	11.0	5.5	75	81	6.8	32.4
1988	85	52	25	2.1	56	23.4	1.0	10	31	3.3	57.4
1987	1	22	20	1.1	24	13.9	0.8	3	4	22.0	115.2
1986	NA	NA	NA	NA	7	18.0	0.1	1	1	11.0	184.1

Data as orig. reptd. NA-Not Available.

Business Summary

Dell Computer Corporation is a direct marketer of high-performance personal computers compatible with industry standards established by IBM. International sales accounted for 36% of the total in 1992-93 and 1991-92.

The company has developed three Dell-branded lines of personal computer systems based on Intel microprocessors. The Performance line, which ranges from notebooks to high-end network file servers, is backed by a comprehensive service and support program. It is marketed directly. The Dimension and Precision lines are comprised of essentially similar desktop and floorstanding products although the Dimension line includes notebooks. The Dimension line is marketed through CompUSA, Staples and Sam's Clubs, and by the company's own sales force. The Precision line is sold through Price Club and Sam's Clubs.

In addition to its own branded products, Dell offers over 4,000 of the most popular software packages and peripheral products through its DellWare program. The company has also enhanced its personal computer systems offerings with a number of specialized services, including custom hardware and software integration and network installation and support.

Manufacturing operations, conducted at facilities in Austin, Tex., and Limerick, Ireland, consist of assembly, testing and quality control of the Performance line. The Precision and Dimension lines, along with certain notebooks, are manufactured by other companies. A flexible production process permits custom configuration of computer systems to specific customer orders.

The company opened its first international sales office in the U.K. in 1987, and has since established subsidiaries in other countries, including Japan.

Dividend Data

No cash dividends have been paid. A three-for-two stock split was effected in April 1992.

Finances

In August 1993, Dell amended its credit facility so that it would not be in default of any covenants despite reporting a loss. At August 1, 1993, the company had $80 million outstanding under the $130 million facility.

In February 1993, Dell withdrew a planned public offering of 4,000,000 common shares, citing unfavorable market conditions. The company currently plans to use debt to finance its growth.

R&D expenses equaled 2.1%, 3.7% and 4.1% of revenues in 1992-93, 1991-92 and 1990-91, respectively.

Capitalization

Long Term Debt: None (8/1/93).

Common Stock: 37,216,485 shs. ($0.01 par).
Officers and directors own 31%, incl. 30% held by M. S. Dell.
Institutions hold 48%.
Shareholders: 3,537 of record (4/93).

Options: To buy 5,043,988 shs. at $0.01 to $36.31 ea.

Office—9505 Arboretum Blvd., Austin, TX 78759-7299. **Tel**—(512) 338-4400. **Chrmn & CEO**—M. S. Dell. **CFO**—T. J. Meredith. **VP & Secy**—R. Salwen. **Dirs**—D. J. Carty, M. S. Dell, P. O. Hirschbiel, Jr., B. R. Inman, M. H. Jordan, G. Kozmetsky, T. Luce, C. B. Malone. **Transfer Agent & Registrar**—American Stock Transfer & Trust Co., NYC. **Incorporated** in Delaware in 1987. **Empl**—4,650.

 Neeraj K. Vohra

Delmarva Power & Light

NYSE Symbol DEW In S&P MidCap 400

Price	Range	P-E Ratio	Dividend	Yield	S&P Ranking	Beta
Jul. 30'93	1993					
23¾	24⅛–21½	14	1.54	6.5%	B+	0.32

Summary

This medium-sized electric and gas utility serves a population of one million on the Delmarva Peninsula, with the major portion of revenues derived from Delaware and lesser amounts from Maryland and Virginia. DEW has pursued a three-pronged strategic plan to meet increasing demand for electricity in its territory: it is building new capacity, purchasing power from others, and working to conserve energy use. Higher profits are expected for 1993, aided by recent base rate increases and well contained power costs.

Current Outlook

Share earnings for 1993 are expected at $1.75, up from the $1.69 of 1992, which included a $0.21 gain from litigation. Earnings in 1994 are projected at $1.75 a share.

The dividend should continue at $0.38½ quarterly.

Modest base rate electric and gas increases coupled with better fuel and maintenance cost controls should benefit earnings in 1993. Earnings quality is anticipated to deteriorate slightly with a stepped-up construction program as noncash credits for interest during construction account for a larger portion of earnings. Nonutility operations should not contribute materially to profits.

Operating Revenues (Million $)

Quarter:	1994	1993	1992	1991
Mar.	---	248.0	225.1	214.1
Jun.	---	214.6	193.8	202.5
Sep.	---	---	237.7	235.6
Dec.	---	---	207.4	192.6
	---	---	864.0	844.8

Operating revenues for the six months ended June 30, 1993, rose 10%, year to year, reflecting customer growth and greater power sales resulting from cooler weather conditions. Despite the absence of an $11.4 million ($0.21 a share) gain on the settlement of the Peach Botttom lawsuit, net income was up 8.4%. Share earnings were $0.85 based on 6.6% more common shares outstanding, versus $0.86.

Common Share Earnings ($)

Quarter:	1994	1993	1992	1991
Mar.	E0.60	0.58	0.62	0.43
Jun.	E0.25	0.27	0.24	0.30
Sep.	E0.65	E0.65	0.59	0.58
Dec.	E0.25	E0.25	0.24	0.13
	E1.75	E1.75	1.69	1.44

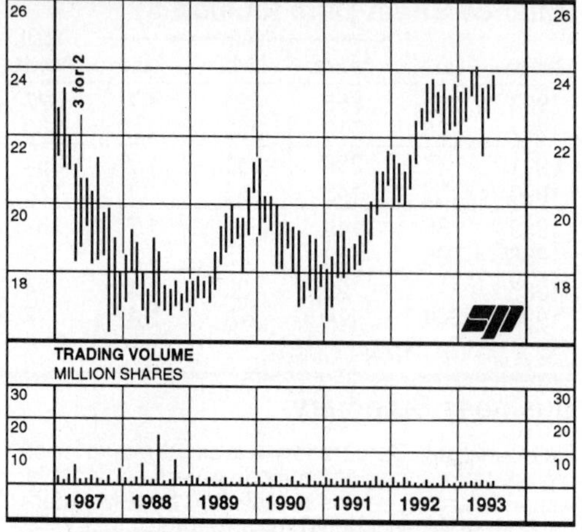

Important Developments

Jun. '93— Delmarva said that as part of its Challenge 2000 strategic plan to "save some, buy some, and build some", the company completed a combined-cycle unit, called Hay Road 4. The plant, which was on time and within budget, has the capacity to generate 170 mw of electricity. In October 1992, DEW filed an application with the Maryland PSC to build a 300-megawatt coal-fired generating station in Dorchester County, Md., at an estimated cost of $600 million by the end of the century. Plans call for the generating station, Dorchester Unit I, to be built on a site about two miles northest of Delmarva's existing Vienna power plant. The company is seeking approval at this time so it can maintain its option to have a power plant on line by year 2000. A decision on the application by the Maryland PSC is expected within two years.

Next earnings report expected in late October.

Per Share Data ($)

Yr. End Dec. 31	1992	1991	1990	1989	1988	1987	1986	1985	1984	1983
Tangible Bk. Val.	**13.14**	13.22	12.63	13.49	13.12	12.87	12.71	12.19	11.70	11.16
Earnings[1]	**1.69**	1.44	0.60	1.80	1.70	1.60	1.94	1.84	1.75	1.63
Dividends	**1.540**	1.540	1.540	1.500	1.460	1.414	1.348	1.280	1.200	1.094
Payout Ratio	**91%**	107%	257%	83%	86%	88%	69%	70%	68%	67%
Prices—High	**23¾**	21⅝	21⅜	21¼	19¼	23⅜	25½	18⅞	14⅞	13⅛
Low	**20**	16⅝	17	17	16½	16¼	16⅞	14	11½	10⅜
P/E Ratio—	**14–12**	15–12	36–28	12–9	11–10	15–10	13–9	10–8	9–7	8–6

Data as orig. reptd. Adj. for stk. div(s). of 50% May 1987. **1.** Bef. spec. item(s) of +0.25 in 1991. d-Deficit. E-Estimated

Income Data (Million $)

Year Ended Dec. 31	Revs.	Depr.	Maint.	Oper. Ratio	[1]Fxd. Chgs. Cover.	Constr. Credits	Eff. Tax Rate	[2]Net Inc.	% Return On— Revs.	[3]Invest. Capital	Com. Equity
1992	**86.4**	**95.3**	**NA**	**83.4%**	**2.89**	**9.7**	**35.8%**	**98.5**	**11.4**	**7.8**	**12.4**
1991	845.0	88.7	NA	83.6%	2.58	7.8	34.9%	80.5	9.5	7.5	11.0
1990	811.0	82.4	NA	82.0%	2.07	5.8	39.7%	37.3	4.5	5.4	4.5
1989	790.0	76.3	65.0	82.3%	2.99	9.6	32.6%	91.3	11.6	8.5	13.4
1988	768.0	71.3	70.3	83.1%	3.04	5.5	36.9%	84.7	11.0	8.4	12.9
1987	712.0	68.0	65.7	82.5%	3.03	4.6	37.9%	79.8	11.2	8.1	12.3
1986	715.0	49.0	62.6	81.2%	3.48	3.5	38.2%	96.1	13.4	9.4	15.4
1985	723.0	54.0	59.4	81.3%	3.69	3.0	43.5%	96.6	13.4	9.6	15.3
1984	703.0	53.7	56.8	81.0%	3.63	3.6	46.2%	92.1	13.1	9.9	15.2
1983	650.0	49.6	53.8	80.1%	3.26	3.2	44.6%	85.1	13.1	10.0	14.9

Balance Sheet Data (Million $)

Dec. 31	[4]Gross Prop.	[5]Capital Expend.	Net Prop.	% Earn. on Net Prop.	Total Cap.	Capitalization— [6]LT Debt	[6]% LT Debt	Pfd.	% Pfd.	Com.	% Com.
1992	**2,862**	**207**	**1,932**	**7.7**	**2,140**	**813**	**46.8**	**176**	**10.2**	**746**	**43.0**
1991	2,667	182	1,817	7.8	2,038	799	48.7	136	8.3	707	43.0
1990	2,533	188	1,721	8.8	1,912	773	50.7	136	9.0	615	40.3
1989	2,204	176	1,588	9.0	1,828	663	45.9	136	9.5	643	44.6
1988	2,204	171	1,502	8.8	1,683	610	45.9	105	7.9	613	46.2
1987	2,080	142	1,432	8.9	1,676	645	47.9	106	7.9	595	44.2
1986	1,965	103	1,377	9.9	1,662	667	49.0	107	7.8	587	43.2
1985	1,889	95	1,353	10.1	1,555	638	48.7	110	8.4	562	42.9
1984	1,810	79	1,321	10.2	1,443	558	44.6	152	12.2	540	43.2
1983	1,738	76	1,298	10.0	1,377	558	45.9	154	12.6	504	41.5

Data as orig. reptd. **1.** Times int. exp. & pfd. divs. covered (pretax basis). **2.** Bef. spec. item(s) in 1991. **3.** Based on income before interest charges. **4.** Utility Plant. **5.** Excl. construction. credits. **6.** Incl. capital lease obligations. NA-Not Available.

Business Summary

Delmarva Power & Light provides electric service to the Delmarva Peninsula, which includes all of Delaware and parts of Maryland and Virginia. Gas service is provided in northern Delaware. Some 90% of operating revenues and 93% of operating income in 1992 was derived from electric sales. Contributions to electric business by class:

	1992	1991	1990	1989
Residential	37%	37%	37%	37%
Commercial	30%	29%	29%	29%
Industrial	19%	19%	20%	20%
Other	14%	15%	14%	14%

The fuel mix in 1992 was 39% coal, 14% oil, 14% nuclear, 4% gas, and 29% purchases and net interchange. DEW has a 7.51% interest in the Peach Bottom Nuclear Station and a 7.41% interest in the Salem Nuclear Power Station. Peak load in 1992 was 2,295 mw and system capability was 2,677 mw, for a capacity margin of 14%. Electricity sales in 1992 were 11,520,811 mwh, up 0.5% from 1991.

Total gas sales in 1992 were 17.01 million Mcf, up 9.2% from 15.57 million Mcf in 1991.

DEW has estimated its capital requirements for 1993-94 at $426 million, including $380 million for construction (excluding AFUDC). Projects include $38 million of capital expenditures related to plans for compliance with provisions of the Clean Air Act Amendments of 1990.

Finances

In June 1993, DEW sold $90 million of 6.40% first mortgage bonds due 2003 through underwriters led by Morgan Stanley & Co., Chemical Securities Inc. and Merrill Lynch & Co. Proceeds were earmarked to redeem higher coupon debt.

Dividend Data

Dividends have been paid since 1921. A dividend reinvestment plan is available.

Amt of Divd. $	Date Decl.	Ex-divd. Date	Stock of Record	Payment Date
0.38½	Sep. 30	Oct. 6	Oct. 13	Oct. 31'92
0.38½	Dec. 29	Jan. 7	Jan. 13	Jan. 30'93
0.38½	Mar. 25	Apr. 6	Apr. 13	Apr. 30'93
0.38½	Jun. 24	Jul. 7	Jul. 13	Jul. 31'93

Capitalization

Long Term Debt: $811,693,000 (3/93), incl. $24.5 million capital lease obligations.

Cum. Preferred Stock: $176,365,000.

Common Stock: 58,091,996 shs. ($2.25 par). Institutions hold about 22%. Shareholders of record: 56,334.

Office—800 King St., (P.O. Box 231) Wilmington, DE 19899. **Tel**—(302) 429-3011. **Chrmn, Pres & CEO**—H. E. Cosgrove. **Secy**—D. P. Connelly. **Investor Contact**—Carol C. Conrad. (800) 365-6495. **Dirs**—M. G. Abercrombie, E. P. Blanchard, Jr., R. D. Burris, H. E. Cosgrove, A. K. Doberstein, J. H. Gilliam, Jr., S. I. Gore, J. C. Johnson III, H. R. Landon, J. T. McKinstry. **Transfer Agents & Registrars**—Wilmington Trust Co., Wilmington; Chemical Bank, NYC. **Incorporated** in Delaware in 1909. **Empl**—2,842.

 Ned Bancroft

Dexter Corp.

NYSE Symbol DEX Options on ASE In S&P MidCap 400

Price	Range	P–E Ratio	Dividend	Yield	S&P Ranking	Beta
Aug. 20'93	1993					
21⅝	28⅞–20⅜	15	0.88	4.1%	B+	0.71

Summary

Dexter is an international producer of specialty materials and services used in the medical, food packaging, electronics, automotive and aerospace markets. It also has a 55% interest in Life Technologies, Inc., a large biotechnology company. In recent years, DEX has completed a number of acquisitions and joint ventures that focused on its strategic global markets, while divesting unprofitable or unrelated businesses. A earnings decline is expected for 1993, reflecting the divestitures of businesses.

Current Outlook

Share earnings for 1993 are projected at about $1.45, down from 1992's $1.58; share earnings for 1994 may reach $1.70, assuming a better economy.

Dividends should remain at $0.22 quarterly.

Sales for 1993 are expected to decline from 1992, reflecting the absence of businesses sold in 1992, soft European markets and adverse currency exchange rates. The May transaction with Akzo will also result in lower annual sales. Electronic, nonwovens, molecular biology and cell culture products should continue to do well, but aerospace and automobile related products are weaker. Operating profits should improve with further benefits of restructuring and cost reductions, including planned plant consolidations.

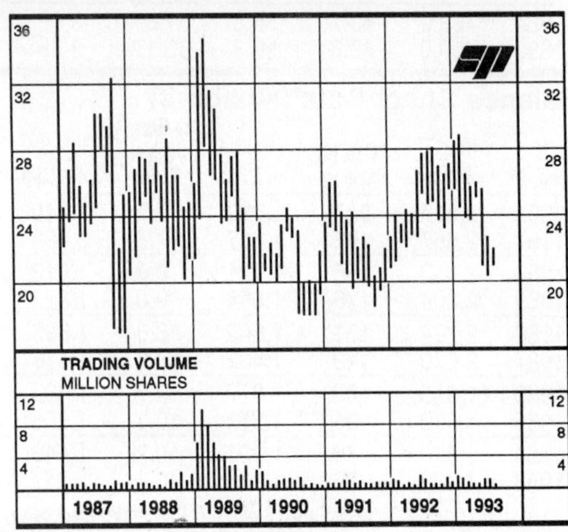

Net Sales (Million $)

Quarter:	1993	1992	1991	1990
Mar.	219	243	235	227
Jun.	229	253	238	225
Sep.		231	229	226
Dec.		225	236	231
		951	938	908

Sales in the first six months of 1993 fell 10%, year to year, reflecting divestitures, unfavorable currency exchange rates, and lower volumes. Net income was off 15%, to $0.72 a share (excluding a net charge of $0.41 for several accounting changes), from $0.85.

Common Share Earnings ($)

Quarter:	1993	1992	1991	1990
Mar.	0.32	0.37	0.29	0.41
Jun.	0.40	0.48	0.20	0.50
Sep.	E0.35	0.37	d0.34	0.44
Dec.	E0.38	0.36	d0.44	0.39
	E1.45	1.58	d0.29	1.74

Important Developments

Jul. '93— Dexter said that second quarter earnings from ongoing operations increased 8% over the 1992 levels despite a 2% drop in sales due to price and volume. The increase was offset by a $0.05 a share reduction from divestitures and a $0.03 a share decrease from the effects of currency exchange rates. Subsequent to the close of the second quarter, there was an explosion and fire at a Japanese plant that is a key source for a raw material for DEX's electronic products.

May '93— Dexter exchanged its coil coatings business with Akzo, the Netherlands, for Akzo's U.S. aerospace coatings business, which was combined with DEX's existing aerospace business. In March, DEX acquired Vernicolor A.G., Switzerland, a food can coatings producer with annual sales of over $20 million.

Next earnings report expected in mid-October.

Per Share Data ($)

Yr. End Dec. 31	1992	1991	[1]1990	[1]1989	1988	1987	[1]1986	[1]1985	[1]1984	[1]1983
Tangible Bk. Val.	**10.69**	10.36	11.53	9.78	8.92	8.27	6.76	8.14	7.07	6.42
Cash Flow	**2.88**	0.95	2.98	2.71	2.61	2.66	2.11	1.83	2.02	1.71
Earnings[2]	**1.58**	d0.29	1.74	1.73	1.61	1.72	1.35	1.15	1.29	1.18
Dividends	**0.880**	0.880	0.880	0.820	0.800	0.600	0.566	0.534	0.508	0.500
Payout Ratio	**56%**	NM	50%	47%	50%	35%	42%	46%	39%	42%
Prices—High	**28⅛**	26⅛	24½	34¾	28¾	32⅜	23⅜	17⅞	16¾	19½
Low	**20⅞**	18½	18	20⅛	20¼	17	16⅞	12½	11⅞	11⅜
P/E Ratio—	**18–13**	NM	14–10	20–12	18–13	19–10	17–13	15–11	13–9	17–10

Data as orig. reptd. Adj. for stk. divs. of 50% Oct. 1986, 66⅔% Oct. 1983. **1.** Refl. merger or acq. **2.** Bef. results of disc. ops. of -0.18 in 1988. d-Deficit. E-Estimated NM-Not Meaningful.

Income Data (Million $)

Year Ended Dec. 31	Revs.	Oper. Inc.	% Oper. Inc. of Revs.	Cap. Exp.	Depr.	Int. Exp.	[3]Net Bef. Taxes	Eff. Tax Rate	Net Inc.	% Net Inc. of Revs.	Cash Flow
1992	**951**	**115**	**12.1**	**52.1**	**31.5**	**18.8**	**73.1**	**37.7%**	**38.2**	**4.0**	**69.7**
1991	938	99	10.5	65.0	30.0	16.8	11.2	109.5%	d7.1	NM	22.9
[1]1990	908	109	12.1	70.3	26.5	16.3	77.4	37.0%	42.2	4.6	72.4
[1]1989	849	99	11.6	95.0	21.9	10.9	77.6	38.0%	43.0	5.1	67.3
[2]1988	827	98	11.8	29.9	20.5	12.2	71.9	38.0%	39.9	4.8	64.8
1987	783	101	12.9	25.8	19.2	14.4	75.9	38.0%	42.8	5.5	66.2
[1]1986	650	83	12.8	38.1	16.8	12.5	56.5	38.0%	33.6	5.2	52.3
[1]1985	633	71	11.2	27.7	16.7	11.9	53.8	35.3%	[4]28.6	4.5	45.3
[1]1984	625	73	11.6	21.9	14.8	11.1	44.9	30.2%	29.7	4.8	46.8
[1]1983	561	64	11.4	39.5	12.2	8.6	48.1	42.3%	27.3	4.9	39.6

Balance Sheet Data (Million $)

Dec. 31	Cash	Curr. Assets	Curr. Liab.	Curr. Ratio	Total Assets	% Ret. on Assets	Long Term Debt	Common Equity	Total Cap.	% LT Debt of Cap.	% Ret. on Equity
1992	**65.0**	**361**	**154**	**2.3**	**782**	**4.9**	**179**	**316**	**584**	**30.6**	**12.1**
1991	39.7	362	169	2.2	784	NM	189	314	586	32.2	NM
1990	81.0	363	148	2.5	762	5.9	160	344	591	27.1	12.8
1989	77.5	336	147	2.3	694	6.5	131	325	535	24.5	13.6
1988	57.6	325	143	2.3	626	6.5	93	307	473	19.6	13.3
1987	71.5	312	131	2.4	606	7.3	106	294	466	22.8	15.5
1986	58.6	267	129	2.1	566	6.4	113	259	429	26.3	13.7
1985	93.0	261	132	2.0	485	6.1	65	233	350	18.7	12.8
1984	28.0	212	102	2.1	426	7.1	74	200	321	23.1	15.4
1983	26.2	199	104	1.9	410	7.3	67	186	302	22.1	15.2

Data as orig. reptd. **1.** Refl. merger or acq. **2.** Excl. disc. ops. **3.** Incl. equity in earns. of nonconsol. subs. **4.** Refl. acctg. change. d-Deficit. NM-Not Meaningful.

Business Summary

Dexter produces specialty materials and chemicals and life science products. Contributions by market group in 1992 were:

	Sales	Profits
Medical	30%	33%
Food packaging	24%	33%
Electronics	15%	8%
Automotive	6%	−1%
Aerospace	5%	−2%
Other	20%	29%

Operations outside North America accounted for 38% of sales and 45% of profits in 1992.

Medical products include nonwoven wraps, drapes, garments and absorbent products. Life Technologies (55% owned) produces cell culture and molecular biology research products. Products for food packaging consist of coatings for food and beverage cans, container sealants, coatings and adhesives for flexible and microwaveable packaging, and nonwoven materials for tea bags, filters and meat casings. Electronics materials include encapsulation compounds, printed wiring board materials (inks, resists, masks and etchants) and magnetic components. Automotive materials consist of polypropylene-based products, acoustical sealants, foam gasketing, adhesives, mold releases and liquid and powder coatings. Aerospace products include adhesives and structural materials (adhesives, primers, composite surfacing films and mold release agents) and coatings (external finishes, coatings and logos).

The other segment includes industrial coatings and wallcover businesses. In 1992, DEX sold the water treatment chemicals, composites and plastisols businesses.

Dividend Data

Dividends have been paid since 1957. A dividend reinvestment plan is available. A "poison pill" stock purchase rights plan was adopted in 1986.

Amt of Divd. $	Date Decl.	Ex–divd. Date	Stock of Record	Payment Date
0.22	Aug. 28	Sep. 9	Sep. 15	Oct. 9'92
0.22	Oct. 23	Dec. 9	Dec. 15	Jan. 11'93
0.22	Feb. 26	Mar. 9	Mar. 15	Apr. 9'93
0.22	Apr. 22	Jun. 9	Jun. 15	Jul. 9'93

Capitalization

Long Term Debt: $197,719,000 (6/93).

Minority Interest: $50,019,000.

Common Stock: 24,312,011 shs. ($1 par).
Institutions hold about 77%.
Shareholders of record: 4,000.

Office—One Elm St., Windsor Locks, CT 06096. **Tel**—(203) 627-9051. **Chrmn, Pres & CEO**—K. G. Walker. **Exec VP-Fin**—R. E. McGill III. **Secy**—B. H. Beatt. **Treas**—D. J. Ribaudo. **VP & Investor Contact**—John D. Thompson. **Dirs**—M. C. Briley, D. L. Coffin, C. H. Curl, B. M. Fox, R. M. Furek, R. E. McGill III, Jean-Francois Saglio, G. L. Urban, K. G. Walker, A. E. Wegner, G. M. Whitesides. **Transfer Agents**—Mellon Securities Trust Co., East Hartford; Mellon Securities Transfer Services, NYC. **Registrar**—Mellon Securities Trust Co., East Hartford. **Incorporated** in Connecticut in 1914. **Empl**—4,800.

 Richard O'Reilly, CFA

Diagnostek, Inc.

NYSE Symbol DXK Options on ASE (Jan-Apr-Jul-Oct) In S&P MidCap 400

Price	Range	P-E Ratio	Dividend	Yield	S&P Ranking	Beta
Oct. 21'93	1993					
15	16¼–5⅞	62	None	None	NR	0.97

Summary

This company manages prescription drug benefits for leading U.S. corporations, managed health care plans and national labor unions. It also provides pharmacy management services to over 212 acute-care hospitals and HMOs nationwide.

Business Summary

Diagnostek is a leading provider of comprehensive pharmacy services designed to contain the costs of dispensing pharmaceuticals. The company dispenses prescription drugs, primarily by mail, to beneficiaries of health benefit plans and provides contract pharmacy management services to hospitals, managed care providers and other institutions. It also leases medical imaging and diagnostic equipment to hospitals. Contributions by business segment (profits in million $) in 1992-93:

	Sales	Profits
Mail service pharmacy	63%	$4.03
Pharmacy management	34%	6.54
Medical imaging	3%	–0.16

Wholly-owned Health Care Services Inc. (HCS) provides mail pharmacy services to corporations, labor unions, government entities and other benefit plan sponsors, including health maintenance (HMO) and preferred provider (PPO) organizations. HCS is one of the largest for-profit providers of prescription drugs by mail. During 1992-93, it dispensed over 3.1 million prescriptions on behalf of about 880 benefit plan sponsors covering over 7.7 million eligible beneficiaries. DXK estimates that its mail pharmacy services generally provide cost savings of 5% to 35% compared with drug plans relying on retail pharmacy dispensing programs.

HPI Health Care Services Inc. (wholly-owned) has been a leading provider of contract pharmacy management services to health care institutions since 1967. These services relieve hospital administrators of daily responsibility for pharmacy operations and provide customers with a more efficient process for dispensing, administering and controlling pharmaceuticals. At March 31, 1993, HPI had about 100 health care institutions, with about 11,400 licensed beds, under contract.

In April 1993, DXK began marketing its new RxChoice product which provides plan administrators and benefit sponsors with integrated pharmacy benefit management services. RxChoice provides plan participants with a choice of prescription benefit delivery method while streamlining pharmacy benefit administration activities.

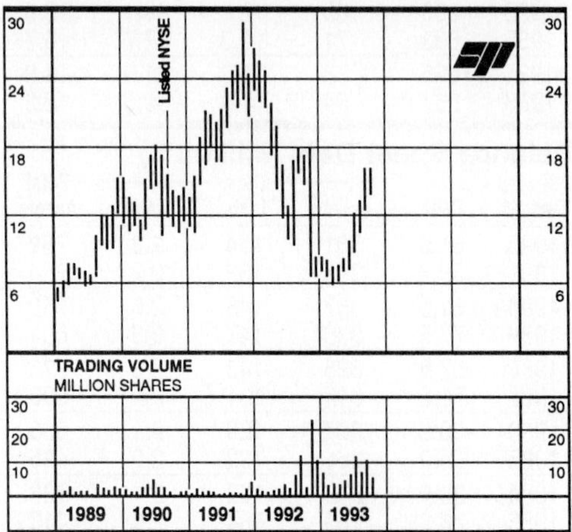

Diagnostek Medical Inc. (100% owned) provides three magnetic resonance imaging (MRI) machines to hospitals on a per-procedure rental basis. Diagnostek of Springfield Inc. (100% owned) is the general partner of a stand-alone out-patient medical diagnostic imaging center in Pennsylvania which houses MRI and other imaging systems.

Important Developments

Oct. '93— DXK agreed to offer integrated prescription drug benefits to the more than ten million individuals insured by American Family Life Assurance Co. of Columbus (AFLAC). Earlier, in September, Diagnostek agreed to provide mail pharmacy services to Utah-based FIRST HEALTH Strategies Inc. (a subsidiary of First Financial Management Corp.), which manages health care benefits for over two million employees.

Next earnings report expected in mid-January.

Per Share Data ($)

Yr. End Mar. 31	1993	1992	[1]1991	1990	1989	[1]1988	[1]1987	1986	[2]1985
Tangible Bk. Val.	**5.22**	5.02	0.86	1.50	1.44	0.83	1.02	0.80	0.72
Cash Flow	**0.32**	0.80	0.54	0.49	0.30	0.05	0.03	0.02	d0.13
Earnings[3]	**0.12**	0.61	0.35	0.38	0.24	0.01	0.02	0.01	d0.13
Dividends	**Nil**	Nil	Nil	Nil	Nil	Nil	Nil	Nil	Nil
Payout Ratio	**Nil**	Nil	Nil	Nil	Nil	Nil	Nil	Nil	Nil
Calendar Years	**1992**	1991	1990	1989	1988	1987	1986	1985	1984
Prices—High	**26¹³⁄₁₆**	29	18¼	15⅝	6⅞	2⅝	2⅞	2½	2⅜
Low	**6⅝**	10½	9¾	4⅜	1	⅞	1½	⅝	⅞
P/E Ratio—	**NM**	48–17	52–28	40–12	29–4	NM	NM	NM	NM

Data as orig. reptd. **1.** Reflects merger or acquisition. **2.** Major merger resulted in formation of new company. **3.** Bef. spec. item(s) of +0.02 in 1988, +0.03 in 1987, +0.01 in 1986. d-Deficit. NM-Not Meaningful.

Income Data (Million $)

Year Ended Mar. 31	Revs.	Oper. Inc.	% Oper. Inc. of Revs.	Cap. Exp.	Depr.	Int. Exp.	Net Bef. Taxes	Eff. Tax Rate	[4]Net Inc.	% Net Inc. of Revs.	Cash Flow
1993	**380**	**7.7**	**2.0**	**1.98**	**4.89**	**3.07**	**[3]4.5**	**40.5%**	**2.8**	**0.7**	**7.7**
1992	290	21.5	7.4	3.55	4.23	3.50	21.0	37.6%	13.1	4.5	17.3
[1]1991	220	15.4	7.0	3.59	3.76	3.95	11.5	38.9%	6.9	3.1	10.6
1990	142	9.6	6.8	7.69	2.06	2.07	12.1	40.2%	7.2	5.1	9.3
1989	80	3.3	4.1	1.31	1.15	0.83	7.1	39.8%	4.1	5.1	5.3
[1]1988	11	d2.0	NM	3.01	0.51	0.19	0.7	74.3%	0.1	0.9	0.6
[1]1987	1	d1.5	NM	1.29	0.09	Nil	[3]0.4	47.8%	0.2	16.4	0.3
1986	Nil	d1.0	NM	0.10	0.02	Nil	[3]0.2	39.9%	0.1	25.9	0.1
[2]1985	Nil	d0.8	NM	0.02	0.01	Nil	d0.9	NM	d0.9	NM	d0.9

Balance Sheet Data (Million $)

Mar. 31	Cash	Curr. Assets	Curr. Liab.	Curr. Ratio	Total Assets	% Ret. on Assets	Long Term Debt	Common Equity	Total Cap.	% LT Debt of Cap.	% Ret. on Equity
1993	**8.4**	**76.4**	**34.7**	**2.2**	**217**	**1.3**	**18.1**	**160**	**182**	**10.0**	**1.8**
1992	6.3	70.8	32.3	2.2	217	7.2	24.0	157	185	13.0	11.6
1991	2.5	57.9	21.1	2.7	118	6.4	37.2	56	96	38.5	13.7
1990	7.2	59.8	16.3	3.7	93	10.4	31.1	43	76	40.9	19.6
1989	14.1	32.3	12.0	2.7	44	9.7	1.5	29	32	4.8	16.8
1988	6.5	21.0	14.0	1.5	32	0.5	2.0	15	17	11.3	0.7
1987	2.6	3.6	0.4	8.0	14	1.6	Nil	13	13	Nil	1.8
1986	6.7	7.6	0.5	14.2	8	1.4	0.2	7	7	2.0	1.6
1985	4.9	5.4	0.5	10.0	7	NA	0.1	6	6	2.1	NA

Data as orig. reptd. **1.** Reflects merger or acquisition. **2.** Major merger resulted in formation of new company. **3.** Inc. equity in earns. of noncon-sol. subs. **4.** Bef. spec. item(s). d-Deficit. NM-Not Meaningful. NA-Not Available.

Net Sales (Million $)

Quarter:	1993–94	1992–93	1991–92	1990–91
Jun.	96.9	84.4	69.8	45.1
Sep.	98.6	96.3	70.1	55.0
Dec.		100.2	73.5	60.8
Mar.		102.6	80.3	64.2
		383.5	293.8	225.1

For the six months ended September 30, 1993, revenues rose 8.2%, year to year, as significantly improved demand at HPI Health Care Services Inc. offset slightly lower revenues from the mail pharmacy services segment. Operating margins widened, and results benefited from the absence of both expenses associated with the aborted merger with Medco Containment Serices Inc., and nonrecurring bad debt provisions of $2.1 million. Net income expanded 184%, to $5,400,000 ($0.23 a share) from $1,900,00 ($0.08, as restated).

Common Share Earnings ($)

Quarter:	1993–94	1992–93	1991–92	1990–91
Jun.	0.11	[1]0.11	0.13	0.11
Sep.	0.12	d0.04	0.14	0.11
Dec.		0.05	0.17	0.03
Mar.		d0.02	0.17	0.11
		0.12	0.61	0.35

Dividend Data

Dividends have never been paid. A "poison pill" stock purchase right was adopted in 1992.

Finances

In November 1992, Medco Containment Services Inc. terminated an agreement to acquire Diagnostek. Both DXK and Medco filed litigation, and in March 1993, the company agreed to settle the litigation and pay Medco $3 million. Diagnostek recorded a pretax charge of $6.8 million ($0.17 a share after taxes) for costs arising from the aborted transaction.

Under a July 1992 program to repurchase up to 1,000,000 DXK common shares, the company acquired 168,726 shares at an average price of $9.44 per share. The program was discontinued in March 1993.

In March 1993, Diagnostek acquired a 15% equity stake in Medical Service Agency Inc., a developer, marketer and administrator of pharmacy benefit plans using card programs through a contractual network of some 30,000 retail pharmacies.

At June 30, 1993, DXK had a $24 million term loan outstanding bearing interest at 10.02%, and had an unused $25 million revolving credit line.

Capitalization

Long Term Debt: $18,129,000 (6/93).

Common Stock: 23,517,206 shs. ($0.01 par). Institutions hold approximately 25%.

1. Restated. d-Deficit.

Office—4500 Alexander Blvd. N.E., Albuquerque, NM 87107. **Tel**—(505) 345-8080. **Chrmn & Pres**—N. P. DeSantis. **EVP-COO**—D. Rodriguez. **EVP-CFO**—W. Barron. **EVP-Secy**—C. Miller. **Investor Contact**—Vincent Villanueva. **Dirs**—N. P. DeSantis, D. G. Devereaux, J. Golden, C. Miller, E. G. Riesenbach, M. Stuchin. **Transfer Agent & Registrar**—American Stock Transfer & Trust Co., NYC. **Incorporated** in Delaware in 1983. **Empl**—1,000.

 Robert M. Gold

Diagnostic Products

NYSE Symbol DP In S&P MidCap 400

Price	Range	P-E Ratio	Dividend	Yield	S&P Ranking	Beta
Aug. 10'93	1993					
20⅝	30¾–17⅛	16	0.40	1.9%	B+	0.57

Summary

This company is the world's leading independent manufacturer of immunodiagnostic test kits and related instrumentation. Derived from immunology and molecular biology, its kits can measure hormones, drugs and other medically important substances present in body fluids and tissues at infinitesimal concentrations. After many years of steady growth, earnings fell in 1992, and recovered only slightly in the 1993 first half.

Business Summary

Diagnostic Products develops, produces and sells medical immunodiagnostic test kits and related instrumentation that utilize state-of-the-art technology based on the immunological reaction between antigens and antibodies.

DP's kits are used by hospitals, clinical, veterinary and forensic laboratories, and doctors' offices to obtain precise and rapid identification and measurement of hormones, drugs, viruses, bacteria and other substances present in body fluids and tissues at infinitesimal concentrations.

The principal clinical applications of the kits relate to in-vitro diagnosis of thyroid conditions and anemia; testing for pregnancy, fertility and fetal well-being; management of diabetes and certain types of cancer; drug abuse testing; rapid diagnosis of infectious diseases (including sexually transmitted diseases); allergy testing; and diagnosis of various disorders due to hormone and steroid imbalances. The company believes it is the market leader in fertility testing.

The kits utilize various techniques to detect and measure substances in a patient's body fluids and tissues. DP has historically concentrated on radioimmunoassay (RIA), the core technology of immunodiagnostics, which utilizes radioisotopes to achieve high levels of test specificity and sensitivity. The company believes it has one of the most extensive RIA product lines of any supplier.

DP also uses various non-isotopic methods of testing to meet other market needs when the superior specificity and sensitivity of the RIA technique is not required. These include: Enzyme Immunoassay (EIA), incorporated into the AlaSTAT EIA product line; Chemiluminescence, used in the IMMULITE System (developed by recently acquired Cirrus Diagnostics Inc.); the latex agglutination technique, used in the PathDx product line; and the immunohistochemical staining technique, used in the ImmuStain line of kits for pathologists to evaluate the nature of tumors and tissue samples.

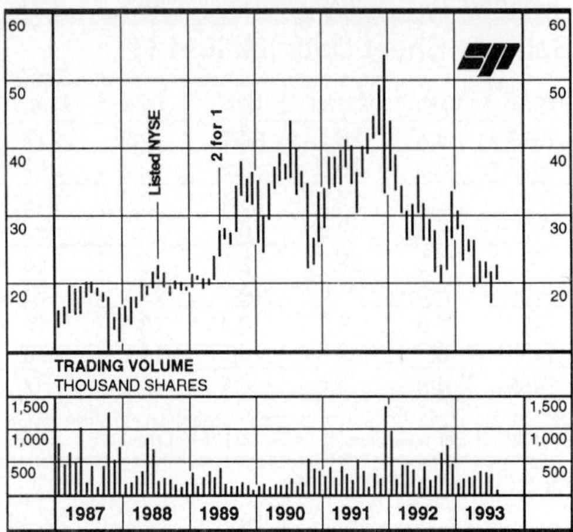

The company's products are sold on a worldwide basis through distributors in over 90 foreign countries. Business in Europe accounted for 54% of net sales in 1992.

DP devotes substantial resources to research and development to update and improve its existing products, and to develop new products. Research and development activities are conducted at facilities located in Los Angeles, the United Kingdom, Germany and Italy (through its 45% owned subsidiary). In 1992 and 1991, R&D outlays totaled $12,845,000 (12% of sales) and $13,517,000 (15%), respectively.

Next earnings report expected in late October.

Per Share Data ($)

Yr. End Dec. 31	[2]1992	[1]1991	[2]1990	[2]1989	1988	1987	1986	1985	1984	1983
Tangible Bk. Val.	**7.92**	7.38	6.51	5.40	4.60	3.95	3.20	1.94	1.55	1.30
Cash Flow	**1.60**	1.79	1.64	1.42	1.14	0.84	0.61	0.44	0.33	0.31
Earnings[3]	**1.26**	1.49	1.35	1.20	1.00	0.75	0.54	0.37	0.27	0.26
Dividends	**0.32**	0.32	0.24	0.20	0.12	Nil	Nil	Nil	Nil	Nil
Payout Ratio	**24%**	20%	17%	16%	11%	Nil	Nil	Nil	Nil	Nil
Prices—High	**44**	53¾	44	38	22¾	20¼	13⅝	7⅞	6⅞	10½
Low	**20⅛**	28¼	22¼	19¼	14	10¼	7⅜	4⅜	3½	5
P/E Ratio—	**35–16**	36–19	33–16	32–16	23–14	27–14	25–14	22–12	25–13	40–19

Data as orig. reptd. Adj. for stk. divs. of 100% Jun. 1989, 50% Sep. 1983. **1.** Reflects accounting change. **2.** Reflects merger or acquisition. **3.** Ful. dil. 1.22 in 1992, 1.44 in 1991, 1.30 in 1990, 1.16 in 1989, 0.97 in 1988, 0.73 in 1987, 0.52 in 1986.

Income Data (Million $)

Year Ended Dec. 31	Revs.	Oper. Inc.	% Oper. Inc. of Revs.	Cap. Exp.	Depr.	Int. Exp.	[3]Net Bef. Taxes	Eff. Tax Rate	Net Inc.	% Net Inc. of Revs.	Cash Flow
[2]1992	**103**	**26.6**	**25.7**	**15.1**	**4.68**	**Nil**	**23.7**	**27.0%**	**17.3**	**16.7**	**22.0**
[1]1991	90	26.2	29.1	9.5	3.95	Nil	27.9	30.9%	19.3	21.5	23.3
[2]1990	76	23.1	30.4	6.0	3.80	Nil	24.5	29.7%	17.3	22.8	21.1
[2]1989	60	20.1	33.3	6.0	2.73	Nil	22.1	31.1%	15.2	25.2	17.9
1988	47	15.2	32.3	4.8	1.77	Nil	17.9	30.6%	12.4	26.4	14.2
1987	37	12.4	33.5	3.9	1.12	Nil	13.4	31.0%	9.3	25.1	10.4
1986	29	8.6	29.7	2.5	0.86	Nil	9.7	34.9%	6.3	21.7	7.2
1985	23	6.0	26.4	0.7	0.80	Nil	6.1	35.9%	3.9	17.2	4.7
1984	18	4.6	25.8	0.8	0.64	Nil	4.4	34.4%	2.9	16.3	3.5
1983	15	4.5	30.0	0.8	0.51	Nil	4.4	37.6%	2.8	18.7	3.3

Balance Sheet Data (Million $)

Dec. 31	Cash	Curr. Assets	Curr. Liab.	Curr. Ratio	Total Assets	% Ret. on Assets	Long Term Debt	Common Equity	Total Cap.	% LT Debt of Cap.	% Ret. on Equity
1992	**22.7**	**70.3**	**14.8**	**4.8**	**134**	**12.6**	**Nil**	**120**	**120**	**Nil**	**14.8**
1991	30.2	76.3	23.9	3.2	131	16.5	Nil	107	107	Nil	19.8
1990	24.3	64.3	15.4	4.2	102	18.5	Nil	87	87	Nil	21.7
1989	20.3	53.4	12.4	4.3	84	20.3	Nil	71	71	Nil	23.5
1988	20.8	44.3	7.6	5.8	65	21.6	Nil	58	58	Nil	23.8
1987	19.6	37.4	3.4	11.0	50	20.8	Nil	47	47	Nil	22.1
1986	18.9	31.1	1.8	16.9	40	19.5	Nil	38	38	Nil	20.8
1985	3.0	13.2	1.7	7.6	23	18.9	Nil	21	21	Nil	20.9
1984	0.3	10.0	1.6	6.3	18	17.1	Nil	17	17	Nil	18.8
1983	3.3	10.2	1.0	10.1	15	20.0	Nil	14	14	Nil	21.8

Data as orig. reptd. **1.** Reflects accounting change. **2.** Reflects merger or acquisition. **3.** Incl. equity in earns. of nonconsol. subs.

Sales (Million $)

Quarter:	1993	1992	1991	1990
Mar.	27.0	24.8	21.4	18.2
Jun.	26.4	25.4	22.1	17.7
Sep.		27.2	22.0	18.9
Dec.		26.1	24.6	21.2
		103.5	90.1	75.9

In the six months ended June 30, 1993, sales rose 6.5%, year to year, despite the negative impact of unfavorable foreign exchange rate fluctuations (which was said to have effectively reduced revenues by about 3%). Gross margins narrowed, and after higher operating costs, and costs associated with the acquisition of Cirrus Diagnostics, pretax income fell 3.0%. After taxes at 30.0%, versus 35.6%, net income was ahead 5.4%, to $8,525,000 ($0.63 a share) from $8,089,000 ($0.59).

Common Share Earnings ($)

Quarter:	1993	1992	1991	1990
Mar.	0.30	0.34	0.38	0.34
Jun.	0.33	0.25	0.39	0.35
Sep.		0.32	0.39	0.31
Dec.		0.35	0.33	0.35
		1.26	1.49	1.35

Finances

In May 1992, the company acquired Cirrus Diagnostics Inc., a development-stage company that developed the IMMULITE System (an integrated instrument/reagent system for the automation of diagnostic immunoassays), for about 786,000 common shares valued at some $28 million. The transaction was accounted for as a pooling of interests.

Dividend Data

Dividends were initiated in 1988.

Amt. of Divd. $	Date Decl.	Ex-divd. Date	Stock of Record	Payment Date
0.08	Oct. 2	Oct. 29	Nov. 4	Nov. 18'92
0.10	Jan. 1	Feb. 4	Feb. 10	Feb. 24'93
0.10	Apr. 1	Apr. 29	May 5	May 19'93
0.10	Jul. 1	Jul. 29	Aug. 4	Aug. 18'93

Capitalization

Long Term Debt: None (6/93).

Common Stock: 13,169,496 shs. (no par).
Officers and directors control about 31%.
Institutions hold some 24%.
Shareholders of record: 649 (2/93).

Office—5700 W. 96th St., Los Angeles, CA 90045. **Tel**—(213) 776-0180. **Chrmn & CEO**—S. Ziering. **Pres & COO**—S. A. Aroesty. **VP-Secy**—M. Ziering. **VP-Fin, CFO & Investor Contact**—Julian R. Bockserman. **Dirs**—S. A. Aroesty, J. Kleiman, M. H. Salter, J. D. Watson, M. Ziering, S. Ziering. **Transfer Agent & Registrar**—First Interstate Bank of California, Los Angeles. **Incorporated** in California in 1971. **Empl**—724.

 Robert M. Gold

Diamond Shamrock, Inc.

NYSE Symbol DRM Options on CBOE (Jan-Apr-Jul-Oct) In S&P MidCap 400

Price	Range	P-E Ratio	Dividend	Yield	S&P Ranking	Beta
Aug. 17'93	1993					
24½	25¾–17	21	0.52	2.1%	NR	0.72

Summary

Diamond Shamrock is a large Southwest regional refiner and marketer of petroleum products, with two Texas refineries, pipelines and terminals and about 2,000 branded stores in eight states. Its activities include crude oil refining, wholesale and retail marketing of refined products, and storage and marketing of natural gas liquids. Earnings for 1992 were down, but rebounded in 1993's first half on strong margins.

Business Summary

Diamond Shamrock, Inc. is engaged in crude oil refining and wholesale marketing of refined petroleum products; retail marketing of refined petroleum products and other merchandise through high-volume gasoline/convenience outlets in the Southwest and Colorado; manufacturing and marketing of petrochemicals; and storage and marketing of natural gas liquids. Revenue and operating profit contributions in 1992:

	Revs.	Profits
Refining & wholesale	50%	49%
Retail marketing	37%	34%
Allied businesses	13%	17%

The company owns and operates two modern refineries. Total processing capacity approximates 200,000 bbls. of crude oil per day: 130,000 bbls. at the McKee, Texas refinery and 70,000 bbls. at the Three Rivers, Texas refinery. Crude throughput was 164,684 barrels daily in 1992, compared with 160,003 in 1991. Wholesale refined product sales were 199,193 barrels daily. Approximately 94% of the refinery outputs are in high value products such as gasoline, diesel, jet fuels, and liquid petroleum gases. DRM ceased operation of its McKee natural gas processing facility in early 1993. The company has no present plans to operate the facility.

DRM transports crude oil to its refineries through owned or leased pipelines. Refined products are distributed through its 2,290 miles of pipelines connected to 15 terminals. DRM markets gasoline, diesel, and convenience merchandise through 761 company-operated retail outlets in Texas, Colorado, Louisiana and New Mexico. Another 1,177 Diamond Shamrock branded stations are supplied with gasoline and diesel by 126 jobbers.

Allied businesses encompass fields where the company has technical, operating or management expertise. DRM is a marketer of natural gas liquids and ammonia fertilizer and offers underground

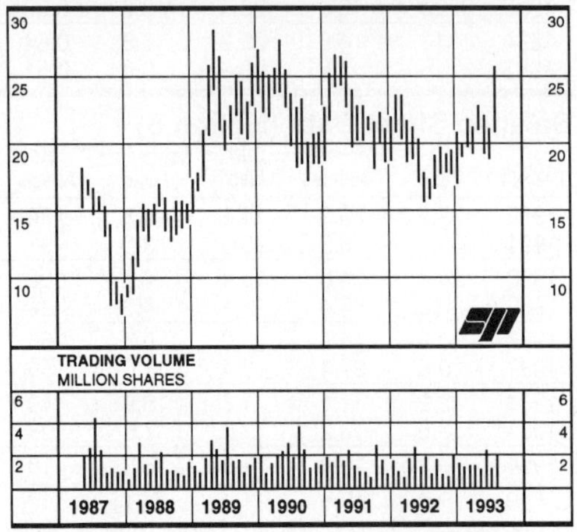

strorage tank services, as well as specialized telephone services. Through a joint venture it explores for, produces and refines oil and gas in South America. At its Mont Belvieu operations, DRM owns and operates the largest commercial underground natural liquids storage facility in the world with about 71 million bbls. of storage.

Important Developments

Jul. '93— DRM announced plans to build a refined products terminal at Colorado Springs, Colo. and extend to Denver its pipeline now under construction from the Texas Panhandle to the Colorado Springs area. The terminal is expected to be completed in the spring of 1994.

Jun. '93— A new hydrocracker began operations at the company's Three Rivers refinery. This expansion will increase gasoline production at the refinery by up to 50%.

Next earnings report expected in late October.

Per Share Data ($)

Yr. End Dec. 31	1992	1991	1990	1989	1988	1987	1986
Tangible Bk. Val.	**15.18**	15.25	13.83	11.11	11.66	10.20	NM
Cash Flow	**2.90**	3.34	4.96	3.91	3.70	1.89	NA
Earnings[1]	**0.92**	[2]1.39	[2]3.04	[2]2.20	[2]2.14	0.41	NA
Dividends	**0.52**	0.52	0.49	0.44	0.40	0.30	Nil
Payout Ratio	**57%**	40%	16%	20%	19%	75%	Nil
Prices—High	**23⅝**	26⅝	27¾	28½	17	18¼	NA
Low	**15⅝**	18⅛	17¼	14⅞	8⅝	7⅜	NA
P/E Ratio—	**26–17**	19–13	9–6	13–7	8–4	45–18	NA

Data as orig. reptd. **1.** Bef. results of disc. opers. of +0.06 in 1987, and spec. items of -0.62 in 1992, -1.30 in 1989, -0.03 in 1988, and -0.40 in 1987. **2.** Ful. dil. EPS: 1.36 in 1991, 2.78 in 1990, 2.10 in 1989, 2.08 in 1988. NM-Not Meaningful. NA-Not Available.

Income Data (Million $)

Year Ended Dec. 31	Revs.	Oper. Inc.	% Oper. Inc. of Revs.	Cap. Exp.	Depr. & Depl.	Int. Exp.	Net Bef. Taxes	Eff. Tax Rate	[2]Net Inc.	% Net Inc. of Revs.	Cash Flow
[3]1992	**2,603**	**132**	**5.1**	**171**	**56.8**	**46.6**	**44**	**40.0%**	**26.4**	**1.0**	**83**
1991	2,576	135	5.2	180	52.3	40.2	58	35.7%	37.1	1.4	89
1990	2,708	199	7.3	86	47.2	38.5	118	34.5%	77.5	2.9	122
1989	2,091	158	7.5	129	41.8	28.7	94	36.0%	60.1	2.9	96
1988	1,804	146	8.1	78	37.4	30.8	84	35.5%	54.3	3.0	89
1987	1,741	78	4.5	45	34.2	35.1	16	39.9%	[3]9.5	0.5	44
[1]1986	1,637	97	5.9	81	33.6	45.7	d30	NM	d24.8	NM	9

Balance Sheet Data (Million $)

Dec. 31	Cash	Curr. Assets	Curr. Liab.	Curr. Ratio	Total Assets	% Ret. on Assets	Long Term Debt	Common Equity	Total Cap.	% LT Debt of Cap.	% Ret. on Equity
1992	**17.5**	**359**	**217**	**1.7**	**1,298**	**2.1**	**534**	**436**	**1,031**	**51.8**	**6.0**
1991	15.7	410	253	1.6	1,222	2.9	442	438	945	46.8	8.9
1990	23.3	449	329	1.4	1,134	7.2	369	338	760	48.5	24.5
1989	26.8	375	224	1.7	1,027	6.4	348	271	744	46.8	19.5
1988	21.9	271	192	1.4	843	6.5	230	279	639	36.0	19.6
1987	14.4	283	178	1.6	825	NM	363	244	634	57.3	NM
1986	20.2	203	268	0.8	725	NA	382	54	457	83.5	NA

Data as orig. reptd. **1.** Excludes discontinued operations. **2.** Bef. results of disc. opers. and spec. item(s). **3.** Reflects accounting changes. d-Deficit. NM-Not Meaningful. NA-Not Available.

Sales & Oper. Revenues (Million $)

Quarter:	1993	1992	1991	1990
Mar.	621	586	640	585
Jun.	657	648	631	567
Sep.		702	668	725
Dec.		667	637	832
		2,603	2,576	2,708

Revenues for the six months ended June 30, 1993, rose 3.6%, year to year, reflecting increased gasoline and merchandise sales. Earnings benefited from strong margins and net income surged 58%, to $0.69 a share from $0.45. A cumulative charge for accounting changes of $17.7 million ($0.62 a share) is excluded from the 1992 period.

Common Share Earnings ($)

Quarter:	1993	1992	1991	1990
Mar.	0.15	d0.38	0.18	0.11
Jun.	0.54	0.82	0.70	0.45
Sep.		0.61	0.61	2.15
Dec.		d0.14	d0.08	0.32
		0.92	1.39	3.04

Finances

During 1993's first half, the company completed the private sale of 1,725,000 shares of 5% convertible preferred stock at $50 per share. Each share is convertible into 1.9 common shares. Net proceeds of $85 million will be used to repay debt and for other corporate purposes.

At March 31, 1993, the company had paid $43.6 million of its potential Maxus Energy Corp. liability of $85.0 million.

DRM's 1993 capital spending budget totals about $140 million, down from $171 million in 1992. The program includes $75 million to complete projects underway, including the expansion at Three Rivers and the diesel desulfurization unit at McKee. In addition, the company plans to open about 12 new U.S. stores in 1993 and 200 new stores in Mexico over the next five years.

In October 1992, DRM announced plans to build a 254 mile refined products pipeline from its McKee refinery in Texas to the Colorado Springs area. About 84 miles of the pipeline was in the ground in late July 1993. The company anticipated completion of the pipeline, with an initial capacity of 32,000 bbl. a day, and a potential capacity of 50,000 bbl. a day, by the end of 1993.

Dividend Data

Dividends were initiated in 1987. A revised "poison pill" stock purchase right was adopted in 1990.

Amt of Divd. $	Date Decl.	Ex–divd. Date	Stock of Record	Payment Date
0.13	Nov. 3	Nov. 16	Nov. 20	Dec. 4'92
0.13	Feb. 2	Feb. 12	Feb. 19	Mar. 5'93
0.13	May 4	May 14	May 20	Jun. 7'93
0.13	Aug. 3	Aug. 16	Aug. 20	Sep. 7'93

Capitalization

Long Term Debt: $549,000,000 (3/93).

5% Conv. Pfd. Stk.: 1,725,000 shs., each initially conv. into com. at $26.50 a sh. after September 8, 1993.

Common Stock: 28,796,522 shs. ($0.01 par). Institutions hold approximately 70%. Shareholders of record: 23,349 (3/93).

d-Deficit.

Office—9830 Colonnade Blvd., P.O. Box 696000, San Antonio, TX 78269-6000. **Tel**—(210) 641-6800. **Chrmn, Pres & CEO**—R. R. Hemminghaus. **VP-Treas**—R. C. Becker. **Secy**—J. D. King. **Investor Contact**—Bill Strain. **Dirs**—B. C. Ames, E. G. Biggs, W. E. Bradford, L. F. Cavazos, W. L. Fisher, R. R. Hemminghaus, B. Marbut, W. S. McConnor, K. D. Ortega. **Transfer Agent**—Society National Bank, Cleveland. **Incorporated** in Delaware in 1987. **Empl**—6,000.

 J.R. Jordan

Dibrell Brothers

NASDAQ Symbol DBRL Options on Options on Phila. (Incl. in Nat'l Market) In S&P MidCap 400

Price	Range	P-E Ratio	Dividend	Yield	S&P Ranking	Beta
Sep. 24'93	1993					
28¼	44–23	10	0.72	2.5%	A–	1.25

Summary

This company redries and packs leaf tobacco for sale to manufacturers of cigarettes and other tobacco products. A large majority of its tobacco revenue is derived from sales to foreign customers. During fiscal 1988, Dibrell entered the international flower brokerage business, which now accounts for about one-third of total sales. An agreement to merge with competitor Standard Commercial was terminated by Standard in April 1993. Dibrell raised the dividend on its common shares by 20% with the June 1993 payment.

Business Summary

Dibrell Brothers' principal business is the buying and processing of leaf tobacco in the U.S. and foreign countries for sale to manufacturers of cigarettes and other tobacco products. The company also derives a significant amount of revenues from the purchase and sale of cut flowers throughout the world (a business it entered in mid-1987). During 1990, Dibrell discontinued its home ice cream freezer and retail flower businesses.

Sales and operating profit by product segment in fiscal 1992 were:

	Sales	Profit
Tobacco	67%	89%
Non–Tobacco	33%	11%

Dibrell and its domestic subsidiaries buy leaf tobacco on auction markets throughout the southeastern U.S. This tobacco is shipped to plants located in North Carolina and Virginia, where it is redried, packed in hogsheads or cases and then stored until shipped to customers. The company also buys, processes and exports tobacco grown in a number of foreign countries that is sold on world markets. Some 70% of the company's tobacco revenues in fiscal 1992 (61% in fiscal 1991) was derived from sales and services to foreign customers.

About 58% of tobacco sales in fiscal 1992 was made to 16 customers controlled by three companies: Philip Morris, Japan Tobacco and RJR Nabisco.

The company's cut flower operations are conducted principally through its Florimex unit, Nuremberg, Germany, which has 50 operations in 18 countries, that import, export and distribute cut flowers to wholesalers and retailers. The flower segment was expanded by the May 1988 acquisition of a 70% interest in Baardse, an exporter of cut flowers purchased primarily from the major flower auctions in the Netherlands. Revenues in the flower segment are derived principally from daily sales of flowers to customers in Europe, North America and Japan (with Europe accounting for most of the revenue).

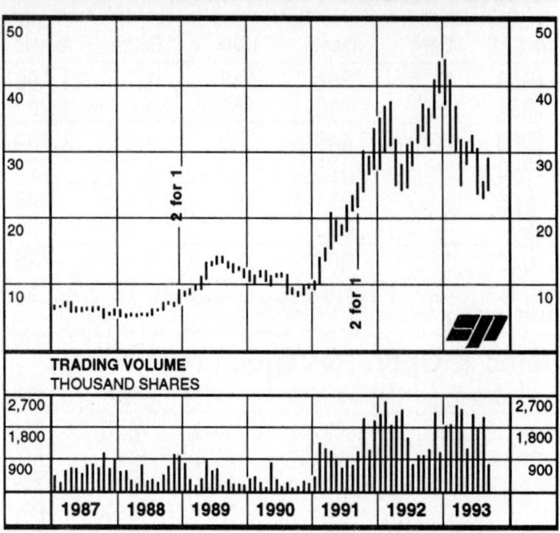

Important Developments

Apr. '93— Dibrell said it was informed by Standard Commercial that Standard's board of directors terminated the previously announced agreement to merge Standard and Dibrell. The merger would have created a new company with annual sales of about $2.3 billion.

Next earnings report expected in mid-November.

Per Share Data ($)

Yr. End Jun. 30	1993	1992	1991	[1]1990	1989	[1]1988	1987	1986	1985	1984
Tangible Bk. Val.	**NA**	4.29	5.37	5.17	4.61	3.97	4.18	4.44	4.36	3.43
Cash Flow	**NA**	3.82	2.46	1.88	1.78	1.45	0.18	0.96	1.27	0.84
Earnings[2]	**2.87**	[3]2.31	[3]1.60	1.11	1.11	0.95	d0.08	0.72	1.09	0.63
Dividends	**0.630**	0.510	0.420	0.360	0.300	0.255	0.230	0.210	0.170	0.137
Payout Ratio	**22%**	22%	26%	33%	27%	27%	NM	26%	15%	21%
Prices[4]—High	**44**	43¾	33¾	12⅛	14¼	9¼	7½	7¼	6¾	4 11/16
Low	**23**	24¼	9¼	8¼	8¼	5 1/16	4 15/16	5¾	4 5/16	3 1/16
P/E Ratio—	**15–8**	19–10	21–6	11–7	13–7	10–5	NM	10–8	6–4	7–5

Data as orig. reptd. Adj. for stk. divs. of 100% Sep. 1991, 100% Dec. 1988, 50% Jun. 1985. **1.** Refl. merger or acq. **2.** Bef. results of disc. ops. of -0.20 in 1990, and spec. items of +0.08 in 1993, -0.02 in 1992. **3.** Ful. dil.: 2.54 in 1993, 2.07 in 1992, 1.59 in 1991. **4.** Cal. yr. d-Deficit. NM-Not Meaningful. NA-Not Available.

Income Data (Million $)

Year Ended Jun. 30	Revs.	Oper. Inc.	% Oper. Inc. of Revs.	Cap. Exp.	Depr.	Int. Exp.	[5]Net Bef. Taxes	Eff. Tax Rate	[6]Net Inc.	% Net Inc. of Revs.	Cash Flow
1992	**1,081**	**87.1**	**8.1**	**32.4**	**20.0**	**26.6**	**47.5**	**35.0%**	**30.6**	**2.8**	**50.7**
1991	1,003	61.0	6.1	19.3	11.4	28.6	34.1	36.4%	21.2	2.1	32.5
[1,2]1990	765	35.4	4.6	12.9	10.3	20.3	20.2	30.9%	14.6	1.9	24.9
1989	685	36.6	5.3	19.6	9.0	17.8	21.5	30.7%	14.6	2.1	23.6
[2]1988	555	33.4	6.0	14.3	6.8	10.0	18.8	28.6%	12.7	2.3	19.5
1987	308	7.3	2.4	5.0	3.7	5.0	d1.8	NM	[3]d1.1	NM	2.6
1986	342	22.2	6.5	6.2	3.7	5.2	16.4	30.6%	11.3	3.3	15.0
1985	382	27.2	7.1	5.5	3.1	5.6	20.3	3.2%	19.2	5.0	22.4
1984	329	23.4	7.1	[4]5.8	3.6	6.2	17.2	33.7%	11.0	3.4	14.6
[3]1983	385	24.7	6.4	3.3	3.3	7.8	17.6	39.1%	10.2	2.6	13.5

Balance Sheet Data (Million $)

Jun. 30	Cash	Curr. Assets	Curr. Liab.	Curr. Ratio	Total Assets	% Ret. on Assets	Long Term Debt	Common Equity	Total Cap.	% LT Debt of Cap.	% Ret. on Equity
1992	**15.2**	**414**	**292**	**1.4**	**630**	**5.2**	**202**	**120**	**329**	**61.5**	**28.1**
1991	29.2	322	222	1.5	539	4.4	203	97	308	65.7	23.7
1990	24.6	271	245	1.1	431	4.0	91	81	178	51.0	18.7
1989	7.2	187	130	1.4	303	4.9	85	75	167	51.0	21.0
1988	19.2	179	130	1.4	290	5.7	84	64	154	54.9	21.3
1987	10.0	112	95	1.2	160	NM	Nil	58	61	Nil	NM
1986	11.4	128	97	1.3	177	7.4	7	64	77	9.7	18.0
1985	15.7	127	71	1.8	159	11.7	Nil	77	84	Nil	28.0
1984	23.8	135	81	1.7	169	6.8	10	60	84	11.8	19.8
1983	12.6	118	65	1.8	153	6.4	20	51	84	23.9	21.7

Data as orig. reptd. **1.** Excl. disc. ops. **2.** Refl. merger or acq. **3.** Refl. acctg. change. **4.** Net. **5.** Incl. equity in earns. of nonconsol. subs. **6.** Bef. spec. items in 1992. d-Deficit. NM-Not Meaningful.

Net Sales (Million $)

Quarter:	1992–93	1991–92	1990–91	1989–90
Sep.	256	219	162	132
Dec.	290	300	302	220
Mar.	259	264	314	242
Jun.	260	298	226	171
	1,065	1,081	1,003	765

Based on a preliminary report, net sales in the year ended June 30, 1993, declined 1.5% from those of the preceding year, as higher flowers sales were outweighed by lower tobacco revenues due to lower average prices. Despite $2.9 million of expenses related to the terminated merger agreement with Standard Commercial, income advanced 25%, to $38,278,395 ($2.87 a share; $2.54 fully diluted), from $30,615,201 ($2.31; $2.07). Per share results exclude a credit of $0.08 and a charge of $0.03 from accounting changes in the respective years.

Common Share Earnings ($)

Quarter:	1992–93	1991–92	1990–91	[1]1989–90
Sep.	0.64	0.47	0.31	0.29
Dec.	0.71	0.54	0.45	0.29
Mar.	0.52	0.66	0.41	0.36
Jun.	0.99	0.63	0.43	0.17
	2.87	2.31	1.60	1.11

1. From contg. ops.

Dividend Data

Cash has been paid each year since 1925.

Amt of Divd. $	Date Decl.	Ex–divd. Date	Stock of Record	Payment Date
0.15	Oct. 30	Nov. 24	Dec. 1	Dec. 15'92
0.15	Mar. 3	Mar. 8	Mar. 13	Mar. 19'93
0.18	May 28	Jun. 2	Jun. 8	Jun. 15'93
0.18	Aug. 27	Aug. 30	Sep. 6	Sep. 15'93

Finances

In April 1992, the company said it had established a $3.6 million loss reserve against tobacco shipments to Iraq for which it hadn't been paid. The charge, which amounted to about $0.27 a share, was recorded in fiscal 1992's third quarter.

Capitalization

Long Term Debt: $202,239,938 (3/93), incl. $56.8 million of 7.75% sub. debs., conv. into com. at $40.31 per sh.

Minority Interest: $1,203,284 (3/93).

Common Stock: 13,300,549 shs. ($1 par). Institutions hold some 42%. Shareholders: 3,727 (8/92).

Office—512 Bridge St., Danville, VA 24541. **Tel**—(804) 792-7511. **Chrmn & CEO**—C. B. Owen Jr. **Pres & COO**—W. G. Barker Jr. **Sr VP & CFO**—T. H. Faucett. **VP & Treas**—J. M. Dall. **VP, Secy & Investor Contact**—John O. Hunnicutt III. **Dirs**—G. L. Baliles, W. G. Barker Jr., L. N. Dibrell III, T. H. Faucett, H. F. Frigon, H. P. Green III, R. J. Holland, J. L. Lanier, T. W. Oakes, C. B. Owen Jr., N. A. Scher, R. M. Simmons Jr. **Registrar & Transfer Agent**—First Union National Bank, Charlotte, NC. **Incorporated** in Virginia in 1904. **Empl**—2,000.

 Gregg W. Bonardi, CFA

Diebold, Inc.

NYSE Symbol DBD Options on CBOE (Feb-May-Aug-Nov) In S&P MidCap 400

Price	Range	P-E Ratio	Dividend	Yield	S&P Ranking	Beta
Oct. 14'93	1993					
57⅞	60⅜–39⅛	24	1.20	2.1%	B+	0.74

Summary

Diebold is a leading manufacturer of automated transaction systems, including automated teller machines and point-of-sale terminals, and security equipment. Propects for continued earnings growth are enhanced by the opportunity to expand into new international markets through InterBold, a joint venture with IBM, and by foreign acquisitions. Results should also continue to benefit from banking industry strength.

Current Outlook

Earnings for 1993 are estimated at $2.40 a share, up from 1992's $2.05 (as adjusted). An advance to $2.75 is possible in 1994.

Dividends should continue at $0.30 quarterly.

DBD should report a strong 1993 fourth quarter, as incoming orders in the third quarter exceeded first and second quarter levels, with improvements in all product areas. Backlog going into the fourth quarter is up from the third quarter level. Beyond 1993, results should benefit from continued expansion in international markets. The company aims for international sales to provide 35% of total revenues within four years, up from 18% in 1992. InterBold, a 70%-owned joint venture with IBM, should continue to expand international sales as the i series of ATMs is rolled out in Europe. Acquisitions and joint ventures, especially in Europe, will aid results. Domestically, DBD should continue to benefit from banking industry strength. Gross margins may narrow slightly, but operating costs should be tightly controlled.

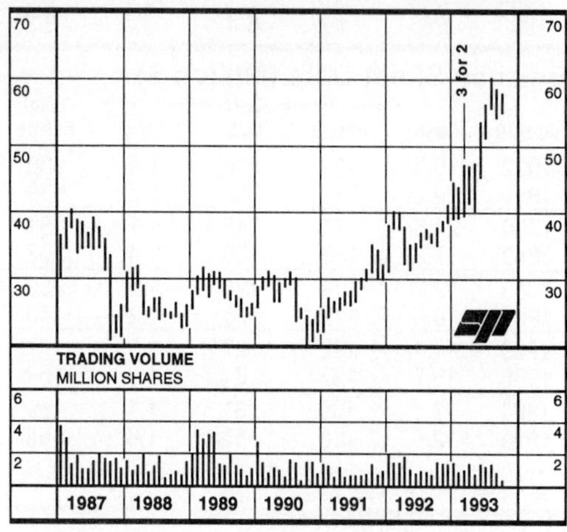

Net Sales (Million $)

Quarter:	1993	1992	1991	1990
Mar.	134.5	121.6	112.8	113.2
Jun.	150.2	134.7	121.5	119.4
Sep.	162.3	133.2	126.7	115.2
Dec.	---	154.4	145.2	128.3
	---	543.9	506.2	476.1

Revenues in the nine months ended September 30, 1993, advanced 15%, year to year. Gross margins narrowed, but operating costs were controlled; pretax income surged 34%. After taxes at 31.4%, versus 28.0%, income was up 27%, to $33.1 million ($1.64 a share), from $26.0 million ($1.30 as adjusted). Results in the 1992 period exclude a charge of $0.89 a share from the cumulative effect of an accounting change.

Common Share Earnings ($)

Quarter:	1993	1992	1991	1990
Mar.	0.43	0.32	0.27	0.40
Jun.	0.58	0.43	0.33	0.39
Sep.	0.63	0.55	0.47	0.11
Dec.	E0.76	0.75	0.73	0.47
	E2.40	2.05	1.80	1.37

Important Developments

Sep. '93— The company signed an agreement with Schlumberger Ltd. (SLB, NYSE) to become the exclusive U.S. distributor of SLB's electronic funds transfer/point-of-sale (EFT/POS) terminals. DBD's current POS debit card products account for more than 10% of installed EFT/POS debit terminals.

Next earnings report expected in mid-January.

Per Share Data ($)

Yr. End Dec. 31	1992	1991	1990	1989	1988	[2]1987	1986	1985	1984	1983
Tangible Bk. Val.[1]	**19.91**	19.88	19.05	19.17	18.27	17.28	16.27	15.26	14.35	12.04
Cash Flow	**2.68**	2.44	2.00	2.43	2.11	2.25	2.15	1.87	3.19	2.79
Earnings[3]	**2.05**	1.80	1.37	1.83	1.59	1.81	1.77	1.55	2.90	2.51
Dividends	**1.120**	1.067	1.000	0.933	0.867	0.800	0.733	0.667	0.533	0.445
Payout Ratio	**55%**	60%	73%	51%	55%	44%	41%	43%	18%	18%
Prices—High	**41⅜**	35 5/16	31 5/16	31 13/16	32	40½	31 5/16	38 5/16	39 5/16	45 5/16
Low	**31⅛**	22 1/16	20	24¼	22 11/16	20¾	23 5/16	21¼	29	32 5/16
P/E Ratio—	**20–15**	20–12	23–15	17–13	20–14	22–11	18–13	25–14	14–10	18–13

Data as orig. reptd. Adj. for stk. divs. of 50% Mar. 1993, 50% Feb. 1985. **1.** Incl. intangibles. **2.** Refl. acctg. change. **3.** Bef. spec. items of -0.89 in 1992, +0.23 in 1988. E-Estimated.

Income Data (Million $)

Year Ended Dec. 31	Revs.	Oper. Inc.	% Oper. Inc. of Revs.	Cap. Exp.	Depr.	Int. Exp.	Net Bef. Taxes	Eff. Tax Rate	[2]Net Inc.	% Net Inc. of Revs.	Cash Flow
1992	**544**	**66**	**12.2**	**12.0**	**12.5**	**0.42**	**57**	**23.9%**	**[1]41.3**	**7.6**	**53.6**
1991	506	57	11.3	9.1	12.8	0.40	52	26.1%	35.7	7.1	48.6
1990	476	51	10.7	22.2	12.6	0.79	40	26.0%	27.1	5.7	39.7
1989	469	58	12.3	9.9	11.9	0.53	54	32.7%	36.2	7.7	48.1
1988	451	47	10.4	18.4	10.3	0.59	44	28.6%	31.3	7.0	41.7
[1]1987	439	55	12.6	8.4	8.7	0.84	55	35.1%	35.8	8.1	44.5
1986	414	54	13.1	14.9	7.4	0.75	57	38.4%	[1]34.9	8.4	42.3
1985	411	44	10.6	9.4	6.4	0.92	50	38.9%	30.4	7.4	36.8
1984	474	100	21.1	10.1	5.8	1.16	108	47.3%	56.9	12.0	62.7
1983	446	89	20.0	8.0	5.5	1.39	94	47.4%	49.1	11.0	54.6

Balance Sheet Data (Million $)

Dec. 31	Cash	Curr. Assets	Curr. Liab.	Curr. Ratio	Total Assets	% Ret. on Assets	Long Term Debt	Common Equity	Total Cap.	% LT Debt of Cap.	% Ret. on Equity
1992	**56**	**292**	**118**	**2.5**	**559**	**7.5**	**Nil**	**400**	**412**	**Nil**	**10.3**
1991	68	321	116	2.8	536	6.8	2.0	397	414	0.5	9.2
1990	85	313	116	2.7	520	5.4	3.3	378	399	0.8	7.1
1989	80	289	90	3.2	490	7.7	4.5	380	397	1.1	9.8
1988	92	299	75	4.0	455	7.0	5.0	361	380	1.3	8.9
1987	84	299	89	3.4	442	8.4	6.0	341	353	1.7	10.8
1986	82	244	77	3.2	409	8.7	7.0	320	332	2.1	11.2
1985	102	267	81	3.3	394	7.8	8.0	300	313	2.6	10.4
1984	77	262	89	3.0	383	15.9	9.0	282	294	3.1	22.0
1983	86	234	80	2.9	331	16.5	11.6	236	250	4.6	22.8

Data as orig. reptd. **1.** Refl. acctg. change. **2.** Before spec. items.

Business Summary

Diebold manufactures a broad line of automated transaction systems and security systems used in financial service and commercial applications. Revenue contributions in recent years were:

	1992	1991	1990
Products	56.5%	55.0%	54.5%
Services	43.5%	45.0%	45.5%

International sales contributed 18% of revenues in 1992, down from 22% in 1990.

In September 1990, the company and IBM formed InterBold, a joint venture that provides automated teller machines and financial self-service systems worldwide. DBD owns 70% of InterBold. The company is the leading provider of ATMs in the U.S. and the second largest in the world, as measured by shipments of new units. AT&T, through its acquisition of NCR, is InterBold's largest competitor in the ATM market. In the fall of 1991, InterBold introduced its current product family, the i Series ATMs.

Electronic security systems include IBM and Tandem host-based and a microprocessor-based monitoring systems. Other products include access control systems, video surveillance systems, film cameras, data line security, alarms, and intrusion detection systems.

Physical security products include a line of modular vault systems as well as vault doors, safe deposit boxes, security lockers, data safes, burglar- and fire-resistive safes, and bullet-resistive barriers.

Dividend Data

Dividends have been paid since 1954. A dividend reinvestment plan is available.

Amt. of Divd. $	Date Decl.	Ex–divd. Date	Stock of Record	Payment Date
0.42	Oct. 30	Dec. 4	Dec. 10	Dec. 31'92
3–for–2 Split	Jan. 27	Mar. 1	Feb. 10	Feb. 26'93
0.30	Jan. 27	Mar. 4	Mar. 10	Mar. 31'93
0.30	Apr. 14	May 14	May 20	Jun. 10'93
0.30	Jul. 14	Aug. 11	Aug. 17	Sep. 7'93

Capitalization

Long Term Debt: None (6/93).

Pensions & Postretirement Benefits: $28,941,000.

Minority Interest: $12,055,000.

Common Stock: 20,190,412 shs. ($1.25 par).
Institutions hold 81%.
Shareholders of record: 2,700 (12/92).

Office—P.O. Box 8230, Canton, OH 44711-8230. **Tel**—(216) 489-4000. **Chrmn Pres & CEO**—R. W. Mahoney. **Vice Chrmn**—R. P. Barone. **VP & Secy**—C. Francis-Vogelsang. **EVP & CFO**—G. F. Morris. **Investor Contact**—Donald Eagon, Jr. **Dirs**—R. P. Baronne, L. V. Bockius III, D. T. Carroll, D. R. Gant, R. Koontz, J. N. Lauer, R. W. Mahoney, W. F. Massy, W. R. Timken, Jr. **Transfer Agent & Registrar**—Society National Bank, Cleveland. **Incorporated** in Ohio in 1876. **Empl**—3,975.

 Neeraj K. Vohra

Dole Food

NYSE Symbol DOL Options on Pacific (Mar-Jun-Sep-Dec) In S&P MidCap 400

Price	Range	P–E Ratio	Dividend	Yield	S&P Ranking	Beta
Jul. 13'93	1993					
35	37⅞–30¼	23	0.40	1.1%	B–	1.21

Summary

The comapny is the largest worldwide producer and marketer of fresh fruits and vegetables, and also sells a growing line of packaged foods. It is also a major real estate developer in Hawaii and California. Earnings from fresh fruit, vegetable and nuts operations are sensitive to fluctuations in market prices for these products. Near-term earnings may be penalized by lower worldwide banana prices.

Current Outlook

Earnings for 1993 are projected at $2.15 a share (including a nonrecurring gain), up from 1992's $1.09. A gain to $2.55 a share is seen for 1994.

The $0.10 quarterly dividend is the minimum expected.

Sales and profits from food operations through 1994 may be penalized by lower worldwide banana prices caused by high volumes of industry shipments and the mid-1993 imposition of banana quotas and tarriffs on Latin American banana shipments to the European Community. Improved earnings are seen for packaged foods. Increased commercial and residential real estate sales and profits are likely to be partially offset by continued high development costs related to the startup of two resorts on Lana'i.

Revenues (Million $)

Weeks:	1993	1992	1991	1990
12 Mar.	766	753	699	658
12 Jun.	864	902	919	792
16 Oct.	---	957	898	879
12 Dec.	---	[1]764	700	674
	---	3,375	3,216	3,003

Revenues in the 24 weeks ended June 19, 1993, decreased 1.5%, year to year. Operating income advanced 11%, reflecting higher real estate development profits, and with a $30.9 million gain on the sale of common stock of a subsidiary, pretax income soared 43%. After taxes at 23.0%, versus 21.0%, income increased to $1.55 a share, from $1.12 (before a charge of $0.83).

Common Share Earnings ($)

Weeks:	1993	1992	1991	1990
12 Mar.	0.89	0.45	0.43	0.30
12 Jun.	0.66	0.67	0.90	0.66
16 Oct.	E0.40	0.36	0.43	0.74
12 Dec.	E0.20	[1]d0.39	0.48	0.33
	E2.15	1.09	2.24	2.03

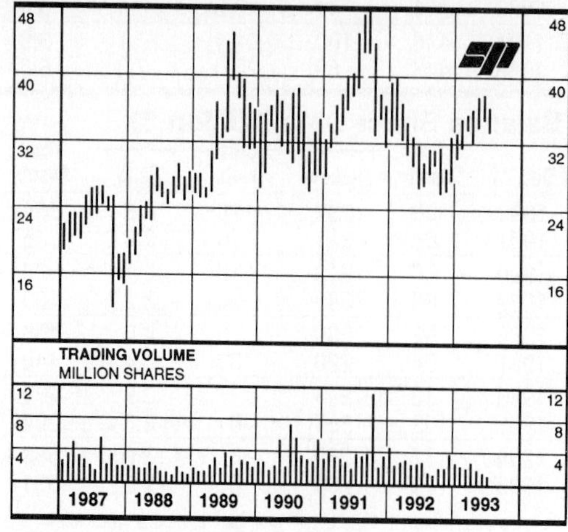

Important Developments

Jul. '93— DOL said 1993 second quarter operating income for food operations slid fractionally, year to year, despite a $9.4 million pretax gain. Lower earnings were attributed primarily to a decline in the price of bananas, partially offset by improved results in the fresh vegetables group, due to stronger overall prices. Operating income for Castle & Cooke Homes Inc. climbed to $8.3 million, from $4.9 million, reflecting more homes delivered in both Hawaii and California. Operating losses before depreciation for the Lana'i resorts narrowed to $4.8 million, from $6.0 million.

Jun. '93— The company registered with the SEC $500 million of debt securities to be offered for public sale. Net proceeds would be used for general corporate purposes, including debt reduction.

Next earnings report expected in mid-November.

Per Share Data ($)

Yr. End Dec. 31[2]	1992	1991	[3]1990	[3]1989	[3,4]1988	[3]1987	1986	1985	[3]1984	[3]1983
Tangible Bk. Val.	**16.80**	17.53	15.67	14.11	12.53	11.22	9.97	8.09	9.39	13.50
Cash Flow	**2.88**	3.63	3.22	2.54	2.86	2.19	2.28	0.43	0.64	d0.39
Earnings[5]	**1.09**	2.24	2.03	1.60	2.05	1.65	1.28	d0.71	d0.30	d1.52
Dividends	**0.40**	0.40	0.10	Nil	Nil	Nil	Nil	Nil	Nil	Nil
Payout Ratio	**36%**	18%	5%	Nil	Nil	Nil	Nil	Nil	Nil	Nil
Prices[6]—High	**40**	48	38⅝	45¼	29⅜	26⅝	20¼	15⅞	19	17⅞
Low	**26**	28	26¼	25⅜	17¼	12	13	9⅝	8⅞	8⅜
P/E Ratio—	**37–24**	21–13	19–13	28–16	14–8	16–7	16–10	NM	NM	NM

Data as orig. reptd. Adj. for stk. div. of 3.2% Jul. 1985. **1.** 13 wks. **2.** Yrs. ended Jun. 30 prior to 1986. **3.** Refl. merger or acq. **4.** Refl. acctg. change. **5.** Bef. results of disc. ops. of +0.13 in 1987, -0.72 in 1986, -0.72 in 1985, -2.73 in 1984, -0.37 in 1983, and spec. item(s) of -0.83 in 1992. **6.** Cal. yr. d-Deficit. E-Estimated. NM-Not Meaningful.

Income Data (Million $)

Year Ended Dec. 31[1]	Revs.	Oper. Inc.	% Oper. Inc. of Revs.	Cap. Exp.	Depr.	Int. Exp.	[6]Net Bef. Taxes	Eff. Tax Rate	[7]Net Inc.	% Net Inc. of Revs.	Cash Flow
1992	**3,375**	**291**	**8.6**	**205**	**107**	**78.2**	**72**	**8.9%**	**[3]65**	**1.9**	**172**
1991	3,216	307	9.5	325	83	73.5	169	21.0%	134	4.2	217
[2]1990	3,003	300	10.0	247	71	72.7	188	36.0%	120	4.0	191
[2]1989	2,718	254	9.4	304	56	60.9	151	37.0%	[3]95	3.5	151
[2,3]1988	2,469	237	9.6	155	41	48.9	175	36.0%	112	4.5	146
[2,4]1987	1,749	156	8.9	268	26	25.8	122	27.2%	89	5.1	104
[4]1986	1,738	176	10.1	40	43	52.6	94	19.6%	[3]76	4.3	99
[4]1985	1,601	76	4.7	30	30	56.7	d11	NM	d10	NM	11
[2,4]1984	1,520	56	3.7	34	27	30.9	d8	NM	1	0.1	18
[2,4]1983	1,552	56	3.6	27	33	[5]37.8	d68	NM	d39	NM	d11

Balance Sheet Data (Million $)

Dec. 31[1]	Cash	Curr. Assets	Curr. Liab.	Curr. Ratio	Total Assets	% Ret. on Assets	Long Term Debt	Common Equity	Total Cap.	% LT Debt of Cap.	% Ret. on Equity
1992	**57**	**981**	**646**	**1.5**	**3,095**	**2.2**	**988**	**1,001**	**2,303**	**42.9**	**6.4**
1991	42	977	565	1.7	2,793	5.1	813	1,041	1,881	43.2	13.6
1990	27	875	616	1.4	2,423	5.1	543	929	1,495	36.3	13.6
1989	44	922	850	1.1	2,270	4.5	245	836	1,121	21.9	12.0
1988	103	866	546	1.6	1,922	5.7	331	743	1,107	29.9	14.9
1987	54	730	429	1.7	1,625	5.6	321	532	991	32.4	15.5
1986	59	524	339	1.5	1,519	4.5	385	470	1,032	37.3	13.2
1985	147	593	391	1.5	1,026	NM	245	215	576	42.6	NM
1984	21	576	302	1.9	1,031	0.1	289	243	655	44.1	NM
1983	14	563	259	2.2	1,043	NM	219	385	734	29.8	NM

Data as orig. reptd. **1.** Yrs. ended Jun. 30 prior to 1986. **2.** Refl. merger or acq. **3.** Refl. acctg. change. **4.** Excl. disc. ops. **5.** Net of int. inc. **6.** Incl. equity in earns. of nonconsol. subs. **7.** Bef. spec. item in 1992. d-Deficit. NM-Not Meaningful.

Business Summary

Dole Food (formerly Castle & Cooke) is a leading worldwide producer, packer and marketer of fresh produce and packaged foods. It also develops real estate. Industry segment contributions (profits in millions) for 1992 were:

	Revs.	Profits
Food products:		
North America	46%	$40
Latin America	22%	64
Far East	15%	83
Europe	11%	10
Real estate	5%	53
Resorts	1%	–41

The Dole Food unit is a major worldwide producer and marketer of branded food products, including Dole fresh fruits, such as pineapples, bananas, table grapes and apples under the Dole label; approximately 30 types of fresh vegetables, including lettuce, celery, cauliflower and broccoli under the Dole and related brand labels; packaged foods, including canned pineapple, frozen novelty items and chilled and frozen juices under various labels; and dried fruit and nuts, such as almonds, pistachios, dates, prunes and raisins under the Dole and other company-owned brand names.

Real estate activities, including residential, resort, commercial and industrial projects in Hawaii, California and Arizona, are conducted under the Castle & Cooke name through the company's real estate group. In March 1993, DOL's homebuilding and residential development subsidiary, Castle & Cooke Homes, Inc., completed an initial public offering of 5.4 million common shares; DOL retained an 80% interest.

Dividend Data

Dividends, omitted since 1982, were resumed in December 1990.

Amt. of Divd. $	Date Decl.	Ex–divd. Date	Stock of Record	Payment Date
0.10	Oct. 9	Nov. 4	Nov. 11	Dec. 16'92
0.10	Feb. 5	Feb. 16	Feb. 22	Mar. 22'93
0.10	Mar. 25	May 5	May 11	Jun. 11'93
0.10	Jul. 8	Aug. 25	Aug. 31	Sep. 30'93

Capitalization

Long Term Debt: $1,073,555,000 (3/93).

Minority Interests: $80,782,000.

Common Stock: 59,426,052 shs. (no par).
D. Murdoch holds 23%.
Institutions own 57%.
Shareholders of record: 17,911.

Office—31355 Oak Crest Drive, Westlake Village, CA 91361. **Tel**—(818) 879-6600. **Chrmn & CEO**—D. H. Murdock. **VP-Fin**—W. J. Hain, Jr. **EVP & CFO**—A. B. Sellers. **VP, Treas & Investor Contact**—David B. Cooper. **Dirs**—E. L. Chao, M. Curb, D. A. DeLorenzo, R. M. Ferry, J. F. Gary, F. J. Hata, D. H. Murdock. **Transfer Agent**—First National Bank of Boston. **Incorporated** in Hawaii in 1894. **Empl**—50,000.

 Kenneth A. Shea

Dollar General

NASDAQ Symbol DOLR (Incl. in Nat'l Market) Options on Pacific In S&P MidCap 400

Price	Range	P–E Ratio	Dividend	Yield	S&P Ranking	Beta
Aug. 18'93	1993					
31½	34¼–21	26	0.20	0.6%	A–	1.36

Summary

This retailer specializes in merchandising inexpensive soft and hard goods to low-, middle- and fixed-income families through more than 1,650 Dollar General Stores in small communities in 24 states. Earnings, which advanced sharply in both 1991-2 and 1992-3, continued to surge in 1993-4's first half, fueled by an aggressive expansion program, higher same store sales and well controlled operating costs.

Business Summary

Dollar General Corporation operates a chain of more than 1,600 small, self-service discount stores. The stores feature, at greatly reduced prices, a focused assortment of both brand-name and irregular soft and hard goods.

Contributions to sales in recent fiscal years were:

	1992–3	1991–2
Soft goods (mainly apparel) .	36%	40%
Hard goods	64%	60%

The company's strategy is to provide a focused assortment of basic quality merchandise at everyday low prices to low-, middle- and fixed-income families. The majority of the products in Dollar General stores are priced at $10 or less, with the most expensive item generally priced at $25. In recent years, the company has shifted its merchandise mix focus to hardgoods, reflecting an increased commitment to be in-stock on basics, a greater emphasis on private label products and an expanded selection of brand-name merchandise.

Irregular, overrun and closeout merchandise accounted for some 20% of soft-goods sales in 1992-3 and about 10% of hard-goods sales, while brandname merchandise represented 30% and 50%, respectively.

During the fiscal year ended January 31, 1993, 146 new stores were opened and 51 were closed, for a total of 1,617 in operation at year-end. The stores were located in 24 states, with the greatest concentrations in Tennessee (151 stores) Florida (141), Kentucky (146), Missouri (112) and Illinois (105). The typical store is relatively small (5,600 sq. ft. average size) and is located in a community of less than 25,000 people. Approximately 55% of the stores are located in strip shopping centers, with the remainder in free-standing and downtown buildings. The average Dollar General store generated annual sales of $600,000 in 1992-3, versus $511,000 in 1991-2.

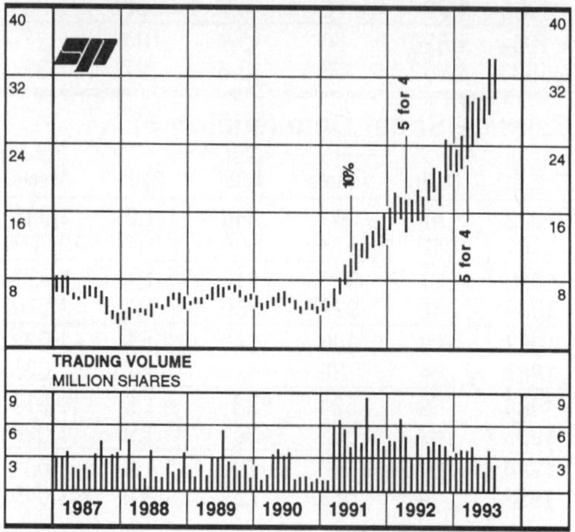

Merchandise is shipped from warehouses in Scottsville, Ky., and Homerville, Ga., or directly from suppliers.

Dollar General's business is seasonal, with significantly higher sales usually recorded in the fourth quarter. The first quarter is historically the least profitable, due largely to the traditionally slow post-Christmas sales period.

Important Developments

Aug. '93— Dollar General said it achieved higher operating profits in 1993-4's second quarter, as well-controlled operating costs and higher sales offset aggressive price reductions. Separately, the company opened 58 new stores and closed 19 stores during the quarter, leaving 1,681 stores in operation as of July 31.

Next earnings report expected in early November.

Per Share Data ($)

Yr. End Jan. 31[1]	1993	1992	1991	1990	1989	1988	1987	[2]1986	1985	[2]1984
Tangible Bk. Val.	**[3]5.80**	[3]4.73	[3]4.18	[3]3.83	[3]3.56	3.44	3.36	3.34	3.54	2.38
Cash Flow	**1.29**	0.86	0.67	0.59	0.51	0.42	0.31	0.69	0.73	0.54
Earnings	**1.05**	0.65	0.46	0.40	0.32	0.21	0.14	0.55	0.64	0.47
Dividends	**0.150**	0.122	0.117	0.117	0.117	0.117	0.117	0.117	0.098	0.078
Payout Ratio	**14%**	19%	25%	30%	36%	57%	87%	21%	15%	17%
Calendar Years	**1992**	1991	1990	1989	1988	1987	1986	1985	1984	1983
Prices—High	**24¾**	15¾	6¾	7⅜	6½	8⅜	14	17⅛	10¼	9¾
Low	**13¾**	4⅜	4¼	5	3¼	2¾	7	10	5	4⅜
P/E Ratio—	**24–13**	24–7	14–9	19–13	20–10	41–14	NM	31–18	16–8	21–9

Data as orig. reptd. Adj. for stk. divs. of 25% Mar. 1993, 25% Apr 1992, 10% Jun. 1991, 20% May 1985. **1.** Dec. 31 of preceding cal. yr. prior to 1989. **2.** Refl. merger or acq. **3.** Incl. intangibles. NM-Not Meaningful.

Income Data (Million $)

Year Ended Jan. 31[1]	Revs.	Oper. Inc.	% Oper. Inc. of Revs.	Cap. Exp.	Depr.	Int. Exp.	Net Bef. Taxes	Eff. Tax Rate	Net Inc.	% Net Inc. of Revs.	Cash Flow
1993	**921**	**69.1**	**7.5**	**24.7**	**8.23**	**2.65**	**58.2**	**38.9%**	**35.6**	**3.9**	**43.8**
1992	754	44.5	5.9	12.8	6.68	3.13	34.7	38.0%	21.5	2.9	28.2
1991	653	34.7	5.3	8.9	6.68	4.95	23.1	36.7%	14.6	2.2	21.3
1990	615	32.3	5.3	17.0	6.03	5.81	20.3	39.1%	12.4	2.0	18.4
1989	613	28.4	4.6	4.5	5.99	6.29	16.2	38.0%	10.0	1.6	16.0
1988	588	25.2	4.3	4.8	6.86	6.77	11.6	44.0%	6.5	1.1	13.4
1987	565	20.4	3.6	12.9	5.90	6.85	7.6	43.4%	4.3	0.8	10.2
[2]1986	584	46.6	8.0	7.3	4.50	7.34	34.8	48.7%	17.8	3.1	22.3
1985	481	47.1	9.8	7.0	2.97	4.15	40.0	48.5%	20.6	4.3	23.6
[2]1984	347	33.6	9.7	2.6	2.15	1.81	29.7	49.0%	15.1	4.4	17.3

Balance Sheet Data (Million $)

Jan. 31[1]	Cash	Curr. Assets	Curr. Liab.	Curr. Ratio	Total Assets	% Ret. on Assets	Long Term Debt	Common Equity	Total Cap.	% LT Debt of Cap.	% Ret. on Equity
1993	**25.0**	**256**	**117.0**	**2.2**	**316**	**12.7**	**7.0**	**190**	**199**	**3.5**	**20.6**
1992	7.9	192	62.4	3.1	237	9.6	21.2	151	175	12.1	15.1
1991	3.9	168	55.1	3.1	208	7.3	19.1	132	153	12.5	11.6
1990	6.5	155	45.1	3.4	194	6.1	26.8	121	149	18.0	10.6
1989	5.7	183	52.4	3.5	210	4.6	45.6	112	158	28.9	9.1
1988	7.3	190	61.4	3.1	225	2.9	48.9	109	163	29.9	6.0
1987	5.2	194	65.2	3.0	232	1.9	52.3	109	167	31.3	4.0
1986	6.8	189	50.2	3.8	228	8.9	64.3	108	177	36.2	17.7
1985	4.7	149	49.3	3.0	174	12.6	27.0	94	125	21.6	24.2
1984	15.9	135	40.2	3.4	154	11.6	35.7	77	114	31.3	21.5

Data as orig. reptd. **1.** Dec. 31 of preceding cal. yr. prior to 1989. **2.** Refl. merger or acq.

Net Sales (Million $)

Quarter:	1993–94	1992–93	1991–92	1990–91
Apr.	222	189	148	134
Jul.	256	217	173	153
Oct.		224	190	165
Jan.		292	243	202
		921	754	653

For the six months ended July 31, 1993, net sales advanced 18%, year to year, reflecting more stores in operation and greater same-store sales. Gross profits widened, benefiting from higher beginning inventory margins and a more profitable product mix. Following well-controlled operating expenses, net income rose 47%, to $15,541,000 ($0.45 a share, based on 2.3% more shares), from $10,578,000 ($0.31).

Common Share Earnings ($)

Quarter:	1993–94	1992–93	1991–92	1990–91
Apr.	0.17	0.11	0.04	0.02
Jul.	0.28	0.20	0.11	0.08
Oct.		0.24	0.13	0.09
Jan.		0.49	0.37	0.29
		1.05	0.65	0.46

Dividend Data

Cash payments were initiated in 1975.

Amt. of Divd. $	Date Decl.	Ex–divd. Date	Stock of Record	Payment Date
0.05	Aug. 18	Aug. 19	Aug. 25	Sep. 11'92
0.05	Nov. 17	Nov. 20	Nov. 27	Dec. 15'92
5–for–4	Feb. 2	Mar. 1	Feb. 12	Feb. 26'93
0.05	Feb. 2	Feb. 17	Feb. 23	Mar. 12'93
0.05	Jun. 7	Aug. 25	Aug. 31	Sep. 17'93

Finances

Capital expenditures during 1993-4 are expected to total between $16 million and $19 million, and will include amounts for opening 185 new stores and installing electronic cash registers and hand-held scanners at all stores.

Capitalization

Long Term Obligs.: $5,974,000 (7/93).

Common Stock: 32,884,157 shs. ($0.50 par). About 26% is owned by the Turner family. Institutions hold about 56%. Shareholders: About 2,950 of record (1/93).

Options: To buy about 2,321,553 shs. at $3.49 to $22.60 ea. (1/93).

Office—104 Woodmont Blvd., Suite 500, Nashville, TN 37205. **Tel**—(615) 386-4000. **Chrmn, Pres & CEO**—C. Turner Jr. **VP & Secy**—B. R. Carpenter. **Investor Contact**—Cabot Pyle (615) 783-2000. **Dirs**—J. L. Clayton, J. D. Cockman, J. B. Holland, W. N. Rasmussen, C. Turner, C. Turner Jr., D. M. Wilds, W. S. Wire II. **Transfer Agent**—Trust Company Bank, Atlanta. **Incorporated** in Kentucky in 1955. **Empl**—10,300.

 John D. Coyle, CFA

Donaldson Co.

NYSE Symbol DCI In S&P MidCap 400

Price	Range	P-E Ratio	Dividend	Yield	S&P Ranking	Beta
Sep. 29'93	1993					
38⅜	40⅜–33¼	19	0.44	1.1%	A	1.01

Summary

Donaldson makes a wide variety of air cleaners, filters and mufflers for use with internal combustion engines. Industrial dust collectors and related products are also produced. International operations are important, contributing some 38% of sales and 58% of operating profits in fiscal 1992. DCI recently decided to exit the diesel exhaust particulate trap business due to a diminished outlook for the worldwide market.

Current Outlook

Share earnings for the fiscal year ending July 31, 1994, may rise to $2.10 from fiscal 1993's $2.03.

The dividend should continue at $0.11 quarterly.

Only a slight rise in sales for fiscal 1994 is anticipated as order backlogs have weakened. Military orders may remain sluggish. Gas turbine filtration sales should continue to rise as a strong order backlog is fulfilled. Margins should benefit from plant capacity utilization increases, continued tight control of selling expenses and the absence of costs related to the diesel particulate trap business which was exited in fiscal 1993. Net income should rise.

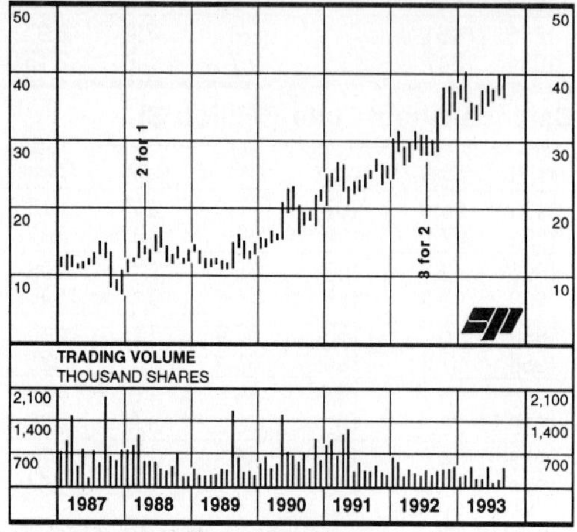

Net Sales (Million $)

Quarter:	1992–93	1991–92	1990–91	1989–90
Oct.	126	113	113	103
Jan.	125	114	116	98
Apr.	133	127	115	112
Jul.	149	128	114	109
	533	482	458	423

Sales (preliminary) for the fiscal year ended July 31, 1993, were up 11% from those of the prior year. Cost of sales rose 9.3%, and operating expenses increased 16%. Following lower other income and higher interest expense, pretax income was up 7.1%. After taxes at 36.9%, against 38.2%, net income rose 9.5%, to $2.03 a share from $1.84 (adjusted).

Common Share Earnings ($)

Quarter:	1992–93	1991–92	1990–91	1989–90
Oct.	0.45	0.43	0.49	0.33
Jan.	0.37	0.35	0.35	0.27
Apr.	0.55	0.52	0.43	0.49
Jul.	0.66	0.53	0.40	0.35
	2.03	1.84	1.67	1.45

Important Developments

Sep. '93— After reassessing their worldwide market potential, DCI decided to exit the business for new and retrofit diesel engine exhaust particulate traps. The company established reserves in fiscal 1993 to cover warranty costs related to particulate traps already in service. Backlogs at July 31, 1993 totaled $130.9 million, down 1% from a year earlier and 5% from April 30, 1993. A 70% rise in gas turbine filtration backlogs offset declines in defense and international engine backlogs. Gas turbine filtration products were in strong demand recently, with sales in the fourth quarter of fiscal 1993 up 70% to a record high of $22.1 million. Hard order backlogs, which are goods scheduled for delivery within 90 days, totaled $88.1 million at July 31, 1993. This was down 8% from the third quarter and 2% lower than a year ago.

Next earnings report expected in late November.

Per Share Data ($)

Yr. End Jul. 31	1993	1992	1991	1990	1989	1988	1987	1986	1985	1984
Tangible Bk. Val.	**NA**	11.63	10.02	8.93	7.49	6.80	6.67	7.16	6.12	5.76
Cash Flow	**NA**	2.85	2.52	2.16	1.79	1.78	1.29	1.45	1.20	1.11
Earnings[1]	**2.03**	1.84	1.67	1.45	1.08	1.11	0.71	0.99	0.73	0.62
Dividends	**0.410**	0.380	0.293	0.263	0.253	0.229	0.220	0.220	0.220	0.220
Payout Ratio	**20%**	21%	18%	18%	24%	21%	31%	22%	30%	36%
Prices[2]—High	**38¼**	38¼	27½	23⅜	16⅛	17⅛	15	13¼	9⅛	8⅛
Low	**24½**	24½	20½	14⅛	11	10½	7⅜	8	5½	5⅜
P/E Ratio—	**18–12**	21–13	16–12	16–10	15–10	16–9	21–10	13–8	13–8	13–9

Data as orig. reptd. Adj. for stk. divs. of 50% Jul. 1992, 100% May 1988. **1.** Bef. spec. items of +0.09 in 1988, +0.09 in 1987. **2.** Cal. yr. NA-Not Available.

Income Data (Million $)

Year Ended Jul. 31	Revs.	Oper. Inc.	% Oper. Inc. of Revs.	Cap. Exp.	Depr.	Int. Exp.	[2]Net Bef. Taxes	Eff. Tax Rate	[3]Net Inc.	% Net Inc. of Revs.	Cash Flow
1992	**482**	**55.3**	**11.5**	**[1]15.5**	**14.0**	**2.68**	**41.7**	**38.2%**	**25.8**	**5.3**	**39.8**
1991	458	53.0	11.6	17.1	11.7	3.53	39.4	38.9%	24.0	5.3	36.2
1990	423	54.8	13.0	16.4	10.4	3.73	34.9	39.7%	21.0	5.0	31.4
1989	398	48.0	12.1	12.1	10.2	3.56	27.7	44.2%	15.4	3.9	25.6
1988	363	44.8	12.3	10.3	10.0	3.23	29.9	45.6%	[4]16.2	4.5	26.2
1987	295	33.3	11.3	15.7	8.9	2.36	21.7	49.6%	11.0	3.7	19.8
1986	271	37.7	13.9	8.3	7.4	2.16	30.9	49.3%	15.6	5.8	23.0
1985	262	32.6	12.4	5.2	7.4	2.50	21.8	47.6%	11.4	4.4	18.8
1984	254	27.8	10.9	5.0	7.7	2.67	20.2	52.1%	9.7	3.8	17.4
1983	204	10.0	4.9	4.6	8.3	2.08	d1.7	NM	d3.5	NM	4.8

Balance Sheet Data (Million $)

Jul. 31	Cash	Curr. Assets	Curr. Liab.	Curr. Ratio	Total Assets	% Ret. on Assets	Long Term Debt	Common Equity	Total Cap.	% LT Debt of Cap.	% Ret. on Equity
1992	**31.1**	**187**	**90.0**	**2.1**	**286**	**9.6**	**23.5**	**160**	**185**	**12.7**	**17.3**
1991	35.1	169	77.5	2.2	253	9.8	25.7	139	165	15.6	18.3
1990	38.4	169	79.9	2.1	246	9.3	28.3	129	157	18.0	17.7
1989	6.2	131	58.0	2.3	205	7.7	30.8	108	138	22.2	15.1
1988	7.3	123	52.1	2.4	194	8.9	33.8	97	131	25.8	16.9
1987	28.9	128	44.6	2.9	201	5.5	35.4	111	146	24.2	9.6
1986	35.8	126	50.5	2.5	191	9.0	16.7	114	130	12.8	14.8
1985	23.8	91	30.7	2.9	154	7.3	17.5	96	114	15.4	12.2
1984	19.5	97	45.0	2.2	161	6.3	19.5	90	110	17.8	11.1
1983	19.6	82	32.8	2.5	148	NM	21.8	85	107	20.4	NM

Data as orig. reptd. **1.** Net. **2.** Incl. equity in earns. of nonconsol. subs. **3.** Bef. spec. items. **4.** Refl. acctg. change. d-Deficit. NM-Not Meaningful.

Business Summary

Donaldson Co. manufactures air cleaners, liquid filtration devices and exhaust products for engines, compressors, mobile equipment and industrial applications. The current focus is on increasing replacement lube filter element market share and marketing diesel particulate traps. Sales and profits by geographic area in fiscal 1992 were:

	Sales	Profits
United States	62.4%	41.6%
Europe	15.5%	21.9%
Japan	13.6%	19.0%
Other countries	8.5%	17.5%

DCI is a major factor in air cleaners and exhaust products for mobile heavy-duty internal combustion engines in the U.S. Related engine products include hydraulic filters, dust control devices for underground mining and special filters for varied purposes, including in-plant air cleaning systems, computer disk drives, clean rooms and respirators.

DCI also makes devices that remove particulate matter from streams of air, gas or liquid, and pulverizing and classifying systems. A lengthy effort to commercialize exhaust after-treatment devices for diesel engines, known as particulate trap oxidizers, was abandoned in the fourth quarter of fiscal 1992-93. The potential for this device over the next few years became severely diminished recently when diesel engine manufacturers were able to comply with new exhaust emission rules for 1993 and 1994 without the need for particulate traps.

Caterpillar (CAT) accounted for 10% of DCI's fiscal 1992 sales, primarily through a joint venture with DCI called AFSI, which manufactures lube, oil and hydraulic filters exclusively for CAT.

Dividend Data

Dividends have been paid since 1956. A dividend reinvestment plan is available. A "poison pill" stock purchase right was adopted in 1986.

Amt of Divd. $	Date Decl.	Ex-divd. Date	Stock of Record	Payment Date
0.10	Nov. 20	Nov. 27	Dec. 3	Dec. 12'93
0.10	Jan. 25	Feb. 22	Feb. 26	Mar. 12'93
0.11	May 21	May 28	Jun. 4	Jun. 14'93
0.11	Jul. 30	Aug. 19	Aug. 25	Sep. 13'93

Capitalization

Long Term Debt: $21,277,000 (4/30/93).

Common Stock: 13,678,231 shs. ($5 par).
Institutions hold about 57% (incl. some shares held by management). The company ESOP holds 12.6%.
Directors & officers own some 9.3%.
Shareholders of record: 1,360.

Office—1400 West 94th St., P.O. Box 1299, Minneapolis, MN 55440. **Tel**—(612) 887-3131. **Chrmn & Pres**— W. A. Hodder. **VP-Secy**—R. F. Vodovnik. **Treas & Investor Contact**—John R. Schweers. **Dirs**—A. G. Ames, M. R. Bonsignore, W. A. Hodder, H. F. Hutter, K. B. Melrose, S. W. Richey, S. W. Sanger, S. G. Shank, P. Townley, C. A. Wurtele. **Transfer Agent & Registrar**—Norwest Bank Minnesota, South St. Paul. **Incorporated** in Delaware in 1936. **Empl**—3,879.

 Joshua M. Harari, CFA

Dreyer's Grand Ice Cream

NASDAQ Symbol DRYR (Incl. in Nat'l Market) Options on Pacific In S&P MidCap 400

Price	Range	P-E Ratio	Dividend	Yield	S&P Ranking	Beta
Sep. 24'93	1993					
26½	31½–19¾	23	0.24	0.9%	B	1.43

Summary

Dreyer's manufactures and distributes premium-quality ice cream and other dairy dessert products; it also distributes frozen dessert products made by others. Following lower earnings in 1992, growth should resume in 1993 on new products and new geographic markets.

Current Outlook

Share earnings are expected to rebound to $1.30 in 1993 and could reach $1.50 in 1994.

The quarterly dividend will likely remain at $0.06 a share.

Revenues in 1993 should benefit from the inclusion of Florida operations for the full year, versus two quarters in 1992, and increased penetration in the eastern U.S. The 1992 acquisitions of T&W and the distribution network of Calip Dairies should provide meaningful gains in the New York metropolitan market. New products for 1993 include six flavors of pint-sized ice cream for distribution to convenience stores, and several flavors of ice cream bars. Margins should rebound somewhat from the depressed level of 1992, which included significant costs for the startup of the Florida operations, though advertising expenditures should remain stable.

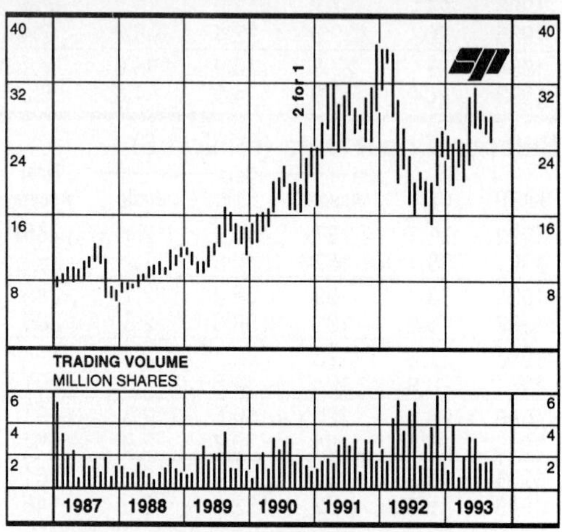

Net Sales (Million $)

13 Weeks:	1993	1992	1991	1990
Mar.	102.3	84.8	72.5	62.8
Jun.	123.5	109.5	97.1	83.5
Sep.	---	120.4	105.5	93.5
Dec.	---	92.4	79.8	68.5
	---	407.0	354.9	308.3

Net sales for the 26 weeks ended June 26, 1993 advanced 16%, year to year. Net income rebounded to $8,993,000 ($0.62 a share), from $6,099,000 ($0.40). Results for the 1992 interim exclude a credit of $0.11 a share from an accounting change.

Common Share Earnings ($)

13 Weeks:	1993	1992	1991	1990
Mar.	0.15	0.02	0.14	0.11
Jun.	0.47	0.38	0.39	0.36
Sep.	E0.48	0.43	0.38	0.32
Dec.	E0.20	0.12	0.14	0.10
	E1.30	0.94	1.05	0.88

Important Developments

Jun. '93— The company executed an agreement to issue $100.8 million face amount of 6.25% debentures to General Electric Capital Corp. and funds managed by GE Investments. Due June 30, 2001, the debentures are convertible into 2.9 million common shares, representing about 16.5% of Dreyer's common shares outstanding. Proceeds were earmarked for the retirement of debt and for general corporate purposes. Separately, the company said that sales growth in 1993's first half was especially strong in Florida and the New York City metropolitan area. On the heels of a very successful entry into the Miami marketplace in mid-1992, Dreyer's expanded into central Florida later in the year; with extensive start-up costs now out of the way, sales and earnings in Florida have begun to contribute significantly to overall corporate growth. In New York, Dreyer's is benefiting from the 1992 acquisitions of the T&W premium ice cream brand and the distribution network of Calip Dairies.

Per Share Data ($)

Yr. End Dec. 31	[1]1992	[1]1991	[1]1990	1989	1988	1987	[1]1986	[1]1985	1984	1983
Tangible Bk. Val.	**2.58**	7.36	6.24	3.34	2.46	2.08	2.37	2.44	2.05	1.79
Cash Flow	**1.69**	1.59	1.42	1.22	1.09	0.67	0.71	0.75	0.61	0.48
Earnings[2]	**0.94**	1.05	[3]0.88	[3]0.69	0.56	0.22	0.40	0.54	0.46	0.35
Dividends	**0.24**	0.20	0.17	Nil	Nil	Nil	Nil	Nil	Nil	Nil
Payout Ratio	**25%**	19%	19%	Nil	Nil	Nil	Nil	Nil	Nil	Nil
Prices—High	**36¼**	36¾	24¼	17	12	12½	16⅛	11 13/16	12⅛	14 11/16
Low	**15**	17¼	12⅝	9	6⅝	5⅝	7 11/16	6 11/16	5⅝	9 3/16
P/E Ratio—	**39–16**	35–16	28–14	25–13	22–12	57–26	40–19	22–12	27–12	42–26

Data as orig. reptd. Adj. for stk. divs. of 100% Oct. 1990, 50% Jun. 1983. **1.** Refl. merger or acq. **2.** Bef. spec. item(s) of +0.12 in 1992, +0.15 in 1989. **3.** Ful. dil.: 0.84 in 1990, 0.68 in 1989. E-Estimated

Income Data (Million $)

Year Ended Dec. 31	Revs.	Oper. Inc.	% Oper. Inc. of Revs.	Cap. Exp.	Depr.	Int. Exp.	[2]Net Bef. Taxes	Eff. Tax Rate	[3]Net Inc.	% Net Inc. of Revs.	Cash Flow
[1]1992	**407**	**38.0**	**9.3**	**29.4**	**11.20**	**5.84**	**22.5**	**37.9%**	**14.0**	**3.4**	**25.2**
[1]1991	355	37.0	10.4	41.6	8.26	5.06	26.1	39.3%	15.9	4.5	24.1
[1]1990	308	30.9	10.0	23.1	7.29	6.13	20.0	40.9%	11.8	3.8	19.1
1989	227	22.9	10.1	12.4	6.54	5.86	13.5	37.0%	8.5	3.7	15.0
1988	189	19.2	10.2	14.1	6.57	5.88	11.3	39.7%	6.8	3.6	13.4
1987	163	11.1	6.8	8.4	5.61	5.75	4.9	43.7%	2.8	1.7	8.4
[1]1986	134	14.1	10.5	11.1	4.52	2.79	11.7	49.5%	5.9	4.4	10.4
[1]1985	103	15.8	15.3	14.2	3.18	0.87	14.0	43.0%	8.0	7.7	11.1
1984	84	14.5	17.2	6.2	2.44	0.35	12.9	44.3%	7.2	8.5	9.6
1983	77	10.8	14.0	7.6	2.02	0.46	9.5	43.5%	5.4	7.0	7.4

Balance Sheet Data (Million $)

Dec. 31	Cash	Curr. Assets	Curr. Liab.	Curr. Ratio	Total Assets	% Ret. on Assets	Long Term Debt	Common Equity	Total Cap.	% LT Debt of Cap.	% Ret. on Equity
1992	**0.6**	**82.3**	**56.5**	**1.5**	**289**	**5.6**	**102.0**	**108**	**232**	**44.0**	**13.0**
1991	3.0	74.0	54.6	1.4	224	7.8	44.3	113	169	26.2	15.2
1990	7.6	68.8	54.9	1.3	180	6.7	21.3	94	124	17.1	16.4
1989	7.1	51.3	22.0	2.3	139	6.5	69.1	41	117	59.1	24.0
1988	5.0	43.4	18.0	2.4	123	5.6	68.6	30	104	65.7	24.6
1987	9.4	48.4	27.4	1.8	124	2.4	65.2	26	96	67.8	9.9
1986	10.6	45.2	16.6	2.7	116	7.0	62.8	32	98	64.0	18.0
1985	10.2	28.3	9.0	3.2	58	15.9	9.4	36	48	19.7	24.6
1984	0.2	12.4	8.4	1.5	44	17.8	2.5	31	35	7.1	23.7
1983	11.1	22.2	5.8	3.9	39	17.7	2.6	30	34	7.8	25.9

Data as orig. reptd. **1.** Refl. merger or acq. **2.** Incl. equity in earns. of nonconsol. subs. prior to 1986. **3.** Bef. spec. item(s).

Business Summary

Dreyer's Grand Ice Cream manufactures and distributes premium-quality ice cream and other dairy dessert products. Its ice cream is the leading premium packaged ice cream product in most areas of the western U.S. In addition, the company's products are sold in various midwestern, mid-Atlantic and southeastern markets and in the New York metropolitan area under the Edy's Grand Ice Cream label (because of an agreement regarding use of the Dreyer's name).

The company's marketing strategy for packaged ice creams is based on maintaining quality. In general, product formulations are developed on the basis of blind taste tests, regardless of the cost of ingredients. Dreyer's tends to resist changes in formulations or production processes even when less expensive alternatives are available.

Dreyer's has responded to a growing customer preference for lower-fat and lower-cholesterol products by introducing several new products in recent years. Grand Light (introduced in 1987 and sold under the Dreyer's and Edy's brand names) is a premium light ice cream that is 93% fat-free and contains as few as 100 calories per serving. Dreyer's and Edy's Frozen Yogurt Inspirations (introduced in 1989) are premium frozen yogurts. Dreyer's Low Fat (1992) has 3% total fat, and Dreyer's Fat Free (reintroduced under the current name in 1992) has no fat and no cholesterol. Grand Delights (1992) is a line of low-calorie ice cream snacks. At 1992 year-end, the various product lines included over 80 flavors.

Dreyer's uses a direct-store delivery system consisting of company-owned and independent distribution operations. To leverage this system, the company also distributes selected branded frozen dessert products manufactured by others, principally Ben & Jerry's Homemade Ice Cream products; Dove brand premium ice cream novelties; and Mocha Mix, manufactured by Dreyer's for Presto Food Products.

Dividend Data

Cash payments were initiated in 1990, and quarterly dividends began in 1991's first quarter.

Amt of Divd. $	Date Decl.	Ex–divd. Date	Stock of Record	Payment Date
0.06	Nov. 16	Dec. 18	Dec. 24	Jan. 6'93
0.06	Mar. 3	Mar. 22	Mar. 26	Apr. 6'93
0.06	May 10	Jun. 21	Jun. 25	Jul. 6'93
0.06	Sep. 9	Sep. 20	Sep. 24	Oct. 5'93

Capitalization

Long Term Debt: $137,650,000 (3/93).

Common Stock: 14,616,977 shs. ($1 par).
Institutions hold about 64%.
Shareholders: 3,166 of record (3/93).

Office—5929 College Ave., Oakland, CA 94618. **Tel**—(510) 652-8187. **Chrmn & CEO**—T. G. Rogers. **Pres**—W. F. Cronk III. **VP & CFO**—P. R. Woodland. **Secy**—E. R. Manwell. **Treas & Investor Contact**—William C. Collett. **Dirs**—W. F. Cronk III, M. M. Halpern, J. L. Katz, E. R. Manwell, T. G. Rogers. **Transfer Agent & Registrar**—First Interstate Bank, San Francisco. **Reincorporated** in Delaware in 1985. **Empl**—1,147.

 Gregg W. Bonardi, CFA

Dreyfus Corp.

NYSE Symbol DRY Options on CBOE (Jan-Apr-Jul-Oct) In S&P MidCap 400

Price	Range	P–E Ratio	Dividend	Yield	S&P Ranking	Beta
Oct. 20'93	1993					
40	44⅜–35¾	15	0.76	1.9%	A	1.58

Summary

Dreyfus Corp. is one of the largest mutual fund management companies in the U.S., with total assets managed, advised or administered of over $80 billion at September 30, 1993. It also owns a savings bank, a trust company, and two insurance companies. Cash and equivalents and marketable securities were over $18 a share at June 30, 1993. Profits in 1993 and 1994 should benefit from the initial assessment of management fees that had been waived on certain funds to attract investors.

Current Outlook

Earnings for 1994 are projected at $2.95 a share, up from the $2.73 estimated for 1993.

The minimum expectation is for dividends to continue at $0.19 quarterly.

DRY's earnings outlook primarily depends on two factors: assets under management and fees received for managing those assets. Assets under management were flat in the first nine months of 1993, but rose 10% in 1992 and 24% in 1991. Growth on the order of 5%-8% is projected for 1994, based on new fund offerings, reinvestment of dividends and interest, and aggressive marketing of employee benefit plans. Total fees, which averaged 0.37% of assets under management in 1993's second quarter, have increased steadily in recent years. The uptrend reflects phase-in of fees on certain funds, which had been waived initially to draw in the assets. As of mid-1993, DRY was waiving fees of about $48 million. Future earnings should benefit from full assessment of management fees, although the timing is uncertain. Share earnings should be aided by stock buybacks. The balance sheet is highly liquid, with cash and marketable securities of about $18.88 per share at June 30, 1993.

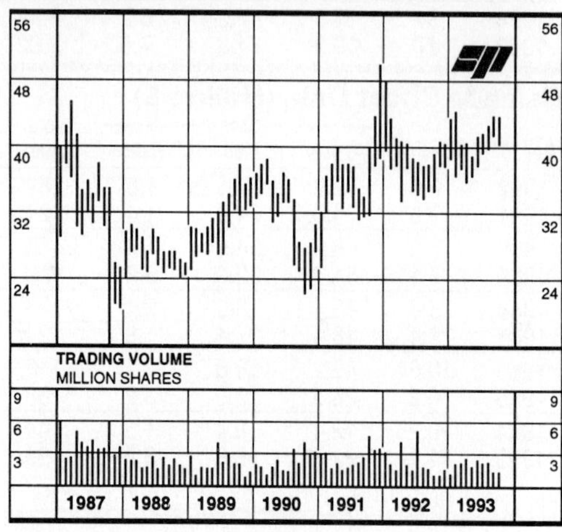

Review of Operations

Revenues in the nine months ended September 30, 1993, rose 12%, year to year, aided by growth of sponsored tax exempt bond funds, reduced fee waivers, and greater gains on investments. Margins widened, and pretax income advanced 14%. After taxes at 37.4%, against 35.0%, net income was up 9.7%. Share earnings were $2.03, on 3.3% fewer shares, versus $1.79.

Common Share Earnings ($)

Quarter:	1994	1993	1992	1991
Mar.	E0.70	0.68	0.60	0.40
Jun.	E0.72	0.68	0.59	0.40
Sep.	E0.75	0.68	0.61	0.48
Dec.	E0.78	E0.69	0.62	0.51
	E2.95	E2.73	2.40	1.77

Important Developments

Oct. '93— Dreyfus attributed its earnings growth for the first nine months of 1993 primarily to an increase in net management fees earned and net gains on investment transactions. Share earnings further benefited from stock buybacks.

Sep. '93— Management announced that DRY had filed a registration statement with the SEC covering the proposed sale of $250 million of debentures due 2003. It is anticipated that the debentures will be offered to the public in late October or early November by undewriters led by Lehman Brothers and Dillon, Read & Co. Proceeds were earmarked for general corporate purposes, including possible acquisitions. DRY is continually evaluating potential acquisitions, certain of which may be material.

Next earnings report expected in early February.

Per Share Data ($)

Yr. End Dec. 31	1992	1991	1990	1989	1988	1987	1986	1985	1984	1983
Tangible Bk. Val.	**20.79**	19.36	17.66	17.67	14.72	12.97	11.52	6.37	3.90	2.98
Earnings[1]	**2.40**	1.77	1.56	3.63	2.21	2.28	1.90	1.60	1.24	1.09
Dividends	**0.640**	0.520	0.520	0.520	0.510	0.480	0.460	0.359	0.334	0.300
Payout Ratio	**27%**	29%	33%	14%	23%	21%	24%	22%	27%	28%
Prices—High	**48**	50	38½	37⅞	30½	45½	39½	30¾	13⅜	11⅝
Low	**33½**	25½	22¼	25⅛	24⅛	16	23⅞	12¼	7¾	6¼
P/E Ratio—	**20–14**	28–14	25–14	10–7	14–11	20–7	21–13	19–8	11–6	11–6

Data as orig. reptd. Adj. for stk. divs. of 200% Jul. 1986, 100% Oct. 1983. **1.** Bef. spec. item of +0.03 in 1988. E-Estimated.

Income Data (Million $)

Year Ended Dec. 31	Mgt. Fees	Int & Div.	Total Revs.	Int. Exp.	% Exp./ Op. Revs.	Net Bef. Taxes	Eff. Tax Rate	[1]Net Inc.	% Return On Revs.	% Return On Assets	% Return On Equity
1992	**278**	**30.6**	**342**	**2.3**	**59.2**	**140**	**34.7%**	**91**	**26.6**	**10.6**	**12.0**
1991	224	41.3	282	4.1	64.0	102	33.2%	68	24.1	8.3	9.6
1990	179	48.5	261	5.1	68.1	83	25.5%	62	23.8	7.2	8.9
1989	183	49.5	272	8.0	61.6	223	33.7%	148	54.3	17.5	22.3
1988	176	39.8	268	5.5	50.4	133	31.5%	91	33.9	12.6	15.9
1987	188	29.9	273	2.0	44.4	152	36.9%	96	35.1	15.6	18.8
1986	173	23.2	232	1.9	37.9	144	44.1%	81	34.8	16.0	22.2
1985	135	23.3	176	9.6	40.2	105	47.1%	56	31.6	15.9	30.8
1984	111	28.7	144	17.7	47.2	76	49.1%	39	26.9	14.2	35.9
1983	104	17.8	127	11.2	46.2	68	50.2%	34	26.8	12.3	41.8

Balance Sheet Data (Million $)

Dec. 31	Total Assets	Cash Items	Rec.	Secs. Owned	Deposits	Due Brokers & Cust.	Other Liabs.	Capitalization Debt	Capitalization Equity	Capitalization Total
1992	**873**	**216**	**43**	**498**	**35.2**	**4.2**	**54**	**Nil**	**780**	**780**
1991	847	228	56	432	47.7	5.8	52	Nil	742	742
1990	793	228	34	408	58.4	Nil	58	Nil	677	677
1989	926	146	180	510	56.6	33.8	118	Nil	717	717
1988	763	193	58	425	76.1	26.1	52	Nil	606	606
1987	624	68	56	442	Nil	21.4	68	Nil	535	535
1986	604	57	73	432	Nil	27.3	90	Nil	487	487
1985	401	100	103	139	Nil	12.2	149	Nil	239	239
1984	297	104	26	153	Nil	3.6	96	75	123	198
1983	247	79	16	144	Nil	Nil	79	75	93	168

Data as orig. reptd. **1.** Bef. spec. items.

Business Summary

Dreyfus Corp. is one of the largest mutual fund organizations in the U.S.; it also owns a savings bank, a trust company and two insurance firms.

At December 31, 1992, total net assets managed, advised or administered of $79.5 billion (up from $76.9 billion a year ago) were divided: Dreyfus Government Cash Management ($6.2 billion), Dreyfus Worldwide Dollar Money Market Fund ($5.6 billion), Dreyfus Liquid Assets ($5.5 billion), Dreyfus Treasury Prime Cash Management ($4.7 billion), Dreyfus Municipal Bond Fund ($4.3 billion), Dreyfus Treasury Cash Management ($3.7 billion), Dreyfus Cash Management ($3.4 billion), Dreyfus Fund ($3.1 billion), Dreyfus 100% U. S. Treasury Money Market Fund ($3.0 billion), Dreyfus Cash Management Plus ($2.5 billion), Dreyfus New York Tax Exempt Bond Fund ($2.0 billion), Premier State Municipal Bond Fund ($1.9 billion), Dreyfus GNMA Fund ($1.8 billion), Dreyfus California Tax Exempt Bond Fund ($1.8 billion), Dreyfus Tax Exempt Cash Management ($1.7 billion) Dreyfus Intermediate Municipal Bond Fund ($1.6 billion), Dreyfus Municipal Money Market Fund ($1.4 billion), General Municipal Bond Fund ($1.1 billion), and other funds ($19.1 billion). Funds jointly advised or administered totaled $3.8 billion, and institutional and individual accounts were $1.3 billion. At 1992 year-end, there were some 1.9 million shareholder accounts in DRY's managed funds.

Dreyfus Service Corp. distributes shares of the Dreyfus group of funds. Dreyfus Management Inc. provides investment advisory and administration services to various pension plans, institutions and individuals. Dreyfus Personal Management, Inc. provides personalized portfolio management to a limited number of clients.

Dividend Data

Dividends have been paid since 1965.

Amt of Divd. $	Date Decl.	Ex–divd. Date	Stock of Record	Payment Date
0.17	Jan. 14	Jan. 26	Feb. 1	Feb. 10'93
0.19	Apr 13	Apr. 27	May 3	May 12'93
0.19	Jul. 15	Jul. 27	Aug. 2	Aug. 11'93
0.19	Oct. 14	Oct. 26	Nov. 1	Nov. 10'93

Finances

DRY repurchased 946,000 shares of its common stock in 1992, 44,000 shares in 1991, 2,242,000 shares in 1990, 671,000 shares in 1989, 286,000 shares in 1988, 1,050,000 in 1987 and 1,640,000 in 1986.

Capitalization

Long Term Debt: $250,000,000, as adj. (9/93).

Common Stock: 36,550,000 shs. ($0.10 par). Some 6.1% owned by officers and directors. Institutions hold approximately 74%. Shareholders of record: 2,800.

Office—200 Park Ave., New York, NY 10166. **Tel**— (212) 922-6000. **Chrmn & CEO**—H. Stein. **Pres**—J. S. DiMartino. **VP-CFO**—A. M. Eisner. **Secy**—M. N. Jacobs. **VP & Investor Contact**—Phillip Toia (212-922-6265). **Dirs**—M. L. Berman, J. S. DiMartino, A. E. Friedman, L. M. Greene, A. Q. McCarthy, J. M. Smerling, H. Stein, D. B. Truman. **Transfer Agent & Registrar**—Bank of New York, NYC. **Incorporated** in New York in 1947. **Empl**—1,800.

 Paul L. Huberman, CFA

Duriron Co.

NASDAQ Symbol DURI (Incl. in Nat'l Market) In S&P MidCap 400

Price	Range	P-E Ratio	Dividend	Yield	S&P Ranking	Beta
Aug. 25'93	1993					
23¾	27¼–20¾	21	0.60	2.5%	B	1.07

Summary

Duriron manufactures equipment and components for the chemical process industries. Earnings fell in 1992, reflecting pressure on gross margins, increased selling and administrative expenses, and restructuring charges. A further decline in the first half of 1993 resulted from continued pressure on margins and higher spending for SG&A. However, earnings for the full year should advance, in the absence of restructuring charges, and sales and earnings should both gain in 1994.

Current Outlook

Earnings for 1994 are projected at $1.50 a share, up from 1993's estimated $1.20.

Dividends should remain at $0.15 quarterly.

Sales in 1994 are expected to grow from 1993 levels, reflecting a forecasted increase in chemical industry spending and a stronger global economy. Firmer pricing and stable raw material costs should boost gross margins. Assuming a moderation in SG&A expense, level interest costs and only a small rise in the tax rate, earnings should post another advance in 1994.

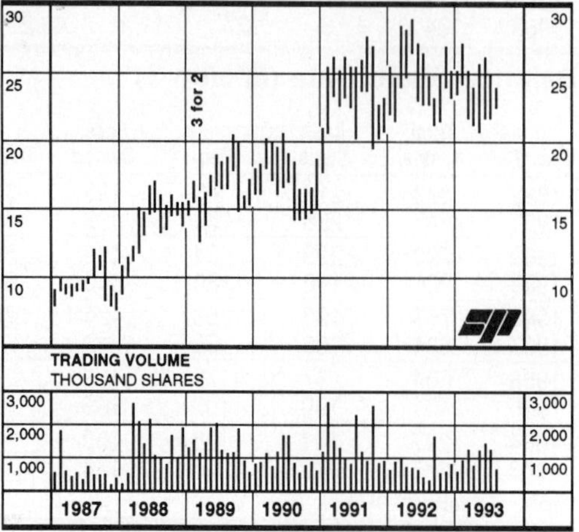

Net Sales (Million $)

Quarter:	1993	1992	1991	1990
Mar.	74.4	73.7	72.2	70.7
Jun.	78.2	72.8	76.1	76.1
Sep.		73.9	72.5	72.2
Dec.		79.9	75.6	77.8
		300.3	296.5	296.8

Net sales in the six months ended June 30, 1993, advanced 4.1%, year to year. Gross margins were flat, but with higher SG&A and increased interest expense, pretax income dropped 27%. After taxes at 37.0%, versus 36.0%, income fell 28%. Share earnings were down to $0.51, from $0.71 (before a charge of $0.95 for an accounting change).

Common Share Earnings ($)

Quarter:	1993	1992	1991	1990
Mar.	0.23	0.36	0.42	0.38
Jun.	0.28	0.35	0.41	0.40
Sep.	E0.31	0.29	0.31	0.42
Dec.	E0.38	0.04	0.41	0.47
	E1.20	1.04	1.55	1.67

Important Developments

Jul. '93— For the 1993 second quarter, DURI reported share earnings of $0.28, on a 7.4% rise in sales, versus $0.35 a year earlier. The company attributed the earnings drop to weak prices, greater interest expense, and increased SG&A spending resulting from the acquisition of Kammer and higher sales commissions. Incoming orders in the quarter reached a record $83.7 million, and totaled $157.1 million for the first half of 1993. Backlog at June 30, 1993, stood at $69.0 million, up $5.7 million from the level at the end of the first quarter.

Sep. '92— The company acquired for $28.5 million Kammer Ventile GmbH of Essen, Germany, and its associated Kammer companies. Kammer is a leading European supplier of automatic control valves.

Next earnings report expected in late October.

Per Share Data ($)

Yr. End Dec. 31	[1]1992	1991	1990	1989	1988	[1]1987	1986	1985	[1]1984	1983
Tangible Bk. Val.	**7.73**	10.89	9.34	8.00	7.01	5.69	5.99	5.96	5.72	6.36
Cash Flow	**1.97**	2.33	2.38	2.16	1.93	1.27	0.75	1.13	0.32	0.77
Earnings[2]	**1.04**	1.55	1.67	1.58	1.30	0.59	0.19	0.57	d0.21	0.29
Dividends	**0.600**	0.560	0.500	0.460	0.394	0.374	0.374	0.374	0.374	0.374
Payout Ratio	**57%**	36%	30%	29%	31%	64%	193%	66%	NM	128%
Prices—High	**29**	27¾	20⅝	20½	17⅛	12¼	9⅞	9⅛	9½	10¾
Low	**21¼**	17¾	14¼	12⅝	8⅞	7⅝	6¼	6½	6⅜	7⅝
P/E Ratio—	**28–20**	18–11	12–9	13–8	13–7	21–13	51–32	16–11	NM	37–26

Data as orig. reptd. Adj. for stk. div. of 50% Mar. 1989. **1.** Refl. merger or acq. **2.** Bef. spec. items of -1.66 in 1992, +0.14 in 1986. E-Estimated. d-Deficit. NM-Not Meaningful.

The Duriron Company, Inc.

Income Data (Million $)

Year Ended Dec. 31	Revs.	Oper. Inc.	% Oper. Inc. of Revs.	Cap. Exp.	Depr.	Int. Exp.	Net Bef. Taxes	Eff. Tax Rate	[2]Net Inc.	% Net Inc. of Revs.	Cash Flow
[1]1992	**300**	**41.9**	**14.0**	**15.3**	**11.80**	**2.92**	**20.7**	**36.0%**	**13.2**	**4.4**	**25.0**
1991	297	44.0	14.8	15.4	9.87	2.95	31.1	37.0%	19.6	6.6	29.5
1990	297	49.3	16.6	16.6	8.90	3.50	33.4	37.4%	20.9	7.0	29.8
1989	281	44.7	15.9	13.4	7.55	3.98	32.4	39.0%	19.7	7.0	27.0
1988	231	38.7	16.8	7.3	7.33	4.12	24.7	39.4%	15.0	6.5	22.3
[1]1987	182	22.6	12.4	4.5	7.27	4.03	10.9	43.5%	6.2	3.4	13.4
1986	144	12.0	8.3	6.5	5.85	1.79	3.6	45.8%	[3]2.0	1.4	7.8
1985	146	17.6	12.0	6.0	5.91	1.85	10.0	40.9%	5.9	4.0	11.8
[1]1984	140	7.1	5.1	7.0	5.50	1.60	d6.8	NM	d2.2	NM	3.3
1983	124	10.5	8.5	5.8	5.03	1.30	4.7	35.7%	3.0	2.4	8.1

Balance Sheet Data (Million $)

Dec. 31	Cash	Curr. Assets	Curr. Liab.	Curr. Ratio	Total Assets	% Ret. on Assets	Long Term Debt	Common Equity	Total Cap.	% LT Debt of Cap.	% Ret. on Equity
1992	**17.3**	**135**	**50.9**	**2.7**	**251**	**5.7**	**42.0**	**120**	**162**	**25.9**	**10.3**
1991	21.6	133	46.3	2.9	213	9.3	21.1	137	167	12.6	15.1
1990	17.0	132	46.6	2.8	206	10.4	26.8	124	158	17.0	18.1
1989	25.2	129	46.4	2.8	194	10.4	31.4	107	144	21.8	19.5
1988	21.2	117	42.8	2.7	178	8.6	35.7	91	133	26.8	17.9
1987	18.1	94	34.0	2.8	150	4.9	41.4	67	115	36.0	9.5
1986	6.9	64	20.0	3.2	103	1.9	16.5	63	83	20.0	3.2
1985	6.1	67	23.3	2.9	101	5.8	11.4	62	78	14.6	9.7
1984	4.2	67	25.7	2.6	101	NM	12.6	59	76	16.7	NM
1983	10.8	66	17.8	3.7	100	3.0	12.2	66	82	14.9	4.5

Data as orig. reptd. **1.** Refl. merger or acq. **2.** Bef. spec. items. **3.** Refl. acctg. change. d-Deficit. NM-Not Meaningful.

Business Summary

The Duriron Company, Inc. is engaged primarily in the design and production of fluid-handling equipment, mainly pumps and valves, for industries that utilize difficult-to-handle and often corrosive fluids in manufacturing processes. The company specializes in the development of precision-engineered equipment that can withstand the severely deteriorating effects associated with the flow of acids, chemical solutions, slurries and gases. Duriron considers itself a leading supplier of such equipment to the chemical process industries.

Sales and operating profits (profits in million $) in 1992 were derived as follows:

	Sales	Profits
U.S.	75%	$22.1
Europe	15%	4.3
Canada	6%	1.2
Other	4%	–1.0

Under the Durco tradename, the company manufactures several lines of centrifugal pumps, used mainly to move liquids during processing activities, as well as in auxiliary services such as waste removal, water treatment and pollution control. Duriron's valves, manufactured under the Durco, Valtek and Atomac tradenames, are used to control the flow of liquids and gases in industrial processing systems. Its Automax actuators are mounted on valves to move them from open to closed positions and vice versa.

Duriron also manufactures complex filtration systems and related spare parts. It produces pressure chamber filters, pressure leaf filters, tubular filters and industrial wastewater treatment packages, marketed to the chemical process industries.

Dividend Data

Cash has been paid in every year since 1935. A dividend reinvestment plan is available.

Amt. of Divd. $	Date Decl.	Ex–divd. Date	Stock of Record	Payment Date
0.15	Oct. 20	Nov. 2	Nov. 6	Dec. 4'92
0.15	Feb. 11	Feb. 22	Feb. 26	Mar. 12'93
0.15	Apr. 23	May 3	May 7	Jun. 4'93
0.15	Jul. 22	Aug. 2	Aug. 6	Sep. 3'93

Capitalization

Long Term Debt: $38,778,000 (6/93).

Common Stock: 12,610,705 shs. ($1.25 par).
Institutions hold 65%.
Shareholders: 2,086 of record (1/93).

Office—3100 Research Blvd., Dayton, OH 45420. **Tel**—(513) 476-6100. **Chrmn**—J. S. Haddick. **Pres & CEO**—W. M. Jordan. **VP & Secy**—R. F. Shuff. **VP-Fin & CFO**—J. E. Johnson. **SVP & Investor Contact**—Bruce E. Hines. **Treas**—G. L. Smith. **Dirs**—C. L. Bates, Jr., R. E. Frazer, H. J. Gazeley, E. Green, J. S. Haddick, W. M. Jordan, S. C. Mason, J. F. Schorr, B. L. Shafer, H. A. Shaw III, K. E. Sheehan. R. E. White. **Transfer Agent**—Bank One, Indianapolis. **Incorporated** in New York in 1912. **Empl**—2,500.

 Leo Larkin

Duty Free International

NYSE Symbol DFI Options on Phila (Feb-May-Aug-Nov) In S&P MidCap 400

Price	Range	P-E Ratio	Dividend	Yield	S&P Ranking	Beta
Oct. 20'93	1993					
16¾	29–14¼	15	0.20	1.2%	NR	NA

Summary

Duty Free is the leading operator of duty-free stores along the U.S./Canadian and U.S./Mexico borders, operates duty-free and retail stores at U.S. international airports, and is the largest supplier of duty-free merchandise to foreign diplomats in the U.S. and to ships engaged in international travel and trade in the northeastern U.S. Earnings in 1992-3 were restricted by $4.4 million of merger-related costs, and by lower than expected Northern Border division sales. Soft Northern Border division sales also hurt operating profits in the 1993-4 first half, and this trend is expected to continue at least through year-end.

Business Summary

Duty Free International, Inc. is the leading operator of duty-free stores along the U.S./Canadian and U.S./Mexico borders, operates duty-free and retail stores in U.S. international airports and is the largest supplier of duty-free merchandise to foreign diplomats in the U.S. and to ships engaged in international travel in the northeastern U.S. Sales contributions by division in recent fiscal years were:

	1992–93	1991–92
Northern border	31%	36%
Southern border	32%	32%
Airport	16%	13%
Diplomatic/wholesale	21%	19%

At January 31, 1993, the Border division was operating 88 duty-free and retail gift stores (which are not duty- or tax-free) along the Canadian (60 stores) and Mexican (28) borders. DFI gained access to the Mexican border with the April 1992 acquisition of UETA, Inc., then the largest operator of duty-free stores along the U.S./Mexican border. Products sold generally consist of luxury items such as perfumes and cosmetics, premium brand liquor, beer, wine and tobacco products and gift merchandise such as scarves and leather goods, at prices generally 20% to 60% below retail prices in the countries of destination.

The Airport division operates 69 duty-free and retail gift stores at 14 international airports, and also owns a 49% equity interest in a company that operates duty free and retail concessions at four Florida international airports. Marketing efforts are directed at affluent international travelers. Merchandise sold includes Cartier watches, Hermes ties, Gucci leather goods, Christian Dior accessories, Mont Blanc pens and Dunhill gift items.

The Diplomatic and Wholesale division operates under the names Samuel Meisel and Co., Lipschutz Brothers, Inc., and Carisam International Corp. The division is the largest supplier of duty-free merchandise to foreign diplomats in the U.S., and also supplies duty-free merchandise to merchant and passenger ships departing the ports of Baltimore, Philadelphia, New York, Miami, Seattle and Carson, Calif.

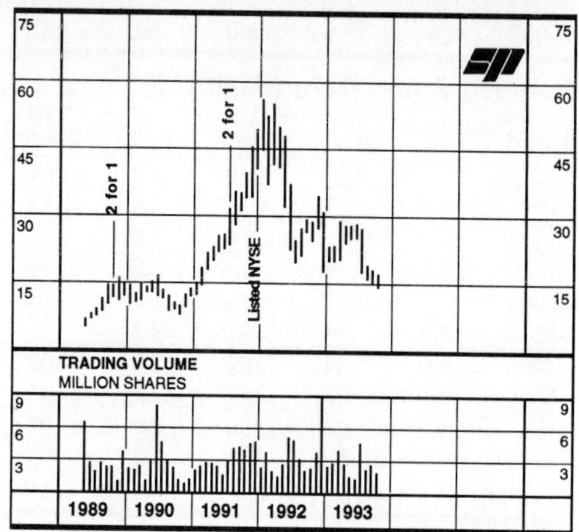

Important Developments

Sep. '93— DFI attributed lower sales in its Northern Border division in the first half of 1993-4 to an ongoing recession in Canada and unfavorable Canadian exchange rates, which have reduced travel across the U.S./Canadian border. The company believes that these trends will continue to hurt sales in the region at least through the end of 1993-4.

Next earnings report expected in late November.

Per Share Data ($)

Yr. End Jan. 31	[1]1993	[1]1992	1991	[1]1990	1989	1988	1987	1986	1985
Tangible Bk. Val.	**5.66**	5.09	3.89	3.37	0.98	0.61	NA	NA	NA
Cash Flow	**1.38**	1.36	0.78	0.67	0.46	NA	NA	NA	NA
Earnings	**1.08**	1.08	0.67	0.56	0.34	0.25	0.18	0.17	0.13
Dividends	**0.15**	Nil	Nil	Nil	Nil	Nil	Nil	Nil	Nil
Payout Ratio	**13%**	Nil	Nil	Nil	Nil	Nil	Nil	Nil	Nil
Calendar Years	**1992**	1991	1990	1989	1988	1987	1986	1985	1984
Prices—High	**56¼**	49⅝	16¾	16¼	NA	NA	NA	NA	NA
Low	**17¾**	12⅜	7⅞	5⅛	NA	NA	NA	NA	NA
P/E Ratio—	**52–16**	46–11	25–12	29–9	NA	NA	NA	NA	NA

Data as orig. reptd. Adj. for stk. divs. of 100% Jul. 1991, 100% Oct. 1989. **1.** Refl. merger or acq. NA-Not Available.

Income Data (Million $)

Year Ended Jan. 31	[1]Revs.	Oper. Inc.	% Oper. Inc. of Revs.	Cap. Exp.	Depr.	Int. Exp.	[3]Net Bef. Taxes	Eff. Tax Rate	Net Inc.	% Net Inc. of Revs.	Cash Flow
[2]1993	**366**	**58.2**	**15.9**	**20.3**	**8.54**	**1.04**	**49.8**	**39.0%**	**30.4**	**8.3**	**38.9**
[2]1992	190	42.7	22.4	5.4	6.21	4.75	37.9	37.1%	23.8	12.5	30.0
1991	107	20.3	19.0	12.0	2.41	0.93	22.8	36.1%	14.6	13.7	17.0
[2]1990	87	16.5	18.8	3.4	2.05	1.08	16.3	38.5%	10.0	11.5	12.1
1989	57	9.4	16.6	5.5	1.65	0.36	8.1	40.9%	4.8	8.5	6.5
1988	46	7.1	15.5	1.0	1.63	0.69	5.3	42.8%	3.0	6.6	NA
1987	30	4.7	15.7	0.9	0.95	0.74	3.4	47.6%	1.8	5.9	NA
1986	16	NA	NA	NA	NA	NA	2.6	37.9%	1.6	10.1	NA
1985	14	NA	NA	NA	NA	NA	1.8	34.3%	1.2	8.6	NA

Balance Sheet Data (Million $)

Jan. 31	Cash	Curr. Assets	Curr. Liab.	Curr. Ratio	Total Assets	% Ret. on Assets	Long Term Debt	Common Equity	Total Cap.	% LT Debt of Cap.	% Ret. on Equity
1993	**38.2**	**129.0**	**38.8**	**3.3**	**256**	**12.7**	**6.3**	**207**	**214**	**2.9**	**15.2**
1992	59.9	96.0	17.9	5.4	199	14.2	8.8	171	180	4.9	17.0
1991	55.2	82.8	12.3	6.7	125	12.7	11.0	100	100	9.9	15.7
1990	64.2	80.4	7.9	10.2	105	13.4	10.0	85	96	10.5	17.6
1989	3.0	13.7	4.7	2.9	29	18.1	5.8	19	24	24.0	29.6
1988	2.9	12.7	4.8	2.6	24	13.2	5.3	14	19	27.3	28.7
1987	NA	NA	NA	NA	22	11.7	10.4	7	17	60.0	31.4
1986	NA	NA	NA	NA	9	23.8	2.1	4	6	32.7	46.2
1985	NA	NA	NA	NA	5	NA	1.6	3	4	37.8	NA

Data as orig. reptd. **1.** Incl. other oper. revs. after 1988. **2.** Refl. merger or acq. **3.** Incl. equity in earns. of nonconsol. subs. NA-Not Available.

Net Sales (Million $)

Quarter:	1993–94	1992–93	1991–92	1990–91
Apr.	77.9	77.2	33.3	18.5
Jul.	99.3	95.5	54.7	29.2
Oct.		103.2	59.8	33.2
Jan.		85.9	40.2	24.1
		361.8	188.0	105.0

Sales in the six months ended July 31, 1993, rose 2.6%, year to year, as gains in the Southern (7.1%), Airport (31%) and Diplomatic and Wholesale (8.9%) divisions outweighed a 17% decline for the Northern Border division. With higher operating costs at new airport locations, operating income fell 16%. Despite a 34% drop in interest income, in the absence of $4.4 million of merger-related expenses, pretax income was down only fractionally. After taxes at 37.0%, versus 43.7%, share earnings rose 11%, to $0.48 (on 4.5% fewer shares), from $0.41.

Common Share Earnings ($)

Quarter:	1993–94	1992–93	1991–92	1990–91
Apr.	0.19	0.06	0.13	0.09
Jul.	0.29	0.35	0.34	0.20
Oct.		0.45	0.43	0.25
Jan.		0.22	0.18	0.13
		1.08	1.08	0.67

Finances

In June 1993, the company acquired a duty free operation in North Dakota, for $8.7 million. In May 1993, DFI purchased a 75% stake in Bared Jewelers, an operator of three stores in the Virgin Islands, for $12.6 million and certain other contingencies.

In April 1992, DFI issued 4,361,941 common shares to acquire UETA, Inc., the largest duty-free retailing company along the U.S./Mexican border.

In a December 1989 public offering, 3,480,000 common shares (including 480,000 for selling stockholders) were sold at $12.50 each (as adjusted). In the company's May 1989 initial public stock offering, underwriters sold 5,750,000 DFI common shares (1,000,000 for stockholders) at $5.125 each (adjusted).

Dividend Data

Quarterly dividends were initiated in July 1992.

Amt. of Divd. $	Date Decl.	Ex-divd. Date	Stock of Record	Payment Date
0.05	Jan. 19	Jan. 25	Jan. 29	Feb. 15'93
0.05	Apr. 15	Apr. 26	Apr. 30	May 14'93
0.05	Jul. 26	Jul. 29	Aug. 4	Aug. 18'93
0.05	Oct. 12	Oct. 25	Oct. 29	Nov. 15'93

Capitalization

Long Term Debt: $4,972,000 (7/93).

Common Stock: 27,236,794 shs. ($0.01 par). Officers and directors control 27%. Gebr. Heinemann (a West German partnership) holds 16%.

Shareholders of record: 440 (2/93).

Office—63 Copps Hill Rd., Ridgefield, CT 06877. **Tel**—(203) 431-6057. **Chrmn**—D. H. Bernstein. **Vice-Chrmn**—J. Africk. **Chrmn & Co-CEO**—J. A. Couri. **Pres & Co-CEO**—A. Carfora. **VP & Treas**—S. S. Yaffe. **VP-Fin & CFO**—G. F. Egan. **Investor Contacts**—Dyan C. Cutro (212-661-2955). **Dirs**—J. Africk, D. H. Bernstein, A. Carfora, J. A. Couri, H. Diehl, W. E. Hurst, Sr., M. W. Offit, C. Reimerdes, S. H. Stackhouse, S. S. Yaffe. **Transfer Agent & Registrar**—First National Bank of Maryland, Baltimore. **Incorporated** in Maryland in 1983. **Empl**—2,000.

 John D. Coyle, CFA

Edison Bros. Stores

NYSE Symbol EBS Options on NYSE (Feb-May-Aug-Nov) In S&P MidCap 400

Price	Range	P-E Ratio	Dividend	Yield	S&P Ranking	Beta
Sep. 14'93	1993					
27⅛	49⅛–26⅜	10	1.24	4.6%	B+	1.63

Summary

This company is primarily a retailer of apparel and women's footwear, and also operates entertainment centers in shopping malls. Operations are conducted through numerous store chains totaling some 2,850 stores in all 50 states. More stores in operation and profit contributions from both core units led to stronger earnings in fiscal 1992-93. Lower sales and rising costs depressed earnings sharply in the first half of fiscal 1993-94.

Business Summary

Edison Brothers Stores is primarily engaged in the retail sale of apparel and shoes through the operation of numerous chains of stores. A total of 2,787 stores were in operation at fiscal year-end 1992-93, consisting of 1,883 apparel stores, 766 footwear stores and departments, and 138 entertainment centers. Business segment contributions in fiscal 1992-93:

	Sales	Profits
Apparel	69%	66%
Footwear	31%	34%

Number of stores in operation (not restated for Handyman spin-off in 1985) at fiscal year-end January 31 (December 31 prior to 1990):

1993	2,787	1990	2,327	1986	2,475
1992	2,781	1988	2,347	1985	2,435
1991	2,733	1987	2,514	1984	2,355

The apparel division includes the following chains: JW/Jeans West (current fashion for young men), Coda (current fashion for young men), Oaktree (leading edge fashion for young men), J. Riggings (traditional apparel for more conservative males), Zeidler & Zeidler/Webster (upscale contemporary for men), Repp Ltd. (big/tall/athletic for men), 5-7-9 Shops (for small size teen girls), and Spirale (sizes 7 to 14 for preteen girls). During 1992-93, the company sold 88 Joan Bari and Cabaret stores.

The shoe store division includes the following chains: Bakers/Leeds, Precis, The Wild Pair, Velocity, and Sacha London.

The entertainment division (acquired in fiscal 1990-91) consists of Time-Out, Space Port, Party Zone and Exhilarama centers (family amusement), Dave & Busters (restaurant/entertainment complexes) and Horizon (exclusive distributor for virtual reality entertainment technology).

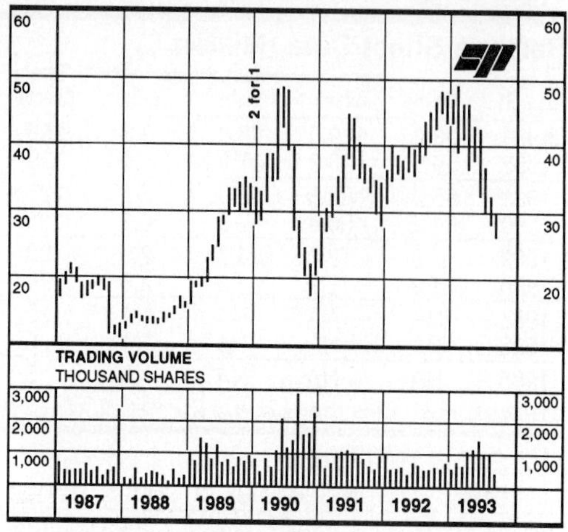

Important Developments

Sep. '93— Sales for the four weeks ended August 28 were $118.7 million, down 5.7%, year to year. For the 30 weeks ended August 28, sales declined 2.0% to $785.7 million. Separately, the company said that its entertaiment group and some of its more traditional fashion chains were performing reasonably well, but that softness in consumer spending had restricted sales in its more fashion-oriented chains.

Next earnings report expected in early December.

Per Share Data ($)

Yr. End Jan. 31[1]	1993	1992	[2]1991	[2]1990	[4]1989	1988	[2]1987	1986	[2]1985	[2]1984
Tangible Bk. Val.	**15.41**	14.26	11.81	9.57	NA	9.71	8.48	10.22	10.64	13.94
Cash Flow	**6.17**	5.60	5.04	4.68	NA	3.38	0.50	2.90	2.18	2.82
Earnings[3]	**3.27**	2.83	2.78	3.04	NA	1.82	d1.06	1.68	1.07	1.60
Dividends	**1.150**	1.060	1.040	0.935	NA	0.900	0.900	0.800	0.800	0.800
Payout Ratio	**36%**	38%	38%	31%	NA	50%	NM	47%	75%	49%
Calendar Years	**1992**	1991	1990	1989	1988	1987	1986	1985	1984	1983
Prices—High	**48¼**	44⅞	48⅞	35⅛	17¼	22	21⅞	19⅛	21½	23⅜
Low	**31⅜**	21¾	17½	16	12⅜	11	16¼	15½	16¼	12⅞
P/E Ratio—	**15–10**	16–8	18–6	12–5	9–7	NM	13–10	18–14	13–10	10–6

Data as orig. reptd. Adj. for stk. div(s) of 100% Jan. 1990. **1.** Yrs. ended Dec. 31 prior to 1990. **2.** Reflects merger or acquisition. **3.** Bef. results of disc. opers. of +0.26 in 1985, and spec. item(s) of -1.06 in 1992, -0.22 in 1990, +0.44 in 1987. **4.** Data deleted due to change in fiscal yr. end. d-Deficit. NM-Not Meaningful. NA-Not Available.

Income Data (Million $)

Year Ended Jan. 31[1]	Revs.	Oper. Inc.	% Oper. Inc. of Revs.	Cap. Exp.	Depr.	Int. Exp.	Net Bef. Taxes	Eff. Tax Rate	[4]Net Inc.	% Net Inc. of Revs.	Cash Flow
1993	**1,509**	**195**	**12.9**	**92.9**	**63.0**	**19.9**	**113.0**	**37.1%**	**71.1**	**4.7**	**134**
1992	1,385	175	12.6	76.7	59.5	20.0	96.5	37.0%	60.8	4.4	120
[2]1991	1,254	155	12.4	83.7	47.8	16.1	93.7	37.0%	59.0	4.7	107
[2]1990	1,074	143	13.3	51.8	33.2	13.2	97.5	37.2%	61.2	5.7	94
1989	NA	NA	NA	NA	NA	NA	NA	NA	NA	NA	NA
1988	919	101	11.0	43.1	31.1	12.8	60.2	39.7%	36.3	4.0	67
[2]1987	931	53	5.7	34.7	30.8	10.2	d34.5	NM	d20.9	NM	10
1986	904	79	8.7	32.4	24.7	8.5	62.4	45.7%	33.9	3.7	59
[3]1985	808	63	7.8	38.5	22.6	6.4	38.1	43.0%	[5]21.7	2.7	44
[2]1984	1,055	82	7.8	56.2	25.3	6.2	58.8	44.0%	32.9	3.1	58

Balance Sheet Data (Million $)

Jan. 31[1]	Cash	Curr. Assets	Curr. Liab.	Curr. Ratio	Total Assets	% Ret. on Assets	Long Term Debt	Common Equity	Total Cap.	% LT Debt of Cap.	% Ret. on Equity
1993	**23**	**404**	**172**	**2.4**	**859**	**8.7**	**194**	**418**	**620**	**31.4**	**17.5**
1992	26	352	214	1.6	769	8.1	120	385	530	22.5	16.6
1991	49	332	189	1.8	734	9.1	145	343	517	28.0	19.7
1990	20	250	191	1.3	533	11.6	52	244	317	16.3	26.7
1989	NA	NA	NA	NA	NA	NA	NA	NA	NA	NA	NA
1988	101	290	145	2.0	513	7.8	102	213	342	29.9	17.8
1987	36	200	123	1.6	419	NM	65	193	286	22.6	NM
1986	80	217	106	2.1	433	8.3	66	225	291	22.7	15.5
1985	48	192	88	2.2	388	5.0	67	216	283	23.6	8.7
1984	29	237	131	1.8	473	7.0	40	283	323	12.3	11.9

Data as orig. reptd. **1.** Prior to 1990 fis. yr. ended Dec. **2.** Reflects merger or acquisition. **3.** Excludes discontinued operations. **4.** Bef. results of disc. opers. and spec. item(s). **5.** Reflects accounting change. d-Deficit. NM-Not Meaningful. NA-Not Available.

Net Sales (Million $)

Quarter:	1993–94	1992–93	1991–92	1990–91
Apr.	329	327	300	248
Jul.	338	349	315	273
Oct.		362	329	311
Jan.		472	441	422
		1,509	1,385	1,254

Sales for the 26 weeks ended July 31, 1993, declined 1.2%, year to year, hurt by soft consumer spending patterns. Total costs and expenses rose 1.7%, and net income fell 55%, to $0.46 a share from $1.03, which was before a $1.06 charge from the cumulative effect of an accounting change.

Common Share Earnings ($)

Quarter:	1993–94	1992–93	1991–92	1990–91
Apr.	0.31	0.44	0.41	0.37
Jul.	0.15	0.59	0.53	0.51
Oct.		0.61	0.54	0.52
Jan.		1.63	1.34	1.38
		3.27	2.83	2.78

Finances

During 1993-94's second quarter, EBS purchased 25 men's big and tall stores, with annual sales of $14 million, from Big & Tall Shoppes of America. The company also acquired 48 men's big and tall apparel stores from two separate sellers, with annual sales of about $31 million.

In February 1992, EBS acquired Harry's Clothing Stores, which sells clothing for big and tall men through a chain of 39 stores. Harry's generated sales of over $21 million in 1991.

Dividend Data

Dividends have been paid since 1934. A "poison pill" stock purchase right was adopted in 1988.

Amt of Divd. $	Date Decl.	Ex-divd. Date	Stock of Record	Payment Date
0.31	Nov. 17	Dec. 15	Dec. 21	Jan. 8'93
0.31	Feb. 22	Mar. 1	Mar. 5	Mar. 12'93
0.31	May 10	May 21	May 27	Jun. 10'93
0.31	Aug. 18	Aug. 25	Aug. 31	Sep. 10'93

Capitalization

Long Term Debt: $194,300,000 (4/93).

Common Stock: 22,043,314 shs. ($1 par).
Institutions hold about 54%.
Officers and directors control 20%.
Shareholders of record: 4,600.

Office—501 North Broadway, St. Louis, MO 63102. **Tel**—(314) 331-6000. **Chrmn**—A. E. Newman. **Pres**—M. K. Sneider. **VP-Secy**—A. A. Sachs. **VP-CFO & Investor Contact**—Lee G. Weeks. **Dirs**—J. I. Edison, P. A. Edison, J. Evans, M. H. Freund, K. W. Michner, A. Miller, A. E. Newman, E. P. Newman, A. A. Sachs, C. D. Schnuck, M. Sneider, R. W. Staley, L. G. Weeks. **Transfer Agent & Registrar**—Boatmen's Trust Co., St. Louis, MO. **Incorporated** in Delaware in 1929. **Empl**—24,000.

 John D. Coyle, CFA

Edwards (A. G.), Inc.

NYSE Symbol AGE Options on CBOE (Feb-May-Aug-Nov) In S&P MidCap 400

Price	Range	P-E Ratio	Dividend	Yield	S&P Ranking	Beta
Oct. 4'93	1993					
29⅝	30½–22½	10	0.60	2.0%	A	2.07

Summary

A. G. Edwards is a holding company whose subsidiaries provide securities and commodities brokerage, investment banking, asset management and insurance services. Its principal subsidiary is A.G. Edwards & Sons, which operates more than 480 locations in 48 states and the District of Columbia. Earnings are subject to wide fluctuations, reflecting the volatile nature of securities markets. Profits in the first six months of fiscal 1993-94 benefited from active trading by individual investors, sparked by a drop in interest rates.

Business Summary

A.G. Edwards, Inc. is a financial services holding company whose primary subsidiary is A.G. Edwards & Sons, a securities broker-dealer based in St. Louis, Mo. The company provides securities and commodities brokerage for individual, corporate and institutional clients. AGE also provides asset management, real estate services, life insurance and annuities, and provides investment banking services for corporate, governmental and municipal clients. Contributions to revenues in the past two fiscal years were:

	1992–93	1991–92
Commissions	56%	55%
Interest	6%	7%
Principal transactions	20%	20%
Investment banking	10%	10%
Other	8%	8%

At February 28, 1993, AGE's 4,887 investment brokers were providing financial products and services to about 1.3 million (up from 1.2 million a year earlier) individual, corporate and institutional clients from more than 470 offices. AGE had the fourth largest branch network in the U. S., based on number of branches.

AGE acts as principal and agent in transactions with customers in the over-the-counter markets. The company also acts as broker in the purchase and sale of options, and, through AGE Commodity Clearing Corp., acts as broker in the purchase and sale of commodity and financial futures contracts. Membership is held in all major securities exchanges in the U.S., The National Association of Securities Dealers, and the Securities Investor Protection Corp.

Investment banking activities include the underwriting of corporate and municipal securities, as well as corporate and municipal unit trusts. AGE also advises clients in mergers and acquisitions, acts as agent in private placements and as consultant. Through AGE Asset Management Inc., the company provides investment advisory services.

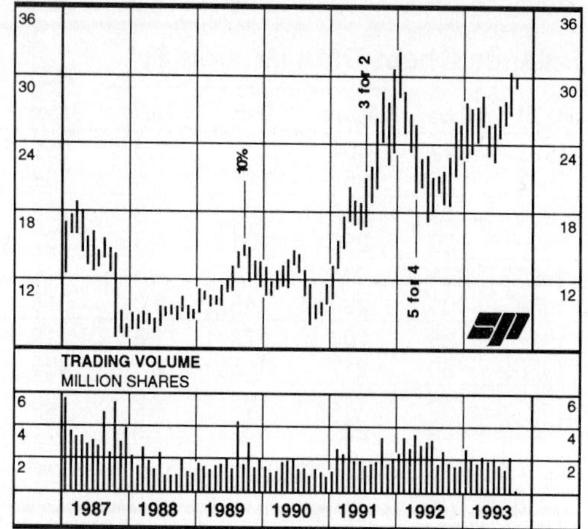

Important Developments

Jul. '93— Management said that earnings for the six months ended August 31, 1993 continued to benefit from a high level of retail investor activity. Earlier, the company announced plans to install new computer-based broker workstations at all of its branch offices that will replace the current branch quote and communications equipment. The estimated cost of these workstations was approximately $39 million. Edwards may also purchase treasury shares for its employee stock plans.

Next earnings report expected in mid-December.

Per Share Data ($)

Yr. End Feb. 28	1993	1992	1991	1990	1989	1988	1987	1986	1985	1984
Tangible Bk. Val.	**13.33**	11.06	9.00	8.07	7.06	6.51	6.06	5.11	4.53	4.13
Earnings	**2.58**	2.35	1.37	1.37	0.82	0.84	1.26	0.90	0.62	0.70
Dividends	**0.520**	0.427	0.362	0.346	0.330	0.330	0.290	0.258	0.258	0.252
Payout Ratio	**20%**	18%	26%	25%	40%	39%	23%	29%	41%	36%
Calendar Years	**1992**	1991	1990	1989	1988	1987	1986	1985	1984	1983
Prices—High	**32¼**	30¹¹⁄₁₆	14⅝	15⅛	10⁷⁄₁₆	18⅞	15	11⁷⁄₁₆	9⁷⁄₁₆	13⅝
Low	**17¼**	10⅜	8⅛	9⅛	7⅜	6¹⁵⁄₁₆	10⁷⁄₁₆	7⅜	6	7⅝
P/E Ratio—	**13–7**	13–4	11–6	11–7	13–9	22–8	12–8	13–8	15–10	20–11

Data as orig. reptd. Adj. for stk. divs. of 25% Apr. 1992, 50% Jul. 1991, 10% Sep. 1989, 50% May 1986. NA-Not Available.

Income Data (Million $)

Year Ended Feb. 28	Commis-sions	Int. Inc.	Total Revs.	Int. Exp.	% Exp./ Op. Revs.	Net Bef. Taxes	Eff. Tax Rate	Net Inc.	% Return On [1]Revs.	% Return On Assets	% Return On [1]Equity
1993	**601**	**64.7**	**1,074**	**1.89**	**82.3**	**190**	**37.1%**	**119**	**11.1**	**6.4**	**21.6**
1992	523	63.9	939	1.19	82.1	168	37.2%	106	11.2	7.1	24.0
1991	345	66.2	675	4.23	86.4	92	35.5%	59	8.8	4.7	16.2
1990	319	65.3	607	1.67	84.9	92	35.7%	59	9.7	5.4	18.3
1989	246	55.6	501	4.26	89.6	52	33.2%	35	7.0	3.6	12.2
1988	324	48.0	505	3.48	88.8	57	36.3%	36	7.1	3.9	13.6
1987	349	41.2	526	2.13	81.3	98	45.4%	54	10.2	5.7	22.8
1986	249	38.2	404	2.41	83.0	69	44.7%	38	9.4	4.5	18.8
1985	170	40.6	309	3.67	85.2	46	41.9%	27	8.6	3.9	14.6
1984	196	36.5	323	0.95	83.8	52	43.9%	29	9.1	5.1	18.1

Balance Sheet Data (Million $)

Feb. 28	Total Assets	Cash Items	Rec.	[2]Secs. Owned	Sec. Borrowed	Due Brokers & Cust.	Other Liabs.	Capitalization Debt	Capitalization Equity	Capitalization Total
1993	**2,111**	**314**	**1,426**	**150**	**Nil**	**1,192**	**304**	**Nil**	**615**	**615**
1992	1,577	255	966	161	Nil	831	254	Nil	492	492
1991	1,403	176	907	139	1	856	160	Nil	386	386
1990	1,126	52	772	144	33	608	141	Nil	344	344
1989	1,063	73	663	179	100	550	112	Nil	301	301
1988	870	43	593	83	Nil	486	110	Nil	274	274
1987	982	67	667	137	Nil	583	142	Nil	257	257
1986	918	114	612	113	Nil	603	100	Nil	215	215
1985	782	33	619	61	Nil	511	80	Nil	191	191
1984	580	35	442	39	Nil	328	77	[3]2.5	172	175

Data as orig. reptd. **1.** As reptd. by co. **2.** At mkt. **3.** Incl. current portion.

Revenues (Million $)

Quarter:	1993–94	1992–93	1991–92	1990–91
May	315	253	219	166
Aug.	314	257	219	173
Nov.		259	232	155
Feb.		306	269	181
		1,074	939	675

Total revenues for the six months ended August 31, 1993, advanced 23%, year to year, reflecting a continuation of strong market conditions. Commissions were up 32%, principal transactions decreased 0.4%, investment banking fees advanced 38%, interest was up 10%, and other revenues rose 14%. Expenses increased at a less rapid rate, and pretax income was up 34%. After taxes at 36.6%, versus 37.1%, net income rose 36%. Share earnings were $1.55 on more shares, versus $1.19.

Common Share Earnings ($)

Quarter:	1993–94	1992–93	1991–92	1990–91
May	0.80	0.60	0.54	0.33
Aug.	0.75	0.59	0.53	0.36
Nov.		0.61	0.60	0.29
Feb.		0.78	0.68	0.39
		2.58	2.35	1.37

Dividend Data

Dividends have been paid since 1971. A "poison pill" stock purchase right was adopted in 1988.

Amt of Divd. $	Date Decl.	Ex-divd. Date	Stock of Record	Payment Date
0.13	Nov. 20	Dec. 7	Dec. 11	Jan. 4'93
0.15	Feb. 19	Mar. 1	Mar. 5	Apr. 1'93
0.15	May 21	May 28	Jun. 4	Jul. 1'93
0.15	Aug. 20	Aug. 30	Sep. 3	Oct. 1'93

Finances

The company is subject to the uniform net capital rule of the SEC. At May 31, 1993, the A. G. Edwards & Sons, Inc. subsidiary had net capital (as defined) of $404.2 million, which was $383.4 million in excess of the minimum required.

Capitalization

Long Term Debt: None (5/93).

Common Stock: 46,658,190 shs. ($1 par). About 4.6% is held by officers and directors. Institutions hold approximately 46%. Shareholders of record: 19,000.

Office—One North Jefferson, St. Louis, MO 63103. **Tel**—(314) 289-3000. **Chrmn & Pres**—B.F. Edwards III. **VP-Treas & Investor Contact**—D.W. Mesker (314) 289-3510. **VP-Secy**—R.E. Buesinger. **Dirs**—R.G. Avis, E.E. Carter, R.C. Dissett, B.F. Edwards III, L. Fernandez, W.S. McEwen, D.W. Mesker, D.M. Sisler, D.C.E. Williamson. **Transfer Agent & Registrar**—Boatmen's Trust Co., St. Louis. **Incorporated** in Delaware in 1967; predecessor founded in 1887. **Empl**—9,487.

 Paul L. Huberman,CFA

El Paso Natural Gas

NYSE Symbol EPG Options on ASE (Jan-Apr-Jul-Oct) In S&P MidCap 400

Price	Range	P-E Ratio	Dividend	Yield	S&P Ranking	Beta
Oct. 21'93	1993					
36¾	40⅜–30¼	16	1.10	3.0%	NR	NA

Summary

This company operates a 17,000 mile natural gas pipeline system from the major producing basins of the Southwest to California and other states. The 1993 second quarter acquisition of the remaining 50% interest in Mojave Pipeline Co. should aid earnings growth in 1993 and 1994. Long-term prospects are enhanced by a low cost structure that should translate into market share growth, and by pipeline system expansion. Although gas marketing activity should increase, margins will remain thin.

Current Outlook

Share earnings for 1994 are projected at $2.65, up from $2.45 estimated for 1993.

The quarterly dividend is expected to be raised from $0.27½ in 1994.

The acquisition of the 50% interest in Mojave that EPG did not already own should boost earnings by $0.10 a share in 1994. Margins will widen on a more favorable rate design at El Paso Natural Gas. Field service operations should benefit from higher throughput. Gas marketing profits are likely to be flat. System expansion into northern Mexico to meet strong growth in gas demand for power generation, and into Northern California, should aid long-term profit gains.

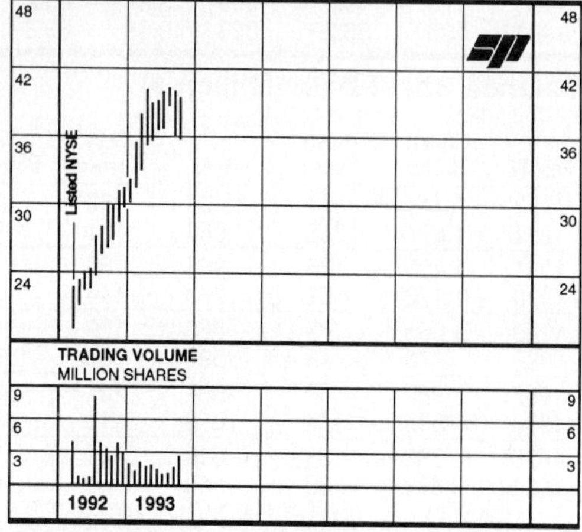

Total Revenues (Million $)

Quarter:	1993	1992	[1]1991
Mar.	210.9	174.4	---
Jun.	220.6	188.4	---
Sep.	245.1	217.2	---
Dec.	---	222.8	---
	---	802.8	729.9

Revenues in the nine months ended September 30, 1993, advanced 17%, year to year, reflecting higher rates and the consolidation of Mojave Pipeline Co. in June 1993. Income from operations climbed 25%. With nonoperating expense, versus nonoperating income, and an increase in both interest expense and the effective tax rate, net income was up only 17%, to $1.87 a share (on 4.3% more shares), from $1.67.

Common Share Earnings ($)

Quarter:	1993	1992	[1]1991
Mar.	0.83	0.87	---
Jun.	0.55	0.46	---
Sep.	0.49	0.38	---
Dec.	E0.58	0.45	---
	E2.45	2.12	1.97

Important Developments

Oct. '93— EPG's 1993 third quarter operating income grew to $55 million, from $40 million in the year-earlier period. The increase reflected greater net revenues from new rates, which became effective in 1993, and from the consolidation of the Mojave Pipeline Co. (effective June 1, 1993, EPG acquired from Enron Corp. the 50% interest in Mojave that it did not already own, for about $40 million in cash). EPG mainline throughput averaged 3.4 Bcf per day in the quarter; field throughput averaged 1.3 Bcf per day. Capital expenditures in the first nine months of 1993 totaled $108 million, down from $169 million in the 1992 period, reflecting the completion of mainline expansion in April 1992. Cash flow from operations decreased to $233 million, from $262 million in the year-earlier period.

Next earnings report expected in mid-Janaury.

Per Share Data ($)

Yr. End Dec. 31	1992	[1]1991
Tangible Bk. Val.	**18.02**	17.38
Cash Flow	**4.15**	3.66
Earnings[2]	**2.12**	1.97
Dividends	**0.75**	NA
Payout Ratio	**35%**	NA
Prices—High	**31½**	NA
Low	**19**	NA
P/E Ratio—	**15–9**	NA

Data as orig. reptd., prior to 1992 data **1.** Pro forma. **2.** Bef. results of disc. ops. in 1991. E-Estimated. NA-Not Available.

Income Data (Million $)

Year Ended Dec. 31[1]	Revs.	Oper. Inc.	% Oper. Inc. of Revs.	Cap. Exp.	Depr.	Int. Exp.	Net Bef. Taxes	Eff. Tax Rate	Net Inc.	% Net Inc. of Revs.	Cash Flow
1992	**803**	**258**	**32.2**	**246**	**73.0**	**68**	**123**	**38.1%**	**76.0**	**9.5**	**150**
1991	730	241	33.0	NA	61.3	103	114	37.0%	[2]71.9	9.9	133

Balance Sheet Data (Million $)

Dec. 31[1]	Cash	Curr. Assets	Curr. Liab.	Curr. Ratio	Total Assets	% Ret. on Assets	Long Term Debt	Common Equity	Total Cap.	% LT Debt of Cap.	% Ret. on Equity
1992	**49**	**364**	**373**	**1.0**	**2,051**	**3.2**	**637**	**669**	**1,508**	**42.2**	**9.4**
1991	170	606	469	1.3	2,094	NA	639	633	1,493	42.8	NA

Data as orig. reptd. **1.** Pro forma. **2.** Bef. results of disc. ops. in 1991. NA-Not Available.

Business Summary

El Paso Natural Gas is engaged in the interstate transportation of natural gas and, to a much lesser extent, gas marketing. The company, formerly wholly owned by Burlington Resources Inc. (BR), sold publicly 5.75 million common shares in March 1992. In June 1992, BR spun off its remaining 85% interest in EPG to BR shareholders. In 1991, the company had conveyed its oil and gas properties, intrastate natural gas transportation properties, and natural gas liquids marketing business to Meridian Oil Holding Inc., a BR subsidiary.

The company owns and operates a 17,000-mile natural gas transmission system connecting the major producing basins of the Southwest to markets in California, Nevada, Arizona, New Mexico and Texas. Through interconnections with other pipelines, access is also provided to most other natural gas producing regions and to most of the significant markets in North America. Natural gas deliveries in recent years were divided as follows:

	1992	1991	1990
California	69%	72%	75%
East–of–California	16%	14%	15%
Off–system	15%	14%	10%

During 1992, EPG delivered 1.4 Tcf (trillion cubic feet) of natural gas, accounting for 7% of total 1992 U.S. consumption; 49% of the natural gas consumed in California in 1992 was delivered by EPG. The company's delivery capacity to California is about 3.3 Bcf per day, and to East-of-California markets about 1.2 Bcf per day; delivery capacity to off-system markets east of EPG's system can be as high as 1.1 Bcf per day depending on the level of demand elsewhere on the sytem. Revenue contributions in recent years were:

	1992	1991	1990
Demand & transportation	61%	57%	57%
Gas & liquid sales	30%	25%	26%
Other	9%	18%	17%

In 1992, natural gas deliveries to Southern California Gas Co., Pacific Gas & Electric Co. and Southwest Gas Corp. accounted for 58% of revenues. The company is the principal interstate natural gas transmission system serving Arizona, southern Nevada, New Mexico and El Paso, Tex. As a result of expansion by EPG and competitors, the capacity to deliver natural gas to California exceeded demand in 1992, and this situation is projected to continue for some time. However, the company expects to remain the lowest-cost transporter of natural gas to California. Its pipeline capacity to California is fully subscribed under long-term contracts that provide for the payment of fixed reservation charges. Through wholly owned Mojave Pipeline Co., EPG transports gas principally for the production of steam for the enhanced oil recovery market of California.

EPG is a member of a five-company consortium that plans to build the proposed Samalayuca II Power Plant near Ciudad Juarez, Mexico. The company has filed for FERC approval to expand its system to provide natural gas service to the plant and to an existing power plant at the same location; the proposed expansion would provide an additional 300 MMcf per day of capacity at an estimated cost of $57 million.

El Paso Gas Marketing Co. conducts all of the company's gas marketing operations, including managing EPG's certificated sales arrangements with utilities and municipalities and remaining long-term gas purchase agreements.

Dividend Data

Dividend payments began in 1992. A "poison pill" stock purchase rights plan was adopted in 1992.

Amt. of Divd. $	Date Decl.	Ex–divd. Date	Stock of Record	Payment Date
0.27½	Jan. 12	Mar. 8	Mar. 12	Apr. 1'93
0.27½	Apr. 13	Jun. 7	Jun. 11	Jul. 1'93
0.27½	Jul. 22	Sep. 3	Sep. 10	Oct. 1'93
0.27½	Oct. 12	Dec. 6	Dec. 10	Jan. 4'94

Finances

Capital spending for 1993 is estimated at $175 million, primarily for maintenance of business, system expansion, and system enhancement. Expenditures totaled $246 million in 1992.

Capitalization

Long Term Debt: $795,752,000 (9/93).

Common Stock: 37,263,825 shs. ($3 par).
Institutions hold 73%.
Shareholders of record: 27,506.

Office—One Paul Kayser Center, 304 Texas Ave., El Paso, TX 79901. **Tel**—(915) 541-2600. **Chrm**—R. M. Bressler. **Pres & CEO**—W. A. Wise. **SVP & CFO**—H. B. Austin. **Secy**—S. J. James. **Investor Contact**—Norma F. Dunn. **Dirs**—B. Allumbaugh, R. M. Bressler, E. G. Laguera, B. F. Love, L. Dell'Osso, Jr., K. L. Smalley, W. A. Wise. **Transfer Agent & Registrar**—First National Bank of Boston. **Incorporated** in Delaware in 1928. **Empl**—2,499.

 Mark Mattke

Ennis Business Forms

NYSE Symbol EBF In S&P MidCap 400

Price	Range	P-E Ratio	Dividend	Yield	S&P Ranking	Beta
Sep. 23'93	1993					
13¼	17⅞–13	11	0.56	4.2%	A	0.97

Summary

Ennis is a leading producer of business forms, most of which are manufactured on a custom or semi-custom basis. Share earnings for 1993-4 are expected to be lower, because of the slow growth of the economy and competitive market conditions. Longer term, the core business will probably grow at close to the GDP rate, with the possibility of additional growth provided by potential acquisitions.

Current Outlook

Earnings for the fiscal year ending February 28, 1994, are estimated at $1.10 a share, down from 1992-3's $1.18 from continuing operations. Earnings of $1.25 a share are estimated for 1994-5.

The dividend was raised 3.7%, to $0.14 quarterly, in mid-1993.

Sales for the fiscal year ending February 28, 1994, should be flat to down, depending mainly on the strength or weakness of the general economy. Competitve market conditions are likely to lead to lower earnings, as higher labor and material costs and little pricing flexibility squeeze margins. To a lesser degree, a higher effective tax rate should also penalize results. Some relief, albeit limited, should come from a reduction in average shares outstanding. Longer term, sales and earnings could get a boost from the company's recently announced aggressive acquisiton strategy, as new products are introduced, and share earnings should continue to benefit from the company's long-standing policy of common stock repurchases.

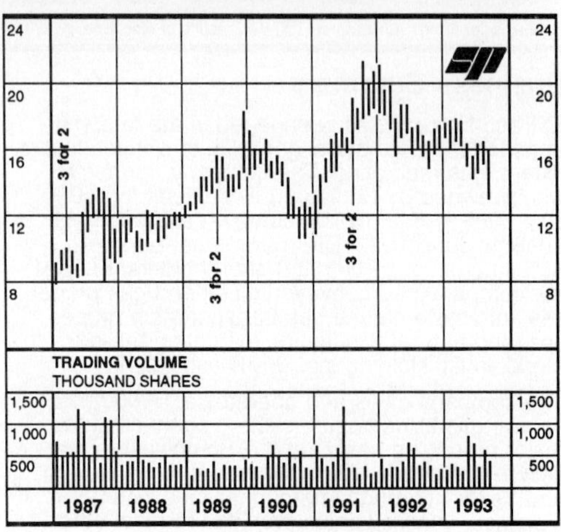

Net Sales (Million $)

Quarter:	1993–4	1992–3	1991–2	1990–1
May	31.3	31.3	31.8	31.9
Aug.	33.8	33.2	33.9	32.4
Nov.	---	33.8	34.3	31.9
Feb.	---	31.1	31.9	30.0
	---	129.3	131.8	126.2

Sales for the six months ended August 31, 1993, rose 1.0%, year to year. Pretax income decreased 6.2%, reflecting higher costs and competitive market conditions. With the passage of the Revenue Reconciliation Act of 1993, the effective tax rate was higher, at 37.6%, versus 36.3%. Income from continuing operations dropped 8.1%. Share earnings of $0.54, based on 5.1% fewer shares, compared with $0.55 (excluding $0.03 from discontinued operations).

Common Share Earnings ($)

Quarter:	1993–4	1992–3	1991–2	1990–1
May	0.27	0.25	0.24	0.25
Aug.	0.27	0.30	0.29	0.27
Nov.	E0.25	0.29	0.27	0.26
Feb.	E0.31	0.34	0.34	0.35
	E1.10	1.18	1.14	1.12

Important Developments

Sep. '93— Ennis said that it decided to temporarily suspend its common stock repurchases, giving investors time to react to the company's recently disclosed forecast of lower 1993-4 earnings. Ennis repurchased more than one million of its common shares at an average cost of a little over $17 each during 1992-3 and an additional 400,000 shares in May 1993.

Next earnings report expected in mid-December.

Per Share Data ($)

Yr. End Feb. 28	1993	[1]1992	1991	1990	1989	1988	1987	1986	1985	1984
Tangible Bk. Val.	**3.28**	3.41	3.05	3.10	2.66	2.37	2.38	1.95	1.73	1.43
Cash Flow	**1.43**	1.38	1.31	1.23	1.09	0.89	0.71	0.63	0.53	0.43
Earnings[2]	**1.18**	1.14	1.12	1.05	0.93	0.74	0.55	0.49	0.41	0.33
Dividends	**0.53**	0.51	0.467	0.409	0.324	0.224	0.149	0.101	0.079	0.064
Payout Ratio	**45%**	45%	40%	38%	35%	29%	26%	20%	19%	19%
Calendar Years	**1992**	1991	1990	1989	1988	1987	1986	1985	1984	1983
Prices—High	**21⅛**	21⅜	17⅛	18⅜	12⅜	13¾	8¼	7⅛	4⅜	4⅛
Low	**14⅞**	10⅞	10⅝	11⅞	9⅝	7⅞	6¼	4¼	2¾	1⅞
P/E Ratio—	**18–13**	19–10	15–10	17–11	13–10	18–11	15–11	14–8	11–7	13–6

Data as orig. reptd. Adj. for stk. divs. of 50% Aug. 1991, 50% Jul. 1989, 50% Mar. 1987, 100% Jul. 1985. **1.** Refl. merger or acq. **2.** Bef. results of disc. ops. of +0.03 in 1993, -0.06 in 1992 & spec. item of +0.08 in 1992. E-Estimated.

Income Data (Million $)

Year Ended Feb. 28	Oper. Revs.	Oper. Inc.	% Oper. Inc. of Revs.	Cap. Exp.	Depr.	Int. Exp.	Net Bef. Taxes	Eff. Tax Rate	[3]Net Inc.	% Net Inc. of Revs.	Cash Flow
[1]1993	**129**	**36.4**	**28.2**	**1.32**	**4.39**	**0.25**	**32.3**	**35.9%**	**20.7**	**16.0**	**25.1**
[1,2]1992	132	36.1	27.4	2.48	4.37	0.34	32.3	35.7%	20.8	15.8	25.1
1991	126	35.0	27.8	3.68	3.69	0.42	32.8	35.6%	21.1	16.7	24.8
1990	130	34.6	26.7	3.64	3.48	0.54	32.7	35.6%	21.0	16.2	24.5
1989	128	31.8	24.8	2.10	3.37	0.60	29.3	35.7%	18.8	14.7	22.2
1988	118	29.0	24.7	2.56	3.25	0.63	25.9	39.1%	[4]15.8	13.4	19.0
1987	112	24.6	22.0	2.91	3.36	0.69	23.1	45.6%	12.6	11.2	15.9
1986	111	23.0	20.8	8.17	3.04	0.76	20.9	45.5%	11.4	10.3	14.4
1985	108	20.6	19.0	3.49	3.07	0.72	17.5	46.3%	9.4	8.7	12.5
1984	96	17.2	17.9	3.43	2.57	0.82	14.6	45.9%	7.9	8.2	10.5

Balance Sheet Data (Million $)

Feb. 28	Cash	Curr. Assets	Curr. Liab.	Curr. Ratio	Total Assets	% Ret. on Assets	Long Term Debt	Common Equity	Total Cap.	% LT Debt of Cap.	% Ret. on Equity
1993	**22.6**	**48.9**	**12.1**	**4.0**	**75.9**	**27.1**	**0.51**	**60.6**	**63.8**	**0.8**	**33.6**
1992	25.1	51.0	9.6	5.3	81.2	26.9	2.40	66.5	68.9	3.5	34.0
1991	25.5	50.9	10.2	5.0	73.2	28.7	3.16	55.8	59.0	5.4	37.5
1990	26.4	55.5	10.1	5.5	79.2	27.7	4.17	60.7	64.9	6.4	37.2
1989	16.0	46.8	10.1	4.6	73.8	25.9	5.84	53.0	58.8	9.9	37.4
1988	19.5	48.7	12.6	3.9	74.2	21.3	6.87	49.6	56.5	12.2	31.6
1987	25.3	53.4	12.6	4.2	79.4	16.5	7.88	54.0	61.8	12.7	24.5
1986	21.0	48.0	11.5	4.2	75.0	15.8	8.84	50.3	59.1	14.9	23.9
1985	9.9	39.3	11.5	3.4	63.9	15.8	7.18	41.6	48.8	14.7	24.5
1984	5.4	32.4	9.8	3.3	57.5	14.5	8.09	36.6	44.7	18.1	23.6

Data as orig. reptd. **1.** Excl. disc. ops. **2.** Refl. merger or acq. **3.** Bef. spec. item in 1992. **4.** Refl. acctg. change.

Business Summary

Ennis Business Forms prints and constructs a broad line of business forms for national distribution. Presentation folders were added to the company's product line through the March 1991 acquisition of Admore Inc., and award ribbons were added through the October 1992 acquisition of Lone Star Ribbon Co. Ennis also manufactures (through its Connolly Tool and Machine Co. subisidiary) tools, dies and special machinery, all to customers' specifications, for clients primarily in the Southwest.

Sales in recent fiscal years were derived as follows:

	1992–3	1991–2
Business products..............	94%	91%
Other	6%	9%

About 85% of the business forms manufactured by Ennis are custom or semi-custom, constructed in a wide variety of sizes, colors, number of parts and quantities on an individual-job basis, depending on customers' specifications.

Distribution of business forms throughout the U.S. is primarily through independent dealers, including business forms distributors, stationers and printers. Distribution of tools, dies and special machinery is on a contract basis with individual customers. No single customer accounts for as much as 10% of consolidated sales.

Ennis believes it is one of the largest producers of business forms in the U.S. and that Connolly Tool is one of the leading independent designers and manufacturers of tools, dies and special machinery in the Southwest.

During the second quarter of 1992-3, the company completed the sale of substantially all the assets of American Business Equipment Inc., which sold copying machine supplies and sold and serviced copying machines.

Dividend Data

Cash has been paid each year since 1973.

Amt. of Divd. $	Date Decl.	Ex–divd. Date	Stock of Record	Payment Date
0.135	Dec. 16	Jan. 11	Jan. 15	Feb. 1'93
0.135	Mar. 26	Apr. 8	Apr. 15	May 3'93
0.14	Jun. 17	Jul. 9	Jul. 15	Aug. 2'93
0.14	Sep. 15	Oct. 8	Oct. 15	Nov. 1'93

Capitalization

Long Term Debt: $505,000 (5/93).

Common Stock: 16,799,045 shs. ($2.50 par). Institutions hold about 43%. Shareholders of record: 2,336.

Office—107 N. Sherman St., Ennis, TX 75119. **Tel**—(214) 875-6581. **Chrmn, CEO & Investor Contact**—Kenneth A. McCrady. **Pres**—C. F. Ray. **VP-Fin, Secy & Treas**—H. Cathey. **Dirs**—H. M. Cornell Jr., J. B. Gardner, H. W. Hartley, J. C. McCormick, K. A. McCrady, R. L. Mitchell, T. R. Price, C. F. Ray, E. L. Tankersley. **Transfer Agent & Registrar**—Ameritrust Corp., Dallas. **Incorporated** in Texas in 1909. **Empl**—1,270.

 M. Graham Hackett

Enterra Corp.

NYSE Symbol EN Options on NYSE & Phila (Jan-Apr-Jul-Oct) In S&P MidCap 400

Price	Range	P–E Ratio	Dividend	Yield	S&P Ranking	Beta
Oct. 7'93	1993					
25⅛	29–17	27	None	None	B–	1.30

Summary

This company provides specialized services and products for drilling onshore and offshore oil and gas wells. It also manufactures, sells and rents specialized equipment used in pipeline construction and rehabilitation. After declining in 1992 on a downturn in oilfield service activity and fewer pipeline construction projects, earnings were level in 1993's first six months.

Business Summary

Enterra Corp. provides specialized services and products to the oil and gas industry through its oilfield services and equipment business, which consists primarily of equipment rental and services for onshore and offshore drilling, and its pipeline construction and rehabilitation equipment business. EN also provides well control assistance and fishing services. Segment contributions in 1992:

	Revs.	Operating Profits
Oilfield services & equipment	59%	58%
Pipeline equipment	41%	42%

In 1992, including exports as foreign sales, the U.S. accounted for 45% of revenues, Canada 11%, and other foreign 44%.

The oilfield services and equipment segment rents specialized equipment used in deep well drilling, generally below 7,500 ft., and in well completion, production and workover activity; provides well control services, which consist of planning and design assistance regarding particular types of equipment needed to control critical wells; and provides fishing services, which require a variety of fishing tools designed to catch or eliminate obstructions lodged in a well. EN's fishing services business increased substantially with the May 1989 acquisition of the fishing tool assets of Donham, Inc. In June 1991, the company acquired Deepwater, a supplier of cut-and-abandonment services in the U.K. sector of the North Sea. The majority of this segment's 1992 revenues were attributable to well completion, production and workover activities.

EN's pipeline equipment business designs, manufactures, services, sells and rents specialized equipment used in the construction and rehabilitation of oil and gas pipelines (ranging from 6 to 120 inches in diameter). The equipment is used for welding, bending and aligning sections of pipe, for cleaning and coating pipe, and for handling pipe in plants and on offshore pipe lay barges, boring under roads, and beveling pipe. EN has expanded this segment through several smaller acquisitions, including 92% of Pipeline Induction Heat Ltd. (heat induction and field coating of pipes), and Canadian Ultra Pressure Services (waterblast cleaning systems). Pipeline equipment is rented primarily in the U.S. and Canada and, with the exception of automatic welding equipment, sold internationally.

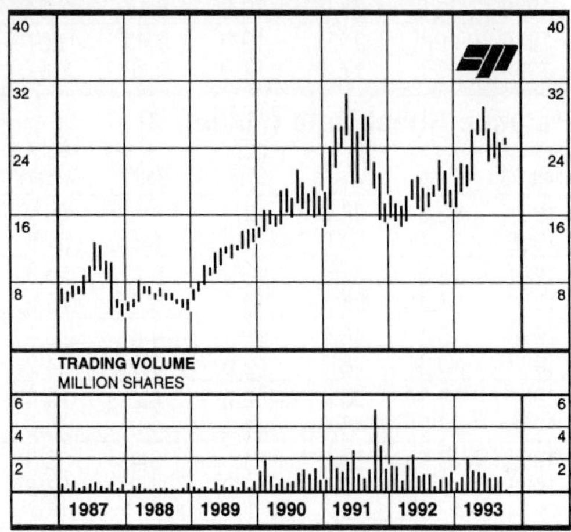

Important Developments

Sep. '93— Enterra is engaged in a contractual disagreement with the Kuwait Oil Co. regarding services rendered in Kuwait. At June 30, 1993, the company had about $10 million of receivables from Kuwait Oil which were involved in the dispute.

Jun. '93— An EN pipeline subsidiary received an offshore equipment order from the Swiss-based Allseas Group. The contract, valued in excess of $10 million, requires deliveries in the first six months of 1994.

Next earnings report expected in early November.

Per Share Data ($)

Yr. End Dec. 31	1992	1991	1990	1989	[1]1988	1987	1986	1985	1984	1983
Tangible Bk. Val.	**12.70**	12.02	10.57	7.82	7.49	8.40	8.05	13.17	14.05	16.28
Cash Flow	**2.03**	2.33	2.13	1.96	1.43	0.73	d1.68	3.54	2.73	2.80
Earnings[2]	**0.92**	1.40	1.21	0.26	d0.43	d1.39	d5.51	d0.73	d2.21	d2.35
Dividends	**Nil**	Nil	Nil	Nil	Nil	Nil	Nil	Nil	0.21	0.84
Payout Ratio	**Nil**	Nil	Nil	Nil	Nil	Nil	Nil	Nil	NM	NM
Prices—High	**22⅝**	30½	21½	14⅜	8¼	12¾	12¼	13⅞	21⅜	25⅝
Low	**14¾**	14¾	13⅜	5⅞	4⅝	4	4½	9⅛	9⅛	14
P/E Ratio—	**25–16**	22–11	18–11	55–23	NM	NM	NM	NM	NM	NM

Data as orig. reptd. **1.** Reflects merger or acquisition. **2.** Bef. results of disc. opers. of +1.48 in 1987. d-Deficit. NM-Not Meaningful.

Income Data (Million $)

Year Ended Dec. 31	Revs.	Oper. Inc.	% Oper. Inc. of Revs.	Cap. Exp.	Depr.	Int. Exp.	Net Bef. Taxes	Eff. Tax Rate	Net Inc.	% Net Inc. of Revs.	Cash Flow
1992	**150**	**34**	**22.4**	**36.2**	**17.9**	**0.6**	**18.5**	**22.2%**	**14.7**	**9.8**	**32.6**
1991	175	45	25.9	25.9	14.9	1.2	34.3	34.9%	22.2	12.7	37.2
1990	144	32	22.4	14.8	13.8	1.2	23.3	21.2%	18.2	12.6	32.1
1989	109	20	18.5	17.9	17.8	2.3	1.6	NM	2.7	2.5	20.6
[1]1988	90	17	19.4	8.2	18.7	4.0	[4]d2.9	NM	d4.3	NM	14.4
[2]1987	42	3	6.7	3.6	18.9	0.8	[4]d12.5	NM	d12.4	NM	6.5
1986	109	11	10.3	6.5	34.2	3.2	[4]d63.8	NM	[5]d49.3	NM	d15.0
1985	142	30	21.3	14.2	38.2	4.7	[4]d12.6	NM	d6.5	NM	31.6
1984	160	32	19.9	15.1	44.2	8.2	[4]d39.6	NM	d19.8	NM	24.4
1983	127	15	11.9	13.1	46.0	[3]7.6	[4]d38.5	NM	d21.0	NM	25.0

Balance Sheet Data (Million $)

Dec. 31	Cash	Curr. Assets	Curr. Liab.	Curr. Ratio	Total Assets	% Ret. on Assets	Long Term Debt	Common Equity	Total Cap.	% LT Debt of Cap.	% Ret. on Equity
1992	**78.8**	**151**	**33.8**	**4.4**	**255**	**5.9**	**Nil**	**210**	**220**	**Nil**	**7.2**
1991	84.3	156	35.4	4.4	246	9.6	Nil	198	208	Nil	11.9
1990	73.1	135	32.9	4.1	214	9.1	Nil	172	179	Nil	12.1
1989	8.8	56	31.0	1.8	123	2.0	Nil	86	90	Nil	3.2
1988	31.2	69	23.3	3.0	142	NM	29.7	82	117	25.4	NM
1987	20.8	42	20.4	2.1	104	NM	4.8	75	82	5.8	NM
1986	14.3	61	23.7	2.6	149	NM	47.9	73	123	39.0	NM
1985	6.4	68	32.2	2.1	230	NM	54.2	123	192	28.2	NM
1984	7.4	84	36.5	2.3	268	NM	74.7	130	227	32.8	NM
1983	6.4	69	33.3	2.1	304	NM	85.0	152	268	31.7	NM

Data as orig. reptd. **1.** Reflects merger or acquisition. **2.** Excludes discontinued operations. **3.** Net of interest income. **4.** Incl. equity in earns. of nonconsol. subs. **5.** Reflects accounting change. d-Deficit. NM-Not Meaningful.

Sales & Revenues (Million $)

Quarter:	1993	1992	1991	1990
Mar.	38.8	33.5	44.1	30.4
Jun.	40.2	40.7	42.9	32.6
Sep.		40.5	48.4	40.4
Dec.		35.5	39.5	41.1
		150.2	174.9	144.5

Revenues in the six months ended June 30, 1993, were up 6.5%, year to year, as increased oilfield services and equipment activity in North America and Kuwait outweighed lower export and U.S. sales of pipeline equipment. Operating expenses rose less rapidly, offsetting lower interest income and greater depreciation charges, and pretax income gained 6.8%. After taxes at 29.8%, versus 24.9%, per share earnings were $0.40 in both periods.

Common Share Earnings ($)

Quarter:	1993	1992	1991	1990
Mar.	0.20	0.17	0.39	0.13
Jun.	0.20	0.24	0.34	0.21
Sep.		0.36	0.42	0.47
Dec.		0.16	0.26	0.38
		0.92	1.40	1.21

Dividend Data

Dividends were omitted in 1984. The most recent payment was $0.10½ on June 1, 1984.

Finances

In April 1993, EN acquired the fishing tool inventory of Yacemientos Petroleos Fiscales (YPF), the national oil company of Argentina, for $5.0 million.

Capital expenditures during 1985-89 were relatively low because of the decrease in demand for most equipment. Since there is still excess equipment, EN's capital expenditures, exclusive of acquisitions, declined to $25.1 million in 1992, from $25.9 million in 1991. During 1993's first six months, capital expenditures, including the acquisition of YPF's inventory, were $18 million.

As of June 30, 1993, there were no borrowings under the company's $40 million line of credit.

Late in 1992's first quarter, EN implemented a cost reduction program, including work force cutbacks, to minimize costs at current industry levels.

Capitalization

Long Term Debt: None (6/93).

Minority Interest: $1,827,000.

Common Stock: 16,316,958 shs. ($1 par).
Institutions hold approximately 85%.
Shareholders of record: 2,100 (3/93).

Office—13100 Northwest Freeway, Sixth Floor, Houston, TX 77040-6310. **Tel**—(713) 462-7300. **Chrmn, Pres & CEO**—D. D. Wood. **VP & CFO**—S. W. Krablin. **Investor Contact**—Steven C. Grant. **Dirs**—J. M. Ballengee, L. Daniel, C. P. Evans, T. L. Kelly, II, R. L. Parker, Sr., R. R. Reinfrank, D. D. Wood. **Transfer Agent & Registrar**—American Stock Transfer and Trust Co., NYC. **Incorporated** in Pennsylvania in 1981; reincorporated in Delaware in 1987. **Empl**—1,250.

 J.R. Jordan

Equifax Inc.

NYSE Symbol EFX Options on Pacific (Jan-Apr-Jul-Oct) In S&P MidCap 400

Price	Range	P–E Ratio	Dividend	Yield	S&P Ranking	Beta
Aug. 24'93	1993					
24	24¾–17⅜	21	0.56	2.3%	A	0.74

Summary

This company provides businesses with information for insurance claims and credit evaluation purposes. Other activities include marketing research and a variety of information services. After rising sharply in 1992, earnings continued to expand in the first half of 1993. In August 1993, the company acquired Integratec, a provider of outsourcing services to the credit industry.

Business Summary

Equifax provides a broad range of information-based administrative services to business, industry and government. Contributions by segment in 1992:

	Revs.	Profits
Credit information services...	39%	66%
Payment services	17%	27%
Insurance information services......................	35%	11%
General business services...	9%	–4%

The credit information segment primarily provides consumer credit services in the U.S., U.K. and Canada, but it also provides other related credit functions. In the U.S., this includes accounts receivable management and collection, locate services, credit fraud detection and prevention, and credit card marketing programs.

The payment segment includes check guarantee functions as well as various credit and debit card processing services for merchants and financial institutions. These services include authorizing card purchases, embossing and issuing cards, and clearing and settling card charges.

The insurance information segment provides all major life insurance companies in North America with various information services for help in determining the classification of applicants as risks for life and health insurance and for assistance in settling health claims. In addition, health data is provided to those companies for their use in underwriting the health aspects of their risks. Also, most of the major fire and casualty companies use information on applicants for such insurance, for reports on the physical characteristics of the property insured, and for an automobile comprehensive loss underwriting exchange (CLUE). This information is used to evaluate applicant risk and to help determine the applicable rates.

The general business segment furnishes a broad range of informational and administrative services that include pre-employment services, market research and analysis, customer opinion surveys, and PC-based marketing systems.

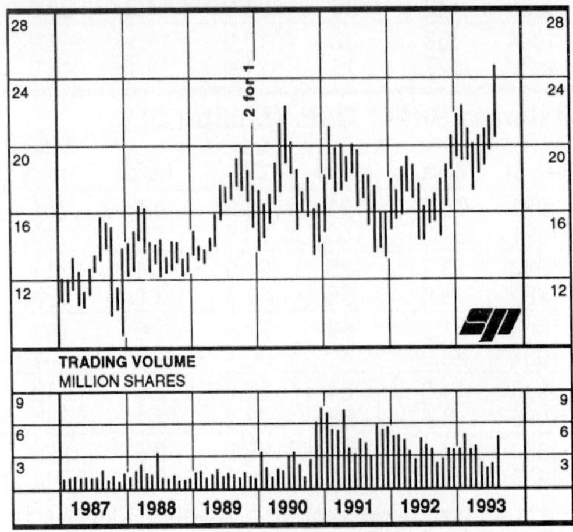

In October 1992, the company acquired Health Economics Corporation (HEC), a provider of health care cost management services.

Important Developments

Aug. '93— EFX acquired Integratec, Inc., one of the nation's largest providers of outsourcing services to the credit industry, for $23 million. Integratec had 1992 revenues of $32 million.

Apr. '93— EFX signed a $650 million agreement with IBM's Integrated Systems Solutions Corp. (ISSC) unit, under which ISSC will operate a portion of EFX's computer data processing operation for 10 years. Separately, the California State Lottery terminated a contract with EFX's High Integrity Systems Inc. unit for non-performance, and will sue the company for breach of contract.

Next earnings report expected in late October.

Per Share Data ($)

Yr. End Dec. 31	1992	1991	[1]1990	1989	[1]1988	1987	1986	1985	1984	1983
Tangible Bk. Val.	**1.93**	2.97	3.25	2.98	2.96	2.32	1.97	1.66	1.45	1.36
Cash Flow	**1.70**	1.34	1.23	1.33	1.26	1.11	0.87	0.71	0.61	0.57
Earnings[2]	**1.04**	0.66	0.79	0.73	0.74	0.72	0.60	0.53	0.44	0.42
Dividends	**0.520**	0.520	0.480	0.430	0.390	0.350	0.318	0.291	0.271	0.243
Payout Ratio	**50%**	79%	61%	59%	56%	49%	53%	55%	62%	58%
Prices—High	**20⅝**	21⅛	22⅜	20	16½	15¾	14¼	10¼	5⅞	6⅜
Low	**14⅜**	13⅜	13½	13	12¼	8¾	9½	5⅜	4	4⅜
P/E Ratio—	**20–14**	32–20	28–17	27–18	22–17	22–12	24–16	19–10	13–9	15–10

Data as orig. reptd. Adj. for stk. divs. of 100% Dec. 1989, 100% Mar. 1986, 50% Mar. 1985. **1.** Reflects merger or acquisition. **2.** Bef. results of disc. opers. of -0.10 in 1985, and spec. items of -0.60 in 1991, +0.12 in 1988.

Income Data (Million $)

Year Ended Dec. 31	Revs.	Oper. Inc.	% Oper. Inc. of Revs.	Cap. Exp.	Depr.	Int. Exp.	Net Bef. Taxes	Eff. Tax Rate	[5]Net Inc.	% Net Inc. of Revs.	Cash Flow
1992	**1,134**	**195**	**17.2**	**34.6**	**53.8**	**4.0**	**[4]145**	**41.1%**	**85.3**	**7.5**	**139**
1991	1,094	181	16.5	23.6	55.9	7.3	[4]94	42.2%	[6]54.1	4.9	110
[1]1990	1,079	173	16.0	45.9	36.0	14.0	[4]113	43.4%	63.9	5.9	100
1989	840	111	13.2	55.7	29.4	12.6	60	40.7%	35.7	4.2	65
[1]1988	743	87	11.7	59.5	24.3	4.4	[4]58	41.5%	34.0	4.6	58
1987	670	75	11.2	27.4	17.1	3.6	[4]56	45.8%	30.6	4.6	48
1986	635	60	9.5	31.9	11.8	3.9	47	45.1%	[6]25.6	4.0	37
[2]1985	564	49	8.8	19.0	7.8	[3]3.7	40	44.4%	22.4	4.0	30
1984	507	42	8.2	16.8	7.4	[3]3.2	33	44.2%	18.6	3.7	26
1983	471	36	7.7	17.3	6.2	[3]2.3	32	44.8%	17.8	3.8	24

Balance Sheet Data (Million $)

Dec. 31	Cash	Curr. Assets	Curr. Liab.	Curr. Ratio	Total Assets	% Ret. on Assets	Long Term Debt	Common Equity	Total Cap.	% LT Debt of Cap.	% Ret. on Equity
1992	**87**	**279**	**129**	**2.2**	**709**	**12.5**	**192**	**258**	**464**	**41.3**	**29.4**
1991	105	304	153	2.0	716	7.3	77	350	447	17.2	14.9
1990	115	324	154	2.1	754	7.7	143	373	570	25.1	16.4
1989	14	178	137	1.3	551	7.3	89	247	384	23.1	15.1
1988	6	149	118	1.3	421	9.3	30	225	295	10.2	18.4
1987	9	125	66	1.9	274	11.7	30	125	198	15.2	26.1
1986	7	114	68	1.7	248	10.9	20	109	172	11.7	25.1
1985	3	103	79	1.3	221	10.7	20	95	138	14.8	24.3
1984	3	98	62	1.6	198	9.9	23	89	132	17.7	21.8
1983	6	88	54	1.6	176	10.8	24	81	120	20.4	23.0

Data as orig. reptd. **1.** Reflects merger or acquisition. **2.** Excludes discontinued operations. **3.** Net of interest income. **4.** Incl. equity in earns. of nonconsol. subs. **5.** Bef. spec. items. **6.** Reflects accounting change.

Oper. Revenues (Million $)

Quarter:	1993	1992	1991	1990
Mar.	276	276	253	253
Jun.	298	276	275	274
Sep.		278	271	268
Dec.		303	295	284
		1,134	1,094	1,079

Revenues in the six months ended June 30, 1993, rose 3.9%, year to year. Margins widened, and despite lower net other income and higher interest expense, pretax income increased 9.8%. After taxes at 40.8%, versus 41.8%, net income rose 12%, to $41,367,000 ($0.55 a share, based on 8.6% fewer shares), from $37,065,000 ($0.45).

Common Share Earnings ($)

Quarter:	1993	1992	1991	1990
Mar.	0.24	0.19	0.01	0.19
Jun.	0.31	0.26	0.24	0.26
Sep.		0.27	0.22	0.24
Dec.		0.32	0.19	0.10
		1.04	0.66	0.79

Dividend Data

Dividends have been paid since 1913. A dividend reinvestment plan is available.

Amt. of Divd. $	Date Decl.	Ex-divd. Date	Stock of Record	Payment Date
0.13	Oct. 28	Nov. 18	Nov. 24	Dec. 15'92
0.14	Jan. 27	Feb. 16	Feb. 22	Mar. 15'93
0.14	Apr. 28	May 19	May 25	Jun. 15'93
0.14	Jul. 27	Aug. 19	Aug. 25	Sep. 15'93

Finances

In June 1993, EFX issued $200 million principal amount of 6.5% senior notes due 2003. Proceeds were used to repay other indebtedness.

In December 1992, EFX repurchased 6,553,000 shares of its common stock at a cost of $126,979,000. In January 1993, directors authorized the repurchase of additional shares at a cost of up to $75,000,000.

Under an August 1988 processing agreement with Computer Sciences Corp. (CSC), EFX has the option to purchase CSC's collection and credit reporting businesses if CSC does not renew the agreement in 1998 or if there is a change in control of CSC. CSC also has the option to sell these businesses to EFX.

Capitalization

Long Term Debt: $203,266,000 (3/93, as adjusted).

Common Stock: 74,896,000 shs. ($2.50 par). Institutions hold about 59%. Shareholders or record: 8,300 (3/93).

Office—1600 Peachtree St., N.W. (P.O. Box 4081), Atlanta, GA 30309 **Tel**—(404) 885-8000. **Chmn & CEO**—C. B. Rogers, Jr. **Pres**—D. W. McGlaughlin. **SVP-CFO**—D. U. Hallman. **VP-Secy**—T. H. Magis. **Investor Contact**—Richard F. Wacht. **Dirs**—L. A. Ault, III, R. D. Barbaro, J. C. Chartrand, J. L. Clendenin, A. W. Dahlberg, L. P. Humann, T. H. Irvin, L. Keith, D. W. McGlaughlin, L. L. Prince, D. R. Riddle, C. B. Rogers, Jr., B. L. Siegel, J. V. White. **Transfer Agent & Registrar**—Trust Co. Bank, Atlanta. **Incorporated** in Georgia in 1913. **Empl**—12,400.

 Kevin J. Gooley

Exabyte Corp.

NASDAQ Symbol EXBT (Incl. in Nat'l Market) Options on ASE & CBOE In S&P MidCap 400

Price	Range	P-E Ratio	Dividend	Yield	S&P Ranking	Beta
Jul. 23'93	1993					
8¾	18⅝–8⅝	38	None	None	NR	NA

Summary

Exabyte designs, develops, manufactures and markets high-capacity 8mm cartridge tape subsystems for cost-effective data storage solutions. Softness in the distribution channel limited growth in recent periods. New products are expected to aid sales in the second half of 1993; however, earnings should remain under pressure on narrower margins, owing to a less favorable product mix, moderate price declines and continued high research and development costs.

Current Outlook

Earnings for 1993 are estimated at $0.70 a share, versus the $0.95 reported for 1992 (which included a $0.62 acquisition-related writeoff). Earnings for 1994 are projected at $1.45 a share.

Initiation of cash dividends is not expected.

Sales should rise in the second half of 1993, spurred by gains in the company's 8mm half-height cartridge tape subsystems, and increased production of its recently acquired 4mm and quarter-inch tape storage devices; 8mm full-height subsystems are expected to continue to decline. While OEM business should remain firm, general economic weakness in Europe will be a restraint. Margins are expected to narrow on declines in average selling prices, a less favorable product mix as manufacturing volumes increase for 4mm and quarter-inch products, and continued high research and development costs.

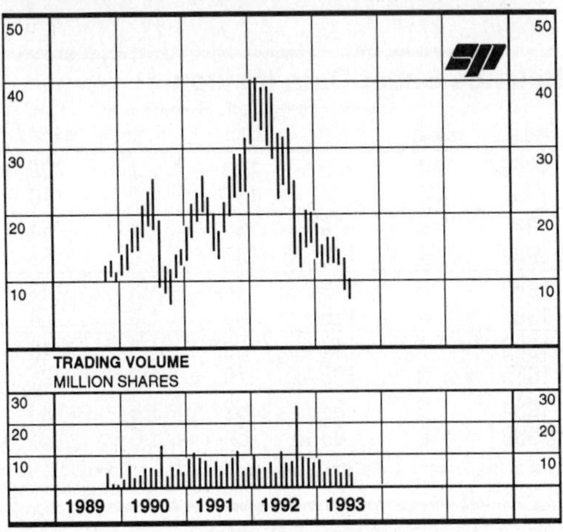

Sales (Million $)

13 Weeks:	1993	1992	1991	1990
Mar.	76.2	76.1	51.6	40.5
Jun.	75.8	76.6	52.5	46.3
Sep.		[1]64.1	58.6	39.2
Dec.		70.6	71.4	44.3
		287.4	234.1	170.3

Sales for the six months ended July 3, 1993, fell fractionally, year to year, as declines in full-height 8mm storage products offset gains in half-height 8mm products and 4mm products. Margins narrowed on moderate pricing pressures, higher manufacturing costs, continued high research and development expense and unfavorable foreign currency movements; pretax profit fell 67%. After taxes at 35.7%, versus 35.8%, net income also declined 67%, to $7,622,000 ($0.36 a share on 1.6% fewer shares), from $23,421,000 ($1.08).

Common Share Earnings ($)

13 Weeks:	1993	1992	1991	1990
Mar.	0.28	0.54	0.34	0.32
Jun.	0.08	0.54	0.30	0.38
Sep.	E0.14	[1]d0.40	0.40	0.29
Dec.	E0.20	0.25	0.47	0.33
	E0.70	0.95	1.51	1.32

Important Developments

Feb. '93— The company acquired the assets of Everex Systems' Mass Storage Division, which makes quarter-inch cartridge tape drives, for $5 million in cash. Separately, EXBT acquired Tallgrass Technologies Corp., a value-added reseller of computer magnetic tape subsystems, for $1.5 million in cash.

Next earnings report expected in mid-October.

Per Share Data ($)

Yr. End Dec. 31	1992	1991	1990	1989	1988	1987
Tangible Bk. Val.	**6.70**	5.51	3.80	[2]2.38	NA	NA
Cash Flow	**1.36**	1.78	1.47	0.73	0.13	d0.19
Earnings[3]	**0.95**	1.51	1.32	0.65	0.10	d0.20
Dividends	**Nil**	Nil	Nil	Nil	Nil	Nil
Payout Ratio	**Nil**	Nil	Nil	Nil	Nil	Nil
Prices—High	**40⅝**	31⅝	25⅜	13⅛	NA	NA
Low	**12**	13⅛	6⅝	10	NA	NA
P/E Ratio—	**43–13**	21–9	19–5	20–15	NA	NA

Data as orig. reptd. **1.** 14 wks. **2.** Incl. intangibles. **3.** Bef. spec. items of +0.07 in 1989, +0.05 in 1988. d-Deficit. E-Estimated. NA-Not Available.

Income Data (Million $)

Year Ended Dec. 31	Revs.	Oper. Inc.	% Oper. Inc. of Revs.	Cap. Exp.	Depr.	Int. Exp.	Net Bef. Taxes	Eff. Tax Rate	[1]Net Inc.	% Net Inc. of Revs.	Cash Flow
1992	**287**	**59.4**	**20.6**	**17.80**	**8.97**	**0.14**	**38.9**	**47.3%**	**20.5**	**7.1**	**29.5**
1991	234	54.2	23.2	6.85	5.73	0.13	50.2	35.9%	32.2	13.8	37.9
1990	170	43.7	25.7	9.26	3.18	0.10	42.9	35.6%	27.6	16.2	30.8
1989	89	19.2	21.7	2.85	1.37	0.13	19.4	36.2%	12.4	13.9	13.7
1988	32	2.8	8.9	0.90	0.55	0.15	2.8	37.6%	1.7	5.6	2.3
1987	3	d4.3	NM	0.87	0.13	0.03	d2.9	NM	d3.0	NM	d2.9

Balance Sheet Data (Million $)

Dec. 31	Cash	Curr. Assets	Curr. Liab.	Curr. Ratio	Total Assets	% Ret. on Assets	Long Term Debt	Common Equity	Total Cap.	% LT Debt of Cap.	% Ret. on Equity
1992	**51.2**	**155**	**42.3**	**3.7**	**183**	**12.1**	**0.50**	**140**	**141**	**0.4**	**16.0**
1991	55.6	135	37.7	3.6	150	25.4	0.14	112	112	0.1	34.0
1990	28.8	89	25.5	3.5	101	33.4	0.22	75	75	0.3	45.2
1989	30.1	58	16.5	3.5	62	30.9	0.17	46	46	0.4	43.9

Data as orig. reptd. **1.** Bef. spec. items. d-Deficit. NM-Not Meaningful.

Business Summary

Exabyte Corp. designs, manufactures and markets cartridge tape subsystems for data storage applications. The company's products are used in a broad spectrum of computer systems ranging from personal computers to supercomputers. A large majority of its units are used with workstations, network file servers and minicomputers. The capacity of these subsystems allows users to back up multiple disk drives and, in many cases, an entire computer system, on a single tape cartridge. Through February 1993, the company had shipped nearly 500,000 tape drives.

The main products, the EXB-8200 and the EXB-8500, are cartridge tape subsystems based upon 8mm helical scan technology. The EXB-8200 can store 2.5 gigabytes (GBs) of data on a single 8mm tape cartridge and has a data transfer rate of 246 kilobytes (KBs) per second. It fits into the 5¼-inch full-height form factor, includes a Small Computer Systems Interface (SCSI) and is offered with a high-speed search feature. The EXB-8200 accounted for 37%, 61% and 85% of sales in 1992, 1991 and 1990, respectively.

Exabyte's EXB-8500 has a 5.0 GB capacity, packaged in the same 5¼-inch form factor, with approximately twice the transfer rate of the EXB-8200. The product's design enables it to be compatible with the EXB-8200 for ease of customer migration, allowing a tape written on either model to be read by the other. The EXB-8500 accounted for about 34%, 21% and less than 1% of sales in 1992, 1991 and 1990, respectively.

Extensions of its mainstay products include standalone versions, half-height offerings, and products with enhanced storage capacities based on data compression technology.

The product line also includes desktop cartridge-handling systems and a robotic tape library, both of which incorporate the EXB-8200 and EXB-8500, as well as recording media, cleaning cartridges, data cartridge holders and other consumables.

Exabyte's 4mm cartridge tape subsystem, the EXB-4200, was initially developed by R-Byte, which was acquired by Exabyte in October 1992. The EXB-4200, which can store up to 2 GBs of data on a single, standard 90 meter DAT cartridge and has a sustained data transfer rate of up to 233 KBs per second, is packaged in the 3½-inch form factor, and includes a SCSI controller.

Sales to OEMs represented 45% and 46% of sales in 1992 and 1991, respectively. IBM accounted for 16% and 20% of total sales in 1992 and 1991. Sales to VARs and system integrators accounted for approximately 37% and 34% of sales in 1992 and 1991. Sales to distributors approximated 18% and 20% in 1992 and 1991, respectively.

International sales were approximately 18% and 15% of total sales in 1992 and 1991, respectively.

Dividend Data

The company has never paid cash dividends on its common stock. A "poison pill" stock purchase right was adopted in 1991.

Finances

In October 1992, EXBT acquired R-Byte Inc., a maker of low-cost, high-capacity digital audio tape (DAT) 4mm computer storage devices, for $12,000,000 in cash and the repayment of $1,750,000 of debt securities. In the third quarter of 1992, Exabyte recorded a $13,469,000 ($0.62 a share) nonrecurring charge to reflect the excess of the purchase price over the net assets acquired.

Capitalization

Long Term Debt: $492,000 of lease obligs. (7/3/93).

Common Stock: 20,965,752 shs. ($0.001 par). Institutions hold about 52%. Shareholders: 1,106 of record (3/93).

Office—1685 38th St., Boulder, CO 80301-9803. **Tel**—(303) 442-4333. **Chrmn, Pres & CEO**—P. D. Behrendt. **VP-Fin, CFO, Treas & Secy**—W. L. Marriner. **Investor Contact**—Susan Merriman (303) 447-7434. **Dirs**—P. D. Behrendt, B. M. Holland, J. M. McCoy, K. Nakao, J. A. Rodriguez, R. Z. Sorenson, T. G. Washing. **Transfer Agent & Registrar**—First National Bank of Boston. **Incorporated** in Delaware in 1985. **Empl**—1,190.

 Peter C. Wood, CFA

FHP International Corp.

NASDAQ Symbol FHPC (Incl. in Nat'l Market) Options on ASE, CBOE In S&P MidCap 400

Price	Range	P-E Ratio	Dividend	Yield	S&P Ranking	Beta
Sep. 15'93	1993					
19	30–17⅜	14	None	None	NR	1.98

Summary

FHP provides comprehensive managed healthcare services through staff and IPA model HMOs in California, Utah, Arizona, New Mexico, Nevada and Guam. Revenues and earnings rose strongly in fiscal 1993, aided by strong IPA model enrollment growth and an 11.6% Medicare rate increase which became effective on January 1, 1993. Further growth is anticipated, though results in the second half of fiscal 1994 will be restricted by a much smaller Medicare rate increase of 2%, which becomes effective January 1, 1994.

Current Outlook

Earnings for the fiscal year ending June 30, 1994, are estimated at $1.65 a share, up from $1.33 in fiscal 1993.

Initiation of cash dividends is not expected.

Revenues will continue to grow strongly in the first half of fiscal 1994, reflecting membership gains estimated in the 13% to 15% range and an 11.5% Medicare rate increase which remains effective through December 31, 1993. Earnings should also be up strongly in the first half, as the medical loss and administrative cost ratios should show some improvement over the year-earlier period. Revenue growth will decelerate during the second half of the year, as gains will be limited by a small 2% Medicare rate increase, effective January 1, 1994. Margins could also be negatively impacted by the small rate increase, but earnings for the full year should still advance nicely.

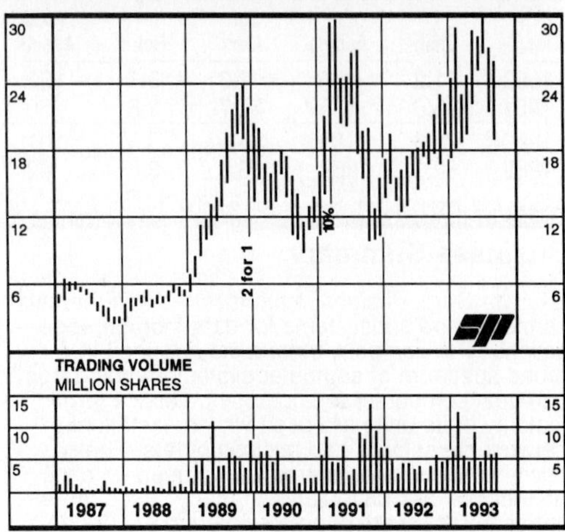

Operating Revenues (Million $)

Quarter:	1992-93	1991-92	1990-91	1989-90
Sep.	444	364	294	210
Dec.	465	375	312	223
Mar.	536	419	338	266
Jun.	561	427	353	281
	2,006	1,586	1,297	980

Based on a preliminary report, revenues in the fiscal year ended June 30, 1993, climbed 26%, year to year, reflecting 26% membership growth in the company's IPA plans (17% overall) and higher premium rates. Aided by improvement in both the medical loss ratio (83.8% versus 84.0%) and the administrative cost ratio (13.4% versus 14.3%), and despite a 33% drop in net interest income, the gain in pretax income was extended to 36%. After taxes at 36.7%, versus 36.1%, net income was up 34%, to $44,166,000 ($1.33 a share), from $32,890,000 ($1.00).

Common Share Earnings ($)

Quarter:	1993-94	1992-93	1991-92	1990-91
Sep.	E0.42	0.20	0.18	0.30
Dec.	E0.43	0.19	0.13	0.29
Mar.	E0.39	0.43	0.45	0.36
Jun.	E0.41	0.51	0.24	0.42
	E1.65	1.33	1.00	1.37

Important Developments

Sep. '93— FHP was informed by the Health Care Financing Administration that it would receive an average Medicare rate increase of 2%, effective January 1, 1994. The company said it hopes to offset the effect of the low rate increase through new products, benefit changes and cost reductions. In addition, a large percentage of the company's providers are paid on a percentage of premium basis, which should also help hold costs in line with revenues.

Next earnings report expected in early November.

Per Share Data ($)

Yr. End Jun. 30	1993	1992	1991	1990	1989	1988	1987	1986
Tangible Bk. Val.	**NA**	9.61	8.38	5.12	4.04	1.61	1.26	0.29
Cash Flow	**NA**	1.70	2.01	1.52	1.40	1.00	0.49	0.63
Earnings	**1.33**	[1]1.00	[1]1.37	[1]1.00	[1]1.00	[1]0.66	[1]0.25	[1]0.44
Dividends	**Nil**	Nil	Nil	Nil	Nil	Nil	Nil	Nil
Payout Ratio	**Nil**	Nil	Nil	Nil	Nil	Nil	Nil	Nil
Prices—High	**30**	[2]23	[2]29¾	[2]20½	[2]24	[2]6	[2]6½	[2]5½
Low	**17⅜**	[2]12½	[2]9⅞	[2]8⅞	[2]5⅜	[2]2¾	[2]2½	[2]3½
P/E Ratio—	**23–13**	23–13	22–7	20–9	24–5	9–4	26–10	13–8

Data as orig. reptd. Adj. for stk. divs. of 10% Mar. 1991, 100% Dec. 1989. **1.** Ful. dil.: 1.36 in 1991, 0.93 in 1989, 0.41 in 1986. **2.** Cal. yr. E-Estimated NA-Not Available.

Income Data (Million $)

Year Ended Jun. 30	Revs.	Oper. Inc.	% Oper. Inc. of Revs.	Cap. Exp.	Depr.	Int. Exp.	Net Bef. Taxes	Eff. Tax Rate	Net Inc.	% Net Inc. of Revs.	Cash Flow
1992	**1,586**	**51.0**	**3.2**	**111**	**23.2**	**3.79**	**51.5**	**36.1%**	**32.9**	**2.1**	**56.1**
1991	1,297	68.6	5.3	61	18.8	4.25	65.7	39.0%	40.1	3.1	58.9
1990	980	56.5	5.8	49	14.9	4.15	45.6	37.0%	28.8	2.9	43.7
1989	699	41.7	6.0	34	11.0	4.81	35.0	37.0%	22.0	3.2	33.0
1988	504	35.5	7.1	24	8.6	5.16	26.6	38.0%	16.5	3.3	25.1
1987	367	18.2	5.0	17	6.6	4.94	10.2	32.0%	6.9	1.9	13.5
1986	265	20.4	7.7	28	4.1	5.71	15.1	39.4%	[1]9.2	3.5	13.3
1985	181	13.5	7.5	29	2.6	0.78	14.8	50.0%	[1]7.4	4.1	NA
1984	123	8.1	6.7	11	1.5	0.93	8.7	50.0%	[1]4.3	3.5	NA
1983	92	3.2	3.5	2	1.1	0.90	2.4	50.0%	[1]1.2	1.3	NA

Balance Sheet Data (Million $)

Jun. 30	Cash	Curr. Assets	Curr. Liab.	Curr. Ratio	Total Assets	% Ret. on Assets	Long Term Debt	Common Equity	Total Cap.	% LT Debt of Cap.	% Ret. on Equity
1992	**239**	**308**	**254**	**1.2**	**616**	**5.7**	**23.3**	**311**	**335**	**7.0**	**11.3**
1991	265	312	207	1.5	529	7.8	29.8	270	300	10.0	18.4
1990	225	259	240	1.1	432	7.6	32.8	142	175	18.8	22.7
1989	158	181	163	1.1	319	8.1	34.4	110	146	23.5	28.7
1988	49	65	92	0.7	182	10.9	43.3	36	82	53.0	51.9
1987	33	49	62	0.8	150	4.4	44.1	35	80	55.1	32.3
1986	19	34	46	0.7	128	7.3	60.5	6	68	89.2	53.1
1985	NA	NA	NA	NA	122	NA	42.4	28	71	60.0	NA

Data as orig. reptd. **1.** Pro forma, aft. giving effect to income tax provision. NA-Not Available.

Business Summary

FHP International Corporation operates a federally qualified multi-state licensed health maintenance organization (HMO) through wholly owned FHP Inc., a California corporation that has been operating managed healthcare programs since 1961. As of June 30, 1993, medical membership approximated 838,000, of which 428,000 were in California, 159,000 in Arizona, 158,000 in Utah, 37,000 on Guam, 36,000 in New Mexico and 20,000 in Nevada.

At June 30, 1993, medical membership by group was as follows: 540,000 (64%) commercial and 298,000 (36%) Senior Plan. Prepaid healthcare contracts with Medicare provided approximately 65%, 65% and 62% of revenues in fiscal 1993, 1992 and 1991, respectively.

Managed healthcare services provided by the company include ambulatory and outpatient physician care, hospital care, pharmacy, dental care, eye care, home health nursing, skilled nursing, physical therapy, psychological counseling and health education. FHP also offers group life insurance products through FHP Life Insurance Co. and workers' compensation and group medical plans through its 24-Hour Managed Care Program, which is offered through arrangements with unaffiliated workers' compensation insurance carriers.

FHP operates primarily through staff model or independent practice association (IPA) model HMOs. In a growing number of service areas, it offers mixed models, where members have a choice of seeing either independent contracting physicians in their offices or staff physicians employed at company-operated medical centers. At June 30, 1993, 499,000 (60%) of the company's members were served through IPA or mixed models and 339,000 (40%) through staff models.

Dividend Data

No cash dividends have been paid. A 10% stock dividend was distributed in 1991, and a two-for-one stock split was effected in 1989.

Finances

In September 1993, the company publicly offered $100 million of senior notes due 2003. Proceeds from the offering will be used to increase the net surplus of a workers' compensation insurance subsidiary ($25 million) and to repay certain debt ($20 million), with the remainder available for general corporate purposes.

Capitalization

Long Term Debt: $20,802,000 (6/93).

Common Stock: 32,763,682 shs. ($0.05 par).
Officers and directors own or control 7.6%.
Institutions hold 74%.
Shareholders: 600 of record (8/92).

Office—9900 Talbert Ave., Fountain Valley, CA 92728-8000. **Tel**—(714) 963-7233. **Chrmn**—R. Gumbiner. **Vice Chrmn, Pres & CEO**—W. W. Price III. **EVP & COO**—J. Massimino. **SVP & Secy**—M. J. Weinstock. **Investor Contact**—Anna Marie Dunlap (714-378-5585). **Dirs**—B. F. Gumbiner, R. Gumbiner, M. B. Hacken, W. Heineman, J. F. Prevratil, W. W. Price III, R. M. Rodnick. **Transfer Agent & Registrar**—American Stock Transfer & Trust Co., NYC. **Incorporated** in Delaware in 1984. **Empl**—9,900.

 Adam J. Penn

Family Dollar Stores

NYSE Symbol FDO Options on Phila (Jan-Apr-Jul-Oct) In S&P MidCap 400

Price	Range	P–E Ratio	Dividend	Yield	S&P Ranking	Beta
Oct. 18'93	1993					
16⅝	23⅝–15⅜	14	0.30	1.8%	A–	1.19

Summary

Family Dollar operates a chain of some 2,055 retail discount stores, located mostly in communities with populations under 50,000. The company takes a no-frills, low-overhead standardized approach to merchandising. Sales gains at existing stores, an aggressive expansion program and a more profitable product mix led to strong earnings growth in recent periods. This trend should continue into fiscal 1994.

Current Outlook

Earnings for the fiscal year ending August 31, 1994, are projected at $1.33 a share, up from fiscal 1993's $1.15.

The quarterly dividend should continue at $0.07½.

Sales are projected to continue double-digit growth in fiscal 1994, spurred by the net addition of 165 stores. Sales at existing stores are expected to rise 4% to 5%. Gross margins should widen on the greater volume, an increased focus on higher-profit apparel and hardline products, and operating efficiencies stemming from recent technology investments. Despite expenses associated with a new distribution center, double-digit share earnings growth is anticipated.

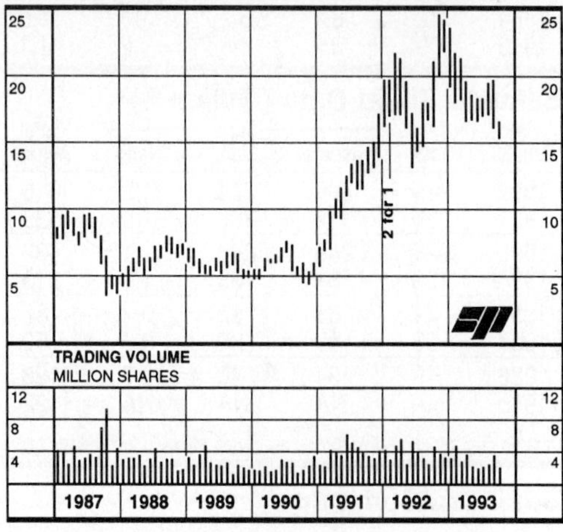

Net Sales (Million $)

Quarter:	1992–93	1991–92	1990–91	1989–90
Nov.	305	264	225	207
Feb.	356	318	257	227
May	310	280	250	218
Aug.	326	297	257	223
	1,297	1,159	989	874

Net sales in the fiscal year ended August 31, 1993 (preliminary), advanced 12% from the preceding year, reflecting a 3.9% gain in same-store sales and more stores in operation. Margins widened on a more favorable product mix, opportunistic purchases of goods from suppliers at closeout prices, and well-controlled SG&A costs. Net income climbed 16%, to $1.15 a share, from $1.00.

Common Share Earnings ($)

Quarter:	1993–94	1992–93	1991–92	1990–91
Nov.	E0.28	0.25	0.21	0.14
Feb.	E0.42	0.37	0.32	0.22
May	E0.35	0.31	0.27	0.22
Aug.	E0.28	0.22	0.20	0.14
	E1.33	1.15	1.00	0.72

Important Developments

Oct. '93— FDO said sales in September 1993 rose 9.1%, year to year; same-store sales were flat. The company indicated that sales in apparel and other softlines departments were softer than sales of hardline merchandise.

Next earnings report expected in January.

Per Share Data ($)

Yr. End Aug. 31	1993	1992	1991	1990	1989	1988	1987	1986	1985	1984
Tangible Bk. Val.	**NA**	4.85	4.08	3.55	3.23	3.02	2.75	2.44	2.01	1.59
Cash Flow	**NA**	1.26	0.96	0.75	0.61	0.67	0.58	0.65	0.57	0.48
Earnings	**1.15**	1.00	0.72	0.52	0.39	0.49	0.43	0.53	0.49	0.42
Dividends	**0.280**	0.240	0.210	0.190	0.170	0.150	0.130	0.110	0.087	0.054
Payout Ratio	**NA**	24%	29%	37%	44%	30%	30%	21%	18%	13%
Prices—High[1]	**24⅝**	24⅝	17⅛	7⅝	7¹⁄₁₆	8	9⅞	14¹⁄₁₆	13½	9¾
Low[1]	**13⅛**	13⅛	5¾	4⁷⁄₁₆	4⅞	4¼	3½	7¹¹⁄₁₆	7¹¹⁄₁₆	15⁷⁄₁₆
P/E Ratio—	**21–11**	25–13	23–8	15–9	18–13	16–9	23–8	27–15	28–16	24–13

Data as orig. reptd. Adj. for stk. divs. of 100% Feb. 1992, 50% Feb. 1985. **1.** Cal. yr. E-Estimated. NA-Not Available.

Income Data (Million $)

Year Ended Aug. 31	Revs.	Oper. Inc.	% Oper. Inc. of Revs.	Cap. Exp.	Depr.	Int. Exp.	Net Bef. Taxes	Eff. Tax Rate	Net Inc.	% Net Inc. of Revs.	Cash Flow
1992	**1,159**	**103**	**8.9**	**30.1**	**14.7**	**Nil**	**88.9**	**37.4%**	**55.7**	**4.8**	**70.4**
1991	989	76	7.7	14.8	13.1	0.41	63.7	36.9%	40.2	4.1	53.3
1990	874	54	6.2	12.5	12.7	1.07	47.6	39.7%	28.7	3.3	41.4
1989	757	43	5.7	18.3	12.0	1.66	35.1	38.7%	21.5	2.8	33.5
1988	669	50	7.5	25.8	10.1	0.85	44.2	38.1%	27.3	4.1	37.5
1987	560	50	8.9	26.0	8.5	Nil	46.8	47.0%	24.8	4.4	33.3
1986	488	56	11.5	20.3	6.8	Nil	57.5	47.0%	30.5	6.3	37.3
1985	410	51	12.5	22.4	4.8	Nil	52.0	46.1%	28.0	6.8	32.8
1984	341	43	12.5	11.1	3.8	Nil	44.5	47.0%	23.6	6.9	27.4
1983	264	30	11.2	8.3	3.0	0.02	30.2	48.0%	15.7	5.9	18.7

Balance Sheet Data (Million $)

Aug. 31	Cash	Curr. Assets	Curr. Liab.	Curr. Ratio	Total Assets	% Ret. on Assets	Long Term Debt	Common Equity	Total Cap.	% LT Debt of Cap.	% Ret. on Equity
1992	**1.7**	**359**	**188**	**1.9**	**478**	**12.7**	**Nil**	**272**	**287**	**Nil**	**22.3**
1991	25.0	294	158	1.9	399	10.6	Nil	227	242	Nil	18.9
1990	4.6	252	144	1.8	355	8.5	Nil	197	211	Nil	15.3
1989	0.7	219	132	1.7	324	7.0	Nil	179	192	Nil	12.4
1988	7.0	192	113	1.7	291	10.5	Nil	167	177	Nil	17.1
1987	13.3	159	75	2.1	242	10.8	Nil	160	167	Nil	16.5
1986	25.0	151	70	2.2	217	15.4	Nil	141	147	Nil	23.7
1985	21.7	125	57	2.2	177	17.7	Nil	116	120	Nil	27.0
1984	32.0	102	44	2.3	138	18.8	Nil	91	94	Nil	29.2
1983	22.4	85	42	2.1	113	15.7	Nil	70	72	Nil	25.1

Data as orig. reptd.

Business Summary

This company operates a chain of self-service retail discount stores under the Family Dollar name. As of August 31, 1993, there were 2,035 stores operating in 31 states, ranging as far northwest as Minnesota, northeast to New Hampshire, southeast to Florida and southwest to Texas. States with significant concentrations of stores include North Carolina, Georgia, South Carolina, Virginia, Tennessee, Alabama, Florida, Kentucky, Louisiana, Ohio and Texas.

The number of stores in operation at the end of recent fiscal years was as follows:

1993....	2,035	1990....	1,680	1987....	1,272
1992....	1,885	1989....	1,580	1986....	1,107
1991....	1,759	1988....	1,429	1985....	920

Each Family Dollar store sells a wide variety of mostly first-quality merchandise, with 46% of sales derived from soft goods, such as apparel, shoes, linen, blankets, bedspreads and curtains; the stores also carry hard goods, including automotive supplies, paints, toys, housewares, school supplies, candy and health and beauty aids.

Merchandise, the majority of which is priced at $17.99 or less, is purchased from about 1,400 suppliers. About 70% of the items carried are manufactured in the U.S.

Stores are located in both rural and urban areas, but most are in communities with populations under 50,000. The units are freestanding or located in shopping centers, with the typical store averaging 6,000 to 8,000 sq. ft. of total area. Most of the stores are leased.

Dividend Data

Cash dividends were initiated in 1976.

Amt of Divd. $	Date Decl.	Ex–divd. Date	Stock of Record	Payment Date
0.06½	Nov. 6	Dec. 9	Dec. 15	Jan. 15'93
0.07½	Jan. 21	Mar. 9	Mar. 15	Apr. 15'93
0.07½	May 14	Jun. 9	Jun. 15	Jul. 15'93
0.07½	Aug. 16	Sep. 9	Sep. 15	Oct. 15'93

Finances

A 540,000-sq.-ft. distribution center in West Memphis, Ark., is expected to be in operation by the Spring of 1994.

In October 1993, FDO announced plans to open about 190 stores and close up to 25 stores during fiscal 1994, for a total of 2,200 stores in operation by August 31, 1994.

Capitalization

Long Term Debt: None (8/93).

Common Stock: 56,344,372 shs. ($0.10 par).
L. Levine controls 28%.
Institutions hold 60%
Shareholders of record: 3,225.

Office—10401 Old Monroe Rd., Charlotte, NC 28201-1017. **Tel**—(704) 847-6961. **Chrmn & Treas**—L. Levine. **Pres**—P. J. Hayes. **EVP, Secy & Investor Contact**—George R. Mahoney, Jr. **SVP-Fin**—C. M. Sowers. **Dirs**—M. R. Bernstein, P. J. Hayes, L. Levine, G. R. Mahoney, Jr., T. R. Payne. **Transfer Agent & Registrar**—Chemical Bank, NYC. **Incorporated** in Delaware in 1969. **Empl**—14,700.

 John D. Coyle, CFA

Federal-Mogul

NYSE Symbol FMO Options on Pacific (Jan-Apr-Jul-Oct) In S&P MidCap 400

Price	Range	P-E Ratio	Dividend	Yield	S&P Ranking	Beta
Sep. 21'93	1993					
25⅝	26½–16	47	0.48	1.9%	B–	0.95

Summary

This leading producer of engine and ball bearings, oil seals, fuel systems and lighting products for automotive original equipment and replacement markets greatly expanded its operations with the 1992 acquisition of TRW's global aftermarket distribution business. FMO is continuing with efforts to reduce inventory and scrappage costs, and raise productivity and profits. In September 1993, the company agreed to buy SPX Corp.'s Sealed Power Replacement division for $150 million in cash.

Current Outlook

Earnings for 1994 may approximate $1.20 a share, versus the $0.95 expected for 1993.

The dividend should continue at $0.12 quarterly.

Sales should advance sharply in 1994, reflecting the addition of the Sealed Power Replacement division of SPX Corp. and higher North American vehicle production. Cost cuts and efforts to improve manufacturing efficiency may be partially offset by weak sales in Europe due to recession. Despite higher interest expense, earnings should rise sharply, reflecting increasing economies of scale stemming from FMO's greatly expanded presence in the aftermarket parts distribution business.

Net Sales (Million $)

Quarter:	1993	1992	1991	1990
Mar.	411	297	278	280
Jun.	402	311	286	289
Sep.	---	298	268	274
Dec.	---	358	267	290
	---	1,264	1,099	1,134

Sales for the six months ended June 30, 1993, increased 34%, year to year, reflecting sales of TRW suspension and engine parts to the aftermarket. Higher domestic original equipment sales were offset by lower sales in Europe. Following a $4.9 million gain on the sale of Westwind Air Bearings, and taxes at 34.7% against 50.5%, net income was $22.8 million ($0.72 a share), up from $5.0 million ($0.15, before an accounting charge of $3.93).

Common Share Earnings ($)

Quarter:	1993	1992	1991	1990
Mar.	0.23	d0.01	d0.09	0.17
Jun.	0.47	0.16	0.05	0.25
Sep.	E0.15	0.10	0.09	0.17
Dec.	E0.10	d0.26	d1.13	d0.39
	E0.95	d0.01	d1.08	0.20

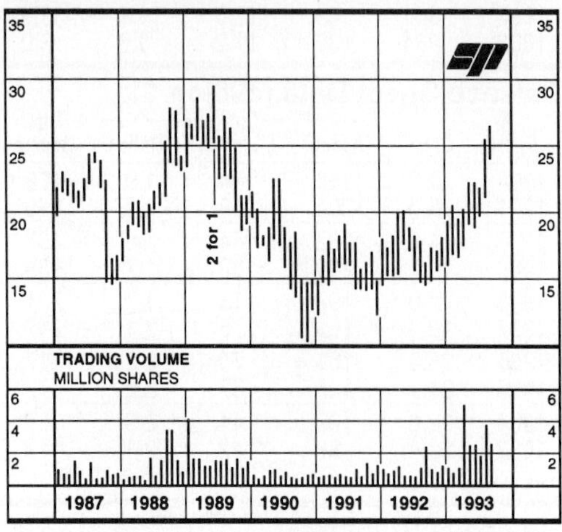

Important Developments

Sep. '93— FMO agreed to acquire the Sealed Power Replacement division of SPX Corp. for $150 million in cash. Sealed Power Replacement, with annual sales of over $163 million, distributes engine and chassis components to the North American automotive aftermarket. FMO will receive a long-term trademark agreement making the company the exclusive distributor of engine and chassis parts sold under the Sealed Power and Speed-Pro brand names in North America. The agreement was expected to be concluded by October 31, 1993.

Jun. '93— FMO acquired the aftermarket business of Brown & Dureau Automotive Pty. Ltd. The unit is a leading Australian importer and distributor of replacement parts and was expected to double FMO's Australian aftermarket sales.

Next earnings report expected in late October.

Per Share Data ($)

Yr. End Dec. 31	[1]1992	1991	[1]1990	1989	1988	1987	[1]1986	[1]1985	1984	1983
Tangible Bk. Val.	**1.76**	7.11	7.74	9.73	13.71	12.72	11.57	12.18	11.38	10.37
Cash Flow	**1.87**	1.03	2.14	3.03	3.46	3.24	1.62	3.23	3.01	2.65
Earnings[2]	**d0.01**	d1.08	0.20	1.26	1.74	1.62	0.20	1.95	1.81	1.47
Dividends	**0.480**	0.920	0.920	0.905	0.860	0.800	0.800	0.770	0.730	0.670
Payout Ratio	**NM**	NM	461%	69%	50%	49%	400%	40%	40%	46%
Prices—High	**20⅛**	19⅛	22½	29½	27⅞	24½	23⅛	19½	18¾	18½
Low	**14½**	12¼	10¼	18⅝	16⅜	14⅝	18¼	15½	14¾	12¾
P/E Ratio—	**NM**	NM	NM	23–15	16–9	15–9	NM	10–8	10–8	13–9

Data as orig. reptd. Adj. for stk. divs. of 100% Jun. 1989. **1.** Reflects merger or acquisition. **2.** Bef. results of disc. ops. of +0.72 in 1991, and spec. items of -3.93 in 1992, -0.07 in 1988, -0.06 in 1986, +0.08 in 1983. d-Deficit. E-Estimated NM-Not Meaningful.

Income Data (Million $)

Year Ended Dec. 31	Revs.	Oper. Inc.	% Oper. Inc. of Revs.	Cap. Exp.	Depr.	Int. Exp.	[3]Net Bef. Taxes	Eff. Tax Rate	[4]Net Inc.	% Net Inc. of Revs.	Cash Flow
[2]1992	**1,264**	**84**	**6.6**	**40**	**43.7**	**27.2**	**9**	**50.5%**	**[5]4.4**	**0.3**	**41.8**
[1]1991	1,099	76	6.9	50	48.7	27.9	d18	NM	d21.0	NM	22.9
[2]1990	1,134	78	6.9	180	43.3	27.1	16	44.5%	9.2	0.8	47.7
1989	1,084	103	9.5	54	40.8	23.7	56	40.3%	33.4	3.1	70.0
1988	1,177	134	11.4	61	43.3	25.7	81	44.9%	43.4	3.7	86.7
1987	1,075	128	11.9	74	41.3	27.8	77	45.4%	41.1	3.8	82.4
[2]1986	942	113	12.0	112	36.4	22.2	18	69.2%	[5]5.1	0.5	41.5
[2]1985	895	131	14.6	72	34.2	21.5	104	48.6%	52.0	5.8	86.2
1984	912	141	15.5	44	32.2	20.6	95	47.7%	48.4	5.3	80.4
1983	747	102	13.7	34	31.1	20.1	69	41.3%	39.0	5.2	69.7

Balance Sheet Data (Million $)

Dec. 31	Cash	Curr. Assets	Curr. Liab.	Curr. Ratio	Total Assets	% Ret. on Assets	Long Term Debt	Common Equity	Total Cap.	% LT Debt of Cap.	% Ret. on Equity
1992	**19**	**488**	**265**	**1.8**	**1,100**	**0.4**	**351**	**142**	**614**	**57.1**	**NM**
1991	45	399	204	2.0	884	NM	304	194	602	50.5	NM
1990	27	507	231	2.2	1,084	1.0	418	228	769	54.3	1.9
1989	10	411	231	1.8	810	4.4	178	237	536	33.1	10.4
1988	18	446	229	1.9	811	5.4	124	362	540	23.0	12.3
1987	15	428	246	1.7	804	5.4	132	342	530	24.9	12.5
1986	4	369	182	2.0	739	0.7	161	320	526	30.6	1.6
1985	102	382	154	2.5	682	8.0	125	339	509	24.5	15.9
1984	47	349	118	3.0	629	8.0	126	323	501	25.1	15.5
1983	23	299	103	2.9	581	6.7	127	298	469	27.1	13.5

Data as orig. reptd. **1.** Excl. disc. ops. **2.** Reflects merger or acquisition. **3.** Incl. equity in earns. of nonconsol. subs. aft. 1984. **4.** Bef. results of disc. ops. and spec. items. **5.** Reflects accounting change. d-Deficit. NM-Not Meaningful.

Business Summary

A leading producer of engine bearings, oil seals and antifriction bearings for motor vehicles, Federal Mogul also produces and distributes other precision parts to the original equipment and replacement motor vehicle parts markets worldwide. Sales by market segment in recent years:

	1992	1991
Aftermarket	55%	53%
Auto & light truck components	25%	25%
Heavy truck, farm & construction equipment components	10%	11%
General industry	10%	11%

Foreign activities accounted for 32% of sales and 22% of operating profits in 1992.

Engine and transmission products accounted for 39% of sales in 1992, ball and roller bearings for 21%, sealing devices 16%, lighting and electrical products 6%, fuel systems 7%, Sinta Forge Parts 4%, and all other 5%.

Major brandnames include Federal Mogul and Glyco engine bearings, Bruss, National and Mather oil seals, BCA ball bearings, Carter fuel systems, Sterling pistons, and Signal-Stat and Switches electrical components. FMO produces all of the original equipment parts it sells. In 1992, FMO acquired TRW's aftermarket parts distribution business and the exclusive right to sell worldwide, TRW brand replacement parts, most of which are purchased from TRW Inc.

Dividend Data

Dividends have been paid since 1936. A dividend reinvestment plan is available. A new "poison pill" stock purchase right was adopted in 1988.

Amt of Divd. $	Date Decl.	Ex-divd. Date	Stock of Record	Payment Date
0.12	Sep. 23	Nov. 16	Nov. 20	Dec. 10'92
0.12	Feb. 3	Feb. 17	Feb. 23	Mar. 10'93
0.12	Mar. 24	May 20	May 26	Jun. 10'93
0.12	Jul. 21	Aug. 19	Aug. 25	Sep. 10'93

Capitalization

Long Term Debt: $235,600,000 (6/93).

Series D Conv. Preferred Stock: $76,600,000. Conv. into 4,255,556 com. shs.

7.5% ESOP Conv. Preferred Stock: $60,900,000. Conv. into 1,908,392 com. shs.

Common Stock: 29,273,104 shs. ($5 par). Institutions hold 61%. Some 7.4% held by Co. stk. purchase plan and 8.5% by a group led by Mario Gabelli.
Shareholders of record: 12,445.

Office—26555 Northwestern Highway, Southfield, MI 48034. **Tel**—(313) 354-7700. **Chrmn & Pres**—D. J. Gormley. **SVP & CFO**—M. E. Welch. **VP & Secy**—G. N. Bashara, Jr. **VP & Treas**—Michael J. Viola. **Investor Contact**—David M. Mestdagh. (800-521-8607). **Dirs**—J. J. Fannon, D. J. Gormley, R. M. Hills, W. J. McCarthy, Jr., R. S. Miller, J. C. Pope, T. F. Russell, H. M. Sekyra, R. W. Skeddle. **Transfer Agent & Registrar**—Bank of New York, New York. **Incorporated** in Michigan in 1924. **Empl**—14,300.

 Joshua M. Harari, CFA

Federal Signal

NYSE Symbol FSS In S&P MidCap 400

Price	Range	P-E Ratio	Dividend	Yield	S&P Ranking	Beta
Jul. 15'93	1993					
24⅝	25½–20⅞	23	0.48	1.9%	A+	0.69

Summary

This company manufactures fire trucks and street sweepers, as well as public safety, signaling and communications equipment, parking gates, signs, electronic displays and perishable tools. Earnings for 1993 should rise on higher shipments of vehicles, signal products and tools. In recent years FSS has expanded into new international markets by acquiring foreign manufacturers of product lines within FSS's fields of expertise. Concurrently, FSS also acquired a number of North American companies that complement its domestic strengths.

Current Outlook

Earnings for 1993 may rise to $1.15 a share from the $1.00 of 1992. A further rise to $1.30 is possible in 1994.

The $0.12 quarterly dividend should continue.

Sales of fire apparatus, street sweepers and signals should grow in 1993, fueled by higher foreign sales and increased penetration of domestic markets. Tool sales should grow as the economy improves, but sign sales may continue to be hampered by a sluggish construction market. Improved operating efficiencies and expense controls should result in higher net income.

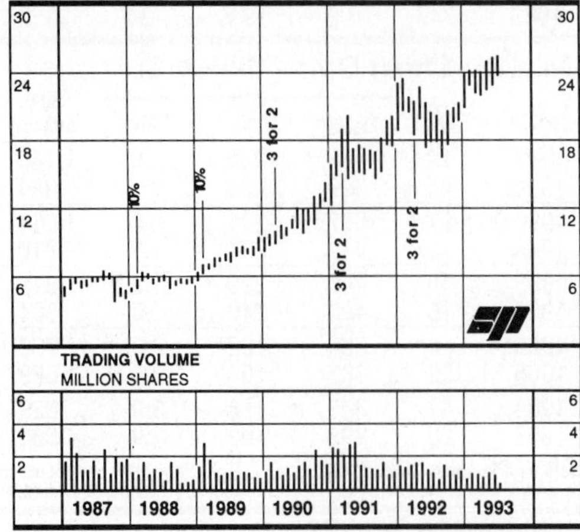

Sales & Revenues (Million $)

Quarter:	1993	1992	1991	1990
Mar.	127.5	119.8	110.5	103.3
Jun.	146.5	131.9	119.4	116.1
Sep.	---	135.5	116.6	109.2
Dec.	---	131.0	120.4	110.7
	---	518.2	466.9	439.4

Sales for the six months ended June 30, 1993 rose 8.8%, year to year, on gains in all four operating groups. Aided by strong gains at Signal and Tool,and a small profit at Sign in place of a loss, net income advanced 14%. Share earnings increased to $0.51, from $0.45.

Common Share Earnings ($)

Quarter:	1993	1992	1991	1990
Mar.	0.21	0.18	0.17	0.15
Jun.	0.31	0.27	0.25	0.23
Sep.	E0.31	0.27	0.24	0.21
Dec.	E0.32	0.28	0.25	0.22
	E1.15	1.00	0.90	0.81

Important Developments

Jul. '93— Second quarter results reflect the acquisition of Guzzler Manufacturing, Inc. from Powerscreen International PLC. With annual sales of $ 24 million, Guzzler manufactures vacuum loader vehicles and systems for the industrial, environmental and municipal markets that are used to clean catch basins and sewers. The backlog of orders rose 3% during the second quarter to $199.1 million. The company expects to begin shipping under a long term contract, its P-23 air crash and rescue vehicle in the third quarter to the U.S. Air Force. The vehicle has been under development for several years and production commenced recently at a rate of six vehicles per week. The company is also developing a civilian version of the vehicle which it believes has strong potential in international markets.

Next earnings report expected in mid-October.

Per Share Data ($)

Yr. End Dec. 31	[1]1992	[1]1991	1990	1989	[2]1988	[1]1987	[1]1986	1985	1984	1983
Tangible Bk. Val.	**3.64**	3.50	3.43	3.13	2.82	2.55	[3]2.89	[3]2.68	2.52	2.47
Cash Flow	**1.25**	1.14	1.04	0.90	0.75	0.58	0.49	0.44	0.42	0.31
Earnings[4]	**1.00**	0.90	0.81	0.67	0.54	0.42	0.34	0.28	0.28	0.21
Dividends	**0.315**	0.360	0.293	0.249	0.215	0.196	0.196	0.196	0.196	0.196
Payout Ratio	**42%**	40%	36%	37%	40%	47%	59%	70%	71%	95%
Prices—High	**23½**	20¼	14 5/16	9½	6 7/16	6 9/16	6 1/16	4 15/16	4 13/16	5⅝
Low	**16½**	12 5/16	8¼	5 11/16	4 11/16	3⅞	4 3/16	3⅝	3⅜	3 13/16
P/E Ratio—	**24–17**	23–14	18–10	14–9	12–9	16–9	18–12	18–13	17–12	27–18

Data as orig. reptd. Adj. for stk. div(s). of 50% Apr. 1992, 50% Feb. 1991, 50% Feb. 1990, 10% Feb. 1989, 10% Feb. 1988, 10% Jan. 1983. **1.** Reflects merger or acquisition. **2.** Reflects accounting change. **3.** Includes intangibles. **4.** Bef. results of disc. opers. of +0.07 in 1990, bef. spec. item(s) of +0.10 in 1985.

Income Data (Million $)

Year Ended Dec. 31	Revs.	Oper. Inc.	% Oper. Inc. of Revs.	Cap. Exp.	Depr.	Int. Exp.	Net Bef. Taxes	Eff. Tax Rate	[4]Net Inc.	% Net Inc. of Revs.	Cash Flow
[2]1992	**518**	**63.9**	**12.3**	**8.8**	**8.73**	**6.47**	**49.9**	**31.0%**	**[1]34.4**	**6.6**	**43.2**
[2]1991	467	58.8	12.6	12.0	8.23	5.65	45.6	31.9%	31.0	6.6	39.3
1990	439	55.4	12.6	8.3	7.78	5.51	42.5	34.0%	28.1	6.4	35.9
1989	414	51.8	12.5	9.5	8.13	7.27	36.0	36.1%	23.0	5.6	31.1
[1]1988	375	42.6	11.4	7.8	7.26	6.50	29.0	35.9%	18.6	4.9	25.8
[2]1987	318	31.8	10.0	7.1	5.72	2.46	[3]24.9	40.2%	[1]14.9	4.7	20.6
[2]1986	283	27.9	9.8	6.7	5.41	3.18	[3]20.5	42.4%	11.8	4.2	17.2
1985	278	28.7	10.3	7.0	5.40	3.52	[3]16.3	41.5%	9.6	3.4	15.0
1984	259	23.9	9.2	4.6	4.89	4.04	[3]15.5	39.6%	9.4	3.6	14.3
1983	226	17.6	7.8	7.4	3.65	3.30	12.0	40.9%	7.1	3.1	10.8

Balance Sheet Data (Million $)

Dec. 31	Cash	Curr. Assets	Curr. Liab.	Curr. Ratio	Total Assets	% Ret. on Assets	Long Term Debt	Common Equity	Total Cap.	% LT Debt of Cap.	% Ret. on Equity
1992	**2.22**	**NA**	**159**	**NA**	**364**	**9.8**	**16.2**	**179**	**205**	**7.9**	**20.0**
1991	0.09	NA	150	NA	341	9.7	15.6	165	191	8.2	19.9
1990	1.51	NA	123	NA	296	10.0	15.8	146	173	9.2	20.4
1989	2.50	NA	115	NA	271	8.8	16.8	130	157	10.7	18.7
1988	0.91	NA	108	NA	251	8.0	18.6	115	143	13.0	16.9
1987	2.36	135	80	1.7	212	7.8	20.8	103	132	15.7	14.8
1986	2.17	121	45	2.7	177	6.6	21.9	102	133	16.5	12.0
1985	2.24	121	47	2.6	175	5.5	28.9	91	128	22.6	10.8
1984	2.06	118	56	2.1	170	5.6	19.4	85	114	17.0	11.1
1983	2.61	114	51	2.2	165	4.6	20.7	85	114	18.2	8.5

Data as orig. reptd.; incl. finance subs. after 1987. **1.** Reflects acctg. change. **2.** Reflects merger or acquisition. **3.** Incl. equity in earnings of nonconsolidated subs. **4.** Bef. spec. items, and bef. results from disc. opers. NA-Not Available.

Business Summary

Contributions of this diversified manufacturer's four segments in 1992 (profits in million $):

	Sales	Profits
Vehicle	51%	$28.3
Tool	19%	21.7
Signal	19%	13.5
Sign	11%	–1.8

In 1992, foreign sales (including exports) accounted for 23.4% of the total, versus 17.1% in 1991, and 12.6% in 1990.

The Vehicle group includes Elgin Sweeper, Emergency One, Ravo International, Superior Emergency Vehicles, Frontline Emergency Vehicles and Guzzler Manufacturing. They manufacture chassis, fire trucks including Class A pumpers, mini-pumpers and tankers, rescue vehicles and aerial ladder trucks, self-propelled street cleaners, vacuum waste removal vehicles, ambulances and mobile communication vehicles.

Signal products includes a variety of visual and audible warning and signaling devices for private industry and governmental agencies; certain communication equipment for government, industrial and transportation related uses; and paging, local signaling and building security. Federal APD offers parking, revenue and access control systems. Aplicaciones Tecnologicas Vama S.L. manufactures emergency vehicle signals in Spain.

Tool products include die components for metal stamping; precision metal products for non-stamping needs; carbide, polycrystalline diamond and cubic boran nitride cutting tools; and industrial grade, high-speed steel and carbide twist drills.

Sign includes illuminated, non-illuminated and electronic advertising sign displays for sale or lease. Contractual maintenance services are provided for Federal's signs as well as for signs made by others.

Dividend Data

Dividends have been paid since 1948. A dividend reinvestment plan is available. A "poison pill" stock purchase right was adopted in 1988.

Amt of Divd. $	Date Decl.	Ex–divd. Date	Stock of Record	Payment Date
0.10½	Oct. 16	Dec. 7	Dec. 11	Jan. 5'93
0.12	Feb. 4	Feb. 8	Feb. 15	Mar. 2'93
0.12	Mar. 26	Apr. 30	May 6	Jun. 1'93
0.12	Jun. 16	Aug. 6	Aug. 12	Sep. 1'93

Capitalization

Long Term Debt: $21,363,000 (3/93).

Common Stock: 34,288,327 shs. ($1 par).
Institutions hold approximately 50%.
Shareholders of record: approximately 9,500.

Office—1415 West 22nd St, Oak Brook, IL 60521-9945. **Tel**—(708) 954-2000. **Chrmn, Pres & CEO**—J. J. Ross. **VP-CFO & Investor Contact**—Charles R. Campbell. **VP-Secy**—K. A. Wehrenberg. **VP-Treas**—R. W. Racic. **Dirs**—J. P. Lannan Jr., J. A. Lovell Jr., T. N. McGowen Jr., W. R. Peirson, J. J. Ross. **Transfer Agent & Registrar**—Harris Trust and Savings Bank, Chicago. **Incorporated** in Illinois in 1901; reincorporated in Delaware in 1969. **Empl**—4,268.

 Joshua M. Harari, CFA

Ferro Corp.

NYSE Symbol FOE Options on Phila In S&P MidCap 400

Price	Range	P-E Ratio	Dividend	Yield	S&P Ranking	Beta
Sep. 14'93	1993					
31⅞	34¾–26⅛	17	0.54	1.7%	B+	1.35

Summary

This company manufactures specialty materials, including coatings, colors, plastics, chemicals and ceramics for the construction, appliance, furnishings, industrial and transportation markets. International business historically has accounted for more than half of net income. Earnings for the past two years have benefited from a restructuring plan implemented in 1991, including workforce cuts and plant consolidations, but the economic downturn in Europe will remain a negative factor for some time.

Current Outlook

Share earnings for 1994 are projected at $2.10, versus the $1.85 expected for 1993.

The quarterly dividend was recently raised 13% to $0.13½ from $0.12.

Sales should advance modestly in 1993 and 1994, due largely to the April 1993 acquisition of a powder coatings business, as well as stronger U.S. sales resulting from the healthier economy and somewhat stronger housing and durable goods markets. European sales may remain weak going into 1994. Profitability is expected to be helped further by the cost reductions and restructuring programs implemented since 1991, with additional plant consolidations planned, especially in Europe.

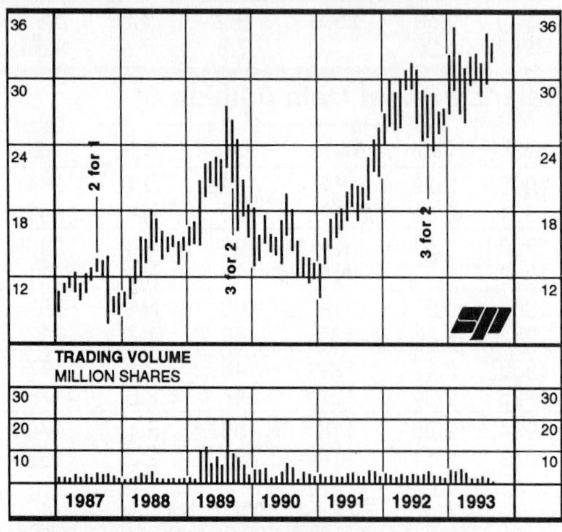

Net Sales (Million $)

Quarter:	1993	1992	1991	1990
Mar.	258	273	263	280
Jun.	281	292	270	282
Sep.	---	272	259	281
Dec.	---	261	265	282
	---	1,098	1,057	1,125

Sales for the first half of 1993 declined 4.6%, year to year, reflecting divestitures; ongoing revenues were down 0.7% on lower European sales. Including a nonrecurring charge of $0.06 a share, net income was down 4.3%, to $0.85 a share, from $0.89, before a net charge of $0.70 a share in 1993 from two accounting changes.

Common Share Earnings ($)

Quarter:	1993	1992	1991	1990
Mar.	0.42	0.42	0.07	0.17
Jun.	0.43	0.47	d0.79	0.22
Sep.	E0.48	0.48	0.37	0.25
Dec.	E0.52	0.53	0.40	d0.09
	E1.85	1.90	0.05	0.55

Important Developments

Jul. '93— Ferro said that second quarter 1993 earnings rose 5% from the year earlier period, excluding a $3.0 million pretax charge associated with acquisition activity, despite lower revenues and a decline in European earnings. A strong U.S. dollar and continued economic recession in Europe combined to reduced second quarter sales by $20 million, with much of the decline offset by acquisitions and improved volumes in the U.S. and Canada.

Jun. '93— FOE purchased the ceramic frit and color operations in Italy of Bayer. In April, FOE acquired Imperial Chemical Industries' powder coatings business in North America and Europe for $51 million. The business has annual sales of about $75 million. FOE said that the purchase made it the world's largest powder coatings producer.

Next earnings report expected in late October.

Per Share Data ($)

Yr. End Dec. 31	1992	1991	1990	1989	1988	1987	1986	1985	1984	[1]1983
Tangible Bk. Val.	**10.49**	8.07	7.81	7.30	9.10	8.11	7.09	6.38	6.17	6.19
Cash Flow	**3.04**	1.19	1.60	2.39	2.31	1.75	1.41	0.87	1.11	1.23
Earnings	**1.90**	0.05	0.55	1.50	1.51	1.02	0.79	0.29	0.57	0.67
Dividends	**0.560**	0.427	0.427	0.400	0.311	0.297	0.267	0.267	0.267	0.267
Payout Ratio	**24%**	NM	75%	25%	21%	29%	34%	91%	48%	42%
Prices—High	**31½**	25¹¹⁄₁₆	19⁹⁄₁₆	27⁹⁄₁₆	18¹⁄₁₆	13¹⁵⁄₁₆	9¼	8¼	8⁹⁄₁₆	8¹³⁄₁₆
Low	**23½**	10³⁄₁₆	11½	14¹⁵⁄₁₆	9⁵⁄₁₆	7¾	6¾	5⁷⁄₁₆	4¹⁵⁄₁₆	5½
P/E Ratio—	**17–12**	NM	35–21	18–10	12–6	14–8	12–9	28–18	15–9	13–8

Data as orig. reptd. Adj. for stk. divs. of 50% Sep. 1992, 50% Sep. 1989, 100% Sep. 1987. **1.** Reflects merger or acquisition. d-Deficit. E-Estimated. NM-Not Meaningful.

Income Data (Million $)

Year Ended Dec. 31	Revs.	Oper. Inc.	% Oper. Inc. of Revs.	Cap. Exp.	Depr.	Int. Exp.	[2]Net Bef. Taxes	Eff. Tax Rate	Net Inc.	% Net Inc. of Revs.	Cash Flow
1992	**1,098**	**137**	**12.5**	**44.8**	**33.5**	**10.0**	**97.7**	**39.8%**	**58.8**	**5.4**	**89.1**
1991	1,057	106	10.0	39.0	32.7	11.6	21.5	72.3%	4.8	0.5	34.3
1990	1,125	96	8.6	61.4	30.4	17.9	45.3	53.2%	19.4	1.7	46.6
1989	1,084	118	10.9	53.5	27.6	19.7	85.6	39.7%	49.7	4.6	73.9
1988	1,009	121	12.0	53.7	24.7	17.3	90.3	46.3%	46.6	4.6	71.3
1987	871	94	10.8	37.3	22.5	14.1	61.2	46.2%	31.7	3.6	54.2
1986	725	74	10.2	23.6	19.2	16.4	44.8	45.6%	[3]24.1	3.3	43.3
1985	651	50	7.7	27.9	17.3	14.1	18.7	50.2%	8.9	1.4	26.2
1984	663	63	9.6	29.4	16.6	14.8	32.8	47.2%	16.9	2.5	33.5
[1]1983	619	64	10.4	20.6	15.7	14.3	39.5	49.8%	19.2	3.1	34.9

Balance Sheet Data (Million $)

Dec. 31	Cash	Curr. Assets	Curr. Liab.	Curr. Ratio	Total Assets	% Ret. on Assets	Long Term Debt	Common Equity	Total Cap.	% LT Debt of Cap.	% Ret. on Equity
1992	**109.0**	**415**	**205**	**2.0**	**697**	**8.5**	**104.0**	**328**	**460**	**22.6**	**17.8**
1991	78.5	406	213	1.9	672	0.7	55.7	235	370	15.0	0.7
1990	21.2	387	221	1.7	686	2.9	58.0	235	385	15.1	7.1
1989	58.2	409	210	1.9	669	8.1	60.8	227	378	16.1	18.4
1988	28.4	357	194	1.8	588	8.3	63.2	295	379	16.7	16.7
1987	43.2	329	175	1.9	532	6.5	64.1	260	346	18.5	13.1
1986	40.5	272	132	2.1	449	5.7	68.1	223	309	22.1	11.4
1985	23.2	227	110	2.1	393	2.3	68.4	196	277	24.7	4.6
1984	14.3	207	95	2.2	362	4.6	61.0	188	261	23.3	9.0
1983	20.5	218	109	2.0	367	5.1	55.9	988	254	22.0	10.4

Data as orig. reptd. **1.** Reflects merger or acquisition. **2.** Incl. equity in earns. of nonconsol. subs. **3.** Reflects accounting change.

Business Summary

Ferro is a worldwide producer of specialty materials. Contributions by business segment in 1992 were:

	Sales	Profits
Coatings, colors & ceramics.	57%	81%
Plastics............................	23%	9%
Chemicals........................	20%	10%

International operations accounted for 55% of sales and 66% of net income in 1992.

Specialty coatings include porcelain enamel frit for appliances, architectural panels and other uses; ceramic glaze frit; organic powder coatings; and engineering services. Specialty colors consists of inorganic color pigments for porcelain enamel and ceramic glaze coatings, plastics and paint; forehearth glass colorants; and enamels for glass decorating. Electronics materials include electronic ceramics, thick-film pastes and sealing glasses and ceramic coated substrates. Ceramic polishing powders are also produced. Specialty ceramics include abrasion-resistant linings, kiln furniture, radiants, refractories, grinding media, and porous ceramics.

Plastics include filled and reinforced thermoplastic compounds, plastic alloys, color and additive concentrates for plastics, gel coats for fiberglass-reinforced plastic products, engineering plastics, liquid and dry colors, and color dispersions (thermoset).

Specialty chemicals include polymer additives such as heat and light stabilizers, antimicrobials, antioxidants and plasticizers; flame retardants; lubricant, engine oil and fuel additives; and solvents, catalysts and intermediate chemicals.

Dividend Data

Dividends have been paid since 1939. A dividend reinvestment plan is available. An amended "poison pill" stock purchase rights plan was adopted in 1989.

Amt of Divd. $	Date Decl.	Ex–divd. Date	Stock of Record	Payment Date
0.12	Oct. 30	Nov. 6	Nov. 13	Dec. 10'92
0.12	Jan. 22	Feb. 8	Feb. 15	Mar. 10'93
0.12	Apr. 23	May 10	May 14	Jun. 10'93
0.13½	Jul. 23	Aug. 9	Aug. 13	Sep. 10'93

Capitalization

Long Term Debt: $79,950,000 (6/93), excl. $47.5 million ESOP loan guarantee.

ESOP 7% Conv. Preferred Stock: $70,500,000.

Common Stock: 29,047,732 shs. ($1 par).
Institutions hold about 85%.
Shareholders of record: 3,132.

Office—1000 Lakeside Ave., Cleveland, OH 44114-1183. **Tel**—(216) 641-8580. **Pres & CEO**—A. C. Bersticker. **Exec VP-Fin**—H. R. Ortino. **Secy**—P. B. Campbell. **Investor Contact**—Patrick Cavanagh. **Dirs**—A. C. Bersticker, P. S. Brentlinger, G. R. Brown, W. F. Bush, W. E. Butler, P. B. Campbell, A. J. Freeman, R. M. Ginn, J. C. Morley, K. O'Donnell, H. R. Ortino, A. Posnick, R. A. Sebastian, D. W. Sullivan. **Transfer Agent & Registrar**—National City Bank, Cleveland. **Incorporated** in Ohio in 1919. **Empl**—6,582.

 Richard O'Reilly, CFA

Fifth Third Bancorp

NASDAQ Symbol FITB (Incl. in Nat'l Market) Options on Phila In S&P MidCap 400

Price	Range	P-E Ratio	Dividend	Yield	S&P Ranking	Beta
Oct. 13'93	1993					
53½	59–49½	18	1.08	2.0%	A+	0.98

Summary

This regional bank holding company, whose largest subsidiary is Fifth Third Bank, has more than 270 offices in Ohio, Indiana and Kentucky. Operations of this well capitalized company have been expanded considerably in recent years through an aggressive acquisition program. Earnings are expected to continue to move higher, reflecting growth in loans and data processing income.

Current Outlook

Earnings for 1994 are projected at $3.66 a share, versus the $3.17 estimated for 1993.

The quarterly dividend is likely to be raised to $0.30 a share, from $0.27, in 1994.

Loans should continue to grow rapidly in 1993 and 1994, reflecting a stronger economy and an increased effort in its strategy of aggressive loan pricing. The company is lending at relatively low rates as it successfully targets the high end of the credit market. The loan loss provision should grow at a somewhat slower pace than loans as FITB has few remaining nonperforming loans to charge off. Noninterest income will likely expand at a similar pace to that of net interest income, as surging business from FITB's data processing subsidiary, Midwest Payment Systems offsets a cyclical slowing of trust income growth. Net interest margins may decline slightly from the recent 4.64% level, given reduced lending rates stemming from the loan growth strategy. Fifth Third is very well capitalized and has consistently generated high returns on assets and on equity.

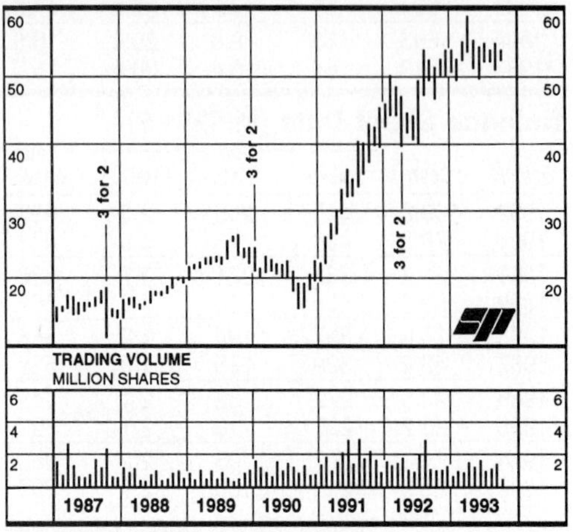

Review of Operations

Net interest income for the six months to June 30, 1993, advanced 15%, year to year, aided by an increase in interest earning assets that was partially offset by a lower net interest margin. The provision for loan losses decreased 16% and, with noninterest income and noninterest expense each rising 13%, pretax income climbed 25%. After taxes at 33.2%, versus 31.0%, net income was up 21%, to $1.55 a share, from $1.29.

Common Share Earnings ($)

Quarter:	1993	1992	1991	1990
Mar.	0.75	0.61	0.52	0.45
Jun.	0.80	0.68	0.58	0.51
Sep.	E0.81	0.72	0.61	0.55
Dec.	E0.81	0.74	0.62	0.54
	E3.17	2.75	2.33	2.05

Important Developments

Oct. '93— FITB's data processing subsidiary, Midwest Payment Systems, is to provide its Jeanie ATM services to four more financial institutions, bringing the total members added in 1993 to 39.

Sep. '93— FITB cancelled its agreement to buy Shelby County Bancorp due to 'environmental issues' concerning property owned by a Shelby subsidiary.

Jul. '93— The company agreed to buy The TriState Bancorp (assets of $375 million), whose subsidiary, First Financial Savings Assoc., is the largest independent thrift in Cincinnati. The transaction calls for Fifth Third to issue about $67.8 million of its common shares to TriState shareholders.

Jun. '93— The company planned to acquire about $139 million of deposits and five branch facilities from World Savings & Loan Association of Ohio, subject to regulatory approval.

Next earnings report expected in mid-October.

Per Share Data ($)

Yr. End Dec. 31	1992	1991	1990	[1]1989	[1]1988	[1]1987	[1]1986	[1]1985	[1]1984	[1]1983
Tangible Bk. Val.	**15.85**	14.21	13.25	11.80	10.36	9.05	7.95	6.68	5.85	5.13
Earnings[2]	**2.75**	2.33	2.05	1.86	1.75	1.35	1.34	1.14	0.96	0.84
Dividends	**0.900**	0.780	0.680	0.600	0.520	0.453	0.391	0.326	0.277	0.243
Payout Ratio	**33%**	33%	33%	32%	30%	33%	29%	29%	29%	29%
Prices—High	**54**	45½	24⅝	26½	20¼	18⅝	19¼	13	7⅝	7⅜
Low	**39¾**	19⅝	15½	19¾	14⅛	13½	12⅝	7½	6⅜	4⅛
P/E Ratio—	**20–14**	20–8	12–8	14–11	12–8	14–10	14–9	11–7	8–7	9–5

Data as orig. reptd. Adj. for stk. divs. of 50% Apr. 1992, 50% Jan. 1990, 50% Oct. 1987, 50% Apr. 1986, 50% Apr. 1985, 100% Mar. 1983.
1. Refl. merger or acq. **2.** Bef. spec. item of +0.17 in 1987. E-Estimated

Income Data (Million $)

Year Ended Dec. 31	Net Int. Inc.	Tax Equiv. Adj.	Non Int. Inc.	Loan Loss Prov.	% Exp./ Op. Revs.	Net Bef. Taxes	Eff. Tax Rate	[2]Net Inc.	% Net Int. Margin	—% Return On— Assets	Equity
1992	**394**	**17.2**	**199**	**65.3**	**47.4**	**240**	**31.5%**	**164**	**4.73**	**1.74**	**17.3**
1991	332	19.1	168	55.7	48.1	199	30.4%	138	4.58	1.68	16.6
[1]1990	293	14.4	138	39.9	50.1	168	28.5%	120	4.56	1.64	16.2
[1]1989	275	15.1	118	36.5	50.9	150	27.6%	108	4.74	1.62	16.5
[1]1988	189	14.8	91	26.1	47.9	112	25.0%	84	4.80	1.80	18.0
[1]1987	143	18.9	73	18.9	48.6	83	27.9%	60	4.83	1.62	16.3
[1]1986	120	27.3	60	14.8	47.7	67	17.2%	55	5.38	1.80	18.5
[1]1985	100	25.0	53	12.5	48.6	56	21.0%	44	5.48	1.74	18.1
[1]1984	73	20.8	44	7.8	47.9	43	19.4%	35	5.40	1.76	17.5
[1]1983	66	15.8	36	5.8	49.2	38	22.6%	30	5.29	1.72	17.3

Balance Sheet Data (Million $)

Dec. 31	Total Assets	———Earning Assets——— Mon. Mkt. Assets	Inv. Secs.	Com'l Loans	Other Loans	% Loan Loss Resv.	——Deposits—— Demand	Time	% Loans/ Deposits	Long Term Debt	Common Equity	% Equity To Assets
1992	**10,213**	**1**	**1,933**	**3,223**	**4,371**	**1.54**	**1,307**	**6,225**	**99.2**	**254**	**1,005**	**10.1**
1991	8,826	192	2,064	2,684	3,228	1.56	1,151	5,536	86.8	13	879	10.1
1990	7,956	336	1,355	2,696	2,912	1.55	989	5,396	86.1	14	783	10.1
1989	7,143	274	1,059	2,547	2,736	1.55	961	4,822	89.3	13	699	9.8
1988	5,246	226	767	2,004	1,845	1.56	784	3,310	91.7	12	509	10.0
1987	4,051	246	628	1,509	1,319	1.56	646	2,538	86.7	13	402	9.9
1986	3,492	414	565	1,171	1,012	1.57	661	1,936	81.7	14	345	9.7
1985	2,761	363	531	897	742	1.62	478	1,528	78.7	55	260	9.6
1984	2,363	355	506	695	584	1.64	430	1,247	72.6	16	222	10.1
1983	1,855	298	413	525	447	1.58	338	918	73.8	20	183	9.9

Data as orig. reptd. **1.** Refl. merger or acq. **2.** Bef. spec. item in 1987.

Business Summary

Fifth Third Bancorp is a regional bank holding company operating through 10 affiliate banks in Ohio, northern Kentucky and Indiana. The company also owns subsidiaries engaged in payment services, discount brokerage, travel and leasing. An aggressive acquisition program has contributed to the expansion of FITB's asset and deposit base. The company has 271 banking offices, including about 62 seven-day-a-week grocery store locations.

At the end of 1992, gross loans and leases outstanding of $7.59 billion were divided: commercial 36.4%, consumer instalment 27.5%, consumer mortgage 25.5%, commercial mortgage 6.5% and construction 4.1%.

Underperforming assets at 1992 year-end amounted to $74.9 million (1.00% of loans, leases and other real estate owned), down from $124.4 million (2.13%) a year earlier. The reserve for loan losses at the end of 1992 was $114.8 million (1.54% of loans and leases outstanding), compared with $90.3 million (1.56%) a year earlier. Net chargeoffs in 1992 totaled $44.7 milllion (0.68% of average loans and leases), versus $50.7 million (0.90%) in 1991.

Average fund sources totaling $8.47 billion in 1992 were divided: demand deposits 13%, interest checking 12%, savings 5%, money market 16%, other time 31%, CDs over $100,000 6% and other 17%.

Fifth Third has pursued an active acquisition policy. Acquisitions in 1989 included First Ohio Bancshares Inc. (assets of $1 billion) and First Security Bank, Hillsboro, Ohio ($136 million). In 1991, FITB acquired Farmers Exchange Bank ($450 million). In 1992, FITB bought Pinnacle Bancorp Inc. of Middletown, Ohio ($215 million) and First Federal S&L of Lima, Ohio ($140 million).

Dividend Data

Cash has been paid each year since 1952. A dividend reinvestment plan is available.

Amt of Divd. $	Date Decl.	Ex–divd. Date	Stock of Record	Payment Date
0.24	Dec. 15	Dec. 24	Dec. 31	Jan. 15'93
0.24	Mar. 16	Mar. 25	Mar. 31	Apr. 15'93
0.24	Jun. 15	Jun. 24	Jun. 30	Jul. 15'93
0.27	Sep. 21	Sep. 24	Sep. 30	Oct. 15'93

Capitalization

Long Term Debt: $254,318,000 (6/93), incl. conv. subordinated notes of $142,456,000.

Common Stock: 59,967,028 shs. (no par). Institutions hold about 46%. Shareholders: 10,437 (12/92).

Office—38 Fountain Square Plaza, Cincinnati, OH 45263. **Tel**—(513) 579-5300. **Chrmn**—C. L. Buenger. **Pres, CEO & COO**—G. A. Schaefer Jr. **Sr VP, CFO & Investor Contact**—P. Michael Brumm (513) 579-4216. **Secy**—P. C. Long. **Treas**—N. E. Arnold. **Dirs**—J. F. Barrett, M. C. Boesel Jr., C. L. Buenger, N. W. Carson, T. L. Dahl, G. V. Dirvin, T. B. Donnell, R. T. Farmer, J. D. Geary, I. W. Gorr, J. H. Head Jr., J. R. Herschede, W. G. Kagler, W. J. Keating, J. D. Kiggen, R. B. Morgan, M. H. Norris, B. H. Rowe, G. A. Schaefer Jr., J. J. Schiff Jr., S. Stranahan, D. J. Sullivan Jr., D. S. Taft. **Transfer Agent & Registrar**—Fifth Third Bank. **Incorporated** in Ohio in 1975. **Empl**—4,661.

 C. Orgielewicz

Fingerhut Companies

NYSE Symbol FHT Options on NYSE In S&P MidCap 400

Price	Range	P-E Ratio	Dividend	Yield	S&P Ranking	Beta
Oct. 29'93	1993					
29	30¼–14 15/16	21	0.16	0.6%	NR	NA

Summary

A leading direct-mail marketer of consumer products, Fingerhut sells general merchandise through catalogs and other direct marketing solicitations. A substantial improvement in customer response and well-controlled operating expenses led to favorable earnings per share comparisons in 1993's first nine months. The shares were split two-for-one in August 1993.

Business Summary

Fingerhut Companies, Inc. is a leading direct-mail marketer of consumer products, using catalogs and membership mailings to sell general merchandise to an active base of about 6.7 million repeat customers. In 1992, the company offered more than 10,000 different products, including a broad mix of brandname and private-label products, many of which are specially manufactured or packaged to appeal to Fingerhut's customers. Much of its merchandise is acquired through opportunistic purchases of product inventories. Most sales are made on credit.

The principal subsidiary, Fingerhut, markets general merchandise—including housewares (20% of the subsidiary's sales in 1992), electronics (19%), home textiles (18%), apparel (11%), jewelry (8%), furniture/home accessories (8%), leisure (8%), tools/automotive/lawn and garden products (5%), financial service products and other (3%)—using catalogs and other direct-mail solicitations. During 1992, FHT mailed about 425 million catalogs and other promotions to existing and prospective customers.

The Figi's subsidiary (which FHT is seeking to sell) is a mail-order retailer of specialty foods (such as quality cheeses, smoked meats, candies and baked goods) and other gifts. Figi's had revenues of $76 million in 1992.

The COMB subsidiary (which was sold in September 1993) uses catalogs and membership mailings to sell general merchandise acquired primarily through opportunistic purchases of product inventories. COMB had revenues of $103 million in 1992.

Montgomery Ward Direct (MWD), a joint venture formed in late 1991 and equally owned by FHT and Montgomery Ward & Co., produces specialty catalogs under the Montgomery Ward name. FHT provides order processing, shipping and computer facilities.

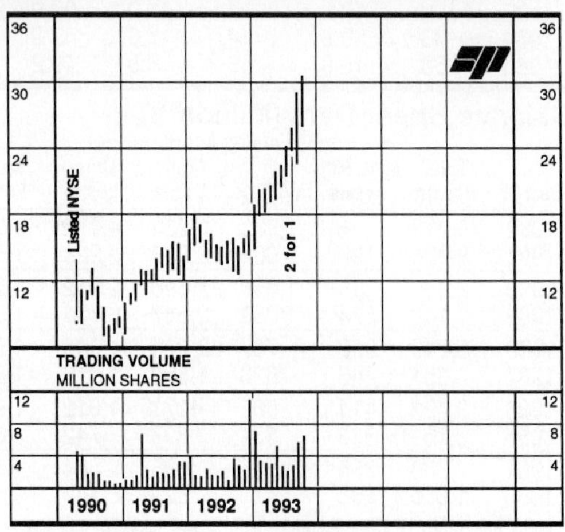

The company derives additional revenues from providing data processing services, manufacturing plastic products and wholesaling excess merchandise. These activities acccounted for about 2% of total revenues in 1992.

Important Developments

Oct. '93— FHT said it was pleased with its performance in 1993's third quarter, citing strong customer response, particularly from existing customers. The company added that it continued to be on target for another record year.

Sep. '93— The company said that it completed the sale of its COMB subsidiary to DAMARK International. Terms were not disclosed, but the sale is not expected to have a material impact on FHT's financial results.

Next earnings report expected in mid-January.

Per Share Data ($)

Yr. End Dec. 31	1992	1991	1990	1989
Tangible Bk. Val.	**7.36**	6.68	5.43	4.66
Cash Flow	**1.52**	1.40	1.28	1.06
Earnings	**1.19**	1.07	0.98	[1]0.79
Dividends	**0.16**	0.16	0.08	Nil
Payout Ratio	**12%**	15%	8%	Nil
Prices—High	**18**	15 9/16	13 3/16	NA
Low	**12⅝**	7 3/16	6⅛	NA
P/E Ratio—	**15–11**	15–7	13–6	NA

Data as orig. reptd., prior to 1990 data as reptd. in prospectus dated Apr. 25, 1990. Adj. for stk. div. of 100% Aug. 1993. **1.** Pro forma. NA-Not Available.

Income Data (Million $)

Year Ended Dec. 31	Revs.	Oper. Inc.	% Oper. Inc. of Revs.	Cap. Exp.	Depr.	[1]Int. Exp.	Net Bef. Taxes	Eff. Tax Rate	Net Inc.	% Net Inc. of Revs.	Cash Flow
1992	**1,606**	**144**	**9.0**	**50.9**	**16.8**	**33.5**	**93.9**	**34.2%**	**61.8**	**3.8**	**78.6**
1991	1,428	122	8.5	71.5	16.5	24.3	81.4	34.2%	53.6	3.7	70.0
1990	1,248	94	7.5	21.1	14.3	16.3	74.1	35.6%	47.7	3.8	62.0
1989	1,111	75	6.7	22.5	11.9	39.9	61.6	36.0%	[2]39.4	3.6	51.3
1988	1,101	62	5.6	7.2	6.4	37.8	52.0	44.2%	29.0	2.8	NA
1987	994	111	11.2	6.3	7.8	28.3	89.9	41.0%	53.1	5.8	NA
1986	901	NA	NA	NA	NA	18.2	58.3	25.8%	43.3	5.1	NA
1985	772	NA	NA	NA	NA	17.9	63.0	47.0%	33.4	4.6	NA

Balance Sheet Data (Million $)

Dec. 31	Cash	Curr. Assets	Curr. Liab.	Ratio	Total Assets	% Ret. on Assets	Long Term Debt	Common Equity	Total Cap.	% LT Debt of Cap.	% Ret. on Equity
1992	**86.70**	**682**	**269**	**2.5**	**926**	**7.3**	**247**	**400**	**653**	**37.9**	**16.1**
1991	9.23	591	293	2.0	802	7.3	119	384	505	23.6	15.0
1990	4.31	489	318	1.5	651	8.5	15	319	334	4.5	15.9
1989	1.75	351	178	2.0	498	NA	22	296	319	6.8	NA
1988	Nil	411	254	1.6	518	5.7	2	254	258	0.7	NA
1987	NA	388	213	1.8	498	9.9	4	NA	232	1.9	NA
1986	NA	465	380	1.2	579	8.2	5	NA	179	2.7	NA
1985	NA	354	301	1.2	471	NA	7	NA	139	5.0	NA

Data as orig. reptd.; prior to 1990 data as reptd. in Prospectus dated Apr. 25, 1990. **1.** Net of interest income for 1985 through 1989. **2.** Pro forma. NA-Not Available.

[1]Total Revenues (Million $)

13 Weeks:	1993	1992	1991	1990
Mar.	372	309	314	221
Jun.	421	359	307	263
Sep.	379	353	309	279
Dec.		584	499	484
		1,606	1,428	1,248

Total revenues for the 39 weeks ended September 24, 1993, advanced 15%, year to year, mainly reflecting improved consumer response, especially from existing customers. Gross margins were restricted by the company's new price/value strategy and, to a lesser extent, higher fulfillment costs. However, other cost and expense categories were well-controlled, and pretax income rose 23%. After taxes at 30.2%, against 34.2%, net income rose 31%. Earnings per share rose to $0.69, reflecting a 4.2% decrease in average shares, from $0.51, as adjusted for the two-for-one stock split in August 1993.

Common Share Earnings ($)

13 Weeks:	1993	1992	1991	1990
Mar.	0.16	0.19	0.18	0.15
Jun.	0.26	0.22	0.20	0.18
Sep.	0.27	0.11	0.17	0.16
Dec.		0.69	0.53	0.50
		1.19	1.07	0.98

Dividend Data

Dividends were initiated in 1990.

Amt of Divd. $	Date Decl.	Ex–divd. Date	Stock of Record	Payment Date
0.08	Jan. 15	Jan. 22	Jan. 28	Feb. 18'93
0.08	Apr. 15	Apr. 23	Apr. 29	May 20'93
2–for–1	Jul. 15	Aug. 20	Jul. 29	Aug. 19'93
0.04	Jul. 15	Jul. 23	Jul. 29	Aug. 19'93
0.04	Oct. 14	Oct. 22	Oct. 28	Nov. 18'93

Finances

In October 1993, FHT said that it reached an agreement with First Deposit Corp. to test a co-branded credit card for selected groups of its customers.

In January 1993, Primerica completed the public sale of 17,012,162 FHT shares (its entire 42% interest) at $15.31 a share (as adjusted).

In December 1992, FHT purchased 3,000,000 of its shares from Primerica at $15 each (as adjusted). In August 1993, it completed a private placement of $45 million of senior notes to refinance the $45 million term loan used to finance the stock repurchase.

Capitalization

Long Term Debt: $247,001,000 (9/93).

Common Stock: 46,117,748 shs. ($0.01 par). Shareholders of record: 412.

Options: To buy 6,344,352 shs. at $5.455 to $17.50 ea. (12/92, as adj.).

1. Incl. finance inc. (net).

Office—4400 Baker Rd., Minnetonka, MN 55343. **Tel**—(612) 932-3100. **Chrmn & Pres**—T. Deikel. **VP-Fin & CFO**—M. A. Qualen. **VP-Secy**—J. K. Ellingboe. **Dirs**—W. R. Anderson, T. Deikel, E. Gage, S. S. Hubbard, R. M. Kovacevich, D. C. Mecum. **Transfer Agent & Registrar**—Norwest Bank Minnesota, South St. Paul. **Incorporated** in Minnesota in 1978; predecessor firm formed in 1948. **Empl**—8,500.

 John D. Coyle, CFA

First Alabama Bancshares

NASDAQ Symbol FABC (Incl. in Nat'l Market) In S&P MidCap 400

Price	Range	P-E Ratio	Dividend	Yield	S&P Ranking	Beta
Sep. 20'93	1993					
31⅞	38⅜–30¼	11	1.04	3.3%	A+	0.92

Summary

This major southeastern bank holding company operates more than 220 offices in Alabama, Florida, Georgia, Tennessee, South Carolina and Mississippi. First Alabama entered the Tennessee banking market in December 1992 with the acquisition of Security Federal Savings and Loan Association. An aggressive acquisition strategy is continuing. A 10% stock dividend was paid in early 1993.

Business Summary

First Alabama Bancshares, Inc. is a southeastern bank holding company that operates 224 offices in Alabama, Florida, Georgia, Tennessee, South Carolina and Mississippi. The lead bank, First Alabama Bank, operates through 163 full-service offices and had assets of $7.1 billion at 1992 year-end.

Consolidated loans aggregated $5.13 billion at December 31, 1992, and were divided:

Commercial	28%
Instalment	28%
Real estate—construction	5%
Real estate—mortgage	39%

At December 31, 1992, the reserve for loan losses totaled $73,619,000 (1.43% of net loans outstanding), compared with $54,769,000 (1.28%) a year earlier. Net chargeoffs in 1992 were $12,584,000 (0.28% of average loans outstanding), versus $14,220,000 (0.35%) in 1991. Nonperforming assets at 1992 year-end amounted to $49,500,000 (0.96% of loans and other real estate), against $43,356,000 (1.01%) a year earlier.

Deposits averaged $6.19 billion in 1992 ($5.56 billion in 1991) and were apportioned: 14% demand, 16% NOW, 16% money market, 8% savings, 7% certificates of $100,000 or more and 39% other interest-bearing deposits.

Interest and fees on loans provided 59% of total income for 1992, interest on investment securities 20%, other interest income 3%, service charges on deposit accounts 6%, trust department income 3% and other noninterest income 9%.

On a tax-equivalent basis, the average yield on total interest-earning assets in 1992 was 8.44% (9.82% in 1991), while the average rate paid on interest-bearing liabilities was 4.09% (5.91%), for a net spread of 4.35% (3.91%).

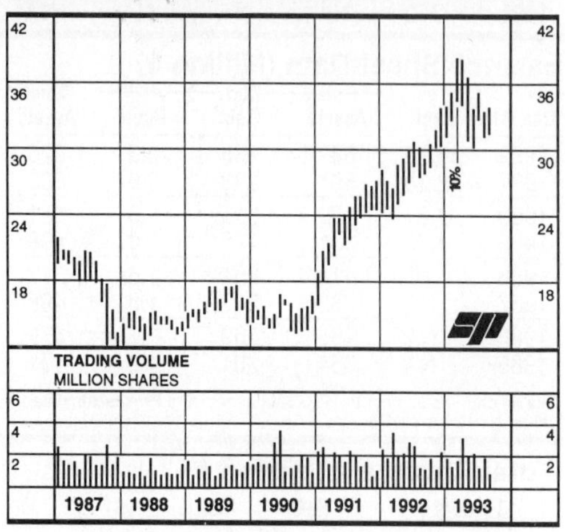

Important Developments

Jun. '93— First Alabama acquired Republic Bancshares and its subsidiary, the Franklin County Bank (assets of $68 million and four offices in middle Tennessee), for 264,470 shares of its common stock.

May '93— The company said it signed a definitive agreement to acquire Secor Bank, FSB of Birmingham, Ala. (assets of $1.9 billion and 42 offices in Alabama, Louisiana and Florida), in a transaction whereby each of Secor's 3,638,524 common shares would be converted into 0.667 of a share of FABC common stock, for an indicated value of $140 million. First Alabama has also entered into agreements in principle to acquire First Federal Savings Bank of Marianna, Fla. (assets of $100 million), in exchange for 454,000 FABC common shares, and First Federal Savings Bank of DeFuniak Springs, Fla. ($91 million), in a transaction that calls for the purchase of all First Federal shares for $15.58 a share.

Next earnings report expected in mid-October.

Per Share Data ($)

Yr. End Dec. 31	[1]1992	1991	1990	[1]1989	[1]1988	[1]1987	[1]1986	[1]1985	1984	1983
Tangible Bk. Val.	**16.60**	14.63	13.38	12.72	11.75	11.64	10.83	10.05	8.54	7.72
Earnings	**2.60**	2.16	1.91	1.73	1.61	1.55	1.52	1.51	1.29	1.17
Dividends	**0.909**	0.873	0.836	0.764	0.727	0.691	0.582	0.509	0.455	0.409
Payout Ratio	**35%**	40%	44%	44%	45%	44%	38%	34%	35%	35%
Prices—High	**33⅞**	27⅛	16⅞	17⅝	15¼	21⅞	24⅛	16⅞	11⅛	8⅞
Low	**23¾**	15⅞	13¼	13¾	12⅛	12	14⅞	9¾	7¾	5⅞
P/E Ratio—	**13–9**	13–7	9–7	10–8	9–8	14–8	16–10	11–6	9–6	8–5

Data as orig. reptd. Adj. for stk. divs. of 10% Mar. 1993, 100% Jun. 1986, 100% Jun. 1984. 1. Refl. merger or acq.

Income Data (Million $)

Year Ended Dec. 31	Net Int. Inc.	Tax Equiv. Adj.	Non Int. Inc.	Loan Loss Prov.	% Exp./ Op. Revs.	Net Bef. Taxes	Eff. Tax Rate	Net Inc.	% Net Int. Margin	—% Return On— Assets	Equity
1992	**313**	**15.6**	**119**	**27.1**	**59.2**	**140**	**32.1%**	**95.0**	**4.98**	**1.34**	**15.6**
1991	265	12.3	102	24.0	60.8	112	30.1%	78.3	4.78	1.23	14.3
1990	222	NA	94	24.2	NA	96	28.3%	68.9	4.40	1.23	13.6
[1]1989	204	NA	71	15.8	NA	84	25.2%	62.6	4.32	1.20	13.2
[1]1988	185	NA	69	10.8	NA	76	23.2%	58.2	4.39	1.24	13.3
[1]1987	170	23.4	66	8.6	59.7	73	23.3%	56.2	5.03	1.31	13.8
[1]1986	162	NA	60	9.1	NA	68	20.5%	54.1	4.56	1.36	14.6
[1]1985	155	NA	53	9.0	NA	63	18.5%	51.1	5.13	1.49	15.8
1984	136	NA	48	7.1	NA	51	13.9%	43.8	4.86	1.38	14.9
1983	133	NA	46	11.5	NA	44	10.5%	39.7	5.06	1.33	14.9

Balance Sheet Data (Million $)

Dec. 31	Total Assets	—Earning Assets— Mon. Mkt. Assets	Inv. Secs.	Com'l Loans	Other Loans	% Loan Loss Resv.	—Deposits— Demand	Time	% Loans/ Deposits	Long Term Debt	Common Equity	% Equity To Assets
1992	**7,881**	**85**	**1,670**	**1,437**	**3,964**	**1.42**	**1,042**	**5,659**	**77.5**	**134**	**657**	**8.59**
1991	6,745	156	1,576	1,328	3,158	1.25	875	5,042	74.3	16	573	8.63
1990	6,344	75	1,489	1,376	2,925	1.07	852	4,501	78.4	20	524	9.03
1989	5,550	155	1,133	1,169	2,607	1.01	836	3,908	77.7	45	489	9.07
1988	5,174	278	1,222	992	2,246	1.11	840	3,491	73.2	21	456	9.31
1987	4,391	51	1,078	874	1,898	1.23	892	2,837	72.8	69	418	9.48
1986	4,397	252	1,091	826	1,743	1.31	963	2,758	67.4	41	387	9.32
1985	3,684	243	901	703	1,424	1.48	818	2,204	68.3	31	342	9.42
1984	3,504	325	974	725	1,111	1.37	798	2,050	62.0	34	307	9.23
1983	3,214	334	1,043	648	850	1.75	749	1,804	55.9	28	279	8.94

Data as orig. reptd. 1. Refl. merger or acq. NA-Not Available.

Review of Operations

Total interest income for the six months ended June 30, 1993, rose 1.6%, year to year. With total interest expense down 12%, net interest income advanced 12%. The provision for loan losses increased 2.3%, and following 10% higher noninterest income and 5.7% greater noninterest expense, pretax income expanded 25%. After taxes at 33.8%, versus 32.5%, net income was up 23%, to $55,363,000 ($1.49 a share), from $45,176,000 ($1.24, as adjusted for the 10% stock dividend in 1993).

Common Share Earnings ($)

Quarter:	1993	1992	1991	1990
Mar.	0.74	0.61	0.52	0.44
Jun.	0.75	0.63	0.54	0.47
Sep.		0.69	0.57	0.51
Dec.		0.67	0.55	0.49
		2.60	2.16	1.91

Finances

In December 1992, the company acquired Security Federal Savings and Loan Association of Nashville, Tenn., which had some $383 million of assets and operated 20 branches throughout the state. Security Federal was converted to First Security Bank of Tennessee at 1992 year-end.

In March 1992, First Alabama acquired $48 million in deposits and five Alabama banking offices formerly operated by Jefferson Federal Savings & Loan, which had been operated in conservatorship by Resolution Trust Corp.

In November 1991, the company's Sunshine Bank unit acquired five banking offices in Pensacola, Fla. (deposits of $146 million).

In July 1991, First Alabama acquired three banking offices of Fulton Federal Savings Association in Columbus, Ga. (deposits of about $110 million).

Dividend Data

Cash has been paid each year since 1968. A dividend reinvestment plan is available.

Amt. of Divd. $	Date Decl.	Ex-divd. Date	Stock of Record	Payment Date
0.25	Nov. 18	Dec. 9	Dec. 15	Jan. 4'93
10% Stk.	Jan. 20	Mar. 1	Mar. 5	Apr. 1'93
0.26	Jan. 20	Mar. 9	Mar. 15	Apr. 1'93
0.26	May 19	Jun. 11	Jun. 17	Jul. 1'93
0.26	Jul. 21	Sep. 9	Sep. 15	Oct. 1'93

Capitalization

Long Term Borrowings: $141,819,000 (6/93).

Common Stock: 37,156,591 shs. ($0.62½ par). Institutions hold about 44%. Shareholders of record: 11,089 (12/92).

Office—417 North 20th St., Birmingham, AL 35202. **Tel**—(205) 832-8450. **Chrmn & CEO**—J. S. Mackin. **Vice Chrmn**—R. D. Horsley. **Secy**—L. B. Barnes III. **Exec VP & Investor Contact**—Robert P. Houston. **Dirs**—S. S. Blair, J. B. Boone Jr., A. P. Brewer, J. S. M. French, W. L. Halsey Jr., R. D. Horsley, C. Jones, O. B. King, N. F. McGowin Jr., H. M. McPhillips Jr., J. S. Mackin, M. L. Salmon, W. W. Shorter, H. E. Simpson, R. E. Steiner III, L. J. Styslinger Jr. **Transfer Agent**—First Alabama Bank, Montgomery. **Incorporated** in Delaware in 1970. **Empl**—4,696.

 Stephen R. Biggar

First of America Bank

NYSE Symbol FOA Options on Phila (Feb-May-Aug-Nov) In S&P MidCap 400

Price	Range	P-E Ratio	Dividend	Yield	S&P Ranking	Beta
Oct. 5'93	1993					
41⅝	43¼–36⅞	12	1.60	3.8%	A	0.67

Summary

This growing multibank holding company, headquartered in Kalamazoo, Mich., has 23 affiliate banks that operate about 561 offices in Michigan, Indiana and Illinois. An aggressive acquisition program has contributed to strong earnings growth in recent years. Security Bancorp, a Michigan bank holding company with assets of $2.7 billion, was acquired in mid-1992. The dividend was recently boosted 14%.

Current Outlook

Earnings for 1994 are projected at $4.60 a share, up from $4.10 expected for 1993 and $2.86 in 1992.

The dividend, recently boosted 14%, is expected to continue at $0.40 a share quarterly.

Earnings in the remainder of 1993 and in 1994 should be fueled by an aggressive acquisition program and ongoing consolidations that have streamlined operations. Profits should also be aided by a strategy of increasing fee income from traditional banking activities, such as credit cards, residential mortgage originations and financial services. Modest loan growth is expected, as gains in consumer lending are offset by flat commercial loan growth. Nonperforming assets are likely to remain flat or decline slightly. Given the bank's healthy risk-based capital ratios and recent acquisitions that have expanded the asset base, earnings gains should continue.

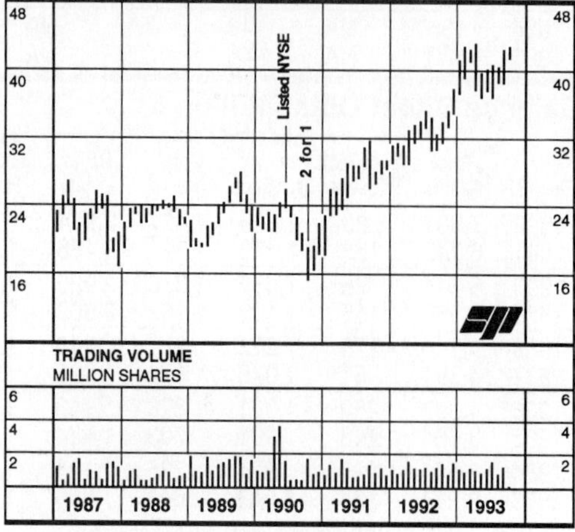

Review of Operations

Net interest income in the six months ended June 30, 1993, increased 5.2%, year to year, largely reflecting growth in earning assets. The net interest margin was 4.92%, down from 4.96%. The provision for loan losses was 14% higher and noninterest income gained 14%. Noninterest expense was 5.7% lower, aided by the absence of charges related to the Security Bancorp acquisition, and pretax income advanced 51%. After taxes at 30.1%, versus 32.3%, income climbed 56%, to $118.2 million ($2.00 a share, on 6.7% more shares), from $75.9 million ($1.27). Results in the 1992 period exclude a charge of $0.41 a share from the cumulative effect of an accounting change.

Common Share Earnings ($)

Quarter:	1993	1992	1991	1990
Mar.	0.99	0.82	0.70	0.79
Jun.	1.01	0.45	0.83	0.79
Sep.	E1.04	0.99	0.89	0.85
Dec.	E1.06	0.61	0.89	0.83
	E4.10	2.86	3.32	3.26

Important Developments

Aug. '93— The company's First of America Mortgage Co. subsidiary acquired Pioneer Mortgage Co., a division of Pioneer Savings Bank, including five North Carolina offices, for an undisclosed amount. Pioneer's mortgage banking operation focuses on residential lending and specializes in government insured loan programs.

Jul. '93— First of America registered for the public sale, on a continuous or delayed basis, of up to $500 million of debt securities, preferred stock and/or common stock. Proceeds are to be used for general corporate purposes, including debt repayment and preferred stock redemption.

Apr. '93— The company acquired Kewanee, Ill.-based Kewanee Investing Co., Inc., a one-bank holding company with $29 million in assets, in exchange for 95,668 First of America common shares.

Next earnings report expected in mid-October.

Per Share Data ($)

Yr. End Dec. 31	[1]1992	[1]1991	[1]1990	[1]1989	[1,2]1988	[1]1987	[1]1986	[1]1985	[1,2]1984	1983
Tangible Bk. Val.	**19.94**	20.84	18.75	17.72	16.23	13.80	12.02	14.49	11.75	9.10
Earnings[3]	**2.86**	3.32	3.26	2.94	3.08	2.97	2.74	2.60	2.29	1.74
Dividends[4]	**1.340**	1.240	1.150	1.075	0.950	0.850	0.750	0.650	0.553	0.583
Payout Ratio	**47%**	37%	35%	37%	31%	29%	27%	25%	24%	34%
Prices—High	**37⅞**	31¾	26	28	25⅛	27	26⅜	22½	13½	9¹⁄₁₆
Low	**29**	18¼	15⅜	19⅛	19	16⅞	20½	13¼	8¹⁵⁄₁₆	6³⁄₁₆
P/E Ratio—	**13–10**	10–5	8–5	10–7	8–6	9–6	10–7	9–5	6–4	5–4

Data as orig. reptd. Adj. for stk. div. of 100% Oct. 1990, 50% Jul. 1984. **1.** Reflects merger or acquisition. **2.** Reflects acctg. change. **3.** Bef. spec. item of -0.40 in 1992. **4.** Divds. declared. E-Estimated

First of America Bank Corporation

Income Data (Million $)

Year Ended Dec. 31	Net Int. Inc.	Tax Equiv. Adj.	Non Int. Inc.	Loan Loss Prov.	% Exp./ Op. Revs.	Net Bef. Taxes	Eff. Tax Rate	Net Inc.	% Net Int. Margin	—% Return On— Assets	Equity
[1]1992	**875**	**25.1**	**246**	**78.8**	**69.5**	**261**	**35.1%**	**169**	**4.98**	**0.87**	**15.2**
[1]1991	606	25.9	170	45.6	68.2	188	28.1%	135	4.92	0.96	17.1
[1]1990	548	28.7	152	29.4	67.7	178	26.1%	132	4.84	1.01	19.2
[1]1989	521	27.7	134	30.5	67.2	165	25.7%	123	4.92	1.00	19.7
[1,2]1988	371	22.2	92	21.6	67.1	116	23.3%	89	4.81	0.99	26.4
[1]1987	322	29.2	82	16.6	65.9	103	23.8%	78	4.76	0.97	31.2
[1]1986	220	36.0	59	16.4	63.6	63	16.0%	53	5.10	0.97	27.7
[1]1985	192	24.8	48	13.7	64.8	55	22.1%	43	5.09	0.93	23.5
[1,2]1984	169	14.9	45	18.0	66.5	44	23.5%	34	4.91	0.83	23.3
1983	148	14.8	40	11.6	73.0	29	10.2%	26	4.65	0.67	20.7

Balance Sheet Data (Million $)

Dec. 31	Total Assets	—Earning Assets— Mon. Mkt. Assets	Inv. Secs.	Com'l Loans	Other Loans	% Loan Loss Resv.	—Deposits— Demand	Time	% Loans/ Deposits	Long Term Debt	Common Equity	% Equity To Assets
1992	**20,147**	**175**	**4,627**	**2,171**	**11,585**	**1.29**	**2,572**	**15,463**	**76.3**	**254**	**1,261**	**5.29**
1991	16,755	170	3,567	2,078	9,394	1.27	2,039	12,982	76.4	221	908	4.97
1990	14,039	42	3,045	2,220	7,281	1.20	1,927	10,614	75.8	137	828	4.59
1989	12,793	290	2,857	2,254	6,092	1.26	1,993	9,373	73.4	137	754	4.31
1988	9,769	187	2,326	1,596	4,648	1.49	1,484	7,192	72.0	108	525	2.93
1987	8,680	292	2,099	1,712	3,722	1.65	1,274	6,281	71.9	119	433	2.36
1986	7,870	417	1,990	1,600	3,080	1.93	1,293	5,635	67.6	124	343	3.14
1985	5,326	85	1,479	979	2,284	1.42	883	3,774	70.1	48	260	3.47
1984	4,261	150	1,100	714	1,910	1.31	700	3,055	69.9	71	186	3.17
1983	4,109	252	1,020	646	1,769	1.14	719	2,778	68.7	93	159	2.80

Data as orig. reptd. **1.** Reflects merger or acquisition. **2.** Reflects acctg. change.

Business Summary

First of America Bank Corp. is a multibank holding company headquartered in Kalamazoo, Mich. with 23 affiliate banks operating about 551 offices in Michigan, Indiana and Illinois. Nonbanking subsidiaries provide mortgage, trust, data processing, pension consulting, revolving credit, discount brokerage and investment advisory services.

Total loans at December 31, 1992, amounted to $13.69 billion, up from $13.23 billion a year earlier, and were divided:

	1992	1991
Real estate–mortgage.........	51%	51%
Consumer........................	31%	28%
Commercial, financial & agricultural..................	16%	18%
Real estate–construction.....	2%	3%

In 1992, loans outstanding accounted for 75% of average earning assets, investment securities 24%, and other 1%. Average sources of funds in 1992 were time deposits 44%, money market and checking accounts 20%, savings and NOW accounts 14%, demand deposits 12%, common shareholders' equity 6%, borrowings 2%, and preferred stock and other 2%.

The allowance for loan losses at 1992 year-end was $176.8 million ($174.9 million a year earlier), or 1.29% (1.32%) of loans outstanding. Net chargeoffs in 1992 were $76.5 million ($60.3 million), or 0.57% (0.53%) of average loans outstanding. Nonperfoming assets at 1992 year-end totaled $196.0 million (1.43% of loans outstanding), against $168.4 million (1.27%) a year earlier.

On a tax-equivalent basis, the average yield on interest-earning assets in 1992 was 8.98% (10.18% in 1991), while the average rate paid on interest-bearing liabilities was 4.57 (5.89%), for a net spread of 4.41% (4.29%).

Dividend Data

Dividends have been paid since 1864. A dividend reinvestment plan is available. A "poison pill" stock purchase right was adopted in 1990.

Amt. of Divd. $	Date Decl.	Ex–divd. Date	Stock of Record	Payment Date
0.35	Nov. 18	Jan. 4	Jan. 8	Jan. 29'93
0.35	Feb. 17	Apr. 2	Apr. 9	Apr. 30'93
0.40	May 19	Jul. 2	Jul. 9	Jul. 30'93
0.40	Aug. 18	Oct. 4	Oct. 8	Oct. 29'93

Capitalization

Long Term Debt: $271,601,000 (6/93).

Common Stock: 57,141,155 shs. ($10 par). Institutions hold 33%. Shareholders of record: 24,000.

Office—211 S. Rose St., Kalamazoo, MI 49007. **Tel**—(616) 376-9000. **Chrmn & CEO**—D. R. Smith. **Pres**—R. F. Chormann. **EVP & Secy**—J. B. Rapp. **SVP & Treas**—S. G. Stone. **EVP, CFO & Investor Contact**—Thomas W. Lambert. **Dirs**—J. W. Brown, R. F. Chormann, E. B. Crouse, J. J. Fitzsimmons, R. E. Fryling, J. N. Goldberg, C. L. Greenwalt, R. L. Hetzler, L. C. Hoff, J. M. Kemp, R. D. Klein, R. Krafft, Jr., F. K. Neumann, G. S. Nugent, D. R. Smith, J. S. Ware, J. W. Wogsland, W. J. Wolpin. **Transfer Agent**—American Stock Transfer and Trust Co., NYC. **Incorporated** in Michigan in 1971. **Empl**—12,940.

 Stephen R. Biggar

First Bank System

NYSE Symbol FBS Options on ASE & CBOE (Mar-Jun-Sep-Dec) In S&P MidCap 400

Price	Range	P-E Ratio	Dividend	Yield	S&P Ranking	Beta
Aug. 13'93	1993					
31⅝	34–25⅞	31	1.00	3.2%	B–	1.31

Summary

This regional bank holding company, headquartered in Minneapolis, had assets of about $23.5 billion at December 31, 1992. The company has been expanding via acquisitions. In May 1993, the company acquired Colorado National Bankshares, the largest independent bank in that state, with assets of about $2.9 billion. While an after tax merger-related charge of $50.0 million penalized second quarter results, earnings should advance in 1993 and 1994.

Current Outlook

Earnings for 1993 could reach $2.25 a share, versus the $1.10 (before an accounting credit) in 1992. Earnings are estimated at $3.20 for 1994.

The $0.25 a share quarterly dividend is the minimum expected.

Earnings should rise in 1993 reflecting improving asset quality, a lower loan loss provision, and wide lending margins. In addition, signs of rising loan growth should also aide profits in the second half of the year and into 1994. While merger-related charges associated with the Western Capital Investment Corp. deal penalized 1992 profits, and second quarter 1993 profits were clipped $50 million due to the Colorado National Bankshares merger, FBS should begin to see gains from these transactions by 1994. Margins have improved as funding costs have declined and as FBS has placed growing emphasis on consumer and middle-market lending. Credit quality is on the rise, as problem asset levels continue to recede. Further improvements are expected, and with reserves at 192% of NPLs, the loan loss provision should decline. A stronger balance sheet has led to some recent acquisitions, and more deals are likely.

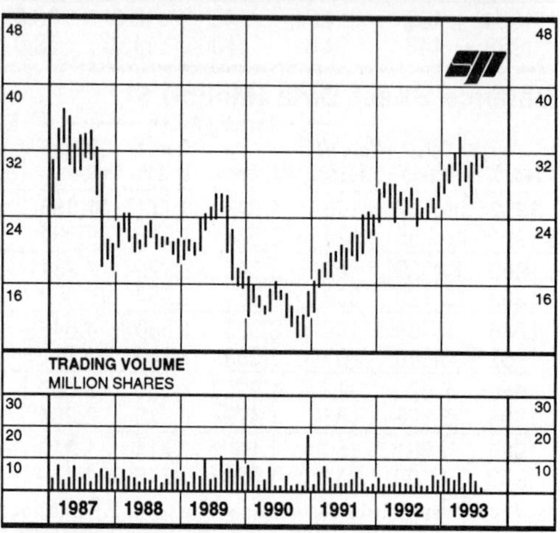

Review of Operations

Net interest income for the six months ended June 30, 1993 rose 14%, year to year (both years restated for acquisitions) primarily reflecting growth in average earning assets and a higher proportion of higher-yielding consumer loans which resulted in a wider net interest margin. The provision for loan losses was 20% lower at $71 million. Net chargeoffs totaled $84 million. Aided by a 16% gain in credit card fees, a 14% increase in trust fees and an 8.6% rise in service charges on deposit accounts, noninterest income advanced 7.5%. Penalized by the $72 million Colorado National merger-related restructuring charge, noninterest expenses increased 19% (up 4.7% excluding the charge). Pretax income exapanded 7.6%. After taxes at 38.0%, versus 33.3%, net income was unchanged. Following preferred dividends, share earnings were $0.85, on 9.0% more shares, versus $0.92, before a special credit of $1.51 in the 1992 period.

Common Share Earnings ($)

Quarter:	1993	1992	1991	1990
Mar.	0.60	d0.38	0.45	0.36
Jun.	0.23	0.51	0.51	0.38
Sep.	E0.70	0.50	0.57	0.39
Dec.	E0.72	d0.47	0.60	0.40
	E2.25	1.10	2.13	1.53

Important Developments

Jul. '93— Included in second quarter results was a $72.2 million charge ($50.0 million after-tax) related to the May 1993 FBS acquisition of Colorado National Bankshares, Inc., a $2.9 billion Colorado-based bank holding company. FBS said excluding the charge earnings would have been $83.5 million ($0.67 per share).

Next earnings report expected in mid-October.

Per Share Data ($)

Yr. End Dec. 31	1992	1991	1990	1989	1988	1987	[1,2]1986	1985	1984	[2]1983
Tangible Bk. Val.	**15.79**	11.90	11.28	10.08	14.37	21.82	22.74	20.47	18.54	16.69
Earnings[4]	**1.10**	2.13	1.53	d0.27	d5.25	0.73	[3]3.42	[3]2.84	[3]2.08	[3]2.12
Dividends	**0.880**	0.820	0.820	1.435	1.640	1.500	0.910	0.800	0.740	0.700
Payout Ratio	**80%**	39%	54%	NM	NM	205%	27%	28%	36%	33%
Prices—High	**28½**	24⅞	17	26⅞	24½	37⅛	29⅞	21½	14¾	15½
Low	**23⅛**	12¾	9⅝	15⅝	18⅝	17⅝	20⅜	12⅝	10⅝	8⅞
P/E Ratio—	**26–21**	12–6	11–6	NM	NM	51–24	9–6	8–4	7–5	7–4

Data as orig. reptd. Adj. for stk. divs. of 100% Dec. 1986, 100% May 1984. 1. Reflects merger or acq. 2. Reflects acctg. change. 3. Ful. dil.: 3.38 in 1986, 2.78 in 1985, 2.03 in 1984, 2.05 in 1983. 4. Bef. spec. item of +1.77 in 1992. d-Deficit. E-Estimated. NM-Not Meaningful.

Income Data (Million $)

Year Ended Dec. 31	Net Int. Inc.	Tax Equiv. Adj.	Non Int. Inc.	Loan Loss Prov.	% Exp./ Op. Revs.	Net Bef. Taxes	Eff. Tax Rate	[3]Net Inc.	% Net Int. Margin	—% Return On— Assets	Equity
1992	**846**	**21.7**	**410**	**164**	**71.0**	**183**	**32.0%**	**124**	**NA**	**0.59**	**NA**
1991	710	32.0	344	153	63.5	213	10.5%	190	4.67	1.09	21.7
1990	639	43.0	326	133	68.2	144	9.6%	131	3.79	0.66	12.0
1989	654	59.0	357	254	72.4	d1	NM	2	3.52	0.01	NM
1988	539	87.0	325	76	65.8	d335	NM	d310	2.60	NM	NM
1987	621	121.0	335	260	58.0	62	19.7%	50	2.88	0.18	3.3
[1,2]1986	686	192.0	320	507	61.7	177	NM	203	3.60	0.76	16.0
1985	640	135.0	300	180	54.0	195	14.5%	167	3.63	0.70	14.6
1984	523	131.0	224	135	55.9	115	NM	131	3.51	0.63	12.0
[2]1983	447	101.0	230	89	57.3	137	5.5%	130	3.45	0.72	13.6

Balance Sheet Data (Million $)

Dec. 31	Total Assets	Earning Assets: Mon. Mkt. Assets	Inv. Secs.	Com'l Loans	Other Loans	% Loan Loss Resv.	Deposits: Demand	Time	% Loans/ Deposits	Long Term Debt	Common Equity	% Equity To Assets
1992	**23,527**	**1,896**	**3,327**	**6,674**	**8,768**	**2.51**	**5,215**	**13,328**	**83.3**	**822**	**1,697**	**NA**
1991	18,301	1,652	1,546	6,589	6,563	2.62	4,020	10,459	90.8	681	1,151	4.38
1990	19,001	1,591	1,780	7,262	6,196	2.68	3,648	10,985	92.0	1,202	1,031	4.58
1989	20,820	567	1,984	9,075	6,639	2.55	3,437	12,316	99.8	1,433	793	4.23
1988	24,248	1,501	2,916	9,823	6,308	2.82	3,369	13,835	93.8	1,545	879	4.82
1987	26,850	3,268	7,823	8,797	4,518	3.21	2,892	12,907	84.3	1,204	1,297	4.63
1986	28,012	2,393	8,079	9,698	5,397	2.35	3,469	12,792	92.2	1,219	1,317	4.62
1985	25,484	2,649	5,696	9,509	5,124	1.58	3,331	12,708	90.3	1,051	1,140	4.53
1984	22,438	3,738	2,867	8,847	4,609	1.30	2,852	11,930	90.2	572	1,012	4.80
1983	20,871	3,344	4,026	7,263	3,967	1.07	2,841	10,590	82.7	432	1,005	5.19

Data as orig. reptd. **1.** Reflects merger or acquisition. **2.** Reflects accounting change. **3.** Bef. spec. item(s). d-Deficit. NA-Not Available. NM-Not Meaningful.

Business Summary

First Bank System is a multi-state bank holding company headquartered in Minneapolis. FBS is comprised of 22 commercial banks and three trust companies with 211 banking offices in Minnesota, Montana, North Dakota, South Dakota, Wisconsin, Washington and Colorado. Together, they provide banking services to consumers and businesses, including lending, corporate finance, trading and selling securities, discount brokerage, and trust and investment management. Nonbank subsidiaries are engaged in commercial finance, insurance, and mortgage banking.

During 1992, average earning assets of $18.4 billion ($18.3 billion in 1991) were divided: commercial and financial loans 35%, commercial real estate loans 8%, consumer loans 36%, foreign and lease financing 1%, investment securities 12%, and temporary investments 8%. Average sources of funds were interest-free deposits 20%, savings deposits 29%, other time deposits 30% (total deposits were $16.2 billion, up 3.6% from 1991), short-term borrowings 5%, long-term debt 4%, equity 9%, and other 3%.

At year-end 1992, nonperforming assets were $358 million (2.30% of loans and related assets), down from $457 million (3.08%) a year earlier, primarily due to a $53 million decline in foreclosed properties and a $27 million decline in nonperforming commercial mortgages. The reserve for loan losses was 2.51% of loans, versus 2.49%. Net chargeoffs in 1992 were 1.25% of average loans, versus 1.39%.

Dividend Data

Dividends have been paid since 1930. A dividend reinvestment plan is available. A "poison pill" stock purchase rights plan was adopted in 1989.

Amt of Divd. $	Date Decl.	Ex-divd. Date	Stock of Record	Payment Date
0.22½	Nov. 18	Nov. 27	Dec. 3	Dec. 15'92
0.25	Feb. 17	Feb. 25	Mar. 3	Mar. 15'93
0.25	May 19	May 26	Jun. 2	Jun. 15'93

Finances

At June 30, 1993 the Tier 1 capital ratio was 9.5%, and the Total capital ratio was 13.0%, compared with 9.5% and 12.6%, respectively at year-end 1992.

Capitalization

Long Term Debt: $857,000,000 (6/93).

Preferred Stock: $379,000,000.

Common Stock: 113,054,767 shs. ($1.25 par). Institutions hold about 49%. Shareholders of record: 21,313.

Office—1200 First Bank Place East, Box 522, Minneapolis, MN 55480. **Tel**—(612) 973-1111. **Chrmn & Pres**—J.F. Grundhofer. **Vice Chrmn & CFO**—R. A. Zona. **VP-Secy**—M. J. O'Rourke. **VP-Investor Contact**—Thomas A. Rice. **Dirs**—C. Bloomfield, J. F. Grundhofer. R. L. Hale, R. J. Haugh, J. H. Kareken, R. L. Knowlton, K. A. Macke, T. F. Madison, M. C. Nelson, E. J. Phillips, J. J. Renier, S. W. Richey, R. L. Schall, W. P. Schmechel, J. E. Schroeder. **Transfer Agent & Registrar**—First Chicago Trust Co., NYC. **Incorporated** in Delaware in 1929. **Empl**—9,875.

 Richard M. Levine, CFA

First Brands

NYSE Symbol FBR In S&P MidCap 400

Price	Range	P-E Ratio	Dividend	Yield	S&P Ranking	Beta
Aug. 27'93	1993					
32⅜	33¾–27⅝	13	0.24	0.7%	NR	NA

Summary

This company makes branded and private label consumer products for the home and automotive markets. Products include Glad plastic bags and related products, automotive performance products sold under the STP and Prestone brand names, and Simoniz cleaners, polishes and waxes. Earnings, which had been in a downtrend since fiscal 1990, advanced in fiscal 1993, benefiting from lower interest expense.

Business Summary

First Brands makes and sells branded and private label consumer products for the home and automotive markets. Its businesses belonged to Union Carbide Corp. prior to their acquisition in July 1986. Sales by class of products in recent fiscal years were divided as follows:

	1993	1992	1991
Plastic wrap & bags and related products	58%	62%	59%
Antifreeze/coolant	16%	16%	23%
Other automotive products	21%	21%	18%
Pet products	5%	1%	Nil

Home products include the most complete line of branded plastic wrap, bags and drinking straws in the U.S. and Canada which is sold under the Glad (and related Glad-lock) brand name. Plastic bags are also sold in Canada under the Surtec brand name. Sales to food outlets account for 71% of domestic sales of plastic wrap and bags and related products. The company's European home products businesses were sold in March 1989.

FBR's automotive products business manufactures branded and private label antifreeze/coolant, antifreeze/coolant for original equipment manufacturers, branded oil and fuel additives, vinyl protectants, a variety of automotive specialty performance products, and cleaners, polishes and waxes. Automotive products include Prestone antifreeze/coolant, automotive specialty performance products sold under the STP and Prestone brand names, and cleaners, polishes and waxes sold under the Simoniz brand name.

Through Himolene, Inc. (acquired 1988), the company is the leading U.S. producer of high molecular weight high density polyethylene plastic trash can liners for institutional and industrial markets.

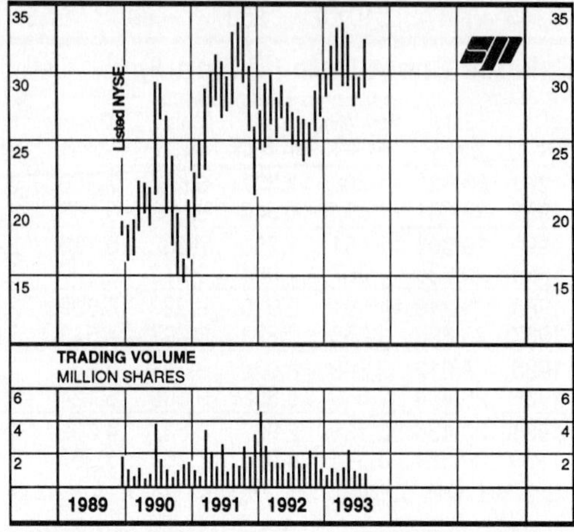

FBR also operates automotive service centers featuring its STP, Prestone and Simoniz brand products. These centers furnish a variety of automotive services to the public, including lube and oil changes, radiator service, tune-ups and car washes.

The company's products are sold directly to retailers and wholesalers. Domestically, the largest 25 customers account for 49% of total sales.

In May 1992, FBR acquired A&M Pet Products, Inc., a manufacturer and seller of two leading clumping cat litter products (Scoop Away and Ever Clean) in the U.S. Texas-based A&M has annual sales in excess of $50 million.

Next earnings report expected in mid-November.

Per Share Data ($)

Yr. End Jun. 30	1993	1992	1991	1990	1989	1988	1987
Tangible Bk. Val.	**NA**	11.88	10.85	8.74	14.94	d8.03	d1.28
Cash Flow	**NA**	3.18	3.82	2.62	3.33	d0.13	0.60
Earnings[1,2]	**2.41**	1.91	2.21	2.40	2.79	d0.75	d0.35
Dividends	**0.19**	0.04	0.04	0.02	Nil	Nil	Nil
Payout Ratio	**8%**	2%	2%	1%	Nil	Nil	Nil
Prices[3]—High	**33¾**	29⅞	35	29⅜	NA	NA	NA
Low	**27⅝**	23½	19⅜	14½	NA	NA	NA
P/E Ratio—	**14–11**	16–12	16–9	12–6	NA	NA	NA

Data as orig reptd.; prior to 1990, data as reptd. in prospectus dated Dec. 13, 1989. **1.** Based on pro forma shs. outstanding prior to 1990. **2.** Bef. spec. items of -0.84 in 1992, -0.08 in 1991, -0.04 in 1990, +0.24 in 1989, -0.04 in 1988. **3.** Cal. yr. d-Deficit. NA-Not Available.

Income Data (Million $)

Year Ended Jun. 30[1]	Revs.	Oper. Inc.	% Oper. Inc. of Revs.	Cap. Exp.	Depr.	Int. Exp.	Net Bef. Taxes	Eff. Tax Rate	[3]Net Inc.	% Net Inc. of Revs.	Cash Flow
1992	**989**	**145**	**14.7**	**97**	**27.9**	**38.7**	**76**	**45.5%**	**41.7**	**4.2**	**69.6**
1991	1,073	164	15.3	48	34.9	47.0	84	43.0%	48.0	4.5	82.9
1990	1,087	154	14.2	40	14.0	52.4	90	44.2%	50.4	4.6	55.0
1989	1,207	186	15.4	39	46.9	60.3	104	45.8%	56.2	4.7	67.2
1988	936	99	10.6	31	44.4	68.4	d12	NM	d15.0	NM	d2.6
1987	837	115	13.8	20	50.4	78.6	d5	NM	d7.0	NM	12.0
[2]1986	370	46	12.3	NA	8.6	Nil	37	49.9%	18.6	5.0	NA
1985	849	90	10.5	NA	16.2	Nil	69	44.8%	37.9	4.5	NA
1984	825	98	11.9	NA	14.9	Nil	82	43.6%	46.4	5.6	NA

Balance Sheet Data (Million $)

Jun. 30	Cash	Curr. Assets	Curr. Liab.	Curr. Ratio	Total Assets	% Ret. on Assets	Long Term Debt	Common Equity	Total Cap.	% LT Debt of Cap.	% Ret. on Equity
1992	**12.5**	**316**	**244**	**1.3**	**836**	**5.0**	**282**	**258**	**567**	**49.8**	**16.9**
1991	13.4	391	213	1.8	816	5.8	318	235	573	55.5	22.6
1990	15.3	401	241	1.7	836	1.2	371	189	566	65.5	16.0
1989	2.5	395	239	1.7	830	6.7	432	44	554	78.0	356.7
1988	7.3	369	235	1.6	852	NM	515	d14	578	89.1	NM

Data as orig. reptd.; prior to 1990, data as reptd. in Prospectus dated Dec. 13, 1989. **1.** Yrs. ended Dec. 31 prior to 1986. **2.** Six mos. **3.** Bef. spec. items. d-Deficit. NM-Not Meaningful. NA-Not Available.

Net Sales (Million $)

Quarter:	1992–93	1991–92	1990–91	1989–90
Sep.	269	261	327	315
Dec.	268	243	254	303
Mar.	220	219	224	221
Jun.	285	265	269	248
	1,042	989	1,073	1,087

Sales for the fiscal year ended June 30, 1993 (preliminary), rose 5.4% from those of fiscal 1992, reflecting the acquisition of A&M Pet Products. Gross margins narrowed, but with a 37% reduction in interest expense, and in the absence of a prior-year restructuring charge of $4.5 million ($0.12 a share, after taxes), pretax income advanced 34%. After taxes at 40.8%, versus 41.0%, net income also was up 34%, to $2.41 a share from $1.79 (restated). Results for fiscal 1992 exclude a $0.72 a share special charge from the repurchase of debt.

Common Share Earnings ($)

Quarter:	1992–93	1991–92	1990–91	1989–90
Sep.	0.66	0.62	0.82	1.01
Dec.	0.68	0.52	0.75	1.09
Mar.	0.41	0.28	0.21	0.16
Jun.	0.63	0.49	0.42	0.20
	2.41	1.91	2.21	[1]2.40

Finances

Capital spending of $31 million was expected for fiscal 1993.

At December 31, 1992, FBR's worldwide credit facilities totaled $196.9 million, of which $82.7 million was available.

During the first quarter of fiscal 1992, the company changed its inventory accounting method from the LIFO to the FIFO method, to better reflect operating results during periods of changing prices, and because overall product costs have declined. The change will result in the restatement of financial statement for prior years.

In May 1992, FBR redeemed the remaining $80.7 million of its 12½% senior subordinated debentures due 1998, using proceeds from a private financing. Net interest savings were expected to total $10 million. Earlier in 1992 and in late 1991, the company retired a total of $170 million of the debentures, partly through the issuance of $100 million of 9⅛% senior notes due 1999.

In March 1991, the company's major shareholder group sold publicly 8,440,000 FBR common shares in the U.S. and Canada, and 2,110,000 shares outside the U.S. and Canada, at $23.875 each. An additional 1,404,000 shares were sold to cover overallotments.

Dividend Data

Dividends were initiated in April 1990.

Amt of Divd. $	Date Decl.	Ex–divd. Date	Stock of Record	Payment Date
0.06	Oct. 22	Dec. 23	Dec. 30	Jan. 20'93
0.06	Mar. 9	Mar. 24	Mar. 30	Apr. 20'93
0.06	May 25	Jun. 23	Jun. 29	Jul. 20'93
0.06	Aug. 10	Sep. 23	Sep. 29	Oct. 20'93

Capitalization

Long Term Debt: $286,526,000 (3/93); incl. $100,000,000 of sr. notes and $45,000,000 of 13.25% sub. notes due 2001.

Common Stock: 21,791,193 shs. ($0.01 par). Institutions hold about 81%.

1. Quarters do not add due to change in number of shs.

Office—83 Wooster Heights Rd., Danbury, CT 06813-1911. **Tel**—(203) 731-2300. **Chrmn**—A. E. Dudley. **Pres**—W. V. Stephenson. **VP-CFO & Investor Contact**—Donald A. DeSantis (203-731-2306). **VP & Secy**—D. Raymond. **Dirs**—A. E. Dudley, A. C. Egler, L. G. Herring, J. R. Maher, J. R. McManus, D. C. Minton, D. Newman, E. R. Shames, W. V. Stephenson, R. G. Tobin. **Transfer Agent & Registrar**—Contintental Stock Transfer & Trust Co., NYC. **Incorporated** in Delaware in 1986. **Empl**—3,800.

 L. Feuer Nelson

First Financial Management

NYSE Symbol FFM Options on NYSE (Jan-Apr-Jul-Oct) In S&P MidCap 400

Price	Range	P–E Ratio	Dividend	Yield	S&P Ranking	Beta
Aug. 6'93	1993					
47¾	48⅛–36	NM	0.10	0.3%	B+	1.80

Summary

First Financial Management is a leading provider of information services, offering a vertically integrated set of data processing, storage and management products. FFM has expanded significantly over the past decade through a combination of internal growth and numerous acquisitions. Cash from the sale of several units leaves FFM in a strong position to make a substantial acquisition.

Current Outlook

Earnings for 1993 are estimated at $2.10 a share, up from 1992's $0.27 from continuing operations, which was after a $1.12 nonrecurring charge. Earnings for 1994 are expected to be $2.55.

Dividends are expected to continue at the current rate of $0.05 semianually.

Earnings for 1993 are likely to rebound sharply from the depressed level of 1992, primarily reflecting the absence of a $79.5 million pretax charge related to the sale of Basis Information Technologies. The sale of this business and Georgia Federal (completed in June 1993) strengthened the company's balance sheet and increased available cash, favorably positioning FFM for additional acquisitions. By selling these businesses, management will focus efforts on its three core segments: merchant services, data imaging, and healthcare services, all of which are expected to see double-digit revenue growth in 1993. Although competition for merchant credit card authorization, processing and settlement services is likely to intensify, FFM's market leadership position in this area is expected to remain intact.

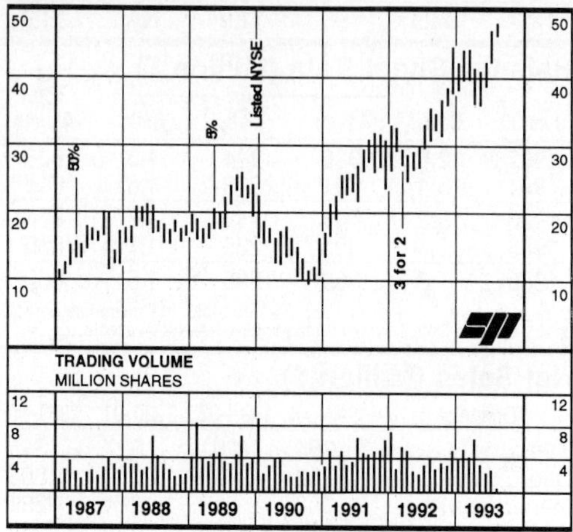

Total Revenues (Million $)

Quarter:	1993	1992	1991	1990
Mar.	344	272	251	192
Jun.	387	328	275	211
Sep.		368	297	231
Dec.		437	352	291
		1,405	1,176	925

Revenues in the six months ended June 30, 1993, climbed 22%, year to year, primarily reflecting gains in merchant services. Margins expanded, and after taxes at 42.2% in both periods, income from continuing operations jumped 51%, to $47.5 million ($0.80 a share), from $31.4 millon ($0.55). Results for the 1992 interim exclude income from discontinued operations totaling $17.9 million ($0.32).

Common Share Earnings ($)

Quarter:	1993	1992	1991	1990
Mar.	0.35	0.24	0.31	0.31
Jun.	0.45	0.31	0.44	0.39
Sep.	E0.55	0.36	0.51	0.43
Dec.	E0.75	d0.62	0.61	0.65
	E2.10	0.27	1.92	1.79

Important Developments

Aug. '93— The company's NaBANCO unit signed an agreement with Sears Merchandise Group to provide MasterCard and Visa credit card authorization, processing, and settlement services for transactions at over 1,800 Sears units.

Next earnings report expected in mid-October.

Per Share Data ($)

Yr. End Dec. 31	1992	1991	[1]1990	[1]1989	[1]1988	[1]1987	[1]1986	[1]1985	[1]1984	1983
Tangible Bk. Val.	**8.50**	8.10	1.98	1.94	2.31	2.29	2.27	2.49	1.49	1.25
Cash Flow	**1.70**	3.50	2.74	2.35	2.00	1.25	0.84	0.61	0.43	0.31
Earnings[2]	**0.27**	[3]1.92	[3]1.79	[3]1.53	[3]1.15	0.73	0.44	0.32	0.25	0.17
Dividends	**0.100**	0.067	0.067	0.065	Nil	Nil	Nil	Nil	Nil	Nil
Payout Ratio	**37%**	3%	4%	4%	Nil	Nil	Nil	Nil	Nil	Nil
Prices—High	**44⅝**	31⅞	22½	26	21¼	20⅛	11¾	10¼	5⅛	7
Low	**24¾**	13½	9⅜	15½	15⅜	10	7⅜	4⅞	3¾	4⅛
P/E Ratio—	**NM**	17–7	13–5	17–10	19–13	27–14	27–17	32–15	21–15	40–24

Data as orig. reptd. Adj. for stk. divs. of 50% Mar.1992, 5% May 1989, 50% Apr. 1987, 50% Jun. 1985. **1.** Reflects merger or acquisition. **2.** Bef. results of disc. opers. of +0.52 in 1992. **3.** Ful. dil.:1.79 in 1991, 1.67 in 1990, 1.43 in 1989, 1.13 in 1988. d-Deficit. E-Estimated. NM-Not Meaningful.

Income Data (Million $)

Year Ended Dec. 31	Revs.	Oper. Inc.	% Oper. Inc. of Revs.	Cap. Exp.	Depr.	Int. Exp.	Net Bef. Taxes	Eff. Tax Rate	Net Inc.	% Net Inc. of Revs.	Cash Flow
[1,4]1992	**1,388**	**217**	**15.6**	**[2]32.3**	**82.4**	**[3]9.0**	**62**	**74.5%**	**15.8**	**1.1**	**98.0**
1991	1,502	345	23.0	[2]31.3	73.6	128.0	149	40.2%	89.0	5.9	163.0
[1]1990	1,266	277	21.9	[2]28.3	38.9	137.0	119	38.7%	72.9	5.8	112.0
[1]1989	870	193	22.2	[2]5.9	30.5	89.3	93	38.8%	56.8	6.6	87.3
[1]1988	416	70	16.9	24.7	21.8	7.0	49	40.0%	29.3	7.0	51.1
[1]1987	172	28	16.5	34.8	8.0	4.4	19	40.1%	11.6	6.8	19.6
[1]1986	68	14	20.7	11.6	5.0	1.1	9	40.3%	5.5	8.1	10.6
[1]1985	52	9	17.2	5.3	3.1	0.9	6	38.8%	3.4	6.6	6.5
[1]1984	35	6	15.8	10.6	1.9	0.3	4	39.0%	2.6	7.3	4.5
1983	23	4	16.1	2.4	1.4	0.2	3	37.2%	1.8	7.5	3.1

Balance Sheet Data (Million $)

Dec. 31	Cash	Curr. Assets	Curr. Liab.	Curr. Ratio	Total Assets	% Ret. on Assets	Long Term Debt	Common Equity	Total Cap.	% LT Debt of Cap.	% Ret. on Equity
1992	**16**	**539**	**377**	**1.4**	**1,546**	**0.4**	**8**	**1,118**	**1,166**	**0.7**	**1.5**
1991	386	NA	NA	NA	5,497	1.4	934	993	1,927	48.5	9.9
1990	417	NA	NA	NA	5,479	1.4	823	601	1,424	57.8	12.9
1989	526	NA	NA	NA	4,941	1.9	1,074	501	1,574	68.2	12.5
1988	175	271	136	2.0	623	5.8	184	278	478	38.5	11.4
1987	39	103	92	1.1	367	4.2	27	223	261	10.4	7.7
1986	16	33	14	2.3	96	7.1	35	39	82	43.3	15.0
1985	20	31	11	2.9	57	7.2	7	33	46	15.3	13.2
1984	7	14	7	2.0	33	9.6	6	16	26	23.1	17.9
1983	9	12	4	3.0	21	10.3	1	13	17	7.3	19.5

Data as orig. reptd. **1.** Reflects merger or acquisition. **2.** Net. **3.** Net of interest income. **4.** Bef. results of disc. opers. NA-Not Available.

Business Summary

First Financial Management provides a variety of information services to a diverse customer base. It offers services for the capture, manipulation and distribution of data for numerous types of financial transactions. The company's continuing operations encompass the areas of merchant services, data imaging services and health care services.

Merchant services consists of NaBANCO, the largest merchant credit card processor in the U.S.; TeleCheck, a leader in check guarantee and verification services; Nationwide Credit, a leading provider of debt collection and accounts receivable management services; and MicroBilt, a major provider of data communications and information processing systems. Serving 205,000 customers through 46 locations with 3,600 employees, this segment had revenues of $841 million in 1992.

First Image Management Company offers a wide array of total data imaging services including computer output micrographics, electronic laser printing, microfilm, demand publishing, high and low speed data capture, direct mail marketing services, and data base management systems. With 3,300 employees and 98 branch locations, First Image provides multiple services to over 12,000 customers. Revenues in 1992 were $222 million.

Health care services are provided by FIRST HEALTH Services and FIRST HEALTH Strategies. Services include Medicaid claims processing, pharmaceutical claims processing, third party administration, psychiatric and chemical dependency managed care, utilization review, provider networks, and data analysis. Services are provided through 36 centers with 3,900 employees to 1,700 customers. Over 165 million health care claims were processed in 1992, representing nearly $15 billion; combined revenues for 1992 were $214 million.

In February 1993, FFM completed the sale of its Basis Information Technologies subsidiary to FIserv Inc. (NASDAQ-FISV) for $96.5 million in cash and FIserv common stock. In June 1993, FFM completed the sale of Georgia Federal Bank, a wholly owned subsidiary of FFM, to First Union Corp. for $269 million in cash. In 1992, the company sold its First Family Financial Services unit (previously wholly owned by Georgia Federal) to Associates Corporation of North America for $247 million in cash.

Dividend Data

Semiannual cash dividends were initiated in mid-1989. Payments in the past 12 months:

Amt. of Divd. $	Date Decl.	Ex-divd. Date	Stock of Record	Payment Date
0.05	Oct. 29	Nov. 25	Dec. 2	Jan. 1'93
0.05	Apr. 29	May 25	Jun. 1	Jul. 1'93

Capitalization

Long Term Debt: $7,569,000 (6/93).

Common Stock: 58,774,910 shs. ($0.10 par). Institutions hold about 80%. Shareholders of record: 1,770 (3/93).

Office—3 Corporate Square, Suite 700, Atlanta, GA 30329. **Tel**—(404) 321-0120. **Chrmn, Pres & CEO**—P.H. Thomas. **Senior Exec VP, CFO & Treas**—M. P. Pittard. **Secy**—R. L. M. Hutto. **Investor Contact**—Donald Y. Sharp (404) 321-0120. **Dirs**—G.L. Cohen, R.E. Coleman, J.R. Kelly Jr., H. A. Leslie., M. T. Pittard, C. B. Presley, J.A. Skarupa, P.H. Thomas, V. R. Williams. **Transfer Agent & Registrar**—Wachovia Bank of North Carolina, Winston-Salem. **Incorporated** in Georgia in 1971. **Empl**—12,600.

 Samuel A. Dedio

First Security Corp. (Utah)

NASDAQ Symbol FSCO (Incl. in Nat'l Market) In S&P MidCap 400

Price	Range	P-E Ratio	Dividend	Yield	S&P Ranking	Beta
Sep. 17'93	1993					
27	30¾–25½	11	0.92	3.4%	B+	0.54

Summary

This holding company, which owns four banks with more than 210 offices in Utah, Idaho, Wyoming and Oregon, continues to pursue an active acquisition program. Earnings for the first half of 1993 continued to benefit from a lower cost of funds, growth in earning assets and a lower loan loss provision.

Current Outlook

Earnings for 1993 are projected at $2.60 a share, up from 1992's $2.22. For 1994, earnings are expected to reach $2.90.

The quarterly cash dividend, raised 21% with the June 1993 payment, will likely be maintained at $0.23 a share.

Earnings for the remainder of 1993 and into 1994 should continue to benefit from growth in interest-earning assets due to acquisitions, a lower cost of funds and a reduced provision for loan losses. The company has made substantial progress in improving credit quality; nonperforming assets at June 30, 1993, were $55.9 million (1.04% of total loans), down 33% from $83.6 million (1.72%) a year earlier. Given the company's aggressive growth prospects, conservative balance sheet, expanding market presence and improving credit quality, the strong earnings momentum should continue.

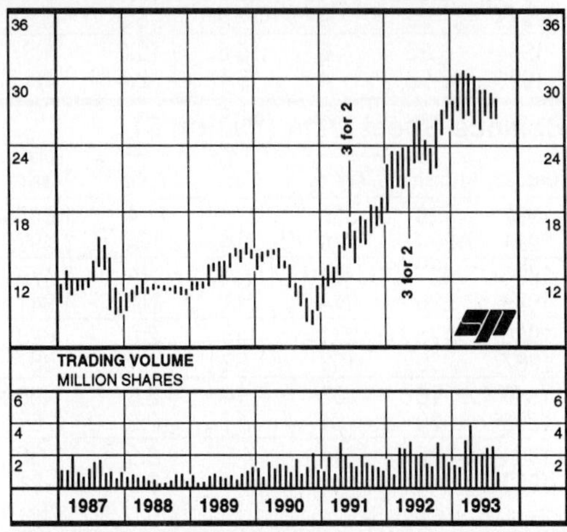

Review of Operations

Net interest income for the six months ended June 30, 1993, rose 7.4%, year to year, primarily reflecting an increase in interest-earning assets and a lower cost of funds. The provision for loan losses was 90% lower, at $1.8 million. Following 18% higher noninterest income and 11% greater noninterest expense, pretax income expanded 38%. After taxes at 38.3%, versus 34.5%, net income was up 30%, to $51,092,000 ($1.27 a share, after preferred dividends), from $39,240,000 ($1.01).

Common Share Earnings ($)

Quarter:	1993	1992	1991	1990
Mar.	0.63	0.48	0.43	0.39
Jun.	0.64	0.53	0.44	0.41
Sep.	E0.66	0.62	0.46	0.37
Dec.	E0.67	0.59	0.43	0.24
	E2.60	2.22	1.76	1.41

Important Developments

Aug. '93— First Security Bank of Utah signed a definitive agreement to purchase certain core banking assets of First Professional Bank for an undisclosed amount. Earlier, First Security Bank of Utah acquired about $8 million in deposits formerly held by Bank of America Arizona at its two branches in Utah for an undisclosed amount.

Jul. '93— The company's First Security Bank of Wyoming (formerly First Security Bank of Rock Springs) signed a definitive agreement to purchase two branches of Equality State Bank of Cheyenne, Wyo. (with combined deposits of $31 million), for an undisclosed amount. Together with the pending acquisition of State Bank of Green River, the new offices will increase First Security's branches to four in southwestern Wyoming.

Jul. '93— During the second quarter of 1993, the company said it acquired Benton County Bank (deposits of $31 million) and First Bankshares, Inc. ($73 million). Other pending acquisitions included Continental Bancorporation ($173 million) and First National Financial, whose First National Bank of Albuquerque ($1.1 billion and 26 branches) will be First Security's first subsidiary in New Mexico.

Next earnings report expected in mid-October.

Per Share Data ($)

Yr. End Dec. 31	[1]1992	[1]1991	[1]1990	1989	[2]1988	1987	1986	1985	[1]1984	[1]1983
Tangible Bk. Val.	**16.53**	15.53	14.81	14.87	13.95	13.29	12.77	13.06	12.86	12.54
Earnings[3]	**2.22**	1.76	1.41	1.55	1.20	0.98	0.18	0.69	0.85	0.78
Dividends	**0.683**	0.602	0.569	0.551	0.500	0.489	0.489	0.489	0.489	0.489
Payout Ratio	**31%**	34%	40%	36%	42%	50%	268%	71%	58%	63%
Prices—High	**28**	19⅜	14¾	15¼	11¹⁵⁄16	15¾	15 9/16	13 1/16	10¼	12 3/16
Low	**18⅛**	9⅞	7 15/16	11	9¼	8 15/16	9 7/16	8 5/16	6 11/16	8¼
P/E Ratio—	**13–8**	11–6	10–6	10–7	10–8	16–9	85–52	19–12	12–8	16–11

Data as orig. reptd. Adj. for stk. divs. of 50% May 1992, 50% Jun. 1991. **1.** Refl. merger or acq. **2.** Refl. acctg. change. **3.** Ful. dil.: 2.21 in 1992, 1.67 in 1991, 1.35 in 1990, 1.15 in 1988, 0.95 in 1987, 0.68 in 1985, 0.81 in 1984, 0.75 in 1983. E-Estimated.

Income Data (Million $)

Year Ended Dec. 31	Net Int. Inc.	Tax Equiv. Adj.	Non Int. Inc.	Loan Loss Prov.	% Exp./ Op. Revs.	Net Bef. Taxes	Eff. Tax Rate	Net Inc.	% Net Int. Margin	—% Return On— Assets	Equity
[1]1992	**330**	**7.9**	**110**	**30**	**62.2**	**132.0**	**34.5%**	**86.6**	**5.19**	**1.20**	**14.2**
[1]1991	274	7.7	103	45	63.6	89.0	33.1%	59.6	4.63	0.88	11.6
[1]1990	251	8.4	89	49	65.0	65.4	30.1%	45.7	4.53	0.72	9.8
1989	220	7.0	68	33	65.9	61.0	29.3%	43.1	4.71	0.80	10.8
[2]1988	199	11.4	59	25	71.2	40.8	19.0%	33.0	4.68	0.66	8.8
1987	184	13.0	55	14	75.7	34.5	21.6%	27.0	4.55	0.55	7.5
1986	179	44.0	97	126	80.4	d51.5	NM	5.1	5.07	0.10	1.4
1985	195	14.0	58	22	80.0	19.2	0.9%	19.0	4.79	0.38	5.4
[1]1984	186	19.4	64	38	71.3	21.5	NM	23.1	4.93	0.48	6.7
[1]1983	189	16.8	41	39	68.6	21.5	1.1%	21.2	5.23	0.46	6.1

Balance Sheet Data (Million $)

Dec. 31	Total Assets	—Earning Assets— Mon. Mkt. Assets	Inv. Secs.	Com'l Loans	Other Loans	% Loan Loss Resv.	—Deposits— Demand	Time	% Loans/ Deposits	Long Term Debt	Common Equity	% Equity To Assets
1992	**7,608**	**564**	**1,349**	**1,535**	**3,470**	**1.98**	**1,149**	**4,536**	**87.8**	**127**	**642**	**8.49**
1991	7,015	394	1,185	1,558	3,196	1.87	968	4,366	88.8	88	568	7.59
1990	6,493	253	1,020	1,484	3,106	1.76	882	4,118	91.4	97	478	7.32
1989	5,795	237	969	1,426	2,646	1.57	752	3,398	97.7	141	415	7.45
1988	5,159	216	714	1,334	2,366	1.56	704	3,198	94.3	153	385	7.48
1987	5,074	398	700	1,304	2,127	1.87	739	3,124	88.5	187	364	7.36
1986	5,080	521	615	1,314	2,142	3.11	755	3,169	87.7	161	350	7.05
1985	5,294	523	475	1,158	2,470	1.34	776	3,055	94.3	248	357	6.91
1984	5,107	551	493	1,144	2,250	1.46	723	3,069	89.1	259	351	7.08
1983	4,944	563	604	1,036	2,140	1.69	721	2,906	87.2	167	340	7.48

Data as orig. reptd. **1.** Refl. merger or acq. **2.** Refl. acctg. change. d-Deficit. NM-Not Meaningful.

Business Summary

First Security Corporation owns four banking affiliates that operate more than 210 offices in Utah, Idaho, southwestern Wyoming and western Oregon. The lead bank, First Security Bank of Utah, Salt Lake City, had deposits of $3.18 billion at 1992 year-end.

Consolidated gross loans and leases at 1992 year-end of $5.01 billion were divided as follows: real estate 39%, commercial, financial & agricultural 26%, consumer auto 21%, other consumer 9% and direct lease financing 5%.

The reserve for possible loan losses was $98,668,000 at the end of 1992 ($88,511,000 a year earlier), equal to 1.98% (1.87%) of loans outstanding. Net loan chargeoffs in 1992 were $23,207,000 (0.48% of average loans), versus $39,127,000 (0.85%) in 1991. Nonperforming assets at 1992 year-end were $64,414,000 (1.29% of loans and other real estate owned), compared with $93,562,000 (1.96%) a year earlier.

Interest and fees on loans contributed 67% of total income in 1992, interest and dividends on investment securities 13%, other interest income 4%, service charges on deposit accounts 6% and other noninterest income 10%.

Consolidated deposits of $5.69 billion at 1992 year-end were divided: noninterest-bearing 20%, savings & NOW 28%, money market 15%, time certificates less than $100,000 32%, and time certificates $100,000 and greater 5%.

On a tax-equivalent basis, the average yield on interest-earning assets was 8.87% in 1992 (10.02% in 1991), while the average rate paid on interest-bearing liabilities was 4.34% (6.19%), for a net spread of 4.53% (3.83%).

Dividend Data

Cash has been paid each year since 1935. A dividend reinvestment plan is available.

Amt of Divd. $	Date Decl.	Ex–divd. Date	Stock of Record	Payment Date
0.19	Oct. 26	Nov. 16	Nov. 20	Dec. 7'92
0.19	Jan. 25	Feb. 8	Feb. 12	Mar. 1'93
0.23	Apr. 26	May 17	May 21	Jun. 7'93
0.23	Jul. 27	Aug. 23	Aug. 27	Sep. 7'93

Capitalization

Long Term Debt: $237,895,000 (6/93).

$3.15 Preferred Stock Series A: 14,000 shs. (no par); each conv. into about 12 com. shs.

Common Stock: 39,271,000 shs. ($1.25 par). Institutions hold about 66%. Shareholders of record: 7,525 (2/93).

Office—79 S. Main St., Salt Lake City, UT 84111; P.O. Box 30006, Salt Lake City, UT 84130. **Tel**—(801) 246-5325. **Chrmn & CEO**—S. F. Eccles. **Pres & COO**—M. J. Evans. **Exec VP, CFO, Treas & Investor Contact**—Scott C. Ulbrich (801-246-5706). **Treas**—J. S. Bachman. **Secy**—A. W. Watson Jr. **Dirs**—M. J. Ashton, J. C. Beardall, R. H. Brady, J. E. Bruce, T. D. Dee II, S. F. Eccles, M. J. Evans, D. P. Gardner, K. D. Garff, U. E. Garrison, D. B. Haight, J. D. Harris, R. T. Heiner, H. W. Hunter, K. H. Huntsman, G. F. Joklik, B. Z. Kastler, S. S. Parker, A. K. Smith, J. L. Sorenson, H. J. Steele. **Transfer Agent & Registrar**—First Security Bank of Utah, N.A., Salt Lake City. **Incorporated** in Delaware in 1959. **Empl**—5,156.

 Stephen R. Biggar

First Tennessee National

NASDAQ Symbol FTEN (Incl. in Nat'l Market) In S&P MidCap 400

Price	Range	P-E Ratio	Dividend	Yield	S&P Ranking	Beta
Aug. 27'93	1993					
39¾	47¼–35¾	11	1.44	3.6%	A–	0.62

Summary

This holding company, whose principal subsidiary is First Tennessee Bank, operates more than 200 offices and is the state's largest banking organization. In late 1992, Home Financial Corp., the parent of a Tennessee bank, was acquired through an exchange of stock. Earnings continued to rise in the first half of 1993, aided by growth in earning assets and a lower loan loss provision.

Current Outlook

Earnings of $4.60 a share are projected for 1994, up from the $4.25 estimated for 1993 and the $3.19 recorded in 1992.

The quarterly cash dividend, increased 20% in late 1992, will likely be maintained at the current level.

Earnings are expected to grow strongly in 1993, aided by continued growth in interest-earning assets, wider net interest margins and a lower loan loss provision. Credit quality has improved markedly, with total nonperforming assets declining 37% in the first half of 1993. Further large loan provisions will not likely be required, as the allowance for loan losses stands at 216% of total nonperformers. The late 1992 acquisition of Home Financial Corp. expanded the company's presence in upper east Tennessee, and consolidations have already begun to help results. Improving credit quality, recent expansion efforts and growth in investment banking income should lead to further earnings progress in 1994.

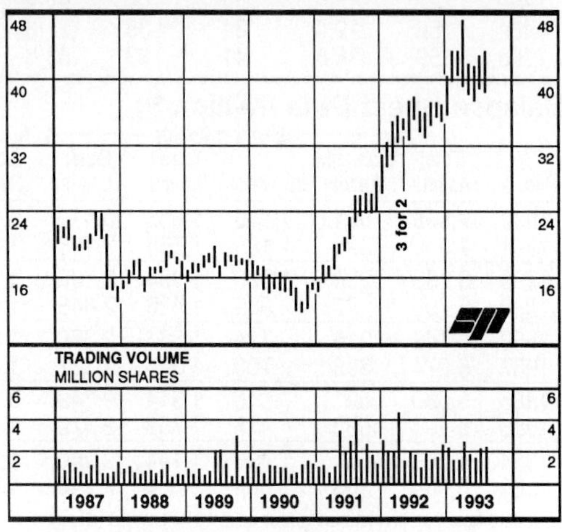

Review of Operations

Total interest income for the six months ended June 30, 1993, declined 5.7%, year to year. With total interest expense down 20%, net interest income rose 7.8%. The provision for loan losses dropped 18% and, following 10% higher noninterest income and 7.3% greater nointerest expense, pretax income expanded 20%. After taxes at 33.4%, versus 32.8%, net income was up 19%, to $60,588,000 ($2.15 a share), from $50,831,000 ($1.82).

Common Share Earnings ($)

Quarter:	1993	1992	1991	1990
Mar.	1.07	0.89	0.59	0.15
Jun.	1.08	0.93	0.66	0.67
Sep.	E1.05	0.95	0.69	0.63
Dec.	E1.05	0.42	0.74	0.56
	E4.25	3.19	2.69	2.01

Important Developments

Aug. '93— The First Tennessee Bank subsidiary signed a definitive agreement to buy Maryland National Mortgage Corp. (MNM), Baltimore, from MNC Financial, Inc. for $115.6 million. MNM originates and services residential mortgages, with a servicing portfolio of about $4 billion and 1992 revenues of $95.6 million.

Jul. '93— First Tennessee National agreed to acquire Cleveland National Bank & Trust Co. (Cleveland, Tenn.), with total assets of $225 million, for 1.1 million FTEN common shares.

Dec. '92— The company acquired Home Financial Corp. (HFC), the parent of Home Federal Bank, with 18 locations in six counties in upper east Tennessee, for nearly 4.2 million FTEN common shares. HFC had assets of $878 million and deposits of $757 million.

Next earnings report expected in mid-October.

Per Share Data ($)

Yr. End Dec. 31	[1]1992	1991	1990	1989	[1]1988	[1]1987	1986	1985	[2]1984	[1]1983
Tangible Bk. Val.	**19.14**	15.64	15.83	14.64	14.15	12.55	12.26	10.48	9.15	7.73
Earnings[3]	**3.19**	2.69	2.01	1.21	[4]2.23	[4]1.46	[4]2.27	[4]1.83	[4]1.79	[4]1.47
Dividends	**1.26**	1.14	1.08	0.967	0.853	0.787	0.753	0.72	0.645	0.583
Payout Ratio	**40%**	42%	54%	80%	38%	54%	33%	39%	36%	40%
Prices—High	**38**	27⅝	18⅛	19⅞	19⅜	24⅛	24⅜	19⅛	13⅝	11⅝
Low	**26¼**	14⅜	11⅞	15⅝	14⅜	13⅛	16⅜	12⅞	9⅜	7⅝
P/E Ratio—	**12–8**	10–5	9–6	16–13	9–6	16–9	11–7	10–7	8–5	8–5

Data as orig. reptd. Adj. for stk. divs. of 50% May 1992, 50% Nov. 1985. **1.** Refl. merger or acq. **2.** Refl. acctg. change. **3.** Bef. results of disc. ops. and/or spec. items of +0.03 in 1984. **4.** Ful. dil.: 2.21 in 1988, 1.43 in 1987, 2.23 in 1986, 1.79 in 1985, 1.76 in 1984, 1.44 in 1983. E-Estimated.

Income Data (Million $)

Year Ended Dec. 31	Net Int. Inc.	Tax Equiv. Adj.	Non Int. Inc.	Loan Loss Prov.	% Exp./ Op. Revs.	Net Bef. Taxes	Eff. Tax Rate	[3]Net Inc.	% Net Int. Margin	—% Return On— Assets	Equity
[1]1992	**323**	**7.7**	**227**	**43.2**	**64.7**	**144**	**38.2%**	**89.2**	**4.37**	**1.07**	**15.4**
1991	265	9.8	177	53.7	67.0	85	24.7%	63.8	4.43	0.93	15.3
1990	243	13.3	142	63.6	64.2	63	24.4%	47.9	4.40	0.74	12.3
1989	225	17.4	125	63.9	68.4	36	20.6%	28.8	4.48	0.47	7.7
[1]1988	214	20.0	110	25.4	67.4	67	22.4%	52.3	4.66	0.90	14.8
[1]1987	192	29.1	120	52.3	66.2	35	5.3%	32.9	4.62	0.58	10.3
1986	169	40.6	116	21.4	65.2	54	11.5%	47.5	4.94	0.93	16.5
1985	169	37.5	103	36.7	64.3	37	NM	37.8	5.22	0.80	14.6
[2]1984	156	33.0	74	13.8	65.6	42	10.6%	37.1	5.15	0.81	15.5
[1]1983	126	24.1	59	11.1	66.2	37	18.7%	30.2	4.61	0.72	13.8

Balance Sheet Data (Million $)

Dec. 31	Total Assets	—Earning Assets— Mon. Mkt. Assets	Inv. Secs.	Com'l Loans	Other Loans	% Loan Loss Resv.	—Deposits— Demand	Time	% Loans/ Deposits	Long Term Debt	Common Equity	% Equity To Assets
1992	**8,926**	**475**	**2,912**	**2,200**	**2,342**	**2.14**	**1,468**	**5,449**	**65.4**	**127**	**598**	**6.96**
1991	7,904	586	2,241	2,231	1,739	2.23	1,403	4,638	65.2	127	438	6.09
1990	6,708	710	1,417	2,107	1,787	2.17	1,117	4,227	71.7	127	398	6.03
1989	6,398	526	1,342	2,031	1,707	1.68	1,051	3,899	74.0	128	381	6.11
1988	5,972	399	1,106	2,071	1,606	1.32	1,187	3,470	76.9	131	372	6.06
1987	5,762	243	1,057	2,161	1,537	1.80	1,229	3,248	80.3	133	327	5.65
1986	5,556	398	819	2,067	1,184	1.27	1,403	2,847	75.0	60	306	5.62
1985	5,249	535	775	1,960	1,037	1.33	1,260	2,623	76.0	61	273	5.47
1984	4,658	518	692	1,737	894	1.22	1,123	2,521	71.1	63	250	5.20
1983	4,617	549	675	1,572	766	1.30	1,155	2,409	64.4	66	229	5.19

Data as orig. reptd. **1.** Refl. merger or acq. **2.** Refl. acctg. change. **3.** Bef. results of disc. ops. and/or spec. items. NM-Not Meaningful.

Business Summary

First Tennessee National Corporation owns First Tennessee Bank, N.A., which operates through 215 locations in Tennessee's major metropolitan areas, and Home Federal Bank (acquired in December 1992), which operates 18 offices in upper east Tennessee.

Consolidated gross loans totaling $4.52 billion at the end of 1992 were divided:

Commercial	48%
Consumer	28%
Real estate	14%
Credit card receivables	9%
Nonperforming	1%

The allowance for loan losses at December 31, 1992, was $96,795,000 (2.10% of loans, net of unearned income), compared with $90,048,000 (1.98%) a year earlier. Net chargeoffs in 1992 were $36,424,000 (0.81% of average loans, net), versus $59,885,000 (1.38%) in 1991. Nonperforming assets at 1992 year-end amounted to $54,686,000 (1.18% of total loans—net, plus foreclosed real estate and other assets), compared with $83,580,000 (1.83%) at the end of 1990.

Interest and fees on loans contributed 48% of total income for 1992, interest on investment securities 23%, other interest income 2%, investment banking income 10%, service charges on deposit accounts 6%, bank card income 3%, trust service income 2% and other noninterest income 6%.

Consolidated deposits of $6.92 billion at year-end 1992 were divided: demand 21%, checking/interest 7%, savings 7%, money market 23%, certificates of deposit (CDs) of $100,000 or more 7% and other CDs and time 35%.

On a tax-equivalent basis, the average yield on total earning assets in 1992 was 8.02% (9.32% in 1991), while the average rate paid on interest-bearing liabilities was 4.40% (6.13%), for a net spread of 3.62% (3.19%).

Dividend Data

Except for 1878 and 1895, dividends have been paid each year from organization in 1864. A dividend reinvestment plan is available.

Amt. of Divd. $	Date Decl.	Ex-divd. Date	Stock of Record	Payment Date
0.36	Oct. 21	Dec. 7	Dec. 11	Jan. 1'93
0.36	Jan. 19	Mar. 8	Mar. 12	Apr. 1'93
0.36	Apr. 21	Jun. 7	Jun. 11	Jul. 1'93
0.36	Jul. 20	Sep. 3	Sep. 10	Oct. 1'93

Capitalization

Long Term Debt: $90,766,000 (6/93).

Common Stock: 28,136,123 shs. ($2.50 par).
Institutions hold about 46%.
Shareholders: 7,837 (12/92).

Office—165 Madison Ave., Memphis, TN 38103. **Tel**—(901) 523-4027. **Chrmn & CEO**—R. Terry. **Pres & COO**—R. Horn. **Exec VP & CFO**—Susan Schmidt Bies. **Sr VP, Treas & Investor Contact**—M. List Underwood Jr. **Dirs**—J. A. Belz, R. C. Blattberg, J. H. Dobbs, R. Horn, J. R. Hyde III, J. Orgill III, C. E. Perry, R. E. Ray, M. D. Rose, W. B. Sansom, G. P. Street Jr., R. Terry, N. R. Turner. **Transfer Agent**—Bank of Boston. **Incorporated** in Tennessee in 1968; bank chartered in 1864. **Empl**—4,440.

 Stephen R. Biggar

First Virginia Banks

NYSE Symbol FVB In S&P MidCap 400

Price	Range	P-E Ratio	Dividend	Yield	S&P Ranking	Beta
Nov. 1'93	1993					
35⅛	41–32½	10	1.12	3.2%	A	1.04

Summary

This multibank holding company, with some $7.0 billion of assets, is the fifth largest banking organization in Virginia, with operations also in Maryland and Tennessee. Its greatest concentration of offices is in the suburbs of Washington, D.C. FVB emphasizes community banking by having affiliate banks retain their management and directors after being acquired. Earnings increased in recent periods, and further growth is projected for 1993 and 1994.

Current Outlook

Earnings for 1993 are estimated at $3.55 a share, versus the $3.02 of 1992. Earnings for 1994 could approximate $3.90.

The $0.28 dividend will likely be raised at least 10% in early 1994.

FVB anticipates at least 7% loan growth in 1993 and 1994, aided by aggressive auto loan pricing, which has become possible because competitors de-emphasized this business, affording FVB the opportunity to lend to the best credits. To grow in the face of renewed competition, FVB targets budding areas like East Tennessee and Frederick, Md. Net interest margins should decline toward 5.0% through the end of 1993 as loans mature and are replaced with new lower rate loans. Margins should remain above 5.0% in 1994. The level of nonperforming assets, which has declined recently, should stablize in 1994; loan loss provisions will grow with loans. The company should continue to benefit from the 1991 completion of an automated branch system which will facilitate further expansion and help reduce overhead.

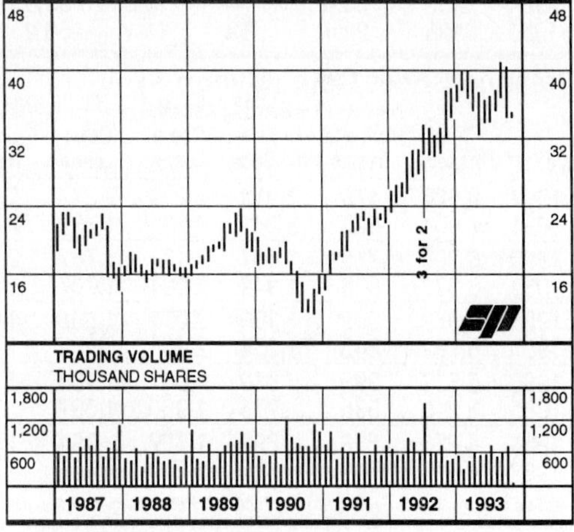

Review of Operations

Net interest income for the nine months ended September 30, 1993, rose 8.9%, year to year, on loan growth and an improved net interest margin. The loan loss provision decreased 62%, and following 6.1% higher noninterest income and 4.0% greater noninterest expense, pretax income advanced 25%. After taxes at 31.9%, versus 30.8%, net income was up 23%. Earnings per share were $2.68, versus $2.20, as adjusted for the 3-for-2 stock split in July, 1992.

Common Share Earnings ($)

Quarter:	1994	1993	1992	1991
Mar.	E0.90	0.90	0.67	0.52
Jun.	E0.95	0.90	0.74	0.51
Sep.	E0.95	0.88	0.79	0.55
Dec.	E1.10	E0.90	0.82	0.58
	E3.90	E3.55	3.02	2.17

Important Developments

Oct. '93— FVB's net interest margin for the first nine months of 1993 rose to 5.53% from 5.39% in the year earlier period.

Oct. '93— The company agreed to acquire FNB Financial Corp. (with assets of $95 million) for a combination of cash and stock. The transaction is subject to various conditions and approvals.

Mar. '93— First Virginia said that directors of United Southern Bank of Morristown, Tenn. (assets of $43 million) approved an agreement for the bank to be acquired by FVB. United Southern shareholders will receive 1.7 FVB common shares for each of their shares, for a total of 196,679 FVB shares. Consistent with First Virginia's community banking philosophy, United Southern will retain its name and directors.

Next earnings report expected in mid-January.

Per Share Data ($)

Yr. End Dec. 31	[1]1992	[1]1991	[1]1990	1989	[1]1988	[1]1987	[1]1986	[1]1985	[1]1984	[1]1983
Tangible Bk. Val.	**18.49**	16.40	15.11	13.91	12.54	11.39	10.71	9.65	8.57	7.73
Earnings[2]	**3.02**	2.17	2.03	2.13	1.93	1.83	1.85	1.73	1.63	1.53
Dividends	**0.99**	0.91	0.85	0.80	0.75	0.69	0.64	0.59	0.53	0.48
Payout Ratio	**33%**	42%	42%	38%	39%	38%	35%	34%	33%	31%
Prices—High	**37⅞**	24	20⅜	23¾	18⅝	23⅜	25	19⅛	13⅜	13⅜
Low	**23⅜**	14⅛	11¼	15⅞	15⅛	14⅛	17	12⅝	9⅞	7½
P/E Ratio—	**13–8**	11–7	10–6	11–7	10–8	13–8	13–9	11–7	8–6	9–5

Data as orig. reptd. Adj. for stk. div. of 50% Jul. 1992. **1.** Reflects merger or acquisition. **2.** Aft. gains/losses on securities trans. of +0.01 in 1987, +0.01 in 1986, +0.02 in 1985, -0.01 in 1984. E-Estimated

Income Data (Million $)

Year Ended Dec. 31	Net Int. Inc.	Tax Equiv. Adj.	Non Int. Inc.	Loan Loss Prov.	% Exp./ Op. Revs.	Net Bef. Taxes	Eff. Tax Rate	Net Inc.	% Net Int. Margin	—% Return On— Assets	Equity
1992	**320**	**8.7**	**77.3**	**17.4**	**58.8**	**141.3**	**31.0%**	**97.5**	**5.46**	**1.50**	**17.1**
1991	256	8.9	72.3	14.0	64.8	95.6	27.2%	69.6	5.03	1.22	13.5
[1]1990	237	8.9	68.0	13.4	64.5	89.5	27.2%	65.1	5.15	1.25	13.6
1989	228	9.4	63.1	11.0	62.5	92.4	27.0%	67.4	5.36	1.39	15.6
[1]1988	209	9.9	61.6	11.4	63.7	80.7	24.5%	60.9	5.19	1.32	15.6
[1]1987	202	14.4	55.3	11.7	61.0	80.2	29.8%	56.3	5.53	1.31	16.2
[1]1986	172	20.3	47.0	10.2	58.9	67.9	29.7%	47.7	5.93	1.35	17.5
[1]1985	143	17.9	41.4	7.7	60.5	54.9	27.0%	40.0	5.98	1.36	17.9
[1]1984	125	16.9	36.0	6.2	60.7	46.4	24.6%	35.0	6.14	1.37	18.7
[1]1983	112	14.6	26.9	5.0	62.0	38.7	25.0%	29.0	6.47	1.34	19.1

Balance Sheet Data (Million $)

Dec. 31	Total Assets	Earning Assets: Mon. Mkt. Assets	Inv. Secs.	Com'l Loans	Other Loans	% Loan Loss Resv.	Deposits: Demand	Time	% Loans/ Deposits	Long Term Debt	Common Equity	% Equity To Assets
1992	**6,841**	**NA**	**2,165**	**382**	**3,812**	**1.28**	**1,012**	**5,001**	**NA**	**5.23**	**607**	**8.8**
1991	6,119	NA	1,813	406	3,487	1.27	835	4,515	NA	11.50	539	9.1
1990	5,384	NA	1,287	434	3,409	1.28	785	3,931	NA	11.80	497	9.2
1989	5,124	NA	1,069	493	3,231	1.23	794	3,633	NA	37.50	453	8.9
1988	4,796	NA	1,091	529	3,034	1.26	807	3,416	NA	38.10	411	8.5
1987	4,433	NA	1,057	522	2,631	1.26	748	3,166	NA	43.70	367	8.1
1986	3,881	NA	946	412	2,150	1.26	695	2,747	NA	43.30	289	7.7
1985	3,144	NA	863	340	1,806	1.24	550	2,215	NA	46.00	237	7.5
1984	2,687	NA	624	311	1,582	1.23	481	1,892	NA	43.70	199	7.3
1983	2,360	NA	640	283	1,318	1.23	408	1,669	NA	45.80	161	6.9

Data as orig. reptd. **1.** Reflects merger or acquisition. NA-Not Available.

Business Summary

First Virginia Banks (formerly First Virginia Bankshares) is a bank holding company controlling 21 member banks with combined assets of approximately $6.8 billion at December 31, 1992. FVB conducts its operations through some 267 offices in Virginia, plus 37 offices in Maryland and 20 in Tennessee. The greatest concentration of offices is in the suburbs of Washington, D.C. Other subsidiaries are engaged in mortgage banking and insurance.

In 1992 (and 1991), average loans outstanding were divided: instalment 66% (67%); real estate 17% (15%); and other 17% (18%).

In 1992, loans outstanding accounted for 61% of average earning assets, investment securities for 35%, and federal funds sold and resale agreements for 4%.

Average sources of funds in 1992 were certificates of deposit 32%, demand deposits 13%, fixed rate transaction accounts 16%, savings accounts 15%, money market accounts 12%, shareholders' equity 9%, and short-term debt and other 3%.

The allowance for loan losses was 1.28% of loans outstanding at year-end 1992, up from 1.27% a year earlier. Net charge-offs were 0.35% of average loans in 1992, down from 0.38% in 1991. At year-end 1992, nonperforming assets (consisting of nonaccruing and restructured loans and foreclosed real estate) were $32.7 million (0.85% of total loans and foreclosed real estate), versus $34.9 million (0.99%) in 1991.

Dividend Data

Dividends have been paid since 1960. A dividend reinvestment plan is available. The company issued a "poison pill" stock purchase right in 1988.

Amt of Divd. $	Date Decl.	Ex-divd. Date	Stock of Record	Payment Date
0.26	Nov. 18	Dec. 24	Dec. 31	Jan. 11'93
0.26	Feb. 24	Mar. 25	Mar. 31	Apr. 19'93
0.28	May 26	Jun. 24	Jun. 30	Jul. 19'93
0.28	Aug. 25	Sep. 24	Sep. 30	Oct. 18'93

Capitalization

Long Term Debt: $1,039,000 of mortgage notes (9/93).

Conv. Preferred Stock: $808,000 (9/93).

Common Stock: 32,208,905 shs. ($1 par).
Institutions hold about 34%.
Shareholders of record: 18,878.

Office—6400 Arlington Blvd., Falls Church, VA 22042-2336. **Tel**—(703) 241-4000. **Chrmn & CEO**—R. H. Zalokar. **Pres**—P. H. Geithner Jr. **VP-Secy**—T. P. Jennings. **VP-Treas & Investor Contact**—Richard F. Bowman. **Dirs**—E. C. Brand, E. L. Breeden III, P. H. Geithner Jr., L. H. Ginn III, G. R. Giordano, T. K. Greer, E. C. Gruver, E. M. Holland, E. C. Kendrick, T. K. Malone Jr., W. L. Phillips Jr., J. P. Rowe III, R. T. Selden, R. H. Zalokar, A. F. Zettlemoyer. **Transfer Agent & Registrar**—Security Trust Co., Baltimore, Md. **Incorporated** in Virginia in 1949. **Empl**—4,652.

 C. Orgielewicz

Flserv, Inc.

NASDAQ Symbol FISV (Incl. in Nat'l Market) In S&P MidCap 400

Price	Range	P-E Ratio	Dividend	Yield	S&P Ranking	Beta
Aug. 13'93	1993					
19¾	21½–16¾	27	None	None	NR	1.03

Summary

This Wisconsin-based company is a leading full-service provider of computerized account processing and integrated information management systems for financial institutions. Flserv posted record revenues and earnings for 1992, aided by acquisitions and internal growth. Acquisitions continue to be an important part of the company's growth strategy, as the purchase of the Basis Information Technologies unit of First Financial Management Corp. was completed in February 1993 for $96.5 million in cash and Flserv common stock. In August 1993, Flserv agreed to acquire two outsourcing units of Mellon Bank Corp.

Business Summary

Flserv, Inc. is an independent provider of data processing outsourcing capabilities and related products and services for financial institutions. The company's system applications are designed to increase the operating efficiency, customer service, and marketing capability of banks, credit unions, mortgage banks, savings institutions and other financial intermediaries.

Since its formation in 1984, the company has grown by developing highly specialized services and products, adding new clients and acquiring firms providing complementary services. At March 31, 1993, the company provided services to more than 5,400 financial institutions worldwide, processing and reporting on daily transactions for about 50 million customer accounts.

Flserve is a full-service resource for the financial industry, with outsourcing of account and transaction processing through its many specialized service bureaus; flexible industry-specific in-house software systems; and resource or facilities management businesses. Complementary products and services include asset/liability management; fund administration and trusteeship of individual or business self-directed retirement plans; forms and graphic design; plastic card products and services; consulting; and disaster recovery services.

The company is a recognized leader in the Electronic Funds Transfer market, providing automated teller machine and point of sale debit support services to both financial institutions and retail clients.

Effective August 1, 1992, Flserv agreed to perform all data processing services for Society for Savings Bancorp, a Connecticut-based savings bank with more than $2.7 billion in assets. The agreement was expected to generate several million dollars per year in recurring revenues for Flserv.

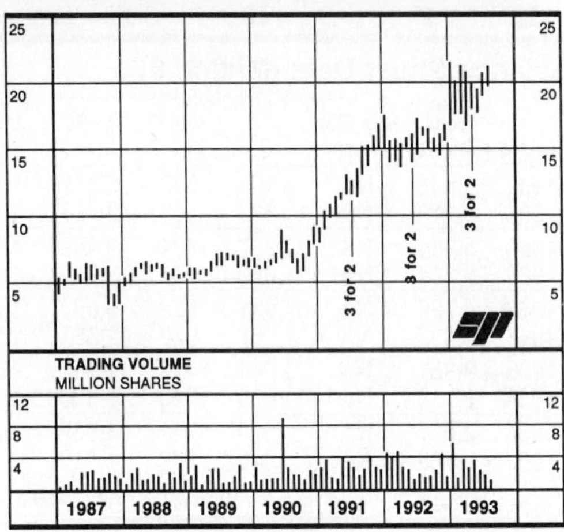

Important Developments

Aug. '93— Flserv entered into a definitive agreement with Mellon Bank Corp. (NYSE: MEL) to purchase two wholly owned outsourcing businesses of Mellon: Financial Institution Outsourcing and Data-Link Systems, Inc. The transaction is expected to be completed by the fourth quarter of 1993. Terms of the agreement were not disclosed, however, the two Mellon technology-based businesses generate annual revenues of about $70 million and provide information processing and mortgage banking services to approximately 200 financial institutions in the U.S. and Canada.

Next earnings report expected in late October.

Per Share Data ($)

Yr. End Dec. 31	[3]1992	[3]1991	[3]1990	[3]1989	[3]1988	[3]1987	[3]1986	[3]1985
Tangible Bk. Val.[1]	**5.70**	5.00	3.45	2.97	2.55	2.14	1.46	0.85
Cash Flow	**1.14**	0.99	0.83	0.73	0.61	0.47	0.42	0.14
Earnings[2]	**0.67**	0.56	0.47	0.39	0.33	0.27	0.22	0.01
Dividends	**Nil**	Nil	Nil	Nil	Nil	Nil	Nil	Nil
Payout Ratio	**Nil**	Nil	Nil	Nil	Nil	Nil	Nil	Nil
Prices—High	**17 19/32**	16 29/32	9¼	7 11/32	6 21/32	6 21/32	4 13/32	NA
Low	**13 21/32**	8	5¾	5¼	4 27/32	3 11/32	3 21/32	NA
P/E Ratio—	**26–21**	30–14	19–12	19–13	20–15	24–12	20–17	NA

Data as orig. reptd. Adj. for stk. divs. of 50% May 1993, Jun. 1992, 50% Jul. 1991. **1.** Incl. intangibles. **2.** Bef. spec. items of +0.05 in 1986, +0.01 in 1985. **3.** Refls. merger or acquis. NA-Not Available.

Income Data (Million $)

Year Ended Dec. 31[3]	Revs.	Oper. Inc.	% Oper. Inc. of Revs.	Cap. Exp.	Depr.	Int. Exp.	Net Bef. Taxes	Eff. Tax Rate	[2]Net Inc.	% Net Inc. of Revs.	Cash Flow
1992	**332**	**55.3**	**16.7**	**19.1**	**16.1**	**5.02**	**37.1**	**38.0%**	**23.0**	**6.9**	**39.1**
1991	281	45.8	16.3	14.3	14.9	3.00	28.7	36.0%	18.3	6.5	32.5
1990	183	33.8	18.4	5.1	10.4	1.91	21.5	36.0%	13.8	7.5	24.1
1989	164	30.3	18.5	14.4	9.5	2.38	18.5	38.5%	11.4	6.9	20.9
1988	125	23.3	18.6	7.2	7.8	[1]0.39	15.1	39.0%	9.2	7.4	17.0
1987	86	17.4	20.3	4.3	5.2	NA	12.4	42.4%	7.2	8.4	12.3
1986	70	13.7	19.4	4.7	4.4	[1]1.17	8.1	41.1%	[4]4.8	6.8	9.2
1985	33	4.4	13.4	1.3	2.7	1.38	0.3	57.3%	0.1	0.4	2.8

Balance Sheet Data (Million $)

Dec. 31	Cash	Curr. Assets	Curr. Liab.	Curr. Ratio	Total Assets	% Ret. on Assets	Long Term Debt	Common Equity	Total Cap.	% LT Debt of Cap.	% Ret. on Equity
1992	**302**	**NA**	**NA**	**NA**	**898**	**2.8**	**50.7**	**192**	**260**	**19.5**	**12.7**
1991	389	NA	NA	NA	740	1.3	51.6	167	230	22.4	6.5
1990	346	NA	NA	NA	565	2.7	34.3	100	143	23.9	14.8
1989	223	NA	NA	NA	443	3.9	25.9	84	116	22.3	14.5
1988	22	50.6	36.0	1.4	134	8.5	21.9	71	98	22.4	14.1
1987	28	44.0	16.0	2.8	79	10.5	3.6	57	63	5.7	15.1
1986	5	18.1	13.0	1.4	51	10.5	3.7	34	38	9.6	17.7
1985	1	8.6	8.9	1.0	33	NA	7.9	17	25	32.1	NA

Data as orig. reptd. **1.** Net of int. inc. **2.** Bef. spec. items in 1986, 1985. **3.** Reflects merger or acquis. **4.** Reflects acct. change. NA-Not Available.

Operating Revenues (Million $)

Quarter:	1993	1992	1991	1990
Mar.	99.7	81.3	47.7	44.4
Jun.	111.2	82.3	71.4	45.4
Sep.		83.7	82.4	46.3
Dec.		84.8	79.9	47.0
		332.1	281.3	183.2

Operating revenues for the six months ended June 30, 1993, advanced 29%, year to year, primarily reflecting acquisition-related growth. Margins remained steady, and pretax income advanced 28%. After taxes at 37.1%, versus 38.0%, net income was up 29%, to $14,451,000 ($0.39 a share, based on 8.7% more shares), from $11,168,000 ($0.32, as adjusted for the three-for-two stock split in 1993).

Common Share Earnings ($)

Quarter:	1993	1992	1991	1990
Mar.	0.19	0.16	0.13	0.11
Jun.	0.20	0.17	0.14	0.11
Sep.		0.17	0.14	0.12
Dec.		0.17	0.15	0.13
		0.67	0.56	0.47

Dividend Data

No cash dividends have been paid on the public shares, and the company intends to retain earnings to support future business opportunities. Three-for-two stock splits were effected in July 1991, June 1992 and May 1993.

Finances

In May 1993, the company completed a public offering of 3,850,000 common shares (1,403,911 sold by Fiserv, 2,446,089 sold by selling shareholders) at $19.25 each. Net proceeds of $23.5 million will be used for general corporate purposes, which could include the repayment of debt and acquisitions.

In February 1993, Fiserv completed the purchase of Basis Information Technologies from First Financial Management Corp. The purchase price of $96.5 million was paid 50% in cash and 50% in Fiserv common stock. Basis provides transaction processing services and related software products to 1,260 financial institutions with more than 20 million customer accounts in 47 states.

In August 1992, the company acquired Performance Analysis, Inc., a Cincinnati-based provider of rate-risk analysis and financial services.

In April 1991, Fiserv acquired the principal financial data processing business units of Citicorp Information Resources, Inc. for $42.7 million in cash and paid an additional $6 million in cash in respect to Citicorp's agreement not to compete with Fiserv. Fiserv and Citicorp also signed a letter of intent with respect to a three-year facilities management contract for Citicorp's payroll processing business.

Capitalization

Debt: $53,678,000 (6/93).

Common Stock: 38,647,352 shs. ($0.01 par).
Institutions hold about 72%.
Shareholders: About 6,750 of record (12/92).

Office—2152 South 114th St., West Allis, WI 53227. **Tel**—(414) 879-5000. **Chrmn & CEO**—G. D. Dalton. **Pres & COO**—L. M. Muma. **Sr Exec VP, CFO & Treas**—K. R. Jensen. **Dirs**—B. K. Anderson, G. D. Dalton, K. R. Jensen, G. J. Levy, L. M. Muma, L. W. Seidman, R. D. Sullivan. **Transfer Agent & Registrar**—First Bank, Milwaukee. **Incorporated** in Delaware in 1984. **Empl**—4,800.

 Samuel A. Dedio

Fisher-Price

NYSE Symbol FPP Options on ASE, NYSE, Pacific (Mar-Jun-Sep-Dec) In S&P MidCap 400

Price	Range	P-E Ratio	Dividend	Yield	S&P Ranking	Beta
Aug. 26'93	1993					
33⅛	33⅜–17⅞	31	0.20	0.6%	NR	NA

Summary

Fisher-Price, which was spun-off by Quaker Oats Co. in July 1991 and is a leading manufacturer of pre-school and infant toys and juvenile products, has agreed to be acquired by Mattel Inc., another leading toy company. Terms call for each share of Fisher-Price common stock to be exchanged for 1.275 shares of Mattel. Shareholder and governmental approvals will be required to complete the transaction.

Current Outlook

As a separate entity, earnings for 1994 should approximate $1.80 a share, up from the $1.50 projected for 1993.

An increase in the $0.05 quarterly dividend is likely in 1993.

Sales for 1994 for Fisher-Price as a separate entity are expected to increase approximately 15%, led by higher international sales. Foreign sales should continue to benefit from a sharp expansion in the company's product line in international markets, which was begun in 1993. Domestic sales should also rise due to an aggressive new product introduction program and a pickup in retail toy sales, which have been sluggish to date in 1993. However, competition will remain intense in the preschool market, especially with demand expected to remain strong for toys bearing the Barney license. Margins should be well maintained as the company focuses on higher margined products and expense control. Long-term propects should be aided by FPP's strong brand name.

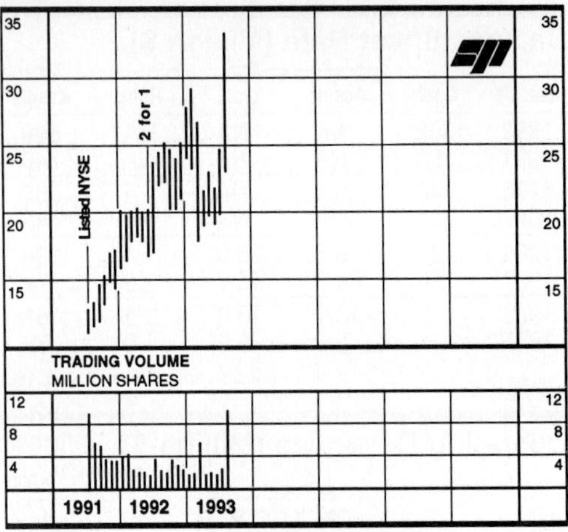

[1]Revenues (Million $)

Quarter:	1993	1992	1991	1990
Mar.	127.4	146.8	122.5	134.9
Jun.	157.4	153.4	144.3	136.2
Sep.	---	186.1	188.0	153.2
Dec.	---	207.6	185.0	183.2
	---	693.9	---	---

Revenues for the six months ended July 4, 1993, declined 5.1%, year to year, reflecting a 6.6% decrease in domestic sales that outweighed a slight increase in international sales. However, before the impact foreign currency translation international sales increased 8.0%. Margins narrowed on the lower volume, and pretax income declined 58%. After taxes at 38.1%, versus 40.6%, net income declined 57%, to $0.17 a share, based on 5.0% fewer shares, from $0.39.

[1]Common Share Earnings ($)

Quarter:	1993	1992	1991	1990
Mar.	d0.03	0.11	---	---
Jun.	0.20	0.28	---	---
Sep.	E0.60	0.45	0.27	---
Dec.	E0.73	0.47	0.13	---
	E1.50	1.30	[2]0.40	---

Important Developments

Aug. '93— FPP and Mattel announced that they had entered into a definitive merger agreement under which each share of Fisher-Price will be exchanged on a tax-free basis for 1.275 shares of NYSE-listed Mattel Inc. common stock (recent price $27⅛). Shareholder and government approval are still required to complete the transaction.

Next earnings report expected in late October.

Per Share Data ($)

Yr. End Dec. 31[3]	1992	1991	[4]1990
Tangible Bk. Val.	**6.30**	5.28	[5]5.25
Cash Flow	**2.02**	NA	d0.24
Earnings	**1.30**	NA	d1.35
Dividends	**0.10**	NA	NA
Payout Ratio	**7%**	NA	NA
Prices[6]—High	**25¼**	17¼	NA
Low	**15⅞**	11	NA
P/E Ratio—	**19–12**	NA	NA

Data as orig. reptd., prior to 1991 data as reptd. in Information Statement dated Jun. 28, 1991. Adj. for stk. div. of 100% Jun. 1992. **1.** Reflects 1991 fiscal yr.-end change to Dec. 31 from Jun. 30. **2.** Six mos. **3.** Yrs. ended Jun. 30 prior to 1992. **4.** Pro forma. **5.** As of Mar. 31, 1991. **6.** Cal. yr. d-Deficit. E-Estimated. NA-Not Available.

Income Data (Million $)

Year Ended Dec. 31[1]	Revs.	Oper. Inc.	% Oper. Inc. of Revs.	Cap. Exp.	Depr.	Int. Exp.	Net Bef. Taxes	Eff. Tax Rate	Net Inc.	% Net Inc. of Revs.	Cash Flow
1992	**694**	**109**	**15.7**	**24.8**	**24.2**	**13.7**	**67.6**	**38.9%**	**41.3**	**6.0**	**65.5**
1991	601	d15	NM	18.1	27.6	9.6	d44.5	NM	d33.6	NM	d6.0
[2]1990	703	9	1.3	NA	34.0	[3]17.9	d62.8	NM	d41.2	NM	d7.2
1989	845	115	13.6	48.6	20.1	[3]10.0	86.7	39.7%	52.3	6.2	72.4
1988	822	121	14.7	37.5	16.3	[3]9.1	96.7	40.2%	57.8	7.0	74.1
1987	597	NA	NA	18.1	15.9	NA	59.7	50.3%	29.7	5.0	45.6
1986	485	NA	NA	17.2	13.1	NA	43.5	46.9%	23.1	4.8	36.2

Balance Sheet Data (Million $)

Dec. 31[1]	Cash	Curr. Assets	Curr. Liab.	Curr. Ratio	Total Assets	% Ret. on Assets	Long Term Debt	Common Equity	Total Cap.	% LT Debt of Cap.	% Ret. on Equity
1992	**32.6**	**301**	**116**	**2.6**	**455**	**9.1**	**98.5**	**232**	**339**	**29.0**	**19.0**
1991	8.7	287	143	2.0	455	NA	98.2	202	312	31.5	NA
[4]1990	31.7	250	105	2.4	421	NA	98.9	202	317	31.2	NA
1989	Nil	412	86	4.8	570	9.3	Nil	465	484	Nil	11.4
1988	8.3	427	84	5.1	556	11.6	Nil	454	472	Nil	NA

Data as orig. reptd.; prior to 1991 data as reptd. in Information Statement dated Jun. 28, 1991. **1.** Yrs. ended Jun. 30 prior to 1992. **2.** Pro forma. **3.** Net of int. inc. **4.** As of Mar. 31, 1991, pro forma. d-Deficit. NM-Not Meaningful. NA-Not Available.

Business Summary

Fisher-Price is one of the world's largest marketers of pre-school and infant toys and juvenile products. The company believes that its strong brand name gives it an advantage over most other toy companies that have a different brand name for each of their products or product lines. Sales contributions by major product categories in 1992 and for the six months ended December 29, 1991:

	1992	1991
Toys	82%	81%
Juvenile products	18%	19%

The Preschool lines includes basics (Bubble Mower, Dino-roarrrrrs, Laundry Center, Flip Track Rail & Road Set, Fun Hydrant Sprinkler, Medical Kit), action tools (Action Workshop, Action Tool Box), playsets (Little People), sports and activites (Basketball, 1-2-3 Roller Shakes), Fun With Food, Kiddicraft and Puffalump Kids. Important preschool lines targeted for increasing market share, include Kidtronics (Tape Recorder), Ride-Ons (Tough Trikes) and Super Toys (Lift & Lock Swing, Picnic Table).

Infant toys and juvenile products remain high priority segments targeted for aggressive product and program development. Infant toys include the Activity Center, Activity Links Gym, Activity Walker, Little Red Ride-On, Pick Up'n Go Dump Truck, Rocking Pony and Baby Basketball. Juvenile products include the Nursery Monitor, 3-in-1 Travel Tender, Car Seats, High Chairs, other Infant Accessories and Nursey Toys. The company also sells a line of youth beds and under-bed storage units, which it acquired from the newborne Company, Inc. in August, 1992.

Additional revenue is generated through various licencing agreements under which Fisher-Price licenses its trademarks for apparel, shoes, books and children's toiletries.

Approximately 65% of Fisher-Price's products are manufactured at production facilities owned or leased by Fisher-Price. Other products are manufactured by subcontract manufacturers, primarily in the Far East.

In fiscal 1992 foreign operations represented 27% of total sales and accounted for 18% of pretax income.

Dividend Data

Common dividends were initiated in July, 1992. A "poison pill" stock purchase right was adopted in 1991.

Amt of Divd. $	Date Decl.	Ex–divd. Date	Stock of Record	Payment Date
0.05	Oct. 26	Nov. 6	Nov. 13	Dec. 3'92
0.05	Feb. 4	Feb. 8	Feb. 15	Mar. 3'93
0.05	Apr. 28	May 10	May 14	Jun. 3'93
0.05	Jul. 30	Aug. 9	Aug. 13	Sep. 3'93

Finances

The company has a three-year revolving credit facility for up to a maximum $175 million limited to a percentage of eligible receivables and inventory and an annual pay down. Additional foreign lines of credit allow maximum borrowings of approximately $90 million. A total of $23.7 million was borrowed under these credit agreements at April 4, 1993.

On July 22, 1991, Quaker Oats distributed 30,474,330 shares of Fisher-Price to its shareholders (data adjusted for 2-for-1 split in June 1992).

Capitalization

Long Term Debt: $98,600,000 (7/4/93).

Common Stock: 30,646,546 shs. ($0.01 par).
Instititions hold approximately 53%.
Shareholders of record: 33,758.

Office—636 Girard Ave., East Aurora, NY 14052 **Tel**—(716) 687-3000. **Chrmn & Pres**—R. J. Jackson. **SVP-CFO**—W. Bingham. **SVP-Secy**—B. J. Oravec. **Investor Contact**—Carol Blackley. **Dirs**—R. J. Jackson, E. R. Kinney, M. E. Moore, J. H. Mullin III, W. F. Pounds, D. E. Virnich. **Transfer Agent & Registrar**—The First National Bank of Boston, Boston, Mass. **Incorporated** in Delaware in 1990. **Empl**—5,642.

 Paul H. Valentine, CFA

FlightSafety Int'l

NYSE Symbol FSI Options on Phila (Feb-May-Aug-Nov) In S&P MidCap 400

Price	Range	P-E Ratio	Dividend	Yield	S&P Ranking	Beta
Aug. 23'93	1993					
36	44–34	15	0.36	1.0%	A	1.22

Summary

FlightSafety provides high technology pilot training programs to industrial corporations, U.S. and foreign commercial airlines, and military and other government agencies. FSI also provides training for ship and steam generating plant personnel, and manufactures sophisticated training equipment. FSI's long-term operating prospects are excellent, but soft demand for initial pilot training is crimping near-term revenue and earnings growth.

Current Outlook

Earnings for 1993 are projected at $2.20 a share, down from the $2.39 reported for 1992, which included a $0.22 nonrecurring gain. About $2.40 is expected for 1994.

No increase is likely in the $0.09 quarterly dividend in 1993.

The improvement in revenues in 1993 will reflect gains in equipment sales as a result of an acquisition. Training, FSI's largest business, is being restricted by the slump plaguing commercial airlines and aircraft manufacturers. The problems facing the major airlines will also limit FSI's profitability, as will increased spending on expansion projects, and higher depreciation and amortization charges. A slowly expanding economy in 1994 should have a positive impact on both revenues and profitability.

Revenues (Million $)

Quarter:	1993	1992	1991	[1]1990
Mar.	73.8	69.9	63.7	64.7
Jun.	78.7	70.9	68.1	70.6
Sep.		69.2	64.3	72.4
Dec.		68.5	71.5	75.7
		278.4	267.6	283.4

Revenues in the six months ended June 30, 1993, rose 8.2%, year to year, despite a 1.0% decline in training revenues. After costs and expenses, including higher noncash charges, pretax earnings declined 8.1%. Following taxes at 35.2%, against 35.8%, net income fell 7.3%. Share earnings were $1.06, down 5.4%, on fewer shares, from $1.12.

Common Share Earnings ($)

Quarter:	1993	1992	1991	1990
Mar.	0.50	0.54	0.52	0.46
Jun.	0.56	0.58	0.53	0.60
Sep.	E0.53	0.75	0.48	0.55
Dec.	E0.61	0.52	0.58	0.61
	E2.20	2.39	2.11	2.22

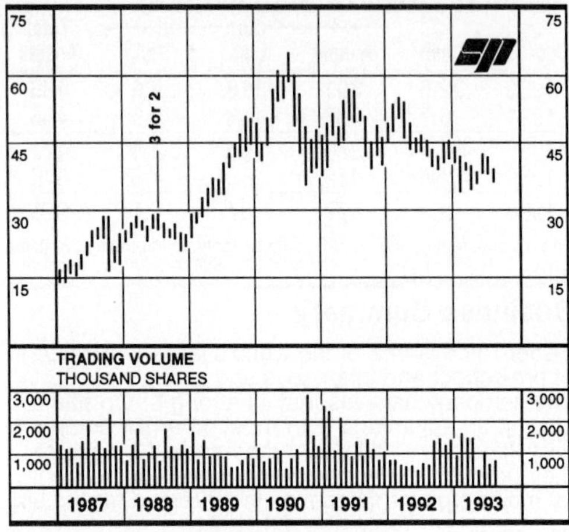

Important Developments

Aug. '93— In commenting on first-half operating results, FSI said that training revenues, which declined 1.0%, year to year, continue to be affected by a decrease in new aircraft deliveries and reduced demand for primary flight training. The 68% advance in equipment sales was largely due to the acquisition of VITAL. The decrease in net income was due to a 13% rise in depreciation and amortization charges.

Feb. '93— Directors authorized a 3 million share buyback program.

Feb. '93— The company acquired the Visual Simulation Systems (VITAL) business unit of McDonnell Douglas Corp. for an undisclosed amount. VITAL systems are incorporated in a wide range of advanced flight simulators, including those produced at FSI's Tulsa facilities.

Next earnings report expected in mid-October.

Per Share Data ($)

Yr. End Dec. 31	1992	1991	1990	1989	1988	1987	1986	1985	1984	1983
Tangible Bk. Val.[2]	**16.38**	14.27	12.36	9.88	8.09	6.77	5.68	4.90	4.06	3.35
Cash Flow	**3.53**	3.13	3.12	2.66	2.14	1.70	1.45	1.44	1.23	1.01
Earnings[3]	**2.39**	2.11	2.22	1.93	1.48	1.25	0.88	0.93	0.81	0.67
Dividends	**0.230**	0.250	0.210	0.170	0.146	0.134	0.114	0.103	0.089	0.075
Payout Ratio	**13%**	12%	9%	9%	10%	11%	13%	11%	11%	11%
Prices—High	**55¼**	57	65¼	51	29¼	28⅞	20⅛	19⅞	15½	17½
Low	**39**	37¾	35½	24⅛	21	14⅛	13⅛	13⅜	8¾	9⅞
P/E Ratio—	**23–16**	27–18	29–16	26–13	20–14	23–11	23–15	21–14	19–11	26–14

Data as orig. reptd. Adj. for stk. divs. of 50% Aug. 1988, 50% May 1985. **1.** Incl. int. & oth. inc. **2.** Includes intangibles. **3.** Bef. spec. item of +0.26 in 1990. E-Estimated.

Income Data (Million $)

Year Ended Dec. 31	Revs.	Oper. Inc.	% Oper. Inc. of Revs.	Cap. Exp.	Depr.	Int. Exp.	²Net Bef. Taxes	Eff. Tax Rate	³Net Inc.	% Net Inc. of Revs.	Cash Flow
1992	**278**	**145**	**52.2**	**68.3**	**39.1**	**5.23**	**13**	**35.7%**	**82.3**	**29.6**	**121**
1991	268	135	50.5	49.5	35.0	5.06	111	34.5%	72.4	27.1	107
1990	273	147	54.0	78.9	30.9	4.80	120	36.8%	75.7	27.7	105
1989	222	122	54.9	68.4	24.9	4.04	104	36.7%	65.6	29.5	91
1988	175	96	54.5	38.7	22.4	3.89	78	36.2%	50.0	28.5	72
1987	130	78	59.9	71.4	¹15.5	2.79	68	38.5%	¹41.8	32.2	57
1986	101	59	58.0	87.7	19.0	1.87	46	36.4%	29.5	29.1	49
1985	104	63	60.9	33.7	17.2	2.19	51	39.0%	30.9	29.7	48
1984	94	57	60.5	42.6	14.0	2.21	46	41.5%	26.8	28.5	41
1983	75	46	61.1	24.2	11.2	2.13	38	41.5%	22.4	27.7	34

Balance Sheet Data (Million $)

Dec. 31	Cash	Curr. Assets	Curr. Liab.	Curr. Ratio	Total Assets	% Ret. on Assets	Long Term Debt	Common Equity	Total Cap.	% LT Debt of Cap.	% Ret. on Equity
1992	**279**	**338**	**107**	**3.2**	**814**	**10.9**	**44.6**	**564**	**701**	**6.4**	**15.6**
1991	205	260	75	3.4	691	11.0	29.7	490	609	4.9	15.8
1990	159	204	78	2.6	621	13.2	35.1	423	537	6.5	19.9
1989	108	146	60	2.4	525	13.4	33.8	337	457	7.4	21.4
1988	72	123	50	2.5	451	11.8	38.8	274	394	9.9	19.9
1987	79	98	42	2.3	391	11.6	39.9	228	340	11.7	19.9
1986	75	89	42	2.1	328	9.7	34.5	191	280	12.3	16.6
1985	89	105	38	2.8	282	12.0	27.1	164	239	11.4	20.7
1984	62	79	33	2.4	234	12.8	29.4	135	196	15.0	21.7
1983	40	57	27	2.1	185	13.2	25.6	111	158	16.2	22.0

Data as orig. reptd. **1.** Reflects accounting change. **2.** Incl. equity in earns. of nonconsol. subs. **3.** Bef. spec. items.

Business Summary

FlightSafety International provides high technology training programs for private, commercial and government aircraft pilots. It also provides training for operators of large ocean-going vessels and for industrial steam generating plant personnel, and manufactures training equipment. FSI operates 38 aviation, marine and power learning centers with over 150 simulators in the U.S., Canada and Europe. FSI began to provide training services and base support to the U.S. military through an August 1988 acquisition, and is an active bidder for government defense training programs.

The most important aspect of the training program is the use of simulators, which reproduce sights, sounds, control responses, and generally the total environment experienced by operators of a particular aircraft. As the authorized training organization for 23 aircraft makers, FSI trains over 37,000 pilots and maintenance technicians a year.

The MarineSafety International subsidiary trains crews of ocean-going vessels in ship, cargo handling and engine room procedures. Customers include the U.S. Navy and Coast Guard.

PowerSafety International, jointly owned with Babcock & Wilcox, trains operator and maintenance personnel of power and industrial steam generating plants. FSI makes training devices and products (including flight simulators) and develops audiovisual programs and training manuals.

Training revenues amounted to 86% of operating revenues in each of the three years through 1992, while sales of manufactured products by the Simulation division to unaffiliated customers were 14% of operating revenues in each of those years.

Dividend Data

Dividends have been paid since 1976.

Amt. of Divd. $	Date Decl.	Ex–divd. Date	Stock of Record	Payment Date
0.09	Sep. 17	Oct. 16	Oct. 22	Nov. 12'92
0.09	Dec. 3	Jan. 8	Jan. 14	Feb. 3'93
0.09	Mar. 9	Apr. 8	Apr. 15	May 4'93
0.09	Jun. 8	Jun. 9	Jul. 15	Aug. 5'93

Finances

Capital expenditures for 1993 were budgeted at $50 million, compared with $68.3 million spent in 1992. In September 1992, directors authorized a $150 million expansion program including the establishment of a training facility in Asia.

Capitalization

Long Term Debt: $42,028,000 (6/93).

Common Stock: 33,238,229 shs. ($0.10 par).
Institutions hold about 49%; A. L. Ueltschi owns 28.7%.
Shareholders of record: 12,500 (1/93).

Office—Marine Air Terminal, La Guardia Airport, Flushing, NY 11371. **Tel**—(718) 565-4100. **Chrmn & Pres**—A. L. Ueltschi. **Secy**—P. P. Mullen. **VP-Treas**—K. W. Motschwiller. **Investor Contact**—B. McDonald. **Dirs**—G. B. Beitzel, E. E. Hood Jr., C. R. Longsworth, J. A. Morgan, A. L. Ueltschi, B. N. Whitman. **Transfer Agent & Registrar**—American Stock Transfer and Trust Co., NYC. **Incorporated** in New York in 1951. **Empl**—2,150.

 William H. Donald

Florida Progress

NYSE Symbol FPC In S&P MidCap 400

Price	Range	P-E Ratio	Dividend	Yield	S&P Ranking	Beta
Sep. 29'93	1993					
35¾	36⅜–31¼	17	1.94	5.4%	A–	0.44

Summary

Florida Progress is the holding company for Florida Power, which provides electric utility services to a growing territory in central and Gulf Coast Florida. Other units are involved in coal mining, leveraged leasing, commercial finance and life insurance. The company's experience diversifying into nonutility businesses has been disappointing and it recently made strategic changes to focus these operations. Modestly higher earnings are expected for 1993, reflecting a significant retail electric rate increase.

Current Outlook

Earnings for 1993 are projected at $2.30 a share, up from $2.06 in 1992. Earnings for 1994 are estimated at $2.35 a share.

The minimum expectation is for dividends to continue at $0.48½ quarterly.

The higher earnings anticipated for 1993 primarily reflect a 9% rate increase (approximately $86 million) to cover the construction of several peaking units, certain post-retirement benefits, and general inflation. FPC last filed an official rate case in 1984. The contribution of the nonutility segment should decline owing to the divestiture of several units and a large balance of problem loans with airline and real estate concerns. Long-term prospects should benefit from a rapidly expanding service territory and customer growth.

Operating Revenues (Million $)

Quarter:	1994	1993	1992	1991
Mar.	---	493	464	457
Jun.	---	553	512	528
Sep.	---	---	627	589
Dec.	---	---	494	501
	---	---	2,095	2,075

Operating revenues for the six months ended June 30, 1993, advanced 7.3%, year to year. Profitability benefited from retail rate increases and customer growth. Net income rose 18%. Share earnings were $0.87 on 4.0% more shares, versus $0.77 (adjusted). Results in 1993 exclude an accounting credit of $0.01 a share.

Common Share Earnings ($)

Quarter:	1994	1993	1992	1991
Mar.	E0.40	0.38	0.36	0.43
Jun.	E0.50	0.49	0.41	0.54
Sep.	E1.00	E0.98	0.86	0.87
Dec.	E0.45	E0.45	0.41	0.32
	E2.35	E2.30	2.06	2.16

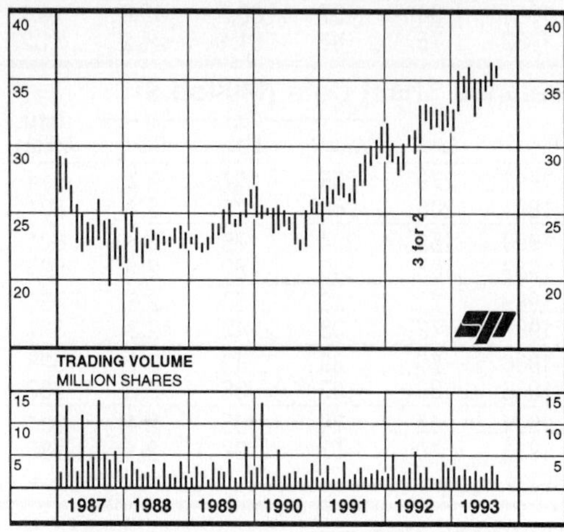

Important Developments

Sep. '93— FPC's Florida Power Corp. unit said its power plant division will reduce its workforce by 20% and close two electric generating plants. Other actions geared toward improving efficiency and competitiveness are anticipated shortly.

Apr. '93— A base rate increase of $10 million in additional annual revenues, the second in a series of three, became effective on April 1, 1993. The Florida Public Service Commission (FPSC) approved a 9% base rate increase of about $86 million for Florida Power Corp. (FP), the principal subsidiary of FPC, in September 1992. The commission granted increases in base rates of approximately $58 million effective November 1992, $10 million in April 1993, and $18 milllion in November 1993. In April 1992, the FPSC allowed FP to begin collecting an interim increase of $31.2 million, subject to refund pending final approval.

Next earnings report expected in mid-October.

Per Share Data ($)

Yr. End Dec. 31	1992	1991	1990	1989	1988	1987	1986	1985	1984	1983
Tangible Bk. Val.	**19.83**	19.15	18.37	17.92	17.20	16.51	[1]15.51	[1]14.42	13.35	13.07
Earnings[2]	**2.06**	2.16	2.33	2.45	2.35	2.49	2.47	2.35	1.81	1.76
Dividends	**1.905**	1.843	1.777	1.720	1.667	1.613	1.540	1.460	1.380	1.300
Payout Ratio	**92%**	88%	77%	70%	71%	65%	63%	64%	79%	78%
Prices—High	**33¼**	31½	27	26$^{13}/_{16}$	25$^{3}/_{16}$	29¼	31$^{5}/_{16}$	20$^{11}/_{16}$	16$^{3}/_{16}$	15
Low	**27⅞**	24$^{7}/_{16}$	22$^{5}/_{16}$	22$^{3}/_{16}$	21$^{5}/_{16}$	19$^{9}/_{16}$	20$^{3}/_{16}$	15½	12$^{7}/_{16}$	12
P/E Ratio—	**16–14**	15–11	12–10	11–9	11–9	12–8	13–8	9–7	9–7	9–7

Data as orig. reptd. Adj. for stk. div. of 50% Jul. 1992. **1.** Incl. intangibles. **2.** Bef. results of disc. opers. of -0.03 in 1992, -0.03 in 1991, -0.19 in 1990. E-Estimated.

Income Data (Million $)

Year Ended Dec. 31	[1]Revs.	Depr.	Maint.	Oper. Ratio	[2]Fxd. Chgs. Cover.	Constr. Credits	Eff. Tax Rate	[3]Net Inc.	% Return On Revs.	% Return On [4]Invest. Capital	% Return On [5]Com. Equity
1992	**1,774**	**210**	**140**	**NA**	**3.00**	**18.7**	**31.5%**	**176**	**9.9**	**6.8**	**10.6**
1991	1,719	206	135	NA	2.74	9.4	32.9%	175	10.2	7.9	11.6
1990	1,709	161	126	NA	2.80	4.2	35.7%	180	10.5	8.8	12.9
1989	1,627	155	138	NA	2.93	5.2	30.3%	187	11.5	9.1	13.9
1988	1,469	137	118	NA	2.87	4.1	24.4%	180	12.2	8.8	13.9
1987	1,472	134	113	NA	3.32	4.3	37.2%	188	12.8	9.3	15.5
1986	1,875	137	108	83.6%	3.59	5.8	43.4%	204	10.9	9.8	16.4
1985	1,653	136	100	81.7%	3.18	7.1	43.5%	186	11.3	9.9	16.8
1984	1,350	112	107	83.9%	2.94	37.6	40.7%	141	10.4	7.7	13.6
1983	1,338	102	89	83.7%	---	29.8	38.8%	129	9.7	8.3	13.5

Balance Sheet Data (Million $)

Dec. 31	[6]Gross Prop.	[6]Capital Expend.	Net Prop.	% Earn. on Net Prop.	Total Cap.	Capitalization LT Debt	% LT Debt	Pfd.	% Pfd.	Com.	% Com.
1992	**5,252**	**494**	**3,442**	**NA**	**4,556**	**1,656**	**45.9**	**216**	**6.0**	**1,738**	**48.1**
1991	4,851	360	3,193	NA	4,367	1,581	46.5	231	6.8	1,588	46.7
1990	4,581	277	3,077	NA	3,955	1,326	44.5	234	7.8	1,424	47.7
1989	4,382	261	2,998	NA	3,690	1,127	41.2	234	8.6	1,372	50.2
1988	4,183	207	2,930	NA	3,538	1,050	40.4	234	9.0	1,317	50.6
1987	4,049	199	2,907	NA	3,485	1,117	42.7	234	8.9	1,265	48.4
1986	3,900	195	2,871	10.8	3,264	1,168	45.7	234	9.1	1,156	45.2
1985	3,751	201	2,836	10.8	3,094	1,151	47.4	265	10.9	1,014	41.7
1984	3,583	285	2,785	8.0	3,005	1,252	52.1	268	11.2	884	36.7
1983	3,342	286	2,642	8.6	2,883	1,208	52.5	274	11.9	818	35.6

Data as orig. reptd. **1.** Utility revs. aft. 1986. **2.** Times int. exp. & pfd. divs. covered (pretax basis). **3.** Bef. results of disc. opers. **4.** Based on income before interest charges. **5.** As rept. by co. prior to 1987. **6.** Utility plant aft. 1986. NA-Not Available.

Business Summary

This holding company owns Florida Power Corp., which provides electric service to over 1.2 million customers located in 32 of Florida's 67 counties. In 1992, Florida Power accounted for 75% of total revenues and 91% of earnings. Nonutility businesses include coal mining, leveraged leasing, commercial finance, life insurance, real estate, and technology. Electric revenues were divided in recent years:

	1992	1991	1990	1989
Residential	53%	53%	53%	51%
Commercial	24%	24%	24%	23%
Industrial	8%	8%	9%	9%
Other	15%	15%	14%	17%

The fuel mix in 1992 was 47% coal, 24% oil, 16% nuclear, 13% purchased power. Peak load in 1992 (winter) was 6,982 mw, and system capability (including purchased power sources) was 7,002 mw, for a capacity margin of 0.3%. Retail electric kwh sales have increased an average of 5.3% during the past ten-year period. Of eight new peaking units planned, totaling 728 mw, four were completed in 1992 with the rest due in 1993.

Crystal River Unit 5, a 717 mw coal-fired plant, began commercial operation in 1984 and completed, along with Crystal River Unit 4, FPC's major base load construction program through the mid-1990s.

Finances

In July 1993, FPC sold $110 million of the $200 million of bonds registered in May. Proceeds were be used to retire higher coupon bonds.

In June 1993, FPC's Progress Rail Services unit acquired Steel Processing Services, Inc., which had sales in excess of $100 million in 1992.

Dividend Data

Dividends have been paid since 1937. A dividend reinvestment plan is available. A "poison pill" stock purchase rights plan was adopted in 1991.

Amt of Divd. $	Date Decl.	Ex-divd. Date	Stock of Record	Payment Date
0.48½	Nov. 19	Nov. 30	Dec. 4	Dec. 20'92
0.48½	Feb. 4	Mar. 1	Mar. 5	Mar. 20'93
0.48½	May 20	May 28	Jun. 4	Jun. 20'93
0.48½	Aug. 19	Aug. 31	Sep. 6	Sep. 20'93

Capitalization

Long Term Debt: $1,885,900,000 (6/93).

Subsid. Cum. Pfd. Stk.: $183,500,000.

Common Stock: 88,419,972 shs. (no par).
Institutions hold about 33%.
Shareholders of record: 44,870.

Office—Barnett Tower, One Progress Plaza, St. Petersburg, FL 33701 (Mail: Box 33028, St. Petersburg, FL 33733). **Tel**—(813) 824-6400. **Chrmn & CEO**—J. R. Critchfield. **Pres**—R. Korpan **SVP & CFO**—D. R. Kuzma. **Secy**—S. D. Purifoy. **Investor Contact**—Richard R. Champion. (813) 824-6428. **Dirs**—J. B. Critchfield, M. P. Graney, A. J. Keesler Jr., R. Korpan, C. V. McKee, V. J. Naimoli, R. A. Nunis, C. B. Reed, J. D. Ruffier, R. T. Stuart Jr., J. G. Wittner. **Transfer Agent & Registrar**—Chemical Bank, NYC. **Incorporated** in Florida in 1899; reincorporated in Florida in 1982. **Empl**—7,301.

 Ned Bancroft

Flowers Industries

NYSE Symbol FLO Options on Phila (Feb-May-Aug-Nov) In S&P MidCap 400

Price	Range	P-E Ratio	Dividend	Yield	S&P Ranking	Beta
Oct. 1'93	1993					
18⅝	20½–16⅜	17	0.76	4.1%	A–	0.85

Summary

This company is a major producer of baked goods, snack products and convenience foods to grocery, food service, restaurant and fast food customers primarily in the Southeast, Central and Western U.S. Near term profitability may be restrained by increased flour costs, but higher profits in fiscal 1994 are expected, led by an improving product mix and further manufacturing efficiency gains.

Current Outlook

Earnings for the fiscal year ending June 30, 1994, are projected to rise to $1.15 a share from fiscal 1993's $1.07.

The dividend is typically raised quarterly. The latest increase was 1.3%, to $0.19 quarterly from $0.18¾, with the August 1993 declaration.

Sales are likely to remain in a firm uptrend in fiscal 1994, led by broad-based volume growth and modestly higher selling prices. Higher raw material costs, most notably flour, may restrain near term profitability, but full year profits should trend higher, however, led by an improving product mix, further production and distribution efficiencies, and cost control.

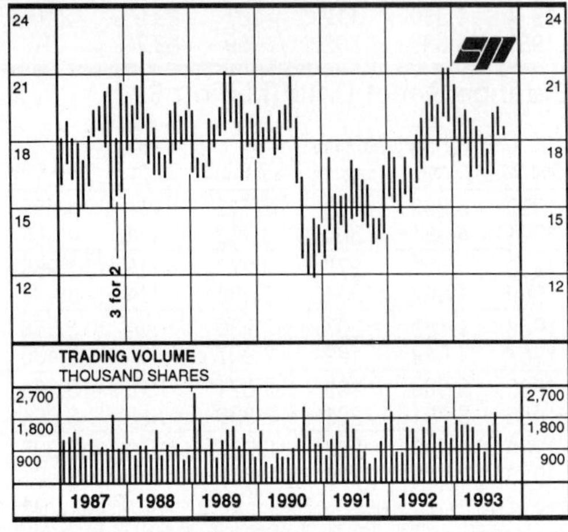

Sales (Million $)

Weeks:	1993–94	1992–93	1991–92	1990–91
12 Wks. Sep. ...	---	210.7	192.3	188.9
12 Wks. Dec.	---	220.0	205.3	195.0
12 Wks. Mar.	---	211.3	201.8	187.1
16 Wks. Jun......	---	[1]320.2	279.8	253.8
	---	962.1	879.2	824.8

Sales for the fiscal year ended July 3, 1993, rose 9.4% from those of the prior year, primarily reflecting increased volume of 7%. Margins narrowed, but following substantially greater other income and a 51% reduction in interest expense, pretax profits advanced 22%. After taxes at 34.8%, versus 35.7%, net income was up 24%, to $1.07 a share (on 6.3% more shares), from $0.92.

Common Share Earnings ($)

Weeks:	1993–94	1992–93	1991–92	1990–91
12 Wks. Sep.	E0.18	0.18	0.11	0.13
12 Wks. Dec.	E0.22	0.20	0.16	0.14
12 Wks. Mar.	E0.25	0.21	0.20	0.13
16 Wks. Jun......	E0.50	[1]0.47	0.44	0.31
	E1.15	1.07	0.92	0.71

Important Developments

Aug. '93— Management attributed the company's growth in sales and profits during fiscal 1993 to strong performances by all three of the company's operating groups, despite "substantial" increases in raw material costs during the second half. FLO noted that volume for the year increased almost 7%, owing to better penetration of the company's existing markets and a broadened product line that is extending its markets geographically as well as by market segment. Management said it expected the improving performance to continue through fiscal 1994 in spite of the "temporary increase in flour costs" due to the recent flooding in the Midwest. Separately, management said that the company's improved balance sheet will allow it to take advantage of acquisition opportunities as they appear.

Next earnings report expected in mid-October.

Per Share Data ($)

Yr. End Jun. 30	1993	1992	1991	1990	1989	1988	[2]1987	[2]1986	1985	[2]1984
Tangible Bk. Val.	**[3]7.43**	[3]6.36	[3]6.14	[3]6.27	5.82	5.60	4.95	4.50	3.97	3.49
Cash Flow	**1.98**	1.88	1.62	1.59	1.86	1.44	1.43	1.25	1.10	0.98
Earnings[4]	**1.07**	0.92	0.71	0.98	0.85	1.18	0.79	0.84	0.73	0.63
Dividends	**0.735**	0.695	0.655	0.590	0.510	0.430	0.368	0.314	0.260	0.218
Payout Ratio	**69%**	76%	92%	60%	59%	36%	46%	37%	35%	35%
Prices[5]—High	**20½**	21¼	17¼	20⅞	21⅛	22	20⅝	19⅜	15¾	11¾
Low	**16⅜**	14¾	12¾	11⅞	16¼	16⅜	14⅝	13⅜	10⅞	7¾
P/E Ratio—	**19–15**	23–16	24–18	21–12	25–19	19–14	26–19	23–16	21–15	19–12

Data as orig. reptd. Adj. for stk. div(s). of 50% Nov. 1987, 50% Oct. 1984. **1.** 17 weeks. **2.** Reflects merger or acquisition. **3.** Includes intangibles. **4.** Bef. spec. item(s) of -0.14 in 1990, +0.05 in 1988. **5.** Cal. yr. E-Estimated NA-Not Available.

Income Data (Million $)

Year Ended Jun. 30	Revs.	Oper. Inc.	% Oper. Inc. of Revs.	Cap. Exp.	Depr.	Int. Exp.	Net Bef. Taxes	Eff. Tax Rate	[2]Net Inc.	% Net Inc. of Revs.	Cash Flow
1993	**962**	**87.2**	**9.1**	**52**	**33.1**	**4.0**	**60.0**	**34.8%**	**39.2**	**4.1**	**72.3**
1992	879	81.3	9.3	33	32.8	8.2	49.2	35.7%	31.7	3.6	65.1
1991	825	73.9	9.0	63	31.0	9.4	39.8	39.6%	24.0	2.9	55.1
1990	835	87.5	10.5	103	31.5	8.5	55.9	38.8%	34.3	4.1	55.3
1989	783	75.8	9.7	103	25.7	9.3	47.5	37.8%	29.6	3.8	65.6
1988	738	83.6	11.3	64	24.1	9.6	62.0	33.1%	41.5	5.6	50.6
[1]1987	797	75.8	9.5	100	23.0	10.5	48.2	42.7%	[3]27.6	3.5	50.1
[1]1986	698	76.8	11.0	97	20.6	10.1	53.7	45.0%	29.5	4.2	43.8
1985	626	70.6	11.3	60	18.2	7.0	47.8	46.3%	25.6	4.1	38.9
[1]1984	603	58.7	9.7	67	16.8	5.2	40.2	44.9%	22.1	3.7	34.0

Balance Sheet Data (Million $)

Jun. 30	Cash	Curr. Assets	Curr. Liab.	Curr. Ratio	Total Assets	% Ret. on Assets	Long Term Debt	Common Equity	Total Cap.	% LT Debt of Cap.	% Ret. on Equity
1993	**17.2**	**151**	**120**	**1.3**	**491**	**7.8**	**36**	**280**	**349**	**10.3**	**15.1**
1992	14.3	143	99	1.4	462	7.0	95	218	344	27.7	14.8
1991	11.0	124	87	1.4	435	5.6	92	206	330	28.0	11.5
1990	17.4	125	77	1.6	439	7.7	92	216	340	26.9	16.2
1989	26.0	137	88	1.5	448	6.7	102	208	340	29.9	14.5
1988	23.6	131	79	1.7	434	10.0	103	198	332	31.0	22.2
1987	21.5	115	77	1.5	399	7.1	108	178	308	35.0	16.3
1986	28.3	124	80	1.5	378	8.3	114	162	277	41.3	19.3
1985	24.7	104	73	1.4	337	8.6	108	143	264	40.8	18.9
1984	23.7	95	65	1.5	263	9.0	57	127	198	29.1	18.4

Data as orig. reptd. **1.** Reflects merger or acquisition. **2.** Bef. spec. item(s) in 1990, 1988. **3.** Reflects accounting change.

Business Summary

Flowers Industries produces and distributes baked foods, snack products and convenience foods to grocery, food service, restaurant and fast food markets in the Southeast, Central and Western U.S. It operates 34 production facilities. Products are distributed through 2,300 company-owned and independent distributor routes, and sold by distributors, salesmen and food brokers. FLO also operates a number of thrift outlets for the sale of surplus product. Sales to Winn-Dixie Stores, Inc. accounted for more than 10% of consolidated sales during fiscal 1993.

Baked foods include a variety of breads, rolls and buns under the company's own brand names (including Flowers, Nature's Own, Breads International, Cobblestone Mill, Rich Grain, Evangeline Maid, Buttermaid, Betsy Ross, Dandee, Purity, Ideal, Holsum) and franchised trademarks (Sunbeam, Bunny).

Snack foods operations include the manufacture of sweet goods, snack cakes, baked and fried pies, doughnuts and potato chips sold under the Beebo, BlueBird and other house brands.

Convenience products include frozen vegetables, batter-dipped and breaded vegetables, fruits, baked goods, pie shells and food ingredient products, sold primarily under the Stilwell brand name.

Dividend Data

Dividends have been paid quarterly since 1971. A dividend reinvestment plan is available. A "poison pill" stock purchase right was adopted in 1989.

Amt of Divd. $	Date Decl.	Ex–divd. Date	Stock of Record	Payment Date
0.18¼	Oct. 16	Oct. 26	Oct. 30	Nov. 13'92
0.18½	Jan. 15	Jan. 15	Jan. 22	Feb. 5'93
0.18¾	Apr. 2	Apr. 12	Apr. 16	Apr. 30'93
0.19	Aug. 6	Aug. 16	Aug. 20	Sep. 3'93

Finances

FLO noted that of the $47,241,000 8.25% convertible subordinated debentures called for redemption by FLO in August 1992, $46,772,000, or 99%, were converted into FLO's common stock at $16 each, or 62.5 million shares for each $1000 face amount of debentures. This conversion resulted in the issuance of 2,923,195 common shares.

Capitalization

Long Term Debt: $35,815,000 (7/3/93).

Common Stock: 37,837,428 shs. ($0.62½ par).
Institutions hold about 43%.
Shareholders of record: 4,811.

Office—U.S. Highway 19 (PO Box 1338), Thomasville, GA 31799. **Tel**—(912) 226-9110. **Chrmn & CEO**—A. R. McMullian. **Pres**—H. Varnedoe III. **Secy**—G. A. Campbell. **VP-CFO & Investor Contact**—C. Martin Wood III. **Dirs**—E. L. Baker, G. A. Campbell, R. P. Crozer, J. B. Ellis, L. S. Flowers, W. H. Flowers Jr., R. M. Fryar, J. L. Lanier Jr., A. R. McMullian, J. V. Shields, H. Varnedoe III, C. M. Wood III. **Transfer Agent & Registrar**—Wachovia Bank of North Carolina, N.A. **Incorporated** in Delaware in 1968; reincorporated in Georgia in 1987. **Empl**—8,400.

 Kenneth A. Shea

Forest Laboratories

ASE Symbol FRX Options on CBOE (Feb-May-Aug-Nov) In S&P MidCap 400

Price	Range	P-E Ratio	Dividend	Yield	S&P Ranking	Beta
Oct. 21'93	1993					
39⅞	43¼–27½	25	None	None	B+	1.28

Summary

This company develops, manufactures and sells both branded and generic forms of ethical drug products which are sold primarily in the U.S., western and eastern Europe, and Puerto Rico. Its leading product, Aerobid, is an inhaled steroid used in the treatment of asthma. U.S. marketing approval was recently received for Flumadine, a drug for the prevention and treatment of Influenza A. Marketing applications are pending for Monuril (an antibiotic for treatment of uncomplicated urinary tract infection) and Infasurf (for treatment of respiratory distress syndrome in premature infants)

Business Summary

Forest Laboratories and subsidiaries develop, make and sell pharmaceutical and related products, both prescription and over-the-counter. Its most important U.S. products consist of branded ethical drug specialties and a controlled release line of generic products.

The company actively promotes in the U.S. those branded products that it believes to have the most growth potential and that enable its salesforce to concentrate on specialty groups of physicians who are high prescribers of its products. Principal products include Aerobid, a metered dose inhaled steroid used to treat asthma (18% of 1992-3 sales); Tessalon, a non-narcotic cough suppresant (11%); and Aerochamber, a spacer device used to improve the delivery of aerosol-administered products, including Aerobid. Other products include the thyroid product Levothroid (acquired from Rhone-Poulenc Rorer in 1990), and the ESGIC and Lorcet lines of analgesics.

Forest's generic product line emphasizes its ability to produce difficult to formulate controlled release products, which are sold in the U.S. by its Inwood Laboratories Inc. unit. Primary products include Propranolol E.R. (14% of 1992-3 sales), a beta blocker used to treat hypertension; Indomethacin E.R., a non-steroidal anti-inflammatory drug useed to treat arthritis; and Theochron, a theophylline tablet used in the treatment of asthma.

The company's U.K. and Ireland subsidiaries sell both ethical products requiring a doctor's prescription and OTC preparations. Chief products include Sudocrem, a topical preparation for the treatment of diaper rash; Colomycin, an antibiotic used in the treatment of Cystic Fibrosis; and Suscard and Sustac, sustained action nitroglycerin tablets in both buccal and oral form used to treat angina pectoris. Sales in the U.K. and Ireland represented 10% of the 1992-3 total, and 6% of operating profits.

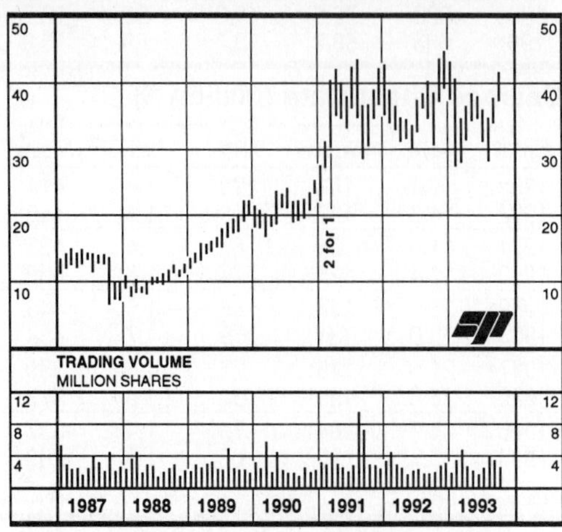

Products in development include Estradiol (in Phase III trials), a transdermally-administered product used for estrogen replacement therapy; Synapton (Phase I), a controlled release formulation of physostigmine that may be useful in treating Alzheimer's disease; and Micturin, a drug for incontinence. Monuril, a single dose antibiotic used to treat uncomplicated urinary tract infections, and Infasurf, a product used to treat respiratory distress syndrome in premature infants, are both awaiting FDA marketing approval, following completion of human clinical studies.

Important Developments

Sep.'93— Forest said it had received U.S. marketing approval for Flumadine (rimantadine HCL), a new antiviral drug for the prophylaxis and treatment of Influenza A. Shipments to wholesalers were expected to begin shortly.

Next earnings report expected in mid-January.

Per Share Data ($)

Yr. End Mar. 31	1993	1992	1991	1990	1989	1988	1987	1986	1985	1984
Tangible Bk. Val.	**7.80**	5.67	3.13	4.19	3.43	3.31	2.06	1.68	1.07	1.23
Cash Flow	**1.65**	1.36	1.08	0.87	0.74	0.59	0.46	0.27	0.21	0.17
Earnings[1,2]	**1.42**	1.13	0.90	0.72	0.60	0.48	0.39	0.25	0.19	0.14
Dividends	**Nil**	Nil	Nil	Nil	Nil	Nil	Nil	Nil	Nil	Nil
Payout Ratio	**Nil**	Nil	Nil	Nil	Nil	Nil	Nil	Nil	Nil	Nil
Calendar Years	**1992**	1991	1990	1989	1988	1987	1986	1985	1984	1983
Prices—High	**44⅞**	43⅝	25⅜	22¼	12¾	15	12⅜	8⅛	8	10¼
Low	**30**	22¼	16¾	12⅛	7⅞	6⅝	6⅞	3⅞	2¾	4½
P/E Ratio—	**32–21**	39–20	28–19	31–17	21–13	31–14	32–18	33–16	44–15	75–34

Data as orig. reptd. Adj. for stk. divs. of 100% Feb. 1991, 100% Apr. 1986. **1.** Bef. spec. item(s) of +0.03 in 1986. **2.** Ful. dil.: 1.41 in 1993, 0.87 in 1991, 0.72 in 1990, 0.59 in 1989.

Income Data (Million $)

Year Ended Mar. 31	Revs.	Oper. Inc.	% Oper. Inc. of Revs.	Cap. Exp.	Depr.	Int. Exp.	Net Bef. Taxes	Eff. Tax Rate	[3]Net Inc.	% Net Inc. of Revs.	Cash Flow
1993	**285**	**102.0**	**35.8**	**[2]6.26**	**10.5**	**1.96**	**101.0**	**36.1%**	**64.3**	**22.5**	**74.8**
1992	240	83.5	34.7	[2]3.64	10.3	3.71	77.5	36.0%	49.6	20.6	59.9
1991	176	55.5	31.5	[2]8.88	7.4	1.19	54.9	31.0%	37.9	21.5	45.3
[1]1990	143	43.3	30.3	[2]4.34	5.9	Nil	41.7	28.8%	29.7	20.8	35.6
1989	97	29.0	30.0	[2]3.85	5.0	Nil	28.8	25.0%	21.6	22.3	26.6
[1]1988	81	22.3	27.3	5.26	3.8	0.16	22.2	24.3%	16.8	20.6	20.6
1987	64	16.8	26.2	4.16	2.9	0.23	16.4	24.3%	12.4	19.2	14.6
[1]1986	40	7.4	18.6	3.07	1.5	0.40	8.2	17.8%	6.8	17.0	7.4
[1]1985	24	3.6	14.9	2.04	0.8	0.19	4.3	3.4%	4.2	17.4	4.7
1984	20	1.9	9.9	2.45	0.7	0.24	3.0	1.4%	2.9	15.0	3.6

Balance Sheet Data (Million $)

Mar. 31	Cash	Curr. Assets	Curr. Liab.	Curr. Ratio	Total Assets	% Ret. on Assets	Long Term Debt	Common Equity	Total Cap.	% LT Debt of Cap.	% Ret. on Equity
1993	**172**	**315**	**41.1**	**7.6**	**521**	**13.3**	**Nil**	**479**	**479**	**Nil**	**14.9**
1992	133	244	55.9	4.4	431	12.6	Nil	373	375	Nil	15.1
1991	60	138	42.0	3.3	331	13.3	23.1	264	289	8.0	15.5
1990	79	133	14.2	9.4	239	13.1	Nil	223	225	Nil	14.0
1989	45	92	8.8	10.3	194	11.7	Nil	185	186	Nil	12.4
1988	53	88	10.2	8.7	173	11.3	Nil	163	163	Nil	12.3
1987	31	58	11.9	4.9	113	11.4	1.1	98	101	1.0	13.0
1986	32	49	10.5	4.6	95	8.5	0.7	75	84	0.8	10.1
1985	18	32	7.0	4.5	49	10.1	1.2	32	42	2.9	12.7
1984	14	25	3.0	8.3	33	10.7	1.5	29	30	5.1	12.7

Data as orig. reptd. **1.** Refl. merger or acq. **2.** Net of curr. yr. retirement and disposals. **3.** Bef. spec. items.

Revenues (Million $)

Quarter:	1993–94	1992–93	1991–92	1990–91
Jun.	81.4	68.6	58.0	41.3
Sep.	85.7	72.7	60.4	42.4
Dec.		78.1	64.9	46.5
Mar.		77.0	65.1	54.0
		296.4	248.4	184.2

In the six months ended September 30, 1993, net revenues climbed 18%, year to year, reflecting increased demand for both principal promoted products and specialty controlled release generic products. Margins widened, and after taxes at 36.0% in each period, net income soared 25%, to $37,091,000 ($0.82 a share), from $29,766,000 ($0.66).

Common Share Earnings ($)

Quarter:	1993–94	1992–93	1991–92	1990–91
Jun.	0.39	0.31	0.25	0.20
Sep.	0.43	0.35	0.28	0.22
Dec.		0.37	0.29	0.23
Mar.		0.39	0.31	0.25
		1.42	1.13	0.90

Dividend Data

No cash dividends have been paid.

Finances

In July 1992, Forest acquired the worldwide rights to Flumadine for $20 million, comprised of $10 million in cash and $10 million payable on the date of the first commercial sale.

In December 1990, the company acquired U.S. rights to the products Armour Thyroid, Levothroid and Thyrolar from Rhone-Poulenc Rorer. The purchase price was $85 million, of which $40 million was paid upon acquisition, $22 million in November 1991, $15 million in December 1992 and $8 million in March 1993.

R&D spending rose to $22,054,000 in 1992-3, from $17,771,000 in 1991-2, reflecting the cost of conducting clinical studies in order to obtain regulatory approval of new products, and the cost of developing products using Forest's controlled release technology. During 1992-3, emphasis was placed on Synapton, fosfomycin trometamol (Monuril) and Infasurf. R&D spending is expected to continue to increase in the future.

Capitalization

Long Term Debt: None (6/93).

Common Stock: 43,114,898 shs. ($0.10 par).
Institutions own 74%.
Shareholders: 3,450 of record (6/93).

Options: To buy 5,585,186 shs. at $6.59 to $42.91 ea. (3/93).

Office—150 E. 58th Street, New York, NY 10155-0015. **Tel**—(212) 421-7850. **Pres & CEO**—H. Solomon. **VP-Fin & Investor Contact**—K. E. Goodman. **Secy**—W. J. Candee III. **Dirs**—W. J. Candee III, G. S. Cohan, D. L. Goldwasser, J. A. Melnick, J. M. Schor, H. Solomon. **Transfer Agent**—Chemical Bank, NYC. **Incorporated** in Delaware in 1956. **Empl**—1,171.

 Robert M. Gold

Franklin Resources

NYSE Symbol BEN Options on Pacific (Feb-May-Aug-Nov) In S&P MidCap 400

Price	Range	P-E Ratio	Dividend	Yield	S&P Ranking	Beta
Oct. 13'93	1993					
51⅝	51¾–32	27	0.28	0.5%	A–	1.74

Summary

Franklin Resources is the largest publicly traded independent mutual fund company in the world, with about $100 billion of assets under management. It owns Templeton, Galbraith & Hansberger Ltd., a leading global investment management firm which is being operated as a separate subsidiary. Favorable long-term prospects reflect the contributions of the Templeton organization, BEN's financial strength, and the company's wide margins.

Current Outlook

Earnings for the fiscal year ending September 30, 1994, are projected at $2.35 a share, up from the $2.00 expected for fiscal 1993.

The minimum expectation is for dividends to continue at $0.07 quarterly.

Profits for fiscal 1994 are expected to benefit from the Templeton acquisition. Templeton's performance record in combination with Franklin's marketing expertise should enhance fund sales to each organization's existing customer base. Fund sales should further benefit from the broadening of both companies' distribution networks and Franklin's stature as a larger, stronger enterprise. A more diversified asset base should help revenue stability across market cycles. Modest cost savings could aid profits. Return on equity, which had been trending down because of a growing equity base, is expected to increase because of debt issued to finance the deal. Both firms as well as their competitors in the industry are aided by the ongoing reinvestment of dividends and interest, an automatic growth factor, and the ability to pass along certain costs to shareholders.

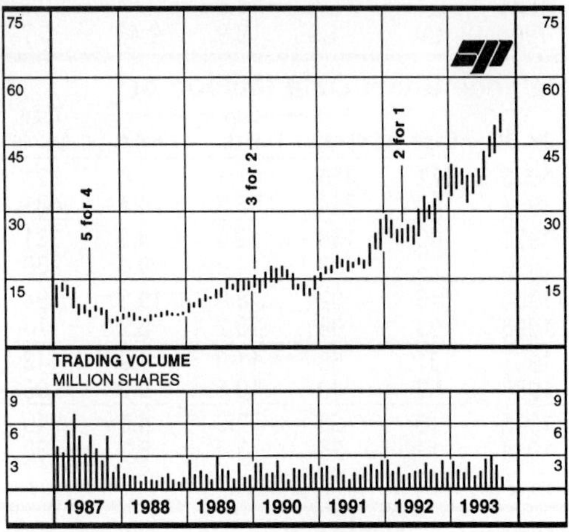

Total Revenues (Million $)

Quarter:	1993–4	1992–93	1991–92	1990–91
Dec.	---	136.7	89.4	73.9
Mar.	---	158.9	95.8	78.0
Jun.	---	172.0	96.6	81.2
Sep.	---	---	103.1	85.4
	---	---	385.0	318.4

Revenues for the nine months ended June 30, 1993, rose 63%, year to year, aided by the Templeton acquisition, reinvestment of dividends and interest, and strong financial markets. Margins narrowed, due to merger-related expenses, and pretax income was held to a 25% increase. After taxes at 35.7%, versus 39.7%, net income advanced 34%. Share earnings were $1.48 on 5.3% more shares, compared with $1.17.

Common Share Earnings ($)

Quarter:	1993–4	1992–93	1991–92	1990–91
Dec.	E0.55	0.43	0.37	0.30
Mar.	E0.58	0.51	0.40	0.30
Jun.	E0.60	0.54	0.40	0.31
Sep.	E0.62	E0.52	0.42	0.35
	E2.35	E2.00	1.59	1.26

Important Developments

Aug. '93— The company said that liquidity has increased since the Templeton acquisition in October 1992 and management anticipates that this trend will continue during the current fiscal year, but at a substantially lower rate than in prior years, until the repayment of acquisition indebtedness has been completed.

Next earnings report expected in late October.

Per Share Data ($)

Yr. End Sep. 30	1992	1991	1990	1989	1988	1987	1986	1985	1984	1983
Tangible Bk. Val.	**5.99**	4.66	3.69	2.77	1.92	1.31	0.67	0.29	0.13	0.06
Earnings	**1.59**	1.26	1.14	1.00	0.84	0.74	0.41	0.17	0.08	0.04
Dividends	**0.260**	0.230	0.200	0.147	0.140	0.072	0.032	0.017	0.010	0.003
Payout Ratio	**16%**	18%	18%	15%	17%	10%	8%	9%	12%	9%
Prices[1]—High	**39**	28¼	17[15]/16	15[1]/16	7[15]/16	14¼	9⅞	5¾	1⅛	⅝
Low	**22¾**	14[11]/16	11¼	7½	5[11]/16	4	5[5]/16	1⅛	9/16	1/16
P/E Ratio—	**25–14**	23–12	16–10	15–8	10–7	19–5	25–13	34–6	14–7	16–2

Data as orig. reptd. Adj. for stk. divs. of 100% Apr. 1992, 50% Jan. 1990, 25% Jul. 1987, 50% Oct. 1986, 100% Jan. 1986, 100% Apr. 1985, 25% Apr. 1984, 100% Jul. 1983. **1.** Cal. yr. E-Estimated.

Income Data (Million $)

Year Ended Sep. 30	Advisor Fee Exp.	[1]Commis-sions	Total Revs.	Exp.	% Exp./ Op. Revs.	Net Bef. Taxes	Eff. Tax Rate	Net Inc.	% Return On Revs.	Assets	[1]Equity
1992	**283**	**30.3**	**385**	**180**	**46.8**	**205**	**39.4%**	**124.1**	**32.2**	**17.6**	**29.9**
1991	230	24.4	318	156	48.9	163	39.6%	98.2	30.9	18.6	30.1
1990	203	23.0	288	143	49.8	144	38.1%	89.4	31.1	20.5	35.4
1989	180	20.4	253	124	48.8	130	39.4%	78.6	31.0	21.9	42.9
1988	155	18.8	203	93	46.0	109	39.3%	66.3	32.7	42.1	52.0
1987	154	29.1	207	93	45.1	113	48.0%	58.9	28.5	52.1	74.9
1986	99	27.1	143	77	53.7	66	51.6%	32.1	22.4	53.2	85.4
1985	42	10.7	63	37	58.8	26	48.5%	13.5	21.2	55.6	82.5
1984	23	5.6	37	24	66.4	12	50.3%	6.1	16.7	49.2	81.6
1983	13	5.1	24	18	76.9	5	43.4%	3.1	13.1	41.9	85.5

Balance Sheet Data (Million $)

Sep. 30	Total Assets	Cash	Rec.	Secs. Owned	Sec. Borrowed	Due Brokers & Cust.	Other Liabs.	Capitalization [2]Debt	[1]Equity	Total
1992	**834**	**2.80**	**171**	**598**	**Nil**	**34.6**	**177**	**155.5**	**467**	**623**
1991	579	3.89	119	408	Nil	35.9	174	5.6	363	369
1990	479	1.70	83	351	Nil	32.0	154	4.2	289	293
1989	394	1.13	85	277	Nil	28.4	143	6.1	217	223
1988	177	0.98	23	120	Nil	6.6	18	2.6	150	153
1987	138	0.39	19	92	Nil	9.0	21	3.6	105	108
1986	88	0.44	18	40	Nil	8.9	20	6.7	53	60
1985	33	0.21	7	20	Nil	8.7	1	0.4	22	23
1984	16	1.47	4	7	Nil	4.2	1	0.4	10	11
1983	9	0.25	2	5	Nil	2.7	1	0.1	5	5

Data as orig. reptd. **1.** Common. **2.** Incl. curr. portion.

Business Summary

Franklin Resources is the largest publicly traded independent asset manager in the world. Operations were significantly expanded with the October 1992 acquisition of Templeton, Galbraith & Hansberger Ltd., a global investment management organization with 13 offices in 10 countries. Templeton is being operated as a separate subsidiary. Assets under management of $99.9 billion at June 30, 1993 were approximately divided as follows (in billion $):

	Amount	%
Franklin:		
Tax–Free Income	$38.7	39%
U. S. government	19.8	20%
Equity/Income	14.1	14%
Money funds	2.4	2%
Templeton:		
Equity	16.7	17%
Fixed Income	1.9	2%
Managed accounts	6.3	6%

As a result of the acquisition, BEN's portfolio mix changed from primarily fixed income oriented to both equity and fixed income. The potential impact of changes in international equity markets on net assets under management also increased with the acquisition. Changes in the amount of net assets under management are the primary factor affecting change in the company's revenues.

The combined company has approximately three million mutual fund accounts worldwide.

Dividend Data

Dividends were initiated in 1981.

Amt. of Divd. $	Date Decl.	Ex–divd. Date	Stock of Record	Payment Date
0.07	Dec. 16	Dec. 24	Dec. 31	Jan. 15'93
0.07	Mar. 18	Mar. 25	Mar. 31	Apr. 15'93
0.07	Jun. 17	Jun. 24	Jun. 30	Jul. 15'93
0.07	Sep. 17	Sep. 24	Sep. 30	Oct. 15'93

Capitalization

Long Term Debt: $496,000,000 incl. $150,000,000 of 6¼% sub. debs. due 2002 (6/93).

Common Stock: 82,098,580 shs. ($0.10 par).
Officers & directors own or control about 55%, incl. some 22% held by C.B. Johnson and about 17% by R.H. Johnson Jr.
Institutions hold approximately 30%.
Shareholders of record: 1,100.

Office—777 Mariners Island Blvd., San Mateo, CA 94404. **Tel**—(415) 312-2000. **Pres & CEO**—C. B. Johnson. **VP-Secy**—H. E. Burns. **SVP-Treas & CFO**—M. L. Flanagan. **SVP & Investor Contact**—Charles E. Johnson (415) 312-3058. **Dirs**—H. E. Burns, J. R. Grosvenor, C. T. L. Hansberger, B. Johnson, R. H. Johnson Jr., H. O. Kline, L. E. Woodworth. **Transfer Agent & Registrar**—Bank of New York, NYC. **Incorporated** in Delaware in 1969. **Empl**—2,520.

 Paul L. Huberman, CFA

Freeport-McMoRan Inc.

NYSE Symbol FTX Options on CBOE (Feb-May-Aug-Nov) In S&P MidCap 400

Price	Range	P-E Ratio	Dividend	Yield	S&P Ranking	Beta
Aug. 2'93	1993					
19	22⅝–17	NM	1.25	6.6%	B+	0.40

Summary

FTX is engaged in the sulphur/phosphate fertilizer business in the U.S. and the copper/gold business in Indonesia. In July 1993, its Resource Partners unit formed a joint venture with IMC Fertilizer Group which combines both companies' phosphate fertilizer businesses. The copper/gold unit raised mill capacity to 57,000 metric tons of ore a day in early 1992, and would optimize throughput to 66,000 tons by mid-1993, and further expand capacity to 90,000 tons by late 1995.

Current Outlook

A loss of $0.50 a share (after a $0.39 a share net charge) is estimated for 1993, versus 1992's $1.17 earnings (after a $0.93 onetime gain).

Dividends should continue at $0.31¼ quarterly.

Metals income in 1993 should fall, as lower copper prices outweigh greater output. Given weak world supply/demand conditions, agriminerals will probably incur a loss instead of making a profit. With full-year absence of spunoff unprofitable oil and gas activities, energy operations are likely to sustain a smaller loss. But with restructuring charges (net of gain on asset sale) replacing 1992's onetime gain and a full year of preferred dividends, a share-loss should be incurred.

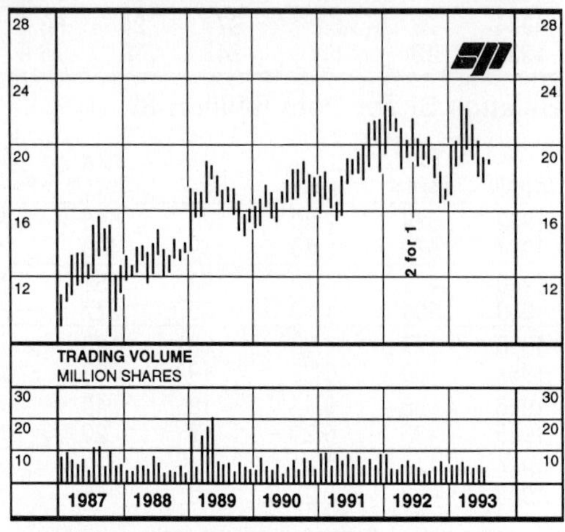

Revenues (Million $)

Quarter:	1993	1992	1991	1990
Mar.	301	363	407	393
Jun.	338	511	390	378
Sep.	---	367	413	421
Dec.	---	413	369	389
	---	1,655	1,579	1,581

First-half 1993 sales fell 27%, year to year. Despite a smaller energy loss, but on lower metals profits, a loss instead of income from agriminerals and a $236.7 million charge in 1993, a pretax loss of $226.0 million contrasted with income of $105.2 million. After a $39.4 million tax credit versus taxes of $31.8 million, and minority interests in loss instead of income of units, a net loss of $114.6 million ($0.88/share on higher preferred dividends) replaced net income of $34.2 million ($0.18).

Common Share Earnings ($)

Quarter:	1993	1992	1991	1990
Mar.	d0.25	0.03	0.21	2.00
Jun.	d0.63	0.16	0.11	0.40
Sep.	E0.25	0.86	0.27	0.27
Dec.	E0.13	0.14	0.09	0.09
	Ed0.50	1.17	0.69	2.61

Important Developments

Jul. '93— Freeport-McMoRan Resource Partners and IMC Fertilizer Group finalized the formation of a joint venture which combines both companies' phosphate fertilizer businesses, for estimated cost savings of at least $95 million a year.

Jul. '93— FTX sold its interests in the recently discovered undeveloped oil, gas and condensate reserves at East Cameron blocks 331/332, offshore Louisiana, for some $95 million cash. The company had drilled seven development wells to delineate the discovery, then sold the reserves before setting permanent production facilities. The sale would result in a third quarter pretax gain of about $70 million.

Feb. '93— FTX announced a new corporate streamlining program that would provide $33 million in annual cost savings.

Next earnings report expected in late October.

Per Share Data ($)

Yr. End Dec. 31	1992	[3]1991	1990	1989	1988	[2]1987	[2]1986	1985	[2]1984	1983
Tangible Bk. Val.	**0.63**	2.61	4.50	1.52	5.91	5.27	4.57	5.38	5.11	5.01
Cash Flow	**2.63**	2.17	4.84	3.34	3.73	3.21	1.09	1.78	1.74	1.89
Earnings[1]	**1.17**	0.69	2.61	1.09	2.07	1.69	0.19	0.83	0.66	0.66
Dividends	**1.25**	1.25	1.25	1.25	0.30	0.30	0.30	0.30	0.30	0.30
Payout Ratio	**104%**	182%	54%	102%	14%	18%	156%	36%	43%	47%
Prices—High	**22½**	21⅝	19	19	14⅞	15¾	10½	11⅛	12⅞	13¾
Low	**16½**	15½	15	13⅝	11⅝	8⅜	7⅛	8	6¾	8⅛
P/E Ratio—	**19–14**	31–23	7–6	18–13	7–6	9–5	55–38	13–10	20–10	21–12

Data as orig. reptd. Adj. for stk. div. of 100% Jun. 1992. **1.** Bef. spec. item of -0.40 in 1991. **2.** Reflects merger or acquisition. **3.** Reflects accounting change. d-Deficit. NM-Not Meaningful. E-Estimated.

Income Data (Million $)

Year Ended Dec. 31	Revs.	Oper. Inc.	% Oper. Inc. of Revs.	Cap. Exp.	Depr.	Int. Exp.	Net Bef. Taxes	Eff. Tax Rate	[4]Net Inc.	% Net Inc. of Revs.	Cash Flow
1992	**1,655**	**463**	**28.0**	**683**	**211**	**136**	**336**	**22.5%**	**188**	**11.3**	**380**
[3]1991	1,579	430	27.2	901	206	165	168	1.8%	97	6.1	302
1990	1,581	557	35.3	702	257	133	719	38.1%	314	19.8	558
1989	1,958	659	33.7	497	271	163	334	22.8%	150	7.7	401
1988	1,945	693	35.6	453	233	102	608	29.3%	310	15.9	521
[1]1987	1,514	492	32.5	250	206	97	430	30.2%	249	16.4	446
[1]1986	630	d57	NM	123	119	77	[2]d12	NM	[3]26	4.1	145
1985	722	261	36.2	207	129	60	[2]149	25.4%	111	15.4	240
[1]1984	842	295	35.0	190	154	36	[2]126	25.0%	94	11.2	248
1983	786	297	37.8	342	173	45	[2]128	26.9%	93	11.9	267

Balance Sheet Data (Million $)

Dec. 31	Cash	Curr. Assets	Curr. Liab.	Curr. Ratio	Total Assets	% Ret. on Assets	Long Term Debt	Common Equity	Total Cap.	% LT Debt of Cap.	% Ret. on Equity
1992	**381**	**984**	**402**	**2.4**	**3,547**	**5.4**	**1,431**	**89**	**2,756**	**51.9**	**74.3**
1991	90	834	369	2.3	3,565	2.5	1,940	379	2,787	69.6	18.6
1990	48	543	424	1.3	3,588	7.9	1,579	580	2,937	53.8	77.5
1989	98	576	357	1.6	3,561	4.6	1,713	161	2,975	57.6	33.1
1988	124	634	389	1.6	3,730	9.1	1,015	802	3,050	33.3	38.1
1987	65	535	377	1.4	3,155	8.9	880	735	2,564	34.3	34.2
1986	33	283	650	0.4	2,359	1.2	765	611	1,587	48.2	3.9
1985	71	289	274	1.1	2,059	5.7	720	718	1,681	42.8	15.9
1984	Nil	214	230	0.9	1,906	5.9	711	691	1,619	43.9	13.8
1983	Nil	199	152	1.3	1,418	5.9	295	735	1,229	24.0	12.4

Data as orig. reptd. **1.** Reflects merger or acq. **2.** Incl. equity in earns. of nonconsol. subs. **3.** Refl. acctg. change. **4.** Bef. spec. items. d-Deficit. NM-Not Meaningful.

Business Summary

FTX is a diversified natural resources company. Contributions by product segment (profits in million $) in 1992:

	Revs.	Profits
Metals	43%	$284
Agricultural minerals	48%	18
Oil & gas	8%	–28
Other	1%	–20

Freeport-McMoRan Copper & Gold (73%-owned) holds an Indonesian unit which is one of the world's largest and lowest cost copper/gold producers. In January 1992, expansion of mill capacity to 57,000 metric tons of ore/day was completed. Throughput would be optimized to 66,000 mt/d by mid-1993 and be expanded again to 90,000 mt/d by late 1995, which would enable annual output nearing 1 billion lbs. of copper and 1.2-1.5 million oz. of gold. Production in 1992 equaled 619.1 million lbs. and 641,000 oz., respectively. Future output from year-end 1992 reserves of 733 million metric tons of ore was estimated at 20.9 billion lbs. of copper and 32.1 million oz. of gold.

Freeport-McMoRan Resource Partners (51%-owned) is the largest integrated and one of the lowest cost phosphate fertilizer producers in the world. It owns 58.3% of the Main Pass sulphur/oil deposit, offshore Louisiana, the largest existing Frasch sulphur reserve in North America with 67 million long tons of recoverable sulphur. This activity became operational in July 1993, and sulphur output was expected to reach a targeted rate of two million long tons/year, when the firm would become the largest U.S. Frasch sulphur producer. Its share of oil production from Main Pass was 4.8 million barrels in 1992 and was estimated at 3.0 million bbls. for 1993. FTX's strategy for oil and gas exploration is to seek opportunities both internationally and domestically that have potential to provide substantial cash flows.

Dividend Data

Freeport Minerals paid cash dividends since 1927. A dividend reinvestment plan is available.

Amt of Divd. $	Date Decl.	Ex–divd. Date	Stock of Record	Payment Date
0.31¼	Aug. 4	Aug. 11	Aug. 17	Sep. 1'92
0.31¼	Nov. 3	Nov. 9	Nov. 16	Dec. 1'92
0.31¼	Feb. 2	Feb. 8	Feb. 15	Mar. 1'93
0.31¼	May 4	May 10	May 14	Jun. 1'93

Capitalization

Long Term Debt: $1,526,066,000 (6/93).

$4.375 Exch. Pfd. Stock: 5,000,000 shs. ($50 par); conv. into com. at $24.66 a sh. Privately held.

Minority Interests: $660,150,000.

Common Stock: 141,092,170 shs. ($1 par). Institutions hold some 61%.

Office—1615 Poydras St., New Orleans, LA 70112. **Tel**—(504) 582-4000. **Chrmn & CEO**—J. R. Moffett. **Pres**—R. L. Latiolais. **SVP-CFO**—R. C. Adkerson. **Secy**—M. C. Kilanowski, Jr. **VP-Investor Contact**—Craig E. Saporito. **Dirs**—R. W. Bruce III, T. B. Coleman, W. H. Cunningham, R. A. Day Jr., J. C. Dudley, W. B. Harrison Jr., H. A. Kissinger, B. L. Lackey, W. K. McWilliams Jr., J. R. Moffett, G. Putnam, B. M. Rankin Jr., B. C. Schmidt, J. T. Wharton, W. W. Woods Jr. **Transfer Agent & Registrar**—Mellon Securities Trust Co., Pittsburgh. **Incorporated** in Delaware in 1980. **Empl**—7,957.

 A.M. Sorrentino, CFA

Fruit of the Loom

ASE Symbol FTL Options on NY (Feb-May-Aug-Nov) In S&P MidCap 400

Price	Range	P–E Ratio	Dividend	Yield	S&P Ranking	Beta
Aug. 24'93	1993					
32⅝	49¼–27¾	13	None	None	NR	1.61

Summary

This company (formerly Farley/Northwest Industries) is a leading international basic apparel manufacturer, emphasizing branded products for consumers of all ages. While major products include underwear and screen print shirts, the company is also deriving higher sales from casualwear, socks, and licensing agreements. Sales and earnings advanced strongly in 1991 and 1992, and further gains are expected in 1993 and 1994. William Farley, the company's chairman, and Farley Inc., which he controls, hold a 33% voting interest.

Current Outlook

Primary earnings for 1993 are projected at $2.75 a share, excluding a $0.04 special credit, up from 1992's $2.48. Earnings for 1994 could reach $3.50.

Dividends are not in prospect.

Sales for 1993 should increase only moderately, reflecting continued retail cautiousness, weak consumer spending, and soft overseas economies. Still, the company should see some market share expansion, as mass merchandisers increasingly demand FTL's brand name products. Sales growth should resume in 1994, assuming stonger consumer spending on apparel. Increased distribution in Europe, expansion of the activewear and casualwear product lines, the introduction of boys' and girls' underwear lines featuring the popular Barney the Dinosaur logo, the introduction of men's fashion underwear, and an expanded offering of socks should all contribute to sales growth. Despite higher marketing and promotional expenses, margins should improve from 1993's expected level on an improved product mix and manufacturing efficiencies. Interest costs should be lower, as debt is cut over the next few years. Over the longer term, FTL will benefit from agreements with Wilson Sporting Goods, Warnaco and others to produce licensed apparel. Within three years, the company plans to have sales totaling $3 billion.

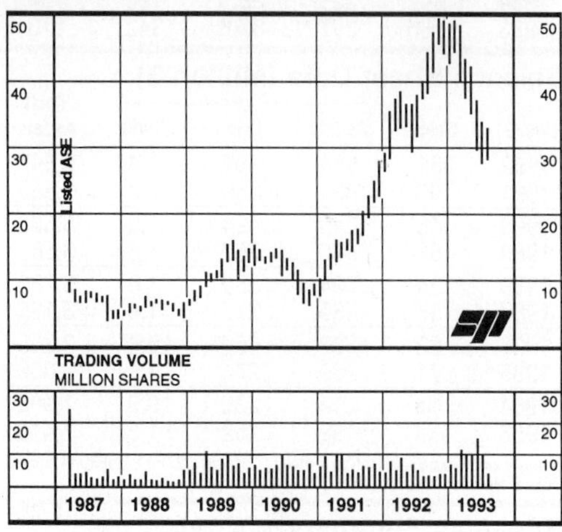

Net Sales (Million $)

Quarter:	1993	1992	1991	1990
Mar.	429	423	349	324
Jun.	523	534	468	443
Sep.	---	451	392	356
Dec.	---	447	419	305
	---	1,855	1,628	1,427

Sales for the first six months of 1993 fell slightly, year to year. Margins widened on lower manufacturing costs, and net income was up 10%, to $1.35 a share (excluding a special credit of $0.04), from $1.23.

Common Share Earnings ($)

Quarter:	1993	1992	1991	1990
Mar.	0.58	0.48	0.26	0.21
Jun.	0.77	0.75	0.55	0.60
Sep.	E0.66	0.61	0.37	0.38
Dec.	E0.74	0.64	0.42	0.06
	E2.75	2.48	1.60	1.25

Important Developments

Jul. '93— FTL noted that second quarter operating results were less than expected due to lower levels of consumer spending and consumer confidence. FTL added that it believed that growth would accelerate in the second half of 1993, spurred by an improved economy, better product availability and aggressive promotion.

Next earnings report expected in mid-October.

Per Share Data ($)

Yr. End Dec. 31	1992	1991	1990	1989	1988	1987	[1]1986
Tangible Bk. Val.	**0.59**	d1.97	d7.18	d9.04	d10.57	d12.00	2.16
Cash Flow	**3.71**	2.81	2.47	2.27	2.16	1.41	0.18
Earnings[2,3]	**2.48**	1.60	1.25	1.17	1.19	0.52	0.32
Dividends	**Nil**	Nil	Nil	Nil	Nil	Nil	Nil
Payout Ratio	**Nil**	Nil	Nil	Nil	Nil	Nil	Nil
Prices—High	**49⅝**	28	15⅜	16	7⅝	9¾	NA
Low	**26½**	7⅝	6⅛	6⅛	4¼	3⅞	NA
P/E Ratio—	**20–11**	18–5	12–5	14–5	6–4	19–7	NA

Data as orig. reptd. **1.** Pro forma, following restructuring & related transactions. **2.** Bef. results of disc. ops. of +0.09 in 1987, +0.38 in 1986, and spec. items of -0.13 in 1992, -0.09 in 1989, -1.01 in 1987. **3.** Ful. dil.: 2.48 in 1992, 1.55 in 1991, 1.18 in 1990, 1.11 in 1989, 1.13 in 1988. E-Estimated. d-Deficit. NA-Not Available.

Income Data (Million $)

Year Ended Dec. 31	Revs.	Oper. Inc.	% Oper. Inc. of Revs.	Cap. Exp.	Depr.	[2]Int. Exp.	Net Bef. Taxes	Eff. Tax Rate	[3]Net Inc.	% Net Inc. of Revs.	Cash Flow
1992	**1,855**	**503**	**27.1**	**189**	**93.2**	**82**	**320**	**41.1%**	**189**	**10.2**	**282**
1991	1,628	403	24.8	74	83.8	115	201	44.8%	111	6.8	195
1990	1,427	376	26.4	158	76.0	129	149	48.1%	77	5.4	153
1989	1,321	333	25.2	85	68.1	124	131	44.8%	72	5.5	140
1988	1,005	291	29.0	160	65.9	105	95	22.8%	73	7.3	133
1987	870	221	25.4	125	49.4	99	78	51.2%	[4]38	4.3	78
[1]1986	693	213	30.7	56	43.0	93	61	70.4%	18	2.6	6

Balance Sheet Data (Million $)

Dec. 31	Cash	Curr. Assets	Curr. Liab.	Curr. Ratio	Total Assets	% Ret. on Assets	Long Term Debt	Common Equity	Total Cap.	% LT Debt of Cap.	% Ret. on Equity
1992	**57.4**	**744**	**434**	**1.7**	**2,282**	**8.5**	**756**	**855**	**1,611**	**46.9**	**24.3**
1991	31.4	656	370	1.8	2,115	4.7	811	689	1,500	54.1	18.6
1990	59.6	629	495	1.3	2,151	3.8	1,014	418	1,432	70.8	20.7
1989	16.7	453	350	1.3	1,878	3.9	988	327	1,445	68.4	24.6
1988	15.4	411	467	0.9	1,830	4.2	905	258	1,290	70.1	32.4
1987	19.4	298	390	0.8	1,610	1.6	62	193	1,111	68.6	59.6
[1]1986	57.9	274	208	1.3	1,541	NA	811	124	936	86.6	NA

Data as orig. reptd. **1.** Pro forma, following restructuring & related transactions. **2.** Net of interest income. **3.** Bef. spec. items & results of disc. opers. **4.** Refl. acctg. change. NA-Not Available.

Business Summary

Fruit of the Loom (FTL) is a leading international producer of casualwear, emphasizing branded products for consumers ranging from infants to senior citizens. It is the largest domestic producer of underwear and activewear for the imprinted market, selling products under the Fruit of the Loom, BVD, Screenstars and Munsingwear brand names. The company is the successor to Northwest Industries, which was acquired by William Farley on July 31, 1985.

FTL offers a broad array of men's and boys' underwear sold under the Fruit of the Loom and BVD names. Products include briefs, boxer shorts, T-shirts and A-shirts, as well as Ribbed Whites, colored and "high fashion" underwear. At the end of 1992, the company had an estimated 39% market share. FTL produces women's briefs, high thigh briefs and bikinis and girls' briefs, all of which are sold under the Fruit of the Loom brand name. FTL had an estimated 17% market share at the end of 1992.

FTL sells blank screen print shirts and fleecewear under the Screen Stars brand name and premium fleecewear and T-shirts under the Fruit of the Loom label. These products are sold to distributors, screen printers and specialty retailers, who generally apply a screen print prior to retail sale. FTL also markets casualwear under the Fruit of the Loom, BVD, and Munsingwear labels; sells socks under the Fruit of the Loom name; and is involved in licensing agreements with Wilson Sporting Goods and Warnaco.

Dividend Data

The company does not anticipate paying dividends in the next several years.

Finances

In December 1992, pursuant to a bankruptcy plan, Farley Inc. publicly sold 861,839 Class B shares that were converted into Class A shares, sold 800,000 Class B shares to William Farley, and distributed 2,138,163 Class B shares. As a result, Farley, Inc. and William Farley reduced their collective interest in FTL from 13.3% to 9.3%, and their collective voting power from 42.7% to about 33.0%.

Capital spending, primarily to expand productive capacity, is expected at $250 million for 1993.

In a May 1991 public offering, a total of 12.75 million Class A common shares (including 5.25 million shares for William Farley and Farley Industries) were sold at $14.25 each. In March 1987, as part of a restructuring plan, underwriters sold 27 million Class A common shares at $9 each, $60 million of 6.75% convertible subordinated debentures due 2002, and $250 million of 10.75% senior subordinated notes due 1995.

Capitalization

Long Term Debt: $687,300,000 (6/93).

Common Stock: 68,957,119 shs. ($0.01 par) Cl. A; 6,690,976 shs. ($0.01 par) Cl. B (five votes ea.).
William Farley and Farley Inc. own 100% of Cl. B, and hold a voting interest of about 33%.
Shareholders of record: 2,437 (3/93).

Office—233 South Wacker Dr., 5000 Sears Tower, Chicago, IL 60606. **Tel**—(312) 876-1724. **Chrmn & CEO**—W. Farley. **Pres**—J. B. Holland. **EVP & CFO**—P. M. O'Hara. **VP & Secy**—K. Greenbaum. **VP & Treas**—E. C. Shanks. **Investor Contact**—Mark Steinkrauss. **Dirs**—D. S. Bookshester, W. Farley, J. B. Holland, L. W. Jennings, H. A. Johnson, R. C. Lappin, A. L. Weil, B. Wolfson. **Transfer Agent & Registrar**—Chemical Bank, NYC. **Incorporated** in Delaware in 1985. **Empl**—31,100.

 Elizabeth Vandeventer

Fuller (H.B.) Co.

NASDAQ Symbol FULL (Incl. in Nat'l Market) In S&P MidCap 400

Price	Range	P-E Ratio	Dividend	Yield	S&P Ranking	Beta
Sep. 27'93	1993					
34	42¾–34¼	16	0.56	1.6%	A–	0.78

Summary

This international manufacturer of adhesives, sealants, coatings, paints, specialty waxes and sanitation chemicals has increased its dividend each year since 1968. Record earnings were posted for fiscal 1991 and 1992, as results benefited from increased sales and aggressive cost controls, but lower earnings will be posted in fiscal 1993, reflecting recessions in foreign economies and possible restructuring charges.

Current Outlook

Share earnings for the fiscal year ending November 30, 1994 are projected at about $2.40, up from the $2.05 (before special charges) expected for fiscal 1993.

The dividend should remain at $0.14 quarterly.

Sales for fiscal 1994 are expected to continue to advance at a moderate rate, reflecting gains in the U.S., Latin America and Asian regions. European sales may remain sluggish well into 1994 due to poor economic conditions. Profitability should benefit from expected restructuring actions, including plant consolidations in Latin America and the reorganization of European operations.

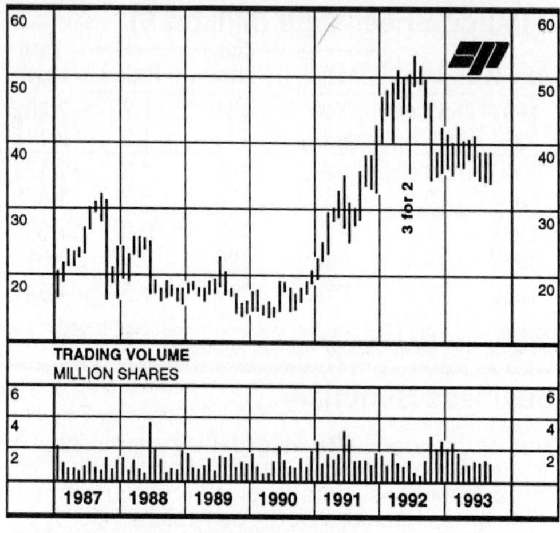

Net Sales (Million $)

Quarter:	1992-93	1992	1991	1990
Feb.	228	219	202	181
May	247	235	216	205
Aug.	252	237	214	203
Nov.		243	221	203
		934	853	792

Sales in the nine months ended August 31, 1993, rose 4.4%, year to year, as a volume gain of 6% outweighed slightly lower prices, unfavorable foreign exchange rates and a negative sales adjustment. Sales rose in all geographical regions except for Europe. Margins narrowed, and net income fell 22%, to $1.47 share, from $1.89.

Common Share Earnings ($)

Period:	1992-93	1992	1991	1990
Feb.	0.21	0.43	0.27	0.01
May	0.63	0.73	0.51	0.47
Aug.	0.63	0.73	0.59	0.47
Nov.	E0.58	0.66	0.63	0.59
	E2.05	2.55	2.00	1.53

Important Developments

Sep. '93— Fuller said its fiscal 1993 third quarter results were not strong and that it expected the fourth quarter would be below the year earlier results. Estimated earnings for fiscal 1993 would be below the previously announced range. The company was also considering a number of major decisions including the early adoption of FAS 106 and 109. In view of the continued depressed economies in several areas of the world, Fuller said that it would be reviewing facilities and operations with possible restructuring actions. Fuller said that both European and Latin American operations in the third quarter experienced lower earnings versus the previous year. European sales declined 8% as a result of the depressed economy, and earnings were down substantially. Latin America had reduced earnings as expenses rose faster than the 11% increase in sales.

Next earnings report due in early January.

Per Share Data ($)

Yr. End Nov. 30	1992	1991	1990	1989	1988	1987	1986	[1]1985	1984	1983
Tangible Bk. Val.	**[2]18.43**	[2]15.96	[2]14.56	[2]13.27	[2]12.56	11.18	9.50	8.10	7.13	6.56
Cash Flow	**4.37**	3.57	3.01	2.25	2.69	2.72	2.13	1.63	1.51	1.49
Earnings[3]	**2.55**	2.00	1.53	1.09	1.47	1.79	1.33	0.96	0.93	0.99
Dividends	**0.463**	0.410	0.397	0.383	0.350	0.270	0.233	0.210	0.197	0.183
Payout Ratio	**18%**	21%	26%	34%	24%	15%	17%	22%	21%	18%
Prices—High[4]	**53¼**	42⅞	20⅞	22⅞	25⅞	32⅜	20⅝	12⅜	13⅜	13⅝
Low[4]	**34½**	19½	13¾	13⅞	15⅝	16⅜	11⅜	9⅛	7⅞	7⅝
P/E Ratio—	**21–14**	21–10	14–9	21–13	18–11	18–9	16–9	13–9	14–8	14–8

Data as orig. reptd. Adj. for stk. divs. of 50% Jun. 1992, 100% Jun. 1984. **1.** Refl. acctg. change. **2.** Incl intangibles. **3.** Bef. results of disc. ops. of -0.03 in 1984 & spec. items of +0.11 in 1985, -0.05 in 1984. **4.** Cal. yr. E-Estimate.

Income Data (Million $)

Year Ended Nov. 30	Revs.	Oper. Inc.	% Oper. Inc. of Revs.	Cap. Exp.	Depr.	Int. Exp.	[3]Net Bef. Taxes	Eff. Tax Rate	[4]Net Inc.	% Net Inc. of Revs.	Cash Flow
1992	**934**	**96.9**	**10.4**	**36.0**	**25.5**	**12.6**	**60.9**	**40.6%**	**35.6**	**3.8**	**61.1**
1991	853	81.6	9.6	30.0	21.8	15.4	47.4	40.4%	27.7	3.2	49.5
1990	792	72.3	9.1	31.5	20.4	15.3	37.1	41.1%	21.1	2.7	41.5
1989	753	70.0	9.3	40.9	23.9	15.7	30.3	46.0%	15.7	2.1	32.2
1988	685	65.3	9.5	40.2	18.8	9.8	36.0	39.8%	21.1	3.1	38.6
1987	597	61.0	10.2	29.2	13.3	5.9	42.9	38.0%	25.8	4.3	39.1
1986	528	50.9	9.6	18.3	11.4	6.2	33.8	41.7%	18.9	3.6	30.3
[1]1985	458	40.1	8.7	15.8	9.3	7.8	23.6	40.3%	13.3	2.9	22.6
[2]1984	448	40.1	8.9	17.0	7.9	9.0	24.1	41.2%	13.0	2.9	20.9
1983	426	40.1	9.4	15.2	6.9	7.4	25.1	41.7%	13.8	3.3	20.7

Balance Sheet Data (Million $)

Nov. 30	Cash	Curr. Assets	Curr. Liab.	Curr. Ratio	Total Assets	% Ret. on Assets	Long Term Debt	Common Equity	Total Cap.	% LT Debt of Cap.	% Ret. on Equity
1992	**29.1**	**299**	**168**	**1.8**	**561**	**6.6**	**53**	**255**	**333**	**16.0**	**15.0**
1991	15.2	260	151	1.7	509	5.5	72	219	313	22.9	13.2
1990	14.0	242	146	1.7	490	4.6	88	197	303	29.1	11.2
1989	10.4	216	120	1.8	455	3.5	101	186	306	32.9	8.6
1988	18.0	218	114	1.9	434	5.5	98	179	295	33.4	12.4
1987	19.9	182	95	1.9	330	8.3	33	161	211	15.7	17.3
1986	14.2	158	84	1.9	291	6.9	37	135	187	19.9	15.1
1985	11.3	137	68	2.0	254	5.4	44	113	170	26.0	12.5
1984	9.7	128	60	2.1	236	5.6	51	100	163	31.5	13.6
1983	12.6	126	61	2.1	226	6.4	52	92	154	33.6	16.0

Data as orig. reptd. **1.** Refl. acctg. change. **2.** Excl. disc. ops. **3.** Incl. equity in earns. of nonconsol. subs. **4.** Bef. spec. items.

Business Summary

H.B. Fuller Company manufactures specialty chemical products, including the formulation, compounding and marketing of adhesives, sealants, coatings, paints, specialty waxes, sanitizing chemicals and other chemical products in the U.S., Canada, Latin America, Europe and the Pacific.

Sales in recent fiscal years were derived from:

	1992	1991
Adhesives, sealants & coatings	84%	84%
Paints	7%	7%
Sanitation chemicals	2%	3%
Specialty waxes	3%	2%
Other	4%	4%

By geographical area, the breakdown of fiscal 1992 results was: U.S. 53% of sales and 41% of operating profits, Europe 24% and 26%, Latin America 15% and 26% and other 8% and 7%.

In the U.S., the company formulates and markets adhesives for packaging, paper converting, structural and other industrial applications, as well as adhesives, sealants and coatings for residential and commercial construction and consumer home improvements. Fuller also markets cleaning and sanitizing chemicals for the dairy, food processing and beverage industries. Principal international subsidaries are HB-Fuller GmbH, Germany, which serves European and worldwide export markets; and Kativo Chemical Industries, S.A., headquartered in Costa Rica and serving Latin American markets. HB-Fuller is a leading supplier of adhesives, specialty waxes, coatings, sealants and specialty products to the packaging, rubber, food, cosmetics, insulating glass, nonwoven, paper converting, automotive and woodworking industries. Kativo produces a general line of paints for residential, commercial and industrial uses, as well as a wide line of industrial and consumer adhesives and other specialty chemicals.

Dividend Data

Cash has been paid each year since 1953. A dividend reinvestment plan is available.

Amt of Divd. $	Date Decl.	Ex–divd. Date	Stock of Record	Payment Date
0.12	Oct. 16	Oct. 20	Oct. 26	Nov. 10'92
0.12	Dec. 3	Jan. 15	Jan. 22	Feb. 10'93
0.14	Apr. 15	Apr. 20	Apr. 26	May 10'93
0.14	Jul. 15	Jul. 21	Jul. 27	Aug. 10'93

Capitalization

Long Term Debt: $56,997,000 (8/93).

$0.50 Cum. Preferred Stock: 45,900 shs. ($10 par); all owned by E.L. Andersen.

Common Stock: 13,883,311 shs. ($1 par).
E.L. Andersen and his family control 22% of the voting power.
Institutions hold 55%.
Shareholders: 3,048 of record (11/92).

Office—2400 Energy Park Drive, St. Paul, MN 55108-1591. **Tel**—(612) 645-3401. **Chrmn & CEO**—A. L. Andersen. **Pres**—W. Kissling. **VP, Treas & CFO**—J. W. Bolanos. **Secy**—L. R. Mitau. **Investor Contact**—Richard Edwards (612-647-3650). **Dirs**—A. L. Andersen, E. L. Andersen, N. R. Berg, E. L. Bronstien, Jr., R. J. Carlson, F. A. Ford, G. Forler, R. C. King, W. Kissling, J. J. Mauriel, Jr., R. B. Schubert, L. C. Webster. **Transfer Agent & Registrar**—Norwest Bank Minnesota, St. Paul. **Incorporated** in Minnesota in 1915. **Empl**—5,800.

 Richard O'Reilly, CFA

GATX Corp.

NYSE Symbol GMT Options on Phila (Mar-Jun-Sep-Dec) In S&P MidCap 400

Price	Range	P-E Ratio	Dividend	Yield	S&P Ranking	Beta
Aug. 13'93	1993					
39¼	40⅛–31⅜	NM	1.40	3.6%	B+	1.42

Summary

GATX is the largest U.S. lessor of rail tank and freight cars, the largest tank terminal operator, the largest contract warehouser, and a leading lessor of commercial aircraft, and provides Great Lakes shipping services. A $37 million net charge ($1.90 a share) was incurred in the 1992 third quarter to increase reserves for potential losses in the real estate and aircraft portfolio. Operating profits are projected to rebound in 1993, reflecting improvement in most business segments. The quarterly dividend was boosted 7.7% with the March 1993 payment.

Current Outlook

Profits for 1993 are estimated at $3.35 a share, up from $0.82 (after a $1.90 charge) reported for 1992. Earnings could reach $3.75 a share in 1994.

Dividends were lifted 7.7% to $0.35 quarterly, from $0.32½, with the March 1993 payment.

Railcar leasing profits should advance moderately in 1993, as utilization rates and the fleet size increase while maintenance and repair costs are flat. Terminal profits should advance as major oil producers require supplemental storage capacity to accommodate reformulated gasolines. Contributions from foreign affiliates should advance, reflecting an upturn in the U.K. economy. GATX Capital will benefit from the absence of substantial loss reserves taken in 1992, plus higher disposal gains in 1993. Warehousing profits may slip reflecting startup costs of new contracts with Atlas Supply and Sears Logistics. Shipping volumes will benefit from rising steel consumption.

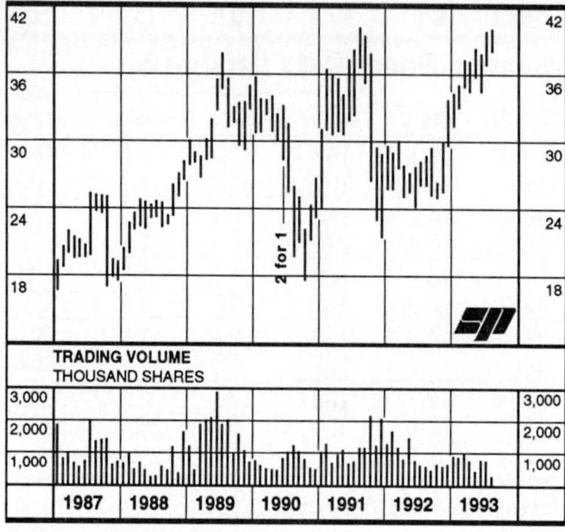

Gross Income (Million $)

Quarter:	1993	1992	1991	1990
Mar.	237	232	212	191
Jun.	289	259	243	213
Sep.	---	273	272	225
Dec.	---	255	263	242
	---	1,019	989	870

Gross income in 1993's first half rose 7.2%, year to year. Net income was up 39%, to $1.92 a share, from $1.32, which was before a $2.36 charge for the cumulative effect of accounting changes.

Common Share Earnings ($)

Quarter:	1993	1992	1991	1990
Mar.	0.77	0.64	0.80	0.86
Jun.	1.15	0.68	0.89	0.75
Sep.	E0.75	d0.96	0.96	0.91
Dec.	E0.68	0.46	0.91	1.09
	E3.35	0.82	3.56	3.61

Important Developments

Jul. '93— Pretax income in 1993's second quarter included a $16 million gain ($0.50 a share after taxes) from an insurance settlement related to certain marine equipment. Offsetting the gain, GMT added $12 million to GATX Capital's reserves for potential losses on aircraft leases. In 1992's third quarter, GMT took a $37 million net charge to increase reserves for potential losses on its real estate and aircraft lease portfolio.

Jun. '93— GMT acquired a 1,500-unit railcar portfolio from Westinghouse Electric Corp. for an undisclosed amount. The relatively new equipment had an original value of $100 million.

Feb. '93— The Unit Companies formed a partnership with Certified Grocers of California to operate a 450,000 sq. ft. warehouse.

Next earnings report expected in late October.

Per Share Data ($)

Yr. End Dec. 31	1992	1991	1990	[1]1989	[1]1988	[1]1987	1986	1985	1984	1983
Book Value	**12.58**	15.38	13.83	[2]17.23	14.43	12.37	11.11	12.73	15.20	14.43
Cash Flow	**7.92**	10.10	9.60	8.23	7.15	6.12	4.43	3.20	4.15	d0.24
Earnings[3]	**0.82**	3.56	3.61	3.18	2.52	1.82	1.10	d0.04	1.19	d3.92
Dividends	**1.300**	1.200	1.100	1.000	0.900	0.750	0.675	0.600	0.600	1.050
Payout Ratio	**159%**	34%	30%	32%	34%	38%	49%	NM	50%	NM
Prices—High	**33¾**	40¼	35¾	37⅞	28¼	25⅜	21	18¾	17¼	18⅜
Low	**24¼**	21½	17⅝	26¾	18½	16⅝	15	13⅞	12⅞	12⅝
P/E Ratio—	**41–30**	11–6	10–5	12–8	11–7	14–9	19–14	NM	15–11	NM

Data as orig. reptd. Adj. for stk. div. of 100% Jun. 1990. **1.** Reflects merger or acquisition. **2.** Incl. intangibles. **3.** Bef. results of disc. ops. of +0.11 in 1986, -1.87 in 1985, and spec. item of -2.36 in 1992. d-Deficit. E-Estimated. NM-Not Meaningful.

Income Data (Million $)

Year Ended Dec. 31	[1]Revs.	Oper. Inc.	% Oper. Inc. of Revs.	Cap. Exp.	Depr.	Int. Exp.	Net Bef. Taxes	Eff. Tax Rate	[4]Net Inc.	% Net Inc. of Revs.	Cash Flow
1992	**1,019**	**389**	**38.2**	**216**	**138**	**180**	**39**	**24.7%**	**29.3**	**2.9**	**154**
1991	989	402	40.6	241	128	187	116	28.9%	82.7	8.4	197
1990	870	389	44.7	310	115	182	118	29.9%	82.9	9.5	185
[2]1989	702	349	49.7	257	98	167	101	35.1%	65.7	9.4	158
[2]1988	564	281	49.8	281	90	144	74	36.2%	47.0	8.2	136
[2]1987	521	250	48.0	104	86	136	56	38.5%	34.7	6.6	120
[3]1986	512	250	48.8	57	81	141	24	NM	26.2	5.1	106
[3]1985	694	260	37.5	56	84	136	1	NM	3.1	0.4	83
1984	847	261	30.9	65	85	141	65	43.8%	36.7	4.3	117
1983	849	247	29.1	69	88	155	d153	NM	d93.1	NM	d6

Balance Sheet Data (Million $)

Dec. 31	Cash	Curr. Assets	Curr. Liab.	Curr. Ratio	Total Assets	% Ret. on Assets	[5]Long Term Debt	Common Equity	Total Inv. Capital	% LT Debt of Cap.	% Ret. on Equity
1992	**22.9**	**NA**	**NA**	**NA**	**3,426**	**0.8**	**1,725**	**385**	**2,516**	**68.5**	**3.9**
1991	25.1	NA	NA	NA	3,514	2.4	1,799	441	2,716	66.2	16.7
1990	76.0	NA	NA	NA	3,310	2.6	1,715	384	2,603	65.9	19.5
1989	20.1	NA	NA	NA	3,060	2.2	1,456	328	2,320	62.8	20.0
1988	21.9	NA	NA	NA	2,605	1.9	1,306	256	1,926	67.8	19.6
1987	20.6	NA	NA	NA	2,200	1.6	1,221	218	1,796	68.0	16.7
1986	84.3	NA	NA	NA	2,234	1.3	1,233	201	1,784	69.1	10.8
1985	51.2	NA	NA	NA	2,392	0.1	1,153	328	1,873	61.6	NM
1984	51.4	NA	NA	NA	2,514	1.5	1,258	403	2,131	59.0	8.1
1983	40.7	NA	NA	NA	2,531	NM	1,281	383	2,122	60.4	NM

Data as orig. reptd. **1.** Incl. other income after 1988. **2.** Reflects merger or acquisition. **3.** Excl. disc. ops. **4.** Bef. spec. items. **5.** Incl. curr. portion. d-Deficit. NM-Not Meaningful. NA-Not Available.

Business Summary

Contributions (million $) by business segment to net income (before corporate charges) in recent years were:

	1992	1991	1990	1989
Railcar leasing.......	$49.4	$55.2	$57.2	$53.0
Financial services...	–16.7	28.5	31.6	27.5
Tank terminals.......	23.4	19.0	19.4	23.8
Shipping...............	6.2	6.3	4.0	2.6
Warehousing.........	0.9	–0.7	–0.4	0.4

General American Transportation Corp. is the largest full-service railcar lessor in the U.S., managing a fleet of 54,388 tank, covered hopper and specialty rail cars at 1992 year-end. The chemical industry generated 55% of railcar lease revenues in 1992. GATX Capital Corp. writes full payout leases for commercial jet aircraft (45% of the lease portfolio at 1992 year-end), rail equipment (16%), real estate (10% but being phased out), production equipment (7%), golf course (7%) and other assets (15%). GATX Terminals Corp. is the world's largest independent bulk liquids storage company, primarily serving the petroleum and chemical industries. At 1992 year-end, it operated 47 terminal facilities and three pipeline systems. Throughput in 1992 was 639 million bbl., versus 650 million bbl. in 1991. GATX Logistics is the largest full service provider of warehousing, distribution and logistics support services in the U.S., operating over 21 million sq. ft. of space at 125 facilities. American Steamship Co., with a fleet of 11 self-unloading vessels on the Great Lakes, transported 23.9 million tons of coal, iron ore, limestone and aggregates in 1992.

Dividend Data

Dividends have been paid since 1919. A dividend reinvestment plan is available. A "poison pill" stock purchase rights plan was adopted in 1986.

Amt. of Divd. $	Date Decl.	Ex–divd. Date	Stock of Record	Payment Date
0.32½	Oct. 30	Dec. 9	Dec. 15	Dec. 31'92
0.35	Jan. 29	Mar. 1	Mar. 5	Mar. 31'93
0.35	Apr. 29	Jun. 9	Jun. 15	Jun. 30'93
0.35	Jul. 30	Sep. 9	Sep. 15	Sep. 30'93

Capitalization

Long Term Debt: $1,701,700,000 (3/93), incl. $283.6 million of capital lease obligs.

$2.50 Conv. Pfd. Stock: 46,454 shs. ($1 par).

$3.875 Conv. Pfd. Stock: 3,395,000 shs. ($1 par).

Common Stock: 19,554,565 shs. ($0.625 par).
Institutions hold 79%.
Shareholders of record: 3,901.

Office—120 South Riverside Plaza, Chicago, IL 60606-3998. **Tel**—(312) 621-6200. **Chrmn & Pres**—J. J. Glasser. **VP-Fin & CFO**—J. F. Chlebowski. **VP-Secy**—P. A. Heinen. **Investor Contact**—G. S. Lowman. **Dirs**—W. R. Christopherson, F. A. Cole, J. W. Cozad, R. J. Day, J. L. Dutt, R. A. Giesen, J. J. Glasser, C. Marshall, M. E. Murphy, M. T. Thompson. **Transfer Agent & Registrar**—Chemical Bank, NYC. **Incorporated** in New York in 1916. **Empl**—5,100.

 Stephen R. Klein

GenCorp Inc.

NYSE Symbol GY Options on CBOE (Mar-Jun-Sep-Dec) In S&P MidCap 400

Price	Range	P-E Ratio	Dividend	Yield	S&P Ranking	Beta
Oct. 13'93	1993					
15⅞	17⅜–11¼	16	0.60	3.8%	B	1.24

Summary

GenCorp is engaged in aerospace and defense work, and manufactures automotive products and polymer products. Fiscal 1993-94 earnings should rise on higher U.S. vehicle production and participation in several new vehicle programs, and despite a continued decline in profits from Aerojet. GY may sell a large part of Aerojet's ordnance division. On December 1, 1993, GY will adopt a new accounting method, which will result in a charge of between $170 million and $195 million and ongoing cost of up to $3 million a year.

Current Outlook

Earnings for the fiscal year ending November 30, 1994, may rise to $1.40 a share from the $1.30 estimated for fiscal 1993. Share earnings for fiscal 1992 were $0.70 after a $0.45 restructuring charge.

The dividend should continue at $0.15 quarterly.

Fiscal 1994 automotive and polymer sales should rise, reflecting an expected increase in motor vehicle build rates and higher sales of commercial wallcovering, latex and tennis balls. Aerojet sales should decline modestly as defense orders continue to fall. Higher profits from automotive and polymer products, along with overhead cost controls, should result in higher earnings for fiscal 1994.

Net Sales (Million $)

Quarter:	1992–93	1992	1991	1990
Feb.	402	461	433	348
May	492	500	500	458
Aug.	482	452	480	463
Nov.		524	580	506
		1,937	1,993	1,775

Sales for the nine months ended August 31, 1993, were down 2.6%, year to year, on a 16% drop in Aerojet sales. Aided by stronger profits at Automotive, which offset a 19% decline at Aerojet, operating profits rose 2.3%. Following 28% lower interest charges, and taxes at 40.0% against 40.7%, net income increased 53%, to $1.00 a share from $0.65.

Common Share Earnings ($)

Quarter:	1992–93	1992	1991	1990
Feb.	0.19	0.07	d0.05	0.71
May	0.56	0.43	0.39	0.32
Aug.	0.25	0.15	0.15	0.08
Nov.	E0.30	0.05	0.51	0.49
	E1.30	0.70	1.00	1.60

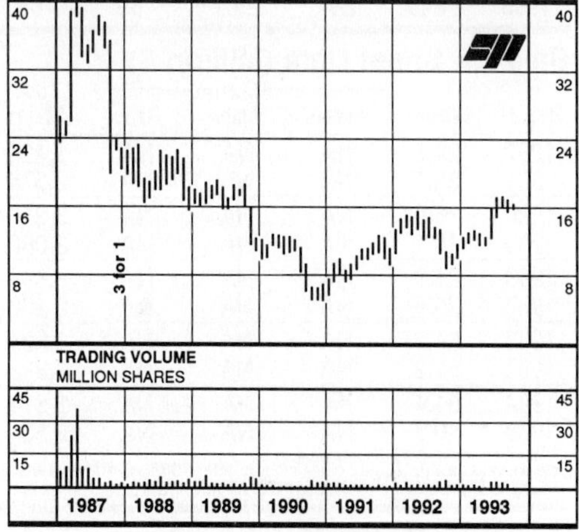

Important Developments

Oct. '93— GY will take a charge of between $170 million and $195 million on December 1, 1993 to adopt a new accounting method, FAS 106, which recognizes the expected future cost of employees' post-retirement benefits. Ongoing cost of up to $3 million a year for FAS 106 is possible.

Sep. '93— GY expected start-up costs for vehicle changeovers to lower fourth quarter earnings to less than the $0.50 a share earned in the year earlier period before a restructuring charge.

Jul. '93— Through a partnership formed with Axel Henniges, GY took a 24.5% interest in a limited partnership with HENNIGES Elastomer-und Kunststofftechnik GmbH & Co., KG, a German rubber products maker with sales of $113 million.

Next earnings report expected in mid-December.

Per Share Data ($)

Yr. End Nov. 30	1992	1991	1990	1989	1988	1987	1986	1985	[2]1984	1983
Tangible Bk. Val.[1]	**6.71**	6.71	6.30	4.88	d1.13	d3.21	14.82	13.35	12.72	13.95
Cash Flow	**3.18**	3.44	3.94	2.46	3.72	1.58	3.51	2.19	1.51	2.10
Earnings[3]	**0.70**	1.00	1.60	0.25	1.72	0.38	1.94	0.73	0.10	1.03
Dividends	**0.600**	0.600	0.600	0.600	0.600	0.500	0.498	0.489	0.479	0.469
Payout Ratio	**86%**	59%	37%	238%	35%	132%	26%	67%	452%	42%
Prices[4]—High	**15⅝**	12¾	12⅞	19⅛	23⅜	40	28¼	22⅞	12½	12½
Low	**8⅞**	5⅝	5	10⅞	15⅝	19⅞	21⅝	10¾	9¾	9⅛
P/E Ratio—	**22–13**	13–6	8–3	77–44	14–9	NM	15–11	32–15	NM	12–9

Data as orig. reptd. Adj. for stk. div(s). of 200% Dec. 1987, 2% Mar. 1986, 2% Feb. 1985, 2% Jan. 1984, 2% Feb. 1983. **1.** Incl. intangibles after 1987. **2.** Reflects acctg. change. **3.** Bef. results from disc. opers. of +0.39 in 1990, +6.36 in 1989, +0.38 in 1988, +9.49 in 1987, +0.40 in 1985, -0.10 in 1983: bef. spec. items of +0.09 in 1988. **4.** Cal. yr. d-Deficit. E-Estimated NM-Not Meaningful.

Income Data (Million $)

Year Ended Nov. 30	Revs.	Oper. Inc.	% Oper. Inc. of Revs.	Cap. Exp.	Depr.	Int. Exp.	Net Bef. Taxes	Eff. Tax Rate	[4]Net Inc.	% Net Inc. of Revs.	Cash Flow
1992	**1,937**	**188**	**9.7**	**96**	**79**	**46**	**37**	**40.5%**	**22**	**1.1**	**101**
1991	1,993	168	8.4	93	77	52	49	34.7%	32	1.6	109
1990	1,775	173	9.7	79	74	62	82	37.8%	51	2.9	125
1989	1,938	170	8.8	111	70	67	8	Nil	8	0.4	78
[1]1988	1,891	195	10.3	131	63	57	73	24.7%	55	2.9	118
[1]1987	1,619	183	11.3	102	58	25	39	53.8%	[2]18	1.1	76
1986	3,099	315	10.2	189	104	26	225	42.2%	130	4.2	235
[1]1985	3,021	266	8.8	161	98	32	76	35.5%	49	1.6	147
[2]1984	2,727	225	8.2	148	94	39	[3]30	75.7%	7	0.3	101
1983	2,184	189	8.7	85	77	28	[3]120	37.7%	75	3.4	152

Balance Sheet Data (Million $)

Nov. 30	Cash	Curr. Assets	Curr. Liab.	Curr. Ratio	Total Assets	% Ret. on Assets	Long Term Debt	Common Equity	Total Cap.	% LT Debt of Cap.	% Ret. on Equity
1992	**34**	**437**	**408**	**1.1**	**1,131**	**2.0**	**344**	**213**	**557**	**61.8**	**10.3**
1991	41	436	379	1.2	1,113	2.9	355	213	582	61.0	15.5
1990	31	415	365	1.1	1,078	4.3	345	200	559	61.7	28.7
1989	45	584	448	1.3	1,270	0.6	496	155	652	76.1	13.4
1988	41	566	401	1.4	1,230	4.7	674	d36	638	NM	NM
1987	41	490	532	0.9	1,108	1.7	473	d97	376	NM	9.0
1986	192	1,096	643	1.7	2,119	6.2	198	1,048	1,316	15.0	13.0
1985	253	1,130	573	2.0	2,073	2.4	255	951	1,353	18.8	5.2
1984	152	949	548	1.7	2,037	0.4	312	910	1,357	23.0	0.8
1983	169	813	452	1.8	1,853	4.4	273	941	1,339	20.4	8.1

Data as orig. reptd. **1.** Excludes discontinued operations. **2.** Reflects accounting change. **3.** Incl. equity in earns. of nonconsol. subs. **4.** Bef. results of disc. opers. and spec. item(s). d-Deficit. NM-Not Meaningful.

Business Summary

This diversified manufacturer is a supplier of space and defense systems, auto parts and polymer products. Sales and operating profits (in millions) for fiscal 1992 were divided:

	Sales	Profits
Aerospace & defense	53%	$71
Polymer products	25%	45
Automotive	22%	9
Restructuring charge	---	–22

Aerojet General is in the aerospace and defense business, selling primarily to the U.S. Government and prime contractors. Aerojet has a diverse product mix in propulsion, defense electronics and ordnance. At the end of fiscal 1992, Aerojet's contract backlog was about $1.3 billion ($900 million funded), down from $1.5 billion ($1.2 billion) a year earlier. Important programs include Peacekeeper, Titan and Delta rocket engines, Advanced Medium Range Air-to-Air Missile (AMRAAM), Sense and Destroy Armor (SADARM), the Advanced Solid Rocket Motor and a variety of programs related to the Strategic Defense Initiative.

GenCorp Automotive is a major supplier of sealing systems, suspension components, reinforced plastic panels for vehicle bodies and other fiber-reinforced plastic components.

Polymer-based product lines include fabricated plastics, latex, wallcovering, tennis balls and racquetballs.

Dividend Data

Dividends have been paid since 1937. A dividend reinvestment plan is available. A "poison pill" stock purchase right was adopted in 1987.

Amt of Divd. $	Date Decl.	Ex-divd. Date	Stock of Record	Payment Date
0.15	Jan. 27	Feb. 2	Feb. 8	Feb. 26'93
0.15	Mar. 31	Apr. 27	May 3	May 31'93
0.15	Jul. 16	Jul. 27	Aug. 2	Aug. 31'93
0.15	Sep. 10	Oct. 26	Nov. 1	Nov. 30'93

Finances

Auditors noted in their opinion on GY's fiscal 1992 financial statements that uncertainties exist regarding the eventual liabilities of Aerojet relating to environmental litigation arising from discharges of chemicals.

Capitalization

Long Term Debt: $416,500,000 (8/93).

Common Stock: 31,729,967 shs. ($0.10 par). Institutions hold about 47%. Shareholders of record: 16,400.

Office—175 Ghent Rd., Fairlawn, OH 44333-3300. **Tel**—(216) 869-4200. **Chrmn & CEO**—A. W. Reynolds. **Pres**—J. L. Heckel. **Secy**—E. R. Dye. **VP-Treas & CFO**—D. M. Steuert. **Investor Contact**—Richard A. Nelson. **Dirs**—J. L. Heckel, R. K. Jaedicke, P. X. Kelley, R. D. Kunisch, J. LaFontant-Mankarious, J. M. Osterhoff, P. J. Phoenix, R. B. Pipes, A. W. Reynolds, H. A. Shaw III, J. R. Stover, W. B. Walsh. **Transfer Agents**—First Chicago Trust Co., NYC; Company's office. **Registrars**—First Chicago Trust Co., NYC; First National Bank of Ohio, Akron. **Incorporated** in Ohio in 1915. **Empl**—13,900.

 Joshua M. Harari, CFA

General Motors Class E Stock

NYSE Symbol GME Options on CBOE, Phila (Mar-Jun-Sep-Dec) In S&P MidCap 400

Price	Range	P-E Ratio	Dividend	Yield	S&P Ranking	Beta
Jul. 29'93	1993					
27⅞	35⅞–26¼	20	[1]0.40	[1]1.4%	NR	0.95

Summary

This common stock was issued by General Motors Corp. (GM) in connection with its 1984 acquisition of Electronic Data Systems (EDS), a leading computer services concern. Class E shares are distinct from GM's regular common stock; EDS's income forms the base out of which dividends may be paid on the shares. Although business with GM may remain flat through 1994, revenues from non-GM customers should return to double digit growth in the second half of 1993 and in 1994, reflecting new sales of $3.3 billion in the first half of 1993.

Current Outlook

Earnings for 1993 are estimated at $1.50 a share, up from 1992's $1.33. An increase to $1.70 is projected for 1994.

The quarterly dividend was increased 11%, to $0.10, with the March 1993 payment.

Revenues are projected to advance about 6.5% in 1993. GM-related revenues should be essentially flat, at about $3.3 billion, while outside customer revenues should increase more than 10%. Base-revenue growth during the first half of 1993 was sluggish, reflecting an unusual number of contract completions in 1992; however, with new sales of $3.3 billion in the first half of 1993, EDS should be able to achieve non-GM revenue growth of 15% in the second half of the year and in 1994. By the end of 1993, services provided to GM should represent 36% of total revenues, down from 41% in 1992. Margins should improve gradually, reflecting continued cost controls. The tax rate is estimated at 36.0% through 1994; however, proposed tax legislation could increase the effective rate in 1994 to 39%.

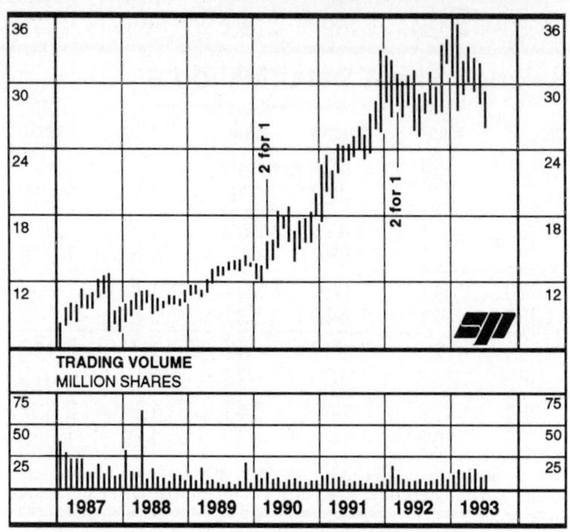

Total Revenues (Million $)

Quarter:	1993	1992	1991	1990
Mar.	2,073	1,995	1,609	1,417
Jun.	2,091	2,017	1,678	1,455
Sep.	---	2,062	1,726	1,530
Dec.	---	2,145	2,086	1,706
	---	8,219	7,099	6,109

Systems and contract revenues in the first half of 1993 rose 3.7%, year to year, with GM-related revenues up 2.1% and non-GM business gaining 4.9%. Costs were well controlled, and net income advanced 14%, to $0.69 a share, from $0.61.

Class E Share Earnings ($)

Quarter:	1993	1992	1991	1990
Mar.	0.32	0.28	0.25	0.23
Jun.	0.37	0.33	0.29	0.26
Sep.	E0.39	0.35	0.30	0.27
Dec.	E0.42	0.37	0.33	0.28
	E1.50	1.33	1.17	1.04

Important Developments

Jul. '93— Baxter Diagnostics Inc. announced the signing of an eight-year strategic alliance with EDS, with a value estimated by Baxter to exceed $250 million. In the partnership, EDS will provide systems development and operations, network management and end-user support for Baxter's new on-line, laboratory information network.

Next earnings report expected in late October.

Per Class E Share Data ($)

Yr. End Dec. 31	1992	1991	[2]1990	[2]1989	[3]1988	1987	1986	1985	1984
Tangible Bk. Val.	**NA**	10.36	9.68	8.17	5.73	5.10	3.75	2.00	NA
Cash Flow	**2.28**	2.11	1.91	1.71	1.60	1.30	1.04	0.54	0.22
Earnings[4]	**1.33**	1.17	1.04	0.91	0.79	0.67	0.54	0.40	[5]0.13
Dividends	**0.360**	0.320	0.280	0.240	0.170	0.130	0.100	0.049	0.012
Payout Ratio	**27%**	27%	27%	27%	22%	20%	19%	12%	9%
Prices—High	**34**	33	20¹⁄₁₆	14⁷⁄₁₆	11¼	12¾	12⁷⁄₁₆	11⅝	6
Low	**25¼**	17½	12³⁄₁₆	10⅝	8⅜	6	6³⁄₁₆	5³⁄₁₆	4⁹⁄₁₆
P/E Ratio—	**26–19**	28–15	19–12	16–12	14–11	19–9	23–12	30–13	NM

Data as orig. reptd.; prior to 1985 pro forma. Adj. for stk. divs. of 100% Mar. 1992, 100% Mar. 1990, 100% Jun. 1985. **1.** Indicated rate. **2.** Refl. merger or acq. **3.** Refl. acctg. change. **4.** Bef. spec. item(s) of -0.03 in 1991. **5.** For period Oct. 18—Dec. 31. NA-Not Available. NM-Not Meaningful. E-Estimated.

General Motors Class E Common Stock

Income Data (Million $)

Year Ended Dec. 31	Revs.	Oper. Inc.	% Oper. Inc. of Revs.	Cap. Exp.	Depr.	Int. Exp.	Net Bef. Taxes	Eff. Tax Rate	[5]Net Inc.	% Net Inc. of Revs.	Cash Flow
1992	**8,155**	**1,438**	**17.6**	**639**	**458**	**61.1**	**1,001**	**36.5%**	**636**	**7.8**	**1,093**
[1]1991	7,029	1,297	18.5	673	446	43.8	[4]894	37.0%	563	8.0	1,009
[1]1990	6,022	1,137	18.9	515	417	30.1	[4]789	37.0%	497	8.3	914
[1]1989	5,374	982	18.3	383	382	24.0	[4]680	36.0%	435	8.1	817
[2]1988	4,745	887	18.7	301	392	18.3	[4]589	34.8%	384	8.1	777
1987	4,324	727	16.8	346	309	2.2	[4]530	39.0%	323	7.5	632
1986	4,321	649	15.0	627	244	2.1	[4]463	43.7%	261	6.0	505
1985	3,406	396	11.6	574	71	4.2	[4]363	47.6%	190	5.6	261
1984	926	[3]118	[3]12.7	NA	NA	NA	[4]139	42.1%	81	8.7	98
1983	702	[3]87	[3]12.4	NA	NA	NA	[4]117	44.2%	65	9.3	81

Balance Sheet Data (Million $)

Dec. 31	Cash	Curr. Assets	Curr. Liab.	Curr. Ratio	Total Assets	% Ret. on Assets	Long Term Debt	Common Equity	Total Cap.	% LT Debt of Cap.	% Ret. on Equity
1992	**588**	**2,157**	**1,903**	**1.1**	**6,124**	**NA**	**561**	**3,063**	**4,220**	**13.3**	**NA**
1991	416	1,946	2,397	0.8	5,703	10.8	276	2,610	3,301	8.4	23.1
1990	715	1,716	1,654	1.0	4,565	11.6	263	2,182	2,889	9.1	24.9
1989	681	1,458	1,495	1.0	3,918	12.1	211	1,764	2,308	9.1	27.9
1988	728	1,339	1,377	1.0	3,416	12.2	89	1,404	1,723	5.1	31.5
1987	965	1,537	1,279	1.2	2,958	12.2	24	1,054	1,171	2.0	35.3
1986	534	1,079	871	1.2	2,410	14.1	20	798	932	2.1	39.3
1985	388	753	655	1.1	1,595	17.7	21	531	633	3.4	42.6
1984	163	391	206	1.9	607	15.0	27	346	388	7.0	25.7
1983	95	235	147	1.6	471	NA	28	281	319	8.9	NA

Data as orig. reptd.; prior to 1985 pro forma data relating to Cl. E com. stock as reptd. in 1984 GM annual report. **1.** Refl. merger or acq. **2.** Refl. acctg. change. **3.** Aft. depr. & interest exp. not separately reptd. **4.** Incl. equity in earns. of nonconsol. subs. prior to 1988. **5.** Bef. spec. item(s). NA-Not Available.

Business Summary

General Motors Class E common stock is distinct from the regular common shares of the U.S. automaker in terms of voting and dividend rights. Class E shares were initially issued in connection with GM's 1984 acquisition of Electronic Data Systems (EDS), a leading computer services company. EDS's income forms the base out of which dividends on the Class E shares may be paid.

EDS, currently a wholly owned GM subsidiary, designs, installs, operates and integrates data processing and communications systems. GM provided 41% of 1992 operating revenues.

In 1985 EDS assumed responsibility for integrating, updating and building GM's worldwide information processing, automated manufacturing, and telecommunication activities. It also continues to expand its business with non-GM customers, including several government agencies and companies in manufacturing, financial, insurance, healthcare, and communications fields.

Dividend Data

GM's directors have adopted a policy whereby annual per share dividends on Class E stock, if declared, equal about 30% of the prior year's Available Separate Consolidated Net Income of EDS, which is equal to the Separate Consolidated Net Income of EDS multiplied by a fraction, the numerator of which is the weighted average of Class E shares outstanding during the period and the denominator of which was 479.3 million shares (adjusted) for 1992. Share earnings on Class E stock are equivalent to earnings available for payment of dividends.

Amt. of Divd. $	Date Decl.	Ex–divd. Date	Stock of Record	Payment Date
0.09	Aug. 10	Aug. 14	Aug. 20	Sep. 10'92
0.09	Nov. 2	Nov. 5	Nov. 12	Dec. 10'92
0.10	Feb. 1	Feb. 5	Feb. 11	Mar. 10'93
0.10	May 3	May 7	May 13	Jun. 10'93

Finances

In January 1992, EDS acquired Energy Management Associates, a provider of planning software and regulatory/management consulting to the electric and gas utilities industry. In November 1991, it purchased McDonnell Douglas Systems Integration Co., a leader in the computer-aided design and manufacturing market. In the 1991 third quarter, EDS acquired SD-Scicon, a leader in the software systems and services field in the U.K.

Capitalization

Notes Payable: $560,600,000, excl. $0.5 million interest-free advances from GM.

Class E Common Stock: 237,119,718 shs. ($0.10 par); has ⅛ voting and liquid. rights relative to GM $1⅔ par com.

Institutions hold 57%.

Shareholders of record: 409,475.

ELECTRONIC DATA SYSTEMS CORP.: Office—7171 Forest Lane, Dallas, TX 75230. **Tel**—(214) 604-6000. **Pres & CEO**—L. M. Alberthal, Jr. **VP & Secy**—J. R. Castle, Jr. **VP & Treas**—A. E. Weynand. **Investor Contact**—Myrna Vance. **Dirs**—L. M. Alberthal, Jr., P. J. Chiaparone, G. J. Fernandes, M. J. Gudis, J. D. Hamlin, J. M. Heller, D. Linderman, R. T. O'Connell, G. S. Reeves, R. J. Schultz, F. A. Smith, R. C. Stempel. **Transfer Agent & Registrar**—First Chicago Trust Co. of New York, NYC. **Empl**—70,000.

Genzyme Corp.

NASDAQ Symbol GENZ (Incl. in Nat'l Market) Options on ASE, CBOE & Phila In S&P MidCap 400

Price	Range	P-E Ratio	Dividend	Yield	S&P Ranking	Beta
Sep. 28'93	1993					
33¾	46¼–27½	22	None	None	C	1.40

Summary

Genzyme develops and manufactures biological products for human healthcare applications. Its lead product, Ceredase, has been marketed for the treament of Type 1 Gaucher disease since receiving FDA approval in April 1991. In May 1993, a New Drug Application was filed with the FDA for a recombinant form of modified GCR enzyme for the treatment of Gaucher disease.

Business Summary

Genzyme Corporation is a human healthcare products company whose activities and products are organized into four major business areas—biotherapeutics, diagnostic products, pharmaceuticals, and fine chemicals.

Genzyme's lead product, Ceredase, is an enzyme used for the treatment of Gaucher disease, a seriously debilitating disorder caused by the inheritance of defective genes for an enzyme called glucocerebrosidase (GCR). Sales of Ceredase were $95 million in 1992, up from $40 million in 1991 (FDA approval was received in April 1991). In May 1993, GENZ filed a New Drug Application with the FDA for a recombinant form of GCR, which is comparable to Ceredase in safety and effectiveness in the treatment of Gaucher disease and would provide the company with an alternate source of supply of GCR. Other products under development include: thyrogen hormone for the diagnosis and therapy of thyroid cancer (Phase III); protein replacement therapy and gene therapy products for the treatment of cystic fibrosis (on behalf of Neozyme II); Vianain debriding agent for the treatment of burns (Phase I/II) and skin ulcers (preclinical); and a line of biomaterial products based on hyaluronic acid to limit the formation of postoperative adhesions (on behalf of the Sugical Aids Partnership).

The diagnostic services business provides a broad range of classical and molecular cytogenetic and biochemical testing services to physicians, hospitals, clinical laboratories, genetic centers and HMO's in the U.S. through 70%-owned IG Laboratories Inc. and wholly-owned Vivigen Inc.

Genzyme's diagnostic products business is the leading independent supplier in the U.S. of diagnostic enzymes and substrates for the manufacture of reagents and clinical diagnostic kits, such as those used for amylase and cholesterol testing, and also sells a line of immunobiologicals to academic, industrial and governmental laboratories for research use. In January 1993, Genzyme's Direct LDL Cholesterol Test for direct measurement of low density lipoprotein cholesterol from blood samples was approved for sale by the FDA.

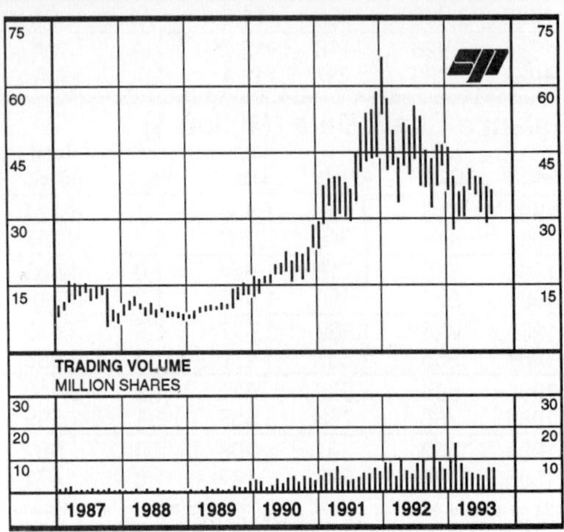

The pharmaceuticals and fine chemicals business develops, produces and sells bulk pharmaceutical intermediaries, active drug substances, fine chemicals and synthetic phospholipids to the pharmaceutical and health care industries.

Important Developments

Aug. '93— Genzyme and Argus Pharmaceuticals entered into an agreement to develop and commercialize Tretinoin (LF), a product for which Argus is conducting Phase I human trials for hematologic malignancies. The agreement includes a $5 million equity investment in Argus by Genzyme, plus milestone payments totaling $1.5 million. Separately, the company and Univax Biologics Inc. formed an alliance to develop and commercialize products for the treatment of infections associated with cystic fibrosis. GENZ agreed to make a $5 million equity investment in Univax, plus license fee and milestone payments of up to $6 million.

Per Share Data ($)

Yr. End Dec. 31	[1]1992	1991	[1]1990	[1]1989	1988	1987	1986	1985	1984	1983
Tangible Bk. Val.	**11.54**	11.90	5.63	6.19	3.90	3.91	3.66	[2]1.07	NA	NA
Cash Flow	**d1.02**	0.75	d1.37	d1.04	0.22	0.13	0.10	d0.34	NA	NA
Earnings[3]	**d1.38**	0.50	d1.70	d1 .32	0.05	0.03	0.01	d0.53	d0.02	d0.29
Dividends	**Nil**	Nil	Nil	Nil	Nil	Nil	Nil	Nil	Nil	Nil
Payout Ratio	**Nil**	Nil	Nil	Nil	Nil	Nil	Nil	Nil	Nil	Nil
Prices—High	**66½**	58¾	28⅝	15½	12⅝	16	14⅜	NA	NA	NA
Low	**32½**	23⅜	12½	7½	7¼	5¾	6⅝	NA	NA	NA
P/E Ratio—	**NM**	NM	NM	NM	NM	NM	NM	NA	NA	NA

Data as orig. reptd. **1.** Refl. merger or acq. **2.** As of 3-31-86, aft. conv. of pfd. stk. & settlement of litigation. **3.** Bef. spec. items of +0.02 in 1992, +0.37 in 1991, +0.03 in 1988, +0.02 in 1987. d-Deficit. NM-Not Meaningful. NA-Not Available.

Income Data (Million $)

Year Ended Dec. 31	Revs.	Oper. Inc.	% Oper. Inc. of Revs.	Cap. Exp.	Depr.	Int. Exp.	Net Bef. Taxes	Eff. Tax Rate	Net Inc.	% Net Inc. of Revs.	Cash Flow
[1]1992	**219**	**47.9**	**21.9**	**61.00**	**8.01**	**7.75**	**[2]d13.2**	**NM**	**d30.8**	**NM**	**d22.8**
1991	109	11.6	10.6	8.03	5.62	1.75	[2]20.6	57.0%	[3]11.2	10.2	16.8
[1]1990	50	d4.4	NM	9.00	5.24	0.39	[2]d27.8	Nil	[3]d27.2	NM	d21.9
[1]1989	33	d3.8	NM	6.17	2.80	0.54	d13.0	Nil	[3]d13.0	NM	d10.2
1988	25	1.4	5.7	6.17	1.49	0.58	0.7	35.3%	[3]0.4	1.8	1.9
1987	17	d1.4	NM	5.69	0.90	0.28	0.4	37.7%	[3]0.3	1.6	1.2
1986	12	0.1	0.6	NA	0.73	0.19	Nil	Nil	[3]Nil	0.3	0.8
1985	10	0.9	9.8	1.67	1.01	0.27	d2.8	Nil	[3]d2.8	NM	d1.9
1984	8	0.4	5.1	0.47	0.30	0.22	Nil	NM	[3]d0.1	NM	NA
1983	5	d0.8	NM	0.56	0.19	0.21	d1.2	Nil	[3]d1.2	NM	NA

Balance Sheet Data (Million $)

Dec. 31	Cash	Curr. Assets	Curr. Liab.	Curr. Ratio	Total Assets	% Ret. on Assets	Long Term Debt	Common Equity	Total Cap.	% LT Debt of Cap.	% Ret. on Equity
1992	**116**	**203**	**36.6**	**5.5**	**481**	**NM**	**105**	**323**	**440**	**23.9**	**NM**
1991	107	159	23.3	6.8	391	4.1	101	260	366	27.6	5.9
1990	43	69	10.4	6.6	118	NM	2	96	106	1.9	NM
1989	53	71	9.9	7.2	109	NM	5	91	96	5.3	NM
1988	11	25	5.3	4.7	42	1.1	3	33	36	7.5	1.3
1987	20	28	4.1	6.8	42	0.7	4	33	38	11.3	0.8
1986	22	29	1.8	16.4	33	0.1	Nil	31	31	0.5	0.4
1985	2	9	4.8	1.9	12	NM	Nil	[4]6	7	5.6	NM
1984	2	6	2.6	2.2	8	NM	Nil	[4]5	5	7.4	NM
1983	NA	NA	NA	NA	5	NM	Nil	[4]3	4	6.3	NM

Data as orig. reptd. **1.** Refl. merger or acq. **2.** Incl. equity in earns. of nonconsol. subs. **3.** Bef. spec. items. **4.** Pro forma, giving effect to conv. of pfd. stk. & related trans. at time of public offering. d-Deficit. NM-Not Meaningful. NA-Not Available.

Operating Revenues (Million $)

Quarter:	1993	1992	1991	1990
Mar.	62.3	45.5	18.9	8.9
Jun.	68.6	56.5	24.8	11.0
Sep.		57.0	29.7	12.7
Dec.		60.1	36.0	17.5
		219.1	109.5	50.1

In the six months ended June 30, 1993, revenues rose 28%, year to year, on increased Ceredase sales, customer additions in the pharmaceuticals and fine chemicals segment, and higher diagnostic product sales. Operating costs rose 34%, but in the absence of a $51.1 million charge related to the purchase of in-house R&D and a $16.9 million writeoff of the value of an option to buy Neozyme II Corp., pretax income replaced a loss. After taxes at 28.4%, versus taxes of $10,872,000, net income of $22,466,000 ($0.86 a share, on 20% more shares) contrasted with a loss of $48,334,000 ($2.20).

Common Share Earnings ($)

Quarter:	1993	1992	1991	1990
Mar.	0.42	0.31	0.20	d1.50
Jun.	0.44	d2.57	0.14	0.36
Sep.		0.37	0.22	d0.06
Dec.		0.33	d0.06	d0.55
		d1.38	0.50	[1]d1.70

1. Does not add due to change in no. of shs. d-Deficit.

Dividend Data

No cash dividends have been paid.

Finances

In July 1993, Genzyme Transgenics Corp. completed an initial public stock offering, thus reducing Genzyme's stake from 100% to 67%. Genzyme Transgenics (NASDAQ: GZTC) applies transgenic technology to the development and production of recombinant proteins for therapeutic and diagnostic uses.

In April 1993, Genzyme acquired Virotech System-Diagnostika GmbH, a German manufacturer of in-vitro diagnostic kits, for about $10 million.

In mid-1992, Genzyme began construction of a new mammalian cell production facility in Boston, which will be used to produce a recombinant form of Ceredase enzyme and other products. The facility is expected to cost over $100 million, and is scheduled for completion during 1994.

Capitalization

Long Term Liabs.: $105,510,000 (6/93), incl. $100,000,000 of 6.75% conv. debs. due 2001.

Common Stock: 23,999,563 shs. ($0.01 par). Institutions hold about 71%.

Options & Warrants: To buy 8,283,246 shs. at $16.01 to $41.31 ea. (12/92).

Office—One Kendall Sq., Cambridge, MA 02139. **Tel**—(617) 252-7500. **Chrmn, Pres & CEO**—H.A. Termeer. **SVP-Fin & CFO**—D.J. McLachlan. **Investor Contact**—Susan P. Cogswell. **Dirs**—C.E. Anagnostopoulos, D.A. Berthiaume, H.E. Blair, C.L. Cooney, H.R. Lewis, H.A. Termeer. **Transfer Agent & Registrar**—American Stock Transfer & Trust Co., NYC. **Incorporated** in Delaware in 1981; reincorp. in Massachusetts in 1991. **Empl**—1,486.

 Robert M. Gold

Georgia Gulf

NYSE Symbol GGC Options on Phila (Feb-May-Aug-Nov) In S&P MidCap 400

Price	Range	P-E Ratio	Dividend	Yield	S&P Ranking	Beta
Jul. 23'93	1993					
18⅜	23½–16½	19	None	None	NR	2.58

Summary

This company is a major producer of several highly integrated lines of commodity chemicals and polymers, including aromatic, natural gas and electrochemical products. Earnings are expected remain under pressure in 1993 due to lower selling prices, despite improved domestic economic conditions.

Current Outlook

Share earnings for 1993 are projected at $1.10, versus the $1.18 of 1992; earnings for 1994 could rise to $1.60 assuming a stronger economy.

Early resumption of cash dividends is unlikely.

Profits for 1993 are expected to decline due to sharply lower prices for caustic soda which has fallen over the past year as a result of high industry production of coproduct chlorine. Prices for PVC resins have been rising since early 1993 on good industry demand through margins still are poor. Interest expense will decline on lower debt resulting from the May 1992 stock offering and the February 1993 debt refinancing. Capital spending for 1993 and 1994 is projected at about $50 million a year, largely for a 240 million pound PVC capacity expansion.

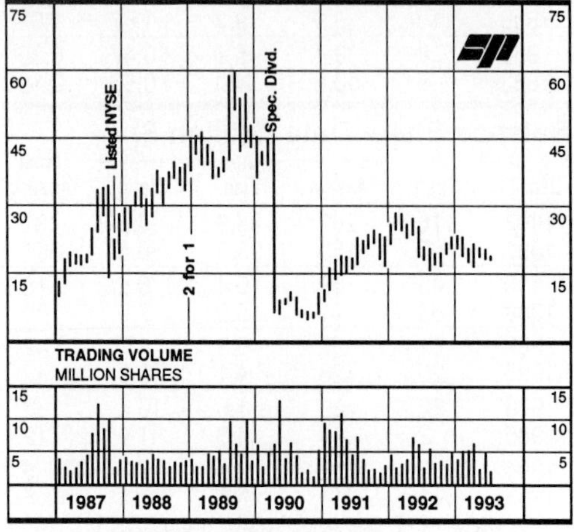

Net Sales (Million $)

Quarter:	1993	1992	1991	1990
Mar.	182	190	236	252
Jun.	195	193	214	219
Sep.	---	200	206	233
Dec.	---	197	182	229
	---	779	838	932

Sales in the first half of 1993 declined 1.4%, year to year, reflecting lower prices. Operating profits fell 22%. On lower interest expense, pretax income was off 16%. After taxes at 33.6%, against 31.9%, income declined 18%, to $0.51 a share, from $0.71. Results exclude both a $0.32 special credit and a $0.32 special charge in the 1993 interim.

Common Share Earnings ($)

Quarter:	1993	1992	1991	1990
Mar.	0.24	0.37	0.49	1.52
Jun.	0.28	0.35	0.48	0.50
Sep.	E0.28	0.26	0.44	0.69
Dec.	E0.30	0.22	0.35	0.56
	E1.10	1.18	1.75	[1]3.07

Important Developments

Jul. '93— GGC said that while overall volumes remained relatively level in the first half, a softening of sales prices and higher raw material costs negatively impacted earnings. The six month comparison was most impacted by a substantial drop in caustic soda prices, which reflected a continued weakness in certain end markets. GGC added that there has been improvement since the first quarter in volumes for some other products, and that it was pleased with the levels of activity for vinyl resin and compounds.

Feb. '93— The company refinanced its credit agreement, replacing a $227 million term loan and $90 million revolving credit facility with a $150 million term loan and a revolving credit facility of up to $150 million. First quarter 1993 earnings exclude an extraordinary charge of $13.3 million in costs related to the early retirement of the facility, largely offset by a $13.0 million credit from the adoption of FAS 109.

Next earnings report expected in late October.

Per Share Data ($)

Yr. End Dec. 31	1992	1991	1990	1989	[2]1988	1987	1986	1985
Tangible Bk. Val.	**[3]d4.00**	[3]d10.61	[3]d12.63	[3]12.80	[3]9.62	5.40	4.51	5.19
Cash Flow	**1.78**	2.34	3.59	8.37	7.30	3.46	1.82	2.48
Earnings[4]	**1.18**	1.75	3.07	7.58	6.75	3.15	1.21	1.11
Dividends	**Nil**	Nil	[5]38.50	1.00	0.65	0.20	Nil	Nil
Payout Ratio	**Nil**	Nil	NM	13%	8%	6%	Nil	Nil
Pric es—High	**28⅝**	24¾	45⅝	59⅞	39⅞	34½	10	NA
Low	**15¾**	8⅞	4⅞	36	24⅜	9¾	9¾	NA
P/E Ratio—	**24–13**	14–5	15–2	8–5	6–4	11–3	8	NA

Data as orig. reptd. Adj. for stk. div.(s) of 100% Jan. 1989. **1.** Does not add due to change in no. of shs. **2.** Reflects merger or acquisition. **3.** Incl. intangibles. **4.** Bef. spec. item(s) of -0.34 in 1987. **5.** Special divd. E-Estimated d-Deficit. NM-Not Meaningful. NA-Not Available.

Income Data (Million $)

Year Ended Dec. 31	Revs.	Oper. Inc.	% Oper. Inc. of Revs.	Cap. Exp.	Depr.	Int. Exp.	Net Bef. Taxes	Eff. Tax Rate	[4]Net Inc.	% Net Inc. of Revs.	Cash Flow
1992	**779**	**152**	**19.6**	**[3]14.3**	**23.6**	**61.2**	**68**	**31.5%**	**46**	**5.9**	**70**
1991	838	191	22.8	27.5	20.8	80.8	90	31.9%	61	7.3	82
1990	932	245	26.3	61.9	16.3	63.2	150	36.5%	95	10.2	112
1989	1,104	318	28.8	[3]54.2	18.7	1.0	300	36.0%	192	17.4	208
[1]1988	1,061	329	31.0	61.4	15.8	3.4	312	38.0%	194	18.3	206
1987	707	181	25.6	9.9	9.0	10.8	163	43.7%	[5]92	13.0	100
1986	583	103	17.6	7.4	17.1	13.2	72	45.9%	39	6.7	51
1985	614	136	22.2	6.2	38.0	24.1	74	50.9%	36	5.9	68
[2]1984	610	100	16.4	NA	66.1	1.2	33	40.2%	19	3.2	NA
[2]1983	446	68	15.3	NA	63.3	1.5	42	44.9%	23	5.2	NA

Balance Sheet Data (Million $)

Dec. 31	Cash	Curr. Assets	Curr. Liab.	Curr. Ratio	Total Assets	% Ret. on Assets	Long Term Debt	Common Equity	Total Cap.	% LT Debt of Cap.	% Ret. on Equity
1992	**2.9**	**193**	**130**	**1.5**	**419**	**10.1**	**409**	**d161**	**290**	**141.3**	**NM**
1991	2.5	176	149	1.2	416	14.1	588	d358	267	220.5	NM
1990	5.5	218	161	1.3	457	17.2	683	d424	295	231.5	NM
1989	46.2	244	106	2.3	473	41.3	1	330	367	0.2	65.6
1988	40.2	260	128	2.0	457	52.1	42	256	329	12.9	99.7
1987	24.2	182	100	1.8	309	25.7	42	143	209	19.9	69.9
1986	3.2	138	69	2.0	265	7.9	83	78	196	42.4	39.8
1985	1.2	153	136	1.1	292	9.1	78	36	156	49.9	NA

Data as orig. reptd. **1.** Reflects merger or acquisition. **2.** Predecessor co. **3.** Net of current year retirement and disposals. **4.** Bef. spec. item(s). **5.** Reflects accounting change. NA-Not Available. d-Deficit. NM-Not Meaningful.

Business Summary

Georgia Gulf is a leading manufacturer of commodity chemicals and plastics, including highly integrated lines comprised of electrochemicals, aromatic chemical products, and natural gas products. Portions of the commodity chemicals produced by the company are used as chemical intermediates for some of its product lines.

Electrochemicals, including chlorine (452,000 tons of annual capacity), caustic soda (501,000) and sodium chloride (27,000), are used in the pulp, paper, aluminum and plastics industries. Chlorine is used to produce vinyl chloride monomer (1.26 billion pounds), which is used to produce polyvinyl chloride resins (898 million pounds) and compounds (290 million pounds). PVC resins and compounds find uses in construction and housing components, packaging, household goods, and molded machine casings. Aromatic chemicals consist of cumene (1,420 million pounds), the feedstock for phenol (600 million) and acetone (370 million), which are used for adhesives, plastics, coatings and solvents. Natural gas products consist of methanol (140 million gallons), used in adhesives, polymers and gasoline additives. These products are manufactured at 12 plants in five locations, with six located at a complex in Plaquemine, La.

Georgia Gulf has a contract to supply, subject to certain limitations, a substantial percentage of Georgia-Pacific Corp.'s requirements for caustic soda, chlorine, methanol, phenol and sodium chlorate. Sales to Georgia-Pacific accounted for about 14% of total sales in 1992. International sales accounted for 15% of GGC's sales in 1992.

Dividend Data

Dividends were omitted in April 1990 after having been initiated in 1987. The most recent payment was $0.25 on January 8, 1990.

Finances

In April 1990, GGC completed a recapitalization, with each common share outstanding exchanged for $30 cash, $8.50 principal amount of 15% senior subordinated notes, and one new share of GGC common stock. Shareholders could elect to receive for each old share (up to 30% of those held) 5.5 shares of new common stock in lieu of cash and securities. Holders of 2,108,600 shares and options took the election, resulting in an increase in the number of shares outstanding of almost 9.5 million (37%). The cash portion of the recapitalization totaled $674 million, with $555 million funded by a bank term loan of $507 million and a revolving credit facility of $160 million. In addition, $191 million of $8.50 principal amount of 15% senior subordinated notes was issued to shareholders.

Capitalization

Long Term Debt: $396,606,000 (6/93).

Common Stock: 40,405,039 shs. ($0.01 par). Some 23% held by directors and officers. Institutions hold approximately 56%. Shareholders of record: 1,224.

Office—400 Perimeter Center Terrace, Suite 595, Atlanta, GA 30346. **Tel**—(404) 395-4500. **Chrmn**—J. R. Kuse. **Pres & CEO**—J. R. Satrum. **VP-CFO**—R. B. Marchese. **VP-Secy**—D. M. Chorba. **Investor Contact**—John. F. Walker. **Dirs**—J. D. Bryan, A. C. Eckert III, R. E. Flowerree, H. T. Green Jr., J. R. Kuse, J. R. Satrum, E. S. Smith. **Transfer Agent & Registrar**—Wachovia Bank, Winston-Salem, N.C. **Incorporated** in Delaware in 1984. **Empl**—1,128.

 Richard O'Reilly, CFA

Gibson Greetings

NASDAQ Symbol GIBG (Incl. in Nat'l Market) Options on Phila In S&P MidCap 400

Price	Range	P–E Ratio	Dividend	Yield	S&P Ranking	Beta
Aug. 16'93	1993					
21¼	22¼–17¾	45	0.40	1.9%	B+	1.07

Summary

This company is a leading U.S. producer of greeting cards and gift wrap. In June 1993 the company acquired The Paper Factory, operator of 106 retail paper goods stores. Earnings growth has resumed in 1993, after having been negatively impacted by writeoffs and other expenses related to the 1992 bankruptcy filing of Phar-Mor, Inc., formerly Gibson's largest customer.

Current Outlook

Earnings in 1993 are expected to rebound to $1.75 a share, from the depressed $0.50 reported for 1992. About $2.00 is anticipated for 1994.

The $0.10 quarterly dividend is expected to be maintained.

Net sales in 1993 are expected to rise moderately, in spite of a sharp drop in sales to Phar-Mor, reflecting strong greeting card gains combined with sales of The Paper Factory. Although expenses associated with The Paper Factory and from start-up operations will hurt profitability, the absence of some $14.4 million of costs related to Phar-Mor and a restructuring will more than compensate.

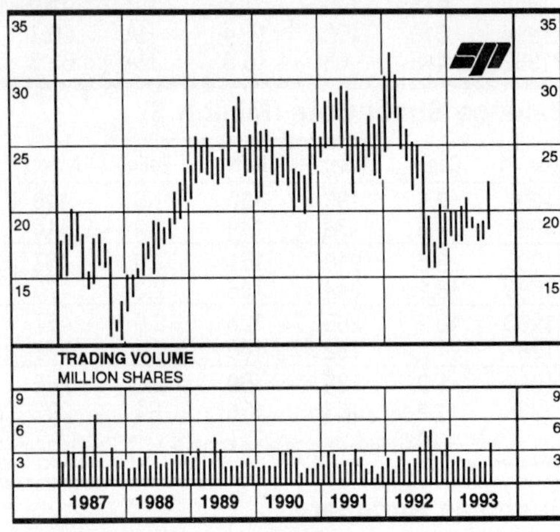

Revenues (Million $)

Quarter:	1993	1992	1991	1990
Mar.	84.9	79.4	84.2	80.9
Jun.	84.0	78.7	85.9	79.6
Sep.		115.6	152.5	145.6
Dec.		212.1	201.8	207.1
		485.8	524.3	513.2

For the six months ended June 30, 1993, revenues rose 6.8%, year to year. Results were penalized by start-up costs of Mexican operations, expenses related to The Paper Factory, higher costs in anticipation of stronger Christmas gift wrap sales, and a higher effective tax rate. Thus, net income fell 17%. Share net was $0.19, versus $0.22.

Common Share Earnings ($)

Quarter:	1993	1992	1991	1990
Mar.	0.11	0.15	0.26	0.39
Jun.	0.08	0.08	0.11	0.13
Sep.	E0.39	d0.75	0.81	0.80
Dec.	E1.17	1.03	1.43	1.19
	E1.75	0.50	2.61	2.51

Important Developments

Jun. '93— Gibson acquired The Paper Factory of Wisconsin, Inc., operator of 106 retail stores in the Midwest, South and West. The stores, located primarily in manufacturers' outlet shopping centers, feature a wide variety of paper party products, gift wrap and related items. Such locations do not compete with the accounts to which Gibson traditionally has marketed its products. Gibson expects the acquisition to accelerate its research efforts regarding merchandising techniques and new product development.

Feb. '93— Gibson said that operating results for 1992 were adversely affected by the August bankruptcy of Phar-Mor Inc. Phar-Mor had been Gibson's largest and fastest growing customer, accounting for about 13% of total revenues in 1991, but 8% in 1992.

Next earnings report expected in early November.

Per Share Data ($)

Yr. End Dec. 31	1992	1991	1990	1989	1988	1987	1986	1985	1984	1983
Tangible Bk. Val.	[2]**18.92**	[2]18.86	[2]16.58	14.15	11.99	10.04	8.81	7.69	5.83	4.28
Cash Flow	**2.04**	3.76	3.46	3.54	3.03	2.23	2.01	2.23	2.03	1.57
Earnings[1]	**0.50**	2.61	2.51	2.68	2.25	1.53	1.43	1.81	1.79	1.44
Dividends	**0.390**	0.355	0.340	0.330	0.288	0.250	0.250	0.240	0.188	0.260
Payout Ratio	**78%**	14%	13%	12%	13%	16%	17%	13%	10%	13%
Prices—High	**32**	29½	26⅞	28¾	23⅜	20¼	29⅜	24⅜	19⅛	18¾
Low	**15¾**	21⅜	19⅞	21	12½	10⅜	14¼	16	12	12⅜
P/E Ratio—	**64–32**	11–8	11–8	11–8	10–6	13–7	21–10	13–9	11–7	13–9

Data as orig. reptd. Adj. for stk. div. of 50% Mar. 1985. **1.** Bef. spec. item(s) of -0.09 in 1992, +0.18 in 1985. **2.** Incl. intangibles. d-Deficit. E-Estimated.

Income Data (Million $)

Year Ended Dec. 31	Revs.	Oper. Inc.	% Oper. Inc. of Revs.	Cap. Exp.	Depr.	Int. Exp.	Net Bef. Taxes	Eff. Tax Rate	[2]Net Inc.	% Net Inc. of Revs.	Cash Flow
1992	**502**	**75.5**	**15.0**	**31.0**	**24.9**	**7.9**	**13.1**	**38.9%**	**[3]8.0**	**1.6**	**32.9**
1991	524	95.7	18.3	31.7	18.5	10.6	68.2	38.6%	41.9	8.0	60.4
1990	513	86.7	16.9	42.7	15.0	10.2	63.9	37.7%	39.8	7.8	54.8
1989	465	80.8	17.4	32.0	13.6	3.9	65.7	35.5%	42.4	9.1	55.9
1988	404	74.4	18.4	17.8	12.2	6.9	56.7	38.3%	35.0	8.7	47.3
1987	360	59.9	16.7	[1]13.7	11.0	6.4	43.4	44.5%	24.1	6.7	35.1
1986	323	55.1	17.0	17.9	9.3	6.1	40.2	43.7%	[3]22.6	7.0	31.9
1985	330	65.6	19.9	18.1	6.5	11.1	51.6	44.4%	28.7	8.7	35.2
1984	302	62.7	20.8	25.2	3.8	10.7	52.5	46.0%	28.3	9.4	32.1
1983	242	51.8	21.4	11.5	1.9	9.6	41.9	46.6%	22.4	9.3	24.3

Balance Sheet Data (Million $)

Dec. 31	Cash	Curr. Assets	Curr. Liab.	Curr. Ratio	Total Assets	% Ret. on Assets	Long Term Debt	Common Equity	Total Cap.	% LT Debt of Cap.	% Ret. on Equity
1992	**9.5**	**334**	**110**	**3.0**	**501**	**1.5**	**70.2**	**303**	**376**	**18.7**	**2.6**
1991	9.8	368	153	2.4	544	7.6	71.1	301	383	18.5	14.8
1990	25.0	379	250	1.5	553	8.0	21.8	261	295	7.4	16.3
1989	5.5	311	164	1.9	439	11.0	30.4	226	265	11.5	20.5
1988	15.4	269	108	2.5	326	11.3	18.6	186	214	8.7	20.5
1987	6.9	236	99	2.4	289	8.6	23.3	154	185	12.6	16.7
1986	16.2	216	93	2.3	275	8.4	28.0	138	175	16.0	17.6
1985	5.5	211	94	2.3	261	11.4	32.7	119	159	20.6	27.3
1984	3.1	174	71	2.5	243	13.2	66.0	91	161	41.1	35.9
1983	0.8	134	71	1.9	182	13.6	30.8	65	98	31.3	51.4

Data as orig. reptd. **1.** Net of cur. yr. retirement and disposals. **2.** Bef. spec. item(s) in 1992, 1985. **3.** Refl. acctg. change.

Business Summary

Gibson Greetings, Inc., whose predecessors date from 1850, is one of the nation's largest manufacturers of greeting cards and gift wrapping paper. The Paper Factory, the operator of 106 paper goods stores, was acquired in June 1993.

Net sales in recent years were derived as follows:

	1992	1991
Greeting cards	50%	52%
Gift wrap..........................	39%	38%
Related products	11%	10%

Of Gibson's greeting card sales in 1992, everyday lines represented about 60% and seasonal lines 40%. Principal tradenames are "Gibson" and "Cleo". A Mexican subsidiary was formed in 1992, which purchased the net assets of a Mexican manufacturer and marketer of greeting cards, to market the company's products primarily in Mexico. During 1991, a subsidiary was formed to market products in the U.K. and in other European countries.

Related products include ribbons and bows, boxes and bags, decorative tags and boxed greeting cards, party goods and holiday decorations. Other products include paper party goods, candles, calendars and gift wrapping accessories.

The company's products often incorporate well-known persons or characters. Net sales associated with licensed properties accounted for 15% of 1992 net sales.

Dividend Data

Dividends have been paid since 1983.

Amt of Divd. $	Date Decl.	Ex–divd. Date	Stock of Record	Payment Date
0.10	Aug. 5	Aug. 25	Aug. 31	Sep. 14'92
0.10	Nov. 20	Nov. 23	Nov. 30	Dec. 14'92
0.10	Feb. 4	Feb. 22	Feb. 26	Mar. 15'93
0.10	Apr. 30	May 24	May 31	Jun. 14'93

Finances

A new $210 million, 3-year revolving credit agreement was consummated in May 1993.

Capitalization

Long Term Debt: $68,833,000 (3/93).

Common Stock: 16,034,075 shs. ($0.01 par).
Institutions hold 98%.
Shareholders: About 9,000 (3/93).

Office—2100 Section Rd., Cincinnati, OH 45237. **Tel**—(513) 841-6600. **Chrmn, Pres & CEO**—B. J. Sottile. **Secy**—H. L. Caldwell. **VP-Fin**—W. A. Cavanaugh. **VP & Treas**—J. H. Johnsen. **Dirs**—T. M. Cooney, J. Koppelman, C. D. Lindberg, R. J. Olson, A. R. Pezzillo, M. A. Pietrangelo, T. J. Smith, B. J. Sottile, B. B. Staniar, F. Stanton, R. T. Staubach, C. A. Wainwright, H. N. Walters. **Transfer Agent & Registrar**—First National Bank of Boston. **Incorporated** in Delaware in 1982. **Empl**—8,800.

Global Marine

NYSE Symbol GLM In S&P MidCap 400

Price	Range	P-E Ratio	Dividend	Yield	S&P Ranking	Beta
Sep. 30'93	1993					
5	5⅝–2⅛	NM	None	None	NR	1.60

Summary

Global Marine is a major international offshore drilling contractor serving the oil and gas industry with a diversified fleet of 23 mobile rigs. The company emerged from bankruptcy in February 1989. Earnings were up sharply in 1992, reflecting one-time gains of $66 million. In the absence of these gains, the first half of 1993 resulted in a loss. GLM anticipates a deficit of $0.20 a share in 1993.

Business Summary

Global Marine, which emerged from three years of Chapter 11 bankruptcy proceedings in February 1989, is primarily a contractor engaged in the operation of offshore oil and gas drilling rigs. Global also participates in oil and gas development and production, and provides offshore drilling management services on a turnkey basis. Revenue and operating income contributions in 1992:

	Revs.	Profits
Marine drilling	93%	89%
Oil, gas & other	7%	11%

In 1992, marine drilling revenues derived outside the U.S. represented 71% of total revenues (65% in 1991).

At June 30, 1993, GLM's fleet consisted of 23 rigs, including 19 jackups, one drillship, two semisubmersibles, and one leased concrete island drilling system (CIDS). CIDS is used to drill in the Beaufort Sea offshore Alaska. The average age of the fleet was approximately 10.9 years. At August 31, 1993, 13 of the company's rigs were employed outside the Gulf of Mexico.

GLM's total fleet rig utilization averaged 78% in 1992, versus 86% a year earlier and 90% in 1990. At December 31, 1992, the worldwide utilization rate for competitive offshore rigs was 77%, versus 76% at year-end 1991. The company's average rig utilization rate for 1993's first half was 81%.

Challenger Minerals Inc. develops and produces oil and gas and participates in various drilling ventures. Activities are conducted throughout the southern and western U.S. and offshore Texas and Louisiana in the Gulf of Mexico. At December 31, 1992, proved reserves totaled 948,000 bbl. of oil and 11.8 Bcf of gas (740,000 bbl. and 18.0 Bcf at 1991 year-end). The estimated present value of future net cash flow from GLM's reserves (discounted at 10%) was $20.5 million, versus $26.1 million at 1991 year-end.

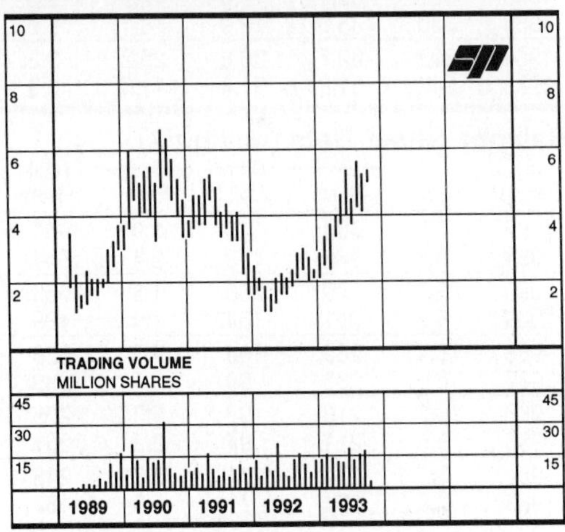

In late 1992, GLM completed a recapitalization that included the sale of 26 million common shares at $2.125 per share and a concurrent sale of $225 million of 12¾% senior secured notes due in 1999. Net proceeds from the offerings of $268 million and available funds of $46 million were used to retire $343 million of long-term debt at a $28 million discount. About $225 million of remaining debt will not be due until December 1999. Separately, in January 1993, GLM sold an additional 3.9 million common shares for net proceeds of $7.8 million.

Important Developments

Aug.'93— The company completed a public offering of 17,250,000 common shares, including 2,250,000 shares through the underwriters' overallotment option, at $4.125 per share. Net proceeds of $67 million will be used to expand GLM's offshore jackup drilling rig fleet, retire about $25 million of long-term debt, finance a four-rig joint venture with Transocean Drilling A.S. of Norway and for rig fleet improvements.

Next earnings report expected in mid-October.

Per Share Data ($)

Yr. End Dec. 31	1992	1991	1990	1989
Tangible Bk. Val.	**1.10**	0.39	0.01	0.13
Cash Flow	**0.64**	0.44	0.06	d0.22
Earnings[1]	**0.24**	0.01	d0.35	d0.61
Dividends	**Nil**	Nil	Nil	Nil
Payout Ratio	**Nil**	Nil	Nil	Nil
Prices—High	**3**	5¼	6⅝	3¾
Low	**1⅛**	1⅝	3	¼
P/E Ratio—	**13–5**	NM	NM	NM

Data as orig. reptd. 1. Bef. spec. item(s) of +0.26 in 1992. d-Deficit. NM-Not Meaningful.

Income Data (Million $)

Year Ended Dec. 31	Revs.	Oper. Inc.	% Oper. Inc. of Revs.	Cap. Exp.	Depr.	Int. Exp.	Net Bef. Taxes	Eff. Tax Rate	[3]Net Inc.	% Net Inc. of Revs.	Cash Flow
1992	**260**	**52**	**19.9**	**21**	**47.1**	**44**	**31**	**10.1%**	**[1]28**	**10.6**	**75**
1991	315	96	30.4	23	46.6	50	4	71.4%	1	0.3	48
1990	282	61	21.5	19	42.2	54	d35	NM	d36	NM	6
1989	188	23	12.1	10	[1]39.1	55	d60	NM	d62	NM	d22
1988	141	3	1.9	43	62.9	75	d156	NM	d156	NM	d108
1987	82	d13	NM	9	48.2	73	d131	NM	[1]d132	NM	d99
1986	186	d12	NM	8	65.0	79	d208	NM	d209	NM	d160
1985	379	8	2.2	36	89.8	151	[2]d222	NM	d220	NM	d146
1984	407	38	9.4	384	89.0	145	[2]d147	NM	d91	NM	d18
1983	447	168	37.6	332	[1]60.6	117	[2]50	1.0%	49	11.0	109

Balance Sheet Data (Million $)

Dec. 31	Cash	Curr. Assets	Curr. Liab.	Curr. Ratio	Total Assets	% Ret. on Assets	Long Term Debt	Common Equity	Total Cap.	% LT Debt of Cap.	% Ret. on Equity
1992	**35**	**91**	**61**	**1.5**	**480**	**4.9**	**225**	**155**	**380**	**59.3**	**26.2**
1991	58	128	40	3.2	524	0.2	386	45	434	89.0	4.4
1990	68	114	43	2.7	544	NM	437	1	441	99.0	NM
1989	74	117	50	2.4	573	NM	443	13	460	96.4	NM
1988	143	183	114	1.6	696	NM	437	81	520	83.9	NM
1987	166	217	142	1.5	1,387	NM	Nil	d208	d50	NM	NM
1986	198	247	127	1.9	1,450	NM	Nil	d61	82	Nil	NM
1985	90	184	1,246	0.1	1,573	NM	Nil	164	291	Nil	NM
1984	181	284	218	1.3	1,847	NM	1,035	400	1,572	65.9	NM
1983	339	441	190	2.3	1,844	3.1	903	513	1,607	56.2	9.7

Data as orig. reptd. **1.** Refl. acctg. change. **2.** Incl. equity in earns. of nonconsol. subs. **3.** Bef. spec. item(s) in 1992. d-Deficit. NM-Not Meaningful.

Revenues (Million $)

Quarter:	1993	1992	1991	1990
Mar.	61.0	68.3	74.5	59.9
Jun.	54.5	69.8	71.4	68.0
Sep.		57.5	81.5	71.4
Dec.		64.7	87.8	82.5
		260.3	315.2	281.8

Revenues for the six months ended June 30, 1993, fell 16%, year to year, as weak North Sea and West African markets offset healthy activity in the U.S. Gulf of Mexico. With operating expenses falling less rapidly and the absence of one-time gains totaling $66 million, a pretax loss of $20.2 million contrasted with income of $50.1 million. After taxes of $1.0 million, versus $1.5 million, a net loss of $21.2 million ($0.15 a share on 25% more shares) replaced income of $48.6 million ($0.42). Results for the 1992 interim exclude a net special credit of $0.01 a share from accounting changes.

Common Share Earnings ($)

Quarter:	1993	1992	1991	1990
Mar.	d0.06	d0.01	d0.02	d0.11
Jun.	d0.08	0.42	d0.02	d0.14
Sep.		d0.09	d0.01	d0.06
Dec.		d0.09	0.06	d0.03
		0.24	0.01	d0.35

d-Deficit.

Dividend Data

No dividends have been paid since the 1989 reorganization. Previously, directors omitted dividends on the old common stock in 1985.

Finances

The company expects to meet all 1993 cash requirements, including debt service, from operating cash flow and cash on hand.

GLM's capital expenditures are expected to total $21 million for 1993.

At December 31, 1992, the company had net operating loss carryforwards of $1.1 billion with expiration dates from 1999 to 2007.

In May 1992, Challenger Minerals fully settled its take-or-pay litigation with Transcontinental Gas Pipe Line Corp., a subsidiary of Transco Energy Co. The company received $20 million in cash and a $20 million long-term, interest bearing note payable. In addition, the company will receive between 750,000 and 1,500,000 shares of Transco, to be placed in escrow. This settlement resulted in a $0.47 a share nonrecurring gain.

Capitalization

Long Term Debt: $225,000,000 (6/93).

Common Stock: 162,560,898 shs. ($0.10 par). Shareholders of record: 10,925.

Office—777 North Eldridge Rd., Houston, TX 77079. **Tel**—(713) 596-5100. **Chrmn, Pres & CEO**—C. R. Luigs. **Sr VP-CFO**—J. C. Martin. **Investor Contact**—David A. Herasimchuk. **Dirs**—P. M. Ahern, D. B. Brown, E. J. Campbell, P. T. Flawn, J. M. Galvin, L. L. Leigh, C. R. Luigs, J. C. Martin, S. A. Shuman, W. R. Thomas, W. C. Walker. **Transfer Agent & Registrar**—Harris Trust & Savings Bank, Chicago. **Incorporated** in Delaware in 1964. **Empl**—1,500.

 J. R. Jordan

Goulds Pumps

NASDAQ Symbol GULD (Incl. in Nat'l Market) Options on NYSE In S&P MidCap 400

Price	Range	P-E Ratio	Dividend	Yield	S&P Ranking	Beta
Oct. 7'93	1993					
25½	26½–21¼	29	0.80	3.1%	B	1.50

Summary

Goulds is a leading manufacturer of centrifugal liquid-handling pumps with industrial, commercial, consumer and agricultural uses. Earnings declined in the first half of 1993, reflecting lower sales and pressure on margins. However, earnings for the full year should increase over 1992 on an acceleration in sales and the absence of charges in the second half. Assuming a continuation of the U. S. recovery and more stable conditions in Europe, sales and earnings should rise in 1994.

Current Outlook

Earnings for 1994 are estimated at $1.45, versus 1993's estimated earnings of $1.25.

Dividends should remain at $0.20 quarterly.

Sales are expected to rise in 1994, reflecting stronger demand in domestic markets and stabilization of European economies. Increased volume, firmer pricing, greater sales of parts and stable raw material costs should lift margins. Assuming a profit contribution by Oil Dynamics equal to 1993's level and only a minimal rise in interest costs, earnings should increase in 1994.

Net Sales (Million $)

Quarter:	1993	1992	1991	1990
Mar.	124	135	132	125
Jun.	152	148	147	142
Sep.		147	149	144
Dec.		129	139	143
		559	567	555

Sales for the six months ended June 30, 1993, declined 2.0%, year to year, reflecting a 3.6% decrease in water technologies; industrial products sales were essentially flat. Margins narrowed, and net income declined 21%, to $11.6 million from $14.6 million. Share earnings were $0.55, versus $0.70 (excluding a charge of $1.42 for accounting changes).

Common Share Earnings ($)

Quarter:	1993	1992	1991	1990
Mar.	0.16	0.34	0.33	0.31
Jun.	0.39	0.36	0.44	0.43
Sep.	E0.41	0.36	0.45	0.45
Dec.	E0.29	d0.02	0.29	0.30
	E1.25	1.04	1.51	1.49

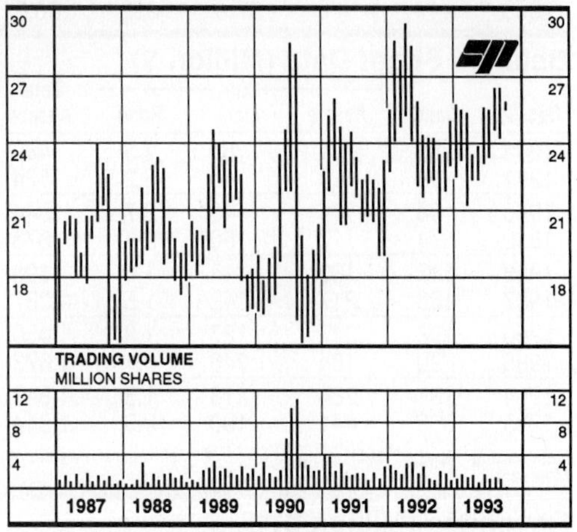

Important Developments

Jul. '93— GULD reported share earnings of $0.39 on a 3.3% increase for 1993's second quarter, versus $0.34 a year earlier. The company attributed the gain to an upturn in parts business, improvement at its Italian subsidiary, lower SG&A expense and a higher contribution from the Oil Dynamics joint venture. Orders at the end of the quarter were $139.5 million, versus $137.5 million in 1992's second quarter; backlog stood at $87.0 million, down from $92.6 million a year-earlier. GULD stated that it expected earnings for 1993's third and fourth quarters to exceed 1992's levels but noted that the magnitude of the improvement was hard to predict because results had become more dependent on short-term order activity.

Next earnings report expected in late October.

Per Share Data ($)

Yr. End Dec. 31	1992	[1,2]1991	1990	1989	1988	1987	1986	[1]1985	1984	1983
Tangible Bk. Val.	**9.08**	10.45	9.94	8.80	9.66	8.45	7.74	7.33	6.80	6.59
Cash Flow	**2.17**	2.60	2.48	2.38	2.17	1.99	1.78	1.70	1.73	1.38
Earnings[3]	**1.04**	1.51	1.49	1.41	1.18	1.03	0.94	1.01	1.16	0.83
Dividends	**0.80**	0.80	0.76	0.76	0.76	0.76	0.76	0.76	0.74	0.68
Payout Ratio	**77%**	53%	51%	54%	64%	75%	81%	78%	63%	82%
Prices—High	**29⅜**	26	28½	24⅝	23⅜	24	19½	18½	21¼	22
Low	**20**	18	15⅛	16½	17¼	15	14¼	14¾	14½	16¾
P/E Ratio—	**20–19**	17–12	19–10	17–12	20–15	23–15	21–15	18–15	18–13	27–20

Data as orig. reptd. **1.** Refl. merger or acq. **2.** Refl. acctg. change. **3.** Bef. results of disc. ops. of -1.47 in 1989, and spec. items of -1.41 in 1992, -0.03 in 1991. d-Deficit. E-Estimated

Income Data (Million $)

Year Ended Dec. 31	Revs.	Oper. Inc.	% Oper. Inc. of Revs.	Cap. Exp.	Depr.	Int. Exp.	[4]Net Bef. Taxes	Eff. Tax Rate	[5]Net Inc.	% Net Inc. of Revs.	Cash Flow
[1,2]1992	**558**	**68.5**	**12.3**	**40.0**	**23.8**	**5.0**	**35.8**	**39.0%**	**21.9**	**3.9**	**45.7**
[1,2]1991	567	76.9	13.6	38.8	22.8	6.4	51.3	39.0%	31.3	5.5	54.1
1990	555	74.7	13.5	28.0	20.4	9.4	48.6	37.0%	30.6	5.5	51.0
[3]1989	507	67.8	13.4	21.3	19.9	9.7	46.1	37.6%	28.8	5.7	48.6
1988	454	59.1	13.0	23.5	19.6	8.9	34.5	32.3%	23.3	5.1	43.0
1987	386	50.0	13.0	17.4	17.3	9.0	28.5	34.9%	18.5	4.8	35.8
1986	356	44.3	12.4	17.1	15.3	10.1	23.4	28.2%	[2]16.8	4.7	32.2
[1]1985	324	43.6	13.5	41.7	11.9	4.1	28.8	39.5%	17.4	5.4	29.3
1984	287	39.9	13.9	21.4	9.9	3.9	31.7	36.4%	20.1	7.0	30.1
1983	275	35.8	13.0	12.0	9.6	4.1	22.6	36.2%	14.4	5.2	24.0

Balance Sheet Data (Million $)

		Curr.									
Dec. 31	Cash	Assets	Liab.	Ratio	Total Assets	% Ret. on Assets	Long Term Debt	Common Equity	Total Cap.	% LT Debt of Cap.	% Ret. on Equity
1992	**13.7**	**237**	**115**	**2.1**	**419**	**5.3**	**40.9**	**193**	**234**	**17.5**	**10.5**
1991	17.3	224	102	2.2	396	7.6	44.4	219	264	16.8	14.6
1990	37.9	256	129	2.0	425	7.4	55.3	207	262	21.1	15.7
1989	28.3	237	110	2.2	394	7.5	70.2	182	252	27.9	15.1
1988	27.4	202	98	2.1	366	6.3	44.8	197	241	18.5	12.7
1987	42.7	184	98	1.9	343	5.6	62.7	156	218	28.7	12.4
1986	38.3	174	99	1.8	308	5.6	42.0	138	180	23.3	12.5
1985	33.6	165	99	1.7	297	6.6	38.5	131	169	22.8	13.8
1984	19.2	121	51	2.4	222	9.4	36.9	117	154	24.0	17.5
1983	20.0	118	41	2.8	209	6.9	39.0	115	154	25.3	12.6

Data as orig. reptd. **1.** Refl. merger or acq. **2.** Refl. acctg. change. **3.** Excl. disc. ops. **4.** Incl. equity in earns. of nonconsol. subs. **5.** Bef. results of disc. ops. and spec. items.

Business Summary

Goulds Pumps designs, manufactures and services pumps, motors and accessories for industrial, agricultural, commercial and consumer markets.

Contributions by segment in 1992 were:

	Sales	Profits
Industrial..........................	60%	53%
Water technologies	40%	47%

The Industrial Products Group manufactures end-suction, double-suction, multistage, axial flow, vertical turbine, sump and slurry pumps for industrial and municipal markets. The segment's long-term plan is to focus on four key markets: chemical, pulp and paper, minerals and energy. Products are sold to U.S. customers through 30 branch sales offices and 90 independent sales representatives and distributors.

The Water Technologies Group makes water pump systems, which include pumps, motors, pressure tanks and related accessories used to supply water for farms, single- and multiple-family residences, office buildings, restaurants and other commercial uses and municipal water supply and sewage treatment facilities. The home water systems market accounts for 60% of segment sales. Products are marketed through 50 water system sales representatives who call on about 400 distributors.

By geographic area in 1992, the U.S. accounted for 71% of total sales and 64% of operating earnings, Europe for 19% (21%), and other foreign for 10% (15%).

Oil Dynamics Inc. (50% owned) makes submersible pumps used principally in secondary oil recovery. The company recognized income from Oil Dynamics of $557,000 in 1992, down from $1,957,000 in 1991.

Dividend Data

Cash has been paid each year since 1948. A dividend reinvestment plan is available. A "poison pill" rights plan was adopted in 1988.

Amt of Divd. $	Date Decl.	Ex-divd. Date	Stock of Record	Payment Date
0.20	Dec. 17	Dec. 31	Jan. 5	Jan. 15'93
0.20	Feb. 12	Mar. 30	Apr. 5	Apr. 15'93
*0.01	Feb. 12	Mar. 30	Apr. 5	Apr. 15'93
0.20	Jun. 22	Jun. 29	Jul. 6	Jul. 15'93
0.20	Sep. 13	Sep. 29	Oct. 5	Oct. 15'93

* Represents redemption of Stk. purchase right.

Capitalization

Long Term Debt: $52,337,000 (6/93).

Common Stock: 21,134,325 shs. ($1 par).
Institutions hold 61%.
Shareholders: 5,805 of record (2/93).

Office—240 Fall St., Seneca Falls, NY 13148. **Tel**—(315) 568-2811. **Chrmn**—R. L. Tarnow. **Pres & CEO**—S. V. Ardia. **VP & Secy**—E. B. Bradshaw. **Treas**—Linda L. Polcaro. **VP, CFO & Investor Contact**—Sean P. Murphy. **Dirs**—S. V. Ardia, W. R. Fenoglio, W. W. Goessel, M. Howard, B. B. Lucas, T. C. McDermott, J. C. Miller III, P. Oddleifson, A. M. Richardson, R. L. Tarnow. **Transfer Agent & Registrar**—American Stock Transfer & Trust Co., New York, NY. **Incorporated** in New York in 1864; reincorporated in Delaware in 1984. **Empl**—4,300.

 Leo Larkin

Granite Construction

NASDAQ Symbol GCCO (Incl. in Nat'l Market) In S&P MidCap 400

Price	Range	P-E Ratio	Dividend	Yield	S&P Ranking	Beta
Aug. 11'93	1993					
18¾	23¾–15½	NM	0.20	1.1%	NR	NA

Summary

This heavy-construction contractor primarily serves the public sector (building highways, dams, airports, etc.), as well as the private sector (site preparation for buildings and plants). It also manufactures asphalt, concrete base rock and other construction materials. Earnings should improve in 1994 from the reduced level expected for 1993, aided by two tollway projects aggregating $162 million. The company's backlog stood at a record level at the end of the second quarter of 1993, even excluding the two projects.

Current Outlook

A loss of about $0.09 a share is expected for 1993 (excluding a special $0.09 a share credit), versus earnings per share of $0.34 in 1992. Earnings should recover in 1994, reaching about $0.75 a share.

Dividends are likely to continue at $0.05 a share quarterly.

Revenues for 1993 are expected to be up about 10%, reflecting contributions of two California branches opened in the second half of 1992. However, competitive pressures in the construction services industry are likely to continue to squeeze margins. Second-half earnings are expected to be about flat, and 1993 earnings per share will be about breakeven (including a $0.09 a share credit from an accounting change). In 1994, results should recover based on higher-margin business booked in 1993. These profitable contracts include a $56 million tollroad project in Orange County, California, and a $106 million expressway contract (North Central Expressway) awarded by the Texas Department of Transportation.

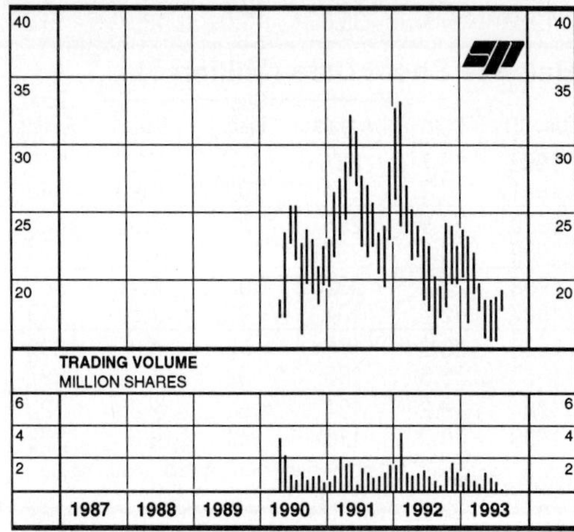

Operating Revenues (Million $)

Quarter:	1993	1992	1991	1990
Mar.	78	68	92	88
Jun.	143	130	149	139
Sep.	---	187	174	173
Dec.	---	136	150	159
	---	518	564	558

Revenues in the six months ended June 30, 1993, rose 11%, year to year. An extremely competitive bidding environment, coupled with sharply lower other income, led to a widening of the loss to $5,205,000 ($0.45 a share), from $1,114,000 ($0.10). Results for 1993 exclude a $0.09 credit from an accounting change.

Common Share Earnings ($)

Quarter:	1993	1992	1991	1990
Mar.	d0.45	d0.33	d0.08	d0.09
Jun.	Nil	0.24	0.53	0.53
Sep.	E0.20	0.37	0.68	0.62
Dec.	E0.16	0.06	0.37	0.58
	Ed0.09	0.34	1.51	[1]1.70

Important Developments

Aug. '93— Granite reported its backlog at June 30, 1993, at a record level of $502 million, up 50% from a year ago. The backlog at June 30, 1993, excluded two recent awards totaling about $162 million. The company also announced that it is targeting more than $1 billion of work on which to bid before the end of the year.

Next earnings report expected in early November.

Per Share Data ($)

Yr. End Dec. 31	[2]1992	1991	1990	1989	1988	1987	1986	1985
Tangible Bk. Val.	**[3]13.83**	13.44	11.62	8.91	7.16	5.33	4.22	2.71
Cash Flow	**2.50**	3.68	3.75	3.36	3.23	2.40	NA	NA
Earnings	**0.34**	1.51	1.70	1.42	1.50	0.85	1.14	0.89
Dividends	**0.20**	0.20	0.15	Nil	Nil	Nil	Nil	Nil
Payout Ratio	**59%**	13%	9%	Nil	Nil	Nil	Nil	Nil
Prices—High	**33¼**	32¼	25½	NA	NA	NA	NA	NA
Low	**16**	19½	16	NA	NA	NA	NA	NA
P/E Ratio—	**98–47**	21–13	15–9	NA	NA	NA	NA	NA

Data as orig. reptd. **1.** Does not reconcile bec. of change in shares. **2.** Refl. merger or acq. **3.** Incl. intangibles. NA-Not Available. E-Estimated. d-Deficit.

Income Data (Million $)

Year Ended Dec. 31	Oper. Revs.	Oper. Inc.	% Oper. Inc. of Revs.	Cap. Exp.	Depr.	Int. Exp.	Net Bef. Taxes	Eff. Tax Rate	Net Inc.	% Net Inc. of Revs.	Cash Flow
[1]**1992**	**518**	**28.9**	**5.6**	**45.4**	**25.3**	**2.20**	**5.5**	**29.3%**	**3.9**	**0.8**	**29.2**
1991	564	48.2	8.5	39.9	25.2	2.08	27.0	34.7%	17.6	3.1	42.9
1990	558	48.9	8.8	29.9	22.8	3.12	29.1	35.2%	18.8	3.4	41.6
1989	504	38.3	7.6	36.6	19.4	4.51	22.0	35.5%	14.2	2.8	33.6
1988	437	39.2	9.0	21.9	17.3	5.63	23.7	36.6%	15.0	3.4	32.3
1987	381	29.6	7.8	15.9	15.4	5.45	13.8	37.6%	8.6	2.3	24.0
1986	374	NA	NA	NA	NA	6.26	20.8	44.7%	11.5	3.1	NA
1985	336	NA	NA	NA	NA	7.12	13.5	33.4%	9.0	2.7	NA

Balance Sheet Data (Million $)

Dec. 31	Cash	Curr. Assets	Curr. Liab.	Curr. Ratio	Total Assets	% Ret. on Assets	Long Term Debt	Common Equity	Total Cap.	% LT Debt of Cap.	% Ret. on Equity
1992	**54.1**	**162**	**109**	**1.5**	**308**	**1.3**	**38.6**	**161**	**200**	**19.3**	**2.5**
1991	55.0	162	104	1.6	275	6.6	14.8	156	171	8.7	12.1
1990	50.5	160	105	1.5	258	7.0	19.1	134	153	12.5	15.9
1989	46.3	152	115	1.3	243	6.4	39.7	89	129	30.8	17.7
1988	19.5	130	87	1.5	203	7.9	44.3	72	116	38.2	24.0
1987	19.8	NA	NA	NA	176	5.0	49.5	53	103	48.2	18.0
1986	16.8	NA	NA	NA	166	7.1	50.2	42	92	54.3	33.2
1985	24.5	NA	NA	NA	155	NA	61.6	27	89	69.4	NA

Data as orig. reptd. **1.** Refl. merger or acquisition. NA-Not Available.

Business Summary

Granite Construction is one of the largest heavy-construction contractors in the U.S. It operates throughout the U.S., focusing primarily on the West and Southwest, and serves both public and private-sector clients. Operating revenues were derived as follows in recent years:

	1992	1991	1990
Contract:			
Private sector	19%	25%	33%
Federal agencies	11%	8%	8%
State agencies	34%	34%	25%
Local public agencies	26%	25%	24%
Construction material	10%	8%	9%

The Branch division (which accounted for 79% of 1992 revenues) has both public and private-sector clients. Public activities include both new construction and improvement of streets, roads, highways and bridges. In the private sector, major contracts include site preparation for housing, including excavation, grading and street paving, and installation of curbs, gutters, sidewalks and underground utilities. Many of the company's 11 branch offices (nine of which are in California) mine aggregates and operate plants that process aggregates into construction materials for internal use and for sale to others.

The Heavy Construction division (21%) undertakes projects that are usually larger and more complex than those performed by the Branch division. In 1992, Heavy Construction projects had a contract amount averaging $36 million in size, with an average duration of 38 months. Large infrastructure projects are undertaken, including construction of major highways, large dams, mass transit facilities, bridges, pipelines, canals, tunnels, waterway locks and dams, and airport runways. Other activities include contract mine stripping and reclamation and large site preparation, as well as demolition, clearing excavation, dewatering, drainage, embankment fill, structural concrete, concrete and asphalt paving and tunneling.

Dividend Data

Cash dividends were initiated in 1990.

Amt. of Divd. $	Date Decl.	Ex-divd. Date	Stock of Record	Payment Date
0.05	Aug. 27	Sep. 24	Sep. 30	Oct. 16'92
0.05	Dec. 21	Dec. 23	Dec. 30	Jan. 22'93
0.05	Mar. 17	Mar. 25	Mar. 31	Apr. 23'93
0.05	May 21	Jun. 24	Jun. 30	Jul. 16'93

Finances

In June 1992, Granite acquired Tarmac California Holdings Inc. for about $44 million and other considerations. The acquisition was financed by $43 million of debt repayable over five years beginning June 30, 1994.

Capitalization

Long Term Debt: $33,608,000 (6/93).

Common Stock: 11,688,272 shs. ($0.01 par). About 39% is held by the company's ESOP. Institutions hold some 39%. Shareholders: 400.

Office—585 W. Beach St., Watsonville, CA 95076. **Tel**—(408) 724-1011. **Chrmn**—R. C. Solari. **Pres & CEO**—D. H. Watts. **VP-CFO**—W. E. Barton. **VP-Secy**—R. L. Reddy. **Investor Contact**—Michael Lawson (408-761-4717). **Dirs**—J. J. Barclay, R. M. Brooks, A. S. Ferrante, D. K. McNear, R. E. Miles, R. H. Roberts, R. C. Solari, D. H. Watts. **Transfer Agent & Registrar**—First Interstate Bank of California, San Francisco. **Incorporated** in Delaware in 1990. **Empl**—2,708.

 M. Graham Hackett

Hancock Fabrics

NYSE Symbol HKF In S&P MidCap 400

Price	Range	P-E Ratio	Dividend	Yield	S&P Ranking	Beta
Jun. 2'93	1993					
10	14½–9⅝	22	0.32	3.2%	NR	1.18

Summary

Hancock Fabrics sells fabrics and related items primarily at retail to the home sewing market through some 492 stores in 33 states. Earnings fell sharply in 1992-93 and the first quarter of 1993-94, as Hancock was hurt by sluggishness in the retail home sewing industry, excess capacity within the industry and pricing pressures from both ready-to-wear apparel retailers and piece goods retailers (poor weather conditions also affected sales and earnings in 1993-94's first quarter). Earnings were expected to remain weak for the remainder of the fiscal year.

Current Outlook

Earnings for the fiscal year ending January 31, 1994, are projected at $0.55 a share, little changed from the depressed level of $0.57 recorded in 1992-93.

The dividend should continue at $0.08 quarterly.

Sales for 1993-94 are expected to be in line with the prior year's level, as Hancock will continue to be affected by sluggishness in the home sewing retail market, which has been brought on by rather weak economic conditions and excessive expansion by fabric retailers. Sales levels will also be held back by deep discounting by ready-to-wear apparel retailers, which will continue to narrow the cost advantage of home sewing. Extreme competitive pressures will persist in hampering margins.

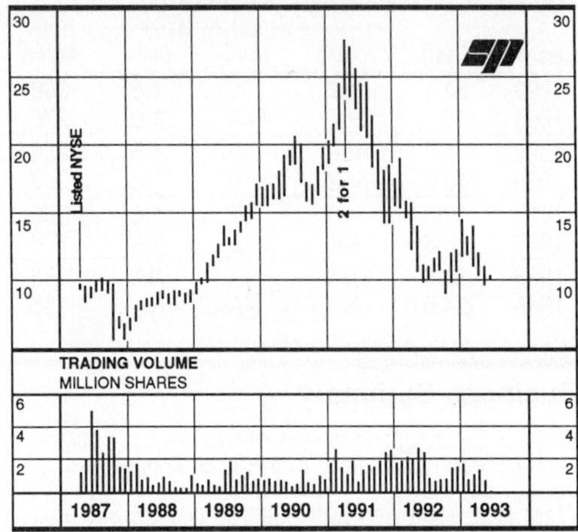

Sales (Million $)

13 Weeks:	1993–94	1992–93	1991–92	1990–91
Apr.	92.8	95.8	101.5	94.4
Jul.	---	87.2	90.1	87.2
Oct.	---	101.2	101.6	100.8
Jan.	---	96.2	94.9	104.5
	---	380.4	388.0	386.9

For the 13 weeks ended May 2, 1993, sales declined 3.1%, year to year, as a 6.9% reduction in same store sales outweighed the addition of new stores. The lower level of same store sales reflected a rather weak retailing climate, excess capacity within the retail home sewing industry, poor weather conditions during a portion of the period and a narrowing of the cost advantage of home sewing. Margins narrowed considerably as a result of extreme competitive pressures, and net income fell 76%, to $0.04 a share, from $0.15.

Common Share Earnings ($)

13 Weeks:	1993–94	1992–93	1991–92	1990–91
Apr.	0.04	0.15	0.29	0.28
Jul.	E0.10	0.10	0.25	0.25
Oct.	E0.20	0.19	0.27	0.32
Jan.	E0.21	0.12	0.22	0.38
	E0.55	0.57	1.03	1.23

Important Developments

May '93— Hancock said that a significant reduction in store concentrations and a contraction in the level of promotional activity would be necessary before the home sewing industry could return to viable profitability.

Next earnings report expected in mid-August.

Per Share Data ($)

Yr. End Jan. 31	1993	1992	1991	1990	1989	1988	1987
Tangible Bk. Val.	**4.44**	4.41	4.18	3.71	4.15	3.48	2.94
Cash Flow	**0.77**	1.21	1.40	1.20	0.99	NA	NA
Earnings[1]	**0.57**	1.03	1.23	1.06	0.86	[2]0.77	0.75
Dividends	**0.32**	0.32	0.28	0.24	0.20	0.15	NA
Payout Ratio	**56%**	31%	22%	21%	23%	18%	NA
Calendar Years	**1992**	1991	1990	1989	1988	1987	1986
Prices—High	**19**	27¾	20⅝	17⅛	9¼	10⅛	NA
Low	**9**	14¼	15½	9	6⅜	5⅝	NA
P/E Ratio—	**33–16**	27–14	17–13	16–9	11–7	13–7	NA

Data as orig. reptd., prior to 1988 pro forma data as reptd. in information statement dated Apr. 24, 1987. Adj. for stk. div(s). of 100% Apr. 1991. **1.** Bef. spec. item(s) of -0.25 in 1992. **2.** Adj. to reflect pro forma effect of recap. E-Estimated. NA-Not Available.

Income Data (Million $)

Year Ended Jan. 31	Revs.	Oper. Inc.	% Oper. Inc. of Revs.	Cap. Exp.	Depr.	Int. Exp.	Net Bef. Taxes	Eff. Tax Rate	[1]Net Inc.	% Net Inc. of Revs.	Cash Flow
1993	**380**	**25.8**	**6.8**	**4.24**	**4.28**	**2.64**	**19.1**	**36.6%**	**12.1**	**3.2**	**16.4**
1992	388	42.6	11.0	6.26	3.95	2.79	36.6	37.2%	[2]23.0	5.9	26.9
1991	387	51.2	13.2	4.93	3.81	3.82	44.5	36.9%	28.1	7.3	31.9
1990	346	46.5	13.5	5.03	3.68	2.89	41.3	37.2%	26.0	7.5	29.6
1989	315	40.1	12.7	5.09	3.43	2.72	35.0	37.2%	22.0	7.0	25.4
1988	298	39.1	13.1	3.56	3.36	2.63	34.9	40.5%	20.8	7.0	24.1
1987	290	45.1	15.5	NA	3.32	0.91	45.7	48.6%	23.5	8.1	26.8
1986	282	NA	NA	NA	NA	NA	36.1	48.6%	18.6	6.6	NA
1985	170	NA	NA	NA	NA	NA	30.4	48.2%	15.7	9.3	NA
1984	162	NA	NA	NA	NA	NA	27.6	48.2%	14.3	8.8	NA

Balance Sheet Data (Million $)

Jan. 31	Cash	Curr. Assets	Curr. Liab.	Curr. Ratio	Total Assets	% Ret. on Assets	Long Term Debt	Common Equity	Total Cap.	% LT Debt of Cap.	% Ret. on Equity
1993	**9.0**	**185**	**47.4**	**3.9**	**214**	**5.7**	**58.0**	**95**	**153**	**38.0**	**12.9**
1992	4.1	189	58.5	3.2	218	11.2	50.3	97	148	34.1	24.3
1991	8.8	173	64.4	2.7	196	15.4	35.5	93	131	27.1	31.9
1990	7.0	154	51.6	3.0	176	15.8	35.8	86	124	29.0	28.6
1989	15.5	150	36.3	4.1	170	13.0	26.1	106	134	19.5	22.6
1988	16.2	150	36.6	4.1	169	0.6	41.4	89	132	31.4	0.8
1987	74.9	198	48.1	4.1	221	NA	1.7	168	171	1.0	NA

Data as orig. reptd., prior to 1988 data as reptd. in information statement dated Apr. 24, 1987. **1.** Bef. spec. item(s) in 1992. **2.** Reflects accounting change. NA-Not Available.

Business Summary

Hancock Fabrics sells fabrics and related items at retail to the home sewing market. It also has wholesale operations which account for a relatively small portion of its total business. As of May 2, 1993, HKF was operating 492 fabric stores in 33 states under the names Hancock Fabrics, Minnesota Fabrics, Fabric Warehouse, and Fabric Market. During the first quarter of 1993-94, Hancock opened 12 new stores, while closing two. It planned a net increase of about 20 stores for the full fiscal year.

Stores added or closed and the number of units in operation at fiscal year-end (January 31):

	1993	1992	1991	1990
Opened/acquired....	37	31	46	43
Closed/relocated....	14	9	11	7
In operation	482	459	437	402

The retail stores, which are located primarily in neighborhood shopping centers and are generally open seven days a week, offer a wide selection of clothing fabrics, notions (including zippers, buttons, threads, and ornamentation), patterns, decorative fabrics (including drapery and upholstery fabrics), craft items, and related supplies. Each store maintains an inventory of cotton, wool, and synthetic staple fabrics such as broadcloth, poplin, gabardine, unbleached muslin, and corduroy, as well as seasonal and current fashion fabrics.

Hancock mainly serves the home sewing market, which consists largely of value-conscious women who sew clothing for themselves and their families. Sales are seasonally highest in the fall and pre-Easter weeks.

Wholesale operations involve the sale of fabrics to about 200 independent retailers in locations in which HKF has elected not to open its own stores. These operations have accounted for less than 5% of Hancock's sales.

Dividend Data

Dividends were initiated in 1987. A "poison pill" stock purchase right was adopted in 1987.

Amt of Divd. $	Date Decl.	Ex-divd. Date	Stock of Record	Payment Date
0.08	Jun. 11	Jun. 25	Jul. 1	Jul. 15'92
0.08	Sep. 10	Sep. 25	Oct. 1	Oct. 15'92
0.08	Dec. 10	Dec. 24	Jan. 1	Jan. 15'93
0.08	Mar. 10	Mar. 26	Apr. 1	Apr. 15'93

Finances

During 1992-93, Hancock repurchased 830,765 of its common shares, under a 1,000,000 share repurchase plan authorized by directors in June 1992. From March 2, 1989, through 1991-92 year-end, HKF had repurchased 4,370,386 of its shares (adjtd.).

Capitalization

Long Term Debt: $58,000,000 (1/93).

Common Stock: 21,362,280 shs. ($0.01 par). Institutions hold about 55%. Shareholders of record: 15,692 (4/15/93).

Office—3406 West Main St, Tupelo, MS 38803. **Tel**—(601) 842-2834. **Chrmn, Pres & CEO**—M. O. Jarvis. **SVP-CFO, Secy & Investor Contact**—Larry G. Kirk. **Dirs**—D. L. Fruge, M. O. Jarvis, L. G. Kirk, I. Owen, D. L. Weaver. **Transfer Agent & Registrar**—Continental Stock Transfer & Trust Co., NYC. **Incorporated** in Delaware in 1987; predecessor businesses incorporated at various times through 1971. **Empl**—7,400.

 Michael W. Jaffe

Hanna (M. A.)

NYSE Symbol MAH Options on NYSE (Mar-Jun-Sep-Dec) In S&P MidCap 400

Price	Range	P-E Ratio	Dividend	Yield	S&P Ranking	Beta
Jul. 28'93	1993					
26	33¼–25¾	17	0.70	2.7%	B–	1.00

Summary

This specialty chemicals company produces polymers and colorants for the plastics and rubber industries, manufactures rubber compounds and plastic products, and distributes plastic shapes and resins. During 1992, MAH expanded in Europe through acquisitions. MAH plans to increase sales abroad to 25% of total sales by 1996. Latin American and the Pacific Rim were targeted for expansion in 1993.

Business Summary

M.A. Hanna Co. (formerly Hanna Mining) is one of North America's largest independent producers of plastic and rubber compounds and a leading producer of color and additive concentrates for plastics. MAH is also an international distributor of engineered plastic shapes and plastic resins, and manufactures polymer products for the printing, textile, construction and automotive industries. During 1991, MAH substantially completed the divestiture of its natural resources and other businesses. Contributions to revenues from continuing operations by product line in recent years:

	1992	1991
Polymer Processing	47%	45%
Polymer Distribution	40%	39%
Manufactured Polymer products	12%	14%
Nonpolymer	1%	2%

Foreign operations accounted for 14% of sales and 13% of profits in 1992.

In polymer processing MAH makes compounds of plastic and rubber polymers, which are plastic resins or rubber mixed with additives that give polymer end products desired physical and aesthetic qualities, which are sold to thousands of manufacturers. MAH also makes custom formulated colorants for the plastics industry. Colorants are produced in concentrate, liquid and powder form, and sold to end users who serve virtually every facet of the plastic manufacturing market. Its 19 facilities have annual capacity of more than 200 million pounds.

With 71 U.S. branch offices and 68 outlets in 13 other countries, MAH distributes plastic shapes, including sheet, rod, tube and film. These plastics are purchased from major producers to be cut, shaped and resold to a wide variety of end users. MAH also distributes in North America plastic resins and other materials manufactured by major producers, as well as plastic compounds made by other MAH units.

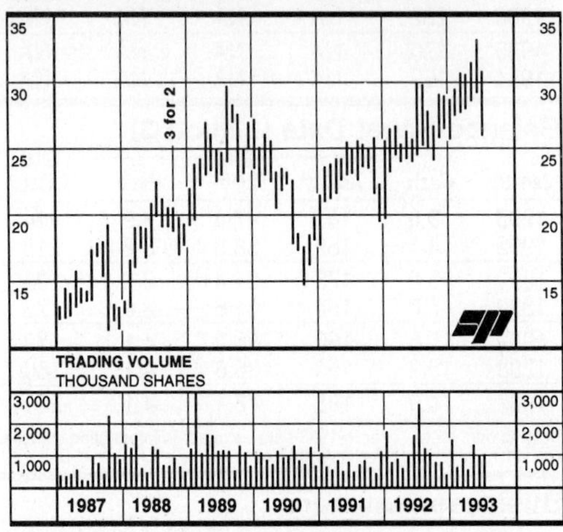

Manufactured polymer products include printing blankets used on offset printing presses to transfer images and cots and aprons used in textile mills, single-ply rubber roofing membrane, and sponge rubber products used as insulation and noise dampening in automobiles.

Important Developments

Jun. '93— MAH completed the acquisition of Texapol Corp. and Monmouth Plastics, which produce engineering thermoplastic compounds and flame retardant compounds, respectively, and have combined annual sales of $32 million. In May, MAH acquired Global Processing Co., a specialty rubber compounder with annual sales of some $10 million. MAH also reached a tentative agreement to acquire the thermoplastic resin distribution business of Plasticos Polisol S.A. de C. V., of Mexico City. MAH also planned to build a polymer processing plant in Mexico in 1993.

Next earnings report expected in mid-October.

Per Share Data ($)

Yr. End Dec. 31	1992	1991	1990	1989	1988	[1]1987	[1]1986	1985	1984	1983
Tangible Bk. Val.	**d0.10**	d0.30	6.23	4.80	0.11	d2.24	8.99	18.50	25.59	24.90
Cash Flow	**3.89**	1.08	3.54	4.90	5.03	2.50	d2.99	d6.98	d0.23	d1.53
Earnings[2]	**1.37**	d0.75	2.03	3.34	3.48	1.65	d3.49	d7.43	d0.59	d1.89
Dividends	**0.663**	0.625	0.550	0.450	0.334	0.266	0.266	0.266	0.266	0.266
Payout Ratio	**59%**	NM	26%	15%	10%	19%	NM	NM	NM	NM
Prices—High	**30**	25⅞	27¼	29¾	22½	19⅜	17⅝	14⅛	16⅛	17½
Low	**19¾**	17¾	14¾	19¼	12⅝	11⅜	10⅜	11	11⅛	12⅜
P/E Ratio—	**22–14**	NM	13–7	9–6	6–4	12–7	NM	NM	NM	NM

Data as orig. reptd. Adj. for stk. div. of 50% Nov. 1988. **1.** Reflects merger or acquisition. **2.** Bef. results of disc. opers. of +1.04 in 1991, -2.76 in 1986, and spec. item(s) of -0.60 in 1992, -0.25 in 1991, +0.63 in 1985, +1.16 in 1984. d-Deficit. NM-Not Meaningful. NA-Not Available.

Income Data (Million $)

Year Ended Dec. 31	Revs.	Oper. Inc.	% Oper. Inc. of Revs.	Cap. Exp.	Depr.	Int. Exp.	[4]Net Bef. Taxes	Eff. Tax Rate	[5]Net Inc.	% Net Inc. of Revs.	Cash Flow
1992	**1,130**	**121**	**9.1**	**19.2**	**47.9**	**32.5**	**42**	**37.0%**	**[6]26**	**2.0**	**74**
[1]1991	1,146	107	9.3	26.8	43.2	23.2	d1	NM	d17	NM	25
1990	1,116	118	10.5	28.3	41.7	18.3	74	25.0%	56	5.0	98
1989	1,110	112	10.1	25.6	39.4	21.3	100	13.4%	87	7.8	124
1988	1,019	99	9.7	38.5	33.4	23.9	90	8.0%	83	8.2	108
[2]1987	459	31	6.9	14.0	15.3	15.4	37	3.2%	36	7.9	45
[3]1986	130	d8	NM	23.9	8.5	7.7	d58	NM	[6]d58	NM	d51
1985	222	d8	NM	10.6	7.5	6.8	d128	NM	d126	NM	d118
1984	200	d6	NM	2.8	5.7	6.0	d8	NM	d10	NM	d4
1983	154	d17	NM	3.6	5.5	9.5	d37	NM	d29	NM	d23

Balance Sheet Data (Million $)

Dec. 31	Cash	Curr. Assets	Curr. Liab.	Curr. Ratio	Total Assets	% Ret. on Assets	Long Term Debt	Common Equity	Total Cap.	% LT Debt of Cap.	% Ret. on Equity
1992	**80.0**	**439**	**252**	**1.7**	**1,178**	**2.3**	**351**	**398**	**749**	**46.9**	**6.7**
1991	24.5	296	202	1.5	1,033	NM	331	380	711	46.5	NM
1990	25.5	292	197	1.5	1,065	5.4	138	568	705	19.5	10.3
1989	18.3	280	182	1.5	1,036	7.6	135	543	677	19.9	16.7
1988	21.6	258	184	1.4	964	8.5	138	369	607	22.7	22.3
1987	16.1	287	212	1.4	1,001	4.7	232	299	630	36.7	10.6
1986	86.0	140	67	2.1	423	NM	28	200	304	9.2	NM
1985	43.6	124	87	1.4	533	NM	61	314	378	16.1	NM
1984	43.3	127	44	2.9	537	NM	26	434	463	5.7	NM
1983	1.9	84	58	1.5	554	NM	80	379	466	17.1	NM

Data as orig. reptd. **1.** Excludes disc. opers. **2.** Reflects merger or acquisition. **3.** Excludes disc. opers. and reflects merger or acquisition. **4.** Incl. equity in earns. of nonconsol. subs. **5.** Bef. results of disc. opers. in 1986, and spec. item(s) in 1985, 1984. **6.** Reflects acctg. change. d-Deficit. NM-Not Meaningful.

Operating Revenues (Million $)

Quarter:	1993	1992	1991	1990
Mar.	370	297	258	268
Jun.	397	333	278	289
Sep.		356	308	290
Dec.		348	303	269
		1,334	1,148	1,116

Revenues for the six months ended June 30, 1993, advanced 22%, year to year, reflecting acquisitions. Margins widened, and with interest and other expense up less sharply, pretax income rose 38%. After taxes at 46.0%, versus 48.5%, income from continuing operations was up 45%, to $12,702,000 ($0.62 a share, before $0.07 of income from discontinued operations) from $8,776,000 ($0.46, before a special charge of $0.60 for the cumulative effect of an accounting change).

Common Share Earnings ($)

Quarter:	1993	1992	1991	1990
Mar.	0.22	0.12	0.13	0.13
Jun.	0.41	0.33	0.22	0.65
Sep.		0.35	d1.21	0.62
Dec.		0.53	0.04	0.63
		1.37	[1]d0.75	2.03

1. Does not reconcile due to changes in number of shs. outstanding. d-Deficit.

Finances

In its 1992 Annual Report, MAH reported that it wanted to increase the percentage of international sales of total sales to one-fourth by 1996. In 1993, MAH was planning on seeking partnerships or alliances with resin producers in the Pacific Rim, as well as establish a business unit in Mexico.

Dividend Data

Amt of Divd. $	Date Decl.	Ex-divd. Date	Stock of Record	Payment Date
0.16¼	Aug. 5	Aug. 11	Aug. 17	Sep. 11'92
0.17½	Nov. 4	Nov. 19	Nov. 25	Dec. 11'92
0.17½	Feb. 3	Feb. 12	Feb. 19	Mar. 12'93
0.17½	May 5	May 17	May 21	Jun. 11'93

Capitalization

Long Term Debt: $339,780,000 (6/93).

Common Stock: 23,469,341 shs. ($1 par).

M.A. Hanna Co. Associates Ownership Trust owns about 14.6%.

Institutions hold approximately 87% (including some closely held shares).

Shareholders of record: 3,225.

Office—1301 East 9th St., Suite 3600, Cleveland, OH 44114-1860. **Tel**—(216) 589-4000. **Chrmn & CEO**—M. D. Walker. **Pres**—D. J. McGregor. **VP-CFO**—R. G. Fountain. **VP-Secy**—J. S. Pyke Jr. **Investor Contact**—Barbara Gould (800) 688-4259. **Dirs**—B. C. Ames, W. R. Embry, J. T. Eyton, G. D. Kirkham, M. L. Mann, P. M. Marshall, D. J. McGregor, R. W. Pogue, M. D. Walker. **Transfer Agent & Registrar**—Ameritrust Company, Cleveland. **Incorporated** in Delaware in 1927. **Empl**—6,333.

 Shayna J. Malnak

Harley-Davidson

NYSE Symbol HDI Options on Phila In S&P MidCap 400

Price	Range	P-E Ratio	Dividend	Yield	S&P Ranking	Beta
Oct. 7'93	1993					
44½	47½–31½	25	0.24	0.5%	B+	1.60

Summary

Harley-Davidson is the world's leading producer of heavyweight touring and custom motorcycles and the only U.S. motorcycle manufacturer. It also produces recreational and commercial vehicles. HDI produced a record 76,495 motorcycles in 1992, and worldwide demand continues to exceed supply. The company's goal is to increase motorcycle production to 100,000 a year by 1996, and it is developing foreign markets to further expand demand. Cash dividends were initiated in 1993.

Current Outlook

Earnings for 1993 may rise to $1.90 a share, from the $1.51 of 1992. An increase to $2.25 is possible in 1994.

Cash dividends were initiated with a $0.06-a-share declaration in May 1993.

After integration of a second assembly line and a new paint shop in 1992, breaking significant bottlenecks, production should range from 345 to 350 units a day in 1993. Over the next few years, HDI expects to develop a market of 100,000 to 120,000 units per year. Aided by manufacturing efficiencies, price increases and a modest turnaround at Holiday Rambler, a sharp rise in earnings is expected in 1993.

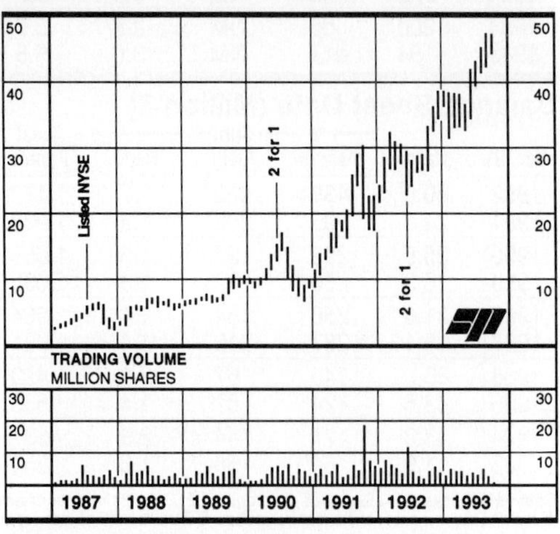

Net Sales (Million $)

Quarter:	1993	1992	1991	1990
Mar.	270	247	196	218
Jun.	334	274	265	250
Sep.	---	272	241	203
Dec.	---	312	238	194
	---	1,105	940	865

Sales for the first half of 1993 rose 16%, year to year, on an 18% increase in motorcycle shipments. Operating profit increased 35%, and interest expense declined. Pretax income rose 48%. After taxes at 40.2%, versus 40.0%, income was up 47%, to $1.03 a share (before a net special charge of $0.80), from $0.73 ($0.01).

Common Share Earnings ($)

Quarter:	1993	1992	1991	1990
Mar.	0.40	0.24	0.13	0.34
Jun.	0.63	0.49	0.45	0.45
Sep.	E0.42	0.36	0.24	0.21
Dec.	E0.45	0.40	0.21	0.09
	E1.90	1.51	1.04	1.08

Important Developments

Jul. '93— Motorcycle shipments in 1993's second quarter rose 22%, to 22,951 units (16,052 domestic; 6,899 export), from 18,771 (13,007; 5,764) in the 1992 second quarter. Operating profit from motorcycles and related products advanced 27%, to $41.6 million, from $32.8 million. For the first half, motorcycle shipments increased 18%, to 42,453 units (29,152; 13,301), from 35,957 (24,118; 11,839) in the 1992 half. Operating profit from motorcycles and related products rose 35%, to $69.1 million, from $51.1 million. Transportation vehicles had a $300,000 profit for the second quarter and a loss of $300,000 for the half year, versus income of $1.1 million in 1992's second quarter and $1.3 million for the 1992 first half. HDI said that it would raise motorcycle production to 350 per day as of September 1, from the current rate of 345.

Next earnings report expected in late October.

Per Share Data ($)

Yr. End Dec. 31	**1992**	1991	1990	1989	1988	1987	[1]1986	1985	1984	1983
Tangible Bk. Val.	**7.36**	5.01	3.82	2.59	1.49	d0.41	d2.47	0.32	NM	NM
Cash Flow	**2.33**	1.68	1.71	1.36	1.35	1.25	0.62	0.69	NA	NA
Earnings[2]	**1.51**	1.04	1.08	0.95	0.86	0.68	0.21	0.18	0.20	0.07
Dividends	**Nil**	Nil	Nil	Nil	Nil	Nil	Nil	Nil	Nil	Nil
Payout Ratio	**Nil**	Nil	Nil	Nil	Nil	Nil	Nil	Nil	Nil	Nil
Prices—High	**38¾**	30⅜	17 3/16	10¾	7½	6⅝	3½	NA	NA	NA
Low	**21¾**	8⅞	6 11/16	6⅛	3	2 5/16	1 13/16	NA	NA	NA
P/E Ratio—	**26–14**	29–9	16–6	11–6	9–3	10–3	17–9	NA	NA	NA

Data as orig. reptd. Adj. for stk. divs. of 100% Jun. 1992, 100% Jun. 1990. **1.** Refl. merger or acq. **2.** Bef. spec. items of -0.01 in 1992, -0.02 in 1990, -0.10 in 1989, -0.11 in 1988, +0.14 in 1987, +0.03 in 1986, +0.50 in 1985, +0.25 in 1984, +0.53 in 1983 & results of disc. ops. of +0.11 in 1989. E-Estimated. d-Deficit. NA-Not Available. NM-Not Meaningful.

Income Data (Million $)

Year Ended Dec. 31	Oper. Revs.	Oper. Inc.	% Oper. Inc. of Revs.	Cap. Exp.	Depr.	Int. Exp.	Net Bef. Taxes	Eff. Tax Rate	[4]Net Inc.	% Net Inc. of Revs.	Cash Flow
1992	**1,105**	**127**	**11.5**	**[3]47.2**	**29.4**	**5.9**	**88.8**	**39.0%**	**54.2**	**4.9**	**83.6**
1991	940	91	9.7	48.2	22.6	9.4	58.1	36.4%	37.0	3.9	59.6
1990	865	107	12.4	38.5	22.4	11.4	62.6	38.8%	38.3	4.4	60.7
[1]1989	791	81	10.2	24.4	14.2	18.0	53.0	38.5%	32.6	4.1	46.8
1988	757	86	11.3	23.8	15.7	24.7	46.0	41.0%	27.2	3.6	42.9
1987	685	68	9.9	17.0	11.8	25.5	30.9	42.7%	17.7	2.6	32.5
[2]1986	295	25	8.4	61.1	8.7	9.5	7.3	41.3%	[5]4.3	1.5	13.0
1985	287	20	7.1	13.1	7.5	9.4	3.2	16.6%	2.6	0.9	10.2
1984	294	23	7.8	8.6	7.4	11.3	4.0	27.2%	2.9	1.0	NA
1983	254	22	8.6	6.3	8.4	11.8	1.9	48.2%	1.0	0.4	NA

Balance Sheet Data (Million $)

Dec. 31	Cash	Total Assets	Net Prop/ Plant/ Equip	Inventories	% Ret. on Assets	Long Term Debt	Total Debt	Common Equity	Total Cap.	% LT Debt of Cap.	% Ret. on Equity
1992	**44.1**	**522**	**184**	**94**	**10.6**	**2**	**19**	**335**	**348**	**0.7**	**18.4**
1991	30.9	474	164	107	8.4	47	88	238	291	16.1	16.9
1990	14.0	407	136	110	9.6	48	72	199	252	19.2	21.4
1989	39.1	379	116	88	8.3	75	102	156	237	31.5	23.4
1988	52.4	401	107	90	6.2	135	168	122	261	51.7	27.1
1987	68.2	381	NA	NA	4.5	179	NA	63	247	72.5	37.3
1986	27.9	327	NA	NA	1.7	192	NA	26	218	88.0	25.9
1985	13.5	114	NA	NA	2.5	52	NA	5	56	91.8	NM
1984	2.1	99	NA	NA	3.1	56	NA	d6	50	112.7	NM
1983	NA	89	NA	NA	1.1	58	NA	d13	45	128.5	NM

Data as orig. reptd. **1.** Excl. disc. ops. **2.** Refl. merger or acq. **3.** Net. **4.** Bef. spec. items. **5.** Refl. acctg. change. NA-Not Available. d-Deficit. NM-Not Meaningful.

Business Summary

Harley-Davidson is a leading producer of heavyweight motorcycles and also makes recreational vehicles and specialized commercial vehicles. Business segment contributions in 1992 were:

	Sales	Profits
Motorcycles & related products	74%	98%
Transportation vehicles	26%	2%

The only U.S. motorcycle manufacturer, HDI competes exclusively in the superheavyweight (those with 850cc engines or larger) market segment. HDI shipped 76,495 superheavyweight touring and custom motorcycles in 1992, versus 68,626 in 1991 and 62,458 in 1990. HDI's share of the U.S. superheavyweight market was 62.9% in 1992 and 63.2% in 1991, versus 46.5% in 1988. HDI sells 20 models, with retail prices ranging from $5,000 to $16,000, through some 600 independent U.S. dealers. Motorcycles are based on five chassis designs and are powered by one of three air-cooled, twin cylinder, "V" configuration engines with displacements of 883cc, 1200cc and 1340cc. HDI's use of advanced manufacturing techniques, including quality circles, just-in-time inventory and statistical process control, has significantly improved productivity and quality. HDI exports about 31% of its motorcycles. Related products, including parts and the merchandising of the Harley Davidson name and trademarks, contributed $155.7 million to sales in 1992, up 19% from 1991.

Holiday Rambler (HR) produces recreational and specialized commercial vehicles. HR is implementing the techniques used in HDI's motorcycle plants. These efforts, along with product development efforts, raised HR's Class A motorhome market share to 5.4% in 1992, from 5.2% in 1991. HR is intent on boosting its competitive position in the travel trailer and fifth-wheel segments of the market. Commercial vehicles include walk-in vans and parcel delivery trucks.

Dividend Data

Cash dividends were initiated in 1993. A dividend reinvestment plan is available. A new "poison pill" stock purchase rights plan was adopted in 1990.

Amt. of Divd. $	Date Decl.	Ex-divd. Date	Stock of Record	Payment Date
0.06	May 8	Jul. 27	Aug. 2	Aug. 16'93

Capitalization

Long Term Liabilities: $12,039,000 (6/93).

Common Stock: 37,957,000 shs. ($0.01 par).
Officers & directors own 3.3%.
Institutions hold about 68%.
Shareholders of record: 13,000.

Office—3700 West Juneau Ave., Milwaukee, WI 53208. **Tel**—(414) 342-4680. **Chrmn**—V. L. Beals Jr. **Pres & CEO**—R. F. Teerlink. **VP-CFO & Investor Contact**—James L. Ziemer. **VP-Secy**—T. K. Hoelter. **Dirs**—B. K. Allen, W. F. Andrews, V. L. Beals Jr., F. L. Brengel, R. Hermon-Taylor, D. A. James, W. B. Potter, R. F. Teerlink. **Transfer Agent & Registrar**—Firstar Trust Co., Milwaukee. **Incorporated** in Delaware in 1981; reincorporated in Wisconsin in 1991. **Empl**—5,800.

 Joshua M. Harari, CFA

Harsco Corp.

NYSE Symbol HSC Options on CBOE (Jan-Apr-Jul-Oct) In S&P MidCap 400

Price	Range	P-E Ratio	Dividend	Yield	S&P Ranking	Beta
Aug. 10'93	1993					
40¾	45–35	11	1.40	3.4%	B+	0.40

Summary

Harsco provides a variety of products and services primarily for defense, industrial, commercial and construction applications. Reflecting the shrinking market for military equipment, Harsco and FMC Corp. have proposed a joint venture combining the company's tracked military vehicle operations with FMC's defense systems group. To expand industrial operations, the company plans to acquire a major metal services firm.

Current Outlook

Earnings for 1993 are estimated at $3.30 a share, versus the $3.52 reported for 1992. For 1994, $3.70 is estimated.

Dividends should continue at the current $0.35 quarterly rate.

Sales for 1993 are expected to decline at least moderately, reflecting a 50% drop in second half defense revenues from first half levels. Industrial services sales should benefit from the Multiserve acquisition before year end, and engineered product sales should continue a moderate pickup. Overall, margins should be stable, excluding possible one-time charges related to the proposed acquisition of MultiServ and the FMC joint venture.

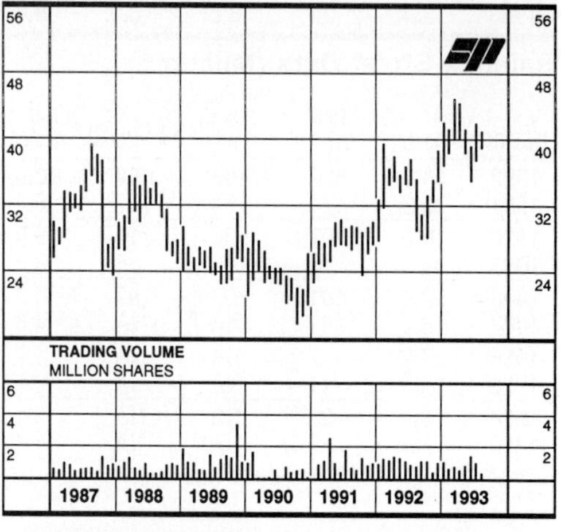

Net Sales & Rentals (Million $)

Quarter:	1993	1992	1991	1990
Mar.	346	408	454	389
Jun.	355	387	455	451
Sep.	---	416	448	414
Dec.	---	414	586	506
	---	1,625	1,943	1,760

Sales in the first six months of 1993 decreased 12%, year to year, primarily reflecting lower defense segment sales. Margins widened on revised truck pricing, and including a gain on sale of an investment equal to $0.21 a share, net income was up 17%, to $1.84 a share from $1.51.

Common Share Earnings ($)

Quarter:	1993	1992	1991	1990
Mar.	0.95	0.79	0.46	0.50
Jun.	0.89	0.72	0.46	0.83
Sep.	E0.70	1.03	0.96	0.69
Dec.	E0.76	0.98	1.03	0.75
	E3.30	3.52	2.91	2.77

Important Developments

Jul. '93— Harsco reached an agreement to acquire Multiserve International N. V. for $380 million. Multiserve is the leader in metal reclamation and steel mill services with operations in 21 countries outside North America. Annual sales are $350 million.

Jul. '93— Justice Dept. approval was expected before the end of 1993 on a proposal to combine Harsco's BMY combat systems division with the defense systems group of FMC Corp., with Harsco's interest at 40% and FMC's at 60%. Harsco would retain its truck operations. The new combined company would have 1993 sales of about $1.2 billion. The FMC group makes the Bradley Fighting Vehicle and other armored vehicles and gun systems.

Next earnings report expected in late October.

Per Share Data ($)

Yr. End Dec. 31	1992	1991	1990	1989	1988	1987	1986	1985	1984	1983
Tangible Bk. Val.	**18.84**	17.59	16.03	14.43	15.28	15.70	15.49	15.00	13.79	13.70
Cash Flow	**5.72**	5.11	4.92	2.57	3.19	4.15	3.41	3.70	3.20	2.52
Earnings[1]	**3.52**	2.91	2.77	0.43	1.17	2.20	1.67	2.03	1.60	0.97
Dividends	**1.320**	1.200	1.200	1.200	1.120	1.000	0.920	0.854	0.800	0.800
Payout Ratio	**38%**	41%	43%	277%	95%	43%	54%	42%	50%	83%
Prices—High	**39½**	30⅜	28¾	31⅛	35⅝	39⅜	28⅞	23⅜	16¾	16¾
Low	**27¾**	22¾	17¾	22½	25	23½	20⅞	15⅝	12¾	11⅞
P/E Ratio—	**11–8**	10–8	10–6	72–52	30–21	18–11	17–13	12–8	10–8	17–12

Data as orig. reptd. Adj. for stk. div. of 50% Mar. 1986. **1.** Bef. spec. items of -0.27 in 1992, -0.11 in 1986. E-Estimated.

Income Data (Million $)

Year Ended Dec. 31	Revs.	Oper. Inc.	% Oper. Inc. of Revs.	Cap. Exp.	Depr.	Int. Exp.	[1]Net Bef. Taxes	Eff. Tax Rate	[2]Net Inc.	% Net Inc. of Revs.	Cash Flow
1992	**1,625**	**205**	**12.6**	**60.3**	**57.1**	**19.2**	**141**	**34.9%**	**[3]91.5**	**5.6**	**149**
1991	1,943	181	9.3	56.8	57.7	18.9	120	36.0%	76.5	3.9	134
1990	1,760	175	9.9	83.9	57.7	17.5	116	37.3%	72.5	4.1	130
1989	1,351	79	5.8	67.6	56.2	16.4	22	48.8%	11.4	0.8	68
1988	1,279	114	8.9	76.0	55.4	16.2	54	42.8%	31.1	2.4	87
1987	1,169	162	13.9	61.0	56.1	8.3	108	41.3%	63.3	5.4	119
1986	1,130	144	12.7	60.6	51.9	12.7	85	41.9%	[3]49.6	4.4	102
1985	1,261	173	13.7	93.5	49.8	14.0	108	44.0%	60.5	4.8	110
1984	1,101	133	12.1	73.3	47.5	14.4	83	42.6%	47.6	4.3	95
1983	839	85	10.1	40.8	44.6	13.6	44	36.7%	27.6	3.3	72

Balance Sheet Data (Million $)

Dec. 31	Cash	Curr. Assets	Curr. Liab.	Curr. Ratio	Total Assets	% Ret. on Assets	Long Term Debt	Common Equity	Total Cap.	% LT Debt of Cap.	% Ret. on Equity
1992	**50**	**598**	**281**	**2.1**	**991**	**9.1**	**120**	**495**	**632**	**19.0**	**19.1**
1991	120	662	377	1.8	1,060	7.5	120	480	624	19.3	16.7
1990	10	593	367	1.6	991	7.4	123	437	582	21.1	17.4
1989	11	599	387	1.5	978	1.2	127	394	538	23.7	2.8
1988	12	547	312	1.8	893	3.7	131	421	570	23.0	7.3
1987	32	463	187	2.5	802	8.4	136	444	606	22.4	14.3
1986	18	426	168	2.5	755	6.3	63	473	576	10.9	10.6
1985	73	473	188	2.5	824	7.3	119	468	619	19.2	13.4
1984	70	505	222	2.3	825	6.2	126	432	575	21.9	11.3
1983	104	403	133	3.0	688	4.1	120	392	530	22.5	7.1

Data as orig. reptd. **1.** Incl. equity in earns. of nonconsol. subs. **2.** Bef. spec. items. **3.** Reflects accounting change.

Business Summary

Harsco's industry segment contributions (pretax profits) in 1992:

	Sales	Profits
Defense	48%	52%
Industrial services/building products	18%	22%
Engineered products	34%	27%

The Defense group provides land defense systems, primarily tracked and wheeled vehicle systems for the U.S. and other governments. Products include a five-ton truck, self-propelled howitzer, a tank recovery vehicle, a field artillery ammunition support vehicle, armored combat earthmovers, and fire direction control vehicles.

The Industrial Services and Building Products group includes metal recovery, scaffolding, shoring and concrete forming equipment, plastic products, mill services, rental of plant equipment, roofing granules and slag abrasives. The company furnishes building products and materials and a wide variety of specialized equipment for construction.

The Engineered Products group includes gas control and containment prod ucts, grating products, pipe fittings, process equipment, railroad equipment, structural composites, specialty metal fabrications, decorative panels, and wear products.

Sales to U.S. government agencies in 1992, 1991, 1990, 1989 and 1988 amounted to 35%, 40%, 36%, 16%, and 22% of total sales, respectively.

Dividend Data

Dividends have been paid since 1939. A dividend reinvestment plan is available. A "poison pill" stock purchase right was issued in 1987.

Amt. of Divd. $	Date Decl.	Ex-divd. Date	Stock of Record	Payment Date
0.33	Sep. 29	Oct. 8	Oct. 15	Nov. 13'92
0.35	Nov. 17	Jan. 11	Jan. 15	Feb. 15'93
0.35	Mar. 18	Apr. 8	Apr. 15	May 14'93
0.35	Jun. 22	Jul. 9	Jul. 15	Aug. 13'93

Finances

At the end of 1992, Harsco took a noncash charge of $7.2 million (after taxes) for the cumulative effect of a change in accounting for post-retirement benefits under SFAS 106.

In early 1992, Harsco authorized the repurchase of 4,000,000 company shares over two years.

Capitalization

Long Term Debt: $119,468,000 (6/93).

Common Stock: 25,379,559 shs. ($1.25 par). Institutions hold about 52%. Shareholders of record: 8,415.

Office—350 Poplar Church Rd., Wormleysburg, PA (Mailing Address: PO Box 8888, Camp Hill, PA 17001-8888.) **Tel**—(717) 763-7064. **Chrmn & CEO**—M. W. Gambill. **Pres**—D. C. Hathaway. **Secy**—P. C. Coppock. **Treas**—R. W. Kaplan. **Investor Contact**—H. R. McIlvaine Jr., **Dirs**—J. J. Burdge, M. W. Gambill, D. C. Hathaway, R. L. Kirk, J. E. Marley, F. E. Masland III, R. F. Nation, N. H. Prater, D. C. Smith Jr., R. C. Smith, A. J. Sordoni III, R. C. Wilburn. **Transfer Agent & Registrar**—Mellon Securities Trust, Ridgefield Park, NJ. **Incorporated** in Pennsylvania in 1899; reincorporated in Delaware in 1956. **Empl**—9,600.

 Thomas Canning, CFA

Hartford Steam Boiler

NYSE Symbol HSB In S&P MidCap 400

Price	Range	P-E Ratio	Dividend	Yield	S&P Ranking	Beta
Sep. 15'93	1993					
45	59⅞–45	22	2.12	4.7%	A–	1.03

Summary

After introducing boiler and machinery insurance in the U.S. in 1866, this company is now the largest underwriter of this type of coverage in North America. It also provides engineering and inspection services. Lower investment income, due mainly to a drop in short-term interest rates, and sharply higher weather-related losses led to lower earnings in 1992. This trend continued into 1993's first half.

Current Outlook

Net operating earnings for 1993 (excluding realized investment gains or losses) are estimated at $2.15 a share, up from 1992's approximate $1.73 (which excluded about $0.98 of investment gains). Operating earnings could rise to $3.00 a share in 1994.

The $0.53 quarterly dividend is the minimum expected.

The forecast of higher earnings for 1993 is predicated on the absence of record catastrophe losses that plagued HSB during 1992. Though not entirely immune to price competition, HSB's dominant market position within this highly focused niche affords it a greater degree of pricing control than most insurers. Engineering services revenue growth will slow to under 10%, but cost cuts and a shift to a higher margin mix of business will aid profits. Investment income growth will slow amid a low interest rate environment, but portfolio writedowns are unlikely. HSB's strategy of holding about 50% of invested assets in equities could increase balance sheet volatility.

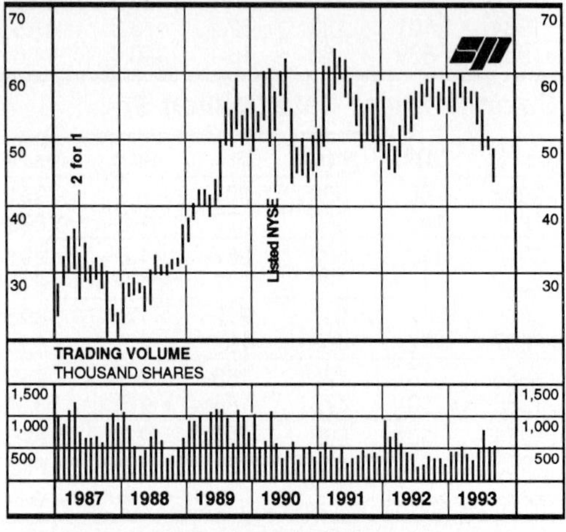

Review of Operations

Revenues in the six months ended June 30, 1993, rose 2.5%, year to year (1992 restated), reflecting 5.6% higher insurance premiums, an 8.0% drop in net investment income and flat engineering revenues and realized investment gains. Margins narrowed, and pretax profits were down 41%. After taxes at 22.6%, versus 28.7%, net income declined 36%, to $1.12 a share (including about $0.49 of net realized investment gains), from $1.74 ($0.48), before a $0.72 special charge in the 1992 interim.

Common Share Earnings ($)

Quarter:	1993	1992	1991	1990
Mar.	0.86	0.85	0.99	0.99
Jun.	0.26	0.89	0.93	0.96
Sep.		0.13	0.89	0.93
Dec.		0.83	0.72	0.93
		2.71	3.53	3.80

Important Developments

Jul. '93— HSB noted that the 5.6% increase in insurance revenues during the first half of 1993 reflected a 1.8% rise in new business and a 3.8% uptick in coverage and prices. But, underwriting results were impaired by an increase in the frequency of large losses, and the adverse development of prior year loss reserves. Underwriting and inspection expenses rose 6.4%, and policy acquisition costs were up 5.3%. As a result, the insurance group incurred a $3.8 million operating loss, versus a year earlier operating profit of $12 million. Engineering revenues were unchanged, at $114.8 million, year to year, as 4.8% higher prices were offset by volume decreases amid a planned shift to a higher-margin mix of business and general weakness in the economy. Margins narrowed on the lower volume, but cost cuts recently undertaken should begin to be felt in the latter half of 1993.

Next earnings report expected in late October.

Per Share Data ($)

Yr. End Dec. 31	1992	1991	1990	1989	[1]1988	1987	1986	1985	[1]1984	1983
Tangible Bk. Val.	**18.08**	19.47	17.05	16.29	13.04	10.65	10.17	7.50	5.58	6.43
Oper. Earnings	**[3]1.73**	NA	NA	NA	NA	NA	NA	NA	NA	NA
Earnings[2]	**2.71**	3.53	3.80	3.78	3.46	2.96	2.50	1.51	0.67	0.94
Dividends	**2.030**	1.850	1.700	1.500	1.150	0.950	0.550	0.419	0.375	0.369
Payout Ratio	**75%**	52%	45%	40%	33%	32%	22%	31%	56%	40%
Prices—High	**59¼**	63¾	62⅛	59¼	37¼	36⅝	25½	15⅞	7½	7¾
Low	**45⅛**	46⅛	43½	34¾	22½	20¼	15⅝	7⅜	6¼	4⅞
P/E Ratio—	**22–17**	18–13	16–11	16–9	11–7	14–8	12–7	12–5	27–22	12–7

Data as orig. reptd. Adj. for stk. divs. of 100% May 1987, 100% Aug. 1986, 100% May 1985. **1.** Reflects accounting change. **2.** Bef. spec. item(s) of -0.73 in 1992. **3.** Approximate. NA-Not Available.

Hartford Steam Boiler Inspection & Insurance Company

Income Data (Million $)

Year Ended Dec. 31	Premium Income	Net Invest. Inc.	Oth. Revs.	Total Revs.	Property & Casualty Underwriting Ratios [2]Loss	[2]Expense	[2]Comb.	Net Bef. Taxes	Net Oper. Inc.	[4]Net Inc.	—% Return On— [3]Revs.	[3]Equity
1992	**350**	**36.5**	**296**	**682**	**50.7**	**49.9**	**100.6**	**73**	**NA**	**56.3**	**8.3**	**14.5**
1991	323	41.4	266	630	43.8	50.1	93.9	101	NA	73.9	11.7	19.3
1990	299	42.4	221	562	37.2	50.8	88.0	110	NA	78.7	14.0	22.8
1989	287	41.7	156	485	33.3	50.6	83.9	110	NA	77.6	16.0	25.8
[1]1988	292	35.8	131	459	35.0	49.0	84.0	96	NA	70.7	15.4	29.1
1987	283	35.5	104	422	35.6	50.1	85.7	75	53.4	60.6	12.7	24.7
1986	269	32.0	88	389	36.5	49.5	86.0	66	45.3	53.1	11.7	24.1
1985	206	25.7	85	317	40.6	54.1	94.7	36	27.7	30.9	8.7	20.4
[1]1984	158	21.5	81	260	52.4	63.5	115.9	NM	6.3	15.1	2.4	4.3
1983	147	17.3	71	235	33.3	64.9	98.2	24	19.0	26.9	11.7	15.4

Balance Sheet Data (Million $)

Dec. 31	Cash & Equiv.	Premiums Due	—Investment Assets— [5]Bonds	Stocks	Loans	Total	% Invest. Yield	Deferred Policy Costs	Total Assets	Debt	Common Equity
1992	**8.7**	**64.8**	**198**	**310**	**Nil**	**508**	**7.0**	**30.6**	**888**	**61.9**	**374**
1991	6.0	61.3	197	333	Nil	530	8.1	28.4	889	68.4	409
1990	11.6	61.1	244	251	Nil	495	8.1	27.8	827	73.9	355
1989	5.6	55.2	250	302	Nil	552	7.8	26.4	795	39.5	335
1988	5.2	58.7	297	225	Nil	522	7.1	24.9	730	51.7	266
1987	17.2	65.8	276	210	Nil	486	7.4	27.1	702	62.6	217
1986	4.0	67.5	240	238	Nil	478	7.3	25.6	670	68.5	216
1985	2.1	59.1	190	196	Nil	387	7.9	23.2	563	71.7	160
1984	5.0	46.8	133	127	Nil	260	7.9	17.1	416	71.7	112
1983	0.4	34.0	97	156	Nil	287	6.4	14.0	396	26.2	185

Data as orig. reptd. **1.** Reflects accounting change. **2.** As reptd. by co. **3.** Based on oper. earns. prior to 1988. **4.** Bef. spec. item(s). **5.** Incl. short-term invest. NA-Not Available. NM-Not Meaningful.

Business Summary

The Hartford Steam Boiler Inspection and Insurance Co. underwrites boiler and machinery insurance and provides engineering services. Contributions to revenues in recent years:

	1992	1991
Premiums earned	51%	51%
Engineering services	39%	37%
Investment income/gains	10%	12%

Boiler and machinery insurance provides for the indemnification of the policyholder for financial loss resulting from destruction or damage to an insured boiler, pressure vessel or other machine caused by an accident. This financial loss can include the cost to repair or replace the damaged equipment, the cost of product spoilage, and lost profits arising from business interruption stemming from an accident. The company provides a high level of loss prevention services with its insurance products. This tends to increase underwriting and inspection expenses, while reducing loss and loss adjustment expenses.

HSB also writes other types of insurance, primarily as an adjunct to its boiler and machinery insurance. Insurance providing other than boiler and machinery coverage accounted for approximately 20% of net earned premiums in 1992.

Engineering services include quality assurance services, training for nondestructive testing, inspections to code standards, and other specialized consulting and inspection services related to the design and applications of boilers, pressure vessels and other types of equipment.

Dividend Data

Dividends have been paid since 1873. A dividend reinvestment plan is available. A "poison pill" stock purchase right was adopted in 1988.

Amt of Divd. $	Date Decl.	Ex-divd. Date	Stock of Record	Payment Date
0.53	Sep. 28	Oct. 5	Oct. 9	Oct. 29'92
0.53	Nov. 23	Jan. 4	Jan. 8	Jan. 28'93
0.53	Mar. 22	Apr. 2	Apr. 9	Apr. 29'93
0.53	Jun. 28	Jul. 2	Jul. 9	Jul. 29'93

Capitalization

Long Term Debt: $40,500,000, incl. $27.7 million of capital lease obligations (6/93).

Common Stock: 20,764,518 shs. (no par).
Institutions hold about 49%.
Shareholders of record: 5,764 (2/93).

Office—One State St., Hartford, CT 06102. **Tel**—(203) 722-1866. **Pres & CEO**—W. Wilde. **SVP-Treas & CFO**—K. S. Hynes. **Secy**—J. J. Kelley. **VP-Investor Contact**—James C. Rowan, Jr. (203) 722-5180. **Dirs**—J. B. Alvord, C. G. Campbell, D. M. Carlton, R. G. Dooley, W. B. Ellis, E. J. Ferland, J. A. Powers, L. D. Rice, P. A. Vatter, J. M. Washburn Jr., W. Wilde. **Transfer Agent & Registrar**—First National Bank of Boston, Boston. **Incorporated** in Connecticut in 1866. **Empl**—4,542.

 Catherine A. Seifert

Hawaiian Electric Industries

NYSE Symbol HE In S&P MidCap 400

Price	Range	P-E Ratio	Dividend	Yield	S&P Ranking	Beta
Oct. 11'93	1993					
38	38⅞–31	15	2.28	6.0%	A–	0.59

Summary

This holding company owns Hawaiian Electric Co., a public utility that provides electric service to 95% of Hawaii's population. Other subsidiaries are engaged in banking, marine freight transportation and real estate development. The company discontinued its property-casualty insurance operations in 1992 after large losses and write-offs associated with Hurricane Iniki. Earnings are expected to improve modestly in 1993, as customer growth, higher subsidiary income, and government spending offset a weak economy.

Current Outlook

Share earnings for 1993 are projected at $2.60, up from 1992's $2.54. Earnings for 1994 are projected at $2.80 a share.

The minimum expectation is for dividends to continue at $0.57 quarterly.

Higher profitability projected for 1993 should primarily reflect an estimated 3% increase in power sales stemming from 1.7% customer growth and continued strong defense spending. Greater subsidiary contributions can be expected, especially from the banking division. Tourism, the state's largest industry, should remain stable. Look for earnings quality to deteriorate slightly with a $1.2 billion construction program over the next five years as noncash credits for interest during construction accounts for a larger portion of earnings.

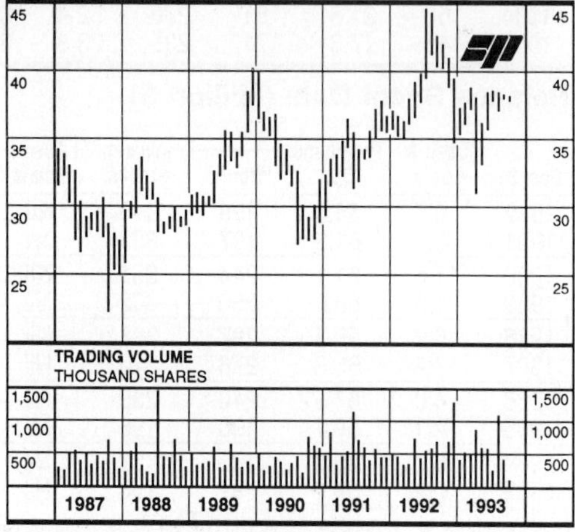

Revenues (Million $)

Quarter:	1994	1993[1]	1992[1]	1991
Mar.	---	279	237	287
Jun.	---	282	241	261
Sep.	---	---	271	274
Dec.	---	---	282	263
	---	---	1,031	1,084

Total revenues for the six months ended June 30, 1993, rose 17%, year to year, reflecting 1992 rate relief and higher nonutility sales. Operating expenses advanced 18%, and after 17% higher interest expense and taxes at 41.5%, versus 35.1%, net income was down 1.5%, to $1.13, from $1.19, based on 3.8% more shares. Results exclude gains of $0.07 and $0.05 a share, respectively, from discontinued operations.

Common Share Earnings ($)

Quarter:	1994	1993[1]	1992[1]	1991
Mar.	E0.60	0.38	0.55	0.58
Jun.	E0.65	0.76	0.64	0.59
Sep.	E0.80	E0.76	0.68	0.64
Dec.	E0.75	E0.70	0.67	0.63
	E2.80	E2.60	2.54	2.40

Important Developments

Jul. '93— The state insurance commissioner filed a lawsuit against HE to recover funds to rehabilitate its insolvent former property-casualty insurance subsidiary. The amount sought was not determined. HE wrote off $59.7 million ($2.46 a share) of losses from its insolvent insurance operations and $13.6 million ($0.56) from its troubled wind farm business in 1992. The company decided to exit the insurance business following policyholder claims of more than $300 million from damage caused by Hurricane Iniki on September 11, 1992. The shortfall in assets available to pay claims was in excees of $80 million, and at least $112 million more would be required if the HIG Group were to continue to write insurance business. In December 1992, HE's directors decided not to contribute the additional capital and to write off HE's remaining investment.

Next earnings report expected in late October.

Per Share Data ($)

Yr. End Dec. 31	1992	1991	1990	1989	1988	1987	1986	1985	1984	1983
Tangible Bk. Val.	**20.06**	21.89	20.33	19.93	18.23	19.59	18.96	17.84	16.99	16.32
Cash Flow	**5.09**	4.95	4.51	5.37	5.21	4.47	4.69	4.38	4.22	3.94
Earnings[2]	**2.54**	2.40	2.02	3.06	2.90	2.20	2.57	2.40	2.25	2.06
Dividends	**2.250**	2.210	2.170	2.070	1.950	1.830	1.740	1.660	1.580	1.515
Payout Ratio	**90%**	96%	109%	69%	73%	85%	69%	70%	72%	75%
Prices—High	**44⅝**	37⅞	40	40¼	33⅝	34¼	35½	25⅜	21¼	16⅞
Low	**34¾**	29⅜	27¼	29⅜	25⅞	22¼	24½	19⅝	15⅜	13⅝
P/E Ratio—	**18–14**	16–12	20–13	13–10	12–9	16–10	14–10	11–8	9–7	8–7

Data as orig. reptd. Adj. for stk. divs. of 100% May 1984. **1.** From continuing ops. **2.** Bef. results of disc. opers. of -3.02 in 1992. E-Estimated.

Income Data (Million $)

Year Ended Dec. 31	Revs.	Oper. Inc.	% Oper. Inc. of Revs.	Cap. Exp.	Depr.	Int. Exp.	Net Bef. Taxes	Eff. Tax Rate	Net Inc.	% Net Inc. of Revs.	Cash Flow
[1]1992	**1,031**	**313**	**30.3**	**191**	**61.9**	**160**	**98.0**	**30.1%**	**68.4**	**6.6**	**124**
1991	1,084	314	29.0	162	58.3	170	91.6	32.7%	61.7	5.7	113
1990	1,011	288	28.5	141	53.6	164	79.7	36.4%	50.7	5.0	97
1989	884	287	32.5	145	48.5	147	97.6	29.6%	68.7	7.8	113
1988	733	211	28.8	121	43.8	86	86.0	30.6%	59.7	8.1	99
1987	635	151	23.8	122	39.1	38	77.2	44.8%	42.6	6.7	77
1986	558	158	28.3	86	35.5	38	86.1	43.2%	49.0	8.8	79
1985	648	145	22.3	77	32.2	34	81.7	44.8%	45.1	7.0	71
1984	673	139	20.7	48	30.9	30	79.8	48.1%	41.4	6.1	66
1983	623	121	19.5	42	28.3	27	69.3	46.3%	37.2	6.0	59

Balance Sheet Data (Million $)

Dec. 31	Cash	Curr. Assets	Curr. Liab.	Curr. Ratio	Total Assets	% Ret. on Assets	Long Term Debt	Common Equity	Total Inv. Capital	% LT Debt of Cap.	% Ret. on Equity
1992	**157**	**NA**	**NA**	**NA**	**4,016**	**1.7**	**727**	**548**	**1,558**	**46.6**	**10.7**
1991	75	NA	NA	NA	3,791	1.6	711	581	1,594	44.6	9.6
1990	129	NA	NA	NA	3,572	1.5	514	511	1,324	38.9	8.6
1989	75	NA	NA	NA	3,057	2.4	507	493	1,311	38.7	13.4
1988	73	NA	NA	NA	2,617	2.9	470	454	1,201	39.2	12.8
1987	63	183	170	1.1	1,218	3.7	360	343	973	37.0	11.2
1986	59	142	108	1.3	1,026	4.7	325	322	907	35.8	13.8
1985	83	199	133	1.5	1,028	4.6	344	296	886	38.8	13.5
1984	38	160	78	2.0	904	4.7	320	272	817	39.2	13.2
1983	10	136	65	2.1	823	4.4	283	252	748	37.9	12.5

Data as orig. reptd. **1.** Excl. disc. opers. NA-Not Available.

Business Summary

Hawaiian Electric Industries is the holding company for Hawaiian Electric Co., which through Maui Electric and Hawaii Electric Light provides electric service on the islands of Oahu, Hawaii, Maui, Lanai and Molokai. Electric sales accounted for 75% of revenues and 76% of operating income in 1992. About 10% of electric revenues in 1992 were derived from federal government agencies. Contributions to electric revenues by customer class:

	1992	1991	1990	1989
Residential	32%	32%	31%	32%
Commercial	31%	30%	30%	30%
Industrial	36%	37%	38%	37%
Other	1%	1%	1%	1%

Fuel used for generation is primarily oil. Peak load in 1992 was 1,493 mw and system capability was 2,046 mw, for a capacity margin of 27%. To meet increases in demand, HE has entered into long-term power purchase agreements with independent suppliers for 406 mw of firm capacity.

The company estimated electric utility capital expenditures for 1993-97 at $1.2 billion, including $240 million for 1993.

Nonutility subsidiaries contributed 24% of operating income in 1992. HE owns American Savings Bank F.S.B., the second largest Hawaii-based savings and loan with 45 branch offices at year-end 1992 and total assets of some $2.5 billion.

Finances

In August 1993, HE sold 1.75 million common shares at $37.25 per share in a public offering. Net proceeds of approximately $63 million were to be used to repay outstanding commercial paper and for general corporate purposes.

Dividend Data

Dividends have been paid since 1901. A dividend reinvestment plan is available.

Amt of Divd. $	Date Decl.	Ex-divd. Date	Stock of Record	Payment Date
0.57	Oct. 20	Nov. 4	Nov. 10	Dec. 10'92
0.57	Jan. 19	Feb. 4	Feb. 10	Mar. 10'93
0.57	Apr. 20	May 4	May 10	Jun. 10'93
0.57	Jul. 20	Aug. 4	Aug. 10	Sep. 10'93

Capitalization

Long Term Debt: $581,686,000 (6/93).

Subsidiary Red. Preferred Stock: $48,270,000.

Subsidiary Preferred Stock: $36,293,000.

Common Stock: 27,052,000 shs. (no par). Institutions hold about 28%. Shareholders of record: 38,196.

Office—900 Richards St., Honolulu, HI 96813. **Tel**—(808) 543-5662. **Pres & CEO**—R. F. Clarke. **VP & CFO**—R. F. Mougeot. **Treas & Investor Contact**—Constance H. Lau (808) 543-7384. **Secy**—B. A. M. Splinter. **Dirs**—E. L. Carter, R. F. Clarke, J. D. Field, W. G. Foster, R. Henderson, B. F. Kaito, V. H. Li, B. D. Mills, A. M. Myers, R. M. Ono, D. J. Plotts, C. D. Pratt Jr., T. Twigg-Smith, J. N. Watanabe, H. D. Williamson. **Transfer Agents**—First Chicago Trust Co. of New York, NYC; Company's office. **Incorporated** in Hawaii in 1891; reincorporated in Hawaii in 1983. **Empl**—3,286.

 Ned Bancroft

HealthCare COMPARE

NASDAQ Symbol HCCC (Incl. in Nat'l Market) Options on CBOE In S&P MidCap 400

Price	Range	P-E Ratio	Dividend	Yield	S&P Ranking	Beta
Sep. 20'93	1993					
16½	31⅞–10½	17	None	None	B–	1.47

Summary

This company is a leading independent provider of healthcare utilization review and payor-based preferred provider organization (PPO) services. Earnings advanced sharply in the first half of 1993, reflecting continued development and expansion of the company's PPO network and the absence of $16 million of charges related to the February 1992 acquisition of Occupational—Urgent Care Health Systems.

Business Summary

HealthCare COMPARE Corp. develops and manages payor-based preferred provider organizations (PPOs) and provides healthcare utilization review services. In addition, through its OUCH Systems subsidiary (acquired in February 1992), the company provides workers' compensation bill review, fee schedule review and claims pricing services. Revenues in recent years were derived as follows:

	1992	1991
PPO & fee schedule services	78%	48%
Utilization review	18%	40%
Govt. contract services	4%	12%

The company assists clients with medical cost management through an array of programs designed to manage specific cost elements. Its various medical review programs help clients manage the number of units of medical services (volume), while its PPO products help manage the cost of such units of service (price). Through its OUCH Sytems capabilities, the company provides workers' compensation bill review services nationally. These services are coupled with the company's review programs and PPO networks in order to provide a comprehensive product offering in the workers' compensation area.

The company's PPO services are offered through its AFFORDABLE Health Care Concepts subsidiary. AFFORDABLE develops and manages payor-based group health and workers' compensation PPO networks throughout the U.S. The AFFORDABLE PPO networks currently serve more than 1,500 clients and contain about 1,250 hospitals, as well as outpatient care networks comprised of physicians, clinical laboratories, surgery centers, radiology facilities and other providers.

HealthCare COMPARE offers several utilization review and cost management programs from which clients may select. Most clients subscribe to the

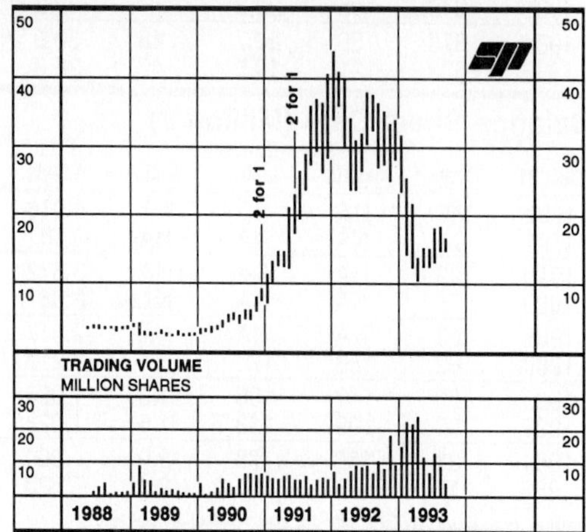

company's medical/surgical hospital review program, which serves as a base to which other programs may be added. About 90% of clients subscribe to at least one additional program. Other cost management programs offered include those concentrating on case management, psychiatric and substance abuse review and disability management, all of which are also offered on a stand-alone basis.

Important Developments

Jul. '93— HealthCare COMPARE signed a letter of agreement to provide PPO services to Wellpoint Health Networks, Inc., the largest for-profit managed healthcare company in California. Separately, the company enhanced its strategic alliance with Employee Benefit Health Plans, Inc. (EBP), agreeing to provide utilization management services in addition to the PPO services already provided to EBP clients on a national basis.

Next earnings report expected in early November.

Per Share Data ($)

Yr. End Dec. 31[1]	[2]1992	1991	1990	1989	[2]1988	1987	1986
Tangible Bk. Val.	[5]**3.75**	2.58	1.86	1.62	1.26	0.79	d0.13
Cash Flow	**0.70**	0.64	0.34	0.22	0.19	0.12	0.05
Earnings[3]	**0.51**	0.50	0.23	0.12	0.13	0.09	0.03
Dividends	**Nil**	Nil	Nil	Nil	Nil	Nil	Nil
Payout Ratio	**Nil**	Nil	Nil	Nil	Nil	Nil	Nil
Prices[4]—High	**44**	40¾	9⁵⁄₁₆	4⅛	4⅜	4¹⁄₁₆	NA
Low	**23¾**	7⅛	2⁹⁄₁₆	2¼	2¹⁵⁄₁₆	1⅞	NA
P/E Ratio—	**86–47**	82–14	40–11	36–20	35–24	46–21	NA

Data as orig. reptd. Adj. for stk. divs. of 100% Jun. 1991, 100% Dec. 1990. **1.** Prior to 1990, yrs. ended Aug. 31; excl. last four mos. of cal. 1989. **2.** Refl. merger or acq. **3.** Bef. spec. items of -0.03 in 1989, +0.01 in 1987, +0.03 in 1986. **4.** Cal. yr. **5.** Incl. intangibles. d-Deficit. NA-Not Available.

Income Data (Million $)

Year Ended Dec. 31[1]	Revs.	Oper. Inc.	% Oper. Inc. of Revs.	Cap. Exp.	Depr.	Int. Exp.	Net Bef. Taxes	Eff. Tax Rate	[3]Net Inc.	% Net Inc. of Revs.	Cash Flow
[2]1992	**134**	**52.5**	**39.4**	**10.2**	**6.61**	**0.13**	**32.3**	**44.0%**	**18.1**	**13.6**	**24.7**
1991	71	21.2	29.9	22.6	3.41	Nil	20.3	37.1%	12.8	18.0	16.2
1990	42	8.6	20.3	3.6	2.67	0.01	8.2	33.0%	5.5	13.1	8.2
1989	31	4.7	14.9	4.2	2.27	0.04	4.1	35.2%	2.6	8.4	4.9
[2]1988	21	4.2	20.2	4.0	1.08	0.02	3.8	39.4%	2.3	11.0	3.3
1987	12	2.3	20.0	1.9	0.42	0.06	2.0	41.3%	1.2	10.1	1.6
1986	6	0.8	14.9	1.0	0.20	0.05	0.6	48.1%	0.3	5.4	0.5

Balance Sheet Data (Million $)

Dec. 31	Cash	Curr. Assets	Curr. Liab.	Curr. Ratio	Total Assets	% Ret. on Assets	Long Term Debt	Common Equity	Total Cap.	% LT Debt of Cap.	% Ret. on Equity
1992	**73.1**	**100**	**15.6**	**6.4**	**146**	**14.7**	**Nil**	**130**	**130**	**Nil**	**16.5**
1991	25.9	40	7.8	5.2	69	20.8	Nil	61	61	Nil	24.1
1990	34.8	42	7.4	5.6	52	10.8	0.07	43	43	0.2	13.7
1989	25.0	40	10.8	3.7	50	5.9	0.23	37	38	0.6	7.3
1988	23.1	27	3.8	7.2	39	7.4	0.27	34	35	0.8	8.6
1987	12.7	14	2.4	5.9	17	9.4	Nil	13	15	Nil	20.3
1986	0.1	1	1.7	0.8	3	NA	Nil	d1	1	Nil	NA

Data as orig. reptd. **1.** Prior to 1990, yrs. ended Aug. 31; excl. last four mos. of cal. 1989. **2.** Refl. merger or acq. **3.** Bef. spec. items. d-Deficit. NA-Not Available.

Revenues (Million $)

Quarter:	1993	1992	1991	1990
Mar.	37.4	31.4	15.5	9.1
Jun.	38.9	32.5	16.9	9.9
Sep.		33.8	18.8	11.2
Dec.		35.8	19.6	12.1
		133.5	70.9	42.2

Revenues in the six months ended June 30, 1993, advanced 19%, year to year, primarily reflecting development and expansion of the company's PPO and fee schedule services; utilization management services gained 7.5%. Margins widened on the higher volume, and operating income climbed 34%. Further aided by the absence of $16 million of merger-related restructuring expenses, pretax income surged to $29,802,000 from $5,657,000. After taxes at 38.9%, versus 70.0%, net income was $18,208,000 ($0.51 a share), versus $1,699,000 ($0.05).

Common Share Earnings ($)

Quarter:	1993	1992	1991	1990
Mar.	0.25	d0.15	0.10	0.04
Jun.	0.26	0.20	0.11	0.05
Sep.		0.22	0.13	0.07
Dec.		0.24	0.17	0.08
		0.51	0.50	0.23

Dividend Data

No cash dividends have been paid, and the company expects to retain earnings for use in the operation and expansion of its business. Two-for-one stock splits were effected in December 1990 and June 1991.

Finances

In June 1993, HealthCare Compare authorized the repurchase of up to 1,500,000 (4.3%) of its common shares from time to time in the open market or private transactions.

In February 1992, HealthCare COMPARE acquired Occupational—Urgent Care Health Systems Inc. (OUCH) in exchange for 9,442,387 common shares. In connection with the merger, the company recorded a one-time charge of $16 million for merger-related costs and expenses incurred by the company and OUCH. As a result of the charge, HealthCare Compare's net income was reduced by $11,500,000 ($0.33 a share).

Capitalization

Long Term Obligations: None (6/93).

Common Stock: 34,755,445 shs. ($0.01 par). Officers and directors own 6.0%. Institutions hold 64%. Shareholders: 1,227 of record (3/93).

Options: To buy 1,399,000 com. shs. at $0.56 to $38.25 ea. (12/92).

d-Deficit.

Office—3200 Highland Ave., Downers Grove, IL 60515. **Tel**—(708) 241-7900. **Chrmn**—T. J. Pritzker. **Pres & CEO**—J. C. Smith. **CFO & Investor Contact**—J. E. Whitters. **EVP & Secy**—R. H. Galowich. **Dirs**—R. J. Becker, D. S. Brunner, R. S. Colman, J. P. Foley, R. H. Galowich, M. Garb, B. W. Kanter, T. J. Pritzker, D. E. Simon, J. C. Smith. **Transfer Agent & Registrar**—LaSalle National Bank of Chicago. **Incorporated** in Delaware in 1982. **Empl**—1,411.

 Adam J. Penn

HEALTHSOUTH Rehabilitation

NYSE Symbol HRC Options on NYSE (Mar-Jun-Sep-Dec) In S&P MidCap 400

Price	Range	P–E Ratio	Dividend	Yield	S&P Ranking	Beta
Aug. 5'93	1993					
14⅜	26⅜–13	12	None	None	NR	2.08

Summary

This company is one of the nation's largest providers of comprehensive rehabilitative healthcare services, operating 75 outpatient and 11 inpatient rehabilitation facilities as of March 1993. Revenues and earnings continued to advance in the first half of 1993, aided by an ongoing expansion program which has increased the company's network of rehabilitation facilities substantially in the past year.

Business Summary

HEALTHSOUTH Rehabilitation provides comprehensive medical rehabilitation services through its outpatient and inpatient facilities. The company offers programs for the rehabilitation of patients experiencing disabilities due to a wide variety of physical conditions, such as stroke, head injury, orthopedic problems, neuromuscular disease and sports-related injuries. HRC services include physical therapy, sports medicine, work hardening, neurorehabilitation, occupational therapy, respiratory therapy, speech-language pathology and rehabilitation nursing. The company also provides general and specialty medical and surgical healthcare services at its medical center facilities.

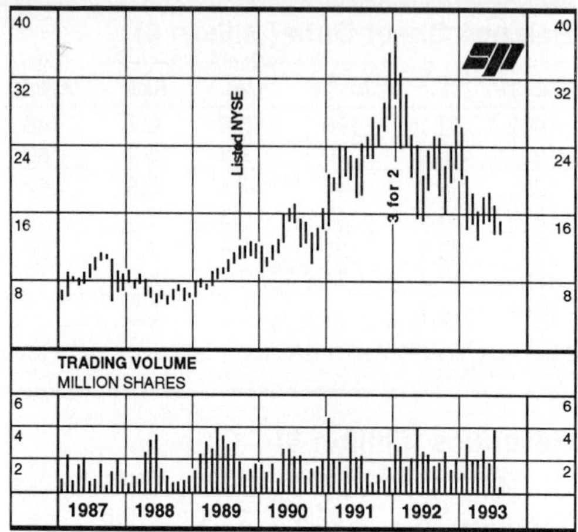

Comprehensive medical rehabilitation concentrates on physical disabilities and impairments utilizing a coordinated interdisciplinary approach to help patients attain measurable goals. The facilities enable patients to receive coordinated care in a single location, rather than the uncoordinated care patients often receive when treated by different therapists in different locations. The professional staff at each facility consists of licensed or credentialed healthcare practitioners who, together with the patient, his family and the referring physician, form the "team" that assists the patient in attaining his rehabilitation goals.

As of March 31, 1993, HRC was operating 75 outpatient facilities, which it believes to be the largest group of affiliated proprietary comprehensive outpatient rehabilitation facilities in the U.S. HRC was also operating 11 inpatient facilities, which generally provide the same professional healthcare services as the outpatient facilities, but on a more intensive level and with the addition of therapeutic recreation and provision of 24-hour nursing care. In addition, the company was operating four specialty medical centers which specialize in orthopedics, sports medicine and rehabilitation.

In June 1992, the company restructured its operations into three divisions— HEALTHSOUTH Outpatient Centers, HEALTHSOUTH Rehabilitation Hospitals and HEALTHSOUTH Medical Centers, each with its own president and controller. The move was meant to strengthen the focus of management on continuing operations and continue the development of market-specific programs. In February 1993, HRC created a new subsidiary to focus on new business ventures.

Important Developments

Jun. '93— HRC announced that it acquired outpatient rehabilitation facilities in Texas, New Jersey and Maryland, bringing to 14 the number of outpatient acquisitions and start-ups since the beginning of 1993. The company also said it was proceeding on schedule with the construction of two new rehabilitation hospitals, scheduled for completion in October 1993 and in late 1994.

Next earnings report expected in late October.

Per Share Data ($)

Yr. End Dec. 31	[2]1992	1991	1990	[2]1989	1988	1987	[2]1986	[2]1985
Tangible Bk. Val.	**10.07**	[1]9.96	[1]6.71	[1]4.27	[1]3.79	[1]3.41	[1]2.09	[1]d1.02
Cash Flow	**1.63**	1.27	1.15	0.81	0.57	0.40	0.13	d0.15
Earnings[3]	**1.00**	0.86	0.71	0.51	0.37	0.27	0.05	d0.19
Dividends	**Nil**	Nil	Nil	Nil	Nil	Nil	Nil	Nil
Payout Ratio	**Nil**	Nil	Nil	Nil	Nil	Nil	Nil	Nil
Prices—High	**37¼**	35⅛	17⅛	12¾	9¼	11⁵⁄₁₆	6¾	NA
Low	**15¼**	14⅝	9⅛	6⅛	5¼	5⁹⁄₁₆	4	NA
P/E Ratio—	**37–15**	41–17	24–13	25–12	25–14	43–21	NM	NA

Data as orig. reptd. Adj. for stk. div(s). of 50% in Jan. 1992. **1.** Incl. intangibles in all yrs. **2.** Reflects merger or acquisition. **3.** Bef. spec. items of +0.04 in 1987, +0.05 in 1986. d-Deficit. NM-Not Meaningful. NA-Not Available.

Income Data (Million $)

Year Ended Dec. 31	Revs.	Oper. Inc.	% Oper. Inc. of Revs.	Cap. Exp.	Depr.	Int. Exp.	Net Bef. Taxes	Eff. Tax Rate	[2]Net Inc.	% Net Inc. of Revs.	Cash Flow
[1]**1992**	**407**	**75.6**	**18.6**	**133**	**18.9**	**12.8**	**46.5**	**33.0%**	**29.7**	**7.3**	**48.7**
1991	225	50.3	22.3	104	10.5	11.9	35.4	32.5%	22.4	9.9	32.8
1990	180	36.5	20.2	39	8.0	12.4	21.1	34.3%	12.9	7.2	20.9
[1]1989	114	21.9	19.2	43	4.9	8.6	13.0	33.6%	8.1	7.1	13.0
1988	75	14.8	19.7	22	3.1	4.3	9.8	33.0%	5.7	7.6	8.9
1987	45	8.6	19.2	19	2.0	2.1	6.2	39.2%	3.8	8.5	5.8
[1]1986	19	2.4	12.7	15	0.8	1.0	1.1	44.5%	0.5	2.6	1.3
[1]1985	5	d1.4	NM	6	0.3	0.2	d1.7	NM	d1.5	NM	d1.2

Balance Sheet Data (Million $)

Dec. 31	Cash	Curr. Assets	Curr. Liab.	Curr. Ratio	Total Assets	% Ret. on Assets	Long Term Debt	Common Equity	Total Cap.	% LT Debt of Cap.	% Ret. on Equity
1992	**86**	**213**	**42.4**	**5.0**	**642**	**5.3**	**300**	**290**	**599**	**50.0**	**10.3**
1991	107	185	19.9	9.3	472	4.9	164	279	444	37.0	9.6
1990	71	128	17.2	7.4	301	4.5	150	128	279	53.7	12.3
1989	32	87	14.9	5.8	219	4.6	133	66	200	66.3	13.1
1988	18	52	13.8	3.8	134	4.9	57	57	117	49.2	10.5
1987	24	44	10.7	4.1	100	5.1	34	51	88	39.1	9.3
1986	9	19	8.8	2.2	52	0.7	15	25	43	36.1	7.5
1985	1	4	1.8	2.5	14	NM	4	d2	12	37.4	NM

Data as orig. reptd. **1.** Reflects merger or acquisition. **2.** Bef. spec. item(s). d-Deficit. NM-Not Meaningful.

Net Revenues (Million $)

Quarter:	1993	1992	1991	1990
Mar.	116.1	93.6	50.6	43.3
Jun.	119.6	102.6	54.4	43.3
Sep.		102.1	55.8	46.1
Dec.		108.7	64.7	47.7
		407.0	225.5	180.5

Revenues for the six months ended June 30, 1993, advanced 20%, year to year, bolstered by the addition of new outpatient facilities. Further aided by the absence of a $3.7 million pretax charge related to a terminated merger agreement, net income increased 47%, to $18,399,000 ($0.62 a share), from $12,520,000 ($0.42).

Common Share Earnings ($)

Quarter:	1993	1992	1991	1990
Mar.	0.30	0.16	0.21	0.16
Jun.	0.33	0.27	0.21	0.17
Sep.		0.28	0.21	0.17
Dec.		0.30	0.23	0.21
		1.00	0.86	0.71

Dividend Data

No cash dividends have been paid. A 3-for-2 stock split was paid December 31, 1991, to shareholders of record December 13.

Finances

HRC intends to pursue the acquisition of additional healthcare operations, including outpatient and inpatient rehabilitation facilities and companies engaged in the provision of rehabilitation-related services, and to expand certain of its existing facilities. In May 1993, the company estimated that it would spend approximately $25 million over the next 12 months for the acquisition and/or development of new comprehensive outpatient rehabilitation facilities and approximately $75 million for the construction of rehabilitation hospitals.

The company has a $390 million revolving line of credit, under which $299 million was outstanding at March 31, 1993.

HRC believes that existing cash, cash flow from operations and borrowings under existing credit facilities will be sufficient to satisfy the company's estimated cash requirements for the foreseeable future.

Capitalization

Long Term Debt: $315,821,000 (3/93).

Minority Interest: $3,676,000.

Common Stock: 28,872,868 shs. ($0.01 par).
Institutions hold about 84%.
Shareholders of record: 653 (3/93).

Office—Two Perimeter Park South, Birmingham, AL 35243. **Tel**—(205) 967-7116. **Chrmn & Pres**—R. M. Scrushy. **Exec VP-CFO & Investor Contact**—A. Beam Jr. **Exec VP & Secy**—A. J. Tanner. **Dirs**—A Beam Jr., J. P. Bennett, R. F. Celeste, C. S. Givens, L. R. House, C. W. Newhall III, R. M. Scrushy, G. H. Strong, A. J. Tanner, P. C. Watkins. **Transfer Agent & Registrar**—Chemical Bank, NYC. **Incorporated** in Delaware in 1984. **Empl**—7,243.

 Adam J. Penn

Heilig-Meyers Co.

NYSE Symbol HMY In S&P MidCap 400

Price	Range	P–E Ratio	Dividend	Yield	S&P Ranking	Beta
Sep. 29'93	1993					
31⅞	33¼–17 5/32	34	0.20	0.6%	A	1.54

Summary

This company is primarily a retailer of home furnishings, with most of its stores located in small and medium-sized towns and cities in the eastern Sunbelt and the Midwest. In September 1993, HMY said that it was discussing the possible acquisition of a company that operates 92 furniture stores in the West and Southwest, which if completed would mark HMY's initial expansion into those areas. The company raised $74.2 million through a public stock offering in May 1993. Earnings remained strong through 1993-94's first half. The shares were split 3-for-2 in July 1993, following two similar splits in 1992.

Current Outlook

Share earnings for the fiscal year ending February 28, 1994, are estimated at $1.07, up from the $0.84 (adjusted) of fiscal 1992-93. Further growth to $1.30 is projected for 1994-95.

Following a 50% stock dividend in July 1993, dividends were raised to $0.05 quarterly from $0.0467 (adjusted).

Sales for the remainder of fiscal 1993-94 should be solidly higher on new store openings and a projected 6% increase in comparable store sales. The higher same store sales would be related to the company's target marketing program and its concentration on regional preferences in its store merchandising. Also contributing will be a weakening of competition, as other less established retailers have had difficulty weathering challenging retail conditions. Margins should remain firm, and interest charges will be lower as proceeds of the May 1993 stock offering are used to repay borrowings. However, more common shares will be outstanding.

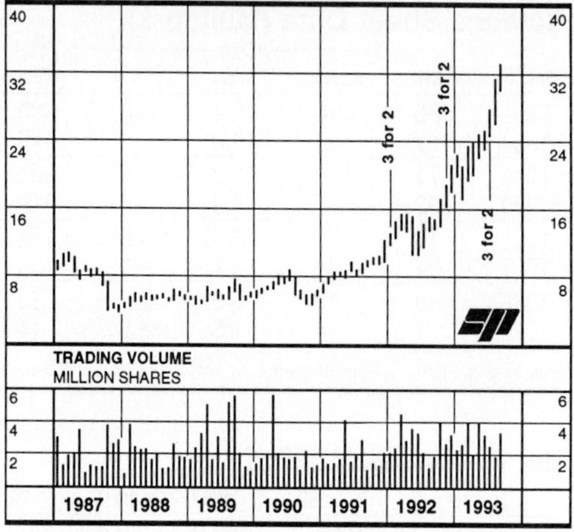

Revenues (Million $)

Quarter:	1993–94	1992–93	1991–92	1990–91
May	186.8	150.9	124.5	112.7
Aug.	204.7	152.5	118.8	109.0
Nov.	---	171.7	129.2	111.9
Feb.	---	182.4	147.4	114.2
	---	657.5	519.9	447.8

Revenues for the six months ended August 31, 1993, advanced 29%, year to year, reflecting a larger number of stores in operation, an 11.8% rise in same store sales, and increased income from financing. Operating margins remained steady, and with interest charges absorbing a smaller proportion of revenues, pretax income was ahead 41%. After taxes at 38.0%, against 35.0%, net income was up 34%. On a larger number of shares, earnings per share were $0.52, versus $0.41 (adjusted).

Common Share Earnings ($)

Quarter:	1993–94	1992–93	1991–92	1990–91
May	0.29	0.23	0.21	0.20
Aug.	0.23	0.17	0.14	0.14
Nov.	E0.27	0.22	0.15	0.14
Feb.	E0.27	0.21	0.15	0.11
	E1.07	0.84	0.65	0.59

Important Developments

Sep. '93— HMY said that it was discussing the possible acquisition of McMahan's Furniture Co., which operates a total of 92 furniture stores in California, Arizona, New Mexico, Texas, Nevada and Colorado, with annual sales of about $100 million. If HMY were to acquire McMahan's, it would mark the company's initial expansion into areas outside the Southeast and Midwest.

Next earnings report expected in mid-December.

Per Share Data ($)

Yr. End Feb. 28[1]	1993	1992	[2]1991	1990	1989	1988	1987	1986	1985	1984
Tangible Bk. Val.	**5.98**	5.29	4.45	4.24	3.79	3.49	3.25	2.42	2.49	2.19
Cash Flow	**1.18**	0.97	0.89	0.84	0.76	0.69	0.59	0.45	0.47	0.39
Earnings[3]	**0.84**	0.65	0.59	0.52	0.48	0.43	0.39	[4]0.31	0.37	0.31
Dividends	**0.160**	0.142	0.130	0.119	0.107	0.095	0.083	0.079	0.071	0.063
Payout R atio	**19%**	23%	22%	23%	22%	22%	22%	25%	19%	20%
Calendar Years	**1992**	1991	1990	1989	1988	1987	1986	1985	1984	1983
Prices—High	**21 11/32**	12⅜	8 25/32	7 23/32	6 15/32	10 25/32	11⅝	6 29/32	4 9/32	4 9/32
Low	**10 21/32**	6⅛	4 23/32	4 23/32	4¼	3 21/32	6 11/32	3 19/32	3 3/32	2 17/32
P/E Ratio—	**25–13**	19–9	15–8	15–9	14–9	25–8	30–16	22–11	12–8	14–8

Data as orig. reptd. Adj. for stk. div(s). of 50% Jul. 1993, 50% Nov. 1992, 50% Jan. 1992, 50% Mar. 1986. **1.** Yrs. ended Mar. 31 prior to 1986. **2.** Reflects accounting change. **3.** Bef. spec. item(s) of -0.07 in 1991, +0.05 in 1990. **4.** Eleven mos. E-Estimated

Income Data (Million $)

Year Ended Feb. 28[1]	[2]Revs.	Oper. Inc.	% Oper. Inc. of Revs.	Cap. Exp.	Depr.	Int. Exp.	Net Bef. Taxes	Eff. Tax Rate	[4]Net Inc.	% Net Inc. of Revs.	Cash Flow
1993	**658**	**98.1**	**14.9**	**27.4**	**15.6**	**23.5**	**59.4**	**36.0%**	**38.0**	**5.8**	**53.6**
1992	520	76.0	14.6	24.0	13.3	21.8	41.2	34.5%	27.0	5.2	40.3
1991	448	68.3	15.2	12.5	11.1	26.4	31.2	33.0%	20.9	4.7	31.9
1990	393	66.7	17.0	18.4	11.5	28.0	27.8	33.6%	18.5	4.7	29.9
1989	352	59.4	16.9	24.0	10.0	23.4	26.5	35.7%	17.1	4.9	27.1
1988	304	51.3	16.9	[3]15.4	9.1	17.7	24.7	37.2%	15.5	5.1	24.6
1987	271	46.4	17.1	30.8	7.3	13.6	26.0	48.0%	13.5	5.0	20.8
1986	182	31.3	17.2	16.4	4.2	8.4	18.9	45.8%	10.2	5.6	14.4
1985	168	32.3	19.2	12.7	3.3	6.8	22.2	47.1%	11.7	7.0	15.0
1984	135	25.5	18.9	10.8	2.5	3.7	19.3	48.5%	10.0	7.4	12.5

Balance Sheet Data (Million $)

Feb. 28[1]	Cash	Curr. Assets	Curr. Liab.	Curr. Ratio	Total Assets	% Ret. on Assets	Long Term Debt	Common Equity	Total Cap.	% LT Debt of Cap.	% Ret. on Equity
1993	**3.87**	**567**	**252**	**2.3**	**741**	**5.5**	**176**	**306**	**489**	**36.1**	**13.2**
1992	2.81	470	120	3.9	618	4.4	226	264	497	45.5	11.0
1991	2.18	380	149	2.5	507	4.1	164	185	358	45.9	11.7
1990	2.43	376	169	2.2	502	3.7	148	171	334	44.5	11.3
1989	5.34	380	171	2.2	499	3.7	154	155	327	47.0	11.5
1988	3.92	314	150	2.1	425	3.9	112	142	274	40.9	11.4
1987	1.90	267	113	2.4	370	3.8	114	131	256	44.5	11.7
1986	3.95	228	140	1.6	304	3.9	69	92	163	42.1	11.8
1985	5.55	175	88	2.0	210	6.4	40	79	120	33.0	15.8
1984	3.95	135	57	2.4	159	7.0	32	69	101	31.7	15.3

Data as orig. reptd. **1.** Years ended Mar. 31 prior to 1986. **2.** Incl. other income. **3.** Net of curr. yr. retirement and disposals. **4.** Bef. spec. item(s).

Business Summary

Heilig-Meyers is primarily engaged in the retail sale of home furnishings. As of August 31, 1993, the company was operating a total of 466 stores in 16 states in the Southeast and Midwest. Stores in operation at fiscal year-end (February 28; March 31 prior to 1986):

1993	425	1990	304	1987	220
1992	374	1989	277	1986	214
1991	322	1988	258	1985	127

Some 90% of all stores are in towns with a population of less than 50,000 and are at least 25 miles from a major population center. The stores generally range in size from 10,000 to 25,000 sq. ft.

In 1992-93, 59% of HMY's revenues were from furniture and accessories (58% in the prior year), 13% from consumer electronics items (13%), 8% from major appliances (8%), 10% from bedding (9%), and 10% from other items, including jewelry, small appliances and seasonal goods (12%).

Some 95% of the merchandise is distributed to the stores through Heilig-Meyers's five distribution centers, which typically are located within 200 miles of a store (the fifth center was opened in Thomasville, Ga., in August 1992). A sixth center, located in Moberly, Mo., was scheduled to open in the fall of 1993, and would be used to support future growth in the Midwest.

Historically over 80% of sales have been made on credit, principally under installment sales.

Dividend Data

Dividends have been paid since 1975. A "poison pill" stock purchase right was adopted in 1988.

Amt of Divd. $	Date Decl.	Ex-divd. Date	Stock of Record	Payment Date
3-for-2	Oct. 14	Nov. 19	Nov. 4	Nov. 18'92
0.06	Oct. 14	Oct. 29	Nov. 4	Nov. 28'92
0.06	Dec. 16	Jan. 15	Jan. 22	Feb. 20'93
0.07	Apr. 7	Apr. 22	Apr. 28	May 22'93
3-for-2	Jun. 17	Jul. 28	Jul. 14	Jul. 27'93
0.05	Jun. 17	Jul. 8	Jul. 14	Aug. 21'93

Finances

In May 1993, HMY sold through underwriters 3,450,000 common shares (including 450,000 to cover overallotments) at $22.58 a share (data adjusted). Net proceeds of some $74.2 million were earmarked to reduce short-term bank borrowings.

Capitalization

Long Term Debt: $171,113,000 (8/93).

Common Stock: 48,007,680 shs. ($2 par).
Institutions hold about 88%.
Shareholders of record: 2,200 (2/93).

Office—2235 Staples Mill Rd, Richmond, VA 23230. **Tel**—(804) 359-9171. **Chrmn & CEO**—W. C. DeRusha. **Pres**—T. A. Peery Jr. **EVP-CFO**—J. R. Jenkins. **VP-Secy & Treas**—R. B. Goodman. **Dirs**—A. Alexander, R. L. Burrus Jr., A. D. Charpentier, W. C. DeRusha, B. F. Edwards III, A. G. Fleischer, N. Krumbein, H. Meyers, S. S. Meyers, T. A. Peery Jr., L. N. Smith, G. A. Thornton III. **Transfer Agent & Registrar**—Wachovia Bank of North Carolina, Winston Salem, N.C. **Incorporated** in 1972 as successor to a partnership founded in 1913. **Empl**—7,850.

 Michael W. Jaffe

Home Shopping Network

NYSE Symbol HSN Options on CBOE (Jan-Apr-Jul-Oct) In S&P MidCap 400

Price	Range	P-E Ratio	Dividend	Yield	S&P Ranking	Beta
Sep. 29'93	1993					
11⅛	15⅛–4⅛	NM	None	None	B–	1.19

Summary

On July 12, 1993, HSN received a proposal from QVC Network, Inc. to merge the two home television shopping companies. Terms of the transaction call for one QVC common share to be exchanged for five HSN shares. On September, 28, however, HSN said that deliberations regarding QVC's proposed merger would be deferred until the status of QVC's recent bid for Paramount Communications, Inc. was clarified. Liberty Media Corp. has a 71% voting stake in HSN and also owns some 22% of QVC Network, Inc.

Current Outlook

Earnings for the calendar year ending December 31, 1993 are estimated at $0.30 a share. The company changed its year-end from August 31, to December 31.

Dividends are not in prospect.

Sales (for the company as a separate entity) in 1993 should be down from a year ago, reflecting weak consumer spending. Gross margins should decline and expenses increase as a percentage of sales. A merger with QVC Network, Inc. would create a $2 billion televised home shopping company.

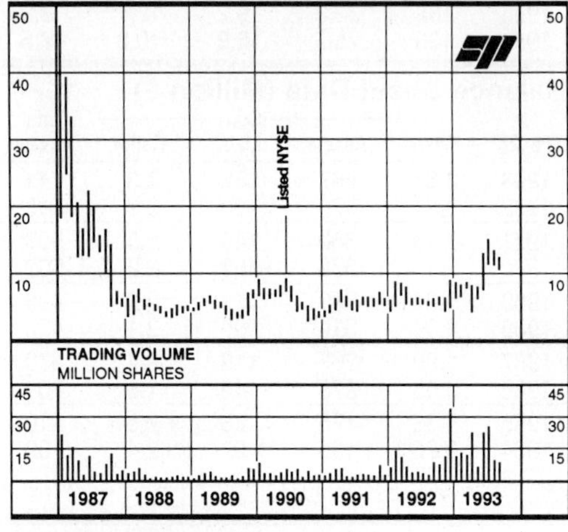

Net Sales (Million $)

Quarter:	1993–94	1992–93	1991–92	1990–91
Nov.	---	266	292	292
Feb.	---	244	276	268
May	---	260	269	263
Aug.	---	---	261	256
	---	---	1,098	1,079

Sales for the nine months ended May 31, 1993, fell 8.0%, year to year. Gross margins narrowed, reflecting the liquidation of merchandise through special sale events and a $22.7 million inventory reserve in the second quarter. Operating income declined significantly, and there was a net loss of $8.1 million ($0.09 a share, on 2% fewer shares), versus net income of $30.0 million ($0.34). Results exclude a special charge of $0.08 a share, due to the early retirement of debt in the fiscal 1993 period.

Common Share Earnings ($)

Quarter:	1993–94	1992–93	1991–92	1990–91
Nov.	---	0.07	0.15	0.13
Feb.	---	d0.23	0.09	d0.28
May	---	0.07	0.10	0.05
Aug.	---	---	0.08	d0.01
	---	---	0.42	d0.11

Merger Proposal

Sep. '93— Management said that directors will temporarily defer consideration of QVC's proposed merger. Negotiations will resume once the status of QVC's bid for NYSE-listed Paramount Communications, Inc. (PCI) is clarified. On September 20, 1993, QVC proposed a merger with PCI. In July, QVC Network, Inc. offered to merge with HSN; under the plan HSN shareholders would receive one common share of QVC for five shares of HSN common stock held. Upon completion of the merger, QVC would be the surviving company. Management also said that although sales for September have strengthened somewhat compared with prior periods, sales for the fiscal year ending December 31, 1993 are expected to be lower than sales for calendar 1992. The company has changed its fiscal year-end from August to December.

Next earnings report expected in mid-October.

Per Share Data ($)

Yr. End Aug. 31[1]	1992	1991	1990	1989	1988	1987	1986	1985	1984	1983
Tangible Bk. Val.	**[5]1.94**	0.63	0.60	0.08	d0.19	1.36	0.50	0.01	0.01	NA
Cash Flow	**0.78**	0.22	0.63	0.02	0.45	0.45	0.25	NA	NA	NA
Earnings[2]	**0.42**	d0.11	0.35	d0.25	0.21	0.33	0.22	[3]Nil	0.01	Nil
Dividends	**Nil**	Nil	Nil	Nil	Nil	Nil	Nil	Nil	Nil	Nil
Payout Ratio	**Nil**	Nil	Nil	Nil	Nil	Nil	Nil	Nil	Nil	Nil
Prices[4]—High	**9**	7⅝	9¼	7⅝	7¾	47	22¼	NA	NA	NA
Low	**4¼**	3½	2⅞	3	3⅜	5	3	NA	NA	NA
P/E Ratio—	**21–10**	NM	26–8	NM	37–16	NM	NM	NA	NA	NA

Data as orig. reptd. Adj. for stk. divs. of 100% Jan. 1987, 200% Sep. 1986. **1.** Yrs. ended Dec. 31 prior to 1985. **2.** Bef. spec. items of +0.01 in 1991, +0.07 in 1990, +0.08 in 1989, +0.01 in 1983. **3.** Eight mos. **4.** Cal. yr. **5.** Includes intangibles. d-Deficit. E-Estimated NM-Not Meaningful. NA-Not Available.

Income Data (Million $)

Year Ended Aug. 31[1]	Revs.	Oper. Inc.	% Oper. Inc. of Revs.	Cap. Exp.	Depr.	Int. Exp.	Net Bef. Taxes	Eff. Tax Rate	[3]Net Inc.	% Net Inc. of Revs.	Cash Flow
1992	**1,098**	**115**	**10.5**	**36**	**32.7**	**22.6**	**64.5**	**42.0%**	**37.4**	**3.4**	**70.1**
1991	1,079	94	8.7	53	29.1	23.8	6.1	256.9%	d9.6	NM	19.5
1990	1,008	103	10.2	35	28.0	26.3	53.4	39.2%	32.5	3.2	60.5
1989	774	56	7.3	30	23.7	30.8	d22.6	NM	d22.1	NM	1.6
1988	730	75	10.3	46	21.5	33.1	28.3	36.5%	18.0	2.5	39.5
1987	582	84	14.4	144	19.8	28.3	55.4	46.7%	29.5	5.1	40.3
1986	160	32	20.0	32	2.0	0.3	30.4	43.9%	17.0	10.6	19.1
[2]1985	11	NM	2.9	2	0.3	0.1	d0.1	Nil	Nil	0.1	NA
1984	11	NM	7.3	1	0.2	0.1	0.5	27.2%	0.4	3.3	NA
1983	4	NM	10.1	Nil	Nil	0.1	0.3	0.2%	0.2	4.3	NA

Balance Sheet Data (Million $)

Aug. 31[1]	Cash	Curr. Assets	Curr. Liab.	Curr. Ratio	Total Assets	% Ret. on Assets	Long Term Debt	Common Equity	Total Cap.	% LT Debt of Cap.	% Ret. on Equity
1992	**53.5**	**202**	**155**	**1.3**	**520**	**6.9**	**173**	**170**	**365**	**47.4**	**22.4**
1991	61.6	229	176	1.3	565	NM	205	162	389	52.7	NM
1990	58.6	230	132	1.7	556	6.0	225	177	424	53.1	20.5
1989	67.6	210	94	2.2	534	NM	285	140	440	64.8	NM
1988	39.7	183	52	3.5	540	3.3	332	143	487	68.2	13.7
1987	59.4	203	84	2.4	547	9.2	336	118	463	72.6	35.4
1986	27.9	54	33	1.6	94	34.3	9	48	57	15.1	71.2
1985	0.4	3	3	0.8	5	NA	1	Nil	2	76.3	NA
1984	0.3	1	2	0.7	2	23.4	Nil	Nil	1	42.5	172.6
1983	NA	NA	NA	NA	1	28.5	Nil	Nil	Nil	84.1	NM

Data as orig. reptd. **1.** Yrs. ended Dec. 31 prior to 1985. **2.** Eight mos. **3.** Bef. spec. items. d-Deficit. NM-Not Meaningful. NA-Not Available.

Business Summary

Home Shopping Network (HSN) is a holding company whose subsidiaries are involved in a variety of direct marketing activities including electronic retail sales, and catalog and mail order sales.

The principal operating subsidiary, Home Shopping Club Inc. (HSC), sells consumer products by means of live, customer-interactive, televised sales programs (primarily Home Shopping Club). The sales programs use the spontaneity of live television, viewer participation, club membership and quality products at bargain prices to attract viewers and promote sales. HSC produces three separate retail sales programming networks: HSN 1, which is carried by cable systems throughout the U.S.; HSN 2, carried primarily by TV broadcast stations owned by or affiliated with HSC as well as by cable systems that retransmit the broadcast TV signal of one of the stations carrying HSN 2; and HSN Spree, which is carried by both cable systems and broadcast TV systems on either a full- or part-time basis and provides system operators and broadcasters with income-producing programming during portions of the day when programming may not otherwise be scheduled. At the end of fiscal 1992, 23.9 million U.S. homes were able to receive HSN 1, 38.7 million could view HSN 2, and HSN Spree was being carried by 101 TV broadcast stations.

The company spun off its Silver King Communications subsidiary to shareholders in December 1992. Silver King owns 12 UHF television stations that primarily broadcast HSN programming.

Dividend Data

No cash dividends have been paid, and the company expects that it will not pay dividends for the foreseeable future.

Finances

In February 1993, the company refinanced $100 million of the $143 million outstanding balance of its senior notes. This resulted in a special charge of $0.08 a share.

Capitalization

Long Term Debt: $142,212,000 (5/31/93).

Common Stock: 68,124,006 shs. ($0.01 par). Liberty Media Corp. owns about 41.5%. Shareholders of record: 9,562.

Cl. B Common Stock: 24,159,456 shs. ($0.01 par); 10 votes ea.; conv. sh.-for-sh. into com.; controlled by Liberty Media Corp.

Options: To buy 7,971,000 com. shs. at $3.33 to $8.43 each.

Office—2501 118th Ave. North, St. Petersburg, FL 33716. **Tel**—(813) 572-8585. **Pres & CEO**—G. Hogan. **VP-CFO, Secy & Treas**—L. R. Wandler. **Dirs**—P. Barton, R. Bennett, J. Draper, J. A. Forstmann, L. J. Hindery, J. J. McNamara, G. C. McNamee, L. R. Wandler. **Transfer Agent & Registrar**—Chase Manhattan Bank, NYC. **Incorporated** in Florida in 1985; reincorporated in Delaware in 1986. **Empl**—5,002.

 Karen J. Sack

HON INDUSTRIES

NASDAQ Symbol HONI (Incl. in Nat'l Market) In S&P MidCap 400

Price	Range	P–E Ratio	Dividend	Yield	S&P Ranking	Beta
Sep. 8'93	1993					
26¾	29¼–21½	22	0.40	1.5%	A–	0.76

Summary

This major manufacturer of wood and metal office furniture also makes fireplaces, woodburning stoves and accessories. Earnings rose only slightly in the first half of 1993, as modest sales gains were largely offset by costs of programs geared towards strengthening future operating performance. Substantial numbers of common shares have been repurchased in recent years.

Business Summary

The principal business of HON INDUSTRIES Inc. is the production of office furniture and products. The company also manufactures prefabricated fireplaces, woodburning stoves and accessories.

In the area of office furniture and products, the company manufactures, through its HON Co. division and BPI Inc., CorryHiebert Corp., Holga Inc., Gunlocke Co. and Chandler Attwood Limited (formed in 1992) subsidiaries, a broad line of metal and wood office furniture. Products include file cabinets, desks, chairs, storage cabinets, combination cabinets, tables, bookcases, machine stands, credenzas, reception area furniture, freestanding office partitions, panel systems, wall systems, office coordinates and stools. These products are available in both contemporary and conventional styles, and are priced to sell in all price ranges. Other units in this product area include XLM Co., which makes a limited line of filing cabinets, desktop systems and hanging file folders designed principally for the home market; and Ring King Visibles, a manufacturer of personal computer and workstation accessories. Ring King was expanded through the $2.4 million acquisition of the rubber band business of ASE-listed Plymouth Rubber Co. in January 1992.

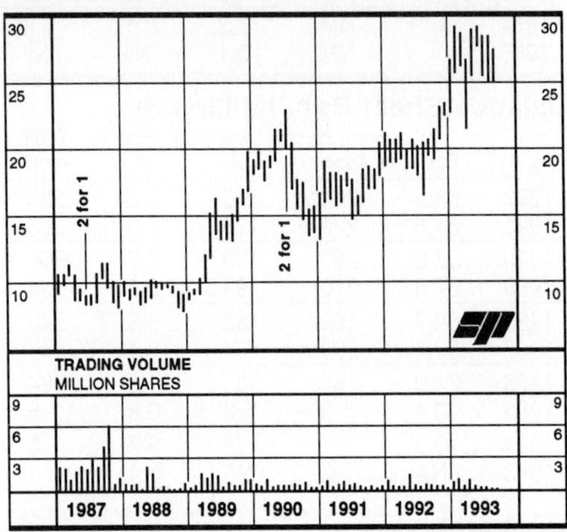

Heatilator Inc. manufactures factory-built fireplaces, fireplace inserts, woodburning stoves and accessories serving the homebuilding products industry. These products account for less than 10% of total revenues.

Office furniture is marketed nationally through more than 13,100 stationery and office furniture retailers and some 200 wholesalers/distributors. HON also makes products for sale by mass-market retailers and office product specialists. Prefabricated fireplaces are distributed through 400 national account locations and 230 distributors, while woodburning stoves are distributed through an estimated 200 dealers.

The company's largest customer in 1992 was United Stationers, accounting for 12% of revenues.

In an effort to strengthen its operating performance, HON has initiated programs to improve all aspects of its business, combined with an ongoing effort to search out new business opportunities.

In January 1992, the company implemented an Employee Stock Ownership Plan, which acquired 916,230 HON common shares, using $17.5 million of company bank borrowings.

Next earnings report expected in mid-October.

Per Share Data ($)

Yr. End Dec. 31	1992	1991	1990	[1]1989	1988	1987	[1,2]1986	1985	1984	1983
Tangible Bk. Val.	**5.04**	4.64	4.06	3.76	3.95	3.33	[3]3.35	2.90	2.59	2.39
Cash Flow	**1.62**	1.43	1.69	1.14	0.99	0.89	0.93	0.81	0.57	0.53
Earnings[4]	**1.18**	1.02	1.30	0.79	0.69	0.62	0.72	0.61	0.39	0.36
Dividends	**0.370**	0.360	0.300	0.240	0.213	0.200	0.160	0.150	0.140	0.140
Payout Ratio	**31%**	35%	23%	30%	31%	32%	22%	24%	36%	39%
Prices—High	**23½**	20½	23	19⅞	10¼	11½	9 15/16	7 13/16	5 13/16	6 5/16
Low	**16½**	13¼	13½	8¾	7⅞	8⅛	7 1/16	4 5/16	3 13/16	5 1/16
P/E Ratio—	**20–14**	20–13	18–10	25–11	15–11	19–13	14–10	13–7	15–10	18–14

Data as orig. reptd. Adj. for stk. divs. of 100% Jul. 1990, 100% Jun. 1987. **1.** Refl. merger or acq. **2.** Refl. acctg. change. **3.** Incl. intangibles. **4.** Bef. results of disc. ops. of +0.26 in 1988.

Income Data (Million $)

Year Ended Dec. 31	Revs.	Oper. Inc.	% Oper. Inc. of Revs.	Cap. Exp.	Depr.	Int. Exp.	Net Bef. Taxes	Eff. Tax Rate	Net Inc.	% Net Inc. of Revs.	Cash Flow
1992	**707**	**76.8**	**10.9**	**36.1**	**14.5**	**3.44**	**61.9**	**37.5%**	**38.7**	**5.5**	**53.2**
1991	608	67.8	11.2	15.2	13.3	3.53	52.7	37.5%	32.9	5.4	46.2
1990	664	81.0	12.2	25.6	12.8	3.71	69.1	37.5%	43.2	6.5	55.9
[1]1989	602	76.5	12.7	32.2	12.2	3.16	44.8	38.4%	27.5	4.6	39.6
[2]1988	532	54.8	10.3	11.2	11.3	4.19	41.5	38.9%	25.8	4.8	37.1
1987	555	55.9	10.1	21.6	10.6	3.51	43.9	44.3%	[3]24.8	4.5	35.4
[1,3]1986	504	62.3	12.4	23.4	9.1	3.51	[4]56.5	48.2%	29.3	5.8	38.4
1985	473	60.8	12.8	10.7	8.8	4.02	[4]50.0	48.0%	26.0	5.5	34.8
1984	397	42.2	10.6	7.5	8.2	4.49	[4]30.8	45.5%	16.8	4.2	25.0
1983	353	40.0	11.3	6.2	7.7	4.08	[4]29.0	46.0%	15.7	4.4	23.3

Balance Sheet Data (Million $)

Dec. 31	Cash	Curr. Assets	Curr. Liab.	Curr. Ratio	Total Assets	% Ret. on Assets	Long Term Debt	Common Equity	Total Cap.	% LT Debt of Cap.	% Ret. on Equity
1992	**45.9**	**171**	**92**	**1.9**	**323**	**12.8**	**54.2**	**163**	**231**	**23.5**	**24.7**
1991	34.6	151	82	1.8	281	11.8	35.7	150	199	18.0	23.5
1990	32.4	147	93	1.6	277	15.8	39.6	132	184	21.6	34.1
1989	37.0	163	106	1.5	284	10.2	38.3	128	178	21.5	20.9
1988	68.1	175	79	2.2	276	9.9	38.7	148	197	19.6	19.0
1987	28.3	142	68	2.1	248	10.2	42.3	126	180	23.6	19.5
1986	36.4	142	69	2.0	256	12.0	38.5	136	187	20.6	23.0
1985	24.5	132	68	1.9	237	11.8	37.8	121	169	22.4	22.8
1984	22.3	119	55	2.2	214	8.2	35.8	112	159	22.6	15.5
1983	16.6	107	51	2.1	200	8.1	33.4	105	149	22.4	15.6

Data as orig. reptd. **1.** Refl. merger or acq. **2.** Excl. disc. ops. **3.** Refl. acctg. change. **4.** Incl. equity in earns. of nonconsol. subs.

Net Sales (Million $)

13 Weeks:	1993	1992	1991	1990
Mar.	186	159	142	174
Jun.	178	164	135	158
Sep.		[1]196	161	163
Dec.		188	170	169
		707	608	664

For the 26 weeks ended July 3, 1993, net sales advanced 13%, year to year. Results were restricted by costs of significant new business venture startups, greater new product development expenditures, and costs of implementing programs to improve all business aspects; the gain in income was held to 2.6%, to $16,353,000 ($0.50 a share), from $15,934,000 ($0.48). Results in the 1993 period exclude a credit of $0.02 a share from the cumulative effect of accounting changes.

Common Share Earnings ($)

13 Weeks:	1993	1992	1991	1990
Mar.	0.25	0.22	0.18	0.34
Jun.	0.25	0.26	0.16	0.25
Sep.		[1]0.38	0.32	0.33
Dec.		0.32	0.36	0.38
		1.18	1.02	1.30

1. 14 wks.

Dividend Data

Cash has been paid each year since 1955.

Amt. of Divd. $	Date Decl.	Ex–divd. Date	Stock of Record	Payment Date
0.10	Nov. 3	Nov. 9	Nov. 16	Dec. 1'92
0.10	Feb. 8	Feb. 11	Feb. 18	Mar. 1'93
0.10	May 10	May 14	May 20	Jun. 1'93
0.10	Aug. 9	Aug. 13	Aug. 19	Sep. 1'93

Finances

During the first 13 weeks of 1993, the company repurchased 47,718 of its common shares at a total cost of $1.3 million. From 1990 through 1992, HON bought 2,396,261 shares at an aggregate cost of $52.3 million; more than 13 million shares have been acquired since 1985. Following a February 1993 authorization to buy an additional $20 million of stock, a total of $28.4 million was available for common purchases.

Capitalization

Long Term Liabs.: $51,884,000 (4/3/93), incl. $7,314,000 of lease obligs.

Common Stock: 32,343,492 shs. ($1 par). Institutions hold 27%. Shareholders: 4,534 of record (12/92).

Office—414 East Third St., P.O. Box 1109, Muscatine, IA 52761-7109. **Tel**—(319) 264-7400. **Chrmn**—S. M. Howe. **Vice Chrmn**—R. H. Stanley. **Pres & CEO**—J. D. Michaels. **SVP-Fin & Investor Contact**—John W. Axel. **Treas**—W. F. Snydacker. **Secy**—R. E. Lasell. **Dirs**—J. W. Axel, W. J. Farrell, S. M. Howe, A. T. Hunt, Jr., L. Liu, J. D. Michaels, C. C. Michalski, M. S. Plunkett, H. J. Schmidt, R. H. Stanley, J. K. Ver Hagen. **Transfer Agent**—Co.'s office. **Incorporated** in Iowa in 1944. **Empl**—5,700.

 Michael W. Jaffe

Houghton Mifflin

NYSE Symbol HTN Options on Pacific (Jan-Apr-Jul-Oct) In S&P MidCap 400

Price	Range	P-E Ratio	Dividend	Yield	S&P Ranking	Beta
Jul. 15'93	1993					
44	44⅝–36⅜	59	0.82	1.9%	A–	1.08

Summary

This well-established publisher derives the bulk of revenues from the sale of textbooks. It also produces general books, educational software, and electronic databases. A strong earnings rebound is expected in 1993. Long-term prospects are favorable, reflecting recent restructurings, rising school enrollments and favorable demographic trends.

Current Outlook

Share earnings for 1993 (including $0.48 of special charges) are projected at $1.70, versus 1992's $1.35. A gain to $2.85 is likely for 1994.

The $0.20½ quarterly dividend could be raised to $0.22 in the near-term.

Revenues are expected to advance about 11% in 1993, aided by the addition of the DLM test line, and by stronger sales opportunities in elementary reading and social studies texts. The division, reference and trade divisions should also do well. Although education development costs will rise sharply, measures taken in 1992 to remove unprofitable operations, ongoing cost controls, and stronger sales of high-margined school texts will boost operating earnings. Unusual costs and expenses should be slightly lower.

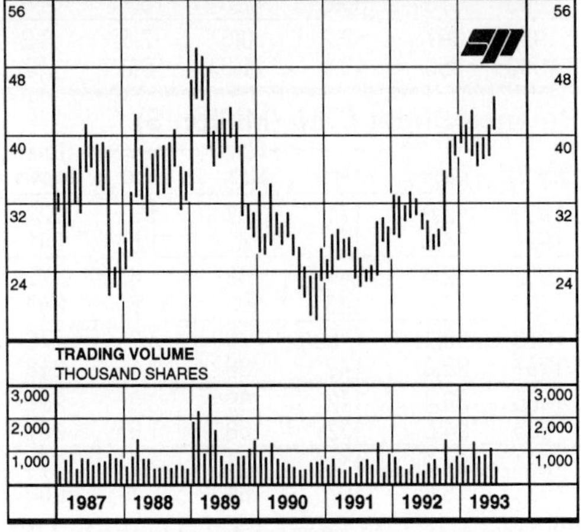

Net Sales (Million $)

Quarter:	1993	1992	1991	1990
Mar.	49.7	52.1	49.9	43.8
Jun.	121.2	125.7	127.2	122.5
Sep.		198.8	211.2	178.8
Dec.		78.2	78.4	76.6
		454.7	466.8	421.6

Net sales in the six months ended June 30, 1993, slid 3.8%, year to year, on declines in educational publishing. Operating costs were also down, but with net restructuring and relocation charges of $6.6 million ($0.48 a share), the seasonal loss widened to $10,451,000 ($0.76 a share), from $2,325,000 ($0.16). Per share results exclude extraordinary charges of $0.07 and $1.03 in the respective periods.

Common Share Earnings ($)

Quarter:	1993	1992	1991	1990
Mar.	d1.08	d0.98	d1.09	d0.85
Jun.	0.32	0.82	0.87	0.81
Sep.	E2.76	2.46	2.36	1.88
Dec.	Ed0.30	d0.92	d0.39	d0.58
	E1.70	1.35	1.75	1.27

Important Developments

Jul. '93— HTN said 1993 second quarter results included charges of $6.6 million ($0.48 a share) for relocation costs, workforce realignment and a warehouse closure, as well as a charge of $1.0 million ($0.07) for early redemption of debt. The company said, in commenting on the outlook for operations, that although 1994 is not a good adoption year, earnings should exceed $2.70 a share. HTN added that net income is expected to increase sharply in 1995, reflecting strong adoption opportunities and the full benefit of a lower cost structure.

Oct. '92— The company acquired a line of 25 clinical/special needs testing instruments from DLM, Inc. for $17 million. HTN said the new list would boost Riverside's sales by 25%, and would increase earnings by $0.11 to $0.13 a share starting in 1993.

Next earnings report expected in mid-October.

Per Share Data ($)

Yr. End Dec.	1992	1991	1990	[1]1989	1988	1987	1986	1985	1984	1983
Tangible Bk. Val.	**12.34**	14.91	13.90	12.82	12.65	11.58	10.49	9.41	8.51	7.68
Cash Flow	**4.33**	4.56	3.67	3.91	3.97	3.95	3.63	2.80	2.37	2.32
Earnings[2]	**1.35**	1.75	1.27	1.62	1.70	1.66	1.61	1.37	1.26	1.08
Dividends	**0.790**	0.770	0.710	0.670	0.630	0.590	0.535	0.490	0.450	0.410
Payout Ratio	**59%**	43%	56%	41%	37%	35%	33%	36%	37%	40%
Prices—High	**39⅞**	30⅜	34⅜	50¼	42½	41⅜	33½	23½	17⅝	15
Low	**26⅝**	22¼	18⅜	28⅛	24⅜	20¾	21	16½	10½	8⅞
P/E Ratio—	**30–20**	17–13	27–14	31–17	25–14	25–13	21–13	17–12	14–8	14–8

Data as orig. reptd. Adj. for stk. divs. of 100% Sep. 1986, 100% Aug. 1983. 1. Refl. merger or acq. 2. Bef. spec. item(s) of -1.04 in 1992. d-Deficit. E-Estimated.

Income Data (Million $)

Year Ended Dec. 31	Revs.	Oper. Inc.	% Oper. Inc. of Revs.	Cap. Exp.	Depr.	Int. Exp.	Net Bef. Taxes	Eff. Tax Rate	[4]Net Inc.	% Net Inc. of Revs.	Cash Flow
1992	**455**	**86.0**	**18.9**	**38.2**	**41.7**	**4.42**	**28.4**	**33.0%**	**[3]19.1**	**4.2**	**60.8**
1991	467	87.7	18.8	41.0	40.3	6.06	40.4	38.0%	25.1	5.4	65.3
1990	422	66.7	15.8	40.2	34.2	5.95	31.3	42.3%	18.0	4.3	52.3
[1]1989	404	72.5	17.9	39.9	32.5	4.34	37.0	37.8%	23.0	5.7	55.6
1988	368	72.8	19.8	38.0	32.2	2.42	38.9	38.0%	24.1	6.5	56.3
1987	343	71.3	20.8	32.6	32.4	2.00	41.8	43.5%	[3]23.6	6.9	56.0
1986	321	64.2	20.0	38.2	28.6	2.18	39.9	43.4%	22.6	7.0	51.2
1985	278	52.1	18.8	30.4	19.8	1.85	32.5	41.8%	18.9	6.8	38.7
1984	249	43.5	17.5	23.0	14.5	2.38	28.7	43.0%	16.4	6.6	30.8
1983	219	39.7	18.1	[2]14.7	15.2	3.02	22.5	41.3%	13.2	6.0	28.4

Balance Sheet Data (Million $)

Dec. 31	Cash	Curr. Assets	Curr. Liab.	Curr. Ratio	Total Assets	% Ret. on Assets	Long Term Debt	Common Equity	Total Cap.	% LT Debt of Cap.	% Ret. on Equity
1992	**68.6**	**234**	**83.9**	**2.8**	**371**	**5.0**	**52.6**	**200**	**253**	**20.8**	**9.0**
1991	92.8	268	92.1	2.9	382	6.7	53.0	223	278	19.0	11.6
1990	77.4	251	92.6	2.7	366	5.2	53.0	210	262	20.2	8.8
1989	37.3	210	81.9	2.6	321	7.9	29.0	200	229	12.7	11.9
1988	22.6	176	66.7	2.6	262	9.4	2.3	185	187	1.2	13.6
1987	35.1	163	68.3	2.4	248	9.8	2.0	169	171	1.2	14.6
1986	24.4	152	70.3	2.2	234	10.1	1.7	154	156	1.1	15.4
1985	28.4	138	61.9	2.2	211	9.2	1.7	139	140	1.2	14.2
1984	30.3	128	55.9	2.3	192	8.8	4.8	123	128	3.8	13.9
1983	31.4	115	44.7	2.6	169	8.0	10.5	106	116	9.0	13.0

Data as orig. reptd. **1.** Refl. merger or acq. **2.** Net of curr. yr. retirement and disposals. **3.** Refl. acctg. change. **4.** Bef. spec. items.

Business Summary

Houghton Mifflin is a leading publisher of textbooks, adult and children's trade and reference books, and testing materials. Contributions to sales in recent years were:

	1992	1991
Textbooks and other educational materials......	60%	62%
College publishing.............	18%	17%
General & reference publishing....................	22%	21%

Elementary and high school texts are sold to school systems, generally on a contract basis for a period of three to six years, with the bulk of deliveries made in the first few years. HTN's major textbook representation is in reading and mathematics; science, social studies, and foreign language texts are also important. College books are sold through school or private book stores. The Riverside Publishing Co. provides educational and psychological test and measurement materials to schools and colleges in addition to providing guidance information and products.

The trade and reference division publishes all types of books for the general reading public. Reference materials are published for six markets: trade, international, college, school, office products and electronic. The software division's language-aid products are licensed to word processing equipment vendors worldwide. The product line includes an electronic dictionary, spelling verifiers, spelling correctors, an electronic thesaurus, a usage alert, and a grammar corrector.

Dividend Data

Dividends have been paid since 1908. A dividend reinvestment plan is available. A "poison pill" stock purchase right was adopted in 1988.

Amt. of Divd. $	Date Decl.	Ex-divd. Date	Stock of Record	Payment Date
0.19½	Jul. 29	Aug. 6	Aug. 12	Aug. 26'92
0.20½	Oct. 28	Nov. 4	Nov. 11	Nov. 25'92
0.20½	Jan. 27	Feb. 4	Feb. 10	Feb. 24'93
0.20½	Apr. 28	May 6	May 12	May 26'93

Finances

In March 1993, directors authorized the repurchase of up to 500,000 HTN common shares.

Capitalization

Long Term Debt: $52,584,000. (3/93).

Long Term Royalties Payable: $2,432,000.

Common Stock: 14,450,853 shs. ($1 par).
Institutions hold 73%.
Shareholders of record: 3,995.

Office—222 Berkeley St, Boston, MA 02116-3764. **Tel**—(617) 725-5000. **Chrmn, Pres & CEO**—N. F. Darehshori. **SVP & Secy**—P. D. Weaver. **EVP, CFO, Treas & Investor Contact**—S. O. Jaeger. **Dirs**—D. Ames, J. A. Baute, N. F. Darehshori, G. Deegan, J. O. Freedman, S. O. Jaeger, M. H. Lindsay, C. R. Longsworth, J. F. Magee, C. B. Malone, G. Putnam, R. Z. Sorenson, D. C. Thomas. **Transfer Agent & Registrar**—Bank of Boston. **Incorporated** in Massachusetts in 1908. **Empl**—2,096.

IBP, inc.

NYSE Symbol IBP Options on ASE, Phila (Feb-May-Aug-Nov) In S&P MidCap 400

Price	Range	P-E Ratio	Dividend	Yield	S&P Ranking	Beta
Jul. 28'93	1993					
21	21¾–17½	15	0.20	1.0%	NR	0.61

Summary

This company is the world's largest producer of both fresh and boxed beef and pork products. To a lesser degree, IBP also produces hides and other allied products used to make leather, animal feeds and pharmaceuticals. Earnings are expected to continue in an uptrend for the remainder of 1993 and into 1994, aided by greater production capacity utilization.

Current Outlook

Earnings are projected to advance to $1.60 a share in 1993, from 1992's $1.34.

The quarterly dividend of $0.05 a share is the minimum expectation.

Sales are projected to continue in a steady uptrend through 1994, led by higher volume and firm selling prices. Increased supplies and lower prices of cattle and hogs should ease cost pressures, while expected growth in production capacity utlization and greater volumes through new plants should generate further operating efficiency gains. Growing export contributions (primarily to Japan) should help sustain future earnings progress.

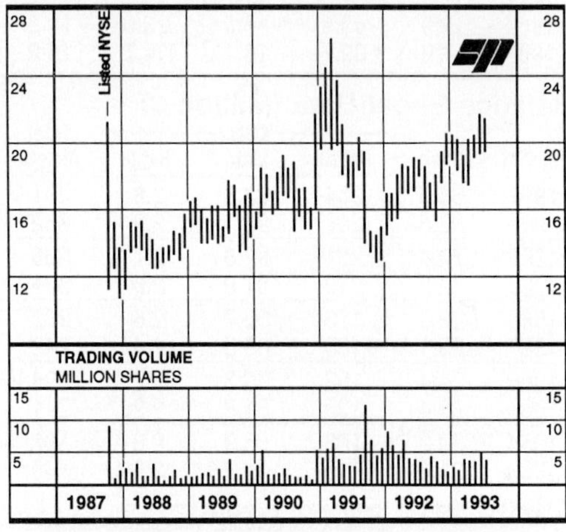

Net Sales (Billion $)

13 Weeks:	1993	1992	1991	1990
Mar.	2.75	2.65	2.54	2.37
Jun.	3.04	2.82	2.67	2.60
Sep.	---	2.87	2.66	2.63
Dec.	---	2.78	2.53	2.58
	---	11.13	10.39	10.19

Sales in the 26 weeks ended June 26, 1993, advanced 5.7%, year to year. Margins narrowed on higher livestock costs, and despite a 17% drop in net interest expense, pretax income was up only fractionally. After taxes at 39.9%, versus 41.5%, income gained 2.8%, to $0.69 a share (before a credit of $0.26 from an accounting change), from $0.67.

Common Share Earnings ($)

13 Weeks:	1993	1992	1991	1990
Mar.	0.26	0.41	d0.19	0.09
Jun.	0.43	0.26	d0.23	0.34
Sep.	E0.45	0.28	0.19	0.34
Dec.	E0.46	0.38	0.25	0.25
	E1.60	1.34	0.03	0.74

Important Developments

Jul. '93— IBP attributed its strong earnings gain in the 1993 second quarter primarily to greater supplies of market-ready cattle and strong retail demand and prices for fresh beef. Pork operations were restricted by competitive market conditions for available hogs. The company said recent Midwest flooding would have no significant short-term effect on the red meat industry; the long-term impact is unclear. Separately, the adoption of FAS 109 increased 1993 first half net income by $0.26 a share, reflecting the adjustment of "pushdown accounting" fixed asset bases resulting from IBP's 1981 acquisition by Occidental Petroleum. The amortization of goodwill and related items from the purchase cut first half income by $0.11 a share.

Next earnings report expected in late October.

Per Share Data ($)

Yr. End Dec. 31	1992	1991	1990	1989	1988	1987	1986
Tangible Bk. Val.	**6.61**	5.39	5.83	5.37	5.06	4.22	NM
Cash Flow	**2.64**	1.38	2.22	1.83	2.36	NA	NA
Earnings[1,2]	**1.34**	0.03	1.01	0.74	1.32	1.10	[3]0.95
Dividends	**0.30**	0.60	0.60	0.60	0.60	0.15	Nil
Payout Ratio	**22%**	NM	59%	80%	46%	14%	Nil
Prices—High	**20⅝**	26¼	21¾	17¾	15¾	20¼	NA
Low	**14½**	12⅞	14¾	13½	11¼	10¾	NA
P/E Ratio—	**15–11**	NM	22–15	24–18	12–9	18–10	NA

Data as orig. reptd. **1.** Bef. spec. item(s) of -0.13 in 1990. **2.** Ful. dil.: 1.00 in 1990, 1.31 in 1988. **3.** Pro forma. d-Deficit. E-Estimated. NA-Not Available. NM-Not Meaningful.

Income Data (Million $)

Year Ended Dec. 31	Revs.	Oper. Inc.	% Oper. Inc. of Revs.	Cap. Exp.	Depr.	Int. Exp.	Net Bef. Taxes	Eff. Tax Rate	[1]Net Inc.	% Net Inc. of Revs.	Cash Flow
1992	**11,128**	**222**	**2.0**	**36**	**62.0**	**54.7**	**109**	**41.4%**	**63.6**	**0.6**	**126**
1991	10,388	126	1.2	25	64.6	61.3	2	39.9%	1.4	NM	66
1990	10,185	182	1.8	126	57.5	59.1	76	36.2%	48.3	0.5	106
1989	9,129	155	1.7	112	51.5	52.3	55	36.0%	35.3	0.4	87
1988	9,066	191	2.1	79	49.6	45.6	101	38.1%	62.3	0.7	112
1987	7,681	180	2.3	51	47.0	19.7	119	43.0%	67.9	0.9	115
1986	6,822	173	2.5	80	43.5	4.1	135	50.4%	[2]66.8	1.0	110
1985	6,509	135	2.1	51	32.8	5.0	101	50.2%	50.5	0.8	83

Balance Sheet Data (Million $)

Dec. 31	Cash	Curr. Assets	Curr. Liab.	Curr. Ratio	Total Assets	% Ret. on Assets	Long Term Debt	Common Equity	Total Cap.	% LT Debt of Cap.	% Ret. on Equity
1992	**25.0**	**702**	**372**	**1.9**	**1,499**	**4.3**	**511**	**534**	**1,111**	**46.0**	**12.5**
1991	22.6	626	388	1.6	1,450	0.1	510	483	1,049	48.6	0.3
1990	15.4	677	443	1.5	1,533	3.3	507	511	1,079	47.0	9.6
1989	19.0	565	382	1.5	1,353	2.6	416	497	961	43.3	7.2
1988	76.5	596	375	1.6	1,324	4.8	402	490	944	42.6	13.2
1987	88.3	548	337	1.6	1,253	NM	417	459	911	45.8	NM
1986	13.7	521	242	2.1	1,222	5.7	27	910	976	2.8	7.6

Data as orig. reptd. **1.** Bef. spec. items. **2.** Refl. acctg. change. NM-Not Meaningful.

Business Summary

IBP, inc. is the world's largest producer of fresh and boxed beef and pork products and of edible and inedible allied products. Segment contributions in recent years were:

	1992	1991
Boxed beef products	67%	64%
Beef carcasses	4%	5%
Pork products	18%	20%
Beef & pork allied products..	11%	11%

The company operates 11 beef slaughtering plants, seven of which have adjoining facilities to reduce carcasses into primal cuts, such as loins, ribs, rounds and chucks, and sub-primal cuts, including sirloins, strips and tenderloins. IBP's carcass and beef processing facilities operated in 1992 at 81% and 80%, respectively, of their production capacities.

Seven of IBP's beef plants include hide treatment facilities. Substantially all hides from its other four beef plants are transported to these facilities, which include brine curing operations and, in four locations, chrome hide tanneries.

The company operates six pork facilities in Iowa and Nebraska. The facilities include both carcass production and processing of fresh pork products, employing a production process similar to that employed in beef operations. The facilities produce fresh boxed pork for shipment to retailers and also produce pork bellies, hams and boneless picnic meat for shipment to customers that further process the pork into bacon, cooked hams, luncheon meats and sausage items. In 1992, IBP's pork plants operated at 87% of production capacity.

Sales to international customers are made through the IBP International, Inc. subsidiary, which has sales offices in London and Tokyo. In 1992, export sales accounted for 12% of total net sales.

Dividend Data

Dividends were initiated in 1987.

Amt. of Divd. $	Date Decl.	Ex-divd. Date	Stock of Record	Payment Date
0.05	Oct. 21	Dec. 9	Dec. 15	Jan. 15'93
0.05	Jan. 27	Mar. 4	Mar. 10	Apr. 15'93
0.05	Apr. 21	Jun. 4	Jun. 10	Jul. 15'93
0.05	Jul. 21	Sep. 3	Sep. 10	Oct. 15'93

Finances

Capital spending in 1992 totaled $36 million, up from 1991's $25 million. Outlays in 1992 included costs associated with construction of a chrome hide tannery at the company's Amarillio, Tex., beef plant; this value-added facility, IBP's fourth hide tannery, began operations in December 1992. For 1993, capital expenditures of about $60 million are projected.

Capitalization

Long Term Debt: $510,900,000 (6/93).

Common Stock: 47,494,159 shs. ($0.05 par).
Institutions hold 83%.
Shareholders of record: 12,800.

Office—IBP Ave., P.O. Box 515, Dakota City, NE 68731. **Tel**—(402) 494-2061. **Chrmn, Pres & CEO**—R. L. Peterson. **EVP-Fin**—L. O. Grigsby. **VP, Treas & Investor Contact**—John N. Borgh. **Dirs**—J. S. Chalsty, A. P. Courtelis, W. L. Gramm, P. V. Haines, E. D. Leman, R. L. Peterson, D. Tinstman. **Transfer Agent & Registrar**—Mellon Securities Trust Co., Pittsburgh. **Incorporated** in Delaware in 1961. **Empl**—27,500.

 Kenneth A. Shea

IMC Fertilizer Group

NYSE Symbol IFL Options on NYSE & Pacific In S&P MidCap 400

Price	Range	P-E Ratio	Dividend	Yield	S&P Ranking	Beta
Sep. 22'93	1993					
29	45⅝–24⅜	NM	None	None	NR	0.42

Summary

This company is one of the world's largest private-enterprise producers of phosphate rock and potash and is a major producer of phosphate chemical fertilizer. In July 1993, IFL and Freeport McMoRan Resource Partners merged their respective phosphate fertilizer businesses in response to depressed fertilizer prices. A loss is expected for fiscal 1994. IFL plans to sell common stock and notes to refinance high-cost debt and to strengthen its balance sheet.

Current Outlook

Without a substantial increase in fertilizer prices, IFL will probably report a loss of at least $0.50 a share for the fiscal year ending June 30, 1994. It posted a loss of $5.44 a share for fiscal 1993.

Near-term resumption of cash dividends is not expected.

With the July 1, 1993, formation of the joint venture combining the phosphate fertilizer businesses of Freeport McMoRan Resource Partners and IFL, annual reported sales for IFL will be about $1.4 billion. The venture is expected to be able to reduce aggregate operating and administrative costs by almost $100 million a year. Depressed fertilizer prices will likely result in continued operating losses in fiscal 1994.

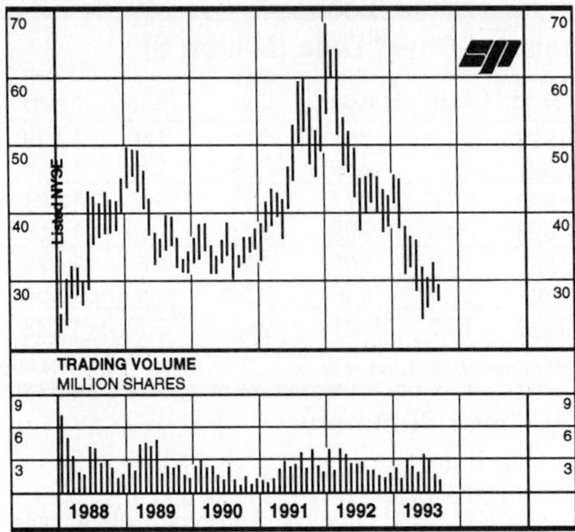

Net Sales (Million $)

Quarter:	1992-3	1991-2	1990-1	1989-90
Sep.	221	259	266	251
Dec.	198	253	276	263
Mar.	223	268	286	284
Jun.	256	280	303	307
	897	1,059	1,131	1,106

Sales for fiscal 1993 (preliminary) fell 15% from those of fiscak 1992, mainly reflecting lower fertilizer prices. Including a net charge of $5.44 a share, versus a gain of $0.82 a share, there was a net loss of $120.0 million ($5.44 a share), versus net income of $90.9 million ($4.12), before per-share charges of $2.13 and $7.50 from accounting changes.

Common Share Earnings ($)

Quarter:	1992-3	1991-2	1990-1	1989-90
Sep.	0.84	0.96	0.87	0.76
Dec.	0.13	1.07	0.94	0.83
Mar.	d5.20	1.74	0.75	0.64
Jun.	d1.21	0.35	1.29	0.90
	d5.44	4.12	3.85	3.13

Important Developments

Sep. '93— IFL planned to sell 2.75 million commmon shares (plus overallotments) and $175 million of notes due 2000. Proceeds will be used to purchase the $220 million of 11.25% notes for about $250 million. In June 1993, IFL completed a financial restructuring. Proceeds from the sale of $260 million of notes were used to pay a $60.6 million portion of a legal settlement with Angus Chemical Co., $100 million to repay bank borrowings and $50 million to repurchase receivables. IFL also entered into a new $100 million credit agreement.

Jul. '93— IFL and Freeport McMoRan Resource Partners formed a joint venture combining their respective phosphate fertilizer businesses, including phosphate rock and uranium. The venture, managed by IFL, expects to reduce aggregate costs by more than $95 million a year.

Next earnings report expected in mid-October.

Per Share Data ($)

Yr. End Jun. 30	1993	1992	1991	1990	[1]1989	1988	1987
Tangible Bk. Val.	**NA**	27.78	32.10	31.13	29.08	22.38	NA
Cash Flow	**NA**	7.89	7.47	6.64	9.10	NA	NA
Earnings[2]	**d5.44**	4.12	3.85	3.13	5.27	3.88	[3]0.10
Dividends	**0.81**	1.08	1.08	1.08	1.02	0.37	Nil
Payout Ratio	**NM**	26%	28%	34%	20%	8%	Nil
Prices[4]—High	**45⅝**	68	60	38⅝	49¾	45⅛	NA
Low	**24⅜**	37¼	33	30⅜	31¼	22½	NA
P/E Ratio—	**NM**	17–9	16–9	12–10	9–6	12–6	NA

Data as orig. reptd. **1.** Refl. acctg. change. **2.** Bef. spec. items of -2.13 in 1993, -7.50 in 1992. **3.** Aft. pro forma adj. **4.** Cal. yr. d-Deficit. NA-Not Available. NM-Not Meaningful.

Income Data (Million $)

Year Ended Jun. 30	Oper. Revs.	Oper. Inc.	% Oper. Inc. of Revs.	Cap. Exp.	Depr.	Int. Exp.	Net Bef. Taxes	Eff. Tax Rate	[2]Net Inc.	% Net Inc. of Revs.	Cash Flow
1992	**1,059**	**248**	**23.4**	**178**	**83.3**	**63.7**	**141**	**35.7%**	**91**	**8.6**	**174**
1991	1,131	266	23.5	169	90.2	51.5	153	37.3%	96	8.5	186
1990	1,106	261	23.6	94	92.5	47.3	128	35.3%	83	7.5	175
[1]1989	1,222	374	30.6	163	99.7	53.3	215	36.1%	137	11.2	237
1988	1,086	300	27.6	26	78.5	36.3	191	41.5%	112	10.3	176
1987	876	116	13.2	110	68.7	8.3	47	43.8%	27	3.0	NA
1986	866	d2	NM	52	68.6	3.5	d71	NM	d35	NM	NA
1985	1,061	216	20.3	64	90.0	0.5	135	38.0%	84	7.9	NA
1984	984	232	23.6	NA	95.6	0.7	150	41.3%	88	9.0	NA
1983	912	185	20.3	NA	79.5	1.3	118	38.0%	73	8.0	NA

Balance Sheet Data (Million $)

Jun. 30	Cash	Curr. Assets	Curr. Liab.	Curr. Ratio	Total Assets	% Ret. on Assets	Long Term Debt	Common Equity	Total Cap.	% LT Debt of Cap.	% Ret. on Equity
1992	**33**	**266**	**186**	**1.4**	**1,778**	**5.1**	**631**	**615**	**1,459**	**43.2**	**13.7**
1991	39	296	248	1.2	1,739	6.3	608	699	1,349	45.0	14.0
1990	30	246	212	1.2	1,585	5.1	385	820	1,234	31.2	10.4
1989	92	395	270	1.5	1,678	7.8	502	765	1,287	39.0	20.3
1988	147	377	231	1.6	1,472	NA	439	476	1,130	38.9	NA
1987	7	245	145	1.7	1,332	2.1	113	804	1,117	10.1	3.3
1986	15	263	117	2.2	1,242	NM	33	829	1,062	3.1	NM

Data as orig. reptd. **1.** Refl. acctg. change. **2.** Bef. spec. item in 1992. d-Deficit. NA-Not Available. NM-Not Meaningful.

Business Summary

On July 1, 1993, IMC Fertilizer Group and Freeport McMoRan Resource Partners (FRP) formed IMC-Agrico Co., a joint venture combining their respective phosphate fertilizer businesses, including phosphate rock and uranium. Distribution from the venture will reflect each partners' contribution to the venture and an equal share of anticipated savings of more than $95 million a year.

IMC Fertilizer Group is the nation's largest producer of phosphate rock and potash, two basic fertilizer materials, and one of the largest producers of phosphate chemical fertilizers. Sales contributions in recent fiscal years:

	1992	1991
Phosphate chemicals	40%	40%
Potash	21%	20%
Phosphate rock	20%	20%
Mixed fertilizers	10%	8%
Uranium	6%	6%
Ammonia	3%	5%
Other	1%	1%

Exports accounted for 25% of sales in fiscal 1992.

IFL owns or operates about 13% of world phosphate rock capacity, 4% of world phosphate chemical capacity and 7% of world potash output. It also produces uranium oxide, which is extracted during the process that produces phosphate chemicals and is sold for upgrading into nuclear power plant fuel. In March 1992, the company sold its ammonia production facility at Sterlington, La.

At June 30, 1992, IFL had proved reserves of 299 million tons of phosphate rock at an average grade of 68% BPL (bone phosphate of lime) in central Florida, 1.6 billion tons of potash at an average K_2O content of 25% in Saskatchewan (Canada) and 183 million tons of potash at an average K_2O content of 10% in New Mexico. IFL's annual production capacity was 23 million tons of phosphate rock, 2.01 million tons of phosphate chemicals, 5.25 million tons of potash and 2.0 million pounds of uranium. A 25% interest is held in a 67-million-ton sulphur deposit and oil and natural gas reserve in the Gulf of Mexico.

FRP's Agrico unit was the world's largest integated phosphate fertilizer producer, with annual production capacity of 4.1 million tons of phosphate fertilizer, 2.0 million tons of phosphoric acid and 8.5 million tons of phosphate rock.

Dividend Data

Dividends were omitted in April 1993, after having been paid since 1988. A "poison pill" stock purchase right was adopted in 1989.

Amt. of Divd. $	Date Decl.	Ex-divd. Date	Stock of Record	Payment Date
0.27	Aug. 20	Sep. 10	Sep. 16	Sep. 30'92
0.27	Oct. 15	Dec. 11	Dec. 17	Dec. 31'92
0.27	Mar. 4	Mar. 11	Mar. 17	Mar. 31'93

Capitalization

Long Term Debt: $893,457,000 (6/93).

Minority Interest: $708,200,000 (pro forma).

Common Stock: 22,050,727 shs. ($1 par). Institutions hold about 90%.

Office—2100 Sanders Rd., Northbrook, IL 60062. **Tel**—(708) 272-9200. **Chrmn**—B. B. Turner. **Pres & CEO**—W. F. Bueche. **Exec VP-CFO**—R. C. Brauneker. **Sr VP & Secy**—M. I. Smith. **VP, Treas & Investor Contact**—John E. Galvin (708) 205-4814. **Dirs**—W. F. Bueche, F. W. Considine, J. M. Davidson, R. C. Frazee, R. A. Lenon, T. H. Roberts Jr., B. B. Turner. **Transfer Agent & Registrar**—First Chicago Trust Co. of New York, NYC. **Incorporated** in Delaware in 1987. **Empl**—5,400.

 Richard O'Reilly, CFA

Idaho Power

NYSE Symbol IDA In S&P MidCap 400

Price	Range	P-E Ratio	Dividend	Yield	S&P Ranking	Beta
Aug. 5'93	1993					
31⅞	32⅝–27¼	17	1.86	5.8%	B	0.56

Summary

This utility provides electric service in southern Idaho and to a much lesser extent in eastern Oregon and northern Nevada. In a normal year, about two-thirds of power generation is hydroelectric; the remainder is mostly coal. Earnings should improve in 1993, based on promising conditions for hydroelectric generation and a 3.9% rate hike. Customer growth of over 3% is among the fastest in the U.S.

Current Outlook

Share earnings for 1993 are estimated at $2.00, up from 1992's $1.55. Earnings for 1994 are projected at $2.05 a share.

Dividends should remain at $0.46½ quarterly.

Profitability in 1993 should benefit from higher streamflow levels which should lead to greater hydroelectric generation and the return to a more normal fuel mix. Cheap hydroelectric power will lower fuel costs by reducing the need for more expensive coal-based generation. Lower-cost electricity also tends to boost sales to other utilities. In May 1992, IDA was granted a rate increase of $15 million for one year. The service territory's economy is experiencing growth rates in some categories among the highest in the country. IDA expects to add some 9,000 new customers in 1993. Estimated construction expenditures should not hinder earnings quality.

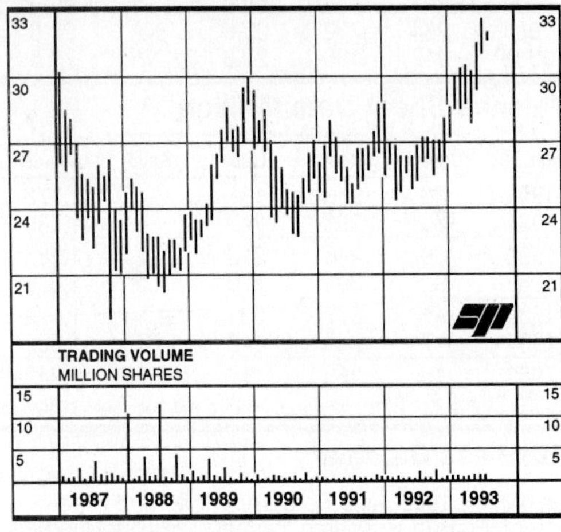

Operating Revenues (Million $)

Quarter:	1993	1992	1991	1990
Mar.	141	115	121	112
Jun.	129	125	111	109
Sep.		129	130	126
Dec.		130	122	118
		498	483	465

Operating revenues for the six months ended March 31, 1993, rose 13%, year to year, reflecting continued strength in the regional economy. Profitability benefited from favorable hydro conditions, and net income increased 55%. After preferred dividends, share earnings were $1.02 on 6.4% more shares, from $0.67

Common Share Earnings ($)

Quarter:	1994	1992	1991	1990
Mar.	E0.55	0.35	0.43	0.46
Jun.	E0.50	0.32	0.26	0.39
Sep.	E0.40	0.38	0.46	0.49
Dec.	E0.60	0.49	0.40	0.58
	E2.05	1.55	1.56	1.91

Important Developments

Jul. '93— IDA said that due to large snowpack accumulation in the Snake River Basin above its hydroelectric facilities hydroelectric generating conditions were extremely favorable in the first half of 1993. With hydro generating 73.5% of the systems' demand during the second quarter of 1993, compared to 30.4% during the same period of 1992, the utility experienced dramatic reductions of $8.3 million in its fuel expense and $14.5 million in purchased power costs, versus these costs in the second quarter of 1992. Bountiful hydro conditions also enabled the company to increase its sales of energy to other utilities by $16.3 million. IDA reiterated that 1992's above average temperatures and below normal precipitation had resulted in reduced water flows into the company's hydro system and produced perhaps the worst water year in the company's history for hydroelectric generation.

Next earnings report expected in late October.

Per Share Data ($)

Yr. End Dec. 31	1992	1991	1990	1989	1988	1987	1986	1985	1984	1983
Tangible Bk. Val.	**17.28**	17.06	17.38	16.69	16.54	16.50	17.31	17.18	16.64	15.68
Earnings[1]	**1.55**	1.56	1.91	2.37	1.32	1.30	2.00	2.16	2.63	2.25
Dividends	**1.86**	1.86	1.86	1.83	1.80	1.80	1.76	1.68	1.59	1.49
Payout Ratio	**120%**	119%	97%	77%	136%	138%	88%	78%	60%	66%
Prices—High	**28¾**	28¾	29⅜	30	25⅝	30¼	30⅞	24½	19⅜	17½
Low	**24⅜**	24¼	22¾	22	20¼	19	22¾	18¾	15½	14⅜
P/E Ratio—	**19–16**	18–16	15–12	13–9	19–15	23–15	15–11	11–9	7–6	8–6

Data as orig. reptd. Adj. for stk. divs. of 100% Jun. 1985. **1.** Bef. spec. item(s) of +0.33 in 1987. E-Estimated.

Income Data (Million $)

Year Ended Dec. 31	Revs.	Depr.	Maint.	Oper. Ratio	[1]Fxd. Chgs. Cover.	Constr. Credits	Eff. Tax Rate	[2]Net Inc.	% Return On Revs.	% Return On [3]Invest. Capital	% Return On Com. Equity
1992	**498**	**59.8**	**35.9**	**79.6%**	**2.33**	**4.9**	**27.9%**	**60**	**12.0**	**6.8**	**9.0**
1991	483	57.6	44.4	78.2%	2.20	4.0	26.8%	58	12.0	7.4	9.0
1990	465	55.1	40.1	76.3%	2.55	1.9	25.1%	69	14.9	8.3	11.0
1989	496	53.1	34.2	74.3%	3.14	3.0	33.2%	85	17.1	9.4	13.9
1988	412	51.7	34.7	76.5%	1.99	4.7	21.7%	49	11.9	6.8	7.7
1987	395	50.9	29.0	76.9%	2.15	5.2	33.8%	48	12.2	6.9	7.4
1986	409	49.3	31.9	71.9%	2.81	7.4	37.4%	78	19.2	8.6	11.5
1985	451	45.6	37.1	74.0%	2.94	13.9	35.2%	85	18.8	8.7	12.7
1984	428	41.0	35.6	69.1%	3.54	20.5	38.1%	100	23.4	9.9	16.2
1983	376	39.0	34.5	68.6%	3.07	12.6	39.5%	88	23.4	9.5	14.6

Balance Sheet Data (Million $)

Dec. 31	[4]Gross Prop.	Capital Expend.	Net Prop.	% Earn. on Net Prop.	Total Cap.	Capitalization LT Debt	% LT Debt	Pfd.	% Pfd.	Com.	% Com.
1992	**2,269**	**119**	**1,585**	**6.5**	**1,719**	**702**	**48.9**	**108**	**7.5**	**625**	**43.6**
1991	2,169	136	1,529	7.1	1,596	630	47.8	108	8.2	580	44.0
1990	2,044	80	1,452	7.7	1,487	562	46.4	59	4.8	591	48.8
1989	1,976	62	1,457	9.0	1,459	543	45.9	59	4.9	589	49.5
1988	1,920	64	1,421	6.8	1,459	556	46.9	59	5.0	571	48.1
1987	1,865	39	1,413	6.4	1,483	567	46.7	59	4.9	587	48.4
1986	1,836	50	1,427	8.0	1,493	586	47.3	59	4.8	593	47.9
1985	1,794	74	1,429	8.3	1,566	616	46.5	124	9.3	586	44.2
1984	1,728	99	1,398	9.6	1,514	605	47.1	124	9.6	556	43.3
1983	1,634	104	1,341	9.0	1,450	579	46.6	150	12.0	513	41.4

Data as orig. reptd. **1.** Times int. exp. & pfd. divs. covered (pretax basis). **2.** Bef. spec. item(s) in 1987. **3.** Based on income before interest charges. **4.** Electric plant.

Business Summary

Idaho Power supplies electricity in an area of 20,000 square miles (Snake River Valley) in southern Idaho, eastern Oregon and northern Nevada with a population of about 632,000 people. About 88% of revenues over the past three years were derived from Idaho, 5% from Oregon and 1% from Nevada. IDA is a combination hydro-thermal utility with 17 hydro power plants, a combustion turbine and part ownership in three coal-fired generating plants. Contributions to revenues by class of customers:

	1992	1991	1990	1989
Commercial–industrial	39%	38%	39%	36%
Residential............	34%	35%	35%	33%
Irrigation/other	19%	16%	17%	17%
Other utilities.........	8%	11%	9%	14%

The fuel mix in 1992 was 35% hydro, 51% coal, and 14% purchased power. Peak load in 1992 was 2,268 mw, and system capacity was 2,987 mw, for a capacity margin of 24%; electricity sales were 13,227,723 mw, down 1% from 1991. IDA estimated its customer energy demand growth at 1.4% per year for the next 20 years. IDA completed the Milner hydroelectric facility in October 1992 and work is under way to double capacity at the Swan Falls plant expected to be completed in 1994. A five-fold capacity expansion project at the Twin Falls facility is slated to begin in late 1993, and renewed operations are expected in 1995.

Finances

In June 1993, IDA sold 250,000 shares of preferred stock at $100 each. In April 1993, IDA offered for public sale $200 million of first mortgage bonds and medium term notes. Proceeds were earmarked to refinance debt and for construction programs.

Dividend Data

Dividends have been paid since 1917. A dividend reinvestment plan is available.

Amt of Divd. $	Date Decl.	Ex–divd. Date	Stock of Record	Payment Date
0.46½	Sep. 10	Oct. 20	Oct. 26	Nov. 20'92
0.46½	Jan. 14	Jan. 19	Jan. 25	Feb. 19'93
0.46½	Mar. 11	Apr. 20	Apr. 26	May 20'93
0.46½	Jul. 8	Jul. 20	Jul. 26	Aug. 20'93

Capitalization

Long Term Debt: $706,307,000 (3/93).

Preferred Stock: $132,856,000.

Common Stock: 36,426,372 shs. ($2.50 par).
Institutions hold 21%.
Shareholders of record: 27,834.

Office—1221 W. Idaho St. (P.O. Box 70), Boise, ID 83707. **Tel**—(208) 383-2200. **Chrmn & CEO**—J. W. Marshall. **Pres & COO**—L. R. Gunnoe. **VP & Treas**—D. K. Bowers. **VP & Secy**—R. W. Stahman. **VP, CFO & Investor Contact**—J. L. Keen. **Dirs**—R. D. Bolinder, R. L. Breezeley, J. B. Carley, G. L. Coiner, A. D. Dunn, J. A. Elorriaga, L. R. Gunnoe, P. T. Johnson, E. Loveless, J. W. Marshall, J. A. McClure, J. H. Miller, R. T. Norman, G. C. Rose, P. Soulen. **Transfer Agents**—Co.'s office; First Chicago Trust Co. of New York, NYC. **Registrars**—First Security Bank of Idaho, Boise; First Chicago Trust Co. of New York, NYC. **Incorporated** in Maine in 1915; reincorporated in Idaho in 1989. **Empl**—1,638.

 Ned Bancroft

Illinois Central

NYSE Symbol IC Options on Phila In S&P MidCap 400

Price	Range	P-E Ratio	Dividend	Yield	S&P Ranking	Beta
Oct. 15'93	1993					
32⅝	33½–23⅝	17	0.68	2.1%	NR	NA

Summary

Illinois Central operates a 2,700-mile midwestern rail system extending from Chicago to the Gulf of Mexico. The railroad traces its origins to 1851, although the present company was formed in mid-1990. Profits should continue to advance in 1994 as IC benefits from a stronger economy, the absence of 1993's coal miners' strike and reduced fixed charges. The quarterly dividend was raised 13% in June 1993.

Current Outlook

Earnings for 1994 are projected at $2.40 a share, versus the $2.10 anticipated for 1993.

Dividends were raised 13%, to $0.17 a share quarterly, with the July 1993 payment.

Continued profit improvement is anticipated for 1994 as rising industrial output fuels gains for chemicals, paper and other cyclical traffic. Coal volumes should advance sharply after being penalized in 1993 by the lengthy miners' strike. Grain traffic could slip as higher movements to poultry breeders are outweighed by lower export movements and the absence of volumes picked up from barge carriers during the 1993 flood. Intermodal traffic will continue to benefit from IC's alliance with M.S. Carriers and Schneider National and the relocation of its Chicago yard. Fuel costs could increase moderately. Interest costs and equipment lease payments could decline. Aiding comparisons will be the absence of 1993's tax adjustment.

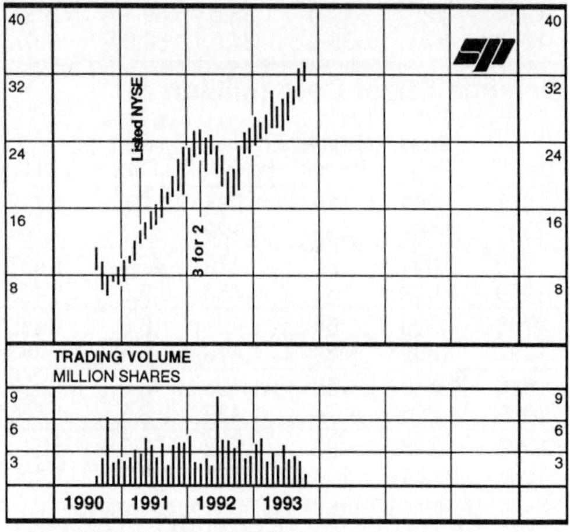

Revenues (Million $)

Quarter:	1993	1992	1991	1990
Mar.	143	139	138	148
Jun.	132	130	131	138
Sep.	147	131	140	130
Dec.	---	147	141	128
	---	547	550	544

Revenues for 1993's first nine months rose 5.6%, year to year. Income before extraordinary items in both periods was up 18%. Share earnings were $1.53, versus $1.31.

Common Share Earnings ($)

Quarter:	1993	1992	1991	1990
Mar.	0.56	0.50	0.43	0.40
Jun.	0.47	0.40	0.35	0.31
Sep.	0.50	0.41	0.41	0.25
Dec.	E0.57	0.39	0.45	0.35
	E2.10	1.70	1.64	1.31

Important Developments

Oct. '93— Net income for 1993's third quarter was reduced by $3.8 million ($0.09 a share) to reflect the increase in the federal corporate tax rate and adjustment to prior years' deferred taxes.

Oct. '93— Coal carloadings for 1993's third quarter fell 23%, year to year, reflecting a strike by the United Mine Workers. IC said the strike, which began in 1993's second quarter, had reduced net income for 1993 by about $2.8 million (or $0.07 a share).

Jul. '93— IC made a $23.4 million ($0.55 a share) extraordinary charge to net income for 1993's second quarter to reflect costs associated with the refinancing of some $145 million face amount of 14.125% senior subordinated debentures due 2001.

Next earnings reported expected in late January.

Per Share Data ($)

Yr. End Dec. 31	1992	1991	1990	[1]1989
Tangible Bk. Val.	**7.94**	6.15	3.61	d0.04
Cash Flow	**2.20**	2.14	1.99	0.66
Earnings[2]	**1.70**	1.64	1.31	0.09
Dividends	**0.50**	Nil	Nil	Nil
Payout Ratio	**29%**	Nil	Nil	Nil
Prices—High	**25⅝**	23⅜	11⅜	NA
Low	**16½**	7⅜	5⅝	NA
P/E Ratio—	**15–10**	14–4	9–4	NA

Data as orig. reptd. Adj. for stk. div. of 50% Mar. 1992. **1.** From 1-27-89. **2.** Bef. spec. item of +0.55 in 1992. d-Deficit. E-Estimated. NA-Not Available.

Income Data (Million $)

Year Ended Dec. 31	Revs.	Oper. Inc.	% Oper. Inc. of Revs.	Cap. Exp.	Depr.	Int. Exp.	[2]Net Bef. Taxes	Eff. Tax Rate	[3]Net Inc.	% Net Inc. of Revs.	Cash Flow
1992	**547**	**182**	**33.2**	**51**	**21.4**	**46.2**	**110**	**34.0%**	**72.5**	**13.2**	**93.9**
1991	550	166	30.1	50	20.0	59.7	96	32.0%	65.4	11.9	85.4
1990	544	155	28.6	89	21.6	75.9	69	32.7%	46.2	8.5	62.7
[1]1989	399	96	24.1	991	16.1	72.8	14	30.6%	10.0	2.5	18.7

Balance Sheet Data (Million $)

Dec. 31	Cash	Curr. Assets	Curr. Liab.	Curr. Ratio	Total Assets	% Ret. on Assets	Long Term Debt	Common Equity	Total Cap.	% LT Debt of Cap.	% Ret. on Equity
1992	**34.6**	**165**	**168**	**1.0**	**1,206**	**6.0**	**367**	**339**	**877**	**41.9**	**24.1**
1991	32.7	180	183	1.0	1,184	5.1	414	260	846	48.9	31.7
1990	13.5	174	218	0.8	1,152	3.5	486	128	774	62.8	NM
1989	27.3	236	309	0.8	1,165	NA	538	d1	773	69.6	NA

Data as orig. reptd. **1.** From 1-27-89. **2.** Incl. equity in earns. of nonconsol. subs. **3.** Bef. spec. item in 1992. d-Deficit. NM-Not Meaningful. NA-Not Available.

Business Summary

Illinois Central Corp. is the parent company of Illinois Central Railroad Co., which traces its origins to 1851. IC was controlled by Whitman Corp. until spun off to Whitman shareholders in January 1989. In September 1989, IC was merged into a unit of Prospect Group, which in 1990 distributed IC common stock to its shareholders.

The Illinois Central Railroad operates some 2,700 miles (including 230 miles of trackage rights), serving shippers in Illinois, Kentucky, Tennessee, Alabama, Mississippi and Louisiana. The northern terminus is at Chicago, while the southernmost point is the Gulf of Mexico. IC also owns 600 miles of secondary main line and 1,900 miles of passing, yard and switching track.

Contributions to freight revenues in recent years:

	1992	1991	1990
Chemicals	24.3%	24.5%	25.3%
Coal	15.3%	15.0%	15.3%
Grain	12.2%	11.7%	10.7%
Paper	12.1%	11.2%	10.7%
Mill/food products	8.8%	8.7%	9.5%
Intermodal	5.4%	5.2%	5.0%
All other	21.9%	23.7%	23.5%

Some 77% of the railroad's traffic originates on its system (of which 32% is forwarded to other railroads), 18% is received from other carriers and terminated by IC and 5% is represented by bridge or through traffic. The average haul in 1992 was 284 miles, compared with 286 miles in 1991. In 1992, IC transported 18.7 billion ton-miles of freight generating average revenue of 2.7 cents per ton-mile, compared with 19.4 billion ton-miles in 1991 earning 2.8 cents. The operating ratio in 1992 was 70.7%, compared with 73.5% in 1991.

IC's equipment fleet at 1992 year-end consisted of 449 locomotives (of which 170 were leased), 15,877 freight cars (7,114 leased) and 903 pieces of work equipment (41 leased) and 203 leased highway trailers and tractors.

Dividend Data

Dividends were initiated in 1992. A dividend reinvestment plan is available.

Amt. of Divd. $	Date Decl.	Ex-divd. Date	Stock of Record	Payment Date
0.15	Nov. 24	Dec. 11	Dec. 17	Jan. 7'93
0.15	Mar. 2	Mar. 19	Mar. 25	Apr. 8'93
0.17	Jun. 3	Jun. 18	Jun. 24	Jul. 8'93
0.17	Sep. 8	Sep. 17	Sep. 23	Oct. 7'93

Finances

IC made an $8.9 million charge against 1992's fourth quarter pretax income ($0.13 a share, net) primarily covering retirement expenses and asset revaluations.

Capital spending for 1993 was projected at $56 million, including $35 million for trackwork and $4.5 million for 17 second-hand locomotives. In 1992, capital outlays totaled $45 million, including $6 million for IC's new intermodal yard in Chicago.

In June 1992, several merchant banking partnerships affiliated with Shearson Lehman Brothers Holding Inc. completed a secondary offering of 9,959,886 shares (23.5%) of IC common stock at $22.625 each. IC said none of the company's officers or directors participated in the offering.

Capitalization

Long Term Debt: $367,800,000 (9/93).

Common Stock: 42,635,566 shs. ($0.001 par).
Officers & directors own 5.8%
Institutions hold about 78%.
Shareholders: 11,000.

Office—455 N. Cityfront Plaza Drive, Chicago, IL 60611-5504. **Tel**—(312) 755-7500. **Chrmn**—G. H. Lamphere. **Pres & CEO**—E. H. Harrison. **VP-Secy**—R. A. Lane. **VP-CFO**—D. W. Phillips. **Investor Contact**—Ann G. Thoma (312) 755-7591. **Dirs**—T. A. Barron, G. D. Gould, E. H. Harrison, W. B. Johnson, G. H. Lamphere, A. P. Lynch, S. F. Prior IV, J. V. Tunney, A. H. Washkowitz. **Transfer Agent & Registrar**—First National Bank of Boston. **Incorporated** in Delaware in 1989. **Empl**—2,917.

 Stephen R. Klein

Illinois Power

NYSE Symbol IPC In S&P MidCap 400

Price	Range	P-E Ratio	Dividend	Yield	S&P Ranking	Beta
Sep. 23'93	1993					
25	25⅞–21¾	16	0.80	3.2%	B	0.73

Summary

This electric and gas utility serves a 15,000-square-mile area composed of parts of northern, central and southern Illinois (outside of Chicago). In September 1993, the Third District Illinois Court of Appeals upheld the Illinois Commerce Commission's decision to deny IPC rate treatment for post-construction costs associated with the Clinton nuclear plant. The decision forced a $195 million writeoff in 1993's third quarter, but should not impair IPC's earnings power. Over the longer term, profits will benefit from an improved cost structure, rate increases and the formation of a nonregulated independent power subsidiary.

Current Outlook

Excluding a $195 million charge for the Clinton nuclear plant, 1993 earnings are projected at $1.60 a share, up from 1992's $1.23. Earnings for 1994 are estimated at $1.80 a share.

Dividends have been predeclared at $0.20 quarterly through the second quarter of 1994.

Earnings for 1993 should benefit from more seasonable weather and $78.5 million in rate hikes approved by regulators in August 1992 related to Clinton Nuclear Station capital expenditures. Other positive factors for 1993 include projected gains in electric kwh sales associated with a predicted rebound in economic activity, lower interest expense from refinancing higher-coupon debt and the passage of an Illinois law enabling the firm to set up a nonregulated subsidiary. The new unit will specialize in independent power production and better position IPC to retain large industrial customers under greater wholesale competition.

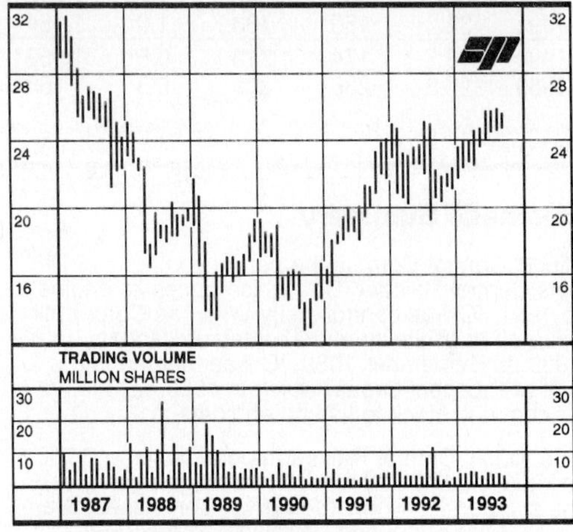

Operating Revenues (Million $)

Quarter:	1994	1993	1992	1991
Mar.	---	395	384	378
Jun.	---	351	336	328
Sep.	---	---	395	403
Dec.	---	---	366	366
	---	---	1,480	1,475

Operating revenues for the six months ended June 30, 1993, rose 3.7%, year to year. Profitability benefited from a return to more normal (cool) weather conditions and continued success controlling costs. Net income advanced 61%. Following preferred dividends, share earnings were $0.57, versus $0.28.

Common Share Earnings ($)

Quarter:	1994	1993	1992	1991
Mar.	E0.30	0.28	0.10	0.01
Jun.	E0.30	0.30	0.18	0.15
Sep.	E0.90	E0.82	0.77	0.74
Dec.	E0.30	E0.20	0.18	0.13
	E1.80	E1.60	1.23	1.04

Important Developments

Sep. '93— IPC said it will take a $195 million aftertax writeoff in the third quarter as a result of a decision by the Illinois Appellate Court to uphold key components of the August 1992 Illinois Commerce Commission's unfavorable rate order that denied IPC recovery of $202 million in Clinton Nuclear Station post-construction costs. The decision will also force the company to refund about $8.5 million to its electric customers. Stock dividends that have been predeclared through the second quarter of 1994 will not be affected. In March 1993, the ICC aproved IPC's plan to predeclare quarterly dividends in order to quell uncertainty arising from the ICC's unfavorable rate order. Dividend policy beyond 1994's second quarter is uncertain. Also in September, the staff of the ICC recommended that IPC be granted an $18.7 million rate increase for its gas operations. A decision on the order could come as soon as year-end 1993, but spring 1994 appears more realistic.

Next earnings report expected in mid-October.

Per Share Data ($)

Yr. End Dec. 31	1992	1991	1990	1989	1988	1987	1986	1985	1984	1983
Tangible Bk. Val.	**17.65**	18.27	17.97	19.77	24.84	25.95	24.99	24.15	23.34	22.60
Earnings[1]	**1.23**	1.04	d1.53	d4.34	1.66	3.75	3.98	3.48	4.02	3.80
Dividends	**0.80**	0.20	Nil	1.32	2.64	2.64	2.64	2.64	2.64	2.48
Payout Ratio	**65%**	19%	Nil	NM	159%	70%	66%	76%	66%	65%
Prices—High	**25⅛**	24⅛	19⅜	21¾	25⅛	31½	32	27½	23⅞	24⅛
Low	**19¼**	15⅜	12¾	13⅜	16½	21¼	23⅛	21⅜	17⅝	19⅜
P/E Ratio—	**20–16**	23–15	NM	NM	15–10	8–6	8–6	8–6	6–4	6–5

Data as orig. reptd. **1.** Bef. spec. item of +0.48 in 1988. d-Deficit. E-Estimated. NM-Not Meaningful.

Income Data (Million $)

Year Ended Dec. 31	Oper. Revs.	Depr.	Maint.	Oper. Ratio	[1]Fxd. Chgs. Cover.	Constr. Credits	Eff. Tax Rate	[2]Net Inc.	% Return On Revs.	% Return On [3]Invest. Capital	% Return On Com. Equity
1992	**1,480**	**161**	**102**	**80.7%**	**1.93**	**5**	**39.4%**	**122**	**8.3**	**6.0**	**6.5**
1991	1,475	177	87	80.2%	1.73	3	40.4%	109	7.4	5.9	5.5
1990	1,396	173	121	81.8%	0.59	3	NM	d78	NM	2.4	NM
1989	1,313	176	89	81.3%	NM	3	20.7%	d288	NM	NM	NM
1988	1,285	184	85	80.9%	2.18	3	29.4%	155	12.1	5.6	6.3
1987	1,220	147	80	80.9%	3.06	110	19.1%	290	23.7	8.2	14.3
1986	1,184	72	59	82.5%	3.25	219	20.5%	293	24.7	9.2	15.9
1985	1,167	70	51	82.5%	3.08	162	26.2%	240	20.6	9.2	14.4
1984	1,281	69	48	82.5%	3.59	119	34.4%	235	18.4	10.2	17.0
1983	1,278	67	45	83.5%	3.89	86	38.3%	208	16.3	10.0	17.1

Balance Sheet Data (Million $)

Dec. 31	Gross Prop.	[4]Capital Expend.	Net Prop.	% Earn. on Net Prop.	Total Cap.	Capitalization LT Debt	% LT Debt	Pfd.	% Pfd.	Com.	% Com.
1992	**6,239**	**244**	**4,429**	**6.5**	**4,753**	**2,017**	**52.5**	**403**	**10.5**	**1,423**	**37.0**
1991	6,056	141	4,371	6.6	4,877	2,153	53.5	413	10.3	1,456	36.2
1990	5,945	131	4,412	5.6	4,877	2,204	54.2	449	11.0	1,415	34.8
1989	6,014	97	4,624	5.0	5,179	2,352	53.7	475	10.8	1,554	35.5
1988	6,408	115	5,154	4.7	5,588	2,341	49.7	475	10.1	1,896	40.2
1987	6,325	264	5,246	4.5	5,387	2,279	49.6	475	10.3	1,841	40.1
1986	5,905	710	4,960	4.5	4,986	2,080	48.6	511	11.9	1,692	39.5
1985	5,209	871	4,325	5.2	4,372	1,837	48.6	401	10.6	1,539	40.8
1984	4,407	553	3,583	6.7	3,699	1,502	47.1	351	11.0	1,337	41.9
1983	3,868	360	3,104	7.1	3,175	1,292	47.3	301	11.0	1,138	41.7

Data as orig. reptd. **1.** Times int. exp. & pfd. divs. covered (pretax basis). **2.** Bef. spec. item in 1988. **3.** Based on inc. bef. int. charges. **4.** Excl. nuclear fuel aft. 1987. d-Deficit. NM-Not Meaningful.

Business Summary

Illinois Power supplies electricity and natural gas to approximately 560,000 customers in a 15,000-square-mile area of Illinois. Electric operations provided 80% of revenues and 94% of operating income in 1992, and gas activities provided 20% and 6%, respectively. Revenues by type of customer were as follows in 1992 :

	Electric	Gas
Residential	37%	63%
Commercial	22%	21%
Industrial	32%	13%
Other	9%	3%

The fuel mix in 1992 was 75% coal and other and 25% nuclear. Peak demand in 1992 was 3,109 mw, and system capacity was 4,052 mw, for a capacity margin of 23.3%. Gas sales in 1992 were 613 million therms, up 7.5% from 570 million therms in 1991.

The cost of the company's construction and capital requirements for the 1993-1997 period was estimated at $1.4 billion. With operation of the 950,000-kilowatt Clinton nuclear unit commencing November 24, 1987, the company expected that additional generating capacity would not be required until after the year 2000.

Finances

IPC plans to refinance $400 million to $500 million before the end of 1993.

In July 1993, Illinois legislators passed a law permitting IPC to fund up to $170 million for a newly formed nonregulated subsidiary, IP Group, Inc., that will build independent power projects.

Dividend Data

Common dividends were paid from 1947 until omission in April 1989 and were resumed in October 1991. In late 1992, the company predeclared its common dividends for 1993.

Amt. of Divd. $	Date Decl.	Ex-divd. Date	Stock of Record	Payment Date
0.20	Dec. 9	Jan. 5	Jan. 11	Feb. 1'93
0.20	Mar. 23	Apr. 2	Apr. 9	May 1'93
0.20	Jun. 21	Jul. 2	Jul. 9	Aug. 1'93
0.20	Oct. 14	---	---	Nov. 1'93

Capitalization

Long Term Debt: $2,033,400,000 (6/93).

Red. Cum. Preferred Stock: $78,000,000.

Cum. Pfd. & Pref. Stock: $346,200,000.

Common Stock: 75,643,937 shs. (no par).
Institutions hold about 54%.
Shareholders of record: 47,807.

Office—500 South 27th St., Decatur, IL 62525. **Tel**—(217) 424-6600. **Chrmn & Pres**—L. D. Haab. **VP-CFO**—L. F. Altenbaumer. **VP-Secy**—L. M. Stetzner. **Investor Contact**—Ann McEvoy (217) 424-8715. **Dirs**—R. R. Berry, L. D. Haab, G. J. Hansen, D. E. Lasater, D. S. Perkins, R. M. Powers, B. F. Schenk, W. D. Scott, R. L. Thompson, W. M. Vannoy, M. von Ferstel, C. W. Wells, V. K. Zimmerman. **Transfer Agent & Registrar**—Company itself. **Incorporated** in Illinois in 1923. **Empl**—4,626.

 Ned Bancroft

Indiana Energy

NYSE Symbol IEI In S&P MidCap 400

Price	Range	P-E Ratio	Dividend	Yield	S&P Ranking	Beta
Aug. 3'93	1993					
34	34¾–28¼	13	1.53	4.5%	B+	0.21

Summary

Through its main subsidiary, Indiana Gas, this holding company distributes natural gas to over 400,000 customers in central, north central, and southern Indiana. The company expects that a growing customer base, normal system enhancements, and repairs will require large capital expenditures in coming years. Operating profits are expected to increase in fiscal 1994, but share earnings will likely decline in the absence of a large nonrecurring gain. IEI sold 1,054,600 common shares at $30.875 each in May 1993, and in July the company declared a 3-for-2 stock split and raised its dividend 3.4%.

Current Outlook

Earnings for the fiscal year ending September 30, 1994, are projected at $2.20 a share, down from an estimated $2.55 (after a $0.51 capital gain) for fiscal 1993, all unadjusted for the pending 3-for-2 stock split.

The quarterly dividend has been was raised 3.4%, to $0.38¼ from $0.37, with the September 1993 payment.

Gas distribution profits should advance in fiscal 1994, assuming a return to normal weather (weather in the first nine months of fiscal 1993 was 3.0% warmer than normal, penalizing earnings by $0.09 a share). Customer growth is expected to be an above average 2.5%. A filing with state regulators is expected to be decided in early fiscal 1994, resulting in recovery of at least some costs associated with a manufactured gas plant site and FASB 106. However, share earnings are expected to decline owing to the absence of the $0.51 a share gain from the sale of IEI's interest in EnTrade Corp. and the larger number of common shares outstanding following the May 1993 public sale of 1,054,600 shares (about an 8% increase).

Operating Revenues (Million $)

Quarter:	1992–93	1991–92	1990–91	1989–90
Dec.	155.5	134.3	124.5	124.7
Mar.	178.3	148.6	165.0	133.1
Jun.	101.3	71.9	55.6	56.7
Sep.	---	56.4	44.4	38.6
	---	411.3	389.6	353.1

Utility operating revenues for the 12 months ended June 30, 1993, rose 23% from those of the preceding 12 months, reflecting higher rates, and colder weather conditions. Benefiting from a $7.1 million ($0.51 a share) gain on the sale of the interest in EnTrade Corp., net income advanced 55%, to $2.69 a share from $1.75.

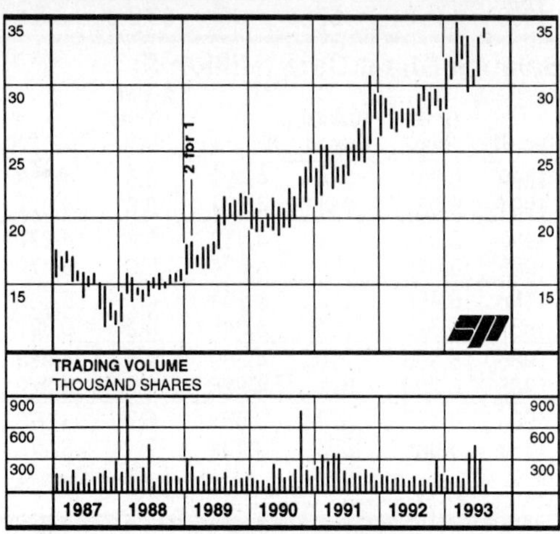

Common Share Earnings ($)

Quarter:	1992–93	1991–92	1990–91	1989–90
Dec.	1.49	0.80	0.66	1.01
Mar.	1.27	1.10	1.30	1.26
Jun.	0.05	d0.07	d0.20	0.02
Sep.	Ed0.26	d0.09	d0.09	d0.27
	E2.55	1.74	1.67	1.90

Important Developments

Jul. '93— IEI's directors declared a 3-for-2 stock split and raised the quarterly dividend 3.4%, to $0.38¼ from $0.37, with the September 1993 payment. In May, IEI sold publicly 1,054,600 common shares at $30.875 each; proceeds were to be used to refinance the December 1992 redemption of preferred stock and to partially finance its continuing construction program.

Next earnings report expected in late October.

Per Share Data ($)

Yr. End Sep. 30	1992	1991	1990	1989	1988	1987	1986	1985	1984	1983
Tangible Bk. Val.	**13.33**	12.76	12.83	12.49	11.77	11.07	10.59	10.45	9.62	8.51
Earnings[1]	**1.74**	1.67	1.90	1.92	1.83	1.29	1.39	1.75	1.94	1.16
Dividends	**1.435**	1.375	1.300	1.240	1.115	1.060	1.030	0.960	0.850	0.775
Payout Ratio	**82%**	82%	68%	65%	61%	82%	74%	55%	44%	67%
Prices[2]—High	**30**	30¾	24¾	21⅞	16⅛	17⅝	18¾	14⅞	10⅝	9¾
Low	**26¼**	21	18¾	15⅞	12¼	11⅞	13½	11	8¼	6⅝
P/E Ratio—	**17–15**	18–13	13–10	11–8	9–7	14–9	14–10	9–6	5–4	8–6

Data as orig. reptd. Adj. for stk. div(s) of 100% Feb. 1989, 100% Oct. 1984. **1.** Bef. spec. item(s) of +0.23 in 1987. **2.** Cal. yr. d-Deficit. E-Estimated.

Income Data (Million $)

Year Ended Sep. 30	Revs.	Depr.	Maint.	Oper. Ratio	[2]Fxd. Chgs. Cover.	Constr. Credits	Eff. Tax Rate	[4]Net Inc.	% Return On Revs.	% Return On [5]Invest. Capital	% Return On [6]Com. Equity
1992	**[1]411**	**[1]25.1**	**NA**	**[1]90.7%**	**[1]3.33**	**NA**	**[3]33.0%**	**[3]24.0**	**[3]5.8**	**NA**	**[3]11.3**
1991	[1]390	[1]23.6	NA	[1]90.9%	[1]3.07	NA	[3]36.3%	[3]23.1	[3]5.9	NA	[3]11.1
1990	[1]353	[1]22.2	NA	[1]91.1%	[1]3.53	NA	[3]34.0%	[3]21.7	[3]6.2	NA	[3]13.5
1989	345	20.7	NA	90.5%	3.50	0.36	33.4%	21.2	6.1	10.3	15.0
1988	323	19.2	9.9	90.0%	3.48	0.23	33.2%	20.1	6.2	10.7	15.0
1987	303	17.3	10.1	91.7%	3.17	0.20	42.5%	14.1	4.7	9.0	13.5
1986	371	15.9	10.4	93.0%	3.55	0.36	44.9%	15.1	4.1	9.6	12.6
1985	420	14.6	9.1	92.8%	4.32	0.20	47.0%	20.7	4.9	11.6	16.9
1984	455	13.5	8.7	92.9%	4.78	0.26	49.7%	22.5	4.9	12.8	20.5
1983	416	12.7	8.8	94.3%	3.08	0.22	47.2%	14.2	3.4	10.1	13.7

Balance Sheet Data (Million $)

Sep. 30	Gross Prop.	Capital Expend.	Net Prop.	% Earn. on Net Prop.	Total Cap.	Capitalization LT Debt	% LT Debt	[7]Pfd.	[7]% Pfd.	Com.	% Com.
1992	**[1]725**	**[1]59.1**	**[1]477**	**[1]8.3**	**[3]453**	**[3]150**	**[3]39.2**	**[3]21.1**	**[3]5.5**	**[3]212**	**[3]55.3**
1991	[1]639	[1]47.9	[1]418	[1]8.8	[3]456	[3]161	[3]41.5	[3]21.5	[3]5.5	[3]206	[3]53.0
1990	[1]598	[1]43.0	[1]391	[1]8.7	[3]392	[3]103	[3]31.6	[3]21.2	[3]6.5	[3]201	[3]61.9
1989	518	38.9	337	10.0	343	121	43.1	20.0	7.1	140	49.8
1988	485	35.7	320	10.3	328	115	43.0	20.0	7.5	132	49.5
1987	447	30.4	302	8.5	281	97	43.8	Nil	Nil	124	56.2
1986	417	35.3	288	9.4	286	100	44.2	8.0	3.5	119	52.3
1985	385	32.1	269	11.6	262	85	41.1	8.0	3.9	114	55.0
1984	357	24.0	251	13.0	256	87	42.1	15.5	7.5	104	50.4
1983	336	21.2	241	10.1	241	88	45.0	17.0	8.7	91	46.3

Data as orig. reptd. **1.** Utility opers. only. **2.** Times int. exp. & pfd. divs. covered (pretax basis). **3.** Consolidated. **4.** Bef. spec. item(s) in 1987. **5.** Based on income before interest charges. **6.** As reptd. by Co. **7.** Incl. minority interest. NA-Not Available.

Business Summary

Indiana Energy is a holding company whose main subsidiary, Indiana Gas, distributes natural gas in north central, central, and southern Indiana; Indiana Gas does not serve Indianapolis. The IEI Investments Inc. subsidiary was formed to control non-regulated investments, including a majority interest in EnTrade Corp. (sold in December 1992), and interest in Loggins, Inc., which distributes products for distributing and using natural gas and propane gas. Revenues by customer class in recent years:

	1992	1991	1990
Residential	56%	57%	58%
Commercial	23%	23%	24%
Industrial–interruptible	11%	9%	7%
Industrial–firm	8%	7%	6%
Other	3%	4%	5%

Gas volumes sold and transported in fiscal 1992 amounted to 102.0 Bcf (97.5 Bcf in fiscal 1991), including residential sales of 41.1 Bcf (38.7 Bcf), commercial sales of 20.4 Bcf (19.4 Bcf), interruptible industrial sales of 17.7 Bcf (12.8 Bcf), firm industrial sales of 9.3 Bcf (7.8), and gas transported 13.4 Bcf (18.4 Bcf). Average revenue per Mcf was $5.75 ($5.72) for residential, $4.69 ($4.65) for commercial, $2.58 ($2.71) for interruptible industrial, and $3.56 ($3.62) for firm industrial customers. Customers served at September 30, 1992, totaled 420,665, up from 411,855 a year earlier. Degree days in fiscal 1992 amounted to 5,071, versus 4,914 in fiscal 1991.

Indiana Gas obtains the majority of its gas supplies through term contracts with producers and gas marketers, and purchases on the spot market.

Dividend Data

Dividends have been paid since 1946. A dividend reinvestment plan is available. A "poison pill" stock purchase right was adopted in 1986.

Amt of Divd. $	Date Decl.	Ex–divd. Date	Stock of Record	Payment Date
0.37	Oct. 30	Nov. 10	Nov. 17	Dec. 1'92
0.37	Jan. 11	Feb. 8	Feb. 15	Mar. 1'93
0.37	Apr. 30	May 12	May 18	Jun. 1'93
0.38¼	Jul. 30	Aug. 12	Aug. 18	Sep. 1'93
3–for–2	Jul. 30	---	Sep. 17	Oct. 1'93

Capitalization

Long Term Debt: $174,901,000 (6/93).

Common Stock: 14,967,638 shs. (no par).
Institutions hold about 17%.
Shareholders of record: 10,650.

Office—1630 N. Meridian St., Indianapolis, IN 46202. **Tel**—(317) 926-3351. **Chrmn**—D. M. Amundson. **Pres & CEO**—L. A. Ferger. **VP, Treas & CFO**—N. C. Ellerbrook. **Secy**—A. E. Ard. **VP-Investor Contact**—Anthony L. Brown (317) 321-0512. **Dirs**—D. M. Amundson, P. T. Baker, G. L. Bepko, H. J. Cofield, N. C. Ellerbrook, L. K. Evans, L. A. Ferger, O. N. Frenzel III, A. H. George, D. E. Marsh, R. P. Rechter, J. C. Shook. **Transfer Agent & Registrar**—First Chicago Trust Co. of New York, NYC. **Incorporated** in Indiana in 1945. **Empl**—1,142.

 Mark Mattke

Information Resources

NASDAQ Symbol IRIC (Incl. in Nat'l Market) Options on CBOE In S&P MidCap 400

Price	Range	P-E Ratio	Dividend	Yield	S&P Ranking	Beta
May 5'93	1993					
31⅞	33½–27	42	None	None	B–	1.65

Summary

This company provides information services to the consumer packaged goods industry in the U.S. and to a wide range of industries worldwide. Services offered assist clients in making better, more cost-effective decisions in selling and marketing their products. In September 1992, the company sold publicly 1.2 million common shares at $24 each.

Business Summary

Information Resources, Inc. (IRIC) develops and maintains computerized proprietary databases, decision support software and analytical models to assist clients, primarily in the consumer packaged goods industry, in testing and evaluating their marketing plans for new products, media advertising, pricing and sales promotions. Total store data are collected from nearly 2,700 retail outlets in 75 markets and in a number of other communities across the U.S., and from nearly 500 drug stores and 250 mass merchandise outlets. Revenues in recent years were derived as follows:

	1992	1991	1990
Information services	70%	68%	69%
Software support services	30%	32%	31%

During 1986, the company introduced InfoScan, which tracks the weekly purchases of every UPC-coded product sold in supermarkets nationwide and promotional activities that motivate consumer spending. Clients periodically receive hard-copy and electronic tracking reports, including scanner-based weekly sales data measuring volume, market share and price, together with information relating weekly store sales to promotional and merchandising conditions. The reports tabulate the purchase data by four-week periods. InfoScan provides data collected from approximately 60,000 households in the company's metro-sampling pods and mini-markets. Weekly InfoScan data may be obtained before printed four-week reports are issued using personal computers and the company's proprietary software.

The company's BehaviorScan system permits clients to measure the effects of different marketing variables on product purchases. The company can target alternate television advertising messages over cable television to groups of pre-selected households; collect household purchase data through the use of supermarket and drugstore point-of-sale scanners; and analyze the effect of client advertising.

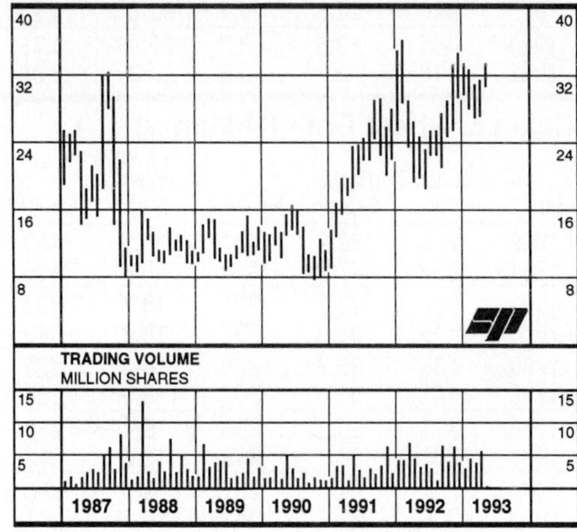

In May 1992, the company acquired Towne-Oller & Associates, Inc. in an exchange of about 690,000 shares of IRIC common stock. Towne-Oller tracks deliveries of health and beauty care products from retailer and wholesaler warehouses to 11,000 individual drug stores and 31,000 individual grocery stores. Towne-Oller represents 80% of total food and drug store health and beauty care sales.

IRIC also designs, develops and markets decision support software and executive information systems to analyze scanner-based data generated through its InfoScan service, and information contained in other databases.

Important Developments

Apr. '93— The company acquired the software and information services business operated by VideOcart Inc. in Australia for approximately $925,000.

Next earnings report expected in late July.

Per Share Data ($)

Yr. End Dec. 31	[2]1992	1991	[1]1990	1989	[2]1988	1987	1986	[2]1985	1984	1983
Tangible Bk. Val.	**7.35**	5.12	2.78	2.88	2.95	[3]3.52	[3]3.77	[3]3.06	[3]2.33	[3]1.88
Cash Flow	**1.54**	1.31	0.82	0.69	0.63	0.46	1.06	0.93	0.72	0.44
Earnings[4]	**0.79**	0.63	0.25	d0.17	0.02	d0.18	0.60	0.53	0.43	0.27
Dividends	**Nil**	Nil	Nil	Nil	Nil	Nil	Nil	Nil	Nil	Nil
Payout Ratio	**Nil**	Nil	Nil	Nil	Nil	Nil	Nil	Nil	Nil	Nil
Prices—High	**36¼**	29¼	16⅝	15⅜	16	32⅜	28½	21⅜	18¾	21⅜
Low	**18½**	9⅛	7¾	8⅞	8⅝	8	16½	14⅛	13⅜	7¾
P/E Ratio—	**46–23**	46–14	67–31	NM	NM	NM	48–28	40–27	43–31	78–28

Data as orig. reptd. Adj. for stk. divs. of 50% Jun. 1986, 100% Aug. 1983, 50% Jan. 1983. **1.** Refl. acctg. change. **2.** Refl. merger or acq. **3.** Incl. intangibles. **4.** Bef. results of disc. ops. of -0.03 in 1990, -0.63 in 1989 & spec. items of -0.07 in 1990, +0.09 in 1989. d-Deficit. NM-Not Meaningful.

Income Data (Million $)

Year Ended Dec. 31	Oper. Revs.	Oper. Inc.	% Oper. Inc. of Revs.	Cap. Exp.	Depr. & Amort.	Int. Exp.	Net Bef. Taxes	Eff. Tax Rate	[5]Net Inc.	% Net Inc. of Revs.	Cash Flow
[3]1992	**276**	**56.2**	**20.3**	**20.0**	**18.5**	**2.54**	**[4]32.2**	**40.2%**	**19.2**	**7.0**	**37.8**
1991	208	38.2	18.4	11.6	15.4	2.64	22.2	35.7%	14.2	6.9	29.6
[1,2]1990	167	24.1	14.5	9.2	10.8	3.43	[4]11.4	57.9%	4.8	2.9	15.5
[2]1989	136	20.6	15.1	7.6	14.7	5.11	[4]d3.8	NM	d2.9	NM	11.8
[3]1988	129	16.7	13.0	8.7	10.8	4.31	[4]0.5	40.7%	0.3	0.2	11.0
1987	105	9.3	8.8	17.6	10.7	1.88	d6.1	NM	d3.0	NM	7.6
1986	94	24.6	26.3	13.9	7.7	0.20	17.9	44.2%	10.0	10.7	17.7
[3]1985	75	21.7	28.9	11.7	6.5	0.13	15.9	45.1%	8.7	11.6	15.2
1984	36	13.7	38.2	12.4	4.1	0.19	10.0	38.8%	6.1	17.1	10.2
1983	21	7.0	33.4	17.2	2.3	0.23	5.4	32.0%	3.7	17.5	6.0

Balance Sheet Data (Million $)

Dec. 31	Cash	Curr. Assets	Curr. Liab.	Curr. Ratio	Total Assets	% Ret. on Assets	Long Term Debt	Common Equity	Total Cap.	% LT Debt of Cap.	% Ret. on Equity
1992	**53.6**	**142**	**53.6**	**2.6**	**264**	**8.0**	**4.7**	**187**	**204**	**2.3**	**12.0**
1991	24.9	105	52.6	2.0	189	8.3	6.6	117	130	5.1	15.3
1990	8.8	62	38.8	1.6	133	3.4	23.5	60	88	26.8	8.4
1989	1.8	51	47.4	1.1	135	NM	29.4	51	87	33.9	NM
1988	4.6	56	42.5	1.3	151	0.2	33.7	59	107	31.5	0.5
1987	7.7	61	35.4	1.7	139	NM	30.1	59	101	29.7	NM
1986	7.4	45	31.0	1.4	99	11.4	0.8	61	68	1.2	18.2
1985	8.7	35	21.5	1.6	75	13.9	0.8	48	53	1.6	20.6
1984	6.8	16	9.1	1.7	46	14.5	0.9	33	37	2.4	20.5
1983	10.1	16	9.3	1.7	38	13.9	1.0	27	29	3.3	25.0

Data as orig. reptd. **1.** Refl. acctg. change. **2.** Excl. disc. ops. **3.** Refl. merger or acq. **4.** Incl. equity in earns. of nonconsol. subs. **5.** Bef. spec. items. d-Deficit. NM-Not Meaningful.

Operating Revenues (Million $)

Quarter:	1993	1992	1991	1990
Mar.	75.7	61.5	48.0	38.3
Jun.		66.2	49.6	39.8
Sep.		71.7	51.2	42.0
Dec.		77.0	58.9	46.7
		276.4	207.7	166.7

Revenues in the three months ended March 31, 1993, advanced 23%, year to year. After a $2.2 million pretax charge for the disposal of certain non-strategic assets, net income declined 3.3%, to $3,927,000 ($0.15 a share, based on 9.2% more shares), from $4,061,000 ($0.17). Results for 1993 exclude a credit from the adoption of FAS 109 of $1,864,000 ($0.07).

Common Share Earnings ($)

Quarter:	1993	1992	1991	1990
Mar.	0.15	0.17	0.12	0.03
Jun.		0.20	0.14	0.07
Sep.		0.24	0.17	0.03
Dec.		0.18	0.20	0.12
		0.78	0.63	0.25

d-Deficit.

Dividend Data

No cash has been paid. In October 1990, the company spun off one common share of VideOcart, Inc. for every two shares of Information Resources held. VideOcart's operations consist of the development of a product that provides point-of-purchase advertising and promotion messages.

Finances

In September 1992, the company issued 1,380,000 shares of its common stock at $24.00 each. Net proceeds amounted to $31.2 million, with a significant portion used to expand the European information services operations and the remainder used for general corporate purposes, including repayment of debt.

In 1992, the company repaid a $12.5 million promissory note payable to Citicorp Credit Service, which it incurred in 1991 when it repurchased from Citicorp Credit warrants to purchase some 2.4 million IRIC common shares at $16 each.

Capitalization

Long Term Obligations: $4,718,000 (12/92).

Common Stock: 24,611,551 shs. ($0.01 par).
Institutions hold about 79%.
Shareholders: 477 of record (2/93).

Office—150 N. Clinton St., Chicago, IL 60661. **Tel**—(312) 726-1221. **Chrmn**—G. M. Fulgoni. **Vice Chrmn**—G. Eskin. **Pres & CEO**—J. Andress. **VP-CFO & Treas**—T. M. Walker. **Secy**—E. S. Berger. **Dirs**—J. G. Andress, T. J. Burrell, G. Eskin, E. E. Epstein, G. M. Fulgoni, J. D. C. Little, L. M. Lodish, E. E. Lucente, E. W. Martin, G. G. Montgomery Jr., G. L. Urban, W. Walter, T. W. Wilson Jr.. **Transfer Agent & Registrar**—Harris Trust & Savings Bank, Chicago. **Incorporated** in Delaware in 1982. **Empl**—4,707.

 Kevin J. Gooley

Intelligent Electronics

NASDAQ Symbol INEL (Incl. in Nat'l Market) In S&P MidCap 400

Price	Range	P-E Ratio	Dividend	Yield	S&P Ranking	Beta
Aug. 27'93	1993					
16¼	17½–12	20	[1]0.32	[1]2.0%	NR	2.84

Summary

This leading wholesale distributor of office productivity solutions sold its BizMart retail subsidiary in March 1993 for $270 million, realizing a gain of $12 million. Renewed focus on the company's wholesale business, together with strong industry fundamentals, should lead to favorable revenue and profit comparisons through 1994-5. Quarterly dividends were initiated in July 1993.

Current Outlook

Earnings for the fiscal year ending January 31, 1994, are estimated at $1.00 a share, up from $0.58 in 1992-3. Profits are expected to reach $1.25 in 1994-5.

In July 1993, an initial $0.08 a share quarterly dividend was declared. A special dividend of $2.00 a share was paid in June 1993.

Revenues are expected to rise sharply in 1993-4, reflecting strong demand for computers and peripherals and sales to new customers. Gross margin improvement will continue to be restricted by industrywide pricing pressures, but operating leverage will be enhanced by the higher sales.

Favorable other income comparisons, along with fewer shares outstanding, should lead to strong earnings growth for the year. Strong industry fundamentals and firmer gross margins are expected to fuel sales and earnings gains in 1994-5.

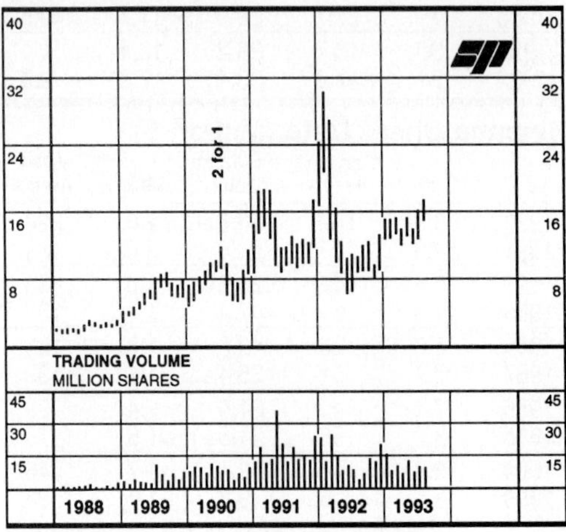

Revenues (Million $)

13 Weeks:	1993–94	1992–93	1991–92
Apr.	617	496	421
Jul.	613	467	426
Oct.		484	474
Jan.		570	516
		2,017	1,838

Net sales in the six months ended July 31, 1993, climbed 28%, year to year, reflecting strong demand for computers and peripherals and expanded systems configuration services. Margins were hurt by industrywide pricing pressures, which offset a 20% decline in SG&A expense. Operating income rose 7.7%. Following a $2.5 million increase in net investment and other income, a 92% drop in interest expense, and a $1.2 million contribution from an equity interest, net income rose 79%, to $0.48 a share on 4.6% fewer shares, from $0.26. Results exclude losses from discontinued operations of $0.06 and $0.19 in the respective periods, and a gain of $0.17 on the sale of BizMart in the 1993 interim.

Common Share Earnings ($)

13 Weeks:	1993–94	1992–93	1991–92
Apr.	0.23	0.21	0.30
Jul.	0.26	0.05	0.24
Oct.	E0.24	0.15	0.25
Jan.	E0.28	0.18	0.25
	E1.00	0.58	1.01

Important Developments

Aug. '93— INEL said it had repurchased 4.2 million shares through July 31, 1993, under two previously announced buyback plans calling for the repurchase of up to 7.5 million shares. The company indicated that the completion of the repurchase program will occur over a reasonable period of time.

Next earnings report expected in late November.

Per Share Data ($)

Yr. End Jan. 31[2]	1993	[3]1991	1990	[3]1989	1988	1987	1986
Tangible Bk. Val.	**5.64**	1.35	0.89	0.24	1.43	1.06	0.19
Cash Flow	**0.81**	1.47	1.28	0.68	0.30	0.19	0.09
Earnings[4,5]	**0.58**	1.11	1.05	0.51	0.30	0.18	0.09
Dividends	**Nil**	Nil	Nil	Nil	Nil	Nil	Nil
Payout Ratio	**Nil**	Nil	Nil	Nil	Nil	Nil	Nil
Calendar Years	**1992**	1991	1990	1989	1988	1987	1986
Prices[6]—High	**30⅜**	18¾	11⅞	8$\frac{13}{16}$	3⅛	3$\frac{5}{16}$	NA
Low	**6¼**	8¾	4$\frac{13}{16}$	2⅞	1$\frac{9}{16}$	1¼	NA
P/E Ratio—	**52–11**	17–8	11–5	17–6	11–5	18–7	NA

Data as orig. reptd. Adj. for stk. divs. of 100% Feb. 1992, 100% Jul. 1990. **1.** See Dividend Data. **2.** Yr. ended Oct. 31 prior to 1993. **3.** Refl. merger or acq. **4.** Bef. results of disc. ops. of -0.53 in 1993, -0.05 in 1986, and spec. items of -0.09 in 1993, +0.01 in 1986. **5.** Ful. dil.: 0.16 in 1987, 0.08 in 1986. **6.** Cal. yr. E-Estimated NA-Not Available.

Income Data (Million $)

Year Ended Jan. 31[1]	Revs.	Oper. Inc.	% Oper. Inc. of Revs.	Cap. Exp.	Depr.	Int. Exp.	Net Bef. Taxes	Eff. Tax Rate	[5]Net Inc.	% Net Inc. of Revs.	Cash Flow
[3]1993	**2,017**	**53.9**	**2.7**	**[4]4.6**	**8.6**	**7.42**	**[5]39.4**	**43.8%**	**22.1**	**1.1**	**30.7**
1992	NA	NA	NA	NA	NA	NA	NA	NA	NA	NA	NA
[2]1991	1,914	78.6	4.1	[4]15.4	12.6	7.23	62.9	39.3%	38.2	2.0	50.8
1990	1,459	59.1	4.1	[4]3.6	6.4	6.17	49.0	40.3%	29.3	2.0	35.6
[2]1989	712	28.4	4.0	[4]1.9	3.5	6.88	18.6	43.1%	10.6	1.5	14.1
1988	129	7.6	5.9	0.2	0.1	0.01	8.0	36.1%	5.1	4.0	5.2
1987	81	4.0	4.9	NM	0.1	0.06	4.1	44.8%	2.2	2.8	2.0
[3]1986	57	2.4	4.1	0.1	NM	0.13	2.2	50.8%	1.1	1.9	0.7

Balance Sheet Data (Million $)

Jan. 31[1]	Cash	Curr. Assets	Curr. Liab.	Curr. Ratio	Total Assets	% Ret. on Assets	Long Term Debt	Common Equity	Total Cap.	% LT Debt of Cap.	% Ret. on Equity
1993	**52**	**526**	**348**	**1.5**	**630**	**3.3**	**Nil**	**281**	**281**	**Nil**	**8.0**
1992	NA	NA	NA	NA	NA	NA	NA	NA	NA	NA	NA
1991	93	439	402	1.1	707	5.8	29.8	274	304	9.8	17.4
1990	121	338	293	1.2	442	7.6	29.5	120	149	19.8	28.5
1989	7	216	170	1.3	295	5.5	47.1	78	125	37.5	18.8
1988	19	50	31	1.6	51	13.9	Nil	20	20	Nil	29.4
1987	7	22	8	2.8	22	7.5	Nil	14	14	Nil	22.8
1986	3	13	9	1.4	13	NA	Nil	1	4	0.6	NA

Data as orig. reptd. **1.** Yr. ended Oct. 31 prior to 1993. **2.** Refl. merger or acq. **3.** Excl. disc. ops. **4.** Net. **5.** Bef. spec. items. NM-Not Meaningful. NA-Not Available.

Summary

Intelligent Electronics, Inc. is a leading wholesale distributor of office productivity solutions, including personal computers and related equipment. It sells primarily to small and medium-size businesses, through a network that consisted of over 1,700 franchised and affiliated customers as of January 30, 1993.

INEL's Reseller Network division provides wholesale distribution of microcomputers to the Intelligent (IE) Network, who in turn, offer value-added systems solutions to end-users. The Reseller Network also provides product selection, technical support, cost-efficient marketing programs and promotions, configuration and identification of marketing opportunities for the Intelligent Network. Centers in the IE Network purchase products from the company on a cost-plus basis, generally at a lower price than could be obtained independently from vendors.

The company began development of the IE Network in 1984 with the establishment of Todays Computers Business Centers, Inc. (TCBC). Operatoons were expanded greatly through the acquisitions of Entré Computer Centers, Inc. in December 1988 and Connecting Point of America, Inc. (CPA) in August 1989.

INEL's InteLogistics division was formed to provide logistics services to unaffiliated third parties. Services being developed and marketed include warehousing, freight consolidation, transportation management, inventory management, invoicing, credit and collection services, returns processing and customized information systems.

In 1992-3, sales of Apple, Hewlett Packard (HP), COMPAQ and IBM products accounted for 22%, 20%, 18% and 18% of total revenues, respectively. The company is also authorized to distribute products of 36 other vendors.

In June 1991, INEL acquired BizMart, Inc., a Texas-based chain of 57 high volume office products supercenters, for $195.8 million. In March 1993, the 105-store chain was sold to Kmart's OfficeMax unit for $270 million cash. A $12 million gain resulted from the transaction.

Dividend Data

INEL paid a special dividend of $2.00 a share on June 1, 1993, to holders of record May 17. Quarterly dividends were implemented in July 1993.

Amt of Divd. $	Date Decl.	Ex–divd. Date	Stock of Record	Payment Date
0.08	Jul. 6	Aug. 12	Aug. 18	Sep. 1'93

Finances

In July 1992, INEL sold its nine remaining company-owned reseller centers in exchange for a 31% equity interest in The Future Now (FNOW, NASDAQ), valued at $16.6 million, and additional cash and warrants.

Capitalization

Long Term Debt: None (7/93).

Common Stock: 35,867,000 shs. ($0.01 par).
Officers and directors own 20%.
Institutions hold 48%.
Shareholders: 1,008 of record (3/17/93).

Options: To buy 4,236,300 shs. at $1.56 to $15.50 ea.

Office—411 Eagleview Blvd., Exton, PA 19341. **Tel**—(215) 458-5500. **Chrmn & CEO**—R. D. Sanford. **Vice Chrmn**—M. R. Shabazian. **Pres & COO**—G. A. Pratt. **VP, CFO & Treas**—E. A. Meltzer. **VP & Secy**—Janice L. M. Longer. **VP & Investor Contact**—Stephanie D. Cohen. **Dirs**—B. M. Abelson, J. M. Ciccarelli, C. T. G. Fish, R. J. Fritz, A. S. Hoffman, W. L. Rulon-Miller, R. D. Sanford, M. R. Shabazian. **Transfer Agent**—Mellon Financial Services, Ridgefield Park, N.J. **Incorporated** in Pennsylvania in 1982. **Empl**—2,956.

 John D. Coyle, CFA

Int'l Dairy Queen

NASDAQ Symbol INDQA (Incl. in Nat'l Market) In S&P MidCap 400

Price	Range	P-E Ratio	Dividend	Yield	S&P Ranking	Beta
Aug. 4'93	1993					
16	21–16	14	None	None	B+	0.99

Summary

This company develops, franchises and services the Dairy Queen, Orange Julius, Karmelkorn Shoppe and Golden Skillet foodservice concepts. Its various chains include about 6,000 retail outlets, nearly all of which are franchises. Moderate earnings improvement is expected in both fiscal 1993 and fiscal 1994. Further repurchase of common shares appears likely.

Current Outlook

Earnings in the fiscal year ending November 30, 1993, are estimated at $1.20 a share, up from fiscal 1992's $1.12. An increase to $1.30 is expected in fiscal 1994.

Near-term initiation of cash dividends is not expected.

Sales and earnings in fiscal 1993 are expected to benefit from a modest improvement in the U.S. economy. The summer's recent extreme heat in the Northeast may help results there, but MidWest sales are likely to be hurt by rain and flooding. In fiscal 1992, service fees were boosted by a full-year contribution from more than 100 units that were converted to the Dairy Queen concept. Long-term growth opportunities include overseas expansion and a gradual upgrading to higher-volume franchise outlets, which may include stronger locations, larger units and fuller menus.

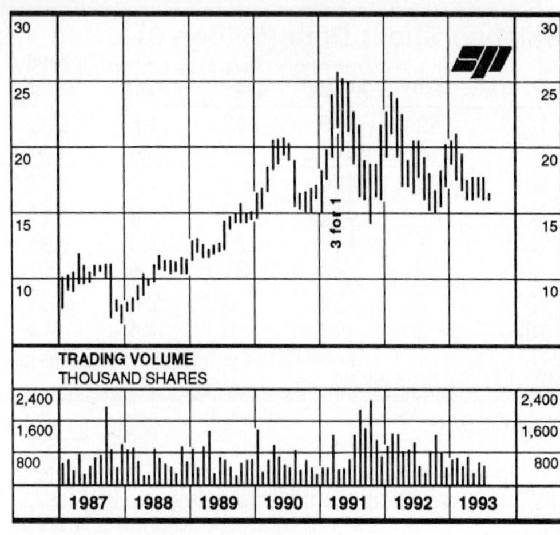

Revenues (Million $)

Quarter:	1992–93	1992	1991	1990
Feb.	58.4	56.7	58.6	57.6
May	87.3	86.5	81.2	83.5
Aug.		91.9	89.2	86.4
Nov.		62.0	59.7	55.5
		297.1	288.8	283.1

Revenues in the six months ended May 28, 1993, increased 1.6%, year to year. Net income was up 1.5%, to $13.3 million ($0.52 a share, on 3.4% fewer shares), from $13.1 million ($0.50).

Common Share Earnings ($)

Quarter:	1992–93	1992	1991	1990
Feb.	0.18	0.17	0.16	0.15
May	0.35	0.33	0.31	0.29
Aug.	E0.44	0.41	0.38	0.36
Nov.	E0.23	0.21	0.20	0.18
	E1.20	1.12	1.05	0.97

Important Developments

Jul. '93— In fiscal 1993's second quarter, service fees from franchisees were flat, year to year, as results were again hurt by inclement weather. Future comparisons are expected to be more favorable, and could benefit from new product rollouts, including a royal fudge soft-serve item and a chicken fingers basket product. At May 28, 1993, the number of INDQA-related outlets (almost all franchises) was 6,034, of which 5,388 were Dairy Queens or Treat Centers. Also, in the first six months of fiscal 1993, INDQA spent $9.4 million on share repurchases. As of July 1 (part way into the third quarter), the total number of shares outstanding was down 552,025 (2.2%) from the number at November 30, 1992. During fiscal 1992, INDQA spent $11.9 million on share repurchases.

Next earnings report expected in early September.

Per Share Data ($)

Yr. End Nov. 30	1992	1991	1990	1989	1988	[1]1987	[1]1986	1985	1984	1983
Tangible Bk. Val.[3]	**4.40**	3.69	3.09	2.70	2.03	1.50	1.00	0.49	0.38	d0.48
Cash Flow	**1.27**	1.20	1.13	0.97	0.82	0.61	0.50	0.40	0.30	0.24
Earnings	**1.12**	1.05	0.97	0.83	0.70	0.51	0.42	0.33	0.24	0.20
Dividends	**Nil**	Nil	Nil	Nil	Nil	Nil	Nil	Nil	Nil	Nil
Payout Ratio	**Nil**	Nil	Nil	Nil	Nil	Nil	Nil	Nil	Nil	Nil
Prices[2]—High	**24¼**	25¾	20¾	15¾	11⅞	11⅞	11⅞	5¾	2¾	2⅝
Low	**15**	14¼	14⅝	11⅜	7½	6⅝	4⅞	2¾	2⅛	1⅜
P/E Ratio—	**22–13**	25–14	21–15	19–14	17–11	23–13	28–12	18–8	11–9	14–7

Data as orig. reptd. Adj. for stk. divs. of 200% Apr. 1991, 400% Feb. 1986. 1. Refl. merger or acq. 2. Cal. yr. 3. Incl. intangibles. E-Estimated d-Deficit.

Income Data (Million $)

Year Ended Nov. 30	Revs.	Oper. Inc.	% Oper. Inc. of Revs.	Cap. Exp.	Depr.	Int. Exp.	Net Bef. Taxes	Eff. Tax Rate	Net Inc.	% Net Inc. of Revs.	Cash Flow
1992	**296**	**50.3**	**17.0**	**0.86**	**4.10**	**3.89**	**47.3**	**38.5%**	**29.1**	**9.8**	**33.2**
1991	287	47.4	16.5	1.61	3.87	3.81	45.4	38.5%	27.9	9.7	31.8
1990	282	46.5	16.5	1.26	4.39	3.01	43.8	39.5%	26.5	9.4	30.9
1989	254	42.1	16.6	2.28	3.96	[2]0.62	38.8	40.0%	23.3	9.2	27.2
1988	242	37.5	15.5	1.31	3.50	[2]1.76	[3]33.5	40.0%	20.1	8.3	23.6
[1]1987	210	30.6	14.6	1.68	2.92	[2]1.96	[3]26.8	44.3%	14.9	7.1	17.8
[1]1986	182	26.6	14.6	2.80	2.55	2.57	23.2	48.1%	12.1	6.6	14.6
1985	158	23.1	14.7	3.16	2.27	2.88	19.2	49.7%	9.7	6.1	11.9
1984	131	19.1	14.5	0.91	1.93	2.77	15.3	49.7%	7.7	5.9	9.6
1983	116	17.6	15.2	1.16	1.76	2.54	14.3	49.7%	7.2	6.2	8.9

Balance Sheet Data (Million $)

Nov. 30	Cash	Curr. Assets	Curr. Liab.	Curr. Ratio	Total Assets	% Ret. on Assets	Long Term Debt	Common Equity	Total Cap.	% LT Debt of Cap.	% Ret. on Equity
1992	**38.3**	**72.1**	**36.5**	**2.0**	**179**	**16.6**	**25.8**	**112.0**	**143**	**18.1**	**28.1**
1991	32.7	64.6	27.9	2.3	175	16.8	46.0	96.8	146	31.4	31.4
1990	28.8	61.4	32.2	1.9	161	18.6	41.8	83.2	129	32.5	34.0
1989	21.9	47.5	27.6	1.7	129	19.2	21.7	75.7	101	21.5	35.1
1988	7.6	33.8	26.1	1.3	115	17.4	27.0	57.7	88	30.5	40.1
1987	15.9	37.9	34.2	1.1	119	14.8	36.8	43.5	84	44.0	41.2
1986	11.8	30.0	21.6	1.4	82	15.7	27.9	29.0	60	46.5	55.7
1985	9.6	25.2	23.8	1.1	70	14.9	29.3	14.0	46	63.5	77.9
1984	5.4	19.2	18.5	1.0	63	13.3	31.1	11.4	45	69.5	59.7
1983	6.3	16.8	16.4	1.0	62	12.3	26.5	16.9	45	58.6	45.4

Data as orig. reptd. **1.** Refl. merger or acq. **2.** Net of int. inc. **3.** Incl. equity in earns. of nonconsol. subs.

Business Summary

INDQ is engaged in developing, licensing and servicing various foodservice concepts, including Dairy Queen, Orange Julius, and Karmelkorn Shoppe. In addition to separate outlets, the company has a Treat Center concept, which combines Dairy Queen menu items with products from the Orange Julius and/or Karmelkorn menus at shopping malls. It is also a franchisor of Golden Skillets in foreign markets. In October 1992, various assets related to the U.S. Golden Skillet business were assigned to a non-affiliated company.

Nearly all of the company's outlets are franchised. A sizable portion of revenue comes from sales of supplies to independently owned warehouses, which in turn sell them to franchisees, and from sales of equipment to franchisees. At November 30, 1992, the number of units open (excluding Golden Skillets in the U.S.), by concept, was:

	U.S.	Foreign	Total
Dairy Queens	4,705	593	5,298
Treat Centers	75	15	90
Subtotal	4,780	608	5,388
Orange Julius	389	133	522
Karmelkorn Shoppes	100	5	105
Golden Skillets	0	19	19
Total	5,269	765	6,034

Most Dairy Queen units are located in smaller towns and suburbs of larger cities. Some franchised units serve only soft-serve dairy products, and others offer some or all of a limited-food menu known as the Brazier product line. The Dairy Queen chain is franchised either directly by INDQ or indirectly through agreements with territorial operators. The level of franchise fees to the company within the system varies.

In 1987 and 1986, respectively, INDQ acquired its Orange Julius chain, which features blended drinks made from orange and other fruit flavors; and the Karmelkorn concept, which sells popcorn, candy and other treat items. In 1989, it acquired a 60% interest in Firstaff, Inc., which is involved in the placement of permanent and temporary office support personnel. Franchising of the Firstaff concept began in 1990.

Dividend Data

No cash dividends have been paid.

Capitalization

Long Term Debt: $24,150,000 (5/28/93).

Class A Common Stock: 15,950,870 shs. ($0.01 par); limited voting rights.
Officers and directors own 16%.
Shareholders of record: About 1,163 (1/93).

Class B Common Stock: 9,073,360 shs. ($0.01 par).
Officers and directors own 39%.
Shareholders of record: About 517 (1/93).

Office—5701 Green Valley Drive, Minneapolis, MN 55437. **Tel**—612-830-0200. **Chrmn**—J. W. Mooty. **Pres & CEO**—M. P. Sullivan. **Secy**—D. M. Bond. **EVP, Treas & Investor Contact**—F. L. Heit. **Dirs**—E. F. Dorn, R. I. Giertsen, F. L. Heit, R. Luther, R. Mithun, J. N. Mooty, J. W. Mooty, R. C. Schweigert, M. P. Sullivan. **Transfer Agent & Registrar**—Norwest Bank Minnesota, South St. Paul. **Empl**—518.

 Tom Graves, CFA

International Game Technology

NYSE Symbol IGT Options on ASE & CBOE In S&P MidCap 400

Price	Range	P-E Ratio	Dividend	Yield	S&P Ranking	Beta
Aug. 27'93	1993					
36⅛	39¾–23¾	42	0.12	0.3%	B	1.54

Summary

This fast-growing company is a leading maker of gaming machines and proprietary software systems for gaming machine networks. The company is in the process of divesting assets outside of its core businesses and had a sizable gain from such a transaction in fiscal 1993's first quarter. Earnings from IGT's primary operations are growing rapidly, aided by the development of new gaming markets. Quarterly dividends were initiated following a 2-for-1 stock split in early 1993.

Current Outlook

Earnings for the fiscal year ending September 30, 1994, are estimated at $1.05 a share (primary), up from the $0.95 expected for fiscal 1993, which includes about $0.15 from asset sale gains.

Dividends were initiated at a $0.03 quarterly rate in April 1993.

Revenues for fiscal 1994 are expected to benefit from development of new gaming markets, the debut of several large new casino/hotels in Las Vegas, replacement of slot machines at existing facilities, and additional use of progressive slot machine systems developed by IGT. Prospective growth markets for IGT machines include water-based casinos in Mississippi, Missouri, Louisiana, and Indiana; casinos on Indian land; and sales to locations in Australia, Japan, and Canada.

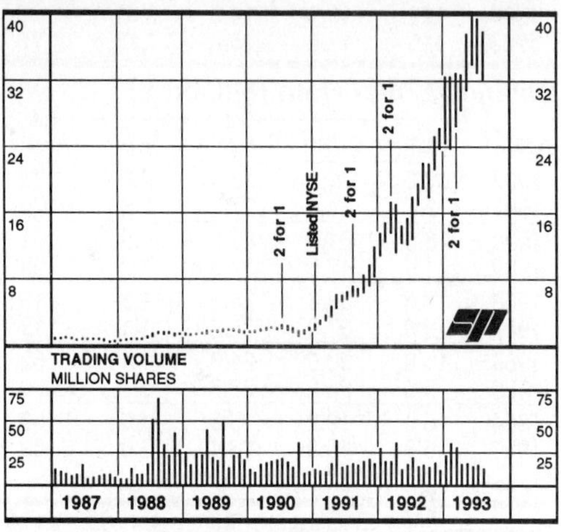

Revenues (Million $)

Quarter:	1992–93	1991–92	1990–91	1989–90
Dec.	96.0	73.6	53.6	47.6
Mar.	106.6	75.2	58.8	47.7
Jun.	141.2	123.3	61.3	58.7
Sep.	---	127.3	63.7	56.2
		399.4	237.4	210.3

Revenues for the nine months ended June 30, 1993, increased 26%, year to year. Including asset sale gains of about $0.15 a share, net income more than doubled, to $0.68 a share (primary) on some 4.1% more shares from $0.35 (adjusted).

Common Share Earnings ($)

Quarter:	1992–93	1991–92	1990–91	1989–90
Dec.	0.29	0.09	0.05	0.04
Mar.	0.15	0.09	0.06	0.04
Jun.	0.24	0.17	0.07	0.06
Sep.	E0.27	0.20	0.09	0.05
	E0.95	0.54	0.26	0.18

Important Developments

Aug. '93— A small company named Casino Data Systems (CSDS) received regulatory approval in Nevada for a new multi-site progressive system that links slot machines throughout the state. While not expected to have a sizable near-term impact on IGT's dominant position in the multi-site progressive slot machine business, CSDS's emergence appears to weaken IGT's competitive position somewhat. Meanwhile, IGT shipped more than 19,000 gaming machines in fiscal 1993's third quarter, compared with 15,000 in the year-ago period. The fiscal 1993 quarter included an initial sale of 2,800 "pachisuro" machines to the Japanese market. On a per unit basis, the Japanese machines are expected to sell for about half as much as a typical U.S. casino slot machine, and have a much lower gross profit.

Next earnings report expected in mid-November.

Per Share Data ($)

Yr. End Sep. 30[1]	1992	1991	[3]1990	[3]1989	1988	1987	1986	1985	1984	1983
Tangible Bk. Val.[2]	**1.84**	1.10	0.83	0.70	0.59	0.36	0.47	0.52	0.51	0.42
Cash Flow	**0.70**	0.36	0.26	0.17	0.15	0.07	[4]0.02	0.05	0.12	0.10
Earnings[5]	**0.54**	0.26	0.18	0.11	0.09	0.01	[4]d0.04	0.02	0.09	0.07
Dividends	**Nil**	Nil	Nil	Nil	Nil	Nil	Nil	Nil	Nil	Nil
Payout Ratio	**Nil**	Nil	Nil	Nil	Nil	Nil	Nil	Nil	Nil	Nil
Prices[6]—High	**26⅜**	11 15/16	2 17/32	2 1/16	1 11/16	1	25/32	1 5/32	1¼	1⅛
Low	**10⅞**	1 27/32	1⅛	1¼	17/32	15/32	½	½	23/32	9/16
P/E Ratio—	**49–20**	46–7	15–7	19–11	20–6	NM	NM	NM	15–8	17–8

Data as orig. reptd. Adj. for stk. divs. of 100% Mar. 1992, 100% Aug. 1991, 100% Jul. 1990. **1.** Yrs. ended Dec. 31 prior to 1986. **2.** Incl. intangibles in all yrs.. **3.** Reflects merger or acquisition. **4.** Nine mos. **5.** Bef. results of disc. opers. of +0.01 in 1989, -0.03 in 1988, and spec. items of +0.04 in 1988, +0.01 in 1987, -0.02 in 1986, +0.02 in 1982. **6.** Cal. yr. E-Estimated d-Deficit. NM-Not Meaningful.

Income Data (Million $)

Year Ended Sep. 30[1]	Revs.	Oper. Inc.	% Oper. Inc. of Revs.	Cap. Exp.	Depr.	Int. Exp.	Net Bef. Taxes	Eff. Tax Rate	[6]Net Inc.	% Net Inc. of Revs.	Cash Flow
1992	**399**	**124**	**31.1**	**33.7**	**19.0**	**13.8**	**[5]108**	**39.3%**	**64.8**	**16.2**	**83.7**
1991	237	57	23.8	22.8	12.0	9.2	[5]48	38.7%	30.2	12.7	42.2
[2]1990	210	39	18.8	14.9	9.4	6.3	30	39.7%	20.0	9.5	29.4
[2]1989	151	28	18.2	16.6	6.6	5.8	22	36.9%	13.2	8.7	19.8
[3]1988	99	18	18.6	8.8	5.5	5.9	[5]12	36.9%	7.7	7.8	13.2
1987	84	13	15.9	9.7	6.7	4.8	[5]3	119.0%	0.5	NM	6.2
[4]1986	42	d2	NM	8.5	7.8	1.2	[5]d9	NM	d5.1	NM	2.6
1985	57	3	5.8	7.9	4.4	1.3	[5]2	20.4%	1.5	2.6	5.9
1984	73	19	26.6	8.5	4.3	0.9	19	41.9%	11.1	15.2	15.4
1983	60	17	27.8	8.9	4.2	1.0	16	45.4%	8.7	14.4	12.9

Balance Sheet Data (Million $)

Sep. 30[1]	Cash	Curr. Assets	Curr. Liab.	Ratio	Total Assets	% Ret. on Assets	Long Term Debt	Common Equity	Total Cap.	% LT Debt of Cap.	% Ret. on Equity
1992	**149**	**323**	**66.1**	**4.9**	**490**	**15.3**	**114**	**214**	**351**	**32.5**	**37.8**
1991	126	227	42.6	5.3	346	10.9	113	124	254	44.6	28.0
1990	22	125	44.2	2.8	209	10.7	28	93	135	20.5	23.3
1989	16	108	39.6	2.7	170	8.8	24	82	115	20.8	17.6
1988	4	79	30.7	2.6	128	5.5	18	67	91	19.9	14.2
1987	3	57	24.9	2.3	109	NM	49	29	82	60.0	NM
1986	2	51	27.1	1.9	95	NM	3	60	68	4.3	NM
1985	0	51	18.1	2.8	94	1.6	2	66	76	3.0	2.3
1984	0	50	18.0	2.8	94	12.9	3	64	76	3.3	19.0
1983	1	40	14.7	2.7	78	12.3	3	52	63	4.4	18.1

Data as orig. reptd. **1.** Yrs. ended Dec. 31 prior to 1986. **2.** Reflects merger or acquisition. **3.** Excl. disc. opers. **4.** Nine mos. **5.** Incl. equity in earns. of nonconsol. subs. **6.** Bef. results of disc. opers. in 1989, 1988, and spec. item(s) in 1988, 1987, 1986, 1982. d-Deficit. NM-Not Meaningful.

Business Summary

IGT is likely the world's largest manufacturer of coin-operated casino products, such as slot and video machines. Also, IGT has developed and has interests in multi-location progressive slot machine systems located in Nevada, Atlantic City, Macau, Mississippi and Deadwood, S.D. In these systems, which link machines at various sites, large jackpots can be won by gamblers. IGT also makes specialized video gaming terminals (VGTs), for lotteries and other applications, and sells proprietary systems that monitor VGTs.

Contributions by business segments in fiscal 1992 (progressive systems included in gaming operations):

	Revs.	Profits
Gaming manufacturing........	59%	59%
Gaming & casino operations	41%	41%

Legalization and use of coin-operated gaming machines is growing in both the U.S. and overseas. In fiscal 1992, IGT sold more than 46,000 gaming machines, up from 31,000 the year before. This included steady demand from Nevada casinos, plus increasing sales to riverboats, Native American casinos and gaming facilities in several small Colorado towns. Also, IGT had higher sales to North American VGT jurisdictions and to Australia, which has been IGT's most important market abroad.

In the U.S., Nevada and Atlantic City have the largest installed base of gaming machines. IGT estimates that it manufactured about 57% of the approximately 151,000 gaming machines in Nevada and about 38% of the approximately 22,000 machines in Atlantic City.

IGT is in the process of divesting other assets, including its majority interest in a relatively small casino business.

Dividend Data

Quarterly dividends were initiated following a 2-for-1 stock split in March 1993.

Amt. of Divd. $	Date Decl.	Ex-divd. Date	Stock of Record	Payment Date
2-for-1	Feb. 23	Mar. 18	Mar. 10	Mar. 17'93
0.03	Apr. 14	Apr. 26	May 1	Jun. 1'93
0.03	Jun. 30	Jul. 27	Aug. 2	Sep. 1'93

Capitalization

Long Term Debt: $92,236,000 (6/93), incl. $73,540,000 of 5½% conv. sub. notes.

Common Stock: 122,571,254 shs. ($0.000625 par).
Officers & directors own about 14%.
Institutions hold some 64%.
Shareholders of record: About 3,516.

Office—520 South Rock Blvd., Reno, NV 89502. **Tel**—(702) 688-0100. **Chrmn & CEO**—C. N. Mathewson. **Pres**—J. J. Russell. **SVP-Secy**—R. D. Pike. **VP-Fin & CFO & Investor Contact**—G. Thomas Baker. **Dirs**—A. J. Crosson, W. K. Keating, C. N. Mathewson, W. L. Nelson, F. B. Rentschler, J. J. Russell, C. B. Williams. **Transfer Agent & Registrar**—Continental Stock Transfer & Trust Co., NYC. **Incorporated** in Nevada in 1980. **Empl**—2,600.

 Tom Graves, CFA

International Multifoods

NYSE Symbol IMC In S&P MidCap 400

Price	Range	P-E Ratio	Dividend	Yield	S&P Ranking	Beta
Sep. 27'93	1993					
21¾	27½–20	NM	0.80	3.7%	B+	1.04

Summary

This diversified food company has evolved into a major processor and distributor of various specialty food products in the U.S., Canada and Venezuela. IMC incurred a $36.3 million ($1.88 per share) after-tax charge in fiscal 1993-94's second quarter in order to better focus on its specialty distribution and bakery businesses. Operating profits in fiscal 1994-95 may continue to be held back by difficult U.S. foodservice industry conditions.

Current Outlook

Share earnings for the fiscal year ending February 28, 1995, are projected at $2.35, up from fiscal 1993-94's estimated $0.22, which includes a $1.88 restructuring charge.

The dividend is expected to remain at $0.20 quarterly.

Sales growth through fiscal 1994-95 is expected to be modest, limited by further pricing pressures in economically sensitive vending and foodservice markets. Canadian businesses may be further restrained by economic weakness and competitive bakery flour markets. Venezuelan profits should benefit from greater volumes, but restricted by pricing pressures for industrial flour.

Net Sales (Million $)

Quarter:	1993-94	1992-93	1991-92	1990-91
May	556	548	553	548
Aug.	522	542	541	525
Nov.	---	597	635	577
Feb.	---	537	552	542
	---	2,224	2,281	2,192

Sales for the six months ended August 31, 1993, were down 1.2%, year to year, reflecting declines in all three business segments. Cost of sales fell 1.5%, and following a restructuring charge of $47.5 million, there was a pretax loss of $34.9 million, versus income of $25.3 million. After tax credits of $14.1 million, against taxes at 39.9%, the net loss was $20.8 million ($1.08 a share), in contrast to net income of $15.2 million ($0.78).

Common Share Earnings ($)

Quarter:	1993-94	1992-93	1991-92	1990-91
May	0.33	0.31	0.31	0.27
Aug.	d1.41	0.47	0.44	0.39
Nov.	E0.78	0.80	0.77	0.72
Feb.	E0.52	0.55	0.48	0.43
	E0.22	2.13	2.00	1.81

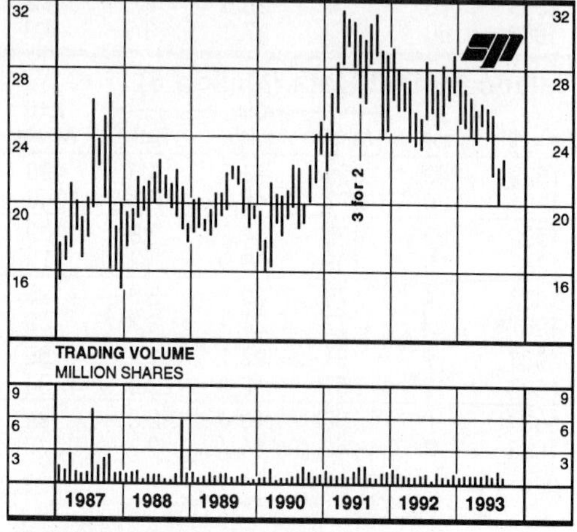

Important Developments

Sep. '93— IMC directors approved several actions to more clearly focus the company's assets and energies on its specialty distribution and bakery businesses, while immediately enhancing shareholder returns. These actions include: the possible divestiture of its Prepared Foods division (approximately 15% of fiscal 1992-93 revenues); the continued investment in internal growth opportunities and acquisitions to bolster core businesses; implementation of a share repurchase program of up to 2.5 million shares (approximately 13% of those outstanding); and the disposal of several underperforming assets and reorganization of remaining businesses to reduce costs. IMC incurred charges of $36.3 million after-tax ($1.88 per share) during fiscal 1993-94's second quarter to reflect these actions.

Next earnings report expected in mid-December.

Per Share Data ($)

Yr. End Feb. 28	1993	[1]1992	[1]1991	[1]1990	[1]1989	[1]1988	[1]1987	[1]1986	1985	1984
Tangible Bk. Val.	**16.64**	[2]16.19	10.50	9.08	9.55	11.99	11.91	8.63	10.92	11.13
Cash Flow	**3.62**	3.66	3.49	2.94	3.06	2.60	1.69	2.13	1.95	2.47
Earnings[3]	**2.13**	2.00	1.81	1.31	1.66	1.51	0.85	1.35	1.18	1.79
Dividends	**0.800**	0.793	0.787	0.787	0.787	0.787	0.784	0.783	0.783	0.770
Payout Ratio	**38%**	40%	46%	61%	43%	52%	95%	58%	66%	43%
Calendar Years	**1992**	1991	1990	1989	1988	1987	1986	1985	1984	1983
Prices—High	**29¼**	31½	24¹⁵⁄₁₆	22¼	22⁹⁄₁₆	26½	20¹⁵⁄₁₆	19¼	14¹¹⁄₁₆	16⁵⁄₁₆
Low	**23¼**	22	16¹⁄₁₆	18³⁄₁₆	17⁵⁄₁₆	15	15	11¼	10¼	12¹⁵⁄₁₆
P/E Ratio—	**14–11**	16–11	14–9	17–14	14–10	18–10	25–18	14–8	12–9	9–7

Data as orig. reptd. Adj. for stk. divs. of 50% Jul. 1991, 50% Jul. 1986. **1.** Refl. merger or acq. **2.** Incl. intangibles. **3.** Bef. results of disc. ops. of +1.57 in 1987, and spec. item(s) of -0.88 in 1992. d-Deficit. E-Estimated.

Income Data (Million $)

Year Ended Feb. 28	Revs.	Oper. Inc.	% Oper. Inc. of Revs.	Cap. Exp.	Depr.	Int. Exp.	[3]Net Bef. Taxes	Eff. Tax Rate	[4]Net Inc.	% Net Inc. of Revs.	Cash Flow
1993	**2,224**	**105**	**4.7**	**45.7**	**28.8**	**14.6**	**66.1**	**37.6%**	**41.2**	**1.9**	**69.8**
[1]1992	2,281	118	5.2	51.2	32.4	21.6	67.4	42.0%	[5]39.1	1.7	71.3
[1]1991	2,192	122	5.5	57.3	32.7	24.5	66.2	46.9%	35.2	1.6	67.7
[1]1990	2,075	101	4.9	69.6	31.6	29.8	45.6	44.5%	25.3	1.2	56.7
[1]1989	1,874	90	4.8	56.0	29.6	23.7	64.1	45.2%	[5]35.1	1.9	64.5
[1]1988	1,698	90	5.3	65.5	23.8	17.5	58.0	43.0%	[5]33.1	1.9	56.7
[1,2]1987	1,403	72	5.1	35.3	17.8	14.1	37.1	50.9%	18.2	1.3	35.8
[1]1986	1,355	68	5.0	43.0	14.3	14.6	44.9	44.4%	24.9	1.8	39.0
1985	1,211	57	4.7	30.5	14.1	15.1	35.6	39.0%	21.7	1.8	35.6
1984	1,067	61	5.7	25.4	12.4	11.9	53.4	38.3%	32.9	3.1	45.2

Balance Sheet Data (Million $)

Feb. 28	Cash	Curr. Assets	Curr. Liab.	Curr. Ratio	Total Assets	% Ret. on Assets	Long Term Debt	Common Equity	Total Cap.	% LT Debt of Cap.	% Ret. on Equity
1993	**11.0**	**416**	**243**	**1.7**	**803**	**5.2**	**167**	**322**	**512**	**32.6**	**12.9**
1992	4.2	413	285	1.4	768	5.0	104	313	436	23.8	12.3
1991	6.0	428	312	1.4	806	4.2	115	321	474	24.3	11.2
1990	17.7	474	348	1.4	844	3.2	135	303	476	28.3	8.4
1989	33.7	396	236	1.7	716	5.0	136	297	466	29.3	11.6
1988	32.8	459	282	1.6	788	4.6	101	350	490	20.6	9.7
1987	50.9	380	224	1.7	645	2.6	42	330	406	10.3	6.0
1986	12.4	348	269	1.3	626	4.4	85	228	345	24.6	10.9
1985	13.3	284	146	1.9	505	4.5	94	224	344	27.2	9.7
1984	8.1	259	109	2.4	460	7.1	95	218	338	28.0	15.1

Data as orig. reptd. **1.** Refl. merger or acq. **2.** Excl. disc. ops. **3.** Incl. equity in earns. of nonconsol. subs. **4.** Bef. results of disc. ops. & spec. item(s). **5.** Refl. acctg. change.

Business Summary

International Multifoods is a diversified international food company. Its North American agriculture segment, which had 1990-1 sales of $252 million, was sold in December 1991, for $146 million in cash. Contributions by market in fiscal 1992-93:

	Sales	Profits
U.S. foodservice	75%	44%
Canadian foods	13%	24%
Venezuelan foods	12%	32%

The U.S. foodservice segment is comprised of the prepared foods group, which processes and sells prepared food products (appetizers, ethnic foods, specialty meats, seafood and bakery products) to commercial and non-commercial customers, convenience stores and warehouse clubs; and the specialty distribution group, which distributes food products to U.S. vending operators (VSA) and specialty ingredients to pizza outlets, Mexican and Italian restaurants, and delicatessens (Pueringer).

Canadian foods include consumer and industrial flour, mixes, oat cereals, pickles and relishes sold under names including Robin Hood, Bick's and Old Mill.

Venezuelan foods consist of consumer and industrial foods such as flours, oat products and specialty spices sold under names including Robin Hood, Juana, Monica, Lassie and Payara; this unit is also a supplier of animal feeds.

Dividend Data

Dividends have been paid since 1923. A dividend reinvestment plan is available. A "poison pill" stock purchase rights plan was adopted in 1986.

Amt of Divd. $	Date Decl.	Ex–divd. Date	Stock of Record	Payment Date
0.20	Dec. 11	Mar. 23	Mar. 29	Apr. 15'93
0.20	May 14	Jun. 22	Jun. 28	Jul. 15'93
0.20	Jun. 25	Sep. 22	Sep. 28	Oct. 15'93
0.20	Sep. 20	Dec. 21	Dec. 28	Jan. 17'94

Capitalization

Long Term Debt: $174,800,000 (8/93).

Red. Preferred Stock: $3,800,000.

Common Stock: 19,451,776 shs. ($0.10 par).
Archer-Daniels-Midland Co. owns 8.3%, FMR Corp. 6.9%, and Hotchkis & Wiley 6.4%.
Institutions hold about 60%.
Shareholders: 5,013.

Office—33 South Sixth St. (P.O. Box 2942), Minneapolis, MN 55402-0942. **Tel**—(612) 340-3300. **Chrmn & Pres**—A. Luiso. **VP & Secy**—F. W. Bonvino. **VP & Treas**—K. M. Erickson. **Investor Contact**—Yolanda Scharton. **Dirs**—W. A. Andres, J. G. Fifield, A. Luiso, R. M. Price, N. L. Reding, J. D. Rehm, L. D. Rice, P. S. Willmott. **Transfer Agent & Registrar**—Norwest Bank Minnesota, South St. Paul. **Incorporated** in Delaware in 1969; business established in 1892. **Empl**—8,341.

 Kenneth A. Shea

International Technology

NYSE Symbol ITX In S&P MidCap 400

Price	Range	P-E Ratio	Dividend	Yield	S&P Ranking	Beta
Oct. 5'93	1993					
4	7⅜–4	NM	None	None	B–	0.94

Summary

This company provides a broad range of environmental management services used for assessment, decontamination and remediation of situations involving hazardous substances. Following a loss in 1992-93, earnings fell sharply in the first quarter of 1993-94 on weak commercial demand. Profitability should continue for the balance of 1993-94, aided by cost control efforts, and earnings should improve in 1994-95.

Current Outlook

Earnings for the fiscal year ending March 31, 1994, are estimated at $0.30 a share, versus the $0.06 loss (excl. a $0.32 a share loss from disc. opers., and a $0.39 credit from an acctg. change) in 1992-93. EPS for 1994-95 are seen at $0.40.

Dividends are not likely to be paid in the foreseeable future.

Sales for the balance of fiscal 1993-94 should improve modestly, reflecting weak demand in the commercial market. An estimated $240 million Hanford cleanup contract and a $218 million analytical services contract are currently under protest by competitors. Profitability should benefit from continued cost-containment efforts, which will offset a higher tax rate. Earnings should continue to improve in 1994-95.

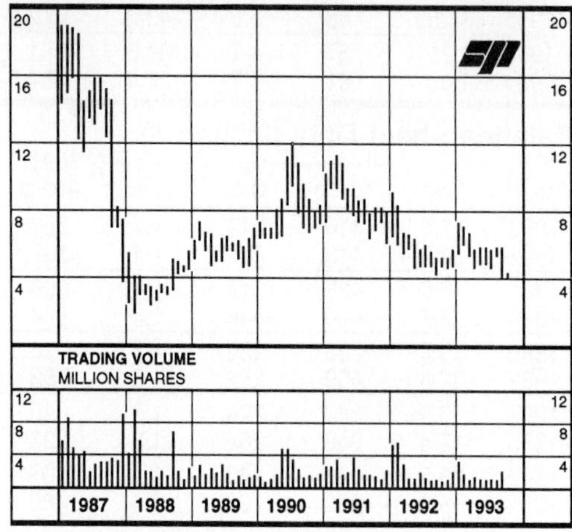

Net Sales (Million $)

Quarter:	1993–94	1992–93	[1]1991–92	1990–91
Jun.	102.5	102.6	96.0	89.4
Sep.		102.8	109.6	100.6
Dec.		101.7	105.9	106.9
Mar.		103.5	109.0	110.3
		410.5	420.5	407.2

Sales for the three months ended June 30, 1993, were virtually flat, year to year. Profitability was penalized by the weak commercial sector and, in the absence of a $3.5 million gain from the sale of stock options, and after taxes at 39.0%, versus 36.0%, earnings per share dropped 57%, to $0.06, from $0.14. Results exclude a $0.39 credit from an accounting change in the 1992-93 interim.

Common Share Earnings ($)

Quarter:	1993–94	1992–93	[1]1991–92	1990–91
Jun.	0.06	0.14	0.08	0.12
Sep.	E0.05	0.06	0.32	0.13
Dec.	E0.08	d0.13	0.07	0.13
Mar.	E0.11	d0.13	d0.20	0.10
	E0.30	d0.06	0.27	0.48

Important Developments

Aug. '93— International Technology received an eight-year, $218 million contract from a unit of Westinghouse Electric (NYSE: WX), for laboratory testing services at the Department of Energy's Hanford site in Richland, Wash. The contract has a five-year option period. Subsequently, a protest was filed by EcoTek Laboratory Services, Inc.

May '93— ITX said that it sold or closed several businesses in Europe, but believes the international market will be strong long term and is pursuing opportunities on a project basis. A realignment and streamlining of ITX's business resulted in a pretax restructuring charge of $8.4 million in the fourth quarter of 1992-93. Management noted that the streamlining, along with reduced costs and increasing marketing efficiency, are key parts of its plan to improve profitability.

Next earnings report expected in late October.

Per Share Data ($)

Yr. End Mar. 31	1993	1992	1991	1990	1989	1988	[2]1987	[2]1986	1985	[2]1984
Tangible Bk. Val.	**2.85**	2.62	2.75	2.19	1.72	1.44	4.00	4.28	2.50	2.15
Cash Flow	**0.51**	0.81	0.82	0.81	0.58	0.38	0.62	0.85	0.50	0.49
Earnings[3]	**d0.06**	0.27	0.48	0.42	0.24	d0.12	0.28	0.58	0.32	0.34
Dividends	**Nil**	Nil	Nil	Nil	Nil	Nil	Nil	Nil	Nil	Nil
Payout Ratio	**Nil**	Nil	Nil	Nil	Nil	Nil	Nil	Nil	Nil	Nil
Calendar Years	**1992**	1991	1990	1989	1988	1987	1986	1985	1984	1983
Prices—High	**9⅛**	11⅜	12⅛	7⅜	5⅝	19	27⅜	15½	6¼	5⅛
Low	**4¼**	6⅛	6⅜	4⅝	1⅞	3¾	13⅜	4⅞	4	4⅞
P/E Ratio—	**NM**	NM	25–13	18–11	23–8	NM	98–48	27–9	19–13	16–15

Data as orig. reptd. Adj. for stk. div(s) of 100% Sep. 1986, 50% May 1985. **1.** From continuing operations. **2.** Reflects merger or acquisition. **3.** Bef. results of disc. opers. of -0.32 in 1993, -0.52 in 1992, -3.68 in 1988, & spec. item(s) of +0.39 in 1993. d-Deficit. E-Estimated NM-Not Meaningful.

Income Data (Million $)

Year Ended Mar. 31	Revs.	Oper. Inc.	% Oper. Inc. of Revs.	Cap. Exp.	Depr.	Int. Exp.	Net Bef. Taxes	Eff. Tax Rate	[4]Net Inc.	% Net Inc. of Revs.	Cash Flow
1993	**411**	**43.6**	**10.6**	**15.6**	**19.2**	**11.7**	**d0.9**	**NM**	**d2.1**	**NM**	**17.1**
[1]1992	420	37.3	8.9	33.2	18.2	11.4	9.7	8.5%	8.9	2.1	27.1
1991	407	38.3	9.4	46.6	11.5	9.7	18.9	16.0%	15.9	3.9	27.4
1990	307	31.4	10.2	22.7	12.8	6.9	15.5	13.0%	13.5	4.4	26.2
1989	265	26.2	9.9	18.2	11.6	6.9	7.9	4.3%	7.6	2.9	18.7
[1]1988	209	13.8	6.6	53.7	15.0	4.7	d5.8	NM	d3.7	NM	11.3
[2]1987	237	27.4	11.6	76.2	10.0	6.5	[3]13.3	40.2%	8.0	3.4	17.9
[2]1986	208	38.9	18.8	51.7	7.2	2.9	[3]29.5	47.6%	15.4	7.4	22.6
1985	144	18.5	12.8	22.5	4.6	3.2	[3]11.5	45.0%	6.3	4.4	9.8
[2]1984	94	13.4	14.3	16.1	3.4	3.3	[3]8.1	44.4%	4.5	4.8	7.6

Balance Sheet Data (Million $)

Mar. 31	Cash	Curr. Assets	Curr. Liab.	Curr. Ratio	Total Assets	% Ret. on Assets	Long Term Debt	Common Equity	Total Cap.	% LT Debt of Cap.	% Ret. on Equity
1993	**8.7**	**155**	**97.9**	**1.6**	**369**	**NM**	**116**	**106**	**222**	**52.2**	**NM**
1992	9.4	162	92.6	1.7	382	2.4	136	99	236	57.9	8.7
1991	14.7	138	88.8	1.5	356	4.8	101	106	208	48.7	16.4
1990	29.2	128	74.0	1.7	307	4.4	76	87	164	46.5	16.9
1989	8.7	80	47.1	1.7	297	2.6	85	72	159	53.7	11.1
1988	8.2	79	39.9	2.0	292	NM	97	65	166	58.5	NM
1987	11.0	79	47.5	1.7	307	3.1	103	132	258	39.7	6.2
1986	6.0	65	35.6	1.8	203	7.3	31	118	167	18.4	16.3
1985	2.9	45	23.0	1.9	130	5.7	39	43	107	36.3	13.1
1984	1.9	24	16.7	1.4	90	4.9	12	37	73	16.6	15.6

Data as orig. reptd. **1.** Excl. disc. opers. **2.** Reflects merger or acquisition. **3.** Incl. equity in earns. of nonconsol. subs. **4.** Bef. spec. item(s). d-Deficit. NM-Not Meaningful.

Business Summary

International Technology provides a broad range of environmental management services, technologies and specialty products used for assessment, decontamination and remediation of situations involving hazardous chemicals and for the detoxification and destruction of hazardous substances. In April 1993, the company realigned its existing business into three areas. Sales in recent years were derived as follows:

	1992–93	1991–92
Environmental services	69%	67%
Construction and Remediation services......	17%	18%
Analytical services	14%	14%

Sales to U.S. government agencies, including the Departments of Defense and Energy, accounted for 45% of total sales in 1992-93, versus 37% in 1991-92.

The company's projects include the cleanup of rivers, streams and groundwater contaminated by chemical substances; buildings, production facilities and storage sites contaminated with hazardous chemical and/or radioactive materials; and land disposal sites.

In May 1992, ITX completed the sale of the manufacturing operations of Pollution Control Systems (PCS) to Koch Engineering for some $21 million. In the fourth quarter of 1991-92, the company realized a $13.1 million net gain from the disposition, and recorded an increase in the loss provision for the disposition of its transportation, treatment and disposal business of $32.7 million, which included the writeoff of its $30.4 million investment in the disposal and transportation operations of Laidlaw Environmental Services of California.

Dividend Data

No dividends have ever been paid. A "poison pill" stock purchase right was issued in 1989.

Finances

In September 1993, ITX completed the public sale of 2.4 million depositary shares (24,000 shares of 7% cumulative convertible exchangeable preferred stock) at $25 each, through lead underwriter Smith Barney Shearson, Inc. The shares will be redeemable on or after September 30, 1996. Net proceeds of $57.9 million will be used to reduce debt by redeeming a portion of its 9⅝% senior notes due 1996 and paying down its credit facility.

Capitalization

Long Term Debt: $114,586,000 (6/93), incl. $75 million of 9⅝% notes. (Excl. $47.3 million of long-term liabilities of discontinued operations.)

Common Stock: 33,273,610 shs. ($1 par). Institutions hold approximately 45%.

7% Cum. Conv. Pfd. Stk.: 24,000 shs. ($100 par). Shareholders: 2,244 of record (6/93).

Office—23456 Hawthorne Blvd., Torrance, CA 90505. **Tel**—(310) 378-9933. **Chrmn**—M. H. Hutchison. **Pres & CEO**—R. B. Sheh. **SVP & CFO**—A. J. DeLuca. **SVP & Secy**—E. Schwartz. **Investor Contact**—Pat Boldt. **Dirs**—D. S. Burns, R. S. Cunningham, R. W. Davis, R. R. Dockson, M. N. Hammes, J. H. Hutchison, M. H. Hutchison, R. R. Knowland, J. C. McGill, R. B. Sheh, J. O. Vance. **Transfer Agent & Registrar**—First National Bank of Boston, Canton, Mass. **Incorporated** in Delaware in 1983. **Empl**—3,477.

 Stewart Scharf

Iowa-Illinois Gas & Electric

NYSE Symbol IWG In S&P MidCap 400

Price	Range	P–E Ratio	Dividend	Yield	S&P Ranking	Beta
Jul. 30'93	1993					
23⅞	24⅜–19	14	1.73	7.2%	B+	0.34

Summary

This company sells gas and electricity in the Quad Cities area of Iowa and Illinois and several other cities in Iowa. The fuel mix during 1992 was 64% coal and 36% nuclear. Earnings should rebound in 1993, owing to higher electric and gas sales, greater contributions from nonregulated operations, and favorable rate relief. Diversified businesses comprised 23% of consoldated 1992 earnings per share and profitability looks even more promising for 1993 with the acquisition of an oil and gas company. With slow sales growth projected, higher earnings in the future will depend on IWG's success in controlling costs.

Current Outlook

Share earnings for 1993 are estimated at $1.80, up from $1.45 in 1992. Earnings for 1994 are projected at $1.85 a share.

The minimum expectation is for dividends to continue at $0.43¼ quarterly.

Anticipated higher earnings for 1993 primarily should reflect the utility operations return to more normal kwh sales levels, as compared to a 3.3% decline in 1992, owing to the mildest summer on record. Profitability should also benefit from 1992 rate increases and an $11.5 million Illinois rate order in July 1993. Diversified operations were expanded with the acquistion of Medallion Petroleum Inc. and the formation of Medallion Production Co. to manage all oil and gas operations.

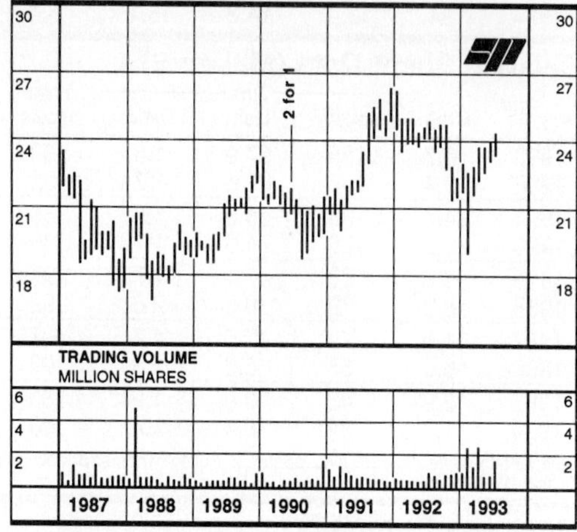

Operating Revenues (Million $)

Quarter:	1994	1993	1992	1991
Mar.	---	162	135	143
Jun.	---	115	107	115
Sep.	---	---	113	123
Dec.	---	---	142	132
	---	---	498	513

Operating revenues for the six months ended June 30, 1993, rose 14%, year to year, reflecting higher natural gas sales and new Iowa electric and gas rates. Operating expenses increased at a slower pace and operating income advanced 17%. Following 48% higher contributions from InterCoast Energy and lower interest charges, net income was up 39%. After preferred and preference dividend requirements, share earnings were $0.99, on 9.3% more shares, versus $0.75.

Common Share Earnings ($)

Quarter:	1994	1993	1992	1991
Mar.	E0.50	0.58	0.41	0.44
Jun.	E0.40	0.41	0.34	0.48
Sep.	E0.70	E0.56	0.46	0.71
Dec.	E0.25	E0.25	0.24	0.23
	E1.85	E1.80	1.45	1.86

Important Developments

Jul. '93— IWG received an order from the Illinois Commerce Commission granting a $9.6 million increase in electric rates and a $1.9 million increase in gas rates. The new rates will be effective in August 1993. Separately, a decision in the May 1993 request for a $14.7 million increase in gas and electric rates from the Iowa Utilities Board (IUB) is expected within 10 months. Also, in January 1993, the IUB approved revised requests which provide for annual increases of $10.4 million in electric revenues and $5.4 million in gas revenues. In May 1993, the Medallion Production Co. subsidiary acquired, for more than $2.5 million, an interest in two wells producing about 620 bbl. of oil per day and 900 Mcf of gas per day, located in Beauregard Parish, LA. Medallion has interests in 480 oil and gas properties and operates 160 wells. Proved reserves now total 14 million bbl. of oil.

Next earnings report expected in late October.

Per Share Data ($)

Yr. End Dec. 31	1992	1991	1990	1989	1988	1987	1986	1985	1984	1983
Tangible Bk. Val.	**16.81**	16.46	16.40	16.08	15.60	15.09	14.46	14.12	13.46	12.76
Earnings[1]	**1.45**	1.86	1.99	2.11	2.10	2.00	1.96	2.04	2.07	2.10
Dividends	**1.73**	1.71	1.67	1.63	1.59	1.52	1.45	1.37	1.30	1.24
Payout Ratio	**119%**	92%	84%	77%	76%	76%	74%	67%	63%	59%
Prices—High	**26¼**	26⅜	23¼	23⅛	20¾	23½	23⅜	18⅛	13$\frac{13}{16}$	13¾
Low	**21⅜**	20	18¾	18$\frac{9}{16}$	16⅞	17¼	17¼	13$\frac{5}{16}$	10¾	10$\frac{9}{16}$
P/E Ratio—	**18–15**	14–11	12–9	11–9	10–8	12–9	12–9	9–7	7–5	7–5

Data as orig. reptd. Adj. for stk. divs. of 100% Jun. 1990. **1.** Bef. spec item(s) of +0.19 in 1987. E-Estimated

Income Data (Million $)

Year Ended Dec. 31	Revs.	Depr.	Maint.	Oper. Ratio	[1]Fxd. Chgs. Cover.	Constr. Credits	Eff. Tax Rate	[2]Net Inc.	% Return On Revs.	% Return On [3]Invest. Capital	% Return On Com. Equity
1992	**498**	**53.9**	**39.5**	**87.2%**	**2.80**	**1.1**	**24.3%**	**45.4**	**9.1**	**5.2**	**8.6**
1991	513	48.5	39.4	85.3%	3.35	1.4	30.7%	54.4	10.6	6.4	11.4
1990	485	48.7	36.7	83.8%	3.50	2.7	27.8%	55.5	11.4	6.9	12.2
1989	494	50.1	29.8	83.8%	3.76	2.9	32.2%	58.5	11.8	7.6	13.2
1988	496	48.1	26.3	83.2%	4.00	1.6	39.3%	58.4	11.8	8.1	13.6
1987	478	46.0	27.0	81.8%	4.40	2.2	44.1%	55.7	11.6	8.5	13.5
1986	538	41.7	24.1	84.0%	3.84	4.2	46.9%	57.8	10.7	9.2	13.8
1985	562	40.1	22.8	83.9%	3.26	5.6	43.3%	59.3	10.5	9.8	14.7
1984	569	37.7	24.1	84.4%	3.20	8.1	43.5%	60.6	10.6	10.2	15.6
1983	514	31.8	20.8	86.4%	3.33	28.2	34.2%	59.5	11.6	9.3	16.9

Balance Sheet Data (Million $)

Dec. 31	Gross Prop.	Capital Expend.	Net Prop.	% Earn. on Net Prop.	Total Cap.	[4]LT Debt	Capitalization [4]% LT Debt	Capitalization Pfd.	Capitalization % Pfd.	Capitalization Com.	Capitalization % Com.
1992	**1,567**	**74**	**998**	**6.5**	**1,434**	**599**	**51.5**	**68**	**5.9**	**496**	**42.6**
1991	1,503	62	969	7.8	1,341	560	52.2	69	6.4	444	41.4
1990	1,464	58	944	8.3	1,247	502	51.5	30	3.1	442	45.4
1989	1,427	51	942	8.4	1,197	479	50.8	30	3.2	433	46.0
1988	1,398	45	952	8.6	1,121	446	49.7	31	3.4	421	46.9
1987	1,378	47	968	8.9	1,036	389	47.0	31	3.8	407	49.2
1986	1,369	44	967	8.9	946	319	43.1	31	4.3	389	52.6
1985	1,329	41	971	9.2	983	349	44.3	68	8.7	371	47.0
1984	1,323	52	998	8.9	946	352	46.1	70	9.1	342	44.8
1983	1,286	92	996	7.2	925	352	46.1	100	13.1	311	40.8

Data as orig. reptd. **1.** Times int. exp. & pfd. divs. covered (pretax basis). **2.** Bef. spec. items. **3.** Based on income bef. interest charges. **4.** Incl. capital lease oblig.

Business Summary

Iowa-Illinois Gas and Electric Company delivers natural gas and electricity in the Quad Cities area (Davenport and Bettendorf, Iowa, and Rock Island, Moline and East Moline, Ill.), Iowa City and Fort Dodge, Iowa. Gas is also delivered to Cedar Rapids and Ottumwa, Iowa. As of June 30, 1993, the company had approximately 202,000 retail electric customers and 242,000 gas customers. Contributions in 1992 were:

	Revs.	Profits
Electric	57%	76%
Gas	33%	15%
InterCoastal	10%	9%

The fuel mix for electric generation in 1992 was 64% coal and 36% nuclear. IWG has a 25% interest in the 1,600-mw Quad Cities Nuclear Power Station. Peak load in 1992 was 952 mw, and net generating capability was 1,429 mw, for a 33% capacity margin. Due to overcapacity, IWG is exploring the possible sale of ownership interests in generation assets. Electric sales during 1992 totaled 5,891 million kwh, down 9.2% from 6,487 million kwh in 1991.

Gas sold and transported in 1992 was 61,710,000 Mcf, up from 59,708,000 Mcf in 1991. The company has numerous long-term gas supply contracts and purchases the rest on the spot market.

InterCoast Energy is a nonregulated subsidiary which holds four energy related businesses.

Finances

In March 1993, IWG refinanced $11.05 million of pollution control bonds and $65 million of first mortgage bonds.

Dividend Data

Dividends have been paid since 1942. A dividend reinvestment plan is available. A "poison pill" stock purchase rights plan was adopted in 1992.

Amt of Divd. $	Date Decl.	Ex–divd. Date	Stock of Record	Payment Date
0.43¼	Oct. 22	Oct. 27	Nov. 2	Dec. 1'92
0.43¼	Jan. 29	Feb. 2	Feb. 8	Mar. 1'93
0.43¼	Apr. 22	Apr. 27	May 3	Jun. 1'93
0.43¼	Jul. 22	Jul. 27	Aug. 2	Sep. 1'93

Capitalization

Long Term Debt: $592,056,000 (3/93).

Red. Cum. Preference Stock: $48,625,000.

Cum. Pfd. & Pref. Stock: $19,829,000.

Common Stock: 29,352,612 shs. ($1 par).
Institutions hold about 15%.
Shareholders of record: 25,180.

Office—206 East Second St., Davenport, IA 52808. **Tel**—(319) 326-7111. **Chrmn & CEO**—S. J. Bright. **VP-Fin & CFO**—L. E. Cooper. **Secy & Treas**—K. M. Giger. **Investor Contact**—Barbara A. Ven Horst. **Dirs**—S. J. Bright, J. W. Colloton, L. E. Cooper, F. S. Cottrel, W. C. Fletcher, M. Foster Jr., N. L. Seifert, S. E. Shelton, W. S. Tinsman, L. L. Woodruff. **Transfer Agents & Registrars**—Chemical Bank, NYC; First Chicago Trust Co. of New York, NYC. **Incorporated** in Illinois in 1940. **Empl**—1,500.

 Ned Bancroft

IPALCO Enterprises

NYSE Symbol IPL In S&P MidCap 400

Price	Range	P-E Ratio	Dividend	Yield	S&P Ranking	Beta
Aug. 26'93	1993					
38⅝	40–34⅝	15	2.04	5.3%	B+	0.46

Summary

On August 23, 1993, this Indiana-based electric utility holding company terminated its hostile tender offer to purchase all of the outstanding common shares of PSI Resources, Inc., which operates the state's largest electric utility, after it became apparent that IPL's nominees for PSI's board of directors would not be elected. PSI's friendly merger with Cincinnati Gas & Electric is continuing.

Current Outlook

Share earnings for 1993 are projected at $2.60, up from the $2.35 recorded in 1992. Share earnings could rise to $2.70 in 1994.

The quarterly dividend was raised 4.1%, to $0.51 from $0.49, with the April 1993 payment.

Share earnings in 1993 should benefit as higher kwh sales, a steam rate hike and the absence of certain one-time charges outweigh higher purchased power capacity payments. A return to more normal weather conditions would further aid results. Share earnings for 1994 should benefit from somewhat higher kwh sales and cost controls. A rate hike is also possible.

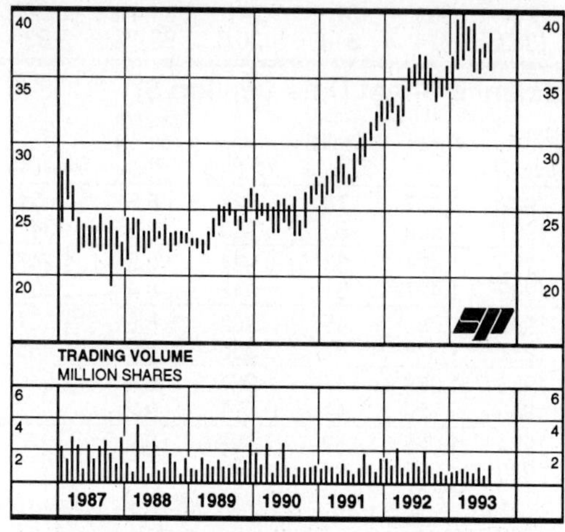

Operating Revenues (Million $)

Quarter:	1993	1992	1991	1990
Mar.	169.0	160.0	162.1	151.4
Jun.	153.1	150.4	154.0	145.2
Sep.	---	166.2	177.7	167.0
Dec.	---	156.6	154.0	147.5
	---	633.2	647.9	611.2

Revenues in the six months ended June 30, 1993, increased 3.8%, year to year. Operating expenses rose 3.3%, and operating income was up 5.8%. After higher other income and almost no change in interest charges, net income was up 14%. Share earnings were $1.23, versus $1.09.

Common Share Earnings ($)

Quarter:	1993	1992	1991	1990
Mar.	0.79	0.73	0.70	0.68
Jun.	0.44	0.36	0.59	0.62
Sep.	E0.82	0.73	0.88	0.80
Dec.	E0.55	0.53	0.55	0.48
	E2.60	2.35	2.72	2.58

Important Developments

Aug. '93— On August 23, the company terminated its hostile tender offer to purchase all of PSI Resources' common stock for $30.50 a share in cash and IPL common stock after it became apparent that IPL's nominees would not be elected to PSI's board of directors. PSI (NYSE, PIN) is the holding company for Indiana's largest public utility (see Standard NYSE Stock Report No. 1735F). On August 17, PSI and Cincinnati Gas & Electric Co. adjusted terms of their merger plan in order to match a previously sweetened IPL bid. Under the revised terms, CIN increased the bid of its friendly buyout offer to $28 a share from $25. However, the offer also presented PSI shareholders with an upside potential of $30.69 a share. The offer was contingent upon the election of PSI's own board of director nominees.

Next earnings report expected in late October.

Per Share Data ($)

Yr. End Dec. 31	1992	1991	1990	1989	1988	1987	1986	1985	1984	1983
Tangible Bk. Val.	**20.26**	19.98	19.26	18.46	17.81	16.80	16.24	14.04	13.47	13.43
Earnings	**2.35**	2.72	2.58	2.54	2.64	2.38	3.27	1.91	2.11	2.09
Dividends	**1.96**	1.88	1.80	1.72	1.64	1.81	1.52	1.52	1.46	1.38
Payout Ratio	**83%**	69%	70%	68%	62%	76%	46%	80%	69%	66%
Prices—High	**36⅞**	33⅜	27½	26⅝	24⅜	28¾	29½	20	16⅞	15⅜
Low	**31½**	25½	23⅛	21¾	21¼	19¼	18½	15¾	13	12⅞
P/E Ratio—	**16–13**	12–9	11–9	10–9	9–8	12–8	9–6	10–8	8–6	7–6

Data as orig. reptd. Adj. for stk. div. of 100% Nov. 1986. E-Estimated

Income Data (Million $)

Year Ended Dec. 31	Revs.	Depr.	Maint.	Oper. Ratio	[1]Fxd. Chgs. Cover.	Constr. Credits	Eff. Tax Rate	Net Inc.	% Return On Revs.	% Return On [2]Invest. Capital	% Return On Com. Equity
1992	**633**	**78.6**	**62.4**	**78.8%**	**4.17**	**5.1**	**31.7%**	**88**	**14.0**	**7.7**	**11.3**
1991	648	78.6	60.5	76.9%	4.12	2.6	30.6%	102	15.7	9.1	13.5
1990	611	76.0	63.8	76.5%	3.86	2.0	31.9%	97	15.9	9.1	13.4
1989	595	74.7	61.4	76.1%	3.64	2.3	30.6%	96	16.1	9.3	13.8
1988	609	70.6	60.8	74.8%	3.67	1.6	31.6%	99	16.3	9.7	15.0
1987	554	64.7	51.8	77.3%	3.52	2.9	34.7%	89	16.1	9.3	14.2
1986	512	52.6	47.2	82.0%	4.88	34.9	34.7%	123	23.9	11.2	20.9
1985	471	45.6	41.7	83.1%	3.47	54.6	33.3%	71	15.0	8.1	13.4
1984	459	44.1	42.7	82.0%	4.25	41.2	34.1%	74	16.0	8.5	15.2
1983	428	42.6	36.4	79.7%	4.24	28.3	37.6%	67	15.8	9.1	15.4

Balance Sheet Data (Million $)

Dec. 31	Gross Prop.	Capital Expend.	Net Prop.	% Earn. on Net Prop.	Total Cap.	Capitalization LT Debt	Capitalization % LT Debt	Capitalization Pfd.	Capitalization % Pfd.	Capitalization Com.	Capitalization % Com.
1992	**2,357**	**118**	**1,538**	**8.9**	**1,735**	**550**	**39.6**	**52**	**3.7**	**788**	**56.7**
1991	2,245	95	1,489	10.2	1,709	547	40.0	52	3.8	770	56.2
1990	2,167	90	1,464	9.9	1,662	537	40.4	52	3.9	738	55.7
1989	2,087	90	1,439	10.0	1,652	539	40.8	72	5.5	709	53.7
1988	2,004	61	1,408	10.9	1,629	552	42.4	72	5.5	678	52.1
1987	1,952	62	1,408	8.9	1,609	555	43.1	92	7.1	641	49.8
1986	1,907	73	1,406	6.6	1,583	563	44.2	92	7.2	619	48.6
1985	1,832	92	1,370	6.0	1,523	603	48.3	92	7.4	554	44.3
1984	1,695	106	1,268	6.8	1,363	534	47.4	92	8.1	502	44.5
1983	1,557	116	1,164	7.7	1,234	468	45.6	92	8.9	467	45.5

Data as orig. reptd. **1.** Times int. exp. & pfd. divs. covered (pretax basis). **2.** Based on income before interest charges.

Business Summary

IPALCO Enterprises is the holding company for Indianapolis Power & Light, which supplies electricity (95% of 1992 revenues) and steam (5%) to more than 390,000 customers. The company also owns Mid-America Capital Resources, Inc., a holding company for IPL's non-regulated businesses. The unit engages in the research and development of energy related projects, investment management, and has a 10% equity interest in Evergreen Media Corp., owner and operator of six radio stations. Nonutility operations experienced a net loss of $0.04 a share in 1992, versus earnings of $0.03 in 1991. Electric revenues by customer class:

	1992	1991	1990	1989
Residential	36%	36%	36%	36%
Small comm'l & ind'l	21%	22%	23%	24%
Large comm'l & ind'l	41%	39%	39%	38%
Other	2%	3%	2%	2%

Peak load in 1992 was 2,505 mw, and system summer capability totaled 2,829 mw, for a capacity margin of 11.4%. For the five-year period 1993-97, IPL has projected that retail kwh sales will increase at a compound annual rate of some 2.3%. To maintain adequate summer capacity margin in the near term, IPL has entered into a five-year firm power purchase agreement with Indiana Michigan Power Co., expiring March 31, 1997.

Nearly all of 1992's generation requirements were derived from coal. IPL utilizes Indiana coal and is subject to the air quality provisions of The Clean Air Act Amendments of 1990. The company estimates that the cost of compliance with the Act through 1997 will be approximately $260 million, including AFUDC, with all such expenditures to be made by December 31, 1997.

Dividend Data

Dividends have been paid since 1934. A dividend reinvestment plan is available. A "poison pill" stock purchase rights plan was adopted in 1990.

Amt of Divd. $	Date Decl.	Ex-divd. Date	Stock of Record	Payment Date
0.49	Aug. 25	Sep. 2	Sep. 9	Oct. 15'92
0.49	Nov. 24	Dec. 3	Dec. 9	Jan. 15'93
0.51	Feb. 23	Mar. 4	Mar. 10	Apr. 15'93
0.51	May 25	Jun. 3	Jun. 9	Jul. 15'93
0.51	Aug. 23	Sep. 7	Sep. 13	Oct. 15'93

Capitalization

Long Term Debt: $549,261,000 (6/93).

Subsid. Cum. Pfd. Stock: $51,898,000.

Common Stock: 37,663,966 shs. (no par). Institutions hold about 37%. Shareholders of record: 25,246.

Office—25 Monument Circle (P.O. Box 1595), Indianapolis, IN 46206-1595. **Tel**—(317) 261-8261. **Chrmn & Pres**—J. R. Hodowal. **Secy**—M. E. Woods. **VP-Treas & Investor Contact**—John R. Brehm. **Dir**—R. A. Borns, M. E. Daniels Jr., O. N. Frenzel III, E. J. Goss, E. B. Herr Jr., J. R. Hodowal, R. L. Humke, S. H. Jones, A. B. Lacy, L. B. Lytle, T. M. Miller, S. W. Rowland, T. H. Sams, Z. G. Todd. **Transfer Agents & Registrars**—Indianopolis Power & Light Shareholder Services, Indianapolis; Chemical Bank, NYC. **Incorporated** in Indiana in 1926. **Empl**—2,435.

 Christopher J. Grant

IVAX Corp.

ASE Symbol IVX Options on CBOE In S&P MidCap 400

Price	Range	P-E Ratio	Dividend	Yield	S&P Ranking	Beta
Sep. 28'93	1993					
27¼	29¾–19¼	27	0.04	0.1%	B–	0.73

Summary

This company generates the majority of its sales from its pharmaceutical operations, and has interests in specialty chemicals and medical diagnostics. During 1992, seven companies were acquired, for a total of $133.5 million (including common stock valued at $99 million). ASE-listed Johnson Products Co. was recently acquired, in exchange for about 2.54 million IVAX common shares.

Current Outlook

Share earnings for 1993 are projected at $1.05, and could reach $1.55 in 1994.

Semi-annual cash dividends of $0.02 a share were initiated in April 1993.

Net revenues should grow at more than 25% for the balance of 1993, in the absence of regulatory approval for competitors' generic versions of verapamil (a hypertension drug that was granted FDA marketing approval in August 1992). Sales of verapamil accounted for 20% of total revenues in the first half of 1993. With improved operating margins, and assuming the successful consolidation of recent acquisitions, profits should continue their impressive expansion through 1994.

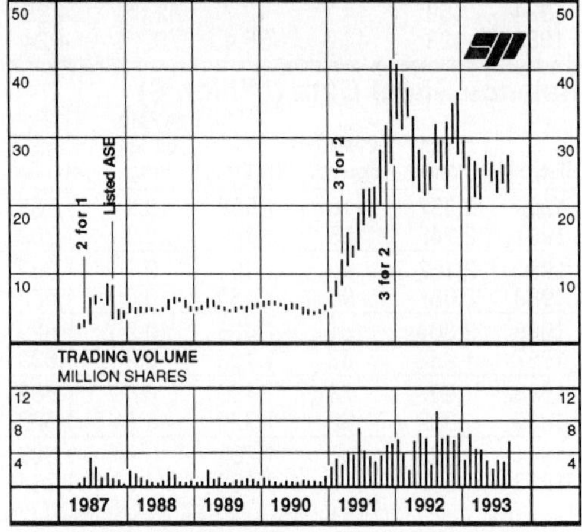

Net Sales (Million $)

Quarter:	1994	1993	1992	1991
Mar.	---	128.0	104.3	43.8
Jun.	---	143.9	97.6	38.7
Sep.	---	---	121.0	41.0
Dec.	---	---	128.2	58.1
	---	---	451.0	181.6

Net revenues in the six months ended June 30, 1993, climbed 36%, year to year, reflecting increased domestic pharmaceutical sales (92% of the total revenue increase). Gross margins widened, and with well-contained operating costs, pretax income soared 370%. After taxes at 38.4%, versus 17.3%, net income was up 251%, to $34,356,000 ($0.49 a share), from $9,770,000 ($0.14).

Common Share Earnings ($)

Quarter:	1994	1993	1992	1991
Mar.	---	0.24	0.06	0.05
Jun.	---	0.26	0.07	0.05
Sep.	---	E0.27	0.32	0.05
Dec.	---	E0.28	0.19	0.04
	E1.55	E1.05	0.65	0.19

Important Developments

Aug. '93— The company acquired ASE-listed Johnson Products Co., a marketer of ethnic personal care products, in exchange for about 2,540,000 IVAX common shares. Johnson Products operations were merged into the Flori Roberts unit, which also focuses parts of its business on African American consumers, and Baker Cummins Dermatologicals. Johnson's products are primarily hair relaxers, conditioners and shampoos, sold to retail consumers and professional hair care customers.

Jun. '93— IVAX acquired certain assets and liabilities of Elf Atochem's janitorial and textiles chemicals businesses in the U.S. and Canada, for $13 million in cash, plus 1,725,000 common shares (valued at $45 million), subject to possible adjustments.

Next earnings report expected in early November.

Per Share Data ($)

Yr. End Dec. 31[1]	[2]1992	[2]1991	[2]1990	1989	[2]1988	1987	1986	1985	1984
Tangible Bk. Val.	**1.71**	1.22	0.67	0.59	0.71	0.33	0.67	0.60	0.37
Cash Flow	**0.87**	0.27	0.07	d0.15	d0.03	d0.07	NA	NA	NA
Earnings[3]	**0.65**	0.19	d0.01	d0.21	d0.08	d0.07	0.08	0.10	0.07
Dividends	**Nil**	Nil	Nil	Nil	Nil	Nil	Nil	Nil	Nil
Payout Ratio	**Nil**	Nil	Nil	Nil	Nil	Nil	Nil	Nil	Nil
Prices[4]—High	**40⅞**	41⅜	6⅛	6½	6⅝	8⅝	2	1⅛	NA
Low	**21⅝**	5⅛	4	4½	4¼	1¼	⅞	⅞	NA
P/E Ratio—	**63–33**	NM	NM	NM	NM	NM	25–11	12–9	NA

Data as orig. reptd. Adj. for stk. divs. of 50% Nov. 1991, 50% Mar. 1991, 100% May 1987. **1.** Yrs. ended Oct. 31 prior to 1987. **2.** Refl. merger or acq. **3.** Bef. spec. item(s) of +0.01 in 1991. **4.** Cal yr. d-Deficit. E-Estimated. NM-Not Meaningful. NA-Not Available.

Income Data (Million $)

Year Ended Dec. 31[1]	Revs.	Oper. Inc.	% Oper. Inc. of Revs.	Cap. Exp.	Depr.	Int. Exp.	Net Bef. Taxes	Eff. Tax Rate	[5]Net Inc.	% Net Inc. of Revs.	Cash Flow
[2]1992	**451**	**70.1**	**15.5**	**20.80**	**15.10**	**11.00**	**[4]54.20**	**17.7%**	**44.60**	**9.9**	**59.70**
[2]1991	182	18.6	10.2	13.19	5.30	3.49	[4]13.64	18.7%	11.09	6.1	16.40
[2]1990	142	10.2	7.2	6.27	4.34	3.43	[4]0.39	NM	d0.76	NM	3.58
1989	63	d5.2	NM	2.21	2.09	1.04	[4]d8.21	NM	d8.21	NM	d6.12
[2]1988	61	0.6	0.9	[3]2.83	1.55	1.13	d2.74	NM	d2.81	NM	d1.26
1987	4	d1.5	NM	8.57	0.22	0.15	d1.45	Nil	d1.45	NM	d1.23
1986	5	0.8	16.2	0.41	0.07	Nil	[4]0.95	32.2%	0.65	13.8	NA
1985	5	0.9	18.7	0.09	0.08	Nil	[4]0.86	42.9%	0.49	10.6	NA
1984	4	0.6	16.4	0.06	0.07	Nil	[4]0.58	46.4%	0.31	8.3	NA

Balance Sheet Data (Million $)

Dec. 31[1]	Cash	Curr. Assets	Curr. Liab.	Curr. Ratio	Total Assets	% Ret. on Assets	Long Term Debt	Common Equity	Total Cap.	% LT Debt of Cap.	% Ret. on Equity
1992	**49.0**	**253.0**	**106.0**	**2.4**	**504**	**9.0**	**133.0**	**259.0**	**392.0**	**33.9**	**18.7**
1991	118.4	267.2	111.3	2.4	449	3.8	135.1	201.1	336.1	40.2	8.2
1990	5.2	64.6	39.4	1.6	117	NM	16.2	58.7	74.9	21.6	NM
1989	5.0	29.7	13.6	2.2	76	NM	7.8	50.9	58.7	13.3	NM
1988	11.5	35.0	11.2	3.1	75	NM	8.6	54.9	63.5	13.5	NM
1987	3.6	14.1	12.1	1.2	46	NM	0.4	33.2	33.7	1.3	NM
1986	3.1	5.0	0.3	15.6	6	11.8	Nil	5.5	5.5	Nil	12.6
1985	3.3	4.8	0.4	11.7	5	10.6	Nil	4.8	4.8	Nil	12.6
1984	0.3	1.6	0.5	3.1	2	NA	Nil	1.5	1.5	Nil	NA

Data as orig. reptd. **1.** Years ended Oct. 31 prior to 1987. **2.** Refl. merger or acq. **3.** Net of curr. yr. retirement and disposals. **4.** Incl. equity in earns. of nonconsol. subs. **5.** Bef. spec. items. d-Deficit. NM-Not Meaningful. NA-Not Available.

Business Summary

IVAX Corp. is a holding company whose primary objective is to become a fully integrated international firm engaged in the research, development, manufacture and sale of pharmaceutical products for human and animal use.

The pharmaceutical group markets several brand pharmaceutical products sold under the Baker Norton trade name. Generic drugs (about 71% of 1992 revenues), are sold in the U.K., Ireland and certain other countries through a U.K. subsidiary, Norton Healthcare Ltd., which makes and markets about 280 generic pharmaceuticals. Through Goldline Laboratories, the company distributes in the U.S. about 700 generic prescription and OTC drugs and vitamin supplements in various dosage forms, strengths and package sizes, constituting an aggregate of some 1,700 products. In August 1992, IVAX received FDA approval to market 240 mg. verapamil HCl ER tablets (for the treatment of hypertension), a generic version of products marketed by G.D. Searle (Calan SR) and by Knoll Pharmaceutical Co. (Isoptin SR).

Under the trade name Baker Cummins Dermatologicals, IVAX produces and sells a line of 22 skin care and dermatological preparations, including medicated shampoos, moisturizers, cleansers, sunscreens and topical anti-inflammatory creams. This unit's product offerings were expanded to the ethnic personal care market through the July 1992 acquisition of Flori Roberts Inc. In addition, wholly owned DVM Pharmaceuticals Inc. formulates, packages and distributes veterinary products.

Specialty chemical operations (7% of 1992 revenues), consist of the manufacture and sale of specialized fluids used vacuum pumps in the semiconductor, aerospace, auto, metallurgical and other industries; chemicals used to prepare, dye and finish textiles; and building maintenance chemicals, supplies and cleaning products.

The medical diagnostics group (5%) develops, produces and sells products for the detection of infectious and auto-immune diseases; to identify elements of the human complement system; and to monitor the level or presence of hormones.

Dividend Data

In April 1993, IVAX initiated semi-annual cash dividends of $0.02 a share. The first dividend was paid June 1, 1993.

Finances

During 1992, the company issued an aggregate of 3.2 million common shares (valued at $99 million at the dates of issuance), and paid a total of $34.5 million in cash, to acquire seven businesses. IVAX intends to continue to expand through internal growth and by acquisitions, and will seek to acquire companies in exchange for common stock.

Capitalization

Long Term Debt: $129,698,000 (6/93).

Common Stock: 69,509,089 shs. ($0.10 par).
Officers and directors control 33%.
Shareholders: about 4,108 of record (3/93).

Office—8800 N.W. 36th St., Miami, FL 33178. **Tel**—(305) 590-2200. **Chrmn, CEO & Pres**—P. Frost. **Deputy CEO**—I. Kaye. **Vice Chrmn**—J. Fishman. **SVP-Fin & Treas**—F. E. Baxter. **Dirs**—M. Andrews, F. Bellini, E. Biekert, D. B. Fascell, J. Fishman, P. Frost, H. S. Geneen, J. Giegel, C. Hsaio, L. Kasprick, I. Kaye, H. M. Krueger, J. H. Moxley III, M. L. Pearce, M. Weintraub. **Transfer Agent & Registrar**—Southeast Bank, Miami. **Reincorporated** in Florida in 1993. **Empl**—2,110.

 Robert M. Gold

Jacobs Engineering Group

NYSE Symbol JEC In S&P MidCap 400

Price	Range	P-E Ratio	Dividend	Yield	S&P Ranking	Beta
Aug. 31'93	1993					
24½	29⅞–20	21	None	None	B	1.22

Summary

This company provides engineering, construction and maintenance services to both private industry and Federal government agencies on a worldwide basis. Earnings have been in a strong uptrend since 1986, with earnings in fiscal 1992 benefiting from continued strong demand for the company's services, an improved mix and a $0.09 a share gain on an asset sale. Revenues and earnings should continue to rise in fiscal 1993 and fiscal 1994.

Current Outlook

Earnings for the fiscal year ended September 30, 1994, are estimated at $1.35 a share, versus earnings of $1.16 estimated for fiscal 1993.

Initiation of cash dividends is not anticipated.

Revenues are expected to rise in fiscal 1994, reflecting acquisitions and an increase in work performed. Benefiting from an improved mix and lower SG&A expense as a percent of revenues, operating income should advance. Assuming flat interest income and a level tax rate, earnings should rise again in fiscal 1994.

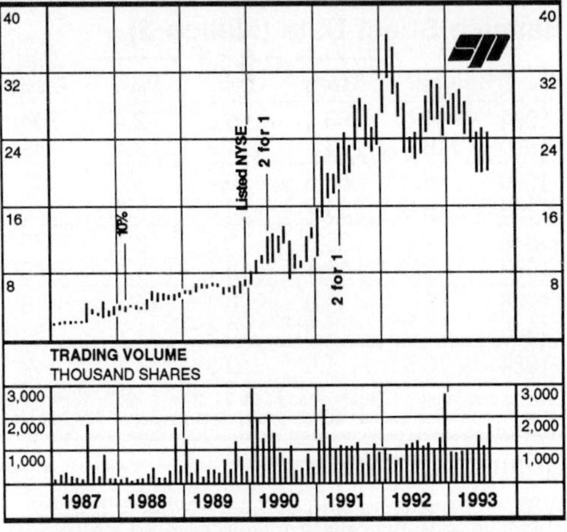

Revenues (Million $)

Quarter:	1992–93	1991–92	1990–91	1989–90
Dec.	285	254	264	212
Mar.	273	270	277	219
Jun.	258	283	264	221
Sep.		299	231	230
		1,106	1,036	882

Revenues for nine months ended June 31, 1993 rose 1.1%, year to year, primarily reflecting gains in the construction and maintainence units. Margins widened, and pretax income rose 3.2%. After taxes at 42.0% in both periods, net income advanced 3.2%. Share earnings were $0.86, versus $0.84.

Common Share Earnings ($)

Quarter:	1992–93	1991–92	1990–91	1989–90
Dec.	0.28	0.24	0.20	0.15
Mar.	0.29	0.34	0.21	0.16
Jun.	0.29	0.26	0.22	0.16
Sep.	E0.30	0.27	0.23	0.17
	E1.16	1.11	0.86	0.64

Important Developments

Jul. '93— JEC reported share earnings of $0.29 on an 8.8% decline in revenues for fiscal 1993's third quarter, versus $0.26 a year-earlier. Net income for the first nine months of fiscal 1992 included a $0.09 a share gain on the sale of securities. Backlog at June 30, 1993 stood at $1.805 billion, an increase of $120 million from $1.685 billion a year-earlier.

Jun. '93— JEC acquired Pennsylvania-based Sigel Group, which provides engineering and design services for projects in the pharmaceutical and biotechnology industries.

Next earnings report expected in early November.

Per Share Data ($)

Yr. End Sep. 30	1992	1991	1990	1989	1988	1987	1986	1985	1984	1983
Tangible Bk. Val.	**5.33**	4.18	3.24	2.46	1.68	1.56	1.35	1.19	1.06	1.44
Cash Flow	**1.43**	1.15	0.89	0.67	0.51	0.30	0.19	0.27	d0.41	d0.08
Earnings[1]	**1.11**	0.86	0.64	0.48	0.34	0.19	0.05	0.11	d0.59	d0.29
Dividends	**Nil**	Nil	Nil	Nil	Nil	Nil	Nil	Nil	0.029	0.114
Payout Ratio	**Nil**	Nil	Nil	Nil	Nil	Nil	Nil	Nil	NM	NM
Prices[2]—High	**36½**	28⅞	13⅝	7¼	5⅞	4⅝	2⁷⁄₁₆	1⅞	2⅜	3¹⁄₁₆
Low	**21⅝**	10⅛	6¹¹⁄₁₆	5⁹⁄₁₆	3⁹⁄₁₆	1¹⁵⁄₁₆	1⁷⁄₁₆	1³⁄₁₆	1¼	1⅞
P/E Ratio—	**33–19**	34–12	21–10	15–12	25–10	53–31	18–11	NM	NM	24–12

Data as orig. reptd. Adj. for stk. divs. of 100% May 1991, 100% Apr. 1990, 10% Feb. 1988. **1.** Bef. spec. item of +0.14 in 1984. **2.** Cal. yr. E-Estimated. d-Deficit. NM-Not Meaningful.

Income Data (Million $)

Year Ended Sep. 30	Revs.	Oper. Inc.	% Oper. Inc. of Revs.	Cap. Exp.	Depr.	Int. Exp.	Net Bef. Taxes	Eff. Tax Rate	[2]Net Inc.	% Net Inc. of Revs.	Cash Flow
1992	**1,106**	**46.2**	**4.2**	**12.10**	**7.73**	**0.34**	**45.9**	**42.0%**	**26.6**	**2.4**	**34.3**
1991	1,036	39.2	3.8	8.54	6.89	0.55	35.1	42.0%	20.4	2.0	27.3
1990	882	27.3	3.1	5.59	5.50	1.22	24.8	42.0%	14.4	1.6	19.9
1989	794	18.8	2.4	6.71	4.07	1.74	17.6	42.0%	10.2	1.3	14.3
[1]1988	757	13.2	1.7	3.86	3.23	1.71	11.0	40.2%	6.6	0.9	9.8
1987	320	6.4	2.0	3.24	2.22	1.28	6.5	46.0%	3.5	1.1	5.7
1986	208	5.3	2.5	1.94	2.68	0.62	1.5	45.1%	0.9	0.4	3.5
1985	220	6.0	2.7	5.07	3.19	2.28	3.6	44.2%	2.0	0.9	5.2
1984	178	d11.7	NM	1.52	3.47	2.32	d21.4	NM	[3]d11.6	NM	d8.1
1983	196	d10.6	NM	1.84	4.07	2.57	d11.1	NM	d5.6	NM	d1.5

Balance Sheet Data (Million $)

Sep. 30	Cash	Curr. Assets	Curr. Liab.	Curr. Ratio	Total Assets	% Ret. on Assets	Long Term Debt	Common Equity	Total Cap.	% LT Debt of Cap.	% Ret. on Equity
1992	**35.1**	**258**	**171**	**1.5**	**317**	**9.2**	**Nil**	**140**	**141**	**Nil**	**21.4**
1991	34.1	207	146	1.4	260	7.8	Nil	107	109	Nil	21.1
1990	22.5	202	163	1.2	254	6.0	Nil	83	84	Nil	19.9
1989	25.5	172	140	1.2	213	4.9	6.3	59	66	9.6	20.2
1988	30.4	144	122	1.2	180	4.4	9.2	38	49	18.8	19.1
1987	27.6	90	64	1.4	117	3.6	12.3	31	44	27.6	12.1
1986	13.1	46	38	1.2	76	1.0	0.9	27	28	3.4	3.2
1985	7.7	65	58	1.1	98	1.9	1.6	27	28	5.8	7.9
1984	7.7	79	71	1.1	111	NM	3.5	24	28	12.6	NM
1983	3.7	47	35	1.4	90	NM	7.7	34	42	18.4	NM

Data as orig. reptd. **1.** Reflects merger or acquisition. **2.** Bef. spec. item(s) in 1984. **3.** Reflects acctg. change. d-Deficit. NM-Not Meaningful.

Business Summary

Jacobs Engineering Group provides engineering, design and consulting services, construction and construction management services, and process plant maintenance services to both private industry and Federal government agencies nationwide. Contributions to revenues by industry in recent fiscal years:

	1992	1991
Chemical and pharmaceutical	32%	40%
Facilities systems	20%	30%
Refining	33%	21%
Environmental	10%	7%
Minerals and fertilizers	5%	2%

Jacobs provides three categories of basic services.

Professional services (32% of fiscal 1992 revenues) include the engineering and design of modern process plants and high technology facilities, as well as remedial engineering and design preparation for major environmental and hazardous waste programs.

Construction services (45%) includes the construction of process plants for industries such as petroleum refining, chemicals and pharmaceuticals; and facility projects, including high technology or special purpose buildings.

Maintenance services (23%) include all tasks required to keep a process plant in day-to-day operations.

In fiscal 1992, some 87% of contracts were cost plus, versus 79% in 1991 and 69% in 1990; 4% were guaranteed maximum, versus 2% in 1991 and 11% in 1990; and 9% were fixed price, against 19% in 1991 and 20% in 1990.

About 9.4% of total revenues were derived from Federal government agencies in fiscal 1992, versus 6.3% in 1991 and 4.9% in 1990.

Revenues from outside North America were some 16% of the total in fiscal 1992, versus 8.4% in fiscal 1991 and 7.1% in 1990.

Dividend Data

Cash dividends were omitted in 1984. The shares were split 2-for-1 in May 1991, 2-for-1 in April 1990, and 3-for-2 in March 1981; a 10% stock dividend was paid in February 1988. A "poison pill" stock purchase rights plan was adopted in 1990.

Capitalization

Long Term Debt: None (6/93).

Common Stock: 24,273,122 shs. ($1 par).
Officers and directors own about 24%.
Institutions hold some 44%.
Shareholders of record: 2,468 (9/92).

Office—251 South Lake Ave., Pasadena, CA 91101. **Tel**—(818) 449-2171. **Chrmn**—J. J. Jacobs. **Pres & CEO**—N. G. Watson. **Secy**—R. M. Barton. **SVP-Fin, Treas & Investor Contact**—John W. Prosser, Jr. **Dirs**—J. F. Alibrandi, R. M. Barton, P. H. Dailey, J. J. Jacobs, L. K. Jacobs, J. C. LaForce, D. M. Petrone, J. Rainey Jr., J. W. Simmons, J. M. Sudarsky, N. G. Watson. **Transfer Agent & Registrar**—First Interstate Bank of California, Los Angeles. **Incorporated** in California in 1957; reincorporated in Delaware in 1987. **Empl**—4,530.

 Leo Larkin

Kansas City Power & Light

NYSE Symbol KLT In S&P MidCap 400

Price	Range	P-E Ratio	Dividend	Yield	S&P Ranking	Beta
Aug. 12'93	1993					
26	26⅛–22	17	1.48	5.7%	B+	0.46

Summary

This midsize electric utility serves over 416,000 customers in 23 counties in western Missouri and eastern Kansas. It derives about 95% of its business from metropolitan Kansas City, which has a diverse economic base. Earnings in 1993 should improve, provided the company enjoys continued success in low cost electric generation at the 47%-owned Wolf Creek Nuclear Station. An extended shutdown of the unit could have a substantial adverse effect on the company's business and financial condition. An improving local economy, load growth and lower interest charges will further support earnings growth.

Current Outlook

Share earnings for 1993 are projected at $1.65, up from 1992's $1.35. Earnings for 1994 are estimated at $1.75 a share.

Directors raised the quarterly cash dividend 2.8%, to $0.37, from $0.36, with the August declaration.

Share earnings should rebound in 1993, reflecting continued low-cost generation at the Wolf Creek Nuclear Station and increased kilowatt-hour sales from higher residential and commercial usage. Improving regional economic conditions and load growth of large customers in the steel, auto manufacturing, grain processing, and plastic container production sectors will further benefit profitability. Interest charges should decline on concerted efforts to refinance higher coupon debt. Wolf Creek was refueled in March and accruing these costs monthly could help smooth earnings.

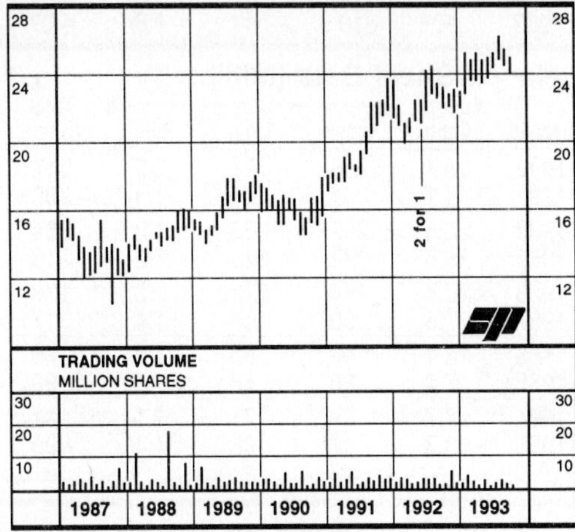

Operating Revenues (Million $)

Quarter:	1993	1992	1991	1990
Mar.	191.4	180.0	181.9	163.6
Jun.	208.3	196.5	208.6	189.8
Sep.	---	229.4	254.4	237.5
Dec.	---	196.7	180.3	170.3
	---	802.7	825.1	761.2

Operating revenues for the six months ended June 30, 1993, rose 6.2%, year to year, reflecting higher power sales from colder weather. In the absence of costs associated with an extended nuclear refueling outage, net income was up 40%, to $41.5 million, from $29.7 million. After higher preferred dividends, share earnings were $0.64 a share, versus $0.46 (adjusted).

Common Share Earnings ($)

Quarter:	1994	1993	1992	1991
Mar.	E0.25	0.24	0.12	0.26
Jun.	E0.45	0.40	0.33	0.44
Sep.	E0.80	E0.81	0.60	0.78
Dec.	E0.25	E0.20	0.29	0.11
	E1.75	E1.65	1.35	1.58

Important Developments

Jun. '93— Wolf Creek Nuclear Station, the company's only nuclear unit, was named the lowest cost U.S. nuclear producer in 1992 at $12.49 per mwh. The plant was efficiently refueled in March and returned to service on-schedule. In 1992, the Wolf Creek station recorded average nuclear fuel costs of $0.32 per million Btu, while the company's fossil-fuel plants (mostly coal) posted averages of $1.03 per million Btu. Management is mindful of the importance of having Wolf Creek on line during the peak summer months, as witnessed by the careful work performed during a delayed first quarter return to service in 1992. These shutdowns lasted over a month for refueling, valve testing, and minor modifications to assure a return to full capacity prior to peak summer demand. The Wolf Creek Nuclear Station finished 1992 with an average 86% availability rating.

Next earnings report expected in early November.

Per Share Data ($)

Yr. End Dec. 31	1992	1991	1990	1989	1988	1987	1986	1985	1984	1983
Tangible Bk. Val.	**13.79**	13.89	13.74	13.49	13.08	14.20	13.87	13.53	12.62	11.73
Earnings	**1.35**	1.58	1.56	1.66	1.60	1.51	1.40	2.21	2.24	2.08
Dividends	**1.430**	1.370	1.310	1.250	1.170	1.060	1.045	1.180	1.165	1.087
Payout Ratio	**106%**	87%	84%	76%	73%	70%	75%	54%	52%	52%
Prices—High	**24½**	23¾	17¹⁵⁄₁₆	18⁷⁄₁₆	16⅛	15⁹⁄₁₆	16⅛	12¼	10¼	11¼
Low	**19¹⁵⁄₁₆**	17⅛	14⁹⁄₁₆	14⁷⁄₁₆	12⁷⁄₁₆	10½	10⁹⁄₁₆	9	7⅛	8⅜
P/E Ratio—	**18–15**	15–11	12–9	11–8	10–8	10–7	12–8	6–4	5–3	5–4

Data as orig. reptd. Adj. for stk. div(s). of 100% Jun. 1992, 50% Nov. 1983. E-Estimated

Income Data (Million $)

Year Ended Dec. 31	Revs.	Depr.	Maint.	Oper. Ratio	[1]Fxd. Chgs. Cover.	Constr. Credits	Eff. Tax Rate	Net Inc.	% Return On Revs.	% Return On [2]Invest. Capital	% Return On Com. Equity
1992	**803**	**88.8**	**81.2**	**82.5%**	**3.24**	**3**	**37.7%**	**86**	**10.8**	**6.0**	**9.7**
1991	825	86.8	80.9	79.5%	3.18	3	36.7%	104	12.6	7.3	11.4
1990	761	85.0	79.5	76.1%	2.88	2	35.7%	103	13.5	7.5	11.4
1989	731	85.4	69.0	74.5%	2.83	2	37.8%	109	14.8	8.0	12.4
1988	737	85.2	85.2	75.5%	2.61	1	34.8%	106	14.3	8.1	12.4
1987	705	83.4	75.1	75.2%	2.52	NM	39.5%	104	14.8	8.0	10.7
1986	665	84.2	73.5	77.0%	2.26	d2	38.4%	106	16.0	8.2	10.2
1985	597	62.4	70.8	82.2%	3.52	111	28.7%	155	26.0	8.7	16.8
1984	583	47.6	57.1	80.7%	4.48	134	31.5%	151	26.0	8.8	18.3
1983	563	46.3	53.4	81.4%	4.12	98	32.9%	126	22.5	8.8	17.5

Balance Sheet Data (Million $)

Dec. 31	[3]Gross Prop.	Capital Expend.	Net Prop.	% Earn. on Net Prop.	Total Cap.	Capitalization LT Debt	% LT Debt	Pfd.	% Pfd.	Com.	% Com.
1992	**3,233**	**130**	**2,285**	**6.2**	**2,401**	**788**	**45.5**	**90.9**	**5.2**	**854**	**49.3**
1991	3,145	122	2,253	7.6	2,373	823	47.7	41.1	2.4	860	49.9
1990	3,051	93	2,221	8.2	2,322	750	44.2	94.2	5.6	851	50.2
1989	2,999	103	2,222	8.4	2,414	879	48.6	94.4	5.2	836	46.2
1988	2,918	95	2,213	8.1	2,416	943	51.0	94.6	5.1	811	43.9
1987	2,986	79	2,357	7.4	2,476	1,020	51.0	99.0	5.0	880	44.0
1986	2,931	71	2,379	6.4	2,499	1,078	52.1	133.0	6.4	860	41.5
1985	2,888	261	2,415	4.6	2,539	1,129	51.8	211.0	9.7	838	38.5
1984	2,648	403	2,224	5.5	2,312	1,032	51.5	220.0	11.0	752	37.5
1983	2,322	305	1,870	6.0	1,944	806	47.8	214.0	12.7	666	39.5

Data as orig. reptd. **1.** Times int. exp. & pfd. divs. covered (pretax basis). **2.** Based on income before interest charges. **3.** Utility plant. d-Deficit. NM-Not Meaningful.

Business Summary

Kansas City Power & Light supplies electricity to over 419,000 customers in a 4,700-square-mile area located in 23 counties in western Missouri and eastern Kansas. Some 95% of the company's business is derived from metropolitan Kansas City. Contributions by customer class in recent years:

	1992	1991	1990	1989
Residential	32%	35%	36%	35%
Commercial	44%	43%	46%	45%
Industrial	15%	14%	15%	15%
Other	9%	8%	3%	4%

The fuel mix in 1992 was 71.1% coal, 28.6% nuclear, 0.2% natural gas, and 0.1% oil. Peak load in 1992 was 2,624 mw and system capacity was 3,089 mw, for a capacity margin of 15.1%. The Wolf Creek nuclear station (47%-owned), which was completed in 1985, provides the company with about 17% of its generating capacity.

The company has estimated construction expenditures (excluding AFUDC) for the 1993-1997 period at $763.2 million. The largest items were for upgrading generating facilities ($311.0 million) and for distribution and general facilities ($323.1 million). Management believed KLT will be able to meet construction outlays through 1994 and a significant portion of the remaining years with internally-generated funds.

Finances

In the first quarter of 1993, the company issued $168 million of medium term notes with a weighted average interest rate of 6.51%. Through April 30, 1993, an additional $65 million of notes had been issued with a weighted average interest rate of 5.03%. After the April issuances, $78 millon of notes remained available for issuance under the series D registration.

Dividend Data

Dividends have been paid since 1921.

Amt of Divd. $	Date Decl.	Ex-divd. Date	Stock of Record	Payment Date
0.36	Nov. 3	Nov. 23	Nov. 30	Dec. 21'92
0.36	Feb. 2	Feb. 22	Feb. 26	Mar. 19'93
0.36	May 4	May 24	May 28	Jun. 21'93
0.37	Aug. 3	Aug. 23	Aug. 27	Sep. 20'93

Capitalization

Long Term Debt: $728,004,000 (3/93).

Red. Preferred Stock: $1,756,000.

Cum. Preferred Stock: $89,000,000.

Common Stock: 61,908,726 shs. (no par).
Institutions hold about 24%.
Shareholders of record: 31,687.

Office—1201 Walnut, Kansas City, MO 64106. **Tel**—(816) 556-2200. **Chrmn & Pres**—A. D. Jennings. **SVP-Fin**—B. J. Beaudoin. **Secy**—J. S. Latz. **Investor Contact**—Robert Levesque (816) 556-2312. **Dirs**—W. H. Clark, R. J. Dineen, A. J. Doyle, W. D. Grant II, A. D. Jennings, G. E. Nettels Jr., G. A. Russell, L. H. Talbott, R. H. West. **Transfer Agent & Registrar**—United Missouri Bank, Kansas City, Mo. **Incorporated** in Missouri in 1922. **Empl**—2,782.

 Ned Bancroft

Kansas City Southern Industries

NYSE Symbol KSU Options on PSE In S&P MidCap 400

Price	Range	P–E Ratio	Dividend	Yield	S&P Ranking	Beta
Aug. 30'93	1993					
39⅞	42¾–23⁷⁄₁₆	23	0.30	0.8%	B	1.13

Summary

Following the acquisition of MidSouth Corp. in June 1993 for $213.5 million, KSU's rail system was expanded 70% to 2,900 miles. KSU derives a rising portion of its income from data processing services and investment management. Strong profit growth is anticipated in 1993, reflecting expansion of assets under management at Janus and a turnaround at DST. The shares were split 2-for-1 in March 1993.

Current Outlook

Earnings for 1993 are projected at $2.05 a share, versus the $1.43 (adjusted) reported for 1992. Profits could reach $2.45 a share in 1994.

Dividends at $0.07½ quarterly could be lifted moderately by late 1993. A 2-for-1 stock split was effected in March 1993.

Profits in 1993 will benefit from a strong performance at Janus Capital, refecting expansion of assets under management. Profits at DST will rebound after being hurt in 1992 by costs to introduce new products and higher ESOP expense. DST also will benefit from growing demand for its new 401(k) and insurance software services. Rail profits will benefit from the inclusion of MidSouth Corp. which should help attract intermodal freight. A stronger economy should help lift shipments of petroleum, ores and forest products. Margins should widen as KSU realizes additional savings under its crew reduction agreement. Restraining profits will be increased interest expense and a higher tax rate.

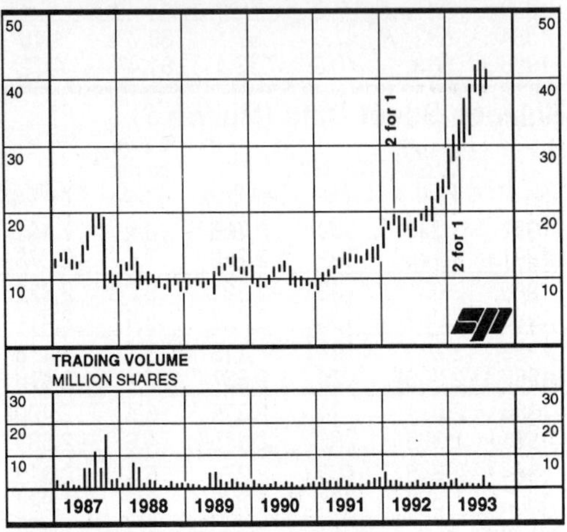

Gross Revenues (Million $)

Quarter:	1993	1992	1991	1990
Mar.	214.6	175.1	142.6	128.3
Jun.	231.7	177.8	149.7	127.0
Sep.	---	189.5	157.5	133.5
Dec.	---	199.0	160.4	139.2
	---	741.4	610.2	528.0

Revenues for 1993's first half rose 26%, year to year. Net income was up 43%, to $0.97 a share (before a $0.14 accounting charge) from $0.68.

Common Share Earnings ($)

Quarter:	1993	1992	1991	1990
Mar.	0.49	0.33	0.23	0.23
Jun.	0.48	0.35	0.24	0.21
Sep.	E0.55	0.36	0.30	0.33
Dec.	E0.53	0.39	0.32	0.23
	E2.05	1.43	1.08	0.99

Important Developments

Jul. '93— DST Systems reported that Kemper Financial Services (representing 10% of DST's shareowner accounts) planned to convert to an internal accounting system. Kemper said the transfer of its business from DST would take place over a two-year period.

Jun. '93— KSU acquired MidSouth Corp (MSC) for $213.5 million. KSU has estimated that the merger of the two rail systems could attract an additional $35 million in traffic after three years. MSC, which operates 1,200 miles of railroad in Alabama, Louisiana, Mississippi and Tennessee, earned $9.0 million in 1992 on revenues of $107.2 million.

Apr. '93— KSU made a $6.5 million ($0.14 a share) charge against 1993 first quarter net income to reflect changes in accounting for deferred taxes and retiree healthcare costs.

Next earnings report expected in late October.

Per Share Data ($)

Yr. End Dec. 31	1992	1991	[1]1990	1989	1988	1987	1986	1985	1984	1983
Tangible Bk. Val.	**9.56**	7.99	7.25	7.45	6.26	8.63	8.51	10.13	[2]4.77	[2]8.82
Cash Flow	**2.84**	2.45	2.24	2.21	0.25	2.32	1.02	2.57	2.33	2.13
Earnings[3]	**1.43**	1.08	0.99	0.89	d1.13	0.83	d0.65	1.23	1.21	1.03
Dividends[4]	**0.300**	0.270	0.270	0.270	0.270	0.270	0.270	0.260	0.183	0.150
Payout Ratio	**20%**	25%	27%	31%	NM	33%	NM	21%	15%	15%
Prices—High	**24⅞**	15	12¹¹⁄₁₆	13¹¹⁄₁₆	14¹³⁄₁₆	19¹⁵⁄₁₆	16¼	14⅝	15	18⅝
Low	**14⅝**	8⅜	8⅝	7⅞	8⅛	8¾	11⅝	11⁵⁄₁₆	9⅛	11
P/E Ratio—	**17–10**	14–8	13–9	15–9	NM	24–11	NM	12–9	12–8	18–11

Data as orig. reptd. Adj. for stk. div(s). of 100% Mar. 1993, 100% Mar. 1992. **1.** Reflects acctg. change. **2.** Incl. intangibles. **3.** Bef. results of disc. opers. of +0.26 in 1989, -0.35 in 1987, -0.43 in 1986; bef. spec. item(s) of -0.09 in 1991, +0.36 in 1988, -0.03 in 1987. **4.** Plus Kemper Corp. com. stk. in 1984 & 1983. E-Estimated d-Deficit. NM-Not Meaningful.

Income Data (Million $)

Year Ended Dec. 31	Revs.	Oper. Inc.	% Oper. Inc. of Revs.	Cap. Exp.	Depr.	Int. Exp.	[3]Net Bef. Taxes	Eff. Tax Rate	[4]Net Inc.	% Net Inc. of Revs.	Cash Flow
1992	**741**	**188**	**25.4**	**174**	**62.4**	**33.1**	**104**	**33.9%**	**63.8**	**8.6**	**126**
1991	610	156	25.5	124	57.5	32.1	74	35.2%	45.7	7.5	103
[1]1990	528	137	26.0	109	49.7	31.4	62	30.4%	41.4	7.8	91
[2]1989	497	137	27.5	101	55.0	30.4	58	34.0%	37.1	7.5	92
1988	507	116	22.9	78	56.6	41.7	d69	NM	d46.3	NM	10
[2]1987	508	144	28.4	87	57.2	25.4	62	43.6%	31.9	6.3	89
[2]1986	479	110	23.0	144	65.7	37.7	d68	NM	d25.3	NM	40
1985	475	120	25.2	155	53.8	22.6	69	21.8%	49.9	10.5	103
1984	476	125	25.5	96	45.7	19.3	76	32.9%	49.1	10.3	94
1983	394	120	29.7	63	[1]44.5	18.9	63	32.0%	41.8	10.6	86

Balance Sheet Data (Million $)

Dec. 31	Cash	Curr. Assets	Curr. Liab.	Curr. Ratio	Total Assets	% Ret. on Assets	Long Term Debt	Common Equity	Total Cap.	% LT Debt of Cap.	% Ret. on Equity
1992	**24**	**246**	**219**	**1.1**	**1,248**	**5.5**	**387**	**456**	**952**	**40.7**	**14.8**
1991	44	232	201	1.2	1,092	4.3	317	405	829	38.3	11.7
1990	87	239	172	1.4	1,034	4.1	345	369	801	43.1	11.7
1989	106	252	200	1.3	965	3.8	283	332	708	40.0	11.9
1988	109	266	258	1.0	979	NM	300	285	664	45.2	NM
1987	87	229	183	1.3	927	3.3	225	354	712	31.6	9.0
1986	74	214	196	1.1	1,006	NM	320	348	790	40.6	NM
1985	93	216	147	1.5	1,066	5.2	302	431	891	33.9	12.0
1984	49	137	122	1.1	854	6.0	173	395	716	24.1	13.0
1983	49	134	133	1.0	773	5.9	138	358	624	22.1	13.5

Data as orig. reptd. **1.** Reflects accounting change. **2.** Excl. disc. oper. **3.** Incl. equity in earns. of nonconsol. subs. **4.** Bef. results of disc. opers. in 1989, 1987, 1986, and spec. item(s) in 1991, 1988, 1987. d-Deficit. NM-Not Meaningful.

Business Summary

Business segment contributions to operating profits (in million $) in recent years:

	1992	1991	1990
Transportation	$75.3	$67.4	$74.3
DST Systems	17.8	26.8	21.6
Janus Capital	45.7	15.8	5.6

Kansas City Southern Railway operates a 1,680-mile rail system spanning Kansas, Missouri, Arkansas, Oklahoma, Louisiana and Texas. The acquisition of MidSouth Corp. for $213.5 million in June 1993 adds 1,200 miles of track in Louisiana, Tennessee, Mississippi and Alabama and reduces KSU's dependence upon coal. In 1992 KSU handled 501,839 carloads of freight, verus 478,503 in 1991, of which coal accounted for 33%. Intermodal shipments accounted for 13.4% of total carloads while chemicals and petroleum generated 12.5% and 10.2% respectively. The average revenue per ton-mile in 1992 was 2.39 cents, versus 2.49 cents in 1991.

DST Systems Inc. primarily provides on-line accounting and recordkeeping services for 22.4 million shareholder accounts at mutual funds, financial services and insurance companies. DST also performs securities transfer services, portfolio accounting, pharmaceutical claims processing and performs administrative services for the insurance industry. Janus Capital Corp. (81%-owned) manages $15.5 billion of funds for 1.5 million shareowners through the Janus and IDEX mutual funds and for private accounts.

Dividend Data

A "poison pill" stock purchase right was adopted in 1986.

Amt of Divd. $	Date Decl.	Ex-divd. Date	Stock of Record	Payment Date
0.15	Nov. 20	Nov. 25	Dec. 2	Dec. 31'92
2-for-1	Jan. 28	Mar. 18	Feb. 19	Mar. 17'93
0.07½	Jan. 28	Feb. 12	Feb. 19	Mar. 17'93
0.07½	May 3	May 10	May 14	Jun. 15'93
0.07½	Aug. 16	Aug. 23	Aug. 27	Sep. 14'93

Capitalization

Long Term Debt: $749,400,000 (6/93).

Minority Interest: $6,700,000.

$1 Non-Cum. Pfd. Stock: 252,000 shs. ($25 par).

Common Stock: 42,131,882 shs. (no par).
Officers & directors own about 8%; employees hold 12% through an ESOP; Hallmark Cards Inc. owns 5%.
Institutions hold about 41%.
Shareholders of record: 2,840.

Office—114 West 11th St., Kansas City, MO 64105. **Tel**—(816) 556-0303. **Chrmn**—P. H. Henson. **Pres & CEO**—L. H. Rowland. **VP-Secy**—A. P. Mauro. **VP-Treas**—A. P. McCarthy. **VP-Contr & Investor Contact**—Joseph D. Monello. **Dirs**—A.E. Allinson, P. F. Balser, J. E. Barnes, T. S. Carter, G. W. Edwards, Jr., M. G. Fitt, P. H. Henson, M. M. Levin, T. A. McDonnell, L. H. Rowland, M. I. Sosland. **Transfer Agents**—United Missouri Bank of Kansas City; Company's office. **Registrar**—United Missouri Bank of Kansas City. **Incorporated** in Del. in 1962. **Empl**—6,071.

 Stephen R. Klein

Kaydon Corp.

NASDAQ Symbol KDON (Incl. in Nat'l Market) In S&P MidCap 400

Price	Range	P-E Ratio	Dividend	Yield	S&P Ranking	Beta
Sep. 10'93	1993					
18¾	32–18½	12	0.36	1.9%	NR	1.24

Summary

Kaydon designs, manufactures and sells anti-friction bearings, bearing systems and components, filters, filter housings and other custom-engineered products. A U.K. manufacturer and distributor of complete bearings and related component parts was acquired in late 1991. Earnings rose in 1992, benefiting from increased sales attributable to the acquisition. The dividend was raised 20% in the second half of 1992.

Business Summary

Kaydon Corporation, which was spun off from Bairnco Corp. in 1984, designs, manufactures and sells custom-engineered products for a broad and diverse customer base. Its principal products include anti-friction bearings, bearing systems, filters, filter housings, high-performance rings, sealing rings, specialty retaining rings, shaft seals and slip-rings. These products are applied in aerospace, defense, instrumentation, medical, construction and other industrial areas. Operations were expanded considerably through several acquisitions since 1985.

Sales in recent years were derived as follows:

	1992	1991
Replacement parts & exports	39%	34%
Aerospace & military equipment	26%	30%
Special industrial machinery	24%	25%
Heavy industrial equipment	11%	11%

The company sells a broad range of custom-engineered products, working closely with its customers to engineer the required solutions to their design problems. Depending on the nature of the application, the design may be used over a protracted time period and in large numbers or for a single use. Kaydon sells its products to more than 1,000 companies throughout the world.

Kaydon's anti-friction bearing products incorporate various types of rolling elements. Its ball, tapered roller, cylindrical roller and needle roller bearings are made in sizes ranging from needle bearings with a ½-inch outside diameter to heavy-duty ball bearings with an outside diameter of 180 inches.

In December 1991, the company acquired for $43.4 million all of the capital stock of Prizerandom

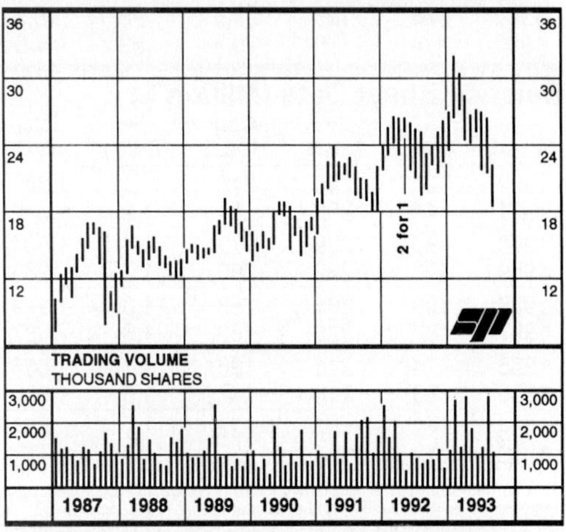

Ltd., the holding company for Cooper Bearings Ltd. Cooper's subsidiaries include Cooper Roller Bearings Ltd., Cooper Split Roller Bearings Corp. and Cooper Geteilte Rollenlager GmbH, all of which either manufacture or distribute complete bearings and related component parts.

Kaydon's 16 facilities are located in Michigan, South Carolina, Georgia, Tennessee, Maryland, Missouri, Virginia, Mexico, Germany and England.

Important Developments

May '93— The company announced that its wholly owned subsidiary, Kaydon Ring & Seal, Inc., elected to temporarily close a chrome plating line as a precautionary measure due to the discovery of a possible wastewater/groundwater interface problem.

Next earnings report expected in late October.

Per Share Data ($)

Yr. End Dec. 31	1992	[1]1991	1990	[1]1989	1988	[1]1987	[1]1986	1985	1984	1983
Tangible Bk. Val.	[2]7.83	[2]7.94	[2]6.63	4.27	3.13	2.00	1.03	0.47	d0.02	d0.71
Cash Flow	2.04	1.98	1.98	1.74	1.57	1.36	0.92	0.74	0.65	NA
Earnings[3]	1.47	1.47	1.51	1.33	1.22	1.00	0.60	0.47	0.35	NA
Dividends	0.315	0.263	0.213	0.163	0.113	0.050	0.025	Nil	Nil	Nil
Payout Ratio	21%	18%	14%	12%	9%	5%	4%	Nil	Nil	Nil
Prices—High	26⅝	23⅞	18⅞	19¼	16¾	17	7⅞	5¾	4⅛	NA
Low	19½	16	13⅝	13⁷⁄₁₆	11⅜	7⁵⁄₁₆	5⅛	3⁷⁄₁₆	1⅞	NA
P/E Ratio—	18–13	16–11	13–9	14–10	14–9	17–7	13–9	12–7	12–5	NA

Data as orig. reptd. Adj. for stk. div(s). of 100% May 1992. **1.** Refl. merger or acq. **2.** Incl. intangibles. **3.** Bef. spec. item(s) of -0.87 in 1992. d-Deficit. NA-Not Available.

Income Data (Million $)

Year Ended Dec. 31	Revs.	Oper. Inc.	% Oper. Inc. of Revs.	Cap. Exp.	Depr.	Int. Exp.	Net Bef. Taxes	Eff. Tax Rate	Net Inc.	% Net Inc. of Revs.	Cash Flow
1992	**184**	**52.5**	**28.4**	**6.1**	**9.99**	**1.82**	**40.8**	**37.1%**	**[3]25.6**	**13.9**	**35.6**
[1]1991	161	48.7	30.2	15.4	8.85	1.59	39.4	35.5%	25.5	15.8	34.3
1990	169	50.8	30.0	6.5	8.11	2.14	40.8	36.2%	26.0	15.3	34.1
[1]1989	151	45.0	29.7	22.4	7.02	2.15	35.9	36.4%	22.8	15.1	29.9
1988	135	41.7	30.9	4.9	6.11	2.52	33.1	36.9%	20.8	15.4	27.0
[1]1987	133	40.0	30.0	3.9	6.11	3.65	29.9	42.8%	[2]17.1	12.8	23.2
[1]1986	113	29.5	26.2	3.0	5.51	5.07	19.7	49.1%	10.0	8.9	15.5
1985	85	24.2	28.6	5.5	4.62	6.01	14.5	46.3%	7.8	9.2	12.4
1984	86	22.1	25.7	4.6	4.89	7.52	10.1	43.6%	5.7	6.6	10.6
1983	72	21.5	29.8	4.3	4.65	7.00	9.9	47.1%	5.3	7.3	9.9

Balance Sheet Data (Million $)

Dec. 31	Cash	Curr. Assets	Curr. Liab.	Curr. Ratio	Total Assets	% Ret. on Assets	Long Term Debt	Common Equity	Total Cap.	% LT Debt of Cap.	% Ret. on Equity
1992	**13.7**	**97.5**	**40.8**	**2.4**	**211**	**11.9**	**8.0**	**136**	**144**	**5.6**	**18.7**
1991	7.9	96.3	37.1	2.6	217	12.9	33.7	138	180	18.7	20.2
1990	17.7	93.1	30.3	3.1	176	15.7	22.6	114	146	15.5	25.4
1989	1.0	70.0	27.0	2.6	154	16.5	27.2	91	127	21.4	28.4
1988	1.5	56.0	24.1	2.3	122	17.1	20.5	70	98	20.8	34.5
1987	1.4	52.2	28.3	1.8	120	14.2	35.0	50	92	38.1	40.6
1986	2.1	52.5	21.6	2.4	120	9.2	60.5	34	98	61.4	34.7
1985	0.8	35.5	15.1	2.4	98	7.8	57.0	24	83	69.1	38.9
1984	0.6	33.9	16.4	2.1	101	5.3	69.0	16	85	81.1	45.2
1983	0.2	33.9	8.4	4.0	88	NA	70.0	7	80	87.5	NA

Data as orig. reptd. **1.** Refl. merger or acq. **2.** Refl. acctg. change. **3.** Bef. spec. items. NA-Not Available.

Net Sales (Million $)

13 Weeks:	1993	1992	1991	1990
Mar.	48.0	45.6	43.1	42.9
Jun.	47.2	48.9	42.6	46.2
Sep.		43.4	36.4	39.8
Dec.		46.0	38.9	40.5
		183.9	161.0	169.4

Based on a brief report, net sales for the six months ended July 3, 1993, rose 0.8%, year to year. Net income rose 0.1%, to $13,783,000 ($0.79 a share), compared with $12,460,000 ($0.71). Results for the 1992 interim exclude a $15,244,000 ($0.87 per share) charge related to an accounting change.

Common Share Earnings ($)

13 Weeks:	1993	1992	1991	1990
Mar.	0.39	0.32	0.37	0.35
Jun.	0.40	0.39	0.41	0.41
Sep.		0.35	0.34	0.37
Dec.		0.41	0.36	0.39
		1.47	1.47	1.51

Finances

In October 1992, Kaydon said it had taken advantage of turmoil in foreign exchange markets and falling interest rates in the U.S. by refinancing its Sterling denominated debt of £5,000,000 associated with the Cooper Bearings acquisition. The long-term Sterling debt was refinanced with short-term dollar denominated debt at a favorable exchange rate.

At September 26, 1992, the company had available under revolving credit agreements $60 million that could be utilized to meet capital, acquisition or liquidity needs.

Dividend Data

Kaydon changed to quarterly payments, from semiannual distributions, in 1987.

Amt. of Divd. $	Date Decl.	Ex-divd. Date	Stock of Record	Payment Date
0.09	Oct. 21	Dec. 8	Dec. 14	Jan. 4'93
0.09	Jan. 27	Mar. 16	Mar. 22	Apr. 5'93
0.09	Apr. 21	Jun. 15	Jun. 21	Jul. 5'93
0.09	Jun. 23	Sep. 14	Sep. 20	Oct. 4'93

Capitalization

Long Term Debt: $8,000,000 (4/93).

Common Stock: 17,435,698 shs. ($0.10 par).
Institutions hold 72%.
Shareholders: 1,929 of record.

Office—19329 U.S. 19 North, Clearwater, FL 34624. **Tel**—(813) 531-1101. **Fax**—(813) 530-9247. **Chrmn & CEO**—L. J. Cawley. **Pres & COO**—S. K. Clough. **Contr**—T. C. Sorrells III. **VP & Secy**—J. F. Brocci. **Investor Contact**—Shelley Schwemley. **Dirs**—G. W. Bailey, G. J. Breen, L. J. Cawley, S. K. Clough, J. H. F. Haskell, Jr., N. Stevens. **Transfer Agent & Registrar**—Continental Stock Transfer & Trust Co., NY. **Incorporated** in Delaware in 1983. **Empl**—1,731.

 M. Graham Hackett

Kelly Services

NASDAQ Symbol KELYA (Incl. in Nat'l Market) In S&P MidCap 400

Price	Range	P-E Ratio	Dividend	Yield	S&P Ranking	Beta
Aug. 27'93	1993					
30¼	36⅝–24¼	28	0.64	2.1%	A	1.06

Summary

This leading supplier of temporary personnel provides services for a diversified group of customers, both domestically and abroad. Revenues are expected to rise strongly in 1993, while earnings, which have been restricted by competitive pressures, should post a more moderate gain. The cash dividend was increased 5.3% in conjunction with a five-for-four stock split in June 1993.

Current Outlook

Share earnings should increase to $1.24 in 1993, from the $1.04 (adjusted) of 1992.

The quarterly dividend was raised 5.3%, to $0.16 a share, in conjunction with a five-for-four stock split in June 1993.

Sales of services should continue to rise strongly in coming quarters, and prices, which have been restricted by the weak economy and intense competitive pressures, should begin to contribute modestly to earnings growth. Margins are likely to improve from current levels, although a return to historical highs is not probable, as competitive pressures—both from other temporary help companies and from stronger customer bargaining power—should persist. Long-term earnings growth should be aided by expansion overseas.

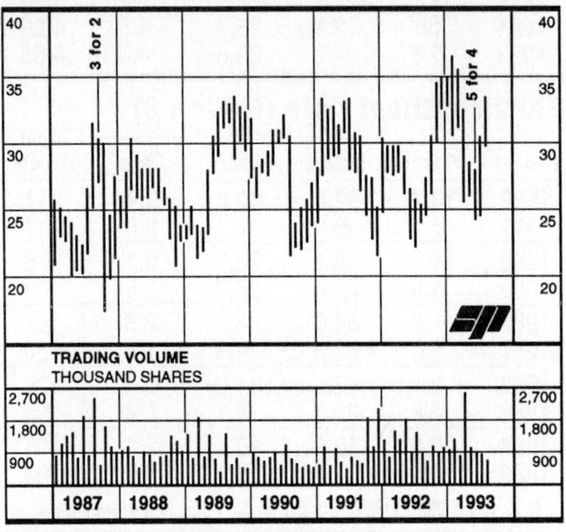

Sales of Services (Million $)

13 Weeks:	1993	1992	1991	1990
Mar.	453	377	330	355
Jun.	484	416	347	368
Sep.	---	452	378	386
Dec.	---	477	382	362
	---	1,723	1,438	1,471

Sales of services for the 26 weeks ended July 4, 1993, advanced 18%, year to year, on strong unit volume. Results were restricted by competitive pricing pressures and higher payroll costs. Net income rose 15%, to $16,888,000 ($0.45 a share, as adjusted), from $14,714,000 ($0.39).

Common Share Earnings ($)

13 Weeks:	1993	1992	1991	1990
Mar.	0.18	0.17	0.22	0.42
Jun.	0.27	0.22	0.26	0.48
Sep.	E0.40	0.30	0.30	0.56
Dec.	E0.39	0.34	0.24	0.43
	E1.24	1.04	1.02	1.90

Important Developments

Jul. '93— Kelly said it believes 1993 will be a good year for the company, despite modest economic forecasts in the U.S. and the continuing recession in Europe.

May '93— The company acquired Karin Lanng AS, a temporary help concern based in Denmark's second largest city, Arhus. Karin will maintain its management and will continue to operate under that name.

Feb. '93— The company acquired Personal Byraet Group, the third largest temporary help company in Norway. The move, which reflects Kelly's emphasis on global expansion, complements its operations in Denmark.

Next earnings report expected in late October.

Per Share Data ($)

Yr. End Dec. 31	1992	1991	1990	1989	1988	1987	1986	1985	1984	1983
Tangible Bk. Val.	**9.42**	9.10	8.70	7.42	6.08	4.91	3.94	3.41	2.86	2.36
Cash Flow	**1.42**	1.29	2.13	2.10	1.81	1.51	1.12	0.98	0.79	0.52
Earnings	**1.04**	1.02	1.90	1.89	1.61	1.34	0.97	[1]0.86	[1]0.70	0.46
Dividends	**0.584**	0.576	0.528	0.462	0.384	0.329	0.278	0.238	0.195	0.162
Payout Ratio	**56%**	56%	28%	24%	24%	24%	29%	28%	28%	35%
Prices—High	**35**	33 13/32	32 3/16	33 19/32	30 13/32	31 19/32	26 3/16	19 13/16	9 5/16	8
Low	**22 3/16**	21 19/32	21 19/32	21 13/32	20 13/16	17 13/32	19 3/16	9	6½	5 5/16
P/E Ratio—	**34–21**	33–21	17–11	18–11	19–13	24–13	27–20	23–11	13–9	18–11

Data as orig. reptd. Adj. for stk. divs. of 25% Jun. 1993, 35% Jun. 1989, 50% Aug. 1987. **1.** Ful. dil.: 0.85 in 1985, 0.70 in 1984. E-Estimated

Income Data (Million $)

Year Ended Dec. 31	Revs.	Oper. Inc.	% Oper. Inc. of Revs.	Cap. Exp.	Depr.	Int. Exp.	Net Bef. Taxes	Eff. Tax Rate	Net Inc.	% Net Inc. of Revs.	Cash Flow
1992	**1,723**	**75**	**4.4**	**32.4**	**14.0**	**Nil**	**61**	**35.7%**	**39.2**	**2.3**	**53.2**
1991	1,438	70	4.9	23.5	9.8	Nil	60	35.9%	38.6	2.7	48.4
1990	1,471	122	8.3	12.0	8.8	Nil	113	37.0%	71.2	4.8	80.0
1989	1,377	119	8.7	11.2	7.9	Nil	113	37.3%	70.8	5.1	78.7
1988	1,269	107	8.4	10.5	7.4	Nil	99	39.3%	60.3	4.8	67.7
1987	1,161	98	8.5	5.7	6.4	Nil	92	45.1%	50.5	4.3	56.8
1986	1,034	78	7.6	7.5	5.6	Nil	73	49.8%	[1]36.4	3.5	42.1
1985	876	69	7.8	8.5	4.6	Nil	64	49.0%	32.6	3.7	37.2
1984	741	56	7.5	8.2	3.4	Nil	52	48.8%	26.7	3.6	30.1
1983	524	37	7.0	2.9	2.4	Nil	35	49.4%	17.5	3.3	19.9

Balance Sheet Data (Million $)

Dec. 31	Cash	Curr. Assets	Curr. Liab.	Curr. Ratio	Total Assets	% Ret. on Assets	Long Term Debt	Common Equity	Total Cap.	% LT Debt of Cap.	% Ret. on Equity
1992	**184**	**409**	**129**	**3.2**	**496**	**8.0**	**Nil**	**367**	**367**	**Nil**	**10.9**
1991	227	411	124	3.3	479	8.4	Nil	355	355	Nil	11.1
1990	217	393	106	3.7	444	17.0	Nil	338	338	Nil	22.9
1989	189	354	111	3.2	394	19.6	Nil	284	284	Nil	27.6
1988	147	292	96	3.0	326	20.5	Nil	230	230	Nil	29.1
1987	101	232	78	3.0	262	21.2	Nil	184	184	Nil	30.4
1986	66	185	66	2.8	213	18.7	Nil	148	148	Nil	26.4
1985	48	152	50	3.1	179	19.9	Nil	129	129	Nil	27.5
1984	40	126	40	3.1	149	19.5	Nil	109	109	Nil	26.9
1983	36	106	35	3.1	124	15.2	Nil	89	89	Nil	20.4

Data as orig. reptd. **1.** Refl. acctg. change.

Business Summary

Kelly Services, Inc. believes that it is the largest supplier of temporary personnel in the U.S. The company provides office/office automation and clerical, marketing, healthcare, technical, light industrial and other help to a diversified group of customers. In recent years, more than 185,000 customers, including the largest industrial corporations in the country, have used Kelly's services.

The company operates through approximately 920 offices in all 50 states, the District of Columbia, Puerto Rico, Mexico, Canada, France, the U.K., Ireland, the Netherlands, Australia, New Zealand, Denmark, Norway, Scotland and Wales. About 98% of Kelly's offices are operated directly by the company; the remainder are operated by licensees.

The Kelly Temporary Services division provides temporary office help to accommodate customer needs caused by absences for vacations or illness, for planned programs and for unexpected work volume increases. The division also supplies marketing support services, semi-skilled light industrial services and technical services. Kelly Assisted Living Services is a subsidiary devoted to assisting clients who need help with their daily living needs.

The company utilizes testing programs to determine a temporary employee's capabilities, particularly in the evaluation of office automation skills. New training programs are continually developed to ensure that employees have the specific skills that customers require.

During 1992, Kelly employed 580,000 people for part-time or temporary periods. As the employer, the company is responsible for Social Security taxes, workers' compensation, liability insurance and similar costs.

Dividend Data

Cash has been paid each year since 1962. Recent dividends on Class A stock were:

Amt of Divd. $	Date Decl.	Ex-divd. Date	Stock of Record	Payment Date
0.19	Nov. 17	Nov. 20	Nov. 27	Dec. 11'92
0.19	Feb. 16	Feb. 22	Feb. 26	Mar. 12'93
5-for-4	May 18	---	May 28	Jun. 11'93
0.16	May 18	May 24	May 28	Jun. 11'93
0.16	Aug. 17	Aug. 23	Aug. 27	Sep. 10'93

Capitalization

Long Term Debt: None (7/93).

Common Stock: 34,120,808 shs. Cl. A ($1 par); 3,603,124 shs. Cl. B ($1 par).

Cl. A shs. are nonvoting; Cl. B are entitled to one vote ea.

Officers & directors hold 55% of Cl. A and 89% of Cl. B (incl. 44% & 61%, respectively, by W.R. Kelly).

Institutions hold about 44% of Cl. A.

Office—999 W. Big Beaver Rd., Troy, MI 48084. **Tel**—(313) 362-4444. **Chrmn**—W. R. Kelly. **Pres & CEO**—T. E. Adderley. **Sr VP & CFO**—R. F. Stoner. **Sr VP & Secy**—E. L. Hartwig. **VP & Treas**—K. S. Ord. **Dirs**—T. E. Adderley, C. V. Fricke, H. E. Guenther, V. G. Istock, W. R. Kelly. **Transfer Agent & Registrar**—NBD Bank, Boston. **Incorporated** in Delaware in 1952. **Empl**—4,000.

 L. Feuer Nelson

Kemper Corp.

NYSE Symbol KEM Options on Phila (Jan-Apr-Jul-Oct) In S&P MidCap 400

Price	Range	P-E Ratio	Dividend	Yield	S&P Ranking	Beta
Aug. 13'93	1993					
38½	43–26⅛	NM	0.92	2.4%	B	1.90

Summary

This major financial services company engages in life insurance, asset management and investment services. To better focus on its core operations, KEM has exited the reinsurance and property-casualty insurance markets. Although operating earnings will trend upward in 1993, the negative effects of underperforming real estate assets will likely lead to a net loss.

Current Outlook

Earnings for 1993 (before realized capital gains or losses) are estimated at $2.75 a share, up from the $0.32 a share reported for 1992. Earnings could rise to $3.50 in 1994.

The $0.23 quarterly dividend is the minimum expected.

Continued robust demand for savings vehicles (such as annuities), together with favorable interest rate spreads and lower operating expenses, will aid life insurance operating margins. Increased productivity, cost cuts and favorable market conditions in the investment unit will be offset by the likelihood of increased litigation reserves. Investment income will be restrained by lower interest rates and the negative effects of underperforming real estate assets. At March 31, 1993, real estate and mortgage loans equaled 26% of invested assets; junk bonds accounted for 4%. Share results will benefit from fewer outstanding shares.

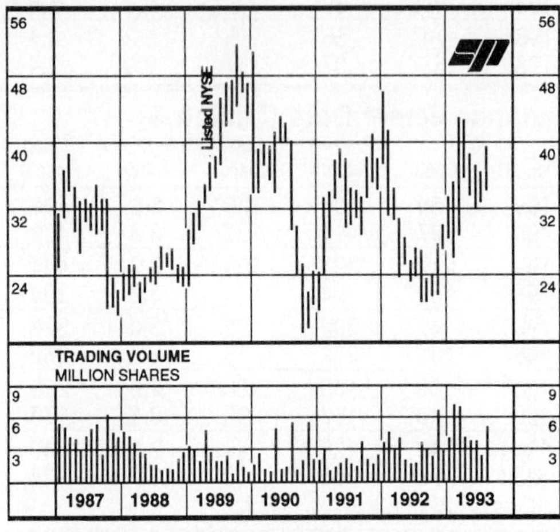

Review of Operations

Revenues in the six months ended June 30, 1993, declined 9.6%, year to year, as restated, reflecting 4.7% higher life insurance revenues, fractionally higher asset management fees, 0.8% lower securities revenue, and sharply higher realized investment losses. Margins narrowed, and the loss from continuing operations widened to $0.60 a share ($0.73 of operating income) from $0.07 ($0.65 of operating income). Share results exclude special charges of $0.24 and $0.30 from an accounting change, and income from discontinued operations of $0.55, compared with $0.19.

Common Share Earnings ($)

Quarter:	1993	1992	1991	1990
Mar.	---	0.40	1.08	0.79
Jun.	[1]d0.60	d0.22	1.10	d2.28
Sep.		d0.11	1.14	0.77
Dec.		d4.32	0.91	0.98
		d4.28	4.25	0.25

Important Developments

Aug. '93— KEM sold Kemper Reinsurance Co. and National Loss Control Services Company to Lumbermens Mutual Casualty Co. In exchange, KEM received 17.4 million of its common shares that were held by Lumbermens. As a result of this tax free transaction, Lumbermens' stake in KEM was reduced to under 4% from 38%, and KEM's outstanding shares were reduced to about 31.9 million from 49.3 million at year end 1992.

Jul. '93— KEM agreed definitively to sell Economy Fire & Casualty Co., one of its discontinued property-casualty units, to The St. Paul Companies for $420 million. The transaction is expected to close during 1993's third quarter. Economy wrote $401 million of personal lines premiums in 1992, and had assets of $733 million and equity of $306 million at March 31, 1993.

Next earnings report expected in early November.

Per Share Data ($)

Yr. End Dec. 31	1992	1991	1990	1989	1988	1987	1986	1985	1984	1983
Tangible Bk. Val.	**33.77**	37.92	34.20	35.25	29.97	26.50	23.48	19.18	17.51	18.32
Oper. Earnings[2]	**0.32**	4.20	d0.15	4.17	3.37	3.19	2.51	1.54	0.57	1.56
Earnings[2,3]	**d4.28**	4.25	0.25	4.44	3.64	4.12	3.40	1.89	1.12	2.27
Dividends	**0.92**	0.92	0.92	0.81	0.72	0.60	0.60	0.60	0.60	0.60
Payout Ratio	**NM**	22%	NM	18%	20%	15%	18%	32%	54%	26%
Prices—High	**46⅛**	41	51	51⅞	27½	38¾	35½	24⅜	15½	17¼
Low	**20¾**	19¾	17⅛	22¾	20¾	19¼	23	14¾	9¾	12
P/E Ratio—[4]	**NM**	10–5	23–8	12–5	8–6	12–6	14–9	16–10	27–17	11–8

Data as orig. reptd. Adj. for stk. div. of 200% in 1986. **1.** Six months. **2.** Bef. results of disc. opers. of +0.45 in 1992, +1.52 in 1989, +0.17 in 1988; and bef. spec. item of -0.33 in 1992. **3.** Aft. gains/losses on securities trans. **4.** Based on oper. earns. prior to 1989. d-Deficit. NM-Not Meaningful.

Income Data (Million $)

Year Ended Dec. 31	Premium Income	Net Invest. Inc.	Total Revs.	Property & Casualty Underwriting Ratios [1]Loss	[1]Expense	[1]Comb.	Net Bef. Taxes	[2]Net Oper. Inc.	[2]Net Inc.	—% Return On— [3]Revs.	[3,4]Equity
1992	**678**	**541**	**2,201**	**NA**	**NA**	**98.7**	**d290**	**16**	**d209**	**NM**	**NM**
1991	1,147	750	3,131	72.5	29.1	101.6	292	202	205	6.5	11.8
1990	936	765	2,929	78.4	28.6	107.0	40	d8	12	0.4	0.7
1989	859	713	2,774	72.9	30.1	103.0	312	216	230	8.3	13.3
1988	1,941	595	3,488	69.3	30.5	99.8	269	198	214	5.7	12.4
1987	2,208	542	3,369	80.1	24.8	104.9	243	195	251	5.3	12.8
1986	2,066	487	3,330	80.1	24.9	105.0	212	148	201	4.4	11.8
1985	1,861	421	2,882	85.6	27.0	112.6	77	76	93	2.6	8.4
1984	1,525	368	2,302	88.7	29.5	118.2	d35	25	48	1.1	3.2
1983	1,532	315	2,222	78.3	31.7	110.0	50	68	100	3.1	9.0

Balance Sheet Data (Million $)

Dec. 31	Cash & Equiv.	Premiums Due	Investment Assets [5]Bonds	Stocks	[6]Loans	Total	% Invest. Yield	Deferred Policy Costs	Total Assets	Debt	Common Equity
1992	**334**	**NA**	**6,119**	**287**	**2,070**	**8,989**	**5.9**	**649**	**14,791**	**659**	**1,665**
1991	254	NA	5,961	405	2,429	9,336	8.2	590	14,697	558	1,838
1990	197	205	6,275	432	2,313	9,020	9.0	510	13,588	523	1,625
1989	245	158	5,837	499	1,626	7,963	9.1	439	12,696	696	1,722
1988	255	345	5,860	487	1,311	7,657	8.3	363	12,078	679	1,737
1987	186	321	5,193	452	1,029	6,675	8.7	332	10,742	554	1,543
1986	163	293	4,666	303	792	5,761	9.2	307	9,735	502	1,417
1985	166	237	4,177	293	407	4,877	9.5	295	9,264	542	994
1984	106	192	3,458	311	263	4,032	9.4	245	7,085	470	746
1983	66	246	3,221	381	192	3,794	8.9	236	6,838	388	789

Data as orig. reptd. **1.** As reptd. by co.; prop.-casualty & reinsurance. **2.** Bef. results of disc. opers. and bef. spec. items. **3.** Based on oper. earns. prior to 1989. **4.** Common. **5.** Incl. short-term invest. **6.** Incl. other invest. d-Deficit. NA-Not Available. NM-Not Meaningful

Business Summary

This diversified financial services holding company is exiting the reinsurance and property casualty insurance market to better focus on its life insurance and asset management operations. Segment contributions (profits in million $) from continuing operations in 1992:

	Revs.	Pretax Inc.
Life Insurance	30%	–$23.6
Securities brokerage	30%	–27.6
Asset management	26%	137.2
Reinsurance	26%	–27.2
Corporate & other	–12%	–349.0

Life insurance operations, conducted by Federal Kemper Life Assurance Co. and Kemper Investors Life Insurance Co., offer an array of term and interest sensitive life insurance, and fixed and variable rate annuities. At year end 1992, life insurance in force equaled $84.2 billion.

The Kemper Securities Group, Inc. is the holding company for five regional securities firms that provide retail and insitiutional securities brokerage and investment banking services through 1,675 brokers in 172 offices throughout the U.S.

Asset management activities are conducted by Kemper Financial Services, Inc. and its 95%-owned INVEST Financial Corp. and Kemper Service Co. At year end 1992, assets under management totaled $69.3 billion. At March 1, 1993, 36 open and closed end mutual funds were being offered.

Kemper Reinsurance Co., which wrote $559 million of net premiums in 1992, was sold in August 1993.

Dividend Data

Cash has been paid each year since 1968. A dividend reinvestment plan is available. A "poison pill" stock purchase right was issued in July 1990.

Amt. of Divd. $	Date Decl.	Ex-divd. Date	Stock of Record	Payment Date
0.23	Sep. 4	Nov. 3	Nov. 9	Nov. 30'92
0.23	Jan. 12	Feb. 1	Feb. 5	Feb. 26'93
0.23	Mar. 18	May 3	May 7	May 28'93
0.23	Jul. 20	Aug. 4	Aug. 10	Aug. 31'93

Capitalization

Total Debt: $709,842,000 (3/93).

Minority Interest: $3,629,000.

Preferred Stock: 2,025,044 shs. (no par).

Common Stock: 31,900,000 shs. ($5 par). Institutions hold some 66%. Shareholders of record: 12,650 (12/92).

Office—One Kemper Dr., Long Grove, IL 60049. **Tel**—(708) 540-2000. **Chrmn & CEO**—D. B. Mathis. **Pres**—S. B. Timbers. **VP-CFO**—J. H. Fitzpatrick. **Secy**—K. A. Gallichio. **Treas**—J. W. Burns. **Investor Contact**—John A. Effrein (708-540-3435). **Dirs**—J. T. Chain, Jr., J. R. Coleman, R. F. Farley, J. H. Fitzpatrick, P. B. Hamilton, G. D. Kennedy, C. M. Kierscht, J. E. Luecke, D. B. Mathis, R. D. Nordman, K. A. Randall, J. C. Stetson, S. B. Timbers, D. R. Toll. **Transfer Agent**—Harris Trust and Savings Bank, Chicago. **Incorporated** in Delaware in 1967. **Empl**—6,090.

 Catherine A. Seifert

Kennametal Inc.

NYSE Symbol KMT In S&P MidCap 400

Price	Range	P-E Ratio	Dividend	Yield	S&P Ranking	Beta
Aug. 27'93	1993					
37	39¾–28	20	1.16	3.1%	B+	1.02

Summary

Kennametal manufactures tools made of cemented carbide, ceramics and other materials, and distributes tooling products and provides supplies and services to the metalworking industry. Following substantially improved earnings for fiscal 1993, profits will probably advance again in fiscal 1994, aided by higher sales. In August 1993, KMT acquired a majority interest in a German tool manufacturer for about $56 million plus the assumption of approximately $57 million in debt.

Current Outlook

Earnings for the fiscal year ending June 30, 1994, are projected at about $2.00 a share (excluding an anticipated substantial charge for the cumulative effect of an accounting change for certain postretirement benefits), up from the $1.85 a share reported for fiscal 1993.

Dividends are expected to continue at the current rate of $0.29 quarterly.

Sales for fiscal 1994 should increase strongly, aided by the recent Hertel acquisition. Metalworking products sales should benefit from full service supply programs, catalog sales, and continued improvement in the U.S. economy. International business is expected to remain weak in Europe in the early part of the fiscal year, with some improvement possible in the second half. Sales of construction tools are likely to continue to increase, benefiting from highway construction projects throughout the world. Profitability will be helped by the higher sales and ongoing cost controls, partially offset by initiation of ongoing expenses related to postretirement benefits.

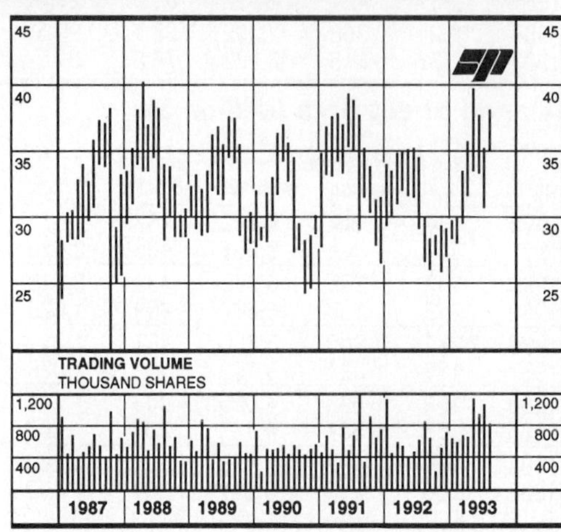

Net Sales (Million $)

Quarter:	1992–93	1991–92	1990–91	1989–90
Sep.	148.8	149.9	152.1	135.7
Dec.	140.7	140.6	152.1	135.5
Mar.	153.7	152.9	157.8	161.5
Jun.	155.3	151.2	155.7	156.4
	598.5	594.5	617.8	589.0

Sales for the fiscal year ended June 30, 1993 (preliminary) were up less than 1%, year to year. Margins widened on a more favorable sales mix and lower production costs. After a decline in interest expenses, and a patent litigation charge of $1.7 million, which was partially offset by a $1.0 million gain, pretax income advanced 63%. Following taxes at 41.1%, versus 38.6%, net income rose 56%, to $1.85 a share (including a $0.10 nonrecurring gain) from $1.20.

Capital Share Earnings ($)

Quarter:	1992–93	1991–92	1990–91	1989–90
Sep.	0.28	0.35	0.66	0.62
Dec.	0.19	0.10	0.60	0.58
Mar.	0.68	0.50	0.56	1.02
Jun.	0.70	0.25	0.18	0.86
	1.85	1.20	2.00	3.08

Important Developments

Aug. '93— KMT said it had acquired an 81% interest in Hertel AG for DM90 million (about $56 million), plus assumed debt of about DM92 million ($57 million). Hertel, based in Furth, Germany, makes cemented carbide tools and tooling systems, and incurred a net loss of $30 million on sales of $259 million for 1991 (latest available). KMT said the acquisition should significantly increase its influence in the European and Asia-Pacific markets. Separately, KMT said its CFO, Henry L. Dykema, had resigned.

Next earnings report expected in late October.

Per Share Data ($)

Yr. End Jun. 30	1993	1992	[1]1991	[1]1990	1989	1988	1987	1986	1985	1984
Tangible Bk. Val.	**NA**	20.19	19.56	18.35	18.77	17.75	15.84	14.73	16.91	16.32
Cash Flow	**NA**	4.12	5.10	5.97	5.43	4.71	3.63	2.17	2.89	2.25
Earnings	**1.85**	1.20	2.00	3.08	2.90	2.37	1.69	0.06	1.51	0.95
Dividends	**1.16**	1.16	1.16	1.16	1.12	1.04	0.97	0.86	0.78	0.72
Payout Ratio	**63%**	97%	59%	38%	39%	44%	58%	NM	52%	76%
Prices[2]—High	**39¾**	35¼	39⅜	37	37⅝	40¼	38¼	26¾	26	35¼
Low	**28**	25⅞	26½	24¼	27¼	28¼	20	20	17½	19⅜
P/E Ratio—	**21–15**	29–22	20–13	12–8	13–9	17–12	23–12	NM	17–12	37–21

Data as orig. reptd. 1. Reflects merger or acquisition. 2. Cal. yr. NM-Not Meaningful. NA-Not Available.

Income Data (Million $)

Year Ended Jun. 30	Revs.	Oper. Inc.	% Oper. Inc. of Revs.	Cap. Exp.	Depr.	Int. Exp.	[3]Net Bef. Taxes	Eff. Tax Rate	Net Inc.	% Net Inc. of Revs.	Cash Flow
1992	**595**	**62.4**	**10.5**	**36.6**	**31.3**	**[2]10.1**	**21.0**	**38.6%**	**12.9**	**2.2**	**44.2**
[1]1991	618	94.1	14.7	55.3	32.7	[2]11.8	38.4	45.1%	21.1	3.4	53.8
[1]1990	589	94.4	16.0	36.0	29.9	[2]10.5	55.1	1.7%	32.1	5.5	62.3
1989	472	81.5	17.3	28.5	25.2	9.0	49.2	39.0%	30.0	6.4	56.2
1988	420	72.4	17.2	46.3	23.1	8.6	41.7	41.7%	24.3	5.8	48.3
1987	354	56.0	15.8	34.1	19.7	7.3	31.6	45.6%	[4]17.2	4.9	36.9
1986	355	48.0	13.5	24.1	21.8	7.7	0.8	25.9%	0.6	0.2	22.4
1985	341	54.1	15.9	24.3	17.3	4.3	34.3	44.6%	19.0	5.6	36.3
1984	319	41.3	12.9	15.5	16.1	4.6	22.9	47.7%	12.0	3.7	28.1
1983	271	4.2	1.6	15.2	15.3	7.0	d19.0	NM	d11.2	NM	4.1

Balance Sheet Data (Million $)

Jun. 30	Cash	Curr. Assets	Curr. Liab.	Curr. Ratio	Total Assets	% Ret. on Assets	Long Term Debt	Common Equity	Total Cap.	% LT Debt of Cap.	% Ret. on Equity
1992	**9.0**	**218**	**110**	**2.0**	**472**	**2.7**	**95.3**	**252**	**355**	**26.9**	**5.2**
1991	11.3	228	139	1.6	476	4.5	73.1	244	328	22.3	8.8
1990	10.3	220	111	2.0	451	7.7	81.3	232	313	26.0	14.7
1989	3.8	193	102	1.9	383	8.0	57.1	204	262	21.8	15.3
1988	8.9	177	77	2.3	359	7.1	74.4	186	261	28.5	13.7
1987	12.3	168	65	2.6	327	5.5	72.1	166	238	30.3	10.7
1986	13.2	157	56	2.8	300	0.2	69.3	153	223	31.1	0.3
1985	7.1	181	56	3.3	327	5.9	34.1	216	250	13.6	8.9
1984	8.8	182	57	3.2	322	3.7	35.2	211	246	14.3	5.7
1983	0.9	175	63	2.8	319	NM	35.9	204	240	15.0	NM

Data as orig. reptd. **1.** Reflects merger or acquisition. **2.** Net. **3.** Incl. equity in earns. of nonconsol. subs. **4.** Reflects acctg. change. d-Deficit. NM-Not Meaningful.

Business Summary

Kennametal manufactures a broad line of cemented carbide and other hard metal products, along with tools and accessories, and provides comprehensive solutions to manufacturing problems of customers in the metalworking indusry. Sales by product line in recent fiscal years:

	1993	1992	1991	1990
Metalworking	80%	81%	83%	84%
Mining and construction	17%	15%	14%	13%
Metallurgical	3%	3%	3%	3%
Other	Nil	1%	Nil	Nom.

Foreign business (primarily to Canada and Western Europe, but also increasingly to Asia) accounted for 27% o sales in fiscal 1993, unchanged from a year before.

The metalworking segment serves the automotive, aerospace, machine tools, farm machinery, fabricated metals, construction machinery, and oil and gas drilling industries. KMT makes a broad line of coated and uncoated carbide, cermet (titanium alloy) and other tools for most metalcutting and metalforming applications. KMT also manufactures a line of toolholders and toolholding systems.

Through GIS and J&L America (acquired in January 1990), KMT provides a complete line of industrial tools and supplies to the metalworking industry. J&L is one of the largest U.S. mail order distributors of industrial products. GIS is one of the leading regional distributors. KMT plans to expand GIS's business nationally as part of a strategy to be a complete source of products and services to the metalworking industry.

Mining and construction products include tungsten carbide tools for mining coal and a line of road construction and maintenance tools.

Metallurgical products comprise proprietary metallurgical powders, and related materials, including intermediate carbide powders and hardfacing materials used in oil and gas drilling equipment.

Dividend Data

Dividends have been paid since 1944. A dividend reinvestment plan is available. A "poison pill" stock purchase rights plan was adopted in 1990.

Amt of Divd. $	Date Decl.	Ex-divd. Date	Stock of Record	Payment Date
0.29	Oct. 26	Nov. 4	Nov. 10	Nov. 25'92
0.29	Jan. 25	Feb. 4	Feb. 10	Feb. 25'93
0.29	Apr. 26	May 4	May 10	May 25'93
0.29	Jul. 26	Aug. 4	Aug. 10	Aug. 25'93

Capitalization

Long Term Debt: $93,395,000 (3/93).

Capital Stock: 10,830,338 shs. ($1.25 par).
Institutions hold approximately 74%.
Shareholders of record: 3,000.

Office—Route 981 at Westmoreland County Airport (PO Box 231), Latrobe, PA 15650. **Tel**—(412) 539-5000. **Chrmn**—Q. C. McKenna. **Pres & CEO**—R. L. McGeehan. **VP-Secy**—D. T. Cofer. **Treas & Acting CFO**—J. E. Morrison. **Investor Contact**—Michael J. Mussog. **Dirs**—R. C. Alberding, P. B. Bartlett, R. N. Eslyn, J. D. Fitzmaurice, W. H. Hollinshead, R. L. McGeehan, Q. C. McKenna, A. T. McLaughlin Jr., W. R. Newlin, E. R. Yost, L. Yost. **Transfer Agent & Registrar**—Mellon Bank N.A., Pittsburgh. **Incorporated** in Pennsylvania in 1943. **Empl**—4,980.

 M. Graham Hackett

KeyCorp

NYSE Symbol KEY Options on Phila (Feb-May-Aug-Nov) In S&P MidCap 400

Price	Range	P–E Ratio	Dividend	Yield	S&P Ranking	Beta
Aug. 17'93	1993					
39⅛	46–34½	11	1.24	3.2%	A	1.22

Summary

This multi-regional bank holding company, with $32 billion in assets at June 30, 1993, has focused its banking activities in the Northeast and the Northwest U.S., and has expanded operations via acquisitions. In January 1993 the company completed the merger of Puget Sound Bancorp, Washington state's largest independent commercial bank holding company (assets of $4.7 billion), for about 26.4 million common shares. Earnings through the first half of 1993 have benefited from growth in earning assets, wide spreads, improving asset quality and gains in fee income.

Business Summary

KeyCorp (formerly Key Banks), a multi-state bank holding company, is among the 30 largest bank holding companies in the U.S. Following its January 1993 acquisition of Puget Sound Bancorp, KEY had assets of almost $32 billion. KEY has approximately 800 banking offices located in New York, Alaska, Idaho, Maine, Oregon, Utah, Washington, and Wyoming. KEY also owns a number of nonbank subsidiaries which provide trust, leasing, credit life reinsurance, investment advisory, data processing, mortgage banking, and other financial-related services.

Loans outstanding at the end of 1992 and 1991 totaled $16.8 billion and $15.4 billion, respectively, and were divided:

	1992	1991
Real estate mortgage	42%	40%
Consumer	31%	34%
Commercial, financial and agricultural	22%	21%
Real estate construction	3%	3%
Lease financing	2%	2%

In 1992 loans outstanding constituted 75% of average earning assets, investment securities 21%, and other earning assets 4%. Average sources of funds in 1992 were noninterest bearing deposits 12%, interest-bearing core deposits 63%, CDs of $100,000 or more 7%, Federal funds purchased, securities sold under repurchase agreements and other short term borrowings 7%, long-term debt 2%, shareholders' equity 7%, and other 2%.

Nonperforming assets amounted to $334.5 million (2.00% of loans and related assets) at December 31, 1992, compared with $369.7 million (2.42%) a year before. The allowance for loan losses amounted to 1.32% of outstanding loans at 1992 year-end, compared with 1.37% a year earlier. Net chargeoffs were 0.96% of average loans in 1992, versus 1.06% in 1991.

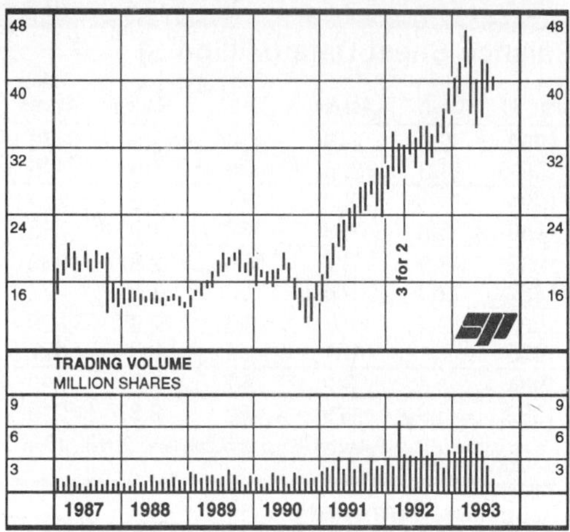

Important Developments

Jul. '93— KEY said that excluding acquisitions, internal loan growth was 5.5% during the quarter (up from 3.5% in the first quarter). KEY noted that loan expansion in the Rocky Mountain banks grew 11%, the Pacific Northwest banks increased loans by 5.4%, while the Eastern banks saw internal loans remain flat. KEY's expected internal loan growth to approximate 5% for 1993. Including acquisitions, growth in the portfolio was estimated at 13%-to-14% for the year (total average loans increased 14.6% through June 30). In January, KEY acquired Puget Sound Bancorp, Washington state's largest independent commercial bank holding company.

Next earnings report expected in mid-October.

Per Share Data ($)

Yr. End Dec. 31	1992	1991	[1]1990	1989	[1]1988	[1]1987	[1]1986	[1]1985	[1]1984	[1]1983
Tangible Bk. Val.	**13.89**	12.27	11.80	11.38	10.17	13.01	12.95	11.09	9.65	8.79
Earnings[2]	**3.17**	2.57	2.31	2.13	1.93	1.50	1.95	1.74	1.47	1.25
Dividends	**1.040**	0.947	0.893	0.840	0.800	0.747	0.667	0.578	0.478	0.434
Payout Ratio	**33%**	37%	39%	39%	41%	50%	34%	33%	33%	35%
Prices—High	**39⅛**	29 11/16	19½	19 13/16	15	20 11/16	20 7/16	17 5/16	10 5/16	9 1/16
Low	**27⅛**	13 13/16	11¼	13 1/16	13	12 7/16	14	10⅝	7 5/16	4⅝
P/E Ratio—	**12–9**	12–5	8–5	9–6	8–7	14–8	10–7	10–6	7–5	7–4

Data as orig. reptd. Adj. for stk. divs. of 50% Apr. 1992, 50% Feb. 1986, 50% May 1984. **1.** Reflects merger or acquisition. **2.** Aft. gains/losses on sec. trans. of +0.25 in 1987, +0.35 in 1986, +0.17 in 1985, +0.05 in 1984, +0.03 in 1983, +0.01 in 1982.

Income Data (Million $)

Year Ended Dec. 31	Net Int. Inc.	Tax Equiv. Adj.	Non Int. Inc.	Loan Loss Prov.	% Exp./ Op. Revs.	[2]Net Bef. Taxes	Eff. Tax Rate	Net Inc.	% Net Int. Margin	—% Return On— Assets	Equity
1992	**1,096**	**35**	**327**	**151**	**61.8**	**375**	**34.4%**	**246**	**5.31**	**1.04**	**16.5**
1991	891	33	303	152	63.4	276	31.8%	188	4.75	0.86	14.7
[1]1990	670	30	209	72	66.2	210	29.2%	148	4.70	0.89	14.5
1989	619	31	204	65	67.9	188	27.0%	137	4.93	0.93	14.5
[1]1988	570	33	167	45	70.6	157	23.8%	120	5.07	0.90	14.4
[1]1987	459	44	145	70	70.4	99	19.3%	80	5.41	0.76	11.8
[1]1986	337	59	108	36	66.1	99	16.8%	82	5.96	1.09	16.3
[1]1985	281	51	77	21	65.7	80	14.5%	68	6.03	1.10	16.9
[1]1984	216	41	49	11	64.8	59	13.6%	51	6.14	1.07	16.0
[1]1983	145	26	29	9	63.9	38	13.8%	33	6.17	1.06	15.0

Balance Sheet Data (Million $)

Dec. 31	Total Assets	—Earning Assets— Mon. Mkt. Assets	Inv. Secs.	Com'l Loans	Other Loans	% Loan Loss Resv.	—Deposits— Demand	Time	% Loans/ Deposits	Long Term Debt	Common Equity	% Equity To Assets
1992	**25,457**	**151**	**5,221**	**4,130**	**13,313**	**1.27**	**3,866**	**17,138**	**81.9**	**655**	**1,475**	**5.83**
1991	23,156	94	4,763	3,559	12,421	1.32	2,936	16,116	82.3	501	1,302	5.53
1990	19,266	46	3,750	3,156	10,333	1.25	2,632	13,350	81.7	382	1,062	6.07
1989	15,461	44	3,484	2,951	7,365	1.28	2,666	9,787	79.8	378	959	6.22
1988	14,646	85	3,454	3,027	6,611	1.28	2,518	9,063	80.5	419	876	5.99
1987	11,596	101	2,515	2,776	5,028	1.27	2,114	7,266	80.6	388	665	6.10
1986	9,073	245	2,086	2,143	3,602	1.26	1,928	5,463	74.8	269	559	6.32
1985	7,122	222	1,743	1,636	2,680	1.22	1,430	4,295	72.3	168	419	5.91
1984	5,620	187	1,406	1,516	1,881	1.07	1,229	3,478	68.6	105	305	5.86
1983	3,492	144	1,028	847	1,136	1.15	809	1,998	65.9	62	220	6.68

Data as orig. reptd. **1.** Reflects merger or acquisition. **2.** Incl. equity in earns. of non consol. subs.

Review of Operations

Net interest income for the six months ended June 30, 1993 rose 13%, year to year, aided by an 11% rise in average earning assets (average loans were up 12%) and a slightly higher net yield on average earning assets (5.36% versus 5.28%). The provision for loan losses fell 22%, to $73.4 million. Aided by significantly higher special asset management fees ($24.0 million versus $1.9 million), a 45% increase in insurance and brokerage revenue and a 16% rise in service charges on deposit accounts, noninterest income was up 25%. Noninterest expense was up 15%. Pretax income advanced 36%. After taxes at 34.8%, versus 32.4%, net income was up 31%. Following preferred dividends, share earnings were $1.86, compared with $1.44 (restated). Results for the 1992 period exclude a $0.07 a share accounting credit.

Common Share Earnings ($)

Quarter:	1993	1992	1991	1990
Mar.	0.91	0.74	0.60	0.57
Jun.	0.95	0.77	0.61	0.58
Sep.		0.82	0.67	0.58
Dec.		0.84	0.68	0.59
		3.17	2.57	2.31

Finances

At December 31, 1992 1992 Tier 1 capital was 8.03% of risk adjusted assets, up from 7.36% at year-end 1991. Total risk adjusted capital was 10.75% at year-end 1992, versus 9.42% at December 31, 1991.

In January 1993, KEY acquired Puget Sound Bancorp, a $4.7 billion bank holding company headquartered in Washington. KEY issued 26.4 million common shares to PSB holders.

In May 1991, KEY acquired some $5.8 billion in assets of 31 branch offices and a mortgage unit of Goldome, a New York stock savings bank.

Dividend Data

Dividends have been paid since 1841. A dividend reinvestment plan is available.

Amt. of Divd. $	Date Decl.	Ex-divd. Date	Stock of Record	Payment Date
0.26	Aug. 21	Sep. 24	Sep. 30	Oct. 15'92
0.26	Oct. 15	Dec. 24	Dec. 31	Jan. 15'93
0.31	Feb. 18	Mar. 25	Mar. 31	Apr. 15'93
0.31	Apr. 23	Jun. 24	Jun. 30	Jul. 15'93

Capitalization

Long Term Debt: $866,000,000 (6/93).

Preferred Stock: $184,000,000.

Common Stock: 101,211,000 shs. ($5 par). Institutions hold about 54%. Shareholders of record: 19,325 (12/92).

Office—One KeyCorp Plaza, P.O. Box 88, Albany, NY 12201-0088. **Tel**—(518) 486-8000. **Chrmn, Pres & CEO**—V.J. Riley Jr. **VP-CFO**—W. H. Dougherty. **VP-Investor Contact**—Don J. Kauth (518) 487-4491. **Dirs**—W.J. Agee, F.A Augsbury Jr., H.D. Barclay, R.H. Bischoff, W.D. Broadnax, C.M. Carlson, K. M. Curtis, J. C. Dimmer, L. J. Fjeldstad, H.S. Hemingway, C. H. Hogan, R.E. Lavoie Jr., V.J. Riley Jr., R.A. Schumacher, R.B. Stafford, P.G. Ten Eyck II, N.B. Veeder. **Transfer Agent & Registrar**—Mellon Securities Trust Co., NYC. **Incorporated** in New York in 1970. **Empl**—17,000.

 Richard M. Levine, CFA

Keystone International

NYSE Symbol KII Options on Pacific (Mar-Jun-Sep-Dec) In S&P MidCap 400

Price	Range	P-E Ratio	Dividend	Yield	S&P Ranking	Beta
Sep. 23'93	1993					
25⅛	29⅛–23	21	0.72	2.9%	A–	0.92

Summary

This company manufactures and distributes worldwide valves and other flow control products for use in a broad range of industries. Earnings in the first half of 1993 were hurt by weakness in overseas markets, and results for the full year will probably trail 1992. Assuming continued economic growth in the U. S. and improvement in foreign economies, sales and earnings should advance in 1994.

Current Outlook

Earnings for 1994 are estimated at $1.40, versus the $1.17 projected for 1993.

The $0.18 quarterly dividend may be increased in 1994.

Sales are expected to rise in 1994, reflecting continued growth in the U.S. and Asia/Pacific and stabilization of sales in Europe. Aided by higher operating rates, firmer pricing and previous restructuring moves, margins should expand. Assuming level interest expense and only a small rise in the tax rate, earnings should advance.

Net Sales (Million $)

Quarter:	1993	1992	1991	1990
Mar................	128.0	128.2	120.4	102.4
Jun................	130.8	135.1	129.7	113.0
Sep................		135.1	132.3	114.3
Dec................		129.9	138.1	116.5
		528.4	520.5	446.2

Sales in the six months ended June 30, 1993, fell 1.7%, year to year, reflecting the adverse impact of currency translation on international operations, and weak overseas markets. Margins were virtually unchanged, but after higher non-operating expense, pretax income fell 8.5%. Following taxes at 38.0%, versus 40.0%, net income declined 5.4%. Share earnings were $0.58 (before a $0.05 gain from an accounting change), versus $0.61.

Common Share Earnings ($)

Quarter:	1993	1992	1991	1990
Mar................	0.28	0.27	0.27	0.30
Jun................	0.30	0.34	0.34	0.34
Sep................	E0.31	0.34	0.27	0.36
Dec................	E0.28	0.27	d0.22	0.31
	E1.17	1.22	0.66	1.31

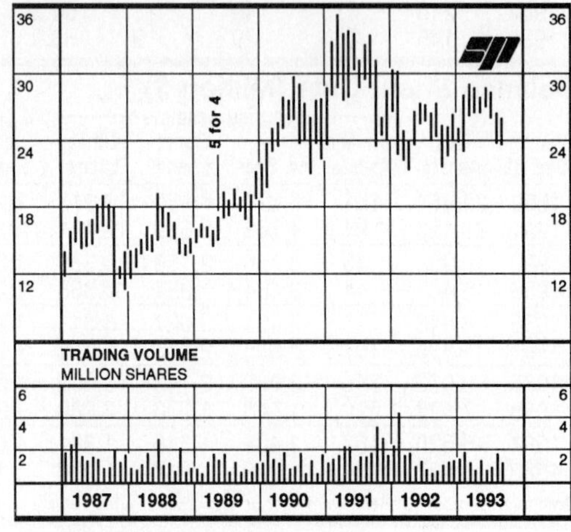

Important Developments

Jul.'93— KII reported share earnings of $0.30 on a 3.2% decline in sales for 1993's second quarter, versus $0.34 a year earlier. Sales and earnings for the quarter and six months were hurt by depressed business conditions in several overseas markets and by the translation effect of weakening foreign currencies. Orders received in the six months ended June 30, 1993, were $263.6 million, essentially unchanged from the comparable period in 1992; orders for the second quarter totaled $130.1 million, a 4.3% increase over 1992's second quarter. Separately, KII stated that 62% of its $20 million restructuring charge had been utilized and that the remaining portion is sufficient to cover the restructuring projects still in progress.

Next earnings report expected in late October.

Per Share Data ($)

Yr. End Dec. 31	1992	1991	1990	1989	1988	1987	[1]1986	1985	1984	1983
Tangible Bk. Val.	**6.47**	6.12	6.02	5.00	4.60	[2]4.92	[2]4.03	[2]3.57	[2]3.20	[2]3.26
Cash Flow	**1.77**	1.17	1.75	1.49	1.34	1.05	0.69	0.80	0.72	0.60
Earnings[3]	**1.22**	0.66	1.31	1.10	0.96	0.68	0.38	0.66	0.61	0.48
Dividends	**0.670**	0.630	0.590	0.533	0.440	0.408	0.379	0.348	0.290	0.275
Payout Ratio	**55%**	96%	45%	48%	46%	61%	103%	52%	45%	58%
Prices—High	**30⅜**	35⅜	29¾	21¼	19¼	19	15¼	12¼	13¼	14¾
Low	**21⅜**	23½	18⅞	14½	11⅝	10	9⅛	9¾	8⅝	10⅛
P/E Ratio—	**25–18**	54–36	23–14	19–13	20–12	28–15	41–24	18–15	22–14	31–21

Data as orig. reptd. Adj. for stk. divs. of 25% May 1989, 5% May 1986, 25% May 1985, 5% May 1984, 5% May 1983. **1.** Reflects merger or acquisition. **2.** Incl. intangibles. **3.** Bef. results of disc. opers. of -0.02 in 1989, +0.03 in 1986, -0.02 in 1985, +0.04 in 1983, & bef. spec. item of -0.14 in 1991. d-Deficit. E-Estimated.

Income Data (Million $)

Year Ended Dec. 31	Revs.	Oper. Inc.	% Oper. Inc. of Revs.	Cap. Exp.	Depr.	Int. Exp.	Net Bef. Taxes	Eff. Tax Rate	[3]Net Inc.	% Net Inc. of Revs.	Cash Flow
1992	**528**	**99.6**	**18.9**	**19.5**	**19.3**	**7.09**	**69.9**	**39.1%**	**42.5**	**8.1**	**61.9**
1991	520	94.3	18.1	35.6	17.7	7.60	43.1	47.0%	[4]22.8	4.4	40.5
1990	446	98.4	22.0	32.5	14.8	7.67	72.1	38.9%	44.0	9.9	58.8
[1]1989	376	84.1	22.4	21.8	13.0	7.72	59.7	38.4%	36.8	9.8	49.8
1988	346	75.1	21.7	10.7	12.8	8.02	51.1	37.6%	31.9	9.2	44.7
1987	292	64.2	22.0	13.6	12.6	8.97	38.2	41.6%	22.3	7.6	34.9
[2]1986	245	52.7	21.5	38.9	11.2	6.95	22.3	47.9%	11.6	4.7	22.8
[1]1985	126	33.4	26.5	12.8	4.5	2.06	30.2	44.8%	16.7	13.2	21.2
1984	124	31.7	25.5	3.4	4.0	2.49	29.3	45.9%	15.9	12.8	19.9
[1]1983	110	27.5	24.9	7.1	4.1	2.69	22.8	44.8%	12.6	11.4	16.7

Balance Sheet Data (Million $)

Dec. 31	Cash	Curr. Assets	Curr. Liab.	Curr. Ratio	Total Assets	% Ret. on Assets	Long Term Debt	Common Equity	Total Cap.	% LT Debt of Cap.	% Ret. on Equity
1992	**29.4**	**278**	**157**	**1.8**	**438**	**9.4**	**14**	**253**	**267**	**5.4**	**17.2**
1991	12.5	290	147	2.0	459	5.1	58	239	298	19.6	9.6
1990	32.3	270	120	2.2	417	11.2	48	231	291	16.6	20.3
1989	29.7	234	103	2.3	366	10.4	51	199	259	19.9	19.3
1988	30.7	221	79	2.8	340	9.5	70	181	261	26.8	18.5
1987	22.9	195	69	2.8	330	6.7	82	163	261	31.6	15.0
1986	26.5	184	68	2.7	321	4.6	116	127	253	45.6	9.7
1985	26.9	98	29	3.4	141	12.6	19	89	113	17.0	19.7
1984	28.9	88	24	3.7	124	12.7	20	80	100	19.7	19.6
1983	33.0	95	24	4.0	131	9.3	20	86	107	19.1	14.7

Data as orig. reptd. **1.** Excl. discontinued operations. **2.** Reflects merger or acquisition. **3.** Bef. spec. items. **4.** Reflects acctg. change.

Business Summary

Keystone International manufactures and distributes valves and other specialized industrial products used to control the flow of liquids, gases, and fibrous and slurry materials for use in a wide variety of industries. Sales and operating profits by geographic area in 1992:

	Sales	Profits
United States	42%	33%
Europe, Middle East & Africa	34%	43%
Asia–Pacific	18%	19%
Canada & South America	6%	5%

In 1992, sales by unit were: industrial valves 40%, safety and environmental products 23%, Keystone controls 20%, specialty valve products 12%, and Keystone Vanessa 5%.

Flow control products include butterfly valves, actuators, electronic controls, and other devices to regulate the movement of liquids, gases and solid materials.

Anderson, Greenwood & Co. designs, engineers, manufactures and markets special-purpose and conventional precision valves for use by the petroleum, chemical, natural gas, pulp and paper, power and other process industries. Yarway Corp. designs, produces and sells specially engineered products and services used in the power generation and process industries.

In 1992, the chemical industry accounted for 11.6% of total sales, OEMs 8.9%, power 8.8%, food and beverage 7.1%, marine and government 9.3%, commercial construction 5.7%, water treatment 5.4%, mining and metals 5.5%, petroleum refining 6.2%, oil and gas pipeline 6.2%, petroleum production 6.0%, industrial plants 5.6%, pulp and paper 3.1%, and other 10.6%.

Dividend Data

Dividends have been paid since 1972. A "poison pill" stock purchase rights plan was adopted in 1990.

Amt. of Divd. $	Date Decl.	Ex–divd. Date	Stock of Record	Payment Date
0.17	Dec. 16	Jan. 27	Feb. 2	Feb. 25'93
0.18	Mar. 17	Apr. 29	May 5	May 19'93
0.18	Jun. 16	Jul. 29	Aug. 4	Aug. 18'93
0.18	Sep. 16	Oct. 27	Nov. 2	Nov. 17'93

Capitalization

Long Term Debt: $14,596,000 (6/93).

Common Stock: 35,057,374 shs. ($1 par).
F.A. Cailloux owns 13.4%.
Institutions hold approximately 59%.
Shareholders of record: about 3,375 (2/93).

d-Deficit.

Office—9600 West Gulf Bank Drive (P.O. Box 40010), Houston, TX 77040. **Tel**—(713) 466-1176. **Chrmn & CEO**—R. A. LeBlanc. **Pres**—M. D. Clark. **VP-CFO & Investor Contact**—Mark E. Baldwin. **Secy**—Donna D. Moore. **Dirs**—F. A. Cailloux, M. D. Clark, B. G. Gower, A. L. French, M. E. Hamilton, F. G. Huber Jr., P. C. Koomey, R. A. LeBlanc, W. W. Patterson, D. F. Raimondi, A. F. Rhodes, W. S. Wilson. **Transfer Agent**—Continental Stock Transfer & Trust Co., NYC. **Incorporated** in Texas in 1947. **Empl**—4,100.

 Leo Larkin

KnowledgeWare

NASDAQ Symbol KNOW (Incl. in Nat'l Market) In S&P MidCap 400

Price	Range	P–E Ratio	Dividend	Yield	S&P Ranking	Beta
Aug. 27'93	1993					
10⅜	15⅞–7¾	NM	None	None	NR	NA

Summary

This Atlanta-based company designs, markets and supports computer-aided software engineering (CASE) products that speed and simplify the process of developing high-quality, well-documented business software applications. A large loss was incurred in the third quarter of fiscal 1993, as well as for the full year, on lower product license revenues and restructuring charges totaling $22 million.

Business Summary

KnowledgeWare, Inc. designs, develops, markets and supports an integrated line of computer-aided software engineering (CASE) products for the planning, analysis, design, construction, maintenance and documentation of complex, computer-based information systems. Revenues in recent fiscal years were derived as follows:

	1993	1992	1991
Software product licenses	62.4%	71.2%	82.4%
Service agreements	27.4%	22.7%	12.2%
Consulting & education	9.2%	5.1%	4.7%
Other	1.0%	1.0%	0.7%

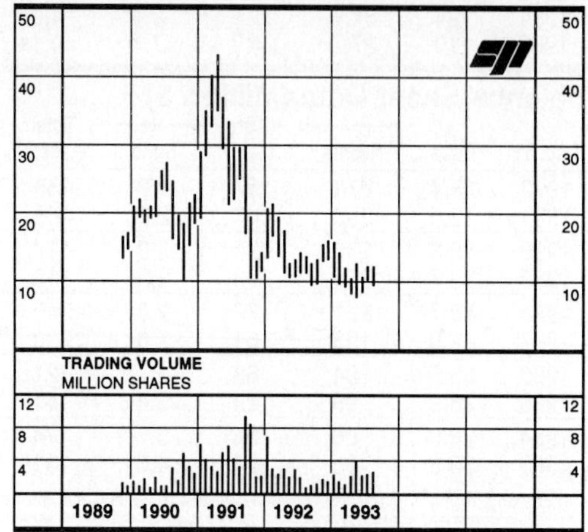

CASE products automate or assist in the information system software development cycle. The principal benefits of CASE are a more consistent development process, reduced development time, higher-quality programs, lower cost, increased end-user involvement and greater standardization of the application software development process.

The company's strategic integrated CASE offering is the Application Development Workbench (ADW), which replaced its older Information Engineering Workbench (IEW) as its premier product line in fiscal 1990. The ADW, which incorporates the significant functions, features and characteristics of the IEW, consists of some 14 personal computer (PC) and mainframe-based tools that capture and analyze enterprise models, business requirements and application designs; and generate application source code for a wide range of computer environments.

KnowledgeWare markets its products principally to information systems departments within financial, governmental, telecommunications, utility and manufacturing organizations worldwide. Through June 30, 1993, it had shipped more than 108,000 copies of its software products to over 4,200 customers throughout the world.

U.S. sales are made through a direct sales force. Foreign sales are made through various member firms of Ernst & Young International. Overseas sources accounted for 27% of revenues in both fiscal 1993 and fiscal 1992.

Important Developments

May '93— In the third quarter of fiscal 1993, KNOW recorded restructuring charges totaling $21,976,000, consisting of about $7 million for the termination of European distribution rights, $7.2 million for the consolidation of real estate, $3.6 million for the reduction and relocation of personnel, $3.5 million for the write-off of capitalized software costs, and $0.6 million related to the acquisition of Matesys Mathematic Systems S.A.

Next earnings report expected in late October.

Per Share Data ($)

Yr. End Jun. 30	1993	[1]1992	1991	1990	1989
Tangible Bk. Val.	**NA**	6.50	6.37	4.64	1.52
Cash Flow	**NA**	0.60	1.55	1.03	0.86
Earnings	**d1.94**	0.02	1.22	0.83	0.75
Dividends	**Nil**	Nil	Nil	Nil	Nil
Payout Ratio	**Nil**	Nil	Nil	Nil	Nil
Prices[2]—High	**15⅞**	21⅜	43¼	27½	17⅛
Low	**7¾**	9½	10½	10	12½
P/E Ratio—	**NM**	NM	35–9	33–12	23–18

Data as orig. reptd. **1.** Refl. merger or acquisition. **2.** Cal. yr. d-Deficit. NM-Not Meaningful. NA-Not Available.

Income Data (Million $)

Year Ended Jun. 30	Revs.	Oper. Inc.	% Oper. Inc. of Revs.	Cap. Exp.	Depr.	Int. Exp.	Net Bef. Taxes	Eff. Tax Rate	Net Inc.	% Net Inc. of Revs.	Cash Flow
[1]1992	**115**	**6.1**	**5.3**	**8.6**	**7.11**	**NA**	**0.9**	**71.6%**	**0.3**	**0.2**	**7.4**
1991	124	26.2	21.1	15.9	4.13	0.02	24.3	37.0%	15.3	12.3	19.5
1990	66	14.6	22.1	11.7	2.32	NM	14.2	31.4%	9.8	14.7	12.1
1989	33	8.7	26.1	2.9	1.01	0.16	7.8	19.2%	6.3	18.9	7.2

Balance Sheet Data (Million $)

Jun. 30	Cash	Curr. Assets	Curr. Liab.	Curr. Ratio	Total Assets	% Ret. on Assets	Long Term Debt	Common Equity	Total Cap.	% LT Debt of Cap.	% Ret. on Equity
1992	**40.1**	**77.9**	**47.7**	**1.6**	**129**	**0.2**	**Nil**	**76.8**	**81.5**	**Nil**	**0.3**
1991	41.4	88.8	45.0	2.0	120	15.7	Nil	74.2	74.8	Nil	23.9
1990	37.1	56.0	19.9	2.8	72	17.9	Nil	51.6	52.0	Nil	28.4
1989	3.7	18.5	12.4	1.5	24	NA	0.52	10.7	11.3	4.6	NA

Data as orig. reptd. **1.** Refl. merger or acquisition. NA-Not Available. NM-Not Meaningful.

Revenues (Million $)

Quarter:	1992–93	1991–92	1990–91	1989–90
Sep.	29.4	21.6	23.5	12.8
Dec.	31.6	32.6	29.7	14.3
Mar.	25.7	26.8	30.8	16.8
Jun.	40.4	34.0	40.3	22.3
	128.8	115.1	124.3	66.2

Based on a preliminary report, revenues for the fiscal year ended June 30, 1993, rose 10% from those of the prior year, as gains of 34% in service agreement revenues and 100% for the consulting and education business outweighed a 3.5% decline in software product licenses. Gross margins narrowed on a less favorable product mix, and following higher R&D expenses and restructuring charges totaling $21,976,000, a pretax loss of $27,199,000 contrasted with a pretax profit of $1,013,000. After tax credits of $1,400,000, versus taxes at 64.9%, the net loss was $25,799,000 ($1.94 a share), against net income of $356,000 ($0.03).

Common Share Earnings ($)

Quarter:	1992–93	1991–92	1990–91	1989–90
Sep.	0.06	d0.42	0.20	0.20
Dec.	0.07	0.11	0.25	0.14
Mar.	d2.34	0.12	0.35	0.20
Jun.	0.21	0.19	0.41	0.29
	d1.94	0.02	1.22	0.83

Dividend Data

No cash dividends have been paid.

Finances

In March 1993, KNOW said it was aggressively refocusing its business on client/server development tools, computing platforms including Windows and UNIX, and consulting services. The company also said the initiation of its own marketing, sales and service organization was expected to spur future revenue growth in Europe.

In March 1993, the company acquired Ernst & Young's European CASE distribution business for between $17 million and $28 million, depending on revenue performance over the next four years. In February 1993, KNOW acquired a client/server development tool vendor, Matesys Mathematic Systems S.A. and its subsidiary, Matesys Corp., for 900,000 of its common shares.

In November 1992, KNOW acquired all of the assets and assumed certain liabilities of Computer & Engineering Consultants Ltd., a Michigan-based applications development consulting and methodology company, for $1,960,000.

In June 1992, KnowledgeWare said IBM had agreed to purchase $25 million of software over three years. IBM accounted for 14% of revenues in fiscal 1992, (12% in fiscal 1991).

In June 1992, the company acquired for $4.5 million, Viewpoint Systems, a maker of PC-based software products for graphical user interface (GUI) development.

In August 1991, KnowledgeWare acquired Language Technology, Inc., a developer of CASE tools for the maintenance and enhancement of existing COBOL systems, for about $6 million in cash.

Research and development expenditures totaled $28,867,000 (22.4% of revenues) in fiscal 1993, compared with $23,672,000 (20.3%) the year before.

Capitalization

Notes Payable: 3,624,000 (6/93).

Common Stock: 13,046,906 shs. (no par).
J. Martin owns 14%, F. Tarkenton 10% and IBM 9%.
Shareholders: About 3,000 (8/92).

Options: To buy 1,856,388 shs. at $1.84 to $39 ea. (6/92).

d-Deficit.

Office—3340 Peachtree Rd., N.E., Atlanta, GA 30326. **Tel**—(404) 231-8575. **Chrmn & CEO**—F. A. Tarkenton. **Pres & COO**—D. P. Addington. **EVP, CFO, Treas & Secy**—R. M. Haddrill. **Dirs**—D. P. Addington, S. A. Brooks, P. E. Sadler, J. W. Scruggs, F. A. Tarkenton. **Transfer Agent & Registrar**—Trust Co. Bank, Atlanta. **Incorporated** in Michigan in 1979; reincorporated in Georgia in 1988. **Empl**—840.

 Peter C. Wood, CFA

LDDS Communications

NASDAQ Symbol LDDSA (Incl. in Nat'l Market) Options on Pacific In S&P MidCap 400

Price	Range	P–E Ratio	Dividend	Yield	S&P Ranking	Beta
Aug. 27'93	1993					
41⅛	42½–28½	NM	None	None	B	1.46

Summary

Among the largest of the second tier long distance carriers, LDDS provides services to customers in 48 states. An agreement has been reached to merge with Metromedia Communications Corp. and Resurgens Communications Group, forming LDDS—Metro Communications, the fourth largest long distance carrier in the U.S., with revenues of over $1.5 billion.

Current Outlook

Earnings for 1993 are estimated at $1.70 a share (before giving effect to the Metromedia and Resurgens merger), versus 1992's $0.05 loss, which included merger-related charges, but excluded a $0.12 special charge. For 1994, earnings are projected at $2.15.

Cash dividends are not likely to be paid for the foreseeable future.

Revenues should expand rapidly in 1993, reflecting volume growth and an aggressive acquisition program; however, average revenues per minute are expected to continue to decline. Margins should widen, benefiting from acquisition synergies and the larger revenue base. Interest costs will grow, reflecting debt related to acquisitions. Profitability should be achieved, in the absence of charges related to the Advanced Telecommunications merger, but share earnings will reflect additional shares outstanding.

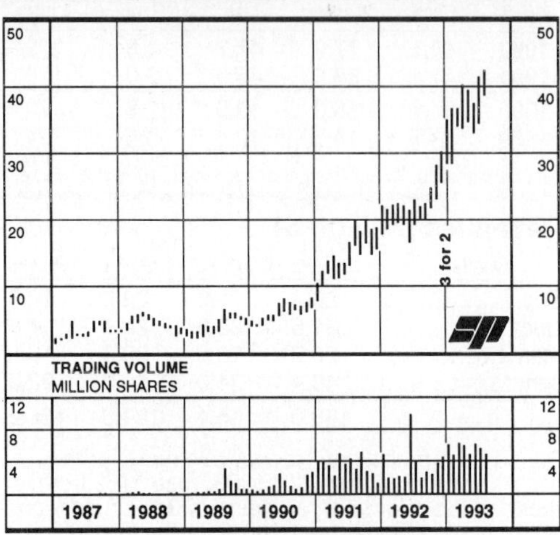

Revenues (Million $)

Quarter:	1993	1992	1991	1990
Mar.	219.0	183.8	43.7	33.8
Jun.	251.5	197.8	57.5	37.4
Sep.		205.8	80.1	42.7
Dec.		213.4	82.1	40.6
		800.8	263.4	154.4

Net revenues for the six months ended June 30, 1993, rose 23%, year to year (as restated for the December 1992 pooling-of-interests acquisition of Advanced Telecommunications), on a 25% advance in minutes billed. Aided by efficiencies achieved with the assimilation of Advanced Telecom., net income advanced 44%. Share earnings were $0.71 (on 5.9% more shares), versus $0.52, as adjusted for a 3-for-2 stock split in January, 1993.

Common Share Earnings ($)

Quarter:	1993	1992	1991	1990
Mar.	0.32	0.25	0.18	0.09
Jun.	0.39	0.27	0.20	0.11
Sep.	E0.45	0.28	0.23	0.15
Dec.	E0.55	d0.85	0.24	0.17
	E1.70	d0.05	0.85	0.52

Important Developments

Aug. '93— LDDS said the planned merger with Metromedia Communiucations Corp. and Resurgens Communications Group, Inc. was expected to be completed in mid-September 1993. Resurgens would be the surviving entity, and would be renamed LDDS—Metro Communications. LDDS shareholders, who would receive 0.9595 of an LDDS—Metro common share for each LDDS share held, would collectively own 68.5% of the fully diluted equity of the new company.

Next earnings report expected in mid-November.

Per Share Data ($)

Yr. End Dec. 31	[2]1992	[2]1991	[2]1990	[3]1989	[2]1988	1987	[2]1986	1985	1984	1983
Tangible Bk. Val.	**d2.24**	d5.55	d3.96	d3.97	NA	d0.13	d0.46	d0.02	d0.01	d0.63
Cash Flow	**1.06**	1.59	1.03	0.77	d0.05	0.11	d0.02	d0.03	d0.20	d0.71
Earnings[1]	**d0.05**	0.85	0.52	0.26	d0.14	0.03	d0.06	d0.06	d0.24	d0.86
Dividends	**Nil**	Nil	Nil	Nil	Nil	Nil	Nil	Nil	Nil	Nil
Payout Ratio	**Nil**	Nil	Nil	Nil	Nil	Nil	Nil	Nil	Nil	Nil
Prices—High	**30¹¹⁄₃₂**	19²⁷⁄₃₂	8¹¹⁄₃₂	6²¹⁄₃₂	6⁵⁄₃₂	4²⁷⁄₃₂	3²¹⁄₃₂	2¼	2²¹⁄₃₂	5⁵⁄₃₂
Low	**16²¹⁄₃₂**	7¾	4	2¼	2²¹⁄₃₂	1½	²⁷⁄₃₂	½	1¼	²⁷⁄₃₂
P/E Ratio—	**NM**	23–9	16–8	26–9	NM	NM	NM	NM	NM	NM

Data as orig. reptd. Adj. for stk. divs. of 50% Jan. 1993, 50% Jun. 1991, 50% Jul. 1990, reverse split May 1987. **1.** Bef. results of disc. ops. of +0.03 in 1988, +0.03 in 1986, -0.14 in 1984, -0.98 in 1983 & spec. items of -0.12 in 1992, -0.37 in 1989, +0.05 in 1987, +0.02 in 1983. **2.** Refl. merger or acq. **3.** Major merger resulted in formation of new co. d-Deficit. E-Estimated NM-Not Meaningful. NA-Not Available.

Income Data (Million $)

Year Ended Dec. 31	Revs.	Oper. Inc.	% Oper. Inc. of Revs.	Cap. Exp.	Depr.	Int. Exp.	Net Bef. Taxes	Eff. Tax Rate	[5]Net Inc.	% Net Inc. of Revs.	Cash Flow
[1]1992	**801**	**172.0**	**21.5**	**[4]57.7**	**53.9**	**23.8**	**8.2**	**102.2%**	**d0.2**	**NM**	**51.6**
[1]1991	263	58.2	22.1	[4]19.0	15.4	13.1	31.1	43.0%	17.7	6.7	33.1
[1]1990	154	36.1	23.4	[4]13.1	9.4	10.5	17.6	44.2%	9.8	6.3	19.2
[2]1989	110	23.1	21.1	[4]9.5	6.4	9.4	7.8	45.2%	4.3	3.9	10.7
[1,3]1988	21	1.4	6.7	1.2	1.4	1.4	d2.0	NM	d2.0	NM	d0.7
1987	16	1.9	11.8	1.1	0.9	0.9	0.6	59.1%	0.3	1.5	1.1
[1,3]1986	6	d0.1	NM	0.1	0.3	0.5	d0.4	NM	d0.4	NM	d0.2
1985	3	d0.3	NM	0.1	0.2	0.4	d0.4	NM	d0.4	NM	d0.2
1984	3	d1.0	NM	0.1	0.2	0.4	d1.2	NM	d1.2	NM	d1.0
[3]1983	3	d0.5	NM	0.1	0.3	0.5	d1.6	NM	d1.6	NM	d1.3

Balance Sheet Data (Million $)

Dec. 31	Cash	Curr. Assets	Curr. Liab.	Curr. Ratio	Total Assets	% Ret. on Assets	Long Term Debt	Common Equity	Total Cap.	% LT Debt of Cap.	% Ret. on Equity
1992	**4.15**	**178.0**	**164.0**	**1.1**	**870**	**NM**	**334**	**296**	**704**	**47.4**	**NM**
1991	4.10	56.0	72.0	0.8	337	6.6	151	100	263	57.2	24.0
1990	1.15	22.6	28.4	0.8	169	6.1	94	39	140	67.0	26.4
1989	0.64	16.4	21.4	0.8	129	NA	77	29	108	71.2	NA
1988	0.47	4.8	7.5	0.6	27	NA	14	6	20	69.2	NA
1987	1.96	6.3	5.8	1.1	24	1.2	10	8	18	56.8	6.0
1986	0.54	2.3	2.9	0.8	10	NM	6	Nil	7	90.8	NM
1985	0.08	1.1	1.8	0.6	5	NM	3	Nil	3	88.3	NM
1984	0.27	1.0	1.3	0.8	5	NM	3	Nil	3	87.2	NM
1983	0.04	0.7	1.9	0.4	5	NM	3	d1	2	129.1	NM

Data as orig. reptd. **1.** Refl. merger or acq. **2.** Major merger resulted in formation of new co. **3.** Excl. disc. ops. **4.** Net. **5.** Bef. spec. items. d-Deficit. NM-Not Meaningful. NA-Not Available.

Business Summary

LDDS Communications, Inc. is one of the largest second-tier long-distance companies in the U.S., providing long-distance telecommunications services throughout the U.S. and many foreign countries to customers in 48 states. The company offers a variety of service options, including "one plus" dialing, inbound "800" service, "800" travel service, operator, private line network and data services.

Customers are charged on the basis of minutes of usage at rates that vary with the distance, duration and time of day of the call. Marketing is directed primarily toward commercial customers, who are typically higher volume users than residential customers, with usage concentrated during peak hours, when rates are highest. The company believes that 87% of total revenues in 1992 were derived from commercial customers.

Traffic is transmitted over a 1,300 mile digital fiber optic network that serves Florida and Georgia, a 400 mile digital microwave network in Texas, and over facilities leased from other carriers on a fixed- or variable-cost (usage-sensitive) basis. LDDS owns or leases computerized network switching equipment that routes all of its customers' long-distance calls over the least expensive transmission facilities available at the time of the call. Profitability is dependent on the company's ability to achieve line costs per minute, including access and transport charges, that are less than its revenues per minute.

The company's expansion strategy involves both internal growth and acquisitions of other interexchange carriers servicing areas adjacent to or within its own service areas. In December 1992, LDDS significantly expanded its operations through a merger with Advanced Telecommunications (revenues of $355 million).

Dividend Data

No cash has been paid. A three-for-two stock split was distributed January 14, 1993, to shareholders of record December 21, 1992. Earlier three-for-two stock splits were effected in July 1990 and June 1991.

Finances

In May 1992, LDDS sold 500,000 shares of 6.5% perpetual preferred stock, for $50 million. Each share is convertible into common stock at $22.67 a share (as adjusted). Proceeds were used to reduce debt.

Capitalization

Long Term Debt: $388,393,000 (3/93).

Conv. Preferred Stock: 500,000 shs.

Class A Common Stock: 51,868,906 shs. ($0.01 par).
Institutions hold about 46%.
Shareholders of record: about 2,912.

Office—Suite 500, LeFleur's Bluff Tower, 4780 I-55 North, Jackson, MS 39211. **Tel**—(601) 364-7000. **Chrmn**—J. A. Porter. **Pres & CEO**—B. J. Ebbers. **EVP & COO**—N. Klugman. **CFO, Treas & Investor Contact**—Charles T. Cannada. **Secy**—C. J. Aycock. **Dirs**—C. J. Aycock, M. E. Bobbit, D. N. Dunnaway, B. J. Ebbers, J. T. Ford, F. Galesi, S. A. Kellett Jr., J. A. Porter, M. E. Thornhill, A. L. Weintraub, D. M. Wilds. **Transfer Agent & Registrar**—First Union National Bank of North Carolina, Charlotte. **Incorporated** in Mississippi in 1983. **Empl**—2,440.

 Susan Stahl Gibney

LG&E Energy

NYSE Symbol LGE In S&P MidCap 400

Price	Range	P–E Ratio	Dividend	Yield	S&P Ranking	Beta
Sep. 9'93	1993					
42¾	43⅛–33¾	17	2.08	4.9%	B+	0.53

Summary

LG&E is an electric and gas utility holding company serving Louisville and adjacent areas of Kentucky. The power plants are primarily coal-fired, scrubber-equipped units, and the company believes they are already in compliance with requirements under the Clean Air Act of 1990. The Energy Systems unit develops independent power projects and in 1992 entered the natural gas marketing business. Earnings should improve in 1993, reflecting increased kilowatt-hour sales and well-contained production costs.

Cuurent Outlook

Share earnings for 1993 are estimated at $2.50, up from 1992's $2.34. Earnings for 1994 are projected at $2.65 a share.

Directors raised the quarterly dividend 3.5%, to $0.52, from $0.50¼, with the September 1, 1993, declaration.

The higher share earnings expected for 1993 would primarily reflect increased kilowatt-hour sales resulting from higher residential usage. In addition, the profit contributions from nonregulated subsidiaries should be even more significant than in 1992. LGE is well positioned to take advantage of opportunities arising from the National Energy Policy Act of 1992, which rewards low-cost generators and encourages competition among natural gas suppliers.

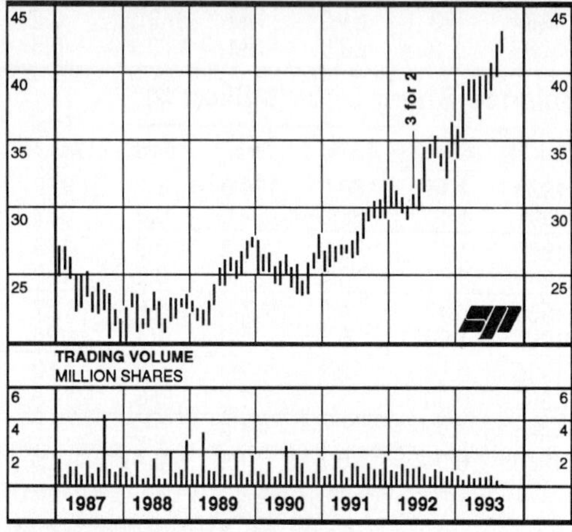

Operating Revenues (Million $)

Quarter:	1994	1993	1992	1991
Mar.	---	238.4	204.9	194.9
Jun.	---	200.4	189.4	161.3
Sep.	---	---	210.0	187.8
Dec.	---	---	230.5	170.9
	---	---	834.7	715.0

Revenues for the six months ended June 30, 1993, rose 11%, year to year, reflecting higher utility sales stemming from colder weather, and greater contributions from nonutility businesses. Expenses grew at a slightly faster pace, but following a 154% increase in equity earnings from the gas marketing units, pretax income advanced 22%. After taxes at 36.8% versus 35.5%, and smaller subsidiary preferred dividends, net income was up 25%, to $1.16 a share from $0.94.

Common Share Earnings ($)

Quarter:	1994	1993	1992	1991
Mar.	E0.65	0.62	0.41	0.69
Jun.	E0.55	0.54	0.53	0.52
Sep.	E1.10	E1.01	0.91	1.05
Dec.	E0.35	E0.33	0.49	0.31
	E2.65	E2.50	2.34	2.57

Important Developments

Apr. '93— The Kentucky Court of Appeals, agreeing with LG&E's arguments, overturned a circuit court ruling that had ordered LGE to refund to customers about $150 million in proceeds from the sale of 25% interest in LG&E's Trimble County generating unit. In February 1993, LGE sold a 12.88% interest in the unit to the Indiana Municipal Power Agency, completing the company's plan to sell 25% of the unit. This transaction replaced the unit power purchase agreement between the two parties signed in December 1991 that included the option for Indiana Municipal to purchase the 12.88% interest. The sale of the 25% capacity was critical to LG&E's growth, as it ensured a market for the portion of the unit's capacity that was not included in retail customer rates. The Trimble County station, like all LG&E's coal-fired generating plants, is equipped with a scrubber system that already complies with the 1990 Clean Air Act Amendments' sulfur-dioxide emissions standard for the year 2000.

Next earnings report expected in late October.

Per Share Data ($)

Yr. End Dec. 31	1992	1991	1990	1989	1988	1987	1986	1985	1984	1983
Tangible Bk. Val.	**20.67**	20.41	19.71	18.75	18.37	17.60	17.05	16.52	16.05	15.15
Earnings[1]	**2.34**	2.57	2.30	2.13	2.47	2.23	2.17	2.10	2.53	1.91
Dividends	**1.981**	1.920	1.873	1.833	1.793	1.753	1.707	1.653	1.600	1.553
Payout Ratio	**85%**	75%	81%	86%	73%	79%	79%	79%	63%	81%
Prices—High	**36⅜**	32	28	27 13/16	23¾	27 3/16	29 9/16	21 13/16	18 13/16	16 11/16
Low	**29⅛**	25⅜	23½	21 5/16	20 3/16	20 1/16	19 5/16	17 1/16	15 1/16	13 7/16
P/E Ratio—	**16–12**	12–10	12–10	13–10	10–8	12–9	14–9	10–8	7–6	9–7

Data as orig. reptd. Adj. for stk. div. of 50% May 1992. **1.** Bef. spec. item of +0.57 in 1990. E-Estimated

Income Data (Million $)

Year Ended Dec. 31	Revs.	Depr.	Maint.	Oper. Ratio	[1]Fxd. Chgs. Cover.	Constr. Credits	Eff. Tax Rate	[2]Net Inc.	% Return On— Revs.	[3]Invest. Capital	Com. Equity
1992	**835**	**79.9**	**NA**	**85.8%**	**3.11**	**NA**	**36.4%**	**75.6**	**9.1**	**7.2**	**11.1**
1991	715	76.7	49.6	80.8%	3.15	NA	37.0%	83.0	11.6	7.9	12.5
1990	699	55.6	48.5	80.4%	2.94	NA	37.3%	73.2	10.5	7.8	11.7
1989	677	55.3	52.0	81.2%	2.85	NA	37.4%	76.1	11.2	7.8	11.3
1988	660	50.7	52.5	80.3%	3.27	NA	31.1%	85.0	12.9	8.4	13.5
1987	631	48.1	53.5	81.1%	3.17	NA	37.1%	76.2	12.1	8.1	12.6
1986	660	45.6	55.2	82.1%	3.25	NA	43.4%	73.3	11.1	8.4	12.8
1985	675	42.5	49.2	83.3%	3.18	NA	43.1%	69.5	10.3	8.4	12.8
1984	676	42.3	38.0	82.0%	3.56	NA	43.6%	79.0	11.7	9.7	16.0
1983	637	41.4	34.5	83.6%	2.86	NA	43.0%	59.7	9.4	8.7	12.7

Balance Sheet Data (Million $)

Dec. 31	Gross Prop.	Capital Expend.	Net Prop.	% Earn. on Net Prop.	Total Cap.	LT Debt	% LT Debt	Capitalization— Pfd.	% Pfd.	Com.	% Com.
1992	**2,373**	**102**	**1,619**	**7.4**	**1,890**	**686**	**46.1**	**117**	**7.9**	**685**	**46.0**
1991	2,285	88	1,592	8.7	1,851	687	46.5	117	7.9	675	45.6
1990	2,215	118	1,584	8.4	1,816	687	47.3	117	8.0	649	44.7
1989	2,277	174	1,695	7.7	1,678	613	46.0	118	8.9	602	45.1
1988	2,110	178	1,602	8.4	1,585	560	44.6	118	9.4	578	46.0
1987	1,941	126	1,477	8.3	1,527	552	45.5	118	9.7	543	44.8
1986	1,830	106	1,400	8.6	1,473	546	46.4	118	10.0	514	43.6
1985	1,736	109	1,338	8.7	1,414	533	46.9	118	10.4	485	42.7
1984	1,655	73	1,261	9.8	1,321	493	46.2	118	11.1	455	42.7
1983	1,617	87	1,229	8.7	1,225	463	46.6	118	11.9	412	41.5

Data as orig. reptd. **1.** Times int. exp. & pfd. divs. covered (pretax basis). **2.** Bef. spec. item in 1990. **3.** Based on inc. bef. int. charges. NA-Not Available.

Business Summary

LG&E Energy is the holding company for Louisville Gas & Electric Co., a public utility that supplies electric and gas service in a 700-square-mile area including Louisville, Ky. The LG&E Energy Systems unit was formed in 1991 to conduct LGE's nonutility operations. In December 1991, LG&E Energy Systems acquired Hadson Power Systems (renamed LG&E Power Systems Inc.), which develops independent power projects. In May 1992, LG&E Energy Systems acquired a one-third interest in Natural Gas Clearinghouse (NGC), a leading gas marketing company. In 1992, electric service accounted for 63% of revenues and 80% of operating profits and gas 21% and 8%. Electric revenues by class of customer were:

	1992	1991	1990
Residential	33%	35%	34%
Large industrial	20%	19%	20%
Large commercial	15%	15%	15%
Small comm'l & ind'l	13%	12%	13%
Other	19%	19%	18%

LGE's electric generating capacity is 90% coal-fired, with the remainder consisting of a hydroelectric plant and combustion turbine peaking units fueled by natural gas and oil. Peak load in 1992 was 2,107 mw, and system capability totaled 2,613 mw, for a capacity margin of 19.4%. Gas sold or transported totaled 48,088,000 Mcf (46,852,000).

Finances

All of LG&E's coal-fired boilers are equipped with sulfur dioxide "scrubbers" and already achieve the final sulfur dioxide emission rates required by the year 2000 under the Clean Air Act Amendments of 1990. Although some construction expenditures may be required, the overall financial effect on the company is expected to be minimal.

Dividend Data

Dividends have been paid since 1913. A dividend reinvestment plan is available. A "poison pill" stock purchase plan was adopted in 1990.

Amt of Divd. $	Date Decl.	Ex-divd. Date	Stock of Record	Payment Date
0.50¼	Dec. 3	Dec. 24	Dec. 31	Jan. 15'93
0.50¼	Mar. 3	Mar. 25	Mar. 31	Apr. 15'93
0.50¼	Jun. 2	Jun. 24	Jun. 30	Jul. 15'93
0.52	Sep. 1	Sep. 24	Sep. 30	Oct. 15'93

Capitalization

Long Term Debt: $661,103,000 (6/93).

Subsid. Cum. Preferred Stock: $116,742,000.

Common Stock: 32,770,016 shs. (no par). Institutions hold about 25%. Shareholders of record: 32,575.

Office—220 West Main Street, P.O. Box 32030, Louisville, KY 40232. **Tel**—(502) 627-2000. **Chrmn & Pres**—R. W. Hale. **Exec VP & CFO**—E. J. Casey Jr. **Investor Contact**—Martha E. Dunbar. **Dirs**—W. C. Ballard Jr., O. Brown II, S. G. Dabney, G. P. Gardner, J. D. Grissom, R. W. Hale, D. B. Lewis, A. H. McNamara, T. B. Morton Jr., D. C. Swain. **Transfer Agents**—Company's office; Continental Stock Transfer & Trust Co., NYC. **Incorporated** in Kentucky in 1913; reincorporated in Kentucky in 1990. **Empl**—3,767.

 Ned Bancroft

LSI Logic

NYSE Symbol LSI Options on CBOE (Jan-Apr-Jul-Oct) In S&P MidCap 400

Price	Range	P-E Ratio	Dividend	Yield	S&P Ranking	Beta
Aug. 27'93	1993					
17½	19¼–10¼	NM	None	None	C	1.66

Summary

LSI Logic is a leading designer and manufacturer of application-specific integrated circuits (ASICs). It also produces standard products, including microprocessors and digital signal processing circuits. Strong industry growth, an aggressive new product introduction program, and savings from a 1992 restructuring, as well as the absence of the restructuring charge itself, should allow substantial profitability to be restored in 1993. Continued industry expansion and well received new products should allow for further growth in 1994.

Current Outlook

Earnings for 1994 should approximate $1.40 a share, up from the $1.05 projected for 1993.

Initiation of cash dividends is not anticipated.

Sales for 1994 are expected to increase more than 20%, aided by a continuation of strong industry conditions and an aggressive new product introduction program. The semiconductor industry is currently in the midst of a strong cyclical rebound that should extend through next year. A recovery in the Japanese market, which has been weak until recently, should give further momentum to the rebound. Growth should also be assisted by the company's expansion of its offerings of 0.60-micron ASICs, as well as by its targeting of networking, digital video and telecommunications markets for additional penetration.

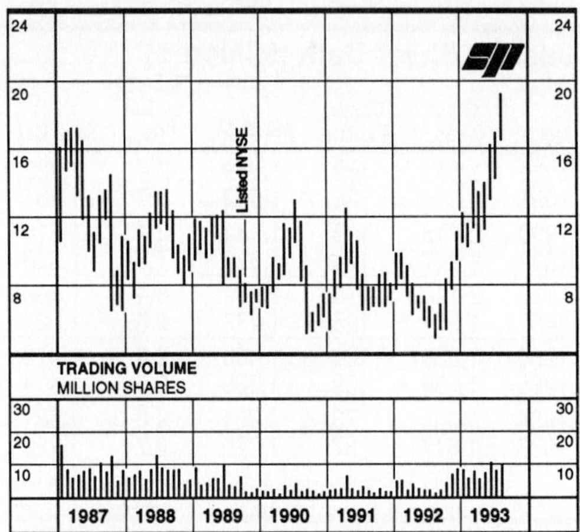

Operating Revenues (Million $)

13 Weeks:	1993	1992	1991	1990
Mar.	168.9	150.5	180.2	139.1
Jun.	177.1	151.8	181.0	159.7
Sep.	---	154.0	172.4	172.5
Dec.	---	161.1	164.3	184.3
	---	617.5	697.8	655.5

Revenues for the six months ended June 30, 1993, increased 14%, year to year, reflecting strong industry conditions and well received new products. Primarily due to the the higher sales, a wider gross profit margin and a decline in expenses, pretax income totaled $36.9 million, versus a loss of $4.9 million. After tax items and minority interest, net income was $23.7 million ($0.49 a share), in contrast to a net loss of $5.5 million ($0.12).

Common Share Earnings ($)

13 Weeks:	1993	1992	1991	1990
Mar.	0.22	0.01	0.05	0.03
Jun.	0.27	d0.13	0.10	0.15
Sep.	E0.26	d2.51	0.02	0.10
Dec.	E0.30	0.15	0.02	d1.08
	E1.05	d2.48	0.19	d0.80

Important Developments

Jul. '93— The company said that design wins involving the 0.60-micron ASIC product families continued on a strong pace during 1993's second quarter. It added that new design wins involving sub-micron ASIC products were roughly half of the total during the quarter.

Next earnings report expected in late October.

Per Share Data ($)

Yr. End Dec. 31	1992	1991	1990	1989	[2]1988	1987	1986	1985	1984	1983
Tangible Bk. Val.	**[1]4.35**	[1]6.70	6.56	[1]7.24	[1]8.20	7.70	6.37	3.97	5.31	4.56
Cash Flow	**d0.88**	2.01	1.60	1.52	1.88	1.23	0.86	0.83	0.65	0.37
Earnings[3]	**d2.48**	0.19	d0.80	d0.60	0.58	0.27	0.10	0.26	0.40	0.29
Dividends	**Nil**	Nil	Nil	Nil	Nil	Nil	Nil	Nil	Nil	Nil
Payout Ratio	**Nil**	Nil	Nil	Nil	Nil	Nil	Nil	Nil	Nil	Nil
Prices—High	**11⅛**	12½	13	12⅜	13⅝	17¼	21⅛	16⅛	15⅞	20½
Low	**4⅞**	5⅜	5⅛	6¼	7¼	6½	8	7⅜	6½	11⅞
P/E Ratio—	**NM**	66–28	NM	NM	23–13	64–24	NM	62–28	40–16	70–40

Data as orig. reptd. Adj. for stk. divs. of 50% Mar. 1986, 50% Apr. 1983. **1.** Incl. intangibles. **2.** Reflects merger or acquisition. **3.** Bef. spec. items of +0.02 in 1990, +0.02 in 1988, +0.01 in 1987, +0.08 in 1983. d-Deficit. E-Estimated. NM-Not Meaningful.

Income Data (Million $)

Year Ended Dec. 31	Revs.	Oper. Inc.	% Oper. Inc. of Revs.	Cap. Exp.	Depr.	Int. Exp.	Net Bef. Taxes	Eff. Tax Rate	[3]Net Inc.	% Net Inc. of Revs.	Cash Flow
1992	**617**	**72**	**11.7**	**[2]143**	**71**	**14.7**	**d99.9**	**NM**	**d110**	**NM**	**d39.1**
1991	698	101	14.5	78	79	19.4	12.3	50.0%	8	1.2	87.1
1990	655	136	20.7	71	101	21.3	d18.5	NM	d34	NM	67.4
1989	547	101	18.4	121	88	17.3	d34.9	NM	d25	NM	62.9
[1]1988	379	79	21.0	110	53	11.3	31.2	41.6%	24	6.3	77.2
1987	262	49	18.5	174	39	9.9	17.3	40.7%	11	4.1	50.2
1986	194	34	17.6	70	31	6.9	8.5	48.2%	4	2.0	34.6
1985	140	33	23.6	40	23	8.1	15.4	30.8%	10	7.2	32.8
1984	84	20	23.2	82	10	6.1	20.5	23.8%	15	18.3	25.5
1983	35	8	23.1	30	3	1.2	14.0	28.7%	10	28.6	12.7

Balance Sheet Data (Million $)

Dec. 31	Cash	Curr. Assets	Curr. Liab.	Curr. Ratio	Total Assets	% Ret. on Assets	Long Term Debt	Common Equity	Total Cap.	% LT Debt of Cap.	% Ret. on Equity
1992	**153**	**350**	**211**	**1.7**	**736**	**NM**	**192**	**198**	**525**	**36.5**	**NM**
1991	157	386	161	2.4	748	1.1	166	293	587	28.3	2.9
1990	159	439	193	2.3	784	NM	190	276	591	32.1	NM
1989	153	392	151	2.6	765	NM	204	297	614	33.3	NM
1988	204	425	130	3.3	787	3.2	192	332	657	29.2	7.4
1987	267	383	72	5.3	699	1.9	188	308	627	30.0	3.8
1986	203	281	32	8.7	451	1.1	107	251	419	25.5	1.9
1985	168	245	33	7.5	372	2.4	82	232	340	24.1	3.7
1984	161	209	31	6.8	318	5.8	67	206	287	23.4	8.1
1983	157	175	12	14.5	211	6.5	21	176	199	10.8	13.4

Data as orig. reptd. **1.** Reflects merger or acquisition. **2.** Net of curr. yr. retirement and disposals. **3.** Bef. spec. items in 1990, 1988, 1987, 1983. d-Deficit. NM-Not Meaningful.

Business Summary

LSI Logic designs, develops, manufactures and markets integrated circuit products and provides computer aided design and technology services and tools based on application-specific integrated circuit (ASIC) technologies. Revenues in recent years were derived as follows:

	1992	1991	1990
Components	83%	85%	85%
Design & services	17%	15%	15%

Foreign sales accounted for 39% of revenues and an $8.8 million operating loss in 1992.

ASICs include metal programmable array, cell-based and Embedded Array architectures. The company offers ASICs that may include both logic and memory elements.

The company offers customers its proprietary Modular Design Environment software that is used to design ASICs for customer's specific functionality and performance requirements. It currently operates on engineering workstations amd comprises libraries of semiconductor macrocells (the basic silicon structures used in the design of logic circuits) and larger predefined functional building blocks, technology bases and design automation programs.

Standard products include 32-bit RISC (reduced instruction set computing) microprocessors, peripheral logic chips and 16-bit microprocessors. The company also offers high-speed digital signal and image processing devices and graphics chips and logic chip sets, as well as video graphics technology board based products.

Products and services are marketed primarily to manufacturers in the electronic data processing, military/aerospace and telecommunications industries.

Dividend Data

LSI has never paid cash dividends. A 3-for-2 stock split was effected in 1986. A "poison pill" stock purchase right was adopted in 1988.

Finances

At June 30, 1993, the company had $172.3 million in cash and short-term investments. There were no short-term borrowings at that time.

Capitalization

Long Term Liabilities: $258,300,000 (6/92).

Minority Interest: $121,600,000.

Common Stock: 46,942,401 shs. ($0.01 par).
Officers & directors own about 11%, incl. some 9% held by W.J. Corrigan.
Institutions hold approximately 55%.
Shareholders of record: About 3,500.

Office—1551 McCarthy Blvd., Milpitas, CA 95035. **Tel**—(408) 433-8000. **Chrmn & CEO**—W. J. Corrigan. **VP-CFO**—A. A. Pimentel. **VP-Secy**—D. E. Sanders. **VP-Investor Contact**—Bruce L. Entin. **Dirs**—T. Z. Chu, W. J. Corrigan, M. R. Currie, J. H. Keyes, R. D. Norby. **Transfer Agent & Registrar**—Bank of Boston, Boston. **Incorporated** in California in 1980; reincorporated in Delaware in 1986. **Empl**—3,450.

 Paul Valentine, CFA

Lac Minerals

NYSE Symbol LAC Options on CBOE, Toronto In S&P MidCap 400

Price	Range	P-E Ratio	Dividend	Yield	S&P Ranking	Beta
Aug. 13'93	1993					
8⅝	10⅝–4¼	NM	[1]0.10	[1]1.2%	B–	0.03

Summary

Lac Minerals, a major Canadian based gold producer, owns eight active gold mines in North America and Chile, and a Chilean zinc mine. The company plans to replace its reserves by entering into joint ventures, making acquisitions, and conducting exploration on a more global basis than in the past. Lac should break even instead of posting a profit in 1993 as expected lower realized gold prices outweigh cost cuts.

Current Outlook

Earnings for 1993 are estimated at breakeven, versus 1992's $0.09 a share.

Semiannual dividends totaled $0.10 (in U.S. funds; before 15% Canadian tax) in the last 12 months.

Revenues for 1993 may decrease moderately, on anticipated lower prices at which Lac sells its gold forward and on expected little change in gold output. In first half 1993, realizations averaged $351 an ounce, off from $396 a year ago. Continued disinflation would probably sustain a downtrend in gold. With anticipated reduced unit production costs outweighed by the lower gold revenues, Lac should break even in 1993.

Revenues (Million U.S. $)

Quarter:	1993	1992	1991	1990
Mar.	120.7	124.5	131.4	111.4
Jun.	103.1	122.1	120.2	118.6
Sep.	---	114.6	121.3	114.9
Dec.	---	125.3	113.6	114.2
	---	486.4	486.6	459.1

First-half 1993 revenues fell 9.2%, year to year, as lower realized gold prices outweighed more gold sold (569,800 oz. versus 553,700). Despite lower unit total costs ($316/oz. against $322) and with other expense instead of income, a pretax loss of $1.8 million contrasted with pretax income of $22.3 million. After a $1.3 million tax credit against taxes of $13.8 million, and minority interest in loss versus earnings, the net loss was $164,000 (Nil per share), against net income of $8.1 million ($0.06).

Common Share Earnings (U.S. $)

Quarter:	1993	1992	1991	1990
Mar.	Nil	0.03	0.02	0.03
Jun.	Nil	0.03	0.04	0.01
Sep.	E0.01	d0.01	0.05	0.06
Dec.	Ed0.01	0.04	0.01	d0.63
	ENil	0.09	0.12	d0.53

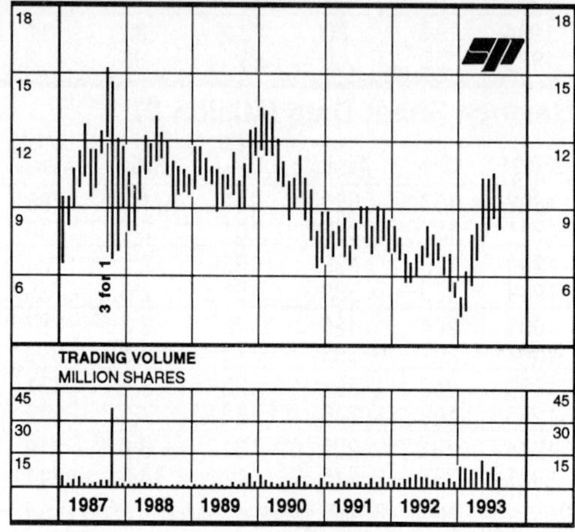

Important Developments

Mar. '93— Lac said that exploration drilling on its 80%-owned Nevada project in Chile continued to outline gold mineralization confirming the potential for a large tonnage, open pit mineable gold deposit. At Lac's Red Mountain property in British Columbia, the company announced in February an indicated and inferred geological resource containing 1,040,000 ounces of gold. In the first quarter, an arbitration hearing was held to decide whether Chevron's intended sale to Lac of its mineral assets in Ireland triggered pre-emption rights in favor of Ivernia Plc. The arbitrator decided in favor of Ivernia.

Oct. '92— Lac increased an existing loan facility by $100 million to $170 million. The expanded five-year loan will mature in October 1997 and will result in a longer average term for Lac's debt. The additional funds would be used for acquisitions.

Next earnings report expected in late October.

Per Share Data (U.S. $)

Yr. End Dec. 31	1992	[2]1991	1990	[2]1989	1988	1987	1986	1985	1984	1983
Tangible Bk. Val.	**5.14**	5.30	4.85	5.54	3.75	3.14	2.50	2.37	NA	NA
Cash Flow	**0.89**	0.94	0.35	0.58	0.60	0.50	0.42	0.19	NA	NA
Earnings[3]	**0.09**	0.12	d0.53	0.31	0.42	0.34	0.16	0.05	0.31	0.31
Dividends	**0.113**	0.192	0.190	0.110	0.100	0.076	0.073	0.036	0.084	0.089
Payout Ratio	**131%**	183%	NM	44%	24%	23%	44%	67%	27%	29%
Prices—High	**8¼**	9⅛	13½	12⅝	13⅛	15¼	9⅞	9⅞	NA	NA
Low	**5⅛**	6½	6⅜	8⅞	8	6½	4¼	7⅝	NA	NA
P/E Ratio—	**92–57**	76–54	NM	41–29	31–19	45–19	61–26	NM	NA	NA

Data as orig. reptd.; prior to 1985 pro forma data as reptd. in prospectus & joint proxy statement dated 6-24-85. Adj. for stk. div(s). of 200% Sep. 1987. **1.** Paid last 12 mos.(approx.), in U.S. funds, bef. 15% Canadian tax on nonresidents. **2.** Reflects merger or acquisition. **3.** Bef. spec. item(s) of +0.04 in 1985, +0.01 in 1983. d-Deficit. NM-Not Meaningful. NA-Not Available. E-Estimated.

Income Data (Million U.S. $)

Year Ended Dec. 31	Revs.	Oper. Inc.	% Oper. Inc. of Revs.	Cap. Exp.	Depr.	Int. Exp.	Net Bef. Taxes	Eff. Tax Rate	[3]Net Inc.	% Net Inc. of Revs.	Cash Flow
1992	**486**	**135**	**27.7**	**44**	**119**	**15.5**	**21.7**	**35.1%**	**12.7**	**2.6**	**131**
[4]1991	487	135	27.7	95	103	18.1	37.8	75.6%	15.4	3.2	119
1990	459	20	4.3	116	106	22.1	d83.6	NM	d64.3	NM	42
[4]1989	186	35	18.9	64	26	7.6	57.3	41.0%	30.5	16.4	57
[1]1988	174	45	25.8	66	17	10.1	[2]59.9	35.7%	38.4	22.1	55
1987	154	51	33.1	81	15	8.4	[2]52.2	43.1%	29.7	19.3	44
1986	182	48	26.7	66	22	7.4	[2]26.2	47.0%	13.9	7.6	36
1985	102	13	12.4	130	11	5.3	[2]11.0	60.3%	4.4	4.3	16
1984	128	49	38.2	NA	16	4.6	42.3	43.2%	24.1	18.7	NA
1983	126	53	41.9	NA	12	0.7	43.6	48.9%	22.3	17.6	NA

Balance Sheet Data (Million U.S. $)

Dec. 31	Cash	Curr. Assets	Curr. Liab.	Curr. Ratio	Total Assets	% Ret. on Assets	Long Term Debt	Common Equity	Total Cap.	% LT Debt of Cap.	% Ret. on Equity
1992	**401**	**542**	**145**	**3.7**	**1,341**	**0.9**	**270**	**756**	**1,043**	**25.9**	**1.7**
1991	311	446	226	2.0	1,346	1.0	167	778	960	17.4	2.1
1990	270	398	221	1.8	1,355	NM	261	588	985	26.5	NM
1989	340	475	314	1.5	1,535	2.5	265	670	1,111	23.9	5.4
1988	265	292	86	3.4	675	6.1	141	346	490	28.8	12.1
1987	203	225	37	6.1	577	5.7	51	288	411	12.3	11.5
1986	98	123	33	3.7	434	3.6	123	212	400	30.8	6.7

Data as orig. reptd.; prior to 1985 pro forma data as reptd. in prospectus & joint proxy statement dated 6-24-85. **1.** Excl. disc. opers. **2.** Incl. equity in earns. of nonconsol. subs. **3.** Bef. spec. item(s). **4.** Refl. merger or acquisition. d-Deficit. NM-Not Meaningful. NA-Not Available.

Business Summary

Lac Minerals owns nine active mines in North America and Chile. Its share of gold output in 1992 was 1,096,384 ounces. Proven and probable reserves at year-end 1992 were estimated at 6.82 million contained ounces of gold.

Operations in Canada include La Mine de Bousquet, an underground gold mine in Quebec. Gold output from Bousquet #2 equaled 149,169 ounces in 1992 at operating costs (including depreciation and amortization) of $261 an ounce. Capital spending for 1993 was planned at about $14 million with some half going towards the East Malartic mill expansion from 1600 tons to 2500 tons a day. Bousquet #1 produced 62,382 oz. of gold at operating costs of $348/oz. Lac's share of 1992 gold output from the Doyon mine (50%-owned) in Quebec was 124,797 oz. at costs of $264/oz. At Lac's Macassa mine, an underground Ontario gold mine, 1992 production was 77,259 oz. at costs of $330/oz. The Golden Patricia mine (Ont.), another underground gold mine, produced 81,465 oz. in 1992 at costs of $340/oz; a new 1100-foot production shaft helped to reduce costs. Milling of tailings from the old Lake Shore mine (Ont.) in 1992 produced 14,846 oz. of gold at costs of $336/oz.

U.S. operations include the Bullfrog open pit gold mine (Nev.), which produced a record 323,825 ounces of gold in 1992 at operating costs of $349/oz. The high level of production reflected higher grades, whose predictability of continuing is uncertain. The Colosseum mine (Cal.), an open pit gold mine, had 1992 output of 44,401 oz. at costs of $397/oz.; mining was completed in July 1992, but output from stockpiles continued to mid-1993.

Lac's Richmond Hill mine (S.D.), a heap leach gold operation, produced 30,373 oz. in 1992 at costs of $510/oz.; last reserves were mined in third quarter 1992, but leaching continued into 1993.

Operations in Chile include Lac's 83%-owned El Indio complex, which consists of the El Indio and Tambo mines; in 1992 they produced 223,688 oz. of gold, 1.5 million oz. of silver and 27,323 tons of copper at operating costs of $297/oz. of gold. After detailed exploration/definition drilling in 1992, proven and probable reserves rose 373,000 oz. at the complex. Potential impact on Lac's reserves led to an acceleration of exploration; 1993 capital and development spending was expected at about $13 million. The Toqui zinc mine produced 31,385 tons of zinc in 1992. At year-end probable reserves were 3.64 million tons grading 8.5% zinc.

Dividend Data

Predecessor companies paid dividends since 1980. Prior to 1993, payments were in Canadian funds. Payments are considered twice yearly.

Amt of Divd. $	Date Decl.	Ex–divd. Date	Stock of Record	Payment Date
*0.09	Nov. 16	Nov. 23	Nov. 30	Dec. 15'92
†0.03	Mar. 30	Apr. 7	Apr. 14	Apr. 23'93

*In Can. funds, bef. 15% Can. tax on nonresidents.
†In U.S. funds, bef. 15% Can. tax on nonresidents.

Capitalization

Long Term Debt: $243,502,000 (6/93).

Common Stock: 147,280,535 shs. (no par).
Institutions hold about 28%.
Shareholders of record: 20,000.

Office—North Tower, 21st Floor, Royal Bank Plaza, P.O. Box 156, Toronto, ON, Canada M5J 2J4. **Tel**—(416) 777-2400. **Pres & CEO**—P. A. Allen. **SVP-Fin & CFO**—J. G. Maw. **Secy**—H. L. Rodrigues. **Investor Contact**—John W. Pearson. **Dirs**—P. A. Allen, J. A. Downing, P. Fortin, W. B. Harris, P. A. Hodges, Z. Merszei, J. E. Mockridge, M. E. Northey, H. E. Rutetzki, R. P. Smith, D. T. Wright. **Transfer Agents**—Montreal Trust Co. of Canada, Toronto; United Missouri Trust Co. of New York, NYC. **Incorporated** in Ontario in 1985. **Empl**—3,200.

 A.M. Sorrentino, CFA

Laidlaw Inc.

NYSE Symbol LDW.B Options on ASE In S&P MidCap 400

Price	Range	P-E Ratio	Dividend	Yield	S&P Ranking	Beta
Oct. 14'93	1993					
6⅝	9½–6	27	[1]0.16	[2]1.8%	A–	0.99

Summary

This Canadian company (the majority of whose operating assets are in the U.S.) is North America's third largest solid waste management firm, the second largest hazardous waste management company and the largest operator of school buses. In fiscal 1993's third quarter, the company recorded a $120 million pretax charge to restructure its solid waste operations, due to fundamental changes in the industry. Earnings are expected to partially recover in fiscal 1994, reflecting improved pricing for solid waste and a better economic environment.

Current Outlook

Share earnings for the fiscal year ending August 31, 1994, are expected to partially recover to $0.65 from the depressed $0.25 (including a $0.27 nonrecurring charge) estimated for fiscal 1993.

Dividends should continue at C$0.04 quarterly.

Revenues for fiscal 1994 are expected to rise about 10%. Gradual improvement is seen for solid waste services, reflecting greater marketing efforts, higher volumes and improved pricing. Hazardous waste should continue to show modest improvement as the economy turns around, waste streams increase and work is performed on projects that were delayed by customers. Acquisitions will also benefit both waste segments. Slow, steady growth is seen for passenger services, also aided by acquisitions. Margins should improve slightly, reflecting cost-cutting programs and the consolidation of certain areas. Longer term, LDW plans to increase its presence in Europe through acquisitions.

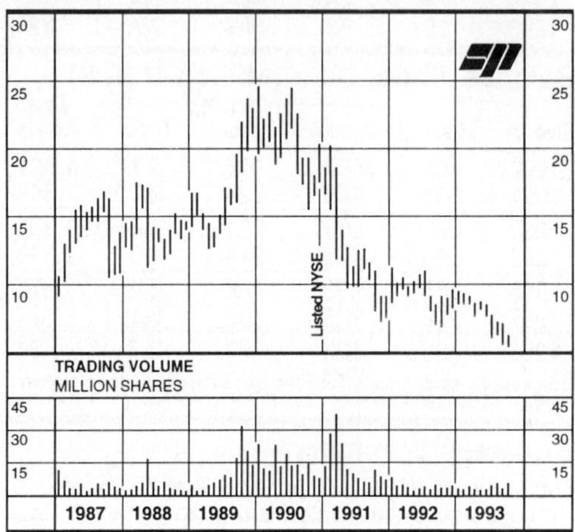

Revenues (Million U.S. $)

Quarter:	1992-93	1991-92	1990-91	1989-90
Nov.	513	521	517	404
Feb.	469	462	455	424
May	544	517	505	494
Aug.	---	424	406	415
	---	1,926	1,882	1,738

Revenues for the nine months ended May 31, 1993, rose 1.6%, year to year, as growth in the hazardous waste and passenger services groups was largely offset by a decline in the solid waste area. Margins narrowed, reflecting lower solid waste prices, and operating income fell 2.4%. Following the recording of a nonrecurring restructuring charge of $120.5 million ($75.0 million after taxes or $0.27 a share), net income plunged 62%. Earnings per share, based on 5.7% more shares, equaled $0.16, against $0.43. Results for the 1991-92 interim exclude a $0.02 special charge.

Common Share Earnings (U.S. $)

Quarter:	1992-93	1991-92	1990-91	1989-90
Nov.	0.18	0.16	0.32	0.27
Feb.	0.10	0.11	0.06	0.25
May	d0.12	0.16	0.16	0.30
Aug.	E0.09	0.09	d1.84	0.28
	E0.25	0.52	[3]d1.35	1.10

Important Developments

Jul. '93— In fiscal 1993's third quarter, the company recorded a nonrecurring pretax charge of $120.5 million ($0.27 a share after taxes) primarily from the restructuring of its U.S. solid waste operations. The restructuring resulted from the continuing decline in solid waste profitability and fundamental changes in the industry.

Next earnings report expected in mid-October.

Per Share Data (U.S. $)

Yr. End Aug. 31	[4]1992	[4]1991	[4]1990	[4]1989	[4]1988	[4]1987	[4]1986	[4]1985	1984
Tangible Bk. Val.	**5.40**	4.82	6.23	4.82	2.74	2.52	0.90	0.77	0.76
Cash Flow	**1.38**	d0.48	1.92	1.70	1.37	1.13	0.61	0.46	0.37
Earnings[5]	**0.52**	d1.35	1.10	1.00	0.76	0.54	0.30	0.24	0.18
Dividends	**0.137**	0.267	0.230	0.193	0.148	0.089	0.056	0.049	0.031
Payout Ratio	**28%**	NM	21%	21%	21%	19%	30%	21%	19%
Prices[6]—High	**11¼**	20¼	24⅝	23¾	17½	16⅞	9¼	5½	NA
Low	**6⅞**	7¼	15½	12⅝	11¼	9⅛	4⅜	3½	NA
P/E Ratio—	**22–13**	NM	22–14	24–13	23–15	31–17	31–15	23–15	NA

Data as orig. reptd. In U.S. funds; based on Canadian GAAP. Adj. for stk. divs. of 50% May 1987, 50% Sep. 1986, 100% Jan. 1985. **1.** In Canadian funds, before 15% tax on nonresidents. **2.** Based on current rate of exchange. **3.** Does not add, due to change in shs. **4.** Refl. merger or acq. **5.** Bef. results of disc. ops. of -0.06 in 1991, -0.08 in 1990 & spec. items of -0.02 in 1992, -0.14 in 1990, +0.07 in 1985. **6.** Cal. yr. d-Deficit. NM-Not Meaningful. NA-Not Available.

Income Data (Million U.S. $)

Year Ended Aug. 31	Revs.	Oper. Inc.	% Oper. Inc. of Revs.	Cap. Exp.	Depr.	Int. Exp.	[2]Net Bef. Taxes	Eff. Tax Rate	[3]Net Inc.	% Net Inc. of Revs.	Cash Flow
[1]1992	**1,926**	**467**	**24.3**	**229**	**230**	**122**	**169**	**18.0%**	**138**	**7.2**	**368**
[1]1991	1,882	463	24.6	248	216	133	d304	NM	d329	NM	d118
[1]1990	1,738	482	27.7	597	190	113	309	14.1%	265	15.3	447
[1]1989	1,413	390	27.6	442	143	65	258	18.2%	211	14.9	346
[1]1988	1,183	314	26.5	416	109	28	198	24.9%	147	12.5	243
[1]1987	909	236	25.9	553	92	31	137	28.5%	94	10.3	175
[1]1986	517	120	23.1	171	43	15	82	36.2%	[4]48	9.2	84
[1]1985	408	97	23.7	110	30	11	64	40.5%	33	8.2	62
1984	325	79	24.4	74	24	8	51	43.4%	24	7.4	47

Balance Sheet Data (Million U.S. $)

Aug. 31	Cash	Curr. Assets	Curr. Liab.	Curr. Ratio	Total Assets	% Ret. on Assets	Long Term Debt	Common Equity	Total Cap.	% LT Debt of Cap.	% Ret. on Equity
1992	**132**	**524**	**349**	**1.5**	**3,659**	**3.6**	**1,261**	**1,950**	**3,310**	**38.1**	**7.3**
1991	125	520	316	1.6	3,595	NM	1,508	1,672	3,279	46.0	NM
1990	208	540	318	1.7	3,895	7.8	1,435	1,907	3,577	40.1	15.3
1989	70	305	211	1.4	2,651	9.3	899	1,330	2,440	36.8	18.4
1988	110	292	172	1.7	1,637	9.9	514	755	1,464	35.1	18.8
1987	119	274	150	1.8	1,248	10.7	179	619	1,098	16.3	19.7
1986	119	214	67	3.2	650	6.6	137	293	583	23.6	14.6
1985	105	170	54	3.2	478	8.3	112	165	424	26.4	21.5
1984	26	90	54	1.7	329	NA	68	137	275	24.5	NA

Data as orig. reptd. In U.S. funds; based on Canadian GAAP. **1.** Refl. merger or acq. **2.** Incl. equity in earns. of nonconsol. subs. **3.** Excl. disc. ops. & spec. items. **4.** Refl. acctg. change. d-Deficit. NM-Not Meaningful. NA-Not Available.

Business Summary

Canada-based Laidlaw Inc. provides solid and hazardous waste services, as well as passenger services. Contributions in fiscal 1992 were:

	Revs.	Profits
Solid waste services...........	42%	35%
Hazardous waste services...	24%	28%
Passenger services............	34%	37%

Operations in the U.S. accounted for 69% of revenues in fiscal 1992 and those in Canada for 31%.

LDW is the third largest solid waste services company in North America, conducting waste collection, transportation, treatment, transfer, recycling and disposal services for commercial, industrial and residential customers in 22 states and seven Canadian provinces. It operates 40 solid waste landfills with unused permitted capacity of about 132 million cubic yards. LDW has contracts with 428 municipalities in 20 states and 192 municipalities in six Canadian provinces, providing solid waste services for some 2.6 million residences, and also collects recyclable products.

Hazardous waste services are provided from 50 locations in 12 states and six Canadian provinces. There are six secure hazardous waste landfills, a land treatment facility for nonhazardous industrial wastes and three incinerators for liquid wastes.

The largest school bus operator in North America, LDW has contracts with 71 school boards and districts in Canada and with 520 in the U.S., as well as other educational institutions, in 23 states, providing transportation for more than 960,000 students per day. It also operates 29 municipal transit systems in Canada and the U.S. LDW also has a 35% fully diluted interest in Attwoods plc, a waste services company, and owns 28% of ADT Ltd., a security and vehicle auction firm.

Dividend Data

Declarations on the Class A and Class B shares in the past 12 months were:

Amt of Divd. $	Date Decl.	Ex–divd. Date	Stock of Record	Payment Date
0.04*	Oct. 16	Oct. 26	Oct. 30	Nov. 15'93
0.04*	Jan. 12	Jan. 25	Jan. 29	Feb. 15'93
0.04	Apr. 8	Apr. 26	Apr. 30	May. 15'93
0.04	Jul. 7	Jul. 26	Jul. 30	Aug. 15'93

***In Canadian funds, bef. 15% tax on nonresidents.**

Capitalization

Long Term Debt: $1,296,292,000 (5/93).

5% Cum. Conv. First Pref. Stock: 653,070 shs. (no par); conv. into 1.5 Cl. B shs. at C$8 ea.

Class A Stock: 47,632,092 shs. (no par).
Canadian Pacific Ltd. owns 47%.
Shareholders of record: 1,871.

Class B Nonvoting Stock: 229,555,668 shs. (no par); has priorities over Cl. A in payment of divds.
Canadian Pacific Ltd. owns 12%.
Institutions hold about 25%.
Shareholders of record: 8,476.

Office—3221 North Service Rd. P.O. Box 5028, Burlington, ON L7R 3Y8, Canada. **Tel**—(416) 336-1800. **Chrmn**—P. N. T. Widdrington. **Pres & CEO**—D. K. Jackson. **Sr VP & CFO**—L. W. Haworth. **VP-Investor Contact**—Tag Watson. **Secy**—W. R. Cottick. **Dirs**—M. A. Ashcroft, J. R. Bullock, W. P. Cooper, R. K. Gamey, D. M. Green, J. F. Hankinson, D. K. Jackson, M. H. Lahn, R. J. Sazio, W. W. Stinson, P. N. T. Widdrington. **Transfer Agents & Registrars**—RM Trust Co., Toronto; Mellon Securities Trust Co., NYC. **Incorporated** in Ontario in 1966. **Empl**—35,345.

 Michael V. Pizzi

Lancaster Colony

NASDAQ Symbol LANC (Incl. in Nat'l Market) Options on NYSE In S&P MidCap 400

Price	Range	P-E Ratio	Dividend	Yield	S&P Ranking	Beta
Sep. 13'93	1993					
37¾	42–27⅝	19	0.52	1.4%	B+	1.19

Summary

Lancaster produces aftermarket and original equipment automotive products, specialty foods and glassware and candle products. Strong earnings growth was recorded in the past three fiscal years, with results for fiscal 1993 boosted by gains in all business segments. A four-for-three stock split was effected in April 1993. Increases in the cash dividend have been frequent.

Business Summary

Lancaster Colony Corporation makes automotive products, specialty foods and glassware and candles. Contributions in fiscal 1992 were:

	Sales	Profits
Automotive	32%	31%
Specialty foods	38%	46%
Glassware & candles	30%	23%

The company produces and markets rubber, vinyl and carpet-insert car mats for both original equipment manufacturers and importers and the auto aftermarket; truck and trailer splash guards; pickup truck bed mats and liners; aluminum running boards for pickup trucks and vans; and a broad line of other auto accessories and components. Auto aftermarket products are marketed primarily through mass merchandisers and automotive outlets under the name Rubber Queen. Ford Motor Co. and General Motors Corp. are significant purchasers of this segment's products.

Specialty food products made and sold by Lancaster include salad dressings and sauces marketed under the Marzetti, Pfeiffer and Girard's brand names; Mountain Top frozen unbaked pies; hearth-baked frozen breads marketed under the New York Frozen Foods name; refrigerated chip and produce dips, dairy snacks and desserts sold under the Oak Lake Farms, Allen and Marzetti names; Inn Maid and Amish Kitchen premium dry egg noodles; and Reames frozen noodles, pastas and breaded specialty items.

In 1986, the company decided to concentrate its resources in the automotive and specialty food product segments. It closed certain manufacturing plants and consolidated its housewares operations. The housewares segment now manufactures a variety of table and giftware items, including domestic glassware, both machine pressed and machine blown, and imported glassware; industrial glass and lighting components; candles in all popular sizes, shapes and scents; and glass florist containers. The segment also distributes a variety of Lancaster's products to commercial markets.

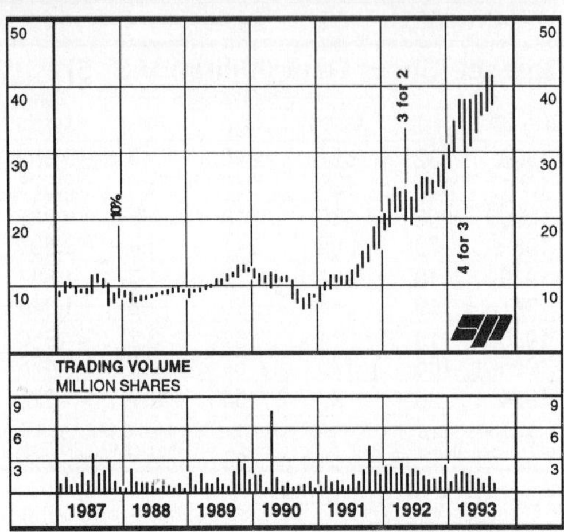

Important Developments

Sep. '93— Despite a difficult business environment, the company reported continued strength in sales and earnings in fiscal 1993's fourth quarter. Lancaster said that it anticipated the same tough climate for growth in fiscal 1994, but it expected to record continued growth in sales and earnings for the year. The company also noted that it was still looking for acquisitions that would help it expand its specialty foods business.

Next earnings report expected in early November.

Per Share Data ($)

Yr. End Jun. 30	1993	1992	1991	[1]1990	1989	1988	[1]1987	1986	1985	[1]1984
Tangible Bk. Val.	**NA**	[2]7.00	[2]6.07	[2]5.57	[2]5.78	[2]5.40	[2]4.95	4.86	4.99	4.76
Cash Flow	**NA**	2.24	1.67	1.40	1.59	1.47	1.22	0.76	1.10	1.18
Earnings[3]	**2.02**	1.42	0.92	0.68	0.91	0.86	0.67	0.12	0.48	0.59
Dividends	**0.498**	0.433	0.395	0.375	0.355	0.325	0.290	0.257	0.248	0.244
Payout Ratio	**25%**	30%	43%	55%	39%	37%	44%	NM	52%	41%
Prices[4]—High	**42**	29⅝	20⅜	12⅝	13¼	9⅞	11⅞	9½	6⅝	7¼
Low	**27⅝**	18⅜	7⅝	6½	8¼	7⅝	7	6⅜	5⅛	5
P/E Ratio—	**21–14**	21–13	22–8	19–10	15–9	11–9	18–11	80–54	14–11	12–8

Data as orig. reptd. Adj. for stk. divs. of 33⅓% Apr. 1993, 50% May 1992, 10% Dec. 1987, 25% Jul. 1986. **1.** Refl. merger or acq. **2.** Incl. intangibles. **3.** Bef. spec. item of -0.05 in 1991. **4.** Cal. yr. NM-Not Meaningful. NA-Not Available.

Income Data (Million $)

Year Ended Jun. 30	Oper. Revs.	Oper. Inc.	% Oper. Inc. of Revs.	Cap. Exp.	Depr.	Int. Exp.	[2]Net Bef. Taxes	Eff. Tax Rate	[3]Net Inc.	% Net Inc. of Revs.	Cash Flow
1992	**556**	**78.5**	**14.1**	**17.0**	**18.8**	**5.58**	**53.9**	**39.9%**	**32.4**	**5.8**	**51.2**
1991	500	62.5	12.5	13.5	17.5	8.74	33.8	37.3%	21.2	4.2	38.7
[1]1990	505	60.6	12.0	21.2	17.2	9.39	27.6	41.9%	16.1	3.2	33.3
1989	492	59.6	12.1	18.1	16.7	8.76	35.1	37.5%	21.9	4.5	38.6
1988	453	56.7	12.5	17.3	15.6	7.05	34.6	37.1%	21.8	4.8	37.4
[1]1987	430	52.9	12.3	21.4	14.3	6.02	33.3	48.3%	17.2	4.0	31.5
1986	423	37.5	8.9	17.1	14.4	6.91	4.7	44.0%	2.6	0.6	17.0
1985	441	40.6	9.2	18.1	13.7	8.67	18.8	43.0%	10.7	2.4	24.4
[1]1984	418	41.6	9.9	21.3	12.9	8.38	22.8	43.1%	13.0	3.1	25.9
1983	361	38.9	10.8	16.0	11.0	6.62	22.7	43.7%	12.8	3.5	23.8

Balance Sheet Data (Million $)

Jun. 30	Cash	Curr. Assets	Curr. Liab.	Curr. Ratio	Total Assets	% Ret. on Assets	Long Term Debt	Common Equity	Total Cap.	% LT Debt of Cap.	% Ret. on Equity
1992	**7.42**	**172**	**75**	**2.3**	**290**	**11.3**	**40.0**	**159**	**206**	**19.4**	**21.7**
1991	5.32	168	75	2.3	287	7.2	57.2	139	204	28.0	15.9
1990	0.72	183	107	1.7	309	5.4	60.2	129	202	29.8	12.2
1989	3.18	172	93	1.9	290	7.8	45.3	138	197	23.0	16.5
1988	4.05	169	89	1.9	286	7.9	49.5	134	197	25.1	17.0
1987	2.25	157	82	1.9	275	6.1	52.1	128	193	27.0	13.4
1986	4.73	152	78	2.0	250	1.0	51.1	113	173	29.5	2.3
1985	3.46	163	82	2.0	263	4.0	58.0	115	182	31.9	9.5
1984	2.41	166	90	1.8	267	5.2	61.2	109	177	34.6	12.4
1983	6.18	139	67	2.1	225	6.1	54.2	98	158	34.3	13.5

Data as orig. reptd. **1.** Refl. merger or acq. **2.** Incl. equity in earns. of nonconsol. subs. **3.** Bef. spec. item in 1991.

Net Sales (Million $)

Quarter:	1992-3	1991-2	1990-1	1989-90
Sep.	152	132	129	127
Dec.	171	147	134	134
Mar.	149	131	110	117
Jun.	159	146	128	126
	631	556	500	505

Based on a preliminary report, net sales for the fiscal year ended June 30, 1993, advanced 13% from those of fiscal 1992, benefiting from strength in all major business segments. Margins widened, and pretax income expanded 38%. After taxes at 37.8%, against 39.9%, net income was ahead 43%, to $46,225,000 ($2.02 a share), from $32,371,000 ($1.42, as adjusted).

Common Share Earnings ($)

Quarter:	1992-3	1991-2	1990-1	1989-90
Sep.	0.46	0.33	0.24	0.25
Dec.	0.53	0.35	0.26	0.23
Mar.	0.42	0.28	0.15	0.18
Jun.	0.61	0.47	0.27	0.02
	2.02	1.42	0.92	0.68

Dividend Data

Cash has been paid in each year since 1963.

Amt. of Divd. $	Date Decl.	Ex-divd. Date	Stock of Record	Payment Date
0.17	Nov. 16	Dec. 4	Dec. 10	Dec. 31'92
0.17	Feb. 25	Mar. 4	Mar. 10	Mar. 31'93
4-for-3	Feb. 25	Apr. 16	Mar. 15	Apr. 15'93
0.13	May 27	Jun. 4	Jun. 10	Jun. 30'93
0.13	Aug. 20	Sep. 3	Sep. 10	Sep. 30'93

Finances

In November 1991, Lancaster acquired substantially all of the assets of a California salad dressing operation from a unit of Kellogg Co. for $5.1 million.

In fiscal 1991, the company recorded a pretax charge of $3 million from the writedown of property held for sale. In fiscal 1990, it recognized a litigation charge of $6.75 million.

In October 1989, Reames Foods, Inc., a manufacturer of frozen food products, was purchased for $5.8 million.

Capitalization

Long Term Debt: $35,215,000 (3/93).

Common Stock: 22,820,000 shs. ($1 par). J. B. Gerlach has voting control of 23%. Institutions hold about 49%. Shareholders: About 10,000 (9/92).

Office—37 W. Broad St., Columbus, OH 43215. **Tel**—(614) 224-7141. **Pres, CEO & CFO**—J. B. Gerlach. **Exec VP & Secy**—J. B. Gerlach Jr. **Treas**—J. L. Boylan. **Dirs**—F. W. Batsch, R. L. Fox, J. B. Gerlach, J. B. Gerlach Jr., M. S. Halpern, R. S. Hamilton, E. H. Jennings, R. R. Murphey Jr., H. M. O'Neill Jr., D. J. Zuver. **Transfer Agent & Registrar**—American Stock Transfer & Trust Co., Brooklyn. **Incorporated** in Delaware in 1961; reincorporated in Ohio in 1992. **Empl**—4,700.

 Michael W. Jaffe

Lance, Inc.

NASDAQ Symbol LNCE (Incl. in Nat'l Market) In S&P MidCap 400

Price	Range	P–E Ratio	Dividend	Yield	S&P Ranking	Beta
Oct. 26'93	1993					
20	24¾–19¾	20	0.96	4.8%	A	0.43

Summary

This manufacturer of snack foods and bakery products derives a significant portion of its total sales from vending machines located in 36 states and the District of Columbia. Sales for 1993 should benefit from the company's entry into the West Coast market and greater emphasis on a marketing program that proved successful in two test markets; however, improvement in margins may be limited by increased supermarket sales, start-up costs at a new bakery facility and the greater marketing outlays.

Current Outlook

Earnings for 1994 are projected at $1.25 a share, up from the $1.04 estimated for 1993.

A modest increase in the $0.24 quarterly dividend is possible by mid-1994.

Sales in 1993 and beyond should benefit from continued slow gains in unit volume, reflecting expanded supermarket distribution, increased emphasis on advertising and entry into the West Coast market. Margins have been weak in recent quarters, but should improve beginning in 1993's fourth quarter as startup costs at a new Vista Bakery plant should be absorbed by greater unit volume. Increased marketing outlays are planned, although preliminary indications are that the additional spending will be outweighed by volume gains. A 2.5 million share buyback authorization may provide some support for this above-average-dividend stock.

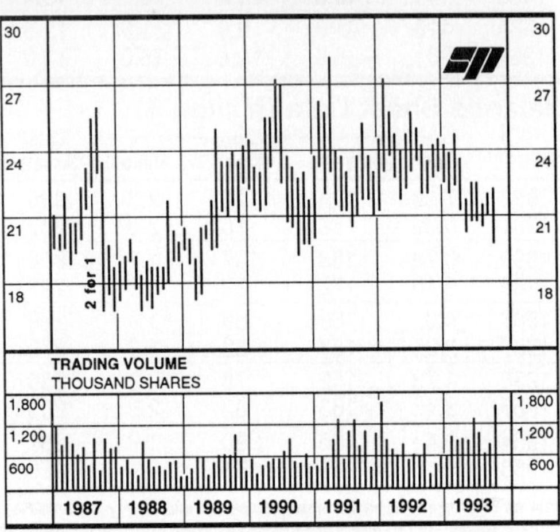

Net Sales (Million $)

Weeks:	1993	1992	1991	1990
12 Mar.	106	105	103	103
12 Jun.	113	110	107	107
12 Sep.	106	105	102	102
16 Dec.	---	141	138	135
	---	461	450	446

Net sales for the 36 weeks ended September 4, 1993, edged up 1.5%, year to year, on continued gains in unit volume. Penalized by start-up costs at a new bakery facility, net income fell 25%, to $21,516,000 ($0.69 a share), from $28,724,000 ($0.92).

Common Share Earnings ($)

Weeks:	1993	1992	1991	1990
12 Mar.	0.24	0.32	0.28	0.34
12 Jun.	0.27	0.32	0.31	0.37
12 Sep.	0.18	0.28	0.26	0.33
16 Dec.	E0.35	0.33	0.36	0.42
	E1.04	1.25	1.21	1.46

Important Developments

Oct. '93— Directors authorized the repurchase of up to 2.5 million of the company's common shares outstanding, with funding for the purchases provided by cash and short term investments. The company said 202,500 shares had been repurchased. Separately, Lance said that weak profitability in 1993's third quarter reflected higher production costs at Vista Bakery, lower sales of higher margin products, increased selling expenses and the impact of the enactment of the new federal tax act. The Vista Bakery costs have restricted profitability for four quarters, and their negative impact on future results should be minimal. The remaining factors, however, will likely continue to affect profitability in the coming periods.

Next earnings report expected in late January.

Per Share Data ($)

Yr. End Dec. 31	1992	1991	1990	1989	1988	1987	1986	1985	1984	1983
Tangible Bk. Val.	**8.06**	7.75	7.42	6.97	6.30	5.88	5.64	5.32	4.79	4.28
Cash Flow	**1.99**	1.90	2.10	2.01	1.77	1.66	1.52	1.42	1.33	1.21
Earnings	**1.25**	1.21	1.46	1.42	1.23	1.17	1.07	1.00	0.94	0.87
Dividends	**0.920**	0.880	0.820	0.720	0.660	0.585	0.520	0.469	0.433	0.395
Payout Ratio	**74%**	73%	58%	51%	54%	50%	48%	47%	46%	46%
Prices—High	**27¼**	28¼	27¼	25	21¾	26	20⅜	16⅛	11¾	11½
Low	**21¼**	20	19¼	17¼	16¾	16¾	15	11⅛	9⅛	9
P/E Ratio—	**22–17**	23–17	19–13	18–12	18–14	22–14	19–14	16–11	12–10	13–10

Data as orig. reptd. Adj. for stk. divs. of 100% Aug. 1987, 33⅓% Apr. 1985. E-Estimated

Income Data (Million $)

Year Ended Dec. 31	Revs.	Oper. Inc.	% Oper. Inc. of Revs.	Cap. Exp.	Depr.	Int. Exp.	Net Bef. Taxes	Eff. Tax Rate	Net Inc.	% Net Inc. of Revs.	Cash Flow
1992	**461**	**77.6**	**16.8**	**51.0**	**23.2**	**Nil**	**60.2**	**34.9%**	**39.1**	**8.5**	**62.4**
1991	450	72.8	16.2	21.4	21.8	Nil	58.7	35.7%	37.7	8.4	59.5
1990	446	82.4	18.5	47.6	20.2	Nil	70.5	35.1%	45.7	10.3	65.9
1989	432	81.9	18.9	30.2	18.6	Nil	69.9	35.8%	44.9	10.4	63.5
1988	408	76.5	18.8	51.5	17.2	Nil	60.4	35.2%	39.1	9.6	56.3
1987	380	75.0	19.7	36.4	16.0	Nil	64.6	41.2%	38.0	10.0	54.0
1986	367	76.2	20.8	19.3	14.8	Nil	66.4	46.4%	35.6	9.7	50.4
1985	355	70.7	19.9	19.2	13.9	0.28	62.0	46.3%	33.3	9.4	47.2
1984	337	66.0	19.6	18.9	12.9	0.29	58.0	46.3%	31.2	9.2	44.1
1983	308	62.2	20.2	16.4	11.6	0.26	53.6	46.4%	28.7	9.3	40.3

Balance Sheet Data (Million $)

Dec. 31	Cash	Curr. Assets	Curr. Liab.	Curr. Ratio	Total Assets	% Ret. on Assets	Long Term Debt	Common Equity	Total Cap.	% LT Debt of Cap.	% Ret. on Equity
1992	**59.0**	**128**	**32.2**	**4.0**	**313**	**12.8**	**Nil**	**252**	**278**	**Nil**	**15.8**
1991	75.9	139	29.5	4.7	300	12.8	Nil	242	268	Nil	15.9
1990	60.7	126	28.6	4.4	289	16.3	Nil	232	257	Nil	20.3
1989	64.4	130	28.7	4.5	276	16.9	Nil	220	245	Nil	21.4
1988	53.2	117	32.0	3.7	256	15.8	Nil	199	221	Nil	20.3
1987	69.0	117	30.7	3.8	242	16.1	Nil	188	209	Nil	20.6
1986	86.8	131	29.7	4.4	237	15.4	Nil	185	205	Nil	19.8
1985	76.5	123	27.2	4.5	227	15.4	1.58	177	198	0.8	19.8
1984	61.0	104	24.9	4.2	204	16.2	1.73	159	177	1.0	20.7
1983	49.1	88	21.5	4.1	182	16.6	1.68	142	158	1.1	21.3

Data as orig. reptd.

Business Summary

Lance, Inc. manufactures and distributes a variety of snacks and bread-basket items.

Principal snack products include cracker sandwiches, cookie sandwiches, peanuts, potato chips, corn chips, popcorn, cakes, cookies, candies, chewing gum, beef snacks and sausages. Principal bread-basket items are wafers, crackers and breadsticks, individually packed and sold to restaurants and similar institutions.

Net sales and other operating revenue in recent years were derived as follows:

	1992	1991	1990
Snack items	88%	88%	87%
Bread–basket items	9%	9%	10%
Other	3%	3%	3%

Snack foods are sold through Lance's own sales force to convenience stores, independent and chain supermarkets, discount stores, military commissaries, restaurants, schools, hospitals, and other customers in 36 states and the District of Columbia, principally east of the Mississippi River and in the midwestern and southwestern U.S.

About 81% of 1992 revenues were derived from company-packaged products, with the balance purchased from others and resold by Lance. A significant portion of output is sold through vending machines, which are made available to customers on a rental, sale or commission basis. Restaurants and similar institutions are the main customers for the bread-basket items.

Midwest Biscuit Co. manufactures cookies and crackers for both private label and its own Vista label. Sales are made primarily to wholesale grocers, supermarket chains and distributors throughout the U.S., with the majority of business in the Midwest.

Wholly owned Caronuts, Inc., is a 12-million-pound peanut-buying station in Boykins, Va.

Dividend Data

Except in 1944, cash has been paid each year since 1935. A dividend reinvestment plan is available.

Amt of Divd. $	Date Decl.	Ex–divd. Date	Stock of Record	Payment Date
0.24	Jan. 12	Jan. 26	Feb. 1	Feb. 15'93
0.24	Apr. 16	Apr. 26	May 1	May 15'93
0.24	Jul. 13	Jul. 26	Aug. 1	Aug. 15'93
0.24	Oct. 5	Oct. 26	Nov. 1	Nov. 15'93

Capitalization

Long Term Debt: None (6/93).

Common Stock: 31,292,851 shs. ($0.83⅓ par).
The Van Every family controls 41%.
Institutions hold about 35%.
Shareholders: 5,524 of record (2/93).

Office—8600 South Boulevard, P.O. Box 32368, Charlotte, NC 28232. **Tel**—(704) 554-1421. **Chrmn, Pres & CEO**—W. Disher. **Treas**—E. D. Leake. **Secy & Investor Contact**—James W. Helms Jr. **Dirs**—A. T. Dickson, J. W. Disher, W. F. Dowd Jr., W. R. Holland, T. B. Horack, E. D. Leake, W. B. Meacham, G. R. Melvin, L. Robinson, R. V. Sisk, A. F. Sloan, G. K. Smith, P. A. Stroup III, V. S. Sutton, R. G. Swain, S. H. Van Every Jr., S. L. Van Every. **Transfer Agent**—Wachovia Bank & Trust Co., Winston-Salem, N.C. **Incorporated** in North Carolina in 1926. **Empl**—5,860.

 Gregg W. Bonardi, CFA

Lands' End

NYSE Symbol LE Options on CBOE (Mar-Jun-Sep-Dec) In S&P MidCap 400

Price	Range	P-E Ratio	Dividend	Yield	S&P Ranking	Beta
Aug. 12'93	1993					
32⅛	32½–23¼	17	0.20	0.6%	NR	1.19

Summary

Lands' End is a specialty mail order retailer of traditionally styled recreational and informal clothing, accessories, shoes, and soft luggage. Improved customer response to new products and higher inventory levels have boosted recent sales and earnings. Earnings gains should continue in fiscal 1993-94, reflecting moderate improvement in consumer spending, good response to specialty catalogs, and better inventory control which should result in fewer markdowns.

Current Outlook

Earnings for the fiscal year ending January 31, 1994, are projected at $2.10 a share, up from the $1.85 of fiscal 1992-93. Earnings could reach $2.40 in fiscal 1994-95.

A $0.20 annual dividend was paid in December 1992.

Sales should increase in fiscal 1993-94 as the economy picks up and consumer spending improves. Gross margins should widen slightly on the higher volume, an improved product mix, and better inventory management. Expense ratios should remain about level.

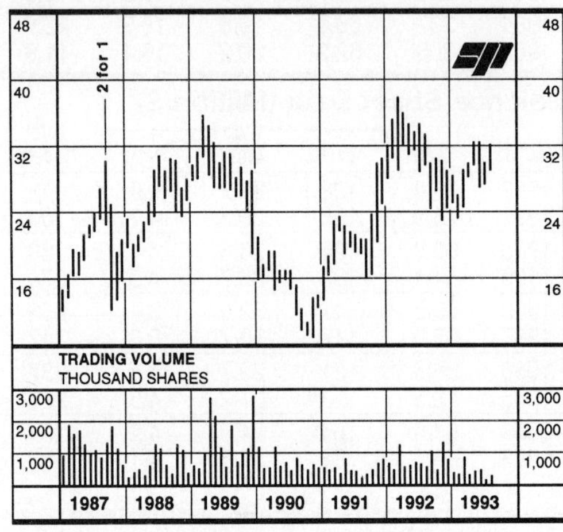

Net Sales (Million $)

Quarter:	1993-94	1992-93	1991-92	1990-91
Apr.	156.3	141.4	128.5	112.2
Jul.	151.1	138.1	122.0	117.1
Oct.	---	174.6	161.4	145.4
Jan.	---	279.5	271.5	229.3
	---	733.6	683.4	604.0

Sales for the six months ended July 30, 1993, advanced 10%, year to year. Gross margins widened, but SG&A expenses rose as a percentage of sales; operating income increased 9.3%. After interest income (net), versus interest expense (net) and higher other income, pretax income rose 17%. Following taxes at 39.0%, versus 38.0%, net income increased 15%. Share earnings were $0.43, (before a $0.07 special credit from an accounting change), against $0.37.

Common Share Earnings ($)

Quarter:	1993-94	1992-93	1991-92	1090-91
Apr.	0.24	0.23	0.08	0.09
Jul.	0.20	0.14	0.06	d0.12
Oct.	E0.36	0.31	0.31	0.02
Jan.	E1.30	1.18	1.10	0.78
	E2.10	1.85	1.53	0.75

Important Developments

Aug. '93— Lands' End said that net sales in the second quarter of fiscal 1993-94 rose mainly because of strong customer reaction to its primary books and increased circulation of specialty catalogs. This was somewhat offset by a later mailing of the spring/summer clearance catalog and a higher percentage of lost sales (orders received for merchandise not in stock and not backordered). Gross profit margin benefited from a higher proportion of sales of full price merchandise, mainly because the later mailing of the spring/summer clearance catalog shifted a substantial portion of lower margin sales from the second quarter to the third. Liquidations of excess inventory declined to 9% of sales, compared with 13% a year ago. Inventory at the end of the second quarter was up only slightly from a year earlier.

Next earnings report expected in mid-November.

Per Share Data ($)

Yr. End Jan. 31	1993	1992	1991	1990	1989	1988	1987	1986	1985	1984
Tangible Bk. Val.	**7.73**	6.86	6.08	5.76	4.59	2.83	1.89	1.49	1.06	1.05
Cash Flow	**2.28**	1.92	1.11	1.71	1.81	1.26	NA	NA	NA	NA
Earnings[1]	**1.85**	1.53	0.75	1.45	1.61	1.11	[2]0.73	[2]0.56	[2]0.36	[2]0.39
Dividends[3]	**0.20**	0.20	0.20	0.20	0.20	0.20	NA	NA	NA	NA
Payout Ratio	**11%**	13%	26%	14%	12%	18%	NA	NA	NA	NA
Calendar Years	**1992**	1991	1990	1989	1988	1987	1986	1985	1984	1983
Prices—High	**37⅞**	30½	21	35¾	30⅞	30¼	15⅛	NA	NA	NA
Low	**23**	13⅜	8⅞	19	17½	12⅛	11⅝	NA	NA	NA
P/E Ratio—	**20–12**	20–9	27–12	25–13	19–11	27–11	21–16	NA	NA	NA

Data as orig. reptd. Adj. for stk. div. of 100% Sep. 1987. **1.** Bef. spec. item(s) of +0.03 in 1988. **2.** Pro forma. **3.** Co. paid cash distributions as an S Corporation in 1987-1984. E-Estimated. NA-Not Available.

Income Data (Million $)

Year Ended Jan. 31	Revs.	Oper. Inc.	% Oper. Inc. of Revs.	Cap. Exp.	Depr.	Int. Exp.	Net Bef. Taxes	Eff. Tax Rate	[2]Net Inc.	% Net Inc.of Revs.	Cash Flow
1993	**734**	**63.5**	**8.7**	**8.6**	**7.90**	**1.33**	**54.0**	**38.0%**	**33.5**	**4.6**	**41.4**
1992	683	56.6	8.3	5.4	7.43	1.55	47.5	39.5%	28.7	4.2	36.2
1991	604	31.6	5.2	17.7	7.04	1.02	24.9	40.9%	14.7	2.4	21.8
1990	545	52.0	9.5	25.2	5.25	1.40	47.3	38.5%	29.1	5.3	34.3
1989	456	54.6	12.0	22.9	3.92	1.23	52.1	38.1%	32.3	7.1	36.2
1988	336	41.4	12.3	5.9	3.19	1.36	38.3	42.3%	22.1	6.6	25.3
1987	265	31.2	11.8	9.6	2.58	1.49	28.5	[1]48.7%	[1]14.6	5.5	21.2
1986	227	23.7	10.4	6.5	1.86	1.58	21.6	[1]47.8%	[1]11.3	5.0	23.4
1985	172	15.0	8.7	2.6	1.44	1.70	12.8	[1]47.4%	[1]6.7	3.9	NA
1984	123	13.7	11.1	8.0	0.84	1.21	12.5	[1]41.5%	[1]7.3	5.9	NA

Balance Sheet Data (Million $)

Jan. 31	Cash	Curr. Assets	Curr. Liab.	Curr. Ratio	Total Assets	% Ret. on Assets	Long Term Debt	Common Equity	Total Inv. Capital	% LT Debt of Cap.	Ret. On Equity
1993	**22.8**	**135**	**67.3**	**2.0**	**209**	**16.3**	**Nil**	**139**	**142**	**Nil**	**25.5%**
1992	1.4	131	74.5	1.8	206	15.0	1.7	127	131	1.3	24.1%
1991	27.3	108	60.8	1.8	185	8.5	3.3	117	125	2.7	13.0%
1990	8.3	100	43.9	2.3	167	18.3	5.0	115	123	4.1	28.2%
1989	32.1	104	51.5	2.0	151	25.0	6.8	92	100	6.8	43.4%
1988	28.2	78	38.9	2.0	107	23.1	8.7	57	68	12.7	46.8%
1987	16.0	58	32.9	1.8	85	20.9	10.6	38	52	20.5	44.9%
1986	3.6	36	18.0	2.0	56	22.3	10.3	27	38	27.5	48.3%
1985	2.0	30	16.2	1.9	46	15.9	10.0	19	29	34.0	36.2%
1984	NA	25	10.6	2.3	39	18.7	[3]10.6	18	28	37.3	57.0%

Data as orig. reptd. **1.** Reflects pro forma provision for income taxes. **2.** Bef. spec. items. **3.** Incl. current portion. NA-Not Available.

Business Summary

Lands' End is a specialty mail order retailer; merchandise is offered through regular mailings of its catalog. The company's products include traditionally styled recreational and informal clothing mostly for men and women, accessories, shoes and soft luggage. Since 1990, Lands' End has mailed a separate children's catalog, a dress shirt and tie catalog, and a specialty catalog focusing on bed and bath products. In 1991, LE formed a foreign subsidiary to manage its growing presence in the U.K.

The growth of the specialty mail order catalog industry can be attributed to more widespread use of credit cards, the use of toll-free telephone lines, the increase in the number of working women with less time to shop in stores, and new applications of computer technology. Customers may purchase merchandise by using a toll-free number 24 hours a day, seven days a week (except Christmas). About 80% of current catalog orders are placed by telephone.

Efforts taken to improve sales have included new products, improving product quality, increasing the number of catalogs mailed, and utilizing computer applications to refine the customer list. The company's mailing list consisted of 15.6 million people at the end of fiscal 1992-93.

During fiscal 1992-93, LE increased the number of catalogs mailed by 11%, to 136 million, while reducing the mailings of its full-size catalogs and increasing mailings of smaller specialty catalogs.

All goods are purchased from independent manufacturers (except for soft luggage, which is made at company facilities), with about 85% (including soft luggage) supplied from U.S. manufacturers. Lands' End determines product specifications, including fibers, fabric construction, and styling. Overstocks and end-of-season close outs are sold at reduced prices to catalog customers and through 12 outlet stores.

Dividend Data

Dividends were initiated in 1987. Payments are on an annual basis.

Amt of Divd. $	Date Decl.	Ex–divd. Date	Stock of Record	Payment Date
0.20	Dec. 8	Dec. 14	Dec. 18	Dec. 29'92

Finances

Capital improvements totaled $10 million in the fiscal year ended January 29, 1993.

In LE's October 1986 initial public offering, underwriters sold 2.8 million common shares (including 1.25 for selling stockholders) at $15 each (data adjusted).

Capitalization

Long Term Debt: None (4/93).

Common Stock: 17,962,059 shs. ($0.01 par). Officers and directors own 65%, incl. 58% by G.C. Comer.
Shareholders of record: 3,461.

Office—Lands' End Lane, Dodgeville, WI 53595. **Tel**—(608) 935-9341. **Chrmn**—G. C. Comer. **Pres & CEO**—W. T. End. **SVP-CFO**—S. A. Orum. **VP & Investor Contact**—Charlotte LaComb. **Dirs**—R. C. Anderson, G. C. Comer, D. F. Dyer, W. T. End, D. B. Heller, H. G. Krane, J. N. Latter. **Transfer Agent & Registrar**—Firstar Trust Co., Milwaukee. **Incorporated** in Delaware in 1986. **Empl**—4,700.

 Karen J. Sack

Lawson Products

NASDAQ Symbol LAWS (Incl. in Nat'l Market) In S&P MidCap 400

Price	Range	P–E Ratio	Dividend	Yield	S&P Ranking	Beta
Jun. 18'93	1993					
25⅞	29¾–23¼	21	0.40	1.5%	A–	0.43

Summary

Ths company distributes replacement fasteners and other expendable parts and supplies used for the repair and maintenance of capital equipment, buildings and automobiles. Lawson has a strong balance sheet, with no long-term debt. Following a decline in 1992, an earnings advance is expected for 1993, based on an anticipated sales increase and efficiencies from a new distribution center.

Current Outlook

Earnings for 1993 are estimated at $1.35 a share, up from the depressed $1.13 reported for 1992.

Dividends are likely to continue at $0.10 quarterly.

Assuming a better economy, net sales for 1993 are expected to show moderate improvement, aided by the introduction of various merchandising programs and a continuing emphasis on developing new business. Profitability should be helped by the higher sales, the absence of expenses related to a new distribution center, efficiencies from the new distribution center, and a nonrecurring gain from the sale of a facility. In addition, the tax rate will benefit from the fact that there is no income tax in Nevada, where the new distribution center came on line in mid-October 1992. There is also the possibility of a tapering off—in the latter part of the year—of charges related to development of the UK market. No permanent outside financing is anticipated for 1993.

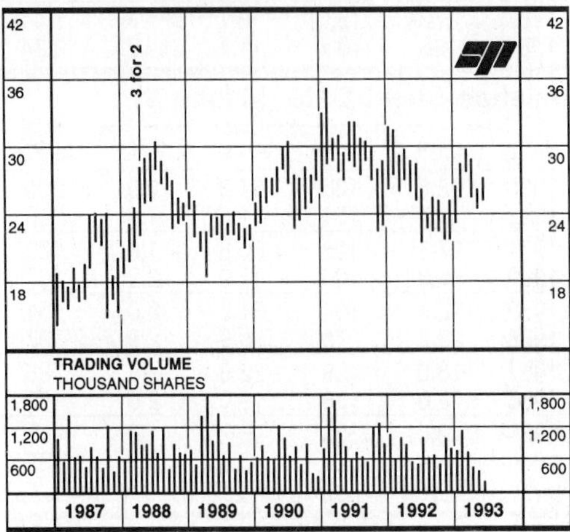

Net Sales (Million $)

Quarter:	1993	1992	1991	1990
Mar.	47.1	45.1	43.7	45.2
Jun.		47.5	46.4	47.3
Sep.		48.1	46.9	47.5
Dec.		45.9	44.7	45.6
		186.7	181.7	185.6

Net sales in the first quarter of 1993 rose 4.3%, year to year, as more orders processed more than offset smaller average order size. Margins widened on the higher sales, and operating profit increased 8.6%. After much larger investment and other income (due primarily to a $1.2 million nonrecurring gain), pretax income moved ahead 34%. With taxes at 35.9%, versus 38.6%, net income was up 40%, to $0.34 a share (before $0.02 credit from cumulative effect of accounting change), from $0.24.

Common Share Earnings ($)

Quarter:	1993	1992	1991	1990
Mar.	0.34	0.24	0.27	0.38
Jun.	E0.32	0.30	0.37	0.48
Sep.	E0.31	0.28	0.32	0.44
Dec.	E0.38	0.31	0.27	0.38
	E1.35	1.13	1.23	1.67

Important Developments

Apr. '93— Lawson noted that results in the 1993 first quarter included a $1.2 million gain—$740,000 after taxes, or about $0.05 a share—from the sale of its Compton, Calif. facility. Separately, Lawson said its adoption of SFAS 109 (accounting for income taxes) resulted in a $0.02 a share credit in the 1993 first quarter, representing the cumulative effect of the accounting change.

Next earnings report expected in late July.

Per Share Data ($)

Yr. End Dec. 31	1992	1991	1990	1989	1988	1987	1986	1985	1984	1983
Tangible Bk. Val.	**9.50**	8.87	8.04	6.74	5.85	5.74	4.82	4.13	3.98	3.83
Cash Flow	**1.35**	1.41	1.82	1.76	1.56	1.36	0.98	0.96	0.88	0.64
Earnings	**1.13**	1.23	1.67	1.61	1.42	1.22	0.85	0.86	0.79	0.54
Dividends	**0.400**	0.400	0.370	0.330	0.254	0.194	0.155	0.129	0.115	0.095
Payout Ratio	**35%**	33%	22%	20%	18%	16%	18%	15%	14%	17%
Prices—High	**31¾**	35¼	30½	26	30½	24⅛	17½	14¼	11¼	11⅛
Low	**21½**	22½	22¾	18½	18⅞	14⅛	12½	10¾	8⅜	7¾
P/E Ratio—	**28–19**	29–18	18–14	16–11	21–13	20–12	21–15	17–12	14–11	20–14

Data as orig. reptd. Adj. for stk. divs. of 50% Apr. 1988, 50% May 1986, 50% Feb. 1984. E-Estimated.

Lawson Products, Inc.

Income Data (Million $)

Year Ended Dec. 31	Revs.	Oper. Inc.	% Oper. Inc. of Revs.	Cap. Exp.	Depr.	Int. Exp.	[1]Net Bef. Taxes	Eff. Tax Rate	Net Inc.	% Net Inc. of Revs.	Cash Flow
1992	**187**	**27.5**	**14.7**	**8.16**	**2.98**	**0.01**	**25.4**	**39.5%**	**15.3**	**8.2**	**18.3**
1991	182	26.7	14.7	4.85	2.44	0.05	26.4	37.0%	16.6	9.2	19.1
1990	186	35.7	19.3	6.39	2.10	0.02	35.2	35.9%	22.6	12.2	24.7
1989	177	34.9	19.7	7.88	1.99	0.03	34.7	37.0%	21.9	12.3	23.9
1988	166	30.4	18.3	1.02	2.03	0.04	31.0	34.3%	20.3	12.2	22.4
1987	147	29.4	19.9	0.81	2.08	0.16	29.1	38.2%	18.0	12.2	20.0
1986	136	24.2	17.8	2.59	1.88	0.08	24.1	48.0%	12.5	9.2	14.4
1985	128	23.5	18.4	3.76	1.55	0.06	24.8	46.7%	13.2	10.3	14.7
1984	121	22.8	18.8	0.34	1.58	0.15	25.1	47.1%	13.3	10.9	14.8
1983	106	17.0	16.0	0.92	1.68	0.11	17.6	47.9%	9.2	8.7	10.9

Balance Sheet Data (Million $)

		Curr.									
Dec. 31	Cash	Assets	Liab.	Ratio	Total Assets	% Ret. on Assets	Long Term Debt	Common Equity	Total Cap.	% LT Debt of Cap.	% Ret. on Equity
1992	**59.6**	**112**	**16.0**	**7.0**	**158**	**10.0**	**Nil**	**129**	**129**	**Nil**	**12.3**
1991	61.3	110	18.4	6.0	150	11.6	Nil	120	120	Nil	14.5
1990	52.3	102	18.7	5.4	138	17.6	Nil	109	109	Nil	22.5
1989	39.1	86	18.8	4.6	119	19.7	Nil	91	92	Nil	25.6
1988	32.5	78	17.1	4.5	106	19.6	Nil	81	81	Nil	25.4
1987	45.0	84	16.3	5.2	107	17.9	Nil	84	85	Nil	23.3
1986	34.1	70	12.9	5.4	95	15.3	Nil	71	76	Nil	19.0
1985	24.8	58	11.6	5.0	81	16.7	Nil	61	65	Nil	22.1
1984	26.7	59	12.6	4.7	82	16.8	Nil	63	66	Nil	21.5
1983	31.3	63	10.2	6.1	81	12.3	Nil	65	67	Nil	15.1

Data as orig. reptd. **1.** Incl. equity in earns. of nonconsol. subs.

Business Summary

Lawson Products distributes expendable maintenance, repair and replacement products to over 180,000 customers. All products are manufactured by others to LAWS's specifications, with about 90% sold under the Lawson label. Revenue contributions:

	1992	1991
Fasteners, fittings & related parts	42%	43%
Industrial supplies	52%	51%
Automotive & equipment maintenance parts	6%	6%

Fasteners, fittings and related parts include screws, nuts, rivets and other fasteners. Industrial supplies include hoses and hose fittings, lubricants, cleansers, adhesives and other chemicals, as well as files, drills, welding products and other shop supplies. Auto and equipment maintenance parts include primary wiring, connectors and other electrical supplies and exhaust and other auto parts. Sales breakdown by markets:

	1992	1991
Heavy–duty equipment maintenance	46%	47%
In–plant & building maintenance	40%	39%
Passenger car maintenance	12%	12%

Heavy-duty equipment maintenance customers include operators of trucks, buses, agricultural implements, construction and road-building equipment, mining, and logging and drilling equipment. The in-plant and building maintenance market includes plants engaged in a broad range of manufacturing and processing activities, as well as institutions such as hospitals, universities, school districts and government agencies. Passenger car maintenance customers include auto service center chains, independent garages, auto dealers, and car rental agencies.

Dividend Data

Cash payments began in 1973.

Amt. of Divd. $	Date Decl.	Ex–divd. Date	Stock of Record	Payment Date
0.10	Aug. 11	Sep. 23	Sep. 29	Oct. 16'92
0.10	Dec. 17	Dec. 28	Jan. 4	Jan. 18'93
0.10	Feb. 18	Mar. 30	Apr. 5	Apr. 19'93
0.10	May 12	Jun. 28	Jul. 2	Jul. 16'93

Capitalization

Long Term Debt: None (3/93).

Common Stock: 13,556,348 shs. ($1 par).
About 38% owned by Mr. & Mrs. Sidney L. Port.
Shareholders of record: 1,546.

Office—1666 E. Touhy Ave., Des Plaines, IL 60018. **Tel**—(708) 827-9666. **Chrmn & CEO**—B. Kalish. **Pres**—P. G. Smith. **VP & Treas**—J. Shaffer. **Secy**—R. J. Washlow. **VP-Controller & Investor Contact**—Joseph L. Pawlick. **Dirs**—J. T. Brophy, L. L. Carrol, B. Kalish, R. B. Port, S. L. Port, R. G. Rettig, J. Shaffer, P. G. Smith, T. W. Smith. **Transfer Agent**—First National Bank of Chicago. **Incorporated** in Illinois in 1952; reincorporated in Delaware in 1982. **Empl**—747.

 N.J. DeVita

Lawter International

NYSE Symbol LAW Options on Phila In S&P MidCap 400

Price	Range	P–E Ratio	Dividend	Yield	S&P Ranking	Beta
Aug. 3'93	1993					
13¾	15½–12⅛	21	0.40	2.9%	A–	0.99

Summary

Lawter manufactures printing ink vehicles, wax compounds and powders, synthetic and hydrocarbon resins, fluorescent pigments and coatings, and thermographic and rota-matic machines. Revenues and earnings reached record levels in 1992, and the company said in early 1993 that improvement should continue as the year progresses. Insiders own about 25% of the shares.

Business Summary

Lawter International, Inc. is engaged principally in the production of specialty chemicals. It also produces thermographic machines. While the graphic arts industry is a major market, Lawter also serves the industrial coatings, adhesives and other industries. Sales contributions in recent years:

	1992	1991	1990
Printing ink vehicles & wax compounds......	49%	46%	48%
Synthetic & hydrocarbon resins..	44%	45%	41%
Fluorescent pigments & coatings, and thermographic machines & compounds............	7%	9%	11%

International operations contributed 45% of sales and 40% of pretax income in 1992.

Printing ink vehicles are fluid and gelled compositions that give printing inks the ability to carry color onto a variety of printing surfaces. Printing ink vehicles influence printing quality, gloss, drying speed, adhesion, rub resistance and press speed. Wax compounds and powders are used in printing inks to provide additional surface slip and rub resistance to the ink film. These products are sold to printing ink manufacturers.

Synthetic and hydrocarbon resins are used to produce adhesives, liquid printing inks and printing ink vehicles, rubber compounds, paints and various coatings to improve durability, chemical resistance, appearance, adhesion and speed of drying.

Fluorescent pigments and coatings are used in the manufacture of paints, printing inks, paper coatings, plastic products, rubber compounds, textile inks and other products where striking color properties are desired. Such fluorescent products are used for greater visibility in safety marking applications, in the plastic industry in toys and bottles and in display advertising.

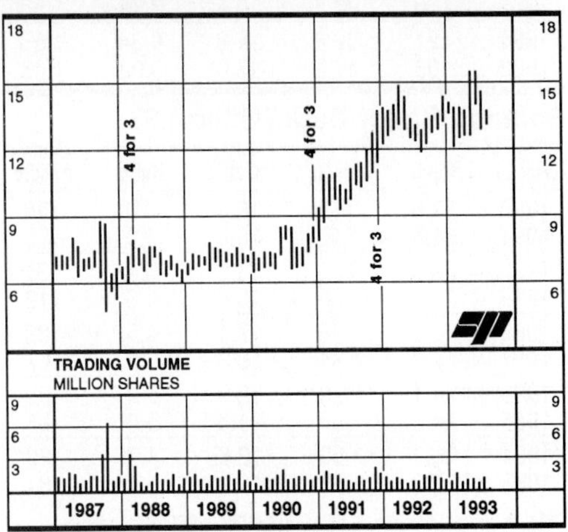

Thermographic machines and compounds are used in the production of thermographic printing, a process that produces raised printing. Rota-matic machines are used to cut, score or perforate paper products. The thermographic printing process and rota-matic machines are used in the manufacture of greeting cards, specialty printing, business cards, stationery and advertising material.

Important Developments

Apr. '93— LAW said that, because of a continuing flow of new products, geographical expansion in Asia and Mexico, the building of additional efficient state of the art plants, and continuing cost control, it expected that both sales and earnings would continue to make gains in the future.

Next earnings report expected in late October.

Per Share Data ($)

Yr. End Dec. 31	1992	1991	1990	1989	1988	1987	1986	1985	1984	1983
Tangible Bk. Val.[1]	**2.83**	2.68	2.44	2.04	1.85	1.67	1.33	1.16	1.41	1.37
Cash Flow	**0.71**	0.70	0.63	0.53	0.58	0.48	0.38	d0.07	0.42	0.41
Earnings	**0.62**	0.61	0.55	0.46	0.50	0.40	0.32	d0.13	0.37	0.35
Dividends	**0.400**	0.345	0.293	0.293	0.293	0.236	0.236	0.236	0.233	0.209
Payout Ratio	**66%**	57%	54%	65%	60%	59%	76%	NM	65%	59%
Prices—High	**14⅞**	13¾	8⁹⁄₁₆	7¹³⁄₁₆	8	8¹³⁄₁₆	7⁵⁄₁₆	5¾	6⅛	5¾
Low	**11⅞**	7⅞	6½	6⁷⁄₁₆	6¹⁄₁₆	4¹³⁄₁₆	4⅞	4⅜	4⁷⁄₁₆	3¹⁄₁₆
P/E Ratio—	**24–19**	23–13	16–12	17–14	16–12	22–12	23–16	NM	17–12	16–9

Data as orig. reptd. Adj. for stk. div(s). of 33⅓% Dec. 1991, 33⅓% Dec. 1990, 33⅓% Mar. 1988, 50% May 1984. **1.** Includes intangibles. d-Deficit. NM-Not Meaningful.

Income Data (Million $)

Year Ended Dec. 31	Revs.	Oper. Inc.	% Oper. Inc. of Revs.	Cap. Exp.	Depr.	Int. Exp.	Net Bef. Taxes	Eff. Tax Rate	Net Inc.	% Net Inc. of Revs.	Cash Flow
1992	**168**	**35.5**	**21.2**	**[2]7.55**	**4.18**	**NA**	**36.6**	**26.1%**	**27.0**	**16.1**	**31.2**
[1]1991	153	34.0	22.3	[2]8.90	3.90	NA	[3]36.4	27.2%	26.5	17.3	30.4
1990	150	31.2	20.8	[2]6.20	3.52	0.76	[3]32.6	28.3%	23.4	15.6	26.9
1989	136	26.1	19.2	[2]3.07	3.55	Nil	[3]26.4	26.3%	19.5	14.4	23.0
1988	126	27.6	21.9	[2]4.52	3.41	Nil	[3]27.4	23.8%	20.9	16.6	24.3
1987	112	25.8	23.0	[2]1.53	3.19	Nil	[3]24.5	32.0%	16.7	14.9	19.9
1986	104	22.6	21.8	1.63	2.89	Nil	[3]20.9	38.0%	12.9	12.5	15.8
1985	97	15.9	16.4	3.26	2.69	NA	[3]14.8	136.7%	d5.4	NM	d2.7
1984	98	23.9	24.3	3.39	2.53	NA	[3]23.3	36.3%	14.9	15.1	17.4
1983	90	21.6	24.0	3.41	2.23	NA	[3]21.8	34.3%	[4]14.3	15.9	16.6

Balance Sheet Data (Million $)

Dec. 31	Cash	Curr. Assets	Curr. Liab.	Curr. Ratio	Total Assets	% Ret. on Assets	Long Term Debt	Common Equity	Total Cap.	% LT Debt of Cap.	% Ret. on Equity
1992	**73.3**	**130**	**36.5**	**3.6**	**187**	**14.6**	**4.86**	**127**	**151**	**3.2**	**21.9**
1991	64.7	124	38.0	3.3	178	15.9	5.24	117	140	3.7	23.8
1990	57.2	108	25.5	4.2	154	16.3	4.35	105	127	3.4	24.2
1989	43.9	94	23.6	4.0	134	15.0	4.40	88	110	4.0	23.3
1988	36.7	86	23.1	3.7	125	17.5	4.45	80	102	4.4	27.6
1987	35.5	78	17.8	4.4	110	16.4	4.50	69	92	4.9	26.8
1986	23.7	62	16.4	3.7	93	14.6	4.55	55	77	5.9	25.1
1985	20.3	53	15.2	3.5	84	NM	4.65	48	69	6.7	NM
1984	23.4	56	11.5	4.9	78	19.3	4.70	58	66	7.0	26.0
1983	23.8	53	12.1	4.4	76	20.2	4.90	56	63	7.4	26.0

Data as orig. reptd. **1.** Refl. merger or acquisition. **2.** Net of curr. yr. retirement and disposals. **3.** Incl. equity in earns. of nonconsol. subs. **4.** Reflects acctg. change. d-Deficit. NA-Not Available. NM-Not Meaningful.

Net Sales (Million $)

Quarter:	1993	1992	1991	1990
Mar.	42.1	41.3	38.2	38.2
Jun.	42.1	40.8	36.3	36.7
Sep.		43.0	37.0	36.6
Dec.		42.5	41.4	38.5
		167.6	152.9	150.0

For the six months ended June 30, 1993, sales were up 2.5%, year to year, and income rose 9.1%, to $15,265,000 ($0.34 a share), from $13,990,000 ($0.32), excluding a $4,025,000 ($0.09) credit from an accounting change in the 1993 period.

Common Share Earnings ($)

Quarter:	1993	1992	1991	1990
Mar.	0.17	0.16	0.15	0.14
Jun.	0.17	0.16	0.15	0.14
Sep.		0.15	0.15	0.14
Dec.		0.15	0.16	0.14
		0.62	0.61	0.55

Finances

Capital expenditures for 1992 were about $7.6 million, used primarily for the construction of a new multipurpose resin facility in Wisconsin, expected to be completed by early 1994. Capital expenditures for 1993 were estimated at $11 million, including continued construction of the U.S. facility, expansion into Mexico and additional modernization of existing facilities elsewhere.

The company has a 27% stake in Hach Co., a world leader in the field of water testing and analysis. As of 1992 year-end, Lawter had an unrecognized gain in Hach of about $50 million.

Dividend Data

Dividends have been paid since 1959.

Amt of Divd. $	Date Decl.	Ex–divd. Date	Stock of Record	Payment Date
0.10	Oct. 30	Nov. 9	Nov. 16	Dec. 1'92
0.10	Jan. 22	Feb. 9	Feb. 16	Mar. 2'93
0.10	May 4	May 10	May 14	Jun. 2'93
0.10	Jul. 26	Aug. 10	Aug. 16	Sep. 1'93

Capitalization

Long Term Obligations: $4,871,000 (3/93).

Common Stock: 44,755,228 shs. ($1 par).
D. J. Terra & family own about 24.5%.
Institutions hold about 43%.
Shareholders of record: 3,800 (3/93).

Office—990 Skokie Blvd., Northbrook, IL 60062. **Tel**—(708) 498-4700. **Chrmn & CEO**—D. J. Terra. **Pres & Investor Contact**—Richard D. Nordman. **VP-Secy & Treas**—W. S. Russell. **Dirs**—W. P. Clark, L. P. Judy, R. D. Nordman, F. G. Steingraber, D. J. Terra. **Transfer Agent & Registrar**—First National Bank of Boston, Boston, Mass. **Incorporated** in Delaware in 1958. **Empl**—485.

 L. Feuer Nelson

LEGENT Corp.

NASDAQ Symbol LGNT Options on CBOE (Incl. in Nat'l Market) In S&P MidCap 400

Price	Range	P-E Ratio	Dividend	Yield	S&P Ranking	Beta
Aug. 26'93	1993					
19¼	54¾–15½	18	None	None	B+	1.73

Summary

This company is a leading supplier of computer system productivity enhancement software for medium and large IBM and IBM-compatible computers. Operations were significantly expanded by the mid-1992 acquisition of Goal Systems, a maker of software for IBM and compatible mainframes, in exchange for about 10 million common shares. Sales and earnings declined in the third quarter of fiscal 1993 on a shortfall of new licence revenue in North America and Germany, however, a resumption of the upward trend in sales and higher margins should benefit earnings in fiscal 1994.

Current Outlook

Earnings for the fiscal year ending September 30, 1994 are projected at $2.00 share, versus the $1.70 estimated for fiscal 1993 and compared with 1992's $0.81 (including $0.90 in acquisition charges).

Initiation of cash dividends is not expected.

Revenues in fiscal 1994 are expected to resume their upward trend, benefitting from the introduction of new products. While the company's pipeline of new business remains strong, customers have slowed purchase decisions as they decide how to utilize and integrate their different computers. In addition, LGNT is increasingly pursuing larger deals encompassing enterprise-wide licenses, which take longer to close. A restructured and more focused sales force should help in these areas. Margins are expected to widen on the higher volume, despite continued investments in software development.

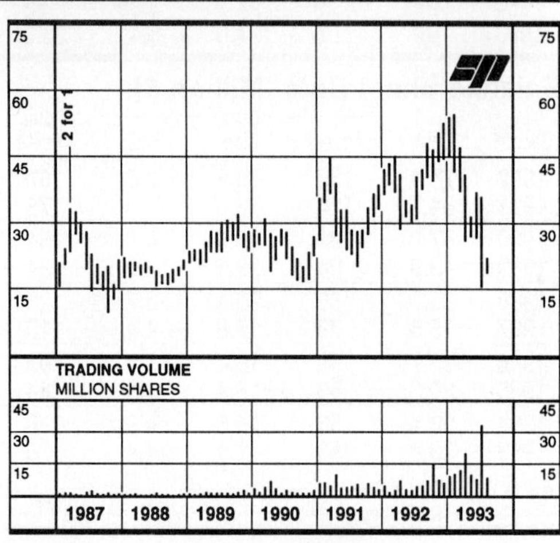

Revenues (Million $)

Quarter:	1992-93	1991-92	1990-91	1989-90
Dec.	116.7	97.3	51.7	40.7
Mar.	102.6	102.4	47.4	40.0
Jun.	100.0	102.6	46.8	42.3
Sep.		124.4	57.3	46.5
		426.7	203.3	169.5

Revenues in the nine months ended June 30, 1993, gained 5.6%, year to year, despite a flat second quarter and a slightly lower third quarter; for the full nine months, new license revenues fell fractionally, while recurring revenues climbed 14%. Despite the lower than expected volume, which particularly penalized third quarter earnings, results benefited from merger-related synergies and tight expense controls, and in the absence of a $3.2 million restructuring charge and merger costs of $7.6 million, pretax income advanced 37%. After taxes at 34.5%, versus 32.2%, net income was up 32%, to $46,733,000 ($1.32 a share, on 3.7% more shares), from $35,424,000 ($1.04).

Common Share Earnings ($)

Quarter:	1992-93	1991-92	1990-91	1989-90
Dec.	0.54	0.37	0.47	0.36
Mar.	0.52	0.29	0.35	0.35
Jun.	0.26	0.38	0.35	0.40
Sep.	E0.38	d0.23	0.38	0.42
	E1.70	0.81	1.54	1.52

Important Developments

Jul. '93— LGNT said that earnings for the third quarter of fiscal 1993 were impacted by a shortfall in expected new license revenue in certain areas of North America and Germany.

Jul. '93— The company announced that its Board of Directors authorized the repurchase of up to 3.5 million LGNT common shares.

Next earnings report expected in late October.

Per Share Data ($)

Yr. End Sep. 30	[1]1992	1991	[2]1990	[1]1989	1988	1987	1986	1985	1984	1983
Tangible Bk. Val.	**8.97**	10.08	7.32	6.10	5.69	4.66	3.86	1.21	0.90	0.27
Cash Flow	**1.14**	1.82	1.73	1.28	1.14	0.84	0.58	0.31	0.22	0.16
Earnings	**0.81**	1.54	[3]1.52	[3]1.15	[3]1.02	[3]0.75	[3]0.53	[3]0.28	[3,4]0.19	[3,4]0.12
Dividends[5]	**Nil**	Nil	Nil	Nil	Nil	Nil	Nil	Nil	Nil	Nil
Payout Ratio	**Nil**	Nil	Nil	Nil	Nil	Nil	Nil	Nil	Nil	Nil
Prices—High[6]	**52¾**	45	31	32	22¼	33¼	17¾	7⅞	3⅞	NA
Low[6]	**28¾**	20¼	16¾	20¾	15¾	9¾	7¼	3⅜	2½	NA
P/E Ratio—	**65–35**	29–13	20–11	28–18	22–15	44–13	34–14	28–12	19–13	NA

Data as orig. reptd. Adj. for stk. divs. of 100% Mar. 1987, 100% Mar. 1986, 50% Oct. 1983. **1.** Major merger resulted in formation of new co. **2.** Refl. merger or acq. **3.** **4.** Pro forma. **5.** To public. **6.** Cal. yr. NA-Not Available. E-Estimated. d-deficit.

Income Data (Million $)

Year Ended Sep. 30	Revs.	Oper. Inc.	% Oper. Inc. of Revs.	Cap. Exp.	Depr.	Int. Exp.	Net Bef. Taxes	Eff. Tax Rate	Net Inc.	% Net Inc. of Revs.	Cash Flow
[1]1992	**427**	**95.1**	**22.3**	**42.0**	**11.30**	**1.79**	**46.8**	**40.6%**	**27.8**	**6.5**	**39.1**
1991	203	52.9	26.0	13.6	6.18	0.15	49.9	32.1%	33.9	16.7	40.0
[2]1990	170	50.8	30.0	13.1	4.45	Nil	50.1	34.3%	32.9	19.4	37.3
[1]1989	125	38.7	31.1	4.6	2.69	Nil	35.2	34.3%	23.1	18.6	25.8
1988	50	15.8	31.4	1.5	1.31	0.01	16.8	34.0%	11.1	22.0	12.4
1987	38	15.6	41.3	2.2	3.50	0.02	13.4	39.5%	8.1	21.6	9.1
1986	24	9.6	39.6	2.1	1.74	0.16	8.8	42.8%	[4]5.0	20.7	5.6
1985	11	3.4	30.4	1.3	0.31	Nil	3.7	35.8%	2.4	21.4	2.6
1984	7	2.1	28.3	0.4	0.11	Nil	2.4	[3]36.4%	[3]1.5	20.1	1.7
1983	5	1.1	23.0	0.3	0.06	Nil	1.2	[3]30.9%	[3]0.8	16.8	1.0

Balance Sheet Data (Million $)

Sep. 30	Cash	Curr. Assets	Curr. Liab.	Curr. Ratio	Total Assets	% Ret. on Assets	Long Term Debt	Common Equity	Total Cap.	% LT Debt of Cap.	% Ret. on Equity
1992	**181**	**355**	**202.0**	**1.8**	**536**	**5.8**	**3.95**	**302**	**311**	**1.3**	**8.7**
1991	151	212	40.3	5.3	274	14.4	4.87	222	234	2.1	17.6
1990	85	141	25.9	5.4	186	19.3	Nil	154	160	Nil	23.3
1989	71	112	18.7	6.0	147	16.9	Nil	121	128	Nil	19.8
1988	25	39	6.1	6.3	68	17.8	Nil	60	62	Nil	20.1
1987	16	25	4.9	5.2	55	16.3	Nil	48	49	Nil	18.4
1986	10	16	3.9	4.2	44	17.3	Nil	39	40	Nil	19.4
1985	3	6	1.3	4.4	11	23.5	Nil	10	10	Nil	26.9
1984	2	4	1.1	3.4	9	28.1	Nil	8	8	Nil	32.8
1983	1	2	0.3	6.1	2	42.0	Nil	2	2	Nil	55.6

Data as orig. reptd. **1.** Major merger resulted in formation of new co. **2.** Refl. merger or acq. **3.** Pro forma. **4.** Refl. acctg. change.

Business Summary

LEGENT Corporation (formerly Duquesne Systems Inc.) provides productivity enhancing software solutions for the management of information systems. Originally targeting large IBM and IBM compatible computers, the company has extended its product line beyond the mainframe environment to distributed and heterogeneous computing platforms including VM, VAX/VMS, DOS, OS/2 and local area networks.

Data center management software is used to increase programming staff productivity, enhance operational and cost efficiencies in the administration and sharing of data center resources, and improve user service. Major segment categories include automated systems operations, output management, network access, production control, security and disaster recovery. Data center management products accounted for 37% and 36% of revenues in fiscal 1992 and 1991, respectively.

Resource management solutions, which accounted for 37% and 38% of revenues in fiscal 1992 and 1991, respectively, optimize the productivity of hardware and software, minimize the costs of expansion, anticipate and plan for future growth, capture and analyze performance and financial data, improve service levels, and ensure that adequate storage is available. Major categories include capacity management, performance management, financial and asset management, storage management, and VSAM storage management.

Application management products, which accounted for 16% and 14% of revenues in fiscal 1992 and 1991, respectively. include software management and distribution management offerings, database tools and employee performance support products. Such products provide integrated solutions for the control of software applications for managing databases more effectively, and for ensuring that employees throughout the organization have the education, training and support resources to effectively learn and use application programs.

Dividend Data

No cash has been paid.

Finances

Fiscal 1992 results included charges totaling $42,150,000 ($0.90 a share) related to acquisitions, including $34,550,000 for the acquisition of Goal Systems, a vendor of software for IBM and compatible mainframes, acquired for about 10 million common shares.

Capitalization

Long Term Capital Leases: $3,947,000 (9/92).

Common Stock: 34,492,020 shs. (no par).
Institutions hold 79%.
Shareholders: About 1,500 of record (9/92).

Office—8615 Westwood Center Dr., Vienna, VA 22182-2218. **Tel**—(703) 734-9494. **Chrmn**—J. M. Henson. **Pres & CEO**—J. F. Burton. **EVP & COO**—D. C. Wetmore. **VP, Secy & Investor Contact**—Richard E. Hanlon. **VP & CFO**—F. M. Smithson. **Dirs**—J. F. Burton, S. A. Denning, D. A. Finley, J. M. Henson, D. C. Wetmore, G. L. Wilson, H. J. Wilson. **Transfer Agent & Registrar**—Mellon Bank, Pittsburgh. **Incorporated** in Delaware in 1989. **Empl**—2,100.

 Peter C. Wood, CFA

Leggett & Platt

NYSE Symbol LEG In S&P MidCap 400

Price	Range	P-E Ratio	Dividend	Yield	S&P Ranking	Beta
Aug. 5'93	1993					
38⅜	40⅞–32¾	21	0.52	1.4%	A	1.09

Summary

This company produces components and related finished products for the home furnishings industry, and also makes diversified products that utilize similar manufacturing technology. Following gains in 1992, earnings continued to advance in the first half of 1993, aided by solid sales growth, cost containment measures and lower interest expense. Further earnings growth is projected through 1994. A planned acquisition would substantially expand the revenue base.

Current Outlook

Earnings for 1994 are projected at $2.40 a share, up from $2.05 estimated for 1993.

Dividends were raised 8.3%, to $0.13 quarterly, with the March 1993 payment.

Solid sales improvement should be seen through 1994, on a stronger housing market and an eventual recovery in consumer confidence. Margins should continue to widen, reflecting emphasis on cost containment measures. The planned acquisition of Hanes Holding is expected to add $0.10 a share to 1994 earnings.

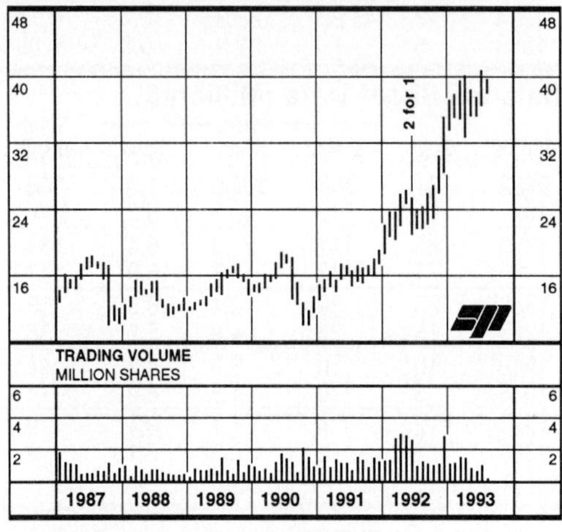

Net Sales (Million $)

Quarter:	1993	1992	1991	1990
Mar.	321	285	263	267
Jun.	334	284	283	277
Sep.	---	304	279	285
Dec.	---	298	257	260
	---	1,170	1,082	1,089

Net sales in the six months ended June 30, 1993, advanced 15%, year to year, benefiting from modest economic growth, acquisitions, increased market share, and gains in the diversified segment. Margins widened on improved operating efficiencies, cost control measures and the reduction of bad debt expense to more normal levels. With sharply lower interest expense, net income soared 35%, to $0.99 a share, from $0.77.

Common Share Earnings ($)

Quarter:	1993	1992	1991	1990
Mar.	0.48	0.38	0.22	0.36
Jun.	0.51	0.39	0.28	0.37
Sep.	E0.55	0.46	0.34	0.30
Dec.	E0.51	0.41	0.28	[1]d0.18
	E2.05	1.64	1.11	0.84

Important Developments

Jul. '93— The company said it plans to acquire privately held Hanes Holding Co. in exchange for $65 million of common stock. Hanes, with annual sales of $150 million, is a leading converter and distributor of woven and nonwoven industrial fabrics, mainly in the home furnishings industry. It is also a commission dye/finisher of non-fashion fabrics for the home furnishings and apparel industries. Its operations would be expanded by its pending acquisition of VWR Textile & Supplies ($70 million in annual sales). The acquisition of Hanes (including VWR) would increase LEG's long term debt by $70 million, raising debt to 25% of total capitalization, from a historically low 16% at March 31, 1993. The transaction, which is subject to various approvals, is expected to close in August 1993, and would be accounted for as a pooling of interests.

Next earnings report expected in late October.

Per Share Data ($)

Yr. End Dec. 31	1992	1991	1990	1989	1988	1987	1986	1985	1984	1983
Tangible Bk. Val.	**9.59**	7.75	7.13	7.41	6.60	6.15	5.41	4.73	3.92	3.49
Cash Flow	**2.65**	2.01	1.69	2.07	1.74	1.65	1.50	1.34	1.09	0.98
Earnings[2,3]	**1.64**	1.11	[1]0.84	1.33	1.11	1.14	1.04	0.88	0.71	0.63
Dividends	**0.460**	0.430	0.420	0.370	0.320	0.280	0.200	0.167	0.147	0.125
Payout Ratio	**28%**	39%	50%	28%	29%	24%	19%	19%	21%	21%
Prices—High	**35¼**	19⅛	18¹⁵⁄₁₆	17⁷⁄₁₆	15½	18⁷⁄₁₆	18³⁄₁₆	11¹⁄₁₆	7¼	8⅛
Low	**18¾**	13	10	11¹³⁄₁₆	10¾	10	10⁵⁄₁₆	6³⁄₁₆	5³⁄₁₆	4¼
P/E Ratio—	**21–11**	17–12	23–12	13–9	14–10	16–9	18–10	13–7	10–7	13–7

Data as orig. reptd. Adj. for stk. divs. of 100% Jun. 1992, 50% Mar. 1986, 100% Aug. 1983. **1.** Incl. restructuring charge of 0.77. **2.** Bef. results of disc. ops. of +0.05 in 1984. **3.** Ful. dil.: 1.63 in 1992, 1.09 in 1991, 1.29 in 1989, 1.09 in 1988, 1.11 in 1987, 1.02 in 1986, 0.82 in 1985, 0.67 in 1984, 0.61 in 1983. d-Deficit. E-Estimated.

Income Data (Million $)

Year Ended Dec. 31	Revs.	Oper. Inc.	% Oper. Inc. of Revs.	Cap. Exp.	Depr.	Int. Exp.	[2]Net Bef. Taxes	Eff. Tax Rate	[3]Net Inc.	% Net Inc. of Revs.	Cash Flow
1992	**1,170**	**143**	**12.2**	**33.2**	**38.2**	**5.8**	**99.8**	**37.4%**	**62.5**	**5.3**	**100.7**
1991	1,082	106	9.8	39.7	31.9	12.3	63.9	38.3%	39.4	3.6	71.3
1990	1,089	118	10.8	42.7	30.2	15.2	50.6	41.8%	29.4	2.7	59.6
1989	992	114	11.5	63.0	25.7	12.7	75.7	39.4%	45.9	4.6	71.6
1988	810	89	10.9	68.6	21.7	7.4	60.0	37.1%	37.7	4.7	59.4
1987	649	83	12.8	32.2	16.7	6.5	64.0	41.5%	37.5	5.8	54.2
1986	586	74	12.6	29.5	15.6	6.4	58.1	40.5%	34.6	5.9	50.2
1985	479	59	12.3	38.5	12.5	6.3	41.1	41.6%	24.0	5.0	36.4
[1]1984	425	45	10.6	19.4	10.3	5.5	31.3	38.1%	19.4	4.6	29.7
1983	354	39	10.9	22.6	8.6	4.6	26.5	41.2%	15.6	4.4	24.1

Balance Sheet Data (Million $)

Dec. 31	Cash	Curr. Assets	Curr. Liab.	Curr. Ratio	Total Assets	% Ret. on Assets	Long Term Debt	Common Equity	Total Cap.	% LT Debt of Cap.	% Ret. on Equity
1992	**4.0**	**340**	**119**	**2.9**	**678**	**9.0**	**101**	**425**	**553**	**18.4**	**15.9**
1991	5.3	322	111	2.9	656	5.9	179	333	539	33.3	12.3
1990	3.3	342	128	2.7	676	4.7	213	303	540	39.4	10.0
1989	2.9	293	113	2.6	568	8.7	147	282	449	32.8	17.3
1988	7.0	250	103	2.4	478	8.5	107	245	368	29.0	16.2
1987	29.6	208	78	2.7	384	10.2	84	209	293	28.5	19.1
1986	35.9	190	67	2.8	349	10.9	88	183	271	32.5	20.1
1985	9.0	138	56	2.5	271	8.8	51	153	204	25.1	17.2
1984	21.8	132	52	2.5	233	8.9	67	108	175	38.4	18.9
1983	18.6	113	46	2.5	202	8.6	54	96	150	36.1	18.0

Data as orig. reptd. **1.** Excl. disc. ops. **2.** Incl. equity in earns. of nonconsol subs. **3.** Bef. results of disc. ops.

Business Summary

Leggett & Platt manufactures components and related finished products for the home furnishings industry, and also makes diversified products with technology similar to its home furnishings operations. Foreign sales are not significant. Business segment contributions in 1992 were:

	Sales	Profits
Home furnishing products....	78%	77%
Diversified........................	22%	23%

The company's component customers manufacture furniture and bedding for homes, offices and institutions. These customers offer their products for sale to wholesalers, retailers, institutions and others. In 1992, bedding components accounted for 33% of sales, with furniture components providing 23%.

LEG also makes finished products for the home furnishings industry (22% of 1992 sales), including sleep-related finished furniture and carpet cushioning materials. Some finished furniture products are sold to bedding and furniture manufacturers, who resell the furniture under their own labels to wholesalers or retailers, while other finished furniture is sold directly to retailers. Carpet cushioning materials are sold primarily to floor covering distributors with some direct contract sales.

Outside of the home furnishings area, the company produces a diversified line of components and other products for home, industrial and commercial uses.

Dividend Data

Dividends have been paid since 1939. A "poison pill" stock purchase rights plan was adopted in 1989.

Amt. of Divd. $	Date Decl.	Ex-divd. Date	Stock of Record	Payment Date
0.12	Aug. 12	Aug. 24	Aug. 28	Sep. 15'92
0.12	Nov. 11	Nov. 20	Nov. 27	Dec. 15'92
0.13	Feb. 10	Feb. 22	Feb. 26	Mar. 15'93
0.13	May 12	May 24	May 28	Jun. 15'93

Finances

LEG's call for redemption in March 1992 of all $40 million of its 6½% debentures due 2006 resulted in the conversion of nearly all of the debt into 2.1 million common shares (as adjusted).

Capitalization

Long Term Debt: $86,766,000 (3/93).

Common Stock: 38,394,507 shs. ($1 par).
Officers and directors own 12%.
Institution hold 57%.
Shareholders: 10,400 of beneficial int. (2/93).

Office—One Leggett Rd., Carthage, MO 64836. **Tel**—(417) 358-8131. **Chrmn & CEO**—H. M. Cornell, Jr. **Pres**—F. E. Wright. **Secy**—T. D. Sherman. **SVP-Fin**—M. A. Glauber. **Treas**—Susan S. Higdon. **Investor Contact**—J. Richard Calhoon. **Dirs**—H. C. Casteel, H. M. Cornell, Jr., R. T. Enloe, III, R. T. Fisher, F. E. Ford, Jr., R. A. Jeffries, Jr., A. M. Levine, J. C. McCormick, R. L. Pearsall, M. E. Purnell, Jr., F. E. Wright. **Transfer Agent & Registrar**—Mellon Securities Trust Co. **Incorporated** in Missouri in 1901. **Empl**—11,400.

 Michael W. Jaffe

Liberty National Bancorp

NASDAQ Symbol LNBC (Incl. in Nat'l Market) In S&P MidCap 400

Price	Range	P–E Ratio	Dividend	Yield	S&P Ranking	Beta
Aug. 27'93	1993					
27	29½–20⅝	14	0.68	2.5%	A	0.55

Summary

Liberty is the largest independent bank holding company based in Kentucky, with more than 100 banking offices throughout the state and southern Indiana. Recent earnings were at record levels, aided by securities gains and wider net interest spreads. Results should continue to trend higher, boosted by acquisitions and a projected decrease in loan loss provisions. A 4-for-3 stock split was effected in May.

Current Outlook

Earnings for 1993 are projected at $2.05 a share, up from 1992's $1.83 (adjusted).

The minimum expectation is for dividends to continue at $0.17 a share quarterly.

Earnings are expected to continue their upward trend in 1993, with returns on equity projected at about 14.0%. Quarterly earnings for the balance of the year will probably fall short of the second quarter's performance, in the anticipated absence of securities gains. At the minimum, net interest margins will remain in the range of 4.65% to 4.75%, as a lower cost of funds continues to offset an expected decrease in income from interest-earning assets. However, the provision for loan losses and net chargeoffs should trend lower, benefiting earnings, and noninterest income, fees and service charges on deposit accounts should make up a larger percentage of total income, although results may feel pressure from lower insurance premiums and commissions earned. The addition of Hardin County Bank & Trust and Farmers Deposit Bank (acquired in March) should add about $0.04 to 1993's results.

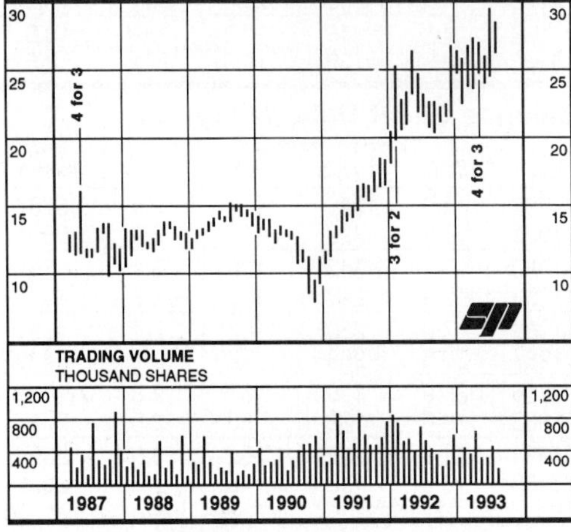

Review of Operations

In the six months ended June 30, 1993, net interest income advanced 15%, year to year, as a result of a 3.2% decline in interest income and a 21% drop in interest expense. The provision for loan losses fell to $11.9 million, from $12.3 million. Noninterest income dropped fractionally, and noninterest expense rose 8.7%; pretax income advanced 20%. After taxes at 27.6%, versus 23.7%, net income was up 14%, to $26.2 million ($1.04 a share), from $23.0 million ($0.92, as adjusted).

Common Share Earnings ($)

Quarter:	1993	1992	1991	1990
Mar.	0.51	0.46	0.36	0.38
Jun.	0.53	0.47	0.41	0.37
Sep.	E0.49	0.45	0.41	0.28
Dec.	E0.52	0.46	0.42	0.40
	E2.05	1.83	1.61	1.43

Important Developments

Jun. '93— LNBC signed a definitive agreement to purchase First Federal Savings Bank, a $64 million in assets thrift with two branches in Hopkinsville, Ky. The transaction, which is subject to regulatory approvals and the approval of First Federal's shareholders, is expected to be completed by year-end 1993.

Mar. 31'93— Liberty National completed its acquisition of Hardin County Bank & Trust Co. and Farmers Deposit Bank of Brandenburg from closely held Financial Dominion of Kentucky Corp. At year-end 1992, the two banks had combined assets of $135 million. Separately, Tier 1 and total risk-based capital ratios were 9.11% and 10.36%, respectively, far exceeding regulatory requirements.

Next earnings report expected in mid-October.

Per Share Data ($)

Yr. End Dec. 31	[1]1992	[1]1991	[1]1990	[1]1989	[1]1988	[2]1987	[1]1986	[1]1985	[2]1984	1983
Tangible Bk. Val.	**12.59**	11.13	10.61	9.64	8.57	9.23	8.31	7.08	6.20	5.57
Earnings[3,4]	**1.83**	1.61	1.43	1.54	1.38	1.24	1.13	1.01	0.86	0.76
Dividends	**0.600**	0.530	0.470	0.410	0.360	0.317	0.285	0.260	0.236	0.216
Payout Ratio	**33%**	33%	33%	27%	26%	26%	25%	26%	27%	29%
Prices—High	**26 13/16**	18½	14¼	15 5/16	13⅞	13 13/16	15⅜	12⅛	6 9/16	6⅛
Low	**18 1/16**	10 13/16	7⅞	11 15/16	10½	9⅞	10 7/16	6½	5⅜	3 11/16
P/E Ratio—	**15–10**	12–7	10–6	10–8	10–8	11–8	14–9	12–6	8–6	8–5

Data as orig. reptd. Adj. for stk. divs. of 33⅓% in 1993, 50% in 1992, 33⅓% in 1987, 50% in 1986, 50% in 1985, 50% in 1983. **1.** Refl. merger or acq. **2.** Refl. acctg. change. **3.** Ful. dil.: 1.55 in 1991, 1.37 in 1990, 1.46 in 1989, 1.31 in 1988, 1.19 in 1987, 1.07 in 1986, 0.99 in 1985. **4.** Bef. spec. item of +0.05 in 1991. E-Estimated.

Liberty National Bancorp, Inc.

Income Data (Million $)

Year Ended Dec. 31	Net Int. Inc.	Tax Equiv. Adj.	Non Int. Inc.	Loan Loss Prov.	% Exp./ Op. Revs.	Net Bef. Taxes	Eff. Tax Rate	Net Inc.	% Net Int. Margin	—% Return On— Assets	Equity
[1]1992	**171**	**9.5**	**54.3**	**26.6**	**60.0**	**60.0**	**24.0%**	**45.6**	**4.60**	**1.06**	**13.6**
[1]1991	149	9.6	52.0	25.6	61.2	49.2	23.2%	37.8	4.48	0.97	13.0
[1]1990	126	9.8	44.8	19.2	61.6	40.3	18.6%	32.8	4.26	0.92	12.5
[1]1989	115	9.8	42.4	13.8	60.9	41.6	20.3%	33.2	4.34	1.03	14.5
[1]1988	102	9.6	36.3	11.4	62.1	35.3	18.1%	28.9	4.37	1.00	14.3
[2]1987	88	13.6	28.9	8.2	61.1	29.8	14.8%	25.4	4.60	1.02	14.3
[1]1986	76	18.6	26.3	9.0	60.3	21.3	NM	22.7	4.50	0.95	14.5
[1]1985	64	13.2	22.8	5.9	63.0	18.4	3.3%	17.8	4.62	0.93	15.4
[2]1984	54	8.7	17.7	4.7	63.6	15.7	11.2%	14.0	4.73	0.92	14.8
1983	48	8.7	14.3	2.8	67.2	12.7	3.4%	12.3	4.49	0.85	14.5

Balance Sheet Data (Million $)

Dec. 31	Total Assets	Earning Assets: Mon. Mkt. Assets	Inv. Secs.	Com'l Loans	Other Loans	% Loan Loss Resv.	Deposits: Demand	Time	% Loans/ Deposits	Long Term Debt	Common Equity	% Equity To Assets
1992	**4,566**	**184**	**769**	**846**	**2,404**	**1.31**	**746**	**3,016**	**85.6**	**39.3**	**353**	**7.75**
1991	4,338	241	675	776	2,197	1.31	787	2,824	81.6	39.1	320	7.46
1990	3,713	22	693	840	1,747	1.21	618	2,424	83.8	37.4	275	7.37
1989	3,536	177	586	797	1,621	1.48	635	2,335	79.6	41.3	248	7.07
1988	3,163	171	498	755	1,425	1.51	502	2,073	82.5	45.2	217	6.96
1987	2,580	142	414	647	1,094	1.47	488	1,616	80.6	29.4	189	7.10
1986	2,600	132	431	654	996	1.50	525	1,541	77.9	32.2	170	6.53
1985	2,147	154	355	586	779	1.59	449	1,203	80.4	24.2	133	6.04
1984	1,622	161	192	485	576	1.61	376	867	82.2	4.4	100	6.19
1983	1,439	171	148	459	494	1.63	313	772	84.8	4.9	90	5.84

Data as orig. reptd. **1.** Refl. merger or acq. **2.** Refl. acctg. change. NM-Not Meaningful.

Business Summary

Liberty National Bancorp, Inc. is the largest multibank holding company in Kentucky, conducting commercial and personal banking services through eight subsidiary banks. At June 30, 1993, Liberty National reported total assets of $4.64 billion, and operated 101 branches in Kentucky and southern Indiana. In addition to commercial and personal banking services, Liberty also provides retail loan services, credit life insurance, leasing and brokerage services through nonbanking subsidiaries. Total loans of $3.25 billion at year-end 1992 were divided:

	1992	1991
Consumer	36%	35%
Real estate – mortgage	35%	35%
Commercial & financial	24%	25%
Real estate – construction	3%	4%
Lease financing	2%	1%

The allowance for possible loan losses was $42.3 million (1.30% of gross loans outstanding) at December 31, 1992, compared with $38.5 million (1.30%) a year earlier. Net chargeoffs in 1992 were $22.8 million (0.75% of average loans), up from $19.9 million (0.72%) in 1991. Total nonperforming assets at December 31, 1992, were $41.9 million (0.92% of total assets), versus $41.4 million (0.95%) at the end of 1991.

In 1992, average deposits of $3.54 billion were divided: interest-bearing demand 14%, noninterest bearing demand 17%, savings 25%, and time 43%. On a taxable-equivalent basis, the average yield on total interest-earning assets was 8.53% in 1992 (9.92% in 1991), and the average rate paid on total interest-bearing liabilities was 4.61% (6.32%), for a net spread of 3.92% (3.60%).

Dividend Data

Cash has been paid each year since 1941. A dividend reinvestment plan is available.

Amt. of Divd. $	Date Decl.	Ex–divd. Date	Stock of Record	Payment Date
0.20	Oct. 14	Oct. 20	Oct. 26	Nov. 1'92
0.22½	Jan. 13	Jan. 19	Jan. 25	Feb. 1'93
0.22½	Apr. 14	Apr. 20	Apr. 26	May 1'93
4–for–3	Apr. 14	May 18	May 3	May 17'93
0.17	Jul. 14	Jul. 20	Jul. 26	Aug. 1'93

Capitalization

Long Term Debt: $103,994,000 (6/93).

Common Stock: 25,440,397 shs. (no par).
Officers & directors own about 11%.
Institutions hold some 38%.
Shareholders of record: 4,100 (12/92).

Office—416 W. Jefferson St., Louisville, KY 40202-3244. **Tel**—(502) 566-2000. **Chrmn, Pres & CEO**—M. B. Chancey Jr. **Secy**—C. R. Page. **Treas & Investor Contact**—Carl E. Weigel (502-566-2510). **Dirs**—D. P. Alagia Jr., M. B. Chancey Jr., S. S. Dickson, C. H. Dishman III, W. H. Dunbar, O. B. Frazier, G. E. Gans III, G. N. Gill, R. K. Guillaume, F. B. Hower Jr., N. Lampton, L. E. Lyles, M. S. Margulis, J. W. McDowell Jr., J. C. Nichols II, G. H. Nixon, J. W. Phelps, C. S. Radford Jr., M. L. Shapira, R. L. Taylor. **Transfer Agent & Registrar**—Liberty National Bank & Trust, Louisville. **Incorporated** in Kentucky in 1854. **Empl**—2,145.

 Barry R. Haas

Lincoln Telecommunications

NASDAQ Symbol LTEC (Incl. in Nat'l Market) In S&P MidCap 400

Price	Range	P-E Ratio	Dividend	Yield	S&P Ranking	Beta
Aug. 27'93	1993					
35	37½–24	18	0.96	2.7%	A	0.87

Summary

This holding company is the parent of Lincoln Telephone and Telegraph Co., which provides local and long-distance telephone service to 22 southeastern Nebraska counties. The company continues to increase its cellular exposure and to install fiber-optic equipment. The conversion of its telecommunications infrastructure to 100% digital, computer-driven switches was completed during 1992. Earnings have been rising in recent periods, and the dividend was recently boosted 9%.

Business Summary

Lincoln Telecommunications Company is a holding company, with Lincoln Telephone and Telegraph Co. (LT&T) its principal subsidiary. Through LT&T and its nonregulated telecommunications subsidiaries, LinTel Systems and Prairie Communications, the company provides local exchange and long distance service, paging and cellular service, and telephone equipment sales and service. Since 1988, telephone operations have provided almost 90% of total revenues, with the balance coming from diversified nonregulated operations.

LT&T operates a telephone system for both local and long-distance service in 22 counties in southeastern Nebraska. At the end of 1992, LT&T had 242,838 access lines in service, up from 233,778 a year earlier. More than 70% of the lines are for residential use, with the balance used by businesses. Lincoln, Neb., the largest city in the company's service area, is a regional retail, financial and insurance center; otherwise, the economies in LT&T's service area are chiefly agricultural.

Lincoln Telephone Cellular operates in the Lincoln-Lancaster County Metropolitan Statistical Area (MSA), which has a population of nearly 200,000. Cellular equipment is sold directly to customers and through sales agents. The unit also operates a wide area paging system covering 138 communities in Nebraska.

In January 1992, the company formed a partnership to hold Centel Corp.'s 55.2% interest in the Omaha Cellular Limited Partnership and assumed operating control of the franchise (subsequently renamed First Cellular Omaha). LTEC purchased a 50% interest in the new partnership for $11.9 million and holds a $23.8 million discount note, with proceeds from the note distributed to Centel; the company will have an option to purchase the remaining 50% over a two-year period beginning December 31, 1996. The number of celllular customers nearly doubled in 1992.

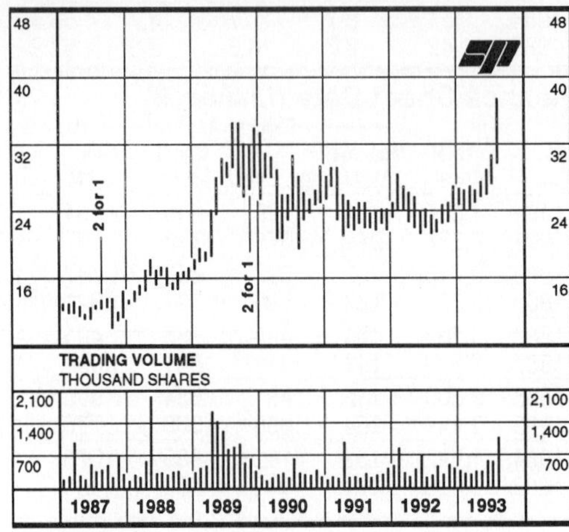

LinTel Systems Inc. provides voice mail, PBX and other systems and services to businesses in the eastern half of Nebraska and in western Iowa. Lincoln Telephone Long Distance provides long-distance discount service plans and regular "1 plus" service to residential and business customers.

Expenditures for network improvements totaled $25.7 in 1992. Spending for 1993 is put at $32.9 million, to be provided from operations.

Important Developments

Apr. '93— LTEC said it expects to install 129 additional miles of fiber optic cable during 1993. The company plans to aggressively invest in its cellular network in order to meet the growing demand for wireless communication. Thirteen new cell sites are planned for the Lincoln and Omaha service areas, and First Cellular Omaha was scheduled to open a new office and service center in Council Bluffs in May.

Next earnings report expected in late October.

Per Share Data ($)

Yr. End Dec. 31	1992	1991	1990	1989	[1]1988	1987	1986	1985	1984	1983
Tangible Bk. Val.	**11.60**	10.83	10.01	9.30	8.59	8.12	7.54	7.03	6.70	6.25
Cash Flow	**3.60**	3.40	3.20	3.17	3.16	2.74	2.84	2.65	2.72	2.51
Earnings[2]	**1.79**	1.66	1.47	1.49	1.49	1.22	1.11	0.88	0.99	0.80
Dividends	**0.860**	0.800	0.740	[3]0.765	0.665	0.583	0.550	0.550	0.538	0.500
Payout Ratio	**48%**	48%	50%	51%	44%	48%	50%	63%	55%	63%
Prices—High	**28½**	29¼	33½	34⅝	18¼	14½	13¾	11⅛	7½	7
Low	**21¼**	21	19½	17⅛	13	10⅛	9¼	7⅜	5¾	6
P/E Ratio—	**16–12**	18–13	23–13	23–11	12–9	12–8	12–8	13–8	7–6	9–7

Data as orig. reptd. Adj. for stk. divs. of 100% Nov. 1989, 100% Aug. 1987. **1.** Refl. acctg. change. **2.** Ful. dil.: 1.06 in 1986, 0.84 in 1985. **3.** Incl. spec.

Income Data (Million $)

Year Ended Dec. 31	Oper. Revs.	Oper. Inc.	% Oper. Inc. of Revs.	Cap. Exp.	Depr.	Int. Exp.	Net Bef. Taxes	Eff. Tax Rate	Net Inc.	% Net Inc. of Revs.	Cash Flow
1992	**176**	**81.0**	**46.0**	**27.3**	**29.5**	**8.8**	**45.7**	**35.2%**	**29.3**	**16.6**	**58.8**
1991	176	78.6	44.6	33.4	28.6	8.7	44.7	37.7%	27.4	15.5	56.0
1990	172	69.7	40.5	35.1	28.6	7.5	36.6	32.5%	24.2	14.1	52.7
[1]1989	170	70.6	41.6	34.3	27.6	5.5	37.5	33.1%	24.6	14.5	52.2
[2]1988	183	69.6	38.1	27.3	27.7	5.5	36.5	30.1%	24.9	13.6	52.8
1987	170	68.2	40.1	29.2	26.2	15.9	35.6	39.1%	21.1	12.4	47.4
1986	159	69.1	43.3	31.1	28.6	7.0	32.2	41.1%	18.3	11.5	47.1
1985	145	62.2	42.8	29.8	30.0	7.1	24.8	38.8%	14.5	10.0	44.0
1984	145	63.8	43.9	26.4	28.3	7.6	27.9	39.5%	16.2	11.2	44.5
1983	134	56.5	42.2	31.8	27.9	7.8	21.9	38.2%	12.8	9.6	40.8

Balance Sheet Data (Million $)

Dec. 31	Cash	Curr. Assets	Curr. Liab.	Curr. Ratio	Total Assets	% Ret. on Assets	Long Term Debt	Common Equity	Total Cap.	% LT Debt of Cap.	% Ret. on Equity
1992	**38.6**	**68.7**	**53.8**	**1.3**	**369**	**8.0**	**73.6**	**189**	**308**	**23.8**	**16.0**
1991	36.2	63.5	50.4	1.3	361	7.7	80.3	178	306	26.3	16.0
1990	63.3	90.5	41.6	2.2	348	7.4	85.8	165	300	28.6	15.2
1989	23.3	51.9	38.9	1.3	305	8.3	55.1	153	261	21.1	16.7
1988	16.1	46.9	27.9	1.7	290	8.8	61.1	142	257	23.7	18.1
1987	15.8	43.7	26.7	1.6	289	7.2	62.6	141	259	24.2	15.5
1986	13.7	41.5	24.9	1.7	286	6.5	76.8	125	258	29.8	15.2
1985	14.5	37.4	27.0	1.4	281	5.2	78.3	117	251	31.2	12.7
1984	6.9	33.9	32.1	1.1	279	5.9	80.7	111	245	32.9	15.2
1983	1.2	20.8	27.2	0.8	269	4.8	82.9	102	239	34.6	12.9

Data as orig. reptd. **1.** Excl. disc. ops. **2.** Refl. acctg. change.

Revenues (Million $)

Quarter:	1993	1992	1991	1990
Mar.	44.7	42.8	42.8	42.6
Jun.	45.3	43.4	43.5	43.5
Sep.		44.5	44.1	42.9
Dec.		45.5	45.9	43.0
		176.2	176.3	172.1

Total operating revenues in the six months ended June 30, 1993, increased 4.8%, year to year, reflecting higher rates and more access lines. Operating expenses rose only fractionally, and pretax income climbed 20%. After taxes at 34.4%, versus 35.7%, income was up 22%, to $16,042,000 ($0.98 a share, after preferred dividends), from $13,137,000 ($0.79). Results in the 1993 period exclude a charge of $1.45 a share for the cumulative effect of an accounting change.

Common Share Earnings ($)

Quarter:	1993	1992	1991	1990
Mar.	0.49	0.37	0.34	0.36
Jun.	0.49	0.42	0.43	0.37
Sep.		0.52	0.45	0.38
Dec.		0.48	0.45	0.36
		1.79	1.66	1.47

Finances

In July 1993, LTEC redeemed $34.75 million outstanding series G, I and J first mortgage bonds with funds from short-term borrowing.

Through March 31, 1993, LTEC had repurchased 179,000 of its common shares, pursuant to an April 1991 authorization to buy up to 300,000 shares.

Dividend Data

Dividends on the common stock have been paid every year since 1937. A dividend reinvestment plan is available.

Amt. of Divd. $	Date Decl.	Ex-divd. Date	Stock of Record	Payment Date
0.22	Sep. 17	Sep. 24	Sep. 30	Oct. 10'92
0.22	Dec. 16	Dec. 24	Dec. 31	Jan. 10'93
0.24	Mar. 17	Mar. 25	Mar. 31	Apr. 10'93
0.24	Jun. 16	Jun. 21	Jun. 25	Jul. 10'93

Capitalization

Long Term Debt: $43,875,000 (6/93).

5% Cum. Pfd. Stock: 44,991 shs. ($100 par); red. at $105.

Common Stock: 16,267,188 shs. ($0.25 par). Institutions hold 33%. Shareholders: 7,800 (12/92).

Office—1440 M Street, Lincoln, NE 68508. **Tel**—(402) 474-2211. **Chrmn & CEO**—J. E. Geist. **Pres & COO**—F. H. Hilsabeck. **VP, Secy, Treas & Investor Contact**—Michael J. Tavlin. **Dirs**—D. W. Acklie, W. W. Cook, Jr., T. L. Fairfield, E. J. Faulkner, J. E. Geist, J. T. Greer, J. Haessler, C. R. Hermes, F. H. Hilsabeck, G. Kelm, D. H. Pegler, Jr., P. C. Schorr III, W. C. Smith, J. W. Strand, C. N. Wheatley, T. C. Woods III, L. W. Ziegenbein. **Transfer Agent & Registrar**—Mellon Security Trust Co., Ridgefield Park, NJ. **Incorporated** in Delaware in 1928; holding co. incorporated in Nebraska in 1981. **Empl**—1,620.

 Ned Bancroft

Linear Technology Corp.

NASDAQ Symbol LLTC (Incl. in Nat'l Market) Options on Pacific In S&P MidCap 400

Price	Range	P-E Ratio	Dividend	Yield	S&P Ranking	Beta
Jun. 4'93	1993					
28½	30¾–20¾	32	0.20	0.7%	B	1.57

Summary

This rapidly growing company manufactures high-performance linear integrated circuits used to bridge real-world phenomena and electronic systems. Markets include computers, cellular telephones, industrial and medical electronic instruments and avionics. Following another substantial increase in earnings for fiscal 1992, further gains are likely in fiscal 1993, reflecting the company's participation in fast-growing market segments, an aggressive new product introduction program and wider margins. Additional growth is projected for fiscal 1994 as industry conditions strengthen further.

Current Outlook

Earnings for the fiscal year ending July 3, 1994, are estimated to reach $1.25 a share, up from the $0.97 projected for fiscal 1993.

The $0.05 quarterly dividend is likely to be increased in October 1993.

Sales for fiscal 1994 are projected to advance approximately 25%. Results should benefit from continued rapid growth of the high-performance linear integrated circuit market, an aggressive new product introduction program and the company's participation in some of the fastest-growing segments of the electronics industry. Stronger industry conditions will also bolster the gain. Somewhat restraining will be weakness in the Japanese market. The company's technological lead and stronger industry conditions allow LLTC to maintain its high gross profit margin. Research and development and selling, general and administrative expenses are likely to remain constant as a percentage of sales. An increase in depreciation due to the addition of a new plant will be partially offsetting.

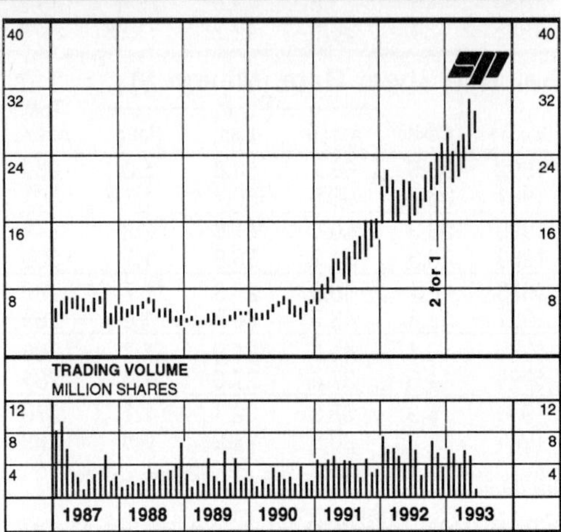

Net Sales (Million $)

13 Weeks:	1992-3	1991-2	1990-1	1989-90
Sep.	33.6	27.4	21.1	17.8
Dec.	35.6	28.9	22.3	17.9
Mar.	38.8	30.6	24.3	19.1
Jun.	---	32.6	26.4	20.8
	---	119.4	94.2	75.6

Net sales for the 39 weeks ended March 28, 1993, increased 24%, year to year. A 3.9 percentage point increase in the gross profit margin and a decline in expenses as a percentage of sales allowed margins to widen. Operating income increased 47%. With a 2.3% decline in net interest income, pretax income was up 43%. After taxes at 34.6%, versus 35.0%, net income rose 44%, to $0.70 a share, from $0.49.

Common Share Earnings ($)

13 Weeks:	1992-3	1991-2	1990-1	1989-90
Sep.	0.21	0.15	0.11	0.08
Dec.	0.23	0.16	0.11	0.08
Mar.	0.26	0.18	0.13	0.09
Jun.	E0.27	0.20	0.14	0.10
	E0.97	0.69	0.48	0.34

Important Developments

Jun. '93— LLTC said that its bookings in the U.S. were broadly higher, led by strong industry growth. Demand was especially strong from makers of notebook, laptop and palmtop computers. Demand in Europe was being led by the telecommunications industry, while business in Asia/Pacific was reasonably good. The Japanese market was flat.

Next earnings report expected in late July.

Per Share Data ($)

Yr. End Jun. 30	1992	1991	1990	1989	1988	1987	1986	1985	1984	1983
Tangible Bk. Val.	**3.53**	2.66	2.10	1.77	1.48	1.19	0.95	NA	NA	NA
Cash Flow	**0.82**	0.59	0.46	0.36	0.28	0.16	0.10	0.06	NA	NA
Earnings[1]	**0.69**	0.48	0.34	0.27	0.21	0.10	0.04	d0.09	d0.51	d0.73
Dividends	**Nil**	Nil	Nil	Nil	Nil	Nil	Nil	Nil	Nil	Nil
Payout Ratio	**Nil**	Nil	Nil	Nil	Nil	Nil	Nil	Nil	Nil	Nil
Prices[2]—High	**25½**	16⅜	7³⁄₁₆	5⁵⁄₁₆	7	8⅛	5	NA	NA	NA
Low	**15¾**	6³⁄₁₆	4⅛	3¹¹⁄₁₆	3⁹⁄₁₆	3⅜	2⅞	NA	NA	NA
P/E Ratio—	**37–23**	34–13	21–12	20–14	34–17	81–34	NM	NM	NM	NM

Data as orig. reptd. Adj. for stk. div. of 100% Nov. 1992. **1.** Bef. spec. items of +0.06 in 1988, +0.09 in 1987. **2.** Cal. yr. E-Estimated. NA-Not Available. d-Deficit. NM-Not Meaningful.

Income Data (Million $)

Year Ended Jun. 30	Oper. Revs.	Oper. Inc.	% Oper. Inc. of Revs.	Cap. Exp.	Depr.	Int. Exp.	Net Bef. Taxes	Eff. Tax Rate	[2]Net Inc.	% Net Inc. of Revs.	Cash Flow
1992	**119**	**40.1**	**33.6**	**[1]9.84**	**4.54**	**1.04**	**38.5**	**35.0%**	**25.0**	**20.9**	**29.6**
1991	94	26.9	28.6	[1]8.16	3.84	1.26	26.2	35.4%	16.9	18.0	20.8
1990	76	19.2	25.4	[1]3.90	4.00	1.46	17.5	35.4%	11.3	14.9	15.3
1989	65	15.8	24.4	6.14	3.32	1.49	14.6	39.0%	8.9	13.8	12.2
1988	51	12.9	25.2	2.87	2.63	1.35	11.3	39.0%	6.9	13.5	9.5
1987	35	7.7	21.8	6.99	1.94	0.78	6.8	51.0%	3.3	9.4	5.2
1986	22	3.1	13.9	0.72	1.69	0.83	1.2	Nil	1.2	5.2	2.9
1985	17	0.9	5.0	1.06	1.37	0.84	d0.8	Nil	d0.8	NM	0.6
1984	7	d3.3	NM	1.41	1.16	0.79	d4.7	Nil	d4.7	NM	NA
1983	NM	d5.6	NM	7.70	0.48	0.47	d5.8	Nil	d5.7	NM	NA

Balance Sheet Data (Million $)

Jun. 30	Cash	Curr. Assets	Curr. Liab.	Curr. Ratio	Total Assets	% Ret. on Assets	Long Term Debt	Common Equity	Total Cap.	% LT Debt of Cap.	% Ret. on Equity
1992	**95.3**	**134**	**33.5**	**4.0**	**160**	**17.5**	**1.73**	**124**	**126**	**1.4**	**23.1**
1991	69.2	100	23.7	4.2	121	15.4	6.44	90	97	6.6	21.1
1990	53.4	80	18.6	4.3	96	12.5	8.17	69	78	10.5	17.8
1989	46.5	70	16.9	4.1	85	11.6	9.00	58	68	13.3	16.7
1988	40.3	57	14.4	4.0	69	11.2	6.68	48	55	12.2	16.0
1987	30.5	42	8.2	5.1	54	7.0	7.28	38	46	16.0	9.6
1986	24.0	33	5.9	5.6	41	3.8	4.27	30	35	12.3	5.7
1985	5.6	12	4.3	2.7	20	NM	5.22	[4]11	16	32.6	NM
1984	2.9	7	3.6	2.0	16	NM	5.58	[4]6	12	46.5	NM
1983	NA	NA	NA	NA	18	NM	[3]6.02	[4]11	17	35.4	NM

Data as orig. reptd. **1.** Net. **2.** Bef. spec. items. **3.** Incl. current portion. **4.** Refl. conv. of pfd. stk. NM-Not Meaningful. d-Deficit. NA-Not Available.

Business Summary

Linear Technology Corporation designs and makes a broad line of standard high-performance linear integrated circuits.

Linear (also called analog) circuits monitor, condition, amplify or transform continuous analog signals associated with such physical properties as temperature, pressure, weight, light, sound and speed, and they play an important role in bridging between real-world phenomena and a variety of electronic systems. Linear circuits also provide voltage regulation to systems.

The company's product line includes operational, instrumentation and audio amplifiers; voltage regulators, references, comparators and converters; switched-capacitor filters; communications interface circuits; one-chip data acquisition systems; pulse-width modulators and sample-and-hold devices. About 2,500 finished part types are offered, of which two-thirds are proprietary.

Linear Technology is targeting the high-performance segments of the linear circuit market, which is characterized by higher precision, both high power or micropower, higher speed, more subsystem integration on a single chip and many other special features. Applications for its products include laptop and desktop computers, computer peripherals, cellular telephones, electronic testers, industrial and medical electronic instruments, automotive controls, process controls, factory automation products and avionics.

Approximately 43% of fiscal 1992 sales stemmed from exports.

Outlays for research and development totaled $12,344,000 (10.3% of net sales) in fiscal 1992, versus $10,219,000 (10.9%) the year before.

Dividend Data

Cash dividends were initiated in October 1992.

Amt. of Divd. $	Date Decl.	Ex–divd. Date	Stock of Record	Payment Date
2–for–1	Oct. 13	Nov. 25	Nov. 3	Nov. 24'92
0.05	Oct. 13	Nov. 19	Nov. 25	Dec. 11'92
0.05	Jan. 12	Jan. 25	Jan. 25	Feb. 10'93
0.05	Apr. 13	Apr. 19	Apr. 23	May 12'93

Finances

At March 28, 1993, the company had cash, cash equivalents and short-term investments of $113.6 million. The current portions of its long-term debt and capital lease obligations were $1.4 million.

Capitalization

Long Term Debt: $641,000 of lease obligs. (3/93).

Common Stock: 35,475,249 shs. (no par).
Institutions hold about 84%.
Shareholders: 497 of record (6/92).

Office—1630 McCarthy Blvd., Milpitas, CA 95035-7487. **Tel**—(408) 432-1900. **Pres & CEO**—R. H. Swanson Jr. **VP & COO**—C. B. Davies. **VP-Fin, CFO & Investor Contact**—Paul Coghlan. **Secy**—A. F. Schneiderman. **Dirs**—D. S. Lee, G. M. Mueller, R. H. Swanson Jr., T. S. Volpe. **Transfer Agent & Registrar**—First National Bank of Boston, Palo Alto, Calif. **Incorporated** in California in 1981. **Empl**—802.

 P. H. Valentine, CFA

Loctite Corp.

NYSE Symbol LOC Options on Phila (Mar-Jun-Sep-Dec) In S&P MidCap 400

Price	Range	P-E Ratio	Dividend	Yield	S&P Ranking	Beta
Oct. 12'93	1993					
36¾	45⅝–35⅛	17	0.80	2.2%	A	1.08

Summary

Loctite manufactures and markets engineering adhesives, sealants, coatings, specialty chemicals and electroluminescent lighting systems for industrial and consumer applications. International business generally accounts for over 50% of sales. Earnings in recent years were at record levels, reflecting strong gains in most international and domestic markets, but the company expects earnings for 1993 to be flat to down from those of 1992, due to business weakness in Europe and the adverse impact of the stronger U.S. dollar. Henkel KGaA of Germany owns about 28.7% of LOC.

Business Summary

Loctite produces high performance adhesives, sealants, coatings, specialized chemicals, and electroluminescent lamps and lighting systems. Products are sold to the industrial and electronics manufacturing and repair, medical products, professional automotive maintenance, and home and car do-it-yourself repair markets.

Contributions by geographic segment in 1992:

	Sales	Profits
Domestic	43%	32%
Europe	39%	65%
Other international	18%	3%

Marketing is effected through the North American industrial group, the North American automotive aftermarket and consumer group, and the international group. Product lines include thread locking sealants, structural adhesives, instant adhesives, gasketing compounds, automotive body repair materials, home care products, sealants for electronics components, lubricating and cleaning compounds, and other specialty chemicals. The principal products are anaerobic sealants and adhesives and cyanoacrylate adhesives. LOC also produces solid state surface electroluminescent lights and lighting systems.

Loctite is believed to be the world's leading manufacturer and marketer of anaerobic sealants and adhesives, which remain liquid while exposed to air and hardening when air is excluded, and cyanoacrylate adhesives, which harden quickly when applied in a thin film and exposed to moisture. Anaerobics are used primarily for locking, sealing and bonding machine elements while cyanoacrylates are used to form structural bonds between parts made of metal, plastic, wood and glass.

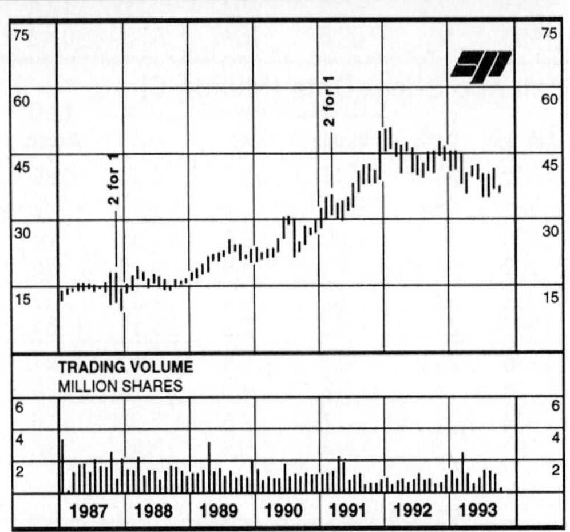

Important Developments

Oct. '93— LOC indicated that third quarter earnings would fall to about $0.45 a share on a modest decline in sales. The company projected that sales growth of 4% to 5% in local currency would be offset by the adverse impact of the stronger U.S. dollar. Good sales growth was seen in the North America and Pacific regions but a modest gain in European sales was offset by much weaker currencies. Latin American sales were down, due to weakness in Brazil. LOC also indicated that it expected stronger sales growth in the fourth quarter and that it was watching expenses carefully. For all of 1993, the company expected share earnings to be flat to down slightly from the $1.99 of 1992 on a modest gain in sales. Second quarter earnings of $0.50 compared with $0.56 from operations in the 1992 period before a $0.24 restructuring charge. The stronger U.S. dollar reduced a 6% local currency sales gain to 3% reported in dollars.

Next earnings report expected in late October.

Per Share Data ($)

Yr. End Dec. 31[1]	1992	1991	1990	1989	1988	[2]1987	1986	1985	1984	1983
Tangible Bk. Val.	**8.39**	7.67	7.10	5.89	5.22	4.61	4.14	3.38	3.41	3.25
Cash Flow	**2.45**	2.38	2.02	1.78	1.42	1.09	0.84	0.73	0.81	0.56
Earnings	**1.99**	1.98	1.70	1.52	1.16	0.85	0.64	0.56	0.67	0.43
Dividends	**0.740**	0.680	0.570	0.450	0.303	0.235	0.205	0.200	0.160	0.140
Payout Ratio	**37%**	34%	34%	30%	26%	28%	32%	35%	24%	33%
Prices[3]—High	**50⅞**	50⅛	30¹¹⁄₁₆	25½	19½	18	12⁷⁄₁₆	9¼	10¾	11¹¹⁄₁₆
Low	**39⅝**	28	20⅝	16⅜	13½	9½	8⁵⁄₁₆	6¾	7¹¹⁄₁₆	7³⁄₁₆
P/E Ratio—	**26–20**	25–14	18–12	17–11	17–12	21–11	19–13	17–12	16–11	27–17

Data as orig. reptd. Adj. for stk. divs. of 100% Mar. 1991, 100% Dec. 1987. **1.** Yrs. end Jun. 30 prior to 1991. **2.** Refl. merger or acq. **3.** Cal. yr.

Income Data (Million $)

Year Ended Dec. 31[1]	Revs.	Oper. Inc.	% Oper. Inc. of Revs.	Cap. Exp.	Depr.	Int. Exp.	[3]Net Bef. Taxes	Eff. Tax Rate	Net Inc.	% Net Inc. of Revs.	Cash Flow
1992	**608**	**130**	**21.3**	**40.2**	**16.8**	**5.6**	**95.1**	**24.0%**	**72.3**	**11.9**	**89.1**
1991	561	114	20.3	33.5	14.7	5.5	95.9	25.0%	71.9	12.8	86.7
1990	510	100	19.7	26.9	11.7	9.1	83.8	26.8%	61.4	12.0	73.1
1989	456	89	19.5	16.0	9.4	5.8	77.8	30.0%	[4]54.5	11.9	63.8
1988	417	75	18.0	14.5	9.3	11.0	61.3	31.8%	41.9	10.0	51.1
[2]1987	338	56	16.6	20.2	8.9	7.7	45.4	32.4%	30.7	9.1	39.5
1986	267	44	16.4	9.3	7.0	7.7	34.0	31.9%	23.2	8.7	30.2
1985	231	41	17.7	11.3	6.0	10.1	31.5	35.1%	20.4	8.8	26.5
1984	242	49	20.1	6.2	5.6	9.3	42.2	37.5%	26.3	10.9	32.0
1983	216	34	15.9	10.0	5.2	7.4	30.1	43.0%	17.1	7.9	22.3

Balance Sheet Data (Million $)

Dec. 31[1]	Cash	Curr. Assets	Curr. Liab.	Curr. Ratio	Total Assets	% Ret. on Assets	Long Term Debt	Common Equity	Total Cap.	% LT Debt of Cap.	% Ret. on Equity
1992	**81.4**	**315**	**137**	**2.3**	**557**	**13.3**	**14.1**	**383**	**398**	**3.6**	**19.4**
1991	84.1	302	128	2.4	529	14.9	25.3	361	387	6.6	22.2
1990	87.8	298	106	2.8	440	15.2	35.8	286	322	11.1	23.7
1989	86.1	257	89	2.9	362	15.4	36.8	229	266	13.8	25.0
1988	76.1	238	96	2.5	347	12.9	39.3	205	245	16.1	21.8
1987	57.2	200	105	1.9	304	11.2	10.6	182	192	5.5	18.3
1986	53.3	170	73	2.3	244	10.0	13.5	154	167	8.1	16.6
1985	58.0	152	76	2.0	219	9.4	14.5	125	140	10.4	16.2
1984	50.1	152	75	2.0	227	12.2	16.0	133	149	10.7	20.3
1983	48.8	137	62	2.2	213	8.3	16.1	133	149	10.8	13.3

Data as orig. reptd. **1.** Yrs. ended Jun. 30 prior to 1991. **2.** Refl. merger or acq. **3.** Incl. equity in earns. of nonconsol. subs. **4.** Refl. acctg. change.

[1]Net Sales (Million $)

Quarter:	1993	1992	1991	1990
Mar.	149.1	147.5	138.3	133.9
Jun.	158.1	154.2	141.0	139.2
Sep.		159.6	140.3	138.9
Dec.		146.7	141.5	143.2
		608.0	561.2	555.2

Sales for the first half of 1993 advanced 1.9%, year to year, reflecting gains in the North American, Latin American, and Pacific regions. European sales fell due to the stronger U.S. dollar, despite a sales increase in local currency. In the absence of a $12.7 million pretax ($0.24 a share after tax) restructuring charge, earnings from operations rose 18%. After higher investment income and lower foreign exchange losses, pretax income was up 22%. Following taxes at 25.0%, versus 23.2%, net income increased 19%, to $1.04 a share from $0.86.

[1]Common Share Earnings ($)

Quarter:	1993	1992	1991	1990
Mar.	0.54	0.54	0.43	0.43
Jun.	0.50	0.32	0.52	0.49
Sep.		0.59	0.53	0.49
Dec.		0.54	0.50	0.45
		1.99	1.98	1.86

Dividend Data

Dividends have been paid since 1962. A dividend reinvestment plan is available.

Amt of Divd. $	Date Decl.	Ex-divd. Date	Stock of Record	Payment Date
0.19	Jul. 22	Sep. 4	Sep. 11	Oct. 1'92
0.19	Sep. 23	Dec. 7	Dec. 11	Jan. 4'93
0.19	Mar. 3	Mar. 8	Mar. 12	Apr. 1'93
0.20	Apr. 23	Jun. 7	Jun. 11	Jul. 1'93
0.20	Jul. 23	Sep. 3	Sep. 10	Oct. 1'93

Finances

In February 1993, LOC said that capital expenditures for 1993 and the next two years were expected to be $50 million-$60 million annually.

In November 1985, the Krieble family sold a 25% equity interest in LOC to Henkel KGaA (Germany), reducing its interest to 14%, to which Henkel was granted a right of first refusal. Henkel agreed to restrict its purchases of LOC stock for 10 years.

Capitalization

Long Term Debt: $15,478,000 (6/93).

Common Stock: 35,381,170 shs. ($0.01 par). Henkel KGaA owns about 28.7%. The Krieble family owns some 9.9%.
Institutions hold approximately 44%.
Shareholders of record: 2,235.

1. Refl. 1991 year-end change from Jun. 30 to Dec. 31.

Office—Ten Columbus Blvd., Hartford, CT 06106. **Tel**—(203) 520-5000. **Chrmn**—K. W. Butterworth. **Pres & CEO**—D. Freeman. **VP-Secy**—E. F. Miller. **SVP-Treas**—R. L. Aller. **Investor Contact**—Western A. Todd. **Dirs**—J. K. Armstrong, W. Barnes, K. W. Butterworth, R. Dohr, D. Freeman, R. E. Ix, F. B. Krieble, J. Manchot, J. H. Schofield, S. J. Trachtenberg. **Transfer Agent & Registrar**—Bank of Boston, Boston, Mass. **Incorporated** in Connecticut in 1953; reincorporated in Delaware in 1987. **Empl**—3,689.

 Richard O'Reilly, CFA

Longview Fibre

NYSE Symbol LFB Options on CBOE (Mar-Jun-Sep-Dec) In S&P MidCap 400

Price	Range	P-E Ratio	Dividend	Yield	S&P Ranking	Beta
Aug. 26'93	1993					
18⅛	20¼–15¾	22	0.40	2.2%	B+	1.18

Summary

This operator of tree farms in the Pacific Northwest produces logs, paper and paperboard, and converted products. Strength in logging operations has offset the adverse effect of intense competition and weak pricing in the paper and converted products segments in recent periods. However, results in the fourth quarter of 1993 may be adversely affected by recent price declines for wood products. Despite the near-term uncertainty, LFB holds valuable timber assets which should grow even more valuable as time passes as a result of environmental restrictions on logging.

Current Outlook

Earnings for the fiscal year ending October 31, 1993, are estimated at $0.87 a share, compared with the $0.62 earned in fiscal 1992. In fiscal 1994, earnings should reach $1.15 a share.

The quarterly dividend is likely to remain at $0.10 a share, although dividends (including extras) should total at least $0.52 in fiscal 1993.

Sales for all of fiscal 1993 are expected to show modest improvement. Logging operations may be hurt in the fourth quarter by recent price declines for wood products, and excess industry capacity is likely to continue to hold down prices for paper and converted products. However, earnings in 1994 are expected to benefit from a gradual improvement in pricing for most of the company's products. Over the long term, the company should be able to capitalize on the value of its timber holdings as a result of increasing environmental restrictions on logging in government-owned forests.

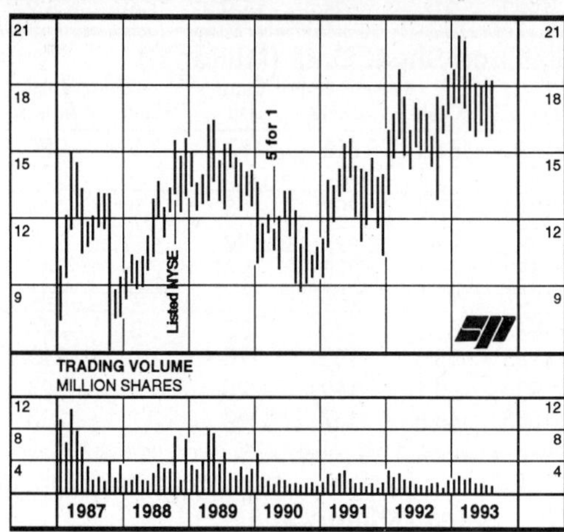

Net Sales (Million $)

Quarter:	1993–94	1992–93	1991–92	1990–91
Jan.	---	156	153	152
Apr.	---	179	173	158
Jul.	---	176	178	161
Oct.	---	---	188	172
	---	---	691	644

Sales for the nine months ended July 31, 1993, rose 1.5%, year to year, as a 61% increase in the average price for logs sold outweighed continued weak demand for paper, paperboard and converted products. Benefiting from sharply higher profits in the log segment and reduced interest expense, pretax income climbed 51%. After taxes at 33.7%, against 32.4%, net income advanced 49%, to $0.64 a share from $0.43.

Common Share Earnings ($)

Quarter:	1993–94	1992–93	1992	1991
Jan.	E0.20	0.10	0.08	0.03
Apr.	E0.30	0.26	0.19	0.06
Jul.	E0.30	0.28	0.17	0.09
Oct.	E0.35	E0.23	0.19	0.14
	E1.15	E0.87	0.62	0.32

Important Developments

Aug. '93— The company anticipated that fourth quarter results for logging operations could deteriorate from third quarter levels due to price declines for logs from peaks reached earlier in the year. Management said the price weakness for wood products was the result of an imbalance in supply and demand.

Next earnings report expected in mid-November.

Per Share Data ($)

Yr. End Oct. 31	1992	1991	1990	1989	1988	1987	1986	1985	1984	1983
Tangible Bk. Val.	**7.39**	7.29	7.49	7.05	6.39	5.06	4.21	3.89	3.74	3.60
Cash Flow	**1.85**	1.44	2.03	1.98	2.33	1.70	1.09	0.86	0.83	0.71
Earnings	**0.62**	0.32	1.13	1.21	1.74	1.17	0.60	0.40	0.40	0.31
Dividends	**0.520**	0.520	0.520	0.480	0.400	0.320	0.280	0.256	0.256	0.240
Payout Ratio	**84%**	162%	44%	39%	23%	27%	46%	63%	64%	77%
Prices[1]—High	**18¾**	15⅝	13⅜	16½	15⅝	15	7⅝	6	6⅛	5¾
Low	**12⅞**	9⅜	8¾	12⅜	8⅜	6⅛	5¼	4	4	4
P/E Ratio—	**30–21**	49–29	12–8	14–10	9–5	13–5	13–9	15–10	15–10	18–13

Data as orig. reptd. Adj. for stk. div. of 400% Apr. 1990. **1.** Cal. yr. E-Estimated

Income Data (Million $)

Year Ended Oct. 31	Revs.	Oper. Inc.	% Oper. Inc. of Revs.	Cap. Exp.	Depr.	Int. Exp.	Net Bef. Taxes	Eff. Tax Rate	Net Inc.	% Net Inc. of Revs.	Cash Flow
1992	**691**	**134**	**19.4**	**74**	**63.4**	**[1]24.4**	**47**	**32.3%**	**32.1**	**4.6**	**95**
1991	644	99	15.4	104	58.0	[1]24.2	23	26.0%	16.6	2.6	75
1990	685	157	23.0	174	48.9	[1]17.1	93	34.1%	61.1	8.9	110
1989	698	152	21.8	136	42.6	16.0	100	33.8%	66.5	9.5	109
1988	657	185	28.2	120	32.4	11.9	146	34.2%	96.3	14.7	129
1987	569	143	25.1	84	29.2	10.8	107	39.0%	65.2	11.4	94
1986	488	89	18.2	27	27.2	15.5	49	31.6%	33.5	6.9	61
1985	459	65	14.1	38	25.2	18.4	26	13.8%	22.4	4.9	48
1984	483	65	13.5	48	24.0	19.9	27	16.6%	22.2	4.6	46
1983	373	51	13.5	45	22.3	20.5	19	10.4%	17.3	4.6	40

Balance Sheet Data (Million $)

		Curr.									
Oct. 31	Cash	Assets	Liab.	Ratio	Total Assets	% Ret. on Assets	Long Term Debt	Common Equity	Total Cap.	% LT Debt of Cap.	% Ret. on Equity
1992	**Nil**	**149**	**118**	**1.3**	**951**	**3.4**	**362**	**382**	**828**	**43.8**	**8.5**
1991	Nil	137	110	1.3	927	1.8	356	377	813	43.8	4.4
1990	0.91	132	105	1.3	874	7.8	303	387	764	39.7	16.3
1989	1.86	126	97	1.3	739	9.7	195	385	642	30.3	18.1
1988	Nil	119	95	1.3	635	16.4	137	353	541	25.3	30.4
1987	Nil	107	85	1.3	541	12.7	133	281	456	29.1	25.3
1986	Nil	100	75	1.3	485	6.9	141	234	410	34.4	14.9
1985	Nil	97	74	1.3	488	4.6	171	216	414	41.2	10.6
1984	Nil	99	79	1.3	481	4.8	169	208	402	42.0	10.9
1983	Nil	91	57	1.6	441	4.0	162	200	384	42.2	8.8

Data as orig. reptd. **1.** Net of int. inc.

Business Summary

Longview Fibre owns and operates tree farms in Oregon and Washington that produce logs for sale. At its mill in Longview, Wash., the company produces pulp that is manufactured into kraft paper and containerboard. Shipping containers and merchandise and grocery bags are produced at 14 converting plants located in 10 states. Segment contributions in fiscal 1992 (profits in millions):

	Sales	Profits
Logs	17%	$61.0
Paper & paperboard	34%	14.4
Converted products	49%	-4.8

Export sales, principally to Japan, Hong Kong, Taiwan, Southeast Asia and Canada, accounted for about 18% of sales in fiscal 1992.

Log sales in fiscal 1992 totaled 243 million board feet, up 11% from fiscal 1991. Most logs produced from the company's timberlands are sold to independent sawmills, plywood plants, U.S. exporters and foreign importers.

Paper sales in fiscal 1992 totaled 253,000 tons, compared with 249,000 a year earlier, and paperboard sales were 174,000 tons, up sharply from 119,000 tons in 1991. Wrapping and converting paper is marketed through the company's sales force and paper merchants. Paper is sold mainly in the domestic market, with some grades sold in the export market, while containerboard is marketed in the export market and in the Pacific Coast states.

Converted product sales in fiscal 1992 totaled 525,000 tons, versus 520,000 tons the year before. The tonnage of paper and containerboard used in the converting plants equals about 63% of the Longview mill's production. Bags are sold directly or through paper merchants. Corrugated and solid-fibre boxes are marketed directly.

At October 31, 1992, the company owned in fee 527,800 acres of tree farms.

Dividend Data

Cash has been paid since 1937. A "poison pill" stock purchase rights plan was adopted in 1989.

Amt of Divd. $	Date Decl.	Ex-divd. Date	Stock of Record	Payment Date
0.10	Sep. 15	Sep. 21	Sep. 25	Oct. 9'92
0.12 Ext	Sep. 15	Sep. 21	Sep. 25	Oct. 9'92
0.10	Dec. 2	Dec. 18	Dec. 24	Jan. 8'93
0.10	Mar. 5	Mar. 19	Mar. 25	Apr. 9'93
0.10	Jun. 14	Jun. 21	Jun. 25	Jul. 9'93

Capitalization

Long Term Debt: $333,111,000 (7/93).

Common Stock: 51,892,732 shs. ($1.50 par). Officers & directors own about 10%. Institutions hold some 41%. Shareholders: About 11,500.

Office—P.O. Box 639, Longview, WA 98632. **Tel**—(206) 425-1550. **Chrmn, Pres & CEO**—R. P. Wollenberg. **SVP-Fin, Treas, Secy & Investor Contact**—Lisa J. Holbrook. **Dirs**—R. B. Arkel, D. L. Bowden, M. A. Dow, L. J. Holbrook, C. H. Monroe, G. E. Schwartz, D. C. Stibich, J. E. Wertheimer, R. E. Wertheimer, D. A. Wollenberg, R. P. Wollenberg. **Transfer Agent**—Chemical Trust Co. of California, San Francisco. **Incorporated** in Delaware in 1926; reincorporated in Washington in 1990. **Empl**—3,450.

 Richard Spiegel

Lubrizol Corp.

NYSE Symbol LZ Options on Phila (Feb-May-Aug-Nov) In S&P MidCap 400

Price	Range	P-E Ratio	Dividend	Yield	S&P Ranking	Beta
Aug. 18'93	1993					
34⅜	34¾–26⅝	23	0.84	2.4%	B+	0.84

Summary

Lubrizol is believed to be the largest supplier to the petroleum industry of chemical additives used in automotive and industrial lubricants. LZ also develops and produces specialty vegetable oils and their chemical derivatives. In December 1992, LZ transferred its Agrigenetics seed business to a 49%-owned partnership with Mycogen Corp. Earnings are expected to begin to improve late in 1993 and in 1994 on increased U.S. shipments of engine oil additives.

Current Outlook

Share earnings for 1994 are projected at about $2.10, up from the $1.85 expected for 1993.

Dividends of $0.21 quarterly are the minimum expected.

Revenues in the 1993 second half and in 1994 should advance on higher shipments and selling prices of specialty additives resulting from the introduction of the new SH standard for engine oils in August, 1993. A new diesel engine oil standard becomes effective in 1994. The acquisition of a French lubricant additive business will be completed in late 1993. Profitability should also benefit from a more favorable product mix and as product development and testing costs begin to level off after substantially growing in recent years.

Revenues (Million $)

Quarter:	1993	1992	1991	1990
Mar.	367	417	374	357
Jun.	394	416	372	358
Sep.		364	359	367
Dec.		356	370	371
		1,552	1,476	1,453

Revenues for the first half of 1993 fell 8.6%, year to year, reflecting the absence of sales from Agrigenetics; ongoing revenues were up 2.0% as higher chemical prices and an acquisition outweighed a volume decline. Margins narrowed and net income fell 25%, to $0.98 a share, from $1.29, excluding a special accounting charge of $0.58 a share in 1993.

Common Share Earnings ($)

Quarter:	1993	1992	1991	1990
Mar.	0.52	0.64	0.51	0.40
Jun.	0.46	0.65	0.40	0.46
Sep.	E0.43	0.28	0.42	1.37
Dec.	E0.44	0.24	0.46	0.46
	E1.85	1.81	1.79	2.67

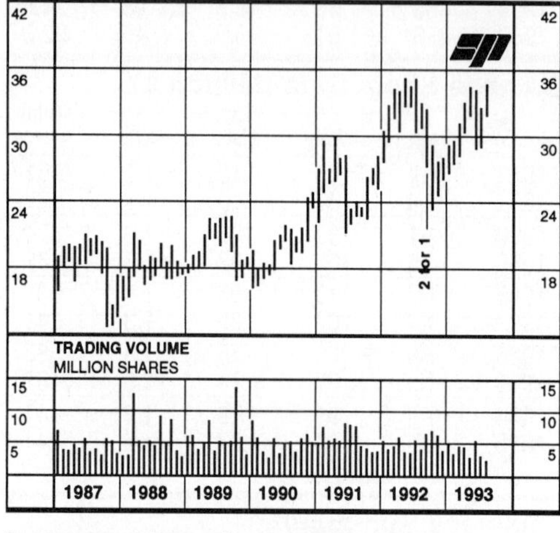

Important Developments

Jul. '93— LZ was optimistic that its second quarter earnings represented the end of a series of unfavorable quarterly comparisons and that it expected conditions to improve and result in sales and earnings growth in 1994. North American shipments declined in the second quarter as customers reduced inventories in anticipation of placing orders for new products for engine oils. LZ repurchased 535,000 common shares during the quarter. In June, directors authorized the repurchase of an additional 4 million shares.

Dec. '92— Lubrizol restructured its agribusiness segment by transferring its Agrigenetics division to a 49%-owned partnership with Mycogen Corp. (MYCO). LZ received 2.29 million MYCO common shares and $39.4 million of convertible preferred stock, boosting its stake in MYCO to 25%. Agrigenetics had 1992 revenues of $86.2 million.

Next earnings report expected in late October.

Per Share Data ($)

Yr. End Dec. 31	1992	1991	1990	1989	1988	1987	1986	[2]1985	1984	1983
Tangible Bk. Val.[1]	**11.74**	11.26	10.36	8.96	8.74	7.98	7.22	6.55	6.07	6.02
Cash Flow	**2.65**	2.58	3.43	2.21	2.30	1.63	1.52	1.30	1.36	1.30
Earnings[3]	**1.81**	1.79	2.67	1.26	1.70	1.03	0.99	0.75	0.87	0.83
Dividends	**0.810**	0.770	0.730	0.690	0.650	0.610	0.585	0.580	0.560	0.540
Payout Ratio	**44%**	43%	27%	55%	38%	58%	59%	78%	65%	65%
Prices—High	**35⁵⁄₁₆**	30	24⅞	22¹¹⁄₁₆	21³⁄₁₆	21¹⁄₁₆	17⁹⁄₁₆	14⁷⁄₁₆	12¼	13¹⁵⁄₁₆
Low	**23⅜**	21¼	16¼	16⅞	15	12⅝	12¹³⁄₁₆	9⅞	9⅛	9¹⁄₁₆
P/E Ratio—	**20–13**	17–12	9–6	18–13	12–9	20–12	18–13	19–13	14–11	17–11

Data as orig. reptd. Adj. for stk. div. of 100% Sep. 1992. **1.** Incl. intangibles before 1989. **2.** Reflects merger or acquisition. **3.** Bef. spec. item(s) of +0.12 in 1988. E-Estimated.

Income Data (Million $)

Year Ended Dec. 31	Revs.	Oper. Inc.	% Oper. Inc. of Revs.	Cap. Exp.	Depr.	Int. Exp.	[2]Net Bef. Taxes	Eff. Tax Rate	[3]Net Inc.	% Net Inc. of Revs.	Cash Flow
1992	**1,552**	**220**	**14.2**	**95.8**	**58.4**	**3.62**	**177**	**29.6%**	**125**	**8.0**	**183**
1991	1,476	222	15.1	82.0	54.6	7.74	178	30.6%	124	8.4	178
1990	1,453	218	15.0	77.0	54.0	6.05	271	29.9%	190	13.1	244
1989	1,228	167	13.6	65.0	48.7	5.44	138	31.8%	94	7.7	165
1988	1,126	162	14.4	55.0	46.6	6.20	186	29.4%	131	11.7	178
1987	1,022	153	15.0	42.0	47.2	6.30	129	37.0%	[4]81	8.0	129
1986	985	152	15.4	41.0	42.6	7.90	129	39.2%	[4]78	7.9	121
[1]1985	913	140	15.4	85.0	44.6	9.50	103	41.8%	60	6.7	105
1984	832	129	15.5	30.0	38.7	5.10	115	41.1%	68	8.1	106
1983	790	125	15.8	26.0	37.0	3.40	114	43.1%	65	8.2	102

Balance Sheet Data (Million $)

Dec. 31	Cash	Curr. Assets	Curr. Liab.	Curr. Ratio	Total Assets	% Ret. on Assets	Long Term Debt	Common Equity	Total Cap.	% LT Debt of Cap.	% Ret. on Equity
1992	**77**	**591**	**206**	**2.9**	**1,127**	**10.9**	**23.3**	**819**	**880**	**2.6**	**15.5**
1991	126	702	262	2.7	1,172	10.8	35.0	794	868	4.0	16.2
1990	76	669	248	2.7	1,115	18.9	54.0	736	827	6.5	28.0
1989	82	543	181	3.0	960	9.9	53.2	663	750	7.1	14.3
1988	124	573	185	3.1	971	13.9	55.3	664	759	7.3	20.7
1987	93	513	169	3.0	939	9.0	56.1	622	746	7.5	13.7
1986	86	463	163	2.8	878	9.0	52.6	573	698	7.5	14.3
1985	63	447	183	2.5	854	7.7	73.4	519	659	11.1	12.0
1984	111	376	132	2.8	702	9.8	30.4	474	558	5.4	14.3
1983	90	362	130	2.8	683	9.8	27.2	472	543	5.0	13.9

Data as orig. reptd. **1.** Reflects merger or acquisition. **2.** Incl. equity in earns. of nonconsol. subs. **3.** Bef. spec. items. **4.** Reflects accounting change.

Business Summary

Lubrizol is a specialty chemical company that serves the transportation, industrial and agricultural markets. Its principal products are chemical additives for lubricants and fuels. It also produces specialty vegetable oils. In December, 1992, LZ transferred its Agrigenetics crop seed business to Mycogen Corp. Contributions by business segment (operating profits in million $) in 1992 were:

	Revs.	Profits
Specialty chemicals............	92%	$185.1
Agribusiness.....................	8%	–11.5

Foreign operations accounted for 53% of revenues and 48% of operating profits in 1992.

Specialty chemicals consist of chemical additives (including detergents, dispersants, oxidation and wear inhibitors, viscosity improvers, and pour depressants) for automotive and industrial lubricants, functional fluids and fuels. Additives are used primarily in engine oils, automotive transmission fluids, gear oils, hydraulic fluids, machine oils, metal working compounds, greases, and gasoline and diesel fuels for use in cars, trucks, buses, off-highway equipment, marine engines, and industrial applications. Additives for engine oil accounted for 48% of revenues in 1992. Other chemical products include paint and coatings additives, and oil field and processing chemicals. About 60% of chemical sales are made to customers outside North America.

SVO Enterprises develops and sells specialty vegetable oils and products derived from oilseed crops, mainly sunflowers, and operates an oilseed crushing and refining facility.

Dividend Data

Dividends have been paid since 1935. An amended "poison pill" stock purchase right was adopted in 1991.

Amt of Divd. $	Date Decl.	Ex–divd. Date	Stock of Record	Payment Date
0.20	Jul. 30	Aug. 4	Aug. 10	Sep. 10'92
0.21	Oct. 26	Nov. 4	Nov. 10	Dec. 10'92
0.21	Jan. 25	Feb. 4	Feb. 10	Mar. 10'93
0.21	Apr. 26	May 4	May 10	Jun. 10'93
0.21	Jul. 26	Aug. 4	Aug. 10	Sep. 10'93

Capitalization

Long Term Debt: $44,581,000 (6/93).

Common Stock: 68,160,152 shs. (no par).
Institutions hold about 69%.
Shareholders of record: 6,860.

Office—29400 Lakeland Blvd., Wickliffe, OH 44092. **Tel**—(216) 943-4200. **Chrmn & CEO**—L. E. Coleman. **Pres**—W. G. Bares. **Secy & Investor Contact**—K. H. Hopping. **Treas**—W. R. Jones. **Dirs**—W. G. Bares, E. F. Bell, L. E. Coleman, P. G. Elliott, A. Gillet, D. H. Hoag, T. C. MacAvoy, W. P. Madar, R. A. Miller, R. A. Mitsch. R. D. Thompson, K. E. Ware. **Transfer Agent & Registrar**—Society National Bank, Cleveland, Ohio. **Incorporated** in Ohio in 1928. **Empl**—4,609.

 Richard O'Reilly, CFA

Lukens Inc.

NYSE Symbol LUC In S&P MidCap 400

Price	Range	P-E Ratio	Dividend	Yield	S&P Ranking	Beta
Sep. 23'93	1993					
39⅛	52⅞–36¼	NA	1.00	2.6%	B	0.84

Summary

Lukens is the third largest U.S. producer of carbon steel plate used in the construction, shipbuilding and transportation markets. In April 1993, it entered the stainless steel market through the acquisition of Washington Steel Co. As part of an effort to focus on its steel businesses, the company has agreed in principle to sell its corrosion protection subsidiaries.

Current Outlook

Earnings for 1994 are estimated at $2.80, up from 1993's estimated $1.95.

Dividends should continue at $0.25 quarterly.

Sales are expected to grow in 1994, reflecting higher volume and prices for carbon and alloy plate and increased volume and firm prices for stainless products. Higher prices, increased operating rates and a more favorable mix should outweigh an expected rise in raw material costs and boost operating profits. Assuming level interest costs, less dilution, and only a small increase in the tax rate, earnings should advance in 1994.

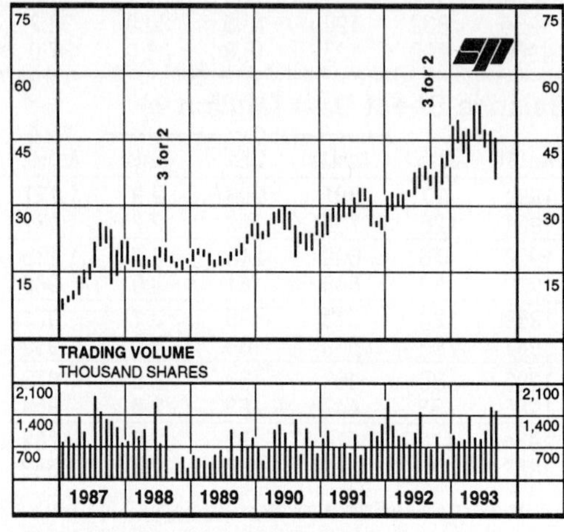

Net Sales (Million $)

13 Weeks:	1993	1992	1991	1990
Mar.	257	140	156	171
Jun.	227	242	178	179
Sep.		254	163	176
Dec.		245	132	158
		881	629	684

Sales from continuing operations in the 26 weeks ended June 26, 1993, climbed 56%, year to year (1992 restated), reflecting the Washington Steel acquisition. Margins narrowed slightly, and with sharply higher interest costs, the gain in income from continuing operations was cut to 32%. After preferred dividends, share earnings, on 15% more shares, were $0.90 (before charges of $4.55 for accounting changes and income of $0.09 from discontinued operations), versus $0.77 (restated).

Common Share Earnings ($)

13 Weeks:	1993	1992	1991	1990
Mar.	0.39	0.38	0.67	0.84
Jun.	0.51	0.76	0.99	0.89
Sep.	E0.45	0.62	0.74	0.95
Dec.	E0.60	0.55	d0.71	0.71
	E1.95	2.31	1.68	3.38

Important Developments

Aug. '93— The company announced plans for Washington Steel Group to begin manufacturing stainless steel cut plate in 1993's fourth quarter. Production and distribution activities associated with the new product line are not expected to have a significant impact on 1993 earnings.

Jul. '93— LUC announced an agreement in principle to sell its corrosion protection subsidiaries to Shaw Industries Ltd., a Canadian company. The agreement was made in connection with a company program to focus resources on its steel businesses. LUC said it would continue to evaluate its other non-steel operations, and may choose to sell some or all such units in due course.

Next earnings report expected in mid-October.

Per Share Data ($)

Yr. End Dec. 31	[3]1992	1991	1990	1989	[2]1988	1987	1986	1985	1984	1983
Tangible Bk. Val.[1]	**18.90**	17.09	16.26	13.73	14.06	11.90	10.49	10.43	10.83	10.65
Cash Flow	**5.20**	3.63	5.35	4.97	4.33	3.37	2.67	1.44	2.07	0.49
Earnings	**2.31**	1.68	3.38	3.15	2.61	1.72	0.77	d0.37	0.41	d1.21
Dividends	**0.990**	0.987	0.947	0.733	0.460	0.303	0.213	0.213	0.177	0.177
Payout Ratio	**43%**	58%	28%	23%	18%	18%	30%	NM	44%	NM
Prices—High	**42⅝**	34	30 3/16	25 15/16	21 15/16	26 1/16	7 5/16	7 1/16	7¼	7¾
Low	**26½**	23	18 11/16	16 5/16	15 9/16	6 9/16	5 3/16	5	4½	5 5/16
P/E Ratio—	**18–11**	20–14	9–6	8–5	8–6	15–4	10–7	NM	18–11	NM

Data as orig. reptd. Adj. for stk. divs. of 50% Sep. 1992, 50% Sep. 1988. **1.** Incl. intangibles prior to 1991. **2.** Refl. acctg. change. **3.** Refl. merger or acq. d-Deficit. E-Estimated. NM-Not Meaningful.

Income Data (Million $)

Year Ended Dec. 31	Revs.	Oper. Inc.	% Oper. Inc. of Revs.	Cap. Exp.	Depr.	Int. Exp.	Net Bef. Taxes	Eff. Tax Rate	Net Inc.	% Net Inc. of Revs.	Cash Flow
[2]**1992**	**881**	**106.0**	**12.0**	**36.0**	**39.2**	**13.6**	**53.9**	**38.7%**	**33.1**	**3.8**	**70.7**
1991	629	61.1	9.7	34.7	24.8	2.3	36.9	37.6%	23.0	3.7	46.2
1990	684	95.6	14.0	35.0	24.8	2.4	70.1	37.0%	44.2	6.5	67.3
1989	645	85.5	13.3	25.5	23.7	3.6	65.9	37.0%	41.5	6.4	63.2
[1]1988	605	77.4	12.8	35.2	22.1	5.8	[3]52.6	36.5%	33.4	5.5	55.5
1987	503	64.7	12.9	24.5	20.8	5.7	[3]38.8	44.2%	21.7	4.3	42.5
1986	405	43.3	10.7	9.7	21.8	8.2	[3]18.1	51.6%	[1]8.8	2.2	30.5
1985	422	26.8	6.4	19.5	20.7	9.0	[3]d9.5	NM	d4.2	NM	16.6
1984	416	38.2	9.2	17.1	19.3	10.4	[3]8.5	44.6%	4.7	1.1	24.0
1983	343	10.0	2.9	8.6	19.7	10.3	d24.3	NM	d14.0	NM	5.7

Balance Sheet Data (Million $)

Dec. 31	Cash	Curr. Assets	Curr. Liab.	Curr. Ratio	Total Assets	% Ret. on Assets	Long Term Debt	Common Equity	Total Cap.	% LT Debt of Cap.	% Ret. on Equity
1992	**15.00**	**294**	**152.0**	**1.9**	**760**	**5.3**	**219.0**	**325**	**577**	**37.9**	**10.4**
1991	59.90	204	99.2	2.1	432	5.4	46.6	215	320	14.6	10.2
1990	35.20	184	87.5	2.1	412	11.1	54.6	203	314	17.4	22.7
1989	4.24	170	82.3	2.1	377	11.6	57.4	170	285	20.1	23.4
1988	3.18	163	93.7	1.7	353	9.8	47.1	181	251	18.8	19.9
1987	4.36	150	85.5	1.8	323	6.8	52.3	151	226	23.1	15.2
1986	4.38	122	77.6	1.6	307	2.7	62.3	129	215	29.0	6.8
1985	6.73	112	68.4	1.6	303	NM	87.4	115	219	39.9	NM
1984	2.75	113	73.3	1.5	308	1.6	69.8	126	219	31.9	3.8
1983	3.72	98	50.4	1.9	296	NM	84.6	123	228	37.0	NM

Data as orig. reptd. **1.** Refl. acctg. change. **2.** Refl. merger or acq. **3.** Incl. equity in earns. of nonconsol. subs. d-Deficit. NM-Not Meaningful.

Business Summary

Lukens is the third largest domestic producer of steel plate, and also provides diverse products and services to industrial, energy, transportation, construction, and defense markets. In April 1992, the company entered the stainless steel market through the acquisition of Washington Steel Co. Contributions in 1992 were as follows:

	Sales	Profits
Lukens Steel	47%	51%
Washington Stainless	32%	29%
Safety products	7%	6%
Corrosion protection	11%	10%
Diversified	3%	4%

Lukens Steel produces a broad range of carbon, alloy, and clad plates for service centers and a wide range of markets in the capital goods sector. Shipments in 1992 totaled 646,100 tons, versus 633,100 tons in 1991. Carbon plate accounted for 63% of the mix, versus 64% in 1991.

Washington Stainless manufactures light-gauge stainless steel sheet, strip, continuous mill plate, hot band and slabs. Shipments from April 1992 to year-end totaled 147,000 tons. Products are sold through its seven service centers.

Safety products include reflective glass beads, tape and sheeting; traffic cones and barrels; flashing lights; safety vests; and warning flags. The segment also provides finished products, equipment and materials for highway maintenance and industrial markets.

Corrosion protection supplies insulative, protective coatings and cathodic protection services for steel pipeline and structural metals. The diversified group includes two materials handling companies, an engineering design company and a real estate development venture.

Dividend Data

Dividends have been paid since 1940. A dividend reinvestment plan is available. A new "poison pill" stock purchase right was adopted in 1990.

Amt. of Divd. $	Date Decl.	Ex-divd. Date	Stock of Record	Payment Date
0.25	Oct. 28	Nov. 3	Nov. 9	Nov. 20'92
0.25	Jan. 27	Feb. 2	Feb. 8	Feb. 19'93
0.25	Apr. 28	May 4	May 10	May 21'93
0.25	Jul. 28	Aug. 3	Aug. 9	Aug. 20'93

Capitalization

Long Term Debt: $211,315,000 (6/93).

8.0% Conv. Preferred Stk: 544,374 shs. (liquid. pref. $60); ea. conv. into 2 com. shs. Held by ESOP.

Common Stock: 14,516,927 shs. ($0.01 par). Institutions hold 79%. Shareholders of record: 4,700 (12/92).

Office—50 South First Ave, Coatesville, PA 19320. **Tel**—(215) 383-2000. **Chrmn & CEO**—R. W. Van Sant. **Pres**—R. E. Heaton. **VP & Secy**—W. D. Sprague. **Investor Contact**—Barbara L. Gaspar. **Dirs**— M. O. Alexander, F. R. Dusto, R. M. Gross, N. H. Hansen, W. H. Nelson III, S. J. Northrop, R. L. Seaman, H. C. Stonecipher, J. L. Thomas, W. P. Tippett, R. W. Van Sant. **Transfer Agent & Registrar**—American Stock Transfer & Trust Co., New Yor, NY. **Incorporated** in Pennsylvania in 1917; reincorporated in Delaware in 1987. **Empl**—4,750.

 Leo Larkin

Lyondell Petrochemical

NYSE Symbol LYO Options on NYSE (Mar-Jun-Sep-Dec) In S&P MidCap 400

Price	Range	P–E Ratio	Dividend	Yield	S&P Ranking	Beta
Oct. 12'93	1993					
19⅜	29½–16¾	NM	0.90	4.6%	NR	NA

Summary

This company is a leading producer of a wide variety of petrochemicals, including ethylene, propylene, methanol, MTBE, aromatics, polyethylene and polypropylene. LYO has a 95% interest in Lyondell-CITGO Refining Co. (formed July 1993) which produces gasoline, heating oil, jet fuel and lubricants. The venture will upgrade its refinery, with CITGO contributing capital in return for a substantial interest in the unit. Earnings will remain depressed for the rest of 1993; the dividend was cut 50% in July 1993.

Current Outlook

Share earnings for 1994 may rise to about $0.50 from the breakeven level expected in 1993.

The quarterly dividend was reduced 50%, to $0.22½ from $0.45, in July 1993.

Petrochemical profits are likely to remain depressed for at least the rest of 1993. Ethylene prices, which declined early in the year, may remain stable in the second half due to lower industry output resulting from temporary plant shutdowns. The increased supply of Venezuelan heavy crude oil will help the refining business; industry refining margins have increased from the very low first quarter levels. The refining venture with CITGO will result in a small minority interest beginning in the second half. Cost reductions and cash conservation measures will be helpful.

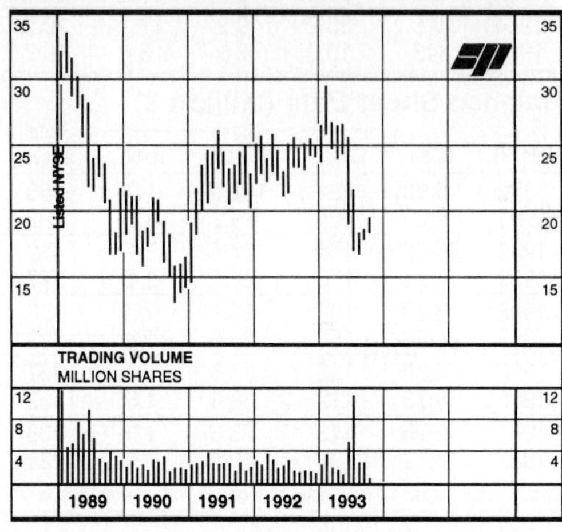

Revenues (Million $)

Quarter:	1993	1992	1991	1990
Mar.	1,064	1,028	1,624	1,488
Jun.	1,080	1,219	1,458	1,403
Sep.		1,335	1,293	1,615
Dec.		1,223	1,354	1,989
		4,805	5,729	6,495

Revenues for the first half of 1993 declined 4.6%, year to year, as lower crude oil resales offset higher refining volumes. On lower petrochemical profits, and despite lower refinery maintenance costs, the net loss increased to $19 million ($0.23 a share) from $4 million ($0.05), before a special credit of $0.27 a share in the 1993 period, versus a charge of $0.12 in the 1992 period, from accounting changes.

Common Share Earnings ($)

Quarter:	1993	1992	1991	1990
Mar.	d0.09	d0.17	1.24	0.98
Jun.	d0.14	0.13	0.86	1.93
Sep.	E0.11	0.15	0.41	0.63
Dec.	E0.12	0.22	0.27	0.91
	ENil	0.32	2.78	4.45

Important Developments

Jul. '93— LYO said that the second quarter loss of $11 million reflected a continuing poor business environment with depressed industry margins in both petrochemicals and Gulf Coast refining. Results were reduced by a $10 million charge, including $6 million for cancellation of a capital project and $2 million related to a workforce reduction. Excluding the charges, there would have been a loss of $1 million ($0.01 a share). Separately, LYO formed a 95%-owned joint venture with CITGO Petroleum Corp., a unit of Petroleos de Venezuela, S.A. (PDVSA), involving LYO's Houston refinery. The venture will significantly expand the heavy crude processing capability of the refinery over the next five years. CITGO will contribute a substantial portion of the estimated $800 million cost of the upgrading project in return for a significant minority interest in the refinery. PDVSA will supply heavy crude oil to the venture.

Next earnings reported expected in late October.

Per Share Data ($)

Yr. End Dec. 31	1992	1991	1990	1989	[1]1988	[1]1987
Tangible Bk. Val.	**d0.08**	1.53	0.48	0.11	2.98	d4.13
Cash Flow	**0.83**	3.29	4.86	4.94	NA	NA
Earnings[3]	**0.32**	2.78	4.45	4.67	6.79	1.05
Dividends	**1.80**	1.75	[2]4.10	1.20	NA	NA
Payout Ratio	**554%**	63%	92%	26%	NA	NA
Prices—High	**25⅞**	26⅛	21½	33½	NA	NA
Low	**21⅛**	14⅝	13⅛	16¾	NA	NA
P/E Ratio—	**80–66**	9–5	5–3	7–4	NA	NA

Data as orig. reptd. **1.** Pro forma. **2.** Incl. 2.50 special divd. **3.** Bef. spec. item(s) of -0.12 in 1992. d-Deficit. E-Estimated NA-Not Available.

Income Data (Million $)

Year Ended Dec. 31	Revs.	Oper. Inc.	% Oper. Inc. of Revs.	Cap. Exp.	Depr. Depl. & Amort.	[1]Int. Exp.	Net Bef. Taxes	Eff. Tax Rate	[3]Net Inc.	% Net Inc. of Revs.	Cash Flow
1992	**4,805**	**121**	**2.5**	**97**	**40**	**79**	**35**	**25.7%**	**[2]26**	**0.5**	**66**
1991	5,729	413	7.2	43	41	74	340	34.7%	222	3.9	263
1990	6,495	634	9.8	145	33	77	537	33.7%	356	5.5	389
1989	5,358	636	11.9	176	21	73	558	33.0%	374	7.0	395
1988	4,696	864	18.4	63	16	26	825	34.2%	543	11.6	559
1987	3,931	275	7.0	29	13	25	205	40.0%	123	3.1	NA
1986	3,010	296	9.8	18	12	30	236	45.8%	128	4.3	NA

Balance Sheet Data (Million $)

Dec. 31	Cash	Curr. Assets	Curr. Liab.	Curr. Ratio	Total Assets	% Ret. on Assets	Long Term Debt	Common Equity	Total Cap.	% LT Debt of Cap.	% Ret. on Equity
1992	**121**	**568**	**345**	**1.6**	**1,215**	**1.9**	**725**	**d6**	**798**	**90.9**	**NM**
1991	307	889	514	1.7	1,479	15.6	710	122	927	76.6	277.5
1990	127	788	550	1.4	1,372	27.0	658	38	773	85.1	NM
1989	245	801	434	1.8	1,267	34.3	714	9	790	90.4	302.8
1988	Nil	609	340	1.8	913	65.3	243	238	538	45.2	291.9
1987	3	493	316	1.6	750	18.3	261	134	395	66.1	NA

Data as orig. reptd.; prior to 1988 data as reptd. in 1988 Annual Report. **1.** Net. **2.** Reflects acctg. change. **3.** Bef. spec. items. NA-Not Available. d-Deficit. NM-Not Meaningful.

Business Summary

Lyondell Petrochemical is an integrated petrochemical and petroleum processor and marketer. The company was formed in 1985 by the combination of Atlantic Richfield Co.'s Channelview, Texas, petrochemical complex and its full conversion Houston Refinery. The Channelview complex and the Houston refinery are linked by pipeline. Contributions by segment in 1992:

	Sales	Profits
Petrochemical	36%	59%
Refined products	64%	41%

The Channelview petrochemical complex consists of two large olefins plants, a methanol plant, a product flexibility unit, and other processing and recovery units. The complex obtains its feedstocks from the Houston refinery and from outside sources. Olefins consists of ethylene (capacity of 3.6 billion pounds per year) used for polyethylene, polyvinyl chloride and polystyrene resins, antifreeze, and detergents; propylene (2.1 billion pounds) for plastics, fibers, and solvents; and butadiene (615 million) for rubber and plastics products. LYO is one of the largest domestic merchant marketer of ethylene and propylene. Methanol (233 million gallons) is used for adhesives, polyester fibers, and as an octane enhancer. The Channelview complex also includes two MTBE units (167 million gallons). LYO manufactures MTBE for ARCO Chemical Co. at one unit, and output from the second plant is used as a gasoline octane enhancer and additive at the Houston refinery.

In February 1990, LYO acquired a low density polyethylene plant (capacity of 140 million pounds a year) and a polypropylene plant (300 million pounds) in Bayport, Texas.

Lyondell-CITGO Refining Co.'s Houston refinery, with operable crude capacity of 265,000 barrels per day, produces gasoline, diesel fuel, heating oil, jet fuels, lubricant oils, chemical feedstocks, aromatics, and industrial products (coke, sulfur, and residual fuel). The company (formed July, 1993) will expand the refinery's heavy crude oil processing capacity to 200,000 barrels a day from the current 130,000 barrels. Aromatics (305 million gallons a year, including those produced at Channelview) include benzene (140 million gallons) used for styrene, fibers and detergents; paraxylene (400 million pounds) for polyester films and fibers; and orthoxylene (270 million pounds) for plasticizers and polyester resins. The refinery has the full conversion capability to process crude oils into a product mix that does not include lower value residual fuels.

Dividend Data

Quarterly dividends were initiated in 1989. A dividend reinvestment plan is available.

Amt. of Divd. $	Date Decl.	Ex-divd. Date	Stock of Record	Payment Date
0.45	Oct. 26	Nov. 6	Nov. 13	Dec. 15'92
0.45	Jan. 25	Feb. 8	Feb. 12	Mar. 15'93
0.45	May 6	May 17	May 21	Jun. 15'93
0.22½	Jul. 23	Aug. 9	Aug. 13	Sep. 15'93

Capitalization

Long Term Debt: $717,000,000 (6/93).

Common Stock: 80,000,000 shs. ($1 par).
Atlantic Richfield owns 49.9%.
Institutions hold about 38%.
Shareholders of record: 3,483.

Office—1221 McKinney Ave., Suite 1600, Houston, TX 77010. **Tel**—(713) 652-7200. **Chrmn**—M. R. Bowlin. **Pres & CEO**—B. G. Gower. **SVP-CFO & Treas**—R. S. Young. **SVP-Secy**—J. R. Pendergraft. **Investor Contact**—David M. Balderston. **Dirs**— M. R. Bowlin, W. T. Butler, A. L. Comstock, T. G. Dallas, B. G. Gower, S. F. Hinchliffe Jr., D. C. Mecum II, W. C. Rusnack, D. F. Smith, P. R. Staley, W. E. Wade. **Transfer Agent & Registrar**—Bank of New York, NYC. **Incorporated** In Delaware in 1985. **Empl**—2,312.

 Richard O'Reilly, CFA

MCN Corp.

NYSE Symbol MCN In S&P MidCap 400

Price	Range	P-E Ratio	Dividend	Yield	S&P Ranking	Beta
Sep. 9'93	1993					
35⅛	35⅝–29	19	1.68	4.8%	NR	NA

Summary

This holding company, through its Michigan Consolidated Gas subsidiary, distributes gas to more than one million customers in the Detroit metropolitan area and various Michigan communities. It is also engaged in data processing, the development of natural gas technologies, and exploration and production. Earnings should benefit in 1993 from higher profits at both utility and nonutility operations. Plans to invest in utility and nonutility projects over the next five years are likely to result in expenditures of more than $1.0 billion, and to lead to strong earnings growth.

Current Outlook

Share earnings for 1993 are estimated at $2.30, up from 1992's $2.11. An increase to $2.45 is projected for 1994.

The $0.42 quarterly dividend may be raised in October 1993.

Utility profits should rise in 1993 on increased gas deliveries, reflecting growth in gas markets served and expansion into new communities. Nonutility profits should benefit from opportunities in gas storage and cogeneration, and higher usage of Saginaw Bay Pipeline. Nonutility operations are expected to perform exceptionally well in the 1993 second half, aided by the signing of computer services contracts and better margins at gas marketing operations. Future results should benefit from increased profits from exploration and production and from gas storage, and greater gas deliveries, assuming normal weather.

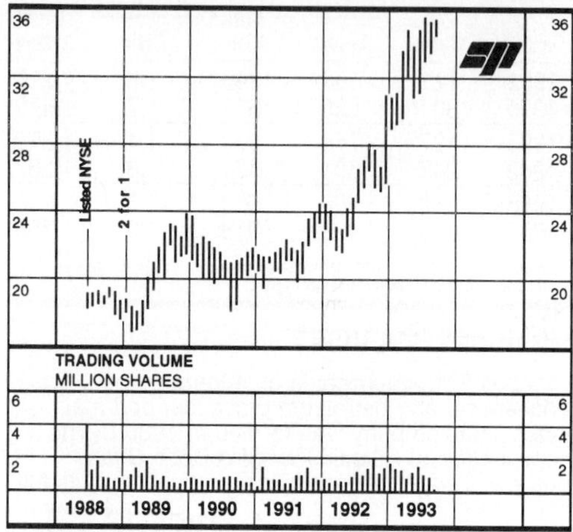

Operating Revenues (Million $)

Quarter:	1993	1992	1991	1990
Mar.	557	535	519	471
Jun.	288	268	211	204
Sep.	---	185	152	145
Dec.	---	450	394	389
	---	1,438	1,276	1,209

Operating revenues in the first half of 1993 rose 5.1%, year to year. After expenses related to refund obligations, and the impact of a sharp increase in spot market gas costs on gas marketing profits, net income declined 4.4%, to $1.92 a share (on 10% more shares), from $2.21.

Common Share Earnings ($)

Quarter:	1993	1992	1991	1990
Mar.	1.85	2.16	2.15	1.85
Jun.	0.07	0.06	d0.01	NM
Sep.	Ed0.50	d0.57	d0.88	d0.89
Dec.	E0.88	0.48	0.19	0.44
	E2.30	2.11	1.42	1.38

Important Developments

Aug. '93— MCN and Destec Energy, Inc. announced plans to jointly build, own and operate a $150 million gas-fueled Michigan cogeneration plant that would sell electricity to Consumers Power Co. and provide steam to a Dow Chemical Co. plant. The facility is expected to begin operations in late 1996.

Jul. '93— MCN said it plans to invest up to $40 million in additional exploration and production projects, primarily in northern Michigan, during 1993. The company plans to drill more than 100 natural gas wells in shallow Devonian shale formations, in partnership with several natural gas producers. The investment is consistent with a five-year strategy to invest $150 million to $300 million in such projects. Separately, MCN said it had signed a number of new computer services clients during 1993, adding more than $12 million in annual revenues.

Next earnings report expected in late October.

Per Share Data ($)

Yr. End Dec. 31	1992	1991	1990	1989	1988	1987	1986	1985	1984	1983
Tangible Bk. Val.	**14.47**	12.67	12.00	12.85	12.06	11.86	11.74	11.62	11.48	11.35
Earnings[1]	**2.11**	1.42	1.38	2.20	2.32	2.28	2.42	2.38	2.22	1.27
Dividends	**1.65**	1.640	1.591	1.575	0.788	NA	NA	NA	NA	NA
Payout Ratio	**78%**	115%	115%	72%	34%	NA	NA	NA	NA	NA
Prices—High	**31**	24½	23¾	23⅞	19½	NA	NA	NA	NA	NA
Low	**21⅝**	19½	18⅛	16⅞	17⅝	NA	NA	NA	NA	NA
P/E Ratio—	**15–10**	17–14	17–13	11–8	9–8	NA	NA	NA	NA	NA

Data as orig. reptd.; prior to 1989, as reptd. in 1988 annual report. Adj. for stk. div. of 100% Jan. 1989. **1.** Bef. spec. item(s) of -0.15 in 1988. NA-Not Available. d-Deficit. NM-Not Meaningful. E-Estimated.

Income Data (Million $)

Year Ended Dec. 31	Oper. Revs.	Depr.	Oper./ Maint.	Oper. Ratio	[1]Fxd. Chgs. Cover.	Int. Exp.	Eff. Tax Rate	[2]Net Inc.	% Return On Revs.	[3]Invest. Capital	Com. Equity
1992	**1,438**	**76.4**	**328**	**93.3%**	**3.16**	**38.9**	**32.7%**	**57.1**	**4.0**	**10.5**	**14.6**
1991	1,276	74.1	323	93.8%	2.32	39.7	34.0%	35.1	2.7	9.4	10.8
1990	1,209	67.2	271	94.4%	2.31	36.4	34.2%	32.3	2.7	9.1	10.8
1989	1,297	64.5	234	94.2%	3.85	24.9	32.2%	49.8	3.8	10.7	18.2
1988	1,281	60.2	225	93.6%	3.44	28.6	30.9%	47.7	3.7	11.4	19.4
1987	1,243	59.0	212	93.6%	3.29	28.5	29.1%	47.0	3.8	11.0	19.3
1986	1,450	57.2	230	95.3%	4.79	23.7	49.3%	49.9	3.4	10.3	20.7
1985	1,846	56.5	224	94.8%	3.31	44.1	53.2%	48.9	2.7	11.8	20.5
1984	2,026	57.7	254	95.7%	2.93	45.4	NA	45.7	2.3	11.1	19.4
1983	1,952	50.2	248	96.5%	2.01	43.1	NA	26.2	1.3	NA	9.6

Balance Sheet Data (Million $)

Dec. 31	Gross Prop.	Capital Expend.	Net Prop.	% Earn. on Net Prop.	Total Invest. Capital	Capitalization LT Debt	% LT Debt	Pfd.	% Pfd.	Com.	% Com.
1992	**2,098**	**171**	**1,115**	**9.0**	**997**	**380**	**46.2**	**9.0**	**1.1**	**434**	**52.7**
1991	1,942	127	1,023	8.0	846	328	47.6	12.0	1.8	349	50.6
1990	1,822	145	965	7.4	779	321	50.3	15.0	2.3	302	47.4
1989	1,684	78	874	8.7	776	307	49.2	18.0	2.9	299	47.9
1988	1,617	72	863	9.6	635	247	48.1	19.5	3.8	247	48.1
1987	1,564	62	854	NA	685	273	50.7	21.0	3.9	244	45.4
1986	1,515	64	854	7.9	718	255	49.1	22.5	4.3	242	46.5
1985	1,463	62	852	11.1	753	301	53.3	24.0	4.3	239	42.4
1984	1,447	58	877	9.8	872	410	58.8	50.3	7.3	237	33.9
1983	1,424	48	886	NA	872	420	59.5	52.0	7.4	234	33.1

Data as orig. reptd.; prior to 1989, as reptd. in 1988 annual report. **1.** Times int. exp. & pfd. divs. covered (pretax basis). **2.** Bef. spec. items. **3.** Based on income bef. interest charges. NA-Not Available.

Business Summary

MCN Corp. is the holding company (formed in 1989) for Michigan Consolidated Gas (MichCon), which distributes natural gas to customers in the Detroit, Grand Rapids, Muskegon and Ann Arbor metropolitan areas and other Michigan communities. Nonutility operations, conducted through MCN Investment, provide gas services, gas storage, gas technology and computer operations services. Contributions (profits in millions) by segment in 1992 were:

	Revs.	Profits
Utility	92%	$110.0
Computer operations services	5%	4.7
Gas services	3%	13.6
Other	---	-2.9

Gas sales and transportation volume in 1992 totaled to 647.6 Bcf (532.9 Bcf in 1991). In 1992, utility customers totaled 1,130,165 (1,124,792). Degree days in 1992 amounted to 6,607 (3.7% warmer than normal), versus 6,092 (10.7% warmer than normal) in 1991. In 1992, the average utility cost of gas purchased per Mcf was $2.74 ($2.69 in 1991).

The company obtains most of its gas supply from gas producers located in Michigan, ANR Pipeline Co. and other intersttate sources and Canadian suppliers. In 1992, MichCon purchased about 7% of its gas supply on the spot market.

Nonutility activities include providing computer processing services through Genix Group, the operation of a gas pipeline in Michigan by Saginaw Bay Pipeline Co. and pursuing energy-related opportunities by Coenergy Trading Co. Other units conduct exploration and production activities, market natural gas technology products for cutting and soldering and are developing storage technologies and combustion applications for natural gas.

Dividend Data

Dividends were initiated in 1988. A dividend reinvestment plan is available. A "poison pill" stock purchase right was adopted in 1989.

Amt. of Divd. $	Date Decl.	Ex-divd. Date	Stock of Record	Payment Date
0.42	Sep. 23	Nov. 6	Nov. 13	Nov. 25'92
0.42	Jan. 27	Feb. 8	Feb. 12	Feb. 25'93
0.42	Apr. 22	May 10	May 14	May 25'93
0.42	Jul. 22	Aug. 9	Aug. 13	Aug. 25'93

Capitalization

Long Term Debt: $376,110,000 (6/93).

Subsid. Red. Cum. Preferred Stock: $5,618,000.

Common Stock: 29,354,659 shs. ($0.01 par). Institutions hold 42%. Shareholders of record: 26,856.

Office—500 Griswold St., Detroit, MI 48226. **Tel**—(313) 256-5500. **Chrmn & Pres**—A. R. Glancy III. **Vice Chrmn & CFO**—W. K. McCrackin. **VP & Secy**—D. L. Schiffer. **Investor Contact**—Sebastian Coppola. **Dirs**—S. E. Ewing, R. Fridholm, A. R. Glancy III, F. M. Hennessey, T. H. Jeffs II, A. L. Johnson, D. A. Johnson, W. K. McCrackin, H. O. Petrauskas, H. F. Sims. **Transfer Agent & Registrar**—NBD Bank, Boston. **Incorporated** in Michigan in 1898. **Empl**—3,968.

 Mark Mattke

MNC Financial

NYSE Symbol MNC Options on ASE (Mar-Jun-Sep-Dec) In S&P MidCap 400

Price	Range	P-E Ratio	Dividend	Yield	S&P Ranking	Beta
Aug. 16'93	1993					
14¾	14⅞–12	9	None	None	C	1.30

Summary

This bank holding company owns Maryland National Bank, the largest bank in that state, smaller banks in Maryland and Washington, D.C., and Virginia Federal S&L. In February 1993, NationsBank Corp., the fourth largest bank holding company in the U.S., decided to exercise its option to acquire the company, in a stock and cash transaction valued at about $1.38 billion. In August, the merger was approved by the Federal Reserve Board and is expected to be completed on October 1, 1993.

Current Outlook

Earnings for the company as currently constituted are estimated at $0.95 a share in 1993, versus the $1.00 recorded in 1992.

The resumption of the dividend, omitted in December 1990, is not expected.

NationsBank, the fourth largest bank in the U.S., feeling that MNC has turned the corner, exercised its option to acquire the company for about $1.38 billion in stock and cash ($15.17 a share). Geographically the merger will extend NB's presence into Maryland, Virginia and the District of Columbia. A key to NB's exercising the option was MNC's ability and willingness to clean up its balance sheet through the sale and charging off of nonperforming assets. Though nonperforming assets have been reduced by 49% in the past year, to $710 million (7.9% of loans and related assets), the drag on performance is still formidable. With problem loans on the decline and with reserves covering 149% of NP loans, the loan loss provision should decline sharply. Excluding the impact of 1992's $51 million in tax benefits, profits should benefit from an eventual pick up in the economy and loan demand, improving credit quality and strong spreads. At June 30, MNC had unrealized gains of $184 million in its investment portfolio which may be harvested.

Review of Operations

Net interest income for the six months ended June 30, 1993, rose 20%, year to year, as a wider net interest margin (3.93% versus 3.26%) outweighed the impact of a marginal decline in earning assets. The provision for loan losses was 57% lower, at $37.7 million. Despite gains in service charges on deposits and other fees, noninterest income declined 24%, largely due to lower investment securities gains ($21.8 million versus $70.9 million). Paced by sharply lower OREO expenses, noninterest income fell 11%. Pretax earnings were $89.80 million versus $4.03 million. After taxes at 25.5%, versus 23.3%, net income was $66.90 million ($0.57 a share), on 26% more shares, compared with $3.09 million (NM).

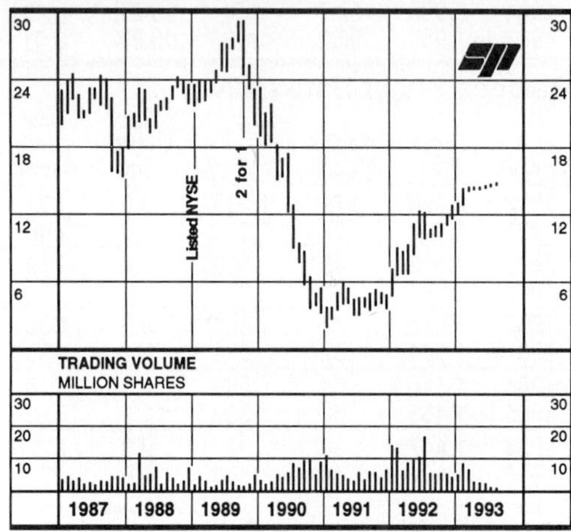

Common Share Earnings ($)

Quarter:	1993	1992	1991	1990
Mar.	0.30	NM	1.75	0.05
Jun.	0.27	NM	d0.96	d0.90
Sep.	E0.18	0.03	d0.70	d2.05
Dec.	E0.20	0.85	d0.96	d2.31
	E0.95	1.00	d0.89	d5.23

Important Developments

Aug. '93— The Federal Reserve Board approved NationsBank's (NB) application to merge with MNC. In February NB exercised its right to acquire MNC. Each MNC holder will receive $15.17 in cash and or stock. Under terms of a purchase-option agreement entered into in July 1992, NB will pay 50.1% of the purchase price for MNC in common stock and 49.9% in cash. MNC holders can elect to receive cash or stock subject to the overall 50.1%-49.9% limit. The transaction is expected to be completed on October 1, 1993.

Per Share Data ($)

Yr. End Dec. 31	1992	1991	1990	1989	1988	[1]1987	1986	[1]1985	1984	1983
Tangible Bk. Val.	**14.74**	10.44	11.37	20.61	18.43	16.55	15.02	13.04	11.68	10.54
Earnings[2]	**1.00**	d0.89	d5.23	3.45	2.93	2.60	2.50	2.06	1.51	1.18
Dividends	**Nil**	Nil	0.870	1.055	0.865	0.715	0.575	0.475	0.370	0.330
Payout Ratio	**Nil**	Nil	NM	31%	30%	28%	23%	23%	25%	28%
Prices—High	**12⅞**	5⅞	23⅜	29⅜	24⅜	24⅝	25½	18⅝	11⅛	8¾
Low	**4¾**	1⅞	3¼	20	18	15⅜	17⅜	10¾	7⅜	5⅞
P/E Ratio—	**13–5**	NM	NM	9–6	8–6	9–6	10–7	9–5	7–5	7–5

Data as orig. reptd. Adj. for stk. div. of 100% Oct. 1989, 100% Mar. 1985. **1.** Reflects merger or acquisition. **2.** Bef. spec. item(s) of +0.21 in 1988. d-Deficit. E-Estimated. NM-Not Meaningful.

Income Data (Million $)

Year Ended Dec. 31	Net Int. Inc.	Tax Equiv. Adj.	Non Int. Inc.	Loan Loss Prov.	% Exp./ Op. Revs.	Net Bef. Taxes	Eff. Tax Rate	[2]Net Inc.	% Net Int. Margin	—% Return On— Assets	Equity
1992	**532**	**Nil**	**320**	**157**	**85.7**	**52**	**NM**	**103**	**3.50**	**0.62**	**9.0**
1991	475	27	710	428	68.7	d107	NM	d70	2.84	NM	NM
1990	819	55	695	975	71.3	d613	NM	d440	3.62	NM	NM
1989	584	43	572	119	60.9	307	30.8%	213	4.14	1.14	17.8
1988	630	46	365	156	58.0	234	27.3%	170	4.31	1.00	16.8
[1]1987	552	63	272	117	57.0	203	26.6%	149	4.47	1.00	17.0
1986	370	61	172	87	55.7	120	23.3%	92	5.71	1.11	18.7
[1]1985	326	43	125	67	57.9	98	25.2%	73	5.90	1.03	17.7
1984	276	28	74	56	60.7	65	24.2%	49	5.98	0.80	14.5
1983	203	24	57	25	66.8	47	18.1%	39	5.55	0.77	12.5

Balance Sheet Data (Million $)

Dec. 31	Total Assets	Earning Assets— Mon. Mkt. Assets	Inv. Secs.	Com'l Loans	Other Loans	% Loan Loss Resv.	—Deposits— Demand	Time	% Loans/ Deposits	Long Term Debt	Common Equity	% Equity To Assets
1992	**16,986**	**712**	**5,226**	**3,190**	**6,424**	**6.34**	**2,277**	**9,373**	**81.5**	**1,350**	**1,322**	**6.44**
1991	17,438	1,092	3,703	4,228	6,239	7.69	1,970	11,923	74.5	742	912	5.58
1990	26,376	2,242	4,480	6,603	10,329	5.62	2,459	18,743	77.5	536	1,076	5.35
1989	20,316	660	2,354	7,284	7,523	2.10	2,145	10,430	113.6	442	1,289	6.41
1988	18,015	726	2,128	6,265	7,025	2.14	2,228	10,081	104.8	500	1,104	5.88
1987	16,658	1,168	2,469	5,497	6,369	1.74	2,221	9,020	102.9	300	942	5.80
1986	9,513	312	1,089	3,210	4,039	1.66	1,863	4,488	112.2	238	542	5.80
1985	7,792	71	840	2,586	3,531	1.53	1,526	3,621	116.8	341	465	5.63
1984	7,286	411	611	2,208	2,812	1.25	1,483	2,890	113.0	213	364	5.26
1983	5,740	826	511	1,712	1,701	1.14	1,179	2,335	95.2	192	328	5.84

Data as orig. reptd. **1.** Reflects merger or acquisition. **2.** Before special item(s) in 1988. d-Deficit. NM-Not Meaningful.

Business Summary

MNC Financial owns Maryland National Bank, the largest bank in that state, Equitable Bancorporation (Baltimore), American Security Bank in Washington, D.C., and Virginia Federal S&L. The company also provides services for smaller corporations, and engages in real estate lending and retail banking. Trust operations are important, with about $35 billion in total trust and custody assets. Nonbank subsidiaries include leasing, mortgage banking, consumer finance and corporate finance. In February 1993 NationsBank Corp., the fourth largest bank holding company in the U.S., decided to exercise it's option under a merger agreement (signed in July 1992) and will acquire MNC for about $1.36 billion in stock and cash. The merger is expected to be completed in the second half of 1993.

During 1992, average earning assets of $15.2 billion (down from 1991's $17.6 billion) were divided: commercial loans and leases 22%, commercial real estate loans 21%, residential mortgages 4%, consumer loans 14%, foreign loans less than 1%, loans held for sale 3%, investment securities 30%, money-market investments 5%. Average sources of funds were: demand deposits 12%, savings and money market accounts 25%, time deposits 38%, short-term borrowings 12%, long-term debt 5%, equity 6% and other 2%.

At year-end 1992, nonperforming assets were $1.11 billion (11.81% of related assets), versus $1.77 billion (16.11%) a year earlier. The reserve for loan losses was 6.73% of loans, versus 7.69%. Net chargeoffs during 1992 of $351 million were 3.70% of average loans, against 3.75% in 1991.

Dividend Data

Common dividends were omitted in December 1990 after having been paid since 1939. The most recent payment on the common was $0.29 on September 28, 1990.

Finances

At December 31, 1992 Tier 1 capital ratio was 10.51% versus 7.02% a year earlier. The total capital ratio was 13.70% versus 10.32%.

Capitalization

Long Term Debt: $1,669,235,000 (6/93).

Preferred Stock: $10,426,200.

Common Stock: 90,787,000 shs. ($2.50 par).
Institutions hold about 33%.
Shareholders of record: 25,415.

Office—100 South Charles St. (PO Box 987), Baltimore, MD 21203. **Tel**—(410) 605-5000. **Chrmn**—A. Lerner. **Pres & CEO**—F. P. Bramble. **VP-Secy**—E. J. Stark. **VP & Investor Contact**—Charles L. Davis. **Dirs**—B. B. Anderson, F. P. Bramble, J. C. Eanes Jr., C. H. Foelber, H. G. Hathaway, A. L. Holton, Jr., R. E. Hug, W. L. Jews, J. S. Keelty, P. X. Kelley, F. X. Knott, A. Lerner, R. L. Leatherwood, F. P. Lucier, G. V. McGowan, F. O. Mitchell, II, J. J. Oliver, Jr., G. G. Radcliffe, S. J. Trachtenberg, O. S. Travers Jr. **Transfer Agent & Registrar**—Security Trust Co., Baltimore. **Incorporated** in Maryland in 1968; bank chartered in 1933. **Empl**—12,000.

 Richard M. Levine, CFA

Mac Frugal's Bargains

NYSE Symbol MFI Options on Pacific (Jan-Apr-Jul-Oct) In S&P MidCap 400

Price	Range	P-E Ratio	Dividend	Yield	S&P Ranking	Beta
Sep. 3'93	1993					
14⅞	20⅛–13⅛	40	None	None	B	1.18

Summary

This retailer operates more than 220 stores, primarily in California and Texas, specializing in the sale of new "close-out" merchandise. Following a sharp drop in 1992-3, earnings were flat in the first half of 1993-4, reflecting lower same-store sales in the second quarter and narrower gross margins. Profitability is expected to rebound in the second half, aided by an ongoing expansion program and improving economic conditions.

Current Outlook

Earnings for the fiscal year ending January 30, 1994, are estimated at $1.35 a share, up from $0.37 in 1992-3. An increase to $1.55 is projected for 1994-5.

Payment of cash dividends is not expected.

Sales are expected to rise about 10% in 1993-4, reflecting modest same-store sales growth and 36 additional units in operation. Gross margins will narrow, as the company continues to shift its merchandise mix to higher-turnover but less-profitable brandname merchandise. The greater volume, combined with well-controlled warehouse and administrative costs, should boost operating profits. Lower interest expense should help to offset a higher effective tax rate. A selective share buyback plan should help share earnings. Further expansion and an improving economy, particularly in California, should boost profits in 1994-5.

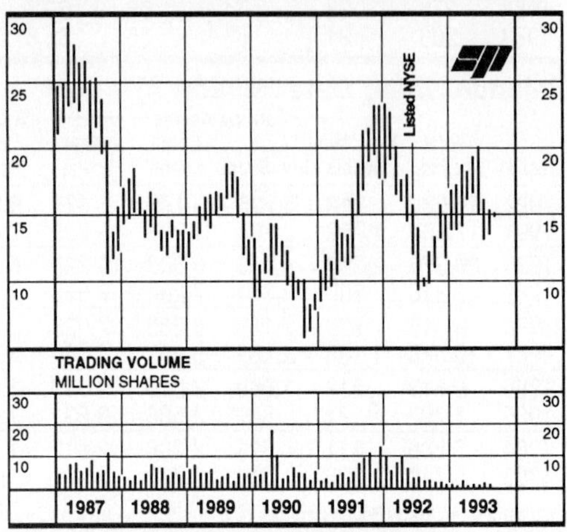

Net Sales (Million $)

13 Weeks:	1993–94	1992–93	1991–92	1990–91
Apr.	127	114	110	119
Jul.	116	109	116	113
Oct.		120	127	105
Jan.		197	189	192
		540	543	529

Sales in the 26 weeks ended August 1, 1993, increased 8.9%, year to year; more stores in operation outweighed a 1.1% decline in same-store sales. Gross margins narrowed, reflecting a planned shift to less profitable brand-name merchandise, and with a 6.2% rise in operating expenses, operating income dropped 5.3%. Interest expense fell 26%. After taxes at 40.0% versus 38.5%, net income was down 2.3%. Share earnings, on 2.4% fewer shares, were flat at $0.27.

Common Share Earnings ($)

13 Weeks:	1993–94	1992–93	1991–92	1990–91
Apr.	0.20	0.18	0.16	0.17
Jul.	0.07	0.09	0.15	d0.27
Oct.	E0.20	d0.66	0.14	0.07
Jan.	E0.88	0.78	0.67	0.60
	E1.35	0.37	1.12	[1]0.52

Important Developments

Sep. '93— MFI said sales in the 30 weeks ended August 29, 1993, gained 9.4%, year to year; comparable-store sales were down 1.1%. Earlier, in August, the company said it was on course to open 36 new stores and 150 temporary Christmas stores in 1993-4.

Next earnings report expected in late November.

Per Share Data ($)

Yr. End Jan. 31[2]	1993	1992	1991	1990	1989	1988	1987	1986	1985	1984
Tangible Bk. Val.	**7.58**	7.38	6.24	6.14	5.27	4.93	3.85	2.84	1.80	2.91
Cash Flow	**0.95**	1.61	0.92	1.20	1.47	1.32	1.10	1.13	0.88	0.82
Earnings	**0.37**	1.12	0.52	0.87	1.24	1.20	1.01	1.04	0.83	0.78
Dividends	**Nil**	Nil	Nil	Nil	Nil	Nil	Nil	Nil	Nil	Nil
Payout Ratio	**Nil**	Nil	Nil	Nil	Nil	Nil	Nil	Nil	Nil	Nil
Calendar Years	**1992**	1991	1990	1989	1988	1987	1986	1985	1984	1983
Prices—High	**23⅜**	23¼	14⅜	18⅞	18½	29½	30⅜	22⅛	16⅛	16⅞
Low	**9⅜**	8½	5¾	11¼	11⅝	10⅝	17⅝	12⅜	9½	11⅛
P/E Ratio—	**63–25**	21–8	28–11	22–13	15–9	25–9	30–17	21–12	19–12	22–14

Data as orig. reptd. Adj. for stk. div. of 50% Jun. 1986. **1.** Sum of quarters does not equal full-year amount, due to change in shs. **2.** Prior to 1991, yrs. ended Dec. 31 of preceding cal. yr. d-Deficit. E-Estimated.

Income Data (Million $)

Year Ended Jan. 31[1]	Revs.	Oper. Inc.	% Oper. Inc. of Revs.	Cap. Exp.	Depr.	Int. Exp.	Net Bef. Taxes	Eff. Tax Rate	Net Inc.	% Net Inc. of Revs.	Cash Flow
1993	**540**	**78.2**	**14.5**	**15.3**	**17.3**	**8.1**	**17.4**	**34.8%**	**11.3**	**2.1**	**28.6**
1992	543	78.4	14.4	9.1	15.2	11.7	54.9	37.7%	34.2	6.3	49.4
1991	529	69.8	13.2	51.8	13.5	12.8	27.7	37.7%	17.2	3.3	30.8
1990	475	67.4	14.2	62.8	12.0	6.2	50.9	39.3%	30.9	6.5	42.8
1989	402	86.4	21.5	49.7	8.7	1.3	77.7	39.7%	46.9	11.7	55.6
1988	362	90.5	25.0	31.5	4.8	0.6	86.6	45.4%	47.3	13.1	52.1
1987	303	84.5	27.9	9.6	3.9	0.1	81.1	51.0%	39.8	13.1	43.7
1986	278	87.0	31.3	9.8	3.4	1.5	82.5	50.2%	41.1	14.8	44.5
1985	232	71.3	30.7	13.1	2.2	2.3	72.3	49.5%	36.5	15.7	38.7
1984	221	68.9	31.2	20.4	1.6	0.2	73.7	50.5%	36.5	16.5	38.0

Balance Sheet Data (Million $)

Jan. 31[1]	Cash	Curr. Assets	Curr. Liab.	Curr. Ratio	Total Assets	% Ret. on Assets	Long Term Debt	Common Equity	Total Cap.	% LT Debt of Cap.	% Ret. on Equity
1993	**21.8**	**188**	**81.7**	**2.3**	**372**	**3.0**	**54.5**	**224**	**290**	**18.8**	**5.1**
1992	41.5	183	78.3	2.3	397	9.2	81.6	226	319	25.6	16.4
1991	18.3	130	75.7	1.7	344	5.7	67.5	190	268	25.2	9.1
1990	6.5	124	60.9	2.0	306	10.9	13.5	221	244	5.5	15.0
1989	19.0	130	56.1	2.3	262	19.5	8.8	190	205	4.3	25.6
1988	53.7	148	40.3	3.7	238	22.3	1.3	192	197	0.7	27.7
1987	58.8	125	30.8	4.1	188	24.0	1.4	152	157	0.9	30.0
1986	37.0	86	28.2	3.0	143	31.6	1.5	112	115	1.3	44.8
1985	22.3	65	22.8	2.8	116	28.4	21.6	71	93	23.2	39.3
1984	88.4	127	29.3	4.4	168	25.0	1.7	136	138	1.3	31.0

Data as orig. reptd. 1. Prior to 1991, yrs. ended Dec. 31 of preceding cal. yr.

Business Summary

This company (formerly Pic 'N' Save Corp.) operates a chain of self-service, cash-and-carry retail stores, under the names Pic 'N' Save and Mac Frugal's Bargains - Close-outs. The stores specialize in the sale of new "close-out" merchandise. At January 31, 1993, the company was operating 205 stores in 12 states, principally in California (109), Texas (36), Arizona (11) and Florida (10). MFI also operates temporary retail locations during the holiday season featuring seasonal merchandise.

"Close-out" merchandise is first-quality merchandise—much of it carrying nationally recognized brandnames—that becomes available at prices less than initial wholesale cost for a variety of reasons, including the inability of suppliers to sell product through normal distribution channels, the discontinuance of merchandise due to a change in style, color, shape or packaging, or the termination of a business by a manufacturer or wholesaler.

The stores offer, on a self-service basis, a wide selection of merchandise, including apparel and accessories, notions, novelties, toys, games, stationery, greeting cards, books, candles, luggage, artificial flowers, beauty aids, candy, snacks, beverages, housewares, domestics, Christmas theme items and giftwares. Merchandise is typically sold at 40% to 70% below regular retail prices.

MFI purchases from more than 2,000 suppliers who can distribute their close-out merchandise through the company's stores without conflict with their normal channels of distribution.

Dividend Data

No cash dividends have been paid. A "poison pill" stock purchase right, issued in March 1988, was redeemed in August 1990.

Finances

During 1992-3, the company repurchased 831,500 of its common shares at an average price of $10.38 per share, pursuant to an August 1992 authorization to buy up to 3,000,000 shares. MFI also acquired 250,000 shares at $21.50 each in a private transaction.

During the 1992-3 third quarter, MFI recorded a $36.6 million charge to better reflect the fair market value of its New Orleans distribution center. The charge stemmed from the company's decision to concentrate future expansion in western markets. The warehouse was servicing 56 MFI stores in the East. In May 1993, the company entered into a letter of intent for the sale/leaseback of the center.

The company's expansion plans call for the opening of 36 stores in each of 1993-4 and 1994-5.

Capitalization

Long Term Debt: $45,306,000 (7/93).

Common Stock: 29,615,727 shs. ($0.02778 par).
Institutions hold 81%.
Shareholders: 1,258 of record (4/23/93).

Office—2430 East Del Amo Blvd., Dominguez, CA 90220-6306. **Tel**—(310) 537-9220. **Chrmn**—P. S. Willmott. **Pres & CEO**—L. S. Williams. **EVP, CFO & Investor Contact**—Philip L. Carter. **Dirs**—D. H. Batchelder, A. Luiso, B. E. Karatz, R. P. Spogli. B. M. Thomas, L. S. Williams, P. S. Willmott, J. J. Zehentbauer. **Transfer Agent & Registrar**—Bank of New York, NYC. **Incorporated** in Delaware in 1971. **Empl**—6,050.

 John D. Coyle, CFA

Magma Power

NASDAQ Symbol MGMA (Incl. in Nat'l Market) In S&P MidCap 400

Price	Range	P-E Ratio	Dividend	Yield	S&P Ranking	Beta
Oct. 5'93	1993					
38¾	41½–29¾	21	None	None	B	−0.23

Summary

Magma has geothermal leaseholds in California and Nevada and owns interests in and manages the operation of four geothermal power plants that generate electricity for sale to Southern California Edison. It also receives royalties and management service fees from the plants and properties. The early 1993 acquisition of certain geothermal assets from Unocal Corp. boosted power generating capacity by about 50%, and has enhanced the company's competitive position and long-term earnings prospects.

Current Outlook

Share earnings for 1993 are estimated at $2.10, up from 1992's $1.59. An increase to $2.60 is projected for 1994.

Dividends are not expected to be initiated in the foreseeable future.

For 1993, contractually guaranteed price increases for energy from the geothermal plants and greater electricity generation (largely reflecting a 50% boost in capacity from the acquisition of geothermal assets) should lead to sharply higher revenues from the sale of electricity (three power plants acquired from Unocal generated about $70 million in revenues for Unocal in 1992). Royalty income from providing geothermal resources to power plants should rise. Earnings for 1994 will likely benefit from greater sales of electricity, partly reflecting full year inclusion of the assets acquired from Unocal, and higher energy payments; an improved cash flow should lead to higher interest income. The acquisition of Unocal assets enhances Magma's competitive position to attract additional contracts with electric utilities in southern California over the next few years.

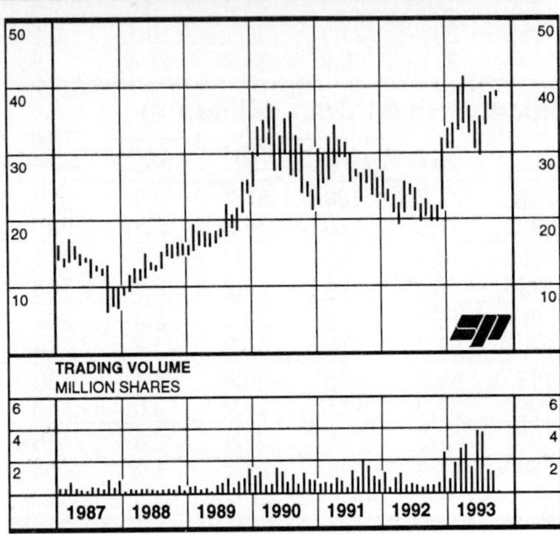

Total Revenues (Million $)

Quarter:	1993	1992	1991	1990
Mar.	22.5	21.5	18.6	19.0
Jun.	45.0	24.2	23.5	17.9
Sep.	---	31.6	29.2	26.7
Dec.	---	31.7	23.5	22.0
	---	109.0	94.9	85.6

Total revenues for the six months ended June 30, 1993, rose 48%, year to year, reflecting the inclusion of the three power plants acquired from Unocal Corp, and higher SO4 contract energy payments at the company's four other power plants. Benefiting from efficiency improvements, net income was up 55%, to $0.79 a share from $0.54 (excluding a credit of $0.77 from an accounting change).

Common Share Earnings ($)

Quarter:	1993	1992	1991	1990
Mar.	0.23	0.25	0.20	0.21
Jun.	0.56	0.32	0.32	0.22
Sep.	E0.71	0.57	0.55	0.50
Dec.	E0.60	0.53	0.37	0.37
	E2.10	1.59	1.44	1.32

Important Developments

Sep. '93— Magma agreed with the Phillippine National Oil Co. to build and operate a 231 mw geothermal power plant. The first phase of the power plant consisting of 77 mw was scheduled for startup in July 1996. In June, in a secondary offering, 4.0 million of the company's common shares were sold at $32 each. Of the total, 3,635,000 shares were sold by Dow Chemical Co. and 365,000 shares by J.P. Morgan & Co. Dow's stake in Magma was cut from 34% to 18%.

Next earnings report expected in late October.

Per Share Data ($)

Yr. End Dec. 31	1992	1991	1990	1989	1988	1987	1986	1985	1984	1983
Tangible Bk. Val.	**11.89**	9.48	7.98	6.35	5.29	5.16	3.45	3.05	2.35	0.37
Cash Flow	**2.11**	1.93	1.80	1.37	0.57	0.36	0.05	0.30	d0.16	d0.36
Earnings[1]	**1.59**	1.44	1.32	1.01	0.43	0.20	d0.13	0.23	d0.20	d0.40
Dividends	**Nil**	Nil	Nil	Nil	Nil	Nil	Nil	Nil	Nil	Nil
Payout Ratio	**Nil**	Nil	Nil	Nil	Nil	Nil	Nil	Nil	Nil	Nil
Prices—High	**32¼**	34¼	37½	26	16¾	17¼	22¼	18⅛	9¼	9
Low	**19¼**	22¼	21½	14⅞	8⅞	6¼	12⅜	6¾	6⅞	5½
P/E Ratio—	**20–12**	24–15	28–16	26–15	39–21	86–31	NM	79–29	NM	NM

Data as orig. reptd. 1. Bef. spec. items of +0.78 in 1992, +0.07 in 1987, +0.04 in 1986, +0.20 in 1985. E-Estimated. d-Deficit. NM-Not Meaningful.

Magma Power Company

Income Data (Million $)

Year Ended Dec. 31	Revs.	Oper. Inc.	% Oper. Inc. of Revs.	Cap. Exp.	Depr.	Int. Exp.	Net Bef. Taxes	Eff. Tax Rate	[1]Net Inc.	% Net Inc. of Revs.	Cash Flow
1992	**100.0**	**59.8**	**59.6**	**11.7**	**11.9**	**6.83**	**49.7**	**26.8%**	**36.4**	**36.2**	**48.3**
1991	84.1	50.6	60.2	15.7	11.7	8.53	41.2	17.6%	33.9	40.3	45.6
1990	76.9	48.4	63.0	7.9	11.0	9.38	36.7	17.8%	30.2	39.2	41.2
1989	57.4	35.6	62.0	43.2	7.8	8.99	26.9	17.1%	22.3	38.8	30.1
1988	20.8	9.2	44.2	98.6	3.1	4.19	11.3	17.5%	9.3	44.5	12.3
1987	17.4	7.7	44.1	62.5	3.1	0.30	6.5	35.3%	4.0	23.1	7.1
1986	12.8	1.4	10.9	10.4	2.9	0.15	d1.4	NM	d2.1	NM	0.8
1985	3.6	d2.0	NM	42.9	1.0	2.17	7.9	53.0%	3.7	101.8	4.7
1984	2.3	d2.3	NM	26.2	0.5	0.84	d2.6	NM	d2.6	NM	d2.2
1983	1.2	d2.7	NM	1.5	0.4	1.22	d4.0	NM	d4.0	NM	d3.6

Balance Sheet Data (Million $)

Dec. 31	Cash	Curr. Assets	Curr. Liab.	Ratio	Total Assets	% Ret. on Assets	Long Term Debt	Common Equity	Total Cap.	% LT Debt of Cap.	% Ret. on Equity
1992	**60.3**	**93**	**18.7**	**5.0**	**397**	**9.7**	**85.8**	**282**	**376**	**22.8**	**14.3**
1991	84.0	110	17.6	6.2	354	9.9	88.6	227	335	26.5	15.7
1990	66.3	91	12.9	7.0	325	9.8	97.2	193	310	31.3	17.3
1989	69.0	83	13.1	6.4	283	8.8	96.3	150	268	36.0	16.1
1988	52.8	58	11.5	5.1	224	4.9	67.9	127	212	32.0	7.7
1987	22.2	27	12.3	2.2	146	3.6	25.5	105	132	19.3	4.5
1986	2.8	4	3.1	1.3	63	NM	Nil	58	59	Nil	NM
1985	4.4	7	3.0	2.4	62	6.3	Nil	49	49	Nil	8.6
1984	1.1	2	1.5	1.1	53	NM	0.5	36	36	1.5	NM
1983	Nil	1	17.6	NM	22	NM	0.4	4	4	10.5	NM

Data as orig. reptd. **1.** Bef. spec. items. d-Deficit. NM-Not Meaningful.

Business Summary

Magma Power Company is engaged in the acquisition, exploration and development of geothermal resources and the leasing, sale and use of such resources for the generation of electricity. In March 1993, the company acquired certain geothermal assets from Unocal Corp. for $225 million; the acquisition boosted generating capacity by 50%. Revenues in recent years were derived as follows:

	1992	1991
Electricity sales	66%	70%
Royalties	21%	14%
Interest & other income	8%	11%
Management services	5%	5%

Geothermal energy is derived from the natural heat of the earth. If a geothermal source has sufficient heat, fluids and pressure, it may be capable of producing steam to drive a turbine, thereby generating electricity without consuming coal, oil, natural gas or nuclear fuel.

Magma operates and holds 50% interests in four plants located in California's Imperial Valley. The Vulcan Plant has a nameplate capacity of 34 megawatts (mw) and a contract capacity of 29.5 mw. The Del Ranch and Elmore geothermal power plants and the Leathers facility each have a nameplate capacity of 38 mw and contract capacity of 34 mw. Mission Energy, an affiliate of Southern California Edison (SCE), owns the remaining 50% interest in each of the plants. In March 1993, three additional plants were acquired from Unocal Corp. All seven plants sell all of their electricity to SCE. Sales by six plants are made under separate 30-year Standard Offer No. 4 (SO4) Power Purchase agreements; the seventh plant makes sales under a negotiated contract. Each agreement sets an annually escalating rate per kilowatt-hour (kwh) to be paid by SCE for the first 10 years. In 1993, payments by SCE under the SO4 contracts will average $0.101 per kwh, up from $0.083 in 1992. In addition, SCE will pay a fixed "capacity payment" based on each plant's contract capacity. The Unocal transaction included a contract option to supply 20 mw of power to SCE.

The company receives royalties for providing geothermal resources to the Del Ranch, Elmore and Leathers plants. It also receives royalty payments from three other geothermal power plants, and owns geothermal leasehold and fee interests in 208,841 acres of land in California and Nevada.

Dividend Data

No cash dividends have been paid.

Capitalization

Loans Payable: $79,829,000 (6/93).

Common Stock: 23,111,380 shs. ($0.10 par).
Dow Chemical owns 18%.
Institutions hold 37%.
Shareholders: 2,378 of record (2/93).

Office—4365 Executive Dr., Suite 900, San Diego, CA 92121. **Tel**—(619) 622-7800. **Chrmn & CEO**—P. M. Pankratz. **Pres**—R. W. Boeker. **VP, Treas & Investor Contact**—Wallace C. Dieckmann. **EVP & Secy**—J. R. Peele. **Dirs**—R. W. Boeker, T. C. Hinrichs, A. W. Hoch, A. L. Johnson, R. Kesseler, W. R. Knee, B. C. McCabe, Jr., P. M. Pankratz, B. Peterson, J. P. Reinhard, J. D. Shepard. **Transfer Agent & Registrar**—Chemical Trust Co. of California, LA. **Incorporated** in Nevada in 1981. **Empl**—238.

 Mark Mattke

MagneTek, Inc.

NYSE Symbol MAG Options on Pacific (Mar-Jun-Sep-Dec) In S&P MidCap 400

Price	Range	P-E Ratio	Dividend	Yield	S&P Ranking	Beta
Aug. 26'93	1992–3					
14¼	25½–13½	13	None	None	B–	NA

Summary

MagneTek manufactures a broad range of electrical equipment products, including lighting ballasts, transformers, motors, generators, drives and controls, and provides repair and rebuilding services to utilities and industrial customers. Sales for fiscal 1993 were up nicely, reflecting a 35% increase in lighting and electronic products, but earnings declined, penalized by a weak fourth quarter.

Business Summary

MagneTek designs, manufactures and markets a broad range of electrical, electronic and industrial components and products, and offers related service and repair support. Contributions by business segment in fiscal 1992 were:

	Sales	Profits
Ballasts and transformers....	53%	68%
Motors and controls............	47%	32%

The Ballasts and transformers segment includes a broad range of equipment in two general product groups: lighting products and transformer products.

Lighting products consist of magnetic fluorescent ballasts, high intensity discharge (HID) ballasts and specialty lines. Transformer products are comprised of electronic power supplies and cast coil distribution transformers. Other products include dry type distribution transformers and various component and specialty transformers.

MagneTek is an industry leader in market share in magnetic fluorescent and HID ballasts. Ballasts are transformers that serve to regulate or alter electrical current for use in a wide range of fluorescent and other lighting applications.

The Motors and controls segment manufactures motors and generators, and systems and controls. Motors and generators include fractional, integral, and specialty industrial electric motors and medium to large output generators. Systems and controls consist of electronic adjustable speed drives and systems, control products, and power conversion systems. The Service group remanufactures and repairs large motors, generators, and transformers for utilities and industrial manufacturers.

In November 1992, MagneTek acquired the INET unit of Teledyne Inc. Terms were not disclosed. INET, which makes electrical and electronic power products and engineers ground support systems for airports, has annual revenues of $45 million.

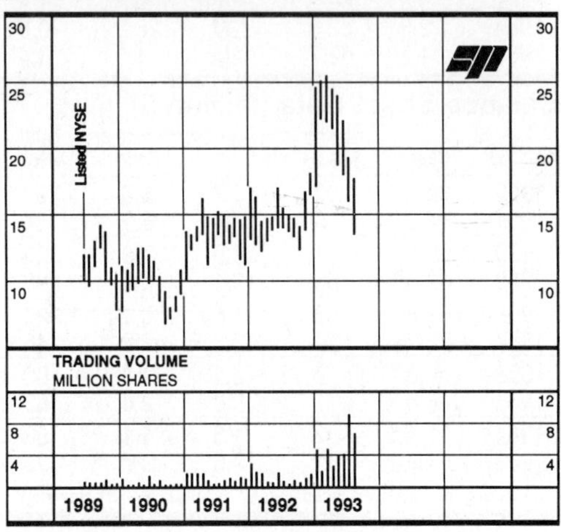

Important Developments

Aug. '93— The 23% sales increase for fiscal 1993 reflected a 35% increase in the lighting and electronic products segment and a 14% rise in the sales of motors, generators and drives. Two acquisitions contributed to the higher revenues.

Mar. '93— Three of MagneTek's shareholders—Magtek Partners, Champlain Associates and Winston Capital Partners—sold publicly 7,000,000 MAG shares at $24 each. Upon completion of the offering, assuming underwriters exercise an overallotment option covering up to 486,649 additional shares, the three stockholders would not own any of the company's shares.

Next earnings report expected in late October.

Per Share Data ($)

Yr. End Jun. 30[1]	1993	1992	[2,3]1991	[3]1990	[3]1989	1988	1987	1986	1985	[4]1984
Tangible Bk. Val.	**NA**	8.24	6.89	5.77	4.34	1.58	0.57	0.39	0.10	NA
Cash Flow	**NA**	2.92	2.98	2.72	2.56	2.50	1.29	0.88	0.33	NA
Earnings[5]	**1.09**	1.22	1.47	1.40	0.97	[6]0.93	0.12	0.27	d0.17	d0.29
Dividends	**Nil**	Nil	Nil	Nil	Nil	Nil	Nil	Nil	Nil	Nil
Payout Ratio	**Nil**	Nil	Nil	Nil	Nil	Nil	Nil	Nil	Nil	Nil
Prices[7]—High	**25½**	18⅛	16¼	12½	14¼	NA	NA	NA	NA	NA
Low	**13½**	12¼	10	6¾	7⅞	NA	NA	NA	NA	NA
P/E Ratio—	**23–12**	15–10	11–7	9–5	15–8	NA	NA	NA	NA	NA

Data as orig. reptd.; prior to 1989 data as reptd. in prospectus dated Jun. 13, 1989. **1.** Prior to 1985 yr. ended Jul. 31. **2.** Refl. accounting change. **3.** Reflects merger or acquisition. **4.** Pro forma. **5.** Bef. spec. items of -1.96 in 1993, -0.30 in 1992, -0.13 in 1989, +0.08 in 1986. **6.** Pro forma to reflect Jun. 1989 stk. offering sh. earns. were 1.00 (bef. 0.06 spec. charge). **7.** Cal. yr. NA-Not Available. d-Deficit.

Income Data (Million $)

Year Ended Jun. 30	Revs.	Oper. Inc.	% Oper. Inc. of Revs.	Cap. Exp.	Depr.	Int. Exp.	Net Bef. Taxes	Eff. Tax Rate	[3]Net Inc.	% Net Inc. of Revs.	Cash Flow
[1,2]1992	**1,230**	**140**	**11.4**	**35.1**	**40.7**	**44.9**	**52.4**	**44.1%**	**29.3**	**2.4**	**70.0**
[1]1991	1,134	145	12.8	28.8	35.7	43.8	61.8	44.0%	34.6	3.1	70.3
[1]1990	1,055	133	12.6	33.3	31.0	45.6	56.3	41.0%	33.2	3.1	63.9
[1]1989	962	114	11.8	25.6	29.4	49.8	34.7	40.3%	20.7	2.2	47.2
[1]1988	910	107	11.8	25.3	27.9	42.9	35.4	44.9%	19.5	2.1	44.5
[1]1987	609	67	10.9	13.9	18.2	29.8	10.8	54.8%	4.9	0.8	20.1
[1]1986	273	31	11.2	4.5	6.5	14.5	8.9	50.4%	4.4	1.6	9.4
1985	195	17	8.6	2.8	5.0	12.0	d0.5	NM	d0.5	NM	2.6

Balance Sheet Data (Million $)

Jun. 30	Cash	Curr. Assets	Curr. Liab.	Ratio	Total Assets	% Ret. on Assets	Long Term Debt	Common Equity	Total Cap.	% LT Debt of Cap.	% Ret. on Equity
1992	**2.03**	**509**	**276**	**1.8**	**917**	**3.4**	**433**	**196**	**641**	**67.6**	**16.2**
1991	7.47	422	244	1.7	785	4.6	365	159	541	67.4	23.8
1990	1.66	391	184	2.1	712	4.9	379	132	528	71.8	28.4
1989	5.49	375	154	2.4	647	3.0	366	99	492	74.4	26.4
1988	3.50	327	168	1.9	580	3.7	357	28	412	86.7	88.1
1987	1.40	276	145	1.9	483	1.4	308	10	339	90.8	23.4
1986	6.42	161	62	2.6	238	1.7	147	7	176	83.7	67.9
1985	1.66	85	34	2.5	131	NA	89	1	96	92.2	NA

Data as orig. reptd.; prior to 1989 data as reptd. in prospectus dated Jun. 13, 1989. **1.** Reflects merger or acquisition. **2.** Reflects accounting change. **3.** Bef. spec. items. d-Deficit. NM-Not Meaningful. NA-Not Available.

Net Sales (Million $)

Quarter:	1992–93	1991–92	1990–91	1989–90
Sep.	336	294	265	238
Dec.	372	284	276	250
Mar.	386	309	293	286
Jun.	419	343	300	281
	1,512	1,230	1,134	1,055

Based on a preliminary report, sales for the fiscal year ended June 30, 1993, advanced 23% from those of fiscal 1992. Margins narrowed sharply, however, particularly in the fourth quarter which was impacted by adverse changes on several fixed-price military contracts, slower sales of large custom motors, and costs relating to the expansion of the electronic ballast business. Net income fell 7.7%, to $1.09 a share ($1.03 fully diluted) on 3.9% more shares, from $1.22 ($1.15). Results exclude charges of $1.96 a share (no dilution) and $0.18 a share ($0.15) in the respective years from the cumulative effects of the adoption of two new accounting standards. Results for fiscal 1992 also exclude an extraordinary loss of $0.12 a share ($0.10) from early retirement of debt.

Common Share Earnings ($)

Quarter:	1992–93	1991–92	1990–91	1989–90
Sep.	0.28	0.28	0.27	0.21
Dec.	0.34	0.28	0.31	0.25
Mar.	0.35	0.27	0.47	0.47
Jun.	0.12	0.38	0.41	0.47
	1.09	1.22	1.47	1.40

Dividend Data

MAG has said that it does not intend to pay cash dividends, but would retain earnings for reinvestment in its business.

Finances

In March 1992, the company acquired May & Christe GmbH for about $42.4 million, comprised of cash, a deferred payment and the assumption of certain long-term debt.

In December 1991, MAG sold $125 million of 10¾% senior subordinated debentures due 1998. Proceeds were used in part to redeem $110 million of 11⅞% first senior subordinated notes at 101.5% of principal amount, with the remainder used to repay borrowings under a revolving credit agreement.

In September 1991, the company sold $75 million of 8% subordinated notes due 2001, convertible into common at $16 a share. Proceeds were used to repay bank debt.

Capitalization

Long Term Debt: $509,431,000 (3/93); incl. $75 million of 8% sub. notes due 2001, conv. into com. at $16 a sh.

Common Stock: 24,104,646 shs. ($0.01 par). Direct accounts holding the stock: 400. Institutions hold about 81%.

Office—11150 Santa Monica Blvd., 15th Floor, Los Angeles, CA 90025. **Tel**—(310) 473-6681. **Chrmn**—A. G. Galef. **Pres & CEO**—F. Perna, Jr. **SVP & CFO**—D. P. Reiland. **VP & Secy**—S. A. Miley. **VP & Treas**—J. P. Colling, Jr. **VP & Investor Contact**—Robert W. Murray. **Dirs**—C. H. Dean, Jr., A. G. Galef, P. K. Kofmehl. C. Kotchian, C. Nevin, F. Perna, Jr. **Transfer Agent & Registrar**—Bank of New York, NYC. **Incorporated** in Delaware in 1984. **Empl**—15,500.

 Samuel A. Dedio

MAPCO Inc.

NYSE Symbol MDA Options on Pacific (Jan-Apr-Jul-Oct) In S&P MidCap 400

Price	Range	P–E Ratio	Dividend	Yield	S&P Ranking	Beta
Aug. 25'93	1993					
63⅛	63⅛–48¾	18	1.00	1.6%	B+	0.57

Summary

This company engages in a broad range of energy-related activities, including refining, gas liquids transmission, coal production, propane distribution, and the operation of retail gasoline outlets in 10 states. MDA made a $20.6 million charge ($0.69 a share) against 1992's fourth quarter net income, in part reflecting costs related to a pipeline explosion in 1992. Operating profits should advance in 1993, reflecting expansion of the Seminole Pipeline and strong refining margins.

Current Outlook

Earnings for 1993 are projected at $4.60 a share, versus the $3.37 (after a $0.69 nonrecurring charge) reported for 1992. Profits could reach $5.30 a share in 1994.

Dividends, currently at $0.25 quarterly, could be lifted moderately by 1993 year-end.

Pipeline profits should advance in 1993, reflecting expansion of the Seminole line, increased movement of gas liquids from Canada to Texas Gulf Coast petrochemical firms, and the absence of costs related to 1992's explosion near Seminole's gas storage facility. Coal profits should improve as increased productivity at Mettiki and absence of nonrecurring charges outweigh lower prices and weak export sales. Refining profits should advance, reflecting wider margins, the absence of operating problems at MDA's Memphis facility, and higher returns from convenience items. Propane volumes will benefit from acquisitions of propane distributors and colder weather. Aiding earnings comparisons will be lower interest costs and the absence of 1992's debt prepayment penalties.

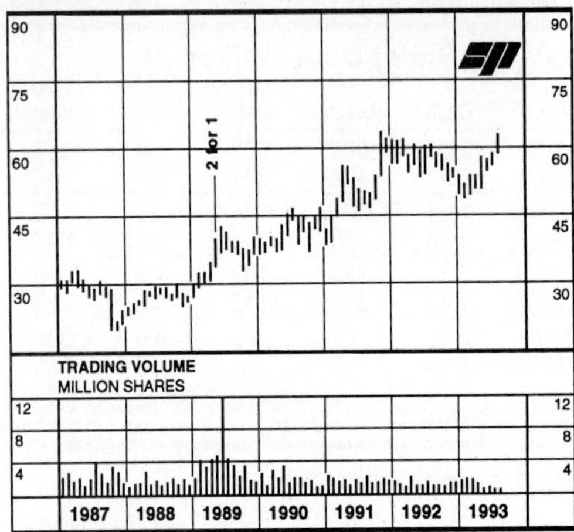

Sales & Oper. Revenues (Million $)

Quarter:	1993	1992	1991	1990
Mar.	692	669	702	636
Jun.	663	675	649	607
Sep.	---	704	699	702
Dec.	---	739	733	878
	---	2,787	2,783	2,823

Revenues for 1993's first half rose 0.8%, year to year. Net income was up 13%, to $2.17 a share from $1.93.

Common Share Earnings ($)

Quarter:	1993	1992	1991	1990
Mar.	1.13	1.16	1.84	1.10
Jun.	1.04	0.78	0.10	1.31
Sep.	E1.25	1.03	1.18	0.81
Dec.	E1.18	0.40	1.04	0.89
	E4.60	3.37	4.20	4.13

Important Developments

Aug. '93— The United Mine Workers (UMW) won a certification vote at MDA's Pontiki mine. Pontiki produced 1.7 million tons of coal in 1992 or 13% of total output. The UMW, which lost a bid to organize MDA's Mettiki mine in August 1992, has indicated that it is preparing to mount another campaign.

May '93— Seminole Pipeline (80%-owned) completed a $120 million expansion project that effectively doubles that line's throughput capacity.

Feb. '93— MDA made a $20.6 million charge ($0.69 a share) against 1992's fourth quarter net income. The largest component of the charge was $10.8 million of insurance costs related to the April 1992 explosion at a pipeline near MDA's underground gas liquids storage facility in Texas. MDA also charged $3.9 million to cover miner retiree costs.

Next earnings report expected in late October.

Per Share Data ($)

Yr. End Dec. 31	1992	[1]1991	1990	1989	1988	1987	1986	1985	1984	1983
Tangible Bk. Val.	[2]15.97	[2]13.76	[2]10.93	[2]11.78	[2]15.31	12.69	11.38	10.16	[2]12.36	11.07
Cash Flow	6.41	7.08	6.61	4.97	4.76	3.50	3.53	2.94	2.08	2.18
Earnings[3]	3.37	4.20	4.13	3.04	2.94	1.38	1.84	1.80	0.68	0.87
Dividends	1.000	1.000	1.000	0.875	0.500	0.500	0.500	0.500	0.500	0.700
Payout Ratio	30%	24%	23%	26%	17%	35%	27%	28%	74%	80%
Prices—High	62⅛	63¾	46⅞	42¾	30¼	33⅜	31⅛	19⅛	15⅜	14⅝
Low	52½	38½	36⅝	27⅛	23⅜	20	18	13⅛	10½	10¾
P/E Ratio—	18–16	15–9	11–9	14–9	10–8	24–15	17–10	11–7	23–15	17–12

Data as orig. reptd. Adj. for stk div(s). of 100% May 1989. **1.** Reflects accounting change. **2.** Incl. intangibles. **3.** Bef. results of disc. opers. of +1.38 in 1984, and spec. item(s) of +1.23 in 1987, -0.10 in 1986, +0.06 in 1983. E-Estimated.

Income Data (Million $)

Year Ended Dec. 31	Revs.	Oper. Inc.	% Oper. Inc. of Revs.	Cap. Exp.	Depr.	Int. Exp.	[3]Net Bef. Taxes	Eff. Tax Rate	[4]Net Inc.	% Net Inc. of Revs.	Cash Flow
1992	**2,640**	**306**	**11.6**	**215**	**91.0**	**52.4**	**145**	**31.1%**	**101**	**3.8**	**192**
[1]1991	2,643	317	12.0	136	86.4	58.3	183	29.7%	126	4.8	212
1990	2,708	306	11.3	315	78.3	60.4	190	31.5%	130	4.8	208
1989	2,019	272	13.5	152	73.7	38.3	174	33.3%	116	5.8	190
1988	1,736	251	14.4	63	72.5	32.3	170	31.0%	117	6.7	190
1987	1,581	207	13.1	64	88.7	37.3	81	29.3%	57	3.6	146
1986	1,570	232	14.7	43	72.2	41.9	128	38.7%	[1]78	5.0	150
1985	1,908	246	12.9	100	65.9	45.5	162	35.8%	104	5.5	170
[2]1984	2,032	199	9.8	98	87.3	49.3	65	36.6%	41	2.0	128
1983	2,065	202	9.8	87	81.4	61.4	80	36.7%	50	2.4	132

Balance Sheet Data (Million $)

Dec. 31	Cash	Curr. Assets	Curr. Liab.	Curr. Ratio	Total Assets	% Ret. on Assets	Long Term Debt	Common Equity	Total Cap.	% LT Debt of Cap.	% Ret. on Equity
1992	**56**	**458**	**393**	**1.2**	**1,912**	**5.6**	**669**	**478**	**1,428**	**46.9**	**22.7**
1991	52	375	308	1.2	1,702	7.4	639	413	1,345	47.5	34.0
1990	78	412	373	1.1	1,700	8.7	654	330	1,282	51.0	37.9
1989	72	349	325	1.1	1,481	8.7	504	408	1,131	44.6	24.8
1988	121	351	247	1.4	1,376	8.5	292	611	1,114	26.2	20.9
1987	138	377	291	1.3	1,365	4.3	318	512	1,041	30.6	11.8
1986	99	387	235	1.6	1,405	5.2	391	490	1,140	34.3	16.9
1985	190	576	523	1.1	1,611	7.3	409	438	1,067	38.3	21.6
1984	93	780	397	2.0	1,793	2.3	428	761	1,369	31.2	5.7
1983	23	415	270	1.5	1,641	2.9	514	643	1,362	37.8	8.1

Data as orig. reptd. **1.** Reflects accounting change. **2.** Excludes discontinued operations. **3.** Incl. equity in earns. of nonconsol. subs. prior to 1991. **4.** Bef. results of disc. opers. in 1984 and spec. item(s) in 1987, 1986, 1983.

Business Summary

MAPCO is a diversified energy concern. Contributions (in million $) to operating profits:

	1992	1991	1990
Gas liquids	$113.7	$140.5	$115.2
Petroleum	73.9	63.6	110.3
Coal	36.0	54.6	49.0

The gas liquids segment includes the Mid-America Pipeline, a 7,166-mile common carrier system extending from Rocky Mountain area and Southwest to markets in the Midwest. A 1,097-mile line moves anhydrous ammonia from the Southwest to Central U.S. MDA also holds an 80% interest in the 740-mile Seminole Pipeline, which transports gas liquids within Texas, and has interests in six underground facilities capable of storing 16.0 million bbls. of natural gas liquids and a 107,000 bbl./day gas liquids fractionator. Thermogas distributes propane and related appliances and liquid fertilizers through 175 outlets in 17 Midwestern and Southeastern states.

MDA operates a 125,000 bbl./day refinery near Fairbanks, Alaska. In Alaska MDA markets petroleum products for both wholesale and retail markets including 21 MAPCO Express convenience outlets in Fairbanks and Anchorage. MDA's Mid-South system includes an 80,000 bbls./day Memphis refinery, which supplies wholesale markets and some 244 gasoline/convenience outlets under the MAPCO Express and Shell brands in nine Southern states. MDA also processes, sells and engages in gas liquids trading.

MDA produced 13.5 million tons of coal in 1992, versus 13.8 million tons in 1991, from eight mine complexes in Kentucky, Maryland, Illinois and Virginia. Coal reserves at 1992 year-end aggregated 372 million tons.

Dividend Data

Dividends have been paid since 1965. A dividend reinvestment plan is available. A "poison pill" stock purchase right, adopted in 1986, was amended in 1989.

Amt of Divd. $	Date Decl.	Ex-divd. Date	Stock of Record	Payment Date
0.25	Dec. 3	Dec. 8	Dec. 14	Dec. 28'92
0.25	Feb. 3	Feb. 23	Mar. 1	Mar. 19'93
0.25	May 27	Jun. 1	Jun. 7	Jun. 18'93
0.25	Jul. 30	Aug. 16	Aug. 20	Sep. 17'93

Capitalization

Long Term Debt: $664,000,000 (6/93).

Minority Interest: $22,600,000.

Common Stock: 30,007,047 shs. ($1 par). Institutions hold approximately 78%. Shareholders of record: 6,000.

Office—1800 South Baltimore Ave., Tulsa, OK 74119. **Tel**—(918) 581-1800. **Chrmn & CEO**—J. E. Barnes. **Pres**—R. M. Howe. **VP-CFO**—F. S. Dickerson III. **VP-Secy**—D. W. Bowman. **VP-Investor Contact**—David S. Leslie. **Dirs**—J. E. Barnes, H. A. Fischer Jr., W. K. Goettsche, D. P. Hodel, M. T. Hopkins, R. M. Howe, P. C. Lauinger Jr., D. L. Mellish, R. L. Parker, H. J. Schmidt, S. F. Segnar. **Transfer Agent**—Harris Trust Co., NYC. **Incorporated** in Delaware in 1958. **Empl**—5,985.

 Stephen R. Klein

Mark IV Industries

NYSE Symbol IV Options on NYSE In S&P MidCap 400

Price	Range	P-E Ratio	Dividend	Yield	S&P Ranking	Beta
Oct. 18'93	1993					
23	23 3/8–15 23/32	19	[1]0.10	[1]0.4%	B	1.32

Summary

This diversified manufacturer operates in three core businesses: power transfer and fluid handling, mass transit and traffic control, and professional audio. Long-term debt has been cut substantially since 1991, and IV is now intent on improving its financial performance by applying stricter cost and quality controls and through selective acquisitions that enhance existing operations. The company recently acquired a European manufacturer of automotive and industrial belts and hydraulic hose.

Current Outlook

Primary share earnings for 1993-4 may rise to $1.35 ($1.22 fully diluted), from 1992-3's $1.15 (1.06), as adjusted. A further rise to $1.55 a share ($1.39 fully diluted) is possible in 1994-95.

The $0.02½ quarterly dividend should continue.

Sales should rise in 1993-4 as the strengthening economy stimulates demand in many of IV's diverse businesses, and reflecting contributions from recent acquisitions. Increased investment in national infrastructure should continue to aid the mass transit and traffic control group, while, overall, margins should benefit from cost controls and a sharp decline in interest expense.

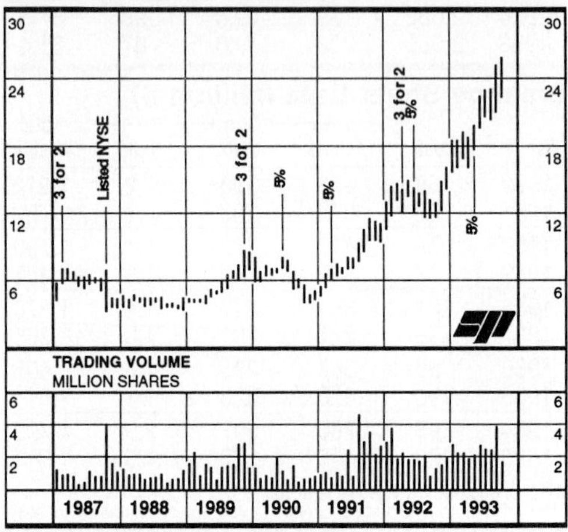

Net Sales (Million $)

Quarter:	1993–94	1992–93	1991–92	1990–91
May	288	309	286	224
Aug.	317	305	284	221
Nov.	---	303	289	228
Feb.	---	305	286	264
	---	1,222	1,146	937

Net sales for the six months ended August 31, 1993, rose 12%, year to year. Aided by contributions by Pirelli Transmissioni Industriali, operating income advanced 18%. With interest costs 6.7% lower, net income was ahead 38%. Share earnings were $0.66 ($0.60 fully diluted) versus $0.48 ($0.45), excluding special charges of $1.18 ($0.99) versus $0.08 ($0.07). Per share amounts are adjusted to reflect the 5% stock dividend in May 1993.

[2]Common Share Earnings ($)

Quarter:	1993–94	1992–93	1991–92	1990–91
May	0.34	0.31	0.31	0.25
Aug.	0.33	0.30	0.30	0.23
Nov.	E0.35	0.30	0.24	0.22
Feb.	E0.33	0.24	0.18	0.20
	E1.35	1.15	0.98	0.86

Important Developments

Sep. '93— IV said that second quarter fiscal 1993-94 earnings reflected a contribution of about $0.02 a share after interest expense, by recently acquired Pirelli Transmissioni Industriali S.p.A. (PTI). IV noted that the summer months are PTI's slowest period of business and that it expected larger contributions from PTI in subsequent quarters due to increasing demand in Europe for automotive air conditioning and power steering components, offsetting lower overall vehicle demand there. IV said that mass transit and traffic control group order rates and shipments continued to rise and that the professional audio segment benefited from improved demand in domestic and Pacific Rim markets, which offset lower demand in Europe.

Next earnings report expected late December.

Per Share Data ($)

Yr. End Feb. 28	1993	[3]1992	[3]1991	1990	[3]1989	[3]1988	[3]1987	[3]1986	1985	1984
Tangible Bk. Val.	**5.17**	4.30	3.35	4.10	[4]3.88	1.22	[4]1.73	1.23	0.61	0.45
Cash Flow	**1.96**	1.79	1.89	1.62	1.31	0.93	0.69	0.38	0.21	0.18
Earnings	**1.15**	[5]0.98	[5]1.04	[5]1.01	[5]0.77	[5]0.63	[5]0.44	[5]0.25	[5]0.17	[5]0.11
Dividends	**0.088**	0.067	0.043	Nil	Nil	Nil	Nil	Nil	Nil	Nil
Payout Ratio	**7%**	9%	4%	Nil	Nil	Nil	Nil	Nil	Nil	Nil
Calendar Years	**1992**	1991	1990	1989	1988	1987	1986	1985	1984	1983
Prices—High	**16 3/16**	11 9/16	8 3/32	8 11/16	4 11/16	7 5/32	6 9/16	3 7/16	15/16	29/32
Low	**10 19/32**	4 21/32	4 1/16	3 1/16	3 11/32	3 7/32	3 3/32	29/32	11/16	7/32
P/E Ratio—	**14–9**	12–5	8–4	9–4	6–4	11–5	15–7	14–3	6–4	8–2

Data as orig. reptd. Adj. for stk. divs. of 5% May 1993, 5% Jun. 1992, 50% April 1992, 5% Mar. 1991, 5% Jun. 1990, 50% Nov. 1989, 50% Feb. 1987, 50% Jun. 1986, 50% Jan. 1985. **1.** Plus stock. **2.** Fully diluted for 1990-91. **3.** Refl. merger or acq. **4.** Incl. intangibles. **5.** Bef. results of disc. ops. of +1.28 in 1990, -0.01 in 1984, and spec. items of -0.14 in 1992, +0.03 in 1991, +0.37 in 1990. E-Estimated

Income Data (Million $)

Year Ended Feb. 28	Revs.	Oper. Inc.	% Oper. Inc. of Revs.	Cap. Exp.	Depr.	Int. Exp.	Net Bef. Taxes	Eff. Tax Rate	[4]Net Inc.	% Net Inc. of Revs.	Cash Flow
[1]1993	**1,222**	**159**	**13.0**	**35**	**32.5**	**56.9**	**70.1**	**34.5%**	**45.9**	**3.8**	**78.4**
[1]1992	1,146	146	12.8	[3]34	25.5	71.8	47.1	34.5%	30.9	2.7	56.4
[1]1991	937	126	13.4	[3]109	20.4	69.7	38.6	35.5%	24.9	2.7	49.3
[2]1990	833	112	13.4	[3]23	16.2	60.6	42.9	36.7%	27.1	3.3	43.4
[1]1989	742	95	12.8	[3]299	16.0	67.8	34.8	34.5%	22.8	3.1	38.8
[1]1988	403	61	15.2	[3]51	8.5	30.8	27.8	38.6%	17.0	4.2	25.5
[1]1987	292	39	13.3	[3]54	5.9	16.5	18.6	45.1%	[5]10.2	3.5	16.1
[1]1986	83	15	18.2	[3]20	2.5	4.0	8.7	45.3%	4.7	5.7	7.2
1985	39	7	17.1	[3]Nil	0.9	0.6	5.1	45.4%	2.8	7.2	3.7
[2]1984	35	5	15.1	[3]Nil	0.2	1.0	3.1	36.0%	2.0	5.7	3.2

Balance Sheet Data (Million $)

Feb. 28	Cash	Curr. Assets	Curr. Liab.	Curr. Ratio	Total Assets	% Ret. on Assets	Long Term Debt	Common Equity	Total Cap.	% LT Debt of Cap.	% Ret. on Equity
1993	**3**	**501**	**209**	**2.4**	**1,095**	**4.2**	**497**	**359**	**856**	**58.1**	**13.4**
1992	5	505	207	2.4	1,090	2.1	525	322	847	62.0	9.9
1991	6	518	161	3.2	1,077	2.7	718	178	895	80.1	15.1
1990	7	399	120	3.3	849	3.0	544	165	709	76.7	20.5
1989	11	546	210	2.6	1,094	2.7	745	115	864	86.3	22.0
1988	193	388	77	5.0	612	3.4	435	93	532	81.8	23.7
1987	86	203	57	3.6	312	4.7	209	40	252	82.9	29.4
1986	1	48	17	2.8	125	5.9	76	29	106	71.7	21.9
1985	Nil	10	4	2.1	26	12.2	9	10	21	42.5	30.6
1984	1	9	5	2.0	19	9.9	5	8	13	39.1	29.3

Data as orig. reptd. **1.** Refl. merger or acq. **2.** Excl. disc. ops. **3.** Net of curr. yr. retirement and disposals. **4.** Bef. results of disc. ops. and spec. items. **5.** Refl. acctg. change.

Business Summary

Mark IV Industries manufactures a wide variety of products. Segment contributions (profits in millions) in 1992-3 were:

	Sales	Profits
Power transfer/fluid handling	57.4%	$72.6
Mass transit/traffic control....	18.0%	32.4
Professional audio	14.5%	22.4
Instrumentation & other.......	10.1%	8.1

Power transfer and fluid handling produces automotive aftermarket and original equipment belts, hoses, couplings, accessory drives, fluid power and transfer assemblies, industrial belts and hydraulic hose, gasoline vapor recovery hose and fittings, temperature controls and protective closures. In June 1993, IV acquired Pirelli Transmissioni Industriali, a European manufacturer of belts and hydraulic hose with sales of $165 million, from Pirelli S.p.A. for $115 million.

Mass transit and traffic control manufactures door controls, information displays, interior lighting and air diffuser systems for buses, rail vehicles and aircraft, vehicle identification and control systems, traffic signs and signals, and other products.

Professional audio produces professional-quality microphones, speakers, mixers and amplifiers, high-fidelity public address musical instrument loudspeaker systems, signal processors and other sound and audio equipment.

Four businesses within the instrumentation products segment with sales of $54 million were sold in early 1993-4. Other non-core businesses with sales of $72 million were discontinued and will be sold. As a result of the divestitures, Mark IV will no longer report instrumentation as a segment.

Dividend Data

Cash dividends were initiated in June 1990.

Amt of Divd. $	Date Decl.	Ex-divd. Date	Stock of Record	Payment Date
0.02¼	Dec. 1	Dec. 7	Dec. 11	Dec. 29'92
0.02½	Mar. 1	Mar. 15	Mar. 19	Apr. 1'93
5% stk	Apr. 28	May 4	May 10	May 20'93
0.02½	Jun. 7	Jun. 14	Jun. 18	Jul. 1'93
0.02½	Sep. 3	Sep. 13	Sep. 17	Oct. 1'93

Capitalization

Long Term Debt: $487,150,000 (5/93).

Common Stock: 40,269,801 shs. ($0.01 par).
Officers & directors own or control 23%.
Institutions hold about 49%.
Shareholders of record: 2,400.

Office—501 John James Audubon Parkway, P.O. Box 810, Amherst, NY 14226-0810. **Tel**—(716) 689-4972. **Chrmn**—S. H. Alfiero. **Pres**—C. R. Arrison. **Exec VP & CFO**—W. P. Montague. **Secy**—G. S. Lippes. **Investor Contact**—Sharlene Vogler. **Dirs**—S. H. Alfiero, C. R. Arrison, J. G. Donohoo, G. S. Lippes, H. Roth Jr. **Transfer Agent**—American Stock Transfer & Trust Co., NYC. **Incorporated** in Delaware in 1970. **Empl**—13,350.

 Joshua M. Harari, CFA

Marshall & Ilsley Corp.

NASDAQ Symbol MRIS (Incl. in Nat'l Market) In S&P MidCap 400

Price	Range	P–E Ratio	Dividend	Yield	S&P Ranking	Beta
Sep. 13'93	1993					
24½	26–20²⁹⁄₃₂	14	0.56	2.3%	A	0.74

Summary

This diversified interstate bank holding company operates 37 banks with 131 offices in Wisconsin, and one bank with 12 offices in the Phoenix, Ariz., metropolitan area. Following strong gains in 1992, earnings continued to rise in the first half of 1993, aided by a favorable interest rate environment and a reduced loan loss provision. A 3-for-1 stock split was effected in May 1993, and the quarterly dividend was subsequently raised 14%. Northwestern Mutual Life Insurance owns 12% of the common stock.

Current Outlook

Earnings for 1993 are projected at $1.85, up from 1992's $1.73, as adjusted.

The minimum expectation is for dividends to continue at $0.14 a share quarterly.

Earnings in 1993 should advance moderately, with growth in noninterest income expected to outpace net interest income growth. Although loan demand has shown some signs of resurgence in Wisconsin, no clear trends can be ascertained. Reinvestment of maturing loans at previous rates of return will prove more difficult, squeezing net interest margins, albeit slightly, as the transition of funds from higher-cost certificates of deposit to lower-cost transaction accounts slows. Revenues from data processing should continue to fuel noninterest income growth in future periods, and expenses are likely to remain well controlled. The level of nonperforming assets peaked during 1992, and loan loss provisions and net loan chargeoffs are expected to continue at the same rate as 1993's first and second quarters. MRIS remains strongly capitalized, with risk-based capital ratios far above federal regulatory minimums.

Review of Operations

In the six months ended June 30, 1993, net interest income edged up 1.9%, year to year, as a 10% drop in interest income was outweighed by a 25% decline in interest expense. The provision for loan losses dropped to $4.4 million, from $7.4 million; pretax income increased 14%. After taxes at 35.1%, versus 33.5%, income was up 11%, to $63.0 million ($0.92 a share; $0.87 fully diluted), from $56.7 million ($0.84; $0.79). Results exclude an $0.11 ($0.10) charge for the cumulative effect of accounting changes in the 1992 interim.

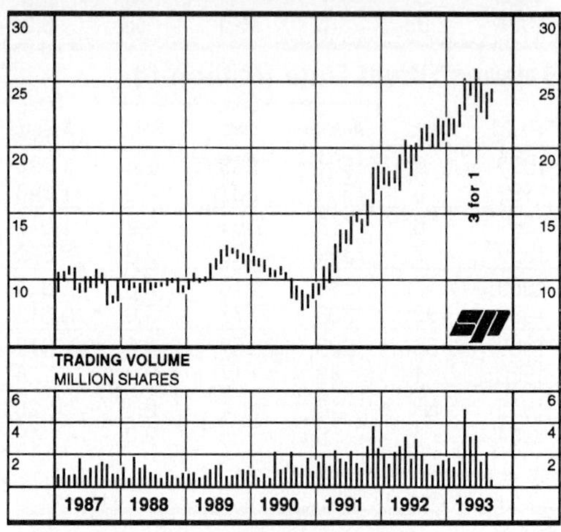

Common Share Earnings ($)

Quarter:	1993	1992	1991	1990
Mar.	0.46	0.41	0.39	0.30
Jun.	0.47	0.43	0.35	0.27
Sep.	E0.46	0.42	0.39	0.28
Dec.	E0.46	0.46	0.37	0.23
	E1.85	1.73	1.50	1.08

Important Developments

Jun. 30'93— MRIS's Tier 1 and total risk-based capital ratios were 13.2% and 15.1%, respectively, far in excess of federal regulatory minimum requirements of 4.0% and 8.0%, respectively.

Next earnings report expected in mid-October.

Per Share Data ($)

Yr. End Dec. 31	1992	1991	[1]1990	1989	[1,2]1988	[2]1987	[1]1986	[1]1985	[1]1984	[1]1983
Tangible Bk. Val.	**11.19**	10.00	8.84	8.13	7.13	6.70	6.01	5.43	5.38	4.96
Earnings[3,4]	**1.73**	1.50	1.08	1.28	1.16	1.05	0.98	0.89	0.74	0.73
Dividends	**0.480**	0.430	0.390	0.350	0.310	0.277	0.262	0.246	0.233	0.218
Payout Ratio	**28%**	29%	36%	27%	27%	26%	27%	28%	32%	30%
Prices—High	**22¼**	18⅝	11⅞	12⅝	10⅛	11	12¹⁵⁄₁₆	9⅛	5⅞	5½
Low	**16⅞**	8¹⁵⁄₁₆	7¾	9⅜	9¹⁄₁₆	8¹⁄₁₆	8½	5⅝	4⅜	3¾
P/E Ratio—	**13–10**	12–6	11–7	10–7	9–8	10–8	13–9	10–6	8–6	8–5

Data as orig. reptd. Adj. for stk. divs. of 200% in May 1993, 200% May 1986. **1.** Refl. merger or acq. **2.** Refl. acctg. change. **3.** Ful. dil.: 1.62 in 1992, 1.40 in 1991, 1.03 in 1990, 1.21 in 1989, 1.10 in 1988, 1.00 in 1987, 0.93 in 1986, 0.87 in 1985, 0.73 in 1984, 0.71 in 1983. **4.** Bef. spec. item of -0.11 in 1992. E-Estimated.

Income Data (Million $)

Year Ended Dec. 31	Net Int. Inc.	Tax Equiv. Adj.	Non Int. Inc.	Loan Loss Prov.	% Exp./ Op. Revs.	Net Bef. Taxes	Eff. Tax Rate	Net Inc.	% Net Int. Margin	—% Return On— Assets	Equity
1992	**308**	**10.8**	**258**	**15.2**	**66.7**	**174**	**33.2%**	**116.6**	**4.68**	**1.56**	**16.2**
1991	289	14.1	223	20.6	66.4	146	32.2%	99.4	4.57	1.36	15.9
[1]1990	275	15.3	190	39.8	67.2	104	31.6%	71.3	4.51	1.00	12.4
1989	254	17.0	168	12.3	65.9	123	30.6%	85.5	4.45	1.23	16.5
[1,2]1988	230	17.2	151	8.3	66.8	108	29.3%	76.2	4.34	1.20	16.7
[2]1987	190	19.3	121	8.7	68.6	81	28.6%	57.9	4.27	1.05	15.9
[1]1986	184	34.3	117	11.1	65.5	72	23.4%	55.0	4.54	1.02	16.6
[1]1985	156	25.2	83	12.7	63.1	61	29.5%	43.0	4.85	1.02	15.6
[1]1984	122	19.0	59	6.3	63.4	48	27.5%	34.7	4.59	1.01	14.5
[1]1983	112	18.3	45	6.3	61.5	43	27.5%	31.5	4.81	1.03	15.5

Balance Sheet Data (Million $)

Dec. 31	Total Assets	Earning Assets: Mon. Mkt. Assets	Inv. Secs.	Com'l Loans	Other Loans	% Loan Loss Resv.	Deposits: Demand	Time	% Loans/ Deposits	Long Term Debt	Common Equity	% Equity To Assets
1992	**7,850**	**138**	**1,882**	**1,947**	**2,932**	**1.76**	**1,636**	**4,576**	**78.5**	**130**	**742**	**9.30**
1991	7,628	321	1,561	2,003	2,812	1.55	1,496	4,637	77.8	182	656	8.50
1990	7,460	153	1,561	1,941	2,866	1.44	1,446	4,533	79.7	178	581	7.97
1989	7,151	55	1,544	1,995	2,665	1.24	1,311	4,274	82.8	149	546	7.60
1988	6,775	136	1,633	1,835	2,271	1.32	1,287	3,924	78.2	187	479	7.11
1987	5,556	237	1,333	1,552	1,557	1.36	1,178	3,141	71.4	163	371	6.60
1986	6,001	400	1,522	1,539	1,360	1.31	1,237	3,095	66.2	153	352	6.19
1985	4,741	266	1,301	1,364	1,079	1.42	1,032	2,558	67.1	169	291	6.55
1984	3,958	400	988	1,081	888	1.18	857	1,969	69.4	53	254	6.97
1983	3,362	254	828	884	777	1.28	694	1,567	73.1	59	216	6.64

Data as orig. reptd. 1. Refl. merger or acq. 2. Refl. acctg. change.

Business Summary

Marshall & Ilsley Corp. owns 37 banks with a total of 131 offices in Wisconsin, one bank with 12 offices in the Phoenix, Ariz., area, and 12 bank-related subsidiaries. The company's lead bank is M&I Marshall & Ilsley Bank which, based on assets of some $2.8 billion at 1992 year end, was the second largest bank in Wisconsin. Consolidated gross loans of $4.88 billion at 1992 year end and $4.82 billion a year earlier were divided:

	1992	1991
Commercial, financial & agricultural	35.2%	35.4%
Real estate—residential	24.6%	25.2%
Real estate—commercial	19.1%	18.7%
Real estate—construction	3.3%	3.4%
Instalment	12.3%	11.5%
Leasing & other	4.7%	6.2%

The allowance for possible loan losses at 1992 year end was $85.9 million (1.76% of gross loans), up from $73.9 million (1.55%) a year earlier. Net chargeoffs during 1992 were $3.2 million (0.07% of average loans), versus $15.4 million (0.32%) during 1991. As of December 31, 1992, nonperforming assets totaled $55.6 million (1.14% of total loans and other real estate owned), down from $71.5 million (1.49%) a year earlier.

Average deposits totaled $5.94 billion in 1992, and were composed: noninterest-bearing demand 23%, money market savings 20%, savings and NOW 24%, and time deposits 34%. On a tax-equivalent basis, the average yield on interest-earning assets in 1992 was 7.97% (9.38% in 1991), while the average rate paid on interest-bearing liabilities was 4.29% (6.03%), for a net spread of 3.66% (3.35%).

Dividend Data

Cash has been paid each year since 1938. A dividend reinvestment plan is available.

Amt. of Divd. $	Date Decl.	Ex–divd. Date	Stock of Record	Payment Date
0.37	Oct. 16	Nov. 23	Nov. 30	Dec. 14'92
0.37	Feb. 16	Feb. 23	Mar. 1	Mar. 12'93
3–for–1	Apr. 27	Jun. 1	May 14	May 28'93
0.14	Apr. 27	May 25	Jun. 1	Jun. 14'93
0.14	Aug. 13	Aug. 25	Aug. 31	Sep. 14'93

Finances

In July 1993, the company issued $100 million of subordinated debt for general corporate purposes and to help finance common stock repurchases.

Capitalization

Long Term Debt: $117,150,000 (6/93).

Conv. Pfd. Stk.: 185,314 shs. ($1.00 par).

Common Stock: 63,445,273 shs. ($1.00 par). Northwestern Mutual Life Insurance owns 12.0%. Institutions hold 37%. Shareholders: 9,381 of record (12/92).

Office—770 North Water St., Milwaukee, WI 53202. **Tel**—(414) 765-7801. **Chrmn & CEO**—J. B. Wigdale. **Pres**—D. J. Kuester. **EVP-CFO**—G. H. Gunnlaugsson. **Secy & Investor Contact**—Michael A. Hatfield. **Dirs**—J. P. Bolduc, W. F. Bueche, J. F. Chait, G. A. Francke, B. E. Jacobs, J. F. Kellner, J. F. Kress, D. R. O'Hare, J. A. Puelicher, S. W. Tisdale, J. B. Wigdale, J. O. Wright. **Transfer Agent & Registrar**—Bank of New York, NYC. **Incorporated** in Wisconsin in 1959. **Empl**—6,315.

 Barry R. Haas

MAXXAM Inc.

ASE Symbol MXM In S&P MidCap 400

Price	Range	P-E Ratio	Dividend	Yield	S&P Ranking	Beta
Sep. 9'93	1993					
28½	35¾–21¾	NM	None	None	B–	1.21

Summary

This company, which holds a 68% interest in Kaiser Aluminum Corp., a fully integrated aluminum company, also has interests in forest products and real estate operations. A large loss is expected for 1993, reflecting competitive pressures in world aluminum markets.

Current Outlook

A loss of $7.50 a share is estimated for 1993 (before charges of $48.80, mostly for the cumulative effect of accounting changes). Earnings of $0.35 are seen for 1994.

Initiation of dividends is not anticipated.

Revenues are likely to decline in 1993, as higher real estate and forest products sales are outweighed by the effects of lower aluminum receipts. Aluminum operating results are expected to reflect lower prices and reduced shipments related to current excess worldwide supply of aluminum. Inventory remains relatively high, and additional contributions are likley from the former Soviet Union, and new supplies from Australia and Bahrain. Potential tax increases may also have a negative effect. Although a $29 million inventory charge will be absent, 1993 results reflect charges of $44.1 million due to the early retirement of debt, and $444 million for accounting changes. Forest products earnings should improve (on favorable price and supply conditions), and real estate operations may become profitable from a loss.

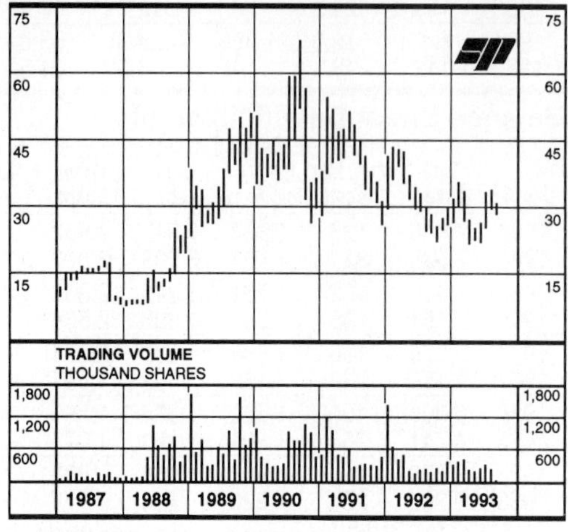

Total Revenues (Million $)

Quarter:	1993	1992	1991	1990
Mar.	514	530	564	572
Jun.	508	564	578	610
Sep.		532	578	601
Dec.		576	536	577
		2,203	2,255	2,361

Revenues in the six months ended June 30, 1993, fell 6.7%, year to year. An operating loss of $2.9 million contrasted with operating income of $78.4 million, as losses at aluminum operations reflected lower shipments and average realized prices. Forest product earnings fell; real estate losses narrowed. A loss of $4.41 a share (before special charges of $48.80) replaced income of $0.24.

Common Share Earnings ($)

Quarter:	1993	1992	1991	1990
Mar.	d2.74	0.10	2.61	2.83
Jun.	d1.67	0.15	1.85	6.06
Sep.	Ed1.50	0.07	0.58	2.94
Dec.	Ed1.50	d1.09	1.04	3.36
	Ed7.50	d0.77	6.08	15.19

Important Developments

Aug. '93— The company said proposed federal legislation would provide for the purchase of 44,000 acres of timberlands from Pacific Lumber in an effort to preserve ancient redwoods.

Aug. '93— MAXXAM estimated that an electric rate increase initiated by Bonneville Power Administration would increase annual costs at its Mead and Tacoma smelters by $15 million.

Next earnings report expected in early November.

Per Share Data ($)

Yr. End Dec. 31	1992	1991	[1]1990	1989	[2]1988	1987	1986	[3]1985	1984	1983
Tangible Bk. Val.	**49.14**	51.90	45.82	27.02	13.66	11.42	11.20	16.26	14.39	12.03
Cash Flow	**10.37**	16.40	25.71	23.13	5.52	0.44	3.26	1.54	5.62	3.48
Earnings[4,5]	**d0.77**	6.08	15.19	12.97	0.48	0.07	d5.16	d1.80	2.59	1.10
Dividends	**Nil**	Nil	Nil	Nil	Nil	Nil	Nil	Nil	Nil	Nil
Payout Ratio	**Nil**	Nil	Nil	Nil	Nil	Nil	Nil	Nil	Nil	Nil
Prices—High	**43½**	54¾	67½	51	25¾	17⅜	16¾	15	15¼	18
Low	**22¼**	26	26⅜	23⅜	7¾	8	8⅞	12¾	11⅝	10¾
P/E Ratio—	**NM**	9–4	4–2	4–2	54–16	NM	NM	NM	6–4	16–10

Data as orig. reptd. **1.** Refl. merger or acq. **2.** Major merger resulted in formation of new company. **3.** Refl. acctg. change. **4.** Bef. results of disc. ops. of +1.81 in 1988, +0.13 in 1987, +3.00 in 1985, and spec. items of +1.84 in 1990. **5.** Ful. dil.: 12.46 in 1989, 0.50 in 1988, 2.37 in 1984, 1.01 in 1983. d-Deficit. E-Estimated. NM-Not Meaningful.

Income Data (Million $)

Year Ended Dec. 31	Revs.	Oper. Inc.	% Oper. Inc. of Revs.	Cap. Exp.	Depr.	Int. Exp.	[5]Net Bef. Taxes	Eff. Tax Rate	[6]Net Inc.	% Net Inc. of Revs.	Cash Flow
1992	**2,203**	**265**	**12.0**	**128**	**105.0**	**201**	**d13**	**NM**	**d7**	**NM**	**98**
1991	2,255	333	14.8	130	98.0	216	67	3.0%	58	2.6	155
[1]1990	2,361	514	21.9	131	100.0	232	222	31.4%	144	6.1	247
1989	2,423	572	23.6	130	91.5	347	227	45.6%	117	4.8	208
[2]1988	519	112	21.6	30	38.4	171	12	21.2%	4	0.7	42
[3]1987	35	d18	NM	5	2.4	24	d7	NM	[4]Nil	1.2	3
1986	108	6	5.6	8	47.4	34	d55	NM	d29	NM	18
[3,4]1985	91	19	21.4	29	23.0	31	d31	NM	d12	NM	11
[1]1984	151	31	20.2	82	21.9	30	28	28.4%	19	12.4	41
1983	134	25	18.4	50	19.9	26	17	38.0%	9	6.9	29

Balance Sheet Data (Million $)

Dec. 31	Cash	Curr. Assets	Curr. Liab.	Curr. Ratio	Total Assets	% Ret. on Assets	Long Term Debt	Common Equity	Total Cap.	% LT Debt of Cap.	% Ret. on Equity
1992	**153**	**1,033**	**561**	**1.8**	**3,125**	**NM**	**1,593**	**444**	**2,213**	**72.0**	**NM**
1991	159	1,093	669	1.6	3,215	1.8	1,552	459	2,191	70.8	13.4
1990	88	1,028	657	1.6	3,028	4.6	1,446	395	1,964	73.6	46.0
1989	289	1,271	844	1.5	3,183	3.2	1,551	233	1,919	80.8	66.7
1988	532	1,818	862	2.1	3,635	0.2	2,307	103	2,569	89.8	3.9
1987	11	113	117	1.0	400	0.1	135	64	219	61.4	0.7
1986	41	153	188	0.8	524	NM	125	63	219	57.3	NM
1985	31	106	150	0.7	649	NM	213	94	351	60.7	NM
1984	11	88	63	1.4	581	3.6	252	89	488	51.7	23.0
1983	12	79	59	1.3	516	2.0	224	84	432	51.9	11.1

Data as orig. reptd. **1.** Refl. merger or acq. **2.** Major merger resulted in formation of new company. **3.** Excl. disc. ops. **4.** Refl. acctg. change. **5.** Incl. equity in earns. of nonconsol. subs. **6.** Bef. spec. item and disc. opers. d-Deficit. NM-Not Meaningful.

Business Summary

MAXXAM (formerly MCO Holdings) is a holding company, with subsidiaries engaged in aluminum production, forest products operations and real estate management and development. Industry segment contributions in 1992 (profits in millions) were:

	Sales	Profits
Aluminum processing	66%	$47.0
Bauxite and alumina	21%	$44.6
Forest products	10%	$65.1
Real estate	3%	–$9.3

International sales were 26% of the total in 1992.

Kaiser Aluminum & Chemical Corp. (68% owned), a fully integrated aluminum company, mines bauxite, refines bauxite into alumina, and produces primary metal and semi-fabricated aluminum products. Bauxite, alumina, and primary, semi-fabricated and fabricated aluminum products are sold to end-users and distributors. Kaiser has five business units: alumina, primary products, flat-rolled products, extruded products/rod-bar-wire, and forgings and castings.

Forest products operations are conducted primarily through Pacific Lumber Co., which owns 187,000 acres of timberland and is engaged in all principal areas of the lumber industry. Britt Lumber produces fence and deck lumber.

Real estate activities are conducted through MAXXAM Property Co. and other units.

Dividend Data

Cash dividends have never been paid.

Finances

In August 1993, the MAXXAM Group Inc. unit (MGI) sold $100 million of 11⅛% senior secured notes due 2003, and $126.7 million of 12¼% senior secured discount notes due 2003.

In June 1993, Kaiser sold 17.25 million depositary shares, each equal to 1/10 of a Series A share. MAXXAM's equity interest in Kaiser was cut to 68%.

In March 1993, Pacific Lumber Co. sold $235 million of 10½% senior notes due 2003, and its subsidiary, Scotia Pacific Holding Co. sold $385 million of 7.95% timber notes due 2015.

Capitalization

Long Term Debt: $1,617,500,000 (6/93).

Minority Interest: $221,500,000.

$0.05 Class A Pfd. Stock: 680,893 shs. ($0.50 par); 10 votes ea.; conv. sh.-for-sh. into com.

Common Stock: 8,698,464 shs. ($0.50 par). C.E. Hurwitz controls 60% of the voting power. Shareholders of record: 6,776.

Office—5847 San Felipe, Suite 2600, Houston, TX 77057. **Tel**—(713) 975-7600. **Chrmn, Pres & CEO**—C. E. Hurwitz. **SVP, CFO, Treas. & Investor Contact**—John T. La Duc. **VP & Secy**—B. L. Wade. **Dirs**—R. J. Cruikshank, C. E. Hurwitz, E. G. Levin, S. D. Rosenberg. **Transfer Agent & Registrar**—The Bank of New York, NYC. **Incorporated** in Delaware in 1955. **Empl**—12,210.

 M. Graham Hackett

McCormick & Co.

NASDAQ Symbol MCCRK (Incl. in Nat'l Market) Options on Phila In S&P MidCap 400

Price	Range	P-E Ratio	Dividend	Yield	S&P Ranking	Beta
Sep. 22'93	1993					
22⅛	29¾–20	19	0.44	2.0%	A–	1.44

Summary

This long-established producer and distributor of spices, extracts, seasonings and convenience foods also makes packaging products and operates a gas-fired cogeneration plant. Earnings should continue to advance in fiscal 1993, aided by moderate sales growth, the sale of lackluster divisions, improved manufacturing efficiency and acquisitions.

Earnings for the fiscal year ending November 30, 1994, are estimated at $1.50 a share, up from $1.25 seen for fiscal 1993.

The quarterly dividend of $0.11 a share is the minimum expected.

Sales growth should continue to reflect increasing unit volume from acquisitions and geographic expansion, especially internationally. Price increases are expected to be minimal at best, due to continued low inflation in the U.S. Margins should benefit from investments in plant efficiency during fiscal 1992, coupled with ongoing improvement in raw material sourcing. Possible restraints on earnings gains include continued emphasis on promotional spending, and the sales mix of high-margin consumer products and lower-margin industrial and foodservice products. Long-term share earnings are seen growing at low double-digit rates.

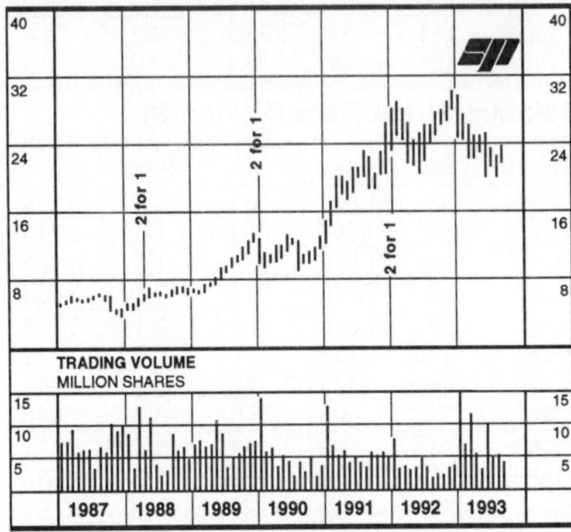

Net Sales (Million $)

Quarter:	1994	1993	1992	1991
Feb.	---	340	322	324
May	---	361	337	333
Aug.	---	395	360	342
Nov.	---	---	452	430
	---	---	1,471	1,428

Net sales in the nine months ended August 31, 1993, increased 7.5%, year to year. Net income edged up 1.1%, to $60,838,000 ($0.74 a share), from $60,195,000 ($0.73).

Common Share Earnings ($)

Quarter:	1994	1993	1992	1991
Feb.	E0.28	0.22	0.21	0.18
May	E0.28	0.22	0.23	0.18
Aug.	E0.40	0.30	0.29	0.25
Nov.	E0.55	E0.51	0.43	0.37
	E1.50	E1.25	1.16	0.98

Important Developments

Sep. '93— McCormick, CPC International Inc. and Rabobank Nederland announced an agreement to form a joint venture in the herb and spice business in Europe. The venture would include the existing retail and catering herb and spice divisions of MCCRK and CPC in Europe, in addition to a German business being acquired. Pursuant to the agreement, McCormick will contribute its retail and catering herb and spice operations in the U.K., Switzerland, Germany and other European countries; CPC will contribute similar businesses located in Germany and Ireland; and Rabobank, a major Dutch bank, will offer its financial expertise and extensive knowledge of the European agribusiness environment. The venture was expected to initially have sales approximating $200 million. Earlier, in June, McCormick directors authorized the repurchase of up to 200,000 of the company's common shares; a previous buyback of like amount was virtually complete.

Per Share Data ($)

Yr. End Nov. 30	1992	1991	1990	1989	1988	[1]1987	1986	[1]1985	[1]1984	1983
Tangible Bk. Val.	**4.36**	4.00	3.61	3.48	2.54	2.36	2.29	2.13	1.96	2.05
Cash Flow	**1.65**	1.43	1.23	0.96	0.72	0.59	0.54	0.51	0.75	0.60
Earnings[2]	**1.16**	0.98	0.83	0.60	0.39	0.33	0.31	0.29	0.55	0.41
Dividends	**0.380**	0.280	0.230	0.170	0.133	0.125	0.110	0.110	0.110	0.110
Payout Ratio	**33%**	28%	28%	27%	35%	38%	36%	39%	20%	27%
Prices[3]—High	**30¼**	26½	13¼	13⁷⁄₁₆	7¼	6½	5¾	4¹³⁄₁₆	4⁵⁄₁₆	4½
Low	**20½**	12¼	9	6⅜	4½	3¾	4¼	3⅞	3⁹⁄₁₆	3⅛
P/E Ratio—	**26–18**	27–13	16–11	22–11	19–12	20–11	19–14	17–14	8–6	11–8

Data as orig. reptd. Adj. for stk. divs. of 100% Jan. 1992, 100% Jan. 1990, 100% Apr. 1988. **1.** Refl. merger or acq. **2.** Bef. results of disc. ops. of +0.95 in 1989, +0.01 in 1988 & spec. item of +0.07 in 1988. **3.** Cal. yr. E-Estimated

Income Data (Million $)

Year Ended Nov. 30	Revs.	Oper. Inc.	% Oper. Inc. of Revs.	Cap. Exp.	Depr.	Int. Exp.	[4]Net Bef. Taxes	Eff. Tax Rate	[5]Net Inc.	% Net Inc. of Revs.	Cash Flow
1992	**1,471**	**207**	**14.1**	**79.4**	**40.0**	**30.9**	**148**	**35.8%**	**95.2**	**6.5**	**135**
1991	1,428	183	12.8	73.5	37.0	27.5	124	34.6%	80.9	5.7	118
1990	1,323	160	12.1	58.5	33.3	29.3	108	35.8%	69.4	5.2	103
[1,2]1989	1,246	134	10.7	55.5	31.9	32.9	82	36.0%	52.5	4.2	84
[1]1988	1,184	110	9.3	53.6	31.6	30.2	58	39.0%	35.6	3.0	67
[3]1987	1,078	88	8.1	43.4	24.5	30.9	49	37.4%	30.6	2.8	55
1986	976	89	9.2	40.4	22.5	19.1	51	41.9%	29.7	3.0	52
[3]1985	873	82	9.4	41.3	21.9	19.6	46	39.5%	27.8	3.2	50
[3]1984	788	85	10.8	31.3	20.0	13.0	79	31.3%	54.6	6.9	75
1983	743	86	11.5	37.2	19.0	10.9	66	39.1%	40.1	5.4	59

Balance Sheet Data (Million $)

Nov. 30	Cash	Curr. Assets	Curr. Liab.	Curr. Ratio	Total Assets	% Ret. on Assets	Long Term Debt	Common Equity	Total Cap.	% LT Debt of Cap.	% Ret. on Equity
1992	**1.8**	**468**	**420**	**1.1**	**1,131**	**8.8**	**201**	**438**	**697**	**28.8**	**22.9**
1991	6.0	445	360	1.2	1,032	8.2	208	389	652	31.8	21.5
1990	5.3	409	306	1.3	947	7.8	211	364	623	34.0	19.9
1989	51.6	427	245	1.7	865	6.7	211	346	606	34.7	17.0
1988	11.3	387	277	1.4	770	4.9	166	294	483	34.3	12.6
1987	7.4	367	272	1.3	718	4.6	139	280	439	31.7	11.2
1986	4.4	325	234	1.4	629	4.9	102	271	388	26.3	11.3
1985	2.6	280	213	1.3	582	4.9	95	261	364	26.1	11.0
1984	4.1	269	193	1.4	542	11.5	97	243	340	28.4	24.1
1983	3.1	228	140	1.6	419	9.7	57	216	273	20.8	19.8

Data as orig. reptd. **1.** Excl. disc. ops. **2.** Refl. acctg. change. **3.** Refl. merger or acq. **4.** Incl. equity in earns. of nonconsol. subs. **5.** Bef. spec. item.

Business Summary

McCormick & Company, Incorporated produces seasonings, flavorings and other specialty food products, which are sold worldwide to the retail food, foodservice and industrial markets under the McCormick and Schilling trademarks. The company also makes plastic bottles and tubes for various industries. Sales in recent fiscal years were derived as follows:

	1992	1991	1990
Consumer Products.....	35%	34%	33%
Foodservice/Industrial..	34%	38%	39%
International...............	21%	21%	19%
Packaging.................	7%	5%	5%
Gilroy Energy............	3%	3%	4%

Consumer products, which are marketed to chain stores, wholesalers, specialty shops and others for retail distribution, include spices, flavorings, extracts, seasonings and cake decorating products. New product development continues to be an important factor in generating sales growth for this division.

The foodservice group is the nation's leading supplier of seasonings, flavorings, dressings and sauces, and specialty frozen products, to the foodservice industry. The industrial group sells similar products to major food manufacturers.

The international division offers a wide variety of retail products, including herbs, spices, seasonings and dressings. The company is seeking an acquisition on the European mainland.

Plastic bottles and tubes are produced in the packaging division for the pharmaceutical, cosmetics and food industries. In addition, McCormick owns a cogeneration facility that supplies power to a subsidiary and to Pacific Gas & Electric Co.

Dividend Data

Cash has been paid each year since 1925. A dividend reinvestment plan is available.

Amt. of Divd. $	Date Decl.	Ex–divd. Date	Stock of Record	Payment Date
0.11	Dec. 21	Dec. 24	Dec. 31	Jan. 15'93
0.11	Mar. 17	Mar. 25	Mar. 31	Apr. 12'93
0.11	Jun. 21	Jun. 25	Jul. 1	Jul. 12'93
0.11	Sep. 17	Sep. 24	Sep. 30	Oct. 11'93

Capitalization

Long Term Debt: $194,346,000 (5/93).

Minority Interest: $1,167,000.

Common Stock: 14,518,000 shs. (no par), plus 66,402,000 nonvoting shs.
Institutions hold 55% of the nonvoting shs.
Shareholders: 11,370 of record (incl. 9,311 nonvoting).

Office—18 Loveton Circle, Sparks, MD 21152-6000. **Tel**—(410) 771-7301. **Chrmn & CEO**—B. A. Thomas. **Pres & COO**—H. E. Blattman. **VP & Secy**—R. W. Single, Sr. **VP & CFO**—J. A. Hooker. **VP & Treas**—D. A. Palumbo. **Dirs**—J. J. Albrecht, H. E. Blattman, J. S. Cook, H. J. Handley, J. A. Hooker, G. W. Koch, C. P. McCormick, Jr., G. V. McGowan, C. D. Nordhoff, R. W. Single, Sr., W. E. Stevens, B. A. Thomas, K. D. Weatherholtz. **Transfer Agent & Registrar**—Co. office. **Co-Transfer Agent**—Security Trust Co., Baltimore. **Incorporated** in Maryland in 1915. **Empl**—8,000.

 Gregg W. Bonardi

Measurex Corp.

NYSE Symbol MX In S&P MidCap 400

Price	Range	P-E Ratio	Dividend	Yield	S&P Ranking	Beta
Sep. 22'93	1993					
18⅝	20–15¾	NM	0.44	2.4%	B	1.16

Summary

Measurex manufactures and services computer integrated manufacturing systems that control continuous batch manufacturing processes primarily for the pulp and paper industries. Profits for the first nine months of fiscal 1993 were down from the year-earlier level, due to lower net interest income and the absence of a $2.4 million nonrecurring gain.

Business Summary

Measurex makes and services computer integrated manufacturing (CIM) systems. These sensor-based computerized systems, which control continuous, batch and discrete manufacturing processes and provide plantwide and millwide information, are designed to increase productivity, reduce raw material usage and energy consumption, and improve product quality and uniformity. Principal industries served are pulp and paper, plastics, metals, rubber and chemicals. The company supports its installed systems with a worldwide sales force of about 1,070 employees (almost half of the total work force). MX offers customers a broad range of on-site and on-call services, including 24-hour-a-day and 365-days-a-year service contracts intended to provide better than 99% system availability.

Revenue contributions in recent years were:

	1992	1991	1990
System sales to:			
Pulp and paper industries	46%	46%	49%
Other industries	13%	12%	16%
Service revenues	41%	42%	36%

Foreign operations accounted for 65% of sales in fiscal 1992, versus 68% in fiscal 1991 and 64% in fiscal 1990.

Products and systems include MXOpen, an integrated information and control system that uses industry-standard computer and communication protocols; Measurex 2002 ET supervisory systems, which are operator stations designed for ease of use with a broad range of graphic displays, fiber optic communications and proprietary software; and SuperVISION 2002 UT, which uses a 32-bit process control computer and provides high-speed machine-direction and high-resolution cross-direction measurements necessary to analyze and reduce variations on paper machines. The company

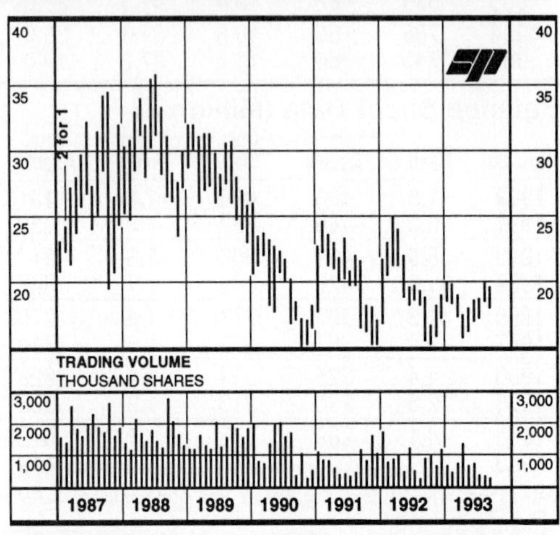

is also a leader in sensor technology for the process industries, currently offering over 70 sensors that monitor various physical properties of products including weight, moisture, gloss, opacity and spacing. In addition, MX is a leader in cross-direction profile controls, a technology that provides manufacturers with precise control over product characteristics during the manufacturing processs.

Important Developments

Sep. '93— MX said system orders in the third quarter of fiscal 1993 were down 6%, to $33 million, from $35 million in the year-earlier period. Pulp and paper system orders were lower in South America, but this decline was offset by gains in other geographic areas, primarily the U.S. System backlog totaled $86 million at August 29, 1993, down 11% from $97 million a year earlier.

Next earnings report expected in mid-December.

Per Share Data ($)

Yr. End Nov. 30	1992	[1]1991	1990	1989	1988	1987	1986	1985	[1]1984	1983
Tangible Bk. Val.	**12.12**	12.82	13.33	12.51	11.02	9.24	8.20	7.15	6.25	5.62
Cash Flow	**0.65**	0.69	1.82	2.64	2.47	1.85	1.51	1.31	1.10	0.71
Earnings[2,3]	**0.04**	0.02	1.26	2.17	1.95	1.39	1.12	0.97	0.73	0.33
Dividends	**0.440**	0.440	0.430	0.370	0.270	0.225	0.165	0.120	0.100	Nil
Payout Ratio	**NM**	NM	34%	17%	14%	15%	15%	12%	14%	Nil
Prices[4]—High	**25**	24⅝	26	32	35⅞	34½	21½	14⅞	11	9½
Low	**15¼**	15¼	15⅛	23	23½	19½	12⅞	8⅜	6½	3⅞
P/E Ratio—	**NM**	NM	21–12	15–11	18–12	25–14	19–12	15–9	15–9	29–12

Data as orig. reptd. Adj. for stk. divs. of 100% Mar. 1987, 100% Jan. 1984. **1.** Refl. merger or acq. **2.** Bef. spec. items of +0.05 in 1992, +0.10 in 1984. **3.** Ful. dil.: 1.11 in 1986. **4.** Cal. yr. NM-Not Meaningful.

Income Data (Million $)

Year Ended Nov. 30	Revs.	Oper. Inc.	% Oper. Inc. of Revs.	Cap. Exp.	Depr.	Int. Exp.	[3]Net Bef. Taxes	Eff. Tax Rate	[4]Net Inc.	% Net Inc. of Revs.	Cash Flow
1992	**253**	**12.5**	**4.9**	**7.8**	**11.3**	**0.81**	**1.7**	**57.4%**	**0.7**	**0.3**	**12.0**
[1]1991	254	15.4	6.0	NA	12.1	0.83	0.5	25.0%	0.4	0.2	12.5
1990	266	29.6	11.1	NA	10.2	0.71	30.4	25.9%	22.5	8.5	32.7
1989	285	46.8	16.4	NA	8.9	0.40	50.9	20.1%	40.7	14.3	49.5
1988	265	49.7	18.7	10.3	9.8	1.14	48.7	24.0%	37.1	14.0	46.9
1987	227	37.8	16.6	6.9	8.7	1.14	37.5	28.6%	26.8	11.8	35.5
1986	193	32.0	16.6	7.3	7.4	1.04	30.9	31.7%	21.1	10.9	28.5
1985	177	29.6	16.8	9.9	6.4	[2]0.78	30.0	41.0%	17.7	10.0	24.1
[1]1984	160	24.4	15.2	7.2	6.4	1.33	25.9	50.8%	[5]12.8	8.0	19.1
1983	123	13.4	10.9	4.9	5.6	1.67	8.9	46.0%	4.8	3.9	10.4

Balance Sheet Data (Million $)

Nov. 30	Cash	Curr. Assets	Curr. Liab.	Curr. Ratio	Total Assets	% Ret. on Assets	Long Term Debt	Common Equity	Total Cap.	% LT Debt of Cap.	% Ret. on Equity
1992	**115**	**218**	**84.8**	**2.6**	**323**	**0.2**	**0.84**	**218**	**238**	**0.4**	**0.3**
1991	127	236	80.8	2.9	340	0.1	4.73	232	259	1.8	0.2
1990	143	255	69.6	3.7	337	6.8	4.85	239	268	1.8	9.7
1989	151	263	76.2	3.5	333	12.8	4.96	230	257	1.9	18.8
1988	148	247	71.7	3.5	303	13.1	5.92	204	232	2.6	19.7
1987	107	204	63.2	3.2	259	11.1	5.94	170	195	3.0	16.7
1986	88	169	47.9	3.5	225	10.0	6.08	152	177	3.4	14.8
1985	71	139	40.5	3.4	193	9.6	6.18	129	153	4.0	14.7
1984	56	123	44.9	2.7	173	7.8	6.47	110	128	5.1	12.2
1983	21	74	32.1	2.3	126	3.9	6.79	81	94	7.2	6.1

Data as orig. reptd. **1.** Refl. merger or acq. **2.** Net of interest income. **3.** Incl. equity in earns. of nonconsol. subs. **4.** Bef. spec. items. **5.** Refl. acctg. change. NA-Not Available.

Revenues (Million $)

Quarter:	1992–93	1991–92	1990–91	1989–90
Feb.	61.8	62.1	63.2	67.8
May	66.1	62.9	65.6	63.4
Aug.	64.3	61.8	63.9	65.9
Nov.		65.8	61.3	69.2
		252.6	254.0	266.2

For the nine months ended August 29, 1993, total revenues climbed 2.9%, year to year, primarily due to increased sales of MXOpen systems; service revenues declined modestly. Operating profits expanded sharply, aided by decreased selling and administrative expenses. Net results were hurt by lower interest income and the absence of a $2.4 million gain on the sale of technology assets; pretax income fell 10%. After taxes at 35.3%, versus 32.0%, net income was off 14%, to $6,253,000 ($0.35 a share), from $7,309,000 ($0.40).

Common Share Earnings ($)

Quarter:	1992–93	1991–92	1990–91	1989–90
Feb.	0.10	0.20	0.26	0.40
May	0.12	0.11	0.12	0.22
Aug.	0.13	0.09	0.11	0.31
Nov.		d0.36	d0.47	0.33
		0.04	0.02	1.26

Dividend Data

Dividends were initiated in 1977, omitted in late 1982, and resumed in late 1983.

Amt of Divd. $	Date Decl.	Ex–divd. Date	Stock of Record	Payment Date
0.11	Dec. 16	Dec. 28	Jan. 4	Jan. 15'93
0.11	Mar. 17	Mar. 25	Mar. 31	Apr. 14'93
0.11	Jun. 16	Jun. 24	Jun. 30	Jul. 14'93
0.11	Sep. 16	Sep. 23	Sep. 29	Oct. 13'93

Finances

In April 1993, MX acquired Finland-based Roibox Oy, a manufacturer of web-inspection technology, for approximately $1.6 million.

In December 1992, the company said it would cut its worldwide work force by about 9%, or approximately 200 people, in the first quarter of fiscal 1993. MX set up related reserves of $9 million in the fiscal 1992 fourth quarter.

Capitalization

Long Term Debt: $18,147,000 (5/93).

Common Stock: 17,782,905 shs. ($0.01 par). Institutions hold 57% incl. 20% by Harnischfeger Industries, Inc.
Shareholders of record: 1,628 (11/92).

d-Deficit.

Office—One Results Way, Cupertino, CA 95014. **Tel**—(408) 255-1500. **Pres & CEO**—D. A. Bossen. **VP-Fin & CFO**—C. A. Thomsen. **Secy**—C. V. Orden. **Treas**—R. W. Hirt. **Investor Contact**—Carol Wilson (408-725-3153). **Dirs**—P. Bancroft III, D. C. Baum, D. A. Bossen, J. T. Grade, O. L. Hoch, J. W. Larson, J. W. McKittrick, G. Tyson. **Transfer Agent & Registrar**—Bank of New York, NYC. **Incorporated** in California in 1968; reincorporated in Delaware in 1984. **Empl**—2,230.

 Samuel A. Dedio

Medco Containment Services

NASDAQ Symbol MCCS (Incl. in Nat'l Market) Options on Pacific In S&P MidCap 400

Price	Range	P-E Ratio	Dividend	Yield	S&P Ranking	Beta
Sep. 13'93	1993					
35½	40–24½	40	0.04	0.1%	NR	1.51

Summary

This company, the largest U.S. provider of prescription drug mail-service programs to employer-funded health plans, recently agreed to be acquired by NYSE-listed Merck & Co. Shareholders would have the option to receive, for each Medco share held, either $39 in cash or 1.21401 Merck shares.

Business Summary

Medco Containment Services, Inc. designs and manages prescription drug benefit plans to control plan sponsors' costs. Through its mail-service pharmacies, the company delivers prescription drugs nationwide to the homes of sponsors' plan participants at a lower cost than is generally available through retail pharmacies. As of September 1, 1992, Medco provided mail-service prescription drug programs through 11 pharmacies in nine states.

Through wholly owned PAID Prescriptions, Inc., the company processes claims for prescription drugs purchased by participants in benefit plans at retail pharmacies in accordance with plan pricing guidelines. At September 1, 1992, PAID had more than 55,000 pharmacies in its network of preferred providers, including all major pharmacy chains.

Medco has designed prescription drug programs that combine its mail-service prescription drug programs with the claims-processing services offered by PAID Prescriptions. By integrating the mail-service delivery system for maintenance prescriptions (covering drugs taken on an ongoing basis) with PAID Prescriptions' network pharmacy system for acute prescriptions (limited-duration), the company is able to offer what it believes to be the industry's most comprehensive prescription drug cost-containment and reporting program.

Medical Marketing Group, Inc. (MMG; 55% owned) licenses aggregated mail-service prescription data and sells information products and marketing programs designed to help pharmaceutical manufacturers efficiently direct their sales and marketing efforts to physicians. MMG's 51%-owned subsidiary, TELERx Marketing, performs promotional programs principally for the healthcare industry.

Synetic, Inc. (60% owned) provides institutional pharmacy services in Connecticut, Massachusetts and Rhode Island and designs, manufactures and distributes porous and solid-plastic components

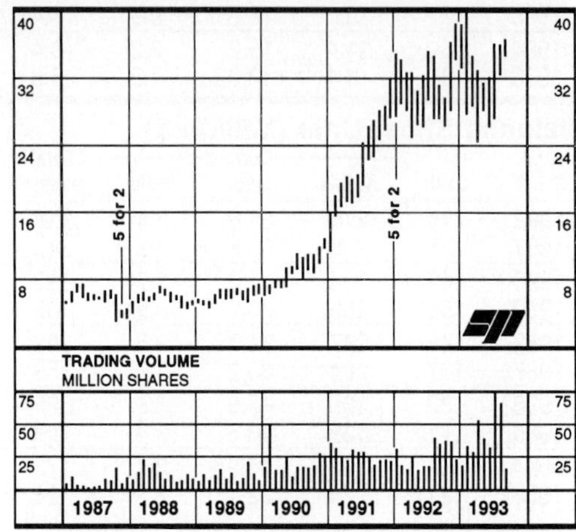

and products used in healthcare, industrial and consumer applications.

In May 1993, the company formed Medco Behavioral Care Corp. (MBCC), the largest U.S. managed behavioral healthcare company. MBCC will serve as the parent company for Personal Performance Consultants Inc. (acquired in April 1992) and American Biodyne Inc. (acquired in December 1992), which together serve more than 10 million managed care lives throughout the U.S.

Important Developments

Jul. '93— Medco agreed to be acquired by NYSE-listed Merck & Co. Medco shareholders would receive, at their option, either $39 in cash or 1.21401 Merck shares for each Medco share held, provided that in the aggregate 60% of Medco shares are converted into Merck stock and 40% are converted into cash.

Next earnings report expected in early November.

Per Share Data ($)

Yr. End Jun. 30	1993	1992	1991	1990	1989	[1]1988	1987	[1]1986	1985
Tangible Bk. Val.	**NA**	3.83	3.20	2.06	2.07	1.70	1.35	1.39	0.39
Cash Flow	**NA**	0.82	0.53	0.04	0.32	0.26	0.14	0.10	0.06
Earnings	**0.88**	0.68	0.43	d0.06	0.24	0.20	0.11	0.08	0.04
Dividends	**0.040**	0.040	0.016	0.016	0.016	0.016	0.016	Nil	Nil
Payout Ratio	**5%**	6%	4%	NM	6%	9%	15%	Nil	Nil
Prices[2]—High	**40**	38⅝	31⅞	12⅞	7½	7¼	7½	6¾	4¾
Low	**24½**	25	11⅜	6⅛	4⅝	4	3	4¼	3¼
P/E Ratio—	**45–28**	57–37	74–27	NM	31–19	37–20	70–28	88–55	NM

Data as orig. reptd. Adj. for stk. divs. of 150% Jan. 1992, 150% Nov. 1987. **1.** Refl. merger or acq. **2.** Cal. yr. d-Deficit. NA-Not Available. NM-Not Meaningful.

Income Data (Million $)

Year Ended Jun. 30	Revs.	Oper. Inc.	% Oper. Inc. of Revs.	Cap. Exp.	Depr.	Int. Exp.	Net Bef. Taxes	Eff. Tax Rate	Net Inc.	% Net Inc. of Revs.	Cash Flow
1992	**1,813**	**159**	**8.7**	**[2]33.1**	**21.4**	**14.3**	**171**	**37.4%**	**103**	**5.7**	**124**
1991	1,343	98	7.3	38.2	14.4	4.0	96	37.5%	58	4.4	73
1990	1,004	66	6.6	15.9	12.6	7.8	12	NM	d8	NM	5
1989	728	47	6.5	19.7	10.1	7.2	[3]45	35.4%	29	4.0	39
[1]1988	503	37	7.4	[2]7.1	7.4	3.9	34	37.3%	[4]22	4.3	29
1987	283	22	7.7	[2]12.1	3.7	NM	25	52.6%	12	4.1	15
[1]1986	136	13	9.5	[2]8.3	2.7	0.7	15	52.2%	7	5.2	10
1985	66	7	10.2	[2]2.4	1.5	Nil	7	51.7%	4	5.4	5

Balance Sheet Data (Million $)

Jun. 30	Cash	Curr. Assets	Curr. Liab.	Curr. Ratio	Total Assets	% Ret. on Assets	Long Term Debt	Common Equity	Total Cap.	% LT Debt of Cap.	% Ret. on Equity
1992	**170**	**672**	**215**	**3.1**	**1,235**	**10.4**	**283**	**665**	**1,003**	**28.2**	**17.4**
1991	201	572	166	3.4	702	8.7	2	496	536	0.4	14.0
1990	198	432	132	3.3	546	NM	103	293	414	24.8	NM
1989	55	289	89	3.2	504	6.8	103	290	415	24.8	10.8
1988	29	184	84	2.2	344	6.7	3	245	260	1.1	9.5
1987	68	195	76	2.6	277	4.4	Nil	193	201	Nil	6.0
1986	102	168	54	3.1	258	4.1	NM	200	204	NM	5.1
1985	1	24	7	3.4	65	NA	Nil	57	59	Nil	NA

Data as orig. reptd. **1.** Refl. merger or acq. **2.** Net. **3.** Incl. equity in earns. of nonconsol. subs. **4.** Refl. acctg. change. d-Deficit. NM-Not Meaningful. NA-Not Available.

Net Sales (Million $)

Quarter:	1992–93	1991–92	1990–91	1989–90
Sep.	566	393	294	219
Dec.	598	422	314	230
Mar.	705	481	358	270
Jun.	756	517	208	284
	2,624	1,813	1,174	1,004

Based on a preliminary report, net sales in the fiscal year ended June 30, 1993, climbed 39% from those of the preceding year, as restated for the acquisition of American Biodyne, reflecting new customers and increased sales to existing customers. Despite lower gains on subsidiary stock issuances ($5.8 million, versus $18.3 million), and acquisition-related charges of $7,041,000, net income gained 34%, to $141,423,000 ($0.88 a share), from $105,792,000 ($0.68).

Common Share Earnings ($)

Quarter:	1992–93	1991–92	1990–91	1989–90
Sep.	0.19	0.15	0.09	d0.05
Dec.	0.20	0.18	0.10	d0.16
Mar.	0.23	0.18	0.12	0.07
Jun.	0.26	0.17	0.12	0.08
	0.88	0.68	0.43	d0.06

Dividend Data

Cash dividends are paid annually.

Amt. of Divd. $	Date Decl.	Ex–divd. Date	Stock of Record	Payment Date
0.04	Apr. 9	Apr. 19	Apr. 23	May 7'93

Finances

In February 1993, majority-owned Synetic, Inc. acquired Reliance Health Services, a provider of pharmacy services to nursing homes and other institutions in Connecticut, in exchange for Synetic common stock valued at $12.5 million.

In December 1992, Medco acquired American Biodyne, Inc., one of the nation's largest providers of managed mental health services, in exchange for 3,963,099 common shares.

Sales to the Service Benefit plan provided by Blue Cross and Blue Shield for federal government employees accounted for 20% of sales in fiscal 1992 (latest available), while sales to federal employee benefit plans accounted for 27%.

Capitalization

Long Term Debt: $281,172,000 (3/93).

Minority Interest: $72,755,000.

Common Stock: 154,655,688 shs. ($0.01 par). Institutions hold 83%. Shareholders: 2,434 of record (9/92).

Options: To purchase 26,148,526 shs. at $0.48 to $34 ea. (6/92).

d-Deficit.

Office—100 Summit Ave., Montvale, NJ 07645. **Tel**—(201) 358-5400. **Chrmn, Pres & CEO**—M. J. Wygod. **SEVP-Fin & Secy**—J. V. Manning. **SEVP & COO**—R. J. Levenson. **Dirs**—T. R. Ferguson, L. R. Lahr, R. J. Levenson, P. G. H. Lofberg, J. V. Manning, B. A. Marden, C. A. Mele, C. Nevin, M. J. Raynes, H. Sarkowsky, A. M. Weis, M. J. Wygod. **Transfer Agent & Registrar**—Citizens & Southern National Bank, Atlanta. **Incorporated** in Delaware in 1983. **Empl**—6,750.

 Adam J. Penn

Media General

ASE Symbol MEG.A In S&P MidCap 400

Price	Range	P-E Ratio	Dividend	Yield	S&P Ranking	Beta
Oct. 14'93	1993					
29⅝	30–17½	33	0.44	1.5%	B	0.55

Summary

This major newspaper publisher and newsprint recycler also owns three TV stations and cable systems in Virginia. Earnings are expected to grow significantly in 1993 and 1994, largely reflecting operating efficiencies and some improvement in newsprint profits.

Current Outlook

Earnings for 1993 are projected at $1.01 a share, up from $0.70 in 1992. A further advance, to about $1.30, is possible for 1994.

The $0.11 quarterly dividend will probably be raised moderately during 1994.

Revenues are expect to show little growth in 1993, as sluggish retail newspaper advertising continues to offset strong gains from cable. A modest revenue increase from television and newsprint is likely. Operating profits should advance, largely reflecting cost controls, a strong rise in newsprint profits, and sharply higher cable profits. Newspaper profitability should be on the upswing by the end of 1994.

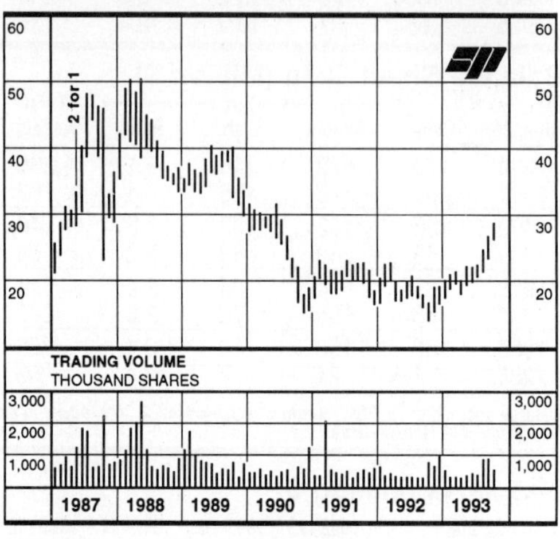

Revenues (Million $)

Quarter:	1993	1992	1990
Mar.	144	142	148
Jun.	153	147	158
Sep.	148	140	152
Dec.	---	149	155
	---	578	613

Revenues in the nine months ended September 30, 1993, edged up 3.6%, year to year. Operating income advanced strongly, as improvement in television, cable and newsprint operations outweighed a drop in newspaper profitability. Despite sharply higher interest costs, income climbed 46%, to $16,648,000 ($0.64), from $11,419,000 ($0.44, before a credit of $0.03 from accounting changes).

Common Share Earnings ($)

Quarter:	1993	1992	1991	1990
Mar.	0.13	0.10	0.09	0.10
Jun.	0.31	0.24	0.20	0.48
Sep.	0.20	0.07	d3.03	0.28
Dec.	E0.37	0.29	0.35	0.12
	E1.05	0.70	d2.39	0.98

Important Developments

Oct. '93— Media General said that a $42 million printing facility currently under construction in Winston-Salem, N.C., marks the final stage of the newspaper division's modernization. The project is expected to be completed by mid-1994. The company also said, in commenting on new FCC cable pricing regulations effective October 1993, that the impact on revenues would be minimal. Softness in retail advertising continues to hurt newspaper advertising revenues, but classified advertising and circulation continue to gain. Media General noted that a 7% reduction in newsprint price discounts announced on March 1, 1993, was not holding, because of continued oversupply and modest demand, but added that year-to-year newsprint revenue comparisons still remained positive in the third quarter.

Next earnings report expected in January.

Per Share Data ($)

Yr. End Dec. 31	1992	1991	1990	1989	1988	1987	1986	1985	1984	1983
Tangible Bk. Val.	**6.24**	5.92	8.80	8.20	7.57	9.27	8.02	7.61	6.76	5.54
Cash Flow	**2.80**	d0.47	2.81	2.56	1.96	3.00	1.93	2.21	2.20	1.90
Earnings[1]	**0.70**	d2.39	0.98	0.80	0.31	1.50	0.60	1.16	1.40	1.27
Dividends	**0.440**	0.440	0.440	0.420	0.385	0.335	0.299	0.290	0.270	0.260
Payout Ratio	**63%**	NM	45%	53%	129%	22%	50%	25%	19%	20%
Prices—High	**22⅞**	23⅛	31¾	40½	50½	48¼	24⅞	21¾	16½	16½
Low	**14**	16½	15¼	29⅞	33½	21⅛	18	15⅞	13	8½
P/E Ratio—	**33–20**	NM	32–16	51–37	NM	32–14	41–30	19–14	12–9	13–8

Data as orig. reptd. Adj. for stk. divs. of 100% May 1987, Nov. 1986. **1.** Bef. spec. item(s) of +0.03 in 1992. d-Deficit. E-Estimated. NM-Not Meaningful.

Income Data (Million $)

Year Ended Dec. 31	Revs.	Oper. Inc.	% Oper. Inc. of Revs.	Cap. Exp.	Depr.	Int. Exp.	[1]Net Bef. Taxes	Eff. Tax Rate	[2]Net Inc.	% Net Inc. of Revs.	Cash Flow
1992	**578**	**97**	**16.8**	**92**	**54.6**	**22.3**	**26.3**	**30.3%**	**[3]18.3**	**3.2**	**72.9**
1991	586	98	16.7	115	49.9	22.1	d52.7	NM	d62.1	NM	d12.1
1990	614	111	18.1	74	47.5	22.6	43.5	41.4%	25.5	4.2	73.0
1989	595	100	16.8	69	45.6	25.4	30.0	30.9%	20.7	3.4	66.4
1988	739	129	17.5	78	47.6	20.3	14.2	37.9%	8.8	1.2	56.5
1987	703	121	17.2	81	43.1	17.5	74.0	42.0%	42.9	6.1	86.0
1986	626	98	15.6	100	38.1	16.1	24.7	30.7%	[3]17.1	2.7	55.2
1985	572	85	14.9	91	30.3	13.6	50.1	34.5%	32.8	5.7	63.1
1984	539	85	15.7	90	22.6	10.8	64.2	38.0%	39.8	7.4	62.4
1983	504	84	16.6	59	18.1	8.2	63.6	43.5%	35.9	7.1	54.0

Balance Sheet Data (Million $)

Dec. 31	Cash	Curr. Assets	Curr. Liab.	Ratio	Total Assets	% Ret. on Assets	Long Term Debt	Common Equity	Total Cap.	% LT Debt of Cap.	% Ret. on Equity
1992	**3.0**	**90**	**80**	**1.1**	**787**	**2.4**	**321**	**210**	**625**	**51.3**	**8.9**
1991	4.6	109	105	1.0	762	NM	276	202	592	46.6	NM
1990	3.1	110	89	1.2	776	3.3	234	274	635	36.9	9.6
1989	8.2	140	78	1.8	783	22.5	276	259	650	42.4	8.1
1988	8.3	207	151	1.4	859	1.1	281	252	659	42.6	3.1
1987	7.7	158	98	1.6	829	5.5	240	348	701	34.2	12.9
1986	7.6	144	92	1.6	740	2.4	203	314	623	32.6	5.5
1985	6.9	147	83	1.8	688	5.2	183	305	584	31.3	11.2
1984	7.1	123	80	1.5	563	7.7	109	278	465	23.3	15.2
1983	5.3	116	67	1.7	475	8.1	84	245	394	21.4	15.6

Data as orig. reptd. **1.** Incl. equity in earns. of nonconsol. subs. **2.** Bef. spec. items. **3.** Refl. acctg. change. d-Deficit. NM-Not Meaningful.

Business Summary

Media General is a major newspaper publisher, recycler of newsprint, and owner of TV and cable systems. Contributions in 1992 were:

	Revs.	Profits
Newspapers	52%	38%
Newsprint	17%	3%
Broadcasting	29%	61%
Other	2%	–2%

Daily and Sunday newspapers are published in Richmond, Va., Tampa, Fla., and Winston-Salem, N.C., with combined circulation of over 600,000 daily and 739,000 Sunday. The company also publishes 14 weekly and semi-weekly neewspapers and shoppers in Florida. Garden State Paper Co. is a major recycler of newsprint. Its patented process is involved in the production of about 10% of U.S. newsprint.

Broadcast operations include one NBC affiliate in Tampa, two ABC affiliates in Charleston and Jacksonville, and four CATV systems in Fairfax County and Fredericksburg, Va., which serve more than 215,000 subscribers. Other operations include products and services in publishing, printing and graphic arts, and financial services.

Media General owns 40% of Garden State Newspapers Inc. (GSN), established in April 1985 to acquire medium-sized newspapers throughout the U.S. At the end of 1992, GSN owned 14 dailies with combined circulation of 498,000, and several weeklies.

Dividend Data

Cash has been paid in each year since 1923. A dividend reinvestment and stock purchase plan is available.

Amt. of Divd. $	Date Decl.	Ex–divd. Date	Stock of Record	Payment Date
0.11	Sep. 24	Nov. 3	Nov. 9	Dec. 11'92
0.11	Jan. 29	Feb. 22	Feb. 26	Mar. 15'93
0.11	Mar. 25	May 24	May 28	Jun. 15'93
0.11	Jul. 29	Aug. 25	Aug. 31	Sep. 15'93
0.11	Sep. 17	Nov. 23	Nov. 30	Dec. 15'93

Capitalization

Long Term Debt: $301,506,000 (6/93).

Class A Common Stock: 25,655,021 shs. ($5 par).
Officers and directors control 15%.
Institutions hold 58%, incl. 30% held by a group led by Mario J. Gabelli.
Shareholders: 2,930 of record.

Class B Common Stock: 557,154 shs. ($5 par).
About 71% is closely held.
Cl. B shs. elect 75% of directors.

Office—333 E. Grace St., Richmond, VA 23219 (P.O. Box C-32333, Richmond 23293). **Tel**—(804) 649-6000. **Chrmn, Pres & CEO**—J. S. Bryan III. **Vice Chrmn**—J. S. Evans. **SVP & CFO**—M. N. Morton. **Investor Contact**— R. W. Pendergast. **Dirs**—R. P. Black, D. T. Bryan, J. S. Bryan III, C. A. Davis, A. S. Donnahoe, J. S. Evans, R. V. Hatcher, T. L. Rankin, H. L. Valentine II. **Transfer Agent & Registrar**—Wachovia Bank of North Carolina, Winston-Salem. **Incorporated** in Virginia in 1969. **Empl**—7,300.

 William H. Donald

Medical Care America

NYSE Symbol MRX Options on CBOE, Pacific (Jan-Apr-Jul-Oct) In S&P MidCap 400

Price	Range	P-E Ratio	Dividend	Yield	S&P Ranking	Beta
Aug. 2'93	1993					
16⅜	27–13¾	22	None	None	NR	1.37

Summary

Medical Care America, formed through the September 1992 merger of Medical Care International and Critical Care America, operates freestanding outpatient surgical centers and provides home infusion therapies. Increased price competition in the home infusion business has led to lower earnings in recent quarters. In response to the increasing presence of managed care, the company is attempting to build volume through contracted business with third-party payors.

Business Summary

Medical Care America was formed in 1992 to combine the outpatient surgical business of Medical Care International, Inc. and the home infusion therapy business of Critical Care America, Inc. Contributions to revenues in recent years (pro forma before 1992) were:

	1992	1991	1990
Surgical centers..........	57%	55%	57%
Infusion therapy..........	43%	45%	43%

The surgical center division operates a network of freestanding outpatient surgical centers, with 91 centers in 25 states as of May 1993. In 1992, its centers handled about 340,000 surgical cases. The centers provide facilities and medical support staff necessary for physicians to perform non-emergency surgical procedures that do not require overnight hospitalization. Centers consist primarily of operating and recovery rooms equipped with the medical instruments required to perform a variety of outpatient procedures. A number are also equipped with post-operative recovery care facilities that allow supervised overnight care after surgery.

The company's home infusion therapy services are provided through 54 regional centers located in major metropolitan areas throughout the U.S. Infusion therapies involve the administration of nutrients, antibiotics and other drugs and fluids intravenously or through a feeding tube. Home infusion therapy generally offers significant cost savings over hospital treatment and enables patients to continue their therapies in a familiar environment. MRX has also developed comprehensive care programs which address complex patient conditions through multiple therapy and service regimens.

MRX also owns or manages five ophthalmic surgical practices, six diagnostic imaging centers, and five physical therapy centers, each of which is located near one of the company's surgical centers, and which in the aggregate contributed 5% of total 1992 revenues.

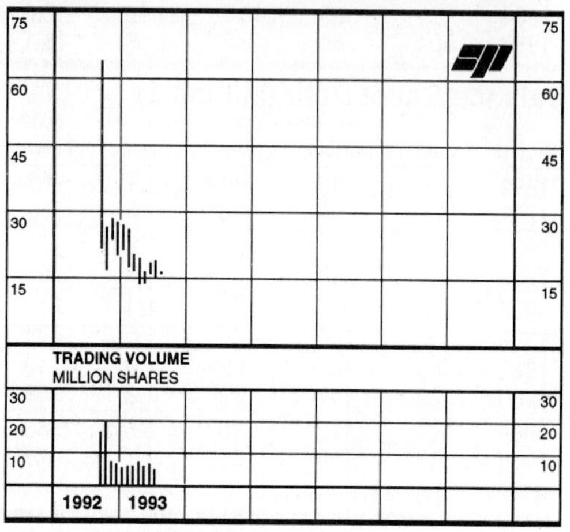

Important Developments

Jul. '93— MRX said it is beginning to see the positive effects of its cost-cutting program in the infusion services division and that it is optimistic that the pricing environment in both the home infusion and surgical center market is stabilizing. The company added that it continues to address the major changes underway in the health care system by increasing volume through contracted business with third-party payors. To accelerate the increased volume, MRX said it is developing a surgical center sales force and redirecting its infusion sales effort to a more balanced effort toward selling to payors as well as physicians.

Next earnings report expected in late October.

Per Share Data ($)

Yr. End Dec. 31	1992	[1]1991	[1]1990	[1]1989
Tangible Bk. Val.	**7.10**	8.55	NA	NA
Cash Flow	**1.79**	1.97	1.80	1.31
Earnings[2]	**1.10**	1.43	1.34	0.93
Dividends	**Nil**	NA	NA	NA
Payout Ratio	**Nil**	NA	NA	NA
Prices—High	**64**	NA	NA	NA
Low	**16⅞**	NA	NA	NA
P/E Ratio—	**58–15**	NA	NA	NA

Data as orig. reptd.; prior to 1992, as reptd. in joint proxy statement/prospectus dated Aug. 3, 1992. **1.** Pro forma. **2.** Bef. spec. items of -0.02 in 1991, -0.04 in 1990, +0.11 in 1989. NA-Not Available.

Income Data (Million $)

Year Ended Dec. 31	Revs.	Oper. Inc.	% Oper. Inc. of Revs.	Cap. Exp.	Depr.	Int. Exp.	Net Bef. Taxes	Eff. Tax Rate	[2]Net Inc.	% Net Inc. of Revs.	Cash Flow
1992	**641**	**168**	**26.2**	**55.1**	**25.6**	**16.4**	**103**	**35.1%**	**41.1**	**6.4**	**66.8**
[1]1991	522	144	27.5	NA	19.5	12.4	87	40.5%	51.6	9.9	71.1
[1]1990	425	108	25.4	NA	16.0	11.0	76	38.9%	46.4	10.9	62.4
[1]1989	278	67	24.0	NA	11.1	7.6	44	37.3%	27.5	9.9	38.6

Balance Sheet Data (Million $)

Dec. 31	Cash	Curr. Assets	Curr. Liab.	Curr. Ratio	Total Assets	% Ret. on Assets	Long Term Debt	Common Equity	Total Cap.	% LT Debt of Cap.	% Ret. on Equity
1992	**179**	**367**	**90.3**	**4.1**	**888**	**4.5**	**229**	**514**	**784**	**29.3**	**8.5**
[1]1991	200	351	63.3	5.5	762	8.0	209	458	668	31.3	13.3
[1]1990	NA	NA	NA	NA	527	9.9	136	317	453	30.0	16.2
[1]1989	NA	NA	NA	NA	406	NA	91	257	347	26.2	NA

Data as orig. reptd.; prior to 1992, as reptd. in joint proxy statement/prospectus dated Aug. 3, 1992. **1.** Pro forma. **2.** Bef. spec. items. NA-Not Available.

Net Revenues (Million $)

Quarter:	1993	1992	[1]1991	[1]1990
Mar.	154	146	114	---
Jun.	160	159	130	---
Sep.		163	133	---
Dec.		173	146	---
		641	522	425

Revenues in the six months ended June 30, 1993, advanced 8.4%, year to year (as reclassified to account for bad debt provision as a reduction in net revenue), limited by declining home infusion revenues. Surgery center revenues climbed 24%. Results were penalized by continuing pricing pressures in infusion services; net income fell 35%, to $24,976,000 ($0.68 a share), from $38,421,000 ($1.02).

Common Share Earnings ($)

Quarter:	1993	1992	[1]1991	[1]1990
Mar.	0.32	0.46	---	---
Jun.	0.36	0.56	[2]0.50	---
Sep.		d0.19	0.45	---
Dec.		0.27	0.48	---
		1.10	1.43	1.34

Dividend Data

The company has not paid cash dividends and does not anticipate paying cash dividends in the foreseeable future. A poison pill" stock purchase right was adopted in 1992.

Finances

In July 1993, MRX said it had repurchased about 200,000 of the 1.8 million shares authorized for repurchase in the first quarter of 1993.

In May 1993, MRX said continuing efforts to improve margins would likely result in additional restructuring charges during 1993, with the extent of the charges not yet determined.

Medical Care America was formed in September 1992 through the merger of Medical Care International, Inc. (MCI) and Critical Care America, Inc. (CCA). Pursuant to the transaction, which became effective September 9, 1992, MCI shareholders received MRX common shares on a one-for-one basis, while CCA shareholders received 0.72 of an MRX common share for each CCA common share held.

Prior to its September 1992 merger with Critical Care America, Medical Care International had outstanding $69 million principal amount of 7% convertible subordinated debentures, due 2015, and $115 principal amount of 6¾% convertible subordinated debentures, due 2006. The 7% debentures and 6¾% debentures were convertible into MCI common stock at $48.375 and $73.375 a share, respectively. Following the merger, the debentures became convertible into MRX stock, with no change in conversion prices, and MRX assumed MCI's obligations with respect to the debentures.

Capitalization

Long Term Debt: $226,495,000 (6/93), incl. $69,000,000 of 7% debs. conv. into com. at $48.375 a sh., and $115,000,000 of 6¾% debs. conv. into com. at $73.375 a sh.

Minority Interest: $35,593,000.

Common Stock: 36,526,714 shs. ($0.01 par). Institutions hold 85%. Shareholders: About 3,000 of record (1/93).

1. Pro forma. **2.** Six mos. d-Deficit.

Office—13455 Noel Rd., Dallas, TX 75240. **Tel**—(214) 701-2200. **Pres & CEO**—D. E Steen. **SVP & CFO**—L. M. Mullen. **SVP & Investor Contact**—J. R. Bond. **Dirs**—J. R. Anderson, T. A. Bosler, J. F. Glenn, B. L. Karns, G. D. Kennedy, M. R. Knapp, D. E. Steen, J. M. Sweeney, W. L. Wearly, W. H. Wilcox, B. L. Wood. **Transfer Agent & Registrar**—Society National Bank. **Incorporated** in Delaware in 1992. **Empl**—5,000.

 Adam J. Penn

Mentor Graphics

NASDAQ Symbol MENT (Incl. in Nat'l Market) Options on ASE & Pacific In S&P MidCap 400

Price	Range	P-E Ratio	Dividend	Yield	S&P Ranking	Beta
Sep. 27'93	1993					
11	12–7⅞	NM	0.24	2.2%	B–	1.33

Summary

Mentor is a worldwide leader in electronic design automation systems. Losses narrowed in 1992, reflecting reduced restructuring charges. Although revenues are expected to remain flat in 1993, with an anticipated increase in software sales offset by a decline in hardware revenues, a return to modest profitability is anticipated.

Current Outlook

Earnings of $0.40 a share are projected for 1994, up from $0.02 estimated for 1993, versus a loss of $1.13 in 1992.

Dividends should continue at $0.06 quarterly.

Revenues are expected to remain flat in 1993, as a planned decline in hardware sales should be offset by higher software sales. Operating margins should improve during the year, as more profitable software sales increase as a percentage of total revenues. The company began distributing version 8.2 of its Software Release tools in March 1993, and initial customer feedback has been favorable. International sales prospects, primarily in Japan and Europe, remain generally weak; foreign sales are expected to hold steady at 46% to 50% of 1993 revenues. Domestic demand for Mentor's software products has shown improvement thus far in 1993. Following a small loss estimated for the third quarter, a seasonally strong fourth quarter should lead to a small profit for the year.

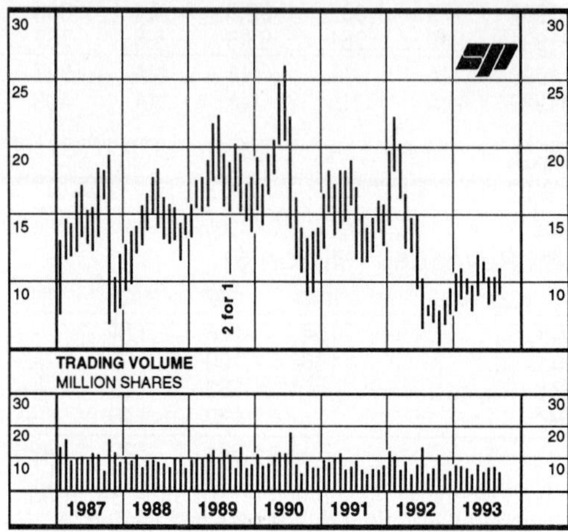

Total Revenues (Million $)

Quarter:	1993	1992	1991	1990
Mar.	83	100	104	117
Jun.	88	89	95	101
Sep.		78	95	104
Dec.		84	107	113
		351	400	435

For the six months ended June 30, 1993, total revenues dropped 9.6%, year to year, reflecting unfavorable worldwide economic conditions, a planned reduction in hardware sales, and slow customer transition to Mentor's version 8 software. Gross margins widened to 63.5% of revenues, from 56.2%, on a greater portion of more profitable software sales. Higher R&D spending was outweighed by lower SG&A costs; the net loss narrowed to $4,008,000 ($0.09 a share), from $5,658,000 ($0.13).

Common Share Earnings ($)

Quarter:	1993	1992	1991	1990
Mar.	d0.09	0.03	d0.09	0.26
Jun.	0.01	d0.15	d0.24	0.08
Sep.	Ed0.02	d1.01	d1.11	0.10
Dec.	E0.12	0.01	0.02	0.09
	E0.02	d1.13	d1.43	0.53

Important Developments

Sep. '93— Mentor said domestic software demand remained firm, but added that weakness in international markets, primarily in Germany and Japan, has restricted revenue gains.

Next earnings report expected in late October.

Per Share Data ($)

Yr. End Dec. 31	1992	1991	[2]1990	1989	1988	1987	1986	1985	[2]1984	[2]1983
Tangible Bk. Val.	[1]**4.86**	[1]6.14	[1]7.70	[1]7.84	6.56	5.70	4.84	4.44	2.69	d0.41
Cash Flow	**d0.56**	d0.74	1.15	1.76	1.39	0.91	0.60	0.45	0.37	NA
Earnings[3]	**d1.13**	d1.43	0.53	1.22	0.96	0.60	0.34	0.26	0.30	d0.05
Dividends	**0.24**	0.24	0.22	0.15	0.05	Nil	Nil	Nil	Nil	Nil
Payout Ratio	**NM**	NM	39%	12%	5%	Nil	Nil	Nil	Nil	Nil
Prices—High	**22¼**	19	26	22⅜	18⅜	19½	9⅞	15⅛	12⅝	NA
Low	**5¼**	11½	9	13⅜	9⅜	6⅞	5⅝	6½	7⅞	NA
P/E Ratio—	**NM**	NM	49–17	18–11	19–10	32–11	29–17	58–25	42–26	NA

Data as orig. reptd. Adj. for stk. div. of 100% Aug. 1989. **1.** Incl. intangibles. **2.** Refl. merger or acq. **3.** Bef. spec. item(s) of +0.06 in 1984. d-Deficit. E-Estimated. NM-Not Meaningful. NA-Not Available.

Income Data (Million $)

Year Ended Dec. 31	Revs.	Oper. Inc.	% Oper. Inc. of Revs.	Cap. Exp.	Depr.	Int. Exp.	Net Bef. Taxes	Eff. Tax Rate	[2]Net Inc.	% Net Inc. of Revs.	Cash Flow
1992	**351**	**d2.1**	**NM**	**24.7**	**25.8**	**5.47**	**d48.3**	**NM**	**d50.9**	**NM**	**d25.1**
1991	400	d3.7	NM	97.0	29.7	5.76	d63.0	NM	d61.6	NM	d31.9
[1]1990	435	52.1	12.0	79.4	27.7	4.51	32.4	27.0%	23.6	5.4	51.4
1989	380	78.7	20.7	39.2	20.0	0.93	66.2	32.4%	44.8	11.8	64.8
1988	301	59.8	19.9	29.3	14.9	0.45	50.6	33.7%	33.5	11.2	48.5
1987	222	38.0	17.1	14.7	10.6	0.98	31.7	36.0%	20.3	9.2	31.0
1986	174	20.5	11.8	10.2	8.5	2.15	16.5	33.5%	[3]11.0	6.3	19.5
1985	137	13.5	9.9	22.5	5.9	1.32	12.1	33.9%	8.0	5.8	13.9
[1]1984	88	11.1	12.6	10.4	2.0	0.13	13.6	38.8%	8.3	9.5	10.4
[1]1983	26	0.7	2.7	6.0	0.9	0.28	d0.2	Nil	d0.2	NM	NA

Balance Sheet Data (Million $)

Dec. 31	Cash	Curr. Assets	Curr. Liab.	Curr. Ratio	Total Assets	% Ret. on Assets	Long Term Debt	Common Equity	Total Cap.	% LT Debt of Cap.	% Ret. on Equity
1992	**109**	**208**	**99**	**2.1**	**379**	**NM**	**55.7**	**221**	**277**	**20.1**	**NM**
1991	144	294	125	2.4	446	NM	50.6	268	318	15.9	NM
1990	162	331	123	2.7	504	5.0	50.2	326	377	13.3	7.2
1989	145	273	79	3.4	362	13.7	7.2	274	281	2.6	17.8
1988	120	224	59	3.8	282	13.0	Nil	222	223	Nil	16.2
1987	98	195	39	5.0	229	9.0	Nil	188	190	Nil	11.7
1986	81	179	57	3.2	215	5.3	Nil	155	157	Nil	7.4
1985	74	158	51	3.1	194	5.0	Nil	140	142	Nil	7.1
1984	37	92	33	2.8	108	12.6	Nil	71	72	Nil	24.3
1983	1	18	14	1.3	24	NM	0.1	d3	10	0.5	NM

Data as orig. reptd. **1.** Refl. merger or acq. **2.** Bef. spec. items. **3.** Refl. acctg. change. d-Deficit. NM-Not Meaningful. NA-Not Available.

Business Summary

Mentor Graphics Corp. designs, manufactures, markets and services electronic design automation systems and software for the integrated circuit (IC) and systems design markets. Its systems enable engineers and designers to analyze, design and test custom ICs, application-specific integrated circuits (ASICs), printed circuit boards and electronic systems and subsystems.

Mentor's Falcon Framework software provides a common foundation for its EDA software products and also allows for the integration of third party software tools developed by other commercial EDA vendors and by customers for their own internal use. The company's products help customers reduce development time in producing innovative hardware products of high quality. In addition to software products, Mentor's service division offers consulting, support and training to enhance customers' success in the design and manufacture of hardware products.

The company's software runs on workstations in a broad range of price and performance levels, including workstations made by Sun Microsystems, Digital Equipment Corp., Hewlett-Packard, NEC Corp., Sony Corp. and IBM. Mentor expects a continuing shift toward more software-only sales and fewer hardware sales.

Products are marketed through a worldwide network of sales and support offices. Customers are in the computer, aerospace, telecommunications, consumer electronics and semiconductor industries. Sales outside of North America represented 48% of revenues in 1992 (51% in 1991).

Dividend Data

Quarterly cash dividends were initiated in 1988.

Amt. of Divd. $	Date Decl.	Ex-divd. Date	Stock of Record	Payment Date
0.06	Oct. 20	Oct. 26	Oct. 30	Nov. 13'92
0.06	Feb. 2	Feb. 8	Feb. 12	Feb. 25'93
0.06	Apr. 20	Apr. 26	Apr. 30	May 13'93
0.06	Jul. 21	Jul. 26	Jul. 30	Aug. 12'93

Finances

A restructuring charge of $12.9 million was recorded in 1992 to cover employee severance payments, facilities consolidation, and costs of resolving contractual issues with third-party software developers.

Capitalization

Long Term Debt: $58,057,000 (6/93).

Common Stock: 46,390,216 shs. (no par).
Institutions hold 65%.
Shareholders: 1,647 of record (12/92).

Options: To buy 6,576,000 shs. at $0.21 to $19.76 ea. (12/92).

Office—8005 S.W. Boeckman Rd., Wilsonville, OR 97070-7777. **Tel**—(503) 685-7000. **Chrmn, Pres & CEO**—T. H. Bruggere. **CFO**—R. D. Norby. **VP & Secy**—F. S. Delia. **Treas & Investor Contact**—Jackie Kraybill. **Dirs**—T. H. Bruggere, M. B. Congdon, D. R. Hathaway, D. C. Moffenbeier, F. K. Richardson, C. J. Santoro, J. A. Shirley, D. N. Strohm. **Transfer Agent & Registrar**—First Interstate Bank of Oregon, Portland. **Incorporated** in Oregon in 1981. **Empl**—2,100.

 Samuel A. Dedio

Mercantile Bancorp.

NYSE Symbol MTL In S&P MidCap 400

Price	Range	P-E Ratio	Dividend	Yield	S&P Ranking	Beta
Jul. 9'93	1993					
50¼	56½–44	11	1.48	2.9%	B+	0.90

Summary

This St. Louis-based holding company owns 39 banks throughout Missouri, southern Illinois and eastern Kansas. Earnings continued their steady advance in the first half of 1993, and further growth is expected. Trading in the shares shifted to the NYSE from the NASDAQ system in March 1993.

Current Outlook

Earnings for 1993 are projected at $4.70 a share, compared with the pro forma $3.80 of 1992. As originally reported, earnings for 1992 were $4.36. Earnings for 1994 are estimated at $5.00 a share.

The $0.37 quarterly dividend is the minimum expectation.

The company sees minimal loan growth in 1993 and 1994, as fears of a slow economic recovery persist. MTL expects to continue to grow its credit card loan portfolio rapidly; it has maintained or improved the quality of these loans, and expects to continue to do so. MTL may see slightly lower net interest margins as rates rise and CDs, which now have relatively short maturities, reprice. The company is targeting loan loss reserves of 150% of nonperforming assets, and expects quarterly provisions to remain at current levels through 1993, when nonperforming assets are expected to improve. Expected lower other real estate expense should aid earnings slightly in 1993 and have a greater impact in 1994.

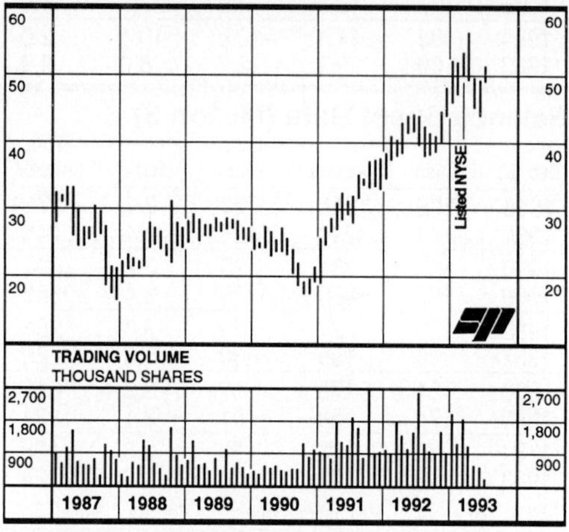

Review of Operations

Net interest income for the six months ended June 30, 1993, rose 16%, year to year, reflecting greater earning assets and wider net interest margin. The provision for loan losses fell 4.1%, and with 13% higher noninterest income and 13% larger noninterest expense, pretax income expanded 31%. After taxes at 37.4%, versus 32.2%, net income was up 21%, to $2.36 a share from $2.08 (restated).

Common Share Earnings ($)

Quarter:	1993	1992	1991	1990
Mar.	1.17	1.04	0.94	0.75
Jun.	1.20	1.08	0.95	0.83
Sep.	E1.13	1.10	0.96	0.93
Dec.	E1.20	1.13	1.00	0.99
	E4.70	4.36	3.85	3.50

Important Developments

Mar. '93— On March 25, the company's common shares began trading on the NYSE. They formerly traded on the NASDAQ under the symbol MTRC.

Mar. '93— MTL agreed to buy Mt. Vernon Bancorp Inc., of Illinois (assets of $117 million), with Mt. Vernon shareholders to receive 144,674 Mercantile common shares and $1.8 million in cash. The transaction was expected to close in the third quarter of 1993 and will be accounted for as a purchase.

Jan. '93— Mercantile acquired three Kansas-based bank holding companies: MidAmerican Corp., Crown Bancshares II, Inc. and Johnson County Bankshares, Inc. (total assets $1.1 billion) for 3,157,616 common shares. The transaction was accounted for as a pooling-of-interests.

Next earnings report expected in mid-October.

Per Share Data ($)

Yr. End Dec. 31	1992	1991	1990	1989	1988	[1,2]1987	1986	[1]1985	[1]1984	[1]1983
Tangible Bk. Val.	**30.86**	27.27	24.66	23.34	24.91	24.59	27.66	25.49	24.11	22.51
Earnings	**4.36**	3.85	3.50	0.03	1.79	d1.53	3.57	3.49	3.13	2.98
Dividends	**1.400**	1.400	1.400	1.400	1.400	1.400	1.400	1.280	1.280	1.191
Payout Ratio	**32%**	36%	40%	NM	78%	NM	39%	37%	41%	40%
Prices—High	**48¼**	37¾	27½	29¼	31¼	33¼	37⅛	27½	22	18¾
Low	**34¾**	19	17½	25	19	16½	27⅛	21¾	15¾	13⅝
P/E Ratio—	**11–8**	10–5	8–5	NM	17–11	NM	10–8	8–6	7–5	6–5

Data as orig. reptd. Adj. for stk. divs. of 50% Apr. 1986, 50% Apr. 1984. **1.** Refl. merger or acq. **2.** Refl. acctg. change. E-Estimated d-Deficit. NM-Not Meaningful.

Mercantile Bancorporation Inc.

Income Data (Million $)

Year Ended Dec. 31	Net Int. Inc.	Tax Equiv. Adj.	Non Int. Inc.	Loan Loss Prov.	% Exp./ Op. Revs.	Net Bef. Taxes	Eff. Tax Rate	Net Inc.	% Net Int. Margin	—% Return On— Assets	Equity
1992	**364**	**6.5**	**142**	**61**	**63.0**	**124.3**	**31.6%**	**85.0**	**4.51**	**0.94**	**13.7**
1991	292	6.5	122	50	64.4	93.9	29.1%	66.6	4.37	0.88	13.6
1990	257	9.9	108	45	64.7	76.9	26.3%	56.7	4.26	0.81	13.4
1989	241	12.9	123	95	73.0	d5.7	NM	0.5	4.34	0.01	0.1
1988	221	15.0	115	60	70.8	29.8	3.9%	28.7	4.05	0.44	6.7
[1,2]1987	234	21.2	113	168	66.5	d64.1	NM	d24.5	4.22	NM	NM
1986	227	39.9	119	63	58.6	64.0	13.7%	55.3	4.52	0.86	12.5
[2]1985	209	32.3	85	36	60.7	61.9	15.7%	52.2	4.63	0.89	13.2
[2]1984	177	28.1	72	25	61.1	55.2	16.5%	46.1	4.52	0.87	12.7
[2]1983	154	21.8	59	16	62.0	50.7	18.1%	41.6	4.07	0.82	12.9

Balance Sheet Data (Million $)

		Earning Assets				% Loan	Deposits			Long		
Dec. 31	Total Assets	Mon. Mkt. Assets	Inv. Secs.	Com'l Loans	Other Loans	Loss Resv.	Demand	Time	% Loans/ Deposits	Term Debt	Common Equity	% Equity To Assets
1992	**9,476**	**265**	**2,423**	**1,741**	**4,159**	**2.37**	**1,244**	**6,288**	**78.3**	**221**	**669**	**6.82**
1991	8,089	406	1,553	1,697	3,693	2.34	1,147	5,334	83.2	116	546	6.49
1990	7,617	224	1,117	1,892	3,531	2.39	1,267	4,895	87.4	117	440	6.06
1989	6,942	150	1,111	1,888	3,018	2.50	1,187	4,260	89.3	118	407	6.47
1988	6,459	157	889	1,968	2,721	1.85	1,114	4,195	87.5	120	429	6.60
1987	6,766	411	977	2,020	2,709	3.82	1,185	4,249	86.1	122	422	6.74
1986	6,586	476	799	2,054	2,433	1.49	1,265	3,792	87.5	123	459	6.90
1985	6,763	1,070	936	1,988	2,053	1.38	1,129	3,857	79.7	144	424	6.72
1984	5,944	687	850	1,880	1,724	1.33	1,231	3,247	78.9	129	374	6.84
1983	5,508	792	885	1,539	1,446	1.33	1,139	2,981	71.1	129	347	6.34

Data as orig. reptd. **1.** Refl. acctg. change. **2.** Refl. merger or acq. d-Deficit. NM-Not Meaningful.

Business Summary

Mercantile Bancorporation is a bank holding company, headquartered in St. Louis, that owns 39 banks in Missouri, southern Illinois and eastern Kansas, including Mercantile Bank N.A., which had deposits totaling $5.08 billion at 1992 year end.

Consolidated total loans of $5.90 billion at the end of 1992 consisted of commercial 30%, real estate 47%, and consumer and credit card 23%.

The reserve for loan losses was $139,857,000 at December 31, 1992 ($126,151,000 a year earlier), equal to 2.37% (2.34%) of loans outstanding. Net chargeoffs in 1992 were $62,988,000 ($55,885,000 in 1991), or 1.08% (1.06%) of average loans. As of 1992 year end, nonperforming loans totaled $95,996,000 (1.6 3% of loans), compared with $112,935,000 (2.10%) a year earlier.

Total deposits of $7.53 billion at the end of 1992 consisted of 17% noninterest-bearing demand, 15% interest-bearing demand, 17% money-market accounts, 8% savings, 37% consumer time CDs under $100,000, 5% time CDs of $100,000 or more, and 1% other time and foreign.

On a tax-equivalent basis, the average yield on interest-earning assets in 1992 was 8.25% (9.66% in 1991), while the average rate paid on interest-bearing liabilities was 4.46% (6.18%), for a net interest spread of 3.79% (3.48%).

Subsidiaries include firms in brokerage services, asset-based lending, investment advisory services, credit card services, general insurance, and credit life insurance.

Mercantile's strategy is to concentrate on growing in Missouri and neighboring states through acquisition while maintaining an emphasis on profitability.

Dividend Data

Dividends, including those of predecessors, have been paid in every year since 1909. A dividend reinvestment plan is available.

Amt of Divd. $	Date Decl.	Ex–divd. Date	Stock of Record	Payment Date
0.35	Oct. 9	Dec. 4	Dec. 10	Jan. 1'93
0.37	Feb. 11	Mar. 4	Mar. 10	Apr. 1'93
0.37	May 13	Jun. 4	Jun. 10	Jul. 1'93
0.37	Jul. 8	Sep. 3	Sep. 10	Oct. 1'93

Capitalization

Long Term Debt: $222,870,000 (6/93).

Common Stock: 23,528,000 shs. ($5 par).
Institutions hold about 47%.
Shareholders: 11,267 (3/93).

Office—Mercantile Tower, P.O. Box 524, St. Louis, MO 63166-0524. **Tel**—(314) 425-2525. **Chrmn, Pres & CEO**—T. H. Jacobsen. **Vice Chrmn, CFO & Investor Contact**—Ralph W. Babb Jr. **Secy**—J. W. Bilstrom. **SVP-Treas**—M. T. Normile. **Dirs**—R. P. Conerly, H. M. Cornell Jr., J. C. Eason, E. K. Dille, B. A. Edison, W. A. Hall, T. A. Hays, W. G. Heckman, T. H. Jacobsen, J. B. Malloy, C. H. Price II, H. Saligman, C. D. Schnuck, R. W. Staley, P. T. Stokes, F. A. Stroble, J. A. Wright. **Transfer Agent & Registrar**—Society National Bank, Cleveland. **Incorporated** in Missouri in 1970; bank founded in 1929. **Empl**—4,839.

 C. Orgielewicz

Mercantile Bankshares

NASDAQ Symbol MRBK (Incl. in Nat'l Market) In S&P MidCap 400

Price	Range	P-E Ratio	Dividend	Yield	S&P Ranking	Beta
Oct. 1'93	1993					
$21\frac{1}{4}$	$23\frac{27}{32}$–$19\frac{11}{32}$	12	[1]0.68	3.2%	A	1.14

Summary

This Maryland holding company owns 19 commercial banks and a mortgage banking firm. Profits improved for the 17th consecutive year in 1992. Earnings continued to grow in 1993's first half, reflecting improvement in the net interest margin. A 3-for-2 stock split was effected in October 1993.

Current Outlook

Earnings for 1993 are projected at $1.85 a share, versus the $1.67 of 1992. Earnings per share in 1994 are expected to reach $2.00.

The $0.17 quarterly dividend is likely to be raised to $0.18 a share in 1994.

The company expects loan growth of about 2.5% in 1993 and 3% in 1994 as the economy slowly improves in Maryland and surrounding areas. MRBK expects the loan loss provision to remain steady for the last half of 1993 as it anticipates a slow decline in nonperforming loans through the rest of the year. The level of nonperforming loans should stablize in 1994 and the loan loss provision should drop as coverage is slowly reduced. The net interest margin rose in the first half of 1993 to 4.79%, from 4.69%. As MRBK has been asset-sensitive in the past few years and maintains a conservative capital base and a high level of non-interest bearing deposits, it expects a moderate rise in net interest margin in 1994 as rates increase. Revenues from trust division services, which represent the largest source of noninterest income, are estimated to grow about 5% in the remainder of 1993 and 6% to 8% in 1994.

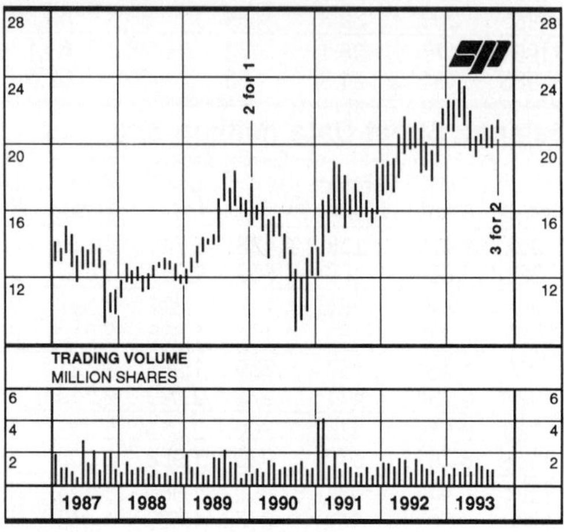

Review of Operations

For the six months ended June 30, 1993, net interest income rose 5.5%, year to year. The provision for loan losses increased 4.9%, to $7,215,000. Noninterest income climbed 3.3% and, with 1.8% higher noninterest expense, pretax income gained 9.2%. After taxes at 38.3%, versus 38.0%, net income rose 8.6%, to $40,906,000 ($1.34 a share), from $37,658,000 ($1.24).

Common Share Earnings ($)

Quarter:	1993	1992	1991	[1]1990
Mar.	0.45	0.41	0.41	0.40
Jun.	0.45	0.41	0.39	0.40
Sep.	E0.47	0.42	0.37	0.37
Dec.	E0.48	0.43	0.39	0.38
	E1.85	1.67	1.56	1.55

Important Developments

Sep. '93— MRBK said it may receive proceeds from the sale of property collateralizing the $21.3 million loan it placed in nonperforming status during 1992's third quarter. However, the assets of the borrower must first be released from bankruptcy court.

Oct. '92— The company reported a $25.1 million increase in nonperforming loans for the quarter ended September 30, 1992, largely attributable to a $21.3 million loan to one borrower. The company increased the provision for loan losses by $28.4 million, which would have resulted in a net loss for the third quarter of 1992 had it not realized pretax gains on the sale of investment securities of $25.9 million. MRBK's investment portfolio was composed mainly of U.S. Treasury securities at June 30, 1993. The fairly short duration and high credit quality of MRBK's investment portfolio provides flexibility should loan demand rise.

Next earnings report expected in mid-October.

Per Share Data ($)

Yr. End Dec. 31	[2]1992	1991	[1]1990	1989	1988	[1]1987	1986	1985	1984	[1]1983
Tangible Bk. Val.	**12.61**	11.46	10.39	9.68	8.49	7.61	6.78	6.03	5.37	4.76
Earnings	**1.67**	1.56	1.55	1.60	1.39	1.20	1.04	0.97	0.86	0.81
Dividends	**0.580**	0.573	0.543	0.483	0.417	0.370	0.330	0.290	0.255	0.232
Payout Ratio	**35%**	37%	35%	30%	30%	31%	32%	30%	30%	29%
Prices—High	**$22\frac{5}{32}$**	19	$17\frac{21}{32}$	$18\frac{13}{32}$	$13\frac{5}{32}$	$15\frac{3}{32}$	$15\frac{3}{4}$	$12\frac{11}{32}$	$7\frac{1}{2}$	$5\frac{27}{32}$
Low	**17**	$12\frac{5}{32}$	$8\frac{27}{32}$	$11\frac{21}{32}$	$10\frac{27}{32}$	$9\frac{11}{32}$	$11\frac{1}{2}$	$7\frac{5}{32}$	$5\frac{11}{32}$	$3\frac{1}{2}$
P/E Ratio—	**13–10**	12–8	11–6	12–7	10–8	13–8	15–11	13–7	9–6	7–4

Data as orig. reptd. Adj. for stk. div. of 100% Dec. 1989, 100% Jan. 1986. **1.** Indicated rate (adj.). **2.** Refl. merger or acq. E-Estimated

Income Data (Million $)

Year Ended Dec. 31	Net Int. Inc.	Tax Equiv. Adj.	Non Int. Inc.	Loan Loss Prov.	% Exp./ Op. Revs.	Net Bef. Taxes	Eff. Tax Rate	Net Inc.	% Net Int. Margin	—% Return On— Assets	Equity
[1]**1992**	**229**	**3.8**	**81.0**	**45.3**	**53.4**	**123**	**37.9%**	**76.3**	**4.70**	**1.50**	**13.3**
1991	209	5.3	71.3	20.9	53.5	112	36.8%	70.6	4.57	1.42	13.6
[1]1990	200	6.8	64.0	15.0	52.4	107	35.7%	68.9	5.00	1.56	14.7
1989	180	8.2	59.1	9.2	54.5	95	34.5%	62.0	5.39	1.66	16.3
1988	153	9.3	53.6	8.7	55.0	79	32.7%	53.4	5.18	1.59	15.9
[1]1987	134	12.9	49.7	5.2	53.3	74	37.6%	46.1	5.20	1.51	15.4
1986	120	15.4	47.0	3.9	54.7	65	39.4%	39.5	5.52	1.48	14.9
1985	116	15.1	42.2	4.7	54.6	59	37.7%	36.7	6.14	1.58	15.5
1984	108	14.4	37.6	4.2	55.7	52	35.4%	33.6	6.42	1.61	15.4
[1]1983	100	12.4	33.6	3.7	56.8	46	35.3%	29.5	6.60	1.59	15.6

Balance Sheet Data (Million $)

Dec. 31	Total Assets	—Earning Assets— Mon. Mkt. Assets	Inv. Secs.	Com'l Loans	Other Loans	% Loan Loss Resv.	—Deposits— Demand	Time	% Loans/ Deposits	Long Term Debt	Common Equity	% Equity To Assets
1992	**5,460**	**122**	**1,505**	**1,126**	**2,363**	**2.57**	**896**	**3,621**	**77.3**	**15.1**	**598**	**10.9**
1991	5,183	142	1,345	1,100	2,275	1.95	802	3,472	79.0	16.6	542	10.5
1990	4,886	279	941	1,142	2,170	1.64	771	3,217	83.1	17.3	487	10.6
1989	4,018	76	707	1,034	1,863	1.60	749	2,618	86.0	23.1	402	10.2
1988	3,642	69	633	890	1,734	1.57	708	2,303	87.1	28.9	353	10.0
1987	3,329	1	667	854	1,491	1.48	724	1,986	86.5	33.9	315	9.8
1986	3,055	78	708	713	1,253	1.56	753	1,814	76.6	40.6	277	9.9
1985	2,568	96	614	553	1,071	1.80	617	1,555	74.7	36.1	249	10.2
1984	2,275	55	550	505	949	1.71	536	1,346	78.0	25.0	229	10.5
1983	2,125	51	637	407	812	1.81	532	1,213	69.4	26.0	210	10.1

Data as orig. reptd. 1. Refl. merger or acq.

Business Summary

Mercantile Bankshares Corporation, headquartered in Baltimore, Md., owns 19 commercial banks and a mortgage banking company. The lead bank is Mercantile-Safe Deposit and Trust Co., which had total assets of $2.22 billion as of December 31, 1992. At June 30, 1993, there were 144 retail banking offices.

Loans outstanding of $3.49 billion at 1992 year-end were divided: commercial, financial and agricultural 32.3%; real estate—mortgage 44.4%; consumer 14.2%; and real estate—construction 9.1%.

The allowance for loan losses at the end of 1992 was $88,261,000 ($65,932,000 a year earlier), equal to 2.6% (2.0%) of loans outstanding. Net chargeoffs in 1992 were $23,017,000 ($9,389,000 in 1991), or 0.67% (0.28%) of average loans outstanding. As of December 31, 1992, nonperforming loans totaled $73,707,000 (2.11% of loans outstanding), compared with $59,627,000 (1.77%) a year earlier.

Average deposits of $4.30 billion in 1992 were apportioned: 27% savings and NOW accounts, 28% CDs and other time deposits of less than $100,000, 8% CDs of $100,000 or more, 20% money market and 17% noninterest-bearing demand.

Total income for 1992 was derived as follows: interest and fees on loans 59%, interest and dividends on investment securities 19%, other interest income 1%, trust division services 8% and other noninterest income 13%.

Trust services are provided throughout Maryland by the trust division of Mercantile-Safe Deposit and Trust Co. Trust division income increased 13% in 1992, to $39.9 million.

Dividend Data

Cash dividends have been paid since 1909. A dividend reinvestment plan is available.

Amt. of Divd. $	Date Decl.	Ex-divd. Date	Stock of Record	Payment Date
0.22½	Dec. 8	Dec. 14	Dec. 18	Dec. 31'92
0.22½	Mar. 9	Mar. 16	Mar. 22	Mar. 31'93
0.22½	Jun. 8	Jun. 14	Jun. 18	Jun. 30'93
0.25½	Sep. 14	Sep. 20	Sep. 24	Sep. 30'93
3–for–2	Sep. 14	Oct. 1	Sep. 24	Sep. 30'93

Capitalization

Long Term Debt: $8,793,000 (6/93).

Common Stock: 45,924,957 shs. ($2 par).
Institutions hold about 42%.
Shareholders: 7,617 of record (2/93).

Office—2 Hopkins Plaza, P.O. Box 1477, Baltimore, MD 21201. **Tel**—(410) 237-5900. **Chrmn & CEO**—H. F. Baldwin. **Vice Chrmn**—D. W. Dodge. **Pres**—E. K. Dunn Jr. **Sr VP-Treas**—C. C. McGuire Jr. **Sr VP-Secy**—J. A. O'Connor Jr. **Investor Contact**—Suzanne Wolff. **Dirs**—H. F. Baldwin, T. M. Bancroft Jr., R. O. Berndt, J. A. Block, G. L. Bunting Jr., D. W. Dodge, E. K. Dunn Jr., B. L. Jenkins, R. D. Kunisch, W. J. McCarthy, M. W. Offit, C. H. Poindexter, W. B. Potter, W. C. Richardson, B. L. Robinson, D. J. Shepard, B. B. Topping, J. M. Wilson, C. J. Zamoiski Jr. **Transfer Agent**—Mercantile-Safe Deposit & Trust Co., Baltimore. **Incorporated** in Maryland in 1969. **Empl**—2,738.

 C. Orgielewicz

Meridian Bancorp

NASDAQ Symbol MRDN (Incl. in Nat'l Market) Options on ASE In S&P MidCap 400

Price	Range	P-E Ratio	Dividend	Yield	S&P Ranking	Beta
Oct. 28'93	1993					
30⅞	35¾–26¾	12	1.28	4.1%	A–	1.14

Summary

With the recent acquisition of Commonwealth Bancshares Corp., this leading Pennsylvania bank holding company now has more than 290 retail branch offices in Pennsylvania, Delaware and New Jersey, with total assets of over $14 billion. Earnings are expected to grow nearly 10% in 1994, from 1993's projected $2.65, benefiting from a greater market presence, lower loan loss provisions and continued cost cutting. Capital ratios at September 30, 1993, were well above federal regulatory minimums.

Current Outlook

Earnings for 1994 are projected at $2.90 a share, up from 1993's expected $2.65.

Dividends are expected to continue at $0.32 quarterly.

Earnings are expected to increase 8% to 10% in 1994, based on cost cutting associated with recent acquisitions and expectations of continued lower loan loss provisions. Core earnings should also benefit from Meridian's decision to refocus its mortgage banking unit on loan origination and away from unprofitable loan servicing, due to the trend of mortgage prepayments and high fixed costs; a related restructuring charge of $0.20 a share was taken in 1993's third quarter. The recent purchase of Commonwealth Bancshares Corp., in addition to agreements to purchase First Bath Corp. and four of Provident Savings Bank's retail branches, will broaden MRDN's geographic scope and considerably strengthen its market presence in Pennsylvania and New Jersey. Continued cost savings should be realized from staff reductions and the streamlining and relocation of data processing operations, combined with higher fee income from trust administration and services units. Credit quality continues to improve, as reflected in the level of nonperforming assets (2.18% of loans at September 30, 1993, versus 2.90% a year earlier). Meridian's total risk-based capital ratio at September 30, 1993, remained above the federal regulatory minimum, at 13.16%.

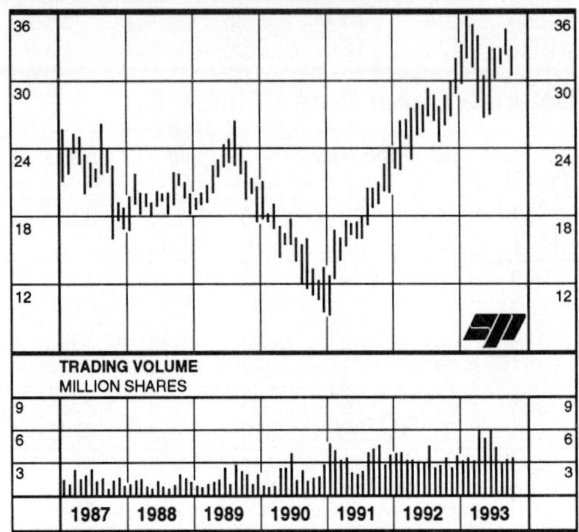

Common Share Earnings ($)

Quarter:	1994	1993[2]	1992	1991
Mar.	E0.70	---	0.61	0.50
Jun.	E0.72	[4]1.28	0.65	0.90
Sep.	E0.73	0.60	0.63	0.64
Dec.	E0.75	E0.77	0.66	0.53
	E2.90	E2.65	2.55	2.56

Review of Operations

For the nine months to September 30, 1993, net interest income advanced 11%, year to year, primarily as a result of wider net interest margins. The provision for loan losses dropped to $43.6 million, from $53.3 million, noninterest income rose 20% and noninterest expense was up 19%. Pretax income rose 9.3%. After taxes at 28.9%, versus 27.9%, income increased 7.8%, to $108.5 million, from a restated $100.6 million. Results for the 1993 period exclude a credit of $7.2 million from the cumulative effect of a change in accounting.

Important Developments

Oct. '93— The Federal Deposit Insurance Corp. approved Meridian Bancorp's application to purchase four southern New Jersey branches and the corresponding deposits of Jersey City-based Provident Savings Bank. Separately, in September, Meridian received regulatory and shareholder approval to acquire First Bath Corp., a bank holding company in Northampton County, Pa. Both transactions are expected to close by year-end 1993.

Next earnings report expected in late January.

Per Share Data ($)

Yr. End Dec. 31	1992	1991	1990	1989	[1,2]1988	[1]1987	[2]1986	[2]1985	[1,2]1984	[2]1983
Tangible Bk. Val.	**19.00**	17.12	16.00	16.33	16.12	17.18	15.65	13.85	11.51	12.49
Earnings[3]	**2.55**	2.56	1.20	2.32	2.21	2.43	2.48	2.34	1.92	1.57
Dividends	**1.20**	1.20	1.20	1.125	1.10	1.00	0.95	0.875	0.75	0.734
Payout Ratio	**47%**	47%	100%	49%	50%	41%	38%	37%	39%	47%
Prices—High	**32**	24⅛	21⅛	26½	21⅞	26¼	27⅝	20⅝	13⅝	11¾
Low	**22⅛**	9¼	9½	17½	16¾	16	19⅛	12⅞	9⅜	8¼
P/E Ratio—	**13–9**	9–4	18–8	11–8	10–8	11–7	11–8	9–6	7–5	7–5

Data as orig. reptd. Adj. for stk. divs. of 100% Aug. 1986, 50% Jun. 1985. **1.** Refl. acctg. change. **2.** Refl. merger or acq. **3.** Bef. results of disc. ops. of -0.16 in 1991, -0.65 in 1990. **4.** Six mos. E-Estimated.

Income Data (Million $)

Year Ended Dec. 31	Net Int. Inc.	Tax Equiv. Adj.	Non Int. Inc.	Loan Loss Prov.	% Exp./ Op. Revs.	Net Bef. Taxes	Eff. Tax Rate	Net Inc.	% Net Int. Margin	—% Return On— Assets	Equity
1992	**495**	**17.5**	**228**	**59.7**	**68.9**	**154**	**25.7%**	**115**	**4.84**	**0.99**	**13.4**
[1]1991	432	23.1	244	99.4	62.3	144	25.6%	107	4.48	0.96	14.6
[1]1990	413	27.9	169	134.7	63.3	68	28.3%	48	4.15	0.42	6.8
1989	371	33.1	183	27.2	70.7	113	19.3%	91	4.32	0.89	13.4
[2,3]1988	333	33.2	172	32.8	69.7	100	14.0%	86	4.58	0.99	13.6
[2]1987	256	39.5	185	20.1	72.8	75	6.2%	70	4.67	1.01	13.8
[3]1986	229	55.4	163	15.8	70.2	71	3.0%	69	4.90	1.09	15.6
[3]1985	209	33.1	101	14.3	68.3	62	7.3%	58	4.72	1.02	16.3
[2,3]1984	156	28.0	43	10.2	65.6	41	0.3%	41	4.58	0.95	15.3
[3]1983	131	26.5	29	8.7	64.5	32	0.5%	32	4.74	0.89	13.2

Balance Sheet Data (Million $)

Dec. 31	Total Assets	—Earning Assets— Mon. Mkt. Assets	Inv. Secs.	Com'l Loans	Other Loans	% Loan Loss Resv.	—Deposits— Demand	Time	% Loans/ Deposits	Long Term Debt	Common Equity	% Equity To Assets
1992	**12,208**	**216**	**2,616**	**3,108**	**4,767**	**2.01**	**1,644**	**8,529**	**77.4**	**206**	**904**	**7.34**
1991	11,337	178	2,184	3,154	4,583	2.14	1,359	8,094	81.4	122	807	6.56
1990	11,866	173	1,776	3,177	5,415	1.71	1,273	7,990	92.5	145	689	6.16
1989	11,925	1,081	1,938	2,928	5,152	1.10	1,183	8,419	83.9	116	713	6.52
1988	9,523	365	1,874	3,395	2,940	1.33	1,260	5,865	88.6	115	627	6.95
1987	7,255	290	1,396	2,843	2,002	1.20	1,019	4,614	85.7	115	498	6.91
1986	6,801	222	1,448	2,686	1,743	1.29	1,074	4,379	80.9	117	453	6.56
1985	6,230	255	1,530	2,223	1,503	1.35	886	3,965	76.2	117	377	5.82
1984	5,494	316	1,323	1,867	1,424	1.34	891	3,689	70.5	127	283	5.95
1983	3,728	127	973	1,427	909	1.34	562	2,528	73.3	57	256	6.75

Data as orig. reptd. **1.** Excl. disc. ops. **2.** Refl. acctg. change. **3.** Refl. merger or acq.

Business Summary

Meridian Bancorp, Inc. is the fourth largest bank holding company based in Pennsylvania, with over $14.3 billion in total assets. Commercial banking operations are conducted through a network of more than 290 branches in Pennsylvania, Delaware and New Jersey; nonbanking subsidiaries offer financial and real estate services. Total loans of $7.38 billion at year-end 1992 were divided:

Commercial, financial & agricultural..	42%
Consumer..................................	27%
Real estate/commercial mortgage....	18%
Real estate/residential..................	9%
Real estate/construction................	4%

At December 31, 1992, the reserve for possible loan losses was $148.0 million (2.00% of gross loans outstanding), down from $165.0 million (2.23%) a year earlier. Net loan chargeoffs in 1992 were $78.9 million (1.08% of average loans), compared with $81.0 million (1.05%) the year before. Nonperforming assets at the end of 1992 amounted to $185.5 million (1.52% of total assets), versus $223.1 million (1.97%) a year earlier.

Total deposits of $10.2 billion at the end of 1992 were divided: money-market 23%, demand 16%, NOW accounts 12%, savings deposits 13%, and time 36%. On a tax-equivalent basis, the average yield on interest-earning assets in 1992 was 8.22% (9.74% in 1991), while the average rate paid on interest-bearing liabilities was 3.89% (5.89%), for a net spread of 4.33% (3.85%).

Dividend Data

Dividends have been paid since 1828. A dividend reinvestment plan is available.

Amt. of Divd. $	Date Decl.	Ex–divd. Date	Stock of Record	Payment Date
0.30	Jan. 26	Feb. 8	Feb. 15	Mar. 1'93
0.32	Apr. 20	May. 10	May. 15	Jun. 1'93
0.32	Jul. 27	Aug. 9	Aug. 15	Sep. 1'93
0.32	Oct. 26	Nov. 8	Nov. 15	Dec. 1'93

Finances

In September 1993, MRDN completed the purchase of Williamsport, Pa.-based Commonwealth Bancshares Corp., a $2.0 billion commercial bank that operates over 60 banking branches in Pennsylvania. MRDN issued about 10.9 million new common shares in the acquisition.

Capitalization

Long Term Debt: $345,510,000 (9/93).

Common Stock: 57,343,118 shs. ($5 par).
Institutions hold about 33%.
Shareholders: 21,826 (12/92).

Office—35 N. Sixth St., P.O. Box 1102, Reading, PA 19603. **Tel**—(215) 655-2000. **Chrmn & CEO**—S. A. McCullough. **Vice Chrmn & CFO**—D. E. Sparks. **Pres & COO**—E. S. Ketchum. **Secy**—W. L. Gaunt. **Investor Contact**—W. Sturgis Corbett. **Dirs**—D. E. Breidegam Jr., T. F. Burke Jr., R. W. Cordy, H. Corless, W. D. Davis, J. W. Erving, F. D. Hafer, J. H. Jones, L. C. Karlson, E. S. Ketchum, S. D. Kline Jr., G. W. Leighow, S. A. McCullough, J. F. Paquette Jr., D. H. Polett, L. R. Pugh, P. R. Roedel, W. R. Schultz, R. B. Seidel, D. E. Sparks, G. Strawbridge Jr., A. A. Summers, J. M. von Seldeneck, E. A. Wooton. **Transfer Agent & Registrar**—Co.'s office. **Formed** in 1969; bank chartered in 1828.

 Barry R. Haas

Merry-Go-Round Enterprises

NYSE Symbol MGR Options on ASE, CBOE, NYSE, Phila (Jan-Apr-Jul-Oct) In S&P MidCap 400

Price	Range	P–E Ratio	Dividend	Yield	S&P Ranking	Beta
Sep. 3'93	1993					
7⅞	17⅝–7⅝	18	0.05	0.6%	B+	1.57

Summary

This specialty retailer operates over 1,450 stores in 44 states. The stores feature moderate- to higher-priced contemporary apparel for young men and women. The number of stores has grown rapidly through internal expansion and acquisitions. Continued weak consumer spending and unseasonable weather have hurt sales in recent periods, and increased promotions have restricted margins. Some improvement should be seen in the second half of 1993-4, reflecting new merchandising and advertising strategies and streamlining of costs.

Current Outlook

Earnings for the fiscal year ending February 1, 1994, are projected at $0.40 a share, down from 1992-3's $0.71. A rebound to $0.85 is seen for 1994-5.

The $0.0133 quarterly dividend is the minimum expected.

Sales should continue to grow in 1993-4, with more stores in operation. Gross margins should narrow, as competitive pricing continues. Expense ratios could rise as a percentage of sales, due to the integration of acquisitions and weak sales gains. Further acquisitions are possible.

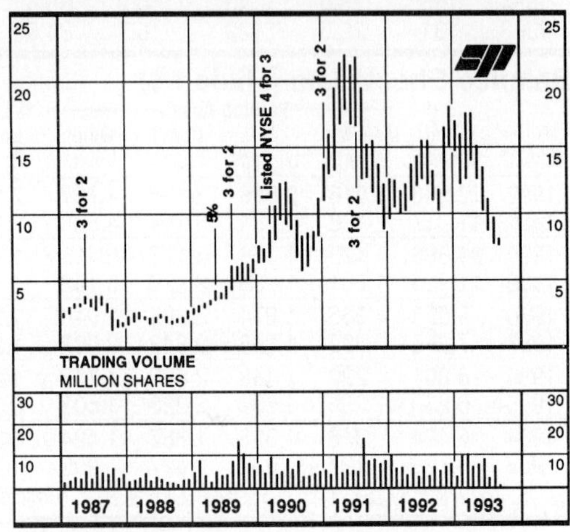

Net Sales (Million $)

13 Weeks:	1993–94	1992–93	1991–92	1990–91
Apr.	185.9	171.4	157.2	121.0
Jul.	214.4	181.6	156.9	124.9
Oct.	---	229.8	197.0	161.5
Jan.	---	294.7	250.0	220.8
	---	887.5	761.2	628.1

Sales in the six months ended July 31, 1993, increased 13%, year to year, reflecting more stores in operation; comparable-store sales dropped 6.6%. Margins narrowed sharply, and a net loss of $544,000 ($0.01) replaced net income of $13.5 million ($0.25).

Common Share Earnings ($)

13 Weeks:	1993–94	1992–93	1991–92	1990–91
Apr.	0.04	0.13	0.17	0.13
Jul.	d0.05	0.12	0.13	0.11
Oct.	E0.15	0.20	0.18	0.22
Jan.	E0.26	0.26	d0.05	0.27
	E0.40	0.71	0.43	0.73

Important Developments

Sep '93— MGR said results continue to be disppointing. Soft sales reflect a lack of consumer confidence and no strong fashion trends. The company has begun to cut operating costs in its corporate headquarters. In addition, a new advertising campaign is planned for the late fall; together with strategic changes in merchandising and marketing plans, this will produce significant cost savings and improved profitability in the second half of 1993-4. Earlier, in May 1993, MGR acquired the Chess King chain (450 stores), which sells young men's fashion sportswear, from Melville Corp. The stores, located in shopping malls throughout the U.S., will continue to be operated under the trade names Chess King and Garage. The company, which has the ability to serve 2,000 stores, has projected sales in excess of $2 billion by the end of the decade, to be achieved by advancing new concepts, making acquisitions, and opening additional stores in each division.

Next earnings report expected in mid-November.

Per Share Data ($)

Yr. End Jan. 31	1993	1992	1991	¹1990	¹1989	1988	1987	1986	1985	1984
Tangible Bk. Val.²	**4.37**	3.70	3.00	2.06	1.41	1.17	0.94	0.77	0.61	0.39
Cash Flow	**1.25**	0.85	1.06	0.74	0.51	0.43	0.31	0.27	0.29	0.29
Earnings	**0.71**	0.43	0.73	0.46	0.25	0.22	0.17	0.17	0.22	0.17
Dividends	**0.053**	0.053	0.033	Nil	Nil	Nil	Nil	Nil	Nil	Nil
Payout Ratio	**8%**	12%	5%	Nil	Nil	Nil	Nil	Nil	Nil	Nil
Calendar Years	**1992**	1991	1990	1989	1988	1987	1986	1985	1984	1983
Prices—High	**18⅛**	22	12⅜	6⅝	2¾	3⅞	3	3	3⅛	2¼
Low	**9⅝**	8⅞	5¾	2½	1¾	1⅜	1⅞	1¾	1¾	1¾
P/E Ratio—	**26–14**	51–21	17–8	14–5	11–7	17–6	18–11	18–10	14–7	13–9

Data as orig. reptd. Adj. for stk. divs. of 50% Jul. 1991, 50% Jan. 1991, 33⅓% Mar. 1990, 50% Aug. 1989, 5% May 1989, 50% May 1987, 50% Jul. 1984. **1.** Refl. merger or acq. **2.** Incl. intangibles. d-Deficit. E-Estimated.

Income Data (Million $)

Year Ended Jan. 31	Revs.	Oper. Inc.	% Oper. Inc. of Revs.	Cap. Exp.	Depr.	Int. Exp.	Net Bef. Taxes	Eff. Tax Rate	Net Inc.	% Net Inc. of Revs.	Cash Flow
1993	**877**	**89.7**	**10.2**	**72.0**	**29.0**	**3.90**	**59.8**	**36.5%**	**38.0**	**4.3**	**67.0**
1992	761	59.1	7.8	84.9	22.6	3.62	36.0	37.0%	22.7	3.0	45.3
1991	628	76.8	12.2	51.3	16.9	2.92	60.0	37.5%	37.5	6.0	54.4
[1]1990	479	52.1	10.9	37.8	13.5	3.70	35.9	38.0%	22.2	4.6	35.8
[1]1989	299	31.6	10.6	34.1	12.4	2.03	18.0	38.0%	11.2	3.7	23.5
1988	255	28.1	11.0	17.5	9.3	1.13	17.8	43.2%	10.1	4.0	19.3
1987	207	22.1	10.6	16.4	6.8	0.75	14.7	49.0%	7.5	3.6	14.2
1986	164	18.4	11.2	14.1	4.7	0.51	13.5	45.8%	7.3	4.4	12.0
1985	158	21.5	13.6	11.6	3.2	0.43	18.7	47.5%	9.8	6.2	13.0
1984	112	15.8	14.2	6.3	2.5	0.32	13.8	47.5%	9.8	8.8	12.3

Balance Sheet Data (Million $)

Jan. 31	Cash	Curr. Assets	Curr. Liab.	Curr. Ratio	Total Assets	% Ret. on Assets	Long Term Debt	Common Equity	Total Cap.	% LT Debt of Cap.	% Ret. on Equity
1993	**40.1**	**137**	**85.8**	**1.6**	**365**	**11.4**	**30.0**	**236**	**270**	**11.1**	**17.5**
1992	39.5	114	62.1	1.8	301	7.8	30.4	197	230	13.2	12.7
1991	82.0	145	77.4	1.9	271	16.3	30.8	156	188	16.4	28.5
1990	46.1	89	48.0	1.9	182	13.7	25.0	103	130	19.3	25.5
1989	21.0	57	33.3	1.7	128	10.7	27.3	64	93	29.5	19.2
1988	6.9	32	23.0	1.4	81	13.1	3.2	53	57	5.7	21.2
1987	3.8	31	25.7	1.2	73	11.4	2.7	42	46	5.9	19.3
1986	7.3	26	19.8	1.3	59	13.5	3.0	35	38	7.8	23.3
1985	9.2	27	16.4	1.6	49	23.5	5.0	28	33	15.2	43.5
1984	10.4	20	12.1	1.6	34	29.8	3.5	18	22	15.8	39.8

Data as orig. reptd. **1.** Refl. merger or acq.

Business Summary

At January 30, 1993, Merry-Go-Round Enterprises operated 989 specialty apparel stores in 39 states and the District of Columbia. The number of outlets was increased to 1,440 through the May 1993 acquisition of the Chess King chain (450 stores), which sells young men's fashion sportswear. Almost all stores are located in enclosed regional malls and offer moderate- to higher-priced contemporary fashions for men and women.

The Merry-Go-Round division operated 496 stores at January 31, 1993, under the names Merry-Go-Round, and The-Go-Round (in Texas only). The stores offer an assortment of apparel for style conscious men and women between the ages of 15 and 25. Fifty stores have been expanded to a new 4,500 sq. ft. of selling format. The Menz division operated 413 young men's stores under the names DJ's, Dejais, Silverman's, His Place and Attivo. These stores cater to young men between the ages of 18 and 35. Club International, a growing new concept, offers tailored clothing and sportswear for men from 25 to 50 years of age.

The Cignal division operated 74 Cignal stores, which averaged about 1,800 sq. ft.. These stores offer high quality contemporary designer sportswear for men and women between the ages of 20 and 40.

Boogies Diner, a destination shopping/dining concept operates at four locations.

The company has increased the use of its private contemporary fashion brand, I.O.U. The brand, introduced in the fall of 1985, now accounts for 25% of sales.

Following an expansion, MGR's new headquarters and distribution center gives the company the capacity to serve over 2,000 stores.

Dividend Data

Cash dividends were initiated in 1990. A"poison pill" stock purchase right was adopted in 1991.

Amt. of Divd. $	Date Decl.	Ex-divd. Date	Stock of Record	Payment Date
0.0133	Oct. 29	Nov. 6	Nov. 13	Nov. 25'92
o.0133	Feb. 2	Feb. 8	Feb. 12	Feb. 26'93
0.0133	May 4	May 10	May 14	May 28'93
0.0133	Aug. 3	Aug. 9	Aug. 13	Aug. 27'93

Finances

MGR sold 4,050,000 common shares at $14.42 each in March 1991, 1,912,500 shares at $11.83 each in June 1990, and 3,000,000 shares at $5.37 each in September 1989, all in conjunction with stockholder sales (as adjusted).

Capitalization

Long Term Debt: $29,787,000 (5/1/93).

Common Stock: 53,913,022 shs. ($0.01 par).
L. Weinglass owns 9.6%, the Estate of H. Goldsmith 9.4%, and N. Ambach 7.1%.
Institutions hold 67%.
Shareholders of record: 1,666.

Office—3300 Fashion Way, Joppa, MD 21085. **Tel**—(410) 538-1000. **Chrmn**—L. Weinglass. **Pres & CEO**—M. D. Sullivan. **SVP, CFO, Secy & Investor Contact**—Isaac Kaufman. **Dirs**—R. A. Altman, R. B. Bank, A. E. Berkowitz, T. J. Byrne, Jr., J. F. Ireton, I. Kaufman, M. D. Sullivan, L. Weinglass. **Transfer Agent & Registrar**—Security Trust Co., Baltimore. **Incorporated** in Maryland in 1971. **Empl**—11,500.

 Karen J. Sack

Michael Foods

NASDAQ Symbol MIKL (Incl. in Nat'l Market) In S&P MidCap 400

Price	Range	P-E Ratio	Dividend	Yield	S&P Ranking	Beta
Aug. 5'93	1993					
9⅛	11½–6½	38	0.20	2.2%	NR	0.72

Summary

This diversified food processor and distributor has interests in eggs and egg products, refrigerator case products, frozen and refrigerated potato products, specialty dairy products and prepared foods. Results in 1993 should benefit from a recovery in refrigerator case distribution volume and a slight improvement in potato prices. The late 1992 introduction of a low-cholesterol liquid egg product, Simply Eggs, should contribute to increased sales in 1993, but profits from the product are not expected until manufacturing and marketing expenses can be offset by increased unit volume.

Current Outlook

Share earnings for 1994 are projected at $0.65, up from the $0.47 estimated for 1993.

Dividends should continue at $0.05 quarterly.

Sales in 1993 should benefit from a turnaround in french fry prices that began in late 1992, initial sales from the rollout of the Simply Eggs low cholesterol liquid egg product, and continued growth in the dairy segment; volume gains at the grocery store distribution unit are also expected, although pricing should remain intensely competitive. Profitability should improve markedly from that of 1992, but continued weakness in the egg and distribution segments will keep margins well below levels achieved in 1991 and earlier.

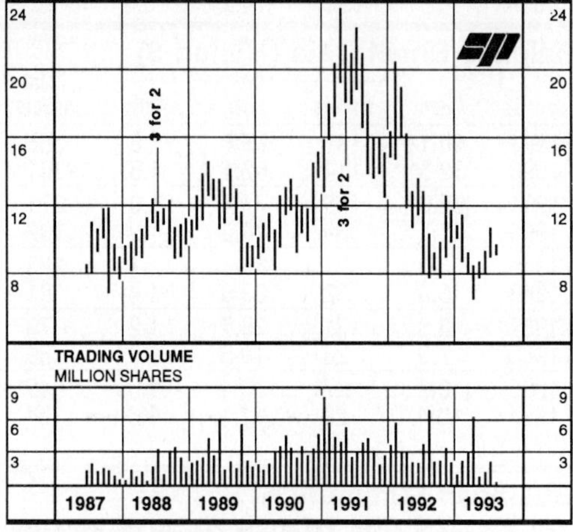

Net Sales (Million $)

Quarter:	1993	1992	1991	1990
Mar.	105	106	114	113
Jun.	119	110	111	120
Sep.	---	110	111	112
Dec.	---	116	119	116
	---	443	455	461

Net sales for the six months ended June 30, 1993, rose 3.7%, year to year. Net income advanced 34%, to $2,645,000 ($0.14 a share), from $1,975,000 ($0.10) in the year-earlier period.

Common Share Earnings ($)

Quarter:	1993	1992	1991	1990
Mar.	0.03	0.07	0.34	0.28
Jun.	0.11	0.03	0.29	0.29
Sep.	E0.13	0.04	0.27	0.27
Dec.	E0.20	0.06	0.18	0.28
	E0.47	0.20	1.07	1.11

Important Developments

Jul. '93— The company said that the strong unit volume for Easy Eggs seen in 1993's second quarter was continuing so far in the third quarter. The low-cholesterol version, Simply Eggs, was no longer being heavily advertised in the retail sector, and was instead being targeted to the foodservice industry. Separately, a U.S. District Court ruled that the patents pertaining to the ultrapasteurization of liquid eggs (Easy Eggs) are valid and enforceable. Michael will be entitled to damages from Papetti's Hygrade Egg Products, which had illegally been using the technology for about three years.

Apr. '93— Michael's directors authorized the purchase of up to $10 million of the company's common shares.

Next earnings report expected in mid-October.

Per Share Data ($)

Yr. End Dec. 31	[1]1992	[1]1991	[1]1990	[2]1989	[2]1988	1987	1986
Tangible Bk. Val.	**6.22**	6.13	3.49	4.47	4.55	2.93	0.59
Cash Flow	**1.30**	2.03	1.89	1.03	1.03	0.98	NA
Earnings[3]	**0.20**	1.07	1.11	0.71	0.80	0.73	0.49
Dividends	**0.200**	0.200	0.217	0.133	0.117	0.036	Nil
Payout Ratio	**100%**	20%	19%	19%	15%	5%	Nil
Prices—High	**20½**	23⅝	15⅛	14$\frac{9}{16}$	12$\frac{7}{16}$	11$\frac{15}{16}$	NA
Low	**7¾**	12½	8¼	8$\frac{3}{16}$	8¼	6¾	NA
P/E Ratio—	**NM**	22–12	14–7	21–12	16–10	16–9	NA

Data as orig. reptd. Adj. for stk. divs. of 50% May 1991, 50% Jul. 1988. **1.** Refl. acctg. change. **2.** Refl. merger or acq. **3.** Bef. spec. item(s) of -0.49 in 1987. E-Estimated NM-Not Meaningful. NA-Not Available.

Income Data (Million $)

Year Ended Dec. 31	Revs.	Oper. Inc.	% Oper. Inc. of Revs.	Cap. Exp.	Depr.	Int. Exp.	Net Bef. Taxes	Eff. Tax Rate	[5]Net Inc.	% Net Inc. of Revs.	Cash Flow
1992	**443**	**37.1**	**8.4**	**32.0**	**21.5**	**10.2**	**6.0**	**36.1%**	**3.9**	**0.9**	**25.3**
[1]1991	455	57.9	12.7	48.4	17.6	10.7	30.7	36.0%	19.7	4.3	37.3
[1]1990	461	55.8	12.1	40.2	13.0	10.9	31.0	36.6%	18.6	4.0	31.6
[2]1989	255	18.2	7.1	35.1	5.5	1.9	[4]16.3	26.1%	12.0	4.7	17.5
[2]1988	189	20.5	10.9	19.8	3.6	0.9	[4]18.3	32.8%	12.3	6.5	15.9
1987	170	19.3	11.3	8.0	3.1	1.5	15.4	41.9%	8.9	5.2	12.0
1986	153	15.0	9.8	3.5	2.5	3.2	9.4	53.1%	4.4	2.9	6.9
1985	102	5.6	5.5	18.4	0.9	0.6	4.2	50.3%	2.1	2.0	NA
1984	98	5.9	6.0	1.2	0.7	0.6	4.7	50.8%	2.3	2.3	NA
1983	45	[3]3.1	[3]6.7	NA	NA	0.4	2.8	52.2%	1.4	3.0	NA

Balance Sheet Data (Million $)

Dec. 31	Cash	Assets	Curr. Liab.	Ratio	Total Assets	% Ret. on Assets	Long Term Debt	Common Equity	Total Cap.	% LT Debt of Cap.	% Ret. on Equity
1992	**6.1**	**93.3**	**38.5**	**2.4**	**370**	**1.1**	**129.0**	**177**	**332**	**38.8**	**2.2**
1991	4.6	98.9	39.9	2.5	357	5.5	115.0	176	317	36.4	12.9
1990	4.0	86.2	72.8	1.2	304	7.6	98.8	111	231	42.7	18.1
1989	7.8	58.1	29.0	2.0	187	7.8	54.6	95	158	34.6	13.3
1988	9.5	38.1	19.6	1.9	123	11.3	8.6	88	104	8.3	17.0
1987	17.4	38.9	17.9	2.2	77	13.3	5.9	47	59	9.9	30.3
1986	0.9	23.3	19.2	1.2	57	7.6	25.2	12	38	66.2	42.5
1985	3.4	25.0	14.8	1.7	58	5.4	34.7	9	44	79.5	25.6
1984	NA	NA	NA	NA	19	11.5	[6]5.6	8	13	41.8	36.9
1983	NA	NA	NA	NA	21	10.1	[6]10.1	4	15	68.5	38.5

Data as orig. reptd. **1.** Refl. acctg. change. **2.** Refl. merger or acq. **3.** Aft. depr. not separately reptd. **4.** Incl. equity in earns. of nonconsol. subs. **5.** Bef. spec. items. **6.** Incl. current portion. NA-Not Available.

Business Summary

Michael Foods, Inc. is a diversified producer and distributor of food products, operating in five basic areas: eggs and egg products, distribution of refrigerator case products, refrigerated and frozen potato products, dairy products and prepared foods.

Through M. G. Waldbaum Co., the company produces, processes and distributes shell eggs and numerous egg products. Principal value-added egg products are ultrapasteurized Easy Eggs, salmonella-free liquid eggs, hard-cooked eggs and 80% cholesterol-reduced Simply Eggs. Products also include frozen and dried egg whites, yolks and whole eggs, frozen whole eggs, pre-cooked egg patties and omelets and frozen breakfast entrees.

Formed in 1989, Crystal Farms Refrigerated Distribution Co. manages the company's refrigerated distribution operations. Distributed products include cheese, bagels, butter, margarine, muffins, potato products, juice, ethnic foods, omelets and a deli line. In 1991, Crystal Farms opened a cheese packaging facility in Lake Mills, Wis.; cheese now accounts for about 50% of Crystal's sales.

The potato products division processes and sells frozen potato products, primarily french fries and refrigerated potato products to both foodservice and retail markets. The refrigerated product line consists of extended shelf-life hash brown, mashed, au gratin and scalloped potatoes.

Kohler Mix Specialties, Inc. processes and sells ice milk mix, ice cream mix, frozen yogurt mix and milk and specialty dairy products, many of which are ultra-high temperature (UHT) pasteurized products. Kohler has about 600 customers, including branded ice cream manufacturers, distributors to fast food businesses and independent ice milk and ice cream retailers.

Dividend Data

Amt of Divd. $	Date Decl.	Ex-divd. Date	Stock of Record	Payment Date
0.05	Oct. 29	Nov. 3	Nov. 9	Nov. 23'92
0.05	Jan. 22	Jan. 27	Feb. 2	Feb. 16'93
0.05	Apr. 27	May 3	May 7	May 21'93
0.05	Jul. 29	Aug. 3	Aug. 9	Aug. 23'93

Capitalization

Long Term Debt: $116,752,000 (3/93).

Common Stock: 19,536,739 shs. ($0.01 par).
North Star Universal, Inc. owns 38%.
Shareholders: 862 of record (12/92).

Office—5353 Wayzata Blvd., Minneapolis, MN 55416. **Tel**—(612) 546-1500. **Chrmn**—J. H. Michael. **Pres & CEO**—R. G. Olson. **VP-Fin, CFO & Treas**—J. D. Reedy. **EVP & Secy**—J. M. Shapiro. **Investor Contact**—Mark Witmer. **Dirs**—R. A. Coonrod, M. E. Efron, O. L. Freeman, A. C. Knudtson, J. D. Marshburn, J. H. Michael, J. J. Michael, R. G. Olson. **Transfer Agent & Registrar**—First National Bank of Boston. **Incorporated** in Delaware in 1987. **Empl**—2,535.

 Gregg W. Bonardi

Micron Technology

NYSE Symbol MU Options on CBOE & Pacific (Jan-Apr-Jul-Oct) In S&P MidCap 400

Price	Range	P-E Ratio	Dividend	Yield	S&P Ranking	Beta
Oct. 13'93	1993					
43⅞	63⅝–18⅛	17	0.05	0.1%	B–	1.83

Summary

This company is a leading manufacturer of dynamic random access memories (DRAMs), static random access memories (SRAMs), video random access memories (VRAMs), and other semiconductor components and board-level products. Following several years of minimal earnings, stronger industry conditions, capacity expansions and yield improvements allowed earnings to rise sharply in fiscal 1993. More than a doubling of earnings is forecast in fiscal 1994 as those factors continue to exert a positive influence.

Current Outlook

Earnings for the fiscal year ending August 31, 1994, are projected at $6.00 a share, up from the $2.57 reported for fiscal 1993.

The annual dividend of $0.05 is likely to be increased.

Sales are likely to advance approximately 45% in fiscal 1994, reflecting a continuation of strong industry conditions and capacity expansions. Prices for the full year should be substantially higher as they stabilize near the levels reached recently due to greater industry demand and panic buying following an explosion at a high-grade epoxy resin factory in Japan that supplied 60% of the world's supply of a resin used in integrated circuit plastic packaging. An aggressive new product introduction program will also boost volume. Margins should widen significantly on the greater volume, firming pricing and yield improvements. However, new capacity coming on stream from competitors and the resumption of more normal market conditions as supplies of epoxy resin increase could put pressure on pricing following the recent surge.

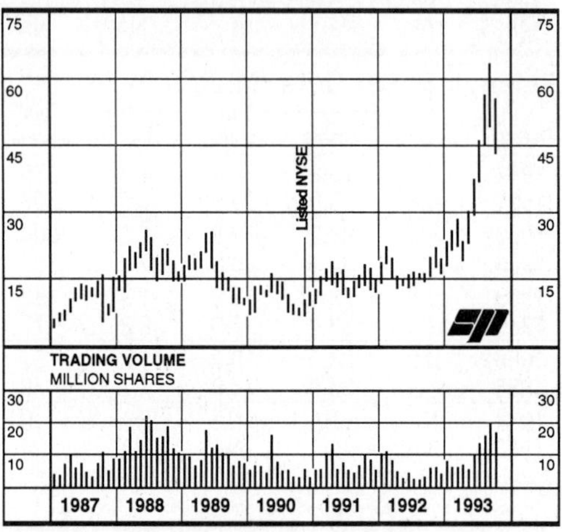

Net Sales (Million $)

Quarter:	1993–94	1992–93	1991–92	1990–91
Nov.	---	131.0	[1]111.8	80.3
Feb.	---	176.4	128.2	94.5
May	---	214.9	131.1	126.8
Aug.	---	306.0	135.2	123.8
	---	828.3	506.3	425.4

Sales for the fiscal year ended September 2, 1993 (preliminary) were up 64% from those of fiscal 1992, principally on greater volumes of semiconductor memory sold. Margins widened on the higher sales, firming prices and improved manufacturing yields, primarily due to reductions in die sizes and increases in wafer output. Pretax income rose to $162.6 million from $9.6 million. After taxes at 36.0%, versus 31.0%, net income was $104.1 million ($2.57 a share), up from $6.6 million ($0.17).

Common Share Earnings ($)

Quarter:	1993–94	1992–93	1991–92	1990–91
Nov.	E1.40	0.07	[1]0.02	d0.25
Feb.	E1.60	0.22	0.04	d0.06
May	E1.65	0.73	0.04	0.18
Aug.	E1.35	1.52	0.07	0.25
	E6.00	2.57	0.17	0.13

Important Developments

Sep. '93— Micron cautioned upon releasing earnings for its fourth quarter that several competitors have recently announced expansions in semiconductor manufacturing capacity. It added that should overall industry production capacity expand faster than market demand, product pricing, which has recently been strong, would likely experience a steep decline.

Next earnings report expected in mid-December.

Per Share Data ($)

Yr. End Aug. 31	1993	1992	1991	1990	1989	1988	1987	1986	1985	1984
Tangible Bk. Val.	**NA**	13.33	13.24	13.12	12.98	8.76	2.82	3.57	4.81	5.09
Cash Flow	**NA**	2.51	2.24	1.77	3.77	4.14	d0.14	d0.79	0.83	0.88
Earnings	**2.57**	0.17	0.13	0.13	2.85	[2]3.38	d0.94	d1.75	0.01	1.50
Dividends	**0.05**	0.05	Nil	Nil	Nil	Nil	Nil	Nil	Nil	Nil
Payout Ratio	**2%**	29%	Nil	Nil	Nil	Nil	Nil	Nil	Nil	Nil
Prices[3]—High	**63⅝**	22⅜	19⅛	16⅜	25¾	26	16⅛	17⅛	27⅝	40½
Low	**18⅛**	12⅞	9½	6¾	9¼	12	4	3⅜	3⅞	14
P/E Ratio—	**25–5**	NM	NM	NM	9–3	6–3	NM	NM	NM	27–9

Data as orig. reptd. **1.** 14 wks. **2.** Ful. dil: 3.25. **3.** Cal. yr. d-Deficit. E-Estimated. NM-Not Meaningful. NA-Not Available.

Income Data (Million $)

Year Ended Aug. 31	[1]Revs.	Oper. Inc.	% Oper. Inc. of Revs.	Cap. Exp.	Depr.	Int. Exp.	Net Bef. Taxes	Eff. Tax Rate	Net Inc.	% Net Inc. of Revs.	Cash Flow
1992	**506**	**105**	**20.7**	**99**	**91.0**	**8.6**	**10**	**31.0%**	**7**	**1.3**	**98**
1991	425	93	21.9	86	81.4	11.2	6	14.0%	5	1.2	86
1990	333	62	18.7	121	61.0	10.6	3	NM	5	1.5	66
1989	446	185	41.4	244	34.6	4.2	166	36.0%	106	23.8	141
1988	301	141	46.9	56	21.9	4.5	118	17.1%	98	32.6	120
1987	91	1	1.5	10	19.5	5.3	d23	Nil	d23	NM	d3
1986	48	d7	NM	12	21.4	5.4	d34	Nil	d34	NM	d15
1985	75	17	22.2	43	18.0	2.1	d7	NM	NM	0.2	16
1984	87	45	51.4	65	5.7	1.8	37	20.7%	29	33.2	35
1983	10	d2	NM	11	1.1	2.1	d3	Nil	d3	NM	d2

Balance Sheet Data (Million $)

Aug. 31	Cash	Curr. Assets	Curr. Liab.	Curr. Ratio	Total Assets	% Ret. on Assets	Long Term Debt	Common Equity	Total Cap.	% LT Debt of Cap.	% Ret. on Equity
1992	**73**	**227**	**106**	**2.1**	**724**	**0.9**	**61.6**	**511**	**609**	**10.1**	**1.3**
1991	68	213	98	2.2	706	0.7	69.6	495	598	11.6	1.0
1990	77	198	101	2.0	697	0.7	74.1	484	590	12.6	1.0
1989	161	279	70	4.0	625	20.0	39.7	477	547	7.3	26.6
1988	164	250	65	3.9	388	35.4	17.7	288	312	5.7	51.5
1987	9	44	19	2.4	129	NM	38.2	73	111	34.5	NM
1986	5	33	10	3.4	132	NM	43.6	79	123	35.5	NM
1985	1	27	5	5.0	133	0.1	35.5	92	128	27.8	0.2
1984	20	43	30	1.4	121	43.1	Nil	89	91	Nil	61.0
1983	6	11	8	1.4	29	NM	9.7	12	22	44.1	NM

Data as orig. reptd. **1.** Net product sales only prior to 1984. d-Deficit. NM-Not Meaningful.

Business Summary

Micron Technology designs, manufactures and markets semiconductor memory components primarily used in various computer applications.

The company's largest product line is Dynamic Random Access Memories (DRAMs), which accounted for 82% of sales in fiscal 1992 (latest available). DRAMs are the highest density, lowest cost per bit random access memory component available, and are the most-widely used semiconductor memory components in computer systems. Although sales of 1 Megabit DRAMs constituted the majority of net sales in fiscal 1992, during the fourth quarter, sales of 4 Megabit DRAMs exceeded those of 1 Megabit DRAMs, as Micron moved to the 4 Megabit DRAM as its primary product. Specialty DRAM memory products are also produced.

Micron also produces Static Random Access Memories (SRAMs), which accounted for 18% of sales in fiscal 1992. SRAMs perform memory functions similar to those of DRAMs, but do not require their memory cells to be electronically refreshed, which generally increases the speed at which they can operate.

The company manufactures and markets a variety of memory intensive board-level products, all of which utilize semiconductor memory components. Memory modules are typically used to increase available memory in upgradable systems.

In November 1991, Micron established a new subsidiary to design and develop new technologies relating to flat panel display technologies.

R&D spending increased to $57.3 million (6.9% of sales) in fiscal 1993, from $47.6 million (9.4%) in fiscal 1992.

Export sales represented 32% of net sales in fiscal 1992 (latest available), up from 26% in fiscal 1991.

Dividend Data

An initial annual dividend of $0.05 was declared in September 1991.

Amt of Divd. $	Date Decl.	Ex–divd. Date	Stock of Record	Payment Date
0.05	Sep. 29	Nov. 27	Dec. 3	Jan. 7'93

Finances

As of September 2, 1993, Micron had cash and liquid investments of $185.8 million.

Capitalization

Long Term Debt: $54,361,000 (9/93).

Common Stock: 39,363,728 shs. ($0.10 par).
Officers and directors own 26%, incl. more than 14% held by Simplot Financial Corp.
Institutions hold 63%.
Shareholders of record: 2,746 (9/92).

Office—2805 E. Columbia Rd., Boise, ID 83706-9698. **Tel**—(208) 368-4000. **Chrmn & CEO**—J. L. Parkinson. **Pres**—J. W. Garrett. **VP-Fin, Treas & CFO**—R. N. Langrill. **Secy**—Cathy L. Smith. **Investor Contact**—Kipp A. Bedard. **Dirs**— J. W. Garrett, R. N. Langrill, T. T. Nicholson, A. T. Noble, J. L. Parkinson, D. J. Simplot, J. R. Simplot, G. C. Smith. **Transfer Agent & Registrar**—West One Bank, Idaho, Boise. **Incorporated** in Delaware in 1984 (successor to a company incorporated in Idaho in 1978). **Empl**—4,300.

 Paul H. Valentine, CFA

Mid-American Waste Systems

NYSE Symbol MAW Options on Phila (Feb-May-Aug-Nov) In S&P MidCap 400

Price	Range	P–E Ratio	Dividend	Yield	S&P Ranking	Beta
Oct. 5'93	1993					
8¾	14⅝–8½	12	0.02	0.2%	NR	NA

Summary

This company is engaged in the nonhazardous solid waste management business in selected markets mainly in Pennsylvania, Ohio, Illinois and Georgia. Rapid growth has been achieved primarily through the acquisition of independent solid waste collection operations and landfills. Although operating results should continue to improve in 1993, aided by further acquisitions and landfill expansion efforts, net income will likely decline as a result of substantially higher interest charges.

Current Outlook

Earnings for 1993 are expected to fall slightly to $0.75 a share (based on more shares outstanding), from 1992's $0.80. A recovery to $0.85 a share is seen for 1994.

Dividends are expected to continue at $0.00½ quarterly.

Revenues are expected to rise about 10% in 1993, with gains seen for both collection and landfill operations. Each segment will benefit from continued acquisition of smaller independent operations, and from price and volume increases. Landfill operations will also be aided by site expansion efforts. However, greater competition in certain markets could limit growth. Margins should be stable, as higher landfill operating costs will offset the greater use of company landfills by its collection operations. However, substantially higher interest and depreciation charges, stemming from projects being taken out of the development stage, will result in a modest decline in net income. Longer term, the company should benefit from continued consolidation in the solid waste disposal industry as a result of the greater financial requirements needed to meet more stringent regulations.

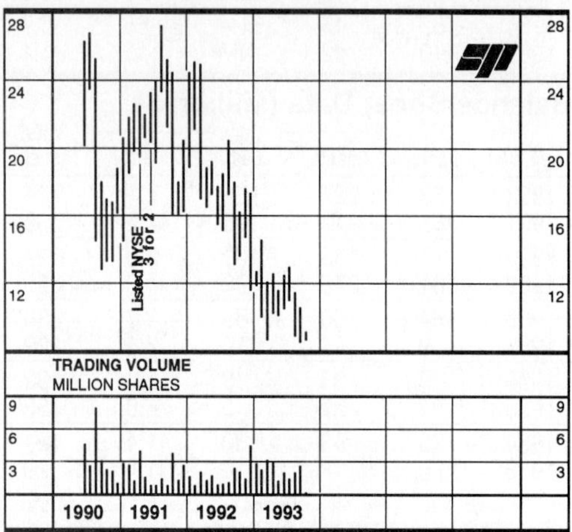

Total Revenues (Million $)

Quarter:	1993	1992	1991	1990
Mar.	38.7	37.7	23.0	15.6
Jun.	44.3	41.2	27.9	20.1
Sep.	---	44.0	32.4	20.9
Dec.	---	44.0	36.2	22.1
	---	166.9	119.4	78.7

Revenues in the six months ended June 30, 1993, rose 5.1%, year to year, reflecting collection and landfill acquisitions, market share growth, and higher landfill volumes. Margins widened, aided by the increased use of company landfills by collection operations, thereby avoiding third-party fees; operating income was up 12%. However, following significantly higher interest and depreciation charges, pretax income declined 3.9%. After taxes at 42.5% in both interims, net income fell 4.0%, to $8,881,000 ($0.36 a share, based on 8.4% more shares) from $9,247,000 ($0.41).

Common Share Earnings ($)

Quarter:	1993	1992	1991	1990
Mar.	0.18	0.20	0.18	0.09
Jun.	0.19	0.22	0.20	0.14
Sep.	E0.19	0.21	0.18	0.17
Dec.	E0.19	0.19	0.27	0.16
	E0.75	0.80	0.83	[1]0.58

Important Developments

Jul. '93— In commenting on 1993's second quarter results, MAW noted it had seen a company-wide firming of prices, including the negative impact of competitive pressures in Pennsylvania and the favorable effect in the West Virginia and Ohio markets, resulting in an overall increase of 5% in the average price charged on a per ton basis.

Next earnings report expected in late October.

Per Share Data ($)

Yr. End Dec. 31	[2]1992	[2]1991	[2]1990	[2]1989	1988	1987	1986
Tangible Bk. Val.	**8.27**	6.81	5.67	0.65	0.69	NA	NA
Cash Flow	**1.96**	1.60	1.28	0.62	0.37	NA	NA
Earnings	**0.80**	0.83	0.58	0.16	0.16	0.03	0.01
Dividends	**Nil**	Nil	Nil	Nil	Nil	Nil	Nil
Pa yout Ratio	**Nil**	Nil	Nil	Nil	Nil	Nil	Nil
Prices—High	**25⅛**	27¼	26⅞	NA	NA	NA	NA
Low	**11⅝**	14½	12⅞	NA	NA	NA	NA
P/E Ratio—	**31–15**	33–17	46–22	NA	NA	NA	NA

Data as orig. reptd. Adj. for stk. div(s). of 50% Jun. 1991. **1.** Does not add due to changes in no. of shs. outstanding. **2.** Reflects merger or acquisition. E-Estimated NA-Not Available.

Income Data (Million $)

Year Ended Dec. 31	Revs.	Oper. Inc.	% Oper. Inc. of Revs.	Cap. Exp.	Depr.	Int. Exp.	Net Bef. Taxes	Eff. Tax Rate	Net Inc.	% Net Inc. of Revs.	Cash Flow
[1]1992	**167**	**63.3**	**37.9**	**204**	**27.1**	**22.5**	**32.5**	**42.5%**	**18.7**	**11.2**	**45.8**
[1]1991	119	41.2	34.5	206	15.8	10.4	29.6	42.3%	17.1	14.3	32.9
[1]1990	79	28.3	36.0	76	10.2	7.7	14.4	41.4%	8.4	10.7	18.4
[1]1989	48	11.2	23.4	44	4.8	4.8	3.3	46.6%	1.8	3.7	6.6
1988	25	7.1	28.1	10	2.4	1.7	3.0	43.1%	1.7	6.8	4.1
1987	8	2.2	26.9	NA	0.9	0.7	0.7	47.6%	0.3	4.1	NA
1986	4	0.8	22.4	NA	0.2	0.3	0.4	50.3%	0.2	4.8	NA

Balance Sheet Data (Million $)

Dec. 31	Cash	Curr. Assets	Curr. Liab.	Curr. Ratio	Total Assets	% Ret. on Assets	Long Term Debt	Common Equity	Total Cap.	% LT Debt of Cap.	% Ret. on Equity
1992	**30.1**	**53.1**	**47.0**	**1.1**	**667**	**3.1**	**316**	**292**	**619**	**51.0**	**6.7**
1991	32.6	50.6	45.0	1.1	478	4.5	193	232	432	44.7	8.8
1990	10.2	22.1	13.6	1.6	195	5.6	66	110	181	36.6	12.4
1989	3.2	9.4	12.0	0.8	104	2.2	65	25	92	70.8	7.4
1988	8.0	12.4	11.9	1.0	60	4.5	24	23	48	50.1	13.5
1987	NA	NA	NA	NA	16	0.3	10	3	13	80.2	18.9
1986	NA	NA	NA	NA	5	NA	2	1	4	65.5	NA

Data as orig. reptd. **1.** Reflects merger or acquisition. NA-Not Available.

Business Summary

Mid-American Waste Systems was organized in 1985 to acquire and consolidate the operations of certain suburban and rural independent solid waste collection businesses and landfills. Currently, the company is active in nonhazardous solid waste management in selected markets in Ohio, Pennsylvania, Indiana, Georgia, West Virginia, Illinois, New Jersey, Colorado, Massachusetts, Kentucky and South Carolina, providing collection, transfer and disposal services to about 375,000 residential, commercial and industrial customers. It designs, constructs, operates and owns solid waste landfills and transfer stations in each of its markets. MAW also offers waste reduction programs such as recycling and composting and is engaged in sludge management. Revenues in recent years were derived as follows:

	1992	1991
Collection services.............	79%	77%
Landfill operations.............	21%	23%

The company owns and operates 18 solid waste landfills; has permits to construct two landfills; operates three municipally owned landfills and one construction and demolition landfill owned by a third party; and is involved in two landfill development projects. Transfer stations, where waste is compacted and transferred to large company-owned vehicles for transport to the landfills, are owned or operated at 11 locations.

As part of its acquisition program, the company has improved the operating efficiencies of acquired operations through the restructuring of route, administrative and management systems; increasing employee productivity; improving equipment utilization; developing marketing programs; and implementing price increases when appropriate. Management's strategy is to continue expanding the business through the acquisition and development of additional landfills in selected markets, as well as through more collection and transfer station acquisitions and growth of the base collection business.

Dividend Data

Cash dividends were initiated in June 1993.

Amt. of Divd. $	Date Decl.	Ex-divd. Date	Stock of Record	Payment Date
0.00½	May 20	May 25	Jun. 1	Jun. 15'93
0.00½	Aug. 18	Aug. 26	Sep. 1	Sep. 15'93

Finances

In May 1993, MAW issued $24.4 million of 4.375% unsecured industrial revenue bonds due 2018. Proceeds were earmarked to reduce debt bearing interest at higher rates.

In May 1992, underwriters sold 1,500,000 MAW common shares at $18 each, including 1,205,000 for the company and 295,000 shares for stockholders. Proceeds to MAW of $20.1 million were used to reduce debt. The offering, which was postponed in April, was reduced from 4,750,000 shares (including 750,000 for stockholders).

Capitalization

Long Term Debt: $323,750,000 (6/93).

Common Stock: 24,453,038 shs. ($1 par).
John L. Kemmerer III and related trusts own 13%.
Institutions hold about 55%.
Stockholders of record: 672.

Office—1006 Walnut St., Canal Winchester, OH 43110. **Tel**—(614) 833-9155. **Chrmn & Pres**—C. L. White. **EVP, Secy & Treas**—D. P. Wilburn. **VP-CFO**—R. A. Widders Jr. **VP & Investor Contact**—Michael Patton. **Dirs**—T. A. Brown, B. H. Love, J. D. Peckskamp Jr., R. J. Roberts, C. L. White, D. P. Wilburn. **Transfer Agent & Registrar**—Provident Bank, Cincinnati. **Incorporated** in Ohio in 1985; reincorporated in Delaware in 1989. **Empl**—1,113.

 Michael V. Pizzi

Miller (Herman)

NASDAQ Symbol MLHR Options on NYSE (Feb-May-Aug-Nov) (Incl. in Nat'l Market) In S&P MidCap 400

Price	Range	P-E Ratio	Dividend	Yield	S&P Ranking	Beta
Aug. 9'93	1993					
28⅜	28⅝–18⅛	32	0.52	1.8%	B	0.99

Summary

This leading designer-manufacturer of office and institutional furniture sells its products nationwide and in Canada and Europe. Operations returned to profitability in 1992-93, on a modest increase in sales volume, cost reduction measures and the absence of $20.6 million (net) of restructuring and other charges.

Business Summary

Herman Miller, Inc. researches, designs, manufactures and sells modular space division, storage and materials handling furniture systems. In each of the past three fiscal years, more than 95% of sales have been for use in office/institution environments, including offices and related conference, lobby and lounge areas, and general public areas such as transportation terminals; most of the remainder have gone to hospitals, laboratories and other health/science environments. Foreign operations contributed about 15% of sales in 1991-92, but had a $6.5 million loss; and about 14% of sales in 1992-93, with a loss of $8.6 million incurred.

Products and systems for the office/institution market consist of the "Action Office" and "Ethospace" systems and a wide selection of seating products, tables and desks. "Action Office" is a freestanding office partition and furnishing system (Miller offers three types of Action Office series), believed to be the first such system to be marketed nationally. The modular systems represent a major portion of Miller's sales. "Ethospace" is a system of movable full- and partial-height walls, with panels and individual wall segments that attach to wall framework.

Health/science products consist of a number of furniture items and systems, including "Co-Struc," a unique, modular system for storing and manually handling materials and supplies within healthcare facilities and laboratories.

The company markets its products through its own sales staff. Some 90% of sales in 1991-2 were made to or through nonexclusive, independent dealers, and the balance directly to end-users, including governmental agencies and major corporations. Foreign sales are made through subsidiaries and dealers. The company has redefined its foreign operations to focus on three major markets: Canada, Europe and the Asia/Pacific region. In certain other foreign markets, the company licenses others to make its products.

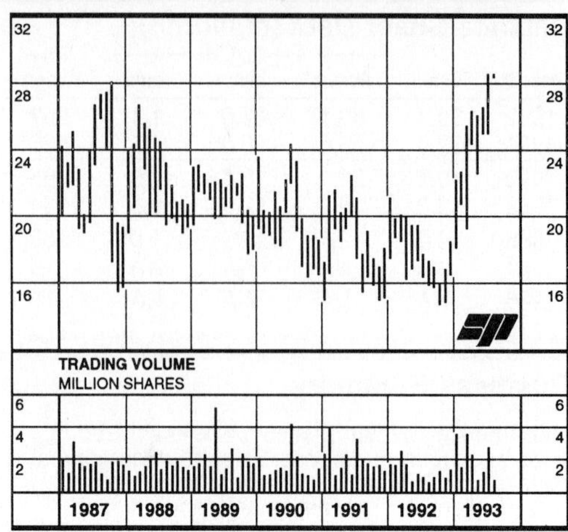

During the fourth quarter of 1991-2, the company recorded restructuring charges of $25 million and charges for additional inventory and accounts receivable reserves of $5.2 million (total after tax charges of $0.82 a share), all of which were related to Miller's refocusing of facility and product strategies and the simplifying of work processes.

Important Developments

Jul. '93— During 1992-93's fourth quarter, the company recorded net charges of $3.2 million ($0.13 a share) for the reconfiguration of manufacturing operations in the U.K. The reconfiguration would result in the consolidation of five facilities into two and the elimination of 90 positions.

Next earnings report expected in late September.

Per Share Data ($)

Yr. End May 31	1993	1992	1991	[1]1990	1989	1988	1987	1986	1985	1984
Tangible Bk. Val.	**NA**	11.14	12.33	11.82	10.65	9.66	8.19	7.83	6.89	5.80
Cash Flow	**NA**	1.05	1.66	2.87	2.62	2.67	2.11	2.20	2.20	1.64
Earnings[2]	**0.88**	d0.14	0.55	1.82	1.71	1.82	1.35	1.53	1.63	1.14
Dividends[3]	**0.520**	0.520	0.520	0.520	0.520	0.440	0.440	0.440	0.348	0.214
Payout Ratio	**59%**	NM	95%	29%	30%	24%	32%	29%	21%	19%
Calendar Years	**1992**	1991	1990	1989	1988	1987	1986	1985	1984	1983
Prices—High	**21⅛**	22½	24⅜	23⅛	26¾	28⅛	31	27⅞	24⅛	18
Low	**14¾**	15	16⅜	17¾	19	15½	19½	18½	13¾	8¼
P/E Ratio—	**24–17**	NM	44–30	13–10	16–11	15–9	23–14	18–12	15–8	16–7

Data as orig. reptd. Adj. for stk. divs. of 50% Sep. 1985, 100% Aug. 1983. **1.** Refl. merger or acq. **2.** Bef. spec. items of -0.42 in 1992, +0.13 in 1989. **3.** Based on ex-dividend date. d-Deficit. NM-Not Meaningful. NA-Not Available.

Income Data (Million $)

Year Ended May 31	Revs.	Oper. Inc.	% Oper. Inc. of Revs.	Cap. Exp.	Depr.	Int. Exp.	Net Bef. Taxes	Eff. Tax Rate	[2]Net Inc.	% Net Inc. of Revs.	Cash Flow
1992	**805**	**57**	**7.1**	**32.8**	**29.9**	**6.9**	**d1.0**	**NM**	**[3]d3.5**	**NM**	**26.4**
1991	879	99	11.3	32.6	28.7	10.3	33.2	57.6%	14.1	1.6	42.8
[1]1990	865	110	12.7	35.0	27.0	12.0	75.0	37.9%	46.6	5.4	73.6
1989	793	92	11.5	57.9	22.4	10.6	66.3	37.6%	[3]41.4	5.2	63.8
1988	714	94	13.1	46.4	21.0	7.6	69.6	35.9%	44.6	6.3	65.6
1987	574	87	15.2	34.2	18.9	5.4	63.3	47.4%	33.3	5.8	52.2
1986	532	88	16.6	19.3	16.8	6.5	66.5	43.1%	[3]37.8	7.1	54.6
1985	492	90	18.2	36.4	14.2	6.7	72.6	43.7%	40.9	8.3	55.1
1984	403	69	17.3	17.8	12.6	7.9	51.4	44.4%	28.6	7.1	41.2
1983	315	46	14.7	12.6	11.0	7.6	30.0	37.1%	18.9	6.0	29.8

Balance Sheet Data (Million $)

May 31	Cash	Curr. Assets	Curr. Liab.	Curr. Ratio	Total Assets	% Ret. on Assets	Long Term Debt	Common Equity	Total Cap.	% LT Debt of Cap.	% Ret. on Equity
1992	**16.9**	**205**	**139**	**1.5**	**471**	**NM**	**29.4**	**280**	**310**	**9.5**	**NM**
1991	15.4	222	108	2.1	493	2.7	54.7	315	382	14.3	4.5
1990	11.8	243	116	2.1	534	8.8	89.0	314	416	21.4	15.5
1989	11.1	225	122	1.8	495	9.0	86.1	270	370	23.3	16.1
1988	9.6	208	103	2.0	434	11.4	66.5	248	328	20.2	19.4
1987	2.6	179	82	2.2	347	10.1	36.5	212	263	13.9	16.5
1986	25.7	185	63	2.9	312	12.6	41.6	192	247	16.8	20.9
1985	26.2	165	59	2.8	290	14.6	48.2	170	229	21.0	26.1
1984	55.9	167	65	2.6	273	11.1	52.3	143	205	25.6	21.7
1983	43.6	134	52	2.6	240	8.0	59.2	119	187	31.6	16.9

Data as orig. reptd. **1.** Refl. merger or acq. **2.** Bef. spec. items in 1992, 1989. **3.** Refl. acctg. change. d-Deficit. NM-Not Meaningful.

Sales (Million $)

13 Weeks:	1992–93	1991–92	1990–91	1989–90
Aug.	200	185	232	205
Nov.	205	206	234	224
Feb.	217	199	207	211
May	234	215	205	224
	856	805	879	865

Based on a preliminary report, net sales for the fiscal year ended May 29, 1993, advanced 6.3% from the prior year's level. Margins benefited from cost reduction measures, a lower fixed cost structure and the absence of $20.6 million of net restructuring and other charges, and despite a net charge of $3.2 million for the reconfiguration of manufacturing operations in the U.K., net income of $22,054,000 ($0.88 a share), contrasted with a net loss of $3,488,000 ($0.14). Results for 1991-92 excluded special charges of $0.11 from the early extinguishment of debt and $0.31 from an accounting change.

Common Share Earnings ($)

13 Weeks:	1992–93	1991–92	1990–91	1989–90
Aug.	0.10	0.09	0.42	0.34
Nov.	0.14	0.21	0.43	0.48
Feb.	0.29	0.16	d0.58	0.47
May	0.35	[1]d0.60	0.28	0.53
	0.88	d0.14	0.55	1.82

1. Incl. restructuring and other charges. d-Deficit.

Dividend Data

Cash has been paid each year since 1945.

Amt of Divd. $	Date Decl.	Ex–divd. Date	Stock of Record	Payment Date
0.13	Oct. 5	Nov. 20	Nov. 27	Jan. 15'93
0.13	Jan. 6	Feb. 22	Feb. 26	Apr. 15'93
0.13	Mar. 24	May 24	May 28	Jul. 15'93
0.13	Jul. 16	Aug. 23	Aug. 27	Oct. 15'93

Finances

In January 1991, directors authorized a two million share repurchase program. Through 1992-93 year-end, Miller had acquired a total of 1,344,000 of its shares at an average cost of $17.07 a share, including 529,000 shares purchased in 1992-93 (all in the first half) at an average cost of $15.43 a share.

During the fourth quarter of 1991-2, Miller recorded a special charge of $0.11 a share from the early retirement of $42.9 million of 10.15% notes.

Capitalization

Long Term Debt: $21,128,000 (5/29/93).

Common Stock: 24,832,042 shs. ($0.20 par). Institutions hold 55%. Shareholders: About 13,000 of record (8/92).

Office—8500 Byron Road, Zeeland, MI 49464. **Tel**—(616) 772-3300. **Chrmn**—M. O. DePree. **Pres & CEO**—J. K. Campbell. **VP-CFO & Investor Contact**—James H. Bloem. **VP-Fin & Treas**—J. G. Schreiber. **Secy**—J. N. DeBoer, Jr. **Dirs**—W. K. Brehm, J. K. Campbell, E. D. Crockett, M. O. DePree, A. M. Fern, B. Griffith, D. L. Nelson, C. W. Pollard, C. D. Ray, R. A. Reister, R. H. Ruch. **Transfer Agent & Registrar**—NBD Bank, Boston. **Incorporated** in Michigan in 1905; reorganized in Delaware in 1970; reorganized in Michigan in 1981. **Empl**—6,001.

 Michael W. Jaffe

Minnesota Power & Light

NYSE Symbol MPL In S&P MidCap 400

Price	Range	P-E Ratio	Dividend	Yield	S&P Ranking	Beta
Sep. 29'93	1993					
35⅝	36½–32⅝	16	1.98	5.6%	A–	0.57

Summary

This moderate-sized electric utility serves an important mining area, which includes the Mesabi Iron Range; taconite and iron producers accounted for 41% of revenues in 1992. Subsidiaries are engaged in coal mining, water utility and wastewater treatment operations, paper manufacturing and recycling, and steam production. Share earnings are expected to improve in 1993, reflecting higher kilowatt-hour sales to the recovering Minnesota mining industry and increased subsidiary contributions to profitability.

Current Outlook

Earnings for 1993 are projected at $2.35 a share, up from 1992's $2.31. Earnings for 1994 are estimated at $2.40 a share.

Directors raised the quarterly dividend 2.1%, to $0.49½ from $0.48½, with the March 1993 payment.

Higher share earnings for 1993 should mainly reflect increased industrial sales, owing to higher usage from the recovering Minnesota mining industry, which accounts for over 40% of electric sales. For 1993 and beyond, incremental contributions to earnings from the company's subsidiary businesses should become more significant. In particular, water utility rate increases and paper manufacturing should improve profitability in 1993.

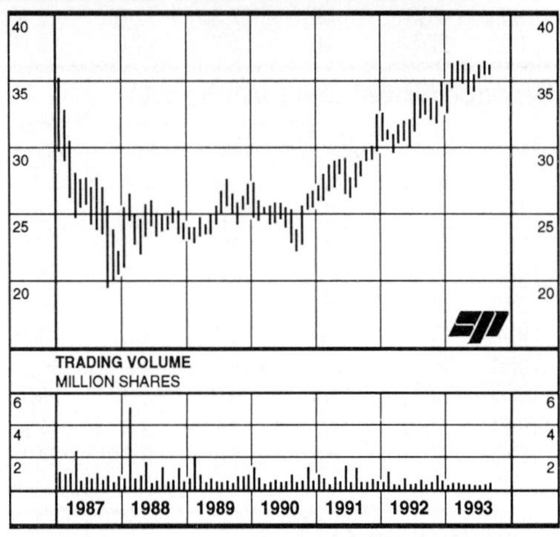

Operating Revenues (Million $)

Quarter:	1994	1993	1992	1991
Mar.	---	127.9	125.1	125.6
Jun.	---	126.3	121.5	120.1
Sep.	---	---	117.1	115.2
Dec.	---	---	125.7	123.2
	---	---	489.4	484.1

Operating revenues for the six months ended June 30, 1993, rose 3.1%, year to year, reflecting 32% higher water utility revenues from increased rates and greater revenues from Florida real estate sales. Operating expenses advanced 3.7%, owing to an increase in purchased power for scheduled plant shutdowns; operating income declined fractionally. Following an 18% decline in other income, and lower interest charges from refinancing debt, net income was down 4.2%. After preferred dividends, share earnings were $1.07, versus $1.19.

Common Share Earnings ($)

Quarter:	1994	1993	1992	1991
Mar.	E0.65	0.62	0.54	0.54
Jun.	E0.45	0.45	0.65	0.42
Sep.	E0.70	E0.68	0.46	0.80
Dec.	E0.60	E0.60	0.66	0.70
	E2.40	E2.35	2.31	2.46

Important Developments

Aug. '93— The Florida Public Service Commission (FPSC) approved a final water and wastewater treatment rate increase of $5.3 million at Marco Island, Fla. Southern States Utilities, a water utility subsidiary, expects the FPSC to implement final rates worth approximately $8.5 million in additional annual revenues on two other cases by year end. MPL's goal for its nonutility businesses is to have them contribute 50% of earnings by the year 2000. These operations contributed 47% of earnings in 1992. Management at the paper subsidiary is concentrating on improving efficiency and productivity to better position itself as the paper industry recovers from its recent recession. MPL's BNI Coal subsidiary supplies mine-mouth lignite coal to two Minnkota Power generating units, which enables them to operate near the lowest cost of any U.S. power plant. MPL buys 71% of the output from one of these stations under a long-term contract which extends until 2007.

Next earnings report expected in late October.

Per Share Data ($)

Yr. End Dec. 31	1992	1991	1990	1989	1988	1987	1986	1985	1984	1983
Tangible Bk. Val.	**19.89**	19.26	19.16	20.30	16.86	16.29	15.62	14.35	13.31	12.55
Earnings[1]	**2.31**	2.46	2.37	2.90	2.35	2.34	2.77	2.34	2.03	1.91
Dividends	**1.94**	1.90	1.86	1.78	1.72	1.66	1.52	1.38	1.28	1.20
Payout Ratio	**84%**	77%	78%	61%	73%	71%	55%	59%	63%	63%
Prices—High	**35**	32½	27⅜	27⅝	26½	35¼	34⅞	20½	15	13⅞
Low	**29⅝**	26	22¼	22⅞	21	19½	19⅛	14⅝	11⅞	11⅝
P/E Ratio—	**15–12**	13–11	12–9	10–8	11–9	15–8	13–7	9–6	7–6	7–6

Data as orig. reptd. Adj. for stk. div(s). of 100% Jul. 1986. **1.** Bef. spec. item(s) of +0.16 in 1992. E-Estimated.

Income Data (Million $)

Year Ended Dec. 31	Revs.	Depr.	Maint.	Oper. Ratio	[1]Fxd. Chgs. Cover.	Constr. Credits	Eff. Tax Rate	[4]Net Inc.	% Return On Revs.	% Return On [2]Invest. Capital	% Return On [3]Com. Equity
1992	**489**	**39.1**	**24.8**	**84.3%**	**2.79**	**Nil**	**26.9%**	**68.5**	**14.0**	**8.1**	**15.3**
1991	484	37.2	26.1	85.7%	2.80	Nil	26.3%	75.5	15.6	8.8	15.4
1990	477	35.7	26.8	84.8%	2.72	Nil	19.2%	74.6	15.6	8.5	13.6
1989	464	36.6	29.0	84.4%	3.31	Nil	25.6%	88.9	19.2	9.6	16.9
1988	460	40.2	26.1	84.1%	2.72	0.3	15.4%	72.9	15.8	8.9	14.1
1987	426	38.7	25.7	84.4%	2.60	0.5	9.8%	70.0	16.4	8.7	14.5
1986	395	37.7	21.4	82.3%	3.37	0.1	23.8%	82.6	20.9	9.9	18.2
1985	413	37.3	23.0	82.2%	3.08	0.2	28.2%	69.4	16.8	9.3	16.7
1984	417	33.9	17.4	82.9%	2.97	0.2	32.6%	59.3	14.2	8.9	15.4
1983	374	31.3	16.3	81.0%	3.24	0.3	43.2%	54.1	14.5	8.9	15.4

Balance Sheet Data (Million $)

Dec. 31	Gross Prop.	Capital Expend.	Net Prop.	% Earn. on Net Prop.	Total Cap.	Capitalization LT Debt	% LT Debt	Pfd.	% Pfd.	Com.	% Com.
1992	**1,553**	**74**	**1,048**	**7.4**	**1,447**	**542**	**50.2**	**49.5**	**4.6**	**488**	**45.2**
1991	1,489	69	1,016	7.0	1,426	534	50.4	52.5	5.0	472	44.6
1990	1,415	69	977	7.3	1,441	520	47.3	56.5	5.2	522	47.5
1989	1,424	67	999	7.4	1,417	517	47.7	58.5	5.4	508	46.9
1988	1,350	85	944	7.9	1,323	509	48.1	60.5	5.7	488	46.2
1987	1,263	44	902	7.4	1,275	489	48.3	66.5	6.6	456	45.1
1986	1,204	39	884	7.9	1,229	461	47.1	83.5	8.6	434	44.3
1985	1,173	30	885	8.2	1,179	459	48.8	83.5	8.9	397	42.3
1984	1,149	28	888	8.3	1,115	456	50.8	83.5	9.3	358	39.9
1983	1,049	26	839	8.5	1,001	403	49.6	83.5	10.3	326	40.1

Data as orig. reptd. **1.** Times int. exp. and pfd. divs. covered (pretax basis). **2.** Based on income bef. interest charges. **3.** As reptd. by Co. **4.** Bef. spec. items.

Business Summary

Minnesota Power & Light provides electric service in a 26,000-square-mile area of central and northeastern Minnesota. The service territory includes the recovering wood-products industry and the Mesabi Iron Range, the major source of taconite pellets used in U.S. steelmaking. Through its Superior Water, Light, & Power (SWL&P) subsidiary, MPL also provides electric, water and gas service in Superior, Wisconsin, and adjacent areas. Other major subsidiaries are engaged in coal mining, paper manufacturing and recycling, steam production and water utility and wastewater treatment plants in Florida and the Carolinas. Contributions to electric revenues (83% of total revenues in 1992) by customer class:

	1992	1991	1990	1989
Industrial	65%	67%	68%	68%
Residential	12%	12%	12%	12%
Commercial	12%	12%	12%	12%
Other	11%	9%	8%	8%

Revenues from sales to taconite and iron mining customers accounted for 41% of electric operating revenues in 1992, compared with 44% in 1991.

The fuel mix in 1992 was 48% steam (mostly coal), 7% hydro and 45% purchased. Peak load in 1992 was 1,299 mw and system capability was 1,495 mw, for a capacity margin of 13%.

Finances

In September 1993, MPL offered 1 million shares of its common stock at $35.875 through underwriters led by PaineWebber Inc. In July 1993, MPL sold $25 million of 6¼% first mortgage bonds.

Dividend Data

Dividends have been paid since 1945. A dividend reinvestment plan is available.

Amt of Divd. $	Date Decl.	Ex–divd. Date	Stock of Record	Payment Date
0.48½	Oct. 21	Nov. 9	Nov. 16	Dec. 1'92
0.49½	Jan. 27	Feb. 9	Feb. 16	Mar. 1'93
0.49½	Apr. 21	May 10	May 14	Jun. 1'93
0.49½	Jul. 21	Aug. 10	Aug. 16	Sep. 1'93

Capitalization

Long Term Debt: $571,909,000 (6/93, adj.).

Red. Cum. Preferred Stock: $21,000,000.

Cum. Preferred Stock: $28,547,000.

Common Stock: 30,934,851 shs. (no par).
Institutions hold about 15%.
Shareholders of record: 29,453.

Office—30 West Superior St., Duluth, MN 55802. **Tel**—(218) 722-2641. **Chrmn, Pres & CEO**—A. J. Sandbulte. **VP-CFO**—R. D. Edwards. **Secy**—P. R. Halverson. **Investor Contact**—Timothy Thorp (212) 723-3953. **Dirs**—M. K. Cragun, D. E. Evans, O. G. Fladmark, M. E. Junck, R. S. Mars Jr., P. F. McQueen, R. S. Nickoloff, J. I. Rajala, C. A. Russell, M. E. Ryland, A. J. Sandbulte, D. C. Wegmiller. **Transfer Agents**—Company's office; Chemical Bank, NYC. **Registrars**—First Bank-Duluth; Chemical Bank, NYC. **Incorporated** in Minnesota in 1906. **Empl**—3,000.

 Ned Bancroft

Mirage Resorts

NYSE Symbol MIR Options on ASE In S&P MidCap 400

Price	Range	P-E Ratio	Dividend	Yield	S&P Ranking	Beta
Sep. 7'93	1993					
53	54½–32¾	32	None	None	B–	2.01

Summary

This major gaming company (formerly Golden Nugget) is expanding its presence in Nevada through the development of a large priate-themed casino/hotel which is expected to open in October 1993. MIR already owns and operates three other Nevada casino/hotels, although ownership of a downtown Las Vegas facility may be spun off or sold. Also, MIR may develop another major new casino/hotel on the Dunes property in Las Vegas, and MIR has been pursuing prospective expansion outside of Nevada.

Current Outlook

Earnings for 1993 are estimated at $2.10 a share, up from 1992's $1.32. An increase to $2.75 is expected in 1994.

Dividends are unlikely over the near term.

Earnings in the second half of 1993 are expected to benefit from an improved third quarter win percentage at table games, and the opening of MIR's new Treasure Island casino/hotel in October. Also, MIR is expected to benefit from the redemption of some of its high-cost debt. In 1994, the full-year presence of Treasure Island is expected to be the principal contributor to higher earnings.

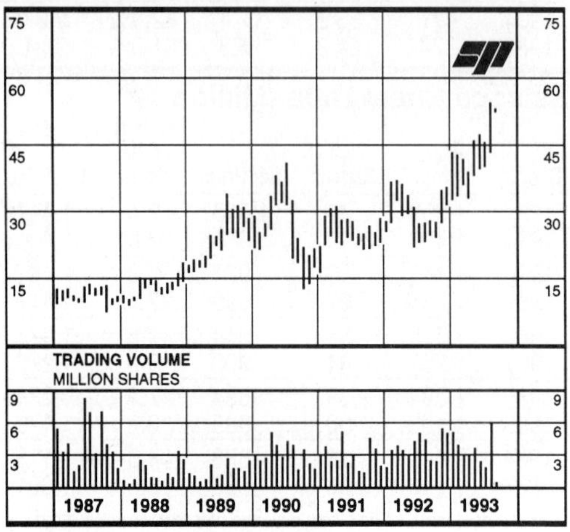

Revenues (Million $)

Quarter:	1993	1992	1991	1990
Mar.	215	216	208	208
Jun.	231	193	213	208
Sep.	---	201	193	214
Dec.	---	223	209	280
	---	833	823	909

Revenues for the six months ended June 30, 1993, increased 9.0%, year to year. Operating profit was up 19%, and with lower interest expense, net income more than doubled, to $28.4 million ($0.89 a share on 23% more shares) from $13.7 million ($0.53). This excludes net adverse effects from special items of $0.07 and $0.23 a share in the respective periods.

Common Share Earnings ($)

Quarter:	1993	1992	1991	1990
Mar.	0.33	0.56	0.55	0.92
Jun.	0.56	d0.01	0.56	0.82
Sep.	E0.51	0.42	0.52	0.27
Dec.	E0.70	0.36	0.36	d0.53
	E2.10	[1]1.32	[1]2.01	[1]1.57

Important Developments

Aug. '93— MIR's management is evaluationg various alternatives that could lead to MIR spinning off or selling ownership of the Golden Nugget casino/hotel in downtown Las Vegas. In 1992, the Golden Nugget had revenues and operating profit (after depreciation) of $190.2 million and $28.6 million, respectively. A recent debt exchange offer related to the downtown facility expired without being completed. Also, MIR is developing long-term plans for the Dunes property in Las Vegas, which MIR acquired in January 1993 for $70 million. A large casino/hotel project may be built on the site, but completion is not likely prior to 1996. MIR already has a large project under way in Las Vegas—the 3,000-room Treasure Island casino/hotel, which is scheduled to open in October 1993. Also, MIR has been pursuing expansion in other areas.

Next earnings report expected in late October.

Per Share Data ($)

Yr. End Dec. 31	1992	1991	1990	1989	[3]1988	1987	1986	1985	1984	1983
Tangible Bk. Val.	**[2]18.55**	[2]13.68	[2]7.32	[2]5.30	6.63	9.63	6.88	6.46	6.37	6.59
Cash Flow	**3.64**	4.80	4.51	0.24	0.48	4.76	0.98	1.48	0.90	1.41
Earnings[4]	**1.32**	2.01	1.57	d1.27	d0.35	4.16	0.10	0.65	0.23	1.09
Dividends	**Nil**	Nil	Nil	Nil	Nil	Nil	Nil	Nil	Nil	Nil
Payout Ratio	**Nil**	Nil	Nil	Nil	Nil	Nil	Nil	Nil	Nil	Nil
Prices—High	**37**	31¼	41⅛	34	18½	13⅞	16⅞	13½	15⅝	19⅜
Low	**22**	16⅜	12¾	16⅜	9⅛	7⅝	9⅛	9¼	8⅛	6¼
P/E Ratio—	**28–17**	16–8	26–8	NM	NM	3–2	NM	21–14	67–35	18–6

Data as orig. reptd. Adj. for stk. div. of 400% Jul. 1983. **1.** Sum of quarters does not equal full-yr. amt., due to change in shs. **2.** Incl. intangibles. **3.** Refl. merger or acq. **4.** Bef. spec. items of -0.30 (net) in 1992, +0.10 in 1991, -0.47 in 1986, -0.05 in 1985, -0.08 in 1984, -0.04 in 1983. d-Deficit. E-Estimated. NM-Not Meaningful.

Income Data (Million $)

Year Ended Dec. 31	Revs.	Oper. Inc.	% Oper. Inc. of Revs.	Cap. Exp.	Depr.	Int. Exp.	Net Bef. Taxes	Eff. Tax Rate	[2]Net Inc.	% Net Inc. of Revs.	Cash Flow
1992	**833**	**191**	**22.9**	**221**	**64.8**	**103**	**46**	**19.0%**	**37**	**4.4**	**102**
1991	823	225	27.4	66	61.8	114	68	34.1%	45	5.4	106
1990	909	223	24.5	129	55.4	116	45	34.3%	30	3.3	85
1989	300	21	7.0	406	25.3	109	d32	NM	d21	NM	4
[1]1988	175	30	17.3	228	18.1	68	d11	NM	d8	NM	11
1987	194	30	15.7	37	19.8	32	179	23.2%	138	70.8	157
1986	382	66	17.4	176	29.9	79	1	NM	3	0.9	33
1985	385	68	17.5	68	29.2	74	30	23.9%	23	5.9	52
1984	385	81	21.0	133	24.4	57	10	21.4%	8	2.1	33
1983	370	115	31.1	107	20.2	45	70	42.3%	41	10.9	61

Balance Sheet Data (Million $)

Dec. 31	Cash	Curr. Assets	Curr. Liab.	Curr. Ratio	Total Assets	% Ret. on Assets	Long Term Debt	Common Equity	Total Cap.	% LT Debt of Cap.	% Ret. on Equity
1992	**143**	**260**	**156**	**1.7**	**1,580**	**2.2**	**831**	**554**	**1,416**	**58.7**	**7.7**
1991	194	278	160	1.7	1,316	2.9	798	301	1,150	69.4	19.3
1990	134	243	134	1.8	1,315	2.4	1,009	122	1,175	85.8	28.3
1989	93	171	124	1.4	1,159	NM	900	88	1,032	87.2	NM
1988	80	101	93	1.1	1,038	NM	749	134	939	79.8	NM
1987	176	193	54	3.6	546	25.1	213	217	489	43.6	74.1
1986	235	272	90	3.0	866	0.4	506	243	776	65.2	1.5
1985	421	454	72	6.3	921	2.8	583	204	850	68.6	11.1
1984	227	334	144	2.3	763	1.1	339	225	619	54.8	3.5
1983	343	370	62	6.0	715	7.3	370	239	654	56.7	23.0

Data as orig. reptd. **1.** Refl. merger or acq. **2.** Bef. spec. items. d-Deficit. NM-Not Meaningful.

Business Summary

This major gaming company (formerly Golden Nugget) operates two casino/hotels in Las Vegas and a casino/hotel in Laughlin, Nev. Also in Las Vegas, MIR is constructing a large, new casino/hotel that is expected to open in October 1993.

In 1992, MIR had $534 million of casino winnings, which represented 64% of total revenues. MIR's largest casino/hotel, The Mirage, accounts for the bulk of MIR's revenue and operating profit. This facility, which opened on the Las Vegas Strip in November 1989, has about 3,030 hotel rooms and suites and 95,500 sq. ft. of casino space. Adjacent to The Mirage, MIR is building a pirate-themed casino/hotel, called Treasure Island, which is expected to have about 3,000 hotel rooms. This is one of three large new gaming facilities (two belonging to other companies) that are expected to open on the Las Vegas Strip in either late 1999 or early 1994. Also, in January 1993, MIR purchased, for $70 million, the 164-acre Dunes property in Las Vegas, on which another major new casino/hotel may be built.

In downtown Las Vegas, MIR's Golden Nugget casino/hotel has 1,907 hotel rooms and suites and about 38,000 sq. ft. of casino space. MIR also owns the Golden Nugget casino/hotel in Laughlin, Nev. Following completion of an expansion in December 1992, the facility now has about 300 hotel rooms and a 32,000 sq. ft. casino. In addition, MIR has been pursuing expansion opportunities in new geographic areas.

Dividend Data

The only cash dividend since 1972 was $0.016 (adjusted) in 1978.

Finances

In April 1992, a public offering of 5.0 million MIR common shares was completed at $35.50 a share. A portion of the net proceeds went toward the redemption of $211 million of relatively high-cost debt.

In May 1991, there was a public offering of 5.0 million MIR common shares at $26 each.

Capitalization

Long Term Debt: $821,399,000 (6/93).

Common Stock: 30,310,386 shs. ($0.02 par).
Institutions hold about 71%.
Shareholders of record: About 12,500 (3/93).

Exercisable Stock Options: To purchase 3.2 million shs. (12/92).

Office—3400 Las Vegas Boulevard South, Las Vegas, NV 89109. **Tel**—(702) 791-7111. **Chrmn, Pres & CEO**—S. A. Wynn. **VP-Secy**—K. R. Wynn. **Sr VP-Fin, CFO, Treas & Investor Contact**—Daniel R. Lee. **Dirs**—R. D. Bronson, G. S. Darman, G. J. Mason, R. M. Popeil, D. B. Wayson, M. B. Wolzinger, E. P. Wynn, K. R. Wynn, S. A. Wynn. **Transfer Agents**—Bank of America Nevada, Las Vegas; First Chicago Trust Co. of New York, NYC. **Registrars**—First Interstate Bank of Nevada, Las Vegas; First Chicago Trust Co. of New York, NYC. **Incorporated** in Nevada in 1949. **Empl**—12,200.

 Tom Graves, CFA

Modine Manufacturing

NASDAQ Symbol MODI (Incl. in Nat'l Market) In S&P MidCap 400

Price	Range	P-E Ratio	Dividend	Yield	S&P Ranking	Beta
Jul. 30'93	1993					
19¾	23½–17½	17	0.46	2.3%	A–	0.29

Summary

Modine makes heat-transfer products for original equipment manufacturers, the automotive aftermarket and nonresidential building markets. Although most of its markets are not growing rapidly, increased penetration in several important markets, including charge-air coolers, Ad-Tech radiators and oil coolers, together with tight cost controls, should lead to higher earnings in 1993-4. The dividend was boosted 9.5% with the June 1993 payment.

Current Outlook

Earnings for 1993-4 are estimated at $1.25 a share, up from $1.12 in 1992-3.

The quarterly dividend was boosted 9.5%, to $0.11½, from $0.10½, with the June 1993 payment.

Sales should rise in 1993-4, reflecting increased sales of radiators and oil coolers to the truck market. Growth will be aided by market share gains and new customer programs. Cost controls and lower interest expense should contribute to higher earnings.

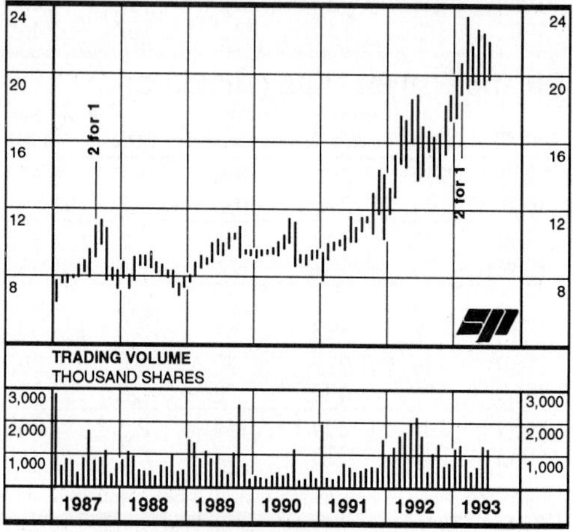

Net Sales (Million $)

13 Weeks:	1993-94	1992-93	1991-92	1990-91
Jun.	148	134	126	114
Sep.		144	133	119
Dec.		147	131	127
Mar.		146	137	123
		571	527	482

Net sales for the quarter ended June 30, 1993, advanced 10%, year to year, on higher sales of parallel-flow products for cars and light trucks and market share gains in medium and heavy-duty truck products. Income from operations climbed 26%. After taxes at 36.8%, versus 37.0%, net income was up 19%, to $0.32 a share, from $0.28, as adjusted. Results exclude a gain of $0.03 a share from an accounting change, versus a charge of $0.46.

Common Share Earnings ($)

13 Weeks:	1993-94	1992-93	1991-92	1990-91
Jun.	0.32	0.28	0.22	0.23
Sep.	E0.31	0.28	0.25	0.24
Dec.	E0.28	0.25	0.22	0.49
Mar.	E0.34	0.31	0.26	0.07
	E1.25	1.12	0.94	1.02

Important Developments

Jul. '93— MODI forecasted an increase in sales of 10% to 15% in fiscal 1993-94, reflecting expected contributions from the planned acquisition of a German limited partnership company, Langerer & Reich, for about one-third of the fiscal year. With annual sales of $120 million, Langerer & Reich produces charge-air coolers, oil coolers, radiators and other heat exchangers in Europe.

May '93— The adoption of FAS 106, a new accounting standard recognizing the expected future costs of postretirement employee health care benefits, resulted in a charge of $0.46 a share in 1992-3. In addition, ongoing costs related to FAS 106 increased net retirement healthcare benefits by $957,000 ($0.03 a share) in 1992-3.

Next earnings report expected in late October.

Per Share Data ($)

Yr. End Mar. 31	**1993**	1992	[1]1991	1990	1989	1988	[1]1987	[1]1986	1985	1984
Tangible Bk. Val.	**7.31**	7.05	6.64	6.05	5.69	5.10	4.44	4.10	3.68	3.13
Cash Flow	**1.96**	1.77	1.74	1.37	1.32	1.30	1.03	0.95	0.99	0.65
Earnings[2]	**1.12**	0.94	1.02	0.84	0.87	0.84	0.66	0.67	0.74	0.44
Dividends	**0.42**	0.38	0.34	0.30	0.26	0.22	0.19	0.17	0.14	0.12
Payout Ratio	**38%**	40%	33%	35%	30%	26%	28%	25%	19%	27%
Calendar Years	**1992**	1991	1990	1989	1988	1987	1986	1985	1984	1983
Prices—High	**18⅞**	14⅜	11½	11	9½	11⅜	7 3/16	5 13/16	3⅝	3
Low	**11¾**	7 13/16	8⅝	7 11/16	6⅞	6½	5⅝	3 9/16	2 7/16	1 11/16
P/E Ratio—	**17–10**	15–8	11–8	13–9	11–8	14–8	11–9	9–5	5–3	7–4

Data as orig. reptd. Adj. for stk. divs. of 100% Feb. 1993, 100% Aug. 1987, 150% Apr. 1985. **1.** Refl. merger or acq. **2.** Bef. spec. items of -0.45 in 1992. E-Estimated NA-Not Available.

Income Data (Million $)

Year Ended Mar. 31	Revs.	Oper. Inc.	% Oper. Inc. of Revs.	Cap. Exp.	Depr.	Int. Exp.	[2]Net Bef. Taxes	Eff. Tax Rate	Net Inc.	% Net Inc. of Revs.	Cash Flow
1993	**571**	**83.1**	**14.6**	**23.6**	**25.5**	**5.95**	**54.1**	**37.7%**	**33.7**	**5.9**	**59.2**
1992	527	69.2	13.1	16.9	25.1	7.12	43.4	35.5%	28.0	5.3	53.1
[1]1991	482	54.8	11.4	28.8	21.3	7.21	48.3	36.9%	30.5	6.3	51.8
1990	436	58.4	13.4	20.5	17.0	5.41	39.7	36.5%	25.2	5.8	41.2
1989	424	58.2	13.7	14.2	14.6	3.95	41.4	36.8%	26.2	6.2	39.9
1988	395	57.5	14.5	14.6	13.9	4.22	41.5	39.8%	25.0	6.3	38.9
[1]1987	349	50.1	14.4	14.4	11.2	3.53	37.5	47.7%	19.6	5.6	30.8
[1]1986	312	48.6	15.6	10.0	8.4	3.88	39.0	47.5%	20.5	6.6	28.9
1985	303	49.8	16.5	12.2	7.4	3.95	38.4	43.9%	21.5	7.1	29.0
1984	225	31.3	13.9	12.2	6.0	3.01	23.2	45.3%	12.7	5.6	18.8

Balance Sheet Data (Million $)

		Curr.									
Mar. 31	Cash	Assets	Liab.	Ratio	Total Assets	% Ret. on Assets	Long Term Debt	Common Equity	Total Cap.	% LT Debt of Cap.	% Ret. on Equity
1993	**33.6**	**221**	**94.7**	**2.3**	**405**	**8.5**	**52.4**	**223**	**287**	**18.3**	**15.3**
1992	18.8	202	75.7	2.7	383	7.2	74.3	215	308	24.1	13.4
1991	27.0	212	88.1	2.4	398	8.4	88.1	205	310	28.4	15.7
1990	27.0	189	73.8	2.6	328	8.2	55.4	184	254	21.8	14.3
1989	24.0	170	71.9	2.4	289	9.4	33.1	171	217	15.2	16.1
1988	15.6	156	61.7	2.5	271	9.8	43.9	154	209	21.0	17.3
1987	4.7	129	62.6	2.1	237	8.7	33.6	131	174	19.3	15.6
1986	13.0	129	58.2	2.2	222	10.0	33.2	125	164	20.2	17.3
1985	3.6	108	38.1	2.8	184	12.4	32.6	110	146	22.3	21.3
1984	5.7	92	37.5	2.4	158	9.0	28.7	89	120	23.9	15.1
1983	7.0	68	19.8	3.5	126	2.9	23.3	81	106	21.9	4.7

Data as orig. reptd. **1.** Refl. merger or acq. **2.** Incl. equity in earns. of nonconsol. subs.

Business Summary

Modine Manufacturing Company is a maker of heat-transfer equipment, serving vehicular, industrial, commercial and building HVAC (heating, ventilating, air-conditioning) and refrigeration equipment markets. The company makes heat exchangers for various original equipment manufacturer applications and for sale to the automotive aftermarket (as replacement parts) and to a wide variety of building markets.

Sales in recent years were derived as follows:

	1993	1992
Radiators/radiator cores	45%	45%
Building HVAC	14%	15%
Oil coolers	13%	13%
Vehicular condensers/ evaporators	12%	13%
Charge air coolers	10%	7%
Miscellaneous	6%	7%

Heat exchangers are supplied for cooling all types of engines, transmissions, auxiliary hydraulic equipment, air-conditioning components used in cars, trucks, farm and construction machinery and equipment, and heating and cooling equipment for residential and commercial building HVAC.

Modine's fastest-growing product grouping is a line of charge-air coolers for turbocharged and supercharged engines. Sales of this product line soared 52% in 1992-3.

In 1992-3, 10 customers accounted in the aggregate for 36% of sales. Shipments of replacement parts to automotive aftermarket customers is the largest single market, at 30% of sales. Export sales accounted for 14% of sales in 1992-3, up from 13% in 1991-2.

Dividend Data

Cash has been paid in each year since 1959. A dividend reinvestment plan is available.

Amt. of Divd. $	Date Decl.	Ex-divd. Date	Stock of Record	Payment Date
0.21	Oct. 21	Nov. 18	Nov. 24	Dec. 4'92
2-for-1 Split	Jan. 20	Feb. 22	Feb. 5	Feb. 19'93
0.10½	Jan. 20	Feb. 23	Mar. 1	Mar. 11'93
0.11½	May 19	May 25	Jun. 1	Jun. 10'93
0.11½	Jul. 21	Aug. 24	Aug. 30	Sep. 9'93

Capitalization

Long Term Debt: $52,496,000 (6/93).

Common Stock: 29,539,000 shs. ($0.62½ par).
Institutions hold 35%.
Shareholders: 2,700 of record (4/1/93).

Office—1500 DeKoven Ave., Racine, WI 53403. **Tel**—(414) 636-1200. **Chrmn**—E. E. Richter. **Pres & CEO**—R. T. Savage. **SVP & Secy**—W. E. Pavlick. **VP-Fin & CFO**—A. D. Reid. **Treas**—R. M. Gunnerson. **Investor Contact**—Gerald J. Sweda. **Dirs**—R. J. Doyle, T. J. Guendel, F. W. Jones, V. L. Martin, G. L. Neale, D. R. O'Hare, J. A. Puelicher, E. E. Richter, W. J. Roper, R. T. Savage, S. W. Tisdale. **Transfer Agent & Registrar**—American Stock Transfer & Trust Co., NYC. **Incorporated** in Wisconsin in 1916. **Empl**—5,348.

 Joshua M. Harari, CFA

Molex Inc.

NASDAQ Symbol MOLX Options on CBOE (Incl. in Nat'l Market) In S&P MidCap 400

Price	Range	P–E Ratio	Dividend	Yield	S&P Ranking	Beta
Aug. 13'93	1993					
34¼	36–25¾	29	0.03	0.1%	A	1.36

Summary

Molex makes electrical and electronic devices such as terminals, connectors and switches which are sold primarily to OEMs in the computer, telecommunications, home appliance and home entertainment industries. Products manufactured and sold outside the U.S. account for over 73% of sales. Revenues and earnings were at record levels in fiscal 1993, aided by strong results in the U.S. and portions of the Far East, which more than offset weakness in Japan & Europe. A 5-for-4 stock split was distributed in late 1992 and the quarterly cash dividend was raised 87.5% in early 1993.

Business Summary

Molex Inc. designs, manufactures and distributes electrical and electronic devices such as terminals, connectors, planer cable, cable assemblies, interconnection systems, fiber optic interconnection systems, backplanes, and mechanical and electronic switches. With a market share of 4%, Molex estimates that it is the second largest connector manufacturer in the world.

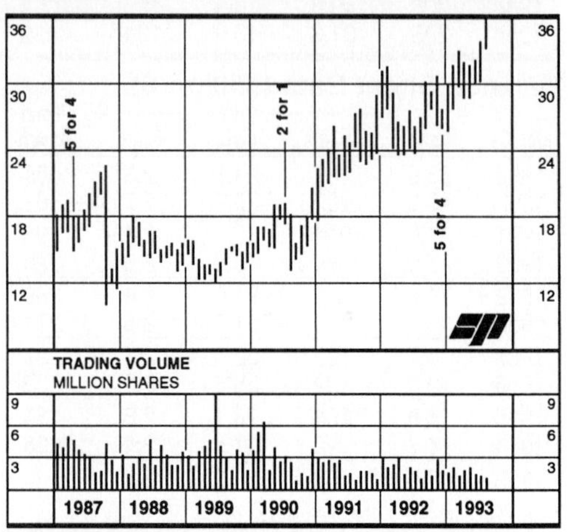

The company's products are sold primarily to original equipment manufacturers and their subcontractors and suppliers. In the U.S. and Canada, it sells through direct sales engineers, manufacturers' representatives and industrial distributors. Internationally, Molex sells its products primarily through distributors and through its own sales organizations. Contributions by geographic area in fiscal 1992 were:

	Sales	Net Inc.
United States	27%	35%
Far East North	35%	49%
Far East South	17%	25%
Europe	18%	10%
Americas (non–U.S.)	2%	1%
Other	1%	–20%

The computer, business equipment and telecommunications markets account for roughly 44% of net revenue, with the balance coming from the home entertainment and home appliance markets, as well as the automotive market. Due to the volatile nature of these markets, the company is uncertain as to what market groups will be its major customers in the future.

Molex's products are typically used in such items as computers, peripheral equipment, calculators, copiers, televisions, stereos, compact disc players, video tape recorders, elecronic games, microwave ovens, refrigerators, freezers, dishwashers, air conditioners, automobiles, farm equipment, electronic medical equipment, vending machines, and security equipment.

Molex continues to expand its operations through selective acquistions within the connector industry. Because of recent competitive pressures, it has been focusing on productivity improvements and reduced spending. During fiscal 1992, the company spent $180.3 million on R&D and capital spending programs, introduced 150 new products and received 140 new patents.

Important Developments

Aug. '93— Molex noted that business in the U.S. and portions of the Far East was strong. However, the company said that overall business continues to be negatively impacted by the economic slowdown in Japan and the recession in Europe. The order backlog stood at $157 million at June 30, 1993, up 6.9% from a year earlier.

Next earnings report expected in late October.

Per Share Data ($)

Yr. End Jun. 30	1993	1992	[1]1991	1990	1989	1988	1987	1986	1985	1984
Tangible Bk. Val.	**NA**	10.50	8.82	7.72	6.79	6.14	4.98	4.03	2.96	2.50
Cash Flow	**NA**	2.15	2.16	1.85	1.71	1.59	1.21	0.93	0.79	0.85
Earnings	**1.19**	1.08	1.04	0.99	0.91	0.94	0.69	0.51	0.50	0.61
Dividends	**0.028**	0.016	0.016	0.017	0.010	0.016	0.008	0.010	0.010	0.010
Payout Ratio	**2%**	1%	2%	2%	1%	2%	1%	2%	2%	2%
Prices[2]—High	**36**	31⅝	29	20⅝	15⅞	18⅛	22⅝	17 15/16	12⅝	13 11/16
Low	**25¾**	23⅝	17⅝	13 3/16	12⅛	13⅛	10	11 11/16	9 1/16	8⅜
P/E Ratio—	**30–22**	29–22	28–17	21–13	17–13	19–14	33–15	35–23	26–18	22–14

Data as orig. reptd. Adj. for stk. divs. of 25% Nov. 1992, 100% Jul. 1990, 25% Apr. 1987, 100% Jan. 1984. **1.** Refl. acctg. change. **2.** Cal. yr. NA-Not Available.

Income Data (Million $)

Year Ended Jun. 30	Revs.	Oper. Inc.	% Oper. Inc. of Revs.	Cap. Exp.	Depr.	Int. Exp.	Net Bef. Taxes	Eff. Tax Rate	Net Inc.	% Net Inc. of Revs.	Cash Flow
1992	**776**	**180**	**23.2**	**133**	**67.6**	**NM**	**117**	**42.4%**	**67.5**	**8.7**	**135**
[1]1991	708	171	24.2	109	58.7	NM	118	45.3%	64.6	9.1	135
1990	594	158	26.6	73	53.6	NM	110	43.2%	62.1	10.4	116
1989	572	160	27.9	94	50.9	NM	105	44.4%	57.7	10.1	109
1988	502	144	28.7	69	41.8	NM	106	43.8%	59.3	11.8	101
1987	387	107	27.6	49	33.2	NM	76	42.2%	43.4	11.2	77
1986	292	78	26.8	40	26.2	2.16	54	39.7%	32.0	11.0	58
1985	253	69	27.3	48	19.1	1.26	53	41.5%	30.9	12.2	50
1984	252	81	32.2	41	14.9	0.87	70	45.4%	38.2	15.2	53
1983	176	53	29.9	19	13.2	NM	42	47.1%	22.0	12.5	35

Balance Sheet Data (Million $)

Jun. 30	Cash	Curr. Assets	Curr. Liab.	Curr. Ratio	Total Assets	% Ret. on Assets	Long Term Debt	Common Equity	Total Cap.	% LT Debt of Cap.	% Ret. on Equity
1992	**157**	**436**	**168**	**2.6**	**850**	**8.6**	**7.9**	**660**	**678**	**1.2**	**11.1**
1991	150	395	144	2.7	710	9.8	9.1	551	563	1.6	12.5
1990	144	355	110	3.2	607	10.9	8.0	481	493	1.6	13.7
1989	124	316	99	3.2	541	11.1	5.8	429	439	1.3	14.1
1988	106	298	96	3.1	499	13.2	6.6	390	399	1.6	16.8
1987	101	229	66	3.5	399	11.9	9.6	316	329	2.9	15.2
1986	73	186	56	3.3	328	11.0	10.1	255	268	3.8	14.5
1985	59	149	50	3.0	255	12.8	8.3	186	202	4.1	18.0
1984	65	146	55	2.7	226	19.4	5.3	157	169	3.1	27.7
1983	50	112	39	2.9	168	14.3	5.5	118	127	4.3	20.7

Data as orig. reptd. **1.** Refl. acctg. change. NM-Not Meaningful.

Net Revenues (Million $)

Quarter:	1992–93	1991–92	1990–91	1989–90
Sep.	215	187	171	143
Dec.	202	189	174	146
Mar.	206	192	177	146
Jun.	236	208	187	159
	859	776	708	594

Based on a preliminary report, revenues in the fiscal year ended June 30, 1993, climbed 11% from those of the prior year. Operating costs were well controlled, and after taxes at 43.7%, versus 42.4%, and higher minority interest, net income was also up 11%, to $74,660,000 ($1.19 a share), from $67,464,000 ($1.08). Results for the 1992-3 period exclude a charge of $3,605,000 ($0.06) from the cumulative effect of an accounting change.

Common Share Earnings ($)

Quarter:	1992–93	1991–92	1990–91	1989–90
Sep.	[1]0.23	0.24	0.27	0.23
Dec.	[1]0.26	0.26	0.25	0.22
Mar.	[1]0.28	0.26	0.24	0.27
Jun.	0.36	0.31	0.28	0.26
	1.19	1.08	1.04	0.99

Dividend Data

Cash dividends have been paid since 1976.

Amt. of Divd. $	Date Decl.	Ex-divd. Date	Stock of Record	Payment Date
0.005	May 29	Sep. 24	Sep. 30	Oct. 26'92
5-for-4	Oct. 26	Dec. 1	Nov. 9	Nov. 30'92
0.0075	Oct. 26	Dec. 24	Dec. 31	Jan. 25'93
0.0075	Oct. 20	Mar. 25	Mar. 31	Apr. 26'93
0.0075	Oct. 26	Jun. 24	Jun. 30	Jul. 26'93

Finances

In fiscal 1993, R&D spending was $56.2 million ($47.6 million in fiscal 1992) and capital expenditures were $93.2 million ($132.7 million).

Capitalization

Long Term Debt: $7,510,000 (6/93).

Minority Interest: $3,851,000.

Common Stock: 31,452,720 shs. ($0.05 par). Institutions hold about 22%.

Cl. A Common: 31,458,190 shs. ($0.05 par); nonvoting; convertible into common stock under certain circumstances.

Cl. B Common: 94,255 shs. ($0.05 par). The Krehbiel family control about 47% of the common, 43% of the Class A common, and 99.8% of the Class B common. Approvals by majorities of the Cl. B shs. (voting separately) and the com. shs. are required for all matters other than the election of directors.

1. Reflects acctg. change.

Office—2222 Wellington Court, Lisle, IL 60532. **Tel**—(708) 969-4550. **Chrmn**—J. H. Krehbiel, Sr. **Vice Chrmn & CEO**—F. A. Krehbiel. **Pres**—J. H. Krehbiel Jr. **VP & Treas**—J. C. Psaltis. **Secy**—L. A. Hecht. **Investor Contact**—Neil Lefort. **Dirs**—R. H. Hayes, E. D. Jannotta, F. A. Krehbiel, J. H. Krehbiel Sr., J. H. Krehbiel Jr., L. E. Platt, R. J. Potter. **Transfer Agent**—Harris Trust & Savings Bank, Chicago. **Reincorporated** in Delaware in 1972. **Empl**—7,483.

 Sam Dedio

Montana Power

NYSE Symbol MTP In S&P MidCap 400

Price	Range	P-E Ratio	Dividend	Yield	S&P Ranking	Beta
Aug. 27'93	1993					
27¼	27⅞–25⅛	14	1.58	5.8%	B+	0.57

Summary

This company, which operates a gas and electric utility in Montana, derives about half of its profits from coal, oil and gas production, cogeneration and telecommunications. In June 1993, a filing was made for a combined $46.5 million annual rate increase for MTP's gas and electric utility. Earnings growth should accelerate in 1994, aided by the proposed rate rise, a greater percentage of cheaper hydroelectric generated power, and higher oil and gas production.

Current Outlook

Earnings for 1993 are estimated at $2.05 a share, up from $2.02 in 1992. A gain to $2.20 is possible for 1994.

Quarterly dividends, at $0.39½ a share, could be raised moderately in early 1994.

Utility profits should rebound in 1993, reflecting colder weather and the benefits of an interim rate hike in the fourth quarter. Margins should widen, as heavy rains allow MTP to generate a greater portion of its power from lower-cost hydroelectric plants. Aiding demand for electric power will be a stronger economy and an expanding population base. Profits from independent power generation will advance, on contributions from new cogeneration facilities in New York and England. Oil and gas profits may be slip, reflecting flat production and lower oil prices. Coal operations will be hurt by losses at the Golden Eagle mine. The sale of the company's waste management unit and lower interest expense will aid comparisons.

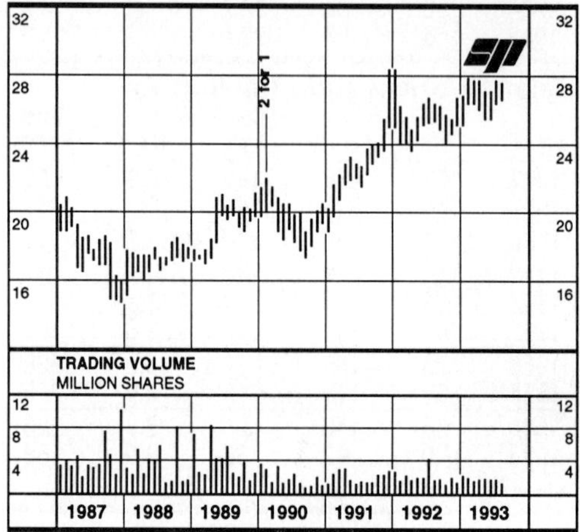

Total Revenues (Million $)

Quarter:	1993	1992	1991	1990
Mar.	303	270	263	236
Jun.	221	201	198	180
Sep.		230	208	174
Dec.		296	269	252
		997	939	842

Revenues in the first half of 1993 advanced 11%, year to year. Net income slipped 3.5%, to $0.83 a share, on 1.7% more shares, from $0.88.

Common Share Earnings ($)

Quarter:	1993	1992	1991	1990
Mar.	0.76	0.80	0.84	0.68
Jun.	0.08	0.08	0.19	0.24
Sep.	E0.35	0.29	0.26	0.13
Dec.	E0.86	0.85	0.74	0.78
	E2.05	2.02	2.03	1.84

Important Developments

Jun. '93— MTP filed a request with the Montana Public Service Commission (MPSC) for a $36.2 million annual rate increase (11.4%) for its electric service and $10.3 million (10.7%) for its gas utility. The company said the increase, the first in three years, is needed to recover higher capital outlays, property taxes and purchased power costs. MTP also requested a $29.1 million combined interim rate hike. The MPSC is expected to issue a decision on the interim request by the end of September 1993, and to decide on the permanent rate increase by early 1994.

May '93— The company sold its Special Resource Management unit to a subsidiary of WMX Technologies Inc. Terms were not disclosed.

Apr. '93— MTP's Entech Coal unit was awarded a 15-year contract to supply Tampa Electric with up to 1.2 million tons of coal annually.

Next earnings report expected in late October.

Per Share Data ($)

Yr. End Dec. 31	1992	1991	1990	1989	1988	1987	1986	1985	1984	1983
Tangible Bk. Val.	**16.82**	16.40	15.78	16.12	16.00	15.87	15.89	15.26	13.84	14.24
Cash Flow	**2.87**	2.85	2.63	2.28	2.24	2.05	2.18	3.42	1.83	2.72
Earnings[1]	**2.02**	2.03	1.84	1.45	1.42	1.26	1.40	2.62	1.03	2.11
Dividends	**1.540**	1.480	1.420	1.380	1.350	1.340	1.255	1.000	1.300	1.455
Payout Ratio	**76%**	74%	78%	95%	95%	106%	90%	38%	127%	69%
Prices—High	**28⅜**	28⅜	22	21⅛	18½	20⅞	21¾	17⅛	15¼	15¼
Low	**23⅝**	18⅞	17⅜	17	15⅛	14¾	15¾	9½	8⅜	12⅝
P/E Ratio—	**14–12**	14–9	12–9	15–12	13–11	17–12	16–11	5–4	15–8	7–6

Data as orig. reptd. Adj. for stk. div. of 100% Feb. 1990. **1.** Bef. spec. item(s) of +0.43 in 1986. E-Estimated.

Income Data (Million $)

Year Ended Dec. 31	[1]Revs.	Oper. Inc.	% Oper. Inc. of Revs.	Cap. Exp.	Depr.	Int. Exp.	Net Bef. Taxes	Eff. Tax Rate	[2]Net Inc.	% Net Inc. of Revs.	Cash Flow
1992	**505**	**170**	**33.8**	**92**	**43.5**	**49.3**	**153**	**29.9%**	**107**	**21.2**	**147**
1991	498	173	34.7	83	41.4	51.9	156	32.3%	106	21.2	143
1990	450	156	34.7	64	39.7	48.7	135	29.7%	95	21.1	131
1989	452	170	37.6	92	40.9	59.1	100	25.9%	74	16.5	112
1988	444	130	29.3	53	39.4	53.5	105	31.5%	72	16.2	107
1987	422	123	29.1	65	37.1	54.0	87	28.2%	62	14.8	96
1986	447	155	34.6	60	35.5	52.2	111	39.7%	67	15.0	99
1985	425	152	35.7	63	34.8	72.2	156	22.1%	122	28.6	149
1984	369	114	31.0	83	33.7	74.9	64	19.4%	51	13.9	77
1983	352	111	31.6	186	23.2	67.6	112	20.6%	89	25.1	103

Balance Sheet Data (Million $)

Dec. 31	Cash	Assets	Curr. Liab.	Ratio	Total Assets	% Ret. on Assets	Long Term Debt	Common Equity	Total Inv. Capital	% LT Debt of Cap.	% Ret. on Equity
1992	**8.9**	**245**	**327**	**0.7**	**2,285**	**4.9**	**581**	**867**	**1,840**	**31.6**	**12.1**
1991	4.7	237	288	0.8	2,085	5.2	603	831	1,686	35.8	12.5
1990	8.5	250	242	1.0	1,985	4.8	600	788	1,635	36.7	11.4
1989	8.7	236	216	1.1	1,946	3.8	563	794	1,606	35.0	8.9
1988	3.1	219	242	0.9	1,926	3.7	551	774	1,580	34.9	8.8
1987	4.5	192	226	0.9	1,863	3.3	562	748	1,555	36.1	7.8
1986	5.5	183	227	0.8	1,836	3.7	568	730	1,530	37.1	8.8
1985	29.4	168	235	0.7	1,743	6.8	581	677	1,435	40.5	17.7
1984	29.1	161	247	0.7	1,765	2.9	706	591	1,500	47.1	7.2
1983	32.7	136	189	0.7	1,692	5.1	688	582	1,490	46.2	14.0

=908M

Data as orig. reptd. **1.** Excl. nonutility opers. **2.** Bef. spec. items.

Business Summary

Montana Power provides electric and gas service in western and central Montana. Nonutility activities such as coal mining, oil and gas production, telecommunications are conducted through Entech, Inc. Contributions to net income (in millions) were:

	1992	1991	1990
Utility........................	$53.1	$53.0	$48.1
Entech......................	50.2	49.4	46.5
Independent power......	3.8	3.4	0.3

Electric utility operations (81% of utility revenues in 1992) serve 213,021 residential and 43,742 commercial and industrial customers Montana. In 1992, 44% of the company's 1,599 mw of system capability was provided from co al, 31% from hydro electric and 25% from purchased power. Peak load in 1992 was 1,436 mw, with a capacity margin of 10%. Total power sales in 1992 were 6.9 billion kilowatt hours. The average residential revenue per kwh in 1992 was 5.75 cents, versus 5.77 cents in 1991.

In 1992, MTP distributed 23.2 Bcf of natural gas to 105,595 residential and 15,394 industrial and commercial customers. Gas sales to other utilities in 1992 were 2.6 Bcf. Average residential revenue per Mcf in 1992 was $4.22, versus $3.96 in 1991.

Entech is one of the nation's largest coal producers. Coal sales in 1992 totaled 22.2 million tons, of which 81% was to unaffiliated utilities. Proved coal reserves at 1992 year-end were 1.84 billion tons. In 1992, Entech produced 4.7 million bbl. of oil and equivalents in Canada and the U.S. Proved reserves at 1992 year-end were 175 Bcf of gas and 10.7 million bbl. of oil and gas liquids. MTP also has interests in telecommunication services and has stakes in six cogeneration plants in Texas, New York and Washington, and in the U.K.

Dividend Data

Dividends have been paid since 1935. A dividend reinvestment plan is available. A "poison pill" stock purchase rights plan was adopted in 1989.

Amt. of Divd. $	Date Decl.	Ex–divd. Date	Stock of Record	Payment Date
0.38½	Sep. 22	Oct. 5	Oct. 9	Oct. 30'92
0.39½	Dec. 22	Jan. 4	Jan. 8	Jan. 29'93
0.39½	Mar. 24	Apr. 2	Apr. 9	Apr. 30'93
0.39½	Jun. 23	Jul. 2	Jul. 9	Jul. 30'93

Capitalization

Long Term Debt: $586,116,000 (6/93).

Cum. Preferred Stock: $51,984,000.

Common Stock: 51,935,730 shs. (no par). Institutions hold 37%. Shareholders of record: 36,069 (12/92).

Office—40 East Broadway, Butte, MT 59701-9989. **Tel**—(406) 723-5421. **Chrmn & CEO**—D. T. Berube. **Vice Chrmn**—J. J. Burke. **VP & Secy**—P. K. Merrell. **VP-Fin & CFO**—J. P. Pederson. **Investor Contact**—Russ J. Cox. **Dirs**—D. T. Berube, J. J. Burke, A. F. Cain, R. D. Corette, K. Foster, R. P. Gannon, B. D. Harris, D. P. Lambros, C. Lehrkind III, J. P. Lucas, S. Miller, A. K. Neill, J. P. Pederson, G. H. Selover, N. E. Vosburg. **Transfer Agents**—Co.'s office; First Chicago Trust Co. of New York, NYC. **Registrars**—First Bank Montana; First Chicago Trust Co. of New York, NYC. **Incorporated** in Montana in 1961. **Empl**—4,139.

 Stephen R. Klein

Morgan Stanley Group

NYSE Symbol MS Options on Phila (Feb-May-Aug-Nov) In S&P MidCap 400

Price	Range	P-E Ratio	Dividend	Yield	S&P Ranking	Beta
Oct. 5'93	1993					
88¼	89⅝–54	11	1.08	1.3%	B+	1.49

Summary

Morgan Stanley Group is a global firm providing a wide range of financial services to corporations, governments, financial institutions, and individual investors. Its businesses include securities underwriting, distribution, and trading; merger, acquisition, restructuring, real estate, project finance, merchant banking and global custody. Managing directors and principals own about 31% of the common stock.

Current Outlook

Earnings for the fiscal year ending January 31, 1994, are projected at $8.60 a share, versus fiscal 1992-93's $5.90. A decline in earnings to $7.20 a share is anticipated for 1994-95.

The minimum expectation is for dividends to continue at $0.27 quarterly.

Earnings for fiscal 1993-94 are expected to rise sharply. Investment banking revenues should benefit from still low interest rates which would encourage further corporate debt issues. Equity deals may also hold up at robust levels. Consistent with the assumption of strong market conditions, interest and dividends and commission income are anticipated to increase. Asset management fees have been rising and the trend is expected to continue. MS has a substantial portfolio of merchant banking investments, but the timing and magnitude of any gains cannot be predicted. Morgan, one of the most consistently profitable companies in the securities industry, benefits from its diversified operations and partnership outlook.

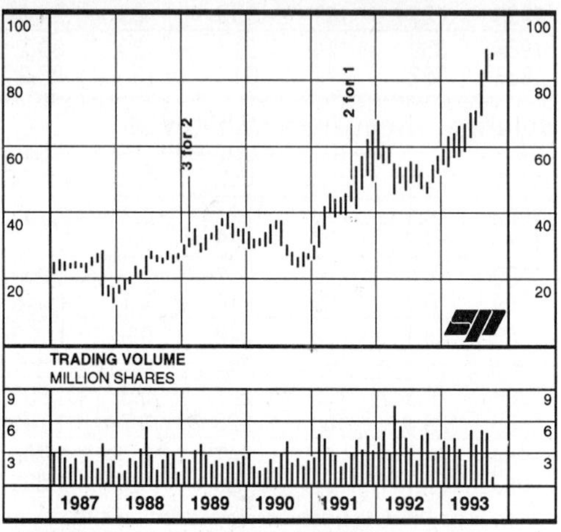

[1]Total Revenues (Million $)

Quarter:	1993-94	1992-93	1991	1990
Apr.	2,187	1,859	1,632	1,397
Jul.	2,489	2,099	1,627	1,446
Oct.	---	1,629	1,738	1,549
Jan.	---	1,795	1,787	1,477
	---	7,382	6,785	5,870

Total revenues for the six months ended July 31, 1993, rose 18%, year to year. Gains of 26% were recorded for investment banking fees, 67% for trading revenues, 19% for commissions, 6.4% for interest and dividends, and 16% for asset management and administration fees. With interest costs up only 3.9%, net revenues increased 40%. Other costs were well controlled, and pretax earnings advanced 60%. After taxes at 37.5%, versus 39.0%, net income rose 64%. Following preferred dividends, share earnings were $5.17, versus $2.98.

[1]Common Share Earnings ($)

Quarter:	1993-94	1992-93	1991	1990
Apr.	2.40	1.62	1.54	1.03
Jul.	2.77	1.36	1.26	0.72
Oct.	E1.80	1.26	1.52	0.91
Jan.	E1.63	1.68	1.61	0.71
	E8.60	5.90	5.93	3.37

Important Developments

Aug. '93— The company reported an agreement, subject to certain conditions, to purchase a building at 1585 Broadway in New York City for $176 million. MS intends to locate its New York Headquarters at this location and to occupy the majority of its 1.3 million square feet of space. Also in August, MS sold $200 million of preferred stock. Separately, during the three months ended July 31 MS repurchased 1.2 million of its common shares for $76.7 million.

Next earnings report expected in early November.

Per Share Data ($)

Yr. End Jan. 31	**1993**	1992	1991	1990	1989	1988	1987	1986	1985	1984
Tangible Bk. Val.	**37.71**	30.13	24.49	23.93	19.09	13.48	10.53	7.46	NA	0.00
Cash Flow	**0.00**	0.00	0.00	0.00	0.00	0.00	0.00	0.00	0.00	0.00
Earnings	**5.90**	5.93	3.37	5.61	5.13	3.00	2.81	[2]1.78	[2]1.02	[2]0.85
Dividends	**0.955**	0.795	0.750	0.500	0.317	0.267	0.117	Nil	Nil	Nil
Payout Ratio	**16%**	13%	22%	9%	6%	9%	4%	Nil	Nil	Nil
Calendar Years	**1992**	1991	1990	1989	1988	1987	1986	1985	1984	1983
Prices—High	**67⅞**	65	37¾	39¾	28 5/16	28⅝	27 5/16	NA	NA	NA
Low	**45⅞**	26	23 9/16	27 7/16	15 9/16	12¾	20 7/16	NA	NA	NA
P/E Ratio—	**12–8**	11–4	11–7	7–5	6–3	10–4	10–7	NA	NA	NA

Data as orig. reptd.; prior to 1986 data reptd. in Prospectus dated Mar. 21, 1986. Adj. for stk. div(s). of 100% Aug. 1991, 50% Feb. 1989.
1. Quarters ended Mar., Jun., Sep., Dec. prior to 1992-93. **2.** Based on pro forma shs. outstanding. E-Estimated NA-Not Available.

Income Data (Million $)

Year Ended Jan. 31	Commis-sions	Int. Inc.	Total Revs.	Int. Exp.	% Exp./ Op. Revs.	Net Bef. Taxes	Eff. Tax Rate	Net Inc.	% Return On Revs.	% Return On Assets	% Return On [1]Equity
1993	**312**	**4,814**	**7,382**	**4,362**	**89.3**	**793**	**35.7%**	**510**	**6.9**	**0.7**	**17.6**
1992	271	4,181	6,785	3,925	88.6	772	38.5%	475	7.0	0.8	21.4
1991	275	3,894	5,870	3,711	92.0	470	42.5%	270	4.6	0.5	13.8
1990	250	3,519	5,831	3,378	87.3	738	40.0%	443	7.6	0.9	27.9
1989	230	2,029	4,109	1,905	84.5	637	38.0%	395	9.6	1.1	32.6
1988	297	1,421	3,148	1,380	88.4	364	36.6%	231	7.3	0.8	25.2
1987	216	1,063	2,463	1,035	86.9	323	37.6%	201	8.2	0.9	32.0
1986	154	938	1,795	900	89.8	183	42.2%	106	5.9	0.7	38.4
1985	130	795	1,340	748	92.1	106	42.1%	61	4.6	0.6	27.4
1984	131	415	860	391	90.0	86	40.6%	51	6.0	0.8	27.1

Balance Sheet Data (Million $)

Jan. 31	Total Assets	Cash Items	Rec.	Secs. Owned	Sec. Borrowed	Due Brokers & Cust.	Other Liabs.	Capitalization Debt	Capitalization [1]Equity	Capitalization Total
1993	**80,353**	**3,558**	**40,390**	**35,662**	**48,206**	**8,306**	**16,448**	**3,960**	**2,813**	**7,394**
1992	63,709	3,827	20,438	26,576	38,710	6,691	12,477	2,837	2,272	5,830
1991	53,526	2,275	17,520	23,393	31,790	5,434	12,749	1,382	1,781	3,553
1990	53,276	872	26,940	16,392	34,768	2,950	12,794	743	1,771	2,764
1989	40,051	1,623	28,765	8,924	26,335	4,002	7,299	815	1,337	2,414
1988	29,663	1,242	20,099	7,678	18,257	3,360	6,353	556	1,001	1,694
1987	29,190	459	18,605	9,511	20,074	3,396	4,541	381	786	1,178
1986	15,794	201	10,410	5,015	8,760	3,290	3,257	172	302	486
1985	13,054	77	8,755	2,885	9,297	1,234	2,041	[2]243	238	481

Data as orig. reptd. Prior to 1986 data reptd. in Prospectus dated Mar. 21, 1986. **1.** Common; as reptd. by Co. **2.** Incl. current portion.

Business Summary

Morgan Stanley Group is a major securities firm whose main subsidiary, Morgan Stanley & Co., is a leading investment banking company. Revenues in recent years were derived as follows:

	1992–93	1991	1990
Investment banking	13%	29%	30%
Principal transaction	15%	47%	42%
Commissions	4%	9%	13%
Net Interest and dividends	65%	9%	8%
Asset mgmt./other	3%	6%	7%

Foreign operations accounted for 40% of net revenues and 37% of pretax earnings in 1992-93.

The company provides a broad range of sales, trading and research services to suppliers of capital worldwide and ranks as one of the largest dealers in equity and fixed income securities. MS is one of 40 primary dealers in U.S. Government securities and is a member of the major U.S. securities and commodities exchanges.

Through its investment banking division, MS provides advice to, and raises capital for, a variety of domestic and international clients. The company participates in the underwriting of public offering of debt, equity and other securities. The company provides advisory services, and is active in corporate merger, acquisition, defense, divestiture and reorganization transactions. MS provides advice and other services related to real estate. MS also manages assets for individuals, and pension and profit sharing funds.

At July 31, 1993, MS's net capital, as defined, totaled $457.4 million, which was $342.0 million in excess of the regulatory minimum requirement.

Dividend Data

Dividends were initiated in 1986.

Amt of Divd. $	Date Decl.	Ex–divd. Date	Stock of Record	Payment Date
0.24	Nov. 19	Nov. 23	Nov. 30	Dec. 17'92
0.27	Feb. 23	Mar. 1	Mar. 5	Mar. 23'93
0.27	May 27	Jun. 1	Jun. 7	Jun. 24'93
0.27	Aug. 23	Aug. 30	Sep. 3	Sep. 23'93

Capitalization

Long Term Debt: $3,899,540,000 (7/93).

Preferred Stock: $819,983,000, incl. $137.5 million conv. into com. at $35.88 a share.

Common Stock: 74,027,880 shs. ($1 par).
Managing directors and principals own about 31%.
Institutions hold approximately 53%.
Shareholders of record: 1,485.

Office—1251 Ave. of the Americas, New York, NY 10020. **Tel**—(212) 703-4000. **Chrmn**—R.B. Fisher. **Pres**—J.J. Mack. **Secy**—J. M. Clark. **CFO**—A.W. Zern. **Treas & Investor Contact**—Charles B. Hintz (212) 703-7178. **Dirs**—A.M. Beard Jr., L. W. Bernard, B.M. Biggs, D. Cheney, R.B. Fisher, S.P. Gilbert, J.J. Mack, R. W. Matschullat, A. E. Murray, P.F. Oreffice. **Transfer Agent & Registrar**—First Chicago Trust Co. of New York, NYC. **Incorporated** in Delaware in 1975. **Empl**—7,421.

 Paul L. Huberman, CFA

Morrison Restaurants

NASDAQ Symbol MORR (Incl. in Nat'l Market) Options on NYSE In S&P MidCap 400

Price	Range	P-E Ratio	Dividend	Yield	S&P Ranking	Beta
Oct. 11'93	1993					
36½	36½–23¾	24	0.50	1.4%	A–	0.97

Summary

Operations of this diversified foodservice company (formerly Morrison Inc.) include a rapidly expanding casual-theme restaurant business, a sizable contract feeding and management division, and a public cafeteria business. In fiscal 1993-94, further earnings growth is projected from each of MORR's business segments. A three-for-two stock split will be effected in October 1993, and the common shares are expected to start trading in October on the NYSE, under the symbol RI.

Current Outlook

Earnings for the fiscal year ending June 4, 1994, are estimated at $1.75 a share, up from fiscal 1992-93's $1.50 (both unadjusted).

Adjusted for the pending stock split, the dividend was raised 4.2%, to $0.08⅓, effective with the October 1993 payment.

The casual-theme restaurant segment is expected to be MORR's fastest growing business in 1993-94, with a profit increase of close to 20% expected to principally come from the Ruby Tuesday chain. An effort is being made to turn around recent weakness in the smaller L&N business. Also, early response to MORR's new Sweetpea's concept is encouraging. Year-ahead earnings from contract services (the hospitality segment) and family dining (largely public cafeterias) are also expected to increase at a double-digit pace.

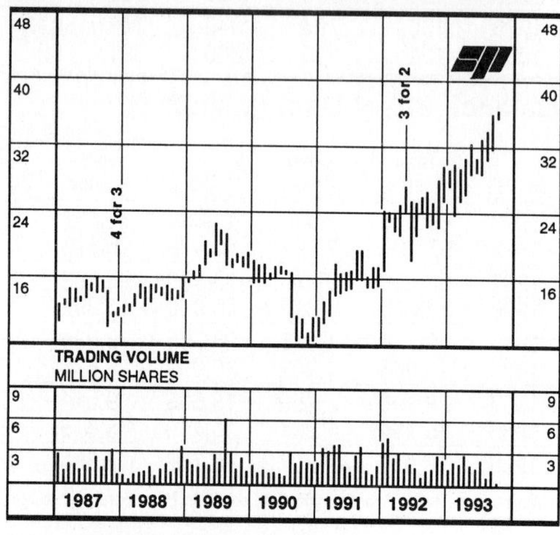

Revenues (Million $)

13 Weeks:	1993–94	1992–93	1991–92	1990–91
Aug.	282	248	242	227
Nov.	---	282	260	246
Feb.	---	284	261	247
May	---	286	[1]276	250
	---	1,100	1,039	971

Revenues for the three months ended September 4, 1993 increased 14%, year to year. Net income rose 16%, to $8.1 million ($0.33 a share), from $7.0 million ($0.28). The 1992-93 period excludes several special items whose net effect was immaterial to per share earnings.

Common Share Earnings ($)

13 Weeks:	1993–94	1992–93	1991–92	1990–91
Aug.	0.33	0.28	0.23	0.19
Nov.	E0.47	0.41	0.36	0.30
Feb.	E0.48	0.41	0.37	0.30
May	E0.47	0.40	[1]0.35	0.28
	E1.75	1.50	1.31	1.07

Important Developments

Sep. '93— In fiscal 1993-94's first quarter, sales and profit from MORR's casual-theme restaurants increased 24% and 20%, respectively. In fiscal 1993-94, about 50 such restaurants are expected to open, most of which would be Ruby Tuesdays. Three or four of the new units are likely to feature MORR's new Sweetpea's concept, which offers relatively high quality cafeteria-style, or "down home," food in a restaurant setting. Meanwhile, first quarter earnings from MORR's hospitality and family dining segments were up 20% and 31%, respectively. In fiscal 1993-94, MORR is expected to open at least 10 family dining units, most of which would be food-court outlets. Also, pending approvals, MORR's stock is expected to start trading on the NYSE, under the symbol RI, on October 21.

Next earnings report expected in late December.

Per Share Data ($)

Yr. End May 31	1993	1992	1991	1990	1989	[2]1988	[2]1987	1986	1985	1984
Tangible Bk. Val.	**[3]9.01**	[3]8.26	[3]7.37	[3]6.90	[3]6.65	[3]6.21	[3]5.76	4.75	4.58	4.20
Cash Flow	**2.94**	2.71	2.35	2.00	2.11	1.83	1.41	1.23	1.15	1.19
Earnings[4]	**1.50**	1.31	1.07	0.89	1.19	0.99	0.75	0.66	0.63	0.71
Dividends	**0.480**	0.440	0.427	0.420	0.387	0.267	0.240	0.229	0.219	0.189
Payout Ratio	**32%**	34%	40%	47%	32%	26%	32%	35%	35%	25%
Calendar Years	**1992**	1991	1990	1989	1988	1987	1986	1985	1984	1983
Prices—High	**29¾**	19½	18⅛	22⅝	15⅞	16¹⁄₁₆	13	10⅝	9⅛	10⅛
Low	**17**	9	8⅛	15⅜	11¾	10	9¼	7¾	6¼	7⅝
P/E Ratio—	**20–11**	15–7	17–8	26–17	13–10	16–10	17–12	16–12	15–10	14–11

Data as orig. reptd. Adj. for stk. divs. of 50% May 1992, 33 1/3% Dec. 1987, 5% Apr. 1986. **1.** 14 wks. **2.** Refl. merger or acq. **3.** Incl. intangibles. **4.** Bef. results of disc. ops. of +0.01 in 1988, +0.03 in 1988, -0.29 in 1986,-0.01 in 1985, -0.01 in 1984 and spec. item(s) of -0.01 in 1993. E-Estimated.

Income Data (Million $)

Year Ended May 31	Revs.	Oper. Inc.	% Oper. Inc. of Revs.	Cap. Exp.	Depr.	Int. Exp.	Net Bef. Taxes	Eff. Tax Rate	[4]Net Inc.	% Net Inc. of Revs.	Cash Flow
1993	**1,098**	**96.1**	**8.8**	**63.0**	**36.5**	**2.79**	**60.9**	**37.3%**	**[5]38.2**	**3.5**	**74.7**
1992	1,039	87.5	8.4	37.8	35.1	4.14	51.4	36.5%	32.7	3.1	67.7
1991	969	74.9	7.7	43.9	31.7	3.33	42.5	37.3%	26.6	2.7	58.3
1990	898	66.7	7.4	55.9	28.7	2.52	35.4	35.2%	23.0	2.6	51.7
[1]1989	825	70.3	8.5	41.8	23.9	2.34	50.4	37.3%	31.6	3.8	56.0
[1,2]1988	686	66.8	9.7	37.2	23.5	2.81	45.8	39.2%	27.8	4.1	51.3
[2]1987	599	56.1	9.4	43.5	18.9	2.33	41.2	47.8%	21.5	3.6	40.4
[1]1986	522	44.1	8.4	28.9	16.6	1.30	30.6	37.5%	19.1	3.7	35.7
[1]1985	479	46.8	9.8	28.4	15.3	2.12	29.1	38.4%	17.9	3.7	33.2
[1]1984	464	45.7	9.8	17.9	14.1	3.46	[3]34.8	40.8%	20.6	4.4	34.7

Balance Sheet Data (Million $)

May 31	Cash	Curr. Assets	Curr. Liab.	Curr. Ratio	Total Assets	% Ret. on Assets	Long Term Debt	Common Equity	Total Cap.	% LT Debt of Cap.	% Ret. on Equity
1993	**31.4**	**105**	**103.0**	**1.0**	**398**	**10.0**	**13.1**	**220**	**256**	**5.1**	**18.1**
1992	50.1	113	90.4	1.3	370	9.3	35.9	204	256	14.0	17.0
1991	22.5	89	76.8	1.2	331	8.2	38.0	181	241	15.8	14.9
1990	15.5	81	70.2	1.1	316	7.7	35.7	176	229	15.6	13.3
1989	17.9	79	70.7	1.1	284	11.1	16.6	174	206	8.1	18.8
1988	16.1	92	64.0	1.4	299	10.2	43.8	169	231	19.0	17.1
1987	10.4	75	57.7	1.3	262	9.1	21.2	166	201	10.6	13.6
1986	15.0	61	39.7	1.5	212	9.1	7.0	151	168	4.1	12.9
1985	15.1	56	36.2	1.5	208	8.8	11.9	146	169	7.0	13.0
1984	10.3	50	38.0	1.3	195	10.7	16.6	127	155	10.7	17.2

Data as orig. reptd. **1.** Excl. disc. ops. **2.** Refl. merger or acq. **3.** Incl. equity in earns. of nonconsol. subs. **4.** Bef. spec. item(s). **5.** Reflects acctg. change.

Business Summary

Morrison Restaurants Inc. (formerly Morrison Inc.) is a diversified foodservice company with operations in more than 35 states. The company was founded in 1920 and had its first and only public stock offering in 1928. MORR currently operates one of the largest public cafeteria chains in the U.S., has more than 250 casual-theme restaurants, and manages foodservice facilities.

Segment contributions in 1992-93 were:

	Revs.	Profits
Casual–theme restaurants ...	34.4%	48.4%
Contract feeding & management.................	39.1%	30.0%
Family dining	26.5%	21.6%

As of June 6, 1993, the company's 247 casual-theme restaurants included 185 Ruby Tuesdays, whose menus include salads, soups, burgers, chicken and ethnic specialties; 42 L&N Seafood Grills, which feature mesquite-grilled, sauteed and fried seafood, regional specials and pasta; and 20 Silver Spoon Cafes, which are casual restaurants aimed at an "upscale" market. Also, the company is developing a new restaurant concept called Sweetpea's, whose first unit opened in early June 1993. Sweetpea's is expected to offer relatively high-quality home-style food. In fiscal 1992-93, MORR opened 38 casual-theme restaurants, and about 50 are expected to debut in fiscal 1993-94.

MORR is also a leading provider of contract food services. Its customer base includes hospitals, schools, office buildings, manufacturing plants, nursing homes, and retirement facilities. As of June 6, 1993, the business held 875 food-service and other management contracts, a net gain of 62 from a year earlier. MORR's family dining business consisted of 151 public cafeterias, seven buffets, and four food-court restaurants. During the past several years, a number of weaker units have been closed, which has helped to improve overall profitability.

Dividend Data

Cash has been paid in each year since 1936.

Amt of Divd. $	Date Decl.	Ex–divd. Date	Stock of Record	Payment Date
0.12	Dec. 22	Jan. 4	Jan. 8	Jan. 29'93
0.12	Mar. 31	Apr. 5	Apr. 9	Apr. 30'93
0.12	Jul. 1	Jul. 6	Jul. 9	Jul. 30'93
3–for–2	Sep. 30	Nov. 1	Oct. 8	Oct. 29'93
0.08333	Sep. 30	Oct. 4	Oct. 8	Oct. 29'93

Capitalization

Long Term Debt: $13,044,000 (9/4/93).

Common Stock: 24,040,332 shs. ($0.01 par).
A.R. Outlaw controls 12%.
Institutions hold about 46%.
Shareholders: 6,550 of record (7/93).

Office—4721 Morrison Dr., Mobile, AL 36609. **Tel**—(205) 344-3000. **Chrmn**—E. E. Bishop. **Pres & CEO**—S. E. Beall III. **Vice Chrmn**—A. R. Outlaw. **SVP & Secy**—P. G. Hunt. **VP & Treas**—J. R. Mothershed. **VP & Investor Contact**—Wyatt Engwall. **Dirs**—S. E. Beall III, E. E. Bishop, W. R. Bunn, J. B. McKinnon, A. R. Outlaw, B. F. Payton, D. Ratajczak, R. J. Theis, Sr., D. W. von Arx. **Transfer Agent & Registrar**—AmSouth Bank, N.A., Birmingham, AL. **Incorporated** in Florida in 1954; reincorporated in Delaware in 1987. **Empl**—37,000.

 Tom Graves, CFA

Multimedia, Inc.

NASDAQ Symbol MMEDC (Incl. in Nat'l Market) Options on Phila In S&P MidCap 400

Price	Range	P-E Ratio	Dividend	Yield	S&P Ranking	Beta
Aug. 16'93	1993					
32⅛	38¾–31½	18	None	None	NR	1.01

Summary

This diversified communications company owns five TV and eight radio stations, owns a video production company, publishes 11 daily and 49 nondaily newspapers, operates cable systems serving some 413,000 subscribers, and produces and syndicates TV programming, including the Donahue, Sally Jessy Raphael, Jerry Springer and Rush Limbaugh shows. Long-term earnings prospects are favorable.

Current Outlook

Earnings for 1993 are projected at $1.95 a share, up from $1.61 in 1992. About $2.25 is expected for 1994.

Directors suspended cash dividend payments following a 1985 recapitalization.

Revenues are expected to advance about 14% in 1993, reflecting strong contributions from entertainment, cable and security systems. Slight gains from newspapers and a slight drop in broadcasting revenues are anticipated. Aided by revenue gains and operating efficiencies, profitability should improve. Interest costs should continue to decrease. Revenues could rise 15% in 1994, assuming slowing in cable and entertainment, but an upturn in newspaper and broadcast advertising.

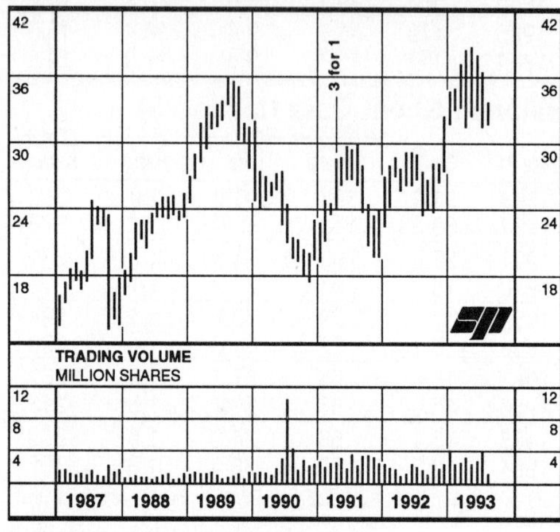

Operating Revenues (Million $)

Quarter:	1993	1992	1991	1990
Mar.	144.1	126.0	119.2	109.8
Jun.	163.5	142.8	134.6	123.9
Sep.	---	140.5	127.4	119.8
Dec.	---	167.4	143.2	127.2
	---	576.8	524.3	480.7

Revenues in the 1993 six months ended June 30, 1993, advanced 14%, year to year, largely boosted by entertainment and cable. Operating profits rose 5.7%. Results benefited from a 16% drop in interest costs. After taxes at 41.0% in each period, and lower minority interest, net income climbed 28%, to $0.88 a share (before a special credit of $0.37), from $0.70.

Common Share Earnings ($)

Quarter:	1993	1992	1991	1990
Mar.	0.40	0.28	0.24	0.16
Jun.	0.48	0.42	0.39	0.34
Sep.	E0.46	0.40	0.28	0.35
Dec.	E0.61	0.51	0.39	0.46
	E1.95	1.61	1.30	1.32

Important Developments

Jul. '93— Multimedia said entertainment revenues in the first half of 1993 climbed 40%, year to year, on gains for the Donahue and Sally Jessy Raphael talk shows; revenues from the Jerry Springer and Rush Limbaugh shows, which premiered nationally in the fall of 1992; and the sale of three TV movies. The company has production orders for 16 hours of made-for-television movies from the networks for 1993, versus 6 hours in 1992. Earlier, Multimedia set up three 50/50 joint ventures, with Tele Munchen in Germany, Tesauro in Spain and Tele Images in France, to develop talk shows in each country based on formats from some of the company's most successful U.S. tabloid interview shows.

Dec. '92— The company purchased cable systems (serving some 28,000 subscribers) adjacent to existing Multimedia systems in Illinois.

Next earnings report expected in mid-October.

Per Share Data ($)

Yr. End Dec. 31	1992	1991	1990	1989	1988	1987	1986	[1]1985	1984	1983
Tangible Bk. Val.	**d15.21**	d17.25	d19.05	d17.79	d19.75	d20.99	d21.47	d21.22	2.37	2.28
Cash Flow	**2.75**	2.33	2.14	1.83	1.52	1.10	0.63	0.99	1.10	1.09
Earnings[2]	**1.61**	1.30	1.32	1.04	0.73	0.34	d0.14	0.47	0.67	0.72
Dividends	**Nil**	Nil	Nil	Nil	Nil	Nil	Nil	0.165	0.200	0.173
Payout Ratio	**Nil**	Nil	Nil	Nil	Nil	Nil	Nil	35%	30%	25%
Prices—High	**32½**	30	32	36	25½	24⅞	15¾	21½	14⅛	14⅝
Low	**22½**	19⅜	17½	24⅝	16⅜	13⅛	9	6¼	9⅞	10⅜
P/E Ratio—	**20–14**	23–15	24–13	35–24	35–22	72–38	NM	46–13	21–15	20–14

Data as orig. reptd. Adj. for stk. div. of 200% April 1991. **1.** Refl. recapitalization. **2.** Bef. spec. item(s) of -0.08 in 1990. E-Estimated. d-Deficit. NM-Not Meaningful.

Income Data (Million $)

Year Ended Dec. 31	Revs.	Oper. Inc.	% Oper. Inc. of Revs.	Cap. Exp.	Depr.	Int. Exp.	Net Bef. Taxes	Eff. Tax Rate	[3]Net Inc.	% Net Inc. of Revs.	Cash Flow
1992	**577**	**216**	**37.5**	**37.5**	**43.0**	**72**	**101.0**	**41.0%**	**60.5**	**10.5**	**103.0**
1991	524	194	37.0	32.2	38.4	79	77.1	39.2%	48.4	9.2	86.8
1990	481	201	41.8	28.5	30.7	88	81.1	40.0%	48.7	10.1	79.3
1989	463	193	41.7	25.5	29.5	102	61.5	37.1%	38.7	8.4	68.2
1988	440	176	40.0	23.4	28.6	108	42.5	36.8%	26.9	6.1	55.4
1987	411	159	38.8	17.4	27.7	111	27.1	54.0%	12.5	3.0	40.2
1986	372	140	37.6	26.6	25.5	112	2.4	NM	[4]d4.7	NM	20.8
[1]1985	336	115	34.2	26.0	24.3	36	47.9	54.8%	21.6	6.4	45.9
1984	304	102	33.6	32.9	21.5	9	64.2	47.5%	33.7	11.1	55.2
1983	270	88	32.8	58.1	18.4	9	[2]65.3	46.1%	35.2	13.0	53.6

Balance Sheet Data (Million $)

Dec. 31	Cash	Curr. Assets	Curr. Liab.	Curr. Ratio	Total Assets	% Ret. on Assets	Long Term Debt	Common Equity	Total Cap.	% LT Debt of Cap.	% Ret. on Equity
1992	**4.6**	**115**	**91**	**1.3**	**628**	**10.0**	**744**	**d291**	**536**	**138.8**	**NM**
1991	6.7	112	101	1.1	556	8.8	743	d375	451	164.9	NM
1990	5.1	105	89	1.2	536	10.3	789	d433	442	178.6	NM
1989	3.4	94	76	1.2	404	9.5	746	d487	325	229.5	NM
1988	3.1	89	78	1.1	405	6.6	792	d537	324	244.8	NM
1987	2.6	82	70	1.2	409	3.1	839	d567	337	249.2	NM
1986	2.6	74	61	1.2	409	NM	877	d580	347	252.9	NM
[1]1985	4.7	69	53	1.3	399	5.4	878	d576	344	255.5	NM
1984	15.2	77	48	1.6	403	8.5	73	249	351	20.9	14.2
1983	50.5	104	54	1.9	387	10.1	80	224	328	24.3	17.8

Data as orig. reptd. **1.** Refl. recapitalization. **2.** Incl. equity in earns. of nonconsol. subs. **3.** Bef. spec. items. **4.** Refl. acctg. change. d-Deficit. NM-Not Meaningful.

Business Summary

Multimedia owns and operates five TV and eight radio stations, cable TV systems and newspapers and produces and syndicates various TV programs.

Contributions by business segment in 1992 were:

	Revs.	Profit
Broadcasting	28%	21%
Newspapers	23%	20%
Cablevision	27%	29%
Entertainment	22%	30%

Broadcast properties include five network-affiliated VHF TV stations, in Cincinnati, Ohio, St. Louis, Mo., Knoxville, Tenn., Cleveland, Ohio (51% owned), and Macon, Ga. Radio stations are in Greenville and Spartanburg, S.C., Macon, Ga., Shreveport, La., and Milwaukee, Wis.

A subsidiary produces and syndicates TV programs, including the Phil Donahue, Sally Jessy Raphael, Jerry Springer and Rush Limbaugh shows, as well as made-for-television movies and other special TV programming.

The cable television division had about 413,000 subscribers at the end of March 1993, in Kansas, Oklahoma, Indiana, Illinois and North Carolina.

Multimedia publishes the only daily and Sunday newspapers in 12 markets, and also publishes 49 nondaily publications.

Dividend Data

Cash dividends were suspended in the fourth quarter of 1985. A shareholder rights plan was adopted in 1989. The shares were split three for one in April 1991.

Finances

Multimedia anticipates 1993 capital spending (which is limited by debt covenants) of $52 million, up from $37.5 million in 1992. Cash interest expense requirements for 1993 are estimated at $66 million, down from $71.8 million in 1992. At year-end 1992, the company was commited to purchase security systems for an aggregate amount of $28 million.

In October 1985, the company completed a merger with an insider group, and a recapitalization of Multimedia was effected. The transaction included the issuance of 11 million common shares (not adjusted), plus cash and debentures valued at a total of $826 million.

Capitalization

Long Term Debt: $683,447,000 (3/93).

Minority Interest: $17,243,000.

Common Stock: 36,885,319 shs. ($0.10 par).
Institutions hold 79%.
Shareholders of record: 1,283 (3/93).

Office—305 South Main St., P.O. Box 1688, Greenville, SC 29602. **Tel**—(803) 298-4373. **Chrmn**—W. E. Bartlett. **Pres & CEO**—J. W. Grimes. **Treas & CFO**—R. E. Hamby, Jr. **Secy**—D. L. Freeman. **VP & Investor Contact**—Elizabeth S. Mills. **Dirs**—W. E. Bartlett, G. H. V. Cecil, R. T. Eskew, D. L. Freeman, J. W. Grimes, R. E. Hamby, Jr., J. T. LaMacchia, L. G. McCraw, D. P. Ramsaur, D. S. Sbarra, E. P. Stall, W. C. Stutt. **Transfer Agent & Registrar**—Wachovia Bank of North Carolina, Winston-Salem. **Incorporated** in South Carolina in 1968. **Empl**—3,800.

Murphy Oil

NYSE Symbol MUR Options on Pacific (Feb-May-Aug-Nov) In S&P MidCap 400

Price	Range	P–E Ratio	Dividend	Yield	S&P Ranking	Beta
Oct. 4'93	1993					
47¼	47⅞–33	26	1.30	2.8%	B–	0.24

Summary

Murphy Oil is an integrated petroleum company. MUR explores for and produces crude oil and natural gas domestically, mostly in the Gulf of Mexico, and internationally in the North Sea and Canada. The company refines and markets petroleum products in the U.S. and the U.K. MUR is emerging from an extensive restructuring program which included the divestiture of its contract drilling unit. Proceeds were used to reduce debt substantially and to fund exploration and production where the company has an established asset base. The dividend was raised 8.3% to $0.32½ quarterly with the September 1993 payment.

Current Outlook

Share earnings for 1994 are projected at $2.10, up slightly from the $2.05 estimated for 1993.

Dividends were increased 8.3%, to $0.32½ quarterly from $0.30, with the September 1993 payment.

Revenues for 1993 and 1994 should improve, owing to increased commodity and refined product volumes. Profitability will increase on greater volumes and net interest income. Longer term, MUR is well positioned to capitalize upon tightening U.S. natural gas and refined product markets.

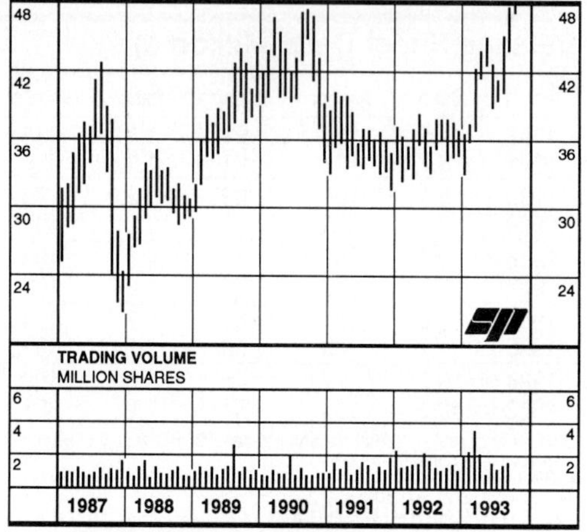

Oper. Revenues (Million $)

Quarter:	1993	1992	1991	1990
Mar.	399	359	414	449
Jun.	430	410	423	397
Sep.	---	415	376	514
Dec.	---	447	387	653
	---	1,631	1,601	2,013

Revenues for the six months ended June 30, 1993, rose 2.9%, year to year, reflecting higher U.S. natural gas prices and increased oil and natural gas output. Margins benefited from improved natural gas markets, and following a lower tax rate, net income advanced 76%. Share earnings for the 1993 period were $1.04, excluding a special credit of $0.34. Share earnings for the 1992 period were $0.59, excluding income from discontinued operations of $0.45 and a special credit of $0.23.

Common Share Earnings ($)

Quarter:	1993	1992	[1]1991	1990
Mar.	0.53	d0.02	0.87	0.53
Jun.	0.51	0.61	d3.07	0.84
Sep.	E0.50	0.33	0.87	1.11
Dec.	E0.51	0.48	0.58	0.52
	E2.05	1.40	d0.24	3.00

Important Developments

Jul. '93— In 1993's second quarter, operating profits were sharply higher, owing to gains in all business segments. U.S. exploration and production profits were boosted by higher natural gas prices and volumes. Crude oil prices and output were lower. Overseas, the company returned to profitability as a result of greater Canadian oil and natural gas volumes, and higher Canadian natural gas prices. In U.S. refining and marketing, profits widened, as refined product sales increased. In foreign refining and marketing, profits were up, reflecting greater Canadian trading activities. Farm, timber, and real estate profits showed improvement. Lumber prices were up sharply while lumber sales increased. Also, there was a sharp increase in the sale of residential lots. Net interest expense declined.

Next earnings report expected in late October.

Per Share Data ($)

Yr. End Dec. 31	1992	1991	1990	1989	1988	1987	1986	1985	1984	1983
Tangible Bk. Val.	**26.76**	26.71	25.76	22.71	22.48	22.15	23.12	29.39	27.61	26.97
Cash Flow	**5.44**	4.63	9.44	7.83	7.76	5.09	2.36	9.45	9.90	10.97
Earnings[2]	**1.40**	d0.24	3.00	1.37	1.14	d1.29	d5.76	2.25	3.21	3.60
Dividends	**1.20**	1.20	1.00	1.00	1.00	1.00	1.00	1.00	1.00	1.00
Payout Ratio	**86%**	NM	33%	73%	87%	NM	NM	43%	31%	28%
Prices—High	**38⅜**	40¼	47½	44¼	35⅛	42¾	31⅞	33¼	38½	38⅞
Low	**32⅜**	31⅝	34	29⅝	23⅛	20¾	20⅜	23½	24½	20¼
P/E Ratio—	**27–23**	NM	16–11	32–22	31–20	NM	NM	15–10	12–8	11–6

Data as orig. reptd. **1.** Quarterly earns. do not reconcile because of change in no. of shs. outstanding. **2.** Bef. results of disc. opers. of +0.53 in 1992, -0.04 in 1991, -0.58 in 1984, and spec. item(s) of +0.42 in 1992, +0.36 in 1990. d-Deficit. E-Estimated. NM-Not Meaningful.

Income Data (Million $)

Year Ended Dec. 31	Revs.	Oper. Inc.	% Oper. Inc. of Revs.	Cap. Exp.	Depr.	Int. Exp.	[2]Net Bef. Taxes	Eff. Tax Rate	[3]Net Inc.	% Net Inc. of Revs.	Cash Flow
[1]1992	**1,631**	**212**	**13.0**	**191**	**182**	**17.1**	**69**	**9.5%**	**63**	**3.8**	**245**
[1]1991	1,601	247	15.4	185	192	31.0	30	123.8%	d10	NM	183
1990	2,013	355	17.6	187	219	36.6	230	48.8%	102	5.1	320
1989	1,653	355	21.5	165	219	45.4	125	64.8%	47	2.8	266
1988	1,474	304	20.6	260	224	36.9	96	72.1%	39	2.6	263
1987	1,474	279	18.9	130	215	27.4	d19	NM	d44	NM	172
1986	1,313	108	8.2	129	275	30.7	d350	NM	[4]d195	NM	80
1985	2,198	571	26.0	257	255	32.5	314	69.1%	80	3.6	335
[1]1984	2,169	600	27.7	317	245	35.1	419	59.5%	[4]118	5.4	363
1983	2,388	771	32.3	347	271	33.1	532	65.0%	132	5.5	402

Balance Sheet Data (Million $)

Dec. 31	Cash	Curr. Assets	Curr. Liab.	Curr. Ratio	Total Assets	% Ret. on Assets	Long Term Debt	Common Equity	Total Cap.	% LT Debt of Cap.	% Ret. on Equity
1992	**378**	**799**	**427**	**1.9**	**1,937**	**3.1**	**25**	**1,200**	**1,269**	**2.0**	**5.2**
1991	242	671	515	1.3	2,175	NM	193	1,201	1,452	13.3	NM
1990	275	724	627	1.2	2,137	4.8	208	873	1,329	15.6	12.4
1989	243	618	482	1.3	2,075	2.2	330	770	1,362	24.3	6.1
1988	235	542	419	1.3	2,068	1.9	382	761	1,423	26.9	5.1
1987	195	510	399	1.3	2,067	NM	340	750	1,387	24.5	NM
1986	163	458	333	1.4	1,980	NM	237	777	1,377	17.2	NM
1985	144	619	529	1.2	2,661	3.1	254	1,014	1,847	13.7	8.1
1984	299	702	579	1.2	2,685	4.3	261	1,006	1,823	14.3	11.8
1983	304	741	626	1.2	2,808	4.6	271	986	1,799	15.1	14.0

Data as orig. reptd. **1.** Excl. disc. opers. **2.** Incl. equity in earns. of nonconsol. subs. **3.** Bef. spec. items. **4.** Reflects accounting change. d-Deficit. NM-Not Meaningful.

Business Summary

Murphy Oil is an integrated crude oil and natural gas company operating in the U.S. and overseas, and has interests in farming, timber, land management and real estate. During the past several years, MUR has been restructuring its businesses. As part of the restructuring, the company sold its contract drilling unit in 1992 and a diving business (for undersea oil and gas activities) in 1990. Profits and losses (million $) in recent years:

	1992	1991
U.S. exploration/production ..	$42.0	$16.0
Foreign exploration/ production	1.2	–21.0
U.S. refining/marketing........	–12.0	20.9
Foreign refining/marketing ...	11.3	22.4
Farm & timber..................	8.4	4.8
Corporate.........................	30.8	52.7

Exploration and production are conducted domestically, onshore and offshore, and overseas, most notably in the U.K. sector of the North Sea and in Canada. Deltic Farm & Timber Co. is engaged in farming, timber, and land management.

In 1992, crude oil and liquids production averaged 30,820 bbl. a day (33,495 b/d in 1991), of which 43% was in the U.S.; natural gas sales were 250,600 Mcf a day (208,397), of which 75% was in the U.S.; oil processed 144,151 b/d (139,254), and petroleum product sales 146,042 b/d (137,506).

Proved reserves at 1992 year-end were estimated at 96.0 million bbl. of crude oil, and 685.3 million Mcf of natural gas. MUR has a 3.94% interest in the Kuvlum discovery in the eastern Beaufort Sea, offshore Alaska, one of the most promising fields since the Prudhoe Bay discovery.

In March 1993, MUR's Canadian affiliate acquired a 6.5% interest in the Hibernia Oil Development Project offshore Newfoundland, while in April the UK subsidiary acquired an 8.52% interest in the UK North Sea "T" Block.

Dividend Data

Dividends have been paid since 1961. A "poison pill" stock purchase right was issued in 1989.

Amt of Divd. $	Date Decl.	Ex-divd. Date	Stock of Record	Payment Date
0.30	Oct. 7	Nov. 9	Nov. 16	Dec. 1'92
0.30	Feb. 3	Feb. 9	Feb. 16	Mar. 1'93
0.30	Apr. 7	May 11	May 17	Jun. 1'93
0.32½	Aug. 4	Aug. 10	Aug. 16	Sep. 1'93

Capitalization

Long Term Debt: $33,392,000, incl. $8,500,000 nonrecourse debt of a subsidiary. (6/93).

Common Stock: 44,806,396 shs. ($1 par).
Institutions hold about 60%, incl. some 26% owned by the Murphy family.
Shareholders of record: 6,522.

Office—200 Peach St., El Dorado, AR 71730-5836. **Tel**—(501) 862-6411. **Chrmn**—C. H. Murphy Jr. **Pres & CEO**—J. W. McNutt. **EVP & COO**—C. P. Deming. **Secy**—W. B. Rowe. **EVP & CFO**—R. M. Murphy. **Contr & Investor Contact**—Ronald W. Herman. **Dirs**—B. R. R. Butler, C. P. Deming, J. W. Deming, H. R. Hart, V. T. Hughes Jr., J. W. McNutt, C. H. Murphy Jr., M. W. Murphy, R. M. Murphy, W. C. Nolan Jr., C. G. Theus, L. C. Webster. **Transfer Agent & Registrar**—Harris Trust Co. of New York, NYC. **Incorporated** in Delaware in 1963. **Empl**—1,787.

 Edward G. Graves

Mylan Laboratories

NYSE Symbol MYL Options on ASE (Jan-Apr-Jul-Oct) In S&P MidCap 400

Price	Range	P-E Ratio	Dividend	Yield	S&P Ranking	Beta
Aug. 19'93	1993					
23⅞	37⅝–19⅝	24	0.16	0.7%	A–	0.76

Summary

This leading manufacturer of generic drugs produces a wide variety of pharmaceuticals for resale by others under their own labels. Over 60 generic drugs in varying strengths are produced, with more than 35 new submissions currently pending before the FDA. Rising contributions from new generic and brand name products enhance longer-range prospects.

Current Outlook

Earnings for the fiscal year ending March 31, 1994, are projected at about $1.15 a share, up from 1992-93's $0.92.

Dividends have been raised to $0.04 quarterly, from $0.03, effective with the October 1993 payment.

Sales for 1993-94 should post further growth, aided by contributions from new products and the full year inclusion of Bertek. Cost-efficient generics should also get a boost from President Clinton's health care reform program. Profitability should benefit from increased volume, operating synergies from Hickam (a drug firm acquired in late 1991) and higher equity earnings from Somerset. Increasing focus on the development of brand-name ethical drugs such as Dotarizine enhances longer-range prospects.

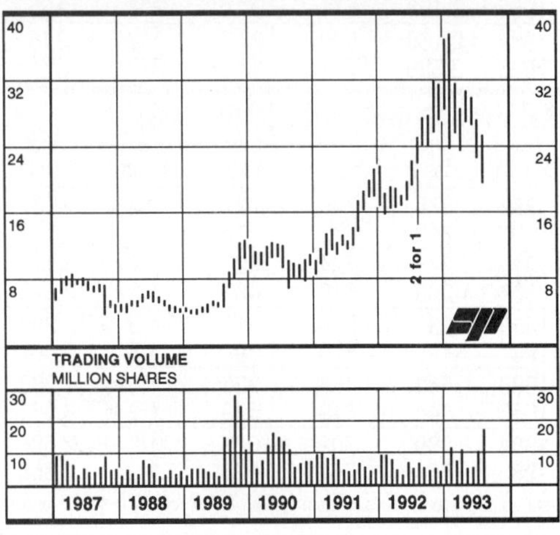

Net Sales (Million $)

Quarter:	1993-94	1992-93	1991-92	1990-91
Jun.	58.5	38.8	27.9	23.3
Sep.	---	51.0	30.4	20.9
Dec.	---	61.1	34.9	22.9
Mar.	---	61.0	38.8	24.0
	---	212.0	131.9	91.1

Sales in the three months ended June 30, 1993, advanced 51%, year to year, aided by new generic drugs. Income before taxes climbed 49%. After taxes at 23.7%, against 20.1%, net income was up 42%. Share profits were $0.21, versus $0.14.

Common Share Earnings ($)

Quarter:	1993-94	1992-93	1991-92	1990-91
Jun.	0.21	0.15	0.12	0.11
Sep.	E0.24	0.22	0.11	0.11
Dec.	E0.34	0.28	0.14	0.12
Mar.	E0.36	0.28	0.16	0.13
	E1.15	0.92	0.53	0.45

Important Developments

Jul. '93— The company received FDA approval to market nortriptyline, the generic equivalent of Sandoz Pharmaceuticals' Pamelor antidepression drug. In June, MYL obtained FDA approval to market the generic equivalents of Merck's Clinoril and McNeil's Tolectin nonsteroidal, anti-inflammatory drugs. The company has some 15 more chemical entities representing over 35 drugs of varying strengths pending before the FDA.

Apr. '93— Mylan arranged an exclusive license agreement with Ferrer Internacional, a Spanish firm, for all rights to its Dotarizine drug for the treatment of migraine and vertigo.

Feb. '93— MYL acquired Bertek, a maker of transdermal drug delivery systems, for 615,880 MYL common shares and the assumption of $8.3 million of debt.

Next earnings report expected in late October.

Per Share Data ($)

Yr. End Mar. 31	[1]1993	1992	1991	1990	1989	1988	1987	1986	1985	1984
Tangible Bk. Val.	**3.30**	2.51	2.12	1.76	1.44	1.24	0.94	0.66	0.41	0.26
Cash Flow	**0.98**	0.59	0.49	0.40	0.29	0.38	0.34	0.30	0.19	0.08
Earnings	**0.92**	0.53	0.45	0.36	0.25	0.35	0.33	0.29	0.18	0.07
Dividends	**0.115**	0.100	0.100	0.050	0.050	0.050	0.042	0.033	0.023	0.006
Payout Ratio	**13%**	19%	22%	14%	20%	14%	13%	12%	13%	6%
Calendar Years	**1992**	1991	1990	1989	1988	1987	1986	1985	1984	1983
Prices—High	**31⅞**	21¼	12⅜	12⅝	6⅝	8 11/16	9 1/16	8¾	6¼	1 13/16
Low	**15¾**	8½	6⅞	3¾	4	3 13/16	5	4	1⅜	11/16
P/E Ratio—	**34–17**	41–16	28–15	35–10	27–16	25–11	28–15	31–14	36–8	27–10

Data as orig. reptd. Adj. for stk. divs. of 100% Jul. 1992, 50% Aug. 1986, 100% Feb. 1985, 50% Aug. 1984, 50% Mar. 1984. **1.** Reflects merger or acq. E-Estimated.

Income Data (Million $)

Year Ended Mar. 31	Revs.	Oper. Inc.	% Oper. Inc. of Revs.	Cap. Exp.	Depr.	Int. Exp.	Net Bef. Taxes	Eff. Tax Rate	Net Inc.	% Net Inc. of Revs.	Cash Flow
[1]1993	**212**	**77.5**	**36.6**	**12.3**	**5.09**	**0.06**	**[2]97.3**	**27.4%**	**70.6**	**33.3**	**75.7**
1992	132	32.1	24.3	10.0	5.06	0.35	[2]50.1	20.0%	40.1	30.4	45.2
[1]1991	91	21.6	23.7	8.4	3.04	0.01	[2]39.0	16.0%	32.7	35.9	35.6
1990	95	22.7	23.8	7.2	2.45	0.01	[2]32.2	18.5%	26.2	27.5	28.7
1989	88	23.4	26.6	7.1	2.20	0.25	[2]23.4	22.0%	18.3	20.8	20.5
1988	96	38.8	40.4	15.3	1.88	0.38	[2]37.4	32.6%	25.2	26.3	27.1
1987	95	43.3	45.5	9.3	1.33	0.14	[2]41.8	44.2%	23.3	24.5	24.6
1986	81	37.2	46.1	5.4	1.02	0.24	38.2	45.8%	20.7	25.6	21.7
1985	54	23.1	43.2	2.4	0.77	0.27	23.0	45.8%	12.5	23.3	13.3
1984	37	9.0	24.4	2.5	0.77	0.22	8.0	41.5%	4.7	12.7	5.5

Balance Sheet Data (Million $)

Mar. 31	Cash	Curr. Assets	Curr. Liab.	Curr. Ratio	Total Assets	% Ret. on Assets	Long Term Debt	Common Equity	Total Cap.	% LT Debt of Cap.	% Ret. on Equity
1993	**98.2**	**180**	**26.5**	**6.8**	**351**	**24.3**	**Nil**	**296**	**298**	**Nil**	**28.1**
1992	60.3	120	17.9	6.7	227	19.7	Nil	203	205	Nil	21.9
1991	37.5	83	11.9	7.0	170	21.3	Nil	153	156	Nil	23.3
1990	21.9	63	7.2	8.7	138	20.9	0.17	127	129	0.1	22.6
1989	29.9	68	6.6	10.3	113	16.5	0.53	104	106	0.2	18.8
1988	38.1	76	11.5	6.6	109	26.7	6.33	90	97	6.5	32.0
1987	26.2	58	6.5	8.8	80	34.2	4.63	68	74	6.3	40.3
1986	15.0	45	5.6	8.0	56	44.7	1.93	48	50	3.8	54.0
1985	5.9	28	4.7	5.9	37	41.0	2.25	29	32	7.0	52.7
1984	2.7	16	3.0	5.4	24	21.2	2.53	18	21	12.0	29.8

Data as orig. reptd. **1.** Reflects merger or acquisition. **2.** Incl. equity in earns. of nonconsol. subs.

Business Summary

Mylan Laboratories Inc. manufactures generic pharmaceutical products in finished tablet, capsule and powder dosage forms for resale by others under their own labels. Some 63 generic drugs in varying strengths are produced.

The company's generic drugs encompass some 21 different therapeutic classes, including analgesics, antianginals, antianxiety agents, antibiotics, antidepressants, antidiabetics, antidiarrheals, an antigout drug, an antihistamine, antihypertensives, anti-inflammatories, antipsychotics, anxiolytics, a bronchial dilator, diuretics, hypnotic agents, a muscle relaxant and a uricosuric. Eldepryl, a treatment for Parkinson's disease, is marketed by Somerset Pharmaceuticals (jointly owned by Mylan and Bolar Laboratories) and by Sandoz Pharmaceuticals. Somerset had sales of $104 million in calendar 1992, up from $85 million in 1991. Eldepryl contributed equity earnings to Mylan equal to $0.24 a share in 1992-93 and $0.22 in 1991-92.

With the exception of Eldepryl and Maxzide, an antihypertensive, all of MYL's products have been previously developed and sold by other concerns. Mylan owns the patent for Maxzide, which is marketed under an exclusive license by the Lederle division of American Cyanamid.

Sales to McKesson and Lederle Laboratories represented 12% and 6%, respectively, of total sales, in 1992-93. Research and development expenses totaled $13.5 million in 1992-93 (equal to 6.4% of sales) and $7.9 million in 1991-92 (6.0%).

Dividend Data

Dividends have been paid each year since 1983.

Amt. of Divd. $	Date Decl.	Ex-divd. Date	Stock of Record	Payment Date
0.03	Dec. 15	Dec. 24	Dec. 31	Jan. 15'93
0.03	Mar. 16	Mar. 25	Mar. 31	Apr. 15'93
0.03	Jun. 14	Jun. 24	Jun. 30	Jul. 15'93
0.04	Jun. 25	Sep. 24	Sep. 30	Oct. 15'93

Capitalization

Long Term Obligations: $5,555,000 (6/93).

Common Stock: 78,977,459 shs. ($0.50 par).
Officers and directors own about 6%.
Institutions hold about 51%.
Shareholders: 59,100.

Office—1030 Century Building, Pittsburgh, PA 15222. **Tel**—(412) 232-0100. **Chrmn & CEO**—R. McKnight. **Pres & Vice Chrmn**—M. Puskar. **Secy**—R. W. Smiley. **Investor Contact**—Patricia Sunseri. **Dirs**—D. G. Barnett, L. S. DeLynn, J. C. Gaisford, R. A. Graciano, R. McKnight, M. Puskar, R. W. Smiley. **Transfer Agent & Registrar**—American Stock Transfer Co., NYC. **Incorporated** in Pennsylvania in 1970. **Empl**—1,037.

 H. Saftlas

NCH Corp.

NYSE Symbol NCH In S&P MidCap 400

Price	Range	P-E Ratio	Dividend	Yield	S&P Ranking	Beta
Oct. 8'93	1993					
57¼	73–55½	14	[1]1.00	1.7%	A–	1.15

Summary

This company is a worldwide distributor of maintenance products, including specialty chemicals, replacement fasteners, welding supplies, and replacement electrical and plumbing parts. Earnings in recent periods have been hurt by lower income from international operations. The Levy family owns more than half the shares.

Business Summary

NCH (formerly National Chemsearch) markets in the U.S. and abroad a wide range of maintenance products, many of which are manufactured by the company. The product line includes specialty chemicals, fasteners, welding supplies, electrical and plumbing parts, and safety supplies. Customers include industry, institutions, and government. Contributions by market sector in 1992-93:

	Sales	Net Inc.
United States	49%	51%
Europe	39%	39%
Other foreign	11%	4%

The original division of NCH, the maintenance chemical group, offers water treatments, fuel supplements, cleaners and degreasers, disinfectants and deodorizers, floor and carpet cleaners, cutting fluids, insecticides, specialty coatings, ground care products, lubricants, skin care products, and adhesives. X-Chem develops and markets oil field production chemicals such as emulsion breakers, water treatments, corrosion controllers, paraffin combatants, cleaners, and production-related products.

The plumbing group offers more than 80,000 parts for plumbing and hardware maintenance. Resource Electronics supplies custom-built cable assemblies, data communication wire, cable and connectors, and devices for computer telecommunications hookups and networks. Safety and identification products include goggles, face shields, first aid kits, first aid supplies, and other equipment.

The Partsmaster companies sell repair and maintenance items including fasteners, welding supplies and electrical products. Industrial and institutional supplies are marketed by Cornerstone Direct, primarily through mail and telemarketing. These products include first-aid kits and supplies, signs and identification items and material handling equipment.

The retail products group sells pet stain removal and deodorizing products through stores, veterinarians and carpet cleaning companies. A line of products for toddler stains and odor control was recently added. Pure Solve creates personalized maintenance programs for automotive and industrial customers who use parts washers, helping customers comply with EPA regulations related to spent solvents.

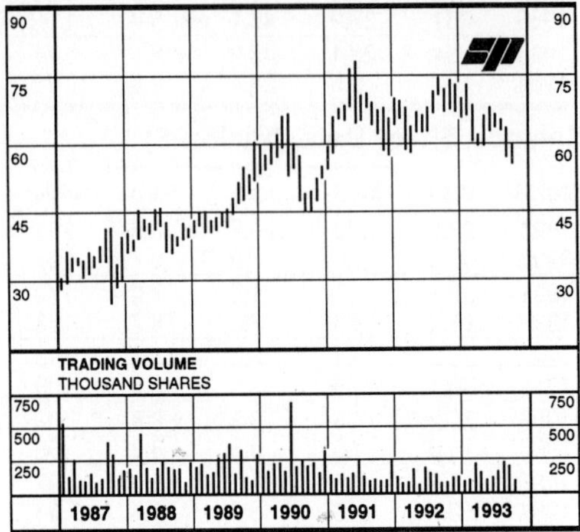

Foreign sales are conducted through subsidiaries in Europe, Canada, Latin America, Australia and the Far East.

Important Developments

Sep. '93— NCH attributed its lower income in the first three months of 1993-94 to lower sales and operating income at international operations. International sales decreased 12% as reported in U.S. dollars, hurt by unfavorable changes in currency translation rates. Margins declined because of lower volumes sold.

Next earnings report expected in early December.

Per Share Data ($)

Yr. End Apr. 30	1993	1992	1991	1990	1989	1988	[2]1987	1986	1985	[2]1984
Tangible Bk. Val.	**34.40**	33.06	30.10	25.36	22.79	20.00	18.07	16.35	15.23	15.13
Cash Flow	**6.04**	6.15	6.53	5.80	5.01	4.14	2.89	2.43	2.18	1.93
Earnings	**4.53**	4.77	5.19	4.69	4.06	3.29	2.12	1.77	1.59	1.35
Dividends	**2.00**	1.00	0.94	0.84	1.12	0.72	0.72	0.72	0.72	0.72
Payout Ratio	**44%**	21%	18%	18%	27%	22%	34%	39%	45%	53%
Calendar Years	**1992**	1991	1990	1989	1988	1987	1986	1985	1984	1983
Prices—High	**74½**	78¼	66¾	60½	46	41¾	33½	26¼	20½	21¼
Low	**58⅛**	54½	45	40½	36	25	24½	17½	16½	15⅞
P/E Ratio—	**16–12**	16–11	13–9	13–9	11–9	13–8	16–12	15–10	13–10	16–12

Data as orig. reptd. **1.** Excl. special. **2.** Reflects merger or acquisition.

Income Data (Million $)

Year Ended Apr. 30	Revs.	Oper. Inc.	% Oper. Inc. of Revs.	Cap. Exp.	Depr.	Int. Exp.	Net Bef. Taxes	Eff. Tax Rate	Net Inc.	% Net Inc. of Revs.	Cash Flow
1993	**680**	**72.8**	**10.7**	**18.0**	**12.5**	**4.70**	**63.5**	**40.8%**	**37.6**	**5.5**	**50.1**
1992	671	79.3	11.8	14.2	11.4	7.97	66.1	40.3%	39.4	5.9	50.8
1991	678	85.8	12.7	16.1	11.1	8.16	71.0	39.2%	43.1	6.4	54.2
1990	628	80.0	12.7	16.5	9.4	7.59	65.0	38.8%	39.8	6.3	49.2
1989	565	74.2	13.1	16.6	8.6	7.41	60.4	39.8%	36.3	6.4	44.9
1988	501	64.0	12.8	10.5	7.8	7.94	49.6	39.5%	30.0	6.0	37.8
[1]1987	427	49.2	11.5	9.1	7.2	7.88	36.1	45.7%	19.6	4.6	26.8
1986	375	43.1	11.5	7.5	6.4	7.43	32.5	47.4%	17.1	4.6	23.5
1985	348	42.5	12.2	6.6	6.1	6.50	33.0	50.1%	16.5	4.7	22.5
[1]1984	320	37.7	11.8	5.2	6.3	4.33	[2]30.0	51.2%	14.6	4.6	21.0

Balance Sheet Data (Million $)

Apr. 30	Cash	Curr. Assets	Curr. Liab.	Curr. Ratio	Total Assets	% Ret. on Assets	Long Term Debt	Common Equity	Total Cap.	% LT Debt of Cap.	% Ret. on Equity
1993	**123**	**335**	**92**	**3.6**	**467**	**8.0**	**8.8**	**286**	**295**	**3.0**	**13.4**
1992	119	342	108	3.2	471	8.7	10.5	274	284	3.7	15.1
1991	89	314	110	2.9	438	10.5	8.2	248	256	3.2	18.9
1990	66	281	106	2.7	394	10.6	11.4	214	225	5.1	19.6
1989	82	272	99	2.7	373	10.2	19.0	203	222	8.5	19.1
1988	78	252	92	2.7	343	9.3	24.8	180	205	12.1	17.5
1987	73	224	82	2.7	309	6.7	21.7	167	189	11.5	12.3
1986	56	196	74	2.6	272	6.9	15.4	151	167	9.2	11.7
1985	63	178	50	3.6	244	6.8	12.2	156	168	7.2	10.6
1984	69	181	55	3.3	251	6.1	10.6	162	175	6.1	9.1

Data as orig. reptd. **1.** Reflects merger or acquisition. **2.** Incl. equity in earns. of nonconsol. subs.

Net Sales (Million $)

Quarter:	1993–94	1992–93	1991–92	1990–91
Jul.	169.7	175.0	169.0	169.3
Oct.		169.4	160.8	169.2
Jan.		168.7	173.0	175.5
Apr.		166.7	168.1	163.7
		679.9	670.8	677.7

Sales in the three months ended July 31, 1993, declined 3.2%, year to year, reflecting lower foreign sales and the negative impact of a strong dollar. Margins narrowed on reduced sales volume in international markets and a change in sales mix, higher marketing expenses, and one-time expenditures for the relocation of a manufacturing facility in the domestic market. Following a 43% plunge in interest and other income (net), pretax income was off 33%. After taxes at 40.3%, versus 41.8%, net income declined 32%, to $7,561,000 ($0.19 a share) from $11,095,000 ($1.34).

Common Share Earnings ($)

Quarter:	1993–94	1992–93	1991–92	1990–91
Jul.	0.91	1.34	1.30	1.30
Oct.		1.18	1.30	1.38
Jan.		0.92	1.24	1.35
Apr.		1.09	0.94	1.16
		4.53	4.77	5.19

Finances

In the first quarter of 1993-94, working capital increased to $251.3 million from $242.9 million at April 30, 1993. The current ratio was unchanged at 3.6 to 1. Net cash flow from operations was $6.3 million, down from $15.8 million. Some $3.4 million was used to repurchase shares.

Dividend Data

Dividends have been paid since 1965.

Amt. of Divd. $	Date Decl.	Ex–divd. Date	Stock of Record	Payment Date
0.25	Jan. 13	Feb. 23	Mar. 1	Mar. 15'93
0.25	Apr. 7	May 25	Jun. 1	Jun. 15'93
0.25	Jul. 29	Aug. 26	Sep. 1	Sep. 15'93
0.25	Sep. 14	Nov. 24	Dec. 1	Dec. 15'93
1.00 Spl.	Sep. 14	Nov. 24	Dec. 1	Dec. 15'93

Capitalization

Long Term Debt: $8,394,000 (7/93).

Common Stock: 8,269,892 shs. ($1 par). About 51% is owned by the Levy family. Institutions hold approximately 40%. Shareholders of record: 783 (6/93).

Office—2727 Chemsearch Blvd., Irving, TX 75062; P. O. Box 152170, Irving, TX 75015-2170. **Tel**—(214) 438-0211. **Chrmn**—L. A. Levy. **Pres**—I. L. Levy. **VP-Secy & Investor Contact**—Joe Cleveland. **VP-Fin & Treas**—G. Sciavally. **Dirs**—R. L. Blumenthal, J. R. Fulgham Jr., I. L. Levy, L. A. Levy, M. P. Levy Jr., J. M. Trim, T. B. Walker Jr. **Transfer Agent & Registrar**—Society Corp. **Incorporated** in Delaware in 1965. **Empl**—10,098.

 Shayna J. Malnak

NIPSCO Industries

NYSE Symbol NI In S&P MidCap 400

Price	Range	P-E Ratio	Dividend	Yield	S&P Ranking	Beta
Sep. 23'93	1993					
34	34⅞–26⅛	15	1.32	3.9%	B	0.60

Summary

This gas and electric utility holding company serves northern Indiana's steel and industrial economy. Coal plants accounted for about 90% of its electric generation in 1992; NI does not expect costs of compliance with the Clean Air Act Amendment of 1990 to be material. Earnings for 1993 should benefit from higher electric sales and improved cost controls. Also, share earnings will be boosted by the company's stock repurchase program. The longer-term outlook is enhanced by NI's strong cash flow and a completed construction program. An increase in the $0.33 quarterly dividend is expected in late 1993.

Current Outlook

Share earnings for 1993 could reach $2.30, up from the $2.00 recorded for 1992. Share earnings could rise to $2.40 in 1994.

The $0.33 quarterly dividend may be raised some 6.1%, effective with the December 1993 declaration.

Share earnings for 1993 should benefit from higher kwh sales, as the service area continues to grow. Also, profits will be boosted by well controlled operating and maintenance expenses and lower interest costs due to refinancings. Fewer shares outstanding will add to per share profits. Share earnings for 1994 are expected to benefit from a continuation of the above positive factors plus profit contributions from the recently acquired Northern Indiana Fuel & Light Co. NI's diversification into a tire-fueled energy plant in England and a pulverized coal injection facility joint venture with Inland Steel (both under construction) bode well for the long term.

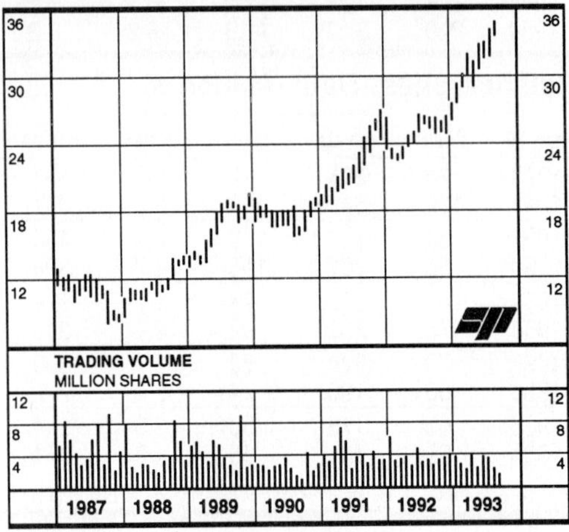

Operating Revenues (Million $)

Quarter:	1993	1992	1991	1990
Mar.	522	474	462	454
Jun.	349	329	320	326
Sep.	---	317	323	318
Dec.	---	463	429	424
	---	1,582	1,535	1,521

Revenues in the six months to June 30, 1993, rose 8.4%, year to year, on greater gas sales. With lower fuel costs, operating income was up 9.9%, and after 6.4% lower interest and other charges, net income rose 20%, to $1.18 per share, from $0.97.

Common Share Earnings ($)

Quarter:	1993	1992	1991	1990
Mar.	0.87	0.70	0.66	0.61
Jun.	0.31	0.26	0.29	0.26
Sep.	E0.39	0.30	0.37	0.36
Dec.	E0.73	0.73	0.61	0.57
	E2.30	2.00	1.94	1.81

Important Developments

Jul. '93— NI reported that gas operating margins were higher in the first half of 1993, year to year, as gas sales rose, reflecting colder weather during 1993's first quarter and the inclusion of Northern Indiana Fuel and Light Co., acquired in March. Electric operating margins also were higher, on increased sales to residential and commercial customers, due to warmer weather in the second quarter and increased industrial demand. Sales to wholesale customers were lower.

Mar. '93— As part of the company's effort to expand its gas business, NI purchased a 202-mile pipeline from Tecumseh Pipeline Co. Earlier, in February, NI acquired Kokomo Gas & Fuel Co. and in January, acquired a controlling interest in Triumph Natural Gas Co. of Dallas, Texas.

Next earnings report expected in late October.

Per Share Data ($)

Yr. End Dec. 31	1992	1991	1990	1989	1988	1987	1986	1985	1984	1983
Tangible Bk. Val.	**15.04**	14.46	13.95	13.19	13.34	12.85	12.87	13.44	15.06	15.08
Earnings[1]	**2.00**	1.94	1.81	1.72	1.41	0.53	d0.57	1.10	1.62	1.73
Dividends	**1.240**	1.160	1.040	0.840	0.600	0.150	Nil	1.170	1.545	1.500
Payout Ratio	**62%**	60%	57%	49%	43%	28%	Nil	106%	95%	87%
Prices—High	**26⅝**	27	19¼	19⅝	14⅛	13	13½	12⅞	15⅛	15½
Low	**22½**	18½	15¾	13⅛	8⅝	8	9⅜	8⅛	10⅞	12
P/E Ratio—	**13–11**	14–10	11–9	11–8	10–6	25–15	NM	12–7	9–7	9–7

Data as orig. reptd. 1. Bef. spec. item(s) of -0.72 in 1989, -1.33 in 1985. d-Deficit. E-Estimated. NM-Not Meaningful.

Income Data (Million $)

Year Ended Dec. 31	Revs.	Depr.	Maint.	Oper. Ratio	[1]Fxd. Chgs. Cover.	Constr. Credits	Eff. Tax Rate	[2]Net Inc.	% Return On Revs.	% Return On [3]Invest. Capital	% Return On Com. Equity
1992	**1,582**	**183**	**85.5**	**84.4%**	**2.87**	**0.6**	**36.0%**	**137**	**8.6**	**8.3**	**13.1**
1991	1,535	176	93.5	83.4%	2.68	1.3	34.2%	133	8.7	8.4	12.9
1990	1,521	171	90.5	83.7%	2.59	1.0	36.4%	125	8.2	8.2	12.7
1989	1,560	166	86.2	83.8%	2.48	0.8	24.6%	124	7.9	8.2	12.4
1988	1,524	155	85.0	83.1%	2.12	0.5	37.1%	103	6.8	8.0	10.4
1987	1,452	144	85.5	86.7%	1.47	22.5	36.0%	65	4.5	6.0	4.1
1986	1,626	133	80.8	88.9%	0.48	49.4	NM	d14	NM	NM	NM
1985	1,909	140	82.1	89.6%	1.98	46.5	3.9%	107	5.6	6.8	7.6
1984	2,001	135	77.0	88.2%	2.39	33.1	44.3%	140	7.0	8.1	10.6
1983	1,956	115	75.2	89.4%	2.48	63.2	41.3%	138	7.0	8.0	11.2

Balance Sheet Data (Million $)

Dec. 31	Gross Prop.	Capital Expend.	Net Prop.	% Earn. on Net Prop.	Total Cap.	LT Debt	% LT Debt	Capitalization Pfd.	% Pfd.	Com.	% Com.
1992	**5,054**	**172**	**3,177**	**7.8**	**2,987**	**1,026**	**45.3**	**204**	**9.0**	**1,035**	**45.7**
1991	4,829	169	3,135	8.1	2,988	1,069	47.1	188	8.3	1,012	44.6
1990	4,672	152	3,145	7.9	3,092	1,166	49.2	194	8.2	1,008	42.6
1989	4,547	151	3,161	8.0	3,097	1,262	52.7	166	6.9	966	40.4
1988	4,417	117	3,178	8.1	3,176	1,308	52.1	175	7.0	1,029	40.9
1987	4,321	157	3,215	6.0	3,330	1,401	52.7	297	11.2	962	36.1
1986	4,154	187	3,166	5.7	3,428	1,552	54.9	314	11.1	963	34.0
1985	3,990	279	3,123	6.5	3,445	1,511	53.2	327	11.5	1,003	35.3
1984	3,733	272	2,969	8.2	3,328	1,318	48.5	333	12.3	1,065	39.2
1983	3,481	267	2,821	7.6	3,256	1,383	50.4	339	12.3	1,023	37.3

Data as orig. reptd. **1.** Times int. exp. & pfd. divs. covered (pretax basis). **2.** Bef. spec. items. **3.** Based on income before interest charges. d-Deficit. NM-Not Meaningful.

Business Summary

NIPSCO Industries is the holding company formed in 1988 by Northern Indiana Public Service Co., which supplies electricity (58% of 1992 revenues) and gas (42%) to the northern third of Indiana with a population of about 2.2 million. Distribution of electric revenues:

	1992	1991	1990	1989
Residential	26%	28%	27%	26%
Commercial	25%	25%	25%	24%
Industrial	43%	40%	45%	44%
Other	6%	7%	3%	6%

Sources of electric generation in 1992 were coal 90%, natural gas 4%, and other 5%. Internal system peak demand in 1992 was 2,496 mw, and capability at peak totaled 2,818 mw, for a capacity margin of 11.4%. Gas sales in 1992 were 265,109,000 dth, up from 243,522,000 dth in 1991.

NI abandoned its nuclear construction program in 1981, and all charges related to the canceled nuclear project were taken by 1989-year-end.

NI's electric system is interconnected with that of Indiana Michigan Power, Commonwealth Edison, Public Service Co. of Indiana, Consumers Power, and Central Illinois Public Service, among others. Electricity is purchased from, sold to, or exchanged with these utilities.

The company estimates that total costs of compliance with the Clean Air Act Amendments of 1990's sulfur dioxide regulations will impact electric rates by less than 5% in the future.

Dividend Data

Common dividends were resumed in August 1987 after having been omitted since December 1985. A dividend reinvestment is available. A "poison pill" stock purchase rights plan was adopted in 1990.

Amt. of Divd. $	Date Decl.	Ex-divd. Date	Stock of Record	Payment Date
0.31	Sep. 22	Oct. 26	Oct. 30	Nov. 20'92
0.33	Dec. 18	Jan. 25	Jan. 29	Feb. 19'93
0.33	Mar. 23	Apr. 26	Apr. 30	May 20'93
0.33	Jun. 22	Jul. 26	Jul. 30	Aug. 20'93

Capitalization

Long Term Debt: $911,137,000 (6/93).

Subsid. Preferred Stock: $167,174,000.

Red. Preferred Stock: $35,000,000.

Common Stock: 66,291,756 shs. (no par).
Institutions hold approximately 56%.
Shareholders of record: 43,659.

Office—5265 Hohman Ave., Hammond, IN 46320. **Tel**—(219) 853-5200. **Chrmn & Pres**—G. L. Neale. **VP-CFO**—S. P. Adik. **Secy**—N. M. Rausch. **Investor Contact**—Dennis E. Senchak. **Dirs**—S. C. Beering, A. J. Decio, C. H. Elliott, G. L. Neale, E. M. Raclin, D. E. Ribordy, I. M. Rolland, E. A. Schroer, R. J. Welsh Jr. **Transfer Agent & Registrar**—Harris Trust and Savings Bank, Chicago. **Incorporated** in Indiana in 1912. **Empl**—4,550.

 Christopher J. Grant

Nabors Industries

ASE Symbol NBR Options on CBOE (Mar-Jun-Sep-Dec) In S&P MidCap 400

Price	Range	P–E Ratio	Dividend	Yield	S&P Ranking	Beta
Oct. 14'93	1993					
9	11–6⅛	16	None	None	B–	0.90

Summary

This company (formerly Anglo Energy) provides contract drilling and oilfield services worldwide. Strong growth in recent years stemmed primarily from acquisitions. Earnings continued to gain in the first nine months of fiscal 1993, reflecting sharply higher other income. The company recently sold 2.0 million NBR common shares, including 200,000 shares for a stockholder, at $9.875 per share.

Business Summary

Nabors Industries, Inc. (formerly Anglo Energy, Inc.) provides contract drilling and other oilfield services, including comprehensive oilfield management, logistics and engineering services. The company is active in North America (Alaska, Canada, the continental U.S. and the Gulf of Mexico), the U.K. North Sea, the Middle East, Asia, South and Central America and Africa. The U.S. and Canada accounted for about 43% of fiscal 1992 revenues. As of August 1993, the company operated about 225 land and 14 offshore drilling rigs.

Nabors emerged from bankruptcy proceedings in May 1988, and in November 1988 acquired the Westburne Group, a Canada-based international drilling contractor, for about $13 million in cash and stock.

In February 1990, Loffland Brothers Co., a U.S.-based international drilling contractor, was acquired for about $58 million in cash. Loffland operated rigs in international markets and had a fleet of modern, mostly diesel electric land drilling rigs in the U.S. that provided most of the equipment subsequently redeployed by the company.

In November 1990, Henley Drilling Co., a subsidiary of Hunt Oil Co., was acquired in exchange for 2,026,000 Nabors common shares and a $2,300,000 note. Henley is engaged in contract drilling and related oilfield services and owns and operates 10 rigs in Texas and Louisiana and one rig in Yemen. In April 1991, Loffland and Henley merged, forming Nabors Loffland Drilling Co.

As of December 1992, the company's regional distribution of operations was as follows: in Alaska, four of eight rigs were under contract; in the North Sea, nine platform rigs were under contract, and during fiscal 1992 Nabors acquired a platform drilling services company; in the Middle East, 21 land rigs and one jackup rig were operating (18 are owned); in the Far East, three of four rigs were under contract; in Canada, 10 of 22 rigs were being actively marketed; in Venezuela, nine rigs were working; in Africa, two rigs were operating: and in the U.S., there were three rigs in the Gulf of Mexico, two of which were under contract, and 39 land rigs. In fiscal 1993, two rigs were shipped to Western Siberia.

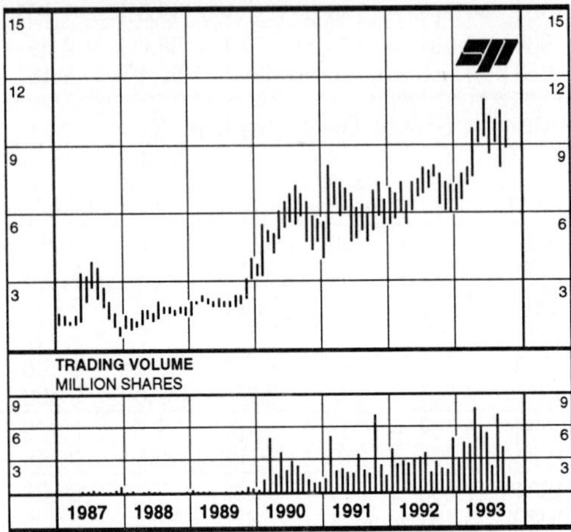

Through 50%-owned Peak Oilfield Services, Nabors also provides, in Alaska, road, pad and pipeline construction and maintenance, general hauling, facilities maintenance, rig moving and warehousing.

Important Developments

Aug. '93— The company sold 2.0 million common shares, including 200,000 shares for a certain shareholder, at $9.875 per share. Total proceeds to NBR were about $18 million, of which $10 million was used to make the final payment on NBR's $32 million acquisition of Grace Drilling's assets. Separately, in 1993's third quarter, Nabors acquired one workover and two drilling rigs in Alaska in exchange for 200,000 NBR common shares.

Next earnings report expected in early December.

Per Share Data ($)

Yr. End Sep. 30	1992	[1]1991	[1]1990	[1]1989	1988	1987	1986	1985	1984	1983
Tangible Bk. Val.	**3.15**	2.52	1.92	1.02	0.83	d2.68	5.79	d0.68	2.20	[4]4.20
Cash Flow	**0.74**	0.58	0.35	0.19	d0.05	d7.99	0.07	d0.49	d0.42	d0.16
Earnings[2]	**0.52**	0.44	0.27	0.12	d0.19	d8.55	d3.01	d2.03	d2.43	d2.57
Dividends	**Nil**	Nil	Nil	Nil	Nil	Nil	Nil	Nil	Nil	Nil
Payout Ratio	**Nil**	Nil	Nil	Nil	Nil	Nil	Nil	Nil	Nil	Nil
Prices[3]—High	**8⅛**	8⅛	7¼	4	2⅛	3⅞	1⅞	2⅜	3	7⅛
Low	**5½**	4	3¼	1½	⅞	⅝	⅜	⅞	⅞	1¼
P/E Ratio—	**16–11**	18–9	27–12	33–13	NM	NM	NM	NM	NM	NM

Data as orig. reptd. **1.** Refl. merger or acq. **2.** Bef. results of disc. ops. of -0.76 in 1985, +0.28 in 1984, -7.50 in 1983, and spec. items of +1.19 in 1988, +20.56 in 1986 (mostly related to Chap. 11 obligs.), +0.33 in 1984. **3.** Cal. year. **4.** Incl. intangibles. d-Deficit. NM-Not Meaningful.

Income Data (Million $)

Year Ended Sep. 30	Revs.	Oper. Inc.	% Oper. Inc. of Revs.	Cap. Exp.	Depr.	Int. Exp.	[4]Net Bef. Taxes	Eff. Tax Rate	[5]Net Inc.	% Net Inc. of Revs.	Cash Flow
1992	**286**	**48.4**	**16.9**	**54.4**	**14.4**	**5.6**	**35.5**	**4.9%**	**33.8**	**11.8**	**48.2**
[1]1991	240	35.3	14.7	80.0	8.5	5.2	29.8	9.3%	27.1	11.3	35.5
[1]1990	139	17.1	12.3	68.5	[3]4.5	3.6	16.9	14.0%	14.6	10.5	19.1
[1]1989	74	6.6	8.8	18.3	3.3	0.8	5.5	0.3%	5.5	7.4	8.7
1988	56	2.1	3.8	6.2	3.1	8.9	d5.2	NM	d4.3	NM	d1.2
1987	29	d4.0	NM	2.7	5.6	20.6	d93.4	NM	d85.6	NM	d80.0
1986	69	10.3	14.9	6.5	9.8	5.9	d9.2	NM	d9.6	NM	0.2
[2]1985	92	11.1	12.1	12.8	12.6	1.4	d17.4	NM	d16.6	NM	d4.0
1984	88	d1.7	NM	3.7	16.4	3.6	d19.5	NM	d19.8	NM	d3.5
[2]1983	150	11.9	7.9	3.0	[3]19.7	17.3	d32.7	NM	d21.0	NM	d1.3

Balance Sheet Data (Million $)

Sep. 30	Cash	Curr. Assets	Curr. Liab.	Curr. Ratio	Total Assets	% Ret. on Assets	Long Term Debt	Common Equity	Total Cap.	% LT Debt of Cap.	% Ret. on Equity
1992	**14.8**	**102**	**65.7**	**1.5**	**309**	**11.6**	**47**	**185**	**234**	**20.0**	**20.3**
1991	16.4	83	67.8	1.2	263	11.3	37	141	180	20.7	21.8
1990	28.8	83	51.9	1.6	209	10.0	38	103	144	26.3	18.4
1989	6.7	25	16.4	1.5	68	8.7	6	45	52	11.3	13.6
1988	13.3	27	17.6	1.5	56	NM	2	35	38	4.3	NM
1987	6.3	16	11.2	1.4	50	NM	49	d27	24	NM	NM
1986	5.2	20	11.8	1.7	120	NM	42	58	108	38.8	NM
1985	50.1	73	21.3	3.4	180	NM	13	d6	16	79.2	NM
1984	46.7	68	18.4	3.7	203	NM	13	18	42	31.8	NM
1983	28.2	77	28.1	2.7	230	NM	15	34	61	25.0	NM

Data as orig. reptd. **1.** Refl. merger or acq. **2.** Excl. disc. ops. **3.** Refl. acctng. change. **4.** Incl. equity in earns. of nonconsol. subs. **5.** Bef. results of disc. ops. and spec. items. d-Deficit. NM-Not Meaningful.

Revenues (Million $)

Quarter:	1992–93	1991–92	1990–91	1989–90
Dec.	69.9	68.4	57.4	18.5
Mar.	78.9	75.3	64.0	31.3
Jun.	83.3	68.9	58.7	41.7
Sep.		73.7	60.1	47.4
		286.3	240.1	138.9

Revenues for the nine months ended June 30, 1993, advanced 9.2%, year to year, reflecting increased activity in Alaska and certain international markets. Operating expenses rose more rapidly, but with sharply higher other income offsetting greater depreciation and interest charges, pretax income gained 14%. After taxes at 8.8%, versus 5.7%, net income was up 11%, to $27,222,000 ($0.41 a share, based on 4.2% more shares; $0.40 fully diluted), from $24,632,000 ($0.38).

Common Share Earnings ($)

Quarter:	1992–93	1991–92	1990–91	1989–90
Dec.	0.12	0.13	0.09	0.04
Mar.	0.13	0.13	0.10	0.06
Jun.	0.16	0.13	0.11	0.07
Sep.		0.14	0.14	0.10
		0.52	0.44	0.27

Dividend Data

Class A dividends were paid from 1973 until omission in July 1982.

Finances

In August 1993, the company received approximately $24 million from warrants exercised in the purchase of about 4.4 million NBR common shares.

In June 1993, Nabors acquired substantially all of the assets of Grace Drilling Co., including 167 land rigs located in 17 states, for about $32 million, consisting of $22 million in cash and a $10 million note, and a three-year warrant to purchase 1.1 million NBR shares at an exercise price of $16.18 a share. Separately, Nabors received about $16 million in cash from the sale of a platform rig in the UK North Sea.

At September 30, 1992, the company had net operating loss carryforwards of about $168 million, expiring from 1999 to 2006.

Capitalization

Long Term Debt: $73,052,000 (6/93).

Common Stock: 69,000,000 shs. ($0.10 par). Officers & directors hold some 34%. Shareholders: 2,031 of record (9/92).

Options: To buy about 1,693,048 shs. at $0.75 to $16.25 ea.

Warrants: To buy 2,600,000 shs. at $5.50 and $16.18 ea.

Office—515 West Greens Rd., Suite 1200, Houston, TX 77067. **Tel**—(713) 874-0035. **Chrmn & CEO**—E. M. Isenberg. **Vice Chrmn**—W. S. Berman, R. A. Stratton. **Pres & COO**—A. G. Petrello. **VP & Secy**—D. McLachlin. **Contr**—B. P. Koch. **Investor Contact**—Harris Kaplan. **Dirs**—W. S. Berman, G. T. Hurford, E. M. Isenberg, A. G. Petrello, H. W. Schmidt, M. M. Sheinfeld, R. A. Stratton, J. Wexler, M. J. Whitman. **Transfer Agent & Registrar**—First Chicago Trust of New York, NYC. **Incorporated** in Delaware in 1978. **Empl**—4,320.

 J. R. Jordan

National Fuel Gas

NYSE Symbol NFG In S&P MidCap 400

Price	Range	P-E Ratio	Dividend	Yield	S&P Ranking	Beta
Sep. 7'93	1993					
36⅝	36⅞–28¾	19	1.54	4.2%	B+	0.39

Summary

This integrated natural gas system serves the Buffalo, N.Y., area and extensive contiguous districts reaching into western Pennsylvania and eastern Ohio. Long-term prospects are enhanced by efforts to expand gas storage and transmission operations geographically, and expected strong gains in exploration and production profits. The quarterly dividend was recently raised 2.7%.

Current Outlook

Share earnings for the fiscal year ending September 30, 1994, are projected at $2.20, up from $2.00 estimated for fiscal 1993.

The quarterly dividend was raised 2.7%, to $0.38½, with the July 1993 payment.

Utility profits for fiscal 1994 are expected to rise, on customer growth of about 1.0%, a $13.9 million rate increase in New York, and, assuming normal weather in Pennsylvania, increased gas usage per customer (in the first nine months of fiscal 1993, weather was 5.5% warmer than normal). Supply, transmission and storage profits are expected to grow, aided by continuing efforts to expand geographically; competition in the Northeast market is likely to remain stiff. Exploration earnings should benefit from greater production and slightly higher wellhead prices. Share earnings growth will be restricted by more shares outstanding.

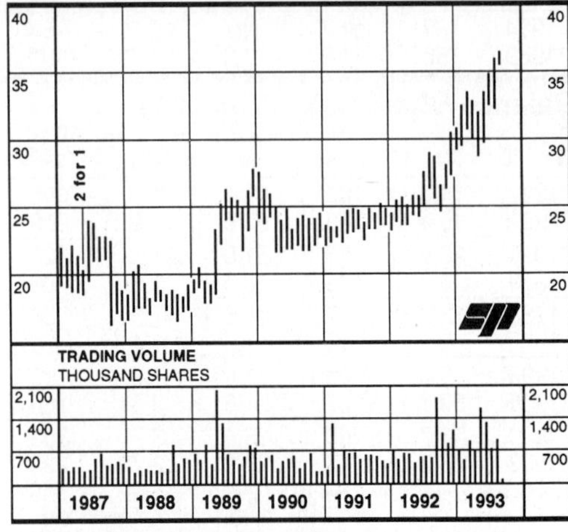

Operating Revenues (Million $)

Quarter:	1992–93	1991–92	1990–91	1989–90
Dec.	294	272	263	291
Mar.	391	346	338	336
Jun.	185	177	147	155
Sep.	---	125	118	110
	---	920	865	892

Operating revenues in the nine months ended June 30, 1993, advanced 9.6% year to year, reflecting increased gas production and higher gas prices. Fewer pipeline construction projects and a reduction in throughput volumes were only partly offset by lower interest expense; the gain in net income was held to 7.6%. Share earnings, on 11% more shares, were down to $2.16, from $2.22.

Common Share Earnings ($)

Quarter:	1992–93	1991–92	1990–91	1989–90
Dec.	0.77	0.87	0.74	0.86
Mar.	1.33	1.29	1.21	1.26
Jun.	0.09	0.06	d0.04	d0.01
Sep.	Ed0.19	d0.28	d0.23	d0.28
	E2.00	1.94	1.63	1.83

Important Developments

Aug. '93— NFG filed with the New York Public Service Commission for a rate increase of $55 million (8.5%), and requested a return on common equity of 12.16%. Included in the request was an initial annual amount of $24.9 million for the recovery of transition costs from pipeline companies that serve the company's distribution operations. The new rates are expected to become effective in July 1994. Separately, in an open season for a 18.1 Bcf natural gas storage project, letters of intent received expressed total interest in 119% of available capacity.

Jul. '93— The company and the Natural Gas Clearinghouse said they expected to begin operation of the Ellisburg-Leidy hub in September 1993, for natural gas buyers and sellers in the Northeast. NFG expects market hubs to create the reliability and efficiency needed under the restructured format of the industry.

Next earnings report expected in late October.

Per Share Data ($)

Yr. End Sep. 30	**1992**	1991	1990	1989	1988	1987	1986	1985	1984	1983
Tangible Bk. Val.	**18.68**	17.53	16.97	16.44	15.66	15.21	14.14	13.53	12.62	11.50
Earnings[1]	**1.94**	1.63	1.83	1.93	1.65	1.49	1.75	1.90	2.05	1.22
Dividends	**1.480**	1.440	1.380	1.300	1.230	1.170	1.090	0.990	0.861	0.750
Payout Ratio	**76%**	88%	75%	67%	75%	79%	62%	52%	42%	62%
Prices[2]—High	**30½**	25¼	27⅝	27⅞	20¾	24	20⅞	15⅝	14⅝	9¼
Low	**23¼**	22⅛	21⅝	17⅞	16½	16¼	14⅜	12½	8⅛	6⅞
P/E Ratio—	**16–12**	15–14	15–12	14–9	13–10	16–11	12–8	8–7	7–4	8–6

Data as orig. reptd. Adj. for stk. divs. of 100% Jun. 1987, 100% May 1984. **1.** Bef. spec. item(s) of +0.27 in 1987. **2.** Cal. yr. d-Deficit. E-Estimated.

National Fuel Gas Company

Income Data (Million $)

Year Ended Sep. 30	Revs.	Depr.	Maint.	Oper. Ratio	[1]Fxd. Chgs. Cover.	Constr. Credits	Eff. Tax Rate	[2]Net Inc.	% Return On Revs.	% Return On [3]Invest. Capital	% Return On [4]Com. Equity
1992	**920**	**55.7**	**22.4**	**87.7%**	**2.62**	**NA**	**36.4%**	**60.3**	**6.6**	**9.6**	**10.3**
1991	865	50.8	20.5	88.6%	2.18	NA	31.5%	49.0	5.7	10.0	9.5
1990	892	43.7	18.7	88.5%	2.38	NA	33.9%	52.0	5.8	10.8	11.0
1989	856	44.4	20.1	88.6%	2.52	NA	32.3%	52.4	6.1	11.4	12.0
1988	769	43.2	21.1	89.7%	2.49	NA	29.6%	42.6	5.5	10.2	10.7
1987	737	36.0	21.4	90.6%	2.54	NA	39.8%	35.9	4.9	9.8	11.6
1986	906	37.4	21.0	92.1%	3.19	1.02	42.1%	43.4	4.8	10.7	12.7
1985	971	31.4	20.4	92.3%	3.31	1.02	41.2%	46.9	4.8	12.0	14.6
1984	1,104	28.7	20.9	93.2%	3.28	0.59	43.9%	49.9	4.5	14.3	17.0
1983	1,011	26.3	19.5	94.4%	2.18	0.55	33.4%	30.2	3.0	12.2	10.7

Balance Sheet Data (Million $)

Sep. 30	Gross Prop.	Capital Expend.	Net Prop.	% Earn. on Net Prop.	Total Cap.	Capitalization LT Debt	% LT Debt	Pfd.	% Pfd.	Com.	% Com.
1992	**1,918**	**158**	**1,416**	**8.3**	**1,310**	**480**	**43.1**	**Nil**	**Nil**	**632**	**56.9**
1991	1,773	156	1,314	7.8	1,170	442	44.9	Nil	Nil	542	55.1
1990	1,625	162	1,206	8.9	1,035	397	45.1	Nil	Nil	484	54.9
1989	1,473	130	1,087	9.4	989	384	45.3	Nil	Nil	464	54.7
1988	1,353	128	1,002	8.2	841	297	42.3	Nil	Nil	406	57.7
1987	1,238	127	919	7.9	800	266	40.4	Nil	Nil	393	59.6
1986	1,133	97	840	8.9	745	274	44.8	Nil	Nil	337	55.2
1985	1,046	88	781	9.9	674	221	39.2	22.5	4.0	321	56.8
1984	961	62	725	10.6	643	238	42.7	24.0	4.3	295	53.0
1983	907	68	692	8.4	562	201	40.9	25.5	5.2	265	53.9

Data as orig. reptd. **1.** Times int. exp. & pfd. divs. covered (pretax basis). **2.** Bef. spec. items. **3.** Based on income before interest charges. **4.** As reptd. by co. NA-Not Available.

Business Summary

National Fuel Gas is a public utility holding company whose main subsidiary distributes natural gas in western New York and northwestern Pennsylvania. Other subsidiaries are engaged in natural gas exploration, production, gathering, purchasing, transmission, storage, natural gas marketing, and pipeline construction. Contributions to revenues and profits by segment in fiscal 1992 were:

	Revs.	Profits
Utility	56%	59%
Supply, trans. & storage	38%	33%
Expl. & prod.	3%	5%
Other	3%	3%

National Fuel Gas Distribution provides retail gas service to the metropolitan areas of Buffalo, Niagara Falls and Jamestown, N.Y., and Erie and Sharon, Pa. Retail customers served during fiscal 1992 averaged 720,129 (714,734 a year earlier). Gas volumes sold and transported totaled 168.5 Bcf in fiscal 1992, up from 154.6 Bcf in fiscal 1991.

Supply Corp. is engaged in the production, purchase, storage, transportation and sale of natural gas; and operates a pipeline from Pennsylvania to the Canadian border. Throughput (excluding intersegment throughput) totaled 132.1 Bcf in fiscal 1992, up from 102.1 Bcf a year earlier. Penn-York provides natural gas storage to 17 utilities in eight northeastern states, and to two interstate pipeline companies.

Other operations include oil and gas exploration and production, pipeline construction, and operation of a saw mill.

Variations in revenues due to abnormal weather during the heating season are largely offset by a weather normalization adjustment in rates in the New York service territory.

Dividend Data

Dividends have been paid since 1903. A dividend reinvestment plan is available.

Amt. of Divd. $	Date Decl.	Ex-divd. Date	Stock of Record	Payment Date
0.37½	Sep. 18	Sep. 24	Sep. 30	Oct. 15'92
0.37½	Dec. 10	Dec. 24	Dec. 31	Jan. 15'93
0.37½	Mar. 16	Mar. 25	Mar. 31	Apr. 15'93
0.38½	Jun. 16	Jun. 24	Jun. 30	Jul. 15'93

Capitalization

Long Term Debt: $448,417,000 (6/93).

Common Stock: 36,580,744 shs. ($1 par).
Institutions hold 24%.
Shareholders of record: 23,218.

Office—30 Rockefeller Plaza, New York, NY 10112. **Tel**—(212) 541-7533. **Chrmn, Pres & CEO**—B. J. Kennedy. **Secy**—R. M. DiValerio. **Treas**—J. P. Pawlowski. **Investor Contact**—Deborah K. Kullander (716-857-7706). **Dirs**—M. L. Antoun, J. M. Brown, D. N. Campbell, L. F. Kahl, B. J. Kennedy, L. R. Reif, L. Rochwarger, G. H. Scofield. **Transfer Agent & Registrar**—Chemical Bank, NYC. **Incorporated** in New Jersey in 1902. **Empl**—3,498.

 Mark Mattke

National Pizza Co.

NASDAQ Symbol PIZA (Incl. in Nat'l Market) In S&P MidCap 400

Price	Range	P-E Ratio	Dividend	Yield	S&P Ranking	Beta
Sep. 23'93	1993					
6	8–5¾	17	None	None	B+	0.52

Summary

This company is the largest Pizza Hut franchisee, operating nearly 360 restaurants and delivery units in 13 states. It also operates and franchises some 206 Skipper's quick-service seafood restaurants. Earnings were flat in the first quarter of 1993-94, despite 10% higher sales.

Business Summary

National Pizza Company is the largest franchisee of PepsiCo, Inc.'s Pizza Hut subsidiary. As of July 1993, National operated 358 Pizza Hut restaurants and delivery kitchens, in Alabama, Arkansas, California, Kansas, Kentucky, Louisiana, Maryland, Mississippi, Missouri, Oklahoma, Tennessee, Virginia and West Virginia. The company also owns Skipper's Inc. (acquired in November 1989), a quick-service seafood restaurant chain, with 206 company-owned or franchised units in 12 western states and British Columbia. In June 1993, the company acquired NRH Corp., owner and franchiser of Tony Roma's, A Place for Ribs, which has 26 company-operated stores in four states.

Pizza Hut restaurants are freestanding, full-table-service units that offer moderately priced pizza, pasta and sandwiches, plus a salad bar with complementary items; most units offer beer. Pizza sales account for about 85% of all revenues and alcoholic beverages less than 2%. The restaurants are substantially uniform in appearance, with a distinctive red roof as an identifying feature. Typical restaurants contain from 1,800 to 3,000 square feet of floor space, including a kitchen area, and have a seating capacity of between 70 and 125. The average cost of a new restaurant, including land, in National's existing territories (excluding California) ranges from $600,000 to $800,000.

At March 30, 1993, the company was providing delivery service from 72 full-service Pizza Hut restaurants and 96 delivery-only outlets (kitchen outlets without restaurant dining areas, salad bars or beer).

National's franchise agreements, which run through 1996-1997 and are renewable for single 15-year terms, require payment of certain initial franchise fees plus varying monthly fees. Total franchise fees paid by the company in 1992-93 were approximately $4,236,000.

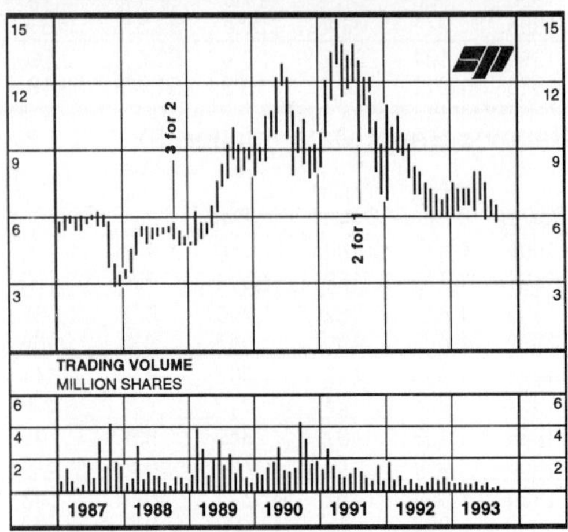

Skipper's Seafood and Chowder House restaurants are freestanding units generally located in commercial/retail areas. The cost of constructing and equiping a unit ranges from $435,000 to $585,000, plus land costs, which range from $150,000 to $400,000. Entrees include fish fillets, oysters, shrimp, clams and chicken; beer and wine are served at most locations. All of Skipper's fried entree items are deep fried in pure vegetable shortening, and the restaurants also serve baked or broiled fish. Other menu offerings include clam chowder, french fried and baked potatoes, coleslaw, entree salads and fish and chicken sandwiches.

Tony Roma's, A Place for Ribs, consists of 26 company-operated restaurants and 127 franchised locations. National Pizza plans to use the Tony Roma's chain as its primary growth vehicle, with five to seven unit openings planned each year.

Next earnings report expected in late October.

Per Share Data ($)

Yr. End Mar. 31	1993	1992	1991	[1]1990	1989	1988	[1]1987	1986	1985	1984
Tangible Bk. Val.	**1.98**	[2]3.30	[2]3.10	[2]2.61	[2]2.06	0.69	d0.05	0.69	0.78	0.26
Cash Flow	**1.00**	0.99	1.07	0.89	0.57	0.54	0.44	0.31	0.23	NA
Earnings	**0.35**	0.40	0.54	0.53	0.36	[3]0.33	[3]0.30	0.24	0.18	[4]0.17
Dividends	**Nil**	Nil	Nil	Nil	Nil	Nil	Nil	Nil	Nil	Nil
Payout Ratio	**Nil**	Nil	Nil	Nil	Nil	Nil	Nil	Nil	Nil	Nil
Calendar Years	**1992**	1991	1990	1989	1988	1987	1986	1985	1984	1983
Prices—High	**11**	14⅞	12⅞	10	5¾	6¼	6⅛	4	2⅜	NA
Low	**6**	7	7¾	4¾	3¼	2⅞	3⅞	1⅞	1⅞	NA
P/E Ratio—	**31–17**	37–18	24–14	19–9	16–9	19–9	21–13	17–8	14–11	NA

Data as orig. reptd. Adj. for stk. divs. of 100% Aug. 1991, 50% Oct. 1988, 33⅓% May 1986. **1.** Refl. merger or acq. **2.** Incl. intangibles. **3.** Ful. dil.: 0.31 in 1988, 0.28 in 1987. **4.** Restated. d-Deficit. NA-Not Available.

Income Data (Million $)

Year Ended Mar. 31	Revs.	Oper. Inc.	% Oper. Inc. of Revs.	Cap. Exp.	Depr.	Int. Exp.	Net Bef. Taxes	Eff. Tax Rate	Net Inc.	% Net Inc. of Revs.	Cash Flow
1993	**285**	**38.0**	**13.3**	**27.2**	**16.7**	**6.39**	**14.7**	**37.8%**	**9.1**	**3.2**	**25.8**
1992	299	43.4	14.5	32.3	15.9	6.69	17.2	36.0%	11.0	3.7	26.9
1991	286	44.4	15.5	44.1	14.7	6.26	23.3	35.4%	15.0	5.3	29.8
[1]1990	198	35.7	18.0	58.1	10.0	3.52	22.6	34.9%	14.7	7.4	24.7
1989	142	25.0	17.7	15.7	7.4	2.63	14.5	32.0%	9.8	6.9	17.2
1988	120	23.6	19.7	13.4	5.4	2.94	14.0	37.2%	8.8	7.3	14.2
[1]1987	96	19.2	19.9	21.0	3.7	2.52	13.8	46.4%	7.4	7.7	11.1
1986	63	11.6	18.3	15.8	1.7	1.20	9.4	43.2%	5.4	8.5	7.0
1985	41	6.7	16.6	7.9	1.0	0.05	6.6	44.8%	3.6	9.0	4.6
1984	36	8.1	22.3	2.9	0.9	0.07	7.5	46.0%	4.0	11.2	4.9

Balance Sheet Data (Million $)

Mar. 31	Cash	Curr. Assets	Curr. Liab.	Curr. Ratio	Total Assets	% Ret. on Assets	Long Term Debt	Common Equity	Total Cap.	% LT Debt of Cap.	% Ret. on Equity
1993	**6.2**	**10.8**	**27.2**	**0.4**	**204**	**4.5**	**79.1**	**89.4**	**169**	**46.9**	**10.6**
1992	6.0	11.0	24.0	0.5	206	5.5	85.8	87.1	173	49.6	13.1
1991	8.4	16.4	21.2	0.8	201	8.1	86.3	85.1	171	50.3	19.2
1990	8.7	13.8	25.1	0.5	172	10.8	66.5	72.0	139	48.0	22.9
1989	6.8	9.2	12.6	0.7	101	10.5	27.7	56.8	89	31.3	19.0
1988	2.9	5.5	9.7	0.6	85	10.4	26.9	45.7	75	35.8	23.4
1987	3.0	4.9	10.0	0.5	75	11.2	37.3	26.4	65	57.1	27.8
1986	17.6	20.2	4.4	4.6	53	14.5	23.0	24.7	48	47.8	24.7
1985	9.3	10.2	2.7	3.9	21	21.9	Nil	18.3	18	Nil	28.4
1984	0.3	3.6	3.9	0.9	10	45.4	Nil	5.9	6	Nil	67.2

Data as orig. reptd. **1.** Refl. merger or acq.

Revenues (Million $)

13 Weeks:	1993–94	1992–93	1991–92	1990–91
Jun.	78.8	71.6	75.9	68.5
Sep.		70.2	74.1	69.1
Dec.		69.1	71.9	68.4
Mar.		74.5	[1]76.8	80.1
		285.4	298.7	286.1

Net revenues for the quarter ended June 29, 1993, rose 10%, year to year. Sales in both divisions were positively impacted by the May 1993 introduction of the Bigfoot pizza and the new battered English Style fish. Same-store sales at Pizza Hut were up 10%, while Skippers sales rose 6%. Net income was up 4.4% to $2,674,000 ($0.11 a share), from $2,562,000 ($0.10).

Common Share Earnings ($)

13 Weeks:	1993–94	1992–93	1991–92	1990–91
Jun.	0.11	0.10	0.15	0.15
Sep.		0.07	0.11	0.14
Dec.		0.09	0.11	0.13
Mar.		0.10	[1]0.03	0.12
		0.35	0.40	0.54

Dividend Data

No cash has been paid. In August 1991, the company paid a dividend of one share of nonvoting Class B common stock for each outstanding share of voting Class A common.

Finances

In August 1993, the company said more than 2.4 million common shares had been repurchased under an authorization to buy back up to 2.5 million shares. The company plans to continue its stock repurchases.

At June 29, 1993, the company had a working capital deficit of $22,814,000. However, as sales are made almost entirely in cash, while credit is received from trade suppliers, National Pizza believes that such deficits will not affect its operations. The company's line of credit was increased to $45 million in June 1993.

Capitalization

Long Term Debt: $97,839,000 (6/93).

Class A Common Stock: 12,621,006 shs. ($0.01 par); controls 100% of voting power.
Institutions hold about 14%.
Shareholders: About 5,200 of record (5/93).

Class B Common Stock: 12,430,487 ($0.01 par); no voting power.

O. Gene Bicknell owns some 62% of the combined shares.

1. 14 wks.

Office—720 W. 20th St., Pittsburg, KS 66762. **Tel**—(316) 231-3390. **Chrmn**—O. G. Bicknell. **Pres & CEO**—J. M. Boyd. **VP-Fin, CFO & Investor Contact**—James K. Schwartz. **Secy**—K. J. Henderson. **Dirs**—O. G. Bicknell, J. M. Boyd, J. W. Carlin, R. E. Cressler, G. W. Elliott, F. D. Jabara. **Transfer Agent & Registrar**—American Stock Transfer & Trust Co., NYC. **Incorporated** in Kansas in 1974. **Empl**—11,200.

 Gregg W. Bonardi

National Presto

NYSE Symbol NPK In S&P MidCap 400

Price	Range	P-E Ratio	Dividend	Yield	S&P Ranking	Beta
Aug. 3'93	1993					
51½	60⅛–49⅞	17	[1]1.80	[1]3.5%	A–	0.87

Summary

This company is a leading manufacturer of comfort appliances, kitchen equipment, and private label consumer products. After eight consecutive years of earnings improvement, profits were considerably lower in 1992, with the decline continuing in 1993's first half. Earnings are projected to be relatively flat for the full year, as NPK should benefit in the second half of the year from a new product introduction.

Current Outlook

Earnings for 1994 are projected at $3.80 a share, up from the $3.55 estimated for 1993.

The annual dividend applicable to 1994 is likely to exceed the $1.80 a share paid in December 1992 applicable to 1993. Extra dividend payments ($2.00 paid during 1992) were expected to continue.

Despite a weak first half performance, sales and earnings are likely to be relatively flat for the full 1993 year. Second half sales levels should be aided by strong shipments of the just introduced ChipShot potato chipper. In addition, with the economic recovery still rather sluggish, consumers should remain attracted to the modest prices of many of NPK's products. Earnings could benefit further from a ruling against Black & Decker in its appeal of the $2.35 million (plus interest) in damages it had been ordered to pay NPK for a patent infringement, and the completion of judgement in a favorable ruling NPK had received in its patent violation suit against West Bend.

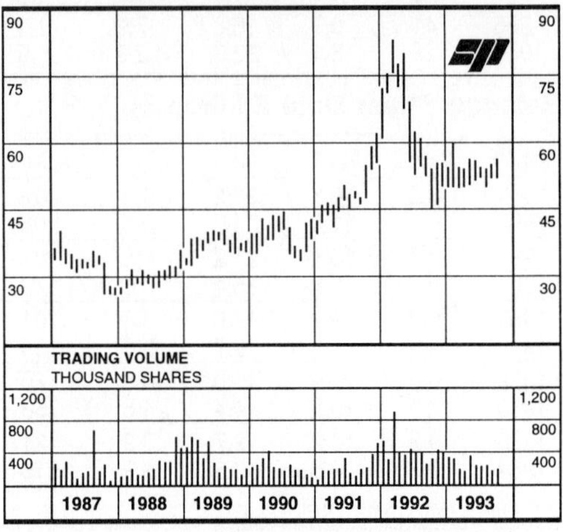

Net Sales (Million $)

Quarter:	1993	1992	1991	1990
Mar.	22.4	24.9	19.5	20.6
Jun.	14.3	17.5	22.5	18.7
Sep.	---	26.8	38.3	28.1
Dec.	---	59.1	81.3	59.7
	---	128.3	161.5	127.0

For the six months ended July 4, 1993, sales declined 14%, year to year, largely as a result of a shift in order patterns. The shift was brought on by customers' adoption of just-in-time inventory controls and strategies adopted to negate the impact of an expected increase in taxes. Also contributing to the decline was inventory carryover. Operating margins narrowed, and hurt by a lower level of interest income, net income fell 35%, to $0.79 a share from $1.20.

Common Share Earnings ($)

Quarter:	1993	1992	1991	1990
Mar.	0.43	0.65	0.61	0.60
Jun.	0.36	0.55	0.65	0.59
Sep.	E0.70	0.74	1.17	0.86
Dec.	E2.06	1.59	2.55	1.89
	E3.55	3.53	4.98	3.94

Important Developments

Aug. '93— The company noted that it had initiated small shipments of the ChipShot potato chipper, a new product that is used to slice potatoes for homemade potato chips. A major fall advertising campaign was planned for the product. NPK could provide a positive earnings surprise in 1993 in the event of a very enthusiastic conusmer reception for ChipShot.

Next earnings report expected in late October.

Per Share Data ($)

Yr. End Dec. 31	1992	1991	1990	1989	1988	1987	1986	1985	1984	1983
Tangible Bk. Val.[2]	**29.53**	29.79	27.48	27.66	25.99	24.49	23.40	22.24	21.00	19.73
Cash Flow	**3.65**	5.11	4.06	3.99	2.86	2.44	2.46	2.42	2.33	2.32
Earnings[3]	**3.53**	4.98	3.94	3.89	2.74	2.28	2.27	2.23	2.17	2.11
Dividends	**3.800**	2.700	4.150	2.250	1.253	1.185	1.120	1.045	0.980	0.890
Payout Ratio	**108%**	54%	104%	57%	45%	52%	49%	47%	45%	42%
Prices—High	**83**	62¼	44½	40⅝	36	40⅜	37⅛	31	29¼	32½
Low	**45¼**	39⅝	33½	32½	26¼	26⅛	27¼	24¾	20¾	20⅝
P/E Ratio—	**24–13**	13–8	11–9	10–8	13–10	18–11	16–12	14–11	13–10	15–10

Data as orig. reptd. Adj. for stk. div(s). of 50% Jul. 1983. **1.** Annual divd. for 1993 paid in Dec. 1992; excl. extras. **2.** Incl. intangibles in all yrs. **3.** Bef. results of disc. opers. of +0.03 in 1985, +0.05 in 1984. E-Estimated

Income Data (Million $)

Year Ended Dec. 31	Revs.	Oper. Inc.	% Oper. Inc. of Revs.	Cap. Exp.	Depr.	Int. Exp.	Net Bef. Taxes	Eff. Tax Rate	[2]Net Inc.	% Net Inc. of Revs.	Cash Flow
1992	**128**	**30.7**	**23.9**	**1.48**	**1.25**	**0.67**	**36.7**	**29.5%**	**25.9**	**20.2**	**27.1**
1991	162	43.8	27.1	0.84	1.28	0.56	52.4	29.9%	36.7	22.7	38.0
1990	127	29.4	23.2	1.20	1.24	0.62	39.6	26.4%	29.1	22.9	30.4
1989	127	28.0	22.0	1.45	1.08	0.60	39.0	26.4%	28.7	22.5	29.8
1988	108	17.5	16.2	1.10	1.19	0.60	26.7	24.0%	20.3	18.8	21.5
1987	102	16.9	16.6	1.15	1.46	0.62	23.9	29.5%	[3]16.9	16.6	18.3
1986	109	18.5	17.1	1.73	1.69	0.63	24.4	31.1%	16.8	15.5	18.5
1985	96	18.3	19.0	1.37	1.73	0.61	24.4	32.3%	16.5	17.2	18.3
[1]1984	89	15.8	17.7	1.97	1.48	0.66	22.4	27.9%	16.2	18.1	17.7
1983	104	17.6	17.0	1.61	1.87	0.68	23.4	33.0%	15.7	15.1	17.5

Balance Sheet Data (Million $)

Dec. 31	Cash	Curr. Assets	Curr. Liab.	Curr. Ratio	Total Assets	% Ret. on Assets	Long Term Debt	Common Equity	Total Cap.	% LT Debt of Cap.	% Ret. on Equity
1992	**206**	**249**	**38.2**	**6.5**	**260**	**9.8**	**5.10**	**217**	**222**	**2.3**	**11.9**
1991	201	259	43.0	6.0	266	14.4	5.10	218	223	2.3	17.5
1990	191	234	35.4	6.6	242	12.0	5.10	201	207	2.5	14.4
1989	179	235	34.1	6.9	243	12.1	6.05	203	209	2.9	14.6
1988	178	224	34.7	6.5	231	9.1	6.05	191	197	3.1	10.9
1987	144	206	26.5	7.8	212	8.0	6.05	180	186	3.3	9.6
1986	145	203	30.4	6.7	209	8.2	6.08	172	179	3.4	10.0
1985	141	192	28.6	6.7	199	8.6	6.10	164	170	3.6	10.4
1984	129	179	25.0	7.2	186	8.9	6.12	155	161	3.8	10.8
1983	115	169	24.9	6.8	176	9.1	6.14	145	152	4.1	11.1

Data as orig. reptd. **1.** Excludes discontinued operations. **2.** Bef. results of disc. opers. in 1985, 1984. **3.** Reflects acctg. change.

Business Summary

National Presto produces and distributes electrical appliances and housewares, including comfort appliances, pressure cookers and canners, private label and premium sales products. It also manufactures defense products on a contract basis, although no production contracts were currently in effect.

Electrical appliances and houseware products consist of pressure cookers and canners; the Presto Control Master single thermostatic control line of fry pans, griddles and combination griddle/warmers, and multi-purpose cookers; deep fryers of various sizes; food processors; can openers; slicer/shredders; curly cutters; ice cream makers; electric shoe polishers; resistance type heaters; corn poppers; coffeemakers; electric tea kettles; electric knife sharpeners; and timers.

In 1992, about 52% of revenues (37% in 1991) was derived from cast products such as frypans, griddles, deep fryers and electric cookers, while 23% (44%) was provided by motorized nonthermal appliances consisting of food processors, can openers, slicer/shredders, curly cutters, ice cream makers, knife sharpeners and shoe polishers.

Sales to Wal-Mart Stores accounted for 31% of revenues in 1992 (24% in 1991) and sales to Kmart 14% (20%).

In the area of defense products, the company has manufactured 105MM projectiles, as well as 8" projectiles, but NPK's standby contract was not renewed after its September 1992 expiration. The company received a storage only contract, which expires in September 1993, and NPK felt that the storage contract would not be extended past that time.

Dividend Data

Dividends have been paid since 1945. Since 1989, directors have been declaring one lump sum annual dividend rather than four quarterly payments; an annual dividend of $1.80 for 1993 was paid in late 1992. Extra dividend payments have also been made since 1989. Payments in the past 12 months:

Amt of Divd. $	Date Decl.	Ex–divd. Date	Stock of Record	Payment Date
1.80	Dec. 4	Dec. 8	Dec. 14	Dec. 28'92
0.75 Ext.	Dec. 4	Dec. 8	Dec. 14	Dec. 28'92

Capitalization

Long Term Debt: $5,103,000 (4/4/93) of 10% senior debs., due Jan. 1996, & conv. into com. at a price based on average daily stock prices for a specified period.

Common Stock: 7,334,001 shs. ($1 par).
Officers & directors control about 30%.
Institutions hold about 50%.
Shareholders of record: 1,445 (12/92).

Office—3925 North Hastings Way, Eau Claire, WI 54703-3703. **Tel**—(715) 839-2121. **Chrmn & CEO**—Melvin S. Cohen. **Pres, CFO & Investor Contact**—Maryjo Cohen. **Secy**—J. F. Bartl. **Dirs**—J. H. Berney, Maryjo Cohen, Melvin S. Cohen, W. G. Ryberg, J. M. Sirianni, R. Strangis. **Transfer Agent & Registrar**—Harris Trust and Savings Bank, Chicago. **Incorporated** in Wisconsin in 1905. **Empl**—609.

 Michael W. Jaffe

Nellcor Inc.

NASDAQ Symbol NELL (Incl. in Nat'l Market) Options on NYSE, Pacific In S&P MidCap 400

Price	Range	P-E Ratio	Dividend	Yield	S&P Ranking	Beta
Sep. 8'93	1993					
20	34¼–17½	13	None	None	NR	1.62

Summary

Nellcor makes and markets electronic patient-monitoring instruments for use primarily in hospital critical-care units. Although higher revenues and earnings are anticipated for fiscal 1994, delays in the receipt of FDA approval for a fetal oximeter and other product line extensions could restrict the rate of sales and earnings growth in coming quarters.

Current Outlook

Earnings for fiscal 1994 are estimated at $1.75 a share, up from fiscal 1993's $1.50.

Initiation of cash dividends is not expected.

Net revenue growth in fiscal 1994 is expected to exceed 10%, reflecting continuing strength in the oximetry business and contributions from product line extensions, such as the N-20 portable oximeter. Increases in the installed base of monitors compatible with the Nellcor's sensor products will provide much of the top-line growth. The company, which relies on new products and product line extensions to fuel revenue gains, is currently awaiting FDA marketing approval for a new fetal oximeter. Dealys in the receipt of approval for product line extensions and for the fetal oximeter could restrict the rate of sales and earnings growth in coming quarters. Long-term prospects remain strong, as the company continues to develop safe, important products for the healthcare industry.

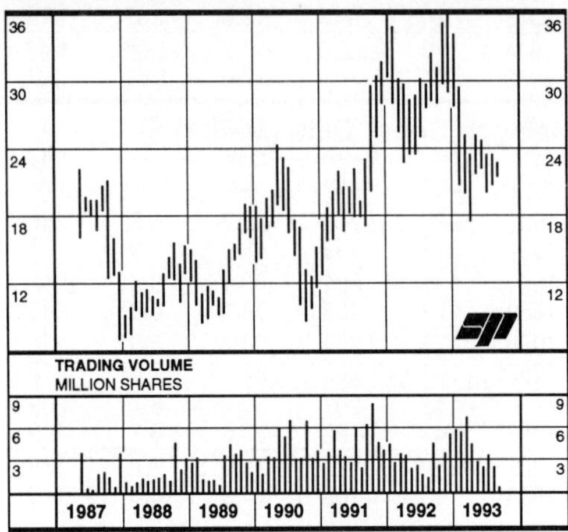

Net Revenues (Million $)

13 Weeks:	1992–93	1991–92	1990–91	1989–90
Sep.	48.6	40.9	34.3	30.3
Dec.	54.0	48.2	[1]40.5	34.0
Mar.	56.2	52.9	41.6	38.5
Jun.	59.4	54.2	42.5	39.8
	218.2	196.2	158.9	142.6

Based on a preliminary report, net revenues in the fiscal year ended July 4, 1993, advanced 11% from those of the preceding year, reflecting continued strength in the oximetry business. Gross margins (as a percentage of revenues) declined modestly, but operating expenses rose less rapidly, and pretax income climbed 19%. After taxes at 38.5%, versus 38.0%, net income was up 18%, to $25,120,000 ($1.50 a share), from $21,293,000 ($1.31).

Common Share Earnings ($)

13 Weeks:	1992–93	1991–92	1990–91	1989–90
Sep.	0.29	0.23	0.17	0.17
Dec.	0.35	0.29	[1]0.20	0.23
Mar.	0.41	0.36	0.31	0.28
Jun.	0.45	0.42	0.36	0.28
	1.50	1.31	1.05	0.96

Important Developments

Aug. '93— FDA marketing approval was received for the Nellcor Stat Cap, a carbon dioxide detection device. Earlier, in July, the FDA notified the company that its N-400 fetal oximeter would be reviewed under Premarket Approval (PMA) Application regulations, requiring clinical studies under Investigational Device Exemption regulatory procedures. Nellcor requested a meeting with the FDA to clarify the agency's position and define steps required to file a PMA for the oximeter.

Next earnings report expected in mid-October.

Per Share Data ($)

Yr. End Jun. 30	1993	[2]1992	1991	1990	1989	1988	1987	1986
Tangible Bk. Val.	**NA**	8.98	7.79	6.47	5.34	4.75	3.99	0.42
Cash Flow	**NA**	1.79	1.62	1.40	0.93	1.02	0.90	0.55
Earnings[3]	**1.50**	1.31	1.05	0.96	0.56	0.73	0.68	0.51
Dividends	**Nil**	Nil	Nil	Nil	Nil	Nil	Nil	Nil
Payout Ratio	**Nil**	Nil	Nil	Nil	Nil	Nil	Nil	Nil
Prices[4]—High	**36**	35⅞	31¾	24⅜	19⅛	15⅝	22¼	NA
Low	**22¾**	22¾	12¾	8⅝	8½	7¼	7	NA
P/E Ratio—	**24–15**	27–17	30–12	25–9	34–15	21–10	33–10	NA

Data as orig. reptd. Adj. for stk. div. of 100% Aug. 1986. **1.** 14 wks. **2.** Refl. merger or acq. **3.** Bef. spec. item(s) of +0.25 in 1986. **4.** Cal. yr. NA-Not Available.

Income Data (Million $)

Year Ended Jun. 30	Revs.	Oper. Inc.	% Oper. Inc. of Revs.	Cap. Exp.	Depr.	Int. Exp.	Net Bef. Taxes	Eff. Tax Rate	[2]Net Inc.	% Net Inc. of Revs.	Cash Flow
[1]1992	**196**	**38.9**	**19.8**	**12.6**	**7.90**	**Nil**	**34.3**	**38.0%**	**21.3**	**10.9**	**29.2**
1991	159	32.6	20.5	7.4	8.72	Nil	25.8	37.0%	16.3	10.2	25.0
[1]1990	143	26.4	18.5	11.5	6.67	Nil	22.9	37.0%	14.4	10.1	21.1
1989	119	15.9	13.4	8.7	5.31	NM	12.8	37.0%	8.1	6.8	13.4
1988	96	19.3	20.2	6.8	4.20	0.02	17.0	38.0%	10.5	11.0	14.7
1987	81	19.7	24.3	7.1	2.86	NM	17.5	49.0%	8.9	11.0	11.8
1986	46	13.1	28.3	3.9	1.47	0.11	12.2	47.5%	6.4	13.9	7.0

Balance Sheet Data (Million $)

Jun. 30	Cash	Curr. Assets	Curr. Liab.	Curr. Ratio	Total Assets	% Ret. on Assets	Long Term Debt	Common Equity	Total Cap.	% LT Debt of Cap.	% Ret. on Equity
1992	**82.6**	**142**	**33.6**	**4.2**	**189**	**12.6**	**Nil**	**154**	**155**	**Nil**	**15.2**
1991	68.3	117	20.6	5.7	143	12.1	Nil	121	122	Nil	14.6
1990	43.5	95	22.3	4.3	121	13.3	0.67	98	99	0.7	16.2
1989	35.6	75	14.8	5.0	90	9.3	Nil	76	76	Nil	11.3
1988	34.9	69	16.1	4.3	81	14.0	Nil	65	65	Nil	17.5
1987	35.0	59	14.3	4.1	68	10.3	0.03	54	54	0.1	30.0
1986	10.6	26	9.4	2.8	31	27.9	0.54	2	22	2.5	NA

Data as orig. reptd. **1.** Refl. merger or acq. **2.** Bef. spec. items. NM-Not Meaningful. NA-Not Available.

Business Summary

Nellcor Incorporated manufactures electronic monitoring instruments and related sensors and airway adapters for patient safety and management throughout the hospital, in emergency care and in the home. The company's products are marketed principally to critical-care units of larger hospitals.

The company's N-200 and N-180 pulse oximeters provide continuous noninvasive measurement of a patient's arterial blood oxygen saturation. Monitoring of this factor is necessary because, left untreated, a severe lack of blood oxygen can cause permanent brain damage or death within minutes. The N-200 product line features Nellcor's proprietary C-LOCK ECG synchronization system, which allows the monitor to improve performance by distinguishing true arterial pulses from motion artifact, as well as by improving signal quality in patients with weak pulses. The company's OXINET pulse oximetry network permits remote monitoring of multiple patients from a central location.

In March 1988, Nellcor began commercial shipments of the N-1000 multifunction monitor, which contains an advanced capnograph to monitor a patient's respiratory gas for carbon dioxide, a pulse oximeter and a nitrous oxide monitoring function. The company's N-2500 anesthesia safety monitor combines an N-1000 monitor with an anesthetic agent analyzer, which may assist medical practitioners in reducing the risk of agent overdose or administration of an inappropriate agent.

The company also produces the N-10 portable pulse oximeter, as well as a variety of disposable and reusable sensors and airway adapters used in conjunction with its monitors. Nellcor's oximetry sensors can also be used with instruments produced under license from the company, and with multiparameter monitors that incorporate Nellcor's OEM module.

Nellcor's EdenTec Corp. subsidiary (acquired in September 1991 for $8.9 million), specializes in infant and adult apnea monitors and diagnostic systems for the home and hospital markets. Through the acquisition of substantially all of the assets of Fenem Inc. (purchased in September 1991 for $8.75 million) the company gained the rights to manufacture and market Fenem's EASY CAP product, a disposable end-tidal carbon dioxide detector used in emergency departments, hospital resuscitation units and ambulances.

Europe accounted for 13% of total revenues, and for operating profit of $651,000, in fiscal 1992.

Dividend Data

No cash has been paid.

Finances

In September 1992, the company filed an action in U.S. District Court for a declaratory judgment against Camino Labs., seeking a judgment that a patent awarded to Camino covering a transducer calibration system is invalid and not infringed by Nellcor. Camino said it would file a counter suit, seeking damages and an injunction prohibiting further infringement by the company.

In its May 1987 initial public stock offering, Nellcor sold 1,600,000 common shares at $16 each.

Capitalization

Long Term Debt: None (7/93).

Common Stock: 16,638,781 shs. ($0.001 par).
Institutions own 82%.
Shareholders: About 786 of record (7/92).

Options: To purchase 2,260,813 shs. at $7.88 to $32.00 ea. (7/5/92).

Office—25495 Whitesell St., Hayward, CA 94545. **Tel**—(510) 887-5858. **Pres & CEO**—C. R. Larkin, Jr. **EVP & COO**—D. L. Schlotterbeck. **VP-Fin, CFO & Investor Contact**—M. P. Downey. **Secy**—Laureen DeBuono. **Dirs**—R. J. Glaser, F. M. Grafton, D. L. Hammond, C. R. Larkin, Jr., W. J. McNerney, E. E. van Bronkhorst. **Transfer Agent & Registrar**—First National Bank of Boston. **Incorporated** in Delaware in 1986. **Empl**—1,512.

 Samuel A. Dedio

Network Systems

NASDAQ Symbol NSCO (Incl. in Nat'l Market) Options on ASE In S&P MidCap 400

Price	Range	P-E Ratio	Dividend	Yield	S&P Ranking	Beta
Aug. 11'93	1993					
7¾	13½–6⅞	NM	None	None	B–	1.19

Summary

This company designs, manufactures and services high-performance data communications equipment and software, mostly for mainframe computers. Sales and earnings declined in the first half of 1993, and the company's CEO recently resigned to join another concern. In May, NSCO completed the acquisition of Bus-Tech, a maker of interconnect controllers.

Business Summary

Network Systems makes and services high-performance data communications equipment that connects a variety of large computers, peripherals and local or wide area networks. Revenues in recent years were derived as follows:

	1992	1991	1990
Products	70%	72%	71%
Services....................	30%	28%	29%

International sales accounted for 42% of revenues in 1992 and 44% in 1991.

Networking products are sold as both separate units and as components of packaged networking solutions, and utilize software and four hardware platforms: HYPERchannel-DX and DXE; Series 6600 single-board internetworking routers; switches that connect to High-Performance Parallel Interface (HIPPI) computer input/output channels; and Vitalink's TransLAN, TransRing, and TransPATH internetworking products. Services include maintenance, training and development of custom networking applications.

In 1992, the bulk of the the company's product revenues were generated by the HYPERchannel-DX platform, a proprietary networking protocol that provides high-speed communications between various types of computers at speeds up to 50 million bits per second. Each HYPERchannel-DX adapter has a nucleus processor, a large high-speed memory capability, a 400 or 800 million-bits-per-second backplane, and interfaces to various computers, media, networking protocols and peripherals. NSCO provides interface boards that allow for a variety of networking configurations, including boards that interface with mainframe computers made by IBM, Amdahl, Unisys and Cray. The DXE platform was introduced at the beginning of 1993 and is expected to gradually replace the DX.

The Series 6600 single-board multi-protocol bridge routers are configured for specific internetworking applications such as the interconnection of ethernet networks. HIPPI switches allow data transmission at 800 million bits per second and provide up to 32 ports for connectivity to supercomputers, workstations, storage devices, and other peripheral devices.

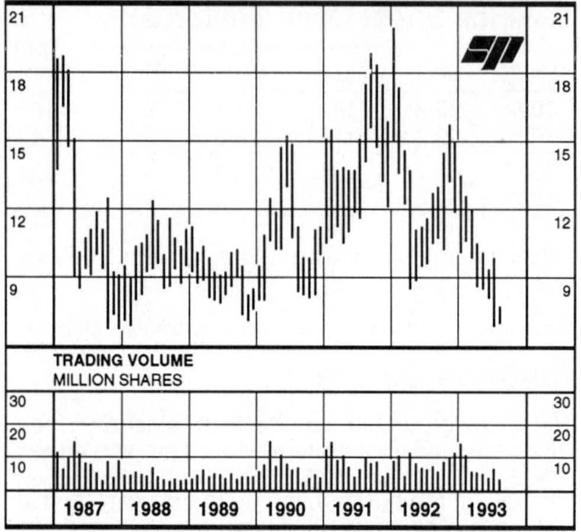

The Vitalink subsidiary (acquired in June 1991) provides products that interconnect local area networks (LANs), including TransLAN, which allows interconnection of ethernet LANs, and TransRING, which facilitates interconnection of Token-Ring LANs. TransPATH products provide routing services between ethernet LANs.

Important Developments

Jul. '93— NSCO president and CEO Michael Fitzpatrick resigned to join Pacific Bell.

May '93— The company completed the acquisition of Bus-Tech, a Burlington, Mass.-based maker of interconnect controllers, for $24.5 million.

Next earnings report expected in late October.

Per Share Data ($)

Yr. End Dec. 31	1992	[1]1991	1990	1989	1988	1987	1986	1985	1984	1983
Tangible Bk. Val.	**7.57**	[2]9.09	8.38	7.53	6.93	6.56	5.87	5.20	3.80	3.16
Cash Flow	**d0.85**	0.85	1.08	0.81	0.60	0.83	0.76	0.67	0.61	0.40
Earnings	**d1.31**	0.50	0.74	0.59	0.39	0.60	0.62	0.59	0.56	0.37
Dividends	**Nil**	Nil	Nil	Nil	Nil	Nil	Nil	Nil	Nil	Nil
Payout Ratio	**Nil**	Nil	Nil	Nil	Nil	Nil	Nil	Nil	Nil	Nil
Prices—High	**20**	18⅞	15¼	11¼	12⅜	18¾	20⅜	27⅜	23¼	28⅝
Low	**8½**	10½	8	7⅛	6⅞	6¾	10⅛	16⅛	12⅝	13½
P/E Ratio—	**NM**	38–21	21–11	19–12	32–18	31–11	33–16	46–27	41–23	78–37

Data as orig. reptd. Adj. for stk. divs. of 25% Apr. 1985, 100% Apr. 1983. **1.** Refl. merger or acq. **2.** Incl. intangibles. d-Deficit. NM-Not Meaningful.

Income Data (Million $)

Year Ended Dec. 31	Revs.	Oper. Inc.	% Oper. Inc. of Revs.	Cap. Exp.	Depr.	Int. Exp.	Net Bef. Taxes	Eff. Tax Rate	Net Inc.	% Net Inc. of Revs.	Cash Flow
1992	**219**	**32.6**	**14.9**	**14.1**	**13.8**	**1.29**	**d34.1**	**NM**	**d39.7**	**NM**	**d25.9**
[1]1991	199	27.8	14.0	13.8	11.0	1.24	23.4	35.0%	15.2	7.7	26.2
1990	164	32.5	19.9	13.5	10.1	0.89	34.0	35.4%	22.0	13.4	32.1
1989	145	24.2	16.7	7.1	6.7	0.68	27.4	36.8%	17.3	12.0	24.0
1988	131	17.5	13.3	8.5	6.4	0.61	18.2	37.4%	11.4	8.6	17.7
1987	121	30.3	25.1	7.1	6.7	0.43	28.9	39.6%	17.5	14.5	24.2
1986	109	29.7	27.3	9.2	4.0	0.44	31.3	42.5%	[2]18.0	16.6	22.0
1985	90	26.2	29.0	10.6	2.5	0.29	30.0	43.2%	17.1	18.9	19.6
1984	71	22.9	32.2	5.1	1.5	0.07	27.4	43.0%	15.6	21.9	17.1
1983	47	12.5	26.7	1.6	1.0	0.07	17.3	42.0%	10.0	21.3	11.1

Balance Sheet Data (Million $)

		Curr.									
Dec. 31	Cash	Assets	Liab.	Ratio	Total Assets	% Ret. on Assets	Long Term Debt	Common Equity	Total Cap.	% LT Debt of Cap.	% Ret. on Equity
1992	**58**	**148**	**45.2**	**3.3**	**293**	**NM**	**1.00**	**230**	**231**	**0.4**	**NM**
1991	69	173	44.6	3.9	343	4.7	2.82	274	280	1.0	5.8
1990	99	179	29.6	6.0	293	7.9	2.86	246	252	1.1	9.4
1989	97	172	25.8	6.7	264	6.9	2.89	220	226	1.3	8.2
1988	114	201	17.6	11.4	240	4.9	2.92	202	210	1.4	5.8
1987	102	188	18.6	10.1	219	8.4	2.95	191	199	1.5	9.6
1986	88	168	17.0	9.9	194	9.8	2.98	171	177	1.7	11.2
1985	75	155	19.2	8.1	173	11.4	1.00	150	153	0.7	13.1
1984	53	110	14.9	7.4	119	14.4	Nil	104	105	Nil	16.5
1983	59	90	10.0	9.0	97	13.9	0.06	86	87	0.1	15.7

Data as orig. reptd. **1.** Refl. merger or acq. **2.** Refl. acctg. change d-Deficit. NM-Not Meaningful.

Total Revenues (Million $)

Quarter:	1993	1992	1991	1990
Mar.	46.1	48.7	33.6	35.7
Jun.	49.1	54.2	45.4	40.4
Sep.		57.3	54.4	40.0
Dec.		58.9	65.3	47.5
		219.1	198.7	163.6

Total revenues in the six months ended June 30, 1993, fell 7.5%, year to year, as product revenues declined 10%, and service revenues were off 1.8%. Gross margins narrowed and operating costs fell only 4.2%. Despite the absence of a $1.6 million charge for amortization of intangibles, and higher net interest income, pretax income fell 17%. After taxes at 36.8%, versus 38.8%, net income declined 14%, to $4,706,000 ($0.16 a share), from $5,482,000 ($0.18).

Common Share Earnings ($)

Quarter:	1993	1992	1991	1990
Mar.	0.08	0.06	0.07	0.13
Jun.	0.08	0.12	0.09	0.18
Sep.		0.16	0.16	0.18
Dec.		d1.65	0.18	0.25
		d1.31	0.50	0.74

Dividend Data

No cash has been paid.

Finances

In February 1993, directors authorized the repurchase of up to 1.5 million Network Systems common shares.

Research and development expenditures equaled 11.4% of revenues in 1992 (10.8% in 1991).

In the 1992 fourth quarter, a restructuring charge of $60.3 million was recorded to write down the entire remaining goodwill and other intangible assets related to the acquisition of Vitalink Communications. Share earnings in the fourth quarter would have been $0.20 without the charge.

In June 1991, Network Systems acquired Vitalink Communications Corp. for a total price, including related costs, of $164 million.

Capitalization

Long Term Debt: $1,000,000 (6/93).

Common Stock: 30,063,151 shs. ($0.02 par).
Institutions hold 74%.
Shareholders: About 1,890 of record (3/93).

Options: To buy 2,682,525 shs. at an avg. price of $10.72 a sh. (12/92).

d-Deficit.

Office—7600 Boone Ave. North, Minneapolis, MN 55428. **Tel**—(612) 424-4888. **Chrmn**—L. D. Altman. **CFO**—Michael Ashby. **VP & Secy**—M. Reid. **Dirs**—L. D. Altman, E. F. Barth, D. W. Feddersen, M. J. Fitzpatrick, D. J. Haggerty, J. E. Thornton. **Transfer Agent & Registrar**—Norwest Bank, Minneapolis. **Incorporated** in Delaware in 1974. **Empl**—1,359.

 Neeraj K. Vohra

Neutrogena Corp.

NASDAQ Symbol NGNA (Incl. in Nat'l Market) Options on Phila In S&P MidCap 400

Price	Range	P-E Ratio	Dividend	Yield	S&P Ranking	Beta
Sep. 22'93	1993					
17½	24½–14¼	21	0.24	1.4%	A–	1.55

Summary

Neutrogena makes and sells high-quality, premium-priced specialty skin-care and hair-care products. Although earnings declined in the first nine months of fiscal 1993, reflecting sluggish worldwide economies, a shift in product mix, and a change in the timing of advertising and promotional campaigns, the company expects improved sales and earnings for the full year. The repurchase of up to 1,000,000 common shares was recently authorized. The family of the chairman controls 45% of the common stock.

Business Summary

Neutrogena Corporation makes and sells high-quality specialty soaps, skin-care products and hair-care products, some of which are used to aid in treating dermatological conditions. Its products are, with one exception, nonprescription items that are sold in drugstores, mass-volume retail stores, food/combination stores, wholesale membership stores, department stores and other retail outlets throughout the U.S. and abroad. Sales by product line in recent fiscal years were:

	1992	1991	1990
Skin–care products......	73%	68%	70%
Hair–care products......	27%	32%	30%

International sales (including U.S. exports) contributed 25% of the total in fiscal 1992, up from 20% the year before and 15% in fiscal 1990. The company sells its products in more than 50 countries, with nearly 80% of international sales generated in England, France, Spain and Germany in fiscal 1992.

Neutrogena's skin-care products include premium-priced soaps specifically formulated to be mild and suitable for normal, sensitive and problem skin. Its line of scented and unscented soaps includes Original Formula, Dry Skin Formula, Baby Cleansing Formula, Cleansing Bar for Acne-prone Skin, Oily Skin Formula, Cleansing Wash and Liquid Neutrogena, an extra-mild facial cleaner.

Other skin-care products include Norwegian Formula Hand Cream, Norwegian Formula Emulsion for longer-lasting moisturization, Rainbath Shower and Bath Gel, Body Lotion, Paba-Free Sunblock (in SPF 8, 15 and 30), Moisture, Moisture SPF 15, Eye Cream, Night Cream, Lip Moisturizer, Drying Gel for Acne-prone Skin, Acne Mask and Cleansing Wash. The skin-care line also contains dermatological products, such as Melanex

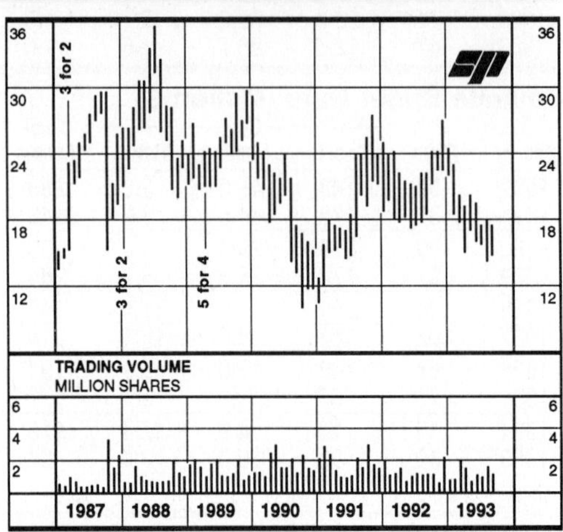

Topical Solution, a prescription item used as an aid in the removal of dark skin spots; Vehicle/N and Vehicle/N Mild; and T/Derm Tar Emollient.

Hair-care products include Neutrogena Shampoo and Neutrogena Conditioner formulated for everyday use; Neutrogena T/Gel Therapeutic Shampoo and Neutrogena T/Gel Conditioner, which are used as aids in the treatment of scalp psoriasis, dandruff and seborrheic dermatitis; and T-Sal Shampoo, for the relief of recurring crusty scalp buildup.

In fiscal 1992, the largest customer accounted for 11% of Neutrogena's sales.

Important Developments

Aug. '93— Neutrogena said it expects strong results in the fiscal 1993 fourth quarter, as well as improved sales and earnings for the full year.

Next earnings report expected in mid-December.

Per Share Data ($)

Yr. End Oct. 31	1992	1991	1990	1989	1988	1987	1986	1985	1984	1983
Tangible Bk. Val.	**[3]4.72**	[3]4.04	[3]3.44	[3]3.00	2.24	1.46	1.01	0.70	0.46	0.40
Cash Flow	**1.08**	0.97	0.79	1.10	0.94	0.62	0.35	0.28	0.20	0.15
Earnings	**0.90**	0.80	0.65	1.00	0.85	0.55	0.30	0.24	[1]0.17	0.12
Dividends	**0.220**	0.200	0.200	0.160	0.113	0.056	0.040	0.033	0.024	0.018
Payout Ratio	**24%**	25%	31%	16%	10%	9%	18%	13%	14%	14%
Prices[2]—High	**27**	27½	29¼	29¾	35⅝	29⅝	15½	10	6⅛	3¼
Low	**17¼**	10½	10	20¾	18¼	11⅝	7⅜	5	2⅞	2¼
P/E Ratio—	**30–19**	34–13	45–15	30–21	42–23	53–24	51–31	42–21	37–18	26–19

Data as orig. reptd. Adj. for stk. divs. 25% Apr. 1989, 50% Jan. 1988, 50% Mar. 1987, 50% Jan. 1986, 50% Jan. 1985, 100% Jan. 1984. **1.** Ful. dil: 0.16. **2.** Cal. yr. **3.** Incl. intangibles.

Income Data (Million $)

Year Ended Oct. 31	Revs.	Oper. Inc.	% Oper. Inc. of Revs.	Cap. Exp.	Depr.	Int. Exp.	Net Bef. Taxes	Eff. Tax Rate	Net Inc.	% Net Inc. of Revs.	Cash Flow
1992	**267**	**41.1**	**15.4**	**6.6**	**5.03**	**Nil**	**37.8**	**36.5%**	**24.0**	**9.0**	**29.1**
1991	231	34.8	15.1	3.5	4.57	Nil	32.8	35.0%	21.3	9.2	25.9
1990	210	30.0	14.3	9.8	3.91	Nil	28.7	40.0%	17.2	8.2	21.1
1989	203	45.6	22.4	16.4	2.81	Nil	44.6	40.0%	26.7	13.2	29.6
1988	179	40.2	22.5	16.2	2.35	Nil	38.9	40.8%	23.0	12.9	25.4
1987	135	28.8	21.3	6.9	1.71	Nil	28.3	47.3%	14.9	11.0	16.6
1986	96	16.9	17.6	3.7	1.33	Nil	16.4	50.6%	8.1	8.5	9.5
1985	75	12.7	17.0	4.6	1.13	Nil	11.8	47.5%	6.2	8.3	7.4
1984	59	8.8	14.9	2.4	0.82	Nil	8.2	48.3%	4.2	7.1	5.1
1983	46	6.7	14.6	1.4	0.63	Nil	6.1	48.2%	3.2	7.0	3.8

Balance Sheet Data (Million $)

Oct. 31	Cash	Curr. Assets	Curr. Liab.	Curr. Ratio	Total Assets	% Ret. on Assets	Long Term Debt	Common Equity	Total Cap.	% LT Debt of Cap.	% Ret. on Equity
1992	**48.5**	**124**	**53.0**	**2.3**	**181**	**14.1**	**Nil**	**124**	**126**	**Nil**	**20.8**
1991	54.7	110	49.6	2.2	160	14.6	Nil	106	109	Nil	21.7
1990	32.2	81	38.4	2.1	132	13.4	Nil	90	92	Nil	20.3
1989	35.7	80	44.3	1.8	125	24.6	Nil	78	80	Nil	39.0
1988	21.8	61	31.7	1.9	93	28.2	Nil	59	60	Nil	47.5
1987	22.8	53	31.5	1.7	71	25.2	Nil	38	39	Nil	46.2
1986	12.5	35	20.3	1.7	47	20.1	Nil	26	27	Nil	36.2
1985	5.3	23	14.3	1.6	33	22.3	Nil	19	19	Nil	40.4
1984	0.6	15	9.9	1.6	22	19.9	Nil	12	13	Nil	37.3
1983	4.2	15	9.3	1.6	20	19.3	Nil	10	11	Nil	35.6

Data as orig. reptd.

Net Sales (Million $)

Quarter:	1992–93	1991–92	1990–91	1989–90
Jan.	70.3	64.0	56.4	55.0
Apr.	66.6	63.3	57.2	46.6
Jul.	61.7	62.9	56.2	52.2
Oct.		77.2	61.5	56.0
		267.5	231.3	209.8

For the nine months ended July 31, 1993, net sales advanced 4.3%, year to year (despite a 2.0% decline in the third quarter), as the introduction of new products domestically outweighed reduced volume for existing products and the discontinuance of two products. Margins narrowed on a shift in sales mix and a change in the timing of advertising and promotional campaigns (although third quarter operating margins benefited from the timing change and continuing cost controls); income dropped 13%, to $14,383,000 ($0.54 a share), from $16,560,000 ($0.62). Results in the fiscal 1993 period exclude a credit of $0.04 a share from an accounting change.

Common Share Earnings ($)

Quarter:	1992–93	1991–92	1990–91	1989–90
Jan.	0.17	0.23	0.20	0.33
Apr.	0.14	0.16	0.14	0.05
Jul.	0.23	0.23	0.28	0.15
Oct.		0.28	0.18	0.12
		0.90	0.80	0.65

Dividend Data

Cash has been paid each year since 1976. In July 1990, directors adopted a shareholder rights plan. The most recent annual cash payment was:

Amt. of Divd. $	Date Decl.	Ex–divd. Date	Stock of Record	Payment Date
0.24	Dec. 3	Dec. 14	Dec. 18	Jan. 8'93

Finances

In August 1993, directors authorized the repurchase of up to 1,000,000 common shares. A December 1989 program to buy 1,000,000 shares has been completed.

In August 1992, a major customer (3% of fiscal 1992 sales) filed for Chapter 11 bankruptcy protection. Based on information available, Neutrogena believed that it was adequately reserved for any potential uncollectible amounts resulting from the bankruptcy.

Capitalization

Long Term Debt: None (7/93).

Common Stock: 25,895,050 shs. ($0.001 par). The Cotsen family owns or controls 45%. Institutions hold 26%. Shareholders: 2,711 of record (12/92).

Options: To buy 1,954,695 shs. at $2.39 to $26.40 ea. (10/92).

Office—5760 West 96th St., Los Angeles, CA 90045. **Tel**—(310) 642-1150. **Chrmn & CEO**—L. E. Cotsen. **Pres & COO**—A. H. Kurtzman. **SVP, CFO & Investor Contact**—Donald R. Schort. **VP, Secy & Treas**—D. Lewin. **Dirs**—R. E. Cape, L. E. Cotsen, C. M. Diker, S. Dworkin, C. L. Firestein, K. Lipper, R. A. McCabe, J. R. McManus. **Transfer Agent & Registrar**—U.S. Stock Transfer, Glendale, CA. **Incorporated** in California in 1962; reincorporated in Delaware in 1988. **Empl**—751.

 Michael W. Jaffe

Nevada Power

NYSE Symbol NVP In S&P MidCap 400

Price	Range	P-E Ratio	Dividend	Yield	S&P Ranking	Beta
Aug. 12'93	1993					
25¾	25¾–22⅝	15	1.60	6.2%	B+	0.40

Summary

This electric utility serves the gaming and tourist economy of Las Vegas. NVP is in the midst of a significantly expanded construction program designed to meet expected continued growth in its service territory. While the regulatory environment has been harsh in the past, the company received a final order for a rate increase of $22.2 million (about 87% of its adjusted request) in August 1992.

Current Outlook

Share earnings for 1993 are projected at $1.65, up from the $1.47 reported for 1992, which includes a $0.13 writeoff of certain deferred amounts that are not likely to be recovered. Share earnings could rise to $1.70 in 1994.

The $0.40 quarterly dividend cannot be considered secure.

Share earnings for 1993 may benefit from higher kwh sales (aided by strong off-system sales in the first quarter) and cost controls, partially offset by higher interest cost and more shares outstanding due to needed construction financings. Share earnings for 1994 should reflect possibly higher kwh sales and cost controls, partially offset by higher interest cost and more shares outstanding. Share earnings in either year could benefit from the reversal of part or all of a $0.46 a share charge taken in 1990 to account for a proposed regulatory order disallowing energy costs arising from the 1985 outage at the Mohave plant.

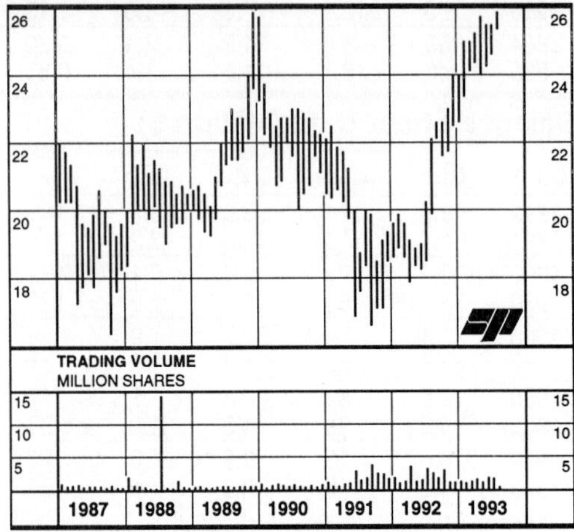

Operating Revenues (Million $)

Quarter:	1993	1992	1991	1990
Mar.	132.8	118.1	109.4	93.8
Jun.	142.3	139.0	121.9	112.1
Sep.	---	204.1	184.4	169.7
Dec.	---	125.6	123.1	105.4
	---	586.9	538.8	481.0

Revenues for the six months to June 30, 1993, rose 4.3%, year to year. Operating costs rose 1.9%, and operating income was up 21%. After higher construction-related credits, which more than offset higher interest expense, net income was up 93%, to $0.57 a share on 9.7% more shares, from $0.29.

Common Share Earnings ($)

Quarter:	1993	[1]1992	[1]1991	1990
Mar.	0.20	0.02	d0.02	0.14
Jun.	0.37	0.26	0.11	0.20
Sep.	E1.05	1.15	0.94	1.09
Dec.	E0.03	0.01	d0.02	d0.65
	E1.65	1.47	1.05	0.78

Important Developments

Aug. '93— The company announced that it plans to construct two 500 kV transmission lines in order to improve the reliability of its system and gain access to economical power from other states. Called the Marketplace-Allen Transmission (MAT) Project, it would be initially owned by NVP and the Los Angeles Department of Water and Power. If approved, the total cost of the 53-mile project would be approximately $121 million. The MAT project could be operational by 1998. In June, NVP sold publicly 2.7 million common shares at $25.125 each. In January, the company filed a request with the Public Service Commission of Nevada (PSCN) to recover energy costs of $46.2 million. The proposed increase represents a 7.9% overall hike in revenues. If approved as submitted, the hike would have no effect on the company's earnings.

Next earnings report expected in early November.

Per Share Data ($)

Yr. End Dec. 31	1992	1991	1990	1989	1988	1987	1986	1985	1984	1983
Tangible Bk. Val.	**13.65**	13.58	13.60	13.87	13.58	13.25	12.58	12.21	11.87	11.58
Earnings	**1.47**	1.05	0.78	1.81	1.78	2.01	1.71	1.62	1.62	1.37
Dividends	**1.60**	1.60	1.58	1.54	1.50	1.46	1.43	1.40	1.37	1.34
Payout Ratio	**109%**	152%	203%	85%	84%	73%	84%	86%	85%	98%
Prices—High	**24**	22½	25¾	25⅞	22¼	22	25¼	16⅞	14⅝	15
Low	**17⅞**	16⅝	20	19¼	18⅜	16⅜	16	13⅝	10⅞	12½
P/E Ratio—	**16-12**	21-16	33-26	14-11	13-10	11-8	15-9	10-8	9-7	11-9

Data as orig. reptd. Adj. for stk. div(s). of 100% Aug. 1986. **1.** Quarterly earns. do not add due to changes in no. of shs. outstanding. d-Deficit. E-Estimated.

Income Data (Million $)

Year Ended Dec. 31	Revs.	Depr.	Maint.	Oper. Ratio	[1]Fxd. Chgs. Cover.	Constr. Credits	Eff. Tax Rate	Net Inc.	% Return On Revs.	[2]Invest. Capital	Com. Equity
1992	**587**	**39.5**	**37.9**	**82.9%**	**2.80**	**12.5**	**34.0%**	**56.8**	**9.7**	**7.6**	**10.6**
1991	539	35.1	47.9	85.6%	2.13	9.0	29.9%	35.2	6.5	6.7	7.5
1990	481	31.0	48.9	84.7%	2.10	10.4	25.4%	25.0	5.2	6.2	5.6
1989	418	27.8	43.9	81.6%	2.79	6.0	27.5%	51.5	12.3	9.0	12.8
1988	409	27.3	40.5	82.0%	3.02	4.5	29.2%	50.2	12.3	9.1	12.9
1987	375	25.9	37.8	79.7%	3.56	6.6	36.3%	56.1	15.0	10.4	15.1
1986	383	24.8	35.7	81.4%	3.03	5.2	37.8%	47.4	12.4	10.3	13.4
1985	361	24.0	32.0	80.9%	3.02	3.5	39.3%	44.1	12.2	10.2	13.1
1984	318	23.4	27.2	78.6%	2.99	4.4	40.5%	42.9	13.5	10.7	13.4
1983	306	23.8	27.6	82.1%	2.34	9.7	35.1%	35.5	11.6	10.4	12.0

Balance Sheet Data (Million $)

Dec. 31	Gross Prop.	Capital Expend.	Net Prop.	% Earn. on Net Prop.	Total Cap.	LT Debt	% LT Debt	Capitalization Pfd.	% Pfd.	Com.	% Com.
1992	**1,740**	**171**	**1,329**	**7.9**	**1,411**	**715**	**55.4**	**42.5**	**3.3**	**532**	**41.3**
1991	1,562	151	1,187	7.1	1,187	579	53.5	42.7	3.9	460	42.6
1990	1,345	156	997	7.9	1,071	521	53.7	42.9	4.4	406	41.9
1989	1,188	121	866	9.4	983	460	51.9	43.1	4.9	383	43.2
1988	1,071	73	766	9.9	908	402	49.2	43.3	5.3	372	45.5
1987	1,008	55	728	10.6	855	369	47.6	43.4	5.6	362	46.8
1986	959	55	702	10.4	793	340	47.5	40.6	5.7	336	46.8
1985	911	33	673	10.3	749	320	47.1	45.2	6.6	314	46.3
1984	882	30	666	10.3	699	295	46.3	47.2	7.4	296	46.3
1983	854	62	660	8.6	661	280	45.9	48.6	8.0	280	46.1

Data as orig. reptd. **1.** Times int. exp. and pfd. divs. covered (pretax basis). **2.** Based on income bef. interest charges.

Business Summary

Nevada Power serves the city of Las Vegas and adjoining areas of Clark County, Nevada, with a population of some 860,000. Revenues by customer class in recent years:

	1992	1991	1990	1989
Residential	42%	40%	41%	44%
Commercial & industrial	52%	53%	53%	51%
Other	6%	7%	6%	5%

Peak demand in 1992 was 2,501 mw and capability totaled 2,989 mw, for a capacity margin of 16%. In 1992, some 49% of kwh sold was company generated, while 4% came from the Hoover Dam, and 47% from purchased power. Sources of company generation were coal 94%, natural gas 5%, and oil 1%.

The Las Vegas economy is characterized by robust growth in the resort, gaming and convention industry. Also, the local economy has experienced a sharp increase in population. Peak demand for electricity in southern Nevada continues its high growth rate. To meet projected demand, the company is constructing two 90 mw combined cycle units, one of which is to be added in 1993 and the other in 1994. NVP is also contructing one 75 mw unit, scheduled to begin operation in 1995, and has the option to construct another 75 mw unit for service in 1996. NVP also intends to meet demand via power purchases from qualifying facilities. In 1992, NVP received 175 mw of such power. NVP intends to purchase 85 mw of such power in 1993 and another 45 mw in 1994. Also, NVP will be increasing its transmission capacity at Hoover Dam to some 235 mw. by mid-1993.

Dividend Data

Dividends have been paid since 1951. A dividend reinvestment plan is available.

Amt of Divd. $	Date Decl.	Ex-divd. Date	Stock of Record	Payment Date
0.40	Oct. 1	Oct. 6	Oct. 13	Nov. 2'92
0.40	Jan. 4	Jan. 8	Jan. 14	Feb. 1'93
0.40	Apr. 1	Apr. 5	Apr. 12	May 3'93
0.40	Jul. 1	Jul. 6	Jul. 12	Aug. 2'93

Capitalization

Long Term Debt: $712,025,000 (6/93).

Red. Cum. Preferred Stock: $4,383,000.

Auction Preferred Stock: $38,000,000.

Common Stock: 40,716,571 shs. ($1 par).
Institutions hold about 14%.
Shareholders of record: 40,921.

Office—6226 West Sahara Ave. (P.O. Box 230), Las Vegas, NV 89102 (89151). **Tel**—(702) 367-5000. **Chrmn & CEO**—C. A. Lenzie. **Pres**—J. C. Holcombe. **VP-Treas & CFO**—S. W. Rigazio. **VP-Secy**—R. L. Hinckley. **Investor Contact**—Robyn A. Warsinske. **Dirs**—J. Cashman III, M. L. Coleman, F. D. Gibson Jr., J. L. Goolsby, J. Herbst, J. C. Holcombe, C. A. Lenzie, C. L. Ryan, F. E. Scott, A. M. Smith, J. A. Tiberti. **Transfer Agents**—Company's office; Manufacturers Hanover Trust, NYC. **Registrars**—First Interstate Bank of Nevada, Las Vegas; Chemical Bank, NYC. **Incorporated** in Nevada in 1929. **Empl**—1,734.

 Christopher J. Grant

New England Electric System

NYSE Symbol NES In S&P MidCap 400

Price	Range	P-E Ratio	Dividend	Yield	S&P Ranking	Beta
Sep. 22'93	1993					
41⅝	43⅜–36⅞	17	2.24	5.4%	A–	0.53

Summary

This utility holding company serves customers throughout Massachusetts, Rhode Island and New Hampshire. NES has a 10% interest in New Hampshire's Seabrook nuclear plant, which began commercial operation on June 30, 1990. Earnings are expected to decline in 1993 as unusual charges from an early retirement program and gas waste liabilities more than offset higher electric rates in Massachusetts. The company may incur additional charges in the future for gas waste liabilities.

Current Outlook

Share earnings for 1993 are estimated at $2.55, including unusual charges of $0.48, down from the $2.85 reported for 1992. Share earnings could rise to $2.95 in 1994.

The quarterly dividend was raised 3.7%, to $0.56 from $0.54, with the July 1993 payment.

Share earnings for 1993 are likely to fall as a one-time charge related to an early retirement program and a charge for gas waste liabilities more than offset a rate hike in Massachusetts (effective October 1, 1992), and lower interest expense. A return to more normal weather conditions would aid 1993 earnings. Share earnings for 1994 should benefit from a full year of cost savings resulting from the early retirement program. Estimates for both years exclude possible additional charges for the cleanup of manufactured gas waste on properties once owned by NES.

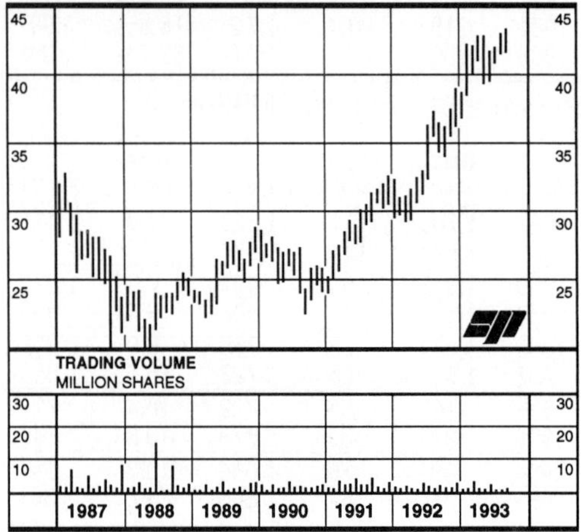

Operating Revenues (Million $)

Quarter:	1993	1992	1991	1990
Mar.	579	575	574	481
Jun.	518	499	475	427
Sep.	---	541	521	476
Dec.	---	567	524	472
	---	2,182	2,094	1,855

Revenues in the six months to June 30, 1993, rose 2.2%, year to year. Results were hurt by a one-time charge of $0.27 a share in the first quarter related to a work force reduction program, and a $0.27 a share charge for gas waste liabilities. Net income fell 23%, to $1.12 a share from $1.46.

Common Share Earnings ($)

Quarter:	1993	1992	1991	1990
Mar.	0.82	0.99	1.14	0.78
Jun.	0.30	0.47	0.29	0.27
Sep.	E0.77	0.74	0.69	2.55
Dec.	E0.66	0.65	0.65	0.51
	E2.55	2.85	2.77	4.11

Important Developments

Jul. '93— NES incurred a $0.21 a share charge in the second quarter of 1993 for potential gas waste liabilities related to 37 manufactured gas locations it once owned. The charge was in addition to reserves in prior periods of $0.18 related to these liabilities. The total reserve reflects preliminary cost estimates to remediate three locations and investigate and monitor 34 locations. NES said there are significant uncertainties as to the potential costs to investigate and, when necessary, remediate the sites. The actual liability, therefore, could be substantially higher than the reserve established. NES intends to review regularly and, when appropriate, revise the reserve level as more information about particular sites becomes available. Earnings for the first half of 1993 also included a one-time charge of $0.27 a share in the first quarter to reflect costs related to an early retirement offer and a special severance program for nonunion employees undertaken by NES units as part of an organizational review.

Next earnings report expected in late October.

Per Share Data ($)

Yr. End Dec. 31	1992	1991	1990	1989	1988	1987	1986	1985	1984	1983
Tangible Bk. Val.	**22.88**	22.05	21.30	19.09	18.17	21.25	20.06	18.68	17.31	16.00
Earnings	**2.85**	2.77	4.11	2.36	d0.94	3.05	3.20	3.15	3.02	2.74
Dividends	**2.140**	2.070	2.040	2.040	2.040	2.010	1.940	1.830	1.725	1.625
Payout Ratio	**75%**	75%	50%	86%	NM	66%	61%	58%	57%	59%
Prices—High	**39**	32⅝	28⅝	28⅞	25½	32⅞	35¼	25¾	20½	21¾
Low	**29¼**	24	22½	22¼	20	20	24⅜	18⅛	14⅜	16½
P/E Ratio—	**14–10**	12–9	7–5	12–9	NM	11–7	11–8	8–6	7–5	8–6

Data as orig. reptd. Adj. for stk. div. of 100% Feb. 1986. E-Estimated. d-Deficit. NM-Not Meaningful.

Income Data (Million $)

Year Ended Dec. 31	Revs.	Depr.	Maint.	Oper. Ratio	[1]Fxd. Chgs. Cover.	Constr. Credits	Eff. Tax Rate	Net Inc.	% Return On Revs.	[2]Invest. Capital	[3]Com. Equity
1992	**2,182**	**302**	**163**	**86.0%**	**3.38**	**4.9**	**36.8%**	**185**	**8.5**	**8.2**	**12.6**
1991	2,094	278	148	86.1%	3.17	4.3	35.9%	180	8.6	7.8	12.6
1990	1,855	259	137	86.3%	3.78	31.9	21.3%	262	14.1	9.8	20.5
1989	1,643	257	122	85.3%	2.49	29.7	19.3%	139	8.4	7.1	12.6
1988	1,520	229	120	85.4%	1.59	3.8	NM	d54	NM	1.5	NM
1987	1,448	179	101	84.3%	3.43	34.9	30.6%	169	11.7	7.6	14.6
1986	1,432	204	89	86.0%	3.65	42.6	38.7%	172	12.0	8.2	16.4
1985	1,444	167	99	86.0%	3.64	53.1	38.1%	164	11.4	8.3	17.3
1984	1,486	151	76	84.8%	3.38	36.2	42.6%	152	10.2	9.0	18.0
1983	1,374	134	82	86.9%	3.49	47.1	41.5%	133	9.7	8.6	17.6

Balance Sheet Data (Million $)

Dec. 31	Gross Prop.	[4]Capital Expend.	Net Prop.	% Earn. on Net Prop.	Total Cap.	Capitalization: LT Debt	% LT Debt	[5]Pfd.	[5]% Pfd.	Com.	% Com.
1992	**4,790**	**242**	**3,375**	**9.1**	**3,969**	**1,533**	**47.3**	**223**	**6.9**	**1,486**	**45.8**
1991	4,666	193	3,321	8.8	3,930	1,548	48.2	226	7.0	1,440	44.8
1990	4,548	218	3,302	8.0	3,991	1,679	51.1	225	6.9	1,380	42.0
1989	4,222	532	3,073	8.4	3,764	1,638	53.4	217	7.1	1,212	39.5
1988	3,733	192	2,661	8.0	3,370	1,434	54.1	163	6.1	1,056	39.8
1987	3,871	165	2,863	8.2	3,573	1,387	50.5	163	5.9	1,200	43.6
1986	3,632	188	2,714	7.6	3,496	1,401	52.1	188	7.0	1,101	40.9
1985	3,413	201	2,565	8.0	3,293	1,364	53.2	205	8.0	993	38.8
1984	3,257	230	2,481	9.5	3,076	1,361	55.4	205	8.4	888	36.2
1983	2,987	231	2,274	8.3	2,752	1,220	55.0	207	9.3	792	35.7

Data as orig. reptd. **1.** Times int. exp. & pfd. divs. covered (pretax basis). **2.** Based on income before interest charges. **3.** As reptd. by co. **4.** Excl. allow. for funds used during constr. **5.** Incl. minority interest aft. 1988. d-Deficit. NM-Not Meaningful.

Business Summary

New England Electric System is a utility holding company that provides electric service to customers in Massachusetts, Rhode Island and New Hampshire. Electric revenues by customer class:

	1992	1991	1990	1989
Residential	40%	40%	39%	40%
Commercial	38%	37%	36%	35%
Industrial	21%	22%	22%	21%
Other	2%	1%	3%	4%

Power sources in 1992 were: coal 41%, nuclear 18%, natural gas 15%, oil 10%, hydro 10% and other 6%. Peak load in 1992 was 3,964 mw, and capability totaled 5,479 mw, for a capacity margin of 28%. NES participates in the Hydro Quebec Interconnection. Phase I was completed in October 1986 and Phase II in November 1990.

NES owns 10% of the Seabrook nuclear facility, located in New Hampshire and operated by the project's largest investor, Public Service of New Hampshire (35.6%). Despite ongoing opposition to its operation, the Seabrook plant received its full power license in March 1990 and began commercial operation on June 30, 1990. In 1988's second quarter, NES resolved its Seabrook prudency issues and wrote off $179 million ($3.14 a share) of plant costs. However, with the operation of the plant in 1990, NES reversed $115 million ($1.80 a share) of the writeoff in 1990's third quarter. NES received a $16.8 million annual rate increase for five years, effective June 30, 1990, Seabrook's in-service date.

Dividend Data

Dividends have been paid since 1947. A dividend reinvestment plan is available.

Amt of Divd. $	Date Decl.	Ex-divd. Date	Stock of Record	Payment Date
0.54	Nov. 24	Dec. 4	Dec. 10	Jan. 2'93
0.54	Feb. 23	Mar. 4	Mar. 10	Apr. 1'93
0.56	May 25	Jun. 4	Jun. 10	Jul. 1'93
0.56	Aug. 24	Sep. 3	Sep. 10	Oct. 1'93

Capitalization

Long Term Debt: $1,570,402,000 (6/93).

Minority Interest: $57,142,000.

Subsid. Red. Preferred Stock: $162,528,000.

Common Stock: 64,969,652 shs. ($1 par).
Institutions hold about 33%.
Shareholders of record: 61,075.

Office—25 Research Drive, Westborough, MA 01582. **Tel**—(508) 366-9011. **Chrmn**—J. T. Bok. **Pres & CEO**—J. W. Rowe. **VP-Secy**—F. E. Greenman. **VP-CFO**— A. D. Houston. **Investor Contact**—Robert G. Seega. **Dirs**—J. T. Bok, P. L. Joskow, J. M. Kucharski, E. H. Ladd, J. A. McClure, M. McLane, F. A. Mirando Jr., J. W. Rowe, G. M. Sage, A. Wexler, J. Q. Wilson, J. R. Winoker. **Transfer Agent & Registrar**—Bank of Boston. **Organized** in Massachusetts in 1926. **Empl**—5,415.

 Christopher J. Grant

N.Y. State Electric & Gas

NYSE Symbol NGE In S&P MidCap 400

Price	Range	P-E Ratio	Dividend	Yield	S&P Ranking	Beta
Oct. 21'93	1993					
32⅞	36½–31⅝	17	2.20	6.7%	B	0.53

Summary

This utility, serving portions of New York's upstate rural economy, owns 18% of the Nine Mile Point 2 nuclear plant. Regulatory issues concerning the plant led to a 24% dividend reduction in 1988; in July 1992, the dividend was raised 1.9%, the fourth consecutive increase. Earnings should rise in 1993, due primarily to favorable rate relief. Continued success controlling costs and the termination of several power purchase contracts should allow NGE to take advantage of opportunities arising from deregulation.

Current Outlook

Share earnings for 1993 are estimated at $2.50, up from 1992's $2.40. Earnings in 1994 are projected to be $2.55 a share.

Directors raised the quarterly cash dividend 1.9%, to $0.55, from $0.54, with the August payment.

Higher earnings projected for 1993 mainly reflect electric and gas rate increases equal to $64.1 million in additional annual revenues. Profitability will benefit from lower interest expense resulting from the refinancing of $250 million of debt in 1992. The cancellation of several unnecessary power purchase contracts should save $1 billion over the term of these agreements. Vision 2000, NGE's comprehensive strategic plan to better position itself for deregulation and greater wholesale competition, has enabled the firm to contain costs and become the region's low-cost power producer.

Operating Revenues (Million $)

Quarter:	1994	1993	1992	1991
Mar.	---	522	490	444
Jun.	---	389	402	373
Sep.	---	396	368	350
Dec.	---	---	432	389
	---	---	1,692	1,556

Operating revenues for the six months ended June 30, 1993, rose 2.2%, year to year, reflecting electric and gas rate increases granted in August 1992. Profitability was penalized by the weak local economy and the negative effect of a change in the timing for revenue recognition. Net income was down 21%. After preferred dividends, share earnings were $1.22 on 1.5% more shares, compared with $1.69.

Common Share Earnings ($)

Quarter:	1994	1993	1992	1991
Mar.	E1.00	0.99	1.10	1.10
Jun.	E0.25	0.23	0.60	0.60
Sep.	E0.55	E0.53	0.31	0.38
Dec.	E0.75	E0.75	0.42	0.28
	E2.55	E2.50	2.40	2.36

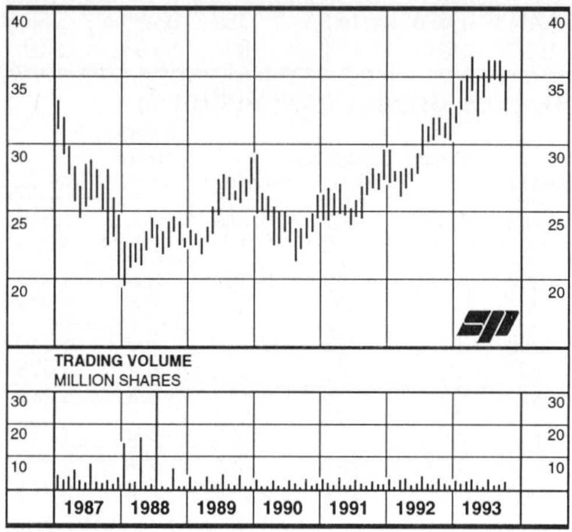

Important Developments

Jul. '93— NGE said that earnings for the six months ended June 30, 1993 would have fallen only 7.6%, year to year, if the new policy recognizing unbilled revenue, authorized by the NYPSC in August 1992, had been in effect in the year earlier period. Earnings for the first half of 1992 would have been $1.32, some $0.37 lower.

Apr. '93— NGE, the staff of the NYPSC, the Independent Power Producers of N.Y., and Cogeneration Partners of America signed a three step, 36-month electric and gas rate settlement agreement. If approved by the NYPSC, $64.1 million in new electric and gas rates would become effective on September 1, 1993. In 1994 and 1995 rate increases of $51.9 million and $53.1 million would become effective on August 1 of the respective years. The rate decision provides for an 11.4% return on common equity.

Next earnings report expected in late October.

Per Share Data ($)

Yr. End Dec. 31	1992	1991	1990	1989	1988	1987	1986	1985	1984	1983
Tangible Bk. Val.	**21.29**	20.59	20.35	19.08	18.17	17.32	22.60	23.53	23.21	22.28
Earnings[1]	**2.40**	2.36	2.48	2.53	2.81	0.70	3.86	3.46	3.68	3.06
Dividends	**2.14**	2.10	2.06	2.02	2.00	2.64	2.60	2.50	2.38	2.26
Payout Ratio	**89%**	89%	83%	80%	71%	377%	67%	72%	65%	74%
Prices—High	**32¾**	29⅝	29¼	29	24⅝	33¼	38½	29¼	23	22⅞
Low	**26⅛**	24	21⅜	21⅞	19½	20⅛	27⅛	21¼	14¾	19⅛
P/E Ratio—	**14–11**	13–10	12–9	11–9	9–7	48–29	10–7	8–6	6–4	7–6

Data as orig. reptd. 1. Bef. spec. item(s) of -4.16 in 1987. E-Estimated.

Income Data (Million $)

Year Ended Dec. 31	Revs.	Depr.	Maint.	Oper. Ratio	[1]Fxd. Chgs. Cover.	Constr. Credits	Eff. Tax Rate	[2]Net Inc.	% Return On Revs.	% Return On [3]Invest. Capital	% Return On [4]Com. Equity
1992	**1,692**	**159**	**103**	**80.9%**	**2.54**	**4**	**32.7%**	**184**	**10.9**	**7.4**	**10.6**
1991	1,556	152	110	80.0%	2.36	8	32.9%	169	10.8	7.5	10.7
1990	1,497	148	107	78.9%	2.30	5	34.7%	158	10.6	7.8	11.4
1989	1,428	148	97	78.1%	2.09	6	27.9%	158	11.1	8.2	11.5
1988	1,340	134	90	75.6%	2.18	26	31.1%	171	12.8	8.9	13.2
1987	1,290	111	93	78.2%	1.86	103	63.9%	52	4.1	5.2	12.2
1986	1,277	101	89	78.0%	2.75	96	34.1%	228	17.9	10.6	15.3
1985	1,242	98	82	80.9%	2.45	76	31.1%	208	16.8	10.9	14.3
1984	1,129	65	69	79.6%	2.46	95	26.1%	211	18.7	11.8	15.9
1983	994	57	62	82.5%	2.45	92	20.8%	157	15.8	10.3	13.5

Balance Sheet Data (Million $)

Dec. 31	[5]Gross Prop.	[6]Capital Expend.	Net Prop.	% Earn. on Net Prop.	Total Cap.	Capitalization LT Debt	% LT Debt	Pfd.	% Pfd.	Com.	% Com.
1992	**5,261**	**243**	**3,833**	**8.5**	**4,618**	**1,777**	**48.9**	**267**	**7.4**	**1,586**	**43.7**
1991	5,063	244	3,753	8.5	4,455	1,789	51.6	269	7.8	1,405	40.6
1990	4,766	211	3,591	8.9	4,254	1,756	53.4	171	5.2	1,364	41.4
1989	4,575	191	3,512	9.0	4,126	1,788	56.1	172	5.4	1,225	38.5
1988	4,409	207	3,453	9.7	4,037	1,824	57.5	174	5.5	1,174	37.0
1987	4,162	185	3,307	8.1	4,185	2,055	61.5	179	5.3	1,107	33.2
1986	4,373	231	3,604	8.1	3,848	1,928	55.0	183	5.2	1,398	39.8
1985	4,055	256	3,368	7.3	3,593	1,749	52.5	248	7.5	1,331	40.0
1984	3,734	350	3,117	7.9	3,269	1,572	51.4	253	8.2	1,235	40.4
1983	3,301	437	2,738	6.9	2,788	1,260	47.7	277	10.5	1,104	41.8

Data as orig. reptd. **1.** Times int. exp. & pfd. divs. covered (pretax basis). **2.** Bef. spec. item(s) in 1987. **3.** Based on income before interest charges. **4.** As reptd. by Co. **5.** Utility plant. **6.** Net.

Business Summary

New York State Electric & Gas Corp. provides electricity to about 784,000 customers and gas to 224,000 customers in the central, eastern and western parts of New York. The upstate New York economy is composed of light industry, high technology businesses, agriculture, recreation facilities, and colleges and universities. In 1992, electric sales accounted for 86% of revenues and gas 14%. Contributions to electric revenues by customer class in recent years:

	1992	1991	1990	1989
Residential	41%	40%	41%	40%
Commercial	22%	21%	21%	21%
Industrial	16%	15%	15%	16%
Other	21%	24%	23%	23%

Power sources in 1992 were coal 80%, nuclear 5%, hydro 1%, and purchased 14%. The 1992-93 winter peak load was 2,517 mw and current system capability totals 3,509 mw for a capacity margin of 28%. Gas sales in 1992 were 56.4 million dth, versus 42.4 million dth in 1991.

NGE has an 18% interest in the Nine Mile Point 2 nuclear plant, operated by Niagara Mohawk Power Corp. No new generating capacity is expected to be required before the year 2008.

Finances

During the first half of 1993, NGE sold $100 million of first mortgage bonds in public offerings through underwriters led by Goldman, Sachs & Co. and Merrill Lynch & Co. Net proceeds were earmarked primarily to repay higher coupon debt.

Dividend Data

Dividends have been paid since 1910. A dividend reinvestment plan is available.

Amt. of Divd. $	Date Decl.	Ex–divd. Date	Stock of Record	Payment Date
0.54	Jan. 15	Jan. 20	Jan. 26	Feb. 15'93
0.54	Apr. 16	Apr. 21	Apr. 27	May 15'93
0.55	Jul. 9	Jul. 21	Jul. 27	Aug. 15'93
0.55	Oct. 8	Oct. 20	Oct. 26	Nov. 15'93

Capitalization

Long Term Debt: $1,739,441,000 (3/93).

Red. Preferred Stock: $106,900,000.

Cum. Preferred Stock: $160,500,000.

Common Stock: 69,720,397 shs. ($6.66⅔ par).
Institutions hold about 34%.
Shareholders of record: 61,183.

Office—4500 Vestal Parkway East (P.O. Box 3607), Binghamton, NY 13902-3607. **Tel**—(607) 729-2551. **Chrmn & Pres**—J. A. Carrigg. **VP-Treas & CFO**—S. J. Rafferty. **VP-Secy**—D. W. Farley. **Investor Contact**—Robert D. Kump (607) 347-4360. **Dirs**—W. P. Allen Jr., J. A. Carrigg, A. P. Casarett, E. A. Gilmour, P. L. Gioia, J. M. Keeler, A. E. Kintigh, B. E. Lynch, A. G. Marshall, D. R. Newcomb, R. A. Plane, C. W. Stuart. **Transfer Agent**—Chemical Bank, NYC. **Incorporated** in New York in 1852. **Empl**—4,888.

 Ned Bancroft

NEXTEL Communications

NASDAQ Symbol CALL Options on CBOE (Feb-May-Aug-Nov) (Incl. in Nat'l Market)

Price	Range	P-E Ratio	Dividend	Yield	S&P Ranking	Beta
Aug. 25'93	1993					
36⅜	38½–17⅞	NM	None	None	NR	NA

Summary

NEXTEL Communications (formerly Fleet Call) is a leading provider of specialized mobile radio (SMR) wireless communications services. CALL is in the process of replacing its current SMR systems with advanced digital mobile networks. In July 1993, CALL greatly expanded its operations with the acquisition of Dispatch Communications for about 16.1 million shares, and it adopted its present corporate title.

Current Outlook

A $0.65 a share loss is projected for fiscal 1993-94, versus fiscal 1992-93's $0.16 loss.

Initiation of cash dividends is not expected.

Revenues in 1993-94 should grow rapidly, reflecting the Dispatch Communications acquisition; however, significant discounting of equipment sales and a decline in average revenues per subscriber as users are migrated to the 900 Mhz systems will hold back revenue growth in original markets. Margins will narrow on a higher proportion of users on the lower-margin 900 Mhz systems, and as costs related to customer acquisition and retention programs rise. Depreciation and amortization costs will increase substantially. Results will reflect sharply higher interest costs and the issuance of approximately 16 million new shares.

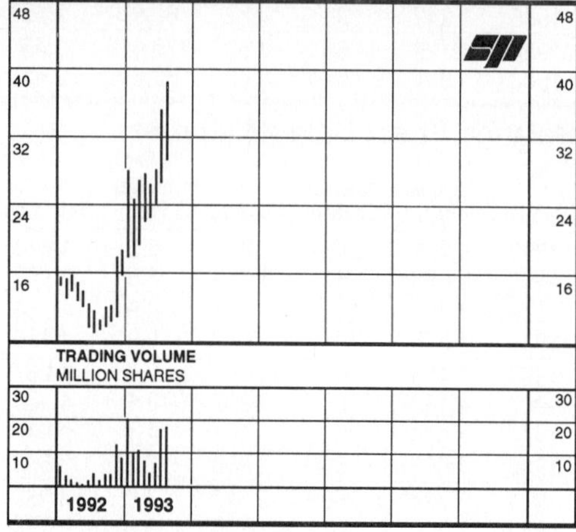

Revenues (Million $)

Quarter:	1993-94	1992-93	1991-92	1990-91
Jun.	12.8	13.3	13.7	13.5
Sep.		13.6	13.6	14.4
Dec.		13.0	12.5	14.2
Mar.		13.2	12.7	11.8
		53.0	52.5	53.9

Revenues for the quarter to June 30, 1993, slipped 3.6%, year to year. Margins narrowed on equipment discounting and higher costs for the 900 Mhz systems. After sharply higher interest costs and expenses related to stock appreciation rights, and in the absence of a $622,000 nonrecurring gain, the net loss rose to $4.9 million ($0.08 a share, on 14% more shares), from $802,000 ($0.01).

Common Share Earnings ($)

Quarter:	1993-94	1992-93	1991-92	1990-91
Jun.	d0.08	d0.01	d0.21	d0.11
Sep.	d0.12	d0.05	d0.15	d0.05
Dec.	d0.20	d0.05	d0.14	0.15
Mar.	d0.25	d0.05	d0.08	d0.29
	Ed0.65	d0.16	d0.58	d0.30

Important Developments

Jul. '93— CALL completed the acquisition of Dispatch Communications, Inc. for about 16.1 million shares. Dispatch operates SMR networks in four regions (Mid-Atlantic, New England, Minnesota and Arizona) covering a population of about 31.8 million. Separately, CALL has entered into agreements to acquire about 745 SMR channels in several major Florida cities for an aggregate price of $52.1 million. CALL has also agreed to acquire a 61% interest in American Mobile Systems (AMS) for $75 million in cash and certain SMR properties in Florida, including those under acquisition agreements. AMS also granted CALL an option to purchase an additional 4% stake for $15.3 million. CALL believes that the regulatory approvals and other steps necessary to complete the Florida acquisitions and AMS transaction will be completed by the end of 1993.

Next earnings report expected in late November.

Per Share Data ($)

Yr. End Mar. 31	1993	1992	1991	1990	1989	1988
Tangible Bk. Val.	**1.75**	0.55	[1]d0.05	NA	NA	NA
Cash Flow	**0.28**	0.30	0.76	0.26	0.09	0.02
Earnings[2]	**d0.16**	d0.65	d0.30	d0.36	d0.20	d0.03
Dividends	**Nil**	Nil	Nil	Nil	Nil	Nil
Payout Ratio	**Nil**	Nil	Nil	Nil	Nil	Nil
Calendar Years	**1992**	1991	1990	1989	1988	1987
Pric es—High	**18¾**	NA	NA	NA	NA	NA
Low	**9**	NA	NA	NA	NA	NA
P/E Ratio—	**NM**	NM	NM	NM	NM	NM

Data as orig. reptd. **1.** Pro forma, as of 9-30-91. **2.** Bef. spec. items of -0.47 in 1992, -0.03 in 1991, -0.08 in 1990. d-Deficit. E-Estimated NM-Not Meaningful. NA-Not Available.

Income Data (Million $)

Year Ended Mar. 31	Revs.	Oper. Inc.	% Oper. Inc. of Revs.	Cap. Exp.	Depr.	Int. Exp.	Net Bef. Taxes	Eff. Tax Rate	[2]Net Inc.	% Net Inc. of Revs.	Cash Flow
1993	**53.0**	**13.0**	**24.5**	**96.80**	**25.9**	**2.6**	**[1]d10.6**	**NM**	**d9.6**	**NM**	**16.3**
1992	52.5	19.1	36.3	7.80	25.7	12.8	[1]d18.9	NM	d15.7	NM	8.2
1991	53.9	19.3	35.7	2.74	24.6	14.2	[1]d15.4	NM	d7.0	NM	17.7
1990	36.3	9.6	26.5	4.16	14.2	7.2	d13.5	NM	d8.2	NM	5.9
1989	17.3	4.7	27.4	3.25	5.9	3.6	d4.6	NM	d4.1	NM	1.8
1988	2.1	0.2	11.2	NA	0.4	0.2	d0.3	NM	d0.3	NM	0.1

Balance Sheet Data (Million $)

Mar. 31	Cash	Curr. Assets	Curr. Liab.	Curr. Ratio	Total Assets	% Ret. on Assets	Long Term Debt	Common Equity	Total Cap.	% LT Debt of Cap.	% Ret. on Equity
1993	**31.9**	**39.9**	**23.3**	**1.7**	**334**	**NM**	**55**	**255**	**310**	**17.7**	**NM**
1992	13.4	20.2	17.5	1.2	211	NM	1	191	193	0.5	NM
1991	0.5	10.1	18.2	0.6	212	NM	106	24	161	66.0	NM
1990	3.2	17.9	15.8	1.1	207	NM	98	28	156	63.0	NM
1989	0.9	13.2	NA	NA	100	NM	47	12	78	60.8	NM
1988	0.5	10.1	NA	NA	38	NM	15	9	24	61.7	NM

Data as orig. reptd. **1.** Incl. equity in earns. of nonconsol. subs. **2.** Bef. spec. items. d-Deficit. NM-Not Meaningful. NA-Not Available.

Business Summary

NEXTEL Communications, Inc. (formerly Fleet Call, Inc.) is a leading provider of specialized mobile radio (SMR) wireless communications services in 12 major U.S. metropolitan areas, providing service to about 189,000 subscriber units (after the Dispatch Communications acquisition). The vast majority of subscribers are dispatch users utilizing the 800/900 megahertz bands of the radio spectrum. The FCC has authorized the company to replace most of its current SMR systems with advanced digital mobile networks that will be constructed using new digital technology developed by Motorola, Inc.

Digital mobile networks will allow CALL to offer high-quality, enhanced mobile communications services, including two-way radio dispatch, paging, data, mobile telephone service and interconnection with the public switched telephone system, comparable to those provided by cellular telephone operators in terms of quality of service, features offered, pricing of system access and airtime utilization, and capability and size of subscriber units. Network services are expected to begin in Los Angeles in August 1993, in San Francisco and the remaining California region in early 1994, in New York and Chicago in mid-1994, in the New England region in late 1994 to early 1995, and in Dallas, Houston, Minneapolis and Phoenix in mid-1995. FCC applications for the New England region and Phoenix are still pending.

Dividend Data

No cash dividends have been paid on the common shares.

Finances

In September 1992, Comcast Corp. bought 3,571,429 CALL common shares at $14 each. Subject to satisfactory technical performance of the company's digital mobile systems in Los Angeles and San Francisco, Comcast will buy an additional $50 million of stock in January 1995, at 90% of the prevailing market price. Comcast also purchased for $20 million a five-year option to buy 25 million shares at $16 each. Comcast has also agreed to purchase about 6.7 million CALL shares in conncection with the Dispatch acquisition to maintain its 30% stake.

In February 1992, Matsushita Communication Industrial Co. completed the purchase of a 5.7% interest in CALL for $45 million.

In CALL's January 1992 initial public offering, 7,500,000 Class A common shares (including 1,500,000 offered outside the U.S.) were sold at $15 each.

CALL has entered into agreements with Motorola regarding the purchase of infrastructure equipment and services related to the construction of the initial phase of the digital mobile networks, the financing by Motorola under a credit facility totaling up to $260 million, the purchase of subscriber equipment and the licensing by Motorola to other subscriber equipment manufacturers of certain rights in connection with the manufacture of such equipment. Northern Telecom, which will manufacture the switch equipment to be provided by Motorola under the purchase agreement, has agreed to provide financing of up to $40 million for the purchase of such equipment.

Capitalization

Long Term Debt: $85,295,000 - pro forma (3/93).

Class A Common Stock: 83,245,884 shs. ($0.001 par).
Institutions hold about 33%.
Shareholders of record: about 667 (7/93).

Class B Common Stock: 2,982,142 shs. ($0.001 par); nonvoting.

Office—201 Route 17 North, Rutherford, NJ 07070. **Tel**—(201) 438-1400. **Chrmn**—M. E. O'Brien. **Pres & CEO**—B. D. McAuley. **Treas & Secy**—E. G. Long. **Investor Contact**—Walt Piecyk. **Dirs**—J. A. Brodsky, R. Cooper, P. J. Finnegan, D. A. Harris, T. Kawada, B. D. McAuley, M. E. O'Brien, J. N. Perry, Jr., J. A. Schleicher. **Transfer Agent & Registrar**—First Chicago Trust Co. of New York, NYC. **Incorporated** in Delaware in 1987. **Empl**—335.

 Susan Stahl Gibney

Noble Affiliates

NYSE Symbol NBL Options on ASE (Feb-May-Aug-Nov) In S&P MidCap 400

Price	Range	P-E Ratio	Dividend	Yield	S&P Ranking	Beta
Aug. 30'93	1993					
30½	31–15¾	60	0.16	0.5%	B	0.38

Summary

This independent energy company explores for and develops crude oil and natural gas throughout the major basins in the U.S., and overseas in Canada, Africa and Indonesia. Earnings for 1993 are expected to decline in the absence of nonrecurring gains, but operating profits are expected to advance, aided by higher production and gas prices. In August 1993, NBL agreed to purchase substantially all of FM Properties Inc.'s oil and gas properties for $305 million; the planned acquisition significantly enhances the long-term profit outlook.

Current Outlook

Share earnings for 1993 are estimated at $0.60, down from the $0.93 (including nonrecurring gains of over $0.40) of 1992. An increase to $1.15 is projected for 1994.

Dividends should continue at $0.04 quarterly.

Higher operating profits are expected in 1993, as an increase in gas prices, and greater production are expected to more than offset higher exploration expenses. Oil production should benefit from startup of production from properties offshore Louisiana and Equatorial Guinea. Earnings should drop in the absence of a contract settlement gain and a gain of about $0.42 a share from the sale of interest in Natural Gas Clearinghouse. Earnings for 1994 should benefit from sharply higher energy production, reflecting the acquisition of assets from FM Properties and higher energy prices.

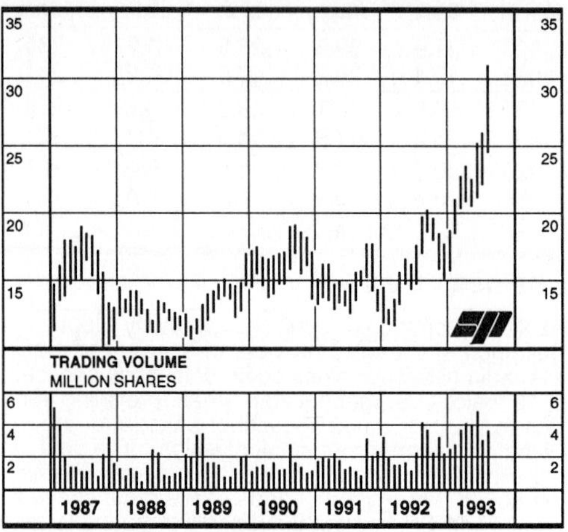

Total Revenues (Million $)

Quarter:	1993	1992	1991	1990
Mar.	69.9	61.5	71.4	66.4
Jun.	66.3	96.9	53.2	46.3
Sep.		68.5	53.8	54.2
Dec.		76.8	72.0	76.3
		303.8	250.4	243.2

Based on a brief report, revenues for the six months ended June 30, 1993, declined 14%, year to year, reflecting the absence of revenues from the sale of interest in Natural Gas Clearinghouse. Without the $18.4 million after-tax gain ($0.42 a share) resulting from the sale, net income dropped 68%, to $0.18 a share from $0.60.

Common Share Earnings ($)

Quarter:	1993	1992	1991	1990
Mar.	0.11	0.06	0.20	0.24
Jun.	0.08	0.54	0.09	0.04
Sep.	E0.12	0.15	0.02	0.13
Dec.	E0.29	0.18	0.12	0.24
	E0.60	0.93	0.44	0.65

Important Developments

Aug. '93— NBL agreed to purchase substantially all of FM Properties Inc.'s oil and gas properties for $305 million in cash, effective October 1, 1993. NBL estimated net proved reserves attributable to the properties to be acquired to be 21.6 million barrels of oil and 253 billion cubic feet of gas. The properties were estimated to be producing about 5,000 barrels of oil and 114 MMcf of gas per day.

Jul. '93— NBL purchased about a 70% interest in oil and gas properties in the Gulf of Mexico from Freeport-McMoRan Inc. for $100 million. The company was evaluating plans for a platform capable of handling daily production of 8,000 barrels of oil and 100,000 mcf of gas. Samedan Oil Corp. sold its interests in 179 nonstrategic Oklahoma properties for $2.8 million.

Next earnings report expected in late October.

Per Share Data ($)

Yr. End Dec. 31	1992	1991	1990	1989	1988	1987	[1]1986	1985	1984	[2]1983
Tangible Bk. Val.	**6.83**	5.99	5.69	5.15	4.55	4.40	4.94	6.65	9.43	9.13
Cash Flow	**3.30**	2.37	2.54	2.36	2.22	2.52	0.97	2.42	2.51	2.33
Earnings[3]	**0.93**	0.44	0.65	0.52	0.27	0.38	d1.45	0.26	0.40	0.52
Dividends	**0.16**	0.16	0.16	0.14	0.12	0.12	0.12	0.12	0.12	0.12
Payout Ratio	**17%**	37%	25%	27%	44%	32%	NM	46%	30%	23%
Prices—High	**20¼**	17¾	19⅛	17	14½	19	14	16½	19	20¾
Low	**11⅝**	12½	13⅝	10⅝	11⅛	10	7⅞	12⅞	12½	11¾
P/E Ratio—	**22–13**	40–28	29–21	33–20	54–41	50–26	NM	63–50	48–31	40–23

Data as orig. reptd. **1.** Reflects merger or acquisition. **2.** Reflects acctg. change. **3.** Bef. results of disc. ops. of -0.28 in 1985, and spec. item(s) of +0.20 in 1989. E-Estimated. d-Deficit. NM-Not Meaningful.

Income Data (Million $)

Year Ended Dec. 31	Revs.	Oper. Inc.	% Oper. Inc. of Revs.	Cap. Exp.	Depr. Depl. & Amort.	Int. Exp.	[4]Net Bef. Taxes	Eff. Tax Rate	[5]Net Inc.	% Net Inc. of Revs.	Cash Flow
1992	**260**	**142**	**54.5**	**66**	**105**	**20.5**	**61**	**32.7%**	**41.2**	**15.9**	**146**
1991	226	117	51.8	123	85	21.0	29	32.5%	19.3	8.5	104
1990	223	123	55.1	97	83	20.5	42	32.2%	28.6	12.8	112
1989	179	100	55.8	97	81	20.6	34	34.1%	22.6	12.6	103
1988	171	102	59.8	56	85	20.8	18	34.7%	11.8	6.9	97
1987	185	121	65.5	28	94	24.9	27	39.3%	16.4	8.9	110
[1]1986	123	60	48.9	240	107	16.1	d114	NM	d64.3	NM	43
[2]1985	170	109	64.3	95	97	12.5	17	31.2%	11.8	7.0	109
1984	271	118	43.5	153	95	15.3	28	35.9%	17.8	6.6	113
[3]1983	270	123	45.4	101	81	13.0	37	37.6%	23.3	8.6	104

Balance Sheet Data (Million $)

Dec. 31	Cash	Curr. Assets	Curr. Liab.	Curr. Ratio	Total Assets	% Ret. on Assets	Long Term Debt	Common Equity	Total Cap.	% LT Debt of Cap.	% Ret. on Equity
1992	**119.0**	**189**	**55.7**	**3.4**	**626**	**6.8**	**225**	**305**	**563**	**39.9**	**14.4**
1991	1.8	78	56.7	1.4	590	3.3	225	265	524	42.9	7.5
1990	39.0	108	64.0	1.7	588	5.0	225	251	514	43.7	11.9
1989	34.6	83	48.0	1.7	544	4.2	225	226	485	46.3	10.6
1988	46.8	101	48.0	2.1	527	2.3	225	199	473	47.5	6.0
1987	15.5	61	40.0	1.5	517	3.0	225	192	468	48.0	8.1
1986	14.1	46	63.0	0.7	590	NM	237	216	505	46.9	NM
1985	35.7	73	59.0	1.3	565	1.8	96	300	501	19.3	3.3
1984	14.4	98	79.0	1.2	768	2.4	108	424	685	15.8	4.3
1983	34.9	93	63.0	1.5	720	3.3	114	408	656	17.4	5.8

Data as orig. reptd. **1.** Reflects merger or acquisition. **2.** Excl. disc. ops. **3.** Reflects accounting change. **4.** Incl. equity in earns. of nonconsol. subs. **5.** Bef. results of disc. ops. and spec. items. d-Deficit. NM-Not Meaningful.

Business Summary

Noble Affiliates is an independent energy company with exploration and production operations, conducted through its Samedan Oil Corp. subsidiary, throughout major basins in the U.S., including the Gulf of Mexico, and in Canada, Africa and Indonesia. An interest in Natural Gas Clearinghouse was sold in May 1992.

Production in 1992 averaged 17,826 bbl. of oil a day (15,001 in 1991) and 204.6 MMcf of gas a day (178.4). Average price per bbl. of oil in 1992 was $18.68, versus $20.39 in 1991. Gas prices averaged $1.81 per Mcf in 1992, versus $1.74. NBL's finding cost per bbl. of oil equivalents (BOE) in 1992 was $3.96, versus $5.32 in 1991. At December 31, 1992, estimated proved reserves amounted to 47,380,000 bbl. of oil and condensate (43,800,000 in 1991) and 372,223 MMcf of natural gas (396,610).

During 1993, the company expected to be active drilling in the Gulf of Mexico, as well as selected onshore areas of the U.S. Internationally, NBL planned to drill two wells in Tunisia and maintain its exploration and development efforts in Canada. The company planned to continue to evaluate opportunities to purchase proved oil and gas reserves that would fit with its existing operations.

In January 1993, NBL set its 1993 capital budget at $125.9 million, which it expected to fund from generated cash flow. The company expected about 40% of the budget to be expended on the acquisition of producing properties. Expenditures for exploration, development, and acquisitions totaled $76 million in 1992.

In May 1992, the company sold its 32% interest in Natural Gas Clearinghouse, which provides energy services, including gas marketing, processing and crude oil trading. After-tax proceeds of $42.2 million from the transaction were expected to be used in the acquisition of proved oil and gas reserves.

Dividend Data

Dividends were initiated in 1975.

Amt. of Divd. $	Date Decl.	Ex-divd. Date	Stock of Record	Payment Date
0.04	Oct. 27	Nov. 3	Nov. 9	Nov. 23'92
0.04	Jan. 26	Feb. 2	Feb. 8	Feb. 23'93
0.04	Apr. 26	May 4	May 10	May 24'93
0.04	Jul. 27	Aug. 3	Aug. 9	Aug. 23'93

Capitalization

Long Term Debt: $125,000,000 (6/93).

Common Stock: 49,700,000 shs. ($3.33⅓ par).
Samuel Roberts Noble Foundation owns 24%.
Institutions hold about 54%.
Shareholders of record: 2,399.

Office—110 West Broadway, Ardmore, OK 73401. **Tel**—(405) 223-4110. **Chrmn, Pres & CEO**—R. Kelley. **VP-Fin, Treas & Investor Contact**—William D. Dickson. **Secy**—O. Walraven. **Dirs**—R. Butler, E. F. Cox, R. Kelley, H. F. Kleinman, G. J. McLeod, G. W. Nichols, J. F. Snodgrass. **Transfer Agent & Registrar**—Liberty National Bank & Trust Co. of Oklahoma City. **Incorporated** in Delaware in 1969. **Empl**—503.

 Mark Mattke

Nordson Corporation

NASDAQ Symbol NDSN (Incl. in Nat'l Market) In S&P MidCap 400

Price	Range	P–E Ratio	Dividend	Yield	S&P Ranking	Beta
Jul. 30'93	1993					
42	48–38¼	22	0.48	1.1%	A	0.51

Summary

This manufacturer and marketer of industrial application equipment has derived more than half of its sales and operating profits in recent years from international business. The earnings advance in fiscal 1992 reflected strength in North American markets, which offset the effects of declining economic activity in Europe and Japan. U.S. demand is still strong, and the company believes the decline in foreign markets has bottomed.

Business Summary

Nordson Corporation is a developer, manufacturer and worldwide marketer of industrial application systems, along with the software and application technologies that enhance their use. Its customers produce consumer and industrial products in which the use of adhesives, sealants, coatings and other technology-oriented materials is critical to the success of their products. More than two-thirds of NDSN's business is attributable to international sales. Contributions by geographic area in fiscal 1992 were:

	Sales	Profits
North America	36%	66%
Europe	42%	23%
Japan	15%	8%
Pacific & Latin America	7%	3%

Markets for NDSN equipment include appliances, automotive, bookbinding, building products, can coating, consumer goods, electronic products, fabricated metal, food and beverage, furniture, machinery, nonwoven products, packaging, paper products and pharmaceuticals. Products are marketed in the U.S. and 46 other countries, mainly through a direct sales force, and in nine countries through qualified distributors.

Hot-melting equipment is used to apply adhesives, sealants, caulking and other thermoplastic materials. Thermoplastic material is applied in heated, liquid form, either by hand-held or automatic guns, to the various package or product surfaces to be closed or fastened. NDSN's adhesive application equipment is used in the packaging market for the fastening of industrial and consumer products and in industrial production applications for the assembly of various items.

NDSN's powder product line consists of application, recovery and recycle equipment that applies both organic and inorganic coating materials to a wide variety of substrates. NDSN also markets air driers, flame detectors, gun movers and programmable controllers, providing the capability to supply a complete powder finishing system to its customers.

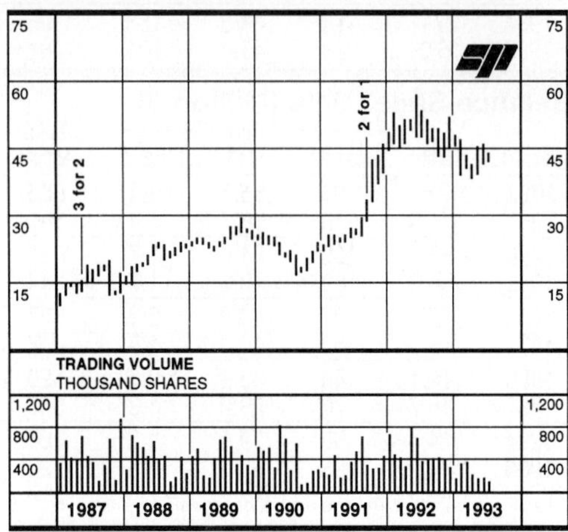

NDSN emphasizes product development through its own research staff. During fiscal 1992, R&D expenditures were approximately $18,431,000 (4.3% of sales), compared with $17,999,000 (4.6%) in fiscal 1991 and $17,620,000 (5.1%) in fiscal 1990.

Important Developments

Jun. '93— NDSN said it was experiencing strong demand for its specialized machinery in the U.S. and believed that the worst of the decline in Europe and Japan was over. If this is the case, NDSN said it could see earnings equal to or possibly exceeding the $2.03 a share earned in fiscal 1992, depending on the direction of foreign exchange rates.

Next earnings report due in mid-September.

Per Share Data ($)

Yr. End Oct. 31	[1]1992	[1]1991	[1]1990	[1]1989	1988	1987	1986	[1]1985	1984	1983
Tangible Bk. Val.	**7.79**	6.87	5.99	4.98	4.57	4.81	3.88	3.37	3.54	3.34
Cash Flow	**2.70**	2.39	2.09	2.15	1.85	1.42	0.89	0.60	0.68	0.55
Earnings[2]	**2.03**	1.77	1.53	1.77	1.56	1.18	0.67	0.44	0.55	0.43
Dividends	**0.440**	0.400	0.360	0.320	0.280	0.240	0.227	0.220	0.200	0.177
Payout Ratio	**22%**	22%	23%	18%	17%	20%	34%	48%	35%	40%
Prices[3]—High	**57**	46	26¼	29½	24⅛	20	10⅜	7³⁄₁₆	6½	6¹⁵⁄₁₆
Low	**43**	22⅛	16¹³⁄₁₆	22	14½	9¹⁵⁄₁₆	6	5	4	5⅛
P/E Ratio—	**28–21**	26–13	17–11	17–12	16–9	17–8	16–9	17–12	12–7	16–12

Data as orig. reptd. Adj. for stk. divs. of 100% Sep. 1991, 50% May 1987, 50% Jan. 1984. **1.** Refl. merger or acq. **2.** Bef. results of disc. ops. of -0.09 in 1984. **3.** Cal. yr.

Income Data (Million $)

Year Ended Oct. 31	Revs.	Oper. Inc.	% Oper. Inc. of Revs.	Cap. Exp.	Depr.	Int. Exp.	Net Bef. Taxes	Eff. Tax Rate	Net Inc.	% Net Inc. of Revs.	Cash Flow
1992	**426**	**80.3**	**18.9**	**17.6**	**13.0**	**6.80**	**60.8**	**34.9%**	**39.5**	**9.3**	**52.5**
[1]1991	388	70.2	18.1	14.2	11.9	7.33	[3]52.0	35.0%	33.8	8.7	45.7
[1]1990	345	60.7	17.6	21.2	10.9	7.10	[3]44.8	34.5%	[4]29.3	8.5	40.3
[1]1989	282	61.2	21.7	35.9	8.4	3.10	[3]51.8	34.0%	34.2	12.1	41.6
1988	245	54.5	22.2	11.9	5.2	2.15	48.6	35.0%	31.6	12.9	37.6
1987	205	44.6	21.8	6.2	5.2	1.76	39.7	37.8%	24.7	12.0	29.9
1986	169	27.1	16.1	7.1	4.6	1.78	22.2	37.6%	[4]13.8	8.2	18.5
[1]1985	140	19.4	13.9	7.9	3.8	1.54	15.9	38.9%	9.7	6.9	13.5
[2]1984	140	26.4	18.9	6.4	3.3	1.85	22.4	40.6%	13.3	9.5	16.6
[2]1983	126	19.2	15.3	5.2	3.0	1.71	16.6	38.0%	10.3	8.2	13.3

Balance Sheet Data (Million $)

Oct. 31	Cash	Curr. Assets	Curr. Liab.	Curr. Ratio	Total Assets	% Ret. on Assets	Long Term Debt	Common Equity	Total Cap.	% LT Debt of Cap.	% Ret. on Equity
1992	**13.0**	**232**	**127**	**1.8**	**346**	**12.3**	**26.8**	**178**	**207**	**12.9**	**23.9**
1991	10.5	194	107	1.8	297	11.9	25.5	153	180	14.2	23.9
1990	8.8	174	108	1.6	270	11.6	25.5	130	158	16.2	24.7
1989	5.8	156	102	1.5	236	17.3	20.1	107	130	15.5	35.1
1988	16.1	120	56	2.1	163	20.1	13.2	89	105	12.6	34.6
1987	42.1	126	46	2.8	164	16.6	12.8	101	116	11.0	27.0
1986	18.1	97	38	2.6	134	11.3	12.6	82	96	13.1	18.2
1985	19.3	78	28	2.9	113	8.7	11.7	72	85	13.7	13.2
1984	31.2	90	24	3.8	120	11.5	11.7	82	95	12.3	16.8
1983	31.7	87	23	3.8	114	8.8	11.8	78	91	12.9	13.9

Data as orig. reptd. **1.** Refl. merger or acq. **2.** Excl. disc. ops. **3.** Incl. equity in earns. of nonconsol. subs. **4.** Refl. acctg. change.

Net Sales (Million $)

13 Weeks:	1992–93	1991–92	1991	1990
Jan.	100.3	93.4	[1]89.0	77.5
Apr.	109.3	106.2	93.7	88.6
Jul.		105.6	99.2	82.7
Oct.		120.5	106.1	96.1
		425.6	388.0	344.9

Net sales in the 26 weeks ended May 2, 1993, rose 5.0%, year to year, with price and volume increases offsetting the effects of a stronger dollar. Margins narrowed on a less favorable sales mix and costs related to geographic expansion. Following an 8.8% decline in net interest and other expense, pretax income fell 13%. After taxes at 34.3%, versus 34.8%, net income fell 12% to $15,470,000 ($0.81 a share) from $17,614,000 ($0.90).

Common Share Earnings ($)

13 Weeks:	1992–93	1991–92	1991	1990
Jan.	0.35	0.38	[1]0.34	0.35
Apr.	0.46	0.52	0.40	0.38
Jul.		0.53	0.46	0.35
Oct.		0.60	0.57	0.45
		2.03	1.77	1.53

Dividend Data

Paid each year since 1969, dividends are targeted at 6% of shareholders' equity at the beginning of each fiscal year. A dividend reinvestment plan is available.

Amt. of Divd. $	Date Decl.	Ex–divd. Date	Stock of Record	Payment Date
0.11	Aug. 19	Aug. 31	Sep. 4	Sep. 28'92
0.12	Nov. 11	Nov. 24	Dec. 1	Jan. 4'93
0.12	Feb. 17	Mar. 1	Mar. 5	Mar. 30'93
0.12	May 19	May 28	Jun. 4	Jun. 29'93

Finances

During 1992, NDSN acquired a U.S. manufacturer of adhesive application equipment for $8,302,000. In 1991, NDSN acquired several European distributors of its equipment for $10,562,000.

At November 1, 1992, NDSN had hedged its foreign receivables and payables with contracts of $12,228,000 in European currencies and $19,928,000 in Japanese yen.

Capitalization

Long Term Debt: $23,234,000 (5/93).

Common Stock: 18,690,659 shs. (no par).
Officers & directors own about 39%.
Institutions hold some 24%.
Shareholders: About 2,485 of record (12/92).

1. 14 weeks.

Office—28601 Clemens Rd., Westlake, OH 44145. **Tel**—(216) 892-1580. **Chrmn**—E. T. Nord. **Pres & CEO**—W. P. Madar. **Secy**—W. D. Ginn. **VP-Fin, Treas & Investor Contact**—Nicholas D. Pellecchia. **Dirs**—G. R. Brown, W. W. Colville, W. D. Ginn, S. R. Hardis, J. O. Kamm, A. O. Krueger, W. P. Madar, E. T. Nord, E. W. Nord. **Transfer Agent & Registrar**—Society National Bank, Cleveland. **Incorporated** in Ohio in 1954. **Empl**—2,937.

 Shayna J. Malnak

Northeast Utilities

NYSE Symbol NU In S&P MidCap 400

Price	Range	P-E Ratio	Dividend	Yield	S&P Ranking	Beta
Aug. 10'93	1993					
28	28⅞–25¼	18	1.76	6.3%	B+	0.31

Summary

This utility holding company serves customers in Connecticut and western Massachusetts. In June 1992, NU acquired financially troubled Public Service Co. of New Hampshire (PNH), which serves about 75% of New Hampshire's population, for $2.3 billion. Included in the acquisition was PNH's 35.6% interest in the Seabrook nuclear plant, which achieved commercial operation on June 30, 1990.

Current Outlook

Share earnings for 1993 could decline to $1.50 from the $2.02 recorded for 1992. Share earnings could increase to $2.15 in 1994.

Dividends are expected to be maintained at $0.44 quarterly.

Share earnings for 1993 should fall as flat kwh sales and higher rates are more than offset by the absence of 1992's one-time gain related to NU's acquisition of PNH, $0.12 of one-time charges in the second quarter of 1993 related to the recent Connecticut rate decision ($0.04 due to a disallowance of recovery of certain prior replacement purchased power costs and $0.08 due to the allocation to customers of a portion of the property tax changes made in the first quarter), and expected workforce reduction charges in 1993's third and fourth quarters (estimated at $0.09 and $0.03, respectively). Share earnings for 1994 should benefit from the Connecticut rate hike decision, aggressive cost cutting, and the possibility of an improved New England economy.

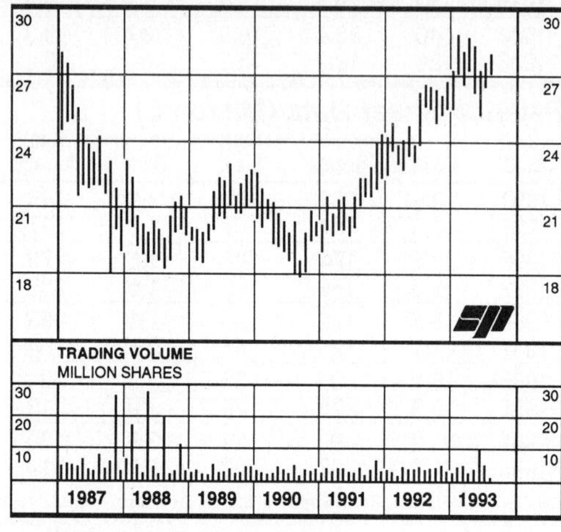

Operating Revenues (Million $)

Quarter:	1993	1992	1991	1990
Mar.	958	763	701	681
Jun.	854	719	637	604
Sep.	---	848	693	675
Dec.	---	888	723	657
	---	3,217	2,754	2,616

Revenues for the six months to June 30, 1993, rose 22%, year to year, on the inclusion of PNH. Net income fell 42%. Share earnings were $0.61 (on 5.5% more average shares) before a $0.39 accounting gain, versus $1.13 in the 1992 period.

Common Share Earnings ($)

Quarter:	1993	1992	1991	1990
Mar.	0.48	0.63	0.63	0.61
Jun.	0.14	[1]0.50	0.46	0.37
Sep.	E0.43	0.47	0.60	0.61
Dec.	E0.45	0.43	0.43	0.35
	E1.50	2.02	2.12	1.94

Important Developments

Jul. '93— NU said it plans to cut its workforce by 600 to 700 persons by 1994 year-end, hopefully via an early retirement program. NU added that it would take an undetermined charge in the third quarter related to the program. If NU has layoffs in November, it expects to take a further, but smaller, charge in the fourth quarter. In June, NU's Connecticut Light & Power Co. unit was granted a $141.3 million (6.2%) rate hike over three years (NU had requested $358 million) by the Department of Public Utility Control (DPUC). The final decision approved hikes of $46.0 million (2.01%), $47.1 million (2.04%) and $48.2 million (2.06%) for 1993, 1994 and 1995, respectively, effective July 1 of each year. The ruling also authorized returns on equity of 11.5%, 11.6% and 11.7% in 1993, 1994 and 1995, respectively. In May, NU postponed any hike in its quarterly dividend, citing the effect on earnings of New England's deep and persistent recession.

Next earnings report expected in late October.

Per Share Data ($)

Yr. End Dec. 31	1992	1991	1990	1989	1988	1987	1986	1985	1984	1983
Tangible Bk. Val.	**15.87**	15.55	16.15	15.94	16.73	16.38	17.21	16.07	14.99	13.74
Earnings[2]	**2.02**	2.12	1.94	1.87	2.07	1.97	2.78	2.72	2.85	2.37
Dividends	**1.76**	1.76	1.76	1.76	1.76	1.76	1.68	1.58	1.48	1.38
Payout Ratio	**87%**	83%	91%	94%	85%	89%	60%	58%	52%	58%
Prices—High	**26¾**	24⅜	22⅝	23	23⅛	28	28¼	18¾	14¾	13⅞
Low	**22½**	19	17⅞	18½	18¼	18	17⅜	13¾	10⅝	11¾
P/E Ratio—	**13–11**	12–9	12–9	12–10	11–9	14–9	10–6	7–5	5–4	6–5

Data as orig. reptd. **1.** Incl. 0.17 one-time gain. **2.** Bef. results of spun-off gas opers. of +0.05 in 1989, +0.08 in 1988, +0.14 in 1987. E-Estimated.

Income Data (Million $)

Year Ended Dec. 31	Revs.	Depr.	Maint.	Oper. Ratio	[1]Fxd. Chgs. Cover.	Constr. Credits	Eff. Tax Rate	[2]Net Inc.	% Return On Revs.	% Return On Invest. Capital	% Return On [3]Com. Equity
1992	**3,217**	**283**	**274**	**86.3%**	**2.56**	**9**	**41.1%**	**256**	**8.0**	**7.8**	**12.7**
1991	2,754	239	230	85.9%	2.77	9	38.5%	237	8.6	8.0	13.0
1990	2,616	212	238	85.5%	2.27	11	31.5%	211	8.1	8.2	12.0
1989	2,206	198	241	82.5%	2.23	9	33.9%	203	9.2	8.0	11.8
1988	2,079	207	191	84.1%	2.57	8	35.4%	225	10.8	7.7	13.0
1987	1,878	192	208	85.2%	2.38	30	30.4%	215	11.4	7.4	12.8
1986	2,032	171	165	85.1%	2.91	99	34.6%	301	14.8	9.2	16.6
1985	2,081	127	181	86.1%	2.89	201	35.0%	289	13.9	9.5	17.4
1984	2,095	121	130	83.6%	3.07	153	38.9%	289	13.8	11.4	19.8
1983	1,889	116	138	84.8%	2.72	122	37.4%	222	11.7	10.6	17.8

Balance Sheet Data (Million $)

Dec. 31	[4]Gross Prop.	Capital Expend.	Net Prop.	% Earn. on Net Prop.	Total Cap.	Capitalization: [5]LT Debt	% LT Debt	Pfd.	% Pfd.	Com.	% Com.
1992	**9,468**	**352**	**6,719**	**7.4**	**8,116**	**4,505**	**61.4**	**654**	**8.9**	**2,174**	**29.7**
1991	7,440	274	5,258	7.4	6,055	2,830	53.7	568	10.7	1,876	35.6
1990	7,299	379	5,265	7.2	5,745	2,713	53.5	569	11.2	1,791	35.3
1989	7,093	293	5,314	7.2	5,736	2,772	54.4	574	11.2	1,752	34.4
1988	6,951	379	5,322	6.3	5,942	3,013	56.8	454	8.6	1,837	34.6
1987	6,732	452	5,265	5.3	5,827	2,901	56.0	488	9.4	1,796	34.6
1986	6,773	489	5,353	5.6	5,750	2,813	54.6	456	8.8	1,884	36.6
1985	6,708	765	5,419	5.6	5,557	2,818	56.0	474	9.4	1,739	34.6
1984	6,043	733	4,855	7.5	5,029	2,550	55.4	477	10.4	1,576	34.2
1983	5,077	581	3,986	7.7	4,240	2,078	53.0	479	12.2	1,362	34.8

Data as orig. reptd. **1.** Times int. exp. & pfd. divs. covered (pretax basis). **2.** Bef. results of gas opers. in 1989, 1988, 1987. **3.** As reptd. by co. **4.** Excl. gas opers. in 1988, 1987. **5.** Incl. capital leases aft. 1983.

Business Summary

Northeast Utilities, the largest utility in New England, is a holding company with three subsidiaries serving some 1.66 million customers in Connecticut, New Hampshire and western Massachusetts. In June 1992, NU acquired Public Service Co. of New Hampshire, which was the largest investor in the Seabrook nuclear plant and emerged from bankruptcy on May 16, 1991. Electric revenues by customer class in recent years:

	1992	1991	1990	1989
Residential	38%	36%	37%	42%
Commercial	29%	30%	31%	32%
Industrial	17%	15%	16%	18%
Other	16%	19%	16%	9%

Power sources in 1992 were nuclear 48%, oil 25%, coal 11%, hydro 5%, gas 3%, and other 8%. Peak demand in 1992 was 5,781 mw and capability at peak totaled 7,800 mw, for a capacity margin of 26%.

NU owns 65% of the 1,150 mw Millstone 3 nuclear plant, which was placed in operation in April 1986. In December 1987, NU wrote off $119.0 million ($1.10 a share) of disallowed Millstone 3 costs retroactive to 1986. NU also has a 39.7% share in the Seabrook nuclear facility (including a 35.6% stake acquired through the June 1992 acquisition of Public Service Co. of New Hampshire). On June 13, 1989, the Seabrook plant achieved its first nuclear reaction. A full power license was awarded in March 1990, and the plant was declared in service and achieved commercial operation on June 30, 1990.

Dividend Data

Dividends have been paid since 1927. A dividend reinvestment plan is available.

Amt of Divd. $	Date Decl.	Ex-divd. Date	Stock of Record	Payment Date
0.44	Oct. 27	Nov. 24	Dec. 1	Dec. 31'92
0.44	Feb. 1	Feb. 23	Mar. 1	Mar. 31'93
0.44	Apr. 28	May 25	Jun. 1	Jun. 30'93
0.44	Jul. 27	Aug. 26	Sep. 1	Sep. 30'93

Capitalization

Long Term Debt: $4,410,763,000 (6/93).

Subsid. Preferred Stock: $647,696,000.

Common Stock: 134,009,097 shs. ($5 par).
Institutions hold about 26%.
Shareholders of record: 147,895.

Office—P.O. Box 270, Hartford, CT 06141. **Tel**—(203) 665-5000. **Chrmn**—W. B. Ellis. **Pres & CEO**—B. M. Fox. **VP-CFO**—R. E. Busch. **VP-Secy**—J. B. Keane. **Investor Contact**—Jeff Kotkin. **Trustees**—C. M. Cleveland, R. L. Creviston, G. David, D. J. Donahue, W. B. Ellis, B. M. Fox, G. B. Harvey, E. D. Jones, E. T. Kennan, D. C. Lunt Jr., B. Marshall, W. J. Pape II, N. C. Rasmussen, J. F. Swope. **Transfer Agents & Registrars**—Northeast Utilities Service Co., Hartford, Conn.; State Street Bank & Trust Co., Boston, Mass. **A Voluntary Association** organized in Massachusetts under a Declaration of Trust in 1927. **Empl**—10,136.

 Christopher J. Grant

Northern Trust Corp.

NASDAQ Symbol NTRS (Incl. in Nat'l Market) Options on CBOE In S&P MidCap 400

Price	Range	P-E Ratio	Dividend	Yield	S&P Ranking	Beta
Sep. 21'93	1993					
40	50½–39¾	14	0.74	1.9%	B+	1.06

Summary

This Chicago-based interstate bank holding company's lead subsidiary is Northern Trust Co., the fourth largest commercial bank in Illinois. Following a gain in 1992, earnings should continue to rise in 1993, aided by higher fee income from trust and cash management operations. Concurrent with a three-for-two stock split in December 1992, the dividend was boosted 16%. Officers and directors hold 7% of the common shares, and a company ESOP owns an additional 21%.

Current Outlook

Earnings for 1993 are projected at $2.95 a share, up from 1992's $2.64.

The minimum expectation is for dividends to continue at $0.18½ quarterly.

Earnings should continue to rise in 1993, based on expected wider interest rate spreads in the lending segment and increased noninterest income from core trust and custody service operations. Noninterest income, which currently accounts for 60% of total taxable equivalent revenue, is expected to advance from 10% to 15% annually over the next several years, as the company continues to emphasize business development efforts and concentrate on its key markets. Most noninterest income is attributable to the trust services division, which administered $448 billion in trust assets as of June 30, 1993, up from $412 billion at year-end 1992. Although only 45% of total corporate assets consist of loans receivable, credit quality appears to be improving: the reserve for loan losses dropped to $145.5 million at June 30, 1993 (1.98% of gross loans outstanding); nonperforming assets now comprise 0.40% of total assets, down from 0.61% at year-end 1992.

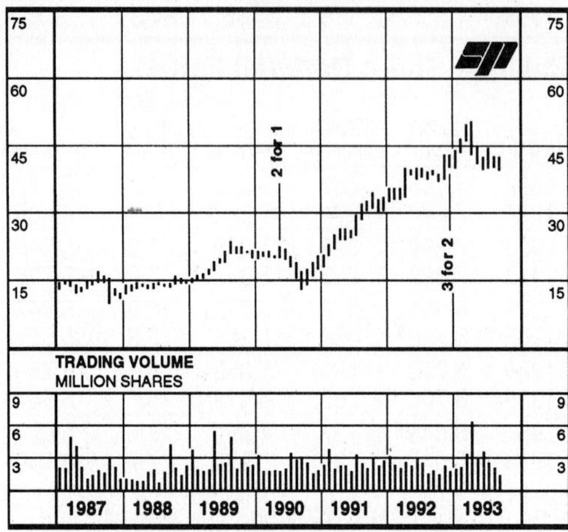

Review of Operations

Net interest income for the six months ended June 30, 1993, advanced 6.3%, year to year, on a 6.5% decrease in interest income and a 15% drop in interest expense. The provision for loan losses fell to $12.0 million, from $16.0 million. Noninterest income was up 9.3%, led by higher trust and cash management fees, while noninterest expense was up only 8.0%; pretax income increased 14%. After taxes at 28.1%, versus 27.0%, net income was up 12%, to $81.8 million ($1.44 a share, after preferred dividends and based on 1.3% more shares; no dilution), from $72.9 million ($1.29).

Common Share Earnings ($)

Quarter:	1993	1992	1991	1990
Mar.	0.71	0.64	0.84	0.69
Jun.	0.73	0.65	0.87	0.77
Sep.	E0.75	0.67	0.84	0.81
Dec.	E0.76	0.68	0.89	0.82
	E2.95	2.64	3.43	3.09

Important Developments

Jun. 30'93— Northern Trust's Tier 1 and total risk-based capital ratios were 8.7% and 11.3%, respectively, both well in excess of federal regulatory minimums.

Next earnings report expected in mid-October.

Per Share Data ($)

Yr. End Dec. 31	1992	[1]1991	[1]1990	[1]1989	[2]1988	1987	[1]1986	1985	1984	[1]1983
Tangible Bk. Val.	**14.37**	12.82	11.04	9.68	8.55	6.66	5.67	8.29	7.97	7.85
Earnings[3]	**2.64**	2.29	2.06	2.08	2.21	d1.59	0.72	0.69	0.45	0.42
Dividends	**0.665**	0.580	0.520	0.413	0.353	0.313	0.203	0.302	0.302	0.302
Payout Ratio	**25%**	25%	25%	20%	16%	NM	28%	44%	67%	72%
Prices—High	**43⅛**	35	22½	23¾	16	17	10⅜	9½	7⅛	7⅛
Low	**32⅝**	18	13	14⅝	12⅛	10	6½	6⅝	6¼	5
P/E Ratio—	**16–12**	15–8	11–6	11–7	7–6	NM	15–9	14–10	16–14	17–12

Data as orig. reptd. Adj. for stk. divs. of 50% Dec. 1992, 100% May 1990, 200% May 1986. **1.** Refl. merger or acq. **2.** Refl. acctg. change. **3.** Ful. dil.: 3.41 in 1991, 3.08 in 1990, 3.02 in 1989, 3.19 in 1988, 1.62 in 1986. E-Estimated d-Deficit. NM-Not Meaningful.

Income Data (Million $)

Year Ended Dec. 31	Net Int. Inc.	Tax Equiv. Adj.	Non Int. Inc.	Loan Loss Prov.	% Exp./ Op. Revs.	Net Bef. Taxes	Eff. Tax Rate	Net Inc.	% Net Int. Margin	—% Return On— Assets	Equity
1992	**311**	**32.5**	**506**	**30**	**68.8**	**207**	**27.6%**	**150**	**2.96**	**1.11**	**18.3**
[1]1991	282	36.0	409	31	68.8	164	22.1%	127	3.00	1.05	19.0
[1]1990	249	38.1	367	14	71.0	140	17.4%	115	2.80	0.99	19.8
[1]1989	237	36.0	330	16	70.7	125	9.4%	113	2.95	1.08	22.8
[2]1988	232	23.8	307	20	68.9	131	16.8%	109	3.20	1.20	28.9
1987	209	28.0	242	179	71.5	d68	NM	d65	3.25	NM	NM
[1]1986	182	37.2	220	55	65.8	61	13.8%	52	3.48	0.70	13.4
1985	172	24.0	176	55	69.7	35	2.3%	34	3.40	0.49	8.6
1984	162	25.1	135	47	71.1	21	NM	22	3.39	0.34	5.6
[1]1983	151	27.0	119	59	68.5	11	NM	18	3.28	0.29	5.4

Balance Sheet Data (Million $)

Dec. 31	Total Assets	—Earning Assets— Mon. Mkt. Assets	Inv. Secs.	Com'l Loans	Other Loans	% Loan Loss Resv.	—Deposits— Demand	Time	% Loans/ Deposits	Long Term Debt	Common Equity	% Equity To Assets
1992	**14,960**	**2,318**	**3,180**	**2,881**	**4,055**	**2.10**	**2,712**	**7,159**	**70.3**	**545**	**841**	**5.83**
1991	13,193	1,710	3,115	3,176	3,104	2.32	1,824	6,737	73.4	266	701	5.24
1990	11,789	1,397	2,194	2,831	2,706	2.67	2,021	6,088	68.3	172	589	4.73
1989	10,938	970	2,244	2,924	2,736	2.65	1,803	5,236	80.4	241	531	4.41
1988	9,904	1,290	2,185	2,660	2,006	3.24	1,965	4,788	69.1	175	410	3.87
1987	9,326	1,654	1,936	2,160	1,803	5.89	2,001	4,846	57.9	175	324	4.58
1986	9,090	1,496	1,634	2,248	1,752	1.90	2,090	4,117	64.5	102	409	4.97
1985	7,500	1,116	1,013	2,162	1,471	1.54	1,871	3,161	72.2	100	371	5.18
1984	7,225	1,258	814	1,925	1,473	1.23	1,706	3,198	69.3	100	353	5.39
1983	6,438	1,508	742	1,633	1,492	1.19	1,442	2,930	71.5	105	346	5.32

Data as orig. reptd. **1.** Refl. merger or acq. **2.** Refl. acctg. change. d-Deficit. NM-Not Meaningful.

Business Summary

Northern Trust Corporation is an interstate bank holding company whose lead bank is Northern Trust Co. of Chicago, the fourth largest bank in Illinois. The company also owns a growing network of smaller banks and nonbanking subsidiaries in Illinois, Florida, Arizona, California, New York and Texas, providing banking, stock brokerage and other services. At December 31, 1992, total assets came to $14.9 billion, and trust assets under administration totaled $412 billion. Gross loans of $6.94 billion at December 31, 1992, were divided:

	1992	1991
Commercial	35%	43%
Real estate–residential	34%	29%
Real estate–commercial	7%	8%
Consumer	7%	7%
Brokerage	5%	5%
International	4%	5%
Leasing & other	8%	1%

The allowance for loan losses at 1992 year-end was $145.5 million (2.10% of gross loans and leases outstanding), down from $145.7 million (2.32%) a year earlier. Net chargeoffs during 1992 amounted to $29.7 million (equal to 0.46% of average loans), up from $33.3 million (0.54%) in 1991. Nonperforming assets at December 31, 1992, totaled $91.2 million (0.61% of total assets), versus $94.2 million (0.70%) at 1991 year-end.

Total deposits of $9.87 billion at year-end 1992 were divided: demand and other noninterest-bearing 27%, savings and money market 37%, savings certificates 13%, other time 4% and foreign 19%. On a tax-equivalent basis, the average yield on interest-earning assets was 6.50% in 1992 (8.33% in 1991), while the average rate paid on interest-bearing liabilities was 4.05% (6.04%), for a net spread of 2.45% (2.29%).

Dividend Data

Cash has been paid each year since 1896.

Amt of Divd. $	Date Decl.	Ex–divd. Date	Stock of Record	Payment Date
3–for–2 Split	Nov. 17	Dec. 10	Nov. 30	Dec. 9'92
0.18½	Nov. 17	Dec. 4	Dec. 10	Jan. 4'93
0.18½	Feb. 17	Mar. 4	Mar. 10	Apr. 1'93
0.18½	May 18	Jun. 4	Jun. 10	Jul. 1'93
0.18½	Aug. 17	Sep. 3	Sep. 10	Oct. 1'93

Capitalization

Notes Payable: $897,100,000 (6/93).

Ser. C Auction Rate Cum. Pfd. Stk.: 600 shs.

Ser. D Flex. Auction Rate Cum. Pfd. Stk.: 600 shs.

Ser. E 6.25% Cum. Conv. Pfd. Stk.: 50,000 shs., ea. conv. into 0.803 com. shs.

Common Stock: 53,039,955 shs. ($1.66⅔ par). Officers and directors hold 7%; ESOP owns 21%. Shareholders: About 2,893 of record (12/92).

Office—50 S. LaSalle St., Chicago, IL 60675. **Tel**—(312) 630-6000. **Chrmn, Pres & CEO**—D. W. Fox. **EVP & CFO**—P. R. Pero. **EVP & Secy**—J. B. Snyder. **Treas & Investor Contact**—David L. Eddy (312-444-7402). **Dirs**—W. H. Clark, D. W. Fox, R. S. Hamada, R. A. Helman, A. L. Kelly, A. Krainik, R. D. Krebs, F. A. Krehbiel, W. G. Mitchell, W. A. Pogue, H. B. Smith, Jr., W. D. Smithburg, B. L. Thomas. **Transfer Agent & Registrar**—Harris Trust & Savings Bank, Chicago. **Incorporated** in Delaware in 1971; bank chartered in Illinois in 1889. **Empl**—5,798.

 Barry R. Haas

NovaCare, Inc.

NYSE Symbol NOV In S&P MidCap 400

Price	Range	P-E Ratio	Dividend	Yield	S&P Ranking	Beta
Aug. 10'93	1993					
12⅞	23⅞–11⅜	14	None	None	NR	2.11

Summary

This company is a leading national provider of comprehensive medical rehabilitation services. The company expanded its operations significantly in March 1992 through the acquisition of Orthopedic Services, Inc., the largest provider of patient care services in the orthotic and prosthetic rehabilitation industry. A pending acquisition will add approximately $50 million to annual revenues.

Business Summary

NovaCare, Inc. is a leading national provider of comprehensive medical rehabilitation services. These services are provided (1) on a contract basis, primarily to long-term health care institutions; (2) through inpatient rehabilitation hospitals and community integrated programs; and (3) through a national network of patient care centers providing orthotic and prosthetic rehabilitation services. The company provides multidisciplinary programs comprising speech-language pathology, occupational therapy and physical therapy to patients experiencing physical disability.

As of March 31, 1993, NOV was providing rehabilitation services under 4,431 contracts in 1,879 facilities located in 40 states. Customers include nursing homes operated by most of the largest nursing home chains in the U.S., with Beverly Enterprises, Inc., accounting for 14% of revenues in each of the last two fiscal years.

Speech-language pathology is the diagnosis and treatment of speech, language, voice and swallowing disorders. Occupational therapy is the evaluation and treatment of physical, cognitive and psychosocial performance deficits. Physical therapy improves muscular and neural responses in an effort to improve patients' physical strength and range of motion.

Rehab Systems Co., acquired in August 1991 for 5,999,993 common shares, provides acute rehabilitation care on a multidisciplinary, physician-directed basis to severely disabled patients through seven acute rehabilitation hospitals. It also operates seven community rehabilitation programs which treat post-acute brain injured patients in community-based settings.

Orthopedic Services, Inc. (OSI), acquired in March 1992 for 10,400,547 common shares, is the largest provider of patient care services in the orthotic and prosthetic rehabilitation industry. As of March 1993, OSI provided services through 105 patient care centers in 23 states. Orthotic rehabilitation is the fitting and fabrication of custom-made braces and support devices for treatment of musculoskeletal conditions. Prosthetic rehabilitation is the fitting and fabrication of custom-made artificial limbs.

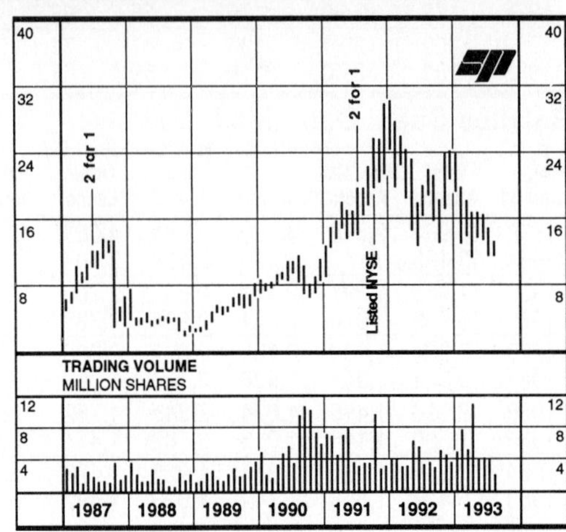

The company's business strategy is to consolidate and integrate selected parts of the medical rehabilitation industry in order to offer a continuum of rehabilitation services and to diversify patient caseload and payors. This strategy is being implemented through a program of disciplined internal growth and acquisitions and is designed to capitalize upon 1) an underserved and growing demand for rehabilitation services; 2) a highly fragmented market in which many competitors lack professional management, information systems and access to capital; and 3) the increasing influence of managed care.

Because of a shortage of qualified therapists, the company has developed career ladder, compensation and management support programs to attract and retain certified therapists.

Next earnings report expected in late October.

Per Share Data ($)

Yr. End Jun. 30	1993	[1]1992	1991	[1]1990	1989	[1]1988	[1]1987	[1]1986
Tangible Bk. Val.	**NA**	2.84	2.67	1.25	[2]1.88	[2]1.68	[2]1.64	[2]d0.05
Cash Flow	**NA**	0.89	0.70	0.49	0.25	0.01	0.13	d0.03
Earnings	**0.93**	[3]0.75	[3]0.64	[3]0.44	[3]0.19	[3]d0.04	[3]0.10	[3]d0.05
Dividends	**Nil**	Nil	Nil	Nil	Nil	Nil	Nil	Nil
Payout Ratio	**Nil**	Nil	Nil	Nil	Nil	Nil	Nil	NM
Prices—High	**23⅞**	[4]30¼	[4]29⅞	[4]11 9/16	[4]8¼	[4]7⅝	[4]13⅝	[4]6 9/16
Low	**11⅜**	[4]12¾	[4]9	[4]6½	[4]2 7/16	[4]1 15/16	[4]3	[4]4¼
P/E Ratio—	**NA**	40–17	47–14	27–15	43–13	NM	NM	NM

Data as orig. reptd. Adj. for stk. divs. of 100% Jul. 1991, 100% Jun. 1987. **1.** Reflects merger or acquisition. **2.** Incl. intangibles. **3.** Bef. spec. item(s) of +0.05 in 1987. **4.** Cal. yr. d-Deficit. NA-Not Available. NM-Not Meaningful.

Income Data (Million $)

Year Ended Jun. 30	Revs.	Oper. Inc.	% Oper. Inc. of Revs.	Cap. Exp.	Depr.	Int. Exp.	Net Bef. Taxes	Eff. Tax Rate	[2]Net Inc.	% Net Inc. of Revs.	Cash Flow
[1]**1992**	**385**	**67.7**	**17.6**	**9.92**	**7.48**	**2.02**	**57.3**	**33.8%**	**37.5**	**9.7**	**45.0**
1991	152	31.4	20.7	1.37	1.88	0.55	30.7	33.7%	20.3	13.4	22.2
[1]1990	102	20.2	19.8	1.18	1.59	1.38	19.0	34.8%	12.4	12.1	14.0
1989	70	9.7	13.8	0.65	1.60	1.64	7.8	34.8%	5.1	7.2	6.7
[1]1988	58	3.6	6.2	0.72	1.30	1.52	d0.3	NM	d1.0	NM	0.3
[1]1987	27	5.1	18.9	1.05	0.58	0.70	4.5	8.6%	2.3	8.6	2.9
[1]1986	8	0.3	3.4	0.14	0.25	0.76	d0.7	NM	d0.7	NM	d0.5

Balance Sheet Data (Million $)

Jun. 30	Cash	Curr. Assets	Curr. Liab.	Curr. Ratio	Total Assets	% Ret. on Assets	Long Term Debt	Common Equity	Total Cap.	% LT Debt of Cap.	% Ret. on Equity
1992	**29.9**	**144**	**46.5**	**3.1**	**292**	**15.4**	**14.3**	**224**	**240**	**6.0**	**18.9**
1991	33.1	80	13.2	6.1	127	17.5	0.4	114	114	0.4	21.6
1990	27.8	55	13.8	4.0	88	15.3	10.9	63	74	14.7	21.9
1989	21.6	41	8.2	5.1	73	7.0	14.5	50	65	22.3	10.8
1988	23.2	41	9.1	4.5	72	NM	17.5	45	63	27.6	NM
1987	1.1	11	6.8	1.6	58	5.7	8.3	43	51	16.2	NM
1986	0.1	4	9.9	0.4	13	NM	3.9	d1	3	122.2	NM

Data as orig. reptd. **1.** Reflects merger or acquisition. **2.** Bef. spec. item(s) in 1987. d-Deficit. NM-Not Meaningful.

Net Revenues (Million $)

Quarter:	1992–93	1991–92	1990–91	1989–90
Sep.	117.3	84.7	31.6	21.7
Dec.	129.5	92.4	35.9	23.6
Mar.	139.3	99.2	39.8	26.7
Jun.	152.9	108.8	44.2	30.2
	539.1	385.1	151.5	102.1

Based on a preliminary report, revenues for the fiscal year ended June 30, 1993, rose 40% from those of the prior year, reflecting continued strong demand for the company's rehabilitation services. Margins were penalized by costs of new programs and training associated with an unusually high number of new hires, which negatively impacted productivity, and by $5.7 million of restructuring charges, which more than offset $4.7 million of merger and other nonrecurring expenses in fiscal 1992. After significantly higher interest expense, net income was up 25%, to $0.93 a share from $0.75.

Common Share Earnings ($)

Quarter:	1992–93	1991–92	1990–91	1989–90
Sep.	0.24	0.18	0.14	0.09
Dec.	0.25	0.13	0.15	0.10
Mar.	0.15	0.21	0.17	0.12
Jun.	0.29	0.23	0.18	0.14
	0.93	0.75	0.64	0.44

Dividend Data

No dividends have been paid. The shares were split 2-for-1 in July 1991 and in June 1987.

Finances

In July 1993, the company acquired two contract services and three orthotic and prosthetics businesses with combined annual revenues of $9 million. Terms of the transactions were not disclosed. Seperately, in June 1993, the company agreed to acquire Rehabilitation Hospital Corp. of America (RHCA), which provides comprehensive medical rehabilitation services through a network of five inpatient hospitals and four outpatient clinics. Under terms of the agreement, NovaCare will pay $31 million in cash for the equity of RHCA, and pay down debt and redeem preferred stock of RHCA totaling approximately $20 million. RHCA has annual revenues of approximately $50 million.

In March 1993, NovaCare recorded a one-time $5.7 million restructuring charge related to the consolidation of certain orthotic and prosthetic patient care and fabrication centers, the closure of selected community integrated programs, and the consolidation of corporate headquarters. In fiscal 1992, the company recorded non-recurring charges of $4.0 million relating primarily to the acquisition of Orthopedic Services, Inc.

In January 1993, the company sold publicly $175 million of 5½% convertible subordinated debentures, due 2000. The debentures are convertible into NOV common stock at $26.65 a share. Net proceeds of approximately $170.3 million were earmarked for general corporate purposes and for acquisitions.

Capitalization

Long Term Debt: $188,517,000 (3/93).

Minority Interest: $1,017,000.

Common Stock: 49,313,816 shs. ($0.01 par).
Institutions hold about 55%.
Shareholders of record: 1,408 (8/92).

Office—1016 W. 9th Ave., King of Prussia, PA 19406. **Tel**—(215) 992-7200. **Chrmn & CEO**—J. H. Foster. **Pres**—F. W. Cash. **SVP-CFO & Secy**—T. E. Foster. **Investor Contact**—Susan J. Campbell. **Dirs**—F. W. Cash, J. H. Foster, T. E. Foster, E. M. Gibson, S. E. O'Neil, C. A. Renschler, G. W. Siguler, D. C. Tosteson, R. Velge. **Transfer Agent & Registrar**—American Stock Transfer Co., NYC. **Incorporated** in Delaware in 1984. **Empl**—5,650.

 Adam J. Penn

OEA, Inc.

NYSE Symbol OEA Options on ASE (Jan-Apr-Jul-Oct) In S&P MidCap 400

Price	Range	P-E Ratio	Dividend	Yield	S&P Ranking	Beta
Oct. 20'93	1993					
28½	32¼–21¾	40	0.12	0.4%	B+	1.01

Summary

This company designs and manufactures propellant and explosive-actuated devices used in space vehicles, military and civilian aircraft and missiles, and is the dominant producer of airbag initiators for automobiles. Although aerospace/defense operations are being affected by the decline in defense spending, the rapid growth of airbag installations expected in the next few years should lead to continued strong earnings gains.

Current Outlook

Earnings for the fiscal year ending July 31, 1994, are estimated at $0.95 a share, up from $0.72 for fiscal 1993.

An increase in the $0.12 annual dividend paid in December 1992 is likely.

Sales for fiscal 1994 could increase in the area of 25%. Revenues from government contracting should be close to year-earlier levels, reflecting an improved order pattern in fiscal 1993 and substantial replacement shipments. Automotive sales will move up strongly, with airbag component shipments likely to rise about 70%. Corporate margins should widen, reflecting cost reduction actions and a larger proportion of higher-margin replacement parts in aerospace volume.

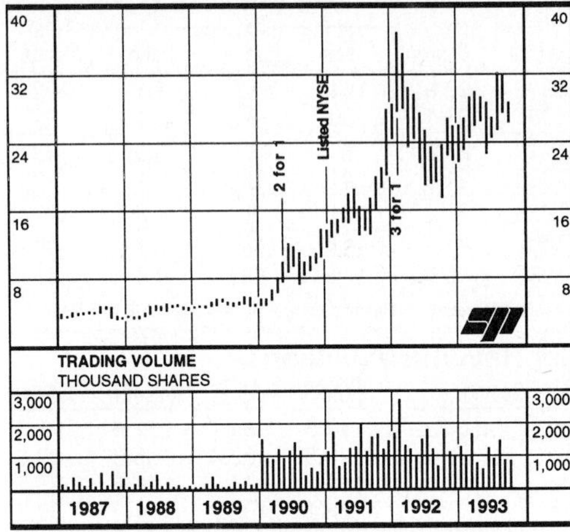

Net Sales (Million $)

Quarter:	1992–93	1991–92	1990–91	1989–90
Oct.	22.4	22.3	18.7	15.4
Jan.	22.2	22.6	20.3	17.0
Apr.	22.0	21.5	21.1	20.9
Jul.	27.5	21.6	23.7	23.5
	94.2	88.1	83.7	76.6

Sales (preliminary) for the year ended July 31, 1993, increased 6.9%, year to year, as a gain for the automotive products segment outweighed a decline for government operations. Margins improved, but smaller nonoperating income ($0.02 a share versus $0.14) held the gain in pretax income to 2.8%. After taxes at 38.5%, versus 34.0%, net income was off 4.4%.

Common Share Earnings ($)

Quarter:	1992–93	1991–92	1990–91	1989–90
Oct.	0.18	0.17	0.14	0.11
Jan.	0.17	0.17	0.14	0.11
Apr.	0.17	0.16	0.14	0.13
Jul.	0.20	0.26	0.18	0.13
	0.72	0.75	0.60	0.47

Important Developments

Oct. '93— OEA reported that in the year ended July 31 sales of automotive safety products increased 34%, while sales of defense related products were off 11%. Operating profit margins increased to 25% from 21%. Record bookings of $98 million during the year resulted in a year-end backlog of $100 million, up from $96 million a year earlier.

Mar. '93— OEA said that its Utah division had become operational, increasing the capacity for air bag initiators to 20 million annually.

Oct. '92— OEA announced that the OEA/Morton hybrid inflator would be installed in passenger-side air bag modules of a Ford vehicle model line. Earlier, the hybrid inflator was selected for Chrysler's new LH vehicles, beginning with the 1994 model year.

Next earnings report expected in early December.

Per Share Data ($)

Yr. End Jul. 31	1993	1992	1991	1990	1989	1988	1987	1986	1985	1984
Tangible Bk. Val.	**NA**	4.65	4.00	3.48	3.01	2.64	2.32	2.06	1.79	1.54
Cash Flow	**NA**	0.88	0.71	0.56	0.44	0.39	0.33	0.33	0.30	0.31
Earnings[1]	**0.72**	0.75	0.60	0.47	0.36	0.31	0.27	0.27	0.24	0.26
Dividends	**0.120**	0.100	0.083	Nil	Nil	Nil	Nil	Nil	Nil	Nil
Payout Ratio	**17%**	13%	14%	Nil	Nil	Nil	Nil	Nil	Nil	Nil
Prices[2]—High	**32¼**	37	28	13⅝	5⅞	5	4¾	4⅜	4⅜	4½
Low	**21¾**	17½	11⅝	4⅝	4½	3¼	3¼	3⅛	2¾	2⅝
P/E Ratio—	**45–30**	49–23	47–19	29–10	16–13	16–11	18–12	16–12	17–12	17–10

Data as orig. reptd. Adj. for stk. divs. of 200% Feb. 1992, 100% May 1990. **1.** Bef. spec. items of +0.01 in 1989, +0.02 in 1988. **2.** Cal. yr. NA-Not Available.

Income Data (Million $)

Year Ended Jul. 31	Revs.	Oper. Inc.	% Oper. Inc. of Revs.	Cap. Exp.	Depr.	Int. Exp.	Net Bef. Taxes	Eff. Tax Rate	[2]Net Inc.	% Net Inc. of Revs.	Cash Flow
1992	**88.1**	**21.0**	**23.9**	**18.4**	**2.55**	**0.05**	**[1]23.1**	**34.0%**	**15.2**	**17.3**	**17.8**
1991	83.7	21.0	25.1	8.2	2.28	0.04	[1]19.2	36.7%	12.1	14.5	14.4
1990	76.6	16.8	21.9	5.3	1.93	0.14	[1]14.9	37.0%	9.4	12.3	11.3
1989	62.0	13.3	21.4	6.2	1.62	0.30	[1]11.5	37.1%	7.3	11.7	8.9
1988	47.3	11.3	24.0	5.0	1.55	0.07	[1]9.9	36.5%	6.3	13.3	7.9
1987	41.9	10.3	24.6	2.1	1.17	Nil	9.6	44.2%	5.4	12.8	6.5
1986	41.0	10.6	25.8	1.5	1.24	0.03	10.0	46.6%	5.3	13.0	6.6
1985	34.3	9.1	26.5	0.9	1.22	0.06	8.6	44.9%	4.7	13.7	5.9
1984	33.4	9.6	28.7	2.9	0.95	0.06	9.1	43.2%	5.2	15.5	6.1
1983	33.0	9.4	28.4	1.6	0.79	0.08	8.8	48.4%	4.5	13.7	5.3

Balance Sheet Data (Million $)

Jul. 31	Cash	Curr. Assets	Curr. Liab.	Curr. Ratio	Total Assets	% Ret. on Assets	Long Term Debt	Common Equity	Total Cap.	% LT Debt of Cap.	% Ret. on Equity
1992	**2.2**	**57.0**	**7.8**	**7.3**	**106**	**15.4**	**Nil**	**94.5**	**97.0**	**Nil**	**17.3**
1991	6.0	61.2	8.6	7.1	92	14.1	0.39	81.0	82.6	0.5	16.0
1990	8.9	56.6	7.9	7.2	80	12.2	0.47	70.2	72.0	0.6	14.4
1989	0.3	53.3	11.2	4.8	74	10.5	0.48	60.5	62.3	0.8	12.8
1988	1.0	48.5	9.7	5.0	64	10.7	0.44	52.9	54.3	0.8	12.7
1987	7.5	43.1	5.9	7.3	54	10.3	0.20	47.1	48.1	0.4	12.1
1986	11.2	39.5	6.3	6.3	49	11.7	0.33	41.1	42.1	0.8	13.9
1985	10.2	34.5	5.6	6.1	43	11.6	0.29	35.7	36.3	0.8	14.1
1984	9.5	30.4	6.1	5.0	39	14.6	0.55	31.0	31.6	1.7	18.2
1983	9.5	26.4	5.6	4.7	33	15.8	0.49	25.8	26.3	1.9	22.1

Data as orig. reptd. **1.** Incl. equity in earns. of nonconsol. subs. **2.** Bef. spec. items in 1989, 1988.

Business Summary

OEA, Inc.'s products have applications mainly in the aerospace industry and in the manufacture of automotive air bags. Segment contributions in fiscal 1992 were:

	Sales	Profits
Government:		
Propellant/explosive.......	50%	46%
Other lines	7%	9%
Commercial	43%	45%

OEA makes propellant and explosive-actuated devices used in personnel escape systems for high-speed aircraft, in separation and release devices for space vehicles and aircraft, and in the control, separation, ejection and jettison of missiles. Its ET, Inc. subsidiary manufactures flexible linear-shaped charges and mild detonating cord systems. The principal customers for these products are the U.S. government and major aircraft and aerospace companies holding prime government contracts. The major portion of the business comes from fixed-price subcontracts. Most military aircraft, missiles/launchers, satellites and the Space Shuttle use these products. Pyrospace, a 45%-owned joint venture, produces pyrotechnic devices in Europe.

Other company products and services include hot gas and explosive initiated valves, fluid control systems, inflatable systems, glass-to-metal sealing, and neutron radiography inspection.

The commercial segment manufactures electric initiators for automobile air bags. OEA had a 70% share of the air bag initiator market at July 1992.

Sales to Morton International (air bag initiators) accounted for 30% of total sales in fiscal 1992, while prime contracts with the U.S. government accounted for 16%.

Dividend Data

Annual cash dividends, omitted in fiscal 1983, were resumed in November 1990.

Amt of Divd. $	Date Decl.	Ex-divd. Date	Stock of Record	Payment Date
0.12	Nov. 20	Dec. 8	Dec. 14	Dec. 21'92

Capitalization

Long Term Debt: None (4/93).

Common Stock: 20,396,000 shs. ($0.10 par).
Kafadar family owns 13%.
Taft-Pierce Manufacturing Co. owns 11%.
Institutions hold 24%.
Shareholders of record: 2,500.

Office—34501 East Quincy Ave (PO Box 100488), Denver, CO 80250. **Tel**—(303) 693-1248. **Chrmn & CEO**—A. D. Kafadar. **Pres**—C. B. Kafadar. **SVP, Secy, Treas & Investor Contact**—John E. Banko. **Dirs**—J. E. Banko, R. A. L. Bogan, Jr., J. R. Burnett, G. B. Huber, P. E. Johnson, T. O. Jones, A. D. Kafadar, C. B. Kafadar, J. G. Maynard, L. W. Watson. **Transfer Agent & Registrar**—Chemical Trust Company of California, San Francisco. **Incorporated** in Delaware in 1969. **Empl**—825.

 T. M. Canning, CFA

Octel Communications

NASDAQ Symbol OCTL (Incl. in Nat'l Market) Options on Pacific In S&P MidCap 400

Price	Range	P-E Ratio	Dividend	Yield	S&P Ranking	Beta
Aug. 11'93	1993					
21½	30–19	18	None	None	B	1.45

Summary

Octel makes voice information processing systems that allow touch-tone telephone users to access, manage and integrate voice, image and data information across the telephone network. Operations continue to grow through acquisitions. The recent acquisitions of Compass Technology Inc. expanded operations to include voice information processing software for PCs, while that of Tigon Corp. added voice processing and networking services. Earnings have been in a long-term uptrend, with profits for fiscal 1993 benefiting from strong growth in net revenues and the consolidation of recent acquisitions.

Business Summary

Octel Communications Corporation designs, makes and markets voice information processing systems that allow users to access, manage and integrate multiple forms of information—voice, image and data—across the telephone network in a single call from any touch-tone telephone in the world. Users with a mailbox on a voice information processing system can send or retrieve voice messages, receive faxes, send or retrieve data and receive notice of electronic mail (E-mail). In fiscal 1991, voice processing capabilities were added, as the company expanded its product line to incorporate data, fax and E-mail. As a result of its 1992 acquisitions of Compass Technology Inc. and Tigon Corp., Octel now designs, manufactures and markets voice processing application software for use with PCs.

The company was founded to develop and market voice processing products; its first system was introduced in 1984. Octel initially focused on serving large corporate customers, but has since expanded its markets to include telephone companies; cellular operators and service bureaus; small and medium-size businesses; federal, state and local governments; medical organizations; and universities and other nonprofit organizations. The product line now covers a range of system sizes and feature functionality.

Octel's three principal customer markets are North American Customer Premise Equipment (CPE) customers, North American voice information services (VIS) providers and international customers (both CPE and VIS). VIS providers buy voice information processing systems and resell their services to customers, generally for a monthly service charge. The VIS market, which accounts for over 70% of the company's total sales, has been growing more rapidly than the CPE market, primarily as a result of growth in international sales.

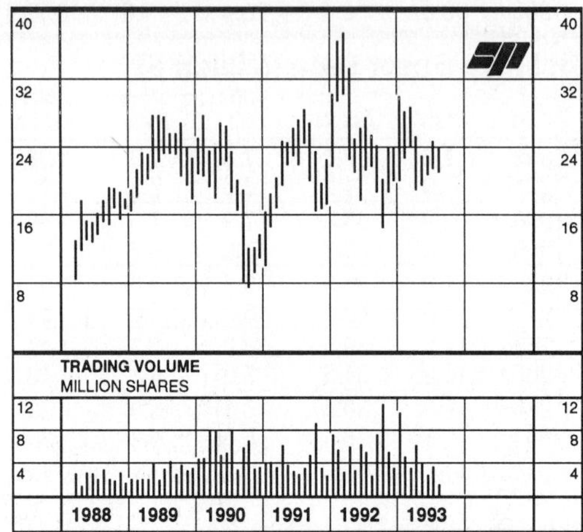

Export sales, primarily to Canada and Western Europe, and to a lesser extent in Mexico, Singapore, Australia, New Zealand, Hong Kong and Taiwan represented 24% of revenues in fiscal 1992, up from 15% in fiscal 1991 and 11% in fiscal 1990.

In July 1991, the company acquired Allegro Intelligent Systems Ltd., which specializes in voice response systems and software, a central resource in delivery of interactive voice response products.

Important Developments

Jun. '93— OCTL announced support for Microsoft's new At Work messaging protocol and Windows telephone applications programming interface (API). OCTL products developed with a library of APIs allow users to visually display, access and manage communications on a desktop computer.

Next earnings report expected in late October.

Per Share Data ($)

Yr. End Jun. 30	1993	1992	1991	1990	1989	1988	1987	1986	1985	1984
Tangible Bk. Val.	**NA**	9.72	8.31	7.25	4.18	2.46	1.22	0.63	0.55	0.17
Cash Flow	**NA**	1.75	1.52	1.40	0.98	0.53	0.11	NA	NA	NA
Earnings[1]	**1.19**	1.14	1.00	1.04	0.78	0.43	0.07	0.03	d0.30	d0.42
Dividends	**Nil**	Nil	Nil	Nil	Nil	Nil	Nil	Nil	Nil	Nil
Payout Ratio	**Nil**	Nil	Nil	Nil	Nil	Nil	Nil	Nil	Nil	Nil
Prices[2]—High	**37½**	37½	28½	27¾	27¾	19¼	NA	NA	NA	NA
Low	**14½**	14½	10⅛	7½	16½	7	NA	NA	NA	NA
P/E Ratio—	**31–12**	33–13	29–10	27–7	36–21	44–16	NA	NA	NM	NM

Data as orig. reptd. **1.** Bef. spec. items of +0.11 in 1988, +0.05 in 1987, +0.02 in 1986. **2.** Cal. yr. d-Deficit. NA-Not Available. NM-Not Meaningful.

Income Data (Million $)

Year Ended Jun. 30	Revs.	Oper. Inc.	% Oper. Inc. of Revs.	Cap. Exp.	Depr.	Int. Exp.	Net Bef. Taxes	Eff. Tax Rate	[1]Net Inc.	% Net Inc. of Revs.	Cash Flow
1992	**189**	**36.2**	**19.2**	**12.1**	**11.6**	**0.10**	**30.5**	**30.0%**	**21.4**	**11.3**	**32.9**
1991	160	31.1	19.4	8.7	9.2	Nil	27.1	34.7%	17.7	11.0	27.0
1990	128	27.8	21.8	11.5	6.0	Nil	27.2	35.0%	17.7	13.8	23.7
1989	87	19.1	21.9	8.7	3.1	0.01	18.7	36.9%	11.8	13.5	14.9
1988	48	9.0	18.8	4.6	1.3	0.03	8.8	37.5%	5.5	11.4	6.8
1987	19	1.8	9.1	1.4	0.5	0.10	1.5	46.4%	0.8	4.2	1.3
1986	10	0.7	6.5	0.8	0.3	0.01	0.7	49.5%	0.4	3.5	0.7
1985	4	d3.6	NM	0.4	0.2	0.01	d3.3	Nil	d3.3	NM	d3.1
1984	NM	NA	NA	NA	NA	NA	d3.4	Nil	d3.4	NM	NA
1983	Nil	NA	NA	NA	NA	NA	d0.9	Nil	d0.9	NM	NA

Balance Sheet Data (Million $)

Jun. 30	Cash	Curr. Assets	Curr. Liab.	Curr. Ratio	Total Assets	% Ret. on Assets	Long Term Debt	Common Equity	Total Cap.	% LT Debt of Cap.	% Ret. on Equity
1992	**108**	**176**	**37.2**	**4.7**	**209**	**11.2**	**Nil**	**172**	**172**	**Nil**	**13.4**
1991	88	142	25.5	5.6	168	11.2	Nil	143	143	Nil	13.3
1990	84	123	22.8	5.4	144	12.3	0.13	121	122	0.1	19.3
1989	40	67	17.5	3.8	80	19.0	0.04	62	62	0.1	24.6
1988	24	39	10.2	3.8	45	17.1	0.01	34	34	NM	22.6
1987	10	18	4.8	3.6	20	5.8	0.36	14	15	2.4	8.0
1986	4	7	2.2	3.4	9	4.8	0.41	6	6	6.6	6.3

Data as orig. reptd. 1. Bef. spec. items. d-Deficit. NM-Not Meaningful. NA-Not Available.

Net Revenues (Million $)

Quarter:	1992–93	1991–92	1990–91	1989–90
Sep.	48.5	42.2	35.2	28.2
Dec.	60.7	45.3	37.5	30.8
Mar.	63.8	48.1	41.0	32.6
Jun.	76.5	53.3	46.6	36.2
	249.6	188.8	160.3	127.8

Based on a preliminary report, net revenues for the fiscal year ended June 30, 1993, advanced 32% from those of the prior year, reflecting the consolidation of the Tigon and Compass acquisitions during the year. Despite higher costs and expenses, operating income rose 20%. With a drop in interest income, and after taxes at 32.5%, versus 30.0%, net income was up 6.1%, to $22,688,000 ($1.19 a share), from $21,356,000 ($1.14). Results in the 1992-3 period exclude a $0.01 a share charge from the cumulative effect of an accounting change.

Common Share Earnings ($)

Quarter:	1992–93	1991–92	1990–91	1989–90
Sep.	0.16	0.20	0.17	0.23
Dec.	0.30	0.27	0.23	0.26
Mar.	0.31	0.30	0.26	0.26
Jun.	0.41	0.37	0.33	0.29
	1.19	1.14	1.00	1.04

Dividend Data

No cash dividends have been paid.

Finances

The primary uses for cash during the first nine months of 1993 were the purchase of property and equipment for $21 million, including land, for approximately $12 million, in relation to the development of the company's new corporate offices; the October 1992 acquisition of Tigon Corp., an independent provider of voice processing and networking services primarily in the U.S., for $12 million in cash; and the purchase of 335,000 shares of OCTL's common stock under a stock repurchase plan for $7.4 million. Earlier, the company had projected expenditures for the corporate office project of $16 million in fiscal 1994 and $4 million in fiscal 1995, for a total cost of about $40 million.

At March 31, 1993, Octel had $81.8 million in cash and cash equivalents, down from $108.4 million at June 30, 1992.

In August 1992, Octel acquired Compass Technology Inc. for about 460,000 of its common shares, valued at $10 million.

Until 1991, Hewlett-Packard Co. (HP) had an OEM agreement to distribute the company's products in Europe; HP purchased and still holds 1,654,119 Octel shares.

Capitalization

Long Term Liabilities: $1,822,000 (3/93).

Common Stock: 17,953,247 shs. ($.001 par).
Hewlett-Packard owns 9.1%.
Institutions hold about 46%.
Shareholders: 2,310 of record (6/92).

Options: To buy 3,218,189 com. shs. at $0.79 to $36.25 a sh.

Office—890 Tasman Dr., Milpitas, CA 95035-7439. **Tel**—(408) 321-2000. **Chrmn**—R. Cohn. **Pres & CEO**—D. C. Chance. **VP & CFO**—G. A. Wetsel. **Secy**—D. S. Daley. **Dirs**— L. J. Chamberlain, D. C. Chance, R. Cohn, J. Freidenrich, R. C. Hawk, D. Tellefsen. **Transfer Agent & Registrar**—Chemical Trust Co. of California, SF. **Incorporated** in California in 1984; reincorporated in Delaware in 1990. **Empl**—1,292.

 Ned Bancroft

Office Depot

NYSE Symbol ODP Options on ASE (Jan-Apr-Jul-Oct) In S&P MidCap 400

Price	Range	P–E Ratio	Dividend	Yield	S&P Ranking	Beta
Sep. 3'93	1993					
32¼	32⅜–17⅞	63	None	None	NR	1.69

Summary

This company operates the largest chain of office products warehouse stores in the U.S., with more than 300 stores in 32 states and Canada selling first-quality branded merchandise primarily to small and medium-size businesses and the home office market. Operations were expanded significantly with the April 1991 acquisition of The Office Club. The opening of new stores and higher same-store sales contributed to higher earnings in recent quarters. A 3-for-2 stock split was effected in June 1993.

Business Summary

Office Depot operates a chain of large volume office products warehouse stores that sell high quality, brand name office products primarily to small and medium-sized businesses. As of year-end 1992, the company was operating a total of 284 stores in 32 states and Canada, with the heaviest concentration in California, Florida and Texas (which together account for about half of the total store network). The company's business was expanded significantly with the April 1991 acquisition of The Office Club, a chain of 59 retail office supply warehouse stores.

Number of stores in operation at year-end:

1992	284	1988	29
1991	228	1987	10
1990	122	1986	3
1989	67		

The stores average between 20,000 and 25,000 sq. ft. in size and use a warehouse format. Each outlet offers about 5,100 brand name office products, including general office supplies, business machines, office furniture and computer hardware and software.

Sales in recent years were derived as follows:

	1992	1991
General office supplies	48%	51%
Business machines & supplies/computer accessories	39%	35%
Office furniture	13%	14%

ODP's merchandising strategy is to offer a wide selection of brand-name office products at everyday low prices. Substantially all inventory is purchased directly from manufacturers in large volumes. The company does not use a central warehouse, but maintains its inventory on the sales floor of its "no frills" stores. ODP feels that its prices are significantly lower than those typically offered to small and medium-sized businesses by their traditional sources of supply.

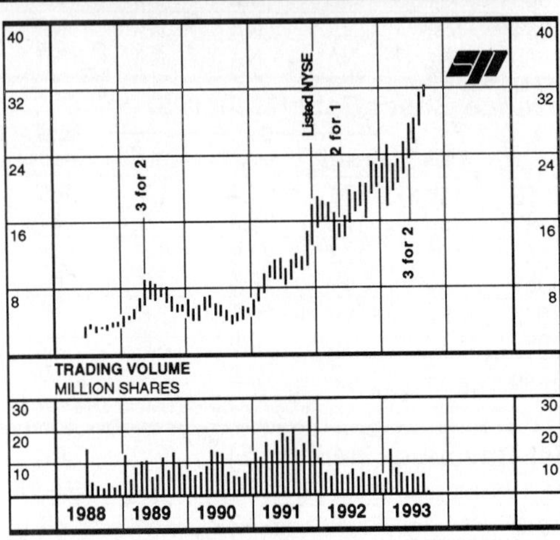

ODP's strategy is to establish itself as a leader in targeted market areas that have a high concentration of small and medium-sized businesses.

Important Developments

Jul. '93— ODP reported that comparable-store sales increased 20% in 1993's second quarter, compared with a 10% gain in the year-earlier quarter. As of June 26, it was operating 313 stores, including 302 in the U.S. and 11 in Canada. Separately, the company agreed to acquire for about $100 million in cash and common stock Eastman Office Products Corp., a leading full service contract stationer and office furniture dealer in the western U.S. with sales of about $295 million in its fiscal year ended June 30, 1992.

Next earnings report expected in mid-October.

Per Share Data ($)

Yr. End Dec. 31	1992	[1]1991	1990	1989	1988	1987	1986
Tangible Bk. Val.	**4.27**	3.57	2.40	2.19	0.85	Nil	Nil
Cash Flow	**0.63**	0.37	0.34	0.20	0.13	NA	NA
Earnings[2]	**0.41**	0.18	0.20	0.13	0.10	d0.16	[3]d0.12
Dividends	**Nil**	Nil	Nil	Nil	Nil	Nil	Nil
Payout Ratio	**Nil**	Nil	Nil	Nil	Nil	Nil	Nil
Prices—High	**23¼**	18	7⁵⁄₃₂	9³⁄₃₂	4¹⁄₃₂	NA	NA
Low	**12½**	4¾	3²¹⁄₃₂	3¹⁷⁄₃₂	2⁷⁄₃₂	NA	NA
P/E Ratio—	**56–30**	NM	36–18	68–27	42–23	NA	NA

Data as orig. reptd. Adj. for stk. divs. of 50% Jun. 1993, 100% May 1992, 50% May 1989. **1.** Reflects merger or acquisition. **2.** Bef. spec. items of +0.02 in 1992, +0.01 in 1991, +0.02 in 1989, +0.02 in 1988. **3.** From inception 3-31-86. d-Deficit. NM-Not Meaningful. NA-Not Available.

Income Data (Million $)

Year Ended Dec. 31	Revs.	Oper. Inc.	% Oper. Inc. of Revs.	Cap. Exp.	Depr.	Int. Exp.	Net Bef. Taxes	Eff. Tax Rate	[4]Net Inc.	% Net Inc. of Revs.	Cash Flow
1992	**1,733**	**82.6**	**4.8**	**61.3**	**20.4**	**1.46**	**62.1**	**39.1%**	**37.8**	**2.2**	**58.2**
[1]1991	1,301	53.5	4.1	56.2	15.4	2.39	26.9	46.5%	14.4	1.1	29.8
1990	626	22.4	3.6	[3]36.3	6.6	0.52	15.8	39.0%	9.7	1.5	16.3
1989	315	10.2	3.2	[3]24.5	2.8	0.10	9.7	38.8%	5.9	1.9	8.8
1988	132	2.3	1.8	[3]9.9	1.0	0.11	3.9	18.3%	3.2	2.4	4.1
1987	34	d2.1	NM	3.2	0.3	0.09	d2.3	Nil	d2.3	NM	NA
[2]1986	2	d1.0	NM	0.7	NM	Nil	d1.0	Nil	d1.0	NM	NA

Balance Sheet Data (Million $)

Dec. 31	Cash	Curr. Assets	Curr. Liab.	Curr. Ratio	Total Assets	% Ret. on Assets	Long Term Debt	Common Equity	Total Cap.	% LT Debt of Cap.	% Ret. on Equity
1992	**130.2**	**664**	**307**	**2.2**	**848**	**5.3**	**154.6**	**382**	**537**	**28.8**	**10.8**
1991	40.2	423	243	1.7	559	2.7	6.5	305	312	2.1	5.6
1990	8.1	207	147	1.4	275	4.2	14.5	111	126	11.5	9.1
1989	28.4	144	81	1.8	182	4.4	0.1	101	101	0.1	8.5
1988	5.1	51	36	1.4	65	7.4	0.3	29	29	1.1	11.9
1987	3.1	15	10	1.5	20	NM	0.2	d3	9	2.3	NM
1986	0.7	3	3	1.1	4	NM	NM	1	1	1.2	NM

Data as orig. reptd. **1.** Reflects merger or acquisition. **2.** From inception 3-31-86. **3.** Net of curr. yr. retirement and disposals. **4.** Bef. spec. items. d-Deficit. NM-Not Meaningful. NA-Not Available.

Net Sales (Million $)

13 Weeks:	1993	1992	1991	1990
Mar.	582	433	325	143
Jun.	528	387	303	137
Sep.		435	332	165
Dec.		478	341	181
		1,733	1,301	626

Sales in the 26 weeks ended June 26, 1993, advanced 35%, year to year, reflecting more stores in operation and an increase in same-store sales. Margins benefited from the higher volume. Despite a $1.7 million unfavorable swing in interest expense (net) because of an increase in debt outstanding, the gain in pretax income was extended to 58%. After taxes at 39.0%, against 39.2%, net income also was up about 58%. Earnings per share were equal to $0.27 based on 2.1% more average shares, versus $0.17 (adjusted).

Common Share Earnings ($)

13 Weeks:	1993	1992	1991	1990
Mar.	0.15	0.10	0.07	0.06
Jun.	0.12	0.07	d0.05	0.03
Sep.		0.11	0.07	0.05
Dec.		0.13	0.08	0.05
		0.41	0.18	0.20

Dividend Data

No cash dividends have been paid. The shares were split 3-for-2 in June 1993, 2-for-1 in May 1992 and 3-for-2 in May 1989.

Finances

Office Depot plans to open a total of about 60 new stores during 1993; it opened 58 new stores in 1991 and 57 stores in 1991. It estimates that its cash requirements, excluding pre-opening expenses of about $125,000, will be about $1.1 million for each additional store.

While the company has the ability to finance its planned expansion through 1993 from cash on hand, funds generated from operations and funds borrowed or equipment leased under its credit facilities, it will also consider alternative financing, such as issuance of equity or convertible debt, depending on market conditions. As of March 27, 1993, there were no borrowings under the $60 million working capital bank line.

In December 1992, ODP sold $275 million of zero coupon convertible LYONs due 2007. Net proceeds of $127 million were used to finance expansion and for working capital.

In May 1993, ODP entered the contract stationery business through the acquisition of Houston-based Wilson Stationery & Printing Co. for about 664,500 common shares (adjusted).

Office Depot acquired The Office Club, Inc. in April 1991 for 25,944,702 (adjusted) common shares. Office Club is a chain of 59 retail office supply warehouses located primarily in the western U.S.

Capitalization

Long Term Debt: $155,873,000 (3/93).

Common Stock: 90,209,559 shs. ($0.01 par). Carrefour (France) owns approximately 18%. Shareholders of record: 2,507.

Options: To purchase 5,824,130 shs. at $0.03 to $22.92 ea.

d-Deficit.

Office—2200 Old Germantown Rd., Delray Beach, FL 33445. **Tel**—(407) 278-4800. **Chrmn & CEO**—D. I. Fuente. **Pres**—M. D. Begelman. **VP-Fin, CFO & Secy**—B. J. Goldstein. **Investor Contacts**—Gary Schweikhart, Barry J. Goldstein. **Dirs**—M. D. Begelman, D. Defforey, D. I. Fuente, W. S. Hedrick, J. B. Mumford, M. J. Myers, P. J. Solomon, A. L. Wurzel. **Transfer Agent**—Mellon Financial Services, Pittsburgh, Pa. **Incorporated** in Delaware in 1986. **Empl**—13,000.

 J. J. Schemitsch

Oklahoma Gas & Electric

NYSE Symbol OGE In S&P MidCap 400

Price	Range	P-E Ratio	Dividend	Yield	S&P Ranking	Beta
Jul. 28'93	1993					
34½	37⅝–33	13	2.66	7.7%	A–	0.37

Summary

This electric utility, which serves a large portion of Oklahoma (including Oklahoma City) and western Arkansas, derives over 60% of its power from coal and the remainder from natural gas. No new base load capacity additions are anticipated for more than 15 years. Approximately 86% of the company's revenues are derived from its regulated electric utility business, and a rate order expected in early 1993 could significantly affect the company's financial results. Sharp rate reductions and large refunds advocated by Oklahoma Commerce Commission staff could jeopardize the modest earnings growth expected for 1993.

Current Outlook

Excluding any large rate reductions and refunds, earnings for 1993 are estimated at $2.70 a share, up from 1992's $2.42. Earnings in 1994 are projected at $2.75 a share.

Quarterly dividends should be maintained at $0.66½ unless an adverse rate order is handed down, then expect dividends in the $0.50 range.

Barring any rate reductions and refunds, being vigorously opposed by OGE, in a rate review currently before the Oklahoma Corporation Commission (OCC), earnings should increase modestly in 1993. Profitability will benefit from customer growth and innovative programs to cut operating costs and improve efficiency. OGE's Business Resource Center and ReSource programs have attracted new businesses to the service area. Uncertainty remains, however, regarding the regulatory environment and its effect on earnings.

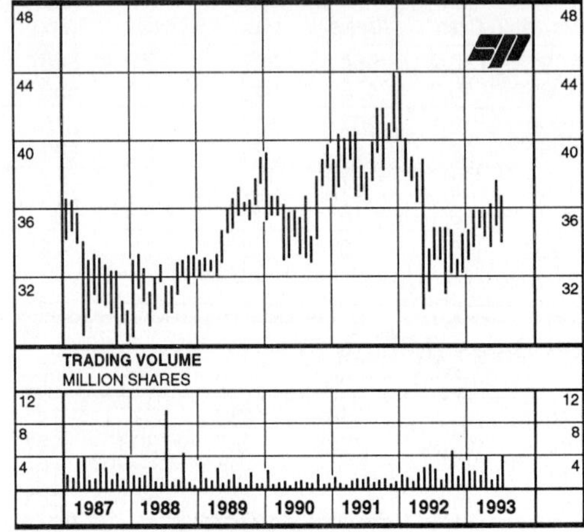

Operating Revenues (Million $)

Quarter:	1994	1993	1992	1991
Mar.	---	303	261	274
Jun.	---	342	306	329
Sep.	---	---	443	427
Dec.	---	---	304	285
	---	---	1,315	1,315

Operating revenues for the six months ended June 30, 1993, rose 14%, year to year, reflecting higher kwh sales from cooler weather and the absence of an $18 million rate refund provision. Operating expenses advanced 12% and operating income rose 28%. After lower interest charges, net income was up 108%, to $0.64 a share, from $0.30.

Common Share Earnings ($)

Quarter:	1994	1993	1992	1991
Mar.	E0.15	0.15	d0.11	0.31
Jun.	E0.50	0.49	0.41	0.82
Sep.	E1.75	E1.75	1.87	1.85
Dec.	E0.35	E0.31	0.25	0.29
	E2.75	E2.70	2.42	3.27

Important Developments

Jul. '93— OCC Chairman J. C. Watts Jr. said he doubted the OCC would be able to issue a rate order in the OGE case before the end of the summer. The commission staff is seeking a $71 million annual reduction in rates and refunds of $173 million, alleging that OGE earned a higher return on equity than authorized. A significant portion of the proposed refund relates to the amounts recovered by OGE through its fuel adjustment clauses for fees paid to its Enogex subsidiary for transporting natural gas to OGE generating plants since June 30, 1989. The company filed testimony supporting a $12 million rate increase, but due to economic conditions, requested no increase. Although OGE feels a rate reduction and refund are inappropriate, the company recorded an $18 million provision for a potential refund earlier in 1992. The OCC is under no time constraint in reaching their decision.

Next earnings report expected in late October.

Per Share Data ($)

Yr. End Dec. 31	1992	1991	1990	1989	1988	1987	1986	1985	1984	1983
Tangible Bk. Val.	**22.35**	22.36	21.68	21.14	20.87	19.97	20.29	18.89	18.52	17.91
Earnings[1]	**2.42**	3.27	3.38	3.05	3.20	2.60	2.75	2.30	2.47	2.68
Dividends	**2.660**	2.580	2.480	2.380	2.280	2.205	2.080	2.000	1.920	1.840
Payout Ratio	**110%**	79%	73%	78%	71%	85%	76%	87%	78%	69%
Prices—High	**44**	44	39¾	39	33⅜	36⅝	38¾	27⅝	23½	21⅞
Low	**30⅛**	36½	32⅞	32	28½	28	26⅛	21½	19⅛	17½
P/E Ratio—	**18–12**	13–11	12–10	13–10	10–9	14–11	14–10	12–9	10–8	8–7

Data as orig. reptd. 1. Bef. spec. item(s) of +0.25 in 1987. d-Deficit. E-Estimated

Income Data (Million $)

Year Ended Dec. 31	Revs.	Depr.	Maint.	Oper. Ratio	[1]Fxd. Chgs. Cover.	Constr. Credits	Eff. Tax Rate	[2]Net Inc.	% Return On Revs.	% Return On [3]Invest. Capital	% Return On Com. Equity
1992	**1,315**	**111**	**72.4**	**86.5%**	**2.99**	**0.81**	**37.3%**	**100**	**7.6**	**7.7**	**10.7**
1991	1,315	108	71.9	83.9%	3.65	2.30	36.4%	134	10.2	9.2	14.7
1990	1,231	104	72.1	82.8%	3.94	3.70	36.8%	139	11.3	9.3	15.6
1989	1,141	101	70.6	82.4%	3.54	4.90	33.8%	129	11.3	8.9	12.1
1988	1,098	98	66.7	81.1%	3.74	4.10	31.5%	138	12.6	9.3	15.5
1987	1,065	96	65.1	82.4%	3.46	2.70	40.6%	114	10.7	8.5	12.5
1986	1,091	93	64.2	82.5%	4.16	2.80	48.2%	126	11.6	9.0	13.8
1985	1,085	79	61.6	85.5%	3.54	14.20	43.8%	109	10.0	8.3	12.3
1984	1,029	70	55.6	85.2%	3.68	24.10	42.9%	113	11.0	8.7	13.5
1983	972	61	52.7	85.1%	3.87	34.50	41.1%	118	12.1	9.1	15.3

Balance Sheet Data (Million $)

Dec. 31	Gross Prop.	Capital Expend.	Net Prop.	% Earn. on Net Prop.	Total Cap.	Capitalization: LT Debt	% LT Debt	Pfd.	% Pfd.	Com.	% Com.
1992	**3,508**	**142**	**2,241**	**7.9**	**2,273**	**839**	**46.8**	**50**	**2.8**	**902**	**50.4**
1991	3,402	115	2,223	9.5	2,302	854	47.0	50	2.8	911	50.2
1990	3,302	117	2,215	9.6	2,283	854	47.8	50	2.8	883	49.4
1989	3,206	109	2,205	9.1	2,279	854	47.9	55	3.1	875	49.0
1988	3,106	94	2,193	9.5	2,291	861	47.7	55	3.0	889	49.3
1987	3,030	99	2,201	8.5	2,189	799	46.9	55	3.2	851	49.9
1986	2,942	98	2,199	9.1	2,230	837	45.9	55	3.0	930	51.1
1985	2,669	136	2,004	8.0	2,063	734	43.3	160	9.5	799	47.2
1984	2,540	139	1,945	8.0	1,994	734	44.2	160	9.6	768	46.2
1983	2,402	169	1,869	8.0	1,929	749	45.8	160	9.8	724	44.4

Data as orig. reptd. **1.** Times int. exp. & pfd. divs. covered (pretax basis). **2.** Bef. spec. item(s). **3.** Based on income before interest charges.

Business Summary

Oklahoma Gas and Electric supplies electricity to a population of about 1,400,000 in Oklahoma and western Arkansas, deriving about 91% of 1992 revenues from Oklahoma. The Enogex Inc. subsidiary owns and operates a gas pipeline system and six gas processing plants. Contributions to total revenues by class of customers:

	1992	1991	1990	1989
Residential	33%	35%	35%	34%
Commercial	21%	22%	22%	23%
Industrial	20%	20%	20%	21%
Other	26%	23%	23%	23%

The fuel mix in 1992 was 30% natural gas and 70% coal. The cost of fuel per million Btu was $3.48 for gas and $1.18 for coal. Peak load in 1992 was 4,550 mw and capacity at time of peak was 5,655 mw, for a capacity margin of 19.5%.

With the commercial operation of the 515-mw, coal-fired Muskogee Unit 6 in 1984, OGE does not anticipate the need to build new base-load generating facilities for more than 15 years. OGE intends to concentrate on updating existing facilities and improving system reliability.

Finances

OGE estimated that construction expenditures (including AFUDC) through 1995 would be $348 million, about $116 million per year. Funding was expected to be internally generated.

Dividend Data

Dividends have been paid since 1908. A dividend reinvestment plan is available. A "poison pill" stock purchase right was adopted in 1991.

Amt of Divd. $	Date Decl.	Ex-divd. Date	Stock of Record	Payment Date
0.66½	Sep. 8	Oct. 5	Oct. 9	Oct. 30'92
0.66½	Dec. 8	Jan. 4	Jan. 8	Jan. 29'93
0.66½	Mar. 9	Apr. 2	Apr. 8	Apr. 30'93
0.66½	Jun. 15	Jul. 2	Jul. 9	Jul. 30'93

Capitalization

Long Term Debt: $838,481,978 (6/93).

Cum. Preferred Stock: $49,973,260.

Common Stock: 40,327,790 shs. ($2.50 par).
Institutions hold about 31%.
Shareholders of record: 37,081.

Office—101 North Robinson, Oklahoma City, OK 73101. **Tel**—(405) 272-3000. **Chrmn & Pres**—J. G. Harlow Jr. **Secy**—I. B. Elliott. **VP-Treas & Investor Contact**—Al M. Strecker (405) 272-3216. **Dirs**—H. H. Champlin, W. E. Durrett, M. W. Griffin, J. G. Harlow Jr., H. L. Hembree III, J. F. Snodgrass, B. Swisher, J. A. Taylor, R. H. White. **Transfer Agent & Registrar**—Liberty National Bank & Trust Co., Oklahoma City. **Incorporated**—in Oklahoma in 1902. **Empl**—3,806.

 Ned Bancroft

Olin Corp.

NYSE Symbol OLN Options on ASE (Feb-May-Aug-Nov) In S&P MidCap 400

Price	Range	P–E Ratio	Dividend	Yield	S&P Ranking	Beta
Aug. 5'93	1993					
42⅜	46¼–40⅜	33	2.20	5.2%	B+	1.08

Summary

Olin is a diversified manufacturer of industrial, specialty and consumer chemicals, metal products, and sporting and defense ammunition, with interests in aerospace and defense. In 1991 OLN implemented a restructuring program to streamline operations and to cut costs through asset sales and personnel reductions. Earnings in recent years have been penalized by weak economic conditions, lower chemical prices, and reduced earnings in the defense and aerospace businesses.

Current Outlook

Share earnings for 1993 are projected at $1.90; earnings in 1994 are expected to improve to about $2.50 a share, assuming a better economy.

Dividends should remain at $0.55 quarterly.

Chemical profits are expected to rebound in 1993 and 1994, aided by lower start-up costs at a new specialty urethanes plant, higher volumes of urethanes and industrial chemicals (despite lower prices), and benefits of favorable 1993 weather on the pool chemicals unit which also bodes well for 1994 prospects. A capacity addition in the metals business will begin to contribute in 1993's second half. The possible acquisition of an ordnance business would have a positive impact but the defense ammunition and aerospace businesses may be affected by a smaller U.S. defense budget.

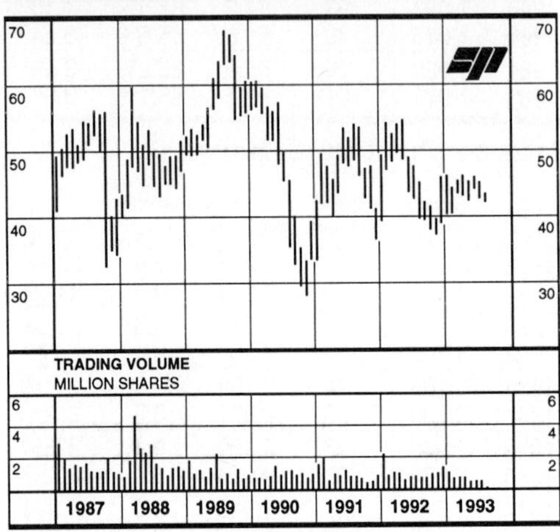

Net Sales (Million $)

Quarter:	1993	1992	1991	1990
Mar.	592	614	561	636
Jun.	626	633	568	660
Sep.		577	551	656
Dec.		552	595	640
		2,376	2,275	2,592

Sales for the first half of 1993 declined 2.3%, year to year, reflecting lower volumes and prices. On lower profits in all three segments, net income fell 42%, to $1.02 a share, from $1.92 (before a special accounting charge of $2.11).

Common Share Earnings ($)

Quarter:	1993	1992	1991	1990
Mar.	0.45	1.04	d3.20	1.60
Jun.	0.57	0.88	0.98	1.41
Sep.	E0.38	0.18	0.70	0.65
Dec.	E0.50	0.07	0.60	0.37
	E1.90	2.17	d0.92	4.03

Important Developments

Jul. '93— Olin said that the modest recovery of the U.S. economy, combined with the economic slowdown in the rest of the world, continued to adversely affect margins in a number of businesses during the second quarter. Earnings rose from the first quarter, aided by the seasonal performance of the pool chemicals business. Chlor-alkali income was significantly behind 1992 levels, due to lower caustic prices. Winchester profits improved on higher commercial sales but ordnance and aerospace earnings lagged modestly. Investments to expand the brass and sulfuric acid regeneration businesses were on track and expected to be fully operational and making a contribution by the end of the third quarter. Separately, OLN was holding discussions regarding the possible purchase of certain assets of GenCorp.'s ordnance division, with 1992 sales of about $130 million.

Next earnings report expected in late October.

Per Share Data ($)

Yr. End Dec. 31	1992	1991	1990	1989	1988	[1]1987	1986	[1]1985	1984	[1]1983
Tangible Bk. Val.	**30.20**	22.88	26.79	23.95	26.44	27.18	26.83	26.33	[2]37.88	[2]35.37
Cash Flow	**7.45**	5.58	10.44	12.10	10.20	8.47	8.46	d2.60	10.03	8.60
Earnings[3]	**2.17**	d0.92	4.03	6.02	4.63	3.38	3.36	d8.28	3.81	3.01
Dividends	**2.200**	2.200	2.150	1.950	1.700	1.600	1.525	1.500	1.365	1.230
Payout Ratio	**101%**	NM	54%	31%	36%	45%	43%	NM	35%	41%
Prices—High	**54¾**	54	60⅝	68¼	60	56¼	53¼	38	33½	34
Low	**37¼**	33½	28⅛	49⅜	40	32⅝	34⅝	28⅜	25⅛	23
P/E Ratio—	**25–17**	NM	15–7	11–8	13–9	17–10	16–10	NM	9–7	11–8

Data as orig. reptd. **1.** Reflects merger or acquisition. **2.** Incl. intangibles. **3.** Bef. results of disc. opers. of +1.09 in 1985 and spec. item of -2.11 in 1992. d-Deficit. E-Estimated NM-Not Meaningful.

Income Data (Million $)

Year Ended Dec. 31	Revs.	Oper. Inc.	% Oper. Inc. of Revs.	Cap. Exp.	Depr.	Int. Exp.	[3]Net Bef. Taxes	Eff. Tax Rate	[4]Net Inc.	% Net Inc. of Revs.	Cash Flow
1992	**2,376**	**240**	**10.1**	**173**	**123**	**43.0**	**88**	**37.5%**	**[5]55**	**2.3**	**161**
1991	2,275	262	11.5	201	127	48.0	d25	NM	d13	NM	106
1990	2,592	274	10.6	187	123	56.0	116	27.6%	84	3.2	199
1989	2,509	345	13.8	142	122	57.0	192	35.2%	124	4.9	242
1988	2,308	297	12.9	147	117	44.0	151	35.1%	98	4.2	215
[1]1987	1,930	267	13.8	115	118	34.0	127	38.6%	78	4.0	196
1986	1,707	195	11.4	128	114	33.0	115	34.5%	[5]75	4.4	189
[2]1985	1,751	187	10.7	203	131	36.4	d282	NM	d190	NM	d60
1984	2,065	269	13.0	165	145	34.8	132	32.7%	89	4.3	234
[1]1983	1,935	225	11.6	123	133	31.6	95	24.6%	72	3.7	205

Balance Sheet Data (Million $)

Dec. 31	Cash	Curr. Assets	Curr. Liab.	Curr. Ratio	Total Assets	% Ret. on Assets	Long Term Debt	Common Equity	Total Cap.	% LT Debt of Cap.	% Ret. on Equity
1992	**4**	**760**	**581**	**1.3**	**2,030**	**2.7**	**477**	**702**	**1,280**	**37.3**	**5.6**
1991	8	768	683	1.1	2,012	NM	520	567	1,210	43.0	NM
1990	6	734	522	1.4	1,866	4.5	466	615	1,229	37.9	12.9
1989	12	790	585	1.4	1,904	6.7	501	565	1,226	40.9	20.0
1988	25	801	617	1.3	1,940	5.6	474	683	1,217	38.9	14.7
1987	34	680	404	1.7	1,685	4.8	392	700	1,141	34.4	11.4
1986	10	601	391	1.5	1,545	5.0	375	654	1,053	35.6	11.6
1985	98	695	391	1.8	1,598	NM	354	687	1,049	33.7	NM
1984	155	806	407	2.0	1,822	5.0	369	867	1,361	27.1	10.6
1983	190	819	413	2.0	1,829	4.1	387	848	1,345	28.8	8.6

Data as orig. reptd. **1.** Reflects merger or acquisition. **2.** Excludes discontinued operations and reflects merger or acquisition. **3.** Incl. equity in earns. of nonconsol. subs. **4.** Bef. results of discontinued operations in 1985. **5.** Reflects acctg. change. d-Deficit. NM-Not Meaningful.

Business Summary

Olin Corp. is a diversified concern with interests in three major areas. Contributions (income in million $) in 1992:

	Sales	Income
Chemicals	42%	$21
Metals	28%	29
Defense & ammunition	30%	29

Foreign operations accounted for 6% of sales in 1992 and $3 million of operating profits.

Chemicals include urethanes (TDI, polyols, urethane systems, isocyanates), electrochemicals (chlorine, caustic soda, reduction and oxidation chemicals), acids, surfactants, functional fluids, hydrazine solutions and propellants, biocides, glycols, pool sanitizers, and electronics (photoresists, acids and solvents, dopants, toners, developers, thick films, coatings and adhesives, and metal packaging systems for integrated circuits) The circuit assembly business was sold in 1993.

The Metals group produces copper and copper alloy sheet, strip, foil, tube and fabricated products, and stainless steel strip for the appliance, automotive, electrical, electronics, plumbing, coinage, and ammunition markets, and includes the A.J. Oster network of metals service centers.

Defense and ammunition include Winchester sporting ammunition, military ammunition (small, medium and large caliber), propellants, and aerospace products (rocket engines, inflation systems, gas generators, power devices, electronic test equipment, anti-armor warheads, and pulsed power systems).

Dividend Data

Dividends have been paid since 1926. A dividend reinvestment plan is available. A "poison pill" stock purchase right was adopted in 1986.

Amt. of Divd. $	Date Decl.	Ex-divd. Date	Stock of Record	Payment Date
0.55	Oct. 29	Nov. 4	Nov. 10	Dec. 10'92
0.55	Jan. 28	Feb. 4	Feb. 10	Mar. 10'93
0.55	Apr. 29	May 4	May 10	Jun. 10'93
0.55	Jul. 29	Aug. 4	Aug. 10	Sep. 10'93

Capitalization

Long Term Debt: $461,100,000 (6/93).

ESOP $5.97 Preferred Stock: $94,100,000.

$3.64 Series A Conversion Preferred Stock: 2,760,000 shs.

Common Stock: 19,075,066 shs. ($1 par). Institutions hold approximately 53%. Shareholders of record: 13,900.

Office—120 Long Ridge Rd., Stamford, CT 06904-1355. **Tel**—(203) 356-2000. **Chrmn & Pres**—J. W. Johnstone Jr. **Secy**—E. M. Cover. **VP & Treas**—J. M. Pierpont. **Investor Contact**—Richard Koch. **Dirs**—R. R. Frederick, D. W. Griffin, W. W. Higgins, R. Holland Jr., J. W. Johnstone Jr., J. D. Kuehler, G. J. Ratcliffe Jr., W. L. Read, J. P. Schaefer, I. Shain, E. F. Williams Jr., R. L. Yohe. **Transfer Agents & Registrars**—Chemical Bank, NYC; Boatmen's Trust Co., St. Louis. **Incorporated** in Virginia in 1892. **Empl**—13,500.

 Richard O'Reilly, CFA

Omnicom Group

NYSE Symbol OMC Options on Pacific In S&P MidCap 400

Price	Range	P-E Ratio	Dividend	Yield	S&P Ranking	Beta
Aug. 23'93	1993					
42⅜	47½–37	16	1.24	2.9%	B+	0.99

Summary

Omnicom, the parent of DDB Needham Worldwide and BBDO Worldwide, two leading full-service international advertising agency networks, acquired its third worldwide agency network, TBWA, in May 1993. OMC also heads a diversified agency services group. The level of billings reflects worldwide economic conditions and success in expanding the agency network and adding clients.

Current Outlook

Earnings for 1993 are projected at $2.75 a share, up 19% from the $2.31 reported for 1992. About $3.20 is anticipated for 1994.

The $0.31-a-share quarterly dividend is expected to be raised in the near term.

Commissions and fees are expected to rise more than 10% in 1993, aided by acquisitions and healthy gains in the Pacific Rim, excluding Japan, and in Latin America. Strength in these areas will offset the impact of sluggish markets in much of Europe and elsewhere. There should be a moderate improvement in margins. Currency fluctuations could have a significant effect on these projections.

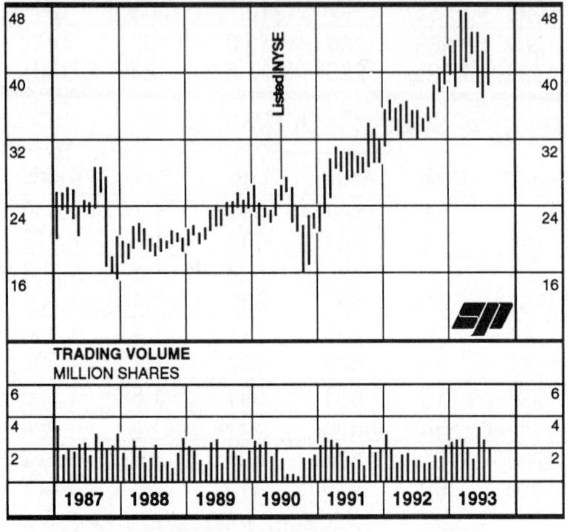

Commissions & Fees (Million $)

Quarter:	1993	1992	1991	1990
Mar.	321	309	283	274
Jun.	382	348	302	299
Sep.		328	275	282
Dec.		401	376	324
		1,385	1,236	1,178

Commission and fee income in the 1993 first half rose 9.8%, year to year. Domestic revenues increased 6.0%, and international advanced 14%. Margins widened as operating and interest expenses rose 9.1%. In the absence of a special $0.13 per share net charge taken in the 1992 first quarter, pretax earnings jumped 30%. After taxes at 42.0%, against 43.4%, a 29% drop in equity earnings and a 21% drop in minority interest deductions, net income advanced 33%. Share earnings were $1.40, up 27% from $1.10.

Common Share Earnings ($)

Quarter:	1993	1992	1991	1990
Mar.	0.52	0.32	0.40	0.42
Jun.	0.90	0.78	0.66	0.67
Sep.	E0.42	0.37	0.28	0.26
Dec.	E0.91	0.84	0.72	0.66
	E2.75	2.31	2.08	2.01

Important Developments

Aug. '93— OMC said that the favorable impact of acquisitions, net of divestitures, on worldwide commission and fee income in the 1993 first half was about 10% compared to 1992. During May, OMC completed the acquisition of TBWA International, which was accounted for as a pooling of interests effective January 1, 1993, in exchange for OMC common stock. TBWA, based in New York, has 14 offices in nine countries and affiliate agencies throughout the world, with annual billings of about $1 billion; it is noted for its Absolut vodka advertising campaign.

Aug. '93— OMC announced plans to redeem its $85.9 million of 7% convertible subordinated debentures on October 8, 1993. Prior to the redemption date, the debentures may be converted into common stock at a conversion price of $25.75 a sh.

Next earnings report expected in early November.

Per Share Data ($)

Yr. End Dec. 31	1992	1991	1990	[1]1989	1988	1987	[2]1986	[3]1985	[3]1984	[3]1983
Tangible Bk. Val.	**d5.96**	d2.85	d6.06	d5.27	2.63	3.22	2.64	NA	NA	NA
Cash Flow	**4.07**	3.77	3.79	3.18	2.74	2.45	0.76	NA	NA	NA
Earnings[4]	**2.31**	2.08	2.01	1.81	1.58	1.41	d0.17	1.27	1.49	1.20
Dividends	**1.205**	1.100	1.070	0.980	0.980	0.980	0.905	0.820	0.730	0.690
Payout Ratio	**52%**	55%	55%	55%	62%	70%	NM	65%	49%	58%
Prices—High	**41⅞**	34	27½	25¾	22	28¾	22	NA	NA	NA
Low	**31¼**	21	16⅛	19⅜	17¼	15⅝	16⅞	NA	NA	NA
P/E Ratio—	**18–14**	16–10	14–8	14–11	14–11	20–11	NM	NA	NA	NA

Data as orig. reptd. 1. Refl. merger or acq. 2. Major merger resulted in formation of new co. 3. Pro forma, BBDO/DDB merger & DDB/NH merger. 4. Bef. spec. items of +0.14 in 1992, +0.17 in 1983. E-Estimated. d-Deficit. NM-Not Meaningful. NA-Not Available.

Income Data (Million $)

Year Ended Dec. 31	Revs.	Oper. Inc.	% Oper. Inc. of Revs.	Cap. Exp.	Depr.	Int. Exp.	[4]Net Bef. Taxes	Eff. Tax Rate	[6]Net Inc.	% Net Inc. of Revs.	Cash Flow
1992	**1,385**	**203**	**14.6**	**34.9**	**49.8**	**40.9**	**132**	**40.4%**	**65.5**	**4.7**	**115**
1991	1,236	181	14.7	32.1	46.2	41.4	121	40.6%	57.1	4.6	103
1990	1,178	173	14.7	32.7	46.4	40.1	112	41.1%	52.0	4.4	98
[1]1989	1,007	138	13.7	33.4	35.7	24.2	99	41.2%	46.8	4.6	82
1988	881	113	12.8	28.4	28.6	15.0	84	42.4%	39.2	4.4	68
1987	811	100	12.3	[5]50.1	25.7	10.3	76	45.8%	34.8	4.3	60
[2]1986	754	84	11.1	[5]28.0	22.6	7.0	26	97.3%	d4.1	NM	19
[1]1985	673	[3]54	[3]8.8	5.9	5.7	7.4	64	53.5%	30.1	4.5	11
1984	631	[3]68	[3]10.7	6.3	4.8	5.8	74	50.3%	36.7	5.8	14
[1]1983	556	[3]56	[4]10.2	8.0	4.1	3.6	62	51.5%	28.7	5.2	10

Balance Sheet Data (Million $)

Dec. 31	Cash	Curr. Assets	Curr. Liab.	Curr. Ratio	Total Assets	% Ret. on Assets	Long Term Debt	Common Equity	Total Cap.	% LT Debt of Cap.	% Ret. on Equity
1992	**131**	**1,137**	**1,311**	**0.9**	**1,952**	**3.4**	**235**	**309**	**589**	**39.9**	**19.4**
1991	157	1,111	1,197	0.9	1,886	3.0	245	366	657	37.3	16.6
1990	123	1,027	1,106	0.9	1,749	3.1	279	298	617	45.2	19.3
1989	126	937	981	1.0	1,548	3.4	267	238	543	49.2	20.5
1988	149	820	761	1.1	1,135	3.6	115	205	354	32.4	19.3
1987	90	763	748	1.0	1,041	3.6	42	203	275	15.3	18.2
1986	84	645	626	1.0	875	NM	35	174	236	15.0	NM

Data as orig. reptd. **1.** Refl. merger or acq. **2.** Major merger resulted in formation of new co. **3.** Aft. depr. not separately reptd. **4.** Incl. equity in earns. of nonconsol. subs. **5.** Net. **6.** Bef. spec. items. d-Deficit. NM-Not Meaningful.

Business Summary

Omnicom Group Inc. was formed in 1986 through the three-way merger of Doyle Dane Bernbach Group Inc., BBDO International Inc. and Needham Harper Worldwide Inc. The company was then reorganized into two major independent ad agency networks—the BBDO Worldwide network and the DDB Needham Worldwide network—plus the Diversified Agency Services group. Omnicom became the third largest advertising agency group worldwide based on combined worldwide billings of roughly $10.8 billion, with its acquisition in May 1993 of TBWA International. In 1992, OMC's 10 largest clients accounted for about 20% of billings, and no client represented more than 5%.

Operations cover the major regions of North America, the United Kingdom, Europe, the Middle East, Africa, Latin America, the Far East and Australia. In 1992, 49% of the company's commissions and fees and 52% of operating profit came from international operations.

The BBDO Worldwide network and the DDB Needham Worldwide network operate globally through subsidiaries. Tracy-Locke Inc., headquartered in Dallas, also operates in Los Angeles and New York. TBWA, based in New York, has 14 offices in nine countries and affiliate agencies worldwide.

The Diversified Agency Services group includes a wide range of general and industry-focused ad agencies and marketing services firms.

Dividend Data

Prior to the business combination in 1986, BBDO had paid cash dividends in each year since 1938 and Doyle Dane Bernbach Group in each year since 1964.

Amt. of Divd. $	Date Decl.	Ex–divd. Date	Stock of Record	Payment Date
0.31	Sep. 15	Sep. 17	Sep. 23	Oct. 2'92
0.31	Dec. 7	Dec. 14	Dec. 18	Jan. 6'93
0.31	Jan. 27	Mar. 8	Mar. 12	Apr. 1'93
0.31	May 14	Jun. 9	Jun. 15	Jul. 2'93

Finances

At March 31, 1993, the company had committed lines of credit totaling $367.1 million, of which $160.3 million was available.

Capitalization

Long Term Debt: $376,111,000 (3/31/93), incl. debs. conv. into some 6,920,900 com. shs. at $25.75 and $28 a sh.

Minority Interests: $36,985,000.

Common Stock: 28,541,000 shs. ($0.50 par).
Institutions hold about 86%.
Shareholders of record: 2,761.

Office—437 Madison Ave., New York, NY 10022. **Tel**—(212) 415-3600. **Pres & CEO**—B. Crawford. **VP-CFO**—F. J. Meyer. **Secy**—R. McGovern. **Investor Contact**—Louis Tripodi. **Dirs**—J. L. Bernbach, M. Boase, R. J. Callander, J. A. Cannon, B. Crawford, P. Jones, R. E. McGovern, F. J. Meyer, J. R. Purcell, K. L. Reinhard, A. Rosenshine, G. L. Roubos, Q. I. Smith Jr., R. B. Smith, E. P. S. Zehnder. **Transfer Agent & Registrar**—Manufacturers Hanover Trust Co., NYC. **Incorporated** in New York in 1986. **Empl**—13,500.

Oregon Steel Mills

NYSE Symbol OS Options on Phila (Feb-May-Aug-Nov) In S&P MidCap 400

Price	Range	P-E Ratio	Dividend	Yield	S&P Ranking	Beta
Sep. 30'93	1993					
22⅝	27½–17½	30	0.56	2.5%	B	0.62

Summary

This company operates the only hot-rolled steel plate minimill located in the eleven western states in the U. S. OS also manufactures large diameter steel pipe. Earnings comparisions for the first half of 1993 were hurt as a less favorable product mix outweighed a sizeable increase in sales. However, the likely absence of charges should enable the company to report higher earnings for the full year.

Current Outlook

Earnings for 1994 are estimated at $1.60, versus 1993's estimated earnings of $1.15.

The dividend should remain at $0.14 quarterly.

Sales are expected to increase in 1994, reflecting better demand for plate and increased shipments from both CF&I and the Camrose pipemaking mill. Profit growth will continue to be limited by a less favorable product mix; but, aided by an improvement in operating rates, moderation in raw material costs and level interest expense, earnings should increase in 1994.

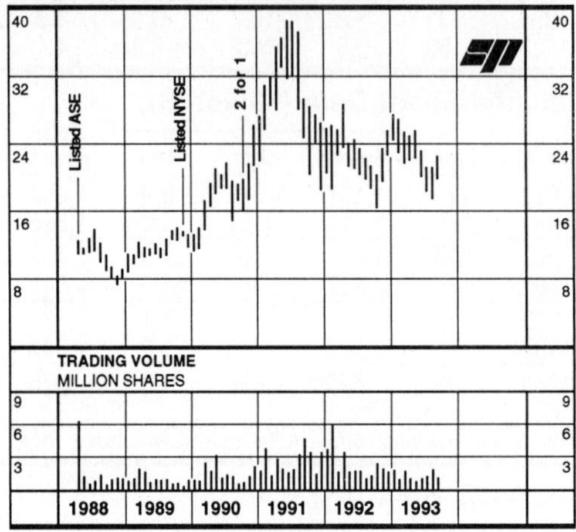

Net Sales (Million $)

Quarter:	1993	1992	1991	1990
Mar.	149.0	126.6	118.9	74.8
Jun.	204.1	125.1	136.9	78.3
Sep.		90.7	125.4	89.7
Dec.		55.4	108.2	91.1
		397.7	489.4	333.9

Sales for the six months ended March 31, 1993, increased 40%, reflecting a 72% rise in tons shipped stemming from the CF&I acquisition. Penalized by lower average selling prices and interest expense in 1993 only, pretax income fell 29%. After taxes at 33.4%, versus 37.0%, net income declined 25%. Earnings on 2.8% more shares were $0.81, versus $1.11.

Common Share Earnings ($)

Quarter:	1993	1992	1991	1990
Mar.	0.35	0.56	0.63	0.45
Jun.	0.46	0.55	0.68	0.51
Sep.	E0.14	0.18	0.26	0.44
Dec.	E0.20	d0.25	0.40	0.39
	E1.15	1.04	1.97	1.78

Important Developments

Jul. '93— OS attributed its lower earnings in 1993's second quarter to a decrease in average selling prices to $485 a ton, from $638 a tons in the year-earlier quarter. Second quarter 1993 shipments rose to 420,800 tons from 196,100 tons in the year-earlier period. The inclusion of CF&I and Camrose Pipe boosted the quarter's total shipment by 229,400 tons. However, profitability was hurt by a decrease in large diameter pipe as a percent of total sales and the lower average selling price of CF&I and Camrose products. OS stated that an expected reduction in pipe shipments in 1993's second half would cause the company to seek new markets in order to keep the melt shop at the Portland steel mill at an efficient production level.

Next earnings report expected in late October.

Per Share Data ($)

Yr. End Dec. 31	1992	1991	1990	1989	1988	1987	1986	1985	1984	1983
Tangible Bk. Val.	**13.41**	12.85	8.44	7.09	6.05	2.99	NA	NA	NA	NA
Cash Flow	**1.89**	2.63	2.33	1.70	1.76	0.48	NA	NA	NA	NA
Earnings[1]	**1.04**	1.97	1.78	1.33	1.43	0.32	d0.05	d0.01	d0.08	d0.08
Dividends	**0.56**	0.50	0.42	0.40	0.20	Nil	Nil	Nil	Nil	Nil
Payout Ratio	**54%**	26%	24%	30%	15%	Nil	Nil	Nil	Nil	Nil
Prices—High	**28¾**	38⅝	26¼	14⅛	13⅞	NA	NA	NA	NA	NA
Low	**16⅜**	18½	11⅜	8⅞	7¼	NA	NA	NA	NA	NA
P/E Ratio—	**26–16**	20–9	15–6	11–7	10–5	NA	NA	NA	NA	NA

Data as orig. reptd. Adj. for stk. div(s). of 100% Oct. 1990. **1.** Bef. spec. item(s) of +0.04 in 1988, +0.05 in 1986, -0.01 in 1985, +0.08 in 1983. d-Deficit. E-Estimated NA-Not Available.

Income Data (Million $)

Year Ended Dec. 31	Revs.	Oper. Inc.	% Oper. Inc. of Revs.	Cap. Exp.	Depr.	Int. Exp.	Net Bef. Taxes	Eff. Tax Rate	[2]Net Inc.	% Net Inc. of Revs.	Cash Flow
1992	**398**	**53.7**	**13.5**	**34.3**	**16.3**	**0.32**	**[1]33.4**	**43.4%**	**[3]20.0**	**5.0**	**36.2**
1991	489	69.5	14.2	38.5	12.4	1.40	[1]58.6	37.0%	36.9	7.5	49.4
1990	334	54.7	16.4	33.3	8.6	2.20	[1]45.9	38.0%	28.5	8.5	37.1
1989	231	36.6	15.8	36.6	5.9	1.91	[1]32.2	35.5%	20.8	9.0	26.6
1988	190	32.6	17.1	16.1	4.8	1.04	[1]30.7	33.4%	20.4	10.7	25.2
1987	127	17.8	14.0	20.8	4.3	1.03	[1]13.5	40.3%	8.0	6.3	12.4
1986	85	5.0	5.9	3.1	4.0	2.30	d2.4	NM	d1.2	NM	NA
1985	85	d2.9	NM	3.9	4.0	2.27	d2.3	NM	d0.3	NM	NA
1984	73	NA	NA	NA	NA	NA	d5.9	NM	d2.8	NM	NA
1983	47	NA	NA	NA	NA	NA	d7.0	NM	d3.3	NM	NA

Balance Sheet Data (Million $)

Dec. 31	Cash	Curr. Assets	Curr. Liab.	Curr. Ratio	Total Assets	% Ret. on Assets	Long Term Debt	Common Equity	Total Cap.	% LT Debt of Cap.	% Ret. on Equity
1992	**5.2**	**155**	**55.7**	**2.8**	**356**	**5.8**	**0.0**	**258**	**285**	**0.0**	**7.9**
1991	14.7	167	43.3	3.9	325	12.0	3.4	246	261	1.3	18.1
1990	2.5	124	86.0	1.4	246	13.8	5.2	137	154	3.4	22.8
1989	8.5	69	27.8	2.5	163	13.7	6.9	112	131	5.3	20.0
1988	31.7	75	18.6	4.0	138	15.9	8.6	95	111	7.8	28.5
1987	1.7	30	19.7	1.5	84	11.3	17.6	35	58	30.3	27.1
1986	0.8	24	15.0	1.6	59	NM	12.1	25	41	29.7	NM
1985	NA	26	15.5	1.7	63	NM	15.4	26	41	37.1	NM
1984	NA	29	13.6	2.2	70	NM	22.0	26	48	45.8	NM
1983	NA	23	7.7	3.0	65	NM	5.2	45	51	10.3	NM

Data as orig. reptd. **1.** Incl. equity in earnings of nonconsol. subs. **2.** Bef. spec. items. **3.** Reflects acctg. change. d-Deficit. NM-Not Meaningful. NA-Not Available.

Business Summary

Oregon Steel Mills makes steel plate at its minimill in Portland, Ore. and steel pipe at its Napa, Calif. facility. It also has a steel plate rolling mill in Fontana, Calif.

Depending upon the product mix, OS had melting and casting capacity of 800,000 tons, rolling capacity of 1,200,000 tons, and steel pipe capacity in excess of 670,000 tons at year-end 1992.

Steel plate products consist of hot-rolled carbon, high-strength low alloy, heat treated and alloy steel plate up to 140 inches wide.

The Napa facility pipe mill produces large diameter steel pipe ranging from 16 to 42 inches in diameter with wall thicknesses of up to 1⅙ inches and lengths of up to 80 feet.

The Fontana plate mill rolls carbon and high-strength low alloy plate up to 140 inches wide and 8 inches thick from semi-finished steel slabs.

Shipments declined to 665,300 tons in 1992, from 762,700 tons in 1991; selling prices averaged $598 a ton, down from $642. Plate shipments came to 379,700 tons in 1992, versus 344,100 in 1991; pipe shipments totaled 285,600 tons, versus 418,600 tons.

In 1992, steel products were sold to more than 300 customers, most of whom were fabricators, manufacturers, steel service centers, and oil and natural gas pipeline companies. A single customer accounted for 45% of sales in 1992.

Standard steel plate products are sold mostly in the Northwest and California. Specialty steel is sold primarily in the West. Large diameter pipe products are sold nationally.

In June 1992, the company acquired a 60% interest in Alberta-based Camrose Pipe Co. The Camrose facility produces large diameter pipe ranging from 20 to 42 inches in diameter, in lengths up to 60 feet. It also makes ERW pipe in sizes 4½ inches through 16 inches.

Dividend Data

Dividends were initiated in 1988.

Amt of Divd. $	Date Decl.	Ex–divd. Date	Stock of Record	Payment Date
0.14	Oct. 29	Nov. 6	Nov. 13	Nov. 30'92
0.14	Jan. 28	Feb. 8	Feb. 12	Feb. 26'93
0.14	Apr. 29	May 10	May 14	May 28'93
0.14	Jul. 28	Aug. 6	Aug. 12	Aug. 31'93

Capitalization

Long Term Debt: $62,122,000 (6/93).

Minority Interest: $13,259,000.

Common Stock: 19,347,781 shs. ($0.01 par).
Employee stock ownership plan owns 16%.
Institutions hold 63%.
Shareholders of record: 970 (12/92).

Offices—1000 Broadway Building, Suite 2200, 1000 S. W. Broadway, Portland, OR 97205. **Tel**—(503) 223-9228. **Chrmn & CEO**—T. B. Boklund. **Pres & COO**—R. J. Sikora. **VP, CFO & Secy**—L. R. Adams. **Investor Contact**—Vicki A. Tagliafico. **Dirs**—T. B. Boklund, C. L. Emerson, V. N. Fulton, A. C. Furth, E. C. Gendron, R. G. Landis, J. A. Maggetti, R. J. Sikora, J. A. Sproul. **Transfer Agent & Registrar**—First Interstate Bank of Oregon, Portland. **Reincorporated** in Delaware in 1974. **Empl**—1,489.

 Leo Larkin

Overseas Shipholding Group

NYSE Symbol OSG In S&P MidCap 400

Price	Range	P-E Ratio	Dividend	Yield	S&P Ranking	Beta
Sep. 1'93	1993					
17⅞	19⅞–15¾	NM	0.60	3.4%	B+	0.99

Summary

This firm is one of the world's largest bulk shipping companies, operating under U.S. and foreign registry a fleet of 59 vessels. In October 1992, OSG entered the cruise ship market through a $220 million investment in a joint venture with Chandris Group. OSG took a $13.1 million charge ($0.40 a share) against 1992's fourth quarter profits to reflect the writedown of its investment in GPA Group. Profits should enjoy a partial rebound in 1993, as increased vessel scrappings and higher OPEC oil production lift tanker rates, and OSG derives greater income from its cruise interests.

Current Outlook

Earnings for 1993 are estimated at $0.55 a share, versus nil in 1992 (after a $0.40 charge). Profits could reach $0.75 in 1994.

Dividends should be maintained at $0.15 quarterly through 1993.

Tanker rates in 1993 for international cargoes will begin to firm as rising oil production from OPEC and increased vessel scrappings help pare industry capacity. In the domestic market, profits could slip reflecting declining Alaskan crude production and drydocking costs for an idle tanker. The dry bulk markets should show improvement reflecting a rebound in rates from depressed levels and increased movement of coal and iron ore to steel producers in Japan, Taiwan and Korea. OSG also will benefit from increased movement of grain to drought-stricken Africa. Trade with the European community will fall as economic activity remains depressed. A positive contribution is anticipated from OSG's new cruise line venture.

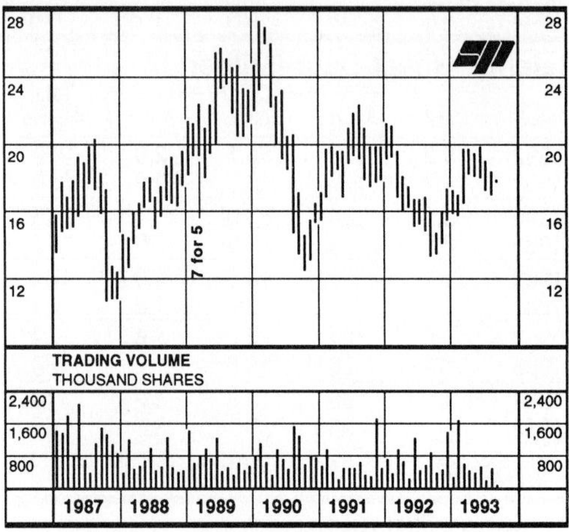

Total Revenues (Million $)

Quarter:	1993	1992	1991	1990
Mar.	102.0	98.9	110.6	99.4
Jun.	94.7	89.6	97.9	94.7
Sep.	---	87.6	110.9	98.7
Dec.	---	94.8	99.6	106.9
	---	370.9	419.1	399.7

Total revenues in 1993's first half rose 4.4%, year to year. Net income fell 12%. Share earnings were $0.32, versus $0.36, which was before a $0.49 special credit from an accounting change.

Common Share Earnings ($)

Quarter:	1993	1992	1991	1990
Mar.	0.15	0.31	0.47	0.38
Jun.	0.17	0.05	0.41	0.54
Sep.	E0.10	0.01	0.43	0.31
Dec.	E0.13	d0.37	0.36	0.40
	E0.55	Nil	1.67	1.63

Important Developments

Aug '93— Second quarter profits for 1993 included a $3.9 million gain ($0.12 a share) from the sale of a foreign-flag tanker and dry bulk carrier. In 1993's first quarter OSG realized a $3.9 million gain ($0.12 a share) from the sale of 97,800 dwt foreign flag tanker. Separately, OSG reported that it had expanded its newbuilding program with the order of two 295,250 dwt. tankers scheduled for delivery in late 1995. OSG will take delivery in 1994 of four foreign-flag tankers aggregating 374,600 dwt. at a cost of $180 million.

Mar. '93— Celebrity Cruise Lines (49%-owned) ordered a 1,740-passenger cruise ship from a German shipyard at a cost of $317.5 million. Delivery is anticipated in 1995. Celebrity said it also committed to purchase a sister ship for delivery in 1996 and has an option on a third vessel of similar size.

Next earnings report expected in early November.

Per Share Data ($)

Yr. End Dec. 31	1992	1991	1990	1989	1988	1987	1986	1985	1984	1983
Tangible Bk. Val.	**23.33**	23.05	21.40	20.09	19.32	18.39	18.30	17.63	16.97	16.19
Cash Flow	**1.72**	3.37	3.25	2.89	2.65	2.35	2.30	2.05	2.39	2.76
Earnings[1]	**Nil**	1.67	1.63	1.46	1.29	0.99	1.04	0.86	1.12	1.31
Divi dends	**0.600**	0.550	0.500	0.500	0.358	0.358	0.358	0.358	0.358	0.358
Payout Ratio	**NM**	33%	30%	34%	28%	36%	35%	42%	32%	27%
Prices—High	**21¼**	22⅜	27⅜	25¾	19⅝	20⅜	21⅝	14⅞	15⅝	17
Low	**13⅜**	15½	12½	18	12	10¾	12¾	9¼	9⅞	10⅞
P/E Ratio—	**NM**	13–9	17–8	18–12	15–9	21–11	21–12	17–11	14–9	13–8

Data as orig. reptd. Adj. for stk. div. of 40% in Mar. 1989. 1. Bef. spec. item of +0.49 in 1992. d-Deficit. E-Estimated. NM-Not Meaningful.

Income Data (Million $)

Year Ended Dec. 31	Revs.	Oper. Inc.	% Oper. Inc. of Revs.	Cap. Exp.	Depr.	Int. Exp.	[1]Net Bef. Taxes	Eff. Tax Rate	[2]Net Inc.	% Net Inc. of Revs.	Cash Flow
1992	**367**	**82**	**22.4**	**81**	**56.5**	**50.7**	**d3.6**	**NM**	**0.1**	**Nil**	**57**
1991	411	150	36.6	69	56.2	56.0	79.8	31.0%	55.1	13.4	111
1990	394	163	41.4	36	55.6	63.2	82.0	30.4%	55.9	14.2	111
1989	308	125	40.7	279	51.1	53.0	75.8	29.3%	52.0	16.9	103
1988	307	123	40.0	125	48.9	44.0	65.8	24.8%	46.4	15.1	95
1987	293	99	33.7	113	49.3	41.7	49.3	23.1%	35.5	12.1	85
1986	292	114	38.9	64	45.9	45.8	54.2	26.2%	37.3	12.8	83
1985	264	106	40.1	125	43.3	50.4	44.9	26.0%	31.0	11.7	74
1984	286	119	41.5	21	45.8	52.8	51.5	17.7%	40.5	14.1	86
1983	300	124	41.5	20	52.6	54.8	54.5	8.3%	47.3	15.8	100

Balance Sheet Data (Million $)

Dec. 31	Cash	Curr. Assets	Curr. Liab.	Curr. Ratio	Total Assets	% Ret. on Assets	Long Term Debt	Common Equity	Total Cap.	% LT Debt of Cap.	% Ret. on Equity
1992	**86**	**160**	**59**	**2.7**	**1,715**	**Nil**	**784**	**762**	**1,645**	**47.7**	**Nil**
1991	114	163	72	2.3	1,546	3.6	576	760	1,456	39.6	7.5
1990	98	147	54	2.7	1,498	3.8	613	707	1,428	42.9	8.1
1989	66	137	57	2.4	1,541	3.7	673	701	1,469	45.8	7.6
1988	110	145	46	3.2	1,318	3.6	478	696	1,258	38.0	6.8
1987	97	140	41	3.4	1,259	2.8	462	662	1,206	38.3	5.4
1986	83	129	40	3.2	1,240	3.0	454	662	1,190	38.1	5.8
1985	91	146	60	2.4	1,265	2.5	481	637	1,193	40.3	5.0
1984	72	133	60	2.2	1,230	3.3	473	613	1,154	41.0	6.8
1983	130	189	123	1.5	1,247	3.7	469	585	1,115	42.1	8.3

Data as orig reptd. **1.** Incl. equity in earns. of nonconsol. subs. **2.** Bef. spec. items. d-Deficit. NM-Not Meaningful.

Business Summary

Overseas Shipholding Group is one of the world's largest bulk shippers of liquid and dry cargos operating in international and U.S. coastal waters. OSG also has a 49% stake in a cruise line venture. At August 10, 1993, OSG's shipping fleet consisted of 59 vessels aggregating 5,661,550 dwt. Contributions to net income (in million $) in recent years:

	1992	1991	1990
Int'l fleet....................	$4.5	$49.6	$62.1
U.S. fleet....................	11.5	5.5	–6.2

OSG operate its fleet without fixed routes or schedules primarily under time or voyage charters where all personnel are supplied by OSG. Some 78% of shipping revenues in 1992 were generated from the movement of crude oil and petroleum products. BP Oil Company, USA, generated 23% of total revenues in 1992. Other bulk commodities transported are coal, iron ore and grain.

The international fleet at August 10, 1993, consisted of 43 vessels aggregating 4,668,200 dwt. and included 16 bulk carriers and 27 tankers or petroleum product carriers. Four 93,650 dwt. tankers are scheduled to be delivered in 1994 and two 295,250 dwt. tankers in 1995. OSG's U.S. fleet at August 10, 1993, consisted of 16 vessels aggregating 993,350 dwt. The U.S. fleet is primarily engaged in the transport of Alaskan oil. OSG also operates a 5,000-unit auto carrier.

OSG has a 49% stake in Celebrity Cruise Lines Inc., which operates five cruise ships aggregating 5,377 berths.

Dividend Data

Dividends were initiated in 1973.

Amt of Divd. $	Date Decl.	Ex–divd. Date	Stock of Record	Payment Date
0.15	Sep. 2	Oct. 27	Nov. 2	Nov. 25'92
0.15	Feb. 2	Feb. 9	Feb. 16	Feb. 26'93
0.15	Apr. 14	Apr. 28	May 4	May 28'93
0.15	Jun. 4	Jul. 27	Aug. 2	Aug. 27'93

Finances

Net income in 1992's fourth quarter was reduced by $13.1 million ($0.40 a share) to reflect the writedown of OSG's investment in GPA Group.

Capitalization

Long Term Debt: $727,949,000 (6/93), incl. $175.2 million of capitalized lease obligations.

Minority Interest: $4,435,000.

Common Stock: 32,676,744 shs. ($1 par).
Archer-Daniels-Midland Co. holds 13.6%.
Officers and directors hold 30%.
Institutions hold approximately 36%.
Shareholders of record: 1,324.

Office—1114 Ave. of the Americas, New York, NY 10036. **Tel**—(212) 869-1222. **Pres**—M. P. Hyman. **SVP-Secy**—R. N. Cowen. **SVP-Treas**—G. Kahana. **Investor Contact**—Catherine J. Mathis. **Dirs**—G. C. Blake, R. N. Cowen, T. H. Dean, M. Fribourg, W. L. Frost, R. Hettena, M. P. Hyman, S. Kamaroff, S. N. Merkin, J. I. Picket, M. A. Recanati, R. Recanati. **Transfer Agent & Registrar**—Mellon Securities Trust Co., NYC. **Incorporated** in Delaware in 1969. **Empl**—2,060.

 Stephen R. Klein

PHH Corporation

NYSE Symbol PHH In S&P MidCap 400

Price	Range	P–E Ratio	Dividend	Yield	S&P Ranking	Beta
Aug. 31'93	1993					
43	43¼–38¾	13	1.20	2.8%	B+	1.11

Summary

This company provides a broad range of integrated management services, including vehicle management and relocation and real estate services, to more than 2,000 corporate clients, as well as mortgage banking services to consumers. Earnings rose strongly in the first quarter of 1993-4, paced by continued strength in vehicle management and mortgage banking.

Business Summary

PHH Corporation (formerly PHH Group), through subsidiaries, offers a broad range of vehicle management and relocation and real estate management services to more than 2,000 corporate clients. It also provides mortgage banking services to consumers. Business segment contributions in 1992-3 were:

	Revs.	Income
Vehicle management	53%	43%
Relocation & real estate	41%	30%
Mortgage banking	6%	27%

International operations, primarily in Europe and Canada, accounted for 15% of consolidated revenues and 6% of operating income in 1992-3.

Vehicle-related services consist of truck and auto fleet management, and leasing and vehicle cost-control services for corporations in the U.S., Canada and the U.K. Services include purchasing and arranging for delivery of new vehicles; fleet financing; registration, title, tax and insurance compliance; used vehicle sales; business travel expense-control programs; fuel purchasing and control programs; and centralized billing programs. The number of vehicles under management was 454,275 at April 30, 1993, down from 466,977 a year earlier.

Relocation services (U.S., Canada and Europe) consist of counseling transferred employees of corporate clients and the purchase, management and resale of their homes. Relocation subsidiaries also provide home marketing, moving services, rental management, spousal career counseling and consulting services for transferred employees. Other subsidiaries provides real estate services to financial institutions and governmental agencies. During

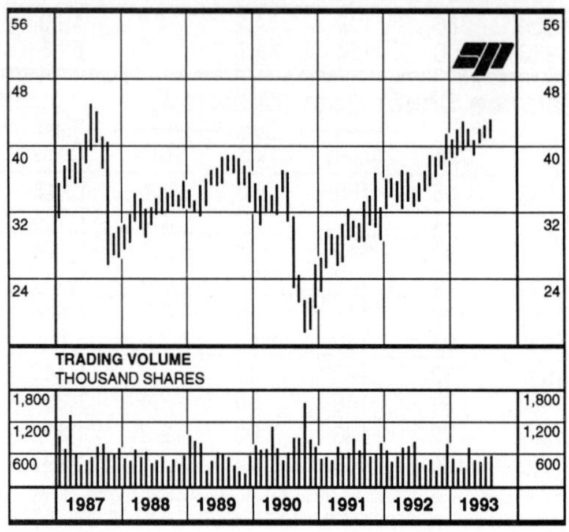

1992-3, the company sold 28,417 homes (28,113 in 1991-2) at an average price of $156,000 ($156,600).

In 1991-2, PHH created a separate operating segment for its mortgage banking subsidiary, PHH US Mortgage Corp. Services consist of the origination, sale and servicing of residential first mortgage loans nationwide. During 1992-3, mortgage loan closings totaled $5.6 billion. The mortgage servicing portfolio amounted to $11.0 billion at 1992-3 year-end.

Important Developments

Aug. '93— PHH said its mortgage servicing portfolio surpassed $12.5 billion during the first quarter of 1993-4.

Next earnings report expected in late November.

Per Share Data ($)

Yr. End Apr. 30	1993	1992	1991	1990	1989	1988	[1]1987	1986	[1]1985	1984
Tangible Bk. Val.	**22.57**	20.72	19.57	17.76	16.84	14.81	11.95	14.01	12.50	13.41
Cash Flow	**45.89**	39.36	39.20	40.00	40.74	32.90	24.08	2.97	2.99	2.64
Earnings[2,3]	**3.26**	2.94	2.78	3.38	2.91	1.12	2.35	2.40	2.56	2.30
Dividends	**1.20**	1.20	1.20	1.16	1.12	1.08	1.04	1.00	0.88	0.84
Payout Ratio	**37%**	41%	43%	34%	38%	97%	44%	42%	34%	36%
Calendar Years	**1992**	1991	1990	1989	1988	1987	1986	1985	1984	1983
Prices—High	**41½**	36¾	37⅛	38⅞	35¾	45	41	39½	36¼	47
Low	**32½**	22½	17⅝	31⅝	27⅝	25¾	29⅛	24⅞	18	29¾
P/E Ratio—	**13–10**	13–8	13–6	12–9	12–9	40–23	17–12	16–10	14–7	20–13

Data as orig. reptd. **1.** Refl. merger or acq. **2.** Bef. results of disc. ops. of -1.09 in 1990, +0.14 in 1989, and spec. item(s) of +1.49 in 1988. **3.** Ful. dil.: 3.25 in 1993, 2.92 in 1992.

Income Data (Million $)

Year Ended Apr. 30	Revs.	Oper. Inc.	% Oper. Inc. of Revs.	Cap. Exp.	Depr.	Int. Exp.	Net Bef. Taxes	Eff. Tax Rate	[4]Net Inc.	% Net Inc. of Revs.	Cash Flow
1993	**2,021**	**1,028**	**50.9**	**[3]20.8**	**738**	**194**	**94.2**	**40.1%**	**56.4**	**2.8**	**794**
1992	1,931	706	36.5	[3]24.0	620	NA	83.1	39.9%	50.0	2.6	670
1991	2,031	683	33.6	[3]26.0	616	NA	77.8	39.5%	47.1	2.3	663
[1]1990	1,911	709	37.1	[3]21.9	620	NA	89.7	36.1%	57.3	3.0	678
[1]1989	1,735	709	40.9	[3]21.7	638	NA	72.7	32.5%	49.1	2.8	687
1988	1,618	593	36.7	25.9	534	NA	38.2	51.0%	18.7	1.2	553
[2]1987	1,362	425	31.2	18.1	364	NA	64.9	39.1%	39.5	2.9	404
1986	866	72	8.3	15.6	9	NA	63.8	39.6%	38.5	4.5	48
[2]1985	700	76	10.9	7.0	7	NA	70.9	42.5%	40.8	5.8	47
1984	538	70	12.9	5.2	5	NA	65.9	44.8%	36.4	6.8	42

Balance Sheet Data (Million $)

Apr. 30	Cash	Curr. Assets	Curr. Liab.	Curr. Ratio	Total Assets	% Ret. on Assets	Long Term Debt	Common Equity	Total Cap.	% LT Debt of Cap.	% Ret. on Equity
1993	**1**	**NA**	**NA**	**NA**	**4,613**	**1.2**	**1,299**	**457**	**1,848**	**70.3**	**12.7**
1992	1	NA	NA	NA	4,365	1.2	1,001	423	1,521	65.8	12.2
1991	Nil	NA	NA	NA	4,199	1.1	823	393	1,315	62.6	12.5
1990	1	NA	NA	NA	4,464	1.3	1,264	363	1,773	71.3	16.1
1989	21	NA	NA	NA	4,231	1.2	1,224	349	1,717	71.3	14.7
1988	152	NA	NA	NA	4,148	0.5	1,178	316	1,648	71.5	6.2
1987	218	NA	NA	NA	3,483	1.2	1,131	289	1,601	70.7	14.0
1986	210	NA	1,554	NA	2,754	1.5	781	262	1,200	65.1	15.3
1985	54	NA	1,196	NA	2,216	2.1	625	239	1,020	61.3	18.0
1984	15	NA	854	NA	1,653	2.4	450	212	800	56.2	18.2

Data as orig. reptd. **1.** Excl. disc. ops. **2.** Refl. merger or acq. **3.** Net. **4.** Bef. spec. items. NA-Not Available.

Revenues (Million $)

Quarter:	1993–94	1992–93	1991–92	1990–91
Jul.	539	513	500	494
Oct.		504	460	502
Jan.		489	477	489
Apr.		515	494	546
		2,021	1,931	2,031

Revenues in the three months ended July 31, 1993, increased 4.9%, year to year, as gains in vehicle management and mortgage banking services outweighed the impact of a weak worldwide economy on relocation services. Results benefited from reduced costs of carrying and reselling homes, and from lower interest expense; net income climbed 17%, to $14,789,000 ($0.84 a share), from $12,639,000 ($0.74).

Common Share Earnings ($)

Quarter:	1993–94	[1]1992–93	[1]1991–92	1990–91
Jul.	0.84	0.74	0.66	0.70
Oct.		0.73	0.62	0.62
Jan.		0.83	0.78	0.71
Apr.		0.95	0.86	0.75
		3.25	2.92	2.78

1. Ful. dil.

Dividend Data

Dividends have been paid since 1959. A "poison pill" stock purchase right was issued in 1986.

Amt. of Divd. $	Date Decl.	Ex-divd. Date	Stock of Record	Payment Date
0.30	Sep. 22	Oct. 5	Oct. 9	Oct. 30'92
0.30	Dec. 9	Jan. 4	Jan. 8	Jan. 29'93
0.30	Feb. 22	Apr. 2	Apr. 8	Apr. 30'93
0.30	Jun. 29	Jul. 2	Jul. 9	Jul. 30'93

Finances

The company maintains $2.4 billion in revolving credit agreements and an additional $300 million in lines of credit. At April 30, 1993, PHH had aggregate commercial paper programs of $1.9 billion, used for the financing of leasing activities, mortgage banking operations and real estate management programs.

Capitalization

Total Debt: $2,900,934,000 (4/93).

Common Stock: 17,319,078 shs. (no par). Institutions hold 83%. Shareholders of record: 2,082 (6/93).

Options: To buy 1,971,570 shs. at $18.13 to $39.63 ea. (4/93).

Office—11333 McCormick Rd., Hunt Valley, MD 21031. **Tel**—(410) 771-3600. **Chrmn, Pres & CEO**—R. D. Kunisch. **SVP & CFO**—R. A. Meierhenry. **SVP & Secy**—E. A. Arbaugh. **VP & Treas**—R. W. Mitchell. **Investor Contact**—Gene Truett (410-771-2463). **Dirs**—J. S. Beard, A. F. Brimmer, G. L. Bunting, Jr., B. S. Feigin, A. P. Hoblitzell, Jr., P. X. Kelley, T. V. King, L. P. Kline, R. D. Kunisch, F. P. Lucier, K. C. Nelson, D. J. Shepard, A. B. Trowbridge. **Transfer Agent**—First Chicago Trust Co. of New York, NYC. **Registrar**—Co.'s office. **Incorporated** in Maryland in 1953. **Empl**—4,900.

 L. Feuer Nelson

PacifiCare Health Systems

NASDAQ Symbol PHSYA (Incl. in Nat'l Market) In S&P MidCap 400

Price	Range	P-E Ratio	Dividend	Yield	S&P Ranking	Beta
Sep. 15'93	1993					
31¾	57½–25½	15	None	None	NR	2.81

Summary

This company operates federally qualified HMOs with over 1,000,000 members in California, Oregon, Washington, Oklahoma and Texas. Revenue and earnings growth in recent periods has been paced by the company's rapidly growing Medicare business. Solid earnings gains are expected to continue despite a lower than expected 2.5% Medicare rate increase which will become effective January 1, 1994.

Current Outlook

Earnings in the fiscal year ending September 30, 1993, are estimated at $2.25 a share, up from $1.78 in fiscal 1992. A further advance to about $2.65 a share is projected for fiscal 1994.

Initiation of cash dividends is not anticipated.

Revenue gains through fiscal 1994 will reflect continued strong growth in the Medicare business, aided by annual membership increases expected to remain above 20%, though total revenue growth will be restricted by a low 2.5% Medicare rate increase which will become effective January 1, 1994. The company should be able to offset most of the lower than expected rate increase with cost controls and/or benefit changes. In addition, the bottom line will benefit from a lower effective tax rate resulting from the adoption of FAS 109, which should help the company to attain its stated goal of 15% to 20% annual earnings growth.

Revenues (Million $)

Quarter:	1992-93	1991-92	1990-91	1989-90
Dec.	485	360	279	204
Mar.	555	425	302	247
Jun.	576	447	319	252
Sep.	---	455	342	272
	---	1,686	1,242	976

For the nine months ended June 30, 1993, revenues climbed 31%, year to year, bolstered by a 36% increase in Medicare enrollment, an 8.5% increase in commercial enrollment, and higher premium rates. A higher commercial medical loss ratio (82.7% versus 80.5%), which resulted primarily from increased hospital capitation, was outweighed by substantial improvement in the administrative cost ratio; net income surged 45%, to $45,585,000 ($1.64 a share, on 16% more shares), from $31,450,000 ($1.31).

Common Share Earnings ($)

Quarter:	1992-93	1991-92	1990-91	1989-90
Dec.	0.39	0.29	0.11	0.13
Mar.	0.54	0.42	0.30	0.17
Jun.	0.71	0.60	0.35	0.21
Sep.	E0.61	0.47	0.35	0.25
	E2.25	1.78	1.10	0.74

Important Developments

Jun. '93— PacifiCare announced that it received approval to begin operation of a workers' compensation HMO product, which it will offer to self-insured companies and insurance carriers. The company will launch the product in Orange County, with six to ten employers participating in the initial phase, and plans to subsequently expand the product statewide. PacifiCare also recently entered the small group market, offering its health plans to businesses from five to 50 employees.

Next earnings report expected in late October.

Per Share Data ($)

Yr. End Sep. 30	[2]1992	[1]1991	1990	1989	1988	1987	[2]1986	1985
Tangible Bk. Val.	**4.52**	4.00	2.95	2.00	1.30	1.20	1.20	1.16
Cash Flow	**2.21**	1.37	0.92	0.59	0.39	0.20	0.18	0.28
Earnings	**1.78**	1.10	0.74	0.48	0.29	0.13	0.13	0.27
Dividends	**Nil**	Nil	Nil	Nil	Nil	Nil	Nil	Nil
Payout Ratio	**Nil**	Nil	Nil	Nil	Nil	Nil	Nil	Nil
Prices[3]—High	**51**	21¼	13¾	15⅛	3⅛	3½	4¼	5¾
Low	**18⅝**	7¼	6	3	1⅜	1¼	2½	3¾
P/E Ratio—	**29–10**	19–7	19–8	32–6	11–5	28–11	35–21	22–14

Data as orig. reptd. Adj. for stk. divs. of 100% Jun. 1992, 100% Sep. 1989, 100% Mar. 1985. **1.** Refl. acctg. change. **2.** Refl. merger or acq. **3.** Cal. yr. E-Estimated.

Income Data (Million $)

Year Ended Sep. 30	Revs.	Oper. Inc.	% Oper. Inc. of Revs.	Cap. Exp.	Depr.	Int. Exp.	Net Bef. Taxes	Eff. Tax Rate	Net Inc.	% Net Inc. of Revs.	Cash Flow
[2]1992	**1,704**	**88.9**	**5.2**	**10.5**	**10.6**	**3.42**	**74.9**	**41.8%**	**43.6**	**2.6**	**54.2**
[1]1991	1,242	36.0	2.9	46.1	6.3	0.17	44.5	42.3%	25.7	2.1	32.0
1990	976	18.7	1.9	10.1	4.3	0.28	29.4	40.1%	17.6	1.8	21.9
1989	650	11.5	1.8	6.0	2.4	0.40	17.7	38.8%	10.9	1.7	13.3
1988	425	5.8	1.4	3.3	2.2	0.54	11.3	43.8%	6.3	1.5	8.6
1987	301	d1.3	NM	2.5	1.7	0.69	4.8	36.8%	3.0	1.0	4.7
[2]1986	167	1.1	0.6	5.3	1.4	0.53	3.9	23.5%	3.0	1.8	4.4
1985	87	9.1	10.5	1.1	0.4	0.38	11.1	48.9%	5.7	6.5	6.0

Balance Sheet Data (Million $)

		Curr.									
Sep. 30	Cash	Assets	Liab.	Ratio	Total Assets	% Ret. on Assets	Long Term Debt	Common Equity	Total Cap.	% LT Debt of Cap.	% Ret. on Equity
1992	**272**	**329**	**280**	**1.2**	**498**	**10.1**	**18.5**	**199**	**218**	**8.5**	**28.0**
1991	206	241	219	1.1	322	9.3	2.3	100	103	2.2	29.5
1990	160	199	156	1.3	232	8.1	0.3	75	76	0.4	29.2
1989	143	174	147	1.2	194	6.6	2.3	44	47	4.9	27.5
1988	107	121	97	1.2	137	5.9	3.3	36	39	8.4	19.2
1987	60	69	47	1.5	85	4.0	4.5	33	38	12.0	9.5
1986	49	55	32	1.7	68	5.3	5.7	31	37	15.7	10.2
1985	37	40	15	2.7	45	NA	2.4	28	31	7.8	NA

Data as orig. reptd. **1.** Refl. acctg. change. **2.** Refl. merger or acq. d-Deficit. NM-Not Meaningful. NA-Not Available.

Business Summary

PacifiCare Health Systems, Inc. is a regionally focused healthcare company with six health maintenance organizations (HMOs) operating in California, Oklahoma, Oregon, Texas and Washington. At June 30, 1993, the geographic membership distribution was:

California	73%
Oklahoma	11%
Oregon & Washington	9%
Texas	7%

PacifiCare serves two types of HMO member groups—commercial members and Medicare beneficiaries. Commercial members join its programs primarily through employer groups, while the company provides healthcare services to individual Medicare beneficiaries through its Secure Horizons programs.

At June 30, 1993, the company's commercial membership had grown to 789,582, from 727,723 a year earlier. Through its HMOs, PacifiCare arranges for the delivery of a comprehensive range of health care services to members, including primary and specialty physician care, hospital care, laboratory and radiology services, prescription drugs, dental care, vision care, skilled nursing care, physical therapy and psychological counseling. The company's Secure Horizons programs, which had 269,135 enrollees at June 30, 1993 (up from 197,729 a year earlier), offer a comprehensive package of benefits extending beyond those to which most beneficiaries are entitled by Medicare.

In December 1991, PacifiCare acquired Health Plan of America, one of California's largest individual practice association HMOs, giving the company rapid access to the Northern California market.

In addition to its core HMO and Secure Horizons operations, the company has units engaged in health and life insurance, behavioral health managed care services, utilization review services, health promotion, and coordination of an alliance of regional HMOs across the U.S.

Dividend Data

The company has never paid cash dividends on its common stock. In June 1992, one new Class B common share was distributed for each common share (reclassified as Class A common), having the effect of a two-for-one stock split.

Finances

In September 1993, the company signed a definitive agreement to acquire California Dental Health Plan, which provides prepaid dental benefits to over 450,000 members and 5,000 employer groups in the western U.S.

Capitalization

Long Term Debt: $18,445,000 (6/93).

Minority Interest: $413,000.

Class A Common Stock: 12,094,334 ($0.01 par). Unihealth America owns 53%. Shareholders: 289 of record (9/92).

Class B Common Stock: 15,238,134 ($0.01 par).; nonvoting. Unihealth America owns 21%. Shareholders: 254 of record (9/92).

Office—5995 Plaza Dr., Cypress, CA 90630. **Tel**—(714) 952-1121. **Chrmn**—T. O. Hartshorn. **Pres & CEO**—A. Hoops. **EVP & CFO**—W. Lowell. **Investor Contact**—David Erickson. **Dirs**—E. Benveniste, D. R. Carpenter, T. O. Hartshorn, G. L. Leary, W. E. Pinckert II, D. A. Reed, L. Ross, D. Strum, S. J. Tibbitts. **Transfer Agent & Registrar**—First Interstate Bank of California, LA. **Incorporated** in Delaware in 1975. **Empl**—2,186.

 Adam J. Penn

Parametric Technology

NASDAQ Symbol PMTC (Incl. in Nat'l Market) In S&P MidCap 400

Price	Range	P-E Ratio	Dividend	Yield	S&P Ranking	Beta
Aug. 27'93	1993					
37¾	40–22½	60	None	None	NR	NA

Summary

This Massachusetts-based company is a leader in the mechanical design automation industry. Steady improvement in and increased acceptance of Parametric's Pro/ENGINEER line of integrated software products led to extremely rapid growth in revenues and earnings in recent years. Continued strong sales and steady margins should aid earnings through fiscal 1994.

Current Outlook

Earnings of $1.00 a share are projected for the fiscal year ending September 30, 1994, up from the $0.70 estimated for fiscal 1993 and the $0.38 recorded in fiscal 1992.

Cash dividends are not currently anticipated.

Revenues through fiscal 1994 are expected to continue their strong upward trend. The company maintains a high level of repeat business and continues to gain new accounts, gaining market share at the expense of its more established competitors. Margins are expected to be maintained as volume efficiencies offset a less favorable revenue mix of services business and additions to its worldwide sales force.

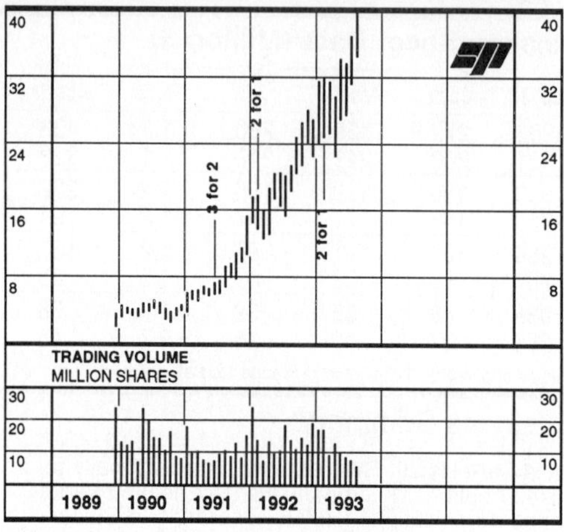

Revenues (Million $)

Quarter:	1992–93	1991–92	1990–91	1989–90
Dec.	32.5	16.5	8.8	4.9
Mar.	38.0	19.2	10.3	5.9
Jun.	43.5	23.5	11.8	6.7
Sep.		27.5	13.7	8.0
		86.7	44.7	25.5

Revenues for the nine months ended July 3, 1993, climbed 93%, year to year, reflecting increased acceptance and market penetration of the company's products, both in the U.S. and abroad. Repeat business from existing customers accounted for over 80% of total revenue. Margins widened on the higher volume, despite a program to expand the worldwide sales force, and pretax profit rose 111%. After taxes at 37.3%, versus 36.4%, net income was up 108%, to $29,527,000, from $14,199,000. Earnings per share were $0.51 and $0.25, respectively, as adjusted for the two-for-one stock split in February 1993.

Common Share Earnings ($)

Quarter:	1992–93	1991–92	1990–91	1989–90
Dec.	0.15	0.07	0.04	0.02
Mar.	0.17	0.08	0.05	0.03
Jun.	0.20	0.10	0.05	0.03
Sep.	E0.18	0.12	0.06	0.04
	E0.70	0.38	0.19	0.11

Important Developments

Jul. '93— The company said that during the third quarter of fiscal 1993 it sold nearly 35,000 software modules for use at some 2,400 workstation seats. Since Pro/ENGINEER was introduced in 1988, a total of 193,000 software modules for use at nearly 16,500 workstation seats have been sold. Its worldwide customer base now totals about 2,900.

Next earnings report expected in mid-November.

Per Share Data ($)

Yr. End Sep. 30	1992	1991	1990	1989	1988
Tangible Bk. Val.	**1.51**	0.85	0.60	d0.12	NA
Cash Flow	**0.40**	0.20	0.12	0.05	NA
Earnings[1]	**0.38**	0.19	0.11	0.04	d0.03
Dividends	**Nil**	Nil	Nil	Nil	Nil
Payout Ratio	**Nil**	Nil	Nil	Nil	Nil
Prices[2]—High	**28⅛**	15⁵⁄₁₆	5¼	3⅝	NA
Low	**12⅝**	3¾	2½	2	NA
P/E Ratio—	**75–34**	81–20	48–23	98–72	NM

Data as orig. reptd. Adj. for stk. divs. of 100% Feb. 1993, 100% Feb. 1992, 50% Jun. 1991, 100% Oct. 1989. **1.** Bef. spec. item of +0.02 in 1989. **2.** Cal. yr. NA-Not Available. d-Deficit. NM-Not Meaningful. E-Estimated.

Income Data (Million $)

Year Ended Sep. 30	Revs.	Oper. Inc.	% Oper. Inc. of Revs.	[1]Cap. Exp.	Depr.	Int. Exp.	Net Bef. Taxes	Eff. Tax Rate	[2]Net Inc.	% Net Inc. of Revs.	Cash Flow
1992	**86.7**	**32.3**	**37.2**	**3.56**	**1.30**	**NM**	**33.2**	**36.6%**	**21.1**	**24.3**	**22.4**
1991	44.7	15.1	33.7	0.82	0.69	0.05	15.9	35.0%	10.3	23.1	11.0
1990	25.5	8.0	31.5	0.47	0.56	0.11	8.6	34.5%	5.6	22.0	6.2
1989	11.0	2.7	24.3	0.05	0.47	0.11	2.3	30.9%	1.6	14.5	1.8
1988	3.3	NA	NA	0.30	NA	0.08	d0.8	Nil	d0.8	NM	NA

Balance Sheet Data (Million $)

Sep. 30	Cash	Curr. Assets	Curr. Liab.	Curr. Ratio	Total Assets	% Ret. on Assets	Long Term Debt	Common Equity	Total Cap.	% LT Debt of Cap.	% Ret. on Equity
1992	**73.5**	**99.2**	**27.0**	**3.7**	**107**	**26.2**	**Nil**	**78.7**	**80.2**	**Nil**	**34.3**
1991	34.5	48.7	7.7	6.3	51	23.9	0.01	42.0	43.2	NM	28.8
1990	24.6	33.1	4.5	7.3	35	13.3	0.22	28.8	30.1	0.7	NM
1989	3.3	6.8	2.2	3.1	8	NA	0.55	d0.9	5.4	10.3	NA

Data as orig. reptd. **1.** Net. **2.** Bef. spec. item in 1989. NA-Not Available. NM-Not Meaningful. d-Deficit.

Business Summary

Parametric Technology Corporation develops, markets and supports a family of fully integrated software products for the automation of the mechanical design-through-manufacturing process—a complex, iterative process encompassing a broad spectrum of distinct engineering disciplines that is essential to the development of virtually all manufactured products, from consumer items to jet aircraft.

Contributions to revenues by geographic area in recent fiscal years were:

	1992	1991	1990
North America	65%	62%	69%
Europe	22%	18%	14%
Far East....................	13%	20%	17%

The company's mechanical design automation (MDA) products enable end-users to reduce the time-to-market and manufacturing costs for their products and, through the easy evaluation of multiple design alternatives, to improve product quality.

Parametric's product line as of late 1992 consisted of its core product, Pro/ENGINEER, and 24 released family modules. First shipped in January 1988, Pro/ENGINEER is a parametric, feature-driven solid modeling system used in the detailed design phase of the MDA cycle. Other modules include Pro/DESIGN, a conceptual design tool; Pro/DETAIL and Pro/DRAFT, which generate detailed manufacturing drawings; and Pro/ASSEMBLY, used to design and manage very complex assemblies. The company's practice has been to issue two major releases of its product line per year, each of which has generally included several new products. Parametric's ability to develop new products rapidly is facilitated by the modular structure of its software code. The company's products run on a wide range of workstations.

Marketing and sales efforts are focused primarily on electronic equipment, aerospace, automotive and consumer products companies, with sales made directly to strategic customers and indirectly through value-added resellers and original equipment manufacturers. Sales and support offices are located in more than 35 cities throughout the U.S. and in Japan, France, Italy, Germany, the U.K., the Netherlands, Hong Kong, Korea and Singapore.

End-users of the company's products range from small companies to some of the world's largest manufacturing organizations.

Dividend Data

No cash dividends have been paid. Two-for-one stock splits were effected in February 1993 and February 1992.

Finances

The company has available a $2 million bank line of credit, none of which was in use at July 3, 1993.

In December 1989, the company, through underwriters led by Alex. Brown & Sons (Baltimore), Hambrecht & Quist (San Francisco) and Wessels, Arnold & Henderson (Minneapolis), sold 9,420,060 (adjusted) common shares at $2 each in Parametric's initial public stock offering. Upon closing of the offering, all of the company's preferred stock was converted into 28,608,000 (adjusted) common shares.

Capitalization

Long Term Debt: None (7/3/93).

Common Stock: 53,981,570 shs. ($0.01 par).
Institutions hold about 83%.
Shareholders: 672 of record (9/92).

Options: To buy 8,119,700 shs. at $0.015 to $22.625 ea. (9/92, as adj.).

Office—128 Technology Drive, Waltham, MA 02154. **Tel**—(617) 894-7111. **Fax**—(617) 891-1069. **Pres & CEO**—S. C. Walske. **Exec VP & Chrmn**—S. P. Geisberg. **VP-Treas & CFO**—M. J. Gallagher. **VP & Investor Contact**—Louis J. Volpe. **Dirs**—D. W. Feddersen, S. P. Geisberg, R. N. Goldman, D. K. Grierson, N. G. Posternak, S. C. Walske. **Transfer Agent & Registrar**—American Stock Transfer & Trust Co., NYC. **Incorporated** in Massachusetts in 1985. **Empl**—820.

 Peter C. Wood, CFA

Parker Drilling

NYSE Symbol PKD In S&P MidCap 400

Price	Range	P-E Ratio	Dividend	Yield	S&P Ranking	Beta
Aug. 3'93	1993					
6¼	7¼–4½	NM	None	None	C	1.01

Summary

This company is a leading land drilling contractor for the oil and gas industry, specializing in deep drilling and remote location drilling worldwide. In fiscal 1992, approximately 76% of revenues were generated from operations outside the United States. Operations have recently been under pressure from low rig utilization in international markets. The longer-term outlook is enhanced by improving utilization rates, a healthy balance sheet and strong niche in difficult geological or operating environments.

Current Outlook

A net loss of $0.20 a share is projected for the fiscal year ending August 31, 1993, versus fiscal 1992's loss of $0.21. Share earnings for fiscal 1994 are estimated at $0.20.

Resumption of dividends is not likely in the foreseeable future.

Revenues for fiscal 1994 are expected to rise, reflecting increased rig utilization attributable to firming international markets and strong gas prices. With drilling's continued movement into remote locations and difficult geological or operating environments, PKD should return to profitability in fiscal 1994.

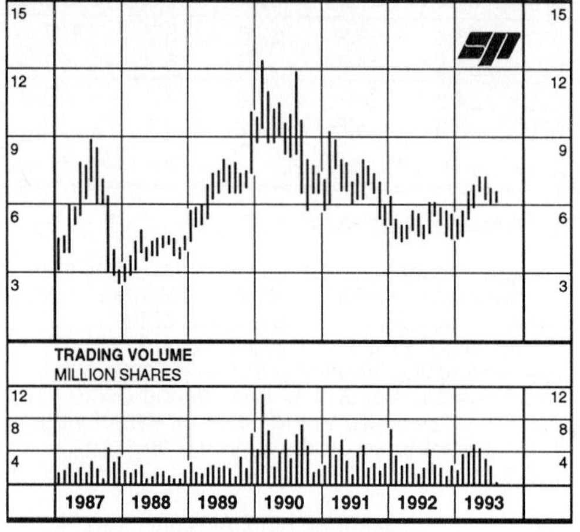

Revenues (Million $)

Quarter:	1992–93	1991–92	1990–91	1989–90
Nov.	23.9	26.7	27.2	28.8
Feb.	25.3	31.9	27.8	25.8
May	25.0	32.3	28.2	26.0
Aug.		32.5	29.6	27.9
		123.3	112.8	108.5

Revenues for the nine months ended May 31, 1993, fell 18%, year to year, reflecting lower rig utilization. Operating expenses declined less rapidly, other income dropped sharply, and depreciation charges increased. In the absence of a $4.0 million gain on a contract settlement, there was a pretax loss of $7.9 million, against pretax earnings of $8.2 million. After taxes of $1.7 million, versus $2.4 million (28.9%), the net loss was $0.18 a share, in contrast to net income of $0.11.

Common Share Earnings ($)

Quarter:	1992–93	1991–92	1990–91	1989–90
Nov.	d0.05	0.03	0.01	d0.04
Feb.	d0.09	0.05	0.01	d0.07
May	d0.04	0.03	0.01	d0.05
Aug.	Ed0.02	d0.33	0.01	d0.21
	Ed0.20	d0.21	0.04	d0.37

Important Developments

Jul. '93— A net loss of $2.1 million in fiscal 1993's third quarter replaced income of $1.8 million in the year-earlier period as the overall utilization rate declined to 24%, from 29%. Eastern Hemisphere revenues were down substantially, reflecting the absence of $4.2 million of revenues from the mobilization/early termination obligations attributable to the cancellation of a three-rig contract in the Russian Republic.

Apr. '93— The company sold its interest in a subsidiary operating in Canada for $2.3 million in cash and $688,000 in notes. Separately, PKD was selected to help develop the Tengiz oilfield, one of the world's most difficult drilling environments, in the former Soviet republic of Kazakhstan.

Next earnings report expected in mid-October.

Per Share Data ($)

Yr. End Aug. 31	1992	1991	1990	1989	1988	1987	1986	1985	1984	1983
Tangible Bk. Val.	**3.89**	4.17	4.06	3.46	4.29	2.05	5.00	7.48	9.81	12.12
Cash Flow	**0.29**	0.38	d0.01	0.18	d1.03	d1.14	d0.01	0.62	0.73	2.21
Earnings[1]	**d0.21**	0.04	d0.37	d0.98	d2.52	d3.02	d2.41	d2.12	d2.18	d0.89
Dividends	**Nil**	Nil	Nil	Nil	Nil	0.02	0.07	0.16	0.16	0.16
Payout Ratio	**Nil**	Nil	Nil	Nil	Nil	NM	NM	NM	NM	NM
Prices[2]—High	**6⅜**	9¼	12⅜	10⅛	4⅞	8⅞	5⅛	7½	12⅝	13¾
Low	**4⅜**	5⅛	5¾	4⅜	2⅝	2½	2⅞	4	6	7½
P/E Ratio—	**NM**	NM	NM	NM	NM	NM	NM	NM	NM	NM

Data as orig. reptd. **1.** Bef. results of disc. opers. of +0.02 in 1991, +0.39 in 1990, and extra. item(s) of +0.11 in 1990, +4.35 in 1988. **2.** Cal. yr.
d-Deficit. E-Estimated. NM-Not Meaningful.

Income Data (Million $)

Year Ended Aug. 31	Revs.	Oper. Inc.	% Oper. Inc. of Revs.	Cap. Exp.	Depr.	Int. Exp.	Net Bef. Taxes	Eff. Tax Rate	[4]Net Inc.	% Net Inc. of Revs.	Cash Flow
1992	**123**	**9**	**7.3**	**28**	**26.1**	**0.4**	**[3]d9**	**NM**	**d11.2**	**NM**	**15**
1991	113	12	10.4	59	17.8	0.9	[3]3	60.6%	2.0	1.8	20
[1]1990	109	d2	NM	13	18.6	1.6	[3]d19	NM	d18.8	NM	Nil
1989	118	7	6.1	20	49.9	5.4	[3]d41	NM	d42.1	NM	8
1988	95	d16	NM	21	50.9	26.0	[3]d86	NM	d86.0	NM	d35
1987	113	d11	NM	21	55.8	27.2	[3]d87	NM	d89.6	NM	d34
1986	196	27	13.6	15	70.7	32.3	[3]d63	NM	d70.8	NM	Nil
1985	255	48	18.7	20	80.3	39.2	d60	NM	d62.1	NM	18
1984	225	10	4.5	27	85.0	[2]43.3	d95	NM	d63.5	NM	21
1983	349	77	22.2	19	89.2	[2]45.2	d34	NM	d25.5	NM	64

Balance Sheet Data (Million $)

Aug. 31	Cash	Curr. Assets	Curr. Liab.	Curr. Ratio	Total Assets	% Ret. on Assets	Long Term Debt	Common Equity	Total Cap.	% LT Debt of Cap.	% Ret. on Equity
1992	**37**	**82**	**23**	**3.5**	**246**	**NM**	**Nil**	**210**	**219**	**0.1**	**NM**
1991	43	92	29	3.2	265	0.7	2	219	230	0.8	0.9
1990	83	130	26	5.0	265	NM	7	210	230	3.1	NM
1989	31	77	31	2.5	245	NM	32	155	209	15.1	NM
1988	38	80	41	1.9	291	NM	30	189	244	12.3	NM
1987	56	102	39	2.6	355	NM	225	62	310	72.6	NM
1986	89	172	38	4.5	445	NM	230	151	407	56.5	NM
1985	103	210	78	2.7	585	NM	262	223	507	51.6	NM
1984	131	236	133	1.8	685	NM	230	289	551	41.7	NM
1983	128	279	70	4.0	805	NM	306	357	735	41.6	NM

Data as orig. reptd. **1.** Excl. disc. opers. **2.** Net of interest income. **3.** Incl. equity in earns. of nonconsol. subs. **4.** Bef. spec. items. d-Deficit. NM-Not Meaningful.

Business Summary

Parker Drilling provides land contract drilling services on a worldwide basis to the oil and gas industry. Customers served by the company include major international oil companies, foreign national oil and gas companies, independent oil companies and industrial users.

The revenue distribution in fiscal 1992 was 24% domestic and 76% foreign. There was a domestic operating loss of $20.0 million and foreign operating income of $2.9 million. Outside the U.S., PKD operates in 15 countries throughout the Far East and Pacific Rim, South America and Africa.

During fiscal 1992, the company decided to dispose of certain parts and rig components, and recorded a $19.3 million provision to reduce the carrying value to the estimated cash proceeds of $2.5 million. Consequently, PKD's fleet of drilling rigs was reduced to 102, from 118, at September 30, 1992. Some 56% of the rigs were located in the U.S., with the remainder primarily located in Southeast Asia, South America, Africa and the Middle East. The company specializes in deep gas, Arctic and remote location drilling, utilizing equipment that is specially designed to be easily transported by helicopter or other vehicles into difficult access areas. Domestically, it specializes in the drilling of deep gas wells (below 15,000 feet). PKD also engages in coring and geothermal operations.

In fiscal 1992, PKD's domestic and foreign rig utilization rates, excluding the 16 rigs to be disposed of and 10 rigs owned by the company's Canadian subsidiary, were 13% and 52%, respectively, versus 20% and 63% the year before.

Parker Technology, Inc. (Partech) designs and constructs specialized rigs and components. In the past three fiscal years, Partech accounted for less than 10% of PKD's revenues.

Parker Kinetic Designs, Inc. develops electric launch technology and other pulse power applications and equipment, and provides specialized engineering services.

Dividend Data

Common dividends were paid from 1976 until they were omitted in 1987.

Finances

At August 31, 1992, PKD had net operating loss carryforwards for tax purposes of about $106.8 million, expiring from 1996 through 2011.

Capitalization

Long Term Debt: None (5/93).

Minority Interest: $3,290,000.

Common Stock: 54,992,182 shs. ($0.16⅔ par).
Robert L. Parker owns 7.7%.
Institutions hold approximately 46%.
Shareholders of record: 5,913.

d-Deficit.

Office—Parker Building, Eight East Third St., Tulsa, OK 74103. **Tel**—(918) 585-8221. **Chrmn**—R. L. Parker Sr. **Pres & CEO**—R. L. Parker Jr. **VP-Fin & CFO**—J. J. Davis. **Secy**—Kathy J. Kucharski. **Investor Contact**—Ed Hendrix. **Dirs**—D. L. Fist, E. F. Gloyna, J. W. Linn, R. L. Parker Sr., R. L. Parker Jr., R. R. Reinfrank, E. L. Swearingen. **Transfer Agent & Registrar**—Chemical Bank, NYC. **Incorporated** in Oklahoma in 1954; reincorporated in Delaware in 1976. **Empl**—1,661.

 J.R. Jordan

Paychex, Inc.

NASDAQ Symbol PAYX (Incl. in Nat'l Market) Options on Phila In S&P MidCap 400

Price	Range	P-E Ratio	Dividend	Yield	S&P Ranking	Beta
Sep. 22'93	1993					
32	33–22½	44	0.16	0.5%	B+	0.93

Summary

The second largest payroll accounting services concern in the U.S., this company primarily provides computerized payroll accounting services to small and medium-sized firms nationwide. Operations have been expanded to include certain fringe benefit products and personnel management services. Earnings continued to advance strongly in the first quarter of 1993-94, and the shares were recently split three for two for the second time in a little more than a year.

Business Summary

Paychex, Inc. was formed in 1979 through the consolidation of 17 corporations providing computerized payroll accounting services. The company concentrates on small and medium-sized firms employing fewer than 200 employees; Paychex believes that there are over 5,000,000 such businesses in the major metropolitan areas across the U.S. The company's 70 branch operating centers were furnishing services to about 167,000 clients as of May 31, 1993, compared with 150,400 clients a year earlier. Paychex believes that it ranks as the second-largest payroll accounting service concern in the U.S.

Services include preparation of paychecks, earnings statements and internal accounting records. Paychex supplies its clients with all required monthly, quarterly and annual payroll tax returns for federal, state and local governments. The market for such services has evolved primarily as a result of legal requirements that employers act as "tax collectors" for the various taxing authorities, making businesses responsible for complying with a wide variety of complex, changing regulations. The computerized Paychex system utilizes proprietary software that is regularly updated to accommodate regulatory changes.

Taxpay, an extension of the payroll service, became available nationwide during 1990-91. Paychex deposits payroll taxes and files returns for its Taxpay clients and assumes full responsibility for accurate and timely filings.

Paychex does not have written contracts with its clients, but some 80% of the businesses served in 1990-91 and 1991-92 continued to be clients in 1992-93. Services are warranted, with the company agreeing to reimburse clients for any penalties and interest incurred as a result of a Paychex error. Warranty expense was $130,000 in 1992-93 and $200,000 the year before.

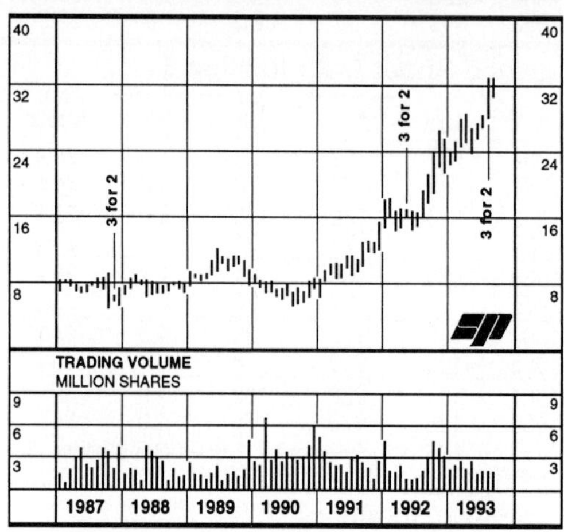

In 1990-91, Paychex established a Human Resources Services division to consolidate its fringe benefit products and personnel management services. Products include group health and disability insurance, workers' compensation and group life, the preparation of employee handbooks and Section 125 Cafeteria Plans. The cafeteria plans allow employees to pay for certain fringe benefits with pretax dollars, with a resultant savings to the employer of Social Security taxes.

Next earnings report expected in mid-December.

Per Share Data ($)

Yr. End May 31	1993	1992	1991	1990	1989	1988	1987	1986	1985	1984
Tangible Bk. Val.	**2.86**	2.27	1.85	[1]1.61	[1]1.37	1.08	0.82	0.64	0.49	0.38
Cash Flow	**1.02**	0.79	0.61	0.54	0.53	0.40	0.29	0.23	0.17	0.11
Earnings[2]	**0.67**	0.47	0.33	0.29	0.33	0.24	0.18	0.15	0.10	0.09
Dividends	**0.147**	0.102	0.085	0.067	0.040	Nil	Nil	Nil	Nil	Nil
Payout Ratio	**22%**	22%	26%	23%	12%	Nil	Nil	Nil	Nil	Nil
Calendar Years	**1992**	1991	1990	1989	1988	1987	1986	1985	1984	1983
Prices—High	**26⅝**	15½	9⅛	12 7/32	9	9 5/32	7⅝	4 5/32	2 15/32	2 25/32
Low	**14½**	6⅜	5 11/32	7 21/32	6 11/32	4 31/32	3 21/32	1 25/32	1 17/32	2 5/32
P/E Ratio—	**40–21**	33–14	28–16	42–26	28–20	38–21	43–21	29–12	23–15	33–26

Data as orig. reptd. Adj. for stk. divs. of 50% Aug. 1993, 50% May 1992, 50% Nov. 1987, 50% May 1986. **1.** Incl. intangibles. **2.** Bef. results of disc. ops. of -0.02 in 1984.

Income Data (Million $)

Year Ended May 31	Revs.	Oper. Inc.	% Oper. Inc. of Revs.	Cap. Exp.	Depr.	Int. Exp.	Net Bef. Taxes	Eff. Tax Rate	Net Inc.	% Net Inc. of Revs.	Cash Flow
1993	**190**	**37.1**	**19.5**	**8.7**	**10.40**	**0.12**	**28.0**	**28.8%**	**20.00**	**10.5**	**30.4**
1992	161	28.4	17.6	[2]13.5	9.57	0.14	19.5	29.9%	13.70	8.5	23.3
1991	137	21.7	15.8	[2]17.4	8.41	0.22	14.0	31.5%	9.62	7.0	18.0
1990	120	19.4	16.2	[2]15.4	7.32	0.18	13.2	35.1%	8.57	7.1	15.9
1989	101	20.0	19.8	9.1	5.92	0.21	15.0	36.9%	9.45	9.3	15.4
1988	79	15.4	19.4	8.1	4.69	0.18	11.2	38.2%	6.94	8.7	11.6
1987	64	13.4	20.9	5.4	3.30	0.18	10.2	50.0%	5.12	8.0	8.4
1986	51	10.3	20.3	3.9	2.55	0.22	7.8	46.4%	4.17	8.2	6.7
1985	41	6.4	15.6	10.0	1.80	0.25	4.8	37.5%	2.98	7.3	4.8
[1]1984	32	4.9	15.5	3.1	0.87	0.03	4.4	45.1%	2.39	7.6	3.3

Balance Sheet Data (Million $)

May 31	Cash	Curr. Assets	Curr. Liab.	Ratio	Total Assets	% Ret. on Assets	Long Term Debt	Common Equity	Total Cap.	% LT Debt of Cap.	% Ret. on Equity
1993	**38.1**	**64.2**	**17.8**	**3.6**	**107.0**	**20.6**	**1.24**	**85.2**	**87.8**	**1.4**	**26.1**
1992	20.0	41.6	13.7	3.0	86.2	17.4	1.63	67.4	70.7	2.3	22.4
1991	11.0	29.7	10.5	2.8	70.4	14.5	2.02	54.5	58.3	3.5	18.9
1990	15.8	31.4	10.2	3.1	62.1	14.6	1.65	47.2	50.6	3.3	19.6
1989	19.4	32.5	9.5	3.4	54.8	19.4	2.14	40.2	44.4	4.8	26.3
1988	13.8	23.3	6.0	3.9	42.5	18.4	2.77	31.5	35.8	7.7	24.9
1987	9.2	16.7	4.7	3.6	32.6	17.3	2.36	24.0	27.5	8.6	24.0
1986	6.2	12.6	4.5	2.8	26.5	17.5	2.57	18.6	22.0	11.7	25.3
1985	3.1	8.6	3.4	2.5	21.1	16.9	2.79	14.3	17.7	15.7	23.2
1984	3.4	7.8	2.6	3.0	14.2	23.0	Nil	11.4	11.5	Nil	34.1

Data as orig. reptd. **1.** Excl. disc. ops. **2.** Net.

Operating Revenues (Million $)

Quarter:	1993–94	1992–93	1991–92	1990–91
Aug.	53.3	45.3	38.0	33.1
Nov.		45.7	39.2	33.5
Feb.		48.6	41.7	35.3
May		50.4	42.4	35.3
		190.0	161.3	137.1

Revenues in the three months ended August 31, 1993, rose 18%, year to year, primarily reflecting an expanded client base and an increase in the number of clients utilizing the Taxpay service. Costs and expenses were well controlled, and net income advanced 30%, to $6,645,000 ($0.22 a share), from $5,099,000 ($0.17, as adjusted for the 3-for-2 stock split effected in August 1993). Results for 1993 exclude a $274,000 ($0.01) credit from a change in the method of accounting for income taxes.

Common Share Earnings ($)

Quarter:	1993–94	1992–93	1991–92	1990–91
Aug.	0.23	0.17	0.11	0.10
Nov.		0.17	0.13	0.10
Feb.		0.15	0.10	0.06
May		0.18	0.12	0.07
		0.67	0.47	0.33

Dividend Data

Cash dividends were initiated in November 1988. Three-for-two stock distributions were effected in 1986, 1987, 1992 and 1993.

Amt of Divd. $	Date Decl.	Ex–divd. Date	Stock of Record	Payment Date
0.06	Oct. 1	Oct. 19	Oct. 23	Nov. 18'92
0.06	Jan. 5	Jan. 22	Jan. 28	Feb. 23'93
0.06	Apr. 8	Apr. 23	Apr. 29	May 25'93
0.06	Jul. 8	Jul. 20	Jul. 26	Aug. 19'93
3–for–2	Jul. 8	Aug. 27	Aug. 2	Aug. 26'93

Finances

As of May 31, 1993, the company had no borrowings outstanding under a $60 million unsecured bank line of credit.

Capital expenditures during 1992-93 were $8,710,000, down from $13,453,000 in 1991-92. Capital expenditures in 1993-94 are expected to total approximately $14,000,000. These expenditures are expected to promote processing efficiencies and support future company growth.

Capitalization

Long Term Debt: $1,193,000 (8/93).

Common Stock: 19,872,051 shs. ($0.01 par).
Directors & officers own some 18%, incl. 14% held by B. T. Golisano.
Institutions hold about 59%.
Shareholders: 1,605 of record (7/93).

Office—911 Panorama Trail South, Rochester, NY 14625-0397. **Tel**—(716) 385-6666. **Chrmn, Pres & CEO**—B. T. Golisano. **VP-Fin, Secy, Treas & Investor Contact**—G. Thomas Clark. **Dirs**—D. W. Brinckman, G. T. Clark, B. T. Golisano, P. Horsley, G. M. Inman, H. P. Messina Jr., J. R. Sebo. **Transfer Agent**—American Stock Transfer & Trust Co., NYC. **Incorporated** in Delaware in 1979. **Empl**—2,800.

 Kevin J. Gooley

Penn Central

NYSE Symbol PC Options on Phila (Mar-Jun-Sep-Dec) In S&P MidCap 400

Price	Range	P-E Ratio	Dividend	Yield	S&P Ranking	Beta
Aug. 18'93	1993					
36	39¾–23½	12	0.84	2.3%	B	1.00

Summary

Penn Central writes insurance primarily in the specialty property and casualty areas, provides systems and software engineering services to defense-related industries, and manufactures and supplies a variety of other products and industrial services. In December 1992, the company said it planned to concentrate its efforts on the insurance business and divest its non-insurance operations. Revenue growth in the insurance segment continued in the first half of 1993, and earnings from continuing operations jumped nearly five-fold, due to investment gains and tax benefits reaped by the company's restructuring. Entities controlled by Carl Lindner recently reduced their stake in PC to nearly 40%, from 51%.

Business Summary

Through subsidiaries, Penn Central Corp. writes property and casualty insurance, provides systems and software engineering services to defense-related government agencies and manufactures and supplies a variety of other products and services. During 1992, PC elected to concentrate its efforts on the property and casualty insurance business, and initiated its planned divestitures with the spinoff of General Cable Corp. (electrical, electronic and communications wire and cable manufacturing operations). Five small industrial businesses in the Diversified Products and Services division remain for sale. Segment contributions in 1992:

	Revs.	Profits
Insurance	63%	86%
Federal Systems	23%	11%
Diversified prods & svcs	14%	3%

Insurance operations consist of Republic Indemnity Co. of America, which sells workers' compensation insurance in California, and Leader National Insurance (acquired in May 1993), Atlanta Casualty, Infinity Insurance and Windsor Insurance, providers of high-risk automobile insurance coverage.

The Federal Systems group provide high-technology systems and software engineering, security and logistics support and technical and management services to the U.S. Department of Defense, NASA, U.S. government agencies and foreign governments.

Diversified products manufactured include aerial lift trucks, safety equipment and mobile tools for installing cable, and commercial batteries. Services provided include onshore contract drilling and well workover services, computerized rail testing services for the railroad industry, the design and installation of communications networks and satellite antennas, and engineering, design and support services for the nuclear and hazardous waste industry.

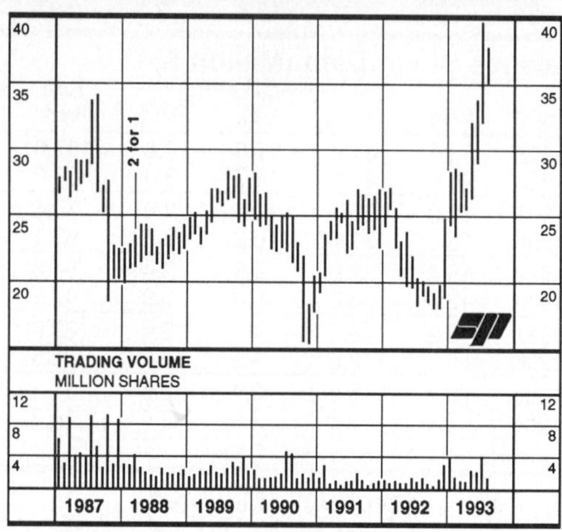

Important Developments

Jul. '93— A subsidiary of American Financial Corp., PC's controlling shareholder, sold 4,400,000 PC common shares in a public offering at $35.25 each. PC received none of the proceeds from the offering. Separately, PC redeemed $133.3 million of its 11% subordinated debentures due 1997.

Jun. '93— As part of its plan to sell its non-insurance operating units, PC signed an agreement to sell Vitro Corp., a defense electronics contractor, to Tracor Inc., for $94 million in cash.

May '93— PC purchased Leader National Insurance Co., which writes non-standard private passenger automobile insurance, from Dyson-Kissner-Moran for $38 million in cash.

Next earnings report expected in late October.

Per Share Data ($)

Yr. End Dec. 31	1992	1991	[1]1990	[1]1989	[1]1988	1987	[1]1986	[1]1985	[1]1984	[1]1983
Tangible Bk. Val.	**23.85**	22.59	20.97	22.76	23.78	21.58	24.20	18.87	16.23	18.18
Cash Flow	**2.18**	2.16	2.67	3.23	1.83	1.08	3.27	2.75	3.88	1.38
Earnings[2]	**1.32**	1.30	1.60	2.48	1.33	0.45	1.93	1.38	2.23	d0.24
Dividends	**0.810**	0.710	0.530	0.420	0.100	0.025	0.025	Nil	Nil	Nil
Payout Ratio	**60%**	53%	29%	16%	8%	5%	1%	Nil	Nil	Nil
Prices—High	**27⅞**	27	28¼	28⅜	24⅜	34¼	31⅜	29⅜	25⅛	20⅝
Low	**18**	19¼	15⅜	22⅞	19⅞	18½	25⅜	22½	18⅜	12⅜
P/E Ratio—	**21–14**	21–15	18–10	11–9	18–15	77–42	16–13	21–16	11–8	NM

Data as orig. reptd. Adj. for stk. div(s). of 100% Mar. 1988. **1.** Reflects merger or acquisition. **2.** Bef. results of disc. opers. of -0.04 in 1992, -1.25 in 1991, +0.13 in 1988, +0.02 in 1987 and spec. item(s) of +5.20 in 1992. d-Deficit. NM-Not Meaningful.

The Penn Central Corporation

Income Data (Million $)

Year Ended Dec. 31	Revs.	Oper. Inc.	% Oper. Inc. of Revs.	Cap. Exp.	Depr.	Int. Exp.	[4]Net Bef. Taxes	Eff. Tax Rate	[5]Net Inc.	% Net Inc. of Revs.	Cash Flow
1992	**1,797**	**181**	**10.1**	**26**	**41**	**69.6**	**102**	**40.3%**	**62**	**3.5**	**103**
[1]1991	1,669	185	11.1	26	42	65.8	105	40.0%	63	3.8	105
[2]1990	2,154	168	7.8	58	66	52.0	155	36.1%	98	4.5	163
[2]1989	1,725	131	7.6	41	53	27.9	241	27.7%	174	10.1	227
[3]1988	1,547	120	7.8	36	36	27.0	146	34.8%	94	6.1	130
[1]1987	1,421	145	10.2	35	50	14.8	78	45.3%	35	2.4	84
[3]1986	2,388	274	11.5	119	108	37.4	292	46.0%	154	6.5	263
[3]1985	2,527	307	12.1	182	111	46.0	213	47.0%	111	4.4	221
[2]1984	2,569	374	14.6	169	104	39.9	318	45.6%	170	6.6	244
[2]1983	2,539	318	12.5	292	103	53.0	55	64.0%	20	0.8	88

Balance Sheet Data (Million $)

Dec. 31	Cash	Curr. Assets	Curr. Liab.	Curr. Ratio	Total Assets	% Ret. on Assets	Long Term Debt	Common Equity	Total Cap.	% LT Debt of Cap.	% Ret. on Equity
1992	**294**	**NA**	**NA**	**NA**	**3,531**	**1.8**	**654**	**1,503**	**2,173**	**30.1**	**4.2**
1991	15	NA	NA	NA	3,383	1.9	654	1,479	2,173	30.1	4.3
1990	35	NA	NA	NA	3,547	3.2	519	1,634	2,210	23.5	6.3
1989	969	NA	NA	NA	3,178	6.5	373	1,827	2,246	16.6	10.1
1988	758	1,274	304	4.2	2,400	3.9	160	1,770	1,973	8.1	5.5
1987	1,072	1,635	421	3.9	2,493	1.3	189	1,657	1,917	9.9	2.0
1986	1,079	1,702	503	3.4	2,933	5.4	87	2,092	2,237	3.9	8.0
1985	193	1,050	539	1.9	2,874	3.9	242	1,826	2,189	11.0	6.4
1984	38	896	539	1.7	2,766	5.3	284	1,619	2,005	14.2	8.4
1983	318	1,096	534	2.1	2,874	0.7	290	1,442	2,132	13.6	NM

Data as orig. reptd. **1.** Excludes discontinued operations. **2.** Reflects merger or acquisition. **3.** Excludes discontinued operations and reflects merger or acquisition. **4.** Incl. equity in earns. of nonconsol. subs. **5.** Bef. results of disc. opers and spec. item(s). NA-Not Available. NM-Not Meaningful.

Revenues (Million $)

Quarter:	1993	1992	1991	1990
Mar.	356	432	407	487
Jun.	397	450	415	555
Sep.		449	422	562
Dec.		467	426	551
		1,797	1,669	2,154

Revenues for the six months ended June 30, 1993, rose 13%, year to year, aided by 24% higher earned premiums from insurance operations. Costs and expenses advanced 12%. After net gains from the sale of equity interests, tax benefits of $33.8 million, versus taxes at 39.3%, income from continuing operations jumped to $106.1 million ($2.27 a share; $2.21 fully diluted), from $21.6 million ($0.45). Results exclude a special credit of $5.33 a share in the 1992 period, and a $0.06 gain and a $0.07 loss from discontinued operations in the 1993 and 1992 interims, respectively.

Common Share Earnings ($)

Quarter:	1993	1992	1991	1990
Mar.	0.67	0.28	0.47	0.38
Jun.	1.60	0.30	0.43	0.40
Sep.		0.30	0.44	0.43
Dec.		0.43	d0.04	0.38
		1.32	1.30	1.60

Dividend Data

Dividends were initiated in 1986 on an annual basis and were placed on a quarterly basis in 1988.

Amt. of Divd. $	Date Decl.	Ex-divd. Date	Stock of Record	Payment Date
0.20	Sep. 14	Sep. 24	Sep. 30	Oct. 14'92
0.21	Dec. 11	Dec. 24	Dec. 31	Jan. 15'93
0.21	Mar. 24	Mar. 29	Apr. 2	Apr. 16'93
0.21	May 24	Jun. 24	Jun. 30	Jul. 14'93

Finances

As part of its plan to concentrate on the insurance business, in 1993's second quarter, PC sold publicly all 2,308,900 limited partnership units (19.0%) it owned of Buckeye Partners, L.P. for net proceeds of about $72 million. PC also announced its intention to sell publicly all 1,982,646 common shares (19.3%) it holds of NYSE-listed Tejas Gas Corp.

Capitalization

Total Debt: $655,900,000 (6/93).

Minority Interest: $16,200,000.

Common Stock: 45,542,115 shs. ($1 par). Institutions hold approximately 76%, incl. 41% held by American Financial Corp. Shareholders: 15,015 of record (7/93).

d-Deficit.

Office—One East Fourth St., Cincinnati, OH 45202. **Tel**—(513) 579-6600. **Chrmn & CEO**—C. H. Lindner. **Pres**—C. H. Lindner III. **VP-Treas & Investor Contact**—Philip A. Hagel. **VP-Secy**—R. W. Olson. **Dirs**—H. F. Culverhouse, T. H. Emmerich, J. E. Evans, N. M. Hahl, R. M. Haverland, T. M. Hunt, C. H. Lindner, C. H. Lindner III, S. C. Lindner, A. W. Martinelli, R. W. Olson. **Transfer Agent & Registrar**—First Chicago Trust Co. of New York, NYC. **Incorporated** in Pennsylvania in 1846; reincorporated in Pennsylvania in 1987. **Empl**—11,100.

 Barry R. Haas

Pentair, Inc.

NASDAQ Symbol PNTA Options on NYSE (Incl. in Nat'l Market) In S&P MidCap 400

Price	Range	P-E Ratio	Dividend	Yield	S&P Ranking	Beta
Oct. 14'93	1993					
33½	41¼–26	14	0.68	2.0%	B+	0.65

Summary

This diversified manufacturer operates businesses that produce and market paper, industrial products and sporting ammunition. Following strong gains in 1991, earnings growth in 1992 was restricted by the impact of the slow economic recovery and operating problems at certain businesses during the second quarter. Earnings improved in the first nine months of 1993 on higher sales and cost control efforts. Results for the balance of 1993 and 1994 should benefit from an improving economy and firming paper prices. A three-for-two stock split was effected in June 1993.

Current Outlook

Primary earnings for 1993 are estimated at $2.25 a share (adjusted for stock split and dil. effect of conversion of pref. shs. into com.), up from $2.15 (adj.) in 1992. Earnings for 1994 are seen at $2.55 a share.

The quarterly dividend was raised 4% effective with the February 1993 payment, and annual dividend hikes are likely to continue.

Sales are expected to continue to rise for the balance of 1993, reflecting new products, a rebound in economic conditions and stronger paper prices. Profitability should continue to benefit from strong results at Myers, Porter-Cable, Delta International and Hoffman Engineering, which will outweigh pricing pressures in publication paper markets. With a lower tax rate in Germany, taxes are expected to fall. Further gains are seen for 1994 as the economy improves. The company plans to acquire an industrial manufacturing firm with annual sales of $100 million to $300 million.

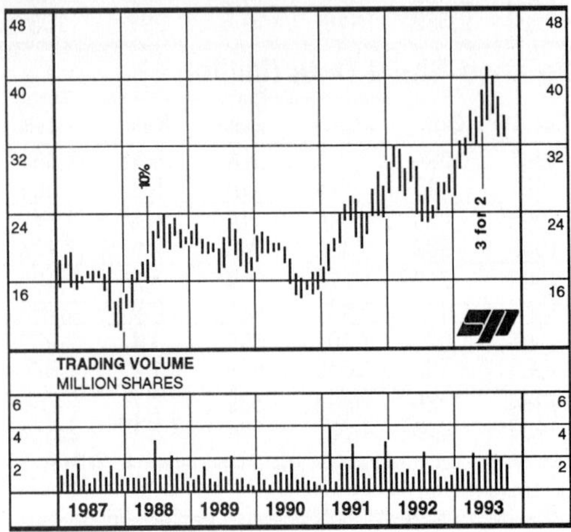

Net Sales (Million $)

Quarter:	1994	1993	1992	1991
Mar.	---	322	293	289
Jun.	---	320	297	284
Sep.	---	346	328	301
Dec.	---	---	321	296
	---	---	1,239	1,169

For the nine months ended September 30, 1993, net sales rose 7.6%, year to year, reflecting increased volume in all three segments. Profitability benefited from the higher volume and efforts to broaden distribution and control costs. Despite a joint venture loss, income advanced 17%, to $32,577,000, from $28,878,000. Earnings per share, after preferred dividends, were $1.57 ($1.53 fully diluted) and $1.35 ($1.30), as adjusted for the 3-for-2 stock split in June 1993), respectively. Results exclude a loss of $2.61 (adj.) due to accounting changes in 1992.

Common Share Earnings ($)

Quarter:	1994	1993	1992	1991
Mar.	E0.50	0.45	0.39	0.37
Jun.	E0.57	0.46	0.36	0.47
Sep.	E0.75	0.66	0.59	0.61
Dec.	E0.73	E0.70	0.80	0.76
	E2.55	E2.25	2.15	2.20

Important Developments

Oct. '93— Pentair said results improved at several of its industrial segments through the first nine months of 1993, but certain areas of its business were affected by softening economic conditions and fluctuating paper prices. PNTA added that it expects its industrial businesses to continue to perform well, but said fourth quarter results will depend on paper pricing trends and the economy.

Next earnings report expected in early February.

Per Share Data ($)

Yr. End Dec. 31	1992	1991	1990	1989	[1]1988	1987	[1]1986	1985	[1]1984	[1]1983
Tangible Bk. Val.	**10.25**	11.25	9.73	8.75	7.37	11.06	10.19	9.48	8.46	7.24
Cash Flow	**5.16**	5.05	4.29	4.33	4.30	3.32	2.74	2.73	2.63	2.04
Earnings[2,3]	**2.15**	2.20	1.69	1.99	2.47	1.37	1.07	1.41	1.51	1.06
Dividends	**0.653**	0.613	0.587	0.533	0.445	0.419	0.399	0.373	0.336	0.300
Payout Ratio	**30%**	28%	35%	27%	19%	31%	37%	26%	22%	28%
Prices—High	**32**	28²⁷⁄₃₂	21²⁷⁄₃₂	23¹³⁄₃₂	23²⁷⁄₃₂	19¹⁹⁄₃₂	19²⁷⁄₃₂	18¹¹⁄₃₂	12²⁹⁄₃₂	12²⁷⁄₃₂
Low	**22²⁹⁄₃₂**	15²⁷⁄₃₂	14	17	12²⁹⁄₃₂	10¹¹⁄₃₂	13⁵⁄₃₂	11½	9²¹⁄₃₂	6¼
P/E Ratio—	**15–11**	13–7	13–8	12–9	10–5	14–8	19–12	13–8	8–6	12–6

Data as orig. reptd. Adj. for stk. divs. of 10% Jun. 1988, 10% Mar. 1986, 25% Apr. 1985, 25% Nov. 1983. **1.** Refl. merger or acq. **2.** Bef. spec. item(s) of -3.92 in 1992. **3.** Ful. dil.: 3.05 in 1992, 3.02 in 1991, 2.43 in 1990, 2.85 in 1989, 3.35 in 1988, 1.95 in 1987, 1.55 in 1986, 2.03 in 1985, 2.25 in 1984, 1.51 in 1983. E-Estimated

Income Data (Million $)

Year Ended Dec. 31	Revs.	Oper. Inc.	% Oper. Inc. of Revs.	Cap. Exp.	Depr.	Int. Exp.	[2]Net Bef. Taxes	Eff. Tax Rate	[4]Net Inc.	% Net Inc. of Revs.	Cash Flow
1992	**1,239**	**140**	**11.3**	**67**	**48.0**	**23.6**	**72.7**	**41.1%**	**42.8**	**3.5**	**82.3**
1991	1,169	132	11.3	49	47.3	22.7	74.1	44.5%	41.1	3.5	79.8
1990	1,176	119	10.1	61	43.9	26.4	57.4	42.5%	33.0	2.8	69.0
1989	1,164	116	10.0	83	37.9	28.1	62.4	41.7%	36.4	3.1	70.1
[1]1988	823	103	12.5	112	27.4	11.5	68.3	41.7%	39.8	4.8	64.3
1987	789	67	8.4	54	28.1	10.7	34.0	35.6%	21.9	2.8	47.7
[1]1986	624	55	8.9	70	23.9	10.5	24.6	38.1%	[3]15.2	2.4	39.1
1985	534	50	9.3	62	18.8	7.5	28.7	30.1%	20.1	3.8	38.8
[1]1984	545	56	10.3	44	15.6	6.8	37.2	42.9%	21.2	3.9	36.6
[1]1983	319	31	9.7	43	10.3	2.8	20.2	40.9%	11.9	3.7	21.4

Balance Sheet Data (Million $)

Dec. 31	Cash	Curr. Assets	Curr. Liab.	Curr. Ratio	Total Assets	% Ret. on Assets	Long Term Debt	Common Equity	Total Cap.	% LT Debt of Cap.	% Ret. on Equity
1992	**8.4**	**399**	**209**	**1.9**	**869**	**5.1**	**212**	**260**	**554**	**38.2**	**12.7**
1991	6.1	373	185	2.0	791	5.2	198	276	568	34.9	12.4
1990	8.8	357	172	2.1	769	4.3	225	195	560	40.1	11.8
1989	8.7	360	168	2.1	781	4.7	251	241	575	43.7	14.1
1988	9.9	375	167	2.2	745	6.4	252	214	550	45.8	18.8
1987	4.7	260	119	2.2	440	4.9	91	159	313	29.0	12.8
1986	9.4	252	127	2.0	445	4.0	143	145	309	46.2	10.9
1985	9.4	158	76	2.1	306	6.8	75	135	226	33.2	15.8
1984	9.8	152	82	1.9	282	8.2	67	119	196	34.1	19.0
1983	10.8	106	68	1.6	209	6.2	28	92	137	20.6	13.2

Data as orig. reptd. **1.** Refl. merger or acq. **2.** Incl. equity in earns. of nonconsol. subs. **3.** Refl. acctg. change. **4.** Bef. spec. items.

Business Summary

Pentair, Inc. is a diversified manufacturing company that conducts operations through three industrial groups; contributions to sales and operating profits in 1992 were as follows:

	Sales	Profits
Specialty products	30%	37%
General industrial	39%	35%
Paper products	31%	28%

The specialty products segment produces woodworking machinery, portable power tools, water pumps, sump and sewage pumps, grinders (for environmental engineering applications) and related systems.

The general industrial segment manufactures electrical enclosures and wireways, material-dispensing equipment, industrial lubrication systems and automotive service (lubricating and lifting) equipment and sporting ammunition.

Paper products, which are sold to the publishing and printing markets, consist primarily of coated publication paper and premium printing papers.

Lake Superior Paper Industries (LSPI), a 50/50 joint venture with Minnesota Power and Light, produces top-grade supercalendered paper. Pentair recognized $1.7 million as its share of LSPI income in 1992.

In September 1992, the company sold its Delta International Machinery Corp.'s Brazilian operation to Brazilian interests. In June 1992, Pentair bought the Automotive Service Equipment unit of ASE-listed Hein-Werner for $9 million.

Dividend Data

A dividend reinvestment plan is available.

Amt of Divd. $	Date Decl.	Ex-divd. Date	Stock of Record	Payment Date
0.25½	Jan. 19	Jan. 25	Jan. 29	Feb. 12'93
0.25½	Apr. 8	Apr. 19	Apr. 23	May 12'93
3–for–2	Apr. 21	Jun. 14	May 14	Jun. 11'93
0.17	Jul. 9	Jul. 19	Jul. 23	Aug. 12'93
0.17	Oct. 8	Oct. 18	Oct. 22	Nov. 12'93

Finances

In March 1993, Pentair redeemed its $1.50 cumulative convertible preferred stock, and substantially all of the shares were converted into 2,175,000 common shares (adjusted).

Capitalization

Long Term Debt: $234,298,000 (6/93).

$7.50 Cum. Conv. Pfd. Stk.: 140,200 shs. ($0.10 par); redeemable; ea. conv. into 3.75 com. shs.

8% Cum. Voting Conv. Pfd. Stk.: 1,841,658 shs.; all held by Pentair's ESOP, conv. into 1.15 com. at $26.22 a sh.

Common Stock: 18,082,721 shs. ($0.16⅔par). Institutions hold 66%.
Shareholders: 3,285 of record (12/92).

Office—Waters Edge Plaza, 1500 County Rd. B2 West, St. Paul, MN 55113-3105. **Tel**—(612) 636-7920. **Chrmn, Pres & CEO**—W. H. Buxton. **SVP, Acting CFO & Investor Contact**—J. R. Collins. **VP & Treas**—R. T. Rueb. **Dirs**—G. N. Butzow, W. H. Buxton, H. V. Haverty, Q. J. Hietpas, B. K. Johnson, W. Kissling, H. W. Lurton, D. E. Nugent. **Transfer Agent & Registrar**—Norwest Bank Minnesota, South St. Paul. **Incorporated** in Minnesota in 1966. **Empl**—8,300.

 Stewart Scharf

Phillips-Van Heusen

NYSE Symbol PVH Options on CBOE (Mar-Jun-Sep-Dec) In S&P MidCap 400

Price	Range	P-E Ratio	Dividend	Yield	S&P Ranking	Beta
Aug. 30'93	1993					
30¼	33⅜–25¾	22	0.15	0.5%	A	1.30

Summary

This company produces a broad range of apparel and shoes which it sells through its own 705 outlets as well as to major department and specialty stores. Earnings have trended upward since 1988, reflecting demand for the company's shoes and men's shirts, efforts to contain costs, successful expansion of its retail outlet stores, and greater market share. Further earnings progress is expected.

Current Outlook

Earnings for the fiscal year ending January 31, 1995, are estimated at $1.95, up from the $1.65 projected for 1993-94.

The $0.03¾ quarterly dividend could be raised this year.

Sales in 1994-95 should advance 10%-15%, reflecting continuing market penetration of PVH's apparel products through J. C. Penney and other major retail outlets, greater sales penetration through factory outlet stores, and new store openings including the launch of Geoffrey Beene Women's stores. New products including Bass dress shirts for men, Bass apparel, and Bass Kids should contribute to sales growth. Margins should continue to benefit from the greater volume, a more profitable product mix including a higher percentage of sales from the profitable retail outlet store business, tighter inventory controls and more rapid inventory turnover, and more efficient manufacturing. Over the longer term, the company hopes to increase sales about 10% annually. Earnings could grow at a slightly faster pace.

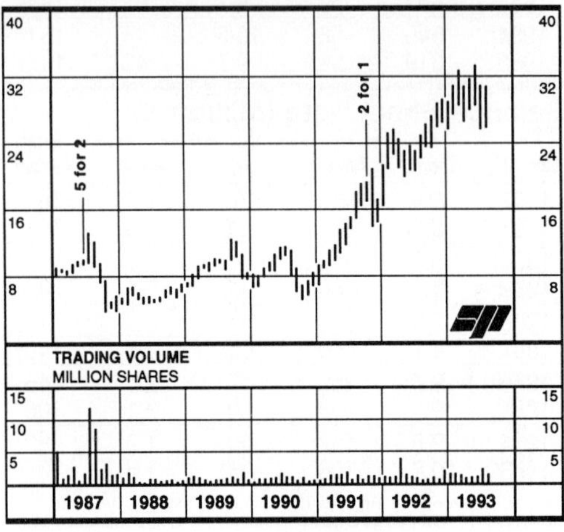

Net Sales (Million $)

13 Weeks:	1993–94	1992–93	1991–92	1990–91
Apr.	222	208	180	155
Jul.	264	240	205	191
Oct.	---	322	286	242
Jan.	---	272	232	218
	---	1,043	904	806

Net sales in the 26 weeks ended August 1, 1993, advanced 8.5%, year to year. Margins narrowed, and after taxes at 31.1%, versus 32.9%, net income fell 12%. In the absence of $2.1 million of preferred dividends, however, income available for common shareholders rose 32%, to $0.21 a share, on 15% more shares, from $0.18.

Common Share Earnings ($)

13 Weeks:	1993–94	1992–93	1991–92	1990–91
Apr.	d0.08	d0.12	d0.16	d0.08
Jul.	0.29	0.24	0.20	0.19
Oct.	E0.95	0.81	0.77	0.68
Jan.	E0.49	0.36	0.32	0.17
	E1.65	[1]1.42	[1]1.15	0.95

Important Developments

Aug. '93— Commenting on its second quarter results, PVH said that despite the very difficult retail environment, it was performing close to its operational plan with sales and earnings improvement in both apparel and footwear. The company added that while it sees no change in the conservative retail environment over the short term, its various new apparel lines should contribute to earnings growth in the future.

Next earnings report expected in late November.

Per Share Data ($)

Yr. End Jan. 31	**1993**	1992	[2]1991	1990	1989	[2]1988	1987	1986	1985	1984
Tangible Bk. Val.	**7.42**	3.50	2.32	2.35	1.61	1.06	5.33	4.82	4.41	3.98
Cash Flow	**2.01**	1.76	1.47	1.22	1.02	0.85	0.80	0.67	0.65	0.75
Earnings[3]	**1.42**	1.15	0.95	0.84	0.68	0.66	0.64	0.51	0.49	0.59
Dividends	**0.150**	0.143	0.140	0.140	0.140	0.125	0.080	0.080	0.080	0.065
Payout Ratio	**11%**	12%	14%	16%	20%	13%	12%	15%	16%	11%
Calendar Years	**1992**	1991	1990	1989	1988	1987	1986	1985	1984	1983
Prices—High	**29¼**	21	11⁹⁄₁₆	12½	7⅛	13¼	8⅞	6⁷⁄₁₆	5¾	4⅝
Low	**16½**	7	5³⁄₁₆	6¹³⁄₁₆	4⅝	3¾	6⁵⁄₁₆	4¹⁄₁₆	3¼	1¾
P/E Ratio—	**21–12**	18–6	12–5	15–8	10–7	20–6	14–10	13–8	12–7	8–3

Data as orig. reptd. Adj. for stk. divs. of 100% Oct. 1991, 150% Jun. 1987, 100% Jan. 1984. **1.** Does not reconcile bec. of change in no. of outstanding shares. **2.** Reflects merger or acquisition. **3.** Bef. results of disc. opers. of -0.02 in 1989, +0.66 in 1988. d-Deficit. E-Estimated.

Income Data (Million $)

Year Ended Jan. 31	Revs.	Oper. Inc.	% Oper. Inc. of Revs.	Cap. Exp.	Depr.	Int. Exp.	Net Bef. Taxes	Eff. Tax Rate	Net Inc.	% Net Inc. of Revs.	Cash Flow
1993	**1,043**	**88.1**	**8.4**	**36.8**	**15.0**	**16.8**	**54.5**	**30.5%**	**37.9**	**3.6**	**50.8**
1992	904	74.1	8.2	21.1	12.1	17.8	44.0	29.3%	31.1	3.4	35.1
[2]1991	806	66.0	8.2	22.2	9.8	20.4	35.2	25.0%	26.4	3.3	28.0
1990	733	59.6	8.1	12.8	7.3	19.1	32.7	26.0%	24.2	3.3	23.3
1989	641	51.9	8.1	13.7	6.2	17.3	27.4	24.0%	20.8	3.2	18.9
[2,3]1988	500	44.7	8.9	7.7	5.2	8.3	36.0	40.7%	21.3	4.3	22.4
1987	[1]514	48.8	9.5	5.7	5.2	4.3	38.5	47.7%	20.1	3.9	25.3
1986	[1]550	44.4	8.1	5.2	5.0	7.9	29.4	45.8%	15.9	2.9	20.9
1985	[1]591	40.7	6.9	8.6	4.9	10.6	26.5	42.2%	15.3	2.6	20.2
1984	[1]506	40.5	8.0	7.0	4.6	5.8	31.2	44.7%	17.3	3.4	21.8

Balance Sheet Data (Million $)

		Curr.									
Jan. 31	Cash	Assets	Liab.	Ratio	Total Assets	% Ret. on Assets	Long Term Debt	Common Equity	Total Cap.	% LT Debt of Cap.	% Ret. on Equity
1993	**77.1**	**411**	**115**	**3.6**	**517**	**7.1**	**170**	**211**	**382**	**44.6**	**21.7**
1992	7.0	303	105	2.9	399	8.0	121	85	280	43.4	30.9
1991	5.8	285	91	3.1	377	7.4	140	62	275	50.9	33.4
1990	6.6	267	84	3.2	333	7.4	119	46	238	50.0	40.7
1989	9.9	265	88	3.0	323	6.5	116	32	222	52.5	46.0
1988	22.6	258	87	3.0	318	9.2	121	22	219	55.3	28.5
1987	26.3	200	63	3.2	245	8.3	9	165	176	5.0	12.8
1986	22.7	196	62	3.1	241	6.1	20	151	172	11.7	11.0
1985	11.7	232	82	2.8	278	5.9	52	138	189	27.2	11.6
1984	16.9	188	79	2.4	236	7.5	27	124	151	17.7	14.7

Data as orig. reptd. **1.** Incl. sales of leased depts. **2.** Reflects merger or acquisition. **3.** Excl. disc. opers.

Business Summary

Phillips-Van Heusen Corp. is a vertically integrated manufacturer, marketer and retailer of men's and women's apparel and men's, women's and children's footwear. Segment contributions in 1992-93:

	Sales	Profits
Apparel	68%	58%
Footwear	32%	42%

Apparel is manufactured domestically and through foreign sources, and marketed through four divisions. Men's traditional dress and sport shirts are produced and sold through the Van Heusen Company to major department and specialty stores. The designer group sells men's designer label dress shirts in the upper moderate to better price range to major department and specialty stores. The private label division produces men's dress and sport shirts for major national retail chains, department stores and catalog merchants. The private label knitwear division sells men's sweaters and golf apparel to department and specialty stores, national retail chains and catalog merchants.

Bass (acquired 1987) makes men's and women's shoes domestically and through foreign sources. Shoes are sold under the Bass, Weejun and Compass names to department and specialty stores.

PVH also operates 705 stores, located primarily in manufacturers' outlet malls, called Van Heusen, Geoffrey Beene, Windsor Shirt, Cape Isle Knitters, and Bass. Plans call for an additional 102 stores (net of store closings) in 1993-94.

Dividend Data

Dividends have been paid since 1970. A "poison pill" stock purchase right was issued in 1986.

Amt. of Divd. $	Date Decl.	Ex-divd. Date	Stock of Record	Payment Date
0.03¾	Sep. 10	Dec. 4	Dec. 10	Jan. 4'93
0.03¾	Feb. 4	Feb. 11	Feb. 18	Mar. 16'93
0.03¾	Mar. 30	May 11	May 17	Jun. 16'93
0.03¾	Jun. 1	Aug. 10	Aug. 16	Sep. 16'93

Capitalization

Long Term Debt: $170,235,000 (5/2/93).

Common Stock: 26,060,219 shs. ($1 par).
Approximately 19% of voting control closely held.
Institutions hold about 75%.
Shareholders of record: 2,084.

Office—1290 Avenue of the Americas, New York, NY 10104. **Tel**—(212) 541-5200. **Chrmn**—L. S. Phillips. **Pres & CEO**—B. J. Klatsky. **VP-CFO**—I. W. Winter. **Dirs**— E. H. Cohen, E. Ellis, J. B. Fuller, B. J. Klatsky, M. E. Lagomasino, B. Maggin, E. E. Meredith, S. L. Osterweis, L. S. Phillips, W. S. Scolnick, P. J. Solomon, I. W. Winter. **Transfer Agent & Registrar**—The Bank of New York, NYC. **Incorporated** in New York in 1919; reincorporated in Delaware in 1976. **Empl**—13,400.

 Elizabeth Vandeventer

Pinnacle West Capital

NYSE Symbol PNW Options on Pacific (Jan-Apr-Jul-Oct) In S&P MidCap 400

Price	Range	P-E Ratio	Dividend	Yield	S&P Ranking	Beta
Sep. 14'93	1993					
24½	25¼–19⅝	13	None	None	B	1.02

Summary

This utility holding company is the parent of Arizona Public Service Co., Arizona's largest electric utility. PNW returned to profitability in 1992, primarily reflecting the absence of 1991's writeoffs of $407 million ($4.68 a share) related to the Palo Verde nuclear plant. The writeoffs were necessitated by a rate settlement approved by the Arizona Corporation Commission in December 1991.

Current Outlook

Share earnings for 1993 could reach $1.90, up from the $1.73 reported for 1992. A further advance to $2.00 is possible in 1994.

Resumption of common dividends, omitted in 1989, is expected in late 1993. A quarterly rate of between $0.20-$0.25 is anticipated.

Share earnings for 1993 should be aided by higher kwh sales due to continued customer growth. Higher income from the accretion of certain temporary writedowns related to the December 1991 rate case settlement may be more than offset by the combination of higher fuel costs and increased O&M costs (due to the adoption of FASB 106). However, earnings should also benefit from lower interest expense due to less debt outstanding. Share earnings for 1994 should reflect customer growth, a possible rate hike, aggressive cost controls, and lower interest expense as PNW continues to refinance debt, partially offset by considerably lower accretion under the aforementioned 1991 rate case settlement.

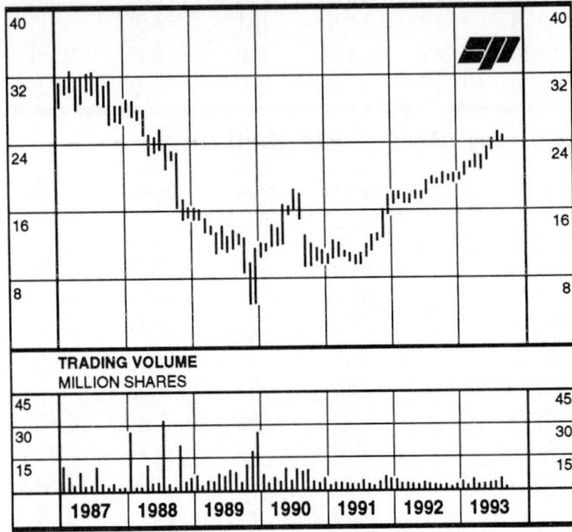

Utility Revenues (Million $)

Quarter:	1993	1992	1991	1990
Mar.	375	345	331	343
Jun.	414	409	358	354
Sep.	---	517	471	472
Dec.	---	399	355	340
	---	1,670	1,515	1,508

Utility revenues in the six months to June 30, 1993, rose 3.8%, year to year. After cost controls and lower interest expense, net income was up 43%. Share earnings were $0.76 (before a $0.22 gain from the cumulative effect of an accounting change), versus $0.53.

Common Share Earnings ($)

Quarter:	1993	1992	1991	1990
Mar.	0.32	0.09	0.06	0.15
Jun.	0.45	0.44	0.16	0.02
Sep.	E0.90	0.98	0.89	0.64
Dec.	E0.23	0.21	d5.02	Nil
	E1.90	1.73	d3.91	0.81

Important Developments

Sep. '93— PNW announced that Palo Verde nuclear Unit 2 returned to service on September 1. Palo Verde Unit 2 had been out of service since it was shut down March 14 when a steam generator tube erupted. A scientific analysis revealed that a phenomenon known as intergranular stress cracking caused the tube break. Defective tubes were plugged in both generators while other maintenance and inspections were preformed. Palo Verde Unit 2 will be shut down again within the next six months to inspect its steam generator tubes once again. Meanwhile, Palo Verde Unit 1 began a similar outage on September 4. During its scheduled 80-day overhaul, about 33% of the nuclear fuel will be replaced, required inspections will be performed and maintenance will be conducted to keep Palo Verde Unit 1 in "prime operating condition."

Next earnings report expected in late October.

Per Share Data ($)

Yr. End Dec. 31	**1992**	1991	1990	1989	1988	1987	1986	1985	1984	1983
Tangible Bk. Val.	**17.00**	15.23	17.40	16.31	19.07	25.98	25.19	25.10	23.96	23.53
Earnings[1]	**1.73**	d3.91	0.81	1.44	0.05	3.21	3.04	3.88	3.65	3.46
Dividends	**Nil**	Nil	Nil	1.20	2.80	2.78	2.72	2.69	2.60	2.56
Payout Ratio	**Nil**	Nil	Nil	83%	NM	87%	89%	69%	71%	74%
Prices—High	**20½**	17⅞	18⅝	16⅜	29¼	32¾	32	28⅛	22¼	26½
Low	**16¾**	9⅝	9⅜	5	15	26⅜	26	20⅝	14½	17¾
P/E Ratio—	**12–10**	NM	23–12	11–3	NM	10–8	11–9	7–5	6–4	8–5

Data as orig. reptd. 1. Bef. results of disc. opers. of +0.07 in 1992, +1.76 in 1991, +0.31 in 1990, -7.80 in 1989, -0.39 in 1984; bef spec. item(s) of +0.19 in 1987. E-Estimated. d-Deficit. NM-Not Meaningful.

Income Data (Million $)

Year Ended Dec. 31	Revs.	Depr.	Maint.	Oper. Ratio	[2]Fxd. Chgs. Cover.	Constr. Credits	Eff. Tax Rate	[4]Net Inc.	% Return On Revs.	% Return On [5]Invest. Capital	% Return On Com. Equity
1992	**1,690**	**220**	**NA**	**76.0%**	**1.93**	**8**	**43.6%**	**150**	**8.9**	**8.3**	**10.7**
1991	1,475	219	116	101.5%	NM	11	NM	d340	NM	0.3	NM
1990	1,597	214	110	76.1%	1.39	13	43.4%	70	4.4	7.3	4.8
1989	1,508	207	121	75.9%	1.80	16	42.7%	125	8.3	7.0	7.2
1988	[1]1,442	[1]194	[1]108	[1]72.1%	NA	[1]22	[3]57.3%	[3]38	[1]18.8	NA	[3]0.2
1987	1,313	161	102	75.4%	3.06	105	36.4%	301	22.9	8.4	12.3
1986	1,250	140	98	78.1%	2.71	132	36.4%	273	21.9	9.0	11.8
1985	1,175	99	89	73.9%	3.05	192	33.7%	324	27.6	10.9	15.6
1984	995	88	68	73.5%	2.89	184	31.5%	298	29.9	11.4	15.2
1983	1,074	90	71	76.3%	---	187	25.3%	265	24.7	10.9	14.6

Balance Sheet Data (Million $)

Dec. 31	Gross Prop.	Capital Expend.	Net Prop.	% Earn. on Net Prop.	Total Cap.	Capitalization LT Debt	% LT Debt	Pfd.	% Pfd.	Com.	% Com.
1992	**6,497**	**224**	**4,524**	**12.2**	**5,547**	**2,774**	**59.6**	**394**	**8.5**	**1,482**	**31.9**
1991	6,410	179	4,487	NM	5,587	2,997	63.5	396	8.4	1,325	28.1
1990	6,797	255	5,126	7.4	6,139	3,218	63.2	361	7.1	1,512	29.7
1989	6,669	294	5,169	7.1	6,168	3,424	65.7	373	7.2	1,414	27.1
1988	[1]6,415	[1]265	[1]5,113	[1]7.9	[3]7,168	[3]3,909	[3]61.8	[3]382	[3]6.0	[3]2,035	[3]32.2
1987	6,229	341	5,093	6.5	6,187	2,782	50.9	391	7.2	2,291	41.9
1986	5,880	459	4,904	5.6	5,308	2,265	47.9	397	8.4	2,069	43.7
1985	5,713	494	4,874	6.7	4,934	2,206	48.7	438	9.7	1,885	41.6
1984	5,088	377	4,344	6.3	4,131	1,685	43.4	501	12.9	1,696	43.7
1983	4,761	577	4,033	6.7	3,853	1,655	44.8	456	12.3	1,587	42.9

Data as orig. reptd. Nonutility opers. consolidated after 1987. **1.** Electric opers. only. **2.** Times int. exp. & pfd. divs. covered (pretax basis). **3.** Consolidated. **4.** Bef. results from disc. opers. and bef. spec. items. **5.** Based on income bef. interest charges. NA-Not Available. NM-Not Meaningful. d-Deficit.

Business Summary

Pinnacle West Capital (previously AZP Group) is a utility holding company whose main subsidiary, Arizona Public Service Co., provides electricity to nearly half the population of Arizona. Other operations include real estate development and venture capital units.

Sources of electric generation in 1992 were coal 56%, nuclear 34%, gas 4%, and purchased and other 6%. Peak demand in 1992 was 3,796 mw, and resources at peak totaled 4,509 mw, for a capacity margin of 16%. PNW has access to 29.1% of the three-unit Palo Verde nuclear project. As part of a December 1991 rate settlement, PNW wrote off $407 million related to the Palo Verde plant, of which $265.2 million was permanent and $141.8 million was temporary.

In January 1990, federal thrift regulators placed in receivership PNW's ailing thrift subsidiary, MeraBank, one of Arizona's largest financial institutions. Pursuant to an agreement with regulators, PNW made an infusion of $465 million ($310 million in cash and a promissory note of $155 million) into MeraBank in March 1990, releasing the company from any further financial obligations to the thrift. During 1991, PNW refinanced the promissory note on more favorable terms. Operations of MeraBank were classified as discontinued effective December 31, 1989, and PNW recorded a $639 million net loss for the unit. In April 1990, PNW sold its Wigwam Resort and certain other properties for $70 million. Malapai Resources, a uranium mining unit, was sold for $38 million in September 1990.

Dividend Data

Common dividends, omitted in 1989 after having been paid since 1920, are expected to be resumed later this year. Subsidiary preferred dividends (Arizona Public Service Co.) have been maintained. A "poison pill" stock purchase rights plan was adopted in 1989.

Capitalization

Long Term Debt: $2,789,071,000 (6/93).

Subsid. Red. Cum. Pfd. Stock: $197,610,000.

Subsid. Cum. Pfd. Stock: $168,561,000.

Common Stock: 87,274,143 shs. (no par).
Institutions hold about 66%.
Shareholders of record: 76,100.

Office—400 East Van Buren St., Phoenix, AZ 85004. **Tel**—(602) 379-2500. **Chrmn & Pres**—R. Snell. **EVP-CFO**—H. B. Sargent. **VP-Secy**—F. Widenmann. **Investor Contact**—Rebecca L. Hickman. **Dirs**—O. M. DeMichele, P. Grant, R. A. Herberger Jr., M. O. Hesse, B. Jamieson Jr., R. Matlock, J. R. Norton III, H. B. Sargent, R. Snell, D. N. Soldwedel, D. J. Wall. **Transfer Agents & Registrars**—Company's office, Phoenix, Ariz.; First National Bank of Boston. **Incorporated** in Arizona in 1920. **Empl**—7,920.

 Christopher J. Grant

Policy Management Systems

NYSE Symbol PMS Options on ASE (Feb-May-Aug-Nov) In S&P MidCap 400

Price	Range	P-E Ratio	Dividend	Yield	S&P Ranking	Beta
Aug. 19'93	1993					
24⅛	87¼–21⅝	10	None	None	NR	1.32

Summary

This company is a leading supplier of standardized software systems and related processing and support services to the insurance industry. In August 1993, auditors said that past financial results should not be relied upon. Sales and earnings are expected to be under pressure in 1993, in part reflecting customer uncertainty about pending changes in government health care regulations as well as expected accounting and legal charges.

Current Outlook

Due to uncertainties attached to the company's financial statements, earnings projections are not feasable at this time.

Initiation of cash dividends is not anticipated in the foreseeable future.

Auditors have said that past financial results should not be relied upon because of uncertainty arising out of an investigation of the company's business and accounting practices; thus, any forecast is not feasible. Nevertheless, strength in the property/casualty and life insurance areas is expected to be offset by weakness in the health care segment, in light of pending changes in government regulations. In addition, a faster than expected wind-down of a major contract with the State of New Jersey will be a restraint. Margins will be penalized by the lower-than-expected volume, and expected charges reflecting accounting restatements as well as for a class action lawsuit. Longer term, however, the company remains the leading vendor of software solutions needed to manage an insurance business.

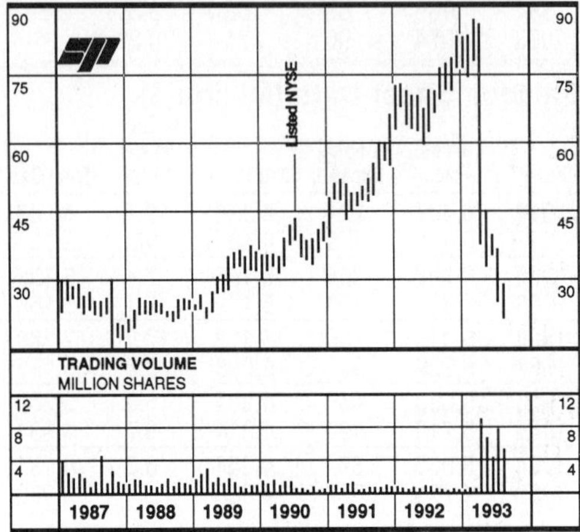

Total Revenues (Million $)

Quarter:	1993	1992	1991	1990
Mar.	120.4	116.1	96.4	80.3
Jun.		123.1	101.6	85.2
Sep.		126.4	105.4	87.5
Dec.		131.5	111.9	93.0
		497.1	415.4	346.1

While results may be restated, revenues for the three months ended March 31, 1993, (latest available) advanced just 3.7%, year to year, which was lower than expected, primarily reflecting weakness in the health care segment. Margins narrowed, and pretax profits declined 31%. After taxes at 32.6%, versus 35.0%, net income fell 29%, to $0.42 a share on 1.8% more shares outstanding, from $0.59.

Common Share Earnings ($)

Quarter:	1993	1992	1991	1990
Mar.	0.42	0.59	0.54	0.45
Jun.	---	0.62	0.54	0.47
Sep.	---	0.65	0.55	0.49
Dec.	---	0.69	0.58	0.51
	---	2.55	2.21	1.92

Important Developments

Aug. '93— Citing uncertainty arising out of an investigation of PMS's business and accounting practices, auditors said that past financial results should not be relied upon. The company changed accounting firms and now engages Coopers and Lybrand as its independent public accountants. Additional audits and a possible restatement of the prior financials will take several months.

Next earnings report expected in mid-October.

Per Share Data ($)

Yr. End Dec. 31[1]	1992	1991	1990	1989	1988	1987	1986	1985	1984	1983
Tangible Bk. Val.	**20.12**	16.96	11.84	10.34	6.07	6.35	6.08	5.86	5.11	4.42
Cash Flow	**3.96**	3.32	2.97	2.57	2.14	1.70	1.48	1.31	1.16	0.84
Earnings	**2.55**	[2]2.21	[2]1.92	[2]1.60	1.30	1.05	0.85	0.89	0.85	0.63
Dividends	**Nil**	Nil	Nil	Nil	Nil	Nil	Nil	Nil	Nil	Nil
Payout Ratio	**Nil**	Nil	Nil	Nil	Nil	Nil	Nil	Nil	Nil	Nil
Prices—High	**83½**	66⅜	43½	37½	26¼	30¼	24½	34¾	31	34⅜
Low	**59¾**	39⅜	30	21¾	18¾	15¼	15	16½	22	18⅛
P/E Ratio—	**32–23**	30–18	23–16	23–14	20–14	29–15	29–18	39–19	36–26	55–29

Data as orig. reptd. Adj. for stk. div. of 100% Oct. 1983. **1.** Reflects merger or acquisition. **2.** Ful. dil.: 2.14 in 1991, 1.80 in 1990, 1.51 in 1989. E-Estimated.

Policy Management Systems Corporation

Income Data (Million $)

Year Ended Dec. 31[1]	Revs.	Oper. Inc.	% Oper. Inc. of Revs.	Cap. Exp.	Depr.	Int. Exp.	Net Bef. Taxes	Eff. Tax Rate	Net Inc.	% Net Inc. of Revs.	Cash Flow
1992	**497**	**112.0**	**22.6**	**56.0**	**32.6**	**NA**	**91.4**	**35.1%**	**59.4**	**11.9**	**92.0**
1991	415	87.9	21.2	20.0	24.1	NA	72.7	34.6%	47.6	11.5	71.7
1990	346	71.5	20.7	35.8	20.3	NA	55.5	33.0%	37.2	10.7	57.5
1989	266	54.6	20.5	21.1	16.3	NA	40.6	34.0%	26.8	10.1	43.0
1988	217	44.8	20.6	15.4	13.3	[2]0.36	31.1	34.2%	20.5	9.4	33.8
1987	180	38.1	21.2	6.1	10.6	[2]0.34	27.1	37.0%	17.1	9.5	27.7
1986	151	32.2	21.4	19.4	10.3	1.20	21.9	37.3%	[3]13.8	9.1	24.1
1985	103	25.4	24.7	25.5	6.8	0.11	20.5	29.8%	14.4	14.0	21.2
1984	85	21.5	25.3	18.9	5.1	Nil	19.5	29.6%	13.7	16.2	18.8
1983	62	14.8	23.8	18.3	3.3	Nil	13.9	30.1%	9.7	15.6	13.0

Balance Sheet Data (Million $)

Dec. 31	Cash	Curr. Assets	Curr. Liab.	Curr. Ratio	Total Assets	% Ret. on Assets	Long Term Debt	Common Equity	Total Cap.	% LT Debt of Cap.	% Ret. on Equity
1992	**239**	**345**	**51.3**	**6.7**	**684**	**9.2**	**6**	**574**	**625**	**1.0**	**11.0**
1991	197	306	48.9	6.2	592	7.9	6	497	535	1.1	10.8
1990	153	246	45.2	5.4	508	7.7	103	325	454	22.6	12.2
1989	144	238	42.2	5.6	461	6.4	103	285	411	25.1	11.5
1988	85	146	28.0	5.2	300	7.1	106	146	272	38.9	14.9
1987	98	150	24.4	6.2	279	7.5	108	131	254	42.6	13.7
1986	13	63	15.2	4.1	180	8.6	28	121	164	17.4	12.0
1985	23	52	17.1	3.0	138	11.4	9	107	121	7.6	14.5
1984	38	54	16.9	3.2	113	13.3	1	92	96	1.5	16.1
1983	44	54	12.4	4.3	93	13.9	1	78	80	1.0	16.9

Data as orig. reptd. **1.** Reflects merger or acquisition. **2.** Net of interest income. **3.** Reflects acctg. change. NA-Not Available.

Business Summary

Policy Management Systems is a leader in providing standardized insurance software systems and related processing support and certain information services to the insurance industry. Prior to 1985, the company primarily served property and casualty insurers. It has since broadened its product and service offerings through internal development and acquisitions and now serves the entire insurance industry. PMS currently offers more than 125 major products and services, including 90 applications software products.

The company's software products automate virtually every insurance processing function, including risk analysis, policy rating, premium calculation, policy issuance and claims management, as well as various accounting, financial reporting and cash management functions. Systems have been designed to permit ease of use and adaptability to a particular customer's requirements. PMS's primary software systems run on medium- and large-scale IBM and IBM-compatible computers utilizing most IBM operating systems. The company also provides software for use with microcomputers and intelligent workstations. Most PMS systems will operate on a stand-alone basis or in conjunction with each other. The company also offers certain processing and professional services to insurance companies.

PMS's new Series III products incorporate as a standard IBM's Systems Applications Architecture. Products are marketed to more than 3,200 property and casualty insurance companies, more than 6,000 life and health providers and independent agents and adjusters in the U.S. and Canada. Software products and related automation support services are also offered in 23 foreign countries. At December 31, 1992, the company was providing information services to more than 9,000 insurance companies, agents and adjusters and had a total of 3,183 software system licenses in force.

Dividend Data

No cash dividends have ever been paid.

Finances

In July 1989, IBM acquired an equity interest in the company by purchasing for $116,775,000 a total of 3,797,561 preferred shares, which were converted share-for-share into common stock in October 1989. IBM may increase its stake to a maximum of 30% by purchasing PMS common shares on the open market.

Capitalization

Long Term Debt: $6,178,000 (3/93).

Common Stock: 22,574,656 shs. ($0.01 par).
IBM owns 16%.
Institutions hold about 82%.
Shareholders of record: 1,327.

Office—One PMS Center, Blythewood, SC 29016 (P.O. Box 10, Columbia, SC 29202). **Tel**—(803) 735-4000. **Chrmn & Pres**—G. L. Wilson. **VP, Treas, Secy & Investor Contact**—Robert L. Gresham. **Dirs**—S. E. Beale, R. L. Faulks, D. W. Feddersen, L. F. Hahne, F. B. Karl, J. M. Palms, J. D. Sargent, J. P. Seibels, R. G. Trub, G. L. Wilson. **Transfer Agent & Registrar**—American Stock Transfer & Trust Co., NYC. **Incorporated** in South Carolina in 1980. **Empl**—4,363.

 Peter C. Wood, CFA

Portland General

NYSE Symbol PGN In S&P MidCap 400

Price	Range	P-E Ratio	Dividend	Yield	S&P Ranking	Beta
Jul. 28'93	1993					
22	22⅝–16	10	1.20	5.5%	B	0.88

Summary

This holding company owns Portland General Electric, a utility providing electric service to a population of about 1.3 million in a 3,170-square-mile area of Oregon. Results in recent years have been erratic as a result of poor operating performance at the company's 67.5%-owned Trojan nuclear plant. The plant was closed permanently in November 1992. After a return to profitability in 1992, earnings should trend higher in 1993 as a result of prospectively improved hydroelectric generating conditions. The $0.30 quarterly dividend should be maintained, based on supportive regulation and PGN's good earnings quality.

Current Outlook

Earnings for 1993 are projected at $1.95 a share, up slightly from 1992's $1.93. Earnings for 1994 are projected at $2.00 a share.

Dividends should be maintained at $0.30 quarterly.

A modest increase in profits is anticipated for 1993, reflecting improved hydroelectric generating condition owing to the accumulation of a large snowpack following severe winter storms. Favorable rate treatment related to the closure of the Trojan nuclear plant will aid profitability. Trojan, which supplied 23% of PGN's firm energy needs, was taken out of service on November 9, 1992, due to the prohibitive expense of repairing its cracked steam generating tubes.

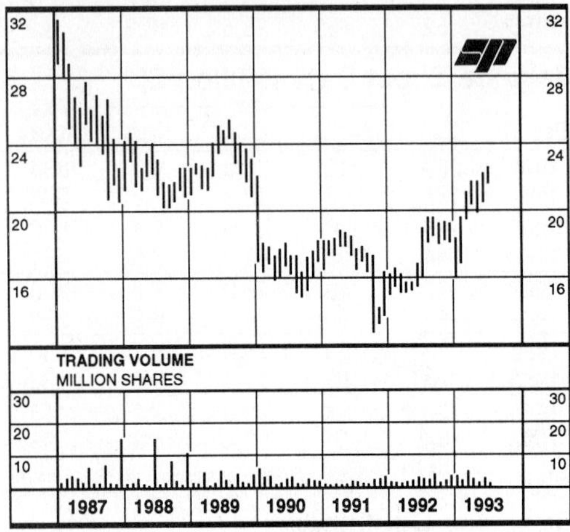

Oper. Revenues (Million $)

Quarter:	1994	1993	1992	1991
Mar.	---	278	238	233
Jun.	---	192	197	200
Sep.	---	---	195	206
Dec.	---	---	254	251
	---	---	884	890

Operating revenues for the six months ended June 30, 1993, rose 7.9%, year to year, as an increase in retail kilowatt-hour sales outweighed a decline in sales to wholesale customers. Operating expenses advanced 7.3%, primarily due to an increase in purchased power costs, and operating income grew 11%. Net income was up 32%, to $49.9 million ($1.05 a share, on 1.2% more common shares outstanding), from $37.9 million ($0.82).

Common Share Earnings ($)

Quarter:	1994	1993	1992	1991
Mar.	E0.80	0.77	0.57	0.69
Jun.	E0.30	0.28	0.25	0.11
Sep.	E0.30	E0.45	0.27	d0.97
Dec.	E0.60	E0.60	0.84	d0.24
	E2.00	E1.95	1.93	d0.43

Important Developments

Jun. '93— PGN received a favorable ruling by the Oregon Public Utility Commission (PUC) on its amended Least Cost Energy Plan, which proposed the permanent closure of its Trojan Nuclear Plant in February 1993. PGN also obtained approval from Nuclear Regulatory Commission for a possession-only license for the plant which allows decommissioning to move forward. In February, the PUC sided with PGN on three accounting issues and granted one declaratory ruling request. PGN can continue to depreciate Trojan and collect decommissioning funds per the 1991 general rate case; can defer 80% of the incremental replacement power cost; and can amortize the costs of an employee retention program. Although these rulings do not constitute a detemination on rate-making treatment of Trojan, they do reduce uncertainty regarding rate-making treatment of the acquisition of new power resources.

Next earnings report expected in late October.

Per Share Data ($)

Yr. End Dec. 31	1992	1991	1990	1989	1988	1987	1986	1985	1984	1983
Tangible Bk. Val.	**15.87**	14.03	16.10	15.94	18.39	18.01	18.26	19.73	18.36	18.18
Earnings[1]	**1.93**	d0.43	2.17	d0.21	2.11	1.69	1.97	3.12	2.80	3.01
Dividends	**1.200**	1.200	1.200	1.960	1.960	1.960	1.945	1.880	1.810	1.770
Payout Ratio	**62%**	NM	55%	NM	93%	116%	99%	60%	65%	59%
Prices—High	**19⅝**	18⅞	22⅛	25½	24¾	31½	36¾	23¼	17½	16⅝
Low	**15**	12¾	14⅞	20⅞	20¼	20⅝	21⅞	16⅛	13	13⅛
P/E Ratio—	**10–8**	NM	10–7	12–10	19–12	19–11	7–5	6–5	6–4	5–4

Data as orig. reptd. 1. Bef. results of disc. oper. of -0.63 in 1991, -0.37 in 1989; bef. spec. item(s) of +0.76 in 1987, -1.63 in 1986, -0.15 in 1985, -1.14 in 1983, -0.64 in 1982. d-Deficit. E-Estimated NM-Not Meaningful.

Income Data (Million $)

Year Ended Dec. 31	Revs.	Depr.	Maint.	Oper. Ratio	[1]Fxd. Chgs. Cover.	Constr. Credits	Eff. Tax Rate	[2]Net Inc.	% Return On Revs.	% Return On [3]Invest. Capital	% Return On Com. Equity
1992	**884**	**99**	**70.5**	**81.4%**	**2.87**	**2.8**	**41.9%**	**90**	**10.1**	**7.8**	**12.8**
[4]1991	890	113	91.3	84.6%	1.25	2.0	45.7%	d21	NM	3.3	NM
1990	852	91	55.5	79.4%	2.81	1.8	46.4%	100	11.7	9.2	13.0
[4]1989	797	92	57.1	79.7%	1.52	3.9	41.9%	d10	NM	3.8	NM
1988	762	98	39.6	74.7%	2.32	3.0	23.1%	109	14.3	9.1	11.1
1987	764	99	41.3	77.7%	2.25	6.2	37.1%	96	12.6	9.5	9.0
1986	760	93	35.0	76.0%	2.53	9.2	49.5%	123	16.3	10.6	10.2
1985	827	87	31.7	75.3%	3.10	26.9	42.5%	176	21.3	12.9	16.0
1984	722	80	34.0	62.4%	2.25	5.9	21.9%	158	21.9	12.8	15.1
1983	586	60	24.1	64.3%	1.84	69.0	25.9%	163	27.8	12.0	16.6

Balance Sheet Data (Million $)

Dec. 31	[5]Gross Prop.	Capital Expend.	Net Prop.	% Earn. on Net Prop.	Total Cap.	[6]LT Debt	% LT Debt	Capitalization Pfd.	% Pfd.	Com.	% Com.
1992	**2,277**	**144**	**1,451**	**8.8**	**2,227**	**874**	**49.9**	**152**	**8.7**	**724**	**41.4**
1991	2,790	139	1,801	7.6	2,208	927	52.8	150	8.5	679	38.7
1990	2,669	109	1,779	9.9	2,126	763	45.3	152	9.0	771	45.7
1989	2,584	119	1,778	9.1	2,100	817	47.1	154	8.9	762	44.0
1988	2,497	86	1,773	10.8	2,168	850	45.1	156	8.3	879	46.6
1987	2,439	76	1,590	10.6	1,905	877	47.2	109	5.9	873	46.9
1986	2,551	82	1,627	10.4	2,079	966	46.9	238	11.5	856	41.6
1985	2,721	109	1,870	10.6	2,075	897	43.4	250	12.1	920	44.5
1984	2,589	129	1,963	13.6	2,114	991	47.1	262	12.5	852	40.4
1983	2,546	191	2,019	10.3	2,062	998	48.6	265	12.9	789	38.5

Data as orig. reptd. **1.** Times int. exp. & pfd. divs. covered (pretax basis). **2.** Bef. spec. items. **3.** Based on income before interest charges. **4.** Excl. disc. ops. **5.** Electric utility plant. **6.** Incl nuclear fuel storage liab. in 1984 & 1983 & capital lease obligs. after 1984. d-Deficit. NM-Not Meaningful.

Business Summary

PGN is the holding company for Portland General Electric, an electric utility supplying a 3,170-square-mile area in Oregon, including Portland and Salem. PGN is phasing out nonutility businesses over the next several years. Utility revenues in recent years were derived as follows:

	1992	1991	1990	1989
Residential............	35%	35%	35%	38%
Commercial	33%	32%	32%	33%
Industrial	16%	15%	16%	17%
Other...................	16%	18%	17%	12%

The fuel mix in 1992 was 10% hydro, 49% thermal (nuclear, coal, and gas) and 41% purchased power. Total kilowatt-hour sales fell 6.0% in 1993, to 18,475 million from 19,654 million in 1991.

With the closure of the Trojan Nuclear plant, PGE must step up its plans for new capacity. Over the next four years, PGE expects to invest $400 million to $600 million to add 600 megawatts of gas-fired combustion turbines and cogeneration projects to PGE's resource base. Capital expenditures of $145 million for 1993 include $89 million for generation, transmission and distribution, and $23 million for energy efficiency.

Finances

The Oregon Attorney General has issued an opinion that the PUC may allow rate recovery of the total Trojan plant closing costs, including the return on the $350 million in undepreciated investment. The opinion does not guarantee cost recovery, but does clarify that the PUC has the authority to allow the recovery of such significant costs in rates.

Dividend Data

Dividends have been paid since 1948. A dividend reinvestment plan is available.

Amt of Divd. $	Date Decl.	Ex-divd. Date	Stock of Record	Payment Date
0.30	Dec. 8	Dec. 21	Dec. 28	Jan. 15'93
0.30	Feb. 23	May 19	May 25	Apr. 15'93
0.30	May 4	Jun. 21	Jun. 25	Jul. 15'93
0.30	Jul. 13	Sep. 20	Sep. 24	Oct. 15'93

Capitalization

Long Term Debt: $872,827,000 (3/93).

Subsid. Red. Cum. Preferred Stock: $81,800,000.

Subsid. Cum. Preferred Stock: $69,704,000.

Common Stock: 47,346,787 shs. ($3.75 par).
Institutions hold about 37%.
Shareholders of record: 51,581.

Office—121 SW Salmon St., Portland, OR 97204. **Tel**—(503) 464-8820. **Chrmn, Pres & CEO**—K. L. Harrison. **VP-Fin & CFO**— J. M. Hirko. **SVP-Secy**—L. A. Girard. **Investor Contact**—Joan Smith (503-464-7120). **Dirs**—G. G. Booth, P. J. Brix, C. Chambers, E. L. Clark Jr., J. W. Creighton Jr., K. L. Harrison, J. E. Hudson, C. C. Knudsen, W. E. McCain, R. L. Miller, J. J. Meyer, R. G. Reiten, R. W. Roth, B. G. Willison. **Transfer Agent & Registrar**—First Chicago Trust Co. of N.Y., NYC. **Incorporated** in Oregon in 1930. **Empl**—3,253.

 Ned Bancroft

Potomac Electric Power

NYSE Symbol POM In S&P MidCap 400

Price	Range	P-E Ratio	Dividend	Yield	S&P Ranking	Beta
Sep. 28'93	1993					
28¾	28⅞–23⅞	15	1.64	5.7%	A–	0.57

Summary

This electric utility serves the government and commercial economy of Washington, D.C., and adjoining parts of Maryland. POM's earnings should rebound in 1993, reflecting rate hikes in Maryland and Washington, D.C., and higher kwh sales due primarily to more favorable summer weather conditions. The dividend may be raised some 2.4% in January 1994.

Current Outlook

Share earnings for 1993 could rebound to $1.90 from the reduced $1.66 recorded for 1992. Share earnings could advance to $1.95 in 1994.

The $0.41 quarterly dividend may be raised some 2.4% with the January 1994 declaration.

Earnings for 1993 should reflect some benefit from the 1992 rate hike in the District of Columbia, a recent rate hike in Maryland, and higher kwh sales due primarily to more favorable summer weather conditions. Income from POM's leasing unit is expected to be approximately flat. The estimate assumes that three aircraft which were returned are leased in the near term. Earnings would further benefit from a return to normal weather conditions. Earnings for 1994 should benefit mostly from a possible rate hike in the District of Columbia, and slightly higher earnings from the leasing unit.

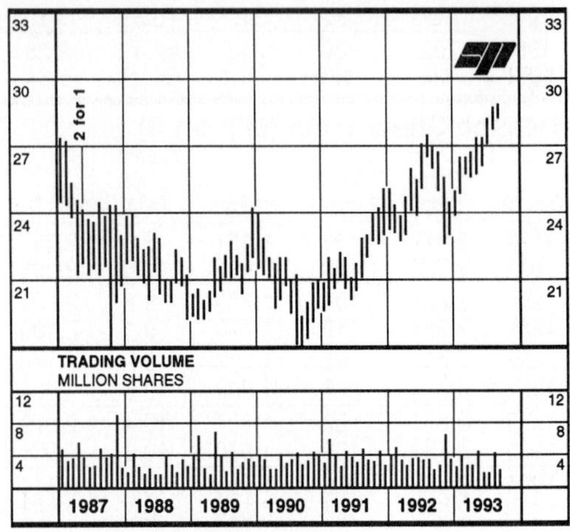

[1]Total Revenues (Million $)

Quarter:	1993	1992	1991	1990
Mar.	339	326	290	283
Jun.	420	391	361	312
Sep.	---	554	563	509
Dec.	---	331	339	307
	---	1,602	1,552	1,412

Total revenue for the six months to June 30, 1993, rose 6.0%, year to year. After 2.9% higher production costs, operating income was up 25%. Following higher nonutility contributions and other income versus expense, but lower construction-related credits, net income rose 57%. After 21% higher preferred dividends, share earnings were $0.71, versus $0.46, which was before a $0.14 gain from an accounting change.

Common Share Earnings ($)

Quarter:	1993	1992	1991	1990
Mar.	0.08	0.04	0.04	0.04
Jun.	0.63	0.41	0.38	0.28
Sep.	E1.09	1.06	1.21	1.13
Dec.	E0.10	0.15	0.22	0.17
	E1.90	1.66	1.87	1.62

Important Developments

Jul. '93— POM said earnings at its aircraft leasing unit almost doubled, year to year, in first six months of 1993, to $21.5 million from $11.1 million. However, POM noted that earnings at the unit are heavily dependent on the timing of individual transactions and do not follow a pattern.

Jun. '93— POM filed for a $72.6 million base rate hike for 1994 in the District of Columbia. The request includes proposals to recover the costs of conservation programs and the resulting lost revenues via surcharges instead of base rates to allow for timely recovery of these costs. POM also requested a surcharge to recover any proposed Federal energy taxes. POM said that if these surcharges were not adopted, the base rate request would have to be raised $29.2 million for a total of $101.8 million. Separately, POM filed for an $81.9 million rate hike for 1994 in Maryland. In December 1992, an $18 million rate hike went into effect in Maryland, and a further $7.2 million hike became effective June 1, 1993.

Next earnings report expected in late October.

Per Share Data ($)

Yr. End Dec. 31	1992	1991	1990	1989	1988	1987	1986	1985	1984	1983
Tangible Bk. Val.	**15.68**	15.31	14.26	14.11	13.11	12.53	11.79	10.66	9.96	9.35
Earnings[2]	**1.66**	1.87	1.62	2.16	2.14	2.11	2.06	1.80	1.62	1.33
Dividends	**1.60**	1.56	1.52	1.46	1.38	1.30	1.18	1.08	0.97	0.89
Payout Ratio	**96%**	83%	94%	68%	64%	62%	57%	60%	60%	67%
Prices—High	**27½**	25⅛	24	24¼	24	27⅜	29⅝	17½	12⅞	11⅛
Low	**22⅝**	19⅝	18	19¼	19¼	18	16⅞	12¼	9⅝	8⅝
P/E Ratio—	**16–13**	13–10	15–11	11–9	11–9	13–9	14–8	10–7	8–6	8–6

Data as orig. reptd. Adj. for stk. div. of 100% May 1987. **1.** Oper. revs. prior to 1992. **2.** Bef. spec. item +0.14 in 1992, +0.23 in 1986. E-Estimated.

Potomac Electric Power Company

Income Data (Million $)

Year Ended Dec. 31	Revs.	Depr.	Maint.	Oper. Ratio	[1]Fxd. Chgs. Cover.	Constr. Credits	Eff. Tax Rate	[2]Net Inc.	% Return On Revs.	% Return On [3]Invest. Capital	% Return On Com. Equity
1992	**1,562**	**150**	**91**	**84.6%**	**2.88**	**29.7**	**30.7%**	**201**	**12.9**	**6.4**	**11.4**
1991	1,552	134	90	81.3%	3.14	32.9	27.8%	210	13.5	7.1	12.6
1990	1,412	124	91	81.9%	2.94	27.2	27.1%	170	12.1	7.0	11.3
1989	1,395	120	93	80.3%	3.69	15.5	31.7%	215	15.4	8.8	15.5
1988	1,350	121	93	79.8%	3.90	8.7	26.8%	211	15.6	9.5	16.5
1987	1,332	116	100	80.3%	4.42	5.3	37.7%	208	15.6	10.3	17.3
1986	1,371	111	96	80.3%	4.25	5.1	43.1%	206	15.0	11.0	18.3
1985	1,316	106	96	80.7%	3.99	2.7	44.3%	184	14.0	10.3	17.3
1984	1,198	102	95	80.4%	3.77	9.1	44.7%	168	14.0	10.1	16.7
1983	1,170	98	83	81.4%	---	4.8	47.6%	140	12.0	9.5	14.5

Balance Sheet Data (Million $)

Dec. 31	Gross Prop.	Capital Expend.	Net Prop.	% Earn. on Net Prop.	Total Cap.	[4]LT Debt	[4]% LT Debt	Pfd.	% Pfd.	Com.	% Com.
1992	**5,368**	**358**	**3,931**	**6.3**	**5,164**	**2,468**	**54.1**	**274**	**6.0**	**1,823**	**39.9**
1991	5,048	432	3,707	8.2	4,982	2,483	56.1	226	5.1	1,716	38.8
1990	4,659	420	3,398	7.9	4,270	2,117	56.8	176	4.7	1,435	38.5
1989	4,271	345	3,098	9.2	3,691	1,639	51.9	126	4.0	1,394	44.1
1988	3,946	273	2,857	9.9	3,433	1,531	52.4	143	4.9	1,249	42.7
1987	3,700	241	2,679	10.0	2,941	1,104	45.3	144	5.9	1,191	48.8
1986	3,497	219	2,543	10.8	2,772	1,028	44.8	150	6.5	1,118	48.7
1985	3,340	192	2,455	10.5	2,721	1,097	48.0	184	8.0	1,008	44.0
1984	3,201	179	2,374	10.1	2,576	1,025	47.1	208	9.5	945	43.4
1983	3,043	161	2,283	9.7	2,510	1,058	49.1	212	9.9	884	41.0

Data as orig. reptd. **1.** Times int. exp. & pfd. divs. covered (pretax basis). **2.** Bef. spec. items. **3.** Based on income bef. interest charges. **4.** Incl. nonutility subs. debt aft. 1987.

Business Summary

Potomac Electric Power provides retail electric service in the Washington metropolitan area, including the District of Columbia and major portions of Montgomery and Prince Georges counties in Maryland, with a population of some 1.9 million. Electricity is also sold at wholesale. POM's unique service territory, with virtually no heavy industry, benefits from economic stability and low unemployment. Electric revenues by customer class in recent years were:

	1992	1991	1990	1989
Residential	28%	29%	28%	28%
Commercial	48%	47%	48%	48%
Federal government	15%	15%	15%	15%
Other	9%	9%	9%	9%

Sources of electric generation in 1992 were coal 75%, oil and natural gas 12%, and purchases 13%. Peak demand in 1992 was 5,546 mw, and capability at peak totaled 6,602 mw, for a capacity margin of 16%.

POM estimates that peak demand will grow at a compound annual rate of about 1% during the period 1993-2002. POM expects annual growth in kwh sales to range between 1% and 2%. The company's ongoing strategies to meet increasing electric demand include conservation and energy use management programs which are designed to curtail growth in peak demand in order to defer construction of additional generating capacity. The company is also expected to rely more heavily on purchased power. POM has a long-term contract with Ohio Edison for a firm supply of 450 mw of capacity which the company expects to utilize in full through the year 2005.

POM's non-utility unit, Potomac Capital Investment Co., primarily leases wide-body commercial aircraft and satellite communications equipment.

Dividend Data

Dividends have been paid since 1904. A dividend reinvestment plan is available.

Amt of Divd. $	Date Decl.	Ex-divd. Date	Stock of Record	Payment Date
0.40	Oct. 22	Nov. 20	Nov. 27	Dec. 31'92
0.41	Jan. 28	Feb. 19	Feb. 25	Mar. 31'93
0.41	Apr. 28	May 21	May 27	Jun. 30'93
0.41	Jul. 22	Aug. 24	Aug. 30	Sep. 30'93

Capitalization

Long Term Debt: $2,754,728,000 (6/93).

Red. Preferred Stock: $147,000,000.

Cum. Preferred Stock: $125,463,000.

Common Stock: 115,331,105 shs. ($1 par).
Institutions hold about 17%.
Shareholders of record: 101,186.

Office—1900 Pennsylvania Ave, N.W., Washington, DC 20068. **Tel**—(202) 872-2456. **Chrmn & CEO**—E. F. Mitchell. **Pres**—J. M. Derrick, Jr. **Vice Chrmn & CFO**—H. L. Davis. **Secy**—B. K. Cauley. **Investor Contact**—Peyton G. Middleton, Jr. **Dirs**—R. R. Blunt Sr., V. C. Burke Jr., A. J. Clark, H. L. Davis, E. K. Hoffman, F. D. McKenzie, A. D. McLaughlin, E. F. Mitchell, P. F. O'Malley, L. A. Simpson, W. R. Thompson, C. E. Walker. **Transfer Agents & Registrars**—Chemical Bank, NYC; Riggs National Bank of Washington, D.C. **Incorporated** in District of Columbia in 1896. **Empl**—5,100.

 Christopher J. Grant

Precision Castparts

NYSE Symbol PCP In S&P MidCap 400

Price	Range	P-E Ratio	Dividend	Yield	S&P Ranking	Beta
Oct. 19'93	1993					
26⅛	27–17⅜	NM	0.12	0.5%	A	0.87

Summary

This leading producer of complex structural investment castings sold primarily to jet aircraft engine makers, is also a large supplier of other investment castings made from stainless steel and various metal alloys, and is one of the two largest manufacturers of precision cast airfoils, consisting primarily of blades and vanes for jet engines. Earnings in recent periods were hurt by order stretch-outs and cancellations by customers, but an improvement is likley for fiscal 1993-94. Backlog at September 26, 1993, was down 36% from a year ago.

Current Outlook

Earnings for 1993-94 are expected to recover somewhat to $1.70 a share, from 1992-93's $0.10, which included nonrecurring charges of $1.29. Earnings for 1994-95 are estimated at $1.75.

Dividends should continue in the near term at $0.03 quarterly.

Sales for 1993-94 will likley be about 10%-15% lower, due to soft demand. While initial sales for the GE-90 products are being recorded, demand will probably not be enough to boost overall revenues for the full year, weakened by the elusiveness of airliner pofitability. Signs of stronger margins, due to restructuring efficiencies, are surfacing, but without the volume gains to fuel real earnings strength going forward, net income growth should only be lackluster. However, per-share earnings will benefit from the 28% reduction in shares outstanding due to PCP's share repurchases. Longer term, growth should come from greater demand, reflecting the development of new designs for aircraft jet engines that meet fuel efficiency and noise reduction requirements and make significantly greater use of the type of structural investment castings produced by PCP than did prior engine designs. However, 1994-95 earnings may only climb to $1.75 a share, due to the absence of 1993-94's $0.18 tax credit.

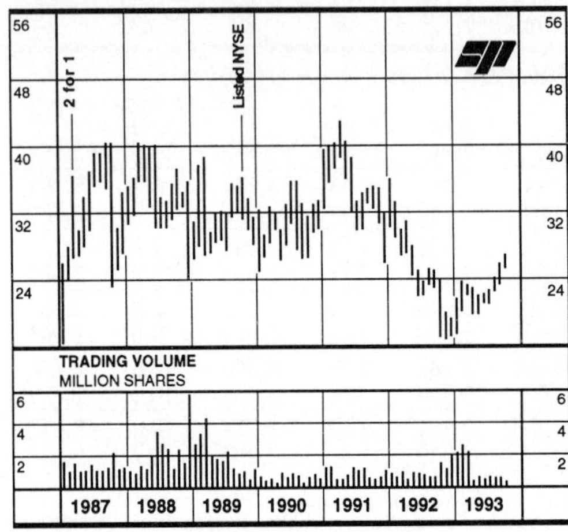

Net Sales (Million $)

13 Weeks:	1993–94	1992–93	1991–92	1990–91
Jun.	101.4	122.5	145.6	129.8
Sep.	107.9	120.0	143.8	130.0
Dec.	---	107.9	149.6	130.0
Mar.	---	111.0	144.3	148.5
	---	461.4	583.3	538.3

Sales for the six months ended September 26, 1993, fell 14%, year to year, on weak demand for jet aircraft engine products. Following narrowed margins and higher interest expense (net), pretax income dropped 2.2%. After taxes at 22.8%, which reflected a $2.4 million tax credit, versus taxes at 35.0%, income fell 15%. Per share earnings of $0.96, based on 27% fewer shares, compared with $0.83. Results for the 1993-94 period exclude a $0.22 a share charge from an acccounting change.

Common Share Earnings ($)

13 Weeks:	1993–94	1992–93	1991–92	1990–91
Jun.	0.54	0.49	0.45	0.43
Sep.	0.42	0.34	0.51	0.46
Dec.	E0.34	d1.06	1.09	0.48
Mar.	E0.40	0.33	0.62	0.55
	E1.70	0.10	2.67	1.92

Important Developments

Mar. '93— PCP repurchased approximately 4.9 million shares, or 28%, of its common stock, in a Dutch auction tender offer.

Next earnings report expected in late January.

Per Share Data ($)

Yr. End Mar. 31	1993	1992[1]	1991	1990	1989	1988	1987[1]	1986	1985[1]	1984
Tangible Bk. Val.	**14.71**	[2]17.91	15.32	13.21	11.40	9.53	5.81	4.28	3.66	3.10
Cash Flow	**1.22**	3.75	2.86	2.56	2.42	2.81	1.78	0.98	0.80	0.52
Earnings	**0.10**	2.67	1.92	1.70	1.75	2.27	1.35	0.63	0.58	0.27
Dividends	**0.120**	0.120	0.120	0.080	0.080	0.080	0.065	0.049	0.033	0.033
Payout Ratio	**120%**	5%	6%	5%	5%	4%	5%	8%	6%	12%
Calendar Years	**1992**	1991	1990	1989	1988	1987	1986	1985	1984	1983
Prices—High	**36**	43	35¾	38¾	40½	40½	16¾	15⅛	8⅞	8½
Low	**16¾**	26	25	26½	24	16⅜	10¼	8½	5⅜	4⅛
P/E Ratio—	**NM**	16–10	19–13	23–16	23–14	18–7	12–8	24–14	16–9	31–15

Data as orig. reptd. Adj. for stk. divs. of 100% Mar. 1987, 25% Mar. 1986, 50% Apr. 1985. **1.** Reflects merger or acquisition. **2.** Incl. intangibles. d-Deficit. E-Estimated. NM-Not Meaningful.

Income Data (Million $)

Year Ended Mar. 31	Revs.	Oper. Inc.	% Oper. Inc. of Revs.	Cap. Exp.	Depr.	Int. Exp.	Net Bef. Taxes	Eff. Tax Rate	Net Inc.	% Net Inc. of Revs.	Cash Flow
1993	**461**	**56.2**	**12.2**	**15.5**	**20.0**	**1.90**	**d0.3**	**NM**	**1.8**	**0.4**	**21.8**
[1]1992	583	75.8	13.0	28.8	19.1	2.20	53.0	10.8%	47.3	8.1	66.4
1991	538	68.5	12.7	28.8	16.3	4.10	49.7	32.8%	33.4	6.2	49.7
1990	457	54.6	11.9	23.0	14.8	5.00	35.4	17.8%	29.1	6.4	43.9
1989	444	59.3	13.4	31.9	11.3	6.16	43.5	32.4%	29.4	6.6	40.7
1988	414	71.7	17.3	26.9	8.8	5.21	59.0	37.7%	36.8	8.9	45.6
[1]1987	326	51.4	15.8	23.4	6.8	6.14	[2]39.4	46.2%	21.2	6.5	28.0
1986	192	25.1	13.0	20.7	5.4	3.76	[2]16.6	43.8%	9.3	4.9	14.7
[1]1985	146	16.8	11.5	17.1	3.4	3.75	[2]10.6	20.9%	8.4	5.8	11.8
1984	94	9.1	9.6	8.2	3.5	1.80	[2]3.9	2.1%	3.8	4.1	7.4

Balance Sheet Data (Million $)

Mar. 31	Cash	Curr. Assets	Curr. Liab.	Curr. Ratio	Total Assets	% Ret. on Assets	Long Term Debt	Common Equity	Total Cap.	% LT Debt of Cap.	% Ret. on Equity
1993	**68.9**	**285**	**150**	**1.9**	**433**	**0.5**	**14.7**	**203**	**233**	**6.3**	**0.8**
1992	25.3	278	93	3.0	443	10.9	18.6	319	350	5.3	16.0
1991	6.1	281	113	2.5	422	8.5	27.4	270	310	8.9	13.3
1990	0.8	230	90	2.6	360	8.2	30.7	229	270	11.4	13.7
1989	2.6	225	91	2.5	347	9.1	52.2	193	256	20.4	16.6
1988	Nil	195	82	2.4	298	12.8	47.2	159	216	21.9	28.7
1987	2.8	170	74	2.3	253	10.7	78.2	89	179	43.8	27.6
1986	0.7	75	31	2.4	141	7.1	35.7	64	110	32.6	15.7
1985	0.1	69	35	2.0	120	8.3	25.3	54	86	29.5	16.7
1984	0.3	43	15	2.9	81	5.1	15.0	45	66	22.9	9.5

Data as orig. reptd. **1.** Reflects merger or acquisition. **2.** Incl. equity in earns. of nonconsol. subs. d-Deficit. NM-Not Meaningful.

Business Summary

Precision Castparts is a leading supplier to the aerospace industry of large, complex structural investment castings, as well as other investment castings from stainless steel and alloys of nickel, cobalt and titanium. PCP also manufactures precision cast airfoils, consisting primarily of blades and vanes used as replacement parts and as original equipment in commercial and military aircraft jet engines. Airfoils are also sold for use in industrial and marine gas turbines.

Contributions to sales in recent fiscal years:

	1992–93	1991–92	1990–91
Aerospace castings.....	86%	88%	89%
Other castings............	14%	12%	11%

Investment casting is a process whereby a ceramic material is invested around a wax pattern of a part that is to be reproduced. The wax is then melted and drained, and molten metal is poured into the resulting cavity. After the metal cools, the ceramic shell is removed and the part cleaned. This method is highly suited to complex patterns and generally produces parts to closer tolerances and with finer surface finishes than other casting methods.

The company's Structurals division manufactures large, complex structural castings that are sold primarily as original equipment to aircraft jet engine manufacturers. PCP's strategy is to develop large castings required for new engine programs, promote the continued substitution of cast parts for fabricated parts, increase the use of castings made from titanium alloys, and increase its participation in the market for smaller castings. The company also manufactures precision cast airfoils for use in aircraft jet engines and in industrial and marine gas turbines. In addition, PCP casts parts for turbochargers used on diesel engines for trucks, buses, off-highway equipment, and a variety of other parts for commercial and industrial use.

In 1992-93, General Electric Co. and the Pratt & Whitney Aircraft division of United Technologies Corp. together accounted for 52% of sales.

Dividend Data

Dividends have been paid since 1978.

Amt of Divd. $	Date Decl.	Ex–divd. Date	Stock of Record	Payment Date
0.03	Nov. 6	Nov. 30	Dec. 4	Jan. 4'93
0.03	Jan. 25	Mar. 1	Mar. 5	Apr. 5'93
0.03	May 21	Jun. 1	Jun. 7	Jul. 6'93
0.03	Aug. 13	Aug. 30	Sep. 3	Oct. 4'93

Capitalization

Long Term Debt: $39,300,000 (6/93).

Common Stock: 12,992,000 shs. (no par).
E. H. Cooley owns about 7.9%.
Institutions hold some 60%.
Shareholders of record: 2,580.

Office—4600 S.E. Harney Drive, Portland, OR 97206. **Tel**—(503) 777-3881. **Chrmn**—E. H. Cooley. **Pres & CEO**—W. C. McCormick. **VP-CFO**—W. D. Larsson. **VP-Secy & Investor Contact**—Roy M. Marvin. **Dirs**—E. H. Cooley, D. C. Frisbee, H. W. Hill, C. M. Martenson, R. M. Marvin, W. C. McCormick, K. H. Pierce, D. A. Sangrey, H. C. Stonecipher. **Transfer Agent**—First Interstate Bank of Oregon. **Incorporated** in Oregon in 1956. **Empl**—4,341.

 M. Graham Hackett

Progressive Corp.

NYSE Symbol PGR Options on Phila (Feb-May-Aug-Nov) In S&P MidCap 400

Price	Range	P-E Ratio	Dividend	Yield	S&P Ranking	Beta
Sep. 23'93	1993					
41⅝	44½–27½	14	0.20	0.5%	B+	0.64

Summary

This holding company is a leading underwriter of nonstandard automobile and other specialty personal lines coverages, including motorcycle, recreational vehicle, motor home, mobile home and boat insurance. Credit related insurance and services are also offered. Earnings in 1993's first half benefited from continued strong premium growth, the positive effects of an aggressive cost-cutting campaign, and sharply higher investment gains. In July 1993, PGR sold publicly 4,950,000 common shares at $37 each.

Current Outlook

Excluding realized investment gains or losses, net operating earnings for 1993 are estimated at $2.35 a share, up from the $1.94 a share (which excluded about $0.15 of net realized gains) reported for 1992. Earnings could rise to $2.75 a share in 1994.

A modest increase in the $0.05 quarterly dividend is likely.

The prospect for higher earnings in coming periods is aided by continued strong written premium growth that will likely exceed 15% in 1993. Tighter underwriting guidelines by many standard and preferred risk insurers increase the market for PGR's core nonstandard (or high risk) coverage. PGR's attempt at expanding its share of the overall auto insurance market is also aided by the pullback of several large carriers from the auto insurance market. The positive effects of an aggressive cost-cutting effort that included a 19% staff reduction will aid margin growth and PGR's competitive stance going forward. Long-term prospects are also aided by the exit from the unprofitable long-haul truck market, and by the settlement of all refund exposure under Proposition 103. Investment income growth will slow amid low interest rates, but asset writedowns are unlikely.

Review of Operations

Revenues in the six months ended June 30, 1993, rose 4.0%, year to year, as the absence of a $103 million Proposition 103 reserve reduction masked a 15% rise in premiums and sharply higher investment gains. Aided by an 8.4% drop in total expenses, pretax profits more than doubled, to $184.4 million from $80.4 million. After taxes at 28.8%, versus 22.9%, net income surged to $131.3 million from $62.0 million. Share earnings were $1.82 on 9.3% more shares (including about $0.53 of net realized investment gains), up from $0.90 ($0.10), before a $0.22 special credit from an accounting change.

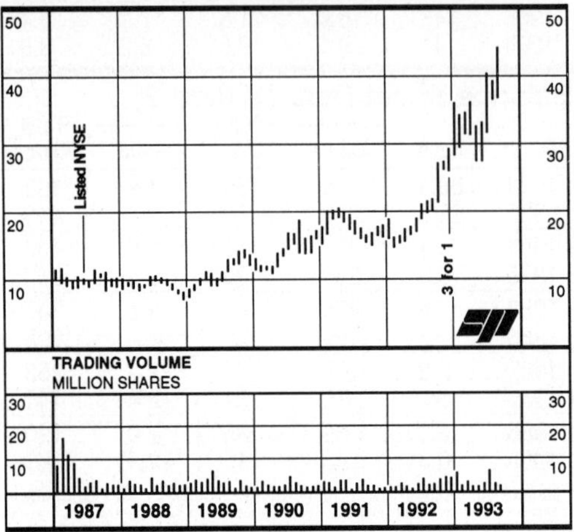

Common Share Earnings ($)

Quarter:	1993	1992	1991	1990
Mar.	0.71	0.31	0.37	0.36
Jun.	1.11	0.60	0.13	0.50
Sep.		0.62	0.14	0.25
Dec.		0.53	d0.26	0.16
		2.09	0.41	1.28

Important Developments

Aug. '93— Commenting on results for the first half of 1993, PGR noted that the 23% rise in net written premiums reflected growth in policy count in the company's core lines of business. The aggressive cost cuts undertaken in 1992 enabled PGR to more aggressively price its products and thus gain market share. Separately, in late July the company sold publicly 4,950,000 common shares at $37 a share.

Next earnings report expected in late October.

Per Share Data ($)

Yr. End Dec. 31	1992	1991	1990	1989	1988	1987	1986	1985	1984	1983
Tangible Bk. Val.	**7.94**	5.83	5.89	5.71	5.13	4.54	3.66	1.75	1.11	1.13
Oper. Earnings[1]	**[4]1.94**	NA	NA	NA	NA	1.05	0.66	0.38	0.28	0.28
Earnings[1,2]	**2.09**	0.41	1.28	0.98	1.29	1.03	0.77	0.52	0.21	0.31
Dividends	**0.190**	0.173	0.160	0.147	0.133	0.077	0.020	0.018	0.016	0.015
Payout Ratio	**9%**	43%	13%	15%	10%	7%	3%	3%	7%	5%
Prices—High	**29⅜**	20¹¹⁄₁₆	18¹³⁄₁₆	14⁷⁄₁₆	10¾	11¹³⁄₁₆	12¹³⁄₁₆	7¹⁄₁₆	3¾	4
Low	**14¾**	15¹⁄₁₆	10¹⁵⁄₁₆	7½	7³⁄₁₆	8½	6¹³⁄₁₆	3⁷⁄₁₆	2¹⁵⁄₁₆	2⁷⁄₁₆
P/E Ratio—[3]	**14–7**	51–37	15–9	15–8	8–6	11–8	19–10	19–9	13–11	14–9

Data as orig. reptd. Adj. for stk. divs. of 200% in Dec. 1992, 125% in May 1986, 50% in May 1985. **1.** Bef. spec. items of +0.23 in 1992, +0.04 in 1987, +0.01 in 1985, +0.05 in 1983. **2.** Aft. gains/losses on security trans. **3.** Based on oper. earns. prior to 1988. **4.** Estimated. d-Deficit. NA-Not Available.

Income Data (Million $)

Year Ended Dec. 31	Premium Income	Net Invest. Inc.	Oth. Revs.	Total Revs.	Property & Casualty Underwriting Ratios [3]Loss	[3]Expense	[3]Comb.	Net Bef. Taxes	[1]Net Oper. Inc.	[1]Net Inc.	—% Return On— [2]Revs.	[3]Equity
1992	**1,451**	**154**	**134**	**1,739**	**68.3**	**29.8**	**98.1**	**179**	**NA**	**140**	**8.0**	**34.7**
1991	1,287	152	54	1,493	65.7	33.5	99.2	33	NA	33	2.2	6.7
1990	1,191	140	45	1,376	62.1	31.1	93.2	88	NA	93	6.8	21.5
1989	1,197	168	28	1,393	67.9	32.6	100.5	86	NA	78	5.6	17.4
1988	1,215	117	13	1,345	62.9	33.2	96.1	132	NA	108	8.0	25.9
1987	994	61	6	1,061	58.3	35.8	94.1	108	91.3	90	8.6	24.3
1986	677	49	6	732	61.0	34.3	95.3	71	55.3	65	7.6	23.0
1985	445	34	12	491	65.6	33.6	99.2	24	25.5	35	5.2	26.3
1984	273	25	10	308	65.0	37.4	102.4	16	18.1	14	5.9	23.5
1983	243	24	8	275	61.3	37.7	99.0	23	20.6	23	7.5	27.1

Balance Sheet Data (Million $)

Dec. 31	Cash & Equiv.	Premiums Due	—Investment Assets— [5]Bonds	Stocks	Loans	Total	[4]% Invest. Yield	Deferred Policy Costs	Total Assets	[6]Debt	Common Equity
1992	**50.0**	**312**	**1,988**	**399**	**Nil**	**2,386**	**6.5**	**101**	**3,005**	**569**	**533**
1991	48.3	323	1,955	349	Nil	2,304	6.9	110	2,979	644	466
1990	52.7	269	1,908	184	Nil	2,093	6.6	105	2,695	644	409
1989	54.5	235	1,885	243	Nil	2,128	6.3	111	2,647	646	435
1988	36.2	225	1,601	252	Nil	1,853	5.9	126	2,307	479	417
1987	35.3	194	1,070	280	Nil	1,351	4.9	124	1,786	217	395
1986	24.4	151	524	430	Nil	954	5.7	85	1,266	101	311
1985	13.0	84	336	282	Nil	619	6.3	60	811	159	118
1984	7.3	44	284	125	Nil	409	7.2	44	538	102	75
1983	7.1	33	237	123	Nil	359	6.6	32	459	55	80

Data as orig. reptd. **1.** Bef. spec. items. **2.** Based on oper. earns. prior to 1988. **3.** As reptd. by co. **4.** As reptd. by co. (aft. taxes at mkt.) prior to 1990. **5.** Incl. short-term invest. **6.** Incl. curr. portion. NA-Not Available.

Business Summary

Progressive Corp. is an insurance holding company with 50 wholly owned operating subsidiaries and one mutual insurance company affiliate. The companies write nonstandard automobile and other specialty property-casualty and credit-related insurance and provide related services throughout the U.S. and Canada. Contributions to premiums in recent years were as follows:

	1992	1991	1990
Personal lines	74%	67%	64%
Commercial lines	26%	33%	36%

PGR's core business (accounting for 93% of 1992's $1.6 billion in net written premiums) consists of underwriting nonstandard private passenger automobile and small commercial vehicle insurance. Nonstandard insurance programs provide coverage for accounts rejected or canceled by other companies. Based on its 1992 written premium volume, PGR was the fourth largest insurer serving this market.

The company's other core personal lines products are dominated by motorcycle insurance, but also include recreational vehicle, motor home, mobile home and boat coverages. As part of a strategy to expand its share of the personal automobile insurance market, the company is selectively underwriting standard and preferred risk automobile coverage.

PGR also provides credit-related insurance and services to lending institutions and risk management services to trade and professional organizations. The Transportation division, which provided insurance coverage and related services primarily to the trucking industry, was discontinued in 1992.

Dividend Data

Cash has been paid each year since 1965.

Amt of Divd. $	Date Decl.	Ex–divd. Date	Stock of Record	Payment Date
3–for–1	Nov. 10	Dec. 9	Nov. 23	Dec. 8'92
0.05	Oct. 23	Nov. 17	Nov. 23	Dec. 31'92
0.05	Feb. 5	Mar. 8	Mar. 12	Mar. 31'93
0.05	Jul. 30	Sep. 3	Sep. 10	Sep. 30'93

Capitalization

Long Term Debt: $568,500,000 (6/93).

9⅜% Cum. Preferred Stock: 4,000,000 shs. ($25 liquid. pref.).

Common Stock: 72,065,544 shs. ($1 par).
Officers and directors own or control about 20%.
Institutions hold approximately 54%.
Shareholders of record: 4,810 (6/93).

Office—6000 Parkland Blvd., Mayfield Heights, OH 44124. **Tel**—(216) 464-8000. **Chrmn, Pres & CEO**—P. B. Lewis. **VP-CFO & Investor Contact**—Charles B. Chokel (216-446-7260). **Secy**—D. M. Schneider. **Treas**—D. R. Lewis. **Dirs**—M. N. Allen, B. C. Ames, S. R. Hardis, P. B. Lewis, N. S. Matthews, D. B. Shackelford, P. B. Sigler. **Transfer Agent & Registrar**—National City Bank, Cleveland. **Incorporated** in Ohio in 1965. **Empl**—5,591.

 Catherine A. Seifert

Provident Life & Accident

NYSE Symbol PVB In S&P MidCap 400

Price	Range	P-E Ratio	Dividend	Yield	S&P Ranking	Beta
Jul. 30'93	1993					
27⅜	31½–25⅝	9	1.04	3.8%	A–	1.80

Summary

This number one provider of individual, non-cancelable disability insurance also offers group disability policies, as well as life and health insurance and pension products. Improved group health underwriting results, contributions from pension operations, and investment gains versus losses offset adverse disability claims development and led to higher first half 1993 earnings.

Current Outlook

Excluding realized investment gains or losses, share earnings of $3.10 are estimated for 1993, up from the approximately $2.94 of operating earnings reported for 1992. Earnings could rise to $3.40 a share in 1994.

A modest increase in the $0.26 quarterly dividend is likely.

Earnings growth in coming periods will be limited by adverse claims development in the individual disability line. The attendant need to bolster reserves for prior years' claims will hurt margins, but steps taken now to tighten underwriting standards aid the long term outlook. The merger of the group and individual disability lines into one segment will also yield cost savings through the consolidation of claims and administrative functions. Group health revenues may decline amid competitive pressures and a weak economy, but improved claims experience and cost cuts will aid profit growth. A pickup in demand for guaranteed investment contracts (GICs) will help offset a decline in sales of single premium annuities (SPA) and limit the drop in pension revenues. Net investment growth may slow amid low interest rates, but favorable spreads on interest sensitive products may offset this decline.

Review of Operations

Based on a brief report, net income in the six months ended June 30, 1993, rose 66%, year to year, to $1.97 a share ($1.32 of operating income), from $1.24 ($1.55).

Revenues in the quarter ended March 31, 1993, declined 1.8%, year to year. Margins widened, and after taxes at 31.5%, versus 30.7%, net income advanced 19%. Following preferred dividends in the 1993 interim only, share earnings were $0.71 ($0.79 of operating income), up from $0.61 ($0.71).

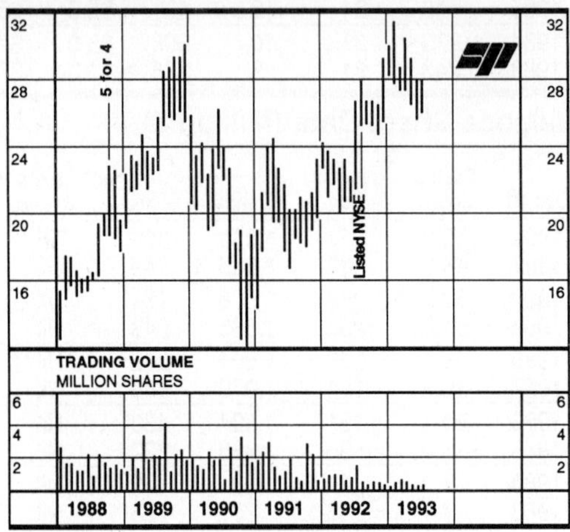

Common Share Earnings ($)

Quarter:	1993	1992	1991	1990
Mar.	0.71	0.61	0.76	0.79
Jun.	1.26	0.63	0.73	0.90
Sep.		0.68	0.51	1.09
Dec.		0.57	0.53	1.07
		2.49	2.53	3.85

Important Developments

May '93— Effective May 27, PVB agreed to pay $27 million to settle a five year dispute with the United States Department of Health and Human Services (HHS) concerning the overpayment by Medicare of certain claims involving working persons covered by both employer-sponsored health plans and Medicare. Funds to cover the settlement fee will come from certain special reserves and from funds in an escrow account established in 1990.

Next earnings report expected in late October.

Per Share Data ($)

Yr. End Dec. 31	1992	1991	1990	[2]1989	1988	1987	1986	1985	1984	1983
Book Value[1]	**30.74**	29.99	28.88	25.88	23.24	21.96	21.60	19.21	16.86	14.72
Oper. Earnings	**2.94**	NA	NA	NA	1.83	0.33	1.72	2.31	2.78	1.91
Earnings[3]	**2.49**	2.53	3.85	3.17	1.95	2.01	3.14	2.67	2.77	1.89
Dividends	**1.000**	0.960	0.830	0.710	0.674	0.673	0.656	0.700	0.563	0.513
Payout Ratio	**40%**	38%	22%	22%	35%	33%	21%	26%	20%	27%
Prices—High	**29¼**	24½	26¼	30⅛	22⅞	23	26⅜	23	16⅝	13¼
Low	**20**	14⅜	12	19⅛	12½	11⅜	18⅜	15⅜	13	9
P/E Ratio—[4]	**12–8**	10–6	7–3	10–6	13–7	70–35	15–11	10–7	6–5	7–5

Data as orig. reptd. Adj. for stk. divs. of 25% (Class A stk.) Oct. 1988, 200% & 33⅓% May 1985. **1.** As reptd. by Co. **2.** Reflects acctg. change. **3.** Bef. spec. item of -0.68 in 1991; aft. gains/losses on security trans. **4.** Based on oper. earns. prior to 1989. NA-Not Available.

Provident Life & Accident Insurance Co. of America

Income Data (Million $)

Year Ended Dec. 31	Life Ins. In Force	-Premium Income- Life	A & H	Net Invest. Inc.	Total Revs.	Net Bef. Taxes	Net Oper. Inc.	[2]Net Inc.	% Return On Revs.	Assets	Equity
1992	**79,956**	**129**	**1,361**	**1,242**	**2,867**	**180**	**133**	**113**	**3.9**	**0.7**	**8.3**
1991	82,434	131	1,406	1,195	2,846	169	NA	117	4.1	0.8	8.6
1990	82,432	136	1,420	1,088	2,751	253	NA	179	6.5	1.4	14.1
[1]1989	80,048	112	1,453	971	2,639	223	NA	148	5.6	1.3	12.0
1988	81,564	595	1,257	889	2,827	128	85	91	3.0	0.8	8.1
1987	96,181	603	1,080	743	2,515	21	15	94	0.9	0.3	2.1
1986	62,526	655	682	613	2,018	125	80	147	4.0	1.2	8.4
1985	58,770	540	631	456	1,688	164	108	125	6.4	2.1	12.8
1984	50,944	445	602	295	1,384	153	130	129	9.4	3.5	17.7
1983	44,348	312	604	196	1,149	126	89	88	7.8	3.0	13.7
1982	43,481	296	572	173	1,067	88	67	69	6.3	2.6	11.4

Balance Sheet Data (Million $)

Dec. 31	Cash & Equiv.	Premiums Due	Investment Assets [3]Bonds	Stocks	Loans	Total	% Invest. Yield	Deferred Policy Costs	Total Assets	Debt	Common Equity
1992	**381**	**93**	**10,602**	**142**	**3,031**	**14,344**	**9.0**	**561**	**15,925**	**206**	**1,388**
1991	326	102	9,439	167	3,179	13,324	9.4	514	14,787	207	1,371
1990	298	119	7,957	143	3,432	12,161	9.6	464	13,522	208	1,343
1989	280	127	6,509	103	3,605	10,539	9.7	424	11,852	215	1,208
1988	267	158	5,648	103	3,488	9,410	10.1	380	10,722	222	1,085
1987	237	164	4,916	115	3,085	8,220	10.0	351	9,455	219	1,025
1986	176	129	3,732	341	2,412	6,571	10.6	320	7,468	Nil	1,009
1985	150	142	2,824	336	1,756	4,991	10.7	295	5,812	Nil	898
1984	133	143	1,996	278	1,199	3,563	9.7	266	4,314	Nil	788
1983	88	161	1,205	265	956	2,487	8.7	245	3,195	Nil	688

Data as orig. reptd. **1.** Reflects acctg. change. **2.** Bef. spec. items. **3.** Incl. short-term invest. NA-Not Available.

Business Summary

Provident Life and Accident Insurance Company of America and its subsidiaries offer accident, health, life and disability insurance on a group and individual basis throughout the United States, Puerto Rico, and parts of Canada.

Segment contributions in 1992 (before investment gains/losses) were derived as follows:

	Revs.	Pretax Profits
Employee benefits	32%	30%
Group Pension	30%	28%
Disability	25%	2%
Individual life	11%	26%
Other	2%	14%

The Employee Benefits division offers group accident and health, including managed care and administrative services only (ASO) plans; as well as term and ordinary life insurance (73% of life insurance in force at year end 1992) to small and large employers. At year-end 1992, the $8.8 billion of group pension funds under management were divided: 84% guaranteed investment contracts and 16% single premium annuities and other funds.

Disability coverage is sold to groups and individuals, mostly on a non-cancelable basis. PVB is the largest underwriter of individual long term, non-cancelable disability insurance in the U.S. Individual life policies (27% of in force life insurance) were divided: 52% universal/interest sensitive, 40% ordinary, 8% other.

Dividend Data

Dividends have been paid since 1925. In 1988, the company distributed one-fourth of a Class A share for each Class B share held. Payments are identical on the Class A and B common.

Amt. of Divd. $	Date Decl.	Ex–divd. Date	Stock of Record	Payment Date
0.25	Jul. 29	Aug. 25	Aug. 31	Sep. 10'92
0.25	Oct. 28	Nov. 23	Nov. 30	Dec. 10'92
0.26	Feb. 11	Feb. 22	Feb. 26	Mar. 10'93
0.26	May 5	May 24	May 28	Jun. 10'93

Capitalization

Long Term Debt: $206,000,000 (3/93).

Preferred Stock: $156,200,000.

Cl. A Common Stock: 8,494,795 shs. ($1 par). Has 0.05 vote per sh. Shareholders: 1,582.

Cl. B Common Stock: 36,666,233 shs. ($1 par). Some 49% controlled by Maclellan family and related trusts. Shareholders: 1,678.

Office—One Fountain Square, Chattanooga, TN 37402. **Tel**—(615) 755-1011. **Pres & CEO**—W. W. Walker (until 10/1/93). **EVP & COO**—T. C. Hardy. **Dirs**—W. L. Armstrong, R. A. Burgin, E. V. Clarke Jr., H. B. Jacks, W. B. Johnson, H. O. Maclellan Sr., H. O. Maclellan Jr., C. W. Pollard, S. L. Probasco Jr., T. F. Reid, B. E. Sorensen, W. W. Walker. **Transfer Agent & Registrar**—First Chicago Trust Co., NYC. **Incorporated** in Tennessee in 1887. **Empl**—4,978.

 Catherine A. Seifert

Public Service of Colorado

NYSE Symbol PSR In S&P MidCap 400

Price	Range	P-E Ratio	Dividend	Yield	S&P Ranking	Beta
Sep. 24'93	1993					
32	33⅜–27½	15	2.00	6.3%	B+	0.23

Summary

This Denver-based utility provides electric and natural gas service throughout most of Colorado, including Denver. PSR plans to decommission the nuclear aspects of its Fort St. Vrain nuclear plant and repower it with natural gas in a phased approach. Share earnings may decline slightly in 1994 from those projected for 1993, reflecting a full year of possibly reduced rates. However, strong cash flow and the resolution of problems posed by Fort St. Vrain enhance the company's longer-term prospects.

Current Outlook

Share earnings for 1993 are projected at $2.40, up from the $2.16 of 1992, which included fourth quarter writedowns totaling $0.44. Share earnings could decline slightly to $2.35 in 1994.

Dividends are currently projected to be maintained at $0.50 quarterly.

Share earnings for 1993 should benefit from the absence of writedowns of $0.44 in the fourth quarter of 1992, partially offset by possibly lower rates (the effective date would be December 1) and a $0.05 writeoff of an investment in the Templeton Gap Methane Recycling Facility (recognized in the second quarter as part of an ongoing effort to focus on its core business). Share earnings for 1994 may reflect a full year of possibly reduced rates.

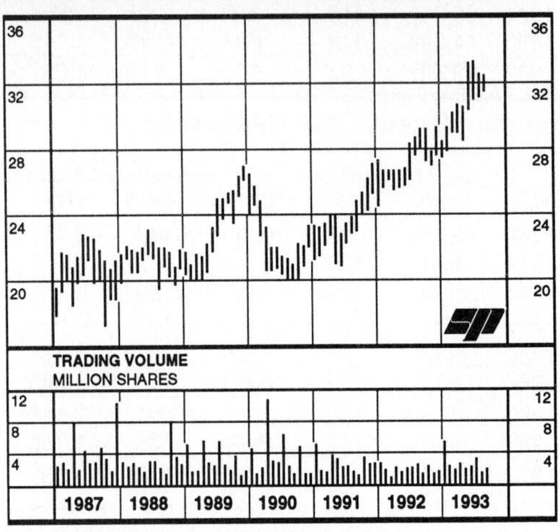

Operating Revenues (Million $)

Quarter:	1993	1992	1991	1990
Mar.	607	527	551	513
Jun.	448	422	391	419
Sep.	---	407	380	364
Dec.	---	506	474	438
	---	1,862	1,795	1,734

Revenues for the six months to June 30, 1993, rose 11%, year to year, primarily reflecting the addition of four wholesale customers previously served by the bankrupt Colorado-Ute Electric Association. After a $3.1 million ($0.05 a share) after-tax write-off of the Templeton Gap Methane Recycling investment, net income was up 5.3%. Share earnings were $1.23, versus $1.21.

Common Share Earnings ($)

Quarter:	1993	1992	1991	1990
Mar.	0.94	0.76	0.77	0.74
Jun.	0.29	0.45	0.16	0.51
Sep.	E0.43	0.46	0.56	0.58
Dec.	E0.74	0.49	0.99	0.67
	E2.40	2.16	2.48	2.49

Important Developments

Jul. '93— PSR said that, pursuant to its request, hearings for its rate case before the Colorado PUC have been scheduled for the weeks beginning August 16, August 23 and September 13. PSR requested the delay because more time was needed to discuss various options, including a possible settlement, with intervenors in the case. Hearings were to have started on July 6. An initial decision is now expected on October 27. The decision should be final on or before November 30. In May, the Colorado Office of Consumer Counsel asked for a $40 million rate reduction, and called for a reduction in the authorized return on equity to 10.75% from the current 14.4%. Also in May, the PUC staff called for a $5.8 million reduction, and asked that the authorized return on equity be lowered to 10.79%. In January, PSR filed a request for an $81.6 million increase, along with an authorized rate of return on equity of 13%.

Next earnings report expected in late October.

Per Share Data ($)

Yr. End Dec. 31	1992	1991	1990	1989	1988	1987	1986	1985	1984	1983
Tangible Bk. Val.	**18.48**	18.02	17.36	16.80	16.14	15.98	14.91	16.96	17.15	16.52
Earnings[1]	**2.16**	2.48	2.49	2.59	2.14	2.49	2.06	1.81	2.55	1.86
Dividends	**2.00**	2.00	2.00	2.00	2.00	2.00	2.00	1.98	1.90	1.82
Payout Ratio	**93%**	81%	80%	77%	93%	80%	97%	109%	75%	98%
Prices—High	**29⅝**	27⅛	26½	27	23⅛	22⅞	22⅜	24¼	19⅝	19
Low	**24½**	20⅞	20	20	19½	17¼	16	18¼	16¼	16⅛
P/E Ratio—	**14–11**	11–8	11–8	10–8	11–9	9–7	11–8	13–10	8–6	10–9

Data as orig. reptd. 1. Bef. spec. items of +0.56 in 1987, -1.93 in 1986. E-Estimated.

Income Data (Million $)

Year Ended Dec. 31	Revs.	Depr.	Maint.	Oper. Ratio	[1]Fxd. Chgs. Cover.	Constr. Credits	Eff. Tax Rate	[2]Net Inc.	% Return On— Revs.	[3]Invest. Capital	[4]Com. Equity
1992	**1,862**	**127**	**72.5**	**86.6%**	**2.33**	**11.3**	**28.0%**	**137**	**7.3**	**9.6**	**11.7**
1991	1,795	112	67.2	86.4%	2.82	9.4	31.6%	150	8.3	10.2	13.8
1990	1,734	107	85.5	86.3%	2.89	6.7	33.6%	146	8.4	10.3	14.3
1989	1,741	103	86.8	85.9%	2.79	3.6	30.9%	149	8.6	10.8	15.4
1988	1,685	101	94.6	87.0%	2.53	0.9	32.8%	125	7.4	9.9	13.0
1987	1,657	105	71.9	86.1%	3.48	2.0	45.5%	144	8.7	10.6	15.7
1986	1,658	105	86.6	85.6%	2.27	4.5	32.6%	124	7.5	10.7	12.7
1985	1,747	101	95.4	89.4%	2.97	6.2	47.8%	111	6.3	8.2	10.5
1984	1,802	97	72.5	88.3%	3.74	9.7	48.6%	145	8.1	10.0	15.0
1983	1,629	92	64.1	89.0%	2.92	8.7	46.8%	106	6.5	8.5	11.2

Balance Sheet Data (Million $)

Dec. 31	Gross Prop.	Capital Expend.	Net Prop.	% Earn. on Net Prop.	Total Cap.	Capitalization— LT Debt	% LT Debt	Pfd.	% Pfd.	Com.	% Com.
1992	**4,814**	**262**	**3,078**	**8.6**	**2,886**	**1,197**	**48.2**	**183**	**7.4**	**1,101**	**44.4**
1991	4,274	261	2,746	9.1	2,505	900	42.5	184	8.7	1,034	48.8
1990	4,039	261	2,609	9.4	2,398	883	43.4	186	9.2	964	47.4
1989	3,825	174	2,468	10.1	2,333	904	45.2	189	9.5	905	45.3
1988	3,702	163	2,413	9.1	2,293	933	46.9	192	9.6	865	43.5
1987	3,592	128	2,379	9.6	2,279	909	46.4	194	9.9	858	43.7
1986	3,552	196	2,411	9.8	2,095	835	45.3	207	11.2	801	43.5
1985	3,498	238	2,474	7.7	2,384	928	45.4	219	10.7	898	43.9
1984	3,282	197	2,355	9.1	2,312	883	44.1	227	11.3	894	44.6
1983	3,065	195	2,233	8.2	2,207	886	45.8	228	11.8	821	42.4

Data as orig. reptd. **1.** Times int. exp. & pfd. divs. covered (pretax basis). **2.** Bef. spec. items. **3.** Based on income before interest charges. **4.** As reptd. by co.

Business Summary

Public Service of Colorado and its subsidiaries supply electric and natural gas service to a population of some 2.7 million throughout Colorado, including Denver. Other interests are primarily in energy-related operations and real estate holdings. Segment contributions in 1992:

	Revs.	Profits
Electric	68%	92%
Gas	31%	4%
Other	1%	4%

In 1992, coal represented some 99% of PSR's generation, and natural gas/oil accounted for 1%. Approximately 32% of the total electric system input was from purchased power. Peak load in 1992 was 3,757 mw and capability was 4,658 mw, for a capacity margin of 19%.

In August 1989, PSR decided to end operations at its Fort St. Vrain nuclear plant. As a consequence of the plant's limited operations and the subsequent removal from rate base of PSR's investment in the facility, several losses have been recognized, including the 1986 writeoff of $101.4 million ($1.93 a share) of unrecoverable costs, and an additional writeoff of $39.6 million ($0.75) in 1988. PSR's remaining investment in the plant at December 31, 1992, was some $62.5 million.

Auditors noted in their report on PSR's 1992 financial statements uncertainties related to the Fort St. Vrain nuclear station, including the ultimate recovery of the company's remaining investment in the facility. Recovery is primarily dependent on PSR's ability to repower the facility with natural gas. PSR intends to repower Fort St. Vrain in a phased approach, with completion of the first phase in 1996 rather than completion of repowering in 1998, as previously disclosed.

Dividend Data

Dividends have been paid since 1907. A dividend reinvestment plan is available.

Amt of Divd. $	Date Decl.	Ex-divd. Date	Stock of Record	Payment Date
0.50	Sep. 22	Oct. 5	Oct. 9	Nov. 1'92
0.50	Dec. 22	Jan. 4	Jan. 8	Feb. 1'93
0.50	Mar. 23	Apr. 2	Apr. 9	May 1'93
0.50	Jun. 22	Jul. 2	Jul. 9	Aug. 1'93

Capitalization

Long Term Debt: $1,139,593,000 (6/93).

Red. Cum. Preferred Stock: $43,078,000.

Cum. Preferred Stock: $140,008,000.

Common Stock: 59,703,821 shs. ($5 par).
Institutions hold about 31%.
Shareholders of record: 56,069.

Office—1225 17th St., Denver, CO 80202. **Tel**—(303) 571-7511. **Chrmn & Pres**—D. D. Hock. **VP-Secy**—J. R. McCotter. **SVP-CFO**—R. C. Kelly. **Investor Contact**—Michael D. Pritchard. **Dirs**—C. P. Chandler Jr., D. M. Drury, T. T. Farley, G. L. Greer, A. B. Hirschfeld, D. D. Hock, G. B. McKinley, W. F. Nicholson Jr., J. M. Powers, T. E. Rodriguez, R. E. Slifer, W. T. Stephens, R. G. Tointon. **Transfer Agent & Registrar**—Co.'s office. **Incorporated** in Colorado in 1924. **Empl**—6,568.

 Christopher J. Grant

Public Service of New Mexico

NYSE Symbol PNM In S&P MidCap 400

Price	Range	P-E Ratio	Dividend	Yield	S&P Ranking	Beta
Aug. 26'93	1993					
11¼	13⅞–9⅞	NM	None	None	B	0.65

Summary

Public Service of New Mexico reported a $104.3 million ($2.67 a share) net loss for 1992, reflecting one-time after-tax charges in the fourth quarter of $126.2 million ($3.02) which were mostly due to a write-down of PNM's investment in Palo Verde nuclear unit 3. The charges were taken to recognize a recent change in PNM's strategy which is designed to restore its financial health, reduce New Mexico electric prices, and meet changing needs for energy services in the future.

Current Outlook

Share earnings for 1993 could reach $1.10, versus 1992's $2.67 loss, which included one-time charges of $3.02 primarily related to Palo Verde Unit 3. Share earnings could rise to $1.25 in 1994.

Early restoration of the common dividend, omitted in April 1989, is unlikely.

Share earnings for 1993 should reflect load growth, the absence of large one-time charges due mostly to writedowns on Palo Verde Unit 3 and a purchased power contract, a lower drag on earnings from excess capacity, an $0.18 gain on the sale of assets in the first quarter and an expected $0.13 gain in the third quarter on the recent sale of 50 mw of San Juan Unit 4 capacity, partly offset by a $0.34 restructuring charge incurred in the first quarter. Share earnings for 1994 should reflect lower kwh sales, a possible slight rate decrease late in the year but much lower operating costs. The estimates exclude a possible a possible write-down on Palo Verde 1 & 2 in either year, and possible additional gains on asset sales during either or both years.

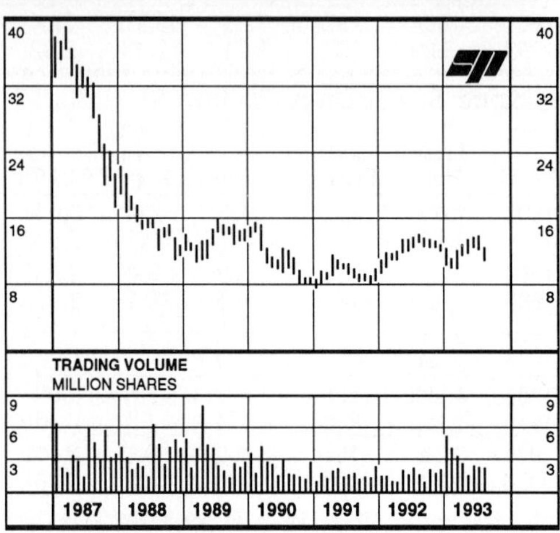

Operating Revenues (Million $)

Quarter:	1993	1992	1991	1990
Mar.	248.6	236.8	248.5	254.4
Jun.	190.8	189.5	194.2	195.7
Sep.	---	206.3	199.2	193.2
Dec.	---	219.5	215.3	211.8
	---	852.0	857.2	855.1

Revenues for the six months to June 30, 1993, rose 3.1%, year to year. However, net income fell 17%, to $0.34 a share from $0.42.

Common Share Earnings ($)

Quarter:	1993	1992	1991	1990
Mar.	0.25	0.34	0.26	d0.17
Jun.	0.09	0.08	d0.10	d0.08
Sep.	E0.46	0.16	0.16	0.13
Dec.	E0.30	d3.25	Nil	d0.11
	E1.10	d2.67	0.32	d0.23

Important Developments

Aug. '93— PNM sold a 50 mw interest in San Jaun Unit 4 to the City of Anaheim. PNM expects to incur fewer losses from its excluded capacity in 1993 than it had in prior years, due to factors including the 50 mw sale to Anaheim (expected to result in a $0.13 a share gain and ongoing annual operating cost savings of $0.06 - $0.08 a share), a pending sale of 30 - 40 mw of San Juan Unit 4 capacity to the Utah Associated Municipal Power System (expected to add $0.04 - $0.06 to share earnings), a one-year contract with Public Service Co. of Colorado (executed in April and expected to add $0.04 - $0.05 to share earnings), and benefits of $0.40 - $0.50 a share from the 1992 writedowns on Palo Verde Unit 3 and a purchased power contract. In July, PNM verbally agreed to sell its Sangre de Cristo Water Co. unit to the city of Santa Fe for $48 million. The sale is not expected to close prior to the second quarter of 1994.

Next earnings report expected in late October.

Per Share Data ($)

Yr. End Dec. 31	1992	1991	1990	1989	1988	1987	1986	1985	1984	1983
Tangible Bk. Val.	**15.00**	17.69	17.36	18.02	18.03	25.68	26.51	25.73	25.28	25.21
Earnings[1]	**d2.67**	0.32	d0.23	1.73	d0.50	2.00	3.29	3.30	3.11	3.53
Dividends	**Nil**	Nil	Nil	0.38	1.87	2.92	2.92	2.89	2.85	2.81
Payout Ratio	**Nil**	Nil	Nil	22%	NM	146%	89%	88%	92%	80%
Prices—High	**14⅛**	11⅝	15½	15⅞	22⅜	39¼	37⅞	30¾	26⅝	29⅝
Low	**9⅜**	7⅝	8	10¾	11	17⅜	28	23⅞	19½	22¾
P/E Ratio—	**NM**	36–24	NM	9–6	NM	20–9	12–9	9–7	9–6	8–6

Data as orig. reptd. **1.** Bef. results of disc. opers. of -4.16 in 1988; bef. spec. item(s) of -1.12 in 1988. d-Deficit. E-Estimated. NM-Not Meaningful.

Income Data (Million $)

Year Ended Dec. 31	Revs.	Depr.	Maint.	Oper. Ratio	[1]Fxd. Chgs. Cover.	Constr. Credits	Eff. Tax Rate	[2]Net Inc.	% Return On— Revs.	[3]Invest. Capital	[4]Com. Equity
1992	**852**	**79.3**	**54.3**	**86.7%**	**NM**	**1.2**	**NM**	**d104.3**	**NM**	**NM**	**NM**
1991	857	76.1	52.2	88.7%	1.36	2.9	30.7%	23.0	2.7	4.7	1.8
1990	855	73.2	56.4	89.2%	0.97	3.5	NM	NM	0.1	3.6	NM
1989	915	72.0	50.8	83.3%	2.14	4.8	27.6%	83.0	9.0	8.0	9.5
1988	842	66.9	46.6	83.4%	0.96	7.1	NM	d10.0	NM	3.5	NM
1987	690	60.3	43.5	80.8%	2.16	34.3	8.2%	95.0	13.8	7.0	7.7
1986	698	60.2	41.9	74.1%	2.24	48.8	41.5%	151.0	21.6	9.3	12.8
1985	749	55.8	43.9	75.1%	2.16	80.8	40.3%	146.0	19.5	9.9	13.2
1984	445	49.0	34.1	67.1%	2.31	76.4	25.9%	133.0	29.8	9.4	12.5
1983	397	47.2	32.0	65.7%	2.48	65.1	27.2%	141.0	35.4	10.2	14.3

Balance Sheet Data (Million $)

Dec. 31	[5]Gross Prop.	Capital Expend.	Net Prop.	% Earn. on Net Prop.	Total Cap.	Capitalization— LT Debt	% LT Debt	Pfd.	% Pfd.	Com.	% Com.
1992	**2,690**	**95**	**1,877**	**5.9**	**1,807**	**911**	**56.2**	**84.7**	**5.2**	**626**	**38.6**
1991	2,665	80	1,905	5.1	1,907	786	48.8	86.0	5.3	739	45.9
1990	2,612	81	1,914	4.8	1,883	790	48.8	105.0	6.4	725	44.8
1989	2,585	74	1,932	8.0	1,926	801	48.2	108.0	6.5	753	45.3
1988	2,454	87	1,885	7.4	2,049	981	53.1	114.0	6.2	753	40.7
1987	2,403	93	1,893	7.0	2,364	891	42.8	120.0	5.7	1,072	51.5
1986	2,366	163	1,903	8.9	2,431	902	42.5	125.0	5.9	1,095	51.6
1985	2,613	263	2,191	8.7	2,612	1,143	48.7	225.0	9.6	977	41.7
1984	2,406	278	2,123	7.3	2,388	1,031	47.5	227.0	10.5	913	42.0
1983	2,140	262	1,900	7.3	2,232	974	47.3	230.0	11.2	856	41.5

Data as orig. reptd. **1.** Times int. exp. & pfd. divs. covered (pretax basis). **2.** Bef. results of disc. opers in 1988; bef. spec. item(s) in 1988. **3.** Based on income before interest charges. **4.** As reptd. by Co. **5.** Utility plant. d-Deficit. NM-Not Meaningful.

Business Summary

Public Service of New Mexico, which operates electric (70.0% of 1992 revenues), gas (28.5%), and water (1.5%) utilities, serves some 1.1 million people primarily in Albuquerque and throughout the state. Electric revenues in recent years (restated to reflect changes in classifications):

	1992	1991	1990	1989
Residential	27%	27%	27%	23%
Commercial	36%	37%	37%	31%
Industrial	12%	12%	12%	10%
Wholesale	21%	19%	18%	31%
Other	4%	5%	6%	5%

Sources of generation in 1992 were coal 69%, and nuclear 31%. Peak demand in 1992 was 1,053 mw and system capability totaled 1,591 mw, for a capacity margin of 34%.

In 1992's fourth quarter PNM incurred one-time charges (net) totaling $126.2 million, due primarily to the writedown of Palo Verde 3 and the provision for loss associated with the Modesto-Santa Clara Redding power purchase contract. PNM had a retained earnings deficit of $52.5 million at December 31, 1992. In 1989's second quarter, the New Mexico Public Service Commission ruled that PNM may seek rate treatment for its 260 mw in units 1 & 2 of the Palo Verde nuclear project and 147 mw from the San Juan 4 coal plant. The decision excluded PNM's 130 mw in Palo Verde 3, 130 mw in San Juan 4, and the 105 mw purchased power contract. As a result of the order, PNM charged off in 1988 $66.6 million (net) for deferred carrying costs of capacity. PNM also wrote off some $38.1 million (net) for an abandoned power project in addition to $10.6 million (net) for miscellaneous operating items. Also in 1988, PNM charged off $173.6 million (net) for nonutility operations. In 1989's second quarter PNM completed a quasi-reorganization which resulted in the transfer of a portion of paid-in capital to retained earnings. The transaction eliminated the retained earnings deficit.

Dividend Data

Common dividends were omitted in April 1989 after having been paid since 1942. Dividends on the preferred stocks have been maintained.

Capitalization

Long Term Debt: $908,843,000 (6/93).

Red. Preferred Stock: $24,400,000.

Cum. Preferred Stock: $59,000,000.

Common Stock: 41,774,083 shs. ($5 par).
Institutions hold about 55%.
Shareholders of record: 27,649.

Office—Alvarado Square, Albuquerque, NM 87158. **Tel**—(505) 848-2700. **Chrmn**—J. T. Ackerman. **Pres & CEO**—B. F. Montoya. **VP-CFO**—M. H. Maerki. **Investor Contact**—Barbara Barsky. **Dirs**—J. T. Ackerman, R. G. Armstrong, V. L. Fisher, J. A. Godwin, L. H. Lattman, C. E. Leyendecker, R. U. Ortiz, R. M. Price, P. F. Roth. **Transfer Agent & Registrar**—Company's office, Albuquerque. **Incorporated** in New Mexico in 1917. **Empl**—3,080.

 Christopher J. Grant

Puget Sound Power & Light

NYSE Symbol PSD In S&P MidCap 400

Price	Range	P-E Ratio	Dividend	Yield	S&P Ranking	Beta
Jul. 28'93	1993					
28½	29⅜–26⅛	14	1.84	6.5%	B+	0.54

Summary

This moderate-size electric utility serves nearly 800,000 customers in the Puget Sound region of Washington State. Hydro is the primary power source, and current generating capacity is adequate for the foreseeable future. Earnings for 1993 should benefit from continued customer growth and base rate increases. The local economy has been strong in recent years due to residential development, but signs that the Pacific Northwest's economy may be slowing could moderate customer growth in the long-term.

Current Outlook

Earnings for 1993 are projected at $2.20 a share, up from 1992's $2.16. Earnings for 1994 are projected at $2.25 a share.

Directors raised the quarterly dividend 2.2%, to $0.46 from $0.45, with the May 15, 1993 payment.

A modest advance in earnings is expected for 1993, reflecting strong customer growth averaging 3% per year (20,000 more customers are projected for 1993) and rate increases from the periodic rate adjustment mechanism (PRAM). Under this cost recovery mechanism, revenues are no longer materially influenced by swings in surplus electricity sales, unseasonally hot or cold weather, and variations in conditions for hydroelectric generation. Future profits should also benefit from a $69 millon request for a general rate increase that could become effective in October 1993.

Operating Revenues (Million $)

Quarter:	1994	1993	1992	1991
Mar.	---	324.0	280.2	276.1
Jun.	---	237.6	240.6	216.8
Sep.	---	---	219.2	208.9
Dec.	---	---	284.9	254.9
	---	---	1,025.0	956.8

Revenues for the six months ended June 30, 1993, rose 7.8%, year to year, reflecting customer growth and a rate increase as a result of the PRAM. Generally higher costs narrowed margins, holding the gain in net income to 4.3%. After significantly higher preferred dividends and on 6.4% more shares, earnings per share were $1.22, versus $1.30.

Common Share Earnings ($)

Quarter:	1994	1993	1992	1991
Mar.	E0.85	0.86	0.83	0.97
Jun.	E0.40	0.37	0.47	0.40
Sep.	E0.35	E0.35	0.25	0.35
Dec.	E0.65	E0.62	0.62	0.49
	E2.25	E2.20	2.16	2.21

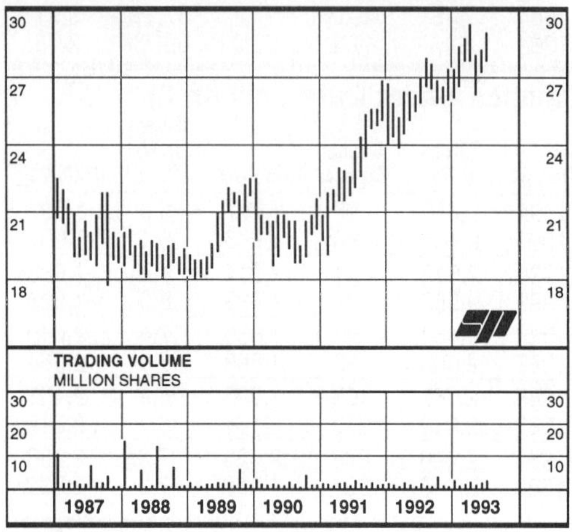

Important Developments

May '93— PSD filed for a $76.2 million rate adjustment under its PRAM to recover the increased costs of power during the severe drought and poor hydro conditions experienced over the last two years. The PRAM recovery is separate from the $69 million general rate increase requested in October 1992 to provide new power supplies. Power supply uncertainties facing the company include the closing of the Trojan nuclear plant. Also, supply uncertainties entail the Endangered Species Act as it relates to the Columbia and Snake River hydro systems. Through 1995, PSD anticipates adding 600 mw of firm power from Washington State cogeneration projects. The company expects to make an $86 million investment during the fall of 1993 in Bonneville Power Administration's construction of a third 500 KV AC tranmission line. PSD has requested 400 mw of firm capacity on the line.

Next earnings report expected in late October.

Per Share Data ($)

Yr. End Dec. 31	1992	1991	1990	1989	1988	1987	1986	1985	1984	1983
Tangible Bk. Val.	**17.57**	16.82	16.37	15.95	15.80	15.30	15.06	15.56	15.27	16.89
Earnings[1]	**2.16**	2.21	2.16	1.88	2.14	2.13	1.74	2.07	1.52	1.93
Dividends	**1.79**	1.76	1.76	1.76	1.76	1.76	1.76	1.76	1.76	1.76
Payout Ratio	**83%**	80%	81%	94%	82%	83%	101%	85%	116%	91%
Prices—High	**27⅞**	26⅞	22½	22½	20¼	22½	25¼	18⅜	15	16½
Low	**23⅞**	19⅛	18⅝	18	18	17¾	17⅝	12⅝	9¼	13⅛
P/E Ratio—	**13–11**	12–9	10–9	12–10	9–8	11–8	15–10	9–8	10–6	9–7

Data as orig. reptd. 1. Bef. spec. item of -1.04 in 1984. E-Estimated

Income Data (Million $)

Year Ended Dec. 31	Revs.	Depr.	Maint.	Oper. Ratio	[1]Fxd. Chgs. Cover.	Constr. Credits	Eff. Tax Rate	[2]Net Inc.	% Return On: Revs.	[3]Invest. Capital	[4]Com. Equity
1992	**1,025**	**123**	**55.7**	**79.1%**	**2.77**	**3.5**	**34.0%**	**136**	**13.2**	**10.2**	**12.6**
1991	957	116	56.2	77.7%	2.85	4.5	29.4%	133	13.9	10.2	13.2
1990	935	111	51.1	77.0%	2.92	4.9	33.0%	132	14.2	10.3	13.3
1989	888	102	50.9	78.7%	2.30	3.9	15.8%	118	13.3	9.6	11.7
1988	791	98	47.3	77.3%	2.40	2.4	12.6%	128	16.2	10.3	13.6
1987	729	94	42.8	77.2%	2.27	1.7	9.2%	120	16.5	9.9	13.9
1986	715	87	35.7	76.4%	2.49	25.8	32.9%	110	15.4	8.7	11.5
1985	714	75	32.4	75.8%	2.97	47.1	38.2%	126	17.6	9.4	13.4
1984	657	62	31.2	76.6%	2.30	40.7	39.0%	95	14.5	8.8	9.2
1983	519	42	28.4	77.4%	2.81	72.0	34.4%	102	19.7	8.1	11.4

Balance Sheet Data (Million $)

Dec. 31	[5]Gross Prop.	[6]Capital Expend.	Net Prop.	% Earn. on Net Prop.	Total Cap.	Capitalization: LT Debt	% LT Debt	Pfd.	% Pfd.	Com.	% Com.
1992	**3,010**	**186**	**1,909**	**11.4**	**2,367**	**1,045**	**44.6**	**259**	**11.0**	**1,040**	**44.4**
1991	2,846	154	1,846	11.8	2,177	1,052	48.8	160	7.4	942	43.8
1990	2,701	132	1,792	12.1	2,119	1,006	48.0	169	8.1	918	43.9
1989	2,586	130	1,766	10.8	2,093	980	47.8	175	8.5	859	43.7
1988	2,474	114	1,738	10.4	2,123	988	48.2	179	8.8	881	43.0
1987	2,371	112	1,721	9.6	2,097	990	52.1	84	4.4	827	43.5
1986	2,295	121	1,732	9.4	2,120	1,015	51.0	189	9.5	787	39.5
1985	2,333	117	1,854	9.5	2,123	1,000	49.8	225	11.2	785	39.0
1984	2,192	143	1,782	8.5	1,972	945	49.6	225	11.8	735	38.6
1983	2,212	202	1,825	6.6	1,920	900	47.9	227	12.1	751	40.0

Data as orig. reptd. **1.** Times int. exp. & pfd. divs. covered (pretax basis). **2.** Bef. spec. item(s). **3.** Based on income before interest charges. **4.** As reptd. by co. **5.** Utility plant. **6.** Excl. allow. for funds used during constr.

Business Summary

Puget Sound Power & Light provides electricity nearly 800,000 customers located in a suburban and rural area of western Washington State. Contributions to revenues by customer class in recent years were:

	1992	1991	1990	1989
Residential	46%	50%	52%	51%
Commercial	34%	32%	33%	30%
Industrial	14%	13%	14%	12%
Other	6%	5%	1%	7%

The fuel mix in 1992 was: 51% hydroelectric and 49% coal. Peak load in 1992 was 3,906 mw and system capability was 5,105 mw, for a capacity margin of 23.5%. Electric sales in 1992 totaled 19,508 kwh, down 3.3% from 1991.

With the placement of the 700-mw coal-fired Colstrip unit 4 (25%-owned) into commercial operation in April 1986, PSD has no plans to build new generating facilities. An identical unit, Colstrip 3 (also 25% owned), was placed into commercial operation in 1984. Construction expenditures for 1993 and 1994 were expected to total $321 million and $256 million, respectively. These expenditures are primarily transmission and distribution-related, designed to meet continuing customer growth.

Finances

On June 24, 1993, PSD offered 3,000,000 common shares for public sale at $27⅞ per share. Net proceeds exceeding $81,000,000 were earmarked to repay debt from PSD's construction program and for other corporate purposes. On October 15, 1992, PSD offered 2,000,000 common shares for public sale at $26.50 per share.

Dividend Data

Dividends have been paid since 1943. A dividend reinvestment plan is available. A preferred stock rights plan was adopted in January 1991.

Amt of Divd. $	Date Decl.	Ex–divd. Date	Stock of Record	Payment Date
0.45	Oct. 8	Oct. 20	Oct. 26	Nov. 15'92
0.45	Jan. 12	Jan. 19	Jan. 25	Feb. 15'93
0.46	Apr. 13	Apr. 20	Apr. 26	May 15'93
0.46	Jul. 13	Jul. 20	Jul. 26	Aug. 15'93

Capitalization

Long Term Debt: $1,064,981,000 (3/93).

Red. Cum. Preferred Stock: $93,222,000.

Cum. Preferred Stock: $115,000,000.

Common Stock: 62,324,321 shs. (no par).
Institutions hold about 15%.
Shareholders of record: 64,554.

Office—411 - 108th Ave. N.E., Bellevue, WA. 98004-5515. **Tel**—(206) 454-6363. **Chrmn**—J. W. Ellis. **Pres & CEO**—R. R. Sonstelie. **Secy**—J. Elredge. **VP-Fin & Investor Contact**—Russel E. Olson (206) 462-3712. **Dirs**—D. P. Beighle, C. W. Bingham, P. J. Campbell, J. H. Dunkak III, J. D. Durbin, J. W. Ellis, D. J. Evans, N. L. Jacob, R. R. Sonstelie, W. S. Weaver, R. K. Wilson. **Transfer Agents & Registrars**—The Bank of New York, NYC; Co.'s office. **Incorporated** in Washington in 1960. **Empl**—2,775.

Ned Bancroft

Puritan-Bennett

NASDAQ Symbol PBEN Options on Pacific (Mar-Jun-Sep-Dec) (Incl. in Nat'l Market) In S&P MidCap 400

Price	Range	P-E Ratio	Dividend	Yield	S&P Ranking	Beta
Sep. 16'93	1993					
17¼	34–13¼	47	0.12	0.7%	B+	1.57

Summary

This company makes a diversified line of respiratory products used in a wide variety of healthcare settings and on aircraft. In September 1992, the company commenced shipments of an intra-arterial blood gas monitoring system, and remains the only company to have introduced and begun shipments of such a product. Restucturing charges of nearly $10 million led to unprofitable results in 1993-94's first half.

Business Summary

Puritan-Bennett develops and makes products related to respiration, used in a wide variety of healthcare settings and on aircraft. The company serves three market segments: the hospital market; the home respiratory care, medical gases and physicians markets; and the aviation markets. Sales contributions for the years ended January 31, 1993 and December 31, 1991 were:

	1993	1991
Home Care	31%	27%
Hospital/Physician	61%	63%
Aviation	8%	10%

International sales represented 18% of total revenues in fiscal 1992-93, up from 16% in 1991.

The Bennett Group provides a microprocessor controlled ventilator to the hospital market, which is designed to ease the work of patient breathing and reduce discomfort. Significant products in this group include the 7200 Series Ventilatory System, PBEN's most advanced ventilator; The PB 3300 Intra-Arterial Blood Gas Monitoring System (shipments commenced in September 1992 in the U.S. and Japan), which measures the levels of oxygen and carbon dioxide in a patient's arterial blood, as well as the blood's pH (relative acidity or alkalinity); and CliniVision, a PC-based patient care and respiratory therapy department management information system that integrates the patient data captured and processed by the 7200 system.

Patients suffering from various severe, chronic respiratory conditions as well as those requiring short-term respiratory therapy due to early hospital discharge are increasingly being cared for at home. In this non-hospital market, the Puritan Group's significant products include oxygen concentrators; liquid oxygen systems; high pressure oxygen systems, portable ventilators; manual resuscitators, sleep apnea systems and medical gases. In addition, the company operates a home health care service business in Southern Florida.

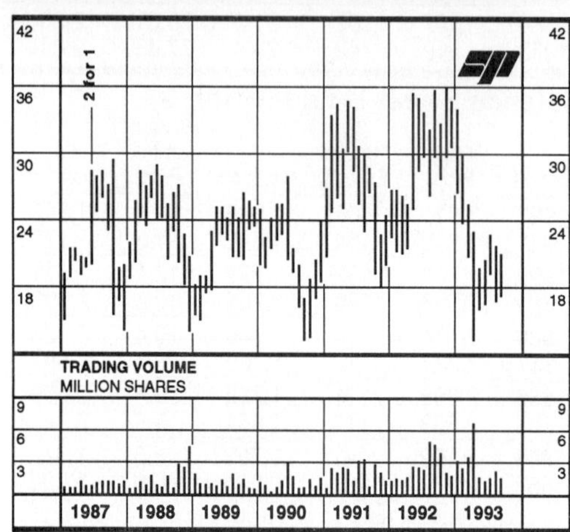

During the first quarter of fiscal 1993-94, the company's physician office business unit was transferred to the Puritan Group. The significant product within this unit is the hand-held PB100 Spirometer for analyzing lung function.

Through Aero Systems, Puritan manufactures high-altitude emergency oxygen equipment and assemblies for commercial jets and private aircraft. Aero is the primary supplier of chemical oxygen generators, passenger masks and passenger air valves for the Boeing 737, 757 and 767 aircraft and for all current models of the European Airbus. In late 1992-3, PBEN acquired proprietary rights and technology related to the manufacture and sale of airborne closed circuit television products.

PBEN also has a 56% stake in Medicomp Inc., a Florida corporation that develops, manufactures and distributes ambulatory cardiac monitors.

Next earnings report expected in late August.

Per Share Data ($)

Yr. End Jan. 31[1]	1993	1991	1990	1989	1988	1987	1986	1985	1984	1983
Tangible Bk. Val.	**10.12**	9.31	9.15	7.70	7.12	5.85	4.95	4.61	4.26	4.89
Cash Flow	**2.17**	0.91	2.15	2.12	1.86	1.51	1.42	0.78	0.02	0.60
Earnings	**1.24**	0.05	1.39	1.42	1.27	1.00	0.99	0.40	d0.38	0.22
Dividends	**0.120**	0.120	0.118	0.110	0.110	0.105	0.100	0.100	0.100	0.100
Payout Ratio	**10%**	NM	8%	8%	9%	11%	10%	26%	NM	46%
Prices—High	**36**	34¾	28	26½	29	29½	15⅞	7⅞	6¾	13½
Low	**21**	18	13¼	15	14	14⅛	7⅝	3⅝	3¼	5⅝
P/E Ratio—	**29–16**	NM	20–10	19–11	23–11	30–14	16–8	20–9	NM	62–26

Data as orig. reptd. Adj. for stk. divs. of 100% Jun. 1987, 100% May 1986. **1.** Prior to 1993 fisc. yr. ended Dec. 31. d-Deficit. NM-Not Meaningful.

Income Data (Million $)

Year Ended Jan. 31[1]	Revs.	Oper. Inc.	% Oper. Inc. of Revs.	Cap. Exp.	Depr.	Int. Exp.	Net Bef. Taxes	Eff. Tax Rate	Net Inc.	% Net Inc. of Revs.	Cash Flow
1993	**300**	**32.2**	**10.7**	**22.7**	**11.00**	**3.72**	**18.4**	**20.7%**	**14.6**	**4.9**	**25.6**
1991	256	10.6	4.1	26.4	9.97	3.81	d2.7	NM	0.6	0.2	10.5
1990	252	32.3	12.8	24.5	8.72	3.27	23.2	31.6%	15.9	6.3	24.6
1989	227	33.5	14.8	12.4	8.27	2.77	24.4	34.4%	16.0	7.1	23.9
1988	204	24.5	12.0	19.0	6.79	1.97	21.6	34.5%	14.1	6.9	20.8
1987	173	25.3	14.7	12.1	5.78	0.95	19.4	42.7%	11.1	6.4	16.7
1986	150	17.6	11.7	8.0	4.84	1.00	18.9	42.1%	[2]10.9	7.3	15.8
1985	124	10.9	8.8	5.1	5.00	1.00	7.3	32.2%	4.9	4.0	9.7
1984	119	2.1	1.8	5.3	4.77	2.14	d7.6	NM	d4.5	NM	0.3
1983	110	8.6	7.9	7.1	4.44	1.35	3.8	32.1%	2.6	2.3	7.0

Balance Sheet Data (Million $)

Jan. 31[1]	Cash	Curr. Assets	Curr. Liab.	Curr. Ratio	Total Assets	% Ret. on Assets	Long Term Debt	Common Equity	Total Cap.	% LT Debt of Cap.	% Ret. on Equity
1993	**0.40**	**127**	**46.3**	**2.8**	**244**	**6.4**	**42.8**	**134**	**178**	**24.1**	**11.4**
1991	0.54	110	38.8	2.8	209	0.3	34.5	121	156	22.1	0.5
1990	0.53	111	29.5	3.8	193	8.9	34.9	117	156	22.4	14.5
1989	0.59	96	31.4	3.1	164	10.4	21.1	100	125	16.9	17.2
1988	3.50	87	26.3	3.3	141	11.0	21.9	84	109	20.1	18.3
1987	0.40	74	32.8	2.3	116	10.4	6.1	69	79	7.8	17.3
1986	2.32	65	26.8	2.4	97	12.4	6.7	58	67	10.0	19.4
1985	0.82	56	20.8	2.7	91	5.3	1.6	63	67	2.3	8.1
1984	0.59	60	23.9	2.5	95	NM	8.3	57	68	12.2	NM
1983	0.76	65	26.4	2.5	100	2.8	9.1	61	74	12.4	4.3

Data as orig. reptd. **1.** Prior to 1993 fisc. yrs. ended December 31. **2.** Refl. acctg. change. d-Deficit. NM-Not Meaningful.

Net Sales (Million $)

[1]Quarter:	1993–94	1992–93	1991	1990
Apr.	75.4	70.5	58.3	61.9
Jul.	77.9	73.5	68.2	63.3
Oct.		76.6	65.0	61.6
Jan.		79.5	64.6	65.1
		300.1	256.1	251.9

Net sales in the six months ended July 31, 1993, rose 6.5%, year to year, as improved performance from the home care business segment outweighed weakness within the aviation business. SG&A costs were ahead 19%, and after restructuring charges of $9,590,000, a pretax deficit replaced income. After tax benefits of $3,163,000, versus taxes of $1,922,000 (21.0%), a net loss of $3,114,000 ($0.26 a share) contrasted with income of $7,232,000 ($0.61), before a charge of $0.23 a share in 1993-94 from the cumulative effect of an accounting change.

Common Share Earnings ($)

[1]Quarter:	1993–94	1992–93	1991	1990
Apr.	0.15	0.29	0.10	0.37
Jul.	d0.41	0.32	0.32	0.32
Oct.		0.33	0.21	0.35
Jan.		0.30	d0.58	0.35
		1.24	0.05	1.39

1. Prior to 1992-93 quarters ended Mar., Jun., Sep., Dec. d-Deficit.

Finances

In 1993-94's first half, PBEN began a restructuring which is expected to reduce annual costs by about $7 million. The actions included: consolidating aviation business facilities; a 15% staff reduction in the ventilator and blood gas monitoring divisions; the move of most blood gas monitoring operations from leased to owned facilities; a writedown of blood gas sensor manufacturing equipment; a reduction of administrative positions; and the consolidation of offices in France.

In April 1993, a joint venture between the company and its hospital products distributor in Germany, began selling, servicing and supporting PBEN's hospital products in Germany.

Dividend Data

Cash has been paid each year since 1976.

Amt. of Divd. $	Date Decl.	Ex–divd. Date	Stock of Record	Payment Date
0.03	Oct. 30	Nov. 9	Nov. 16	Nov. 30'92
0.03	Jan. 29	Feb. 9	Feb. 16	Feb. 28'93
0.03	Apr. 30	May 10	May 14	May 31'93
0.03	Jul. 30	Aug. 10	Aug. 16	Aug. 31'93

Capitalization

Long Term Debt: $42,840,000 (4/93).

Common Stock: 11,960,006 shs. ($1 par). Institutions hold about 66%. Shareholders: 3,300 of record (1/93).

Office—9401 Indian Creek Parkway, P.O. Box 25905, Overland Park, KS 66225-5905. **Tel**—(913) 661-0444. **Chrmn, Pres & CEO**—B.A. Dole Jr. **EVP-COO**—J.H. Morrow. **VP-CFO & Contr**—L.A. Robbins. **Secy**—D.C. Weary. **Treas**—D.S. Treff. **Dirs**—B.A. Dole Jr., C. Duboc, C.P. Larson Jr., A.F. Marion, T.A. Reed, D.C. Weary, F.P. Wilton. **Transfer Agent & Registrar**—United Missouri Bank, Kansas City. **Incorporated** in Delaware in 1968. **Empl**—2,600.

 Robert M. Gold

Quaker State

NYSE Symbol KSF Options on ASE (Mar-Jun-Sep-Dec) In S&P MidCap 400

Price	Range	P-E Ratio	Dividend	Yield	S&P Ranking	Beta
Jul. 29'93	1993					
12¾	14¼–11⅛	28	0.40	3.1%	B–	0.67

Summary

This company is a major producer of branded motor oils, and makes other automotive products including filters, anti-freeze and coatings. It also provides nationwide fast lube services, and owns a credit insurance company. Operations are being restructured and KSF is exiting those areas that don't provide long-term profit opportunities. Earnings should recover in 1993 and 1994, benefiting from an improved cost structure, international expansion, and the recovery in the domestic economy. As part of the restructuring, KSF has cut the quarterly dividend 50% with the September 1993 payment.

Current Outlook

Share earnings for 1994 are projected at $0.95, up from 1993's estimated $0.75.

The quarterly dividend was cut 50%, to $0.10 from $0.20, with the July 1993 declaration.

Revenues should firm in 1993 and 1994 as the economic recovery gains momentum, aiding consumer product sales. Intense competitive pressures in KSF's lubricant and refined products business will limit increases in retail prices, volumes and margins. The long-term outlook is enhanced by expansion in foreign markets.

[4]Revenues (Million $)

Quarter:	1993	1992	1991	1990
Mar.	181.7	173.4	188.5	209.0
Jun.	197.2	189.7	211.7	222.8
Sep.	---	187.2	212.7	225.1
Dec.	---	174.0	200.8	217.3
	---	724.4	813.6	874.1

Revenues for the six months ended June 30, 1993, rose 3.5%, year to year, as gains in insurance and vehicular lighting offset a decline in refining and marketing revenues. Lower selling, general and administrative expenses and reduced noncash charges led to wider margins, and net income increased 50%, to $0.29 a share from $0.19. Results for the 1992 period are before a $0.06 a share loss from the discontinued coal operations and a $2.30 accounting charge.

Capital Share Earnings ($)

Quarter:	1993	1992	1991	1990
Mar.	0.13	0.04	0.01	0.09
Jun.	0.16	0.15	0.22	0.31
Sep.	E0.20	0.10	0.21	0.15
Dec.	E0.26	0.06	0.14	0.17
	E0.75	0.35	0.58	0.72

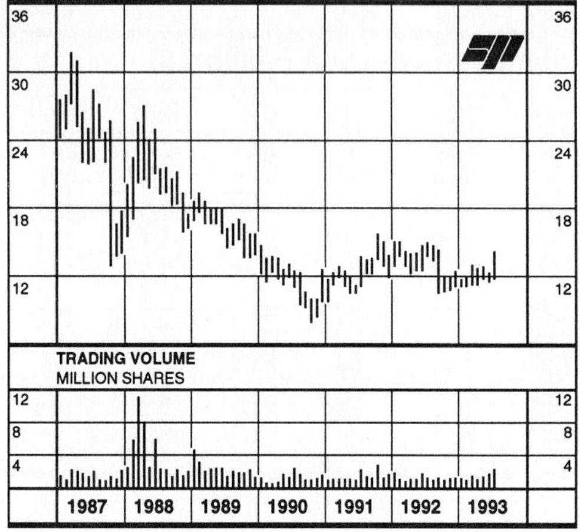

Important Developments

Jul. '93— Operating profits in 1993's second quarter inched higher, year to year, reflecting gains in the oil and gas production segment, insurance, and the Truck-Lite vehicular lighting unit. However, KSF's principal business, refining and marketing, reported lower earnings. Refined product sales volumes were lower while the unit was able to maintain some price increases. The fast lube business reported lower income due to a reduced number stores. In the oil and gas sector, higher natural gas prices accounted for improved profitability. Heritage insurance profits were aided by increase premiums and substantial capital gains. At Truck-Lite, increased sales to heavy duty truck markets and automobile manufacturers led to greater profitability. Separately, directors authorized the repurchase from time to time of up to 2 million of the company's common shares.

Next earnings report expected in late October.

Per Share Data ($)

Yr. End Dec. 31	1992	1991	1990	1989	[1]1988	1987	1986	[2]1985	1984	1983
Tangible Bk. Val.	**7.04**	11.34	11.18	11.32	11.93	12.15	14.83	13.05	12.29	12.90
Cash Flow	**1.42**	1.82	2.04	1.78	2.05	d0.33	3.44	3.43	2.41	3.22
Earnings[3]	**0.35**	0.58	0.72	0.44	0.57	d1.82	2.01	1.91	0.82	1.66
Dividends	**0.80**	0.80	0.80	0.80	0.80	0.80	0.85	0.85	0.80	0.85
Payout Ratio	**231%**	140%	111%	183%	141%	NM	45%	44%	98%	51%
Prices—High	**15⅛**	15¾	14¾	19⅜	27⅛	31¾	30	25	19⅞	20½
Low	**10½**	9¾	7⅞	13⅝	15½	12⅞	23	17⅜	15	15¼
P/E Ratio—	**43–30**	27–17	20–11	44–31	48–27	NM	15–11	13–9	24–18	12–9

Data as orig. reptd. **1.** Reflects acctg. change. **2.** Reflects merger or acquisition. **3.** Bef. results of disc. opers. of -1.50 in 1992, and spec. items of -2.30 in 1992, +0.26 in 1991. **4.** Sales and Oper. Revs. prior to 1993. d-Deficit. E-Estimated NM-Not Meaningful.

Income Data (Million $)

Year Ended Dec. 31	Revs.	Oper. Inc.	% Oper. Inc. of Revs.	Cap. Exp.	Depr.	Int. Exp.	Net Bef. Taxes	Eff. Tax Rate	[5]Net Inc.	% Net Inc. of Revs.	Cash Flow
[1]1992	**724**	**41**	**5.7**	**25.7**	**29.3**	**4.8**	**10**	**7.4%**	**[2]9.4**	**1.3**	**38.7**
1991	814	52	6.5	32.0	33.9	6.7	20	22.0%	15.5	1.9	49.5
1990	874	54	6.2	40.2	35.7	7.6	27	26.9%	19.6	2.2	55.3
1989	819	42	5.2	37.9	36.4	10.6	15	21.8%	11.8	1.4	48.2
[2]1988	869	52	6.0	47.2	39.2	9.0	18	15.3%	14.9	1.7	54.1
1987	848	52	6.2	77.7	39.5	7.0	[4]d104	NM	d48.1	NM	d8.6
1986	899	116	12.9	71.0	35.7	8.9	[4]90	44.1%	[2]50.3	5.6	86.0
[3]1985	974	111	11.4	64.9	36.4	13.5	[4]82	43.8%	45.9	4.7	82.3
1984	925	89	9.6	68.2	34.8	12.9	[4]27	33.6%	17.8	1.9	52.5
1983	903	95	10.5	50.1	34.2	9.7	63	41.6%	36.6	4.1	70.8

Balance Sheet Data (Million $)

Dec. 31	Cash	Curr. Assets	Curr. Liab.	Curr. Ratio	Total Assets	% Ret. on Assets	Long Term Debt	Common Equity	Total Cap.	% LT Debt of Cap.	% Ret. on Equity
1992	**50.0**	**NA**	**NA**	**NA**	**793**	**1.2**	**74**	**191**	**265**	**27.8**	**3.8**
1991	25.4	NA	NA	NA	751	2.1	84	308	413	20.4	5.1
1990	31.3	NA	NA	NA	757	2.6	67	303	414	16.3	6.4
1989	40.6	NA	NA	NA	765	1.6	97	307	456	21.4	3.8
1988	24.4	NA	NA	NA	740	2.2	94	315	457	20.5	4.7
1987	12.8	186	98	1.9	613	NM	105	320	469	22.3	NM
1986	9.1	201	108	1.9	665	7.3	64	391	557	11.6	13.7
1985	13.7	220	127	1.7	649	7.3	112	312	522	21.5	15.2
1984	14.5	186	106	1.8	573	3.1	110	276	468	23.5	6.3
1983	36.9	219	93	2.3	552	6.8	91	284	459	19.9	13.4

Data as orig. reptd. **1.** Excl. disc. opers. **2.** Reflects acctg. change. **3.** Reflects merger or acquisition. **4.** Incl. equity in earns. of nonconsol. subs. **5.** Bef. results of disc. opers. and spec. items. d-Deficit. NM-Not Meaningful. NA-Not Available.

Business Summary

Quaker State's principal business is the manufacturing and marketing of motor oils under its own brand name. The company positions the Quaker State brand as a premium line, and seeks to avoid discounting. Overall market share is second to the Pennzoil brand. KSF also sells a variety of refined products and products for the auto aftermarket, including filters, anti-freeze, brake and power-steering fluids, chemicals and coatings. The company operates a nationwide network of fast lube centers (434 stores), which provide car care service including oil changes, filter replacement, and maintenance of power steering, brake and transmission fluids. Fast lube centers are operated under the Quaker State Q Lube, Minit-Lube, Inc. and McQuik's Oilube, Inc. names. Profits (in million $) by segment in recent years:

	1992	1991
Refining & marketing	$23.3	$36.8
Oil & gas	3.8	2.8
Fast lube	2.0	–1.1
Insurance	6.1	3.0
Other	–1.5	1.6

In late 1992, KSF announced plans to exit the coal mining business, and sold assets related to its Valley Camp Coal Co. The company plans to sell the remaining coal assets in 1993. During 1992, the coal unit was classified as discontinued, and results for 1991 were restated. KSF has considered selling its lighting unit, Truck-Lite Co.

The Heritage Insurance Group primarily writes credit life insurance and credit accident and health insurance issued in connection with the purchase of automobiles and other durable consumer goods.

The Quaker State Oil Refining Corp., formed in January 1990, manufactures and markets the branded motor oil and other auto care products. The unit offers a synthetic motor oil. The company also has a small crude oil and natural gas exploration and production business.

Dividend Data

Dividends have been paid since 1931. A dividend reinvestment plan is available.

Amt of Divd. $	Date Decl.	Ex–divd. Date	Stock of Record	Payment Date
0.20	Oct. 29	Nov. 6	Nov. 13	Dec. 15'92
0.20	Jan. 28	Feb. 8	Feb. 15	Mar. 15'93
0.20	Apr. 29	May 10	May 14	Jun. 15'93
0.10	Jul. 29	Aug. 9	Aug. 13	Sep. 15'93

Capitalization

Long Term Debt: $59,704,000 (3/93).

Capital Stock: 27,152,185 shs. ($1 par).
Institutions hold 34%.
Shareholders of record: 12,606.

Office—255 Elm Street (P.O. Box 989), Oil City, PA 16301. **Tel**—(814) 676-7676. **Chrmn & CEO**—H. M. Baum. **Pres**—C. A. Conrad. **VP-CFO**—R. S. Keefer. **VP-Secy**—G. W. Callahan. **Investor Contact**—Benton H. Faulkner. **Dirs**—H. M. Baum, L. M. Carroll, C. A. Conrad, J. W. Corn, H. M. Ellenburg, C. F. Fetterolf, T. A. Gardner, H. B. Jordan, W. C. McClelland, D. J. McQuaide, R. A. Ross Jr. **Transfer Agent & Registrar**—Mellon Securities Trust Co., NYC. **Incorporated** in Del. in 1931. **Empl**—3,715.

 Edward G. Graves

Quantum Corp.

NASDAQ Symbol QNTM (Incl. in Nat'l Market) Options on NYSE In S&P MidCap 400

Price	Range	P-E Ratio	Dividend	Yield	S&P Ranking	Beta
Aug. 23'93	1993					
12¾	17¾–9½	8	None	None	B	1.97

Summary

Quantum is a leading supplier of 3½-inch and 2½-inch hard disk drives to OEMs for use in personal computers and desktop workstations, as well as storage enhancement products for personal computers. Higher earnings in 1992-3 reflected strong sales and improved margins. However, despite higher unit shipments, earnings for 1993-4 will be penalized by intense pricing pressures.

Current Outlook

Earnings for the fiscal year ending March 31, 1994, are estimated at $0.70 a share, down from the $2.05 reported for 1992-3.

Initiation of cash dividends is not expected.

Sales are expected to rise in 1993-4, as greater unit volume outweighs competitive pricing pressures. Strong personal computer demand will spur ongoing demand for disk drives. However, a faster-than-normal shift to higher-capacity drives has resulted in oversupply and rapid price deterioration, particularly in lower-end drives with capacities below 200 MBs. Margins should narrow on pricing pressures, despite stringent cost controls. While the pricing environment may begin to ease somewhat in coming months, a loss is expected for the second quarter of 1993-4. The shipment of new, low-cost drives should return results to profitability in the December quarter. The effective tax rate should drop to between 33% and 35% in 1993-4 and continue to decline somewhat thereafter, reflecting benefits from increased factory operations in Switzerland.

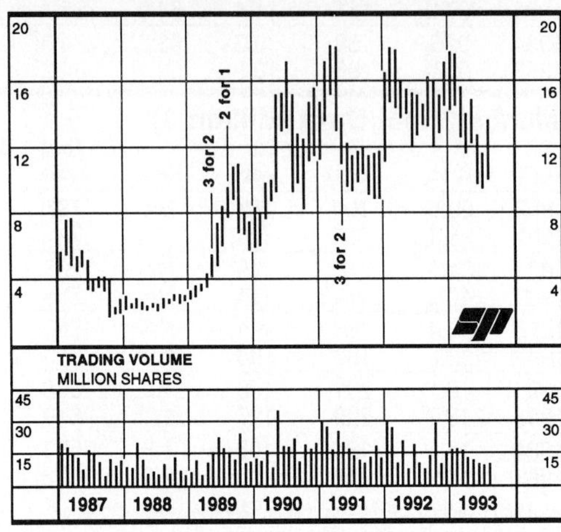

Sales (Million $)

13 Weeks:	1993-4	1992-3	1991-2	1990-1
Jun.	479	369	251	163
Sep.	---	363	245	192
Dec.	---	459	287	232
Mar.	---	507	345	291
	---	1,697	1,128	878

Sales for the quarter ended July 4, 1993, rose 30%, year to year, as strong unit volume outweighed competitive pricing pressures. Margins narrowed sharply in the lower pricing environment, and high G&A costs reflected continued investments in the Swiss operation. Pretax income fell 85%. After taxes at 33.0%, versus 36.0%, net income was down 84%, to $3,373,000 ($0.08 a share, based on 2.1% fewer shares), from $21,492,000 ($0.47; $0.41 fully diluted).

Common Share Earnings ($)

13 Weeks:	1993-4	1992-3	1991-2	1990-1
Jun.	0.08	0.47	0.28	0.40
Sep.	Ed0.10	0.39	0.17	0.43
Dec.	E0.30	E0.30	0.21	0.41
Mar.	E0.42	E0.42	0.38	0.45
	E0.70	2.05	1.05	1.69

Important Developments

Aug. '93— The company said it believed pricing and margin pressures would continue through the September quarter and expected to report a loss for the second quarter of 1993-4. In addition, Quantum said it would take a charge for a planned 5%-7% workforce reduction in the second quarter.

Next earnings report expected in early November.

Per Share Data ($)

Yr. End Mar. 31	1993	1992	1991	1990	1989	1988	1987	1986	1985	1984
Tangible Bk. Val.	**9.01**	[1]7.19	[1]6.09	3.90	2.55	2.36	2.64	2.48	1.96	1.45
Cash Flow	**2.64**	1.68	2.00	1.27	0.40	0.06	0.33	0.59	0.54	0.28
Earnings	**2.05**	1.05	1.69	1.14	0.30	d0.08	0.21	0.51	0.49	0.25
Dividends	**Nil**	Nil	Nil	Nil	Nil	Nil	Nil	Nil	Nil	Nil
Payout Ratio	**Nil**	Nil	Nil	Nil	Nil	Nil	Nil	Nil	Nil	Nil
Calendar Years	**1992**	1991	1990	1989	1988	1987	1986	1985	1984	1983
Prices—High	**18**	18⅛	17⅛	11	3⅛	7¾	6	6¾	5¼	7¾
Low	**11⅛**	8⅞	5⅞	2⅞	2⅛	1¾	3½	4	3⅜	3½
P/E Ratio—	**9-5**	17-8	10-3	10-2	10-7	NM	28-17	13-8	11-7	31-14

Data as orig. reptd. Adj. for stk. divs. of 50% Apr. 1991, 100% Aug. 1989, 50% May 1989. **1.** Incl. intangibles. d-Deficit. E-Estimated. NM-Not Meaningful.

Income Data (Million $)

Year Ended Mar. 31	Oper. Revs.	Oper. Inc.	% Oper. Inc. of Revs.	Cap. Exp.	Depr.	Int. Exp.	Net Bef. Taxes	Eff. Tax Rate	Net Inc.	% Net Inc. of Revs.	Cash Flow
1993	**1,697**	**176**	**10.4**	**36.1**	**26.9**	**14.4**	**147**	**36.0%**	**93.8**	**5.5**	**121**
1992	1,128	103	9.2	37.8	28.1	7.8	74	37.0%	46.8	4.2	75
1991	878	121	13.8	46.0	13.2	5.2	116	36.3%	73.9	8.4	87
1990	446	70	15.7	16.7	5.3	1.8	72	34.5%	47.2	10.6	53
1989	208	17	8.0	6.4	4.3	0.6	18	26.6%	12.9	6.2	17
1988	189	11	5.6	4.5	5.8	Nil	d4	NM	d3.2	NM	3
1987	121	15	12.3	6.4	5.1	Nil	11	19.0%	8.8	7.3	14
1986	121	25	20.7	8.7	3.6	Nil	32	30.1%	22.2	18.3	26
1985	120	31	26.0	6.8	2.5	Nil	31	31.6%	21.0	17.4	23
1984	67	17	25.5	6.3	1.3	Nil	19	44.5%	10.7	15.9	12

Balance Sheet Data (Million $)

Mar. 31	Cash	Curr. Assets	Curr. Liab.	Curr. Ratio	Total Assets	% Ret. on Assets	Long Term Debt	Common Equity	Total Cap.	% LT Debt of Cap.	% Ret. on Equity
1993	**289**	**830**	**316**	**2.6**	**927**	**12.7**	**213**	**398**	**611**	**34.8**	**26.4**
1992	145	453	236	1.9	547	8.7	Nil	308	311	Nil	16.5
1991	115	396	248	1.6	489	19.8	Nil	238	242	Nil	36.9
1990	79	185	83	2.2	243	23.2	Nil	154	160	Nil	36.6
1989	51	110	53	2.1	157	9.5	Nil	100	104	Nil	13.4
1988	59	96	24	4.1	142	NM	Nil	114	118	Nil	NM
1987	77	118	19	6.3	137	6.8	Nil	108	119	Nil	8.4
1986	78	107	13	8.2	126	19.6	Nil	106	113	Nil	23.5
1985	47	86	14	6.1	100	23.9	Nil	82	86	Nil	29.2
1984	19	47	14	3.4	75	16.2	Nil	60	61	Nil	19.5

Data as orig. reptd. d-Deficit. NM-Not Meaningful.

Business Summary

Quantum Corporation designs, manufactures and markets small-form-factor hard disk drives for use in desktop personal computers (PCs), workstations and notebook computers.

The company's primary product line is the ProDrive Series of high-performance, 3½-inch hard disk drives designed for the desktop PC and workstation marketplace. Drive capacities range from 85 megabytes (MBs) to 1.2 gigabytes (GBs) and are available with imbedded Small Computer Systems Interface (SCSI) or AT-bus controllers.

The Go-Drive line of 2½-inch hard disk drives is designed for the notebook computer market. Capacities range from 84 to 169 MBs, and they also are available with imbedded SCSI or AT-bus controllers.

High-volume drives, such as the ProDrive models with capacities between 85 and 245 MBs, as well as all Go-Drives, are made by Quantum's Japanese partner, Matsushita-Kotobuki Electronics, which manufactured products contributing more than 90% of the company's sales in 1992-3. Higher-capacity, more technically complex products are made in Quantum's California manufacturing facility.

Drives are sold to original equipment manufacturers (OEMs) and distributors through a worldwide sales force.

Quantum also designs and markets storage enhancement products that upgrade the capacity of existing desktop PCs, including the Hardcard drive, which fits into a PC expansion slot, and the Passport XL removable drive. Such products are marketed through retail distribution channels to end-users.

In 1992-3, Apple Computer accounted for 20% of sales (25% in 1991-2). International sales provided 48% (52%) of the total.

Dividend Data

No cash has been paid on the common stock.

Finances

In August 1993, the company said it had repurchased 1,812,000 of its common shares since October 1992, under authorizations to buy back up to 4.5 million QNTM shares.

R&D spending totaled $63,019,000 (3.7% of sales) in 1992-3, versus $59,255,000 (5.3%) in 1991-2.

Capitalization

Long Term Debt: $212,500,000 of 6⅜% sub. debs. due 2002 & conv. into com. at $18.15 a sh. (6/93).

Common Stock: 44,957,470 shs. (no par). Institutions hold about 77%.

Options: To buy 6,985,000 shs. (3/93).

Office—500 McCarthy Blvd., Milpitas, CA 95035. **Tel**—(408) 894-4000. **Chrmn**—S. M. Berkley. **CEO**—W. J. Miller. **Exec VP**—M. A. Brown. **Exec VP-Fin, CFO & Secy**—J. T. Rodgers. **Dirs**—S. M. Berkley, D. A. Brown, E. M. Esber Jr., W. J. Miller, S. C. Wheelwright. **Transfer Agent**—Harris Trust Co. of California (c/o Harris Trust & Savings Bank, Chicago). **Incorporated** in California in 1980; reincorporated in Delaware in 1987. **Empl**—2,455.

 Peter C. Wood, CFA

Questar Corp.

NYSE Symbol STR In S&P MidCap 400

Price	Range	P-E Ratio	Dividend	Yield	S&P Ranking	Beta
Aug. 5'93	1993					
36¼	36¼–25⅝	17	1.10	3.0%	A–	0.25

Summary

This diversified holding company is engaged in natural gas transmission, distribution and storage primarily in Utah, Wyoming and Colorado; in oil and gas exploration and production in the western U.S.; and in property management. Earnings have grown steadily since 1988 and are expected to increase again in 1993 and 1994. Long-term prospects are enhanced by the expected development of nontraditional markets and wider margins at production operations.

Current Outlook

Share earnings for 1993 are estimated at $2.10, up from 1992's $1.79. An increase to $2.20 is projected for 1994.

Dividends should continue at $0.27½ quarterly.

Utility profits should rise in 1993, in part reflecting increased spaceheating sales; the 1993 first half was 25% colder than the year-earlier period. Transmission profits should advance, with higher volumes delivered; projects to increase gas storage capacity should enhance future profits. Exploration and production earnings should benefit from higher average gas prices. Greater production from tight-sands projects will lead to higher tax credits. Earnings for 1994 are expected to benefit from a continued uptrend in average wellhead price for natural gas, and from greater production. Pipeline profits are expected to be higher; a restructuring of pipeline operations to comply with FERC's Order 636 will reduce risk associated with volume fluctuations. Assuming normal weather conditions, distribution profits should rise fractionally as favorable economic conditions in STR's service are expected to lead to customer growth, which should more than offset a slight decline in gas usage per customer.

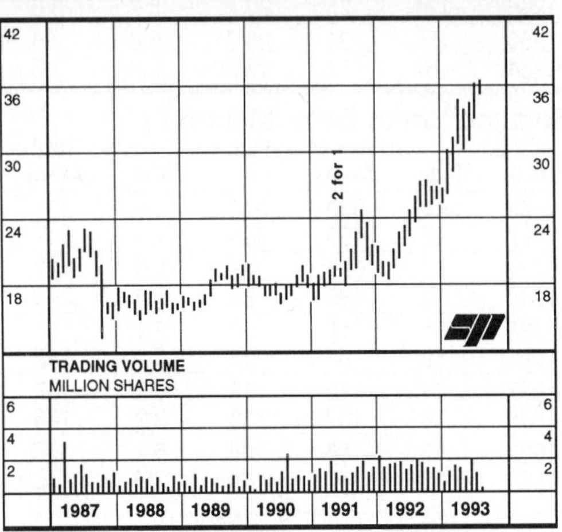

Revenues (Million $)

Quarter:	1993	1992	1991	1990
Mar.	249.8	225.8	236.3	201.0
Jun.	136.8	109.6	133.0	101.8
Sep.	---	90.5	90.1	72.7
Dec.	---	179.0	173.0	160.9
	---	604.8	632.3	536.3

Revenues for the six months ended June 30, 1993, rose 15%, year to year, reflecting increases in gas distribution and transmission deliveries, natural gas production, and natural gas prices. Benefiting from sharply higher exploration and production and distribution profits, net income advanced 39%, to $1.25 a share from $0.91, which was before a credit of $0.23 from an accounting change.

Common Share Earnings ($)

Quarter:	1993	1992	1991	1990
Mar.	0.88	0.76	0.85	0.73
Jun.	0.37	0.15	0.22	0.11
Sep.	E0.12	0.15	0.04	0.05
Dec.	E0.72	0.73	0.52	0.57
	E2.10	1.79	1.63	1.46

Important Developments

Aug.'93— Questar Pipeline Co. expected to be able to make the transition to operations under FERC's Order 636 by September 1, 1993. Also, STR and Fidelity Capital agreed to combine their western U.S. specialized mobile radio (SMR) activities, creating the nation's third largest SMR operation. Questar Telecom Inc. and Advanced MobileComm Inc. planned to form a new corporation that would serve metropolitan areas with a combined population of 24.5 million.

Next earnings report expected in late October.

Per Share Data ($)

Yr. End Dec. 31	1992	1991	1990	1989	1988	[1]1987	1986	1985	1984	[2]1983
Tangible Bk. Val.	**13.55**	12.49	11.76	11.54	11.88	12.24	11.86	11.60	10.94	9.82
Cash Flow	**3.80**	3.45	3.16	2.91	2.38	2.59	2.89	3.18	2.93	2.64
Earnings[3]	**1.79**	1.63	1.46	1.28	0.64	0.67	1.20	1.60	1.58	1.52
Dividends	**1.040**	1.010	0.970	0.945	0.940	0.910	0.870	0.815	0.740	0.668
Payout Ratio	**59%**	63%	66%	75%	145%	143%	73%	51%	47%	47%
Prices—High	**27½**	24¾	19⅞	19¹³⁄₁₆	17¹³⁄₁₆	23³⁄₁₆	19⁹⁄₁₆	17⅜	16⁷⁄₁₆	17⅛
Low	**18½**	16⅝	16⁵⁄₁₆	15¾	14¹⁵⁄₁₆	13¼	12¹¹⁄₁₆	13½	11½	8⁷⁄₁₆
P/E Ratio—	**15–10**	15–10	14–11	16–12	28–23	35–20	16–11	11–8	10–7	11–6

Data as orig. reptd. Adj. for stk. div(s). of 100% Jun. 1991, 100% Sep. 1983. **1.** Reflects merger or acquisition. **2.** Reflects accounting change. **3.** Bef. spec. item(s) of +0.24 in 1992, +0.26 in 1984. E-Estimated.

Income Data (Million $)

Year Ended Dec. 31	Revs.	Oper. Inc.	% Oper. Inc. of Revs.	Cap. Exp.	Depr.	Int. Exp.	Net Bef. Taxes	Eff. Tax Rate	[5]Net Inc.	% Net Inc. of Revs.	Cash Flow
1992	**605**	**213**	**35.3**	**169**	**79.4**	**36.9**	**[4]105**	**31.8%**	**70.5**	**11.7**	**150**
1991	632	200	31.6	133	70.3	37.1	[4]101	36.8%	63.1	10.0	133
1990	536	182	34.0	138	66.4	36.9	[4]91	36.6%	56.5	10.5	123
1989	509	169	33.1	92	63.4	33.0	80	36.7%	49.6	9.7	113
1988	486	161	33.2	79	66.9	[3]29.6	39	33.2%	24.6	5.1	91
[1]1987	493	175	35.5	122	71.2	29.8	46	43.2%	25.9	5.0	96
1986	528	180	34.0	71	59.1	26.2	81	47.0%	43.2	8.2	101
1985	644	180	27.9	104	56.6	27.8	108	42.9%	61.7	9.6	114
1984	687	178	26.0	112	48.4	25.6	110	43.7%	62.0	9.0	105
[2]1983	567	157	27.7	107	37.1	26.9	99	43.5%	55.7	9.8	87

Balance Sheet Data (Million $)

Dec. 31	Cash	Curr. Assets	Curr. Liab.	Curr. Ratio	Total Assets	% Ret. on Assets	Long Term Debt	Common Equity	Total Cap.	% LT Debt of Cap.	% Ret. on Equity
1992	**7.3**	**177**	**215**	**0.8**	**1,324**	**5.5**	**365**	**554**	**1,095**	**33.3**	**13.3**
1991	6.0	165	173	1.0	1,220	5.3	354	502	1,033	34.3	13.0
1990	11.1	165	173	1.0	1,151	5.1	328	460	965	34.0	12.5
1989	22.5	163	164	1.0	1,075	4.6	276	456	898	30.7	10.7
1988	15.1	143	156	0.9	1,026	2.4	249	451	859	29.0	5.4
1987	20.5	143	136	1.1	1,047	2.3	255	472	901	28.3	5.5
1986	21.7	150	179	0.8	968	4.4	200	414	782	25.5	10.4
1985	30.9	181	162	1.1	1,005	6.2	244	414	815	30.0	14.3
1984	50.8	209	157	1.3	991	6.4	246	395	811	30.3	15.1
1983	19.2	199	145	1.4	927	5.8	244	350	765	31.9	15.2

Data as orig. reptd. **1.** Reflects merger or acquisition. **2.** Reflects acctg. change. **3.** Net of interest income. **4.** Incl. equity in earns. of noncon-sol. subs. **5.** Bef. spec. items.

Business Summary

Questar is a holding company whose subsidiaries are engaged in the natural gas, oil, telecommunications and property development businesses in the western U.S. Contributions (profits in million $) by business segment in 1992:

	Revs.	Profits
Gas distribution	44%	$44.4
Expl. & prod.	28%	42.2
Gas transmission	24%	47.4
Other	4%	–0.2

Natural gas distribution operations are conducted by Mountain Fuel Supply, which at 1992 year-end served 532,109 customers, with 96% in Utah and the remainder in southwestern Wyoming and southeastern Idaho. Gas deliveries in 1992 totaled 125.6 million decatherms, down from 129.6 million in 1991. The number of heating degree days in 1992 amounted to 5,235, versus 6,084 in 1992.

Oil and gas exploration and production operations are conducted through Celsius Energy Co. mainly in the Rocky Mountain region; Universal Resources Corp. in Midcontinent areas; and Wexpro Co., which develops gas reserves owned by Mountain Fuel Supply. Total proved reserves at year-end 1992 were estimated at 11.2 million bbl. of oil and 197.7 million Mcf of gas.

Questar Pipeline Co. owns and operates interstate pipeline systems in Utah, Wyoming and Colorado, and operates gas storage facilities in Utah and Wyoming. It also has an 18% interest in and operates the 88-mile Overthrust segment of the 800-mile Trailblazer Pipeline running between Wyoming and Nebraska.

Other units include Questar Development Corp., Questar Telecom Inc., and Questar Service Corp.

Dividend Data

Dividends have been paid since 1935. A "poison pill" stock purchase rights plan was adopted in 1986.

Amt of Divd. $	Date Decl.	Ex–divd. Date	Stock of Record	Payment Date
0.26½	Aug. 11	Aug. 17	Aug. 21	Sep. 14'92
0.26½	Oct. 30	Nov. 16	Nov. 20	Dec. 14'92
0.26½	Feb. 9	Feb. 12	Feb. 19	Mar. 15'93
0.27½	May 18	May 24	May 28	Jun. 21'93

Capitalization

Long Term Debt: $377,473,000 (3/93).

Cum. Red. Preferred Stock: $8,726,000.

Common Stock: 39,950,100 shs. (no par).
Institutions hold 66%.
Shareholders of record: 11,303.

Office—180 East First South St., Salt Lake City, UT 84147. **Tel**—(801) 534-5000. **Chrmn, Pres & CEO**—R. D. Cash. **SVP & CFO**—W. F. Edwards. **VP & Secy**—Connie. C. Holbrook. **VP & Treas**—S. E. Parks. **Investor Contact**—R. Curtis Burnett. **Dirs**—R. H. Bischoff, R. D. Cash, U. E. Garrison, J. A. Harmon, W. W. Hawkins, W. N. Jones, R. E. Kadlec, D. L. Leavitt, N. A. Maxwell, M. Mead, D. N. Rose, H. H. Simmons. **Transfer Agents**—First Chicago Trust Co. of New York; Co.'s office. **Registrars**—Mellon Bank, Pittsburgh; Zions First National Bank, Salt Lake City. **Incorporated** in Utah in 1935. **Empl**—2,659.

 Mark Mattke

RPM, Inc.

NASDAQ Symbol RPOW (Incl. in Nat'l Market) Options on CBOE In S&P MidCap 400

Price	Range	P-E Ratio	Dividend	Yield	S&P Ranking	Beta
Sep. 10'93	1993					
18⅛	19⅜–16¼	22	0.48	2.6%	A+	1.13

Summary

This company manufactures specialty coatings and products for the structural waterproofing and corrosion control markets, as well as products for the consumer, do-it-yourself and hobby and craft markets. RPM actively seeks to acquire companies in targeted niche areas. Higher sales and earnings have been achieved for 46 consecutive years, and further gains are expected in 1993-4. The dividend has been raised regularly.

Current Outlook

Earnings for the fiscal year ending May 31, 1994, are projected at $0.90 a share, up from $0.83 in 1992-3.

Dividends, currently at $0.12 quarterly, have been raised regularly.

Sales are expected to grow more than 10% in 1993-4, reflecting stable demand for industrial and consumer niche coatings, the acquisition of Dynatron/Bondo, and improving market conditions in Europe in the latter part of the year. Margins are expected to be maintained, aided by a strict planning process and traditional margin leverage enjoyed by RPM's high-end market brand franchises. Traditionally high margins are also supported by a policy of divesting products that are believed to have become commodities. Interest expense will be lower, following the conversion of debentures in early August 1993. Despite an expected rise in the effective tax rate, to 42.0%, and more shares outstanding, earnings should advance.

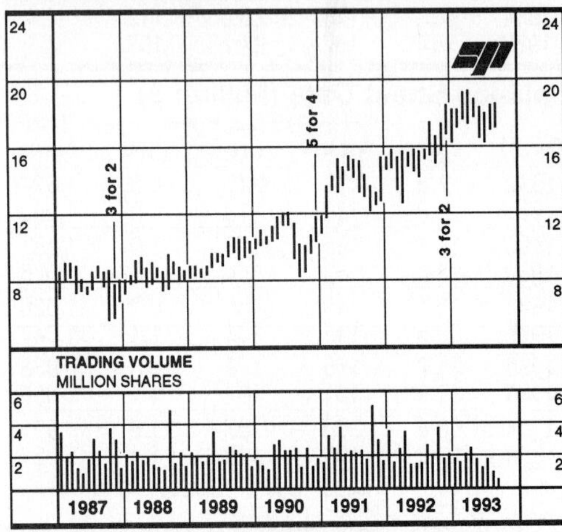

Net Sales (Million $)

Quarter:	1992–93	1991–92	1990–91	1989–90
Aug.	166	130	135	108
Nov.	153	139	134	110
Feb.	139	126	104	101
May	167	157	128	126
	626	552	500	445

Net sales in the fiscal year ended May 31, 1993, increased 13% from those of the preceding year. Margins narrowed on a less favorable product mix, but with lower net interest and other expense, pretax income gained 15%. After taxes at 40.4%, versus 39.8%, net income was up 14%, to $39,376,000 ($0.83 a share), from $34,466,000 ($0.73).

Common Share Earnings ($)

Quarter:	1993–94	1992–93	1991–92	1990–91
Aug.	E0.27	0.25	0.21	0.25
Nov.	E0.24	0.23	0.21	0.22
Feb.	E0.11	0.10	0.09	0.07
May	E0.28	0.25	0.21	0.15
	E0.90	0.83	0.73	0.69

Important Developments

Jun. '93— RPM called for redemption August 2, 1993, all $50 million of its 6¾% subordinated debentures, noting that it expected the debentures to be converted into common stock at $13.60 a share. Separately, the company acquired Dynatron/Bondo Corp., a supplier of specialty automotive repair material and associated products with annual revenues of $45 million.

Next earnings report expected in early October.

Per Share Data ($)

Yr. End May 31	[1]1993	[1]1992	[1]1991	[1]1990	1989	[1]1988	[1]1987	[1]1986	[1]1985	1984
Tangible Bk. Val.	**2.12**	1.68	2.43	1.43	2.08	1.96	1.61	1.76	1.81	1.72
Cash Flow	**1.28**	1.15	0.99	0.95	0.81	0.71	0.60	0.55	0.50	0.43
Earnings[2]	**0.83**	0.73	0.69	0.65	0.57	0.51	0.42	0.37	0.37	0.31
Dividends	**0.473**	0.443	0.398	0.354	0.322	0.288	0.257	0.215	0.180	0.143
Payout Ratio	**57%**	60%	58%	54%	56%	57%	60%	58%	49%	46%
Calendar Years	**1992**	1991	1990	1989	1988	1987	1986	1985	1984	1983
Prices—High	**18½**	15½	12⅛	11	9½	9⅛	8½	6⅞	5	4¾
Low	**12⅝**	10⅞	8¼	8⅛	7¼	5¾	6¼	4¾	3½	3⅜
P/E Ratio—	**22–15**	21–15	18–12	16–13	17–13	18–11	21–15	18–13	14–10	15–11

Data as orig. reptd. Adj. for stk. divs. of 50% Dec. 1992, 25% Dec. 1990, 50% Nov. 1987, 25% Dec. 1984. **1.** Refl. merger or acq. **2.** Ful. dil.: 0.79 in 1993, 0.72 in 1992, 0.67 in 1991, 0.63 in 1990, 0.55 in 1989, 0.49 in 1988, 0.41 in 1987, 0.36 in 1985, 0.31 in 1984. E-Estimated.

Income Data (Million $)

Year Ended May 31	Revs.	Oper. Inc.	% Oper. Inc. of Revs.	Cap. Exp.	Depr.	Int. Exp.	[2]Net Bef. Taxes	Eff. Tax Rate	Net Inc.	% Net Inc. of Revs.	Cash Flow
[1]1993	**626**	**100.9**	**16.1**	**18.4**	**21.4**	**9.8**	**66.1**	**40.4%**	**39.4**	**6.3**	**60.8**
[1]1992	552	88.1	16.0	17.1	19.4	13.9	57.3	39.8%	34.8	6.2	53.9
[1]1991	500	70.6	14.1	16.4	14.4	9.7	51.7	38.4%	31.8	6.4	46.2
[1]1990	445	66.5	14.9	10.7	12.2	8.9	45.0	38.3%	27.7	6.2	39.9
1989	376	60.2	16.0	8.9	10.1	7.0	39.1	37.8%	24.2	6.4	34.4
[1]1988	342	50.3	14.7	6.5	8.9	7.1	35.3	39.5%	[3]21.4	6.2	30.3
[1]1987	291	41.5	14.3	9.8	7.5	6.3	29.4	45.6%	15.9	5.5	23.4
[1]1986	251	29.6	11.8	4.5	6.1	6.6	19.3	34.6%	12.6	5.0	18.7
[1]1985	203	24.8	12.2	7.0	4.1	4.9	18.2	40.5%	10.7	5.3	14.8
[1]1984	154	18.3	11.9	3.8	3.2	3.2	13.7	38.9%	8.4	5.4	11.5

Balance Sheet Data (Million $)

May 31	Cash	Curr. Assets	Curr. Liab.	Curr. Ratio	Total Assets	% Ret. on Assets	Long Term Debt	Common Equity	Total Cap.	% LT Debt of Cap.	% Ret. on Equity
1993	**24.8**	**281**	**117.9**	**2.4**	**585**	**6.9**	**221**	**239**	**467**	**47.3**	**17.1**
1992	27.3	263	90.1	2.9	559	7.1	239	222	467	51.1	16.0
1991	18.6	205	75.7	2.7	401	7.8	114	206	324	35.3	16.6
1990	2.5	186	63.2	2.9	375	8.4	145	161	311	46.7	18.0
1989	6.0	150	56.8	2.6	286	8.9	77	147	229	33.6	17.1
1988	6.4	133	44.4	3.0	261	8.2	75	136	216	34.9	16.1
1987	3.0	110	43.1	2.6	242	6.8	76	118	199	38.3	13.8
1986	2.2	106	41.9	2.5	219	6.3	62	110	177	35.0	13.1
1985	2.5	86	30.7	2.8	141	7.9	42	64	110	37.9	17.4
1984	2.5	74	22.1	3.4	120	7.7	40	55	97	40.8	15.8

Data as orig. reptd. **1.** Refl. merger or acq. **2.** Incl. equity in earns. of nonconsol. subs. **3.** Refl. acctg. change.

Business Summary

RPM, Inc. derives the vast majority of its revenues from the production of a wide variety of protective coatings. It also manufactures a line of non-apparel fabrics and wall coverings. The company participates in five broad market categories worldwide: industrial waterproofing and general maintenance; industrial corrosion-control; specialty chemicals; consumer do-it-yourself; and consumer hobby and leisure. Industrial sources account for about 60% of sales, with consumer-oriented products targeted at the do-it-yourself and hobby markets contributing the remaining 40%.

The protective coating products manufactured by RPM are used primarily to provide waterproofing and corrosion control to existing goods or structures and are generally not affected by cyclical movements in the economy.

The company has pursued an aggressive acquisition policy. In June 1991, RPM acquired the Rust-Oleum Europe operation in the Netherlands and France and obtained a license from Rust-Oleum International Corp. to use the trademark and other marks in Europe, the former USSR and certain North African countries. In October 1991, Day-Glo Color Corp., an Ohio manufacturer and marketer of fluorescent pigments and colorants, was acquired. In March 1992, the company purchased, through its wholly owned Belgian subsidiary Radiant Color N.V., all of the outstanding shares of Martin Mathys N.V., a Belgian manufacturer and seller of specialized protective coatings. In May 1992, RPM bought Sentry Polymers, a manufacturer of high performance concrete coatings.

International operations currently account for about 12% of sales, although RPM also receives license fees and royalty income from numerous license agreements and joint ventures in other countries. The company markets its products in more than 110 countries, and operates more than 39 plants worldwide.

Dividend Data

Cash has been paid each year since 1969. A dividend reinvestment plan is available.

Amt. of Divd. $	Date Decl.	Ex-divd. Date	Stock of Record	Payment Date
0.18	Oct. 9	Oct. 13	Oct. 19	Oct. 30'92
3-for-2 Split	Oct. 9	Dec. 7	Nov. 20	Dec. 4'92
0.12	Jan. 8	Jan. 11	Jan. 18	Jan. 29'93
0.12	Apr. 7	Apr. 12	Apr. 16	Apr. 30'93
0.12	Jul. 8	Jul. 13	Jul. 19	Jul. 30'93

Capitalization

Long Term Debt: $220,942,000 (5/93).

Common Stock: 53,120,465 shs. (no par).
Shareholders: 19,226 of record (8/93).

Office—2628 Pearl Rd., P.O. Box 777, Medina, OH 44258. **Tel**—(216) 273-5090. **Fax**—(216) 225-8743. **Chrmn & CEO**—T. C. Sullivan. **Pres, COO & CFO**—J. A. Karman. **VP & Secy**—P. A. Granzier. **VP & Treas**—R. E. Klar. **Dirs**—E. B. Brandon, L. Gustin, R. H. Holdt, E. B. Jones, J. A. Karman, D. K. Miller, J. H. Morris, Jr., K. O'Donnell, W. A. Papenbrock, S. Stranahan, T. C. Sullivan. **Registrar & Transfer Agent**—Society Corp., Cleveland. **Incorporated** in Ohio in 1947. **Empl**—3,500.

 Shayna J. Malnak

Ranger Oil

NYSE Symbol RGO Options on Toronto (Jan-Apr-Jul-Oct) In S&P MidCap 400

Price	Range	P-E Ratio	Dividend	Yield	S&P Ranking	Beta
Sep. 30'93	1993					
5⅜	6–4¼	26	[1]0.08	[1]1.5%	B	0.37

Summary

This Canadian company primarily engages in the exploration and production of crude oil and natural gas in the UK, both on and offshore, the Netherlands' sectors of the North Sea, Africa and North America, primarily Canada. Earnings were down in 1993's first six months, despite higher oil and gas production, as Ranger had tax expense versus a recovery.

Business Summary

Ranger Oil Ltd. engages in the exploration, development and production of crude oil and natural gas in the UK, both offshore and onshore, the Netherlands' sectors of the North Sea, North America and Africa. Other activities include a 50% interest in offshore drilling equipment used in the North Sea. The company's 1992 exploration program concentrated on the North Sea. Going forward, RGO will remain focused on the North Sea while increasing North American production and expanding exploration in other international areas.

RGO's principal producing property in the UK is its interest in the Ninian field in the British sector of the North Sea, in which it holds an 11.5% interest. In November 1991, the company's first operated North Sea development project, the Anglia Field, began production. All RGO's UK oil production is sold to British Petroleum PLC.

Daily production in 1992 (before royalties) totaled 13,860 bbl. of crude oil and natural gas liquids (12,763 in 1991) and 94,100 Mcf of natural gas (58,300). The increased production reflects 1991 acquisitions and the 1992 acquisition of MLC Oil and Gas Ltd.

Proved reserves, net of royalties, at December 31, 1992, amounted to 39,664,000 bbl. of oil and natural gas liquids (24,428,000 bbl. in 1991) of which 76% was in the North Sea and 24% was in North America; and 309.2 Bcf of natural gas (312.9 Bcf in 1991), with 34% in the North Sea and 66% in North America. The estimated present value of future net cash flows of RGO's reserves (discounted at 10%) was $342.4 million, versus $339.8 million at year-end 1991.

At 1992 year-end RGO had 839,602 gross (248,480 net) developed acres, mostly in Canada, and 7,870,000 gross (3,259,000 net) undeveloped acres, primarily in the North Sea and other foreign areas. During 1992, the company spent $179 million on oil and gas property acquisition, exploration and development activities, up 16% from 1991.

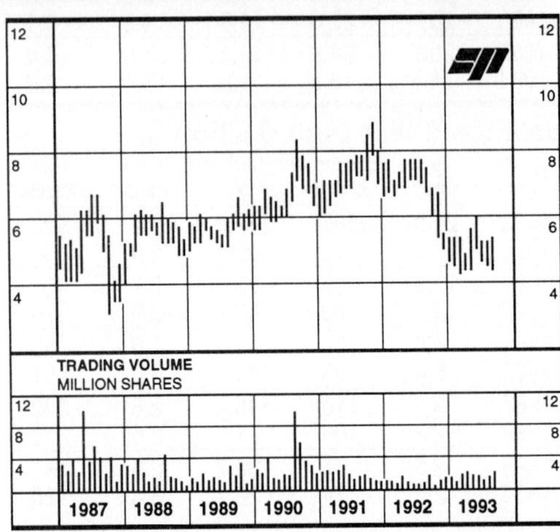

In July 1992, the company acquired the oil and gas assets of MLC Oil and Gas Ltd. for $57.4 million, increasing its proved and probable reserves by 7,900,000 bbl. of oil and natural gas liquids and 89,000,000 Mcf of natural gas. If this acquisition, the largest in RGO's history, had occurred on January 1, 1991, pro forma 1992 per share earnings would have been $0.24.

Important Developments

Aug. '93— Ranger announced the successful result of its first exploration well in Angola, Block 4. RGO plans to spend about $25 million during the next two years on oil exploration offshore Angola.

Apr. '93— The company and its partners approved development of the Forth oil field in the U.K. sector of the North Sea. Total development costs are estimated at $600 million and production is expected to begin in early 1996.

Next earnings report expected in early November.

Per Share Data (U.S. $)

Yr. End Dec. 31	[6]1992	1991	1990	1989	1988	>1987	[2]1986	1985	1984	1983
Tangible Bk. Val.	**4.55**	4.39	4.36	3.69	2.71	2.52	2.22	3.03	3.34	3.52
Cash Flow	**0.93**	0.53	1.11	0.84	0.68	0.66	0.72	0.42	0.32	1.13
Earnings[3]	**0.24**	0.06	[4]0.46	[4]0.27	0.12	0.20	0.06	d0.35	d0.23	[4]0.61
Dividends[5]	**0.08**	0.08	0.06	Nil	Nil	Nil	Nil	Nil	Nil	Nil
Payout Ratio	**34%**	146%	14%	Nil	Nil	Nil	Nil	Nil	Nil	Nil
Prices—High	**7¾**	8⅞	8⅜	6⅝	6½	6¾	5⅛	5½	11⅜	13⅛
Low	**5**	6	5⅝	5	4	3⅛	2⅝	2½	4½	5⅝
P/E Ratio—	**32–21**	NM	18–12	25–19	54–33	34–16	85–44	NM	NM	22–9

Data as orig. reptd. **1.** Annual divd. paid in Apr. 1993; in U.S. funds, bef. 15% Canadian tax to U.S. residents. **2.** Reflects merger or acquisition and acctg. change. **3.** Bef. spec item(s) of +0.36 in 1989, +0.07 in 1988, +0.10 in 1987, -0.95 in 1986, +0.02 in 1985. **4.** Ful. Dil. EPS: 0.45 in 1990, 0.26 in 1989, 0.60 in 1983. **5.** Bef. 15% Canadian tax to U.S. residents. **6.** Reflects merger or acquisition. d-Deficit. NM-Not Meaningful.

Income Data (Million U.S. $)

Year Ended Dec. 31	[1]Revs.	Oper. Inc.	% Oper. Inc. of Revs.	Cap. Exp.	Depr.	Int. Exp.	[3]Net Bef. Taxes	Eff. Tax Rate	[4]Net Inc.	% Net Inc. of Revs.	Cash Flow
[6]1992	**144**	**76**	**52.9**	**185**	**68.3**	**1.3**	**16.4**	**NM**	**23.5**	**16.3**	**91.8**
1991	112	54	48.5	157	46.4	1.8	4.5	NM	5.8	5.2	51.8
1990	144	87	60.6	89	57.2	5.2	41.2	NM	[5]42.4	29.5	98.3
1989	118	69	58.6	110	45.1	6.3	32.6	28.7%	23.2	19.7	67.0
1988	85	55	64.4	100	42.0	9.5	13.0	21.6%	10.2	12.0	50.8
1987	80	51	64.3	28	34.6	7.8	25.6	35.7%	16.5	20.6	49.7
[2]1986	77	50	64.0	66	48.3	5.1	7.7	28.8%	5.5	7.1	52.3
1985	142	62	43.3	49	53.8	7.9	d26.6	NM	d23.9	NM	28.9
1984	126	42	33.6	46	37.9	13.4	d4.5	NM	d15.9	NM	22.1
1983	151	92	60.9	132	33.0	4.7	62.8	39.3%	38.1	25.3	71.1

Balance Sheet Data (Million U.S. $)

Dec. 31	Cash	Curr. Assets	Curr. Liab.	Curr. Ratio	Total Assets	% Ret. on Assets	Long Term Debt	Common Equity	Total Cap.	% LT Debt of Cap.	% Ret. on Equity
1992	**13**	**57**	**29**	**2.0**	**641**	**3.8**	**33**	**448**	**567**	**5.8**	**5.3**
1991	58	93	44	2.1	590	1.0	3	432	506	0.6	1.3
1990	168	197	47	4.2	589	6.9	6	423	506	1.2	10.5
1989	156	184	48	3.8	565	4.3	82	312	485	16.9	8.1
1988	116	140	31	4.5	459	2.2	82	202	402	20.3	4.5
1987	186	208	45	4.6	471	3.7	87	188	405	21.6	8.5
1986	118	154	57	2.7	420	1.1	37	166	345	10.6	2.1
1985	90	136	43	3.2	504	NM	50	210	446	11.2	NM
1984	76	120	45	2.7	564	NM	76	235	501	15.1	NM
1983	61	111	46	2.4	557	6.6	75	243	495	15.2	19.7

Data as orig. reptd. **1.** Excl. other income. **2.** Refl. merger or acquisition and acctg. change. **3.** Incl. equity in earn. of nonconsol. subs. **4.** Bef. spec. items in 1989, 1988, 1987, 1986, 1985. **5.** Refl. accounting change. **6.** Refl. merger or acquisition. d-Deficit. NM-Not Meaningful.

[1]Total Revenues (Million U.S. $)

Quarter:	1993	1992	1991	1990
Mar.	43.3	34.2	34.6	35.8
Jun.	38.0	38.0	26.0	35.4
Sep.		40.6	27.3	39.0
Dec.		41.0	32.8	50.1
		153.7	120.7	160.3

Total revenues for the six months ended June 30, 1993, advanced 13%, year to year, reflecting higher oil and gas production in North America and increased gas production in the North Sea. Operating expenses rose less rapidly and future site restoration costs were down, partially offsetting greater depreciation and interest charges. Pretax income was up 19%. After taxes at 8.9%, versus tax credits of $4,077,000, share earnings were $0.12, against $0.15.

Common Share Earnings (U.S. $)

Quarter:	1993	1992	1991	1990
Mar.	0.07	0.08	0.04	0.09
Jun.	0.05	0.08	0.03	0.13
Sep.		0.02	0.06	0.06
Dec.		0.07	d0.07	0.18
		0.24	0.06	0.46

Dividend Data

An annual dividend on the common stock was initiated in 1990. Payment for 1992:

Amt of Divd. $	Date Decl.	Ex–divd. Date	Stock of Record	Payment Date
0.08*	Feb. 26	Mar. 22	Mar. 26	Apr. 15'93

***U.S. funds bef. 15% Canadian tax to U.S. residents.**

Finances

In September 1993, Ranger privately placed $50 million of 6.95% senior notes due 2003. Proceeds will be used to repay bank debt and fund acquisitions and North Sea development.

In February 1992, the company redeemed $2.3 million of its 8.5% convertible subordinated debentures. The remaining outstanding debentures were redeemed in September 1992.

During 1992, RGO received Petroleum Revenue Tax and income tax refunds of $38 million. Also, at December 31, 1992, the company had tax credits available to offset future taxable income in the U.K. ($137 million), Canada ($150 million) and Netherlands ($4.0 million).

Capitalization

Long Term Debt: $26,400,000 (6/93).

Common Stock: 98,485,689 shs. (no par).
Institutions hold approximately 21%.
Shareholders of record: 9,265.

1. Includes other income. d-Deficit.

Office—2700 Esso Plaza East, 425 First St. SW, Calgary, AB T2P 3L8, Canada. **Tel**—(403) 232-5200. **Chrmn**—S. S. Reisman. **Pres & CEO**—F. J. Dyment. **VP-Fin & CFO**—J. M. D'Aguiar. **VP & Secy**—J. E. Fletcher. **Dirs**—E. M. Bronfman, R. W. Campbell, F. J. Dyment, T. Enger, W. A. Gatenby, F. R. Matthews, P. H. Morrison, S. S. Reisman. **Transfer Agents & Registrars**—The R-M Trust Co., Montreal, Calgary, Vancouver, Toronto, London (UK); Mellon Securities Trust Co., NYC. **Incorporated** in Ontario in 1950. **Empl**—185.

 J.R. Jordan

Reynolds & Reynolds

NYSE Symbol REY In S&P MidCap 400

Price	Range	P-E Ratio	Dividend	Yield	S&P Ranking	Beta
Jul. 23'93	1993					
40¼	41⅜–24⅛	18	0.52	1.3%	B+	1.77

Summary

This company is a major supplier of information processing systems, including standard and custom business forms and computer systems, to automotive, professional, medical and general business markets. Emphasis on profitability and cost controls, a recovery in the automotive industry, and gains in market share are contributing to strong earnings advances.

Current Outlook

Earnings for the fiscal year to end September 30, 1994, are projected at $3.00 a share, up 22% from the $2.45 estimated for fiscal 1993.

The $0.13 quarterly dividend is likely to be raised to $0.15 or more in 1994.

Revenues are expected to rise sharply in fiscal 1994, boosted by the acquisition of COIN, and by gains in market share and improved market conditions. Profitability will benefit from ongoing operating efficiencies and savings realized from the consolidation of COIN's operations, a lower bad-debt reserve, and a shift toward higher-margin lines.

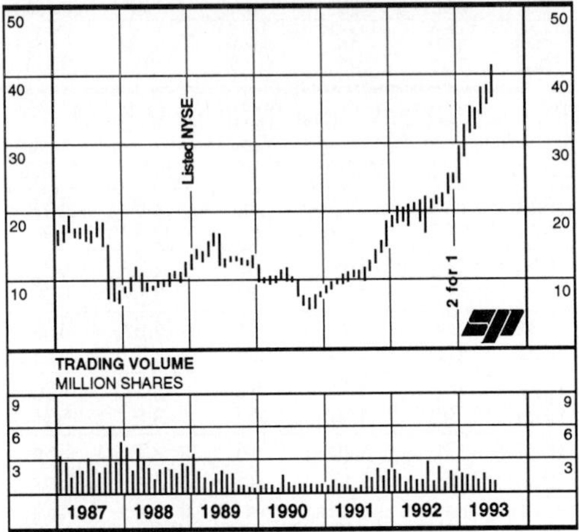

Revenues (Million $)

Quarter:	1992–93	1991–92	1990–91	1989–90
Dec.	163.5	151.7	151.4	139.4
Mar.	171.1	161.7	154.7	151.0
Jun.	169.8	159.8	141.3	149.4
Sep.	---	171.7	151.9	155.5
	---	644.8	599.3	595.3

Revenues in the nine months ended June 30, 1993, advanced 6.6%, year to year. Operating income climbed 40%, reflecting strong performance for the automotive computer systems business and significantly lower bad debt expense. With lower interest costs, net income soared 44%. Share earnings rose to $1.80, on 6.7% fewer shares, from $1.16 (before a credit of $0.05 from an accounting change).

Common Share Earnings ($)

Quarter:	1992–93	1991–92	1990–91	1989–90
Dec.	0.55	0.35	0.21	0.29
Mar.	0.62	0.40	0.25	0.31
Jun.	0.63	0.41	0.25	0.30
Sep.	E0.68	0.46	0.35	0.25
	E2.50	1.62	1.06	1.15

Important Developments

Jul. '93— REY said it had acquired Atlanta-based COIN Inc., a provider of automobile dealer computer systems, in June 1993, for about $30 million. The company said that the integration of COIN's operations is proceeding smoothly, and added that although no material impact from the acquisition is likely in fiscal 1993, a meaningful contribution to profitability is anticipated for fiscal 1994.

May '93— The company announced a program to buy back up to 500,000 common shares, in addition to a program announced in February 1993. Over the past 12 months, the company has repurchased over 2 million shares.

Apr. '93— REY said that with impending reform certain to impact health providers, its NMC Services unit is well positioned to profit from the need to improve efficiency and increase cash flow in physicians' practices.

Next earnings report expected in late October.

Per Share Data ($)

Yr. End Sep. 30	[3]1992	1991	1990	1989	1988	[3]1987	[3]1986	1985	1984	1983
Tangible Bk. Val.	**8.45**	8.40	7.42	6.45	[4]9.42	[4]8.69	[4]8.07	[4]6.09	[4]5.27	[4]4.73
Cash Flow	**2.66**	2.10	2.22	2.23	1.80	1.76	1.90	1.76	1.57	1.24
Earnings[2]	**1.62**	1.07	1.15	1.27	0.84	0.96	1.22	1.12	0.90	0.63
Dividends	**0.45**	0.42	0.40	0.38	0.38	0.38	0.35	0.31	0.27	0.27
Payout Ratio	**26%**	39%	35%	30%	45%	40%	29%	28%	30%	43%
Prices[1]—High	**25½**	18½	12¼	16⅞	12½	19½	20¾	14⅜	10	13⅛
Low	**16¾**	8	5¾	11½	8⅛	6¾	12½	7¾	6½	7½
P/E Ratio—	**16–10**	17–8	11–5	13–9	15–10	21–7	17–10	13–7	11–7	21–12

Data as orig. reptd. Adj. for stk. divs. of 100% Dec. 1992, 100% Apr. 1986. **1.** Cal. yr. **2.** Bef. spec. items of +0.05 in 1992, +0.37 in 1988. **3.** Refl. merger or acq. **4.** Incl. intangibles. E-Estimated.

Income Data (Million $)

Year Ended Sep. 30	Revs.	Oper. Inc.	% Oper. Inc. of Revs.	Cap. Exp.	Depr.	Int. Exp.	Net Bef. Taxes	Eff. Tax Rate	[3]Net Inc.	% Net Inc. of Revs.	Cash Flow
[1]**1992**	**645**	**91.7**	**14.2**	**17.4**	**24.4**	**5.1**	**64.4**	**40.9%**	**38.1**	**5.9**	**62.5**
1991	599	68.5	11.4	15.6	22.0	8.3	38.6	41.7%	22.5	3.8	44.5
1990	595	69.8	11.7	19.6	22.8	10.9	41.7	41.5%	24.4	4.1	47.2
1989	602	74.7	12.4	18.2	20.8	10.4	46.1	40.9%	[4]27.2	4.5	48.1
1988	600	46.5	7.7	22.3	20.5	11.9	[2]27.5	34.2%	18.1	3.0	38.6
[1]1987	563	58.9	10.5	33.9	17.9	8.5	[2]39.1	45.7%	[4]21.2	3.8	39.1
[1]1986	404	56.2	13.9	48.8	13.3	5.7	[2]41.5	42.6%	23.9	5.9	37.2
1985	325	46.8	14.4	21.0	12.1	2.0	[2]37.7	44.1%	21.1	6.5	33.1
1984	290	44.0	15.2	19.4	12.7	2.0	[2]29.7	42.3%	17.1	5.9	29.8
1983	252	32.3	12.8	18.4	11.6	2.3	[2]19.8	39.8%	11.9	4.7	23.5

Balance Sheet Data (Million $)

Sep. 30	Cash	Curr. Assets	Curr. Liab.	Curr. Ratio	Total Assets	% Ret. on Assets	Long Term Debt	Common Equity	Total Cap.	% LT Debt of Cap.	% Ret. on Equity
1992	**23.8**	**NA**	**NA**	**NA**	**522**	**7.2**	**69**	**257**	**380**	**18.0**	**14.8**
1991	27.7	NA	NA	NA	515	4.4	82	248	388	21.2	9.3
1990	30.2	NA	NA	NA	515	4.9	103	235	396	26.0	10.8
1989	28.7	NA	NA	NA	487	6.2	114	221	389	29.3	12.9
1988	2.7	163	68.9	2.4	399	4.7	98	202	317	30.9	9.3
1987	3.3	153	77.7	2.0	381	6.0	88	193	292	30.0	11.4
1986	7.8	141	54.6	2.6	324	9.1	75	178	261	28.6	15.3
1985	3.4	89	37.0	2.4	173	12.7	8	114	129	6.5	19.8
1984	2.8	77	42.6	1.8	159	11.4	7	99	111	6.2	18.3
1983	3.7	69	29.3	2.4	144	8.6	12	90	107	10.9	13.8

Data as orig. reptd. **1.** Refl. merger or acq. **2.** Incl. equity in earns. of nonconsol. subs. **3.** Bef. spec. items. **4.** Refl. acctg. change. NA-Not Available.

Business Summary

Reynolds & Reynolds is a major information systems company. Business segment contributions in fiscal 1992 were:

	Revs.	Profits
Business forms	58%	45%
Computer systems	42%	55%

Foreign operations accounted for 9% of revenues and 8% of operating income in fiscal 1992.

The business systems division manufactures standard, imprint and custom business forms for automobile dealers and related vehicle, parts and service businesses. The division also markets its products to office products dealers, other small businesses, financial institutions and hospitals. The company's Arnold Corp. unit produces continuous and snap-out custom forms, computer stock forms, and entertainment, sporting event and lottery tickets. Arnold also markets forms management services to financial institutions, insurance companies, hospitals and other large corporations.

The computer systems division sells turnkey computer systems, primarily to automobile dealers, markets computer hardware and software to office-based physicians, and sells microcomputer peripherals, supplies and accessories.

Dividend Data

Cash dividends have been paid each year since 1953. A "poison pill" stock purchase right was issued in 1991. A dividend reinvestment plan is available.

Amt. of Divd. $	Date Decl.	Ex-divd. Date	Stock of Record	Payment Date
0.24	Aug. 11	Aug. 20	Aug. 26	Sep. 11'92
2-for-1 Split	Nov. 17	Dec. 11	Nov. 30	Dec. 10'92
0.13	Nov. 17	Dec. 17	Dec. 23	Jan. 13'93
0.13	Feb. 11	Mar. 15	Mar. 19	Apr. 13'93
0.13	May 3	May 17	May 21	Jun. 11'93

Finances

Capital spending for fiscal 1993 was budgeted at $17 million, versus $18 million in fiscal 1992.

Capitalization

Long Term Debt: $28,284,000 (3/93).

Cl. A Common Stock: 21,068,603 shs. ($0.625 par).
Institutions hold 69%.
Shareholders of record: 1,728.

Cl. B Common Stock: 6,000,000 shs. ($0.03125 par); ea. conv. into 0.05 of a Cl. A sh.
R. H. Grant III owns all Cl. B shs. and controls over 20% of the total voting power.

Office—115 South Ludlow St., Dayton, OH 45402; P. O. Box 2608, Dayton 45401. **Tel**—(513) 443-2000. **Chrmn & Pres**—D.R. Holmes. **VP, CFO & Investor Contact**—Dale L. Medford (513-449-4099). **Secy**—A. M. Lutynski. **Dirs**—J. N. Bausman, D. E. Fry, R. H. Grant, Jr., R. H. Grant III, D. R. Holmes, D. L. Medford, R. C. Nevin, G. B. Price, Jr., W. H. Seall, K. W. Thiele, M. D. Walker. **Transfer Agent & Registrar**—Bank One, Indianapolis. **Incorporated** in Ohio in 1889. **Empl**—4,995.

 William H. Donald

Rochester Telephone

NYSE Symbol RTC In S&P MidCap 400

Price	Range	P-E Ratio	Dividend	Yield	S&P Ranking	Beta
Sep. 16'93	1993					
48	48–34⅝	21	1.58	3.3%	B+	0.81

Summary

This company provides telephone service in the City of Rochester and adjacent areas in New York and in 14 other states. It also distributes telecommunications equipment and provides long-distance and cellular telephone services. In September 1993, RTC filed with New York regulators the final details of its plan to open its Rochester local telephone market to full competition.

Current Outlook

Earnings for 1993 are forecast at $2.30 a share, versus 1992's $2.08. For 1994, earnings are projected to reach $2.55.

The $0.39½ quarterly dividend is the minimum expectation.

The rate of growth from telephone revenues will slow in 1993, reflecting a less aggressive acquisition schedule. Telephone margins should widen, aided by cost-control efforts. Contributions from network services and systems should increase, on good growth prospects for the long-distance unit. Revenues and earnings from cellular operations are expected to rise strongly. Interest costs will benefit from stabilization of the acquisition and network modernization programs. Share earnings will reflect additional shares outstanding.

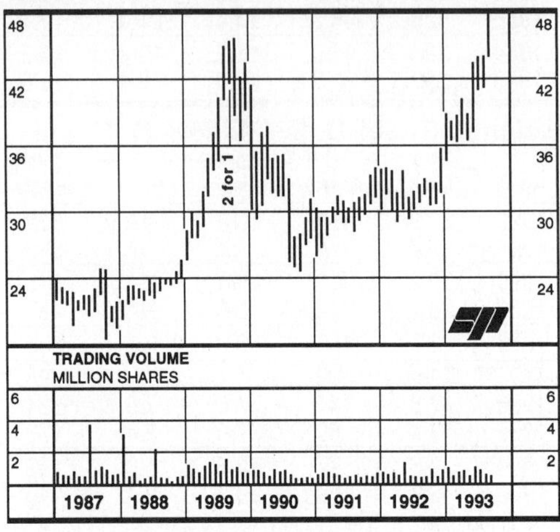

Total Revenues (Million $)

Quarter:	1993	1992	1991	1990
Mar.	211.0	193.5	160.2	146.6
Jun.	222.9	198.5	164.2	145.3
Sep.		201.6	184.2	150.4
Dec.		210.5	194.6	157.7
		804.0	703.2	600.0

Revenues for the six months ended June 30, 1993, rose 11%, year to year, aided by strong growth from the long-distance and wireless segments. Margins widened, and operating income was up 12%. Lower interest charges offset higher net other expenses, and pretax earnings advanced 17%. After taxes at 37.9%, versus 39.2%, net income was up 19%. Following preferred dividends, share earnings were $1.11, against $0.94.

Common Share Earnings ($)

Quarter:	1993	1992	1991	1990
Mar.	0.53	0.45	0.44	0.42
Jun.	0.58	0.49	0.92	0.42
Sep.	E0.58	0.54	0.48	0.44
Dec.	E0.61	0.60	0.52	0.44
	E2.30	2.08	2.36	1.72

Important Developments

Sep. '93— RTC filed with the New York Public Service Commission the final details of its proposal to open its Rochester local telephone market to full competition. The filing included the proposed prices for the split of the local telco into two separate companies, one acting as a wholesaler of telephone services ("R-Net") and the other as a retailer ("R-Com"). The wholesaler would remain a fully regulated subsidiary. R-Net's basic network services would be unbundled into functional elements which would be sold to competitive retailers at wholesale prices, allowing for discounts to stimulate usage. Customers would be allowed to choose among various service providers, including R-Com, for residential and business services; the proposal would also allow the retail company to bundle local, long-distance and cellular services. The plan includes a rate stabilization scheme with residential flat rate service rates frozen and wholesale rates increases limited to the inflation rate.

Next earnings report expected in mid-October.

Per Share Data ($)

Yr. End Dec. 31	1992	1991	1990	1989	1988	1987	1986	1985	1984	1983
Tangible Bk. Val.[1]	**13.79**	13.05	13.46	15.56	14.50	14.25	14.00	13.56	12.84	12.12
Earnings[2]	**2.08**	2.36	1.72	2.00	2.17	1.60	1.78	1.96	1.90	1.72
Dividends	**1.54**	1.50	1.46	1.42	1.36	1.32	1.28	1.22	1.14	1.08
Payout Ratio	**74%**	64%	85%	71%	63%	83%	72%	62%	60%	63%
Prices—High	**35¾**	34	41½	45¾	25¾	24⅞	26	21⅛	16⅝	16¾
Low	**29⅛**	26	24⅝	25¾	20⅜	18½	18	16⅛	13¾	13½
P/E Ratio—	**17–14**	14–11	24–14	23–13	12–9	16–12	15–10	11–8	9–7	10–8

Data as orig. reptd. Adj. for stk. div. of 100% Sep. 1989. **1.** Incl. intangibles prior to 1990. **2.** Bef. spec. items of -0.03 in 1992, +0.12 in 1991, +0.82 in 1989, +0.27 in 1987. NA-Not Available. E-Estimated.

Income Data (Million $)

Year Ended Dec. 31	[1]Access Lines	Util. Revs.	Non Util. Revs.	Total Revs.	Constr. Credits	Eff. Tax Rate	[2]Net Inc.	% Return On Revs.	% Return On Assets	% Return On [3]Equity
1992	**896**	**567**	**237**	**804**	**1.31**	**34.2%**	**70.5**	**8.8**	**4.7**	**11.6**
1991	853	487	216	703	1.57	35.1%	73.3	10.4	5.5	15.0
1990	674	407	193	600	2.03	35.7%	49.7	8.3	4.4	11.2
1989	610	360	202	562	1.89	32.4%	51.5	9.2	5.2	18.9
1988	559	322	157	479	1.86	33.5%	50.9	10.6	5.8	15.4
1987	508	291	148	439	2.02	44.9%	36.2	8.2	4.7	13.3
1986	478	279	122	401	2.28	44.5%	37.7	9.4	5.6	12.9
1985	467	272	132	405	1.87	43.9%	41.1	10.1	6.8	14.8
1984	455	257	101	358	0.56	48.8%	39.9	11.1	7.4	15.2
1983	NA	238	52	290	0.37	47.0%	36.0	12.4	7.2	14.5

Balance Sheet Data (Million $)

Dec. 31	[4]Gross Prop.	Depr. Reserve	Net Prop.	Capital Expend.	Total Invest. Capital	LT Debt	% LT Debt	Capitalization Pfd.	% Pfd.	Com.	% Com.
1992	**1,615**	**658**	**957**	**124**	**1,269**	**526**	**45.8**	**22.8**	**2.0**	**599**	**52.2**
1991	1,514	587	928	106	1,290	591	50.2	22.8	1.9	564	47.9
1990	1,190	423	767	106	981	363	43.5	22.8	2.7	449	53.8
1989	1,025	340	685	105	898	338	44.8	22.8	3.0	395	52.2
1988	903	286	617	106	734	244	40.7	22.8	3.8	333	55.5
1987	802	243	559	99	710	255	43.3	22.8	3.9	310	52.8
1986	733	222	512	105	572	182	36.9	22.8	4.6	288	58.5
1985	704	229	475	133	541	183	37.9	22.8	4.7	277	57.4
1984	645	217	428	73	477	151	34.6	22.9	5.3	262	60.1
1983	605	196	409	44	449	148	35.4	22.6	5.4	247	59.2

Data as orig reptd. **1.** In thousands. **2.** Bef. spec. items. **3.** Common; as reptd. by co. **4.** Utility plant. NA-Not Available.

Business Summary

Rochester Telephone provides telephone service in the city of Rochester, N.Y., and adjacent areas. It also owns 37 small telephone companies operating in 15 states. Unregulated businesses are provided through the Telecommunications Services group. Business segment contributions in 1992:

	Revs.	Profits
Telephone........................	70%	87%
Network services & systems	27%	11%
Wireless communications....	3%	2%

At December 31, 1992, telephone operations served a total of 895,971 access lines, up 5.1% from a year earlier. Over 36% of access lines are outside New York State.

The Telecommunications Services Group consists of the Network Services and Systems and the Wireless Communications segments. Network Services and Systems includes the long-distance operations, serving parts of the Northeast, Mid-Atlantic and Canada; and Rotelcom, which sells and maintains business communications equipment and systems.

Rochester Tel Mobile Communications provides cellular telephone and paging services in New York State. The company expected implementation of its New York State supersystem in the first quarter of 1994; the 50/50 joint venture with NYNEX Mobile Communications would provide cellular customers in upstate and western New York with expanded geographic coverage. RTC would be the managing partner of the venture which would serve 2.86 million POPs (adjusted).

Dividend Data

Dividends have been paid since 1926. A dividend reinvestment plan is available.

Amt of Divd. $	Date Decl.	Ex-divd. Date	Stock of Record	Payment Date
0.38½	Sep. 21	Oct. 8	Oct. 15	Nov. 1'92
0.39½	Dec. 22	Jan. 11	Jan. 15	Feb. 1'93
0.39½	Mar. 15	Apr. 8	Apr. 15	May 1'93
0.39½	Jun. 21	Jul. 9	Jul. 15	Aug. 1'93

Capitalization

Long Term Debt: $510,000,000 (6/93).

Minority Interests: $2,902,000.

Preferred Stock: $22,785,000.

Common Stock: 33,823,423 shs. ($1 par).
Institutions hold about 27%.
Shareholders of record: 20,131.

Office—180 South Clinton Ave., Rochester, NY 14646-0700. **Tel**—(716) 777-1000. **Pres & CEO**—R. L. Bittner. **VP-Fin & Treas**—L. L. Massaro. **Secy**—J. S. Trubek. **Investor Contact**—Kristen Jenks. **Dirs**—P. C. Barron, R. L. Bittner, J. R. Block, H. D. Calkins, B. Evans Edgerton, J. A. Estrada, D. E. Gill, A. C. Hasselwander, W. J. Humphrey Jr., D. H. McCorkindale, R. P. Miller Jr., G. D. O'Brien, L. J. Thomas, M. T. Tomaino. **Transfer Agent & Registrar**—First Chicago Trust Co. of New York, NYC. **Incorporated** in New York in 1920. **Empl**—4,701.

 Susan Stahl Gibney

Rohr, Inc.

NYSE Symbol RHR Options on Phila (Mar-Jun-Sep-Dec) In S&P MidCap 400

Price	Range	P-E Ratio	Dividend	Yield	S&P Ranking	Beta
Sep. 17'93	1993					
7	13⅛–6½	NM	None	None	B–	1.69

Summary

Sales of this leading supplier of jet engine nacelle assemblies are likely to reflect declining deliveries of commercial jet transports to major airlines expected over the next few years. RHR has taken substantial writeoffs and adopted new acccounting standards to reflect this environment, which resulted in a loss for fiscal 1993. Some earnings recovery could develop in fiscal 1994.

Current Outlook

Earnings for the fiscal year ending July 31, 1994, are projected at $0.75 a share, versus a deficit of $1.71 for fiscal 1993, which included substantial writedowns and restructuring charges.

Resumption of dividends is not expected in the near future.

Sales for fiscal 1994 could decline approximately 15%-20%, following an 8% drop for fiscal 1993. Delivery rates on a number of commercial programs are decreasing to reflect stretchouts and cancellations of orders by airline customers. Some recovery in operating margins could be seen as the result of production efficiencies and a reduction in restructuring and other unusual costs. A decline in interest expense could also develop.

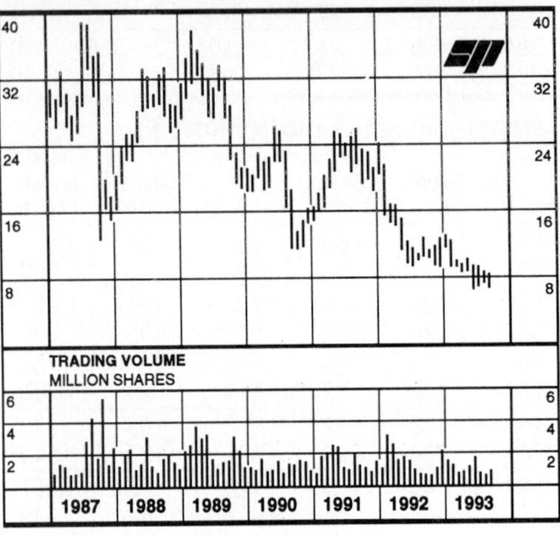

Net Sales (Million $)

Quarter:	1992–93	1991–92	1990–91	1989–90
Oct.	284	325	321	234
Jan.	342	307	301	227
Apr.	297	299	358	298
Jul.	252	349	405	318
	1,175	1,280	1,385	1,078

Sales (preliminary) for the fiscal year ended July 31, 1993, decreased 8.2% from the prior year, primarily reflecting declining commercial delivery rates. Margins narrowed, in part as a result of substantial nonrecurring charges in both years. There was a net loss of $30.6 million ($1.71 a share, before special charges of $12.50 from accounting changes), versus a profit of $1.45 million ($0.08 a share).

Common Share Earnings ($)

Quarter:	1992–93	1991–92	1990–91	1989–90
Oct.	0.20	0.50	0.26	d0.64
Jan.	d0.68	0.48	0.33	Nil
Apr.	d1.24	d1.42	0.51	0.25
Jul.	0.01	0.52	0.64	0.39
	d1.71	0.08	1.74	Nil

Important Developments

Sep. '93— Rohr said it would defer a proposed public offering of $125 million of senior subordinated notes.

May '93— The company said that it had adopted new accounting methods for long-term programs and contracts, which reduce the number of units and spares used to calculate overall profit margins. Resultant after-tax charges for the nine months ended May 2 were $22.5 million; cumulative charges through July 31, 1992, were $219.7 million. Also, in fiscal 1993, there were after-tax charges of $15.4 million for restructuring and other costs.

Jan. '93— Pratt & Whitney signed an agreement with Rohr extending through 2002 the contract for nacelles and thrust reversers for the PW4000 engine used on MD-11, A300 and A310 aircraft.

Next earnings report expected in late November.

Per Share Data ($)

Yr. End Jul. 31	1993	1992	1991	1990	[1]1989	1988	1987	1986	1985	1984
Tangible Bk. Val.	**NA**	25.17	25.23	23.42	23.34	21.34	19.54	17.84	15.14	12.22
Cash Flow	**NA**	1.66	3.32	1.52	3.30	3.18	2.45	3.55	3.69	3.30
Earnings[3]	**d1.71**	0.08	1.74	Nil	1.90	1.85	1.53	2.70	2.89	2.46
Dividends	**Nil**	Nil	Nil	Nil	Nil	Nil	Nil	Nil	Nil	Nil
Payout Ratio	**Nil**	Nil	Nil	Nil	Nil	Nil	Nil	Nil	Nil	Nil
Prices[2]—High	**13⅛**	24¼	26	26¼	37⅞	33½	39	36⅜	35	23⅛
Low	**6½**	9¼	14⅞	11½	18⅞	16⅜	12¾	25½	20⅞	13⅝
P/E Ratio—	**NM**	NM	15–9	NM	20–10	18–9	25–8	13–9	12–7	9–6

Data as orig. reptd. Adj. for stk. div. of 100% Dec. 1985. **1.** Reflects accounting change. **2.** Cal. yr. **3.** Bef. spec. items of -12.50 in 1993. d-Deficit. NM-Not Meaningful. NA-Not Available.

Income Data (Million $)

Year Ended Jul. 31	Revs.	Oper. Inc.	% Oper. Inc. of Revs.	Cap. Exp.	Depr.	Int. Exp.	Net Bef. Taxes	Eff. Tax Rate	Net Inc.	% Net Inc. of Revs.	Cash Flow
1992	**1,280**	**73**	**5.7**	**62.9**	**27.9**	**67.0**	**d17.8**	**NM**	**1.5**	**0.1**	**29.3**
1991	1,385	128	9.3	32.4	27.7	54.8	46.9	34.9%	30.5	2.2	58.2
1990	1,079	59	5.4	28.9	27.0	53.8	d9.0	NM	Nil	NM	27.1
[1]1989	1,045	100	9.6	39.0	24.8	32.0	46.1	27.3%	33.5	3.2	58.3
1988	907	84	9.3	51.2	23.4	23.8	[3]46.4	30.0%	[1]32.5	3.6	55.8
1987	663	67	10.1	37.3	16.1	10.0	[3]44.6	39.7%	26.9	4.1	43.0
1986	626	87	13.9	35.0	15.0	3.3	[3]77.7	39.1%	47.3	7.6	62.3
1985	[2]607	95	15.7	30.2	13.2	4.2	[3]78.4	39.7%	47.3	7.8	60.5
1984	[2]614	90	14.6	19.8	12.9	6.9	70.5	46.4%	37.8	6.2	50.6
1983	569	60	10.5	24.8	12.0	7.2	41.5	41.9%	24.1	4.2	34.1

Balance Sheet Data (Million $)

Jul. 31	Cash	Curr. Assets	Curr. Liab.	Curr. Ratio	Total Assets	% Ret. on Assets	Long Term Debt	Common Equity	Total Cap.	% LT Debt of Cap.	% Ret. on Equity
1992	**21**	**1,008**	**308**	**3.3**	**1,364**	**0.1**	**525**	**449**	**1,017**	**51.6**	**0.3**
1991	26	1,050	337	3.1	1,408	2.2	542	441	1,036	52.3	7.2
1990	26	982	346	2.8	1,320	0.0	484	414	959	50.5	0.0
1989	51	878	323	2.7	1,165	3.3	361	412	833	43.3	8.5
1988	87	694	197	3.5	883	4.1	296	375	674	43.9	9.0
1987	100	561	188	3.0	707	4.4	154	346	503	30.6	8.1
1986	79	362	154	2.3	502	10.0	21	313	334	6.3	16.4
1985	108	329	142	2.3	438	10.7	23	264	288	8.1	19.8
1984	92	277	154	1.8	396	10.3	50	191	240	20.7	21.7
1983	49	245	105	2.3	322	6.6	59	149	208	28.2	15.8

Data as orig. reptd. **1.** Reflects accounting change. **2.** Incl. other inc. **3.** Incl. equity in earns. of nonconsol. subs. d-Deficit. NM-Not Meaningful.

Business Summary

Rohr Inc., (formerly Rohr Industries) is primarily engaged in the manufacture of systems for commercial, military and business aircraft, and for space vehicles.

The manufacture of components for and the assembly of nacelles (pods that surround aircraft engines), pylons (which attach the propulsion system to the aircraft) and thrust reversers (which aid aircraft deceleration after landing) comprise the bulk of the company's sales. Complete nacelle systems, which usually include the cowling, nozzle systems and thrust reversers, are made for commercial, military and general aviation aircraft under contracts with major airframe and engine manufacturers. Other products include noise suppression systems, engine components, and structures for high-temperature environments.

McDonnell Douglas accounted for 18% of sales in fiscal 1992 (versus 14% in fiscal 1991), Pratt & Whitney for 15% (16%), Boeing Co. for 15% (14%), General Electric for 12% (12%), Airbus Industrie for 8% (12%) and Rolls-Royce for 7% (8%). Direct or indirect sales to the U.S. government (including some overlap with the above) accounted for about 14% of the total (20%).

Space operations, which account for a small part of sales, consist primarily of the manufacture of solid rocket motor nozzles and insulated cases for the Titan Space Launch Vehicle.

Dividend Data

No cash dividends have been paid since October, 1975. A "poison pill" stock purchase right was issued in 1986.

Finances

The company reported that the cash balance as of July 31, 1993 was $42.2 million compared with $21.1 million at the end of the 1992 fiscal year. The firm backlog was $1.4 billion, down from $1.9 billion a year earlier.

Capitalization

Long Term Debt: $480,889,000 (7/93).

Common Stock: 17,906,631 shs. ($1 par). Institutions hold about 57%. Shareholders of record: 3,789.

Office—Foot of H Street, Chula Vista, CA 91910. **Tel**—(619) 691-4111. **Chrmn**—J. J. Kerley. **Pres & CEO**—R. H. Rau. **VP & Secy**—R. W. Madsen. **VP & Treas**—R. Miller. **Investor Contact**—J. F. Walsh. **Dirs**—W. Barnes, W. W. Booth, E. E. Covert, R. H. Goldsmith, K. R. Hahn, W. M. Hoffman, J. J. Kerley, D. L. Moore, R. M. Price, R. H. Rau, W. P. Sommers, J. D. Steele. **Transfer Agent & Registrar**—First Chicago Trust Co. of New York. **Incorporated** in California in 1949; reincorporated in Delaware in 1969. **Empl**—7,450.

 T.M. Canning, CFA

Rollins, Inc.

NYSE Symbol ROL In S&P MidCap 400

Price	Range	P-E Ratio	Dividend	Yield	S&P Ranking	Beta
Oct. 21'93	1993					
23⅜	26⅞–21⅜	20	0.44	1.9%	NR	0.69

Summary

Rollins derives most of its revenues from its Orkin termite and pest control business, one of the largest in the world. It also provides lawn care and interior landscaping services and is engaged in the residential and commercial protective services business. Revenues and earnings advanced, year to year, in 1993's first half, benefiting primarily from gains in the Orkin businesses.

Business Summary

Rollins, Inc. provides termite and pest control, lawn care and interior landscaping services under the Orkin name and security-related products and services. Contributions in 1992 by business segment:

	Revs.	Profits
Orkin	87%	87%
Rollins Protective	11%	8%
Other	2%	5%

The company's Orkin Exterminating Co. subsidiary is one of the world's largest termite and pest control service concerns. Continuous protection against insects and rodents through periodic preventive treatments is provided to homes, hotels and motels, office buildings and warehouses, food and drug stores, restaurants, food processing plants and hospitals and aboard aircraft and ships. Operations are conducted from 349 company-owned and operated branches in 49 states, the District of Columbia, Canada, Mexico and Puerto Rico. The seasonal nature of this business has historically resulted in higher revenues and income in the spring and summer.

Orkin Lawn Care provides residential lawn care services on a contractual basis through 32 branches in 14 states. ROL entered the West Coast market through a 1989 acquisition with operations in California, Oregon and Washington.

Orkin Plantscaping was added in 1990, also through acquisitions. From 10 branches and one supply outlet, Plantscaping provides interior landscaping services in 16 states to commercial businesses such as hotels, shopping malls, restaurants and office buildings.

The Rollins Protective Services subsidiary offers a full range of protective services to residential and commercial clients. Operations are conducted from 44 company-owned branches serving customers in 33 states and the District of Columbia. In addition to designing and installing wireless and wired protection systems, the company provides guaranteed routine maintenance programs, as well as 24-hour emergency repair and 24-hour monitoring services.

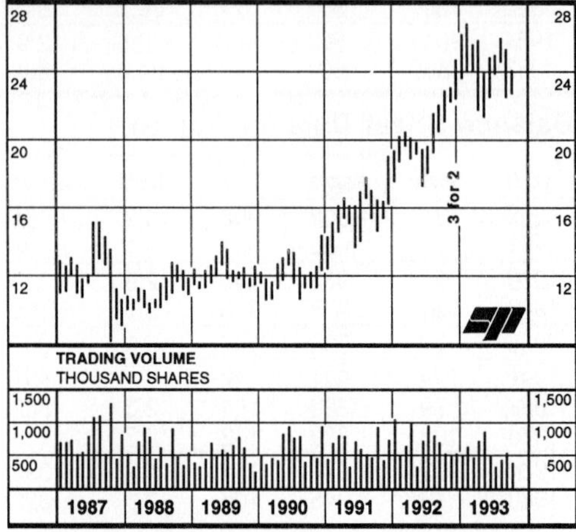

Important Developments

Sep. '93— The company acquired Allied Pest Control Inc. of Indiana and Bugco, Inc. of Texas. Terms were not disclosed.

Jul. '93— ROL said sales and operating income gains for the pest control and termite businesses in the first half of 1993 reflected increased customer retention, improved employee productivity, effective cost control measures, new services and a good termite season. The company added that, after the first quarter of 1993, the protective services division refocused its sales attention to the core residential market through the introduction of the midrange priced Protector Security System, which contributed to improved results in the second quarter of 1993.

Next earnings report expected in late October.

Per Share Data ($)

Yr. End Dec. 31[1]	1992	[2]1991	1990	1989	1988	1987	1986	1985	1984	1983
Tangible Bk. Val.	**2.46**	1.79	1.27	0.90	0.59	0.16	d0.07	d0.30	d0.15	NA
Cash Flow	**1.29**	1.11	0.99	0.87	0.89	0.76	0.71	0.63	0.57	1.31
Earnings	**1.07**	0.89	0.77	0.67	0.70	0.57	0.53	0.46	0.42	0.23
Dividends	**0.400**	0.387	0.373	0.357	0.337	0.323	0.310	0.307	NA	NA
Payout Ratio	**37%**	44%	48%	54%	48%	58%	58%	66%	NA	NA
Prices[3]—High	**24¾**	19⅛	14⅜	14	12⅞	15⅛	12⅛	8¼	9	NA
Low	**17 11/32**	12⅜	10⅝	11¼	9⅞	8⅛	8⅜	6¼	4⅝	NA
P/E Ratio—	**23–16**	22–14	19–14	21–17	18–14	27–14	23–16	18–14	21–11	NA

Data as orig. reptd.; prior to 1984 data as reptd. in RPC Energy Services prospectus dated 6-1-84, adjusted to exclude RPC Energy Services and Rollins Communications. Adj. for stk. div. of 50% in Dec. 1992. **1.** Yr. ended Jun. 30 prior to 1988. **2.** Refl. merger or acquisition. **3.** Cal. yr. d-Deficit. NA-Not Available.

Income Data (Million $)

Year Ended Dec. 31[1]	Revs.	Oper. Inc.	% Oper. Inc. of Revs.	Cap. Exp.	Depr.	[3]Int. Exp.	Net Bef. Taxes	Eff. Tax Rate	Net Inc.	% Net Inc. of Revs.	Cash Flow
1992	**528**	**68.9**	**13.1**	**6.6**	**8.0**	**Nil**	**62.8**	**39.5%**	**38.0**	**7.2**	**46.0**
[2]1991	476	58.0	12.1	8.0	7.8	Nil	52.1	39.5%	31.5	6.6	39.3
1990	436	50.0	11.5	8.0	7.5	Nil	45.4	39.5%	27.4	6.3	34.9
1989	402	44.0	11.0	9.0	7.5	Nil	38.8	39.3%	23.5	5.8	31.0
1988	381	47.0	12.3	8.0	7.0	Nil	41.5	40.5%	[4]24.7	6.5	31.7
1987	337	46.0	13.7	7.0	6.7	0.40	39.6	49.8%	19.9	5.9	26.5
1986	308	43.0	14.1	5.0	6.1	0.68	36.7	49.2%	18.6	6.0	24.7
1985	281	39.0	14.0	10.0	6.0	1.42	31.8	48.9%	16.3	5.8	22.3
1984	262	36.0	13.8	7.0	5.7	1.01	29.7	47.3%	15.6	6.0	21.3
1983	246	34.0	13.7	3.0	6.5	1.34	15.7	42.0%	9.1	3.7	51.3

Balance Sheet Data (Million $)

Dec. 31[1]	Cash	Curr. Assets	Curr. Liab.	Curr. Ratio	Total Assets	% Ret. on Assets	Long Term Debt	Common Equity	Total Cap.	% LT Debt of Cap.	% Ret. on Equity
1992	**50.7**	**152**	**62.1**	**2.4**	**236**	**17.2**	**Nil**	**130**	**151**	**Nil**	**32.3**
1991	41.2	121	56.4	2.1	205	16.5	Nil	105	126	Nil	32.8
1990	31.8	95	49.6	1.9	178	16.2	Nil	87	105	Nil	34.5
1989	26.0	84	40.4	2.1	160	15.3	Nil	72	97	Nil	35.3
1988	16.9	74	37.6	2.0	147	17.8	Nil	61	88	Nil	46.4
1987	11.0	60	42.6	1.4	132	15.9	Nil	45	74	Nil	47.7
1986	5.9	50	34.0	1.5	117	15.7	4.0	38	72	5.6	55.8
1985	11.2	50	41.6	1.2	120	14.3	18.6	29	69	26.9	52.6
1984	4.2	39	47.7	0.8	112	7.5	12.0	34	65	18.6	12.9
1983	14.1	47	39.1	1.2	117	7.3	3.5	92	114	3.0	9.2

Data as orig. reptd.; prior to 1984 data reptd. in RPC Energy Services prospectus dated 6-1-84, adj. to excl. RPC Energy Services and Rollins Communications. 1. Yr. ended Jun. 30 prior to 1988. 2. Refl. merger or acq. 3. Net of interest income prior to 1987. 4. Refl. acctg. change.

Revenues (Million $)

Quarter:	1993	1992	1991	1990
Mar.	127	117	105	98
Jun.	163	150	136	124
Sep.		138	125	113
Dec.		122	111	102
		528	4 76	436

For the six months ended June 30, 1993, revenues rose 8.6%, year to year, primarily reflecting growth at the Orkin businesses. Protective services revenues were up marginally, while other businesses gained 17%. Operating income increased 14% at Orkin, 4.3% at Rollins Protective and 23% for other businesses, and pretax income expanded 14%. After taxes at 38.5%, versus 39.5%, consolidated net income was up 16%, to $24.9 million ($0.70 a share), from $21.5 million ($0.61).

Common Share Earnings ($)

Quarter:	1993	1992	1991	1990
Mar.	0.16	0.14	0.11	0.10
Jun.	0.54	0.47	0.39	0.35
Sep.		0.28	0.24	0.21
Dec.		0.18	0.15	0.12
		1.07	0.89	0.77

Dividend Data

Dividends have been paid since 1961. A dividend reinvestment plan is available.

Amt. of Divd. $	Date Decl.	Ex–divd. Date	Stock of Record	Payment Date
0.15	Oct. 27	Nov. 4	Nov. 10	Dec. 10'92
3–for–2 Split	Oct. 27	Dec. 11	Nov. 10	Dec. 10'92
0.11	Jan. 26	Feb. 4	Feb. 10	Mar. 10'93
0.11	Apr. 27	May 4	May 10	Jun. 10'93
0.11	Jul. 27	Aug. 4	Aug. 10	Sep. 10'93

Finances

At June 30, 1993, the company had working capital of $104.8 million ($89.9 million at December 31, 1992) and cash, short-term investments and marketable securities of $58.9 million ($50.7 million).

Capitalization

Long Term Debt: None (6/93).

Common Stock: 35,635,459 shs. ($1 par).
The Rollins family controls about 41%.
Institutions hold about 44% (incl. some Rollins family shares).
Shareholders of record: 4,076 (12/92).

Office—2170 Piedmont Rd., N.E., Atlanta, GA 30324. **Tel**—(404) 888-2000. **Chrmn & CEO**—R. R. Rollins. **Pres**—G. W. Rollins. **CFO, Secy, Treas & Investor Contact**—Gene L. Smith **Dirs**—B. J. Dismuke, W. Looney, G. W. Rollins, J. W. Rollins, R. R. Rollins, H. B. Tippie, J. B. Williams. **Transfer Agent & Registrar**—Trust Co. Bank, Atlanta. **Incorporated** in Delaware in 1948. **Empl**—8,633.

 L. Feuer Nelson

Ruddick Corp.

NYSE Symbol RDK In S&P MidCap 400

Price	Range	P–E Ratio	Dividend	Yield	S&P Ranking	Beta
Sep. 9'93	1993					
20½	22⅝–18⅝	15	[4]0.28	[4]1.4%	A	0.52

Summary

This diversified holding company derives about half of its profits from supermarket operations, with most of the balance from manufacturing thread and yarn. The company also makes and distributes business forms and related products. Earnings have been in an uptrend since 1985; increased earnings in fiscal 1993's first nine months reflected higher sales and profits in both supermarket and thread and yarn operations.

Business Summary

Ruddick Corporation is a diversified holding company whose subsidiaries operate supermarkets, manufacture yarn and thread and business forms and make venture capital investments. Contributions by subsidiary in fiscal 1992 were:

	Sales	Profits
Harris Teeter	81%	49%
American & Efird	16%	45%
Jordan Graphics	3%	6%

The Harris Teeter (HT) subsidiary operates supermarkets, with a total of 135 stores in operation as of fiscal 1992 year-end, in North Carolina (95), South Carolina (18), Virginia (19), Georgia (two) and Tennessee (one). The stores carry typical food items sold by supermarkets, as well as non-food items such as health and beauty aids.

Most HT stores feature a full-service deli, bakery, fresh seafood and meat counters, wine and floral departments. HT's policy is have each store undergo a major remodel every eight years.

The number of HT stores in operation at recent fiscal year-ends were:

1992	135	1989	128
1991	132	1988	123
1990	130		

American & Efird (A&E) makes industrial sewing thread from natural and synthetic fibers for use by clothing, automotive, furniture, upholstery and footwear manufacturers. It also manufactures sales yarn used by the knitting and weaving industries and consumer sewing thread for home sewing.

Jordan Graphics (formerly Jordan Business Forms) produces and distributes a broad line of business forms, labels, envelopes, special items and laser printed products.

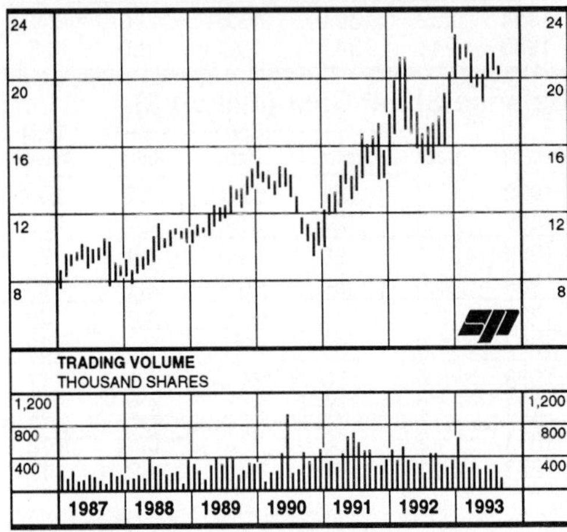

Ruddick Investment Co. is a wholly owned venture-capital concern. Capital gains are its principal objective.

Important Developments

Aug. '93— Ruddick acquired five grocery stores from Bruno's Inc., all of which are located in or around Columbia, S.C. Terms were not disclosed.

Jul. '93— The company attributed the higher sales and operating profits in fiscal 1993's third quarter to improved results at both A&E and Harris. A&E benefited from strong U.S. industrial thread sales, mainly reflecting quality improvements. Profits at Harris Teeter were up on a 6.0% gain in same-store sales, strong feature oriented merchandising and increased advertising. Ruddick believed that earnings in fiscal 1993's fourth quarter would continue to improve and that sales and earnings for the year would exceed those of fiscal 1992.

Next earnings report expected in mid-October.

Per Share Data ($)

Yr. End Sep. 30	1992	1991	1990	1989	1988	[2]1987	1986	1985	[2]1984	1983
Tangible Bk. Val.[1]	**11.03**	10.10	9.30	8.37	7.61	6.93	6.38	5.98	5.52	5.21
Cash Flow	**2.74**	2.65	2.61	2.39	1.98	1.67	1.54	1.38	1.36	1.18
Earnings	**1.30**	1.24	1.19	1.04	0.95	0.75	0.70	0.65	0.75	0.66
Dividends	**0.390**	0.370	0.350	0.310	0.285	0.225	0.210	0.193	0.215	0.193
Payout Ratio	**29%**	32%	29%	29%	29%	29%	29%	30%	29%	26%
Prices[3]—High	**21¼**	17⅜	15⅛	14¹¹⁄₁₆	11⁷⁄₁₆	10⁹⁄₁₆	9⁵⁄₁₆	8½	7⁷⁄₁₆	7⁷⁄₁₆
Low	**14⅞**	10	9½	10⁵⁄₁₆	7⅞	7⅝	5⅞	5¾	5	4⁷⁄₁₆
P/E Ratio—	**16–11**	14–8	13–8	14–10	12–8	14–10	13–8	13–9	10–7	11–7

Data as orig. reptd. Adj. for stk. divs. of 100% Jul. 1991, 100% Jul. 1986. **1.** Incl. intangibles. **2.** Reflects merger or acquisition. **3.** Cal. yr. **4.** Excl. extra.

Income Data (Million $)

Year Ended Sep. 30[1]	Revs.	Oper. Inc.	% Oper. Inc. of Revs.	Cap. Exp.	Depr.	Int. Exp.	[4]Net Bef. Taxes	Eff. Tax Rate	Net Inc.	% Net Inc. of Revs.	Cash Flow
1992	**1,569**	**93.9**	**6.0**	**48.6**	**34.3**	**9.5**	**50.4**	**38.4%**	**30.8**	**2.0**	**65.0**
1991	1,478	87.0	5.9	43.2	30.6	13.2	43.6	37.6%	26.8	1.8	57.3
1990	1,422	81.0	5.7	48.1	28.7	12.6	40.3	38.1%	24.0	1.7	52.6
1989	1,301	74.0	5.7	50.6	26.7	13.8	33.9	38.3%	20.2	1.6	46.8
1988	1,104	59.7	5.4	84.8	20.2	8.6	30.6	39.9%	18.4	1.7	38.5
[2]1987	971	50.2	5.2	32.3	17.6	6.0	27.5	47.8%	14.4	1.5	31.9
1986	884	39.9	4.5	24.6	16.2	4.7	22.3	39.7%	13.4	1.5	29.5
1985	882	39.3	4.5	27.7	14.2	4.7	22.0	43.0%	12.6	1.4	26.6
[2]1984	730	35.1	4.8	44.9	11.1	5.0	22.5	41.1%	13.2	1.8	24.1
1983	541	27.6	5.1	18.8	8.7	[3]3.9	17.0	37.8%	10.6	2.0	19.0

Balance Sheet Data (Million $)

Sep. 30	Cash	Curr. Assets	Curr. Liab.	Curr. Ratio	Total Assets	% Ret. on Assets	Long Term Debt	Common Equity	Total Cap.	% LT Debt of Cap.	% Ret. on Equity
1992	**20.4**	**242**	**144**	**1.7**	**542**	**5.9**	**89**	**254**	**386**	**23.1**	**12.6**
1991	10.8	216	136	1.6	498	5.1	74	232	351	21.2	12.0
1990	11.4	199	124	1.6	468	5.2	109	183	333	32.7	13.8
1989	10.5	183	123	1.5	439	4.8	112	157	307	36.6	13.4
1988	10.2	169	122	1.4	402	5.2	101	142	245	41.1	13.4
1987	10.4	141	86	1.6	304	5.0	60	129	191	31.2	11.5
1986	13.3	117	75	1.6	264	5.3	47	116	166	28.5	11.8
1985	5.3	101	64	1.6	238	5.4	45	106	155	29.0	12.1
1984	4.8	102	69	1.5	227	5.9	42	97	143	29.1	13.7
1983	15.1	87	42	2.1	175	6.2	45	74	133	33.6	14.6

Data as orig. reptd. **1.** Refl. merger or acq. **2.** Reflects merger or acquisition. **3.** Net of int. inc. **4.** Incl. equity in earns. of nonconsol. subs.

Net Sales (Million $)

Quarter:	1992–93	1991–92	1990–91	1989–90
Dec.	422	389	363	353
Mar.	418	387	362	353
Jun.	424	400	378	358
Sep.		393	375	358
		1,569	1,478	1,422

Net sales for the nine months ended June 27, 1993, rose 7.5%, year to year, led by gains of 7.1% for A&E and 7.9% for HT. Operating profits were up 5.3%, reflecting a 5.5% increase for A&E and a 8.1% rise at HT. Profits at Jordan Graphics fell 27%, owing to lower sales of custom and stock forms and higher paper prices. Following an 11% decline in interest expense (net), pretax income rose 7.5%. After taxes at 38.7%, versus 38.6%, net income was up 7.5%, to $24,781,000 ($1.04 a share), from $23,050,000 ($0.97).

Common Share Earnings ($)

Quarter:	1992–93	1991–92	1990–91	1989–90
Dec.	0.34	0.32	0.28	0.29
Mar.	0.33	0.31	0.31	0.30
Jun.	0.37	0.34	0.34	0.32
Sep.		0.33	0.31	0.29
		1.30	1.24	1.19

Dividend Data

Dividends have been paid since 1976. A "poison pill" stock purchase right was adopted in 1990.

Amt of Divd. $	Date Decl.	Ex–divd. Date	Stock of Record	Payment Date
0.06	Nov. 19	Dec. 1	Dec. 7	Dec. 31'92
0.06	Feb. 18	Mar. 8	Mar. 12	Apr. 1'93
0.07	May 20	Jun. 7	Jun. 11	Jul. 1'93
0.07	Aug. 19	Sep. 13	Sep. 17	Oct. 1'93
0.17 Ext.	Aug. 19	Sep. 13	Sep. 17	Oct. 1'93

Finances

In April 1992, Ruddick secured a 15-year, $70 million bank loan and used the proceeds to pay off an existing $38.5 million loan and a portion of a $45 million revolving credit facility.

Capitalization

Long Term Debt: $75,421,000 (6/93).

$0.56 Noncum. Conv. Pref. Stock: 102,800 shs. ($5 par); red. at $10; ea. conv. into 4 com. shs.

Common Stock: 23,153,000 shs. ($1 par).
Ruddick ESOP holds 31%.
A. T. Dickson & R. S. Dickson together own 16%.
Shareholders of record: 2,038 (11/92).

Office—2000 Two First Union Center, Charlotte, NC 28282. **Tel**—(704) 372-5404. **Chrmn**—R. S. Dickson. **Pres**—A. T. Dickson. **VP-Fin & Investor Contact**—Richard N. Brigden. **Secy**—D. B. Williford. **Treas**—D. A. Stephenson. **Dirs**—T. M. Belk, E. B. Borden Jr., J. W. Copeland, A. T. Dickson, R. S. Dickson, B. F. Dolan, R. Dowd, J. E. S. Hynes, H. L. McColl Jr., E. C. Wall Jr. **Transfer Agent & Registrar**—Wachovia Bank of North Carolina, Winston-Salem. **Incorporated** in North Carolina in 1968. **Empl**—14,100.

 John D. Coyle, CFA

Savannah Foods & Industries

NYSE Symbol SFI In S&P MidCap 400

Price	Range	P–E Ratio	Dividend	Yield	S&P Ranking	Beta
Sep. 23'93	1993					
15⅞	17⅞–13½	21	0.54	3.4%	B+	0.66

Summary

This company refines both beet and cane sugar for sale in a variety of forms to consumers and processors. Sales and earnings declined in the past two years, and management expected negative earnings comparisons to continue at least through 1993's first three quarters and possibly into the fourth. Competitive pricing pressures are largely to blame for the weakness.

Business Summary

Savannah Foods & Industries is one of the nation's largest refined cane and beet sugar producers. Products are marketed primarily in the eastern half of the U.S. The company operates three cane sugar refineries, five sugar beet processing plants and a raw-sugar mill.

The Savannah Sugar Refinery division refines and processes sugar and sugar products (including blends with corn syrups) and liquid animal feeds produced at a refinery near Savannah, Ga. Output is marketed mainly in the Southeast under the brand name Dixie Crystals, considered the leading brand of sugar marketed in the area. Packaged sugars are also distributed under other brand names and private labels.

Wholly-owned Everglades Sugar produces bulk, liquid (including corn syrup blends) and a limited line of packaged sugars under the names Evercane and Dixie Crystals. Grocery sugars are marketed both directly and through brokers in Florida. Industrial sugars are marketed throughout the East and Midwest.

Colonial Sugars refines sugar and sugar products (including blends) and by-products of the sugar refining process. It markets a complete line of bulk, packaged and liquid sugars under the Colonial name.

Michigan Sugar Co. processes sugar beets into refined sugar and produces beet pulp and molasses. Products are sold under the Pioneer brand name primarily in Michigan, and to a lesser extent in the midwestern and eastern portions of the U.S.

A line of sugar envelopes and portion-control items, consisting of individual servings of salt, pepper, nondairy creamers, etc., is produced by wholly-owned Savannah Foodservice Inc., and is sold under the trade names Dixie Crystals and Pioneer and various private labels. Saccharin- and aspartame-based sweeteners are marketed under the Sweet Thing and Sweet Thing II brand names, respectively.

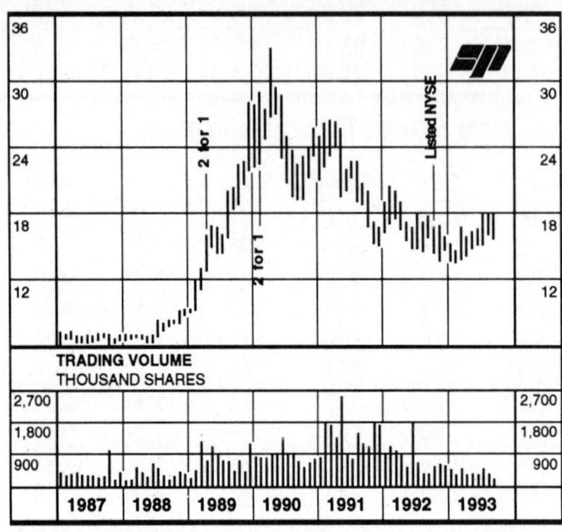

Other subsidiaries include Phoenix Packaging, which packages powdered and brown sugars; Raceland Sugars (acquired in 1991 for $18.5 million), a producer of raw sugar and by-products; and Food Carrier Inc., an irregular-route transporter of sugar products and general commodities.

Important Developments

Jul. '93— Savannah acquired King Packaging Co., with annual sales of about $20 million, for an undisclosed amount. Separately, the company said that weather conditions in the sugar beet growing regions appeared to be producing an average crop in 1993, which would be down from the record crop of 1992. Savannah believes that if the 1993 crop does decline from the prior year and government marketing allocations are kept in place through most of the 1993 crop year, earnings for 1994 should exceed those of 1993.

Per Share Data ($)

Yr. End Dec. 31	1992	1991	1990	[1]1989	1988	1987	[1]1986	1985	[1]1984	1983
Tangible Bk. Val.	**[3]8.03**	8.39	7.50	6.24	5.05	4.49	4.22	4.01	3.63	3.29
Cash Flow	**1.88**	2.15	2.41	2.08	1.26	1.02	0.79	0.98	0.86	0.82
Earnings[2]	**1.03**	1.43	1.80	1.53	0.75	0.53	0.39	0.66	0.65	0.67
Dividends	**0.525**	0.490	0.390	0.293	0.240	0.225	0.220	0.223	0.206	0.213
Payout Ratio	**50%**	34%	22%	19%	32%	43%	56%	34%	32%	32%
Prices—High	**20½**	26½	33	28⅛	9⅜	7⅜	9⅜	7⅞	5⅝	5
Low	**13⅝**	15	19¼	9	6⅜	6	5½	4¼	4⅛	2⅞
P/E Ratio—	**20–13**	19–10	18–11	18–6	13–8	14–11	24–14	12–6	9–6	8–4

Data as orig. reptd. Adj. for stk. divs. of 100% Feb. 1990, 100% Apr. 1989, 100% Oct. 1985. **1.** Refl. merger or acq. **2.** Bef. results of disc. ops. of +0.27 in 1983 & spec. item(s) of -0.69 in 1992. **3.** Incl. intangibles.

Income Data (Million $)

Year Ended Dec. 31	Revs.	Oper. Inc.	% Oper. Inc. of Revs.	Cap. Exp.	Depr.	Int. Exp.	Net Bef. Taxes	Eff. Tax Rate	[4]Net Inc.	% Net Inc. of Revs.	Cash Flow
1992	**1,138**	**71.5**	**6.3**	**45.3**	**22.4**	**10.50**	**41.0**	**33.3%**	**[3]27.3**	**2.4**	**49.7**
1991	1,200	86.2	7.2	55.7	19.4	9.82	60.1	36.3%	38.3	3.2	57.6
1990	1,214	97.4	8.0	41.6	16.5	9.67	74.9	35.1%	48.6	4.0	65.2
[1]1989	1,097	80.6	7.3	34.5	15.0	8.01	60.7	32.4%	41.1	3.7	56.0
1988	917	46.3	5.0	16.6	13.6	6.60	30.6	34.4%	20.1	2.2	33.7
1987	879	37.4	4.3	13.7	13.3	6.77	22.6	37.9%	[3]14.0	1.6	27.3
[1]1986	635	26.1	4.1	45.4	10.5	6.29	17.2	39.7%	10.4	1.6	20.9
1985	629	42.6	6.8	25.0	8.5	4.89	29.6	41.6%	17.3	2.7	25.8
[1]1984	591	34.4	5.8	43.0	5.7	3.80	29.0	40.3%	17.3	2.9	23.0
[2]1983	488	33.8	6.9	7.6	4.4	1.94	32.6	42.9%	18.6	3.8	23.0

Balance Sheet Data (Million $)

Dec. 31	Cash	Curr. Assets	Curr. Liab.	Curr. Ratio	Total Assets	% Ret. on Assets	Long Term Debt	Common Equity	Total Cap.	% LT Debt of Cap.	% Ret. on Equity
1992	**8.0**	**371**	**234**	**1.6**	**636**	**4.5**	**126.0**	**211**	**346**	**36.6**	**12.7**
1991	59.6	357	223	1.6	582	7.1	94.4	224	339	27.8	18.0
1990	26.4	310	179	1.7	496	10.0	77.4	201	302	25.6	26.4
1989	52.9	319	201	1.6	482	9.3	76.4	170	269	28.4	26.8
1988	24.7	260	166	1.6	395	5.3	58.6	134	218	26.9	15.8
1987	7.8	229	143	1.6	359	4.0	60.4	119	206	29.3	12.1
1986	8.4	204	123	1.7	343	3.2	69.5	112	211	32.9	9.5
1985	10.1	198	124	1.6	307	6.2	48.2	106	177	27.2	17.1
1984	7.8	166	102	1.6	252	8.2	34.4	96	146	23.6	18.9
1983	23.4	93	64	1.5	179	10.8	17.0	92	115	14.7	22.7

Data as orig. reptd. **1.** Refl. merger or acq. **2.** Excl. disc. ops. **3.** Refl. acctg. change. **4.** Bef. spec. item(s).

Net Sales (Million $)

13 Weeks:	1993	1992	1991	1990
Mar.	255	254	291	273
Jun.	271	282	305	292
Sep.		298	310	331
Dec.		305	294	317
		1,138	1,200	1,214

Net sales for the 26 weeks ended July 4, 1993, declined 1.8%, year to year, as a decrease in average sugar sales prices was partially offset by increased raw sugar sales by Raceland Sugars. Operating earnings were higher in all but one segment, though a sharp drop in cane sugar sales prices led to a 52% fall in income from operations. Results were further penalized by higher interest expense, and net income fell 66%, to $4,144,000 ($0.16 a share) from $12,144,000 ($0.45). Per-share results exclude a special credit of $0.02 and a special charge of $0.68 from accounting changes in the respective interims.

Common Share Earnings ($)

13 Weeks:	1993	1992	1991	1990
Mar.	0.10	0.17	0.33	0.32
Jun.	0.06	0.28	0.39	0.46
Sep.		0.21	0.37	0.55
Dec.		0.37	0.35	0.47
		1.03	1.43	1.80

Finances

In July 1993, directors approved a change in the company's fiscal year to the Sunday nearest September 30, from December, to coincide with the sugar crop year.

Savannah Foods has revolving credit facilities that aggregate $135 million, of which $23.2 million was in use at July 4, 1993.

Pursuant to a November 1991 authorization to buy back up to two million of the company's common shares, Savannah repurchased 600,000 shares during 1992.

Dividend Data

Dividends have been paid since 1924. A dividend reinvestment plan is available.

Amt of Divd. $	Date Decl.	Ex-divd. Date	Stock of Record	Payment Date
0.13½	Oct. 16	Dec. 7	Dec. 11	Dec. 30'92
0.13½	Feb. 18	Mar. 8	Mar. 12	Apr. 1'93
0.13½	May 27	Jun. 7	Jun. 11	Jul. 1'93
0.13½	Jul. 21	Sep. 3	Sep. 10	Oct. 1'93

Capitalization

Long Term Debt: $126,036,000 (7/4/93).

Common Stock: 26,238,196 shs. ($0.25 par).
Institutions hold about 33%.
Shareholders of record: 3,582 (12/92).

Office—P.O. Box 339, Savannah, GA 31402. **Tel**—(912) 234-1261. **Chrmn & CEO**—W. W. Sprague, Jr. **Pres**—W. W. Sprague III. **SVP-Fin**—W. R. Steinhauer. **Secy**—J. M. Tatum. **Dirs**—W. W. Bradley, J. D. Carswell, D. C. Critz, L. B. Durham Jr., F. S. Exley, G. Fawcett, E. Flegenheimer, A. M. Gignilliat Jr., R. L. Harrison, W. W. Sprague, Jr., W. W. Sprague III, H. M. Tarbutton, A. Tenenbaum. **Transfer Agent & Registrar**—Wachovia Bank of North Carolina, Winston-Salem. **Incorporated** in New York in 1916; reincorporated in Delaware in 1969. **Empl**—2,137.

 Gregg W. Bonardi

Sbarro, Inc.

ASE Symbol SBA Options on ASE, Phila (Mar-Jun-Sep-Dec) In S&P MidCap 400

Price	Range	P-E Ratio	Dividend	Yield	S&P Ranking	Beta
Aug. 10'93	1993					
43⅛	44⅜–30⅛	21	0.20	0.5%	B+	1.49

Summary

This company operates and franchises a national chain of cafeteria-style Italian restaurants under the Sbarro name. As of mid-July 1993, 616 restaurants (478 company-operated) were in operation. An improvement in general retail activity would likely help comparable-unit sales, since most of SBA's restaurants are located in shopping malls.

Current Outlook

Including some potential effects of a higher tax rate, earnings for 1993 are estimated at $2.10 a share, up from 1992's $1.78. An increase to $2.40 is projected for 1994.

Quarterly dividends of $0.20 a share were initiated with the April 1993 payment.

Revenue growth in 1993 is expected to come largely from the opening of more units, with some improvement in comparable-unit sales. Results should also reflect cost-cutting efforts in 1992, and the absence of severance charges. However, comparisons will restricted by one week fewer in the 1993 fourth quarter. With most units located in shopping malls, general improvement in retail traffic would be helpful.

[1]Revenues (Million $)

Weeks:	1993	1992	1991	1990
16 Apr.	69.2	61.8	54.0	48.6
12 Jul.	56.3	48.3	42.9	40.3
12 Oct.	---	55.6	51.3	46.4
12 Dec.	---	[2]71.9	61.7	56.0
	---	237.6	209.8	191.2

Revenues in the 28 weeks ended July 18, 1993, increased 14%, year to year. Income soared 50% from the depressed level of the year-earlier period, to $10.8 million ($0.80 a share), from $7.2 million ($0.53). Results in the 1993 period exclude a credit of $0.07 a share from an accounting change.

Common Share Earnings ($)

Weeks:	1993	1992	1991	1990
16 Apr.	0.43	0.28	0.36	0.28
12 Jul.	0.37	0.26	0.31	0.26
12 Oct.	E0.50	0.45	0.41	0.37
12 Dec.	E0.80	[2]0.79	[3]0.53	0.61
	E2.10	1.78	1.61	1.52

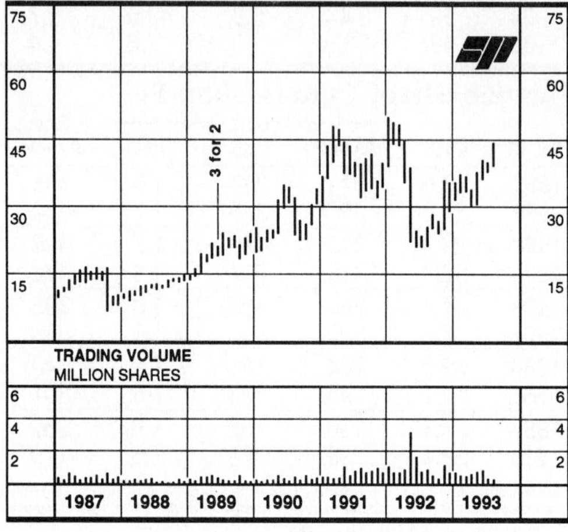

Important Developments

Jul. '93— In the 12 weeks ended July 18, 1993, comparable-unit sales were up 2.5%. Transaction levels likely benefited from customers seeking air conditioning at shopping malls during a recent heat wave. Profitability improved sharply, aided by a decline in food and paper costs as a percentage of sales. Results reflected payroll reductions effected in 1992, and the absence of some severance costs. Year-to-year earnings comparisons are expected to become more difficult in the second half of 1993, which includes one fewer week in the fourth quarter. In the first 28 weeks of 1993, there was a net increase (including closings) of 22 company restaurants, to a total of 478; the number of franchise units rose by seven, to 138.

Next earnings report expected in early November.

Per Share Data ($)

Yr. End Dec. 31	1992	1991	1990	1989	1988	1987	1986	1985	1984	1983
Tangible Bk. Val.	**10.36**	8.58	6.96	5.41	4.33	3.51	2.95	1.26	0.39	0.15
Cash Flow	**2.84**	2.54	2.29	1.71	1.29	0.89	0.61	0.46	0.31	NA
Earnings	**1.78**	1.61	1.52	1.08	0.81	0.55	0.39	0.33	0.23	0.08
Dividends	**Nil**	Nil	Nil	Nil	Nil	Nil	Nil	Nil	Nil	Nil
Payout Ratio	**Nil**	Nil	Nil	Nil	Nil	Nil	Nil	Nil	Nil	Nil
Prices—High	**50⅛**	48	34⅞	24¼	14⅞	16½	13⅜	6¾	NA	NA
Low	**21**	30¼	19⅞	13⅞	9	6¾	5⅞	3¾	NA	NA
P/E Ratio—	**28–12**	30–19	23–13	22–13	18–11	30–12	35–24	21–11	NA	NA

Data as orig. reptd. Adj. for stk. divs. of 50% Jun. 1989, 100% Jun. 1986. **1.** Incl. int. inc. **2.** 13 wks. **3.** After 0.09 charge. E-Estimated. NA-Not Available.

Income Data (Million $)

Year Ended Dec. 31	Revs.	Oper. Inc.	% Oper. Inc. of Revs.	Cap. Exp.	Depr.	Int. Exp.	Net Bef. Taxes	Eff. Tax Rate	Net Inc.	% Net Inc. of Revs.	Cash Flow
1992	**236**	**50.7**	**21.4**	**30.1**	**14.4**	**Nil**	**38.8**	**38.0%**	**24.1**	**10.2**	**38.5**
1991	208	47.7	22.9	23.5	12.6	0.01	36.0	39.4%	21.8	10.5	34.4
1990	190	42.2	22.2	21.3	10.4	0.04	33.9	39.5%	20.5	10.8	30.9
1989	148	30.9	20.9	28.5	8.5	0.04	24.0	39.5%	14.5	9.8	23.0
1988	117	23.2	19.9	18.0	6.5	0.06	[1]17.8	39.5%	10.8	9.2	17.3
1987	86	16.7	19.4	18.8	4.5	0.07	[1]13.1	43.5%	7.4	8.6	11.9
1986	58	11.5	19.8	18.9	2.8	0.17	[1]9.0	45.9%	4.9	8.4	7.7
1985	35	7.2	20.6	10.8	1.5	0.31	[1]5.5	37.9%	3.4	9.8	4.9
1984	20	4.8	23.7	5.1	1.0	0.35	[1]3.4	41.0%	2.0	10.1	2.8
1983	11	1.8	16.6	2.0	0.5	0.19	1.1	36.4%	0.7	6.5	NA

Balance Sheet Data (Million $)

Dec. 31	Cash	Curr. Assets	Curr. Liab.	Curr. Ratio	Total Assets	% Ret. on Assets	Long Term Debt	Common Equity	Total Cap.	% LT Debt of Cap.	% Ret. on Equity
1992	**61.9**	**66.6**	**25.2**	**2.6**	**183**	**14.1**	**Nil**	**140**	**158**	**Nil**	**18.8**
1991	51.0	55.3	25.9	2.1	159	15.0	Nil	116	133	Nil	20.8
1990	35.9	40.2	22.7	1.8	133	17.0	Nil	94	110	Nil	24.6
1989	20.3	25.3	22.7	1.1	108	14.8	0.07	72	85	0.1	22.3
1988	21.4	24.4	19.6	1.2	87	14.1	0.12	57	66	0.2	20.8
1987	14.1	16.5	13.5	1.2	66	12.6	0.20	46	52	0.4	17.3
1986	13.5	14.8	6.7	2.2	50	13.1	0.36	39	43	0.8	17.7
1985	2.0	3.2	4.8	0.7	22	19.5	0.65	14	17	3.9	36.3
1984	0.7	1.9	6.3	0.3	11	25.3	0.13	4	4	3.1	80.6
1983	0.6	1.2	3.4	0.3	5	16.4	0.11	NA	2	5.9	61.7

Data as orig. reptd. **1.** Incl. equity in earns. of nonconsol. subs. NA-Not Available.

Business Summary

Sbarro, Inc. operates and franchises a chain of family-style Italian restaurants, under the "Sbarro," "Sbarro the Italian Eatery" and "Cafe Sbarro" names. At July 18, 1993, there were 478 company-owned restaurants and 138 franchised units in operation. Restaurants were located in the U.S., Australia, Canada, the U.K., and the Philippines.

The company's restaurants are cafeteria-style units, featuring a menu of popular Italian food, including pizza with a variety of toppings, a selection of pasta dishes, other hot and cold Italian entrees, salads, sandwiches, cheesecake and other desserts. Sbarro believes that pizza, which is sold largely by the slice, account for about 50% of restaurant sales.

Most Sbarro restaurants are located in enclosed shopping malls. The restaurants are primarily in one of two categories— either "in-line" restaurants (self-contained units with capacity to seat about 60-120 people), or "food-court" units, which share a common dining area provided by a mall. In fiscal 1992, 84 restaurants were opened, including 58 company-owned units. A total of 27 units were closed or terminated, of which 13 were company restaurants; one additional restaurant was sold to a franchisee. In 1992, systemwide sales, including franchises, totaled $309 million. Comparable-unit sales at company-owned restaurants were down slightly from the 1991 level.

Dividend Data

Quarterly dividends were initiated with the April 1993 payment. A three-for-two stock split was effected in 1989.

Amt. of Divd. $	Date Decl.	Ex-divd. Date	Stock of Record	Payment Date
0.20	Feb. 17	Mar. 16	Mar. 22	Apr. 5'93
0.20	May 14	Jun. 16	Jun. 22	Jul. 6'93

Finances

The 1991 fourth quarter included a charge of $0.09 a share for the closing in early 1992 of certain restaurants that had not met performance criteria. These units had a loss totaling $0.03 a share in 1991.

The company's basic franchise agreement generally requires a $35,000 initial license fee and royalty payments totaling 5% to 7% of gross revenues.

Sbarro's business has some seasonality. In the past, the fourth quarter has accounted for about 40% of annual earnings, reflecting higher sales in shopping malls during the holidays.

Capitalization

Long Term Debt: None (4/25/93).

Common Stock: 13,515,632 shs. ($0.01 par).
The Sbarro family owns 43%.
Institutions hold 46%.
Shareholders: About 547 of record (3/93).

Office—763 Larkfield Rd., Commack, NY 11725. **Tel**—(516) 864-0200. **Fax**—(516) 462-9058. **Chrmn & Pres**—M. Sbarro. **EVP & Secy**—J. Sbarro. **EVP & Treas**—A. Sbarro. **VP-Fin, CFO & Investor Contact**—Robert S. Koebele. **Dirs**—H. L. Kestenbaum, R. A. Mandell, T. J. Sandleitner, A. Sbarro, J. Sbarro, M. Sbarro, P. A. Vatter, T. Vince, B. Zimmerman. **Transfer Agent**—Chemical Bank, NYC. **Incorporated** in New York in 1977. **Empl**—7,400.

 Tom Graves, CFA

SCANA Corp.

NYSE Symbol SCG In S&P MidCap 400

Price	Range	P-E Ratio	Dividend	Yield	S&P Ranking	Beta
Jul. 28'93	1993					
48⅜	49–40⅛	15	2.74	5.7%	A–	0.53

Summary

SCANA is the holding company for South Carolina Electric & Gas, which furnishes electric and gas service to a population of some 3 million primarily in the central and southern half of South Carolina. To meet continued customer growth of nearly 2% annually, the company broke ground for the 385 mw Cope generating station in November 1992. Profitability in 1993 should benefit from a two-phase rate increase, continued success controlling costs and economic growth prompted by the state's pro-business climate.

Current Outlook

Earnings for 1993 are projected at $3.40 a share, up from 1992's $2.84. Earnings for 1994 are projected at $3.50 a share.

Dividends were raised 2.2%, to $0.68½ quarterly from $0.67, with the April 1, 1993, payment.

Earnings for 1993 are expected to benefit from an improving regional economy and a $60.5 million rate order apporved in two-step. SCG's service area continues to be an attractive location for new and expanding industry. An excellent transportation network, pre-employment training programs, dependable sources of energy, and a pro-business climate are major factors in South Carolina's continued economic growth. SCG should benefit from better cost structure and is well positioned to benefit from increased competition.

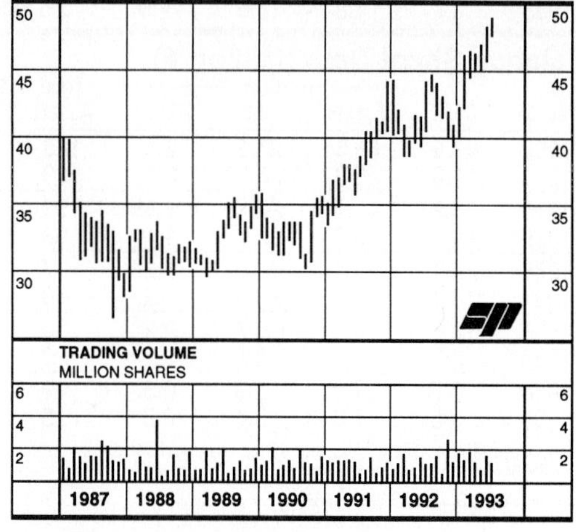

Operating Revenues (Million $)

Quarter:	1993	1992	1991	1990
Mar.	322	297	298	287
Jun.	280	255	256	261
Sep.		306	310	308
Dec.		280	284	277
		1,138	1,148	1,133

Operating revenues for the six months ended June 30, 1993, rose 8.9%, year to year, reflecting improved contributions from the electric utility, retail propane, and natural gas exploration units. Net income increased 42%. Share earnings were $1.62 on 8.2% more shares, versus $1.24.

Common Share Earnings ($)

Quarter:	1993	1992	1991	1990
Mar.	1.02	0.83	0.94	0.84
Jun.	0.61	0.41	0.60	0.67
Sep.	E1.25	0.96	1.25	2.50
Dec.	E0.52	0.64	0.58	0.43
	E3.40	2.84	3.37	4.44

Important Developments

May '93— SCG received a $60.5 million, or 7.4%, increase in retail electric rates from the South Carolina Public Service commission. The rate order proposes a two phase increase: Phase I, with new rates effective June 1, 1993, will produce additional revenues of approximately $42.0 million annually; and Phase 2 (based on additional construction expenditures for the Cope plant), effective June 1, 1994, will produce extra revenues of about $18.5 million annually. Also in May, the FERC accepted a rate request of $7.4 million, or 20%, for wholsale electric rates. FERC has set up an expedited schedule for this case, and the ruling will take effect, subject to refund, on October 23, 1993. Wholesale electric customers include three municipalities, two cooperatives and one public power authority. Those customers accounted for about 4% of total 1992 electric sales revenues.

Next earnings report expected in late October.

Per Share Data ($)

Yr. End Dec. 31	1992	1991	1990	1989	1988	1987	1986	1985	1984	1983
Tangible Bk. Val.	**26.15**	24.91	24.36	22.58	22.03	21.42	20.62	19.82	19.80	18.15
Earnings	**2.84**	3.37	4.44	3.04	3.00	3.20	3.03	2.82	3.05	2.29
Dividends	**2.68**	2.62	2.52	2.46	2.40	2.32	2.24	2.16	2.05	2.00
Payout Ratio	**94%**	78%	57%	81%	80%	73%	74%	77%	67%	87%
Prices—High	**44¾**	44¼	35⅞	35¾	33¾	40	42⅞	28⅛	23⅝	21¼
Low	**38⅝**	33½	30¼	29⅝	28½	26½	27⅛	22⅛	17¼	17½
P/E Ratio—	**16–14**	13–10	8–7	12–10	11–10	13–8	14–9	10–8	8–6	9–8

Data as orig. reptd. E-Estimated.

Income Data (Million $)

Year Ended Dec. 31	Revs.	Depr.	Maint.	Oper. Ratio	1Fxd. Chgs. Cover.	Constr. Credits	Eff. Tax Rate	Net Inc.	% Return On Revs.	% Return On 2Invest. Capital	% Return On Com. Equity
1992	**1,138**	**108**	**65.4**	**81.6%**	**2.72**	**9.8**	**32.7%**	**118**	**10.3**	**7.4**	**10.7**
1991	1,148	103	61.6	80.6%	3.17	8.3	34.6%	136	11.8	8.5	13.4
1990	1,133	98	67.5	80.1%	3.61	5.1	36.5%	182	16.0	10.7	18.9
1989	1,123	102	69.3	81.0%	2.93	6.2	29.5%	123	10.9	8.7	13.5
1988	1,083	97	54.1	81.1%	3.15	6.2	34.4%	121	11.1	8.6	13.7
1987	1,116	93	58.0	81.7%	3.73	3.9	40.6%	129	11.5	9.1	15.1
1986	1,102	91	56.9	82.0%	3.79	3.3	46.1%	122	11.1	9.3	14.9
1985	1,110	87	60.8	82.2%	3.20	3.5	46.1%	114	10.2	9.4	14.3
1984	1,128	75	52.6	82.3%	3.42	14.2	44.9%	122	10.8	10.0	16.4
1983	975	45	36.3	84.6%	3.10	48.2	41.5%	87	8.9	8.0	12.7

Balance Sheet Data (Million $)

Dec. 31	3Gross Prop.	Capital Expend.	Net Prop.	% Earn. on Net Prop.	Total Cap.	Capitalization LT Debt	% LT Debt	Pfd.	% Pfd.	Com.	% Com.
1992	**4,003**	**278**	**2,810**	**7.7**	**3,087**	**1,205**	**49.2**	**82**	**3.4**	**1,162**	**47.4**
1991	3,789	239	2,665	8.5	2,874	1,122	50.1	88	3.9	1,029	46.0
1990	3,587	230	2,550	9.0	2,647	939	46.2	90	4.4	1,004	49.4
1989	3,400	182	2,444	8.8	2,615	1,004	49.8	94	4.7	918	45.5
1988	3,258	183	2,385	8.7	2,450	886	47.0	103	5.5	896	47.5
1987	3,100	173	2,302	9.0	2,403	887	47.5	111	5.9	872	46.6
1986	2,959	144	2,236	8.9	2,234	745	43.2	144	8.3	837	48.0
1985	2,859	129	2,214	9.0	2,243	785	44.4	179	10.1	806	45.5
1984	2,765	284	2,198	9.5	2,285	894	48.2	183	9.9	778	41.9
1983	2,510	182	2,011	7.6	2,051	789	46.8	187	11.1	710	42.1

Data as orig. reptd. **1.** Times int. exp. & pfd. divs. covered (pretax basis). **2.** Based on income before interest charges. **3.** Utility plant.

Business Summary

SCANA Corp. is the holding company for South Carolina Electric & Gas, a utility serving about 462,000 electric customers in a 15,000 square-mile territory in central, southern, and southwestern South Carolina. Urban bus service is provided in the metropolitan areas of Columbia and Charleston. Business segment contributions (operating income in million $) in 1992:

	Revs.	Profit
Electric	72.9%	$180.6
Gas	26.8%	34.9
Transportation	0.3%	–5.7

The fuel mix in 1992 was 64% coal, 29% nuclear, and 7% hydro and other. Peak load in 1992 was 3,380 mw and system capacity was 3,912 mw, for a capacity margin of 13.6%. Gas sales in 1992 totaled 761.7 million therms, up 9.6% from 1991.

In November 1992, construction began on the 385 mw coal-fired Cope electric generating plant, with commercial operations expected to begin in the spring of 1996. The new plant, estimated to cost $450 million, will have the ability to burn either coal or natural gas.

Finances

On July 12, 1993, SCG registered with the SEC to sell 1,300,000 common shares. Net proceeds will be used for the acquisition of producing oil and gas properties by SCANA Petroluem Resources. In June 1993, SCG refinanced approximately $400 million of long-term debt with lower coupon bonds.

Dividend Data

Dividends have been paid since 1946. A dividend reinvestment plan is available.

Amt of Divd. $	Date Decl.	Ex–divd. Date	Stock of Record	Payment Date
0.67	Aug. 26	Sep. 3	Sep. 10	Oct. 1'92
0.67	Oct. 20	Dec. 4	Dec. 10	Jan. 1'93
0.68½	Feb. 16	Mar. 4	Mar. 10	Apr. 1'93
0.68½	Apr. 29	Jun. 4	Jun. 10	Jul. 1'93

Capitalization

Long Term Debt: $1,147,454,000 (3/93).

Subsidiary Red. Pfd. Stk.: $54,394,000.

Subsidiary Pfd. Stk.: $26,027,000.

Common Stock: 44,545,784 shs. (no par).
Institutions hold about 44%.
Shareholders of record: 42,937.

Office—1426 Main Street, Columbia, SC 29201. **Tel**—(803) 748-3000. **Chrmn & CEO**—L. M. Gressette Jr. **Secy**—K. B. Marsh. **SVP-CFO**—W. B. Timmerman. **Investor Contact**—H. J. Winn III (803) 748-3240. **Dirs**—B. L. Amick, W. B. Bookhart Jr., W. T. Cassels Jr., H. M. Chapman, J. B. Edwards, E. T. Freeman, L. M. Gressette Jr., B. A. Hagood, W. H. Hipp, B. D. Kenyon, F. C. McMaster, H. Ponder, J. B. Rhodes, W. B. Timmerman, E. C. Wall Jr., J. A. Warren. **Transfer Agents**—Chemical Bank, NYC. **Registrars**—Chemical Bank, NYC. **Incorporated** in South Carolina in 1924. **Empl**—4,849.

 Ned Bancroft

Schulman (A.), Inc.

NASDAQ Symbol SHLM (Incl. in Nat'l Market) In S&P MidCap 400

Price	Range	P–E Ratio	Dividend	Yield	S&P Ranking	Beta
Jul. 28'93	1993					
29¾	32–26	22	0.32	1.1%	A+	0.85

Summary

This company, one of the largest independent manufacturers of plastic compounds, is also an international merchant of plastic resins. With foreign operations accounting for more than 70% of sales and profits, results are significantly affected by foreign exchange fluctuations. Lower earnings are expected for fiscal 1993, reflecting soft European market conditions.

Business Summary

A. Schulman, Inc., founded in 1928, formulates and manufactures proprietary plastic compounds engineered to fulfill customers' requirements, acts as a merchant, buying plastic resins and reselling them to a variety of users, and distributes certain plastic products and synthetic rubber for major producers in the U.S. and abroad.

For the fiscal year ended August 31, 1992, sales and income (before taxes, foreign currency translation gains or losses and corporate expense) were:

	Sales	Income
Manufacturing	58%	66%
Merchant activities	20%	18%
Distribution	22%	16%

Foreign operations, primarily in Europe, accounted for 70% of sales and 75% of operating income in fiscal 1992.

Proprietary plastic compounds are formulated in the company's laboratories and manufactured in Schulman's eight plastics compounding plants in the U.S., Europe and Canada. Basic resins purchased from other producers are combined with various additives to achieve desired properties in the resulting compounds.

Compounds are sold to manufacturers and suppliers in markets that include consumer products, for writing instruments, shelving, video tape cassettes, batteries, outdoor furniture, lawn sprinklers, artificial turf, skateboards, toys, games and plastic parts for household appliances; the electrical/electronics industry, for outdoor lighting, parts for telephones, connector blocks, transformers, capacitor housings and wire and cable insulation for power generation systems; the packaging industry, for plastic bags and packaging materials for various household necessities; the office equipment industry, for cases and housings for computers, folders and binders, stack trays and drawers for copying machines; the automotive industry, for side moldings, window seals, bumper guards, air ducts, steering wheels and fan shrouds; and the agricultural industry, for greenhouse coverings, protective film for animal feed and agricultural mulch. Schulman also makes flame-retardant engineered compounds used in telephone system terminal blocks and color television tube covers.

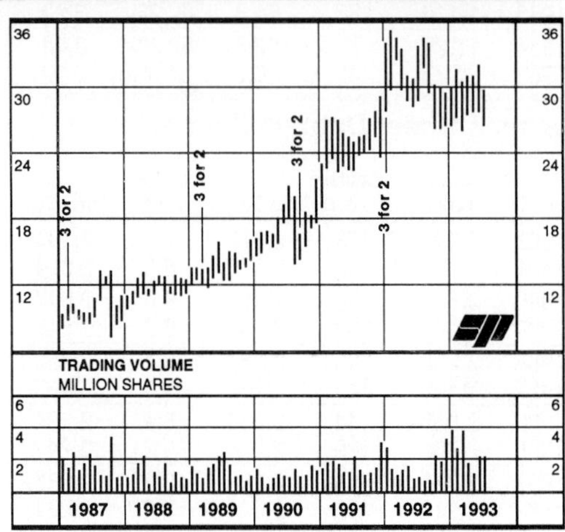

Important Developments

Jul. '93— Schulman attributed its earnings decline in the first nine months of fiscal 1993 to the recession in Europe, and said it expects earnings for the year to be lower than those of fiscal 1992. Demand in Europe remains strong, but oversuppy of plastic resin has held down prices. The company added that recent strengthening of European operations and growing profits in North America should aid fiscal 1994 results.

Next earnings report due in late November.

Per Share Data ($)

Yr. End Aug. 31	1992	1991	1990	1989	1988	1987	1986	1985	1984	1983
Tangible Bk. Val.	[1]**10.33**	[1]7.83	7.39	5.49	4.78	4.14	3.35	2.51	2.15	1.93
Cash Flow	**1.97**	1.87	1.55	1.31	1.19	0.89	0.69	0.53	0.51	0.45
Earnings	**1.48**	1.43	1.19	1.02	0.91	0.65	0.51	0.39	0.38	0.34
Dividends	**0.270**	0.233	0.191	0.169	0.166	0.107	0.084	0.071	0.062	0.052
Payout Ratio	**18%**	16%	16%	17%	18%	16%	16%	18%	17%	15%
Prices[2]—High	**35¼**	29⅛	21⅝	16⅛	13⅛	13⅜	8⅞	5⅝	3⅜	3⅝
Low	**26¼**	19	13⅞	11¾	9⅞	7⅜	5½	2⅞	2¾	2⅛
P/E Ratio—	**24–18**	20–13	18–12	16–12	14–11	20–11	17–11	14–7	9–7	10–6

Data as orig. reptd. Adj. for stk. divs. of 50% Jan. 1992, 50% Sep. 1990, 50% Mar. 1989, 50% Feb. 1987, 10% Nov. 1985, 100% Dec. 1983, 10% Jan. 1983. **1.** Incl. intangibles. **2.** Cal. yr.

Income Data (Million $)

Year Ended Aug. 31	Revs.	Oper. Inc.	% Oper. Inc. of Revs.	Cap. Exp.	Depr.	Int. Exp.	Net Bef. Taxes	Eff. Tax Rate	Net Inc.	% Net Inc. of Revs.	Cash Flow
1992	**732**	**81.8**	**11.2**	**15.8**	**14.6**	**1.37**	**73.2**	**40.1%**	**43.8**	**6.0**	**58.3**
1991	736	80.7	11.0	18.0	13.0	1.38	70.0	39.8%	42.3	5.8	55.2
1990	679	73.3	10.8	17.7	10.8	1.02	63.2	43.4%	36.1	5.3	46.8
1989	624	63.2	10.1	26.0	8.7	1.51	54.8	43.8%	30.8	4.9	39.4
1988	598	58.7	9.8	11.7	8.2	1.27	50.4	45.2%	27.6	4.6	35.8
1987	464	44.9	9.7	11.2	7.0	1.27	37.8	47.5%	19.8	4.3	26.7
1986	388	34.8	9.0	11.9	5.4	1.04	28.7	47.1%	15.2	3.9	20.5
1985	319	27.7	8.7	6.9	4.2	1.19	22.6	48.1%	11.7	3.7	15.8
1984	314	26.1	8.3	7.3	4.0	1.38	20.8	46.8%	11.1	3.5	15.0
1983	263	21.2	8.0	8.6	3.0	0.95	17.5	42.3%	10.1	3.8	13.0

Balance Sheet Data (Million $)

Aug. 31	Cash	Curr. Assets	Curr. Liab.	Curr. Ratio	Total Assets	% Ret. on Assets	Long Term Debt	Common Equity	Total Cap.	% LT Debt of Cap.	% Ret. on Equity
1992	**82.9**	**327**	**83.6**	**3.9**	**428**	**11.3**	**10.1**	**307**	**327**	**3.1**	**16.2**
1991	44.6	255	81.5	3.1	344	12.7	9.0	231	250	3.6	18.8
1990	19.2	241	76.5	3.2	328	12.3	7.0	223	240	2.9	18.5
1989	18.2	187	64.8	2.9	258	12.4	10.0	166	185	5.4	19.9
1988	16.3	185	71.5	2.6	240	12.1	9.6	144	162	5.9	20.5
1987	15.9	163	64.3	2.5	215	10.2	11.2	125	144	7.8	17.5
1986	17.3	129	51.9	2.5	174	9.5	10.1	101	118	8.6	17.2
1985	4.9	110	51.7	2.1	144	8.6	8.8	75	89	9.9	16.8
1984	3.9	95	45.5	2.1	126	9.2	9.7	63	78	12.5	18.3
1983	4.7	85	37.9	2.2	114	9.6	13.1	57	74	17.8	18.7

Data as orig. reptd.

Sales & Other Income (Million $)

Quarter:	1992–93	1991–92	1990–91	1989–90
Nov.	184	188	215	165
Feb.	162	174	193	160
May	187	193	178	182
Aug.		184	153	175
		739	740	681

For the nine months ended May 31, 1993, revenues declined 3.9%, year to year, reflecting recessionary conditions in Europe, especially in Germany. Lower profits from European operations, due to an oversupply of plastic resins, outweighed improvements in North American operations; pretax income fell 15%. After taxes at 38.9%, versus 41.3%, net income decreased 12%, to $27,310,000 ($0.91 a share, after preferred dividends), from $31,002,000 ($1.05).

Common Share Earnings ($)

Quarter:	1992–93	1991–92	1990–91	1989–90
Nov.	0.30	0.32	0.33	0.25
Feb.	0.27	0.33	0.33	0.27
May	0.34	0.40	0.33	0.32
Aug.		0.43	0.44	0.36
		1.48	1.43	1.19

Dividend Data

Cash has been paid each year since 1968.

Amt. of Divd. $	Date Decl.	Ex–divd. Date	Stock of Record	Payment Date
0.07	Oct. 9	Oct. 20	Oct. 26	Nov. 4'92
0.08	Jan. 12	Jan. 21	Jan. 27	Feb. 5'93
0.08	Apr. 14	Apr. 23	Apr. 29	May 7'93
0.08	Jul. 12	Jul. 21	Jul. 27	Aug. 5'93

Finances

Capital spending totaled $15.8 million in fiscal 1992. In fiscal 1993, Schulman was scheduled to install new lines in South Wales and Belgium at a total cost of $9.8 million. The company expected to spend $15 to $20 million to increase efficiency in fiscal 1993.

In fiscal 1992, translation effects from the weaker U.S. dollar increased sales by $9.1 million, versus by $27.2 million in fiscal 1991. The cumulative foreign currency translation adjustment account on stockholders equity increased by $38.2 million in fiscal 1992.

Capitalization

Long Term Debt: $10,171,000 (5/93).

Minority Interest: $1,500,000 (2/93).

$5 Cum. Pfd. Stock: 10,707 shs. ($100 par).

Common Stock: 29,910,852 shs. ($1 par). Institutions hold 61%. Shareholders: 1,421 of record.

Office—3550 W. Market St., PO Box 1710, Akron, OH 44333. **Tel**—(216) 666-3751. **Chrmn & CFO**—R. A. Stefanko. **Pres & CEO**—T. L. Haines. **Secy**—J. H. Berick. **Treas**—B. R. Colbow. **Dirs**—J. H. Berick, L. G. Ford, T. L. Haines, G. E. Heffern, L. A. Kushkin, F. A. Loehr, A. L. Ockene, C. J. Pilliod, Jr., P. C. Roberts, R. C. Rombouts, R. A. Stefanko, R. G. Wallace. **Transfer Agent & Registrar**—Ameritrust Co., Cleveland. **Incorporated** in Delaware in 1969. **Empl**—1,587.

 Shayna J. Malnak

Schwab (Charles)

NYSE Symbol SCH Options on CBOE (Mar-Jun-Sep-Dec) In S&P MidCap 400

Price	Range	P-E Ratio	Dividend	Yield	S&P Ranking	Beta
Sep. 1'93	1993					
33⅞	34–16⅝	20	0.20	0.6%	NR	2.49

Summary

This company's Charles Schwab & Co. subsidiary is the largest discount brokerage firm in the U.S., with more than 175 branch offices and two million active customer accounts. The company estimates that it serves over 44% of the discount brokerage market. Earnings are subject to wide fluctuations, reflecting the volatile nature of the securities markets. Record profits in 1993's first half reflected higher trading activity and record growth in new client accounts. The shares were split 3-for-2 in May 1993.

Business Summary

The Charles Schwab Corp. and its subsidiaries provide brokerage and related investment services to 2.0 million active investors, whose assets entrusted to the company totaled $66 billion at December 31, 1992. The company's principal subsidiary, Charles Schwab & Co., Inc. serves over 44% of the discount brokerage market. With a network of 175 branch offices, Schwab is represented in 46 states. The company acquired Schwab from BankAmerica Corp. in a management-led leveraged buyout in 1987. Mayer & Schweitzer, Inc., a market maker in over-the-counter securities, provides trade execution services to institutional and broker-dealer clients. Operating revenues in recent years were derived as follows:

	1992	1991	1990
Commissions	49%	44%	39%
Interest	28%	38%	49%
Principal transactions	14%	8%	1%
Mutual fund service fees	7%	7%	7%
Other	2%	3%	4%

Schwab primarily serves investors who wish to conduct their own research and make their own investment decisions and do not wish to pay, through brokerage commissions, for research or portfolio management. To attract and accommodate investors who want such services, Schwab offers a variety of fee-based (primarily third-party) research and portfolio management products. SCH does not generally maintain inventories of securities for sale to its customers or engage in principal transactions with its customers.

Commission revenues in 1992 were derived as follows: 52% listed securities (52% in 1991), 33% over-the-counter securities (32%), 8% mutual funds (7%), and 7% options (9%). Interest revenues in 1992 were derived 57% from investments and 42% from margin loans.

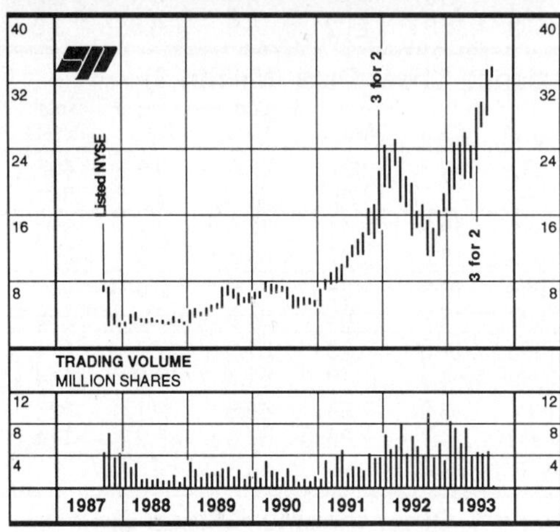

For a given number of new accounts, trading is at its highest initially, then declines over time. Advertising plays a crucial role in obtaining new customers. The company opened 562,000 new accounts in 1992, 384,000 new accounts in 1991, 300,000 in 1990 and 273,000 in 1989.

Important Developments

Jul. '93— The company said that during the first half of 1993 it opened a record 358,000 new accounts, 30% more than those added during the same period last year. Assets in client accounts increased by $13.6 billion since the beginning of the year, totaling a record $79.2 billion at June 30, 1993.

Next earnings report expected in mid-October.

Per Share Data ($)

Yr. End Dec. 31	1992	1991	1990	1989	1988	1987	1986
Tangible Bk. Val.	**3.69**	2.33	1.25	1.09	0.94	0.48	NA
Cash Flow	**NA**	2.33	NA	NA	NA	NA	NA
Earnings	**1.39**	0.85	0.27	0.30	0.12	0.39	0.23
Dividends	**0.120**	0.085	0.058	0.040	Nil	Nil	Nil
Payout Ratio	**11%**	10%	21%	13%	Nil	Nil	Nil
Prices—High	**25⁵⁄₃₂**	21¹¹⁄₃₂	7³¹⁄₃₂	7¹⁷⁄₃₂	4⁹⁄₃₂	7¹⁷⁄₃₂	NA
Low	**11³⁄₃₂**	5	4²³⁄₃₂	3	2⅝	2¹⁷⁄₃₂	NA
P/E Ratio—	**18–8**	25–6	29–17	25–10	36–22	20–7	NA

Data as orig. reptd; pro forma data prior to 1988. Adj. for stk. div(s) of 50% May 1993, 50% Dec. 1991. NA-Not Available.

Income Data (Million $)

Year Ended Dec. 31	Commis-sions	Int. Inc.	Total Revs.	Int. Exp.	% Exp./ Op. Revs.	Net Bef. Taxes	Eff. Tax Rate	Net Inc.	% Return On Revs.	% Return On Assets	% Return On Equity
1992	**441**	**251**	**909**	**159**	**83.9**	**146.2**	**44.5%**	**81.2**	**8.9**	**1.5**	**35.4**
1991	349	302	795	226	88.9	88.1	43.8%	49.5	6.2	1.1	28.0
1990	244	310	626	238	95.3	29.1	42.4%	16.8	2.7	0.4	10.3
1989	229	273	553	207	94.0	33.2	43.0%	18.9	3.4	0.6	11.4
1988	205	168	392	126	96.6	13.3	44.3%	7.4	1.9	0.3	4.8
1987	317	133	465	93	90.1	46.0	47.0%	24.4	5.3	1.4	21.8
1986	214	87	308	63	90.1	30.4	51.6%	14.7	4.8	NA	NA

Balance Sheet Data (Million $)

Dec. 31	Total Assets	Cash Items	Rec.	Secs. Owned	Sec. Borrowed	Due Brokers & Cust.	Other Liabs.	Capitalization Debt	Capitalization Equity	Capitalization Total
1992	**5,905**	**3,714**	**1,952**	**Nil**	**Nil**	**5,376**	**118**	**152**	**259**	**410**
1991	5,026	3,467	1,350	Nil	Nil	4,605	102	119	200	319
1990	4,188	3,141	842	Nil	Nil	3,856	52	126	154	280
1989	3,480	2,335	932	Nil	Nil	3,121	57	131	172	302
1988	2,533	1,572	745	Nil	Nil	2,201	41	132	159	291
1987	2,020	995	783	Nil	Nil	1,606	77	188	150	338

Data as orig. reptd. Pro forma data prior to 1988. NA-Not Available.

Total Revenues (Million $)

Quarter:	1993	1992	1991	1990
Mar.	270.0	265.0	186.2	149.7
Jun.	264.6	219.1	183.6	154.7
Sep.		196.8	202.3	164.8
Dec.		228.1	223.1	156.7
		909.0	795.2	625.9

Total revenues for the six months ended June 30, 1993, rose 10%, year to year, reflecting a 17% increase in commissions, 9.4% lower interest income, 12% greater principal transaction revenues, and 53% higher mutual fund service fees. Margins widened on the greater volume, and pretax income advanced 32%. After taxes at 40.9%, versus 43.9%, net income was up 39%, to $1.13 a share from $0.81 (adjusted).

Common Share Earnings ($)

Quarter:	1993	1992	1991	1990
Mar.	0.60	0.50	0.18	0.06
Jun.	0.53	0.31	0.17	0.07
Sep.		0.13	0.23	0.12
Dec.		0.43	0.27	0.02
		1.39	0.85	0.27

Dividend Data

Dividends were initiated in 1989. A dividend reinvestment plan is available.

Amt of Divd. $	Date Decl.	Ex-divd. Date	Stock of Record	Payment Date
0.06	Oct. 21	Oct. 27	Nov. 2	Nov. 16'92
0.06	Jan. 14	Jan. 26	Feb. 1	Feb. 16'93
0.07½	Mar. 25	Apr. 27	May 3	May 17'93
3-for-2	Mar. 25	Jun. 2	May 3	Jun. 1'93
0.05	Jul. 14	Jul. 27	Aug. 2	Aug. 16'93

Finances

Management's goal is to increase the value of the company by achieving over the long term a 20% annual net revenue growth while maintaining an after-tax profit margin of 10% and a return on stockholders' equity of 20%.

At March 31, 1993, SCH's regulatory net capital was $221 million (10.5% of aggregate debit balances), which was $179 million in excess of the minimum required net capital.

During July 1992, Schwab introduced nationally its No Transaction Fee (NTF) Mutual Fund Service, which enables customers to invest in 90 no-load mutual funds offered by nine fund families without incurring transaction fees. Mutual fund trades placed through NTF grew from an average of 3,200 per day in 1992's third quarter to an average of 5,800 per day in 1993's second quarter.

Transaction-based revenues represent the majority of the company's revenues. Since these revenues are heavily influenced by fluctuations in volumes and price levels of securities transactions, it is not unusual for the company to experience significant variations in quarterly net revenue levels. Most of the company's expenses do not vary directly, at least in the short-run, with fluctuations in securities trading volumes.

Capitalization

Long Term Debt: $152,638,000 (3/93).

Common Stock: 57,474,783 shs. ($0.01 par). Officers & directors own about 43%, incl. 26% held by Charles R. Schwab. An ESOP owns about 10.7%.

Institutions hold approximately 36%.

Shareholders of record: 1,429.

Office—101 Montgomery St., San Francisco, CA 94104. **Tel**—(415) 627-7000. **Chrmn & CEO**—C. R. Schwab. **Pres**—D. S. Pottruck. **VP-Fin & CFO**—A. J. Gambs. **Secy**—M. B. Templeton. **Investor Contact**—Mark Thompson (415) 627-7810. **Dirs**—N. H. Bechtle, C. P. Butcher, D. G. Fisher, A. M. Frank, J. R. Harvey, S. T. McLin, C. R. Schwab, L. J. Stupski, R. O. Walther. **Transfer Agent & Registrar**—Harris Trust Co., Chicago, IL. **Incorporated** in California in 1971. **Empl**—4,500.

 Paul L. Huberman, CFA

SciMed Life Systems

NASDAQ Symbol SMLS (Incl. in Nat'l Market) Options on CBOE In S&P MidCap 400

Price	Range	P–E Ratio	Dividend	Yield	S&P Ranking	Beta
Sep. 27'93	1993					
51⅜	68–33¼	13	None	None	B–	2.26

Summary

SciMed is a leading producer of disposable medical devices, principally coronary angioplasty catheters for the treatment of coronary artery disease. Greater penetration of overseas markets, contributions from new angioplasty products, and expansion into other cardiac-related products enhance long-term prospects. An important catheter patent litigation case with Pfizer Inc. recently went to trial.

Current Outlook

Earnings in the fiscal year ending February 28, 1995, are projected at $5.50 a share, up from $4.00 estimated for 1993-4.

Initiation of cash dividends is not anticipated.

Sales are expected post another strong advance in 1994-5, aided by a shift from distributor to direct sales operations in Japan and Europe, and by new products such as the Rally rapid-exchange angioplasty catheter. Despite startup costs associated with expansion abroad, margins should widen on the greater volume, lower royalty payments and cost efficiencies. New interventional cardiology products currently under development enhance long-term prospects.

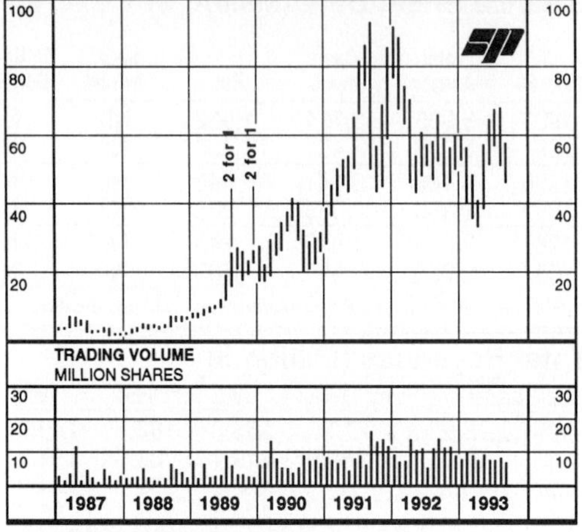

Net Sales (Million $)

Quarter:	1993–94	1992–93	1991–92	1990–91
May	65.8	51.3	42.0	24.4
Aug.	67.7	54.4	44.6	25.9
Nov.	---	56.8	49.1	28.7
Feb.	---	60.3	48.3	32.8
	---	222.7	183.9	111.8

Net sales in the six months ended August 31, 1993, climbed 26%, year to year, reflecting new products and strong foreign sales. Pretax income soared 35%. After taxes at 36.5%, versus 35.5%, net income was up 33%, to $1.96 a share, from $1.49.

Common Share Earnings ($)

Quarter:	1993–94	1992–93	1991–92	1990–91
May	0.99	0.70	0.78	0.45
Aug.	0.97	0.79	0.78	0.49
Nov.	E0.80	0.87	d0.12	0.50
Feb.	E1.24	1.02	0.81	0.53
	E4.00	3.37	2.27	1.98

Important Developments

Sep. '93— An important patent litigation case with Pfizer Inc. went to trial September 27, 1993. Pfizer alleged that SciMed's Express and Rally catheter products infringe upon patents held by Pfizer units.

Aug. '93— International sales in the 1993-4 second quarter soared over 50%, aided by a conversion from distributors to direct sales operations in Germany and the U.K., and by contract manufacturing revenues from a new plant in Belgium. The company is also shifting to direct sales in Japan. A reserve against orders from its Japanese distributor cut second quarter sales by $2.6 million, and could lower third quarter revenues by $5 to $8 million.

Next earnings report expected in mid-December.

Per Share Data ($)

Yr. End Feb. 28	1993	1992	1991	1990	1989	1988	1987	1986	1985	1984
Tangible Bk. Val.	[1]**12.28**	[1]8.58	[1]5.97	3.89	1.08	0.61	0.64	0.61	0.62	0.69
Cash Flow	**3.70**	2.49	2.13	1.37	0.39	0.03	0.07	0.03	d0.03	0.11
Earnings[2,3]	**3.37**	2.27	1.98	1.29	0.33	d0.03	0.02	d0.02	d0.07	0.08
Dividends	**Nil**	Nil	Nil	Nil	Nil	Nil	Nil	Nil	Nil	Nil
Payout Ratio	**Nil**	Nil	Nil	Nil	Nil	Nil	Nil	Nil	Nil	Nil
Calendar Years	**1992**	1991	1990	1989	1988	1987	1986	1985	1984	1983
Prices—High	**91¾**	93	41¾	27¼	7¼	7⅛	3½	2⅝	1⅝	3¼
Low	**43¼**	28¼	17½	6¾	1⅞	1½	1	⅝	⅝	1½
P/E Ratio—	**27–12**	41–12	21–9	21–5	22–6	NM	NM	NM	NM	41–19

Data as orig. reptd. Adj. for stk. divs. of 100% Dec. 1989, 100% Aug. 1989, 100% Dec. 1986. **1.** Incl. intangibles. **2.** Bef. spec. items of +0.01 in 1987, +0.01 in 1984. **3.** Ful. dil.: 2.25 in 1992, 1.90 in 1991, 1.21 in 1990, 0.31 in 1989. d-Deficit. E-Estimated. NM-Not Meaningful.

Income Data (Million $)

Year Ended Feb. 28	Revs.	Oper. Inc.	% Oper. Inc. of Revs.	Cap. Exp.	Depr.	Int. Exp.	Net Bef. Taxes	Eff. Tax Rate	[1]Net Inc.	% Net Inc. of Revs.	Cash Flow
1993	**223**	**81.5**	**36.6**	**18.40**	**4.95**	**0.97**	**79.7**	**35.5%**	**51.4**	**23.1**	**56.3**
1992	184	79.5	43.2	8.77	3.40	0.26	51.9	33.9%	34.3	18.7	37.7
1991	112	44.5	39.8	5.95	2.14	0.17	45.7	37.1%	28.8	25.7	30.9
1990	67	26.3	39.0	5.11	0.99	0.26	26.2	35.6%	16.9	25.0	17.9
1989	27	5.9	21.5	1.61	0.64	0.26	5.3	25.7%	3.9	14.3	4.6
1988	14	0.3	1.8	0.55	0.63	0.11	d0.3	Nil	d0.3	NM	0.3
1987	10	0.6	6.0	0.57	0.60	Nil	0.2	43.3%	0.1	1.2	0.7
1986	9	d0.3	NM	0.61	0.48	Nil	d0.2	NM	d0.2	NM	0.3
1985	7	d0.9	NM	0.96	0.36	Nil	d0.8	NM	d0.7	NM	d0.3
1984	9	1.0	11.1	0.43	0.29	Nil	1.0	22.8%	0.7	7.8	1.0

Balance Sheet Data (Million $)

Feb. 28	Cash	Curr. Assets	Curr. Liab.	Curr. Ratio	Total Assets	% Ret. on Assets	Long Term Debt	Common Equity	Total Cap.	% LT Debt of Cap.	% Ret. on Equity
1993	**117.0**	**161**	**44.1**	**3.6**	**230**	**25.6**	**Nil**	**186**	**186**	**Nil**	**32.6**
1992	76.5	114	31.4	3.6	169	25.2	Nil	128	128	Nil	31.7
1991	55.0	79	13.8	5.7	102	33.5	Nil	87	87	Nil	39.9
1990	37.7	52	8.0	6.5	63	39.2	3.2	51	54	5.9	51.8
1989	7.5	15	4.6	3.2	21	23.5	3.2	13	16	20.2	40.1
1988	1.7	6	1.9	3.3	11	NM	3.2	6	9	33.9	NM
1987	1.4	6	1.3	4.4	8	1.7	Nil	7	7	Nil	2.0
1986	1.0	5	1.3	4.0	7	NM	Nil	6	6	Nil	NM
1985	3.2	6	2.0	3.1	8	NM	Nil	6	6	Nil	NM
1984	4.0	8	2.6	3.2	9	10.0	Nil	7	7	Nil	13.7

Data as orig. reptd. 1. Bef. spec. items. d-Deficit. NM-Not Meaningful.

Business Summary

SciMed Life Systems designs and produces disposable medical products, principally coronary angioplasty catheters used by cardiologists in the interventional treatment of coronary artery disease. Products are sold primarily to hospitals and medical supply distributors.

Exports accounted for 20% of 1992-3 total sales, up from 17% in 1991-2. R&D spending equalled 7.6% of sales in 1992-3, up from 6.2% in 1991-2.

The most important angioplasty product is the balloon or percutaneous transluminal coronary angioplasty (PTCA) catheter. The PTCA procedure involves inserting a balloon-tipped catheter into a major artery through an incision in the leg or arm and guiding it through the arteries to the site of blockage or occlusion. The balloon is then inflated and deflated to widen the artery and improve blood flow. PTCA has grown dramatically since the early 1980s, reflecting its success as an effective alternative to drug and surgical therapies.

SciMed's line of PTCA products includes 19 different models, including over-the-wire systems such as its Shadow and Cobra catheters; fixed wire systems represented by the Ace line; and rapid exchange systems such as the Express and Rally lines. The company's PTCA products are believed to account for about 40% of the U.S. balloon catheter market and 30% of the international market. SciMed's PTCA products are subject to royalties, pursuant to a 1991 settlement of patent litigation with Eli Lilly & Co. The Express catheter is manufactured in the U.S. under a limited license granted by Lilly, expiring November 30, 1993 (sales of the product outside of the U.S. are not affected). The Rally catheter was designed as a replacement for Express. The company is still engaged in patent litigation with Pfizer Inc., and is a defendant in lawsuits alleging violations of state and federal securities laws.

Related products include guide catheters, guide wires, inflation devices and other ancillary products. The company is also developing non-balloon, catheter-based products for the treatment of cardiovascular disease, as well as products to treat peripheral vascular disease affecting the legs and kidneys.

Dividend Data

No cash has been paid.

Capitalization

Long Term Liabs.: $328,000 (8/93).

Common Stock: 15,134,246 shs. ($0.05 par). Institutions hold 80%. Shareholders: 1,535 of record (2/93).

Office—6655 Wedgwood Rd., Maple Grove, MN 55369. **Tel**—(612) 420-0700. **Pres & CEO**—D. A. Spencer. **SVP & CFO**—Craig R. Dvorak. **Investor Contact**—Karen J. Kelsey. **Dirs**—R. C. Alberding, R. F. Bellows, R. B. Emmitt, D. C. Harrison, L. L. Horsch, D. A. Spencer. **Transfer Agent**—Norwest Bank Minnesota, South St. Paul. **Incorporated** in Minnesota in 1972. **Empl**—1,315.

 H. B. Saftlas

Seagate Technology

NASDAQ Symbol SGAT (Incl. in Nat'l Market) Options on ASE In S&P MidCap 400

Price	Range	P–E Ratio	Dividend	Yield	S&P Ranking	Beta
Aug. 5'93	1993					
19⅞	21¾–13⅛	7	None	None	B	2.18

Summary

Seagate is one of the leading makers of rigid magnetic disk drives for computer systems ranging from personal computers to supercomputers. Earnings rose sharply in fiscal 1993, aided by increased unit sales, despite the onset of severe pricing pressures in the second half. While sales in fiscal 1994 are expected to benefit from higher unit demand, earnings growth should be restricted by continued price pressures.

Current Outlook

Earnings in the fiscal year ending June 30, 1994, are projected at $2.80 a share, flat with the $2.80 recorded in fiscal 1993.

Initiation of cash dividends is not expected.

Revenues in fiscal 1994 are expected to continue to advance, reflecting a higher level of unit shipments. PC price wars have spurred demand for desktop and other small computers, which should aid unit sales of disk drives and other PC components. Continued increases in demand for storage will aid the high end of the market as well. However, margins are expected to narrow, restricted by competitive pricing pressures caused in large part by industry-wide excess manufacturing capacity in drives under 200MBs.

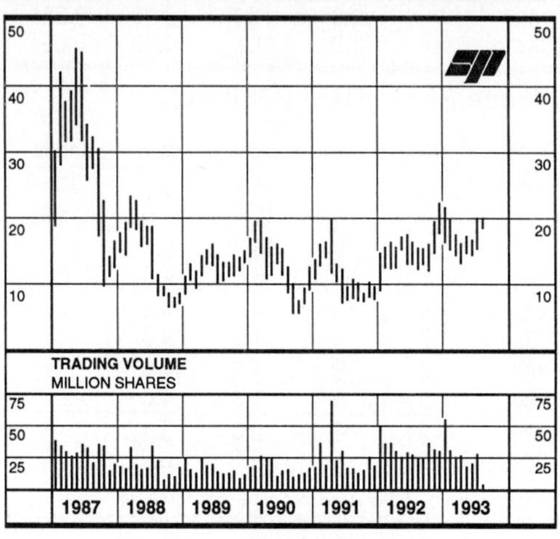

Net Sales (Million $)

Quarter:	1992–93	1991–92	1990–91	1989–90
Sep.	743	620	630	379
Dec.	777	695	693	690
Mar.	754	780	677	676
Jun.	770	780	677	668
	3,044	2,875	2,677	2,413

Based on a preliminary report, net sales in the fiscal year ended July 2, 1993, climbed 5.9% from those of the prior year, reflecting increased unit shipments. Margins widened on the higher volume and a more favorable product mix, despite competitive pricing pressures which were particularly intense in the second half of fiscal 1993 for drives with storage capacities below 200 MBs. Following net interest and other income, contrasted with net expense, and restructuring charges of $15,000,000, versus $33,865,000, pretax income surged to $271,436,000, from $85,382,000. After taxes at 28.0%, versus 26.0%, net income rose to $195,434,000 ($2.80 a share; $2.71 fully diluted) from $63,183,000 ($0.92).

Common Share Earnings ($)

Quarter:	1992–93	1991–92	1990–91	1989–90
Sep.	0.86	d0.72	0.22	0.45
Dec.	0.91	0.17	0.36	0.56
Mar.	0.56	0.59	0.38	0.44
Jun.	0.48	0.84	0.01	0.46
	2.80	[1]0.92	[1]0.95	1.92

Important Developments

Jul. '93— Price erosion for disk drive products in the first six months of 1993 was much more severe than usual. Although pricing is expected to return to more normal rates of decline later this year or early in 1994, near-term pricing pressures are likely to continue.

Next earnings report expected in mid-October.

Per Share Data ($)

Yr. End Jun. 30	1993	1992	1991	[2]1990	1989	1988	1987	1986	[2]1985	1984
Tangible Bk. Val.	**NA**	[5]12.63	[5]11.76	[5]10.64	8.85	8.89	7.36	4.41	3.66	3.74
Cash Flow	**NA**	3.37	3.04	3.84	1.55	2.54	3.36	1.11	0.28	1.13
Earnings	**2.80**	0.92	[3]0.95	1.92	0.01	1.54	2.81	0.72	0.02	0.95
Dividends	**Nil**	Nil	Nil	Nil	Nil	Nil	Nil	Nil	Nil	Nil
Payout Ratio	**NA**	Nil	Nil	Nil	Nil	Nil	Nil	Nil	Nil	Nil
Prices—High	**22⅜**	[4]22⅜	[4]19⅞	[4]19¾	[4]16⅛	[4]23⅜	[4]45¾	[4]21	[4]8¾	[4]17
Low	**9**	[4]9	[4]7⅛	[4]5⅝	[4]8½	[4]6½	[4]9¾	[4]7⅛	[4]4¾	[4]4
P/E Ratio—	**7–3**	24–10	21–8	10–3	NM	15–4	16–3	29–10	NM	18–4

Data as orig. reptd. Adj. for stk. div. of 100% Jun. 1983. **1.** Sum of qtrs. does not equal full-yr. amt., due to change in shs. **2.** Refl. merger or acq. **3.** Bef. spec. item(s) of +0.07 in 1991. **4.** Cal. yr. **5.** Incl. intangibles. d-Deficit. NM-Not Meaningful. NA-Not Available.

Income Data (Million $)

Year Ended Jun. 30	Revs.	Oper. Inc.	% Oper. Inc. of Revs.	Cap. Exp.	Depr.	Int. Exp.	Net Bef. Taxes	Eff. Tax Rate	[3]Net Inc.	% Net Inc. of Revs.	Cash Flow
1992	**2,875**	**309**	**10.7**	**82**	**169**	**34.0**	**85**	**26.0%**	**63**	**2.2**	**232**
1991	2,677	256	9.5	99	138	42.5	82	22.9%	63	2.3	201
[1]1990	2,413	297	12.3	58	118	48.7	150	22.0%	117	4.9	235
1989	1,372	91	6.6	63	78	24.1	NM	26.1%	NM	NM	78
1988	1,266	151	11.9	208	50	21.9	99	21.9%	77	6.1	128
1987	958	208	21.7	65	28	5.1	186	24.8%	140	14.6	167
1986	460	58	12.7	38	19	2.9	36	4.4%	35	7.5	54
[1]1985	215	NM	NM	28	12	1.8	[2]d10	NM	1	0.5	13
1984	344	64	18.5	34	8	0.9	[2]65	35.6%	42	12.2	50
1983	110	19	17.0	38	3	0.4	[2]18	29.2%	13	11.9	16

Balance Sheet Data (Million $)

Jun. 30	Cash	Curr. Assets	Curr. Liab.	Curr. Ratio	Total Assets	% Ret. on Assets	Long Term Debt	Common Equity	Total Cap.	% LT Debt of Cap.	% Ret. on Equity
1992	**504**	**1,259**	**502**	**2.5**	**1,817**	**3.3**	**321**	**862**	**1,280**	**25.0**	**7.6**
1991	252	1,184	591	2.0	1,880	3.3	393	766	1,254	31.4	8.6
1990	263	1,139	550	2.1	1,851	7.3	510	675	1,269	40.2	19.0
1989	190	652	265	2.5	1,077	NM	305	442	812	37.6	0.1
1988	93	685	288	2.4	1,094	8.0	304	436	806	37.8	19.4
1987	396	647	109	6.0	814	24.8	302	354	705	42.8	49.4
1986	47	183	67	2.7	305	11.9	15	208	238	6.3	18.1
1985	7	169	68	2.5	275	0.4	18	172	207	8.6	0.6
1984	14	127	31	4.1	215	22.5	10	165	184	5.3	29.3
1983	24	110	27	4.0	157	12.6	7	121	130	5.6	16.1

Data as orig. reptd. **1.** Refl. merger or acq. **2.** Incl. equity in earns. of nonconsol. subs. **3.** Bef. spec. items. d-Deficit. NM-Not Meaningful.

Business Summary

Seagate Technology, Inc. designs and manufactures a broad line of rigid magnetic disk drives and related products for use in a wide range of computer systems to record, store and retrieve digital information that cannot be stored entirely in the system's central processing unit. Products are sold to original equipment manufacturers (OEMs) for inclusion in their computer systems or subsystems, to distributors, value-added resellers (VARs) and dealers that service the add-in and add-on computer market and to system integrators.

SGAT's strategy is to produce disk drive products to meet the performance, size and volume requirements of the following major computer system markets: personal computers (including desktop, laptop and notebook microcomputers); midrange systems (including high-performance microcomputers, workstations and minicomputers); and mainframes/supercomputers.

The company offers over 150 disk drive models with form factors of 1.8, 2½, 3½, 5¼, eight and nine inches, and capacities ranging from 20 megabytes (MBs) to 3.2 gigabytes (GBs). Products are differentiated by form factor and on a price/performance basis.

SGAT pursues a strategy of vertical integration and is a major designer and manufacturer of disk drive components. It also sells spare parts, repair services and components. Products are manufactured primarily in the Far East and the U.S.

Dividend Data

No cash has been paid.

Finances

In January 1993, the company agreed to acquire a 25% interest in Sundisk Corp. SGAT will market certain storage products worldwide, under both the Seagate and Sundisk brand names and the companies will jointly develop data storage products.

During fiscal 1992, SGAT recorded restructuring and other charges totaling $33,865,000.

In October 1989, the company acquired Imprimis Technology, the data storage products subsidiary of Control Data Corp. (CDC), for about $450 million.

Capitalization

Long Term Debt: $281,276,000 (6/93); incl. $266.8 million of 6.75% sub. debs. conv. into com. at $42.50 per sh.

Common Stock: 67,903,232 shs. ($0.01 par). Institutions hold 75%. Stockholders of record: 7,017 (6/92).

Office—920 Disc Drive, Scotts Valley, CA 95066. **Tel**—(408) 438-6550. **Chrmn, Pres & CEO**—A. F. Shugart. **SVP-Fin, CFO & Secy**—D. L. Waite. **Investor Contact**—Jon van Bronkhorst. **Dirs**—G. B. Filler, K. E. Haughton, B. C. Hegarty, R. A. Kleist, L. Perlman, A. F. Shugart, T. P. Stafford. **Transfer Agent & Registrar**—Chemical Trust Co. of California, SF. **Incorporated** in California in 1978; reincorporated in Delaware in 1986. **Empl**—43,000.

 Peter C. Wood, CFA

Seagull Energy

NYSE Symbol SGO Options on Phila (Feb-May-Aug-Nov) In S&P MidCap 400

Price	Range	P-E Ratio	Dividend	Yield	S&P Ranking	Beta
Sep. 29'93	1993					
30⅝	32⅞–14⅞	NM	None	None	B	0.53

Summary

Seagull is primarily engaged in natural gas exploration, development, and production. The December 1992 acquisition of Arkla Exploration Co. for $397 million made exploration and production the company's largest segment and enhanced long-term earnings prospects due to the favorable outlook for natural gas prices. Activities also include operations of pipelines and transmission and distribution of natural gas in Alaska. Earnings for 1993 and 1994 should benefit from higher production and natural gas prices.

Current Outlook

Share earnings for 1993 are estimated at $0.55, up from the depressed $0.17 of 1992, as adjusted for the 2-for-1 split in June 1993. An increase to $0.85 a share is projected for 1994.

Dividends are not expected to be initiated in the foreseeable future.

With the outlook for natural gas prices positive, long-term earnings growth prospects were enhanced by the acquisition of Arkla Exploration. Exploration and production profits should be up sharply in 1993, aided by the acquisition. Transmission and distribution profits are likely to decline on warmer weather conditions. Higher pipeline profits are expected, as increased gas demand should lead to greater gas marketing activity. Interest costs will rise, and share earnings will be restricted by more shares. Earnings for 1994 should benefit from a sharp increase in natural gas production and delivery capability largely due to exploitation efforts of onshore operating areas in 1993, nearly a 10% increase in natural gas prices, and (assuming normal weather) higher transmission and distribution earnings.

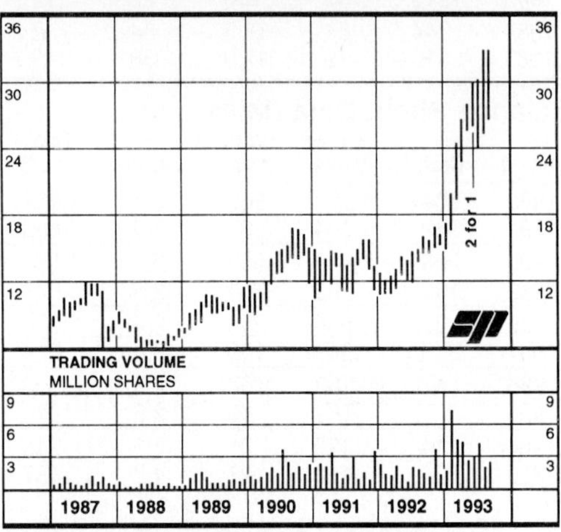

Total Revenues (Million $)

Quarter:	1993	1992	1991	1990
Mar.	103.2	67.5	73.1	63.0
Jun.	87.0	49.2	55.3	38.5
Sep.	---	48.9	48.0	43.5
Dec.	---	73.2	72.2	75.0
	---	238.8	248.5	219.9

Revenues for the six months ended June 30, 1993, rose 63%, year to year, reflecting higher energy prices and the Mid-South Inc. acquisition. Benefiting from wider pipeline margins and greater volumes delivered, net income advanced 128%, to $0.22 a share (on 32% more shares) from $0.13 (adjusted), which was before a $0.09 credit from an accounting change.

Common Share Earnings ($)

Quarter:	1993	1992	1991	1990
Mar.	0.12	0.03	0.28	0.52
Jun.	0.10	0.10	d0.07	0.16
Sep.	E0.03	d0.09	d0.13	d0.02
Dec.	E0.30	0.14	0.15	0.47
	E0.55	0.17	0.23	1.11

Important Developments

Sep. '93— SGO entered into a definitive agreement to purchase an interest in a natural gas field in East Texas for $26.6 million. Independent engineers estimated the interest SGO planned to purchase contained proved reserves equivalent to 29.4 Bcf of gas. Daily production from the field's 50 wells, net to the interest SGO was purchasing, totaled about 7.5 MMcf of gas and 54 barrels of condensate. Separately, SGO announced a natural gas discovery off the coast of Louisiana.

Next earnings report expected in late October.

Per Share Data ($)

Yr. End Dec. 31	1992	1991	1990	1989	1988	1987	1986	1985	1984	1983
Tangible Bk. Val.	**9.51**	9.23	8.59	5.50	5.63	5.57	5.92	6.20	5.28	4.71
Cash Flow	**2.65**	2.56	2.72	2.12	1.32	1.70	0.98	1.57	1.21	1.81
Earnings[1]	**0.17**	0.23	1.11	0.70	0.08	0.40	d0.17	0.58	0.58	1.13
Dividends	**Nil**	Nil	Nil	Nil	Nil	Nil	Nil	Nil	Nil	Nil
Payout Ratio	**Nil**	Nil	Nil	Nil	Nil	Nil	Nil	Nil	Nil	Nil
Prices—High	**16⅞**	15¾	16¹³⁄₁₆	11½	9⁵⁄₁₆	12¹⁄₁₆	8⁹⁄₁₆	9¹¹⁄₁₆	10¾	11⁹⁄₁₆
Low	**10¹³⁄₁₆**	10½	9¹⁄₁₆	7⅜	6	6¹⁄₁₆	6¹⁄₁₆	7¾	6¼	4½
P/E Ratio—	**99–64**	70–47	15–8	16–11	NM	30–15	NM	17–13	19–11	10–4

Data as orig. reptd., adjtd. for stk divd. of 100% Jun. 1993. 1. Bef. spec. item(s) of +0.09 in 1992. d-Deficit. E-Estimated. NM-Not Meaningful.

Income Data (Million $)

Year Ended Dec. 31	Revs.	Oper. Inc.	% Oper. Inc. of Revs.	Cap. Exp.	Depr.	Int. Exp.	Net Bef. Taxes	Eff. Tax Rate	[1]Net Inc.	% Net Inc. of Revs.	Cash Flow
1992	**239**	**93.1**	**39.0**	**510**	**63.2**	**18.5**	**6.9**	**36.2%**	**4.4**	**1.8**	**67.6**
1991	249	83.1	33.4	274	52.9	19.6	5.3	3.8%	5.1	2.1	58.0
1990	220	64.1	29.2	99	30.1	10.0	30.8	33.2%	20.6	9.4	50.7
1989	178	47.1	26.4	35	19.1	12.4	19.6	34.9%	12.8	7.2	28.6
1988	162	33.3	20.6	27	18.5	10.2	6.8	32.8%	4.6	2.8	19.6
1987	153	44.0	28.8	15	19.3	10.7	15.8	38.7%	9.7	6.3	25.3
1986	156	6.0	3.9	13	14.8	14.1	d1.4	NM	0.2	0.1	12.6
1985	96	27.2	28.4	186	12.5	8.3	9.1	11.2%	8.1	8.5	19.8
1984	59	15.7	26.5	30	6.8	0.5	9.3	33.3%	6.2	10.5	13.0
1983	54	9.5	17.5	10	7.3	1.3	20.0	39.6%	12.1	22.2	19.4

Balance Sheet Data (Million $)

Dec. 31	Cash	Curr. Assets	Curr. Liab.	Curr. Ratio	Total Assets	% Ret. on Assets	Long Term Debt	Common Equity	Total Cap.	% LT Debt of Cap.	% Ret. on Equity
1992	**3.9**	**98.8**	**144**	**0.7**	**1,103**	**0.5**	**608**	**244**	**878**	**69.2**	**1.8**
1991	6.2	90.9	105	0.9	619	1.0	219	236	485	45.2	2.2
1990	5.2	85.7	98	0.9	386	4.5	49	193	271	18.2	13.0
1989	14.1	90.9	77	1.2	331	4.1	114	77	236	48.3	12.1
1988	1.2	67.6	75	0.9	308	1.5	85	83	219	38.8	1.3
1987	1.3	61.5	67	0.9	292	3.2	84	83	216	39.1	6.9
1986	1.9	50.3	49	1.0	264	0.1	83	76	203	41.0	NM
1985	6.7	45.6	57	0.8	301	3.8	131	79	233	56.3	10.0
1984	0.3	26.1	23	1.1	101	7.3	12	57	78	15.4	11.6
1983	2.3	18.0	13	1.4	70	17.7	Nil	51	56	Nil	28.2

Data as orig. reptd. **1.** Bef. spec. item(s). d-Deficit. NM-Not Meaningful.

Business Summary

Seagull Energy is an independent energy company primarily engaged in natural gas exploration, development and production. The December 31, 1992 acquisition of Arkla Exploration Co. (renamed Seagull Mid-South Inc.) made exploration and production SGO's largest segment and more than doubled proved natural gas reserves from 313 Bcf to 884 Bcf. Activities also include pipeline operations, principally the southwestern U.S, and gas transmission and distribution in Alaska. Segment contributions in 1992 (operating profits in million $) were:

	Revs.	Profits
Exploration & production	38%	–$1.6
Alaska transmission & distribution....................	46%	22.4
Pipeline operations.............	16%	9.1

Exploration and production efforts are concentrated in the Gulf of Mexico offshore Texas and Louisiana and onshore in the Mid-Continent and Mid-South regions. At year-end 1992, total net proved reserves totaled 884 Bcf of gas (335 Bcf in 1991) and 18 million bbl. of crude oil, condensate and natural gas liquids (11 million in 1991). Production in 1992 totaled 38.14 Bcf of gas (32.90 Bcf in 1991) and 1.28 million bbl. of oil (1.34 million). Adjusted for the acquisition of Arkla Exploration, gas production in 1992 was 93.01 Bcf and oil production was 2.10 million bbl.

ENSTAR Alaska engages in transmission and distribution of natural gas in south-central Alaska, including Anchorage (about 86,400 customers are served in the Anchorage area). Gas volumes delievered in 1992 totaled 41,168 MMcf, up from 39,625 MMcf in 1991. Degree days in 1992 totaled 10,653, versus 10,178 in 1991.

Pipeline operations transport natural gas, hydrocarbon products, and petrochemicals in Texas and Louisiana. SGO is also involved in pipeline engineering, design, construction and operation, as well as natural gas processing, third-party natural gas marketing, and the marketing of all uncommitted natural gas and liquids production.

Dividend Data

No cash dividends have ever been paid on the common stock. A "poison pill" stock purchase right was adopted in 1989.

Amt of Divd. $	Date Decl.	Ex–divd. Date	Stock of Record	Payment Date
2–for–1	Mar. 19	Jun. 7	May 21	Jun. 4'93

Capitalization

Long Term Debt: $428,716,000 (6/93).

Common Stock: 35,827,622 shs. ($0.10 par). Institutions hold about 80%. Shareholders of record: 3,000.

Office—1700 First City Tower, 1001 Fannin, Houston, TX 77002-6714. **Tel**—(713) 951-4700. **Chrmn, Pres & CEO**—B. J. Galt. **SVP & CFO**—R. W. Shower. **Treas**—R. M. King. **Investor Contact**—Alan Payne. **Dirs**—J. E. Attwell, J. B. Brock, J. W. Elias, P. J. Fluor, B. J. Galt, W. R. Grant, D. P. Guerin, R. M. Morrow, D. S. Osborne, S. F. Segnar, R. W. Shower, G. M. Sullivan. **Transfer Agent & Registrar**—Bank of Boston. **Incorporated** in Texas in 1973. **Empl**—704.

 Mark Mattke

Sealed Air

NYSE Symbol SEE In S&P MidCap 400

Price	Range	P-E Ratio	Dividend	Yield	S&P Ranking	Beta
Oct. 20'93	1993					
28⅞	30⅜–21	23	None	None	A–	1.06

Summary

This company is primarily a manufacturer of protective packaging materials and systems and selected food packaging products. Principal products include air cellular cushioning materials and foam-in-place packaging systems. Despite the recessionary business environment, which limited sales growth in 1991 and 1992, earnings benefited from reduced interest expense and a lower tax rate. Earnings growth continued in the first nine months of 1993, and should continue for the rest of the year and into 1994 on improving economic conditions, new products, lower interest expense and a tax rate reduction.

Current Outlook

Earnings for 1993 are estimated at $1.30 a share, versus the $1.08 reported for 1992. Earnings for 1994 are seen at $1.50 a share.

No dividends have been paid since a $20 a share (adjusted) special distribution in 1989. Resumption of dividends is unlikely in the near future.

Sales for the remainder of 1993 and through 1994 are expected to improve based on a rebound in economic conditions and more favorable exchange rates. Sales of food packaging products, which fell in the first nine months of 1993, should begin to rise during the fourth quarter on an improving product mix, while unit volume of Instapak products and polyethylene foams should advance at a more rapid pace. Profitability is seen benefiting from the increased volume, new product development and marketing programs, expansion overseas, lower interest expense, and a tax rate reduction.

Net Sales (Million $)

Quarter:	1994	1993	1992	1991
Mar.	---	109.2	110.0	103.5
Jun.	---	113.7	112.1	108.9
Sep.	---	110.2	110.2	105.8
Dec.	---	---	113.7	116.9
	---	---	446.1	435.1

Net sales in the nine months ended September 30, 1993, rose fractionally, year to year, as slightly higher engineered products volume offset lower sales for surface protection and other cushioning products, and food packaging products, reflecting unfavorable exchange rates and lower selling prices. Profitability improved on lower operating expenses, and following a decline in interest expense, pretax earnings were up 17%. After taxes at 44.0%, versus 46.5%, net income rose 23%. On a per share basis, earnings were $0.97, compared with $0.80 (adj.). Results exclude an $0.08 a share gain from an accounting change in the 1993 interim.

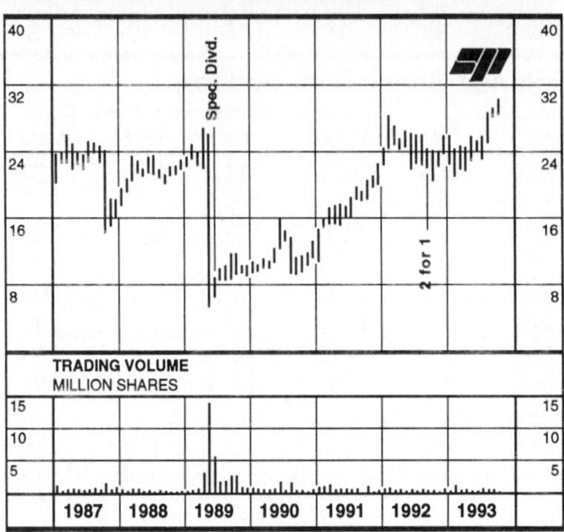

Common Share Earnings ($)

Quarter:	1994	1993	1992	1991
Mar.	E0.35	0.31	0.26	0.20
Jun.	E0.42	0.36	0.30	0.24
Sep.	E0.35	0.30	0.24	0.20
Dec.	E0.38	E0.33	0.28	0.24
	E1.50	E1.30	1.08	0.88

Important Developments

Oct. '93— Sealed Air said sales in the third quarter of 1993 were favorably impacted by increased unit volume in its major classes of products and the additional sales of Shurtuff durable mailer products, resulting from the recent acquisition of the Shurtuff division.

Jun. '93— Sealed Air said it expects to be on track soon toward double-digit sales growth and plans to focus on expanding abroad, specifically in Asia.

Next earnings report expected in late January.

Per Share Data ($)

Yr. End Dec. 31	1992	[1]1991	1990	1989	1988	[1]1987	1986	1985	1984	[1]1983
Tangible Bk. Val.[3]	**d3.45**	d4.99	d7.50	d9.56	9.91	8.70	7.62	6.45	5.42	4.82
Cash Flow	**1.81**	1.54	1.29	1.05	2.16	1.90	1.54	1.36	1.18	0.87
Earnings	**1.08**	0.88	0.65	0.44	1.55	1.30	1.08	0.98	0.86	0.65
Dividends	**Nil**	Nil	Nil	[2]20.080	0.290	0.260	0.235	0.210	0.190	0.165
Payout Ratio	**Nil**	Nil	Nil	NM	19%	21%	22%	22%	22%	26%
Prices—High	**28½**	22⅝	16	26 15/16	23⅜	26⅛	21⅞	18 7/16	14⅜	12½
Low	**20½**	10 13/16	9¼	5⅜	17 9/16	14¼	16 9/16	11¼	9 7/16	6 13/16
P/E Ratio—	**26–19**	26–12	25–14	61–12	15–11	20–11	20–15	19–12	17–11	19–10

Data as orig. reptd. Adj. for stk. div(s). of 100% Sep. 1992, Sep. 1983. **1.** Reflects merger or acquisition. **2.** Incl. 20.00 (adj.) spec. divd. **3.** Incl. intangibles. E-Estimated d-Deficit. NM-Not Meaningful.

Income Data (Million $)

Year Ended Dec. 31	Revs.	Oper. Inc.	% Oper. Inc. of Revs.	Cap. Exp.	Depr.	Int. Exp.	Net Bef. Taxes	Eff. Tax Rate	Net Inc.	% Net Inc. of Revs.	Cash Flow
1992	**446**	**86.3**	**19.3**	**12.4**	**14.1**	**31.1**	**[2]38.8**	**46.5%**	**20.8**	**4.7**	**34.8**
[1]1991	435	81.8	18.8	43.1	12.3	35.3	[2]31.5	48.6%	16.2	3.7	28.5
1990	413	78.5	19.0	12.1	11.1	41.4	24.5	53.5%	11.4	2.8	22.4
1989	385	67.8	17.6	13.8	10.1	31.8	24.1	69.8%	7.3	1.9	17.4
1988	346	52.3	15.1	18.2	9.9	3.6	41.8	39.6%	25.3	7.3	35.2
[1]1987	303	45.5	15.0	15.2	9.5	3.6	34.2	40.4%	20.4	6.7	29.9
1986	207	35.7	17.3	14.5	6.7	2.1	27.4	43.2%	15.5	7.5	22.3
1985	183	31.1	17.0	10.6	5.6	1.9	24.5	42.7%	14.0	7.6	19.6
1984	166	26.5	15.9	14.4	4.4	1.6	21.4	44.3%	11.9	7.2	16.3
[1]1983	124	19.3	15.5	6.2	2.9	1.1	15.8	44.5%	8.8	7.0	11.7

Balance Sheet Data (Million $)

Dec. 31	Cash	Curr. Assets	Curr. Liab.	Curr. Ratio	Total Assets	% Ret. on Assets	Long Term Debt	Common Equity	Total Cap.	% LT Debt of Cap.	% Ret. on Equity
1992	**26.0**	**123**	**93.4**	**1.3**	**268**	**7.6**	**225**	**d66**	**159**	**141.7**	**NM**
1991	20.2	118	99.9	1.2	275	6.2	254	d95	159	159.5	NM
1990	17.2	107	84.5	1.3	225	4.9	259	d132	128	203.2	NM
1989	24.4	111	77.0	1.4	229	3.0	302	d160	141	NM	242.5
1988	54.3	150	65.3	2.3	256	10.4	19	162	181	10.5	16.6
1987	46.6	127	57.8	2.2	228	9.8	21	141	162	13.0	15.4
1986	40.6	93	35.5	2.6	168	9.8	14	110	124	11.3	15.3
1985	34.3	80	33.5	2.4	148	10.3	15	93	108	13.9	16.4
1984	18.7	63	27.0	2.3	121	10.5	14	76	89	15.3	16.7
1983	12.8	53	26.3	2.0	104	9.4	8	66	74	11.1	14.0

Data as orig. reptd. **1.** Reflects merger or acquisition. **2.** Incl. equity in earns. of nonconsol. sub. d-Deficit. NM-Not Meaningful.

Business Summary

Sealed Air produces a wide variety of protective packaging materials and systems. In 1987, SEE significantly expanded its protective packaging operations with the acquisition of Jiffy Packaging Corp., a manufacturer of padded shipping envelopes and other protective packaging products. Business segment contributions in recent years:

	1992	1991	1990
Surface protection/ cushioning products.	46%	46%	45%
Engineered products....	40%	38%	39%
Food packaging products................	12%	11%	11%
Other products	2%	5%	5%

Foreign operations accounted for 30% of sales and 25% of operating profits in 1992.

The company's surface protection and other cushioning products include SEE's air cellular packaging materials, which are plastic sheets containing encapsulated air bubbles that protect products from damage through shock or vibration during shipment. Also included in this group are tear-resistant shipping envelopes, thin polyethylene foams and cellulose wadding. SEE's engineered products are its Instapak foam-in-place packaging systems, consisting of a proprietary blend of polyurethane chemicals which when mixed together and dispensed react to form a foam cushion.

These systems provide protective packaging for a variety of products, including computer, electronic, office, medical and communications equipment, furniture and spare parts, and void-fill packaging of office supplies, books, cosmetics and other small products for distribution.

Food Packaging products consist of absorbent pads and supermarket display case liners used in the display of meat, fish and poultry. Other products include those designed to control static electricity, and recreation and energy conservation products.

In August 1993, the company acquired the Shurtuff unit of Shuford Mills, Inc. Management said this will broaden its line of Jiffy Mailer products.

Dividend Data

Dividends were initiated in 1975 and discontinued in May 1989 following payment of a $20 a share (adjusted) special dividend. The shares were split 2-for-1 in September 1992.

Capitalization

Long Term Debt: $195,888,000 (9/93); incl. $170 million of 12⅝% sr. sub. notes due July 1, 1999.

Common Stock: 19,515,432 shs. ($0.01 par).
Officers and directors control some 6.8%.
Institutions hold about 70%.
Shareholders of record: 1,254 (3/93).

Office—Park 80 Plaza East, Saddle Brook, NJ 07662-5291. **Tel**—(201) 791-7600. **Pres & CEO**—T. J. D. Dunphy. **SVP-Fin & CFO**—W. V. Hickey. **Secy**—R. M. Grace Jr. **Investor Contact**—Mary A. Coventry. **Dirs**—J. K. Armstrong, J. K. Castle, T. J. D. Dunphy, C. F. Farrell Jr., S. A. Jackson, A. H. Miller, R. L. San Soucie. **Transfer Agent**—First Chicago Trust Co., NYC. **Incorporated** in New Jersey in 1960; reincorporated in Delaware in 1969. **Empl**—2,720.

 Stewart Scharf

Sensormatic Electronics

NYSE Symbol SRM Options on ASE (Jan-Apr-Jul-Oct) In S&P MidCap 400

Price	Range	P-E Ratio	Dividend	Yield	S&P Ranking	Beta
Sep. 3'93	1993					
43	46⅛–30	30	0.30	0.7%	B+	0.82

Summary

This company makes and services electronic and video surveillance equipment used to deter theft in retail stores and other environments. Earnings rose strongly in fiscal 1993, on record sales and wider gross margins.

Current Outlook

Earnings in the fiscal year ending June 30, 1994, are estimated at $1.73 a share, up from $1.45 in fiscal 1993.

Dividends should continue at $0.07½ quarterly.

Revenues will climb about 20% in fiscal 1994. Margins should remain stable. Long-term prospects should benefit from SRM's strong market position, continued growth in the retail hard goods and industrial sectors, and recent acquisitions that will expand the company's presence in newer, faster growing markets.

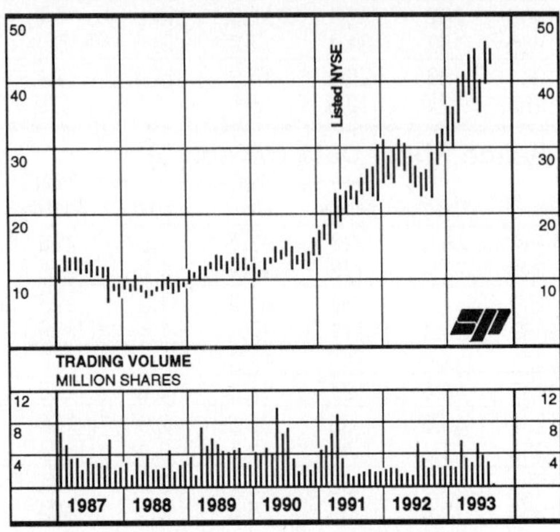

[1]Revenues (Million $)

Quarter:	1993-94	1992-93	1991-92	1990-91
Sep.	---	119.7	69.0	54.7
Dec.	---	122.1	78.1	57.2
Mar.	---	114.5	73.0	54.5
Jun.	---	131.0	89.7	72.8
	---	487.3	309.9	239.2

Based on a preliminary report, revenues in the fiscal year ended June 30, 1993, soared 57% from those of the year ended May 31, 1992. Results benefited from strong sales to the retail hard goods sector and the inclusion of ALPS. Gross margins widened, and net income soared 72%, to $54,084,000 ($1.45 a share, on 30% more shares; $1.40 fully diluted), from $31,526,000 ($1.10; no dilution).

[1]Common Share Earnings ($)

Quarter:	1993-94	1992-93	1991-92	1990-91
Sep.	E0.38	0.31	0.24	0.20
Dec.	E0.45	0.36	0.28	0.23
Mar.	E0.39	0.46	0.21	0.17
Jun.	E0.51	E0.42	0.37	0.30
	E1.73	1.45	1.10	0.90

Important Developments

Aug. '93— The company agreed to acquire Robot Research, a manufacturer of closed circuit television products. Separately, SRM introduced the VRS 2000, a visual reality security system that integrates various features on a computer-based graphical workstation.

Jun. '93— SRM said it would pay Checkpoint Systems, Inc. $3.5 million to terminate a European distribution agreement. The payment is covered by previously established reserves. The company and Checkpoint also agreed to cross-license their Ultra-Max and radio frequency technologies to each other, subject to certain restrictions. Separately, SRM said it believes that its new prototype deactivator, which is being evaluated by music manufacturers, overcomes concerns regarding the effect of deactivation on audio cassettes.

Mar. '93— The National Association of Recording Merchandisers (NARM) recommended the company's acousto-magnetic Ultra-Max technology as the industry standard for source labeling of music products with electronic anti-theft labels.

Next earnings report expected in late October.

Per Share Data ($)

Yr. End May 31[7]	1993	1992	[2]1991	1990	1989	[3]1988	1987	1986	1985	1984
Tangible Bk. Val.	**NA**	7.17	6.21	6.07	5.91	[4]6.52	[4]7.19	[4]6.69	[4]6.82	[4]6.69
Cash Flow	**NA**	1.60	1.33	1.06	0.93	d0.38	0.78	0.06	0.46	0.84
Earnings[5,6]	**1.45**	1.10	0.90	0.72	0.60	d0.63	0.48	d0.15	0.27	0.65
Dividends	**0.300**	0.300	0.300	0.125	0.050	0.025	0.050	0.050	0.050	0.050
Payout Ratio	**21%**	27%	33%	17%	8%	NM	10%	NM	19%	8%
Calendar Years	**1992**	1991	1990	1989	1988	1987	1986	1985	1984	1983
Prices—High	**32⅞**	30½	16⅜	14	10⅞	13⅞	11¾	9⅝	24½	42½
Low	**22½**	13⅞	9⅜	9½	7⅜	6¾	7⅛	6¼	5⅝	22⅝
P/E Ratio—	**23–16**	28–13	18–10	19–13	18–12	NM	24–15	NM	91–21	65–35

Data as orig. reptd. **1.** Quarters ended Aug., Nov., Feb. and May prior to 1992-93. **2.** Refl. merg. or acq. **3.** Refl. acctg. chg. **4.** Incl. intangibles. **5.** Bef. results of disc. ops. of +0.07 in 1991, and spec. item(s) of -0.07 in 1991. **6.** Ful. dil.: 1.40 in 1993. **7.** Yrs. ended May 31 prior to 1993. E-Estimated. d-Deficit. NM-Not Meaningful. NA-Not Available.

Income Data (Million $)

Year Ended May 31	Revs.	Oper. Inc.	% Oper. Inc. of Revs.	Cap. Exp.	Depr.	Int. Exp.	[3]Net Bef. Taxes	Eff. Tax Rate	[4]Net Inc.	% Net Inc. of Revs.	Cash Flow
1992	**310**	**58.1**	**18.7**	**39.0**	**14.5**	**11.4**	**41.0**	**23.2%**	**31.5**	**10.2**	**46.1**
[1]1991	239	43.3	18.1	35.6	11.8	2.8	31.2	20.8%	24.7	10.3	36.5
[2,5]1990	191	34.0	17.8	25.4	9.4	1.4	25.0	20.0%	20.0	10.5	29.4
1989	151	27.4	18.1	92.4	9.2	1.0	21.1	20.8%	16.7	11.1	25.9
1988	123	25.8	21.0	66.3	7.1	0.7	d11.9	NM	d17.7	NM	d10.6
1987	98	23.0	23.4	39.6	8.4	1.4	21.3	35.3%	13.8	14.0	22.2
1986	89	8.2	9.2	37.9	5.9	1.5	d6.1	NM	d4.3	NM	1.6
1985	91	16.9	18.5	38.0	5.4	1.9	9.3	19.9%	7.5	8.2	12.9
1984	94	26.6	28.4	54.8	5.1	1.2	25.2	27.8%	18.2	19.5	23.4
1983	86	36.9	42.9	43.2	5.3	6.1	33.1	30.9%	[5]22.9	26.6	28.2

Balance Sheet Data (Million $)

May 31	Cash	Curr. Assets	Curr. Liab.	Curr. Ratio	Total Assets	% Ret. on Assets	Long Term Debt	Common Equity	Total Cap.	% LT Debt of Cap.	% Ret. on Equity
1992	**63**	**NA**	**NA**	**NA**	**462**	**7.0**	**134**	**256**	**390**	**34.4**	**13.0**
1991	102	NA	62.5	NA	422	7.2	137	222	359	38.1	11.6
1990	27	NA	49.5	NA	265	7.8	9	200	216	4.3	10.4
1989	53	NA	47.4	NA	255	7.0	10	192	208	4.9	9.0
1988	67	NA	39.0	NA	227	NM	3	180	188	1.4	NM
1987	89	NA	35.0	NA	247	5.5	3	203	212	1.2	7.0
1986	75	NA	34.4	NA	248	NM	11	187	213	4.9	NM
1985	62	NA	24.9	NA	244	3.1	12	190	219	5.4	4.0
1984	47	NA	28.6	NA	241	7.6	11	186	213	5.2	11.5
1983	62	NA	29.4	NA	208	14.0	53	114	179	29.9	23.0

Data as orig. reptd. **1.** Refl. merger or acq. **2.** Excl. disc. ops. **3.** Incl. equity in earns. of nonconsol. subs. **4.** Bef. results of disc. ops. and spec. items. **5.** Refl. acctg. change. d-Deficit. NM-Not Meaningful. NA-Not Available.

Business Summary

Sensormatic Electronics produces and services electronic article surveillance (EAS) systems and microprocessor-controlled closed-circuit television systems (CCTV) used to deter shoplifting and internal theft in retail stores, as well as in nonretail environments. Foreign operations provided 37% of 1991-2 revenues.

The standard EAS system, used primarily by clothing retailers, consists of sensitized tags, and/or disposable labels which are attached to merchandise and then removed using a detaching or deactivator device when the item is purchased. If an item is taken through the controlled exit with the label attached, an alarm is activated. A similar EAS system is designed for various hard goods in drug stores, discount stores, record and video stores, supermarkets, and auto parts and hardware stores.

The company's industrial division markets EAS, CCTV and access control systems for the protection and control of assets and people in warehouses, hospitals, airports, office complexes, and power plants.

SRM's point-of-sale exception monitoring systems consist of proprietary software interfaces that link retail cash registers with CCTV systems, which are programmed to record predetermined types of transactions. These systems allow store management to deter and detect internal theft.

Dividend Data

Dividends have been paid since 1978.

Amt. of Divd. $	Date Decl.	Ex–divd. Date	Stock of Record	Payment Date
0.07½	Oct. 6	Oct. 9	Oct. 16	Oct. 27'92
0.07½	Dec. 29	Jan. 26	Feb. 1	Feb. 15'93
0.07½	Mar. 31	Apr. 27	May 3	May 14'93
0.07½	Jul. 20	Jul. 27	Aug. 2	Aug. 11'93

Finances

In June 1993, SRM acquired the 70% of Security Tag Systems that it did not already own, for about $40 million of common stock.

In July 1992, the company acquired the European EAS and CCTV businesses (ALPS) of Automated Security (Holdings) PLC for £150 million ($280 million) in cash.

Capitalization

Long Term Debt: $303,123,000 (3/93).

Common Stock: 38,700,890 shs. ($0.01 par).
Institutions hold 87%.
Shareholders of record: 3,392 (5/92).

Office—500 N.W. 12th Ave, Deerfield Beach, FL 33442. **Tel**—(305) 420-2000. **Chrmn, Pres & CEO**—R. G. Assaf. **EVP, COO & Investor Contact**—Michael E. Pardue. **Secy & Treas**—M. A. Flores. **Dirs**—R. G. Assaf, T. V. Buffet, J. M. LeWine, J. E. Lineberger, A. G. Milnes, M. E. Pardue, J. T. Ray, Jr. **Transfer Agent & Registrar**—First National Bank of Boston. **Incorporated** in Delaware in 1968. **Empl**—2,889.

 Kevin J. Gooley

Sequa Corp.

NYSE Symbol SQA.A In S&P MidCap 400

Price	Range	P-E Ratio	Dividend	Yield	S&P Ranking	Beta
Sep. 3'93	1993					
31⅝	33½–17⅞	NM	5---	5---	C	0.71

Summary

Sequa Corp. is a diversified industrial company engaged in a broad range of products and services. Following the recent discontinuation and sale of several units, it focuses on four technology-oriented operations: aerospace, metals and machinery, specialty chemicals, and professional services. A loss is likely for 1993, reflecting a second-quarter suspension of jet-engine repair operations by the FAA. A gradual recovery in aerospace operations should lead to a profits recovery in 1994. In August 1993 directors suspended dividends on the company's common and preferred shares.

Current Outlook

A loss of $1.70 a share is projected for 1993, versus income from continuing operations of $1.53 in 1992. For 1994, earnings of $2.75 are estimated.

Dividends on Class A and B common and preferred shares were suspended in August 1993.

Revenues are likely to decline at least moderately in 1993. With the engine repair plant recertified in June, it is expected that aerospace operations will begin a gradual recovery following a large first-half loss. Machinery and metal coatings should also rebound in the second half, reflecting plant consolidation and increasing sales. Some improvement should be seen for specialty chemicals, with international results recovering by the fourth quarter. Extension of strong first half improvement for services is expected.

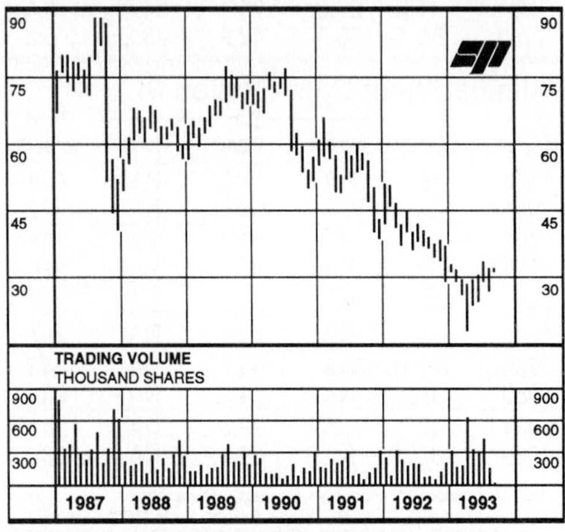

Revenues (Million $)

Quarter:	1993	1992	1991	1990
Mar.	427	461	451	534
Jun.	412	474	449	568
Sep.	---	469	473	543
Dec.	---	464	506	565
	---	1,868	1,879	2,211

Revenues for the six months ended June 30, 1993, decreased 10.2%, year to year. Results were hurt by large aerospace losses primarily resulting from charges related to the suspension of engine repair operations. There was a net loss of $22.0 million ($2.45 a share), in contrast to net income of $8.5 million ($0.72).

Common Share Earnings ($)

Quarter:	1993	1992	1991	1990
Mar.	d0.44	0.27	0.55	1.78
Jun.	d2.00	0.45	0.40	1.94
Sep.	E0.25	0.48	0.26	1.65
Dec.	E0.50	0.33	0.03	d2.38
	Ed1.70	1.53	1.24	3.03

Important Developments

Aug. '93— By August 1 approvals had been obtained from the Federal Aviation Administration (FAA) for the repair of parts that represent approximately 40% of repair revenues at the Orangeburg , N.Y. plant of the Gas Turbine division. Work on aircraft engines was suspended in the April-June period because of allegations of defective repair work on parts at the plant. Severance payments and a $2.5 million payment to the government reduced second quarter results by about $25 million. Sequa said that gradual improvement in results was expected to begin in the second half.

Mar. '93— Sequa said it expected to dispose of two additional discontinued operations during 1993.

Next earnings report expected in early November.

Per Share Data ($)

Yr. End Dec. 31	1992	1991	1990	1989	[2]1988	[3]1987	[2]1986	1985
Tangible Bk. Val.[1]	**27.23**	31.17	32.27	28.27	25.68	25.71	42.57	NA
Cash Flow[1]	**13.78**	11.80	13.22	13.43	13.25	8.58	4.46	NA
Earnings[1,4]	**1.53**	1.24	3.03	5.55	6.31	4.28	3.24	3.41
Dividends	**0.60**	0.60	0.60	0.60	0.60	0.60	0.48	NA
Payout Ratio	**39%**	48%	20%	10%	9%	14%	20%	NA
Prices—High	**51**	66⅛	77	77½	68¾	88⅜	84¾	NA
Low	**29**	38¾	50	56⅝	49⅝	40¾	34¾	NA
P/E Ratio—	**33–19**	53–31	25–17	14–10	11–8	21–10	13–12	NA

Data as orig. reptd. **1.** Combined Class A and B. **2.** Reflects accounting change. **3.** Reflects merger or acquisition. **4.** Bef. results of disc. opers. of -2.26 in 1992, -2.27 in 1991, -0.45 in 1989, -0.17 in 1988, -0.33 in 1987, +16.66 in 1986 and spec. item(s) of -0.76 in 1992. **5.** Dirs. omitted divd. Aug. 12, 1993. d-Deficit. E-Estimated NA-Not Available. NM-Not Meaningful.

Income Data (Million $)

Year Ended Dec. 31	Revs.	Oper. Inc.	% Oper. Inc. of Revs.	Cap. Exp.	Depr.	Int. Exp.	Net Bef. Taxes	Eff. Tax Rate	Net Inc.	% Net Inc. of Revs.	Cash Flow
1992	**1,868**	**242**	**13.0**	**93**	**118**	**73**	**44**	**59.1%**	**[6]17.9**	**1.0**	**133**
[1]1991	1,879	218	11.6	124	101	83	36	53.2%	[6]15.0	0.8	112
1990	2,211	342	15.5	170	98	109	75	54.2%	32.7	1.5	127
[1]1989	1,959	303	15.4	121	80	88	[5]112	45.7%	60.5	3.1	137
[1,2]1988	1,713	265	15.5	99	74	76	[5]120	40.3%	71.5	4.2	142
[1,3]1987	1,133	169	14.9	101	47	34	[5]79	35.5%	50.9	4.5	94
[1,2]1986	371	41	11.1	17	10	20	[5]29	9.3%	26.1	7.0	36
1985	884	85	9.7	45	25	[4]20	[5]12	66.6%	4.1	0.5	29

Balance Sheet Data (Million $)

Dec. 31	Cash	Curr. Assets	Curr. Liab.	Curr. Ratio	Total Assets	% Ret. on Assets	Long Term Debt	Common Equity	Total Cap.	% LT Debt of Cap.	% Ret. on Equity
1992	**15**	**679**	**350**	**1.9**	**1,912**	**0.9**	**690**	**625**	**1,383**	**49.9**	**2.3**
1991	16	779	403	1.9	2,108	0.6	825	670	1,571	52.6	1.7
1990	51	941	449	2.1	2,517	1.4	1,101	690	1,896	58.0	4.3
1989	87	945	451	2.1	2,344	2.9	923	673	1,712	53.9	8.6
1988	69	786	424	1.9	1,959	4.0	631	667	1,382	45.6	10.5
1987	86	777	396	2.0	1,663	3.3	493	641	1,182	41.7	7.6
1986	489	870	413	2.1	1,395	2.2	273	598	922	29.7	6.0

Data as orig. reptd.; finance subs. consol. after 1987. **1.** Excludes disc. opers. **2.** Reflects accounting change. **3.** Reflects merger or acquisition. **4.** Net of interest income. **5.** Incl. equity in earns. of nonconsol. subs. **6.** Bef. spec. items.

Business Summary

Sequa Corp. is a multi-industry company that provides a broad range of products and services. Contributions by segment in 1992 were:

	Sales	Profits
Aerospace	63%	50%
Machinery & metal coatings	13%	18%
Specialty chemicals	12%	26%
Professional services/other	12%	6%

European operations accounted for 22% of sales and 23% of profits in 1992.

Aerospace includes the manufacture and repair of blades, vanes and other components of gas turbine engines used for commercial and military jet aircraft. The segment also makes electro-optical and electronic devices for the military as well as avionic instruments and test equipment. Through Atlantic Research, it manufactures rocket propulsion systems.

Machinery is comprised of the manufacture of equipment for the two-piece food and beverage can industry and the web offset printing industry. The company also coats metal coils for the building, container and appliance industries.

Specialty chemicals makes products for the overseas detergent industry and the domestic textile and paper industries.

Professional services provides consulting and technical services for systems engineering and facility management. Other operations include manufacture of automotive products such as cigarette lighters and sensing devices, can making, a real estate holding company and an insurance company.

During 1992, Sequa sold the Valley Line, Sabine Towing, its engineered services operations, its men's apparel unit, and part of its financial services operations.

Dividend Data

As a result of deficiencies under covenants of the senior notes, payments on Class A and B common shares and the $5 cumulative preferred shares were suspended in August 1993. Payments on Class A shares in the past 12 months:

Amt of Divd. $	Date Decl.	Ex-divd. Date	Stock of Record	Payment Date
0.15	Oct. 23	Dec. 9	Dec. 15	Dec. 31'92
0.15	Feb. 25	Mar. 9	Mar. 15	Apr. 1'93
0.15	May 17	Jun. 9	Jun. 15	Jul. 1'93

Directors omitted the dividend August 12, 1993.

Capitalization

Long Term Debt: $539,073,000 (6/93).

$5 Cum. Conv. Preferred Stock: 633,511 shs. ($1 par); ea. conv. into 1.3219 Cl. A com. shs.

Class A Common Stock: 6,181,018 shs. (no par). N.E. Alexander owns 30%.

Class B Common Stock: 3,473,578 shs. (no par). Has 10 votes per sh.; conv. sh.-for-sh. into Cl. A. N.E. Alexander owns 51%.

Office—200 Park Ave., New York, NY 10166. **Tel**—(212) 986-5500. **Chrmn & CEO**—N. E. Alexander. **Pres & COO**—J. J. Quicke. **VP & Secy**—I. A. Schreger. **VP & Treas**—K. A. Drucker. **Investor Contact**—L. G. Kyriakou. **Dirs**—N. E. Alexander, A. Dworman, A. L. Fergenson, R. Frankel, D. S. Gottesman, S. Z. Krinsly, D. D. Kummerfeld, R. S. LeFrak, J. J. Quicke, F. R. Sullivan, G. Tsai, Jr. **Transfer Agent & Registrar**—Continental Stock Transfer & Trust Co., NYC. **Incorporated** in Delaware in 1929. **Empl**—13,800.

 T. Canning, CFA

Sequent Computer Systems

NASDAQ Symbol SQNT (Incl. in Nat'l Market) Options on ASE In S&P MidCap 400

Price	Range	P-E Ratio	Dividend	Yield	S&P Ranking	Beta
Oct. 13'93	1993					
17¼	24–11¼	34	None	None	C	1.87

Summary

Sequent is a leading supplier of high-performance, multi-user computer systems, used mainly for on-line transaction processing applications in commercial markets. Despite disappointing results for the 1993 second quarter, due largely to transitions in the company's organization and product mix, earnings should grow strongly in 1994.

Current Outlook

Earnings for 1993 are estimated at $0.50 a share, down from $0.55 in 1992. Share earnings of $0.90 are possible in 1994.

Initiation of dividend payments is not expected.

Despite a setback during the second quarter, due largely to transitions in the company's organizational and product mix, Sequent appears well situated for growth in upcoming periods. The company has positioned itself to take advantage of the current shift by large computer users towards open-systems client/server computing. The company's products also incorporate symmetric multiprocessing, a concept that is gaining adherents. In addition, SQNT recently started shipping Windows NT-based computers. These factors, together with a refocused and expanded sales force, should spur revenue growth in 1994. Gross margins should be relatively stable, despite severe price competition, as Sequent markets its products as complete solutions, rather than as commodity-like boxes. Despite a major advertising campaign that began during the second quarter, operating expenses should be controlled.

Operating Revenues (Million $)

13 Weeks:	1993	1992	1991	1990
Mar.	77.6	64.5	47.9	50.7
Jun.	80.8	72.2	50.1	58.2
Sep.	---	81.9	53.8	66.5
Dec.	---	88.7	61.5	73.3
	---	307.3	213.3	248.8

Total revenues in the six months ended July 3, 1993, advanced 16%, year to year, as product revenues rose 11% and service revenues climbed 40%. Gross margins widened, and following a 20% increase in operating costs, operating income rose 4.8%. After higher net interest and other expense, and taxes at 19.7%, versus 10.8%, net income slid 7.7%, to $3,667,000 ($0.12 a share, on 19% more shares), from $3,974,000 ($0.16).

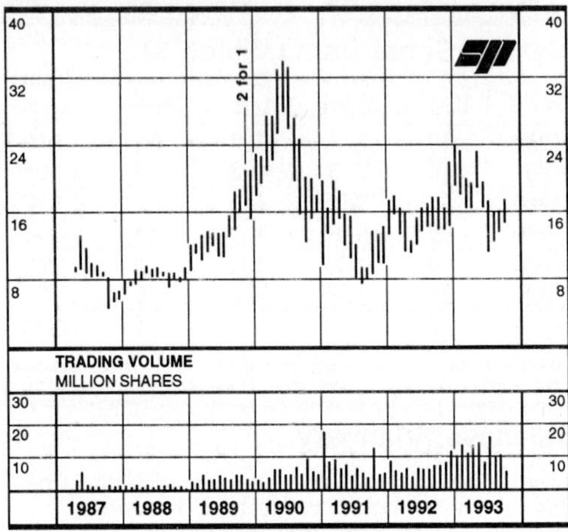

Common Share Earnings ($)

13 Weeks:	1993	1992	1991	1990
Mar.	0.12	0.04	d0.30	0.22
Jun.	0.01	0.12	d0.86	0.24
Sep.	E0.08	0.16	d0.99	0.25
Dec.	E0.29	0.23	0.04	0.11
	E0.50	0.55	d2.10	0.81

Important Developments

Oct. '93— SQNT received a contract to provide client/server consulting services and hardware to Thrift Drug, a subsidiary of J.C. Penney (NYSE: JCP). Separately, SQNT won a five-year contract from the National Association of Securities Dealers, valued at $3 million for the first year, to provide client/server services and systems.

Next earnings report expected in late October.

Per Share Data ($)

Yr. End Dec. 31	1992	1991	1990	1989	[2]1988	1987	1986	1985	1984	1983
Tangible Bk. Val.	[1]7.68	[1]7.25	[1]9.82	[1]6.65	[1]3.35	2.78	1.02	0.24	0.03	0.59
Cash Flow	1.49	d1.16	1.40	1.07	0.56	0.34	0.02	NA	NA	NA
Earnings[3]	0.55	d2.10	0.81	0.70	0.34	0.20	d0.09	d0.86	d1.16	d0.52
Dividends	Nil	Nil	Nil	Nil	Nil	Nil	Nil	Nil	Nil	Nil
Payout Ratio	Nil	Nil	Nil	Nil	Nil	Nil	Nil	Nil	Nil	Nil
Prices—High	22	19¾	34	21	9⅝	13⅜	NA	NA	NA	NA
Low	11⅛	7½	12½	9⅛	6⅜	4¾	NA	NA	NA	NA
P/E Ratio—	40–20	NM	42–15	30–13	28–19	65–23	NM	NM	NM	NM

Data as orig. reptd. Adj. for stk. div. of 100% Nov. 1989. **1.** Incl. intangibles. **2.** Refl. merger or acq. **3.** Bef. spec. items of +0.11 in 1989, +0.06 in 1988, +0.06 in 1987. d-Deficit. E-Estimated. NM-Not Meaningful. NA-Not Available.

Income Data (Million $)

Year Ended Dec. 31	Revs.	Oper. Inc.	% Oper. Inc. of Revs.	Cap. Exp.	Depr.	Int. Exp.	Net Bef. Taxes	Eff. Tax Rate	[2]Net Inc.	% Net Inc. of Revs.	Cash Flow
1992	**307**	**54.4**	**17.7**	**47.5**	**24.6**	**4.92**	**15.9**	**9.1%**	**14.4**	**4.7**	**39.0**
1991	213	d6.1	NM	33.5	21.8	4.03	d52.4	NM	d48.7	NM	d26.9
1990	249	38.4	15.4	59.8	13.8	1.09	26.2	28.0%	18.8	7.6	32.6
1989	146	25.0	17.1	24.3	7.2	0.74	18.5	25.6%	13.8	9.5	20.9
[1]1988	76	10.4	13.7	12.4	3.6	0.32	7.2	22.7%	5.5	7.3	9.1
1987	38	5.4	14.0	5.3	1.9	0.40	4.2	28.0%	3.0	7.9	5.0
1986	20	0.6	3.1	2.6	1.1	0.61	d0.9	Nil	d0.9	NM	0.2
1985	4	d7.1	NM	1.1	0.7	0.26	d7.8	Nil	d7.8	NM	NA
1984	NM	d7.2	NM	1.7	0.6	0.20	d7.7	Nil	d7.7	NM	NA
1983	NA	NA	NA	NA	NA	NA	d2.5	Nil	d2.5	NM	NA

Balance Sheet Data (Million $)

Dec. 31	Cash	Assets	Curr. Liab.	Ratio	Total Assets	% Ret. on Assets	Long Term Debt	Common Equity	Total Cap.	% LT Debt of Cap.	% Ret. on Equity
1992	**44.4**	**168**	**81.1**	**2.1**	**279**	**5.5**	**24.0**	**173**	**197**	**12.2**	**9.0**
1991	36.0	153	86.8	1.8	246	NM	7.2	149	157	4.6	NM
1990	37.0	164	40.2	4.1	251	8.9	13.6	195	209	6.5	11.5
1989	28.1	103	32.7	3.2	147	12.2	1.8	111	113	1.6	16.4
1988	0.2	50	19.2	2.6	76	8.5	0.8	54	55	1.4	11.2
1987	18.6	42	7.6	5.5	52	4.4	1.0	43	44	2.3	7.0
1986	7.5	18	9.8	1.9	23	NM	1.6	[3]12	13	11.7	NM
1985	0.3	4	2.6	1.5	7	NM	1.7	[3]2	4	44.3	NM
1984	NA	NA	NA	NA	6	NM	1.7	[3]NM	29	89.9	NM
1983	NA	NA	NA	NA	4	NM	0.8	[3]3	4	23.2	NM

Data as orig. reptd. **1.** Refl. merger or acq. **2.** Bef. spec. items. **3.** Refl. conv. of pfd. stk. upon completion of public offering. d-Deficit. NM-Not Meaningful. NA-Not Available.

Business Summary

Sequent Computer Systems makes high-performance symmetric multiprocessing computer systems and parallel-enabled software for the commercial open systems marketplace. Its Symmetry 2000 system incorporates up to 30 Intel i486 microprocessors to provide superior price/performance and scalability for open systems on-line transaction processing (OLTP), relational database management software (RDBMS) and network and client server applications. Revenue contributions in recent years were as follows:

	1992	1991	1990
End–user products	68%	70%	66%
OEM products	14%	13%	26%
Service & other	18%	16%	8%

International sales accounted for 49% of 1992 revenues (46% in 1991); OEM customer Unisys provided 12% (8%). OEM revenues in 1993 are expected to be below 1992 levels.

The company's symmetric multiprocessor architecture and DYNIX/ptx, its enhanced version of the UNIX operating system, have been designed to maximize OLTP applications using RDBMS. Its systems support large numbers of concurrent users with high throughput, fast response times, ease of use, high system uptime, configurability to current needs, easy on-site expansion and a growing library of applications. The Symmetry product family, based on the Intel i486 microprocessor, offers up to 618 transactions per second of performance at prices ranging from $50,000 for a dual-processor system to over $2 million for a 30-processor system serving several hundred active users in a database environment.

R&D costs of $28.1 million (9% of revenues) were expensed in 1992, versus $25.8 million (12%) in 1991.

Dividend Data

No cash dividends have been paid. A two-for-one stock split was effected in 1989.

Finances

In a February 1993 public offering, 4.6 million shares (including 1.6 million for selling shareholders) were sold at $21.125. Net proceeds to Sequent totaled $60 million. In connection with the offering, the 1.5 million outstanding shares of Series A Preferred Stock were converted into 3 million common shares and $9.9 million of the convertible debentures were converted into 626,092 common shares.

Capitalization

Long Term Debt: $12,618,000 (7/3/93); incl. $2,164,000 of cap. leases.

Common Stock: 29,897,054 shs. ($0.01 par). Institutions hold 92%.
Shareholders: 1,420 of record (1/93).

Office—15450 S.W. Koll Pkwy., Beaverton, OR 97006-6063. **Tel**—(503) 626-5700. **Chrmn, Pres & CEO**—K. C. Powell, Jr. **VP-Fin, Treas & CFO**—R. S. Gregg. **SVP & Secy**—M. D. Simon. **Dirs**—D. R. Hathaway, R. C. Mathis, M. S. S. Morton, R. C. Palermo, K. C. Powell, Jr., R. W. Wilmot. **Transfer Agent & Registrar**—Chemical Trust Co. of Calif., San Francisco. **Incorporated** in Delaware in 1983. **Empl**—1,629.

 Neeraj K. Vohra

Service Merchandise

NYSE Symbol SME Options on Phila In S&P MidCap 400

Price	Range	P-E Ratio	Dividend	Yield	S&P Ranking	Beta
Jul. 26'93	1993					
11⅝	15⅜–10	14	None	None	B	1.65

Summary

This retailer conducts a general merchandise business on high-volume, low-margin principles through a chain of more than 370 catalog stores in 37 states. The company promotes its merchandise through a 560-page annual catalog mailed in the fall of each year, smaller spring and Christmas catalogs, and seasonal flyers and newspaper inserts. Earnings improved in 1992 on higher sales and lower interest expense.

Business Summary

Service Merchandise Company, Inc. is a catalog showroom merchandiser that was operating 372 catalog stores and two Kids Central USA stores in 37 states as of June 1993. The stores offer a wide variety of jewelry, diamonds, housewares, small appliances, giftware, silverware, cameras, luggage, radios, televisions, other home electronics, sporting goods, toys and patio, lawn and garden products. SME believes its prices are competitive with those of other retailers selling similar lines of merchandise and operating on high-volume, low-profit-margin principles.

The company's stores are divided into several departments. Only the jewelry and sight-and-sound departments require personnel for customer assistance. In those departments, the merchandise is displayed in showcases, and sales personnel deliver it to the customer and accept payment. In self-service sections, customers select the merchandise from a shelf and take it to a checkout counter to complete the purchase. In the remainder of the store, only a sample of the merchandise is displayed and order forms are available at various locations. After the customer orders the merchandise by filling out the form, a store cashier is paid and the merchandise is delivered to a pickup station. Management believes this merchandising technique reduces selling space requirements, handling and payroll costs and provides greater control over customer-related inventory shrinkage.

Customers may also phone in orders for mail delivery 24 hours a day, seven days a week, fax an order to the company's mail-order department or call a store to pick up an order.

Principal promotional efforts are made through an annual fall catalog of approximately 560 pages and a spring catalog of about 170 pages. SME also distributes a 100-page Christmas catalog, as well as with seasonal flyers and newspaper inserts.

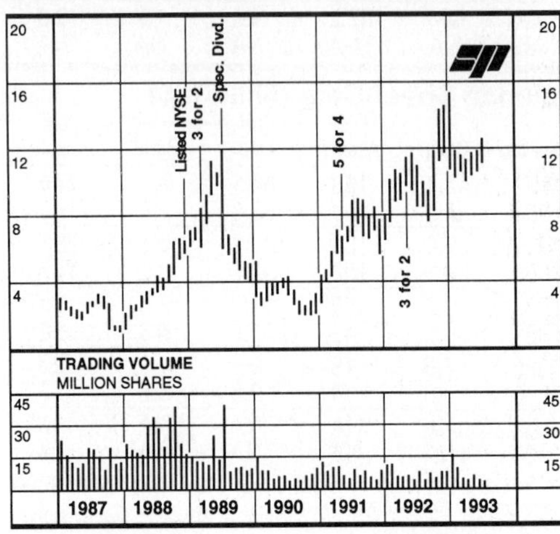

Most of the company's stores display and maintain an inventory of substantially all of the catalog items and some merchandise not described in the published catalogs in warehouse space contiguous to the sales area. Merchandise is purchased from about 2,100 suppliers. SME monitors inventory through an extensive on-line data processing network consisting of computerized terminals located in each store connected by satellite or phone lines to a central host computer.

Important Developments

Jul. '93— The company said it planned to open a net 17 new stores in the second half of 1993, compared with nine in the year-earlier period. It expected the increased pace of store openings to improve sales growth in future quarters.

Next earnings report expected in mid-October.

Per Share Data ($)

Yr. End Dec. 31	1992	1991	1990	1989	1988	1987	1986	[1]1985	1984	1983
Tangible Bk. Val.	**1.96**	1.06	0.26	d0.43	4.06	3.27	2.97	3.50	3.42	2.97
Cash Flow	**1.41**	1.32	1.17	1.30	1.37	0.87	0.42	0.58	0.81	0.75
Earnings[2]	**0.83**	0.76	0.62	0.74	0.81	0.27	d0.18	0.11	0.52	0.53
Dividends	**Nil**	Nil	Nil	[3]5.349	0.028	0.028	0.028	0.028	0.028	0.028
Payout Ratio	**Nil**	Nil	Nil	NM	3%	11%	NM	25%	6%	5%
Prices—High	**14⅝**	9	5¼	11⅞	6⅝	3⅜	5⅜	5⅞	5⅞	9⅝
Low	**6½**	2¾	2	4⅛	1¼	1⅛	2⅝	3⅞	3¾	4⅝
P/E Ratio—	**18–8**	12–4	9–3	16–5	8–2	13–4	NM	51–34	11–7	18–9

Data as orig. reptd. Adj. for stk. divs. of 50% May 1992, 25% May 1991, 50% Mar. 1989, 100% May 1983. **1.** Refl. merger or acq. **2.** Bef. results of disc. ops. of -0.32 in 1986 & spec. item of +0.07 in 1987. **3.** Incl. 5.33 special. d-Deficit. NM-Not Meaningful.

Income Data (Million $)

Year Ended Dec. 31	Oper. Revs.	Oper. Inc.	% Oper. Inc. of Revs.	Cap. Exp.	Depr.	Int. Exp.	Net Bef. Taxes	Eff. Tax Rate	[4]Net Inc.	% Net Inc. of Revs.	Cash Flow
1992	**3,713**	**285**	**7.7**	**70**	**58.7**	**93**	**139**	**39.0%**	**84.5**	**2.3**	**143**
1991	3,400	285	8.4	63	56.2	[3]109	125	39.0%	76.1	2.2	132
1990	3,435	275	8.0	56	54.7	[3]126	98	38.0%	60.7	1.8	115
1989	3,307	263	8.0	90	54.2	[3]102	111	35.0%	72.0	2.2	126
1988	3,093	251	8.1	35	53.6	[3]82	121	37.0%	76.5	2.5	130
1987	2,719	178	6.5	42	56.2	[3]86	44	44.0%	24.9	0.9	81
[1]1986	2,527	91	3.6	71	56.7	68	d29	NM	[5]d17.1	NM	40
[2]1985	2,526	105	4.2	394	44.0	57	10	NM	10.7	0.4	55
1984	1,657	126	7.6	127	25.0	21	85	47.4%	44.6	2.7	70
1983	1,458	118	8.1	48	18.4	18	88	48.7%	44.9	3.1	63

Balance Sheet Data (Million $)

Dec. 31	Cash	Curr. Assets	Curr. Liab.	Curr. Ratio	Total Assets	% Ret. on Assets	Long Term Debt	Common Equity	Total Cap.	% LT Debt of Cap.	% Ret. on Equity
1992	**165**	**1,099**	**809**	**1.4**	**1,709**	**5.1**	**697**	**194**	**900**	**77.4**	**56.5**
1991	111	965	744	1.3	1,573	4.7	715	104	829	86.2	117.2
1990	208	1,040	787	1.3	1,653	3.7	827	25	866	95.5	NM
1989	198	1,046	754	1.4	1,664	4.2	930	d42	910	NM	40.3
1988	337	1,148	731	1.6	1,711	4.7	574	381	980	58.6	22.3
1987	250	962	593	1.6	1,553	1.6	622	307	959	64.8	8.5
1986	146	897	450	2.0	1,525	NM	770	279	1,075	71.6	NM
1985	48	812	625	1.3	1,459	0.9	492	328	834	59.1	3.3
1984	90	561	368	1.5	867	5.3	185	309	498	37.1	15.5
1983	189	556	348	1.6	756	6.6	154	252	408	37.7	19.3

Data as orig. reptd. **1.** Excl. disc. ops. **2.** Refl. merger or acq. **3.** Net of int. inc. **4.** Bef. spec. item in 1987. **5.** Refl. acctg. change. d-Deficit. NM-Not Meaningful.

Net Sales (Million $)

Quarter:	1993	1992	1991	1990
Mar.	673	665	608	625
Jun.	803	781	748	749
Sep.		698	656	658
Dec.		1,568	1,388	1,402
		3,713	3,400	3,435

Sales for the six months ended June 30, 1993, were up 2.1%, year to year, reflecting an increase in comparable-store sales of 1.6% and the opening of new stores. Gross margins benefited from an increase in jewelry sales as a percentage of total sales and improved margins for hardline goods. Higher SG&A expenses, due largely to a planned increase in advertising costs, were somewhat offset by reduced interest expense, and the seasonal loss was trimmed to $2,437,000 ($0.03 a share, before a net special credit of $0.01), from $3,356,000 ($0.03, as adjusted).

Common Share Earnings ($)

Quarter:	1993	1992	1991	1990
Mar.	d0.11	d0.09	d0.13	d0.15
Jun.	0.08	0.06	0.05	0.01
Sep.		d0.02	d0.05	d0.08
Dec.		0.88	0.88	0.84
		0.83	0.76	0.62

d-Deficit.

Dividend Data

SME discontinued its quarterly cash dividend in conjunction with the payment in July 1989 of a special distribution of $5.33 a share (adjusted). Previously, dividends had been paid since 1977. The shares were split three for two in 1992.

Finances

In April 1993, SME amended its credit agreement, reducing the contractual rate for its $157,000,000 million term loan and its $475,000,000 revolving credit to prime plus 0.05%, including facility fees. In February 1993, SME issued $300 million of 9% subordinated debentures due 2004, using the net proceeds and existing cash to retire its 11¾% debentures due in 1996.

The company historically has incurred a net loss in the first nine months of the year, due to the seasonality of the retail catalog store business.

Capitalization

Long Term Debt: $692,764,000 (3/93), incl. $87,912,000 of lease obligs.

Common Stock: 99,225,286 shs. ($0.50 par) The Zimmerman family owns about 8.2%. Institutions hold some 58%. Shareholders of record: 5,947.

Office—7100 Service Mechandise Drive, Brentwood, TN 37027. **Tel**—(615) 660-6000. **Chrmn & Pres**—R. Zimmerman. **VP, CFO & Investor Contact**—Sam Cusano. **VP-Treas**—S. P. Braud. **VP-Secy**—G. A. Bodzy. **Dirs**—R. P. Crane Jr., R. M. Holt, C. V. Moore, J. E. Poole, H. Roitenberg, R. Zimmerman. **Transfer Agent**—Harris Trust & Savings Bank, Chicago. **Incorporated** in Tennessee in 1970. **Empl**—22,200.

 Jane Collin

Shaw Industries

NYSE Symbol SHX Options on CBOE (Feb-May-Aug-Nov) In S&P MidCap 400

Price	Range	P-E Ratio	Dividend	Yield	S&P Ranking	Beta
Aug. 23'93	1993					
43	46½–28⅛	31	0.36	0.9%	A–	1.60

Summary

This company is the world's largest carpet manufacturer, producing tufted carpet for residential and commercial use. A long earnings uptrend was broken in fiscal 1991, reflecting the impact of the recession and efforts to increase market share, but progress resumed in fiscal 1992. Further gains are expected for fiscal 1993 and 1994, on improved carpet demand, greater volume, and synergies from acquisitions. A formal response was recently filed to a lawsuit charging SHX with violations of federal antitrust laws and state laws.

Current Outlook

Earnings for the fiscal year ending June 30, 1994, are projected at $2.00 a share, up from fiscal 1993's $1.43.

The $0.09 quarterly dividend should be increased this year.

Fiscal 1994 sales should advance 10% to 15% from those of fiscal 1993, reflecting acquisitions, increased market share (SHX aims for a 40% share by 1995, up from 30%), and greater demand for carpets as the economy improves and the housing market strengthens. Housing turnover and consumer confidence levels typically drive sales of rugs and carpets. Margins should widen on the greater volume, manufacturing efficiencies, a more favorable product mix, and more timely distribution. Interest costs may be slightly higher. In the long-term, earnings will benefit from efforts to expand overseas.

Net Sales (Million $)

Quarter:	1992–93	1991–92	1990–91	1989–90
Sep.	547	437	420	332
Dec.	585	411	416	321
Mar.	519	404	341	395
Jun.	669	500	430	427
	2,321	1,751	1,608	1,475

Sales in the fiscal year ended July 3, 1993 (preliminary), climbed 33% from those of the preceding year. Margins widened, and net income surged 73%, to $1.43 a share, on 12% more shares, from $0.93.

Common Share Earnings ($)

Quarter:	1992–93	1991–92	1990–91	1989–90
Sep.	0.32	0.24	0.23	0.24
Dec.	0.36	0.20	0.16	0.23
Mar.	0.23	0.14	Nil	0.25
Jun.	0.52	0.36	0.18	0.35
	1.43	0.93	0.58	1.06

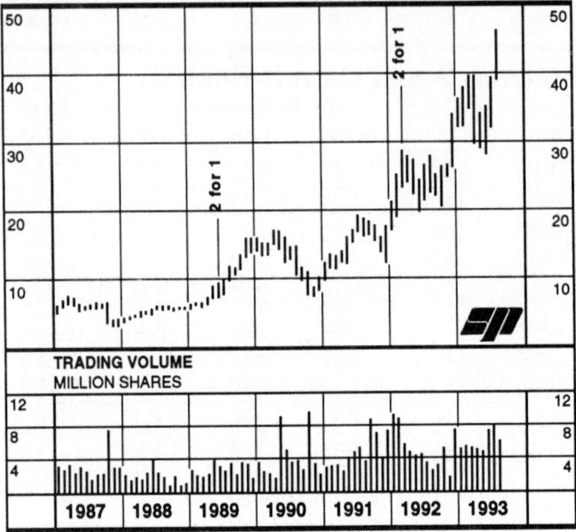

Important Developments

Jul. '93— The company filed a formal response to a law suit against it by Diamond Rug and Carpet Mills. The response included a motion to dismiss and for partial summary judgment, and a counterclaim for unspecified monetary and punitive damages and injunctive relief. In its May 1993 lawsuit, Diamond charged that SHX had violated federal antitrust laws and state laws.

Jul. '93— SHX agreed to acquire Abingdon Carpets of Gwent, England. Separately, it formed a joint venture with Capital Carpet Industries Pty., Ltd. of Melbourne, Australia, to participate in a government-supported rationalization of the Australian carpet industry. Subsequently, the company agreed to acquire the remaining joint venture interest.

Next earnings report expected in mid-October.

Per Share Data ($)

Yr. End Jun. 30	1993	[1]1992	1991	1990	1989	[1]1988	1987	1986	1985	1984
Tangible Bk. Val.	**NA**	6.59	3.81	3.95	3.08	2.56	2.31	2.08	1.80	1.49
Cash Flow	**NA**	1.94	1.62	1.81	1.44	1.07	0.79	0.63	0.62	0.51
Earnings	**1.43**	0.93	0.58	1.06	0.79	0.54	0.43	0.36	0.38	0.34
Dividends	**0.330**	0.275	0.250	0.225	0.183	0.158	0.125	0.082	0.069	0.059
Payout Ratio	**23%**	31%	41%	21%	23%	29%	29%	23%	18%	18%
Prices[2]—High	**34⅛**	34⅛	19¼	17³⁄₁₆	16¹⁄₁₆	6¼	7¹¹⁄₁₆	5¹³⁄₁₆	3½	2⅞
Low	**28⅛**	17	9¹¹⁄₁₆	7⅜	5⁹⁄₁₆	3¹¹⁄₁₆	3⁹⁄₁₆	2¹⁵⁄₁₆	2⁵⁄₁₆	1⅜
P/E Ratio—	**32–20**	37–18	33–17	16–7	20–7	12–7	18–7	17–8	9–6	8–4

Data as orig. reptd. Adj. for stk. divs. of 100% Mar. 1992, 100% May 1986, 33⅓% Oct. 1983. **1.** Refl. merger or acq. **2.** Cal. yr. NA-Not Available.

Income Data (Million $)

Year Ended Jun. 30	Revs.	Oper. Inc.	% Oper. Inc. of Revs.	Cap. Exp.	Depr.	[2]Int. Exp.	Net Bef. Taxes	Eff. Tax Rate	Net Inc.	% Net Inc. of Revs.	Cash Flow
[1]**1992**	**1,751**	**183**	**10.4**	**51**	**63.2**	**25.5**	**94**	**38.4%**	**58.0**	**3.3**	**121**
1991	1,608	147	9.2	78	59.3	35.2	53	38.2%	33.1	2.1	92
1990	1,475	179	12.1	168	46.3	27.2	106	38.2%	65.4	4.4	112
1989	1,176	138	11.7	27	39.2	22.4	77	38.1%	47.6	4.0	87
[1]1988	958	107	11.1	109	34.0	18.9	54	37.3%	33.8	3.5	68
1987	694	87	12.5	55	24.0	8.0	55	48.0%	28.5	4.1	53
1986	550	67	12.1	33	18.8	4.7	44	44.5%	24.1	4.4	43
1985	519	68	13.2	21	16.1	5.9	47	44.5%	25.9	5.0	42
1984	454	58	12.7	43	11.4	4.9	41	44.2%	22.9	5.0	34
1983	302	30	10.0	11	8.1	4.4	18	43.9%	10.0	3.3	18

Balance Sheet Data (Million $)

Jun. 30	Cash	Curr. Assets	Curr. Liab.	Curr. Ratio	Total Assets	% Ret. on Assets	Long Term Debt	Common Equity	Total Cap.	% LT Debt of Cap.	% Ret. on Equity
1992	**16.7**	**677**	**286**	**2.4**	**1,090**	**5.6**	**316**	**456**	**797**	**39.6**	**16.4**
1991	10.8	475	219	2.2	814	4.3	357	205	589	60.7	15.8
1990	4.5	483	225	2.1	794	9.8	304	237	564	53.9	31.1
1989	7.9	348	138	2.5	538	8.9	197	185	397	49.5	28.5
1988	3.5	343	142	2.4	546	7.7	230	157	402	57.2	22.6
1987	6.1	234	92	2.5	363	9.0	105	153	269	39.0	19.7
1986	2.5	181	62	2.9	279	9.4	64	141	215	29.6	18.3
1985	4.1	150	54	2.8	236	11.4	51	123	182	28.2	23.1
1984	4.0	136	55	2.5	217	11.6	52	102	162	32.2	25.6
1983	8.5	115	39	3.0	168	6.1	49	73	129	37.6	15.3

Data as orig. reptd. **1.** Refl. merger or acq. **2.** Net of interest income.

Business Summary

Shaw Industries is the world's largest carpet manufacturer. It is a fully integrated maker of tufted carpet for residential and commercial use. The company broadened its operations through the 1987 acquisition of the carpet and rug division of West Point Pepperell, the 1989 purchase of the carpet division of Armstrong World Industries, and the 1992 acquisitions of Salem Carpet Mills and Amoco Fabric and Fibers Co.'s polpropylene fiber manufacturing facilities.

Products include 800 styles of tufted carpet sold under the Philadelphia, Cabin Crafts, Shaw Commercial Carpets, Stratton, Networx, Shawmark, Evans Black, Salem and Sutton trade names and under certain private labels.

Carpet is sold in a broad range of prices, patterns and textures, with the majority of sales in the medium to high retail price range. Shaw sells to retailers, distributors and commerical users throughout the U.S. and in certain foreign markets. Marketing is influenced significantly by trends in style and fashion, principally color trends. The company believes that it has been a leader in the development of color technology.

Product marketing is conducted through 1,010 salaried sales personnel through retailers and distributors and directly to large national accounts. The company's 13 regional service centers and six redistribution centers enable it to provide prompt delivery of its products.

The carpet industry is somewhat cyclical, with the level of business tending to reflect fluctuations in consumer durable goods spending, interest rates, and turnover in housing and the residential construction industry.

Dividend Data

Dividends have been paid in each year since 1972. Two quarterly payments were omitted in 1982. A "poison pill" stock purchase right was adopted in 1989.

Amt. of Divd. $	Date Decl.	Ex–divd. Date	Stock of Record	Payment Date
0.07½	Oct. 21	Oct. 28	Nov. 3	Nov. 17'92
0.09	Jan. 20	Feb. 1	Feb. 5	Feb. 17'93
0.09	Apr. 20	Apr. 28	May 4	May 18'93
0.09	Jul. 29	Aug. 5	Aug. 11	Aug. 25'93

Capitalization

Long Term Debt: $268,217,000 (3/93).

Common Stock: 71,484,398 shs. (no par).
Officers and directors own 17%.
Institutions hold 64%.
Shareholders of record: 2,206.

Office—616 East Walnut Ave, Dalton, GA 30720. **Tel**—(706) 278-3812. **Chrmn**—J. C. Shaw. **Pres & CEO**—R. E. Shaw. **SVP & Treas**—W. C. Lusk, Jr. **Secy**—B. M. Laughter. **VP & Investor Contact**—W. M. Sims, Jr. **Dirs**—T. G. Cousins, S. T. Grigg, R. R. Harlin, C. M. Kirtland, J. H. Lanier, W. N. Little, W. C. Lusk, Jr., R. J. McCamy, J. C. Shaw, R. E. Shaw. **Transfer Agent & Registrar**—Wachovia Bank of North Carolina, N.A. **Incorporated** in Georgia in 1967. **Empl**—19,100.

 Elizabeth Vandeventer

Sigma-Aldrich Corp.

NASDAQ Symbol SIAL (Incl. in Nat'l Market) Options on CBOE In S&P MidCap 400

Price	Range	P-E Ratio	Dividend	Yield	S&P Ranking	Beta
Aug. 13'93	1993					
47	58–44 1/2	23	0.29	0.6%	A+	1.19

Summary

This company manufactures and distributes an extensive line of biochemicals, organic and inorganic chemicals, diagnostic reagents and related products for use in research and development, in the diagnosis of disease, and for manufacturing purposes. It also manufactures and sells metal components. In May 1993, Sigma acquired a supplier of chromatography products for $55 million.

Business Summary

Sigma-Aldrich Corporation is engaged in two lines of business: the production and sale of biochemicals, organic and inorganic chemicals, radiolabeled chemicals, diagnostic reagents and related products; and the manufacture and sale of metal components for strut, cable tray, pipe support and telecommunication systems. Contributions to sales and pretax income in 1992 were:

	Sales	Income
Chemical products	85%	91%
Metal products	15%	9%

In both 1992 and 1991, about 52% of chemical product sales were to foreign customers.

The company distributes about 61,000 chemical products for use primarily in research and development, in the diagnosis of disease and as specialty chemicals for manufacturing. In laboratory applications, the products are used in biochemistry, synthetic chemistry, quality control and testing, immunology, hematology, pharmacology, microbiology, neurology and endocrinology and in studies of life processes. Its diagnostic products are used to detect liver and kidney diseases, heart attacks and various metabolic disorders.

In addition, Sigma offers about 38,000 esoteric chemicals as a special service to customers interested in screening them for application in many areas (such as medicine and agriculture). It also engages in organic chemical contract research for the U.S. Government and for private companies.

Of the approximately 61,000 listed chemical products, Sigma-Aldrich produced some 26,000 that accounted for 42% of its 1992 chemical product sales; the remaining products were purchased from numerous outside sources. Sales were made to about 125,000 customers in 1992, with the majority of sales representing small orders in laboratory quantities averaging less than $200.

B-Line Systems (wholly owned) makes and markets a line of products for use in electrical, mechanical and telecommunications applications.

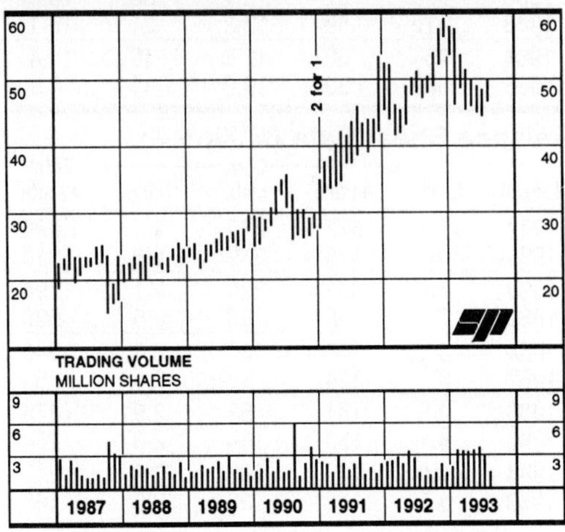

These include strut and pipe support systems, which are metal frameworks and related accessories used in industry to support pipes, lighting fixtures and conduit; cable tray systems, which are continuous networks of ventilated or solid trays used primarily in the routing of power cables and control wiring in power plant or industrial installations; and components and complete systems used to support telecommunications apparatus and cabling.

Important Developments

Jun '93— The B-Line Systems subsidiary acquired Circle A W Products Co. (1992 sales of $21 million), for $10.6 million in cash. Circle A W supplies electrical and electronic enclosures to industrial, residential and commercial markets. Separately, in May, SIAL acquired Supelco Inc. (1992 sales of $48 million), a worldwide supplier of chromatography products used in chemical research and production, for $55 million in cash.

Next earnings report due in mid-November.

Per Share Data ($)

Yr. End Dec. 31	1992	1991	[2]1990	[2]1989	1988	1987	[2]1986	1985	[2]1984	1983
Tangible Bk. Val.[1]	**10.28**	8.86	7.42	6.04	4.94	3.98	3.17	2.58	2.50	2.12
Cash Flow	**2.47**	2.12	1.91	1.62	1.40	1.08	0.85	0.67	0.56	0.47
Earnings	**1.92**	1.60	1.44	1.30	1.15	0.85	0.69	0.57	0.47	0.38
Dividends	**0.260**	0.228	0.205	0.185	0.165	0.145	0.125	0.105	0.088	0.076
Payout Ratio	**14%**	14%	14%	14%	14%	17%	18%	19%	19%	20%
Prices—High	**59 1/4**	53 1/2	35 7/8	29 3/4	25 5/8	25 5/16	20 1/8	14 3/16	8 5/8	8 5/8
Low	**41 3/4**	27 3/4	25	21 7/8	19 7/8	15 1/8	13 3/8	8 9/16	7 3/16	6 7/16
P/E Ratio—	**31–22**	33–17	25–17	23–17	22–17	30–18	29–19	25–15	18–15	23–17

Data as orig. reptd. Adj. for stk. divs. of 100% Jan. 1991, 200% Jan. 1986, 100% Jan. 1982. **1.** Incl. intangibles aft. 1983. **2.** Refl. merger or acq.

Income Data (Million $)

Year Ended Dec. 31	Revs.	Oper. Inc.	% Oper. Inc. of Revs.	Cap. Exp.	Depr.	Int. Exp.	Net Bef. Taxes	Eff. Tax Rate	Net Inc.	% Net Inc. of Revs.	Cash Flow
1992	**654**	**180**	**27.5**	**30.9**	**27.4**	**5.38**	**147**	**35.2%**	**95.5**	**14.6**	**123**
1991	589	158	26.7	26.1	25.8	7.99	124	35.6%	79.8	13.5	106
[1]1990	529	142	26.8	32.5	23.6	8.25	110	35.2%	71.2	13.5	95
[1]1989	441	123	27.8	51.7	16.1	6.83	100	36.0%	64.0	14.5	80
1988	375	105	28.0	35.6	12.6	3.83	89	36.2%	56.5	15.0	69
1987	305	86	28.3	20.6	11.1	3.14	72	42.0%	[2]41.9	13.7	53
[1]1986	253	72	28.6	35.6	7.6	2.41	62	45.5%	34.0	13.4	42
1985	215	58	27.1	17.4	5.4	NA	53	45.4%	28.9	13.4	34
[1]1984	180	48	26.9	11.9	4.7	NA	44	44.5%	24.2	13.5	29
1983	151	39	26.0	7.9	4.3	NA	35	43.4%	19.7	13.1	24

Balance Sheet Data (Million $)

Dec. 31	Cash	Curr. Assets	Curr. Liab.	Curr. Ratio	Total Assets	% Ret. on Assets	Long Term Debt	Common Equity	Total Cap.	% LT Debt of Cap.	% Ret. on Equity
1992	**44.9**	**416**	**66.2**	**6.3**	**616**	**15.7**	**18.7**	**512**	**543**	**3.5**	**20.0**
1991	28.1	391	70.9	5.5	597	14.0	69.3	441	520	13.3	19.7
1990	6.6	341	92.9	3.7	546	14.0	70.8	368	448	15.8	21.3
1989	9.7	284	98.6	2.9	472	15.3	61.5	299	367	16.7	23.5
1988	5.7	233	88.2	2.6	360	17.5	15.7	244	265	5.9	25.7
1987	3.4	186	60.6	3.1	285	15.8	15.5	196	219	7.1	23.8
1986	5.2	154	59.0	2.6	245	15.7	16.3	156	180	9.0	24.1
1985	2.8	123	33.5	3.7	187	16.4	14.4	126	148	9.8	23.2
1984	21.9	122	21.6	5.6	174	15.4	13.3	130	149	8.9	20.2
1983	14.5	97	16.6	5.8	141	15.3	7.2	110	122	5.9	19.3

Data as orig. reptd. **1.** Refl. merger or acq. **2.** Refl. acctg. change. NA-Not Available.

Net Sales (Million $)

Quarter:	1993	1992	1991	1990
Mar.	180	169	152	132
Jun.	184	162	146	129
Sep.		166	147	133
Dec.		158	144	134
		654	589	529

Based on a brief report, net sales for the six months ended June 30, 1993, advanced 10%, year to year. Net income was up 12%, to $53,860,000 ($1.08 a share), from $47,994,000 ($0.96). Results in the 1993 period exclude a charge of $10,806,000 ($0.22) from the cumulative effect of an accounting change.

Common Share Earnings ($)

Quarter:	1993	1992	1991	1990
Mar.	0.54	0.48	0.41	0.37
Jun.	0.54	0.48	0.40	0.37
Sep.		0.50	0.40	0.36
Dec.		0.46	0.39	0.35
		1.92	1.60	1.44

Dividend Data

Cash has been paid each year since 1970.

Amt. of Divd. $	Date Decl.	Ex–divd. Date	Stock of Record	Payment Date
0.07¼	Nov. 10	Dec. 15	Dec. 21	Jan. 4'93
0.07¼	Feb. 16	Feb. 23	Mar. 1	Mar. 15'93
0.07¼	May 4	May 25	Jun. 1	Jun. 15'93
0.07¼	Aug. 10	Aug. 26	Sep. 1	Sep. 15'93

Finances

During 1992, SIAL repaid SwFr66,000,000 ($46,200,000) of borrowings that were outstanding under unsecured credit facilities with three Swiss banks. The company retained commitments totaling SwFr46,000,000, which expire in December 1994, unless extended by mutual agreement. In addition, Sigma has domestic credit commitments of $44 million and German agreements for $12 million.

Capital expenditures for 1993 are expected to rise to $40-45 million, up from $31 million in 1992, as the company continues to expand its foreign operations and invest in selected domestic improvements.

Capitalization

Long Term Debt: $19,363,000 (3/93).

Common Stock: 49,800,799 shs. ($1 par).
Members of the Bader, Broida & Fischer families own about 16%.
Institutions hold some 61%.
Shareholders: 2,234 of record (3/93).

Office—3050 Spruce St., St. Louis, MO 63103. **Tel**—(314) 771-5765. **Chrmn, Pres & CEO**—C. T. Cori. **EVP & COO**—D. R. Harvey. **VP-Secy**—P. A. Gleich. **Contr & Investor Contact**—Kirk A. Richter. **VP & Treas**—T. M. Tallarico. **Dirs**—D. N. Brandin, C. T. Cori, D. R. Harvey, R. J. Hurst, D. M. Kipnis, A. E. Newman, W. C. O'Neil Jr., J. W. Sandweiss, T. N. Urban Jr. **Transfer Agent**—Boatmen's Trust Co., St. Louis. **Incorporated** in Delaware in 1975. **Empl**—4,291.

 Robert M. Gold

Silicon Graphics

NYSE Symbol SGI Options on ASE (Feb-May-Aug-Nov) In S&P MidCap 400

Price	Range	P-E Ratio	Dividend	Yield	S&P Ranking	Beta
Aug. 5'93	1993					
35¼	39¾–23½	29	None	None	C	1.62

Summary

This company makes high performance workstations and computing systems for the design, analysis and simulation of three-dimensional objects. MIPS Computer Systems was acquired in June 1992. Following a loss in fiscal 1992, earnings rebounded in fiscal 1993, aided by new product introductions and controlled operating costs. Although a further earnings gain is expected for fiscal 1994, SGI will face increasing competition from both workstation and PC makers.

Current Outlook

Earnings for the fiscal year ending June 30, 1994, are estimated at $1.50 a share, up from fiscal 1993's $1.20 (before tax loss carryforward credits of $0.10).

Initiation of cash dividends is not expected.

Capitalizing on its image as the leading 3D graphics and imaging computer maker, SGI should experience strong revenue growth in fiscal 1994. With the recent addition of the low-priced Indy workstation, total revenues could soar 30%. However, gross margins may narrow, restricted by increasing competition from both workstation and PC makers. R&D spending should equal 12% of sales, while SG&A costs will be about 27%. The company seeks to achieve operating margins of 13% to 14%. Although share earnings could climb 25% in fiscal 1994 if SGI's plans are realized, results might be weaker if increased competition forces gross margins from 53% toward the workstation industry norm of 42%. The company's engagement in interactive TV is unlikely to contribute materially to fiscal 1994 earnings.

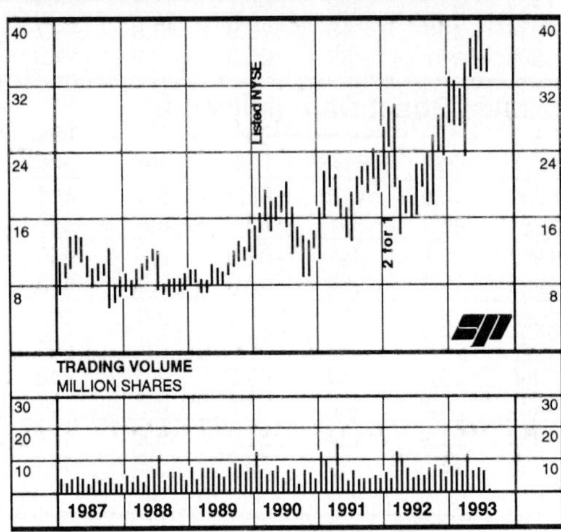

Net Revenues (Million $)

Quarter:	1993-94	1992-93	1991-92	1990-91
Sep.	E267.7	231.1	184.1	115.8
Dec.	E315.1	270.2	234.9	136.0
Mar.	E311.3	270.7	207.7	133.1
Jun.	E370.4	319.3	239.8	165.1
	E1,264.5	1,091.2	866.6	549.9

Based on a preliminary report, total revenues in the fiscal year ended June 30, 1993, climbed 26% from those of the preceding year; product revenues advanced 25%, and service revenues soared 35%. Gross margins widened, and operating costs rose less rapidly. In the absence of $110 million in merger-related costs and a $23.4 million restructuring charge, pretax income contrasted with a pretax loss. After taxes at 30.0%, versus taxes of $15.8 million, income of $87.7 million ($1.20 a share, on 29% more shares, before tax loss carryforward credits of $0.10) replaced a loss of $124 million ($2.19).

Common Share Earnings ($)

Quarter:	1993-94	1992-93	1991-92	1990-91
Sep.	E0.25	0.19	d0.50	0.22
Dec.	E0.40	0.31	0.23	0.25
Mar.	E0.36	0.28	d0.02	0.07
Jun.	E0.49	0.43	d1.88	0.19
	E1.50	1.20	d2.19	0.73

Important Developments

Jul. '93— SGI unveiled the Indy, a low-priced workstation that features on-line videoconferencing and a graphical user interface. The company said that the Indy offers more interactive media, visual computing and workgroup collaboration capabilites in a PC-priced desktop system than any other computer.

Next earnings report expected in late October.

Per Share Data ($)

Yr. End Jun. 30	1993	[1]1992	1991	1990	1989	1988	1987	1986	1985	1984
Tangible Bk. Val.	NA	[2]7.21	[2]7.94	6.03	4.86	4.47	2.13	1.08	NM	NM
Cash Flow	NA	d1.07	1.36	1.36	0.77	0.66	0.37	0.14	NA	NA
Earnings[3]	1.20	d2.19	0.73	0.85	0.34	0.43	0.23	0.05	d0.27	d0.46
Dividends	Nil	Nil	Nil	Nil	Nil	Nil	Nil	Nil	Nil	Nil
Payout Ratio	NA	Nil	Nil	Nil	Nil	Nil	Nil	Nil	Nil	Nil
Prices[4]—High	NA	29¾	24⅜	20⁷⁄₁₆	14¹¹⁄₁₆	12⅜	14⅛	7⅛	NA	NA
Low	NA	14⅛	11⅛	9	7⅛	6¾	5⅜	5⅝	NA	NA
P/E Ratio—	NA	NM	33–15	24–11	44–21	29–16	63–24	NM	NA	NA

Data as orig. reptd. Adj. for stk. div. of 100% Feb. 1992. 1. Refl. merger or acq. 2. Incl. intangibles. 3. Bef. spec. items of +0.10 in 1993, +0.01 in 1988, +0.19 in 1987, +0.05 in 1986. 4. Cal. yr. d-Deficit. E-Estimated. NM-Not Meaningful. NA-Not Available.

Income Data (Million $)

Year Ended Jun. 30	Revs.	Oper. Inc.	% Oper. Inc. of Revs.	Cap. Exp.	Depr.	Int. Exp.	Net Bef. Taxes	Eff. Tax Rate	[2]Net Inc.	% Net Inc. of Revs.	Cash Flow
[1]1992	**867**	**88.2**	**10.2**	**67.0**	**63.4**	**2.77**	**d103**	**NM**	**d118**	**NM**	**d60.3**
1991	550	74.8	13.6	47.2	31.3	3.21	48	31.0%	33	6.0	62.5
1990	420	69.3	16.5	29.6	22.3	5.59	48	33.0%	32	7.7	54.3
1989	264	29.7	11.3	23.3	15.1	2.25	16	30.0%	11	4.4	26.6
1988	153	22.2	14.6	21.1	6.7	2.19	17	28.5%	12	8.0	19.0
1987	86	13.7	15.9	9.9	3.5	0.69	11	50.3%	6	6.5	9.1
1986	42	3.6	8.7	3.5	2.0	0.14	2	49.3%	1	2.4	3.0
1985	22	d3.3	NM	2.4	1.5	0.21	d5	Nil	d5	NM	NA
1984	5	d6.2	NM	1.9	0.5	0.21	d7	Nil	d7	NM	NA
1983	NM	NA	NA	NA	NA	0.05	d2	Nil	d2	NM	NA

Balance Sheet Data (Million $)

Jun. 30	Cash	Curr. Assets	Curr. Liab.	Curr. Ratio	Total Assets	% Ret. on Assets	Long Term Debt	Common Equity	Total Cap.	% LT Debt of Cap.	% Ret. on Equity
1992	**183**	**578**	**217**	**2.7**	**758**	**NM**	**27.3**	**446**	**507**	**5.4**	**NM**
1991	196	480	116	4.1	642	6.1	27.8	329	523	5.3	10.8
1990	86	298	83	3.6	364	9.5	36.4	210	281	13.0	16.9
1989	94	238	46	5.1	291	4.6	87.8	157	245	35.9	7.6
1988	76	170	32	5.3	207	7.1	35.1	140	175	20.1	11.8
1987	58	94	20	4.7	107	4.9	35.6	52	87	40.8	15.7
1986	7	24	8	3.0	29	4.1	1.1	[3]20	21	5.1	5.6
1985	4	15	3	4.8	19	NM	0.8	[3]15	16	4.7	NM
1984	NA	NA	NA	NA	15	NM	0.5	[3]13	13	3.6	NM
1983	NA	NA	NA	NA	4	NM	0.2	[3]3	3	5.0	NM

Data as orig. reptd. **1.** Refl. merger or acq. **2.** Bef. spec. items. **3.** Incl. pfd. stk. (conv. into com. upon public offering). d-Deficit. NM-Not Meaningful. NA-Not Available.

Business Summary

Silicon Graphics designs, manufactures, markets and services a family of computer systems that are used by engineers, scientists and other creative professionals to develop, analyze and simulate complex three-dimensional objects. MIPS Computer Systems was acquired in June 1992.

The company's product line includes the Personal IRIS (integrated real-time interactive system) workstations, the IRIS Indigo workstations and servers, the IRIS Crimson workstations and compute servers, and the IRIS POWER Series workstations, project supercomputers and compute servers. These computers, all part of the IRIS 4D product family, use RISC microprocessors developed by MIPS, and are binary-compatible, allowing software to be run without modification across the entire product line.

As a result of the acquisition of MIPS, SGI obtained the MIPS product line of stand-alone and network-configurable Magnum workstations and Millennium workstation servers.

IRIS worksations use IRIX, an enhanced version of UNIX, as their operating system software. The IRIS Graphics Library provides application software that support common 3D graphic manipulations. Over 1,200 application software programs are available for use on SGI workstations.

Customers include end-users—typically large manufacturers such as automotive and aerospace companies—VARs, OEMs, and the U.S. government. Sales outside North America accounted for 50% of revenues in fiscal 1993.

Dividend Data

No dividends have ever been paid. The shares were split two-for-one in February 1992.

Finances

In June 1993, SGI and Time Warner Cable announced a relationship to develop technology for a full service interactive digital cable television network in Orlando, Fla., based on the MIPS microprocessor architecture.

In June 1992, the company aquired MIPS Computer Systems for 13,387,290 SGI common shares. As a result of the transaction, which was accounted for as a pooling of interests, the company incurred expenses totaling $110 million.

Capitalization

Long Term Debt: $25,989,000 (6/93).

Conv. Preferred Stock: $33,996,000.
Held by NKK Corp.

Common Stock: 65,412,000 shs. ($0.001 par).
Institutions hold 67%.
Shareholders of record: 3,697 (6/92).

Office—2011 N. Shoreline Blvd, Mountain View, CA 94039-7311. **Tel**—(415) 960-1980. **Chrmn**—J. H. Clark. **Pres & CEO**—E. R. McCracken. **SVP-Fin & CFO**—S. J. Meresman. **Secy**—R. L. Smith McKeithen. **Investor Contact**—Marilyn Lattin. **Dirs**—J. H. Clark, A. F. Jacobson, C. R. Kramlich, E. R. McCracken, J. A. McDivitt, R. C. Miller, J. A. Mollica, G. M. Mueller, M.W. Perry, L. Shapiro, J. G. Treybig, R. T. Wall. **Transfer Agent & Registrar**—First National Bank of Boston, Boston. **Incorporated** in California in 1981; reincorporated in Delaware in 1990. **Empl**—3,575.

 Neeraj K. Vohra

Sizzler International

NYSE Symbol SZ Options on CBOE In S&P MidCap 400

Price	Range	P–E Ratio	Dividend	Yield	S&P Ranking	Beta
Sep. 22'93	1993					
10	10½–7	83	0.16	1.6%	NR	1.53

Summary

Recent earnings of this large restaurant company were hurt by weak sales in U.S. operations, unfavorable currency fluctuations and several unusual charges. In addition to the Sizzler chain, SZ's operations include about 80 Kentucky Fried Chicken units in Australia. Formerly known as Collins Foods, the company changed its name to Sizzler International in May 1991. A sizable common stock repurchase authorization was reactivated in July 1993.

Current Outlook

Fiscal 1993-4 earnings are estimated at $0.40 a share, in contrast to 1992-3's loss of $0.33 a share, which included $0.52 of unusual charges.

Near term, the dividend is expected to remain at $0.04 quarterly.

In 1993-4, international operations are expected to provide the bulk of SZ's earnings; however, the level of profit is projected to decline somewhat from 1992-3's $22.1 million. From the U.S., no more than a modest profit is expected in 1993-4. Although near-term U.S. results are likely to be hurt by recent adverse publicity, benefits are expected during the year from closing some weaker units and from efforts to attract more family-oriented business. SZ's development of a new steakhouse concept offers long-term growth potential.

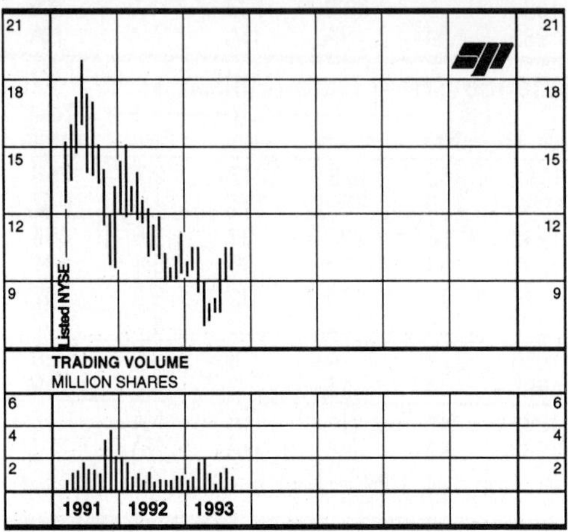

Total Revenues (Million $)

Weeks:	1993–4	1992–3	1991–2	[1]1990–1
12 Jul.	118.2	122.7	126.5	112.9
12 Oct.	---	118.5	124.5	114.7
16 Jan.	---	147.5	158.7	142.5
12 Apr.	---	115.4	[2]133.5	121.2
	---	504.2	543.2	491.4

Revenues for the 12 weeks ended July 25, 1993, were down 3.2%, year to year. Net income was $4.0 million ($0.14 a share), in contrast to a year-earlier loss of $9.1 million ($0.31 a share, including $0.42 related to an unusual charge).

Common Share Earnings ($)

Weeks:	1993–4	1992–3	1991–2	[1]1990–91
12 Jul.	0.14	d0.31	0.24	0.24
12 Oct.	E0.05	0.05	0.19	0.27
16 Jan.	E0.10	0.01	0.16	0.24
12 Apr.	E0.11	d0.07	[2]0.17	0.10
	E0.40	d0.33	0.75	0.85

Important Developments

Sep. '93— Recent adverse publicity is likely to have some negative effect on SZ's near-term operating results. There were reports of bacterial infection whose occurrence may be related to people having eaten at either a Sizzler franchise restaurant in Oregon or a franchise unit in Seattle, Wash. Earlier, in March, there was an isolated outbreak of food-borne illness among a small number of patrons of two other franchise Sizzler restaurants in Oregon. In connection with the March events, SZ had a charge of $0.10 a share in 1992-3's fourth quarter, a portion of which was to support family-centered programs, including rollout of a "Just for Kids" food bar. Also, in 1993-4's first quarter, SZ reactivated a plan to repurchase up to 1.4 million of its common shares, or about 5% of the number currently outstanding.

Next earnings report expected in late November.

Per Share Data ($)

Yr. End Apr. 30	1993	1992	1991	1990
Book Value[3]	**9.60**	10.21	9.69	NA
Cash Flow	**0.68**	1.68	NA	NA
Earnings	**d0.33**	0.75	[1]0.85	[1]1.06
Dividends	**0.16**	0.16	0.04	NM
Payout Ratio	**NM**	21%	NM	NM
Calendar Years	**1992**	1991	1990	1989
Prices—High	**15⅛**	18⅞	NM	NM
Low	**9**	9⅝	NM	NM
P/E Ratio—	**NM**	25–13	NM	NM

Data as orig. reptd. **1.** Pro forma. **2.** 13 wks. **3.** Incl. intangibles. d-Deficit. E-Estimated. NM-Not Meaningful. NA-Not Available.

Income Data (Million $)

Year Ended Apr. 30	Revs.	Oper. Inc.	% Oper. Inc. of Revs.	Cap. Exp.	Depr.	Int. Exp.	Net Bef. Taxes	Eff. Tax Rate	Net Inc.	% Net Inc. of Revs.	Cash Flow
1993	**504**	**38.7**	**7.7**	**29**	**29.2**	**1.70**	**[2]d16.4**	**NM**	**d9.5**	**NM**	**19.7**
1992	543	65.2	12.0	55	27.5	2.90	[2]37.5	41.0%	22.1	4.1	49.6
[1]1991	491	NA	NA	NA	NA	NA	43.0	41.2%	25.3	5.1	NA
[1]1990	429	74.9	17.5	NA	24.1	2.11	53.4	40.7%	31.6	7.4	55.8

Balance Sheet Data (Million $)

Apr. 30	Cash	Curr. Assets	Curr. Liab.	Curr. Ratio	Total Assets	% Ret. on Assets	Long Term Debt	Common Equity	Total Cap.	% LT Debt of Cap.	% Ret. on Equity
1993	**11.4**	**31.0**	**55.1**	**0.6**	**413**	**NM**	**21.0**	**280**	**341**	**6.0**	**NM**
1992	9.7	30.0	63.1	0.5	443	5.0	16.8	298	365	4.6	7.6
1991	27.3	47.3	72.5	0.7	446	6.2	24.3	288	312	7.8	10.4
[1]1990	38.8	63.0	50.4	1.2	369	NA	25.6	198	270	9.5	NA

Data as orig. reptd. **1.** Pro forma. **2.** Incl. equity in earns. of nonconsol. subs. d-Deficit. NM-Not Meaningful. NA-Not Available.

Business Summary

Sizzler International (SZ) was formed through a series of transactions that occurred in the first half of 1991. SZ was formerly known as Collins Foods Inc., which was a successor company to the old Collins Foods International.

As of April 30, 1993, the company's Sizzler restaurant business included 700 company-operated, franchised and joint-venture units. Of these, about 600 were in the U.S. and approximately 100 were in other countries (principally Australia). In the U.S., about 40% of the Sizzler restaurants were company-operated. Domestic Sizzler restaurants serve moderately priced meals from a menu that includes steak, chicken, seafood, sandwiches and a fruit and salad bar. About 44% of all Sizzler's U.S. restaurants were in California. The company has closed some weaker U.S. company units, and SZ is developing a new restaurant concept called Buffalo Ranch Steakhouses. The first such unit opened in December 1992 in Mission Viejo, Calif., and there are expected to be eight to 10 open by the end of 1993-4. In 1992-3, SZ's overall U.S. activities had an operating loss of $35.5 million, including $26.1 million of unusual charges.

SZ's international business is primarily in Australia. At April 30, 1993, it included approximately 100 Sizzler restaurants, of which about 43 were company-operated, and most of the remainder were franchises. SZ also operated 80 Kentucky Fried Chicken units in Australia. In 1992-3, SZ had international operating profit of $22.1 million, down 13% from the year before. In 1992-3, there was a net increase of 24 international units, and an increase of about 15 to 20 is expected in 1993-4.

Dividend Data

Cash dividends were initiated in 1991.

Amt. of Divd. $	Date Decl.	Ex–divd. Date	Stock of Record	Payment Date
0.04	Nov. 20	Dec. 15	Dec. 21	Jan. 11'93
0.04	Mar. 22	Mar. 29	Apr. 2	Apr. 14'93
0.04	Jun. 16	Jun. 22	Jun. 28	Jul. 16'93
0.04	Aug. 25	Sep. 22	Sep. 28	Oct. 12'93

Finances

SZ's 1992-3 first quarter included a $0.42-a-share charge related to closing some underperforming Sizzler units and costs of developing a new restaurant concept. Since that time, SZ has closed 22 restaurants and, as of mid-1993, five former Sizzler units had been converted to SZ's new Buffalo Ranch Steakhouse concept. Earlier, SZ's 1990-1 fourth quarter included about $0.10 a share (pro forma) of unusual charges.

SZ in its current form was created through a series of transactions in the first half of 1991. The company was formerly known as Collins Foods, Inc. (CF), which was a successor to the old Collins Foods International (CFI). A portion of the old CFI—primarily its domestic Kentucky Fried Chicken (KFC) franchise business—was acquired by PepsiCo Inc. (PEP) in March 1991 in exchange for about 4.9 million PEP common shares. These PEP shares were distributed to shareholders of the old CFI, who received about 0.215 of a PEP share for each CFI share owned. The assets and liabilities of the old CFI not acquired by PEP were spun off to the successor company. CFI shareholders of record March 15, 1991, received a share-for-share distribution of CF common stock. In April 1991, the current company acquired the remaining minority interest in Sizzler Restaurants International (SIZZ). In this transaction, 1.25 common shares of the company were exchanged for each SIZZ share not already owned. This completed a two-part acquisition of SIZZ shares, in which 6,929,674 new CF (now SZ) shares were issued.

Capitalization

Long Term Debt: $15,497,000 (7/93).

Common Stock: 29,130,311 shs. (6/93) ($0.01 par).

Institutions hold about 57%.

James A. Collins owns about 14%.

Shareholders of record: About 3,415.

Office—12655 West Jefferson Blvd., Los Angeles, CA 90066. **Tel**—(310) 827-2300. **Chrmn**—J. A. Collins. **Pres & CEO**—R. P. Bermingham. **Exec VP-Fin & CFO**—C. R. Thomas. **Treas & Investor Contact**—John Bayley (ext. 3326). **Secy**—M. D. Weisberger. **Dirs**—R. P. Bermingham, J. A. Collins, P. H. Dailey, T. L. Gregory, W. S. Hansen, W. G. Kees, H. W. Merryman, R. K. Montgomery, C. A. Scott, D. L. Tilton. **Transfer Agent**—Bank of New York, NYC. **Incorporated** in Delaware in 1991. **Empl**—16,600.

 Tom Graves, CFA

Smith International

NYSE Symbol SII Options on Phila (Jan-Apr-Jul-Oct) In S&P MidCap 400

Price	Range	P-E Ratio	Dividend	Yield	S&P Ranking	Beta
Sep. 29'93	1993					
10¼	10⅞–7⅞	NM	None	None	C	0.55

Summary

This company is an international supplier of drilling tools and services to the oil and gas and mining industries. In March 1993, the company sold its directional drilling and services business for some $270 million. Proceeds were earmarked to pay down debt and fund possible acquisitions. Smith anticipates a loss in the third quarter of 1993, despite improved operating results, owing to an unusual charge of $19.5 million to cover the settlement of a lawsuit alleging price fixing.

Business Summary

Smith International, Inc. is a worldwide supplier to the oil and gas industry of drill bits and related drilling tools and services. The company sold its directional drilling and services business in March 1993 and reported the segment's 1992 results as discontinued operations. Substantially all of the company's products and services are used in the process of drilling oil and natural gas wells, with the remainder used in the mining industry. Revenues from continuing operations by product group in recent years were:

	1992	1991
Drill bits	69%	66%
Downhole tools & remedial services	31%	34%

International markets accounted for 58% of 1992's total revenues from continuing operations, versus 56% in 1991. About 53% of Smith's revenues are denominated in U.S. dollars.

The company offers more than 900 drill bits, consisting mainly of three-cone drill bits for the petroleum and mining industries. It also makes drill bits featuring inserts made of polycrystalline diamond cutters or natural diamonds.

Smith provides a full line of downhole tools and remedial services. Downhole tools include tubular drill string components, stabilizers and reamers. Various remedial tools are manufactured for use in the drill string for specialized drilling and workover operations. Field service centers provide inspection and repair services for the drill string components, customer-owned tubular goods and the company's own rental tools.

The company has 16 field service centers in the U.S. and Canada and 27 centers elsewhere worldwide. Smith has four principal production facilities in the U.S. and Italy, which at year-end 1992 were operating at 60% of capacity.

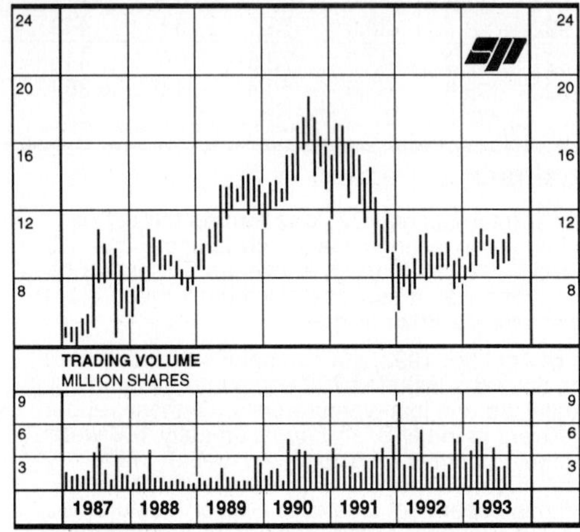

SII restructured its worldwide operations during 1991 and 1992. The company closed certain manufacturing and service locations, downsized other operations and reduced the worldwide workforce by about 27%.

On December 31, 1987, Smith emerged from Chapter 11 bankruptcy proceedings that arose from an adverse court patent judgment.

Important Developments

Sep. '93— The company said it has been successful in raising certain drill bit prices and expects that 1994 will see an improvement over 1993.

Jul. '93— SII announced a stock repurchase program whereby it may repurchase up to 3.0 million common shares.

Next earnings report expected in early November.

Per Share Data ($)

Yr. End Dec. 31	1992	1991	1990	1989	1988	1987	1986	1985	1984	1983
Tangible Bk. Val.[1]	**3.58**	3.78	3.42	2.83	2.98	3.95	1.47	8.07	19.80	23.99
Cash Flow	**0.61**	0.46	0.88	0.58	0.04	3.20	d4.58	d9.28	d0.66	d1.55
Earnings[2]	**d0.02**	d0.38	0.21	d0.18	d0.86	1.78	d6.56	d11.66	d3.01	d4.17
Dividends	**Nil**	Nil	Nil	Nil	Nil	Nil	0.08	0.32	0.96	0.96
Payout Ratio	**Nil**	Nil	Nil	Nil	Nil	Nil	NM	NM	NM	NM
Prices—High	**10⅝**	17⅛	18¾	14⅛	10⅞	10⅞	7½	14¼	21⅜	31¼
Low	**6⅛**	6¾	11	8½	5¾	4	1¼	6¾	9¾	18½
P/E Ratio—	**NM**	NM	89–52	NM	NM	6–2	NM	NM	NM	NM

Data as orig. reptd. **1.** Incl. intangibles. **2.** Bef. results of disc. ops. of -0.08 in 1992, -1.80 in 1987 & spec. items of +0.25 in 1990, +1.31 in 1987. d-Deficit. NM-Not Meaningful.

Income Data (Million $)

Year Ended Dec. 31	[1]Revs.	Oper. Inc.	% Oper. Inc. of Revs.	Cap. Exp.	Depr.	Int. Exp.	[4]Net Bef. Taxes	Eff. Tax Rate	[5]Net Inc.	% Net Inc. of Revs.	Cash Flow
[2]1992	**211**	**33**	**15.7**	**27**	**22.7**	**10.6**	**NM**	**NM**	**1**	**0.6**	**22**
1991	403	62	15.4	43	25.2	21.4	d4	NM	d10	NM	14
1990	388	67	17.3	41	20.2	21.0	22	62.8%	8	2.1	27
1989	312	41	13.0	22	21.6	21.1	1	NM	d3	NM	17
1988	321	48	15.0	20	25.9	[3]18.4	d20	NM	d23	NM	1
[2]1987	264	d5	NM	14	32.7	2.3	58	28.8%	[6]41	15.5	74
1986	415	d43	NM	17	44.9	1.2	d136	NM	d149	NM	d104
1985	697	51	7.3	52	54.1	26.8	d247	NM	d265	NM	d211
1984	747	105	14.1	46	53.4	36.9	d107	NM	d68	NM	d15
1983	697	57	8.2	46	59.5	22.1	d175	NM	d95	NM	d35

Balance Sheet Data (Million $)

Dec. 31	Cash	Curr. Assets	Curr. Liab.	Curr. Ratio	Total Assets	% Ret. on Assets	Long Term Debt	Common Equity	Total Cap.	% LT Debt of Cap.	% Ret. on Equity
1992	**16**	**296**	**214**	**1.4**	**370**	**0.3**	**2**	**130**	**156**	**1.1**	**NM**
1991	18	240	132	1.8	397	NM	100	137	263	38.0	NM
1990	30	257	125	2.1	396	2.3	146	98	267	54.5	7.3
1989	17	211	83	2.6	325	NM	138	81	242	57.1	NM
1988	25	227	98	2.3	347	NM	140	85	249	56.3	NM
1987	28	242	93	2.6	372	6.8	143	112	280	51.2	53.3
1986	130	443	150	2.9	674	NM	1	33	40	1.3	NM
1985	27	520	173	3.0	817	NM	Nil	183	212	NM	NM
1984	32	624	280	2.2	991	NM	235	450	711	33.1	NM
1983	21	514	224	2.3	1,035	NM	245	545	811	30.3	NM

Data as orig. reptd. **1.** Incl. other inc. **2.** Excl. disc. ops. **3.** Net of int. inc. **4.** Incl. equity in earns. of nonconsol. subs. **5.** Bef. spec. items. **6.** Refl. acctg. change. d-Deficit. NM-Not Meaningful.

Sales & Revenues (Million $)

Quarter:	1993	[1]1992	1991	1990
Mar.	50	54	101	79
Jun.	53	50	108	86
Sep.		53	101	98
Dec.		53	93	125
		211	403	388

Revenues for the six months ended June 30, 1993, declined 1.1%, year to year, reflecting reduced drilling activity outside North America. Earnings benefited from lower interest expense and sharply higher other income, and pretax income was up 54%. After taxes at 2.7%, versus 28.8%, net income from continuing operations surged 110%, to $3,978,000 ($0.08 a share, after preferred dividends), from $1,894,000 ($0.02). Results in 1993 exclude a gain of $2.02 a share (versus a loss of $0.02 in 1992) from discontinued operations and a loss of $0.04 from an accounting change.

Common Share Earnings ($)

Quarter:	1993	[1]1992	1991	1990
Mar.	0.03	0.05	0.10	d0.01
Jun.	0.06	d0.01	0.16	0.04
Sep.		d0.02	0.10	0.02
Dec.		d0.02	d0.66	0.18
		[2]d0.02	[2]d0.38	0.21

Dividend Data

Common dividends were omitted in 1986, after having been paid since 1956. A "poison pill" stock purchase right was adopted in 1990.

Finances

In June 1993, the company converted 798,800 preferred shares into 2.5 million common shares. The redemption will save SII $1.8 million per year in dividends.

During 1993's first quarter, SII sold its directional drilling and services business (DDS) to Halliburton Co. (HAL) for 6.9 million HAL shares. In April 1993, Smith sold the HAL shares in a public offering priced at $36.125 per share, and recorded a gain of $2.02 per share on the sale. A portion of the proceeds was used to substantially reduce debt.

At March 31, 1993, Smith had domestic net operating loss carryforwards of about $88 million, expiring between 2001 and 2007.

Capitalization

Long Term Debt: 46,000,000 (6/93).

Common Stock: 39,299,994 shs. ($1 par). Institutions hold approximately 69%. Shareholders of record: 5,750.

Warrants: To buy 2,097,844 shs. at $8.28-$15 ea.

1. Restated. 2. Sum of quarters does not equal full-year amount, due to change in shares. d-Deficit.

Office—16740 Hardy St., Houston, TX 77032. **Tel**—(713) 443-3370. **Chrmn, Pres, COO & CEO**—D. L. Rock. **EVP & CFO**—L. K. Carroll. **VP & Secy**—N. S. Sutton. **Dirs**—B. J. Bailar, G. C. Buck, L. K. Carroll, J. R. Gibbs, J. W. Neely, D. L. Rock, H. M. Rollins. **Transfer Agent & Registrar**—First Chicago Trust Co. of New York, NYC. **Incorporated** in California in 1937; reincorporated in Delaware in 1983. **Empl**—1,800.

 J. R. Jordan

Smucker (J.M.)

NYSE Symbol SJM.A In S&P MidCap 400

Price	Range	P–E Ratio	Dividend	Yield	S&P Ranking	Beta
Aug. 25'93	1993					
23⅞	32⅜–20¼	19	0.46	1.9%	A	0.66

Summary

This leading producer of jellies and preserves has achieved a degree of diversification through product line extensions and the production of related food products. Earnings, which have been rising for more than a decade, should continue to advance in fiscal 1993-94, reflecting benefits from favorable raw material costs and steady demand for the company's products.

Current Outlook

Earnings for the fiscal year to April 30, 1994, are projected at $1.35 a share, up from 1992-93's $1.27, which was before a $0.15 accounting charge.

The quarterly dividend was boosted 9.5%, to $0.11½ from $0.10½, with the June 1993 payment.

Sales in fiscal 1993-94 are expected to approximate those of the preceding year, reflecting only modest volume growth in both consumer and industrial businesses. Profitability should benefit from favorable raw material costs and volume-based cost efficiencies, but higher merchandising spending may restrict near-term earnings progress. Expansion into international markets augurs well for the future.

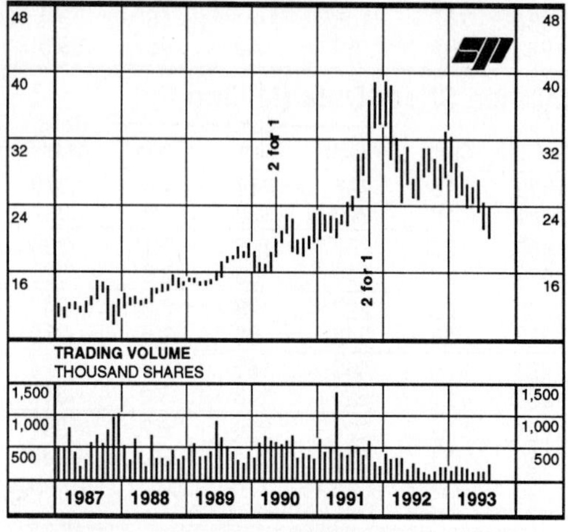

Net Sales (Million $)

Quarter:	1993–94	1992–93	1991–92	1990–91
Jul.	118	125	120	111
Oct.	---	134	131	125
Jan.	---	110	112	102
Apr.	---	122	121	117
	---	491	483	455

Sales for the three months ended July 31, 1993 declined 5.2%, year to year, reflecting lower fruit spread volume and unfavorable currency translations. Margins narrowed, and pretax income fell 6.8%. After taxes at 39.0%, versus 39.3%, income was down 6.4%, to $0.31 a share from $0.32 (before a $0.15 accounting charge).

Common Share Earnings ($)

Quarter:	1993–94	1992–93	1991–92	1990–91
Jul.	0.31	0.32	0.30	0.29
Oct.	E0.38	0.35	0.32	0.30
Jan.	E0.28	0.25	0.23	0.21
Apr.	E0.39	0.35	0.31	0.29
	E1.35	1.27	1.16	1.08

Important Developments

Aug. '93— SJM attributed the 5.2% year-to-year sales decline in fiscal 1993-94 to weakened currencies in Australia, Canada, and the U.K.; "substantially" lower frozen fruit sales (as a result of the company's decision to eliminate certain unprofitable lines); and a decline in fruit spread volume, which management attributed largely to the efforts of retailers to reduce inventories. SJM said that its fruit spread market share continued to grow during the quarter, and consumer fruit spread purchases appeared to be up slightly as well. International sales were up despite the adverse impact of currency fluctuations. Marketing and administrative expenses were higher during the quarter due primarily to marketing expenditures in support of two new product introductions, "Super Spreaders" and Sundae Syrups".

Next earnings report expected in mid-November.

Per Share Data ($)

Yr. End Apr. 30	1993	1992	1991	1990	1989	[1]1988	1987	1986	1985	1984
Tangible Bk. Val.	**6.76**	6.47	5.68	4.87	4.44	3.87	3.38	2.93	2.67	2.61
Cash Flow	**1.64**	1.52	1.40	1.32	1.21	1.01	0.80	0.71	0.68	0.59
Earnings[2]	**1.27**	1.16	1.08	1.03	0.94	0.78	0.61	0.54	0.54	0.47
Dividends	**0.420**	0.380	0.340	0.260	0.220	0.180	0.150	0.143	0.120	0.100
Payout Ratio	**33%**	33%	32%	25%	23%	23%	25%	26%	22%	21%
Calendar Years	**1992**	1991	1990	1989	1988	1987	1986	1985	1984	1983
Prices—High	**39**	38⅞	23³⁄₁₆	19½	15¹¹⁄₁₆	15	12½	12¹⁵⁄₁₆	7¹⁄₁₆	5¹³⁄₁₆
Low	**24½**	20	16¹⁄₁₆	14⁷⁄₁₆	11¹¹⁄₁₆	9¾	9⁵⁄₁₆	6½	4⁹⁄₁₆	3⅞
P/E Ratio—	**31–19**	34–17	22–15	19–14	17–12	19–13	21–15	24–12	13–8	12–8

Data as orig. reptd. Adj. for stk. divs. of 100% (Cl. B com.) Oct. 1991, 100% May 1990, 100% Dec. 1985. **1.** Refl. merger or acq. **2.** Bef. spec. item(s) of -0.15 in 1993. E-Estimated.

Income Data (Million $)

Year Ended Apr. 30	Revs.	Oper. Inc.	% Oper. Inc. of Revs.	Cap. Exp.	Depr.	Int. Exp.	Net Bef. Taxes	Eff. Tax Rate	[3]Net Inc.	% Net Inc. of Revs.	Cash Flow
1993	**491**	**70.9**	**14.4**	**21.0**	**11.1**	**0.39**	**61.5**	**39.2%**	**[2]37.4**	**7.6**	**48.5**
1992	483	65.2	13.5	17.4	10.8	0.45	56.1	39.2%	34.1	7.1	44.9
1991	455	61.1	13.4	17.3	9.5	0.79	52.6	39.6%	31.7	7.0	41.3
1990	422	57.7	13.7	18.1	8.7	1.09	49.9	39.6%	30.2	7.1	38.9
1989	367	50.7	13.8	13.2	7.9	0.42	44.6	38.2%	27.6	7.5	35.5
[1]1988	314	44.4	14.1	10.5	6.9	1.01	38.6	40.7%	22.9	7.3	29.7
1987	288	40.0	13.9	9.8	5.9	1.17	34.7	49.1%	17.7	6.1	23.6
1986	263	34.3	13.0	8.4	5.3	1.24	30.1	47.3%	[2]15.9	6.0	21.1
1985	230	30.8	13.4	9.8	4.2	1.11	28.9	45.1%	15.9	6.9	20.0
1984	215	27.5	12.8	7.5	3.4	0.81	26.2	47.0%	13.9	6.5	17.2

Balance Sheet Data (Million $)

		Curr.									
Apr. 30	Cash	Assets	Liab.	Ratio	Total Assets	% Ret. on Assets	Long Term Debt	Common Equity	Total Cap.	% LT Debt of Cap.	% Ret. on Equity
1993	**50.4**	**168**	**56.5**	**3.0**	**295**	**13.1**	**Nil**	**220**	**224**	**Nil**	**17.4**
1992	36.3	162	53.6	3.0	278	12.9	3.83	212	223	1.7	17.0
1991	24.5	141	50.0	2.8	252	13.3	4.27	190	201	2.1	17.8
1990	18.4	120	45.7	2.6	225	14.2	4.28	167	178	2.4	19.3
1989	36.7	118	41.9	2.8	198	15.0	4.95	145	155	3.2	20.4
1988	27.1	102	35.6	2.9	170	14.2	3.08	125	133	2.3	19.6
1987	25.2	96	35.6	2.7	153	12.4	4.15	108	116	3.6	17.5
1986	18.1	80	28.3	2.8	132	12.4	4.50	94	102	4.4	17.5
1985	25.5	76	27.6	2.8	126	13.4	6.17	88	97	6.4	19.1
1984	34.1	79	23.5	3.4	112	13.1	7.00	78	88	8.0	19.0

Data as orig. reptd. **1.** Refl. merger or acq. **2.** Refl. acctg. change. **3.** Bef. spec. item(s).

Business Summary

J.M. Smucker Co. manufactures and markets food products, including preserves, jams, jellies, all-fruit spreads, marmalades, toppings, fruit butters, low-calorie spreads, fruit syrups, breakfast syrups, fruit and fruit products, fruit puree, fruit juice concentrates, peanut butter, industrial fruit products (such as bakery fillings, dairy fillings and cereal fillings), honey, fruit and vegetable juices, carbonated juice beverages, gift packages, condiments and frozen, whipped dessert products.

The products are sold under the Smucker label mainly through grocery stores but also to foodservice customers (restaurants, hotels, etc.), industrial customers and by direct order as gift packages. A small portion of sales is under private label and the R.W. Knudsen Family Label, and some of the foodservice sales are under the Dickinson's name. International sales account for approximately 8% of the total.

Ingredients used in the company's products are usually purchased from independent growers and suppliers, although Smucker does grow some of the fruit that it uses. Because of the seasonal nature of most of the crops on which the company depends, it is necessary to prepare and freeze stocks of fruit, fruit juices, berries and other food products and to maintain them in cold storage warehouses. Sweeteners, peanuts and other ingredients are obtained from various sources.

Dividend Data

Dividends have been paid since 1949. A dividend reinvestment plan is available. Payments on the Class A and Class B common shares in the past 12 months:

Amt of Divd. $	Date Decl.	Ex-divd. Date	Stock of Record	Payment Date
0.10½	Oct. 22	Nov. 10	Nov. 17	Dec. 1'92
0.10½	Jan. 15	Feb. 8	Feb. 15	Mar. 1'93
0.11½	Apr. 16	May 12	May 18	Jun. 1'93
0.11½	Jul. 21	Aug. 12	Aug. 18	Sep. 1'93

Capitalization

Long Term Debt: None (7/93).

Class A Common Stock: 14,413,693 shs. (no par); one vote per sh. (10 votes per sh. on shs. held for four yrs.).
Shareholders of record: 6,805.

Class B Common Stock: 14,791,173 shs. (no par); nonvoting; divd. at least equal to Cl. A divd.
The Smucker family controls 27% of both Cl. A and Cl. B com.
Shareholders of record: 5,355.

Office—Strawberry Lane, Orrville, OH 44667-0280. **Tel**—(216) 682-3000. **Chrmn**—T. P. Smucker. **Chrmn Exec Comm & CEO**—P. H. Smucker. **Pres**—R. K. Smucker. **Secy & Investor Contact**—Steven J. Ellcessor. **Treas**—P. P. Yuschak. **Dirs**—L. C. Bailey, W. P. Boyle, Jr., R. G. Mawby, C. S. Mechem, Jr., R. R. Morrison, V. D. Netzly, P. H. Smucker, R. K. Smucker, T. P. Smucker, B. B. Tregoe, Jr., B. Trueman, W. Wrigley, Jr. **Transfer Agent & Registrar**—National City Bank, Cleveland. **Incorporated** in Ohio in 1921. **Empl**—1,950.

 Kenneth A. Shea

Sonoco Products

NASDAQ Symbol SONO (Incl. in Nat'l Market) In S&P MidCap 400

Price	Range	P-E Ratio	Dividend	Yield	S&P Ranking	Beta
Aug. 25'93	1993					
21¼	24⅞–20½	21	0.54	2.5%	A–	0.93

Summary

This international manufacturer of paper and plastic packaging products, which serves a variety of industries and markets worldwide, has more than 250 operations in 22 countries. Acquisitions have been an important part of its growth strategy, and are likely to continue to boost results. Sales and earnings are expected to reach record levels in 1993, and long-term prospects are favorable.

Current Outlook

Earnings for 1993 are estimated at $1.44 a share, up from $0.94 in 1992 (as adjusted). A gain to $1.65 is seen for 1994.

The quarterly dividend, which was boosted 8% with the June 1993 payment, should remain at $0.13½.

Sales are expected to increase moderately in 1993, aided by acquisitions and a slowly recovering economy. Margins should continue to widen as a result of restructuring and cost containment efforts. Purchases of compatible businesses will help fuel future growth; approximately 40% of SONO's growth in the 1980s came as a result of acquisitions. As foreign markets recover, earnings are likely to resume a steady uptrend.

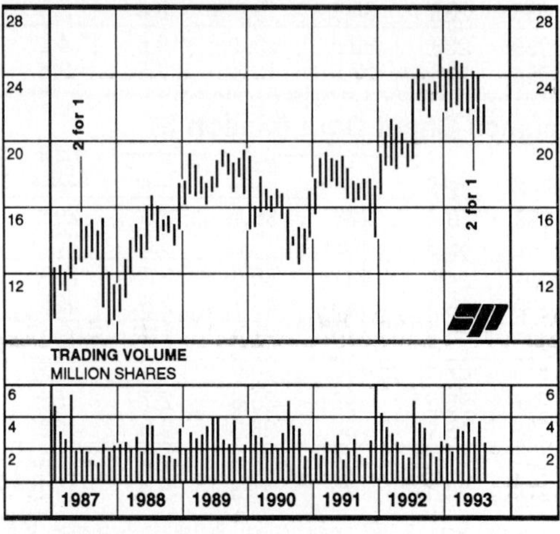

Net Sales (Million $)

13 Weeks:	1993	1992	1991	1990
Mar.	467	430	408	404
Jun.	479	462	422	421
Sep.	---	463	421	416
Dec.	---	484	446	429
	---	1,838	1,697	1,669

Sales in the six months ended July 4, 1993, advanced 6.1%, year to year. Results benefited from restructuring and cost containment measures; pretax income climbed 15%. After taxes at 39.4%, versus 40.1%, and lower equity in earnings of affiliates, income was also up 15%, to $0.67 a share, from $0.59 (as adjusted). Results in the 1992 period exclude a charge of $0.44 a share related to accounting changes.

Common Share Earnings ($)

13 Weeks:	1994	1993	1992	1991
Mar.	E0.35	0.31	0.26	0.27
Jun.	E0.41	0.36	0.33	0.26
Sep.	E0.42	E0.37	0.32	0.29
Dec.	E0.47	E0.40	0.04	0.29
	E1.65	E1.44	0.94	1.10

Important Developments

Aug. '93— SONO said its first quarter purchase of OPV-Durener group, Germany's second largest producer of tubes and cores ($25 million in sales), had enabled it to close or consolidate a number of European plants. The company also said operations sold recently or to be sold in the near-term had generated losses of $8.6 million in 1992. The sale of these businesses is expected to raise $50 million in cash. SONO added that the combination of Crellin Holding, Inc., a manufacturer of injection molded plastics (annual sales $75 million), acquired in the 1993 first quarter, with the company's molded plastic operations would allow SONO to provide customers with a broader range of plastic carriers. SONO also expects its R&D efforts to provide new competitive advantages and enhance product quality.

Next earnings report expected in mid-October.

Per Share Data ($)

Yr. End Dec. 31	1992	1991	1990	1989	1988	[1]1987	1986	[1]1985	1984	1983
Tangible Bk. Val.	**11.54**	5.80	5.30	5.03	4.66	3.85	3.34	2.97	2.77	2.51
Cash Flow	**3.79**	1.99	1.41	1.95	1.89	1.35	1.03	0.92	0.80	0.73
Earnings[2]	**0.94**	1.10	0.58	1.18	1.10	0.70	0.63	0.57	0.49	0.43
Dividends	**0.490**	0.460	0.450	0.405	0.320	0.250	0.205	0.180	0.157	0.138
Payout Ratio	**52%**	42%	78%	34%	29%	36%	33%	32%	32%	32%
Prices—High	**25¼**	19⅜	19⅛	19½	17½	15⅜	10¼	7¹⁵⁄₁₆	5⅞	5¹⁵⁄₁₆
Low	**16⅞**	14¼	12⅝	16¼	9¾	9	7⁵⁄₁₆	4¹⁵⁄₁₆	4¾	3⅝
P/E Ratio—	**27–18**	18–13	33–22	17–14	16–9	22–13	16–12	14–9	12–10	14–8

Data as orig. reptd. Adj. for stk. divs. of 100% Jun. 1993, 100% Jun. 1987, 100% Jun. 1985. **1.** Refl. merger or acq. **2.** Bef. results of disc. ops. of -0.05 in 1983, and spec. item(s) of -0.44 in 1992. E-Estimated.

Income Data (Million $)

Year Ended Dec. 31	Revs.	Oper. Inc.	% Oper. Inc. of Revs.	Cap. Exp.	Depr.	Int. Exp.	[3]Net Bef. Taxes	Eff. Tax Rate	[5]Net Inc.	% Net Inc. of Revs.	Cash Flow
1992	**1,838**	**280**	**15.2**	**109**	**83.8**	**30.4**	**133**	**38.9%**	**81**	**4.4**	**165**
1991	1,697	252	14.8	91	76.6	28.2	158	40.2%	95	5.6	171
1990	1,669	262	15.7	118	72.2	28.1	94	46.6%	50	3.0	123
1989	1,656	255	15.4	109	67.3	29.4	164	37.0%	104	6.3	171
1988	1,600	256	16.0	94	69.1	25.2	163	41.0%	96	6.0	165
[1]1987	1,312	195	14.9	105	57.1	18.6	110	44.2%	61	4.7	119
1986	964	141	14.7	45	35.7	8.6	99	44.8%	[4]55	5.7	90
[1]1985	870	129	14.8	38	31.2	8.7	91	45.9%	49	5.7	81
1984	741	108	14.5	34	27.3	4.4	78	45.3%	43	5.7	70
[2]1983	669	94	14.1	33	26.1	5.1	65	43.0%	37	5.6	63

Balance Sheet Data (Million $)

Dec. 31	Cash	Curr. Assets	Curr. Liab.	Curr. Ratio	Total Assets	% Ret. on Assets	Long Term Debt	Common Equity	Total Cap.	% LT Debt of Cap.	% Ret. on Equity
1992	**38.1**	**465**	**312**	**1.5**	**1,247**	**6.8**	**241**	**562**	**803**	**30.0**	**14.4**
1991	28.6	421	257	1.6	1,136	8.4	228	562	790	28.8	17.6
1990	39.9	432	248	1.7	1,114	4.8	279	513	866	32.2	9.9
1989	25.7	376	183	2.1	995	10.5	226	512	812	27.9	21.4
1988	20.4	378	190	2.0	977	10.4	276	454	788	35.0	23.1
1987	14.4	322	178	1.8	878	8.6	263	380	700	37.6	17.3
1986	20.3	223	118	1.9	559	10.3	58	333	441	13.2	17.4
1985	19.1	199	94	2.1	501	10.9	73	296	406	18.1	17.7
1984	17.8	169	78	2.2	408	10.7	32	261	330	9.5	17.1
1983	9.7	148	69	2.2	383	10.0	42	237	315	13.4	16.4

Data as orig. reptd. **1.** Refl. merger or acq. **2.** Excl. disc. ops. **3.** Incl. equity in earns. of nonconsol. subs. **4.** Refl. acctg. change. **5.** Bef. spec. items.

Business Summary

Sonoco Products Company is a major manufacturer of paper and plastic packaging products. It has expanded and diversified from its original product line of paper cones for the southern textile market to serve a large variety of industries and markets worldwide. At the end of 1992, the company had more than 250 operations in 22 countries. Sales to unaffiliated customers and operating profits (in millions) for 1992 were derived as follows:

	Sales	Profits
Converted products	53%	$94.4
Paper	14%	65.4
International	22%	−12.4
Miscellaneous	11%	23.5

The largest subsidiaries abroad are in the U.K., Canada, France, Mexico, Australia and Germany.

The company is the U.S. market leader in most of its traditional businesses, including the manufacture of tubes, cores and cones; fibre and plastic drums; and nailed wood and metal reels. It is the second leading producer of fibre partitions. The paper division is a leading producer of recycled paperboard. Industrial markets, including paper, chemical, pharmaceutical and textile manufacturers and the construction industry, accounted for 65% of sales in 1992.

SONO's consumer packaging businesses, which represented 35% of 1992 sales, serve most of the world's major food processors and grocery chains. The company makes composite containers used for frozen-juice concentrate, baked products, snacks, powdered beverages, cleansers and many other items. SONO is the leading producer of plastic grocery sacks in the U.S. with a market share of over 40%. It is also the only U.S. supplier of caulk and grease cartridges.

Dividend Data

Cash has been paid each year since 1925. A dividend reinvestment plan is available.

Amt. of Divd. $	Date Decl.	Ex-divd. Date	Stock of Record	Payment Date
0.25	Oct. 21	Nov. 16	Nov. 20	Dec. 10'92
0.25	Feb. 3	Feb. 12	Feb. 19	Mar. 10'93
0.27	Apr. 21	May 17	May 21	Jun. 10'93
2–for–1 Split	Apr. 21	Jun. 11	May 21	Jun. 10'93
0.13½	Jul. 21	Aug. 16	Aug. 20	Sep. 19'93

Capitalization

Long Term Debt: $307,482,000 (7/93).

Common Stock: 87,259,527 shs. (no par).
Officers and directors own 7.4%.
Institutions hold 32%.
Shareholders: 31,000.

Office—North Second St., Hartsville, SC 29550-0160. **Tel**—(803) 383-7000. **Chrmn & CEO**—C. W. Coker. **Pres & COO**—R. C. King, Jr. **Secy**—J. L. Coker. **Treas**—C. J. Hupfer. **Investor Contact**—Dick Puffer (803-383-7425). **Dirs**—C. J. Bradshaw, R. J. Brown, C. W. Coker, F. L. H. Coker, J. L. Coker, T. C. Coxe III, A. T. Dickson, R. E. Elberson, J. C. Fort, P. Fulton, R. C. King, Jr., E. H. Lawton, Jr., H. L. McColl, Jr., E. C. Wall, Jr. **Transfer Agent**—Wachovia Bank & Trust Co., Winston-Salem, NC. **Registrar**—Co.'s office. **Incorporated** in South Carolina in 1899. **Empl**—15,780.

 Richard Spiegel

Sotheby's Holdings

NYSE Symbol BID Options on ASE, CBOE, Pacific (Jan-Apr-Jul-Oct) In S&P MidCap 400

Price	Range	P-E Ratio	Dividend	Yield	S&P Ranking	Beta
Aug. 24'93	1993					
12½	14⅞–10¾	74	0.24	1.9%	NR	1.72

Summary

This company is the world's largest auctioneer of fine art, primarily paintings, and of jewelry and decorative art. Auction sales totaled $1.13 billion in 1992, with fine art accounting for 43% and decorative art for 38%. Earnings for 1993's first half were enhanced by increases in auction sales volume and the buyer's premium. In August 1993, the quarterly dividend was cut 60%.

Business Summary

Sotheby's Holdings is the world's largest auctioneer of fine art, specializing in paintings, and of jewelry, decorative art, and a wide range of other property. It is also engaged in art-related financing and the luxury real estate business. Revenue and pretax profit contributions by business segment in 1992:

	Revs.	Profits
Auction	89%	36%
Financial services	6%	46%
Real estate	4%	18%

Operations in North America accounted for 48% of revenues and operating income of $13.6 million in 1992, Europe 48% of revenues and a loss of $8.2 million, and Asia 4% of revenues and a loss of $0.4 million.

The worldwide auction business is conducted through a division known as Sotheby's and consists of three principal operating units: Sotheby's, Inc., encompassing North and South American operations and headquartered in New York City, Sotheby's Europe, and Sotheby's Asia.

Auction sales totaled $1.13 billion in 1992 ($1.10 billion the year before), of which fine art accounted for 43%; decorative art 38%; and jewelry, rare books and other property 19%. BID identifies, evaluates and authenticates works of art, uses marketing techniques to stimulate purchaser interest, and matches sellers and buyers through the auction process.

Sotheby's normally functions as an agent accepting property on consignment from its selling clients. It bills and receives payments from buyers and remits the proceeds to the consignor. Buyers pay a premium to the company on auction purchases, which in most locations is 15% of the hammer price of the property. In addition, the seller is charged a commission. Business is seasonal with peak revenues generally occurring in the second and fourth quarters.

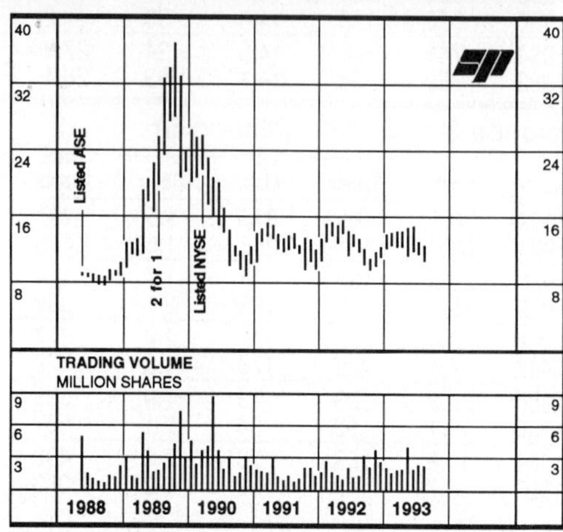

Financial services primarily involve making loans secured by consigned art and loans to collectors or dealers secured by property not intended for sale. In January 1990, BID discontinued financing auction purchases.

Real estate operations involve acting as an exclusive marketing agent providing services to licensed real estate brokerage offices, and operating its own real estate brokerage offices.

Important Developments

Aug. '93— BID attributed its improved earnings for the first half of 1993 to an increase in auction sales volume combined with the increase in the buyer's premium that became effective in January 1993. Sales of Impressionist and Modern art for the spring season increased 87%. BID added that the renewed activity in the spring season and the property that it has secured for the fall season provide evidence of improvement in a number of the major segments of the auction market.

Next earnings report expected in late October.

Per Share Data ($)

Yr. End Dec. 31	1992	1991	1990	[1]1989	1988	1987	1986	1985	1984	1983
Tangible Bk. Val.	**3.03**	4.21	4.90	4.34	2.64	1.62	0.62	NA	NA	NA
Cash Flow	**0.22**	0.39	1.79	2.18	1.33	1.01	NA	NA	NA	NA
Earnings[2]	**0.07**	0.25	1.66	1.96	1.12	0.78	0.27	Nil	d0.13	[3]d0.21
Dividends	**0.600**	0.950	1.450	0.613	0.063	Nil	Nil	Nil	Nil	Nil
Payout Ratio	**831%**	373%	77%	31%	5%	Nil	Nil	Nil	Nil	Nil
Prices—High	**15⅝**	15¼	26½	37	10½	NA	NA	NA	NA	NA
Low	**9⅝**	9⅝	8⅞	9⅞	7¾	NA	NA	NA	NA	NA
P/E Ratio—	**NM**	61–39	16–5	19–5	9–7	NA	NA	NA	NA	NA

Data as orig. reptd. Adj. for stk. div. of 100% in Jul. 1989. **1.** Reflects accounting change. **2.** Bef. spec. item(s) of -0.02 in 1988, -0.01 in 1987, +0.08 in 1986, +0.07 in 1985. **3.** Four mos. d-Deficit. NM-Not Meaningful. NA-Not Available.

Income Data (Million $)

Year Ended Dec. 31	Revs.	Oper. Inc.	% Oper. Inc. of Revs.	Cap. Exp.	Depr.	Int. Exp.	Net Bef. Taxes	Eff. Tax Rate	[2]Net Inc.	% Net Inc. of Revs.	Cash Flow
[3]1992	**225**	**16**	**7.0**	**9.9**	**8.2**	**6.2**	**[4]6**	**39.0%**	**4**	**1.8**	**12**
1991	222	17	7.5	11.3	7.4	10.8	21	39.0%	13	5.9	21
1990	378	128	33.8	13.5	7.2	13.0	155	38.7%	95	25.0	102
[1]1989	445	208	46.8	9.2	12.6	11.8	188	40.0%	113	25.3	125
1988	349	121	34.7	10.9	11.9	7.5	99	36.8%	63	17.9	75
1987	279	97	34.6	7.6	11.3	11.7	73	46.4%	39	14.0	50
1986	191	45	23.2	5.3	11.5	8.3	23	42.9%	13	7.0	NA
1985	141	23	16.1	5.4	11.4	8.2	3	95.9%	Nil	0.1	NA
1984	124	NA	NA	NA	NA	NA	d2	NM	d6	NM	NA

Balance Sheet Data (Million $)

Dec. 31	Cash	Curr. Assets	Curr. Liab.	Curr. Ratio	Total Assets	% Ret. on Assets	Long Term Debt	Common Equity	Total Cap.	% LT Debt of Cap.	% Ret. on Equity
1992	**85.7**	**488**	**396**	**1.2**	**595**	**0.6**	**Nil**	**198**	**199**	**Nil**	**1.7**
1991	43.3	553	415	1.3	665	1.8	Nil	246	249	Nil	4.9
1990	66.4	702	530	1.3	811	10.4	0.1	278	281	Nil	36.2
1989	31.1	908	755	1.2	1,000	14.1	0.8	243	246	0.3	55.1
1988	46.3	507	434	1.2	604	11.3	0.8	166	169	0.5	44.3
1987	42.9	402	341	1.2	503	8.8	37.2	117	162	23.0	41.6
1986	52.0	277	273	1.0	385	4.1	38.3	71	112	34.3	21.9
1985	NA	NA	NA	NA	268	0.1	NA	52	NA	NA	0.3
1984	NA	NA	NA	NA	237	NM	NA	40	NA	NA	NM

Data as orig. reptd. **1.** Reflects accounting change. **2.** Bef. spec. items. **3.** Reflects merger or acquis. **4.** d-Deficit. NA-Not Available. NM-Not Meaningful.

Operating Revenues (Million $)

Quarter:	1993	1992	1991	1990
Mar.	37	36	32	61
Jun.	87	78	76	176
Sep.		26	25	24
Dec.		84	89	117
		225	222	378

For the six months ended June 30, 1993, auction revenues rose 13%, year to year, reflecting increased auction sales volume and an increase in the buyer's premium, partially offset by unfavorable exchange rates. Following flat operating expenses, pretax income for the division more than doubled, to $19.0 million from $9.1 million. Lower pretax income for financial services was offset by higher pretax income for real estate. Consolidated net income increased to $11.4 million ($0.21 a share on 2.7% more shares) from $5.5 million ($0.10).

Common Share Earnings ($)

Quarter:	1993	1992	1991	1990
Mar.	d0.09	d0.11	d0.10	0.10
Jun.	0.30	0.20	0.19	1.12
Sep.		d0.25	d0.22	d0.06
Dec.		0.21	0.33	0.49
		0.07	0.25	1.66

Finances

Capital expenditures, consisting primarily of office and auction facility refurbishment and the acquisition of computer equipment, totaled $9.9 million in 1992, and are anticipated to approximate $8 million in 1993.

In BID's May 1988 initial public offering, 11,006,214 Class A shares were sold at $9 each (adjusted). All shares were offered by selling shareholders and no proceeds were received by BID.

Dividend Data

Payments in the past 12 months:

Amt of Divd. $	Date Decl.	Ex-divd. Date	Stock of Record	Payment Date
0.15	Nov. 2	Nov. 23	Nov. 30	Dec. 16'92
0.15	Jan. 28	Feb. 19	Feb. 25	Mar. 15'93
0.15	Apr. 30	May 19	May 25	Jun. 15'93
0.06	Aug. 19	Sep. 10	Sep. 16	Oct. 7'93

Capitalization

Long Term Debt: $38,000 capital lease obligations (6/93).

Class A Common Stock: 34,093,730 shs. ($0.10 par); one vote per sh.
Shareholders of record: 1,573 (3/93).

Class B Common Stock: 21,220,129 shs. ($0.10 par); 10 votes per sh.; conv. sh.-for-sh. into Class A com. Alfred A. Taubman controls about 62%.
Shareholders of record: 54 (3/93).

Options: To purchase 3,817,659 shs. at $1.50 to $22.62 each.

d-Deficit.

Office—500 North Woodward Ave., Bloomfield Hills, MI 48304. **Tel**—(313) 646-2400. **Chrmn**—A. A. Taubman. **Pres & CEO**—M. L. Ainslie. **SVP-CFO**—K. A. Bousquette. **VP-Treas & Investor Contact**—Mary A. Walling (212-606-7040). **Dirs**—M. L. Ainslie, Viscount Blakenham, D. D. Brooks, W. J. P. Curley, M. M. Fisher, The Earl of Gowrie, A. A. Taubman, R. J. de la M. Thompson, L. H. Wexner. **Transfer Agent & Registrar**—Chemical Bank, NYC. **Incorporated** in Michigan in 1983; predecessor firm founded in 1744. **Empl**—1,494.

 L. Feuer Nelson

Southdown, Inc.

NYSE Symbol SDW In S&P MidCap 400

Price	Range	P-E Ratio	Dividend	Yield	S&P Ranking	Beta
Aug. 2'93	1993					
17¼	17¾–9⅝	NM	None	None	C	0.96

Summary

This company is one of the leading U.S. cement and ready-mix concrete producers, and also provides environmental services. In 1993's second quarter, the company recorded its first profitable quarter since 1990. In February 1993, SDW sold one of four hazardous waste processors it plans to sell. In April 1993, a proxy battle was avoided when the company reached a settlement agreement with its principal shareholder which expanded board of directors.

Business Summary

Southdown is one of the leading U.S. cement and ready-mixed concrete producers. It is also engaged in hazardous waste processing, recycling and resource recovery. Business segment contributions in 1992 (profits in millions):

	Sales	Profits
Cement	63%	$59.0
Concrete products	29%	-11.6
Environmental services	8%	-10.6

The company operates eight quarrying and manufacturing facilities and a network of 18 terminals for the production and distribution of portland and masonry cement, primarily in the southwestern, southeastern and Ohio valley regions of the U.S. The principal raw material used in the production of portland cement is calcium carbonate found in the form of limestone. The company's total estimated recoverable reserves of limestone are approximately 960 million tons located on about 32,700 acres, most of which are owned in fee. Cement sales are made generally within a radius of 300 miles of each plant, principally to ready-mixed concrete producers and manufacturers of concrete products such as blocks, roof tile, pipe and prefabricated building components.

The company has vertically integrated its operations in the areas surrounding its two largest cement plants, which are located in southern California and in Florida. SDW's Transmix division is a major producer of ready-mixed concrete and a supplier of aggregates in the southern California counties of Los Angeles and Orange. The Florida Mining & Materials division produces and supplies ready-mixed concrete and concrete products in Florida and southeastern Georgia. Concrete products operations consist of approximately 600 ready-mixed concrete trucks, 65 batch plants, two aggregate quarries and 11 concrete block plants.

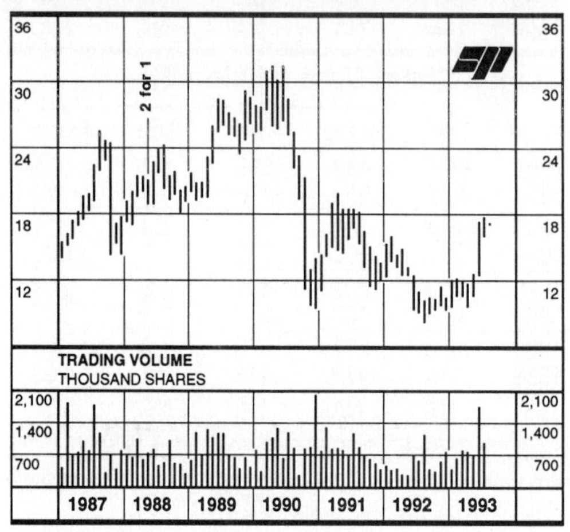

Waste processing facilities located in Alabama, California, Illinois, Tennessee and Texas collect, recycle, treat and arrange for the disposal of solid and liquid hazardous wastes, and blend waste derived fuels for burning in SDW's and other cement kilns. The company sold its Ohio plant in February 1993, and plans to sell three additional plants.

Important Developments

Apr. '93— The Carpenters Pension Trust for Southern California and Richard C. Blum & Associates (RCBA), the investment advisor to the trust, which owns 2,521,000 shares of SDW common stock, initiated a proxy contest, proposing three different nominees for election as directors. A settlement agreement had been reached in April 1993 under which SDW, the trust and RCBA agreed to nominate three additional directors to the board, expand membership of the nominating committee and SDW agreed to dismiss its lawsuit against the trust and RCBA.

Next earnings report expected in late October.

Per Share Data ($)

Yr. End Dec. 31	1992	1991	1990	1989	[2]1988	1987	[3]1986	1985	1984	1983
Tangible Bk. Val.	**10.17**	11.48	14.69	15.70	12.61	13.61	12.38	13.60	12.91	11.53
Cash Flow	**d0.07**	d0.24	2.87	4.84	5.97	5.77	1.32	3.51	4.02	3.98
Earnings[1]	**d2.74**	d2.86	0.44	0.99	2.33	3.25	d0.73	1.52	1.92	1.87
Dividends	**Nil**	0.125	0.500	0.500	0.500	0.500	0.476	0.680	0.219	0.214
Payout Ratio	**Nil**	NM	111%	50%	25%	15%	NM	45%	12%	11%
Prices—High	**16**	19⅞	31½	29¼	24¼	25½	21⅛	22½	21⅛	19
Low	**8¼**	11⅛	9½	19¼	17	14	13½	17½	16¾	12⅝
P/E Ratio—	**NM**	NM	72–22	30–19	10–7	8–4	NM	15–11	11–9	10–7

Data as orig. reptd. Adj. for stk. div(s). of 100% Jun. 1988, 5% Nov. 1986, 5% Nov. 1985, 4% Nov. 1984, 3% Oct. 1983. **1.** Bef. results of disc. opers. of +0.05 in 1992, +2.67 in 1989 and spec. item(s) of -0.08 in 1991, +1.39 in 1988, -0.02 in 1987. **2.** Reflects merger or acquisition. **3.** Reflects accounting change. d-Deficit. NM-Not Meaningful.

Income Data (Million $)

Year Ended Dec. 31	Revs.	Oper. Inc.	% Oper. Inc. of Revs.	Cap. Exp.	Depr.	Int. Exp.	Net Bef. Taxes	Eff. Tax Rate	[5]Net Inc.	% Net Inc. of Revs.	Cash Flow
1992	**[6]507**	**49**	**9.7**	**17**	**45.3**	**45.0**	**d59.0**	**NM**	**d41.4**	**NM**	**d1.1**
1991	505	33	6.6	31	44.2	41.0	[4]d70.6	NM	d43.2	NM	d4.1
1990	562	94	16.7	43	41.5	31.9	[4]19.0	13.2%	13.4	2.4	49.1
[1]1989	587	117	19.9	37	39.8	53.4	[4]38.0	30.5%	23.0	3.9	81.6
[2]1988	600	155	25.9	84	51.4	57.6	[4]63.4	36.5%	37.1	6.2	84.4
1987	339	91	26.9	47	34.5	26.0	[4]75.9	40.3%	[3]45.4	13.4	78.9
[3]1986	338	75	22.1	39	37.0	18.8	[4]d26.7	NM	d13.1	NM	23.9
1985	325	90	27.7	64	35.9	20.8	[4]41.2	33.3%	27.5	8.5	63.4
1984	314	90	28.8	146	36.3	18.9	50.7	34.5%	33.2	10.6	69.5
1983	238	85	35.9	94	36.3	9.9	46.1	30.4%	32.1	13.5	68.3

Balance Sheet Data (Million $)

Dec. 31	Cash	Curr. Assets	Curr. Liab.	Curr. Ratio	Total Assets	% Ret. on Assets	Long Term Debt	Common Equity	Total Cap.	% LT Debt of Cap.	% Ret. on Equity
1992	**13**	**171**	**98**	**1.7**	**911**	**NM**	**307**	**248**	**785**	**39.1**	**NM**
1991	15	194	104	1.9	986	NM	323	294	852	37.9	NM
1990	18	199	92	2.2	1,040	1.3	308	342	909	33.8	2.2
1989	108	280	159	1.8	1,064	2.0	254	343	858	29.6	5.2
1988	11	196	197	1.0	1,211	3.9	359	286	952	37.7	13.0
1987	25	117	68	1.7	566	9.3	174	178	495	35.1	26.1
1986	15	117	63	1.9	566	NM	161	225	498	32.2	NM
1985	7	119	79	1.5	620	4.5	167	246	535	31.3	11.4
1984	12	117	73	1.6	586	6.2	174	229	505	34.4	15.3
1983	43	108	58	1.9	462	7.8	126	195	404	31.3	17.6

Data as orig. reptd. **1.** Excludes discontinued operations. **2.** Reflects merger or acquisition. **3.** Reflects accounting change. **4.** Includes equity in earns. of nonconsol. subs. **5.** Bef. spec. items and disc. opers. **6.** Incl. other inc. d-Deficit. NM-Not Meaningful.

Total Revenues (Million $)

Quarter:	1993	1992	1991	1990
Mar.	106	108	104	129
Jun.	144	137	137	151
Sep.		139	141	153
Dec.		124	124	134
		507	507	566

Revenues for the six months ended June 30, 1993, rose 2.6%, year to year. Results benefited from the profitable cement segment, which reflected gains in volume and pricing; operating losses narrowed at both concrete products and environmental services on restructuring efforts undertaken at 1992 year-end. Despite expenses associated with postretirement health care benefits and costs related to a proxy contest, the net loss narrowed to $1.8 million ($0.26 a share, after preferred dividends), from $14.4 million ($1.00). Results for the 1993 period exclude a $2.86 a share charge from the cumulative effect of an accounting change.

Common Share Earnings ($)

Quarter:	1993	1992	1991	1990
Mar.	d0.34	d0.51	d0.52	0.28
Jun.	0.08	d0.49	d0.21	0.38
Sep.		d0.10	d0.65	d0.25
Dec.		d1.64	d1.48	0.03
		d2.74	d2.86	0.44

d-Deficit.

Dividend Data

Dividends were omitted in April 1991 after having been resumed in 1975. A "poison pill" stock purchase right was adopted in 1991.

Finances

In February 1993, SDW sold its Ohio hazardous waste processing facility to Clean Harbors, Inc. for $7 million, of which 20% was paid in cash and the balance in a preferred issue of Clean Harbors. SDW recorded a $17 million charge in 1992 to write down the value of its four processors to be sold.

In December 1992, SDW entered into an amended bank credit facility agreement, to avoid violation of loan covenants, which reduced the facility to $200 million from $250 million.

Capitalization

Long Term Debt: $304,500,000 (3/93).

Minority Interest: $30,100,000.

$0.70 Series A Cum. Conv. Pfd. Stk.: 1,999,000 shs. ($10 stated val.); conv. into 0.5 com.

$3.75 Series B Cum. Exch. Pfd. Stk.: 959,000 shs. ($50 stated val.); conv. into 2.5 com.

Common Stock: 16,945,000 shs. ($1.25 par). Richard C. Blum & Associates Inc. owns 15%. Institutions hold approximately 63%. Shareholders of record: 2,101.

Office—1200 Smith St., Suite 2400, Houston, TX 77002-4486. **Tel**—(713) 650-6200. **Chrmn**—G. W. Loewenbaum II. **Pres & CEO**—C.C. Comer. **SVP-CFO & Investor Contact**—James L. Persky. **Secy**—W.E. Phillips II. **Dirs**—F. Bracewell, C.C. Comer, W.J. Conway, K.L. Huger, Jr., G.W. Loewenbaum II, E.J. Marston III, M.A. Nicolais, F.J. Ryan, R.J. Slater, R.N. Tutor, V.H. Van Horn III, S.B. Wolitzer. **Transfer Agent & Registrar**—Chemical Bank, NYC. **Incorporated** in Louisiana in 1930. **Empl**—2,600.

 M. Graham Hackett

Southern New England Telecom.

NYSE Symbol SNG Options on NYSE (Jan-Apr-Jul-Oct) In S&P MidCap 400

Price	Range	P-E Ratio	Dividend	Yield	S&P Ranking	Beta
Oct. 4'93	1993					
36	38⅜–33⅝	14	1.76	4.9%	A	0.75

Summary

This holding company for Southern New England Telephone (SNET) provides telephone service to virtually all of Connecticut, and has moved into nonregulated telecommunications businesses. Revenues and earnings in recent periods have been impacted by the weak regional economy.

Current Outlook

Earnings for 1993 are estimated at $2.50 a share, versus 1992's $2.56. For 1994, earnings are projected to reach $2.65.

The dividend should continue at $0.44 quarterly.

Telephone revenues for 1993 are expected to rise moderately, as a state rate increase will be offset by increased competition and softness in the regional economy; the unit should be aided by the reorganization of SNET Systems. Margins will narrow on higher depreciation charges. Publishing revenues and earnings will continue to be soft, lagging improvement in the economy. Nonregulated operations should benefit from growth of cellular and paging operations, but will be impacted by a downward trend in set rentals at SNET Diversified Group and the SNET Systems reorganization.

Revenues (Million $)

Quarter:	1993	1992	1991	1990
Mar.	402	398	395	402
Jun.	411	405	412	404
Sep.		405	417	408
Dec.		406	410	406
		1,614	1,633	1,619

Revenues for the six months to June 30, 1993, rose 1.2%, year to year, as higher telephone revenues offset a decline in sales from non-telephone operations. Margins narrowed on higher depreciation expense; operating income was up marginally. Following a 6.5% reduction in interest charges, pretax income advanced 2.8%. After taxes at 43.2%, versus 39.7%, net income was down 3.1%. Share earnings were $1.22 (before a special charge of $3.47), against $1.29 (before income from discontinued operations of $0.03).

Common Share Earnings ($)

Quarter:	1993	1992	1991	1990
Mar.	0.58	0.63	0.61	0.62
Jun.	0.64	0.66	0.28	0.61
Sep.	E0.63	0.63	0.62	0.35
Dec.	E0.65	0.64	0.55	0.59
	E2.50	2.56	2.06	2.17

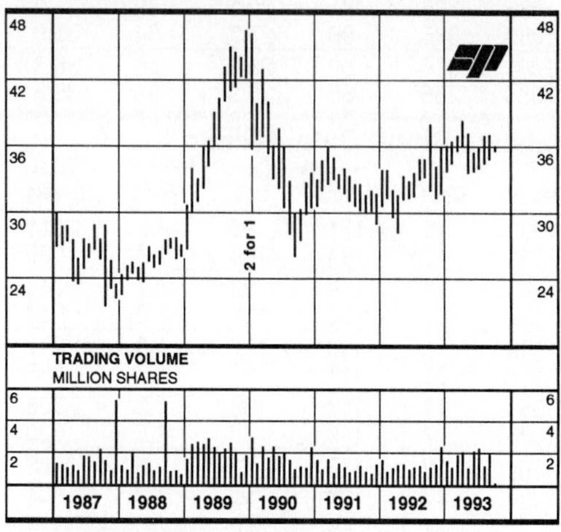

Important Developments

Aug. '93— The Connecticut Department of Public Utility Control (DPUC) gave SNET final approval to implement new residential and business basic service rates. The new rates will replace an interim increase in effect since July when the DPUC granted a rate increase of $37.5 million; in January the company had requested an increase of $133 million. The DPUC did not approve an incentive regulation plan and lowered SNET's allowed rate of return to 11.65%, from the prior 12.75%. The revenue increase authorized was insufficent to cover the $40 million increase in depreciation expense authorized by the DPUC in May 1993. In its telecommunications policy decision, the DPUC allowed competition for intrastate long-distance calling, set SNET's planned technological development plan (with some modifications) as the minimum modernization target over the next four-year, endorsed the concept of price cap regulation and said that pricing of all telecommunications services must be moved closer to the actual costs of providing those services.

Next earnings report expected in late October.

Per Share Data ($)

Yr. End Dec. 31	1992	1991	1990	1989	1988	1987	1986	1985	1984	1983
Tangible Bk. Val.	**19.79**	18.78	18.19	19.56	18.48	17.44	16.52	15.62	15.03	14.30
Earnings[1]	**2.56**	2.06	2.17	3.04	2.50	2.27	2.23	1.91	2.02	1.98
Dividends	**1.760**	1.760	1.760	1.640	1.515	1.455	1.410	1.370	1.330	1.275
Payout Ratio	**69%**	85%	81%	54%	61%	64%	63%	72%	66%	64%
Prices—High	**38**	35⅞	46¼	46½	27¾	30	30¾	23½	18⅛	20
Low	**28¼**	29	26	26¾	22⅝	21½	21½	17½	13⅞	14¾
P/E Ratio—	**15–11**	17–14	21–12	15–9	11–9	13–9	14–10	12–9	9–7	10–7

Data as orig. reptd. Adj. for stk. divs. of 100% Jan. 1990, 100% Oct. 1983. **1.** Bef. results of disc. opers of -0.08 in 1992, and spec. items of -0.04 in 1992, -0.04 in 1991, -0.09 in 1990. E-Estimated

Southern New England Telecommunications Corporation

Income Data (Million $)

Year Ended Dec. 31	[1]Revs.	Depr.	Maint.	Oper. Ratio	[2]Fxd. Chgs. Cover.	Constr. Credits	Eff. Tax Rate	[3]Net Inc.	% Return On Revs.	% Return On [4]Invest. Capital	% Return On [5]Com. Equity
1992	**1,614**	**250**	**308**	**84.1%**	**3.76**	**NA**	**40.9%**	**159**	**9.9**	**8.8**	**12.5**
1991	1,633	254	316	85.5%	2.92	NA	41.2%	126	7.7	8.3	10.8
1990	1,619	253	322	85.5%	3.13	NA	39.3%	132	8.2	8.6	11.2
1989	1,671	232	329	86.6%	5.39	2.9	43.1%	189	11.3	10.1	15.8
1988	1,583	215	313	84.8%	3.98	3.9	28.5%	155	9.8	9.9	13.9
1987	1,470	206	290	86.7%	4.75	7.1	33.6%	140	9.5	9.2	13.3
1986	1,433	197	253	87.3%	5.46	4.5	38.0%	139	9.7	9.1	13.8
1985	1,304	182	245	84.8%	4.35	2.6	37.5%	120	9.2	8.6	12.4
1984	1,273	166	233	84.5%	4.83	2.5	41.1%	125	9.8	9.2	13.7
1983	1,183	149	220	85.1%	4.82	2.7	39.7%	121	10.2	9.3	14.2

Balance Sheet Data (Million $)

Dec. 31	Gross Prop.	Capital Expend.	Net Prop.	% Earn. on Net Prop.	Total Cap.	Capitalization [6]LT Debt	% LT Debt	Pfd.	% Pfd.	Com.	% Com.
1992	**4,069**	**290**	**2,767**	**9.4**	**2,954**	**1,048**	**45.5**	**Nil**	**Nil**	**1,254**	**54.5**
1991	3,917	321	2,713	8.9	2,916	1,107	48.5	Nil	Nil	1,176	51.5
1990	3,762	393	2,644	9.1	2,785	1,022	47.5	Nil	Nil	1,128	52.5
1989	3,753	390	2,502	9.3	2,689	879	42.2	Nil	Nil	1,203	57.8
1988	3,486	328	2,312	10.7	2,569	855	42.6	Nil	Nil	1,155	57.4
1987	3,226	381	2,127	9.6	2,244	648	37.5	Nil	Nil	1,080	62.5
1986	2,968	289	1,942	9.6	2,159	646	39.0	Nil	Nil	1,011	61.0
1985	2,768	244	1,856	10.8	2,065	573	36.2	68.7	4.3	944	59.5
1984	2,599	212	1,804	11.0	1,960	564	36.9	69.2	4.5	895	58.6
1983	2,475	177	1,782	10.0	1,882	577	38.9	70.2	4.7	837	56.4

Data as orig. reptd. **1.** Aft. prov. for uncollectible accounts. **2.** Times int. exp. & pfd. divs. covered (pretax basis). **3.** Bef. results of disc. opers. and spec. items. **4.** Based on income bef. interest charges. **5.** As reptd. by Co. **6.** Incl. capital lease obligations. NA-Not Available.

Business Summary

Southern New England Telecommunications is the holding company for Southern New England Telephone (SNET), which provides local telephone service throughout most of Connecticut. At June 30, 1993, SNET served 1,947,000 customer access lines. Contributions to revenues by type of service in recent years:

	1992	1991	1990
Local service	32%	31%	29%
Intrastate toll	22%	22%	22%
Network access	20%	19%	21%
Sales	14%	15%	15%
Publ. & other	12%	13%	13%

In addition to providing telephone service, SNET publishes and distributes telephone directories throughout Connecticut and certain adjacent communities.

The company also engages in various nonregulated telecommunications businesses, including: SNET Cellular, SNET MobileCom and SNET Paging, which provide wholesale and retail cellular mobile telephone and paging services; and SNET Diversified Group, which sells and leases communications equipment to residential and small business customers. The company plans to disband its SNET Systems unit, which distributes telecommunications equipment, during 1993; telecommunications equipment will continue as a product line, but the reorganization would change the focus to the telco's central office-based solutions. Nonregulated telecommunications subsidiaries had a net loss of $4.7 million in 1992, versus a $7.4 million loss in 1991, on sales of $218.6 million ($212.3 million).

Dividend Data

Dividends have been paid since 1891. A dividend reinvestment plan is available. A "poison pill" stock purchase right was adopted in 1987.

Amt of Divd. $	Date Decl.	Ex-divd. Date	Stock of Record	Payment Date
0.44	Dec. 9	Dec. 15	Dec. 21	Jan. 15'93
0.44	Mar. 10	Mar. 16	Mar. 22	Apr. 15'93
0.44	Jun. 9	Jun. 15	Jun. 21	Jul. 15'93
0.44	Sep. 8	Sep. 14	Sep. 20	Oct. 15'93

Capitalization

Long Term Debt: $1,034,000,000 (6/93).

Common Stock: 63,746,034 shs. ($1 par). Institutions hold approximately 31%. Shareholders of record: 59,089.

Office—227 Church St., New Haven, CT 06510. **Tel**—(203) 771-5200. **Chrmn**—W. H. Monteith, Jr. **Pres & CEO**—D. J. Miglio. **VP-Secy**—M. M. DeMatteo. **VP-Treas**—J. J. Miller. **Investor Contact**—James A. Magrone. **Dirs**—F. G. Adams, W. F. Andrews, R. H. Ayers, Z. Baird, B. M. Bloom, F. J. Connor, W. F. Fenoglio, C. L. Gaudiani, J. R. Greenfield, N. L. Greenman, W. Loomis, B. G. Malkiel, D. J. Miglio, W. H. Monteith, Jr., F. R. O'Keefe, Jr. **Transfer Agent**—Company's office. **Registrar**—Union Trust Co., New Haven. **Incorporated** in Connecticut in 1882. **Empl**—11,216.

 Susan Stahl Gibney

SouthTrust Corp.

NASDAQ Symbol SOTR (Incl. in Nat'l Market) Options on Pacific In S&P MidCap 400

Price	Range	P-E Ratio	Dividend	Yield	S&P Ranking	Beta
Sep. 20'93	1993					
19⅝	22⁵⁄₃₂–16¹⁹⁄₃₂	11	0.60	3.1%	A	1.00

Summary

This regional bank holding company, headquartered in Birmingham, Ala., operates 40 banks with more than 375 offices in Alabama, Florida, Georgia, North Carolina, South Carolina and Tennessee. Expansion is continuing through acquisitions. A three-for-two stock split was effected in May 1993.

Business Summary

SouthTrust Corporation is a regional multibank holding company headquartered in Birmingham, Ala. At December 31, 1992, the company had subsidiary banks in Alabama, Florida, Georgia, South Carolina, North Carolina and Tennessee, as well as eight bank-related affiliates. The lead bank is the $4.4-billion-asset SouthTrust Bank of Alabama. SouthTrust is pursuing an aggressive policy of expansion through acquisitions.

Loans outstanding increased to $7.62 billion at the end of 1992, from $6.04 billion a year earlier, and were divided as follows:

	1992	1991
Commercial, financial & agricultural	31%	32%
Real estate:		
Construction	4%	6%
Commercial mortgage	27%	26%
Residential mortgage	23%	19%
Consumer	15%	17%

The allowance for loan losses was $103,770,000 (1.38% of net loans outstanding) at the end of 1992, up from $80,393,000 (1.35%) a year earlier. Net loans charged off in 1992 were $31,538,000 (0.49% of average loans), down from $31,691,000 (0.55%) in 1991. At December 31, 1992, nonperforming assets (including nonaccrual and restructured loans and other real estate owned) amounted to $128.8 million (1.69% of loans, net of unearned income), down from $142.6 million (2.36%) a year earlier.

Average deposits of $9.00 billion in 1992 were apportioned: 69% time deposits, 14% noninterest-bearing demand, 11% interest-bearing demand and 6% savings.

In 1992, interest and fees on loans accounted for 59% of total income, interest on investment securities 26%, other interest income 1%, service charges on deposit accounts 7% and other noninterest income 7%.

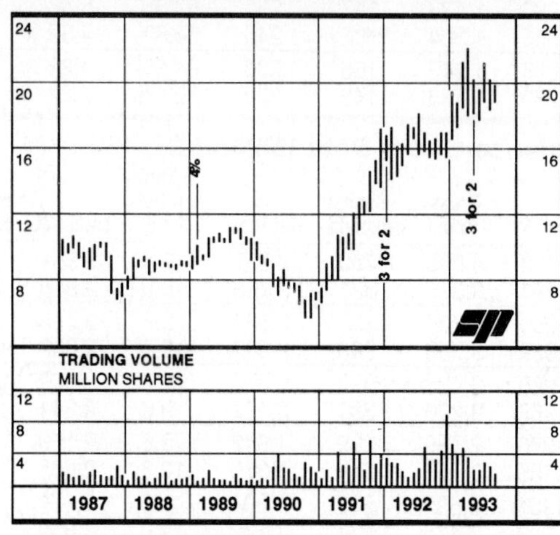

On a tax-equivalent basis, the average yield on total interest-earning assets was 8.44% in 1992 (9.88% in 1991), while the average rate paid on interest-bearing liabilities was 4.33% (6.19%), for a net spread of 4.11% (3.69%).

Important Developments

Jul. '93— SouthTrust received Federal Reserve Board approval to acquire County Bancshares Inc. of Troy, Ala. (deposits of $86.2 million).

Jun. '93— The company reached a definitive agreement to acquire BMR Financial Group, Inc. (OTC: BMRG) in a transaction whereby each of the approximately 2,540,000 BMR common shares outstanding would be purchased by SouthTrust for $6.30 in cash. BMR, the parent of Ameribank in Clearwater and Community First Bank of Central Florida in Winter Garden, had total assets of $97.4 million at March 31, 1993. The acquisition was expected to be completed by 1993 year-end.

Next earnings report expected in mid-October.

Per Share Data ($)

Yr. End Dec. 31	1992	1991	[1]1990	1989	[1]1988	[1]1987	[1]1986	[1]1985	1984	[1]1983
Tangible Bk. Val.	**11.55**	10.06	8.98	8.31	7.20	6.79	6.10	5.15	4.43	3.90
Earnings	**1.66**	1.42	1.14	1.21	1.14	1.04	0.97	0.85	0.76	0.63
Dividends	**0.520**	0.480	0.462	0.427	0.376	0.342	0.291	0.256	0.226	0.205
Payout Ratio	**31%**	34%	40%	35%	33%	33%	30%	30%	30%	33%
Prices—High	**18⅛**	17¼	10⅜	11¼	9½	10⅝	11	8¼	6	4⅜
Low	**14⅛**	6⅝	5¾	8⅞	7⅜	6⅞	8⅛	5¾	3¾	2½
P/E Ratio—	**11–9**	12–5	9–5	9–7	8–7	10–7	11–8	10–7	8–5	7–4

Data as orig. reptd. Adj. for stk. divs. of 50% May 1993, 50% Jan. 1992, 4% Jan. 1989, 66⅔% Jun. 1985, 50% Nov. 1983. **1.** Refl. merger or acq.

SouthTrust Corporation

Income Data (Million $)

Year Ended Dec. 31	Net Int. Inc.	Tax Equiv. Adj.	Non Int. Inc.	Loan Loss Prov.	% Exp./ Op. Revs.	Net Bef. Taxes	Eff. Tax Rate	Net Inc.	% Net Int. Margin	—% Return On— Assets	Equity
1992	**449**	**19.6**	**132**	**43.3**	**62.2**	**165**	**30.7%**	**114**	**4.65**	**1.04**	**15.7**
1991	353	22.5	105	38.0	61.8	123	27.0%	90	4.36	0.96	15.2
[1]1990	282	24.3	87	44.6	59.7	90	22.6%	70	4.08	0.85	13.3
1989	238	27.6	75	21.2	58.8	92	20.8%	73	4.12	1.03	15.4
[1]1988	216	27.8	65	19.1	58.1	83	18.9%	68	4.26	1.08	16.1
[1]1987	182	35.6	57	18.2	54.5	73	16.8%	60	4.51	1.15	16.3
[1]1986	159	47.6	52	22.2	51.8	55	3.0%	54	4.95	1.18	17.1
[1]1985	140	37.4	45	21.0	51.9	49	10.8%	44	5.46	1.21	17.7
1984	113	26.6	39	9.9	56.6	40	13.4%	34	5.11	1.12	18.5
[1]1983	99	23.0	34	10.4	57.5	30	7.4%	28	5.26	1.05	17.0

Balance Sheet Data (Million $)

		—Earning Assets—					—Deposits—					
Dec. 31	Total Assets	Mon. Mkt. Assets	Inv. Secs.	Com'l Loans	Other Loans	% Loan Loss Resv.	Demand	Time	% Loans/ Deposits	Long Term Debt	Common Equity	% Equity To Assets
1992	**12,714**	**103**	**3,756**	**2,378**	**5,442**	**1.34**	**1,598**	**8,484**	**76.8**	**258**	**860**	**6.62**
1991	10,158	164	3,104	1,911	4,127	1.35	1,106	7,172	72.1	140	662	6.29
1990	9,006	145	2,449	1,900	3,707	1.28	1,053	6,175	76.5	149	550	6.37
1989	7,763	259	2,068	1,716	3,048	1.27	929	5,126	77.5	145	507	6.66
1988	6,645	203	1,747	1,503	2,642	1.28	849	4,270	79.6	147	446	6.73
1987	5,924	341	1,447	1,458	2,178	1.26	842	3,860	76.1	139	396	7.04
1986	5,101	384	1,245	1,396	1,682	1.28	748	3,225	76.0	47	351	6.89
1985	4,210	232	1,046	1,299	1,262	1.24	693	2,546	77.1	47	271	6.86
1984	3,423	291	758	1,001	1,003	1.25	647	1,945	75.0	47	202	6.03
1983	3,002	327	741	741	864	1.36	584	1,614	70.2	47	177	6.17

Data as orig. reptd. 1. Refl. merger or acq.

Review of Operations

Total interest income for the six months ended June 30, 1993, advanced 12%, year to year. With a 0.7% drop in total interest expense, net interest income climbed 23%. The provision for loan losses increased 8.8%, and following 32% higher noninterest income and 20% greater noninterest expense, pretax income expanded 40%. After taxes at 32.7%, versus 30.2%, net income was up 35%, to $72,084,000 ($0.94 a share, based on 15% more shares), from $53,247,000 ($0.80).

Common Share Earnings ($)

Quarter:	1993	1992	1991	1990
Mar.	0.46	0.39	0.33	0.21
Jun.	0.48	0.41	0.37	0. 31
Sep.		0.42	0.37	0.31
Dec.		0.44	0.36	0.31
		1.66	1.42	1.14

Finances

In May 1993, SouthTrust completed an offering of $100 million of 7% subordinated notes due 2003.

Acquisitions in 1992 included Mid-States Federal (assets of $12 million), 1st American Bank of Georgia ($842 million), Carolina Financial Corp. ($134 million), Citizens Federal ($18 million), Bank South ($60 million), Colony Bank ($21 million) and CK Federal Savings Bank ($403 million).

During 1992, the company sold publicly 4,571,250 (adjusted) SouthTrust common shares, at $16 each, through underwriters led by Merrill Lynch & Co., J.C. Bradford & Co. and Sterne, Agee & Leach, Inc.

Dividend Data

Cash dividends, paid since 1944, have been increased each year since 1971. A dividend reinvestment plan is available.

Amt of Divd. $	Date Decl.	Ex-divd. Date	Stock of Record	Payment Date
0.19½	Oct. 21	Nov. 23	Nov. 30	Jan. 1'93
0.22	Jan. 20	Feb. 22	Feb. 26	Apr. 1'93
3-for-2	Apr. 14	May 20	Apr. 23	May 19'93
0.15	Apr. 14	May 24	May 28	Jul. 1'93
0.15	Jul. 21	Aug. 23	Aug. 27	Oct. 1'93

Capitalization

Long Term Debt: $488,832,000 (6/93).

Common Stock: 77,294,694 shs. ($2.50 par). Institutions hold about 42%. Shareholders: 8,500 of record (11/92).

Office—420 N. 20th St., Birmingham, AL 35203. **Tel**—(205) 254-5509. **Chrmn & CEO**—W. D. Malone Jr. **Pres & COO**—R. W. Gilbert Jr. **Secy, Treas, Contr & Investor Contact**—Aubrey D. Barnard. **Dirs**—J. M. Bradford, R. W. Gilbert Jr., B. L. Harbert, W. C. Hulsey, A. J. Keesler Jr., W. D. Malone Jr., C. E. McNeil, T. W. Mitchell, H. Stockham, C. G. Taylor, W. K. Upchurch Jr. **Transfer Agent & Registrar**—SouthTrust Bank of Alabama, Birmingham. **Incorporated** in Delaware in 1968. **Empl**—6,500.

 Stephen R. Biggar

Southwest Airlines

NYSE Symbol LUV Options on CBOE (Mar-Jun-Sep-Dec) In S&P MidCap 400

Price	Range	P–E Ratio	Dividend	Yield	S&P Ranking	Beta
Oct. 13'93	1993					
35⅞	37⅝–18⅛	43	0.04	0.1%	B	1.37

Summary

This airline, with operating costs among the lowest in the industry, has grown rapidly in recent years through expansion of its low-fare, high-frequency service into new markets, primarily in the West and Midwest. Continued expansion of the fleet is planned, and the company made its initial entry to the East Coast in September with service to Baltimore. Strong traffic growth should lead to substantial earnings improvement in 1993 and 1994. The shares were split 3-for-2 in July, 1993.

Current Outlook

Earnings for 1993 are estimated at $1.00 a share, up from the $0.65 (excluding a $0.09 special credit) of 1992, as adjusted for the July 1993 3-for-2 split. Earnings for 1994 are projected at $1.35.

Dividends should continue at least at the recently increased $0.01 quarterly rate.

Revenues should advance strongly throughout 1993. Southwest is adding three new cities during the year, and service expansion is in place in a number of older locations. Strong traffic growth is producing substantially higher load factors. Yields should improve moderately, despite an increased amount of lower-priced leisure travel. Although costs will reflect startup at new locations, margins should widen, aided by customary strong expense control.

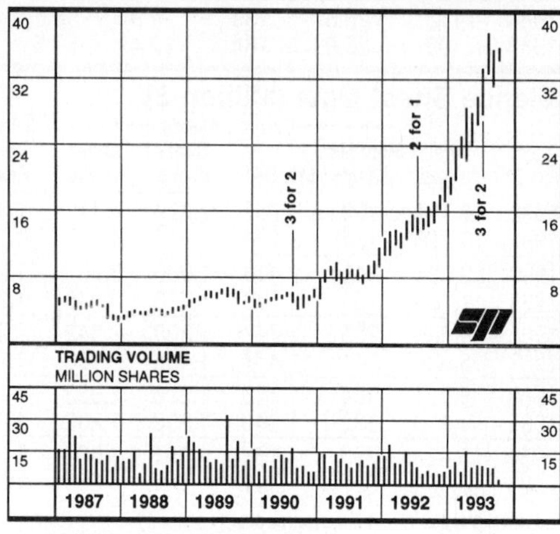

Revenues (Million $)

Quarter:	1993	1992	1991	1990
Mar.	454	374	283	261
Jun.	520	417	325	308
Sep.		447	355	316
Dec.		447	351	302
		1,685	1,314	1,187

Revenues for the first six months of 1993 increased 23%, year to year, reflecting strong passenger traffic (up 18%) and higher yield. Operating costs rose 20%. Net income (excluding special credits from accounting changes) advanced 75%, to $0.45 a share from $0.27 (both adjusted).

Common Share Earnings ($)

Quarter:	1993	1992	1991	1990
Mar.	0.16	0.10	d0.07	0.04
Jun.	0.29	0.17	0.09	0.19
Sep.	E0.35	0.19	0.13	0.18
Dec.	E0.20	0.19	0.07	d0.04
	E1.00	0.65	0.21	0.37

Important Developments

Oct. '93— Passenger traffic in the third quarter of 1993 was up 22.6%, year to year. With capacity up 14.8%, the load factor rose to 69.8% from 65.4%. For the first nine months of the year, traffic increased 21.5% and the load factor was 68.1%, against 64.9%.

Sep. '93— Southwest began service at Baltimore/Washington International on September 15 with five daily flights to Chicago (Midway) and five to Cleveland. In July it began service at San Jose with flights to Burbank and Las Vegas, and additional destinations were added in August. In May it added Louisville to its route system, with service to Chicago, St. Louis and Birmingham.

Next earnings report expected in late October.

Per Share Data ($)

Yr. End Dec. 31	**1992**	1991	1990	1989	1988	1987	1986	[1]1985	1984	1983
Tangible Bk. Val.	**6.16**	4.97	4.79	4.47	4.03	3.65	3.41	3.07	2.73	2.37
Cash Flow	**1.41**	0.89	0.98	1.06	0.88	0.60	0.81	0.73	0.64	0.54
Earnings[2]	**0.65**	0.21	0.37	0.53	0.41	0.14	0.35	0.35	0.38	0.31
Dividends	**0.035**	0.033	0.033	0.031	0.029	0.029	0.029	0.029	0.029	0.029
Payout Ratio	**5%**	16%	9%	6%	7%	20%	8%	8%	8%	9%
Prices—High	**19²⁹⁄₃₂**	11²¹⁄₃₂	6²¹⁄₃₂	6²⁷⁄₃₂	4¹⁹⁄₃₂	5¹⁹⁄₃₂	6³⁄₃₂	6²⁹⁄₃₂	6½	7²⁷⁄₃₂
Low	**10²⁵⁄₃₂**	5½	4¼	4¹³⁄₃₂	2²⁹⁄₃₂	2²¹⁄₃₂	4³⁄₃₂	4¾	3¹¹⁄₃₂	4½
P/E Ratio—	**30–16**	56–26	18–12	13–8	11–7	40–19	18–12	20–14	17–9	25–14

Data as orig. reptd. Adj. for stk. div(s). of 50% Jul. 1993, 100% Jul. 1992, 50% Aug. 1990, 25% Jan. 1984, 100% Jan. 1983. **1.** Reflects merger or acquisition. **2.** Bef. spec. item(s) of +0.09 in 1992. d-Deficit. E-Estimated.

Income Data (Million $)

Year Ended Dec. 31	Revs.	Oper. Inc.	% Oper. Inc. of Revs.	Cap. Exp.	Depr.	Int. Exp.	Net Bef. Taxes	Eff. Tax Rate	[2]Net Inc.	% Net Inc. of Revs.	Cash Flow
1992	**1,685**	**291**	**17.3**	**533**	**108.0**	**58.9**	**147**	**38.0%**	**91.0**	**5.4**	**199**
1991	1,314	149	11.4	341	86.2	43.9	44	38.6%	26.9	2.0	113
1990	1,187	161	13.6	318	79.4	32.0	75	37.0%	47.1	4.0	127
1989	1,015	170	16.7	262	72.3	33.5	111	35.5%	71.6	7.0	144
1988	860	152	17.7	389	66.2	29.2	85	32.1%	58.0	6.7	124
1987	778	97	12.5	235	66.6	30.7	29	30.7%	20.2	2.6	87
1986	769	156	20.3	195	67.9	37.3	65	23.5%	50.0	6.5	118
[1]1985	680	132	19.4	445	53.9	26.9	61	22.2%	47.3	7.0	101
1984	536	103	19.3	185	34.9	16.1	68	26.7%	49.7	9.3	85
1983	448	98	21.9	127	29.9	12.4	64	35.7%	40.9	9.1	71

Balance Sheet Data (Million $)

Dec. 31	Cash	Curr. Assets	Curr. Liab.	Curr. Ratio	Total Assets	% Ret. on Assets	Long Term Debt	Common Equity	Total Cap.	% LT Debt of Cap.	% Ret. on Equity
1992	**411**	**506**	**368**	**1.4**	**2,293**	**4.2**	**699**	**854**	**1,687**	**41.4**	**11.8**
1991	261	340	260	1.3	1,837	1.6	617	629	1,351	45.7	4.4
1990	88	158	225	0.7	1,471	3.3	327	605	1,041	31.4	8.1
1989	146	204	196	1.0	1,415	5.4	354	587	1,060	33.4	12.8
1988	210	265	153	1.7	1,308	4.9	370	567	1,038	35.6	10.7
1987	143	201	112	1.8	1,043	1.9	251	514	851	29.5	4.0
1986	75	128	83	1.5	1,078	4.8	339	512	960	35.3	10.2
1985	69	118	72	1.6	1,022	5.5	381	466	946	40.3	11.0
1984	26	63	47	1.3	646	8.1	153	362	597	25.7	14.7
1983	131	153	48	3.2	587	7.9	159	315	537	29.6	14.4

Data as orig. reptd. **1.** Reflects merger or acquisition. **2.** Bef. spec. items.

Business Summary

Southwest Airlines is a scheduled air carrier operating primarily in Southwestern, Western and Midwestern states. In Texas, it serves the cities of Dallas, Houston, San Antonio, Harlingen (Rio Grande Valley), Corpus Christi, Midland-Odessa, Lubbock, El Paso, Amarillo, and Austin. As of January 1993, cities served in other states included New Orleans, Tulsa, Oklahoma City, Albuquerque, Kansas City, Little Rock, Las Vegas, Reno, Phoenix, San Diego, Los Angeles, San Francisco, Oakland, Sacramento, Ontario, Burbank, St. Louis, Nashville, Birmingham, Indianapolis, Detroit, Cleveland, Columbus and Chicago (Midway).

Operating data in recent years (passenger- and seat-miles in billions):

	1992	1991	1990
Rev. pass–miles	13.79	11.30	9.96
Avail. seat–miles	21.37	18.49	16.41
Load factor %	64.5	61.1	60.7
Rev. per RPM(¢)	11.78	11.22	11.49
Cost per ASM(¢)	7.03	6.76	6.73

The company offers frequent flights made possible by a short average hop and a quick turnaround of aircraft. All flights provide a single class of service utilizing a peak/off-peak coach fare structure. Two types of discount fares are also offered.

Southwest has maintained a competitive advantage by being able to utilize smaller airports closer to the city center in several locations than those used by other carriers.

At June 30, 1993, the Southwest fleet consisted of 150 737 aircraft.

Dividend Data

Dividends were initiated in 1976. A "poison pill" stock purchase right was adopted in 1986.

Amt of Divd. $	Date Decl.	Ex-divd. Date	Stock of Record	Payment Date
0.014	Nov. 18	Dec. 1	Dec. 7	Dec. 28'92
0.014	Jan. 20	Feb. 26	Mar. 4	Mar. 26'93
0.014	May 19	May 28	Jun. 4	Jun. 25'93
3–for–2	May 19	Jul. 16	Jul. 1	Jul. 15'93
0.01	Jul. 21	Aug. 30	Sep. 6	Sep. 27'93

Finances

In September 1992, the company sold publicly $100,000,000 of 7.875% debentures due 2007. On March 1, 1993, it redeemed $100 million of 9% notes due in 1996.

Capitalization

Long Term Debt: $594,963,000 (6/93).

Common Stock: 138,976,000 shs. ($1 par). Institutions hold about 63%. Shareholders of record: 5,679.

Office—P.O. Box 36611, Love Field, Dallas, TX 75235. **Tel**—(214) 904-4000. **Chrmn & Pres**—H. D. Kelleher. **EVP-Secy**—C. C. Barrett. **VP-CFO**—G. C. Kelly. **Dirs**—S. E. Barshop, G. H. Bishop, W. P. Hobby Jr., T. C. Johnson, H. D. Kelleher, R. W. King, W. M. Mischer Sr. **Transfer Agent & Registrar**—Continental Stock Transfer & Trust Co., NYC. **Incorporated** in Texas in 1967. **Empl**—12,595.

 T.M. Canning, CFA

Southwestern Public Service

NYSE Symbol SPS In S&P MidCap 400

Price	Range	P-E Ratio	Dividend	Yield	S&P Ranking	Beta
Sep. 29'93	1993					
32¼	33⅝–30	13	2.20	6.8%	A–	0.43

Summary

This utility supplies electricity to a population of about one million in a 52,000-square-mile area of the Panhandle and south plains of Texas and parts of New Mexico, Oklahoma and Kansas. No new generating capacity is expected to be required until the mid 1990s. The ability to consistently produce low cost electricity has allowed the company to negotiate off-system sales agreements. Moderately higher earnings are expected for fiscal 1994, primarily reflecting electric sales growth. A U.S. bankruptcy court judge recently denied a request by SPS to file a $2.2 billion reorganization plan to acquire El Paso Electric Co.

Current Outlook

Earnings for the fiscal year ending August 31, 1994, are projected at $2.55 a share, up from the $2.45 estimated for fiscal 1993.

Dividends should continue at $0.55 quarterly.

Earnings should improve modestly in fiscal 1994, reflecting sales growth of about 5.5% for wholesale sales (excluding non-firm sales) and 1.8% for retail sales. Profitability should benefit from continued success at low cost production, and from current and future off-system sales contracts with neighboring utilities. Detriments to earnings are seen as the weak oil and gas industry and a 2% rate reduction ordered in September 1993. The acquisition of El Paso Electric Co. would have provided direct access to the fast growing Mexican market, but would also have entailed the assumption of a large amount of debt.

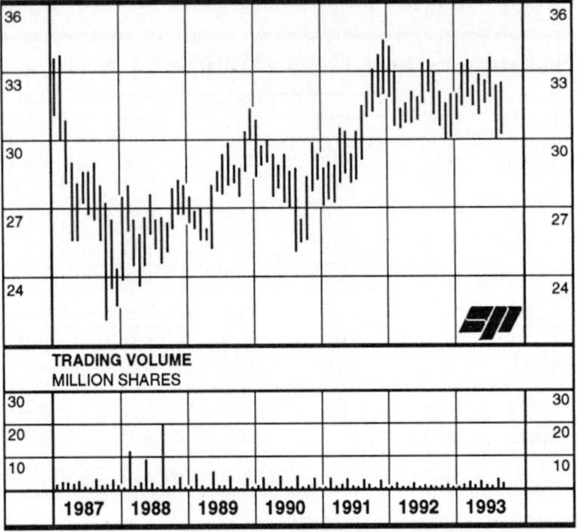

Operating Revenues (Million $)

Quarter:	1993–94	1992–93	1991–92	1990–91
Nov.	---	192	184	183
Feb.	---	180	173	167
May	---	193	176	172
Aug.	---	---	217	203
	---	---	749	725

Operating revenues for the 12 months ended May 31, 1993, rose 6.3% from those of the preceding 12 months, reflecting higher kilowatt-hour sales to all customer classes. Aided by a $0.05 a share franchise tax refund and lower interest charges, net income advanced marginally, to $2.39 a share after lower preferred dividends from $2.36.

Common Share Earnings ($)

Quarter:	1993–94	1992–93	1991–92	1990–91
Nov.	E0.60	0.55	0.57	0.69
Feb.	E0.55	0.50	0.46	0.54
May	E0.55	0.51	0.49	0.54
Aug.	E0.85	E0.89	0.82	0.86
	E2.55	E2.45	2.34	2.63

Important Developments

Sep. '93— A U.S. Bankruptcy Court judge for the Western District of Texas in Austin denied a motion by SPS to file a competing plan of reorganization that would have provided for the acquisition of El Paso Electric Co. (ELPAQ) for an approximate value of $2.2 billion. ELPAQ said it would begin solicitation of approval on or before September 21 for its third amended reorganization plan, under which it would emerge from bankruptcy as a subsidiary of Central & South West Corp. Also in September 1993, SPS agreed with the staff of the Public Utilities Commission of Texas to reduce its electric rates by 2% on an annual basis to settle litigation concerning a rate case hearing. The rate reduction will lower annual net income by about $0.16 a share. The company said it will consider more cost controls and certain reductions in company operations to mitigate the effect of the rate reduction on earnings.

Next earnings report expected in late October.

Per Share Data ($)

Yr. End Aug. 31	1992	1991	1990	1989	1988	1987	1986	1985	1984	1983
Tangible Bk. Val.	**16.57**	16.47	16.04	15.51	15.12	14.73	14.67	13.86	12.79	11.71
Earnings[1]	**2.34**	2.63	2.73	2.45	2.50	2.18	2.27	2.72	2.57	2.36
Dividends	**2.20**	2.20	2.20	2.20	2.12	2.12	2.02	1.88	1.74	1.62
Payout Ratio	**94%**	84%	81%	90%	85%	97%	89%	69%	68%	69%
Prices[2]—High	**34⅛**	34⅜	30⅞	31⅜	28¼	33¾	37⅞	26⅞	22	19¾
Low	**30**	27⅛	25⅛	25¼	23⅝	22⅛	25¼	20	17	15⅝
P/E Ratio—	**15–13**	13–10	11–9	13–10	11–9	15–10	17–11	10–7	9–7	8–7

Data as orig. reptd. 1. Bef. spec. item(s) of +0.48 in 1986. 2. Cal. yrs. E-Estimated.

Income Data (Million $)

Year Ended Aug. 31	Revs.	Depr.	Maint.	Oper. Ratio	[1]Fxd. Chgs. Cover.	Constr. Credits	Eff. Tax Rate	[2]Net Inc.	% Return On Revs.	% Return On [3]Invest. Capital	% Return On [4]Com. Equity
1992	**749**	**59.1**	**25.8**	**81.6%**	**4.04**	**4.5**	**34.3%**	**103**	**13.7**	**9.5**	**14.2**
1991	725	57.1	24.1	79.3%	4.16	3.8	33.1%	115	15.8	10.5	16.2
1990	769	56.3	24.4	81.1%	3.64	1.4	33.7%	119	15.5	11.1	17.3
1989	799	55.6	21.6	81.2%	3.66	1.0	34.5%	108	13.5	10.5	15.9
1988	794	54.5	21.2	80.2%	3.71	1.5	35.5%	110	13.8	10.8	16.6
1987	772	53.7	22.0	81.0%	3.71	2.2	43.9%	97	12.5	10.2	14.7
1986	808	55.5	24.3	82.2%	3.44	3.1	42.4%	102	12.6	11.2	15.8
1985	832	49.5	23.9	82.6%	4.11	27.3	37.7%	118	14.2	12.2	20.2
1984	806	45.5	25.1	82.8%	3.98	26.1	36.5%	109	13.5	12.0	20.6
1983	726	44.0	23.9	84.3%	3.04	12.5	22.5%	95	13.1	12.0	20.6

Balance Sheet Data (Million $)

Aug. 31	[5]Gross Prop.	[6]Capital Expend.	Net Prop.	% Earn. on Net Prop.	Total Cap.	Capitalization LT Debt	% LT Debt	Pfd.	% Pfd.	Com.	% Com.
1992	**2,146**	**73**	**1,448**	**9.6**	**1,538**	**513**	**39.8**	**99**	**7.6**	**679**	**52.6**
1991	2,080	80	1,429	10.6	1,529	520	40.2	100	7.7	674	52.1
1990	2,006	50	1,401	10.4	1,505	520	40.7	101	7.9	656	51.4
1989	1,967	46	1,410	10.6	1,532	564	43.3	102	7.9	635	48.8
1988	1,941	41	1,423	11.0	1,515	570	44.0	103	7.9	625	48.1
1987	1,908	51	1,436	10.2	1,487	572	44.5	103	8.0	609	47.5
1986	1,868	63	1,439	10.0	1,457	569	44.5	103	8.0	607	47.5
1985	1,826	101	1,442	10.3	1,413	570	45.5	115	9.2	566	45.3
1984	1,737	133	1,371	10.6	1,328	562	47.3	115	9.7	511	43.0
1983	1,595	135	1,259	9.5	1,240	551	49.0	115	10.2	458	40.8

Data as orig. reptd. **1.** Times int. exp. & pfd. divs. covered (pretax basis). **2.** Bef. spec. items. **3.** Based on income before interest charges. **4.** Based on mean common equity. **5.** Utility plant. **6.** As reptd. by co.

Business Summary

Southwestern Public Service provides electricity to a population of some one million in the Panhandle and south plains region of Texas (about 58% of revenues) and parts of Kansas, Oklahoma and New Mexico. Contributions by class of customer in recent fiscal years:

	1992	1991	1990	1989
Residential	20%	20%	20%	19%
Commercial	18%	18%	18%	18%
Industrial	35%	34%	34%	35%
Other	27%	28%	28%	28%

Some 26% of fiscal 1992 kwh sales were derived from industrial customers engaged in oil and gas production and petroleum refining.

The fuel mix in 1992 was 73.1% coal, 25.5% gas, and 1.4% other. Peak load in 1991 was 3,205 mw and system capability was 4,062 mw, for a capacity margin of 21.1%. Sales of electricity were 18,259 mw, up 2.7% from 17,772 mw the year before.

In November 1992, management estimated the company's construction expenditures, excluding AFUDC, at $98.2 million for fiscal 1993 and $481.4 million for fiscal 1993-1997. SPS does not expect new base-load generating facilities will be needed until after the mid-1990s.

Finances

In the nine months ended May 31, 1993, SPS spent $76.3 million on capital expenditures and expects all financing for the 1993 capital expenditure budget to be internally generated.

Dividend Data

Dividends have been paid since 1942. A dividend reinvestment plan is available. A "poison pill" stock purchase rights plan was adopted in 1991.

Amt of Divd. $	Date Decl.	Ex–divd. Date	Stock of Record	Payment Date
0.55	Oct. 27	Nov. 9	Nov. 16	Dec. 1'92
0.55	Jan. 13	Feb. 9	Feb. 16	Mar. 1'93
0.55	Apr. 27	May 10	May 14	Jun. 1'93
0.55	Jul. 27	Aug. 10	Aug. 16	Sep. 1'93

Capitalization

Long Term Debt: $522,959,000 (5/93).

Cum. Preferred Stock: $72,680,000.

Common Stock: 40,917,908 shs. ($1 par).
Institutions hold about 25%.
Shareholders of record: 34,619.

Office—SPS Tower, 6th and Tyler Streets, Amarillo, TX 79101. **Tel**—(806) 378-2121. **Chrmn & CEO**—B. D. Helton. **Pres**—C. Webb. **VP-CFO**—D. R. Bunch II. **Secy-Treas**—R. D. Dickerson. **Investor Contact**—Louise Ross. **Group Mgr.-Finance**—J. Steinhilper. **Dirs**—G. H. Bishop, J. C. Chambers, D. H. Conklin, G. M. Forbess, B. D. Helton, D. Maddox, J. H. Mock, S. B. Perry, J. A. Rush Jr., C. Webb, G. W. Wolf. **Transfer Agent & Registrar**—Society National Bank. **Incorporated** in New Mexico in 1921. **Empl**—2,030.

 Ned Bancroft

Standard Register

NASDAQ Symbol SREG (Incl. in Nat'l Market) In S&P MidCap 400

Price	Range	P–E Ratio	Dividend	Yield	S&P Ranking	Beta
Aug. 10'93	1993					
19¾	21¾–16	15	0.64	3.3%	A	1.12

Summary

This leading manufacturer of business forms also produces data systems and forms-handling equipment. Following an expected earnings gain in 1992, further progress has been realized during 1993, but has been dampened somewhat by the slow growth of the economy. Long term prospects are enhanced by a strategy of using electronics to improve both efficiency and customer service.

Current Outlook

Earnings for 1993 are tentatively projected at about $1.45 a share, up from $1.37 (excluding extraordinary items) in 1992.

The dividend was recently increased 6.7% to $0.16 quarterly.

Revenues for 1993 are likely to increase only moderately, reflecting the slow growth of the economy. Despite strength in sales for the company's Communicolor and Business Equipment and Systems products, business forms sales were lower and results by Advanced Medical Systems (AMS) continues to disappoint. However, AMS is expected to return to profitability in 1994, as productivity benefits are achieved under its current reorganization efforts. The company noted that in February 1993, the paper industry increased certain paper costs about 16%, and instituted a second increase in April of 6.5%. The company said that it expected to recover the higher paper costs. Part of the company's long term strategy is to focus resources on its most rapidly growing products and to invest in electronics to aid in cutting costs and improving customer service.

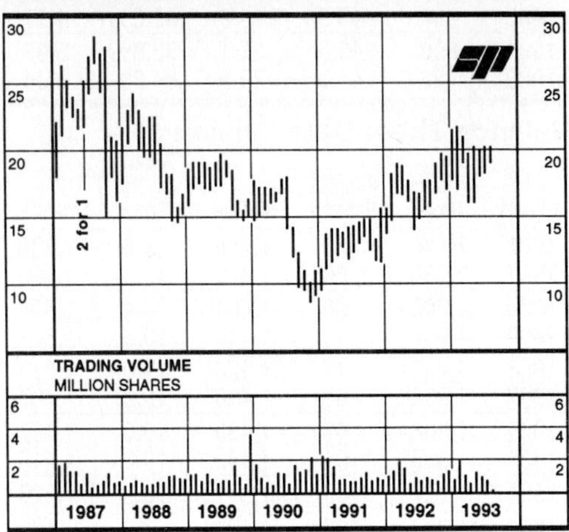

Revenues (Million $)

13 Weeks:	1993	1992	1991	1990
Mar.	169	169	172	175
Jun.	175	173	174	179
Sep.		170	164	175
Dec.		193	184	189
		705	694	716

In the 26 weeks ended July 4, 1993, revenues rose 0.7%, year to year, on strong sales growth from its Communicolor and Business Equipment and Systems products, offsetting lower sales by business forms. Pretax income rose 7.5%, benefiting from sharply reduced interest expense. After taxes at 38.5% versus 36.4%, net income rose 4.0% to $18,912,000 ($0.66 a share) from $18,190,000 ($0.63). Results for 1992 exclude a $0.47 a share charge from the cumulative effect of accounting changes.

Common Share Earnings ($)

13 Weeks:	1993	1992	1991	1990
Mar.	0.33	0.30	0.21	0.32
Jun.	0.33	0.33	0.24	0.30
Sep.	E0.33	0.31	0.24	0.19
Dec.	E0.46	0.43	0.45	d0.07
	E1.45	1.37	1.14	0.74

Important Developments

May '93— Standard Register said it entered into a joint venture to make business forms with Russia's Techpol PC, based in St. Petersburg. Under the agreement, expected to close by year-end, the company said it will own nearly 50% of the firm for an investment of less than $10 million.

May '93— SPEG said it may buy back up to $20 million of its outstanding common stock in the open market or in private transactions, depending on market conditions.

Next earnings report expected in late October.

Per Share Data ($)

Yr. End Dec. 31	1992	1991	1990	1989	1988	1987	[1]1986	1985	1984	[1]1983
Tangible Bk. Val.	[2]11.78	[2]11.49	[2]10.92	[2]10.71	[2]9.88	[2]9.11	[2]8.17	6.44	5.54	4.87
Cash Flow	2.15	1.89	1.44	1.98	1.84	1.91	1.69	1.51	1.22	1.04
Earnings[3]	1.37	1.14	0.74	1.35	1.28	1.36	1.21	1.21	0.93	0.77
Dividends	0.600	0.560	0.560	0.520	0.470	0.430	0.360	0.298	0.250	0.217
Payout Ratio	44%	49%	76%	38%	37%	32%	30%	25%	27%	28%
Prices—High	19¾	15⅝	18	19¾	24¼	28½	25⅛	19½	11⅛	8⅝
Low	13¾	9½	8⅝	14¾	14⅝	15	15¾	10⅞	7⅜	5⅛
P/E Ratio—	14–10	14–8	24–12	15–11	19–11	21–11	21–13	16–9	12–8	11–7

Data as orig. reptd. Adj. for stk. divs. of 100% Jun. 1987, 100% Jun. 1985, 200% Jun. 1983. **1.** Refl. merger or acq. **2.** Incl. intangibles. **3.** Bef. spec. item(s) of -0.47 in 1992. d-Deficit. E-Estimated

Income Data (Million $)

Year Ended Dec. 31	Revs.	Oper. Inc.	% Oper. Inc. of Revs.	Cap. Exp.	Depr.	Int. Exp.	Net Bef. Taxes	Eff. Tax Rate	[3]Net Inc.	% Net Inc. of Revs.	Cash Flow
1992	**705**	**89.3**	**12.7**	**22.7**	**22.3**	**2.12**	**61.9**	**36.3%**	**[2]39.4**	**5.6**	**61.7**
1991	694	75.4	10.9	28.0	21.4	3.01	51.0	35.9%	32.7	4.7	54.1
1990	716	72.1	10.1	24.7	20.7	4.46	33.0	33.9%	21.8	3.0	42.5
1989	709	86.3	12.2	33.8	18.7	5.57	62.0	34.9%	40.4	5.7	59.1
1988	675	83.2	12.3	23.4	16.6	5.32	61.3	37.9%	38.1	5.6	54.7
1987	667	91.7	13.8	31.7	16.4	5.70	69.6	41.8%	[2]40.5	6.1	56.9
[1]1986	562	81.2	14.4	80.7	12.9	5.55	62.7	47.9%	32.7	5.8	45.6
1985	441	70.0	15.9	17.3	8.0	0.89	61.1	48.0%	31.8	7.2	39.8
1984	412	54.1	13.2	13.6	7.6	1.11	47.4	48.3%	24.5	6.0	32.1
[1]1983	363	45.7	12.6	12.1	7.1	1.56	39.1	48.3%	20.2	5.6	27.3

Balance Sheet Data (Million $)

Dec. 31	Cash	Curr. Assets	Curr. Liab.	Curr. Ratio	Total Assets	% Ret. on Assets	Long Term Debt	Common Equity	Total Cap.	% LT Debt of Cap.	% Ret. on Equity
1992	**86.2**	**312**	**81.0**	**3.9**	**482**	**8.3**	**24.5**	**338**	**377**	**6.5**	**11.8**
1991	61.7	293	75.1	3.9	464	7.1	35.2	329	389	9.1	10.2
1990	41.4	289	74.1	3.9	454	4.9	41.9	313	380	11.0	7.0
1989	56.2	301	67.9	4.4	459	8.9	48.7	319	391	12.5	13.2
1988	61.8	299	72.2	4.1	444	8.8	55.3	294	372	14.9	13.5
1987	62.7	291	71.1	4.1	425	9.7	62.0	271	354	17.5	15.7
1986	55.8	262	70.0	3.7	407	9.5	75.0	243	337	22.2	15.0
1985	42.5	169	42.0	4.0	251	13.6	21.8	170	209	10.4	20.1
1984	21.7	151	42.2	3.6	216	11.9	14.4	146	174	8.3	17.9
1983	19.5	134	37.7	3.6	195	11.0	16.4	128	157	10.5	16.7

Data as orig. reptd. **1.** Refl. merger or acq. **2.** Refl. acctg. change. **3.** Bef. spec. item(s).

Business Summary

The Standard Register Company manufactures business forms and printed promotional direct-mail material. It also produces and services financial, bar-coding and document-processing equipment. SREG is the second largest company in the U.S. forms industry, which includes roughly 500 firms. Sales by product category in recent years:

	1992	1991	1990
Business forms..........	78%	89%	89%
Other.......................	22%	11%	11%

SREG produces forms that range from commodity-type stock continuous forms to complex custom forms designed to meet specific needs of individual customers. Other printed products and services include personalized mail promotional materials and pressure-sensitive labels. High-value-added business forms are emphasized, designed to satisfy customers' desire to simplify paperwork and thus improve efficiency.

Products are marketed by direct sales and service organizations that operate in principal cities throughout the U.S. Forms are produced at plants in the U.S. and shipped directly to the customer or stored in warehouses for subsequent on-demand delivery. The management of forms inventories to provide timely, cost-effective delivery is a major element of customer service.

Engineering and research spending is focused on the development of new products and on the improvement of existing products and services.

The Stanfast unit operates print centers that manufacture business forms for customers requiring relatively small quantities on a quick-turnaround basis.

Dividend Data

Cash has been paid each year since 1927.

Amt of Divd. $	Date Decl.	Ex–divd. Date	Stock of Record	Payment Date
0.15	Oct. 15	Nov. 6	Nov. 13	Nov. 27'92
0.16	Dec. 10	Feb. 22	Feb. 26	Mar. 12'93
0.16	Apr. 21	May 17	May 21	Jun. 4'93
0.16	Jul. 22	Aug. 16	Aug. 20	Sep. 3'93

Capitalization

Long Term Debt: $20,781,000 (6/93).

Class A Stock: 4,725,000 shs. ($1 par); conv. sh.-for-sh. into com.; five votes ea.

Common Stock: 24,036,796 shs. ($1 par); one vote ea.
Sherman Trusts have 72% of the combined voting power.
Shareholders: 3,565 of record.

d-Deficit.

Office—600 Albany St., Dayton, OH 45401. **Tel**—(513) 443-1000. **Chrmn**—P. H. Granzow. **Pres & CEO**—J. K. Darragh. **Secy**—R. A. Kagan. **VP-Fin & Treas**—C. J. Brown. **Dirs**—R. R. Burchenal, F. D. Clarke, III, J. K. Darragh, P. H. Granzow, M. C. Nushawg, P. S. Redding, J. J. Schiff, Jr., C. F. Sherman, J. L. Sherman, W. P. Sherman. **Transfer Agent & Registrar**—Wachovia Bank of North Carolina, N.A., Winston-Salem, N.C. **Incorporated** in Ohio in 1912. **Empl**—5,724.

 M. Graham Hackett

Stanhome Inc.

NYSE Symbol STH Options on ASE In S&P MidCap 400

Price	Range	P-E Ratio	Dividend	Yield	S&P Ranking	Beta
Aug. 2'93	1993					
28¼	34⅝–26⅞	18	1.00	3.5%	A	0.77

Summary

Stanhome imports and distributes giftware to a diverse group of retailers; sells giftware and collectibles directly to consumers through advertising and direct-mail marketing; and manufactures home and personal care products distributed through direct sales demonstrations. Earnings fell in 1993's first half, hurt largely by weak European economic conditions and a net restructuring charge of $11.5 million. A pick up in earnings is projected for 1994.

Current Outlook

Earnings for 1994 are projected at $2.60 a share, up from the $1.65 estimated for 1993, which includes a $0.58 restructuring charge.

Dividends should remain at $0.25 quarterly.

Sales and earnings for the remainder of 1993 are expected to rise only slightly, as continued strength in the direct response segment and a small improvement in the giftware segment are largely offset by continued weakness in the direct selling segment (as the European economy remains weak). Earnings should strengthen in 1994, when STH is likely to benefit from more favorable worldwide economic conditions, and savings of $0.15 a share from the recently initiated restructuring program.

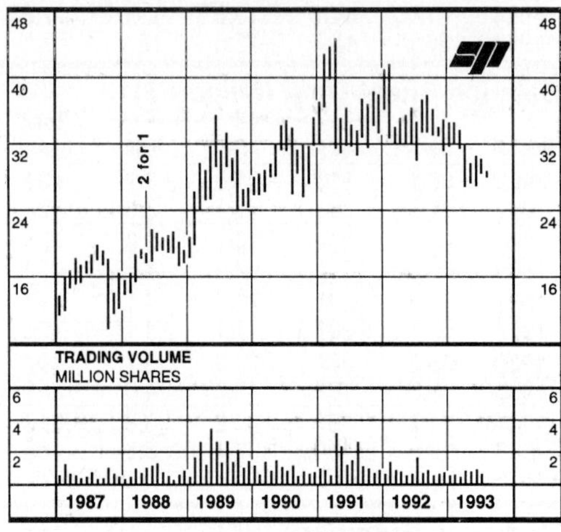

Net Sales (Million $)

Quarter:	1993	1992	1991	1990
Mar.	164	169	157	151
Jun.	187	185	171	164
Sep.	---	182	173	155
Dec.	---	208	209	206
	---	744	710	676

Sales for the six months ended June 30, 1993, declined fractionally, year to year, as weakness in the direct selling segment, outweighed a strong sales improvement in the direct response segment and a modest increase in giftware sales. The lower sales levels in the direct selling area were mainly related to poor European economic conditions, while the strength in direct response sales primarily reflected strong demand for collectible plates. Margins narrowed on the weak direct selling revenues, unfavorable foreign exchange rates, and the absence of a $0.04 a share gain on the sale of a Brazilian facility, and following a net restructuring charge of $11.5 million, net income fell 74%, to $0.25 a share, from $0.97.

Common Share Earnings ($)

Quarter:	1993	1992	1991	1990
Mar.	0.31	0.41	0.34	0.50
Jun.	d0.06	0.57	0.47	0.61
Sep.	E0.60	0.58	0.58	0.52
Dec.	E0.80	0.76	0.83	0.93
	E1.65	2.32	2.22	2.55

Important Developments

Aug. '93— STH reported that it had commenced a restructuring program designed to increase its operating efficiencies and productivity worldwide. The program, which would include a workforce reduction of about 10%, was expected to result in annual cost savings of $11 million ($7 million net) by the time of its completion in 1996. STH recorded a net restructuring charge of $11.5 million ($0.58 a share) in 1993's second quarter.

Next earnings report expected in late October.

Per Share Data ($)

Yr. End Dec. 31	1992	1991	1990	[1]1989	1988	1987	1986	1985	1984	[1]1983
Tangible Bk. Val.	**10.96**	10.20	9.14	7.07	7.28	6.16	4.81	4.77	[2]4.49	[2]4.12
Cash Flow	**2.80**	2.67	2.98	2.60	2.31	1.87	1.44	1.08	1.01	0.58
Earnings	**2.32**	2.22	2.55	2.23	1.97	1.59	1.18	0.86	0.78	0.38
Dividends	**0.960**	0.920	0.830	0.710	0.615	0.470	0.400	0.300	0.289	0.275
Payout Ratio	**41%**	40%	32%	31%	30%	28%	30%	35%	37%	73%
Prices—High	**41⅝**	44¾	35¼	35½	21¾	19⅞	13½	6⅞	5⅞	6
Low	**30⅛**	30¾	25⅝	18⅜	13⅞	9¾	6½	5¼	4⅜	4⅛
P/E Ratio—	**18–13**	20–14	14–10	16–8	11–7	13–6	11–6	8–6	7–5	16–11

Data as orig. reptd. Adj. for stk. divs. of 100% Jun. 1988, 100% Sep. 1986, 100% Nov. 1984. **1.** Refl. merger or acq. **2.** Incl. intangibles. d-Deficit. E-Estimated.

Income Data (Million $)

Year Ended Dec. 31	Revs.	Oper. Inc.	% Oper. Inc. of Revs.	Cap. Exp.	Depr.	Int. Exp.	Net Bef. Taxes	Eff. Tax Rate	Net Inc.	% Net Inc. of Revs.	Cash Flow
1992	**744**	**91.0**	**12.2**	**6.9**	**9.80**	**3.35**	**87.0**	**46.3%**	**46.7**	**6.3**	**56.5**
1991	710	86.4	12.2	7.8	9.20	5.02	81.1	44.5%	45.1	6.3	54.3
1990	676	94.3	14.0	10.9	7.65	5.40	90.3	43.4%	51.1	7.6	59.6
[1]1989	571	86.2	15.1	5.1	6.73	5.95	79.7	44.0%	44.6	7.8	52.4
1988	480	80.0	16.6	5.1	6.66	8.14	71.8	43.4%	40.6	8.5	47.7
1987	433	68.8	15.9	7.0	5.77	6.15	62.4	47.6%	32.7	7.6	38.5
1986	381	56.1	14.8	11.2	5.52	3.38	50.5	49.3%	25.6	6.7	31.2
1985	328	38.9	11.9	7.1	4.77	3.77	34.7	48.0%	18.1	5.5	22.8
1984	333	37.9	11.4	11.8	4.86	4.47	32.8	50.4%	16.3	4.9	21.1
[1]1983	277	17.3	6.2	13.8	4.31	3.72	[2]14.4	45.6%	7.8	2.8	12.2

Balance Sheet Data (Million $)

Dec. 31	Cash	Curr. Assets	Curr. Liab.	Curr. Ratio	Total Assets	% Ret. on Assets	Long Term Debt	Common Equity	Total Cap.	% LT Debt of Cap.	% Ret. on Equity
1992	**42.3**	**298**	**143**	**2.1**	**416**	**11.2**	**0.91**	**257**	**258**	**0.4**	**18.8**
1991	52.2	294	159	1.8	419	11.0	1.17	241	242	0.5	19.8
1990	51.8	271	162	1.7	392	14.0	1.42	211	213	0.7	26.6
1989	43.8	219	150	1.5	335	14.8	1.44	170	172	0.8	27.6
1988	65.6	182	104	1.7	276	15.5	1.60	158	160	1.0	27.9
1987	44.7	149	100	1.5	244	14.4	2.00	131	133	1.5	27.9
1986	25.1	110	90	1.2	202	13.9	1.83	101	103	1.8	25.8
1985	26.3	103	68	1.5	187	9.7	1.71	110	111	1.5	17.6
1984	19.0	96	75	1.3	180	9.3	6.24	94	100	6.3	18.1
1983	15.7	88	73	1.2	171	4.7	6.59	86	92	7.1	8.9

Data as orig. reptd. **1.** Refl. merger or acq. **2.** Incl. equity in earns. of nonconsol. subs.

Business Summary

Stanhome is a worldwide marketer of consumer products. Its key product segments include quality designed giftware and collectibles sold to retailers; collectible dolls, plates and figurines sold through direct response; and household, personal care and giftware items sold through direct selling. Business segment contributions in 1992 were:

	Sales	Profits
Giftware	47%	57%
Direct response	13%	8%
Direct selling	40%	35%

In 1992, international operations (principally in Europe) accounted for 43% of sales.

Giftware operations are led by the Enesco unit, a leading importer and distributor of giftware items, licensed lines and collectibles. Products include porcelain figurines, decoupage, miniatures, jack-in-the-boxes, tinware, music boxes, dolls and ornaments produced mostly by independent manufacturers in the Far East. The licensed Precious Moments line accounted for about 23% of Stanhome's sales in 1992.

The direct response segment (established in 1989 through an acquisition) consists of the Hamilton Collection subsidiary, which sells collectible plates, dolls and figurines directly to consumers through advertising and direct mail marketing in the U.S., the U.K. and Canada.

The direct selling division manufactures a broad line of home care, personal care and giftware items, sold and distributed in the U.S., Europe and Latin America. Sales of products generally result from the "Party Plan," under which a hostess invites friends and neighbors to her home to view a demonstration of products by an independent Stanhome dealer, who solicits orders following the demonstration.

Dividend Data

Cash has been paid each year since 1943. A dividend reinvestment plan is available. A "poison pill" stock purchase right was adopted in 1988.

Amt of Divd. $	Date Decl.	Ex-divd. Date	Stock of Record	Payment Date
0.25	Sep. 2	Sep. 10	Sep. 16	Oct. 1'92
0.25	Dec. 2	Dec. 10	Dec. 16	Jan. 1'93
0.25	Mar. 3	Mar. 11	Mar. 17	Apr. 1'93
0.25	Jun. 2	Jun. 10	Jun. 16	Jul. 1'93

Capitalization

Long Term Debt: $875,395 (3/93).

Common Stock: 19,798,907 shs. ($0.12½ par).
Institutions hold about 69%.
Shareholders of record: 3,787 (12/92).

Options: To buy 1,399,477 shs. at $4.97 to $41.12 ea. (12/92).

Office—333 Western Ave., Westfield, MA 01085. **Tel**—(413) 562-3631. **Chrmn**—H. L. Tower. **Pres & CEO**—A. D. Vargas. **Exec VP & CFO**—A. G. Keirstead. **Treas**—C. J. Mascaro. **VP & Secy**—B. H. Wyatt. **Asst Treas & Investor Contact**—Gerald W. Tower. **Dirs**— J. F. Cauley Jr., T. R. Horton, A. G. Keirstead, A. O'Brien, H. G. Perkins, G. W. Seawright, H. L. Tower, A. D. Vargas, A. L. Verville, R. G. Widham. **Transfer Agent & Registrar**—Mellon Securities Trust Co., East Hartford, Conn. **Incorporated** in Massachusetts in 1931. **Empl**—4,400.

 Michael W. Jaffe

State Street Boston

NASDAQ Symbol STBK (Incl. in Nat'l Market) Options on Phila In S&P MidCap 400

Price	Range	P-E Ratio	Dividend	Yield	S&P Ranking	Beta
Jul. 23'93	1993					
33	49⅛–29¼	15	0.52	1.6%	A+	1.65

Summary

This bank holding company, among the largest in Massachusetts, provides commercial banking services and is the leading mutual fund custodian in the U.S., with about 40% of the industry's assets in custody. It also offers master trust services to large pension funds and institutional investors. Fee income from a rapidly growing mutual funds industry has fueled earnings gains in recent years.

Current Outlook

Earnings for 1993 could reach $2.30 a share, versus 1992's $2.10. Earnings could rise to $2.55 in 1994.

The quarterly dividend was increased 8.3%, to $0.13 a share, with the June 1993 payment.

Earnings growth will likely slow moderately in 1993 and 1994 as STBK has stepped up its investment spending to support future business. Nonetheless earnings are expected to rise about 10% over the near-term. As STBK derives the vast majority of net revenues from fees (73% in the first six months of 1993), particularly from its mutual funds processing business, it has been relatively unscathed by the struggling regional economy and weak real estate market. STBK is likely to gain market share in servicing mutual funds, reflecting its ability to efficiently process transactions through its investment in technology. In addition, growth of fiduciary compensation should benefit from a growing international market. While the regional economy will likely remain stagnant, the $2.4 billion loan portfolio accounts for only 13% of assets. Credit quality appears to be improving, and with reserves of about $56 million, (161% of problem loans) a modest decline in the loan loss provision is likely.

Review of Operations

Net interest income for the six months ended June 30, 1993 rose 12%, year to year, primarily reflecting strong growth in average earning assets. The provision for loan losses declined 29%, to $5.6 million. While the largest revenue source, fiduciary compensation rose 12%, a 68% advance in foreign exchange revenues and an 88% rise in processing service fees, led to an 18% gain in total non-interest income. Paced by a 56% rise in equipment expense due to the addition of a second data center to support future business, noninterest expenses expanded 21%, limiting the gain in pretax earnings to 7.8%. After taxes at 34.3%, versus 38.2%, net income increased 15%. Share earnings were $1.13 ($1.11 fully diluted), up from $0.99 ($0.97).

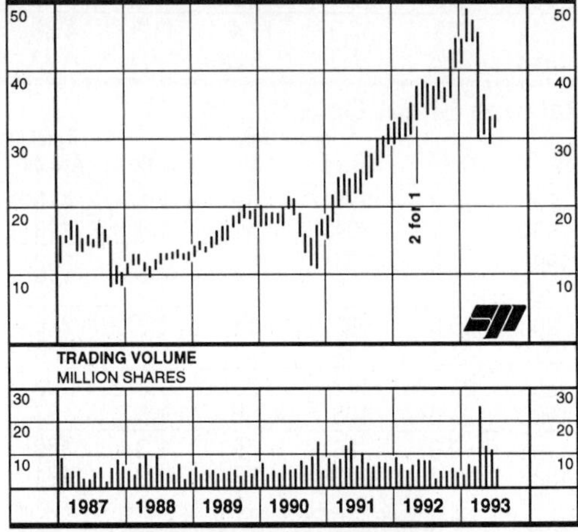

Common Share Earnings ($)

Quarter:	1993	1992	1991	1990
Mar.	0.56	0.48	0.78	0.38
Jun.	0.57	0.51	0.35	0.39
Sep.	E0.58	0.55	0.37	0.41
Dec.	E0.59	0.57	0.38	0.43
	E2.30	2.10	1.86	1.59

Important Developments

Jul. '93— STBK said higher second quarter earnings reflected revenue growth of 18%, partially offset by increased expenses for strategic investments. Fiduciary compensation rose 14% for the quarter, primarily due to the growth of mutual fund assets and additional mutual funds serviced. At June 30, assets under custody totaled $1.4 trillion, up 28% from a year earlier, and assets under management were $128 billion, up 23%.

Next earnings report expected in mid-October.

Per Share Data ($)

Yr. End Dec. 31	1992	1991	1990	1989	1988	1987	[1]1986	1985	1984	1983
Tangible Bk. Val.	**12.70**	10.97	9.51	8.29	7.22	6.45	5.60	4.74	4.05	3.48
Earnings[2]	**2.10**	1.86	1.59	1.42	1.26	1.12	0.99	0.80	0.71	0.56
Dividends	**0.455**	0.390	0.340	0.300	0.260	0.220	0.180	0.148	0.125	0.113
Payout Ratio	**22%**	21%	21%	21%	21%	20%	18%	19%	18%	20%
Prices—High	**44⅞**	32⅛	21⅝	20 7/16	13⅞	18 1/16	14 7/16	10 7/16	5 13/16	5 15/16
Low	**29¼**	15 7/16	10 15/16	12¾	9 11/16	8¼	9⅝	5 11/16	3 9/16	3 5/16
P/E Ratio—	**21–14**	17–8	14–7	14–9	11–8	16–7	15–10	13–7	8–5	11–6

Data as orig. reptd. Adj. for stk. divs. of 100% May 1992, 100% Aug. 1986, 100% Aug. 1985, 100% May 1983. **1.** Refl. acctg. change. **2.** Bef. results of disc. ops. and/or spec. items of -0.04 in 1983; ful. dil.: 2.07 in 1992, 1.81 in 1991, 1.55 in 1990, 1.38 in 1989, 1.20 in 1988, 1.06 in 1987, 0.92 in 1986, 0.73 in 1985, 0.65 in 1984, 0.53 in 1983. E-Estimated.

Income Data (Million $)

Year Ended Dec. 31	Net Int. Inc.	Tax Equiv. Adj.	Non Int. Inc.	Loan Loss Prov.	% Exp./ Op. Revs.	Net Bef. Taxes	Eff. Tax Rate	[3]Net Inc.	% Net Int. Margin	—% Return On— Assets	Equity
1992	**282**	**13.6**	**691**	**12.2**	**72.6**	**257**	**37.5%**	**160**	**2.14**	**1.04**	**18.1**
1991	274	18.8	617	60.0	66.9	225	38.1%	139	2.89	1.20	18.0
1990	271	20.8	503	45.7	68.6	183	36.1%	117	3.26	1.15	18.1
[1]1989	217	15.5	447	19.4	70.3	163	36.3%	104	3.34	1.29	18.7
[1]1988	200	16.1	396	15.6	71.4	145	36.1%	92	3.51	1.27	18.7
1987	197	25.5	329	22.6	67.2	133	37.5%	83	3.89	1.20	19.2
[1]1986	181	31.1	247	17.9	65.5	110	35.2%	71	4.27	1.14	20.0
[2]1985	155	29.1	178	12.5	64.3	89	37.6%	55	4.66	1.12	18.9
1984	132	25.0	144	4.0	64.8	77	36.2%	49	5.08	1.26	19.6
1983	133	19.5	117	4.7	66.3	65	41.1%	39	4.84	0.97	17.2

Balance Sheet Data (Million $)

Dec. 31	Total Assets	Earning Assets— Mon. Mkt. Assets	Inv. Secs.	Com'l Loans	Other Loans	% Loan Loss Resv.	—Deposits— Demand	Time	% Loans/ Deposits	Long Term Debt	Common Equity	% Equity To Assets
1992	**16,490**	**8,224**	**4,092**	**1,771**	**233**	**2.89**	**4,374**	**6,687**	**18.1**	**146**	**953**	**5.72**
1991	15,046	8,113	3,250	1,623	282	3.46	3,564	5,168	21.8	147	817	6.68
1990	11,651	4,278	2,842	1,738	803	2.01	3,236	4,422	33.2	112	695	6.32
1989	9,983	3,262	2,515	1,632	833	2.04	3,263	2,915	39.9	115	597	6.86
1988	8,372	2,481	2,367	1,472	707	2.30	2,775	2,613	40.4	123	506	6.81
1987	6,955	1,683	1,942	1,309	834	2.18	2,606	1,932	47.2	125	471	6.26
1986	7,190	1,536	1,622	1,332	837	1.95	3,406	1,863	41.2	136	392	5.69
1985	6,653	1,873	1,307	1,290	742	1.78	2,696	1,874	44.5	70	323	5.94
1984	4,744	1,113	799	1,106	448	1.75	1,808	1,403	48.3	82	267	6.45
1983	4,044	1,040	783	944	431	1.93	1,208	1,277	55.2	82	241	5.63

Data as orig. reptd. **1.** Refl. acctg. change. **2.** Refl. merger or acq. **3.** Bef. results of disc. ops. and spec. items.

Business Summary

State Street Boston Corp., the holding company for State Street Bank & Trust, is among the largest bank holding companies in Massachusetts. It is the leading mutual fund custodian in the U.S., providing securities custody and recordkeeping services to approximately 1,698 mutual funds with assets totaling $560 billion at December 31, 1992 (up 12% from the level at December 31, 1991). Master trust ($466 billion in assets) and other services brought total assets in custody to $1.29 trillion (up 23%). In addition, trust assets under management were $111 billion (up 25%). The company provides corporate banking services, primarily to New England middle market companies, as well as specialized lending and international banking services. Boston Financial Services, a joint venture, provides recordkeeping services for shareholders.

During 1992, average earning assets of $13.85 billion (up 37% from 1991) were divided: commercial and financial loans 11%; real estate, consumer and other loans 4%; investment securities 25%; trading account assets 2%; money market investments 37%; and federal funds sold and securities purchased under resale agreements 21%. Average sources of funds were: noninterest-bearing deposits 19%, other domestic deposits 15%, other foreign deposits 25% (total deposits were $9.2 billion, up from $7.2 billion), short term debt 31%, long term debt 1%, equity 6% and other 3%.

At year-end 1992, nonperforming assets amounted to $56.3 million (2.62% of related assets), versus $56.3 million (2.93%) a year earlier. The allowance for loan losses was 2.89% of loans, down from 3.46%. Net chargeoffs during 1992 were 0.97% of average loans, versus 2.14% in 1991.

Dividend Data

Cash has been paid each year since 1910.

Amt. of Divd. $	Date Decl.	Ex-divd. Date	Stock of Record	Payment Date
0.11	Sep. 17	Sep. 25	Oct. 1	Oct. 15'92
0.12	Dec. 17	Dec. 28	Jan. 4	Jan. 15'93
0.12	Mar. 18	Mar. 26	Apr. 1	Apr. 15'93
0.13	Jun. 17	Jun. 25	Jul. 1	Jul. 15'93

Capitalization

Long Term Debt: $106,562,000 (6/93), incl. $10.3 million of sub. debs. conv. into com. at $5.75 a sh.

Common Stock: 75,359,000 shs. ($1 par). Institutions hold 68%. Shareholders of record: 5,011 (12/92).

Office—225 Franklin St., Boston, MA 02110. **Tel**—(617) 786-3000. **Chrmn & CEO**—M. N. Carter. **Secy**—R. J. Malley. **Treas & CFO**—G. J. Fesus. **Investor Contact**—Susanne G. Clark. **Dirs**—T. E. Albright, J. A. Baute, I. M. Booth, M. N. Carter, J. I. Cash Jr., T. S. Casner, G. H. Conrades, N. F. Darehshori, J. B. Gray, L. D. Juliber, C. F. Kaye, A. J. Kelley, N. O. Keohane, G. H. Kidder, J. M. Kucharski, C. R. LaMantia, D. B. Perini, D. J. Picard, B. W. Reznicek, D. A. Spina, M. Tanenbaum, R. E. Weissman. **Transfer Agent**—State Street Bank & Trust, Boston. **Registrar**—Bank of Boston. **Formed** in 1970; bank incorporated in Massachusetts in 1891. **Empl**—9,338.

 Richard M. Levine, CFA

Sterling Chemicals

NYSE Symbol STX In S&P MidCap 400

Price	Range	P-E Ratio	Dividend	Yield	S&P Ranking	Beta
Sep. 10'93	1993					
3½	5–3⅛	NM	[4]---	[4]---	NR	NA

Summary

Sterling Chemicals is a major manufacturer of commodity chemicals, the most important of which is styrene monomer, which accounts for a large percentage of operating earnings. STX also makes pulp chemicals and related equipment. Earnings fell significantly in fiscal 1992, and a loss was incurred in the first nine months of fiscal 1993, reflecting the impact of the slow economy and industry overcapacity on the styrene monomer business. In July 1993, STX omitted its quarterly dividend due to the continuance of problems in styrene markets and events in China that have disrupted the acrylonitrile market.

Business Summary

Sterling Chemicals is a major producer of seven intermediate petrochemicals, which are sold to others for use in the manufacture of other chemicals which in turn are used to produce a wide range of finished goods. STX also makes pulp chemicals and related equipment.

The company is the largest producer (14% of domestic capacity) of styrene monomer, a clear liquid used in the production of a variety of consumer goods, including foam products and housing for kitchen appliances. It is the second largest domestic producer (25%) of acrylonitrile, the principal raw material for synthetic fibers. It is a major producer of acetic acid (16%), used in a great variety of pharmaceuticals, adhesives, coatings and paints, and of plasticizers (22%), which enhance the flexibility and strength of vinyl products. It is the only U.S. producer of lactic acid, used in food additives and preservatives, pharmaceuticals and in surface coatings, and of TBA, used in silicone caulk, tires and hoses. Sterling operates a 100 million pound-a-year sodium cyanide project owned by duPont that was built in fiscal 1990; sodium cyanide is used in precious metals recovery and electroplating. Manufacturing facilities are located in Texas City, Texas, on a 250-acre site on Galveston Bay.

In August 1992, Sterling Canada purchased the pulp chemicals business of Albright & Wilson from Tenneco Canada. The plants include four that produce sodium chlorate, which is used to produce chlorine dioxide and is sold primarily as a bleaching agent for kraft pulp manufacturing, and one for sodium chlorite, used primarily as an antimicrobial agent and disinfectant. STX owns about 20% of North American sodium chlorate capacity. Considered more environmentally friendly than elemental chlorine in paper bleaching, chlorine dioxide demand has risen with its use as a substitute. The unit also licenses and constructs large-scale generators to convert sodium chlorate to chlorine dioxide for pulp bleaching.

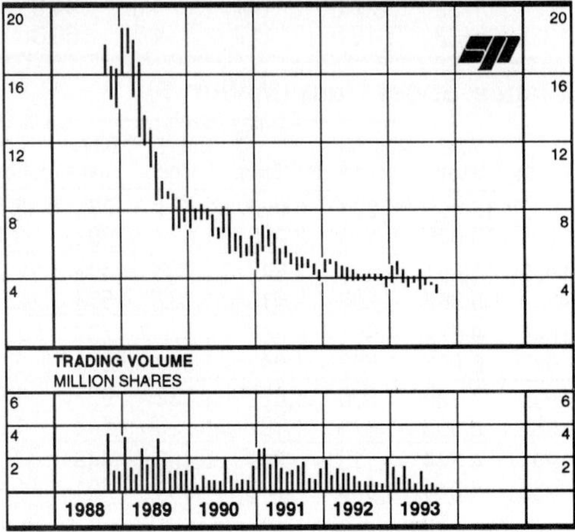

Export sales accounted for approximately 43% of total sales in fiscal 1992, versus 45% in fiscal 1991 and 35% in 1990.

Important Developments

Jul '93— The company reported that directors had omitted the quarterly dividend due to the continued performance by the petrochemicals business at a lower level than previously expected. STX's styrene unit operated at slightly more than 70% of capacity in the first nine months of fiscal 1993, compared with 80% in the prior-year period. STX did not anticipate a sustainable improvement in stryrene's supply/demand balance for the next few years as additional worldwide capacity is scheduled. Acrylonitrile sales volumes to export customers declined as a result of weaker demand from customers shipping to China, which reflected continued concern over China's currency valuation and free market reform policies.

Next earnings report expected in December.

Per Share Data ($)

Yr. End Sep. 30	1992	1991	1990	1989	1988	1987
Tangible Bk. Val.	**[3]1.59**	1.95	1.96	1.97	1.51	1.39
Cash Flow	**0.53**	1.03	1.41	2.01	3.78	1.40
Earnings[1]	**0.08**	0.67	1.07	1.77	3.56	0.86
Dividends	**0.245**	0.650	1.000	0.750	Nil	Nil
Payout Ratio	**297%**	97%	93%	40%	Nil	Nil
Prices[2]—High	**5⅛**	7⅛	8⅝	18¾	17¾	NA
Low	**3½**	3⅞	5¼	6⅞	14⅛	NA
P/E Ratio—	**64–44**	11–6	8–5	11–4	5–4	NA

Data as orig. reptd.; prior to 1988 data as reptd. in prospectus dated Oct. 12, 1988. **1.** Bef. spec. item(s) of -0.19 in 1992, -0.01 in 1988, -0.07 in 1987. **2.** Cal. yr. **3.** Incl. intangibles. **4.** Dirs. omitted divd. Jul. 1, 1993. NA-Not Available.

Income Data (Million $)

Year Ended Sep. 30	Revs.	Oper. Inc.	% Oper. Inc. of Revs.	Cap. Exp.	Depr.	[1]Int. Exp.	Net Bef. Taxes	Eff. Tax Rate	[2]Net Inc.	% Net Inc. of Revs.	Cash Flow
[4]1992	**431**	**42**	**9.8**	**138**	**24.5**	**9.3**	**9**	**51.0%**	**[3]5**	**1.1**	**29**
1991	543	81	14.9	35	20.1	7.6	55	32.5%	37	6.8	57
1990	492	87	17.8	20	18.9	9.4	88	33.2%	59	12.0	78
1989	581	176	30.4	58	14.1	6.4	156	33.5%	104	17.9	118
1988	699	335	47.9	17	13.2	9.5	312	31.5%	214	30.6	227
1987	413	123	29.7	13	11.6	21.1	90	43.0%	51	12.4	62

Balance Sheet Data (Million $)

Sep. 30	Cash	Curr. Assets	Curr. Liab.	Curr. Ratio	Total Assets	% Ret. on Assets	Long Term Debt	Common Equity	Total Cap.	% LT Debt of Cap.	% Ret. on Equity
1992	**2.63**	**172**	**115**	**1.5**	**600**	**0.9**	**292**	**87**	**423**	**69.1**	**4.5**
1991	3.01	118	89	1.3	361	10.3	71	112	224	31.7	33.4
1990	0.18	124	91	1.4	352	17.5	64	108	214	29.8	54.5
1989	0.43	108	72	1.5	329	34.4	66	110	211	31.6	106.6
1988	0.45	116	77	1.5	294	57.2	86	91	207	41.6	245.4
1987	3.00	110	81	1.4	283	19.7	116	52	197	58.9	176.1
1986	7.64	67	34	2.0	239	NA	185	5	199	93.3	NA

Data as orig. reptd.; prior to 1988 data as reptd. in prospectus dated Oct. 12, 1988. **1.** Net of interest inc. **2.** Bef. spec. item(s) in 1988, 1987. **3.** Reflects acctg. change. **4.** Reflects merger or acquisition. NA-Not Available.

Revenues (Million $)

Quarter:	1992–93	1991–92	1990–91	1989–90
Dec.	137.8	115.9	182.4	88.0
Mar.	113.0	89.3	147.2	117.1
Jun.	132.3	120.9	110.2	139.2
Sep.		104.4	102.8	161.8
		430.5	542.7	506.1

Revenues for the nine months ended June 30, 1993, advanced 17%, year to year, reflecting the acquisition of the Canadian chemical pulp business. Margins narrowed due to lower operating income from acrylonitrile and stryrene operations. Following 254% greater interest and debt related expenses, there was a pretax loss of $3,485,000, in contrast to income of $7,771,000. After a tax credit of $530,000, versus taxes at 38.1%, the net loss was $2,955,000 ($0.05 a share), against net income of $4,813,000 ($0.09, before a $0.19 charge for the cumulative effect of an accounting change).

Common Share Earnings ($)

Quarter:	1992–93	1991–92	1990–91	1989–90
Dec.	Nil	0.01	0.44	0.08
Mar.	d0.05	d0.04	0.13	0.20
Jun.	d0.01	0.12	0.05	0.34
Sep.		Nil	0.06	0.45
		0.08	0.67	1.07

Finances

The company sells its products pursuant to long-term contracts and through its direct sales force. Most of the contracts are structured as conversion agreements, by which the customer furnishes raw materials which the company processes. Novacor Chemicals, a subsidiary of NOVA Corp. of Alberta, purchases some one-third of STX's styrene capacity. Its contract, which expires at the end of fiscal 1993, was expected to be renegotiated at substantially lower volumes.

In August 1992, STX purchased the assets of the pulp chemicals business of Albright & Wilson Americas of Canada from Tenneco Inc. for $202 million. The purchase was financed through additional debt, including a term loan of $41.25 million under an $80 million revolving credit agreement; a loan to Sterling Canada of $148.75 million; and an unsecured note of $44 million of Sterling Canada to Tenneco Credit Corp. Also, Sterling Canada obtained a C$20 million revolving credit facility.

STX expected capital outlays to total $8 million in fiscal 1993 and $12 million for fiscal 1994 and 1995.

In October 1988, in STX's initial public offering, certain shareholders sold 11 million common shares at $16 a share. STX was formed in May 1986 to purchase six petrochemicals manufacturing facilities of Monsanto Co.

Dividend Data

Payments were initiated in 1989 and were omitted in July 1993. Payments in the past 12 months:

Amt of Divd. $	Date Decl.	Ex–divd. Date	Stock of Record	Payment Date
0.02	Oct. 1	Oct. 6	Oct. 13	Oct. 28'92
0.02	Jan. 4	Jan. 11	Jan. 15	Jan. 27'93
0.02	Apr. 2	Apr. 7	Apr. 14	Apr. 28'93

Capitalization

Long Term Debt: $262,067,000 (6/93).

Common Stock: 55,347,383 shs. ($0.01 par).
Officers and directors own about 26%.
Institutions hold approximately 27%.
Shareholders of record: 15,000.

Office—1200 Smith St., Suite 1900, Houston, TX 77002. **Tel**—(713) 650-3700. **Chrmn**—G. A. Cain. **Pres & CEO**—J. V. Waggoner. **VP-CFO & Investor Contact**—J. David Heaney. **Secy**—F. M. Evans. **Dirs**—G.A. Cain, J.J. Kerley, R. R. Knowland, W.A. McMinn, F. J. Pizzitola, G.M.A. Portal, J.V. Waggoner. **Transfer Agent & Registrar**—Society National Bank, Houston. **Incorporated** in Delaware in 1986. **Empl**—1,225.

 Shayna J. Malnak

Stewart & Stevenson Services

NASDAQ Symbol SSSS (Incl. in Nat'l Market) Options on Pacific In S&P MidCap 400

Price	Range	P-E Ratio	Dividend	Yield	S&P Ranking	Beta
Sep. 3'93	1993					
50	51¾–28	32	0.24	0.5%	B	0.84

Summary

This leading manufacturer of custom diesel and gas turbine power systems and tactical military vehicles is also a distributor of industrial equipment. Sales and earnings rose in 1992-3, mostly reflecting a strong gain in gas turbines. Assuming continued strong growth in gas turbines, together with an upturn in distribution and truck sales, sales and earnings should maintain their uptrend through 1994-5.

Current Outlook

Earnings for the fiscal year ending January 31, 1995, are projected at $2.05 a share, up from 1993-4's estimated $1.70.

The dividend was increased 20%, to $0.06 quarterly, with the August 1993 payment.

Sales are expected to rise in 1994-5 from the levels of 1993-4, reflecting continued growth in power systems, another advance in distribution and increased deliveries of trucks. Higher volume and an increase in the operating rate should lead to better margins. Assuming flat interest costs and only a small rise in the tax rate, earnings should continue their uptrend in 1994-5. Long-term sales and earnings growth will benefit from a worldwide trend toward smaller scale production of electric power.

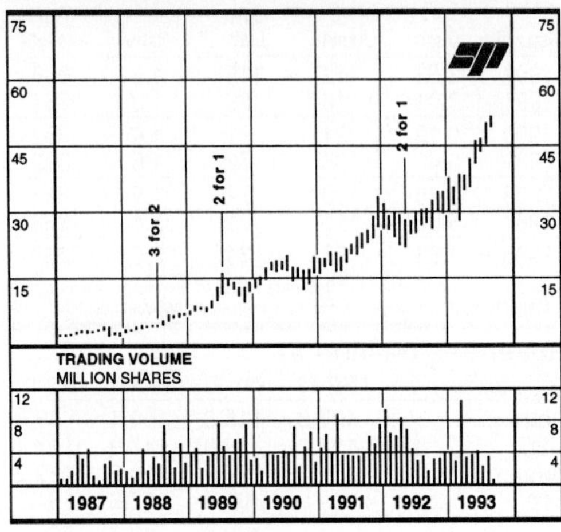

Net Sales (Million $)

Quarter:	1993-94	1992-93	1991-92	1990-91
Apr.	220	182	154	144
Jul.	258	200	160	160
Oct.		208	187	174
Jan.		222	186	169
		813	686	646

Net sales in the six months ended July 31, 1993, advanced 25%, year to year, reflecting gains in all segments. Margins widened, and net income increased 34%. Share earnings rose to $0.79, on 1.2% more shares, from $0.60, as adjusted. Results for the 1992 interim exclude a charge of $0.29 a share for an accounting change.

Common Share Earnings ($)

Quarter:	1993-94	1992-93	1991-92	1990-91
Apr.	0.37	0.28	0.26	0.25
Jul.	0.42	0.33	0.28	0.26
Oct.	E0.44	0.36	0.31	0.27
Jan.	E0.47	0.40	0.33	0.22
	E1.70	1.35	1.18	0.99

Important Developments

Aug. '93— SSSS signed a letter of intent with Devtek Corp. to form an equally owned company to make and distribute an advanced gaseous fuel-injection system for automobiles and light trucks. The new company will be known as GFI Control Systems Inc. and will produce alternate fuel equipment for orginal equipment manufacturers and aftermarket customers worldwide.

Next earnings report expected in late November.

Per Share Data ($)

Yr. End Jan. 31	1993	1992	1991	1990	1989	1988	1987	1986	1985	1984
Tangible Bk. Val.	**9.33**	8.40	6.09	5.22	3.74	3.01	2.56	2.56	3.25	3.12
Cash Flow	**1.73**	1.46	1.25	1.23	1.03	0.71	0.20	d0.52	0.39	0.22
Earnings[1]	**1.35**	1.18	0.99	0.97	0.76	0.46	Nil	d0.69	0.13	d0.06
Dividends	**0.190**	0.140	0.110	0.073	0.025	Nil	Nil	Nil	Nil	0.025
Payout Ratio	**14%**	12%	11%	8%	3%	Nil	Nil	Nil	Nil	NM
Calendar Years	**1992**	1991	1990	1989	1988	1987	1986	1985	1984	1983
Prices—High	**34¾**	33⅝	20¼	16¼	7¼	4⁵⁄₁₆	2¹³⁄₁₆	3¹⁄₁₆	2⅝	2¾
Low	**22**	16⅛	12⅜	6¹⁵⁄₁₆	2⅞	2⅛	1¹¹⁄₁₆	1¹⁵⁄₁₆	1⅝	1⅞
P/E Ratio—	**25–16**	28–14	21–13	17–7	10–4	9–5	NM	NM	21–13	NM

Data as orig. reptd. Adj. for stk. divs. of 100% May 1992, 100% Jul. 1989, 50% Jul. 1988. **1.** Bef. spec. item of -0.29 in 1992. E-Estimated. d-Deficit. NM-Not Meaningful.

Income Data (Million $)

Year Ended Jan. 31	Revs.	Oper. Inc.	% Oper. Inc. of Revs.	Cap. Exp.	Depr.	Int. Exp.	[1]Net Bef. Taxes	Eff. Tax Rate	[3]Net Inc.	% Net Inc. of Revs.	Cash Flow
1993	**813**	**77.8**	**9.6**	**75.1**	**12.3**	**3.7**	**64.6**	**31.9%**	**[4]44.0**	**5.4**	**56.3**
1992	686	64.3	9.4	26.2	8.3	7.0	52.5	32.0%	35.7	5.2	44.0
1991	646	55.0	8.5	11.6	7.8	6.0	43.2	32.0%	29.4	4.6	37.2
1990	605	52.1	8.6	7.7	7.4	7.6	39.7	31.4%	27.3	4.5	34.7
1989	474	41.2	8.7	12.0	7.5	5.6	29.7	29.9%	20.8	4.4	28.3
1988	343	25.3	7.4	8.0	6.9	4.7	14.5	13.2%	12.6	3.7	19.5
1987	249	8.6	3.5	6.6	5.5	4.7	Nil	Nil	Nil	Nil	5.5
1986	269	9.8	3.7	5.9	4.7	5.5	d25.5	NM	[2]d19.0	NM	d14.3
1985	257	12.9	5.0	3.6	7.2	7.1	d0.7	NM	3.4	1.3	10.6
1984	237	12.6	5.3	4.4	7.4	9.2	d3.6	NM	d1.5	NM	5.9

Balance Sheet Data (Million $)

Jan. 31	Cash	Curr. Assets	Curr. Liab.	Curr. Ratio	Total Assets	% Ret. on Assets	Long Term Debt	Common Equity	Total Cap.	% LT Debt of Cap.	% Ret. on Equity
1993	**21.9**	**436**	**199**	**2.2**	**573**	**8.3**	**44.5**	**306**	**356**	**12.5**	**15.1**
1992	6.5	413	166	2.5	478	7.9	27.9	272	309	9.0	15.2
1991	3.3	344	166	2.1	394	8.3	38.0	182	225	16.9	17.4
1990	7.4	261	122	2.1	311	9.2	23.5	155	186	12.6	20.4
1989	4.8	211	106	2.0	261	9.1	39.5	103	152	26.0	22.4
1988	11.0	153	83	1.8	197	6.9	24.4	83	111	22.0	16.4
1987	19.8	126	61	2.1	169	NM	29.8	70	105	28.3	NM
1986	32.0	131	59	2.2	175	NM	37.0	70	113	32.7	NM
1985	7.1	125	47	2.6	197	1.7	42.5	89	147	28.8	3.9
1984	0.9	137	52	2.6	206	NM	47.5	86	152	31.4	NM

Data as orig. reptd. **1.** Incl. equity in earns. of nonconsol. subs. **2.** Refl. acctg. change. **3.** Bef. spec. items. **4.** Reflects acctg. change. d-Deficit. NM-Not Meaningful.

Business Summary

Stewart & Stevenson Services, Inc. manufactures custom diesel and gas turbine power systems and tactical military vehicles and distributes industrial equipment.

Revenue and profit contributions in 1992-3 were:

	Revs.	Profits
Engineered power systems..	62.6%	80.7%
Distribution	33.1%	16.9%
Tactical vehicle sytems	4.2%	2.2%
Corporate services	0.1%	0.2%

SSSS engineers and sells generator sets and mechanical drive packages that are driven by diesel or gas turbine engines supplied by independent manufacturers and are designed to meet specific requirements of customers in various applications. The gas turbine generator sets range from 20 Mw to 50 Mw and are sold to independent power producers and public utilities. Gas turbine-driven products and services accounted for 50.5% of 1992-3 sales. The company also makes military vehicles, power systems for military and commercial marine applications, aircraft ground support equipment, and equipment for the oilfield service industry.

The distribution division markets industrial equipment and related parts manufactured by others and provides in-shop and on-site repair services for such products. Principal products include Detroit Diesel engines, General Motors Electro-Motive diesel engines, Allison automatic transmissions, Thermo King transport refrigeration units, and John Deere equipment.

The Tactical Vehicle Systems unit manufactures tactical vehicles, primarily 2½ and 5-ton trucks under contract with the U. S. Army. The division has a contract to produce 7,738 2½-ton trucks and 3,105 5-ton trucks over a five-year period beginning in 1992. The contract is valued at $1.2 billion.

Dividend Data

Cash dividends, which had been paid in each year since 1976, were omitted in 1983 and resumed in 1988.

Amt. of Divd. $	Date Decl.	Ex–divd. Date	Stock of Record	Payment Date
0.05	Dec. 8	Jan. 25	Jan. 29	Feb. 17'93
0.05	Apr. 15	Apr. 26	Apr. 30	May 13'93
0.06	Jun. 10	Jul. 26	Jul. 31	Aug. 12'93

Capitalization

Long Term Debt: $46,228,000 (4/93).

Common Stock: 32,788,938 shs. (no par).
Stewart and Stevenson families own 16.5%
Institutions hold 65%.
Shareholders: 825 of record (2/93).

Office—2707 North Loop West, P.O. Box 1637, Houston, TX 77008. **Tel**—(713) 868-7700. **Pres & CEO**—B. H. O'Neal. **VP, Treas & CFO**—R. L. Hargrave. **VP & Secy**—L. E. Wilson. **Investor Contact**—David R. Stewart. **Dirs**—J. T. Currie, J. H. Elder, Jr., W. E. Greehey, R. L. Hargrave, J. E. Knott, J. W. Lander, J. C. Manning, B. H. O'Neal, R. H. Parsley, D. E. Stevenson, C. J. Stewart II, R. S. Sullivan. **Transfer Agent & Registrar**—Bank of New York, NYC. **Incorporated** in Texas in 1947. **Empl**—2,852.

 Leo Larkin

Storage Technology

NYSE Symbol STK Options on CBOE (Mar-Jun-Sep-Dec) In S&P MidCap 400

Price	Range	P-E Ratio	Dividend	Yield	S&P Ranking	Beta
Jul. 28'93	1993					
25½	45–18	NM	None	None	B–	0.59

Summary

Storage Technology manufactures and markets high-performance disk and tape subsystems and high speed impact printers, and markets non-impact printers. STK emerged from Chapter 11 bankruptcy proceedings in 1987. Earnings in recent periods were penalized by slower product sales owing to general economic weakness and narrower margins. While a continuation of the difficult business climate, particularly in Europe, will restrain earnings through 1993, the introduction of new products should benefit results in 1994.

Current Outlook

A $0.10 a share loss is estimated for 1993, versus the $0.37 profit recorded in 1992. Earnings for 1994 are projected at $2.00.

Payment of cash dividends is not expected.

Revenue growth should be sluggish in the second half of 1993, owing to weak economic conditions in Europe and ongoing competitive price pressures. Margins are expected to narrow, despite expense controls, on weak volume, new product launch costs and acquisition related expenses. The company plans to introduce several major new products in the second half of 1993, including the much anticipated Iceberg data storage subsystem (expected late in the year), as well as line extensions to its current mainstay of tape libraries, which should benefit results in 1994.

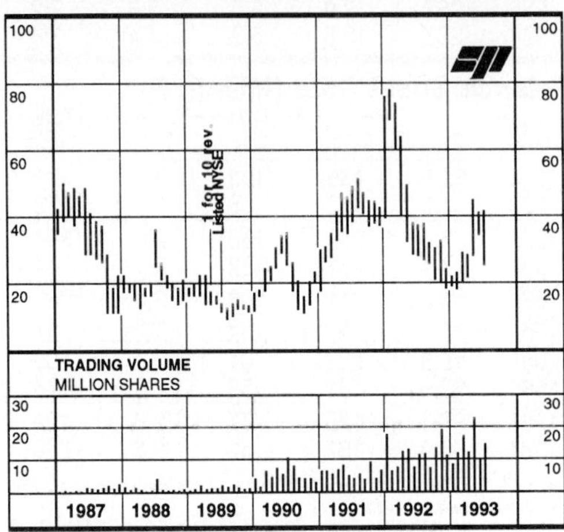

Total Revenues (Million $)

Quarter:	1993	1992	1991	1990
Mar.	333	334	361	260
Jun.	335	386	360	276
Sep.		387	387	265
Dec.		414	476	339
		1,521	1,585	1,141

Revenues for the six months ended June 25, 1993, fell 4.4%, year to year, as an 11% decline in product sales outweighed a 10% gain in service and rentals. Sales of automated tape library products slowed on global economic weakness, particularly in Europe. Margins narrowed on the lower volume, a less favorable product mix, and competitive pricing pressures, despite well controlled expenses; pretax income declined 55%. After taxes at 32.0%, versus 24.5%, net income was down 60%. After preferred dividends, per share earnings were $0.09 versus $0.45. Results in the 1993 interim exclude a $40,000,000 ($0.95 a share) gain from the cumulative effect of an accounting change.

Common Share Earnings ($)

Quarter:	1993	1992	1991	1990
Mar.	0.14	0.30	0.36	0.34
Jun.	d0.04	0.16	0.47	0.47
Sep.	Ed0.30	0.10	0.59	0.36
Dec.	E0.10	d0.18	0.88	1.00
	Ed0.10	0.37	[1]2.33	[1]2.22

Important Developments

Jul. '93— The company acquired Sceptre Corp., a supplier of software to manage cartridge-tape information storage in open-systems computing environments, for an undisclosed amount. In May, STK executed a letter of intent to acquire Amperif Corp., a manufacturer of high-performance, random-access storage subsystems, for about 1.3 million common shares.

Next earnings report expected in mid-October.

Per Share Data ($)

Yr. End Dec. 31	[2]1992	[2]1991	1990	[2]1989	1988	1987	1986	[3]1985	1984	1983
Tangible Bk. Val.	**[5]22.25**	[5]21.80	[5]16.14	[5]13.12	12.46	10.23	d5.20	d15.69	0.81	NM
Cash Flow	**3.58**	5.05	4.78	4.39	4.59	3.29	21.90	7.79	d115.07	23.50
Earnings[4]	**0.37**	2.33	2.22	1.40	1.90	0.80	4.80	d12.60	d146.20	d2.80
Dividends	**Nil**	Nil	Nil	Nil	Nil	Nil	Nil	Nil	Nil	Nil
Payout Ratio	**Nil**	Nil	Nil	Nil	Nil	Nil	Nil	Nil	Nil	Nil
Prices—High	**78**	51½	35¼	22½	36¼	50	73¾	38¾	146¼	250
Low	**18⅜**	17¾	11	9¼	12½	11¼	17½	10	20	135
P/E Ratio—	**NM**	22–8	16–5	16–7	19–7	63–14	15–4	NM	NM	NM

Data as orig. reptd. Adj. for a 1-for-10 reverse stk split May 1989. **1.** Does not add due to change in no. of shs. **2.** Reflects merger or acquisition. **3.** Reflects acctg. change. **4.** Bef. results of disc. opers. of +0.49 in 1987, -9.22 in 1983, bef. spec. item(s) of -0.04 in 1990, +0.43 in 1989, -0.18 in 1987, +5.54 in 1986, -3.96 in 1985. **5.** Includes intangibles. d-Deficit. E-Estimated NM-Not Meaningful.

Income Data (Million $)

Year Ended Dec. 31	Revs.	Oper. Inc.	% Oper. Inc. of Revs.	Cap. Exp.	Depr.	Int. Exp.	[4]Net Bef. Taxes	Eff. Tax Rate	[5]Net Inc.	% Net Inc. of Revs.	Cash Flow
1992	**1,521**	**150**	**9.8**	**105**	**135**	**47.6**	**34**	**54.6%**	**15**	**1.0**	**150**
[1]1991	1,585	198	12.5	111	109	51.4	106	12.0%	93	5.9	202
1990	1,141	162	14.2	141	81	41.2	76	6.5%	71	6.2	152
[1]1989	983	134	13.7	240	78	49.4	39	5.4%	36	3.7	114
1988	874	119	13.6	209	63	49.1	41	NM	44	5.1	107
1987	750	91	12.1	160	57	40.0	25	22.8%	19	2.5	76
1986	696	64	9.2	110	60	6.3	35	51.3%	17	2.4	76
[2]1985	673	12	1.8	70	71	7.2	d39	NM	d44	NM	27
1984	809	d107	NM	142	108	65.0	d532	NM	d505	NM	d398
[3]1983	887	77	8.7	105	90	55.6	d32	NM	d9	NM	80

Balance Sheet Data (Million $)

Dec. 31	Cash	Curr. Assets	Curr. Liab.	Curr. Ratio	Total Assets	% Ret. on Assets	Long Term Debt	Common Equity	Total Cap.	% LT Debt of Cap.	% Ret. on Equity
1992	**118**	**768**	**413**	**1.9**	**1,710**	**0.9**	**370**	**919**	**1,297**	**28.5**	**1.7**
1991	175	866	439	2.0	1,700	6.2	372	884	1,261	29.5	12.1
1990	64	515	300	1.7	1,048	6.1	216	530	748	28.9	14.7
1989	61	478	276	1.7	977	3.8	360	337	698	51.5	11.1
1988	127	430	204	2.1	847	5.4	345	284	631	54.7	17.1
1987	78	378	195	1.9	786	0.6	334	233	577	58.0	33.1
1986	244	509	216	2.4	880	1.9	9	d18	d4	NM	NM
1985	230	487	202	2.4	919	NM	18	d54	d34	NM	NM
1984	79	476	170	2.8	973	NM	13	3	19	70.6	NM
1983	8	623	271	2.3	1,266	NM	412	503	995	41.4	NM

Data as orig. reptd. **1.** Reflects merg. or acq. **2.** Reflects acctg. change. **3.** Excl. disc. opers. **4.** Incl. equity in earns. of nonconsol. subs. prior to 1987. **5.** Bef. results of disc. opers. and spec. items. d-Deficit. NM-Not Meaningful.

Business Summary

Storage Technology is a supplier of high performance computer information storage and retrieval subsystems, primarily for use with mainframe and midrange computer systems as well as for computer networks. On July 28, 1987, the company emerged from Chapter 11 of the Federal Bankruptcy Code. Revenue in recent years:

	1992	1991	1990
Serial Access Sub.......	62%	57%	48%
Random Access Sub ...	11%	12%	12%
Midrange Systems	21%	25%	32%
Printer & Other...........	6%	6%	8%

International revenue accounted for 41% of total revenue in 1992, compared to 39% in 1991 and 33% in 1990.

Serial Access (or tape) subsystems include the 4400 Automatic Cartridge System (ACS) library which automates the process of locating, transporting and mounting storage tapes in STK's 18-track cartridge drive products. Initially designed for mainframes, STK has introduced software and hardware which permit connectivity with other computer environments. Through 1992 year-end, over 5,000 ACS libraries had been shipped. STK plans to ship several major ACS upgrade and enhancement products in 1993.

Random Access Subsystems include high-performance solid-state memory devices such as the 4080, which uses semiconductor memory and emulates a disk drive, but provides very rapid access to stored information. In anticipation of STK's Iceberg 9200 Disk Array Subsystem, expected by late 1993, the company discontinued its 8380 family of rotating, magnetic disk subsystems in late 1992.

Through its Datacomp subsidiary (acquired in November 1991) STK serves the IBM midrange market through the distribution of used equipment; sale of the company's own new peripheral equipment; and a comprehensive array of hardware and software support services.

STK offers high speed, impact printers and non-impact printers. STK also offers software enhancement products for data management and access.

Dividend Data

No cash dividends have ever been paid. A 1-for-10 reverse split was effected in May, 1989. A "poison pill" stock purchase right was renewed in 1990.

Capitalization

Long Term Debt: $348,936,000 (6/93), incl. $115.3 million of nonrecourse borrowings.

$3.50 Conv. Exch. Preferred Stock: 3,450,000 shares (liquid. pref. $50).

Common Stock: 41,333,199 shs. ($0.10 par). Institutions hold about 54%. Shareholders of record: 25,430.

Office—2270 South 88th St., Louisville, CO 80028-4309. **Tel**—(303) 673-5151. **Chrmn & Pres**—R. R. Poppa. **VP-Fin & Treas**—R. J. Luth. **Investor Contact**—Michael Klatman. **Dirs**—J. E. N. Albino, W. L. Armstrong, R. A. Burgin, P. Friedman, S. J. Keane, R. E. LaBlanc, R. E. Lee, R. R. Poppa, H. Shull, R. C. Steadman, R. C. Wilson. **Transfer Agent**—American Stock Transfer, NYC. **Incorporated** in Delaware in 1969. **Empl**—10,100.

 Peter C. Wood, CFA

Stratus Computer

NYSE Symbol SRA Options on Pacific (Jan-Apr-Jul-Oct) In S&P MidCap 400

Price	Range	P-E Ratio	Dividend	Yield	S&P Ranking	Beta
Oct. 13'93	1993					
26⅝	41¼–20¼	12	None	None	B+	2.00

Summary

The fault-tolerant computer systems made by this company are designed to provide continuous, normal operations despite the failure of hardware components. Sales to IBM accounted for 13% of product revenues in 1992. Earnings for the second half of 1993 will be penalized by intense competition and the slow global economy.

Current Outlook

Earnings for 1993 are projected at $2.15 a share, down from 1992's $2.43. Earnings of $2.60 are estimated for 1994.

Initiation of cash dividends is not expected.

Earnings for 1993 are expected to decline, due to increasing competition in the fault-tolerant marketplace as well as continued economic sluggishness. SRA will face greater competition from market-leader Tandem, as well as general-purpose computer firms that keep adding fault-tolerance features to their offerings. Management has responded by introducing lower priced products and cutting costs. SRA is also attempting to diversify into other sectors of the computer industry: in September the company agreed to buy Shared Financial Systems, a software and services firm, for $15 million. In addition, the company is becoming less reliant on IBM's resale of SRA systems and such sales accounted for 3.4% of the total during the first half of 1993.

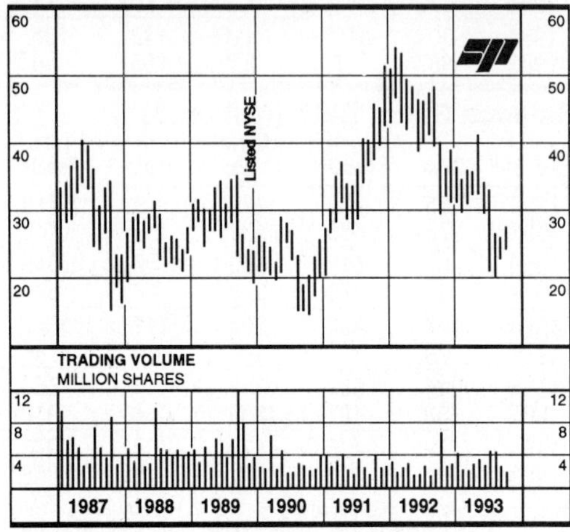

Revenues (Million $)

13 Weeks:	1993	1992	1991	1990
Mar.	114.6	110.2	101.0	87.1
Jun.	124.1	117.4	107.1	94.1
Sep.	---	123.8	112.5	104.1
Dec.	---	134.9	128.0	118.5
	---	486.3	448.6	403.9

Revenues for the six months ended July 4, 1993, advanced 4.9%, year to year, as product revenue rose 0.6% and service revenue increased 22%. Gross margins narrowed on the lower product volume and operating costs rose 3.3%. Following 46% higher other income, pretax income fell 10%. After taxes at 21.0% in both periods, net income was also down 10%, to $0.94 a share from $1.06.

Common Share Earnings ($)

13 Weeks:	1993	1992	1991	1990
Mar.	0.37	0.49	0.35	0.32
Jun.	0.57	0.58	0.47	0.34
Sep.	E0.43	0.63	0.61	0.47
Dec.	E0.78	0.73	0.79	0.64
	E2.15	2.43	2.22	1.77

Important Developments

Oct. '93— SRA signed a definitive agreement to acquire Atlanta-based BellSouth Systems Integration Inc., a unit of BellSouth Business Systems, for $15 million. Separately, SRA said it will eliminate 80 engineering and manufacturing positions in a move to cut costs. The company also expects to eliminate a similar number of jobs in other departments by the end of 1993. These actions will result in a one-time charge of some $3.5 million for the third quarter.

Next earnings report expected in late October.

Per Share Data ($)

Yr. End Dec. 31	1992	1991	1990	1989	1988	1987	1986	1985	1984	1983
Tangible Bk. Val.	**17.03**	14.18	11.15	9.12	7.08	5.34	4.05	3.24	2.73	2.42
Cash Flow	**3.78**	3.51	2.72	2.52	1.97	1.37	0.98	0.60	0.30	0.14
Earnings[1]	**2.43**	2.22	1.77	1.71	1.45	0.97	0.70	0.45	0.22	0.10
Dividends	**Nil**	Nil	Nil	Nil	Nil	Nil	Nil	Nil	Nil	Nil
Payout Ratio	**Nil**	Nil	Nil	Nil	Nil	Nil	Nil	Nil	Nil	Nil
Prices—High	**54¼**	51½	29	35¼	31½	40½	24¾	26	13¾	16¾
Low	**29½**	20⅜	14⅝	19¼	19½	15¼	17¼	9	7¾	9¾
P/E Ratio—	**22-12**	23-9	16-8	21-11	22-13	42-16	35-25	58-20	63-35	NM

Data as orig. reptd. Adj. for stk. divs. of 100% Jul. 1983, 100% Dec. 1982. **1.** Bef. spec. items of +0.06 in 1984, +0.03 in 1983. E-Estimated NM-Not Meaningful.

Income Data (Million $)

Year Ended Dec. 31	Revs.	Oper. Inc.	% Oper. Inc. of Revs.	[1]Cap. Exp.	Depr.	Int. Exp.	Net Bef. Taxes	Eff. Tax Rate	[2]Net Inc.	% Net Inc. of Revs.	Cash Flow
1992	**486**	**100**	**20.6**	**60.8**	**31.8**	**1.00**	**72.1**	**21.0%**	**56.9**	**11.7**	**88.7**
1991	449	91	20.3	31.5	28.9	1.86	65.4	24.0%	49.7	11.1	78.6
1990	404	71	17.6	27.4	19.9	NA	51.4	28.0%	37.0	9.2	56.9
1989	341	71	20.7	37.0	16.9	NA	55.3	36.0%	35.4	10.4	52.3
1988	265	56	21.0	17.8	10.5	NA	45.8	36.0%	29.3	11.1	39.9
1987	184	39	21.1	13.8	8.1	NA	31.6	38.7%	19.4	10.5	27.5
1986	125	28	22.2	15.6	5.5	Nil	23.5	42.5%	13.5	10.9	19.0
1985	80	15	19.1	9.1	2.9	Nil	14.7	41.5%	8.6	10.7	11.5
1984	42	6	13.4	5.1	1.4	NA	7.0	39.8%	4.2	10.0	5.6
1983	21	2	8.4	2.4	0.7	0.02	2.2	23.2%	1.7	8.3	2.4

Balance Sheet Data (Million $)

Dec. 31	Cash	Curr. Assets	Curr. Liab.	Curr. Ratio	Total Assets	% Ret. on Assets	Long Term Debt	Common Equity	Total Cap.	% LT Debt of Cap.	% Ret. on Equity
1992	**135**	**351**	**73.6**	**4.8**	**467**	**13.2**	**0.5**	**390**	**390**	**0.1**	**16.0**
1991	98	306	64.1	4.8	385	13.6	2.6	314	317	0.8	17.7
1990	43	242	71.9	3.4	321	12.3	14.3	230	245	5.8	17.7
1989	32	197	60.7	3.2	274	14.8	29.4	184	213	13.8	21.7
1988	28	152	50.6	3.0	200	16.8	10.2	139	149	6.8	24.1
1987	32	114	36.9	3.1	145	15.2	6.2	102	109	5.7	21.6
1986	23	83	25.8	3.2	107	14.2	5.7	76	81	7.0	19.8
1985	30	69	20.2	3.4	82	12.1	2.6	59	62	4.2	15.7
1984	28	53	9.0	5.9	60	7.9	1.5	49	51	2.9	9.0
1983	32	44	3.0	14.6	47	7.5	0.3	43	44	0.6	8.6

Data as orig. reptd. **1.** Net of curr. yr. retirement and disposals prior to 1988. **2.** Bef. spec. items in 1984. 1983. NA-Not Available.

Business Summary

Stratus Computer manufactures fault-tolerant computer systems designed for normal and continuous operation despite failure of hardware or software components. International revenues represented 44% of total revenues in 1992, unchanged from 1991. Sales to IBM, which resells Stratus systems under the IBM label as System 88, accounted for 13%, down from 23% in 1991.

Stratus systems are used primarily for on-line transaction processing (OLTP) and other interactive applications where data integrity, system availability and rapid, high-volume processing are critical, such as in securities quotation and trading, stock exchange control, electronic funds transfer, automated teller machines, retail point-of-sale and distribution, plant management control, hotel reservations and communications switching.

The company's proprietary architecture uses comparative circuitry, duplication of inexpensive off-the-shelf microprocessors and the proprietary Virtual Operating System (VOS) designed specifically for OLTP or Stratus FTX, the company's UNIX System V.4-based operating system. The multiprocessor architecture allows the system to handle heavy transaction loads efficiently with multiple users accessing data simultaneously. To increase capacity, users can add more processors without rewriting software.

The Stratus XA/R Continuous Processing System product line, based on the Intel i860 RISC microprocessor, was rolled out in 1992. Offering up to two and one-half times the performance of Stratus' previous XA2000 generation of systems, the XA/R line is the only continuous availability line that runs both proprietary and industry-standard operating systems.

A Stratus Continuous Processing System consists of up to 32 processing modules (containing as many as 192 processors) connected via StrataLINK, a high-speed communications link. Through StrataNET, thousands of modules can be linked in a wide area network.

Stratus systems can identify and isolate their own failures and automatically dial in to a customer assistance center to report interruptions and order replacement parts.

At 1992 year-end, the company had an installed base of 6,213 systems, up from 5,257 systems a year earlier.

Dividend Data

Stratus has never paid cash dividends. A "poison pill" stock purchase right was adopted in 1990.

Capitalization

Long Term Debt: $423,000 (6/93).

Common Stock: 23,368,162 shs. ($0.01 par).
Officers and directors own about 4%.
Institutions hold some 90%.
Shareholders of record: 1,959 (2/93).

Office—55 Fairbanks Blvd., Marlborough, MA 01752. **Tel**—(508) 460-2000. **Pres & CEO**—W. E. Foster. **VP-CFO**—R. E. Donahue. **Clerk**—F. S. Prifty. **Treas & Investor Contact**—Michael McConnell. **Dirs**—A. V. d'Arbeloff, A. Carr, P. J. Ferri, W. E. Foster, G. C. Hendrie, R. M. Morrill. **Transfer Agent**—First National Bank of Boston, Boston, Mass. **Incorporated** in Massachusetts in 1980. **Empl**—2,622.

 Neeraj K. Vohra

Structural Dynamics Research

NASDAQ Symbol SDRC (Incl. in Nat'l Market) In S&P MidCap 400

Price	Range	P-E Ratio	Dividend	Yield	S&P Ranking	Beta
Aug. 26'93	1993					
20¼	21⅝–9⅝	53	None	None	NR	1.84

Summary

This company is a leading supplier of mechanical design automation software and engineering services used by automotive, aerospace and industrial manufacturers for the design, analysis, testing and manufacturing of sophisticated mechanical products. Earnings have declined in recent periods, on lower than expected sales, higher R&D spending, and unfavorable foreign currency swings, however, the release of a new version of SDRC's flagship I-DEAS software product should aid sales and earnings through 1994.

Current Outlook

Earnings for 1994 are projected at $0.85 a share versus the $0.65 estimated for 1993 and compared to the $0.48 recorded in 1992.

Initiation of cash dividends is not expected.

Revenues are expected to advance through 1994, spurred by the newest release of the company's flagship I-DEAS mechanical design automation software product. Margins should be aided by the higher volume, despite continued marketing programs, as the company's sales force is largely in place. The demand for mechanical design related products is associated with general business conditions, thus, results would be aided by improving economies in such key markets as Germany in Europe and Japan in the Far East.

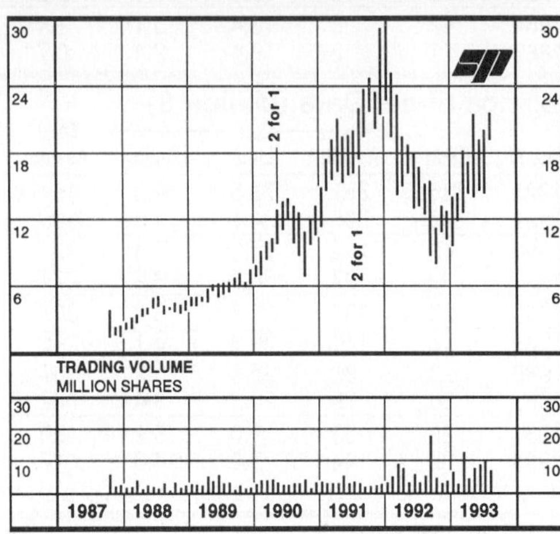

Revenues (Million $)

Quarter:	1993	1992	1991	1990
Mar.	39.1	38.0	31.9	25.2
Jun.	49.6	42.4	36.3	28.6
Sep.		37.7	36.9	29.9
Dec.		45.5	41.2	34.9
		163.6	146.3	118.6

Revenues in the six months ended June 30, 1993, rose 10%, year to year, as a 13% gain for software products and services outweighed a 4.6% drop in engineering services, as declines in certain industrial markets resulted from general market-related and economic weakness in the U.S., Japan and certain European countries. Profitability was hurt by sluggish first quarter volume in anticipation of the new release of the I-DEAS Master Series, and with 22% higher R&D expense, pretax earnings fell 25%. After taxes at 35.6%, versus 32.8%, net income declined 28%, to $6,994,000 ($0.23 a share), from $9,761,000 ($0.33).

Common Share Earnings ($)

Quarter:	1993	1992	1991	1990
Mar.	0.10	0.16	0.12	0.09
Jun.	0.14	0.17	0.15	0.11
Sep.	E0.18	0.10	0.16	0.12
Dec.	E0.23	0.07	0.20	0.16
	E0.65	0.48	0.63	0.49

Important Developments

Jul. '93— SDRC said that despite uncertain economic conditions it expected the pace of business in the second half of 1993 to improve over the year-earlier period.

Jun. '93— The company began shipping a new release of its flagship I-DEAS mechanical design automation software product, the I-DEAS Master Series, which offers ease-of-use and enhanced functionality.

Next earnings report expected in mid-October.

Per Share Data ($)

Yr. End Dec. 31	1992	1991	1990	1989	1988	1987	1986	1985	1984
Tangible Bk. Val.	**4.19**	3.59	2.67	2.11	1.69	1.42	0.90	0.79	0.71
Cash Flow	**0.71**	0.87	0.70	0.57	0.42	0.42	0.31	NA	NA
Earnings[1,2]	**0.48**	0.63	0.49	0.37	0.24	0.18	0.10	0.08	0.11
Dividends	**Nil**	Nil	Nil	Nil	Nil	Nil	Nil	Nil	Nil
Payout Ratio	**Nil**	Nil	Nil	Nil	Nil	Nil	Nil	Nil	Nil
Prices—High	**30**	29¼	13⅞	7½	5⅛	3¹³⁄₁₆	NA	NA	NA
Low	**8**	11⅜	6⅞	4¼	2⅛	1⅜	NA	NA	NA
P/E Ratio—	**63–17**	46–18	29–14	20–11	22–9	22–8	NA	NA	NA

Data as orig. reptd. Adj. for stk. divs. of 100% Aug. 1991, 100% May 1990. **1.** Bef. spec. item(s) of +0.04 in 1984. **2.** Ful. dil.: 0.60 in 1991, 0.48 in 1990, 0.37 in 1989, 0.23 in 1988. E-Estimated NA-Not Available.

Income Data (Million $)

Year Ended Dec. 31	Revs.	Oper. Inc.	% Oper. Inc. of Revs.	Cap. Exp.	Depr.	Int. Exp.	Net Bef. Taxes	Eff. Tax Rate	[2]Net Inc.	% Net Inc. of Revs.	Cash Flow
1992	**164**	**26.2**	**16.0**	**9.1**	**6.92**	**Nil**	**[1]21.4**	**32.3%**	**14.5**	**8.9**	**21.4**
1991	146	32.0	21.9	11.3	6.89	0.10	[1]27.8	35.6%	17.9	12.2	24.8
1990	119	24.1	20.3	7.0	5.94	0.29	[1]20.7	36.0%	13.3	11.2	19.2
1989	94	17.2	18.4	6.8	5.24	0.30	[1]15.2	35.6%	9.8	10.4	15.0
1988	75	12.7	16.9	4.8	4.68	0.40	9.2	35.6%	5.9	7.9	10.6
1987	61	11.5	18.7	5.0	5.11	0.51	6.4	44.3%	3.6	5.9	8.7
1986	52	7.7	15.0	5.7	3.86	0.54	3.3	43.9%	1.9	3.6	5.7
1985	40	4.6	11.4	3.7	2.25	0.52	1.8	16.4%	1.5	3.8	NA
1984	36	6.4	17.6	2.9	1.75	0.56	4.1	51.2%	2.0	5.5	NA

Balance Sheet Data (Million $)

Dec. 31	Cash	Curr. Assets	Curr. Liab.	Curr. Ratio	Total Assets	% Ret. on Assets	Long Term Debt	Common Equity	Total Cap.	% LT Debt of Cap.	% Ret. on Equity
1992	**53.8**	**114.0**	**37.2**	**3.1**	**158**	**9.7**	**Nil**	**118.0**	**121**	**Nil**	**13.3**
1991	47.8	98.8	32.5	3.0	134	14.5	Nil	97.1	102	Nil	21.2
1990	43.2	79.0	29.5	2.7	107	13.6	2.60	68.4	77	3.4	21.7
1989	36.0	61.8	25.2	2.5	86	12.5	2.75	52.5	61	4.5	20.7
1988	24.2	46.4	18.9	2.5	68	9.2	2.82	41.0	49	5.7	15.7
1987	23.2	38.6	17.0	2.3	59	6.5	3.13	33.7	42	7.4	13.0
1986	5.3	19.7	14.5	1.4	40	5.0	3.86	16.8	25	15.2	11.9
1985	2.4	16.2	10.5	1.5	35	4.5	4.20	14.6	24	17.3	10.9
1984	NA	NA	NA	NA	31	6.8	4.63	12.9	17	26.5	17.4

Data as orig. reptd. **1.** Incl. equity in earns. of nonconsol. subs. **2.** Bef. spec. item. NA-Not Available.

Business Summary

Structural Dynamics Research Corporation (SDRC) is a leading international supplier of mechanical design automation software and engineering services used by automotive, aerospace and industrial manufacturers for the design, analysis, testing and manufacturing of sophisticated mechanical products. The company's software and services are intended to reduce product development time and costs, and to improve product quality by enabling customers to optmize product designs prior to production.

Revenues and operating profit in 1992 were derived as follows:

	Revs.	Profit
Software products & services	82%	100%
Engineering services	18%	Nil

In 1992, foreign sales (in Europe and the Far East) accounted for 67% of revenues and 83% of operating profit, compared with 62% and 84%, respectively, in 1991.

I-DEAS, SDRC's mechanical design automation software system, provides design engineers with solid modeling, finite-element modeling and analysis, computer-aided testing, drafting and manufacturing. The I-DEAS system, which allows all members of a product development team to evaluate multiple designs and manufacturing processes before final production, is available on leading engineering workstations, minicomputers and mainframes.

Software products are sold to end-users primarily through a direct sales force. The company also markets its products by means of original equipment manufacturers, distributors, value added resellers and hardware suppliers

SDRC's engineering services division provides mechanical engineering consulting services to improve the design of its customers' products, as well as its customers' engineering and manufacturing processes. The company also offers its clients advanced training and technology transfer. Engineering services are offered in the areas of design audits, product design, engineering process development and troubleshooting.

Dividend Data

No cash dividends have been paid. A "poison pill" stock purchase right was adopted in 1988.

Finances

At December 31, 1992, SDRC's principal sources of liquidity were $53.8 million of cash and equivalents and an unsecured and unused $10 million bank line of credit.

Capitalization

Long Term Debt: None (6/93).

Common Stock: 28,415,358 shs. ($0.0069 stated value).
Directors and officers control 9.7%.
Institutions hold 70%.
Shareholders of record: About 14,700 (12/92).

Office—2000 Eastman Dr., Milford, OH 45150. **Tel**—(513) 576-2400. **Chrmn, Pres & CEO**—R. J. Friedsam. **SVP-Fin, CFO & Treas**—R. H. Hoffman. **VP & Secy**—J. A. Mongelluzzo. **Investor Contact**—Jere Hunter. **Dirs**—W. P. Conlin, R. J. Friedsam, R. P. Henderson, T. H. McCourtney, Jr., J. E. McDowell, A. F. Peter, G. R. Whitaker, Jr. **Transfer Agent**—Fifth Third Bank, Cincinnati. **Empl**—1,130.

 Peter C. Wood, CFA

Stryker Corporation

NASDAQ Symbol STRY (Incl. in Nat'l Market) Options on Phila In S&P MidCap 400

Price	Range	P–E Ratio	Dividend	Yield	S&P Ranking	Beta
Jul. 22'93	1993					
25½	39¾–21	23	[1]0.06	[1]0.2%	A–	1.60

Summary

This company develops, manufactures and sells specialty surgical and medical products, including powered surgical instruments, orthopedic implants, endoscopic systems and patient-handling equipment. A subsidiary operates 44 outpatient physical therapy clinics. In 1992, Stryker continued to exceed its goal of 20% annual earnings growth, with earnings up 44%; profits advanced 29% in the first half of 1993.

Business Summary

Stryker Corporation develops, manufactures and markets specialty surgical and medical products, including endoscopic systems, otrhopaedic implants, powered surgical instruments, and patient-handling equipment. Sales contributions by product segment in recent years were:

	1992	1991	1990	1989
Surgical	83%	83%	82%	81%
Medical	17%	17%	18%	19%

The company's products are sold in more than 100 countries, with international sales accounting for about 31% of total revenues and 14% of operating profits in each of 1992 and 1991.

In the area of surgical products, Stryker's principal specialty is orthopaedics. Artificial joint replacements, medical video cameras, arthroscopes, heavy-duty powered instruments, and pulsating irrigation systems are manufactured and marketed for use by the orthopaedic surgeon. The company specializes in the design and production of innovative total and partial hip and knee replacements.

The company's broad line of drills, saws, fixation and reaming equipment and other powered surgical instruments is used primarily by orthopedic surgeons for varied procedures; its small "micro" powered tools are used in oral and maxillofacial surgery, otology, neurosurgery and podiatry. Endoscopic systems, used in less-invasive surgery such as arthroscopy and laparoscopy, include miniature video cameras, a light source, endoscopes, powered and manual instruments.

Other operating room products include the CBC-Constavac system, a post-operative wound drainage and blood repurfusion device that enables joint replacement patients to receive their own blood rather than donor blood; the Haemocell system (FDA marketing approval was received in late 1992), an intraoperative blood filtration system to recover and reinfuse patient blood lost during surgery; and the High Vacuum Cement Injection System, used to mix and inject cement for implant applications.

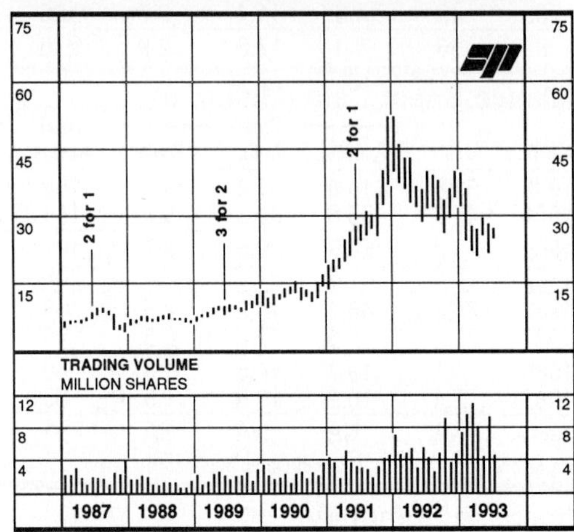

The Medical product line consists primarily of patient-handling equipment, mainly specialty stretcher-beds used in hospital departments, including emergency, recovery, intensive-care, surgery and birthing rooms. Beds can be customized to incorporate features such as hydraulic jacks, removable top sections, built-in scales and on-board x-ray equipment. Through wholly owned Physiotherapy Associates Inc., Stryker operates 44 physical therapy clinics in nine states.

During 1992, the Stryker Biotech unit began human clinical trials of the Osteogenic Protein Device (developed by Creative BioMolecules Inc. as part of a long-term research program funded by Stryker since 1985). In preclinical studies, the Device induced the formation of new bone when implanted into bone defect sites.

Next earnings report expected in mid-October.

Per Share Data ($)

Yr. End Dec. 31	1992	1991	1990	1989	1988	1987	1986	1985	1984	1983
Tangible Bk. Val.	**4.61**	3.69	3.25	2.30	1.84	1.48	1.22	1.06	0.86	0.70
Cash Flow	**1.24**	0.94	0.65	0.54	0.47	0.39	0.31	0.26	0.20	0.17
Earnings[2]	**1.00**	0.70	0.50	0.41	0.34	0.27	0.23	0.19	0.16	0.13
Dividends	**0.06**	0.05	Nil	Nil	Nil	Nil	Nil	Nil	Nil	Nil
Payout Ratio	**6%**	7%	Nil	Nil	Nil	Nil	Nil	Nil	Nil	Nil
Prices—High	**52¼**	52¼	16⅞	12½	8¼	9⅝	7⅜	4⅛	3⅜	4⅜
Low	**26¼**	13¾	9⅝	6½	5⅞	4¼	3⅞	2¾	2⅛	2⅜
P/E Ratio—	**52–26**	75–20	34–19	30–16	24–17	35–15	33–17	22–14	22–13	34–19

Data as orig. reptd. Adj. for stk. divs. of 100% Jun. 1991, 50% Jun. 1989, 100% Jun. 1987, 50% Aug. 1985. **1.** See Dividend Data. **2.** Bef. spec. item(s) of +0.21 in 1990.

Income Data (Million $)

Year Ended Dec. 31	Revs.	Oper. Inc.	% Oper. Inc. of Revs.	Cap. Exp.	Depr.	Int. Exp.	[2]Net Bef. Taxes	Eff. Tax Rate	[3]Net Inc.	% Net Inc. of Revs.	Cash Flow
1992	**477**	**85.1**	**17.8**	**31.6**	**11.4**	**0.41**	**76.9**	**38.0%**	**47.7**	**10.0**	**59.1**
1991	365	63.4	17.4	16.6	11.8	0.66	53.3	38.0%	33.1	9.1	44.9
1990	281	42.8	15.3	11.9	7.1	0.51	38.1	38.0%	23.6	8.4	30.7
1989	226	37.9	16.8	7.1	6.3	0.69	31.0	38.0%	19.2	8.5	25.5
1988	179	32.4	18.1	8.0	6.0	0.59	26.0	39.0%	15.9	8.9	21.9
1987	148	27.4	18.5	[1]4.1	5.4	0.46	22.0	42.2%	12.7	8.6	18.1
1986	121	22.1	18.3	[1]5.3	3.8	0.38	18.5	45.5%	10.1	8.3	13.9
1985	102	17.5	17.3	[1]6.8	3.0	0.33	15.1	44.5%	8.4	8.3	11.4
1984	84	13.7	16.3	[1]4.5	1.9	0.05	12.6	45.0%	6.9	8.2	8.9
1983	70	11.2	15.9	[1]2.3	1.6	0.05	10.3	44.2%	5.8	8.2	7.4

Balance Sheet Data (Million $)

Dec. 31	Cash	Curr. Assets	Curr. Liab.	Curr. Ratio	Total Assets	% Ret. on Assets	Long Term Debt	Common Equity	Total Cap.	% LT Debt of Cap.	% Ret. on Equity
1992	**91.8**	**270**	**101**	**2.7**	**340**	**15.5**	**1.43**	**232**	**234**	**0.6**	**23.0**
1991	80.0	229	88	2.6	270	13.8	1.40	180	182	0.8	20.2
1990	54.1	176	58	3.0	210	13.0	1.90	148	152	1.3	18.2
1989	19.3	125	36	3.5	152	13.8	2.66	112	117	2.3	18.9
1988	4.6	99	29	3.4	125	13.8	3.12	91	96	3.2	19.1
1987	6.0	81	25	3.3	105	13.1	3.70	75	80	4.6	18.6
1986	8.4	64	21	3.1	86	12.8	3.95	60	65	6.1	18.6
1985	12.1	54	17	3.2	71	13.2	4.24	49	54	7.9	19.0
1984	11.0	43	12	3.5	57	13.9	3.64	40	44	8.2	19.2
1983	10.4	33	10	3.3	43	14.8	0.05	32	33	0.1	19.5

Data as orig. reptd. **1.** Net. **2.** Incl. equity in earns. of nonconsol. subs. **3.** Bef. spec. items.

Net Sales (Million $)

Quarter:	1993	1992	1991	1990
Mar.	135	113	86	68
Jun.	140	117	89	68
Sep.		117	90	68
Dec.		130	101	78
		477	365	281

Sales in the six months ended June 30, 1993, advanced 20%, year to year, as surgical product sales gained 18% and sales of medical products soared 32%. Results benefited from the greater volume, and net income climbed 29%, to $28,450,000 ($0.59 a share), from $22,080,000 ($0.46).

Common Share Earnings ($)

Quarter:	1993	1992	1991	1990
Mar.	0.30	0.23	0.16	0.14
Jun.	0.29	0.23	0.16	0.12
Sep.		0.23	0.16	0.12
Dec.		0.31	0.22	0.13
		1.00	0.70	0.50

Dividend Data

A year-end dividend of $0.06 a share was paid January 29, 1993.

Finances

R&D spending totaled $32,313,000 (6.8% of sales) in 1992, up from $23,703,000 (6.5%) in 1991. Expenses in 1992 and 1991 reflected development of new product designs (the Series 7000 Total Knee System introduced in 1992); further applications of hydroxylapatite (HA) technology for arthroplasty; development of advanced powered instruments and video technology (SE4 Arthroscopy Power System in 1991, and the third generation 3-Chip and 1-Chip Camera Systems in 1992); development of patient care equipment (a warming stretcher for the recovery room in 1992, a general patient hospital bed scheduled for 1993); and preclinical trials for the Osteogenic Protein Device.

In 1992, Stryker entered into a worldwide licensing agreement with Haemocell plc to jointly develop and market the Haemocell system.

During 1991, the company's Osteonics subsidiary launched the Omniflex hip presthesis, the first hydroxylapatite (HA)-coated hip stem to be released in the U.S.

Capitalization

Long Term Debt: $2,213,000 (6/93).

Common Stock: 48,311,949 shs. ($0.10 par).
Officers and directors own 18%.
Institutions hold 67%.
Shareholders: 3,512 of record (12/92).

Office—P.O. Box 4085, Kalamazoo, MI 49003-4085. **Tel**—(616) 385-2600. **Chrmn, Pres & CEO**—J. W. Brown. **VP, Secy & CFO**—D. J. Simpson. **Treas, Contr & Asst Secy**—R. D. Monk. **Dirs**—J. W. Brown, H. E. Cox Jr., D. M. Engelman, J. H. Grossman, J. S. Lillard, W. U. Parfet, R. E. Stryker, G. Thomas. **Transfer Agent & Registrar**—First National Bank of Chicago. **Incorporated** in Michigan in 1946. **Empl**—2,906.

 Robert M. Gold

Sundstrand Corp.

NYSE Symbol SNS Options on NYSE & Pacific In S&P MidCap 400

Price	Range	P–E Ratio	Dividend	Yield	S&P Ranking	Beta
Aug. 25'93	1993					
41⅞	44¾–35	14	1.20	2.9%	B	1.47

Summary

Sundstrand is a major manufacturer of aircraft and aerospace components; transmissions and related products for use in construction and agricultural equipment; heavy-duty gears; and pumps and compressors used in fluid transfer. Sales of aerospace products in 1993 are under pressure from the weak market for commercial aircraft, but industrial sales should benefit from recovery in the economy. Earnings should improve in 1993 and 1994 through cost cutting and restructuring of operations.

Current Outlook

Earnings for 1993 are estimated at $3.20 a share, versus the $2.31 (including restructuring charges of $0.67) of 1992. For 1994, $3.55 is estimated.

Dividends should continue at the current $0.30 quarterly rate.

Sales for 1993 should decline slightly. Aerospace sales during the second half will continue to reflect weakness in original equipment and aftermarkets, as a result of airline postponements and cancellations, and the soft military market. Industrial sales reflect the slow expansion in the economy. Sundstrand expects persisting market weakness at least into early 1994. Margins in both segments should show improvement primarily as a result of continuing cost-reduction efforts.

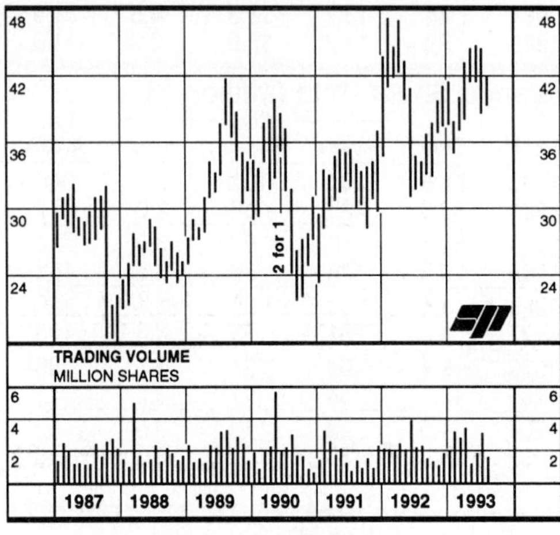

Net Sales (Million $)

Quarter:	1993	1992	1991	1990
Mar.	341	383	403	387
Jun.	342	413	407	390
Sep.	---	417	406	384
Dec.	---	460	454	439
	---	1,673	1,669	1,600

Sales from continuing operations (excluding Data Control) for the first six months of 1993 decreased 2.7%, year to year, reflecting softness in commercial aerospace markets. Margins improved as a result of restructuring measures, and income from continuing operations was up 189%, to $1.24 a share, from $0.42 (which included a restructuring charge of $0.57).

Common Share Earnings ($)

Quarter:	1993	1992	1991	1990
Mar.	0.70	0.50	0.66	0.74
Jun.	0.54	d0.01	0.24	0.59
Sep.	E0.70	0.73	0.76	0.90
Dec.	E1.26	1.09	1.36	0.94
	E3.20	2.31	3.02	3.15

Important Developments

Jul. '93— Sundstrand reached an agreement for the sale of the Data Control division to AlliedSignal for $195 million. In 1992, the division had sales of $194 million. The transaction, expected to be completed in September, should result in a nonrecurring gain.

Apr. '93— Total backlog on March 31, 1992, was $859 million, compared with $914 million at the end of 1992. Acquisition of Westinghouse ESD in May added $86 million to the year-end 1992 backlog.

Feb. '93— Sundstrand authorized the repurchase of up to 4,000,000 shares of its common stock.

Next earnings report expected in mid-October.

Per Share Data ($)

Yr. End Dec. 31	[1]1992	[1]1991	1990	1989	1988	1987	1986	[1]1985	[1]1984	[1]1983
Tangible Bk. Val.	**6.19**	13.03	13.76	12.63	10.30	13.01	12.73	12.51	12.63	[2]13.68
Cash Flow	**4.34**	4.90	5.19	5.43	0.99	3.04	3.26	3.77	3.38	2.62
Earnings[3]	**2.31**	3.02	3.15	3.09	d1.36	0.93	1.21	2.01	1.82	1.21
Dividends	**1.175**	1.10	1.10	0.90	0.90	0.90	0.90	0.90	0.90	0.90
Payout Ratio	**51%**	37%	34%	29%	NM	96%	74%	45%	50%	74%
Prices—High	**47¼**	37	39⅞	41¾	29	32¼	32⅛	27⅜	26	25⅞
Low	**31⅛**	23⅜	21¾	25⅛	21⅛	18	24⅝	20	17¼	19
P/E Ratio—	**20–13**	12–8	13–7	14–8	NM	35–19	27–20	14–10	14–9	21–16

Data as orig. reptd. Adj. for stk. div. of 100% Jun. 1990. **1.** Refl. merger or acq. **2.** Incl. intangibles. **3.** Bef. results of disc. ops. of -0.04 in 1990 & spec. items of -5.68 in 1992, -0.72 in 1988. d-Deficit. E-Estimated. NM-Not Meaningful.

Income Data (Million $)

Year Ended Dec. 31	Oper. Revs.	Oper. Inc.	% Oper. Inc. of Revs.	Cap. Exp.	Depr.	Int. Exp.	[3]Net Bef. Taxes	Eff. Tax Rate	[4]Net Inc.	% Net Inc. of Revs.	Cash Flow
[1]1992	**1,673**	**286**	**17.1**	**81**	**73.2**	**63**	**130**	**36.0%**	**[5]83**	**5.0**	**157**
[1]1991	1,669	299	17.9	72	67.7	78	174	37.5%	109	6.5	177
[2]1990	1,600	302	18.9	93	65.3	96	190	39.0%	116	7.2	181
1989	1,595	317	19.9	81	86.6	101	201	39.8%	121	7.6	201
1988	1,477	197	13.4	88	86.8	108	d80	NM	d50	NM	37
1987	1,365	201	14.7	119	79.1	70	56	37.8%	35	2.5	114
1986	1,434	223	15.6	119	76.7	56	66	31.6%	45	3.2	122
[1]1985	1,284	203	15.8	162	65.3	39	120	37.8%	74	5.8	140
[1]1984	1,042	172	16.5	121	57.3	25	112	40.5%	66	6.4	124
[1]1983	909	150	16.4	88	51.5	23	71	37.3%	44	4.9	96

Balance Sheet Data (Million $)

Dec. 31	Cash	Curr. Assets	Curr. Liab.	Curr. Ratio	Total Assets	% Ret. on Assets	Long Term Debt	Common Equity	Total Cap.	% LT Debt of Cap.	% Ret. on Equity
1992	**5.2**	**915**	**425**	**2.2**	**1,804**	**4.7**	**400**	**530**	**939**	**42.6**	**13.6**
1991	8.4	945	301	3.1	1,720	6.6	455	692	1,340	33.9	16.5
1990	5.9	897	326	2.7	1,582	7.6	370	625	1,189	31.1	19.6
1989	18.0	895	438	2.0	1,503	7.9	234	573	1,033	22.7	21.4
1988	36.7	851	512	1.7	1,567	NM	259	490	1,055	24.6	NM
1987	13.5	739	356	2.1	1,480	2.4	279	595	1,074	26.0	5.8
1986	16.3	669	255	2.6	1,399	3.3	297	605	1,082	27.4	7.6
1985	2.7	621	333	1.9	1,311	6.2	225	589	978	23.0	13.2
1984	6.7	536	257	2.1	1,090	6.6	161	536	833	19.4	12.8
1983	16.0	491	184	2.7	917	4.9	119	500	732	16.3	8.9

Data as orig. reptd.; finance subs. consol. after 1987. **1.** Refl. merger or acq. **2.** Excl. disc. ops. **3.** Incl. equity in earns. of nonconsol. subs. before 1990. **4.** Bef. spec. items. **5.** Refl. acctg. change. d-Deficit. NM-Not Meaningful.

Business Summary

Sundstrand is a major manufacturer of aircraft and aerospace components and industrial parts and equipment. Through Milton Roy Co. (acquired in January 1991), it produces precision pumps and analytical instruments. By product segment, sales and operating profits for 1992 were:

	Sales	Profits
Aerospace	62%	58%
Industrial	38%	42%

In 1992, exports of domestically manufactured products represented 26% and military sales (primarily to the U.S. Government) 22% of total sales.

The Aerospace group produces electrical, mechanical and hydraulic components used in commercial and military jets, including constant-speed drives and electric power regulators, actuation systems, fuel pumps and air valves, and other products used in engine starting, environmental control and navigation systems. A substantial portion of sales is to the aftermarket.

The Industrial group produces power transmissions and couplings for basic industries; pumps, compressors and blowers for processing industries; rotary-screw air and gas compressors for construction and general industry; and scientific instruments for chemical analysis and measurement.

Dividend Data

Dividends have been paid since 1940. A dividend reinvestment plan is available. A "poison pill" stock purchase right was adopted in 1986.

Amt. of Divd. $	Date Decl.	Ex-divd. Date	Stock of Record	Payment Date
0.30	Oct. 20	Nov. 24	Dec. 1	Dec. 15'92
0.30	Feb. 16	Feb. 24	Mar. 2	Mar. 16'93
0.30	Apr. 20	May 25	Jun. 1	Jun. 15'93
0.30	Jun. 15	Aug. 31	Sep. 7	Sep. 21'93

Capitalization

Long Term Debt: $399,100,000 (3/93).

Common Stock: 35,819,438 shs. ($0.50 par).
Institutions hold about 79%.
Shareholders of record: 4,300.

Office—4949 Harrison Ave., P.O. Box 7003, Rockford, IL 61125-7003. **Tel**—(815) 226-6000. **Chrmn & Pres**—H. C. Stonecipher. **Exec VP-CFO**—P. Donovan. **VP-Secy**—R. M. Schilling. **Dirs**—J. P. Bolduc, G. Grinstein, C. Marshall, K. H. Murmann, D. E. Nordlund, D. R. O'Hare, T. G. Pownall, J. A. Puelicher, W. Smith, R. J. Smuland, H. C. Stonecipher. **Transfer Agent & Registrar**—First Chicago Trust Co. of New York, NYC. **Incorporated** in Illinois in 1910; reincorporated in Delaware in 1966. **Empl**—12,300.

 T. Canning, CFA

Surgical Care Affiliates

NYSE Symbol SCA Options on NYSE (Jan-Apr-Jul-Oct) In S&P MidCap 400

Price	Range	P-E Ratio	Dividend	Yield	S&P Ranking	Beta
Aug. 4'93	1993					
15⅝	28⅜–14¾	19	0.16	1.0%	B	1.31

Summary

This Nashville-based outpatient surgery center operator currently operates 51 surgery centers in 21 states. Through a subsidiary, the company also holds majority interests in two health maintenance organizations (HMOs) in Lexington, Ky., and Baltimore, Md. SCA intends to spin off its HMO operations to stockholders in late 1993.

Business Summary

Surgical Care Affiliates primarily develops, owns and operates outpatient surgical care centers. The company intends to spin off its health maintenance organization (HMO) operations in late 1993. Revenues and operating income in 1992 were derived as follows:

	Revs.	Profits
Outpatient centers	71%	88%
HMOs	29%	12%

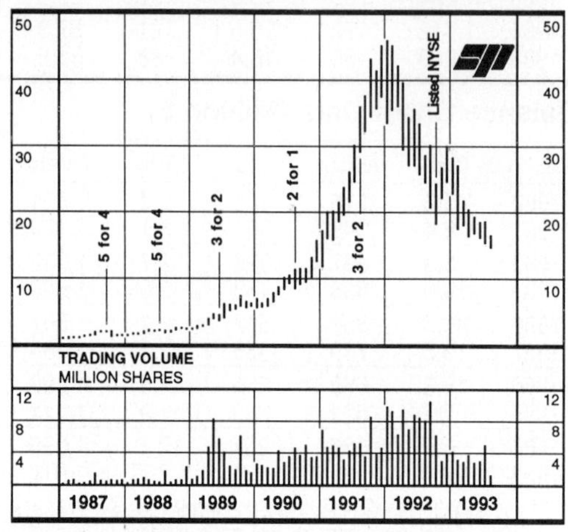

An outpatient or ambulatory surgical care center is a facility that is designed, equipped and staffed to perform surgical procedures that generally do not require overnight hospitalization and that the treating physician chooses not to or cannot perform in the office. Approximately 475 types of surgical procedures can be performed in SCA's centers, usually at lower cost than similar procedures performed by hospitals on an outpatient basis.

As of July 1993, the company was operating 51 centers in 21 states, up from 26 centers at the end of 1989. SCA's ownership interest in surgical care centers typically consists of all the capital stock of corporations that are general partners of a limited or general partnership that owns and operates a center. The other general or limited partners of the partnerships are physicians who practice in the communities where the surgical care center is located or, in the case of joint ventures, other local health care providers. SCA and participating partners share the center's operating income or loss and depreciation deductions, and receive quarterly distributions of any excess cash.

The typical SCA surgical care center is a free-standing facility of about 8,500 to 12,500 sq. ft., with three to six fully equipped operating rooms and ancillary areas for reception, preparation, recovery and administration. Centers are normally open weekdays from 6 A.M. to 4 P.M. The company estimates that a four-room operating center can accommodate up to 6,000 procedures per year. Fees for use of the centers generally range from $600 to $4,000; some 43% of patients are covered by commercial insurance (including HMOs), 33% by Medicare, 18% by Blue Cross, and 6% self pay.

Through a subsidiary, SCA also owns a 51% interest in an individual practice association (IPA)-type health maintenance organization (HMO) that provides health services to approximately 50,000 members in central Kentucky, and an 81% interest (acquired in February 1993) in an IPA-type HMO providing services to 26,000 members in Baltimore, Md. The company intends to spin off its HMO subsidiary to its shareholders in late 1993.

Next earnings report expected in late October.

Per Share Data ($)

Yr. End Dec. 31	[1]1992	[1]1991	[1]1990	1989	1988	1987	1986	[1]1985	1984	[1]1983
Tangible Bk. Val.	**1.93**	1.73	1.38	1.01	0.75	0.61	0.53	0.53	0.57	0.03
Cash Flow	**1.02**	0.74	0.45	0.29	0.21	0.13	0.08	0.02	d0.01	d0.05
Earnings[2]	**0.78**	0.57	0.33	0.19	0.11	0.05	0.01	d0.03	d0.02	d0.06
Dividends	**0.147**	0.094	0.043	0.007	Nil	Nil	Nil	Nil	Nil	Nil
Payout Ratio	**19%**	16%	13%	3%	Nil	Nil	Nil	Nil	Nil	Nil
Prices—High	**46**	45¼	15⅞	7½	2¹¹⁄₁₆	2⁷⁄₁₆	1⁷⁄₁₆	1⁹⁄₁₆	2	NA
Low	**18¼**	11⅞	5⅝	2⁷⁄₁₆	1⁷⁄₁₆	²⁷⁄₃₂	¾	¾	1¹⁄₁₆	NA
P/E Ratio—	**59–23**	79–21	48–17	39–13	23–12	44–18	NM	NM	NM	NA

Data as orig. reptd. Adj. for stk. divs. of 50% Aug. 1991, 100% Aug. 1990, 50% Jun. 1989, 25% Jul. 1988, 25% Sep. 1987, 220% Sep. 1983. **1.** Refl. merger or acq. **2.** Bef. spec. items of +0.02 in 1987, +0.01 in 1986. d-Deficit. NM-Not Meaningful. NA-Not Available.

Income Data (Million $)

Year Ended Dec. 31	Revs.	Oper. Inc.	% Oper. Inc. of Revs.	Cap. Exp.	Depr.	Int. Exp.	Net Bef. Taxes	Eff. Tax Rate	[2]Net Inc.	% Net Inc. of Revs.	Cash Flow
[1]**1992**	**225**	**81.1**	**36.0**	**34.8**	**8.99**	**3.41**	**73.1**	**24.2%**	**28.8**	**12.8**	**37.8**
[1]1991	170	60.9	35.8	25.3	6.29	3.97	55.7	23.2%	20.7	12.2	27.0
[1]1990	124	38.6	31.2	13.5	4.47	4.35	33.4	22.9%	11.5	9.3	16.0
1989	82	22.4	27.2	11.6	3.42	3.99	17.8	21.4%	6.3	7.7	9.7
1988	53	14.3	27.0	3.4	3.05	3.58	9.3	20.4%	3.5	6.6	6.6
1987	35	8.2	23.5	7.4	2.62	3.44	3.3	26.8%	1.3	3.8	3.9
1986	23	4.9	21.2	8.9	2.07	3.04	0.6	32.4%	0.3	1.2	2.4
[1]1985	13	1.4	10.8	15.1	1.34	2.29	d1.1	NM	d0.8	NM	0.6
1984	5	d0.7	NM	11.9	0.35	0.60	d0.5	NM	d0.6	NM	d0.2
[1]1983	2	d0.2	NM	6.7	0.10	0.28	d0.5	NM	d0.6	NM	d0.5

Balance Sheet Data (Million $)

Dec. 31	Cash	Curr. Assets	Curr. Liab.	Curr. Ratio	Total Assets	% Ret. on Assets	Long Term Debt	Common Equity	Total Cap.	% LT Debt of Cap.	% Ret. on Equity
1992	**52.6**	**82.1**	**42.1**	**2.0**	**248**	**13.0**	**35.4**	**136**	**206**	**17.2**	**25.3**
1991	61.0	83.1	32.1	2.6	188	12.7	40.0	89	156	25.7	28.8
1990	47.8	64.4	25.4	2.5	131	9.4	36.8	53	106	34.8	24.9
1989	32.4	44.9	19.7	2.3	107	6.6	38.3	38	87	44.1	20.0
1988	21.0	29.9	12.8	2.3	76	4.8	33.7	23	64	53.0	16.8
1987	15.2	20.2	8.7	2.3	68	2.0	36.1	18	59	61.1	7.5
1986	16.2	20.2	5.9	3.4	64	0.5	38.3	16	58	66.2	1.7
1985	9.5	16.4	6.7	2.4	52	NM	27.7	16	45	61.6	NM
1984	12.9	14.3	3.6	4.0	35	NM	14.7	16	32	46.7	NM
1983	1.6	2.2	0.9	2.4	10	NM	6.6	1	9	70.1	NM

Data as orig. reptd. **1.** Refl. merger or acq. **2.** Bef. spec. items. d-Deficit. NM-Not Meaningful.

Net Revenues (Million $)

Quarter:	[1]1993	1992	1991	1990
Mar.	45.4	51.1	37.6	27.6
Jun.	48.5	54.2	42.3	29.9
Sep.		55.4	42.2	31.1
Dec.		64.5	48.2	35.2
		225.3	170.3	123.8

Revenues in the six months ended June 30, 1993, advanced 27%, year to year (restated to reflect HMO operations as discontinued), reflecting both same-center sales growth and additional surgery centers in operation. Higher general, administrative and development expenses were offset by lower interest expense and by a relatively small increase in minority interest; net income was up 28%, to $15,381,438 ($0.41 a share), from $12,021,306 ($0.33), excluding income from discontinued operations of $0.06 and $0.04 a share in the respective periods.

Common Share Earnings ($)

Quarter:	[1]1993	1992	1991	1990
Mar.	0.21	0.18	0.11	0.07
Jun.	0.20	0.19	0.14	0.08
Sep.		0.20	0.15	0.09
Dec.		0.21	0.17	0.09
		0.78	0.57	0.33

1. From continuing ops.

Dividend Data

Cash dividends were initiated in late 1989.

Amt of Divd. $	Date Decl.	Ex-divd. Date	Stock of Record	Payment Date
0.04	Nov. 2	Nov. 20	Nov. 27	Dec. 10'92
0.04	Feb. 24	Feb. 26	Mar. 4	Mar. 10'93
0.04	May 18	May 24	May 28	Jun. 10'93
0.04	Jul. 22	Aug. 23	Aug. 27	Sep. 10'93

Finances

In May 1993, SCA said it plans to build six to eight new surgery centers in 1993 at a cost of approximately $3 million each, funds for which will be provided by the company's $18 million of lines of credit and from cash on hand. SCA also expects to purchase at least four centers in 1993 with a combination of cash and stock.

Capitalization

Long Term Debt: $47,102,785 (6/93), incl. $9,977,312 of capital lease obligations.

Minority Interest: $28,495,448.

Common Stock: 37,846,668 shs. ($0.25 par).
Officers and directors own some 13%.
Institutions hold approximately 57%.
Shareholders of record: 2,378 (12/92).

Office—102 Woodmont Blvd., Suite 610, Nashville, TN 37205. **Tel**—(615) 385-3541. **Chrmn & CEO**—J. C. Gordon. **Vice Chrmn**—K. J. Melkus. **Pres & COO**—W. J. Hamburg. **SVP, CFO & Investor Contact**—Tarpley B. Jones. **Dirs**—D. E. Bruhl, Jr., L. Burch III, R. J. Fraiman, J. C. Gordon, W. J. Hamburg, K. J. Melkus, A. W. Miller, E. J. Nighbert, M. J. Schaeffer. **Transfer Agent & Registrar**—Trust Co. Bank, Atlanta. **Incorporated** in Tennessee in 1982; reincorporated in Delaware in 1986. **Empl**—1,200.

 Adam J. Penn

Symantec Corp.

NASDAQ Symbol SYMC (Incl. in Nat'l Market) Options on Pacific In S&P MidCap 400

Price	Range	P–E Ratio	Dividend	Yield	S&P Ranking	Beta
Aug. 20'93	1993					
14⅞	18⅝–9¼	NM	None	None	NR	NA

Summmary

This leading international software company provides application and system software products for IBM PC and Apple Macintosh computer users. Revenues declined and a loss was sustained in 1992-3 on the market's rapid shift from DOS to Windows and restructuring and other charges. Higher revenues, spurred by contributions from new products, and strict cost containment should return Symantec to profitability in 1993-4.

Current Outlook

Earnings for the fiscal year ending March 31, 1994, are estimated at $0.30 a share (including nonrecurring charges totaling $0.32), in contrast to the $0.49 loss sustained in 1992-3 (including nonrecurring charges of $0.34).

Initiation of cash dividends is not expected.

Revenues are expected to rise in 1993-4, reflecting contributions from new products, including new development tools and network utilities and updated versions of old products. A leading vendor of PC utilities software for the DOS operating system, Symantec has been hurt by the market's rapid move to Windows. However, the company is now particularly focused on the Windows market for new product development. Margins should widen on progressively higher volume, as costs are expected to be well controlled.

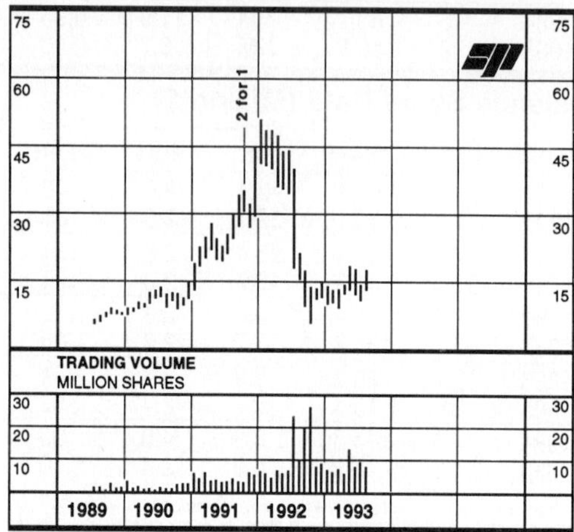

Net Revenues (Million $)

Quarter:	1993–4	1992–3	1991–2	1990–1
Jun.	59.1	61.5	43.2	22.9
Sep.	---	44.5	54.3	27.5
Dec.	---	48.7	56.8	30.9
Mar.	---	51.3	62.3	35.0
	---	206.0	216.6	116.3

Net revenues for the three months ended June 30, 1993, fell 8.9%, year to year (as restated), penalized by the software market's rapid transition from the DOS to the Windows operating environment. Results were hurt by the lower volume and, following a $12,100,000 charge for acquisition and restructuring expenses, a pretax loss contrasted with income. After net tax credits of $3,185,000, versus taxes at 36.3%, the net loss was $7,090,000 ($0.27 a share, based on 6.0% fewer shares), against restated net income of $5,073,000 ($0.18).

Common Share Earnings ($)

Quarter:	1993–4	1992–3	1991–2	1990–1
Jun.	d0.27	0.20	0.16	0.09
Sep.	E0.12	d0.48	0.11	d0.05
Dec.	E0.20	d0.17	0.26	0.20
Mar.	E0.25	d0.06	0.06	0.22
	E0.30	d0.49	0.77	0.47

Important Developments

Jul. '93— During the first quarter of 1993-4, SYMC recorded charges totaling $12.1 million ($0.32 a share) as follows: $7.4 million for the acquisition of Contact Software International Inc., a vendor of contact management software, for about 2.6 million common shares, and $4.7 million for the relocation of the company's technical support and customer service departments.

Next earnings report expected in late October.

Per Share Data ($)

Yr. End Mar. 31	[1]1993	[1]1992	[1]1991	1990	1989
Tangible Bk. Val.	**2.91**	3.35	2.10	1.77	d1.53
Cash Flow	**d0.05**	0.98	0.63	0.65	0.04
Earnings[2]	**d0.49**	0.77	0.47	0.53	d0.04
Dividends	**Nil**	Nil	Nil	Nil	Nil
Payout Ratio	**Nil**	Nil	Nil	Nil	Nil
Calendar Years	**1992**	1991	1990	1989	1988
Prices—High	**51**	44¾	14¾	9	NA
Low	**5⅞**	13	7½	5½	NA
P/E Ratio—	**NM**	46–13	32–16	17–10	NA

Data as orig. reptd. Adj. for stk. div. of 100% Oct. 1991. **1.** Refl. merger or acq. **2.** Ful. dil.: 0.76 in 1992, 0.45 in 1991, 0.52 in 1990. d-Deficit. E-Estimated. NM-Not Meaningful. NA-Not Available.

Income Data (Million $)

Year Ended Mar. 31	Oper. Revs.	Oper. Inc.	% Oper. Inc. of Revs.	Cap. Exp.	Depr.	Int. Exp.	Net Bef. Taxes	Eff. Tax Rate	Net Inc.	% Net Inc. of Revs.	Cash Flow
[1]1993	**206**	**4.6**	**2.3**	**15.4**	**10.4**	**NA**	**d17.2**	**NM**	**d11.5**	**NM**	**d1.1**
[1]1992	217	40.2	18.5	12.7	5.2	0.46	28.8	35.1%	18.7	8.6	23.9
[1]1991	116	22.9	19.7	5.5	3.3	0.46	14.3	34.4%	9.4	8.1	12.7
1990	50	9.7	19.4	2.8	1.6	0.86	8.7	23.3%	6.7	13.4	8.3
1989	40	5.2	13.1	1.8	0.9	0.11	4.1	23.1%	3.2	7.9	0.4

Balance Sheet Data (Million $)

Mar. 31	Cash	Curr. Assets	Curr. Liab.	Curr. Ratio	Total Assets	% Ret. on Assets	Long Term Debt	Common Equity	Total Cap.	% LT Debt of Cap.	% Ret. on Equity
1993	**53.3**	**110**	**45.9**	**2.4**	**142**	**NM**	**26.2**	**69.6**	**95.8**	**27.4**	**NM**
1992	31.9	96	45.5	2.1	123	18.8	1.6	75.6	77.3	2.1	30.4
1991	24.9	53	22.8	2.3	65	14.8	1.6	41.0	42.6	3.8	24.9
1990	21.5	31	10.8	2.8	38	15.7	6.1	21.3	27.4	22.3	NM
1989	4.3	12	5.5	2.1	18	20.8	1.3	d7.1	12.5	10.4	NM

Data as orig. reptd. **1.** Refl. merger or acq. d-Deficit. NA-Not Available. NM-Not Meaningful.

Business Summary

Symantec Corporation designs, markets and supports a diverse line of microcomputer software products for the information management, productivity enhancement, software development and software utility needs of business and professional users. More than half of the company's 1992-3 revenues came from products that operate on the MS-DOS operating system; its other software products utilize the MS-Windows, Apple Macintosh and IBM's OS/2 operating systems. Products are organized into four groups: utilities, productivity applications, project management and development tools.

Utilities software, which represented about 75% of 1992-3 revenues, includes offerings (sold primarily under the Norton brand name) designed to provide disk and data recovery, security, performance optimization, preventive maintenance, virus protection, hard disk backup, ASCII editing and remote computing capabilities.

Productivity applications, representing about one-tenth of total revenues in 1992-3, include Q&A, an integrated database management and word processing , word processing, desktop presentations and financial charting; and >GreatWorks, an integrated program offering eight different applications.

Project management products, which accounted for about one-tenth of 1992-3 revenues, consist of Time Line, a project organizing, scheduling and resource allocation program; and On Target, a project planning tool for use with Microsoft Windows.

Development tools, accounting for less than one-tenth of 1992-3 revenues, include THINK C, THINK Pascal, THINK Reference and Zortech C++.

International revenues accounted for about 35% of the total in 1992-3, versus 31% in 1991-2. In 1992-3, 34% of net revenues (37% in 1991-2) came from the company's three largest accounts—Ingram Micro D, Merisel and Egghead.

Dividend Data

No cash dividends have been paid.

Finances

During 1992-3, SYMC recorded charges totaling $12.1 million ($0.34 a share) for acquisition costs, a restructuring program and other one-time items.

In 1992-3, R&D spending totaled $39,762,000 (19% of sales), up from $33,189,000 (15%) in 1991-2.

In February 1993, SYMC placed privately $25 million of 7¾% subordinated notes due 2001 and convertible into common stock at $12 a share.

In November 1992, SYMC acquired Certus International, a maker of antivirus and systems security products, for 368,141 common shares. In September 1992, the company acquired software application development tool vendors MultiScope Inc. and Whitewater Group Inc. in exchange for 253,075 and 69,740 common shares, respectively.

In 1991-2, the company recorded a $6.8 million ($0.20 a share) charge associated with the acquisitions of Zortech Inc., Leonard Development Group, Dynamic Microprocessor Associates Inc. and Symantec (UK) Ltd.

Capitalization

Long Term Obligs.: $26,153,000 (6/93), incl. $25 million of 7¾% sub. notes due 2001 & conv. into com. at $12 a sh.

Common Stock: 26,917,316 shs. ($0.01 par). Institutions hold about 64%. Shareholders: 655 of record (3/93).

Office—10201 Torre Ave., Cupertino, CA 95014-2132. **Tel**—(408) 253-9600. **Chrmn, Pres & CEO**—G. E. Eubanks Jr. **Exec VP-Fin & CFO**—R. R. B. Dykes. **Secy**—G. K. Davidson. **Dirs**—W. W. Bregman, C. D. Carman, L. J. Doerr, G. E. Eubanks Jr., P. Norton, L. L. Vadasz. **Transfer Agent**—Bank of Boston. **Incorporated** in Delaware in 1988. **Empl**—1,012.

 Peter C. Wood, CFA

Symbol Technologies

NYSE Symbol SBL Options on ASE (Jan-Apr-Jul-Oct) In S&P MidCap 400

Price	Range	P–E Ratio	Dividend	Yield	S&P Ranking	Beta
Sep. 13'93	1993					
12	15⅞–11¼	NM	None	None	B–	2.80

Summary

This company develops, manufactures and sells portable bar code scanning equipment that employs laser technology to read data encoded in bar code symbols. Symbol is currently in the process of consolidating the engineering and manufacturing operations of its two product divisions, which it expects to complete by the end of 1993's third quarter. Earnings fell sharply in 1993's first half, reflecting a decline in revenues, lower gross margins and higher engineering expenses.

Business Summary

Symbol Technologies develops, manufactures and sells bar code reading equipment, portable data collection systems, and radio frequency data communications products. These data collection systems are used in retail, manufacturing, distribution, military, healthcare and other industries. The company also manufactures film masters for printing bar code symbols, and Lasercheck, a bar code quality control system.

The Bar Code Scanner division, which accounted for more than one-half of revenues in 1992, develops, manufactures, sells and services portable bar code reading equipment that employs laser technology to read data encoded in bar code symbols. The company's portable bar code scanning equipment is compatible with a wide variety of data collection systems, including computers, electronic cash registers and portable data collection terminals. The scanner may be used as a portable hand-held unit, or it may be placed in a stationary mount. The largest selling hand-held laser scanner is the LS 2000, sold primarily to point-of-sale customers and for use in conjunction with portable data collection terminals. The company's "hands-free" scanners are usually triggered by an object sensor to enable use in "hands-free" situations.

Through its Portable Data Collection Systems division, which accounted for approximately 40% of revenues in 1992, SBL designs, manufactures, sells and services a family of hand-held portable data collection systems. These systems consist of hand-held terminals, peripheral devices, software and programming tools, and are designed to provide solutions to specific customer needs in data collection.

In 1988, through the acquisition of Vectran Corp., SBL acquired technology related to data radio systems. In 1989, SBL introduced the portable radio terminal, a narrow band radio frequency version of the portable data terminal product line. In 1990, the company introduced the laser radio terminal and the laser data terminal, which both contain visible laser diode scanning technology.

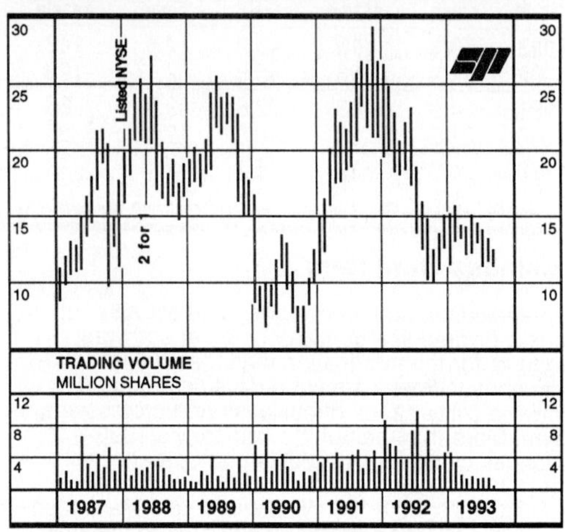

In December 1992, SBL adopted a plan of restructuring which called for consolidation of engineering and manufacturing operations its two product divisions—the Portable Systems division (located in in Costa Mesa, Calif.) and the Bar Code Scanning division (located in Bohemia, NY), into a single Products Group to be located in Bohemia.

Important Developments

Jul. '93— In reporting operating results for 1993's second quarter, Symbol said that execution of its restructuring and consolidation plan was on schedule, and is expected to be substantially completed by the end of 1993's third quarter.

Next earnings report expected in late October.

Per Share Data ($)

Yr. End Dec. 31[1]	1992	1991	1990	1989	1988	1987	1986	1985	1984	1983
Tangible Bk. Val.	**[2]5.95**	[2]11.12	[2]10.14	[2]9.83	[2]6.15	[2]4.94	1.69	1.18	0.30	0.09
Cash Flow	**0.10**	1.51	0.87	1.37	1.18	0.48	0.17	0.08	d0.21	d0.29
Earnings[3]	**d0.65**	0.91	0.33	0.91	1.07	0.42	0.12	0.04	d0.25	d0.31
Dividends	**Nil**	Nil	Nil	Nil	Nil	Nil	Nil	Nil	Nil	Nil
Payout Ratio	**Nil**	Nil	Nil	Nil	Nil	Nil	Nil	Nil	Nil	Nil
Prices[4]—High	**26½**	29⅜	16⅝	25⅝	27⅛	21⅝	9⅝	7	6⅛	9⅛
Low	**10**	10¾	5⅜	15⅛	14¾	8⅝	5⅛	4⅛	3	3⅞
P/E Ratio—	**NM**	32–12	50–16	28–17	25–14	52–21	80–43	NM	NM	NM

Data as orig. reptd. Adj. for stk. div(s). of 100% Jun. 1988. **1.** Yr. ended Jun. 30 prior to 1989. **2.** Incl. intangibles. **3.** Bef. spec. items of -0.03 in 1992, +0.17 in 1987, +0.10 in 1986, +0.03 in 1985. **4.** Cal. yr. d-Deficit. NM-Not Meaningful.

Income Data (Million $)

Year Ended Dec. 31[1]	Revs.	Oper. Inc.	% Oper. Inc. of Revs.	Cap. Exp.	Depr.	Int. Exp.	Net Bef. Taxes	Eff. Tax Rate	[3]Net Inc.	% Net Inc. of Revs.	Cash Flow
1992	**345**	**39.5**	**11.5**	**15.0**	**17.9**	**2.07**	**d22.5**	**NM**	**d15.5**	**NM**	**2.4**
1991	319	53.7	16.8	17.2	15.1	2.82	36.7	38.0%	22.8	7.1	37.8
1990	231	26.9	11.6	15.3	12.3	2.82	12.8	41.0%	7.6	3.3	19.9
1989	222	45.9	20.7	14.1	9.6	5.24	31.6	39.9%	19.0	8.5	28.6
1988	89	30.2	34.0	[2]11.9	1.9	1.09	30.7	34.1%	20.2	22.7	22.1
1987	45	10.5	23.0	8.4	0.9	0.09	10.5	45.9%	5.7	12.5	6.5
1986	23	2.8	12.1	1.1	0.6	0.63	2.4	45.5%	1.3	5.5	1.9
1985	14	1.4	10.1	0.6	0.4	0.82	0.5	48.8%	0.3	1.9	0.7
1984	9	d0.6	NM	1.2	0.3	0.86	d1.5	Nil	d1.5	NM	d1.3
1983	3	d1.2	NM	0.2	0.1	0.28	d1.7	Nil	d1.7	NM	d1.6

Balance Sheet Data (Million $)

Dec. 31[1]	Cash	Curr. Assets	Curr. Liab.	Curr. Ratio	Total Assets	% Ret. on Assets	Long Term Debt	Common Equity	Total Cap.	% LT Debt of Cap.	% Ret. on Equity
1992	**6.9**	**185**	**96.2**	**1.9**	**379**	**NM**	**14.6**	**245**	**260**	**5.6**	**NM**
1991	17.3	171	48.2	3.5	354	6.6	21.7	263	284	7.6	9.0
1990	19.0	146	46.7	3.1	315	2.5	24.8	226	251	9.9	3.4
1989	21.9	134	39.6	3.4	294	8.3	23.7	217	241	9.9	10.8
1988	71.7	114	14.8	7.7	137	16.7	9.2	112	122	7.5	19.9
1987	68.7	90	9.8	9.2	101	8.3	4.3	87	91	4.7	9.7
1986	9.5	19	2.8	7.0	23	5.7	0.8	19	20	4.2	8.0
1985	9.1	17	2.4	6.9	20	1.6	5.8	12	18	32.9	3.5
1984	1.5	7	2.0	3.5	10	NM	5.5	2	8	70.1	NM
1983	3.9	6	1.3	4.7	8	NM	5.8	1	6	90.7	NM

Data as orig. reptd. **1.** Fiscal yr. ended Jun. 30 prior to 1989. **2.** Net of curr. yr. retirement and disposals. **3.** Bef. spec. item(s). d-Deficit. NM-Not Meaningful.

Net Revenues (Million $)

Quarter:	1993	1992	1991	1990
Mar.	83.7	89.0	70.6	51.1
Jun.	89.9	94.9	77.6	55.2
Sep.		78.4	87.3	62.3
Dec.		82.6	83.8	62.9
		344.9	319.4	231.5

Net revenues for the six months ended June 30, 1993, declined 5.6%, year to year, as a decrease in worldwide scanner sales outweighed higher sales volume of portable terminal units. Gross margins fell to 46% of revenues, from 50%, and with higher engineering costs, total operating expenses edged up 1.4%. Pretax income fell 70%. After taxes at 43.0%, versus 33.8%, net income was down 75%, to $2,975,000 ($0.12 a share), from $11,683,000 ($0.47). Results for the 1992 interim exclude a special charge of $0.03 per share for an accounting change.

Common Share Earnings ($)

Quarter:	1993	1992	1991	1990
Mar.	0.03	0.22	0.17	0.01
Jun.	0.09	0.25	0.23	0.06
Sep.		d0.14	0.28	0.15
Dec.		d0.99	0.23	0.11
		d0.65	0.91	0.33

Dividend Data

No cash dividend has ever been paid. The shares were split 2-for-1 in June 1988.

Finances

In March 1993, Symbol issued $25 million of its Series A Senior Notes due February 15, 2003 and $25 million of its Series B Senior Notes due February 15, 2003 to four insurance companies for working capital and general corporate purposes. The Series A Notes will be repaid in equal annual installments beginning in February, 1995. The Series B Notes will be repaid in equal annual installments beginning in February 1997.

In December 1992, SBL announced a restructuring of its operations which resulted in a $34 million pretax charge to fourth quarter earnings. The charge covered costs associated with consolidation of engineering and manufacturing operations and the streamlining of sales, marketing, finance and administrative departments. Symbol expects to realize annual savings of about $16 million as a result of the restructuring.

Capitalization

Long Term Debt: $64,483,000 (6/93).

Common Stock: 24,433,000 shs. ($0.01 par). Reliance Financial Services owns some 14.2%. Institutions hold approximately 62%. Shareholders of record: 2,167 (2/93).

d-Deficit.

Office—116 Wilbur Place, Bohemia, NY 11716. **Tel**—(516) 563-2400. **Chrmn & CEO**—J. Swartz. **Pres**—R. R. Martino. **SVP-CFO**—T. G. Amato. **Investor Contact**—Michael Archambault. **SVP-Secy**—L. H. Goldner. **Dirs**—G. Bugliarello, L. C. Freiberg, F. P. Heiman, H. P. Mallement, R. R. Martino, S. P. Steinberg, J. Swartz. **Transfer Agent & Registrar**—Continental Stock Transfer & Trust Co., NYC. **Incorporated** in New York in 1973; reincorporated in Delaware in 1987. **Empl**—2,192.

 Samuel A. Dedio

Synergen, Inc.

NASDAQ Symbol SYGN (Incl. in Nat'l Market) Options on Pacific, Phila In S&P MidCap 400

Price	Range	P-E Ratio	Dividend	Yield	S&P Ranking	Beta
Sep. 24'93	1993					
11	65–8	NM	None	None	C	2.63

Summary

Synergen develops protein-based human pharmaceuticals, focusing on inflammatory diseases and neurological disorders. Revenues consist of payments by others to fund sponsored research, payments under joint development agreements, and interest and other income. The company recently commenced a follow-up Phase III clinical study of its sepsis drug, Antril; disappointing results from a previous Phase III study were released in February.

Current Outlook

A large loss is seen again for 1993, following 1992's loss of $1.66 share.

Initiation of cash dividends is not expected.

Total revenues in 1993 are expected to drop sharply from 1992's $51.4 million, reflecting reduced funds from R&D contracts and lower interest and other income. Despite disappointing test results for Antril, the company has initiated follow-up clinical trials on Antril for sepsis and other conditions, and is also developing other compounds. Long-term prospects depend significantly upon the outcome of these programs.

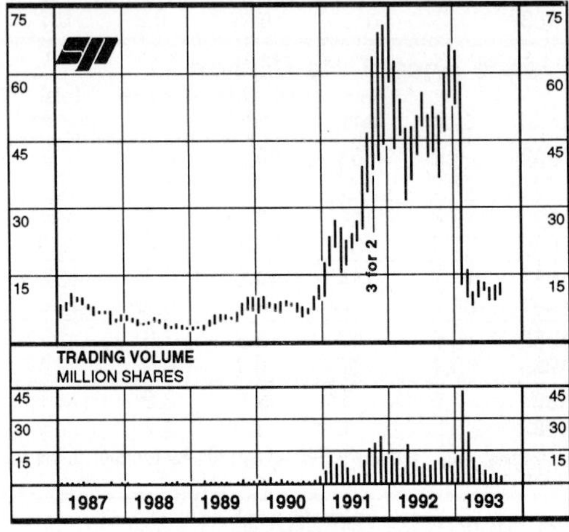

Revenues (Million $)

Quarter:	1993	[1]1992	[1]1991	1990
Mar.	9.4	10.5	3.0	2.0
Jun.	3.6	13.0	5.3	2.1
Sep.	---	16.5	6.8	3.8
Dec.	---	11.4	8.7	0.8
	---	51.4	23.8	8.7

In the six months ended June 30, 1993, revenues fell 45%, year to year, reflecting both lower sponsored R&D revenues and a lesser amount of interest and other income. Research and development expenditures surged to $47.2 million, from $21.2 million, and after higher general and administrative costs, and a restructuring charge of $2.0 million, the net loss widened to $46.2 million ($1.84 a share) from $3.4 million ($0.14).

Common Share Earnings ($)

Quarter:	1993	1992	1991	1990
Mar.	d0.82	d0.02	d0.13	d0.09
Jun.	d1.01	d0.12	d0.07	d0.08
Sep.	---	d0.09	d0.07	NM
Dec.	---	d1.43	d0.09	d0.25
	---	d1.66	d0.36	d0.42

Important Developments

Aug. '93— Synergen announced that the first patient was enrolled in its Antril follow-up severe sepsis (Phase III) clinical trial. The primary objective of this study is to provide further evidence of the efficacy and safety of Antril compared to placebo in increasing survival time in patients with presumed severe sepsis. The company is hopeful that this study will generate the data necessary to apply for a license application with the FDA.

Aug. '93— Synergen said that it began the drug treatment portion of its Phase II/III trial (being conducted along with Syntex Inc.) to evaluate the safety and efficacy of CNTF for amyotrophic lateral sclerosis (ALS, or Lou Gherig's Disease).

Next earnings report expected in early November.

Per Share Data ($)

Yr. End Dec. 31	1992	1991	1990	1989	1988	1987	1986	1985	1984	1983
Tangible Bk. Val.	**13.62**	14.66	3.45	3.05	3.13	3.49	2.72	1.60	1.53	0.56
Cash Flow	**d1.51**	d0.27	d0.33	Nil	d0.28	0.07	0.11	0.14	NA	NA
Earnings[2]	**d1.66**	d0.36	d0.42	d0.10	d0.37	d0.01	0.03	0.06	0.06	d0.14
Dividends	**Nil**	Nil	Nil	Nil	Nil	Nil	Nil	Nil	Nil	Nil
Payout Ratio	**Nil**	Nil	Nil	Nil	Nil	Nil	Nil	Nil	Nil	Nil
Prices—High	**75**	70¾	12⅞	10⅛	6⅛	11	12¼	NA	NA	NA
Low	**31¾**	10⅜	5⅝	2¾	2⅞	4	5⅛	NA	NA	NA
P/E Ratio—	**NM**	NM	NM	NM	NM	NM	NM	NA	NA	NA

Data as orig. reptd. Adj. for stk. div. of 50% Oct. 1991. **1.** Incl. int. inc. **2.** Bef. spec. items of +0.02 in 1986, +0.02 in 1985, +0.02 in 1984. d-Deficit. NM-Not Meaningful. NA-Not Available.

Synergen, Inc.

Income Data (Million $)

Year Ended Dec. 31	Revs.	Oper. Inc.	% Oper. Inc. of Revs.	Cap. Exp.	Depr.	Int. Exp.	Net Bef. Taxes	Eff. Tax Rate	[3]Net Inc.	% Net Inc. of Revs.	Cash Flow
1992	**31.6**	**d38.8**	**NM**	**51.5**	**3.81**	**0.35**	**[2]d41.20**	**NM**	**d41.20**	**NM**	**d37.40**
1991	14.2	d14.3	NM	21.2	1.90	0.47	[2]d7.12	Nil	d7.12	NM	d5.22
1990	8.7	d8.6	NM	4.2	1.34	0.48	d6.41	Nil	d6.41	NM	d5.08
1989	11.9	d2.4	NM	0.9	1.29	0.49	d1.31	Nil	d1.31	NM	d0.02
1988	4.2	d6.5	NM	4.2	1.25	0.48	d5.16	Nil	d5.16	NM	d3.92
1987	6.8	d1.4	NM	[1]1.5	0.99	0.40	[2]d0.12	Nil	d0.12	NM	0.87
1986	5.9	d0.2	NM	0.6	0.96	0.44	0.43	31.3%	0.29	5.0	1.25
1985	5.4	0.5	9.2	3.3	0.76	0.52	0.69	21.6%	0.54	10.0	1.30
1984	4.0	0.2	6.0	3.6	0.51	Nil	0.60	24.5%	0.46	11.3	NA
1983	1.3	d1.2	NM	0.8	0.29	Nil	d1.07	Nil	d1.07	NM	NA

Balance Sheet Data (Million $)

Dec. 31	Cash	Curr. Assets	Curr. Liab.	Ratio	Total Assets	% Ret. on Assets	Long Term Debt	Common Equity	Total Cap.	% LT Debt of Cap.	% Ret. on Equity
1992	**239**	**262**	**11.60**	**22.6**	**359**	**NM**	**6**	**342**	**348**	**1.7**	**NM**
1991	321	330	7.34	45.0	374	NM	6	361	367	1.6	NM
1990	44	47	3.47	13.5	65	NM	6	55	61	9.8	NM
1989	29	34	1.56	21.6	48	NM	6	41	47	12.9	NM
1988	31	33	1.00	33.0	48	NM	6	41	47	12.8	NM
1987	43	45	0.79	57.3	57	NM	6	50	56	10.7	NM
1986	31	32	1.23	25.7	40	0.5	6	33	39	15.3	1.9
1985	12	13	1.30	10.1	23	2.4	6	15	21	28.3	3.6
1984	11	12	1.30	9.0	22	3.3	6	15	21	29.3	NA

Data as orig. reptd. **1.** Net. **2.** Incl. equity in earns. of nonconsol. subs. **3.** Bef. spec. items. d-Deficit. NM-Not Meaningful. NA-Not Available.

Business Summary

Synergen is a biotechnology company engaged in the discovery, development and production of protein-based pharmaceuticals. Its research focus is targeted primaily toward products to treat inflammatory diseases and neurological disorders. Revenues consist of payments to the company by others to fund sponsored research, benchmark payments under joint development agreements, and interest and other income. R&D spending totaled $60.3 million in 1992, up from $24.1 million in 1991.

The company's lead product, Antril, is a genetically engineered version of interleukin-1 receptor antagonist, a natural protein involved in regulating the extent and duration of the human inflammatory response. In February, 1993, Synergen released results of a Phase III clinical trial that tested Antril's efficacy in treating sepsis. The study did not confirm a reduction in mortality seen in an earlier Phase II trial. However, it did show a benefit from Antril in the more severely ill patients. The company subsequently commenced a follow-up study on severely ill patients. Antril is also being evaluated as a treatment for rheumatoid arthritis, psoriasis, asthma and several other inflammatory conditions.

Other products in the R&D pipeline include elastase inhibitor (SLPI) for the treatment of cystic fibrosis, genetic emphysema and chronic bronchitis; and several neurotrophic factors which are being developed through a joint venture with Syntex Inc. These include ciliary neurotrophic factor (CNTF) for amyotrophic lateral sclerosis (Lou Gehrig's disease) and others which are being evaluated for the treatment of strokes, Alzheimer's disease and Parkinson's disease.

Dividend Data

No cash dividends have been paid.

Finances

In December, 1992, the company completed the buyout of its first sponsored R&D partnership, Synergen Development Partners Ltd. (SDPL) in exchange for 255,750 Synergen common shares, plus warrants to buy an additional 209,250 shares. The company now owns exclusive rights to products previously owned by SDPL, including SLPI, an elastase inhibitor. The transaction resulted in a charge of $0.73 a share in the fourth quarter of 1992.

Capitalization

Long Term Debt: $6,000,000 of indust. rev. bonds (6/93).

Common Stock: 25,225,399 shs. ($0.01 par). Officers and directors own or control 10%. Institutions hold about 60%.
Shareholders: About 2,250 of record.

Office—1885 33rd St., Boulder, CO 80301. **Tel**—(303) 938-6200. **Chrmn & CEO**—L. Soll. **EVP-Fin**—K. J. Collins. **EVP & Secy**—G. B. Abbott. **EVP-Research**—R. C. Thompson. **Treas**—S. S. Tetlow. **Investor Contact**—Debra Bannister (303-938-6292). **Dirs**—G. B. Abbott, A. H. Hayes, Jr., D. I. Hirsh, B. MacTaggart, L. Soll, R. C. Thompson, G. S. Utt, Jr. **Transfer Agent & Registrar**—Manufacturers Hanover Trust Co., NYC. **Incorporated** in Delaware in 1982. **Empl**—591.

 Robert M. Gold

SynOptics Communications

NASDAQ Symbol SNPX (Incl. in Nat'l Market) Options on CBOE, NY, Phila In S&P MidCap 400

Price	Range	P-E Ratio	Dividend	Yield	S&P Ranking	Beta
Aug. 23'93	1993					
$28\frac{1}{4}$	$42\frac{3}{4}$–$23\frac{13}{32}$	25	None	None	NR	NA

Summary

SynOptics provides high-speed networking solutions that distribute management and processing power throughout the network at the intelligent hub, allowing efficient and reliable delivery of data across a local area network (LAN). Its products include connectivity, internetworking and network management options for Ethernet, Token Ring and FDDI. Record earnings in 1992 reflected continued rapid growth in the computer networking industry. Rapid earnings growth should continue in 1993 before moderating in 1994.

Current Outlook

Earnings for 1993 are estimated at $1.40 a share, up from 1992's $0.66, as adjusted. Share earnings for 1994 are projected at $1.75.

Initiation of dividends is not expected.

SNPX hopes to increase sales in the next several quarters at a rate somewhat faster than the expected annualized industry growth rate of 35% to 40%. The local area networking (LAN) market is projected to grow at this rapid clip because, according to one estimate, only 63% of corporate personal computers were attached to LANs at the end of 1992. The aggressive introduction of new products should help the company grow faster than the LAN industry as a whole. However, increasing competition and a shift in product mix will continue to slowly erode gross margins — a decrease to the 51% range is likely by the end of 1994. To arrest the effects of lower gross margins on earnings, the company plans to continue controlling operating costs. Nevertheless, lower gross margins will mean that earnings will grow slower than sales: we are estimating that per share earnings will rise some 25% in 1994.

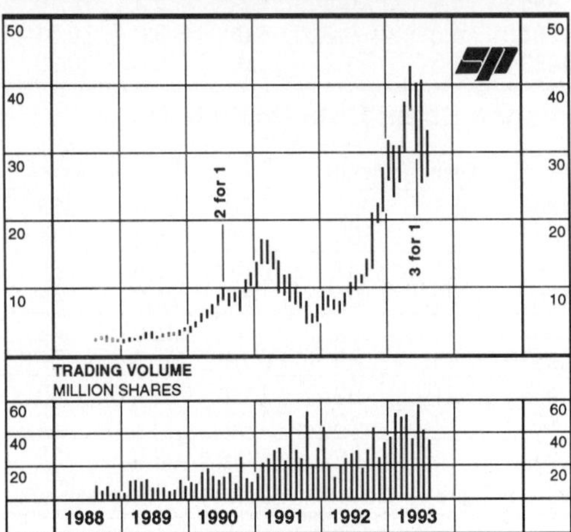

Revenues (Million $)

13 Weeks:	1993	1992	1991	1990
Mar.	153	68	61	30
Jun.	180	82	64	41
Sep.	E190	108	59	48
Dec.	E202	130	64	56
	E725	389	248	176

Revenues in the 26 weeks ended July 2, 1993, soared 122%, year to year, as the networking market continued to grow. Gross margins narrowed, but operating costs rose just 64%; operating income quadrupled. After taxes at 36.5% in both periods, net income was up 3.8-fold, to $46,426,000 ($0.67 a share, on 12% more shares), from $12,080,000 ($0.20, as adjusted).

Common Share Earnings ($)

13 Weeks:	1993	1992	1991	1990
Mar.	0.32	0.08	0.15	0.07
Jun.	0.35	0.11	0.14	0.11
Sep.	E0.35	0.21	0.07	0.14
Dec.	E0.38	0.25	0.08	0.15
	E1.40	0.66	0.44	0.47

Important Developments

Jul. '93— The company said that the strong financial results for the second quarter were led by increased shipments of Token Ring modular and non-modular hub products. These products play a crucial role as organizations transition from host-based environments to distributed, client/server computing. Also during the quarter, SNPX said it made substantial progress in bringing down the long lead times it had been experiencing on some of its products.

Next earnings report expected in mid-October.

Per Share Data ($)

Yr. End Dec. 31	1992	1991	1990	1989	1988	1987
Tangible Bk. Val.	**3.39**	2.37	1.80	1.25	0.62	d0.06
Cash Flow	**0.93**	0.64	0.59	0.26	0.18	NM
Earnings	**0.66**	0.44	0.47	0.20	0.15	d0.01
Dividends	**Nil**	Nil	Nil	Nil	Nil	Nil
Payout Ratio	**Nil**	Nil	Nil	Nil	Nil	Nil
Prices—High	**$27\frac{27}{32}$**	$17\frac{5}{32}$	$12\frac{1}{4}$	$4\frac{7}{32}$	$3\frac{1}{32}$	NA
Low	**$6\frac{1}{4}$**	$4\frac{3}{4}$	$3\frac{1}{2}$	$1\frac{31}{32}$	$2\frac{1}{8}$	NA
P/E Ratio—	**42–9**	39–11	26–7	21–10	20–14	NA

Data as orig. reptd. Adj. for stk. divs. of 300% Jun. 1993, 100% Jul. 1990, 100% Jan. 1988. d-Deficit. NM-Not Meaningful. NA-Not Available. E-Estimated.

Income Data (Million $)

Year Ended Dec. 31	Revs.	Oper. Inc.	% Oper. Inc. of Revs.	Cap. Exp.	Depr.	Int. Exp.	Net Bef. Taxes	Eff. Tax Rate	Net Inc.	% Net Inc. of Revs.	Cash Flow
1992	**389**	**82.8**	**21.3**	**18.8**	**16.7**	**0.20**	**66.8**	**36.5%**	**42.4**	**10.9**	**59.1**
1991	248	52.3	21.1	20.9	12.1	0.32	42.9	37.5%	26.8	10.8	38.9
1990	176	49.9	28.4	21.2	6.9	0.51	46.3	39.0%	28.2	16.0	35.1
1989	77	17.4	22.5	5.3	2.6	0.47	15.5	39.0%	9.4	12.2	12.1
1988	40	9.8	24.4	5.7	0.9	0.21	9.2	36.3%	5.9	14.7	6.8
1987	6	d0.1	NM	0.4	0.3	0.09	d0.3	NM	d0.3	NM	NM

Balance Sheet Data (Million $)

Dec. 31	Cash	Curr. Assets	Curr. Liab.	Curr. Ratio	Total Assets	% Ret. on Assets	Long Term Debt	Common Equity	Total Cap.	% LT Debt of Cap.	% Ret. on Equity
1992	**92.1**	**222**	**56.8**	**3.9**	**260**	**19.6**	**0.44**	**203**	**203**	**0.2**	**24.6**
1991	61.8	129	27.3	4.7	164	18.1	1.22	136	137	0.9	22.5
1990	49.0	102	24.4	4.2	128	26.4	1.90	100	102	1.9	33.4
1989	42.4	74	12.7	5.8	86	14.1	3.73	69	73	5.1	18.4
1988	13.9	30	9.1	3.3	39	20.2	2.43	27	30	8.2	NM
1987	1.6	4	1.1	3.6	5	NM	0.74	d1	4	18.1	NM

Data as orig. reptd. d-Deficit. NM-Not Meaningful.

Business Summary

SynOptics Communications designs, manufactures, markets and supports diverse, high-performance local area network (LAN) systems. Its systems distribute management and processing power through intelligent hubs to provide efficient, reliable delivery of data across LANs. The company focuses on integrating connectivity, network management and internetworking products into a complete networking solution that stresses management and expansion of increasingly large and complex LANs. In 1992, export sales accounted for 31% of the total.

The company's product strategy focuses on the concentrator, or intelligent hub, as a central control point for network management and growth. The intelligent hub provides connections to various cabling types and media-access methods, and integrates bridging, routing and switching functions. All functions are coordinated through open, standards-based, network management products. SNPX's products provide options for future network expansion.

Connectivity products, which enable computing devices to communicate over networks, include concentrators or intelligent hubs (both the modular 3000 line and the stackable 2000 line), related concentrator communications modules (host modules) and transceivers. Network management products distribute management intelligence through geographically dispersed LANs as, through a combination of hardware and software, data is gathered, monitored, controlled and analyzed. SNPX's internetworking products include local and remote bridges, local and remote routers and terminal servers.

One reseller accounted for 19% and 16% of the company's revenues in 1992 and 1991, respectively.

Research and development costs expensed in 1992 equaled $43 million (11% of revenue), compared to $32 million (13%) in 1991.

Dividend Data

No cash dividends have been paid. A three-for-one stock split was effected June 11, 1993.

Finances

In the 1992 fourth quarter, the company recorded a $2.25 million charge related to the settlement of two consolidated class action stockholder suits.

Capitalization

Long Term Debt: $110,126,000 (7/2/93), incl. cap. leases.

Common Stock: 60,000,000 shs. ($0.01 par).
Officers and directors control 13%.
Institutions own 89%.
Shareholders: 975 of record (12/92).

Office—4401 Great America Parkway, Santa Clara, CA 95054. **Tel**—(408) 988-2400. **Pres & CEO**—A. K. Ludwick. **VP & CFO**—W. J. Ruehle. **Secy**—M. Kersten. **Investor Contact**—Linda Fellows. **Dirs**—S. H. Carter, Jr., J. C. Lewis, J. S. Lewis, A. K. Ludwick, F. J. Pipp, R. V. Schmidt. **Transfer Agent & Registrar**—First National Bank of Boston. **Incorporated** in California in 1985; reincorporated in Delaware in 1990. **Empl**—1,255.

 Neeraj K. Vohra

T2 Medical

NYSE Symbol TSQ Options on Pacific (Feb-May-Aug-Nov) In S&P MidCap 400

Price	Range	P-E Ratio	Dividend	Yield	S&P Ranking	Beta
Sep. 10'93	1993					
6¼	25⅞–5¾	5	0.10	1.6%	NR	2.44

Summary

This company provides alternate site health care treatment services, including a broad range of home and outpatient infusion therapy services. Results in recent periods were restricted by increased price competition in the home infusion business. In August 1993, previously reported earnings for the first and second quarters of fiscal 1993 were restated downward, reflecting recently discovered accounting irregularities. T² recently announced that a group of current and former officers had terminated its efforts to formulate an acquisition proposal for the company.

Business Summary

T² Medical, Inc. is a leading provider of alternate site health care treatment services, including a broad range of infusion therapy services administered at a patient's home or at one of the company's ambulatory infusion therapy ("IntraCare") facilities. Contributions to revenues (as adjusted for acquisitions) in recent fiscal years were:

	1992	1991	1990
Home infusion	79%	84%	91%
IntraCare	16%	10%	6%
Lithotripsy	3%	1%	Nil
Other	3%	5%	3%

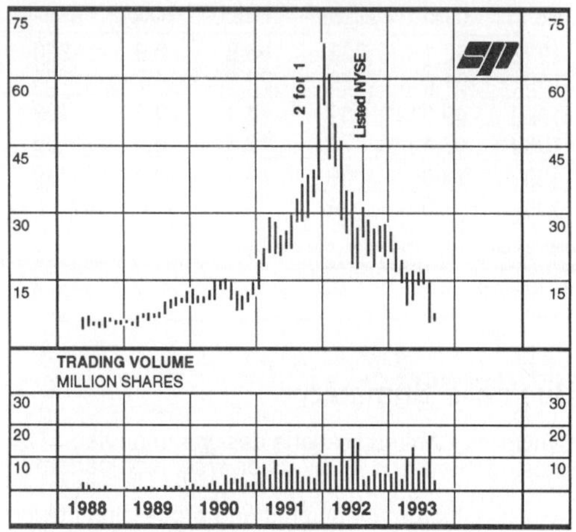

Infusion therapy is the intravenous administration of anti-infective, cancer chemotherapy, pharmaceutical nutrients and other pharmaceutical treatments. The alternate site infusion therapy industry has grown markedly in recent years, reflecting cost savings and quality of life advantages of alternate site care versus hospital care, as well as advances in medical technology allowing treatment of more disease states through infusion therapy. As of April 1993, the company provided home infusion therapy in 94 cities in 34 states and operated 52 IntraCare facilities in 37 cities in 17 states.

The company has begun expanding its operations into other alternate site health care services, including lithotripsy services (a non-invasive technique that uses shock waves to break up kidney stones), maternity risk management services through a joint venture with Tokos Medical Corp., and specialized pediatric treatment services through Pediatric Partners, Inc. (acquired in October 1992; doing business as Kids Medical Club). In addition, the company has begun developing a practice management service to be marketed to physicians who practice alone or in small groups.

In February 1993, T² entered the ambulatory surgery market by establishing a relationship with Surgex Inc., a Ft. Worth-based manager and developer of ambulatory surgery centers. The relationship will allow the company to acquire a substantial majority interest in Surgex.

About 94% of billings in fiscal 1992 were attributable to private third-party payors, which tend to pay more quickly, pay a higher percentage of billed services, and provide broader coverage than Medicare (6%).

Important Developments

Sep. '93— T² announced that a group that includes certain current and former company managers had terminated its efforts to formulate a proposal to acquire T². The company also said it is continuing to seek a new CEO and a new CFO, following the August 1993 departures of the former holders of these positions.

Next earnings report due in late December.

Per Share Data ($)

Yr. End Sep. 30	[1]1992	[1]1991	[1]1990	[1]1989	1988	[1]1987	1986	1985	1984
Tangible Bk. Val.	**3.08**	1.88	1.81	[2]d0.66	1.13	d0.15	0.12	0.10	NA
Cash Flow	**1.74**	1.15	0.68	0.49	0.34	0.29	NA	NA	NA
Earnings	**1.55**	1.02	0.57	0.40	0.33	0.27	0.12	0.02	[2]d0.04
Dividends	**0.025**	Nil	Nil	Nil	Nil	Nil	Nil	Nil	Nil
Payout Ratio	**2%**	Nil	Nil	Nil	Nil	Nil	Nil	Nil	Nil
Prices[3]—High	**67¾**	58½	15⅜	12½	7¹⁄₁₆	NA	NA	NA	NA
Low	**17¾**	13⅛	8⅜	4¹³⁄₁₆	4	NA	NA	NA	NA
P/E Ratio—	**44–11**	57–13	27–15	31–12	22–12	NA	NA	NA	NA

Data as orig. reptd. Adj. for stk. div. of 100% Sep. 1991. **1.** Refl. merger or acq. **2.** From inception 4-30-84. **3.** Cal. yr. d-Deficit. NA-Not Available.

Income Data (Million $)

Year Ended Sep. 30	Revs.	Oper. Inc.	% Oper. Inc. of Revs.	Cap. Exp.	Depr.	Int. Exp.	²Net Bef. Taxes	Eff. Tax Rate	Net Inc.	% Net Inc. of Revs.	Cash Flow
¹1992	**242**	**96.4**	**39.8**	**5.74**	**7.33**	**1.53**	**91.5**	**35.1%**	**59.3**	**24.5**	**66.7**
¹1991	142	50.4	35.5	5.38	4.59	2.17	52.5	34.2%	34.6	24.3	39.2
¹1990	71	24.6	34.9	4.76	3.09	2.54	24.5	37.0%	15.4	21.8	18.5
¹1989	38	15.3	40.2	1.23	1.72	2.38	12.5	36.7%	7.9	20.8	9.7
1988	11	5.4	49.8	0.07	0.09	0.24	5.8	39.0%	3.5	32.7	3.6
¹1987	5	1.2	25.0	0.59	0.06	0.07	1.3	28.9%	0.9	18.9	1.0
1986	1	0.3	21.1	0.13	0.04	0.02	0.2	Nil	0.2	16.6	NA
1985	NM	0.1	13.6	0.10	0.01	0.01	NM	Nil	NM	8.4	NA

Balance Sheet Data (Million $)

Sep. 30	Cash	Curr. Assets	Curr. Liab.	Curr. Ratio	Total Assets	% Ret. on Assets	Long Term Debt	Common Equity	Total Cap.	% LT Debt of Cap.	% Ret. on Equity
1992	**69.4**	**127.0**	**29.9**	**4.3**	**280**	**23.7**	**4.2**	**244**	**248**	**1.7**	**27.9**
1991	47.3	87.9	28.8	3.1	201	18.5	0.3	164	165	0.2	22.1
1990	44.4	66.8	10.3	6.5	150	12.2	11.2	128	139	8.1	16.5
1989	0.4	14.6	8.0	1.8	73	15.2	22.6	42	65	34.6	24.3
1988	13.6	18.4	3.0	6.1	19	31.4	1.5	15	16	9.3	55.9
1987	0.1	1.7	1.8	1.0	2	61.9	1.9	d1	1	NM	NM
1986	0.1	0.4	0.3	1.6	1	50.9	0.1	NM	NM	35.5	99.7
1985	NA	NA	NA	NA	NM	NA	0.1	NM	NM	58.3	NA

Data as orig. reptd. **1.** Refl. merger or acq. **2.** Incl. equity in earns. of nonconsol. subs. NA-Not Available. NM-Not Meaningful. d-Deficit.

Total Revenues (Million $)

Quarter:	1992–93	1991–92	1990–91	1989–90
Dec.	74.6	56.6	28.5	14.7
Mar.	69.4	57.8	33.8	16.2
Jun.	66.6	62.5	41.0	19.6
Sep.		65.2	44.3	21.6
		242.1	147.6	73.1

Total revenues in the nine months ended June 30, 1993, advanced 13%, year to year, spurred by 31% growth in outpatient infusion, resulting from the development of additional IntraCare centers, and a 704% surge in lithotripsy revenues, reflecting acquisitions. Home infusion revenues were down 4.4%, penalized by increased competition and discounts granted to third-party payors. Stricter reimbursement patterns by insurance carriers resulted in increased provisions for doubtful accounts and lower margins; despite a nonrecurring gain of $0.10 a share on the sale of assets, net income fell 26%, to $34,706,347 ($0.86 a share), from $46,775,277 ($1.15).

Common Share Earnings ($)

Quarter:	1992–93	1991–92	1990–91	1989–90
Dec.	0.36	0.35	0.20	0.13
Mar.	0.28	0.36	0.25	0.14
Jun.	0.25	0.41	0.27	0.15
Sep.		0.43	0.29	0.16
		1.55	1.02	0.57

Finances

In August 1993, T² announced that it had become aware of certain accounting irregularities and errors related to the timing of revenue recognition and the writeoff of doubtful accounts that would result in adjustments to previously announced results for the first and second quarters of fiscal 1993. Consequently, fiscal 1993 first quarter earnings were later restated to $0.35 a share, from $0.44, and second quarter earnings to $0.25 a share, from $0.47.

In August 1993, the U.S. Department of Health and Human Services confirmed that the company is one of several targets of investigations into possible Medicare fraud involving possible kickbacks to doctors.

Dividend Data

Quarterly dividends were initiated in September 1992.

Amt. of Divd. $	Date Decl.	Ex-divd. Date	Stock of Record	Payment Date
0.02½	Nov. 12	Dec. 9	Dec. 15	Dec. 31'92
0.02½	Feb. 16	Mar. 9	Mar. 15	Mar. 31'93
0.02½	Jun. 3	Jun. 9	Jun. 15	Jun. 30'93
0.02½	Sep. 9	Sep. 10	Sep. 16	Sep. 30'93

Capitalization

Long Term Debt: $4,094,353 (6/93) of cap. lease obligs.

Common Stock: 40,486,387 shs. ($0.01 par).
Institutions hold 44%.
Shareholders of record: 2,285 (11/92).

Options: To buy 3,437,807 shs. at $0.50 to $58.125 ea. (9/92).

Office—1121 Alderman Dr., Alpharetta, GA 30202. **Tel**—(404) 442-2160. **Chrmn**—T. E. Haire. **VP & Investor Contact**—Dale R. Benzine. **Dirs**—B. D. Fielitz, T. E. Haire, A. C. Smith, S. S. Trotman. **Transfer Agent & Registrar**—Trust Co. Bank, Atlanta. **Incorporated** in Florida in 1984; reincorporated in Delaware in 1988. **Empl**—1,285.

 Adam J. Penn

TCA Cable TV

NASDAQ Symbol TCAT (Incl. in Nat'l Market) In S&P MidCap 400

Price	Range	P-E Ratio	Dividend	Yield	S&P Ranking	Beta
Sep. 13'93	1993					
26⅛	26½–18½	35	0.40	1.5%	B+	0.85

Summary

This cable television company operates mostly in smaller markets in Texas, Louisiana and Arkansas. As of September 1993, TCA owned or managed 53 systems with about 449,000 subscribers. Although fiscal 1994 revenues are expected to decline fractionally, due to the implementation of new FCC regulations, earnings should continue to rise, and the longer-term outlook is favorable. The dividend was boosted 18% in early 1993.

Earnings for fiscal 1993 are projected at $0.80 a share, up 31% from the $0.61 for 1992. Another rise, to about $0.90 is anticipated for 1994.

An increase in the $0.10 quarterly dividend is possible in early 1994.

Revenues for fiscal 1994 are expected to decline by less than 1%, reflecting compliance with new FCC regulations requiring rebates, rollbacks and price freezes for basic cable service and for certain ancillary charges. Nevertheless, cash flow should rise modestly. The rise in net income will largely stem from lower interest expense. Revenues and cash flow are expected to advance in fiscal 1995.

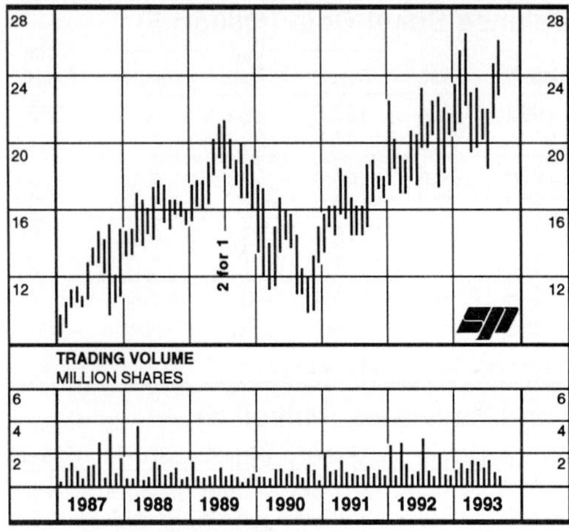

Revenues (Million $)

Quarter:	1992–93	1992	1991	1990
Jan.	36.7	33.6	30.3	27.0
Apr.	37.8	34.6	31.8	28.1
Jul.	38.3	35.1	32.2	28.7
Oct.	---	35.6	32.8	30.0
	---	138.8	127.1	113.7

Based on a brief report, revenues for the nine months ended July 31, 1993, advanced 9.2%, year to year, aided by a continued increase in subscribers. Operating income (before depreciation) was up 9.1% from the year earlier period. After other items, including sharply lower interest expense, and taxes, net income climbed 32%. Share earnings were $0.60, up 30% from $0.46.

Common Share Earnings ($)

Quarter:	1992–93	1992	1991	1990
Jan.	0.19	0.14	0.08	0.04
Apr.	0.21	0.16	0.08	0.05
Jul.	0.20	0.16	0.09	0.04
Oct.	E0.20	0.15	0.10	0.07
	E0.80	0.61	0.35	0.20

Important Developments

Sep. '93— TCAT announced its finalized schedule for upgrading its cable systems with fiber optics in order to have state-of-the-art infrastructure for enhanced video signal delivery. The system upgrades, which will take three to five years to complete, at a cost of about $100 million, will vastly expand channel capacity, and will be able to provide telecommunications and high speed data transmission to include virtually any interconnection of computers, schools, houses and businesses. TCAT also reported that it has completed the restructuring of rates and channel line ups as provided for under FCC rules which went into effect on September 1, 1993. The company estimates that revenues in fiscal 1994 will decline by less than 1%, under the new regulations.

Next earnings report expected in early December.

Per Share Data ($)

Yr. End Oct. 31	1992	1991	1990	[1]1989	1988	[1]1987	[1]1986	[1]1985	[1]1984	[1]1983
Tangible Bk. Val.	**d4.15**	d4.91	d5.57	d5.66	0.56	[4]2.22	0.62	0.81	0.75	0.57
Cash Flow	**1.95**	1.27	1.06	1.19	0.97	0.78	0.71	0.66	0.57	0.42
Earnings[2]	**0.61**	0.35	0.20	0.45	0.40	0.23	0.27	0.30	0.25	0.20
Dividends	**0.340**	0.280	0.240	0.200	0.160	0.120	0.076	0.064	0.048	0.040
Payout Ratio	**56%**	80%	120%	44%	40%	57%	28%	21%	19%	20%
Prices[3]—High	**23**	19	17½	21⅜	17¾	15⅛	11⅛	11¼	6⅛	6
Low	**17**	13½	9⅞	15⅜	13¼	8½	7¾	5½	4½	4⅝
P/E Ratio—	**38–28**	54–39	88–49	48–34	45–34	66–37	41–29	38–19	25–18	31–23

Data as orig. reptd. Adj. for stk. divs. of 100% Jul. 1989, 25% Apr. 1986. **1.** Refl. merger or acq. **2.** Bef. spec. items of -0.03 in 1986, -0.02 in 1984. **3.** Cal. yr. **4.** Incl. intangibles. E-Estimated. d-Deficit.

Income Data (Million $)

Year Ended Oct. 31	Revs.	Oper. Inc.	% Oper. Inc. of Revs.	Cap. Exp.	Depr.	Int. Exp.	Net Bef. Taxes	Eff. Tax Rate	[2]Net Inc.	% Net Inc. of Revs.	Cash Flow
1992	**139**	**70.4**	**50.7**	**16.5**	**32.8**	**13.2**	**24.7**	**39.2%**	**15.0**	**10.8**	**47.8**
1991	127	53.9	42.4	11.9	22.5	17.9	13.9	38.8%	8.5	6.7	31.0
1990	114	49.4	43.4	20.2	20.8	20.7	8.2	42.1%	4.8	4.2	25.6
[1]1989	79	41.1	52.0	49.9	18.0	5.4	18.0	40.0%	10.8	13.7	28.9
1988	69	33.1	48.1	12.1	13.8	4.6	15.7	38.9%	9.6	13.9	23.4
[1]1987	60	28.6	47.4	26.5	12.2	6.4	10.2	50.3%	5.1	8.4	17.3
[1]1986	48	24.1	50.0	17.1	9.5	3.7	11.1	46.8%	5.9	12.2	15.4
[1]1985	44	21.5	49.3	22.4	7.9	4.1	10.0	35.7%	6.4	14.8	14.3
[1]1984	28	14.2	50.8	19.8	5.4	2.5	6.4	35.2%	4.2	14.9	9.6
[1]1983	22	10.8	49.8	14.6	3.7	1.7	5.4	42.1%	3.1	14.4	6.8

Balance Sheet Data (Million $)

Oct. 31	Cash	Curr. Assets	Curr. Liab.	Curr. Ratio	Total Assets	% Ret. on Assets	[3]Long Term Debt	Common Equity	Total Cap.	% LT Debt of Cap.	% Ret. on Equity
1992	**0.82**	**NA**	**48.8**	**NA**	**290**	**5.0**	**130**	**78.0**	**241**	**54.0**	**20.1**
1991	0.99	NA	40.5	NA	306	2.7	165	70.8	265	62.0	12.4
1990	0.73	NA	27.9	NA	325	1.5	205	64.9	297	69.1	7.3
1989	1.01	NA	22.2	NA	328	4.7	216	65.8	305	70.8	17.3
1988	0.81	NA	18.5	NA	135	7.0	37	59.5	117	31.8	16.9
1987	0.69	NA	15.8	NA	138	4.2	52	53.7	122	42.3	12.2
1986	0.91	NA	NA	NA	90	6.8	43	26.3	82	52.0	24.3
1985	9.40	NA	NA	NA	84	8.6	41	22.1	73	55.9	29.7
1984	0.45	NA	NA	NA	51	9.6	26	16.4	47	55.2	28.1
1983	0.45	NA	3.3	NA	36	10.8	18	13.1	34	54.3	31.8

Data as orig. reptd. **1.** Refl. merger or acq. **2.** Bef. spec. items. **3.** Incl. current portion. NA-Not Available.

Business Summary

Formed in 1981, TCA Cable TV, Inc. develops, operates and manages cable television systems. As of June 1993, TCA owned or managed 53 cable systems with a combined total of nearly 449,000 subscribers. The systems are located primarily in smaller markets in Arkansas, Louisiana and Texas where over-the-air television reception is unsatisfactory.

Basic service includes signals of nearby over-the-air TV stations carrying the commercial networks; independent, specialty and educational stations; sports and educational programming; and additional satellite programming such as signals of distant independent stations and continuous time, news and weather information. Expanded basic service includes a variety of packaged programming, purchased from independent suppliers and combined in different formats to appeal to different tastes. TCA also offers premium services such as The Movie Channel, HBO, Showtime, and The Disney Channel. The average charge for basic and expanded basic service during fiscal 1992 was $19.71 per subscriber. A one-time installation fee of up to $35 is usually charged to new subscribers. The company charges an additional $8 to $10 per month for each premium service.

During fiscal 1992, the company derived about 6% of its revenues from sales of blocks of advertising time, home shopping channels and "pay-per-view" services. TCA expects these to contribute a growing share to revenues in future periods.

Dividend Data

Cash has been paid each year since 1982.

Amt of Divd. $	Date Decl.	Ex-divd. Date	Stock of Record	Payment Date
0.10	Dec. 2	Dec. 29	Jan. 5	Jan. 19'93
0.10	Mar. 30	Apr. 7	Apr. 14	Apr. 28'93
0.10	Jun. 30	Jul. 9	Jul. 15	Jul. 29'93
0.10	Sep. 7	Sep. 16	Sep. 22	Oct. 6'93

Finances

Capital expenditures are mainly for cable system construction, upgrading and rebuilding, acquisitions of other cable systems and purchases of converters to be furnished to subscribers. Approximately $16.3 million of internally generated funds were spent for system upgrading and expansion in fiscal 1992. In September 1993, TCAT said it plans to spend some $100 million over the next three to five years to complete an extensive system upgrade.

Capitalization

Debt: $154,056,179 (4/93).

Common Stock: 24,635,332 shs. ($0.10 par).
Officers & directors own about 32%, incl. some 24% held by Robert M. Rogers.
Institutions hold about 62%.
Shareholders: About 1,800 (1/93).

Office—3015 SSE Loop 323, Tyler, TX 75701. **Tel**—(903) 595-3701. **Chrmn & CEO**—R. M. Rogers. **Pres & COO**—F. R. Nichols. **VP, CFO, Treas & Investor Contact**—Jimmie F. Taylor. **Secy**—Martha Sue Hensley. **Dirs**—J. F. Ackerman, B. R. Fisch, K. S. Gunter, W. J. McKinney, F. R. Nichols, A. W. Riter Jr., R. K. Rogers, R. M. Rogers. **Transfer Agent & Registrar**—First National Bank of Chicago. **Incorporated** in Texas in 1981. **Empl**—772.

TECO Energy

NYSE Symbol TE In S&P MidCap 400

Price	Range	P-E Ratio	Dividend	Yield	S&P Ranking	Beta
Sep. 23'93	1993					
25¼	25⅞–20⁹⁄₁₆	19	0.96	3.8%	A	0.41

Summary

TECO Energy owns the Tampa Electric Co. utility, serving the growing Tampa Bay region in west central Florida. The company also has significant diversified operations related to its core business including river barging, coal mining, natural gas production and independent power production. Long-term prospects are enhanced by expected higher profit contributions from the non-regulated businesses and growth in energy sales. On August 30, 1993, the shares were split 2-for-1.

Current Outlook

Earnings for 1994 are projected at $1.43 a share, after a $0.05 one-time charge, up from 1993's estimated $1.37.

The quarterly dividend was raised 5.5%, to $0.24 from $0.22¾(both adjusted), with the May 1993 payment. Over the longer term, annual dividend hikes should average about 5.0%.

Share earnings from operations for 1993 should benefit from gains from diversified operations and greater utility rates and power sales. Net earnings will be restricted by a coal settlement charge. Share earnings for 1994 should benefit from a rate hike and higher kwh sales. Also, profits will be boosted by greater profits at the independent power facilities and gains in coal operations.

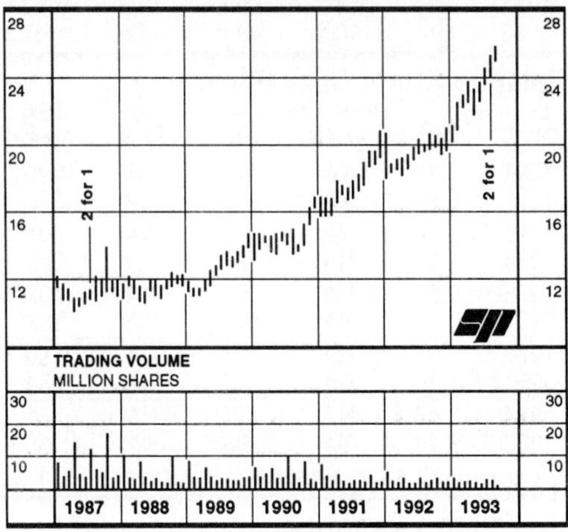

Operating Revenues (Million $)

Quarter:	1993	1992	1991	1990
Mar.	282	263	253	236
Jun.	315	284	291	278
Sep.	---	341	324	309
Dec.	---	296	286	273
	---	1,183	1,154	1,097

Revenues in the six months to June 30, 1993, advanced 9.3%, year to year. Higher diversified business profits more than offset a pretax charge of $10 million ($0.05 a share after taxes) that resulted from a coal pricing settlement agreement. Net income rose 3.3%. Share earnings were $0.55 (before a $0.10 credit from adoption of FAS 109) versus $0.54. All per share figures are adjusted to reflect the August 1993 2-for-1 stock split.

Common Share Earnings ($)

Quarter:	1993	1992	1991	1990
Mar.	0.22	0.23	0.23	0.24
Jun.	0.33	0.31	0.34	0.34
Sep.	E0.50	0.47	0.43	0.40
Dec.	E0.32	0.30	0.28	0.25
	E1.37	1.30	1.28	1.23

Important Developments

Jul. '93— The company reported that operating income for the diversified companies in the second quarter of 1993 rose to $19.5 million on revenues of $116.3 million, from $13.1 million on revenues of $89.7 million in the 1992 interim. The improvement was due mostly to higher gas prices and production at TECO Coalbed Methane. Also contributing to the gains were the initial contribution from TECO Power Services' Hardee Power Station and higher third party business at TECO Transport. Tampa Electric's second quarter operating income was $51.3 million on revenues of $259.3 million, versus $51.9 million on revenues of $243.8 million. Revenues were boosted by higher rates while earnings were limited by increased operating and maintenance costs and greater non-cash charges.

Next earnings report expected in late October.

Per Share Data ($)

Yr. End Dec. 31	1992	1991	1990	1989	1988	1987	1986	1985	1984	1983
Tangible Bk. Val.	**8.32**	7.81	7.31	7.73	7.30	6.99	6.67	6.43	6.07	5.63
Cash Flow	**2.55**	2.44	2.29	2.17	2.00	1.87	1.69	1.64	1.47	1.33
Earnings[1]	**1.30**	1.28	1.23	1.18	1.07	0.98	0.87	0.90	0.93	0.79
Dividends	**0.898**	0.848	0.798	0.748	0.700	0.660	0.620	0.580	0.540	0.500
Payout Ratio	**69%**	67%	65%	63%	66%	68%	72%	66%	60%	66%
Prices—High	**21¹⁄₁₆**	20⅞	16¹⁵⁄₁₆	14¾	12⁷⁄₁₆	13¹⁵⁄₁₆	13¾	9³⁄₁₆	7⅝	6¾
Low	**18**	15¾	13⅛	11	10⅝	10¹⁄₁₆	8½	6¹⁵⁄₁₆	6	5³⁄₁₆
P/E Ratio—	**16–14**	16–12	14–11	13–9	12–10	14–10	16–10	10–8	8–6	9–7

Data as orig. reptd. Adj. for stk. div(s). of 100% Aug. 1993, 100% Aug. 1987. **1.** Bef. spec. item(s) of -0.06 in 1988. E-Estimated.

Income Data (Million $)

Year Ended Dec. 31	Revs.	Oper. Inc.	% Oper. Inc. of Revs.	Cap. Exp.	Depr.	Int. Exp.	Net Bef. Taxes	Eff. Tax Rate	[1]Net Inc.	% Net Inc. of Revs.	Cash Flow
1992	**1,183**	**412**	**34.8**	**255**	**142**	**65.6**	**209**	**27.0%**	**153**	**12.9**	**292**
1991	1,154	395	34.2	410	133	66.1	202	26.4%	149	12.9	278
1990	1,097	379	34.6	253	121	60.3	206	30.6%	143	13.0	260
1989	1,060	366	34.5	159	112	58.8	209	33.8%	138	13.0	246
1988	1,034	340	32.9	136	106	63.1	186	32.2%	126	12.2	227
1987	970	352	36.3	133	101	60.5	195	39.8%	117	12.1	212
1986	902	327	36.3	164	93	55.2	187	44.4%	104	11.5	191
1985	886	323	36.5	141	82	59.4	192	45.2%	105	11.9	181
1984	717	249	34.8	260	56	54.0	176	40.8%	104	14.5	154
1983	677	216	32.0	272	51	47.4	139	41.8%	81	11.9	125

Balance Sheet Data (Million $)

Dec. 31	Cash	Curr. Assets	Curr. Liab.	Curr. Ratio	Total Assets	% Ret. on Assets	Long Term Debt	Common Equity	Total Inv. Capital	% LT Debt of Cap.	% Ret. on Equity
1992	**183**	**451**	**420**	**1.1**	**3,024**	**5.2**	**1,048**	**956**	**2,583**	**40.6**	**16.1**
1991	161	436	444	1.0	2,834	5.6	908	891	2,367	38.4	16.8
1990	95	370	329	1.1	2,513	5.8	763	831	2,156	35.4	16.3
1989	135	387	236	1.6	2,387	5.9	675	877	2,107	32.0	15.7
1988	86	334	211	1.6	2,315	5.5	684	828	2,064	33.1	14.9
1987	78	319	235	1.4	2,270	5.3	660	792	2,011	32.8	14.3
1986	45	268	136	2.0	2,113	5.0	685	755	1,953	35.1	13.2
1985	21	241	133	1.8	2,039	5.2	644	725	1,883	35.3	14.0
1984	59	276	177	1.6	1,921	5.6	648	655	1,730	37.4	15.5
1983	34	204	167	1.2	1,649	4.9	542	548	1,468	36.9	13.9

Data as reptd. 1. Bef. results of disc. opers. and spec. item(s) in 1988.

Business Summary

TECO Energy's principal subsidiary is Tampa Electric, which serves Tampa, Florida and adjacent communities. TE has diversified extensively into nonregulated businesses, including transportation, energy production and real estate. Contributions (in million $) to operating income in recent years:

	1992	1991
Regulated utility	$215.0	$210.3
Energy services	60.3	52.8
Other	5.7	6.5

Tampa Electric Co. serves some 475,000 customers in west central Florida, including Hillsborough, Polk, Pasco and Pinellas counties. In 1992, Tampa sold 13.55 million megawatt hours (mwh) of power, versus 13.45 mwh sold in 1991. TE's customer mix in 1992 (based on revenues) was: residential (44%); commercial (29%); industrial (12%); and other (15%). TE derives about 98% of its power needs from coal. The total generating capability of TE's 19 power units at 1992 year-end was 3,312 mw, while peak usage in 1992 was 2,771 mw.

TE's diversified operations include: TECO Coal, whose subsidiaries sold about 60% of their 1992 production to Tampa Electric from properties in Kentucky and Tennessee containing 175 million tons of coal; TECO Coalbed Methane, which participates in the production of natural gas from coalbeds located in Alabama's Black Warrior Basin; TECO Transport, which consists of four subsidiaries that transport, store and transfer coal and other bulk commodities to Tampa Electric and other customers; and TECO Power Services, which seeks opportunities both in and outside Florida to develop, own and operate cogeneration and independent power projects. TE also has interests in real estate development and financial investments.

Dividend Data

Dividends have been paid since 1900. A dividend reinvestment plan is available. A "poison pill" stock purchase right plan was adopted in 1989.

Amt of Divd. $	Date Decl.	Ex-divd. Date	Stock of Record	Payment Date
0.45½	Oct. 20	Oct. 26	Oct. 30	Nov. 15'92
0.45½	Jan. 19	Jan. 25	Jan. 29	Feb. 15'93
0.48	Apr. 20	Apr. 26	Apr. 30	May 15'93
0.48	Jul. 20	Jul. 26	Jul. 30	Aug. 15'93
2-for-1	Jul. 20	Aug. 31	Jul. 30	Aug. 30'93

Capitalization

Long Term Debt: $1,058,233,000 (6/93).

Subsidiary Preferred Stock (Tampa Electric Co.): $54,956,000.

Common Stock: 115,396,232 shs. ($1 par).
Institutions hold about 39%.
Shareholders of record: 29,789.

Office—702 North Franklin St., Tampa, FL 33602. **Tel**—(813) 228-4111. **Chrmn & CEO**—T. L. Guzzle. **SVP-Fin & Treas**—A. D. Oak. **VP-Secy**—R. H. Kessel. **Investor Contact**—Sandra Callahan. **Dirs**—C. D. Ausley, S. L. Baldwin, H. L. Culbreath, J. L. Ferman Jr., E. L. Flom, H. R. Guild Jr., T. L. Guzzle, C. H. Ross Jr., R. L. Ryan, J. T. Touchton, J. A. Urquhart, J. O. Welch Jr. **Transfer Agent & Registrar**—First National Bank of Boston. **Incorporated** in Florida in 1899; reincorporated in 1949. **Empl**—4,744.

 Christopher J. Grant

Tambrands Inc.

NYSE Symbol TMB Options on NYSE (Jan-Apr-Jul-Oct) In S&P MidCap 400

Price	Range	P–E Ratio	Dividend	Yield	S&P Ranking	Beta
Oct. 5'93	1993					
43	65–39½	18	1.68	3.9%	B+	0.66

Summary

This company is the leading producer of tampons, its Tampax line accounting for about 52% of the domestic market and its tampon products sold abroad in some 150 countries. In accordance with a 1989 restructuring plan, TMB has sold various nontampon businesses, reduced its workforce, and consolidated plants. Nevertheless, earnings in 1993 will be hurt by increased competition, higher marketing expenses, and a one-time after tax restructuring charge of $20.3 million. Profit growth is expected to rebound somewhat in 1994. In June 1993, Martin Emmett abruptly resigned as chairman and CEO.

Current Outlook

Earnings for 1994 could reach $2.85 a share, up from the $2.11 estimated for 1993 (including a one-time $0.53 restructuring charge).

The quarterly dividend was increased 10.5%, to $0.42 from $0.38, with the September 1993, declaration.

Despite efforts to restage its product line since 1991, including new packaging and product improvements, sales for 1994 should be flat or advance only moderately, reflecting stable to declining market share and increased competition. Further declines in the U.S. could be offset by increased volume overseas, due to greater market penetration, particularly in newer growth countries such as the People's Republic of China and Russia, and emphasis on new marketing strategies. Despite higher costs associated with marketing programs, margins are expected to expand on improved operating efficiencies and efforts to reduce operating expenses. Earnings comparisons will benefit from the absence of a one time $20.3 million after tax restructuring charge.

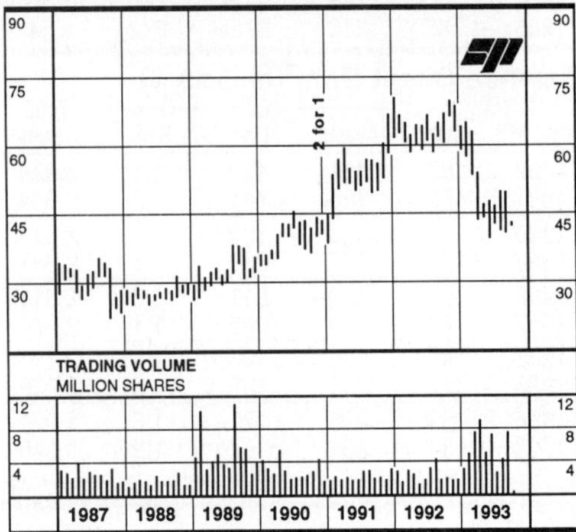

Net Sales (Million $)

Quarter:	1993	1992	1991	1990
Mar.	154.4	174.9	156.7	159.3
Jun.	149.0	169.4	178.4	169.3
Sep.		174.5	151.8	152.1
Dec.		165.3	173.8	150.9
		684.1	660.7	631.5

Sales for the first six months of 1993 declined 12%, year to year, reflecting the sale of Maxithins in 1992, the sale of the sanitary pad and diaper businesses in Brazil and Mexico, adverse currency exchanges, and lower volume in the U.S. Costs fell more rapidly, and after a one-time restructuring charge of $30 million, a decline in net interest income, and a higher tax rate, net income was off 50%. Share earnings, based on 3.0% fewer shares, totaled $0.74, down from $1.44 which excludes a $0.03 special charge.

Common Share Earnings ($)

Quarter:	1993	1992	1991	1990
Mar.	0.82	0.73	0.61	0.51
Jun.	d0.09	0.72	0.87	0.75
Sep.	E0.62	0.85	0.34	0.61
Dec.	E0.76	0.80	0.09	0.43
	E2.11	3.09	1.92	2.30

Important Developments

Sep. '93— TMB announced that its board decided unanimously that the company would continue to operate as an independent entity, versus trying to find a buyer of the company.

Jul. '93— TMB took a $20.3 million after tax restructuring charge in the second quarter as part of an ongoing program to become more competitive, reduce operating costs and increase efficiency.

Next earnings report expected in late October.

Per Share Data ($)

Yr. End Dec. 31	1992	1991	1990	1989	1988	1987	1986	[1]1985	1984	1983
Tangible Bk. Val.	**4.09**	5.22	5.74	5.69	6.40	5.53	5.28	4.51	4.34	3.90
Cash Flow	**3.49**	2.26	2.56	0.33	2.23	2.02	1.81	1.58	1.42	1.25
Earnings[2]	**3.09**	1.92	2.30	0.04	1.92	1.73	1.56	1.41	1.28	1.15
Dividends	**1.400**	1.240	1.110	1.035	0.975	0.915	0.863	0.813	0.763	0.713
Payout Ratio	**45%**	64%	47%	NM	51%	53%	55%	58%	60%	62%
Prices—High	**70½**	66⅞	45½	38¼	31⅝	35 9/16	30 7/16	22 15/16	15 7/16	15 7/16
Low	**58⅝**	38⅝	33¾	26 5/16	25¼	22⅜	21¾	14 3/16	11 11/16	11¼
P/E Ratio—	**23–19**	35–20	20–15	NM	17–13	21–13	20–14	16–10	12–9	13–10

Data as orig. reptd. Adj. for stk. div(s). of 100% Dec. 1990, 100% Dec. 1986. **1.** Reflects merger or acquisition. **2.** Bef. spec. item(s) of -0.03 in 1992, -0.10 in 1985, +0.06 in 1984. d-Deficit. E-Estimated NM-Not Meaningful.

Income Data (Million $)

Year Ended Dec. 31	Revs.	Oper. Inc.	% Oper. Inc. of Revs.	Cap. Exp.	Depr.	Int. Exp.	[2]Net Bef. Taxes	Eff. Tax Rate	[3]Net Inc.	% Net Inc. of Revs.	Cash Flow
1992	**684**	**210**	**30.8**	**55.1**	**15.7**	**8.6**	**192**	**36.2%**	**[4]122**	**17.9**	**138**
1991	661	175	26.4	46.0	14.1	8.9	132	40.0%	79	12.0	93
1990	632	161	25.5	43.7	11.1	12.4	155	36.8%	98	15.5	109
1989	583	123	21.0	14.9	13.0	8.8	31	94.4%	2	0.3	15
1988	563	150	26.7	16.8	13.9	9.7	134	36.4%	85	15.1	99
1987	539	139	25.8	22.2	12.9	6.2	126	39.2%	77	14.2	89
1986	487	123	25.4	28.1	11.2	2.6	117	41.0%	[4]69	14.2	80
[1]1985	420	104	24.8	48.0	7.7	Nil	106	41.1%	62	14.8	70
1984	390	96	24.6	14.8	6.5	Nil	99	43.1%	57	14.5	63
1983	346	88	25.3	18.7	5.3	Nil	91	43.9%	51	14.7	56

Balance Sheet Data (Million $)

		Curr.									
Dec. 31	Cash	Assets	Liab.	Ratio	Total Assets	% Ret. on Assets	Long Term Debt	Common Equity	Total Cap.	% LT Debt of Cap.	% Ret. on Equity
1992	**24**	**197**	**184**	**1.1**	**373**	**32.7**	**1.03**	**168**	**189**	**0.5**	**63.9**
1991	73	234	153	1.5	390	20.7	2.07	223	237	0.9	33.9
1990	100	250	117	2.1	381	25.5	2.38	249	264	0.9	37.8
1989	115	249	113	2.2	411	0.4	Nil	284	298	Nil	0.5
1988	88	239	83	2.9	465	19.5	Nil	353	382	Nil	25.5
1987	57	189	62	3.1	408	19.8	Nil	314	347	Nil	26.7
1986	90	198	71	2.8	364	20.0	Nil	260	292	Nil	28.4
1985	72	177	80	2.2	328	20.8	Nil	226	248	Nil	29.3
1984	100	179	56	3.2	269	22.0	Nil	198	214	Nil	30.0
1983	93	163	59	2.8	245	22.8	Nil	179	186	Nil	29.2

Data as orig. reptd. **1.** Reflects merger or acquisition. **2.** Incl. equity in earns. of nonconsol. subs. prior to 1991. **3.** Bef. spec. items. **4.** Reflects accounting change.

Business Summary

Tambrands Inc. (formerly Tampax Inc.) is the leading international manufacturer and marketer of tampons. As part of a restructuring program announced in 1989, TMB has divested various divisions in order to focus on becoming the leading supplier of tampons worldwide. Between 1989 and the end of 1992, TMB has sold its cosmetics, diagnostics and Maxithins pad and panty shield businesses; its headquarters in Lake Success, NY; its non-tampon business in Spain; its interest in a joint venture in Turkey; its disposable diaper and external pad business in Brazil; and its alcohol and external pad business in Mexico. Contributions to sales and pretax earnings by regions in 1992:

	Sales	Profits
U.S.	58%	77%
Europe	30%	22%
Other foreign	13%	1%

TMB's largest selling product is the Tampax flushable applicator tampon, which became commercially available in 1936. TMB also sells Tampax tampons with plastic applicators in the U.S. and Tampax Compak tampons, with a compact all-plastic applicator in the U.S., Canada and parts of Europe. Recent new products include a Tampax comfort shaped flushable applicator tampon that has an all-paper rounded-end applicator and a slimmer design; a Tampax Satin Touch tampon which offers the ease and comfort of a plastic applicator but has an all-paper applicator that is flushable and biodegradable; and Tampax Tampets non-applicator tampons.

TMB sells its products in the U.S. and some 150 countries. TMB's foreign subsidiaries and joint ventures operate in Canada, Europe, Eastern Europe, South Africa, Latin America, and the Ukraine. The company owns an 80% joint venture in the The People's Republic of China.

Dividend Data

Dividends have been paid since 1942. A new "poison pill" stock purchase right was adopted in 1989. A dividend reinvestment plan is available.

Amt of Divd. $	Date Decl.	Ex-divd. Date	Stock of Record	Payment Date
0.38	Feb. 23	Mar. 1	Mar. 5	Mar. 15'93
0.38	May 5	Jun. 1	Jun. 7	Jun. 15'93
0.38	Aug. 24	Aug. 31	Sep. 7	Sep. 15'93
0.42	Sep. 21	Dec. 1	Dec. 7	Dec. 15'93

Capitalization

Long Term Debt: $747,000 of capital lease obligations (6/93).

Common Stock: 38,444,939 shs. ($0.25 par).
Institutions hold about 69%.
Shareholders of record: 6,255.

Office—777 Westchester Ave., White Plains, NY 10604. **Tel**—(914) 696-6000. **Chrmn**—H. B. Wentz, Jr. **Pres**—C. J. Chapman. **SVP-Secy & Investor Contact**—Paul E. Konney. **SVP-CFO & Treas**—R. F. Wright. **Dirs**—L. H. Affinito, C. J. Chapman, P. S. Doherty, F. Hall, B. Healey, R. P. Kiley, J. Loudon, R. M. Manton, J. A. Meyers, H. L. Tower, H. B. Wentz Jr., R. M. Williams. **Transfer Agent & Registrar**—First Chicago Trust Co.of New York, NYC. **Incorporated** in Delaware in 1936. **Empl**—3,300.

 E.A. Vandeventer

Teleflex Inc.

ASE Symbol TFX In S&P MidCap 400

Price	Range	P–E Ratio	Dividend	Yield	S&P Ranking	Beta
Aug. 24'93	1993					
32⅜	33⅝–27¾	17	0.46	1.4%	A+	0.97

Summary

This diversified manufacturer, which serves the aerospace, commercial and medical markets, has compiled an outstanding record of sales, earnings and dividend growth over the past decade. Earnings gains in 1993 should reflect strong auto, marine and industrial markets, outweighing weakness in the aerospace area and the impact of soft European economies on the medical unit. Further growth is expected for 1994.

Current Outlook

Earnings for 1993 are estimated at $2.05 a share, up from $1.87 in 1992. An increase to $2.35 is seen for 1994.

Dividends should continue at no less than the current $0.11½ quarterly rate.

Sales should rise about 15% in 1993 from 1992 levels. Aerospace revenues will provide most of the gain, reflecting the acquistion of The Engineering Group. The commercial segment should continue to gain in the second half of 1993 and in 1994, benefiting from improved auto and marine markets. Medical sales are expected to remain soft in the second half of 1993, reflecting weak European economies. Second half margins will narrow, restricted by declines for the aerospace and medical groups. For 1994, these groups should have moderate sales growth, with margins improving on cost cutting moves.

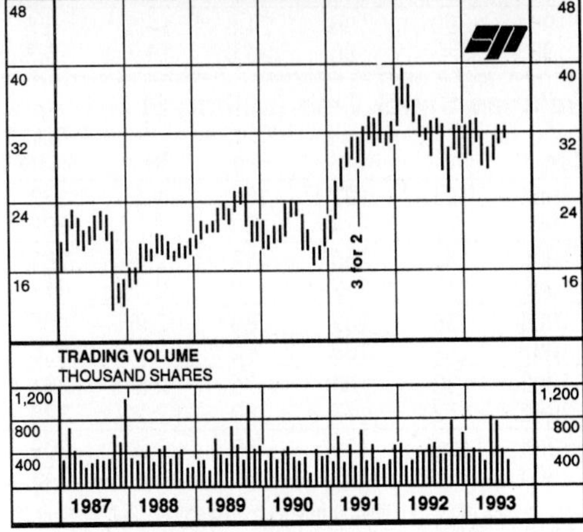

Revenues (Million $)

13 Weeks:	1993	1992	1991	1990
Mar.	157	133	112	109
Jun.	175	149	117	116
Sep.	---	138	116	102
Dec.	---	151	138	117
	---	570	483	444

Sales in the 26 weeks ended June 27, 1993, climbed 18%, year to year, as strong gains for commercial business and an aerospace acquisition outweighed a decline in medical operations. Margins narrowed, and the gain in net income was held to 7.8%, to $1.04 a share, from $0.97.

Common Share Earnings ($)

13 Weeks:	1993	1992	1991	1990
Mar.	0.50	0.47	0.45	0.44
Jun.	0.54	0.50	0.47	0.46
Sep.	E0.40	0.36	0.35	0.35
Dec.	E0.61	0.54	0.50	0.48
	E2.05	1.87	1.77	1.73

Important Developments

Jun. '93— The company's Sermatech International division acquired the Advanced Welding and Coating Services operation of Metallurgical Industries, Inc.

Mar. '93— Teleflex acquired The Engineering Group, a privately held company that makes aircraft engine parts and performs heat treating, surface finishing and testing of parts, for net cash of $38 million, plus the assumption of certain liabilities. The Engineering Group had 1992 sales of $57 million.

Jan. '93— The company purchased the remaining shares of Techsonic Industries, a maker of marine information systems. A minority interest had been acquired in 1991.

Next earnings report expected in mid-October.

Per Share Data ($)

Yr. End Dec. 31	1992	[1]1991	1990	[1]1989	1988	[2]1987	1986	1985	1984	1983
Tangible Bk. Val.	[4]14.25	[4]12.73	[4]11.45	[4]9.87	8.49	7.25	6.25	5.36	4.64	[4]4.08
Cash Flow	3.13	2.81	2.72	2.38	2.12	1.76	1.45	1.13	0.95	0.82
Earnings[3]	1.87	1.77	1.73	1.63	1.48	1.19	1.01	0.84	0.72	0.61
Dividends	0.415	0.390	0.350	0.307	0.257	0.217	0.182	0.153	0.137	0.123
Payout Ratio	22%	22%	20%	19%	17%	18%	18%	18%	19%	20%
Prices—High	39½	34⅜	24⅛	25⅞	20⅜	23¼	20	13⁹⁄₁₆	10¹¹⁄₁₆	13
Low	25	19⅝	16⅝	18¾	14¼	11⁹⁄₁₆	13¼	8¹⁵⁄₁₆	7¹⁄₁₆	9⁷⁄₁₆
P/E Ratio—	21–13	19–11	14–10	16–11	14–10	19–10	20–13	16–11	15–10	21–15

Data as orig. reptd. Adj. for stk. divs. of 50% Jun. 1991, 100% May 1986. **1.** Refl. merger or acq. **2.** Refl. acctg. change. **3.** Bef. spec. item(s) of +0.05 in 1992. **4.** Incl. intangibles. E-Estimated.

Income Data (Million $)

Year Ended Dec. 31	Revs.	Oper. Inc.	% Oper. Inc. of Revs.	Cap. Exp.	Depr.	Int. Exp.	[3]Net Bef. Taxes	Eff. Tax Rate	[4]Net Inc.	% Net Inc. of Revs.	Cash Flow
[1]1992	**567**	**82.5**	**14.5**	**19.3**	**21.6**	**15.5**	**48.7**	**34.2%**	**32.0**	**5.6**	**53.6**
[1]1991	480	73.1	15.2	42.4	17.5	13.8	45.3	34.3%	29.8	6.2	47.3
1990	441	68.4	15.5	17.5	16.2	12.4	42.9	33.4%	28.6	6.5	44.7
[1]1989	356	54.0	15.2	64.8	12.3	6.9	39.2	31.7%	26.8	7.5	39.1
1988	324	48.5	15.0	27.5	10.5	6.2	36.4	34.0%	24.0	7.4	34.5
[2]1987	270	43.9	16.3	16.7	9.3	4.9	31.7	37.9%	[2]19.7	7.3	29.0
1986	214	33.8	15.8	43.3	7.1	3.7	26.9	39.0%	16.4	7.7	23.6
1985	172	25.3	14.7	10.1	4.7	1.6	22.2	40.1%	13.3	7.7	18.0
1984	153	21.8	14.2	7.3	3.7	1.4	19.1	40.8%	11.3	7.4	15.0
1983	129	19.4	15.0	7.6	3.3	1.5	16.1	41.0%	9.5	7.3	12.8

Balance Sheet Data (Million $)

		Curr.									
Dec. 31	Cash	Assets	Liab.	Ratio	Total Assets	% Ret. on Assets	Long Term Debt	Common Equity	Total Cap.	% LT Debt of Cap.	% Ret. on Equity
1992	**36.3**	**290**	**123**	**2.4**	**535**	**6.3**	**135**	**240**	**402**	**33.5**	**14.1**
1991	24.5	255	123	2.1	478	6.6	119	212	342	34.9	14.8
1990	44.3	237	103	2.3	425	7.2	113	188	311	36.4	16.3
1989	18.4	194	82	2.4	367	8.5	106	160	275	38.6	18.0
1988	33.2	161	62	2.6	264	9.8	57	136	201	28.5	19.0
1987	26.2	140	50	2.8	226	9.6	55	116	176	31.2	18.3
1986	24.2	112	42	2.7	185	10.1	38	101	143	26.3	17.6
1985	31.0	92	25	3.6	137	10.8	24	84	111	21.1	16.9
1984	21.5	76	20	3.8	109	10.8	14	73	90	15.8	16.6
1983	16.4	69	20	3.4	100	10.3	14	64	80	17.7	17.6

Data as orig. reptd. **1.** Refl. merger or acq. **2.** Refl. acctg. chg. **3.** Incl. equity in earns. of nonconsol. subs. **4.** Bef. spec. items.

Business Summary

Teleflex Inc., originally a manufacturer of push/pull controls for military aircraft, has diversified over the years in specific market niches in the aerospace, commercial and medical markets. Contributions by business segment in 1992 were:

	Sales	Profits
Commercial products..........	37%	38%
Medical products	32%	38%
Aerospace products	31%	24%

The U.S. government accounted for 9% of 1992 sales (12% in 1991). Foreign operations, principally in Europe, provided 30% of total sales in 1992 (32% in 1991); export sales accounted for 11% (10%).

Commercial products made for the automotive industry include automatic and manual transmission shift controls, accelerator and cruise controls, trunk and hood release cables, and fuel system hose. Marine products include mechanical and hydraulic steering systems, electrical gauges and instrumentation, and electronic navigation systems. Industrial products include cables for outdoor power equipment, hose used in underground fuel tank connectors and other applications, and heat-shrinkable tubing for home appliances.

The aerospace products and services segment consists of two major product lines: aerospace/defense and Sermatech International Inc. The aerospace/defense group designs and makes mechanical and electromechanical controls; it participates in major military and commercial programs. Sermatech offers technical services and repairs to the gas turbine market worldwide.

The TFX Medical group makes invasive disposable products and devices for the anesthesiological, urological, cardiovascular, gastroenterological and general surgical markets. Rusch International, a German manufacturer of disposable and reusable medical products, was acquired in 1989.

Dividend Data

Quarterly dividends have been paid since 1977.

Amt. of Divd. $	Date Decl.	Ex–divd. Date	Stock of Record	Payment Date
0.10½	Nov. 4	Nov. 19	Nov. 25	Dec. 15'92
0.10½	Feb. 2	Feb. 19	Feb. 25	Mar. 15'93
0.11½	Apr. 30	May 19	May 25	Jun. 15'93
0.11½	Aug. 3	Aug. 19	Aug. 25	Sep. 15'93

Capitalization

Long Term Debt: $142,440,000 (6/93).

Common Stock: 16,952,934 shs. ($1 par).
Nearly 9% is held by Woelm Holding Co. Ltd.
L. K. Black controls 14%.
Institutions hold 56%.
Shareholders: About 1,700 of record (2/93).

Office—630 W. Germantown Pike, Plymouth Meeting, PA 19462. **Tel**—(215) 834-6301. **Fax**—(215) 834-8228. **Chrmn & CEO**—L. K. Black. **Pres**—D. S. Boyer. **VP & CFO**—H. L. Zuber, Jr. **VP & Secy**—S. K.Chance. **Investor Contact**—Janine Dusossoit (215-834-6362). **Dirs**—D. Beckman, L. K. Black, L. W. Bluemle, Jr., L. E. Hatch, Jr., P. Hutchinson, S. W. W. Lubsen, J. H. Remer, P. E. Retzlaff J. W. Stratton. **Transfer Agent & Registrar**—Mellon Securities Trust Co., Ridgefield, NJ. **Incorporated** in Delaware in 1943. **Empl**—7,400.

 T. M. Canning

Telephone and Data Systems

ASE Symbol TDS Options on Pacific (Feb-May-Aug-Nov) In S&P MidCap 400

Price	Range	P-E Ratio	Dividend	Yield	S&P Ranking	Beta
Aug. 26'93	1993					
48½	49–33¼	66	0.34	0.7%	B+	1.39

Summary

TDS is the 17th largest telephone holding company in the U.S., providing local telephone service in 29 states, as well as cellular telephone service and paging services. Rapid growth of revenues and operating earnings has reflected an aggressive acquisition program. The company anticipates that in five years over half of revenues will come from wireless services.

Current Outlook

Earnings for 1993 are estimated at $0.75 a share, down from 1992's $0.91 (including a gain of $0.19 from the sale of a cellular interest). An increase to $1.00 is projected for 1994.

The $0.08½ quarterly dividend should be maintained.

Telephone revenues are expected to rise 10% to 15% in 1993, aided by internal growth and acquisitions. Margins should be stable, as higher depreciation charges are offset by operating efficiencies. Cellular operations should continue to grow rapidly; operations are expected to approach positive operating margins during the year, aided by economies and efficiencies resulting from the clustering strategy. Contributions from paging operations are expected to improve. Earnings will reflect higher interest costs and more shares outstanding as a result of the company's aggressive acquisition program. Comparisions with 1992 will reflect the absence of a gain of $0.19 a share from the sale of a cellular interest.

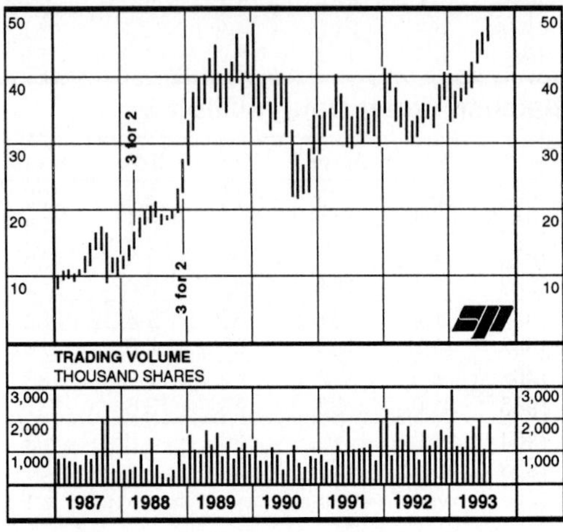

Operating Revenues (Million $)

Quarter:	1993	1992	1991	1990
Mar.	126.7	100.6	77.2	67.4
Jun.	144.8	111.0	86.4	71.9
Sep.		118.4	92.7	75.0
Dec.		126.1	98.3	80.4
		456.1	354.0	294.6

Revenues in the six months ended June 30, 1993, jumped 28%, year to year, with growth in all segments. With improved performance at all units, operating income advanced 24%. With a 13% rise in interest expense, and in the absence of a $6.9 million net gain on the sale of cellular properties, net income fell 21%. After preferred dividends, share earnings decreased to $0.32 (on 20% more shares), from $0.50 (before a charge of $0.18 for an accounting change).

Common Share Earnings ($)

Quarter:	1993	1992	1991	1990
Mar.	0.14	0.35	0.18	0.18
Jun.	0.18	0.16	0.17	0.20
Sep.	E0.19	0.15	0.17	0.21
Dec.	E0.24	0.26	0.07	0.27
	E0.75	0.91	0.59	0.86

Important Developments

Aug. '93— TDS signed a network modernization agreement with AT&T's Network Systems unit. The agreement, valued at about $100 million, calls for modernization of the company's telephone networks in 29 states over a seven-year period. The modernization will allow TDS to provide customers with advanced service offerings such as telemedicine, distance learning and video entertainment.

Next earnings report expected in late October.

Per Share Data ($)

Yr. End Dec. 31	1992	1991	1990	1989	1988	1987	1986	1985	1984	1983
Book Value[1]	**21.27**	18.42	14.17	12.00	7.81	5.89	4.83	4.28	4.09	3.98
Cash Flow	**3.44**	2.91	2.93	2.29	2.20	2.18	2.01	1.69	1.68	1.38
Earnings[2]	**0.91**	0.59	0.86	0.35	0.40	0.47	0.42	0.41	0.45	0.41
Dividends	**0.320**	0.300	0.280	0.260	0.240	0.230	0.211	0.194	0.176	0.156
Payout Ratio	**35%**	51%	33%	74%	60%	49%	51%	47%	39%	38%
Prices—High	**41¼**	40⅜	48	46½	27¾	17⅝	9⅝	6⅛	6⅛	7⅜
Low	**30⅛**	28½	21¾	26⅞	11¼	8⅛	5⅝	4⅛	3⅝	4¾
P/E Ratio—	**45–33**	68–48	56–25	NM	69–28	38–18	21–12	15–10	14–8	18–12

Data as orig. reptd. Adj. for stk. divs. of 50% Dec. 1988, 50% Mar. 1988. **1.** As reptd. by co. **2.** Bef. results of disc. ops. of +0.03 in 1988, +0.05 in 1987, +0.22 in 1986, -0.03 in 1985, -0.11 in 1984, and spec. items of -0.19 in 1992, -0.15 in 1991. E-Estimated. NM-Not Meaningful.

Income Data (Million $)

Year Ended Dec. 31	Oper. Revs.	Depr.	Maint.	Oper. Ratio	[1]Fxd. Chgs. Cover.	Constr. Credits	Eff. Tax Rate	[2]Net Inc.	—% Return On— Revs.	[3]Invest. Capital	Com. Equity	Cash Flow
1992	**456**	**98.9**	**46.9**	**94.7%**	**2.04**	**Nil**	**43.6%**	**38.5**	**8.4**	**5.2**	**4.8**	**135.3**
1991	354	76.8	42.5	92.8%	1.63	Nil	41.4%	21.1	6.0	5.0	3.6	96.3
1990	295	62.9	35.9	89.6%	2.09	Nil	37.6%	27.2	9.2	6.8	6.6	89.0
1989	240	53.3	29.5	91.6%	1.43	Nil	41.8%	11.1	4.6	5.4	3.6	63.0
1988	196	44.1	22.9	88.4%	1.43	Nil	40.8%	10.6	5.4	6.8	6.3	53.7
1987	175	27.2	17.8	87.1%	1.51	Nil	42.1%	11.3	6.5	8.2	9.6	48.9
1986	155	25.8	16.6	85.1%	1.42	Nil	33.5%	9.8	6.3	8.3	9.3	42.8
1985	119	20.8	15.4	81.8%	1.47	0.80	27.5%	9.3	7.8	8.5	10.1	34.9
1984	99	18.2	14.3	79.4%	1.73	0.89	31.0%	8.6	8.7	8.2	10.6	29.2
1983	88	16.8	14.2	78.9%	1.50	1.14	29.8%	7.8	8.9	8.0	11.0	23.5

Balance Sheet Data (Million $)

Dec. 31	Gross Prop.	Capital Expend.	Net Prop.	% Earn. on Net Prop.	Total Invest. Capital	—Capitalization— LT Debt	% LT Debt	[4]Pfd.	[4]% Pfd.	Com.	% Com.
1992	**1,571**	**162**	**1,178**	**2.3**	**1,511**	**405**	**27.8**	**174.3**	**12.0**	**877**	**60.2**
1991	1,225	169	898	3.5	1,232	381	32.2	155.6	13.2	645	54.6
1990	831	152	564	6.0	789	255	34.5	54.4	7.4	430	58.1
1989	706	157	463	4.8	694	256	39.3	40.5	6.2	355	54.5
1988	584	86	379	6.5	504	235	50.3	38.7	8.3	194	41.4
1987	497	77	319	7.4	403	217	59.0	14.9	4.0	136	37.0
1986	445	63	293	8.3	358	210	63.8	14.5	4.4	105	31.8
1985	398	53	267	9.7	326	198	66.9	10.9	3.7	87	29.4
1984	354	46	239	9.0	307	175	65.9	9.6	3.6	81	30.5
1983	328	46	227	8.6	275	173	69.0	12.2	4.9	66	26.1

Data as orig. reptd. **1.** Times int. exp. & pfd. divs. covered (aft. taxes). **2.** Bef. pfd. divs. of subs. cos.; bef. results of disc. ops. and spec. items. **3.** Based on income bef. interest charges. **4.** Incl. minority interest.

Business Summary

Telephone and Data Systems (TDS) is a diversified telecommunications service company with established local telephone operations and developing cellular telephone and radio paging operations. Contributions to revenues in recent years were:

	1992	1991	1990
Telephone	52%	60%	66%
Cellular mobile telephone	36%	28%	21%
Radio paging	12%	12%	13%

As of June 30, 1993, TDS provided local telephone service through 92 telephone companies serving 344,600 access lines in rural and suburban areas in 29 states. Operations have been expanded through an aggressive acquisition program.

Radio paging services, or beepers, are offered through wholly owned American Paging, Inc. At June 30, 1993, nearly 400,000 pagers were in service in 14 states. American is expanding the geographic coverage of its paging systems and is initiating new services, such as voice mail, as they become practical.

TDS conducts virtually all of its cellular operations through 83%-owned United States Cellular Corp. (USM, ASE). The company and USM own or have the right to acquire cellular interests in metropolitan rural service areas representing 22.3 million POPs. At June 30, 1993, USM served 189,100 customers in 107 majority-owned and managed systems.

Dividend Data

Dividends have been paid since 1974.

Amt. of Divd. $	Date Decl.	Ex–divd. Date	Stock of Record	Payment Date
0.08	Sep. 3	Sep. 4	Sep. 11	Sep. 29'92
0.08	Dec. 2	Dec. 9	Dec. 15	Dec. 29'92
0.08½	Mar. 2	Mar. 11	Mar. 17	Mar. 31'93
0.08½	Jun. 8	Jun. 14	Jun. 18	Jun. 30'93

Capitalization

Long Term Debt: $490,472,000 (3/93).

Minority Interest: $146,831,000.

Red. Preferred Stock: $27,257,000.

Nonred. Preferred Stock: $16,883,000.

Series A Common Stock: 6,900,000 shs. ($1 par); conv. sh.-for-sh. into com. About 96% is closely held.
Shareholders: 113 of record (2/93).

Common Stock: 40,500,000 shs. ($1 par).
Institutions own 75%.
Shareholders: 3,703 of record (2/93).

Office—30 North LaSalle St., Chicago, IL 60602. **Tel**—(312) 630-1900. **Chrmn**—L. T. Carlson. **Pres & CEO**—L. T. Carlson, Jr. **EVP-Fin & CFO**—M. L. Swanson. **Secy**—M. G. Hron. **Treas**—R. D. Webster. **Investor Contact**—Julie Mathews. **Dirs**—J. Barr III, D. R. Brown, L. T. Carlson, L. T. Carlson, Jr., W. C. D. Carlson, R. J. Collins, R. E. Hornacek, L. O. Johnson, D. C. Nebergall, M. L. Swanson, H. S. Wander. **Transfer Agent**—Harris Trust & Savings Bank, Chicago. **Incorporated** in Iowa in 1968. **Empl**—3,803.

 Susan Stahl Gibney

Teradyne, Inc.

NYSE Symbol TER Options on Pacific (Jan-Apr-Jul-Oct) In S&P MidCap 400

Price	Range	P–E Ratio	Dividend	Yield	S&P Ranking	Beta
Aug. 25'93	1993					
28½	29–13	41	None	None	B–	2.25

Summary

This leading manufacturer of automatic test equipment used primarily by the semiconductor and telecommunications industries also makes backplane connectors. Earnings are likely to increase for the third consecutive year in 1993, reflecting strong demand for semiconductor testers and telecommunications products, as well as the absence of non-recurring charges; however, board test demand remains weak. Extremely strong growth in semiconductor testers and a rebound in other operations resulting from a stronger economy should produce sharply higher earnings in 1994.

Current Outlook

Earnings for 1994 should approximate $1.40, up from $0.92 projected for 1993.

Cash dividends have never been paid.

Revenues are expected to climb about 25% in 1994, paced by surging demand for semiconductor testers. The semiconductor industry is in the midst of a strong cyclical rebound that is expected to last through 1994, and that is leading to capacity additions and greater demand for semiconductor testers. Manufacturers are also ordering semiconductor testers to meet technological changes resulting from the introduction of more sophisticated semiconductors. Telecommunications sales are also likely to rise substantially, reflecting strong industry growth and receipt of a large order from Germany. Backplane connections sales should benefit from strength in the electronics industry, which should also assist growth in board test. Margins should widen substantially on the greater volume and well controlled costs.

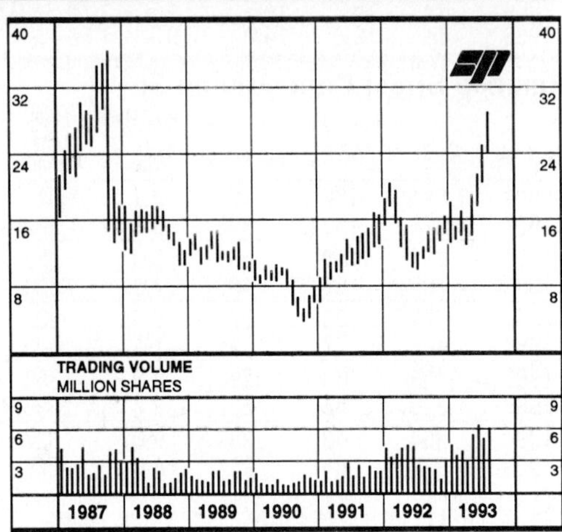

Net Sales (Million $)

Quarter:	1993	1992	1991	1990
Mar.	127.8	133.9	117.6	113.2
Jun.	139.3	134.8	130.5	108.5
Sep.	---	131.5	130.3	117.0
Dec.	---	129.4	130.5	120.3
	---	529.6	508.9	458.9

Sales in the six months ended July 4, 1993, declined fractionally, year to year, as weakness in board test and telecommunications demand offset increased sales of semiconductor testers. Results benefited from cost controls, and in the absence of $3 million of restructuring charges, pretax income soared 22%. After taxes at 30.0%, versus 20.0%, net income was up 12%, to $0.37 a share, from $0.35.

Common Share Earnings ($)

Quarter:	1993	1992	1991	1990
Mar.	0.16	0.21	d0.02	d0.16
Jun.	0.21	0.14	0.14	d0.23
Sep.	E0.25	0.17	0.23	d0.26
Dec.	E0.30	0.15	0.23	d0.06
	E0.92	0.67	0.58	d0.71

Important developments

Jul. '93— The company said it was experiencing a surge in semiconductor tester orders greater than demand at any time in the past 10 years. TER added that orders for other products were also strong, with the exception of board test, where demand remained sluggish.

May '93— Directors authorized the purchase of up to one million TER common share in the open market.

Next earnings report expected in late October.

Per Share Data ($)

Yr. End Dec. 31	1992	1991	1990	1989	1988	[1]1987	1986	1985	1984	1983
Tangible Bk. Val.	**10.43**	9.78	[2]9.26	[2]10.01	[2]9.68	9.63	[2]11.20	[2]11.14	[2]10.17	[2]8.13
Cash Flow	**1.58**	1.60	0.57	1.63	1.05	0.39	1.11	1.98	2.70	1.81
Earnings[3]	**0.67**	0.58	d0.71	0.35	d0.11	d0.76	0.01	0.87	1.87	1.08
Dividends	**Nil**	Nil	Nil	Nil	Nil	Nil	Nil	Nil	Nil	Nil
Payout Ratio	**Nil**	Nil	Nil	Nil	Nil	Nil	Nil	Nil	Nil	Nil
Prices—High	**20⅜**	16⅞	11⅛	14¾	17¾	36½	29⅝	32⅝	39⅜	39⅜
Low	**10**	6⅛	3¾	9⅞	10⅝	13⅜	15⅝	17⅛	21¼	13⅝
P/E Ratio—	**30–15**	29–11	NM	42–28	NM	NM	NM	38–20	21–11	36–13

Data as orig. reptd. Adj. for stk. div. of 100% Aug. 1983. **1.** Refl. merger or acq. **2.** Incl. intangibles. **3.** Bef. spec. item(s) of +0.01 in 1987. d-Deficit. E-Estimated. NM-Not Meaningful.

Income Data (Million $)

Year Ended Dec. 31	Revs.	Oper. Inc.	% Oper. Inc. of Revs.	Cap. Exp.	Depr.	Int. Exp.	Net Bef. Taxes	Eff. Tax Rate	[3]Net Inc.	% Net Inc. of Revs.	Cash Flow
1992	**530**	**58.7**	**11.1**	**19.5**	**31.1**	**4.11**	**26.1**	**13.5%**	**22.5**	**4.3**	**53.6**
1991	509	56.2	11.0	14.6	32.1	5.21	20.3	10.0%	18.3	3.6	50.3
1990	459	17.6	3.8	23.9	38.4	6.01	d27.9	NM	d21.3	NM	17.0
1989	484	55.5	11.5	28.3	37.8	6.95	13.9	27.0%	10.2	2.1	48.0
1988	462	53.3	11.5	19.8	33.5	7.09	0.1	NM	d3.3	NM	30.2
[1]1987	378	11.4	3.0	40.9	32.5	3.80	d33.2	NM	d21.5	NM	11.0
1986	306	19.8	6.5	18.0	26.3	NA	[2]d2.7	NM	[4]0.2	0.1	26.6
1985	336	45.1	13.4	19.7	25.9	1.72	[2]27.5	26.7%	20.2	6.0	46.1
1984	389	91.3	23.5	36.9	19.3	5.32	[2]66.8	35.4%	43.2	11.1	62.5
1983	251	51.3	20.4	20.6	14.6	6.51	[2]30.5	30.0%	21.4	8.5	36.0

Balance Sheet Data (Million $)

Dec. 31	Cash	Curr. Assets	Curr. Liab.	Curr. Ratio	Total Assets	% Ret. on Assets	Long Term Debt	Common Equity	Total Cap.	% LT Debt of Cap.	% Ret. on Equity
1992	**67.4**	**261**	**92.4**	**2.8**	**461**	**5.0**	**23.6**	**345**	**369**	**6.4**	**6.8**
1991	35.4	218	86.9	2.5	421	4.4	24.3	306	331	7.3	6.1
1990	7.4	173	84.9	2.0	389	NM	25.0	275	301	8.3	NM
1989	3.9	194	75.2	2.6	418	2.4	38.4	293	339	11.3	3.5
1988	10.9	220	79.9	2.8	434	NM	66.0	278	350	18.9	NM
1987	11.1	180	66.8	2.7	398	NM	43.4	279	327	13.3	NM
1986	33.1	157	40.9	3.8	335	0.1	12.3	264	294	4.2	0.1
1985	24.8	156	42.5	3.7	327	5.9	12.6	254	284	4.4	8.3
1984	0.8	190	53.4	3.6	350	14.2	63.9	227	305	20.9	21.2
1983	0.1	126	36.8	3.4	253	8.3	28.3	176	216	13.1	14.3

Data as orig. reptd. **1.** Refl. merger or acq. **2.** Incl. equity in earns. of nonconsol. subs. **3.** Bef. spec. items. **4.** Refl. acctg. change. d-Deficit. NM-Not Meaningful. NA-Not Available.

Business Summary

Teradyne, Inc. is a manufacturer of electronic systems and software and backplane connection systems used in the electronics and telecommunications industries. Contributions by industry segment in 1992 were:

	Sales	Profits
Electronic test systems and software	84%	84%
Backplane connection systems	16%	16%

Exports contributed 42% of sales in 1992, down from 47% in 1991.

TER designs, manufactures, markets, and services electronic systems and software used by component manufacturers in the design and testing of their products and by electronic manufacturers for the incoming inspection of components and for the design and testing of circuit boards and other assemblies. The company's electronic systems and software are also used by telephone operating companies for maintenance of their subscriber telephone lines and related equipment.

Electronic systems and software produced by the company include test systems for a wide variety of semiconductors, including digital and analog integrated circuits, test systems for circuit boards and other assemblies, test systems for telephone lines and networks, and computer-aided engineering software used in the design of electronic components and assemblies. Systems are computer-controlled and require extensive software support by both the customer and TER. Prices range from below $100,000 to over $5 million; software prices typically range from $10,000 to $500,000.

TER also makes backplane connection systems, principally for the military/aerospace, telecommunications, and computer industries.

Engineering and development expenditures amounted to $62.0 million (11.7% of sales) in 1992, essentially unchanged from 1991's $62.0 million (12.2%).

Dividend Data

No cash dividends have ever been paid. A "poison pill" stock purchase right was adopted in 1990.

Capitalization

Long Term Debt: $23,812,000 (7/93), incl. $14.4 million of 9¼% debs. due 2012; conv. into com. at $23.50 a sh.

Common Stock: 34,427,272 shs. ($0.125 par).
Institutions hold 72%.
Shareholders of record: 4,289.

Office—321 Harrison Ave, Boston, MA 02118. **Tel**—(617) 482-2700. **Chrmn & Pres**—A. V. d'Arbeloff. **EVP-Fin**—O. W. Robbins. **Clerk**—R. J. Testa. **VP & Investor Contact**—Frederick T. Van Veen. **Dirs**—A. V. d'Arbeloff, E. L. Artzt, D. S. Gregory, D. H. Hibbard, F. P. Johnson, Jr., J. H. McArthur, J. P. Mulroney, J. Prestridge, O. Robbins, R. J. Testa, H. M. Watts, Jr. **Transfer Agent & Registrar**—Bank of Boston. **Incorporated** in Massachusetts in 1960. **Empl**—4,100.

 Paul H. Valentine, CFA

Thermo Electron

NYSE Symbol TMO Options on NYSE (Mar-Jun-Sep-Dec) In S&P MidCap 400

Price	Range	P-E Ratio	Dividend	Yield	S&P Ranking	Beta
Sep. 16'93	1993					
61⅞	64⅞–47	25	None	None	B+	1.25

Summary

This company manufactures environmental and analytical instruments, biomedical equipment, cogeneration systems and process equipment. Sales and earnings are expected to continue to rise rapidly, reflecting acquisitions, new product development and market growth. TMO owns majority interests in eight publicly traded subsidiaries, a strategy management believes encourages entrepreneurial effort. A 3-for-2 stock split is to be distributed October 28, 1993.

Current Outlook

Share earnings for 1994 are expected to advance to $3.10 from the $2.55 expected for 1993, both unadjusted for the pending 3-for-2 stock split.

TMO does not plan to pay dividends in the foreseeable future.

Sales and contract revenues are expected to continue to rise at a rapid pace. Thermo Instrument's business will benefit from the passage of the second stage of the Clean Air Act, anticipated in early 1994. Thermo Process and Thermo Power are seen continuing steady growth in their environmentally related businesses. The cyclical product lines of Thermo Fibertek are expected to begin to turn around in 1994, benefiting from large orders from U.S. paper makers. Thermotrex and Thermedics (including Thermo Cardio and Thermo Voltek) should see continued growth in newly-developed products and the continued success of recent acquisitions. Nonpublic subsidiaries should grow mostly on contributions from high-growth medical products and as operations improve at Thermo Energy. With gains on the sale of stock in subsidiaries expected to be a smaller percentage of net income, the quality of earnings will improve.

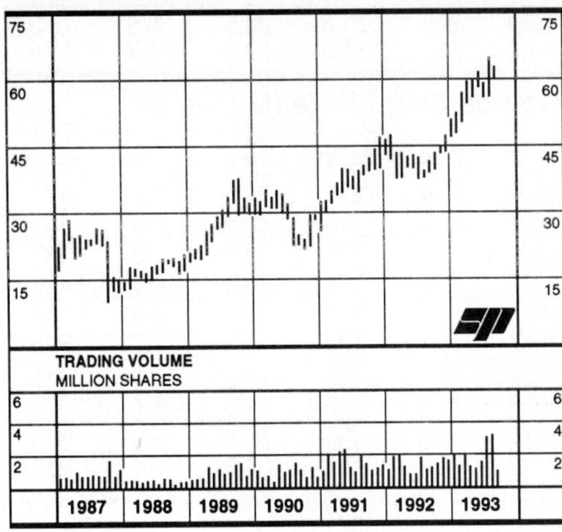

Sales & Contract Revs. (Million $)

Quarter:	1993	1992	1991	1990
Mar.	292.8	204.4	195.5	142.8
Jun.	300.4	210.1	197.8	170.2
Sep.	---	242.9	192.0	181.5
Dec.	---	291.6	220.2	213.5
	---	949.0	805.5	708.0

Revenues for the six months ended April 3, 1993, increased 43%, year to year, reflecting acquisitions in the analytical and environmental monitoring, process equipment and biomedical products businesses. After taxes at 23.6%, versus 29.8%, and minority interests, net income grew 25%, to $1.22 a share from $1.00, which was before a $0.05 charge for a change in accounting.

Common Share Earnings ($)

Quarter:	1993	1992	1991	1990
Mar.	0.57	0.48	0.39	0.32
Jun.	0.65	0.52	0.48	0.38
Sep.	E0.67	0.58	0.54	0.46
Dec.	E0.74	0.69	0.55	0.48
	[1]E2.55	2.27	1.97	1.65

Important Developments

Aug. '93— Thermo Instruments (THI) sold $210 million of convertible debt, of which TMO purchased $140 million. THI will pay $100 million of the proceeds to TMO to reduce debt. In July, TMO sold 4,500,000 shares of common stock at $57 a share, raising net proceeds of $246 million. TMO expected to use these funds and others, totaling some $500 million in all, on acquisitions in the next two years.

Next earnings report expected in November.

Per Share Data ($)

Yr. End Dec. 31	[2]1992	[2]1991	[2]1990	1989	[2]1988	1987	[2]1986	1985	1984	1983
Tangible Bk. Val.	**[3]20.47**	[3]18.62	[3]14.66	7.86	6.96	6.81	5.83	4.96	4.24	3.79
Cash Flow	**3.36**	2.95	2.57	2.05	1.71	1.51	1.26	1.13	0.91	0.48
Earnings[4]	**2.27**	1.97	1.65	1.35	1.15	1.00	0.83	0.67	0.45	0.01
Dividends	**Nil**	Nil	Nil	Nil	Nil	Nil	Nil	Nil	Nil	Nil
Payout Ratio	**Nil**	Nil	Nil	Nil	Nil	Nil	Nil	Nil	Nil	Nil
Prices—High	**47½**	47	35¼	37⅞	20¾	28⅝	23	15½	9⅞	9⅞
Low	**37½**	25⅞	21¾	19⅛	12¾	10	13⅜	8	6⅛	4⅝
P/E Ratio—	**21–17**	24–13	21–13	28–14	18–11	29–10	28–16	23–12	22–14	NM

Data as orig. reptd. Adj. for stk. divs. of 50% Nov. 1986, 50% Sep. 1985, 50% Jan. 1984. **1.** Does not add due to changes in no. of shs. outstanding. **2.** Reflects merger or acquisition. **3.** Incl. intangibles. **4.** Bef. spec. item of -0.05 in 1992. E-Estimated NM-Not Meaningful.

Income Data (Million $)

Year Ended Dec. 31	Revs.	Oper. Inc.	% Oper. Inc. of Revs.	Cap. Exp.	Depr.	Int. Exp.	Net Bef. Taxes	Eff. Tax Rate	Net Inc.	% Net Inc. of Revs.	Cash Flow
[1]1992	**947**	**95.5**	**10.1**	**193**	**29.2**	**31.4**	**[3]102**	**26.9%**	**[2]60.6**	**6.4**	**89.8**
[1]1991	805	65.3	8.1	33	23.4	18.3	[3]79	31.4%	47.1	5.8	70.4
[1]1990	708	56.9	8.0	24	18.8	13.9	[3]58	29.5%	33.9	4.8	52.6
1989	579	32.6	5.6	20	12.7	11.6	[3]37	25.6%	24.6	4.2	37.3
[1]1988	501	30.0	6.0	24	9.9	10.2	29	24.9%	20.1	4.0	30.0
1987	383	22.1	5.8	14	9.2	7.7	25	18.8%	18.1	4.7	27.3
[1]1986	332	19.9	6.0	16	7.5	4.4	18	16.4%	[2]14.3	4.3	21.8
1985	266	17.8	6.7	7	6.5	4.6	12	18.6%	9.6	3.6	16.1
1984	235	16.9	7.2	7	6.3	4.9	6	1.4%	6.1	2.6	12.3
[2]1983	182	6.5	3.6	10	6.4	4.8	0	81.0%	0.1	Nil	6.4

Balance Sheet Data (Million $)

Dec. 31	Cash	Curr. Assets	Curr. Liab.	Curr. Ratio	Total Assets	% Ret. on Assets	Long Term Debt	Common Equity	Total Cap.	% LT Debt of Cap.	% Ret. on Equity
1992	**369**	**830**	**326**	**2.5**	**1,818**	**3.9**	**694**	**553**	**1,451**	**47.8**	**11.5**
1991	422	763	297	2.6	1,199	4.1	255	481	869	29.4	10.9
1990	178	494	254	1.9	898	4.2	210	307	614	34.2	12.3
1989	210	416	153	2.7	624	4.3	172	211	450	38.2	12.3
1988	136	331	123	2.7	490	4.4	148	182	357	41.6	11.7
1987	144	296	95	3.1	426	5.0	132	162	320	41.2	11.9
1986	64	194	767	2.6	309	5.0	58	146	225	26.0	10.7
1985	30	131	58	2.3	222	4.5	45	102	159	28.5	10.1
1984	11	103	55	1.9	194	3.2	44	84	135	32.6	7.4
1983	16	88	439	2.1	181	Nil	48	79	136	35.0	0.1

Data as orig. reptd. **1.** Reflects merger or acquisition. **2.** Reflects accounting change. **3.** Incl. equity in earns. of nonconsol. subs.

Business Summary

Thermo Electron has developed businesses from its existing technologies or through acquisition. It has focused on new technologies that it believes will provide long-term growth. To help finance its growth, TMO has sold minority positions in internally grown businesses once they have been judged sufficiently viable to stand alone. This strategy is believed to add incentive to the subsidiaries' managements to grow the businesses. Segment contributions in 1992:

	Sales	Profits
Instruments	37%	69%
Alternative energy systems	23%	2%
Process equipment	17%	16%
Services	12%	10%
Biomedical products	6%	1%
Advanced technologies	5%	2%

Thermo Instrument Systems Inc. (82%-owned) makes instruments for detecting and measuring air pollution, nuclear radioactivity, toxic substances, trace quantities of metals, and other elements and compounds. The 52%-owned Thermo Power (formerly Tecogen) develops and manufactures packaged cogeneration and cooling systems fueled principally by natural gas. Thermo Process Systems (71%-owned) produces custom-engineerd thermal processing systems to treat primary metals and metal parts. Thermo Fibertek (80%-owned) makes processing machinery and accessories for the paper-making and recycling industries.

Thermedics Inc. (53%-owned) manufactures biomedical products and instruments used to detect trace quantities of explosives and narcotics. Combined with Thermedics' stakes, TMO owns 58% of Thermo Cardiosystems, a producer of ventricular-assist devices, and 62% of Thermo Voltek., a maker of high-voltage equipment. In the advanced technology area, Thermotrex Corp. (62%-owned) conducts research in electro-optical and electro-acoustic systems, advanced laser systems, thermodynamics, heat transfer, materials technology and advanced parallel and signal processing.

Other nonpublic operations could be spun off in the future. The largest is 87%-owned Thermo Energy Systems Corp., which develops and operates alternative-energy power plants owned by third parties, including waste-to-energy electric power plants and fossil fuel cogeneration plants.

Dividend Data

No cash dividends have been paid. A "poison pill" stock purchase rights plan was adopted in 1988. A 3-for-2 stock split is payable October 28, 1993, to shareholders of record October 14.

Capitalization

Long Term Debt: $440,729,000 (6/93).

Minority Interest: $219,439,000.

Common Stock: 31,597,343 shs. ($1 par).
Institutions hold some 54%.
Shareholders of record: 5,832.

Office—81 Wyman St. (P.O. Box 9046), Waltham, MA 02254-9046. **Tel**—(617) 622-1000. **Chrmn & Pres**—G. N. Hatsopoulos. **EVP-CFO & Investor Contact**—John N. Hatsopoulos (617-622-1111). **Secy**—S. L. Lambert. **Dirs**—J. M. Albertine, P. O. Crisp, E. P. Gyftopoulos, G. N. Hatsopoulos, F. Jungers, R. A. McCabe, F. E. Morris, D. E. Noble, H. S. Olayan, R. D. Wellington. **Transfer Agent & Registrar**—Bank of Boston. **Incorporated** in Delaware in 1956; reincorporated in 1960. **Empl**—8,000.

 Shayna J. Malnak

Thiokol Corp.

NYSE Symbol TKC Options on Phila (Jan-Apr-Jul-Oct) In S&P MidCap 400

Price	Range	P-E Ratio	Dividend	Yield	S&P Ranking	Beta
Oct. 19'93	1993					
25⅝	25⅞–15¾	8	0.68	2.7%	NR	–0.77

Summary

This company is the leading maker of solid rocket propulsion systems used in the Space Shuttle and other space vehicles, as well as in strategic and tactical missiles. The company is attempting to offset a decline in defense spending by commercial acquisitions. Huck Manufacturing, a maker of fastener systems, was purchased in late 1991, and other acquisitions are likely. Thiokol has a share repurchase program, and recently increased the dividend substantially. Relatively stable earnings are expected for fiscal 1994.

Current Outlook

Earnings for the fiscal year ending June 30, 1994, are estimated at $3.00 a share, versus the $3.13 reported for fiscal 1993.

Dividends should continue at the current $0.17 quarterly rate.

Sales for fiscal 1994 are likely to drop about 13%-15%. Space revenues should be down slightly on lower shuttle sales and unmanned vehicle motor revenues. Strategic sales are likely to be down, reflecting the end of a major program. Lower tactical sales will reflect reductions in several programs, and ordnance revenues will fall. Improving industrial markets should produce a pickup for Huck fastener sales. Overall margins should improve, reflecting improved shuttle rates, improvement at Huck, and restructuring and cost cutting moves.

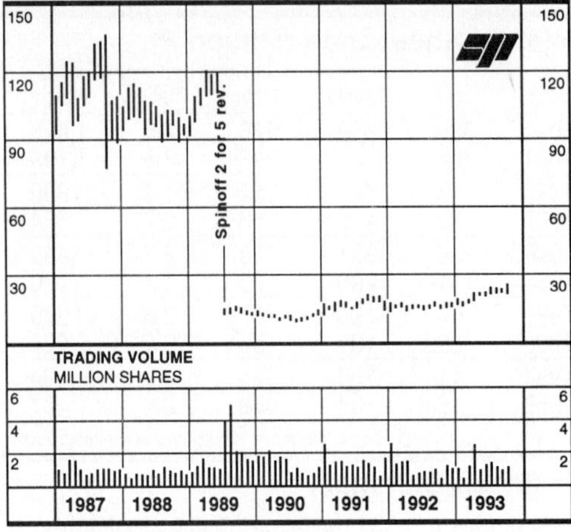

Net Sales (Million $)

Quarter:	1992-93	1991-92	1990-91	1989-90
Sep.	289	290	293	268
Dec.	307	329	299	289
Mar.	278	341	308	286
Jun.	327	352	355	339
	1,202	1,312	1,255	1,181

Sales in the year ended June 30, 1993, fell 8.4%, as lower defense-related sales offset the Huck contribution. Operating margins widened, and net income was up 1.3%.

Common Share Earnings ($)

Quarter:	1992-93	1991-92	1990-91	1989-90
Sep.	0.67	0.66	0.60	0.46
Dec.	0.72	0.72	0.61	0.51
Mar.	0.76	0.75	0.60	0.54
Jun.	0.98	0.99	0.94	0.64
	3.13	3.12	2.75	2.15

Important Developments

Aug. '93— Thiokol commented that the absence of tax recoveries, which benefited fiscal 1993 results, would be offset by potentially higher margins on some programs and improved performance in the fastener business.

Aug. '93— The company said that during the June 1993 quarter it repurchased 505,600 shares of its common stock under a 2.5 million share buyback program authorized in April. It plans to complete the program by June 30, 1994.

May '93— Lockheed Missiles and Space selected the company's new Castor 120 solid rocket motor to power a new family of launch vehicles under development.

Next earnings report expected in late October.

Per Share Data ($)

Yr. End Jun. 30	1993	[1]1992	1991	1990	[2]1989	1988	1987	1986	1985	1984
Tangible Bk. Val.	**18.09**	15.31	13.57	11.01	9.08	11.03	NA	NA	NA	NA
Cash Flow	**5.02**	5.06	4.64	4.19	3.00	NA	NA	NA	NA	NA
Earnings[3]	**[5]3.13**	3.12	2.75	2.15	0.92	2.25	1.73	2.28	2.10	1.53
Dividends	**0.47**	0.36	0.30	0.30	Nil	NA	NA	NA	NA	NA
Payout Ratio	**15%**	11%	11%	14%	Nil	NA	NA	NA	NA	NA
Prices[4]—High	**25⅞**	17¾	21¼	14½	16	NA	NA	NA	NA	NA
Low	**15¾**	13⅝	12⅛	9⅛	12⅜	NA	NA	NA	NA	NA
P/E Ratio—	**8–5**	6–4	8–4	7–4	17–13	NA	NA	NA	NA	NA

Data as orig. reptd.; prior to 1989 data as reptd. in prospectus dated May 22, 1989. Adj. for 2-for-5 reverse split Jul. 1989. **1.** Reflects merger or acquisition. **2.** Reflects accounting change. **3.** Bef. spec. item of -0.55 in 1988. **4.** Cal yr. **5.** Ful. dil.: 3.08. NA-Not Available.

Income Data (Million $)

Year Ended Jun. 30	Revs.	Oper. Inc.	% Oper. Inc. of Revs.	Cap. Exp.	Depr.	Int. Exp.	Net Bef. Taxes	Eff. Tax Rate	[3]Net Inc.	% Net Inc. of Revs.	Cash Flow
1993	**1,202**	**158**	**13.1**	**20**	**38.6**	**25.5**	**102**	**37.3%**	**64**	**5.3**	**102**
[1]1992	1,312	155	11.8	37	39.0	24.2	102	38.1%	63	4.8	102
1991	1,255	133	10.6	41	36.7	22.3	88	39.3%	53	4.3	90
1990	1,181	122	10.3	30	39.3	24.8	68	39.3%	41	3.5	81
[2]1989	1,168	116	9.9	37	39.8	21.4	38	53.1%	18	1.5	58
1988	1,068	117	11.0	65	36.3	15.1	69	37.2%	43	4.0	NA
1987	893	109	12.2	58	28.2	8.9	67	50.5%	33	3.7	NA
1986	927	119	12.8	36	24.3	20.8	83	48.3%	43	4.7	NA
1985	863	NA	NA	48	NA	NA	NA	NA	41	4.8	NA
1984	734	NA	NA	34	NA	NA	NA	NA	31	4.2	NA

Balance Sheet Data (Million $)

		Curr.									
Jun. 30	Cash	Assets	Liab.	Ratio	Total Assets	% Ret. on Assets	Long Term Debt	Common Equity	Total Cap.	% LT Debt of Cap.	% Ret. on Equity
1993	**31**	**400**	**184**	**2.2**	**841**	**7.0**	**88**	**443**	**594**	**14.8**	**15.3**
1992	136	499	360	1.4	962	6.9	123	387	547	22.5	17.5
1991	198	490	134	3.7	849	6.4	220	326	672	32.7	17.7
1990	113	468	150	3.1	816	5.3	220	274	621	35.5	16.1
1989	15	378	120	3.2	729	1.3	220	238	568	38.7	2.7
1988	6	384	213	1.8	741	6.2	126	275	523	24.1	16.0
1987	12	338	272	1.2	657	5.4	26	275	368	7.0	NA
1986	NA	NA	NA	NA	564	7.8	26	NA	NA	NA	NA
1985	NA	NA	NA	NA	543	8.1	146	NA	NA	NA	NA
1984	NA	NA	NA	NA	466	NA	146	NA	NA	NA	NA

Data as orig. reptd.; prior to 1989 data as reptd. in prospectus dated May 22, 1989. **1.** Reflects merger or acquisition. **2.** Reflects accounting change. **3.** Bef. spec. items. NA-Not Available.

Business Summary

The business of Thiokol Corp. consists of the aerospace operations of the former Morton Thiokol, following the spin-off of nonaerospace businesses in July 1989, and the fastener operations of Huck Manufacturing, acquired in November 1991. Segment contributions in fiscal 1993 were:

	Sales	Profits
Propulsion systems	87%	94%
Fastening systems	13%	6%

Propulsion operations consist of the development and production of solid propellant rocket motor systems for space vehicles, such as the booster motors for the Space Shuttle and the Delta, Scout and other launch vehicles. Placement motors are produced for satellites such as Westar, Telesat Satcom and Intelsat. Strategic systems include propulsion for the MX Peacekeeper and the submarine-launched Trident. Tactical missile propulsion systems include the Maverick, HARM, Hellfire, Standard (MK-70 and MK-104) and Patriot. With 40% of the market, Thiokol is the largest producer of solid rocket propulsion systems in the U.S.

Gas generator operations consist of the production of generator components for missile applications, including thrust vector control actuators, launch eject systems, attitude control and ordnance dispensers.

Ordnance operations consist of production of air- and ground-launched flares, munitions simulators for training, and conventional artillery munitions, mines and mine clearing and demolition charges.

Fastening systems include specialty fasteners used in aerospace and other transportation and industrial markets.

Services include launch and recovery operations for the Space Shuttle.

Dividend Data

Following the spinoff of Morton International and a 2-for-5 reverse split in July 1989, dividends on Thiokol Corp. were initiated in August 1989. A "poison pill" stock purchase rights plan was adopted in 1989.

Amt. of Divd. $	Date Decl.	Ex–divd. Date	Stock of Record	Payment Date
0.10	Oct. 15	Nov. 23	Nov. 30	Dec. 8'92
0.10	Jan. 21	Feb. 22	Feb. 26	Mar. 9'93
0.17	Apr. 14	May 24	May 31	Jun. 11'93
0.17	Aug. 19	Aug. 25	Aug. 31	Sep. 10'93

Capitalization

Long Term Debt: $87,900,000 (6/93).

Common Stock: 20,403,697 shs. ($1 par).
Institutions hold about 69%.
Shareholders of record: 8,533.

Office—2475 Washington Blvd., Ogden, UT 84401-2398. **Tel**—(801) 629-2270. **Chrmn**—U. E. Garrison. **Pres & CEO**—J. R. Wilson. **Secy**—E. M. North. **Treas**—S. E. George. **Dirs**—N. A. Armstrong, J. R. Burnett, U. E. Garrison, L. D. Kozlowski, C. S. Locke, R. T. Marsh, J. A. Rice, J. S. Ringler, D. C. Trauscht. **Transfer Agent & Registrar**—First Chicago Trust Company of New York. **Incorporated** in New York in 1890; reincorporated in Delaware in 1969. **Empl**—9,300.

T.M. Canning, CFA

Tidewater Inc.

NYSE Symbol TDW Options on NYSE, Phila (Jan-Apr-Jul-Oct) In S&P MidCap 400

Price	Range	P–E Ratio	Dividend	Yield	S&P Ranking	Beta
Oct. 25'93	1993					
23⅜	27–16⅜	46	0.40	1.7%	B–	0.98

Summary

This company owns and operates the largest fleet of vessels serving the international offshore energy industry following the January 1992 acquisition of Zapata Gulf Marine Corp.; the transaction increased the number of common shares outstanding by more than 80%. TDW also owns and operates one of the largest fleets of natural gas and air compressors in the U.S. Earnings for fiscal 1993-94 and 1994-95 are expected to benefit from higher natural gas prices leading to an increase in demand for TDW's services.

Current Outlook

Share earnings for the fiscal year ending March 31, 1994, are estimated at $0.80, up from fiscal 1992-93's $0.53. An increase to $1.25 is projected for fiscal 1994-95.

Dividends should continue at $0.10 quarterly.

Marine services profits for fiscal 1993-94 should benefit from an increase in utilization and day rates, as strong gas prices should lead to higher activity in the Gulf of Mexico. Gains are likely to be restricted by weakness in activity overseas. Compression services profits should increase slightly on increased demand for gas compressors. Profits in 1994-95 should benefit from higher gas prices leading to increased activity, and improved activity in the West African market.

Revenues (Million $)

Quarter:	1993–94	1992–93	1991–92	1990–91
Jun.	129.2	110.6	139.1	55.8
Sep.	134.2	120.3	140.8	60.3
Dec.	---	124.5	138.1	64.4
Mar.	---	120.1	128.5	65.8
	---	475.5	546.5	246.2

Revenues for the six months ended September 30, 1993, rose 14%, year to year, reflecting strength at marine operations. Penalized by lower compression profits and a $1.9 million ($0.04 a share) tax-related charge, net income from continuing operations declined 3.9%, to $0.32 a share from $0.34.

Common Share Earnings ($)

Quarter:	1993–94	1992–93	1991–92	1990–91
Jun.	0.15	0.13	0.24	0.22
Sep.	0.17	0.21	0.40	0.26
Dec.	E0.28	0.14	0.22	0.38
Mar.	E0.20	0.05	d0.36	0.25
	E0.80	0.53	0.50	1.11

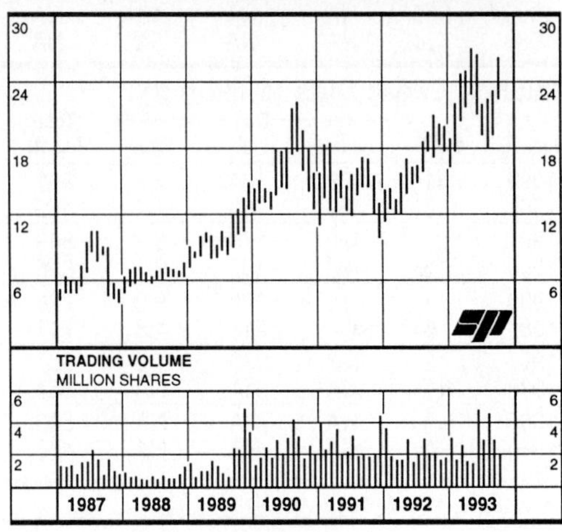

Important Developments

Oct. '93— TDW's revenues increased to $134.2 million in the fiscal 1993-94 second quarter from $129.1 million in the prior quarter, reflecting high activity levels and rising day rates for TDW's vessels operating in the U.S. Gulf of Mexico. The improvements largely offset the softer level of activity outside the U.S., though some foreign areas, such as the Middle East, experienced strengthening during the period. Tidewater's natural gas compressor rentals recorded high levels of utilization throughout the period, typically a slack time for compression activities; revenues benefited from the acquisition of 113 units in July.

Sep. '93— TDW prepaid $51.1 million of loans, eliminating its senior debt and increasing its financial flexibility.

Next earnings report expected in late January.

Per Share Data ($)

Yr. End Mar. 31	1993	[3]1992	1991	1990	1989	1988	1987	1986	1985	1984
Tangible Bk. Val.	[1]**10.36**	[1]10.22	9.03	7.90	6.88	7.43	8.86	12.56	[1]14.88	[1]18.95
Cash Flow	**2.03**	2.01	2.50	1.42	1.47	d0.03	d0.43	0.62	0.51	3.56
Earnings[2]	**0.53**	0.50	1.11	d0.38	d0.58	d2.13	d2.62	d2.01	d3.13	0.08
Dividends	**0.325**	Nil	Nil	Nil	Nil	Nil	Nil	0.725	0.900	0.900
Payout Ratio	**43%**	Nil	Nil	Nil	Nil	Nil	Nil	NM	NM	NM
Calendar Years	**1992**	1991	1990	1989	1988	1987	1986	1985	1984	1983
Prices—High	**21**	18½	22¼	14⅞	7⅝	10½	13⅜	20⅝	29½	31¼
Low	**11⅜**	9⅞	12⅜	7¼	4⅞	4	3	12⅛	17¾	20¼
P/E Ratio—	**40–21**	37–20	20–11	NM	NM	NM	NM	NM	NM	NM

Data as orig. reptd. **1.** Incl. intangibles. **2.** Bef. results of disc. opers. of +0.06 in 1993, +0.65 in 1988, and spec. item(s) of -0.13 in 1993, +0.75 in 1986. **3.** Refl. merger or acq. d-Deficit. E-Estimated. NM-Not Meaningful.

Income Data (Million $)

Year Ended Mar. 31	Revs.	Oper. Inc.	% Oper. Inc. of Revs.	Cap. Exp.	Depr.	Int. Exp.	[3]Net Bef. Taxes	Eff. Tax Rate	[4]Net Inc.	% Net Inc. of Revs.	Cash Flow
[1]1993	**476**	**130**	**27.3**	**52.4**	**79.9**	**12.3**	**42.7**	**28.9%**	**[5]27.8**	**0.8**	**108**
[6]1992	547	141	25.8	39.0	79.6	18.6	43.0	39.4%	26.3	4.8	106
1991	246	78	31.8	42.0	40.1	10.3	35.0	8.2%	31.8	12.9	72
1990	203	50	24.5	17.0	40.9	18.6	d7.0	NM	d8.1	NM	32
1989	183	40	22.1	23.0	46.2	19.3	d17.0	NM	d12.5	NM	33
[1]1988	151	16	10.5	8.0	46.6	[2]18.6	d45.0	NM	d46.8	NM	d1
1987	166	12	7.3	5.0	47.9	[2]19.8	d53.0	NM	d56.7	NM	d9
1986	238	35	14.7	48.0	47.0	[2]19.2	d50.0	NM	[5]d32.0	NM	11
1985	303	78	25.9	79.0	61.1	23.6	d71.0	NM	d47.4	NM	9
1984	321	85	26.5	97.0	58.1	25.8	d3.0	NM	1.6	0.5	59

Balance Sheet Data (Million $)

Mar. 31	Cash	Curr. Assets	Curr. Liab.	Curr. Ratio	Total Assets	% Ret. on Assets	Long Term Debt	Common Equity	Total Cap.	% LT Debt of Cap.	% Ret. on Equity
1993	**109**	**297**	**96**	**3.1**	**839**	**3.3**	**96**	**548**	**699**	**13.7**	**5.1**
1992	113	289	111	2.6	846	3.4	124	536	718	17.3	5.2
1991	54	147	44	3.3	391	8.3	84	257	341	24.5	13.2
1990	45	125	45	2.8	370	NM	92	224	317	29.1	NM
1989	45	123	65	1.9	397	NM	167	154	330	50.5	NM
1988	29	101	47	2.2	405	NM	177	166	356	49.6	NM
1987	21	92	47	2.0	447	NM	184	197	394	46.7	NM
1986	12	107	71	1.5	530	NM	178	245	455	39.0	NM
1985	31	153	90	1.7	628	NM	201	249	523	38.5	NM
1984	37	184	76	2.4	722	0.2	202	316	632	32.0	0.4

Data as orig. reptd. **1.** Excl. disc. operations. **2.** Net of interest income. **3.** Incl. equity in earns. of nonconsol. subs. **4.** Bef. results of disc. opers. and spec. item(s). **5.** Refl. acctg. change. **6.** Refl. merger or acq. d-Deficit. NM-Not Meaningful.

Business Summary

Tidewater is an international energy service company which provides various support services, engineered products and technical services to the oil and gas industry. The company owns and operates the world's largest fleet of vessels primarily serving the international offshore energy industry, and one of the largest fleets of natural gas and air compressors in the U.S. In January 1992, TDW acquired Zapata Gulf Marine Corp. in exchange for 23,786,000 common shares, which increased the number of TDW shares outstanding by over 80%. Business segment contributions in fiscal 1992-93:

	Revs.	Profits
Marine services	87%	84%
Compression services	13%	16%

Marine service and support functions include towing and anchor-handling for mobile drilling rigs and equipment; transporting supplies necessary to sustain exploration, development, production and workover drilling operations; and supporting pipelaying and construction activities. At March 31, 1993, TDW's fleet, including joint-venture holdings, consisted of 611 vessels, up from 577 at 1991-92 year-end. In 1992-93, the company derived about 68% of its marine equipment revenues from foreign marine operations, compared with 65% in 1991-92. Vessel utilization in 1992-93 declined to 82% from 84% a year earlier.

The company provides gas and air compression equipment and services for a variety of industries. The compressors are used to boost natural gas from the wellhead to feed it into nearby gas processing plants or into high pressure pipelines. Compression equipment also is used in production of coalbed methane, cogeneration facilities, and enhanced recovery projects. At March 31, 1993, there were 840 gas compressor units and 118 air compressor units, which had utilization rates in 1992-93 of 79% and 41%, respectively.

The company also operates two shipyards which build repair, modify, and drydock vessels.

Dividend Data

Dividends, omitted in 1986, were resumed in 1992. A "poison pill" stock purchase right was adopted in 1990.

Amt. of Divd. $	Date Decl.	Ex–divd. Date	Stock of Record	Payment Date
0.07½	Dec. 17	Dec. 29	Jan. 5	Jan. 19'93
0.10	Mar. 25	Apr. 2	Apr. 8	Apr. 22'93
0.10	Jul. 22	Jul. 30	Aug. 5	Aug. 12'93
0.10	Oct. 21	Nov. 1	Nov. 5	Nov. 12'93

Capitalization

Long Term Debt: $48,000,000 (9/93).

Common Stock: 53,300,000 shs. ($0.10 par).
Institutions hold approximately 64%.
Shareholders of record: 2,845.

Office—1440 Canal St., New Orleans, LA 70112. **Tel**—(504) 568-1010. **Chrmn, Pres & CEO**—J. P. Laborde. **VP-CFO & Investor Contact**—Ken C. Tamblyn. **VP-Secy**—V. I. Koock. **Dirs**—R. H. Boh, D. T. Bollinger, A. R. Carlson, H. J. Kelly, J. P. Laborde, R. C. Lassiter, P. W. Murrill, L. Pollack, J. H. Roff, Jr., W. W. Woods, Jr. **Transfer Agents & Registrars**—Whitney National Bank, New Orleans; Chemical Bank, NYC. **Incorporated** in Delaware in 1956. **Empl**—6,864.

 Mark Mattke

Tiffany & Co.

NYSE Symbol TIF Options on Phila (Feb-May-Aug-Nov) In S&P MidCap 400

Price	Range	P–E Ratio	Dividend	Yield	S&P Ranking	Beta
Aug. 30'93	1993					
29⅞	35⅜–24⅛	NM	0.28	0.9%	NR	1.44

Summary

This company is an international retailer, designer, manufacturer and distributor of fine jewelry and gift items. Jewelry accounted for 60% of sales in fiscal 1992-93; some 29% of total sales were of products made by the company. In July 1993, the company assumed full marketing and merchandising responsibility for retail activities at 29 boutiques operated by Mitsukoshi Ltd. in Japan.

Business Summary

Tiffany & Co. is engaged in the design, manufacture and distribution of fine jewelry, gift and fashion accessory items.

Jewelry (60% of sales in fiscal 1992-93) is offered in an extensive selection at a wide range of prices. All jewelry products are constructed of gold, platinum or sterling silver with or without precious gems or colored stones. TIF crafts certain of its jewelry in its workshops, but much is made by others to its specifications.

TIF is well known for its sterling silver merchandise such as flatware, hollowware (tea and coffee services, bowls, cups and trays), trophies, key holders, picture frames and desk accessories. Other products include decorative crystal, serving pieces, vases, decanters, glassware, china and other tableware, watches, clocks, handbags, wallets, scarves, ties, fashion accessories, writing instruments, stationery, and fragrances.

Tiffany produced 29% of the merchandise offered for sale in 1992-93, while 71% was purchased from other sources. Approximately 42% of the purchased merchandise purchased was made outside the U.S.

Products are sold through three channels of distribution: U.S. retail, direct marketing, and international retail. U.S. retail consists primarily of the New York flagship store, branch stores (14 at year-end 1992-93), and a network of selected independent retailers authorized under Tiffany's wholesale trade program. Tiffany's New York flagship store accounted for 24% of total company sales in 1992-93 (versus 23% the year before).

Direct marketing involves the sale of products and services to businesses (through business-to-business selling specialists, advertising, and special catalogs) and to nonbusiness customers (through the mailing of catalogs based on both a proprietary list of mail and telephone customers and rented mailing lists).

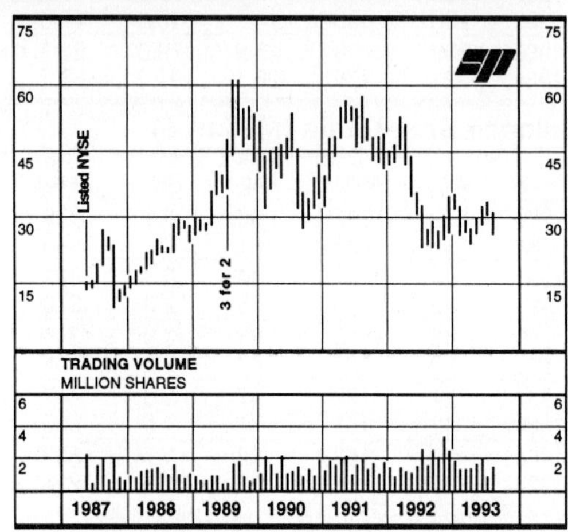

International business includes sales of merchandise at wholesale to Mitsukoshi Ltd. in Hong Kong, Taipei, Hawaii and Guam; to Heiwado & Co. in Japan; and to Lotte Trading Co., Ltd. in Korea. TIF also sells at retail through stores in London, Munich, Zurich, Hong Kong, Taipei, Singapore, Frankfurt and Toronto. Mitsukoshi manages TIF's boutiques in Japan, but TIF assumed merchandising responsibility for the stores in mid-1993.

In the fiscal year ended January 31, 1993, sales to Mitsukoshi Ltd., owner of 13.7% of TIF common, constituted 15% of total sales, versus 23% the year before. Mitsukoshi's holdings may not exceed 19.99% of TIF total shares outstanding.

Important Developments

Jul. '93— TIF assumed full marketing and merchandising responsibility for retail activities at 29 Tiffany & Co. boutiques in Japan.

Next earnings report expected in mid-November.

Per Share Data ($)

Yr. End Jan. 31[1]	1993	1992	1991	1990	[2]1989	1988	1987	1986
Tangible Bk. Val.	**12.64**	12.37	11.06	8.48	6.46	5.70	1.48	0.49
Cash Flow	**1.72**	2.52	2.69	2.36	1.73	1.25	0.64	NA
Earnings[3]	**1.00**	2.01	2.34	2.13	1.63	1.17	0.56	0.12
Dividends	**0.280**	0.280	0.260	0.183	0.100	Nil	Nil	Nil
Payout Ratio	**28%**	14%	11%	8%	6%	Nil	Nil	Nil
Calendar Years	**1992**	1991	1990	1989	1988	1987	1986	1985
Prices—High	**52⅞**	57½	53¾	61¼	29⅝	27⅜	NA	NA
Low	**23**	32⅝	27½	26	14	9⅝	NA	NA
P/E Ratio—	**53–23**	29–16	23–12	29–12	18–9	23–8	NA	NA

Data as orig. reptd., prior to 1988 data as reptd. in prospectus dated May 5, 1987. Adj. for stk. div(s) of 50% in Jul., 1989. **1.** Yr. ended Jun. 30 prior to 1987. **2.** Reflects accounting change. **3.** Bef. spec. item(s) of -0.40 in 1992, -0.04 in 1988, +0.05 in 1987, +0.05 in 1986. NA-Not Available.

Income Data (Million $)

Year Ended Jan. 31[1]	Revs.	Oper. Inc.	% Oper. Inc. of Revs.	Cap. Exp.	Depr.	Int. Exp.	Net Bef. Taxes	Eff. Tax Rate	[4]Net Inc.	% Net Inc. of Revs.	Cash Flow
1993	**486**	**38.2**	**7.8**	**22.8**	**11.40**	**7.23**	**19.9**	**21.1%**	**15.7**	**3.2**	**27.1**
1992	493	69.2	7.8	41.4	8.13	6.34	55.1	42.2%	[2]31.8	6.5	39.9
1991	456	73.1	16.0	24.8	5.30	4.48	63.5	42.2%	36.7	8.0	42.1
1990	384	64.1	16.7	14.0	3.15	2.58	58.4	43.0%	33.3	8.7	36.8
[2]1989	290	45.8	15.8	9.7	1.63	0.83	[3]43.0	42.1%	24.9	8.6	26.5
1988	230	34.7	15.1	1.9	1.02	2.17	[3]31.2	46.1%	16.8	7.3	17.8
1987	183	22.9	12.6	1.2	1.02	8.92	[3]12.8	46.9%	6.8	3.7	7.8
1986	154	13.2	8.6	1.4	1.39	10.20	1.6	26.9%	1.2	0.8	NA

Balance Sheet Data (Million $)

Jan. 31[1]	Cash	Curr. Assets	Curr. Liab.	Curr. Ratio	Total Assets	% Ret. on Assets	Long Term Debt	Common Equity	Total Cap.	% LT Debt of Cap.	% Ret. on Equity
1993	**6.7**	**292**	**92**	**3.2**	**418**	**3.9**	**102.0**	**205**	**310**	**32.7**	**7.7**
1992	4.0	282	122	2.3	395	9.0	50.0	200	258	19.4	16.8
1991	4.6	234	103	2.3	307	13.4	18.2	176	201	9.0	23.4
1990	2.6	187	74	2.5	237	16.6	18.2	136	161	11.3	28.2
1989	1.6	137	56	2.5	163	15.8	Nil	99	105	Nil	26.9
1988	12.9	114	47	2.4	127	12.5	Nil	72	78	Nil	37.3
1987	1.9	85	29	2.9	99	NA	49.6	13	68	73.1	NA
1986	1.2	83	30	2.8	95	NA	59.4	4	64	93.2	NA

Data as orig. reptd.; prior to 1988 data as reptd. in prospectus dated May 5, 1987. **1.** Yr. ended Jun. 30 prior to 1987. **2.** Reflects accounting change. **3.** Incl. equity in earns. of nonconsol. subs. **4.** Bef. spec. item(s). NA-Not Available.

Net Sales (Million $)

Quarter:	1993–94	1992–93	1991–92	1990–91
Apr.	109.5	107.2	97.1	93.2
Jul.	114.2	120.8	119.4	107.3
Oct.		105.9	126.4	113.2
Jan.		152.4	149.0	142.0
		486.4	491.9	445.7

Sales for the six months ended July 31, 1993, fell 1.9%, year to year, as gains of 9% for U.S. retail and 1% for direct marketing were offset by a 15% reduction in international sales (reflecting a decline in wholesale shipments to Mitsukoshi). Following a product return reserve of $57.5 million related to the purchase of inventory previously sold to Mitsukoshi, and higher SG&A expenses, there was a net loss of $31.5 million ($2.00 a share), in contrast to net income of $7.0 million ($0.44).

Common Share Earnings ($)

Quarter:	1993–94	1992–93	1991–92	1990–91
Apr.	0.07	0.20	0.28	0.35
Jul.	d2.06	0.25	0.46	0.45
Oct.		Nil	0.51	0.58
Jan.		0.55	0.76	0.96
		1.00	2.01	2.34

Finances

In January 1993, in order to secure additional long term borrowings, the company completed a $51.5 million private placement of 7.52% senior notes due 2003. Proceeds were used to replace a portion of borrowings under a revolving credit facility.

In March 1991, TIF sold in Europe $50 million of 6⅜% subordinated debentures due 2001 and convertible into common at $56 a share. Proceeds were used to refinance borrowings under a multi-bank, multi-currency revolving credit facility.

Dividend Data

Dividends were initiated in May 1988. A "poison pill" stock purchase right was adopted in 1988.

Amt of Divd. $	Date Decl.	Ex-divd. Date	Stock of Record	Payment Date
0.07	Nov. 19	Dec. 14	Dec. 18	Jan. 8'93
0.07	Feb. 18	Mar. 15	Mar. 19	Apr. 9'93
0.07	May 20	Jun. 14	Jun. 18	Jul. 9'93
0.07	Aug. 19	Sep. 14	Sep. 20	Oct. 8'93

Capitalization

Long Term Debt: $101,500,000 (7/93), incl. $50 million of 6⅜% Eurobond sub. debs. due 2001, conv. into com. at $56 a sh.

Common Stock: 15,626,562 shs. ($0.01 par).
Mitsukoshi Ltd. owns about 14%; institutions hold about 79%.
Shareholders of record: 2,315 (3/93).

d-Deficit.

Office—727 Fifth Ave., New York, NY 10022. **Tel**—(212) 755-8000. **Chrmn & Pres**—W. R. Chaney. **SVP-Fin & CFO**—J. N. Fernandez. **SVP-Secy**—P. B. Dorsey. **Investor Contact**—Mark L. Aaron. **Dirs**—W. R. Chaney, J. Dudley, S. L. Hayes III, C. K. Marquis, Y. Sakakura, W. A. Shutzer, G. Stutz. **Transfer Agent & Registrar**—Chemical Bank, NYC. **Founded** in 1837; incorporated in Delaware in 1984. **Empl**—2,865.

 L. Feuer Nelson

Topps Co.

NASDAQ Symbol TOPP (Incl. in Nat'l Market) Options on Phila In S&P MidCap 400

Price	Range	P-E Ratio	Dividend	Yield	S&P Ranking	Beta
Sep. 8'93	1993					
9⅛	14–6¼	27	0.28	3.1%	NR	0.97

Summary

Best known for its baseball picture cards and "Bazooka" bubble gum products, Topps also produces other collectible picture, gum and candy items. In early 1992, the company formed a unit to create and market high-quality comic books. The stock price dropped sharply following a decline in sales and earnings in 1992-93's third quarter and the subsequent announcement of a fourth quarter loss. Topps continues to face the difficulties of a contracting sports card market. A 5,000,000 share repurchase program was authorized in late 1992.

Business Summary

The Topps Company, Inc. was incorporated as a holding company in February 1987 as the successor to Topps Chewing Gum Inc. The company is best known for its Topps Baseball Bubble Gum picture cards and its "Bazooka" bubble gum. It is also the leader in marketing other collectible picture products, primarily bubble gum picture cards, featuring sports figures, popular television and movie characters, significant events of national interest, and parodies of popular trends or recognized products. In addition, Topps manufactures and distributes other gums, candy novelties and candy-coated gums, usually in packaging that has entertainment value, and distributes Topps Magazine, which covers the sports card collecting hobby. In 1992, Topps formed a unit to create comic books.

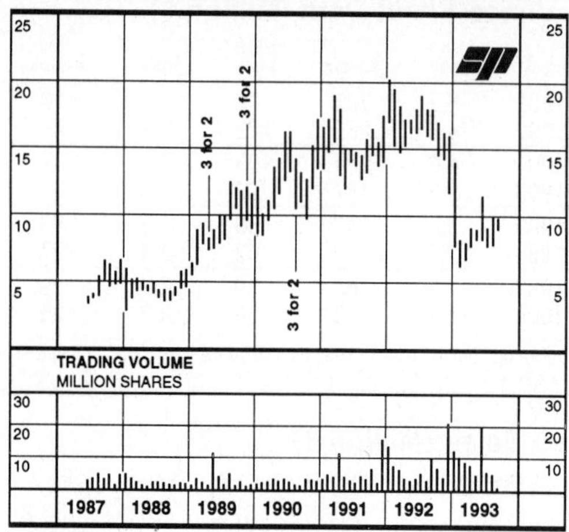

Sales conttributions in recent fiscal years:

	1992–93	1991–92
Collectible picture products:		
Sports	65%	67%
Entertainment & other....	5%	9%
Bazooka–brand gums.........	11%	11%
Lollipops & other candy.......	19%	13%

Topps' sports and entertainment picture products are sold in various packages, with or without bubble gum. The most popular sports packages contain 15 cards and a promotional insert card. In May 1991, Topps introduced "Stadium Club" sports cards—premium-quality cards, manufactured using laminated paperboard, state-of-the-art reproduction techniques, dramatic photography and unusual statistics. Topps has exclusive license arrangements with virtually every major league baseball and professional football, basketball and hockey player, while it also holds a variety of licenses with the entertainment media. License royalties and fees paid or accrued in 1992-93 approximated $36.8 million.

In April 1992, the company announced the formation of Topps Comics, Inc. to create and market high-quality comic books. The unit's debut title, "Dracula," was released in the fall of 1992.

Important Developments

May '93— The company reported that, as a result of a contraction in the sports card industry, it had found it necessary to make a variety of cost reductions. This included trimming 300 employees from its work force to bring manufacturing costs in line with current volume expectations.

Next earnings report expected in mid-September.

Per Share Data ($)

Yr. End Feb. 28	1993	1992	1991	1990	1989	1988	1987	1986	1985
Tangible Bk. Val.	**0.57**	0.56	d0.41	d1.48	d2.23	d2.68	d0.39	d0.90	NA
Cash Flow	**0.50**	1.29	1.28	0.98	0.74	0.70	NA	NA	NA
Earnings[1]	**0.40**	1.15	1.15	0.80	0.59	0.56	0.33	0.01	d0.14
Dividends[2]	**0.280**	0.240	0.190	0.151	0.119	0.051	Nil	Nil	Nil
Payout Ratio	**70%**	21%	17%	19%	20%	9%	Nil	Nil	Nil
Calendar Years	**1992**	1991	1990	1989	1988	1987	1986	1985	1984
Prices—High	**20¼**	19	17¼	12½	6	6⅝	NA	NA	NA
Low	**11¾**	12	8½	5½	2⅞	3¼	NA	NA	NA
P/E Ratio—	**51–29**	17–10	15–7	16–7	10–5	12–6	NA	NA	NA

Data as orig. reptd. Adj. for stk. divs. of 50% Aug. 1990, 50% Nov. 1989, 50% Apr. 1989. **1.** Bef. spec. item of +0.06 in 1987. **2.** Pd. 2.96 (adj.) spec. in Jan. 1988. d-Deficit. NA-Not Available.

The Topps Company, Inc.

Income Data (Million $)

Year Ended Feb. 28	Revs.[1]	Oper. Inc.	% Oper. Inc. of Revs.	Cap. Exp.	Depr.	Int. Exp.	Net Bef. Taxes	Eff. Tax Rate	Net Inc.[3]	% Net Inc. of Revs.	Cash Flow
1993	**268**	**37.5**	**14.0**	**3.81**	**4.69**	**[2]Nil**	**32.8**	**41.9%**	**19.0**	**7.1**	**23.7**
1992	309	97.6	31.6	2.22	6.50	[2]1.9	89.3	39.0%	54.5	17.6	61.0
1991	290	96.4	33.2	3.91	6.30	[2]5.8	90.0	39.9%	54.1	18.7	60.4
1990	251	86.3	34.4	2.70	8.30	12.2	65.8	42.9%	37.6	15.2	45.9
1989	199	69.8	35.1	2.99	6.70	14.0	49.2	43.1%	28.0	14.1	34.6
1988	169	56.0	33.2	3.12	6.30	3.6	47.5	45.5%	25.9	15.3	32.2
1987	149	41.2	27.6	1.79	7.40	7.0	27.3	44.5%	15.1	10.2	NA
1986	75	14.6	19.8	1.05	7.10	10.0	0.6	Nil	0.6	0.8	NA
1985	79	16.1	20.3	0.60	11.50	11.0	d6.3	Nil	d6.3	NM	NA
1984	74	NA	NA	NA	NA	1.1	13.4	47.5%	7.0	9.5	NA

Balance Sheet Data (Million $)

Feb. 28	Cash	Curr. Assets	Curr. Liab.	Curr. Ratio	Total Assets	% Ret. on Assets	Long Term Debt	Common Equity	Total Cap.	% LT Debt of Cap.	% Ret. on Equity
1993	**13.8**	**86.5**	**80.9**	**1.1**	**142**	**13.4**	**Nil**	**54.4**	**58.5**	**Nil**	**34.9**
1992	10.9	87.2	80.8	1.1	143	40.6	Nil	55.1	60.3	Nil	163.6
1991	7.7	64.3	65.5	1.0	125	43.9	40	11.4	56.8	70.4	NM
1990	6.7	57.9	63.7	0.9	121	30.8	85	d35.5	54.5	156.0	NM
1989	6.1	54.7	52.4	1.0	123	23.3	127	d66.6	67.6	187.9	NM
1988	7.4	44.8	53.7	0.8	117	22.4	144	d88.2	60.6	237.6	NM
1987	12.9	41.9	42.1	1.0	114	13.6	44	22.5	68.4	64.4	114.5
1986	2.5	32.1	23.8	1.3	109	0.5	78	4.0	82.0	95.2	19.8
1985	2.3	NA	NA	NA	104	NM	83	1.9	85.0	97.8	NM
1984	3.7	NA	NA	NA	42	9.6	1	21.5	22.0	2.5	36.9

Data as orig. reptd. **1.** Incl. royalties. **2.** Net of int. inc. **3.** Bef. spec. items. d-Deficit. NA-Not Available. NM-Not Meaningful.

Net Sales (Million $)

13 Weeks:	1993–94	1992–93	1991–92	1990–91
May	76.3	76.4	68.1	86.2
Aug................		83.8	76.3	71.2
Nov................		62.6	74.1	65.0
Feb................		40.4	84.7	67.5
		263.2	303.2	290.0

In the 13 weeks ended May 29, 1993, net sales declined fractionally, year to year, as reduced production of baseball cards (related to market contraction) and lower sales of entertainment picture products ("Batman Returns" picture cards were shipped in the 1992-93 period) were largely offset by the inclusion of basketball product sales. Gross margins narrowed on an increase in general reserves and higher product development expenses, and pretax income fell 22%. After taxes at 42.0%, against 40.0%, net income was off 25%, to $9,439,000 ($0.20 a share), from $12,504,000 ($0.26).

Common Share Earnings ($)

13 Weeks:	1993–94	1992–93	1991–92	1990–91
May	0.20	0.26	0.28	0.29
Aug................		0.35	0.30	0.30
Nov................		0.24	0.30	0.26
Feb................		d0.45	0.27	0.29
		0.40	1.15	1.15

d-Deficit.

Dividend Data

Cash payments were initiated in July 1987. A "poison pill" stock purchase rights plan was adopted in December 1991.

Amt. of Divd. $	Date Decl.	Ex–divd. Date	Stock of Record	Payment Date
0.07	Sep. 23	Oct. 9	Oct. 16	Oct. 31'92
0.07	Dec. 16	Jan. 12	Jan. 19	Feb. 1'93
0.07	Mar. 30	Apr. 12	Apr. 16	Apr. 30'93
0.07	Jun. 23	Jul. 12	Jul. 16	Jul. 30'93

Finances

In December 1992, the repurchase of up to five million Topps common shares was authorized (455,000 shares were acquired in 1992-93's final quarter).

In February 1984, the Topps business, then publicly owned, was acquired for some $98 million in a leveraged buyout led by Forstmann Little & Co. and members of the existing management. The return to public ownership took place with a common stock offering in May 1987. In December 1991, Forstmann Little & Co. distributed its remaining 53% interest in Topps to the partners who invested in the leveraged buyout.

Capitalization

Long Term Debt: None (5/29/93).

Common Stock: 47,029,048 shs. ($0.01 par).
Shareholders: About 5,000 of record (4/15/93).

Office—254 36th St., Brooklyn, NY 11232. **Tel**—(718) 768-8900. **Chrmn & CEO**—A. T. Shorin. **Pres & COO**—J. J. Langdon. **VP-CFO & Contr**—J. Perillo. **Dirs**—S. P. Berger, A. A. Feder, N. C. Forstmann, T. J. Forstmann, S. D. Greenberg, J. J. Langdon, W. B. Little, J. H. Nusbaum, A. T. Shorin, J. A. Sprague, S. Tulchin. **Transfer Agent & Registrar**—Chemical Banking Corp., NYC. **Incorporated** in Delaware in 1987.

 Michael W. Jaffe

Tosco Corp.

NYSE Symbol TOS Options on ASE (Jan-Apr-Jul-Oct) In S&P MidCap 400

Price	Range	P-E Ratio	Dividend	Yield	S&P Ranking	Beta
Sep. 1'93	1993					
26	26⅜–18⅞	31	0.60	2.3%	B–	0.88

Summary

This independent refiner processes and markets over 400,000 bbl. per day of petroleum products, with operations on both the East Coast and the West Coast. During the first half of 1993, production more than doubled with the acquisition of the Bayway refinery, located in Linden, N.J. In addition, the principal operating assets of wholly owned Seminole Fertilizer Corp. were sold for $128 million. Following a drop in 1992, reflecting weak refining margins and a $25 million environmental reserve, earnings rebounded in the first half of 1993, aided by the addition of the Bayway refinery.

Business Summary

Tosco Corp. is an independent petroleum refiner engaged in the refining of crude oil and marketing of wholesale petroleum products, primarily transportation fuels, on both the East Coast and the West Coast. The company processes and markets more than 400,000 bbl. per day of petroleum products.

The company owns and operates through its Tosco Refining division a petroleum refinery in Avon, Calif., and related distribution facilities. The refinery is equipped with coking, catalytic cracking, hydrocracking and hydrosulfurizing units. During 1992, the refinery produced an average of 151,130 bbl. of petroleum products per day, of which 61% was gasoline and 22% was diesel, compared 1991's 137,150 bbls. per day in 1991 (58% gasoline and 20% diesel). Average refinery gross margins (the difference between realized product prices and crude costs) were $7.98 in 1992 and $8.16 in 1991. Five domestic oil companies supplied TOS with most of its crude oil needs; the remainder was purchased on the spot market.

In April 1993, TOS acquired the Bayway refinery, located in Linden, N.J., for $175 million, plus about $158 million for inventory. The transaction, Financed by a private placement of $150 million of first mortgage bonds, borrowings under the company's credit facility, and available cash, more than doubled production of refined petroleum products. TOS increased the crude and intermediate feedstock processed at the refinery to 240,000 bbl. per day, from 180,000.

The company has interests in 23,100 acres of oil shale properties in Colorado and 20,525 acres in Utah.

Important Developments

Jul. '93— The company settled outstanding litigation regarding environmental issues at its Avon, Calif., refinery. For the next four years, the previous owners will pay up to $18 million for 50% of the environmental compliance costs, and will also provide TOS with a $6 million credit for past expenses.

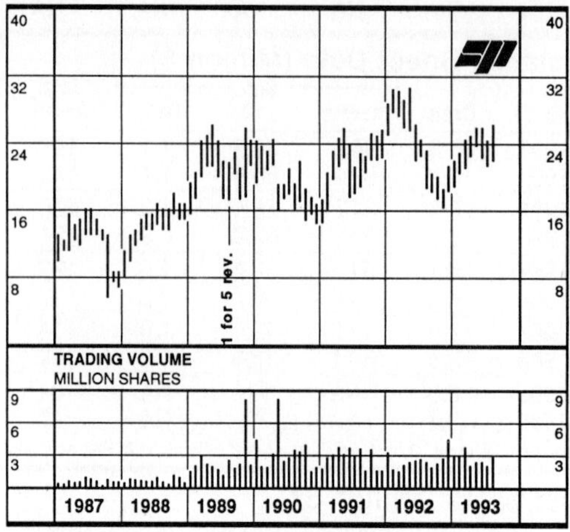

May '93— TOS sold the principal operating assets of wholly owned Seminole Fertilizer Corp., for $128 million. Seminole's interest in the Fort Meade Chemical Products partnership, which is still for sale, was not included in the transaction.

Mar. '93— The company entered into an agreement to acquire 60,000 bbl. per day of crude oil from Statoil, representing about 25% of the daily necessary crude and feedstock supply of the Bayway refinery.

Next earnings report expected in early November.

Per Share Data ($)

Yr. End Dec. 31	1992	1991	1990	[1]1989	1988	1987	1986	1985	1984	[2]1983
Tangible Bk. Val.	**9.10**	12.78	11.15	7.00	5.29	d3.51	d11.40	d69.06	d75.24	d26.44
Cash Flow	**1.55**	4.04	7.52	4.32	5.40	2.83	d6.86	5.90	d44.26	d97.57
Earnings[3,4]	**0.68**	2.39	5.37	1.71	3.25	0.65	d10.85	1.45	d50.95	d106.75
Dividends	**0.60**	0.60	0.60	0.30	Nil	Nil	Nil	Nil	Nil	Nil
Payout Ratio	**87%**	25%	15%	21%	Nil	Nil	Nil	Nil	Nil	Nil
Prices—High	**30¾**	25⅞	24⅝	26¼	18⅛	16¼	23⅛	25	25⅝	73⅛
Low	**16⅜**	14⅝	14½	15⅝	8⅛	5⅝	8⅛	5	5	22½
P/E Ratio—	**45–24**	11–6	5–3	15–9	6–3	25–9	NM	17–3	NM	NM

Data as orig. reptd. Adj. for 1-for-5 reverse split Jul. 1989. **1.** Refl. merger or acq. **2.** Refl. acctg. change. **3.** Bef. results of disc. ops. of -5.53 in 1992, and spec. items of +2.00 in 1992. +3.38 in 1988, +2.51 in 1987, +3.50 in 1986. **4.** Ful. dil.: 2.35 in 1991, 3.94 in 1990, 1.24 in 1989, 1.65 in 1988. d-Deficit. NM-Not Meaningful.

Income Data (Million $)

Year Ended Dec. 31	Revs.	Oper. Inc.	% Oper. Inc. of Revs.	Cap. Exp.	Depr.	Int. Exp.	[3]Net Bef. Taxes	Eff. Tax Rate	[4]Net Inc.	% Net Inc. of Revs.	Cash Flow
[5]1992	**1,861**	**120**	**64.0**	**69**	**[2]25.7**	**[6]20.3**	**51**	**40.7%**	**[2]30**	**1.6**	**46**
1991	1,980	155	7.8	60	49.6	43.2	78	3.8%	75	3.8	121
1990	2,158	249	11.5	29	46.3	62.8	142	13.3%	123	5.7	162
[1]1989	1,441	110	7.6	24	34.8	46.1	33	NM	40	2.8	58
1988	1,142	136	11.9	23	22.5	25.7	97	42.9%	55	4.8	56
1987	1,187	99	8.3	22	22.1	[6]28.4	55	49.1%	[2]28	2.3	28
1986	780	d14	NM	15	21.8	28.7	d56	NM	d56	NM	d38
1985	1,513	67	4.4	27	21.0	47.4	8	NM	9	0.6	28
1984	1,899	d14	NM	18	27.9	66.9	d213	NM	d211	NM	d185
[2]1983	2,494	d35	NM	145	32.6	92.5	d470	NM	d378	NM	d346

Balance Sheet Data (Million $)

Dec. 31	Cash	Curr. Assets	Curr. Liab.	Curr. Ratio	Total Assets	% Ret. on Assets	Long Term Debt	Common Equity	Total Cap.	% LT Debt of Cap.	% Ret. on Equity
1992	**103.0**	**439**	**168**	**2.6**	**963**	**3.2**	**357**	**266**	**745**	**47.9**	**6.3**
1991	50.7	273	171	1.6	970	7.9	266	382	778	34.2	20.0
1990	53.2	291	188	1.5	949	9.1	398	333	743	53.6	42.7
1989	30.1	232	143	1.6	938	4.0	496	112	778	63.7	23.2
1988	34.5	189	97	1.9	556	9.2	166	44	450	36.9	NM
1987	84.7	189	95	2.0	559	4.7	233	d26	450	51.7	NM
1986	16.0	115	67	1.7	492	NM	240	d66	407	58.9	NM
1985	23.6	163	125	1.3	629	1.3	531	d346	431	123.3	NM
1984	30.3	228	123	1.9	695	NM	603	d358	493	122.4	NM
1983	16.9	316	173	1.8	954	NM	805	d95	768	104.7	NM

Data as orig. reptd. **1.** Refl. merger or acq. **2.** Refl. acctg. change. **3.** Incl. equity in earns. of nonconsol. subs. prior to 1987. **4.** Bef. results of disc. ops. and spec. items. **5.** Excl. disc. ops. **6.** Net of interest income. d-Deficit. NM-Not Meaningful.

Revenues (Million $)

Quarter:	1993	1992	1991	1990
Mar.	416	332	496	424
Jun.	956	477	506	541
Sep.		516	494	557
Dec.		535	485	636
		1,861	1,980	2,158

Revenues in the six months ended June 30, 1993, soared 70%, year to year, reflecting the inclusion of the Bayway refinery. Operating expenses rose more rapidly, and interest expense was up sharply. After taxes at 40.4%, versus 40.3%, the gain in income was held to 11%. After preferred dividends, share earnings increased to $1.09, on 2.6% fewer shares, from $0.93. Per share results in the 1992 period exclude a loss of $0.15 from discontinued operations, as well as a credit of $0.54 from accounting changes.

Common Share Earnings ($)

Quarter:	1993	[1]1992	1991	1990
Mar.	0.42	d0.13	0.65	d0.66
Jun.	0.67	1.06	0.68	2.62
Sep.		0.25	0.03	3.05
Dec.		d0.53	1.03	0.45
		0.68	2.39	[2]5.37

1. Restated. **2.** Does not reconcile because of changes in no. of shs. outstanding. d-Deficit.

Finances

In August 1993, TOS redeemed $50 million of 8% convertible subordinated debentures due 1995.

In the 1993 first quarter, the company submitted applications for projects to supply significant volumes of California-mandated gasoline beginning in April 1996. The projects would involve an investment of about $300 million.

At December 31, 1992, TOS had $200 million of federal net operating loss carryforwards, expiring from 1997 through 2001.

Dividend Data

In July 1989, a 1-for-5 reverse stock split was effected.

Amt. of Divd. $	Date Decl.	Ex-divd. Date	Stock of Record	Payment Date
0.15	Sep. 8	Sep. 14	Sep. 18	Sep. 30'92
0.15	Dec. 8	Dec. 14	Dec. 18	Dec. 30'92
0.15	Mar. 9	Mar. 15	Mar. 19	Mar. 31'93
0.15	Jun. 8	Jun. 14	Jun. 18	Jun. 30'93

Capitalization

Long Term Debt: $506,865,000 (6/93).

$4.375 Cum. Conv. Preferred Stock: 2,300,000 shs. ($50 liq. pref.); conv. into 2.0833 com. shs.

Common Stock: 29,272,138 shs. ($0.75 par). Institutions own 59%.
Shareholders of record: 13,770 (2/93).

Office—72 Cummings Point Rd., Stamford, CT 06902. **Tel**—(203) 977-1000. **Chrmn, Pres & CEO**—T. D. O'Malley. **EVP, CFO & Treas**—J. F. Allen. **VP & Secy**—W. McClave III. **Investor Contact**—Daniel P. Mulderry. **Dirs**—J. F. Allen, H. I. Flournoy, C. G. Frame, E. A. Hajim, J. P. Ingrassia, C. J. Luellen, T. D. O'Malley. **Transfer Agent & Registrar**—First Interstate Bank, Ltd., LA. **Incorporated** in Nevada in 1955. **Empl**—994.

 J.R. Jordan

Transatlantic Holdings

NYSE Symbol TRH In S&P MidCap 400

Price	Range	P–E Ratio	Dividend	Yield	S&P Ranking	Beta
Oct. 11'93	1993					
54¾	61½–49	17	0.28	0.5%	NR	NA

Summary

Transatlantic Holdings provides property and casualty reinsurance in domestic and international markets through its wholly owned subsidiaries Transatlantic Reinsurance Co. and Putnam Reinsurance Co. The sluggish growth in net income during 1993's first half largely reflected sharply lower realized investment gains. Operating earnings rose amid a competitive pricing environment that is showing signs of improving. American International Group holds about 45% of the stock.

Current Outlook

Excluding net realized investment gains or losses, earnings for 1993 are estimated at $3.50 a share, up from the $2.74 a share reported for 1992. Earnings could rise to $4.25 a share in 1994.

The $0.07 quarterly dividend will likely be increased.

While near-term operating earnings growth will be limited by competitive pricing conditions and record catastrophe losses that have plagued primary insurers and reinsurers lately, longer-term prospects are bolstered by an expected firming of rates in the wake of these losses. Since 1987, primary insurers have been retaining a larger portion of their risks. These higher retention levels have hampered reinsurers' premium growth, but TRH's refusal to write subpar business for the sake of near-term premium growth leaves it better positioned to capitalize on a market turn that is beginning to emerge, particularly in property lines. Because it takes a year for higher prices to translate into higher profits, earnings growth will be moderate until 1994. As the seventh largest reinsurer, TRH is also well positioned to capitalize on a consolidation trend in the reinsurance market. While investment income growth will be modest, writedowns are unlikely.

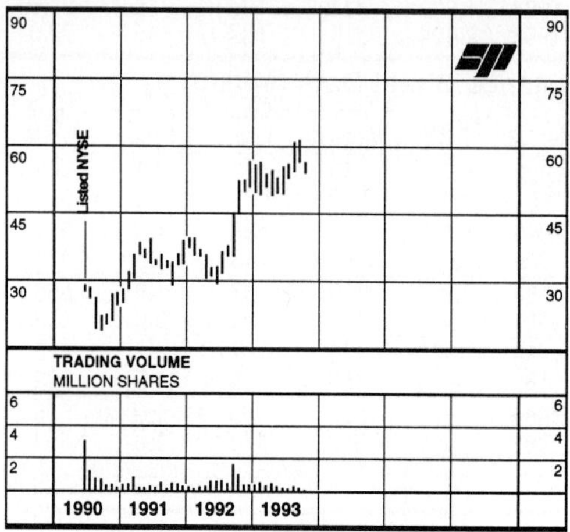

Common Share Earnings ($)

Quarter:	1993	1992	1991	1990
Mar.	0.85	0.96	0.80	0.67
Jun.	0.94	0.80	0.74	0.64
Sep.		0.30	0.72	0.63
Dec.		1.07	0.83	0.76
		3.13	3.09	2.71

Review of Operations

Revenues in the six months ended June 30, 1993, rose 11%, year to year, reflecting 12% higher earned premiums and a 6.7% increase in investment income. Following a 13% rise in expenses, and an 84% plunge in pretax realized investment gains, pretax profits were off 5.6%. After taxes at 9.0%, versus 15.5%, net income rose 1.6%. Share earnings were $1.79 ($1.77 of operating income), versus $1.76 ($1.56), before a $2.02 special credit from an accounting change in the 1993 interim.

Important Developments

Jul. '93— TRH noted that the 19% rise in first half 1993 net written premiums largely reflected increased demand for and better pricing of certain types of property coverage, particulary in certain overseas markets. Despite $8.5 million of charges from the March storm, the World Trade Center bombing, and a large London bomb blast, the combined ratio for the first half of 1993 was 108.2%, versus 108.3% in the 1992 interim.

Next earnings report expected in early November.

Per Share Data ($)

Yr. End Dec. 31	1992	1991	1990	1989	1988	1987	1986	1985
Tangible Bk. Val.	**24.52**	21.80	18.38	16.28	13.98	NA	NA	NA
Oper. Earnings	**2.74**	2.96	NA	NA	NA	NA	NA	NA
Earnings[1,2]	**3.13**	3.09	2.71	2.44	1.97	1.74	0.35	d0.44
Dividends	**0.24**	0.20	0.05	Nil	Nil	Nil	Nil	Nil
Payout Ratio	**8%**	6%	2%	Nil	Nil	Nil	Nil	Nil
Prices—High	**56¾**	39⅜	29⅛	NA	NA	NA	NA	NA
Low	**29⅜**	25	18⅞	NA	NA	NA	NA	NA
P/E Ratio—	**18–9**	13–8	11–7	NA	NA	NA	NA	NA

Data as orig. reptd. **1.** Bef. spec. item(s) of +0.14 in 1988, +0.27 in 1987, +0.28 in 1986. **2.** Aft. gains/losses on security transactions. d-Deficit. NA-Not Available.

Income Data (Million $)

Year Ended Dec. 31	Premium Income	Net Invest. Inc.	Oth. Revs.	Total Revs.	Property & Casualty Underwriting Ratios Loss	Expense	Comb.	Net Bef. Taxes	Net Oper. Inc.	[1]Net Inc.	—% Return On— Revs.	Equity
1992	**478**	**130**	**11.1**	**619**	**86.0**	**25.6**	**111.6**	**83.8**	**62.8**	**71.7**	**11.6**	**13.5**
1991	497	121	3.7	623	81.4	26.2	107.6	84.1	67.5	70.5	11.3	15.3
1990	472	104	4.5	580	79.8	25.9	105.7	75.8	NA	61.9	10.7	15.6
1989	486	91	4.0	581	79.7	27.2	106.9	64.3	NA	55.7	9.6	16.0
1988	426	73	3.0	502	80.6	23.9	104.5	53.5	NA	44.9	8.9	15.2
1987	446	57	7.1	510	82.7	22.1	104.8	47.7	NA	39.8	7.8	16.1
1986	370	41	3.5	414	86.4	17.4	103.8	17.8	NA	7.9	1.9	4.7
1985	170	32	1.0	203	98.3	24.3	122.6	d10.6	NA	d10.1	NM	NA

Balance Sheet Data (Million $)

Dec. 31	Cash & Equiv.	Premiums Due	—Investment Assets— [2]Bonds	Stocks	[3]Loans	Total	% Invest. Yield	Deferred Policy Costs	Total Assets	Debt	Common Equity
1992	**155**	**Nil**	**1,768**	**124**	**19.7**	**1,912**	**7.2**	**21.7**	**2,432**	**Nil**	**562**
1991	111	21.2	1,604	107	13.6	1,725	7.6	21.5	2,204	Nil	500
1990	126	22.1	1,383	57	20.8	1,461	7.6	26.4	1,993	Nil	421
1989	99	13.6	1,177	63	8.9	1,249	8.1	26.8	1,735	Nil	374
1988	77	40.8	936	31	34.9	1,002	NA	25.9	1,499	Nil	321
1987	NA	NA	NA	NA	NA	NA	NA	NA	1,261	Nil	270
1986	NA	NA	NA	NA	NA	NA	NA	NA	1,044	Nil	224
1985	NA	NA	NA	NA	NA	NA	NA	NA	553	Nil	114

Data as orig. reptd. **1.** Bef. spec. items. **2.** Fixed maturities. **3.** Short term invest. d-Deficit. NA-Not Available. NM-Not Meaningful.

Business Summary

Transatlantic Holdings provides property and casualty reinsurance, directly and through brokers, to insurance and reinsurance companies in both the domestic and international markets through its wholly owned subsidiaries Transatlantic Reinsurance Co. and Putnam Reinsurance Co. Contributions to net premiums earned by line of reinsurance in recent years:

	1992	1991	1990
General liability...........	48%	58%	62%
Medical malpractrice....	14%	12%	6%
Fire..........................	9%	7%	7%
Inland marine.............	4%	5%	7%
Workers' compensation	5%	5%	5%
Automobile liability	12%	5%	5%
Other........................	8%	8%	8%

Based upon 1992 statutory net premiums written of $482 million, Transatlantic Reinsurance and Putnam Reinsurance together would have ranked as the seventh largest domestic reinsurer.

About 40% of 1992 gross premiums written resulted from reinsurance business with American International Group, Inc. (AIG), which has informed the company that it intends to continue to provide TRH with a right of first acceptance to participate in substantially all property and casualty reinsurance purchased by AIG through at least 1995. Non-U.S. business accounted for 13% of 1992 net premiums written.

TRH seeks to focus a significant part of its business on the reinsurance of more complex risks within the broad range of insurance lines it writes, requiring a relatively high degree of underwriting, actuarial and claims expertise.

Dividend Data

Dividends have been paid since 1990. Payments in the past 12 months:

Amt of Divd. $	Date Decl.	Ex-divd. Date	Stock of Record	Payment Date
0.07	Dec. 2	Feb. 24	Mar. 2	Mar. 9'93
0.07	Mar. 26	Jun. 2	Jun. 8	Jun. 22'93
0.07	May 21	Aug. 31	Sep. 7	Sep. 21'93
0.07	Sep. 24	Dec. 1	Dec. 7	Dec. 21'93

Capitalization

Long Term Debt: None (6/93).

Common Stock: 22,886,903 shs. ($1 par). American International Group holds about 45%. Shareholders of record: 2,471 (1/93).

Office—80 Pine St., New York, NY 10005. **Tel**—(212) 770-2000. **Chrmn**—M. R. Greenberg. **Pres**—J. V. Taranto. **Secy**—E. M. Tuck. **VP & Investor Contact**—David W. Smith. **Dirs**—J. Balog, J. M. Fowler, H. Freeman, M. R. Greenberg, J. J. Mackowski, E. E. Matthews, J. F. Murphy, Y. Sato, J. V. Taranto, T. R. Tizzio. **Transfer Agent & Registrar**—Harris Trust Co. of New York, NYC. **Incorporated** in Delaware in 1986. **Empl**—240.

 Catherine A. Seifert

Trinity Industries

NYSE Symbol TRN Options on ASE (Jan-Apr-Jul-Oct) In S&P MidCap 400

Price	Range	P-E Ratio	Dividend	Yield	S&P Ranking	Beta
Sep. 2'93	1993					
36½	36½–24¾	25	0.68	1.9%	B+	1.32

Summary

This company is a leading railcar manufacturer, a major producer of marine vessels, and fabricates a variety of metal products. In February 1993, TRN issued some 4,341,000 common shares (adjusted) on the conversion of $91.4 million of called debentures. Profits in fiscal 1993-94 will benefit from increased railcar production, rising demand for highway-related products, and better margins on marine contracts. The dividend was lifted 27.5% in conjunction with a 3-for-2 stock split distributed in August 1993.

Current Outlook

Profits for the fiscal year ending March 31, 1994, are estimated at $1.80 a share (on 13% more shares), versus the $1.27 of fiscal 1992-93 (adjusted for the recent 3-for-2 split) .

The quarterly dividend has been lifted 27.5%, to $0.17 from $0.13⅓ (adjusted), with the October 1993 payment.

Profit growth in fiscal 1993-94 will be paced by sharp gains in the railcar segment as railroads rebuild their aging fleets. Profits for the marine segment should advance as margins widen on new orders for military, commercial and specialty vessels. While increased housing construction will boost demand for LPG tanks, competitive pressure will hurt margins. Metal components will benefit from a gradual increase in capital spending by the chemical industry. The construction segment will benefit from the full integration of Syro Steel and increased infrastructure spending.

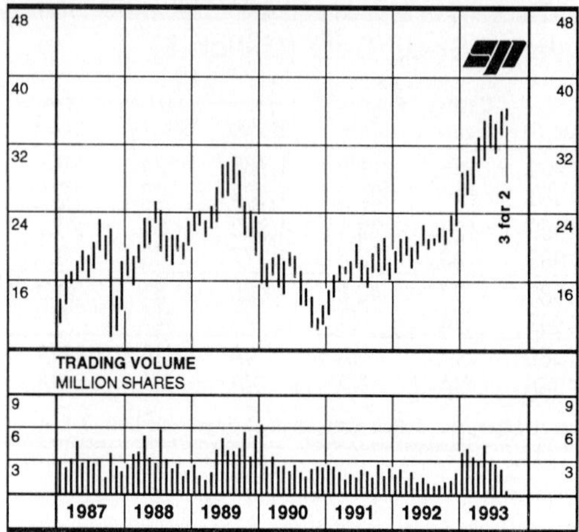

Revenues (Million $)

Quarter:	1993-94	1992-93	1991-92	1990-91
Jun.	402	365	300	283
Sep.	---	394	304	318
Dec.	---	393	302	361
Mar.	---	389	287	301
	---	1,540	1,192	1,263

Revenues for the three months ended June 30, 1993, rose 10%, year to year. Net income was up 102%. Share earnings were $0.42 (before a $0.20 accounting credit), versus $0.24 (all adjusted).

Common Share Earnings ($)

Quarter:	1993-94	1992-93	1991-92	1990-91
Jun.	0.42	0.24	0.19	0.19
Sep.	E0.45	0.28	0.17	0.29
Dec.	E0.45	0.35	0.19	0.33
Mar.	E0.48	0.40	0.15	0.14
	E1.80	1.27	0.69	0.95

Important Developments

Jul. '93— TRN took a $7.9 million credit ($0.20 a share, adjusted) in the fiscal 1993-94 first quarter to reflect the cumulative effect of a change in accounting for deferred taxes.

May '93— Capital outlays for fiscal 1993-94 were projected at $32.4 million, versus $36.2 million in fiscal 1992-93. Outlays for 1992-93 exclude the issuance of 2,432,172 common shares (adjusted) to acquire Syro Steel Corp. Syro, which produces a variety of steel products, generates about $100 million in annual revenues.

Feb. '93— TRN issued some 4,341,000 common shares (13%, adjusted) on the conversion of $84.4 million of its called 6.75% debentures due 2012 and $7 million of variable-rate debentures due 2004.

Next earnings report expected in mid-October.

Per Share Data ($)

Yr. End Mar. 31	[1]1993	1992	1991	1990	[1]1989	[1]1988	[1]1987	1986	1985	1984
Tangible Bk. Val.	**12.97**	10.91	10.74	9.79	8.40	7.58	6.72	6.81	7.13	7.73
Cash Flow	**2.95**	2.19	2.26	2.67	5.10	1.07	0.77	0.61	0.34	0.67
Earnings[2]	**1.27**	0.69	0.95	1.37	1.11	0.49	0.23	0.03	d0.25	0.20
Dividends	**0.533**	0.533	0.533	0.433	0.333	0.333	0.333	0.333	0.333	0.333
Payout Ratio	**46%**	76%	56%	33%	30%	68%	142%	NM	NM	167%
Calendar Years	**1992**	1991	1990	1989	1988	1987	1986	1985	1984	1983
Prices—High	**26½**	21⅛	21⅞	30⅝	25¼	23⅛	13⅜	11⅜	17	17⅛
Low	**17⅛**	12⅛	10⅝	19⅛	15½	9½	8⅞	8⅜	8⅞	8
P/E Ratio—	**21–13**	30–18	23–11	22–14	23–14	47–19	57–38	NM	NM	85–40

Data as orig. reptd. Adj. for stk. div(s). Of 50% Sep. 1993. **1.** Reflects merger or acquisition. **2.** Bef. spec. item(s) of -0.07 in 1987. E-Estimated. d-Deficit. NM-Not Meaningful.

Income Data (Million $)

Year Ended Mar. 31	Revs.	Oper. Inc.	% Oper. Inc. of Revs.	Cap. Exp.	Depr.	Int. Exp.	Net Bef. Taxes	Eff. Tax Rate	[3]Net Inc.	% Net Inc. of Revs.	Cash Flow
[1]1993	**1,540**	**162**	**10.5**	**111**	**59.3**	**32.6**	**72.1**	**37.6%**	**45.0**	**2.9**	**104**
1992	1,192	113	9.5	112	47.4	32.9	36.3	39.1%	22.1	1.9	70
1991	1,263	123	9.8	91	41.8	34.8	48.3	37.7%	30.1	2.4	72
1990	1,310	137	10.4	57	35.8	43.7	60.3	36.7%	38.2	2.9	74
[1,2]1989	1,001	116	11.5	70	31.5	39.0	46.7	35.1%	30.3	3.0	62
[1]1988	633	33	5.1	19	15.3	19.9	20.5	36.4%	13.0	2.1	28
[1]1987	490	19	3.9	42	12.9	15.1	10.1	43.9%	5.7	1.2	19
1986	436	d13	NM	4	13.9	15.3	1.0	15.8%	[2]0.9	0.2	15
1985	453	d3	NM	31	14.1	12.7	d13.6	NM	d6.0	NM	8
[1]1984	380	6	1.7	76	11.3	7.8	7.4	36.4%	4.7	1.2	16

Balance Sheet Data (Million $)

Mar. 31	Cash	Curr. Assets	Curr. Liab.	Curr. Ratio	Total Assets	% Ret. on Assets	Long Term Debt	Common Equity	Total Inv. Capital	% LT Debt of Cap.	% Ret. on Equity
1993	**7.5**	**NA**	**NA**	**NA**	**1,089**	**3.9**	**257**	**507**	**850**	**30.2**	**9.6**
1992	4.5	NA	NA	NA	975	2.3	326	346	754	43.2	6.4
1991	5.9	NA	NA	NA	929	3.2	291	340	721	40.3	9.3
1990	7.4	NA	NA	NA	875	4.2	333	285	702	47.4	14.4
1989	6.4	NA	NA	NA	878	4.1	382	228	683	56.0	14.0
1988	7.2	271	112	2.4	579	2.3	199	201	400	49.7	6.9
1987	15.3	212	74	2.9	505	1.2	207	162	370	56.1	3.5
1986	7.5	208	68	3.1	464	0.2	176	162	338	52.0	0.5
1985	4.6	220	107	2.1	471	NM	132	169	301	43.8	NM
1984	10.8	194	69	2.8	425	1.2	100	183	284	35.4	2.6

Data as orig. reptd. **1.** Reflects merger or acquisition. **2.** Reflects acctg. change. **3.** Bef. spec. item(s). d-Deficit. NM-Not Meaningful. NA-Not Available.

Business Summary

Contributions by business segment to operating profits (in million $) in recent fiscal years:

	1992–93	1991–92	1990–91
Railcars	$26.9	$12.7	$31.6
Containers	15.0	15.3	21.1
Construction products	22.6	19.2	16.8
Marine products	30.8	5.5	–0.5
Metal components	13.8	15.4	17.6
Leasing	7.5	6.8	0.4

TRN is the largest railcar manufacturer in the U.S. It produces a variety of car types including pressure and non-pressure tank cars and intermodal freight cars, as well as rail components, and performs repair services.

The container group produces heavy pressure vessels used to store and transport liquefied petroleum gas; precision welded products including industrial silencers, desalinization equipment, heat exchangers, evaporators and gas processing systems.

The construction segment produces highway guardrail and bridge beams and girders, steel framing used in the construction of commercial and industrial buildings and airport passenger boarding bridges and conveyor systems. TRN also produces concrete and aggregates in Texas.

TRN is a leading fabricator of marine vessels for inland waterways and offshore applications. Its product line includes tug boats, barges, military vessels, patrol and service vessels and commercial and private transport and pleasure vessels.

Metal components include elbow, flanges and other weld fittings, as well as forges, used by the petrochemical, process and power industries.

TRN's leasing operations include a fleet of 9,589 railcars and 220 river hopper barges.

Dividend Data

Dividends have been paid since 1964. A "poison pill" stock purchase right was adopted in 1989.

Amt of Divd. $	Date Decl.	Ex-divd. Date	Stock of Record	Payment Date
0.20	Dec. 10	Jan. 11	Jan. 15	Jan. 29'93
0.20	Mar. 11	Apr. 8	Apr. 15	Apr. 30'93
0.20	Jun. 8	Jul. 9	Jul. 15	Jul. 30'93
3–for–2	Jul. 21	Sep. 1	Aug. 16	Aug. 31'93
0.17	Jul. 21	Oct. 8	Oct. 15	Oct. 29'93

Capitalization

Long Term Debt: $303,000,000 (6/93).

Common Stock: 39,452,578 shs. ($1 par).
Officers & directors own 5.0%.
Institutions hold about 70%.
Shareholders of record: 2,700 (3/93).

Office—2525 Stemmons Freeway, Dallas, TX 75207-2401. **Tel**—(214) 631-4420. **Chrmn & Pres**—W. R. Wallace. **Secy**—J. J. French Jr. **Treas**—N. O. Shoop. **VP & Investor Contact**—F. Dean Phelps. **Dirs**—D. W. Biegler, B. J. Galt, D. P. Guerin, J. T. Hay, E. M. Hoffman, R. J. Pulley, T. R. Wallace, W. R. Wallace. **Transfer Agent & Registrar**—Bank of New York, NYC. **Incorporated** in Texas in 1933; reincorporated in Delaware in 1987. **Empl**—12,600.

 Stephen R. Klein

Tyson Foods

NASDAQ Symbol TYSNA (Incl. in Nat'l Market) Options on Pacific In S&P MidCap 400

Price	Range	P–E Ratio	Dividend	Yield	S&P Ranking	Beta
Aug. 4'93	1993					
20¼	27⅛–19¼	16	0.04	0.2%	A	1.28

Summary

Tyson is one of the world's leading producers, processors and marketers of poultry-based food products. Acquisitions, including that of Holly Farms Corp. in 1989, have contributed to growth in recent years. In October 1992, Arctic Alaska Fisheries Corp. was acquired. Earnings are expected to continue to advance through fiscal 1994, aided by favorable poultry product consumption trends.

Current Outlook

Earnings for fiscal 1994 are projected at $1.50 a share, up from fiscal 1993's estimated $1.32.

Quarterly dividends should be no less than the current $0.01.

Sales should continue in a firm uptrend through fiscal 1994, reflecting modest increases for consumer poultry sales prices and tonnage, as well as acquisitions. Recent weather-related crop damage may raise near-term poultry production costs, but profitability levels should remain favorable, aided by further emphasis on higher-profit, value-enhanced poultry products. Share earnings gains may be restricted by more shares outstanding.

Net Sales (Million $)

13 Weeks:	1992-93	1991-92	1990-91	1989-90
Dec.	1,083	957	901	901
Mar.	1,170	1,041	932	932
Jun.	1,217	1,022	1,017	979
Sep.	---	[1]1,150	1,072	1,013
	---	4,169	3,922	3,825

Sales in the 39 weeks ended July 3, 1993, advanced 15%, year to year. Margins widened, and with lower interest and other expense, pretax income climbed 21%. After taxes at 38.0%, versus 39.0%, net income soared 23%, to $139,195,000 ($0.94 a share, on 7.2% more shares), from $112,976,000 ($0.82).

Common Share Earnings ($)

13 Weeks:	1992-93	1991-92	1990-91	1989-90
Dec.	0.27	0.23	0.21	0.18
Mar.	0.31	0.27	0.24	0.20
Jun.	0.36	0.32	0.29	0.26
Sep.	E0.38	[1]0.34	0.31	0.27
	E1.32	1.16	1.05	0.91

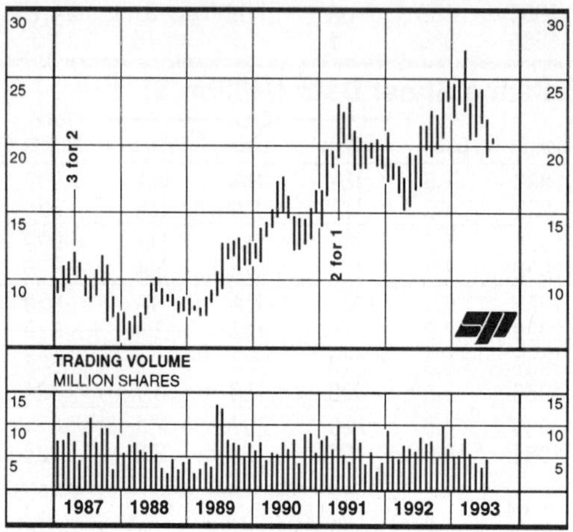

Important Developments

Jul. '93— At July 3, 1993, Tyson's current ratio was 1.3-to-1, versus 1.5-to-1 at the end of fiscal 1992. Long term debt accounted for 32.6% of total capitalization, down from 33.8% at fiscal 1992 year end.

Oct. '92— The company acquired Arctic Alaska Fisheries Corp., a vertically integrated seafood products company with fiscal 1993 sales estimated at $250 million. The total cost of the acquisition was $242.7 million, consisting of $37.4 million in cash, plus 9,548,153 Tyson Class A common shares. Separately, the company acquired certain assets of Louis Kemp Seafood Co., a processor of seafood products, for $19.3 million in cash.

Next earnings report expected in early November.

Per Share Data ($)

Yr. End Sep. 30	1992	1991	1990	[2]1989	1988	1987	[2]1986	[2]1985	1984	1983
Tangible Bk. Val.	**1.72**	0.43	d0.89	d2.31	2.64	2.06	1.55	1.17	0.69	0.57
Cash Flow	**2.24**	2.04	1.78	1.43	1.19	1.00	0.72	0.53	0.28	0.19
Earnings	**1.16**	1.05	0.91	0.78	0.64	0.53	0.40	0.30	0.16	0.10
Dividends	**0.040**	0.035	0.020	0.020	0.020	0.018	0.012	0.008	0.006	0.006
Payout Ratio	**3%**	3%	2%	3%	3%	4%	3%	3%	3%	6%
Prices[3]—High	**24⅞**	23¼	17¾	13⅛	10⅛	12	12¾	4¾	2⅜	1⅛
Low	**15¼**	14	11⅜	7⅜	5½	5⅜	4¼	1⅞	1	¾
P/E Ratio—	**21–13**	22–13	20–13	17–10	16–9	23–10	32–11	16–6	15–6	12–7

Data as orig. reptd. Adj. for stk. divs. of 100% Apr. 1991, 50% Apr. 1987, 100% Apr. 1986, 150% Apr. 1985, 100% Apr. 1983. **1.** 14 wks. **2.** Refl. merger or acq. **3.** Cal. yr. E-Estimated. d-Deficit.

Income Data (Million $)

Year Ended Sep. 30	Revs.	Oper. Inc.	% Oper. Inc. of Revs.	Cap. Exp.	Depr.	Int. Exp.	Net Bef. Taxes	Eff. Tax Rate	Net Inc.	% Net Inc. of Revs.	Cash Flow
1992	**4,169**	**481**	**11.5**	**108**	**149**	**78**	**261**	**38.5%**	**161**	**3.9**	**309**
1991	3,922	469	12.0	214	136	97	243	40.0%	145	3.7	281
1990	3,825	444	11.6	164	117	130	200	40.0%	120	3.1	237
[1]1989	2,538	291	11.5	129	81	46	164	38.5%	101	4.0	185
1988	1,936	195	10.1	86	70	21	104	22.0%	81	4.2	152
1987	1,786	207	11.6	133	60	25	123	45.0%	68	3.8	128
[1]1986	1,504	157	10.4	169	42	22	98	48.6%	50	3.3	92
[1]1985	1,136	117	10.3	128	28	20	70	50.4%	35	3.1	63
1984	750	58	7.7	36	14	12	33	44.4%	18	2.4	32
1983	604	41	6.8	20	12	10	20	45.9%	11	1.8	23

Balance Sheet Data (Million $)

Sep. 30	Cash	Curr. Assets	Curr. Liab.	Curr. Ratio	Total Assets	% Ret. on Assets	Long Term Debt	Common Equity	Total Cap.	% LT Debt of Cap.	% Ret. on Equity
1992	**27**	**680**	**466**	**1.5**	**2,618**	**6.1**	**727**	**980**	**2,152**	**33.8**	**17.8**
1991	25	662	550	1.2	2,646	5.6	846	822	2,096	40.4	19.5
1990	17	586	483	1.2	2,501	4.6	950	663	2,018	47.1	21.1
1989	56	750	470	1.6	2,586	5.8	1,319	448	2,116	62.3	25.3
1988	19	436	181	2.4	889	9.6	206	341	708	29.1	26.7
1987	22	379	308	1.2	807	8.6	211	269	499	42.4	28.6
1986	108	398	332	1.2	761	8.2	212	204	429	49.4	28.0
1985	5	235	191	1.2	471	8.7	119	155	280	42.3	28.3
1984	13	161	121	1.3	298	6.6	87	84	178	49.1	24.0
1983	1	133	103	1.3	255	4.5	81	67	152	53.6	18.0

Data as orig. reptd. **1.** Refl. merger or acq.

Business Summary

Tyson Foods, the largest poultry processor in the U.S., produces fresh, frozen and precooked poultry, as well as pork, beef and other foods.

Contributions to sales in recent fiscal years were:

	1992	1991
Value–enhanced poultry......	73%	71%
Basic poultry....................	8%	11%
Tortillas, beef, pork & other prepared foods.............	14%	13%
Live pork & related............	3%	2%
Animal foods & other..........	2%	3%

Value-enhanced poultry products include chicken patties and nuggets, pre-cooked chicken, individually-quick-frozen chicken segments, pre-packaged and pre-priced poultry, and cornish game hens. Basic poultry includes chilled and prepackaged fresh chicken. Products are sold primarily to foodservice, retail and wholesale club markets under labels including Tyson, Holly Farms and Weaver.

Flour and corn tortillas, corn chips and taco shells are sold to U.S. retail and foodservice markets. Beef, pork and other prepared foods sold under the Harker's, Henry House and Quik-to-Fix labels are also produced for these markets. The company also breeds and finishes live pork for regional and national packers.

Export sales accounted for 4.6% of the total in fiscal 1992.

Dividend Data

Cash has been paid each year since 1976.

Amt. of Divd. $	Date Decl.	Ex–divd. Date	Stock of Record	Payment Date
0.01	Aug. 21	Nov. 24	Dec. 1	Dec. 15'92
0.01	Dec. 18	Feb. 23	Mar. 1	Mar. 15'93
0.01	Mar. 1	May 25	Jun. 1	Jun. 15'93
0.01	Apr. 23	Aug. 26	Sep. 1	Sep. 15'93

Finances

A 19.5% drop in interest expense in fiscal 1992 resulted primarily from reduced average debt and lower overall interest rates. As a percent of sales, interest expense decreased to 1.8% in fiscal 1992, from 2.4% in fiscal 1991. The average interest rate on the company's total debt at the end of fiscal 1992 was 7.87%, down from 8.69% at fiscal 1991 year end.

Capitalization

Long Term Debt: $854,540,000 (7/3/93).

Class B Common Stock: 68,457,178 shs. ($0.10 par); 10 votes per sh.; 99.9% owned by the Tyson family.

Class A Common Stock: 79,682,066 shs. ($0.10 par).

Officers and directors control 12%.

Institutions hold 32%.

Shareholders of record: 36,830 (11/92).

Office—2210 W. Oaklawn Dr., P.O. Drawer E, Springdale, AR 72764. **Tel**—(501) 756-4000. **Chrmn**—D. Tyson. **Pres & CEO**—L. E. Tollett. **EVP-Fin**—G. Johnston. **VP, Treas & Investor Contact**—Wayne Britt. **Secy**—Mary Rush. **Dirs**—N. Cassady, L. V. Hackley, R. R. Jensen, S. D. Massey, J. F. Starr, L. E. Tollett, B. Tyson, D. Tyson, J. H. Tyson, F. Vorsanger. **Transfer Agent**—First Chicago Trust Co. of New York, NYC. **Incorporated** in Arkansas in 1947; reincorporated in Delaware in 1986. **Empl**—47,950.

 Kenneth A. Shea

UJB Financial

NYSE Symbol UJB Options on CBOE (Jan-Apr-Jul-Oct) In S&P MidCap 400

Price	Range	P-E Ratio	Dividend	Yield	S&P Ranking	Beta
Sep. 27'93	1993					
30	33½–21½	21	0.64	2.1%	A–	1.29

Summary

This bank holding company, the fourth largest in New Jersey, has six member banks and nine nonbank subsidiaries with over 250 offices in New Jersey and eastern Pennsylvania. Earnings in 1993 should continue to benefit from an improved net interest margin and reductions in the loan loss provision. The company recently announced a comprehensive restructuring program aimed at focusing on profitable core businesses and bank consolidations. The quarterly dividend was raised 6.7% in early 1993.

Current Outlook

Earnings for 1993 are projected at $1.70 a share (before a restructuring charge), up from 1992's $1.09. For 1994, share earnings are expected to reach $2.35.

Dividends, raised 6.7% in early 1993, are expected to continue at $0.16 quarterly.

Earnings for the balance of 1993 should continue to benefit from an improved net interest margin and reductions in the loan loss provision made possible by further declines in nonperforming loans (which fell 27%, year to year, to $296 million at June 30, 1993). Longer term, a recent restructuring plan that will focus on profitable core businesses and consolidate statewide member banks should begin to yield substantial savings in the latter half of 1994. Given adequate reserves, healthy capital levels and recent increases in residential mortgage lending, UJB's earnings should advance in 1994.

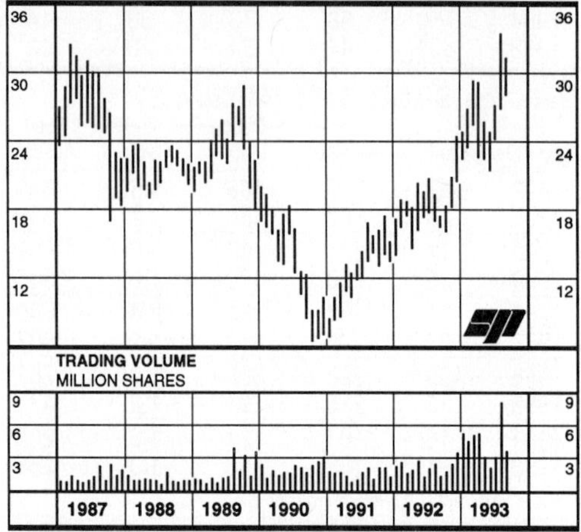

Review of Operations

Net interest income in the six months ended June 30, 1993, rose 6.8%, year to year, primarily benefiting from a wider interest margin (3.98% versus 3.76%). The provision for loan losses was 39% lower, made possible by a decline in the level of nonperforming loans. Following 0.6% lower noninterest income and 7.9% greater noninterest expense, pretax income expanded 122%. After taxes at 26.0%, versus 16.5%, net income was up 97%. Share earnings were $0.75 on 11% more shares, compared with $0.41. Results for the 1993 period exclude a credit of $0.07 a share from the cumulative effect of an accounting change.

Common Share Earnings ($)

Quarter:	1993	1992	1991	1990
Mar.	0.32	0.20	0.03	0.55
Jun.	0.43	0.21	0.08	0.13
Sep.	E0.45	0.33	0.16	d0.46
Dec.	E0.50	0.35	0.18	d0.39
	E1.70	1.09	0.45	d0.17

Important Developments

Sep. '93— The company announced a comprehensive restructuring program designed to enhance shareholder value and improve its competitive position. The program will focus on a new management structure centered on four primary lines of business (wholesale lending, retail banking, mortgage banking, and investment management), enhanced customer service, the establishment of new financial goals, and the statewide consolidation of member banks into a single bank in New Jersey worth $11 billion and a single bank in Pennsylvania worth $3 billion. Consolidations would be completed by the third quarter of 1994. The company said that it would take a restructuring charge in 1993, but that the quarter in which it was taken would remain profitable.

May '93— UJB said it completed its first bulk sale of $45 million of accruing and non-accruing real estate loans during the first quarter of 1993.

Next earnings report expected in mid-October.

Per Share Data ($)

Yr. End Dec. 31	1992	1991	1990	1989	1988	[1,2]1987	[1]1986	1985	1984	1983
Tangible Bk. Val.	**16.88**	16.26	16.45	18.28	16.60	15.47	14.84	14.67	13.23	12.03
Earnings	**1.09**	0.45	d0.17	2.62	2.58	2.31	2.17	2.17	1.92	1.62
Dividends	**0.600**	0.600	1.160	0.820	1.010	0.910	0.816	0.906	0.640	0.431
Payout Ratio	**55%**	133%	NM	31%	39%	39%	38%	42%	33%	27%
Prices—High	**24½**	17½	20	28⅞	23¾	32½	31½	26¾	15⅝	14¾
Low	**14**	6⅞	6½	18	19	17	22⅛	14¼	11⅜	7⅝
P/E Ratio—	**22–12**	39–15	NM	11–7	9–7	14–7	15–10	12–7	8–6	9–5

Data as orig. reptd. Adj. for stk. div(s). of 50% Sep. 1986, 50% Sep. 1985. **1.** Reflects merger or acquisition. **2.** Reflects acctg. change. d-Deficit. E-Estimated NM-Not Meaningful.

Income Data (Million $)

Year Ended Dec. 31	Net Int. Inc.	Tax Equiv. Adj.	Non Int. Inc.	Loan Loss Prov.	% Exp./ Op. Revs.	Net Bef. Taxes	Eff. Tax Rate	Net Inc.	% Net Int. Margin	—% Return On— Assets	Equity
1992	**538**	**19.1**	**158**	**139**	**70.4**	**71.9**	**25.1%**	**53.8**	**4.52**	**0.40**	**6.31**
1991	491	23.0	136	167	69.0	25.0	10.9%	22.0	4.22	0.17	2.60
1990	485	27.0	171	246	62.9	d22.0	NM	d6.0	4.33	NM	NM
1989	470	31.0	108	53	62.2	160.0	25.9%	119.0	4.84	1.05	14.30
1988	431	32.0	112	40	61.0	154.0	24.7%	116.0	4.93	1.13	15.90
[1]1987	390	43.0	103	33	60.2	139.0	26.2%	103.0	5.05	1.09	15.40
[2]1986	322	49.0	55	36	61.7	89.0	19.4%	72.0	5.71	1.00	15.30
1985	177	26.0	35	18	64.1	38.0	6.8%	36.0	5.44	0.87	15.40
1984	160	22.0	26	17	63.6	32.0	5.1%	30.0	5.44	0.82	15.10
1983	135	22.0	19	11	66.3	22.0	NM	24.0	5.13	0.71	13.50

Balance Sheet Data (Million $)

Dec. 31	Total Assets	———Earning Assets——— Mon. Mkt. Assets	Inv. Secs.	Com'l Loans	Other Loans	% Loan Loss Resv.	——Deposits—— Demand	Time	% Loans/ Deposits	Long Term Debt	Common Equity	% Equity To Assets
1992	**13,771**	**270**	**3,515**	**3,314**	**5,468**	**3.13**	**2,587**	**9,200**	**74.5**	**216.0**	**890**	**6.14**
1991	13,378	72	3,377	4,586	4,183	3.29	2,097	9,217	77.5	66.6	782	5.94
1990	12,818	95	2,944	3,358	5,325	2.99	2,008	8,621	81.5	72.2	777	6.55
1989	12,172	156	2,589	3,327	5,032	1.46	2,043	7,293	89.3	81.1	823	7.09
1988	10,888	312	2,204	2,826	4,513	1.47	2,156	6,738	82.3	87.9	740	6.77
1987	10,139	262	2,330	2,779	3,808	1.46	2,039	5,837	83.4	89.2	661	6.71
1986	8,024	260	1,750	2,193	2,871	1.45	2,149	4,524	75.8	84.7	480	6.30
1985	4,428	336	994	1,191	1,440	1.65	1,097	2,513	72.8	40.3	220	5.10
1984	4,051	539	838	1,021	1,242	1.51	977	2,231	70.5	40.4	191	4.73
1983	3,635	476	917	770	1,079	1.42	882	2,122	61.4	33.2	160	4.67

Data as orig. reptd. **1.** Reflects merger or acquisition and acctg. change. **2.** Reflects merger or acquisition. d-Deficit. NM-Not Meaningful.

Business Summary

UJB Financial Corp. is a bank holding company with 259 banking offices in New Jersey and eastern Pennsylvania. It owns six subsidiary banks and nine active non-bank subsidiaries engaged in discount brokerage, venture capital, commercial finance, lease finance and credit insurance.

Average earning assets in 1992 of $12.3 billion (up 1.2% from 1991) were divided: commercial loans 36%, mortgage loans 18%, instalment loans 16%, investment securities 27%, and 3% other. Average sources of funds were savings deposits 37%, other time deposits 29%, other borrowed funds 7%, demand deposits 16%, shareholders' equity 6%, and other 5%. The average yield on interest earning assets in 1992 was 7.88% (9.26% in 1991), and the average cost of interest-bearing liabilities was 4.04% (5.92%), for a spread of 3.84% (3.34%).

At year-end 1992, nonperforming loans were $361.8 million (4.12% of total loans), down from $444.7 million (5.07%) a year earlier. The reserve for loan losses was $275.3 million (3.13%), against $288.8 million (3.29%). Net charge-offs in 1992 were $152.5 million (1.73% of average loans), up from $137.3 million (1.53%) in 1990.

Finances

In December 1992, UJB completed a public offering of $175 million of 8⅝% subordinated notes, maturing in December 2002. About $100 million of the proceeds was to be used to purchase subordinated notes from subsidiary banks, which will raise their capital levels and allow the units to qualify for a rating of well capitalized.

In August 1992, UJB sold publicly 4,000,000 common shares at $17.875 each. Net proceeds amount to about $68.3 million.

Dividend Data

Dividends have been paid since 1935. A dividend reinvestment plan is available. A "poison pill" stock purchase rights plan was adopted in 1989.

Amt. of Divd. $	Date Decl.	Ex-divd. Date	Stock of Record	Payment Date
0.15	Dec. 17	Dec. 31	Jan. 7	Feb. 1'93
0.16	Mar. 16	Apr. 10	Apr. 7	May 3'93
0.16	Jun. 17	Jun. 30	Jul. 7	Aug. 2'93
0.16	Sep. 21	Oct. 1	Oct. 7	Nov. 1'93

Capitalization

Long Term Debt: $195,151,000 (6/93).

Adjust. Rate Cum. Preferred Stock: 600,166 shs. ($50 stated value).

Common Stock: 51,252,235 shs. ($1.20 par). Officers & directors own about 4.5%. Institutions hold about 31%. Shareholders of record: 21,376.

Office—301 Carnegie Center, P.O. Box 2066, Princeton, NJ 08543-2066. **Tel**—(609) 987-3200. **Chrmn, Pres & CEO**—T. J. Semrod. **EVP-Secy**—R. F. Ober, Jr. **VP-CFO**—J. R. Haggerty. **VP-Investor Contact**—William J. Healy (609-987-3220). **Dirs**—R. L. Boyle, J. G. Collins, T. J. D. Dunphy, E. J. Ferdon, F. G. Harvey, J. R. Howell, F. J. Mertz, H. S. Patterson II, T. J. Semrod, R. Silverstein, J. A. Skidmore, Jr., J. M. Tabak. **Transfer Agents**—First Chicago Trust Co. of New York, NYC; United Jersey Bank, Hackensack. **Registrar**—First Chicago Trust Co. of New York, NYC. **Incorporated** in New Jersey in 1969. **Empl**—6,326.

 Stephen R. Biggar

Unifi, Inc.

NYSE Symbol UFI In S&P MidCap 400

Price	Range	P-E Ratio	Dividend	Yield	S&P Ranking	Beta
Oct. 5'93	1993					
23¼	38⅜–20	12	0.56	2.4%	B+	1.37

Summary

Unifi's business, which had historically consisted solely of texturizing and producing polyester yarn, was expanded by the August 1991 acquisition of Macfield, Inc. into the areas of nylon texturizing, dyed yarns and spandex yarns; the acquisition also doubled Unifi's revenue base. Through the April 1993 acquisition of Vintage Yarns, Inc. for some eight million UFI common shares, Unifi expanded its business to include the production of yarn from staple fibers. Yarn operations were further enlarged through the August 1993 acquisition of the group of Pioneer Corporations. The quarterly dividend was raised 27% in August 1993.

Business Summary

Unifi, Inc. is one of the world's largest texturizers and dyers of polyester and nylon filament fibers. Its business primarily involves the purchase of partially oriented yarn (POY), either raw polyester or nylon filament, and the processing of the POY to give it bulk, strength, stretch, consistent dyeability and a soft feel, thereby making it suitable for use in the weaving and knitting of fabrics. The company's revenue base was doubled by the August 1991 acquisition of Macfield, Inc.

UFI's texturizing process involves the use of high-speed machines to draw, heat and twist the POY to produce yarns having various physical characteristics, depending upon their ultimate use.

The company's business, which had consisted solely of texturizing and producing polyester yarn, was expanded by the August 1991 acquisition of Macfield, Inc. into the areas of nylon texturizing, dyed yarns and spandex yarns. Through the April 1993 acquisition of Vintage Yarns, Unifi also manufactures yarn from staple fibers. Yarn operations were further expanded through the August 1993, acquisition of the group of Pioneer Corporations.

UFI sells its textured polyester and nylon, both domestically and internationally, to weavers and knitters that produce fabrics for the apparel, industrial, hosiery, home furnishings and auto upholstery markets.

At fiscal 1992 year-end, the company owned 12 manufacturing and warehousing facilities with an aggregate of 3.8 million sq. ft. of floor space. In fiscal 1993's third quarter, UFI completed construction of a new polyester texturizing plant in Yadkinville, N.C.

In fiscal 1992, Unifi's largest customer accounted for 11% of total sales. UFI's international subsidiaries, which operate mainly in Europe, contributed 19% of fiscal 1992 sales.

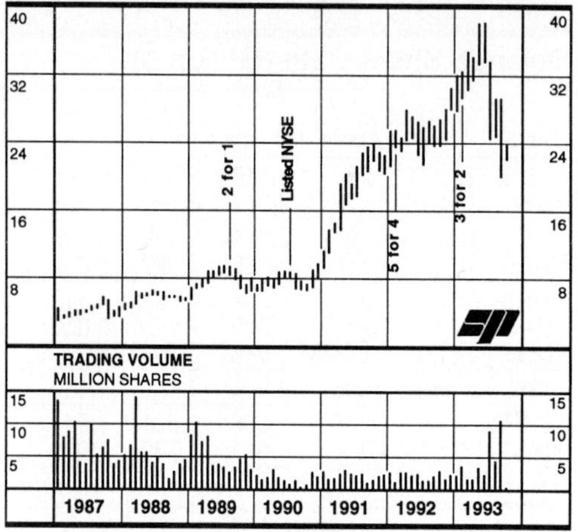

Important Developments

Sep. '93— The company reported that as the first quarter of fiscal 1994 unfolded, it had experienced a slowing of domestic business and the resultant adverse impact on domestic margins. It added that in Europe, while volumes were "satisfactory," margins remained under pressure. As such, UFI expected earnings for the quarter to fall below the level of the year-earlier period; it added that it did not anticipate a change in this business environment in the near-term.

Aug. '93— The company completed the acquisition of the group of Pioneer Corporations, whose primary products include open-end spun yarns made solely of cotton, in exchange for some 2.7 million UFI common shares. The acquisition was to be accounted for on a pooling-of-interests basis.

Next earnings report expected in late October.

Per Share Data ($)

Yr. End Jun. 30	1993	[1]1992	1991	1990	1989	1988	1987	1986	1985	1984
Tangible Bk. Val.	**NA**	[2]6.79	[2]4.29	[2]4.15	[2]3.33	3.07	2.70	2.40	2.03	1.85
Cash Flow	**NA**	1.67	1.59	1.15	1.07	0.93	0.59	0.47	0.36	0.33
Earnings[3]	**1.87**	1.04	1.08	0.71	0.68	0.63	0.31	0.29	0.18	0.19
Dividends	**0.42**	0.360	0.213	Nil	Nil	Nil	Nil	Nil	Nil	Nil
Payout Ratio	**22%**	34%	18%	Nil	Nil	Nil	Nil	Nil	Nil	Nil
Prices[4]—High	**38⅜**	30⅝	24⅛	9⅞	9⅝	6⅝	5⅞	4¾	2⅝	3⅜
Low	**20**	21⅜	9⅜	6½	5½	4¼	2⅞	2½	1½	1⅜
P/E Ratio—	**21–11**	29–21	22–9	14–9	14–8	11–7	19–9	17–9	15–8	18–7

Data as orig. reptd. Adj. for stk. divs. of 50% Feb. 1993, 25% Feb. 1992, 100% Aug. 1989, 50% Feb. 1986, 25% Feb. 1983. **1.** Major merger resulted in formation of new co. **2.** Incl. intangibles. **3.** Bef. spec. items of +0.05 in 1990, -0.11 in 1983. **4.** Cal. yr. NA-Not Available.

Income Data (Million $)

Year Ended Jun. 30	Revs.	Oper. Inc.	% Oper. Inc. of Revs.	Cap. Exp.	Depr.	Int. Exp.	Net Bef. Taxes	Eff. Tax Rate	[3]Net Inc.	% Net Inc. of Revs.	Cash Flow
[1]1992	**1,091**	**168**	**15.4**	**66.9**	**37.4**	**9.66**	**[2]103**	**39.0%**	**62.6**	**5.7**	**100**
1991	442	70	15.9	17.3	17.9	0.86	56	31.1%	38.3	8.7	56
1990	399	55	13.9	19.8	16.7	0.93	39	33.0%	26.4	6.6	43
1989	392	59	15.0	41.3	17.2	0.90	41	35.7%	26.2	6.7	42
1988	298	45	15.1	7.2	12.5	0.79	38	34.8%	24.8	8.3	37
1987	276	36	13.0	1.8	11.8	2.76	22	46.4%	12.0	4.4	24
1986	249	24	9.7	47.4	8.3	3.37	17	37.4%	10.4	4.2	19
1985	216	19	8.6	6.1	6.5	3.84	11	43.3%	6.3	2.9	13
1984	217	21	9.6	17.2	5.9	3.91	13	45.4%	7.4	3.4	13
1983	176	18	10.4	3.0	5.6	4.06	13	38.8%	8.3	4.7	14

Balance Sheet Data (Million $)

Jun. 30	Cash	Curr. Assets	Curr. Liab.	Curr. Ratio	Total Assets	% Ret. on Assets	Long Term Debt	Common Equity	Total Cap.	% LT Debt of Cap.	% Ret. on Equity
1992	**262**	**505**	**132**	**3.8**	**805**	**10.8**	**251**	**404**	**673**	**37.3**	**19.0**
1991	17	120	52	2.3	197	20.0	Nil	140	145	Nil	27.7
1990	36	129	47	2.8	208	13.3	4	152	161	2.7	19.3
1989	2	109	59	1.8	187	15.3	Nil	121	128	Nil	22.4
1988	21	78	35	2.3	144	18.4	Nil	104	109	Nil	25.3
1987	12	70	30	2.3	133	8.8	1	97	103	1.0	13.2
1986	1	73	23	3.2	146	7.8	29	89	123	23.9	12.7
1985	26	78	23	3.4	114	5.5	16	71	90	17.3	9.3
1984	30	86	29	2.9	122	6.5	22	68	93	24.0	11.4
1983	32	79	19	4.1	104	7.8	22	61	85	25.6	15.7

Data as orig. reptd. **1.** Major merger resulted in formation of new co. **2.** Incl. equity in earns. of nonconsol. subs. **3.** Bef. spec. items.

Net Sales (Million $)

13 Weeks:	1992–93	1991–92	1990–91	1989–90
Sep.	---	261	[1]104	94
Dec.	---	261	103	99
Mar.	[2]988	280	112	99
Jun.	344	289	122	108
	1,332	1,091	442	399

Based on a preliminary report, net sales for the fiscal year ended June 27, 1993, advanced 5.6% from the prior year's level, both as restated for the pooling-of-interests acquisition of Vintage Yarns in April 1993. Operating margins widened, and benefiting from a considerably higher level of other income and the absence of a $24.8 million charge (gross) related to merger expenses, net income rose 44%, to $128,053,000 ($1.87 a share), from $88,847,000 ($1.31).

Common Share Earnings ($)

Quarter:	1992–93	1991–92	1990–91	1989–90
Sep.	---	d0.04	[1]0.22	0.12
Dec.	---	0.29	0.24	0.17
Mar.	[2]1.37	0.36	0.29	0.17
Jun.	0.50	0.43	0.33	0.24
	1.87	1.04	1.08	0.71

Dividend Data

Quarterly dividends were resumed in August 1990, marking the first payment since 1977.

Amt of Divd. $	Date Decl.	Ex-divd. Date	Stock of Record	Payment Date
0.15	Oct. 22	Oct. 30	Nov. 5	Nov. 12'92
0.16½	Jan. 21	Feb. 1	Feb. 5	Feb. 16'93
3–for–2	Jan. 21	Feb. 17	Feb. 5	Feb. 16'93
0.11	Apr. 15	May 4	May 10	May 17'93
0.14	Jul. 15	Jul. 26	Jul. 30	Aug. 6'93

Finances

In April 1993, Unifi acquired Vintage Yarns, Inc. in exchange for 8,388,637 UFI common shares (including 496,387 shares reserved for issuance upon the exercise of certain stock options). The acquisition of Vintage, which had sales of some $170 million in its fiscal 1992 year, was accounted for on a pooling-of-interests basis.

Macfield, Inc. was acquired in August 1991 for about 20,325,000 (adjusted) common shares. In June 1991, UFI sold publicly 5,849,250 (adjusted) common shares at $17.73 each; proceeds were used to retire Macfield long-term debt.

Capitalization

Long Term Debt: $245,436,000 (3/93); incl. $230 million of sub. notes due 2002 & conv. into com. at $29.67 a sh.

Common Stock: 67,591,000 shs. ($0.10 par). Institutions hold about 62%. Shareholders of record: 1,162 (8/92).

1. 14 wks. **2.** 39 wks. d-Deficit.

Office—7201 W. Friendly Rd., P.O. Box 19109, Greensboro, NC 27419. **Tel**—(919) 294-4410. **Pres & CEO**—W. T. Kretzer. **Exec VP, CFO & Investor Contact**—Robert A. Ward. **Secy**—C. C. Frazier Jr. **Dirs**—W. G. Armfield IV, C. R. Carter, J. W. Eller, W. D. Kimbrell, W. T. Kretzer, K. G. Langone, D. L. McMichael Sr., G. A. Mebane, D. F. Orr, T. R. Pohl, E. Sharp, R. A. Ward, G. A. Webster. **Transfer Agent & Registrar**—First Union National Bank, Charlotte, N.C. **Incorporated** in New York in 1969. **Empl**—5,200.

 Michael W. Jaffe

United HealthCare

NYSE Symbol UNH Options on ASE, CBOE, NYSE, Phila (Mar-Jun-Sep-Dec) In S&P MidCap 400

Price	Range	P-E Ratio	Dividend	Yield	S&P Ranking	Beta
Oct. 13'93	1993					
67⅞	70⅝–40	34	0.03	0.1%	B	1.96

Summary

UNH is a national leader in health care cost management, serving both providers and purchasers of health care. It owns and manages health maintenance organizations and provides specialty managed care services. Growing acceptance of cost-effective managed care health plans and growth in related specialty services enhance long-term prospects.

Current Outlook

Earnings for 1994 are projected at $2.85 a share, up from the $2.30 indicated for 1993.

Dividends should continue at $0.03 annually.

Total revenues for 1994 are expected to show another strong advance. Revenues from owned and managed health plans should rise, aided by acquisitions, enrollment growth and higher premium rates. Gains are also forecast for UNH's specialty services, reflecting rising enrollment and higher rates. Margins should be well maintained on the greater volume and cost efficiencies. Efficient HMO firms such as UNH should be net beneficiaries under the new Clinton health care reform program.

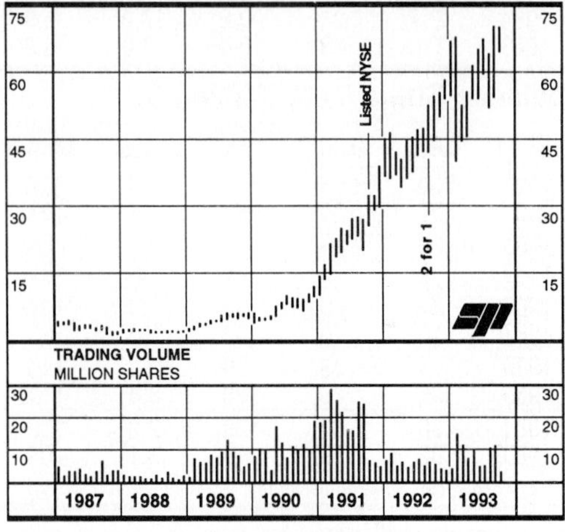

Total Revenues (Million $)

Quarter:	1993	1992	1991	1990
Mar.	475	335	179	130
Jun.	514	351	187	150
Sep.	---	367	221	157
Dec.	---	388	260	169
	---	1,442	847	605

Total revenues in the six months ended June 30, 1993, rose 44%, year to year, reflecting strong gains in premiums, management service revenues and investment income. Pretax income gained 53%. After taxes at 36.0%, versus 35.0%, and higher minority interest, net income was up 51%. Share profits were $1.12, against $0.77, as adjusted for the 2-for-1 split in September 1992.

Common Share Earnings ($)

Quarter:	1993	1992	1991	1990
Mar.	0.54	0.38	0.27	0.14
Jun.	0.58	0.39	0.29	0.16
Sep.	E0.58	0.42	0.31	0.16
Dec.	E0.60	0.46	0.33	0.18
	E2.30	1.65	1.20	0.64

Important Developments

Aug. '93— UNH acquired HMO America Inc. for about 7.4 million UNH common shares. HMO America, a Chicago-based HMO with about 300,000 members, earned $11.4 million on revenues of $318 million in 1992. In July, UNH sold a 26,800-member HMO in Iowa for $19.8 million. In January, UNH acquired Western Ohio Health Care Corp., an HMO with 182,600 members, for about $100 million.

Jun. 30'93— Enrollment in the company's owned and managed health plans totaled 2,017,000, up 22% from the level a year earlier. For the company's owned plans (excluding Western Ohio Health Care), first half enrollment on a "same store" basis rose 19%, year to year. Specialty managed care products and services covered 28.2 million persons, up 50%, year to year.

Next earnings report expected in early November.

Per Share Data ($)

Yr. End Dec. 31	[1]1992	[1]1991	[1]1990	1989	1988	1987	[1]1986	[1]1985	1984	1983
Tangible Bk. Val.	**7.61**	4.14	1.88	1.03	[2]0.17	[2]1.30	[2]1.79	[2]0.65	0.49	0.07
Cash Flow	**2.04**	1.43	1.35	0.51	d0.89	d0.25	0.32	0.15	0.13	0.04
Earnings[3]	**1.65**	1.20	0.65	0.32	d1.15	d0.50	0.21	0.09	0.10	0.02
Dividends	**0.015**	0.015	0.015	Nil	Nil	Nil	Nil	Nil	Nil	Nil
Payout Ratio	**1%**	1%	2%	Nil	Nil	Nil	Nil	Nil	Nil	Nil
Prices—High	**58⅜**	39⅛	12	6⅜	2¾	4½	8	6	2⅜	NA
Low	**34¼**	10	3⅞	2½	1¾	1⅜	3½	2	1¾	NA
P/E Ratio—	**35–20**	33–8	18–6	20–8	NM	NM	38–17	67–13	24–18	NA

Data as orig. reptd. Adj. for stk. div. of 100% Sep. 1992. **1.** Refl. merger or acq. **2.** Incl. intangibles. **3.** Bef. spec. items of +0.03 in 1986, +0.04 in 1985. E-Estimated. d-Deficit. NM-Not Meaningful. NA-Not Available.

Income Data (Million $)

Year Ended Dec. 31	Revs.	Oper. Inc.	% Oper. Inc. of Revs.	Cap. Exp.	Depr.	Int. Exp.	Net Bef. Taxes	Eff. Tax Rate	[4]Net Inc.	% Net Inc. of Revs.	Cash Flow
[1]1992	**1,442**	**205**	**14.2**	**[2]22.4**	**27.0**	**0.94**	**177**	**35.0%**	**114.0**	**7.9**	**141.0**
[1]1991	847	129	15.3	[2]15.1	14.3	1.25	114	34.0%	74.8	8.8	89.2
[1]1990	605	66	10.9	[2]2.7	10.6	3.34	[3]52	34.0%	33.9	5.6	44.6
1989	412	34	8.2	[2]3.7	7.8	4.29	[3]22	36.0%	13.7	3.3	21.5
1988	440	19	4.2	[2]4.4	8.3	4.51	[3]d34	NM	d36.8	NM	d28.4
1987	440	7	1.6	[2]4.9	7.8	4.98	[3]d21	NM	d15.8	NM	d8.0
[1]1986	216	15	7.0	[2]10.6	3.5	0.94	[3]13	47.3%	6.3	2.9	9.8
[1]1985	101	7	6.5	[2]6.2	1.6	0.06	[3]4	49.5%	2.1	2.0	3.6
1984	13	3	19.5	1.3	0.4	0.14	2	42.4%	1.2	8.9	1.6
1983	8	2	23.4	1.6	0.3	0.07	Nil	NM	0.2	2.6	0.5

Balance Sheet Data (Million $)

Dec. 31	Cash	Curr. Assets	Curr. Liab.	Curr. Ratio	Total Assets	% Ret. on Assets	Long Term Debt	Common Equity	Total Cap.	% LT Debt of Cap.	% Ret. on Equity
1992	**242**	**320**	**333**	**1.0**	**994**	**14.1**	**0.4**	**656**	**658**	**0.1**	**22.7**
1991	251	301	235	1.3	574	16.4	3.4	319	331	1.0	32.2
1990	113	142	139	1.0	293	10.9	7.0	126	145	4.8	34.5
1989	152	175	103	1.7	237	6.2	58.3	50	127	46.0	48.0
1988	95	113	81	1.4	169	NM	60.0	5	81	73.9	NM
1987	61	95	97	1.0	210	NM	52.9	42	105	50.2	NM
1986	49	86	71	1.2	198	5.0	52.9	55	119	44.3	16.9
1985	18	25	26	1.0	42	7.3	Nil	15	16	Nil	15.3
1984	2	5	1	4.4	8	17.5	Nil	6	7	Nil	31.9
1983	Nil	2	3	0.5	4	6.4	Nil	1	1	Nil	28.8

Data as orig. reptd. **1.** Refl. merger or acq. **2.** Net. **3.** Incl. equity in earns. of nonconsol. subs. **4.** Bef. spec. items. d-Deficit. NM-Not Meaningful.

Business Summary

United HealthCare Corporation serves nearly two million members through owned and managed health plans, and provides specialty managed care products and services to more than 28 million additional individuals through employers, employee groups, insurers, HMO operators and other health care providers. Contributions in 1992 were:

	Revenues	Profits
Owned health plans	82.0%	59.6%
Managed plans/specialty managed care services ...	17.3%	29.5%
Corporate/eliminations	0.7%	10.9%

At year-end 1992, the company was providing management services to nine owned health plans with 815,000 members (94% commercial; 6% Medicare) and 10 managed or minority-owned plans with 910,700 members (91%; 9%). During 1992, 15% of total revenues was associated with Medicare and 9% with Medicaid.

UNH provides, for both owned and managed health plans, computerized management information systems, claims processing and marketing, contracting, and financial and accounting services. For management services provided to health plans, it receives fees based on a percentage of gross revenues and may receive additional fees based on performance.

Specialty managed care services offered to HMOs, PPOs, insurers, providers, Blue Cross/Blue Shield plans, third-party administrators and employers include prescription drug benefit programs, case management, and benefit administration services, mental health/substance abuse programs, workers' compensation services and geriatric care management. As of June 30, 1993, specialty managed care products were provided to 28.2 million participants.

Dividend Data

Annual dividend payments of $0.03 a share (not adjusted) have been made since 1990, and UNH intends to maintain a $0.03 annual dividend.

Amt. of Divd. $	Date Decl.	Ex-divd. Date	Stock of Record	Payment Date
2-for-1 Split	Aug. 12	Sep. 16	Sep. 1	Sep. 15'92
0.03	Feb. 16	Mar. 26	Apr. 1	Apr. 16'93

Capitalization

Long Term Liabilities: $406,000 (12/92).

Minority Interest: $1,655,000.

Common Stock: 69,400,467 shs. ($0.01 par).
Institutions hold 90%.
Shareholders of record: 2,375.

Office—300 Opus Center, 9900 Bren Road East, Minnetonka, MN 55343. **Tel**—(612) 936-1300. **Chrmn & Pres**—W. W. McGuire. **EVP & CFO**—G. B. Borkow. **VP, Treas & Investor Contact**—David P. Koppe (612-939-7760). **Secy**—K. Roche. **Dirs**—W. C. Ballard, G. B. Borkow, R. T. Burke, R. K. Ditmore, T. H. Kean, D. W. Leatherdale, E. J. McCormack, W. W. McGuire, E. J. McKinley, J. L. Seiberlich, W. G. Spears, G. R. Wilensky. **Transfer Agent & Registrar**—Norwest Bank Minnesota, South St. Paul. **Incorporated** in Minnesota in 1977. **Empl**—4,800.

 H. B. Saftlas

U.S. Healthcare, Inc.

NASDAQ Symbol USHC (Incl. in Nat'l Market) Options on ASE In S&P MidCap 400

Price	Range	P-E Ratio	Dividend	Yield	S&P Ranking	Beta
Sep. 8'93	1993					
44	59¾–36¾	20	0.64	1.5%	B+	1.45

Summary

This company owns and operates health maintenance organizations that serve more than 1,500,000 members in the mid-Atlantic, Greater New York and New England regions. Revenues and earnings have grown strongly in recent years, and should continue to benefit from increased use of managed care by employer groups seeking to control rising medical costs. Despite the company's favorable outlook, the shares continue to trade well below their early 1993 highs, hurt by healthcare reform uncertainties.

Current Outlook

Earnings for 1993 are projected at $2.40 a share, up from $1.85 in 1992. A further advance to about $2.85 is estimated for 1994.

The quarterly dividend will be raised 23% with the September 1993 payment.

Revenues should continue to show healthy gains in the remainder of 1993 and 1994, aided by higher premium rates and further growth in membership enrollment. Membership growth, which should exceed 10% annually, will reflect a continuing trend among employer groups to turn to managed care in an attempt to control rising medical costs. Premium rate increases are expected to slow in 1994, but well controlled medical and administrative costs should spur strong earnings growth.

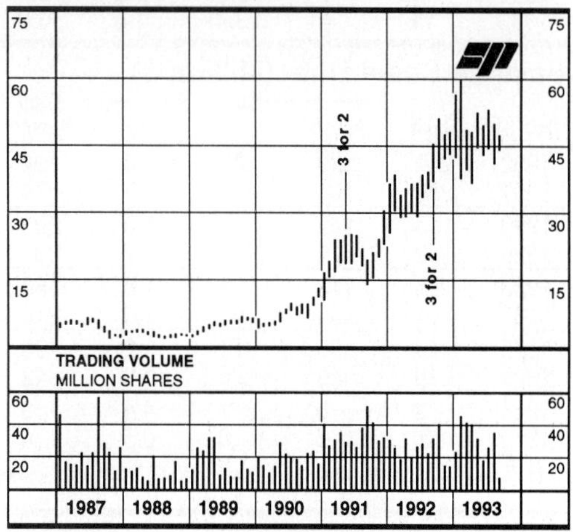

Total Revenues (Million $)

Quarter:	1993	1992	1991	1990
Mar.	622	523	401	321
Jun.	650	532	414	325
Sep.	---	560	435	335
Dec.	---	573	459	349
	---	2,189	1,709	1,330

Total revenues in the six months ended June 30, 1993, climbed 22%, year to year, reflecting increased membership and higher premium rates. The medical loss ratio improved to 75.2%, from 77.5%, and with administrative and marketing costs stable as a percentage of sales (10.5% in each period), pretax income soared 41%. After taxes at 39.5% in each period, net income was also up 41%, to $130,204,000 ($1.20 a share), from $92,392,000 ($0.85, as adjusted).

Common Share Earnings ($)

Quarter:	1993	1992	1991	1990
Mar.	0.58	0.42	0.31	0.11
Jun.	0.62	0.43	0.32	0.13
Sep.	E0.60	0.44	0.36	0.18
Dec.	E0.60	0.55	0.40	0.30
	E2.40	1.85	1.39	0.72

Important Developments

Aug. '93— USHC received approval from the Health Care Financing Administration to offer its Medicare plan in New Jersey. The company's Medicare plan currently covers 25,000 Medicare members in southeastern Pennsylvania, Pittsburgh and New York.

Next earnings report expected in late October.

Per Share Data ($)

Yr. End Dec. 31	1992	1991	1990	1989	1988	1987	1986	1985	1984	1983
Tangible Bk. Val.	**[1]4.70**	[1]3.28	[1]2.21	[1]1.58	[1]1.37	[1]1.37	1.70	1.13	0.49	0.39
Cash Flow	**1.99**	1.48	0.78	0.31	0.07	0.04	0.69	0.06	0.11	0.03
Earnings[2]	**1.85**	1.39	0.72	0.27	0.04	0.01	0.66	0.23	0.10	0.04
Dividends	**0.410**	0.240	0.153	0.095	0.071	0.071	0.053	0.017	Nil	Nil
Payout Ratio	**22%**	17%	21%	35%	NM	NM	8%	7%	Nil	Nil
Prices—High	**51¼**	30½	13¼	6 15/16	3 15/16	6½	10 3/16	10 1/16	4 11/16	2 7/16
Low	**25⅝**	10 9/16	4¼	2 5/16	1 15/16	1 15/16	4 15/16	3 13/16	1½	27/32
P/E Ratio—	**28–14**	22–8	18–6	26–9	NM	NM	15–8	45–17	47–15	74–24

Data as orig. reptd. Adj. for stk. divs. of 50% Sep. 1992, 50% May 1991, 50% Nov. 1985, 50% Jul. 1985, 50% Jan. 1985, 50% Aug. 1984, 50% Sep. 1983, 50% Jun. 1983. **1.** Incl. intangibles. **2.** Ful. dil.: 2.08 in 1991, 1.07 in 1990. E-Estimated. NM-Not Meaningful.

Income Data (Million $)

Year Ended Dec. 31	[1]Revs.	Oper. Inc.	% Oper. Inc. of Revs.	Cap. Exp.	Depr.	Int. Exp.	Net Bef. Taxes	Eff. Tax Rate	Net Inc.	% Net Inc. of Revs.	Cash Flow
1992	**2,129**	**285**	**13.4**	**43.2**	**15.00**	**Nil**	**[2]330**	**39.4%**	**200**	**9.4**	**215**
1991	1,664	211	12.7	17.1	9.73	Nil	[2]247	38.9%	151	9.1	161
1990	1,292	89	6.9	44.9	6.04	Nil	[2]124	37.5%	78	6.0	84
1989	976	26	2.7	18.3	4.50	Nil	[2]45	36.4%	28	2.9	33
1988	720	d3	NM	6.0	6.66	Nil	[2]5	29.5%	4	0.5	8
1987	598	d29	NM	4.7	5.11	Nil	[2]d5	NM	1	0.2	4
1986	502	48	9.6	4.0	4.65	Nil	[2]131	42.2%	76	15.1	79
1985	351	39	11.1	14.7	2.82	Nil	48	49.1%	25	7.0	26
1984	199	16	8.1	8.0	1.17	Nil	21	49.3%	11	5.4	12
1983	93	4	4.0	1.2	0.50	Nil	6	49.2%	3	3.5	4

Balance Sheet Data (Million $)

Dec. 31	Cash	Curr. Assets	Curr. Liab.	Curr. Ratio	Total Assets	% Ret. on Assets	Long Term Debt	Common Equity	Total Cap.	% LT Debt of Cap.	% Ret. on Equity
1992	**179**	**277**	**463**	**0.6**	**981**	**22.8**	**Nil**	**505**	**505**	**Nil**	**46.7**
1991	90	175	401	0.4	758	22.0	Nil	347	347	Nil	52.0
1990	314	391	374	1.0	613	15.0	Nil	234	234	Nil	38.7
1989	206	278	245	1.1	414	8.2	Nil	164	164	Nil	18.6
1988	81	132	128	1.0	271	1.4	Nil	140	142	Nil	2.6
1987	130	188	118	1.6	261	0.4	Nil	139	141	Nil	0.7
1986	164	215	86	2.5	280	32.0	Nil	189	192	Nil	47.1
1985	118	142	60	2.4	197	16.0	0.91	135	137	0.7	25.5
1984	44	60	48	1.2	103	13.3	0.19	54	55	0.3	22.3
1983	48	56	17	3.4	60	9.0	0.20	43	43	0.4	14.7

Data as orig. reptd. **1.** Premiums & other revs.; excl. invest. inc. **2.** Incl equity in earns. of nonconsol. subs. d-Deficit. NM-Not Meaningful.

Business Summary

U.S. Healthcare, Inc. (formerly U.S. Health Care Systems, Inc.) provides comprehensive managed healthcare services through health maintenance organizations (HMOs) in Pennsylvania, New Jersey, New York, Delaware, Connecticut, Massachusetts, New Hampshire and Maryland. At June 30, 1993, the company's HMOs served 1,523,000 members, up from 1,405,000 at 1992 year-end and 1,240,000 at December 31, 1991.

USHC's HMOs generally operate under the individual-practice model, in which the HMO contracts with independent physicians who are broadly dispersed throughout a community and who care for patients in their own offices. In exchange for a fixed monthly payment, members receive virtually complete healthcare coverage with minimal out-of-pocket expenditures, unlike conventionally designed health plans that frequently require substantial copayments and deductibles. When an individual enrolls in one of the company's HMOs, he or she selects a primary-care physician from among those physicians who have contracted with that HMO.

The services of the company's HMOs are marketed primarily to employer groups. In addition to comprehensive primary-physician care, specialist care and hospital services, USHC makes available home healthcare and other outpatient services, as well as optional prescription drug, vision care and dental plans.

USHC also provides managed care administrative services to self-insured and other employees. Membership in employer-insured plans for which the company provides such services was 119,000 at June 30, 1993, up from 91,000 at December 31, 1992, and 53,000 at December 31, 1991.

Dividend Data

Cash dividends are paid quarterly. A 3-for-2 stock split was effected in September 1992.

Amt. of Divd. $	Date Decl.	Ex–divd. Date	Stock of Record	Payment Date
0.13	Mar. 2	Mar. 10	Mar. 16	Mar. 23'93
0.13	Jun. 4	Jun. 10	Jun. 16	Jun. 23'93
0.16	Aug. 4	Sep. 2	Sep. 9	Sep. 23'93
0.16	Aug. 4	Dec. 3	Dec. 9	Dec. 23'93

Capitalization

Long Term Liabs.: $14,299,000 (6/93).

Common Stock: 97,304,109 shs. ($0.005 par). Institutions hold 76%.

Cl. B. Stock: 10,525,555 shs. (L. Abramson holds 99.8%); conv. sh.-for-sh. into com.; ea. sh. entitled to 50 voting rights.

Office—980 Jolly Rd., P.O. Box 1109, Blue Bell, PA 19422-0770. **Tel**—(215) 628-4800. **CEO**—L. Abramson. **EVP & CFO**—C. C. Nicolaides. **Secy**—A. R. Letofsky. **Dirs**—L. Abramson, J. S. Goodman, A. Misher, D. B. Soll, T. T. Weglicki. **Transfer Agent**—American Stock Transfer & Trust Co. NYC. **Incorporated** in Pennsylvania in 1982. **Empl**—2,538.

 Adam J. Penn

U.S. Shoe

NYSE Symbol USR Options on Phila (Jan-Apr-Jul-Oct) In S&P MidCap 400

Price	Range	P-E Ratio	Dividend	Yield	S&P Ranking	Beta
Oct. 18'93	1993					
11	12¾–8⅝	NM	0.32	2.8%	B–	1.79

Summary

This leading retailer of women's apparel and eyewear also manufactures and retails brand name footwear. Despite ongoing efforts to restructure the company, including closing or selling unprofitable and marginally profitable women's apparel stores, earnings were disappointing in 1992-93, mainly reflecting soft women's apparel sales. A loss is expected in 1993-94, but some improvement is expected in 1994-95. In May 1993, directors cut the quarterly dividend 38% to conserve cash.

Current Outlook

A loss for the fiscal year ending January 29, 1994, is projected at $0.33 a share, including a $0.22 one-time charge, compared with share earnings of $0.10 in 1992-93. Earnings for 1994-95 could rebound to $0.50.

Directors cut the quarterly dividend 38%, from $0.13 to $0.08, with the May 1993 declaration.

Sales for 1993-94 could decline moderately, reflecting the continued closing or divestiture of unprofitable or marginally profitable women's apparel stores, and lower sales at the remaining apparel stores reflecting a change in the product mix and soft consumer demand. Sales at the footwear division could also decline because of increased competition. Despite the planned divestiture of seven Lenscrafter stores in the UK, the optical retail division should post higher sales, reflecting acquisitions and expansion of Sight & Save, a chain offering value-priced optical wear. Margins may remain under pressure with continued losses at the women's apparel stores, and one-time charges of $25 million for divestitures.

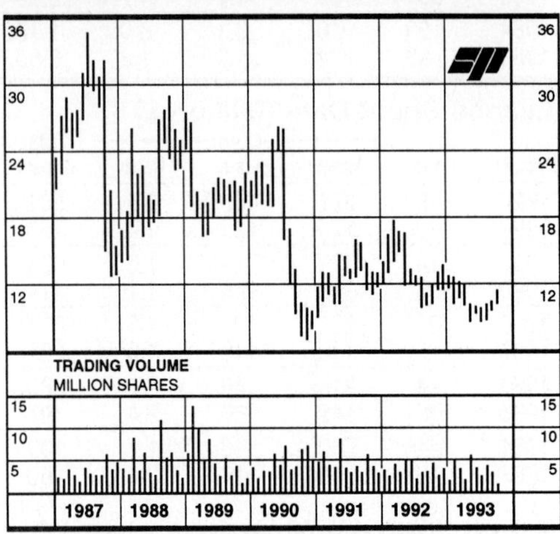

Net Sales (Million $)

13 Weeks:	1993-94	1992-93	1991-92	1990-91
Apr.	640	648	675	667
Jul.	640	640	677	671
Oct.		675	679	675
Jan.		688	694	706
		2,651	2,726	2,719

Sales in the first six months ended July 31, 1993, fell fractionally, year to year, on lower sales in the women's apparel and footwear divisions. Higher operating income at the optical retailing division was more than offset by a wider operating loss at the women's apparel group and a loss at the footwear division, versus operating income. As a result, the consolidated operating loss widened to $32.4 million ($0.71 a share), from $4.7 million ($0.10).

Common Share Earnings ($)

13 Weeks:	1993-94	1992-93	1991-92	1990-91
Apr.	d0.21	0.06	0.27	0.39
Jul.	d0.50	d0.16	0.14	0.04
Oct.	E0.13	0.18	0.19	0.20
Jan.	E0.25	0.02	0.28	d1.24
	Ed0.33	0.10	0.88	d0.61

Important Developments

Oct. '93— USR said it would charge $3.8 million ($0.08 a share) against third quarter earnings to sell its United Kingdom Lenscrafters division. In August, it recorded a $10.6 million charge to divest the unprofitable Ups 'N Downs and Caren Charles apparel divisions and said it was recruiting new executive leadership in footwear and apparel, and reducing corporate expenses.

Next earnings report expected in late November.

Per Share Data ($)

Yr. End Jan. 31	1993	1992	[1]1991	1990	1989	1988	1987	1986	1985	1984
Tangible Bk. Val.	**10.22**	10.96	10.81	11.75	11.17	11.29	10.57	10.38	9.32	8.53
Cash Flow	**1.93**	2.72	1.16	2.73	1.76	2.01	1.54	2.22	1.83	2.20
Earnings[2]	**0.10**	0.88	d0.61	1.10	0.29	0.80	0.57	1.46	1.21	1.71
Dividends	**0.520**	0.520	0.505	0.460	0.460	0.460	0.460	0.445	0.419	0.370
Payout Ratio	**543%**	59%	NM	42%	158%	56%	80%	30%	34%	21%
Calendar Years	**1992**	1991	1990	1989	1988	1987	1986	1985	1984	1983
Prices—High	**NA**	16	26¼	27½	29	34¾	27⅜	23	18⅞	24½
Low	**NA**	9	7	16⅜	14	12¾	19½	12⅛	11½	12⅜
P/E Ratio—	**NA**	18–10	NM	25–15	NM	43–16	48–34	16–8	16–10	14–7

Data as orig. reptd. Adj. for stk. divs. of 100% Jun. 1986, 100% Jun. 1983. **1.** Refl. acctg. change. **2.** Bef. spec. items of -0.19 in 1992, -0.08 in 1991, +0.36 in 1988. d-Deficit. E-Estimated NM-Not Meaningful. NA-Not Available.

Income Data (Million $)

Year Ended Jan. 31	Revs.	Oper. Inc.	% Oper. Inc. of Revs.	Cap. Exp.	Depr.	[2]Int. Exp.	Net Bef. Taxes	Eff. Tax Rate	[3]Net Inc.	% Net Inc. of Revs.	Cash Flow
1993	**2,651**	**108**	**4.1**	**72**	**83.5**	**16.9**	**8**	**43.0%**	**4.4**	**0.2**	**88**
1992	2,726	169	6.2	60	83.2	17.1	68	41.0%	[1]50.0	1.5	123
[1]1991	2,719	148	5.4	109	80.1	23.3	d39	NM	d27.7	NM	52
1990	2,557	187	7.3	70	73.6	25.1	82	40.2%	49.2	1.9	123
1989	2,343	138	5.9	93	65.9	27.2	21	37.5%	13.0	0.6	79
1988	2,168	124	5.7	165	54.8	17.4	61	40.9%	36.0	1.7	91
1987	2,003	119	5.9	149	44.0	18.1	49	48.5%	[1]25.5	1.3	70
1986	1,920	183	9.5	79	33.7	15.9	124	47.6%	64.9	3.4	99
1985	1,717	144	8.4	66	27.4	15.9	100	46.6%	53.4	3.1	81
1984	1,508	173	11.5	54	21.8	10.1	143	47.4%	75.2	5.0	97

Balance Sheet Data (Million $)

Jan. 31	Cash	Curr. Assets	Curr. Liab.	Curr. Ratio	Total Assets	% Ret. on Assets	Long Term Debt	Common Equity	Total Cap.	% LT Debt of Cap.	% Ret. on Equity
1993	**159.0**	**705**	**427**	**1.6**	**1,166**	**0.4**	**192**	**489**	**695**	**27.6**	**0.9**
1992	83.6	680	444	1.5	1,152	3.3	144	507	671	21.5	7.9
1991	59.5	721	450	1.6	1,236	NM	245	498	766	32.0	NM
1990	21.3	661	374	1.8	1,164	4.3	178	549	774	23.0	9.2
1989	10.1	580	324	1.8	1,111	1.2	202	517	776	26.1	2.5
1988	22.1	584	369	1.6	1,101	3.6	154	518	724	21.3	7.2
1987	16.0	505	229	2.2	923	2.9	144	489	632	22.7	5.2
1986	14.7	534	232	2.3	850	7.8	92	477	570	16.2	14.3
1985	12.0	532	295	1.8	807	7.2	46	428	473	9.6	13.0
1984	2.5	439	199	2.2	670	11.9	50	390	440	11.3	20.7

Data as orig. reptd. **1.** Refl. acctg. change. **2.** Net of int. inc. **3.** Bef. spec. items. d-Deficit. NM-Not Meaningful.

Business Summary

U.S. Shoe is a consumer goods company with operations in women's apparel retailing, optical retailing, and footwear manufacturing and distribution. As of 1992-93 year-end, the company was operating 2,468 retail locations and leased departments. During the second quarter of 1993-94, the company sold its Caren Charles and Ups 'N Downs divisions. Segment contributions in 1992-93 (profits in millions):

	Sales	Profits
Women's specialty retailing..	48%	$12.1
Optical retailing	25%	40.4
Footwear	27%	–5.5

As of January 31, 1993, the women's specialty retailing group had 1,523 stores (including those sold during the second quarter of 1993-94), located mainly in malls, consisting of 735 Casual Corner stores, 340 Petite Sophisticate stores, 165 Ups 'N Downs/Capezio stores, 170 Caren Charles/Pappagallo stores, 105 August Max Woman stores, and eight Career Image stores.

Optical retailing consisted of 429 LensCrafters optical superstores in the U.S. and 54 in Canada, and 19 Sight & Save stores. In October 1993, USR agreed to sell its seven remaining Lenscrafter stores in the United Kingdom.

Footwear consists of the manufacture, importing, wholesaling and retailing of women's footwear. Major brands include Amalfi, Bandolino, Capezio, Cobbie, Easy Spirit, Evan-Picone, Joyce, Pappagallo, Selby and Vittorio Ricci Studio. The group also produces boots under various brand names. In addition, USR operates 292 shoe stores, as well as various outlet stores and concept shoe stores. It also operates 142 leased shoe departments.

Dividend Data

Dividends have been paid since 1932. A dividend reinvestment plan is available. A "poison pill" stock purchase rights plan was adopted in 1986.

Amt of Divd. $	Date Decl.	Ex–divd. Date	Stock of Record	Payment Date
0.13	Dec. 2	Dec. 21	Dec. 28	Jan. 14'93
0.13	Feb. 12	Mar. 9	Mar. 15	Apr. 5'93
0.08	May 20	Jun. 15	Jun. 21	Jul. 12'93
0.08	Sep. 15	Sep. 27	Oct. 1	Oct. 15'93

Capitalization

Long Term Debt: $190,012,000 (7/93).

Common Stock: 45,629,897 shs. (no par). Institutions hold approximately 70%. Shareholders of record: 11,376 (3/93).

Office—One Eastwood Drive, Cincinnati, OH 45227. **Tel**—(513) 527-7000. **Pres & CEO**—B. B. Hudson. **VP-Secy**—J. J. Crowe. **Investor Contact**—Robert Burton. **Dirs**—J. H. Anderer, P. E. Beekman, G. Hahn Jr., R. L. Howe, B. B. Hudson, L. T. Kellar, A. M. Kronick, T. Laco, C. S. Mechem Jr. (Chrmn), J. L. Roy, P. S. Sewell. **Transfer Agent & Registrar**—The Bank of New York, NYC. **Incorporated** in Ohio in 1931. **Empl**—41,000.

 Elizabeth Vandeventer

Universal Corp.

NYSE Symbol UVV In S&P MidCap 400

Price	Range	P-E Ratio	Dividend	Yield	S&P Ranking	Beta
Oct. 4'93	1993					
23	33¾–21¾	10	0.88	3.9%	A–	0.91

Summary

Universal Corp. is the holding company for Universal Leaf Tobacco Co., the world's largest independent leaf tobacco dealer. Other subsidiaries are engaged in the agri-products and lumber and building products businesses. Restrained by a worldwide surplus of tobacco and related softening of prices, profits are expected to rise only modestly in fiscal 1994. A strong profit upturn is projected in fiscal 1995.

Current Outlook

Earnings for the fiscal year ending June 30, 1994, are projected at $2.50 a share, up from fiscal 1993's $2.39. $3.00 is seen for fiscal 1995.

The $0.22 quarterly dividend is likely to be raised in early 1994.

Profits in fiscal 1994 are projected to rise only modestly from year earlier levels, held by high levels of unsold tobacco stocks worldwide and legislative limitations on U.S. tobacco imports. Lumber and building profits should be enhanced by growing operating efficiency, while agri-products' profits should benefit from greater tea volumes. A profit upturn in all three units is projected for fiscal 1995.

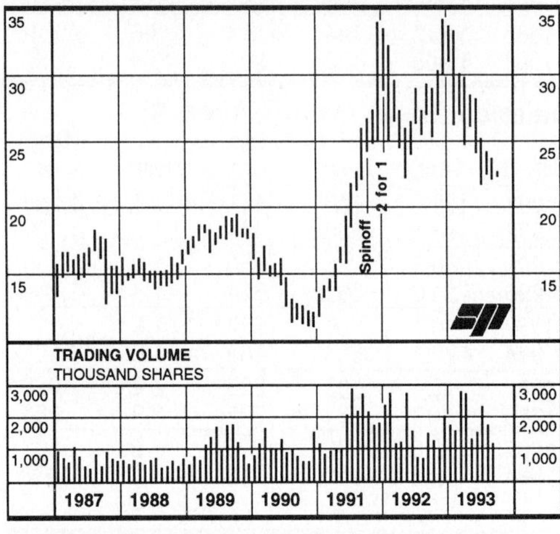

Gross Revenues (Million $)

Quarter:	1993-94	1992-93	1991-92	1990-91
Sep.	---	827	695	644
Dec.	---	888	874	915
Mar.	---	837	942	828
Jun.	---	496	478	509
	---	3,047	2,989	2,896

Sales for the fiscal year ended June 30, 1993 rose 1.9% from those of the preceding year. Margins widened and, following a 7.5% reduction in interest expense, pretax profits advanced 17%. After taxes at 36.8%, versus 34.9%, net income was up 13%, to $2.39 a share (on 2.4% more shares) from $2.15.

Common Share Earnings ($)

Quarter:	1993-94	1992-93	1991-92	1990-91
Sep.	E0.75	0.72	0.61	0.28
Dec.	E1.00	1.08	0.89	0.80
Mar.	E0.65	0.58	0.57	0.54
Jun.	E0.10	0.06	0.08	0.11
	E2.50	[1]2.39	2.15	1.72

Important Developments

Aug. '93— UVV reported that results of U.S. tobacco operations were up slightly in fiscal 1993 due to increased processing efficiencies and shipments delayed to the first quarter of fiscal 1993. Total volume of U.S. tobacco bought and processed was down from year ago levels, principally reflecting burley tobacco, where orders were down almost 15%. International tobacco operations represented the major part of UVV's increased earnings, reflecting improvements for Brazil and Africa, while European affiliates lagged. The lumber and building products operating results were little changed from the year earlier level, held by recessionary conditions in Europe. Agri-products earnings rose significantly, reflecting improved results in principal segments and the sale of the unprofitable peanut shelling operation.

Next earnings report expected in mid-October.

Per Share Data ($)

Yr. End Jun. 30	1993	1992	1991	1990	1989	1988	[2]1987	[3]1986	[3]1985	1984
Tangible Bk. Val.	**7.81**	8.75	11.43	11.10	10.57	9.68	8.60	7.72	6.77	6.74
Cash Flow	**3.36**	3.04	2.51	1.92	2.35	2.43	2.20	1.73	1.66	1.53
Earnings[4]	**2.39**	2.15	1.72	1.11	1.60	1.78	1.63	1.37	1.33	1.11
Dividends	**0.840**	0.790	0.755	0.730	0.685	0.625	0.560	0.520	0.480	0.450
Payout Ratio	**37%**	37%	44%	65%	43%	35%	34%	38%	36%	41%
Prices—High[5]	**34¼**	34¼	34	18 1/16 4	19½	16⅞	18⅜	15½	12¼	11
Low[5]	**22¼**	22¼	11 13/16	11	16½	13 15/16	12 13/16	11⅝	9⅜	7⅝
P/E Ratio—	**14-9**	16–10	20–7	16–10	12–10	9–8	11–8	11–8	9–7	10–7

Data as orig. reptd. Adj. for stk. divs. of 100% Jan. 1992, 100% Mar. 1984. **1.** Does not add due to chg. in no. of shares outstanding. **2.** Refl. acctg. change. **3.** Refl. merger or acq. **4.** Bef. results of disc. ops. of -0.99 in 1991, +0.02 in 1985, and spec. items of -0.12 in 1991, +0.24 in 1990. **5.** For prev. cal. yr. E-Estimated NA-Not Available.

Income Data (Million $)

Year Ended Jun. 30	Revs.	Oper. Inc.	% Oper. Inc. of Revs.	Cap. Exp.	Depr.	Int. Exp.	[5]Net Bef. Taxes	Eff. Tax Rate	[6]Net Inc.	% Net Inc. of Revs.	Cash Flow
[1]1992	**[4]2,989**	**180**	**6.0**	**47.1**	**29.2**	**49.8**	**106**	**33.4%**	**70.7**	**2.4**	**99.9**
[1]1991	[4]2,896	160	5.5	44.6	25.8	58.0	81	30.1%	56.4	1.9	82.2
1990	[4]2,815	107	3.8	31.8	27.1	33.7	50	27.0%	37.1	1.3	64.2
1989	[4]2,920	131	4.5	37.7	25.6	29.6	79	30.9%	54.0	1.9	79.7
1988	[4]2,420	126	5.2	48.3	22.0	32.5	78	22.6%	60.7	2.5	82.7
[2]1987	2,116	139	6.6	24.8	19.6	31.1	90	38.0%	56.0	2.7	75.6
[3]1986	1,145	77	6.7	15.8	12.5	7.0	66	28.6%	47.1	4.2	59.6
[1,3]1985	1,079	70	6.5	23.3	11.3	10.4	59	22.4%	45.9	4.3	57.2
1984	1,019	73	7.1	20.0	14.8	11.2	59	34.1%	38.3	3.8	53.1
1983	1,082	68	6.3	19.5	12.6	10.3	56	32.6%	36.6	3.4	49.2

Balance Sheet Data (Million $)

Jun. 30	Cash	Curr. Assets	Curr. Liab.	Curr. Ratio	Total Assets	% Ret. on Assets	Long Term Debt	Common Equity	Total Cap.	% LT Debt of Cap.	% Ret. on Equity
1992	**82.7**	**970**	**697**	**1.4**	**1,261**	**5.6**	**190**	**302**	**522**	**36.4**	**20.4**
1991	59.5	877	654	1.3	1,276	4.6	160	390	578	27.7	14.4
1990	50.8	717	453	1.6	1,171	3.4	144	397	576	25.1	9.6
1989	68.4	639	438	1.5	1,062	5.2	85	386	505	16.9	14.6
1988	53.1	610	429	1.4	1,007	6.3	88	357	474	18.6	17.9
1987	42.7	571	399	1.4	943	7.2	93	326	448	20.8	18.1
1986	24.0	234	150	1.6	604	8.6	73	294	383	19.1	17.0
1985	31.0	189	149	1.3	488	9.7	8	261	284	3.0	18.6
1984	3.1	270	160	1.7	459	8.9	31	233	299	10.4	17.1
1983	0.7	224	126	1.8	404	8.9	31	215	277	11.3	17.8

Data as orig. reptd. **1.** Excl. disc. ops. **2.** Refl. acctg. change. **3.** Refl. merger or acq. **4.** Incl. other inc. **5.** Incl. equity in earns. of nonconsol. subs. **6.** Bef. results of disc. ops. and spec. items.

Business Summary

Universal Corp. is the holding company for Universal Leaf Co., the world's largest independent leaf tobacco dealer. Through other subsidiaries, it is engaged in the agri-products and lumber and buildings products businesses. Insurance operations were spun off in October 1991. Contributions from continuing operations in fiscal 1993 were:

	Revenues	Profits
Tobacco	75%	84%
Lumber & building products	13%	10%
Agri–products	12%	6%

In fiscal 1993, the U.S. accounted for 56% of revenues, Western Europe for 33%, South and Central America 6%, and other 5%.

Tobacco operations involve selecting, buying, shipping, processing, packing, storing and financing leaf tobacco in the U.S. and other tobacco growing countries for the account of, or resale to, manufacturers of tobacco products throughout the world. In August 1991, the company acquired Kliemann, S.A.-Commercio Industria e Agricultura, a Brazilian leaf tobacco dealer. Most foreign customers are long-established firms or government monopolies.

The Deli Universal subsidiary in engaged in the buying, processing and selling of dark air cured tobacco, as well as a number of other agricultural products including coffee, tea, rubber and sunflower seeds. UVV's peanut business was discontinued during fiscal 1992.

UVV also distributes lumber and related building products to the construction market in Europe, primarily in Holland; and manufactures laminated wood products in the U.S.

Dividend Data

Dividends have been paid since 1927. A dividend reinvestment plan is available. A "poison pill" stock purchase right was adopted in 1989.

Amt of Divd. $	Date Decl.	Ex–divd. Date	Stock of Record	Payment Date
0.22	Dec. 3	Jan. 5	Jan. 11	Feb. 8'93
0.22	Feb. 4	Apr. 5	Apr. 12	May 10'93
0.22	May 6	Jul. 6	Jul. 12	Aug. 9'93
0.22	Aug. 6	Oct. 5	Oct. 12	Nov. 8'93

Capitalization

Long Term Debt: $281,807,000 (6/93).

Minority Interest: $2,452,000.

Common Stock: 35,631,485 shs. (no par). Institutions hold 69%. Shareholders of record: 4,132.

Office—1501 North Hamilton St., Richmond, VA 23260. **Tel**—(804) 359-9311. **Chrmn & CEO**—H. H. Harrell. **Pres**—A. B. King. **VP & Secy**—J. M. White III. **VP & CFO**—H. H. Roper. **VP, Treas & Investor Contact**—O. Kemp Dozier (804-254-3720). **Dirs**—W. W. Berry, R. E. Carrier, W. L. Chandler, L. S. Eagleburger, A. P. Funkhouser, J. Godthelp, E. T. Gray, H. H. Harrell, R. G. Holder, A. B. King, J. D. Munford, H. R. Stallard, T. R. Towers. **Transfer Agent & Registrar**—Wachovia Bank of North Carolina, N.A., Winston-Salem. **Incorporated** in Virginia in 1918. **Empl**—25,000.

 Kenneth A. Shea

Universal Foods

NYSE Symbol UFC Options on Phila (Mar-Jun-Sep-Dec) In S&P MidCap 400

Price	Range	P–E Ratio	Dividend	Yield	S&P Ranking	Beta
Jul. 20'93	1993					
35⅛	37¼–31⅝	21	0.88	2.5%	A–	0.40

Summary

Universal Foods is an international manufacturer and marketer of value-added food products sold primarily to the food manufacturing and food service industries. Products include food flavors and colors, frozen french fried potatoes, yeast products, and dehydrated vegetables. Earnings are expected to continue to advance through fiscal 1994, benefiting from improving market conditions for the core frozen potato division.

Current Outlook

Earnings for the fiscal year ending September 30, 1994, are projected at $2.40 a share, up from fiscal 1993's estimated $2.25.

The $0.22 quarterly dividend is likely to be raised in the second half of 1993.

Sales are projected to rise modestly through fiscal 1994, restrained by competitive industry pricing and weakness in European markets. Improving U.S. market conditions for frozen french fry products, combined with recent cost cutting measures in that segment, are expected to aid overall profitability and lead to higher earnings.

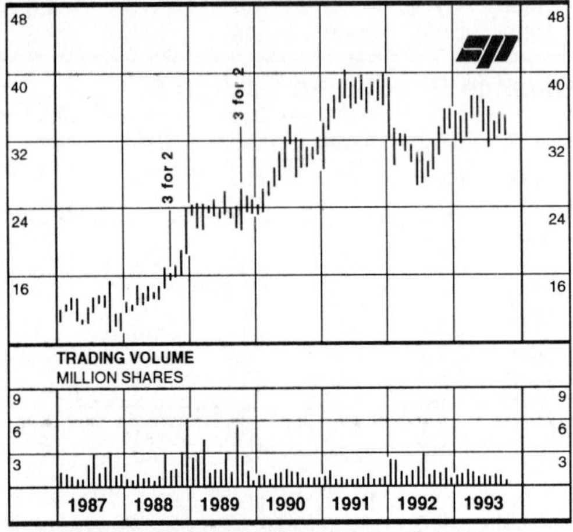

Total Revenues (Million $)

Quarter:	1993-94	1992-93	1991-92	1990-91
Dec.	---	209	206	198
Mar.	---	217	223	200
Jun.	---	228	223	221
Sep.	---	---	231	215
	---	---	883	834

Revenues in the nine months ended June 30, 1993, edged up fractionally, year to year. Results benefited from cost controls and stronger pricing in several divisions, and with a 1.3% decline in interest expense, pretax income advanced 7.7%. After taxes at 37.5%, versus 37.7%, net income was up 8.1%, to $1.64 a share (on 1.3% fewer shares), from $1.50.

Common Share Earnings ($)

Quarter:	1993-94	1992-93	1991-92	1990-91
Dec.	E0.59	0.55	0.55	0.54
Mar.	E0.56	0.53	0.47	0.47
Jun.	E0.60	0.56	0.48	0.52
Sep.	E0.65	E0.61	0.07	0.65
	E2.40	E2.25	1.57	2.18

Important Developments

Jul. '93— UFC said the Frozen Foods division contributed significantly to gains in the first nine months of fiscal 1993, aided by price increases for frozen french fry products. Third quarter profits for the Flavor and Color divisions were restrained by weak demand in Europe. The Dehydrated Products and Red Star Yeast and Products divisions were lower, held by competitive pressures. Separately, during the fiscal 1993 third quarter, the company acquired Spectrum S.A., a Mexican food color distributor with a 20% share of the Mexican market. Spectrum has annual sales of about $8 million, principally in Mexico, with some export sales to other Latin American countries. UFC also acquired certain assets related to the biotechnological research program of Zeagen, Inc., a subsidiary of ACX Technologies, Inc.

Next earnings report expected in mid-October.

Per Share Data ($)

Yr. End Sep. 30	[1]1992	[1]1991	[1]1990	[1]1989	[1]1988	1987	[1]1986	[1]1985	[1]1984	1983
Tangible Bk. Val.	**7.42**	7.38	6.10	5.19	5.14	5.01	4.34	4.74	4.99	4.69
Cash Flow	**2.62**	3.09	2.99	2.42	1.85	1.58	1.21	1.28	1.12	1.36
Earnings[2]	**1.57**	2.18	1.95	1.60	1.12	0.93	0.63	0.74	0.69	0.86
Dividends	**0.840**	0.760	0.680	0.534	0.409	0.364	0.338	0.314	0.309	0.309
Payout Ratio	**54%**	35%	35%	34%	37%	39%	58%	42%	44%	36%
Prices[3]—High	**39½**	40⅜	33⅞	26¼	24	15⅜	12⅜	9⅛	8⅛	9¼
Low	**26⅝**	28⅝	23¼	21⅜	11⅝	9⅜	8⅜	6⅞	5⅝	6⅝
P/E Ratio—	**25–17**	19–13	17–12	16–13	22–10	16–10	20–13	12–9	12–8	11–8

Data as orig. reptd. Adj. for stk. divs. of 50% Oct. 1989, 50% Oct. 1988, 50% Aug. 1986. **1.** Refl. merger or acq. **2.** Bef. results of disc. ops. of -0.18 in 1984. **3.** Cal. yr. E-Estimated.

Income Data (Million $)

Year Ended Sep. 30	Revs.	Oper. Inc.	% Oper. Inc. of Revs.	Cap. Exp.	Depr.	Int. Exp.	Net Bef. Taxes	Eff. Tax Rate	[3]Net Inc.	% Net Inc. of Revs.	Cash Flow
[1]1992	**883**	**131**	**14.8**	**51.5**	**28.1**	**17.1**	**67.0**	**37.8%**	**41.7**	**4.7**	**69.8**
[1]1991	834	130	15.6	54.8	24.2	14.8	92.3	37.4%	57.8	6.9	81.9
[1]1990	839	118	14.0	69.6	26.4	13.2	82.6	40.1%	49.4	5.9	75.9
[1]1989	837	98	11.7	46.6	20.6	11.5	66.6	40.0%	40.0	4.8	60.6
[1]1988	721	81	11.2	26.2	18.3	10.0	49.6	44.3%	27.6	3.8	46.0
1987	711	74	10.4	16.2	17.1	10.7	46.4	46.5%	[4]24.8	3.5	42.0
[1]1986	604	61	10.1	52.5	14.2	9.6	29.1	47.0%	15.4	2.6	29.7
[1]1985	492	49	9.9	30.3	12.4	5.3	31.3	44.5%	17.4	3.5	29.8
[1,2]1984	430	44	10.2	31.5	10.5	5.4	28.5	42.2%	16.5	3.8	26.9
1983	520	53	10.1	32.4	12.0	5.1	36.2	43.1%	20.6	4.0	32.6

Balance Sheet Data (Million $)

Sep. 30	Cash	Curr. Assets	Curr. Liab.	Curr. Ratio	Total Assets	% Ret. on Assets	Long Term Debt	Common Equity	Total Cap.	% LT Debt of Cap.	% Ret. on Equity
1992	**11.0**	**300**	**185**	**1.6**	**702**	**6.2**	**168**	**303**	**495**	**33.9**	**14.1**
1991	13.2	284	157	1.8	653	9.4	152	292	466	32.6	21.1
1990	8.2	226	135	1.7	549	9.5	117	243	374	31.3	22.0
1989	3.9	214	121	1.8	489	8.9	126	203	352	35.6	20.8
1988	2.6	189	99	1.9	404	7.2	85	178	288	29.6	15.9
1987	14.9	184	89	2.1	392	6.2	85	183	295	28.9	14.2
1986	8.9	191	94	2.0	400	4.2	111	165	299	37.3	9.9
1985	9.2	154	69	2.2	292	6.5	74	129	220	33.5	14.1
1984	5.9	138	61	2.3	246	6.8	47	119	180	26.1	14.0
1983	4.5	127	58	2.2	242	8.9	53	119	183	28.9	18.3

Data as orig. reptd. **1.** Refl. merger or acq. **2.** Excl. disc. ops. **3.** Bef. results of disc. ops. **4.** Refl. acctg. change.

Business Summary

Universal Foods makes and distributes a wide range of food products. Foreign operations accounted for 15% and 21% of revenue and profits, respectively, in 1991-2. Sales by segment were derived as follows:

	1992
Frozen Foods	32%
Flavor	28%
Red Star Yeast & Products	17%
Color	13%
Dehydrated Products	8%
Red Star Specialty Products	2%

Frozen foods products, sold mostly to the food service industry, consist of branded and private label french fried potatoes, including regular cuts, hash browns, patties, wedges, pancakes and specialty fries. Consumer brands include Inland Valley.

Flavoring products are sold as ingredients to the dairy, food processor and beverage industries worldwide. UFC operates in the marketplace as Universal Flavors, Bowey KrimKo, BlankeBaer, Flavorshades, Felton and Fantasy Flavors.

The yeast division specializes in the production of compressed, active dry and nutritional yeast products for sale to industrial, institutional, and retail accounts under the Red Star trademark.

Food color products, sold under the brand names of Red Seal and Spectracoat, are used by producers of soft drinks, bakery products, processed foods, confections, pet foods, alcoholic beverages and pharmaceuticals.

Dehydrated onion and garlic products are marketed under the Rogers trademark and private labels. UFC also produces and distributes chili powder and pepper, paprika, and dehydrated vegetables.

Specialty products consist of all-natural, fermentation-derived flavor enhancers, yeast peptones and yeast extracts.

Dividend Data

Dividends have been paid since 1934. A dividend reinvestment plan is available. A "poison pill" stock purchase right was adopted in 1988.

Amt of Divd. $	Date Decl.	Ex-divd. Date	Stock of Record	Payment Date
0.22	Oct. 7	Oct. 16	Oct. 22	Nov. 5'93
0.22	Jan. 21	Feb. 5	Feb. 11	Feb. 25'93
0.22	Apr. 8	May. 5	May. 11	Jun. 1'93
0.22	Jun. 10	Jul. 29	Aug. 4	Sep. 1'93

Capitalization

Long Term Debt: $181,979,000 (3/93).

Common Stock: 26,351,627 shs. ($0.10 par).
Institutions hold 65%.
Shareholders of record: 6,956.

Office—433 East Michigan St, Milwaukee, WI 53202. **Tel**—(414) 271-6755. **Chrmn & CEO**—G. A. Osborn. **Treas**—D. Krzykowski. **VP & Secy**—T. M. O'Reilly. **VP-Finance & Investor Contact**—Geoffrey J. Hibner. **Dirs**—A. R. Anderson, M. E. Batten, J.L. Forbes, O. D. Forker, L. T. Kendall, J. H. Keyes, P.L. Kohnstamm, K. P. Manning, C. S. McNeer, J. L. Murray, G. A. Osborn, C. I. Waslien-Ghazaii, E. Whitelaw. **Transfer Agent & Registrar**—Firstar Trust Co., Milwaukee. **Incorporated** in Wisconsin in 1882. **Empl**—5,400.

 Kenneth A. Shea

UtiliCorp United

NYSE Symbol UCU In S&P MidCap 400

Price	Range	P-E Ratio	Dividend	Yield	S&P Ranking	Beta
Aug. 3'93	1993					
30	29¾–27⅛	17	1.60	5.3%	A–	0.63

Summary

This electric and gas utility operates in nine states and one Canadian province, serving over 1,000,000 customers. Its growth strategy is to balance its services by product, region, climate and regulatory jurisdiction, and to be in the forefront of utility deregulation. Profitability should rebound in 1993 primarily on recent rate increases and the utility operations' return to more normal sales levels. Strategic acquisitions and the careful placement of the energy related businesses should enable the company to take advantage of the opportunities provided by the National Energy Policy Act of 1992 and FERC Order 636.

Current Outlook

Share earnings for 1993 are projected at $2.05, up from 1992's depressed $1.32. Earnings for 1994 are projected at $2.25 a share.

The minimum expectation is for dividends to continue at $0.40 quarterly.

Higher earnings in 1993 should reflect rate increases of $17.5 million and $23.2 million in pending rate requests. The company's electric sales are estimated to advance 2.4% for each of the next five years. Through its refocused Aquila Energy and UtilCo Group subsidiaries, UCU is well positioned to take advantage of the opportunities presented by domestic deregulation of the gas and electric business. Internationally, the company has found ways to enter overseas markets where privitization of utilities is starting to take place.

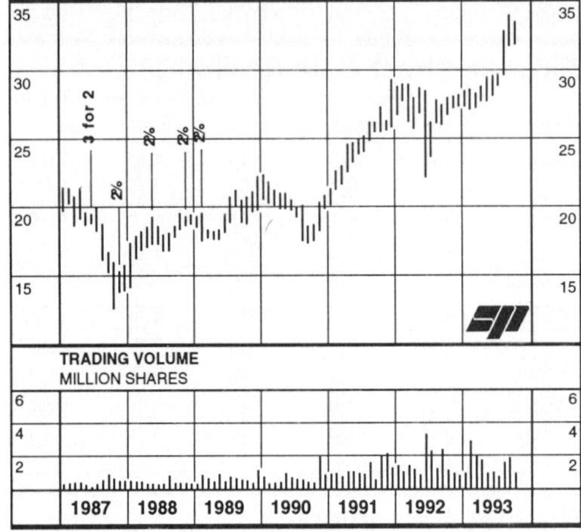

Operating Revenues (Million $)

Quarter:	1994	1993	1992	1991
Mar.	---	481	366	317
Jun.	---	329	254	189
Sep.	---	---	275	194
Dec.	---	---	405	375
	---	---	1,299	1,075

Revenues for the six months ended June 30, 1993, rose 31%, year to year, reflecting rate relief, better contributions from Aquila Energy and higher sales as a result of normal weather conditions. Following greater expenses, and taxes at 38.4% versus 36.4%, net income was up 88%. Share earnings were $0.97 on 14% more shares, compared with $0.54.

Common Share Earnings ($)

Quarter:	1994	1993	1992	1991
Mar.	E0.95	0.87	0.77	0.95
Jun.	E0.15	0.13	d0.23	0.15
Sep.	E0.35	E0.35	0.10	0.36
Dec.	E0.80	E0.70	0.68	0.75
	E2.25	E2.05	1.32	2.23

Important Developments

May '93— UCU signed a definitive agreement to purchase Kansas transmission and distribution facilities serving 22,600 customers from Arkla for $25 million. The acquisition is expected to close in three to six months. In addition, in February, UCU purchased the Nebraska gas distribution system of Arkla's Minnegasco division for approximately $78 million. The system, which serves about 124,000 gas customers in 63 eastern Nebraska communities, will be merged with UCU's Peoples Natural Gas division. Separately, as part of its global investment strategy, UtiliCorp agreed to enter a joint venture arrangement through the planned acquisition of a 33% interest in WEL Energy Group Ltd. from the Waikato Electricity Authority in New Zealand for about $20 million. WEL is an electric utility serving 60,000 customers in the New Zealand region of Waikato with gross revenues in 1991 of approximately $41 million.

Next earnings report expected in late October.

Per Share Data ($)

Yr. End Dec. 31	1992	1991	1990	1989	1988	1987	1986	1985	1984	1983
Tangible Bk. Val.	**18.66**	19.45	17.49	16.58	15.54	14.19	13.29	11.75	10.49	9.47
Earnings[1]	**1.32**	2.23	2.13	2.04	1.98	1.79	1.72	1.83	1.75	1.67
Dividends	**1.600**	1.540	1.460	1.414	1.028	0.934	0.874	0.783	0.661	0.616
Payout Ratio	**121%**	69%	69%	69%	52%	52%	51%	43%	37%	37%
Prices—High	**29**	29⅜	22⅜	22¼	19½	21⅛	21	16⅜	11¼	9⅞
Low	**22⅛**	20⅛	17⅜	17½	14⅛	12½	13⅜	11⅛	8⅜	7¼
P/E Ratio—	**22–17**	13–9	11–8	11–9	10–7	12–7	12–8	9–6	6–5	6–4

Data as orig. reptd. Adj. for stk. divs. of 2% Feb. 1989, 50% Jul. 1987, & 4% annually in 1983-1988. **1.** Bef. spec. item(s) of -0.17 in 1987. d-Deficit. E-Estimated

Income Data (Million $)

Year Ended Dec. 31	Revs.	Depr.	Maint.	Oper. Ratio	[1]Fxd. Chgs. Cover.	Constr. Credits	Eff. Tax Rate	[2]Net Inc.	% Return On Revs.	% Return On [3,4]Invest. Capital	% Return On [4]Com. Equity
1992	**1,299**	**123.0**	**40.5**	**89.4%**	**1.73**	**NA**	**37.4%**	**52.9**	**4.1**	**8.2**	**7.0**
1991	1,075	53.9	37.1	86.3%	2.20	NA	36.0%	73.5	6.8	9.4	11.3
1990	894	49.2	29.2	87.1%	2.21	NA	33.4%	58.9	6.6	9.5	11.8
1989	732	44.2	31.7	88.1%	2.17	NA	32.6%	48.3	6.6	10.4	12.2
1988	673	38.9	29.8	88.5%	2.37	NA	33.4%	40.9	6.1	10.4	13.1
1987	595	34.2	21.2	89.6%	2.39	0.66	45.1%	33.2	5.6	10.2	11.9
1986	596	29.9	21.2	91.2%	2.26	0.57	35.8%	29.7	5.0	10.5	13.6
1985	243	15.6	17.2	83.5%	3.53	0.54	45.8%	26.9	11.1	9.4	15.2
1984	234	14.6	16.0	83.0%	3.28	1.02	45.2%	25.8	11.0	11.4	17.4
1983	217	13.3	14.8	82.3%	2.96	2.12	42.7%	23.6	10.9	11.3	18.2

Balance Sheet Data (Million $)

Dec. 31	Gross Prop.	Capital Expend.	Net Prop.	[4]% Earn. on Net Prop.	Total Cap.	LT Debt	% LT Debt	Capitalization Pfd.	% Pfd.	Com.	% Com.
1992	**2,221**	**150**	**1,454**	**9.7**	**1,830**	**891**	**54.1**	**95.1**	**5.8**	**661**	**40.1**
1991	2,088	134	1,366	12.0	1,873	928	54.8	97.1	5.7	670	39.5
1990	1,591	119	1,084	11.1	1,415	668	53.2	86.8	6.9	491	23.2
1989	1,479	98	1,003	9.6	1,059	438	47.9	97.4	10.7	378	41.4
1988	1,199	79	813	9.8	828	358	50.1	35.1	4.9	322	45.0
1987	1,113	57	575	9.2	710	318	52.3	25.0	4.1	264	43.6
1986	855	47	577	9.5	582	261	51.6	33.0	6.5	212	41.9
1985	787	32	537	9.0	503	226	52.2	41.8	9.6	166	38.2
1984	504	24	360	11.2	360	128	42.5	43.0	14.2	131	43.3
1983	477	27	348	11.2	339	133	46.0	43.3	15.0	112	39.0

Datas as orig. reptd. **1.** Times int. exp. and pfd. divs. covered (pretax basis). **2.** Bef. spec. items. **3.** Based on income bef. interest charges. **4.** Based on year-end averages. NA-Not Available.

Business Summary

UtiliCorp United (formerly Missouri Public Service) provides electric and/or gas service to nine states and British Columbia, Canada, through seven operating divisions and West Kootenay Power, Ltd., a Canadian subsidiary acquired in 1987. In 1992, electric operations accounted for 39% of revenues and 65% of operating income, gas operations for 40% and 25%, respectively, and energy related businesses for 21% and 10%. Contributions to electric revenues by customer class:

	1992	1991	1990	1989
Residential............	42%	46%	47%	46%
Commercial	29%	27%	26%	26%
Industrial	14%	12%	12%	12%
Other....................	15%	15%	15%	15%

In 1992, 71% of the company's produced electricity was generated from coal, 29% from hydro sources, and 3% from natural gas and oil. Total system capability at year-end 1992 was 2,605 mw, at which date 410,826 electric customers were being served.

With the February 1993 acquisition of a Nebraska gas distribution system, UCU supplies gas to approximately 723,000 customers in nine states.

Nonregulated businesses are Aquila Energy, which produces, processes and markets natural gas, and UtilCo Group, which invests in independent power projects. The company markets natural gas in the United Kingdom through several joint ventures.

Finances

In July 1993, UCU registered $100 million of unsecured senior notes with the SEC to be offered for public sale on a delayed or continuous basis. Net proceed will be used to refinance higher coupon debt and for general corporate purposes.

Dividend Data

Dividends have been paid since 1939. A dividend reinvestment plan is available.

Amt of Divd. $	Date Decl.	Ex-divd. Date	Stock of Record	Payment Date
0.40	Aug. 5	Aug. 14	Aug. 20	Sep. 12'92
0.40	Nov. 4	Nov. 13	Nov. 19	Dec. 12'92
0.40	Feb. 3	Feb. 22	Feb. 26	Mar. 12'93
0.40	May 5	May 14	May 20	Jun. 12'93
0.40	May 5	May 14	May 20	Jun. 12'93

Capitalization

Long Term Debt: 1,019,500,000 (3/93).

Subsid. Preferred Stock: $9,600,000.

Preference Stock: $85,500,000.

Common Stock: 40,990,873 shs. ($1 par).
Institutions hold approximately 17%.
Shareholders of record: 31,906.

Office—3000 Commerce Tower, 911 Main, Kansas City, MO 64105. **Tel**—(816) 421-6600. **Chrmn & Pres**—R. C. Green Jr. **SVP-Fin & CFO**—H. L. Winn Jr. **VP-Fin & Secy**—D. J. Wolf. **Investor Contact**—Phil Hermanson (816-691-3541). **Dirs**—D. R. Armacost, J. R. Baker, H. Cain, R. C. Green Jr., S. O. Ikenberry, R. F. Jackson Jr., L. P. Kline, A. G. Tucker. **Transfer Agent & Registrar**—First Chicago Trust Co. of New York, NYC. **Incorporated** in Missouri in 1950; reincorporated in Delaware in 1986. **Empl**—4,361.

 Ned Bancroft

Valero Energy

NYSE Symbol VLO Options on ASE (Mar-Jun-Sep-Dec) In S&P MidCap 400

Price	Range	P-E Ratio	Dividend	Yield	S&P Ranking	Beta
Sep. 22'93	1993					
24⅝	26⅛–20⅞	14	0.52	2.1%	B	0.85

Summary

This company is primarily engaged in refining and marketing unleaded gasoline and other petroleum products. It holds a 49% interest in Valero Natural Gas Partners, L.P., which is engaged in pipeline operations in Texas, owns gas processing facilities, and markets natural gas liquids. In April 1993, VLO began operating a facility that converts butane into a gasoline component mandated by the Clean Air Act. Long-term prospects are enhanced by an expected shortage of domestic refining capacity.

Current Outlook

Share earnings for 1993 are estimated at $2.05, up from 1992's $1.94. An increase to $2.40 is projected for 1994.

The quarterly dividend was raised 18%, to $0.13 from $0.11, with the December 1993 payment.

Refining and marketing profits should advance in 1993, on growth in volumes largely attributable to the April 1993 startup of an MTBE production facility. Margins are expected to narrow, despite expected improvement in the 1993 second half. Comparisons in the 1993 fourth quarter should benefit from the absence of a charge related to an early retirement program and a scheduled turnaround of the refinery's hydro-desulfurization unit. In 1994, and for several subsequent years, margins should widen, aided by a reduction in industry refining capacity. Economic growth and full-year operation of the MTBE plant should contribute to throughput volumes growth and higher profits in 1994. Equity in earnings of Valero Natural Gas Partners is expected to rise, on increased gas and gas liquids deliveries; competition at pipeline operations and higher gas prices are likely to restrict margins and profit growth.

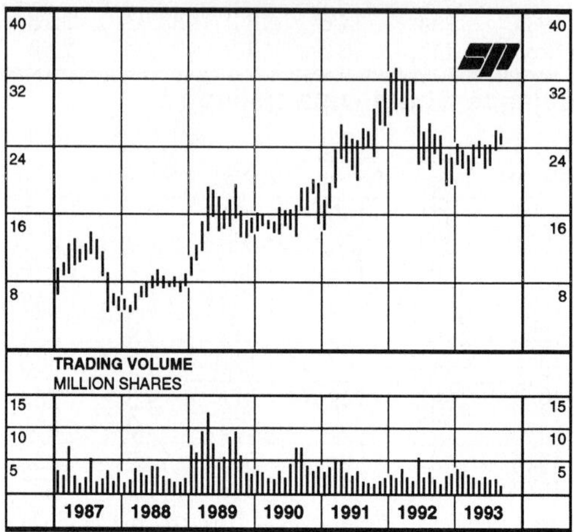

Operating Revenues (Million $)

Quarter:	1993	1992	1991	1990
Mar.	296	275	287	260
Jun.	321	319	273	276
Sep.	---	337	256	297
Dec.	---	304	195	336
	---	1,235	1,012	1,169

Revenues in the six months ended June 30, 1993, rose 3.8%, year to year, on a 13% increase in throughput volumes. A 19% drop in throughput margin per bbl. outweighed higher profits at Valero Natural Gas Partners; net income decreased 15%, to $0.92 a share, from $1.11.

Common Share Earnings ($)

Quarter:	1993	1992	1991	1990
Mar.	0.36	0.48	0.47	0.22
Jun.	0.56	0.63	0.58	0.51
Sep.	E0.57	0.65	0.70	0.76
Dec.	E0.56	0.18	0.53	0.78
	E2.05	1.94	2.28	2.31

Important Developments

Sep. '93— VLO agreed to sell Rio Grande Valley Gas Co. to Southern Union Co., for about $30 million. The sale includes 1,552 miles of distribution lines serving about 75,000 customers in South Texas. Separately, the company said the price of residual fuel oil in Asia was hurt in the 1993 second quarter by down-time of several Korean refineries. As a result, the average throughput margin in the quarter was $6.94 per bbl., down from $8.32 in the 1992 period.

Next earnings report expected in mid-October.

Per Share Data ($)

Yr. End Dec. 31	1992	1991	1990	1989	1988	[1]1987	1986	1985	1984	1983
Tangible Bk. Val.	**19.09**	16.90	15.20	13.16	13.56	13.14	13.34	17.84	17.89	18.57
Cash Flow	**3.07**	3.19	3.25	2.17	1.83	2.10	1.93	3.83	0.76	3.05
Earnings[2]	**1.94**	2.28	2.31	0.98	0.54	0.80	d4.36	1.06	d1.14	1.57
Dividends	**0.42**	0.34	0.26	0.15	Nil	Nil	Nil	Nil	0.33	0.41
Payout Ratio	**22%**	15%	12%	19%	Nil	Nil	Nil	Nil	NM	26%
Prices—High	**33⅜**	31	20¼	19⅝	9½	13⅞	14¼	14¾	23⅞	36¾
Low	**19½**	14¼	13½	8⅞	4½	4½	6⅝	6	5⅞	17¾
P/E Ratio—	**17–10**	14–6	9–6	20–9	18–8	17–6	NM	14–6	NM	23–11

Data as orig. reptd. **1.** Refl. acctg. change. **2.** Bef. results of disc. ops. of -0.56 in 1987, and spec. item(s) of -0.18 in 1987. E-Estimated. d-Deficit. NM-Not Meaningful.

Income Data (Million $)

Year Ended Dec. 31	Revs.	Oper. Inc.	% Oper. Inc. of Revs.	Cap. Exp.	Depr. & Depl.	Int. Exp.	Net Bef. Taxes	Eff. Tax Rate	[4]Net Inc.	% Net Inc. of Revs.	Cash Flow
1992	**1,235**	**182**	**14.8**	**283**	**48.2**	**46**	**[3]131**	**36.1%**	**83.9**	**6.8**	**131**
1991	1,012	156	15.4	230	36.6	38	[3]146	32.6%	98.7	9.8	129
1990	1,169	170	14.5	138	35.6	25	[3]146	35.0%	94.7	8.1	123
1989	941	104	11.1	37	34.4	25	[3]59	30.0%	41.5	4.4	63
1988	771	72	9.4	14	33.7	24	[3]34	11.1%	30.6	4.0	48
[1,2]1987	629	d24	NM	18	33.3	45	[3]23	NM	31.9	5.1	54
1986	1,880	100	5.3	42	64.2	117	d182	NM	d99.9	NM	48
1985	2,662	196	7.3	60	65.3	126	66	47.7%	[2]34.7	1.3	90
1984	2,308	144	6.3	118	42.1	92	[3]d4	NM	[2]d16.1	NM	17
1983	1,495	137	9.2	175	32.8	58	[3]71	37.0%	44.7	3.0	68

Balance Sheet Data (Million $)

Dec. 31	Cash	Curr. Assets	Curr. Liab.	Curr. Ratio	Total Assets	% Ret. on Assets	Long Term Debt	Common Equity	Total Cap.	% LT Debt of Cap.	% Ret. on Equity
1992	**8.2**	**305**	**175**	**1.7**	**1,759**	**5.0**	**482**	**821**	**1,544**	**31.2**	**10.7**
1991	13.9	288	168	1.7	1,481	7.2	380	687	1,269	29.9	14.2
1990	51.7	315	149	2.1	1,254	7.9	247	618	1,064	23.2	15.2
1989	15.1	247	122	2.0	1,018	3.6	222	472	849	26.1	5.9
1988	20.9	166	77	2.1	927	3.2	186	355	793	23.5	4.0
1987	23.3	168	98	1.7	965	2.4	214	340	803	26.6	6.0
1986	19.6	312	323	1.0	1,697	NM	825	314	1,348	61.2	NM
1985	71.5	503	361	1.4	1,995	1.6	904	455	1,614	56.0	5.5
1984	43.8	460	387	1.2	1,998	NM	981	399	1,603	61.2	NM
1983	11.0	353	298	1.2	1,477	3.3	489	414	1,171	41.7	8.8

Data as orig. reptd. **1.** Excl. disc. ops. **2.** Refl. acctg. change. **3.** Incl. equity in earns. of nonconsol. subs. **4.** Bef. results of disc. ops. and spec.items. d-Deficit. NM-Not Meaningful.

Business Summary

Valero Energy owns a specialized oil refinery and engages in petroleum refining, and marketing. It also owns a 49% interest in Valero Natural Gas Partners, L.P. (VLP). Other operations include pipeline and distribution operations not transfered to VLP in March 1987. Business segment contributions in 1992 (profits in million $) were:

	Revs.	Profits
Refining and marketing	86%	$137.2
Other	14%	– 3.2

Refining operations through VLO's Corpus Christi, Tex., refinery process high-sulfur atmospheric tower bottoms, a type of residual fuel oil, into products including unleaded gasoline and middle distillates. Refining and marketing sales volume in 1992 totaled 45.2 million bbl. (35.5 million bbl. in 1991); average sales price per bbl. was $23.14, versus $24.99. Refinery throughput amounted to 43.6 million bbl. (29.9 million) and throughput margin per bbl. was $7.00 ($8.84). Productos Ecologicos S.A. de C.V. (35% owned) is proceeding with plans to construct a plant in Mexico with capacity to produce 12,700 bbl. per day; the plant is estimated to cost $350 million. The company believes that by 1995, U.S. gasoline capacity will become increasingly limited, due to the high cost of refinery construction and expense associated with compliance with regulations.

Through 49%-owned Valero Natural Gas Partners, L.P., the company is engaged in pipeline operations primarily in Texas, consisting of transporting, purchasing, gathering and selling natural gas, and owns ten gas processing facilities and markets natural gas liquids.

Dividend Data

Common dividends, omitted in late 1984, were resumed in 1989. A "poison pill" stock purchase right was adopted in 1985.

Amt. of Divd. $	Date Decl.	Ex–divd. Date	Stock of Record	Payment Date
0.11	Jan. 21	Jan. 26	Feb. 1	Mar. 9'93
0.11	Apr. 29	May 10	May 14	Jun. 11'93
0.11	Jul. 15	Jul. 21	Jul. 27	Sep. 8'93
0.13	Sep. 16	Oct. 26	Nov. 1	Dec. 7'93

Capitalization

Long Term Debt: $513,649,000 (6/93).

Red. Preferred Stock: $14,950,000.

Common Stock: 43,103,413 shs. ($1 par).
Institutions hold 70%.
Shareholders of record: 10,204.

Office—530 McCullough Ave., San Antonio, TX 78215. **Tel**—(210) 246-2000. **Chrmn & CEO**—W. E. Greehey. **VP & CFO**—E. C. Benninger. **Secy**—R. C. Schmidt. **VP & Investor Contact**—Keith Booke (800-531-7911). **Dirs**—E. C. Benninger, R. G. Dettmer, A. R. Dudley, W. E. Greehey, J. L. Johnson, L. H. Lebermann, S. A. Shelton, P. K. Verleger, Jr. **Transfer Agents & Registrars**—Co.'s office; Norwest Trust Co., NYC. **Incorporated** in Delaware in 1955. **Empl**—1,890.

 Mark Mattke

Vanguard Cellular Systems

NASDAQ Symbol VCELA (Incl. in Nat'l Market) Options on CBOE In S&P MidCap 400

Price	Range	P-E Ratio	Dividend	Yield	S&P Ranking	Beta
Aug. 9'93	1993					
29	30–20½	NM	None	None	NR	2.17

Summary

Vanguard, which is among the three largest independent nonwireline cellular operators in the U.S., operates five cellular networks throughout the East. A continuing acquisition program has raised the company's population base to 6.2 million (adjusted for percentage ownership). Although losses continue, operating cash flow has been positive since the second quarter of 1991. Losses are expected to narrow in 1993, as results benefit from strong subscriber growth and efforts to control costs.

Current Outlook

Losses are expected to narrow to $0.70 a share in 1993, from 1992's $1.08. For 1994, the loss is expected to be cut to $0.35.

Initiation of cash dividends is not expected in the foreseeable future.

Revenues should climb about 25% in 1993, reflecting rapid subscriber growth. Additional revenues from outside subscribers using the company's systems should offset an expected decline in average revenues per subscriber as lower-usage customers are added to the subscriber base. Losses from cellular equipment sales are expected to continue. Vanguard should achieve operating profits for the year, aided by the increased revenue base, despite continued high marketing costs. Interest charges should decline slightly, as lower interest rates are largely offset by the cost of additional debt to finance acquisitions. Share earnings will reflect additional shares outstanding.

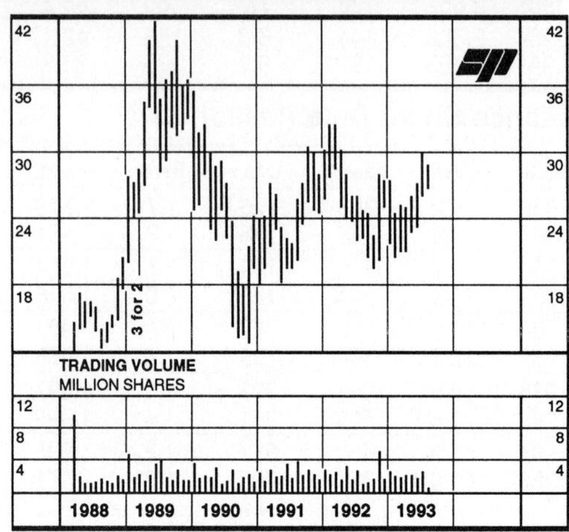

Operating Revenues (Million $)

Quarter:	1993	1992	1991	1990
Mar.	24.4	18.5	14.9	14.4
Jun.	30.1	22.4	17.2	16.2
Sep.		24.4	19.0	16.9
Dec.		24.3	18.3	16.8
		89.6	69.4	64.2

Revenues in the six months ended June 30, 1993, soared 34%, year to year, primarily reflecting higher service fees resulting from a 39% increase in the number of subscribers. Aided by increased use of the network, operating costs and expenses rose less rapidly, and the operating loss narrowed. After lower interest expense, the loss was cut to $9.4 million ($0.37 a share), from $13.5 million ($0.55). Results in the 1993 period exclude an extraordinary charge of $0.15 a share.

Common Share Earnings ($)

Quarter:	1993	1992	1991	1990
Mar.	d0.22	d0.33	d0.48	d0.53
Jun.	d0.16	d0.21	d0.43	d0.47
Sep.	Ed0.17	d0.29	d0.28	d0.54
Dec.	Ed0.15	d0.24	d0.28	[1]0.12
	Ed0.70	d1.08	d1.44	d1.42

Important Developments

Jul. '93— Vanguard achieved an operating profit in the 1993 second quarter. Average monthly revenue per subscriber was $90, up from $80 in the first quarter, primarily due to seasonal factors; average revenue was $93 in the year-earlier period reflecting additional non-business subscribers. Marketing and selling costs (including equipment subsidies) per net new addition were slashed 28% from the level of the 1992 second quarter, to $722.

Next earnings report expected in late October.

Per Share Data ($)

Yr. End Dec. 31	1992	1991	1990	1989	1988	[3]1987
Tangible Bk. Val.[2]	**1.20**	2.11	0.45	1.74	1.91	0.63
Cash Flow	**d0.38**	d0.79	d0.91	0.12	d1.10	d0.77
Earnings	**d1.08**	d1.44	d1.42	d0.31	d1.37	d1.03
Dividends	**Nil**	Nil	Nil	Nil	Nil	Nil
Payout Ratio	**Nil**	Nil	Nil	Nil	Nil	Nil
Prices—High	**32½**	30½	35½	41¾	20½	NA
Low	**19½**	18	12¾	20	12	NA
P/E Ratio—	**NM**	NM	NM	NM	NM	NM

Data as orig. reptd. Adj. for stk. div. of 50% Mar. 1989. **1.** Incl. 0.65 gain on contrib. of cellular interests to joint venture. **2.** Incl. intangibles. **3.** Refl. acctg. change. d-Deficit. E-Estimated NM-Not Meaningful. NA-Not Available.

Income Data (Million $)

Year Ended Dec. 31	Revs.	Oper. Inc.	% Oper. Inc. of Revs.	Cap. Exp.	Depr.	Int. Exp.	[2]Net Bef. Taxes	Eff. Tax Rate	Net Inc.	% Net Inc. of Revs.	Cash Flow
1992	**89.6**	**9.2**	**10.3**	**18.2**	**17.3**	**16.4**	**d27.0**	**NM**	**d26.7**	**NM**	**d9.3**
1991	69.4	NM	NM	16.5	14.7	20.0	d33.0	NM	d32.7	NM	d18.0
1990	64.2	d16.2	NM	37.4	10.5	20.8	d29.7	NM	d29.3	NM	d18.9
1989	46.6	d26.2	NM	21.2	8.9	16.2	d7.6	NM	d6.4	NM	2.5
1988	22.9	d19.0	NM	30.9	5.3	7.8	d27.6	NM	d26.6	NM	d21.4
[1]1987	10.9	d8.3	NM	7.6	3.3	3.6	d14.5	NM	d13.0	NM	d9.7

Balance Sheet Data (Million $)

Dec. 31	Cash	Curr. Assets	Curr. Liab.	Curr. Ratio	Total Assets	% Ret. on Assets	Long Term Debt	Common Equity	Total Cap.	% LT Debt of Cap.	% Ret. on Equity
1992	**9.5**	**19.6**	**20.7**	**0.9**	**252**	**NM**	**195**	**30.3**	**231**	**84.4**	**NM**
1991	11.0	22.2	14.3	1.5	256	NM	184	51.7	241	76.1	NM
1990	12.7	26.2	24.8	1.1	237	NM	198	9.3	212	93.2	NM
1989	15.8	31.6	18.6	1.7	202	NM	146	35.6	183	79.6	NM
1988	10.7	19.8	15.2	1.3	138	NM	83	39.1	122	68.1	NM
1987	3.4	6.5	16.3	0.4	56	NM	30	9.2	40	76.7	NM

Data as orig. reptd. **1.** Refl. acctg. change. **2.** Incl. equity in earns. of nonconsol. subs. d-Deficit. NM-Not Meaningful.

Business Summary

Vanguard Cellular Systems owns interests in and operates cellular telephone systems, primarily in the eastern U.S. The company believes that it is one of the three largest independent U.S. nonwireline cellular providers, with operations covering 6.2 million pops. At June 30, 1993, it had 107,500 subcribers in its majority-owned markets.

Vanguard's growth strategy has been to expand the scope of operations through the acquisition of some or all of the assets of corporations or partnerships owning cellular telephone license interests. Its goal has been to obtain controlling interests in cellular markets that can be efficiently managed and easily integrated into existing operations within concentrated geographic areas. The company has concentrated on acquiring licenses adjacent to its existing markets in order to build market clusters.

Through a series of acquisitions and exchanges of certain of its license interests, the company has created five regional metro-clusters, located in Pennsylvania, Florida, the Carolinas, New England and West Virginia.

Vanguard generally offers customers several pricing options, most of which consist of a fixed monthly access charge plus additional variable charges per minute of telephone or airtime usage. The company has also implemented automatic roaming agreements with other cellular operators throughout the U.S. With automatic roaming, subscribers are preregistered in other cellular systems and receive service automatically while they are outside their home system for a daily fee and usage charges.

Dividend Data

No cash dividends have been paid. A three-for-two stock split was effected in 1989.

Finances

The company has entered into agreements to acquire additional interests in markets within its Pennsylvannia regional cluster for interests in exchange for minority-owned cellular markets outside its clusters and $27.2 million in cash and common shares; the transactions are expected to be completed during 1993.

During 1992, Vanguard acquired an additional 5.88% interest in the Harrisburg, Pa., MSA for $2.5 million in cash; and a Pennsylvannia rural cellular service area, in exchange for certain minority interests and $2.6 million in cash and Class A shares.

During 1992, capital spending totaled $18 million, primarily to expand coverage and capacity in existing markets. An additional $26 million of spending for capital equipment is expected for 1993.

In June and July 1991, the company sold publicly 3.5 million Class A common shares, at $20.25 each, through underwriters led by Lehman Brothers and Salomon Brothers Inc. Proceeds were earmarked for the retirement of debt.

During the 1990 third quarter, Vanguard completed a transfer of its ownership interests in the Wilmington and Jacksonville, N.C., cellular markets to a 50-50 joint venture with GTE Mobilnet, Inc. The transfer resulted in a net gain of $13,365,000 ($0.65 a share) in 1990.

Capitalization

Long Term Debt: $218,651,000 (6/93).

Minority Interests: $5,760,000.

Cl. A Common Stock: 25,232,667 shs. ($0.01 par). Officers and directors control 15%. Institutions hold 46%. Shareholders: 1,150 of record (3/93).

Office—2002 Pisgah Church Rd., Suite 300, Greensboro, NC 27408. **Tel**—(919) 282-3690. **Chrmn**—S. S. Richardson. **Vice-Chrmn, EVP & Treas**—L. R. Preyer, Jr. **Pres & CEO**—H. G. Griffin. **EVP, COO & Secy**—S. R. Leeolou. **SVP & CFO**—S. L. Holcombe. **Investor Contact**—Stanley Haines. **Dirs**—R. M. DeMichele, J. F. Dille, Jr., H. G. Griffin, S. R. Leeolou, L. R. Preyer, Sr., L. R. Preyer, Jr., S. S. Richardson, R. A. Silverberg, T. I. Storrs. **Transfer Agent**—First Union National Bank of North Carolina, Charlotte. **Reincorporated** in North Carolina in 1987. **Empl**—650.

 Susan Stahl Gibney

Varco International

NYSE Symbol VRC In S&P MidCap 400

Price	Range	P-E Ratio	Dividend	Yield	S&P Ranking	Beta
Oct. 1,93	1993					
7½	8½–4⅛	NM	None	None	B–	1.56

Summary

Varco is a leading manufacturer of products used in the drilling industry worldwide. The company also develops equipment and systems which enhance the safety and productivity of the drilling process. After suffering through historically low levels of domestic drilling activity in 1992, VRC should benefit from the start of a modest drilling industry recovery in 1993 which should last for at least several years.

Current Outlook

Share earnings for 1993 are estimated at $0.20, up from 1992's $0.01 (before a special credit of $0.06). An increase to $0.30 is projected for 1994.

Dividends are not expected to be resumed in the foreseeable future.

Profits for 1993 at Varco Drilling Systems should rise slightly on an increase in orders for drilling equipment. Profitability at Varco BJ Oil Tools should benefit from the absence of the $4.9 million charge associated with closing a manufacturing plant. Although drilling activity is expected to increase, the low level of activity will likely prevent significant improvement in demand at Drilling Systems and Oil Tools. Earnings for 1994 are expected to benefit from a slight improvement in the level of drilling activity and better margins.

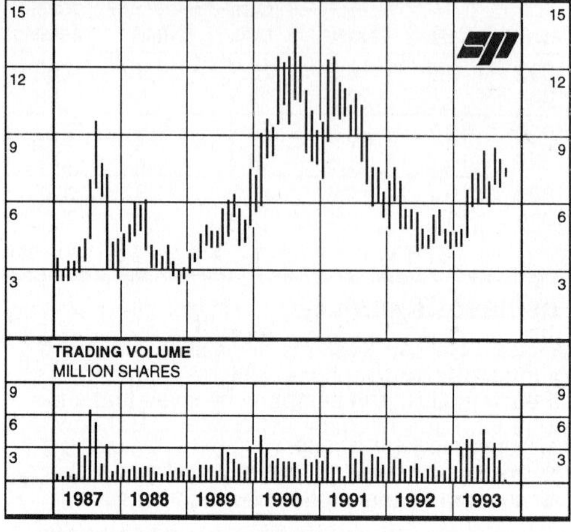

[1]Revenues (Million $)

Quarter:	1993	1992	1991	1990
Mar.	45.8	47.3	46.3	22.9
Jun.	48.7	37.4	55.9	27.3
Sep.	---	37.8	56.7	36.4
Dec.	---	50.5	57.4	44.4
	---	173.1	216.2	130.9

Revenues for the six months ended June 30, 1993, rose 11%, year to year, reflecting the Shaffer division acquisition in July 1992. Costs were well controlled, and pretax income was up 22%. After taxes at 37.1%, versus 26.0%, net income was up 3.5%. Share earnings were $0.08 in both interims (excluding a special credit of $0.06 in the 1992 period).

Common Share Earnings ($)

Quarter:	1993	1992	1991	1990
Mar.	0.04	0.07	0.11	0.05
Jun.	0.04	0.01	0.12	0.07
Sep.	E0.05	d0.16	0.12	0.08
Dec.	E0.07	0.09	0.11	0.13
	E0.20	0.01	0.45	0.33

Important Developments

Aug. '93— VRC said it had acquired all the outstanding stock of Metrox Inc., a designer and manufacturer of instrumentation used in the oil and gas industry, as well as in general commercial and industrial applications. For the year ended September 30, 1992, Metrox had revenues of about $3.5 million.

Aug. '93— VRC said incoming orders totaled $37.1 million, down from $42.3 million in the 1993 first quarter, but up from $33.7 in the 1992 second quarter; backlog at June 30, 1993 totaled about $26.1 million. Management said worldwide drilling activity continued to be relatively weak, particularly in the international markets. As a result the company planned to remain focused on cost containment and cash flow. In the uncertain market, VRC expected those strategies would continue to serve it well.

Next earnings report expected in early November.

Per Share Data ($)

Yr. End Dec. 31	[2]1992	1991	[2]1990	1989	[2]1988	1987	1986	1985	1984	1983
Tangible Bk. Val.	**3.26**	3.18	2.11	2.31	1.93	1.53	0.79	1.69	1.92	3.59
Cash Flow	**0.28**	0.73	0.55	0.26	0.28	d0.17	d0.53	0.14	d1.21	d0.57
Earnings[3]	**0.01**	0.45	0.33	0.09	0.10	d0.42	d0.91	d0.24	d1.69	d1.10
Dividends	**Nil**	Nil	Nil	Nil	Nil	Nil	Nil	Nil	Nil	Nil
Payout Ratio	**Nil**	Nil	Nil	Nil	Nil	Nil	Nil	Nil	Nil	Nil
Prices—High	**7⅝**	12½	13¾	7½	6⅛	9⅝	5	5¾	7¼	9⅜
Low	**3⅞**	5⅜	5⅝	2⅞	2⅜	2½	1⅞	2¼	2¼	5
P/E Ratio—	**NM**	28–12	42–17	83–32	61–24	NM	NM	NM	NM	NM

Data as orig. reptd. **1.** Incl. other inc. aft. 1991; incl. rental inc. aft. 1990. **2.** Reflects merger or acquisition. **3.** Bef. spec. item(s) of +0.06 in 1992. d-Deficit. E-Estimated. NM-Not Meaningful.

Income Data (Million $)

Year Ended Dec. 31	Revs.	Oper. Inc.	% Oper. Inc. of Revs.	Cap. Exp.	Depr.	Int. Exp.	Net Bef. Taxes	Eff. Tax Rate	[2]Net Inc.	% Net Inc. of Revs.	Cash Flow
[1]1992	**172**	**18.0**	**10.4**	**4.6**	**8.95**	**3.9**	**0.9**	**62.2%**	**0.3**	**0.2**	**9.2**
1991	216	29.8	13.8	7.9	8.74	4.5	16.9	17.1%	14.0	6.5	22.7
[1]1990	131	18.2	13.9	4.0	5.80	3.7	9.8	11.2%	8.7	6.7	14.5
1989	85	8.7	10.2	2.5	4.30	3.2	2.6	8.8%	2.4	2.8	6.6
[1]1988	68	8.1	11.9	0.7	3.78	2.7	2.5	10.6%	2.3	3.3	6.0
1987	37	Nil	NM	0.1	3.90	3.0	d5.9	NM	d6.0	NM	d2.6
1986	42	d2.0	NM	0.7	4.32	3.3	d9.0	NM	d9.2	NM	d5.9
1985	59	7.1	12.1	0.3	4.25	5.0	d1.5	NM	d1.7	NM	1.6
1984	59	d3.2	NM	0.3	5.42	6.4	d17.6	NM	d17.9	NM	d13.4
1983	55	d1.6	NM	3.3	5.90	7.2	d18.1	NM	d11.8	NM	d6.3

Balance Sheet Data (Million $)

Dec. 31	Cash	Curr. Assets	Curr. Liab.	Curr. Ratio	Total Assets	% Ret. on Assets	Long Term Debt	Common Equity	Total Cap.	% LT Debt of Cap.	% Ret. on Equity
1992	**26.9**	**136**	**33.5**	**4.1**	**232**	**0.1**	**52.4**	**144**	**199**	**26.3**	**0.2**
1991	4.8	118	36.1	3.3	204	6.8	25.6	141	167	15.3	11.3
1990	4.1	98	39.7	2.5	186	5.8	51.8	94	146	35.5	10.7
1989	23.4	65	13.6	4.7	101	2.3	26.5	60	87	30.3	4.2
1988	9.9	64	16.5	3.9	102	2.5	36.3	48	85	42.6	5.1
1987	13.3	37	9.9	3.7	69	NM	25.9	33	59	43.6	NM
1986	6.5	26	8.1	3.2	63	NM	32.0	10	55	58.3	NM
1985	5.3	35	12.0	2.9	76	NM	31.8	21	64	49.9	NM
1984	6.1	42	18.9	2.2	97	NM	44.7	23	78	57.1	NM
1983	5.6	51	18.9	2.7	118	NM	46.7	41	99	47.2	NM

Data as orig. reptd. **1.** Reflects merger or acquisition. **2.** Bef. spec. item(s). d-Deficit. NM-Not Meaningful.

Business Summary

Varco International, Inc. is a leader in the design and manufacture of drilling equipment and machinery and rig instrumentation for oil and gas drilling worldwide. It is widely recognized for the development of equipment and systems which enhance the safety and productivity of the drilling process. In 1992, Varco Drilling Systems accounted for 33% of revenues, Varco BJ Oil Tools for 31%, Martin-Decker/TOTCO Instrumentation for 27%, and Shaffer for 9%.

Products are sold for use in about 80 countries, and international sales contributed about 72% of revenues in 1992, versus 71% in 1991.

Varco Drilling Systems designs and manufactures drilling equipment which mechanizes or automates drilling and pipe handling operations and enhances their efficiency and safety. Principal products are Top Drive Drilling Systems, pipe racking and handling systems, and the Automated Roughneck, which combines the functions of the spinning wrench and torque wrench in a single tool.

Varco BJ Oil Tools produces a wide variety of conventional tools and equipment used on drilling rigs, including pipe handling tools, hoisting equipment and rotary equipment. Replacement and spare parts represent a substantial portion of sales.

MD/TOTCO designs, manufactures and sells or rents instrumentation, primarily for use in oil and gas well drilling operations; to a lesser extent instrumentation is provided to certain industrial markets and for use in non-drilling oilfield applications. Shaffer (acquired in July 1992) designs, manufactures, sells and distributes pressure control equipment.

Sales of VRC's drilling equipment, and sales and rentals of instrumentation products depend on the level of construction of new drilling rigs and the replacement and upgrading of equipment for existing rigs.

Dividend Data

Common stock dividends were omitted in late 1982 after having been paid since 1974.

Capitalization

Long Term Debt: $52,142,000 (6/93).

Common Stock: 33,205,774 shs. (no par).
Officers & directors control about 10%; Baker Hughes Inc. owns about 19%.
Institutions hold approximately 36%.
Shareholders of record: 2,373.

Office—743 North Eckhoff St, Orange, CA 92668. **Tel**—(714) 978-1900. **Chrmn**—W. B. Reinhold. **Pres & CEO**—G. Boyadjieff. **Treas**—D. L. Stichler. **VP-Fin, CFO & Investor Contact**—Richard A. Kertson. **Dirs**—G. Boyadjieff, T. R. Embry, A. R. Horn, M. E. Jacques, J. W. Knowlton, L. J. Pircher, W. B. Reinhold, R. A. Teitsworth, E. R. White, J. D. Woods. **Transfer Agent & Registrar**—Harris Trust Co. of California, Los Angeles. **Incorporated** in California in 1911. **Empl**—1,198.

 M.Mattke

Varian Associates

NYSE Symbol VAR Options on ASE (Feb-May-Aug-Nov) In S&P MidCap 400

Price	Range	P-E Ratio	Dividend	Yield	S&P Ranking	Beta
Jul. 12'93	1993					
52¾	54–38	25	0.40	0.8%	B–	1.04

Summary

Varian produces a broad line of medical equipment, analytical instruments, electron tubes and semiconductor production equipment. Earnings declined in fiscal 1992, penalized by weak sales of semiconductor production equipment and electron devices. Higher earnings are likely in fiscal 1993, reflecting cost reductions and a stronger economy; medical equipment and instruments sales should benefit from well received new products. Further growth is likely for fiscal 1994, as the economy strengthens. The dividend was boosted 11% in early 1993.

Current Outlook

Earnings for the fiscal year ending September 30, 1994, are likely to reach $3.40 a share, up from the $2.50 projected for fiscal 1993.

The quarterly dividend was boosted 11%, to $0.10 from $0.09, with the April 1993 payment.

Sales should rise significantly in fiscal 1994, reflecting gains in all segments. Following several years of disappointing results, sales of semiconductor production equipment should advance strongly, as recent substantial growth in the semiconductor industry fuels increased capital spending; a new physical vapor deposition product should also help results. Medical equipment sales should continue to increase, benefiting from well received new products, especially in cancer treatment. Stronger economic conditions in the U.S. and Europe should allow instruments to post improved comparisons. Electron devices sales are likely to grow only modestly, despite the stronger economy, reflecting the maturity of this business. Margins should widen on the greater volume, an improved product mix, manufacturing efficiencies and well controlled costs.

Net Sales (Million $)

Quarter:	1992–93	1991–92	1990–91	1989–90
Dec.	291	304	316	285
Mar.	325	315	360	301
Jun.	---	311	363	345
Sep.	---	359	339	334
	---	1,288	1,378	1,265

Sales in the six months ended April 2, 1993, decreased fractionally, year to year, on a 2.2% decline in electron devices. Results benefited from cost reductions, and pretax income increased 2.8%. After taxes at 38.0% in each period, net income was also up 2.8%, to $0.86 a share, from $0.80.

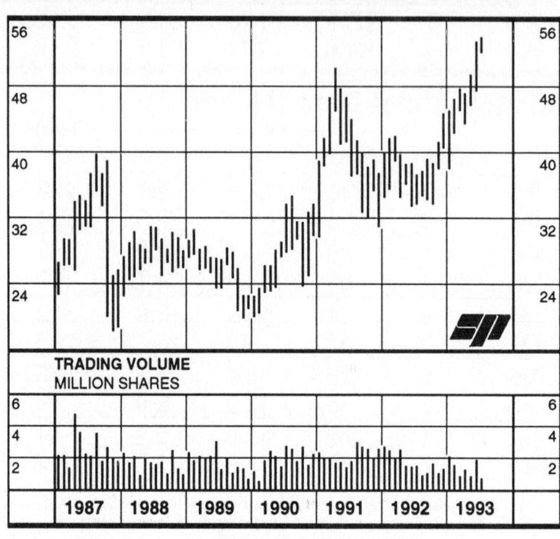

Common Share Earnings ($)

Quarter:	1992–93	1991–92	1990–91	1989–90
Dec.	0.36	0.40	0.64	0.42
Mar.	0.51	0.41	0.81	0.45
Jun.	E0.70	0.54	0.82	d0.98
Sep.	E0.92	0.71	0.67	0.75
	E2.50	2.04	2.95	0.64

Important Developments

Jun. '93— VAR said it had acquired Helsinki-based Dosetek OY, a major supplier of radiotherapy systems and associated equipment in the European market. Earlier, in April, the company had said that medical equipment results were benefiting from well received new products, while a stronger economy had stabilized results at electron devices. Results of instruments and semiconductor production equipment were below plan.

Next earnings report expected in late July.

Per Share Data ($)

Yr. End Sep. 30	1992	1991	1990	1989	1988	1987	1986	1985	1984	1983
Book Value	[1]**23.57**	[1]22.71	[1]20.75	[1]21.48	[1]20.81	[1]19.95	[1]19.16	20.14	19.57	16.93
Cash Flow	**4.62**	5.27	2.80	3.60	3.30	3.05	1.09	3.06	3.65	2.98
Earnings[2]	**2.04**	2.95	0.64	1.53	1.27	0.98	d0.70	1.81	2.72	2.14
Dividends	**0.34**	0.29	0.26	0.26	0.26	0.26	0.26	0.26	0.26	0.26
Payout Ratio	**16%**	10%	40%	16%	20%	27%	NM	14%	9%	12%
Prices—High[3]	**44¾**	50¼	34¾	30½	31	39¾	30½	42⅜	58½	63⅜
Low[3]	**33½**	29¾	20	19⅞	22½	18¼	22⅜	22½	30¼	30½
P/E Ratio—	**22–16**	17–10	54–31	20–13	24–18	41–19	NM	23–12	22–11	30–14

Data as orig. reptd. Adj. for stk. div. of 100% Mar. 1983. **1.** Incl. intangibles. **2.** Bef. results of disc. ops. of -0.85 in 1990, -0.62 in 1985. **3.** Cal. yr. E-Estimated. d-Deficit. NM-Not Meaningful.

Income Data (Million $)

Year Ended Sep. 30	Revs.	Oper. Inc.	% Oper. Inc. of Revs.	Cap. Exp.	Depr.	Int. Exp.	[2]Net Bef. Taxes	Eff. Tax Rate	[3]Net Inc.	% Net Inc. of Revs.	Cash Flow
1992	**1,288**	**114**	**8.9**	**48.6**	**48.9**	**5.9**	**62.4**	**38.0%**	**38.7**	**3.0**	**88**
1991	1,378	146	10.6	59.7	45.4	8.4	92.8	38.0%	57.5	4.2	103
[1]1990	1,265	129	10.0	54.9	42.2	13.0	20.7	39.0%	12.6	1.0	55
1989	1,344	109	8.1	49.4	42.9	10.8	50.8	38.0%	31.5	2.3	74
1988	1,171	114	9.8	48.2	44.7	7.9	43.4	36.0%	27.8	2.4	72
1987	983	73	7.4	46.2	44.7	6.6	31.9	33.0%	21.4	2.2	66
[1]1986	891	19	2.2	50.0	38.0	8.4	d40.2	NM	d14.9	NM	23
[1]1985	973	85	8.7	94.1	27.4	8.5	56.8	30.0%	39.8	4.1	67
1984	929	115	12.4	60.6	20.5	6.1	98.3	39.1%	59.9	6.4	80
1983	760	85	11.2	33.7	17.5	12.0	72.4	38.0%	44.9	5.9	62

Balance Sheet Data (Million $)

Sep. 30	Cash	Curr. Assets	Curr. Liab.	Curr. Ratio	Total Assets	% Ret. on Assets	Long Term Debt	Common Equity	Total Inv. Capital	% LT Debt of Cap.	% Ret. on Equity
1992	**67**	**604**	**384**	**1.6**	**893**	**4.5**	**49.7**	**428**	**509**	**9.8**	**9.2**
1991	54	595	350	1.7	884	6.4	68.0	434	535	12.7	13.8
1990	26	668	408	1.6	924	1.4	76.8	400	516	14.9	3.1
1989	Nil	643	414	1.6	931	3.7	54.9	427	517	10.6	7.5
1988	12	590	336	1.8	856	3.3	35.2	451	519	6.8	6.3
1987	28	537	328	1.6	830	2.6	38.1	438	502	7.6	5.0
1986	8	505	304	1.7	790	NM	50.8	411	486	10.5	NM
1985	13	474	247	1.9	745	5.5	46.2	429	498	9.3	9.4
1984	65	514	231	2.2	721	9.0	43.0	427	489	8.8	15.0
1983	101	446	182	2.4	599	7.7	42.3	362	416	10.2	13.5

Data as orig. reptd. **1.** Excl. disc. ops. **2.** Incl. equity in earns. of nonconsol. subs. **3.** Bef. results of disc. ops. d-Deficit. NM-Not Meaningful.

Business Summary

Varian Associates produces equipment and components for communications, scientific, medical, industrial, and defense markets. Segment contributions (profits in million $) in fiscal 1992 were:

	Sales	Profits
Medical equipment	21%	$47
Instruments	23%	35
Semiconductor equipment	21%	–4
Electron devices	28%	20
Eliminations and other	7%	–12

Foreign business accounted for 33% of sales and 22% of pretax income in fiscal 1992.

The company is one of the world's leading suppliers of equipment and services for treating cancer with high-energy radiation therapy. Products include medical linear accelerators, which generate the radiation, simulators for treatment planning, and ancillary equipment aimed at therapy management and enhanced precision.

The instrument group supplies analytical instruments for the determination of chemical structure, chemical composition, or both. The instruments are used in industrial, academic, and governmental laboratories.

The semiconductor equipment group makes semiconductor fabrication equipment, with leadership positions in ion implantation and sputtering systems.

VAR is the world's largest manufacturer of microwave, power-grid, and X-ray tubes and related equipment such as amplifiers and power supplies. Primary markets include medical, communications, defense, industrial, and energy research.

Dividend Data

Dividends were initiated in 1973. A dividend reinvestment plan is available. A "poison pill" stock purchase right was adopted in 1986.

Amt of Divd. $	Date Decl.	Ex–divd. Date	Stock of Record	Payment Date
0.09	May 15	Jul. 14	Jul. 20	Jul. 31'92
0.09	Aug. 14	Oct. 13	Oct. 19	Nov. 2'92
0.09	Nov. 20	Jan. 15	Jan. 22	Feb. 1'93
0.10	Feb. 19	Apr. 13	Apr. 19	Apr. 30'93
0.10	May 21	Jul. 19	Jul. 23	Aug. 2'93

Capitalization

Long Term Debt: $63,600,000 (4/93).

Common Stock: 17,997,000 shs. ($1 par).
Institutions hold 72%.
Shareholders of record: 7,203.

Office—3100 Hansen Way, Palo Alto, CA 94304. **Tel**—(415) 493-4000. **Chrmn & CEO**—J. T. O'Rourke. **VP-Fin & CFO**—R. A. Lemos. **VP & Secy**—J. B. Phair. **Investor Contact**—Allen Jones. **Dirs**—R. M. Davis, S. Hellman, T. Kubo, A. A. MacNaughton, J. G. McDonald, W. F. Miller, G. E. Moore, D. E. Mundell, J. T. O'Rourke, D. O. Pederson, P. J. Quigley, B. Richter, T. D. Sege, P. G. Stern, R. W. Vieser. **Transfer Agent & Registrar**—First National Bank of Boston. **Incorporated** in California in 1948; reincorporated in Delaware in 1976. **Empl**—8,100.

 Paul H. Valentine, CFA

VeriFone, Inc.

NASDAQ Symbol VFIC (Incl. in Nat'l Market) Options on CBOE In S&P MidCap 400

Price	Range	P–E Ratio	Dividend	Yield	S&P Ranking	Beta
Aug. 6'93	1993					
26½	30–20¼	25	None	None	NR	NA

Summary

This company is the leading supplier of transaction automation systems for the payment processing market, with more than three million systems sold worldwide. It also produces such systems for electronic benefits transfer. Earnings for the first half of 1993 rose, as higher sales and wider gross margins outweighed increased operating expenses.

Business Summary

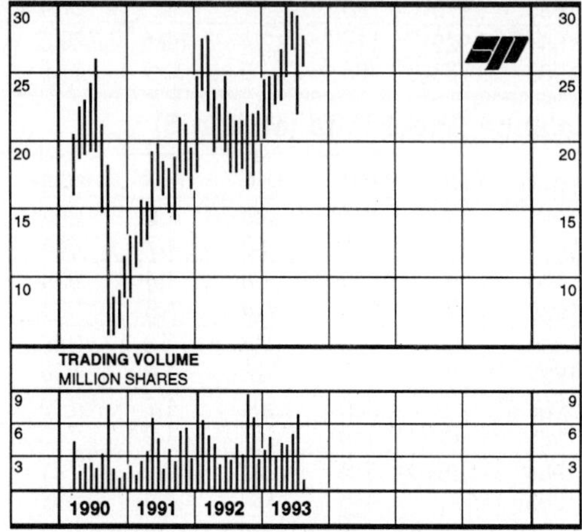

VeriFone, Inc. designs, manufactures, markets and supports transaction automation solutions used by retailers, petroleum service station and convenience store operators, healthcare providers and government agencies to electronically automate the processing of payments, benefits and information transactions. The company played a major role in expanding transaction automation in the payment processing market by offering the first low-cost systems for electronic credit card authorization, and is now the leading supplier of transaction automation systems for the payment processing market.

As of mid-1993, VeriFone had shipped more than 3.0 million systems to customers in more than 70 countries. A majority of the shipments were to retailers. In 1992, sales outside the U.S. represented 21% of consolidated revenue, up from 16% in 1991.

The company's product line is organized into five classes: transaction systems, which are flexible platforms designed to support a variety of application programs, including credit and debit card sales authorization, draft capture and settlement, healthcare insurance eligibility verification and government benefits disbursement; transaction supersystems, which extend the payment processing capabilities of transaction automation systems to provide multiple payment options; ValuCard systems that allow consumers to use a prepaid card to buy products from vending machines; network systems used to expedite the delivery of automated transactions between the point of sale and wide area networks; and application software.

Since 1989, products have been manufactured primarily at a VeriFone facility in Taiwan. The company markets its products mainly through resellers, such as banks, independent sales organizations and industry service providers, and also directly to selected end-users.

VeriFone believes that the quality and reliability of its systems and the ongoing support of such systems are important elements of its strategy. Support includes pre-sales consulting, application software development and support, site survey, deployment, field maintenance, 24-hour hotline service, expedited system replacement programs, and repair. Research and development outlays expensed in 1992 equaled 12.4% of net revenues, compared to 13.4% in 1991 and 10.9% in 1990.

Important Developments

Jul. '93— VeriFone introduced PNC+Plus, a software application that links DOS-based personal computers with the company's PNC 330 Transaction Automation Systems.

Jun. '93— VeriFone and Gemplus SCA announced the formation of a joint venture, called VeriGem, which will develop and market SmartCash electronic currency solutions based on smart cards with stored value that can be used in place of cash.

Next earnings report expected in late October.

Per Share Data ($)

Yr. End Dec. 31	1992	1991	1990	1989	1988	1987	1986	1985
Tangible Bk. Val.[1]	**7.48**	6.37	5.53	2.29	NA	NA	NA	NA
Cash Flow	**1.32**	1.09	0.73	0.60	0.43	NA	NA	NA
Earnings	**1.02**	0.82	0.55	0.50	0.36	0.01	NM	0.13
Dividends	**Nil**	Nil	Nil	Nil	Nil	Nil	Nil	Nil
Payout Ratio	**Nil**	Nil	Nil	Nil	Nil	Nil	Nil	Nil
Prices—High	**27¾**	21¾	26	NA	NA	NA	NA	NA
Low	**16½**	8½	5¾	NA	NA	NA	NA	NA
P/E Ratio—	**27–16**	27–10	47–11	NA	NA	NA	NA	NA

Data as orig. reptd. 1. Incl. intangibles. NA-Not Available. NM-Not Meaningful.

Income Data (Million $)

Year Ended Dec. 31	Revs.	Oper. Inc.	% Oper. Inc. of Revs.	Cap. Exp.	Depr.	Int. Exp.	Net Bef. Taxes	Eff. Tax Rate	Net Inc.	% Net Inc. of Revs.	Cash Flow
1992	**226**	**38.2**	**16.9**	**6.7**	**7.22**	**0.84**	**33.3**	**28.0%**	**24.0**	**10.6**	**31.2**
1991	188	29.8	15.9	11.2	6.19	0.51	27.1	31.0%	18.7	10.0	24.9
1990	155	19.9	12.9	10.9	4.19	0.75	18.3	33.5%	12.2	7.8	16.3
1989	123	16.4	13.3	8.5	2.12	0.65	15.8	36.5%	10.1	8.1	12.0
1988	73	10.7	14.5	1.9	1.14	0.57	10.3	38.0%	6.4	8.7	7.5
1987	44	1.7	3.9	1.1	0.94	0.70	0.1	25.9%	0.1	0.2	NA
1986	31	NA	NA	NA	NA	NA	NM	NM	NM	NM	NA
1985	15	NA	NA	NA	NA	NA	0.9	4.7%	0.9	5.6	NA

Balance Sheet Data (Million $)

Dec. 31	Cash	Curr. Assets	Curr. Liab.	Curr. Ratio	Total Assets	% Ret. on Assets	Long Term Debt	Common Equity[1]	Total Cap.	% LT Debt of Cap.	% Ret. on Equity
1992	**82.5**	**197**	**43.0**	**4.6**	**240**	**11.1**	**2.22**	**174**	**197**	**1.1**	**14.9**
1991	74.0	153	31.2	4.9	189	10.8	2.38	144	158	1.5	13.9
1990	61.9	124	23.9	5.2	151	6.4	1.40	119	127	1.1	14.4
1989	20.2	71	21.2	3.4	93	12.2	1.22	68	72	1.7	16.3
1988	35.9	68	13.8	4.9	73	12.1	0.03	55	59	0.1	17.3
1987	NA	NA	NA	NA	33	0.4	0.09	19	19	0.5	0.7
1986	NA	NA	NA	NA	23	NM	0.60	11	12	5.1	NM
1985	NA	NA	NA	NA	8	NA	0.20	5	5	4.1	NA

Data as orig. reptd. **1.** Refl. conv. of pfd. stk. upon public offering. NA-Not Available. NM-Not Meaningful.

Net Oper. Revenues (Million $)

Quarter:	1993	1992	1991	1990
Mar.	54.7	46.9	37.5	33.0
Jun.	65.5	58.7	47.4	41.1
Sep.		58.0	50.0	39.7
Dec.		62.6	[1]53.0	41.2
		226.2	187.9	155.0

Net revenues in the six months ended July 2, 1993 rose 14%, year to year. Gross margins widened, but an 18% increase in operating expenses limited the gain in pretax income to 6.4%. After taxes at 29.7%, versus 31.0%, net income was up 8.5%, to $10,398,000 ($0.44 a share), from $9,582,000 ($0.41).

Common Share Earnings ($)

Quarter:	1993	1992	1991	1990
Mar.	0.18	0.15	0.12	0.11
Jun.	0.26	0.26	0.20	0.17
Sep.		0.29	0.25	0.10
Dec.		0.32	[1]0.25	0.16
		1.02	0.82	0.55

Dividend Data

No cash dividends have been paid on the common shares, and VeriFone does not expect to pay any dividends in the foreseeable future.

Finances

In April 1993, VeriFone announced an increase from 19.9% to 48.9% in its ownership of VeriFone Finance, a privately held corporation offering flexible financing and leasing exclusively for VeriFone systems. Beginning in the second quarter of 1993, VFIC will report VeriFone Finance results on a consolidated basis.

The company has secured and unsecured credit lines of $10 million and $30 million, respectively—both unused at April 2, 1993. VeriFone also has a $2 million unsecured line of credit for foreign exchange transactions. At April 2, 1993, there were no borrowings outstanding under this line of credit.

On March 13, 1990, in its initial public stock offering, VeriFone, Inc. sold 4,485,000 common shares, at $16 per share, through underwriters led by Morgan Stanley & Co. Inc., Robertson, Stephens & Co. and Dean Witter Reynolds Inc. Of the shares, 2,500,000 were sold for VeriFone's account and 1,985,000 for stockholders, and 3,885,000 were offered in the U.S. and Canada and 600,000 elsewhere.

Capitalization

Long Term Debt: $1,875,000 (4/2/93), incl. lease obligations.

Common Stock: 23,443,227 shs. ($0.01 par).
Officers & directors own about 6.6%.
Institutions hold some 39%.
Shareholders: 1,318 of record (1/93).

Options: To purchase 1,585,853 shs. at $1 to $24.25 ea. (12/92).

1. 14 weeks.

Office—Three Lagoon Dr., Redwood City, CA 94065. **Tel**—(415) 591-6500. **Chrmn, Pres & CEO**—H. A. Tyabji. **VP-Fin, CFO & Secy**—T. W. Hubbs. **Dirs**—F. J. Caufield, K. B. Geeslin, W. F. Gorog, H. H. Haight IV, B. J. McMurtry, W. N. Melton, J. R. C. Porter, A. M. Spence, H. A. Tyabji. **Transfer Agent & Registrar**—First National Bank of Boston. **Incorporated** in Delaware in 1986. **Empl**—1,600.

 Kevin J. Gooley

Vons Companies

NYSE Symbol VON Options on NYSE & Pacific (Mar-Jun-Sep-Dec) In S&P MidCap 400

Price	Range	P-E Ratio	Dividend	Yield	S&P Ranking	Beta
Aug. 2'93	1993					
19⅝	26⅜–19½	10	None	None	B–	1.04

Summary

This company operates supermarkets and drug stores in southern California. While sales growth has been limited by the soft economy and price deflation in certain product categories, earnings since 1990 have benefited from the company's ongoing remodeling program, promotional buying opportunities, pricing flexibility, and lower interest expense. In July 1993, the company expressed continued reservations about the near term sales outlook.

Business Summary

The Vons Companies is the largest supermarket chain in southern California, owning and operating a total of 345 stores (218 Vons supermarkets, 86 Vons Food and Drug stores, 32 Pavilions, and 9 Tianguis) as of January 3, 1993. Store data for recent years (in operation as of year end):

	1992	1991	1990	1989
Opened or acquired	26	6	2	6
Closed or sold.......	1	6	10	28
In operation	345	320	320	328

The company's traditional supermarkets offer dry groceries, wine and liquor, produce, meat, fish, dairy products, and limited assortments of general merchandise and health and beauty aids. Many Vons supermarkets also have in-store bakeries, service delicatessens with fresh and prepared foods, and service seafood departments.

Vons Food and Drug stores combine traditional supermarket offerings and service departments with a pharmacy that is supported by a wide assortment of health and beauty care items, cosmetics and other typical drug store merchandise.

Pavilions stores offer expanded selections of food products and a variety of service departments.

Tianguis units offer foods and merchandise targeted to Hispanics, as well as traditional supermarket items.

The company also operates a fluid milk processing facility, an ice cream plant, a central bakery, a delicatessan kitchen and a meat grinding and frozen meat-patty making facility.

In 1988, Vons acquired the southern California operations of Safeway Stores, consisting of 162 stores (net of stores sold to comply with FTC requirements) plus distribution and processing operations. In January 1992, Vons acquired 18 Williams Bros. supermarkets.

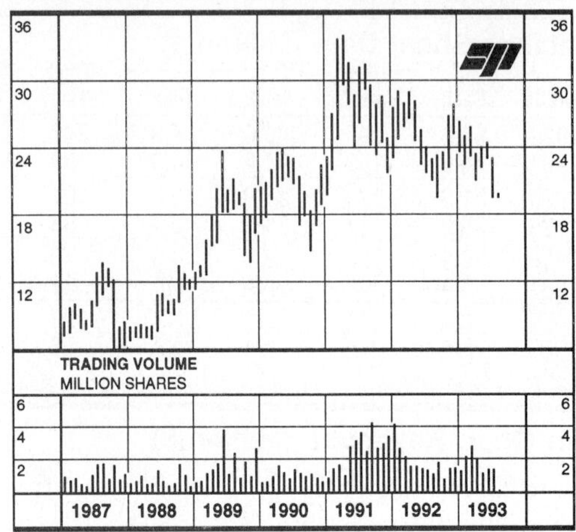

Important Developments

Jul. '93— Vons said it did not expect a material near term sales improvement, reflecting the soft economic conditions in Southern California. Looking ahead, the company's long term strategy is to invest in existing stores and in both consumer and cost-saving technology. Towards that end, Vons expects to open 14 new stores and remodel 50 to 60 stores in 1993.

Mar. '93— The company said it had been named in a number of lawsuits in state and federal courts in Washington, Nevada and California arising from claims of food-borne illness caused by food served at several Jack-In-The-Box restaurants. Vons is a processor of frozen hamburger patties for Foodmaker, the parent company of Jack-In-The-Box. Vons added that it intends to vigorously defend these lawsuits.

Next earnings report expected in late October.

Per Share Data ($)

Yr. End Dec. 31[1]	[3]1992	1991	1990	1989	[3]1988	[3]1987	1986	1985	1984	1983
Tangible Bk. Val.	**[2]11.38**	[2]11.05	[2]7.04	[2]4.91	[2]5.53	d6.74	7.62	6.69	7.23	7.44
Cash Flow	**3.97**	3.40	3.08	1.19	0.99	NA	NA	NA	NA	NA
Earnings[4]	**1.89**	1.56	1.28	d0.65	d0.77	d1.04	0.34	NM	d0.25	0.26
Dividends	**Nil**	Nil	Nil	Nil	Nil	Nil	Nil	Nil	Nil	Nil
Payout Ratio	**Nil**	Nil	Nil	Nil	Nil	Nil	Nil	Nil	Nil	Nil
Prices[5]—High	**29⅛**	34⅛	23⅞	23¾	13½	13¾	10⅛	6	3⅝	4⅞
Low	**19½**	19¾	14¾	11⅜	6¾	6	5½	2¼	2⅛	3⅛
P/E Ratio—	**15–10**	22–13	19–12	NM	NM	NM	30–16	NM	NM	19–12

Data as orig. reptd. **1.** Prior to 1988 yrs. ended Jun. 30. **2.** Includes intangibles. **3.** Reflects merger or acquisition. **4.** Bef. spec. items of -0.65 in 1992, +0.84 in 1990, +0.31 in 1986, +0.01 in 1985, +1.05 in 1983. **5.** Cal. yr. d-Deficit. NM-Not Meaningful. NA-Not Available.

Income Data (Million $)

Year Ended Dec. 31[1]	[2]Revs.	Oper. Inc.	% Oper. Inc. of Revs.	Cap. Exp.	Depr.	Int. Exp.	Net Bef. Taxes	Eff. Tax Rate	[6]Net Inc.	% Net Inc. of Revs.	Cash Flow
[3]1992	**5,596**	**310**	**5.5**	**261**	**90.6**	**[5]72**	**148**	**44.4%**	**[7]82.1**	**1.5**	**173**
1991	5,350	276	5.2	157	76.2	[5]86	113	42.7%	65.0	1.2	141
1990	5,334	253	4.8	126	69.8	[5]98	86	42.3%	49.7	0.9	120
1989	5,221	170	3.3	64	71.0	103	d24	NM	d25.1	NM	46
[3]1988	3,917	116	3.0	263	54.6	73	d22	NM	d23.9	NM	31
1987	421	12	2.9	[4]26	5.0	13	d14	NM	d14.4	NM	NA
1986	386	8	1.9	16	2.6	3	8	46.0%	4.4	1.1	NA
1985	480	2	0.4	6	3.7	1	NM	43.1%	0.2	Nil	NA
1984	530	d2	NM	11	3.8	1	d3	NM	d2.6	NM	NA
1983	576	4	0.7	6	3.6	1	6	45.5%	3.1	0.5	NA

Balance Sheet Data (Million $)

Dec. 31[1]	Cash	Curr. Assets	Curr. Liab.	Curr. Ratio	Total Assets	% Ret. on Assets	Long Term Debt	Common Equity	Total Cap.	% LT Debt of Cap.	% Ret. on Equity
1992	**8.3**	**465**	**557**	**0.8**	**2,066**	**4.2**	**788**	**493**	**1,375**	**57.3**	**16.9**
1991	6.7	448	523	0.9	1,803	3.5	691	478	1,169	59.1	16.6
1990	6.4	428	549	0.8	1,713	3.0	775	273	1,047	74.0	21.5
1989	6.9	419	511	0.8	1,655	NM	839	190	1,029	81.5	NM
1988	6.6	409	549	0.7	1,673	NM	800	214	1,014	78.9	NM
1987	3.3	233	310	0.7	149	NM	543	154	696	77.9	NM
1986	122.0	164	31	5.2	204	2.7	91	77	171	53.4	5.7
1985	37.0	73	31	2.4	95	0.2	6	52	61	9.7	NM
1984	19.0	74	39	1.9	108	NM	12	52	67	17.5	NM
1983	26.0	85	42	2.0	112	2.9	9	56	68	13.4	5.8

Data as orig. reptd. **1.** Prior to 1988 yrs. ended Jun. 30. **2.** Includes other income after 1985. **3.** Reflects merger or acquisition. **4.** Net of curr. yr. retirement and disposals. **5.** Net of interest income. **6.** Bef. spec. items. **7.** Reflects acctg. change. d-Deficit. NM-Not Meaningful. NA-Not Available.

Revenues (Million $)

Weeks:	1993	1992	1991	1990
12 Wks. Mar.	1,194	1,268	1,223	1,212
12 Wks. Jun......	1,175	1,286	1,251	1,222
16 Wks. Oct......		1,682	1,636	1,639
12 Wks. Dec. ...		[1]1,360	1,240	1,262
		5,596	5,350	5,334

Sales in the 24 weeks ended June 20, 1993, declined 7.2%, year to year, hurt by poor economic conditions, competitive pressures and the residual impact of the Foodmaker food poisoning epidemic. Ongoing remodel and new store programs, pricing flexibility and favorable buying opportunities held the decline in operating income to 4.0%. Following an 18% decline in net interest expense, net income was up 4.3%, to $0.77 a share, from $0.75, as restated for an income tax accounting change. Results in 1992 exclude special charges of $0.65 a share.

Common Share Earnings ($)

Weeks:	1993	1992	1991	1990
12 Wks. Mar.	0.37	0.35	0.33	0.21
12 Wks. Jun......	0.40	0.40	0.40	0.27
16 Wks. Oct......		0.51	0.42	0.34
12 Wks. Dec.		[1]0.63	0.42	0.46
		1.89	1.56	1.28

Dividend Data

No cash has been paid on the common since 1970.

Finances

Vons expects capital expenditures in 1993 to approximate $250 million.

During 1992, Vons redeemed $114 million of 12¾% senior discount debentures, $85.1 million of 13% subordinated debentures, and $83.1 million of 12⅞% reset notes. In March 1992, Vons issued $150 million of 9⅝% senior subordinated notes.

In May 1991, underwriters sold publicly 10,964,348 Vons common shares at $28 each, of which 4,500,000 were sold by Vons and the balance by selling shareholders.

Capitalization

Long Term Debt: $835,700,000 (6/93; incl. capital lease obligations).

Common Stock: 43,335,176 shs. ($0.10 par). About 35% is owned by Safeway Inc. Institutions hold 40%.

Shareholders: 6,341 of record (3/8/93).

1. 13 weeks.

Office—618 Michillinda Ave., Arcadia, CA 91007. **Tel**—(818) 821-7000. **Chrmn & CEO**—R. E. Stangeland. **Pres**—D. K. Eck. **EVP & CFO**—M. F. Henn. **SVP-Secy**—T. J. Wallock. **Investor Contact**—Mary M. McAboy (818-821-7897). **Dirs**—W. S. Davila, F. L. Duda, D. K. Eck, H. E. James, R. I. MacDonnell, P. A. Magowan, C. E. Rickershauser, E. A. Sanders, J. C. Shewmaker, R. E. Stangeland, W. Y. Tauscher. **Transfer Agent**—Bank of New York, NYC. **Incorporated** in Delaware in 1926. **Empl**—32,300.

 John D. Coyle, CFA

WPL Holdings

NYSE Symbol WPH In S&P MidCap 400

Price	Range	P-E Ratio	Dividend	Yield	S&P Ranking	Beta
Oct. 12'93	1993					
35⅛	36¾–32½	17	1.90	5.5%	A	0.43

Summary

WPL Holdings is the holding company for Wisconsin Power and Light, which supplies electric, gas and water service in south-central Wisconsin. The main fuel for electricity generation is coal, with nuclear used to a lesser extent. Plans call for three 82-megawatt combustion-turbine generators to become operational in 1994 through 1996. Earnings for 1993 should benefit from customer growth at the utility units, the acquisition and proper placement of consulting operations, and a prospective rate increase.

Current Outlook

Share earnings for 1993 are estimated at $2.35, up from 1992's $2.11. Earnings in 1994 are projected at $2.40 a share.

Dividends should be maintained at $0.47½ quarterly.

Higher earnings for 1993 should reflect customer growth at the utility operations, the expansion of consulting services through acquisition, and a favorable rate ruling likely to be ordered later in the year. WPL's generating stations already meet the 1990 Clean Air Act Amendment's emissions standards and the company became the first utility in the U.S. to sell emission credits. Subsidiary businesses are well positioned to profit from opportunities arising from utility deregulation and in environmental services. The construction of two 86 mw combustion-turbines to match sales growth should not materially effect earnings quality.

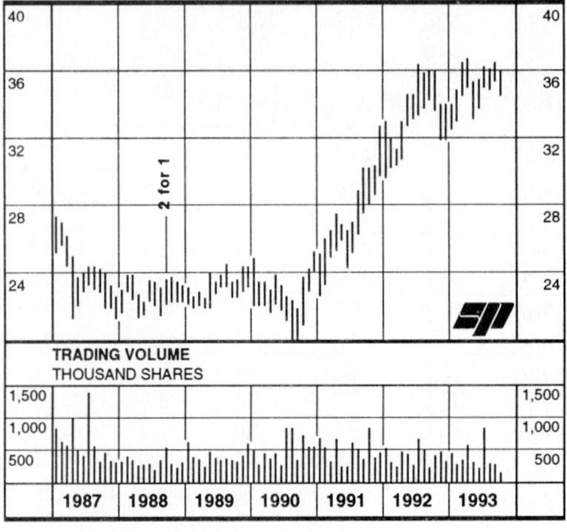

Operating Revenues (Million $)

Quarter:	1994	1993	1992	1991
Mar.	---	204	178	177
Jun.	---	169	140	148
Sep.	---	---	151	152
Dec.	---	---	182	172
	---	---	652	649

Revenues for the six months ended June 30, 1993, rose 16%, year to year, as gas and electric sales increased due to cooler weather. Total operating expenses grew 18% and operating income advanced 5.1%. Following lower other income and greater interest expense, pretax net rose 3.3%. After taxes at 24.7%, against 25.3%, net income was up 4.4%. Per share income was $0.94, on 5.9% more shares, versus $0.95.

Common Share Earnings ($)

Quarter:	1994	1993	1992	1991
Mar.	E0.70	0.71	0.69	0.71
Jun.	E0.30	0.24	0.26	0.39
Sep.	E0.65	E0.70	0.45	0.67
Dec.	E0.75	E0.70	0.71	0.67
	E2.40	E2.35	2.11	2.43

Important Developments

Jul. '93— WPL requested a freeze of electric, natural gas and water rates until January 1, 1997 contingent upon the favorble resolution of the rate case presently before the Public Service Commission of Wisconsin (PSCW). In January 1993, WPL filed a rate request to increase residential electric rates by 6.4% and residential gas rates by 2.9%. WPL expects a decision in August 1993.

Apr. '93— WPL acquired A&C Enercom Consultants, Inc. (A&C) and transferred ownership to its recently incorporated Heartland Development Corp. subsidiary. Heartland will broker natural gas and electricity as a commodity. A&C provides demand side management and energy efficiency services, as well as customer service, marketing information systems, advertising and promotion, training and market research. A&C's gross revenues in 1992 were about $35 million.

Next earnings report expected in late October.

Per Share Data ($)

Yr. End Dec. 31	1992	1991	1990	1989	1988	1987	1986	1985	1984	1983
Tangible Bk. Val.	**17.55**	17.02	16.31	15.85	15.59	14.98	14.44	13.76	12.99	12.17
Earnings	**2.11**	2.43	2.23	1.93	2.18	2.08	2.14	2.13	2.06	1.99
Dividends	**1.86**	1.80	1.74	1.68	1.62	1.54	1.45	1.35	1.26	1.18
Payout Ratio	**88%**	74%	78%	87%	74%	74%	68%	63%	61%	59%
Prices—High	**36⅜**	32¾	25¼	24½	23⅞	27⅜	30⅛	20¼	16	14⅝
Low	**29⅝**	22⅝	20	21⅞	21⅜	21¼	19½	14⅝	12⅞	11½
P/E Ratio—	**17–14**	13–9	11–9	13–11	11–10	13–10	14–9	10–7	8–6	7–6

Data as orig. reptd. Adj. for stk. div. of 100% Sep. 1988. E-Estimated

Income Data (Million $)

Year Ended Dec. 31	Revs.	Depr.	Maint.	Oper. Ratio	[1]Fxd. Chgs. Cover.	Constr. Credits	Eff. Tax Rate	Net Inc.	% Return On— Revs.	[2]Invest. Capital	Com. Equity
1992	**652**	**59.5**	**45.1**	**85.6%**	**2.92**	**3.7**	**28.4%**	**57.0**	**8.7**	**8.6**	**12.1**
1991	649	53.0	42.9	84.7%	3.51	2.0	32.9%	64.9	10.0	9.6	14.5
1990	618	55.3	41.7	84.2%	3.45	1.3	32.4%	59.5	9.6	9.1	13.8
1989	605	54.6	40.6	85.2%	3.67	1.8	34.3%	51.5	8.5	9.4	12.2
1988	601	52.3	39.8	85.1%	3.69	1.6	35.0%	57.9	9.6	10.7	14.2
1987	549	58.7	36.3	84.0%	3.50	1.0	38.3%	55.0	10.0	10.5	14.1
1986	569	58.6	34.8	84.4%	3.59	1.3	43.5%	60.5	10.6	11.0	15.1
1985	589	63.5	33.7	86.3%	4.68	5.8	44.7%	60.7	10.3	10.2	15.9
1984	575	54.1	30.8	86.8%	4.12	13.8	44.4%	58.3	10.1	11.0	16.3
1983	556	48.0	29.9	86.5%	4.14	7.3	47.9%	54.6	9.8	11.0	16.8

Balance Sheet Data (Million $)

Dec. 31	[3]Gross Prop.	Capital Expend.	Net Prop.	% Earn. on Net Prop.	Total Cap.	Capitalization— LT Debt	% LT Debt	Pfd.	% Pfd.	Com.	% Com.
1992	**1,853**	**125**	**1,133**	**8.5**	**1,184**	**418**	**43.5**	**60.0**	**6.3**	**481**	**50.2**
1991	1,747	93	1,072	9.4	1,098	367	41.5	60.0	6.8	458	51.7
1990	1,682	74	1,041	9.4	1,076	360	42.0	60.0	7.0	437	51.0
1989	1,622	97	882	10.3	857	321	39.9	60.0	7.4	424	52.7
1988	1,549	103	853	10.7	855	323	40.4	60.0	7.5	417	52.1
1987	1,465	80	821	10.8	838	398	51.0	60.0	7.7	323	41.3
1986	1,404	85	809	11.1	837	333	42.9	60.0	7.7	384	49.4
1985	1,336	88	791	10.3	822	333	43.9	60.0	7.9	366	48.2
1984	1,269	106	776	10.1	773	299	42.1	66.7	9.4	345	48.5
1983	1,178	100	733	10.5	721	287	43.0	68.2	10.2	312	46.8

Data as orig. reptd. **1.** Times int. exp. & pfd. divs. covered (pretax basis). **2.** Based on income before interest charges. **3.** Utility plant.

Business Summary

WPL Holdings is the holding company for Wisconsin Power and Light, which supplies electric, gas and water service to some 378,600 customers in a 16,000-square-mile service area in south-central Wisconsin. Electric sales accounted for 80% of operating revenues in 1992, gas sales for 19%, and nonutility operations and water for the remainder. Contributions to electric revenues by class of customer in recent years:

	1992	1991	1990	1989
Residential/rural	36%	37%	36%	36%
Industrial	27%	25%	27%	27%
Commercial	19%	19%	19%	19%
Wholesale	14%	14%	14%	14%
Other	4%	5%	4%	4%

At year-end 1992, WPL served 354,705 electric customers, up 2.0% from 347,908 a year before. In 1992, 80% of electricity was coal generated, 17% nuclear, and 3% was hydro and other.

The company provided retail natural gas service to 131,669 customers at December 31, 1992, up 2.8% from 128,027 at the end of 1991.

Heartland Development Corp. manages nonutility operations engaged in real estate development, and environmental, energy, and utility consulting.

Finances

On April 20, 1993, the company sold through underwriters 1.65 million common shares at $35.50 a share, generating $56.9 million. The company anticipated using $45 million of the net proceeds to repay Wisconsin Power and Light debt and to finance construction. Remaining proceeds would be used for general corporate purposes.

Dividend Data

Dividends have been paid since 1946. A dividend reinvestment plan is available. A "poison pill" stock purchase rights plan was adopted in 1989.

Amt of Divd. $	Date Decl.	Ex–divd. Date	Stock of Record	Payment Date
0.47½	Jan. 13	Jan. 25	Jan. 29	Feb. 13'93
0.47½	Apr. 14	Apr. 26	Apr. 30	May 15'93
0.47½	Jul. 14	Jul. 26	Jul. 30	Aug. 14'93
0.47½	Oct. 13	Oct. 25	Oct. 29	Nov. 15'93

Capitalization

Long Term Debt: $422,798,000 (6/93).

Subsid. Cum. Preferred Stock: $59,963,000.

Common Stock: 29,753,052 shs. ($0.01 par).
Institutions hold about 14%.
Shareholders of record: 37,600 (3/93).

Office—222 West Washington Ave., Madison, WI 53703. **Tel**—(608) 252-4888. **Pres & CEO**—E. B. Davis Jr. **Treas & Secy**—J. G. Fabie. **Investor Contact**—Susan J. Kosmo. **Dirs**—E. B. Davis Jr., R. G. Flowers, A. M. Nemirow, M. E. Neshek, H. C. Prange, J. D. Pyle, J. R. Underkofler. **Transfer Agent & Registrar**—WPL Holdings, Inc. **Incorporated** in Wisconsin in 1917. **Empl**—2,673.

 Ned Bancroft

Waban Inc.

NYSE Symbol WBN Options on CBOE (Mar-Jun-Sep-Dec) In S&P MidCap 400

Price	Range	P-E Ratio	Dividend	Yield	S&P Ranking	Beta
Sep. 21'93	1993					
14⅛	18⅜–11¾	11	None	None	NR	NA

Summary

This company is a major participant in the rapidly growing field of warehouse merchandising through its HomeBase and BJ's Wholesale Club businesses. HomeBase operates 87 units offering home improvement products, while BJ's is a 46-unit chain of self-service, food and general merchandise membership warehouse clubs. Earnings should remain about level in fiscal 1993-94, reflecting increased competition and continued weakness in the California economy.

Current Outlook

Earnings for the fiscal year ending January 31, 1994, are expected to increase only slightly, to about $1.35 a share from the $1.33 of 1992-93. Earnings could rise to $1.60 in fiscal 1994-95.

Early initiation of dividends is not in prospect.

Sales for fiscal 1993-94 should increase moderately, mainly reflecting gains at new outlets partially offset by weakness in comparable units. Operating income at HomeBase should improve, but gains will be tempered by the weak California economy. BJ's operating income gains will come from a larger store base, and over the longer term will benefit from less competition as the industry consolidates.

Net Sales (Million $)

13 Weeks:	1993-94	1992-93	1991-92	1990-91
Apr.	834	736	617	546
Jul.	967	864	736	623
Oct.	---	821	694	606
Jan.	---	938	737	635
	---	3,358	2,784	2,410

Sales for the 26 weeks ended July 31, 1993, rose 13%, year to year, reflecting a 15% gain at BJ's and an 11% increase at HomeBase. Gross margins narrowed slightly but SG&A expenses declined as a percentage of sales. Operating income advanced 12%. Following a more than 4-fold increase in net interest expense, pretax income fell 3.9% After taxes at 39.0%, versus 38.7%, net income declined 4.4%, to $0.54 a share (before a $0.03 credit from an accounting change) from $0.57.

Common Share Earnings ($)

13 Weeks:	1993-94	1992-93	1991-92	1990-91
Apr.	0.13	0.19	0.15	0.05
Jul.	0.41	0.38	0.33	0.24
Oct.	E0.38	0.35	0.19	0.24
Jan.	E0.43	0.42	0.33	0.12
	E1.35	1.33	1.01	0.64

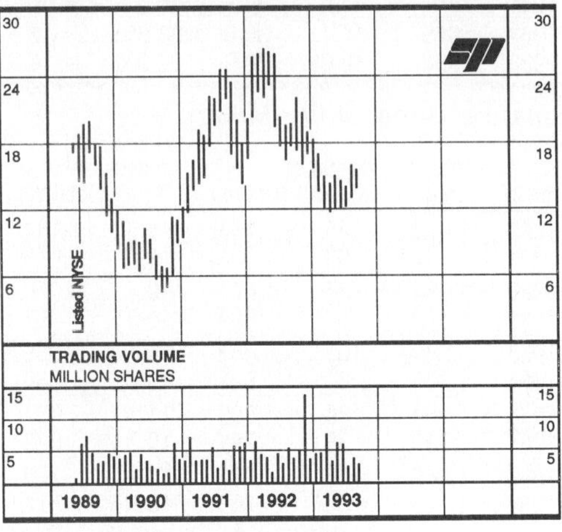

Important Developments

Aug. '93— Waban said that sales in the second quarter of fiscal 1993-94 continued at the disappointing levels seen in the first quarter, but that the steps taken to control expenses, manage inventories and operate more efficiently improved profitability at both HomeBase and BJ's. Sales at HomeBase increased 6%, year to year, in the second quarter and 11% year-to-date; operating income rose 12% and 10%, respectively. Sales were up 19% at BJ's during the quarter and 15% in the first half, while operating income rose 40% and 18%, respectively. In July, management said that same store sales declines at BJ's reflected deflation, increased competition from other clubs, new units built in close proximity to older ones, and the weak Northeast economy. Fifteen new BJ's were slated to open in fiscal 1993-94 and six HomeBase units.

Next earnings report expected in mid-November.

Per Share Data ($)

Yr. End Jan. 31	1993	1992	1991	1990	1989
Tangible Bk. Val.	**13.23**	11.87	9.94	9.29	8.70
Cash Flow	**2.23**	1.75	1.28	1.54	1.15
Earnings	**1.33**	1.01	0.64	1.01	0.80
Dividends	**Nil**	Nil	Nil	Nil	NA
Payout Ratio	**Nil**	Nil	Nil	Nil	NA
Calendar Years	**1992**	1991	1990	1989	1988
Prices—High	**26½**	24⅝	12	20	NA
Low	**16⅛**	9½	4⅝	10	NA
P/E Ratio—	**20–12**	24–9	19–7	20–10	NA

Data as orig. reptd. Prior to 1990 pro forma data as reptd. in information statement dated May 12, 1989. E-Estimated NA-Not Available.

Income Data (Million $)

Year Ended Jan. 31	Revs.	Oper. Inc.	% Oper. Inc. of Revs.	Cap. Exp.	Depr.	Int. Exp.	Net Bef. Taxes	Eff. Tax Rate	Net Inc.	% Net Inc. of Revs.	Cash Flow
1993	**3,358**	**104.0**	**3.1**	**165.0**	**29.8**	**13.5**	**68.3**	**35.2%**	**44.2**	**1.3**	**74.1**
1992	2,784	83.2	2.7	68.6	22.1	[1]7.7	48.9	38.7%	30.0	1.1	52.1
1991	2,410	64.1	2.7	35.8	18.1	[1]5.8	30.7	40.0%	18.4	0.8	36.5
1990	2,057	66.6	3.2	41.8	15.0	[1]4.0	48.5	40.7%	28.8	1.4	43.7
1989	1,652	50.8	3.1	NA	9.7	[1]3.6	37.5	40.2%	22.4	1.4	27.7

Balance Sheet Data (Million $)

Jan. 31	Cash	Curr. Assets	Curr. Liab.	Curr. Ratio	Total Assets	% Ret. on Assets	Long Term Debt	Common Equity	Total Cap.	% LT Debt of Cap.	% Ret. on Equity
1993	**53**	**638**	**352**	**1.8**	**1,007**	**4.9**	**193**	**437**	**639**	**30.2**	**10.7**
1992	116	556	288	1.9	786	4.1	87	389	485	17.9	8.4
1991	13	400	246	1.6	580	3.3	29	284	323	9.0	6.7
1990	15	362	224	1.6	537	5.8	31	265	305	10.3	18.4
1989	30	306	175	1.7	456	NA	31	245	281	10.9	NA

Data as orig. reptd. Prior to 1990 pro forma data as reptd. in Information Statement dated May 12, 1989. **1.** Net. NA-Not Available.

Business Summary

Waban Inc. consists of HomeBase (formerly HomeClub), one of the leading U.S. merchandisers of home improvement products at everyday low prices, and BJ's Wholesale Club, a chain of membership warehouse clubs. The company was spun off to shareholders of Zayre Corp. (now TJX Companies) in June 1989 as part of a corporate restructuring.

HomeBase sells home improvement products in warehouse outlets targeted to the contractor and the do-it-yourselfer. In recent years, HomeBase has expanded its strategic and marketing focus to more effectively target the DIY market. HomeBase launched a number of customer service programs and promotional campaigns designed to enhance its appeal to casual do-it-yourselfers. In the spring of 1991, HomeBase discontinued its membership program, under which members paid annual fees and non-members paid a 5% surcharge on all purchases. In the spring of 1992, HomeBase changed its name from HomeClub to eliminate any remaining perception that it maintained a membership prigram. As of January 30, 1993, HomeBase operated 86 units in 13 states in the West and Southwest, including 49 in California. The average size is about 102,000 sq. ft.

BJ's is a membership warehouse club for food and general merchandise. Shopping is limited to members only. Its membership base consists primarily of small businesses and individual members. BJ's membership fees are generally $25 per annum for business and individual members; supplemental business memberships are available for $10 a year. BJ's membership strategy is designed to attract a clientele who find it advantageous to purchase large volumes of merchandise at attractive prices. Merchandise assortments include selected frozen foods, meats, dairy products, dry groceries and canned products, as well as office equipment and supplies, hardware, electronics, appliances, auto accessories and tires and some apparel. BJ's offers fresh meat and bakery departments and food courts in nearly all of its clubs. The average size of BJ's 39 warehouse clubs is about 108,000 sq. ft. The clubs are located mostly in Massachusetts, New York and other eastern Seaboard states.

Waban's business is subject to seasonal influences, with HomeBase experiencing higher sales levels during the spring building season and BJ's experiencing its heaviest sales volume during the Christmas season.

Dividend Data

No dividends have yet been paid. A "poison pill" stock purchase right was adopted in 1989.

Finances

In July 1992, the company completed a public offering of $108.6 million of 6.5% subordinated debentures due 2002, convertible into common stock at $24.75 a share.

Zayre Corp. (now TJX Companies) on June 14, 1989, spun off to its shareholders of record June 1 its HomeClub and BJ's Wholesale Club as part of a major restructuring. Zayre Corp. shareholders received one Waban share for every two shares of Zayre Corp. held.

Capitalization

Long Term Debt: $178,260,000 (7/93), incl. some $108.6 million of 6.5% debs. due 2002, conv. into com. at $24.75 a sh.

Common Stock: 33,032,550 shs. ($0.01 par).
Institutions hold approximately 79%.
Shareholders of record: 5,000.

Office—One Mercer Rd., P. O. Box 9600, Natick, MA 01760. **Tel**—(508) 651-6500. **Chrmn**—S. L. Feldberg. **Pres & CEO**—H. J. Zarkin. **CFO**—D. N. Garth. **VP-Treas**—G. Freeman. **Secy**—Sarah M. Gallivan. **Investor Contact**—Jane W. McCahon. **Dirs**—S. H. Feldberg, S. L. Feldberg, J. M. Henson, J. F. Levy, A. F. Loewy, W. J. Salmon, T. J. Shields, L. R. Waxlax, H. J. Zarkin. **Transfer Agent & Registrar**—First Chicago Trust Co. of New York, NYC. **Incorporated** in California in 1983; reincorporated in Delaware in 1985. **Empl**—17,200.

 Karen J. Sack

Wallace Computer Services

NYSE Symbol WCS Options on Phila (Mar-Jun-Sep-Dec) In S&P MidCap 400

Price	Range	P-E Ratio	Dividend	Yield	S&P Ranking	Beta
Sep. 14'93	1993					
24⅝	29½–22⅞	13	0.58	2.4%	A	0.99

Summary

This leading manufacturer of business forms—primarily continuous forms for computer applications—also engages in commercial printing and direct marketing of small business computers and computer and office supplies. Following earnings gains in fiscal 1993, earnings are expected to continue to advance in fiscal 1994, aided by anticipated sales gains and cost controls.

Current Outlook

Earnings for the fiscal year ending July 31, 1994, are projected at about $2.05 a share (excluding a one time charge for the cumulative effect of an accounting change related to post-retirement benefits), up from $1.84 in fiscal 1993.

Some increase in the quarterly dividend rate of $0.14½ is likely during fiscal 1994.

Net sales are likely to improve in fiscal 1994, as contributions by the company's new added-value services continue and Colorforms and TOPS sales return to normal. Profitability should benefit from the increased sales, implementation of strict cost controls (designed to manage operating expenses in line with sales), efficiencies from the integration/reorganization of manufacturing and sales at the Colorforms division. A limiting factor may be continuing price competition at TOPS. Initiation of ongoing expenses for post-retirement benefits will probably not have a material impact. Long-term strategy includes opening additional sales offices to increase market share (particularly in secondary markets), spending on projects designed to improve efficiency, and increased use of high technology to provide better products.

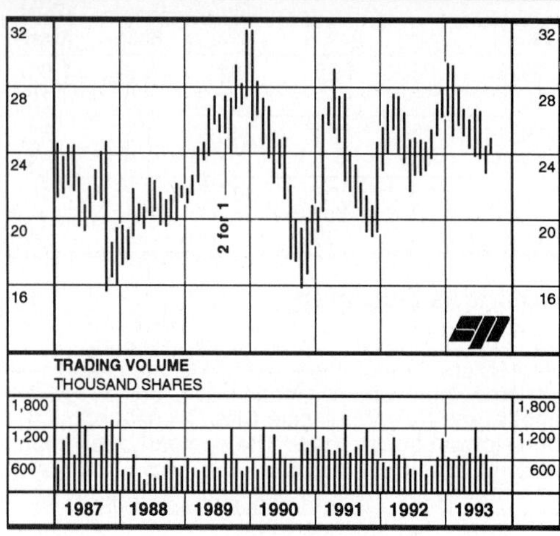

Net Sales (Million $)

Quarter:	1992–93	1991–92	1990–91	1989–90
Oct.	133.9	125.4	112.1	110.2
Jan.	138.1	132.2	122.2	117.9
Apr.	131.8	120.2	110.3	108.4
Jul.	141.6	133.8	114.3	112.1
	545.3	511.6	458.8	448.7

Based on a preliminary report, sales in the fiscal year ended July 31, 1993, advanced 6.6%, from those of the prior year. Despite disappointing Tops and Colorform results, operating income rose 11%, but after sharply lower interest income, pretax income climbed 4.3%. After taxes at 34.0% in both periods, net income also increased 4.3%, to $1.84 a share, from $1.76.

Common Share Earnings ($)

Quarter:	1992–93	1991–92	1990–91	1989–90
Oct.	0.44	0.41	0.43	0.43
Jan.	0.52	0.49	0.46	0.48
Apr.	0.43	0.43	0.40	0.45
Jul.	0.45	0.43	0.34	0.50
	1.84	1.76	1.63	1.86

Important Developments

Sep. '93— The company reported improved earnings for fiscal 1993 despite sharply higher employee healthcare costs and supplier paper prices, and lower investment income.

Jun. '93— WCS said it had repurchased 631,300 of its shares through April 30 at an average of $25.98 each, under a 1,000,000 share repurchase program. Subsequent to April 30 an additional 252,250 shares were acquired at an average price of $25.78.

Next earnings report expected in November.

Per Share Data ($)

Yr. End Jul. 31	1993	1992	1991	1990	[1]1989	1988	[1]1987	1986	1985	1984
Tangible Bk. Val.	**NA**	15.00	14.15	12.97	11.46	10.03	8.76	7.69	6.68	5.68
Cash Flow	**NA**	3.03	2.67	2.65	2.49	2.17	1.80	1.63	1.46	1.27
Earnings	**1.84**	1.76	1.63	1.86	1.76	1.53	1.27	1.20	1.10	0.95
Dividends	**0.570**	0.530	0.490	0.445	0.383	0.323	0.288	0.244	0.219	0.195
Payout Ratio	**31%**	30%	30%	24%	22%	21%	23%	20%	20%	21%
Prices[2]—High	**29½**	28	29⅛	31½	31½	22½	24¾	25⅛	20⅜	16⅛
Low	**22⅞**	21¾	19	15⅞	21	17¼	15¾	18½	15⅛	11⅞
P/E Ratio—	**16–12**	16–12	18–12	17–9	18–12	14–11	19–12	21–15	18–14	17–13

Data as orig. reptd. Adj. for stk. divs. of 100% Aug. 1989, 100% May 1983. **1.** Reflects merger or acquisition. **2.** Cal. yr. NA-Not Available.

Income Data (Million $)

Year Ended Jul. 31	Revs.	Oper. Inc.	% Oper. Inc. of Revs.	Cap. Exp.	Depr.	Int. Exp.	Net Bef. Taxes	Eff. Tax Rate	Net Inc.	% Net Inc. of Revs.	Cash Flow
1992	**512**	**83.4**	**16.3**	**33.5**	**28.6**	**2.62**	**59.8**	**34.0%**	**39.5**	**7.7**	**68.0**
1991	459	71.6	15.6	40.5	22.5	1.84	53.9	35.0%	35.0	7.6	57.5
1990	449	70.7	15.8	49.8	18.4	1.79	60.9	35.0%	39.6	8.8	56.3
[1]1989	429	68.8	16.0	30.7	15.4	1.74	56.5	34.8%	36.9	8.6	52.3
1988	383	60.8	15.9	24.9	13.4	1.19	48.6	35.0%	31.6	8.3	45.0
[1]1987	341	57.6	16.9	30.0	10.8	0.59	48.2	46.0%	26.0	7.6	36.8
1986	305	52.3	17.1	27.5	8.7	0.61	45.1	46.0%	24.4	8.0	33.1
1985	275	47.0	17.1	24.9	7.2	0.65	41.6	47.0%	22.0	8.0	29.2
1984	243	40.1	16.5	14.9	6.3	0.64	35.2	47.0%	18.6	7.7	24.9
[1]1983	210	34.9	16.6	12.6	5.6	0.68	30.7	48.0%	16.0	7.6	21.6

Balance Sheet Data (Million $)

Jul. 31	Cash	Curr. Assets	Curr. Liab.	Curr. Ratio	Total Assets	% Ret. on Assets	Long Term Debt	Common Equity	Total Cap.	% LT Debt of Cap.	% Ret. on Equity
1992	**55.1**	**205**	**53.0**	**3.9**	**467**	**8.9**	**26.0**	**356**	**405**	**6.4**	**11.7**
1991	52.3	184	42.9	4.3	399	9.0	19.8	309	349	5.7	11.8
1990	54.4	187	49.0	3.8	375	11.1	20.2	279	320	6.3	15.0
1989	60.9	179	40.9	4.4	332	11.8	20.5	244	286	7.2	16.1
1988	39.4	154	36.7	4.2	292	11.4	20.8	211	252	8.3	16.0
1987	24.4	135	34.4	3.9	260	10.7	21.2	182	223	9.5	15.2
1986	30.8	127	36.6	3.5	225	11.5	14.5	158	189	7.7	16.5
1985	31.8	113	32.0	3.5	195	12.4	14.8	136	163	9.1	17.5
1984	21.7	96	26.1	3.7	157	12.6	7.1	115	131	5.4	17.4
1983	23.9	83	24.4	3.4	136	12.2	7.4	97	112	6.6	17.3

Data as orig. reptd. **1.** Reflects merger or acquisition.

Business Summary

Wallace Computer Services manufactures and supplies business forms, industrial and consumer catalogs, directories and price lists, pressure sensitive labels, computer and business machine ribbons, a standard line of office products forms, and direct mail promotional printing. In addition, it markets computer accessories supplies, office supplies, and computer hardware and software. Sales breakdown by product category:

	1992	1991	1990
Printed products	89%	90%	88%
Other........................	11%	10%	12%

The Business Forms division produces customized and standard forms primarily for use on computers. Major products include custom continuous forms, unit set forms, and mailer forms. The division also markets Barcode Asset Management, a hardware/software system for inventory and asset control.

The TOPS Business Forms division is a leading manufacturer of office forms and systems, offering over 1,000 products that are manufactured and distributed from four U.S. locations.

The Label division has four units: Datamark, a manufacturer of computer generated pressure sensitive labels; Continental Ribbon & Carbon, which makes computer ribbons; Business Data, a supplier of computer hardware and proprietary software; and Apollo Labeling Systems, a producer of prime pressure sensitive labels.

Visible Computer Supply Corp. sells computer supplies and office products via catalogs mailed directly to users. The catalogs carry more than 8,000 items that are available to order by telephone, fax or mail.

The Wallace Press division produces a wide variety of catalogs, price guides and directories using computerized typesetting and page makeup.

The Colorforms division (acquired August 1991) provides printing, personalization and mailing services to the direct mail advertising industry.

Dividend Data

Dividends have been paid since 1933. A "poison pill" stock purchase rights plan was adopted in 1990.

Amt of Divd. $	Date Decl.	Ex-divd. Date	Stock of Record	Payment Date
0.14½	Nov. 11	Nov. 24	Dec. 1	Dec. 21'92
0.14½	Jan. 20	Feb. 23	Mar. 1	Mar. 22'93
0.14½	Mar. 11	May 26	Jun. 1	Jun. 21'93
0.14½	Jun. 16	Aug. 26	Sep. 1	Sep. 20'93

Capitalization

Long Term Debt: $25,210,000 (7/93).

Common Stock: 22,258,127 shs. ($1 par). Institutions hold approximately 77%. Shareholders of record: 4,435.

Office—4600 West Roosevelt Rd., Hillside, IL 60162-2079. **Tel**—(312) 626-2000. **Chrmn**—T. Dimitriou. **Pres & CEO**—R. J. Cronin. **VP-CFO, Secy & Investor Contact**—Michael J. Halloran (708) 449-8600. **Treas**—L. J. Hauskey. **Dirs**—F. F. Canning, R. J. Cronin, T. Dimitriou, R. F. Doyle, R. D. Ewers, W. N. Lane III, W. E. Olsen, N. E. Stearns Jr. **Transfer Agent & Registrar**—State Street Bank & Trust, Boston. **Incorporated** in Illinois in 1908; reincorporated in Delaware in 1963. **Empl**—3,386.

 M. Graham Hackett

Washington Gas Light

NYSE Symbol WGL In S&P MidCap 400

Price	Range	P-E Ratio	Dividend	Yield	S&P Ranking	Beta
Aug. 5'93	1993					
43¾	45¾–37	16	2.18	5.0%	A	0.28

Summary

This natural gas distributor serves Washington, D.C., and areas of Maryland and Virginia. To a much lesser extent, it is also engaged in gas exploration and production and the manufacture of conservation products. Long-term prospects are enhanced by an improving residential market share and expected growth in gas sales volumes to the fleet vehicle market. In July 1993, WGL was granted a $10.6 million base rate hike in Maryland; a $24.5 million rate hike application in the District of Columbia was pending.

Current Outlook

Share earnings for the fiscal year ending September 30, 1993, are projected at $2.85, up from an estimated $2.75 for fiscal 1993.

The $0.54½ quarterly dividend is expected to be raised at the March 1994 meeting.

Utility profits for fiscal 1994 should advance slightly, reflecting expected approval by September 1993 of a portion of the $24.5 million rate increase in the District of Columbia, a $10.6 million rate hike in Maryland, and customer growth of about 2.5%, a rate above the industry average. Assuming weather conditions in fiscal 1994 return to normal (weather was 8.5% colder than normal in the first nine months of fiscal 1993) gas sales volumes to residential customers may decline marginally as a decline in gas usage per customer should exceed benefits from the customer growth. Gas deliveries for nonspaceheating purposes should increase; gas sales to the natural gas vehicle market will grow but remain at an insignificant level in fiscal 1994. Large volume industrial customers are expected to be retained, but margins on service to those customers are likely to remain small.

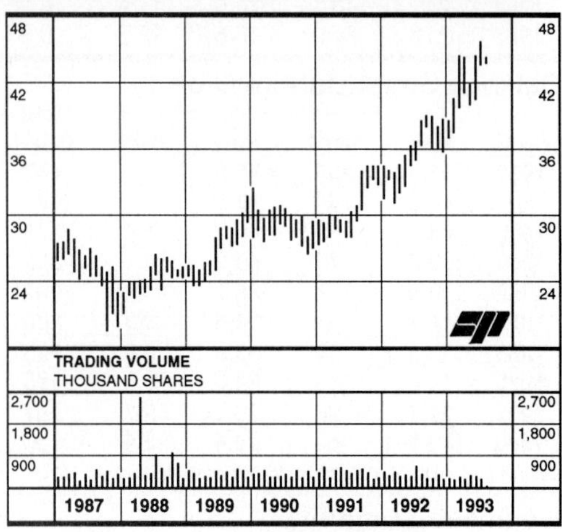

Oper. Revenues (Million $)

Quarter:	1992–93	1991–92	1990–91	1989–90
Dec.	273.1	230.5	223.1	274.9
Mar.	383.8	305.0	287.5	249.0
Jun.	139.8	115.1	99.7	111.7
Sep.	---	95.6	87.6	100.0
	---	746.2	697.9	735.5

Revenues for the nine months ended June 30, 1993, rose 22%, year to year, reflecting increased gas sales volumes from 7.9% colder weather, and customer growth of 2.7%. Cost of gas increased 40%, but other operating expenses were up only 5.7%, and net income advanced 8.1%, to $3.43 a share from $3.23.

Common Share Earnings ($)

Quarter:	1992–93	1991–92	1990–91	1989–90
Dec.	1.36	1.24	1.22	1.64
Mar.	2.39	2.14	2.14	1.59
Jun.	d0.31	d0.15	d0.29	d0.25
Sep.	Ed0.69	d0.69	d0.59	d0.46
	E2.75	2.53	2.28	2.51

Important Developments

Jul. '93— The Public Service Commission of Maryland granted WGL a $10.6 million increase in base rate revenues and about $1.0 million in additional revenues resulting from the modification to, or the addition of, certain service related charges; the new rates would be effective August 1, 1993. WGL expected District of Columbia regulators to decide on its $24.5 million, or 13.2%, rate hike application by September 1993.

Next earnings report expected in late October.

Per Share Data ($)

Yr. End Sep. 30[1]	1992	1991	1990	1989	1988	1987	1986	1985	1984	1983
Tangible Bk. Val.	**21.28**	20.61	20.25	19.62	19.83	18.73	18.21	17.89	16.99	16.10
Earnings	**2.53**	2.28	2.51	2.43	2.52	2.27	2.29	2.46	2.45	2.14
Dividends	**2.120**	2.070	2.000	1.920	1.860	1.790	1.735	1.635	1.518	1.425
Payout Ratio	**84%**	91%	80%	79%	74%	79%	76%	66%	62%	67%
Prices[2]—High	**39⅛**	34½	32½	31¾	26½	28¾	30⅝	23½	18½	15⅞
Low	**31⅛**	27⅜	26½	23⅝	21⅛	19½	20⅛	17¼	14¾	12½
P/E Ratio—	**15–12**	15–12	13–11	13–10	11–8	13–9	13–9	10–7	8–6	7–6

Data as orig. reptd. Adj. for stk. div(s). of 100% Nov. 1984. **1.** Yrs. ended Dec. 31 prior to 1989. **2.** Cal. yr. d-Deficit. E-Estimated.

Income Data (Million $)

Year Ended Sep. 30[1]	Revs.	Depr.	Maint.	Oper. Ratio	[2]Fxd. Chgs. Cover.	Constr. Credits	Eff. Tax Rate	Net Inc.	% Return On Revs.	% Return On [3]Invest. Capital	% Return On Com. Equity
1992	**746**	**37.2**	**31.4**	**89.0%**	**3.81**	**0.16**	**37.1%**	**52.2**	**7.0**	**9.8**	**12.0**
1991	698	36.1	30.9	89.9%	3.51	0.50	36.8%	46.4	6.6	9.5	11.1
1990	736	36.1	32.3	89.7%	3.63	0.46	36.6%	50.2	6.8	10.1	12.5
1989	756	32.8	31.4	90.9%	3.74	0.40	36.8%	47.3	6.3	9.9	13.0
1988	698	29.4	30.0	90.6%	3.86	0.50	37.0%	43.7	6.3	9.8	12.5
1987	684	30.8	30.1	91.4%	4.05	0.39	42.5%	39.4	5.8	9.4	12.2
1986	722	27.9	28.6	92.2%	4.37	0.26	45.2%	39.3	5.4	9.4	12.8
1985	764	23.8	27.4	92.3%	4.12	NA	42.6%	41.8	5.5	9.8	14.0
1984	801	23.3	27.0	92.7%	3.92	NA	43.8%	40.8	5.1	10.0	14.6
1983	816	27.0	24.9	93.3%	2.95	NA	45.9%	30.6	3.7	9.7	12.3

Balance Sheet Data (Million $)

Sep. 30[1]	Gross Prop.	Capital Expend.	Net Prop.	% Earn. on Net Prop.	Total Cap.	Capitalization LT Debt	% LT Debt	Pfd.	% Pfd.	Com.	% Com.
1992	**1,313**	**88**	**865**	**9.8**	**852**	**294**	**38.9**	**28.6**	**3.8**	**433**	**57.3**
1991	1,240	82	821	8.8	783	263	37.4	28.6	4.1	412	58.5
1990	1,186	94	783	10.0	776	280	39.6	28.6	4.0	399	56.4
1989	1,109	116	729	10.0	779	297	42.0	28.6	4.1	381	54.0
1988	1,038	107	676	10.3	734	253	38.1	28.7	4.3	382	57.6
1987	954	79	600	10.2	645	227	39.5	28.7	5.0	319	55.5
1986	882	59	554	10.5	622	222	40.0	28.8	5.2	305	54.8
1985	831	51	535	11.2	640	251	43.7	28.9	5.0	295	51.3
1984	791	41	510	11.7	630	264	46.0	33.9	5.9	276	48.1
1983	761	33	495	11.1	616	275	48.6	34.7	6.1	256	45.3

Data as orig. reptd. **1.** Years ended Dec. 31 prior to 1989. **2.** Times int. exp. & pfd. divs. covered (pretax basis). **3.** Based on income before interest charges. NA-Not Available.

Business Summary

Washington Gas Light distributes natural gas in suburban Maryland, northern Virginia, and the District of Columbia. Through its Shenandoah Gas Co. and Frederick Gas Co. units, the company provides gas service in the Shenandoah Valley region of Virginia and West Virginia and in Frederick County, Md. Crab Run Gas Co. is engaged in exploration activities and Hampshire Gas Co. operates an underground gas storage field. WGL's wholly owned subsidiary, Washington Resources Group, Inc. holds and manages non-gas investments (except for Crab Run), including supplying and installation of energy conservation products, and real estate and venture capital investments. Gas volumes delivered contributions in recent years:

	1992	1991
Residential	45%	42%
Commercial & industrial:		
Firm	30%	29%
Interruptible & elec. gen.	24%	28%
Transportation	1%	1%

Gas sales in fiscal 1992 amounted to 1,339.5 million therms, compared with 1,249.4 million therms a year earlier. Gas transportation volumes in fiscal 1992 totaled 13.3 million therms, down from 13.9 million in fiscal 1991. Of the total 1,352.8 million therms delivered in fiscal 1992 44% were delivered to customers in Maryland, 30% to Virginia, 24% to the District of Columbia, and 2% to West Virginia. During fiscal 1992, customers served (as measured by the number of customers' meters) totaled 683,277, versus 667,114 in fiscal 1991. Degree days in fiscal 1992 amounted to 3,946 (1.8% colder than normal) versus 3,370 in fiscal 1991.

Dividend Data

Dividends have been paid since 1852. A dividend reinvestment plan is available.

Amt of Divd. $	Date Decl.	Ex-divd. Date	Stock of Record	Payment Date
0.53½	Sep. 30	Oct. 5	Oct. 12	Nov. 1'92
0.53½	Dec. 10	Jan. 5	Jan. 11	Feb. 1'93
0.54½	Mar. 31	Apr. 5	Apr. 12	May 1'93
0.54½	Jun. 30	Jul. 6	Jul. 12	Aug. 1'93

Capitalization

Long Term Debt: $342,588,000 (6/93).

Serial Preferred Stock: $28,521,000.

Common Stock: 20,669,861 shs. (no par).
Institutions hold about 21%.
Shareholders of record: 21,501.

Office—1100 H St., NW, Washington, DC 20080. **Tel**—(202) 750-4440. **Chrmn & CEO**—P. J. Maher. **Pres**—J. K. Hughitt. **VP-CFO**—E. W. Smallwood. **Secy**—D. V. Pope. **Treas**—E. M. Arnold. **Investor Contact**—Maria Frazzini. **Dirs**—M. Barnes, F. J. Brinkman, D. J. Callahan III, O. W. Darden, M. J. Estrin, S. W. Fantle, J. K. Hughitt, P. J. Maher, K. H. Williams, S. G. Yeonas. **Transfer Agent & Registrar**—Riggs National Bank, Washington, D.C. **Incorporated** in Washington, D.C. in 1848 & in Virginia in 1953. **Empl**—2,724.

 Mark Mattke

Washington Post

NYSE Symbol WPO In S&P MidCap 400

Price	Range	P–E Ratio	Dividend	Yield	S&P Ranking	Beta
Sep. 23'93	1993					
216½	244–212	20	4.20	1.9%	B+	0.75

Summary

This company publishes The Washington Post and Newsweek magazine. It also operates four television stations, has cable TV systems, is involved in education and database services and has significant interests in several newsprint companies. Lingering weakness in advertising is limiting the earnings recovery that began in 1992.

Current Outlook

Earnings for 1993 are projected at $11.80 a share, up 9.3% from the $10.80 reported for 1992. About $13.00 is estimated for 1994.

The $1.05 quarterly dividend is likely to be raised in 1994.

Revenues for 1993 are expected to rise moderately, aided by gains in circulation and subscriber revenues and improved television advertising revenues. Ongoing cost controls and operating efficiencies will boost profitability. The absence of U.K. cable operations will reduce capital spending requirements, but cable margins will be restricted nonetheless by new FCC restrictions on certain subscriber charges. An increase in newsprint pricing should lead to a sharp improvement in equity contributions.

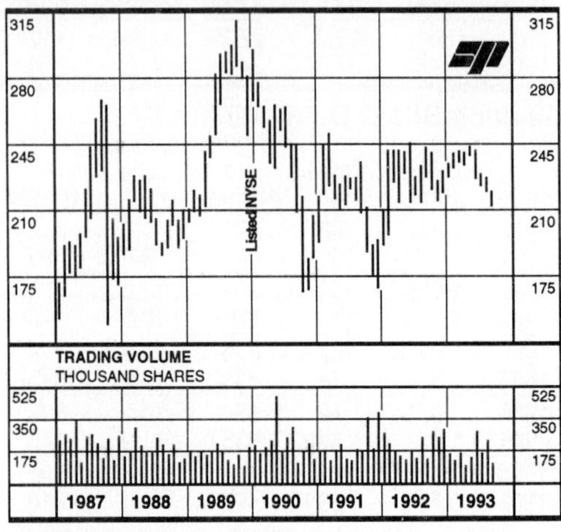

Revenues (Million $)

Quarter:	1993	1992	1991	1990
Mar.	362	329	317	341
Jun.	377	377	357	380
Sep.	---	351	340	349
Dec.	---	394	367	369
	---	1,451	1,380	1,439

Revenues for 1993's first half rose 4.6%, year to year. Operating income declined 4.3%, reflecting a weak local economy and softness in national advertising at Newsweek. With sharply lower equity losses, pretax earnings declined less than 1%. Following taxes at 42.0%, versus 43.0%, income rose 1.6%. Share earnings were $5.65 (before a $0.98 special credit), up from $5.53.

Common Share Earnings ($)

Quarter:	1993	1992	1991	1990
Mar.	2.42	1.66	1.06	3.16
Jun.	3.23	3.87	2.86	4.60
Sep.	E2.65	2.33	2.12	3.14
Dec.	E3.50	2.94	3.96	4.55
	E11.80	10.80	10.00	14.45

Important Developments

Sep. '93— WPO reported that it completed the sale of its cable franchises in the U.K. and would realize an aftertax gain on the transaction of $5 million to $10 million.

Jul. '93— The company said newspaper division revenues gained 4% in the first half, as higher prices more than offset reduced demand for ad space. Daily circulation at The Post was up 1%, year to year, while Sunday circulation declined 1%. Broadcast revenues gained 7%, and magazine revenues fell 3%, but circulation revenues gained 5%. Cable division revenue was up 11%, boosted by an acquisition. Revenues from other businesses climbed 20%, largely reflecting the acquisition of Pro Am Sports System (PASS), a Detroit-area cable sports network. Better results at newsprint operations helped reduce equity losses to $2.4 million, from $6.6 million.

Next earnings report expected in late October.

Per Share Data ($)

Yr. End Dec. 31	1992	1991	[1]1990	1989	1988	1987	1986	1985	1984	[1]1983
Tangible Bk. Val.	**56.58**	51.02	48.16	49.14	40.94	19.90	5.70	19.74	21.68	16.92
Cash Flow	**17.09**	16.23	20.12	20.12	20.40	25.49	18.85	11.65	10.75	7.82
Earnings[2]	**10.80**	10.00	14.45	[3]15.50	[3]20.91	[3]14.52	7.80	[3]8.66	6.11	4.82
Dividends	**4.20**	4.20	4.00	1.84	1.56	1.28	1.12	0.96	0.80	0.66
Payout Ratio	**39%**	42%	27%	12%	7%	9%	14%	11%	13%	14%
Prices—High	**246**	251	295½	311	229	269	184½	130	85	73¼
Low	**191½**	169	167	204	186½	150	115	77¾	60¾	54½
P/E Ratio—	**23–18**	25–17	20–12	20–13	11–9	19–10	24–15	15–9	14–10	15–11

Data as orig. reptd. **1.** Refl. merger or acq. **2.** Bef. spec. item of -4.04 in 1991. **3.** Incl. gains on sale of assets. E-Estimated.

Income Data (Million $)

Year Ended Dec. 31	Revs.	Oper. Inc.	% Oper. Inc. of Revs.	Cap. Exp.	Depr.	[2]Int. Exp.	[3]Net Bef. Taxes	Eff. Tax Rate	[4]Net Inc.	% Net Inc. of Revs.	Cash Flow
1992	**1,451**	**306**	**21.1**	**59**	**74.3**	**6.4**	**224**	**43.0%**	**128**	**8.8**	**202**
1991	1,380	273	19.8	56	74.1	17.8	190	37.6%	[5]119	8.6	193
[1]1990	1,439	350	24.3	72	68.5	16.7	291	40.1%	175	12.1	243
1989	1,444	376	26.0	81	62.5	17.0	334	40.7%	198	13.7	260
1988	1,368	313	22.9	59	59.0	16.9	435	38.2%	269	19.7	328
1987	1,315	313	23.8	84	55.6	26.2	331	43.7%	187	14.2	242
1986	1,215	278	22.9	162	49.4	35.5	205	51.0%	[5]100	8.2	150
1985	1,079	232	21.5	44	27.6	9.7	221	48.4%	114	10.6	142
1984	984	190	19.3	34	24.0	1.8	166	48.3%	86	8.7	110
[1]1983	878	155	17.6	23	22.3	2.7	135	49.2%	68	7.8	91

Balance Sheet Data (Million $)

Dec. 31	Cash	Curr. Assets	Curr. Liab.	Curr. Ratio	Total Assets	% Ret. on Assets	Long Term Debt	Common Equity	Total Cap.	% LT Debt of Cap.	% Ret. on Equity
1992	**328**	**525**	**282**	**1.9**	**1,568**	**8.4**	**52**	**993**	**1,092**	**4.7**	**13.3**
1991	280	472	288	1.6	1,488	8.0	52	924	1,024	5.1	13.0
1990	277	472	296	1.6	1,497	11.8	127	905	1,114	11.4	19.4
1989	365	553	270	2.0	1,532	13.6	152	942	1,166	13.0	22.2
1988	303	494	192	2.6	1,422	20.6	155	868	1,086	14.2	36.3
1987	21	227	215	1.1	1,194	16.0	156	614	834	18.7	35.5
1986	38	219	185	1.2	1,145	9.9	336	437	829	40.6	25.5
1985	203	359	157	2.3	885	15.5	222	350	603	36.9	32.7
1984	74	219	114	1.9	646	14.2	6	380	413	1.5	24.7
1983	69	191	109	1.8	571	12.7	9	319	357	2.4	23.6

Data as orig. reptd. **1.** Refl. merger or acq. **2.** Net of int. inc. prior to 1986. **3.** Incl. equity in earns. of nonconsol. subs. **4.** Bef. spec. item in 1991. **5.** Refl. acctg. change.

Business Summary

Contributions by business segment in 1992 were:

	Sales	Profits
Newspaper publishing.........	47%	52%
Magazine publishing...........	24%	10%
Cable television................	12%	17%
Broadcasting....................	11%	24%
Other	6%	–3%

The Newspaper division publishes The Washington Post, the largest newspaper in Washington, D.C., with an average circulation of 824,000 daily and 1,159,000 Sunday in 1992, the Washington Post national weekly edition, the Gaithersburg Gazette (84%-owned), which publishes 11 weeklies in Maryland, and the Everett Herald (Everett, Wash.). The division also includes newspaper feature syndication and other publications and a 94%-owned newsprint warehousing firm.

The Magazine division publishes Newsweek, with weekly average circulation of about 3.2 million. It also publishes three international editions.

The Broadcast division operates four VHF network-affiliated television stations: WFSB-TV in Hartford, Conn.; WDIV in Detroit, Mich.; WPLG-TV in Miami, Fla.; and WJXT-TV in Jacksonville, Fla.

The Cable Television division includes 53 systems serving over 470,000 subscribers in 15 midwestern, western and southern states. The company also owns the Stanley H. Kaplan Educational Centers and Legi-Slate, a database service. Interests are owned in two newsprint concerns, a timberlands company, The International Herald Tribune (50%), the Los Angeles Times-Washington Post News Service (50%) and Cowles Media (28%).

Dividend Data

Cash has been paid each year since 1956.

Amt. of Divd. $	Date Decl.	Ex–divd. Date	Stock of Record	Payment Date
1.05	Jan. 14	Jan. 15	Jan. 22	Feb. 12'93
1.05	Mar. 11	Apr. 2	Apr. 9	May 7'93
1.05	Jul. 8	Jul. 19	Jul. 23	Aug. 6'93
1.05	Sep. 9	Oct. 4	Oct. 8	Nov. 5'93

Capitalization

Long Term Debt: $51,805,000 (6/93).

Class A Common Stock: 1,843,250 shs. ($1 par); conv. sh. for sh. into Class B com.; elects 70% of directors; owned by the Graham family & related trusts.

Class B Common Stock: 9,906,666 shs. ($1 par); limited voting rights.

Berkshire Hathaway Inc. owns about 17%.

Institutions hold approximately 64%.

Shareholders of record: 1,667.

Office—1150 15th St., N.W., Washington, D.C. 20071. **Tel**—(202) 334-6000. **Chrmn & CEO**—D. E. Graham. **Pres**—A. G. Spoon. **VP-Secy**—D. M. Daniels. **VP-Fin & Investor Contact**—John B. Morse (202) 334-6662. **Dirs**—B. C. Bradlee, J. E. Burke, M. Cohen, G. J. Gillespie III, R. E. Gomory, D. E. Graham, K. Graham, N. deB. Katzenbach, D. R. Keough, A. J. F. O'Reilly, B. S. Preiskel, W. J. Ruane, R. D. Simmons, A. G. Spoon, G. W. Wilson. **Transfer Agents & Registrars**—First Chicago Trust Co. of New York, NYC; Riggs National Bank of Washington, D.C. **Incorporated** in Delaware in 1947. **Empl**—6,400.

 William H. Donald

Watts Industries

NASDAQ Symbol WATTA (Incl. in Nat'l Market) In S&P MidCap 400

Price	Range	P-E Ratio	Dividend	Yield	S&P Ranking	Beta
Aug. 20'93	1993					
37	48½–33¾	18	0.36	1.0%	A–	0.96

Summary

This long-established, Massachusetts-based company makes an extensive line of valves for the water safety and flow control, water quality, industrial and other markets. Acquisitions are an important element in the company's growth strategy. Earnings in fiscal 1993 were adversely affected by nonrecurring charges, a narrowing of gross margins and higher SG&A. Earnings are expected to rise in fiscal 1994, reflecting moderation of SG&A expense, less dilution and improvement in margins.

Current Outlook

Earnings for the fiscal year ending June 30, 1994, are estimated at $2.40 a share, up from fiscal 1993's $2.02.

The dividend was increased 29%, to $0.09 quarterly from $0.07, with the March 1993 payment.

Sales for fiscal 1994 are expected to rise, reflecting acquisitions and an increase in sales from existing units. Gross margins are expected to improve on higher volume and firmer prices. Assuming a moderation of SG&A expense as acquisitions are integrated and the absence of nonrecurring charges, profits should advance. Benefiting further from flat interest expense and less dilution, earnings should increase from fiscal 1993's reduced level.

Net Sales (Million $)

Quarter:	1992-93	1991-92	1990-91	1989-90
Sep.	110	94	81	68
Dec.	114	108	88	71
Mar.	120	110	95	79
Jun.	122	111	87	74
	466	424	351	292

Based on a brief report, sales for the fiscal year year ended June 30, 1993 (preliminary) rose 10% from those of fiscal 1992, reflecting the favorable impact of acquisitions. However, gross margins narrowed, and penalized further by increased SG&A and a $4.3 million after-tax charge, net income fell 17%. Share earnings on 6.2% more shares were $2.02 (before a $0.21 special charge for FASB 106), versus $2.59.

Common Share Earnings ($)

Quarter:	1992-93	1991-92	1990-91	1989-90
Sep.	0.66	0.66	0.60	0.55
Dec.	0.33	0.65	0.62	0.56
Mar.	0.57	0.72	0.68	0.62
Jun.	0.46	0.56	0.53	0.45
	2.02	2.59	2.43	2.18

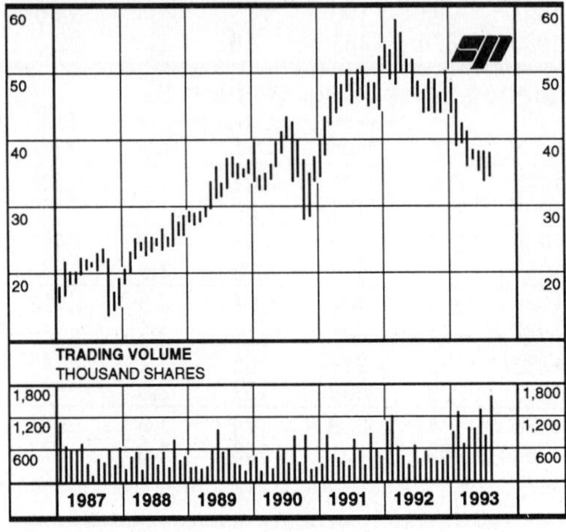

Important Developments

Jul. '93— Watts announced that it had completed the acquisition of LeHage Industries Inc., a manufacturer of floor and roof drains, backwater valves, yard hydrants and stainless and carbon steel specialty products used in construction applications. LeHage, based in Ontario, Canada, had sales of about $10 million.

Jun. '93— Watts announced that directors had authorized the repurchase of up to 500,000 Class A common shares over the next six months through open market and private purchases.

May '93— Watts said that it had completed the acquisition of Edward Barber Ltd, a U.K.-based maker of municipal water valves and meters with sales of $11.5 million.

Next earnings report expected in late October.

Per Share Data ($)

Yr. End Jun. 30	1993	[1]1992	[1]1991	[1]1990	1989	1988	[1]1987	1986
Tangible Bk. Val.	**NA**	17.19	15.11	11.76	10.63	9.49	8.15	6.39
Cash Flow	**NA**	3.62	3.47	3.02	2.48	2.04	1.59	1.48
Earnings[2]	**2.02**	2.59	2.43	2.18	1.82	1.50	1.15	1.10
Dividends	**0.30**	0.26	0.22	0.18	0.14	0.10	0.06	Nil
Payout Ratio	**15%**	11%	9%	8%	8%	7%	5%	Nil
Prices—High[3]	**48½**	58	52½	43½	37½	29	23¾	16¾
Low[3]	**33¾**	44	34½	28	27¼	18½	13¾	12½
P/E Ratio—	**24–17**	22–17	22–14	20–13	21–15	19–12	21–12	15–11

Data as orig. reptd. **1.** Refl. merger or acq. **2.** Ful. dil.: 2.53 in 1992, 2.35 in 1991, 2.13 in 1990 and bef. spec. item(s) of -0.21 in 1993. **3.** Cal. yr. E-Estimated. NA-Not Available.

Income Data (Million $)

Year Ended Jun. 30	Oper. Revs.	Oper. Inc.	% Oper. Inc. of Revs.	Cap. Exp.	Depr.	Int. Exp.	Net Bef. Taxes	Eff. Tax Rate	Net Inc.	% Net Inc. of Revs.	Cash Flow
[1]**1992**	**424**	**79.2**	**18.7**	**29.4**	**14.7**	**7.88**	**59.9**	**38.9%**	**36.6**	**8.6**	**51.3**
[1]1991	351	67.8	19.3	14.1	13.6	5.85	51.3	38.3%	31.7	9.0	45.3
[1]1990	292	57.3	19.6	33.1	10.7	5.92	44.2	37.4%	27.7	9.5	38.4
1989	224	46.5	20.8	16.5	8.4	3.06	37.8	39.0%	23.0	10.3	31.4
1988	181	38.9	21.5	15.4	6.8	2.13	31.1	39.1%	18.9	10.4	25.7
[1]1987	146	33.4	23.0	11.4	5.4	1.84	27.6	48.2%	[2]14.3	9.8	19.7
1986	137	28.4	20.7	11.7	4.4	1.86	24.2	47.2%	12.8	9.3	16.9

Balance Sheet Data (Million $)

Jun. 30	Cash	Curr. Assets	Curr. Liab.	Curr. Ratio	Total Assets	% Ret. on Assets	Long Term Debt	Common Equity	Total Cap.	% LT Debt of Cap.	% Ret. on Equity
1992	**109**	**295**	**54.9**	**5.4**	**469**	**8.6**	**95.6**	**315**	**412**	**23.2**	**12.8**
1991	76	230	44.8	5.1	353	9.6	65.3	236	307	21.3	15.1
1990	42	181	42.4	4.3	287	10.4	65.4	171	243	26.9	17.6
1989	79	175	30.0	5.8	247	10.9	65.2	144	216	30.2	17.3
1988	40	119	23.2	5.1	177	11.6	23.7	123	153	15.5	16.6
1987	42	100	15.2	6.6	148	10.4	22.7	105	133	17.1	15.3
1986	17	72	12.8	5.6	115	NA	22.9	76	102	22.4	NA

Data as orig. reptd. **1.** Refl. merger or acq. **2.** Refl. acctg. change. NA-Not Available.

Business Summary

Formed in 1874 to design and produce steam regulators for New England textile mills, Watts Industries, Inc. now designs, manufactures and sells an extensive line of valves for the water plumbing and heating, water quality, flow control, steam, industrial and oil and gas markets. The company believes that it is the market leader in most of its water service and water quality valve products, which account for more than half of its sales.

Product lines include: 1) safety relief valves, regulators, ball valves and flow control valves for water service primarily in residential and commercial environments and specialty bronze valves and fittings used in underground water service connections; 2) backflow preventers for preventing contamination of potable water; 3) steam regulators and control devices for industrial HVAC and naval/marine applications; 4) ball valves, pneumatic and electric actuators, relief valves, check valves and butterfly valves for industrial applications; 5) valves for the oil and gas industry; and 6) butterfly valves used in water distribution, treatment and wastewater management.

Watts operates its own automated foundries for casting bronze component parts and has extensive facilities for machining bronze, brass, iron and steel components and assembling them into finished valves. The company operates manufacturing plants, warehouses, product development facilities or sales offices at 19 locations in the U.S., three in Canada and one each in the Netherlands, France and Germany, manufacturing about 90,000 valves a day. Approximately 11% of sales and 12% of operating income in fiscal 1992 were derived from Canada and Europe.

The company relies primarily on commissioned representative organizations to market its product lines. These organizations, which accounted for about 68% of fiscal 1992 sales, sell primarily to plumbing and heating wholesalers and industrial, steam and oil and gas distributors for resale to end-users. Watts also sells directly to certain large original equipment manufacturers and private-label accounts.

An important element of Watts' growth strategy is to acquire companies and product lines in related businesses. In September 1991, Watts acquired Henry Pratt Co. (Aurora, Ill.), a manufacturer of AWWA-approved butterfly valves and other valve products used in water distribution, water treatment, wastewater management, fire protection and power generation. The purchase price consisted of $57.2 million in cash, plus contingent deferred payments.

Dividend Data

Cash dividends have been paid since 1986.

Amt of Divd. $	Date Decl.	Ex–divd. Date	Stock of Record	Payment Date
0.07	Oct. 20	Nov. 24	Dec. 1	Dec. 15'92
0.09	Jan. 27	Feb. 23	Mar. 1	Mar. 15'93
0.09	Apr. 15	May 24	May 30	Jun. 15'93
0.09	Aug. 10	Aug. 30	Sep. 3	Sep. 17'93

Capitalization

Long Term Debt: $96,164,000 (3/93).

Class A Common Stock: 9,225,570 shs. ($0.10 par); one vote per sh.
Institutions hold approximately 87%.
Shareholders of record: 292.

Class B Common Stock: 5,744,635 shs. ($0.10 par); conv. sh.-for-sh. into Cl. A; 10 votes per sh.
Officers & directors control about 85% of the company's voting power.

Office—Route 114 & Chestnut St., North Andover, MA 01845. **Tel**—(508) 688-1811. **Chrmn & CEO**—T. P. Horne. **Pres & COO**—C. W. Grigg. **VP, CFO, Secy, Treas & Investor Contact**—Kenneth J. McAvoy. **Dirs**—C. W. Grigg, N. T. Herndon, F. B. Horne, T. P. Horne, G. W. Moran, D. J. Murphy III. **Registrar & Transfer Agent**—First National Bank of Boston. **Incorporated** in Delaware in 1985. **Empl**—3,000.

 Leo Larkin

Wausau Paper Mills

NASDAQ Symbol WSAU (Incl. in Nat'l Market) In S&P MidCap 400

Price	Range	P-E Ratio	Dividend	Yield	S&P Ranking	Beta
Sep. 28'93	1993					
38	39½–29	19	0.28	0.7%	A	1.18

Summary

Wausau manufactures a wide range of fine writing, printing and specialty papers. Earnings declined in fiscal 1993, mostly due to weakness early in the year, but higher profits are expected in fiscal 1994. Over the next few years, added capacity and new product offerings should contribute to steadily growing earnings. The company is also expected to benefit from cost control efforts.

Current Outlook

Earnings for the fiscal year ending August 31, 1994, are projected at $2.30 a share, compared with the $1.95 recorded for fiscal 1993.

The $0.07 quarterly dividend may be increased later in calendar 1993.

Paper product sales should rise moderately in fiscal 1994, aided by a recovering U.S. economy and the addition of newly acquired production facilities. Pricing should be somewhat firmer, helping Wausau's margins. Cost control efforts will also boost margins. Steady earnings growth is likely over the next few years.

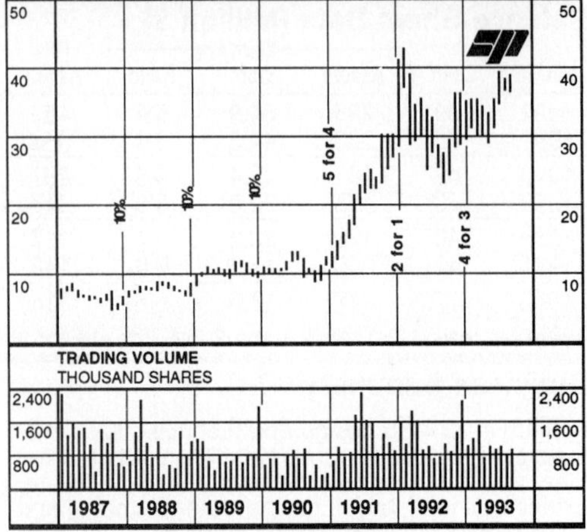

Net Sales (Million $)

Quarter:	1993–94	1992–93	1991–92	1990–91
Nov.	---	94.8	96.3	89.3
Feb.	---	87.3	87.0	81.3
May	---	100.3	95.0	88.2
Aug.	---	99.5	92.7	91.5
	---	381.8	370.9	350.4

Sales for the fiscal year ended August 31, 1993 (preliminary) rose 2.9% from those of the preceding year, reflecting higher shipments. Cost and expenses increased more rapidly than sales, and pretax income was up only fractionally. After taxes at 36.3%, against 34.7%, net income fell 1.6%, to $1.95 a share from $1.98 (as adjusted for the 4-for-3 stock split in January 1993). Results for fiscal 1993 exclude a special charge of $0.83 a share related to an accounting change.

Common Share Earnings ($)

Quarter:	1993–94	1992–93	1991–92	1990–91
Nov.	E0.46	0.40	0.50	0.30
Feb.	E0.48	0.42	0.43	0.33
May	E0.68	0.59	0.53	0.41
Aug.	E0.68	0.54	0.53	0.47
	E2.30	1.95	1.98	1.51

Important Developments

Sep. '93— WSAU reported a 3.6% earnings increase for the fourth quarter of fiscal 1993 (before a $0.01 a share special charge related to an accounting change) on a 7.3% sales gain. Shipments for the period were up 13% from the fourth quarter of fiscal 1992. Separately, Wausau said that future earnings would benefit substantially from the acquisition of manufacturing facilities in Groveton, N.H., from James River Corp. earlier in the year. These facilities have an annual production capacity of 90,000 tons of printing and writing papers, boosting WSAU's total capacity by over 50%. The purchase included two paper machines, a finishing operation and a warehouse/distribution center. Wausau also expected to benefit from the building of a new cogeneration plant next to its Rhinelander, Wisc., paper mill, which will reduce the plant's energy costs, and the introduction of more than 20 new products.

Next earnings report expected in mid-December.

Per Share Data ($)

Yr. End Aug. 31	1993	1992	1991	1990	1989	1988	1987	1986	1985	1984
Tangible Bk. Val.	**NA**	[1]8.21	[1]6.46	[1]5.18	4.60	3.73	3.06	2.56	2.13	1.88
Cash Flow	**NA**	2.66	2.17	1.35	1.41	1.15	0.94	0.87	0.62	0.58
Earnings[3]	**1.95**	1.98	1.51	0.79	1.05	0.80	0.60	0.57	0.33	0.32
Dividends	**0.280**	0.256	0.226	0.249	0.156	0.124	0.104	0.087	0.074	0.068
Payout Ratio	**14%**	13%	15%	32%	15%	16%	17%	15 %	22%	21%
Prices[2]—High	**39½**	43 1/32	30 7/16	13 5/16	11 15/16	9 1/32	8 11/16	7 3/32	4 9/16	2 25/32
Low	**29**	23 5/16	11	8 27/32	8 3/8	6 23/32	4 7/8	4 13/32	1 15/32	1 9/16
P/E Ratio—	**20–15**	22–12	20–7	17–11	11–8	11–8	14–8	12–8	14–5	9–5

Data as orig. reptd. Adj. for stk. divs. of 33 1/3% Jan. 1993, 100% Jan. 1992, 25% Jan. 1991, 10% Dec. 1989, 10% Dec. 1988, 10% Dec. 1987, 10% Dec. 1986, 10% Dec. 1985. **1.** Incl. intangibles. **2.** Cal. yr. **3.** Excl. spec. item(s) of -0.83 in 1993. E-Estimated. NA-Not Available.

Income Data (Million $)

Year Ended Aug. 31	Revs.	Oper. Inc.	% Oper. Inc. of Revs.	Cap. Exp.	Depr.	Int. Exp.	Net Bef. Taxes	Eff. Tax Rate	Net Inc.	% Net Inc. of Revs.	Cash Flow
1992	**371**	**76.1**	**20.5**	**59**	**13.7**	**1.28**	**61.3**	**34.7%**	**40.0**	**10.8**	**53.7**
1991	350	63.2	18.1	53	13.1	4.05	47.0	35.2%	30.5	8.7	43.5
1990	340	36.9	10.8	98	11.3	4.45	24.2	34.3%	15.9	4.7	27.2
1989	317	39.2	12.3	108	7.4	2.31	32.2	35.1%	20.9	6.6	28.3
1988	284	33.2	11.7	25	7.1	2.01	24.4	34.3%	16.0	5.6	23.1
1987	251	29.4	11.7	19	6.8	2.42	20.9	42.5%	12.0	4.8	18.9
1986	225	28.4	12.6	27	6.1	2.46	20.8	44.8%	11.5	5.1	17.6
1985	205	20.3	9.9	17	6.0	2.80	10.9	37.3%	6.8	3.3	12.8
1984	214	17.5	8.2	14	5.4	3.07	10.6	38.0%	6.6	3.1	11.9
1983	185	13.1	7.1	8	5.0	3.63	5.8	37.3%	3.6	2.0	8.7

Balance Sheet Data (Million $)

Aug. 31	Cash	Curr. Assets	Curr. Liab.	Curr. Ratio	Total Assets	% Ret. on Assets	Long Term Debt	Common Equity	Total Cap.	% LT Debt of Cap.	% Ret. on Equity
1992	**2.0**	**72.5**	**38.2**	**1.9**	**267**	**15.8**	**22.7**	**166**	**222**	**10.2**	**27.0**
1991	3.5	63.3	43.7	1.5	240	13.3	30.7	130	189	16.3	26.0
1990	2.0	54.8	31.3	1.8	217	8.0	55.4	104	181	30.5	16.1
1989	1.9	49.4	28.4	1.7	178	13.2	37.5	92	148	25.3	25.0
1988	10.6	59.6	29.9	2.0	138	12.2	15.8	75	106	14.9	23.5
1987	13.7	54.8	26.5	2.1	124	10.0	20.3	61	97	21.0	21.3
1986	11.3	52.1	26.7	2.0	116	10.3	24.1	52	89	27.0	24.4
1985	13.2	51.1	26.1	2.0	108	6.5	26.4	43	81	32.4	16.6
1984	10.1	47.8	23.3	2.1	102	6.5	29.1	39	78	37.2	18.0
1983	7.3	46.9	25.2	1.9	100	3.6	30.7	34	74	41.5	10.9

Data as orig. reptd.

Business Summary

Wausau Paper Mills Company manufactures and sells paper through its Brokaw division and Rhinelander Paper Co. subsidiary. In addition, wholly owned Wausau Papers International Inc. acts as a foreign sales corporation and markets Wausau's products outside the U.S.

The Brokaw division produces fine printing, writing and specialty papers at a mill in Brokaw, Wisconsin. These papers are sold to a large network of paper distributors, which in turn sell these products to commercial printers, in-plant print shops and quick print copy centers. End-uses for Brokaw's paper products include printed advertising, office papers and converted products such as envelopes and announcement cards. During 1991, Brokaw introduced a product line with 50% recycled fibers, with 10% of the total fiber content from post-consumer waste. Approximately 70% of this division's fine printing and writing paper is colored paper.

The Rhinelander Paper Co. subsidiary manufactures lightweight dense technical specialty papers, sold directly to converters. Rhinelander custom engineers and manufactures dense, lightweight, technical specialty paper, and is the leading U.S. manufacturer of release papers for the pressure-sensitive labeling industry. Its other products include lightweight papers used for sterilized medical packaging, and specialty papers used in food packaging such as microwavable popcorn and other convenience food packaging.

Approximately 55% of the pulp consumed by the Brokaw division is produced internally from aspen, which is in abundant supply. The balance used by Wausau is purchased from pulp mills throughout the U.S. and Canada.

In October 1992, WSAU projected that it would spend over $100 million on capital improvements in the next three fiscal years. Company spending on capital improvements totaled $31.8 million in fiscal 1992, versus $24.9 million in 1991 and $43.9 million in 1990.

Dividend Data

Cash has been paid each year since 1960.

Amt of Divd. $	Date Decl.	Ex–divd. Date	Stock of Record	Payment Date
4–for–3	Dec. 15	Jan. 14	Dec. 30	Jan. 13'93
0.07	Dec. 15	Dec. 23	Dec. 30	Jan. 13'93
0.07	Feb. 17	Mar. 8	Mar. 12	Apr. 1'93
0.07	May 28	Jun. 14	Jun. 18	Jul. 1'93
0.07	Aug. 16	Aug. 30	Sep. 3	Oct. 1'93

Capitalization

Long Term Debt: $35,735,000 (5/93).

Common Stock: 20,214,157 shs. (no par).
Descendants of A.P. Woodson and family own 23%; trustees of the David B. Smith Family Trust control about 9%; officers and directors hold approximately 10%.
Institutions hold some 53%.
Shareholders of record: 1,511.

Office—One Clark's Island, P.O. Box 1408, Wausau, WI 54402-1408. **Tel**—(715) 845-5266. **Chrmn**—S. W. Orr Jr. **Pres & CEO**—A. M. Nemirow. **VP-Fin, Secy, Treas & Investor Contact**—Steven A. Schmidt. **Dirs**—H. R. Baker, A. M. Nemirow, S. W. Orr Jr., D. B. Smith Jr., S. F. Staples Jr. **Transfer Agent**—Harris Trust & Savings Bank, Chicago. **Incorporated** in Wisconsin in 1899. **Empl**—1,352.

 Richard Spiegel

Wellman, Inc.

NYSE Symbol WLM Options on NYSE (Mar-Jun-Sep-Dec) In S&P MidCap 400

Price	Range	P–E Ratio	Dividend	Yield	S&P Ranking	Beta
Aug. 6'93	1993					
19	24⅞–18⅛	11	0.20	1.1%	NR	1.67

Summary

Wellman, Inc. manufactures polyester textile fibers under the Fortrel brand name and produces recycled polyester and nylon fibers and plastic resins. WLM also builds and operates materials recovery facilities. The company is the largest domestic recycler of plastic, fiber and film wastes, which are used in its manufacturing operations. Operating earnings in 1993 will be limited by reduced selling prices for polyester fibers and startup costs associated with major capital projects.

Current Outlook

Share earnings for 1993 are estimated at about $1.75; earnings for 1994 are projected at $1.70.

The quarterly dividend was raised 67% to $0.05 from $0.03, with the June 1993 payment.

Sales for 1993 are projected to rise modestly, reflecting the late 1992 acquisition of Creative Forming and gains in the polymer, resins and wool units. The New England CRInc. business should advance with the start-up of four materials recovery facilities. Higher imports of polyester fibers have resulted in lower selling prices; the late 1993 startup of new industry capacity may put additional pressure on prices. PET bottle recycling and polyester yarn capacities will be increased by early 1994. Startup costs related to major capital projects will continue to impact earnings going into 1994.

Net Sales (Million $)

Quarter:	1993	1992	1991	1990
Mar.	208.0	207.5	191.6	208.6
Jun.	214.0	205.4	215.8	209.4
Sep.		212.4	199.1	205.4
Dec.		202.9	199.2	204.4
		828.2	805.7	827.8

Sales for 1993's first half rose 2.2%, year to year, reflecting higher sales in the wool and resins units, and acquisitions. Operating profit fell 5.3% due to lower fiber prices. On lower net interest expense and a nonrecurring gain of $0.22 a share, net income rose 28%, to $1.05 a share from $0.82.

Common Share Earnings ($)

Quarter:	1993	1992	1991	1990
Mar.	0.66	0.38	0.32	0.55
Jun.	0.39	0.44	0.36	0.56
Sep.	E0.35	0.39	0.31	0.43
Dec.	E0.35	0.39	0.42	0.35
	E1.75	1.60	1.39	1.90

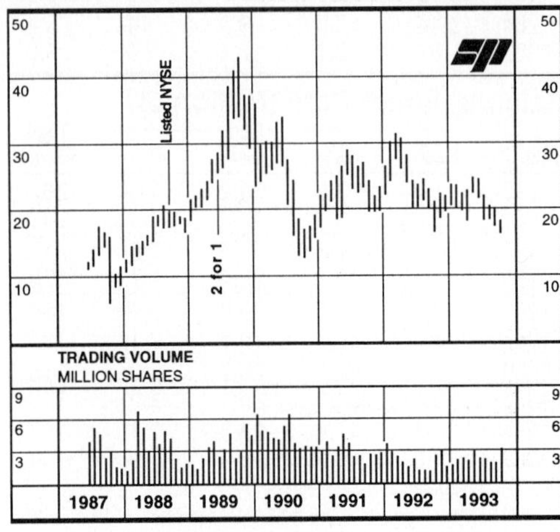

Important Developments

Jul. '93— WLM said that second quarter earnings declined from the 1992 period due to lower domestic polyester staple fiber prices, resulting from price competition, and increased project expense, resulting from its capital investment program. WLM was negotiating for the purchase of BASF's polyester business at Lowland, Tenn.

Jan. '93— As part of a $240 million multi-year capital investment program, WLM announced plans to expand PET resin capacity at its Darlington plant by 120 million pounds (55%) by early 1995. It will also build a 400 million pound monomer unit to support the resin expansion. WLM is also installing equipment by year end 1993 to solid-state 75 million pounds a year of PET resin. WLM will expand POY capacity by 30% by 1994 and increase PET bottle recycling capacity by 70%.

Next earnings report expected in late October.

Per Share Data ($)

Yr. End Dec. 31	[2]1992	1991	[2]1990	[2]1989	1988	[3]1987	[4]1986
Tangible Bk. Val.[1]	**14.86**	13.44	12.11	9.97	5.29	4.07	[5]2.52
Cash Flow	**3.18**	2.71	2.80	2.21	1.54	1.07	0.70
Earnings[6]	**1.60**	1.39	1.90	1.84	1.32	0.87	0.64
Dividends	**0.120**	0.120	0.120	0.115	0.025	Nil	Nil
Payout Ratio	**7%**	9%	6%	7%	2%	Nil	Nil
Prices—High	**31½**	29	36	43	20¾	17⅝	NA
Low	**16½**	17¼	12¾	18½	10¾	6	NA
P/E Ratio—	**20–10**	21–12	19–7	23–10	16–8	20–7	NA

Data as orig. reptd. Adj. for stk. div. of 100% June 1989. **1.** Includes intangibles. **2.** Reflects merger or acquisition. **3.** Reflects acctg. change. **4.** Pro forma, reflects acquisition of WIL and related financial transactions. **5.** As of 3-31-87. **6.** Bef. spec. items of -0.36 in 1987, -0.29 in 1986. E-Estimated NA-Not Available.

Income Data (Million $)

Year Ended Dec. 31	Revs.	Oper. Inc.	% Oper. Inc. of Revs.	Cap. Exp.	Depr.	Int. Exp.	Net Bef. Taxes	Eff. Tax Rate	[7]Net Inc.	% Net Inc. of Revs.	Cash Flow
[1]1992	**828**	**163**	**19.7**	**62**	**51.7**	**23.0**	**[6]88**	**40.6%**	**52.3**	**6.3**	**104**
1991	806	154	19.1	26	43.1	[5]29.4	[6]82	44.6%	45.3	5.6	88
[1]1990	828	176	21.3	31	29.0	43.1	105	41.1%	61.6	7.4	101
[1]1989	438	102	23.4	246	11.0	[5]12.3	[6]80	32.3%	54.5	12.4	68
1988	315	67	21.2	27	6.3	[5]5.2	[6]57	33.0%	38.0	12.1	46
[2]1987	261	52	20.0	34	5.2	9.3	[6]38	39.0%	22.3	8.5	27
[3]1986	239	[4]42	17.3	NA	3.7	8.9	34	45.7%	18.3	7.6	15

Balance Sheet Data (Million $)

Dec. 31	Cash	Curr. Assets	Curr. Liab.	Curr. Ratio	Total Assets	% Ret. on Assets	Long Term Debt	Common Equity	Total Cap.	% LT Debt of Cap.	% Ret. on Equity
1992	**1.7**	**252**	**110**	**2.3**	**997**	**5.6**	**300**	**483**	**783**	**38.3**	**11.4**
1991	0.7	232	111	2.1	865	5.2	270	435	705	38.2	10.9
1990	5.4	227	109	2.1	891	7.0	342	392	734	46.6	17.2
1989	7.8	221	121	1.8	861	9.6	396	319	714	55.4	22.3
1988	19.9	138	43	3.2	243	17.0	37	151	199	18.4	28.5
1987	8.4	117	32	3.6	203	11.3	46	116	170	27.1	28.3
[8]1986	1.6	99	26	3.9	179	NA	51	95	146	35.1	NA

Data as orig. reptd. **1.** Reflects merger or acquisition. **2.** Reflects acctg. change. **3.** Pro forma, reflects acquisition of WIL and related financial transactions. **4.** Aft. depr. **5.** Net of interest income. **6.** Incl. equity in earns. of nonconsol. subs. **7.** Bef. spec. item(s) in 1987, 1986. **8.** Pro forma, 3-31-87. NA-Not Available.

Business Summary

Wellman manufactures polyester textile fibers and also produces recycled polyester and nylon fibers and plastic resins. The company is the largest domestic recycler of plastic, fiber and film wastes, and is the only major fiber manufacturer using waste products as a primary feedstock. The waste products utilized are post consumer polyethylene terephthalate (PET) soft drink bottles, reclaimed fiber producer wastes, and PET film wastes. Contributions to sales:

	1992	1991
Fibers	81.4%	80.8%
Polymer products	6.5%	6.4%
Engineering resins	3.1%	3.0%
Nonwovens	2.8%	3.0%
Wool	3.5%	3.0%
Creative Forming	0.3%	---
CRInc.	2.4%	3.7%

Western Europe accounted for 12% of sales and 5% of operating profits in 1992.

The Fibers division produces from petrochemicals polyester textile staple in Darlington, S.C. (annual capacity of 450 million pounds) and partially oriented yarn (100 million pounds) in Fayetteville, N.C., which are marketed under the Fortrel brand name and used in apparel, home furnishings and industrial uses. WLM also recycles fiber and plastic wastes to produce polyester and nylon staple fibers at plants in Johnsonville (255 million pounds) and Marion (32 million pounds), S.C., for fiberfill, furniture, home furnishings, carpet, and industrial uses. Wellman International Ltd., Republic of Ireland, conducts a similar business serving the U.K. and Western Europe with annual capacity of 154 million pounds.

WLM also producers PET resin for polyester resins and bottles and packaging uses, makes recycled nylon engineering resins for automobile, consumer and industrial uses, and markets recycled high density polyethylene (HDPE) for use in the packaging industry. The company converts polyester fiber into high-loft nonwoven batting used as filling for home furnishings and manufactures geotextile fabrics for various geotextile and civil engineering uses. WLM also processes raw wool to produce wool blends used by worsted fabric manufacturers. Creative Forming, Inc. (acquired in November 1992) produces thermoformed plastics packaging products.

New England CRInc. (acquired August, 1990) designs, builds and operates materials recycling facilities for mixed recyclables. There were ten operating facilities at year-end 1992.

Dividend Data

Dividends were initiated in 1988. A "poison pill" stock purchase right was adopted in 1991.

Amt of Divd. $	Date Decl.	Ex–divd. Date	Stock of Record	Payment Date
0.03	Nov. 12	Nov. 23	Nov. 30	Dec. 15'92
0.03	Feb. 18	Mar. 1	Mar. 5	Mar. 17'93
0.05	May 18	May 25	Jun. 1	Jun. 15'93
0.05	Jul. 20	Aug. 25	Aug. 31	Sep. 15'93

Capitalization

Long Term Debt: $298,198,000 (6/93).

Common Stock: 32,720,386 shs. ($0.001 par). Institutions hold about 87%. Shareholders of record: 1,856.

Office—1040 Broad St., Suite 302, Shrewsbury, NJ 07702. **Tel**—(908) 542-7300. **Pres & CEO**—T. M. Duff. **VP, CFO & Treas**—C. J. Christenson. **Secy**—D. K. Duffell. **Investor Contact**—Jill M. Rea. **Dirs**—C. W. Beckwith, P. H. Conze, A. R. Dragone, T. M. Duff, R. F. Heitmiller, J. M. Nelson, R. C. Tower, R. A. Vandenberg. **Transfer Agent & Registrar**—Continental Stock Transfer and Trust Co., NYC. **Incorporated** in Delaware in 1985. **Empl**—3,600.

 Richard O'Reilly, CFA

West One Bancorp

NASDAQ Symbol WEST (Incl. in Nat'l Market) In S&P MidCap 400

Price	Range	P-E Ratio	Dividend	Yield	S&P Ranking	Beta
Oct. 4'93	1993					
31⅜	31⅜–22⅞	14	0.62	2.0%	B+	0.61

Summary

This Idaho-based regional multibank holding company, with assets of $7.1 billion, operates more than 200 offices in Idaho, Utah, Oregon and Washington. West One entered the Washington market through an acquisition in 1988 and has been pursuing an aggressive expansion program in that state. Recent earnings have been strong, reflecting favorable demographic and economic trends in West One's market area. In August 1993, the shares were split two-for-one.

Business Summary

West One Bancorp (formerly Moore Financial Group Inc.) is a regional bank holding company serving four western states through more than 200 offices, mainly in Idaho and in Utah, Oregon and Washington. The company's lead bank is West One Bank, Idaho, the largest in that state.

Loans totaled $4.5 billion (net of unearned income) at the end of 1992, up from $3.5 billion a year earlier, divided as follows:

	1992	1991
Commercial	32%	30%
Agricultural	8%	9%
Real estate	38%	34%
Consumer	19%	23%
Leases	3%	4%

The allowance for credit losses was $68,243,000 (1.51% of loans outstanding) at the end of 1992, compared with $53,048,000 (1.52%) a year earlier. Net loan chargeoffs totaled $9,821,000 (0.26% of average loans) in 1992, versus $24,455,000 (0.73%) the year before. As of December 31, 1992, nonperforming assets (including nonaccrual loans and restructured loans and other real estate owned) totaled $31,101,000 (0.68% of loans and other real estate owned), against $53,971,000 (1.54%) a year earlier.

As of December 31, 1992, deposits totaled $5.64 billion, comprised of noninterest-bearing 20%, interest-bearing demand 12%, regular and money-market savings 31%, time certificates 29%, and time certificates of $100,000 and more 8%.

Interest on loans accounted for 65% of total income for 1992, interest on short-term investments for 2%, interest on investment securities for 17%, trust fees and commissions for 2%, service charges on deposit accounts for 6%, other service charges, fees and commissions for 6% and other noninterest income for 2%.

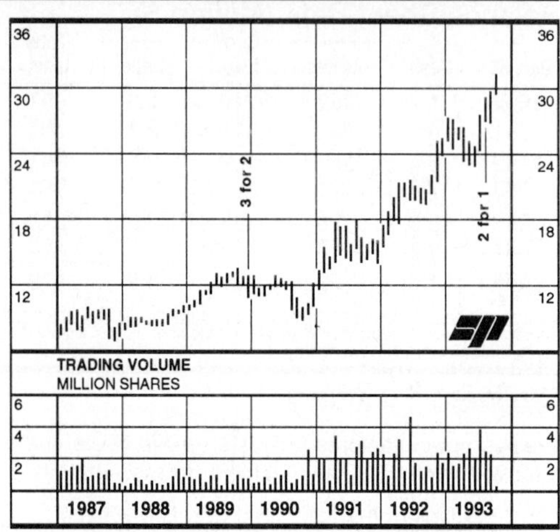

The average yield on total interest-earning assets was 8.44% in 1992 (9.81% in 1991), while the average rate paid on total interest-bearing liabilities was 3.68% (5.33%), for a net spread of 4.76% (4.48%).

Important Developments

Jun. '93— The company acquired Ben Franklin National Bank of Pasco, Wash. (assets of $35 million) for 206,254 (adjusted) WEST common shares. The transaction was accounted for as a pooling of interests. Ben Franklin National Bank's three branches were merged with the four branches of recently acquired Yakima Valley Bank to form West One Bank, Eastern Washington.

Apr. '93— West One signed a definitive agreement to acquire Idaho State Bank, a seven-branch, $50-million asset institution. The agreement, subject to regulatory approval, would involve the issuance of 133,332 (adjusted) WEST common shares.

Next earnings report expected in mid-October.

Per Share Data ($)

Yr. End Dec. 31	[1]1992	[1]1991	[1]1990	[1]1989	[1,2]1988	1987	1986	[1]1985	1984	[1]1983
Tangible Bk. Val.	**15.14**	13.08	12.11	10.98	10.19	9.52	9.32	9.89	9.29	8.61
Earnings[3]	**2.09**	1.47	1.67	1.36	1.09	0.75	d0.16	1.01	1.07	1.12
Dividends	**0.520**	0.480	0.440	0.410	0.400	0.400	0.400	0.400	0.373	0.364
Payout Ratio	**25%**	33%	26%	30%	37%	53%	NM	40%	35%	33%
Prices—High	**25½**	17⅞	12⅞	13⁹⁄₁₆	10⁹⁄₁₆	10	11⅜	8¹⁵⁄₁₆	8⁵⁄₁₆	8⁷⁄₁₆
Low	**15½**	11⅝	8¹³⁄₁₆	9¾	7¹⁵⁄₁₆	6¹⁵⁄₁₆	7³⁄₁₆	7¹³⁄₁₆	5⁷⁄₁₆	5¹⁵⁄₁₆
P/E Ratio—	**12–7**	12–8	8–5	10–7	9–7	13–9	NM	9–8	8–5	8–5

Data as orig. reptd. Adj. for stk. divs. of 100% Aug. 1993, 50% Dec. 1989, 10% Oct. 1984. **1.** Refl. merger or acq. **2.** Refl. acctg. change. **3.** Ful. dil.: 1.99 in 1992, 1.44 in 1991, 1.66 in 1990, 1.34 in 1989, 1.09 in 1988. d-Deficit. NM-Not Meaningful.

Income Data (Million $)

Year Ended Dec. 31	Net Int. Inc.	Tax Equiv. Adj.	Non Int. Inc.	Loan Loss Prov.	% Exp./ Op. Revs.	Net Bef. Taxes	Eff. Tax Rate	Net Inc.	% Net Int. Margin	—% Return On— Assets	Equity
[1]1992	**239**	**13.1**	**81.8**	**14.3**	**64.9**	**91.3**	**30.6%**	**63.4**	**4.76**	**1.08**	**14.9**
[1]1991	198	12.2	70.5	29.7	65.4	57.5	28.3%	41.2	4.48	0.80	11.8
[1]1990	164	11.4	57.9	10.7	64.9	59.6	28.6%	42.6	4.45	0.97	14.7
[1]1989	143	9.6	48.8	6.8	69.2	45.6	26.3%	33.6	4.23	0.84	13.1
[1,2]1988	122	5.5	39.2	10.9	67.9	36.8	30.8%	25.5	3.98	0.72	11.2
1987	109	4.7	46.6	20.8	69.9	23.4	27.7%	16.9	3.73	0.50	8.1
1986	107	9.9	44.2	53.5	70.6	d3.9	NM	d3.3	3.72	NM	NM
[1]1985	112	12.0	33.0	25.6	62.8	26.2	21.5%	20.6	4.33	0.65	10.6
1984	99	14.3	24.4	11.5	66.9	25.1	13.1%	21.8	4.31	0.75	12.0
[1]1983	93	15.2	20.8	8.3	63.3	26.0	12.7%	22.7	4.76	0.90	13.4

Balance Sheet Data (Million $)

Dec. 31	Total Assets	—Earning Assets— Mon. Mkt. Assets	Inv. Secs.	Com'l Loans	Other Loans	% Loan Loss Resv.	—Deposits— Demand	Time	% Loans/ Deposits	Long Term Debt	Common Equity	% Equity To Assets
1992	**7,134**	**191**	**1,657**	**1,923**	**2,609**	**1.51**	**1,136**	**4,500**	**80.4**	**118**	**490**	**7.26**
1991	5,417	205	1,220	1,521	1,976	1.52	669	3,375	86.5	112	367	6.75
1990	4,587	102	998	1,411	1,576	1.55	692	2,847	84.4	71	309	6.63
1989	4,350	192	996	1,246	1,353	1.82	656	2,585	80.2	62	272	6.41
1988	3,906	425	810	1,047	1,169	2.29	588	2,448	72.3	62	239	6.45
1987	3,519	358	837	962	977	2.38	509	2,164	71.9	65	220	6.22
1986	3,412	296	812	849	1,073	2.42	519	2,216	69.8	65	194	5.66
1985	3,459	373	635	1,033	999	1.34	452	2,295	73.4	66	203	6.16
1984	2,980	162	622	1,001	865	1.13	366	2,021	77.6	31	190	6.28
1983	2,767	125	668	743	798	1.10	354	1,786	71.3	30	175	6.69

Data as orig. reptd. **1.** Refl. merger or acq. **2.** Refl. acctg. change. d-Deficit. NM-Not Meaningful.

Review of Operations

Net interest income in the six months ended June 30, 1993, climbed 34%, year to year, and the provision for loan losses fell 28%, to $6,506,000, aided by an improved economy in the company's operating region of Idaho, Washington, Oregon and Utah. With 22% higher other income and 35% greater other expense, pretax income grew 32%. After taxes at 31.1%, versus 31.0%, net income also was up 32%. Adjusted share earnings were $1.18, based on 14.2% more shares ($1.13 fully diluted), compared to $1.03 ($0.98).

Common Share Earnings ($)

Quarter:	1993	1992	1991	1990
Mar.	0.55	0.50	0.40	0.35
Jun.	0.63	0.53	0.42	0.41
Sep.		0.52	0.22	0.48
Dec.		0.54	0.43	0.44
		2.09	1.47	1.67

Finances

At June 30, 1993, the company had leverage, tier I and total capital ratios of 6.79%, 8.56% and 10.98%, all of which were well in excess of regulatory requirements.

In September 1992, the company purchased 38 branches and seven specialty branches from Security Pacific Corp. in Washington. The transaction included the purchase of about $837 million of loans, and about $1.2 billion of deposit liabilities.

In June 1992, West One sold 3 million (adjusted) common shares at $21 each through Merrill Lynch & Co. and Salomon Brothers Inc. Net proceeds of $60.9 million were used to enhance capital at West One, Washington, which was acquiring branches from Security Pacific.

Dividend Data

Cash has been paid each year since 1935. A dividend reinvestment plan is available.

Amt of Divd. $	Date Decl.	Ex-divd. Date	Stock of Record	Payment Date
0.26	Oct. 15	Dec. 24	Dec. 31	Jan. 21'93
0.31	Dec. 17	Mar. 25	Mar. 31	Apr. 15'93
0.31	Apr. 15	Jun. 24	Jun. 30	Jul. 15'93
2-for-1	Jul. 16	Aug. 16	Jul. 23	Aug. 13'93
0.155	Jul. 16	Sep. 24	Sep. 30	Oct. 21'93

Capitalization

Long Term Debt: $119,714,000 (6/93).

Common Stock: 32,729,056 shs. ($1 par).
Harry Bettis holds 6.5%.
Institutions hold about 53%.
Shareholders: 4,544 of record (12/92).

Office—101 S. Capitol Blvd., Boise, ID 83733. **Tel**—(208) 383-7000. **Chrmn & CEO**—D. R. Nelson. **Pres**—D. M. Jones. **EVP & CFO**—S. M. Hayes. **SVP & Secy**—D. V. Board. **VP-Investor Contact**—Linda Blount-Strauss. **Dirs**—H. Bettis, W. J. Deasy, J. B. Fery, S. A. Hall, J. S. Hay, D. M. Jones, J. B. Little, W. E. McCain, D. W. McCallum, D. R. Nelson, A. T. Noble, P. B. Soulen. **Transfer Agent & Registrar**—West One Bank. **Incorporated** in Idaho in 1981. **Empl**—4,500.

Western Publishing Group

NASDAQ Symbol WPGI (Incl. in Nat'l Market) In S&P MidCap 400

Price	Range	P-E Ratio	Dividend	Yield	S&P Ranking	Beta
Sep. 27'93	1993					
15¼	21–13¼	NM	None	None	NR	1.23

Summary

This company, known for the "Golden" trademark, is the largest U.S. publisher of children's books. Significant revenues are also come from the sale of other consumer products and from printing and sponsored publishing services. A loss is anticipated for 1993-4, reflecting writedowns, as well as costs of expanding the Books "R" Us program and starting "shop within a store" programs in Wal-Mart and other stores.

Current Outlook

A loss of about $1.00 a share is likely for the year ending January 31, 1994, versus earnings of $0.80 in 1992-3. Earnings of about $1.40 are anticipated for 1994-5.

No cash dividends have been paid on the common shares.

Revenue should begin to advanced in the second half of 1993-4, boosted by aggressive expansion and product development programs. Startup and development costs, as well as higher interest expense, will hamper profitability through 1994-5. Measures currently being taken are expected to result in accelerating revenue and earnings gains in subsequent years.

Revenues (Million $)

13 Weeks:	1993-94	1992-93	1991-92	1990-91
Apr.	111.0	121.5	98.7	104.3
Jul.	131.3	124.4	109.9	107.9
Oct.		228.9	191.5	155.7
Jan.		177.4	154.4	125.8
		652.2	554.5	493.6

Revenues in the six months ended July 31, 1993, declined 1.5%, year to year. Results were restricted by expansion and development costs and higher interest expense, and after a $21.8 million ($1.04) asset writedown, a loss of $34,278,000 ($1.65) replaced income of $3,509,000 ($0.15). Results in the 1993 period exclude a charge of $0.71 a share from the cumulative effect of an accounting change.

Common Share Earnings ($)

13 Weeks:	1993-94	1992-93	1991-92	1990-91
Apr.	d1.45	0.09	d0.11	0.09
Jul.	d0.20	0.06	0.01	0.04
Oct.	E0.48	0.61	0.58	0.39
Jan.	E0.17	0.04	0.14	d0.16
	Ed1.00	0.80	0.62	0.36

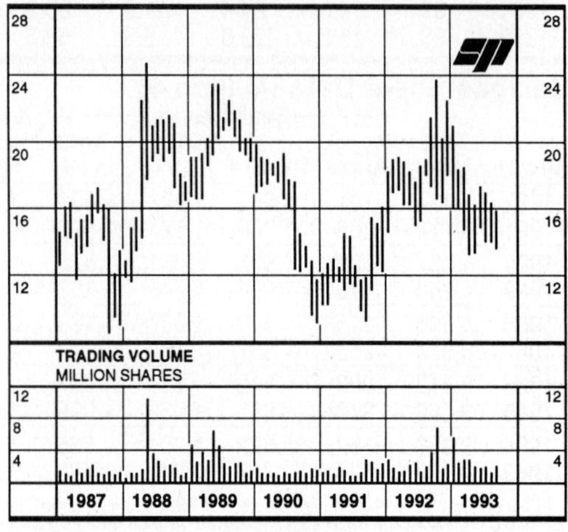

Important Developments

Sep. '93— Western said that in addition to a $21.8 million writedown at its Penn Ad Specialty division, it incurred an operating loss in the first half of 1993-4, reflected costs of in-store merchandising personnel and category management programs. Results were also hurt by poor retail sales, adverse weather in the first quarter, acceleration of just-in-time inventory management, and pessimism among retailers. The company noted, however, that two-thirds of sales and 95% of profits are generated in the second half of the year. Western also said that its "Storyland" children's book program was scheduled to open in about 100 Wal-Mart stores in the fall of 1993, and that another program with a major national discount chain would be announced shortly.

Next earnings report due in mid-December.

Per Share Data ($)

Yr. End Jan. 31	1993	1992	1991	1990	1989	1988	[1]1987	1986	1985
Tangible Bk. Val.	**8.23**	7.76	7.06	6.72	5.39	3.54	1.98	1.50	0.36
Cash Flow	**1.43**	1.25	0.97	1.71	2.10	1.74	1.18	1.14	NA
Earnings[2]	**0.80**	0.62	0.36	1.05	1.45	1.08	0.88	1.10	[3]0.39
Dividends	**Nil**	Nil	Nil	Nil	Nil	Nil	Nil	Nil	Nil
Payout Ratio	**Nil**	Nil	Nil	Nil	Nil	Nil	Nil	Nil	Nil
Calendar Years	**1992**	1991	1990	1989	1988	1987	1986	1985	1984
Prices—High	**23¾**	16⅛	19⅞	23½	24¾	17¼	21⅛	NA	NA
Low	**14⅝**	9¼	9⅛	16⅝	11⅝	8½	11⅞	NA	NA
P/E Ratio—	**30–18**	26–15	55–25	22–16	17–8	16–8	24–13	NA	NA

Data as orig. reptd. **1.** Refl. merger or acq. **2.** Bef. spec. item(s) of -0.24 in 1987. **3.** 11 mos. d-Deficit. NM-Not Meaningful. NA-Not Available.

Income Data (Million $)

Year Ended Jan. 31	Revs.	Oper. Inc.	% Oper. Inc. of Revs.	Cap. Exp.	Depr.	Int. Exp.	Net Bef. Taxes	Eff. Tax Rate	[4]Net Inc.	% Net Inc. of Revs.	Cash Flow
1993	**651**	**50.7**	**7.8**	**22.8**	**13.3**	**10.4**	**28.4**	**38.3%**	**17.5**	**2.7**	**30.0**
1992	553	40.7	7.4	11.9	13.3	6.3	22.3	38.5%	13.7	2.5	26.2
[1]1991	492	33.4	6.8	14.4	12.8	7.5	13.7	39.1%	8.3	1.7	20.3
1990	493	52.5	10.6	13.2	13.3	7.8	33.8	35.5%	21.8	4.4	34.3
1989	549	70.0	12.8	9.8	13.0	8.7	50.7	41.1%	29.9	5.4	42.0
1988	455	58.6	12.9	10.2	13.1	8.3	39.5	45.2%	21.6	4.8	34.8
1987	319	37.0	11.6	5.2	5.7	3.5	30.8	45.4%	16.8	5.3	22.5
[1]1986	308	35.1	11.4	4.9	0.7	10.7	28.9	39.0%	17.6	5.7	18.3
[2]1985	263	19.7	7.5	4.9	0.1	13.1	8.1	23.1%	6.3	2.4	NA
[3]1984	241	NA	NA	NA	NA	4.1	7.8	46.4%	4.2	1.7	NA

Balance Sheet Data (Million $)

Jan. 31	Cash	Curr. Assets	Curr. Liab.	Curr. Ratio	Total Assets	% Ret. on Assets	Long Term Debt	Common Equity	Total Cap.	% LT Debt of Cap.	% Ret. on Equity
1993	**10.40**	**375**	**93**	**4.0**	**509**	**3.9**	**180.0**	**215**	**414**	**43.4**	**8.0**
1992	8.77	282	176	1.6	391	3.8	Nil	199	213	Nil	6.6
1991	7.49	232	129	1.8	339	2.5	Nil	190	207	Nil	3.9
1990	8.17	206	109	1.9	310	7.0	Nil	183	199	Nil	12.1
1989	5.78	208	131	1.6	311	9.8	Nil	163	178	Nil	19.6
1988	4.84	194	149	1.3	299	7.6	Nil	133	143	Nil	17.7
1987	3.14	160	141	1.1	268	8.4	Nil	111	123	Nil	25.0
1986	6.32	123	31	3.0	135	13.1	[5]55.0	24	89	61.9	118.9
1985	4.45	126	42	4.1	134	NA	[5]82.6	6	98	84.0	NA

Data as orig. reptd. **1.** Refl. merger or acq. **2.** 11 mos. **3.** Predecessor co. **4.** Bef. spec. items. **5.** Excl. lease obligs. NA-Not Available.

Business Summary

Western Publishing Group, Inc. is the nation's largest publisher of children's story books, (primarily under the "Golden" trademark), and produces other leisure-time and commercial products. Contributions (profits in million $) by business segment in 1992-3 were:

	Sales	Profits
Consumer products	83.7%	$53.6
Commercial products	16.3%	–3.6

Western creates and publishes story books, coloring books, activity books and games and puzzles for children, as well as puzzles, games and special-interest books for adults. Products are marketed primarily through mass merchandising chains, bookstores and toy stores.

About half of consumer product sales are from juvenile products using characters and properties from the company's five largest licensors: The Walt Disney Co., Children's Television Workshop (Sesame Street), Mattel Inc., International Design Workshop Inc. and Warner Brothers Inc.

The Diversified Products division provides graphic services, commercial and specialty printing, game manufacturing, and custom publishing services.

In March 1993, Western and Toys "R" Us agreed to expand the Books "R" Us shop-within-a-store program from 30 to 200 stores. The company recorded a related charge in the 1993-4 first quarter.

Dividend Data

No cash dividends have been paid on the common shares, and Western does not expect to make such payments in the foreseeable future.

Finances

In November 1992, Western obtained a $200 million unsecured bank revolving credit agreement, expiring in May 1996. The agreement and the September 1992 sale of $150 million of 10-year senior notes completed a program to raise additional capital.

Capitalization

Long Term Debt: $224,800,000 (5/1/93).

Preferred Stock: 19,970 shs. (no par); ea. conv. into 28 com. shs.; entitled to cum. divds. at annual rate of $42.50 per sh.; red. at $500 per sh. no later than Mar. 31'96.

Common Stock: 20,955,924 shs. ($0.01 par).
Directors, officers and key employees hold 24%, incl. 20% by R.A. Bernstein.
The Gabelli Group controls 20%.

Office—444 Madison Ave., New York, NY 10022. **Tel**—(212) 688-4500. **Chrmn & CEO**—R. A. Bernstein. **Pres & COO**—F. P. DiPrima. **EVP, CFO & Treas**—S. Turner. **VP & Secy**—J. A. Cohen. **Dirs**—R. A. Bernhard, R. A. Bernstein, F. P. DiPrima, S. B. Fortenbaugh III, A. S. Gordon, J. Morgenthau, M. A. Pietrangelo. **Transfer Agent & Registrar**—First Chicago Trust Co. of New York, NYC. **Incorporated** in Delaware in 1984. **Empl**—3,800.

Willamette Industries

NASDAQ Symbol WMTT (Incl. in Nat'l Market) Options on NYSE In S&P MidCap 400

Price	Range	P–E Ratio	Dividend	Yield	S&P Ranking	Beta
Jul. 16'93	1993					
37	44½–34	22	0.88	2.4%	B+	1.22

Summary

This integrated forest products company manufactures and sells particleboard, plywood, corrugated containers, bleached pulp, grocery bags, and other wood and paper products. Operations were significantly expanded by the late 1991 acquisition of Bohemia Inc. and the June 1992 purchase of 11 corrugated container plants from Boise Cascade. Earnings in recent years were depressed by cyclical weakness in the paper industry, but future prospects are bolstered by the company's efforts to be among the industry's lowest cost producers.

Current Outlook

Earnings for 1993 are projected at $2.10 a share, up from the $1.52 recorded in 1992. In 1994, earnings are expected to reach $2.80 a share.

Quarterly dividends, which were increased 4.8% with the March 1993 payment, should continue at $0.22 for the remainder of the year.

Sales are expected to rise at least 10% in 1993, aided by increased prices for building products and some recovery in paper product pricing. Margins are likely to widen, aided by strong cost control efforts. Though earnings are expected to fall well short of peak levels reached in the late 1980s, they should increase significantly in 1993 and 1994 over the depressed results of the past two years. Longer term, Willamette's highly efficient operations will probably enable the company to outperform its peers in the industry and generate high levels of profitability.

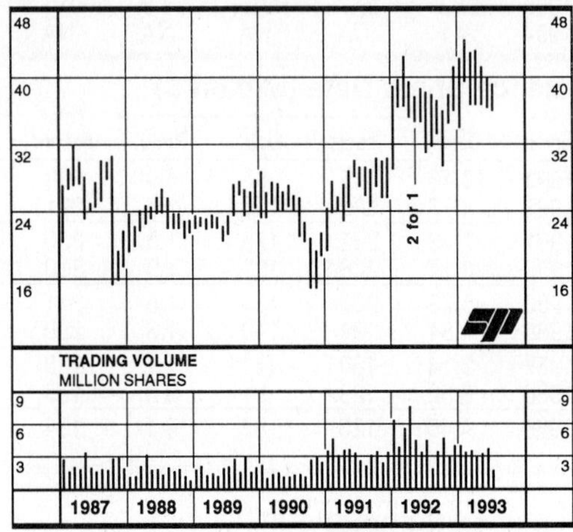

Net Sales (Million $)

Quarter:	1994	1993	1992	1991
Mar.	---	633	561	461
Jun.	---	654	592	495
Sep.	---	---	623	505
Dec.	---	---	597	543
	---	---	2,372	2,005

Sales for the six months ended June 30, 1993, rose 12%, year to year, reflecting strong lumber and particleboard prices and firmer prices for certain bleached paper grades. Benefiting from reduced manufacturing costs and increased manufacturing efficiencies, pretax income advanced 19%. After taxes at 38.0% in each period, net income was also up 19%, to $1.05 a share from $0.91. Results for the 1993 period exclude a credit of $0.48 a share related to accounting changes.

Common Share Earnings ($)

Quarter:	1994	1993	1992	1991
Mar.	E0.65	0.56	0.46	0.11
Jun.	E0.70	0.49	0.45	0.23
Sep.	E0.75	E0.55	0.37	0.27
Dec.	E0.70	E0.50	0.24	0.30
	E2.80	E2.10	1.52	0.90

Important Developments

Jul. '93— Willamette reported that plywood prices weakened substantially in the second quarter from first quarter levels due to disappointing housing starts. The company said it was continuing to focus on lowering manufacturing costs.

Apr. '93— Management said capital investment decisions were being complicated by uncertainty over the federal timber supply in the Northwest.

Next earnings report expected in mid-October.

Per Share Data ($)

Yr. End Dec. 31	1992	[1]1991	[1]1990	1989	1988	1987	[1]1986	1985	1984	1983
Tangible Bk. Val.	**21.27**	19.52	[2]19.42	17.72	14.69	12.12	10.27	9.31	8.62	7.87
Cash Flow	**4.75**	3.87	4.67	5.82	5.06	4.09	2.88	2.45	2.51	1.59
Earnings[3]	**1.52**	0.90	2.55	3.76	3.17	2.39	1.47	1.19	1.31	0.44
Dividends	**0.840**	0.800	0.800	0.725	0.600	0.540	0.510	0.498	0.453	0.453
Payout Ratio	**56%**	89%	31%	19%	19%	23%	35%	42%	35%	103%
Prices—High	**42½**	30⅜	28¾	27¾	26¾	32	23	15⅝	11¾	14
Low	**29**	19⅜	14⅞	20½	19¼	15⅜	14¾	10⅛	7	9½
P/E Ratio—	**28–19**	34–22	11–6	7–5	8–6	13–6	16–10	13–9	9–5	32–22

Data as orig. reptd. Adj. for stk. divs. of 100% May 1992, 66⅔% May 1986. **1.** Refl. merger or acq. **2.** Incl. intangibles. **3.** Bef. spec. item of -0.10 in 1984. E-Estimated.

Income Data (Million $)

Year Ended Dec. 31	Revs.	Oper. Inc.	% Oper. Inc. of Revs.	Cap. Exp.	Depr.	Int. Exp.	Net Bef. Taxes	Eff. Tax Rate	[3]Net Inc.	% Net Inc. of Revs.	Cash Flow
1992	**2,372**	**371**	**15.7**	**[2]367**	**174**	**73.8**	**129**	**37.0%**	**82**	**3.4**	**255**
[1]1991	2,005	295	14.7	[2]244	151	64.0	74	37.8%	46	2.3	197
[1]1990	1,905	347	18.2	[2]347	108	52.0	209	37.9%	130	6.8	237
1989	1,892	439	23.2	280	104	42.1	308	38.0%	191	10.1	296
1988	1,716	382	22.3	278	95	35.1	255	36.7%	161	9.4	257
1987	1,432	317	22.2	129	86	31.1	201	39.6%	121	8.5	208
[1]1986	1,200	206	17.1	243	71	25.9	112	33.2%	[4]75	6.2	146
1985	1,152	177	15.3	95	64	19.9	95	36.9%	60	5.2	124
1984	1,182	188	15.9	59	61	26.2	101	34.6%	66	5.6	127
1983	1,046	111	10.6	55	58	28.6	36	38.8%	22	2.1	80

Balance Sheet Data (Million $)

Dec. 31	Cash	Curr. Assets	Curr. Liab.	Curr. Ratio	Total Assets	% Ret. on Assets	Long Term Debt	Common Equity	Total Cap.	% LT Debt of Cap.	% Ret. on Equity
1992	**9.0**	**481**	**323**	**1.5**	**2,527**	**3.3**	**844**	**1,165**	**2,191**	**38.5**	**7.3**
1991	2.2	439	292	1.5	2,219	2.2	747	994	1,912	39.0	4.6
1990	21.1	402	246	1.6	1,965	7.3	565	987	1,717	32.9	13.7
1989	11.4	349	167	2.1	1,604	12.6	388	901	1,437	27.0	23.2
1988	33.2	344	152	2.3	1,430	12.3	391	747	1,275	30.7	23.6
1987	8.9	273	142	1.9	1,181	10.6	294	616	1,035	28.4	21.3
1986	1.3	231	143	1.6	1,100	7.4	314	522	954	32.9	15.0
1985	8.1	211	125	1.7	884	6.5	185	473	791	27.8	13.2
1984	17.1	232	174	1.3	882	7.1	183	438	757	31.6	15.8
1983	9.7	210	150	1.4	866	2.4	238	400	769	38.6	5.6

Data as orig. reptd. **1.** Refl. merger or acq. **2.** Net. **3.** Bef. spec. items. **4.** Refl. acctg. change.

Business Summary

Willamette Industries grows and harvests timber and manufactures paper and building products. The company owns or controls 1.2 million acres of forests. Segment contributions in 1992:

	Sales	Profits
Paper Group.....................	62%	49%
Building Materials Group	38%	51%

In 1992, the company accounted for 6.1% of U.S. production of bleached hardwood market pulp and 5.0% of U.S. fine paper production. Four Willamette paper mills manufactured 4.2% of the country's production of linerboard, corrugating medium and bag paper, most of which is used by WMTT's box and bag manufacturing plants or traded for their needs. Recycled fiber provides about 47% of the company's fiber needs.

Seven Willamette plants manufactured 5.4% of 1992 U.S. production of business forms. The company's continuous computer forms, photocopy and printer paper are marketed through 46 sales and distribution centers nationwide. Corrugated containers are made at 31 facilities, accounting for 4.8% of U.S. production in 1992, while five bag plants produced 10.1% of the nation's paper bags.

Willamette manufactured 7.4% of the plywood produced in the U.S. in 1992 at 11 plants, and its seven sawmills produced 1.1% of the nation's lumber output. Lumber and plywood products are marketed through independent wholesalers and distributors. Five Willamette facilities produced 13.9% of 1992 U.S. particleboard output, and two plants accounted for 17.8% of the nation's medium density fiberboard production. Composite board products are sold nationwide to distributors and cabinet and furniture makers. The company also accounted for 29% of U.S. laminated beam production in 1992.

Willamette supplies 40% of its own long-term log needs, with the remainder purchased through government and private sales and open market purchases.

Dividend Data

Amt of Divd. $	Date Decl.	Ex-divd. Date	Stock of Record	Payment Date
0.21	Aug. 7	Aug. 25	Aug. 31	Sep. 14'92
0.21	Nov. 12	Nov. 23	Nov. 30	Dec. 14'92
0.22	Feb. 11	Feb. 16	Feb. 22	Mar. 12'93
0.22	Apr. 13	May 24	May 31	Jun. 14'93

Capitalization

Long Term Debt: $873,302,000 (3/93).

Common Stock: 54,788,000 shs. ($0.50 par). Officers and directors control about 10%. Institutions hold approximately 61%. Shareholders: 11,500 (12/92).

Office—3800 First Interstate Tower, 1300 S.W. Fifth Ave., Portland, OR 97201. **Tel**—(503) 227-5581. **Chrmn & CEO**—W. Swindells. **Pres**—S. R. Rogel. **EVP, CFO, Secy, Treas & Investor Contact**—J. A. Parsons. **Dirs**—C. M. Bishop Jr., G. K. Drummond, E. B. Hart, C. W. Knodell, P. N. McCracken, S. J. Shelk Jr., R. Smelick, W. Swindells, S. C. Wheeler, B. R. Whiteley. **Transfer Agent & Registrar**—First Interstate Bank of Oregon, Portland. **Incorporated** in Oregon in 1906. **Empl**—12,000.

 Richard Spiegel

Wilmington Trust

NASDAQ Symbol WILM (Incl. in Nat'l Market) In S&P MidCap 400

Price	Range	P–E Ratio	Dividend	Yield	S&P Ranking	Beta
Sep. 30'93	1993					
30⅜	31–25½	14	1.00	3.3%	A+	0.97

Summary

This bank holding company, through its Wilmington Trust Co. subsidiary, operates more than 60 offices offering a broad variety of services, mainly in Wilmington, Del., and nearby counties. Earnings rose in each of the past 13 years. Both regulatory and shareholder approval has been received for the acquisition of Freedom Valley Bank of Pennsylvania.

Current Outlook

Earnings for 1994 are projected at $2.50 a share, up from the $2.28 estimated for 1993.

The quarterly dividend is likely to be raised to $0.27 a share in early 1994.

Loans should grow nearly 6% in 1993 and at least 6% in 1994, as commercial lending continues to increase, aided by the inclusion of Sussex Trust Co. and increased market share from existing operations in northern Delaware. The loan loss provision is likely to remain at current levels, as the company reduces total nonperforming assets and other real estate owned at a pace similar to its expected loan growth. The company sees a slight narrowing in net interest margins, as it plans to reduce the maturity length of its investment portfolio. Wilmington is selling its 30-year fixed mortgages, as the expense of hedging against increases in long-term rates continues to rise. Wilmington expects growth of at least 10% for nationwide corporate trust and investment management operations. The company plans to open a third office in Florida, in addition to two existing high-growth offices, and is opening two personal investment centers in Delaware, bringing the total there to eight.

Review of Operations

For the six months to June 30, 1993, net interest income gained 7.2%, year to year. The provision for loan losses fell 38%, to $5.0 million, and with a 3.1% increase in noninterest income, constrained by lower securities gains, and 5.3% greater noninterest expense, pretax income climbed 13%. After taxes at 30.2%, versus 26.9%, income was up 7.6%, to $40,093,000 ($1.08 a share), from $37,256,000 ($0.98). Results for the 1992 period exclude a charge of $0.39 a share from an accounting change.

Common Share Earnings ($)

Quarter:	1994	1993	[2]1992	1991
Mar.	E0.55	0.53	[1]0.47	0.44
Jun.	E0.60	0.55	0.51	0.48
Sep.	E0.65	E0.60	0.55	0.54
Dec.	E0.70	E0.60	0.56	0.55
	E2.50	E2.28	2.09	2.04

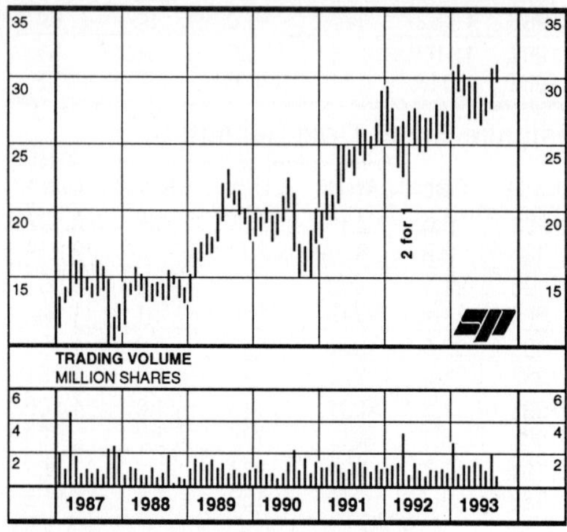

Important Developments

Sep. '93— The company said the purchase of Freedom Valley Bank, which has received approval from both regulators and Freedom Valley's shareholders, is expected to be completed early in the fourth quarter of 1993. It had previously agreed to buy Freedom Valley Bank (assets of $110 million) for $11.85 million in cash. Freedom Valley has branches in four Pennsylvania towns.

Dec. '92— As a result of the adoption of SFAS No. 106 (accounting for postretirement benefits), Wilmington recorded a net charge of $14.7 million ($0.39 a share), retroactive to the 1992 first quarter. The company elected to incur the charge in a single period, instead of amortizing it over future years, reflecting Wilmington's strong financial condition.

Next earnings report expected in mid-October.

Per Share Data ($)

Yr. End Dec. 31	[2]1992	[2]1991	[2]1990	1989	1988	1987	1986	1985	[2]1984	1983
Tangible Bk. Val.	**10.12**	9.72	8.41	7.45	6.53	5.56	4.84	4.17	3.65	3.27
Earnings[1]	**2.09**	2.04	1.90	1.70	1.49	1.23	0.98	0.79	0.64	0.50
Dividends	**0.88**	0.795	0.72	0.59	0.46	0.39	0.315	0.275	0.22	0.193
Payout Ratio	**42%**	39%	38%	35%	31%	32%	32%	35%	34%	39%
Prices—High	**29⅜**	29⅜	22½	23⅛	15¾	18	12¾	9½	5½	3 15/16
Low	**22⅝**	18	15⅛	13¼	11½	10	9⅛	5½	3⅞	2½
P/E Ratio—	**14–11**	14–9	12–8	14–8	11–8	15–8	13–9	12–7	9–6	8–5

Data as orig. reptd. Adj. for stk. divs. of 100% Apr. 1992, Nov. 1986, 100% Aug. 1985, 100% Nov. 1983. **1.** Bef. spec. item of -0.39 in 1992. **2.** Refl. merger or acq. E-Estimated.

Income Data (Million $)

Year Ended Dec. 31	Net Int. Inc.	Tax Equiv. Adj.	Non Int. Inc.	Loan Loss Prov.	% Exp./ Op. Revs.	Net Bef. Taxes	Eff. Tax Rate	[2]Net Inc.	% Net Int. Margin	—% Return On— Assets	Equity
[1]1992	**165**	**12.1**	**108**	**13.0**	**53.9**	**109**	**27.5%**	**78.8**	**4.62**	**1.90**	**21.5**
[1]1991	142	16.1	96	13.3	51.4	94	23.9%	71.9	4.47	1.91	22.7
[1]1990	126	18.5	90	10.5	52.0	84	20.2%	67.0	4.32	1.88	24.5
1989	114	18.9	75	10.3	52.3	73	18.4%	59.4	4.62	1.91	24.4
1988	99	16.4	71	10.3	52.8	64	18.9%	51.8	4.54	1.87	25.2
1987	86	21.4	69	10.7	52.3	55	20.7%	43.4	4.33	1.61	23.7
1986	73	33.0	59	8.3	52.3	38	10.5%	34.0	4.58	1.37	21.8
1985	68	23.8	46	6.8	55.3	28	3.2%	27.0	5.01	1.36	20.4
[1]1984	61	14.1	40	4.4	57.4	26	18.8%	21.5	4.82	1.27	19.1
1983	53	10.2	30	2.7	62.8	20	18.4%	16.3	4.31	1.02	16.3

Balance Sheet Data (Million $)

Dec. 31	Total Assets	—Earning Assets— Mon. Mkt. Assets	Inv. Secs.	Com'l Loans	Other Loans	% Loan Loss Resv.	—Deposits— Demand	Time	% Loans/ Deposits	Long Term Debt	Common Equity	% Equity To Assets
1992	**4,285**	**147**	**802**	**867**	**2,142**	**1.57**	**528**	**2,746**	**91.5**	**Nil**	**377**	**8.88**
1991	4,061	141	828	842	1,932	1.46	424	2,623	90.7	Nil	346	8.41
1990	3,834	117	835	791	1,824	1.46	392	2,461	91.3	Nil	296	7.67
1989	3,703	237	793	739	1,642	1.45	452	2,162	90.8	Nil	258	7.83
1988	2,982	191	482	676	1,369	1.51	421	1,871	89.3	3.3	228	7.43
1987	2,891	361	528	659	1,112	1.46	543	1,851	74.0	3.5	193	6.82
1986	2,778	377	522	607	1,023	1.53	696	1,534	73.1	3.7	170	6.25
1985	2,328	235	437	534	884	1.37	480	1,350	77.5	17.1	144	6.65
1984	2,085	470	298	405	700	1.24	601	1,013	68.5	19.6	123	6.64
1983	1,795	456	299	306	558	1.35	392	891	67.3	22.2	106	6.27

Data as orig. reptd. **1.** Refl. merger or acq. **2.** Bef. spec. item in 1992.

Business Summary

Wilmington Trust Corporation conducts commercial banking, savings, trust, investment management and other financial activities through its Wilmington Trust Co. subsidiary, which operates a main office and seven branches in Wilmington, Del., 23 in New Castle County, 11 in Kent County, 19 in Sussex County and one in Chester County, Pa. Operations were expanded with the acquisition of Sussex Trust Co. in January 1992.

At 1992 year-end, the gross loan portfolio of $3.01 billion ($3.03 billion at 1991 year-end) was divided: mortgage 44% (45% in 1991); commercial, financial and agricultural 29% (28%); consumer 23% (23%); and construction 4% (4%).

The reserve for possible loan losses at December 31, 1992, was $46,962,000 ($44,996,000 a year earlier), equal to 1.59% (1.54%) of average loans outstanding. Net chargeoffs in 1992 amounted to $11,034,000 ($13,111,000 in 1991), equal to 0.37% (0.45%) of average loans. Nonaccruing loans, restructured loans and loans past due 90 days or more totaled $32,019,000 (1.07% of loans outstanding) at 1992 year-end, compared with $42,361,000 (1.40%) a year earlier.

Total deposits at 1992 year-end amounted to $3.27 billion, of which demand deposits represented about 16%, savings 9%, interest checking 14%, money market 19%, certificates of under $100,000 35% and certificates of $100,000 and more 7%.

On a tax-equivalent basis, the average yield on total interest-earning assets was 8.54% in 1992 (9.82% in 1991), while the average rate paid on total interest-bearing liabilities was 4.61% (6.33%), for a net interest spread of 3.93% (3.49%).

Dividend Data

Cash has been paid each year since 1914. A dividend reinvestment plan is available.

Amt. of Divd. $	Date Decl.	Ex–divd. Date	Stock of Record	Payment Date
0.225	Oct. 15	Nov. 6	Nov. 2	Nov. 16'92
0.225	Jan. 21	Jan. 26	Feb. 1	Feb. 16'93
0.25	Apr. 15	Apr. 26	May 3	May 17'93
0.25	Jul. 15	Jul. 27	Aug. 2	Aug. 16'93

Capitalization

Long Term Debt: None (6/93).

Common Stock: 37,069,411 shs. ($1 par).
Institutions hold about 41%.
Shareholders: 8,261 (12/92).

Office—Rodney Sq. North, Wilmington, DE 19890. **Tel**—(302) 651-1000. **Chrmn, Pres, & CEO**—L. W. Quill. **Exec VP & CFO**—T. T. Cecala. **Exec VP & Treas**—R. V. A. Harra Jr. **VP & Secy**—T. P. Collins. **Investor Contact**—Charles W. King (302) 651-8069. **Dirs**—R. H. Bolling Jr., C. S. Burger, J. E. Burris, R. R. Collins Jr., C. S. Crompton Jr., N. M. Curtis, E. B. duPont, H. S. Dunn Jr., G. P. Edmonds, R. C. Forney, T. L. Gossage, A. B. Kirkpatrick Jr., W. F. Laird, R. L. Mears, H. E. Miller, S. J. Mobley, L. W. Quill, D. P. Roselle, T. P. Sweeney, B. J. Taylor II, M. J. Theisen, R. W. Tunnell Jr. **Transfer Agent & Registrar**—Co. itself. **Incorporated** in Delaware in 1901; reincorporated in 1985. **Empl**—2,188.

 C. Orgielewicz

Wisconsin Energy

NYSE Symbol WEC In S&P MidCap 400

Price	Range	P-E Ratio	Dividend	Yield	S&P Ranking	Beta
Aug. 26'93	1993					
28½	28¾–24¾	17	1.36	4.8%	A	0.45

Summary

This electric and gas utility holding company, one of the most financially sound power companies in the U.S., derives its power requirements primarily from coal and to a lesser extent from nuclear facilities. WEC's coal plants are expected to exceed national emission control standards. The longer-term outlook is enhanced by a supportive regulatory climate, nonutility ventures, and excellent cash flow.

Current Outlook

Share earnings for 1993 are estimated at $1.85, up from the $1.67 reported for 1992. Share earnings could rise to $1.95 in 1994.

The quarterly dividend was raised 4.2%, to $0.33⅞ from $0.32½, effective with the June 1993 payment. WEC is expected to maintain above-average dividend growth for the next several years.

Share earnings for 1993 should benefit from rate hikes and the likelihood of both a return to more normal weather conditions and a stronger economic recovery. Share earnings for 1994 should be aided by higher kwh sales as the economy continues to strengthen, aggressive cost controls, and improved results from nonutility ventures, partially offset by slight increases in interest expense and shares outstanding.

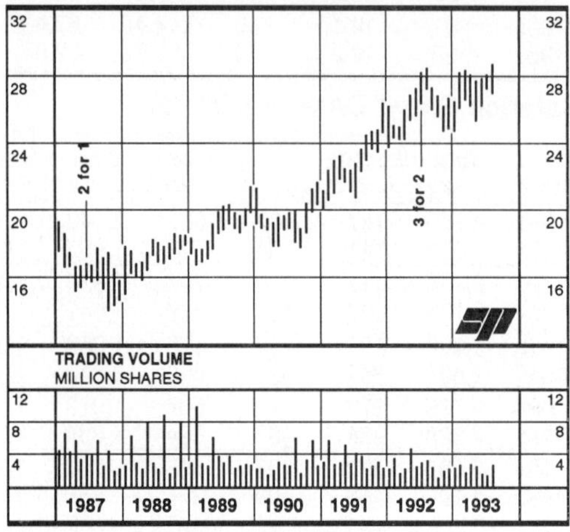

Operating Revenues (Million $)

Quarter:	1993	1992	1991	1990
Mar.	443	422	418	391
Jun.	375	357	355	338
Sep.	---	358	364	341
Dec.	---	414	402	372
	---	1,552	1,539	1,443

Revenues for the six months to June 30, 1993, rose 5.0%, year to year. After 4.7% higher operating expenses, operating income increased 7.1%. Higher other income (net) was more than offset by increased interest charges. Net income was up 2.5%. With 2.5% more average shares outstanding, share earnings were unchanged at $0.83.

Common Share Earnings ($)

Quarter:	1993	1992	1991	1990
Mar.	0.56	0.53	0.54	0.53
Jun.	0.28	0.30	0.37	0.38
Sep.	E0.51	0.37	0.50	0.48
Dec.	E0.50	0.46	0.48	0.46
	E1.85	1.67	1.87	1.85

Important Developments

Aug. '93— WEC entered into a definitive agreement to acquire Wisconsin Southern Gas Co., Inc., in an exchange of stock valued at about $46 million.

Feb. '93— The Public Service Commission of Wisconsin (PSCW) authorized an annualized retail electric base rate hike of $26.7 million (2.3%), effective February 17, 1993, which includes the elimination of the $24.2 million fuel adjustment rate reduction in effect since May 29, 1992. The hike is based on an authorized regulatory return on common equity of 12.3%, down from 12.8% authorized for 1992. In January, the Federal Energy Regulatory Commission authorized a hike in WEC's wholesale rates by $8.5 million (15%) on an annual basis, effective June 9, 1993. The hike is subject to refund pending an investigation, hearing and final order.

Next earnings report expected in late October.

Per Share Data ($)

Yr. End Dec. 31	1992	1991	1990	1989	1988	1987	1986	1985	1984	1983
Tangible Bk. Val.	**14.78**	14.25	13.63	13.41	12.56	11.71	10.98	10.30	9.47	8.77
Earnings	**1.67**	1.87	1.85	1.92	1.82	1.70	1.58	1.59	1.45	1.33
Dividends	**1.285**	1.223	1.157	1.087	1.010	0.943	0.877	0.810	0.746	0.687
Payout Ratio	**77%**	65%	63%	57%	55%	55%	55%	51%	51%	52%
Prices—High	**28½**	26⁷⁄₁₆	21¹¹⁄₁₆	21⁷⁄₁₆	18⁹⁄₁₆	19¼	21⁹⁄₁₆	13⁹⁄₁₆	11¼	9⁹⁄₁₆
Low	**23¾**	20	17¾	16¾	15	14	12¹³⁄₁₆	10⁵⁄₁₆	8⁹⁄₁₆	7⁵⁄₁₆
P/E Ratio—	**17–14**	14–11	12–10	11–9	10–8	11–8	14–8	9–6	8–6	7–6

Data as orig. reptd. Adj. for stk. div(s). of 50% Jul. 1992, 100% Jul. 1987. E-Estimated.

Income Data (Million $)

Year Ended Dec. 31	Revs.	Depr.	Maint.	Oper. Ratio	[1]Fxd. Chgs. Cover.	Constr. Credits	Eff. Tax Rate	Net Inc.	% Return On Revs.	% Return On [2]Invest. Capital	% Return On Com. Equity
1992	**1,552**	**163**	**150**	**84.6%**	**3.71**	**12.1**	**33.8%**	**170**	**10.9**	**8.1**	**11.3**
1991	1,539	147	142	83.7%	4.18	13.4	33.8%	189	12.3	9.1	13.4
1990	1,442	145	134	83.3%	4.25	12.2	34.5%	187	12.9	9.3	13.8
1989	1,493	154	150	82.3%	4.15	9.1	34.4%	194	13.0	11.1	15.2
1988	1,541	146	171	83.1%	3.93	5.4	34.4%	183	11.9	11.4	15.5
1987	1,365	139	139	81.5%	4.04	3.4	41.0%	170	12.4	11.5	15.5
1986	1,411	143	121	84.4%	4.96	5.5	46.8%	158	11.2	10.9	15.4
1985	1,441	141	121	84.9%	5.45	7.0	46.8%	167	11.6	11.6	16.6
1984	1,435	125	125	86.0%	5.06	16.2	46.0%	163	11.3	11.4	16.8
1983	1,418	108	111	85.5%	4.27	13.2	46.3%	150	10.6	11.5	16.4

Balance Sheet Data (Million $)

Dec. 31	[3]Gross Prop.	Capital Expend.	Net Prop.	% Earn. on Net Prop.	Total Cap.	Capitalization LT Debt	% LT Debt	Pfd.	% Pfd.	Com.	% Com.
1992	**4,463**	**344**	**2,629**	**9.4**	**3,402**	**1,210**	**42.4**	**98**	**3.5**	**1,543**	**54.1**
1991	4,170	268	2,466	10.4	3,180	1,094	41.4	100	3.8	1,450	54.8
1990	3,977	238	2,374	10.3	3,003	990	40.0	100	4.1	1,384	55.9
1989	3,805	230	2,060	12.9	2,585	1,004	41.4	100	4.2	1,314	54.3
1988	3,676	180	2,025	12.8	2,545	1,044	44.0	100	4.2	1,230	51.8
1987	3,598	401	2,040	13.1	2,227	849	40.9	100	4.8	1,128	54.3
1986	3,203	150	1,768	12.4	2,228	886	43.4	100	4.9	1,057	51.7
1985	3,105	162	1,788	12.2	1,979	702	39.3	100	5.6	986	55.1
1984	2,984	153	1,796	11.2	1,896	634	37.0	160	9.4	919	53.6
1983	2,872	163	1,795	11.5	1,918	692	39.7	185	10.6	868	49.7

Data as orig. reptd. **1.** Times int. exp. & pfd. divs. covered (pretax). **2.** Based on income before interest charges. **3.** Utility plant.

Business Summary

Wisconsin Energy is the holding company for Wisconsin Electric Power and Wisconsin Natural Gas, which supply electricity (84% of 1992 revenues), gas (15%) and steam service (1%) in Milwaukee, northern Wisconsin and the Upper Peninsula of Michigan. WEC also owns five nonregulated businesses. Electric revenues by class:

	1992	1991	1990	1989
Residential	34%	35%	34%	33%
Small comm'l & ind'l	29%	28%	29%	28%
Large comm'l & ind'l	30%	29%	29%	30%
Other	7%	8%	8%	9%

Some 61% of WEC's generating capability was derived from coal in 1992, 28% from nuclear, 10% from purchased power, and 1% from other sources. WEC's nuclear capacity is composed of the two-unit Point Beach nuclear station. Future generation will be derived from purchased power and combustion turbine units. Peak load in 1992 was 4,640 mw, and capability at peak totaled 5,255 mw, for a capacity margin of 12%. Gas deliveries in 1992 totaled 670,687,000 therms, versus 669,328,000 therms in 1991.

WEC plans to complete a total of 600 mw of natural gas-fired combustion turbine peaking capacity by the summer of 1995 with about 200 mw of additional generating capacity to be provided by a WEC-owned cogeneration facility planned for completion in 1994. Construction of additional generating capacity is planned for later in the 1990s, including about 225 mw scheduled for completion in 1997. However, WEC is evaluating whether intermediate load capacity would better fit the anticipated growth in future demand requirements.

Dividend Data

Dividends have been paid since 1939. A dividend reinvestment plan is available.

Amt of Divd. $	Date Decl.	Ex-divd. Date	Stock of Record	Payment Date
0.32½	Oct. 29	Nov. 3	Nov. 9	Dec. 1'92
0.32½	Jan. 27	Feb. 2	Feb. 8	Mar. 1'93
0.33⅞	Apr. 28	May 4	May 10	Jun. 1'93
0.33⅞	Jul. 29	Aug. 3	Aug. 9	Sep. 1'93

Capitalization

Long Term Debt: $1,227,272,000 (6/93).

Subsid. Preferred Stock: $98,351,000.

Common Stock: 104,259,613 shs. ($0.01 par). Institutions hold about 30%. Shareholders of record: 79,478.

Office—231 West Michigan St. (P.O. Box 2949), Milwaukee, WI 53201. **Tel**—(414) 221-2590. **Chrmn & Pres**—R. A. Abdoo. **Secy**—J. H. Goetsch. **Treas**—J. G. Remmel. **Investor Contact**—Charles Ziegler (414) 221-4444. **Dirs**—R. A. Abdoo, J. F. Bergstrom, J. W. Boston, G. B. Johnson, J. L. Murray, M. W. Reid, F. P. Stratton Jr., J. G. Udell. **Transfer Agents**—First Chicago Trust Co. of New York, NYC; Company's office. **Registrars**—First Wisconsin Trust Co., Milwaukee; First Chicago Trust Co. of New York, NYC. **Incorporated** in Wisconsin in 1896; reincorporated in Wisconsin in 1986. **Empl**—5,656.

 Christopher J. Grant

Witco Corp.

NYSE Symbol WIT Options on NYSE (Jan-Apr-Jul-Oct) In S&P MidCap 400

Price	Range	P-E Ratio	Dividend	Yield	S&P Ranking	Beta
Sep. 13'93	1993					
60⅝	62¾–48	28	2.00	3.3%	B+	0.92

Summary

This company produces a wide range of specialty chemical and petroleum products and engineered materials and parts for industrial and consumer use. The November 1992 acquisition of the natural substances and industrial chemicals divisions of Schering AG greatly increased Witco's sales and doubled its international revenues. The dividend was recently raised 8.7% and a 2-for-1 stock split is pending.

Current Outlook

Share earnings for 1993 are estimated at $3.15, up from 1992's $2.38. For 1994, share earnings could reach $3.75. (All figures unadjusted for the pending 2-for-1 stock split.)

The quarterly dividend on present shares was recently raised 8.7%, to $0.50 from $0.46.

Sales for 1993 are projected at about $2.3 billion, reflecting the November 1992 purchase of the natural substances and industrial chemicals divisions of Schering AG, which has greatly expanded WIT's surfactants, oleochemicals and polymer additives businesses. The healthier U.S. economy will also boost sales, but European markets may remain soft. The integration of the two businesses and a corporate reorganization should result in significant cost savings, especially beginning in the 1993 second half. There will be about 10% more shares following the March 1993 stock offering.

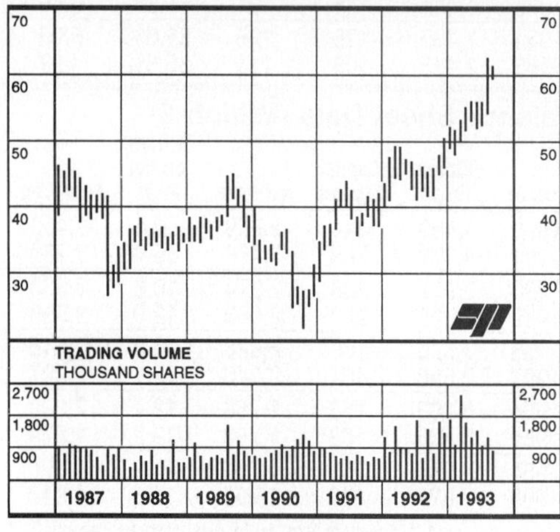

Net Sales (Million $)

Quarter:	1993	1992	1991	1990
Mar.	553	420	398	395
Jun.	549	427	421	403
Sep.	---	425	420	419
Dec.	---	456	391	414
	---	1,729	1,631	1,631

Sales for the first half of 1993 rose 30%, year to year, primarily reflecting the Schering acquisitions in late 1992. Including in 1993 a nonrecurring charge of $0.23 a share, net income fell 8.7%, to $1.36 a share from $1.59, which was before an accounting charge of $0.59.

Common Share Earnings ($)

Quarter:	1993	1992	1991	1990
Mar.	0.80	0.82	0.74	0.63
Jun.	0.58	0.78	0.70	0.98
Sep.	E0.85	0.81	0.92	0.85
Dec.	E0.92	d0.03	0.85	0.49
	E3.15	2.38	3.21	2.95

Important Developments

Jul. '93— Second quarter 1993 earnings included an after-tax charge of $6.06 million ($0.23 a share) for the sublease arrangements of existing offices to be vacated when WIT's relocates to its new world headquarters in 1994.

Mar. '93— Witco sold publicly 2.875 million common shares at $51.25 per share and $275 million of debt securities. Proceeds from the offerings were used to repay most of the $440 million of debt incurred in the November 1992 purchase of the industrial chemicals and natural substances divisions of Schering AG. The 1992 fourth quarter loss included a charge of $13.3 million ($0.53 a share) for the consolidation of offices, and a loss of $2.8 million ($0.11) related to the acquisition of the Schering units. In December 1992, WIT announced a restructuring that recasted the company along business lines.

Next earnings report expected in late October.

Per Share Data ($)

Yr. End Dec. 31	[2]1992	1991	1990	1989	1988	1987	1986	1985	1984	1983
Tangible Bk. Val.	**16.37**	25.52	25.11	24.54	24.96	22.11	20.16	18.05	16.27	14.57
Cash Flow	**4.86**	5.41	4.96	3.46	4.77	4.58	5.18	4.75	4.74	4.19
Earnings[1]	**2.38**	3.21	2.95	1.60	3.05	2.72	2.93	2.57	2.85	2.40
Dividends	**1.840**	1.810	1.720	1.665	1.445	1.200	1.086	0.988	0.960	0.860
Payout Ratio	**77%**	56%	55%	107%	47%	42%	34%	38%	34%	36%
Prices—High	**50⅝**	44	39⅞	45⅛	38⅜	47⅜	40	27⅞	26⅜	24⅞
Low	**40**	28⅞	21¾	34⅝	30⅝	26⅝	26⅜	22	18½	11½
P/E Ratio—	**21–17**	14–9	14–7	28–22	13–10	17–10	14–9	11–9	9–6	10–5

Data as orig. reptd. Adj. for stk. divs. of 50% Jul. 1986, 50% Jul. 1983. **1.** Bef. spec. item of -0.59 in 1992, +0.80 in 1988. **2.** Reflects merger or acquisition. d-Deficit. E-Estimated

Income Data (Million $)

Year Ended Dec. 31	Revs.	Oper. Inc.	% Oper. Inc. of Revs.	Cap. Exp.	Depr.	Int. Exp.	[1]Net Bef. Taxes	Eff. Tax Rate	[2]Net Inc.	% Net Inc. of Revs.	Cash Flow
[4]1992	**1,729**	**174**	**10.1**	**72.6**	**67.1**	**17.3**	**82**	**34.4%**	**[3]53.9**	**3.1**	**121**
1991	1,631	173	10.6	74.3	59.6	17.2	110	33.1%	73.5	4.5	133
1990	1,631	149	9.1	90.8	55.3	18.2	106	35.8%	68.0	4.2	123
1989	1,588	155	9.7	70.4	52.7	17.6	53	34.5%	35.0	2.2	88
1988	1,586	176	11.1	72.1	48.8	18.0	116	38.0%	71.6	4.5	120
1987	1,428	153	10.7	69.1	50.0	17.3	100	36.8%	63.3	4.4	113
1986	1,355	162	12.0	60.1	50.8	13.6	108	39.8%	[3]65.2	4.8	116
1985	1,449	141	9.7	71.1	48.3	14.0	94	39.4%	56.8	3.9	105
1984	1,496	144	9.6	65.7	41.6	16.0	92	32.2%	62.6	4.2	104
1983	1,386	133	9.6	44.9	39.0	15.4	90	42.3%	52.0	3.8	91

Balance Sheet Data (Million $)

Dec. 31	Cash	Curr. Assets	Curr. Liab.	Curr. Ratio	Total Assets	% Ret. on Assets	Long Term Debt	Common Equity	Total Cap.	% LT Debt of Cap.	% Ret. on Equity
1992	**134**	**747**	**769**	**1.0**	**1,812**	**3.5**	**173**	**614**	**896**	**19.3**	**8.6**
1991	139	577	256	2.3	1,198	6.2	179	625	878	20.4	12.1
1990	116	563	204	2.8	1,179	6.0	230	587	878	26.2	12.0
1989	213	636	180	3.5	1,139	3.1	236	571	858	27.4	6.1
1988	194	635	196	3.2	1,115	6.6	241	578	888	27.1	13.1
1987	227	620	203	3.1	1,056	6.7	243	513	823	29.5	12.9
1986	68	412	165	2.5	820	8.0	96	464	626	15.3	14.8
1985	83	408	174	2.3	810	7.2	136	414	604	22.5	14.4
1984	34	367	164	2.2	756	8.4	143	373	518	27.7	17.6
1983	56	380	177	2.1	733	7.4	147	334	484	30.4	16.3

Data as orig. reptd. **1.** Incl. equity in earns. of nonconsol. subs. **2.** Bef. spec. items. **3.** Refl. acctg. change. **4.** Reflects merger or acquisition.

Business Summary

Witco Corp. (formerly Witco Chemical) produces a wide range of specialty chemical and petroleum products and engineered materials and parts. Contributions by industry segment in 1992:

	Sales	Profits
Petroleum	42%	40%
Chemical	48%	57%
Diversified	10%	3%

Foreign operations accounted for 22% of sales in 1992 and 24% of profits.

Petroleum consists of petroleum specialties (white mineral oils, petrolatums, sulfonates, microcrystalline waxes, refrigeration and ink oils, cable fillers) and lubricants (lubricants, greases and equipment, naphthenic oils, asphalt, road treatment products, and Kendall and Amalie brand motor oils and lubricants) produced from refined or semi-refined oils.

Chemicals include oleochemicals (fatty acids, glycerines, amines, amides, esters), surfactants (surfactants, emulsifiers, detergents and cleaners), plastic additives (stabilizers, plasticizers, lubricants, anti-oxidants, catalysts, stearates, organic peroxides), polyester and urethane resins and intermediates, epoxy resins, polyamide and polyamine resins, and curing agents.

Diversified products include metal cleaning, plating and corrosion resistant products, carbon black, and lightweight conveyor belts, molded industrial diaphragms and coated fabrics. Witco is the leading independent producer of plastic and hard rubber battery containers, covers and parts.

Dividend Data

Dividends have been paid since 1950. A dividend reinvestment plan is available.

Amt of Divd. $	Date Decl.	Ex–divd. Date	Stock of Record	Payment Date
0.46	Dec. 3	Dec. 8	Dec. 14	Jan. 5'93
0.46	Mar. 2	Mar. 5	Mar. 11	Apr. 1'93
0.46	Jun. 9	Jun. 14	Jun. 18	Jul. 1'93
0.50	Sep. 2	Sep. 10	Sep. 16	Oct. 5'93
2–for–1	Sep. 2	Oct. 6	Sep. 16	Oct. 5'93

Capitalization

Long Term Debt: $488,326,000 (6/93).

$2.65 Conv. Preferred Stock: 9,361 shs. ($1 par); red. at $66; conv. into 8.4037 com.

Common Stock: 25,219,870 shs. ($5 par). Institutions hold about 69%. Shareholders of record: 5,262.

Office—520 Madison Ave., New York, NY 10022-4236. **Tel**—(212) 605-3800. **Chrmn & CEO**—W. R. Toller. **EVP-CFO**—M. D. Fullwood. **VP-Secy**—D. McCoy. **SVP & Investor Contact**—C. R. Soderlind. **Dirs**—D. Andreuzzi, W. J. Ashe, S. Brinberg, W. G. Burns, W. R. Grant, R. M. Hayden, H. G. Hohn, W. E. Mahoney, L. J. Polite Jr., D. J. Samuel, L. Scheinbart, H. Sonneborn III, W. R. Toller, B. F. Wesson, W. Wishnick. **Transfer Agent & Registrar**—First Chicago Trust Co. of New York, NYC. **Incorporated** in Delaware in 1968. **Empl**—8,400.

 Richard O'Reilly, CFA

XOMA Corp.

NASDAQ Symbol XOMA (Incl. in Nat'l Market) Options on ASE, CBOE, NYSE In S&P MidCap 400

Price	Range	P-E Ratio	Dividend	Yield	S&P Ranking	Beta
Sep. 2'93	1993					
6⅛	10½–5	NM	None	None	C	2.00

Summary

This company is developing pharmaceutical products based on recombinant DNA and other technologies for the targeted treatment of infectious and immune system diseases and other serious disorders. Efforts to obtain FDA approval for a septic shock drug and for a product to treat graft versus host disease are continuing. A major restructuring was undertaken in late 1992, and a related $10 million charge was recorded.

Business Summary

XOMA Corp. is a leading developer of biotechnology and other technologies for the targeted treatment of infectious and immune system diseases and other serious disorders. In October 1992, the company refocused its R&D strategy to emphasize products based on recombinantly-derived human bactericidal/permeability increasing protein (rBPI), as well as new T lymphocyte-targeted products for autoimmune disease therapy, while continuing development of E5 for treatment of gram-negative sepsis and CD5 Plus for graft versus host disease (GvHD).

XOMA was evaluating, in mid-1993, potential indications for efficacy testing in Phase II studies on rBPI-23, a naturally occurring protein isolated from certain immune cells, as a potential treatment of bacterial infections and other indications. It is part of the body's natural defense against infection, and has both endotoxin-binding and bactericidal properties against a broad range of gram-negative bacteria. It may also have anti-inflammatory and other potentially useful clinical properties.

The company has completed several clinical trials (including two Phase III studies) of E5, a murine monoclonal antibody that neutralizes the effects of endotoxin, a poison released from most clinically relevant species of gram-negative bacteria. In October 1992, XOMA said that because of FDA notification that earlier Phase III trials were not sufficient to warrant marketing approval, it intended to conduct a third Phase III trial, to be managed and co-funded by Pfizer Inc. This trial commenced in June 1993

CD5 Plus is an immunoconjugate that has the targeting specificity of a monoclonal antibody and the cell-killing capacity of a cytotoxic enzyme. XOMA is continuing to seek FDA approval of the product for graft versus host Disease (GvHD) in bone marrow patients. However, in October 1992, the company decided to cease development of CD5 Plus for autoimmune diseases.

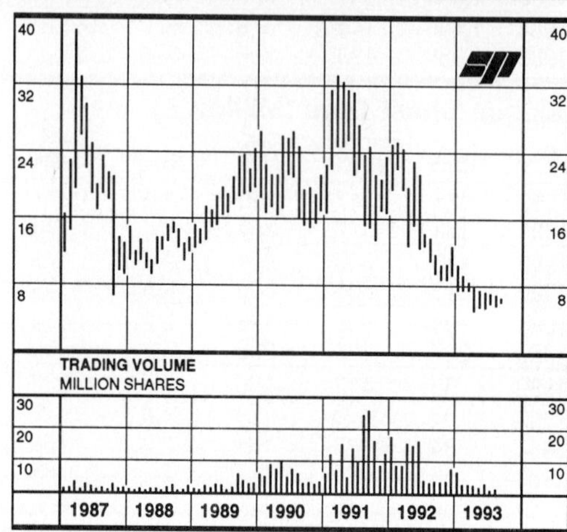

The company is using its experience with CD5 Plus to develop and evaluate several proprietary variants of genetically engineered T lymphocyte-targeted proteins that incorporate CD5's targeting specificity and cell-killing properties, while possibly offering greater potency, opportunities for chronic administration, and simplified manufacturing processes. XOMA is also investigating a series of novel synthetic peptides (derived from T lymphocytes) that appear to be associated with specific autoimmune disease processes and may be capable of inducing tolerance to or reversing the disease.

XOMA continues to explore alternatives, including corporate alliances, for development of additional products outside the scope of its core research efforts, involving immunoconjugates for melanoma and colorectal cancer, osteoinductive proteins for bone repair, and non-cariogenic proteins for low-calorie flavor enhancement.

Next earnings report expected in early November.

Per Share Data ($)

Yr. End Dec. 31	1992	1991	1990	[1]1989	1988	1987	[2]1986	1985
Tangible Bk. Val.	**4.12**	6.28	1.78	2.02	2.74	3.63	1.37	d9.57
Cash Flow	**d2.06**	d1.67	d1.56	d1.32	d1.04	d1.05	d7.97	d2.38
Earnings	**d2.20**	d1.77	d1.68	d1.43	d1.12	d1.24	d6.36	d1.01
Dividends	**Nil**	Nil	Nil	Nil	Nil	Nil	Nil	Nil
Payout Ratio	**Nil**	Nil	Nil	Nil	Nil	Nil	Nil	Nil
Prices—High	**25¼**	33¼	26½	24½	15½	38⅝	17½	NA
Low	**8¾**	13½	15	12½	9¼	6¾	8	NA
P/E Ratio—	**NM**	NM	NM	NM	NM	NM	NM	NA

Data as orig. reptd. 1. Refl. merger or acq. 2. Refl. acctg. change. d-Deficit. NM-Not Meaningful. NA-Not Available.

Income Data (Million $)

Year Ended Dec. 31	Revs.	Oper. Inc.	% Oper. Inc. of Revs.	Cap. Exp.	Depr.	Int. Exp.	Net Bef. Taxes	Eff. Tax Rate	Net Inc.	% Net Inc. of Revs.	Cash Flow
1992	**5.1**	**d35.9**	**NM**	**6.82**	**3.00**	**NA**	**d47.1**	**NM**	**d47.1**	**NM**	**d44.1**
1991	17.1	d39.3	NM	6.42	1.94	1.73	[3]d34.3	NM	d34.3	NM	d32.4
1990	20.5	d22.0	NM	1.59	1.69	5.87	[3]d23.7	NM	d23.7	NM	d22.0
[1]1989	10.4	d21.2	NM	2.05	1.44	5.06	[3]d18.9	NM	d18.9	NM	d17.4
1988	5.0	d13.4	NM	4.63	0.82	1.60	[3]d12.0	NM	d12.0	NM	d11.2
1987	5.8	d11.7	NM	0.98	1.90	2.12	[3]d12.2	NM	d12.2	NM	d10.3
[2]1986	0.1	d13.1	NM	1.62	1.98	1.26	[3]d46.6	NM	d46.7	NM	d44.7
1985	7.3	d4.2	NM	2.67	1.40	Nil	[3]d4.8	NM	d4.8	NM	d3.4

Balance Sheet Data (Million $)

Dec. 31	Cash	Curr. Assets	Curr. Liab.	Curr. Ratio	Total Assets	% Ret. on Assets	Long Term Debt	Common Equity	Total Cap.	% LT Debt of Cap.	% Ret. on Equity
1992	**83.0**	**91.0**	**9.90**	**9.2**	**109**	**NM**	**1.1**	**88.0**	**90**	**1.2**	**NM**
1991	124.3	139.5	18.33	7.6	154	NM	1.5	134.0	136	1.1	NM
1990	72.1	85.2	11.70	7.3	97	NM	58.9	26.4	85	69.0	NM
1989	91.3	98.7	6.72	14.7	111	NM	76.7	27.1	104	73.9	NM
1988	45.3	47.5	3.41	13.9	55	NM	21.8	29.8	52	42.2	NM
1987	60.2	62.2	3.36	18.5	66	NM	24.7	38.5	63	39.1	NM
1986	40.5	41.8	3.23	13.0	47	NM	32.2	12.0	44	72.9	NM
1985	8.5	9.0	1.32	6.9	15	NM	0.2	d14.4	14	1.7	NM

Data as orig. reptd. **1.** Refl. merger or acq. **2.** Refl. acctg. change. **3.** Incl. equity in earns. of nonconsol. subs. d-Deficit. NM-Not Meaningful. NA-Not Available.

Total Revenues (Million $)

Quarter:	1993	1992	1991	1990
Mar.	0.29	1.95	5.13	7.53
Jun.	0.15	1.86	4.93	4.14
Sep.		0.72	4.25	4.15
Dec.		0.58	2.83	4.65
		5.11	17.14	20.48

Revenues in the six months ended June 30, 1993, fell 88%, year to year, on a lower level of R&D fees from both Pfizer Inc. (XOMA's marketing partner for its E5 product) and from Ortho Biotech Inc. (its marketing partner for CD5 Plus). Operating costs fell less rapidly, and other income was down 40%, but in the absence of a $3.3 million litigation charge, the net loss narrowed to $15,748,000 ($0.73 a share) from $19,202,000 ($0.90).

Common Share Earnings ($)

Quarter:	1993	1992	1991	1990
Mar.	d0.34	d0.36	d0.44	d0.25
Jun.	d0.40	d0.54	d0.41	d0.44
Sep.		d0.89	d0.42	d0.50
Dec.		d0.42	d0.50	d0.49
		d2.20	d1.77	d1.68

Dividend Data

No cash dividends have been paid.

Finances

During 1993's second quarter, XOMA issued warrants to buy 2.2 million company common shares at $7.26 per share. The warrants were issued in partial settlement of securities class action lawsuits filed against the company in 1991. In 1992's second quarter, XOMA recorded a one-time $3.3 million charge related to the settlement of such litigation.

At June 30, 1993, the company had cash and short-term investments of $67.2 million, down from $83.4 million at December 31, 1992.

At December 31, 1992, XOMA had $216 million of net operating loss carryforwards (NOL's) for financial reporting purposes.

During 1992's third quarter, the company took a charge of $10 million, consisting of $1.5 million of personnel termination costs, $2.5 million in future idle production capacity costs, and a $6.0 million reserve for a portion of XOMA's E5 raw materials inventory.

During 1991 and 1990, sales of purified E5 bulk to Pfizer Inc. amounted to $6.5 million and $7.4 million, respectively. There were no sales in 1992, because product inventories had reached appropriate levels for product launch and beyond.

R&D spending fell to $30.1 million in 1992 from $30.5 million in 1991, reflecting reduced clinical activity for both E5 and CD5 Plus, partially offset by increased spending on BPI and second generation recombinant products for treatment of immune related disorders.

Capitalization

Long Term Liabilities: $9,911,000 (6/93).

Common Stock: 21,469,880 shs. ($0.0005 par).
Institutions hold 14%.
Shareholders: About 3,439 of record (2/93).

d-Deficit.

Office—2910 Seventh St., Berkeley, CA 94710. **Tel**—(510) 644-1170. **Chrmn, Pres & CEO**—J. T. Castello. **SVP-Fin & Treas**—C. L. Dellio. **VP & Secy**—C. J. Margolin. **Dirs**—W. K. Bowes, Jr., J. L. Castello, A. Kornberg, S. C. Mendell, Y. H. Robert, P. J. Scannon, W. D. Van Ness, G. Wilcox. **Transfer Agent & Registrar**—First Interstate Bank of California, SF. **Incorporated** in Delaware in 1981. **Empl**—235.

 Robert M. Gold

Xilinx, Inc.

NASDAQ Symbol XLNX (Incl. in Nat'l Market) Options on CBOE & Pacific In S&P MidCap 400

Price	Range	P-E Ratio	Dividend	Yield	S&P Ranking	Beta
Jul. 26'93	1993					
39½	40¾–23½	31	None	None	NR	NA

Summary

Xilinx markets field programmable gate arrays (FPGAs) and associated development system software. The company has experienced rapid earnings growth in recent years, reflecting strong expansion of its market and well-received products. Another substantial earnings gain is projected for 1993-4, despite increasing competition and high spending levels.

Current Outlook

Earnings for the fiscal year ending April 2, 1994, are estimated to reach $1.50 a share, up from the $1.15 of 1992-3.

Initiation of dividends, which have never been paid, is unlikely.

Sales for 1993-4 are expected to rise about 35%, reflecting continued strong growth of the programmable logic market, a rebound in Europe and a ramping-up of the XC4000 Family. Growth in the U.S. should be led by networking and telecommunications markets, while greater demand from telecommunications markets will lead European sales. The Japanese market is likely to be flat. Margins should be well maintained, due to high gross margins on the XC4000 Family and efforts to restrain marketing, general and administrative expenses. However, research and development spending is likely to remain high. Longer term, competition in the field programmable gate array market is likely to increase.

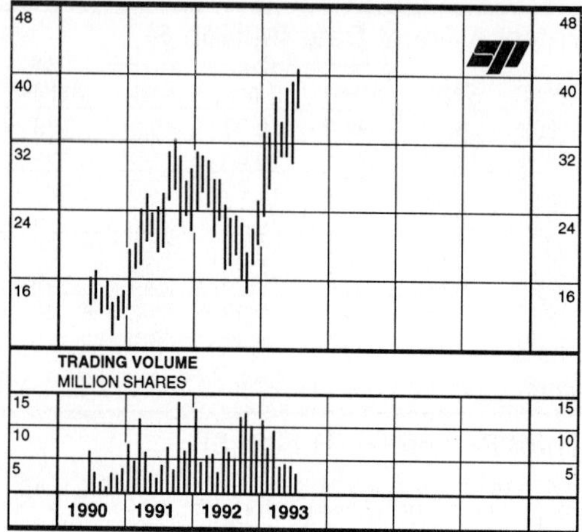

Net Revenues (Million $)

13 Weeks:	1993-94	1992-93	1991-92	1990-91
Jun.	54.4	39.0	33.2	18.5
Sep.	---	[1]42.5	35.0	23.1
Dec.	---	46.2	32.2	26.3
Mar.	---	50.2	35.4	29.7
	---	178.0	135.8	97.6

Net revenues for the three months ended July 3, 1993, increased 39%, year to year, reflecting strong industry growth and the acceptance of new products. Geographically, revenue growth resulted largely from the sustained strength in the North American and European markets, while Japan and the rest of the world continued to be weak. Costs and expenses were up 34% and after taxes at 38.0%, versus 37.0%, net income advanced 49%, to $0.37 a share from $0.25.

Common Share Earnings ($)

13 Weeks:	1993-94	1992-93	1991-92	1990-91
Jun.	0.37	0.25	0.24	0.14
Sep.	E0.36	[1]0.26	0.26	0.16
Dec.	E0.38	0.30	0.24	0.18
Mar.	E0.39	0.34	0.15	0.22
	E1.50	1.15	0.89	0.70

Important Developments

Jul. '93— Xilinx said that during its first quarter its XC3000 product revenues, including XC3100 products, rose 9% to over $30 million from its foruth quarter, while the XC4000 Family increased 28% to nearly $12 million sequentially. Sales of the new high speed XC3100 Family doubled from the previous quarter and represented 4% of integrated circuit revenues.

Next earnings report expected in mid-October.

Per Share Data ($)

Yr. End Mar. 31	1993	1992	1991	1990	1989	1988	1987	1986
Tangible Bk. Val.	**5.50**	4.73	3.68	d0.01	NA	NA	NA	NA
Cash Flow	**1.52**	1.12	0.83	0.40	0.23	d0.05	NA	NA
Earnings[2]	**1.15**	0.89	0.70	0.33	0.17	d0.10	d0.34	d0.51
Dividends	**Nil**	Nil	Nil	Nil	Nil	Nil	Nil	Nil
Payout Ratio	**Nil**	Nil	Nil	Nil	Nil	Nil	Nil	Nil
Calendar Years	**1992**	1991	1990	1989	1988	1987	1986	1985
Prices—High	**31**	32½	17	NA	NA	NA	NA	NA
Low	**14½**	12½	9½	NA	NA	NA	NA	NA
P/E Ratio—	**27–13**	37–14	24–14	NA	NA	NA	NA	NA

Data as orig. reptd. **1.** 14 wks. **2.** Bef. spec. items of +0.13 in 1990, +0.08 in 1989. E-Estimated. d-Deficit. NA-Not Available.

Income Data (Million $)

Year Ended Mar. 31	Revs.	Oper. Inc.	% Oper. Inc. of Revs.	Cap. Exp.	Depr.	Int. Exp.	Net Bef. Taxes	Eff. Tax Rate	[1]Net Inc.	% Net Inc. of Revs.	Cash Flow
1993	**178**	**50.2**	**28.2**	**9.81**	**8.62**	**0.66**	**43.6**	**37.6%**	**27.2**	**15.3**	**35.9**
1992	136	39.2	28.9	7.24	5.56	0.65	33.8	37.0%	21.3	15.7	26.8
1991	98	25.8	26.4	4.08	3.14	0.55	25.7	38.1%	15.9	16.3	19.1
1990	50	10.2	20.5	1.95	1.38	0.30	9.4	35.1%	6.1	12.2	7.5
1989	30	5.7	18.8	0.50	1.19	0.26	4.9	40.0%	2.9	9.6	4.1
1988	14	d1.1	NM	0.11	0.87	0.22	d1.7	Nil	d1.7	NM	d0.8
1987	4	NA	NA	NA	NA	NA	d5.1	Nil	d5.1	NM	NA
1986	1	NA	NA	NA	NA	NA	d4.9	Nil	d4.9	NM	NA

Balance Sheet Data (Million $)

Mar. 31	Cash	Curr. Assets	Curr. Liab.	Curr. Ratio	Total Assets	% Ret. on Assets	Long Term Debt	Common Equity	Total Cap.	% LT Debt of Cap.	% Ret. on Equity
1993	**84.8**	**137**	**35.7**	**3.8**	**163**	**17.6**	**3.91**	**123**	**127**	**3.1**	**23.5**
1992	81.3	121	33.0	3.7	147	16.4	4.96	109	114	4.4	22.0
1991	71.8	100	24.6	4.1	112	10.8	3.81	83	87	4.4	30.1
1990	13.1	29	9.8	3.0	35	21.2	1.98	23	25	8.0	33.2
1989	9.5	20	7.3	2.7	23	16.9	1.67	14	16	10.7	29.2
1988	NA	NA	NA	NA	12	NM	1.28	6	7	17.5	NM
1987	NA	NA	NA	NA	11	NM	1.01	7	8	13.2	NM
1986	NA	NA	NA	NA	9	NM	1.41	6	8	18.4	NM

Data as orig. reptd. 1. Bef. spec. items. d-Deficit. NM-Not Meaningful. NA-Not Available.

Business Summary

Xilinx, Inc. is the leading supplier of field programmable gate arrays (FPGAs) and related development system software used by electronic system manufacturers for bringing complex products rapidly to market.

Net revenues in recent fiscal years were derived as follows:

	1992–3	1991–2
FPGAs	93%	91%
Development system software & miscellaneous	7%	9%

U.S. export revenue from shipments to Europe represented 19% of product revenue in 1992-3, while exports to Japan and the Pacific Rim accounted for 11%.

The company's FPGAs are proprietary integrated circuits designed by Xilinx; they provide a unique combination of the high logic density usually associated with custom gate arrays, the time-to-market advantages of programmable logic and the availability of a standard product. The company offers three families of FPGAs, ranging from 1,200 to 13,000 usable gates.

To implement the FPGA solution, system designers use proprietary Xilinx development system software, together with industry standard CAE software, to develop FPGA applications. At the end of 1992-3, Xilinx had about 14,500 development systems installed.

The company's product line was expanded with the February 1992 acquisition of Plus Logic Inc., a producer of less complex programmable logic devices.

In 1992-3, research and development outlays totaled $24.3 million (13.7% of revenues), up from $17.7 million (13.0%) in 1991-2.

Dividend Data

No cash dividends have been paid, and Xilinx does not expect to pay any in the foreseeable future.

Finances

At July 3, 1993, the company had $98.6 million of cash, cash equivalents and short-term investments.

In its June 1990 initial public stock offering, Xilinx sold 2,875,000 common shares (including 1,778,485 for stockholders) at $10 each. Simultaneously with the closing of the offering, Advanced Micro Devices (AMD) purchased 3,411,772 common shares at $11 each, which it subsequently sold. In exchange for a payment of $5,000,000 by the company, AMD's rights to use certain technology were suspended or limited.

Capitalization

Long Term Debt: $3,302,000 of lease obligs. (7/3/93).

Common Stock: 22,414,000 shs. ($0.01 par).
Institutions hold about 87%.
Shareholders of record: 589.

Options: To buy 2,132,000 shs. at an avg. price of $13.16 per sh. (4/3/93).

Office—2100 Logic Dr., San Jose, CA 95124. **Tel**—(408) 559-7778. **Fax**—(408) 559-7114. **Pres**—B. V. Vonderschmitt. **VP-Fin & CFO**—G. M. Steel. **Secy**—L. W. Sonsini. **Investor Contact**—Maria Quillard (408) 879-4988. **Dirs**—M. D. Burkett, P. T. Gianos, H. A. Marshall, B. V. Vonderschmitt. **Transfer Agent & Registrar**—First National Bank of Boston. **Incorporated** in Delaware in 1990. **Empl**—544.

 Paul H. Valentine, CFA

York International

NYSE Symbol YRK In S&P MidCap 400

Price	Range	P–E Ratio	Dividend	Yield	S&P Ranking	Beta
Aug. 17'93	1993					
37	41½–31½	19	0.08	0.3%	NR	NA

Summary

This company is a full-line, global manufacturer of heating, ventilating, air-conditioning and refrigeration products. York derives about half of its sales from service, repairs and replacement parts, which provides a relatively stable components to sales. Earnings for the first half of 1993 benefited from improved demand, cost reductions, and decreased interest expense. The outlook for the balance of 1993 and for 1994 is favorable.

Current Outlook

Earnings for 1994 could rise to $2.25 a share from the $2.05 expected for 1993.

The $0.02 quarterly dividend should continue.

Sales for 1994 should rise as the economic recovery in the U.S. gathers speed and the recession in many European markets eases. Sales will benefit from increased capital spending for modernization projects, as well as stronger demand for residential products. Improvment in domestic construction related markets is not expected. Aided by operating cost reductions, improved efficiencies and lower interest expense, income should increase.

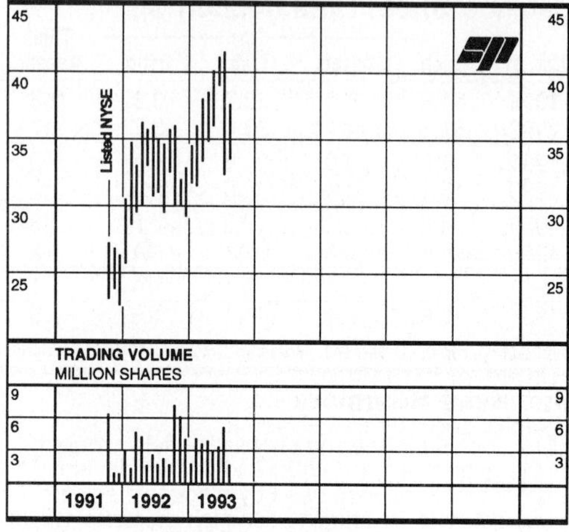

Net Sales (Million $)

Quarter:	1993	1992	1991
Mar.	447	439	350
Jun.	531	518	428
Sep.	---	475	414
Dec.	---	507	461
		1,939	1,653

Sales for the six months ended June 30, 1993, increased 2.2%, year to year. Benefiting from cost reductions and lower interest expense, net income advanced 14%, to $1.04 a share on 7.3% more shares from $0.98. Results are before before special charges of $1.38 a share, versus $0.52.

Common Share Earnings ($)

Quarter:	1993	1992	1991
Mar.	0.35	0.33	Nil
Jun.	0.70	0.63	0.26
Sep.	E0.53	0.48	0.06
Dec.	E0.47	0.44	0.21
	E2.05	1.90	[1]0.56

Important Developments

Jul. '93— The net special charge for the first half of 1993 of $51.9 million ($1.38 a share) reflected the cumulative effect of the adoption of two new accounting standards. The company took a pretax charge of $85.2 million ($51.1 million, $1.36 a share aftertax) for FAS 106, which recognizes the expected cost for future employee postretirement benefits, primarily healthcare. Ongoing costs related to FAS 106 will reduce annual earnings by about $5.3 million or $0.14 a share after taxes. The second accounting change regarded accounting for income taxes and resulted in a charge of $0.8 million or $0.02 a share. Separately,YRK said that it expected its 1993 operating performance to better 1992 by between 5% and 10%.

Next earnings report expected in mid-October.

Per Share Data ($)

Yr. End Dec. 31	1992	1991	[2]1990
Tangible Bk. Val.	**2.10**	d4.17	NA
Cash Flow	**2.72**	1.83	2.18
Earnings[3]	**1.90**	0.56	1.21
Dividends	**0.04**	0.01	NA
Payout Ratio	**2%**	2%	NA
Prices—High	**36¼**	27¼	NA
Low	**25¾**	22⅝	NA
P/E Ratio—	**19–13**	49–40	NA

Data as orig. reptd. **1.** Does not add bec. of change in no. of shares outstanding. **2.** Pro forma. **3.** Bef. spec. item(s) of -0.50 in 1992, -0.74 in 1991, +0.29 in 1990. d-Deficit. NA-Not Available.

Income Data (Million $)

Year Ended Dec. 31	Revs.	Oper. Inc.	% Oper. Inc. of Revs.	Cap. Exp.	Depr.	Int. Exp.	Net Bef. Taxes	Eff. Tax Rate	[3]Net Inc.	% Net Inc. of Revs.	Cash Flow
1992	**1,939**	**204**	**10.5**	**37.0**	**29.9**	**42**	**[4]123.0**	**43.9%**	**69.3**	**3.6**	**99.1**
1991	1,653	177	10.7	37.7	30.0	99	[4]36.8	64.7%	13.0	0.8	42.6
[1]1990	1,601	162	10.1	21.8	30.0	[2]60	82.7	55.0%	37.2	2.3	67.2

Balance Sheet Data (Million $)

Dec. 31	Cash	Curr. Assets	Curr. Liab.	Curr. Ratio	Total Assets	% Ret. on Assets	Long Term Debt	Common Equity	Total Cap.	% LT Debt of Cap.	% Ret. on Equity
1992	**5.1**	**579**	**414**	**1.4**	**1,164**	**5.1**	**227**	**455**	**699**	**32.5**	**17.7**
1991	2.5	612	432	1.4	1,206	0.9	458	254	723	63.4	NM
[5]1990	NA	NA	NA	NA	1,172	NA	488	214	NA	NA	NA

Data as reptd. **1.** Pro forma. **2.** Net. **3.** Bef. spec. items. **4.** Incl. equity in earns. of nonconsol. subs. **5.** As of Jun. 30, 1991; pro forma. NM-Not Meaningful. NA-Not Available.

Business Summary

York International Corp. is a full-line, manufacturer of heating, ventilating, air-conditioning and refrigeration products. The company believes that it is the third largest manufacturer of such products in the U.S. and one of the leaders internationally. YRK's air-conditioning systems range from a one-ton small residence unit to the 49,000-ton system installed in the New York World Trade Center. Products are sold in 110 countries through over 700 sales and distribution centers. Contributions by geographic segment in 1992 were:

	Sales	Profits
U.S.	65.6%	78.2%
Europe	23.7%	14.4%
Other	8.9%	6.3%
Canada	1.8%	1.1%

The company's products fall into three general categories: commercial products (45% of sales in 1992), which include heating, air-conditioning, process cooling and thermal storage equipment designed for commercial applications in retail stores, office buildings, shopping malls, manufacturing facilities, airports and marine vessels; residential products (31%), which consist of central air-conditioning and heat pumps, furnace units and hermetic compressors designed for use in residential applications; and refrigeration products and gas compression equipment (24%), designed for use in the food, beverage, chemical and petrochemical processing industries.

The company has 2,300 company technicians stationed in offices throughout the world who generate 49% of YRK's revenues through the sale of replacement parts and by providing routine and emergency service for air conditioning and refrigeration equipment manufactured by York and its competitors.

The company markets its residential products throughout the U.S. and internationally through 42 exclusive distributors, 16 company-owned distribution centers and more than 226 nonexclusive distributors and wholesalers. Other products are marketed directly to contractors, distributors, architects, engineers and building owners domestically and around the world. The company's products are in use in such diverse locations as the British Houses of Parliament, the World Trade Center, NASA's Vehicle Assembly Building at Cape Canaveral, the Los Angeles International Airport, the Jeddah Airport, the Overseas Union Bank Centre in Singapore, the Sydney Opera House, the National Library Complex in Beijing and the Hong Kong Exposition Centre.

Dividend Data

The company paid its initial quarterly dividend of $0.01 on December 26, 1991.

Amt of Divd. $	Date Decl.	Ex-divd. Date	Stock of Record	Payment Date
0.01	Aug. 21	Sep. 1	Sep. 8	Sep. 25'92
0.01	Dec. 10	Dec. 15	Dec. 21	Dec. 29'92
0.02	Mar. 4	Mar. 9	Mar. 15	Mar. 25'93
0.02	Jun. 3	Jun. 8	Jun. 14	Jun. 24'93

Finances

On April 30, 1993, YRK acquired Email York, a division of Email Ltd. in Australia and New Zealand. Email York is the leading Australian manufacturer of air conditioning chillers which are produced at a factory near Sydney, operates one of the largest HVAC service operations in Australia and conducts sales and service operations in New Zealand. The acquisition complements the 1992 acquisition of Tempmaster-AustraliaAsia which produces air distribution products in Perth, Australia. YRK expects these additions to broaden its base in the Asia-Pacific area and allow it to ship locally manufactured products to the region.

Capitalization

Long Term Debt: $241,734,000 (3/93).

Common Stock: 37,116,837 shs. ($0.005 par).
Officers & directors control 12%.
Institutions hold about 87%.
Shareholders of record: 1,121.

Office—631 South Richland Ave., York, PA 17403. **Tel**—(717) 771-7890. **Chrmn & Pres**—R. N. Pokelwaldt. **VP-CFO**—D. T. DuCray. **VP-Secy**—T. D. Washburn. **Investor Contact**—Helen S. Marsteller (717) 771-7451. **Dirs**—J. T. Dresher, R. F. B. Logan, G. C. McDonough, R. N. Pokelwaldt, D. M. Roberts, J. A. Urry, J. E. Welsh III, W. B. Wriston. **Transfer Agent & Registrar**—Chemical Bank, NYC. **Incorporated** in Delaware in 1988. **Empl**—12,500.

 Joshua M. Harari, CFA